A

DICTIONARY OF LAW

CONTAINING

DEFINITIONS OF THE TERMS AND PHRASES OF AMERICAN AND ENGLISH JURISPRUDENCE, ANCIENT AND MODERN

INCLUDING

THE PRINCIPAL TERMS OF INTERNATIONAL, CONSTITUTIONAL, AND COMMERCIAL LAW; WITH A COLLECTION OF LEGAL MAXIMS AND NUMEROUS SELECT TITLES FROM THE CIVIL LAW AND OTHER FOREIGN SYSTEMS

BY HENRY CAMPBELL BLACK, M.A.

Author of Treatises on "JUDGMENTS," "TAX-TITLES," "CONSTITUTIONAL PROHIBITIONS," etc.

THE LAWBOOK EXCHANGE, LTD.
1991

ISBN-13: 978-0-9630106-05
ISBN-10: 0-9630106-0-3

Library of Congress Catalog Card Number 91-62383

The quality of this reprint is equivalent to the quality of the original work.

THE LAWBOOK EXCHANGE, LTD.
33 Terminal Avenue
Clark, New Jersey 07066-1321

Please see our website for a selection of our other publications and fine facsimile reprints of classic works of legal history:
www.lawbookexchange.com

Printed in the United States of America on acid-free paper

A
DICTIONARY OF LAW

CONTAINING

DEFINITIONS OF THE TERMS AND PHRASES OF AMERICAN AND ENGLISH JURISPRUDENCE, ANCIENT AND MODERN

INCLUDING

THE PRINCIPAL TERMS OF INTERNATIONAL, CONSTITUTIONAL, AND COMMERCIAL LAW; WITH A COLLECTION OF LEGAL MAXIMS AND NUMEROUS SELECT TITLES FROM THE CIVIL LAW AND OTHER FOREIGN SYSTEMS

BY HENRY CAMPBELL BLACK, M.A.

Author of Treatises on "JUDGMENTS," "TAX-TITLES," "CONSTITUTIONAL PROHIBITIONS," etc.

ST. PAUL, MINN.

WEST PUBLISHING CO.

1891

PREFACE.

THE dictionary now offered to the profession is the result of the author's endeavor to prepare a concise and yet comprehensive book of definitions of the terms, phrases, and maxims used in American and English law and necessary to be understood by the working lawyer and judge, as well as those important to the student of legal history or comparative jurisprudence. It does not purport to be an epitome or compilation of the body of the law. It does not invade the province of the text-books, nor attempt to supersede the institutional writings. Nor does it trench upon the field of the English dictionary, although vernacular words and phrases, so far as construed by the courts, are not excluded from its pages. Neither is the book encyclopædic in its character. It is chiefly required in a dictionary that it should be comprehensive. Its value is impaired if any single word that may reasonably be sought between its covers is not found there. But this comprehensiveness is possible (within the compass of a single volume) only on condition that whatever is foreign to the true function of a lexicon be rigidly excluded. The work must therefore contain nothing but the legitimate matter of a dictionary, or else it cannot include all the necessary terms. This purpose has been kept constantly in view in the preparation of the present work. Of the most esteemed law dictionaries now in use, each will be found to contain a very considerable number of words not defined in any other. None is quite comprehensive in itself. The author has made it his aim to include *all* these terms and phrases here, together with some not elsewhere defined.

For the convenience of those who desire to study the law in its historical development, as well as in its relations to political and social philosophy, place has been found for numerous titles of the old English law, and words used in old European and feudal law, and for the principal terminology of the Roman law. And in view of the modern interest in comparative jurisprudence and similar studies, it has seemed necessary to introduce a considerable vocabulary from the civil, canon, French, Spanish, Scotch, and Mexican law and other foreign systems. In order to further adapt the work to the advantage and convenience of all classes of users, many terms of political or public law are here defined, and such as are employed in trade, banking, and commerce, as also the principal phraseology of international and maritime law and forensic medicine. There have also been included numerous words taken from the vernacular, which, in consequence of their interpretation by the courts or in statutes, have acquired a quasi-technical meaning, or which, being frequently used in laws or private documents, have often been referred to the courts for construction. But the main body of the work is given to the definition of the technical terms and phrases used in modern American and English jurisprudence.

In searching for definitions suitable to be incorporated in the work, the author has carefully examined the codes, and the compiled or revised statutes, of the various states, and from these sources much valuable matter has been obtained. The definitions thus enacted by law are for the most part terse, practical, and of course authoritative. Most, if not all, of such statutory interpretations of words and phrases will be found under their appropriate titles. Due prominence has also been given to definitions formulated by the appellate courts and embodied in the reports. Many of these judicial definitions have been literally copied and adopted as the author's definition of the particular term, of course with a proper reference. But as the constant aim has been to present a definition at once concise, comprehensive, accurate, and lucid, he has not felt bound to copy the language of the courts in any instance where, in his judgment, a better definition could be found in treatises of acknowledged authority, or could be framed by adaptation or re-arrangement. But many judicial interpretations have been added in the way of supplementary matter to the various titles.

The more important of the synonyms occurring in legal phraseology have been carefully discriminated. In some cases, it has only been necessary to point out the correct and incorrect uses of these pairs and groups of words. In other cases, the distinctions were found to be delicate or obscure, and a more minute analysis was required.

A complete collection of legal maxims has also been included, comprehending as well those in English and Law French as those expressed in the Latin. These have not been grouped in one body, but distributed in their proper alphabetical order through the book. This is believed to be the more convenient arrangement.

It remains to mention the sources from which the definitions herein contained have been principally derived. For the terms appertaining to old and middle English law and the feudal polity, recourse has been had freely to the older English law dictionaries,(such as those of Cowell, Spelman, Blount, Jacob, Cunningham, Whishaw, Skene, Tomlins, and the "Termes de la Ley,") as also to the writings of Bracton, Littleton, Coke, and the other sages of the early law. The authorities principally relied on for the terms of the Roman and modern civil law are the dictionaries of Calvinus, Scheller, and Vicat, (with many valuable suggestions from Brown and Burrill,) and the works of such authors as Mackeldey, Hunter, Browne, Hallifax, Wolff, and Maine, besides constant reference to Gaius and the *Corpus Juris Civilis.* In preparing the terms and phrases of French, Spanish, and Scotch law, much assistance has been derived from the treatises of Pothier, Merlin, Toullier, Schmidt, Argles, Hall, White, and others, the commentaries of Erskine and Bell, and the dictionaries of Dalloz, Bell, and Escriche. For the great body of terms used in modern English and American law, the author, besides searching the codes and statutes and the reports, as already mentioned, has consulted the institutional writings of Blackstone, Kent, and Bouvier, and a very great number of text-books on special topics of the law. An examination has also been made of the recent English law dictionaries of Wharton, Sweet, Brown, and Mozley & Whitley, and of the American lexicographers, Abbott, Anderson, Bouvier, Burrill, and Rapalje & Lawrence. In each case where aid is directly levied from these sources, a suitable acknowledgment has been made. This list of authorities is by no means exhaustive, nor does it make mention of the many cases in which the definition had to be written entirely *de novo;* but it will suffice to show the general direction and scope of the author's researches.

H. C. B.

WASHINGTON, D. C., August 1, 1891.

A TABLE

OF

BRITISH REGNAL YEARS.

Sovereign.	Accession.	Length of reign.
William I	Oct. 14, 1066	21
William II	Sept. 26, 1087	13
Henry I	Aug. 5, 1100	36
Stephen	Dec. 26, 1135	19
Henry II	Dec. 19, 1154	35
Richard I	Sept. 23, 1189	10
John	May 27, 1199	18
Henry III	Oct. 28, 1216	57
Edward I	Nov. 20, 1272	35
Edward II	July 8, 1307	20
Edward III	Jan. 25, 1326	51
Richard II	June 22, 1377	23
Henry IV	Sept. 30, 1399	14
Henry V	March 21, 1413	10
Henry VI	Sept. 1, 1422	39
Edward IV	March 4, 1461	23
Edward V	April 9, 1483	
Richard III	June 26, 1483	3
Henry VII	Aug. 22, 1485	24
Henry VIII	April 22, 1509	38
Edward VI	Jan. 28, 1547	7
Mary	July 6, 1553	6
Elizabeth	Nov. 17, 1558	45
James I	March 24, 1603	23
Charles I	March 27, 1625	24
The Commonwealth	Jan. 30, 1649	11
Charles II	May 29, 1660	37
James II	Feb. 6, 1685	4
William and Mary	Feb. 13, 1689	14
Anne	March 8, 1702	13
George I	Aug. 1, 1714	13
George II	June 11, 1727	34
George III	Oct. 25, 1760	60
George IV	Jan. 29, 1820	11
William IV	June 26, 1830	7
Victoria	June 20, 1837	

BIBLIOGRAPHICAL LIST

OF THE

PRINCIPAL LAW DICTIONARIES

IN

ENGLISH AND FOREIGN LANGUAGES.

ABBOTT, Benj. Vaughan. Dictionary of terms and phrases used in American or English Jurisprudence. 2 vols. 8vo. Boston, 1879.

ADAMS, Henry C. A juridical glossary; being an exhaustive compilation of the most celebrated maxims, aphorisms, doctrines, precepts, technical phrases and terms employed in the Roman, Civil, Feudal, Canon, and Common Law, and quoted in the standard elementary works and reports of the British and American courts. Vol. 1, A to E. 8vo. Albany, 1886.

ANDERSON, William C. A dictionary of law, consisting of judicial definitions and explanations of words, phrases, and maxims, and an exposition of the principles of law; comprising a dictionary and compendium of American and English jurisprudence. 1 vol. 8vo. Chicago, 1889.

BACON, Francis, Lord. The maxims of the law. [Printed in Bacon's Law Tracts, 1 vol. 12mo. London, 1737.]

BADEN, Gustav Ludvig. Forsög til et dansk-norsk juridisk ord- og sag-leksikon. 1 vol. 16mo. Odense, 1814.

BELL, William. A dictionary and digest of the law of Scotland, with short explanations of the most ordinary English law terms. 1 vol. 8vo. Edinburgh, 1861.

BIRET, Aimé Charles Louis Modeste. Vocabulaire des Cinq Codes, ou definitions simplifiées des termes de droit et de jurisprudence exprimés dans ces codes. 1 vol. 8vo. Paris, 1826.

BLOUNT, Thomas. A law dictionary and glossary, interpreting such difficult and obscure words and terms as are found either in our common or statute, ancient or modern, laws. 3d Edn. 1 vol. folio. London, 1717.

BOUSQUET, J. Nouveau dictionaire de droit. 2d Edn. 1 vol. 4to. Paris, 1847.

BOUVIER, John. A law dictionary adapted to the constitution and laws of the United States of America and of the several states of the American Union, with references to the civil and other systems of foreign law. 1st Edn. 2 vols. 8vo. Philadelphia, 1839.

——, **Same.** 14th Edn. 2 vols. 8vo. Philadelphia, 1882.

BRILLON, Pierre Jacques. Nouveau dictionaire civil et canonique de droit et de pratique. 1 vol. 4to. Paris, 1707.

BRISSONIUS, Barnabas. De verborum quæ ad jus civile pertinent significatione. 1st Edn. 1 vol. folio. Leyden, 1559. [Other editions, 1578, 1683, 1697, 1721.]

——, **Same.** 6th Edn. By J. G. Heineccius. 1 vol. folio. Halae Magdeburgicae, 1743.

BROOM, Herbert. A selection of legal maxims, classified and illustrated. 2d Edn. 1 vol. 8vo. London, 1848.

——, **Same.** 8th Edn.

BROWN, Archibald. A new law dictionary and institute of the whole law, for the use of students, the legal profession, and the public. 1 vol. 8vo. London, 1874.

——, **Same.** American edition, by **A. P.** Sprague. 1 vol. 8vo. Albany, 1875.

BURN, Richard and John. A new law dictionary, intended for general use as well as for gentlemen of the profession. 2 vols. 8vo. London, 1792.

BURRILL, Alexander M. A new law dictionary and glossary, containing full definitions of the principal terms of the common and civil law, together with translations and explanations of the various technical phrases in different languages occurring in the ancient and modern reports and standard treatises; embracing also all the principal common and civil law maxims. 1st Edn. 2 vols. 8vo. New York, 1850.

——, **Same.** 2d Edn. 2 vols. 8vo. New York, 1867.

CALVINUS, (or Kahl,) John. Lexicon juridicum juris Cæsarei, simul et canonici, feudalis, item, civilis, criminalis, theoretici ac practici, et in schola et in foro usitatarum. 1 vol. folio. ——, 1669.

COWELL, John. Nomothetes: The Interpreter, containing the genuine signification of such obscure words and terms used either in the common or statute laws of this realm. 1st Edn. 1 vol. folio. Cambridge, 1607.

——, **Same.** 2d Edn. London, 1672. 3d Edn. London, 1708.

CRAMER, Andreas Wilhelm. Supplementi ad Barnabæ Brissonii opus, De verborum quæ ad jus civile pertinent significatione, specimen. 1 vol. 4to. Kiliae, 1813.

CUNNINGHAM, T. A new and complete law dictionary or general abridgment of the law. 3d Edn. 2 vols. 4to. London, 1783.

DALLOZ, Armand. Dictionnaire general et raisonné de legislation, de doctrine, et de jurisprudence, en matière civile, commerciale, criminelle, administrative, et de droit public. 4 vols. 4to. Paris, 1835.

ESCRICHE, Joaquin. Diccionario razonado de legislacion y jurisprudencia. 3d Edn. 2 vols. 4to. Madrid, 1847.

FERRIÈRE, Claude Joseph. Dictionnaire de droit et de pratique. 1st Edn. 1734. 2d Edn. 1740. 3d Edn. 2 vols. 4to. Paris, 1762.

GOIRAND, Leopold. Glossary of French judicial terms. [In his work on the French Code of Commerce. 1 vol. 8vo. London, 1880.]

HALKERSTON, Peter. A collection of Latin maxims and rules in law and equity, selected from the most eminent authors on the civil, canon, feudal, English, and Scots law, with an English translation. 1 vol. 8vo. Edinburgh, 1823.

HOLTHOUSE, Henry James. A new law dictionary, containing explanations of such technical terms and phrases as occur in the works of legal authors, in the practice of the courts, and in the parliamentary proceedings of the houses of Lords and Commons. 1st Edn. London, 1839.

——, **Same.** American edn. from 2d English edn. 1 vol. 12mo. Philadelphia, 1847.

HOLTZENDORFF, Franz von. Rechts-Lexicon. [Part second of his Encyclopædie der Rechts-wissenschaft.] 2 vols. 8vo. Leipsic, 1875.

JACOB, Giles. A new law dictionary, containing the interpretation and definition of words and terms used in the law, as also the law and practice under the proper heads and titles; together with such learning as explains the history and antiquity of the law, our manners, customs, and original government. 10th Edn. By J. Morgan. 1 vol. folio. London, 1782.

——, **Same.** 1st American edn. from [Tomlin's] 2d English edn. 6 vols. 8vo. Philadelphia, 1811.

KELHAM, Robert. A dictionary of the Norman or old French language. 1 vol. 8vo. London, 1779.

LAWSON, John D. A concordance of words and phrases construed in the judicial reports, and of legal definitions contained therein. 1 vol. 8vo. St. Louis, 1883.

LEE, Thomas. A dictionary of the practice in civil actions in the courts of King's Bench and Common Pleas, with practical directions and forms, arranged under each title. 2d Edn. 2 vols. 8vo. London, 1825.

LLOYD, A. Parlett. Glossary of words and terms frequently used by builders, architects, etc. [Printed in his Treatise on the Law of Building. 1 vol. 8vo. Boston, 1888.]

LOFFT, Capel. Maxims and rules of the law of England and principles of equity. [In his reports of cases adjudged in the court of King's Bench. 1 vol. folio. London, 1776. Same, 1 vol. 8vo. Dublin, 1790.]

MAXWELL, John Irwing. A pocket dictionary of the law of bills of exchange, promissory notes, bank notes, checks, etc. 1 vol. 12mo. Philadelphia, 1808.

MONTEFIORE, Joshua. A commercial dictionary, containing the present state of mercantile law, practice, and custom. 1st Amer. Edn. 3 vols. 8vo. Philadelphia, 1804.

MOZLEY (Herbert Newman) and WHITLEY, (George Crispe.) A concise law dictionary. 1 vol. 8vo. London, 1876.

OSTERSEN, Christian. Glossarium juridico-Danicum. 1 vol. 4to. Kjöbenhavn, 1641. *Note.* A second, revised edition was printed in 1652, and this was reprinted in 1665 and subsequently.

POTTS, Thomas. A compendious law dictionary, containing both an explanation of the terms and the law itself. Intended for the use of the country gentleman, the merchant, and the professional man. 1 vol. 16mo. London, 1803.

RAPALJE (Stewart) and LAWRENCE, (Robert L.) A dictionary of American and English law. 2 vols. 8vo. Jersey City, 1883.

RASTELL, John. Terms of the law; or certain difficult and obscure words and terms of the common and statute laws expounded and explained in French and English. 1 vol. 16mo. London, 1721. *Note.* This work is also known as "Termes de la Ley."

RAWSON, Henry Gilbert. The pocket law lexicon, explaining technical words, phrases, and maxims of the English, Scotch, and Roman law. 2d Edn. 1 vol. 16mo. London, 1884.

SCHLYTER, Carl Johan. Glossarium ad corpus juris Sueo-Gotorum antiqui. Ordbok till Samlingen of Sweriges Gamla Lagar. 1 vol. 4to. Lund, 1877.

SKENE, John. De verborum significatione; the exposition of the termes and difficill wordes conteined in the foure buiks of "Regiam Majestatem" and uthers, in the acts of parliament, etc. 1 vol. 4to. London, 1641.

——, Same. Printed at the end of the collection of the laws of James I. Folio. Edinburgh, 1597.

SPELMAN, Sir Henry. Glossarium archaiologicum; continens Latino-Barbara, peregrina, obsoleta, et novatæ significationis vocabula. 1st Edn. 1 vol. 4to. London, 1626.

——, Same. 3d Edn. 1 vol. folio. London, 1687.

STIMSON, F. J. Glossary of technical terms, phrases, and maxims of the common law. 1 vol. 12mo. Boston, 1881.

SWEET, Charles. A dictionary of English law, containing definitions of the technical terms in modern use and a concise statement of the rules of law affecting the principal subjects, with historical and etymological notes. 1 vol. 8vo. London, 1882.

TAYLER, Thomas. A law-glossary of the Latin, Greek, Norman, French, and other languages, interspersed in the commentaries by Sir W. Blackstone, Knt., and various law treatises upon each branch of the profession, translated into English and alphabetically arranged. 1 vol. 8vo. London, 1819.

——, Same. American edition. Albany, 1833.

TERMES DE LA LEY. See RASTELL.

TOLLUIRE (R. S.) and BOULET (J. B. E.) Nouveau dictionnaire des termes de droit et de pratique; ou *Ferrière* moderne. 1 vol. 8vo. Paris, 1841.

TOMLINS, Sir Thomas E. The law dictionary, explaining the rise, progress, and present state of the British law, defining and interpreting the terms or words of art. 4th Edn. 2 vols. 4to. London, 1835.

——, **Same.** 1st American from 4th English Edn. 3 vols. 8vo. Philadelphia, 1836.

TRAYNER, John. Latin phrases and maxims, collected from the institutional and other writers on Scotch law, with translations and illustrations. 2d Edn. 1 vol. 12mo. Edinburgh, 1876.

VICAT, Philip. Vocabularium juris utriusque, ex variis ante editis. 2d Edn. 4 vols. 8vo. Naples, 1760.

WHARTON, J. J. S. The law lexicon, forming an epitome of the law of England, and containing full explanations of the technical terms and phrases thereof, both ancient and modern. 1st Edn. 1 vol. 8vo. London, 1848.

WHARTON, J. J. S. Same. 7th Edn. by J. M. Lely. 1 vol. 8vo. London, 1883.

——, **Same.** 1st American from 1st English Edn. 1 vol. 8vo. Philadelphia, 1854.

WHISHAW, James. A new law dictionary, containing a concise exposition of the mere terms of art and such obsolete words as occur in old legal, historical, and antiquarian writers. 1 vol. 8vo. London, 1829.

WILLIAMS, Thomas Walter. A compendious and comprehensive law dictionary, elucidating the terms and general principles of law and equity. 1 vol. 8vo. London, 1816.

WINFIELD, Charles H. Adjudged words and phrases, being a collection of adjudicated definitions of terms used in the law, with references to authorities. 1 vol. 8vo. Jersey City, 1882.

WINGATE, Edmond. Maxims of reason, or the reason of the common law of England. 1 vol. 4to. London, 1658.

BLACK'S DICTIONARY OF LAW.

A.

A. The first letter of the English alphabet; used to distinguish the first page of a folio from the second, marked b, or the first page of a book, the first foot-note on a printed page, the first of a series of subdivisions, etc., from the following ones, which are marked b, c, d, e, etc.

A. Lat. The letter marked on the ballots by which, among the Romans, the people voted against a proposed law. It was the initial letter of the word "*antiquo*," I am for the old law. Tayl. Civil Law, 191.

A. Lat. The letter inscribed on the ballots by which, among the Romans, jurors voted to acquit an accused party. It was the initial letter of "*absolvo*," I acquit. Tayl. Civil Law, 192.

"A." The English indefinite article. This particle is not necessarily a singular term; it is often used in the sense of "any," and is then applied to more than one individual object. 141 Mass. 266, 4 N. E. Rep. 794; 101 N. Y. 458, 5 N. E. Rep. 322; 60 Iowa, 223, 14 N. W. Rep. 247.

A. D. Lat. Contraction for *Anno Domini*, (in the year of our Lord.)

A. R. *Anno regni*, the year of the reign; as, A. R. V. R. 22, (*Anno Regni Victoriæ Reginæ cicesimo secundo*,) in the twenty-second year of the reign of Queen Victoria.

A 1. Of the highest qualities. An expression which originated in a practice of underwriters of rating vessels in three classes,—A, B, and C; and these again in ranks numbered. Abbott.

A AVER ET TENER. L. Fr. (L. Lat. *habendum et tenendum*.) To have and to hold. Co. Litt. §§ 523, 524. *A aver et tener a luy et a ses heires, a touts jours*,—to have and to hold to him and his heirs forever. Id. § 625. See AVER ET TENER.

A CŒLO USQUE AD CENTRUM. From the heavens to the center of the earth.

A communi observantia non est recedendum. From common observance there should be no departure; there must be no departure from common usage. 2 Coke, 74; Co. Litt. 186*a*, 229*b*, 365*a*; Wing. Max. 752, max. 203. A maxim applied to the practice of the courts, to the ancient and established forms of pleading and conveyancing, and to professional usage generally. Id. 752–755. Lord Coke applies it to common professional opinion. Co. Litt. 186*a*, 364*b*.

A CONSILIIS. (Lat. *consilium*, advice.) Of counsel; a counsellor. The term is used in the civil law by some writers instead of *a responsis*. Spelman, "*Apocrisarius*."

A CUEILLETTE. In French law. In relation to the contract of affreightment, signifies when the cargo is taken on condition that the master succeeds in completing his cargo from other sources. Arg. Fr. Merc. Law, 543.

A DATU. L. Lat. From the date. 2 Salk. 413. *A die datûs*, from the day of the date. Id.; 2 Crabb, Real Prop. p. 248, § 1301; 1 Ld. Raym. 84, 480; 2 Ld. Raym. 1242. *A dato*, from the date. Cro. Jac. 135.

A digniori fieri debet denominatio. Denomination ought to be from the more worthy. The description (of a place) should be taken from the more worthy subject, (as from a will.) Fleta, lib. 4, c. 10, § 12.

A digniori fieri debet denominatio et resolutio. The title and exposition of a thing ought to be derived from, or given, or made with reference to, the more worthy degree, quality, or species of it. Wing. Max. 265, max. 75.

A FORFAIT ET SANS GARANTIE. In French law. A formula used in indorsing commercial paper, and equivalent to "without recourse."

A FORTIORI. By a stronger reason. A term used in logic to denote an argument to the effect that because one ascertained fact exists, therefore another, which is included in it, or analogous to it, and which is less improbable, unusual, or surprising, must also exist.

A GRATIA. From grace or favor; as a matter of indulgence, not of right.

A LATERE. Lat. From the side. In connection with the succession to property, the term means "collateral." Bract. fol. 20*b*. Also, sometimes, "without right." Id. fol. 42*b*. In ecclesiastical law, a legate *a latere* is one invested with full apostolic powers; one authorized to represent the pope as if the latter were present. Du Cange.

A LIBELLIS. L. Lat. An officer who had charge of the *libelli* or petitions addressed to the sovereign. Calvin. A name sometimes given to a chancellor, (*cancellarius*,) in the early history of that office. Spelman, "*Cancellarius*."

A l'impossible nul n'est tenu. No one is bound to do what is impossible.

A ME. (Lat. *ego*, I.) A term denoting direct tenure of the superior lord. 2 Bell, H. L. Sc. 133. Unjustly detaining from me. He is said to withhold *a me* (from me) who has obtained possession of my property unjustly. Calvin.

A MENSA ET THORO. From bed and board. Descriptive of a limited divorce or separation by judicial sentence.

A NATIVITATE. From birth, or from infancy. Denotes that a disability, status, etc., is congenital.

A non posse ad non esse sequitur argumentum necessarie negative. From the impossibility of a thing to its non-existence, the inference follows necessarily in the negative. That which cannot be done is not done. Hob. 336*b*. Otherwise, in the affirmative. Id.

A PALATIO. L. Lat. From *palatium*, (a palace.) Counties palatine are hence so called. 1 Bl. Comm. 117. See PALATIUM.

A piratis aut latronibus capti liberi permanent. Persons taken by pirates or robbers remain free. Dig. 49, 15, 19, 2; Gro. de J. B. lib. 3, c. 3, § 1.

A piratis et latronibus capta dominium non mutant. Things taken or captured by pirates and robbers do not change their ownership. Bynk. bk. 1, c. 17; 1 Kent, Comm. 108, 184. No right to the spoil vests in the piratical captors; no right is derivable from them to any recaptors in prejudice of the original owners. 2 Wood. Lect. 428.

A POSTERIORI. A term used in logic to denote an argument founded on experiment or observation, or one which, taking ascertained facts as an effect, proceeds by synthesis and induction to demonstrate their cause.

A PRENDRE. L. Fr. To take. *Bref à prendre la terre*, a writ to take the land. Fet Ass. § 51. A right to take something out of the soil of another is a profit *à prendre*, or a right coupled with a profit. 1 Crabb, Real Prop. p. 125, § 115. Distinguished from an easement. 5 Adol. & E. 758. Sometimes written as one word, *apprendre*, *apprender*.

A PRIORI. A term used in logic to denote an argument founded on analogy, or abstract considerations, or one which, positing a general principle or admitted truth as a cause, proceeds to deduce from it the effects which must necessarily follow.

A QUO. A term used, with the correlative *ad quem*, (to which,) in expressing the computation of time, and also of distance in space. Thus, *dies à quo*, the day from which, and *dies ad quem*, the day to which, a period of time is computed. So, *terminus à quo*, the point or limit from which, and *terminus ad quem*, the point or limit to which, a distance or passage in space is reckoned.

A QUO; A QUA. From which. The judge or court from which a cause has been brought by error or appeal, or has otherwise been removed, is termed the judge or court *a quo; a qua*. Abbott.

A RENDRE. (Fr. to render, to yield.) That which is to be rendered, yielded, or paid. *Profits à rendre* comprehend rents and services. Ham. N. P. 192.

A rescriptis valet argumentum. An argument drawn from original writs in the register is good. Co. Litt. 11*a*.

A RESPONSIS. L. Lat. In ecclesiastical law. One whose office it was to give or convey answers; otherwise termed *responsalis*, and *apocrisiarius*. One who, being consulted on ecclesiastical matters, gave answers, counsel, or advice; otherwise termed *a consiliis*. Spelman, "*Apocrisiarius*."

A RETRO. L. Lat. Behind; in arrear. *Et reditus proveniens inde à retro fuerit*, and the rent issuing therefrom be in arrear. Fleta, lib. 2, c. 55, § 2.

A RUBRO AD NIGRUM. Lat. From the red to the black; from the rubric or title of a statute, (which, anciently, was in *red* letters,) to its body, which was in the ordinary *black*. Tray. Lat. Max.; Bell, "*Rubric*."

A summo remedio ad inferiorem actionem non habetur regressus, neque auxilium. From (after using) the highest remedy, there can be no recourse (going back) to an inferior action, nor assistance, (derived from it.) Fleta, lib. 6, c. 1, § 2. A maxim in the old law of real actions, when there were grades in the remedies given; the rule being that a party who brought a writ of right, which was the highest writ in the law, could not afterwards resort or descend to an inferior remedy. Bract. 112*b*; 3 Bl. Comm. 193, 194.

A TEMPORE CUJUS CONTRARII MEMORIA NON EXISTET. From time of which memory to the contrary does not exist.

A verbis legis non est recedendum. From the words of the law there must be no departure. 5 Coke, 119; Wing. Max. 25. A court is not at liberty to disregard the express letter of a statute, in favor of a supposed intention. 1 Steph. Comm. 71; Broom, Max. 268.

A VINCULO MATRIMONII. (Lat. from the bond of matrimony.) A term descriptive of a kind of divorce, which effects a complete dissolution of the marriage contract. See DIVORCE.

Ab abusu ad usum non valet consequentia. A conclusion as to the use of a thing from its abuse is invalid. Broom, Max. 17.

AB ACTIS. Lat. An officer having charge of *acta*, public records, registers, journals, or minutes; an officer who entered on record the *acta* or proceedings of a court; a clerk of court; a notary or actuary. Calvin. Lex. Jurid. See "*Acta*." This, and the similarly formed epithets *à cancellis*, *à secretis*, *à libellis*, were also anciently the titles of a chancellor, (*cancellarius*,) in the early history of that office. Spelman, "*Cancellarius*."

AB AGENDO. Disabled from acting; unable to act; incapacitated for business or transactions of any kind.

AB ANTE. In advance. Thus, a legislature cannot agree *ab ante* to any modification or amendment to a law which a third person may make. 1 Sum. 308.

AB ANTECEDENTE. Beforehand; in advance.

AB ANTIQUO. Of old; of an ancient date.

Ab assuetis non fit injuria. From things to which one is accustomed (or in which there has been long acquiescence) no legal injury or wrong arises. If a person neglect to insist on his right, he is deemed to have abandoned it. Amb. 645; 3 Brown, Ch. 639.

AB EPISTOLIS. Lat. An officer having charge of the correspondence (*epistolæ*) of his superior or sovereign; a secretary. Calvin.; Spiegelius.

AB EXTRA. (Lat. *extra*, beyond, without.) From without. 14 Mass. 151.

AB INCONVENIENTI. From hardship, or inconvenience. An argument founded upon the hardship of the case, and the inconvenience or disastrous consequences to which a different course of reasoning would lead.

AB INITIO. L. Lat. From the beginning; from the first act. A party is said to be a trespasser *ab initio*, an estate to be good *ab initio*, an agreement or deed to be void *ab initio*, a marriage to be unlawful *ab initio*, and the like. Plow. 6*a*, 16*a*; 1 Bl. Comm. 440.

AB INITIO MUNDI. Lat. From the beginning of the world. *Ab initio mundi usque ad hodiernum diem*, from the beginning of the world to this day. Y. B. M. 1 Edw. III. 24.

AB INTESTATO. Lat. In the civil law. From an intestate; from the intestate; in case of intestacy. *Hæreditas ab intestato*, an inheritance derived from an intestate. Inst. 2, 9, 6. *Successio ab intestato*, succession to an intestate, or in case of intestacy. Id. 3, 2, 3; Dig. 38, 6, 1. This answers to the descent or inheritance of real estate at common law. 2 Bl. Comm. 490, 516; Story, Confl. Laws, § 480. "Heir *ab intestato*."

1 Burr. 420. The phrase "*ab intestato*" is generally used as the opposite or alternative of *ex testamento*, (from, by, or under a will.) *Vel ex testamento, vel ab intestato* [*hæreditates*] *pertinent*,—inheritances are derived either from a will or from an intestate, (one who dies without a will.) Inst. 2, 9, 6; Dig. 29, 4; Cod. 6, 14, 2.

AB INVITO. Lat. By or from an unwilling party. A transfer *ab invito* is a compulsory transfer.

AB IRATO. By one who is angry. A devise or gift made by a man adversely to the interest of his heirs, on account of anger or hatred against them, is said to be made *ab irato*. A suit to set aside such a will is called an action *ab irato*. Merl. Repert. "*Ab irato.*"

ABACTOR. In Roman law. A cattle thief; a driver away of cattle and other animals; one who stole cattle in numbers; one who abstracted cattle from the herd, intending to steal them. Also called *abigeus*. Blount; Cowell.

ABADENGO. In Spanish law. Land owned by an ecclesiastical corporation, and therefore exempt from taxation. In particular, lands or towns under the dominion and jurisdiction of an abbot.

ABALIENATIO. In Roman law. The perfect conveyance or transfer of property from one Roman citizen to another. This term gave place to the simple *alienatio*, which is used in the Digest and Institutes, as well as in the feudal law, and from which the English "alienation" has been formed. Inst. 2, 8, pr.; Id. 2, 1, 40; Dig. 50, 16, 28.

ABAMITA. Lat. In the civil law. A great-great-grandfather's sister, (*abavi soror*.) Inst. 3, 6, 6; Dig. 38, 10, 3. Called *amita maxima*. Id. 38, 10, 10, 17. Called, in Bracton, *abamita magna*. Bract. fol. 68*b*.

ABANDON. To desert, surrender, relinquish, give up, or cede. See ABANDONMENT.

ABANDONEE. A party to whom a right or property is abandoned or relinquished by another. Applied to the insurers of vessels and cargoes. Lord Ellenborough, C. J., 5 Maule & S. 82; Abbott, J., Id. 87; Holroyd, J., Id. 89.

ABANDONMENT. The surrender, relinquishment, disclaimer, or cession of property or of rights.

The giving up a thing absolutely, without reference to any particular person or purpose; as throwing a jewel into the highway; leaving a thing to itself, as a vessel at sea; desertion, or dereliction. (2 Bl. Comm. 9, 10.) Burrill.

In marine insurance. A relinquishment or cession of property by the owner to the insurer of it, in order to claim as for a total loss, when in fact it is so by construction only. 2 Steph. Comm. 178. The exercise of a right which a party having insured goods or vessels has to call upon the insurers, in cases where the property insured has, by perils of the sea, become so much damaged as to be of little value, to accept of what is or may be saved, and to pay the full amount of the insurance, as if a total loss had actually happened. Park, Ins. 143; 2 Marsh. Ins. 559; 3 Kent, Comm. 318-335, and notes.

Abandonment is the act by which, after a constructive total loss, a person insured by contract of marine insurance declares to the insurer that he relinquishes to him his interest in the thing insured. Civil Code Cal. § 2716.

The term is used only in reference to risks in navigation; but the principle is applicable in fire insurance, where there are remnants, and sometimes, also, under stipulations in life policies in favor of creditors.

In maritime law. The surrender of a vessel and freight by the owner of the same to a person having a claim thereon arising out of a contract made with the master. See Poth. Chart. § 2, art. 3, § 51.

By husband or wife. The act of a husband or wife who leaves his or her consort willfully, and with an intention of causing perpetual separation.

"Abandonment, in the sense in which it is used in the statute under which this proceeding was commenced, may be defined to be the act of willfully leaving the wife, with the intention of causing a palpable separation between the parties, and implies an actual desertion of the wife by the husband." 60 Ind. 279.

In French law. The act by which a debtor surrenders his property for the benefit of his creditors. Merl. Repert. "Abandonment."

ABANDONMENT FOR TORTS. In the civil law. The act of a person who was sued in a noxal action, *i. e.*, for a tort or trespass committed by his slave or his animal, in relinquishing and abandoning the slave or animal to the person injured, whereby he saved himself from any further responsibility. See Inst. 4, 8, 9; 11 La. Ann. 396.

ABANDUN, or ABANDUM. Anything sequestered, proscribed, or abandoned. *Abandon, i. e., in bannum res missa,* a thing banned or denounced as forfeited or lost, whence to *abandon, desert,* or *forsake,* as lost and gone. Cowell.

ABARNARE. Lat. To detect or discover, and disclose to a magistrate, any secret crime. Leges Canuti, cap. 10.

ABATAMENTUM. L. Lat. In old English law. An abatement of freehold; an entry upon lands by way of interposition between the death of the ancestor and the entry of the heir. Co. Litt. 277*a;* Yel. 151.

ABATEMENT. **In pleading.** The effect produced upon an action at law, when the defendant pleads matter of fact showing the writ or declaration to be defective and incorrect. This defeats the action for the time being, but the plaintiff may proceed with it after the defect is removed, or may recommence it in a better way. In England, in equity pleading, declinatory pleas to the jurisdiction and dilatory to the persons were (prior to the judicature act) sometimes, by analogy to common law, termed "pleas in abatement."

In chancery practice. The determination, cessation, or suspension of all proceedings in a suit, from the want of proper parties capable of proceeding therein, as upon the death of one of the parties pending the suit. See 2 Tidd, Pr. 932; Story, Eq. Pl. § 354.

In mercantile law. A drawback or rebate allowed in certain cases on the duties due on imported goods, in consideration of their deterioration or damage suffered during importation, or while in store. A diminution or decrease in the amount of tax imposed upon any person.

In contracts. A reduction made by the creditor for the prompt payment of a debt due by the payor or debtor. Wesk. Ins. 7.

Of legacies and debts. A proportional diminution or reduction of the pecuniary legacies, when the funds or assets out of which such legacies are payable are not sufficient to pay them in full. Ward, Leg. p. 369, c. 6, § 7; 1 Story, Eq. Jur. § 555; 2 Bl. Comm. 512, 513. In equity, when equitable assets are insufficient to satisfy fully all the creditors, their debts must abate in proportion, and they must be content with a dividend; for *æquitas est quasi æqualitas.*

ABATEMENT OF A NUISANCE. The removal, prostration, or destruction of that which causes a nuisance, whether by breaking or pulling it down, or otherwise removing, disintegrating, or effacing it.

The remedy which the law allows a party injured by a nuisance of destroying or removing it by his own act, so as he commits no riot in doing it, nor occasions (in the case of a private nuisance) any damage beyond what the removal of the inconvenience necessarily requires. 3 Bl. Comm. 5, 168; 3 Steph. Comm. 361; 2 Salk. 458.

ABATEMENT OF FREEHOLD. This takes place where a person dies seised of an inheritance, and, before the heir or devisee enters, a stranger, having no right, makes a wrongful entry, and gets possession of it. Such an entry is technically called an "abatement," and the stranger an "abator." It is, in fact, a figurative expression, denoting that the rightful possession or freehold of the heir or devisee is overthrown by the unlawful intervention of a stranger. *Abatement* differs from *intrusion,* in that it is always to the prejudice of the *heir* or immediate *devisee,* whereas the latter is to the prejudice of the *reversioner* or *remainder-man;* and *disseisin* differs from them both, for to *disseise* is to put forcibly or fraudulently a person seised of the freehold out of possession. 1 Co. Inst. 277*a;* 3 Bl. Comm. 166. By the ancient laws of Normandy, this term was used to signify the act of one who, having an apparent right of possession to an estate, took possession of it immediately after the death of the actual possessor, before the heir entered. (Howard, Anciennes Lois des Français, tome 1, p. 539.) Bouvier.

ABATOR. In real property law, a stranger who, having no right of entry, contrives to get possession of an estate of freehold, to the prejudice of the heir or devisee, before the latter can enter, after the ancestor's death. Litt. § 397. In the law of torts, one who abates, prostrates, or destroys a nuisance.

ABATUDA. Anything diminished. *Moneta abatuda* is money clipped or diminished in value. Cowell; Dufresne.

ABAVIA. Lat. In the civil law. A great-great-grandmother. Inst. 3, 6, 4; Dig. 38, 10, 1, 6; Bract. fol. 68*b*.

ABAVITA. A great-great-grandfather's sister. Bract. fol. 68*b*. This is a misprint for *abamita*, (q. v.) Burrill.

ABAVUNCULUS. Lat. In the civil law. A great-great-grandmother's brother, (*abaviæ frater*.) Inst. 3, 6, 6; Dig. 38, 10, 3. Called *avunculus maximus*. Id. 38, 10, 10, 17. Called by Bracton and Fleta *abavunculus magnus*. Bract. fol. 68*b*; Fleta, lib. 6, c. 2, § 19.

ABAVUS. Lat. In the civil law. A great-great-grandfather. Inst. 3, 6, 4; Dig. 38, 10, 1, 6; Bract. fol. 67*a*.

ABBACY. The government of a religious house, and the revenues thereof, subject to an abbot, as a bishopric is to a bishop. Cowell. The rights and privileges of an abbot.

ABBEY. A society of religious persons, having an abbot or abbess to preside over them.

ABBOT. The spiritual superior or governor of an abbey or monastery. Feminine, *Abbess*.

ABBREVIATE OF ADJUDICATION. In Scotch law. An abstract of the decree of adjudication, and of the lands adjudged, with the amount of the debt. Adjudication is that diligence (execution) of the law by which the real estate of a debtor is adjudged to belong to his creditor in payment of a debt; and the abbreviate must be recorded in the register of adjudications.

ABBREVIATIO PLACITORUM. An abstract of ancient judicial records, prior to the Year Books. See Steph. Pl. Append. xvi.

ABBREVIATIONS. Shortened conventional expressions, employed as substitutes for names, phrases, dates, and the like, for the saving of space, of time in transcribing, etc. Abbott.

Abbreviationum, ille numerus et sensus accipiendus est, ut concessio non sit inanis. In abbreviations, such number and sense is to be taken that the grant be not made void. 9 Coke, 48.

ABBREVIATORS. In ecclesiastical law. Officers whose duty it is to assist in drawing up the pope's briefs, and reducing petitions into proper form to be converted into papal bulls. Bouvier.

ABBROCHMENT, or ABBROACHMENT. The act of forestalling a market, by buying up at wholesale the merchandise intended to be sold there, for the purpose of selling it at retail. See FORESTALLING.

ABDICATION. The act of a sovereign in renouncing and relinquishing his government or throne, so that either the throne is left entirely vacant, or is filled by a successor appointed or elected beforehand.

Also, where a magistrate or person in office voluntarily renounces or gives it up before the time of service has expired. It differs from resignation, in that resignation is made by one who has received his office from another and restores it into his hands, as an inferior into the hands of a superior; abdication is the relinquishment of an office which has devolved by act of law. It is said to be a renunciation, quitting, and relinquishing, so as to have nothing further to do with a thing, or the doing of such actions as are inconsistent with the holding of it. Chambers.

ABDUCTION. In criminal law. The offense of taking away a man's wife, child, or ward, by fraud and persuasion, or open violence. 3 Bl. Comm. 139-141.

The unlawful taking or detention of any female for the purpose of marriage, concubinage, or prostitution.

ABEARANCE. Behavior; as a recognizance to be of good abearance signifies to be of good behavior. 4 Bl. Comm. 251, 256

ABEREMURDER. (From Sax. *abere*, apparent, notorious; and *mord*, murder.) Plain or downright murder, as distinguished from the less heinous crime of manslaughter, or chance medley. It was declared a capital offense, without fine or commutation, by the laws of Canute, c. 93, and of Hen. I. c. 13. Spelman.

ABESSE. Lat. In the civil law. To be absent; to be away from a place. Said of a person who was *extra continentia urbis*, (beyond the suburbs of the city.)

ABET. In criminal law. To encourage, incite, or set another on to commit a crime. To abet another to commit a murder is to command, procure, or counsel him to commit it. Old Nat. Brev. 21; Co. Litt. 475.

ABETTATOR. L. Lat. In old English law. An abettor. Fleta, lib. 2, c. 65, § 7. See ABETTOR.

ABETTOR. In criminal law. An instigator, or setter on; one who promotes or procures a crime to be committed; one who commands, advises, instigates, or encourages another to commit a crime; a person who, being present or in the neighborhood, incites another to commit a crime, and thus becomes a principal.

The distinction between abettors and accessaries is the presence or absence at the commission of the crime. Cowell; Fleta, lib. 1, c. 34. Presence and participation are necessary to constitute a person an abettor. 4 Shars. Bl. Comm. 33; Russ. & R. 99; 9 Bing. N. C. 440; 13 Mo. 382; 1 Wis. 159; 10 Pick. 477.

ABEYANCE. In the law of estates. Expectation; waiting; suspense; remembrance and contemplation in law. Where there is no person in existence in whom an inheritance can vest, it is said to be in *abeyance*, that is, in expectation; the law considering it as always potentially existing, and ready to vest whenever a proper owner appears. 2 Bl. Comm. 107. Or, in other words, it is said to be in the remembrance, consideration, and intendment of the law. Co. Litt. §§ 646, 650. The term "abeyance" is also sometimes applied to personal property. Thus, in the case of maritime captures during war, it is said that, until the capture becomes invested with the character of prize by a sentence of condemnation, the right of property is in *abeyance*, or in a state of legal sequestration. 1 Kent, Comm. 102. It has also been applied to the franchises of a corporation. "When a corporation is to be brought into existence by some future acts of the corporators, the franchises remain in *abeyance*, until such acts are done; and, when the corporation is brought into life, the franchises instantaneously attach to it." Story, J., 4 Wheat. 691.

ABIATICUS, or Aviaticus. L. Lat. In feudal law. A grandson; the son of a son. Spelman; Lib. Feud., Baraterii, tit. 8, cited Id.

ABIDE. To "abide the order of the court" means to perform, execute, or conform to such order. 8 Cush. 297; 7 Tex. App. 38; 108 Mass. 585.

A stipulation in an arbitration bond that the parties shall "abide by" the award of the arbitrators means only that they shall await the award of the arbitrators, without revoking the submission, and not that they shall acquiesce in the award when made. 6 N. H. 162; 48 N. H. 40.

ABIDING BY. In Scotch law. A judicial declaration that the party abides by the deed on which he founds, in an action where the deed or writing is attacked as forged. Unless this be done, a decree that the deed is false will be pronounced. Pat. Comp. It has the effect of pledging the party to stand the consequences of founding on a forged deed. Bell.

ABIGEATORES. In the civil law. Cattle stealers; those who drove away cattle or other animals, with the intention of stealing them. A rarer form of *abigei*, (q. v.) Calvin.

ABIGEATUS. Lat. (From *abigere*, to drive away.) In the civil law. The offense of stealing or driving away cattle. Dig. 47, 14, 2.

ABIGEI. Lat. In the civil law. Cattle stealers. Dig. 47, 14, 1, 1. Calvin.; Brissonius; 4 Bl. Comm. 239. See ABIGEUS.

ABIGERE. Lat. (From *ab*, from; and *agere*, to drive.) In the civil law. To drive away. Applied to those who drove away animals with the intention of stealing them. Dig. 47, 14, "*De abigeis.*" Applied, also, to the similar offense of cattle stealing on the borders between England and Scotland. Scott's Minstrelsy of the Scottish Border, Introd. Append. No. vii.

ABIGERE. To drive out; to expel by force; to produce abortion. Dig. 47, 11, 4.

ABIGEUS. Lat. (From *abigere*, to drive away.) In the civil law. A stealer of cattle; one who drove or drew away (*subtraxit*) cattle from their pastures, as horses or oxen from the herds, and made booty of them, and who followed this as a business or trade. Dig. 47, 14, 1, 1. The term was applied also to those who drove away the smaller animals, as swine, sheep, and goats. Id. 47, 14, 1, 2. In the latter case, it depended on the *number* taken, whether the offender was *fur* (a common thief) or *abigeus*. Id. 47, 14, 3. But the taking of a single horse or ox seems to have constituted the crime of *abigeatus*. Dig. 47, 14, 3. And those who *frequently* did this were clearly *abigei*, though they took but an animal or two at a time. Id. 47, 14, 3, 2. See Cod. 9, 37; Nov. 22, c. 15, § 1.

ABILITY. When a statute makes it a ground of divorce that the husband has neglected to provide for his wife the common necessaries of life, having the ability to provide the same, the word "ability" has reference to the possession by the husband of the means in property to provide such necessaries, not to his capacity of acquiring such means by labor. 9 Cal. 476.

ABISHERING, or ABISHERSING. Quit of amercements. It originally signified a forfeiture or amercement, and is more properly *mishering, mishersing,* or *miskering,* according to Spelman. It has since been termed a liberty of freedom, because, wherever this word is used in a grant, the persons to whom the grant is made have the forfeitures and amercements of all others, and are themselves free from the control of any within their fee. Termes de la Ley, 7.

ABJUDICATIO. In old English law. The depriving of a thing by the judgment of a court; a putting out of court; the same as *forisjudicatio,* forjudgment, forjudger. Co. Litt. 100*a, b;* Townsh. Pl. 49.

ABJURATION OF ALLEGIANCE. One of the steps in the process of naturalizing an alien. It consists in a formal declaration, made by the party under oath before a competent authority, that he renounces and abjures all the allegiance and fidelity which he owes to the sovereign whose subject he has theretofore been.

ABJURATION OF THE REALM. In ancient English law. A renunciation of one's country, a species of self-imposed banishment, under an oath never to return to the kingdom unless by permission. This was formerly allowed to criminals, as a means of saving their lives, when they had confessed their crimes, and fled to sanctuary. See 4 Bl. Comm. 332.

ABJURE. To renounce, or abandon, by or upon oath. See ABJURATION.

"The decision of this court in Arthur v. Broadnax, 3 Ala. 557, affirms that if the husband has *abjured* the state, and remains abroad, the wife, meanwhile trading as a *feme sole,* could recover on a note which was given to her as such. We must consider the term 'abjure,' as there used, as implying a total abandonment of the state; a departure from the state without the intention of returning, and not a renunciation of one's country, upon an oath of perpetual banishment, as the term originally implied." 15 Ala. 148.

ABLE-BODIED. As used in a statute relating to service in the militia, this term does not imply an absolute freedom from all physical ailment. It imports an absence of those palpable and visible defects which evidently incapacitate the person from performing the ordinary duties of a soldier. 10 Vt. 152.

ABLEGATI. Papal ambassadors of the second rank, who are sent to a country where there is not a nuncio, with a less extensive commission than that of a nuncio.

ABLOCATIO. A letting out to hire, or leasing for money. Calvin. Sometimes used in the English form "ablocation."

ABMATERTERA. Lat. In the civil law. A great-great-grandmother's sister, (*abaviæ soror.*) Inst. 3, 6, 6; Dig. 38, 10, 3. Called *matertera maxima.* Id. 38, 10, 10, 17. Called, by Bracton, *abmatertera magna.* Bract. fol. 68*b*.

ABNEPOS. Lat. A great-great-grandson. The grandson of a grandson or granddaughter. Calvin.

ABNEPTIS. Lat. A great-great-granddaughter. The granddaughter of a grandson or granddaughter. Calvin.

ABODE. The place where a person dwells.

ABOLITION. The destruction, abrogation, or extinguishment of anything; also the leave given by the sovereign or judges to a criminal accuser to desist from further prosecution. 25 Hen. VIII. c. 21.

ABORDAGE. Fr. In French commercial law. Collision of vessels.

ABORTION. In criminal law. The miscarriage or premature delivery of a woman who is quick with child. When this is brought about with a malicious design, or for an unlawful purpose, it is a crime in law.

The act of bringing forth what is yet imperfect; and particularly the delivery or expulsion of the human *fœtus* prematurely, or before it is yet capable of sustaining life. Also the thing prematurely brought forth, or product of an untimely process. Sometimes loosely used for the offense of procuring a premature delivery; but, strictly, the early delivering is the abortion; causing or procuring abortion is the full name of the offense. Abbott.

ABORTIVE TRIAL. A term descriptive of the result when a case has gone off, and no verdict has been pronounced, without the fault, contrivance, or management of the parties. Jebb & B. 51.

ABORTUS. Lat. The fruit of an abortion; the child born before its time, incapable of life.

ABOUT. Nearly; approximating to; in the neighborhood of; not much more or less than. An expression constantly used where a time or sum cannot be precisely stated, importing the possibility of a small variation from it.

ABOUTISSEMENT. Fr. An abuttal or abutment. See Guyot, Répert. Univ. "*Aboutissans.*"

ABOVE. (Lat. *super, supra.*) In practice. Higher; superior. The court to which a cause is removed by appeal or writ of error is called the court *above*. Principal; as distinguished from what is auxiliary or instrumental. Bail to the action, or special bail, is otherwise termed bail *above*. 3 Bl. Comm. 291. See BELOW.

ABOVE CITED or MENTIONED. Quoted before. A figurative expression taken from the ancient manner of writing books on scrolls, where whatever is mentioned or cited before in the same roll must be *above*. Encyc. Lond.

ABPATRUUS. Lat. In the civil law. A great-great-grandfather's brother, (*abavi frater.*) Inst. 3, 6, 6; Dig. 38, 10, 3. Called *patruus maximus*. Id. 38, 10, 10, 17. Called, by Bracton and Fleta, *abpatruus magnus*. Bract. fol. 68*b*; Fleta, lib. 6, c. 2, § 17.

ABRIDGE. To reduce or contract; usually spoken of written language.

In copyright law, to abridge means to epitomize; to reduce; to contract. It implies preserving the substance, the essence, of a work, in language suited to such a purpose. In making *extracts* there is no condensation of the author's language, and hence no abridgment. To abridge requires the exercise of the mind; it is not *copying*. Between a compilation and an abridgment there is a clear distinction. A compilation consists of selected extracts from different authors; an abridgment is a condensation of the views of one author. 4 McLean, 306, 310.

In practice. To shorten a declaration or count by taking away or severing some of the substance of it. Brooke, Abr. "Abridgment."

ABRIDGMENT. An epitome or compendium of another and larger work, wherein the principal ideas of the larger work are summarily contained.

Abridgments of the law are brief digests of the law, arranged alphabetically. The oldest are those of Fitzherbert, Brooke, and Rolle; the more modern those of Viner, Comyns, and Bacon. (1 Steph. Comm. 51.) The term "digest" has now supplanted that of "abridgment." Sweet.

ABRIDGMENT OF DAMAGES. The right of the court to reduce the damages in certain cases. *Vide* Brooke, tit. "Abridgment."

ABROGATE. To annul, repeal, or destroy; to annul or repeal an order or rule issued by a subordinate authority; to repeal a former law by legislative act, or by usage.

ABROGATION. The annulment of a law by constitutional authority. It stands opposed to *rogation;* and is distinguished from *derogation*, which implies the taking away only some part of a law; from *subrogation*, which denotes the adding a clause to it; from *dispensation*, which only sets it aside in a particular instance; and from *antiquation*, which is the refusing to pass a law. Encyc. Lond.

ABSCOND. To go in a clandestine manner out of the jurisdiction of the courts, or to lie concealed, in order to avoid their process.

To hide, conceal, or absent oneself clandestinely, with the intent to avoid legal process. 2 Sneed, 153. See, also, 8 Kan. 262; 1 Ala. 200.

ABSCONDING DEBTOR. One who absconds from his creditors.

An absconding debtor is one who lives without the state, or who has intentionally concealed himself from his creditors, or withdrawn himself from the reach of their suits, with intent to frustrate their just demands. Thus, if a person departs from his usual residence, or remains absent therefrom, or conceals himself in his house, so that he cannot be served with process, with intent unlawfully to delay or defraud his creditors, he is an absconding debtor; but if he departs from the state or from his usual abode, with the intention of again returning, and without any fraudulent design, he has not absconded, nor absented himself, within the intendment of the law. 5 Conn. 121.

A party may abscond, and subject himself to the operation of the attachment law against absconding debtors, without leaving the limits of the state. 7 Md. 209.

A debtor who is shut up from his creditors in his own house is an absconding debtor. 2 Root, 133.

ABSENCE. The state of being absent, removed, or away from one's domicile, or usual place of residence.

Absence is of a fivefold kind: (1) A *necessary absence*, as in banished or transported persons; this is entirely necessary. (2) *Necessary and voluntary*, as upon the account of the commonwealth, or in the service of the church. (3) A *probable absence*, according to the civilians, as that of students on the score of study. (4) *Entirely voluntary*, on account of trade, merchandise, and the like. (5) *Absence cum dolo et culpâ*, as not appearing to a writ, *subpœna*, citation, etc., or to delay or defeat creditors, or avoiding arrest, either on civil or criminal process. Ayliffe.

Where the statute allows the vacation of a judgment rendered against a defendant "in his absence," the term "absence" means non-appearance to the action, and not merely that the party was not present in court. 12 Neb. 423, 11 N. W. Rep. 867.

ABSENCE. In Scotch law. Want or default of appearance. A decree is said to be *in absence* where the defender (defendant) does not appear. Ersk. Inst. bk. 4, tit. 3, § 6. See DECREET.

ABSENTE. Lat. (Abl. of *absens.*) Being absent. A common term in the old reports. "The three justices, *absente* North, C. J., were clear of opinion." 2 Mod. 14.

ABSENTEE. One who dwells abroad; a landlord who resides in a country other than that from which he draws his rents. The discussions on the subject have generally had reference to Ireland. McCul. Pol. Econ.; 33 Brit. Quar. Rev. 455.

One who is absent from his usual place of residence or domicile.

In Louisiana law and practice. A person who has resided in the state, and has departed without leaving any one to represent him. Also, a person who never was domiciliated in the state and resides abroad. Civil Code La. art. 3556; 18 La. Ann. 696; 30 La. Ann. 880.

ABSENTEES, or DES ABSENTEES. A parliament so called was held at Dublin, 10th May, 8 Hen. VIII. It is mentioned in letters patent 29 Hen. VIII.

Absentem accipere debemus eum qui non est eo loci in quo petitur. We ought to consider him absent who is not in the place where he is demanded. Dig. 50, 16, 199.

Absentia ejus qui reipublicæ causâ abest, neque ei neque alii damnosa esse debet. The absence of him who is away in behalf of the republic (on business of the state) ought neither to be prejudicial to him nor to another. Dig. 50, 17, 140.

ABSOILE—ASSOILE. To pardon or set free; used with respect to deliverance from excommunication. Cowell; Kelham.

Absoluta sententia expositore non indiget. An absolute sentence or proposition (one that is plain without any scruple, or absolute without any saving) needs not an expositor. 2 Inst. 533.

ABSOLUTE. Unconditional; complete and perfect in itself, without relation to, or dependence on, other things or persons,—as an *absolute* right; without condition, exception, restriction, qualification, or limitation, —as an *absolute* conveyance, an *absolute* estate; final, peremptory,—as an *absolute* rule.

ABSOLUTE CONVEYANCE. A conveyance by which the right or property in a thing is transferred, free of any condition or qualification, by which it might be defeated or changed; as an ordinary deed of lands, in contradistinction to a mortgage, which is a conditional conveyance. Burrill.

ABSOLUTE COVENANT. A covenant which is unconditional or unqualified.

ABSOLUTE ESTATE. An estate in lands not subject to be defeated upon any condition.

In this phrase the word "absolute" is not used legally to distinguish a fee from a life-estate, but a qualified or conditional fee from a fee-simple. 71 Pa. St. 483.

ABSOLUTE INTEREST. That is an absolute interest in property which is so completely vested in the individual that he can by no contingency be deprived of it without his own consent. So, too, he is the owner of such absolute interest who must necessarily sustain the loss if the property is destroyed. The terms "interest" and "title" are not synonymous. A mortgagor in possession, and a purchaser holding under a deed defectively executed, have, both of them, absolute, as well as insurable, interests in the property, though neither of them has the legal title. "Absolute" is here synonymous with "vested," and is used in contradistinction to contingent or conditional. 29 Conn. 20.

ABSOLUTE LAW. The true and proper law of nature, immutable in the abstract or in principle, in theory, but not in application; for very often the object, the reason, situation, and other circumstances, may vary its exercise and obligation. 1 Steph. Comm. 21 et seq.

ABSOLUTE PROPERTY. Absolute property is where a man hath solely and exclusively the right, and also the occupation, of movable chattels; distinguished from a qualified property, as that of a bailee. 2 Bl. Comm. 388; 2 Kent, Comm. 347.

ABSOLUTE RIGHTS. Absolute rights are such as appertain and belong to particular persons merely as individuals or single persons, as distinguished from relative rights, which are incident to them as members of society. 1 Bl. Comm. 123; 1 Chit. Pl. 364; 1 Chit. Pr. 32.

ABSOLUTE RULE. In practice. A rule of court commanding something to be done *absolutely*, and at all events, as distinguished from a rule *nisi*, which commands something to be done, *unless* cause be shown against it; or, as the latter is more commonly called, a rule to *show cause* why a thing should not be done. 3 Steph. Comm. 680.

ABSOLUTE WARRANDICE. In Scotch law. A warranting or assuring of property against all mankind. It is, in effect, a covenant of title.

ABSOLUTELY. Completely; wholly; without qualification; without reference or relation to, or dependence upon, any other person, thing, or event.

ABSOLUTION. In the civil law. A sentence whereby a party accused is declared innocent of the crime laid to his charge.

In canon law. A juridical act whereby the clergy declare that the sins of such as are penitent are remitted.

In French law. The dismissal of an accusation. The term "acquitment" is employed when the accused is declared not guilty and "absolution" when he is recognized as guilty but the act is not punishable by law, or he is exonerated by some defect of intention or will. Merl. Repert.; Bouvier.

ABSOLUTISM. Any system of government, be it a monarchy or democracy, in which one or more persons, or a class, govern absolutely, and at pleasure, without check or restraint from any law, constitutional device, or co-ordinate body.

ABSOLVITOR. In Scotch law. An acquittal; a decree in favor of the defender in any action.

ABSQUE. Without. Occurs in phrases taken from the Latin; such as the following:

ABSQUE ALIQUO INDE REDENDO. (Without rendering anything therefrom.) A grant from the crown reserving no rent. 2 Rolle, Abr. 502.

ABSQUE CONSIDERATIONE CURIÆ. In old practice. Without the consideration of the court; without judgment. Fleta, lib. 2, c. 47, § 13.

ABSQUE HOC. Without this. These are technical words of denial, used in pleading at common law by way of special traverse, to introduce the negative part of the plea, following the affirmative part or inducement.

ABSQUE IMPETITIONE VASTI. Without impeachment of waste; without accountability for waste; without liability to suit for waste. A clause anciently often inserted in leases, (as the equivalent English phrase sometimes is,) signifying that the tenant or lessee shall not be liable to suit, (*impetitio*,) or challenged, or called to account, for committing waste. 2 Bl. Comm. 283; 4 Kent, Comm. 78; Co. Litt. 220*a*; Litt. § 352.

ABSQUE TALI CAUSA. (Lat. without such cause.) Formal words in the now obsolete replication *de injuria*. Steph. Pl. 191.

ABSTENTION. In French law. Keeping an heir from possession; also tacit renunciation of a succession by an heir. Merl. Repert.

ABSTRACT. An abstract is a less quantity containing the virtue and force of a greater quantity. A transcript is generally defined a copy, and is more comprehensive than an abstract. 10 S. C. 283.

ABSTRACT OF A FINE. In old conveyancing. One of the parts of a fine, being an abstract of the writ of covenant, and the concord, naming the parties, the parcels of land, and the agreement. 2 Bl. Comm. 351; Shep. Touch. 3. More commonly called the "note" of the fine. See FINE; CONCORD.

ABSTRACT OF TITLE. A condensed history of the title to land, consisting of a synopsis or summary of the material or operative portion of all the conveyances, of whatever kind or nature, which in any manner affect said land, or any estate or interest therein, together with a statement of all liens, charges, or liabilities to which the same may be subject, and of which it is in any way material for purchasers to be apprised. Warv. Abst. § 2.

An abstract of a judgment or title is not the same as a copy of a judgment or title. An "abstract of a title" is a brief account of all the deeds upon which the title rests; a synopsis of the distinctive portions of the various instruments which constitute the muniments of title. See Prest. Abst.; Whart. Law Dict. (2d Lond. Ed.;) Bouv.

Law Dict. 47. An abstract, ordinarily, means a mere brief, and not a copy of that from which it is taken. 7 W. Va. 413.

Abundans cautela non nocet. Extreme caution does no harm. 11 Coke, 6*b*. This principle is generally applied to the construction of instruments in which superfluous words have been inserted more clearly to express the intention.

ABUSE, *v.* To make excessive or improper use of a thing, or to employ it in a manner contrary to the natural or legal rules for its use; to make an extravagant or excessive use, as to abuse one's authority.

In the civil law, the borrower of a chattel which, in its nature, cannot be used without consuming it, such as wine or grain, is said to abuse the thing borrowed if he uses it.

ABUSE, *n.* Everything which is contrary to good order established by usage. Merl. Repert. Departure from use; immoderate or improper use.

The "abuse or misuse" of its franchises by a corporation signifies any positive act in violation of the charter and in derogation of public right, willfully done, or caused to be done, by those appointed to manage the general concerns of the corporation. 3 Pittsb. R. 20; 26 Pa. St. 318.

Abuse of judicial discretion, and especially gross and palpable abuse of discretion, which are the terms ordinarily employed to justify an interference with the exercise of discretionary power, implies not merely error of judgment, but perversity of will, passion, prejudice, partiality, or moral delinquency. The exercise of an honest judgment, however erroneous it may appear to be, is not an abuse of discretion. 29 N. Y. 431.

ABUSE OF A FEMALE CHILD. An injury to the genital organs in an attempt at carnal knowledge, falling short of actual penetration. 58 Ala. 376.

ABUSE OF DISTRESS. The using an animal or chattel distrained, which makes the distrainer liable as for a conversion.

ABUSE OF PROCESS. There is said to be an abuse of process when an adversary, through the malicious and unfounded use of some regular legal proceeding, obtains some advantage over his opponent. Wharton.

A malicious abuse of legal process is where the party employs it for some unlawful object, not the purpose which it is intended by the law to effect; in other words, a perversion of it. 64 Pa. St. 285.

ABUT. To reach, to touch. In old law, the ends were said to abut, the sides to adjoin. Cro. Jac. 184.

ABUTMENTS. The ends of a bridge, or those parts of it which touch the land.

ABUTTALS. (From *abut,* q. v.) Commonly defined "the buttings and boundings of lands, east, west, north, and south, showing on what other lands, highways, or places they *abut,* or are limited and bounded." Cowell; Toml.

AC ETIAM. (Lat. And also.) Words used to introduce the statement of the real cause of action, in those cases where it was necessary to allege a fictitious cause of action to give the court jurisdiction, and also the real cause, in compliance with the statutes.

AC SI. (Lat. As if.) Townsh. Pl. 23, 27. These words frequently occur in old English statutes. Lord Bacon expounds their meaning in the statute of uses: "The statute gives entry, not *simpliciter,* but with an *ac si.*" Bac. Read. Uses, Works, iv. 195.

ACADEMY. In its original meaning, an association formed for mutual improvement, or for the advancement of science or art; in later use, a species of educational institution, of a grade between the common school and the college.

ACAPTE. In French feudal law. A species of relief; a seignorial right due on every change of a tenant. A feudal right which formerly prevailed in Languedoc and Guyenne, being attached to that species of heritable estates which were granted on the contract of *emphyteusis.* Guyot, Inst. Feod. c. 5, § 12.

ACCEDAS AD CURIAM. An original writ out of chancery, directed to the sheriff, for the removal of a replevin suit from a hundred court or court baron to one of the superior courts. See Fitzh. Nat. Brev. 18; 3 Bl. Comm. 34; 1 Tidd, Pr. 38.

ACCEDAS AD VICE COMITEM. L. Lat. (You go to the sheriff.) A writ formerly directed to the coroners of a county in England, commanding them to go to the sheriff, where the latter had suppressed and neglected to return a writ of *pone,* and to deliver a writ to him requiring him to return it. Reg. Orig. 83. See PONE.

ACCELERATION. The shortening of the time for the vesting in possession of an expectant interest.

ACCEPT. To receive with approval or satisfaction; to receive with intent to retain. Also, in the capacity of drawee of a bill, to recognize the draft, and engage to pay it when due.

ACCEPTANCE. The taking and receiving of anything in good part, and as it were a tacit agreement to a preceding act, which might have been defeated or avoided if such acceptance had not been made. Brooke, Abr.

The act of a person to whom a thing is offered or tendered by another, whereby he receives the thing with the intention of retaining it, such intention being evidenced by a sufficient act.

The acceptance of goods sold under a contract which would be void by the statute of frauds without delivery and acceptance involves something more than the act of the vendor in the delivery. It requires that the vendee should also act, and that his act should be of such a nature as to indicate that he receives and accepts the goods delivered as his property. He must receive and retain the articles delivered, intending thereby to assume the title to them, to constitute the acceptance mentioned in the statute. 40 N. Y. 524. See, also, 10 Metc. 132.

In marine insurance, the acceptance of an abandonment by the underwriter is his assent, either express or to be implied from the surrounding circumstances, to the sufficiency and regularity of the abandonment. Its effect is to perfect the insured's right of action as for a total loss, if the cause of loss and circumstances have been truly disclosed. Rap. & Law.

Acceptance of a bill of exchange. In mercantile law. The act by which the person on whom a bill of exchange is drawn (called the "drawee") assents to the request of the drawer to pay it, or, in other words, engages, or makes himself liable, to pay it when due. 4 East, 57, 72; 2 Bl. Comm. 469. It may be by parol or in writing, and either general or special, absolute or conditional; and it may be impliedly, as well as expressly, given. 3 Kent, Comm. 83, 85; Story, Bills, §§ 238, 251. But the usual and regular mode of acceptance is by the drawee's writing across the face of the bill the word "acceptance," and subscribing his name; after which he is termed the *acceptor*. Id. § 243.

The following are the principal varieties of acceptances:

Absolute. An express and positive agreement to pay the bill according to its tenor.

Conditional. An engagement to pay the bill on the happening of a condition.

Express. An absolute acceptance.

Implied. An acceptance inferred by law from the acts or conduct of the drawee.

Partial. An acceptance varying from the tenor of the bill.

Qualified. One either conditional or partial, and which introduces a variation in the sum, time, mode, or place of payment.

Special. One which specifies a particular place for payment.

Supra protest. An acceptance by a third person, after protest of the bill for non-acceptance by the drawee, to save the honor of the drawer or some particular indorser.

ACCEPTANCE AU BESOIN. Fr. In French law. Acceptance in case of need; an acceptance by one on whom a bill is drawn *au besoin*, that is, in case of refusal or failure of the drawee to accept. Story, Bills, §§ 65, 254, 255.

ACCEPTARE. Lat. In old pleading. To accept. *Acceptavit*, he accepted. 2 Strange, 817. *Non acceptavit*, he did not accept. 4 Man. & G. 7.

In the civil law. To accept; to assent; to assent to a promise made by another. Gro. de J. B. lib. 2, c. 11, § 14.

ACCEPTEUR PAR INTERVENTION. In French law. Acceptor of a bill for honor.

ACCEPTILATION. In the civil and Scotch law. A release made by a creditor to his debtor of his debt, without receiving any consideration. Ayl. Pand. tit. 26, p. 570. It is a species of donation, but not subject to the forms of the latter, and is valid unless in fraud of creditors. Merl. Repert.

The verbal extinction of a verbal contract, with a declaration that the debt has been paid when it has not; or the acceptance of something merely imaginary in satisfaction of a verbal contract. Sanders' Just. Inst. (5th Ed.) 386.

ACCEPTOR. The person who accepts a bill of exchange, (generally the drawee,) or who engages to be primarily responsible for its payment.

ACCEPTOR SUPRA PROTEST. One who accepts a bill which has been protested, for the honor of the drawer or any one of the indorsers.

ACCESS. Approach; or the means, power, or opportunity of approaching. Sometimes importing the occurrence of sexual intercourse; otherwise as importing opportunity of communication for that purpose as between husband and wife.

In real property law, the term "access" denotes the right vested in the owner of land which adjoins a road or other highway to go and return from his own land to the highway without obstruction.

ACCESSARY. In criminal law. Contributing to or aiding in the commission of a crime. One who, without being present at the commission of a felonious offense, becomes guilty of such offense, not as a chief actor, but as a participator, as by command, advice, instigation, or concealment; either before or after the fact or commission; a *particeps criminis*. 4 Bl. Comm. 35; Cowell.

An accessary is one who is not the chief actor in the offense, nor present at its performance, but in some way concerned therein, either *before* or *after* the act committed. Code Ga. 1882, § 4306.

ACCESSARY AFTER THE FACT. An accessary after the fact is a person who, having full knowledge that a crime has been committed, conceals it from the magistrate, and harbors, assists, or protects the person charged with, or convicted of, the crime. Code Ga. 1882, § 4308.

All persons who, after the commission of any felony, conceal or aid the offender, with knowledge that he has committed a felony, and with intent that he may avoid or escape from arrest, trial, conviction, or punishment, are accessaries. Pen. Code Dak. § 28.

All persons who, after full knowledge that a felony has been committed, conceal it from the magistrate, or harbor and protect the person charged with or convicted thereof, are accessaries. Pen. Code Cal. § 32.

An accessary *after the fact* is a person who, knowing a felony to have been committed by another, receives, relieves, comforts or assists the felon, in order to enable him to escape from punishment, or the like. 1 Russ. Crimes, 171; Steph. 27; 39 Miss. 702.

ACCESSARY BEFORE THE FACT. In criminal law. One who, being absent at the time a crime is committed, yet procures, counsels, or commands another to commit it; and, in this case, absence is necessary to constitute him an accessary, for, if he be present at any time during the transaction, he is guilty of the crime as principal. Plow. 97. 1 Hale, P. C. 615, 616; 4 Steph. Comm. 90, note *n*.

An accessary before the fact is one who, being absent at the time of the crime committed, doth yet procure, counsel, or command another to commit a crime. Code Ga. 1882, § 4307.

ACCESSARY TO ADULTERY. A phrase used in the law of divorce, and derived from the criminal law. It implies more than connivance, which is merely knowledge with consent. A conniver abstains from interference; an accessary directly commands, advises, or procures the adultery. A husband or wife who has been accessary to the adultery of the other party to the marriage cannot obtain a divorce on the ground of such adultery. 20 & 21 Vict. c. 85, §§ 29, 31. See Browne, Div.

ACCESSIO. In Roman law. An increase or addition; that which lies next to a thing, and is supplementary and necessary to the principal thing; that which arises or is produced from the principal thing. Calvin. Lex. Jurid.

One of the modes of acquiring property, being the extension of ownership over that which grows from, or is united to, an article which one already possesses.

ACCESSION. The right to all which one's own property produces, whether that property be movable or immovable; and the right to that which is united to it by accession, either naturally or artificially. 2 Kent, 360; 2 Bl. Comm. 404.

A principle derived from the civil law, by which the owner of property becomes entitled to all which it produces, and to all that is added or united to it, either naturally or artificially, (that is, by the labor or skill of another,) even where such addition extends to a change of form or materials; and by which, on the other hand, the possessor of property becomes entitled to it, as against the original owner, where the addition made to it by his skill and labor is of greater value than the property itself, or where the change effected in its form is so great as to render it impossible to restore it to its original shape. Burrill.

In international law. The absolute or conditional acceptance by one or several states of a treaty already concluded between other sovereignties. Merl. Repert. Also the commencement or inauguration of a sovereign's reign.

ACCESSION, DEED OF. In Scotch law. A deed executed by the creditors of a bankrupt or insolvent debtor, by which they approve of a trust given by their debtor for the general behoof, and bind themselves to concur in the plans proposed for extricating his affairs. Bell, Dict.

Accessorium non ducit, sed sequitur suum principale. Co. Litt. 152. That which is the accessory or incident does not lead, but follows, its principal.

Accessorius sequitur naturam sui principalis. An accessary follows the nature of his principal. 3 Inst. 139. One who is accessary to a crime cannot be guilty of a higher degree of crime than his principal.

ACCESSORY. Anything which is joined to another thing as an ornament, or to render it more perfect, or which accompanies it, or is connected with it as an incident, or as subordinate to it, or which belongs to or with it.

In criminal law. An accessary. The latter spelling is preferred. See that title.

ACCESSORY ACTION. In Scotch practice. An action which is subservient or auxiliary to another. Of this kind are actions of "proving the tenor," by which lost deeds are restored; and actions of "transumpts," by which copies of principal deeds are certified. Bell, Dict.

ACCESSORY CONTRACT. In the civil law. A contract which is incident or auxiliary to another or principal contract; such as the engagement of a surety. Poth. Obl. pt. 1, c. 1, § 1, art. 2.

A principal contract is one entered into by both parties on their own accounts, or in the several qualities they assume. An accessory contract is made for assuring the performance of a prior contract, either by the same parties or by others; such as suretyship, mortgage, and pledge. Civil Code La. art. 1771.

ACCESSORY OBLIGATION. In the civil law. An obligation which is incident to another or principal obligation; the obligation of a surety. Poth. Obl. pt. 2, c. 1, § 6.

In Scotch law. Obligations to antecedent or primary obligations, such as obligations to pay interest, etc. Ersk. Inst. lib. 3, tit. 3, § 60.

ACCIDENT. An unforeseen event, occurring without the will or design of the person whose mere act causes it; an unexpected, unusual, or undesigned occurrence; the effect of an unknown cause, or, the cause being known, an unprecedented consequence of it; a casualty.

There is nothing in the definition of the word "accident" that excludes the negligence of the injured party as one of the elements contributing to produce the result. A very large proportion of those events which are universally called "accidents" happen through some carelessness of the party injured, which contributes to produce them. Thus, men are injured by the careless use of fire-arms, of explosive substances, of machinery, the careless management of horses, and in a thousand ways, where it can readily be seen afterwards that a little greater care on their part would have prevented it. Yet such injuries, having been unexpected, and not caused intentionally or by design, are always called "accidents," and properly so. 24 Wis. 28.

In equity practice. Such an unforeseen event, misfortune, loss, act, or omission as is not the result of any negligence or misconduct in the party. Fran. Max. 87; Story, Eq. Jur. § 78.

The meaning to be attached to the word "accident," in relation to equitable relief, is any unforeseen and undesigned event, productive of disadvantage. Wharton.

An accident relievable in equity is such an occurrence, not the result of negligence or misconduct of the party seeking relief in relation to a contract, as was not anticipated by the parties when the same was entered into, and which gives an undue advantage to one of them over another in a court of law. Code Ga. 1882, § 3112.

Accipere quid ut justitiam facias, non est tam accipere quam extorquere. To accept anything as a reward for doing justice is rather extorting than accepting. Lofft, 72.

ACCIPITARE. To pay relief to lords of manors. *Capitali domino accipitare, i. e.*, to pay a relief, homage, or obedience to the chief lord on becoming his vassal. Fleta, lib. 2, c. 50.

ACCOLA. In the civil law. One who inhabits or occupies land near a place, as one who dwells by a river, or on the bank of a river. Dig. 43, 13, 3, 6.

In feudal law. A husbandman; an agricultural tenant; a tenant of a manor. Spelman. A name given to a class of villeins in Italy. Barr. St. 302.

ACCOMENDA. In maritime law. A contract between the owner of goods and the master of a ship, by which the former intrusts the property to the latter to be sold by him on their joint account.

In such case, two contracts take place: First, the contract called *mandatum*, by which the owner of the property gives the master power to dispose of it; and the contract of partnership, in virtue of which the profits are to be divided between them. One party runs the risk of losing his capital; the other, his labor. If the sale produces no more than first cost, the owner takes all the proceeds. It is only the profits which are to be divided. Emerig. Mar. Loans, § 5.

ACCOMMODATION. An arrangement or engagement made as a favor to another, not upon a consideration received; something done to oblige, usually spoken of a loan of money or commercial paper; also a friendly agreement or composition of differences. Abbott.

ACCOMMODATION LANDS. Land bought by a builder or speculator, who erects houses thereon, and then leases portions thereof upon an improved ground-rent.

ACCOMMODATION PAPER. An accommodation bill or note is one to which the accommodating party, be he acceptor, drawer, or indorser, has put his name, without consideration, for the purpose of benefiting or accommodating some other party who desires to raise money on it, and is to provide for the bill when due.

ACCOMMODATION WORKS. Works which a railway company is required to make and maintain for the accommodation of the owners or occupiers of land adjoining the railway, *e. g.*, gates, bridges, culverts, fences, etc. 8 Vict. c. 20, § 68.

ACCOMPLICE. (From *ad*, to, and *complicare*, to fold up, or wrap together.) In criminal law. One who is joined or united with another; one of several concerned in a felony; an associate in a crime; one who cooperates, aids, or assists in committing it. Tomlins; Jacob. This term includes all the *participes criminis*, whether considered in strict legal propriety as principals or as accessaries. 1 Russ. Crimes, 26. It is generally applied to those who are admitted to give evidence against their fellow criminals. 4 Bl. Comm. 331; Hawk. P. C. bk. 2, c. 37, § 7.

One who is in some way concerned in the commission of a crime, though not as a principal; and this includes all persons who have been concerned in its commission, whether they are considered, in strict legal propriety, as principals in the first or second degree, or merely as accessaries before or after the fact. 47 Ill. 152; 71 Cal. 20, 11 Pac. Rep. 799.

ACCORD, *v.* In practice. To agree or concur, as one judge with another. "I accord." Eyre, C. J., 12 Mod. 7. "The rest accorded." 7 Mod. 361.

ACCORD, *n.* A satisfaction agreed upon between the party injuring and the party injured which, when performed, is a bar to all actions upon this account. 75 N. Y. 576.

ACCORD AND SATISFACTION. An agreement between two persons, one of whom has a right of action against the other, that the latter should do or give, and the former accept, something in satisfaction of the right of action different from, and usually less than, what might be legally enforced. When the agreement is executed, and satisfaction has been made, it is called "accord and satisfaction."

An accord and satisfaction may be briefly defined as "the settlement of a dispute or the satisfaction of a claim, by an executed agreement between the party injuring and the party injured;" or, to give a definition indicating more definitely its peculiar nature, it is "something of legal value to which the creditor before had no right, received in full satisfaction of the debt, without regard to the magnitude of the satisfaction." 1 Smith, Lead. Cas. (10th Amer. Ed.,) 558; 43 Conn. 462.

Accord and satisfaction is the substitution of another agreement between the parties in satisfaction of the former one, and an execution of the latter agreement. Such is the definition of this sort of defense, usually given. But a broader application of the doctrine has been made in later times, where one promise or agreement is set up in satisfaction of another. The rule is that an agreement or promise of the same grade will not be held to be in satisfaction of a prior one, unless it has been expressly accepted as such; as, where a new promissory note has been given in lieu of a former one, to have the effect of a satisfaction of the former, it must have been accepted on an express agreement to that effect. 50 Miss. 257.

An accord is an agreement to accept, in extinction of an obligation, something different from or less than that to which the person agreeing to accept is entitled. Civil Code Cal. § 1521; Civil Code Dak. § 859.

ACCORDANT. Fr. and Eng. Agreeing; concurring. "Baron Parker, *accordant*," Hardr. 93; "Holt, C. J., *accordant*," 6 Mod. 299; "Powys, J., *accord*," "Powell, J., *accord*," Id. 298.

ACCOUCHEMENT. The act of a woman in giving birth to a child. The fact of the accouchement, proved by a person who was present, is often important evidence in proving the parentage of a person.

ACCOUNT. A detailed statement of the mutual demands in the nature of debt and credit between parties, arising out of contracts or some fiduciary relation. 1 Metc. (Mass.) 216; 1 Hemp. 114; 32 Pa. St. 202.

A statement in writing, of debts and credits, or of receipts and payments; a list of items of debts and credits, with their respective dates. 5 Cow. 593.

The word is sometimes used to denote the balance, or the right of action for the balance, appearing due upon a statement of dealings; as where one speaks of an assignment of accounts; but there is a broad distinction between an account and the mere balance of an account, resembling the distinction in logic between the premises of an argument and the conclusions drawn therefrom. A balance is but the conclusion or result of the debit and credit sides of an account. It implies mutual dealings, and the existence of debt and credit, without which there could be no balance. 45 Mo. 574.

The word is often used in the sense of "behalf," or "charge;" as in saying that an agent acts upon account of his principal; that a policy is issued on account of whom it may concern. Abbott.

ACCOUNT. In practice. A writ or action at common law, (sometimes called "account render,") which lies against a person who, by reason of his office or business as bailiff, receiver, or guardian, ought to render an account to another, but refuses to do so. Fitzh. Nat. Brev. 116; Co. Litt. 172.

Account is a writ or action brought against a person who, by means of his office as a guardian, or for some business he has undertaken as an agent, or some money he has received for another, ought to render an account to him, and refuses to do it; and he that calls him to an account shall recover of him not only what shall be found due, but also damages for the wrong done him. 1 Amer. & Eng. Enc. Law, 128.

ACCOUNT-BOOK. A book kept by a merchant, trader, mechanic, or other person, in which are entered from time to time the transactions of his trade or business. Such books, when regularly kept, may be admitted in evidence. Greenl. Ev. §§ 115-118.

ACCOUNT CURRENT. An open or running or unsettled account between two parties.

ACCOUNT DUTIES. Duties payable by the English customs and inland revenue act, 1881, (44 Vict. c. 12, § 38,) on a *donatio mortis causa,* or on any gift, the donor of which dies within three months after making it, or on joint property voluntarily so created, and taken by survivorship, or on property taken under a voluntary settlement in which the settlor had a life-interest.

ACCOUNT RENDERED. An account made out by the creditor, and presented to the debtor for his examination and acceptance. When accepted, it becomes an account stated.

ACCOUNT STATED. The settlement of an account between the parties, with a balance struck in favor of one of them; an account rendered by the creditor, and by the debtor assented to as correct, either expressly, or by implication of law from the failure to object.

This was also a common count in a declaration upon a contract under which the plaintiff might prove an absolute acknowledgment by the defendant of a liquidated demand of a fixed amount, which implies a promise to pay on request. It might be joined with any other count for a money demand. The acknowledgment or admission must have been made to the plaintiff or his agent. Wharton.

ACCOUNTABLE. Subject to pay; responsible; liable. Where one indorsed a note "A. C. accountable," it was held that, under this form of indorsement, he had waived demand and notice. 42 N. H. 74.

ACCOUNTABLE RECEIPT. An instrument acknowledging the receipt of money or personal property, coupled with an obligation to account for or pay or deliver the whole or some part of it to some person. 27 Minn. 315, 7 N. W. Rep. 262.

ACCOUNTANT. One who keeps accounts; a person skilled in keeping books or accounts; an expert in accounts or bookkeeping.

A person who renders an account. When an executor, guardian, etc., renders an account of the property in his hands and his administration of the trust, either to the beneficiary or to a court, he is styled, for the purpose of that proceeding, the "accountant."

ACCOUNTANT GENERAL, or ACCOMPTANT GENERAL. An officer of the court of chancery, appointed by act of parliament to receive all money lodged in court, and to place the same in the Bank of England for security. 12 Geo. I. c. 32; 1 Geo. IV. c. 35; 15 & 16 Vict. c. 87, §§ 18-22, 39. See Daniell, Ch. Pr. (4th Ed.) 1607 et seq. The office, however, has been abolished by 35 & 36 Vict. c. 44, and the duties transferred to her majesty's paymaster general.

ACCOUNTING. The making up and rendition of an account, either voluntarily or by order of a court.

ACCOUPLE. To unite; to marry. *Ne unques accouple*, never married.

ACCREDIT. In international law. (1) To receive as an envoy in his public character, and give him credit and rank accordingly. Burke. (2) To send with credentials as an envoy. Webst. Dict.

ACCREDULITARE. L. Lat. In old records. To purge an offense by oath. Blount; Whishaw.

ACCRESCERE. In the civil and old English law. To grow to; to pass to, and become united with, as soil to land *per alluvionem*. Dig. 41, 1, 30, pr.

ACCRETION. The act of growing to a thing; usually applied to the gradual and imperceptible accumulation of land by natural causes, as out of the sea or a river. Accretion of land is of two kinds: By *alluvion*, *i. e.*, by the washing up of sand or soil, so as to form firm ground; or by *dereliction*, as when the sea shrinks below the usual watermark.

The increase of real estate by the addition of portions of soil, by gradual deposition through the operation of natural causes, to that already in possession of the owner. 2 Washb. Real Prop. 451.

ACCROACH. To encroach; to exercise power without due authority.

To attempt to exercise royal power. 4 Bl. Comm. 76. A knight who forcibly assaulted and detained one of the king's subjects till he paid him a sum of money was held to have committed treason, on the ground of accroachment. 1 Hale, P. C. 80.

ACCROCHER. Fr. In French law. To delay; retard; put off. *Accrocher un procès*, to stay the proceedings in a suit.

ACCRUE. To grow to; to be added to; to attach itself to; as a subordinate or accessory claim or demand arises out of, and is joined to, its principal; thus, costs accrue to a judgment, and interest to the principal debt.

The term is also used of independent or original demands, and then means to arise, to happen, to come into force or existence; as in the phrase, "The right of action did not *accrue* within six years."

ACCRUER, CLAUSE OF. An express clause, frequently occurring in the case of gifts by deed or will to persons as tenants in common, providing that upon the death of one or more of the beneficiaries his or their shares shall go to the survivor or survivors. Brown. The share of the decedent is then said to *accrue* to the others.

ACCRUING. Inchoate; in process of maturing. That which will or may, at a future time, ripen into a vested right, an available demand, or an existing cause of action. 13 Ohio St. 382.

ACCRUING COSTS. Costs and expenses incurred after judgment.

ACCUMULATED SURPLUS. In statutes relative to the taxation of corporations, this term refers to the fund which the company has in excess of its capital and liabilities. 34 N. J. Law, 493; 35 N. J. Law, 577.

ACCUMULATIONS. When an executor or other trustee masses the rents, dividends, and other income which he receives, treats it as a capital, invests it, makes a new capital of the income derived therefrom, invests that, and so on, he is said to accumulate the fund, and the capital and accrued income thus procured constitute *accumulations*.

ACCUMULATIVE. That which accumulates, or is heaped up; additional. Said of several things heaped together, or of one thing added to another.

ACCUMULATIVE JUDGMENT. Where a person has already been convicted and sentenced, and a second or additional judgment is passed against him, the execution of which is postponed until the completion of the first sentence, such second judgment is said to be *accumulative*.

ACCUMULATIVE LEGACY. A second, double, or additional legacy; a legacy given in addition to another given by the same instrument, or by another instrument.

Accusare nemo se debet, nisi coram Deo. No one is bound to accuse himself, except before God. See Hardres, 139.

ACCUSATION. A formal charge against a person, to the effect that he is guilty of a punishable offense, laid before a court or magistrate having jurisdiction to inquire into the alleged crime.

Accusator post rationabile tempus non est audiendus, nisi se bene de omissione excusaverit. Moore, 817. An accuser ought not to be heard after the expiration of a reasonable time, unless he can account satisfactorily for the delay.

ACCUSE. To bring a formal charge of crime against a person, before a competent court or officer. 30 Mich. 468. See 5 Rich. 492.

ACCUSED. The person against whom an accusation is made.

"Accused" is the generic name for the defendant in a criminal case, and is more appropriate than either "prisoner" or "defendant." 1 Car. & K. 131.

ACCUSER. The person by whom an accusation is made.

ACEPHALI. The levelers in the reign of Hen. I., who acknowledged no head or superior. Leges H. 1; Cowell. Also certain ancient heretics, who appeared about the beginning of the sixth century, and asserted that there was but one substance in Christ, and one nature. Wharton.

ACEQUIA. In Mexican law. A ditch, channel, or canal, through which water, diverted from its natural course, is conducted, for use in irrigation or other purposes.

ACHAT. Fr. A purchase or bargain. Cowell.

ACHERSET. In old English law. A measure of corn, conjectured to have been the same with our quarter, or eight bushels. Cowell.

ACKNOWLEDGE. To own, avow, or admit; to confess; to recognize one's acts, and assume the responsibility therefor.

ACKNOWLEDGMENT. In conveyancing. The act by which a party who has executed an instrument of conveyance as grantor goes before a competent officer or court, and declares or acknowledges the same as his genuine and voluntary act and deed. The certificate of the officer on such instrument that it has been so acknowledged.

The term is also used of the act of a person who avows or admits the truth of certain facts which, if established, will entail a civil liability upon him. Thus, the debtor's *acknowledgment* of the creditor's demand or right of action will toll the statute of limitations. *Admission* is also used in this sense. To denote an avowal of criminal acts, or the concession of the truth of a criminal charge, the word "confession" seems more appropriate.

ACKNOWLEDGMENT MONEY. A sum paid in some parts of England by copyhold tenants on the death of their lords, as a recognition of their new lords, in like manner as money is usually paid on the attornment of tenants. Cowell.

ACOLYTE. An inferior ministrant or servant in the ceremonies of the church, whose duties are to follow and wait upon the priests and deacons, etc.

ACQUEST. An estate acquired newly, or by purchase. 1 Reeve, Eng. Law, 56.

ACQUETS. In the civil law. Property which has been acquired by purchase, gift, or otherwise than by succession. Immovable property which has been acquired otherwise than by succession. Merl. Repert.

Profits or gains of property, as between husband and wife. Civil Code La. § 2369.

ACQUIESCE. To give an implied consent to a transaction, to the accrual of a right, or to any act, by one's mere silence, or without express assent or acknowledgment.

ACQUIESCENCE. Acquiescence is where a person who knows that he is entitled to impeach a transaction or enforce a right neglects to do so for such a length of time that, under the circumstances of the case, the other party may fairly infer that he has waived or abandoned his right. Sweet.

ACQUIETANDIS PLEGIIS. A writ of justices, formerly lying for the surety against a creditor who refuses to acquit him after the debt has been satisfied. Reg. Writs, 158; Cowell; Blount.

ACQUIRE. In the law of contracts and of descents; to become the owner of property; to make property one's own.

ACQUIRED. Coming to an intestate in any other way than by gift, devise, or descent from a parent or the ancestor of a parent. 2 Lea, 54.

ACQUISITION. The act of becoming the owner of certain property; the act by which one acquires or procures the property in anything. Used also of the thing acquired.

Original acquisition is where the title to the thing accrues through occupancy or accession, (*q. v.*,) or by the creative labor of the individual, as in the case of patents and copyrights.

Derivative acquisition is where property in a thing passes from one person to another. It may transpire by the act of the law, as in cases of forfeiture, insolvency, intestacy, judgment, marriage, or succession, or by the act of the parties, as in cases of gift, sale, or exchange.

ACQUIT. To release, absolve, or discharge one from an obligation or a liability; or to legally certify the innocence of one charged with crime.

ACQUIT À CAUTION. In French law. Certain goods pay higher export duties when exported to a foreign country than when they are destined for another French port. In order to prevent fraud, the administration compels the shipper of goods sent from one French port to another to give security that such goods shall not be sent to a foreign country. The certificate which proves the receipt of the security is called "*acquit à caution.*" Argles, Fr. Merc. Law, 543.

ACQUITTAL. In contracts. A release, absolution, or discharge from an obligation, liability, or engagement.

In criminal practice. The legal and formal certification of the innocence of a person who has been charged with crime; a deliverance or setting free a person from a charge of guilt.

The absolution of a party accused on a trial before a traverse jury. 1 Nott & McC. 36; 3 McCord, 461.

Acquittals in fact are those which take place when the jury, upon trial, finds a verdict of not guilty.

Acquittals in law are those which take place by mere operation of law; as where a man has been charged merely as an accessary, and the principal has been acquitted. 2 Co. Inst. 364.

In feudal law. The obligation on the part of a mesne lord to protect his tenant from any claims, entries, or molestations by lords paramount arising out of the services due to them by the mesne lord. See Co. Litt. 100*a*.

ACQUITTANCE. In contracts. A written discharge, whereby one is freed from an obligation to pay money or perform a duty. It differs from a *release* in not requiring to be under seal.

This word, though perhaps not strictly speaking synonymous with "receipt," includes it. A receipt is one form of an acquittance; a discharge is another. A receipt in full is an acquittance, and a receipt for a part of a demand or obligation is an acquittance *pro tanto*. 51 Vt. 104.

ACQUITTED. Released; absolved; purged of an accusation; judicially discharged from accusation; released from debt, etc. Includes both civil and criminal prosecutions. 26 Wend. 383, 399.

ACRE. A quantity of land containing 160 square rods of land, in whatever shape. Serg. Land Laws Pa. 185; Cro. Eliz. 476, 665; 6 Coke, 67; Poph. 55; Co. Litt. 5*b*.

Originally the word "acre" (*acer*, *aker*, or Sax. *æcer*) was not used as a measure of land, or to signify any determinate quantity of land, but to denote any open ground, (*latum quantumvis agrum*,) wide champaign, or field; which is still the meaning of the German *acker*, derived probably from the same source, and is preserved in the names of some places in England, as Castle Acre, South Acre, etc. Burrill.

ACREFIGHT, or ACRE. A camp or field fight; a sort of duel, or judicial combat, anciently fought by single combatants, English and Scotch, between the frontiers of the two kingdoms with sword and lance. Called "campfight," and the combatants "champions," from the open *field* that was the stage of trial. Cowell.

ACROSS. Under a grant of a right of way *across* the plaintiff's lot of land, the grantee has not a right to enter at one place, go partly across, and then come out at another place on the same side of the lot. 5 Pick. 163. See 10 Me. 391.

ACT, *n*. In its most general sense, this noun signifies something done voluntarily by a person; the exercise of an individual's power; an effect produced in the external world by an exercise of the power of a person objectively, prompted by intention, and proximately caused by a motion of the will. In a more technical sense, it means something done voluntarily by a person, and of such a nature that certain legal consequences attach to it. Thus a grantor acknowledges the conveyance to be his "*act* and deed," the terms being synonymous.

In the civil law. An *act* is a writing which states in a legal form that a thing has been said, done, or agreed. Merl. Repert.

In practice. Anything done by a court and reduced to writing; a decree, judgment, resolve, rule, order, or other judicial proceeding. In Scotch law, the orders and decrees of a court, and in French and German law, all the records and documents in an action, are called "acts."

In legislation. A written law, formally ordained or passed by the legislative power of a state, called in England an "act of parliament," and in the United States an "act of congress," or of the "legislature;" a statute.

Acts are either public or private. Public acts (also called general acts, or general statutes, or statutes at large) are those which relate to the community generally, or establish a universal rule for the governance of the whole body politic.

Private acts (formerly called special, Co. Litt. 126*a*) are those which relate either to particular persons (personal acts) or to particular places, (local acts,) or which operate only upon specified individuals or their private concerns.

In Scotch practice. An abbreviation of *actor*, (proctor or advocate, especially for a plaintiff or pursuer,) used in records. "*Act*. A. *Alt*. B." an abbreviation of *Actor*, A. *Alter*, B.; that is, for the pursuer or plaintiff, A., for the defender, B. 1 Broun, 336, note.

ACT, *v*. In Scotch practice. To do or perform judicially; to enter of record. Surety "acted in the Books of Adjournal." 1 Broun, 4.

ACT BOOK. In Scotch practice. The minute book of a court. 1 Swin. 81.

ACT IN PAIS. An act done or performed out of court, and not a matter of record.

A deed or an assurance transacted between two or more private persons in the country, that is, according to the old common law, upon the very spot to be transferred, is matter *in pais*. 2 Bl. Comm. 294.

ACT OF ATTAINDER. A legislative act, attainting a person. See ATTAINDER.

ACT OF BANKRUPTCY. Any act which renders a person liable to be proceeded against as a bankrupt, or for which he may be adjudged bankrupt. These acts are usually defined and classified in statutes on the subject.

ACT OF CURATORY. In Scotch law. The act extracted by the clerk, upon any one's acceptance of being curator. Forb. Inst. pt. 1, b. 1, c. 2, tit. 2. 2 Kames, Eq. 291. Corresponding with the order for the appointment of a guardian, in English and American practice.

ACT OF GOD. Inevitable accident; *vis major*. Any misadventure or casualty is said to be caused by the "act of God" when it happens by the direct, immediate, and exclusive operation of the forces of nature, uncontrolled or uninfluenced by the power of man and without human intervention, and is of such a character that it could not have been prevented or escaped from by any amount of foresight or prudence, or by any reasonable degree of care or diligence, or by the aid of any appliances which the situation of the party might reasonably require him to use.

Inevitable accident, or casualty; any accident produced by any physical cause which is irresistible, such as lightning, tempests, perils of the seas, an inundation, or earthquake; and also the sudden illness or death of persons. Story, Bailm. § 25; 2 Bl. Comm. 122; Broom, Max. 108.

Under the term "act of God" are comprehended all misfortunes and accidents arising from inevitable necessity, which human prudence could not foresee or prevent. 1 Conn. 491.

ACT OF GRACE. In Scotch law. A term applied to the act of 1696, c. 32, by which it was provided that where a person imprisoned for a civil debt is so poor that he cannot aliment [maintain] himself, and will make oath to that effect, it shall be in the power of the magistrates to cause the creditor by whom he is incarcerated to provide an aliment for him, or consent to his liberation; which, if the creditor delay to do for 10 days, the magistrate is authorized to set the debtor at liberty. Bell.

The term is often used to designate a general act of parliament, originating with the crown, such as has often been passed at the commencement of a new reign, or at the close of a period of civil troubles, declaring pardon or amnesty to numerous offenders. Abbott.

ACT OF HONOR. When a bill has been protested, and a third person wishes to take it up, or accept it, for honor of one or more of the parties, the notary draws up an instrument, evidencing the transaction, called by this name.

ACT OF INDEMNITY. A statute by which those who have committed illegal acts which subject them to penalties are protected from the consequences of such acts.

ACT OF INSOLVENCY. Within the meaning of the national currency act, an act of insolvency is an act which shows the bank to be insolvent; such as non-payment of its circulating notes, bills of exchange, or certificates of deposit; failure to make good the impairment of capital, or to keep good its surplus or reserve; in fact, any act which shows that the bank is unable to meet its liabilities as they mature, or to perform those duties which the law imposes for the purpose of sustaining its credit. 5 Biss. 504.

ACT OF LAW. The operation of fixed legal rules upon given facts or occurrences, producing consequences independent of the design or will of the parties concerned; as distinguished from "act of parties."

ACT OF PARLIAMENT. A statute, law, or edict, made by the British sovereign, with the advice and consent of the lords spiritual and temporal, and the commons, in parliament assembled. Acts of parliament form the *leges scriptæ, i. e.*, the written laws of the kingdom.

ACT OF SETTLEMENT. The statute (12 & 13 Wm. III. c. 2) limiting the crown to the Princess Sophia of Hanover, and to the heirs of her body being Protestants.

ACT OF STATE. An act done by the sovereign power of a country, or by its delegate, within the limits of the power vested in him. An act of state cannot be questioned or made the subject of legal proceedings in a court of law.

ACT OF SUPREMACY. The statute (1 Eliz. c. 1) by which the supremacy of the British crown in ecclesiastical matters within the realm was declared and established.

ACT OF UNIFORMITY. In English law. The statute of 13 & 14 Car. II. c. 4, enacting that the book of common prayer, as then recently revised, should be used in every parish church and other place of public worship, and otherwise ordaining a uniformity in religious services, etc. 3 Steph. Comm. 104.

ACT OF UNION. In English law. The statute of 5 Anne, c. 8, by which the articles of union between the two kingdoms of England and Scotland were ratified and confirmed. 1 Bl. Comm. 97.

ACT ON PETITION. A form of summary proceeding formerly in use in the high court of admiralty, in England, in which the parties stated their respective cases briefly, and supported their statements by affidavit. 2 Dod. Adm. 174, 184; 1 Hagg. Adm. 1, note.

ACTA DIURNA. Lat. In the Roman law. Daily acts; the public registers or journals of the daily proceedings of the senate, assemblies of the people, courts of justice, etc. Supposed to have resembled a modern newspaper. Brande.

Acta exteriora indicant interiora secreta. 8 Coke, 146*b*. External acts indicate undisclosed thoughts.

Acta in uno judicio non probant in alio nisi inter easdem personas. Things done in one action cannot be taken as evidence in another, unless it be between the same parties. Tray. Lat. Max. 11.

ACTA PUBLICA. Lat. Things of general knowledge and concern; matters transacted before certain public officers. Calvin.

ACTE. In French law, denotes a document, or formal, solemn writing, embodying a legal attestation that something has been done, corresponding to one sense or use of the English word "act." Thus, *actes de naissance* are the certificates of birth, and must contain the day, hour, and place of birth, together with the sex and intended christian name of the child, and the names of the parents and of the witnesses. *Actes de mariage* are the marriage certificates, and contain names, professions, ages, and places of birth and domicile of the two persons marrying, and of their parents; also the consent of these latter, and the mutual agreements of the intended husband and wife to take each other for better and worse, together with the usual attestations. *Actes de décès* are the certificates of death, which are required to be drawn up before any one may be buried. *Les actes de l' état civil* are public documents. Brown.

ACTE AUTHENTIQUE. In French law. A deed, executed with certain prescribed formalities, in the presence of a notary, mayor, *greffier, huissier*, or other functionary qualified to act in the place in which it is drawn up. Argles, Fr. Merc. Law, 50.

ACTE DE FRANCISATION. In French law. The certificate of registration of a ship, by virtue of which its French nationality is established.

ACTE D' HÉRITIER. In French law. Act of inheritance. Any action or fact on the part of an heir which manifests his intention to accept the succession; the acceptance may be express or tacit. Duverger.

ACTE EXTRAJUDICIAIRE. In French law. A document served by a *huissier*, at the demand of one party upon another party, without legal proceedings.

ACTING. A term employed to designate a *locum tenens* who is performing the duties of an office to which he does not himself claim title; *e. g.*, "*Acting* Supervising Architect." 16 Ct. of Cl. 514.

ACTIO. Lat. In the civil law. An action or suit; a right or cause of action. It should be noted that this term means both the proceeding to enforce a right in a court and the right itself which is sought to be enforced.

ACTIO AD EXHIBENDUM. In the civil law. An action for the purpose of compelling a defendant to exhibit a thing or title in his power. It was preparatory to another action, which was always a real action in the sense of the Roman law; that is, for the recovery of a thing, whether it was movable or immovable. Merl. Quest. tome i. 84.

ACTIO ÆSTIMATORIA. ACTIO QUANTI MINORIS. In the civil law. Two names of an action which lay in behalf of a buyer to reduce the contract price, not to cancel the sale; the *judex* had power, however, to cancel the sale. Hunter, Rom. Law, 332.

ACTIO ARBITRARIA. In the civil law. Action depending on the discretion of the judge. In this, unless the defendant would make amends to the plaintiff as dictated by the judge in his discretion, he was liable to be condemned. Hunter, Rom. Law, 825.

ACTIO BONÆ FIDEI. (Lat. An action of good faith.) In the civil law. A class of actions in which the judge might at the trial, *ex officio*, take into account any equitable circumstances that were presented to him affecting either of the parties to the action. 1 Spence, Eq. Jur. 218.

ACTIO CALUMNIÆ. In the civil law. An action to restrain the defendant from prosecuting a groundless proceeding or trumped-up charge against the plaintiff. Hunter, Rom. Law, 859.

ACTIO CIVILIS. In the common law. A civil action, as distinguished from a criminal action. Bracton divides personal actions into *criminalia et civilia*, according as they grow out of crimes or contracts, (*secundum quod descendunt ex maleficiis vel contractibus.*) Bract. fol. 101*b*.

ACTIO COMMODATI. In the civil law. Included several actions appropriate to enforce the obligations of a borrower or a lender. Hunter, Rom. Law, 305.

ACTIO COMMODATI CONTRARIA. In the civil law. An action by the borrower against the lender, to compel the execution of the contract. Poth. *Prêt à Usage*, n. 75.

ACTIO COMMODATI DIRECTA. In the civil law. An action by a lender against a borrower, the principal object of which is to obtain a restitution of the thing lent. Poth. *Prêt à Usage*, nn. 65, 68.

ACTIO COMMUNI DIVIDUNDO. In the civil law. An action to procure a judicial division of joint property. Hunter, Rom. Law, 194. It was analogous in its object to proceedings for partition in modern law.

ACTIO CONDICTIO INDEBITATI. In the civil law. An action by which the plaintiff recovers the amount of a sum of money or other thing he paid by mistake. Poth. Promutuum, n. 140; Merl. Repert.

ACTIO CONFESSORIA. In the civil law. An affirmative petitory action for the recognition and enforcement of a servitude. So called because based on the plaintiff's affirmative allegation of a right in defendant's land. Distinguished from an *actio negatoria*, which was brought to repel a claim of the defendant to a servitude in the plaintiff's land. Mackeld. Rom. Law, § 324.

ACTIO DAMNI INJURIA. In the civil law. The name of a general class of actions for damages, including many species of suits for losses caused by wrongful or negligent acts. The term is about equivalent to our "action for damages."

ACTIO DE DOLO MALO. In the civil law. An action of fraud; an action which lay for a defrauded person against the defrauder and his heirs, who had been enriched by the fraud, to obtain the restitution of the thing of which he had been fraudulently deprived, with all its accessions (*cum omni causa;*) or, where this was not practicable, for compensation in damages. Mackeld. Rom. Law, § 227.

ACTIO DE PECULIO. In the civil law. An action concerning or against the *peculium*, or separate property of a party.

ACTIO DE PECUNIA CONSTITUTA. In the civil law. An action for money engaged to be paid; an action which lay against any person who had engaged to pay money for himself, or for another, without any formal stipulation, (*nulla stipulatione interposita.*) Inst. 4, 6, 9; Dig. 13, 5; Cod. 4, 18.

ACTIO DEPOSITI CONTRARIA. In the civil law. An action which the depositary has against the depositor, to compel him to fulfil his engagement towards him. Poth. *Du Dépôt*, n. 69.

ACTIO DEPOSITI DIRECTA. In the civil law. An action which is brought by the depositor against the depositary, in order to get back the thing deposited. Poth. *Du Dépôt*, n. 60.

ACTIO DIRECTA. In the civil law. A direct action; an action founded on strict law, and conducted according to fixed forms; an action founded on certain legal obligations which from their origin were accurately defined and recognized as actionable.

ACTIO EMPTI. In the civil law. An action employed in behalf of a buyer to compel a seller to perform his obligations or pay compensation; also to enforce any special agreements by him, embodied in a contract of sale. Hunter, Rom. Law, 332.

ACTIO EX CONDUCTO. In the civil law. An action which the bailor of a thing for hire may bring against the bailee, in order to compel him to redeliver the thing hired.

ACTIO EX CONTRACTU. In the civil and common law. An action of contract; an action arising out of, or founded on, contract. Inst. 4, 6, 1; Bract. fol. 102; 3 Bl. Comm. 117.

ACTIO EX DELICTO. In the civil and common law. An action of tort; an action arising out of fault, misconduct, or malfeasance. Inst. 4, 6, 15; 3 Bl. Comm. 117. *Ex maleficio* is the more common expression of the civil law; which is adopted by Bracton. Inst. 4, 6, 1; Bract. fols. 102, 103.

ACTIO EX LOCATO. In the civil law. An action upon letting; an action which the person who let a thing for hire to another might have against the hirer. Dig. 19, 2; Cod. 4, 65.

ACTIO EX STIPULATU. In the civil law. An action brought to enforce a stipulation.

ACTIO EXERCITORIA. In the civil law. An action against the *exercitor* or employer of a vessel.

ACTIO FAMILIÆ ERCISCUNDÆ. In the civil law. An action for the partition of an inheritance. Inst. 4, 6, 20; Id. 4, 17, 4. Called, by Bracton and Fleta, a mixed action, and classed among actions arising *ex quasi contractu.* Bract. fol. 100*b;* Id. fols. 443*b*, 444; Fleta, lib. 2, c. 60, § 1.

ACTIO FURTI. In the civil law. An action of theft; an action founded upon theft. Inst. 4, 1, 13–17; Bract. fol. 444. This could only be brought for the penalty attached to the offense, (*tantum ad pœnæ persecutionem pertinet,*) and not to recover the thing stolen itself, for which other actions were provided. Inst. 4, 1, 19.

ACTIO HONORARIA. In the civil law. An honorary, or prætorian action. Dig. 44, 7, 25, 35.

ACTIO IN FACTUM. In the civil law. An action adapted to the particular case, having an analogy to some *actio in jus*, the latter being founded on some subsisting acknowledged law. Spence, Eq. Jur. 212. The origin of these actions is similar to that of actions on the case at common law.

ACTIO IN PERSONAM. In the civil law. An action against the person, founded on a personal liability; an action seeking redress for the violation of a *jus in personam* or right available against a particular individual.

In admiralty law. An action directed against the particular person who is to be charged with the liability. It is distinguished from an *actio in rem*, which is a suit directed against a specific *thing* (as a vessel) irrespective of the ownership of it, to enforce a claim or lien upon it, or to obtain, out of the thing or out of the proceeds of its sale, satisfaction for an injury alleged by the claimant.

ACTIO IN REM. In the civil and common law. An action *for a thing;* an action for the recovery of a thing possessed by another. Inst. 4, 6, 1. An action for the enforcement of a right (or for redress for its invasion) which was originally available against all the world, and not in any special sense against the individual sued, until he violated it. See IN REM.

ACTIO JUDICATI. In the civil law. An action instituted, after four months had elapsed after the rendition of judgment, in which the judge issued his warrant to seize, first, the movables, which were sold within eight days afterwards; and then the immovables, which were delivered in pledge to the creditors, or put under the care of a curator, and if, at the end of two months, the debt was not paid, the land was sold. Dig. 42, 1; Code, 8, 34.

ACTIO LEGIS AQUILIÆ. In the civil law. An action under the Aquilian law; an action to recover damages for maliciously or injuriously killing or wounding the slave or beast of another, or injuring in any way a thing belonging to another. Otherwise called *damni injuriæ actio.*

ACTIO MANDATI. In the civil law. Included actions to enforce contracts of mandate, or obligations arising out of them. Hunter, Rom. Law, 316.

ACTIO MIXTA. In the civil law. A mixed action; an action brought for the recovery of a thing, or compensation for damages, and also for the payment of a penalty; partaking of the nature both of an *actio in rem* and *in personam.* Inst. 4, 6, 16, 18, 19, 20; Mackeld. Rom. Law, § 209.

ACTIO NEGATORIA. In the civil law. An action brought to repel a claim of the defendant to a servitude in the plaintiff's land. Mackeld. Rom. Law, § 324.

ACTIO NEGOTIORUM GESTORUM. In the civil law. Included actions between principal and agent and other parties to an engagement, whereby one person undertook the transaction of business for another.

ACTIO NON. In pleading. The Latin name of that part of a special plea which follows next after the statement of appearance and defense, and declares that the plaintiff "ought not to have or maintain his aforesaid action," etc.

ACTIO NON ACCREVIT INFRA SEX ANNOS. The name of the plea of the statute of limitations, when the defendant alleges that the plaintiff's action has not accrued within six years.

Actio non datur non damnificato. An action is not given to one who is not injured. Jenk. Cent. 69.

Actio non facit reum, nisi mens sit rea. An action does not make one guilty, unless the intention be bad. Lofft. 37.

ACTIO NON ULTERIUS. In English pleading. A name given to the distinctive clause in the plea to the *further maintenance* of the action, introduced in place of the plea *puis darrein continuance;* the averment being that the plaintiff ought not *further* (*ulterius*) to have or maintain his action. Steph. Pl. 64, 65, 401.

ACTIO NOXALIS. In the civil law. A noxal action; an action which lay against a master for a crime committed or injury done by his slave; and in which the master had the alternative either to pay for the damage done or to deliver up the slave to the complaining party. Inst. 4, 8, pr.; Heinecc. Elem. lib. 4, tit. 8. So called from *noxa,* the offense or injury committed. Inst. 4, 8, 1.

ACTIO PERSONALIS. In the civil and common law. A personal action. The ordinary term for this kind of action in the civil law is *actio in personam,* (*q. v.,*) the word *personalis* being of only occasional occurrence. Inst. 4, 6, 8, *in tit.;* Id. 4, 11, pr. 1. Bracton, however, uses it freely, and hence the *personal action* of the common law. Bract. fols. 102*a*, 159*b*. See PERSONAL ACTION.

Actio personalis moritur cum persona. A personal right of action dies with the person. Noy, Max. 14.

ACTIO PIGNORATITIA. In the civil law. An action of pledge; an action founded on the contract of pledge, (*pignus.*) Dig. 13, 7; Cod. 4, 24.

Actio pœnalis in hæredem non datur, nisi forte ex damno locupletior hæres factus sit. A penal action is not given against an heir, unless, indeed, such heir is benefited by the wrong.

ACTIO PRÆJUDICIALIS. In the civil law. A preliminary or preparatory action. An action instituted for the determination of some preliminary matter on which other litigated matters depend, or for the determination of some point or question arising in another or principal action; and so called from its being *determined before*, (*prius*, or *præ judicari*.)

ACTIO PRÆSCRIPTIS VERBIS. In the civil law. A form of action which derived its force from continued usage or the *responsa prudentium*, and was founded on the unwritten law. 1 Spence, Eq. Jur. 212.

ACTIO PRÆTORIA. In the civil law. A prætorian action; one introduced by the prætor, as distinguished from the more ancient *actio civilis*, (*q. v.*) Inst. 4, 6, 3; Mackeld. Rom. Law, § 207.

ACTIO PRO SOCIO. In the civil law. An action of partnership. An action brought by one partner against his associates to compel them to carry out the terms of the partnership agreement.

ACTIO PUBLICIANA. In the civil law. An action which lay for one who had lost a thing of which he had *bona fide* obtained possession, before he had gained a property in it, in order to have it restored, under color that he had obtained a property in it by prescription. Inst. 4, 6, 4; Heinecc. Elem. lib. 4, tit. 6, § 1131; Halifax, Anal. b. 3, c. 1, n. 9. It was an honorary action, and derived its name from the prætor Publicius, by whose edict it was first given. Inst. 4, 6, 4.

Actio quælibet it sua via. Every action proceeds in its own way. Jenk. Cent. 77.

ACTIO QUOD JUSSU. In the civil law. An action given against a master, founded on some business done by his slave, acting under his *order*, (*jussu*.) Inst. 4, 7, 1; Dig. 15, 4; Cod. 4, 26.

ACTIO QUOD METUS CAUSA. In the civil law. An action granted to one who had been compelled by unlawful force, or fear (*metûs causa*) that was not groundless, (*metus probabilis* or *justus*,) to deliver, sell, or promise a thing to another. Bract. fol. 103*b*; Mackeld. Rom. Law, § 226.

ACTIO REALIS. A real action. The proper term in the civil law was *Rei Vindicatio*. Inst. 4, 6, 3.

ACTIO REDHIBITORIA. In the civil law. An action to cancel a sale in consequence of defects in the thing sold. It was prosecuted to compel complete restitution to the seller of the thing sold, with its produce and accessories, and to give the buyer back the price, with interest, as an equivalent for the restitution of the produce. Hunter, Rom. Law, 332.

ACTIO RERUM AMOTARUM. In the civil law. An action for things removed; an action which, in cases of divorce, lay for a husband against a wife, to recover things carried away by the latter, in contemplation of such divorce, (*divortii consilio*.) Dig. 25, 2; Id. 25, 2, 25, 30. It also lay for the wife against the husband in such cases. Id. 25, 2, 7, 11; Cod. 5, 21.

ACTIO RESCISSORIA. In the civil law. An action for restoring the plaintiff to a right or title which he has lost by prescription, in a case where the equities are such that he should be relieved from the operation of the prescription. Mackeld. Rom. Law, § 226.

ACTIO SERVIANA. In the civil law. An action which lay for the lessor of a farm, or rural estate, to recover the goods of the lessee or farmer, which were pledged or bound for the rent. Inst. 4, 6, 7.

ACTIO STRICTI JURIS. In the civil law. An action of strict right. The class of civil law personal actions, which were adjudged only by the strict law, and in which the judge was limited to the precise language of the formula, and had no discretionary power to regard the *bona fides* of the transaction. See Inst. 4, 6, 28; Gaius, iii. 137; Mackeld. Rom. Law, § 210.

ACTIO TUTELÆ. In the civil law. Action founded on the duties or obligations arising on the relation analogous to that of guardian and ward.

ACTIO UTILIS. In the civil law. A beneficial action or equitable action. An action founded on equity instead of strict law, and available for those who had equitable rights or the beneficial ownership of property.

Actions are divided into *directæ* or *utiles* actions. The former are founded on certain legal obligations which from their origin were accurately defined and recognized as actionable. The latter were formed analogically in imitation of the former. They were permitted in legal obligations for which the *actiones directæ* were not originally intended, but which resembled the legal obligations which formed the basis of the direct action. Mackeld. Rom. Law, § 207.

ACTIO VENDITI. In the civil law. An action employed in behalf of a seller, to compel a buyer to pay the price, or perform any special obligations embodied in a contract of sale. Hunter, Rom. Law, 332.

ACTIO VI BONORUM RAPTORUM. In the civil law. An action for goods taken by force; a species of mixed action, which lay for a party whose goods or movables (*bona*) had been taken from him by force, (*vi*) to recover the things so taken, together with a penalty of triple the value. Inst. 4, 2; Id. 4, 6, 19. Bracton describes it as lying *de rebus mobilibus vi ablatis sive robbatis*, (for movable things taken away by force, or robbed.) Bract. fol. 103*b*.

ACTIO VULGARIS. In the civil law. A legal action; a common action. Sometimes used for *actio directa*. Mackeld. Rom. Law, § 207.

ACTION. Conduct; behavior; something done; the condition of acting; an act or series of acts.

In practice. The legal and formal demand of one's right from another person or party made and insisted on in a court of justice.

An action is an ordinary proceeding in a court of justice by which one party prosecutes another for the enforcement or protection of a right, the redress or prevention of a wrong, or the punishment of a public offense. Code Civil Proc. Cal. § 22; Code N. Y. § 2; Code N. C. 1883, § 126.

An action is merely the judicial means of enforcing a right. Code Ga. 1882, § 3151.

Action is the form of a suit given by law for the recovery of that which is one's due; the lawful demand of one's right. Co. Litt. 284*b*, 285*a*.

Classification of actions. *Civil* actions are such as lie in behalf of persons to enforce their rights or obtain redress of wrongs in their relation to individuals.

Criminal actions are such as are instituted by the sovereign power, for the purpose of punishing or preventing offenses against the public.

Penal actions are such as are brought, either by the state or by an individual under permission of a statute, to enforce a penalty imposed by law for the commission of a prohibited act.

Common law actions are such as will lie, on the particular facts, at common law, without the aid of a statute.

Statutory actions are such as can only be based upon the particular statutes creating them.

Popular actions, in English usage, are those actions which are given upon the breach of a penal statute, and which any man that will may sue on account of the king and himself, as the statute allows and the case requires. Because the action is not given to one especially, but generally to any that will prosecute, it is called "action popular;" and, from the words used in the process, (*qui tam pro domino rege sequitur quam pro se ipso*, who sues as well for the king as for himself,) it is called a *qui tam* action. Tomlins.

Real, personal, mixed. Actions are divided into real, personal, and mixed; real actions being those brought for the specific recovery of lands or other realty; personal actions, those for the recovery of a debt, personal chattel, or damages; and mixed actions, those for the recovery of real property, together with damages for a wrong connected with it. Litt. § 494; 3 Bl. Comm. 117.

Local actions are those founded upon a cause of action which necessarily refers to, and could only arise in, some particular place, *e. g.*, trespass to land.

Transitory actions are those founded upon a cause of action not necessarily referring to or arising in any particular locality.

Actions are called, in common-law practice, *ex contractu*, when they are founded on a contract; *ex delicto*, when they arise out of a wrong.

"Action" and "Suit." The terms "action" and "suit" are now nearly, if not entirely synonymous. (3 Bl. Comm. 3, 116, et passim.) Or, if there be a distinction, it is that the term "action" is generally confined to proceedings in a court of law, while "suit" is equally applied to prosecutions at law or in equity. Formerly, however, there was a more substantial distinction between them. An *action* was considered as terminating with the giving of judgment, and the execution formed no part of it. (Litt. § 504; Co. Litt. 289*a*.) A *suit*, on the other hand, included the execution. (Id. 291*a*.) So, an action is termed by Lord Coke, "the *right* of a *suit*." (2 Inst. 40.) Burrill.

In French commercial law. Stock in a company, or shares in a corporation.

ACTION FOR POINDING OF THE GROUND. A term of the Scotch law. See POINDING.

ACTION OF A WRIT. A phrase used when a defendant pleads some matter by which he shows that the plaintiff had no cause to have the writ sued upon, although it may be that he is entitled to another writ or action for the same matter. Cowell.

ACTION OF ABSTRACTED MULTURES. In Scotch law. An action for multures or tolls against those who are thirled to a mill, *i. e.*, bound to grind their corn at a certain mill, and fail to do so. Bell.

ACTION OF ADHERENCE. In Scotch law. An action competent to a husband or wife, to compel either party to adhere in case of desertion. It is analogous to the English suit for restitution of conjugal rights. Wharton.

ACTION OF BOOK DEBT. A form of action for the recovery of claims, such as are usually evidenced by a book-account; this action is principally used in Vermont and Connecticut.

ACTION ON THE CASE. A species of personal action of very extensive application, otherwise called "trespass on the case," or simply "case," from the circumstance of the plaintiff's whole *case* or cause of complaint being set forth at length in the original writ by which formerly it was always commenced. 3 Bl. Comm. 122.

ACTION REDHIBITORY. In the civil law. An action instituted to avoid a sale on account of some vice or defect in the thing sold, which renders it either absolutely useless or its use so inconvenient and imperfect that it must be supposed the buyer would not have purchased it had he known of the vice. Civil Code La. art. 2496.

ACTIONABLE. That for which an action will lie; furnishing legal ground for an action; *e. g.*, words are *actionable per se*, in slander, when an action may be brought upon them without alleging special damage.

ACTIONARE. L. Lat. (From *actio*, an action.) In old records. To bring an action; to prosecute, or sue. Thorn's Chron.; Whishaw.

ACTIONARY. A foreign commercial term for the proprietor of an *action* or share of a public company's stock; a stockholder.

ACTIONES LEGIS. In the Roman law. Legal or lawful actions; actions of or at law, (*legitimæ actiones.*) Dig. 1, 2, 2, 6.

ACTIONES NOMINATÆ. In the English chancery. Writs for which there were precedents. The statute of Westminster, 2, c. 24, gave chancery authority to form new writs *in consimili casu;* hence the action on the case.

ACTIONS ORDINARY. In Scotch law. All actions which are not rescissory. Ersk. Inst. 4, 1, 18.

ACTIONS RESCISSORY. In Scotch law. These are either (1) actions of proper improbation for declaring a writing false or forged; (2) actions of reduction-improbation for the production of a writing in order to have it set aside or its effect ascertained under the certification that the writing if not produced shall be declared false or forged; and (3) actions of simple reduction, for declaring a writing called for null until produced. Ersk. Prin. 4, 1, 5.

ACTIVE. That is in action; that demands action; actually subsisting; the opposite of passive. An active debt is one which draws interest. An active trust is a confidence connected with a duty. An active use is a present legal estate.

ACTON BURNEL, Statute of. In English law. A statute, otherwise called "*Statutum de Mercatoribus*," made at a parliament held at the castle of Acton Burnel in Shropshire, in the 11th year of the reign of Edward I. 2 Reeves, Eng. Law, 158-162.

ACTOR. In Roman law. One who acted for another; one who attended to another's business; a manager or agent. A slave who attended to, transacted, or superintended his master's business or affairs, received and paid out moneys, and kept accounts. Burrill.

A plaintiff or complainant. In a civil or private action the plaintiff was often called by the Romans "*petitor;*" in a public action (*causa publica*) he was called "*accusator.*" The defendant was called "*reus,*" both in private and public causes; this term, however, according to Cicero, (*De Orat.* ii. 43,) might signify either party, as indeed we might conclude from the word itself. In a private action, the defendant was often called "*adversarius,*" but either party might be called so.

Also, the term is used of a party who, for the time being, sustains the burden of proof, or has the initiative in the suit.

In old European law. A proctor, advocate, or pleader; one who acted for another in legal matters; one who represented a party and managed his cause. An attorney, bailiff, or steward; one who managed or acted for another. The Scotch "doer" is the literal translation.

Actor qui contra regulam quid adduxit, non est audiendus. A plaintiff is not to be heard who has advanced anything against authority, (or against the rule.)

Actor sequitur forum rei. According as *rei* is intended as the genitive of *res*, a thing, or *reus*, a defendant, this phrase means: The plaintiff follows the forum of the property in suit, or the forum of the defendant's residence. Branch, Max. 4.

Actore non probante reus absolvitur. When the plaintiff does not prove his case the defendant is acquitted. Hob. 103.

Actori incumbit onus probandi. The burden of proof rests on the plaintiff, (or on the party who advances a proposition affirmatively.) Hob. 103.

ACTORNAY. In old Scotch law. An attorney. Skene.

ACTRIX. Lat. A female actor; a female plaintiff. Calvin.

Acts indicate the intention. 8 Co. 146*b;* Broom, Max. 301.

ACTS OF COURT. Legal memoranda made in the admiralty courts in England, in the nature of pleas.

ACTS OF SEDERUNT. In Scotch law. Ordinances for regulating the forms of proceeding, before the court of session, in the administration of justice, made by the judges, who have the power by virtue of a Scotch act of parliament passed in 1540. Ersk. Prin. § 14.

ACTUAL. Real; substantial; existing presently in act; having a valid objective existence; as opposed to that which is merely theoretical or possible.

Something real, in opposition to constructive or speculative; something existing in act. 31 Conn. 213.

ACTUAL CASH VALUE. In insurance. The sum of money the insured goods would have brought for cash, at the market price, at the time when and place where they were destroyed by fire. 4 Fed. Rep. 59.

ACTUAL COST. The actual price paid for goods by a party, in the case of a real *bona fide* purchase, and not the market value of the goods. 2 Story, 422, 429; 2 Mas. 48; 9 Gray, 226.

ACTUAL DAMAGES. Real, substantial, and just damages. The amount adjudged to a complainant in compensation for his actual and real loss or damage; opposed to "nominal damages," which is a trifling sum awarded as a matter of course, and not in compensation, but merely in recognition of the fact that his right has been technically violated; and opposed also to "exemplary" or "punitive" damages, the latter being in excess of the real loss, and intended as a punishment to the wrong-doer, or (from motives of public policy) to discourage a repetition of such acts.

ACTUAL DELIVERY. In the law of sales, actual delivery consists in the giving real possession of the thing sold to the vendee or his servants or special agents who are identified with him in law and represent him. Constructive delivery is a general term, comprehending all those acts which, although not truly conferring a real possession of the thing sold on the vendee, have been held, by construction of law, equivalent to acts of real delivery. In this sense constructive delivery includes symbolical delivery and all those *traditiones fictæ* which have been admitted into the law as sufficient to vest the absolute property in the vendee and bar the rights of lien and stoppage *in transitu*, such as marking and setting apart the goods as belonging to the vendee, charging him with warehouse rent, etc. 1 Rawle, 19.

ACTUAL FRAUD. Actual fraud implies deceit, artifice, trick, design, some direct and active operation of the mind. Constructive fraud is indirect, and may be implied from some other act or omission to act, which may be, in moral contemplation, entirely innocent, but which, without the explanation or actual proof of its innocence, is evidence of fraud. 35 Barb. 457.

ACTUAL NOTICE. A notice expressly and actually given, and brought home to the party directly, in distinction from one inferred or imputed by the law on account of the existence of means of knowledge.

ACTUAL OCCUPATION. An open, visible occupancy as distinguished from the constructive one which follows the legal title.

ACTUAL OUSTER. By "actual ouster" is not meant a physical eviction, but a possession attended with such circumstances as to evince a claim of exclusive right and title, and a denial of the right of the other tenants to participate in the profits. 45 Iowa, 287.

ACTUAL POSSESSION. This term, as used in the provisions of Rev. St. N. Y.

p. 312, § 1, authorizing proceedings to compel the determination of claims to real property, means a possession in fact effected by actual entry upon the premises; an actual occupation. 59 N. Y. 134.

It means an actual occupation or possession in fact, as contradistinguished from that constructive one which the legal title draws after it. The word "actual" is used in the statute in opposition to virtual or constructive, and calls for an open, visible occupancy. 7 Hun, 616.

ACTUAL SALE. Lands are "actually sold" at a tax sale, so as to entitle the treasurer to the statutory fees, when the sale is completed; when he has collected from the purchaser the amount of the bid. 5 Neb. 272.

ACTUAL TOTAL LOSS. In marine insurance. The total loss of the vessel covered by a policy of insurance, by its real and substantive destruction, by injuries which leave it no longer existing *in specie*, by its being reduced to a wreck irretrievably beyond repair, or by its being placed beyond the control of the insured and beyond his power of recovery. Distinguished from a *constructive* total loss, which occurs where the vessel, though injured by the perils insured against, remains *in specie* and capable of repair or recovery, but at such an expense, or under such other conditions, that the insured may claim the whole amount of the policy upon abandoning the vessel to the underwriters.

"An *actual* total loss is where the vessel ceases to exist *in specie*,—becomes a 'mere congeries of planks,' incapable of being repaired; or where, by the peril insured against, it is placed beyond the control of the insured and beyond his power of recovery. A *constructive* total loss is where the vessel remains *in specie*, and is susceptible of repairs or recovery, but at an expense, according to the rule of the English common law, exceeding its value when restored, or, according to the terms of this policy, where 'the injury is equivalent to fifty per cent. of the agreed value in the policy,' and where the insured abandons the vessel to the underwriter. In such cases the insured is entitled to indemnity as for a total loss. An exception to the rule requiring abandonment is found in cases where the loss occurs in foreign ports or seas, where it is impracticable to repair. In such cases the master may sell the vessel for the benefit of all concerned, and the insured may claim as for a total loss by accounting to the insurer for the amount realized on the sale. There are other exceptions to the rule, but it is sufficient now to say that we have found no case in which the doctrine of constructive total loss without abandonment has been admitted, where the injured vessel remained *in specie* and was brought to its home port by the insured. A well marked distinction between an actual and a constructive total loss is therefore found in this: that in the former no abandonment is necessary, while in the latter it is essential, unless the case be brought within some exception to the rule requiring it. A *partial* loss is where an injury results to the vessel from a peril insured against, but where the loss is neither actually nor constructively total." 25 Ohio St. 64. See, also, 96 U. S. 645; 9 Hun, 383.

ACTUARIUS. In Roman law. A notary or clerk. One who drew the acts or statutes, or who wrote in brief the public acts.

ACTUARY. In English ecclesiastical law. A clerk that registers the acts and constitutions of the lower house of convocation; or a registrar in a court christian.

Also an officer appointed to keep savings banks accounts; the computing officer of an insurance company; a person skilled in calculating the value of life interests, annuities, and insurances.

ACTUM. A deed; something done.

ACTUS. **In the civil law.** A species of right of way, consisting in the right of driving cattle, or a carriage, over the land subject to the servitude. Inst. 2, 3, pr. It is sometimes translated a "road," and included the kind of way termed "*iter*," or path. Lord Coke, who adopts the term "*actus*" from Bracton, defines it a foot and horse way, vulgarly called "pack and prime way;" but distinguishes it from a cart-way. Co. Litt. 56*a*.

In old English law. An act of parliament; a statute. A distinction, however, was sometimes made between *actus* and *statutum*. *Actus parliamenti* was an act made by the lords and commons; and it became *statutum*, when it received the king's consent. Barring. Obs. St. 46, note *b*.

ACTUS. In the civil law. An act or action. *Non tantum verbis, sed etiam actu;* not only by words, but also by act. Dig. 46, 8, 5.

Actus curiæ neminem gravabit. An act of the court shall prejudice no man. Jenk. Cent. 118. Where a delay in an action is the act of the court, neither party shall suffer for it.

Actus Dei nemini est damnosus. The act of God is hurtful to no one. 2 Inst. 287.

Actus Dei nemini facit injuriam. The act of God does injury to no one. 2 Bl. Comm. 122. A thing which is inevitable by the act of God, which no industry can avoid, nor policy prevent, will not be construed to the prejudice of any person in whom there was no laches. Broom, Max. 230.

Actus inceptus, cujus perfectio pendet ex voluntate partium, revocari potest; si autem pendet ex voluntate tertiæ personæ, vel ex contingenti, revocari non potest. An act already begun, the completion of which depends on the will of the parties, may be revoked; but if it depend on the will of a third person, or on a contingency, it cannot be revoked. Bac. Max. reg. 20.

Actus judiciarius coram non judice irritus habetur, de ministeriali autem a quocunque provenit ratum esto. A judicial act by a judge without jurisdiction is void; but a ministerial act, from whomsoever proceeding, may be ratified. Lofft, 458.

Actus legis nemini est damnosus. The act of the law is hurtful to no one. An act in law shall prejudice no man. 2 Inst. 287.

Actus legis nemini facit injuriam. The act of the law does injury to no one. 5 Coke, 116.

Actus legitimi non recipiunt modum. Acts required to be done by law do not admit of qualification. Hob. 153; Branch, Princ.

Actus me invito factus non est meus actus. An act done by me, against my will, is not my act. Branch, Princ.

Actus non facit reum, nisi mens sit rea. An act does not make [the doer of it] guilty, unless the mind be guilty; that is, unless the intention be criminal. 3 Inst. 107. The intent and the act must both concur to constitute the crime. Lord Kenyon, C. J., 7 Term 514; Broom, Max. 306.

Actus repugnus non potest in esse produci. A repugnant act cannot be brought into being, *i. e.*, cannot be made effectual. Plowd. 355.

Actus servi in iis quibus opera ejus communiter adhibita est, actus domini habetur. The act of a servant in those things in which he is usually employed, is considered the act of his master. Lofft, 227.

AD. Lat. At; by; for; near; on account of; to; until; upon.

AD ABUNDANTIOREM CAUTELAM. L. Lat. For more abundant caution. 2 How. State Tr. 1182. Otherwise expressed, *ad cautelam ex superabundanti.* Id. 1163.

AD ADMITTENDUM CLERICUM. For the admitting of the clerk. A writ in the nature of an execution, commanding the bishop to admit his clerk, upon the success of the latter in a *quare impedit.*

AD ALIUD EXAMEN. To another tribunal; belonging to another court, cognizance, or jurisdiction.

AD ALIUM DIEM. At another day. A common phrase in the old reports. Yearb. P. 7 Hen. VI. 13.

AD ASSISAS CAPIENDAS. To take assises; to take or hold the assises. Bract. fol. 110*a;* 3 Bl. Comm. 185. *Ad assisam capiendam;* to take an assise. Bract. fol. 110*b*.

AD AUDIENDUM ET TERMINANDUM. To hear and determine. St. Westm. 2, cc. 29, 30.

AD BARRAM. To the bar; at the bar. 3 How. State Tr. 112.

AD CAMPI PARTEM. For a share of the field or land, for champert. Fleta, lib. 2, c. 36, § 4.

AD CAPTUM VULGI. Adapted to the common understanding.

AD COLLIGENDUM BONA DEFUNCTI. To collect the goods of the deceased. Special letters of administration granted to one or more persons, authorizing them to *collect* and preserve the goods of the deceased, are so called. 2 Bl. Comm. 505; 2 Steph. Comm. 241. These are otherwise termed "letters *ad colligendum,*" and the party to whom they are granted, a "collector."

AD COMMUNEM LEGEM. At common law. The name of a writ of entry (now obsolete) brought by the reversioners after the death of the life tenant, for the recovery of lands wrongfully alienated by him.

AD COMPARENDUM. To appear. *Ad comparendum, et ad standum juri,* to appear and to stand to the law, or abide the judgment of the court. Cro. Jac. 67.

AD COMPOTUM REDDENDUM. To render an account. St. Westm. 2, c. 11.

AD CURIAM. At a court. 1 Salk. 195. To court. *Ad curiam vocare,* to summon to court.

AD CUSTAGIA. At the costs. Toullier; Cowell; Whishaw.

AD CUSTUM. At the cost. 1 Bl. Comm. 314.

AD DAMNUM. In pleading. "To the damage." The technical name of that clause of the writ or declaration which contains a statement of the plaintiff's money loss, or the damages which he claims.

AD DEFENDENDUM. To defend. 1 Bl. Comm. 227.

AD DIEM. At a day; at the day. Townsh. Pl. 23. *Ad certum diem*, at a certain day. 2 Strange, 747. *Solvit ad diem;* he paid at or on the day. 1 Chit. Pl. 485.

Ad ea quæ frequentius accidunt jura adaptantur. Laws are adapted to those cases which most frequently occur. 2 Inst. 137; Broom, Max. 43.

Laws are adapted to cases which frequently occur. A statute, which, construed according to its plain words, is, in all cases of ordinary occurrence, in no degree inconsistent or unreasonable, should not be varied by construction in every case, merely because there is one possible but highly improbable case in which the law would operate with great severity and against our notions of justice. The utmost that can be contended is that the construction of the statute should be varied in that particular case, so as to obviate the injustice. 7 Exch. 549; 8 Exch. 778.

AD EFFECTUM. To the effect, or end. Co. Litt. 204*a;* 2 Crabb, Real Prop. p. 802, § 2143. *Ad effectum sequentem*, to the effect following. 2 Salk. 417.

AD EXCAMBIUM. For exchange; for compensation. Bract. fol. 12*b*, 37*b*.

AD EXHÆREDATIONEM. To the disherison, or disinheriting; to the injury of the inheritance. Bract. fol. 15*a;* 3 Bl. Comm. 288. Formal words in the old writs of waste.

AD EXITUM. At issue; at the end (of the pleadings.) Steph. Pl. 24.

AD FACIENDUM. To do. Co. Litt. 204*a*. *Ad faciendum, subjiciendum et recipiendum;* to do, submit to, and receive. *Ad faciendam juratam illam;* to make up that jury. Fleta, lib. 2, c. 65, § 12.

AD FACTUM PRÆSTANDUM. In Scotch law. A name descriptive of a class of obligations marked by unusual severity. A debtor who is under an obligation of this kind cannot claim the benefit of the act of grace, the privilege of sanctuary, or the *cessio bonorum*. Ersk. Inst. lib. 3, tit. 3, § 62.

AD FEODI FIRMAM. To fee farm. Fleta, lib. 2, c. 50, § 30.

AD FIDEM. In allegiance. 2 Kent, Comm. 56. Subjects born *ad fidem* are those born in allegiance.

AD FILUM AQUÆ. To the thread of the water; to the central line, or middle of the stream. *Usque ad filum aquæ*, as far as the thread of the stream. Bract. fol. 208*b;* 235*a*. A phrase of frequent occurrence in modern law; of which *ad medium filum aquæ* (*q. v.*) is another form.

AD FILUM VIÆ. To the middle of the way; to the central line of the road. 8 Metc. (Mass.) 260.

AD FINEM. Abbreviated *ad fin.* To the end. It is used in citations to books, as a direction to read from the place designated to the end of the chapter, section, etc. *Ad finem litis*, at the end of the suit.

AD FIRMAM. To farm. Derived from an old Saxon word denoting rent. *Ad firmam noctis* was a fine or penalty equal in amount to the estimated cost of entertaining the king for one night. Cowell. *Ad feodi firmam*, to fee farm. Spelman.

AD GAOLAS DELIBERANDAS. To deliver the gaols; to empty the gaols. Bract. fol. 109*b*. *Ad gaolam deliberandam;* to deliver the gaol; to make gaol delivery. Bract. fol. 110*b*.

AD GRAVAMEN. To the grievance, injury, or oppression. Fleta, lib. 2, c. 47, § 10.

AD HOMINEM. To the person. A term used in logic with reference to a personal argument.

AD HUNC DIEM. At this day. 1 Leon. 90.

AD IDEM. To the same point, or effect. *Ad idem facit*, it makes to or goes to establish the same point. Bract. fol. 27*b*.

AD INDE. Thereunto. *Ad inde requisitus*, thereunto required. Townsh. Pl. 22.

AD INFINITUM. Without limit; to an infinite extent; indefinitely.

AD INQUIRENDUM. To inquire; a writ of inquiry; a judicial writ, commanding inquiry to be made of any thing relating to a cause pending in court. Cowell.

AD INSTANTIAM. At the instance. 2 Mod. 44. *Ad instantiam partis*, at the instance of a party. Hale, Com. Law, 28.

AD INTERIM. In the mean time. An officer *ad interim* is one appointed to fill a temporary vacancy, or to discharge the duties of the office during the absence or temporary incapacity of its regular incumbent.

AD JUDICIUM. To judgment; to court. *Ad judicium provocare;* to summon to court; to commence an action; a term of the Roman law. Dig. 5, 1, 13, 14.

AD JUNGENDUM AUXILIUM. To joining in aid; to join in aid. See AID PRAYER.

AD JURA REGIS. To the rights of the king; a writ which was brought by the king's clerk, presented to a living, against those who endeavored to eject him, to the prejudice of the king's title. Reg. Writs, 61.

AD LARGUM. At large; at liberty; free, or unconfined. *Ire ad largum*, to go at large. Plowd. 37.

At large; giving details, or particulars; *in extenso.* A special verdict was formerly called a verdict at large. Plowd. 92.

AD LITEM. For the suit; for the purposes of the suit; pending the suit. A guardian *ad litem* is a guardian appointed to prosecute or defend a suit on behalf of a party incapacitated by infancy or otherwise.

AD LUCRANDUM VEL PERDENDUM. For gain or loss. Emphatic words in the old warrants of attorney. Reg. Orig. 21, et seq. Sometimes expressed in English, "to lose and gain." Plowd. 201.

AD MAJOREM CAUTELAM. For greater security. 2 How. State Tr. 1182.

AD MANUM. At hand; ready for use. *Et querens sectam habeat ad manum;* and the plaintiff immediately have his suit ready. Fleta, lib. 2, c. 44, § 2.

AD MEDIUM FILUM AQUÆ. To the middle thread of the stream.

AD MEDIUM FILUM VIÆ. To the middle thread of the way.

AD MELIUS INQUIRENDUM. A writ directed to a coroner commanding him to hold a second inquest. See 45 Law J. Q. B. 711.

AD MORDENDUM ASSUETUS. Accustomed to bite. Cro. Car. 254. A material averment in declarations for damage done by a dog to persons or animals. 1 Chit. Pl. 388; 2 Chit. Pl. 597.

AD NOCUMENTUM. To the nuisance, or annoyance. Fleta, lib. 2, c. 52, § 19. *Ad nocumentum liberi tenementi sui*, to the nuisance of his freehold. Formal words in the old assise of nuisance. 3 Bl. Comm. 221.

Ad officium justiciariorum spectat, unicuique coram eis placitanti justitiam exhibere. It is the duty of justices to administer justice to every one pleading before them. 2 Inst. 451.

AD OSTENDENDUM. To show. Formal words in old writs. Fleta, lib. 4, c. 65, § 12.

AD OSTIUM ECCLESIÆ. At the door of the church. One of the five species of dower formerly recognized by the English law. 1 Washb. Real Prop. 149; 2 Bl. Comm. 132.

Ad proximum antecedens fiat relatio nisi impediatur sententiâ. Relative words refer to the nearest antecedent, unless it be prevented by the context. Jenk. Cent. 180.

AD QUÆRIMONIAM. On complaint of.

AD QUEM. To which. A term used in the computation of time or distance, as correlative to *a quo;* denotes the end or terminal point. See A QUO.

Ad questiones facti non respondent judices; ad questiones legis non respondent juratores. Judges do not answer questions of fact; juries do not answer questions of law. 8 Coke, 308; Co. Litt. 295.

AD QUOD CURIA CONCORDAVIT. To which the court agreed. Yearb. P. 20 Hen. VI. 27.

AD QUOD DAMNUM. The name of a writ formerly issuing from the English chancery, commanding the sheriff to make inquiry "to what damage" a specified act, if done, will tend. *Ad quod damnum* is a writ which ought to be sued before the king grants certain liberties, as a fair, market, or such like, which may be prejudicial to others, and thereby it should be inquired whether it will be a prejudice to grant them, and to whom it will be prejudicial, and what prejudice will come thereby. There is also another writ of *ad quod damnum*, if any one will turn a common highway and lay out another way as beneficial. Termes de la Ley.

AD QUOD NON FUIT RESPONSUM. To which there was no answer. A phrase used in the reports, where a point advanced in argument by one party was not denied by the other; or where a point or argument of counsel was not met or noticed by the court; or where an objection was met by the court, and not replied to by the counsel who raised it. 3 Coke, 9; 4 Coke, 40.

AD RATIONEM PONERE. A technical expression in the old records of the Exchequer, signifying, to put to the bar and interrogate as to a charge made; to arraign on a trial.

AD RECOGNOSCENDUM. To recognize. Fleta, lib. 2, c. 65, § 12. Formal words in old writs.

Ad recte docendum oportet, primum inquirere nomina, quia rerum cognitio a nominibus rerum dependet. In order rightly to comprehend a thing, inquire first into the names, for a right knowledge of things depends upon their names. Co. Litt. 68.

AD REPARATIONEM ET SUSTENTATIONEM. For repairing and keeping in suitable condition.

AD RESPONDENDUM. For answering; to make answer; words used in certain writs employed for bringing a person before the court to make answer in defense in a proceeding. Thus there is a *capias ad respondendum, q. v.;* also a *habeas corpus ad respondendum.*

AD SATISFACIENDUM. To satisfy. The emphatic words of the writ of *capias ad satisfaciendum*, which requires the sheriff to *take* the person of the defendant *to satisfy* the plaintiff's claim.

AD SECTAM. At the suit of. Commonly abbreviated to *ads.* Used in entering and indexing the names of cases, where it is desired that the name of the defendant should come first. Thus, "B. *ads.* A." indicates that B. is defendant in an action brought by A., and the title so written would be an inversion of the more usual form "A. *v.* B."

An affidavit of merits, on the same paper with the pleas, by a defendant, entitled "C. D. *ads.* A. B.," is the same in law as if entitled "A. B. *v.* C. D.," and is properly entitled, and it is error to strike the pleas from the files as for want of a sufficient affidavit. 86 Ill. 11.

AD STUDENDUM ET ORANDUM. For studying and praying; for the promotion of learning and religion. A phrase applied to colleges and universities. 1 Bl. Comm. 467; T. Raym. 101.

AD TERMINUM ANNORUM. For a term of years.

AD TERMINUM QUI PRETERIT. For a term which has passed. Words in the Latin form of the writ of entry employed at common law to recover, on behalf of a landlord, possession of premises, from a tenant holding over after the expiration of the term for which they were demised. See Fitzh. Nat. Brev. 201.

Ad tristem partem strenua est suspicio. Suspicion lies heavy on the unfortunate side.

AD TUNC ET IBIDEM. In pleading. The Latin name of that clause of an indictment containing the statement of the subject-matter "then and there being found."

AD ULTIMAM VIM TERMINORUM. To the most extended import of the terms; in a sense as universal as the terms will reach. 2 Eden, 54.

AD USUM ET COMMODUM. To the use and benefit.

AD VALENTIAM. To the value. See AD VALOREM.

AD VALOREM. According to value. Duties are either *ad valorem* or *specific;* the former when the duty is laid in the form of a percentage on the value of the property; the latter where it is imposed as a fixed sum on each article of a class without regard to its value.

The term *ad valorem* tax is as well defined and fixed as any other used in political economy or legislation, and simply means a tax or duty upon the value of the article or thing subject to taxation. 24 Miss. 501.

AD VENTREM INSPICIENDUM. To inspect the womb. A writ for the summoning of a jury of matrons to determine the question of pregnancy.

Ad vim majorem vel ad casus fortuitus non tenetur quis, nisi sua culpa intervenerit. No one is held to answer for the effects of a superior force, or of accidents, unless his own fault has contributed. Fleta, lib. 2, c. 72, § 16.

AD VITAM. For life. Bract. fol. 13*b*. *In feodo, vel ad vitam;* in fee, or for life. Id.

AD VITAM AUT CULPAM. For life or until fault. This phrase describes the tenure of an office which is otherwise said to be held "for life or during good behavior." It is equivalent to *quamdiu bene se gesserit.*

AD VOLUNTATEM. At will. Bract. fol. 27*a*. *Ad voluntatem domini,* at the will of the lord.

AD WARACTUM. To fallow. Bract. fol. 228*b*. See WARACTUM.

ADAWLUT. Corrupted from *Adalat,* justice, equity; a court of justice. The terms "Dewanny Adawlut" and "Foujdarry Adawlut" denote the civil and criminal courts of justice in India. Wharton.

ADCORDABILIS DENARII. Money paid by a vassal to his lord upon the selling or exchanging of a feud. Enc. Lond.

ADDICERE. Lat. In the civil law. To adjudge or condemn; to assign, allot, or deliver; to sell. In the Roman law, *addico* was one of the three words used to express the extent of the civil jurisdiction of the prætors.

ADDICTIO. In the Roman law. The giving up to a creditor of his debtor's person by a magistrate; also the transfer of the debtor's goods to one who assumes his liabilities.

Additio probat minoritatem. An addition [to a name] proves or shows minority or inferiority. 4 Inst. 80; Wing. Max. 211, max. 60. This maxim is applied by Lord Coke to courts, and terms of law; *minoritas* being understood in the sense of difference, inferiority, or qualification. Thus, the style of the king's bench is *coram rege,* and the style of the court of chancery is *coram domino rege in cancellaria;* the addition showing the difference. 4 Inst. 80. By the word "fee" is intended *fee-simple,* fee-tail not being intended by it, unless there be added to it the *addition* of the word "tail." 2 Bl. Comm. 106; Litt. § 1.

ADDITION. Whatever is added to a man's name by way of title or description, as additions of mystery, place, or degree. Cowell.

In English law, there are four kinds of *additions,*—additions of *estate,* such as yeoman, gentleman, esquire; additions of *degree,* or names of dignity, as knight, earl, marquis, duke; additions of *trade,* mystery, or occupation, as scrivener, painter, mason, carpenter; and additions of *place* of residence, as London, Chester, etc. The only additions recognized in American law are those of mystery and residence.

In the law of liens. Within the meaning of the mechanic's lien law, an "addition" to a building must be a lateral addition. It must occupy ground without the limits of the building to which it constitutes an addition, so that the lien shall be upon the building formed by the addition and the land upon which it stands. An alteration in a former building, by adding to its height, or to its depth, or to the extent of its interior accommodations, is merely an "alteration," and not an "addition." Putting a new story on an old building is not an addition. 27 N. J. Law, 132.

In French law. A supplementary process to obtain additional information. Guyot, Repert.

ADDITIONAL. This term embraces the idea of joining or uniting one thing to another, so as thereby to form one aggregate. Thus, "additional security" imports a security, which, united with or joined to the former one, is deemed to make it, as an aggregate, sufficient as a security from the beginning. 53 Miss. 626.

ADDITIONALES. In the law of contracts. Additional terms or propositions to be added to a former agreement.

ADDONE, Addonne. L. Fr. Given to. Kelham.

ADDRESS. That part of a bill in equity wherein is given the appropriate and technical description of the court in which the bill is filed.

The word is sometimes used as descriptive of a formal document, embodying a request, presented to the governor of a state by one or both branches of the legislative body, desiring him to perform some executive act.

A place of business or residence.

ADDUCED. "The word 'adduced' is broader in its signification than the word 'offered,' and, looking to the whole statement in relation to the evidence below, we think it sufficiently appears that all of the evidence is in the record." 106 Ind. 84, 5 N. E. Rep. 882.

ADEEM. To take away, recall, or revoke. To satisfy a legacy by some gift or substituted disposition, made by the testator, in advance. See ADEMPTION.

ADELANTADO. In Spanish law. A governor of a province; a president or president judge; a judge having jurisdiction over a kingdom, or over certain provinces only. So called from having authority over the judges of those places. Las Partidas, pt. 3, tit. 4, l. 1.

ADELING or ATHELING. Noble; excellent. A title of honor among the Anglo-Saxons, properly belonging to the king's children. Spelman.

ADEMPTIO. Lat. In the civil law. A revocation of a legacy; an ademption. Inst. 2, 21, pr. Where it was expressly transferred from one person to another, it was called *translatio.* Id. 2, 21, 1; Dig. 34, 4.

ADEMPTION. The revocation, recalling, or cancellation of a legacy, according to the apparent intention of the testator, implied by the law from acts done by him in his life, though such acts do not amount to an express revocation of it.

"The word 'ademption' is the most significant, because, being a term of art, and never used for any other purpose, it does not suggest any idea foreign to that intended to be conveyed. It is used to describe the act by which the testator pays to his legatee, in his life-time, a general legacy which by his will he had proposed to give him at his death. (1 Rop. Leg. p. 365.) It is also used to denote the act by which a specific legacy has become inoperative on account of the testator having parted with the subject." 16 N. Y. 40.

Ademption, in strictness, is predicable only of specific, and satisfaction of general legacies. 9 Barb. 35, 56; 3 Duer, 477, 541.

ADEO. Lat. So, as. *Adeo plene et integre,* as fully and entirely. 10 Coke, 65.

"ADEQUATE CAUSE." In criminal law. Adequate cause for the passion which reduces a homicide committed under its influence from the grade of murder to manslaughter, means such cause as would commonly produce a degree of anger, rage, resentment, or terror, in a person of ordinary temper, sufficient to render the mind incapable of cool reflection. Insulting words or gestures, or an assault and battery so slight as to show no intention to inflict pain or injury, or an injury to property unaccompanied by violence are not adequate causes. 2 Tex. App. 100; 7 Tex. App. 396; 10 Tex. App. 421.

ADEQUATE CONSIDERATION. One which is equal, or reasonably proportioned, to the value of that for which it is given. 1 Story, Eq. Jur. §§ 244-247.

ADEQUATE REMEDY. One vested in the complainant, to which he may at all times resort at his own option, fully and freely, without let or hindrance. 54 Conn. 249.

ADESSE. In the civil law. To be present; the opposite of *abesse.* Calvin.

ADFERRUMINATIO. In the civil law. The welding together of iron; a species of *adjunctio,* (*q. v.*) Called also *ferruminatio.* Mackeld. Rom. Law, § 276; Dig. 6, 1, 23, 5.

ADHERENCE. In Scotch law. The name of a form of action by which the mutual obligation of marriage may be enforced by either party. Bell. It corresponds to the English action for the restitution of conjugal rights.

ADHERING. Joining, leagued with, cleaving to; as, "adhering to the enemies of the United States."

Rebels, being citizens, are not "enemies," within the meaning of the constitution; hence a conviction for treason, in promoting a rebellion, cannot be sustained under that branch of the constitutional definition which speaks of "adhering to their enemies, giving them aid and comfort." 2 Abb. (U. S.) 364.

ADHIBERE. In the civil law. To apply; to employ; to exercise; to use. *Adhibere diligentiam,* to use care. *Adhibere vim,* to employ force.

ADIATION. A term used in the laws of Holland for the application of property by an executor. Wharton.

ADIEU. L. Fr. Without day. A common term in the Year Books, implying final dismissal from court.

ADIRATUS. Lost; strayed; a price or value set upon things stolen or lost, as a recompense to the owner. Cowell.

ADIT. In mining law. A lateral entrance or passage into a mine; the opening by which a mine is entered, or by which water and ores are carried away; a horizontal excavation in and along a lode. 9 Colo. 207, 11 Pac. Rep. 80; 6 Colo. 278.

ADITUS. An approach; a way; a public way. Co. Litt. 56*a*.

ADJACENT. Lying near or close to; contiguous. The difference between *adjacent* and *adjoining* seems to be that the former implies that the two objects are not widely separated, though they may not actually touch, while *adjoining* imports that they are so joined or united to each other that no third object intervenes.

ADJECTIVE LAW. The aggregate of rules of procedure or practice. As opposed to that body of law which the courts are established to administer, (called "substantive law,") it means the rules according to which the substantive law is administered. That part of the law which provides a method for enforcing or maintaining rights, or obtaining redress for their invasion.

ADJOINING. The word "adjoining," in its etymological sense, means touching or contiguous, as distinguished from lying near to or adjacent. And the same meaning has been given to it when used in statutes. 52 N. Y. 397. See ADJACENT.

ADJOURN. To put off; defer; postpone. To postpone action of a convened court or body until another time specified, or indefinitely, the latter being usually called to adjourn *sine die*.

The primary signification of the term "adjourn" is to put off or defer to another day specified. But it has acquired also the meaning of suspending business for a time,—deferring, delaying. Probably, without some limitation, it would, when used with reference to a sale on foreclosure, or any judicial proceeding, properly include the fixing of the time to which the postponement was made. 14 How. Pr. 58. See, also, 5 N. Y. 22.

ADJOURNAL. A term applied in Scotch law and practice to the records of the criminal courts. The original records of criminal trials were called "bukis of adiornale," or "books of adjournal," few of which are now extant. An "act of adjournal" is an order of the court of justiciary entered on its minutes.

Adjournamentum est ad diem dicere seu diem dare. An adjournment is to appoint a day or give a day. 4 Inst. 27. Hence the formula "*eat sine die.*"

ADJOURNATUR. L. Lat. It is adjourned. A word with which the old reports very frequently conclude a case. 1 Ld. Raym. 602; 1 Show. 7; 1 Leon. 88.

ADJOURNED SUMMONS. A summons taken out in the chambers of a judge, and afterwards taken into court to be argued by counsel.

ADJOURNED TERM. In practice. A continuance, by adjournment, of a regular term. 4 Ohio St. 473. Distinguished from an "additional term," which is a distinct term. Id. An *adjourned term* is a continuation of a previous or regular term; it is the same term prolonged, and the power of the court over the business which has been done, and the entries made at the regular term, continues. 22 Ala. 57.

ADJOURNMENT. A putting off or postponing of business or of a session until another time or place; the act of a court, legislative body, public meeting, or officer, by which the session or assembly is dissolved, either temporarily or finally, and the business in hand dismissed from consideration, either definitively or for an interval. If the adjournment is final, it is said to be *sine die*.

In the civil law. A calling into court; a summoning at an appointed time. Du Cange.

ADJOURNMENT DAY. A further day appointed by the judges at the regular sittings at *nisi prius* to try issues of fact not then ready for trial.

ADJOURNMENT DAY IN ERROR. In English practice. A day appointed some days before the end of the term at which matters left undone on the affirmance day are finished. 2 Tidd, Pr. 1176.

ADJOURNMENT IN EYRE. The appointment of a day when the justices in eyre mean to sit again. Cowell; Spelman.

ADJUDGE. To pass upon judicially; to decide, settle, or decree; to sentence or condemn.

ADJUDICATAIRE. In Canadian law. A purchaser at a sheriff's sale. See 1 Low. Can. 241; 10 Low. Can. 325.

ADJUDICATE. To settle in the exercise of judicial authority. To determine finally. Synonymous with *adjudge* in its strictest sense.

ADJUDICATIO. In the civil law. An adjudication. The judgment of the court that the subject-matter is the property of one of the litigants; confirmation of title by judgment. Mackeld. Rom. Law, § 204.

ADJUDICATION. The giving or pronouncing a judgment or decree in a cause; also the judgment given. The term is principally used in bankruptcy proceedings, the adjudication being the order which declares the debtor to be a bankrupt.

In French law. A sale made at public auction and upon competition. Adjudications are voluntary, judicial, or administrative. Duverger.

In Scotch law. A species of diligence, or process for transferring the estate of a debtor to a creditor, carried on as an ordinary action before the court of session. A species of judicial sale, redeemable by the debtor. A decreet of the lords of session, adjudging and appropriating a person's lands, hereditaments, or any heritable right to belong to his creditor, who is called the "adjudger," for payment or performance. Bell; Ersk. Inst. c. 2, tit. 12, §§ 39-55; Forb. Inst. pt. 3, b. 1, c. 2, tit. 6.

ADJUDICATION CONTRA HÆREDITATEM JACENTEM. In Scotch law. When a debtor's heir apparent renounces the succession, any creditor may obtain a decree *cognitionis causâ*, the purpose of which is that the amount of the debt may be ascertained so that the real estate may be adjudged.

ADJUDICATION IN IMPLEMENT. In Scotch law. An action by a grantee against his grantor to compel him to complete the title.

ADJUNCTIO. In the civil law. Adjunction; a species of *accessio*, whereby two things belonging to different proprietors are brought into firm connection with each other; such as interweaving, (*intertextura;*) welding together, (*adferruminatio;*) soldering together, (*applumbatura;*) painting, (*pictura;*) writing, (*scriptura;*) building, (*inædificatio;*) sowing, (*satio;*) and planting, (*plantatio.*) Inst. 2, 1, 26-34; Dig. 6, 1, 23; Mackeld. Rom. Law, § 276. See ACCESSIO.

ADJUNCTS. Additional judges sometimes appointed in the English high court of delegates. See Shelf. Lun. 310.

ADJUNCTUM ACCESSORIUM. An accessory or appurtenance.

ADJURATION. A swearing or binding upon oath.

ADJUST. To bring to proper relations; to settle; to determine and apportion an amount due.

ADJUSTMENT. In the law of insurance, the adjustment of a loss is the ascertainment of its amount and the ratable distribution of it among those liable to pay it; the settling and ascertaining the amount of the indemnity which the assured, after all allowances and deductions made, is entitled to receive under the policy, and fixing the proportion which each underwriter is liable to pay. Marsh. Ins. (4th Ed.) 499; 2 Phil. Ins. §§ 1814, 1815.

Adjuvari quippe nos, non decipi, beneficio oportet. We ought to be favored, not injured, by that which is intended for our benefit. (The species of bailment called "loan" must be to the advantage of the borrower, not to his detriment.) Story, Bailm. § 275. See 8 El. & Bl. 1051.

ADLAMWR. In Welsh law. A proprietor who, for some cause, entered the service of another proprietor, and left him after the expiration of a year and a day. He was liable to the payment of 30 pence to his patron. Wharton.

ADLEGIARE. To purge one's self of a crime by oath.

ADMANUENSIS. A person who swore by laying his hands on the book.

ADMEASUREMENT. Ascertainment by measure; measuring out; assignment or apportionment by measure, that is, by fixed quantity or value, by certain limits, or in definite and fixed proportions.

ADMEASUREMENT, WRIT OF. It lay against persons who usurped more than their share, in the two following cases: Admeasurement of dower, where the widow held from the heir more land, etc., as dower, than rightly belonged to her; and admeasurement of pasture, which lay where any one having common of pasture surcharged the common. Termes de la Ley.

ADMEASUREMENT OF DOWER. In practice. A remedy which lay for the heir on reaching his majority to rectify an assignment of dower made during his minority, by which the doweress had received more than she was legally entitled to. 2 Bl. Comm. 136; Gilb. Uses, 379.

In some of the states the statutory proceeding enabling a widow to compel the assignment of dower is called "admeasurement of dower."

ADMEASUREMENT OF PASTURE. In English law. A writ which lies between those that have common of pasture appendant, or by vicinage, in cases where any one or more of them surcharges the common with more cattle than they ought. Bract. fol. 229*a;* 1 Crabb, Real Prop. p. 318, § 358.

ADMENSURATIO. In old English law. Admeasurement. Reg. Orig. 156, 157.

ADMEZATORES. In old Italian law. Persons chosen by the consent of contending parties, to decide questions between them. Literally, mediators. Spelman.

ADMINICLE. In Scotch law. An aid or support to something else. A collateral deed or writing, referring to another which has been lost, and which it is in general necessary to produce before the tenor of the lost deed can be proved by parol evidence. Ersk. Inst. b. 4, tit. 1, § 55.

Used as an English word in the statute of 1 Edw. IV. c. 1, in the sense of aid, or support.

In the civil law. Imperfect proof. Merl. Repert.

ADMINICULAR. (From *adminiculum, q. v.*) Auxiliary to. "The murder would be *adminicular* to the robbery," (*i. e.*, committed to accomplish it.) 3 Mason, 121.

ADMINICULAR EVIDENCE. In ecclesiastical law. Auxiliary or supplementary evidence; such as is presented for the purpose of explaining and completing other evidence.

ADMINICULATE. To give adminicular evidence.

ADMINICULATOR. An officer in the Romish church, who administered to the wants of widows, orphans, and afflicted persons. Spelman.

ADMINICULUM. An adminicle; a prop or support; an accessory thing. An aid or support to something else, whether a right or the evidence of one. It is principally used to designate evidence adduced in aid or support of other evidence, which without it is imperfect. Brown.

ADMINISTER. To discharge the duties of an office; to take charge of business; to manage affairs; to serve in the conduct of affairs, in the application of things to their uses; to settle and distribute the estate of a decedent.

In physiology, and in criminal law, to administer means to cause or procure a person to take some drug or other substance into his or her system; to direct and cause a medicine, poison, or drug to be taken into the system. 8 Ohio St. 131; 34 N. Y. 223; 11 Fla. 247; 1 Moody, 114.

Neither fraud nor deception is a necessary ingredient in the act of administering poison. To force poison into the stomach of another; to compel another by threats of violence to swallow poison; to furnish poison to another for the purpose and with the intention that the person to whom it is delivered shall commit suicide therewith, and which poison is accordingly taken by the suicide for that purpose; or to be present at the taking of poison by a suicide, participating in the taking thereof, by assistance, persuasion, or otherwise,—each and all of these are forms and modes of "administering" poison. 23 Ohio St. 146.

ADMINISTRATION. In public law. The administration of government means the practical management and direction of the executive department, or of the public machinery or functions, or of the operations of the various organs of the sovereign. The term "administration" is also conventionally applied to the whole class of public functionaries, or those in charge of the management of the executive department.

ADMINISTRATION OF ESTATES. The management and settlement of the estate of an intestate, or of a testator who has no executor, performed under the supervision of a court, by a person duly qualified and legally appointed, and usually involving (1) the collection of the decedent's assets; (2) payment of debts and claims against him and expenses; (3) distributing the remainder of the estate among those entitled thereto.

The term is applied broadly to denote the management of an estate by an executor, and also the management of estates of minors, lunatics, etc., in those cases where trustees have been appointed by authority of law to take charge of such estates in place of the legal owners. Bouvier.

Administration is principally of the following kinds, viz.:

Ad colligendum. That which is granted temporarily, for the purpose of collecting and preserving property of a perishable nature.

Ancillary administration is auxiliary and subordinate to the administration at the place of the decedent's domicile; it may be taken out in any foreign state or country where assets are locally situated, and is merely for the purpose of collecting such assets and paying debts there.

Cum testamento annexo. Administration with the will annexed. Administration granted in cases where a testator makes a will, without naming any executors; or where the executors who are named in the will are incompetent to act, or refuse to act; or in case of the death of the executors, or the survivor of them. 2 Bl. Comm. 503, 504.

De bonis non. Administration of the goods not administered. Administration granted for the purpose of administering such *of the goods* of a deceased person as were *not administered* by the former executor or administrator. 2 Bl. Comm. 506.

De bonis non cum testamento annexo. That which is granted when an executor dies leaving a part of the estate unadministered. 3 Cush. 28; 4 Watts, 34, 38, 39.

Durante absentia. That which is granted during the absence of the executor and until he has proved the will.

Durante minori ætate. Where an infant is made executor; in which case administration with will annexed is granted to another, during the minority of such executor, and until he shall attain his lawful age to act. See Godo. 102.

Foreign administration. That which is exercised by virtue of authority properly conferred by a foreign power.

Pendente lite. Administration during the suit. Administration granted during the pendency of a suit touching the validity of a will. 2 Bl. Comm. 503.

Public administration is such as is conducted (in some jurisdictions) by an officer called the public administrator, who is appointed to administer in cases where the intestate has left no person entitled to apply for letters.

ADMINISTRATION SUIT. In English practice. A suit brought in chancery, by any one interested, for administration of a decedent's estate, when there is doubt as to its solvency. Stimson.

ADMINISTRATIVE LAW. That branch of public law which deals with the various organs of the sovereign power considered as in motion, and prescribes in detail the manner of their activity, being concerned with such topics as the collection of the revenue, the regulation of the military and naval forces, citizenship and naturalization, sanitary measures, poor laws, coinage, police, the public safety and morals, etc. See Holl. Jur. 305–307.

ADMINISTRATOR, in the most usual sense of the word, is a person to whom letters of administration, that is, an authority to administer the estate of a deceased person, have been granted by the proper court. He resembles an executor, but, being appointed by the court, and not by the deceased, he has to give security for the due administration of the estate, by entering into a bond with sureties, called the administration bond. (Browne, Prob. Pr. 150.) Sweet.

By the law of Scotland the father is what is called the "administrator-in-law" for his children. As such, he is *ipso jure* their tutor while they are pupils, and their curator during their minority. The father's power extends over whatever estate may descend to his children, unless where that estate has been placed by the donor or grantor under the charge of special trustees or managers. This power in the father ceases by the child's discontinuing to reside with him, unless he continues to live at the father's expense; and with regard to daughters, it ceases on their marriage, the husband being the legal curator of his wife. Bell.

A public administrator is an officer authorized by the statute law of several of the states to superintend the settlement of estates of persons dying without relatives entitled to administer.

ADMINISTRATOR. In the civil law. A manager or conductor of affairs, especially the affairs of another, in his name or behalf. A manager of public affairs in behalf of others. Calvin. A public officer, ruler, or governor. Nov. 95, gl.; Cod. 12, 8.

ADMINISTRATRIX. A female who administers, or to whom letters of administration have been granted.

ADMIRAL. **In European law.** An officer who presided over the *admiralitas*, or *collegium ammiralitatis*. Locc. de Jur. Mar. lib. 2, c. 2, § 1.

In English law. A high officer or magistrate that hath the government of the king's navy, and the hearing of all causes belonging to the sea. Cowell.

In the navy. Admiral is also the title of high naval officers; they are of various grades, —rear admiral, vice-admiral, admiral, admiral of the fleet, the latter being the highest.

ADMIRALITAS. L. Lat. Admiralty; the admiralty, or court of admiralty.

In European law. An association of private armed vessels for mutual protection and defense against pirates and enemies.

ADMIRALTY. A court exercising jurisdiction over maritime causes, both civil and criminal, and marine affairs, commerce and navigation, controversies arising out of acts done upon or relating to the sea, and over questions of prize.

Also, the system of jurisprudence relating to and growing out of the jurisdiction and practice of the admiralty courts.

In English law. The executive department of state which presides over the naval forces of the kingdom. The normal head is the lord high admiral, but in practice the functions of the great office are discharged by several commissioners, of whom one is the chief, and is called the "First Lord." He is assisted by other lords and by various secretaries. Also, the court of the admiral.

The building where the lords of the admiralty transact business.

In American law. A tribunal exercising jurisdiction over all maritime contracts, torts, injuries, or offenses. 2 Pars. Mar. Law, 508.

ADMISSIBLE. Proper to be received. As applied to evidence, the term means that it is of such a character that the court or judge is bound to receive it; that is, allow it to be introduced.

ADMISSIBILITY. An objection to the *admissibility* of evidence in any cause can only be properly founded on the hypothesis that such testimony violates the law of evidence in this: that the law prohibits the proof of the particular fact in the manner proposed, or because of its irrelevancy to the subject-matter of the inquiry. 7 Md. 87.

ADMISSION. In evidence. A voluntary acknowledgment, confession, or concession of the existence of a fact or the truth of an allegation made by a party to the suit.

In pleading. The concession or acknowledgment by one party of the truth of some matter alleged by the opposite party, made in a pleading, the effect of which is to narrow the area of facts or allegations requiring to be proved by evidence.

In practice. The formal act of a court, by which attorneys or counsellors are recognized as officers of the court and are licensed to practice before it.

In corporations. The act of a corporation or company by which an individual acquires the rights of a member of such corporation or company.

In English ecclesiastical law. The act of the bishop, who, on approval of the clerk presented by the patron, after examination, declares him fit to serve the cure of the church to which he is presented, by the words "*admitto te habilem,*" I admit thee able. Co. Litt. 344*a;* 4 Coke, 79; 1 Crabb, Real Prop. p. 138, § 123.

ADMISSIONALIS. In European law. An usher. Spelman.

ADMIT. To allow, receive, or take; to suffer one to enter; to give possession; to license. See ADMISSION.

ADMITTANCE. In English law. The act of giving possession of a copyhold estate. It is of three kinds: (1) Upon a *voluntary grant by the lord,* where the land has escheated or reverted to him. (2) Upon *surrender* by the former tenant. (3) Upon *descent,* where the heir is tenant on his ancestor's death.

ADMITTENDO CLERICO. A writ of execution upon a right of presentation to a benefice being recovered in *quare impedit,* addressed to the bishop or his metropolitan, requiring him to *admit* and institute the clerk or presentee of the plaintiff. Reg. Orig. 33*a*.

ADMITTENDO IN SOCIUM. A writ for associating certain persons, as knights and other gentlemen of the county, to justices of assize on the circuit. Reg. Orig. 206.

ADMONITIO TRINA. A triple or threefold warning, given, in old times, to a prisoner standing mute, before he was subjected to the *peine forte et dure.* 4 Bl. Comm. 325; 4 Steph. Comm. 391.

ADMONITION. In ecclesiastical law, this is the lightest form of punishment, consisting in a reprimand and warning administered by the judge to the defendant. If the latter does not obey the admonition, he may be more severely punished, as by suspension, etc.

ADMORTIZATION. The reduction of property of lands or tenements to mortmain, in the feudal customs.

ADNEPOS. The son of a great-great-grandson. Calvin.

ADNEPTIS. The daughter of a great-great-granddaughter. Calvin.

ADNICHILED. Annulled, cancelled, made void. 28 Hen. VIII.

ADNIHILARE. In old English law. To annul; to make void; to reduce to nothing; to treat as nothing; to hold as or for nought.

ADNOTATIO. In the civil law. The subscription of a name or signature to an instrument. Cod. 4, 19, 5, 7.

A rescript of the prince or emperor, signed with his own hand, or sign-manual. Cod. 1, 19, 1. "In the imperial law, casual homicide was excused by the indulgence of the emperor, signed with his own sign-manual, *annotatione principis.*" 4 Bl. Comm. 187.

ADOLESCENCE. That age which follows puberty and precedes the age of majority. It commences for males at 14, and for females at 12 years completed, and continues till 21 years complete.

ADOPT. To accept, appropriate, choose, or select; to make that one's own (property or act) which was not so originally; to take another's child and give him the rights and duties of one's own.

To adopt a route for the transportation of the mail means to take the steps necessary to cause the mail to be transported over that route. Dev. Ct. Cl. 47.

To adopt a contract is to accept it as binding, notwithstanding some defect which entitles the party to repudiate it. Thus, when a person affirms a voidable contract, or ratifies a contract made by his agent beyond his authority, he is said to adopt it. Sweet.

ADOPTION. The act of one who takes another's child into his own family, treating him as his own, and giving him all the rights and duties of his own child.

A juridical act creating between two persons certain relations, purely civil, of paternity and filiation. 6 Demol. § 1.

ADOPTIVE ACT. An act of parliament which comes into operation within a limited area upon being adopted, in manner prescribed therein, by the inhabitants of that area.

ADOPTIVUS. Lat. Adoptive. Applied both to the parent adopting, and the child adopted. Inst. 2, 13, 4; Id. 3, 1, 10–14.

ADPROMISSOR. In the civil and Scotch law. A guarantor, surety, or cautioner; a peculiar species of *fidejussor;* one who adds his own promise to the promise given by the principal debtor, whence the name.

ADQUIETO. Payment. Blount.

ADRECTARE. To do right, satisfy, or make amends.

ADRHAMIRE. In old European law. To undertake, declare, or promise solemnly; to pledge; to pledge one's self to make oath. Spelman.

ADRIFT. Sea-weed, between high and low water-mark, which has not been deposited on the shore, and which during flood-tide is moved by each rising and receding wave, is *adrift*, although the bottom of the mass may touch the beach. 2 Allen, 549.

ADROGATION. In the civil law. The adoption of one who was *impubes;* that is, if a male, under fourteen years of age; if a female, under twelve. Dig. 1, 7, 17, 1.

ADSCENDENTES. Lat. In the civil law. Ascendants. Dig. 23, 2, 68; Cod. 5, 5, 6.

ADSCRIPTI GLEBÆ. Slaves who served the master of the soil, who were annexed to the land, and passed with it when it was conveyed. Calvin.

In Scotland, as late as the reign of George III., laborers in collieries and salt works were bound to the coal-pit or salt work in which they were engaged, in a manner similar to that of the *adscripti* of the Romans. Bell.

ADSCRIPTUS. In the civil law. Added, annexed, or bound by or in writing; enrolled, registered; united, joined, annexed, bound to, generally. *Servus colonæ adscriptus*, a slave annexed to an estate as a cultivator. Dig. 19, 2, 54, 2. *Fundus adscriptus*, an estate bound to, or burdened with a duty. Cod. 11, 2, 3.

ADSESSORES. Side judges. Assistants or advisers of the regular magistrates, or appointed as their substitutes in certain cases. Calvin.

ADSTIPULATOR. In Roman law. An accessory party to a promise, who received the same promise as his principal did, and could equally receive and exact payment; or he only stipulated for a part of that for which the principal stipulated, and then his rights were co-extensive with the amount of his own stipulation. Sandars, Just. Inst. (5th Ed.) 348.

ADULT. In the civil law. A male infant who has attained the age of fourteen; a female infant who has attained the age of twelve. Dom. Liv. Prel. tit. 2, § 2, n. 8.

In the common law. One of the full age of twenty-one. Swanst. Ch. 533.

"The authorities all agree, so far as we are advised, that at common law the word 'adult' signifies a person who has attained the full age of 21 years. The word 'adult' seems to have a well-defined meaning, both in law and in common acceptation. Mr. Bouvier defines the meaning of the word in the civil law, with which we have no present concern, and says: 'In the common law an adult is considered one of full age.' Mr. Wharton defines the word as signifying 'a person of full age.' Mr. Webster gives as one of the meanings 'one who has reached the years of manhood.'" 10 Tex. App. 411; 11 Tex. App. 95.

ADULTER. Lat. One who corrupts; one who seduces another man's wife. *Adulter solidorum.* A corruptor of metals; a counterfeiter. Calvin.

ADULTERA. In the civil law. An adulteress; a woman guilty of adultery. Dig. 48, 5, 4, pr.; Id. 48, 5, 15, 8.

ADULTERATION. The act of corrupting or debasing. The term is generally applied to the act of mixing up with food or drink intended to be sold other matters of an inferior quality, and usually of a more or less deleterious quality.

It is not clear that the addition of a wholesome article, as of pure water to milk, is adulterating. 5 Park. Crim. R. 311.

ADULTERATOR. Lat. In the civil law. A forger; a counterfeiter. *Adulteratores monetæ*, counterfeiters of money. Dig. 48, 19, 16, 9.

ADULTERINE. Begotten in an adulterous intercourse. In the Roman and canon law, adulterine bastards were distinguished from such as were the issue of two unmarried persons, and the former were treated with more severity, not being allowed the *status* of natural children, and being ineligible to holy orders.

ADULTERINE GUILDS. Traders acting as a corporation without a charter, and paying a fine annually for permission to exercise their usurped privileges. Smith, Wealth Nat. b. 1, c. 10.

ADULTERIUM. A fine anciently imposed as a punishment for the commission of adultery.

ADULTEROUS BASTARDY. Adulterous bastards are those produced by an unlawful connection between two persons, who, at the time when the child was conceived, were, either of them or both, connected by marriage with some other person. Civil Code La. art. 182.

ADULTERY. Adultery is the voluntary sexual intercourse of a married person with a person other than the offender's husband or wife. Civil Code Cal. § 93; 1 Bish. Mar. & Div. § 703; 6 Metc. 243; 36 Me. 261; 11 Ga. 56.

Adultery is the unlawful voluntary sexual intercourse of a married person with one of the opposite sex, and when the crime is committed between parties, only one of whom is married, both are guilty of adultery. Pen. Code Dak. § 333.

It is to be observed, however, that in some of the states it is held that this crime is committed only when the *woman* is married to a third person, and the unlawful commerce of a married man with an unmarried woman is not of the grade of adultery. In some jurisdictions, also, a distinction is made between double and single adultery, the former being committed where both parties are married to other persons, the latter where one only is so married.

ADVANCE, *v.* To pay money or render other value before it is due; or to furnish capital in aid of a projected enterprise, in expectation of return from it.

ADVANCEMENT. Money or property given by a father to his child or presumptive heir, or expended by the former for the latter's benefit, by way of anticipation of the share which the child will inherit in the father's estate and intended to be deducted therefrom. It is the latter circumstance which differentiates an advancement from a gift or a loan.

Advancement, in its legal acceptation, does not involve the idea of obligation or future liability to answer. It is a pure and irrevocable gift made by a parent to a child in anticipation of such child's future share of the parent's estate. 13 Pa. St. 580.

An advancement is any provision by a parent made to and accepted by a child out of his estate, either in money or property, during his life-time, over and above the obligation of the parent for maintenance and education. Code Ga. 1882, § 2579.

An "advancement by portion," within the meaning of the statute, is a sum given by a parent to establish a child in life, (as by starting him in business,) or to make a provision for the child, (as on the marriage of a daughter.) L. R. 20 Eq. 155.

ADVANCES. Moneys paid before or in advance of the proper time of payment; money or commodities furnished on credit; a loan or gift, or money advanced to be repaid conditionally. See 51 Barb. 597, 612; 10 Barb. 73.

This word, when taken in its strict legal sense, does not mean gifts, (advancements,) and does mean a sort of loan; and, when taken in its ordinary and usual sense, it includes both loans and gifts, — loans more readily, perhaps, than gifts. 25 Ga. 355.

Payments advanced to the owner of property by a factor or broker on the price of goods which the latter has in his hands, or is to receive, for sale.

ADVANTAGIUM. In old pleading. An advantage. Co. Ent. 484; Townsh. Pl. 50.

ADVENA. In Roman law. One of foreign birth, who has left his own country and settled elsewhere, and who has not acquired citizenship in his new locality; often called *albanus*. Du Cange.

ADVENT. A period of time recognized by the English common and ecclesiastical law, beginning on the Sunday that falls either upon St. Andrew's day, being the 30th of November, or the next to it, and continuing to Christmas day. Wharton.

ADVENTITIOUS. That which comes incidentally, fortuitously, or out of the regular course.

ADVENTITIUS. Lat. Fortuitous; incidental; that which comes from an unusual source. *Adventitia bona* are goods which fall to a man otherwise than by inheritance. *Adventitia dos* is a dowry or portion given by some friend other than the parent.

ADVENTURA. An adventure. 2 Mon. Angl. 615; Townsh. Pl. 50. Flotson, jetson, and lagon are styled *adventuræ maris*, (adventures of the sea.) Hale, De Jure Mar. pt. 1, c. 7.

ADVENTURE. **In mercantile law.** Sending goods abroad under charge of a supercargo or other agent, at the risk of the sender, to be disposed of to the best advantage for the benefit of the owners.

The goods themselves so sent.

In marine insurance. A very usual word in policies of marine insurance, and everywhere used as synonymous, or nearly so, with "perils." It is often used by the writers to describe the enterprise or voyage as a "marine adventure" insured against. 14 Fed. Rep. 233.

ADVENTURE, BILL OF. In mercantile law. A writing signed by a merchant, stating that the property in goods shipped in his name belongs to another, to the adventure or chance of which the person so named is to stand, with a covenant from the merchant to account to him for the produce.

ADVERSARIA. (From Lat. *adversa*, things remarked or ready at hand.) Rough memoranda, common-place books.

ADVERSARY. A litigant-opponent, the opposite party in a writ or action.

ADVERSARY PROCEEDING. One having opposing parties; contested, as distinguished from an *ex parte* application; one of which the party seeking relief has given legal warning to the other party, and afforded the latter an opportunity to contest it.

ADVERSE. Opposed; contrary; in resistance or opposition to a claim, application, or proceeding.

ADVERSE CLAIM. A claim set up by a stranger to goods upon which the sheriff has levied an execution or attachment.

ADVERSE ENJOYMENT. The possession or exercise of an easement, under a claim of right against the owner of the land out of which such easement is derived. 2 Washb. Real Prop. 42.

ADVERSE POSSESSION. The possession and enjoyment of real property, or of any estate lying in grant, continued for a certain length of time, held adversely and in denial and opposition to the title of another claimant, or under circumstances which indicate an assertion or color of right or title on the part of the person maintaining it, as against another person who is out of possession.

ADVERSE USER. An adverse user is such a use of the property as the owner himself would make, asking no permission, and disregarding all other claims to it, so far as they conflict with this use. 63 Me. 434.

ADVERSE VERDICT. Where a party, appealing from an allowance of damages by commissioners, recovers a verdict in his favor, but for a less amount of damages than had been originally allowed, such verdict is *adverse* to him, within the meaning of his undertaking to pay costs if the verdict should be adverse to him. 16 Gray, 256.

ADVERSE WITNESS. A witness whose mind discloses a bias hostile to the party examining him; not a witness whose evidence, being honestly given, is adverse to the case of the examinant. Brown.

ADVERSUS. In the civil law. Against, (*contra*.) *Adversus bonos mores*, against good morals. Dig. 47, 10, 15.

ADVERTISEMENT. Notice given in a manner designed to attract public attention; information communicated to the public, or to an individual concerned, by means of handbills or the newspaper.

A sign-board, erected at a person's place of business, giving notice that lottery tickets are for sale there, is an "advertisement," within the meaning of a statute prohibiting the advertising of lotteries. In such connection the meaning of the word is not confined to notices printed in newspapers. 5 Pick. 42.

ADVERTISEMENTS OF QUEEN ELIZABETH. Certain articles or ordinances drawn up by Archbishop Parker and some of the bishops in 1564, at the request of Queen Elizabeth, the object of which was to enforce decency and uniformity in the ritual of the church. The queen subsequently refused to give her official sanction to these advertisements, and left them to be enforced by the bishops under their general powers. Phillim. Ecc. Law, 910; 2 Prob. Div. 276; Id. 354.

ADVICE. View; opinion; the counsel given by lawyers to their clients; an opinion expressed as to wisdom of future conduct.

The instruction usually given by one merchant or banker to another by letter, informing him of shipments made to him, or of bills or drafts drawn on him, with particulars of date, or sight, the sum, and the payee. Bills presented for acceptance or payment are frequently dishonored for *want of advice.*

ADVISARE, ADVISARI. To consult, deliberate, consider, advise; to be advised. Occurring in the phrase *curia advisari vult,* (usually abbreviated *cur. adv. vult,* or *C. A. V.,*) the court wishes to be advised, or to consider of the matter.

ADVISE. To give an opinion or counsel, or recommend a plan or course of action; also to give notice.

This term is not synonymous with "direct" or "instruct." Where a statute authorizes the trial court to *advise* the jury to acquit, the court has no power to *instruct* the jury to acquit. The court can only counsel, and the jury are not bound by the advice. 70 Cal. 17, 11 Pac. Rep. 470.

ADVISED. Prepared to give judgment, after examination and deliberation. "The court took time to be advised." 1 Leon. 187.

ADVISEMENT. Deliberation, consideration, consultation; the consultation of a court, after the argument of a cause by counsel, and before delivering their opinion.

ADVISORY. Counselling, suggesting, or advising, but not imperative. A verdict on an issue out of chancery is advisory. 101 U. S. 252.

ADVOCARE. Lat. To defend; to call to one's aid; to vouch; to warrant.

ADVOCASSIE. L. Fr. The office of an advocate; advocacy. Kelham.

ADVOCATA. In old English law. A patroness; a woman who had the right of presenting to a church. Spelman.

ADVOCATE. One who assists, defends, or pleads for another; one who renders legal advice and aid and pleads the cause of another before a court.

A person learned in the law, and duly admitted to practice, who assists his client with advice, and pleads for him in open court. Holthouse.

The *College or Faculty of Advocates* is a corporate body in Scotland, consisting of the members of the bar in Edinburgh. A large portion of its members are not active practitioners, however. 2 Bankt. Inst. 486.

In the civil and ecclesiastical law. An officer of the court, learned in the law, who is engaged by a suitor to maintain or defend his cause.

ADVOCATE GENERAL. The adviser of the crown in England on questions of naval and military law.

ADVOCATE, LORD. The principal crown lawyer in Scotland, and one of the great officers of state of Scotland. It is his duty to act as public prosecutor; but private individuals injured may prosecute upon obtaining his concurrence. He is assisted by a solicitor general and four junior counsel, termed "advocates-depute." He has the power of appearing as public prosecutor in any court in Scotland, where any person can be tried for an offense, or in any action where the crown is interested. Wharton.

ADVOCATE, QUEEN'S. A member of the College of Advocates, appointed by letters patent, whose office is to advise and act as counsel for the crown in questions of civil, canon, and international law. His rank is next after the solicitor general.

ADVOCATI. In Roman law. Patrons; pleaders; speakers. Anciently, any one who lent his aid to a friend, and who was supposed to be able in any way to influence a judge, was called *advocatus.*

ADVOCATI ECCLESIÆ. A term used in the ecclesiastical law to denote the patrons of churches who presented to the living on an avoidance. This term was also applied to those who were retained to argue the cases of the church.

ADVOCATI FISCI. In the civil law. Advocates of the fisc, or revenue; fiscal advocates, (*qui causam fisci egissent.*) Cod. 2,

9, 1; Id. 2, 7, 13. Answering, in some measure, to the king's counsel in English law. 3 Bl. Comm. 27.

ADVOCATIA. In the civil law. The quality, function, privilege, or territorial jurisdiction of an advocate.

ADVOCATION. In Scotch law. A process by which an action may be carried from an inferior to a superior court before final judgment in the former.

ADVOCATIONE DECIMARUM. A writ which lay for tithes, demanding the fourth part or upwards, that belonged to any church.

ADVOCATOR. In old practice. One who called on or vouched another to warrant a title; a voucher. *Advocatus;* the person called on, or vouched; a vouchee. Spelman; Townsh. Pl. 45.

In Scotch practice. An appellant. 1 Broun, R. 67.

ADVOCATUS. In the civil law. An advocate; one who managed or assisted in managing another's cause before a judicial tribunal. Called also "*patronus.*" Cod. 2, 7, 14. But distinguished from *causidicus.* Id. 2, 6, 6.

ADVOCATUS DIABOLI. The devil's advocate; the advocate who argues against the canonization of a saint.

Advocatus est, ad quem pertinet jus advocationis alicujus ecclesiæ, ut ad ecclesiam, nomine proprio, non alieno, possit præsentare. A patron is he to whom appertains the right of presentation to a church, in such a manner that he may present to such a church in his own name, and not in the name of another. Co. Litt. 119.

ADVOWEE, or AVOWEE. The person or patron who has a right to present to a benefice. Fleta, lib. 5, c. 14.

ADVOWEE PARAMOUNT. The sovereign, or highest patron.

ADVOWSON. In English ecclesiastical law. The right of presentation to a church or ecclesiastical benefice; the right of presenting a fit person to the bishop, to be by him admitted and instituted to a certain benefice within the diocese, which has become vacant. 2 Bl. Comm. 21; Co. Litt. 119*b*, 120*a*. The person enjoying this right is called the "patron" (*patronus*) of the church, and was formerly termed "*advocatus,*" the advocate or defender, or in English, "*advowee.*" Id.; 1 Crabb, Real Prop. p. 129, § 117.

Advowsons are of the following several kinds, viz.:

Advowson appendant. An advowson annexed to a manor, and passing with it, as incident or appendant to it, by a grant of the manor only, without adding any other words. 2 Bl. Comm. 22; Co. Litt. 120, 121; 1 Crabb, Real Prop. p. 130, § 118.

Advowson collative. Where the bishop happens himself to be the patron, in which case (presentation being impossible, or unnecessary) he does by one act, which is termed "*collation,*" or conferring the benefice, all that is usually done by the separate acts of presentation and institution. 2 Bl. Comm. 22, 23; 1 Crabb, Real Prop. p. 131, § 119.

Advowson donative. Where the patron has the right to put his clerk in possession by his mere gift, or deed of donation, without any presentation to the bishop, or institution by him. 2 Bl. Comm. 23; 1 Crabb, Real Prop. p. 131, § 119.

Advowson in gross. An advowson separated from the manor, and annexed to the person. 2 Bl. Comm. 22; Co. Litt. 120; 1 Crabb, Real Prop. p. 130, § 118; 3 Steph. Comm. 116.

Advowson presentative. The usual kind of advowson, where the patron has the right of *presentation* to the bishop, or ordinary, and moreover to demand of him to institute his clerk, if he finds him canonically qualified. 2 Bl. Comm. 22; 1 Crabb, Real Prop. p. 131, § 119.

ADVOWTRY, or ADVOUTRY. The offense, by an adulteress, of continuing to live with the man with whom she committed the adultery. Cowell; Termes de la Ley.

ÆDES. Lat. In the civil law. A house, dwelling, place of habitation, whether in the city or country. Dig. 30, 41, 5. In the country everything upon the surface of the soil passed under the term "*ædes.*" Du Cange; Calvin.

ÆDIFICARE. Lat. In civil and old English law. To make or build a house; to erect a building. Dig. 45, 1, 75, 7.

Ædificare in tuo proprio solo non licet quod alteri noceat. 3 Inst. 201. To build upon your own land what may injure another is not lawful. A proprietor of land has no right to erect an edifice on his own ground, interfering with the due enjoyment of adjoining premises, as by overhanging them, or by throwing water from the roof and eaves upon them, or by obstructing ancient lights and windows. Broom, Max. 369.

Ædificatum solo solo cedit. What is built upon land belongs to or goes with land. Broom, Max. 172; Co. Litt. 4*a*.

Ædificia solo cedunt. Buildings belong to [go with] the soil. Fleta, lib. 3, c. 2, § 12.

ÆDILE. In Roman law. An officer who attended to the repairs of the temples and other public buildings; the repairs and cleanliness of the streets; the care of the weights and measures; the providing for funerals and games; and regulating the prices of provisions. Ainsw. Lex.; Smith, Lex.; Du Cange.

ÆDILITUM EDICTUM. In the Roman law. The Ædilitian Edict; an edict providing remedies for frauds in sales, the execution of which belonged to the curule ædiles. Dig. 21, 1. See Cod. 4, 58.

ÆFESN. In old English law. The remuneration to the proprietor of a domain for the privilege of feeding swine under the oaks and beeches of his woods.

ÆGROTO. Lat. Being sick or indisposed. A term used in some of the older reports. "Holt *ægroto.*" 11 Mod. 179.

ÆGYLDE. Uncompensated, unpaid for, unavenged. From the participle of exclusion, *a*, *æ*, or *ex*, (Goth.,) and *gild*, payment, requital. Anc. Inst. Eng.

ÆL. A Norman French term signifying "grandfather." It is also spelled "*aieul*" and "*ayle.*" Kelham.

Æquior est dispositio legis quam hominis. The disposition of the law is more equitable than that of man. 8 Coke, 152.

ÆQUITAS. In the civil law. Equity, as opposed to *strictum* or *summum jus*, (*q. v.*) Otherwise called *æquum*, *æquum bonum*, *æquum et bonum*, *æquum et justum*. Calvin.

Æquitas agit in personam. Equity acts upon the person. 4 Bouv. Inst. n. 3733.

Æquitas est correctio legis generaliter latæ, qua parte deficit. Equity is the correction of that wherein the law, by reason of its generality, is deficient. Plowd. 375.

Æquitas est correctio quædam legi adhibita, quia ab eâ abest aliquid propter generalem sine exceptione comprehensionem. Equity is a certain correction applied to law, because on account of its general comprehensiveness, without an exception, something is absent from it. Plowd. 467.

Æquitas est perfecta quædam ratio quæ jus scriptum interpretatur et emendat; nulla scriptura comprehensa, sed solum in verâ ratione consistens. Equity is a certain perfect reason, which interprets and amends the written law, comprehended in no writing, but consisting in right reason alone. Co. Litt. 24*b*.

Æquitas est quasi æqualitas. Equity is as it were equality; equity is a species of equality or equalization. Co. Litt. 24.

Æquitas ignorantiæ opitulatur, oscitantiæ non item. Equity assists ignorance, but not carelessness.

Æquitas non facit jus, sed juri auxiliatur. Equity does not make law, but assists law. Lofft, 379.

Æquitas nunquam contravenit leges. Equity never counteracts the laws.

Æquitas sequitur legem. Equity follows the law. Gilb. 186.

Æquitas supervacua odit. Equity abhors superfluous things. Lofft, 282.

Æquitas uxoribus, liberis, creditoribus maxime favet. Equity favors wives and children, creditors most of all.

Æquum et bonum est lex legum. What is equitable and good is the law of laws. Hob. 224.

ÆRA, or ERA. A fixed point of chronological time, whence any number of years is counted; thus, the Christian era began at the birth of Christ, and the Mohammedan era at the flight of Mohammed from Mecca to Medina. The derivation of the word has been much contested. Wharton.

ÆRARIUM. Lat. In the Roman law. The treasury, (*fiscus.*) Calvin.

ÆS. Lat. In the Roman law. Money, (literally, brass;) metallic money in general, including gold. Dig. 9, 2, 2, pr.; Id. 9, 2, 27, 5; Id. 50, 16, 159.

ÆS ALIENUM. A civil law term signifying a debt; the property of another; borrowed money, as distinguished from *æs suum*, one's own money.

ÆS SUUM. One's own money. In the Roman law. Debt; a debt; that which others owe to us, (*quod alii nobis debent.*) Dig. 50, 16, 213.

ÆSNECIA. In old English law. Esnecy; the right or privilege of the eldest born. Spelman; Glanv. lib. 7, c. 3; Fleta, lib. 2, c. 66, §§ 5, 6.

ÆSTIMATIO CAPITIS. In Saxon law. The estimation or valuation of the head; the price or value of a man. By the laws of Athelstan, the life of every man, not excepting that of the king himself, was estimated at a certain price, which was called the *were*, or *æstimatio capitis*. Crabb, Eng. Law, c. 4.

Æstimatio præteriti delicti ex postremo facto nunquam crescit. The weight of a past offense is never increased by a subsequent fact. Bacon.

ÆTAS INFANTIÆ PROXIMA. In the civil law. The age next to infancy; the first half of the period of childhood, (*pueritia,*) extending from seven years to ten and a half. Inst. 3, 20, 9; 4 Bl. Comm. 22.

ÆTAS LEGITIMA. In the civil law. Lawful age; the age of twenty-five. Dig. 3, 5, 27, pr.; Id. 26, 2, 32, 2; Id. 27, 7, 1, pr.

ÆTAS PERFECTA. In the civil law, Complete age; full age; the age of twenty-five. Dig. 4, 4, 32; Id. 22, 3, 25, 1.

ÆTAS PRIMA. In the civil law. The first age; infancy, (*infantia.*) Cod. 6, 61, 8, 3.

ÆTAS PUBERTATI PROXIMA. In the civil law. The age next to puberty; the last half of the period of childhood, (*pueritia,*) extending from ten years and a half to fourteen. Inst. 3, 20, 9; 4 Bl. Comm. 22.

ÆTATE PROBANDA. A writ which inquired whether the king's tenant holding in chief by chivalry was of full age to receive his lands. It was directed to the escheater of the county. Now disused.

ÆTHELING. In Saxon law. A noble; generally a prince of the blood.

AFFAIRS. A person's concerns in trade or property; business.

AFFECT. This word is often used in the sense of acting injuriously upon persons and things. 93 U. S. 84.

Affectio tua nomen imponit operi tuo. Your disposition (or intention) gives name (or character) to your work or act. Bract. fol. 2*b*, 101*b*.

AFFECTION. The making over, pawning, or mortgaging a thing to assure the payment of a sum of money, or the discharge of some other duty or service. Crabb, Technol. Dict.

AFFECTUS. Disposition; intention, impulse or affection of the mind. One of the causes for a challenge of a juror is *propter affectum*, on account of a suspicion of *bias* or favor. 3 Bl. Comm. 363; Co. Litt. 156.

Affectus punitur licet non sequatur effectus. The intention is punished although the intended result does not follow. 9 Coke, 55.

AFFEER. To assess, liquidate, appraise, fix in amount.

To affeer an amercement. To establish the amount which one amerced in a court-leet should pay.

To affeer an account. To confirm it on oath in the exchequer. Cowell; Blount; Spelman.

AFFEERORS. Persons who, in court-leets, upon oath, settle and moderate the fines and amercements imposed on those who have committed offenses arbitrarily punishable, or that have no express penalty appointed by statute. They are also appointed to moderate fines, etc., in courts-baron. Cowell.

AFFERMER. L. Fr. To let to farm. Also to make sure, to establish or confirm. Kelham.

AFFIANCE. A plighting of troth between man and woman. Litt. § 39. An agreement by which a man and woman promise each other that they will marry together. Poth. Traité du Mar. n. 24.

AFFIANT. The person who makes and subscribes an affidavit. The word is used, in this sense, interchangeably with "deponent." But the latter term should be reserved as the designation of one who makes a deposition.

AFFIDARE. To swear faith to; to pledge one's faith or do fealty by making oath. Cowell.

AFFIDARI. To be mustered and enrolled for soldiers upon an oath of fidelity.

AFFIDATIO. A swearing of the oath of fidelity or of fealty to one's lord, under whose protection the quasi-vassal has voluntarily come. Brown.

AFFIDATIO DOMINORUM. An oath taken by the lords in parliament.

AFFIDATUS. One who is not a vassal, but who for the sake of protection has connected himself with one more powerful. Spelman; 2 Bl. Comm. 46.

AFFIDAVIT. A written or printed declaration or statement of facts, made voluntarily, and confirmed by the oath or affirmation of the party making it, taken before an officer having authority to administer such oath.

An affidavit is a written declaration under oath, made without notice to the adverse party. Code Civil Proc. Cal. § 2003; Code Civil Proc. Dak. § 464.

An affidavit is an oath in writing, sworn before and attested by him who hath authority to administer the same. 1 Mich. N. P. 189.

An affidavit is always taken *ex parte*, and in this respect it is distinguished from a deposition, the matter of which is elicited by questions, and which affords an opportunity for cross-examination.

AFFIDAVIT OF DEFENSE. An affidavit stating that the defendant has a good defense to the plaintiff's action on the merits of the case. Also called an affidavit of merits.

AFFIDAVIT OF SERVICE. An affidavit intended to certify the service of a writ, notice, or other document.

AFFIDAVIT TO HOLD TO BAIL. An affidavit made to procure the arrest of the defendant in a civil action.

AFFILARE. L. Lat. To file or affile. *Affiletur*, let it be filed. 8 Coke, 160. *De recordo affilatum*, affiled of record. 2 Ld. Raym. 1476.

AFFILE. A term employed in old practice, signifying to put on file. 2 Maule & S. 202. In modern usage it is contracted to *file*.

AFFILIATION. The fixing any one with the paternity of a bastard child, and the obligation to maintain it.

In French law. A species of adoption which exists by custom in some parts of France. The person affiliated succeeded equally with other heirs to the property acquired by the deceased to whom he had been affiliated, but not to that which he inherited. Bouvier.

In ecclesiastical law. A condition which prevented the superior from removing the person affiliated to another convent. Guyot, Repert.

AFFINAGE. A refining of metals. Blount.

AFFINES. In the civil law. Connections by marriage, whether of the persons or their relatives. Calvin.

Neighbors, who own or occupy adjoining lands. Dig. 10, 1, 12.

Affinis mei affinis non est mihi affinis. One who is related by marriage to a person related to me by marriage, has no affinity to me. Shelf. Mar. & Div. 174.

AFFINITAS. In the civil law. Affinity; relationship by marriage. Inst. 1, 10, 6.

AFFINITAS AFFINITATIS. Remote relationship by marriage. That connection between parties arising from marriage which is neither consanguinity nor affinity.

AFFINITY. Relationship by marriage between the husband and the blood relations of the wife, and between the wife and the blood relations of the husband. 1 Bl. Comm. 434. Affinity is distinguished into three kinds: (1) *Direct*, or that subsisting between the husband and his wife's relations by blood, or between the wife and the husband's relations by blood; (2) *secondary*, or that which subsists between the husband and his wife's relations by marriage; (3) *collateral*, or that which subsists between the husband and the relations of his wife's relations. Wharton.

The connection which arises by marriage between each person of the married pair and the kindred of the other. Mackeld. Rom. Law, § 147. A husband is related by affinity to all the *consanguinei* of his wife, and *vice versa*, the wife to the husband's *consanguinei*; for the husband and wife being considered one flesh, those who are related to the one by blood are related to the other by affinity. Gib. Cod. 412; 1 Bl. Comm. 435.

In a larger sense, consanguinity or kindred. Co. Litt. 157*a*.

Affinity means the tie which arises from the marriage between the husband and the blood relations of the wife, and between the wife and the blood relations of the husband. 45 N. Y. Super. Ct. 84.

AFFIRM. To ratify, make firm, confirm, establish, reassert.

To ratify or confirm a former law or judgment. Cowell.

In the practice of appellate courts, to *affirm* a judgment, decree, or order, is to declare that it is valid and right, and must stand as rendered below; to ratify and reassert it; to concur in its correctness and confirm its efficacy.

In pleading. To allege or aver a matter of fact; to state it affirmatively; the opposite of *deny* or *traverse.*

In practice. To make affirmation; to make a solemn and formal declaration or asseveration that an affidavit is true, that the witness will tell the truth, etc., this being substituted for an oath in certain cases. Also, to give testimony on affirmation.

In the law of contracts. A party is said to affirm a contract, the same being voidable at his election, when he ratifies and accepts it, waives his right to annul it, and proceeds under it as if it had been valid originally.

AFFIRMANCE. In practice. The confirming, or ratifying a former law, or judgment. Cowell; Blount.

The confirmation and ratification by an appellate court of a judgment, order, or decree of a lower court brought before it for review. See AFFIRM.

A dismissal of an appeal for want of prosecution is not an "affirmance" of the judgment. 14 N. Y. 60.

The ratification or confirmation of a voidable contract or act by the party who is to be bound thereby.

The term is in accuracy to be distinguished from *ratification*, which is a recognition of the validity or binding force as against the party ratifying, of some act performed by another person; and from *confirmation*, which would seem to apply more properly to cases where a doubtful authority has been exercised by another in behalf of the person ratifying; but these distinctions are not generally observed with much care. Bouvier.

AFFIRMANCE DAY GENERAL. In the English court of exchequer, is a day appointed by the judges of the common pleas, and barons of the exchequer, to be held a few days after the beginning of every term for the general affirmance or reversal of judgments. 2 Tidd, Pr. 1091.

AFFIRMANT. A person who testifies on affirmation, or who affirms instead of taking an oath. See AFFIRMATION. Used in affidavits and depositions which are *affirmed*, instead of sworn to, in place of the word "deponent."

Affirmanti, non neganti incumbit probatio. The [burden of] proof lies upon him who affirms, not upon one who denies. Steph. Pl. 84.

Affirmantis est probare. He who affirms must prove. 9 Cush. 535.

AFFIRMATION. In practice. A solemn and formal declaration or asseveration that an affidavit is true, that the witness will tell the truth, etc., this being substituted for an oath in certain cases.

A solemn religious asseveration in the nature of an oath. 1 Greenl. Ev. § 371.

AFFIRMATIVE. That which declares positively; that which avers a fact to be true; that which establishes; the opposite of negative.

The party who, upon the allegations of pleadings joining issue, is under the obligation of making proof, in the first instance, of matters alleged, is said to hold the affirmative, or, in other words, to sustain the burden of proof. Abbott.

AFFIRMATIVE PREGNANT. In pleading. An affirmative allegation implying some negative in favor of the adverse party.

AFFIRMATIVE STATUTE. In legislation. A statute couched in affirmative or mandatory terms; one which directs the doing of an act, or declares what shall be done; as a *negative* statute is one which prohibits a thing from being done, or declares what shall not be done. Blackstone describes affirmative acts of parliament as those "wherein justice is directed to be done according to the law of the land." 1 Bl. Comm. 142.

AFFIRMATIVE WARRANTY. In the law of insurance, warranties may be either affirmative or promissory. Affirmative warranties may be either express or implied, but they usually consist of positive representations in the policy of the existence of some fact or state of things at the time, or previous to the time, of the making of the policy; and they are, in general, conditions precedent, which, if untrue, whether material to the risk or not, the policy does not attach, as it is not the contract of the insurer. 4 Cliff. 281.

AFFIXUS. In the civil law. Affixed, fixed, or fastened to.

AFFORARE. To set a price or value on a thing. Blount.

AFFORATUS. Appraised or valued, as things vendible in a market. Blount.

AFFORCE. To add to; to increase; to strengthen; to add force to.

AFFORCE THE ASSISE. In old English practice. A method of securing a verdict, where the jury disagreed, by adding other jurors to the panel until twelve could be found who were unanimous in their opinion. Bract. fol. 185*b*, 292*a;* Fleta, lib. 4, c. 9, § 2; 2 Reeve, Hist. Eng. Law, 267.

AFFORCIAMENTUM. In old English law. A fortress or stronghold, or other fortification. Cowell.

The calling of a court upon a solemn or extraordinary occasion. Id.

AFFOREST. To convert land into a forest in the legal sense of the word.

AFFOUAGE. In French law. The right of the inhabitants of a commune or section of a commune to take from the forest the fire-wood which is necessary for their use. Duverger.

AFFRANCHIR. L. Fr. To set free. Kelham.

AFFRANCHISE. To liberate; to make free.

AFFRAY. In criminal law. The fighting of two or more persons in some public place to the terror of the people.

It differs from a riot in not being premeditated; for if any persons meet together upon any lawful or innocent occasion, and happen on a sudden to engage in fighting, they are not guilty of a riot, but an affray only; and in that case none are guilty except those actually engaged in it. Hawk. P. C. bk. 1, c. 65, § 3; 4 Bl. Comm. 146; 1 Russ. Crimes, 271.

If two or more persons voluntarily or by agreement engage in any fight, or use any blows or violence towards each other in an angry or quarrelsome manner, in any public place to the disturbance of others, they are guilty of an affray, and shall be punished by imprisonment in the county jail not exceeding thirty days, or by fine not exceeding one hundred dollars. Rev. Code Iowa 1880, § 4065.

AFFRECTAMENTUM. Affreightment; a contract for the hire of a vessel. From the Fr. *fret*, which, according to Cowell, meant tons or tonnage.

AFFREIGHTMENT. A contract of affreightment is a contract with a ship-owner to hire his ship, or part of it, for the carriage of goods. Such a contract generally takes the form either of a charter-party or of a bill of lading. Maude & P. Mer. Shipp. 227; Smith, Merc. Law. 295.

In French law, freighting and affreighting are distinguished. The owner of a ship freights it, (*le frete;*) he is called the freighter, (*freteur;*) he is the letter or lessor, (*locateur, locator.*) The merchant affreights (*affrete*) the ship, and is called the affreighter, (*affreteur;*) he is the hirer, (*locataire, conductor.*) Emerig. Tr. des Ass. c. 11, § 3.

AFFRETEMENT. Fr. In French law. The hiring of a vessel; affreightment. Called also *nolissement.* Ord. Mar. liv. 1, tit. 2, art. 2; Id. liv. 3, tit. 1, art. 1.

AFFRI. In old English law. Plow cattle, bullocks or plow horses. *Affri,* or *afri carucæ;* beasts of the plow. Spelman.

AFORESAID. Before, or already said, mentioned, or recited; premised. Plowd. 67. *Foresaid* is used in Scotch law.

Although the words "preceding" and "aforesaid" generally mean next before, and "following" means next after, yet a different signification will be given to them if required by the context and the facts of the case. 35 Ga. 180.

AFORETHOUGHT. In criminal law. Deliberate; planned; premeditated; prepense.

AFTER-ACQUIRED. Acquired after a particular date or event. Thus, a judgment is a lien on after-acquired realty, *i. e.*, land acquired by the debtor after entry of the judgment.

AFTER-DISCOVERED. Discovered or made known after a particular date or event.

AFTERMATH. A second crop of grass mown in the same season; also the right to take such second crop. See 1 Chit. Gen. Pr. 181.

AFTERNOON. This word has two senses. It may mean the whole time from noon to midnight; or it may mean the earlier part of that time, as distinguished from the evening. When used in a statute, its meaning must be determined by the context and the circumstances of the subject-matter. 2 El. & Bl. 451.

AGAINST THE FORM OF THE STATUTE. When the act complained of is prohibited by a statute, these technical words must be used in an indictment under it. The Latin phrase is *contra formam statuti.*

AGAINST THE PEACE. A technical phrase used in alleging a breach of the peace. See CONTRA PACEM.

AGAINST THE WILL. Technical words which must be used in framing an indictment for robbery from the person. 1 Chit. Crim. Law, 244.

AGALMA. An impression or image of anything on a seal. Cowell.

AGARD. L. Fr. An award. *Nul fait agard;* no award made.

AGARDER. L. Fr. To award, adjudge, or determine; to sentence, or condemn.

AGE. Signifies those periods in the lives of persons of both sexes which enable them to do certain acts which, before they had arrived at those periods, they were prohibited from doing.

The length of time during which a person has lived or a thing has existed.

In the old books, "age" is commonly used to signify "full age;" that is, the age of twenty-one years. Litt. § 259.

AGE, Awe, Aive. L. Fr. Water. Kelham.

AGE PRAYER. A suggestion of nonage, made by an infant party to a real action, with a prayer that the proceedings may be deferred until his full age. It is now abolished. St. 11 Geo. IV.; 1 Wm. IV. c. 37, § 10; 1 Lil. Reg. 54; 3 Bl. Comm. 300.

AGENCY. The contract of agency may be defined to be a contract by which one of the contracting parties confides the management of some affair, to be transacted on his account, to the other party, who undertakes to do the business and render an account of it. 1 Liverm. Prin. & Ag. 2.

A contract by which one person, with greater or less discretionary power, undertakes to represent another in certain business relations. Whart. Ag. 1.

A relation between two or more persons, by which one party, usually called the agent or attorney, is authorized to do certain acts for, or in relation to the rights or property of the other, who is denominated the principal, constituent, or employer. Bouvier, quoting Prof. Joel Parker, MS. Lect. 1851.

AGENCY, DEED OF. A revocable and voluntary trust for payment of debts. Wharton.

AGENFRIDA. Sax. The true master or owner of a thing. Spelman.

AGENHINA. In Saxon law. A guest at an inn, who, having stayed there for three nights, was then accounted one of the family. Cowell.

AGENS. Lat. An agent, a conductor, or manager of affairs. Distinguished from *factor*, a workman. A plaintiff. Fleta, lib. 4, c. 15, § 8.

AGENT. One who undertakes to transact some business, or to manage some affair, for another, by the authority and on account of the latter, and to render an account of it. 1 Liverm. Prin. & Ag. 67; 2 Bouv. Inst. 3.

An agent is one who represents another called the "principal," in dealings with third persons. Such representation is called agency. Civil Code Dak. § 1337.

The terms "agent" and "attorney" are often used synonymously. Thus, a letter c power of attorney is constantly spoken of a the formal instrument by which an agency is created. Paley, Ag. (Dunl. Ed.) 1, n.

Classification. Agents are either general or special. A general agent is one employed in his capacity as a professional man or master of an art or trade, or one to whom the principal confides his whole business or all transactions or functions of a designated class. A special agent is one employed to conduct a particular transaction or authorized to perform a specified act.

Agents employed for the sale of goods or merchandise are called "mercantile agents," and are of two principal classes,—brokers and factors, (*q. v.;*) a factor is sometimes called a "commission agent," or "commission merchant." Russ. Merc. Ag. 1.

Synonyms. The term "agent" is to be distinguished from its synonyms "servant," "representative," and "trustee." A servant acts in behalf of his master and under the latter's direction and authority, but is regarded as a mere instrument, and not as the substitute or proxy of the master. A representative (such as an executor or an assignee in bankruptcy) owes his power and authority to the law, which puts him in the place of the person represented, although the latter may have designated or chosen the representative. A trustee acts in the interest and for the benefit of one person, but by an authority derived from another person.

In international law. A diplomatic *agent* is a person employed by a sovereign to manage his private affairs, or those of his subjects in his name, at the court of a foreign government. Wolff, Inst. Nat. § 1237.

In the practice of the house of lords and privy council. In appeals, solicitors and other persons admitted to practise in those courts in a similar capacity to that of solicitors in ordinary courts, are technically called "agents." Macph. Priv. Coun. 65.

AGENT AND PATIENT. A phrase indicating the state of a person who is required to do a thing, and is at the same time the person to whom it is done.

Agentes et consentientes pari pœna plectentur. Acting and consenting parties are liable to the same punishment. 5 Coke, 80.

AGER. Lat. **In the civil law.** A field; land generally. A portion of land inclosed by definite boundaries.

In old English law. An acre. Spelman.

AGGER. Lat. In the civil law. A dam, bank or mound. Cod. 9, 38; Townsh. Pl. 48.

AGGRAVATED ASSAULT. An assault with circumstances of aggravation, or of a heinous character, or with intent to commit another crime. See ASSAULT.

Defined in Pennsylvania as follows: "If any person shall unlawfully and maliciously inflict upon another person, either with or without any weapon or instrument, any grievous bodily harm, or unlawfully cut, stab, or wound any other person, he shall be guilty of a misdemeanor," etc. Brightly, Purd. Dig. p. 434, § 167.

AGGRAVATION. Any circumstance attending the commission of a crime or tort which increases its guilt or enormity or adds to its injurious consequences, but which is above and beyond the essential constituents of the crime or tort itself.

Matter of aggravation, correctly understood, does not consist in acts of the same kind and description as those constituting the gist of the action, but in something done by the defendant, on the occasion of committing the trespass, which is, to some extent, of a different legal character from the principal act complained of. 19 Vt. 107.

In pleading. The introduction of matter into the declaration which tends to increase the amount of damages, but does not affect the right of action itself. Steph. Pl. 257; 12 Mod. 597.

AGGREGATE. Composed of several; consisting of many persons united together. 1 Bl. Comm. 469.

AGGREGATIO MENTIUM. The meeting of minds. The moment when a contract is complete. A supposed derivation of the word "agreement."

AGGRESSOR. The party who first offers violence or offense. He who begins a quarrel or dispute, either by threatening or striking another.

AGGRIEVED. Having suffered loss or injury; damnified; injured.

AGGRIEVED PARTY. Under statutes granting the right of appeal to the party aggrieved by an order or judgment, the party aggrieved is one whose pecuniary interest is directly affected by the adjudication; one whose right of property may be established or divested thereby. 6 Metc. (Mass.) 197; 16 Pick. 264; 6 N. H. 116; 25 N. J. Eq. 505; 64 N. C. 110. Or one against whom error has been committed. 67 Mo. 99. See, also, 27 Wis. 670; 2 Paine, 315; 17 Cal. 250; 3 Allen, 556.

AGILD. In Saxon law. Free from penalty, not subject to the payment of *gild*, or *weregild;* that is, the customary fine or pecuniary compensation for an offense. Spelman; Cowell.

AGILER. In Saxon law. An observer or informer.

AGILLARIUS. L. Lat. In old English law. A hayward, herdward, or keeper of the herd of cattle in a common field. Cowell.

AGIO. In commercial law. A term used to express the difference in point of value between metallic and paper money, or between one sort of metallic money and another. McCul. Dict.

AGIOTAGE. A speculation on the rise and fall of the public debt of states, or the public funds. The speculator is called "*agioteur.*"

AGIST. **In ancient law.** To take in and feed the cattle of strangers in the king's forest, and to collect the money due for the same to the king's use. Spelman; Cowell.

In modern law. To take in cattle to feed, or pasture, at a certain rate of compensation. Jacob; 13 East, 159.

AGISTATIO ANIMALIUM IN FORESTA. The drift or numbering of cattle in the forest.

AGISTERS or GIST TAKERS. Officers appointed to look after cattle, etc. See Williams, Common, 232.

AGISTMENT. The taking in of another person's cattle to be fed, or to pasture, upon one's own land, in consideration of an agreed price to be paid by the owner. Also the profit or recompense for such pasturing of cattle.

There is also agistment of sea-banks, where lands are charged with a tribute to keep out the sea; and *terræ agistatæ* are lands whose owners must keep up the sea-banks. Holthouse.

AGISTOR. One who takes in horses or other animals to pasture at certain rates. Story, Bailm. § 443.

AGNATES. In the law of descents. Relations by the father. This word is used in the Scotch law, and by some writers as an English word, corresponding with the Latin *agnati*, (*q. v.*) Ersk. Inst. b. 1, tit. 7, § 4.

AGNATI. In Roman law. The term included "all the cognates who trace their connection exclusively through males. A table of *cognates* is formed by taking each lineal ancestor in turn and including all his descendants of both sexes in the tabular view. If, then, in tracing the various branches of such a genealogical table or tree, we stop whenever we come to the name of a female, and pursue that particular branch or ramification no further, all who remain after the descendants of women have been excluded are *agnates*, and their connection together is agnatic relationship." Maine, Anc. Law, 142.

All persons are agnatically connected together who are under the same *patria potestas*, or who have been under it, or who might have been under it if their lineal ancestor had lived long enough to exercise his empire. Maine, Anc. Law, 144.

The agnate family consisted of all persons, living at the same time, who would have been subject to the *patria potestas* of a common ancestor, if his life had been continued to their time. Hadl. Rom. Law, 131.

Between *agnati* and *cognati* there is this difference: that, under the name of agnati, *cognati* are included, but not *è converso;* for instance, a father's brother, that is, a paternal uncle, is both *agnatus* and *cognatus*, but a mother's brother, that is, a maternal uncle, is a *cognatus* but not *agnatus*. (Dig. 38, 7, 5, pr.) Burrill.

AGNATIC. [From *agnati, q. v.*] Derived from or through males. 2 Bl. Comm. 236.

AGNATIO. In the civil law. Relationship on the father's side; agnation. *Agnatio a patre est.* Inst. 3, 5, 4; Id. 3, 6, 6.

AGNATION. Kinship by the father's side. See AGNATES; AGNATI.

AGNOMEN. Lat. An additional name or title; a nickname. A name or title which a man gets by some action or peculiarity; the last of the four names sometimes given a Roman. Thus, Scipio *Africanus*, (the African,) from his African victories. Ainsworth; Calvin.

AGNOMINATION. A surname; an additional name or title; agnomen.

AGNUS DEI. Lat. Lamb of God. A piece of white wax, in a flat, oval form, like a small cake, stamped with the figure of a lamb, and consecrated by the pope. Cowell.

AGRARIAN. Relating to land, or to a division or distribution of land; as an agrarian law.

AGRARIAN LAWS. In Roman law. Laws for the distribution among the people, by public authority, of the lands constituting the public domain, usually territory conquered from an enemy.

In common parlance the term is frequently applied to laws which have for their object the more equal division or distribution of landed property; laws for subdividing large properties and increasing the number of landholders.

AGRARIUM. A tax upon or tribute payable out of land.

AGREAMENTUM. In old English law. Agreement; an agreement. Spelman.

AGREE. To concur; to come into harmony; to give mutual assent; to unite in mental action; to exchange promises; to make an agreement.

To assent to a thing, or undertake to do it; to promise. 1 Denio, 226, 228, 229. This is a loose and incorrect sense of the term. 5 East, 11.

To concur or acquiesce in; to approve or adopt. *Agreed, agreed to,* are frequently used in the books, (like *accord*,) to show the concurrence or harmony of cases. *Agreed per curiam* is a common expression.

To harmonize or reconcile. "You will *agree* your books." 8 Coke, 67.

AGRÉÉ. In French law. A solicitor practising solely in the tribunals of commerce.

AGREEANCE. In Scotch law. Agreement; an agreement or contract.

AGREED. Settled or established by agreement. This word in a deed creates a covenant.

This word is a technical term, and it is synonymous with "contracted." Meigs, 433. It means, *ex vi termini*, that it is the agreement of both parties, whether both sign it or not, each and both consenting to it. 26 Barb. 298.

AGREED STATEMENT OF FACTS. A statement of facts, agreed on by the parties as true and correct, to be submitted to a court for a ruling on the law of the case.

AGREEMENT. A concord of understanding and intention, between two or more parties, with respect to the effect upon their relative rights and duties, of certain past or future facts or performances. The act of two or more persons, who unite in expressing a mutual and common purpose, with the view of altering their rights and obligations.

A coming together of parties in opinion or determination; the union of two or more minds in a thing done or to be done; a mutual assent to do a thing. Com. Dig. "Agreement," A 1.

The consent of two or more persons concurring, the one in parting with, the other in receiving, some property, right, or benefit. Bac. Abr.

A promise, or undertaking. This is a loose and incorrect sense of the word. 5 East, 11. See 3 Brod. & B. 14; 3 N. Y. 335.

The writing or instrument which is evidence of an agreement.

Agreements are of the following several descriptions, viz.:

Conditional agreements, the operation and effect of which depend upon the existence of a supposed state of facts, or the performance of a condition, or the happening of a contingency.

Executed agreements, which have reference to past events, or which are at once closed and where nothing further remains to be done by the parties.

Executory agreements are such as are to be performed in the future. They are commonly preliminary to other more formal or important contracts or deeds, and are usually evidenced by memoranda, parol promises, etc.

Express agreements are those in which the terms and stipulations are specifically declared and avowed by the parties at the time of making the agreement.

Implied agreements are those which the law infers the parties to have made, although the terms were not openly expressed.

Synonyms distinguished. The term "agreement" is often used as synonymous with "contract." Properly speaking, however, it is a wider term than "contract" (Anson, Cont. 4.) An agreement might not be a contract, because not fulfilling some requirement of the law of the place in which it is made. So, where a contract embodies a series of mutual stipulations or constituent clauses, each of these clauses might be denominated an "agreement."

"*Agreement*" is seldom applied to specialties; "*contract*" is generally confined to simple contracts; and "*promise*" refers to the engagement of a party without reference to the reasons or considerations for it, or the duties of other parties. Pars. Cont. 6.

"Agreement" is more comprehensive than "promise;" signifies a mutual contract, on consideration, between two or more parties. A statute (of frauds) which requires the agreement to be in writing includes the consideration. 5 East, 10.

"Agreement" is not synonymous with "promise" or "undertaking," but, in its more proper and correct sense, signifies a mutual contract, on consideration, between two or more parties, and implies a consideration. 24 Wend. 285.

• **AGREEMENT FOR INSURANCE.** A brief agreement entered into between the insurer and insured, preliminary to the filling up and delivery of a policy.

AGREER. Fr. In French marine law. To rig or equip a vessel. Ord. Mar. liv. 1, tit. 2, art. 1.

AGREZ. Fr. In French marine law. The rigging or tackle of a vessel. Ord. Mar. liv. 1, tit. 2, art. 1; Id. tit. 11, art. 2; Id. liv. 3, tit. 1, art. 11.

AGRI. Arable lands in common fields.

AGRI LIMITATI. In Roman law. Lands belonging to the state by right of conquest, and granted or sold in plots. Sandars, Just. Inst. (5th Ed.) 98.

AGRICULTURE. A person actually engaged in the "science of agriculture" (within the meaning of a statute giving him special exemptions) is one who derives the support of himself and his family, in whole or in part, from the tillage and cultivation of fields. He must cultivate something more than a garden, although it may be much less than a farm. If the area cultivated can be called a field, it is agriculture, as well in contemplation of law as in the etymology of the word. And if this condition be fulfilled, the uniting of any other business, not inconsistent with the pursuit of agriculture, does not take away the protection of the statute. 22 Pa. St. 193. See, also, 7 Heisk. 515; 62 Me. 526; 64 Ga. 128.

AGUSADURA. In ancient customs, a fee, due from the vassals to their lord for sharpening their plowing tackle.

AHTEID. In old European law. A kind of oath among the Bavarians. Spelman. In Saxon law. One bound by oath, *q. d.* "oath-tied." From *ath*, oath, and *tied*. Id.

AID, *v.* To support, help, or assist. This word must be distinguished from its synonym "encourage," the difference being that the former connotes active support and assistance, while the latter does not; and also from "abet," which last word imports necessary criminality in the act furthered, while "aid," standing alone, does not.

AID AND COMFORT. Help; support; assistance; counsel; encouragement.

As an element in the crime of treason, the giving of "aid and comfort" to the enemy may consist in a mere attempt. It is not essential to constitute the giving of aid and comfort that the enterprise commenced should be successful and actually render assistance. 4 Sawy. 472; 97 U. S. 62.

AID OF THE KING. The king's tenant prays this, when rent is demanded of him by others.

AID PRAYER. In English practice. A proceeding formerly made use of, by way of petition in court, praying in aid of the tenant for life, etc., from the reversioner or remainder-man, when the title to the inheritance was in question. It was a plea in suspension of the action. 3 Bl. Comm. 300.

AIDER BY VERDICT. The healing or remission, by a verdict rendered, of a defect or error in pleading which might have been objected to before verdict.

The presumption of the proof of all facts necessary to the verdict as it stands, coming to the aid of a record in which such facts are not distinctly alleged.

AIDING AND ABETTING. In criminal law. That kind of connection with the commission of a crime which, at common law, rendered the person guilty as a principal in the second degree. It consisted in being present at the time and place, and doing some act to render aid to the actual perpetrator of the crime, though without taking a direct share in its commission. See 4 Bl. Comm. 34.

AIDS. In feudal law, originally mere benevolences granted by a tenant to his lord, in times of distress; but at length the lords claimed them as of right. They were principally three: (1) To ransom the lord's person, if taken prisoner; (2) to make the lord's eldest son and heir apparent a knight; (3) to give a suitable portion to the lord's eldest daughter on her marriage. Abolished by 12 Car. II. c. 24.

Also, extraordinary grants to the crown by the house of commons, and which were the origin of the modern system of taxation. 2 Bl. Comm. 63, 64.

AIEL, Aieul, Aile, Ayle. L. Fr. A grandfather.

A writ which lieth where the grandfather was seised in his demesne as of fee of any lands or tenements in fee-simple the day that he died, and a stranger abateth or entereth the same day and dispossesseth the heir. Fitzh. Nat. Brev. 222; Spelman; Termes de la Ley; 3 Bl. Comm. 186.

AIELESSE. A Norman French term signifying "grandmother." Kelham.

AINESSE. In French feudal law. The right or privilege of the eldest born; primogeniture; esnecy. Guyot, Inst. Feud. c. 17.

AIR. That fluid transparent substance which surrounds our globe.

AIRE. In old Scotch law. The court of the justices itinerant, corresponding with the English *eyre*, (*q. v.*) Skene de Verb. Sign. voc. *Iter.*

AIRT AND PAIRT. In old Scotch criminal law. Accessary; contriver and partner. 1 Pitc. Crim. Tr. pt. 1, p. 133; 3 How. State Tr. 601. Now written *art and part*, (*q. v.*)

AIR-WAY. In English law. A passage for the admission of air into a mine. To maliciously fill up, obstruct, or damage, with intent to destroy, obstruct, or render useless the air-way to any mine, is a felony punishable by penal servitude or imprisonment at the discretion of the court. 24 & 25 Vict. c. 97, § 28.

AISIAMENTUM. In old English law. An easement. Spelman.

AISNE or EIGNE. In old English law, the eldest or first born.

AJOURNEMENT. In French law. The document pursuant to which an action or suit is commenced, equivalent to the writ of summons in England. Actions, however, are in some cases commenced by *requête* or petition. Arg. Fr. Merc. Law, 545.

AJUAR. In Spanish law. Paraphernalia. The jewels and furniture which a wife brings in marriage.

AJUTAGE. A tube, conical in form, intended to be applied to an aperture through which water passes, whereby the flow of the water is greatly increased. See 2 Whart. 477.

AKIN. In old English law. Of kin. "Next-a-kin." 7 Mod. 140.

AL. L. Fr. At the; to the. *Al barre;* at the bar. *Al huis d'esglise;* at the church-door.

ALÆ ECCLESIÆ. The wings or side aisles of a church. Blount.

ALANERARIUS. A manager and keeper of dogs for the sport of hawking; from *alanus*, a dog known to the ancients. A falconer. Blount.

ALARM LIST. The list of persons liable to military watches, who were at the same time exempt from trainings and musters. See Prov. Laws 1775-76, c. 10, § 18; Const. Mass. c. 11, § 1, art. 10; Pub. St. Mass. 1882, p. 1287.

ALBA FIRMA. In old English law. White rent; rent payable in silver or white money, as distinguished from that which was anciently paid in corn or provisions, called black mail, or black rent. Spelman; Reg. Orig. 319*b*.

ALBANAGIUM. In old French law. The state of alienage; of being a foreigner or alien.

ALBANUS. In old French law. A stranger, alien, or foreigner.

ALBINATUS. In old French law. The state or condition of an alien or foreigner.

ALBINATUS JUS. In old French law. The *droit d'aubaine* in France, whereby the king, at an alien's death, was entitled to all his property, unless he had peculiar exemption. Repealed by the French laws in June, 1791.

ALBUM BREVE. A blank writ; a writ with a blank or omission in it.

ALBUS LIBER. The white book; an ancient book containing a compilation of the law and customs of the city of London. It has lately been reprinted by order of the master of the rolls.

ALCABALA. In Spanish law. A duty of a certain per cent. paid to the treasury on the sale or exchange of property.

ALCALDE. The name of a judicial officer in Spain, and in those countries which have received their laws and institutions from Spain. His functions somewhat resembled those of mayor in small municipalities on the continent, or justice of the peace in England and most of the United States.

ALDERMAN. A judicial or administrative magistrate. Originally the word was synonymous with "elder," but was also used to designate an earl, and even a king.

In English law. An associate to the chief civil magistrate of a corporate town or city.

In American cities. The aldermen are generally a legislative body, having limited judicial powers as a body, as in matters of internal police regulation, laying out and repairing streets, constructing sewers, and the like; though in many cities they hold separate courts, and have magisterial powers to a considerable extent. Bouvier.

ALDERMANNUS CIVITATIS VEL BURGI. L. Lat. Alderman of a city or borough, from which the modern office of alderman has been derived. T. Raym. 435, 437.

ALDERMANNUS COMITATUS. The alderman of the county. According to Spelman, he held an office intermediate between that of an earl and a sheriff. According to other authorities, he was the same as the earl. 1 Bl. Comm. 116.

ALDERMANNUS HUNDREDI SEU WAPENTACHII. Alderman of a hundred or wapentake. Spelman.

ALDERMANNUS REGIS. Alderman of the king. So called, either because he received his appointment from the king or because he gave the judgment of the king in the premises allotted to him.

ALDERMANNUS TOTIUS ANGLIÆ. Alderman of all England. An officer among the Anglo-Saxons, supposed by Spelman to be the same with the chief justiciary of England in later times. Spelman.

ALE-CONNER. An officer appointed by the court-leet, sworn to look to the assise and goodness of ale and beer within the precincts of the leet. Kitch. Courts, 46; Whishaw.

An officer appointed in every court-leet, and sworn to look to the assise of bread, ale, or beer within the precincts of that lordship. Cowell.

ALE-HOUSE. A place where ale is sold to be drunk on the premises where sold.

ALE SILVER. A rent or tribute paid annually to the lord mayor of London, by those who sell ale within the liberty of the city.

ALE-STAKE. A maypole or long stake driven into the ground, with a sign on it for the sale of ale. Cowell.

ALEA. Lat. In the civil law. A game of chance or hazard. Dig. 11, 5, 1. See Cod. 3, 43. The chance of gain or loss in a contract.

ALEATOR. Lat. (From *alea*, *q. v.*) In the civil law. A gamester; one who plays at games of hazard. Dig. 11, 5; Cod. 3, 43.

ALEATORY CONTRACT. A mutual agreement, of which the effects, with respect both to the advantages and losses, whether to all the parties or to some of them, depend on an uncertain event. Civil Code La. art. 2982.

A contract, the obligation and performance of which depend upon an uncertain event, such as insurance, engagements to pay annuities, and the like.

A contract is aleatory or hazardous when the performance of that which is one of its objects depends on an uncertain event. It is certain when the thing to be done is supposed to depend on the will of the party, or when in the usual course of events it must happen in the manner stipulated. Civil Code La. art. 1776.

ALER A DIEU. L. Fr. In old practice. To be dismissed from court; to go quit. Literally, "to go to God."

ALER SANS JOUR. In old practice, a phrase used to indicate the final dismissal of a case from court without continuance. "To go without day."

ALEU. Fr. In French feudal law. An allodial estate, as distinguished from a feudal estate or benefice.

ALFET. A cauldron into which boiling water was poured, in which a criminal plunged his arm up to the elbow, and there held it for some time, as an ordeal. Du Cange.

ALGARUM MARIS. Probably a corruption of *Laganum maris*, *lagan* being a right, in the middle ages, like *jetsam* and *flotsam*, by which goods thrown from a vessel in distress became the property of the king, or the lord on whose shores they were stranded. Spelman; Jacob; Du Cange.

ALGO. Span. In Spanish law. Property. White, Nov. Recop. b. 1, tit. 5, c. 3, § 4.

ALIA ENORMIA. Other wrongs. The name given to a general allegation of injuries caused by the defendant with which the plaintiff in an action of trespass under the common law practice concluded his declaration. Archb. Crim. Pl. 694.

ALIAMENTA. A liberty of passage, open way, water-course, etc., for the tenant's accommodation. Kitchen.

ALIAS. In practice. Formerly; hitherto; at another time. An *alias* writ is a second writ issued in the same cause, where a former writ of the same kind had been issued without effect. In such case, the language of the second writ is, "We command you, as we have *before* [*sicut alias*] commanded you," etc.

ALIAS DICTUS. "Otherwise called." This phrase (or its shorter and more usual form, *alias*,) when placed between two names in a pleading or other paper, indicates that the same person is known by both those names. A fictitious name assumed by a person is colloquially termed an "*alias*."

ALIBI. Lat. In criminal law. Elsewhere; in another place. A term used to express that mode of defense to a criminal prosecution, where the party accused, in order to prove that he could not have committed the crime with which he is charged, offers evidence to show that he was *in another place* at the time; which is termed setting up an *alibi*. Tomlins.

ALIEN, *n.* A foreigner; one born abroad; a person resident in one country, but owing allegiance to another. In England, one born out of the allegiance of the king. In the United States, one born out of the jurisdiction of the United States, and who has not been naturalized under their constitution and laws. 2 Kent, Comm. 50.

ALIEN AMY. In international law. Alien friend. An alien who is the subject or citizen of a foreign government at peace with our own.

ALIEN AND SEDITION LAWS. Acts of congress of July 6 and July 14, 1798. See Whart. State Tr. 22.

ALIEN ENEMY. In international law. An alien who is the subject or citizen of some hostile state or power. See Dyer, 2*b;* Co. Litt. 129*b*. A person who, by reason of owing a permanent or temporary allegiance to a hostile power, becomes, in time of war, impressed with the character of an enemy, and, as such, is disabled from suing in the courts of the adverse belligerent. See 1 Kent, Comm. 74; 2 Id. 63; 10 Johns. 183.

ALIEN FRIEND. The subject of a nation with which we are at peace; an *alien amy.*

ALIEN NEE. A man born an alien.

ALIEN or ALIENE. *v.* To transfer or make over to another; to convey or transfer the property of a thing from one person to another; to alienate. Usually applied to the transfer of lands and tenements. Co. Litt. 118; Cowell.

Aliena negotia exacto officio geruntur. The business of another is to be conducted with particular attention. Jones, Bailm. 83; 79 Pa. St. 118.

ALIENABLE. Proper to be the subject of alienation or transfer.

ALIENAGE. The condition or state of an alien.

ALIENATE. To convey; to transfer the title to property. Co. Litt. 118*b*. *Alien* is very commonly used in the same sense. 1 Washb. Real Prop. 53.

"Sell, *alienate,* and dispone" are the formal words of transfer in Scotch conveyances of heritable property. Bell.

"The term *alienate* has a technical legal meaning, and any transfer of real estate, short of a conveyance of the title, is not an alienation of the estate. No matter in what form the sale may be made, unless the title is conveyed to the purchaser, the estate is not alienated." 11 Barb. 630.

Alienatio licet prohibeatur, consensu tamen omnium, in quorum favorem prohibita est, potest fieri, et quilibet potest renunciare juri pro se introducto. Although alienation be prohibited, yet, by the consent of all in whose favor it is prohibited, it may take place; for it is in the power of any man to renounce a law made in his own favor. Co. Litt. 98.

Alienatio rei præfertur juri accrescendi. Alienation is favored by the law rather than accumulation. Co. Litt. 185.

ALIENATION. **In real property law.** The transfer of the property and possession of lands, tenements, or other things, from one person to another. Termes de la Ley. It is particularly applied to absolute conveyances of real property. 1 N. Y. 290, 294.

The act by which the title to real estate is voluntarily resigned by one person to another and accepted by the latter, in the forms prescribed by law. See 24 N. H. 558; 11 Barb. 629; 31 Ill. 119.

In medical jurisprudence. A generic term denoting the different kinds of aberration of the human understanding. 1 Beck, Med. Jur. 535.

ALIENATION OFFICE. In English practice. An office for the recovery of fines levied upon writs of covenant and entries.

Alienation pending a suit is void. 2 P. Wms. 482; 2 Atk. 174; 3 Atk. 392; 11 Ves. 194; 1 Johns. Ch. 566, 580.

ALIENEE. One to whom an alienation, conveyance, or transfer of property is made.

ALIENI GENERIS. Lat. Of another kind. 3 P. Wms. 247.

ALIENI JURIS. Under the control, or subject to the authority, of another person; *e. g.*, an infant who is under the authority of his father or guardian; a wife under the power of her husband. The term is contrasted with SUI JURIS, (*q. v.*)

ALIENIGENA. One of foreign birth; an alien. 7 Coke, 31.

ALIENISM. The state, condition, or character of an alien. 2 Kent, Comm. 56, 64, 69.

ALIENOR. He who makes a grant, transfer of title, conveyance, or alienation.

ALIENUS. Lat. Another's; belonging to another; the property of another. *Alienus homo,* another's man, or slave. Inst. 4, 3, pr. *Aliena res,* another's property. Bract. fol. 13*b*.

ALIMENT. In Scotch law. To maintain, support, provide for; to provide with necessaries. As a noun, maintenance, support; an allowance from the husband's estate for the support of the wife. Paters. Comp. §§ 845, 850, 893.

ALIMENTA. Lat. In the civil law. Aliments; means of support, including food, (*cibaria,*) clothing, (*vestitus,*) and habitation, (*habitatio.*) Dig. 34, 1, 6.

ALIMONY. The allowance made to a wife out of her husband's estate for her support, either during a matrimonial suit, or at its termination, when she proves herself entitled to a separate maintenance, and the fact of a marriage is established.

Alimony is an allowance out of the husband's estate, made for the support of the wife when living separate from him. It is either temporary or permanent. Code Ga. 1882, § 1736.

The allowance which is made by order of court to a woman for her support out of her husband's estate, upon being separated from him by divorce, or pending a suit for divorce. Pub. St. Mass. 1882, p. 1287.

By *alimony* we understand what is necessary for the nourishment, lodging, and support of the person who claims it. It includes education, when the person to whom the alimony is due is a minor. Civil Code La. art. 230.

The term is commonly used as equally applicable to all allowances, whether annual or in gross, made to a wife upon a decree in divorce. 107 Mass. 432.

Alimony pendente lite is that ordered during the pendency of a suit.

Permanent alimony is that ordered for the use of the wife after the termination of the suit during their joint lives.

ALIO INTUITU. Lat. In a different view; under a different aspect. 4 Rob. Adm. & Pr. 151.

With another view or object. 7 East, 558; 6 Maule & S. 234.

Aliquid conceditur ne injuria remaneat impunita, quod alias non concederetur. Something is (will be) conceded, to prevent a wrong remaining unredressed, which otherwise would not be conceded. Co. Litt. 197*b*.

ALIQUID POSSESSIONIS ET NIHIL JURIS. Somewhat of possession, and nothing of right, (but no right.) A phrase used by Bracton to describe that kind of possession which a person might have of a thing as a guardian, creditor, or the like; and also that kind of possession which was granted for a term of years, where nothing could be demanded but the usufruct. Bract. fols. 39*a*, 160*a*.

Aliquis non debet esse judex in propriâ causâ, quia non potest esse judex et pars. A person ought not to be judge in his own cause, because he cannot act as judge and party. Co. Litt. 141; 3 Bl. Comm. 59.

ALITER. Lat. Otherwise. A term often used in the reports.

Aliud est celare, aliud tacere. To conceal is one thing; to be silent is another thing. Lord Mansfield, 3 Burr. 1910.

Aliud est distinctio, aliud separatio. Distinction is one thing; separation is another. It is one thing to make things distinct, another thing to make them separable.

Aliud est possidere, aliud esse in possessione. It is one thing to possess; it is another to be in possession. Hob. 163.

Aliud est vendere, aliud vendenti consentire. To sell is one thing; to consent to a sale (seller) is another thing. Dig. 50, 17, 160.

ALIUD EXAMEN. A different or foreign mode of trial. 1 Hale, Com. Law, 38.

ALIUNDE. Lat. From another source; from elsewhere; from outside. Evidence *aliunde* (*i. e.*, from without the will) may be received to explain an ambiguity in a will. 1 Greenl. Ev. § 291.

"ALL FAULTS." A sale of goods with "all faults" covers, in the absence of fraud on the part of the vendor, all such faults and defects as are not inconsistent with the identity of the goods as the goods described. 118 Mass. 242.

ALL FOURS. Two cases or decisions which are alike in all material respects, and precisely similar in all the circumstances affecting their determination, are said to be or to run on "all fours."

ALL THE ESTATE. The name given in England to the short clause in a conveyance or other assurance which purports to convey "all the estate, right, title, interest, claim, and demand" of the grantor, lessor, etc., in the property dealt with. Dav. Conv. 93.

Allegans contraria non est audiendus. One alleging contrary or contradictory things (whose statements contradict each other) is not to be heard. 4 Inst. 279. Applied to the statements of a witness.

Allegans suam turpitudinem non est audiendus. One who alleges his own infamy is not to be heard. 4 Inst. 279.

Allegari non debuit quod probatum non relevat. That ought not to be alleged which, if proved, is not relevant. 1 Ch. Cas. 45.

ALLEGATA. In Roman law. A word which the emperors formerly signed at the bottom of their rescripts and constitutions; under other instruments they usually wrote *signata* or *testata*. Enc. Lond.

ALLEGATA ET PROBATA. Lat. Things alleged and proved. The allegations made by a party to a suit, and the proof adduced in their support.

Allegatio contra factum non est admittenda. An allegation contrary to the deed (or fact) is not admissible.

ALLEGATION. The assertion, declaration, or statement of a party to an action, made in a pleading, setting out what he expects to prove.

A material allegation in a pleading is one essential to the claim or defense, and which could not be stricken from the pleading without leaving it insufficient. Code Civil Proc. Cal. § 463.

In ecclesiastical law. The statement of the facts intended to be relied on in support of the contested suit.

In English ecclesiastical practice the word seems to designate the pleading as a whole; the three pleadings are known as the allegations; and the defendant's plea is distinguished as the defensive, or sometimes the responsive, allegation, and the complainant's reply as the rejoining allegation.

ALLEGATION OF FACULTIES. A statement made by the wife of the property of her husband, in order to her obtaining alimony. 11 Ala. 763; 3 Tex. 168.

ALLEGE. To state, recite, assert, or charge; to make an allegation.

ALLEGED. Stated; recited; claimed; asserted; charged.

ALLEGIANCE. By allegiance is meant the obligation of fidelity and obedience which the individual owes to the government under which he lives, or to his sovereign in return for the protection he receives. It may be an absolute and permanent obligation, or it may be a qualified and temporary one. The citizen or subject owes an absolute and permanent allegiance to his government or sovereign, or at least until, by some open and distinct act, he renounces it and becomes a citizen or subject of another government or another sovereign. The alien, while domiciled in the country, owes a local and temporary allegiance, which continues during the period of his residence. 16 Wall. 154.

"The tie or *ligamen* which binds the subject [or citizen] to the king [or government] in return for that protection which the king [or government] affords the subject, [or citizen."] 1 Bl. Comm. 366. It consists in "a true and faithful obedience of the subject due to his sovereign." 7 Coke, 4*b*.

Allegiance is the obligation of fidelity and obedience which every citizen owes to the state. Pol. Code Cal. § 55.

In Norman French. Alleviation; relief; redress. Kelham.

ALLEGIARE. To defend and clear one's self; to wage one's own law.

ALLEGING DIMINUTION. The allegation in an appellate court, of some error in a subordinate part of the *nisi prius* record.

ALLEVIARE. L. Lat. In old records. To levy or pay an accustomed fine or composition; to redeem by such payment. Cowell.

ALLIANCE. The relation or union between persons or families contracted by intermarriage.

In international law. A union or association of two or more states or nations, formed by league or treaty, for the joint prosecution of a war, or for their mutual assistance and protection in repelling hostile attacks. The league or treaty by which the association is formed. The act of confederating, by league or treaty, for the purposes mentioned.

If the alliance is formed for the purpose of mutual aid in the prosecution of a war against a common enemy, it is called an "offensive" alliance. If it contemplates only the rendition of aid and protection in resisting the assault of a hostile power, it is called a "defensive" alliance. If it combines both these features, it is denominated an alliance "offensive and defensive."

ALLISION. The running of one vessel into or against another, as distinguished from a collision, *i. e.*, the running of two vessels against each other.

ALLOCATION. An allowance made upon an account in the English exchequer. Cowell.

ALLOCATIONE FACIENDA. In old English practice. A writ for allowing to an accountant such sums of money as he hath lawfully expended in his office; directed to the lord treasurer and barons of the exchequer upon application made. Jacob.

ALLOCATO COMITATU. In old English practice. In proceedings in outlawry, when there were but two county courts holden between the delivery of the writ of *exigi facias* to the sheriff and its return, a special *exigi facias*, with an *allocato comitatu* issued to the sheriff in order to complete the proceedings. See EXIGENT.

ALLOCATUR. Lat. It is allowed. A word formerly used to denote that a writ or order was allowed.

A word denoting the allowance by a master or prothonotary of a bill referred for his consideration, whether touching costs, damages, or matter of account. Lee.

ALLOCATUR EXIGENT. A species of writ anciently issued in outlawry proceedings, on the return of the original writ of exigent. 1 Tidd, Pr. 128.

ALLOCUTUS. In criminal procedure, when a prisoner is convicted on a trial for treason or felony, the court is bound to demand of him what he has to say as to why the court should not proceed to judgment against him; this demand is called the "*allocutus*," and is entered on the record. Archb. Crim. Pl. 173.

ALLODARII. Owners of allodial lands. Owners of estates as large as a subject may have. Co. Litt. 1; Bac. Abr. "*Tenure*," A.

ALLODIAL. Free; not holden of any lord or superior; owned without obligation of vassalage or fealty; the opposite of feudal.

ALLODIUM. Land held absolutely in one's own right, and not of any lord or superior; land not subject to feudal duties or burdens.

An estate held by absolute ownership, without recognizing any superior to whom any duty is due on account thereof. 1 Washb. Real Prop. 16.

ALLOGRAPH. A document not written by any of the parties thereto; opposed to autograph.

ALLONGE. When the indorsements on a bill or note have filled all the blank space, it is customary to annex a strip of paper, called an "*allonge*," to receive the further indorsements.

ALLOT. To apportion, distribute; to divide property previously held in common among those entitled, assigning to each his ratable portion, to be held in severalty; to set apart specific property, a share of a fund, etc., to a distinct party.

In the law of corporations, to allot shares, debentures, etc., is to appropriate them to the applicants or persons who have applied for them; this is generally done by sending to each applicant a letter of allotment, informing him that a certain number of shares have been allotted to him. Sweet.

ALLOTMENT. Partition, apportionment, division; the distribution of land under an inclosure act, or shares in a public undertaking or corporation.

ALLOTMENT NOTE. A writing by a seaman, whereby he makes an assignment of part of his wages in favor of his wife, father or mother, grandfather or grandmother, brother or sister. Every allotment note must be in a form sanctioned by the board of trade. The allottee, that is, the person in whose favor it is made, may recover the amount in the county court. Mozley & Whitley.

ALLOTMENT SYSTEM. Designates the practice of dividing land in small portions for cultivation by agricultural laborers and other cottagers at their leisure, and after they have performed their ordinary day's work. Wharton.

ALLOTMENT WARDEN. By the English general inclosure act, 1845, § 108, when an allotment for the laboring poor of a district has been made on an inclosure under the act, the land so allotted is to be under the management of the incumbent and church warden of the parish, and two other persons elected by the parish, and they are to be styled "the allotment wardens" of the parish. Sweet.

ALLOTTEE. One to whom an allotment is made, who receives a ratable share under an allotment; a person to whom land under an inclosure act or shares in a public undertaking are allotted.

ALLOW. To grant, approve, or permit; as to allow an appeal or a marriage; to allow an account. Also to give a fit portion out of a larger property or fund.

ALLOWANCE. A deduction, an average payment, a portion assigned or allowed; the act of allowing.

ALLOWANCE PENDENTE LITE. In the English chancery division, where property which forms the subject of proceedings is more than sufficient to answer all claims in the proceedings, the court may allow to the parties interested the whole or part of the income, or (in the case of personalty) part of the property itself. St. 15 & 16 Vict. c. 86, § 57; Daniell, Ch. Pr. 1070.

ALLOY. An inferior or cheaper metal mixed with gold or silver in manufacturing or coining. As respects coining, the amount of alloy is fixed by law, and is used to increase the hardness and durability of the coin.

ALLOYNOUR. L. Fr. One who conceals, steals, or carries off a thing privately. Britt. c. 17.

ALLUVIO MARIS. Lat. In the civil and old English law. The washing up of the sea; formation of soil or land from the sea; maritime increase. Hale, Anal. § 8. "*Alluvio maris* is an increase of the land adjoining, by the projection of the sea, casting up and adding sand and slubb to the adjoining land, whereby it is increased, and for the most part by insensible degrees." Hale, de Jure Mar. pt. 1, c. 6.

ALLUVION. That increase of the earth on a shore or bank of a river, or to the shore of the sea, by the force of the water, as by a current or by waves, which is so gradual that no one can judge how much is added at each moment of time. Inst. l. 2, t. 1, § 20. Ang. Watercourses, 53.

The term is chiefly used to signify a gradual increase of the shore of a running stream, produced by deposits from the waters.

By the common law, alluvion is the addition made to land by the washing of the sea, or a navigable river or other stream, whenever the increase is so gradual that it cannot be perceived in any one moment of time. 64 Ill. 58.

Alluvion differs from avulsion in this: that the latter is sudden and perceptible. 23 Wall. 46. See AVULSION.

ALLY. A nation which has entered into an alliance with another nation. 1 Kent, Comm. 69.

A citizen or subject of one of two or more allied nations.

ALMANAC. A publication, in which is recounted the days of the week, month, and year, both common and particular, distinguishing the fasts, feasts, terms, etc., from the common days by proper marks, pointing out also the several changes of the moon, tides, eclipses, etc.

ALMESFEOH. In Saxon law. Alms-fee; alms-money. Otherwise called "Peter-pence." Cowell.

ALMOIN. Alms; a tenure of lands by divine service. See FRANKALMOIGNE.

ALMOXARIFAZGO. In Spanish law. A general term, signifying both export and import duties, as well as excise.

ALMS. Charitable donations. Any species of relief bestowed upon the poor. That which is given by public authority for the relief of the poor.

ALNAGER or ULNAGER. A sworn officer of the king whose duty it was to look to the assise of woolen cloth made throughout the land, and to the putting on the seals for that purpose ordained, for which he collected a duty called "alnage." Cowell; Termes de la Ley.

ALNETUM. In old records, a place where alders grow, or a grove of alder trees. Doomsday Book; Co. Litt. 4*b*.

ALODE, Alodes, Alodis. L. Lat. In feudal law. Old forms of *alodium*, or *allodium*, (*q. v.*)

ALONG. This term means "by," "on," or "over," according to the subject-matter and the context. 34 Conn. 425; 1 Barn. & Adol. 448; 67 Mo. 58.

ALT. In Scotch practice. An abbreviation of *Alter*, the other: the opposite party; the defender. 1 Broun, 336, note.

ALTA PRODITIO. L. Lat. In old English law. High treason. 4 Bl. Comm. 75. See HIGH TREASON.

ALTA VIA. L. Lat. In old English law. A highway; the highway. 1 Salk. 222. *Alta via regia;* the king's highway; "the king's high street." Finch, Law, b. 2. c. 9.

ALTARAGE. In ecclesiastical law. Offerings made on the altar; all profits which accrue to the priest by means of the altar. Ayliffe, Parerg. 61.

ALTER. To make a change in; to modify; to vary in some degree; to change some of the elements or ingredients or details, without substituting an entirely new thing or destroying the identity of the thing affected.

This term is to be distinguished from its synonyms "change" and "amend." To change may import the substitution of an entirely different thing, while to alter is to operate upon a subject-matter which continues objectively the same while modified in some particular. If a check is raised, in respect to its amount, it is altered; if a new check is put in its place, it is changed. To "amend" implies that the modification made in the subject improves it, which is not necessarily the case with an alteration. An amendment always involves an alteration, but an alteration does not always amend.

ALTERATION. Variation; changing; making different.

An act done upon a written instrument, which, without destroying the identity of the document, introduces some change into its terms, meaning, language, or details. This may be done either by the mutual agreement of the parties concerned, or by a person interested under the writing without the consent, or without the knowledge, of the others. In either case it is properly denominated an alteration; but if performed by a mere stranger, it is more technically described as a spoliation or mutilation. The term is not properly applied to any change which involves the substitution of a practically new document. And it should in strictness be reserved for the designation of changes in form or language, and not used with reference to modifications in matters of substance.

An alteration is an act done upon the instrument by which its meaning or language is changed. If what is written upon or erased from the instrument has no tendency to produce this result, or to mislead any person, it is not an alteration. 5 Neb. 444.

An alteration is said to be *material* when it affects, or may possibly affect, the rights of the persons interested in the document.

Alterius circumventio alii non præbet actionem. The deceiving of one person does not afford an action to another. Dig. 50, 17, 49.

ALTERNAT. A usage among diplomatists by which the rank and places of different powers, who have the same right and pretensions to precedence, are changed from time to time, either in a certain regular order or one determined by lot. In drawing up treaties and conventions, for example, it is the usage of certain powers to alternate, both in the preamble and the signatures, so that each power occupies, in the copy intended to be delivered to it, the first place. Wheat. Int. Law, § 157.

ALTERNATIM. L. Lat. Interchangeably. Litt. § 371; Townsh. Pl. 37.

Alternativa petitio non est audienda. An alternative petition or demand is not to be heard. 5 Coke, 40.

ALTERNATIVE. One or the other of two things; giving an option or choice; allowing a choice between two or more things or acts to be done.

ALTERNATIVE OBLIGATION. An obligation allowing the obligor to choose which of two things he will do, the performance of either of which will satisfy the instrument.

Where the things which form the object of the contract are separated by a disjunctive, then the obligation is *alternative*. A promise to deliver a certain thing or to pay a specified sum of money, is an example of this kind of obligation. Civil Code La. art. 2066.

ALTERNATIVE REMEDY. Where a new remedy is created in addition to an existing one, they are called "alternative" if only one can be enforced; but if both, "cumulative."

ALTERNATIVE WRIT. A writ commanding the person against whom it is issued to do a specified thing, or show cause to the court why he should not be compelled to do it.

ALTERNIS VICIBUS. L. Lat. By alternate turns; at alternate times; alternately. Co. Litt. 4*a;* Shep. Touch. 206.

ALTERUM NON LÆDERE. Not to injure another. This maxim, and two others, *honeste vivere*, and *suum cuique tribuere*, (*q. v.*,) are considered by Justinian as fundamental principles upon which all the rules of law are based. Inst. 1, 1, 3.

ALTIUS NON TOLLENDI. In the civil law. A servitude due by the owner of a house, by which he is restrained from building beyond a certain height. Dig. 8, 2, 4; Sandars, Just. Inst. 119.

ALTIUS TOLLENDI. In the civil law. A servitude which consists in the right, to him who is entitled to it, to build his house as high as he may think proper. In general, however, every one enjoys this privilege, unless he is restrained by some contrary title. Sandars, Just. Inst. 119.

ALTO ET BASSO. High and low. This phrase is applied to an agreement made between two contending parties to submit all matters in dispute, *alto et basso*, to arbitration. Cowell.

ALTUM MARE. L. Lat. In old English law. The high sea, or seas. Co. Litt. 260*b*. The deep sea. *Super altum mare*, on the high seas. Hob. 212*b*.

ALUMNUS. A child which one has nursed; a foster-child. Dig. 40, 2, 14. One educated at a college or seminary is called an "*alumnus*" thereof.

ALVEUS. The bed or channel through which the stream flows when it runs within its ordinary channel. Calvin.

Alveus derelictus, a deserted channel. Mackeld. Rom. Law, § 274.

AMALGAMATION. A term applied in England to the merger or consolidation of two incorporated companies or societies.

In the case of the Empire Assurance Corporation, (1867,) L. R. 4 Eq. 347, the vice-chancellor said: "It is difficult to say what the word 'amalgamate' means. I confess at this moment I have not the least conception of what the full legal effect of the word is. We do not find it in any law dictionary, or expounded by any competent authority. But I am quite sure of this: that the word 'amalgamate' cannot mean that the execution of a deed shall make a man a partner in a firm in which he was not a partner before, under conditions of which he is in no way cognizant, and which are not the same as those contained in the former deed."

AMALPHITAN CODE. A collection of sea-laws, compiled about the end of the eleventh century, by the people of Amalphi. It consists of the laws on maritime subjects, which were or had been in force in countries bordering on the Mediterranean; and was for a long time received as authority in those countries. Azuni; Wharton.

AMANUENSIS. One who writes on behalf of another that which he dictates.

AMBACTUS. A messenger; a servant sent about; one whose services his master hired out. Spelman.

AMBASCIATOR. A person sent about in the service of another; a person sent on a service. A word of frequent occurrence in the writers of the middle ages. Spelman.

AMBASSADOR. In international law. A public officer, clothed with high diplomatic powers, commissioned by a sovereign prince or state to transact the international business of his government at the court of the country to which he is sent.

Ambassador is the commissioner who represents one country in the seat of government of another. He is a public minister, which, usually, a consul is not. Brown.

Ambassador is a person sent by one sovereign to another, with authority, by letters of credence, to treat on affairs of state. Jacob.

The United States have always been represented by ministers plenipotentiary, never having sent a person of the rank of an ambassador, in the diplomatic sense. 1 Kent, Comm. 39, note.

AMBER, or AMBRA. In old English law. A measure of four bushels.

AMBIDEXTER. Skillful with both hands; one who plays on both sides. Applied anciently to an attorney who took pay from both sides, and subsequently to a juror guilty of the same offense. Cowell.

Ambigua responsio contra proferentem est accipie da. An ambiguous answer is to be taken against (is not to be construed in favor of) him who offers it. 10 Coke, 59.

Ambiguis casibus semper præsumitur pro rege. In doubtful cases, the presumption always is in behalf of the crown. Lofft, Append. 248.

AMBIGUITAS. Lat. From *ambiguus*, doubtful, uncertain, obscure. Ambiguity; uncertainty of meaning.

Ambiguitas verborum latens verificatione suppletur; nam quod ex facto oritur ambiguum verificatione facti tollitur. A latent ambiguity in the language may be removed by evidence; for whatever ambiguity arises from an extrinsic fact may be explained by extrinsic evidence. Bac. Max. reg. 23.

Ambiguitas verborum patens nullâ verificatione excluditur. A patent ambiguity cannot be cleared up by extrinsic evidence. Lofft, 249.

AMBIGUITY. Doubtfulness; doubleness of meaning; indistinctness or uncertainty of meaning of an expression used in a written instrument.

Latent ambiguity is where the language employed is clear and intelligible and suggests but a single meaning, but some extrinsic fact or evidence *aliunde*, creates a necessity for interpretation or a choice among two or more possible meanings.

Patent ambiguity is that which appears on the face of the instrument, and arises from the defective, obscure, or insensible language used.

Ambiguity of language is to be distinguished from unintelligibility and inaccuracy, for words cannot be said to be ambiguous unless their signification seems doubtful and uncertain to persons of competent skill and knowledge to understand them. Story, Contr. 272.

The term "ambiguity" does not include mere *inaccuracy*, or such uncertainty as arises from the use of peculiar words, or of common words in a peculiar sense. Wig. Wills, 174.

Ambiguum pactum contra venditorem interpretandum est. An ambiguous contract is to be interpreted against the seller.

Ambiguum placitum interpretari debet contra proferentem. An ambiguous plea ought to be interpreted against the party pleading it. Co. Litt. 303*b*.

AMBIT. A boundary line, as going around a place; an exterior or inclosing line or limit.

The limits or circumference of a power or jurisdiction; the line circumscribing any subject-matter.

AMBITUS. In the Roman law. A going around; a path worn by going around. A space of at least two and a half feet in width, between neighboring houses, left for the convenience of going around them. Calvin.

The procuring of a public office by money or gifts; the unlawful buying and selling of a public office. Inst. 4, 18, 11; Dig. 48, 14.

Ambulatoria est voluntas defuncti usque ad vitæ supremum exitum. The will of a deceased person is ambulatory until the latest moment of life. Dig. 34, 4, 4.

AMBULATORY. Movable; revocable; subject to change.

Ambulatoria voluntas (a changeable will) denotes the power which a testator possesses of altering his will during his life-time.

The court of king's bench in England was formerly called an "ambulatory court," because it followed the king's person, and was held sometimes in one place and sometimes in another. So, in France, the supreme court or parliament was originally *ambulatory*. 3 Bl. Comm. 38, 39, 41.

The return of a sheriff has been said to be *ambulatory* until it is filed. Wilmot, J., 3 Burr. 1644.

AMBUSH. The noun "ambush" means (1) the act of attacking an enemy unexpectedly from a concealed station; (2) a concealed station, where troops or enemies lie in wait to attack by surprise, an ambuscade; (3) troops posted in a concealed place for attacking by surprise. The verb "ambush" means to lie in wait, to surprise, to place in ambush. 46 Ala. 142.

AMELIORATIONS. Betterments; improvements. 6 Low. Can. 294; 9 Id. 503.

AMENABLE. Subject to answer to the law; accountable; responsible; liable to punishment.

Also means tractable, that may be easily led or governed; formerly applied to a wife who is governable by her husband. Cowell.

AMEND. To improve; to make better by change or modification. See ALTER.

AMENDE HONORABLE. In old English law. A penalty imposed upon a person by way of disgrace or infamy, as a punishment for any offense, or for the purpose of making reparation for any injury done to another, as the walking into church in a white sheet, with a rope about the neck and a torch in the hand, and begging the pardon of God, or the king, or any private individual, for some delinquency. Bouvier.

In French law. A species of punishment to which offenders against public decency or morality were anciently condemned.

AMENDMENT. **In practice.** The correction of an error committed in any process, pleading, or proceeding at law, or in equity, and which is done either of course, or by the consent of parties, or upon motion to the court in which the proceeding is pending. 3 Bl. Comm. 407, 448; 1 Tidd, Pr. 696.

Any writing made or proposed as an improvement of some principal writing.

In legislation. A modification or alteration proposed to be made in a bill on its passage, or an enacted law; also such modification or change when made.

AMENDS. A satisfaction given by a wrong-doer to the party injured, for a wrong committed. 1 Lil. Reg. 81.

AMENTIA. In medical jurisprudence. Insanity; idiocy.

AMERALIUS. L. Lat. A naval commander, under the eastern Roman empire, but not of the highest rank; the origin, according to Spelman, of the modern title and office of admiral. Spelman.

AMERCE. To impose an amercement or fine; to punish by a fine or penalty.

AMERCEMENT. A pecuniary penalty, in the nature of a fine, imposed upon a person for some fault or misconduct, he being "in mercy" for his offense. It was assessed by the peers of the delinquent, or the affeerors, or imposed arbitrarily at the discretion of the court or the lord.

The difference between *amercements* and *fines* is as follows: The latter are certain, and are created by some statute; they can only be imposed and assessed by courts of record; the former are arbitrarily imposed by courts not of record, as courts-leet. Termes de la Ley, 40.

The word "amercement" has long been especially used of a mulct or penalty, imposed by a court upon its own officers for neglect of duty, or failure to pay over moneys collected. In particular, the remedy against a sheriff for failing to levy an execution or make return of proceeds of sale is, in several of the states, known as "amercement." In others, the same result is reached by process of attachment. Abbott.

AMERICAN CLAUSE. In marine insurance. A proviso in a policy to the effect that, in case of any subsequent insurance, the insurer shall nevertheless be answerable for the full extent of the sum subscribed by him, without right to claim contribution from subsequent underwriters. 14 Wend. 399.

AMEUBLISSEMENT. In French law. A species of agreement which by a fiction gives to immovable goods the quality of movable. Merl. Repert.; 1 Low. Can. 25, 58.

AMI; AMY. A friend; as *alien ami*, an alien belonging to a nation at peace with us; *prochein ami*, a next friend suing or defending for an infant, married woman, etc.

AMICABLE ACTION. In practice. An action between friendly parties. An action brought and carried on by the mutual consent and arrangement of the parties, in order to obtain the judgment of the court on a doubtful question of law, the facts being usually settled by agreement.

AMICABLE COMPOUNDERS. In Louisiana law and practice. "There are two sorts of arbitrators,—the arbitrators properly so called, and the amicable compounders. The arbitrators ought to determine as judges, agreeably to the strictness of law. Amicable compounders are authorized to abate something of the strictness of the law in favor of natural equity. Amicable compounders are in other respects subject to the same rules which are provided for the arbitrators by the present title." Civil Code La. arts. 3109, 3110.

AMICABLE SUIT. The words "arbitration" and "amicable lawsuit," used in an obligation or agreement between parties, are not convertible terms. The former carries with it the idea of settlement by disinterested third parties, and the latter by a friendly submission of the points in dispute to a judicial tribunal to be determined in accordance with the forms of law. 20 La. Ann. 535.

AMICUS CURIÆ. Lat. A friend of the court. A by-stander (usually a counsellor) who interposes and volunteers information upon some matter of law in regard to which the judge is doubtful or mistaken, or upon a matter of which the court may take judicial cognizance.

When a judge is doubtful or mistaken in matter of law, a by-stander may inform the court thereof as *amicus curiæ*. Counsel in court frequently act in this capacity when they happen to be in possession of a case which the judge has not seen, or does not at the moment remember. Holthouse.

It is also applied to persons who have no right to appear in a suit, but are allowed to introduce evidence to protect their own interests. 11 Tex. 699, 701, 702.

AMIRAL. Fr. In French maritime law. Admiral. Ord. de la Mar. liv. 1, tit. 1, § 1.

AMITA. Lat. A paternal aunt. An aunt on the father's side. *Amita magna.* A great-aunt on the father's side. *Amita* *major.* A great-great aunt on the father's side. *Amita maxima.* A great-great-great aunt, or a great-great-grandfather's sister. Calvin.

AMITINUS. The child of a brother or sister; a cousin; one who has the same grandfather, but different father and mother. Calvin.

AMITTERE. Lat. In the civil law. To lose. Hence the old Scotch "amitt."

AMITTERE CURIAM. To lose the court; to be deprived of the privilege of attending the court.

AMITTERE LEGEM TERRÆ. To lose the protection afforded by the law of the land.

AMITTERE LIBERAM LEGEM. To lose one's frank-law. A term having the same meaning as *amittere legem terræ,* (*q. v.*) He who lost his law lost the protection extended by the law to a freeman, and became subject to the same law as thralls or serfs attached to the land.

AMNESTY. A sovereign act of pardon and oblivion for past acts, granted by a government to all persons (or to certain persons) who have been guilty of crime or delict, generally political offenses,—treason, sedition, rebellion,—and often conditioned upon their return to obedience and duty within a prescribed time.

A declaration of the person or persons who have newly acquired or recovered the sovereign power in a state, by which they pardon all persons who composed, supported, or obeyed the government which has been overthrown.

The word "amnesty" properly belongs to international law, and is applied to treaties of peace following a state of war, and signifies there the burial in oblivion of the particular cause of strife, so that that shall not be again a cause for war between the parties; and this signification of "amnesty" is fully and poetically expressed in the Indian custom of burying the hatchet. And so amnesty is applied to rebellions which by their magnitude are brought within the rules of international law, and in which multitudes of men are the subjects of the clemency of the government. But in these cases, and in all cases, it means only "oblivion," and never expresses or implies a grant. 10 Ct. of Cl. 407.

"Amnesty" and "pardon" are very different. The former is an act of the sovereign power, the object of which is to efface and to cause to be forgotten a crime or misdemeanor; the latter is an act of the same authority, which exempts the individual on whom it is bestowed from the punishment the law inflicts for the crime he has committed. Bouvier.

AMONG. Intermingled with. "A thing which is *among* others is intermingled with them. Commerce *among* the states cannot stop at the external boundary line of each state, but may be introduced into the interior." 9 Wheat. 194.

Where property is directed by will to be distributed *among* several persons, it cannot be all given to one, nor can any of the persons be wholly excluded from the distribution. 6 Munf. 352.

AMORTIZATION. An alienation of lands or tenements in mortmain. The reduction of the property of lands or tenements to mortmain.

In its modern sense, amortization is the operation of paying off bonds, stock, or other indebtedness of a state or corporation. Sweet.

AMORTIZE. To alien lands in mortmain.

AMOTIO. In the civil law. A moving or taking away. "The slightest *amotio* is sufficient to constitute theft, if the *animus furandi* be clearly established." 1 Swint. 205.

AMOTION. A putting or turning out; dispossession of lands. Ouster is an *amotion* of possession. 3 Bl. Comm. 199, 208.

A moving or carrying away; the wrongful taking of personal chattels. Archb. Civil Pl. Introd. c. 2, § 3.

In corporation law. The act of removing an officer, or official representative, of a corporation from his office or official station, before the end of the term for which he was elected or appointed, but without depriving him of membership in the body corporate. In this last respect the term differs from "disfranchisement," (or expulsion,) which imports the removal of the party from the corporation itself, and his deprivation of all rights of membership.

AMOUNT COVERED. In insurance. The amount that is insured, and for which underwriters are liable for loss under a policy of insurance.

AMOUNT OF LOSS. In insurance. The diminution, destruction, or defeat of the value of, or of the charge upon, the insured subject to the assured, by the direct consequence of the operation of the risk insured against, according to its value in the policy, or in contribution for loss, so far as its value is covered by the insurance.

AMOVEAS MANUS. Lat. That you remove your hands. After office found, the king was entitled to the things forfeited, either lands or personal property; the remedy for a person aggrieved was by "petition," or "*monstrans de droit,*" or "*traverses,*" to establish his superior right. Thereupon a writ issued, *quod manus domini regis amoveantur.* 3 Bl. Comm. 260.

AMPARO. In Spanish-American law. A document issued to a claimant of land as a protection to him, until a survey can be ordered, and the title of possession issued by an authorized commissioner. 1 Tex. 790.

AMPLIATION. In the civil law. A deferring of judgment until a cause be further examined. Calvin.; Cowell. An order for the rehearing of a cause on a day appointed, for the sake of more ample information. Halifax, Anal. b. 3, c. 13, n. 32.

In French law. A duplicate of an acquittance or other instrument. A notary's copy of acts passed before him, delivered to the parties

AMPLIUS. In the Roman law. More; further; more time. A word which the prætor pronounced in cases where there was any obscurity in a cause, and the *judices* were uncertain whether to condemn or acquit; by which the case was deferred to a day named. Adam, Rom. Ant. 287.

AMPUTATION OF RIGHT HAND. An ancient punishment for a blow given in a superior court; or for assaulting a judge sitting in the court.

AMY. See AMI; PROCHEIN AMY.

AN ET JOUR. Fr. Year and day; a year and a day.

AN, JOUR, ET WASTE. In feudal law. Year, day, and waste. A forfeiture of the lands to the crown incurred by the felony of the tenant, after which time the land escheats to the lord. Termes de la Ley, 40.

ANACRISIS. In the civil law. An investigation of truth, interrogation of witnesses, and inquiry made into any fact, especially by torture.

ANAGRAPH. A register, inventory, or commentary.

ANALOGY. In logic. Identity or similarity of proportion. Where there is no precedent in point, in cases on the same subject, lawyers have recourse to cases on a different subject-matter, but governed by the same general principle. This is reasoning by analogy. Wharton.

ANARCHY. The destruction of government; lawlessness; the absence of all political government; by extension, confusion in government. See 122 Ill. 253.

ANATHEMA. An ecclesiastical punishment by which a person is separated from the body of the church, and forbidden all intercourse with the members of the same.

ANATHEMATIZE. To pronounce anathema upon; to pronounce accursed by ecclesiastical authority; to excommunicate.

ANATOCISM. In the civil law. Repeated or doubled interest; compound interest; usury. Cod. 4, 32, 1, 30.

ANCESTOR. One who has preceded another in a direct line of descent; a lineal ascendant.

A former possessor; the person last seised. Termes de la Ley; 2 Bl. Comm. 201.

A deceased person from whom another has inherited land. A former possessor.

The term differs from "predecessor," in that it is applied to a natural person and his progenitors, while the latter is applied also to a corporation and those who have held *offices* before those who now fill them. Co. Litt. 78*b*.

ANCESTRAL. Relating to ancestors, or to what has been done by them; as *homage ancestrel.*

Derived from ancestors. Ancestral estates are such as are transmitted by descent, and not by purchase. 4 Kent, Comm. 404.

ANCHOR. A measure containing ten gallons.

ANCHOR WATCH. A watch, consisting of a small number of men, (from one to four,) kept constantly on deck while the vessel is riding at single anchor, to see that the stoppers, painters, cables, and buoy-ropes are ready for immediate use. 2 Low. 220.

ANCHORAGE. In English law. A prestation or toll for every anchor cast from a ship in a port; and sometimes, though there be no anchor. Hale, de Jure Mar. pt. 2, c. 6. See 1 W. Bl. 413 et seq.; 4 Term, 262.

ANCIENT. Old; that which has existed from an indefinitely early period, or which by age alone has acquired certain rights or privileges accorded in view of long continuance.

ANCIENT DEMESNE. Manors which in the time of William the Conqueror were in the hands of the crown, and are so recorded in the Domesday Book. Fitzh. Nat. Brev. 14, 56.

Tenure in *ancient demesne* may be pleaded in abatement to an action of ejectment. 2 Burr. 1046.

Also a species of copyhold, which differs, however, from common copyholds in certain privileges, but yet must be conveyed by surrender, according to the custom of the manor. There are three sorts: (1) Where the lands are held freely by the king's grant; (2) customary freeholds, which are held of a manor in ancient demesne, but not at the lord's will, although they are conveyed by surrender, or deed and admittance; (3) lands held by copy of court-roll at the lord's will, denominated copyholds of base tenure.

ANCIENT HOUSE. One which has stood long enough to acquire an easement of support against the adjoining land or building. 3 Kent, Comm. 437; 2 Washb. Real Prop. 74, 76.

In England this term is applied to houses or buildings erected before the time of legal memory, (Cooke, Incl. Acts, 35, 109,) that is, before the reign of Richard I., although practically any house is an ancient messuage if it was erected before the time of living memory, and its origin cannot be proved to be modern.

ANCIENT LIGHTS. Lights or windows in a house, which have been used in their present state, without molestation or interruption, for twenty years, and upwards. To these the owner of the house has a right by prescription or occupancy, so that they cannot be obstructed or closed by the owner of the adjoining land which they may overlook.

ANCIENT READINGS. Readings or lectures upon the ancient English statutes, formerly regarded as of great authority in law. Litt. § 481; Co. Litt. 280.

ANCIENT RENT. The rent reserved at the time the lease was made, if the building was not then under lease. 2 Vern. 542.

ANCIENT SERJEANT. In English law. The eldest of the queen's serjeants.

ANCIENT WALL. A wall built to be used, and in fact used, as a party-wall, for more than twenty years, by the express permission and continuous acquiescence of the owners of the land on which it stands. 4 Duer, 53, 63.

ANCIENT WRITINGS. Wills, deeds, or other documents upwards of thirty years old. These are presumed to be genuine without express proof, when coming from the proper custody.

ANCIENTS. In English law. Gentlemen of the inns of court and chancery. In Gray's Inn the society consists of benchers, ancients, barristers, and students under the bar; and here the ancients are of the oldest barristers. In the Middle Temple, those who had passed their readings used to be termed "ancients." The Inns of Chancery consist of ancients and students or clerks; from the ancients a principal or treasurer is chosen yearly. Wharton.

ANCIENTY. Eldership; seniority. Used in the statute of Ireland, 14 Hen. VIII. Cowell.

ANCILLARY. Aiding; auxiliary; attendant upon; subordinate; a proceeding attendant upon or which aids another proceeding considered as principal.

ANCILLARY ADMINISTRATION. When a decedent leaves property in a foreign state, (a state other than that of his domicile,) administration may be granted in such foreign state for the purpose of collecting the assets and paying the debts there, and bringing the residue into the general administration. This is called "ancillary" (auxiliary, subordinate) administration.

ANCIPITIS USUS. Lat. In international law. Of doubtful use; the use of which is doubtful; that may be used for a civil or peaceful, as well as military or warlike, purpose. Gro. de Jure B. lib. 3, c. 1, § 5, subd. 3; 1 Kent, Comm. 140.

ANDROCHIA. In old English law. A dairy-woman. Fleta, lib. 2, c. 87.

ANDROGYNUS. An hermaphrodite.

ANDROLEPSY. The taking by one nation of the citizens or subjects of another, in order to compel the latter to do justice to the former. Wolffius, § 1164; Moll. de Jure Mar. 26.

ANECIUS. L. Lat. Spelled also *æsnecius, enitius, æneas, eneyus.* The eldest-born; the first-born; senior, as contrasted with the *puis-ne,* (younger.) Spelman.

ANGARIA. A term used in the Roman law to denote a forced or compulsory service exacted by the government for public purposes; as a forced rendition of labor or goods for the public service. See Dig. 50, 4, 18, 4.

In maritime law. A forced service, (*onus,*) imposed on a vessel for public purposes; an impressment of a vessel. Locc. de Jure Mar. lib. 1, c. 5, §§ 1-6.

In feudal law. Any troublesome or vexatious personal service paid by the tenant to his lord. Spelman.

ANGEL. An ancient English coin, of the value of ten shillings sterling. Jacob.

ANGILD. In Saxon law. The single value of a man or other thing; a single weregild; the compensation of a thing according to its single value or estimation. Spelman. The double gild or compensation was called "*twigild,*" the triple, "*trigild,*" etc. Id.

ANGLESCHERIA. In old English law. Englishery; the fact of being an Englishman.

Angliæ jura in omni casu libertatis dant favorem. The laws of England in every case of liberty are favorable, (favor liberty in all cases.) Fortes. c. 42.

ANGLICE. In English. A term formerly used in pleading when a thing is described both in Latin and English, inserted immediately after the Latin and as an introduction of the English translation.

ANGLO - INDIAN. An Englishman domiciled in the Indian territory of the British crown.

ANGYLDE. In Saxon law. The rate fixed by law at which certain injuries to person or property were to be paid for; in injuries to the person, it seems to be equivalent to the "were," *i. e.,* the price at which every man was valued. It seems also to have been the fixed price at which cattle and other goods were received as currency, and to have been much higher than the market price, or *ceapgild.* Wharton.

ANHLOTE. In old English law. A single tribute or tax, paid according to the custom of the country as scot and lot.

ANIENS, or ANIENT. Null, void, of no force or effect. Fitzh. Nat. Brev. 214.

ANIMAL. Any animate being which is endowed with the power of voluntary motion. In the language of the law the term includes all living creatures not human.

Domitæ are those which have been tamed by man; domestic.

Feræ naturæ are those which still retain their wild nature.

Mansuetæ naturæ are those gentle or tame by nature, such as sheep and cows.

Animalia fera, si facta sint mansueta et ex consuetudine eunt et redeunt, volant et revolant, ut cervi, cygni, etc., eo usque nostra sunt, et ita intelliguntur quamdiu habuerunt animum revertendi. Wild animals, if they be made tame, and are accustomed to go out and return, fly away and fly back, as stags, swans, etc., are considered to belong to us so long as they have the intention of returning to us. 7 Coke, 16.

ANIMALS OF A BASE NATURE. Animals in which a right of property may be acquired by reclaiming them from wildness, but which, at common law, by reason of their base nature, are not regarded as possible subjects of a larceny. 3 Inst. 109; 1 Hale, P. C. 511, 512.

ANIMO. Lat. With intention, disposition, design, will. *Quo animo,* with what intention. *Animo cancellandi,* with intention to cancel. 1 Pow. Dev. 603. *Furandi,* with intention to steal. 4 Bl. Comm. 230; 1 Kent, Comm. 183. *Lucrandi,* with intention to gain or profit. 3 Kent, Comm. 357. *Manendi,* with intention to remain. 1 Kent, Comm. 76. *Morandi,* with intention to stay, or delay. *Republicandi,* with intention to republish. 1 Pow. Dev. 609. *Revertendi,* with intention to return. 2 Bl. Comm. 392. *Revocandi,* with intention to revoke. 1 Pow. Dev. 595. *Testandi,* with intention to make a will. See ANIMUS and the titles which follow it.

ANIMO ET CORPORE. By the mind, and by the body; by the intention and by the physical act. Dig. 50, 17, 153; Id. 41, 2, 3, 1; Fleta, lib. 5, c. 5, §§ 9, 10.

ANIMO FELONICO. With felonious intent. Hob. 134.

ANIMUS. Lat. Mind; intention; disposition; design; will. *Animo,* (*q. v.;*) with the intention or design. These terms are derived from the civil law.

Animus ad se omne jus ducit. It is to the intention that all law applies. Law always regards the intention.

ANIMUS CANCELLANDI. The intention of destroying or canceling, (applied to wills.)

ANIMUS CAPIENDI. The intention to take or capture. 4 C. Rob. Adm. 126, 155.

ANIMUS DEDICANDI. The intention of donating or dedicating.

ANIMUS DEFAMANDI. The intention of defaming. The phrase expresses the malicious intent which is essential in every case of verbal injury to render it the subject of an action for libel or slander.

ANIMUS DERELINQUENDI. The intention of abandoning. 4 C. Rob. Adm. 216.

ANIMUS DIFFERENDI. The intention of obtaining delay.

ANIMUS DONANDI. The intention of giving. Expressive of the intent to give which is necessary to constitute a gift.

ANIMUS ET FACTUS. Intention and act; will and deed. Used to denote those acts which become effective only when accompanied by a particular intention.

ANIMUS FURANDI. The intention to steal.

Animus hominis est anima scripti. The intention of the party is the soul of the instrument. 3 Bulst. 67; Pitm. Prin. & Sur. 26. In order to give life or effect to an instrument, it is essential to look to the intention of the individual who executed it.

ANIMUS LUCRANDI. The intention to make a gain or profit.

ANIMUS MANENDI. The intention of remaining; intention to establish a permanent residence. 1 Kent, Comm. 76. This is the point to be settled in determining the domicile or residence of a party. Id. 77.

ANIMUS MORANDI. The intention to remain, or to delay.

ANIMUS POSSIDENDI. The intention of possessing.

ANIMUS QUO. The intent with which.

ANIMUS RECIPIENDI. The intention of receiving.

ANIMUS RECUPERANDI. The intention of recovering. Locc. de Jure Mar. lib. 2, c. 4, § 10.

ANIMUS REPUBLICANDI. The intention to republish.

ANIMUS RESTITUENDI. The intention of restoring. Fleta, lib. 3, c. 2, § 3.

ANIMUS REVERTENDI. The intention of returning. A man retains his domicile if he leaves it *animo revertendi*. 3 Rawle, 312; 4 Bl. Comm. 225; 2 Russ. Crimes, 18; Poph. 42, 52; 4 Coke, 40.

Also, a term employed in the civil law, in expressing the rule of ownership in tamed animals.

ANIMUS REVOCANDI. The intention to revoke.

ANIMUS TESTANDI. An intention to make a testament or will.

ANKER. A measure containing ten gallons.

ANN. In Scotch law. Half a year's stipend, over and above what is owing for the incumbency, due to a minister's relict, or child, or next of kin, after his decease. Whishaw.

ANNA. In East Indian coinage, a piece of money, the sixteenth part of a rupee.

ANNALES. Lat. Annuals; a title formerly given to the Year Books.

In old records. Yearlings; cattle of the first year. Cowell.

ANNALY. In Scotch law. To alienate; to convey.

ANNATES. In ecclesiastical law. First-fruits paid out of spiritual benefices to the pope, so called because the value of one year's profit was taken as their rate.

ANNEX. To add to; to unite; to attach one thing permanently to another. The word expresses the idea of joining a smaller or subordinate thing with another, larger, or of higher importance.

In the law relating to fixtures, the expression "annexed to the freehold" means fastened to or connected with it; mere juxtaposition, or the laying of an object, however heavy, on the freehold, does not amount to annexation. 14 Cal. 64.

ANNEXATION. The act of attaching, adding, joining, or uniting one thing to another; generally spoken of the connection of a smaller or subordinate thing with a larger or principal thing. The attaching an illustrative or auxiliary document to a deposition, pleading, deed, etc., is called "annexing" it. So the incorporation of newly-acquired territory into the national domain, as an integral part thereof, is called "annexation," as in the case of the addition of Texas to the United States.

In the law relating to fixtures: *Actual annexation* includes every movement by which a chattel can be joined or united to the freehold. *Constructive annexation* is the union of such things as have been holden parcel of the realty, but which are not actually annexed, fixed, or fastened to the freehold. Shep. Touch. 469; Amos & F. Fixt. 2.

In Scotch law. The union of lands to the crown, and declaring them inalienable. Also the appropriation of the church-lands by the crown, and the union of lands lying at a distance from the parish church to which they belong, to the church of another parish to which they are contiguous.

ANNI ET TEMPORA. Lat. Years and terms. An old title of the Year Books.

ANNI NUBILES. A woman's marriageable years. The age at which a girl becomes by law fit for marriage; the age of twelve.

ANNICULUS. A child a year old. Calvin.

Anniculus trecentesimo sexagesimo-quinto die dicitur, incipiente plane non exacto die, quia annum civiliter non ad momenta temporum sed ad dies numeramur. We call a child a year old on the three hundred and sixty-fifth day, when the day is fairly begun but not ended, because we calculate the civil year not by moments, but by days. Dig. 50, 16, 134; Id. 132; Calvin.

ANNIENTED. Made null, abrogated, frustrated, or brought to nothing. Litt. c. 3, § 741.

ANNIVERSARY. An annual day, in old ecclesiastical law, set apart in memory of a deceased person. Also called "year day" or "mind day." Spelman.

ANNO DOMINI. In the year of the Lord. Commonly abbreviated A. D. The computation of time, according to the Christian era, dates from the birth of Christ.

ANNONA. Grain; food. An old English and civil law term to denote a yearly contribution by one person to the support of another.

ANNONÆ CIVILES. A species of yearly rents issuing out of certain lands, and payable to certain monasteries.

ANNOTATIO. In the civil law. The sign-manual of the emperor; a rescript of the emperor, signed with his own hand. It is distinguished both from a rescript and pragmatic sanction, in Cod. 4, 59, 1.

ANNOTATION. A remark, note, or commentary on some passage of a book, intended to illustrate its meaning. Webster.

In the civil law. An imperial rescript signed by the emperor. The answers of the prince to questions put to him by private persons respecting some doubtful point of law.

Summoning an absentee. Dig. 1, 5.

The designation of a place of deportation. Dig. 32, 1, 3.

Annua nec debitum judex non separat ipsum. A judge (or court) does not divide annuities nor debt. 8 Coke, 52; 1 Salk. 36, 65. Debt and annuity cannot be divided or apportioned by a court.

ANNUA PENSIONE. An ancient writ to provide the king's chaplain, if he had no preferment, with a pension. Reg. Orig. 165, 307.

ANNUAL ASSAY. An annual trial of the gold and silver coins of the United States, to ascertain whether the standard fineness and weight of the coinage is maintained. See Rev. St. U. S. § 3547.

ANNUAL INCOME. Annual income is annual receipts from property. Income means that which comes in or is received from any business, or investment of capital, without reference to the outgoing expenditures. 4 Abb. N. C. 400.

ANNUAL PENSION. In Scotch law. A yearly profit or rent.

ANNUALLY. The meaning of this term, as applied to interest, is not an undertaking to pay interest at the end of one year only, but to pay interest at the end of each and every year during a period of time, either fixed or contingent. 6 Gray, 164. See, also, 19 S. C. 89; 16 Ohio St. 348.

ANNUITANT. The recipient of an annuity; one who is entitled to an annuity.

ANNUITIES OF TIENDS. In Scotch law; annuities of tithes; 10*s*. out of the boll of tiend wheat, 8*s*. out of the boll of beer, less out of the boll of rye, oats, and peas, allowed to the crown yearly of the tiends not paid to the bishops, or set apart for other pious uses.

ANNUITY. A yearly sum stipulated to be paid to another in fee, or for life, or years, and chargeable only on the person of the grantor. Co. Litt. 144*b*.

An annuity is different from a rent-charge, with which it is sometimes confounded, the annuity being chargeable on the person merely, and so far personalty; while a rent-charge is something reserved out of realty, or fixed as a burden upon an estate in land. 2 Bl. Comm. 40; Rolle, Abr. 226; 10 Watts, 127.

The contract of *annuity* is that by which one party delivers to another a sum of money, and agrees not to reclaim it so long as the receiver pays the rent agreed upon. This annuity may be either perpetual or for life. Civil Code La. arts. 2793, 2794.

The name of an action, now disused, (L. Lat. *breve de annuo redditu*,) which lay for the recovery of an annuity. Reg. Orig. 158*b*; Bract. fol. 203*b*; 1 Tidd, Pr. 3.

ANNUITY-TAX. An impost levied annually in Scotland for the maintenance of the ministers of religion.

ANNUL. To cancel; make void; destroy. To annul a judgment or judicial proceeding is to deprive it of all force and operation, either *ab initio* or prospectively as to future transactions.

ANNULUS. Lat. In old English law. A ring; the ring of a door. *Per haspam vel annulum hostii exterioris*; by the hasp or ring of the outer door. Fleta, lib. 3, c. 15, § 5.

ANNULUS ET BACULUS. (Lat. ring and staff.) The investiture of a bishop was *per annulum et baculum*, by the prince's delivering to the prelate a ring and pastoral staff, or crozier. 1 Bl. Comm. 378; Spelman.

ANNUS. Lat. In civil and old English law. A year; the period of three hundred and sixty-five days. Dig. 40, 7, 4, 5; Calvin.; Bract. fol. 359*b*.

ANNUS DELIBERANDI. In Scotch law. A year of deliberating; a year to deliberate. The year allowed by law to the heir to deliberate whether he will enter and represent his ancestor. It commences on the death of the ancestor, unless in the case of a posthumous heir, when the year runs from his birth. Bell.

ANNUS, DIES, ET VASTUM. In old English law. Year, day, and waste. See Year, Day, and Waste.

Annus est mora motus quo suum planeta pervolvat circulum. A year is the duration of the motion by which a planet revolves through its orbit. Dig. 40, 7, 4, 5; Calvin.; Bract. 359*b*.

ANNUS ET DIES. A year and a day.

Annus inceptus pro completo habetur. A year begun is held as completed. Tray. Lat. Max. 45.

ANNUS LUCTUS. The year of mourning. It was a rule among the Romans, and also the Danes and Saxons, that widows should not marry *infra annum luctûs*, (within the year of mourning.) Code 5, 9, 2; 1 Bl. Comm. 457.

ANNUS UTILIS. A year made up of available or serviceable days. Brissonius; Calvin. In the plural, *anni utiles* signifies the years during which a right can be exercised or a prescription grow.

ANNUUS REDITUS. A yearly rent; annuity. 2 Bl. Comm. 41; Reg. Orig. 158*b*.

ANON., AN., A. Abbreviation for anonymous.

ANONYMOUS. Nameless; wanting a name or names. A publication, withholding the name of the author, is said to be anonymous. Cases are sometimes reported anonymously, *i. e.*, without giving the names of the parties. Abbreviated to "*Anon.*"

ANOYSANCE. Annoyance; nuisance. Cowell; Kelham.

ANSEL, ANSUL, or AUNCEL. In old English law. An ancient mode of weighing by hanging scales or hooks at either end of a beam or staff, which, being lifted with one's finger or hand by the middle, showed the equality or difference between the weight at one end and the thing weighed at the other. Termes de la Ley, 66.

ANSWER. In pleading. Any pleading setting up matters of fact by way of defense. In chancery pleading, the term denotes a defense in writing, made by a defendant to the allegations contained in a bill or information filed by the plaintiff against him.

In pleading, under the Codes of Civil Procedure, the answer is the formal written statement made by a defendant setting forth the grounds of his defense; corresponding to what, in actions under the common-law practice, is called the "plea."

In Massachusetts, the term denotes the statement of the matter intended to be relied upon by the defendant in avoidance of the plaintiff's action, taking the place of special pleas in bar, and the general issue, except in real and mixed actions. Pub. St. Mass. 1882, p. 1287.

In matrimonial suits in the (English) probate, divorce, and admiralty division, an answer is the pleading by which the respondent puts forward his defense to the petition. Browne, Div. 223.

Under the old admiralty practice in England, the defendant's first pleading was called his "answer." Williams & B. Adm. Jur. 246.

In practice. A reply to interrogatories; an affidavit in answer to interrogatories. The declaration of a fact by a witness after a question has been put, asking for it.

As a verb, the word denotes an assumption of liability, as to "answer" for the debt or default of another.

ANTAPOCHA. In the Roman law. A transcript or counterpart of the instrument called "*apocha*," signed by the debtor and delivered to the creditor. Calvin.

ANTE. Lat. Before. Usually employed in old pleadings as expressive of time, as *præ* (before) was of place, and *coram* (before) of person. Townsh. Pl. 22.

Occurring in a report or a text-book, it is used to refer the reader to a previous part of the book.

ANTE EXHIBITIONEM BILLÆ. Before the exhibition of the bill. Before suit begun.

ANTE-FACTUM or ANTE-GESTUM. Done before. A Roman law term for a previous act, or thing done before.

ANTE LITEM MOTAM. Before suit brought; before controversy instituted.

ANTECESSOR. An ancestor, (*q. v.*)

ANTEDATE. To date an instrument as of a time before the time it was written.

ANTEJURAMENTUM. In Saxon law. A preliminary or preparatory oath, (called also "*præjuramentum*," and "*juramentum calumniæ*,") which both the accuser and accused were required to make before any trial or purgation; the accuser swearing that he would prosecute the criminal, and the accused making oath on the very day that he was to undergo the ordeal that he was innocent of the crime with which he was charged. Whishaw.

ANTENATUS. Lat. From *ante* and *natus*. Born before. A person born before another person or before a particular event. The term is particularly applied to one born in a country before a revolution, change of government or dynasty, or other political event, such that the question of his rights, *status*, or allegiance will depend upon the date of his birth with reference to such event. In England, the term commonly denotes one born before the act of union with Scotland; in America, one born before the declaration of independence. Its opposite is *postnatus*, one born after the event.

ANTENUPTIAL. Made or done before a marriage. *Antenuptial settlements* are settlements of property upon the wife, or upon her and her children, made before and in contemplation of the marriage.

ANTI MANIFESTO. A term used in international law to denote a proclamation or manifesto published by one of two belligerent powers, alleging reasons why the war is defensive on its part.

ANTICHRESIS. In the civil law. A species of mortgage, or pledge of immovables. An agreement by which the debtor gives to the creditor the income from the property which he has pledged, in lieu of the interest on his debt. Guyot, Repert.

A debtor may give as security for his debt any immovable which belongs to him, the creditor having the right to enjoy the use of it on account of the interest due, or of the capital if there is no interest due; this is called "anticresis." Civil Code Mex. art. 1927.

By the law of Louisiana, there are two kinds of pledges,—the pawn and the antichresis. A pawn relates to movables, and the antichresis to immovables. The antichresis must be reduced to writing; and the creditor thereby acquires the right to the fruits, etc., of the immovables, deducting yearly their proceeds from the interest, in the first place, and afterwards from the principal of his debt. He is bound to pay taxes on the property, and keep it in repair, unless the contrary is agreed. The creditor does not become the proprietor of the property by failure to pay at the agreed time, and any clause to that effect is void. He can only sue the debtor, and obtain sentence for sale of the property. The possession of the property is, however, by the contract, transferred to the creditor. 11 Pet. 351.

ANTICIPATION. The act of doing or taking a thing before its proper time.

In conveyancing, anticipation is the act of assigning, charging, or otherwise dealing with income before it becomes due.

In patent law, a person is said to have been anticipated when he patents a contrivance already known within the limits of the country granting the patent.

ANTIGRAPHUS. In Roman law. An officer whose duty it was to take care of tax money. A comptroller.

ANTIGRAPHY. A copy or counterpart of a deed.

ANTINOMIA. In Roman law. A real or apparent contradiction or inconsistency in the laws. Merl. Repert. Conflicting laws or provisions of law; inconsistent or conflicting decisions or cases.

ANTINOMY. A term used in logic and law to denote a real or apparent inconsistency or conflict between two authorities or propositions; same as *antinomia*, (*q. v.*)

ANTIQUA CUSTUMA. In English law. Ancient custom. An export duty on wool, wool-felts, and leather, imposed during the reign of Edw. I. It was so called by way of distinction from an increased duty on the same articles, payable by foreign merchants, which was imposed at a later period of the same reign and was called "*custuma nova.*" 1 Bl. Comm. 314.

ANTIQUA STATUTA. Also called "*Vetera Statuta.*" English statutes from the time of Richard I. to Edward III. 1 Reeve, Eng. Law, 227.

ANTIQUARE. In Roman law. To restore a former law or practice: to reject or vote against a new law; to prefer the old law. Those who voted against a proposed law wrote on their ballots the letter "A," the initial of *antiquo*, I am for the old law. Calvin.

ANTIQUUM DOMINICUM. In old English law. Ancient demesne.

ANTITHETARIUS. In old English law. A man who endeavors to discharge himself of the crime of which he is accused, by retorting the charge on the accuser. He differs from an approver in this: that the latter does not charge the accuser, but others. Jacob.

ANTRUSTIO. In early feudal law. A confidential vassal. A term applied to the followers or dependents of the ancient German chiefs, and of the kings and counts of the Franks. Burrill.

ANUELS LIVRES. L. Fr. The Year Books. Kelham.

APANAGE. In old French law. A provision of lands or feudal superiorities assigned by the kings of France for the maintenance of their younger sons. An allowance assigned to a prince of the reigning house for his proper maintenance out of the public treasury. 1 Hallam, Mid. Ages, pp. ii, 88; Wharton.

APARTMENT. A part of a house occupied by a person, while the rest is occupied by another, or others. As to the meaning of this term, see 7 Man. & G. 95; 6 Mod. 214; 42 Ala. 356; 10 Pick. 293; 10 Mass. 190; 38 Cal. 137.

APATISATIO. An agreement or compact. Du Cange.

APERTA BREVIA. Open, unsealed writs.

APERTUM FACTUM. An overt act.

APERTURA TESTAMENTI. In the civil law. A form of proving a will, by the witnesses acknowledging before a magistrate their having sealed it.

APEX. The summit or highest point of anything; the top; *e. g.*, in mining law, "apex of a vein." See 26 N. W. Rep. 887.

APEX JURIS. The summit of the law; a legal subtlety; a nice or cunning point of law; close technicality; a rule of law carried to an extreme point, either of severity or refinement.

Apices juris non sunt jura, [jus.] Extremities, or mere subtleties of law, are not rules of law, [are not law.] Co. Litt. 304*b*; 10 Coke, 126; Wing. Max. 19, max. 14; Broom, Max. 188.

APICES LITIGANDI. Extremely fine points, or subtleties of litigation. Nearly equivalent to the modern phrase "sharp practice." "It is unconscionable in a defendant to take advantage of the *apices litigandi*, to turn a plaintiff around and make him pay costs when his demand is just." Per Lord Mansfield, in 3 Burr. 1243.

APOCHA. Lat. In the civil law. A writing acknowledging payments; acquittance. It differs from acceptilation in this: that acceptilation imports a complete discharge of the former obligation whether payment be made or not; *apocha*, discharge only upon payment being made. Calvin.

APOCHÆ ONERATORIÆ. In old commercial law. Bills of lading.

APOCRISARIUS. In ecclesiastical law. One who answers for another. An officer whose duty was to carry to the emperor messages relating to ecclesiastical matters, and to take back his answer to the petitioners. An officer who gave advice on questions of ecclesiastical law. An ambassador or legate of a pope or bishop. Spelman.

APOCRISARIUS CANCELLARIUS. In the civil law. An officer who took charge of the royal seal and signed royal dispatches.

APOGRAPHIA. A civil law term signifying an inventory or enumeration of things in one's possession. Calvin.

APOPLEXY. In medical jurisprudence. The failure of consciousness and suspension of voluntary motion from suspension of the functions of the cerebrum.

APOSTACY. In English law. The total renunciation of Christianity, by embracing either a false religion or no religion at all. This offense can only take place in such as have once professed the Christian religion. 4 Bl. Comm. 43; 4 Steph. Comm. 231.

APOSTATA. In civil and old English law. An apostate; a deserter from the faith; one who has renounced the Christian faith. Cod. 1, 7; Reg. Orig. 71*b*.

APOSTATA CAPIENDO. An obsolete English writ which issued against an apostate, or one who had violated the rules of his religious order. It was addressed to the sheriff, and commanded him to deliver the defendant into the custody of the abbot or prior. Reg. Orig. 71, 267; Jacob; Wharton.

APOSTILLE, Appostille. L. Fr. An addition; a marginal note or observation. Kelham.

APOSTLES. In English admiralty practice. A term borrowed from the civil law, denoting brief dismissory letters granted to a party who appeals from an inferior to a superior court, embodying a statement of the case and a declaration that the record will be transmitted.

This term is still sometimes applied in the admiralty courts of the United States to the papers sent up or transmitted on appeals.

APOSTOLI. In the civil law. Certificates of the inferior judge from whom a cause is removed, directed to the superior. Dig. 49, 6. See APOSTLES.

APOSTOLUS. A messenger; an ambassador, legate, or nuncio. Spelman.

APOTHECA. In the civil law. A repository; a place of deposit, as of wine, oil, books, etc. Calvin.

APOTHECARY. Any person who keeps a shop or building where medicines are compounded or prepared according to prescriptions of physicians, or where medicines are sold. Act Cong. July 13, 1866, § 9; 14 St. at Large, 119.

The term "druggist" properly means one whose occupation is to buy and sell drugs without compounding or preparing them. The term therefore has a much more limited and restricted meaning than the word "apothecary," and there is little difficulty in concluding that the term "druggist" may be applied in a technical sense to persons who buy and sell drugs. 28 La. Ann. 767.

APPARATOR. A furnisher or provider. Formerly the sheriff, in England, had charge of certain county affairs and disbursements, in which capacity he was called "*apparator comitatus*," and received therefor a considerable emolument. Cowell.

APPARENT. That which is obvious, evident, or manifest; what appears, or has been made manifest. In respect to facts involved in an appeal or writ of error, that which is stated in the record.

APPARENT DANGER, as used with reference to the doctrine of self-defense in homicide, means such overt actual demonstration, by conduct and acts, of a design to take life or do some great personal injury, as would make the killing apparently necessary to self-preservation. 44 Miss. 762.

APPARENT DEFECTS, in a thing sold, are those which can be discovered by simple inspection. Code La. art. 2497.

APPARENT EASEMENT. Apparent or continuous easements are those depending upon some artificial structure upon, or natural formation of, the servient tenement, obvious and permanent, which constitutes the easement or is the means of enjoying it; as the bed of a running stream, an overhanging roof, a pipe for conveying water, a drain, or a sewer. Non-apparent or non-continuous easements are such that have no means specially constructed or appropriated to their enjoyment, and that are enjoyed at intervals, leaving between these intervals no visible sign of their existence, such as a right of way, or right of drawing a seine upon the shore. 18 N. J. Eq. 262.

APPARENT HEIR. **In English law.** One whose right of inheritance is indefeasible, provided he outlive the ancestor. 2 Bl. Comm. 208.

In Scotch law. He is the person to whom the succession has actually opened. He is so called until his regular entry on the lands by service or infeftment on a precept of *clare constat*.

APPARENT MATURITY. The apparent maturity of a negotiable instrument payable at a particular time is the day on which, by its terms, it becomes due, or, when that is a holiday, the next business day. Civil Code Cal. § 3132.

APPARITIO. In old practice. Appearance; an appearance. *Apparitio in judicio*, an appearance in court. Bract. fol. 344. *Post apparitionem*, after appearance. Fleta, lib. 6, c. 10, § 25.

APPARITOR. An officer or messenger employed to serve the process of the spiritual courts in England and summon offenders. Cowell.

In the civil law. An officer who waited upon a magistrate or superior officer, and executed his commands. Calvin.; Cod. 12, 53–57.

APPARLEMENT. In old English law. Resemblance; likelihood; as apparlement of war. St. 2 Rich. II. st. 1, c. 6; Cowell.

APPARURA. In old English law the apparura were furniture, implements, tackle, or apparel. *Carucarum apparura*, plow-tackle. Cowell.

APPEAL. **In civil practice.** The complaint to a superior court of an injustice done or error committed by an inferior one, whose judgment or decision the court above is called upon to correct or reverse.

The removal of a cause from a court of inferior to one of superior jurisdiction, for the purpose of obtaining a review and retrial. 3 Dall. 321; 7 Cranch, 110; 10 Pet. 205; 14 Mass. 414; 1 Serg. & R. 78; 1 Bin. 219; 3 Bin. 48.

The distinction between an appeal and a writ of error is that an appeal is a process of civil law origin, and removes a cause entirely, subjecting the facts, as well as the law, to a review and revisal; but a writ of error is of common law origin, and it removes nothing for re-examination but the law. 3 Dall. 321; 7 Cranch, 108.

But appeal is sometimes used to denote the nature of appellate jurisdiction, as distinguished from original jurisdiction, without any particular regard to the mode by which a cause is transmitted to a superior jurisdiction. 1 Gall. 5, 12.

In criminal practice. A formal accusation made by one private person against another of having committed some heinous crime. 4 Bl. Comm. 312.

Appeal was also the name given to the proceeding in English law where a person, indicted of treason or felony, and arraigned for the same, confessed the fact before plea pleaded, and *appealed*, or accused others, his accomplices in the same crime, in order to obtain his pardon. In this case he was called an "approver" or "prover," and the party appealed or accused, the "*appellee*." 4 Bl. Comm. 330.

In legislation. The act by which a member of a legislative body who questions the correctness of a decision of the presiding officer, or "chair," procures a vote of the body upon the decision.

In old French law. A mode of proceeding in the lords' courts, where a party was dissatisfied with the judgment of the peers, which was by accusing them of having given a false or malicious judgment, and offering to make good the charge by the duel or combat. This was called the "appeal of false judgment." Montesq. Esprit des Lois, liv. 28, c. 27.

APPEAL BOND. The bond given on taking an appeal, by which the appellant binds himself to pay damages and costs if he fails to prosecute the appeal with effect.

APPEALED. In a sense not strictly technical, this word may be used to signify the exercise by a party of the right to remove a litigation from one forum to another; as where he removes a suit involving the title to real estate from a justice's court to the common pleas. 8 Metc. (Mass.) 166.

APPEAR. In practice. To be properly before a court; as a fact or matter of which it can take notice. To be in evidence; to be proved. "Making it *appear* and proving are the same thing." Freem. 53.

To be regularly in court; as a defendant in an action. See APPEARANCE.

APPEARANCE. In practice. A coming into court as party to a suit, whether as plaintiff or defendant.

The formal proceeding by which a defendant submits himself to the jurisdiction of the court.

According to Bouvier, appearance may be of the following kinds:

Compulsory. That which takes place in consequence of the service of process.

Conditional. One which is coupled with conditions as to its becoming general.

De bene esse. One which is to remain an appearance, except in a certain event. See DE BENE ESSE.

General. A simple and absolute submission to the jurisdiction of the court.

Gratis. One made before the party has been legally notified to appear.

Optional. One made where the party is not under any obligation to appear, but does so to save his rights. It occurs in chancery practice, especially in England.

Special. That which is made for certain purposes only, and does not extend to all the purposes of the suit.

Subsequent. An appearance by the defendant after one has already been entered for him by the plaintiff. See Daniell, Ch. Pr.

Voluntary. That which is made in answer to a *subpœna* or summons without process. 1 Barb. Ch. Pr. 77.

APPEARANCE DAY. The day for appearing; that on which the parties are bound to come into court.

APPEARAND HEIR. In Scotch law. An apparent heir. See APPARENT HEIR.

APPELLANT. The party who takes an appeal from one court or jurisdiction to another.

APPELLATE. Pertaining to or having cognizance of appeals and other proceedings for the judicial review of adjudications.

APPELLATE COURT. A court having jurisdiction of appeal and review; a court to which causes are removable by appeal, *certiorari*, or error.

APPELLATE JURISDICTION. Jurisdiction on appeal; jurisdiction to revise or correct the proceedings in a cause already instituted and acted upon by an inferior court, or by a tribunal having the attributes of a court. 6 Kan. 505.

APPELLATIO. Lat. An appeal.

APPELLATOR. An old law term having the same meaning as "appellant," (*q. v.*) In the civil law, the term was applied to the judge *ad quem*, or to whom an appeal was taken. Calvin.

APPELLEE. The party in a cause against whom an appeal is taken; also called the "respondent."

APPELLO. Lat. In the civil law. I appeal. The form of making an appeal *apud acta*. Dig. 49, 1, 2.

APPELLOR. In old English law. A criminal who accuses his accomplices, or who challenges a jury.

APPENDAGE. Something added as an accessory to or the subordinate part of another thing. 28 N. J. Law, 26; 30 N. W. Rep. (Iowa,) 633.

APPENDANT. A thing annexed to or belonging to another thing and passing with it; a thing of inheritance belonging to another inheritance which is more worthy; as an advowson, common, etc., which may be appendant to a manor, common of fishing to a freehold, a seat in a church to a house, etc. It differs from appurtenance, in that appendant must ever be by prescription, *i. e.*, a personal usage for a considerable time, while an appurtenance may be created at this day; for if a grant be made to a man and his heirs, of common in such a moor for his beasts levant or couchant upon his manor, the commons are appurtenant to the manor, and the grant will pass them. Co. Litt. 121*b*. See APPURTENANCE.

APPENDITIA. The appendages or appurtenances of an estate or house. Cowell.

APPENDIX. A printed volume, used on an appeal to the English house of lords or privy council, containing the documents and other evidence presented in the inferior court and referred to in the cases made by the parties for the appeal. Answering in some respects to the "paper-book" or "case" in American practice.

APPENSURA. Payment of money by weight instead of by count. Cowell.

APPERTAINING. Belonging to; appurtenant. See APPURTENANT.

APPLICABLE. When a constitution or court declares that the common law is in force in a particular state so far as it is *applicable*, it is meant that it must be applicable to the habits and conditions of the community, as well as in harmony with the genius, the spirit, and the objects of their institutions. 3 Iowa, 402; 3 Scam. 121; 5 Gilman, 130.

When a constitution prohibits the enactment of local or special laws in all cases where a general law would be *applicable*, a general law should always be construed to be applicable, in this sense, where the entire people of the state have an interest in the subject, such as regulating interest, statutes of frauds or limitations, etc. But where only a portion of the people are affected, as in locating a county-seat, it will depend upon the facts and circumstances of each particular case whether such a law would be applicable. 8 Nev. 322.

APPLICARE. Lat. In old English law. To fasten to; to moor (a vessel.) Anciently rendered, "to apply." Hale, de Jure Mar.

Applicatio est vita regulæ. Application is the life of a rule. 2 Bulst. 79.

APPLICATION. A putting to, placing before, preferring a request or petition to or before a person. The act of making a request for something.

A written request to have a certain quantity of land at or near a certain specified place. 3 Bin. 21; 5 Id. 151.

The use or disposition made of a thing.

A bringing together, in order to ascertain some relation or establish some connection; as the *application* of a rule or principle to a case or fact.

In insurance. The preliminary request, declaration, or statement made by a party applying for an insurance on life, or against fire.

Of purchase money. The disposition made of the funds received by a trustee on a sale of real estate held under the trust.

APPLICATION OF PAYMENTS. Appropriation of a payment to some particular debt; or the determination to which of several demands a general payment made by a debtor to his creditor shall be applied.

APPLY. 1. To make a formal request or petition, usually in writing, to a court, officer, board, or company, for the granting of some favor, or of some rule or order, which is within his or their power or discretion. For example, to apply for an injunction, for a pardon, for a policy of insurance.

2. To use or employ for a particular purpose; to appropriate and devote to a particular use, object, demand, or subject-matter. Thus, to apply payments to the reduction of interest.

3. To put, use, or refer, as suitable or relative; to co-ordinate language with a particular subject-matter; as to apply the words of a statute to a particular state of facts.

APPOINTEE. A person who is appointed or selected for a particular purpose; as the appointee under a power is the person who is to receive the benefit of the power.

APPOINTMENT. In chancery practice. The exercise of a right to designate the person or persons who are to take the use of real estate. 2 Washb. Real Prop. 302.

The act of a person in directing the disposition of property, by limiting a use, or by substituting a new use for a former one, in pursuance of a power granted to him for that purpose by a preceding deed, called a "power of appointment;" also the deed or other instrument by which he so conveys.

Where the power embraces several permitted objects, and the appointment is made to one or more of them, excluding others, it is called "exclusive."

Appointment may signify an appropriation of money to a specific purpose. 3 N. Y. 93, 119.

In public law. The selection or designation of a person, by the person or persons having authority therefor, to fill an office or public function and discharge the duties of the same.

The term "appointment" is to be distinguished from "election." The former is an executive act, whereby a person is named as the incumbent of an office and invested therewith, by one or more individuals who have the sole power and right to select and constitute the officer. Election means that the person is chosen by a principle of selection in the nature of a vote, participated in by the public generally or by the entire class of persons qualified to express their choice in this manner.

APPOINTOR. The person who appoints, or executes a power of appointment; as *appointee* is the person to whom or in whose favor an appointment is made. 1 Steph. Comm. 506, 507; 4 Kent, Comm. 316.

One authorized by the donor, under the statute of uses, to execute a power. 2 Bouv. Inst. n. 1923.

APPORT. L. Fr. In old English law. Tax; tallage; tribute; imposition; payment; charge; expenses. Kelham.

APPORTIONMENT. The division, partition, or distribution of a subject-matter in proportionate parts. Co. Litt. 147; 1 Swanst. 37, n.; 1 Story, Eq. Jur. 475*a*.

Of contracts. The allowance, in case of a severable contract, partially performed, of a part of the entire consideration proportioned to the degree in which the contract was carried out.

Of rent. The allotment of their shares in a rent to each of several parties owning it. The determination of the amount of rent to be paid when the tenancy is terminated at some period other than one of the regular intervals for the payment of rent.

Of incumbrances. Where several persons are interested in an estate, apportionment, as between them, is the determination of the respective amounts which they shall contribute towards the removal of the incumbrance.

Of corporate shares. The *pro tanto* division among the subscribers of the shares allowed to be issued by the charter, where more than the limited number have been subscribed for.

Of common. A division of the right of common between several persons, among whom the land to which, as an entirety, it first belonged has been divided.

Of representatives. The determination upon each decennial census of the number of representatives in congress which each state shall elect, the calculation being based upon the population. See Const. U. S. art. 1, § 2.

APPORTS EN NATURE. In French law. That which a partner brings into the partnership other than cash; for instance, securities, realty or personalty, cattle, stock, or even his personal ability and knowledge. Argl. Fr. Merc. Law, 545.

APPORTUM. In old English law. The revenue, profit, or emolument which a thing brings to the owner. Commonly applied to a corody or pension. Blount.

APPOSAL OF SHERIFFS. The charging them with money received upon their account in the exchequer. St. 22 & 23 Car. II.; Cowell.

APPOSER. An officer in the exchequer, clothed with the duty of examining the sheriffs in respect of their accounts. Usually called the "foreign apposer." Termes de la Ley.

APPOSTILLE, or APOSTILLE. In French law, an addition or annotation made in the margin of a writing. Merl. Repert.

APPRAISE. In practice. To fix or set a price or value upon; to fix and state the true value of a thing, and, usually, in writing.

APPRAISEMENT. A just and true valuation of property. A valuation set upon property under judicial or legislative authority.

APPRAISER. A person appointed by competent authority to make an appraisement, to ascertain and state the true value of goods or real estate.

APPREHEND. To take hold of, whether with the mind, and so to conceive, believe, fear, dread; or actually and bodily, and so to take a person on a criminal process; to seize; to arrest. 1 Amer. & Eng. Enc. Law, 636.

APPREHENSIO. Lat. In the civil and old English law. A taking hold of a person or thing; apprehension; the seizure or capture of a person. Calvin.

One of the varieties or subordinate forms of *occupatio*, or the mode of acquiring title to things not belonging to any one.

APPREHENSION. In practice. The seizure, taking, or arrest of a person on a criminal charge. The term "apprehension" is applied exclusively to criminal cases, and "arrest" to both criminal and civil cases.

In the civil law. A physical or corporal act, (*corpus*,) on the part of one who intends to acquire possession of a thing, by which he brings himself into such a relation to the thing that he may subject it to his exclusive control; or by which he obtains the physical ability to exercise his power over the thing whenever he pleases. One of the requisites to the acquisition of judicial possession, and by which, when accompanied by intention, (*animus*,) possession is acquired. Mackeld. Rom. Law, §§ 248, 249, 250.

APPRENDRE. A fee or profit taken or received. Cowell.

APPRENTICE. A person, usually a minor, bound in due form of law to a master, to learn from him his art, trade, or business, and to serve him during the time of his apprenticeship. 1 Bl. Comm. 426; 2 Kent, Comm. 211; 3 Rawle, 307; 4 Term. 735.

APPRENTICE EN LA LEY. An ancient name for students at law, and afterwards applied to counselors, *apprentici ad barras*, from which comes the more modern word "barrister."

APPRENTICESHIP. A contract by which one person, usually a minor, called the "apprentice," is bound to another person, called the "master," to serve him during a prescribed term of years in his art, trade, or business, in consideration of being instructed by the master in such art or trade, and (commonly) of receiving his support and maintenance from the master during such term.

The term during which an apprentice is to serve.

The *status* of an apprentice; the relation subsisting between an apprentice and his master.

APPRENTICIUS AD LEGEM. An apprentice to the law; a law student; a counselor below the degree of serjeant; a barrister. See APPRENTICE EN LA LEY.

APPRIZING. In Scotch law. A form of process by which a creditor formerly took possession of the estates of the debtor in payment of the debt due. It is now superseded by adjudications.

APPROACH. In international law. The right of a ship of war, upon the high sea, to visit another vessel for the purpose of ascertaining the nationality of the latter. 1 Kent, Comm. 153, note.

APPROBATE AND REPROBATE. In Scotch law. To approve and reject; to take advantage of one part, and reject the rest. Bell. Equity suffers no person to *approbate and reprobate* the same deed. 1 Kames, Eq. 317; 1 Bell, Comm. 146.

APPROPRIATE. 1. To make a thing one's own; to make a thing the subject of property; to exercise dominion over an object to the extent, and for the purpose, of making it subserve one's own proper use or pleasure. The term is properly used in this sense to denote the acquisition of property and a right of exclusive enjoyment in those things which before were without an owner or were *publici juris*.

2. To prescribe a particular use for particular moneys; to designate or destine a fund or property for a distinct use, or for the payment of a particular demand.

In its use with reference to payments or moneys, there is room for a distinction between this term and "apply." The former properly denotes the setting apart of a fund or payment for a particular use or purpose, or the mental act of resolving that it shall be so employed, while "apply" signifies the actual expenditure of the fund, or using the payment, for the purpose to which it has been appropriated. Practically, however, the words are used interchangeably.

3. To *appropriate* is also used in the sense of to distribute; in this sense it may denote the act of an executor or administrator who distributes the estate of his decedent among the legatees, heirs, or others entitled, in pursuance of his duties and according to their respective rights.

APPROPRIATION. The act of appropriating or setting apart; prescribing the destination of a thing; designating the use or application of a fund.

In public law. The act by which the legislative department of government designates a particular fund, or sets apart a specified portion of the public revenue or of the money in the public treasury, to be applied to some general object of governmental expenditure, (as the civil service list, etc.,) or to some individual purchase or expense.

When money is appropriated (*i. e.*, set apart) for the purpose of securing the payment of a specific debt or class of debts, or for an individual purchase or object of expense, it is said to be specifically appropriated for that purpose.

A specific appropriation is an act of the legislature by which a named sum of money has been set apart in the treasury, and devoted to the payment of a particular demand. 45 Cal. 149.

Appropriation of payments. This means the application of a payment to the discharge of a particular debt. Thus, if a creditor has two distinct debts due to him from his debtor, and the latter makes a general payment on account, without specifying at the time to which debt he intends the payment to apply, it is optional for the creditor to *appropriate* (apply) the payment to either of the two debts he pleases. (1 Mer. 585.) Brown.

In English ecclesiastical law. The perpetual annexing of a benefice to some spiritual corporation either sole or aggregate, being the patron of the living. 1 Bl. Comm. 384; 3 Steph. Comm. 70–75; 1 Crabb, Real Prop. p. 144, § 129. Where the annexation is to the use of a lay person, it is usually called an "impropriation." 1 Crabb, Real Prop. p. 145, § 130.

APPROPRIATOR. In English ecclesiastical law. A spiritual corporation entitled to the profits of a benefice.

APPROVAL. The act of a judge or magistrate in sanctioning and accepting as satisfactory a bond, security, or other instrument which is required by law to pass his inspection and receive his approbation before it becomes operative.

APPROVE. To take to one's proper and separate use. To improve; to enhance the value or profits of anything. To inclose and cultivate common or waste land.

To *approve common* or waste land is to inclose and convert it to the purposes of husbandry, which the owner might always do, provided he left common sufficient for such as were entitled to it. St. Mert. c. 4; St. Westm. 2, c. 46; 2 Bl. Comm. 34; 3 Bl. Comm. 240; 2 Steph. Comm. 7; 3 Kent, Comm. 406.

In old criminal law. To accuse or prove; to accuse an accomplice by giving evidence against him.

APPROVED INDORSED NOTES. Notes indorsed by another person than the maker, for additional security.

APPROVEMENT. By the common law, approvement is said to be a species of confession, and incident to the arraignment of a prisoner indicted for treason or felony, who confesses the fact before plea pleaded, and appeals or accuses others, his accomplices in the same crime, in order to obtain his own pardon. In this case he is called an "approver," or "prover," "probator," and the party appealed or accused is called the "appellee." Such approvement can only be in capital offenses, and it is, as it were, equivalent to an indictment, since the appellee is equally called upon to answer it. 26 Ill. 347.

APPROVER. Approvement; improvement. "There can be no *approver* in derogation of a right of common of turbary." 1 Taunt. 435.

APPROVER. L. Fr. To approve or prove; to vouch. Kelham.

APPROVER. In criminal law. An accomplice in crime who accuses others of the same offense, and is admitted as a witness at the discretion of the court to give evidence against his companions in guilt. He is vulgarly called "Queen's Evidence."

He is one who confesses himself guilty of felony and accuses others of the same crime to save himself from punishment. 26 Ill. 175.

In old English law. Certain men sent into the several counties to increase the farms (rents) of hundreds and wapentakes, which formerly were let at a certain value to the sheriff. Cowell.

APPROVERS. In old English law. Bailiffs of lords in their franchises. Sheriffs were called the king's "approvers" in 1 Edw. III. st. 1, c. 1. Termes de la Ley, 49.

Approvers in the Marches were those who had license to sell and purchase beasts there.

APPRUARE. To take to one's use or profit. Cowell.

APPULSUS. In the civil law. A driving to, as of cattle to water. Dig. 8, 3, 1, 1.

APPURTENANCE. That which belongs to something else; an adjunct; an appendage; something annexed to another thing more worthy as principal, and which passes as incident to it, as a right of way or other easement to land; an out-house, barn, garden, or orchard, to a house or messuage. Webster.

Appurtenances of a ship include whatever is on board a ship for the objects of the voyage and adventure in which she is engaged, belonging to her owner.

Appurtenant is substantially the same in meaning as *accessory*, but it is more technically used in relation to property, and is the more appropriate word for a conveyance.

APPURTENANT. Belonging to; accessory or incident to; adjunct, appended, or annexed to; answering to *accessorium* in the civil law. 2 Steph. Comm. 30 note.

A thing is deemed to be incidental or *appurtenant* to land when it is by right used with the land for its benefit, as in the case of a way, or water-course, or of a passage for light, air, or heat from or across the land of another. Civil Code Cal. § 662.

In common speech, appurtenant denotes annexed or belonging to; but in law it denotes an annexation which is of convenience merely and not of necessity, and which may have had its origin at any time, in both which respects it is distinguished from appendant, (*q. v.*)

APT TIME. Apt time sometimes depends upon *lapse* of time; as, where a thing is required to be done at the first term, or within a given time, it cannot be done afterwards. But the phrase more usually refers to the *order* of proceedings, as fit or suitable. 74 N. C. 383.

APT WORDS. Words proper to produce the legal effect for which they are intended; sound technical phrases.

APTA VIRO. Fit for a husband; marriageable; a woman who has reached marriageable years.

APUD ACTA. Among the acts; among the recorded proceedings. In the civil law, this phrase is applied to appeals taken orally, in the presence of the judge, at the time of judgment or sentence.

AQUA. In the civil and old English law. Water; sometimes a stream or water-course.

AQUA ÆSTIVA. In Roman law. Summer water; water that was used in summer only. Dig. 43, 20, 1, 3, 4.

Aqua cedit solo. Water follows the land. A sale of land will pass the water which covers it. 2 Bl. Comm. 18; Co. Litt. 4.

AQUA CURRENS. Running water.

Aqua currit et debet currere, ut currere solebat. Water runs, and ought to run, as it has used to run. 3 Bulst. 339; 3 Kent, Comm. 439. A running stream should be left to flow in its natural channel, without alteration or diversion. A fundamental maxim in the law of water-courses.

AQUÆ DUCTUS. In the civil law. A servitude which consists in the right to carry water by means of pipes or conduits over or through the estate of another. Dig. 8, 3, 1; Inst. 2, 3.

AQUA DULCIS or FRISCA. Fresh water. Reg. Orig. 97; Bract. fols. 117, 135.

AQUA FONTANEA. Spring water. Fleta, lib. 4, c. 27, § 8.

AQUÆ HAUSTUS. In the civil law. A servitude which consists in the right to draw water from the fountain, pool, or spring of another. Inst. 2, 3, 2; Dig. 8, 3, 1, 1.

AQUÆ IMMITTENDÆ. A civil law easement or servitude, consisting in the right of one whose house is surrounded with other buildings to cast waste water upon the adjacent roofs or yards. Similar to the common law easement of drip. 15 Barb. 96.

AQUA PROFLUENS. Flowing or running water. Dig. 1, 8, 2.

AQUA QUOTIDIANA. In Roman law. Daily water; water that might be drawn at all times of the year, (*qua quis quotidie possit uti, si vellet.*) Dig. 43, 20, 1–4.

AQUA SALSA. Salt water.

AQUAGIUM. A canal, ditch, or water-course running through marshy grounds. A mark or gauge placed in or on the banks of a running stream, to indicate the height of the water, was called "*aquagaugium.*" Spelman.

AQUATIC RIGHTS. Rights which individuals have to the use of the sea and rivers, for the purpose of fishing and navigation, and also to the soil in the sea and rivers.

ARABANT. They plowed. A term of feudal law, applied to those who held by the tenure of plowing and tilling the lord's lands within the manor. Cowell.

ARAHO. In feudal law. To make oath in the church or some other holy place. All oaths were made in the church upon the relics of saints, according to the Ripuarian laws. Cowell; Spelman.

ARALIA. Plow-lands. Land fit for the plow. Denoting the character of land, rather than its condition. Spelman.

ARATOR. A plow-man; a farmer of arable land.

ARATRUM TERRÆ. In old English law. A plow of land; a plow land; as much land as could be tilled with one plow. Whishaw.

ARATURA TERRÆ. The plowing of land by the tenant, or vassal, in the service of his lord. Whishaw.

ARATURIA. Land suitable for the plow; arable land. Spelman.

ARBITER. A person chosen to decide a controversy; an arbitrator, referee.

A person bound to decide according to the rules of law and equity, as distinguished from an arbitrator, who may proceed wholly at his own discretion, so that it be according to the judgment of a sound man. Cowell.

According to Mr. Abbott, the distinction is as follows: "Arbitrator" is a technical name of a person selected with reference to an established system for friendly determination of controversies, which, though not judicial, is yet regulated by law; so that the powers and duties of the arbitrator, when once he is chosen, are prescribed by law, and his doings may be judicially revised if he has exceeded his authority. "Arbiter" is an untechnical designation of a person to whom a controversy is referred, irrespective of any law to govern the decision; and is the proper word to signify a referee of a question outside of or above municipal law.

But it is elsewhere said that the distinction between arbiters and arbitrators is not observed in modern law. Russ. Arb. 112.

In the Roman law. A judge invested with a discretionary power. A person appointed by the prætor to examine and decide that class of causes or actions termed "*bonæ fidei,*" and who had the power of judging according to the principles of equity, (*ex æquo et bono;*) distinguished from the *judex,* (*q. v.,*) who was bound to decide according to strict law. Inst. 4, 6, 30, 31.

ARBITRAMENT. The award or decision of arbitrators upon a matter of dispute, which has been submitted to them. Termes de la Ley.

ARBITRAMENT AND AWARD. A plea to an action brought for the same cause which had been submitted to arbitration and on which an award had been made. Wats. Arb. 256.

Arbitramentum æquum tribuit cuique suum. A just arbitration renders to every one his own. Noy, Max. 248.

ARBITRARY. Not supported by fair, solid, and substantial cause, and without reason given. L. R. 9 Exch. 155.

ARBITRARY PUNISHMENT. That punishment which is left to the decision of the judge, in distinction from those defined by statute.

ARBITRATION. In practice. The investigation and determination of a matter or matters of difference between contending parties, by one or more unofficial persons, chosen by the parties, and called "arbitrators," or "referees." Worcester; 3 Bl. Comm. 16.

Compulsory arbitration is that which takes place when the consent of one of the parties is enforced by statutory provisions.

Voluntary arbitration is that which takes place by mutual and free consent of the parties.

In a wide sense, this term may embrace the whole method of thus settling controversies, and thus include all the various steps. But in more strict use, the decision is separately spoken of, and called an "award," and the "arbitration" denotes only the submission and hearing.

ARBITRATION OF EXCHANGE. This takes place where a merchant pays his debts in one country by a bill of exchange upon another.

ARBITRATOR. A private, disinterested person, chosen by the parties to a disputed question, for the purpose of hearing their contention, and giving judgment between them; to whose decision (award) the litigants submit themselves either voluntarily, or, in some cases, compulsorily, by order of a court.

"Referee" is of frequent modern use as a synonym of arbitrator, but is in its origin of broader signification and less accurate than arbitrator.

ARBITRIUM. The decision of an arbiter, or arbitrator; an award; a judgment.

Arbitrium est judicium. An award is a judgment. Jenk. Cent. 137.

Arbitrium est judicium boni viri, secundum æquum et bonum. An award is the judgment of a good man, according to justice. 3 Bulst. 64.

ARBOR. Lat. A tree; a plant; something larger than an herb; a general term including vines, osiers, and even reeds. The mast of a ship. Brissonius. Timber. Ainsworth; Calvin.

ARBOR CONSANGUINITATIS. A table, formed in the shape of a tree, showing the genealogy of a family. See the *arbor civilis* of the civilians and canonists. Hale, Com. Law, 335.

Arbor dum crescit, lignum cum crescere nescit. [That which is] a tree while it grows, [is] wood when it ceases to grow. Cro. Jac. 166; Hob. 77*b*, in marg.

ARBOR FINALIS. In old English law. A boundary tree; a tree used for making a boundary line. Bract. fols. 167, 207*b*.

ARCA. Lat. In the civil law. A chest or coffer; a place for keeping money. Dig. 30, 30, 6; Id. 32, 64. Brissonius.

ARCANA IMPERII. State secrets. 1 Bl. Comm. 337.

ARCARIUS. In civil and old English law. A treasurer; a keeper of public money. Cod. 10, 70, 15; Spelman.

ARCHAIONOMIA. A collection of Saxon laws, published during the reign of Queen Elizabeth, in the Saxon language, with a Latin version by Lambard.

ARCHBISHOP. In English ecclesiastical law. The chief of the clergy in his province, having supreme power under the king or queen in all ecclesiastical causes.

ARCHDEACON. A dignitary of the church who has ecclesiastical jurisdiction immediately subordinate to that of the bishop, either throughout the whole of his diocese or in some particular part of it.

ARCHDEACON'S COURT. In English ecclesiastical law. A court held before a judge appointed by the archdeacon, and called his official. Its jurisdiction comprises the granting of probates and administrations, and ecclesiastical causes in general, arising within the archdeaconry. It is the most inferior court in the whole ecclesiastical polity of England. 3 Bl. Comm. 64; 3 Steph. Comm. 430.

ARCHDEACONRY. A division of a diocese, and the circuit of an archdeacon's jurisdiction.

ARCHERY. In feudal law. A service of keeping a bow for the lord's use in the defense of his castle. Co. Litt. 157.

ARCHES COURT. In English ecclesiastical law. A court of appeal belonging to the Archbishop of Canterbury, the judge of which is called the "Dean of the Arches," because his court was anciently held in the church of Saint Mary-le-Bow, (*Sancta Maria de Arcubus*,) so named from the steeple, which is raised upon pillars built archwise. The court was until recently held in the hall belonging to the College of Civilians, commonly called "Doctors' Commons." It is now held in Westminster Hall. Its proper jurisdiction is only over the thirteen peculiar parishes belonging to the archbishop in London, but, the office of Dean of the Arches having been for a long time united with that of the archbishop's principal official, the Judge of the Arches, in right of such added office, it receives and determines appeals from the sentences of all inferior ecclesiastical courts within the province. 3 Bl. Comm. 64.

ARCHETYPE. The original copy.

ARCHICAPELLANUS. L. Lat. In old European law. A chief or high chancellor, (*summus cancellarius*.) Spelman.

ARCHIVES. The Rolls; any place where ancient records, charters, and evidences are kept. In libraries, the private depository. Cowell; Spelman.

The derivative meaning of the word (now the more common) denotes the writings themselves thus preserved; thus we say the archives of a college, of a monastery, etc.

ARCHIVIST. The custodian of archives.

ARCTA ET SALVA CUSTODIA. Lat. In strict and safe custody or keeping. When a defendant is arrested on a *capias ad satisfaciendum*, (*ca. sa.*,) he is to be kept *arcta et salva custodia*. 3 Bl. Comm. 415.

ARDENT SPIRITS. This phrase, in a statute, does not include alcohol, which is not a liquor of any kind. 34 Ark. 340.

ARDOUR. In old English law. An incendiary; a house burner.

ARE. A surface measure in the French law, in the form of a square, equal to 1076.441 square feet.

AREA. An inclosed yard or opening in a house; an open place adjoining a house. 1 Chit. Pr. 176.

In the civil law. A vacant space in a city; a place not built upon. Dig. 50, 16, 211.

The site of a house; a site for building; the space where a house has stood. The ground on which a house is built, and which remains after the house is removed. Brissonius; Calvin.

ARENALES. In Spanish law. Sandy beaches; or grounds on the banks of rivers. White, Recop. b. 2, tit. 1, c. 6.

ARENIFODINA. In the civil law. A sand-pit. Dig. 7, 1, 13, 5.

ARENTARE. Lat. To rent; to let out at a certain rent. Cowell. *Arentatio*. A renting.

AREOPAGITE. In ancient Greek law. A lawyer or chief judge of the Areopagus in capital matters in Athens; a tribunal so called after a hill or slight eminence, in a street of that city dedicated to Mars, where the court was held in which those judges were wont to sit. Wharton.

ARETRO. In arrear; behind. Also written *a retro*.

ARG. An abbreviation of *arguendo*.

ARGENT. In heraldry. Silver.

ARGENTARIUS. In the Roman law, a money lender or broker; a dealer in money; a banker. *Argentarium*, the instrument of the loan, similar to the modern word "bond" or "note."

ARGENTARIUS MILES. A money porter in the English exchequer, who carries the money from the lower to the upper exchequer to be examined and tested. Spelman.

ARGENTEUS. An old French coin, answering nearly to the English shilling. Spelman.

ARGENTUM. Silver; money.

ARGENTUM ALBUM. Bullion; uncoined silver; common silver coin; silver coin worn smooth. Cowell; Spelman.

ARGENTUM DEI. Lat. God's money; God's penny; money given as earnest in making a bargain. Cowell.

ARGUENDO. In arguing; in the course of the argument. A statement or observation made by a judge as a matter of argument or illustration, but not directly bearing upon the case at bar, or only incidentally involved in it, is said (in the reports) to be made *arguendo*, or, in the abbreviated form, *arg.*

ARGUMENT. In rhetoric and logic, an inference drawn from premises, the truth of which is indisputable, or at least highly probable.

The argument of a demurrer, special case, appeal, or other proceeding involving a question of law, consists of the speeches of the opposed counsel; namely, the "opening" of the counsel having the right to begin, (*q. v.*,) the speech of his opponent, and the "reply" of the first counsel. It answers to the trial of a question of fact. Sweet.

ARGUMENT AB INCONVENIENTI. An argument arising from the inconvenience which the proposed construction of the law would create.

ARGUMENTATIVE. In pleading. Indirect; inferential. Steph. Pl. 179.

A pleading is so called in which the statement on which the pleader relies is implied instead of being expressed, or where it contains, in addition to proper statements of facts, reasoning or arguments upon those facts and their relation to the matter in dispute, such as should be reserved for presentation at the trial.

Argumentum a communiter accidentibus in jure frequens est. An argument drawn from things commonly happening is frequent in law. Broom, Max. 44.

Argumentum a divisione est fortissimum in jure. An argument from division [of the subject] is of the greatest force in law. Co. Litt. 213*b*; 6 Coke, 60.

Argumentum a majori ad minus negative non valet; valet e converso. An argument from the greater to the less is of no force negatively; affirmatively it is. Jenk. Cent. 281.

Argumentum a simili valet in lege. An argument from a like case (from analogy) is good in law. Co. Litt. 191.

Argumentum ab auctoritate est fortissimum in lege. An argument from authority is the strongest in the law. "The book cases are the best proof of what the law is." Co. Litt. 254*a*.

Argumentum ab impossibili valet in lege. An argument drawn from an impossibility is forcible in law. Co. Litt. 92*a*.

Argumentum ab inconvenienti est validum in lege; quia lex non permittit aliquod inconveniens. An argument drawn from what is inconvenient is good in law, because the law will not permit any inconvenience. Co. Litt. 66*a*, 258.

Argumentum ab inconvenienti plurimum valet [est validum] in lege. An argument drawn from inconvenience is of the greatest weight [is forcible] in law. Co. Litt. 66*a*, 97*a*, 152*b*, 258*b*; Broom, Max. 184. If there be in any deed or instrument equivocal expressions, and great inconvenience must necessarily follow from one construction, it is strong to show that such construction is not according to the true intention of the grantor; but where there is no equivocal expression in the instrument, and the words used admit only of one meaning, arguments of inconvenience prove only want of foresight in the grantor. 3 Madd. 540; 7 Taunt. 496.

ARIBANNUM. In feudal law. A fine for not setting out to join the army in obedience to the summons of the king.

ARIERBAN, or ARRIERE-BAN. An edict of the ancient kings of France and Germany, commanding all their vassals, the noblesse, and the vassals' vassals, to enter the army, or forfeit their estates on refusal. Spelman.

ARIMANNI. A mediæval term for a class of agricultural owners of small allodial farms, which they cultivated in connection with larger farms belonging to their lords, paying rent and service for the latter, and being under the protection of their superiors. Military tenants holding lands from the emperor. Spelman.

ARISTOCRACY. A government in which a class of men rules supreme.

A form of government which is lodged in a council composed of select members or nobles, without a monarch, and exclusive of the people.

A privileged class of the people; nobles and dignitaries; people of wealth and station.

ARISTO-DEMOCRACY. A form of government where the power is divided between the nobles and the people.

ARLES. Earnest. Used in Yorkshire in the phrase "Arles-penny." Cowell. In Scotland it has the same signification. Bell.

ARM OF THE SEA. A portion of the sea projecting inland, in which the tide ebbs and flows. 5 Coke, 107.

An arm of the sea is considered as extending as far into the interior of a country as the water of fresh rivers is propelled backwards by the ingress of the tide. Ang. Tide-waters, 73.

ARMA. Lat. Arms; weapons, offensive and defensive; armor; arms or cognizances of families.

ARMA DARE. To dub or make a knight.

Arma in armatos sumere jura sinunt. The laws permit the taking up of arms against armed persons. 2 Inst. 574.

ARMA MOLUTA. Sharp weapons that cut, in contradistinction to such as are blunt, which only break or bruise. Fleta, lib. 1, c. 33, par. 6.

ARMA REVERSATA. Reversed arms. a punishment for a traitor or felon. Cowell.

ARMATA VIS. In the civil law. Armed force. Dig. 43, 16, 3; Fleta, lib. 4, c. 4.

ARMED. A vessel is "armed" when she is fitted with a full armament for fighting purposes. She may be equipped for warlike purposes, without being "armed." By "armed" it is ordinarily meant that she has cannon, but if she had a fighting crew, muskets, pistols, powder, shot, cutlasses, and boarding appliances, she might well be said to be equipped for warlike purposes, though not armed. 2 Hurl. & C. 537; 2 Cranch, 121.

ARMIGER. An armor-bearer; an esquire. A title of dignity belonging to gentlemen authorized to bear arms. Cowell.

In its earlier meaning, a servant who carried the arms of a knight. Spelman.

A tenant by scutage; a servant or valet; applied, also, to the higher servants in convents. Spelman.

ARMISCARA. An ancient mode of punishment, which was to carry a saddle at the back as a token of subjection. Spelman.

ARMISTICE. A suspending or cessation of hostilities between belligerent nations or forces for a considerable time.

ARMORIAL BEARINGS. In English law. A device depicted on the (now imaginary) shield of one of the nobility, of which gentry is the lowest degree. The criterion of nobility is the bearing of arms, or armorial bearings, received from ancestry.

Armorum appellatione, non solum scuta et gladii et galeæ, sed et fustes et lapides continentur. Under the name of arms are included, not only shields and swords and helmets, but also clubs and stones. Co. Litt. 162.

ARMS. Anything that a man wears for his defense, or takes in his hands, or uses in his anger, to cast at or strike at another. Co. Litt. 161*b*, 162*a;* Cromp. Just. Peace, 65.

This term, as it is used in the constitution, relative to the right of citizens to bear arms, refers to the arms of a militiaman or soldier, and the word is used in its military sense. The arms of the infantry soldier are the musket and bayonet; of cavalry and dragoons, the sabre, holster pistols, and carbine; of the artillery, the field-piece, siege-gun, and mortar, with side arms. The term, in this connection, cannot be made to cover such weapons as dirks, daggers, slung-shots, sword-canes, brass knuckles, and bowie-knives. These are not military arms. 37 Tex. 476; 3 Heisk. 179.

Arms, or coat of arms, signifies *insignia, i. e.*, ensigns of honor, such as were formerly assumed by soldiers of fortune, and painted on their shields to distinguish them; or nearly the same as armorial bearings, (*q. v.*)

ARMY. The armed forces of a nation intended for military service on land.

"The term 'army' or 'armies' has never been used by congress, so far as I am advised, so as to include the navy or marines, and there is nothing in the act of 1862, or the circumstances which led to its passage, to warrant the conclusion that it was used therein in any other than its long established and ordinary sense,—the land force, as distinguished from the navy and marines." 2 Sawy. 205.

AROMATARIUS. A word formerly used for a grocer. 1 Vent. 142.

AROMATIC. This word, when employed to express one of the qualities of a liquor, cannot be protected as a trade-mark. 45 Cal. 467.

ARPEN, Arpent. A measure of land of uncertain quantity, mentioned in Domesday and other old books; by some called an "acre," by others "half an acre," and by others a "furlong." Spelman; Cowell; Blount.

A measure of land in Louisiana. 6 Pet. 763.

A French measure of land, containing one hundred square perches, of eighteen feet each, or about an acre. But the quantity varied in different provinces. Spelman.

ARPENTATOR. A measurer or surveyor of land. Cowell; Spelman.

ARRA. In the civil law. Earnest; earnest-money; evidence of a completed bargain. Used of a contract of marriage, as well as any other. Spelled, also, *Arrha*, *Arrœ*. Calvin.

ARRACK. A spirit procured from distillation of the cocoa-nut tree, rice, or sugar-cane, and imported from India.

ARRAIGN. In criminal practice. To bring a prisoner to the bar of the court to answer the matter charged upon him in the indictment. The arraignment of a prisoner consists of calling upon him by name, and reading to him the indictment, (in the English tongue,) and demanding of him whether he be guilty or not guilty, and entering his plea.

In old English law. To order, or set in order; to conduct in an orderly manner; to prepare for trial. *To arraign an assise* was to cause the tenant to be called to make the plaint, and to set the cause in such order as the tenant might be enforced to answer thereunto. Litt. § 442; Co. Litt. 262*b*.

ARRAIGNMENT. In criminal practice. Calling the defendant to the bar of the court, to answer the accusation contained in the indictment.

ARRAIGNS, CLERK OF. In English law. An assistant to the clerk of assise.

ARRAMEUR. In old French law. An officer employed to superintend the loading of vessels, and the safe stowage of the cargo. 1 Pet. Adm. Append. XXV.

ARRAS. In Spanish law. The donation which the husband makes to his wife, by reason or on account of marriage, and in consideration of the *dote*, or portion, which he receives from her. Aso & M. Inst. b. 1, t. 7, c. 3.

ARRAY. The whole body of jurors summoned to attend a court, as they are *arrayed* or arranged on the panel. Dane, Abr. Index; 1 Chit. Crim. Law, 536; Com. Dig. "Challenge," B.

A ranking, or setting forth in order; the order in which jurors' names are ranked in the panel containing them. Co. Litt. 156*a;* 3 Bl. Comm. 359.

ARREARS, or ARREARAGES. Money unpaid at the due time, as rent behind; the remainder due after payment of a part of an account; money in the hands of an accounting party. Cowell.

ARRECT. To accuse or charge with an offense. *Arrectati*, accused or suspected persons.

ARRENDAMIENTO. In Spanish law. The contract of letting and hiring an estate or land, (*heredad.*) White, Recop. b. 2, tit. 14, c. 1.

ARREST. In criminal practice. The stopping, seizing, or apprehending a person by lawful authority; the act of laying hands upon a person for the purpose of taking his body into custody of the law; the restraining of the liberty of a man's person in order to compel obedience to the order of a court of justice, or to prevent the commission of a crime, or to insure that a person charged or suspected of a crime may be forthcoming to answer it.

Arrest is well described in the old books as "the beginning of imprisonment, when a man is first taken and restrained of his liberty, by power of a lawful warrant." 2 Shep. Abr. 299; Wood, Inst. Com. Law, 575.

In civil practice. The apprehension of a person by virtue of a lawful authority to answer the demand against him in a civil action.

In admiralty practice. In admiralty actions a ship or cargo is *arrested* when the marshal has served the writ in an action *in rem*. Williams & B. Adm. Jur. 193.

Synonyms distinguished. The term "apprehension" seems to be more peculiarly appropriate to seizure on criminal process; while "arrest" may apply to either a civil or criminal action, but is perhaps better confined to the former.

As ordinarily used, the terms "arrest" and "attachment" coincide in meaning to some extent, though in strictness, as a distinction, an arrest may be said to be the act resulting from the service of an attachment; and, in the more extended sense which is sometimes given to attachment, including the act of taking, it would seem to differ from arrest, in that it is more peculiarly applicable to a taking of property, while *arrest* is more commonly used in speaking of persons. Bouvier.

By *arrest* is to be understood to take the party into custody. To *commit* is the separate and distinct act of carrying the party to prison, after having taken him into custody by force of the execution. 1 Metc. (Mass.) 502.

ARREST OF INQUEST. Pleading in arrest of taking the inquest upon a former issue, and showing cause why an inquest should not be taken.

ARREST OF JUDGMENT. In practice. The act of staying a judgment, or refusing to render judgment in an action at law, after verdict, for some matter intrinsic appearing on the face of the record, which would render the judgment, if given, erroneous or reversible. 3 Bl. Comm. 393; 3 Steph. Comm. 628; 2 Tidd, Pr. 918.

ARRESTANDIS BONIS NE DISSIPENTUR. In old English law. A writ which lay for a person whose cattle or goods were taken by another, who during a contest was likely to make away with them, and who had not the ability to render satisfaction. Reg. Orig. 126.

ARRESTANDO IPSUM QUI PECUNIAM RECEPIT. In old English law. A writ which issued for apprehending a person who had taken the king's prest money to serve in the wars, and then hid himself in order to avoid going.

ARRESTATIO. In old English law. An arrest, (*q. v.*)

ARRESTEE. In Scotch law. The person in whose hands the movables of another, or a debt due to another, are arrested by the creditor of the latter by the process of *arrestment.* 2 Kames, Eq. 173, 175.

ARRESTER. In Scotch law. One who sues out and obtains an arrestment of his debtor's goods or movable obligations. Ersk. Inst. 3, 6, 1.

ARRESTMENT. In Scotch law. Securing a criminal's person till trial, or that of a debtor till he give security *judicio sisti.* The order of a judge, by which he who is debtor in a movable obligation to the arrester's debtor is prohibited to make payment or delivery till the debt due to the arrester be paid or secured. Ersk. Inst. 3, 6, 2.

ARRESTMENT JURISDICTIONIS FUNDANDÆ CAUSÂ. In Scotch law. A process to bring a foreigner within the jurisdiction of the courts of Scotland. The warrant attaches a foreigner's goods within the jurisdiction, and these will not be released unless caution or security be given.

ARRESTO FACTO SUPER BONIS MERCATORUM ALIENIGENORUM. In old English law. A writ against the goods of aliens found within this kingdom, in recompense of goods taken from a denizen in a foreign country, after denial of restitution. Reg. Orig. 129. The ancient civilians called it "*clarigatio,*" but by the moderns it is termed "*reprisalia.*"

ARRÊT. Fr. A judgment, sentence, or decree of a court of competent jurisdiction. The term is derived from the French law, and is used in Canada and Louisiana. *Saisie arrêt* is an attachment of property in the hands of a third person. Code Prac. La. art. 209; 2 Low. Can. 77; 5 Low. Can. 198, 218.

ARRETTED. Charged; charging. The convening a person charged with a crime before a judge. Staundef. P. C. 45. It is used sometimes for *imputed* or *laid unto;* as no folly may be *arretted* to one under age. Cowell.

ARRHABO. In the civil law. Earnest; money given to bind a bargain. Calvin.

ARRHÆ. In the civil law. Money or other valuable things given by the buyer to the seller, for the purpose of evidencing the contract; earnest.

ARRIAGE AND CARRIAGE. In English and Scotch law. Indefinite services formerly demandable from tenants, but prohibited by statute, (20 Geo. II. c. 50, §§ 21, 22.) Holthouse; Ersk. Inst. 2, 6, 42.

ARRIER BAN. A second summons to join the lord, addressed to those who had neglected the first. A summons of the inferiors or vassals of the lord. Spelman.

ARRIERE FIEF, or FEE. In feudal law. A fief or fee dependent on a superior one; an inferior fief granted by a vassal of the king, out of the fief held by him. Montesq. Esprit des Lois, liv. 31, cc. 26, 32.

ARRIERE VASSAL. In feudal law. The vassal of a vassal.

ARRIVAL. In marine insurance. The arrival of a vessel means an arrival for purposes of business, requiring an entry and clearance and stay at the port so long as to require some of the acts connected with business, and not merely touching at a port for advices, or to ascertain the state of the market, or being driven in by an adverse wind and sailing again as soon as it changes. 9 How. 372. See, also, 1 Ware, 281; 1 Mason, 482; 2 Sum. 422; 2 Cush. 453; 15 Fed. Rep. 265.

"A vessel arrives at a port of discharge when she comes, or is brought, to a place where it is intended to discharge her, and where is the usual and customary place of discharge. When a vessel is insured to one or two ports, and sails for one, the risk terminates on her arrival there. If a vessel is insured to a particular port of discharge, and is destined to discharge cargo successively at two different wharves, docks, or places, within that port, each being a distinct place for the delivery of cargo, the risk ends when she has been moored twenty-four hours in safety at the first place. But if she is destined to one or more places for the delivery of cargo, and delivery or discharge of a portion of her cargo is necessary, not by reason of her having reached any destined place of delivery, but as a necessary and usual nautical measure, to enable her to reach such usual and destined place of delivery, she cannot properly be considered as having arrived at the usual and customary place of discharge, when she is at anchor for the purpose only of using such means as will better enable her to reach it. If she cannot get to the destined and usual place of discharge in the port because she is too deep, and must be lightered to get there, and, to aid in prosecuting the voyage, cargo is thrown overboard or put into lighters, such discharge does not make that the place of arrival; it is only a stopping-place in the voyage. When the vessel is insured to a particular port of discharge, arrival within the limits of the harbor does not terminate the risk, if the place is not one where vessels are discharged and voyages completed. The policy covers the vessel through the port navigation, as well as on the open sea, until she reaches the destined place." 1 Holmes, 137.

ARRIVE. To reach or come to a particular place of destination by traveling towards it. 1 Brock. 411.

In insurance law. To reach that particular place or point in a harbor which is the ultimate destination of a vessel. 2 Cush. 439, 453.

The words "arrive" and "enter" are not always synonymous; there certainly may be an arrival without an actual entry or attempt to enter. 5 Mason, 120, 132. See, also, 1 Brock. 407, 411.

ARROGATION. In the civil law. The adoption of a person who was of full age or *sui juris*. 1 Browne, Civil & Adm. Law, 119; Dig. 1, 7, 5; Inst. 1, 11, 3.

ARRONDISSEMENT. In France, one of the subdivisions of a department.

ARSÆ ET PENSATÆ. Burnt and weighed. A term formerly applied to money tested or assayed by fire and by weighing.

ARSENALS. Store-houses for arms; dock-yards, magazines, and other military stores.

ARSER IN LE MAIN. Burning in the hand. The punishment by burning or branding the left thumb of lay offenders who claimed and were allowed the benefit of clergy, so as to distinguish them in case they made a second claim of clergy. 5 Coke, 51; 4 Bl. Comm. 367.

ARSON. Arson, at common law, is the act of unlawfully and maliciously burning the *house* of another man. 4 Steph. Comm. 99; 2 Russ. Crimes, 896; Steph. Crim. Dig. 298.

Arson, by the common law, is the willful and malicious burning of the house of another. The word "house," as here understood, includes not merely the dwelling-house, but all outhouses which are parcel thereof. 20 Conn. 246.

Arson is the malicious and willful burning of the house or outhouse of another. Code Ga. 1882, § 4375.

Arson is the willful and malicious burning of a building with intent to destroy it. Pen. Code Cal. § 447.

ARSURA. The trial of money by heating it after it was coined.

The loss of weight occasioned by this process. A pound was said to *burn* so many pence (*tot ardere denarios*) as it lost by the fire. Spelman. The term is now obsolete.

ART. A principle put in practice and applied to some art, machine, manufacture, or composition of matter. 4 Mason, 1. See Act Cong. July 8, 1870.

In the law of patents, this term means a useful art or manufacture which is beneficial, and which is described with exactness in its mode of operation. Such an art can be protected only in the mode and to the extent thus described. 1 Fish. Pat. Cas. 64. See, also, 15 How. 267; 7 Wall. 295.

ART, WORDS OF. Words used in a technical sense; words scientifically fit to carry the sense assigned them.

ART AND PART. In Scotch law. The offense committed by one who aids and assists the commission of a crime, but who is not the principal or chief actor in its actual commission. An accessary. A principal in the second degree. Paters. Comp.

ARTHEL, ARDHEL, or ARDDELIO. To avouch; as if a man were taken with stolen goods in his possession he was allowed a lawful *arthel, i. e.*, vouchee, to clear him of the felony; but provision was made against it by 28 Hen. VIII. c. 6. Blount.

ARTICLE. A separate and distinct part of an instrument or writing comprising two or more particulars; one of several things presented as connected or forming a whole.

In English ecclesiastical law. A complaint exhibited in the ecclesiastical court by way of libel. The different parts of a libel, responsive allegation, or counter allegation in the ecclesiastical courts. 3 Bl. Comm. 109.

In Scotch practice. A subject or matter; competent matter. "Article of dittay." 1 Broun, 62. A "point of dittay." 1 Swint. 128, 129.

ARTICLED CLERK. In English law. A clerk bound to serve in the office of a solicitor in consideration of being instructed in the profession.

ARTICLES. 1. A connected series of propositions; a system of rules. The subdivisions of a document, code, book, etc. A specification of distinct matters agreed upon or established by authority or requiring judicial action.

2. A statute; as having its provisions articulately expressed under distinct heads. Several of the ancient English statutes were called "articles," (*articuli.*)

3. A system of rules established by legal authority; as *articles* of war, *articles* of the navy, *articles* of faith, (*q. v.*)

4. A contractual document executed between parties, containing stipulations or terms of agreement; as *articles* of agreement, *articles* of partnership.

It is a common practice for persons to enter into articles of agreement, preparatory to the execution of a formal deed, whereby it is stipulated that one of the parties shall convey to the other certain lands, or release his right to them, or execute some other disposition of them.

5. In chancery practice. A formal written statement of objections filed by a party, after depositions have been taken, showing ground for discrediting the witnesses.

ARTICLES APPROBATORY. In Scotch law. That part of the proceedings which corresponds to the answer to the charge in an English bill in chancery. Paters. Comp.

ARTICLES IMPROBATORY. In Scotch law. Articulate averments setting forth the facts relied upon. Bell. That part of the proceedings which corresponds to the charge in an English bill in chancery to set aside a deed. Paters. Comp. The answer is called "articles approbatory."

ARTICLES, LORDS OF. A committee of the Scottish parliament, which, in the mode of its election, and by the nature of its powers, was calculated to increase the influence of the crown, and to confer upon it a power equivalent to that of a negative before debate. This system appeared inconsistent with the freedom of parliament, and at the revolution the convention of estates declared it a grievance, and accordingly it was suppressed by Act 1690, c. 3. Wharton.

ARTICLES OF AGREEMENT. A written memorandum of the terms of an agreement. See ARTICLES, 4.

ARTICLES OF ASSOCIATION. Articles subscribed by the members of a joint-stock company or corporation organized under a general law, and which create the corporate union between them. Such articles are in the nature of a partnership agreement, and commonly specify the form of organization, amount of capital, kind of business to be pursued, location of the company, etc. Articles of association are to be distinguished from a charter, in that the latter is a grant of power from the sovereign or the legislature.

ARTICLES OF CONFEDERATION. The name of the instrument embodying the compact made between the thirteen original states of the Union, before the adoption of the present constitution.

ARTICLES OF FAITH. In English law. The system of faith of the Church of England, more commonly known as the "Thirty-Nine Articles."

ARTICLES OF IMPEACHMENT. A formal written allegation of the causes for impeachment; answering the same office as an indictment in an ordinary criminal proceeding.

ARTICLES OF PARTNERSHIP. A written agreement by which the parties enter into a copartnership upon the terms and conditions therein stipulated.

ARTICLES OF RELIGION. In English ecclesiastical law. Commonly called the "Thirty-Nine Articles;" a body of divinity drawn up by the convocation in 1562, and confirmed by James I.

ARTICLES OF ROUP. In Scotch law. The terms and conditions under which property is sold at auction.

ARTICLES OF SET. In Scotch law. An agreement for a lease. Paters. Comp.

ARTICLES OF THE CLERGY. The title of a statute passed in the ninth year of Edward II. for the purpose of adjusting and settling the great questions of cognizance then existing between the ecclesiastical and temporal courts. 2 Reeve, Hist. Eng. Law, 291-296.

ARTICLES OF THE NAVY. A system of rules prescribed by act of parliament for the government of the English navy; also, in the United States, there are articles for the government of the navy.

ARTICLES OF THE PEACE. A complaint made or exhibited to a court by a person who makes oath that he is in fear of death or bodily harm from some one who has threatened or attempted to do him injury. The court may thereupon order the person complained of to find sureties for the peace, and, in default, may commit him to prison. 4 Bl. Comm. 255.

ARTICLES OF UNION. In English law. Articles agreed to, A. D. 1707, by the parliaments of England and Scotland, for the union of the two kingdoms. They were twenty-five in number. 1 Bl. Comm. 96.

ARTICLES OF WAR. Codes framed for the government of a nation's army are commonly thus called.

ARTICULATE ADJUDICATION. In Scotch law. Where the creditor holds several distinct debts, a separate adjudication for each claim is thus called.

ARTICULATELY. Article by article; by distinct clauses or articles; by separate propositions.

ARTICULI. Lat. Articles; items or heads. A term applied to some old English statutes, and occasionally to treatises.

ARTICULI CLERI. Articles of the clergy, (*q. v.*)

ARTICULI DE MONETA. Articles concerning money, or the currency. The title of a statute passed in the twentieth year of Edward I. 2 Reeve, Hist. Eng. Law, 228; Crabb, Eng. Law, (Amer. Ed.) 167.

ARTICULI MAGNÆ CHARTÆ. The preliminary articles, forty-nine in number, upon which the *Magna Charta* was founded.

ARTICULI SUPER CHARTAS. Articles upon the charters. The title of a statute passed in the twenty-eighth year of Edward I. st. 3, confirming or enlarging many particulars in *Magna Charta*, and the *Charta de Foresta*, and appointing a method for enforcing the observance of them, and for the punishment of offenders. 2 Reeve, Hist. Eng. Law, 103, 233.

ARTICULO MORTIS. (Or more commonly *in articulo mortis.*) In the article of death; at the point of death.

ARTIFICER. One who buys goods in order to reduce them, by his own art or industry, into other forms, and then to sell them. 3 T. B. Mon. 335.

One who is actually and personally engaged or employed to do work of a mechanical or physical character, not including one who takes contracts for labor to be performed by others. 7 El. & Bl. 135.

One who is master of his art, and whose employment consists chiefly in manual labor. Wharton; Cunningham.

ARTIFICIAL. Created by art, or by law; existing only by force of or in contemplation of law.

ARTIFICIAL PERSONS. Persons created and devised by human laws for the purposes of society and government, as distinguished from natural persons. Corporations are examples of artificial persons. 1 Bl. Comm. 123.

ARTIFICIAL PRESUMPTIONS. Also called "legal presumptions;" those which derive their force and effect from the law, rather than their natural tendency to produce belief. 3 Starkie, Ev. 1235.

ARTIFICIALLY. Technically; scientifically; using terms of art. A will or contract is described as "artificially" drawn if it is couched in apt and technical phrases and exhibits a scientific arrangement.

ARURA. An old English law term, signifying a day's work in plowing.

ARVIL-SUPPER. A feast or entertainment made at a funeral in the north of England; *arvil bread* is bread delivered to the poor at funeral solemnities, and *arvil*, *arval*, or *arfal*, the burial or funeral rites. Cowell.

AS. Lat. In the Roman and civil law. A pound weight; and a coin originally weighing a pound, (called also "*libra;*") divided into twelve parts, called "*unciæ.*"

Any integral sum, subject to division in certain proportions. Frequently applied in the civil law to inheritances; the whole inheritance being termed "as," and its several proportionate parts "*sextans,*" "*quadrans,*" etc. Burrill.

The term "as," and the multiples of its *unciæ,* were also used to denote the rates of interest. 2 Bl. Comm. 462, note *m.*

AS AGAINST; AS BETWEEN. These words contrast the relative position of two persons, with a tacit reference to a different relationship between one of them and a third person. For instance, the temporary bailee of a chattel is entitled to it *as between* himself and a stranger, or *as against* a stranger; reference being made by this form of words to the rights of the bailor. Wharton.

ASCEND. To go up; to pass up or upwards; to go or pass in the ascending line. 4 Kent, Comm. 393, 397.

ASCENDANTS. Persons with whom one is related in the ascending line; one's parents, grandparents, great-grandparents, etc.

ASCENDIENTES. In Spanish law. Ascendants; ascending heirs; heirs in the ascending line. Schm. Civil Law, 259.

ASCENT. Passage upwards; the transmission of an estate from the ancestor to the heir in the ascending line. See 4 Kent, Comm. 393, 397.

ASCERTAIN. To fix; to render certain or definite; to estimate and determine; to clear of doubt or obscurity.

ASCRIPTITIUS. In Roman law. A foreigner who had been registered and naturalized in the colony in which he resided. Cod. 11, 47.

ASPECT. View; object; possibility. Implies the existence of alternatives. Used in the phrases "bill with a double aspect" and "contingency with a double aspect."

ASPHYXIA. In medical jurisprudence. Swooning, suspended animation, produced by the non-conversion of the venous blood of the lungs into arterial.

ASPORTATION. The removal of things from one place to another. The carrying away of goods; one of the circumstances requisite to constitute the offense of larceny. 4 Bl. Comm. 231.

ASPORTAVIT. He carried away. Sometimes uses as a noun to denote a carrying away. An "*asportavit* of personal chattels." 2 H. Bl. 4.

ASSACH. In old Welsh law. An oath made by compurgators. Brown.

ASSART. In English law. The offense committed in the forest, by pulling up the trees by the roots that are thickets and coverts for deer, and making the ground plain as arable land. It differs from waste, in that waste is the cutting down of coverts which may grow again, whereas assart is the plucking them up by the roots and utterly destroying them, so that they can never afterward grow. This is not an offense if done with license to convert forest into tillage ground. Consult *Manwood's Forest Laws,* pt. I. p. 171. Wharton.

ASSASSINATION. Murder committed for hire, without provocation or cause of resentment given to the murderer by the person upon whom the crime is committed. Ersk. Inst. 4, 4, 45.

A murder committed treacherously, or by stealth or surprise, or by lying in wait.

ASSATH. An ancient custom in Wales, by which a person accused of crime could clear himself by the oaths of three hundred men. It was abolished by St. 1 Hen. V. c. 6. Cowell; Spelman.

ASSAULT. An unlawful attempt or offer, on the part of one man, with force or violence, to inflict a bodily hurt upon another.

An attempt or offer to beat another, without touching him; as if one lifts up his cane or his fist in a threatening manner at another; or strikes at him, but misses him. 3 Bl. Comm. 120; 3 Steph. Comm. 469.

Aggravated assault is one committed with the intention of committing some additional crime; or one attended with circumstances of peculiar outrage or atrocity. *Simple assault* is one committed with no intention to do any other injury.

An assault is an unlawful attempt, coupled with a present ability, to commit a violent injury on the person of another. Pen. Code Cal. § 240.

An assault is an attempt to commit a violent injury on the person of another. Code Ga. 1882, § 4357.

An assault is any willful and unlawful attempt or offer, with force or violence, to do a corporal hurt to another. Pen. Code Dak. § 305.

An assault is an offer or an attempt to do a corporal injury to another; as by striking at him with the hand, or with a stick, or by shaking the fist at him, or presenting a gun or other weapon within such distance as that a hurt might be given, or drawing a sword and brandishing it in a menacing manner; provided the act is done with intent to do some corporal hurt. 2 Wash. C. C. 435.

An assault is an attempt, with force or violence, to do a corporal injury to another, and may consist of any act tending to such corporal injury, accompanied with such circumstances as denote at the time an intention, coupled with the present ability, of using actual violence against the person. 1 Hill, 351.

An assault is an attempt or offer, with force or violence, to do a corporal hurt to another, whether from malice or wantonness, with such circumstances as denote, at the time, an intention to do it, coupled with a present ability to carry such intention into effect. 43 Ala. 354.

An assault is an intentional attempt, by violence, to do an injury to the person of another. It must be *intentional;* for, if it can be collected, notwithstanding appearances to the contrary, that there is not a *present* purpose to do an injury, there is no assault. 1 Ired. 127.

In order to constitute an assault there must be something more than a mere menace. There must be violence begun to be executed. But, where there is a clear intent to commit violence, accompanied by acts which if not interrupted will be followed by personal injury, the violence is commenced and the assault is complete. 27 Cal. 633.

ASSAY. The proof or trial, by chemical experiments, of the purity or fineness of metals,—particularly of the precious metals, gold and silver.

A trial of weights and measures by a standard; as by the constituted authorities, clerks of markets, etc. Reg. Orig. 280.

A trial or examination of certain commodities, as bread, cloths, etc. Cowell; Blount.

ASSAY OFFICE. The staff of persons by whom (or the building in which) the process of assaying gold and silver, required by government, incidental to maintaining the coinage, is conducted.

ASSAYER. One whose business it is to make assays of the precious metals.

ASSAYER OF THE KING. An officer of the royal mint, appointed by St. 2 Hen. VI. c. 12, who received and tested the bullion taken in for coining; also called "*assayator regis.*" Cowell; Termes de la Ley.

ASSECURARE. To assure, or make secure by pledges, or any solemn interposition of faith. Cowell; Spelman.

ASSECURATION. In European law. Assurance; insurance of a vessel, freight, or cargo. Ferriere.

ASSECURATOR. In maritime law. An insurer, (*aversor periculi.*) Locc. de Jure Mar. lib. 2, c. 5, § 10.

ASSEDATION. In Scotch law. An old term, used indiscriminately to signify a lease or feu-right. Bell; Ersk. Inst. 2, 6, 20.

ASSEMBLY. The concourse or meeting together of a considerable number of persons at the same place. Also the persons so gathered.

Popular assemblies are those where the people meet to deliberate upon their rights; these are guaranteed by the constitution. Const. U. S. Amend. art. 1.

The lower or more numerous branch of the legislature in many of the states is also called the "Assembly" or "House of Assembly," but the term seems to be an appropriate one to designate any political meeting required to be held by law.

ASSEMBLY GENERAL. The highest ecclesiastical court in Scotland, composed of a representation of the ministers and elders of the church, regulated by Act 5th Assem. 1694.

ASSEMBLY, UNLAWFUL. In criminal law. The assembling of three or more persons together to do an unlawful act, who separate without actually doing it, or making any motion towards it. 3 Inst. 176; 4 Bl. Comm. 146.

It differs from a riot or rout, because in each of the latter cases there is some act done besides the simple meeting. See 1 Ired. 30; 9 Car. & P. 91, 431; 5 Car. & P. 154; 1 Bish. Crim. Law, § 535; 2 Bish. Crim. Law, §§ 1256, 1259.

ASSENT. Compliance; approval of something done; a declaration of willingness to do something in compliance with a request.

ASSERTORY COVENANT. One which affirms that a particular state of facts exists; an affirming promise under seal.

ASSESS. 1. To ascertain, adjust, and settle the respective shares to be contributed by several persons toward an object beneficial to them all, in proportion to the benefit received.

2. To adjust or fix the proportion of a tax which each person, of several liable to it, has to pay; to apportion a tax among several; to distribute taxation in a proportion founded on the proportion of burden and benefit.

3. To place a valuation upon property for the purpose of apportioning a tax.

4. To impose a pecuniary payment upon persons or property; to tax.

ASSESSED. Where the charter of a corporation provides for the payment by it of a state tax, and contains a proviso that "no other tax or impost shall be levied or assessed upon the said company," the word "assessed" in the proviso cannot have the force and meaning of describing special levies for public improvements, but is used merely to describe the act of levying the tax or impost. 42 N. J. Law, 97.

ASSESSMENT. In a general sense, denotes the process of ascertaining and adjusting the shares respectively to be contributed by several persons towards a common beneficial object according to the benefit received.

In taxation. The listing and valuation of property for the purpose of apportioning a tax upon it, either according to value alone or in proportion to benefit received. Also determining the share of a tax to be paid by each of many persons; or apportioning the entire tax to be levied among the different taxable persons, establishing the proportion due from each.

Assessment, as used in juxtaposition with taxation in a state constitution, includes all the steps necessary to be taken in the legitimate exercise of the power to tax. 4 Neb. 336.

Assessment is also popularly used as a synonym for taxation in general,—the authoritative imposition of a rate or duty to be paid. But in its technical signification it denotes only taxation for a special purpose or local improvement; local taxation, as distinguished from general taxation; taxation on the principle of apportionment according to the relation between burden and benefit.

As distinguished from other kinds of taxation, assessments are those special and local impositions upon property in the immediate vicinity of municipal improvements which are necessary to pay for the improvement, and are laid with reference to the special benefit which the property is supposed to have derived therefrom. 29 Wis. 599.

Assessment and tax are not synonymous. An assessment is doubtless a tax, but the term implies something more; it implies a tax of a particular kind, predicated upon the principle of equivalents, or benefits, which are peculiar to the persons or property charged therewith, and which are said to be assessed or appraised, according to the measure or proportion of such equivalents; whereas a simple tax is imposed for the purpose of supporting the government generally, without reference to any special advantage which may be supposed to accrue to the persons taxed. Taxes must be levied, without discrimination, equally upon all the subjects of property; whilst assessments are only levied upon lands, or some other specific property, the subjects of the supposed benefits; to repay which the assessment is levied. 1 Handy, 464.

In corporations. Instalments of the money subscribed for shares of stock, called for from the subscribers by the directors, from time to time as the company requires money, are called "assessments," or, in England, "calls."

The periodical demands made by a mutual insurance company, under its charter and by-laws, upon the makers of premium notes, are also denominated "assessments."

Of damages. Fixing the amount of damages to which the successful party in a suit is entitled after an interlocutory judgment has been taken.

Assessment of damages is also the name given to the determination of the sum which a corporation proposing to take lands for a public use must pay in satisfaction of the demand proved or the value taken.

In insurance. An apportionment made in general average upon the various articles and interests at risk, according to their value at the time and place of being in safety, for contribution for damage and sacrifices purposely made, and expenses incurred for escape from impending common peril. 2 Phil. Ins. c. xv.

ASSESSOR. An officer chosen or appointed to appraise, value, or assess property.

In civil and Scotch law. Persons skilled in law, selected to advise the judges of the inferior courts. Bell; Dig. 1, 22; Cod. 1, 51.

A person learned in some particular science or industry, who sits with the judge on the trial of a cause requiring such special knowledge and gives his advice.

In England it is the practice in admiralty business to call in assessors, in cases involving questions of navigation or seamanship. They are called "nautical assessors," and are always Brethren of the Trinity House.

ASSETS. In probate law. Property of a decedent available for the payment of debts and legacies; the estate coming to the heir or personal representative which is chargeable, in law or equity, with the obligations which such heir or representative is required, in his representative capacity, to discharge.

In an accurate and legal sense, all the personal property of the deceased which is of a salable nature, and may be converted into ready money, is deemed *assets.* But the word is not confined to such property; for all other property of the deceased which is chargeable with his debts or legacies, and is applicable to that purpose, is, in a large sense, *assets.* 1 Story, Eq. Jur. § 531.

Assets per descent. That portion of the ancestor's estate which descends to the heir, and which is sufficient to charge him, as far as it goes, with the specialty debts of his ancestors. 2 Williams, Ex'rs, 1011.

Equitable assets. The term includes equities of any sort and rights and claims which are available only by the aid of a court of equity, and which are to be divided, *pari passu*, among all the creditors.

Legal assets. Such as constitute the fund, for the payment of debts, that can be reached in an action at law.

Personal assets. Goods and personal chattels to which the executor or administrator is entitled.

Real assets. Such as descend to the heir, as an estate in fee-simple.

In commercial law. The aggregate of available property, stock in trade, cash, etc., belonging to a merchant or mercantile company.

The word "assets," though more generally used to denote everything which comes to the representatives of a deceased person, yet is by no means confined to that use, but has come to signify everything which can be made available for the payment of debts, whether belonging to the estate of a deceased person or not. Hence we speak of the assets of a bank or other monied corporation, the assets of an insolvent debtor, and the assets of an individual or private copartnership; and we always use this word when we speak of the means which a party has, as compared with his liabilities or debts. 26 Conn. 449.

The property or effects of a bankrupt or insolvent, applicable to the payment of his debts.

The term "assets" includes all property of every kind and nature, chargeable with the debts of the bankrupt, that comes into the hands of and under the control of the assignee; and the value thereof is not to be considered a less sum than that actually realized out of said property, and received by the assignee for it. 16 N. B. R. 351.

ASSETS ENTRE MAINS. L. Fr. Assets in hand; assets in the hands of executors or administrators, applicable for the payment of debts. Termes de la Ley; 2 Bl. Comm. 510; 1 Crabb, Real Prop. 23.

ASSEVERATION. An affirmation; a positive assertion; a solemn declaration. This word is seldom, if ever, used for a declaration made under oath, but denotes a declaration accompanied with solemnity or an appeal to conscience.

ASSEWIARE. To draw or drain water from marsh grounds. Cowell.

ASSIGN, *v*. In conveyancing. To make or set over to another; to transfer; as to assign property, or some interest therein. Cowell; 2 Bl. Comm. 326.

In practice. To appoint, allot, select, or designate for a particular purpose, or duty. Thus, in England, justices are said to be "*assigned* to take the assises," "*assigned* to hold pleas," "*assigned* to make gaol delivery," "*assigned* to keep the peace," etc. St. Westm. 2, c. 30; Reg. Orig. 68, 69; 3 Bl. Comm. 58, 59, 353; 1 Bl. Comm. 351.

To transfer persons, as a sheriff is said to assign prisoners in his custody.

To point at, or point out; to set forth, or specify; to mark out or designate; as to *assign errors* on a writ of error; to *assign breaches* of a covenant. 2 Tidd, Pr. 1168; 1 Tidd, 686.

ASSIGNABLE. That may be assigned or transferred; transferable; negotiable, as a bill of exchange. Comb. 176; Story, Bills, § 17.

ASSIGNATION. A Scotch law term equivalent to assignment, (*q. v.*)

Assignatus utitur jure auctoris. An assignee uses the right of his principal; an assignee is clothed with the rights of his principal. Halk. Max. p. 14; Broom, Max. 465.

ASSIGNAY. In Scotch law. An assignee.

ASSIGNEE. A person to whom an assignment is made. The term is commonly used in reference to personal property; but it is not incorrect, in some cases, to apply it to realty, *e. g.*, "assignee of the reversion."

Assignee in fact is one to whom an assignment has been made in fact by the party having the right.

Assignee in law is one in whom the law vests the right; as an executor or administrator.

The word has a special and distinctive use as employed to designate one to whom, under an insolvent or bankrupt law, the whole estate of a debtor is transferred to be administered for the benefit of creditors.

In old law. A person deputed or appointed by another to do any act, or perform any business. Blount. An *assignee*, however, was distinguished from a *deputy*, being said to occupy a thing in his own right, while a deputy acted in right of another. Cowell.

ASSIGNMENT. In contracts. 1. The act by which one person transfers to another, or causes to vest in that other, the whole of the right, interest, or property which he has in any realty or personalty, in possession or in action, or any share, interest, or subsidiary estate therein. More particularly, a *written* transfer of property, as distinguished from a transfer by mere delivery.

2. In a narrower sense, the transfer or making over of the estate, right, or title which one has in lands and tenements; and, in an especially technical sense, the transfer of the unexpired residue of a term or estate for life or years.

Assignment does not include testamentary transfers. The idea of an assignment is essentially that of a transfer by one existing party to another existing party of some species of property or valuable interest, except in the case of an executor. 34 N. Y. 447.

3. A transfer or making over by a debtor of all his property and effects to one or more *assignees* in trust for the benefit of his creditors. 2 Story, Eq. Jur. § 1036.

4. The instrument or writing by which such a transfer of property is made.

5. A transfer of a bill, note, or check, not negotiable.

6. In bankruptcy proceedings, the word designates the setting over or transfer of the bankrupt's estate to the assignee.

ASSIGNMENT FOR BENEFIT OF CREDITORS. An assignment whereby a debtor, generally an insolvent, transfers to another his property, in trust to pay his debts or apply the property upon their payment.

ASSIGNMENT OF DOWER. Ascertaining a widow's right of dower by laying out or marking off one-third of her deceased husband's lands, and setting off the same for her use during life.

ASSIGNMENT OF ERRORS. In practice. The statement of the plaintiff's case on a writ of error, setting forth the errors complained of; corresponding with the declaration in an ordinary action. 2 Tidd, Pr. 1168; 3 Steph. Comm. 644.

There is not, in the strict common-law sense of the term, any assignment of errors required to be filed by the appellant. What is meant by the term, as heretofore used by this court, is that a specification must be filed of the errors upon which the appellant will rely, with such fullness as to give aid to the court in the examination of the transcript. 10 Cal. 298.

ASSIGNMENT WITH PREFERENCES. An assignment for the benefit of creditors, with directions to the assignee to prefer a specified creditor or class of creditors, by paying their claims in full before the others receive any dividend, or in some other manner. More usually termed a "preferential assignment."

ASSIGNOR. One who makes an assignment of any kind; one who assigns or transfers property.

ASSIGNS. Assignees; those to whom property shall have been transferred. Now seldom used except in the phrase, in deeds, "heirs, administrators, and assigns." 8 R. I. 36.

ASSISA. In old English and Scotch law. An assise; a kind of jury or inquest; a writ; a sitting of a court; an ordinance or statute; a fixed or specific time, number, quantity, quality, price, or weight; a tribute, fine, or tax; a real action; the name of a writ. See ASSISE.

ASSISA ARMORUM. Assise of arms. A statute or ordinance requiring the keeping of arms for the common defense. Hale, Com. Law, c. 11.

ASSISA CADERE. To fail in the assise; *i. e.*, to be nonsuited. Cowell; 3 Bl. Comm. 402.

ASSISA CADIT IN JURATUM. The assise falls (turns) into a jury; hence to submit a controversy to trial by jury.

ASSISA CONTINUANDA. An ancient writ addressed to the justices of assise for the continuation of a cause, when certain facts put in issue could not have been proved in time by the party alleging them. Reg. Orig. 217.

ASSISA DE CLARENDON. The assise of Clarendon. A statute or ordinance passed in the tenth year of Henry II., by which those that were accused of any heinous crime, and not able to purge themselves, but must abjure the realm, had liberty of forty days to stay and try what succor they could get of their friends towards their sustenance in exile. Bract. fol. 136; Co. Litt. 159*a;* Cowell.

ASSISA DE FORESTA. Assise of the forest; a statute concerning orders to be observed in the royal forests.

ASSISA DE MENSURIS. Assise of measures. A common rule for weights and measures, established throughout England by Richard I., in the eighth year of his reign. Hale, Com. Law, c. 7.

ASSISA DE NOCUMENTO. An assise of nuisance; a writ to abate or redress a nuisance.

ASSISA DE UTRUM. An obsolete writ, which lay for the parson of a church whose predecessor had alienated the land and rents of it.

ASSISA FRISCÆ FORTIÆ. Assise of fresh force, which see.

ASSISA MORTIS D'ANCESTORIS. Assise of *mort d'ancestor*, which see.

ASSISA NOVÆ DISSEYSINÆ. Assise of novel disseisin, which see.

ASSISA PANIS ET CEREVISIÆ. Assise of bread and ale, or beer. The name of a statute passed in the fifty-first year of Henry III., containing regulations for the sale of bread and ale; sometimes called the "statute of bread and ale." Co. Litt. 159*b*; 2 Reeve, Hist. Eng. Law, 56; Cowell; Bract. fol. 155.

ASSISA PROROGANDA. An obsolete writ, which was directed to the judges assigned to take assises, to stay proceedings, by reason of a party to them being employed in the king's business. Reg. Orig. 208.

ASSISA ULTIMÆ PRÆSENTATIONIS. Assise of darrein presentment, (*q. v.*)

ASSISA VENALIUM. The assise of salable commodities, or of things exposed for sale.

ASSISE, or ASSIZE. 1. An ancient species of court, consisting of a certain number of men, usually twelve, who were summoned together to try a disputed cause, performing the functions of a jury, except that they gave a verdict from their own investigation and knowledge and not upon evidence adduced. From the fact that they sat together, (*assideo*,) they were called the "assise." See Bract. 4, 1, 6; Co. Litt. 153*b*, 159*b*.

A court composed of an assembly of knights and other substantial men, with the baron or justice, in a certain place, at an appointed time. Grand Cou. cc. 24, 25.

2. The verdict or judgment of the jurors or recognitors of assise. 3 Bl. Comm. 57, 59.

3. In modern English law, the name "assises" or "assizes" is given to the court, time, or place where the judges of assise and *nisi prius*, who are sent by special commission from the crown on circuits through the kingdom, proceed to take indictments, and to try such disputed causes issuing out of the courts at Westminster as are then ready for trial, with the assistance of a jury from the particular county; the regular sessions of the judges at *nisi prius*.

4. Anything reduced to a certainty in respect to time, number, quantity, quality, weight, measure, etc. Spelman.

5. An ordinance, statute, or regulation. Spelman gives this meaning of the word the first place among his definitions, observing that *statutes* were in England called "assises" down to the reign of Henry III.

6. A species of writ, or real action, said to have been invented by Glanville, chief justice to Henry II., and having for its object to determine the right of possession of lands, and to recover the possession. 3 Bl. Comm. 184, 185.

7. The whole proceedings in court upon a writ of assise. Co. Litt. 159*b*. The verdict or finding of the jury upon such a writ. 3 Bl. Comm. 57.

ASSISE OF CLARENDON. See ASSISA DE CLARENDON.

ASSISE OF DARREIN PRESENTMENT. A writ of assise which formerly lay when a man or his ancestors under whom he claimed presented a clerk to a benefice, who was instituted, and afterwards, upon the next avoidance, a stranger presented a clerk and thereby disturbed the real patron. 3 Bl. Comm. 245; St. 13 Edw. I. (Westm. 2) c. 5. It has given way to the remedy by *quare impedit*.

ASSISE OF FRESH FORCE. In old English practice. A writ which lay by the usage and custom of a city or borough, where a man was disseised of his lands and tenements in such city or borough. It was called "fresh force," because it was to be sued within forty days after the party's title accrued to him. Fitzh. Nat. Brev. 7 C.

ASSISE OF MORT D'ANCESTOR. A real action which lay to recover land of which a person had been deprived on the death of his ancestor by the abatement or intrusion of a stranger. 3 Bl. Comm. 185; Co. Litt. 159*a*. It was abolished by St. 3 & 4 Wm. IV. c. 27.

ASSISE OF NOVEL DISSEISIN. A writ of assise which lay for the recovery of lands or tenements, where the claimant had been lately disseised.

ASSISE OF NUISANCE. A writ of assise which lay where a nuisance had been committed to the complainant's freehold; either for abatement of the nuisance or for damages.

ASSISE OF THE FOREST. A statute touching orders to be observed in the king's forests. Manwood, 35.

ASSISE RENTS. The certain established rents of the freeholders and ancient copyholders of a manor; so called because they are *assised*, or made precise and certain.

ASSISER. An assessor; juror; an officer who has the care and oversight of weights and measures.

ASSISORS. In Scotch law. Jurors; the persons who formed that kind of court which in Scotland was called an "assise," for the purpose of inquiring into and judging divers civil causes, such as perambulations, cognitions, molestations, purprestures, and other matters; like jurors in England. Holthouse.

ASSISTANCE. The name of a writ which issues from the court of chancery, in aid of the execution of a judgment at law, to put the complainant into possession of lands adjudged to him, when the sheriff cannot execute the judgment.

ASSISTANT JUDGE. A judge of the English court of general or quarter sessions in Middlesex. He differs from the other justices in being a barrister of ten years' standing, and in being salaried. St. 7 & 8 Vict. c. 71; 22 & 23 Vict. c. 4; Pritch. Quar. Sess. 31.

ASSISUS. Rented or farmed out for a specified assise; that is, a payment of a certain assessed rent in money or provisions.

ASSITHMENT. Weregeld or compensation by a pecuniary mulct. Cowell.

ASSIZE. In the practice of the criminal courts of Scotland, the fifteen men who decide on the conviction or acquittal of an accused person are called the "assize," though in popular language, and even in statutes, they are called the "jury." Wharton. See ASSISE.

ASSIZES. Sessions of the justices or commissioners of assize. See ASSISE.

ASSIZES DE JERUSALEM. A code of feudal jurisprudence prepared by an assembly of barons and lords A. D. 1099, after the conquest of Jerusalem.

ASSOCIATE. An officer in each of the English courts of common law, appointed by the chief judge of the court, and holding his office during good behavior, whose duties were to superintend the entry of causes, to attend the sittings of *nisi prius*, and there receive and enter verdicts, and to draw up the posteas and any orders of *nisi prius*. The associates are now officers of the Supreme Court of Judicature, and are styled "Masters of the Supreme Court." Wharton.

A person associated with the judges and clerk of assise in the commission of general jail delivery. Mozley & Whitley.

The term is frequently used of the judges of appellate courts, other than the presiding judge or chief justice.

ASSOCIATION. The act of a number of persons who unite or join together for some special purpose or business. The union of a company of persons for the transaction of designated affairs, or the attainment of some common object.

An unincorporated society; a body of persons united and acting together without a charter, but upon the methods and forms used by incorporated bodies for the prosecution of some common enterprise.

In English law. A writ directing certain persons (usually the clerk and his subordinate officers) to associate themselves with the justices and sergeants for the purposes of taking the assises. 3 Bl. Comm. 59, 60.

ASSOCIÉ EN NOM. In French law. In a *société en commandité* an *associé en nom* is one who is liable for the engagements of the undertaking to the whole extent of his property. This expression arises from the fact that the names of the *associés* so liable figure in the firm-name or form part of the *société en nom collectif*. Arg. Fr. Merc. Law, 546.

ASSOIL. To absolve; acquit; to set free; to deliver from excommunication. St. 1 Hen. IV. c. 7; Cowell.

ASSOILZIE. In Scotch law. To acquit the defendant in an action; to find a criminal not guilty.

ASSUME. To undertake; engage; promise. 1 Ld. Raym. 122; 4 Coke, 92.

A stipulation in a deed, accepted by the grantee, that he shall "assume" an outstanding mortgage on the premises conveyed, is broken by a failure to pay the mortgage debt within a reasonable time after its maturity. 12 Cush. 227.

ASSUMPSIT. Lat. He undertook; he promised. A promise or engagement by which one person assumes or undertakes to do some act or pay something to another. It may be either oral or in writing, but is not under seal. It is *express* if the promisor puts his engagement in distinct and definite language; it is *implied* where the law infers a promise (though no formal one has passed) from the conduct of the party or the circumstances of the case.

In practice. A form of action which lies for the recovery of damages for the non-performance of a parol or simple contract; or a contract that is neither of record nor under seal. 7 Term, 351; 3 Johns. Cas. 60.

The ordinary division of this action is into (1) common or *indebitatus assumpsit*, brought for the most part on an implied promise; and (2) special *assumpsit*, founded on an express promise. Steph. Pl. 11, 13.

The action of *assumpsit* differs from *trespass* and *trover*, which are founded on a tort, not upon a contract; from *covenant* and *debt*, which are appropriate where the ground of recovery is a sealed instrument, or special obligation to pay a fixed sum; and from *replevin*, which seeks the recovery of specific property, if attainable, rather than of damages.

ASSURANCE. In conveyancing. A deed or instrument of conveyance. The legal evidences of the transfer of property are in England called the "common assurances" of the kingdom, whereby every man's estate is *assured* to him, and all controversies, doubts, and difficulties are either prevented or removed. 2 Bl. Comm. 294.

In contracts. A making secure; insurance. The term was formerly of very frequent use in the modern sense of insurance, particularly in English maritime law, and still appears in the policies of some companies, but is otherwise seldom seen of late years. There seems to be a tendency, however, to use *assurance* for the contracts of life insurance companies, and *insurance* for risks upon property.

ASSURED. A person who has been insured by some insurance company, or underwriter, against losses or perils mentioned in the policy of insurance.

ASSURER. An insurer against certain perils and dangers; an underwriter; an indemnifier.

ASSYTHEMENT. In Scotch law. Damages awarded to the relative of a murdered person from the guilty party, who has not been convicted and punished. Paters. Comp.

ASTIPULATION. A mutual agreement, assent, and consent between parties; also a witness or record.

ASTITRARIUS HÆRES. An heir apparent who has been placed, by conveyance, in possession of his ancestor's estate during such ancestor's life-time. Co. Litt. 8.

ASTITUTION. An arraignment, (*q. v.*)

ASTRARIUS. In old English law. A householder; belonging to the house; a person in actual possession of a house.

ASTRER. In old English law. A householder, or occupant of a house or hearth.

ASTRICT. In Scotch law. To assign to a particular mill.

ASTRICTION TO A MILL. A servitude by which grain growing on certain lands or brought within them must be carried to a certain mill to be ground, a certain multure or price being paid for the same. Jacob.

ASTRIHILTET. In Saxon law. A penalty for a wrong done by one in the king's peace. The offender was to replace the damage twofold. Spelman.

ASTRUM. A house, or place of habitation. Bract. fol. 267*b*; Cowell.

ASYLUM. 1. A sanctuary, or place of refuge and protection, where criminals and debtors found shelter, and from which they could not be taken without sacrilege. 6 Neb. 291.

2. Shelter; refuge; protection from the hand of justice. The word includes not only place, but also shelter, security, protection; and a fugitive from justice, who has committed a crime in a foreign country, "seeks an asylum" at all times when he claims the use of the territories of the United States. 12 Blatchf. 395.

3. An institution for the protection and relief of unfortunates, as asylums for the poor, for the deaf and dumb, or for the insane.

AT ARM'S LENGTH. Beyond the reach of personal influence or control. Parties are said to deal "at arm's length" when each stands upon the strict letter of his rights, and conducts the business in a formal manner, without trusting to the other's fairness or integrity, and without being subject to the other's control or overmastering influence.

AT BAR. Before the court. "The case at bar," etc. Dyer, 31.

AT LARGE. (1) Not limited to any particular place, district, person, matter, or question. (2) Free; unrestrained; not under corporal control; as a ferocious animal so free from restraint as to be liable to do mischief. (3) Fully; in detail; in an extended form.

AT LAW. According to law; by, for, or in law; particularly in distinction from that which is done in or according to equity; or in titles such as sergeant at law, barrister at law, attorney or counsellor at law.

AT SEA. Out of the limits of any port or harbor on the sea-coast. 1 Story, 251.

ATAMITA. In the civil law. A great-great-great-grandfather's sister.

ATAVIA. In the civil law. A great-grandmother's grandmother.

ATAVUNCULUS. The brother of a great-grandfather's grandmother.

ATAVUS. The great-grandfather's or great-grandmother's grandfather; a fourth grandfather. The ascending line of lineal ancestry runs thus: *Pater, Avus, Proavus, Abavus, Atavus, Tritavus.* The seventh generation in the ascending scale will be *Tritavipater*, and the next above it *Proavi-atavus.*

ATHA. In Saxon law. An oath; the power or privilege of exacting and administering an oath. Spelman.

ATHEIST. One who does not believe in the existence of a God.

ATIA. Hatred or ill-will. See DE ODIO ET ATIA.

ATILIUM. The tackle or rigging of a ship; the harness or tackle of a plow. Spelman.

ATMATERTERA. A great-grandfather's grandmother's sister, (*ataviæ soror;*) called by Bracton "*atmatertera magna.*" Bract. fol. 68*b*.

ATPATRUUS. The brother of a great-grandfather's grandfather.

ATTACH. To take or apprehend by commandment of a writ or precept.

It differs from *arrest*, because it takes not only the body, but sometimes the goods, whereas an arrest is only against the person; besides, he who attaches keeps the party attached in order to produce him in court on the day named, but he who arrests lodges the person arrested in the custody of a higher power, to be forthwith disposed of. Fleta, lib. 5, c. 24. See ATTACHMENT.

ATTACHÉ. A person attached to the suite of an ambassador or to a foreign legation.

ATTACHIAMENTA BONORUM. A distress formerly taken upon goods and chattels, by the legal *attachiators* or bailiffs, as security to answer an action for personal estate or debt.

ATTACHIAMENTA DE SPINIS ET BOSCIS. A privilege granted to the officers of a forest to take to their own use thorns, brush, and windfalls, within their precincts. Kenn. Par. Antiq. 209.

ATTACHMENT. The act or process of taking, apprehending, or seizing persons or property, by virtue of a writ, summons, or other judicial order, and bringing the same into the custody of the law; used either for the purpose of bringing a person before the court, of acquiring jurisdiction over the property seized, to compel an appearance, to furnish security for debt or costs, or to arrest a fund in the hands of a third person who may become liable to pay it over.

Also the writ or other process for the accomplishment of the purposes above enumerated, this being the more common use of the word.

Of persons. A writ issued by a court of record, commanding the sheriff to bring before it a person who has been guilty of contempt of court, either in neglect or abuse of its process or of subordinate powers. 3 Bl. Comm. 280; 4 Bl. Comm. 283.

Of property. A species of mesne process, by which a writ is issued at the institution or during the progress of an action, commanding the sheriff to seize the property, rights, credits, or effects of the defendant to be held as security for the satisfaction of such judgment as the plaintiff may recover. It is principally used against absconding, concealed, or fraudulent debtors.

To give jurisdiction. Where the defendant is a non-resident, or beyond the territorial jurisdiction of the court, his goods or land within the territory may be seized upon process of attachment; whereby he will be compelled to enter an appearance, or the court acquires jurisdiction so far as to dispose of the property attached. This is sometimes called "foreign attachment."

Domestic and foreign. In some jurisdictions it is common to give the name "domestic attachment" to one issuing against a resident debtor, (upon the special ground of fraud, intention to abscond, etc.,) and to designate an attachment against a non-resident, or his property, as "foreign." But the term "foreign attachment" more properly belongs to the process otherwise familiarly known as "garnishment." It was a peculiar and ancient remedy open to creditors within the jurisdiction of the city of London, by which they were enabled to satisfy their own debts by attaching or seizing the money or goods of the debtor in the hands of a third person within the jurisdiction of the city. This power and process survive in modern law, in all common-law jurisdictions, and are variously denominated "garnishment," "trustee process," or "factorizing."

ATTACHMENT OF PRIVILEGE. In English law. A process by which a man, by virtue of his privilege, calls another to litigate in that court to which he himself belongs, and who has the privilege to answer there.

A writ issued to apprehend a person in a privileged place. Termes de la Ley.

ATTACHMENT OF THE FOREST. One of the three courts formerly held in forests. The highest court was called "justice in eyre's seat;" the middle, the "swainmote;" and the lowest, the "attachment." Manwood, 90, 99.

ATTAINDER. That extinction of civil rights and capacities which takes place whenever a person who has committed treason or felony receives sentence of death for his crime. 1 Steph. Comm. 408; 1 Bish. Crim. Law, § 641.

It differs from conviction, in that it is *after* judgment, whereas conviction is upon the verdict of guilty, but *before* judgment pronounced, and may be quashed upon some point of law reserved, or judgment may be arrested. The consequences of attainder are forfeiture of property and corruption of blood. 4 Bl. Comm. 380.

At the common law, attainder resulted in three ways, viz.: *by confession, by verdict,* and *by process* or *outlawry.* The first case was where the prisoner pleaded guilty at the bar, or having fled to sanctuary, confessed his guilt and abjured the realm to save his life. The second was where the prisoner pleaded not guilty at the bar, and the jury brought in a verdict against him. The third, when the person accused made his escape and was outlawed.

ATTAINDER, BILL OF. See BILL OF ATTAINDER.

ATTAINT. In old English practice. A writ which lay to inquire whether a jury of twelve men had given a false verdict, in order that the judgment might be reversed. 3 Bl. Comm. 402; Bract. fol. 288*b*–292. This inquiry was made by a grand assise or jury of twenty-four persons, and, if they found the verdict a false one, the judgment was that the jurors should become infamous, should forfeit their goods and the profits of their lands, should themselves be imprisoned, and their wives and children thrust out of doors, should have their houses razed, their trees extirpated, and their meadows plowed up, and that the plaintiff should be restored to all that he lost by reason of the unjust verdict. 3 Bl. Comm. 404; Co. Litt. 294*b*.

A person was said to be attaint when he was under attainder, (*q. v.*) Co. Litt. 390*b*.

ATTAINT D'UNE CAUSE. In French law. The gain of a suit.

ATTEMPT. In criminal law. An effort or endeavor to accomplish a crime, amounting to more than mere preparation or planning for it, and which, if not prevented, would have resulted in the full consummation of the act attempted, but which, in fact, does not bring to pass the party's ultimate design.

An intent to do a particular criminal thing combined with an act which falls short of the thing intended. 1 Bish. Crim. Law, § 728.

There is a marked distinction between "attempt" and "intent." The former conveys the idea of physical effort to accomplish an act; the latter, the quality of mind with which an act was done. To charge, in an indictment, an assault with an attempt to murder, is not equivalent to charging an assault with intent to murder. 14 Ala. 411.

ATTENDANT. One who owes a duty or service to another, or in some sort depends upon him. Termes de la Ley. One who follows and waits upon another.

ATTENDANT TERMS. In English law. Terms, (usually mortgages,) for a long period of years, which are created or kept outstanding for the purpose of *attending* or waiting upon and protecting the inheritance. 1 Steph. Comm. 351.

A phrase used in conveyancing to denote estates which are kept alive, after the objects for which they were originally created have ceased, so that they might be deemed merged or satisfied, for the purpose of protecting or strengthening the title of the owner. Abbott.

ATTENTAT. Lat. He attempts. In the civil and canon law. Anything wrongfully innovated or *attempted* in a suit by an inferior judge, (or judge *a quo,*) pending an appeal. 1 Addams, 22, note; Shelf. Mar. & Div. 562.

ATTERMINARE. In old English law. To put off to a succeeding term; to prolong the time of payment of a debt. St. Westm. 2, c. 4; Cowell; Blount.

ATTERMINING. In old English law. A putting off; the granting of a time or term, as for the payment of a debt. Cowell.

ATTERMOIEMENT. In canon law. A making terms; a composition, as with creditors. 7 Low. Can. 272, 306.

ATTEST. To witness the execution of a written instrument, at the request of him who makes it, and subscribe the same as a witness. This is also the technical word by which, in the practice in many of the states, a certifying officer gives assurance of the genuineness and correctness of a copy.

An "attested" copy of a document is one which has been examined and compared with the original, with a certificate or memorandum of its correctness, signed by the persons who have examined it.

ATTESTATION. The act of witnessing an instrument in writing, at the request of the party making the same, and subscribing it as a witness. 3 P. Wms. 254; 2 Ves. Sr. 454; 17 Pick. 373.

Execution and *attestation* are clearly distinct formalities; the former being the act of the *party*, the latter of the *witnesses* only.

ATTESTATION CLAUSE. That clause wherein the witnesses certify that the instrument has been executed before them, and the manner of the execution of the same.

ATTESTING WITNESS. One who signs his name to an instrument, at the request of the party or parties, for the purpose of proving and identifying it.

ATTESTOR OF A CAUTIONER. In Scotch practice. A person who attests the sufficiency of a cautioner, and agrees to become *subsidiarie* liable for the debt. Bell.

ATTILE. In old English law. Rigging; tackle. Cowell.

ATTORN. In feudal law. To transfer or turn over to another. Where a lord aliened his seigniory, he might, with the consent of the tenant, and in some cases without, *attorn* or transfer the homage and service of the latter to the alienee or new lord. Bract. fols. 81*b*, 82.

In modern law. To consent to the transfer of a rent or reversion. A tenant is said to *attorn* when he agrees to become the tenant of the person to whom the reversion has been granted. See ATTORNMENT.

ATTORNARE. In feudal law. To attorn; to transfer or turn over; to appoint an attorney or substitute.

ATTORNARE REM. To turn over money or goods, *i. e.*, to assign or appropriate them to some particular use or service.

ATTORNATO FACIENDO VEL RECIPIENDO. In old English law. An obsolete writ, which commanded a sheriff or steward of a county court or hundred court to receive and admit an attorney to appear for the person who owed suit of court. Fitzh. Nat. Brev. 156.

ATTORNE. L. Fr. In old English law. An attorney. Britt. c. 126.

ATTORNEY. In the most general sense this term denotes an agent or substitute, or one who is appointed and authorized to act in the place or stead of another.

It is "an ancient English word, and signifieth one that is set in the turne, stead, or place of another; and of these some be private * * * and some be publike, as attorneys at law." Co. Litt. 51*b*, 128*a*; Britt. 285*b*.

One who is appointed by another to do something in his absence, and who has authority to act in the place and turn of him by whom he is delegated.

Attorneys, in the modern use, are of two sorts, attorneys at law and attorneys in fact, as to which see those titles.

ATTORNEY AT LARGE. In old practice. An attorney who practised in all the courts. Cowell.

ATTORNEY AT LAW. An advocate, counsel, official agent employed in preparing, managing, and trying cases in the courts. An officer in a court of justice, who is employed by a party in a cause to manage the same for him.

In English law. An attorney at law was a public officer belonging to the superior courts of common law at Westminster, who conducted legal proceedings on behalf of others, called his clients, by whom he was retained; he answered to the solicitor in the courts of chancery, and the proctor of the admiralty, ecclesiastical, probate, and divorce courts. An attorney was almost invariably also a solicitor. It is now provided by the judicature act, 1873, § 87, that solicitors, attorneys, or proctors of, or by law empowered to practise in, any court the jurisdiction of which is by that act transferred to the high court of justice or the court of appeal, shall be called "solicitors of the supreme court." Wharton.

The term is in use in America, and in most of the states includes "barrister," "counsellor," and "solicitor," in the sense in which those terms are used in England. In some states, as well as in the United States supreme court, "attorney" and "counsellor" are distinguishable, the former term being applied to the younger members of the bar, and to those who carry on the practice and formal parts of the suit, while "counsellor" is the adviser, or special counsel retained to try the cause. In some jurisdictions one must have been an attorney for a given time before he can be admitted to practise as a counsellor. Rap. & L.

ATTORNEY GENERAL. In English law. The chief law officer of the realm, being created by letters patent, whose office is to exhibit informations and prosecute for the crown in matters criminal, and to file bills in the exchequer in any matter concerning the king's revenue.

In American law. The attorney general of the United States is the head of the department of justice, appointed by the president, and a member of the cabinet. He appears in behalf of the government in all cases in the supreme court in which it is interested, and gives his legal advice to the president and heads of departments upon questions submitted to him.

In each state also there is an attorney general, or similar officer, who appears for the people, as in England the attorney general appears for the crown.

ATTORNEY IN FACT. A private attorney authorized by another to act in his place and stead, either for some particular purpose, as to do a particular act, or for the transaction of business in general, not of a legal character. This authority is conferred by an instrument in writing, called a "letter of attorney," or more commonly a "power of attorney." Bac. Abr. "Attorney;" Story, Ag. § 25.

ATTORNEY OF THE WARDS AND LIVERIES. In English law. This was the third officer of the Duchy court. Bac. Abr. "Attorney."

ATTORNEY'S CERTIFICATE. In English law. A certificate that the attorney named has paid the annual tax or duty. This is required to be taken out every year by all practising attorneys under a penalty of fifty pounds.

ATTORNEYSHIP. The office of an agent or attorney.

ATTORNMENT. In feudal and old English law. A turning over or transfer by a lord of the services of his tenant to the grantee of his seigniory.

Attornment is the act of a person who holds a leasehold interest in land, or estate for life or years, by which he agrees to become the tenant of a stranger who has acquired the fee in the land, or the remainder or reversion, or the right to the rent or services by which the tenant holds.

AU BESOIN. In case of need. A French phrase sometimes incorporated in a bill of exchange, pointing out some person from whom payment may be sought in case the drawee fails or refuses to pay the bill. Story, Bills, § 65.

AUBAINE. See DROIT D'AUBAINE.

AUCTION. A public sale of land or goods, at public outcry, to the highest bidder.

A sale by auction is a sale by public outcry to the highest bidder on the spot. Civil Code Cal. § 1792; Civil Code Dak. § 1022.

The sale by auction is that which takes place when the thing is offered publicly to be sold to whoever will give the highest price. Civil Code La. art. 2601.

Auction is very generally defined as a sale to the *highest* bidder, and this is the usual meaning. There may, however, be a sale to the *lowest* bidder, as where land is sold for non-payment of taxes to whomsoever will take it for the shortest term; or where a contract is offered to the one who will perform it at the lowest price. And these appear fairly included in the term "auction." Abbott.

AUCTIONARIÆ. Catalogues of goods for public sale or auction.

AUCTIONARIUS. One who bought and sold again at an increased price; an auctioneer. Spelman.

AUCTIONEER. A person authorized or licensed by law to sell lands or goods of other persons at public auction; one who sells at auction.

Auctioneers differ from *brokers*, in that the latter may both buy and sell, whereas auctioneers can only sell; also brokers may sell by private contract only, and auctioneers by public auction only. Auctioneers can only sell goods for ready money, but factors may sell upon credit.

AUCTOR. In the Roman law. An auctioneer.

In the civil law. A grantor or vendor of any kind.

In old French law. A plaintiff. Kelham.

AUCTORITAS. In the civil law. Authority.

In old European law. A diploma, or royal charter. A word frequently used by Gregory of Tours and later writers. Spelman.

Auctoritates philosophorum, medicorum, et poetarum, sunt in causis allegandæ et tenendæ. The opinions of philosophers, physicians, and poets are to be alleged and received in causes. Co. Litt. 264.

Aucupia verborum sunt judice indigna. Catching at words is unworthy of a judge. Hob. 343.

Audi alteram partem. Hear the other side; hear both sides. No man should be condemned unheard. Broom, Max. 113. See L. R. 2 P. C. 106.

AUDIENCE. In international law. A hearing; interview with the sovereign. The king or other chief executive of a country grants an audience to a foreign minister who comes to him duly accredited; and, after the recall of a minister, an "audience of leave" ordinarily is accorded to him.

AUDIENCE COURT. In English law. A court belonging to the Archbishop of Canterbury, having jurisdiction of matters of form only, as the confirmation of bishops, and the like. This court has the same authority with the Court of Arches, but is of inferior dignity and antiquity. The Dean of the Arches is the official auditor of the Audience court. The Archbishop of York has also his Audience court.

AUDIENDO ET TERMINANDO. A writ or commission to certain persons to appease and punish any insurrection or great riot. Fitzh. Nat. Brev. 110.

AUDIT. As a verb; to make an official investigation and examination of accounts and vouchers.

As a noun; the process of auditing accounts; the hearing and investigation had before an auditor.

AUDITA QUERELA. The name of a writ constituting the initial process in an action brought by a judgment defendant to obtain relief against the consequences of the judgment, on account of some matter of defense or discharge, arising since its rendition, and which could not be taken advantage of otherwise. See 1 Amer. & Eng. Enc. Law, 1003; Bac. Abr. *sub voce;* 3 Bl. Comm. 405.

AUDITOR. A public officer whose function is to examine and pass upon the accounts and vouchers of officers who have received and expended public money by lawful authority.

In practice. An officer (or officers) of the court, assigned to state the items of debit and credit between the parties in a suit where accounts are in question, and exhibit the balance. 1 Metc. (Mass.) 218.

In English law. An officer or agent of the crown, or of a private individual, or corporation, who examines periodically the accounts of under officers, tenants, stewards, or bailiffs, and reports the state of their accounts to his principal.

AUDITOR OF THE RECEIPTS. An officer of the English exchequer. 4 Inst. 107.

AUDITORS OF THE IMPREST. Officers in the English exchequer, who formerly had the charge of auditing the accounts of the customs, naval and military expenses, etc., now performed by the commissioners for auditing public accounts.

AUGMENTATION. The increase of the crown's revenues from the suppression of religious houses and the appropriation of their lands and revenues.

Also the name of a court (now abolished) erected 27 Hen. VIII., to determine suits and controversies relating to monasteries and abbey-lands.

Augusta legibus soluta non est. The empress or queen is not privileged or exempted from subjection to the laws. 1 Bl. Comm. 219; Dig. 1, 3, 31.

AULA. In old English law. A hall, or court; the court of a baron, or manor; a court baron. Spelman.

AULA ECCLESIÆ. A nave or body of a church where temporal courts were anciently held.

AULA REGIS. The chief court of England in early Norman times. It was established by William the Conqueror in his own hall. It was composed of the great officers of state, resident in the palace, and followed the king's household in all his expeditions.

AULNAGE. See ALNAGE.

AULNAGER. See ALNAGER.

AUMEEN. In Indian law. Trustee; commissioner; a temporary collector or supervisor, appointed to the charge of a country on the removal of a zemindar, or for any other particular purpose of local investigation or arrangement.

AUMIL. In Indian law. Agent; officer; native collector of revenue; superintendent of a district or division of a country, either on the part of the government zemindar or renter.

AUMILDAR. In Indian law. Agent; the holder of an office; an intendant and collector of the revenue, uniting civil, military, and financial powers under the Mohammedan government.

AUMONE, SERVICE IN. Where lands are given in alms to some church or religious house, upon condition that a service or prayers shall be offered at certain times for the repose of the donor's soul. Britt. 164.

AUNCEL WEIGHT. In English law. An ancient mode of weighing, described by Cowell as "a kind of weight with scales hanging, or hooks fastened to each end of a staff, which a man, lifting up upon his forefinger or hand, discerneth the quality or difference between the weight and the thing weighed."

AUNT. The sister of one's father or mother, and a relation in the third degree, correlative to niece or nephew.

AURES. A Saxon punishment by cutting off the ears, inflicted on those who robbed churches, or were guilty of any other theft.

AURUM REGINÆ. Queen's gold. A royal revenue belonging to every queen consort during her marriage with the king.

AUTER, Autre. L. Fr. Another; other.

AUTER ACTION PENDANT. L. Fr. In pleading. Another action pending. A species of plea in abatement. 1 Chit. Pl. 454.

AUTER DROIT. In right of another, *e. g.*, a trustee holds trust property in right of his *cestui que trust*. A *prochein amy* sues in right of an infant. 2 Bl. Comm. 176.

AUTHENTIC. Genuine; true; having the character and authority of an original; duly vested with all necessary formalities and legally attested; competent, credible, and reliable as evidence.

AUTHENTIC ACT. In the civil law. An act which has been executed before a notary or other public officer authorized to execute such functions, or which is testified by a public seal, or has been rendered public by the authority of a competent magistrate, or which is certified as being a copy of a public register. Nov. 73, c. 2; Cod. 7, 52, 6, 4, 21; Dig. 22, 4.

The *authentic act*, as relates to contracts, is that which has been executed before a notary public or other officer authorized to execute such functions, in presence of two witnesses, free, male, and aged at least fourteen years, or of three witnesses, if the party be blind. If the party does not know how to sign, the notary must cause him to affix his mark to the instrument. All *procès verbals* of sales of succession property, signed by the sheriff or other person making the same, by the purchaser and two witnesses, are authentic acts. Civil Code La. art. 2234.

AUTHENTICATION. In the law of evidence. The act or mode of giving authority or legal authenticity to a statute, record, or other written instrument, or a certified copy thereof, so as to render it legally admissible in evidence.

An attestation made by a proper officer by which he certifies that a record is in due form of law, and that the person who certifies it is the officer appointed so to do.

AUTHENTICS. In the civil law. A Latin translation of the Novels of Justinian by an anonymous author; so called because the Novels were translated *entire*, in order to distinguish it from the epitome made by Julian.

There is another collection so called, compiled by Irnier, of incorrect extracts from the Novels and inserted by him in the Code, in the places to which they refer.

AUTHENTICUM. In the civil law. An original instrument or writing; the original of a will or other instrument, as distinguished from a copy. Dig. 22, 4, 2; Id. 29, 3, 12.

AUTHOR. One who produces, by his own intellectual labor applied to the materials of his composition, an arrangement or compilation new in itself. 2 Blatchf. 39.

AUTHORITIES. Citations to statutes, precedents, judicial decisions, and text-books of the law, made on the argument of questions of law or the trial of causes before a court, in support of the legal positions contended for.

AUTHORITY. In contracts. The lawful delegation of power by one person to another.

In the English law relating to public administration, an authority is a body having jurisdiction in certain matters of a public nature.

In governmental law. Legal power; a right to command or to act; the right and power of public officers to require obedience to their orders lawfully issued in the scope of their public duties.

Authority to execute a deed must be given by deed. Com. Dig. "Attorney," C, 5; 4 Term, 313; 7 Term, 207; 1 Holt, 141; 9 Wend. 68, 75; 5 Mass. 11; 5 Bin. 613.

AUTO ACORDADO. In Spanish colonial law. An order emanating from some superior tribunal, promulgated in the name and by the authority of the sovereign. Schm. Civil Law, 93.

AUTOCRACY. The name of an unlimited monarchical government. A government at the will of one man, (called an "autocrat,") unchecked by constitutional restrictions or limitations.

AUTOGRAPH. The handwriting of any one.

AUTONOMY. The political independence of a nation; the right (and condition) of self-government.

AUTOPSY. The dissection of a dead body for the purpose of inquiring into the cause of death. Pub. St. Mass. 1882, p. 1288.

AUTRE. L. Fr. Another.

AUTRE VIE. L. Fr. Another's life. A person holding an estate for or during the life of another is called a tenant "*pur autre vie*," or "*pur terme d'autre vie.*" Litt. § 56; 2 Bl. Comm. 120.

AUTREFOIS. At another time; formerly; before; heretofore.

AUTREFOIS ACQUIT. In criminal law. Formerly acquitted. The name of a plea in bar to a criminal action, stating that the defendant has been once already indicted and tried for the same alleged offense and has been acquitted.

AUTREFOIS ATTAINT. In criminal law. Formerly attainted. A plea that the defendant has already been attainted for one felony, and therefore cannot be criminally prosecuted for another. 4 Bl. Comm. 336.

AUTREFOIS CONVICT. Formerly convicted. In criminal law. A plea by a criminal in bar to an indictment that he has been formerly convicted of the same identical crime. 4 Bl. Comm. 336; 4 Steph. Comm. 404.

AUXILIUM. In feudal and old English law. Aid; a kind of tribute paid by the vassal to his lord, being one of the incidents of the tenure by knight's service. Spelman.

AUXILIUM AD FILIUM MILITEM FACIENDUM ET FILIAM MARITANDAM. An ancient writ which was addressed to the sheriff to levy compulsorily an aid towards the knighting of a son and the marrying of a daughter of the tenants *in capite* of the crown.

AUXILIUM CURIÆ. In old English law. A precept or order of court citing and convening a party, at the suit and request of another, to warrant something.

AUXILIUM REGIS. In English law. The king's aid or money levied for the royal use and the public service, as taxes granted by parliament.

AUXILIUM VICE COMITI. An ancient duty paid to sheriffs. Cowell.

AVAIL OF MARRIAGE. In feudal law. The right of marriage, which the lord or guardian in chivalry had of disposing of his infant ward in matrimony. A guardian in socage had also the same right, but not attended with the same advantage. 2 Bl. Comm. 88.

In Scotch law. A certain sum due by the heir of a deceased ward vassal, when the heir became of marriageable age. Ersk. Inst. 2, 5, 18.

AVAILABLE MEANS. This phrase, among mercantile men, is a term well understood to be anything which can readily be converted into money; but it is not necessarily or primarily money itself. 13 N. Y. 219; 32 N. Y. 224.

AVAILS. Profits, or proceeds. This word seems to have been construed only in reference to wills, and in them it means the *corpus* or proceeds of the estate after the payment of the debts. 1 Amer. & Eng. Enc. Law, 1039. See 3 N. Y. 276; 34 N. Y. 201.

AVAL. In French law. The guaranty of a bill of exchange; so called because usually placed at the foot or bottom (*aval*) of the bill. Story, Bills, § 394, 454.

The act of subscribing one's signature at

the bottom of a promissory note or of a bill of exchange; properly an act of suretyship, by the party signing, in favor of the party to whom the note or bill is given. 1 Low. Can. 221.

AVANTURE. Chance; hazard; mischance.

AVARIA, AVARIE. Average; the loss and damage suffered in the course of a navigation. Poth. Mar. Louage, 105.

AVENAGE. A certain quantity of oats paid by a tenant to his landlord as rent, or in lieu of some other duties.

AVENTURE, or ADVENTURE. A mischance causing the death of a man, as where a person is suddenly drowned or killed by any accident, without felony. Co. Litt. 391.

AVER. In pleading. To declare or assert; to set out distinctly and formally; to allege.

In old pleading. To avouch or verify. Litt. § 691; Co. Litt. 362*b*. To make or prove true; to make good or justify a plea.

AVER. In old English and French. A working beast; a horse or bullock.

AVER CORN. A rent reserved to religious houses, to be paid by their tenants in corn.

AVER ET TENER. In old conveyancing. To have and to hold.

AVER LAND. In feudal law. Land plowed by the tenant for the proper use of the lord of the soil.

AVER PENNY. Money paid towards the king's averages or carriages, and so to be freed thereof.

AVER SILVER. A custom or rent formerly so called.

AVERAGE. A medium, a mean proportion.

In old English law. A service by horse or carriage, anciently due by a tenant to his lord. Cowell. A labor or service performed with working cattle, horses, or oxen, or with wagons and carriages. Spelman.

Stubble, or remainder of straw and grass left in corn-fields after harvest. In Kent it is called "*gratten*," and in other parts "*roughings*."

In maritime law. Loss or damage accidentally happening to a vessel or to its cargo during a voyage.

Also a small duty paid to masters of ships, when goods are sent in another man's ship, for their care of the goods, over and above the freight.

In marine insurance. Where loss or damage occurs to a vessel or its cargo at sea, *average* is the adjustment and apportionment of such loss between the owner, the freight, and the cargo, in proportion to their respective interests and losses, in order that one may not suffer the whole loss, but each contribute ratably. It is of the following kinds:

General average (also called "gross") consists of expense purposely incurred, sacrifice made, or damage sustained for the common safety of the vessel, freight, and cargo, or the two of them, at risk, and is to be contributed for by the several interests in the proportion of their respective values exposed to the common danger, and ultimately surviving, including the amount of expense, sacrifice, or damage so incurred in the contributory value. 2 Phil. Ins. § 1269 et seq.

Particular average is a loss happening to the ship, freight, or cargo which is not to be shared by contribution among all those interested, but must be borne by the owner of the subject to which it occurs. It is thus called in contradistinction to *general* average.

Petty average is a term sometimes applied to small charges which were formerly assessed upon the cargo, viz., pilotage, towage, light-money, beaconage, anchorage, bridge-toll, quarantine, pier-money.

AVERAGE CHARGES. "Average charges for toll and transportation" are understood to mean, and do mean, charges made at a mean rate, obtained by dividing the entire receipts for toll and transportation by the whole quantity of tonnage carried, reduced to a common standard of tons moved one mile. 74 Pa. St. 190.

AVERAGE LOSS. In maritime law. A partial loss of goods or vessels insured, for which the insurers are bound to compensate the insured in the proportion which the loss bears to the whole insurance. 2 Steph. Comm. 178.

AVERAGE PRICES. Such as are computed on all the prices of any articles sold within a certain period or district.

AVERIA. In old English law. This term was applied to working cattle, such as horses, oxen, etc.

AVERIA CARRUCÆ. Beasts of the plow.

AVERIIS CAPTIS IN WITHERNAM. A writ granted to one whose cattle were unlawfully distrained by another and driven out of the county in which they were taken, so that they could not be replevied by the sheriff. Reg. Orig. 82.

AVERMENT. **In pleading.** A positive statement of facts, in opposition to argument or inference. 1 Chit. Pl. 320.

In old pleading. An offer to prove a plea, or pleading. The concluding part of a plea, replication, or other pleading, containing new affirmative matter, by which the party offers or declares himself "ready to *verify*."

AVERRARE. In feudal law. A duty required from some customary tenants, to carry goods in a wagon or upon loaded horses.

AVERSIO. In the civil law. An averting or turning away. A term applied to a species of sale in gross or bulk. Letting a house altogether, instead of in chambers. 4 Kent, Comm. 517.

AVERSIO PERICULI. A turning away of peril. Used of a contract of insurance. 3 Kent, Comm. 263.

AVERUM. Goods, property, substance; a beast of burden. Spelman.

AVET. A term used in the Scotch law, signifying to abet or assist.

AVIA. In the civil law. A grandmother. Inst. 3, 6, 3.

AVIATICUS. In the civil law. A grandson.

AVIZANDUM. In Scotch law. To make *avizandum* with a process is to take it from the public court to the private consideration of the judge. Bell.

AVOCAT. Fr. Advocate; an advocate.

AVOID. To annul; cancel; make void; to destroy the efficacy of anything.

AVOIDANCE. A making void, or of no effect; annulling, cancelling; escaping or evading.

In English ecclesiastical law. The term describes the condition of a benefice when it has no incumbent.

In parliamentary language, avoidance of a decision signifies evading or superseding a question, or escaping the coming to a decision upon a pending question. Holthouse.

In pleading. The allegation or statement of new matter, in opposition to a former pleading, which, admitting the facts alleged in such former pleading, shows cause why they should not have their ordinary legal effect.

AVOIRDUPOIS. The name of a system of weights (sixteen ounces to the pound) used in weighing articles other than medicines, metals, and precious stones.

AVOUCHER. The calling upon a warrantor of lands to fulfil his undertaking.

AVOUÉ. In French law. A barrister, advocate, attorney. An officer charged with representing and defending parties before the tribunal to which he is attached. Duverger.

AVOW. In pleading. To acknowledge and justify an act done.

To make an avowry. For example, when replevin is brought for a thing distrained, and the party taking claims that he had a right to make the distress, he is said to avow.

AVOWANT. One who makes an avowry.

AVOWEE. In ecclesiastical law. An advocate of a church benefice.

AVOWRY. A pleading in the action of replevin, by which the defendant *avows*, that is, acknowledges, the taking of the distress or property complained of, where he took it in his own right, and sets forth the reason of it; as for rent in arrear, damage done, etc. 3 Bl. Comm. 149; 1 Tidd, Pr. 645.

Avowry is the setting forth, as in a declaration, the nature and merits of the defendant's case, showing that the distress taken by him was lawful, which must be done with such sufficient authority as will entitle him to a *retorno habendo*. 6 Hill, 284.

An avowry must be distinguished from a *justification*. The former species of plea admits the plaintiff's ownership of the property, but alleges a right in the defendant sufficient to warrant him in taking the property and which still subsists. A justification, on the other hand, denies that the plaintiff had the right of property or possession in the subject-matter, alleging it to have been in the defendant or a third person, or avers a right sufficient to warrant the defendant in taking it, although such right has not continued in force to the time of making answer.

AVOWTERER. In English law. An adulterer with whom a married woman continues in adultery. Termes de la Ley.

AVOWTRY. In old English law. Adultery. Termes de la Ley.

AVULSION. The removal of a considerable quantity of soil from the land of one man, and its deposit upon or annexation to the land of another, suddenly and by the perceptible action of water. 2 Washb. Real Prop. 452.

The property of the part thus separated continues in the original proprietor, in which respect avulsion differs from alluvion, by which an addition is insensibly made to a property by the gradual washing down of the river, and which addition becomes the property of the owner of the lands to which the addition is made. Wharton.

AVUNCULUS. In the civil law. A mother's brother. 2 Bl. Comm. 230. *Avunculus magnus*, a great-uncle. *Avunculus major*, a great-grandmother's brother. *Avunculus maximus*, a great-great-grandmother's brother. See Dig. 38, 10, 10; Inst. 3, 6, 2.

AVUS. In the civil law. A grandfather. Inst. 3, 6, 1.

AWAIT. A term used in old statutes, signifying a lying in wait, or waylaying.

AWARD, *v.* To grant, concede, adjudge to. Thus, a jury *awards* damages; the court *awards* an injunction.

AWARD, *n.* The decision or determination rendered by arbitrators or commissioners, or other private or extrajudicial deciders, upon a controversy submitted to them; also the writing or document embodying such decision.

AWAY-GOING CROP. A crop sown before the expiration of a tenancy, which cannot ripen until after its expiration, to which, however, the tenant is entitled. Broom, Max. 412.

AWM. In old English statutes. A measure of wine, or vessel containing forty gallons.

AXIOM. In logic. A self-evident truth; an indisputable truth.

AYANT CAUSE. In French law. This term signifies one to whom a right has been assigned, either by will, gift, sale, exchange, or the like; an assignee. An *ayant cause* differs from an heir who acquires the right by inheritance. 8 Toullier, n. 245. The term is used in Louisiana.

AYLE. See AIEL.

AYRE. In old Scotch law. Eyre; a circuit, eyre, or iter.

AYUNTAMIENTO. In Spanish law. A congress of persons; the municipal council of a city or town. 1 White, Coll. 416; 12 Pet. 442, notes.

AZURE. A term used in heraldry, signifying blue.

B.

B. The second letter of the English alphabet; is used to denote the second of a series of pages, notes, etc.; the subsequent letters, the third and following numbers.

B. C. An abbreviation for "before Christ," "bail court," and "bankruptcy cases."

B. E. An abbreviation for "Baron of the Court of Exchequer."

B. F. An abbreviation for *bonum factum*, a good or proper act, deed, or decree; signifies "approved."

B. R. An abbreviation for *Bancus Regis*, (King's Bench,) or *Bancus Reginæ*, (Queen's Bench.) It is frequently found in the old books as a designation of that court. In more recent usage, the initial letters of the English names are ordinarily employed, *i. e.*, K. B. or Q. B.

B. S. *Bancus Superior*, that is, upper bench.

"BABY ACT." A plea of infancy, interposed for the purpose of defeating an action upon a contract made while the person was a minor, is vulgarly called "pleading the baby act." By extension, the term is applied to a plea of the statute of limitations.

BACHELERIA. In old records. Commonalty or yeomanry, in contradistinction to baronage.

BACHELOR. The holder of the first or lowest degree conferred by a college or university, *e. g.*, a bachelor of arts, bachelor of law, etc.

A kind of inferior knight; an esquire.

A man who has never been married.

BACKWATER. Water in a stream which, in consequence of some dam or obstruction below, is detained or checked in its course, or flows back.

Water caused to flow backward from a steam-vessel by reason of the action of its wheels or screw.

BACKBEAR. In forest law. Carrying on the back. One of the cases in which an offender against vert and venison might be arrested, as being taken with the mainour, or manner, or found carrying a deer off on his *back*. Manwood; Cowell.

BACKBEREND. Sax. Bearing upon the back or about the person. Applied to a thief taken with the stolen property in his immediate possession. Bract. 1, 3, tr. 2, c. 32. Used with *handhabend*, having in the hand.

BACKBOND. In Scotch law. A deed attaching a qualification or condition to the terms of a conveyance or other instrument. This deed is used when particular circumstances render it necessary to express in a separate form the limitations or qualifications of a right. Bell. The instrument is equivalent to a declaration of trust in English conveyancing.

BACKING. Indorsement; indorsement by a magistrate.

BACKING A WARRANT. The warrant of a justice of the peace cannot be enforced or executed outside of his territorial jurisdiction unless a magistrate of the jurisdiction where it is to be executed indorses or writes on the back of such warrant an authority for that purpose, which is thence termed "backing the warrant."

BACKSIDE. In English law. A term formerly used in conveyances and also in pleading; it imports a yard at the back part of or behind a house, and belonging thereto.

BACKWARDATION. In the language of the stock exchange, this term signifies a consideration paid for delay in the delivery of stock contracted for, when the price is lower for time than for cash. Dos Passos, Stock-Brok. 270.

BACKWARDS. In a policy of marine insurance, the phrase "forwards and backwards at sea" means from port to port in the course of the voyage, and not merely from one terminus to the other and back. 1 Taunt. 475.

BACULUS. A rod, staff, or wand, used in old English practice in making livery of seisin where no building stood on the land, (Bract. 40;) a stick or wand, by the erection of which on the land involved in a real action the defendant was summoned to put in his appearance; this was called "*baculus nuntiatorius*." 3 Bl. Comm. 279.

BAD, (in substance.) The technical word for unsoundness in pleading.

BADGE. A mark or cognizance worn to show the relation of the wearer to any person or thing; the token of anything; a distinctive mark of office or service.

BADGE OF FRAUD. A term used relatively to the law of fraudulent conveyances made to hinder and defraud creditors. It is defined as a fact tending to throw suspicion upon a transaction, and calling for an explanation. Bump, Fraud. Conv. 31.

BADGER. In old English law. One who made a practice of buying corn or victuals in one place, and carrying them to another to sell and make profit by them.

BAG. A certain and customary quantity of goods and merchandise in a sack. Wharton.

BAGA. In English law. A bag or purse. Thus there is the petty-bag-office in the common-law jurisdiction of the court of chancery, because all original writs relating to the business of the crown were formerly kept in a little sack or bag, *in parvâ bagâ.* 1 Madd. Ch. 4.

BAGGAGE. In the law of carriers. This term comprises such articles of personal convenience or necessity as are usually carried by passengers for their personal use, and not merchandise or other valuables, although carried in the trunks of passengers, which are not designed for any such use, but for other purposes, such as a sale and the like. Story, Bailm. § 499. See, also, Hutch. Carr. § 679; L. R. 6 Q. B. 612; 6 Hill, 586; 9 Humph. 621; 23 Fed. Rep. 765. See cases collected in 1 Amer. & Eng. Enc. Law, 1042.

The term includes whatever the passenger takes with him for his personal use or convenience according to the habits or wants of the particular class to which he belongs, either with reference to the immediate necessities or ultimate purpose of the journey. L. R. 6 Q. B. 612.

BAHADUM. A chest or coffer. Fleta.

BAIL, *v.* To procure the release of a person from legal custody, by undertaking that he shall appear at the time and place designated and submit himself to the jurisdiction and judgment of the court.

To set at liberty a person arrested or imprisoned, on security being taken for his appearance on a day and a place certain, which security is called "bail," because the party arrested or imprisoned is delivered into the hands of those who bind themselves for his forthcoming, (that is, become bail for his due appearance when required,) in order that he may be safely protected from prison. Wharton.

BAIL, *n.* **In practice.** The sureties who procure the release of a person under arrest, by becoming responsible for his appearance at the time and place designated. Those persons who become sureties for the appearance of the defendant in court.

Upon those contracts of indemnity which are taken in legal proceedings as security for the performance of an obligation imposed or declared by the tribunals, and known as undertakings or recognizances, the sureties are called "bail." Civil Code Cal. § 2780.

The taking of bail consists in the acceptance by a competent court, magistrate, or officer, of sufficient bail for the appearance of the defendant according to the legal effect of his undertaking, or for the payment to the state of a certain specified sum if he does not appear. Code Ala. 1886, § 4407.

Bail is of various kinds, such as:

Civil bail. That taken in civil actions.

Special bail, being persons who undertake that if the defendant is condemned in the action he shall pay the debt or surrender himself for imprisonment.

Bail in error. That given by a defendant who intends to bring error on the judgment and desires a stay of execution in the mean time.

See, further, the following titles.

In Canadian law. A lease. *Bail emphytéotique.* A lease for years, with a right to prolong indefinitely. 5 Low. Can. 381. It is equivalent to an alienation. 6 Low. Can. 58.

BAIL À CHEPTEL. In French law. A contract by which one of the parties gives to the other cattle to keep, feed, and care for, the borrower receiving half the profit of increase, and bearing half the loss. Duverger.

BAIL À FERME. In French law. A contract of letting lands.

BAIL À LOYER. In French law. A contract of letting houses.

BAIL À RENTE. In French law. A contract partaking of the nature of the contract of sale, and that of the contract of lease; it is translative of property, and the rent is essentially redeemable. 4 La. 286; Poth. Bail à Rente, 1, 3.

BAIL ABSOLUTE. Sureties whose liability is conditioned upon the failure of the principal to duly account for money coming to his hands as administrator, guardian, etc.

BAIL-BOND. In practice. A bond executed by a defendant who has been arrested, together with other persons as sureties, naming the sheriff, constable, or marshal as obligee, in a penal sum proportioned to the damages claimed or penalty denounced, conditioned that the defendant shall duly appear to answer to the legal process in the officer's hands, or shall cause special bail to be put in, as the case may be.

BAIL, COMMON. In practice. A fictitious proceeding, intended only to express the appearance of a defendant, in cases where special bail is not required. It is put in in the same form as special bail, but the sureties are merely nominal or imaginary persons, as John Doe and Richard Roe. 3 Bl. Comm. 287.

BAIL COURT. In English law and practice. An auxiliary court of the court of queen's bench at Westminster, wherein points connected more particularly with pleading and practice are argued and determined. Holthouse.

BAIL PIECE. In practice. A formal entry or memorandum of the recognizance or undertaking of special bail in civil actions, which, after being signed and acknowledged by the bail before the proper officer, is filed in the court in which the action is pending. 3 Bl. Comm. 291; 1 Tidd, Pr. 250.

BAIL TO THE ACTION, BAIL ABOVE, OR SPECIAL BAIL. In practice. Persons who undertake jointly and severally in behalf of a defendant arrested on mesne process in a civil action that, if he be condemned in the action, he shall pay the costs and condemnation, (that is, the amount which may be recovered against him,) or render himself a prisoner, or that they will pay it for him. 3 Bl. Comm. 291; 1 Tidd, Pr. 245.

BAIL TO THE SHERIFF, OR BAIL BELOW. In practice. Persons who undertake that a defendant arrested upon mesne process in a civil action shall duly appear to answer the plaintiff; such undertaking being in the form of a bond given to the sheriff, termed a "bail-bond," (*q. v.*) 3 Bl. Comm. 290; 1 Tidd, Pr. 221.

BAILABLE. Capable of being bailed; admitting of bail; authorizing or requiring bail. A bailable *action* is one in which the defendant cannot be released from arrest except on furnishing bail. Bailable *process* is such as requires the officer to take bail, after arresting the defendant. A bailable *offense* is one for which the prisoner may be admitted to bail.

BAILEE. In the law of contracts. One to whom goods are bailed; the party to whom personal property is delivered under a contract of bailment.

BAILIE. In the Scotch law. A bailie is (1) a magistrate having inferior criminal jurisdiction, similar to that of an alderman, (*q. v.*;) (2) an officer appointed to confer infeoffment, (*q. v.*;) a bailiff, (*q. v.*;) a server of writs. Bell.

BAILIFF. In a general sense, a person to whom some authority, care, guardianship, or jurisdiction is delivered, committed, or intrusted; one who is deputed or appointed to take charge of another's affairs; an overseer or superintendent; a keeper, protector, or guardian; a steward. Spelman.

A sheriff's officer or deputy. 1 Bl. Comm. 344.

A magistrate, who formerly administered justice in the parliaments or courts of France, answering to the English sheriffs as mentioned by Bracton.

In the action of account render. A person who has by delivery the custody and administration of lands or goods for the benefit of the owner or bailor, and is liable to render an account thereof. Co. Litt. 271; Story, Eq. Jur. § 446.

A bailiff is defined to be "a servant that has the administration and charge of lands, goods, and chattels, to make the best benefit for the owner, against whom an action of account lies, for the profits which he has raised or made, or might by his industry or care have raised or made." 25 Conn. 149.

BAILIFF-ERRANT. A bailiff's deputy.

BAILIFFS OF FRANCHISES. In English law. Officers who perform the duties of sheriffs within liberties or privileged jurisdictions, in which formerly the king's writ could not be executed by the sheriff. Spelman.

BAILIFFS OF HUNDREDS. In English law. Officers appointed over hundreds, by the sheriffs, to collect fines therein, and summon juries; to attend the judges and justices at the assises and quarter sessions; and also to execute writs and process in the several hundreds. 1 Bl. Comm. 345; 3 Steph. Comm. 29; Bract. fol. 116.

BAILIFFS OF MANORS. In English law. Stewards or agents appointed by the lord (generally by an authority under seal) to superintend the manor, collect fines, and quit rents, inspect the buildings, order repairs, cut down trees, impound cattle trespassing, take an account of wastes, spoils, and misdemeanors in the woods and demesne lands, and do other acts for the lord's interest. Cowell.

BAILIVIA. In old law. A bailiff's jurisdiction, a bailiwick; the same as *bailium*. Spelman. See BAILIWICK.

In old English law. A liberty, or exclusive jurisdiction, which was exempted from the sheriff of the county, and over which the lord of the liberty appointed a bailiff with such powers within his precinct as an under-sheriff exercised under the sheriff of the county. Whishaw.

BAILIWICK. The territorial jurisdiction of a sheriff or bailiff. 1 Bl. Comm. 344.

BAILLEUR DE FONDS. In Canadian law. The unpaid vendor of real estate.

BAILLI. In old French law. One to whom judicial authority was assigned or delivered by a superior.

BAILMENT. A delivery of goods or personal property, by one person to another, in trust for the execution of a special object upon or in relation to such goods, beneficial either to the bailor or bailee or both, and upon a contract, express or implied, to perform the trust and carry out such object, and thereupon either to redeliver the goods to the bailor or otherwise dispose of the same in conformity with the purpose of the trust. See Code Ga. 1882, § 2058.

A delivery of goods in trust upon a contract, expressed or implied, that the trust shall be faithfully executed on the part of the bailee. 2 Bl. Comm. 455.

Bailment, from the French *bailler*, to deliver, is a delivery of goods for some purpose, upon a contract, express or implied, that, after the purpose has been fulfilled, they shall be redelivered to the bailor, or otherwise dealt with, according to his directions, or (as the case may be) kept till he reclaims them. 2 Steph. Comm. 80.

A delivery of goods in trust upon a contract, expressed or implied, that the trust shall be duly executed, and the goods restored by the bailee as soon as the purposes of the bailment shall be answered. 2 Kent, Comm. 559.

Bailment is a delivery of a thing in trust for some special object or purpose, and upon a contract, express or implied, to conform to the object or purpose of the trust. Story, Bailm. 3.

A delivery of goods in trust on a contract, either expressed or implied, that the trust shall be duly executed, and the goods redelivered as soon as the time or use for which they were bailed shall have elapsed or be performed. Jones, Bailm. 117.

Bailment is a word of French origin, significant of the curtailed transfer, the delivery or mere handing over, which is appropriate to the transaction. Schouler, Pers. Prop. 695.

The test of a bailment is that the identical thing is to be returned; if another thing of equal value is to be returned, the transaction is a sale. 6 Thomp. & C. 29; 3 Hun, 550.

Sir William Jones has divided bailments into five sorts, namely: *Depositum*, or deposit; *mandatum*, or commission without recompense; *commodatum*, or loan for use without pay; *pignori acceptum*, or pawn; *locatum*, or hiring, which is always with reward. This last is subdivided into *locatio rei*, or hiring, by which the hirer gains a temporary use of the thing; *locatio operis faciendi*, when something is to be done to the thing delivered; *locatio operis mercium vehendarum*, when the thing is merely to be carried from one place to another. Jones, Bailm. 36.

Lord Holt divided bailments thus:

(1) *Depositum*, or a naked bailment of goods, to be kept for the use of the bailor.

(2) *Commodatum*. Where goods or chattels that are useful are lent to the bailee *gratis*, to be used by him.

(3) *Locatio rei*. Where goods are lent to the bailee to be used by him for hire.

(4) *Vadium*. Pawn or pledge.

(5) *Locatio operis faciendi*. Where goods are delivered to be carried, or something is to be done about them, for a reward to be paid to the bailee.

(6) *Mandatum*. A delivery of goods to somebody who is to carry them, or do something about them, *gratis*. 2 Ld. Raym. 909.

Another division, suggested by Bouvier, is as follows: *First*, those bailments which are for the benefit of the bailor, or of some person whom he represents; *second*, those for the benefit of the bailee, or some person represented by him; *third*, those which are for the benefit of both parties.

BAILOR. The party who *bails* or delivers goods to another, in the contract of bailment.

BAIR-MAN. In old Scotch law. A poor insolvent debtor, left bare and naked, who was obliged to swear in court that he was not worth more than five shillings and fivepence.

BAIRNS. In Scotch law. A known term, used to denote one's whole issue. Ersk. Inst. 3, 8, 48. But it is sometimes used in a more limited sense. Bell.

BAIRN'S PART. In Scotch law. Children's part; a third part of the defunct's free movables, debts deducted, if the wife survive, and a half if there be no relict.

BAITING ANIMALS. In English law. Procuring them to be worried by dogs. Punishable on summary conviction, under 12 & 13 Vict. c. 92, § 3.

BALÆNA. A large fish, called by Blackstone a "whale." Of this the king had the head and the queen the tail as a perquisite whenever one was taken on the coast of England. 1 Bl. Comm. 222.

BALANCE. The amount remaining due from one person to another on a settlement of the accounts involving their mutual dealings; the difference between the two sides (debit and credit) of an account.

A balance is the conclusion or result of the debit and credit sides of an account. It implies mutual dealings, and the existence of debt and credit, without which there could be no balance. 45 Mo. 574. See, also, 71 Pa. St. 69.

The term is also frequently used in the sense of residue or remainder; as when a will speaks of "the balance of my estate." 3 Ired. 155; 23 S. C. 269.

BALANCE OF TRADE. The difference between the value of the exports from and imports into a country.

BALANCE-SHEET. When it is desired to ascertain the exact state of a merchant's business, or other commercial enterprise, at a given time, all the ledger accounts are closed up to date and balances struck; and these balances, when exhibited together on a single page, and so grouped and arranged as to close into each other and be summed up in one general result, constitute the "balance-sheet."

BALCANIFER, or BALDAKINIFER. The standard-bearer of the Knights Templar.

BALCONIES. Small galleries of wood or stone on the outside of houses. The erection of them is regulated in London by the building acts.

BALDIO. In Spanish law. Waste land; land that is neither arable nor pasture. White, New Recop. b. 2, tit. 1, c. 6, § 4, and note.

BALE. A pack or certain quantity of goods or merchandise, wrapped or packed up in cloth and corded round very tightly, marked and numbered with figures corresponding to those in the bills of lading for the purpose of identification. Wharton.

A bale of cotton is a certain quantity of that commodity compressed into a cubical form, so as to occupy less room than when in bags. 2 Car. & P. 525.

BALISE. Fr. In French marine law. A buoy.

BALIUS. In the civil law. A teacher; one who has the care of youth; a tutor; a guardian. Du Cange; Spelman.

BALIVA. L. Lat. In old English law. A bailiwick, or jurisdiction.

BALLAST. In marine insurance. There is considerable analogy between *ballast* and *dunnage*. The former is used for trimming the ship, and bringing it down to a draft of water proper and safe for sailing. Dunnage is placed under the cargo to keep it from being wetted by water getting into the hold, or between the different parcels to keep them from bruising and injuring each other. 13 Wall. 674.

BALLASTAGE. A toll paid for the privilege of taking up ballast from the bottom of a port or harbor.

BALLIVO AMOVENDO. An ancient writ to remove a bailiff from his office for want of sufficient land in the bailiwick. Reg. Orig. 78.

BALLOT. In the law of elections. A slip of paper bearing the names of the offices to be filled at the particular election and the names of the candidates for whom the elector desires to vote; it may be printed, or written, or partly printed and partly written, and is deposited by the voter in a "ballot-box" which is in the custody of the officers holding the election.

Also the act of voting by balls or tickets.

A ballot is a ticket folded in such a manner that nothing written or printed thereon can be seen. Pol. Code Cal. § 1186.

A ballot is defined to be "a paper ticket containing the names of the persons for whom the elector intends to vote, and designating the office to which each person so named is intended by him to be chosen." Thus a ballot, or a ticket, is a single piece of paper containing the names of the candidates and the offices for which they are running. If the elector were to write the names of the candidates upon his ticket twice or three or more times, he does not thereby make it more than one ticket. 28 Cal. 136.

BALLOT-BOX. A case made of wood for receiving ballots.

BALNEARII. In the Roman law. Those who stole the clothes of bathers in the public baths. 4 Bl. Comm. 239.

BAN. 1. In old English and civil law. A proclamation; a public notice; the announcement of an intended marriage. Cowell. An excommunication; a curse, publicly pronounced. A proclamation of silence made by a crier in court before the meeting of champions in combat. Id. A statute, edict, or command; a fine, or penalty.

2. In French law. The right of announcing the time of mowing, reaping, and gathering the vintage, exercised by certain seignorial lords. Guyot, Repert. Univ.

3. An expanse; an extent of space or territory; a space inclosed within certain limits; the limits or bounds themselves. Spelman.

4. A privileged space or territory around a town, monastery, or other place.

5. In old European law. A military standard; a thing unfurled, a banner. Spelman. A summoning to a standard; a calling out of a military force; the force itself so summoned; a national army levied by proclamation.

BANAL. In Canadian and old French law. Pertaining to a *ban* or privileged place; having qualities or privileges derived from a *ban*. Thus, a banal mill is one to which the lord may require his tenant to carry his grain to be ground.

BANALITY. In Canadian law. The right by virtue of which a lord subjects his vassals to grind at his mill, bake at his oven, etc. Used also of the region within which this right applied. Guyot, Repert. Univ.

BANC. Bench; the seat of judgment; the place where a court permanently or regularly sits.

The full bench, full court. A "sitting *in banc*" is a meeting of all the judges of a court, usually for the purpose of hearing arguments on demurrers, points reserved, motions for new trial, etc., as distinguished from the sitting of a single judge at the assises or at *nisi prius* and from trials at bar.

BANCI NARRATORES. In old English law. Advocates; countors; serjeants. Applied to advocates in the common pleas courts. 1 Bl. Comm. 24; Cowell.

BANCO. Ital. See BANC. A seat or bench of justice; also, in commerce, a word of Italian origin signifying a bank.

BANCUS. In old English law and practice. A bench or seat in the king's hall or palace. Fleta, lib. 2, c. 16, § 1.

A high seat, or seat of distinction; a seat of judgment, or tribunal for the administration of justice.

The English court of common pleas was formerly called "*Bancus.*"

A sitting *in banc;* the sittings of a court with its full judicial authority, or in full form, as distinguished from sittings at *nisi prius.*

A stall, bench, table, or counter, on which goods were exposed for sale. Cowell.

BANCUS REGINÆ. L. Lat. The queen's bench. See QUEEN'S BENCH.

BANCUS REGIS. Lat. The king's bench; the supreme tribunal of the king after parliament. 3 Bl. Comm. 41.

BANCUS SUPERIOR. The upper bench. The king's bench was so called during the Protectorate.

BAND. In old Scotch law. A proclamation calling out a military force.

BANDIT. An outlaw; a man *banned*, or put under a ban; a brigand or robber. *Banditti*, a band of robbers.

BANE. A malefactor. Bract. l. 1, t. 8, c. 1.

Also a public denunciation of a malefactor; the same with what was called "*hutesium*," hue and cry. Spelman.

BANERET, or BANNERET. In English law. A knight made in the field, by the ceremony of cutting off the point of his standard, and making it, as it were, a banner. Knights so made are accounted so honorable that they are allowed to display their arms in the royal army, as barons do, and may bear arms with supporters. They rank next to barons; and were sometimes called "*vexillarii.*" Wharton.

BANI. Deodands, (*q. v.*)

BANISHMENT. In criminal law. A punishment inflicted upon criminals, by compelling them to quit a city, place, or country for a specified period of time, or for life. See 4 Dall. 14.

It is inflicted principally upon political offenders, "transportation" being the word used to express a similar punishment of ordinary criminals. Banishment, however, merely forbids the return of the person banished before the expiration of the sentence, while transportation involves the idea of deprivation of liberty after the convict arrives at the place to which he has been carried. Rap. & L.

BANK. 1. A bench or seat; the bench or tribunal occupied by the judges; the seat of judgment; a court. The full bench, or full court; the assembly of all the judges of a court. A "sitting *in bank*" is a meeting of all the judges of a court, usually for the purpose of hearing arguments on demurrers, points reserved, motions for new trial, etc., as distinguished from the sitting of a single judge at the assises or at *nisi prius* and from trials at bar. But, in this sense, *banc* is the more usual form of the word.

2. An institution, of great value in the commercial world, empowered to receive deposits of money, to make loans, and to issue its promissory notes, (designed to circulate as money, and commonly called "bank-notes" or "bank-bills,") or to perform any one or more of these functions.

The term "bank" is usually restricted in its application to an incorporated body; while a private individual making it his business to conduct banking operations is denominated a "banker."

Also the house or place where such business is carried on.

Banks in the commercial sense are of three kinds, to-wit: (1) Of deposit; (2) of discount; (3) of circulation. Strictly speaking, the term "bank" implies a place for the deposit of money, as that is the most obvious purpose of such an institution. Originally the business of banking consisted only in receiving deposits, such as bullion, plate, and the like, for safe-keeping until the depositor should see fit to draw it out for use, but the business, in the progress of events, was extended, and bankers assumed to discount bills and notes, and to loan money upon mortgage, pawn, or other security, and, at a still later period, to issue notes of their own, intended as a circulating currency and a medium of exchange, instead of gold and silver. Modern bankers frequently exercise any two or even all three of those functions, but it is still true that an institution prohibited from exercising any more than one of those functions is a bank, in the strictest commercial sense. 17 Wall. 118; Rev. St. U. S. § 3407.

3. An acclivity; an elevation or mound of earth; usually applied in this sense to the raised earth bordering the sides of a watercourse.

BANK-ACCOUNT. A sum of money placed with a bank or banker, on deposit, by a customer, and subject to be drawn out on the latter's check. The statement or computation of the several sums deposited and those drawn out by the customer on checks, entered on the books of the bank and the depositor's pass-book.

BANK-BILLS. Promissory notes issued by a bank designed to circulate as money, and payable to the bearer on demand.

The term "bank-bills" is familiar to every man in this country, and conveys a definite and certain meaning. It is a written promise on the part of the bank to pay to the bearer a certain sum of money, on demand. This term is understood by the community generally to mean a written promise for the payment of money. So universal is this understanding that the term "bank-bills" would be rendered no more certain by adding the words "for the payment of money." 3 Scam. 328.

The words "bank-bill" and "bank-note," in their popular sense, are used synonymously. 21 Ind. 176; 2 Park. Crim. R. 37.

Bank-notes, bank-bills, and promissory notes, such as are issued by the directors of a bank incorporated by the legislature of Vermont, mean the same thing; so that the expression in a statute "bank-bill or promissory note" is an evident tautology. 17 Vt. 151.

BANK-BOOK. A book kept by a customer of a bank, showing the state of his account with it.

BANK-CREDITS. Accommodations allowed to a person on security given to a bank, to draw money on it to a certain extent agreed upon.

BANK-NOTE. A promissory note issued by a bank or authorized banker, payable to bearer on demand, and intended to circulate as money.

BANK-STOCK. Shares in the capital of a bank; shares in the property of a bank.

BANKABLE. In mercantile law Notes, checks, bank-bills, drafts, and other securities for money, received as cash by the banks. Such commercial paper as is considered worthy of discount by the bank to which it is offered is termed "bankable."

BANKER. A private person who keeps a bank; one who is engaged in the business of banking.

BANKER'S NOTE. A commercial instrument resembling a bank-note in every particular except that it is given by a private banker or unincorporated banking institution.

BANKEROUT. O. Eng. Bankrupt; insolvent; indebted beyond the means of payment.

BANKING. The business of receiving money on deposit, loaning money, discounting notes, issuing notes for circulation, collecting money on notes deposited, negotiating bills, etc.

BANKRUPT. A person who has committed an act of bankruptcy; one who has done some act or suffered some act to be done in consequence of which, under the laws of his country, he is liable to be proceeded against by his creditors for the seizure and distribution among them of his entire property.

A trader who secretes himself or does certain other acts tending to defraud his creditors. 2 Bl. Comm. 471.

In a looser sense, an insolvent person; a broken-up or ruined trader. 3 Story, 453.

A person who, by the formal decree of a court, has been declared subject to be proceeded against under the bankruptcy laws, or entitled, on his voluntary application, to take the benefit of such laws.

BANKRUPT LAW. A law relating to bankrupts and the procedure against them in the courts. A law providing a remedy for the creditors of a bankrupt, and for the relief and restitution of the bankrupt himself.

A law which, upon a bankrupt's surrendering all his property to commissioners for the benefit of his creditors, discharges him from the payment of his debts, and all liability to arrest or suit for the same, and secures his future acquired property from a liability to the payment of his past debts. Webster.

A bankrupt law is distinguished from the ordinary law between debtor and creditor, as involving these three general principles: (1) A summary and immediate seizure of all the debtor's property; (2) a distribution of it among the creditors in general, instead of merely applying a portion of it to the payment of the individual complainant; and (3) the discharge of the debtor from future liability for the debts then existing.

The leading distinction between a bankrupt law and an insolvent law, in the proper technical sense of the words, consists in the character of the persons upon whom it is designed to operate,—the former contemplating as its objects bankrupts only, that is, traders of a certain description; the latter, insolvents in general, or persons unable to pay their debts. This has led to a marked separation between the two systems, in principle and in practice, which in England has always been carefully maintained, although in the United States it has of late been effectually disregarded. In further illustration of this distinction, it may be observed that a bankrupt law, in its proper sense, is a remedy intended primarily for the benefit of creditors; it is set in motion at their instance, and operates upon the debtor against his will, (*in invitum*,) although in its result it effectually discharges him from his debts. An insolvent law, on the other hand, is chiefly intended for the benefit of the debtor, and is set in motion at his instance, though less effective as a discharge in its final result. 5 Hill, 327.

The only substantial difference between a strictly bankrupt law and an insolvent law lies in the circumstance that the former affords relief upon the application of the creditor, and the latter upon the application of the debtor. In the general character of the remedy, there is no difference, however much the modes by which the remedy may be administered may vary. 37 Cal. 222.

BANKRUPTCY. 1. The state or condition of one who is a bankrupt; amenability to the bankrupt laws; the condition of one who has committed an act of bankruptcy, and is liable to be proceeded against by his creditors therefor, or of one whose circumstances are such that he is entitled, on his voluntary application, to take the benefit of the bankrupt laws. The term is used in a looser sense as synonymous with "insolvency,"—inability to pay one's debts; the stopping and breaking up of business because the trader is broken down, insolvent, ruined. See 2 Story, 354, 359.

2. The term denotes the proceedings taken, under the bankrupt law, against a person (or firm or company) to have him adjudged a bankrupt, and to have his estate administered for the benefit of the creditors, and divided among them.

3. That branch of jurisprudence, or system of law and practice, which is concerned with the definition and ascertainment of acts of bankruptcy and the administration of bankrupts' estates for the benefit of their creditors and the absolution and restitution of bankrupts.

As to the distinction between bankruptcy and insolvency, it may be said that insolvent laws operate at the instance of an imprisoned debtor; bankrupt laws, at the instance of a creditor. But the line of partition between bankrupt and insolvent laws is not so distinctly marked as to define what belongs exclusively to the one and not to the other class of laws. 4 Wheat. 122.

Insolvency means a simple inability to pay, as debts should become payable, whereby the debtor's business would be broken up; bankruptcy means the particular legal *status*, to be ascertained and declared by a judicial decree. 2 Ben. 196.

BANKRUPTCY COURTS. Courts for the administration of the bankrupt laws. The present English bankruptcy courts are the London bankruptcy court, the court of appeal, and the local bankruptcy courts created by the bankruptcy act, 1869.

BANLEUCA. An old law term, signifying a space or tract of country around a city, town, or monastery, distinguished and protected by peculiar privileges. Spelman.

BANLIEU, or BANLIEUE. A French and Canadian law term, having the same meaning as *banleuca*, (*q. v.*)

BANNERET. See BANERET.

BANNI OR BANNITUS. In old law, one under a ban, (*q. v.*;) an outlaw or banished man. Britt. cc. 12, 13; Calvin.

BANNI NUPTIARUM. L. Lat. In old English law. The bans of matrimony.

BANNIMUS. We ban or expel. The form of expulsion of a member from the University of Oxford, by affixing the sentence in some public places, as a promulgation of it. Cowell.

BANNIRE AD PLACITA, AD MOLENDINUM. To summon tenants to serve at the lord's courts, to bring corn to be ground at his mill.

BANNUM. A ban, (*q. v.*)

BANNUS. In old English law. A proclamation. *Bannus regis;* the king's proclamation, made by the voice of a herald, forbidding all present at the trial by combat to interfere either by motion or word, whatever they might see or hear. Bract. fol. 142.

BANQUE. A bench; the table or counter of a trader, merchant, or banker. *Banque route;* a broken bench or counter; bankrupt.

BANS OF MATRIMONY. A public announcement of an intended marriage, required by the English law to be made in a church or chapel, during service, on three consecutive Sundays before the marriage is celebrated. The object is to afford an opportunity for any person to interpose an objection if he knows of any impediment or other just cause why the marriage should not take place. The publication of the bans may be dispensed with by procuring a special license to marry.

BANYAN. In East Indian law. A Hindoo merchant or shop-keeper. The word is used in Bengal to denote the native who manages the money concerns of a European, and sometimes serves him as an interpreter.

BAR. 1. A partition or railing running across a court-room, intended to separate the general public from the space occupied by the judges, counsel, jury, and others concerned in the trial of a cause. In the English courts it is the partition behind which all outer-barristers and every member of the public must stand. Solicitors, being officers of the court, are admitted within it; as are also queen's counsel, barristers with patents of precedence, and serjeants, in virtue of their ranks. Parties who appear in person also are placed within the bar on the floor of the court.

2. The term also designates a particular part of the court-room; for example, the place where prisoners stand at their trial, whence the expression "prisoner at the bar."

3. It further denotes the presence, actual or constructive, of the court. Thus, a trial *at bar* is one had before the full court, distinguished from a trial had before a single judge at *nisi prius.* So the "case at bar" is the case now before the court and under its consideration; the case being tried or argued.

4. In the practice of legislative bodies, the *bar* is the outer boundary of the house, and therefore all persons, not being members, who wish to address the house, or are summoned to it, appear *at the bar* for that purpose.

5. In another sense, the whole body of attorneys and counsellors, or the members of the legal profession, collectively, are figuratively called the "bar," from the place which they usually occupy in court. They are thus distinguished from the "bench," which term denotes the whole body of judges.

6. In the law of contracts, "bar" means an impediment, an obstacle, or preventive barrier. Thus, relationship within the prohibited degrees is a *bar* to marriage.

7. It further means that which defeats, annuls, cuts off, or puts an end to. Thus, a provision "in bar of dower" is one which has the effect of defeating or cutting off the dower-rights which the wife would otherwise become entitled to in the particular land.

8. In pleading, it denoted a special plea, constituting a sufficient answer to an action at law; and so called because it *barred, i. e.,* prevented, the plaintiff from further prosecuting it with effect, and, if established by proof, defeated and destroyed the action altogether. Now called a special "plea in bar." See PLEA IN BAR.

BAR FEE. In English law. A fee taken by the sheriff, time out of mind, for every prisoner who is acquitted. Bac. Abr. "Extortion." Abolished by St. 14 Geo. III. c. 26; 55 Geo. III. c. 50; 8 & 9 Vict. c. 114.

BARAGARIA. Span. A concubine, whom a man keeps alone in his house, unconnected with any other woman. Las Partidas, pt. 4, tit. 14.

Baratriam committit qui propter pecuniam justitiam baractat. He is guilty of barratry who for money sells justice. Bell.

BARBANUS. In old Lombardic law. An uncle, (*patruus.*)

BARBICANAGE. In old European law. Money paid to support a barbican or watch-tower.

BARE TRUSTEE. A person to whose fiduciary office no duties were originally attached, or who, although such duties were originally attached to his office, would, on the requisition of his *cestuis qui trust*, be compellable in equity to convey the estate to them or by their direction. 1 Ch. Div. 279.

BARET. L. Fr. A wrangling suit. Britt. c. 92; Co. Litt. 368*b*.

BARGAIN. A mutual undertaking, contract, or agreement.

A contract or agreement between two parties, the one to sell goods or lands, and the other to buy them. 5 Mass. 360. See, also, 6 Conn. 91; 5 East, 10; 6 East, 307.

"If the word 'agreement' imports a mutual act of two parties, surely the word 'bargain' is not less significative of the consent of two. In a popular sense, the former word is frequently used as declaring the engagement of one only. A man may agree to pay money or to perform some other act, and the word is then used synonymously with 'promise' or 'engage.' But the word 'bargain' is seldom used, unless to express a mutual contract or undertaking." 17 Mass. 131.

BARGAIN AND SALE. In conveyancing. The transferring of the property of a thing from one to another, upon valuable consideration, by way of sale. Shep. Touch. (by Preston,) 221.

A contract or bargain by the owner of land, in consideration of money or its equivalent paid, to sell land to another person, called the "bargainee," whereupon a use arises in favor of the latter, to whom the seisin is transferred by force of the statute of uses. 2 Washb. Real Prop. 128.

The expression "bargain and sale" is also applied to transfers of personalty, in cases where there is first an executory agreement for the sale, (the bargain,) and then an actual and completed sale.

The proper and technical words to denote a bargain and sale are "bargain and sell;" but any other words that are sufficient to raise a use upon a valuable consideration are sufficient. 2 Wood. Conv. 15; 3 Johns. 484.

BARGAINEE. The party to a bargain to whom the subject-matter of the bargain or thing bargained for is to go; the grantee in a deed of bargain and sale.

BARGAINOR. The party to a bargain who is to perform the contract by delivery of the subject-matter.

BARK. Is sometimes figuratively used to denote the mere words or letter of an instrument, or outer covering of the ideas sought to be expressed, as distinguished from its inner substance or essential meaning. "If the *bark* makes for them, the pith makes for us." Bacon.

BARLEYCORN. In linear measure. The third of an inch.

BARMOTE COURTS. Courts held in certain mining districts belonging to the Duchy of Lancaster, for regulation of the mines, and for deciding questions of title and other matters relating thereto. 3 Steph. Comm. 347, note b.

BARNARD'S INN. An inn of chancery. See INNS OF CHANCERY.

BARO. An old law term signifying, originally, a "man," whether slave or free. In later usage, a "freeman," a "strong man," a "good soldier," a "baron;" also a "vassal," or "feudal tenant or client," and "husband," the last being the most common meaning of the word.

BARON. A lord or nobleman; the most general title of nobility in England. 1 Bl. Comm. 398, 399.

A particular degree or title of nobility, next to a viscount.

A judge of the court of exchequer. 3 Bl. Comm. 44; Cowell.

A freeman. Co. Litt. 58*a*. Also a vassal holding directly from the king.

A husband; occurring in this sense in the phrase "*baron et feme*," husband and wife.

BARON AND FEME. Husband and wife. A wife being under the protection and influence of her *baron*, lord, or husband, is styled a "*feme-covert*," (*fœmina viro cooperta*,) and her state of marriage is called her "coverture."

BARONAGE. In English law. The collective body of the barons, or of the nobility at large. Spelman.

BARONET. An English name or title of dignity, (but not a title of nobility,) established A. D. 1611 by James I. It is created by letters patent, and descends to the male heir. Spelman.

BARONS OF THE CINQUE PORTS. Members of parliament from these ports, viz.: Sandwich, Romney, Hastings, Hythe, and Dover. Winchelsea and Rye have been added.

BARONS OF THE EXCHEQUER. The six judges of the court of exchequer in England, of whom one is styled the "chief baron;" answering to the justices and chief justice of other courts.

BARONY. The dignity of a baron; a species of tenure; the territory or lands held by a baron. Spelman.

BARONY OF LAND. In England, a quantity of land amounting to 15 acres. In Ireland, a subdivision of a county.

BARRA, or BARRE. In old practice. A plea in bar. The bar of the court. A barrister.

BARRATOR. One who is guilty of the crime of barratry.

BARRATROUS. Fraudulent; having the character of barratry.

BARRATRY. In maritime law. An act committed by the master or mariners of a vessel, for some unlawful or fraudulent purpose, contrary to their duty to the owners, whereby the latter sustain injury. It may include negligence, if so gross as to evidence fraud. 8 Cranch, 49; 2 Cush. 511; 3 Pet. 230.

Barratry is some fraudulent act of the master or mariners, tending to their own benefit, to the prejudice of the owner of the vessel, without his privity or consent. 2 Caines, 67.

Barratry is a generic term, which includes many acts of various kinds and degrees. It comprehends any unlawful, fraudulent, or dishonest act of the master or mariners, and every violation of duty by them arising from gross and culpable negligence contrary to their duty to the owner of the vessel, and which might work loss or injury to him in the course of the voyage insured. A mutiny of the crew, and forcible dispossession by them of the master and other officers from the ship, is a form of barratry. 9 Allen, 217.

In criminal law. Common barratry is the practice of exciting groundless judicial proceedings. Pen. Code Cal. § 158; Pen. Code Dak. § 191.

Also spelled "Barretry," which see.

In Scotch law. The crime committed by a judge who receives a bribe for his judgment. Skene; Brande.

BARREL. A measure of capacity, equal to thirty-six gallons.

In agricultural and mercantile parlance, as also in the inspection laws, the term "barrel" means, *prima facie*, not merely a certain quantity, but, further, a certain state of the article; namely, that it is in a cask. 11 Ired. 72.

BARREN MONEY. In the civil law. A debt which bears no interest.

BARRENNESS. Sterility; the incapacity to bear children.

BARRETOR. In criminal law. A common mover, exciter, or maintainer of suits and quarrels either in courts or elsewhere in the country; a disturber of the peace who spreads false rumors and calumnies, whereby discord and disquiet may grow among neighbors. Co. Litt. 368.

BARRETRY. In criminal law. The act or offense of a barretor, (*q. v.;*) usually called "common barretry." The offense of frequently exciting and stirring up suits and quarrels, either at law or otherwise. 4 Bl. Comm. 134; 4 Steph. Comm. 262.

BARRIER. In mining law and the usage of miners, is a wall of coal left between two mines.

BARRISTER. In English law. An advocate; one who has been called to the bar. A counsellor learned in the law who pleads at the bar of the courts, and who is engaged in conducting the trial or argument of causes. To be distinguished from the *attorney*, who draws the pleadings, prepares the testimony, and conducts matters out of court.

Inner barrister. A serjeant or king's counsel who pleads within the bar.

Ouster barrister. One who pleads "ouster" or without the bar.

Vacation barrister. A counsellor newly called to the bar, who is to attend for several long vacations the exercise of the house.

BARTER. A contract by which parties exchange goods or commodities for other goods. It differs from *sale*, in this: that in the latter transaction goods or property are always exchanged for money.

This term is not applied to contracts concerning land, but to such only as relate to goods and chattels. Barter is a contract by which the parties exchange goods. 4 Biss. 123.

BARTON. In old English law. The demesne land of a manor; a farm distinct from the mansion.

BAS CHEVALIERS. In old English law. Low, or inferior knights, by tenure of a base military fee, as distinguished from *barons* and *bannerets*, who were the chief or superior knights. Cowell.

BAS VILLE. In French law. The suburbs of a town.

BASE COURT. In English law. Any inferior court that is not of record, as a court baron, etc. Kitch. 95, 96; Cowell.

BASE ESTATE. The estate which "base tenants" (*q. v.*) have in their land. Cowell.

BASE FEE. In English law. An estate or fee which has a qualification subjoined thereto, and which must be determined whenever the qualification annexed to it is at an end. 2 Bl. Comm. 109.

BASE-INFEFTMENT. In Scotch law. A disposition of lands by a vassal, to be held of himself.

BASE RIGHT. In Scotch law. A subordinate right; the right of a subvassal in the lands held by him. Bell.

BASE SERVICES. In feudal law. Such services as were unworthy to be performed by the nobler men, and were performed by the peasants and those of servile rank. 2 Bl. Comm. 61.

BASE TENANTS. Tenants who performed to their lords services in villenage; tenants who held at the will of the lord, as distinguished from *frank* tenants, or freeholders. Cowell.

BASE TENURE. A tenure by villenage, or other customary service, as distinguished from tenure by military service; or from tenure by free service. Cowell.

BASILEUS. A Greek word, meaning "king." A title assumed by the emperors of the Eastern Roman Empire. It is used by Justinian in some of the Novels; and is said to have been applied to the English kings before the Conquest. See 1 Bl. Comm. 242.

BASILICA. The name given to a compilation of Roman and Greek law, prepared about A. D. 880 by the Emperor Basilius, and published by his successor, Leo the Philosopher. It was written in Greek, was mainly an abridgment of Justinian's *Corpus Juris*, and comprised sixty books, only a portion of which are extant. It remained the law of the Eastern Empire until the fall of Constantinople, in 1453.

BASILS. In old English law. A kind of money or coin abolished by Henry II.

BASIN. In admiralty law and marine insurance. A part of the sea inclosed in rocks. 13 Amer. Jur. 286.

BASKET TENURE. In feudal law. Lands held by the service of making the king's baskets.

BASSE JUSTICE. In feudal law. Low justice; the right exercised by feudal lords of personally trying persons charged with trespasses or minor offenses.

BASTARD. An illegitimate child; a child born of an unlawful intercourse, and while its parents are not united in marriage.

A child born after marriage, but under circumstances which render it impossible that the husband of his mother can be his father. 6 Bin. 283.

One begotten and born out of lawful wedlock. 2 Kent, Comm. 208.

One born of an illicit union. Civil Code La. arts. 29, 199.

A bastard is a child born out of wedlock, and whose parents do not subsequently intermarry, or a child the issue of adulterous intercourse of the wife during wedlock. Code Ga. 1882, § 1797.

BASTARD EIGNE. In old English law. Bastard elder. If a child was born of an illicit connection, and afterwards the parents intermarried and had another son, the elder was called "*bastard eigne,*" and the younger "*mulier puisne,*" *i. e.*, afterwards born of the wife. See 2 Bl. Comm. 248.

BASTARDA. In old English law. A female bastard. Fleta, lib. 5, c. 5, § 40.

BASTARDIZE. To declare one a bastard, as a court does. To give evidence to prove one a bastard. A mother (married) cannot bastardize her child.

Bastardus nullius est filius, aut filius populi. A bastard is nobody's son, or the son of the people.

Bastardus non potest habere hæredem nisi de corpore suo legitime procreatum. A bastard can have no heir unless it be one lawfully begotten of his own body. Tray. Lat. Max. 51.

BASTARDY. The offense of begetting a bastard child. The condition of a bastard.

BASTARDY PROCESS. The method provided by statute of proceeding against the putative father to secure a proper maintenance for the bastard.

BASTON. In old English law, a baton, club, or staff. A term applied to officers of the wardens of the prison called the "Fleet," because of the staff carried by them. Cowell; Spelman; Termes de la Ley.

BATABLE-GROUND. Land that is in controversy, or about the possession of which there is a dispute, as the lands which were situated between England and Scotland before the Union. Skene.

BATAILLE. In old English law. Battel; the trial by combat or *duellum.*

BATH, KNIGHTS OF THE. In English law. A military order of knighthood, instituted by Richard II. The order was newly regulated by notifications in the London Gazette of 25th May, 1847, and 16th August, 1850. Wharton.

BATIMENT. In French marine law. A vessel or ship.

BATONNIER. The chief of the French bar in its various centres, who presides in the council of discipline. Arg. Fr. Merc. Law, 546.

BATTEL. Trial by combat; wager of battel.

BATTEL, WAGER OF. In old English law. A form of trial anciently used in military cases, arising in the court of chivalry and honor, in appeals of felony, in criminal cases, and in the obsolete real action called a "writ of action." The question at issue was decided by the result of a personal combat between the parties, or, in the case of a writ of right, between their champions.

BATTERY. Any unlawful beating, or other wrongful physical violence or constraint, inflicted on a human being without his consent. 2 Bish. Crim. Law, § 71.

A battery is a willful and unlawful use of force or violence upon the person of another. Pen. Code Cal. § 242; Pen. Code Dak. § 306.

The actual offer to use force to the injury of an other person is *assault;* the use of it is *battery;* hence the two terms are commonly combined in the term "assault and battery."

BATTURE. In Louisiana. A marine term used to denote a bottom of sand, stone, or rock mixed together and rising towards the surface of the water; an elevation of the bed of a river under the surface of the water, since it is rising towards it; sometimes, however, used to denote the same elevation of the bank when it has risen above the surface of the water, or is as high as the land on the outside of the bank. In this latter sense it is synonymous with "alluvion." It means, in common-law language, land formed by accretion. 2 Amer. & Eng. Enc. Law, 157. See 6 Mart. (La.) 216; 3 Woods, 117.

BAWD. One who procures opportunities for persons of opposite sexes to cohabit in an illicit manner; who may be, while exercising the trade of a bawd, perfectly innocent of committing in his or her own proper person the crime either of adultery or of fornication. See 4 Mo. 216.

BAWDY-HOUSE. A house of prostitution; a brothel. A house or dwelling maintained for the convenience and resort of persons desiring unlawful sexual connection.

BAY. A pond-head made of a great height to keep in water for the supply of a mill, etc., so that the wheel of the mill may be turned by the water rushing thence, through a passage or flood-gate. St. 27 Eliz. c. 19. Also an arm of the sea surrounded by land except at the entrance.

In admiralty law and marine insurance. A bending or curving of the shore of the sea or of a lake. 14 N. H. 477. An opening into the land, where the water is shut in on all sides except at the entrance. 13 Amer. Jur. 286.

BAYLEY. In old English law. Bailiff. This term is used in the laws of the colony of New Plymouth, Mass., A. D. 1670, 1671. Burrill.

BAYOU. A species of creek or stream common in Louisiana and Texas. An outlet from a swamp, pond, or lagoon, to a river, or the sea. See 8 How. 48, 70.

BEACH. This term, in its ordinary signification, when applied to a place on tidewaters, means the space between ordinary high and low water mark, or the space over which the tide usually ebbs and flows. It is a term not more significant of a sea margin than "shore." 13 Gray, 257.

The term designates land washed by the sea and its waves; is synonymous with "shore." 28 Me. 180.

When used in reference to places near the sea, beach means the land between the lines of high water and low water, over which the tide ebbs and flows. 48 Me. 68.

Beach means the shore or strand. 15 Me. 237.

Beach, when used in reference to places anywhere in the vicinity of the sea, means the territory lying between the lines of high water and low water, over which the tide ebbs and flows. It is in this respect synonymous with "shore," "strand," or "flats." 5 Gray, 328, 335.

Beach generally denotes land between high and low water mark. 6 Hun, 257.

To "beach" a ship is to run it upon the beach or shore; this is frequently found necessary in case of fire, a leak, etc.

BEACON. A light-house, or sea-mark, formerly used to alarm the country, in case of the approach of an enemy, but now used for the guidance of ships at sea, by night, as well as by day.

BEACONAGE. Money paid for the maintenance of a beacon or signal-light.

BEADLE. In English ecclesiastical law. An inferior parish officer, who is chosen by the vestry, and whose business is to attend the vestry, to give notice of its meetings, to execute its orders, to attend upon inquests, and to assist the constables. Wharton.

BEAMS AND BALANCE. Instruments for weighing goods and merchandise.

BEAR. In the language of the stock exchange, this term denotes one who speculates for a fall in the market.

BEARER. One who carries or holds a thing. When a check, note, draft, etc., is payable to "bearer," it imports that the contents thereof shall be payable to any person who may present the instrument for payment.

BEARERS. In old English law. Those who bore down upon or oppressed others; maintainers. Cowell.

BEARING DATE. Disclosing a date on its face; having a certain date. These words are often used in conveyancing, and in pleading, to introduce the date which has been put upon an instrument.

BEAST. An animal; a domestic animal; a quadruped, such as may be used for food or in labor or for sport.

BEASTGATE. In Suffolk, England, imports land and common for one beast. 2 Strange, 1084; Rosc. Real Act. 485.

BEASTS OF THE CHASE. In English law. The buck, doe, fox, martin, and roe. Co. Litt. 233*a*.

BEASTS OF THE FOREST. In English law. The hart, hind, hare, boar, and wolf. Co. Litt. 233*a*.

BEASTS OF THE PLOW. An old term for animals employed in the operations of husbandry.

BEASTS OF THE WARREN. In English law. Hares, coneys, and roes. Co. Litt. 233; 2 Bl. Comm. 39.

BEAT. To beat, in a legal sense, is not merely to whip, wound, or hurt, but includes any unlawful imposition of the hand or arm. The slightest touching of another in anger is a battery. 60 Ga. 511.

BEAU-PLEADER, (to plead fairly.) In English law. An obsolete writ upon the statute of Marlbridge, (52 Hen. III. c. 11,) which enacts that neither in the circuits of the justices, nor in counties, hundreds, or courts-baron, any fines shall be taken for fair-pleading, *i. e.*, for not pleading fairly or aptly to the purpose; upon this statute, then, this writ was ordained, addressed to the sheriff, bailiff, or him who shall demand such fine, prohibiting him to demand it; an *alias, pluries*, and attachment followed. Fitzh. Nat. Brev. 596.

BED. The hollow or channel of a water-course; the depression between the banks worn by the regular and usual flow of the water.

"The *bed* is that soil so usually covered by water as to be distinguishable from the banks by the character of the soil, or vegetation, or both, produced by the common presence and action of flowing water." Curtis, J., 13 How. 426.

The term also occurs in the phrase "divorce from bed and board," *a mensa et thoro;* where it seems to indicate the right of cohabitation or marital intercourse.

BED OF JUSTICE. In old French law. The seat or throne upon which the king sat when personally present in parliament; hence it signified the parliament itself.

BEDEL. In English law. A crier or messenger of court, who summons men to appear and answer therein. Cowell.

An officer of the forest, similar to a sheriff's special bailiff. Cowell.

A collector of rents for the king. Plowd. 199, 200.

A well-known parish officer. See BEADLE.

BEDELARY. The jurisdiction of a bedel, as a bailiwick is the jurisdiction of a bailiff. Co. Litt. 234*b;* Cowell.

BEDEREPE. A service which certain tenants were anciently bound to perform, as to reap their landlord's corn at harvest. Said by Whishaw to be still in existence in some parts of England. Blount; Cowell; Whishaw.

BEER. A liquor compounded of malt and hops.

In its ordinary sense, denotes a beverage which is intoxicating, and is within the fair meaning of the words "strong or spirituous liquors," used in the statutes on this subject. 3 Park. Crim. R. 9; 3 Denio, 437; 21 N. Y. 173. To the contrary, 20 Barb. 246.

BEER-HOUSE. In English law. A place where beer is sold to be consumed on the premises; as distinguished from a "beer-shop," which is a place where beer is sold to be consumed off the premises. 16 Ch. Div. 721.

BEFORE. Prior to; preceding. In the presence of; under the official purview of; as in a magistrate's jurat, "*before* me personally appeared," etc.

In the absence of any statutory provision governing the computation of time, the authorities are uniform that, where an act is required to be done a certain number of days or weeks *before* a certain other day upon which another act is to be done, the day upon which the first act is done is to be excluded from the computation, and the whole number of the days or weeks must intervene before the day fixed for doing the second act. 63 Wis. 44, 22 N. W. Rep. 844, and cases cited.

BEG. To solicit alms or charitable aid. The act of a cripple in passing along the sidewalk and silently holding out his hand and receiving money from passers-by is "begging for alms," within the meaning of a statute which uses that phrase. 3 Abb. N. C. 65.

BEGA. A land measure used in the East Indies. In Bengal it is equal to about a third part of an acre.

BEGGAR. One who lives by begging charity, or who has no other means of support than solicited alms.

BEGUM. In India. A lady, princess, woman of high rank.

BEHALF. A witness testifies on "behalf" of the party who calls him, notwithstanding his evidence proves to be adverse to that party's case. 65 Ill. 274. See, further, 12 Q. B. 693; 18 Q. B. 512.

BEHAVIOR. Manner of behaving, whether good or bad; conduct; manners; carriage of one's self, with respect to propriety and morals; deportment. Webster.

Surety to be of good *behavior* is said to be a larger requirement than surety to keep the peace.

BEHETRIA. In Spanish law. Lands situated in places where the inhabitants had the right to select their own lords.

BEHOOF. Use; benefit; profit; service; advantage. It occurs in conveyances, *e. g.*, "to his and their use and behoof."

BELIEF. A conviction of the truth of a proposition, existing subjectively in the mind, and induced by argument, persuasion, or proof addressed to the judgment. Belief is to be distinguished from "proof," "evidence," and "testimony." See EVIDENCE.

With regard to things which make not a very deep impression on the memory, it may be called "belief." "Knowledge" is nothing more than a man's firm belief. The difference is ordinarily merely in the degree; to be judged of by the court, when addressed to the court; by the jury, when addressed to the jury. 9 Gray, 274.

The distinction between the two mental conditions seems to be that knowledge is an assurance of a fact or proposition founded on perception by the senses, or intuition; while belief is an assurance gained by evidence, and from other persons. Abbott.

BELLIGERENT. In international law. A term used to designate either of two nations which are actually in a state of war with each other, as well as their allies actively co-operating; as distinguished from a nation which takes no part in the war and maintains a strict indifference as between the contending parties, called a "neutral."

Bello parta cedunt reipublicæ. Things acquired in war belong or go to the state. 1 Kent, Comm. 101; 5 C. Rob. Adm. 173, 181; 1 Gall. 558. The right to all captures vests primarily in the sovereign. A fundamental maxim of public law.

BELLUM. In public law. War. An armed contest between nations; the state of those who forcibly contend with each other. *Jus belli*, the law of war.

BELOW. In practice. Inferior; of inferior jurisdiction, or jurisdiction in the first instance. The court from which a cause is removed for review is called the "court *below.*"

Preliminary; auxiliary or instrumental. Bail to the sheriff is called "bail *below*," as being preliminary to and intended to secure the putting in of bail above, or special bail.

BENCH. A seat of judgment or tribunal for the administration of justice; the seat occupied by judges in courts; also the court itself, as the "King's Bench," or the aggregate of the judges composing a court, as in the phrase "before the full bench."

The collective body of the judges in a state or nation, as distinguished from the body of attorneys and advocates, who are called the "bar."

In English ecclesiastical law. The aggregate body of bishops.

BENCH WARRANT. Process issued by the court itself, or "from the bench," for the attachment or arrest of a person; either in case of contempt, or where an indictment has been found, or to bring in a witness who does not obey the *subpœna*. So called to distinguish it from a warrant issued by a justice of the peace, alderman, or commissioner.

BENCHERS. In English law. Seniors in the inns of court, usually, but not necessarily, queen's counsel, elected by co-optation, and having the entire management of the property of their respective inns.

BENE. Lat. Well; in proper form; legally; sufficiently.

Benedicta est expositio quando res redimitur à destructione. 4 Coke, 26. Blessed is the exposition when anything is saved from destruction. It is a laudable interpretation which gives effect to the instrument, and does not allow its purpose to be frustrated.

BENEFICE. In ecclesiastical law. In its technical sense, this term includes ecclesiastical preferments to which rank or public office is attached, otherwise described as ecclesiastical dignities or offices, such as bishoprics, deaneries, and the like; but in popular acceptation, it is almost invariably appropriated to rectories, vicarages, perpetual curacies, district churches, and endowed chapelries. 3 Steph. Comm. 77.

"Benefice" is a term derived from the feudal law, in which it signified a permanent stipendiary estate, or an estate held by feudal tenure. 3 Steph. Comm. 77, note *i;* 4 Bl. Comm. 107.

BÉNÉFICE DE DISCUSSION. In French law. Benefit of discussion. The right of a guarantor to require that the creditor should exhaust his recourse against the principal debtor before having recourse to the guarantor himself.

BÉNÉFICE DE DIVISION. In French law. Benefit of division; right of contribution as between co-sureties.

BÉNÉFICE D'INVENTAIRE. In French law. A term which corresponds to the *beneficium inventarii* of Roman law, and substantially to the English law doctrine that the executor properly accounting is only liable to the extent of the assets received by him.

BÉNÉFICIAIRE. In French law. The person in whose favor a promissory note or bill of exchange is payable; or any person in whose favor a contract of any description is executed. Arg. Fr. Merc. Law, 547.

BENEFICIAL. Tending to the benefit of a person; yielding a profit, advantage, or benefit; enjoying or entitled to a benefit or profit. This term is applied both to estates (as a "beneficial interest") and to persons, (as "the beneficial owner.")

BENEFICIAL ENJOYMENT. The enjoyment which a man has of an estate in his own right and for his own benefit, and not as trustee for another. 11 H. L. Cas. 271.

BENEFICIAL INTEREST. Profit, benefit, or advantage resulting from a contract, or the ownership of an estate as distinct from the legal ownership or control.

BENEFICIAL POWER. In New York law and practice. A power which has for its object the donee of the power, and which is to be executed solely for his benefit; as distinguished from a trust power, which has for its object a person other than the donee, and is to be executed solely for the benefit of such person. 73 N. Y. 234; Rev. St. N. Y. § 79.

BENEFICIARY. A term suggested by Judge Story as a substitute for *cestui que trust*, and adopted to some extent. 1 Story, Eq. Jur. § 321.

He that is in possession of a benefice; also a *cestui que trust*, or person having the enjoyment of property, of which a trustee, executor, etc., has the legal possession.

BENEFICIO PRIMO [ECCLESIASTICO HABENDO.] In English law. An ancient writ, which was addressed by the king to the lord chancellor, to bestow the benefice that should *first* fall in the royal gift, above or under a specified value, upon a person named therein. Reg. Orig. 307.

BENEFICIUM. In early feudal law. A benefice; a permanent stipendiary estate; the same with what was afterwards called a "fief," "feud," or "fee." 3 Steph. Comm. 77, note *i;* Spelman.

In the civil law. A benefit or favor; any particular privilege. Dig. 1, 4, 3; Cod. 7, 71; Mackeld. Rom. Law, § 196.

A general term applied to ecclesiastical livings. 4 Bl. Comm. 107; Cowell.

BENEFICIUM ABSTINENDI. In Roman law. The power of an heir to abstain from accepting the inheritance. Sandars, Just. Inst. (5th Ed.) 214.

BENEFICIUM CEDENDARUM ACTIONUM. In Roman law. The privilege by which a surety could, before paying the creditor, compel him to make over to him the actions which belonged to the stipulator, so as to avail himself of them. Sandars, Just. Inst. (5th Ed.) 332, 351.

BENEFICIUM CLERICALE. Benefit of clergy, which see.

BENEFICIUM COMPETENTIÆ. In Scotch law. The privilege of competency. A privilege which the grantor of a gratuitous obligation was entitled to, by which he might retain sufficient for his subsistence, if, before fulfilling the obligation, he was reduced to indigence. Bell.

In the civil law. The right which an insolvent debtor had, among the Romans, on making cession of his property for the benefit of his creditors, to retain what was required for him to live honestly according to his condition. 7 Toullier, n. 258.

BENEFICIUM DIVISIONIS. In civil and Scotch law. The privilege of one of several co-sureties (cautioners) to insist upon paying only his *pro rata* share of the debt. Bell.

BENEFICIUM INVENTARII. See BENEFIT OF INVENTORY.

Beneficium non datum nisi propter officium. Hob. 148. A remuneration not given, unless on account of a duty performed.

BENEFICIUM ORDINIS. In civil and Scotch law. The privilege of order. The privilege of a surety to require that the creditor should first proceed against the principal and exhaust his remedy against him, before resorting to the surety. Bell.

BENEFICIUM SEPARATIONIS. In the civil law. The right to have the goods of an heir separated from those of the testator in favor of creditors.

BENEFIT BUILDING SOCIETY. The original name for what is now more commonly called a "building society," (*q. v.*)

BENEFIT OF CESSION. In the civil law. The release of a debtor from future imprisonment for his debts, which the law operates in his favor upon the surrender of his property for the benefit of his creditors. Poth. Proc. Civil, pt. 5, c. 2, § 1.

BENEFIT OF CLERGY. In its original sense, the phrase denoted the exemption which was accorded to clergymen from the jurisdiction of the secular courts, or from arrest or attachment on criminal process issuing from those courts in certain particular cases. Afterwards, it meant a privilege of exemption from the punishment of death accorded to such persons as were *clerks*, or who could read.

This privilege of exemption from capital punishment was anciently allowed to clergymen only, but afterwards to all who were connected with the church, even to its most subordinate officers, and at a still later time to all persons who could read, (then called "clerks,") whether ecclesiastics or laymen. It does not appear to have been extended to cases of high treason, nor did it apply to mere misdemeanors. The privilege was claimed after the person's conviction, by a species of motion in arrest of judgment, technically called "praying his clergy." As a means of testing his clerical character, he was given a psalm to read, (usually, or always, the fifty-first,) and, upon his reading it correctly, he was turned over to the ecclesiastical courts, to be tried by the bishop or a jury of twelve clerks. These heard him on oath, with his witnesses and compurgators, who attested their belief in his innocence. This privilege operated greatly to mitigate the extreme rigor of the criminal laws, but was found to involve such gross abuses that parliament began to enact that certain crimes should be felonies "without benefit of clergy," and finally, by St. 7 Geo. IV. c. 28, § 6, it was altogether abolished. The act of congress of April 30, 1790, § 30, provided that there should be no benefit of clergy for any capital crime against the United States, and, if this privilege formed a part of the common law of the several states before the Revolution, it no longer exists.

BENEFIT OF DISCUSSION. In the civil law. The right which a surety has to cause the property of the principal debtor to be applied in satisfaction of the obligation in the first instance. Civil Code La. arts. 3014–3020.

In Scotch law. That whereby the antecedent heir, such as the heir of line in a pursuit against the heir of tailzie, etc., must be first pursued to fulfill the defunct's deeds and pay his debts. This benefit is likewise competent in many cases to cautioners.

BENEFIT OF DIVISION. Same as *beneficium divisionis*, (*q. v.*)

BENEFIT OF INVENTORY. In the civil law. The privilege which the heir obtains of being liable for the charges and debts of the succession, only to the value of the effects of the succession, by causing an inventory of these effects within the time and manner prescribed by law. Civil Code La. art. 1032.

BENEFIT SOCIETIES. Under this and several similar names, in various states, corporations exist to receive periodical payments from members, and hold them as a fund to be loaned or given to members needing pecuniary relief. Such are beneficial societies of Maryland, fund associations of Missouri, loan and fund associations of Massachusetts, mechanics' associations of Michigan, protection societies of New Jersey. Friendly societies in Great Britain are a still more extensive and important species belonging to this class. Abbott.

BENERTH. A feudal service rendered by the tenant to his lord with plow and cart. Cowell.

BENEVOLENCE. The doing a kind or helpful action towards another, under no obligation except an ethical one.

Is no doubt distinguishable from the words "liberality" and "charity;" for, although many charitable institutions are very properly called "benevolent," it is impossible to say that every object of a man's benevolence is also an object of his charity. 3 Mer. 17.

In public law. Nominally a voluntary gratuity given by subjects to their king, but in reality a tax or forced loan.

BENEVOLENT. This word is certainly more indefinite, and of far wider range, than "charitable" or "religious;" it would include all gifts prompted by good-will or kind feeling towards the recipient, whether an object of charity or not. The natural and usual meaning of the word would so extend it. It has no legal meaning separate from its usual meaning. "Charitable" has acquired a settled limited meaning in law, which confines it within known limits. But in all the decisions in England on the subject it has been held that a devise or bequest for benevolent objects, or in trust to give to such objects, is too indefinite, and therefore void. 19 N. J. Eq. 307, 313; 20 N. J. Eq. 489.

This word, as applied to objects or purposes, may refer to those which are in their nature charitable, and may also have a broader meaning and include objects and purposes not charitable in the legal sense of that word. Acts of kindness, friendship, forethought, or good-will might properly be described as benevolent. It has therefore been held that gifts to trustees to be applied for "benevolent purposes" at their discretion, or to such "benevolent purposes" as they could agree upon, do not create a public charity. But where the word is used in connection with other words explanatory of its meaning, and indicating the intent of the donor to limit it to purposes strictly charitable, it has been held to be synonymous with, or equivalent to, "charitable." 132 Mass. 413. See, also, 111 Mass. 268; 31 N. J. Eq. 695; 23 Minn. 92.

BENEVOLENT SOCIETIES. In English law. Societies established and registered under the friendly societies act, 1875, for any charitable or benevolent purposes.

Benigne faciendæ sunt interpretationes chartarum, ut res magis valeat quam pereat; et quælibet concessio fortissime contra donatorem interpretanda est. Liberal interpretations are to be made of deeds, so that the purpose may rather stand than fall; and every grant is to be taken most strongly against the grantor. 4 Mass. 134; 1 Sandf. Ch. 258, 268.

Benigne faciendæ sunt interpretationes, propter simplicitatem laicorum, ut res magis valeat quam pereat. Constructions [of written instruments] are to be made liberally, on account of the simplicity of the laity, [or common people,] in order that the thing [or subject-matter] may rather have effect than perish, [or become void.] Co. Litt. 36*a;* Broom, Max. 540.

Benignior sententia in verbis generalibus seu dubiis, est præferenda. 4 Coke, 15. The more favorable construction is to be placed on general or doubtful expressions.

Benignius leges interpretandæ sunt quo voluntas earum conservetur. Laws are to be more liberally interpreted, in order that their intent may be preserved. Dig. 1, 3, 18.

BEQUEATH. To give personal property by will to another. 13 Barb. 106. The word may be construed *devise*, so as to pass real estate. Wig. Wills, 11.

BEQUEST. A gift by will of personal property; a legacy.

A *specific* bequest is one whereby the testator gives to the legatee all his property of a certain class or kind; as all his pure personalty.

A *residuary* bequest is a gift of all the remainder of the testator's personal estate, after payment of debts and legacies, etc.

An *executory* bequest is the bequest of a future, deferred, or contingent interest in personalty.

BERCARIA. In old English law, a sheepfold; also a place where the bark of trees was laid to tan.

BERCARIUS, OR BERCATOR. A shepherd.

BEREWICHA, or BEREWICA. In old English law. A term used in Domesday for a village or hamlet belonging to some town or manor.

BERGHMAYSTER. An officer having charge of a mine. A bailiff or chief officer among the Derbyshire miners, who, in addition to his other duties, executes the office of coroner among them. Blount; Cowell.

BERGHMOTH, or BERGHMOTE. The ancient name of the court now called "barmote," (*q. v.*)

BERNET. In Saxon law. Burning; the crime of house burning, now called "arson." Cowell; Blount.

BERRA. In old law. A plain; open heath. Cowell.

BERRY, or BURY. A villa or seat of habitation of a nobleman; a dwelling or mansion house; a sanctuary.

BERTON. A large farm; the barn-yard of a large farm.

BES. Lat. In the Roman law. A division of the *as*, or pound, consisting of eight *unciæ*, or duodecimal parts, and amounting to two-thirds of the *as*. 2 Bl. Comm. 462, note *m*.

Two-thirds of an inheritance. Inst. 2, 14, 5.

Eight per cent. interest. 2 Bl. Comm. ubi supra.

BESAILE, BESAYLE. The great-grandfather, *proavus*. 1 Bl. Comm. 186.

BESAYEL, Besaiel, Besayle. In old English law. A writ which lay where a great-grandfather died seised of lands and tenements in fee-simple, and on the day of his death a stranger abated, or entered and kept out the heir. Reg. Orig. 226; Fitzh. Nat. Brev. 221 D; 3 Bl. Comm. 186.

BEST EVIDENCE. Primary evidence, as distinguished from secondary; original, as distinguished from substitutionary; the best and highest evidence of which the nature of the case is susceptible. A written instrument is itself always regarded as the primary or best possible evidence of its existence and contents; a copy, or the recollection of a witness, would be secondary evidence.

BESTIALITY. Bestiality is the carnal knowledge and connection against the order of nature by man or woman in any manner with a beast. Code Ga. 1882, § 4354.

We take it that there is a difference in signification between the terms "bestiality," and the "crime against nature." *Bestiality* is a connection between a human being and a brute of the opposite sex. *Sodomy* is a connection between two human beings of the same sex,—the male,—named from the prevalence of the sin in *Sodom*. Both may be embraced by the term "crime against nature," as felony embraces murder, larceny, etc., though we think that term is more generally used in reference to sodomy. *Buggery* seems to include both sodomy and bestiality. 10 Ind. 356.

BET. Bet and wager are synonymous terms, and are applied both to the contract of betting or wagering and to the thing or sum bet or wagered. For example, one bets or wagers, or lays a bet or wager of so much, upon a certain result. But these terms cannot properly be applied to the act to be done, or event to happen, upon which the bet or wager is laid. Bets or wagers may be laid upon acts to be done, events to happen, or facts existing or to exist. The bets or wagers may be illegal, and the acts, events, or facts upon which they are laid may not be. Bets or wagers may be laid upon games, and things that are not games. Everything upon which a bet or wager may be laid is not a game. 11 Ind. 16. See, also, 81 N. Y. 539.

BETROTHMENT. Mutual promise of marriage; the plighting of troth; a mutual promise or contract between a man and woman competent to make it, to marry at a future time.

BETTER EQUITY. The right which, in a court of equity, a second incumbrancer has who has taken securities against subsequent dealings to his prejudice, which a prior incumbrancer neglected to take although he had an opportunity. 1 Ch. Prec. 470, n.; 4 Rawle, 144. See 3 Bouv. Inst. n. 2462.

BETTERMENTS. Improvements put upon an estate which enhance its value more than mere repairs. The term is also applied to denote the additional value which an estate acquires in consequence of some public improvement, as laying out or widening a street, etc.

BETWEEN. As a measure or indication of distance, this word has the effect of excluding the two termini. 1 Mass. 93; 12 Me. 366. Compare 31 N. J. Law, 212.

If an act is to be done "between" two certain days, it must be performed before the commencement of the latter day. In computing the time in such a case, both the days named are to be excluded. 14 Ill. 332; 16 Barb. 352.

In case of a devise to A. and B. "between them," these words create a tenancy in common. 2 Mer. 70.

BEVERAGE. This term is properly used to distinguish a sale of liquors to be drunk for the pleasure of drinking, from liquors to be drunk in obedience to a physician's advice. 142 Mass. 469, 8 N. E. Rep. 327.

BEWARED. O. Eng. Expended. Before the Britons and Saxons had introduced the general use of money, they traded chiefly by exchange of wares. Wharton.

BEYOND SEA. Beyond the limits of the kingdom of Great Britain and Ireland; outside the United States; out of the state.

Beyond sea, beyond the four seas, beyond the seas, and out of the realm, are synonymous. Prior to the union of the two crowns of England and Scotland, on the accession of James I., the phrases "beyond the four seas," "beyond the seas," and "out of the realm," signified out of the limits of the realm of England. 1 Har. & J. 350.

In Pennsylvania, it has been construed to mean "without the limits of the United States," which approaches the literal signification. 2 Dall. 217; 1 Yeates, 329; 6 Pet. 291, 300. The same construction has been given to it in Missouri. 20 Mo. 530. See Ang. Lim. §§ 200, 201.

The term "beyond seas," in the proviso or saving clause of a statute of limitations, is equivalent to without the limits of the state where the statute is enacted; and the party who is without those limits is entitled to the benefit of the exception. 3 Cranch, 174; 3 Wheat. 541; 11 Wheat. 361; 1 McLean, 146; 2 McCord, 331; 8 Ark. 488; 26 Ga. 182; 13 N. H. 79.

BIAS. This term is not synonymous with "prejudice." By the use of this word in a statute declaring disqualification of jurors, the legislature intended to describe another and somewhat different ground of disqualification. A man cannot be prejudiced against another without being biased against him; but he may be biased without being prejudiced. Bias is "a particular influential power, which sways the judgment; the inclination of the mind towards a particular object." It is not to be supposed that the legislature expected to secure in the juror a state of mind absolutely free from all inclination to one side or the other. The statute means that, although a juror has not formed a judgment for or against the prisoner, before the evidence is heard on the trial, yet, if he is under such an influence as so sways his mind to the one side or the other as to prevent his deciding the cause according to the evidence, he is incompetent. 12 Ga. 444.

BID. An offer by an intending purchaser to pay a designated price for property which is about to be sold at auction.

BIDAL, or BIDALL. An invitation of friends to drink ale at the house of some poor man, who hopes thereby to be relieved by charitable contribution. It is something like "house-warming," *i. e.*, a visit of friends to a person beginning to set up house-keeping. Wharton.

BIDDER. One who offers to pay a specified price for an article offered for sale at a public auction. 11 Ill. 254.

BIDDINGS. Offers of a designated price for goods or other property put up for sale at auction.

BIELBRIEF. Germ. In European maritime law. A document furnished by the builder of a vessel, containing a register of her admeasurement, particularizing the length, breadth, and dimensions of every part of the ship. It sometimes also contains the terms of agreement between the party for whose account the ship is built, and the ship-builder. It has been termed in English the "grand bill of sale;" in French, "*contrat de construction ou de la vente d'un vaisseau*," and corresponds in a great degree with the English, French, and American "register," (*q. v.*,) being an equally essential document to the lawful ownership of vessels. Jac. Sea Laws, 12, 13, and note. In the Danish law, it is used to denote the contract of bottomry.

BIENNIALLY. This term, in a statute, signifies, not duration of time, but a period for the happening of an event; once in every two years. 9 Hun, 573; 68 N. Y. 479.

BIENS. In English law. Property of every description, except estates of freehold and inheritance. Sugd. Vend. 495; Co. Litt. 119*b*.

In French law. This term includes all kinds of property, real and personal. *Biens* are divided into *biens meubles*, movable property; and *biens immeubles*, immovable property. The distinction between movable and immovable property is recognized by the continental jurists, and gives rise, in the civil as well as in the common law, to many important distinctions as to rights and remedies. Story, Confl. Laws, § 13, note 1.

BIGA, or BIGATA. A cart or chariot drawn with two horses, coupled side to side; but it is said to be properly a cart with two wheels, sometimes drawn by one horse; and in the ancient records it is used for any cart, wain, or wagon. Jacob.

BIGAMUS. In the civil law. A man who was twice married; one who at different times and successively has married two wives. 4 Inst. 88. One who has two wives living. One who marries a widow.

Bigamus seu trigamus, etc., est qui diversis temporibus et successivè duas seu tres uxores habuit. 4 Inst. 88. A bigamus or trigamus, etc., is one who at different times and successively has married two or three wives.

BIGAMY. The criminal offense of willfully and knowingly contracting a second marriage (or going through the form of a second marriage) while the first marriage, to the knowledge of the offender, is still subsisting and undissolved.

The state of a man who has two wives, or of a woman who has two husbands, living at the same time.

The offense of having a plurality of wives at the same time is commonly denominated "polygamy;" but the name "bigamy" has been more frequently given to it in legal proceedings. 1 Russ. Crimes, 185.

The use of the word "bigamy" to describe this offense is well established by long usage, although often criticised as a corruption of the true meaning of the word. Polygamy is suggested as the correct term, instead of bigamy, to designate the offense of having a plurality of wives or husbands at the same time, and has been adopted for that purpose in the Massachusetts statutes. But as the substance of the offense is marrying a second time, while having a lawful husband or wife living, without regard to the number of marriages that may have taken place, bigamy seems not an inappropriate term. The objection to its use urged by Blackstone (4 Bl. Comm. 163) seems to be founded not so much upon considerations of the etymology of the word as upon the propriety of distinguishing the ecclesiastical offense termed "bigamy" in the canon law, and which is defined below, from the offense known as "bigamy" in the modern criminal law. The same distinction is carefully made by Lord Coke, (4 Inst. 88.) But, the ecclesiastical offense being now obsolete, this reason for substituting polygamy to denote the crime here defined ceases to have weight. Abbott.

In the canon law, the term denoted the offense committed by an ecclesiastic who married two wives successively. It might be committed either by marrying a second wife after the death of a first or by marrying a widow.

BIGOT. An obstinate person, or one that is wedded to an opinion, in matters of religion, etc.

BILAGINES. By-laws of towns; municipal laws.

BILAN. A term used in Louisiana, derived from the French. A book in which bankers, merchants, and traders write a statement of all they owe and all that is due them; a balance-sheet. See 3 Mart. (N. S.) 446.

BILANCIIS DEFERENDIS. In English law. An obsolete writ addressed to a corporation for the carrying of weights to such a haven, there to weigh the wool anciently licensed for transportation. Reg. Orig. 270.

BILATERAL CONTRACT. A term, used originally in the civil law, but now generally adopted, denoting a contract in which both the contracting parties are bound to fulfill obligations reciprocally towards each other; as a contract of sale, where one becomes bound to deliver the thing sold, and the other to pay the price of it.

"Every convention properly so called consists of a promise or mutual promises proffered and accepted. Where one only of the agreeing parties gives a promise, the convention is said to be 'unilateral.' Wherever mutual promises are proffered and accepted, there are, in strictness, two or more conventions. But where the performance of either of the promises is made to depend on the performance of the other, the several conventions are commonly deemed one convention, and the convention is then said to be 'bilateral.'" Aust. Jur. § 308.

BILGED. In admiralty law and marine insurance. That state or condition of a vessel in which water is freely admitted through holes and breaches made in the planks of the bottom, occasioned by injuries, whether the ship's timbers are broken or not. 3 Mass. 39.

BILINE. A word used by Britton in the sense of "collateral." *En line biline*, in the collateral line. Britt. c. 119.

BILINGUIS. Of a double language or tongue; that can speak two languages. A term applied in the old books to a jury composed partly of Englishmen and partly of foreigners, which, by the English law, an alien party to a suit is, in certain cases, entitled to; more commonly called a "jury *de medietate linguæ*." 3 Bl. Comm. 360; 4 Steph. Comm. 422.

BILL. A formal declaration, complaint, or statement of particular things in writing. As a legal term, this word has many meanings and applications, the more important of which are enumerated below.

1. A formal written statement of complaint to a court of justice.

In the ancient practice of the court of king's bench, the usual and orderly method of beginning an action was by a *bill*, or original bill, or plaint. This was a written statement of the plaintiff's cause of action, like a declaration or complaint, and always alleged a trespass as the ground of it, in order to give the court jurisdiction. 3 Bl. Comm. 43.

2. A formal written declaration by a court to its officers, in the nature of process; as the old *bill of Middlesex*.

3. A record or certified written account of the proceedings in an action, or a portion of the same; as *a bill of exceptions*.

4. **In equity practice.** A formal written complaint, in the nature of a petition, addressed by a suitor in chancery to the chancellor or to a court of equity or a court having equitable jurisdiction, showing the names of the parties, stating the facts which make up the case and the complainant's allegations, averring that the acts disclosed are contrary to equity, and praying for process and for specific relief, or for such relief as the circumstances demand.

Bills are said to be original, not original, or in the nature of original bills. They are original when the circumstances constituting the case are not already before the court, and relief is demanded, or the bill is filed for a subsidiary purpose.

5. In legislation and constitutional law, the word means a draft of an act of the legislature before it becomes a law; a proposed or projected law. A draft of an act presented to the legislature, but not enacted. An *act* is the appropriate term for it, after it has been acted on by, and passed by, the legislature. 26 Pa. St. 450.

Also a special act passed by a legislative body in the exercise of a *quasi* judicial power. Thus, bills of attainder, bills of pains and penalties, are spoken of.

In England, "bill" also signifies the draft of a patent for a charter, commission, dignity, office, or appointment; such a bill is drawn up in the attorney general's patent bill office, is submitted by a secretary of state for her majesty's signature, when it is called the "queen's bill;" it is countersigned by the secretary of state, and sealed by the privy seal, and then the patent is prepared and sealed. Sweet.

6. A solemn and formal legislative declaration of popular rights and liberties, promulgated on certain extraordinary occasions; as the famous *Bill of Rights* in English history.

7. **As a contract.** An obligation; a deed, whereby the obligor acknowledges himself to owe unto the obligee a certain sum of money or some other thing, in which, besides the names of the parties, are to be considered the sum or thing due, the time, place, and manner of payment or delivery thereof. It may be indented or poll, and with or without a penalty. West, Symb. §§ 100, 101.

8. A written statement of the terms of a contract, or specification of the items of a demand, or counter-demand.

Also the creditor's written statement of his claim, specifying the items.

9. By the English usage, it is applied to the statement of the charges and disbursements of an attorney or solicitor incurred in the conduct of his client's business, and which might be taxed upon application, even though not incurred in any suit. Thus, conveyancing costs might be taxed. Wharton.

BILL-BOOK. In mercantile law. A book in which an account of bills of exchange and promissory notes, whether payable or receivable, is stated.

BILL CHAMBER. In Scotch law. A department of the court of session in which petitions for suspension, interdict, etc., are entertained. It is equivalent to sittings in chambers in the English and American practice. Paters. Comp.

BILL FOR A NEW TRIAL. In equity practice. A bill in equity in which the specific relief asked is an injunction against the execution of a judgment rendered at law and a new trial in the action, on account of some fact which would render it inequitable to enforce the judgment, but which was not available to the party on the trial at law, or which he was prevented from presenting by fraud or accident, without concurrent fraud or negligence on his own part.

BILL FOR FORECLOSURE. In equity practice. One which is filed by a mortgagee against the mortgagor, for the purpose of having the estate sold, thereby to obtain the sum mortgaged on the premises, with interest and costs. 1 Madd. Ch. Pr. 528.

BILL-HEAD. A printed form on which merchants and traders make out their bills and render accounts to their customers.

BILL IN CHANCERY. See BILL, 4.

BILL IN EQUITY. See BILL, 4.

BILL IN NATURE OF A BILL OF REVIEW. A bill in equity, to obtain a re-examination and reversal of a decree, filed by one who was not a party to the original suit, nor bound by the decree.

BILL IN NATURE OF A BILL OF REVIVOR. Where, on the abatement of a suit, there is such a transmission of the interest of the incapacitated party that the title to it, as well as the person entitled, may be the subject of litigation in a court of chancery, the suit cannot be continued by a mere bill of revivor, but an original bill upon which the title may be litigated must be filed. This is called a "bill in the nature of a bill of revivor." It is founded on privity of estate or title by the act of the party. And the nature and operation of the whole act by which the privity is created is open to controversy. Story, Eq. Pl. §§ 378-380; 2 Amer. & Eng. Enc. Law, 271.

BILL IN NATURE OF A SUPPLEMENTAL BILL. A bill filed when new parties, with new interests, arising from events happening since the suit was commenced, are brought before the court; wherein it differs from a supplemental bill, which is properly applicable to those cases only where the same parties or the same interests remain before the court. Story, Eq. Pl. (5th Ed.) § 345 *et seq.*

BILL OBLIGATORY. A bond absolute for the payment of money. It is called also a "single bill," and differs from a promissory note only in having a seal. 2 Serg. & R. 115.

BILL OF ADVENTURE. A written certificate by a merchant or the master or owner of a ship, to the effect that the property and risk in goods shipped on the vessel in his own name belong to another person, to whom he is accountable for the proceeds alone.

BILL OF ADVOCATION. In Scotch practice. A bill by which the judgment of an inferior court is appealed from, or brought under review of a superior. Bell.

BILL OF APPEAL. An ancient, but now abolished, method of criminal prosecution. See BATTEL.

BILL OF ATTAINDER. A legislative act, directed against a designated person, pronouncing him guilty of an alleged crime, (usually treason,) without trial or conviction according to the recognized rules of procedure, and passing sentence of death and attainder upon him.

"Bills of attainder," as they are technically called, are such special acts of the legislature as inflict capital punishments upon persons supposed to be guilty of high offenses, such as treason and felony, without any conviction in the ordinary course of judicial proceedings. If an act inflicts a milder degree of punishment than death, it is called a "bill of pains and penalties," but both are included in the prohibition in the Federal constitution. Story, Const. § 1344.

BILL OF CERTIORARI. A bill, the object of which is to remove a suit in equity from some inferior court to the court of chancery, or some other superior court of equity, on account of some alleged incompetency of the inferior court, or some injustice in its proceedings. Story, Eq. Pl. (5th Ed.) § 298.

BILL OF CONFORMITY. In equity practice. One filed by an executor or administrator, who finds the affairs of the deceased so much involved that he cannot safely administer the estate except under the direction of a court of chancery. This bill is filed against the creditors, generally, for the purpose of having all their claims adjusted, and procuring a final decree settling the order of payment of the assets. 1 Story, Eq. Jur. § 440.

BILL OF COSTS. A certified, itemized statement of the amount of costs in an action or suit.

BILL OF CREDIT. In constitutional law. A bill or promissory note issued by the government of a state or nation, upon its faith and credit, designed to circulate in the community as money, and redeemable at a future day.

In mercantile law. A license or authority given in writing from one person to another, very common among merchants, bankers, and those who travel, empowering a person to receive or take up money of their correspondents abroad.

BILL OF DEBT. An ancient term including promissory notes and bonds for the payment of money. Com. Dig. "Merchant," F. 2.

BILL OF DISCOVERY. A bill in equity filed to obtain a discovery of facts resting in the knowledge of the defendant, or of deeds or writings, or other things in his custody or power. Story, Eq. Pl. (5th Ed.) § 311.

BILL OF ENTRY. An account of the goods entered at the custom house, both incoming and outgoing. It must state the name of the merchant exporting or importing, the quantity and species of merchandise, and whither transported, and whence.

BILL OF EXCEPTIONS. A formal statement in writing of the objections or exceptions taken by a party during the trial of a cause to the decisions, rulings, or instructions of the trial judge, stating the objection, with the facts and circumstances on which it is founded, and, in order to attest its accuracy, signed and sealed by the judge; the object being to put the controverted rulings or decisions upon the record for the information of the appellate court. 2 Dak. 470, 11 N. W. Rep. 497; Pow. App. Proc. 211.

BILL OF EXCHANGE. A written order from A. to B., directing B. to pay to C. a certain sum of money therein named. Byles, Bills, 1.

An open (that is, unsealed) letter addressed by one person to another directing him, in effect, to pay, absolutely and at all events, a certain sum of money therein named, to a third person, or to any other to whom that third person may order it to be paid, or it may be payable to bearer or to the drawer himself. 1 Daniel, Neg. Inst. 27.

A bill of exchange is an instrument, negotiable in form, by which one, who is called the "drawer," requests another, called the "drawee," to pay a specified sum of money. Civil Code Cal. § 3171.

A bill of exchange is an order by one person, called the "drawer" or "maker," to another, called the "drawee" or "acceptor," to pay money to another, (who may be the drawer himself,) called the "payee," or his order, or to the bearer. If the payee, or a bearer, transfers the bill by indorsement, he then becomes the "indorser." If the drawer or drawee resides out of this state, it is then called a "foreign bill of exchange." Code Ga. 1882, § 2773.

BILL OF GROSS ADVENTURE. In French maritime law. Any written instrument which contains a contract of bottomry, *respondentia*, or any other kind of maritime loan. There is no corresponding English term. Hall, Marit. Loans, 182, n.

BILL OF HEALTH. An official certificate, given by the authorities of a port from which a vessel clears, to the master of the ship, showing the state of the port, as respects the public health, at the time of sailing, and exhibited to the authorities of the port which the vessel next makes, in token that she does not bring disease. If the bill alleges that no contagious or infectious disease existed, it is called a "clean" bill; if it admits that one was suspected or anticipated, or that one actually prevailed, it is called a "touched" or a "foul" bill.

In Scotch law. An application of a person in custody to be discharged on account of ill health. Where the health of a prisoner requires it, he may be indulged, under proper regulations, with such a degree of liberty as may be necessary to restore him. 2 Bell, Comm. (5th Ed.) 549; Paters. Comp. § 1129.

BILL OF INDEMNITY. In English law. An act of parliament, passed every session until 1869, but discontinued in and after that year, as having been rendered unnecessary by the passing of the promissory oaths act, 1868, for the relief of those who have unwittingly or unavoidably neglected to take the necessary oaths, etc., required for the purpose of qualifying them to hold their respective offices. Wharton.

BILL OF INDICTMENT. A formal written document accusing a person or persons named of having committed a felony or misdemeanor, lawfully laid before a grand jury for their action upon it. If the grand jury decide that a trial ought to be had, they indorse on it "a true bill;" if otherwise, "not a true bill" or "not found."

BILL OF INFORMATION. In chancery practice. Where a suit is instituted on behalf of the crown or government, or of those of whom it has the custody by virtue of its prerogative, or whose rights are under its particular protection, the matter of complaint is offered to the court by way of information by the attorney or solicitor general, instead of by petition. Where a suit immediately concerns the crown or government alone, the proceeding is purely by way of information, but, where it does not do so immediately, a relator is appointed, who is answerable for costs, etc., and, if he is interested in the matter in connection with the crown or government, the proceeding is by information and bill. Informations differ from bills in little more than name and form, and the same rules are substantially applicable to both. See Story, Eq. Pl. 5; 1 Daniell, Ch. Pr. 2, 8, 288; 3 Bl. Comm. 261.

BILL OF INTERPLEADER. The name of a bill in equity to obtain a settlement of a question of right to money or other property adversely claimed, in which the party filing the bill has no interest, although it may be in his hands, by compelling such adverse claimants to litigate the right or title between themselves, and relieve him from liability or litigation.

BILL OF LADING. In common law. The written evidence of a contract for the carriage and delivery of goods sent by sea for a certain freight. 1 H. Bl. 359.

A written memorandum, given by the person in command of a merchant vessel, acknowledging the receipt on board the ship of certain specified goods, in good order or "apparent good order," which he undertakes, in consideration of the payment of freight, to deliver in like good order (dangers of the sea excepted) at a designated place to the consignee therein named or to his assigns.

The term is often applied to a similar receipt and undertaking given by a carrier of goods by land.

A bill of lading is an instrument in writing, signed by a carrier or his agent, describing the freight so as to indentify it, stating the name of the consignor, the terms of the contract for carriage, and agreeing or directing that the freight be delivered to the order or assigns of a specified person at a specified place. Civil Code Cal. § 2126; Civil Code Dak. § 1229.

BILL OF MIDDLESEX. An old form of process similar to a *capias*, issued out of the court of king's bench in personal actions, directed to the sheriff of the county of Middlesex, (hence the name,) and commanding him to take the defendant and have him before the king at Westminster on a day named, to answer the plaintiff's complaint.

BILL OF MORTALITY. A written statement or account of the number of deaths which have occurred in a certain district during a given time. In some places, births as well as deaths are included.

BILL OF PAINS AND PENALTIES. A special act of the legislature which inflicts a punishment, less than death, upon persons supposed to be guilty of treason or felony, without any conviction in the ordinary course of judicial proceedings. It differs from a bill of attainder in this: that the punishment inflicted by the latter is death.

BILL OF PARCELS. A statement sent to the buyer of goods, along with the goods, exhibiting in detail the items composing the parcel and their several prices, to enable him to detect any mistake or omission; an invoice.

BILL OF PARTICULARS. In practice. A written statement or specification of the particulars of the demand for which an action at law is brought, or of a defendant's set-off against such demand, (including dates, sums, and items in detail,) furnished by one of the parties to the other, either voluntarily or in compliance with a judge's order for that purpose. 1 Tidd, Pr. 596-600; 2 Archb. Pr. 221.

BILL OF PEACE. In equity practice. One which is filed when a person has a right which may be controverted by various persons, at different times, and by different actions.

BILL OF PRIVILEGE. In old English law. A method of proceeding against attorneys and officers of the court not liable to arrest. 3 Bl. Comm. 289.

BILL OF PROOF. In English practice. The name given, in the mayor's court of London, to a species of intervention by a third person laying claim to the subject-matter in dispute between the parties to a suit.

BILL OF REVIVOR. In equity practice. One which is brought to continue a suit which has abated before its final consummation, as, for example, by death, or marriage of a female plaintiff.

BILL OF REVIVOR AND SUPPLEMENT. In equity practice. One which is a compound of a supplemental bill and bill of revivor, and not only continues the suit, which has abated by the death of the plaintiff, or the like, but supplies any defects in the original bill arising from subsequent events, so as to entitle the party to relief on the whole merits of his case. 5 Johns. Ch. 334; Mitf. Eq. Pl. 32, 74.

BILL OF REVIEW. In equity practice. One which is brought to have a decree of the court reviewed, corrected, or reversed.

BILL OF RIGHTS. A formal and emphatic legislative assertion and declaration of popular rights and liberties usually promulgated upon a change of government; particularly the statute 1 W. & M. St. 2, c. 2. Also the summary of the rights and liberties of the people, or of the principles of constitutional law deemed essential and fundamental, contained in many of the American state constitutions.

BILL OF SALE. In contracts. A written agreement under seal, by which one person assigns or transfers his right to or interest in goods and personal chattels to another.

An instrument by which, in particular, the property in ships and vessels is conveyed.

BILL OF SIGHT. When an importer of goods is ignorant of their exact quantity or quality, so that he cannot make a perfect entry of them, he may give to the customs officer a written description of them, according to the best of his information and belief. This is called a "bill of sight."

BILL OF STORE. In English law. A kind of license granted at the custom-house to merchants, to carry such stores and provisions as are necessary for their voyage, custom free. Jacob.

BILL OF SUFFERANCE. In English law. A license granted at the custom-house to a merchant, to suffer him to trade from one English port to another, without paying custom. Cowell.

BILL PAYABLE. In a merchant's accounts, all bills which he has accepted, and promissory notes which he has made, are called "bills payable," and are entered in a ledger account under that name, and recorded in a book bearing the same title.

BILL PENAL. In contracts. A written obligation by which a debtor acknowledges himself indebted in a certain sum, and binds himself for the payment thereof, in a larger sum, called a "penalty."

BILL QUIA TIMET. A bill invoking the aid of equity "because he fears," that is, because the complainant apprehends an injury to his property rights or interests, from the fault or neglect of another. Such bills are entertained to guard against possible or prospective injuries, and to preserve the means by which existing rights may be protected from future or contingent violations; differing from injunctions, in that the latter correct past and present or imminent and certain injuries. Bisp. Eq. § 568; 2 Story, Eq. Jur. § 826.

BILL RECEIVABLE. In a merchant's accounts, all notes, drafts, checks, etc., payable to him, or of which he is to receive the proceeds at a future date, are called "bills receivable," and are entered in a ledger-account under that name, and also noted in a book bearing the same title.

BILL RENDERED. A bill of items rendered by a creditor to his debtor; an "account rendered," as distinguished from "an account stated."

BILL SINGLE. A written promise to pay to a person or persons named a stated sum at a stated time, without any condition. When under seal, as is usually the case, it is sometimes called a "bill obligatory," (*q. v.*) It differs from a "bill penal," (*q. v.*,) in that it expresses no penalty.

BILL TO CARRY A DECREE INTO EXECUTION. In equity practice. One which is filed when, from the neglect of parties or some other cause, it may become impossible to carry a decree into execution without the further decree of the court. Hind, Ch. Pr. 68; Story, Eq. Pl. § 42.

BILL TO PERPETUATE TESTIMONY. A bill in equity filed in order to procure the testimony of witnesses to be taken as to some matter not at the time before the courts, but which is likely at some future time to be in litigation. Story, Eq. Pl. (5th Ed.) § 300 et seq.

BILL TO SUSPEND A DECREE. In equity practice. One brought to avoid or suspend a decree under special circumstances.

BILL TO TAKE TESTIMONY DE BENE ESSE. In equity practice. One which is brought to take the testimony of witnesses to a fact material to the prosecution of a suit at law which is actually commenced, where there is good cause to fear that the testimony may otherwise be lost before the time of trial. 2 Story, Eq. Jur. § 1813, n.

BILLA. L. Lat. A bill; an original bill.

BILLA CASSETUR, or QUOD BILLA CASSETUR. (That the bill be quashed.) In practice. The form of the judgment rendered for a defendant on a plea in abatement, where the proceeding is *by bill;* that is, where the suit is commenced by *capias*, and not by original writ. 2 Archb. Pr. K. B. 4.

BILLA EXCAMBII. A bill of exchange.

BILLA EXONERATIONIS. A bill of lading.

BILLA VERA. (A true bill.) In old practice. The indorsement anciently made on a bill of indictment by a grand jury, when they found it sufficiently sustained by evidence. 4 Bl. Comm. 306.

BILLET. A soldier's quarters in a civilian's house; or the ticket which authorizes him to occupy them.

In French law. A bill or promissory note. *Billet à ordre*, a bill payable to order. *Billet à vue*, a bill payable at sight. *Billet de complaisance*, an accommodation bill.

BILLET DE CHANGE. In French law. An engagement to give, at a future time, a bill of exchange, which the party is not at the time prepared to give. Story, Bills, § 2, n.

BILLETA. In old English law. A bill or petition exhibited in parliament. Cowell.

BILLETING SOLDIERS. Quartering them in the houses of private citizens; finding quarters for them.

BI-METALLIC. Pertaining to, or consisting of, two metals used as money at a fixed relative value.

BI-METALLISM. The legalized use of two metals in the currency of a country at a fixed relative value.

BIND. To obligate; to bring or place under definite duties or legal obligations, particularly by a bond or covenant; to affect one in a constraining or compulsory manner with a contract or a judgment. So long as a contract, an adjudication, or a legal relation remains in force and virtue, and continues to impose duties or obligations, it is said to be "*binding.*" A man is *bound* by his contract or promise, by a judgment or decree against him, by his bond or covenant, by an estoppel, etc.

BIND OUT. To place one under a legal obligation to serve another; as to *bind out* an apprentice.

BINDING OVER. The act by which a court or magistrate requires a person to enter into a recognizance or furnish bail to appear for trial, to keep the peace, to attend as a witness, etc.

BIPARTITE. Consisting of, or divisible into, two parts. A term in conveyancing descriptive of an instrument in two parts, and executed by both parties.

BIRRETUM, BIRRETUS. A cap or coif used formerly in England by judges and serjeants at law. Spelman.

BIRTH. The act of being born or wholly brought into separate existence.

BIS. Lat. Twice.

Bis idem exigi bona fides non patitur; et in satisfactionibus non permittitur amplius fieri quam semel factum est. Good faith does not suffer the same thing to be demanded twice; and in making satisfaction [for a debt or demand] it is not allowed to be done more than once. 9 Coke, 53.

BISAILE. The father of one's grandfather or grandmother.

BISANTIUM, BESANTINE, BEZANT. An ancient coin, first issued at Constantinople; it was of two sorts,—gold, equivalent to a ducat, valued at 9s. 6d.; and silver, computed at 2s. They were both current in England. Wharton.

BI-SCOT. In old English law. A fine imposed for not repairing banks, ditches, and causeways.

BISHOP. An English ecclesiastical dignitary, being the chief of the clergy within his diocese, subject to the archbishop of the province in which his diocese is situated. Most of the bishops are also members of the house of lords.

A bishop has three powers: (1) A power of ordination, gained on his consecration, by which he confers orders, etc., in any place throughout the world; (2) a power of jurisdiction throughout his see or his bishopric; (3) a power of administration and government of the revenues thereof, gained on confirmation. He has, also, a consistory court, to hear ecclesiastical causes, and visits and superintends the clergy of his diocese. He consecrates churches and institutes priests, confirms, suspends, excommunicates, and grants licenses for marriages. He has his archdeacon, dean, and chapter, chancellor, who holds his courts and assists him in matters of ecclesiastical law, and vicar-general. He grants leases for three lives, or twenty-one years, reserving the accustomed yearly rent. Wharton.

BISHOPRIC. In ecclesiastical law. The diocese of a bishop, or the circuit in which he has jurisdiction; the office of a bishop. 1 Bl. Comm. 377-382.

BISHOP'S COURT. In English law. An ecclesiastical court, held in the cathedral of each diocese, the judge whereof is the bishop's chancellor, who judges by the civil canon law; and, if the diocese be large, he has his commissaries in remote parts, who hold *consistory courts*, for matters limited to them by their commission.

BISSEXTILE. The day which is added every fourth year to the month of February, in order to make the year agree with the course of the sun.

Leap year, consisting of 366 days, and happening every fourth year, by the addition of a day in the month of February, which in that year consists of twenty-nine days.

BLACK ACRE and WHITE ACRE. Fictitious names applied to pieces of land, and used as examples in the old books.

BLACK ACT. The statute 9 Geo. I. c. 22, so called because it was occasioned by the outrages committed by persons with their faces blacked or otherwise disguised, who appeared in Epping Forest, near Waltham, in Essex, and destroyed the deer there, and committed other offenses. Repealed by 7 & 8 Geo. IV. c. 27.

BLACK ACTS. Old Scotch statutes passed in the reigns of the Stuarts and down to the year 1586 or 1587, so called because printed in black letter. Bell.

BLACK BOOK OF HEREFORD. In English law. An old record frequently referred to by Cowell and other early writers.

BLACK BOOK OF THE ADMIRALTY. A book of the highest authority in admiralty matters, generally supposed to have been compiled during the reign of Edward III. with additions of a later date. It contains the laws of Oleron, a view of crimes and offenses cognizable in the admiralty, and many other matters. See 2 Gall. 404.

BLACK BOOK OF THE EXCHEQUER. The name of an ancient book kept in the English exchequer, containing a collection of treaties, conventions, charters, etc.

BLACK CAP. It is a vulgar error that the head-dress worn by the judge in pronouncing the sentence of death is assumed as an emblem of the sentence. It is part of the judicial full dress, and is worn by the judges on occasions of especial state. Wharton.

BLACK GAME. In English law. Heath fowl, in contradistinction to red game, as grouse.

BLACK-LIST. A list of persons marked out for special avoidance, antagonism, or enmity on the part of those who prepare the list or those among whom it is intended to circulate; as where a trades-union "black-lists" workmen who refuse to conform to its rules, or where a list of insolvent or untrustworthy persons is published by a commercial agency or mercantile association.

BLACK-MAIL. 1. In one of its original meanings, this term denoted a tribute paid by English dwellers along the Scottish border to influential chieftains of Scotland, as a condition of securing immunity from raids of marauders and border thieves.

2. It also designated rents payable in cattle, grain, work, and the like. Such rents were called "black-mail," (*reditus nigri,*) in distinction from white rents, (*blanche firmes,*) which were rents paid in silver.

3. The extortion of money by threats or overtures towards criminal prosecution or the destruction of a man's reputation or social standing.

In common parlance, the term is equivalent to, and synonymous with, "extortion,"—the exaction of money, either for the performance of a duty, the prevention of an injury, or the exercise of an influence. It supposes the service to be unlawful, and the payment involuntary. Not infrequently it is extorted by threats, or by operating upon the fears or the credulity, or by promises to conceal, or offers to expose, the weaknesses, the follies, or the crimes of the victim. 26 How. Pr. 431; 17 Abb. Pr. 226.

BLACK MARIA. A closed wagon or van in which prisoners are carried to and from the jail, or between the court and the jail.

BLACK RENTS. In old English law. Rents reserved in work, grain, provisions, or baser money, in contradistinction to those which were reserved in *white* money or silver, which were termed "white rents," (*reditus albi,*) or blanch farms. Tomlins; Whishaw.

BLACK-ROD, GENTLEMAN USHER OF. In England, the title of a chief officer of the queen, deriving his name from the *Black Rod* of office, on the top of which reposes a golden lion, which he carries.

BLACK WARD. A subvassal, who held ward of the king's vassal.

"BLACKLEG." "The word 'blackleg' has been used long enough to be understood, not only by experts in slang, but by the public at large, and therefore it was for the judge to expound its meaning. I have always understood the word 'blackleg' to mean a person who gets his living by frequenting race-courses and places where games of chance are played, getting the best odds, and giving the least he can, but not necessarily cheating. That is not indictable either by statute or at common law." Pollock, C. B., 3 Hurl. & N. 379.

BLADA. In old English law. Growing crops of grain of any kind. Spelman. All manner of annual grain. Cowell. Harvested grain. Bract. 217*b;* Reg. Orig. 94*b*, 95.

BLADARIUS. In old English law. A corn-monger; meal-man or corn-chandler; a bladier, or engrosser of corn or grain. Blount.

BLANC SEIGN. In Louisiana, a paper signed at the bottom by him who intends to bind himself, give acquittance, or compromise, at the discretion of the person whom he intrusts with such *blanc seign*, giving him power to fill it with what he may think proper, according to agreement. 6 Mart. (La.) 718.

BLANCH HOLDING. An ancient tenure of the law of Scotland, the duty payable being trifling, as a penny or a pepper-corn, etc., if required; similar to free and common socage.

BLANCHE FIRME. White rent; a rent reserved, payable in silver.

BLANCUS. In old law and practice. White; plain; smooth; blank.

BLANK. A space left unfilled in a written document, in which one or more words or marks are to be inserted to complete the sense.

Also a skeleton or printed form for any legal document, in which the necessary and invariable words are printed in their proper order, with blank spaces left for the insertion of such names, dates, figures, additional clauses, etc., as may be necessary to adapt the instrument to the particular case and to the design of the party using it.

BLANK ACCEPTANCE. An acceptance of a bill of exchange written on the paper before the bill is made, and delivered by the acceptor.

BLANK BAR. Also called the "common bar." The name of a plea in bar which in an action of trespass is put in to oblige the plaintiff to assign the certain place where the trespass was committed. It was most in practice in the common bench. See Cro. Jac. 594.

BLANK BONDS. Scotch securities, in which the creditor's name was left blank, and which passed by mere delivery, the bearer being at liberty to put in his name and sue for payment. Declared void by Act 1696, c. 25.

BLANK INDORSEMENT. The indorsement of a bill of exchange or promissory note, by merely writing the name of the indorser, without mentioning any person to whom the bill or note is to be paid; called "blank," because a blank or space is left *over* it for the insertion of the name of the indorsee, or of any subsequent holder. Otherwise called an indorsement "in blank." 3 Kent, Comm. 89; Story, Prom. Notes, § 138.

BLANKET POLICY. In the law of fire insurance. A policy which contemplates that the risk is shifting, fluctuating, or varying, and is applied to a class of property, rather than to any particular article or thing. 1 Wood, Ins. § 40. See 93 U. S. 541.

BLANKS. A kind of white money, (value 8d.,) coined by Henry V. in those parts of France which were then subject to England; forbidden to be current in that realm by 2 Hen. VI. c. 9. Wharton.

BLASARIUS. An incendiary.

BLASPHEMY. In English law. Blasphemy is the offense of speaking matter relating to God, Jesus Christ, the Bible, or the Book of Common Prayer, intended to wound the feelings of mankind or to excite contempt and hatred against the church by law established, or to promote immorality. Sweet.

In American law. Any oral or written reproach maliciously cast upon God, his name, attributes, or religion. 2 Bish. Crim. Law, § 76; 2 Har. (Del.) 553; 20 Pick. 206; 11 Serg. & R. 394; 8 Johns. 290.

Blasphemy consists in wantonly uttering or publishing words casting contumelious reproach or profane ridicule upon God, Jesus Christ, the Holy Ghost, the Holy Scriptures, or the Christian religion. Pen. Code Dak., § 31.

In general, blasphemy may be described as consisting in speaking evil of the Deity with an impious purpose to derogate from the divine majesty, and to alienate the minds of others from the love and reverence of God. It is purposely using words concerning God calculated and designed to impair and destroy the reverence, respect, and confidence due to him as the intelligent creator, governor, and judge of the world. It embraces the idea of detraction, when used towards the Supreme Being, as "calumny" usually carries the same idea when applied to an individual. It is a willful and malicious attempt to lessen men's reverence of God by denying his existence, or his attributes as an intelligent creator, governor, and judge of men, and to prevent their having confidence in him as such. 20 Pick. 211, 212.

The use of this word is, in modern law exclusively confined to sacred subjects; but *blasphemia* and *blasphemare* were anciently used to signify the reviling by one person of another. Nov. 77, c. 1, § 1; Spelman.

BLEES. Grain; particularly corn.

BLENCH, BLENCH HOLDING. See BLANCH HOLDING.

BLENDED FUND. In England, where a testator directs his real and personal estate to be sold, and disposes of the proceeds as forming one aggregate, this is called a "blended fund."

BLIND. One who is deprived of the sense or faculty of sight.

BLINKS. In old English law. Boughs broken down from trees and thrown in a way where deer are likely to pass. Jacob.

BLOCKADE. In international law. A marine investment or beleaguering of a town or harbor. A sort of circumvallation round a place by which all foreign connection and correspondence is, as far as human power can effect it, to be cut off. 1 C. Rob. Adm. 151. It is not necessary, however, that the place should be invested by land, as well as by sea, in order to constitute a legal blockade; and, if a place be blockaded by sea only, it is no violation of belligerent rights for the neutral to carry on commerce with it by inland communications. 1 Kent, Comm. 147.

The actual investment of a port or place by a hostile force fully competent, under ordinary circumstances, to cut off all communication therewith, so arranged or disposed as to be able to apply its force to every point of practicable access or approach to the port or place so invested. Bouvier.

It is called a "blockade *de facto*" when the usual notice of the blockade has not been given to the neutral powers by the government causing the investment, in consequence of which the blockading squadron has to warn off all approaching vessels.

BLOOD. Kindred; consanguinity; family relationship; relation by descent from a common ancestor. One person is "of the blood" of another when they are related by lineal descent or collateral kinship.

Brothers and sisters are said to be of the whole blood if they have the same father and mother, and of the half blood if they have only one parent in common. 5 Whart. 477.

BLOOD MONEY. A weregild, or pecuniary mulct paid by a slayer to the relatives of his victim.

Also used, in a popular sense, as descriptive of money paid by way of reward for the apprehension and conviction of a person charged with a capital crime.

BLOODWIT. An amercement for bloodshed. Cowell.

The privilege of taking such amercements. Skene.

A privilege or exemption from paying a fine or amercement assessed for bloodshed. Cowell.

BLOODY HAND. In forest law. The having the hands or other parts bloody, which, in a person caught trespassing in the forest against venison, was one of the four kinds of circumstantial evidence of his having killed deer, although he was not found in the act of chasing or hunting. Manwood.

BLUE LAWS. A supposititious code of severe laws for the regulation of religious and personal conduct in the colonies of Connecticut and New Haven; hence any rigid Sunday laws or religious regulations. The assertion by some writers of the existence of the blue laws has no other basis than the adoption, by the first authorities of the New Haven colony, of the Scriptures as their code of law and government, and their strict application of Mosaic principles. Century Dict.

BOARD. A committee of persons organized under authority of law in order to exercise certain authorities, have oversight or control of certain matters, or discharge certain functions of a magisterial, representative, or fiduciary character. Thus, "board of aldermen," "board of health," "board of directors," "board of works."

Also lodging, food, entertainment, furnished to a guest at an inn or boarding-house.

BOARD OF HEALTH. A board or commission created by the sovereign authority or by municipalities, invested with certain powers and charged with certain duties in relation to the preservation and improvement of the public health.

General boards of health are usually charged with general and advisory duties, with the collection of vital statistics, the investigation of sanitary conditions, and the methods of dealing with epidemic and other diseases, the quarantine laws, etc. Such are the national board of health, created by act of congress of March 3, 1879, (20 St. at Large, 484,) and the state boards of health created by the legislatures of most of the states.

Local boards of health are charged with more direct and immediate means of securing the public health, and exercise inquisitorial and executive powers in relation to sanitary regulations, offensive nuisances, markets, adulteration of food, slaughterhouses, drains and sewers, and similar subjects. Such boards are constituted in most American cities either by general law, by their charters, or by municipal ordinance, and in England by the statutes, 11 & 12 Vict.

c. 63, and 21 & 22 Vict. c. 98, and other acts amending the same.

BOARD OF SUPERVISORS. Under the system obtaining in some of the northern states, this name is given to an organized committee, or body of officials, composed of delegates from the several townships in a county, constituting part of the county government, and having special charge of the revenues of the county.

BOARD OF TRADE. An organization of the principal merchants, manufacturers, tradesmen, etc., of a city, for the purpose of furthering its commercial interests, encouraging the establishment of manufactures, promoting trade, securing or improving shipping facilities, and generally advancing the prosperity of the place as an industrial and commercial community.

In England, one of the administrative departments of government, being a committee of the privy council which is appointed for the consideration of matters relating to trade and foreign plantations.

BOARD OF WORKS. The name of a board of officers appointed for the better local management of the English metropolis. They have the care and management of all grounds and gardens dedicated to the use of the inhabitants in the metropolis; also the superintendence of the drainage; also the regulation of the street traffic, and, generally, of the buildings of the metropolis. Brown.

BOARDER. One who, being the inhabitant of a place, makes a special contract with another person for food with or without lodging. 7 Cush. 424; 36 Iowa, 651.

One who has food and lodging in the house or with the family of another for an agreed price, and usually under a contract intended to continue for a considerable period of time. 1 Tex. App. 220; 7 Rob. (N. Y.) 561.

The distinction between a guest and a boarder is this: The guest comes and remains without any bargain *for time*, and may go away when he pleases, paying only for the actual entertainment he receives; and the fact that he may have remained a long time in the inn, in this way, does not make him a boarder, instead of a guest. 25 Iowa, 553.

BOARDING-HOUSE. A boarding-house is not in common parlance, or in legal meaning, every private house where one or more boarders are kept occasionally only and upon special considerations. But it is a *quasi* public house, where boarders are generally and habitually kept, and which is held out and known as a place of entertainment of that kind. 1 Lans. 486.

A boarding-house is not an inn, the distinction being that a boarder is received into a house by a voluntary contract, whereas an innkeeper, in the absence of any reasonable or lawful excuse, is bound to receive a guest when he presents himself. 2 El. & Bl. 144.

The distinction between a boarding-house and an inn is that in a boarding-house the guest is under an express contract, at a certain rate for a certain period of time, while in an inn there is no express agreement; the guest, being on his way, is entertained from day to day, according to his business, upon an implied contract. 2 E. D. Smith, 148.

BOAT. A small open vessel, or water-craft, usually moved by oars or rowing. It is commonly distinguished in law from a ship or vessel, by being of smaller size and without a deck. 5 Mason, 120, 137.

BOC. In Saxon law. A book or writing; a deed or charter. *Boc land*, deed or charter land. *Land boc*, a writing for conveying land; a deed or charter; a land-book.

BOC HORDE. A place where books, writings, or evidences were kept. Cowell.

BOC LAND. In Saxon law. Allodial lands held by deed or other written evidence of title.

BOCERAS. Sax. A scribe, notary, or chancellor among the Saxons.

BODMERIE, BODEMERIE, BODDEMEREY. Belg. and Germ. Bottomry, (*q. v.*)

BODY. A person. Used of a natural body, or of an artificial one created by law, as a corporation.

Also the main part of any instrument; in deeds it is spoken of as distinguished from the recitals and other introductory parts and signatures; in *affidavits*, from the title and jurat.

The main part of the human body; the trunk. 22 N. Y. 149.

BODY CORPORATE. A corporation.

BODY OF A COUNTY. A county at large, as distinguished from any particular place within it. A county considered as a territorial whole.

BODY OF AN INSTRUMENT. The main and operative part; the substantive provisions, as distinguished from the recitals, title, jurat, etc.

BODY OF LAWS. An organized and systematic collection of rules of jurisprudence; as, particularly, the body of the civil law, or *corpus juris civilis.*

BODY POLITIC. A term applied to a corporation, which is usually designated as a "body corporate and politic."

The term is particularly appropriate to a *public* corporation invested with powers and duties of government. It is often used, in a rather loose way, to designate the state or nation or sovereign power, or the government of a county or municipality, without distinctly connoting any express and individual corporate character.

BOILARY. Water arising from a salt well belonging to a person who is not the owner of the soil.

BOIS, or BOYS. Wood; timber; brush.

BOLHAGIUM, or BOLDAGIUM. A little house or cottage. Blount.

BOLT. The desertion by one or more persons from the political party to which he or they belong; the permanent withdrawal before adjournment of a portion of the delegates to a political convention. Rap. & L.

BOLTING. In English practice. A term formerly used in the English inns of court, but more particularly at Gray's Inn, signifying the private arguing of cases, as distinguished from *mooting,* which was a more formal and public mode of argument. Cowell; Tomlins; Holthouse.

BOMBAY REGULATIONS. Regulations passed for the presidency of Bombay, and the territories subordinate thereto. They were passed by the governors in council of Bombay until the year 1834, when the power of local legislation ceased, and the acts relating thereto were thenceforth passed by the governor general of India in council. Mozley & Whitley.

BON. Fr. In old French law. A royal order or check on the treasury, invented by Francis I. *Bon pour mille livres,* good for a thousand livres. Step. Lect. 387.

In modern law. The name of a clause (*bon pour* ——, good for so much) added to a cedule or promise, where it is not in the handwriting of the signer, containing the amount of the sum which he obliges himself to pay. Poth. Obl. part 4, ch. 1, art. 2, § 1.

BONA. Goods; property; possessions. In the Roman law, this term was used to designate all species of property, real, personal, and mixed, but was more strictly applied to real estate. In modern civil law, it includes both personal property (technically so called) and chattels real, thus corresponding to the French *biens.* In the common law, its use was confined to the description of movable goods.

BONA CONFISCATA. Goods confiscated or forfeited to the imperial *fisc* or treasury. 1 Bl. Comm. 299.

BONA ET CATALLA. Goods and chattels. Movable property.

This expression includes all personal things that belong to a man. 16 Mees. & W. 68.

BONA FELONUM. In English law. Goods of felons; the goods of one convicted of felony. 5 Coke, 110.

BONA FIDE. In or with good faith; honestly, openly, and sincerely; without deceit or fraud.

Truly; actually; without simulation or pretense.

Innocently; in the attitude of trust and confidence; without notice of fraud, etc.

The phrase "*bona fide*" is often used ambiguously; thus, the expression "a *bona fide* holder for value" may either mean a holder for real value, as opposed to a holder for pretended value, or it may mean a holder for real value without notice of any fraud, etc. Byles, Bills, 121.

Bona fide possessor facit fructus consumptos suos. By good faith a possessor makes the fruits consumed his own. Tray. Lat. Max. 57.

BONA FIDE PURCHASER. A purchaser for a valuable consideration paid or parted with in the belief that the vendor had a right to sell, and without any suspicious circumstances to put him on inquiry. 12 Barb. 605.

One who acts without covin, fraud, or collusion; one who, in the commission of or connivance at no fraud, pays full price for the property, and in good faith, honestly, and in fair dealing buys and goes into possession. 42 Ga. 250.

A *bona fide* purchaser is one who buys property of another without notice that some third person has a right to, or interest in, such property, and pays a full and fair price for the same, at the time of such purchase, or before he has notice of the claim or interest of such other in the property. 65 Barb. 231.

BONA FIDES. Good faith; integrity of dealing; honesty; sincerity; the opposite of *mala fides* and of *dolus malus.*

Bona fides exigit ut quod convenit fiat. Good faith demands that what is agreed upon shall be done. Dig. 19, 20, 21; Id. 19, 1, 50; Id. 50, 8, 2, 13.

Bona fides non patitur ut bis idem exigatur. Good faith does not allow us to demand twice the payment of the same thing. Dig. 50, 17, 57; Broom, Max. 338, note; 4 Johns. Ch. 143.

BONA FORISFACTA. Goods forfeited.

BONA FUGITIVORUM. In English law. Goods of fugitives; the proper goods of him who flies for felony. 5 Coke, 109*b*.

BONA GESTURA. Good abearance or behavior.

BONA GRATIA. In the Roman law. By mutual consent; voluntarily. A term applied to a species of divorce where the parties separated by mutual consent; or where the parties renounced their marital engagements without assigning any cause, or upon mere pretexts. Tayl. Civil Law, 361, 362; Calvin.

BONA MEMORIA. Good memory. Generally used in the phrase *sanæ mentis et bonæ memoriæ*, of sound mind and good memory, as descriptive of the mental capacity of a testator.

BONA MOBILIA. In the civil law. Movables. Those things which move themselves or can be transported from one place to another, and not permanently attached to a farm, heritage, or building.

BONA NOTABILIA. In English probate law. Notable goods; property worthy of notice, or of sufficient value to be accounted for, that is, amounting to £5.

Where a decedent leaves goods of sufficient amount (*bona notabilia*) in different dioceses, administration is granted by the metropolitan, to prevent the confusion arising from the appointment of many different administrators. 2 Bl. Comm. 509; Rolle, Abr. 908.

BONA PATRIA. In the Scotch law. An assize or jury of good neighbors. Bell.

BONA PERITURA. Goods of a perishable nature; such goods as an executor or trustee must use diligence in disposing of and converting them into money.

BONA UTLAGATORUM. Goods of outlaws; goods belonging to persons outlawed.

BONA VACANTIA. Vacant, unclaimed, or stray goods. Those things in which nobody claims a property, and which belong to the crown, by virtue of its prerogative. 1 Bl. Comm. 298.

BONA WAVIATA. In English law. Waived goods; goods stolen and *waived*, that is, thrown away by the thief in his flight, for fear of being apprehended, or to facilitate his escape; and which go to the sovereign. 5 Coke, 109*b*; 1 Bl. Comm. 296.

BONÆ FIDEI. In the civil law. Of good faith; in good faith. This is a more frequent form than *bona fide.*

BONÆ FIDEI CONTRACTS. In civil and Scotch law. Those contracts in which equity may interpose to correct inequalities, and to adjust all matters according to the plain intention of the parties. 1 Kames, Eq. 200.

BONÆ FIDEI EMPTOR. A purchaser in good faith. One who either was ignorant that the thing he bought belonged to another or supposed that the seller had a right to sell it. Dig. 50, 16, 109. See Id. 6, 2, 7, 11.

BONÆ FIDEI POSSESSOR. A possessor in good faith. One who believes that no other person has a better right to the possession than himself. Mackeld. Rom. Law, § 243.

Bonæ fidei possessor in id tantum quod sese pervenerit tenetur. A possessor in good faith is only liable for that which he himself has obtained. 2 Inst. 285.

BONANZA. In mining parlance, the widening out of a vein of silver, suddenly, and extraordinarily; hence any sudden, unexpected prosperity in mining. Webster.

BOND. A contract by specialty to pay a certain sum of money; being a deed or instrument under seal, by which the maker or obligor promises, and thereto *binds* himself, his heirs, executors, and administrators, to pay a designated sum of money to another; usually with a clause to the effect that upon performance of a certain condition (as to pay another and smaller sum) the obligation shall be void.

The word "bond" shall embrace every written undertaking for the payment of money or acknowledgment of being bound for money, conditioned to be void on the performance of any duty, or the occurrence of anything therein expressed, and subscribed and delivered by the party making it, to take effect as his obligation, whether it be sealed or unsealed; and, when a bond is required by law, an undertaking in writing without seal shall be sufficient. Rev. Code Miss. 1880, § 19.

The word "bond" has with us a definite legal signification. It has a clause, with a sum fixed as a penalty, binding the parties to pay the same, conditioned, however, that the payment of the penalty may be avoided by the performance by some one or more of the parties of certain acts. 3 Redf. Sur. 459.

Bonds are either single (simple) or double, (conditional.)

A *single* bond is one in which the obligor binds himself, his heirs, etc., to pay a certain sum of money to another person at a specified day.

A *double* (or conditional) bond is one to which a condition is added that if the obligor does or forbears from doing some act the obligation shall be void. Formerly such a condition was sometimes contained in a separate instrument, and was then called a "defeasance."

The term is also used to denote debentures or certificates of indebtedness issued by public and private corporations, governments, and municipalities, as security for the repayment of money loaned to them. Thus, "railway aid bonds" are bonds issued by municipal corporations to aid in the construction of railroads likely to benefit them, and exchanged for the company's stock.

BOND. In old Scotch law. A bond-man; a slave. Skene.

BOND, *v.* To give bond for, as for duties on goods; to secure payment of duties, by giving bond. *Bonded,* secured by bond. Bonded goods are those for the duties on which bonds are given.

BOND AND DISPOSITION IN SECURITY. In Scotch law. A bond and mortgage on land.

BOND AND MORTGAGE. A species of security, consisting of a bond conditioned for the repayment of a loan of money, and a mortgage of realty to secure the performance of the stipulations of the bond.

BOND CREDITOR. A creditor whose debt is secured by a bond.

BOND TENANTS. In English law. Copyholders and customary tenants are sometimes so called. 2 Bl. Comm. 148.

BONDAGE. Slavery; involuntary personal servitude; captivity. In old English law, villenage, villein tenure. 2 Bl. Comm. 92.

BONDED WAREHOUSE. See WAREHOUSE SYSTEM.

BONDSMAN. A surety; one who has entered into a bond as surety. The word seems to apply especially to the sureties upon the bonds of officers, trustees, etc., while *bail* should be reserved for the sureties on recognizances and bail-bonds.

BONES GENTS. L. Fr. In old English law. Good men, (of the jury.)

BONI HOMINES. In old European law. Good men; a name given in early European jurisprudence to the tenants of the lord, who judged each other in the lord's courts. 3 Bl. Comm. 349.

Boni judicis est ampliare jurisdictionem. It is the part of a good judge to enlarge (or use liberally) his remedial authority or jurisdiction. Ch. Prec. 329; 1 Wils. 284.

Boni judicis est ampliare justitiam. It is the duty of a good judge to enlarge or extend justice. 1 Burr. 304.

Boni judicis est judicium sine dilatione mandare executioni. It is the duty of a good judge to cause judgment to be executed without delay. Co. Litt. 289.

Boni judicis est lites dirimere, ne lis ex lite oritur, et interest reipublicæ ut sint fines litium. It is the duty of a good judge to prevent litigations, that suit may not grow out of suit, and it concerns the welfare of a state that an end be put to litigation. 4 Coke, 15*b;* 5 Coke, 31*a*.

BONIS CEDERE. In the civil law. To make a transfer or surrender of property, as a debtor did to his creditors. Cod. 7, 71.

BONIS NON AMOVENDIS. A writ addressed to the sheriff, when a writ of error has been brought, commanding that the person against whom judgment has been obtained be not suffered to remove his goods till the error be tried and determined. Reg. Orig. 131.

BONITARIAN OWNERSHIP. In Roman law. A species of equitable title to things, as distinguished from a title acquired according to the strict forms of the municipal law; the property of a Roman citizen in a subject capable of quiritary property, acquired by a title not known to the civil law, but introduced by the prætor, and protected by his *imperium* or supreme executive power, *e. g.*, where *res mancipi* had been transferred by mere tradition. Poste's Gaius Inst. 187. See QUIRITARIAN OWNERSHIP.

BONO ET MALO. A special writ of jail delivery, which formerly issued of course for each particular prisoner. 4 Bl. Comm. 270.

Bonum defendentis ex integra causa; malum ex quolibet defectu. The success of a defendant depends on a perfect case; his loss arises from some defect. 11 Coke, 68*a*.

Bonum necessarium extra terminos necessitatis non est bonum. A good thing required by necessity is not good beyond the limits of such necessity. Hob. 144.

BONUS. A gratuity. A premium paid to a grantor or vendor.

An extra consideration given for what is received.

Any premium or advantage; an occasional extra dividend.

A premium paid by a company for a charter or other franchises.

"A definite sum to be paid at one time, for a loan of money for a specified period, distinct from and independently of the interest." 24 Conn. 147.

A bonus is not a gift or gratuity, but a sum paid for services, or upon some other consideration, but in addition to or in excess of that which would ordinarily be given. 16 Wall. 452.

Bonus judex secundum æquum et bonum judicat, et æquitatem stricto juri præfert. A good judge decides according to what is just and good, and prefers equity to strict law. Co. Litt. 34.

BOOK. 1. A general designation applied to any literary composition which is printed, but appropriately to a printed composition bound in a volume.

2. A bound volume consisting of sheets of paper, not printed, but containing manuscript entries; such as a merchant's account-books, dockets of courts, etc.

3. A name often given to the largest subdivisions of a treatise or other literary composition.

4. In practice, the name of "book" is given to several of the more important papers prepared in the progress of a cause, though entirely written, and not at all in the book form; such as demurrer-books, error-books, paper-books, etc.

BOOK DEBT. In Pennsylvania practice. The act of 28th March, 1835, § 2, in using the words, "book debt" and "book entries," refers to their usual signification, which includes goods sold and delivered, and work, labor, and services performed, the evidence of which, on the part of the plaintiff, consists of entries in an original book, such as is competent to go to a jury, were the issue trying before them. 2 Miles, 102.

BOOK OF ACTS. A term applied to the records of a surrogate's court. 8 East, 187.

BOOK OF ADJOURNAL. In Scotch law. The original records of criminal trials in the court of justiciary.

BOOK OF RATES. An account or enumeration of the duties or tariffs authorized by parliament. 1 Bl. Comm. 316.

BOOK OF RESPONSES. In Scotch law. An account which the directors of the chancery kept to enter all non-entry and relief duties payable by heirs who take precepts from chancery.

BOOKLAND. In English law. Land, also called "charter-land," which was held by deed under certain rents and free services, and differed in nothing from free socage land. 2 Bl. Comm. 90.

BOOKS. All the volumes which contain authentic reports of decisions in English courts, from the earliest times to the present, are called, *par excellence*, "The Books." Wharton.

BOOKS OF ACCOUNT. The books in which merchants, traders, and business men generally keep their accounts.

BOOM. An inclosure formed upon the surface of a stream or other body of water, by means of piers and a chain of spars, for the purpose of collecting or storing logs or timber.

BOOM COMPANY. A company formed for the purpose of improving streams for the floating of logs, by means of booms and other contrivances, and for the purpose of running, driving, booming, and rafting logs.

BOON DAYS. In English law. Certain days in the year (sometimes called "due days") on which tenants in copyhold were obliged to perform corporal services for the lord. Whishaw.

BOOT, or BOTE. An old Saxon word, equivalent to "estovers."

BOOTING, or BOTING, CORN. Certain rent corn, anciently so called. Cowell.

BOOTY. Property captured from the enemy in war, on land, as distinguished from "prize," which is a capture of such property on the sea.

BORD. An old Saxon word, signifying a cottage; a house; a table.

BORDAGE. In old English law. A species of base tenure, by which certain lands (termed "bord lands,") were anciently held in England, the tenants being termed "*bordarii;*" the service was that of keeping the lord in small provisions.

BORDARIA. A cottage.

BORDARII, or BORDIMANNI. In old English law. Tenants of a less servile condition than the *villani*, who had a bord or cottage, with a small parcel of land, allowed to them, on condition they should supply the lord with poultry and eggs, and other small provisions for his board or entertainment. Spelman.

BORD-BRIGCH. In Saxon law. A breach or violation of suretyship; pledge-breach, or breach of mutual fidelity.

BORDER WARRANT. A process granted by a judge ordinary, on either side of the border between England and Scotland, for arresting the person or effects of a person living on the opposite side, until he find security, *judicio sisti.* Bell.

BORDEREAU. In French law. A note enumerating the purchases and sales which may have been made by a broker or stockbroker. This name is also given to the statement given to a banker with bills for discount or coupons to receive. Arg. Fr. Merc. Law, 547.

BORD-HALFPENNY. A customary small toll paid to the lord of a town for setting up boards, tables, booths, etc., in fairs or markets.

BORDLANDS. The demesnes which the lords keep in their hands for the maintenance of their board or table. Cowell.

Also lands held in bordage. Lands which the lord gave to tenants on condition of their supplying his table with small provisions, poultry, eggs, etc.

BORDLODE. A service anciently required of tenants to carry timber out of the woods of the lord to his house; or it is said to be the quantity of food or provision which the *bordarii* or bordmen paid for their bordlands. Jacob.

BORDSERVICE. A tenure of bordlands.

BOREL-FOLK. Country people; derived from the French *bourre*, (Lat. *floccus*,) a lock of wool, because they covered their heads with such stuff. Blount.

BORG. In Saxon law. A pledge, pledge giver, or surety. The name given among the Saxons to the head of each family composing a tithing or decennary, each being the pledge for the good conduct of the others. Also the contract or engagement of suretyship; and the pledge given.

BORGBRICHE. A breach or violation of suretyship, or of mutual fidelity. Jacob.

BORGESMON. In Saxon law. The name given to the head of each family composing a tithing.

BORGH OF HAMHALD. In old Scotch law. A pledge or surety given by the seller of goods to the buyer, to make the goods forthcoming as his own proper goods, and to warrant the same to him. Skene.

BOROUGH. In English law. A town, a walled town. Co. Litt. 108*b*. A town of note or importance; a fortified town. Cowell. An ancient town. Litt. 164. A corporate town that is not a city. Cowell. An ancient town, corporate or not, that sends burgesses to parliament. Co. Litt. 109*a;* 1 Bl. Comm. 114, 115. A city or other town sending burgesses to parliament. 1 Steph. Comm. 116. A town or place organized for local government.

A parliamentary borough is a town which returns one or more members to parliament.

In Scotch law. A corporate body erected by the charter of the sovereign, consisting of the inhabitants of the territory erected into the borough. Bell.

In American law. In Pennsylvania, the term denotes a part of a township having a charter for municipal purposes; and the same is true of Connecticut. 23 Conn. 128. See, also, 1 Dill. Mun. Corp. § 41, n.

"Borough" and "village" are duplicate or cumulative names of the same thing; proof of either will sustain a charge in an indictment employing the other term. 18 Ohio St. 496.

BOROUGH COURTS. In English law. Private and limited tribunals, held by prescription, charter, or act of parliament, in particular districts for the convenience of the inhabitants, that they may prosecute small suits and receive justice at home.

BOROUGH ENGLISH. A custom prevalent in some parts of England, by which the youngest son inherits the estate in preference to his older brothers. 1 Bl. Comm. 75.

BOROUGH FUND. In English law. The revenues of a municipal borough derived from the rents and produce of the land, houses, and stocks belonging to the borough in its corporate capacity, and supplemented where necessary by a borough rate.

BOROUGH-HEADS. Borough-holders, bors-holders, or burs-holders.

BOROUGH-REEVE. The chief muncipal officer in towns unincorporated before the municipal corporations act, (5 & 6 Wm. IV. c. 76.)

BOROUGH SESSIONS. Courts of limited criminal jurisdiction, established in English boroughs under the municipal corporations act.

BORROW. This word is often used in the sense of returning the thing borrowed *in specie*, as to borrow a book or any other thing to be returned again. But it is evident that where money is borrowed, the identical money loaned is not to be returned, because, if this were so, the borrower would derive no benefit from the loan. In the broad sense of the term, it means a contract for the use of money. 13 Neb. 88, 12 N. W. Rep. 812; 39 Leg. Int. 98; 78 N. Y. 177.

BORROWE. In old Scotch law. A pledge.

BORROWER. One to whom money or other property is loaned at his request.

BORSHOLDER. In Saxon law. The borough's ealder, or headborough, supposed to be the discreetest man in the borough, town, or tithing.

BOSCAGE. In English law. The food which wood and trees yield to cattle; browsewood, mast, etc. Spelman.

An ancient duty of wind-fallen wood in the forest. Manwood.

BOSCARIA. Wood-houses, or ox-houses.

BOSCUS. Wood; growing wood of any kind, large or small, timber or coppice. Cowell; Jacob.

BOTE. In old English law. A recompense or compensation, or profit or advantage. Also reparation or amends for any damage done. Necessaries for the maintenance and carrying on of husbandry. An allowance; the ancient name for estovers.

House-bote is a sufficient allowance of wood from off the estate to repair or burn in the house, and sometimes termed "fire-bote;" *plow-bote* and *cart-bote* are wood to be employed in making and repairing all instruments of husbandry; and *hay-bote* or *hedge-bote* is wood for repairing of hays, hedges, or fences. The word also signifies reparation for any damage or injury done, as *man-bote*, which was a compensation or amends for a man slain, etc.

BOTELESS. In old English law. Without amends; without the privilege of making satisfaction for a crime by a pecuniary payment; without relief or remedy. Cowell.

BOTHA. In old English law. A booth, stall, or tent to stand in, in fairs or markets. Cowell.

BOTHAGIUM, or BOOTHAGE. Customary dues paid to the lord of a manor or soil, for the pitching or standing of booths in fairs or markets.

BOTHNA, or BUTHNA. In old Scotch law. A park where cattle are inclosed and fed. Bothna also signifies a barony, lordship, etc. Skene.

BOTTOMAGE. L. Fr. Bottomry.

BOTTOMRY. In maritime law. A contract in the nature of a mortgage, by which the owner of a ship borrows money for the use, equipment, or repair of the vessel, and for a definite term, and pledges the ship (or the keel or *bottom* of the ship, *pars pro toto*) as a security for its repayment, with maritime or extraordinary interest on account of the marine risks to be borne by the lender; it being stipulated that if the ship be lost in the course of the specified voyage, or during the limited time, by any of the perils enumerated in the contract, the lender shall also lose his money. 2 Hagg. Adm. 48, 53; 2 Sum. 157.

Bottomry is a contract by which a ship or its freightage is hypothecated as security for a loan, which is to be repaid only in case the ship survives a particular risk, voyage, or period. Civil Code Cal. § 3017; Civil Code Dak. § 1783.

When the loan is not made upon the ship, but on the goods laden on board, and which are to be sold or exchanged in the course of the voyage, the borrower's personal *responsibility* is deemed the principal security for the performance of the contract, which is therefore called "*respondentia*," which see. And in a loan upon *respondentia* the lender must be paid his principal and interest though the ship perish, provided the goods are saved. In most other respects the contracts of *bottomry* and of *respondentia* stand substantially upon the same footing. Bouvier.

BOTTOMRY BOND. The instrument embodying the contract or agreement of bottomry.

The true definition of a bottomry bond, in the sense of the general maritime law, and independent of the peculiar regulations of the positive codes of different commercial nations, is that it is a contract for a loan of money on the bottom of the ship, at an extraordinary interest, upon maritime risks, to be borne by the lender for a voyage, or for a definite period. 2 Sum. 157.

BOUCHE. Fr. The mouth. An allowance of provision. *Avoir bouche à court;* to have an allowance at court; to be in ordinary at court; to have meat and drink scot-free there. Blount; Cowell.

BOUCHE OF COURT, or BUDGE OF COURT. A certain allowance of provision from the king to his knights and servants, who attended him on any military expedition.

BOUGH OF A TREE. In feudal law. A symbol which gave seisin of land, to hold of the donor *in capite*.

BOUGHT AND SOLD NOTES. When a broker is employed to buy and sell goods, he is accustomed to give to the buyer a note of the sale, commonly called a "sold note," and to the seller a like note, commonly called a "bought note," in his own name, as agent of each, and thereby they are respectively bound, if he has not exceeded his authority. Story, Ag. § 28.

BOULEVARD. The word "boulevard," which originally indicated a bulwark or rampart, and was afterwards applied to a public walk or road on the site of a demolished fortification, is now employed in the same sense as public drive. A park is a piece of ground adapted and set apart for purposes of ornament, exercise, and amusement. It is not a street or road, though carriages may pass through it.

So a boulevard or public drive is adapted and set apart for purposes of ornament, exercise, and amusement. It is not technically a street, avenue, or highway, though a carriage-way over it is a chief feature. 52 How. Pr. 445.

BOUND. As an *adjective*, denotes the condition of being constrained by the obligations of a bond or a covenant. In the law of shipping, "bound to" or "bound for" denotes that the vessel spoken of is intended or designed to make the voyage to the place named.

As a *noun*, the term denotes a limit or boundary, or a line inclosing or marking off a tract of land. In the familiar phrase "metes and bounds," the former term properly denotes the measured distances, and the latter the natural or artificial marks which indicate their beginning and ending. A distinction is sometimes taken between "bound" and "boundary," to the effect that, while the former signifies the limit itself, (and may be an imaginary line,) the latter designates a visible mark which indicates the limit. But no such distinction is commonly observed.

BOUND BAILIFFS. In English law. Sheriffs' officers are so called, from their being usually *bound* to the sheriff in an obligation with sureties, for the due execution of their office. 1 Bl. Comm. 345, 346.

BOUNDARY. By boundary is understood, in general, every separation, natural or artificial, which marks the confines or line of division of two contiguous estates. Trees or hedges may be planted, ditches may be dug, walls or inclosures may be erected, to serve as boundaries. But we most usually understand by boundaries stones or pieces of wood inserted in the earth on the confines of the two estates. Civil Code La. art. 826.

Boundaries are either natural or artificial. Of the former kind are water-courses, growing trees, beds of rock, and the like. Artificial boundaries are landmarks or signs erected by the hand of man, as a pole, stake, pile of stones, etc.

BOUNDED TREE. A tree marking or standing at the corner of a field or estate.

BOUNDERS. In American law. Visible marks or objects at the ends of the lines drawn in surveys of land, showing the courses and distances. Burrill.

BOUNDS. In the English law of mines, the trespass committed by a person who excavates minerals under-ground beyond the boundary of his land is called "working out of bounds."

BOUNTY. A gratuity, or an unusual or additional benefit conferred upon, or compensation paid to, a class of persons.

A premium given or offered to induce men

to enlist into the public service. The term is applicable only to the payment made to the enlisted man, as the inducement for his service, and not to a premium paid to the man through whose intervention, and by whose procurement, the recruit is obtained and mustered. 39 How. Pr. 488.

It is not easy to discriminate between bounty, reward, and bonus. The former is the appropriate term, however, where the services or action of many persons are desired, and each who acts upon the offer may entitle himself to the promised gratuity, without prejudice from or to the claims of others; while reward is more proper in the case of a single service, which can be only once performed, and therefore will be earned only by the person or co-operating persons who succeed while others fail. Thus, bounties are offered to all who will enlist in the army or navy; to all who will engage in certain fisheries which government desire to encourage; to all who kill dangerous beasts or noxious creatures. A reward is offered for rescuing a person from a wreck or fire; for detecting and arresting an offender; for finding a lost chattel.

Bonus, as compared with bounty, suggests the idea of a gratuity to induce a money transaction between individuals; a percentage or gift, upon a loan or transfer of property, or a surrender of a right. Abbott.

BOUNTY LANDS. Portions of the public domain given to soldiers for military services, by way of bounty.

BOUNTY OF QUEEN ANNE. A name given to a royal charter, which was confirmed by 2 Anne, c. 11, whereby all the revenue of first-fruits and tenths was vested in trustees, to form a perpetual fund for the augmentation of poor ecclesiastical livings. Wharton.

BOURG. In old French law. An assemblage of houses surrounded with walls; a fortified town or village.

In old English law. A borough, a village.

BOURGEOIS. In old French law. The inhabitant of a *bourg*, (*q. v.*)

A person entitled to the privileges of a municipal corporation; a burgess.

BOURSE. Fr. An exchange; a stock-exchange.

BOURSE DE COMMERCE. In the French law. An aggregation, sanctioned by government, of merchants, captains of vessels, exchange agents, and courtiers, the two latter being nominated by the government, in each city which has a *bourse*. Brown.

BOUSSOLE. In French marine law. A compass; the mariner's compass.

BOUWERYE. Dutch. In old New York law. A farm; a farm on which the farmer's family resided.

BOUWMEESTER. Dutch. In old New York law. A farmer.

BOVATA TERRÆ. As much land as one ox can cultivate. Said by some to be thirteen, by others eighteen, acres in extent. Skene; Spelman; Co. Litt. 5*a*.

BOW-BEARER. An under-officer of the forest, whose duty it is to oversee and true inquisition make, as well of sworn men as unsworn, in every bailiwick of the forest; and of all manner of trespasses done, either to vert or venison, and cause them to be presented, without any concealment, in the next court of attachment, etc. Cromp. Jur. 201.

BOWYERS. Manufacturers of bows and shafts. An ancient company of the city of London.

BOYCOTT. In criminal law. A conspiracy formed and intended directly or indirectly to prevent the carrying on of any lawful business, or to injure the business of any one by wrongfully preventing those who would be customers from buying anything from or employing the representatives of said business, by threats, intimidation, or other forcible means. 11 Va. Law J. 329.

BOZERO. In Spanish law. An advocate; one who pleads the causes of others, or his own, before courts of justice, either as plaintiff or defendant.

BRACHIUM MARIS. An arm of the sea.

BRACINUM. A brewing; the whole quantity of ale brewed at one time, for which *tolsestor* was paid in some manors. *Brecina*, a brew-house.

BRAHMIN, BRAHMAN, or BRAMIN. In Hindu law. A divine; a priest; the first Hindu caste.

BRANCH. A branch of a family stock is a group of persons, related among themselves by descent from a common ancestor, and related to the main stock by the fact that that common ancestor descends from the original founder or progenitor.

BRAND. To stamp; to mark, either with a hot iron or with a stencil plate. 11 Hun, 575.

BRANDING. An ancient mode of punishment by inflicting a mark on an offender with a hot iron. It is generally disused in civil law, but is a recognized punishment for some military offenses.

BRANKS. An instrument formerly used in some parts of England for the correction of scolds; a scolding bridle. It inclosed the head and a sharp piece of iron entered the mouth and restrained the tongue.

BRASIATOR. A maltster, a brewer.

BRASIUM. Malt.

BRAWL. The popular meanings of the words "brawls" and "tumults" are substantially the same and identical. They are correlative terms, the one employed to express the meaning of the other, and are so defined by approved lexicographers. Legally, they mean the same kind of disturbance to the public peace, produced by the same class of agents, and can be well comprehended to define one and the same offense. 42 N. H. 464.

Brawling is quarrelling or chiding, or creating a disturbance, in a church, or churchyard, (4 Bl. Comm. 146; 4 Steph. Comm. 253.) Mozley & Whitley.

BREACH. The breaking or violating of a law, right, or duty, either by commission or omission.

In contracts. The violation or non-fulfilment of an obligation, contract, or duty.

A *continuing* breach occurs where the state of affairs, or the specific act, constituting the breach, endures for a considerable period of time, or is repeated at short intervals.

A *constructive* breach of contract takes place when the party bound to perform disables himself from performance by some act, or declares, before the time comes, that he will not perform.

In pleading. This name is sometimes given to that part of the declaration which alleges the violation of the defendant's promise or duty, immediately preceding the *ad damnum* clause.

BREACH OF CLOSE. The unlawful or unwarrantable entry on another person's soil, land, or close. 3 Bl. Comm. 209.

BREACH OF COVENANT. The nonperformance of any covenant agreed to be performed, or the doing of any act covenanted not to be done. Holthouse.

BREACH OF DUTY. In a general sense, any violation or omission of a legal or moral duty. More particularly, the neglect or failure to fulfill in a just and proper manner the duties of an office or fiduciary employment.

BREACH OF POUND. The breaking any pound or place where cattle or goods distrained are deposited, in order to take them back. 3 Bl. Comm. 146.

BREACH OF PRISON. The offense of actually and forcibly breaking a prison or gaol, with intent to escape. 4 Chit. Bl. 130, notes; 4 Steph. Comm. 255. The escape from custody of a person lawfully arrested on criminal process.

BREACH OF PRIVILEGE. An act or default in violation of the privilege of either house of parliament, of congress, or of a state legislature.

BREACH OF PROMISE. Violation of a promise; chiefly used as an elliptical expression for "breach of promise of marriage."

BREACH OF THE PEACE. A violation of the public tranquillity and order. The offense of breaking or disturbing the public peace by any riotous, forcible, or unlawful proceeding. 4 Bl. Comm. 142, et seq.; 4 Steph. Comm. 273, et seq.

A *constructive* breach of the peace is an unlawful act which, though wanting the elements of actual violence or injury to any person, is yet inconsistent with the peaceable and orderly conduct of society. Various kinds of misdemeanors are included in this general designation, such as sending challenges to fight, going armed in public without lawful reason and in a threatening manner, etc.

An *apprehended* breach of the peace is caused by the conduct of a man who threatens another with violence or physical injury, or who goes about in public with dangerous and unusual weapons in a threatening or alarming manner, or who publishes an aggravated libel upon another, etc.

BREACH OF TRUST. Any act done by a trustee contrary to the terms of his trust, or in excess of his authority and to the detriment of the trust; or the wrongful omission by a trustee of any act required of him by the terms of the trust.

Also the wrongful misappropriation by a trustee of any fund or property which had been lawfully committed to him in a fiduciary character.

BREAD ACTS. Laws providing for the sustenance of persons kept in prison for debt.

BREAKING. Forcibly separating, parting, disintegrating, or piercing any solid substance. In the law as to housebreaking and burglary, it means the tearing away or removal of any part of a house or of the locks, latches, or other fastenings intended to secure it, or otherwise exerting force to gain an entrance, with the intent to commit a felony; or violently or forcibly breaking out of a house, after having unlawfully entered it, in the attempt to escape.

BREAKING A CASE. The expression by the judges of a court, to one another, of their views of a case, in order to ascertain how far they are agreed, and as preliminary to the formal delivery of their opinions. "We are breaking the case, that we may show what is in doubt with any of us." Holt, C. J., addressing Dolbin, J., 1 Show. 423.

BREAKING BULK. The offense committed by a bailee (particularly a carrier) in opening or unpacking the chest, parcel, or case containing goods intrusted to his care, and removing the goods and converting them to his own use.

BREAKING DOORS. Forcibly removing the fastenings of a house, so that a person may enter.

BREAKING JAIL. The act of a prisoner in effecting his escape from a place of lawful confinement. *Escape*, while denoting the offense of the prisoner in unlawfully leaving the jail, may also connote the fault or negligence of the sheriff or keeper, and hence is of wider significance than "breaking jail" or "prison-breach."

BREAKING OF ARRESTMENT. In Scotch law. The contempt of the law committed by an arrestee who disregards the arrestment used in his hands, and pays the sum or delivers the goods arrested to the debtor. The breaker is liable to the arrester in damages. See ARRESTMENT.

BREAST OF THE COURT. A metaphorical expression, signifying the conscience, discretion, or recollection of the judge. During the term of a court, the record is said to remain "in the breast of the judges of the court and in their remembrance." Co. Litt. 260*a;* 3 Bl. Comm. 407.

BREATH. In medical jurisprudence. The air expelled from the lungs at each expiration.

BREDWITE. In Saxon and old English law. A fine, penalty, or amercement imposed for defaults in the assise of bread. Cowell.

BREHON. In old Irish law. A judge. 1 Bl. Comm. 100. Brehons, (*breitheamhuin,*) judges.

BREHON LAW. The name given to the ancient system of law of Ireland as it existed at the time of its conquest by Henry II.; and derived from the title of the judges, who were denominated "Brehons."

BRENAGIUM. A payment in bran, which tenants anciently made to feed their lords' hounds.

BREPHOTROPHI. In the civil law. Persons appointed to take care of houses destined to receive foundlings.

BRETHREN. This word, in a will, may include sisters, as well as brothers, of the person indicated; it is not necessarily limited to the masculine gender. 1 Rich. Eq. 78.

BRETTS AND SCOTTS, LAWS OF THE. A code or system of laws in use among the Celtic tribes of Scotland down to the beginning of the fourteenth century, and then abolished by Edward I. of England.

BRETTWALDA. In Saxon law. The ruler of the Saxon heptarchy.

BREVE. L. Lat. A writ. An original writ. A writ or precept of the king issuing out of his courts.

A writ by which a person is summoned or attached to answer an action, complaint, etc., or whereby anything is commanded to be done in the courts, in order to justice, etc. It is called "*breve,*" from the brevity of it, and is addressed either to the defendant himself, or to the chancellors, judges, sheriffs, or other officers. Skene.

BREVE DE RECTO. A writ of right, or license for a person ejected out of an estate, to sue for the possession of it.

BREVE INNOMINATUM. A writ making only a general complaint, without the details or particulars of the cause of action.

Breve ita dicitur, quia rem de qua agitur, et intentionem petentis, paucis verbis breviter enarrat. A writ is so called because it briefly states, in few words, the matter in dispute, and the object of the party seeking relief. 2 Inst. 39.

Breve judiciale debet sequi suum originale, et accessorium suum principale. Jenk. Cent. 292. A judicial writ ought to follow its original, and an accessory its principal.

Breve judiciale non cadit pro defectu formæ. Jenk. Cent. 43. A judicial writ fails not through defect of form.

BREVE NOMINATUM. A named writ. A writ stating the circumstances or details of the cause of action, with the time, place, and demand, very particularly.

BREVE ORIGINALE. An original writ; a writ which gave *origin* and commencement to a suit.

BREVE PERQUIRERE. To purchase a writ or license of trial, in the king's courts, by the plaintiff, *qui breve perquisivit.*

BREVE TESTATUM. A written memorandum introduced to perpetuate the tenor of the conveyance and investiture of lands. 2 Bl. Comm. 307.

In Scotch law. A similar memorandum made out at the time of the transfer, attested by the *pares curiæ* and by the seal of the superior. Bell.

BREVET. In military law. A commission by which an officer is promoted to the next higher rank, but without conferring a right to a corresponding increase of pay.

In French law. A privilege or warrant granted by the government to a private person, authorizing him to take a special benefit or exercise an exclusive privilege. Thus a *brevet d'invention* is a patent for an invention.

BREVIA. Lat. Writs. The plural of *breve*, which see.

BREVIA ADVERSARIA. Adversary writs; writs brought by an adversary to recover land. 6 Coke, 67.

BREVIA AMICABILIA. Amicable or friendly writs; writs brought by agreement or consent of the parties.

BREVIA ANTICIPANTIA. At common law. Anticipating or preventive writs. Six were included in this category, viz.: Writ of *mesne; warrantia chartæ; monstraverunt; audita querela; curia claudenda;* and *ne injuste vexes.*

BREVIA DE CURSU. Writs of course. Formal writs issuing as of course.

BREVIA FORMATA. Certain writs of approved and established form which were granted of course in actions to which they were applicable, and which could not be changed but by consent of the great council of the realm. Bract. fol. 413*b*.

BREVIA JUDICIALIA. Judicial writs. Auxiliary writs issued from the court during the progress of an action, or in aid of the judgment.

BREVIA MAGISTRALIA. Writs occasionally issued by the *masters* or clerks of chancery, the form of which was varied to suit the circumstances of each case. Bract. fol. 413*b*.

BREVIA SELECTA. Choice or selected writs or processes. Often abbreviated to Brev. Sel.

Brevia, tam originalia quam judicialia, patiuntur Anglica nomina. 10 Coke, 132. Writs, as well original as judicial, bear English names.

BREVIA TESTATA. The name of the short memoranda early used to show grants of lands, out of which the deeds now in use have grown. Jacob.

BREVIARIUM ALARICIANUM. A compilation of Roman law made by order of Alaric II., king of the Visigoths, in Spain, and published for the use of his Roman subjects in the year 506.

BREVIARIUM ANIANI. Another name for the Brevarium Alaricianum, (*q. v.*) Anian was the referendery or chancellor of Alaric, and was commanded by the latter to authenticate, by his signature, the copies of the breviary sent to the *comites.* Mackeld. Rom. Law, § 68.

BREVIATE. A brief; brief statement, epitome, or abstract. A short statement of contents, accompanying a bill in parliament. Holthouse.

BREVIBUS ET ROTULIS LIBERANDIS. A writ or mandate to a sheriff to deliver to his successor the county, and appurtenances, with the rolls, briefs, remembrance, and all other things belonging to his office. Reg. Orig. 295.

BREWER. One who manufactures fermented liquors of any name or description, for sale, from malt, wholly or in part, or from any substitute therefor. Act July 13, 1866, § 9, (14 St. at Large, 117.)

BRIBE. Any valuable thing given or promised, or any preferment, advantage, privilege, or emolument, given or promised corruptly and against the law, as an inducement to any person acting in an official or public capacity to violate or forbear from his duty, or to improperly influence his behavior in the performance of such duty.

The term "bribe" signifies any money, goods, right in action, property, thing of value, or advantage, present or prospective, or any promise or undertaking to give any, asked, given, or accepted, with a corrupt intent to influence unlawfully the person to whom it is given, in his action, vote, or opinion, in any public or official capacity. Pen. Code Dak. § 774.

BRIBERY. In criminal law. The receiving or offering any undue reward by or to any person whomsoever, whose ordinary profession or business relates to the administration of public justice, in order to influence his behavior in office, and to incline him to act contrary to his duty and the known rules of honesty and integrity. 1 Russ. Crimes, 154; 1 Hawk. P. C. 414; 3 Co. Inst. 149; 29 Ark. 302.

The term "bribery" now extends further, and includes the offense of giving a bribe to many other classes of officers; it applies both to the actor and receiver, and extends to voters, cabinet ministers, legislators, sheriffs, and other classes. 2 Whart. Crim. Law, § 1858.

The offense of taking any undue reward by a judge, juror, or other person concerned in the administration of justice, or by a public officer, to influence his behavior in his office. 4 Bl. Comm. 139, and note.

Bribery is the giving or receiving any undue reward to influence the behavior of the person receiving such reward in the discharge of his duty, in any office of government or of justice. Code Ga. 1882, § 4469.

The crime of offering any undue reward or remuneration to any public officer of the crown, or other person intrusted with a public duty, with a view to influence his behavior in the discharge of his duty. The taking such reward is as much bribery as the offering it. It also sometimes signifies the taking or giving a reward for public office. The offense is not confined, as some have supposed, to judicial officers. Brown.

BRIBERY AT ELECTIONS. The offense committed by one who gives or promises or offers money or any valuable inducement to an elector, in order to corruptly induce the latter to vote in a particular way or to abstain from voting, or as a reward to the voter for having voted in a particular way or abstained from voting.

BRIBOUR. One that pilfers other men's goods; a thief.

BRICOLIS. An engine by which walls were beaten down. Blount.

BRIDEWELL. In England. A house of correction.

BRIDGE. A structure erected over a river, creek, stream, ditch, ravine, or other place, to facilitate the passage thereof; including by the term both arches and abutments. 40 N. J. Law, 305.

A building of stone or wood erected across a river, for the common ease and benefit of travelers. Jacob.

Bridges are either public or private. Public bridges are such as form a part of the highway, common, according to their character as foot, horse, or carriage bridges, to the public generally, with or without toll. 2 East, 342.

A private bridge is one erected by one or more private persons for their own use and convenience.

BRIDGE-MASTERS. Persons chosen by the citizens, to have the care and supervision of bridges, and having certain fees and profits belonging to their office, as in the case of London Bridge.

BRIDLE ROAD. In the location of a private way laid out by the selectmen, and accepted by the town, a description of it as a "bridle road" does not confine the right of way to a particular class of animals or special mode of use. 16 Gray, 175.

BRIEF. **In general.** A written document; a letter; a writing in the form of a letter. A summary, abstract, or epitome. A condensed statement of some larger document, or of a series of papers, facts, or propositions.

An epitome or condensed summary of the facts and circumstances, or propositions of law, constituting the case proposed to be set up by either party to an action about to be tried or argued.

In English practice. A document prepared by the attorney, and given to the barrister, before the trial of a cause, for the instruction and guidance of the latter. It contains, in general, all the information necessary to enable the barrister to successfully conduct their client's case in court, such as a statement of the facts, a summary of the pleadings, the names of the witnesses, and an outline of the evidence expected from them, and any suggestions arising out of the peculiarities of the case.

In American practice. A written or printed document, prepared by counsel to serve as the basis for an argument upon a cause in an appellate court, and usually filed for the information of the court. It embodies the points of law which the counsel desires to establish, together with the arguments and authorities upon which he rests his contention.

A brief, within a rule of court requiring counsel to furnish briefs, before argument, implies some kind of statement of the case for the information of the court. 43 Ind. 356.

In Scotch law. Brief is used in the sense of "writ," and this seems to be the sense in which the word is used in very many of the ancient writers.

In ecclesiastical law. A papal rescript sealed with wax. See BULL.

BRIEF A L'EVESQUE. A writ to the bishop which, in *quare impedit,* shall go to remove an incumbent, unless he recover or be presented *pendente lite.* 1 Keb. 386.

BRIEF OF TITLE. In practice. A methodical epitome of all the patents, conveyances, incumbrances, liens, court proceedings, and other matters affecting the title to a certain portion of real estate.

BRIEF OUT OF THE CHANCERY. In Scotch law. A writ issued in the name of the sovereign in the election of tutors to minors, the cognoscing of lunatics or of idiots, and the ascertaining the widow's terce; and sometimes in dividing the property belonging to heirs-portioners. In these cases only brieves are now in use. Bell.

BRIEF, PAPAL. In ecclesiastical law. The pope's letter upon matters of discipline.

BRIEVE. In Scotch law. A writ. 1 Kames, Eq. 146.

BRIGA. In old European law. Strife, contention, litigation, controversy.

BRIGANDINE. A coat of mail or ancient armour, consisting of numerous jointed scale-like plates, very pliant and easy for the body, mentioned in 4 & 5 P. & M. c. 2.

BRIGBOTE. In Saxon and old English law. A tribute or contribution towards the repairing of bridges.

BRINGING MONEY INTO COURT. The act of depositing money in the custody of a court or of its clerk or marshal, for the purpose of satisfying a debt or duty, or to await the result of an interpleader.

BRIS. In French maritime law. Literally, breaking; wreck. Distinguished from *naufrage,* (*q. v.*)

BRISTOL BARGAIN. In English law. A contract by which A. lends B. £1,000 on good security, and it is agreed that £500, together with interest, shall be paid at a time stated; and, as to the other £500, that B., in consideration thereof, shall pay to A. £100 *per annum* for seven years. Wharton.

BRITISH COLUMBIA. The territory on the north-west coast of North America, once known by the designation of "New Caledonia." Its government is provided for by 21 & 22 Vict. c. 99. Vancouver Island is united to it by the 29 & 30 Vict. c. 67. See 33 & 34 Vict. c. 66.

BROCAGE. The wages, commission, or pay of a broker, (also called "brokerage.") Also the avocation or business of a broker.

BROCARIUS, BROCATOR. In old English and Scotch law. A broker; a middleman between buyer and seller; the agent of both transacting parties. Bell; Cowell.

BROCELLA. In old English law. A wood, a thicket or covert of bushes and brushwood. Cowell; Blount.

BROKEN STOWAGE. In maritime law. That space in a ship which is not filled by her cargo.

BROKER. An agent employed to make bargains and contracts between other persons, in matters of trade, commerce, or navigation, for a compensation commonly called "brokerage." Story, Ag. § 28.

Those who are engaged for others in the negotiation of contracts relative to property, with the custody of which they have no concern. Paley, Prin. & Ag. 13.

The *broker* or *intermediary* is he who is employed to negotiate a matter between two parties, and who, for that reason, is considered as the mandatary of both. Civil Code La. art. 3016.

One whose business is to negotiate purchases or sales of stocks, exchange, bullion, coined money, bank-notes, promissory notes, or other securities, for himself or for others. Ordinarily, the term "broker" is applied to one acting for others; but the part of the definition which speaks of purchases and sales for himself is equally important as that which speaks of sales and purchases for others. 91 U. S. 710.

A broker is a mere negotiator between

other parties, and does not act in his own name, but in the name of those who employ him. 50 Ind. 234.

Brokers are persons whose business it is to bring buyer and seller together; they need have nothing to do with negotiating the bargain. 68 Pa. St. 42.

The difference between a *factor* or commission merchant and a *broker* is this: A factor may buy and sell in his own name, and he has the goods in his possession; while a broker, as such, cannot ordinarily buy or sell in his own name, and has no possession of the goods sold. 23 Wall. 321, 330.

The legal distinction between a broker and a factor is that the factor is intrusted with the property the subject of the agency; the broker is only employed to make a bargain in relation to it. 50 Ala. 154, 156.

Brokers are of many kinds, the most important being enumerated and defined as follows:

Exchange brokers, who negotiate foreign bills of exchange.

Insurance brokers, who procure insurances for those who employ them and negotiate between the party seeking insurance and the companies or their agents.

Merchandise brokers, who buy and sell goods and negotiate between buyer and seller, but without having the custody of the property.

Note brokers, who negotiate the discount or sale of commercial paper.

Pawnbrokers, who lend money on goods deposited with them in pledge, taking high rates of interest.

Real-estate brokers, who procure the purchase or sale of land, acting as intermediary between vendor and purchaser to bring them together and arrange terms; and who negotiate loans on real-estate security, manage and lease estates, etc.

Ship-brokers, who transact business between the owners of ships and freighters or charterers, and negotiate the sale of vessels.

Stock-brokers, who are employed to buy and sell for their principals all kinds of stocks, corporation bonds, debentures, shares in companies, government securities, municipal bonds, etc.

BROKERAGE. The wages or commissions of a broker; also, his business or occupation.

BROSSUS. Bruised, or injured with blows, wounds, or other casualty. Cowell.

BROTHEL. A bawdy-house; a house of ill fame; a common habitation of prostitutes.

BROTHER. One person is a brother "of the whole blood" to another, the former being a male, when both are born from the same father and mother. He is a brother "of the half blood" to that other (or half-brother) when the two are born to the same father by different mothers or by the same mother to different fathers.

In the civil law, the following distinctions are observed: Two brothers who descend from the same father, but by different mothers, are called "consanguine" brothers. If they have the same mother, but are begotten by different fathers, they are called "uterine" brothers. If they have both the same father and mother, they are denominated brothers "germane."

BROTHER-IN-LAW. A wife's brother or a sister's husband. There is not any relationship, but only affinity, between brothers-in-law.

BRUARIUM. In old English law. A heath ground; ground where heath grows. Spelman.

BRUGBOTE. See BRIGBOTE.

BRUILLUS. In old English law. A wood or grove; a thicket or clump of trees in a park or forest. Cowell.

BRUISE. In medical jurisprudence. A contusion; an injury upon the flesh of a person with a blunt or heavy instrument, without solution of continuity, or without breaking the skin.

BRUKBARN. In old Swedish law. The child of a woman conceiving after a rape, which was made legitimate. Literally, the child of a struggle. Burrill.

BRUTUM FULMEN. An empty noise; an empty threat.

BUBBLE. An extravagant or unsubstantial project for extensive operations in business or commerce, generally founded on a fictitious or exaggerated prospectus, to ensnare unwary investors. Companies formed on such a basis or for such purposes are called "bubble companies." The term is chiefly used in England.

BUBBLE ACT. The statute 6 Geo. I. c. 18, "for restraining several extravagant and unwarrantable practices herein mentioned," was so called. It prescribed penalties for the formation of companies with little or no capital, with the intention, by means of, alluring advertisements, of obtaining money from the public by the sale of shares. Such undertakings were then commonly called "bubbles." This legislation was prompted by the collapse of the "South Sea Project," which, as Blackstone says, "had beggared half the nation." It was mostly repealed by the statute 6 Geo. IV. c. 91.

BUCKSTALL. A toil to take deer. 4 Inst. 306.

BUDGET. A name given in England to the statement annually presented to parliament by the chancellor of the exchequer, containing the estimates of the national revenue and expenditure.

BUGGERY. A carnal copulation against nature; and this is either by the confusion of species,—that is to say, a man or a woman with a brute beast,—or of sexes, as a man with a man, or man unnaturally with a woman. 3 Inst. 58; 12 Coke, 36.

BUILDING. A structure or edifice erected by the hand of man, composed of natural materials, as stone or wood, and intended for use or convenience.

BUILDING LEASE. A lease of land for a long term of years, usually 99, at a rent called a "ground rent," the lessee covenanting to erect certain edifices thereon according to specification, and to maintain the same, etc., during the term.

BUILDING SOCIETY. An association in which the subscriptions of the members form a capital stock or fund out of which advances may be made to members desiring them, on mortgage security.

BUL. In the ancient Hebrew chronology, the eighth month of the ecclesiastical, and the second of the civil, year. It has since been called "*Marshevan,*" and answers to our October.

BULK. Unbroken packages. Merchandise which is neither counted, weighed, nor measured.

Bulk is said of that which is neither counted, weighed, nor measured. A sale by the bulk is the sale of a quantity such as it is, without measuring, counting, or weighing. Civil Code La. art. 3556, par. 6.

BULL. In ecclesiastical law. An instrument granted by the pope of Rome, and sealed with a seal of lead, containing some decree, commandment, or other public act, emanating from the pontiff. Bull, in this sense, corresponds with edict or letters patent from other governments. Cowell; 4 Bl. Comm. 110; 4 Steph. Comm. 177, 179.

This is also a cant term of the Stock Exchange, meaning one who speculates for a rise in the market.

BULLA. A seal used by the Roman emperors, during the lower empire; and which was of four kinds,—gold, silver, wax, and lead.

BULLETIN. An officially published notice or announcement concerning the progress of matters of public importance. In France, the registry of the laws.

BULLETIN DES LOIS. In France, the official sheet which publishes the laws and decrees; this publication constitutes the promulgation of the law or decree.

BULLION. Gold and silver intended to be coined. The term is usually applied to a quantity of these metals ready for the mint, but as yet lying in bars, plates, lumps, or other masses; but it may also include ornaments or dishes of gold and silver, or foreign coins not current as money, when intended to be descriptive of its adaptability to be coined, and not of other purposes to which it may be put.

BULLION FUND. A fund of public money maintained in connection with the mints, for the purpose of purchasing precious metals for coinage.

BUM-BAILIFF. A person employed to dun one for a debt; a bailiff employed to arrest a debtor. Probably a vulgar corruption of "bound-bailiff," (*q. v.*)

BUNDA. In old English law. A bound, boundary, border, or limit, (*terminus, limes.*)

BUNGALOW. A country-house in the East Indies.

BUOY. In maritime law. A piece of wood or cork, or a barrel, raft, or other thing, made secure and floating upon a stream or bay, intended as a guide and warning to mariners, by marking a spot where the water is shallow, or where there is a reef or other danger to navigation, or to mark the course of a devious channel.

BURDEN OF PROOF. (Lat. *onus probandi.*) In the law of evidence. The necessity or duty of affirmatively proving a fact or facts in dispute on an issue raised between the parties in a cause.

The term "burden of proof" is not to be confused with "*prima facie* case." When the party upon whom the burden of proof rests has made out a *prima facie* case, this will, in general, suffice to shift the burden.

In other words, the former expression denotes the necessity of establishing the latter.

BUREAU. An office for the transaction of business. A name given to the several departments of the executive or administrative branch of government, or to their larger subdivisions.

BUREAUCRACY. A system in which the business of government is carried on in departments, each under the control of a chief, in contradistinction from a system in which the officers of government have a coordinate authority.

BURG, BURGH. A term anciently applied to a castle or fortified place; a borough, (*q. v.*) Spelman.

BURGAGE. A name anciently given to a dwelling-house in a borough town. Blount.

BURGAGE-HOLDING. A tenure by which lands in royal boroughs in Scotland were held of the sovereign. The service was watching and warding, and was done by the burgesses within the territory of the borough, whether expressed in the charter or not.

BURGAGE-TENURE. In English law. One of the three species of free socage holdings; a tenure whereby houses and lands which were formerly the site of houses, in an ancient borough, are held of some lord by a certain rent. There are a great many customs affecting these tenures, the most remarkable of which is the custom of Borough English. See Litt. § 162; 2 Bl. Comm. 82.

BURGATOR. One who breaks into houses or inclosed places, as distinguished from one who committed robbery in the open country. Spelman.

BURGBOTE. In old English law. A term applied to a contribution towards the repair of castles or walls of defense, or of a borough.

BURGENSES. In old English law. Inhabitants of a *burgus* or borough; burgesses. Fleta, lib. 5, c. 6, § 10.

BURGERISTH. A word used in Domesday, signifying a breach of the peace in a town. Jacob.

BURGESS. In English law. An inhabitant or freeman of a borough or town; a person duly and legally admitted a member of a municipal corporation. Spelman; 3 Steph. Comm. 188, 189.

A magistrate of a borough. Blount.

An elector or voter; a person legally qualified to vote at elections. The word in this sense is particularly defined by the statute 5 & 6 Wm. IV. c. 76, §§ 9, 13. 3 Steph. Comm. 192.

A representative of a borough or town, in parliament. Co. Litt. 109*a;* 1 Bl. Comm. 174.

In American law. The chief executive officer of a borough, bearing the same relation to its government and affairs that the *mayor* does to those of a city. So used in Pennsylvania.

BURGESS ROLL. A roll, required by the St. 5 & 6 Wm. IV. c. 76, to be kept in corporate towns or boroughs, of the names of burgesses entitled to certain new rights conferred by that act.

BURGH-BRECHE. A fine imposed on the community of a town, for a breach of the peace, etc.

BURGH ENGLISH. See BOROUGH ENGLISH.

BURGH ENGLOYS. Borough English, (*q. v.*)

BURGHMAILS. Yearly payments to the crown of Scotland, introduced by Malcolm III., and resembling the English fee-farm rents.

BURGHMOTE. In Saxon law. A court of justice held semi-annually by the bishop or lord in a *burg*, which the thanes were bound to attend without summons.

BURGLAR. One who commits burglary. One who breaks into a dwelling-house in the night-time with intent to commit a felony.

BURGLARIOUSLY. In pleading. A technical word which must be introduced into an indictment for burglary at common law.

BURGLARITER. L. Lat. (Burglariously.) In old criminal pleading. A necessary word in indictments for burglary.

BURGLARY. In criminal law. The breaking and entering the house of another in the night-time, with intent to commit a felony therein, whether the felony be actually committed or not. 3 Inst. 63; 1 Hale, P. C. 549; 1 Hawk. P. C. c. 38, § 1.

Burglary is the breaking and entering the dwelling-house of another, in the night-time, with intent to commit a felony. 29 Ind. 80; 1 N. J. Law, 441; 9 Ired. 463; 1 Dev. 253; 7 Mass. 247.

The common-law definition has been much modified by statute in several of the states.

For example: "Every person who enters any house, room, apartment, tenement, shop, warehouse, store, mill, barn, stable, outhouse, or other building, tent, vessel, or railroad car, with intent to commit grand or petit larceny, or any felony, is guilty of burglary." Pen. Code Cal. § 459.

BURGOMASTER. The title given in Germany to the chief executive officer of a borough, town, or city; corresponding to our "mayor."

BURGUNDIAN LAW. See LEX BURGUNDIONUM.

BURGWHAR. A burgess, (*q. v.*)

BURIAL. Sepulture; the act of interring dead human bodies.

BURKISM, (from the name of its first perpetrator.) The practice of killing persons for the purpose of selling their bodies for dissection.

BURLAW COURTS. In Scotch law. Courts consisting of neighbors selected by common consent to act as judges in determining disputes between neighbor and neighbor.

BURLAWS. In Scotch law. Laws made by neighbors elected by common consent in the burlaw courts. Skene.

BURN. To consume with fire. The verb "to burn," in an indictment for arson, is to be taken in its common meaning of "to consume with fire." 17 Ga. 130.

Burning and *setting fire to* are not legal synonyms. 5 Grat. 664.

BURNING FLUID. As used in policies of insurance, this term does not mean any fluid which will burn, but it means a recognized article of commerce, called by that name, and which is a different article from naphtha or kerosene. 4 Fed. Rep. 766; 24 Hun, 569.

BURNING IN THE HAND. In old English criminal law, laymen, upon being accorded the benefit of clergy, were burned with a hot iron in the brawn of the left thumb, in order that, being thus marked, they could not again claim their clergy. 4 Bl. Comm. 367.

BURROCHIUM. A burroch, dam, or small wear over a river, where traps are laid for the taking of fish. Cowell.

BURROWMEALIS. In Scotch law. A term used to designate the rents paid into the king's private treasury by the burgesses or inhabitants of a borough.

BURSA. A purse.

BURSAR. A treasurer of a college.

BURSARIA. The exchequer of collegiate or conventual bodies; or the place of receiving, paying, and accounting by the bursars. Also stipendiary scholars, who live upon the burse, fund, or joint-stock of the college.

BURYING ALIVE. In English law. The ancient punishment of sodomites, and those who contracted with Jews. Fleta, lib. 1, c. 27, § 3.

BURYING-GROUND. A place set apart for the interment of the dead; a cemetery.

BUSCARL. In Saxon and old English law. Seamen or marines. Spelman.

BUSHEL. A dry measure, containing four pecks, eight gallons, or thirty-two quarts. But the dimensions of a bushel, and the weight of a bushel of grain, etc., vary in the different states in consequence of statutory enactments.

BUSINESS. This word embraces everything about which a person can be employed. 23 N. Y. 242, 244.

That which occupies the time, attention, and labor of men for the purpose of a livelihood or profit. The doing of a single act pertaining to a particular business will not be considered engaging in or carrying on the business; yet a series of such acts would be so considered. 50 Ala. 130. See, also, 2 Allen, 395; 38 N. J. Law, 237.

Labor, business, and work are not synonyms. Labor may be business, but it is not necessarily so; and business is not always labor. Making an agreement for the sale of a chattel is not within a prohibition of labor upon Sunday, though it is (if by a merchant in his calling) within a prohibition upon business. 2 Ohio St. 387.

BUSINESS HOURS. Those hours of the day during which, in a given community, commercial, banking, professional, public, or other kinds of business are ordinarily carried on.

This phrase is declared to mean not the time during which a principal requires an employee's services, but the business hours of the community generally. 18 Minn. 133, (Gil. 119.)

BUSONES COMITATUS. In old English law. The barons of a county.

BUSSA. A term used in the old English law, to designate a large and clumsily constructed ship.

BUTLERAGE. A privilege formerly allowed to the king's butler, to take a certain part of every cask of wine imported by an alien.

BUTLER'S ORDINANCE. In English law. A law for the heir to punish waste in the life of the ancestor. "Though it be on record in the parliament book of Edward I., yet it never was a statute, nor ever so received; but only some constitution of the king's council, or lords in parliament, which never obtained the strength or force of an act of parliament." Hale, Hist. Eng. Law, p. 18.

BUTT. A measure of liquid capacity, equal to one hundred and eight gallons; also a measure of land.

BUTTALS. The bounding lines of land at the end; abuttals, which see.

BUTTED AND BOUNDED. A phrase sometimes used in conveyancing, to introduce the boundaries of lands. See BUTTS AND BOUNDS.

BUTTS. In old English law. Short pieces of land left unplowed at the *ends* of fields, where the plow was turned about, (otherwise called "headlands,") as sidelings were similar unplowed pieces on the sides. Burrill.

Also a place where bowmen meet to shoot at a mark.

BUTTS AND BOUNDS. A phrase used in conveyancing, to describe the end lines or circumscribing lines of a certain piece of land. The phrase "metes and bounds" has the same meaning.

BUTTY. A local term in the north of England, for the associate or deputy of another; also of things used in common.

BUY. To acquire the ownership of property by giving an accepted price or consideration therefor; or by agreeing to do so; to acquire by the payment of a price or value; to purchase. Webster.

BUY IN. To purchase, at public sale, property which is one's own or which one has caused or procured to be sold.

BUYER. One who buys; a purchaser, particularly of chattels.

BUYING TITLES. The purchase of the rights or claims to real estate of a person who is not in possession of the land or is disseised. Void, and an offense, at common law.

BY. This word, when descriptively used in a grant, does not mean "in immediate contact with," but "near" to, the object to which it relates; and "near" is a relative term, meaning, when used in land patents, very unequal and different distances. 6 Gill, 121; 48 N. H. 491.

A contract to complete work *by* a certain time, means that it shall be done before that time. 3 Pen. & W. 48.

By an acquittance for the last payment all other arrearages are discharged. Noy, 40.

BY-BIDDING. In the law relating to sales by auction, this term is equivalent to "puffing." The practice consists in making fictitious bids for the property, under a secret arrangement with the owner or auctioneer, for the purpose of misleading and stimulating other persons who are bidding in good faith.

BY BILL, BY BILL WITHOUT WRIT. In practice. Terms anciently used to designate actions commenced by original *bill*, as distinguished from those commenced by original *writ*, and applied in modern practice to suits commenced by *capias ad respondendum*. 1 Arch. Pr. pp. 2, 337; 5 Hill, 213.

BY ESTIMATION. In conveyancing. A term used to indicate that the quantity of land as stated is estimated only, not exactly measured; has the same meaning and effect as the phrase "more or less."

BY GOD AND MY COUNTRY. In old English criminal practice. The established formula of reply by a prisoner, when arraigned at the bar, to the question, "Culprit, how wilt thou be tried?"

BY-LAWS. Regulations, ordinances, or rules enacted by a private corporation for its own government.

A by-law is a rule or law of a corporation, for its government, and is a legislative act, and the solemnities and sanction required by the charter must be observed. A resolution is not necessarily a by-law, though a by-law may be in the form of a resolution. 7 Barb. 508.

"That the reasonableness of a by-law of a corporation is a question of law, and not of fact, has always been the established rule; but in the case of State v. Overton, 24 N. J. Law, 435, a distinction was taken in this respect between a by-law and a regulation, the validity of the former being a judicial question, while the latter was regarded as a matter *in pais*. But although, in one of the opinions read in the case referred to, the view was clearly expressed that the reasonableness of a corporate regulation was properly for the consideration of the jury, and not of the court, yet it was nevertheless stated that the point was not involved in the controversy then to be decided. There is no doubt that the rule thus intimated is in opposition to recent American authorities. Nor have I been able to find in the English books any such distinction as that above stated between a by-law and a regulation of a corporation." 34 N. J. Law, 135.

The word has also been used to designate the local laws or municipal statutes of a city or town. But of late the tendency is to employ the word "ordinance" exclusively for this class of enactments, reserving "by-law" for the rules adopted by private corporations.

BY LAW MEN. In English law. The chief men of a town, representing the inhabitants.

BY-ROAD. The statute law of New Jersey recognizes three different kinds of roads:

A public road, a private road, and a by-road. A by-road is a road used by the inhabitants, and recognized by statute, but not laid out. Such roads are often called "drift-ways." They are roads of necessity in newly-settled countries. 29 N. J. Law, 516. See, also, Id. 68.

An obscure or neighborhood road in its earlier existence, not used to any great extent by the public, yet so far a public road that the public have of right free access to it at all times. 34 N. J. Law, 89.

BY THE BY. Incidentally; without new process. A term used in former English practice to denote the method of filing a declaration against a defendant who was already in the custody of the court at the suit of a different plaintiff or of the same plaintiff in another cause.

BYE-BIL-WUFFA. In Hindu law. A deed of mortgage or conditional sale.

C.

C. The initial letter of the word "*Codex*," used by some writers in citing the Code of Justinian. Tayl. Civil Law, 24.

It was also the letter inscribed on the ballots by which, among the Romans, jurors voted to condemn an accused party. It was the initial letter of *condemno*, I condemn. Tayl. Civil Law, 192.

C, as the third letter of the alphabet, is used as a numeral, in like manner with that use of A and B, (*q. v.*)

The letter is also used to designate the *third* of a series of propositions, sections, etc., as A, B, and the others are used as numerals.

It is used as an abbreviation of many words of which it is the initial letter; such as cases, civil, circuit, code, common, court, criminal, chancellor, crown.

C. A. V. An abbreviation for *curia advisari vult*, the court will be advised, will consider, will deliberate.

C. B. In reports and legal documents, an abbreviation for common bench. Also an abbreviation for chief baron.

C. C. Various terms or phrases may be denoted by this abbreviation; such as circuit court, (or city or county court;) criminal cases, (or crown or civil or chancery cases;) civil code; chief commissioner; and the return of *cepi corpus*.

C. C. P. An abbreviation for Code of Civil Procedure; also for court of common pleas.

C. J. An abbreviation for chief justice; also for circuit judge.

C. L. An abbreviation for civil law.

C. L. P. Common law procedure, in reference to the English acts so entitled.

C. O. D. "Collect on delivery." These letters are not cabalistic, but have a determinate meaning. They import the carrier's liability to return to the consignor either the goods or the charges. 59 Ind. 263.

C. P. An abbreviation for common pleas.

C. R. An abbreviation for *curia regis;* also for chancery reports.

C. T. A. An abbreviation for *cum testamento annexo*, in describing a species of administration.

CABAL. A small association for the purpose of intrigue; an intrigue. This name was given to that ministry in the reign of Charles II. formed by Clifford, Ashley, Buckingham, Arlington, and Lauderdale, who concerted a scheme for the restoration of popery. The initials of these five names form the word "cabal;" hence the appellation. Hume, Hist. Eng. ix. 69.

CABALIST. In French commercial law. A factor or broker.

CABALLARIA. Pertaining to a horse. It was a feudal tenure of lands, the tenant furnishing a horseman suitably equipped in time of war, or when the lord had occasion for his service.

CABALLERIA. In Spanish law. An allotment of land acquired by conquest, to a horse soldier. It was a strip one hundred feet wide by two hundred feet deep. The term has been sometimes used in those parts of the United States which were derived from Spain. See 12 Pet. 444, note.

CABALLERO. In Spanish law. A knight. So called on account of its being more honorable to go on horseback (*à caballo*) than on any other beast.

CABINET. The advisory board or council of a king or other chief executive. In the government of the United States the cabinet is composed of the secretary of state, the secretary of the treasury, the secretary of the interior, the secretary of war, the secretary of the navy, the secretary of agriculture, the attorney general, and the postmaster general.

The select or secret council of a prince or executive government; so called from the apartment in which it was originally held. Webster.

CABINET COUNCIL. In English law. A private and confidential assembly of the most considerable ministers of state, to concert measures for the administration of public affairs; first established by Charles I. Wharton.

CABLE. The great rope of a ship, to which the anchor is fastened.

CABLISH. Brush-wood, or more properly windfall-wood.

CACHEPOLUS, or CACHERELLAS. An inferior bailiff, or catchpoll. Jacob.

CACHET, LETTRES DE. Letters issued and signed by the kings of France, and countersigned by a secretary of state, authorizing the imprisonment of a person. Abolished during the revolution of 1789.

CACICAZGOS. In Spanish-American law. Property entailed on the *caciques*, or heads of Indian villages, and their descendants. Schm. Civil Law, 309.

CADASTRE. In Spanish law. An official statement of the quantity and value of real property in any district, made for the purpose of justly apportioning the taxes payable on such property. 12 Pet. 428, note.

CADASTU. In French law. An official statement of the quantity and value of realty made for purposes of taxation; same as *cadastre*, (*q. v.*)

CADERE. Lat. To end; cease; fail. As in the phrases *cadit actio*, (or *breve*,) the action (or writ) fails; *cadit assisa*, the assise abates; *cadit quæstio*, the discussion ends, there is no room for further argument.

To be changed; to be turned into. *Cadit assisa in juratum*, the assise is changed into a jury.

CADET. In the United States laws, students in the military academy at West Point are styled "cadets;" students in the naval academy at Annapolis, "cadet midshipmen." Rev. St. §§ 1309, 1512.

In England. The younger son of a gentleman; particularly applied to a volunteer in the army, waiting for some post. Jacob.

CADI. The name of a Turkish civil magistrate.

CADIT. It falls, abates, fails, ends, ceases. See CADERE.

CADUCA. In the civil law. Property of an inheritable quality; property such as descends to an heir. Also the lapse of a testamentary disposition or legacy. Also an escheat; escheated property.

CADUCARY. Relating to or of the nature of escheat, forfeiture, or confiscation. 2 Bl. Comm. 245.

CÆDUA. In the civil and old common law. Kept for cutting; intended or used to be cut. A term applied to wood.

CÆSAR. In the Roman law. A cognomen in the Gens Julia, which was assumed by the successors of Julius. Tayl. Civil Law, 31.

CÆSAREAN OPERATION. A surgical operation whereby the fœtus, which can neither make its way into the world by the ordinary and natural passage, nor be extracted by the attempts of art, whether the mother and fœtus be yet alive, or whether either of them be dead, is, by a cautious and well-timed operation, taken from the mother, with a view to save the lives of both, or either of them. If this operation be performed after the mother's death, the husband cannot be tenant by the curtesy; since his right begins from the birth of the issue, and is consummated by the death of the wife; but, if mother and child are saved, then the husband would be entitled after her death. Wharton.

CÆTERIS PARIBUS. Other things being equal.

CÆTERIS TACENTIBUS. Lat. The others being silent; the other judges expressing no opinion. Comb. 186.

CÆTERORUM. When a limited administration has been granted, and all the property cannot be administered under it, administration *cæterorum* (as to the residue) may be granted.

CAHIER. In old French law. A list of grievances prepared for deputies in the states-general. A petition for the redress of grievances enumerated.

CAIRNS' ACT. An English statute for enabling the court of chancery to award damages. 21 & 22 Vict. c. 27.

CALCETUM, CALCEA. A causeway, or common hard-way, maintained and repaired with stones and rubbish.

CALE. In old French law. A punishment of sailors, resembling the modern "keel-hauling."

CALEFAGIUM. In old law. A right to take fuel yearly. Cowell.

CALENDAR. The established order of the division of time into years, months, weeks, and days; or a systematized enumeration of such arrangement; an almanac.

CALENDAR MONTH. One of the months of the year as enumerated in the calendar, — January, February, March, etc.,— without reference to the number of days it may contain; as distinguished from a lunar month, of twenty-eight days, or a month for business purposes, which may contain thirty, at whatever part of the year it occurs.

CALENDAR OF CAUSES. In practice. A list of the causes instituted in the particular court, and now ready for trial, drawn up by the clerk shortly before the beginning of the term, exhibiting the titles of the suits, arranged in their order for trial, with the nature of each action, the date of issue, and the names of the counsel engaged; designed for the information and convenience of the court and bar. It is sometimes called the "trial-list," or "docket."

CALENDAR OF PRISONERS. In English practice. A list kept by the sheriffs containing the names of all the prisoners in their custody, with the several judgments against each in the margin. Staundef. P. C. 182; 4 Bl. Comm. 403.

CALENDS. Among the Romans the first day of every month, being spoken of by itself, or the very day of the new moon, which usually happen together. And if *pridie*, the day before, be added to it, then it is the last day of the foregoing month, as *pridie calend. Septemb.* is the last day of August. If any number be placed with it, it signifies that day in the former month which comes so much before the month named, as the tenth calends of October is the 20th day of September; for if one reckons backwards, beginning at October, that 20th day of September makes the 10th day before October. In March, May, July, and October, the calends begin at the sixteenth day, but in other months at the fourteenth; which calends must ever bear the name of the month following, and be numbered backwards from the first day of the said following months. Jacob.

CALENDS, GREEK. A metaphorical expression for a time never likely to arrive.

CALL. 1. In English law. The election of students to the degree of barrister at law, hence the ceremony or epoch of election, and the number of persons elected.

2. In conveyancing. A visible natural object or landmark designated in a patent, entry, grant, or other conveyance of lands, as a limit or boundary to the land described, with which the points of surveying must correspond. Also the courses and distances designated.

3. In corporation law. A demand made by the directors of a stock company upon the persons who have subscribed for shares, requiring a certain portion or installment of the amount subscribed to be paid in. The word, in this sense, is synonymous with "assessment," (*q. v.*)

A call is an assessment on shares of stock, usually for unpaid installments of the subscription thereto. The word is said to be capable of three meanings: (1) The resolution of the directors to levy the assessment; (2) its notification to the persons liable to pay; (3) the time when it becomes payable. 4 Exch. 543.

4. In the language of the stock exchange, a "call" is an option to claim stock at a fixed price on a certain day. Bid. Stock-Brok. 70.

CALL OF THE HOUSE. A call of the names of all the members of a legislative body, made by the clerk in pursuance of a resolution requiring the attendance of members. The names of absentees being thus ascertained, they are imperatively summoned (and, if necessary, compelled) to attend the session.

CALLING A SUMMONS. In Scotch practice. See this described in Bell, Dict.

CALLING THE JURY. Successively drawing out of a box into which they have been previously put the names of the jurors on the panels annexed to the *nisi prius* record, and calling them over in the order in which they are so drawn. The twelve persons whose names are first called, and who appear, are sworn as the jury, unless some just cause of challenge or excuse, with respect to any of them, shall be brought forward.

CALLING THE PLAINTIFF. In practice. A formal method of causing a nonsuit to be entered.

When a plaintiff or his counsel, seeing that sufficient evidence has not been given to maintain the issue, withdraws, the crier is ordered to call or demand the plaintiff, and if neither he, nor any person for him, appear, he is nonsuited, the jurors are discharged without giving a verdict, the action is at an end, and the defendant recovers his costs.

CALLING TO THE BAR. In English practice. Conferring the dignity or degree of barrister at law upon a member of one of the inns of court. Holthouse.

CALLING UPON A PRISONER. When a prisoner has been found guilty on an indictment, the clerk of the court addresses him and calls upon him to say why judgment should not be passed upon him.

CALPES. In Scotch law. A gift to the head of a clan, as an acknowledgment for protection and maintenance.

CALUMNIA. In the civil law. Calumny, malice, or ill design; a false accusation; a malicious prosecution.

In the old common law. A claim, demand, challenge to jurors.

CALUMNIÆ JURAMENTUM. In the old canon law. An oath similar to the *calumniæ jusjurandum*, (*q. v.*)

CALUMNIÆ JUSJURANDUM. The oath of calumny. An oath imposed upon the parties to a suit that they did not sue or defend with the intention of calumniating, (*calumniandi animo*,) *i. e.*, with a malicious design, but from a firm belief that they had a good cause. Inst. 4, 16.

CALUMNIATOR. In the civil law. One who accused another of a crime without cause; one who brought a false accusation. Cod. 9, 46.

CALUMNY. Defamation; slander; false accusation of a crime or offense. "There was a word called 'calumny' in the civil law, which signified an unjust prosecution or defense of a suit, and the phrase is said to be still used in the courts of Scotland and the ecclesiastical and admiralty courts of England, though we do not find cases of the kind in the reports." 30 Ohio St. 117.

CAMARA. In Spanish law. A treasury. Las Partidas, pt. 6, tit. 3, l. 2.

The exchequer. White, New Recop. b. 3, tit. 8, c. 1.

CAMBELLANUS, or CAMBELLARIUS. A chamberlain. Spelman.

CAMBIATOR. In old English law. An exchanger. *Cambiatores monetæ*, exchangers of money; money-changers.

CAMBIO. In Spanish law. Exchange. Schm. Civil Law, 148.

CAMBIPARTIA. Champerty; from *campus*, a field, and *partus*, divided. Spelman.

CAMBIPARTICEPS. A champertor.

CAMBIST. In mercantile law. A person skilled in exchanges; one who trades in promissory notes and bills of exchange.

CAMBIUM. In the civil law. Change or exchange. A term applied indifferently to the exchange of land, money, or debts.

Cambium reale or *manuale* was the term generally used to denote the technical common-law exchange of lands; *cambium locale*, *mercantile*, or *trajectitium*, was used to designate the modern mercantile contract of exchange, whereby a man agrees, in consideration of a sum of money paid him in one place, to pay a like sum in another place. Poth. *de Change*, n. 12; Story, Bills, § 2, et seq.

CAMERA. In old English law. A chamber, room, or apartment; a judge's chamber; a treasury; a chest or coffer. Also, a stipend payable from vassal to lord; an annuity.

CAMERA REGIS. In old English law. A chamber of the king; a place of peculiar privileges especially in a commercial point of view.

CAMERA SCACCARII. The old name of the exchequer chamber, (*q. v.*)

CAMERA STELLATA. The star chamber, (*q. v.*)

CAMERALISTICS. The science of finance or public revenue, comprehending the means of raising and disposing of it.

CAMERARIUS. A chamberlain; a keeper of the public money; a treasurer.

Also a bailiff or receiver.

CAMINO. In Spanish law. A road or highway. Las Partidas, pt. 3, tit. 2, l. 6.

CAMPANA. In old European law. A bell. Spelman.

CAMPANA BAJULA. A small hand-bell used in the ceremonies of the Romish church; and, among Protestants, by sextons, parish clerks, and criers. Cowell.

CAMPANARIUM, CAMPANILE. A belfry, bell tower, or steeple; a place where bells are hung. Spelman; Townsh. Pl. 191, 213.

CAMPARTUM. A part of a larger field or ground, which would otherwise be in gross or in common.

CAMPBELL'S (LORD) ACTS. English statutes, for amending the practice in prosecutions for libel, 9 & 10 Vict. c. 93; also 6 & 7 Vict. c. 96, providing for compensation to relatives in the case of a person having been killed through negligence; also 20 & 21 Vict. c. 83, in regard to the sale of obscene books, etc.

CAMPERS. A share; a champertor's share; a champertous division or sharing of land.

CAMPERTUM. A corn-field; a field of grain. Blount; Cowell; Jacob.

CAMPFIGHT. In old English law. The fighting of two champions or combatants in the field; the judicial combat, or *duellum*. 3 Inst. 221.

CAMPUS. **In old European law.** An assembly of the people; so called from being anciently held in the open air, in some *plain* capable of containing a large number of persons.

In feudal and old English law. A field, or plain. The field, ground, or lists marked out for the combatants in the *duellum*, or trial by battle.

CAMPUS MAII. L. Lat. The field of May. An anniversary assembly of the Saxons, held on May-day, when they confederated for the defense of the kingdom against all its enemies.

CAMPUS MARTII. The field of March. See CHAMP DE MARS.

CAN. A promise to pay as soon as the debtor possibly *can* is in contemplation of law a promise to pay presently; the law supposes every man able to pay his debts. 1 Bibb, 396.

CANA. A distance in the measure of ground.

CANAL. An artificial ditch or trench in the earth, for confining water to a defined channel, to be used for purposes of transportation.

The meaning of this word, when applied to artificial passages for water, is a trench or excavation in the earth, for conducting water and confining it to narrow limits. It is unlike the words "river," "pond," "lake," and other words used to designate natural bodies of water, the ordinary meaning of which is confined to the water itself; but it includes also the banks, and has reference rather to the excavation or channel as a receptacle for the water; it is an artificial thing. 18 Conn. 394. See, also, 103 U. S. 604.

CANCEL. To obliterate, strike, or cross out; to destroy the effect of an instrument by defacing, obliterating, expunging, or erasing it. See 18 Cal. 451.

In equity. Courts of equity frequently cancel instruments which have answered the end for which they were created, or instruments which are void or voidable, in order to prevent them from being vexatiously used against the person apparently bound by them. Snell, Eq. 498.

CANCELLARIA. Chancery; the court of chancery. *Curia cancellaria* is also used in the same sense. See 4 Bl. Comm. 46; Cowell.

Cancellarii Angliæ dignitas est, ut secundus a rege in regno habetur. The dignity of the chancellor of England is that he is deemed the second from the sovereign in the kingdom. 4 Inst. 78.

CANCELLARIUS. A chancellor; a scrivener, or notary. A janitor, or one who stood at the door of the court and was accustomed to carry out the commands of the judges.

CANCELLATION. The act of crossing out a writing. The manual operation of tearing or destroying a written instrument. 1 Eq. Cas. Abr. 409; Rob. Wills, 367, n.

According to Bartolus, an expunging or wiping out of the contents of an instrument by two lines drawn in the manner of a cross; also used to signify any manner of obliteration and defacement.

CANCELLATURA. In old English law. A cancelling. Bract. 398*b*.

CANCELLI. The rails or lattice work or balusters inclosing the bar of a court of justice or the communion table. Also the lines drawn on the face of a will or other writing, with the intention of revoking or annulling it.

CANDIDATE. A person who offers himself, or is presented by others, to be elected to an office. Derived from the Latin *candidus*, (white,) because in Rome it was the custom for those who sought office to clothe themselves in white garments.

One who seeks or aspires to some office or privilege, or who offers himself for the same. A man is a candidate for an office when he is seeking such office. It is not necessary that he should have been *nominated* for the office. 112 Pa. St. 624, 4 Atl. Rep. 607.

CANDLEMAS-DAY. A festival appointed by the church to be observed on the second day of February in every year, in honor of the purification of the Virgin Mary, being forty days after her miraculous delivery. At this festival, formerly, the Protestants went, and the Papists now go, in procession with lighted candles; they also consecrate candles on this day for the service of the ensuing year. It is the fourth of the four cross quarter-days of the year. Wharton.

CANFARA. In old records. A trial by hot iron, formerly used in England. Whishaw.

CANON. A law, rule, or ordinance in general, and of the church in particular. An ecclesiastical law or statute.

One of the dignitaries of the English church; being a prebendary or member of a chapter.

In the civil, Spanish, and Mexican law. An annual charge or rent; an emphyteutic rent. See 15 Cal. 556.

In old English records. A prestation, pension, or customary payment. Cowell.

CANON LAW. A body of ecclesiastical jurisprudence which, in countries where the Roman Catholic church is established, is composed of maxims and rules drawn from patristic sources, ordinances and decrees of general councils, and the decretals and bulls of the popes. In England, according to Blackstone, there is a kind of national canon law, composed of legatine and provincial constitutions enacted in England prior to the reformation, and adapted to the exigencies of the English church and kingdom. 1 Bl. Comm. 82.

The canon law consists partly of certain rules taken out of the Scripture, partly of the writings of the ancient fathers of the church, partly of the ordinances of general and provincial councils, and partly of the decrees of the popes in former ages; and it is contained in two principal parts,—the decrees and the decretals. The decrees are ecclesiastical constitutions made by the popes and cardinals. The decretals are canonical epistles written by the pope, or by the pope and cardinals, at the suit of one or more persons, for the ordering and determining of some matter of controversy, and have the authority of a law. As the decrees set out the origin of the canon law, and the rights, dignities, and decrees of ecclesiastical persons, with their manner of election, ordination, etc., so the decretals contain the law to be used in the ecclesiastical courts. Jacob.

CANON RELIGIOSORUM. Lat. In ecclesiastical records. A book wherein the religious of every greater convent had a fair transcript of the rules of their order, frequently read among them as their local statutes. Kennett, Gloss.; Cowell.

CANONICAL. Pertaining to, or in conformity to, the canons of the church.

CANONICAL OBEDIENCE. That duty which a clergyman owes to the bishop who ordained him, to the bishop in whose diocese he is beneficed, and also to the metropolitan of such bishop. Wharton.

CANONICUS. In old English law. A canon. Fleta, lib. 2, c. 69, § 2.

CANONIST. One versed and skilled in the canon law; a professor of ecclesiastical law.

CANONRY. In English ecclesiastical law. An ecclesiastical benefice, attaching to the office of canon. Holthouse.

CANONS OF DESCENT. The legal rules by which inheritances are regulated, and according to which estates are transmitted by descent from the ancestor to the heir.

CANONS OF INHERITANCE. The legal rules by which inheritances are regulated, and according to which estates are transmitted by descent from the ancestor to the heir. 2 Bl. Comm. 208.

CANT. In the civil law. A method of dividing property held in common by two or more joint owners. See 9 Mart. (La.) 87.

CANTEL, or CANTLE. A lump, or that which is added above measure; also a piece of anything, as "cantel of bread," or the like. Blount.

CANTERBURY, ARCHBISHOP OF. In English ecclesiastical law. The primate of all England; the chief ecclesiastical dignitary in the church. His customary privilege is to crown the kings and queens of England; while the Archbishop of York has the privilege to crown the queen consort, and be her perpetual chaplain. The Archbishop of Canterbury has also, by 25 Hen. VIII. c. 21, the power of granting dispensations in any case not contrary to the holy scriptures and the law of God, where the pope used formerly to grant them, which is the foundation of his granting special licenses to marry at any place or time; to hold two livings, (which must be confirmed under the great seal,) and the like; and on this also is founded the right he exercises of conferring degrees in prejudice of the two universities. Wharton.

CANTRED. A district comprising a hundred villages; a hundred. A term used in Wales in the same sense as "hundred" is in England. Cowell; Termes de la Ley.

CANUM. In feudal law. A species of duty or tribute payable from tenant to lord, usually consisting of produce of the land.

CANVASS. The act of examining and counting the returns of votes cast at a public election.

CAP OF MAINTENANCE. One of the regalia or ornaments of state belonging to the sovereigns of England, before whom it is carried at the coronation and other great solemnities. Caps of maintenance are also carried before the mayors of several cities in England. Enc. Lond.

CAPACITY. Legal capacity is the attribute of a person who can acquire new rights, or transfer rights, or assume duties, according to the mere dictates of his own will, as manifested in juristic acts, without any restraint or hindrance arising from his *status* or legal condition.

Ability; qualification; legal power or right. Applied in this sense to the attribute of persons (natural or artificial) growing out of their *status* or juristic condition, which enables them to perform civil acts; as capacity to hold lands, capacity to devise, etc.

CAPAX DOLI. Lat. Capable of committing crime, or capable of criminal intent. The phrase describes the condition of one who has sufficient intelligence and comprehension to be held criminally responsible for his deeds.

CAPAX NEGOTII. Competent to transact affairs; having business capacity.

CAPE. In English practice. A judicial writ touching a plea of lands or tenements, divided into *cape magnum*, or the *grand cape*, which lay before appearance to summon the tenant to answer the default, and also over to the demandant; the *cape ad valentiam* was a species of grand cape; and *cape parvum*, or *petit cape*, after appearance or view granted, summoning the tenant to answer the default only. Termes de la Ley; 3 Steph. Comm. 606, note.

CAPE AD VALENTIAM. A species of *cape magnum*. See CAPE.

CAPELLA. In old records. A box, cabinet, or repository in which were preserved the relics of martyrs. Spelman. A small building in which relics were preserved; an oratory or chapel. Id.

In old English law. A chapel. Fleta, lib. 5, c. 12, § 1; Spelman; Cowell.

CAPERS. Vessels of war owned by private persons, and different from ordinary privateers only in size, being smaller. Beawes, Lex Merc. 230.

CAPIAS. Lat. "That you take." The general name for several species of writs, the common characteristic of which is that they require the officer to take the body of the defendant into custody; they are writs of attachment or arrest.

In English practice. A *capias* is the process on an indictment when the person charged is not in custody, and in cases not otherwise provided for by statute. 4 Steph. Comm. 383.

CAPIAS AD AUDIENDUM JUDICIUM. In practice. A writ issued, in a case of misdemeanor, after the defendant has appeared and is found guilty, to bring him to hear judgment if he is not present when called. 4 Bl. Comm. 368.

CAPIAS AD COMPUTANDUM. In the action of account render, after judgment of *quod computet*, if the defendant refuses to appear personally before the auditors and make his account, a writ by this name may issue to compel him.

CAPIAS AD RESPONDENDUM. In practice. A judicial writ, (usually simply termed a "*capias*,") by which actions at law were frequently commenced; and which commands the sheriff to *take* the defendant, and him safely keep, so that he may have his body before the court on a certain day, to *answer* the plaintiff in the action. 3 Bl. Comm. 282; 1 Tidd, Pr. 128. The name of this writ is commonly abbreviated to *ca. resp.*

CAPIAS AD SATISFACIENDUM. In practice. A writ of execution, (usually termed, for brevity, a "*ca. sa.*,") which a party may issue after having recovered judgment against another in certain actions at law. It commands the sheriff to *take* the party named, and keep him safely, so that he may have his body before the court on a certain day, *to satisfy* the party by whom it is issued, the damages or debt and damages recovered by the judgment. Its effect is to deprive the party taken of his liberty until he makes the satisfaction awarded. 3 Bl. Comm. 414, 415; 2 Tidd, Pr. 993, 1025; Litt. § 504; Co. Litt. 289*a*.

CAPIAS EXTENDI FACIAS. A writ of execution issuable in England against a debtor to the crown, which commands the sheriff to "take" or arrest the body, and "cause to be extended" the lands and goods of the debtor. Man. Exch. Pr. 5.

CAPIAS IN WITHERNAM. A writ, in the nature of a reprisal, which lies for one whose goods or cattle, taken under a distress, are removed from the county, so that they cannot be replevied, commanding the sheriff to seize other goods or cattle of the distrainor of equal value.

CAPIAS PRO FINE. (That you take for the fine or in mercy.) Formerly, if the verdict was for the defendant, the plaintiff was adjudged to be amerced for his false claim; but, if the verdict was for the plaintiff, then in all actions *vi et armis*, or where the defendant, in his pleading, had falsely denied his own deed, the judgment contained an award of a *capiatur pro fine;* and in all other cases the defendant was adjudged to be amerced. The insertion of the *misericordia* or of the *capiatur* in the judgment is now unnecessary. Wharton.

CAPIAS UTLAGATUM. (You take the outlaw.) In English practice. A writ which lies against a person who has been *outlawed* in an action, by which the sheriff is commanded to *take* him, and keep him in custody until the day of the return, and then present him to the court, there to be dealt with for his contempt. Reg. Orig. 138*b;* 3 Bl. Comm. 284.

CAPIATUR PRO FINE. (Let him be taken for the fine.) In English practice. A clause inserted at the end of old judgment records in actions of debt, where the defendant denied his deed, and it was found against him upon his false plea, and the jury were troubled with the trial of it. Cro. Jac. 64.

CAPITA. Heads, and, figuratively, entire bodies, whether of persons or animals. Spelman.

Persons individually considered, without relation to others, (polls;) as distinguished from *stirpes* or stocks of descent. The term in this sense, making part of the common phrases, *in capita, per capita,* is derived from the civil law. Inst. 3, 1, 6.

CAPITA, PER. By heads; by the poll; as individuals. In the distribution of an intestate's personalty, the persons legally entitled to take are said to take *per capita* when they claim, each in his own right, as in equal degree of kindred; in contradistinction to claiming by right of representation, or *per stirpes.*

CAPITAL, *n.* In political economy, that portion of the produce of industry existing in a country, which may be made directly available, either for the support of human existence, or the facilitating of production; but, in commerce, and as applied to individuals, it is understood to mean the sum of money which a merchant, banker, or trader adventures in any undertaking, or which he contributes to the common stock of a partnership. Also the fund of a trading company or corporation, in which sense the word "stock" is generally added to it. McCul. Dict.; 2 Bouv. Inst. 1458.

The actual estate, whether in money or property, which is owned by an individual or a corporation. In reference to a corporation, it is the aggregate of the sum subscribed and paid in, or secured to be paid in, by the shareholders, with the addition of all gains or profits realized in the use and investment of those sums, or, if losses have been incurred, then it is the residue after deducting such losses. 23 N. Y. 219.

When used with respect to the property of a corporation or association, the term has a settled meaning. It applies only to the property or means contributed by the stockholders as the fund or basis for the business or enterprise for which the corporation or association was formed. As to them the term does not embrace temporary loans, though the moneys borrowed be directly appropriated in their business or undertakings. And, when used with respect to the property of individuals in any particular business, the term has substantially the same import; it then means the property taken from other investments or uses and set apart for and invested in the special business, and in the increase, proceeds, or earnings of which property beyond expenditures incurred in its use consist the profits made in the business. It does not, any more than when used with respect to corporations, embrace temporary loans made in the regular course of business. 21 Wall. 286.

The principal sum of a fund of money; money invested at interest.

Also the political and governmental metropolis of a state or country; the seat of government; the place where the legislative department holds its sessions, and where the chief offices of the executive are located.

CAPITAL, *adj.* Affecting or relating to the head or life of a person; entailing the ultimate penalty. Thus, a capital crime is one punishable with death. See Bract. fol. 101*b*.

Also principal; leading; chief; as "capital burgess." 10 Mod. 100.

CAPITAL CRIME. A crime for which the punishment of death is provided by law.

CAPITAL PUNISHMENT. The punishment of death.

CAPITAL STOCK. The common stock or fund of a corporation. The sum of money raised by the subscriptions of the stockholders, and divided into shares. It is said to be the sum upon which calls may be made upon the stockholders, and dividends are to be paid. 1 Sandf. Ch. 280; Ang. & A. Corp. §§ 151, 556.

Originally "the capital stock of the bank" was all the property of every kind, everything, which the bank possessed. And this "capital stock," all of it, in reality belonged to the contributors, it being intrusted to the bank to be used and traded with for their exclusive benefit; and thus the bank became the agent of the contributors, so that the transmutation of the money originally advanced by the subscribers into property of other kinds, though it altered the form of the investment, left its beneficial ownership unaffected; and every new acquisition of property, by exchange or otherwise, was an acquisition for the original subscribers or their representatives, their respective interests in it all always continuing in the same proportion as in the aggregate capital originally advanced. So that, whether in the form of money, bills of exchange, or any other property in possession or in action into which the money originally contributed has been changed, or which it has produced, all is, as the original contribution was, the capital stock of the bank, held, as the original contribution was, for the exclusive benefit of the original contributors and those who represent them. The original contributors and those who represent them are the stockholders. 31 Conn. 109.

Capital stock, as employed in acts of incorporation, is never used to indicate the value of the property of the company. It is very generally, if not universally, used to designate the amount of capital prescribed to be contributed at the outset by the stockholders, for the purposes of the corporation. The value of the corporate assets may be greatly increased by surplus profits, or be diminished by losses, but the amount of the capital stock remains the same. The funds of the company may fluctuate; its capital stock remains invariable, unless changed by legislative authority. 23 N. J. Law, 195.

CAPITALE. A thing which is stolen, or the value of it. Blount.

CAPITALE VIVENS. Live cattle. Blount.

CAPITALIS. In old English law. Chief, principal; at the *head*. A term applied to persons, places, judicial proceedings, and some kinds of property.

CAPITALIS BARO. In old English law. Chief baron. *Capitalis baro scaccarii domini regis*, chief baron of the exchequer. Townsh. Pl. 211.

CAPITALIS CUSTOS. Chief warden or magistrate; mayor. Fleta, lib. 2, c. 64, § 2.

CAPITALIS DEBITOR. The chief or principal debtor, as distinguished from a surety, (*plegius*.)

CAPITALIS DOMINUS. Chief lord. Fleta, lib. 1, c. 12, § 4; Id. c. 28, § 5.

CAPITALIS JUSTICIARIUS. The chief justiciary; the principal minister of state, and guardian of the realm in the king's absence.

This office originated under William the Conqueror; but its power was greatly diminished by *Magna Charta*, and finally distributed among several courts by Edward I. Spelman; 3 Bl. Comm. 38.

CAPITALIS JUSTICIARIUS AD PLACITA CORAM REGE TENENDA. Chief justice for holding pleas before the king. The title of the chief justice of the king's bench, first assumed in the latter part of the reign of Henry III. 2 Reeve, Eng. Law, 91, 285.

CAPITALIS JUSTICIARIUS BANCI. Chief justice of the bench. The title of the chief justice of the (now) court of common pleas, first mentioned in the first year of Edward I. 2 Reeve, Eng. Law, 48.

CAPITALIS JUSTICIARIUS TOTIUS ANGLIÆ. Chief justice of all England. The title of the presiding justice in the court of *aula regis*. 3 Bl. Comm. 38; 1 Reeve, Eng. Law, 48.

CAPITALIS PLEGIUS. A chief pledge; a head borough. Townsh. Pl. 35.

CAPITALIS REDITUS. A chief rent.

CAPITALIS TERRA. A head-land. A piece of land lying at the head of other land.

CAPITANEUS. A tenant *in capite*. He who held his land or title directly from the king himself. A captain; a naval commander.

CAPITARE. In old law and surveys. To head, front, or abut; to touch at the head, or end.

CAPITATIM. Lat. By the head; by the poll; severally to each individual.

CAPITATION. (Lat. *caput*, head.) A poll-tax. An imposition periodically laid upon each person.

A tax or imposition raised on each person in consideration of his labor, industry, office, rank, etc. It is a very ancient kind of tribute, and answers to what the Latins called "*tributum,*" by which taxes on persons are distinguished from taxes on merchandise, called "*vectigalia.*" Wharton.

CAPITATION TAX. One which is levied upon the person simply, without any reference to his property, real or personal, or to any business in which he may be engaged, or to any employment which he may follow. Phillips, 22.

CAPITE. By the head. Tenure *in capite* was an ancient feudal tenure, whereby a man held lands of the king immediately. It was of two sorts,—the one, principal and general, or of the king as the source of all tenure; the other, special and subaltern, or of a particular subject. It is now abolished. Jacob. As to distribution *per capita*, see CAPITA.

CAPITE MINUTUS. In the civil law. One who had suffered *capitis diminutio*, one who lost *status* or legal attributes. See Dig. 4. 5.

CAPITIS DIMINUTIO. In Roman law. A diminishing or abridgment of personality. This was a loss or curtailment of a man's *status* or aggregate of legal attributes and qualifications, following upon certain changes in his civil condition. It was of three kinds, enumerated as follows:

Capitis diminutio maxima. The highest or most comprehensive loss of *status.* This occurred when a man's condition was changed from one of freedom to one of bondage, when he became a slave. It swept away with it all rights of citizenship and all family rights.

Capitis diminutio media. A lesser or medium loss of *status.* This occurred where a man lost his rights of citizenship, but without losing his liberty. It carried away also the family rights.

Capitis diminutio minima. The lowest or least comprehensive degree of loss of *status.* This occurred where a man's family relations alone were changed. It happened upon the arrogation of a person who had been his own master, (*sui juris,*) or upon the emancipation of one who had been under the *patria potestas.* It left the rights of liberty and citizenship unaltered. See Inst. 1, 16, pr.; 1, 2, 3; Dig. 4, 5, 11; Mackeld. Rom Law, § 144.

CAPITITIUM. A covering for the head, mentioned in St. 1 Hen. IV. and other old statutes, which prescribe what dresses shall be worn by all degrees of persons. Jacob.

CAPITULA. Collections of laws and ordinances drawn up under heads of divisions. Spelman.

The term is used in the civil and old English law, and applies to the ecclesiastical law also, meaning chapters or assemblies of ecclesiastical persons. Du Cange.

CAPITULA CORONÆ. Chapters of the crown. Chapters or heads of inquiry, resembling the *capitula itineris,* (*q.v.,*) but of a more minute character.

CAPITULA DE JUDÆIS. A register of mortgages made to the Jews. 2 Bl. Comm. 343; Crabb, Eng. Law, 130, et seq.

CAPITULA ITINERIS. Articles of inquiry which were anciently delivered to the justices in eyre when they set out on their circuits. These schedules were designed to include all possible varieties of crime. 2 Reeve, Eng. Law, p. 4, c. 8.

CAPITULA RURALIA. Assemblies or chapters, held by rural deans and parochial clergy, within the precinct of every deanery; which at first were every three weeks, afterwards once a month, and subsequently once a quarter. Cowell.

CAPITULARY. In French law. A collection and code of the laws and ordinances promulgated by the kings of the Merovingian and Carlovingian dynasties.

Any orderly and systematic collection or code of laws.

In ecclesiastical law. A collection of laws and ordinances orderly arranged by divisions. A book containing the beginning and end of each Gospel which is to be read every day in the ceremony of saying mass. Du Cange.

CAPITULATION. In military law. The surrender of a fort or fortified town to a besieging army; the treaty or agreement between the commanding officers which embodies the terms and conditions on which the surrender is made.

In the civil law. An agreement by which the prince and the people, or those who have the right of the people, regulate the manner in which the government is to be administered. Wolffius, § 989.

CAPITULI AGRI. Head-fields; lands lying at the head or upper end of furrows, etc.

Capitulum est clericorum congregatio sub uno decano in ecclesia cathedrali. A chapter is a congregation of clergy under one dean in a cathedral church. Co. Litt. 98.

CAPPA. In old records. A cap. *Cappa honoris*, the cap of honor. One of the solemnities or ceremonies of creating an earl or marquis.

CAPTAIN. A head-man; commander; commanding officer. The captain of a war-vessel is the officer first in command. In the United States navy, the rank of "captain" is intermediate between that of "commander" and "commodore." The governor or controlling officer of a vessel in the merchant service is usually styled "captain" by the inferior officers and seamen, but in maritime business and admiralty law is more commonly designated as "master." In foreign jurisprudence his title is often that of "patron." In the United States army (and the militia) the captain is the commander of a company of soldiers, one of the divisions of a regiment. The term is also used to designate the commander of a squad of municipal police.

CAPTATION. In French law. The act of one who succeeds in controlling the will of another, so as to become master of it; used in an invidious sense.

CAPTATOR. A person who obtains a gift or legacy through artifice.

CAPTIO. In old English law and practice. A taking or seizure; arrest; receiving; holding of court.

CAPTION. In practice. That part of a legal instrument, as a commission, indictment, etc., which shows where, when, and by what authority it is taken, found, or executed.

When used with reference to an indictment, caption signifies the style or preamble or commencement of the indictment; when used with reference to a commission, it signifies the certificate to which the commissioners' names are subscribed, declaring when and where it was executed. Brown.

The caption of a pleading, deposition, or other paper connected with a case in court, is the heading or introductory clause which shows the names of the parties, name of the court, number of the case on the docket or calendar, etc.

Also signifies a taking, seizure, or arrest of a person. 2 Salk. 498. The word in this sense is now obsolete in English law.

In Scotch law. Caption is an order to incarcerate a debtor who has disobeyed an order, given to him by what are called "letters of horning," to pay a debt or to perform some act enjoined thereby. Bell.

CAPTIVES. Prisoners of war. As in the goods of an enemy, so also in his person, a sort of qualified property may be acquired, by taking him a prisoner of war, at least till his ransom be paid. 2 Bl. Comm. 402.

CAPTOR. In international law. One who takes or seizes property in time of war; one who takes the property of an enemy. In a stricter sense, one who takes a prize at sea. 2 Bl. Comm. 401; 1 Kent, Comm. 86, 96, 103.

CAPTURE. In international law. The taking or wresting of property from one of two belligerents by the other. It occurs either on land or at sea. In the former case, the property captured is called "booty;" in the latter case, "prize."

Capture, in technical language, is a taking by military power; a seizure is a taking by civil authority. 35 Ga. 344.

In some cases, this is a mode of acquiring property. Thus, every one may, as a general rule, on his own land, or on the sea, capture any wild animal, and acquire a qualified ownership in it by confining it, or absolute ownership by killing it. 2 Steph. Comm. 79.

CAPUT. A head; the head of a person; the whole person; the life of a person; one's personality; *status;* civil condition.

At common law. A head.

Caput comitatis, the head of the county; the sheriff; the king. Spelman.

A person; a life. The upper part of a town. Cowell. A castle. Spelman.

In the civil law. It signified a person's civil condition or *status*, and among the Romans consisted of three component parts or elements,—*libertas*, liberty; *civitas*, citizenship; and *familia*, family.

CAPUT ANNI. The first day of the year.

CAPUT BARONIÆ. The castle or chief seat of a baron.

CAPUT JEJUNII. The beginning of the Lent fast, *i. e.*, Ash Wednesday.

CAPUT LOCI. The head or upper part of a place.

CAPUT LUPINUM. In old English law. A wolf's head. An outlawed felon was said to be *caput lupinum*, and might be knocked on the head, like a wolf.

CAPUT MORTUUM. A dead head; dead; obsolete.

CAPUT PORTUS. In old English law. The head of a port. The town to which a port belongs, and which gives the denomination to the port, and is the head of it. Hale de Jure Mar. pt. 2, (*de portubus maris,*) c. 2.

CAPUT, PRINCIPIUM, ET FINIS. The head, beginning, and end. A term applied in English law to the king, as head of parliament. 4 Inst. 3; 1 Bl. Comm. 188.

CAPUTAGIUM. In old English law. Head or poll money, or the payment of it. Cowell; Blount.

CAPUTIUM. In old English law. A head of land; a headland. Cowell.

CARABUS. In old English law. A kind of raft or boat. Spelman.

CARAT. A weight of four grains, used in weighing diamonds. Webster. A weight equal to three and one-sixth grains. Wharton.

CARCAN. In French law. An instrument of punishment, somewhat resembling a pillory. It sometimes signifies the punishment itself. Biret, Vocab

CARCANUM. A gaol; a prison.

CARCARE. In old English law. To load; to load a vessel; to freight.

CARCATUS. Loaded; freighted, as a ship.

CARCEL-AGE. Gaol-dues; prison-fees.

CARCER. A prison or gaol. Strictly, a place of detention and safe-keeping, and not of punishment. Co. Litt. 620.

Carcer ad homines custodiendos, non ad puniendos, dari debet. A prison should be used for keeping persons, not for punishing them. Co. Litt. 260*a*.

Carcer non supplicii causâ sed custodiæ constitutus. A prison is ordained not for the sake of punishment, but of detention and guarding. Lofft, 119.

CARDINAL. In ecclesiastical law. A dignitary of the court of Rome, next in rank to the pope.

CARDS. In criminal law. Small papers or pasteboards of an oblong or rectangular shape, on which are printed figures or points, used in playing certain games. See 2 Humph. 496; 4 Pick. 251; 19 Mo. 377; 12 Wis. 434.

CARE. As a legal term, this word means diligence, prudence, discretion, attentiveness, watchfulness, vigilance. It is the opposite of negligence or carelessness.

There are three degrees of care in the law, corresponding (inversely) to the three degrees of negligence, viz.: slight care, ordinary care, and great care.

Slight care or diligence is such as persons of ordinary prudence usually exercise about their own affairs of slight importance; ordinary care or diligence is such as they usually exercise about their own affairs of ordinary importance; and great care or diligence is such as they usually exercise about their own affairs of great importance. Civil Code Dak. § 2100.

The exact boundaries between the several degrees of care, and their correlative degrees of carelessness, or negligence, are not always clearly defined or easily pointed out. We think, however, that by "ordinary care" is meant that degree of care which may reasonably be expected from a person in the party's situation,—that is, "reasonable care;" and that "gross negligence" imports not a malicious intention or design to produce a particular injury, but a thoughtless disregard of consequences, the absence, rather than the actual exercise, of volition with reference to results. 23 Conn. 443.

Slight care is such as is usually exercised by persons of common sense, but careless habits, under circumstances similar to those of the particular case in which the question arises, and where their own interests are to be protected from a similar injury.

Ordinary care is such as is usually exercised in the like circumstances by the majority of the community, or by persons of careful and prudent habits.

Great care is such as is exercised under such circumstances by persons of unusually careful and prudent habits. Abbott.

CARENA. A term used in the old ecclesiastical law to denote a period of forty days.

CARENCE. In French law. A *procès-verbal de carence* is a document setting out that the *huissier* attended to issue execution upon a judgment, but found nothing upon which to levy. Arg. Fr. Merc. Law, 547.

CARETA, (spelled, also, *Carreta* and *Carecta.*) A cart; a cart-load.

CARETORIUS, or CARECTARIUS. A carter. Blount.

CARGA. In Spanish law. An incumbrance; a charge. White, New Recop. b. 2, tit. 13, c. 2, § 2.

CARGAISON. In French commercial law. Cargo; lading.

CARGARE. In old English law. To charge. Spelman.

CARGO. In mercantile law. The load or lading of a vessel; goods and merchandise put on board a ship to be carried to a certain port.

The lading or freight of a ship; the goods, merchandise, or whatever is conveyed in a ship or other merchant vessel. See 1 Mason, 142; 4 Pick. 429; 9 Metc. (Mass.) 366; 103 Mass. 406.

A cargo is the loading of a ship or other vessel, the bulk of which is to be ascertained from the capacity of the ship or vessel. The word embraces all that the vessel is capable of carrying. 3 Rob. (N. Y.) 173.

The term may be applied in such a sense as to include passengers, as well as freight, but in a technical sense it designates goods only.

CARIAGIUM. In old English law. Carriage; the carrying of goods or other things for the king.

CARISTIA. Dearth, scarcity, dearness. Cowell.

CARK. In old English law. A quantity of wool, whereof thirty make a sarplar. (The latter is equal to 2,240 pounds in weight.) St. 27 Hen. VI. c. 2. Jacob.

CARLISLE TABLES. Life and annuity tables, compiled at Carlisle, England, about 1780. Used by actuaries, etc.

CARMEN. In the Roman law. Literally, a verse or song. A formula or form of words used on various occasions, as of divorce. Tayl. Civil Law, 349.

CARNAL. Of the body; relating to the body; fleshly; sexual.

CARNAL KNOWLEDGE. The act of a man in having sexual bodily connection with a woman.

Carnal knowledge and sexual intercourse held equivalent expressions. 22 Ohio St. 541.

From very early times, in the law, as in common speech, the meaning of the words "carnal knowledge" of a woman by a man has been sexual bodily connection; and these words, without more, have been used in that sense by writers of the highest authority on criminal law, when undertaking to give a full and precise definition of the crime of rape, the highest crime of this character. 97 Mass. 61.

CARNALITER. In old criminal law. Carnally. *Carnaliter cognovit,* carnally knew. Technical words in indictments for rape, and held essential. 1 Hale, P. C. 637-639.

CARNALLY KNEW. In pleading. A technical phrase essential in an indictment to charge the defendant with the crime of rape.

CARNO. In old English law. An immunity or privilege. Cowell.

CAROOME. In English law. A license by the lord mayor of London to keep a cart.

CARPEMEALS. Cloth made in the northern parts of England, of a coarse kind, mentioned in 7 Jac. I. c. 16. Jacob.

CARRERA. In Spanish law. A carriage-way; the right of a carriage-way. Las Partidas, pt. 3, tit. 31, l. 3.

CARRIAGE. A vehicle used for the transportation of persons either for pleasure or business, and drawn by horses or other draught animals over the ordinary streets and highways of the country; not including cars used exclusively upon railroads or street railroads expressly constructed for the use of such cars. 63 Wis. 97, 23 N. W. Rep. 425; 8 Kan. 84; 47 N. Y. 122; 46 N. H. 523; 5 Q. B. Div. 176.

The act of carrying, or a contract for transportation of persons or goods.

The contract of carriage is a contract for the conveyance of property, persons, or messages from one place to another. Civil Code Cal. § 2085; Civil Code Dak. § 1208.

CARRICLE, or CARRACLE. A ship of great burden.

CARRIER. One who undertakes to transport goods from one place to another. 1 Pars. Cont. 632.

One who carries or agrees to carry the goods of another, from one place to another, for hire, or without hire.

Carriers are either common or private. Private carriers are persons who undertake for the transportation in a particular instance only, not making it their vocation, nor holding themselves out to the public as ready to act for all who desire their services.

To bring a person within the description of a common carrier, he must exercise it as a public employment; he must undertake to carry goods for persons generally; and he must hold himself out as ready to transport goods for hire, as a business, not as a casual occupation, *pro hâc vice.*

"CARRY AWAY." A technical phrase in an indictment for larceny, translating the Lat. *asportavit.* 7 Gray, 45.

CARRYING AWAY. In criminal law. The act of removal or asportation, by which the crime of larceny is completed, and which is essential to constitute it.

CARRYING AWAY INFANT FEMALES. See ABDUCTION.

CARRYING COSTS. A verdict is said to carry costs when the party for whom the verdict is given becomes entitled to the payment of his costs as incident to such verdict.

CART. A carriage for luggage or burden, with two wheels, as distinguished from a wagon, which has four wheels. The vehicle in which criminals are taken to execution.

This word, in its ordinary and primary acceptation, signifies a carriage with two wheels; yet it has also a more extended signification, and may mean a carriage in general. 22 Ala. 624.

CART BOTE. Wood or timber which a tenant is allowed by law to take from an estate, for the purpose of repairing instruments, (including necessary vehicles,) of husbandry. 2 Bl. Comm. 35.

CARTA. In old English law. A charter, or deed. Any written instrument.

In Spanish law. A letter; a deed; a power of attorney. Las Partidas, pt. 3, tit. 18, l. 30.

CARTA DE FORESTA. In old English law. The charter of the forest. More commonly called "*Charta de Foresta,*" (*q. v.*)

CARTE. In French marine law. A chart.

CARTE BLANCHE. A white sheet of paper; an instrument signed, but otherwise left blank. A sheet given to an agent, with the principal's signature appended, to be filled up with any contract or engagement as the agent may see fit. Hence, metaphorically, unlimited authority.

CARTEL. An agreement between two hostile powers for the delivery of prisoners or deserters. Also a written challenge to fight a duel.

CARTEL-SHIP. A vessel commissioned in time of war to exchange the prisoners of any two hostile powers; also to carry any particular proposal from one to another. For this reason, the officer who commands her is particularly ordered to carry no cargo, ammunition, or implements of war, except a single gun for the purpose of signals. Enc. Lond.

CARTMEN. Carriers who transport goods and merchandise in carts, usually for short distances, for hire.

CARTULARY. A place where papers or records are kept.

CARUCA, or CARUA. A plow.

CARUCAGE. In old English law. A kind of tax or tribute anciently imposed upon every plow, (*carue* or plow-land,) for the public service. Spelman.

CARUCATA. A certain quantity of land used as the basis for taxation. As much land as may be tilled by a single plow in a year and a day. Also, a team of cattle, or a cart-load.

CARUCATARIUS. One who held lands in *carvage*, or plow-tenure. Cowell.

CARUE. A carve of land; plow-land. Britt. c. 84.

CARVAGE. The same as carucage, (*q. v.*) Cowell.

CARVE. In old English law. A carucate or plow-land.

CAS FORTUIT. Fr. In the law of insurance. A fortuitous event; an inevitable accident.

CASATA. In old English law. A house with land sufficient for the support of one family. Otherwise called "*hida,*" a hide of land, and by Bede, "*familia.*" Spelman.

CASATUS. A vassal or feudal tenant possessing a *casata;* that is, having a house, household, and property of his own.

CASE. 1. A general term for an action, cause, suit, or controversy, at law or in equity. A question contested before a court of justice.

The primary meaning of "case" is "cause." When applied to legal proceedings, it imports a state of facts which furnishes occasion for the exercise of the jurisdiction of a court of justice. In its generic sense, the word includes all cases, special or otherwise. 12 N. Y. 592, 596.

2. A statement of the facts involved in a transaction or series of transactions, drawn up in writing in a technical form, for submission to a court or judge for decision or opinion. Under this meaning of the term are included a "case made" for a motion for new trial, a "case reserved" on the trial of

a cause, an "agreed case" for decision without trial, etc.

3. A form of action which lies to recover damages for injuries for which the more ancient forms of action will not lie. Steph. Pl. 15. See TRESPASS ON THE CASE.

CASE AGREED ON. A formal written enumeration of the facts in a case, assented to by both parties as correct and complete, and submitted to the court by their agreement, in order that a decision may be rendered, without a trial, upon the court's conclusions of law upon the facts as stated.

CASE FOR MOTION. In English divorce and probate practice, when a party desires to make a motion, he must file, among other papers, a case for motion, containing an abstract of the proceedings in the suit or action, a statement of the circumstances on which the motion is founded, and the prayer, or nature of the decree or order desired. Browne, Div. 251; Browne, Prob. Pr. 295.

CASE LAW. A professional name for the aggregate of reported cases as forming a body of jurisprudence; or for the law of a particular subject as evidenced or formed by the adjudged cases; in distinction to statutes and other sources of law.

CASE ON APPEAL. In American practice. Before the argument in the appellate court of a case brought there for review, the appellant's counsel prepares a document or brief, bearing this name, for the information of the court, detailing the testimony and the proceedings below.

In English practice. The "case on appeal" is a printed statement prepared by each of the parties to an appeal to the house of lords or the privy council, setting out methodically the facts which make up his case, with appropriate references to the evidence printed in the "appendix." The term also denotes a written statement, prepared and transmitted by an inferior court or judge, raising a question of law for the opinion of a superior court.

CASE RESERVED. A statement in writing of the facts proved on the trial of a cause, drawn up and settled by the attorneys and counsel for the respective parties under the supervision of the judge, for the purpose of having certain points of law, which arose at the trial, and could not then be satisfactorily decided, determined upon full argument before the court in *banc*. This is otherwise called a "special case;" and it is usual for the parties, where the law of the case is doubtful, to agree that the jury shall find a general verdict for the plaintiff, subject to the opinion of the court upon such a case to be made, instead of obtaining from the jury a special verdict. 3 Bl. Comm. 378; 3 Steph. Comm. 621; Steph. Pl. 92, 93; 1 Burrill, Pr. 242, 463.

CASE STATED. In practice. An agreement in writing, between a plaintiff and defendant, that the facts in dispute between them are as therein agreed upon and set forth. 3 Whart. 143. A case agreed upon. See CASE AGREED ON.

CASE TO MOVE FOR NEW TRIAL. In practice. A case prepared by the party against whom a verdict has been given, upon which to move the court to set aside the verdict and grant a new trial.

CASH. Ready money; whatever can be used as money without being converted into another form; that which circulates as money, including bank-bills.

Cash payment means the opposite of credit. 6 Md. 37; 24 N. J. Law. 96.

CASH-ACCOUNT. A record, in bookkeeping, of all cash transactions; an account of moneys received and expended.

CASH-BOOK. In book-keeping, an account-book in which is kept a record of all cash transactions, or all cash received and expended. The object of the cash-book is to afford a constant facility to ascertain the true state of a man's cash. Pardessus, n. 87.

CASH-NOTE. In England. A bank-note of a provincial bank or of the Bank of England.

CASH-PRICE. A price payable in cash at the time of sale of property, in opposition to a barter or a sale on credit.

CASHIER, *n.* An officer of a moneyed institution, or commercial house, or bank, who is intrusted with, and whose duty it is to take care of, the cash or money of such institution or bank.

The cashier of a bank is the executive officer, through whom the whole financial operations of the bank are conducted. He receives and pays out its moneys, collects and pays its debts, and receives and transfers its commercial securities. Tellers and other subordinate officers may be appointed, but they are under his direction, and are, as it were, the arms by which designated portions of his various functions are discharged. The directors may limit his authority as they deem proper, but this would not affect those to whom the limitation was unknown. 10 Wall. 650.

CASHIER, *v.* In military law. To deprive a military officer of his rank and office.

CASHLITE. An amercement or fine; a mulct.

CASSARE. To quash; to render void; to break.

CASSATION. In French law. Annulling; reversal; breaking the force and validity of a judgment. A decision emanating from the sovereign authority, by which a decree or judgment in the court of last resort is broken or annulled. Merl. Repert.

CASSATION, COURT OF. (Fr. *cour de cassation.*) The highest court in France; so termed from possessing the power to quash (*casser*) the decrees of inferior courts. It is a court of appeal in criminal as well as civil cases.

CASSETUR BILLA. (Lat. That the bill be quashed.) In practice. The form of the judgment for the defendant on a plea in abatement, where the action was commenced by bill, (*billa.*) 3 Bl. Comm. 303; Steph. Pl. 128, 131. The form of an entry made by a plaintiff on the record, after a plea in abatement, where he found that the plea could not be confessed and avoided, nor traversed, nor demurred to; amounting in fact to a discontinuance of the action. 2 Archb. Pr. K. B. 3, 236; 1 Tidd, Pr. 683.

CASSETUR BREVE. (Lat. That the writ be quashed.) In practice. The form of the judgment for the defendant on a plea in abatement, where the action was commenced by original writ, (*breve.*) 3 Bl. Comm. 303; Steph. Pl. 107, 109.

CASSOCK, or CASSULA. A garment worn by a priest.

CAST, *v.* In old English practice. To allege, offer, or present; to proffer by way of excuse, (as to "cast an essoin.")

This word is now used as a popular, rather than a technical, term, in the sense of to overcome, overthrow, or defeat in a civil action at law.

CAST, *p. p.* Overthrown, worsted, or defeated in an action.

CASTEL, or CASTLE. A fortress in a town; the principal mansion of a nobleman. 3 Inst. 31.

CASTELLAIN. In old English law. The lord, owner, or captain of a castle; the constable of a fortified house; a person having the custody of one of the crown mansions; an officer of the forest.

CASTELLANUS. A castellain; the keeper or constable of a castle. Spelman.

CASTELLARIUM, CASTELLATUS. In old English law. The precinct or jurisdiction of a castle. Blount.

CASTELLORUM OPERATIO. In Saxon and old English law. Castle work. Service and labor done by inferior tenants for the building and upholding castles and public places of defense. One of the three necessary charges, (*trinoda necessitas,*) to which all lands among the Saxons were expressly subject. Cowell.

CASTIGATORY. An engine used to punish women who have been convicted of being common scolds. It is sometimes called the "trebucket," "tumbrel," "ducking-stool," or "cucking-stool."

CASTING. Offering; alleging by way of excuse. Casting an essoin was alleging an excuse for not appearing in court to answer an action. Holthouse.

CASTING VOTE. Where the votes of a deliberative assembly or legislative body are equally divided on any question or motion, it is the privilege of the presiding officer to cast one vote (if otherwise he would not be entitled to any vote) on either side, or to cast one additional vote, if he has already voted as a member of the body. This is called the "casting vote."

By the common law, a casting vote sometimes signifies the single vote of a person who never votes; but, in the case of an equality, sometimes the double vote of a person who first votes with the rest, and then, upon an equality, creates a majority by giving a second vote. 48 Barb. 606.

CASTLEGUARD. In feudal law. An imposition anciently laid upon such persons as lived within a certain distance of any castle, towards the maintenance of such as watched and warded the castle.

CASTLEGUARD RENTS. In old English law. Rents paid by those that dwelt within the precincts of a castle, towards the maintenance of such as watched and warded it.

CASTRATION. The act of depriving a man of the testicles.

CASTRENSIS. In the Roman law. Relating to the camp or military service.

Castrense peculium, a portion of property which a son acquired in war, or from his connection with the camp. Dig. 49, 17.

CASTRUM. Lat. In Roman law. A camp.

In old English law. A castle. Bract. fol. 69*b*. A castle, including a manor. 4 Coke, 88.

CASU CONSIMILI. In old English law. A writ of entry, granted where tenant by the curtesy, or tenant for life, alienated in fee, or in tail, or for another's life, which was brought by him in reversion against the party to whom such tenant so alienated to his prejudice, and in the tenant's life-time. Termes de la Ley.

CASU PROVISO. A writ of entry framed under the provisions of the statute of Gloucester, (6 Edw. I.,) c. 7, which lay for the benefit of the reversioner when a tenant in dower aliened in fee or for life.

CASUAL. That which happens accidentally, or is brought about by causes unknown; fortuitous; the result of chance.

CASUAL EJECTOR. In practice. The nominal defendant in an action of ejectment; so called because, by a fiction of law peculiar to that action, he is supposed to come *casually* or by accident upon the premises, and to turn out or eject the lawful possessor. 3 Bl. Comm. 203; 3 Steph. Comm. 670.

CASUAL EVIDENCE. A phrase used to denote (in contradistinction to "preappointed evidence") all such evidence as happens to be adducible of a fact or event, but which was not prescribed by statute or otherwise arranged beforehand to be the evidence of the fact or event. Brown.

CASUAL PAUPER. A poor person who, in England, applies for relief in a parish other than that of his settlement. The ward in the work-house to which they are admitted is called the "casual ward."

CASUAL POOR. In English law. Those who are not settled in a parish.

Such poor persons as are suddenly taken sick, or meet with some accident, when away from home, and who are thus providentially thrown upon the charities of those among whom they happen to be. 17 N. J. Law, 405.

CASUALTIES OF SUPERIORITY. In Scotch law. Payments from an inferior to a superior, that is, from a tenant to his lord, which arise upon uncertain events, as opposed to the payment of rent at fixed and stated times. Bell.

CASUALTIES OF WARDS. In Scotch law. The mails and duties due to the superior in ward-holdings.

CASUALTY. Inevitable accident; an event not to be foreseen or guarded against. A loss from such an event or cause; as by fire, shipwreck, lightning, etc. Story, Bailm. § 240.

CASUS. Lat. Chance; accident; an event; a case; a case contemplated.

CASUS BELLI. An occurrence giving rise to or justifying war.

CASUS FŒDERIS. In international law. The case of the treaty. The particular event or situation contemplated by the treaty, or stipulated for, or which comes within its terms.

In commercial law. The case or event contemplated by the parties to an individual contract, or stipulated for by it, or coming within its terms.

CASUS FORTUITUS. Lat. An inevitable accident, a chance occurrence, or fortuitous event. A loss happening in spite of all human effort and sagacity. 3 Kent, Comm. 217, 300; Whart. Neg. §§ 113, 553.

Casus fortuitus non est sperandus, et nemo tenetur devinare. A fortuitous event is not to be expected, and no one is bound to foresee it. 4 Coke, 66.

Casus fortuitus non est supponendus. A fortuitous event is not to be presumed. Hardr. 82, arg.

CASUS MAJOR. In the civil law. A casualty; an extraordinary casualty, as fire, shipwreck, etc. Dig. 44, 7, 1, 4.

CASUS OMISSUS. A case omitted; an event or contingency for which no provision is made; particularly a case not provided for by the statute on the general subject, and which is therefore left to be governed by the common law.

Casus omissus et oblivioni datus dispositioni juris communis relinquitur. A case omitted and given to oblivion (forgotten) is left to the disposal of the common law. 5 Coke, 38. A particular case, left unprovided for by statute, must be disposed of according to the law as it existed prior to such statute. Broom, Max. 46.

Casus omissus pro omisso habendus est. A case omitted is to be held as (intentionally) omitted. Tray. Lat. Max. 67.

CAT. An instrument with which criminals are flogged. It consists of nine lashes of whip-cord, tied on to a wooden handle.

CATALLA. In old English law. Chattels. The word among the Normans primarily signified only beasts of husbandry, or, as they are still called, "cattle," but, in a secondary sense, the term was applied to all movables in general, and not only to these, but to whatever was not a fief or feud. Wharton.

Catalla juste possessa amitti non possunt. Chattels justly possessed cannot be lost. Jenk. Cent. 28.

CATALLA OTIOSA. Dead goods or chattels, as distinguished from animals. Idle cattle, that is, such as were not used for working, as distinguished from beasts of the plow; called also *animalia otiosa.* Bract. fols. 217, 217*b;* 3 Bl. Comm. 9.

Catalla reputantur inter minima in lege. Chattels are considered in law among the least things. Jenk. Cent. 52.

CATALLACTICS. The science of political economy.

CATALLIS CAPTIS NOMINE DISTRICTIONIS. An obsolete writ that lay where a house was within a borough, for rent issuing out of the same, and which warranted the taking of doors, windows, etc., by way of distress.

CATALLIS REDDENDIS. For the return of the chattels; an obsolete writ that lay where goods delivered to a man to keep till a certain day were not upon demand redelivered at the day. Reg. Orig. 39.

CATALLUM. A chattel. Most frequently used in the plural form, *catalla,* (*q. v.*)

CATALS. Goods and chattels. See CATALLA.

CATANEUS. A tenant *in capite.* A tenant holding immediately of the crown. Spelman.

CATAPULTA. A catapult. A warlike engine to shoot darts; a cross-bow.

CATASCOPUS. An old name for an archdeacon.

CATCHING BARGAIN. A bargain by which money is loaned, at an extortionate or extravagant rate, to an heir or any one who has an estate in reversion or expectancy, to be repaid on the vesting of his interest; or a similar unconscionable bargain with such person for the purchase outright of his expectancy.

CATCHINGS. Things caught, and in the possession, custody, power, and dominion of the party, with a present capacity to use them for his own purposes. The term includes blubber, or pieces of whale flesh cut from the whale, and stowed on or under the deck of a ship. A policy of insurance upon outfits, and catchings substituted for the outfits, in a whaling voyage, protects the blubber. 1 Story, 603; 4 Law Rep. 297.

CATCHLAND. Land in Norfolk, so called because it is not known to what parish it belongs, and the minister who first seizes the tithes of it, by right of preoccupation, enjoys them for that year. Cowell.

CATCHPOLL. A name formerly given to a sheriff's deputy, or to a constable, or other officer whose duty it is to arrest persons. He was a sort of serjeant. The word is not now in use as an official designation. Minshew.

CATEGORICAL. A term of logic, meaning direct; unqualified; unconditional.

CATEGORY. In logic. A series or order of all the predicates or attributes contained under a genus.

CATER COUSIN. A expression used to designate a very distant relation.

CATHEDRAL. In English ecclesiastical law. The church of the bishop of the diocese, in which is his *cathedra,* or throne, and his special jurisdiction; in that respect the principal church of the diocese.

CATHEDRAL PREFERMENTS. In English ecclesiastical law. All deaneries, archdeaconries, and canonries, and generally all dignities and offices in any cathedral or collegiate church, below the rank of a bishop.

CATHEDRATIC. In English ecclesiastical law. A sum of 2s. paid to the bishop by the inferior clergy; but from its being usually paid at the bishop's *synod,* or visitation, it is commonly named *synodals.* Wharton.

CATHOLIC CREDITOR. In Scotch law. A creditor whose debt is secured on all or several distinct parts of the debtor's property. Bell.

CATHOLIC EMANCIPATION ACT. The statute of 10 Geo. IV. c. 7, by which Roman Catholics were restored, in general, to the full enjoyment of all civil rights, except that of holding ecclesiastical offices, and certain high appointments in the state. 3 Steph. Comm. 109.

CATONIANA REGULA. In Roman law. The rule which is commonly expressed in the maxim, *Quod ab initio non valet tractu temporis non convalebit,* meaning that what is at the beginning void by reason of some technical (or other) legal defect will not become valid merely by length of time. The rule applied to the institution of *hæredes,* the bequest of legacies, and such like. The rule is not without its application also in English law; *e. g.;* a married woman's will (being void when made) is not made valid merely because she lives to become a widow. Brown.

CATTLE. A term which includes the domestic animals generally; all the animals used by man for labor or food.

Animals of the bovine genus. In a wider sense, all domestic animals used by man for labor or food, including sheep, (2 Sawy. 148,) and hogs, (21 Wall. 294.)

CATTLE-GATE. In English law. A right to pasture cattle in the land of another. It is a distinct and several interest in the land, passing by lease and release. 13 East, 159; 5 Taunt. 811.

CATTLE-GUARD. A device to prevent cattle from straying along a railroad-track at a highway-crossing. Century Dict. See 31 Kan. 337, 2 Pac. Rep. 800.

CAUDA TERRÆ. A land's end, or the bottom of a ridge in arable land. Cowell.

CAULCEIS. Highroads or ways pitched with flint or other stones.

CAUPO. In the civil law. An innkeeper. Dig. 4, 9, 4, 5.

CAUPONA. In the civil law. An inn or tavern. Inst. 4, 5, 3.

CAUPONES. In the civil law. Innkeepers. Dig. 4, 9; Id. 47, 5; Story, Ag. § 458.

CAURSINES. Italian merchants who came into England in the reign of Henry III., where they established themselves as money lenders, but were soon expelled for their usury and extortion. Cowell; Blount.

CAUSA. 1. A cause, reason, occasion, motive, or inducement.

2. **In the civil law and in old English law.** The word signified a source, ground, or mode of acquiring property; hence a title; one's title to property. Thus, "*Titulus est justa causa possidendi id quod nostrum est;*" title is the lawful ground of possessing that which is ours. 8 Coke, 153. See Mackeld. Rom. Law, §§ 242, 283.

3. A condition; a consideration; motive for performing a juristic act. Used of contracts, and found in this sense in the Scotch law also. Bell.

4. **In old English law.** A cause; a suit or action pending. *Causa testamentaria,* a testamentary cause. *Causa matrimonialis,* a matrimonial cause. Bract. fol. 61.

5. **In old European law.** Any movable thing or article of property.

6. Used with the force of a preposition, it means by virtue of, on account of. Also with reference to, in contemplation of. *Causa mortis,* in anticipation of death.

Causa causæ est causa causati. The cause of a cause is the cause of the thing caused. 12 Mod. 639. The cause of the cause is to be considered as the cause of the effect also.

CAUSA CAUSANS. The immediate cause; the last link in the chain of causation.

Causa causantis, causa est causati. The cause of the thing causing is the cause of the effect. 4 Camp. 284; 4 Gray, 398.

CAUSA DATA ET NON SECUTA. In the civil law. Consideration given and not followed, that is, by the event upon which it was given. The name of an action by which a thing given in the view of a certain event was reclaimed if that event did not take place. Dig. 12, 4; Cod. 4, 6.

Causa ecclesiæ publicis æquiparatur; et summa est ratio quæ pro religione facit. The cause of the church is equal to public cause; and paramount is the reason which makes for religion. Co. Litt. 341.

Causa et origo est materia negotii. The cause and origin is the substance of the thing; the cause and origin of a thing are a material part of it. The law regards the original act. 1 Coke, 99.

CAUSA HOSPITANDI. For the purpose of being entertained as a guest. 4 Maule & S. 310.

CAUSA JACTITATIONIS MARITAGII. A form of action which anciently lay against a party who boasted or gave out that he or she was married to the plaintiff, whereby a common reputation of their marriage might ensue. 3 Bl. Comm. 93.

CAUSA MATRIMONII PRÆLOCUTI. A writ lying where a woman has given lands to a man in fee-simple with the intention that he shall marry her, and he refuses so to do within a reasonable time, upon suitable request. Cowell. Now obsolete. 3 Bl. Comm. 183, note.

CAUSA MORTIS. In contemplation of approaching death. In view of death. Commonly occurring in the phrase *donatio causa mortis*, (*q. v.*)

CAUSA PATET. The reason is open, obvious, plain, clear, or manifest. A common expression in old writers. Perk. c. 1, §§ 11, 14, 97.

CAUSA PROXIMA. The immediate, nearest, or latest cause.

Causa proxima, non remota, spectatur. The immediate, not the remote, cause, is looked at, or considered. 12 East, 648; 3 Kent, Comm. 302; Story, Bailm. § 515; Bac. Max. reg. 1.

CAUSA REI. In the civil law. The accessions, appurtenances, or fruits of a thing; comprehending all that the claimant of a principal thing can demand from a defendant in addition thereto, and especially what he would have had, if the thing had not been withheld from him. Inst. 4, 17, 3; Mackeld. Rom. Law, § 166.

CAUSA REMOTA. A remote or mediate cause; a cause operating indirectly by the intervention of other causes.

CAUSA SCIENTIÆ PATET. The reason of the knowledge is evident. A technical phrase in Scotch practice, used in depositions of witnesses.

CAUSA SINE QUA NON. A necessary or inevitable cause; a cause without which the effect in question could not have happened.

CAUSA TURPIS. A base (immoral or illegal) cause or consideration.

Causa vaga et incerta non est causa rationabilis. 5 Coke, 57. A vague and uncertain cause is not a reasonable cause.

Causæ dotis, vitæ, libertatis, fisci sunt inter favorabilia in lege. Causes of dower, life, liberty, revenue, are among the things favored in law. Co. Litt. 341.

CAUSAM NOBIS SIGNIFICES QUARE. A writ addressed to a mayor of a town, etc., who was by the king's writ commanded to give seisin of lands to the king's grantee, on his delaying to do it, requiring him to show cause why he so delayed the performance of his duty. Blount; Cowell.

CAUSARE. In the civil and old English law. To be engaged in a suit; to litigate; to conduct a cause.

CAUSATOR. In old European law. One who manages or litigates another's cause. Spelman.

CAUSE. That which produces an effect; whatever moves, impels, or leads. The origin or foundation of a thing, as of a suit or action; a ground of action. 1 N. Y. 47.

The consideration of a contract, that is, the inducement to it, or motive of the contracting party for entering into it, is, in the civil and Scotch law, called the "cause."

The civilians use the term "cause," in relation to obligations, in the same sense as the word "consideration" is used in the jurisprudence of England and the United States. It means the motive, the inducement to the agreement,—*id quod inducet ad contrahendum.* In contracts of mutual interest, the cause of the engagement is the thing given or done, or engaged to be given or done, or the risk incurred by one of the parties. 1 La. Ann. 192.

In pleading. Reason; motive; matter of excuse or justification.

In practice. A suit, litigation, or action. Any question, civil or criminal, contested before a court of justice.

Cause imports a judicial proceeding entire, and is nearly synonymous with *lis* in Latin, or suit in English. Although allied to the word "case," it differs from it in the application of its meaning. A cause is pending, postponed, appealed, gained, lost, etc.; whereas a case is made, rested, argued, decided, etc. Case is of a more limited signification, importing a collection of facts, with the conclusion of law thereon. Both terms may be used with propriety in the same sentence; *e. g.*, on the trial of the *cause*, the plaintiff introduced certain evidence, and there rested his *case*. 18 Conn. 10.

A distinction is sometimes taken between "cause" and "action." Burrill observes that a cause is not, like an action or suit, said to be commenced, nor is an action, like a cause, said to be tried. But, if there is any substantial difference between these terms, it must lie in the fact that "action" refers more peculiarly to the *legal procedure* of a controversy; "cause" to its *merits* or the state of facts involved. Thus, we cannot say "the *cause* should have been replevin." Nor would it be correct to say "the plaintiff pleaded his own *action.*"

CAUSE-BOOKS. Books kept in the central office of the English supreme court, in which are entered all writs of summons issued in the office. Rules of Court, v 8.

CAUSE LIST. In English practice. A printed roll of actions, to be tried in the order of their entry, with the names of the solicitors for each litigant. Similar to the calendar of causes, or docket, used in American courts.

CAUSE OF ACTION. Matter for which an action may be brought. The ground on which an action may be sustained. The right to bring a suit.

Cause of action is properly the ground on which an action can be maintained; as when we say that such a person has no cause of action. But the phrase is often used to signify the matter of the complaint or claim on which a given action is in fact grounded, whether or not legally maintainable. Mozley & Whitley.

It sometimes means a person having a right of action. Thus, where a legacy is left to a married woman, and she and her husband bring an action to recover it, she is called in the old books the "meritorious cause of action." 1 H. Bl. 108.

The term is synonymous with right of action, right of recovery. 26 How. Pr. 501.

Cause of action is not synonymous with chose in action; the latter includes debts, etc., not due, and even stocks. 10 How. Pr. 1.

CAUSES CÉLÈBRES. Celebrated cases. A work containing reports of the decisions of interest and importance in French courts in the seventeenth and eighteenth centuries.

Secondarily a single trial or decision is often called a "*cause célèbre,*" when it is remarkable on account of the parties involved, or the unusual, interesting, or sensational character of the facts.

CAUSIDICUS. In the civil law. A pleader; one who argued a cause *ore tenus.*

CAUTELA. Lat. Care; caution; vigilance; prevision.

CAUTIO. **In the civil and French law.** Security given for the performance of any thing; bail; a bond or undertaking by way of surety. Also the person who becomes a surety.

In Scotch law. A pledge, bond, or other security for the performance of an obligation, or completion of the satisfaction to be obtained by a judicial process. Bell.

CAUTIO FIDEJUSSORIA. Security by means of bonds or pledges entered into by third parties. Du Cange.

CAUTIO PIGNORATITIA. Security given by pledge, or deposit, as plate, money, or other goods.

CAUTIO PRO EXPENSIS. Security for costs, charges, or expenses.

CAUTIO USUFRUCTUARIA. Security, which tenants for life give, to preserve the property rented free from waste and injury. Ersk. Inst. 2, 9, 59.

CAUTION. In Scotch law, and in admiralty law. Surety; security; bail; an undertaking by way of surety. 6 Mod. 162. See CAUTIO.

CAUTION JURATORY. In Scotch law. Security given by oath. That which a suspender swears is the best he can afford in order to obtain a suspension. Ersk. Pract. 4, 3, 6.

CAUTIONARY. In Scotch law. An instrument in which a person binds himself as surety for another.

CAUTIONE ADMITTENDA. In English ecclesiastical law. A writ that lies against a bishop who holds an excommunicated person in prison for contempt, notwithstanding he offers sufficient caution or security to obey the orders and commandment of the church for the future. Reg. Orig. 66; Cowell.

CAUTIONER. In Scotch law. A surety; a bondsman. One who binds himself in a bond with the principal for greater security. He is still a cautioner whether the bond be to pay a debt, or whether he undertake to produce the person of the party for whom he is bound. Bell.

CAUTIONNEMENT. In French law. The same as becoming surety in English law.

CAUTIONRY. In Scotch law. Suretyship.

CAVEAT. Lat. Let him beware. A formal notice or warning given by a party interested to a court, judge, or ministerial officer against the performance of certain acts within his power and jurisdiction. This process may be used in the proper courts to prevent (temporarily or provisionally) the proving of a will or the grant of administration, or to arrest the enrollment of a decree in chancery when the party intends to take an appeal, to prevent the grant of letters patent, etc. It is also used, in the American practice, as a kind of equitable process, to stay the granting of a patent for lands.

In patent law. A caveat is a formal written notice given to the officers of the patent-office, requiring them to refuse letters patent on a particular invention or device to to any other person, until the party filing the caveat (called the "caveator") shall have an opportunity to establish his claim to priority of invention.

CAVEAT ACTOR. Let the doer, or actor, beware.

CAVEAT EMPTOR. Let the buyer take care. This maxim summarizes the rule that the purchaser of an article must examine, judge, and test it for himself, being bound to discover any obvious defects or imperfections. Hob. 99; Co. Litt. 102*a*.

Caveat emptor, qui ignorare non debuit quod jus alienum emit. Hob. 99. Let a purchaser beware, who ought not to be ignorant that he is purchasing the rights of another.

CAVEAT VENDITOR. In Roman law. A maxim, or rule, casting the responsibility for defects or deficiencies upon the *seller* of goods, and expressing the exact opposite of the common law rule of *caveat emptor*. See 18 Wend. 449.

In English and American jurisprudence. *Caveat venditor* is sometimes used as expressing, in a rough way, the rule which governs all those cases of sales to which *caveat emptor* does not apply.

CAVEAT VIATOR. Let the traveler beware. This phrase has been used as a concise expression of the duty of a traveler on the highway to use due care to detect and avoid defects in the way. 10 Exch. 771, 774.

CAVEATOR. One who files a caveat.

Cavendum est a fragmentis. Beware of fragments. Bac. Aph. 26.

CAVERE. In the civil and common law. To take care; to exercise caution; to take care or provide for; to provide by law; to provide against; to forbid by law; to give security; to give caution or security on arrest.

CAVERS. Persons stealing ore from mines in Derbyshire, punishable in the berghmote or miners' court; also officers belonging to the same mines. Wharton.

CAYA. In old English law. A quay, kay, key, or wharf. Cowell.

CAYAGIUM. In old English law. Cayage or kayage; a toll or duty anciently paid for landing goods at a quay or wharf. Cowell.

CEAP. A bargain; anything for sale; a chattel; also cattle, as being the usual medium of barter. Sometimes used instead of ceapgild, (*q. v.*)

CEAPGILD. Payment or forfeiture of an animal. An ancient species of forfeiture.

CEDE. To yield up; to assign; to grant. Generally used to designate the transfer of territory from one government to another.

CEDENT. In Scotch law. An assignor. One who transfers a chose in action.

CEDO. I grant. The word ordinarily used in Mexican conveyances to pass title to lands. 26 Cal. 88, 108.

CEDULA. In old English law. A schedule.

In Spanish law. An act under private signature, by which a debtor admits the amount of the debt, and binds himself to discharge the same on a specified day or on demand.

Also the notice or citation affixed to the door of a fugitive criminal requiring him to appear before the court where the accusation is pending.

CEDULE. In French law. The technical name of an act under private signature. 3 La. Ann. 458.

CELATION. In medical jurisprudence. Concealment of pregnancy or delivery.

CELDRA. In old English law, a chaldron. In old Scotch law, a measure of grain, otherwise called a "chalder." See 1 Kames, Eq. 215.

CELEBRATION OF MARRIAGE. The formal act by which a man and woman take each other for husband and wife, according to law; the solemnization of a marriage. The term is usually applied to a marriage ceremony attended with ecclesiastical functions.

CELIBACY. The condition or state of life of an unmarried person.

CELLERARIUS. A butler in a monastery; sometimes in universities called "manciple" or "caterer."

CEMETERY. A place of burial, differing from a churchyard by its locality and incidents,—by its locality, as it is separate and apart from any sacred building used for the performance of divine service; by its incidents that, inasmuch as no vault or burying-place in an ordinary churchyard can be purchased for a perpetuity, in a cemetery a permanent burial place can be obtained. Wharton.

Six or more human bodies being buried at one place constitutes the place a cemetery. Pol. Code Cal. § 3106.

CENDULÆ. Small pieces of wood laid in the form of tiles to cover the roof of a house; shingles. Cowell.

CENEGILD. In Saxon law. An expiatory mulct or fine paid to the relations of a murdered person by the murderer or his relations. Spelman.

CENELLÆ. In old records. Acorns.

CENNINGA. A notice given by a buyer to a seller that the things which had been sold were claimed by another, in order that he might appear and justify the sale. Blount; Whishaw.

CENS. In French Canadian law. An annual tribute or due reserved to a seignior or lord, and imposed merely in recognition of his superiority. Guyot, Inst. c. 9.

CENSARIA. In old English law. A farm, or house and land let at a standing rent. Cowell.

CENSARII. In old English law. Farmers, or such persons as were liable to pay a census, (tax.) Blount; Cowell.

CENSERE. In the Roman law. To ordain; to decree. Dig. 50, 16, 111.

CENSITAIRE. In Canadian law. A tenant by *cens*, (*q. v.*)

CENSIVE. In Canadian law. Tenure by *cens*, (*q. v.*)

CENSO. In Spanish and Mexican law. An annuity. A ground rent. The right which a person acquires to receive a certain annual pension, for the delivery which he makes to another of a determined sum of money or of an immovable thing. Civil Code Mex. art. 3206. See Schm. Civil Law, 149, 309; White, New Recop. bk. 2, c. 7, § 4; 13 Tex. 655.

CENSO CONSIGNATIVO. In Spanish and Mexican law. A *censo* (*q. v.*) is called "*consignatico*" when he who receives the money assigns for the payment of the pension (annuity) the estate the fee in which he reserves. Civil Code Mex. art. 3207.

CENSO ENFITEUTICO. In Spanish and Mexican law. An emphyteutic annuity. That species of *censo* (annuity) which exists where there is a right to require of another a certain canon or pension annually, on account of having transferred to that person forever certain real estate, but reserving the fee in the land. The owner who thus transfers the land is called the "*censualisto*," and the person who pays the annuity is called the "*censatario*." Hall, Mex. Law, § 756.

CENSUALES. In old European law. A species of *oblati* or voluntary slaves of churches or monasteries; those who, to procure the protection of the church, bound themselves to pay an annual tax or quit-rent only of their estates to a church or monastery.

CENSUERE. In Roman law. They have decreed. The term of art, or technical term for the judgment, resolution, or decree of the senate. Tayl. Civil Law, 566.

CENSUMETHIDUS, or CENSUMORTHIDUS. A dead rent, like that which is called "mortmain." Blount; Cowell.

CENSURE. In ecclesiastical law. A spiritual punishment, consisting in withdrawing from a baptized person (whether belonging to the clergy or the laity) a privilege which the church gives him, or in wholly expelling him from the Christian communion. The principal varieties of censures are admonition, degradation, deprivation, excommunication, penance, sequestration, suspension. Phillim. Ecc. Law, 1367.

A custom observed in certain manors in Devon and Cornwall, where all persons above the age of sixteen years are cited to swear fealty to the lord, and to pay 11d. per poll, and 1d. per annum.

CENSUS. The official counting or enumeration of the people of a state or nation, with statistics of wealth, commerce, education, etc.

In Roman law. A numbering or enrollment of the people, with a valuation of their fortunes.

In old European law. A tax, or tribute; a toll. Montesq. Esprit des Lois, liv. 30, c. 14.

CENSUS REGALIS. In English law. The annual revenue or income of the crown.

CENT. A coin of the United States, the least in value of those now minted. It is the one-hundredth part of a dollar. Its weight is 72 gr., and it is composed of copper and nickel in the ratio of 88 to 12.

CENTENA. A hundred. A district or division containing originally a hundred freemen, established among the Goths, Germans, Franks, and Lombards, for military and civil purposes, and answering to the Saxon "hundred." Spelman; 1 Bl. Comm. 115.

Also, in old records and pleadings, a hundred weight.

CENTENARII. Petty judges, under-sheriffs of counties, that had rule of a hundred, (*centena*,) and judged smaller matters among them. 1 Vent. 211.

CENTENI. The principal inhabitants of a *centena*, or district composed of different villages, originally in number a hundred, but afterwards only called by that name.

CENTESIMA. In Roman law. The hundredth part.

Usuriæ centesimæ. Twelve per cent. per annum; that is, a hundredth part of the principal was due each month,—the month being the unit of time from which the Romans reckoned interest. 2 Bl. Comm. 462, note.

CENTIME. The name of a denomination of French money, being the one-hundredth part of a franc.

CENTRAL CRIMINAL COURT. An English court, having jurisdiction for the trial of crimes and misdemeanors committed in London and certain adjoining parts of Kent, Essex, and Sussex, and of such other criminal cases as may be sent to it out of the queen's bench, though arising beyond its proper jurisdiction. It was constituted by the acts 4 & 5 Wm. IV. c. 36, and 19 & 20 Vict. c. 16, and superseded the "Old Bailey."

CENTRAL OFFICE. The central office of the supreme court of judicature in England is the office established in pursuance of the recommendation of the legal departments commission in order to consolidate the offices of the masters and associates of the common-law divisions, the crown office of the queen's bench division, the record and writ clerk's report, and enrollment offices of the chancery division, and a few others. The central office is divided into the following departments, and the business and staff of the office are distributed accordingly: (1) Writ, appearance, and judgment; (2) summons and order, for the common-law divisions only; (3) filing and record, including the old chancery report office; (4) taxing, for the common-law divisions only; (5) enrollment; (6) judgments, for the registry of judgments, executions, etc.; (7) bills of sale; (8) married women's acknowledgments; (9) queen's remembrancer; (10) crown office; and (11) associates. Sweet.

CENTRALIZATION. This word is used to express the system of government prevailing in a country where the management of local matters is in the hands of functionaries appointed by the ministers of state, paid by the state, and in constant communication and under the constant control and inspiration of the ministers of state, and where the funds of the state are largely applied to local purposes. Wharton.

CENTUMVIRI. In Roman law. The name of an important court consisting of a body of one hundred and five judges. It was made up by choosing three representatives from each of the thirty-five Roman tribes. The judges sat as one body for the trial of certain important or difficult questions, (called, "*causæ centumvirales*,") but ordinarily they were separated into four distinct tribunals.

CENTURY. One hundred. A body of one hundred men. The Romans were divided into *centuries*, as the English were divided into hundreds.

Also a cycle of one hundred years.

CEORL. In Anglo Saxon law. The freemen were divided into two classes,—thanes and ceorls. The thanes were the proprietors of the soil, which was entirely at their disposal. The ceorls were men personally free, but possessing no landed property. Guizot, Rep. Govt.

A tenant at will of free condition, who held land of the thane on condition of paying rent or services. Cowell.

A freeman of inferior rank occupied in husbandry. Spelman.

CEPI. Lat. I have taken. This word was of frequent use in the returns of sheriffs when they were made in Latin.

CEPI CORPUS. I have taken the body. The return of a sheriff who has arrested a person upon a *capias*.

CEPI CORPUS ET PARATUM HABEO. I have taken the body and have it ready. A return made by the sheriff upon an attachment, *capias*, etc., when he has the person against whom the process was issued in custody.

CEPIT. In civil practice. He took. This was the characteristic word employed in (Latin) writs of trespass for goods taken, and in declarations in trespass and replevin.

Replevin *in the cepit* is a form of replevin which is brought for carrying away goods merely. Wells, Repl. § 53.

In criminal practice. This was a technical word necessary in an indictment for larceny. The charge must be that the defendant took the thing stolen with a felonious design. Bac. Abr. "Indictment," G, 1.

CEPIT ET ABDUXIT. He took and led away. The emphatic words in writs in trespass or indictments for larceny, where the thing taken was a living chattel, *i. e.*, an animal.

CEPIT ET ASPORTAVIT. He took and carried away. Applicable in a declaration in trespass or an indictment for larceny where the defendant has carried away goods without right. 4 Bl. Comm. 231.

CEPIT IN ALIO LOCO. In pleading. A plea in replevin, by which the defendant alleges that he took the thing replevied in another place than that mentioned in the declaration. 1 Chit. Pl. 490.

CEPPAGIUM. In old English law. The stumps or roots of trees which remain in the ground after the trees are felled. Fleta, lib. 2, c. 41, § 24.

CERA, or CERE. In old English law. Wax; a seal.

CERAGRUM. In old English law. A payment to provide candles in the church. Blount.

CEREVISIA. In old English law. Ale or beer.

CERT MONEY. In old English law. Head money or common fine. Money paid yearly by the residents of several manors to the lords thereof, for the certain keeping of the leet, (*pro certo letæ;*) and sometimes to the hundred. Blount; 6 Coke, 78.

Certa debet esse intentio, et narratio, et certum fundamentum, et certa res quæ deducitur in judicium. The design and narration ought to be certain, and the foundation certain, and the matter certain, which is brought into court to be tried. Co. Litt. 303*a*.

CERTA RES. In old English law. A certain thing. Fleta, lib. 2, c. 60, §§ 24, 25.

CERTAIN SERVICES. In feudal and old English law. Such services as were stinted (limited or defined) in quantity, and could not be exceeded on any pretense; as to pay a stated annual rent, or to plow such a field for three days. 2 Bl. Comm. 61.

CERTAINTY. In pleading. Distinctness; clearness of statement; particularity. Such precision and explicitness in the statement of alleged facts that the pleader's averments and contention may be readily understood by the pleader on the other side, as well as by the court and jury.

This word is technically used in pleading in two different senses, signifying either distinctness, or particularity, as opposed to undue generality.

Certainty is said to be of three sorts: (1) *Certainty to a common intent* is such as is attained by using words in their ordinary meaning, but is not exclusive of another meaning which might be made out by argument or inference. (2) *Certainty to a certain intent in general* is that which allows of no misunderstanding if a fair and reasonable construction is put upon the language employed without bringing in facts which are possible, but not apparent. (3) *Certainty to a certain intent in particular* is the highest degree of technical accuracy and precision. Co. Litt. 303; 2 H. Bl. 530; 9 Johns. 317.

In contracts. The quality of being specific, accurate, and distinct.

A thing is certain when its essence, quality, and quantity are described, distinctly set forth, etc. Dig. 12, 1, 6. It is uncertain when the description is not that of an individual object, but designates only the kind. Civil Code La. art. 3522, no. 8; 5 Coke, 121.

CERTIFICANDO DE RECOGNITIONE STAPULÆ. In English law. A writ commanding the mayor of the staple to certify to the lord chancellor a statute-staple taken before him where the party himself detains it, and refuses to bring in the same. There is a like writ to certify a statute-merchant, and in divers other cases. Reg. Orig. 148, 151, 152.

CERTIFICATE. A written assurance, or official representation, that some act has or has not been done, or some event occurred, or some legal formality been complied with. Particularly, such written assurance made or issuing from some court, and designed as a notice of things done therein, or as a warrant or authority, to some other court, judge, or officer.

A document in use in the English custom-house. No goods can be exported *by certificate*, except foreign goods formerly imported, on which the whole or a part of the customs paid on importation is to be drawn back. Wharton.

CERTIFICATE FOR COSTS. In English practice. A certificate or memorandum drawn up and signed by the judge before whom a case was tried, setting out certain facts the existence of which must be thus proved before the party is entitled, under the statutes, to recover costs.

CERTIFICATE INTO CHANCERY. In English practice. This is a document containing the opinion of the common-law judges on a question of law submitted to them for their decision by the chancery court.

CERTIFICATE OF DEPOSIT. In the practice of bankers. This is a writing acknowledging that the person named has deposited in the bank a specified sum of money, and that the same is held subject to be drawn out on his own check or order, or that of some other person named in the instrument as payee.

CERTIFICATE OF HOLDER OF ATTACHED PROPERTY. A certificate required by statute, in some states, to be given by a third person who is found in possession of property subject to an attachment in the sheriff's hands, setting forth the amount and character of such property and the nature of the defendant's interest in it. Code Civil Proc. N. Y. § 650.

CERTIFICATE OF REGISTRY. In maritime law. A certificate of the registration of a vessel according to the registry acts, for the purpose of giving her a national character. 3 Steph. Comm. 274; 3 Kent, Comm. 139-150.

CERTIFICATE OF STOCK. A certificate of a corporation or joint-stock company that the person named is the owner of a designated number of shares of its stock; given when the subscription is fully paid and the "scrip-certificate" taken up.

CERTIFICATE, TRIAL BY. This is a mode of trial now little in use; it is resorted to in cases where the fact in issue lies out of the cognizance of the court, and the judges, in order to determine the question, are obliged to rely upon the solemn averment or information of persons in such a station as affords them the clearest and most competent knowledge of the truth. Brown.

CERTIFICATION. In Scotch practice. This is the assurance given to a party of the course to be followed in case he does not appear or obey the order of the court.

CERTIFICATION OF ASSISE. In English practice. A writ anciently granted for the re-examining or retrial of a matter passed by assise before justices, now entirely superseded by the remedy afforded by means of a new trial.

CERTIFICATS DE COÛTUME. In French law. Certificates given by a foreign lawyer, establishing the law of the country to which he belongs upon one or more fixed points. These certificates can be produced before the French courts, and are received as evidence in suits upon questions of foreign law. Arg. Fr. Merc. Law, 548.

CERTIFIED CHECK. In the practice of bankers. This is a depositor's check recognized and accepted by the proper officer of the bank as a valid appropriation of the amount specified to the payee named, and as drawn against funds of such depositor held by the bank. The usual method of certification is for the cashier or teller to write his name across the face of the check.

CERTIFIED COPY. A copy of a document, signed and certified as a true copy by the officer to whose custody the original is intrusted.

CERTIORARI. Lat. (To be informed of, to be made certain in regard to.) The name of a writ issued by a superior court directing an inferior court to send up to the former some pending proceeding, or all the record and proceedings in a cause before verdict, with its certificate to the correctness and completeness of the record, for review or trial; or it may serve to bring up the record of a case already terminated below, if the inferior court is one not of record, or in cases where the procedure is not according to the course of the common law.

Originally, and in English practice, a *certiorari* is an original writ, issuing out of the court of chancery or the king's bench, and directed in the king's name to the judges or officers of inferior courts, commanding them to certify or to return the records or proceedings in a cause depending before them, for the purpose of a judicial review of their action. Jacob.

In Massachusetts it is defined by statute as a writ issued by the supreme judicial court to any inferior tribunal, commanding it to certify and return to the supreme judicial court its records in a particular case, in order that any errors or irregularities which appear in the proceedings may be corrected. Pub. St. Mass. 1882, p. 1288.

CERTIORARI, BILL OF. In English chancery practice. An original bill praying relief. It was filed for the purpose of removing a suit pending in some inferior court of equity into the court of chancery, on account of some alleged incompetency or inconvenience.

Certum est quod certo reddi potest. That is certain which can be reduced to a certainty. 3 Rep. Ch. 142.

Certum est quod certum reddi potest. That is certain which can be rendered certain. 9 Coke, 47; Broom, Max. 623.

CERURA. A mound, fence, or inclosure.

CERVISARII. In Saxon law. Tenants who were bound to supply drink for their lord's table. Cowell.

CERVISIA. Ale, or beer. Sometimes spelled "*cerevisia.*"

CERVISIARIUS. In old records. An ale-house keeper. A beer or ale brewer. Blount.

CERVUS. Lat. A stag or deer.

CESIONARIO. In Spanish law. An assignee. White, New Recop. b. 3, tit. 10, c. 1, § 3.

CESS, *v.* In old English law. To cease, stop, determine, fail.

CESS, *n.* An assessment or tax. In Ireland, it was anciently applied to an exaction of victuals, at a certain rate, for soldiers in garrison.

Cessa regnare, si non vis judicare. Cease to reign, if you wish not to adjudicate. Hob. 155.

Cessante causa, cessat effectus. The cause ceasing, the effect ceases. Broom, Max. 160.

Cessante ratione legis, cessat et ipsa lex. The reason of the law ceasing, the law itself ceases also. Co. Litt. 70*b;* 2 Bl. Comm. 390, 391; Broom, Max. 159.

Cessante statu primitivo, cessat derivativus. When the primitive or original estate determines, the derivative estate determines also. 8 Coke, 34; Broom, Max. 495.

CESSARE. L. Lat. To cease, stop, or stay.

CESSAVIT PER BIENNIUM. In practice. An obsolete writ, which could formerly have been sued out when the defendant had for two years *ceased* or neglected to perform such service or to pay such rent as he was bound to do by his tenure, and had not upon his lands sufficient goods or chattels to be distrained. Fitzh. Nat. Brev. 208. It also lay where a religious house held lands on condition of performing certain spiritual services which it failed to do. 3 Bl. Comm. 232.

CESSE. (1) An assessment or tax; (2) a tenant of land was said to *cesse* when he neglected or *ceased* to perform the services due to the lord. Co. Litt. 373*a*, 380*b*.

CESSER. Neglect; a ceasing from, or omission to do, a thing. 3 Bl. Comm. 232.

The determination of an estate. 1 Coke, 84; 4 Kent, Comm. 33, 90, 105, 295.

The "cesser" of a term, annuity, or the like, takes place when it determines or comes to an end. The expression is chiefly used (in England) with reference to long terms of a thousand years or some similar period, created by a settlement for the purpose of securing the income, portions, etc., given to the objects of the settlement. When the trusts of a term of this kind are satisfied, it is desirable that the term should be put an end to, and with this object it was formerly usual to provide in the settlement itself that, as soon as the trusts of the term had been satisfied, it should cease and determine. This was called a "proviso for cesser." Sweet.

CESSER, PROVISO FOR. Where terms for years are raised by settlement, it is usual to introduce a proviso that they shall *cease* when the trusts end. This proviso generally expresses three events: (1) The trusts never arising; (2) their becoming unnecessary or incapable of taking effect; (3) the performance of them. Sugd. Vend. (14th Ed.) 621-623.

CESSET EXECUTIO. (Let execution stay.) In practice. A stay of execution; or an order for such stay; the entry of such stay on record. 2 Tidd, Pr. 1104.

CESSET PROCESSUS. (Let process stay.) A stay of proceedings entered on the record.

CESSIO. Lat. A cession; a giving up, or relinquishment; a surrender; an assignment.

CESSIO BONORUM. In Roman law. Cession of goods. A surrender, relinquishment, or assignment of all his property and effects made by an insolvent debtor for the benefit of his creditors. The effect of this voluntary action on the debtor's part was to secure him against imprisonment or any bodily punishment, and from infamy, and to cancel his debts to the extent of the property ceded. It much resembled our voluntary bankruptcy or assignment for creditors. The term is commonly employed in modern continental jurisprudence to designate a bankrupt's assignment of property to be distributed among his creditors, and is used in the same sense by some English and American writers, but here rather as a convenient than as a strictly technical term. See 2 Bl. Comm. 473; 1 Kent, Comm. 247, 422; Ersk. Inst. 4, 3, 26.

CESSIO IN JURE. In Roman law. A fictitious suit, in which the person who was to acquire the thing claimed (*vindicabat*) the thing as his own, the person who was to transfer it acknowledged the justice of the claim, and the magistrate pronounced it to be the property (*addicebat*) of the claimant. Sandars' Just. Inst. (5th Ed.) 89, 122.

CESSION. The act of ceding; a yielding or giving up; surrender; relinquishment of property or rights.

In the civil law. An assignment. The act by which a party transfers property to another. The surrender or assignment of property for the benefit of one's creditors.

In ecclesiastical law. A giving up or vacating a benefice, by accepting another without a proper dispensation. 1 Bl. Comm. 392; Latch, 234.

In public law. The assignment, transfer, or yielding up of territory by one state or government to another.

CESSION DES BIENS. In French law. The surrender which a debtor makes of all his goods to his creditors, when he finds himself in insolvent circumstances. It is of two kinds, either voluntary or compulsory, (*judiciaire*,) corresponding very nearly to liquidation by arrangement and bankruptcy in English and American law.

CESSION OF GOODS. The surrender of property; the relinquishment that a debtor makes of all his property to his creditors, when he finds himself unable to pay his debts. Civil Code La. art. 2170.

CESSIONARY. In Scotch law. An assignee. Bell.

CESSIONARY BANKRUPT. One who gives up his estate to be divided among his creditors.

CESSMENT. An assessment, or tax.

CESSOR. One who ceases or neglects so long to perform a duty that he thereby incurs the danger of the law. O. N. B. 136.

CESSURE. L. Fr. A receiver; a bailiff. Kelham.

C'EST ASCAVOIR. L. Fr. That is to say, or to-wit. Generally written as one word, *cestascavoir*, *cestascavoire*.

C'est le crime qui fait la honte, et non pas l'echafaud. It is the offense which causes the shame, and not the scaffold.

CESTUI, CESTUY. He. Used frequently in composition in law French phrases.

CESTUI QUE TRUST. He who has a right to a beneficial interest in and out of an estate the legal title to which is vested in another. 2 Washb. Real Prop. 163.

The person who possesses the equitable right to property and receives the rents, issues, and profits thereof, the legal estate of which is vested in a trustee.

It has been proposed to substitute for this uncouth term the English word "beneficiary," and the latter, though still far from universally adopted, has come to be quite frequently used. It is equal in precision to the antiquated and unwieldy Norman phrase, and far better adapted to the genius of our language.

CESTUI QUE USE. He for whose use and benefit lands or tenements are held by another. The *cestui que use* has the right to receive the profits and benefits of the estate, but the legal title and possession (as well as the duty of defending the same) reside in the other.

CESTUI QUE VIE. He whose life is the measure of the duration of an estate. 1 Washb. Real Prop. 88.

The person for whose life any lands, tenements, or hereditaments are held.

Cestuy que doit inheriter al père doit inheriter al fils. He who would have been heir to the father of the deceased shall also be heir of the son. Fitzh. Abr. "Descent," 2; 2 Bl. Comm. 239, 250.

CF. An abbreviated form of the Latin word *conferre*, meaning "compare." Directs the reader's attention to another part of the work, to another volume, case, etc., where contrasted, analogous, or explanatory views or statements may be found.

CH. This abbreviation most commonly stands for "chapter," or "chancellor," but it may also mean "chancery," or "chief."

CHACE. L. Fr. A chase or hunting ground.

CHACEA. In old English law. A station of game, more extended than a park, and less than a forest; also the liberty of chasing or hunting within a certain district; also the way through which cattle are driven to pasture, otherwise called a "drove-way." Blount.

Chacea est ad communem legem. A chase is by common law. Reg. Brev. 806.

CHACEABLE. L. Fr. That may be chased or hunted.

CHACER. To drive, compel, or oblige; also to chase or hunt.

CHACURUS. A horse for the chase, or a hound, dog, or courser.

CHAFEWAX. An officer in the English chancery whose duty was to fit the wax to seal the writs, commissions, and other instruments thence issuing. The office was abolished by St. 15 & 16 Vict. c. 87, § 23.

CHAFFERS. An ancient term for goods, wares, and merchandise.

CHAFFERY. Traffic; the practice of buying and selling.

CHAIN. A measure used by engineers and surveyors, being twenty-two yards in length.

CHAIRMAN. A name given to the presiding officer of an assembly, public meeting, convention, deliberative or legislative body, board of directors, committee, etc.

CHAIRMAN OF COMMITTEES OF THE WHOLE HOUSE. In English parliamentary practice. In the commons, this officer, always a member, is elected by the house on the assembling of every new parliament. When the house is in committee on bills introduced by the government, or in committee of ways and means, or supply, or in committee to consider preliminary resolutions, it is his duty to preside.

CHALDRON, CHALDERN, or CHALDER. Twelve sacks of coals, each holding three bushels, weighing about a ton and a half. In Wales they reckon 12 barrels or pitchers a ton or chaldron, and 29 cwt. of 120 lbs. to the ton. Wharton.

CHALKING, or CAULKING. The process or method of stopping the seams in a ship or a vessel.

CHALLENGE. 1. To object or except to; to prefer objections to a person, right, or instrument; to formally call into question the capability of a person for a particular function, or the existence of a right claimed, or the sufficiency or validity of an instrument.

2. As a noun, the word signifies the objection or exception so advanced.

3. An exception taken against legal documents, as a declaration, count, or writ. But this use of the word is now obsolescent.

4. An exception or objection preferred against a person who presents himself at the polls as a voter, in order that his right to cast a ballot may be inquired into.

5. An objection or exception to the personal qualification of a judge or magistrate about to preside at the trial of a cause; as on account of personal interest, his having been of counsel, bias, etc.

6. An exception or objection taken to the jurors summoned and returned for the trial of a cause, either individually, (to the polls,) or collectively, (to the array.)

AT COMMON LAW. The causes for principal challenges fall under four heads: (1) *Propter honoris respectum*. On account of respect for the party's social rank. (2) *Propter defectum*. On account of some legal disqualification, such as infancy or alienage. (3) *Propter affectum*. On account of partiality; that is, either expressed or implied bias or prejudice. (4) *Propter delictum*. On account of crime; that is, disqualification arising from the conviction of an infamous crime.

CHALLENGE FOR CAUSE. A challenge to a juror for which some cause or reason is alleged. Termes de la Ley; 4 Bl. Comm. 353. Thus distinguished from a peremptory challenge.

CHALLENGE PEREMPTORY. A privilege allowed to a prisoner in criminal cases, of challenging peremptorily a certain number of jurors, without assigning any cause. Termes de la Ley; 4 Bl. Comm. 353; Co. Litt. 156*b*.

CHALLENGE, PRINCIPAL. Such as is made for a cause which when substantiated is of itself sufficient evidence of bias in favor of or against the party challenging. Co. Litt. 156*b*. See 3 Bl. Comm. 363; 4 Bl. Comm. 353.

CHALLENGE TO FIGHT. A summons or invitation, given by one person to another, to engage in a personal combat; a request to fight a duel. A criminal offense. See Steph. Crim. Dig. 40; 3 East, 581; 6 Blackf. 20.

CHALLENGE TO THE ARRAY. An exception to the whole panel in which the jury are *arrayed*, or set in order by the sheriff in his return, upon account of partiality, or some default in the sheriff, coroner, or other officer who arrayed the panel or made the return. 3 Bl. Comm. 359; Co. Litt. 155*b*.

CHALLENGE TO THE FAVOR. Is where the party has no principal challenge, but objects only some probable circumstances of suspicion, as acquaintance, and the like, the validity of which must be left to the determination of triors, whose office it is to decide whether the juror be favorable or unfavorable. 3 Bl. Comm. 363; 4 Bl. Comm. 353.

CHALLENGE TO THE POLL. A challenge made separately to an individual juror; as distinguished from a challenge to the array.

CHAMBER. A room or apartment in a house. A private repository of money; a treasury. Sometimes used to designate a court, a commission, or an association of persons habitually meeting together in an apartment, *e. g.*, the "star chamber," "chamber of deputies," "chamber of commerce."

CHAMBER OF ACCOUNTS. In French law. A sovereign court, of great antiquity, in France, which took cognizance of and registered the accounts of the king's revenue; nearly the same as the English court of exchequer. Enc. Brit.

CHAMBER OF COMMERCE. An association (which may or may not be incorporated) comprising the principal merchants, manufacturers, and traders of a city, designed for convenience in buying, selling, and exchanging goods, and to foster the commercial and industrial interests of the place.

CHAMBER, WIDOW'S. A portion of the effects of a deceased person, reserved for the use of his widow, and consisting of her apparel, and the furniture of her bed-chamber, is called in London the "widow's chamber." 2 Bl. Comm. 518.

CHAMBERDEKINS, or CHAMBER DEACONS. In old English law. Certain poor Irish scholars, clothed in mean habit, and living under no rule; also beggars banished from England. (1 Hen. V. cc. 7, 8.) Wharton.

CHAMBERLAIN. Keeper of the chamber. Originally the chamberlain was the keeper of the treasure chamber (*camera*) of the prince or state; otherwise called "treasurer." Cowell.

The name of several high officers of state in England, as the lord great chamberlain of England, lord chamberlain of the household, chamberlain of the exchequer. Cowell; Blount.

The word is also used in some American cities as the title of an officer corresponding to "treasurer."

CHAMBERLARIA. Chamberlainship; the office of a chamberlain. Cowell.

CHAMBERS. In practice. The private room or office of a judge; any place in which a judge hears motions, signs papers, or does other business pertaining to his office, when he is not holding a session of court. Business so transacted is said to be done "in chambers." The term is also applied, in England, to the private office of a barrister.

In international law. Portions of the sea cut off by lines drawn from one promontory to another, or included within lines extending from the point of one cape to the next, situate on the sea-coast of the same nation, and which are claimed by that nation as asylums for merchant vessels, and exempt from the operations of belligerents.

CHAMBIUM. In old English law. Change, or exchange. Bract. fols. 117, 118.

CHAMBRE DEPEINTE. A name anciently given to St. Edward's chamber, called the "Painted Chamber," destroyed by fire with the houses of parliament.

CHAMP DE MAI. (Lat. *Campus Maii.*) The field or assembly of May. The national assembly of the Franks, held in the month of May.

CHAMP DE MARS. (Lat. *Campus Martii.*) The field or assembly of March.

The national assembly of the Franks, held in the month of March, in the open air.

CHAMPART. In French law. The grant of a piece of land by the owner to another, on condition that the latter would deliver to him a portion of the crops. 18 Toullier, n. 182.

CHAMPERT. In old English law. A share or division of land; champerty.

In old Scotch law. A gift or bribe, taken by any great man or judge from any person, for delay of just actions, or furthering of wrongous actions, whether it be lands or any goods movable. Skene.

CHAMPERTOR. In criminal law. One who makes pleas or suits, or causes them to be moved, either directly or indirectly, and sues them at his proper costs, upon condition of having a part of the gain. One guilty of champerty. St. 33 Edw. I. c. 2.

CHAMPERTOUS. Of the nature of champerty; affected with champerty.

CHAMPERTY. A bargain made by a stranger with one of the parties to a suit, by which such third person undertakes to carry on the litigation at his own cost and risk, in consideration of receiving, if he wins the suit, a part of the land or other subject sought to be recovered by the action.

The purchase of an interest in a thing in dispute, with the object of maintaining and taking part in the litigation. 7 Bing. 378.

The act of assisting the plaintiff or defendant in a legal proceeding in which the person giving the assistance has no valuable interest, on an agreement that, if the proceeding is successful, the proceeds shall be divided between the plaintiff or defendant, as the case may be, and the assisting person. Sweet.

Champerty is the carrying on a suit in the name of another, but at one's own expense, with the view of receiving as compensation a certain share of the avails of the suit. 4 Duer, 275.

The distinction between *champerty* and *maintenance* lies in the interest which the interfering party is to have in the issue of the suit. In the former case, he is to receive a share or portion of what may be recovered; in the latter case, he is in no way benefited by the success of the party aided, but simply intermeddles officiously. Thus every champerty includes maintenance, but not every maintenance is champerty. See 2 Inst. 208.

CHAMPION. A person who fights a combat in his own cause, or in place of another. The person who, in the trial by battel, fought either for the tenant or demandant. 3 Bl. Comm. 339.

CHAMPION OF THE KING OR QUEEN. An ancient officer, whose duty it was to ride armed *cap-à-piè*, into Westminster Hall at the coronation, while the king was at dinner, and, by the proclamation of a herald, make a challenge "that, if any man shall deny the king's title to the crown, he is there ready to defend it in single combat." The king drank to him, and sent him a gilt cup covered, full of wine, which the champion drank, retaining the cup for his fee. This ceremony, long discontinued, was revived at the coronation of George IV., but not afterwards. Wharton.

CHANCE. In criminal law. An accident; an unexpected, unforeseen, or unintended consequence of an act; a fortuitous event. The opposite of intention, design, or contrivance.

There is a wide difference between *chance* and *accident*. The one is the intervention of some unlooked-for circumstance to prevent an expected result; the other is the uncalculated effect of mere luck. The shot discharged at random strikes its object by chance; that which is turned aside from its well-directed aim by some unforeseen circumstance misses its mark by accident. Pure chance consists in the entire absence of all the means of calculating results; accident, in the unusual prevention of an effect naturally resulting from the means employed. Morris, (Iowa,) 173.

CHANCE-MEDLEY. In criminal law. A sudden affray. This word is sometimes applied to any kind of homicide by misadventure, but in strictness it is applicable to such killing only as happens in defending one's self. 4 Bl. Comm. 184.

CHANCEL. In ecclesiastical law. The part of a church in which the communion table stands; it belongs to the rector or the impropriator. 2 Broom & H. Comm. 420.

CHANCELLOR. In American law, this is the name given in some states to the judge (or the presiding judge) of a court of chancery. In England, besides being the designation of the chief judge of the court of chancery, the term is used as the title of several judicial officers attached to bishops or other high dignitaries and to the universities. (See the following titles.) In Scotch practice, it denotes the foreman of an assise or jury.

CHANCELLOR OF A CATHEDRAL. In English ecclesiastical law. One of the *quatuor personæ*, or four chief dignitaries of the cathedrals of the old foundation. The duties assigned to the office by the statutes of the different chapters vary, but they are chiefly of an educational character, with a special reference to the cultivation of theology.

CHANCELLOR OF A DIOCESE. In ecclesiastical law. Is the officer appointed to assist a bishop in matters of law, and to hold his consistory courts for him. 1 Bl. Comm. 382; 2 Steph. Comm. 672.

CHANCELLOR OF A UNIVERSITY. In English law. The official head of a university. His principal prerogative is to hold a court with jurisdiction over the members of the university, in which court the vice-chancellor presides. The office is for the most part honorary.

CHANCELLOR OF THE DUCHY OF LANCASTER. In English law. An officer before whom, or his deputy, the court of the duchy chamber of Lancaster is held. This is a special jurisdiction concerning all manner of equity relating to lands holden of the king in right of the duchy of Lancaster. Hob. 77; 3 Bl. Comm. 78.

CHANCELLOR OF THE EXCHEQUER. In English law. A high officer of the crown, who formerly sat in the exchequer court, and, together with the regular judges of the court, saw that things were conducted to the king's benefit. In modern times, however, his duties are not of a judicial character, but such as pertain to a minister of state charged with the management of the national revenue and expenditure.

CHANCELLOR OF THE ORDER OF THE GARTER, and other military orders, in England, is an officer who seals the commissions and the mandates of the chapter and assembly of the knights, keeps the register of their proceedings, and delivers their acts under the seal of their order.

CHANCELLOR, THE LORD HIGH. In England, this is the highest judicial functionary in the kingdom, and superior, in point of precedency, to every temporal lord. He is appointed by the delivery of the queen's great seal into his custody. He may not be a Roman Catholic. He is a cabinet minister, a privy counsellor, and prolocutor of the house of lords by prescription, (but not necessarily, though usually, a peer of the realm,) and vacates his office with the ministry by which he was appointed. To him belongs the appointment of all justices of the peace throughout the kingdom. Being, in the earlier periods of English history, usually an ecclesiastic, (for none else were then capable of an office so conversant in writings,) and presiding over the royal chapel, he became keeper of the sovereign's conscience, visitor, in right of the crown, of the hospitals and colleges of royal foundation, and patron of all the crown livings under the value of twenty marks *per annum* in the king's books. He is the general guardian of all infants, idiots, and lunatics, and has the general superintendence of all charitable uses, and all this, over and above the vast and extensive jurisdiction which he exercises in his judicial capacity in the supreme court of judicature, of which he is the head. Wharton.

CHANCELLOR'S COURTS IN THE TWO UNIVERSITIES. In English law. Courts of local jurisdiction in and for the two universities of Oxford and Cambridge in England.

CHANCERY. Equity; equitable jurisdiction; a court of equity; the system of jurisprudence administered in courts of equity. See COURT OF CHANCERY.

CHANGE. 1. An alteration; substitution of one thing for another. This word does not connote either improvement or deterioration as a result. In this respect it differs from *amendment*, which, in law, always imports a change for the better.

2. Exchange of money against money of a different denomination. Also small coin. Also an abbreviation of *exchange.*

CHANGER. An officer formerly belonging to the king's mint, in England, whose business was chiefly to *exchange* coin for bullion brought in by merchants and others.

CHANNEL. This term refers rather to the bed in which the main stream of a river flows than to the deep water of the stream as followed in navigation. 55 Iowa, 558, 8 N. W. Rep. 443.

The "main channel" of a river is that bed of the river over which the principal volume of water flows. Many great rivers discharge themselves into the sea through more than one channel. They all, however, have a main channel, through which the principal volume of water passes. 31 Fed. Rep. 757.

CHANTER. The chief singer in the choir of a cathedral. Mention d in 13 Eliz. c. 10.

CHANTRY. A church or chapel endowed with lands for the maintenance of priests to say mass daily for the souls of the donors. Termes de la Ley; Cowell.

CHAPEL. A place of worship; a lesser or inferior church, sometimes a part of or subordinate to another church. Webster.

CHAPEL OF EASE. In English ecclesiastical law. A chapel founded in general at some period later than the parochial church itself, and designed for the accommodation of such of the parishioners as, in course of time, had begun to fix their residence at some distance from its site; and so termed because built *in aid* of the original church. 3 Steph. Comm. 151.

CHAPELRY. The precinct and limits of a chapel. The same thing to a chapel as a parish is to a church. Cowell; Blount.

CHAPERON. A hood or bonnet anciently worn by the Knights of the Garter, as part of the habit of that order; also a little escutcheon fixed in the forehead of horses drawing a hearse at a funeral. Wharton.

CHAPITRE. A summary of matters to be inquired of or presented before justices in eyre, justices of assise, or of the peace, in their sessions. Also articles delivered by the justice in his charge to the inquest. Brit. c. iii.

CHAPLAIN. An ecclesiastic who performs divine service in a chapel; but it more commonly means one who attends upon a king, prince, or other person of quality, for the performance of clerical duties in a private chapel. 4 Coke, 90.

A clergyman officially attached to a ship of war, to an army, (or regiment,) or to some public institution, for the purpose of performing divine service. Webster.

CHAPMAN. An itinerant vendor of small wares. A trader who trades from place to place. Say. 191, 192.

CHAPTER. In ecclesiastical law. A congregation of ecclesiastical persons in a cathedral church, consisting of canons, or prebendaries, whereof the dean is the head, all subordinate to the bishop, to whom they act as assistants in matters relating to the church, for the better ordering and disposing the things thereof, and the confirmation of such leases of the temporalty and offices relating to the bishopric, as the bishop shall make from time to time. And they are termed "*capitulum*," as a kind of head, instituted not only to assist the bishop in manner aforesaid, but also anciently to rule and govern the diocese in the time of vacation. Burn, Dict.

CHARACTER. The aggregate of the moral qualities which belong to and distinguish an individual person; the general result of the one's distinguishing attributes.

That moral predisposition or habit, or aggregate of ethical qualities, which is believed to attach to a person, on the strength of the common opinion and report concerning him.

The opinion generally entertained of a person derived from the common report of the people who are acquainted with him. 3 Serg. & R. 336; 3 Mass. 192.

Character and *reputation* are not synonymous terms. Character is what a man or woman is morally, while reputation is what he or she is reputed to be. Yet reputation is the estimate which the community has of a person's character; and it is the belief that moral character is wanting in an individual that renders him unworthy of belief; that is to say, that reputation is evidence of character, and if the reputation is bad for truth, or reputation is bad in other respects affecting the moral character, then the jury may infer that the character is bad and the witness not reliable. General character has always been proved by proving general reputation. 6 Or. 213.

The word "character" no doubt has an objective and subjective import, which are quite distinct. As to the object, character is its quality. As to man, it is the quality of his mind, and his affections, his capacity and temperament. But as a subjective term, certainly in the minds of others, one's character is the aggregate, or the abstract, of other men's opinions of one. And in this sense, when a witness speaks of the character of another witness for truth, he draws not upon his memory alone, but his judgment also. It is the conclusion of the mind of the witness, in summing up the amount of all the reports he has heard of the man, and declaring his character for truth, as held in the minds of his neighbors and acquaintances, and in this sense character, general character, and general report or reputation are the same, as held in the books. 26 Vt. 278.

CHARGE, *v.* To impose a burden, obligation, or lien; to create a claim against property; to claim, to demand; to accuse; to instruct a jury on matters of law.

CHARGE, *n.* **In general.** An incumbrance, lien, or burden; an obligation or duty; a liability; an accusation.

In contracts. An obligation, binding upon him who enters into it, which may be removed or taken away by a discharge. Termes de la Ley.

An undertaking to keep the custody of another person's goods.

An obligation entered into by the owner of an estate, which binds the estate for its performance. Com. Dig. "Rent," c. 6; 2 Ball & B. 223.

In the law of wills. A responsibility or liability imposed by the testator upon a devisee personally, or upon the land devised.

In equity pleading. An allegation in the bill of matters which disprove or avoid a defense which it is alleged the defendant is supposed to pretend or intend to set up. Story, Eq. Pl. § 31.

In equity practice. A paper presented to a master in chancery by a party to a cause, being a written statement of the items with which the opposite party should be debited or should account for, or of the claim of the party making it. It is more comprehensive than a *claim*, which implies only the amount due to the person producing it, while a charge may embrace the whole liabilities of the accounting party. Hoff. Mast. 36.

In common-law practice. The final address made by a judge to the jury trying a case, before they make up their verdict, in which he sums up the case, and instructs the jury as to the rules of law which apply to its various issues, and which they must observe, in deciding upon their verdict, when they shall have determined the controverted matters of fact. The term also applies to the address of the court to a grand jury, in which the latter are instructed as to their duties.

In Scotch law. The command of the king's letters to perform some act; as a *charge* to enter heir. Also a messenger's execution, requiring a person to obey the order of the king's letters; as a *charge* on letters of horning, or a *charge* against a superior. Bell.

CHARGE AND DISCHARGE. Under the former system of equity practice, this phrase was used to characterize the usual method of taking an account before a master. After the plaintiff had presented his "charge," a written statement of the items of account for which he asked credit, the defendant filed a counter-statement, called a "discharge," exhibiting any claims or demands he held against the plaintiff. These served to define the field of investigation, and constituted the basis of the report.

CHARGÉ DES AFFAIRES, or CHARGÉ D'AFFAIRES. The title of a diplomatic representative of inferior rank. He has not the title or dignity of a minister, though he may be charged with the functions and offices of the latter, either as a temporary substitute for a minister or at a court to which his government does not accredit a minister.

CHARGE-SHEET. A paper kept at a police-station to receive each night the names of the persons brought and given into custody, the nature of the accusation, and the name of the accuser in each case. It is under the care of the inspector on duty. Wharton.

CHARGE TO ENTER HEIR. In Scotch law. A writ commanding a person to enter heir to his predecessor within forty days, otherwise an action to be raised against him as if he had entered.

CHARGEABLE. This word, in its ordinary acceptation, as applicable to the imposition of a duty or burden, signifies capable of being charged, subject to be charged, liable to be charged, or proper to be charged. 46 Vt. 625; 107 Mass. 419.

CHARGEANT. Weighty; heavy; penal; expensive. Kelham.

CHARGES. The expenses which have been incurred, or disbursements made, in connection with a contract, suit, or business transaction. Spoken of an action, it is said that the term includes more than what falls under the technical description of "costs."

CHARGING ORDER. The name bestowed, in English practice, upon an order allowed by St. 1 & 2 Vict. c. 110, § 14, and 3 & 4 Vict. c. 82, to be granted to a judgment creditor, that the property of a judgment debtor in government stock, or in the stock of any public company in England, corporate or otherwise, shall (whether standing in his own name or in the name of any person in trust for him) stand charged with the payment of the amount for which judgment shall have been recovered, with interest. 3 Steph. Comm. 587, 588.

CHARITABLE USES, CHARITIES. Gifts to general public uses, which may extend to the rich, as well as the poor. Amb. 651; 2 Sneed, 305.

Gifts to such purposes as are enumerated in the act 43 Eliz. c. 4, or which, by analogy, are deemed within its spirit or intendment. Boyle, Char. 17.

CHARITY. Subjectively, the sentiment or motive of benevolence and philanthropy; the disposition to relieve the distressed. Objectively, alms-giving; acts of benevolence; relief, assistance, or services accorded to the needy without return. Also gifts for the promotion of philanthropic and humanitarian purposes.

The meaning of the word "charity," in its legal sense, is different from the signification which it ordinarily bears. In its legal sense, it includes not only gifts for the benefit of the poor, but endowments for the advancement of learning, or institutions for the encouragement of science and art, and, it is said, for any other useful and public purpose. 25 Ohio St. 243.

Charity, in its widest sense, denotes all the good affections men ought to bear towards each other; in a restricted and common sense, relief of the poor. 9 Ves. 399.

Charity, as used in the Massachusetts Sunday law, includes whatever proceeds from a sense of moral duty or a feeling of kindness and humanity, and is intended wholly for the purpose of the relief or comfort of another, and not for one's own benefit or pleasure. 118 Mass. 195, 197.

CHARRE OF LEAD. A quantity consisting of 36 pigs of lead, each pig weighing about 70 pounds.

CHART. The word "chart," as used in the copyright law, does not include sheets of paper exhibiting tabulated or methodically arranged information. 24 Fed. Rep. 632.

CHARTA. In old English law. A charter or deed; an instrument written and sealed; the formal evidence of conveyances and contracts. Also any signal or token by which an estate was held. The term came to be applied, by way of eminence, to such documents as proceeded from the sovereign, granting liberties or privileges, and either where the recipient of the grant was the whole nation, as in the case of *Magna Charta*, or a public body, or private individual, in which case it corresponded to the modern word "charter."

In the civil law. Paper, suitable for the inscription of documents or books; hence, any instrument or writing. See Dig. 32, 52, 6; Nov. 44, 2.

CHARTA COMMUNIS. In old English law. A common or mutual charter or deed; one containing mutual covenants, or involving mutuality of obligation; one to which both parties might have occasion to refer, to establish their respective rights. Bract. fols. 33*b*, 34.

CHARTA CYROGRAPHATA. In old English law. A chirographed charter; a charter executed in two parts, and cut through the middle, (*scinditur per medium*,) where the word "*cyrographum*," or "*chirographum*," was written in large letters. Bract. fol. 34; Fleta, lib. 3, c. 14, § 3.

CHARTA DE FORESTA. A collection of the laws of the forest, made in the 9th Hen. III., and said to have been originally a part of *Magna Charta*.

Charta de non ente non valet. Co. Litt. 36. A charter concerning a thing not in existence avails not.

CHARTA DE UNA PARTE. A deed-poll.

Charta non est nisi vestimentum donationis. A deed is nothing else than the vestment of a gift. Co. Litt. 36.

CHARTA PARTITA. (Literally, a deed divided.) A charter-party. 3 Kent, Comm. 201.

CHARTÆ LIBERTATUM. These are *Magna Charta* and *Charta de Foresta*.

Chartarum super fidem, mortuis testibus, ad patriam de necessitudine recurrendum est. Co. Litt. 36. The witnesses being dead, the truth of charters must of necessity be referred to the country, *i. e.*, a jury.

CHARTE. A chart, or plan, which mariners use at sea.

CHARTE-PARTIE. Fr. In French marine law. A charter-party.

CHARTEL. A challenge to a single combat; also an instrument or writing between two states for settling the exchange of prisoners of war.

CHARTER, *v*. In mercantile law. To hire or lease a vessel for a voyage. A "chartered" is distinguished from a "seeking" ship. 7 East, 24.

CHARTER, *n*. An instrument emanating from the sovereign power, in the nature of a grant, either to the whole nation, or to a class or portion of the people, or to a colony or dependency, and assuring to them certain rights, liberties, or powers. Such was the "Great Charter" or "*Magna Charta*," and such also were the charters granted to certain of the English colonies in America. See Story, Const. § 161.

An act of the legislative department of government, creating a corporation, is called the "charter" of the corporation.

In old English law. The term denoted a deed or other written instrument under seal; a conveyance, covenant, or contract.

In old Scotch law. A disposition made by a superior to his vassal, for something to be performed or paid by him. 1 Forb. Inst. pt. 2, b. 2, c. 1, tit. 1. A writing which contains the grant or transmission of the feudal right to the vassal. Ersk. Inst. 2, 3, 19.

CHARTER-HOUSE. Formerly a convent of Carthusian monks in London; now a college founded and endowed by Thomas Sutton. The governors of the charter-house are a corporation aggregate without a head, president, or superior, all the members being of equal authority. 3 Steph. Comm. (7th Ed.) 14, 97.

CHARTER-LAND. Otherwise called "book-land," is property held by deed under certain rents and free services. It, in effect, differs nothing from the free socage lands, and hence have arisen most of the freehold tenants, who hold of particular manors, and owe suit and service to the same. 2 Bl. Comm. 90.

CHARTER OF PARDON. In English law. An instrument under the great seal, by which a pardon is granted to a man for a felony or other offense.

CHARTER OF THE FOREST. See CHARTA DE FORESTA.

CHARTER-PARTY. A contract by which an entire ship, or some principal part thereof, is let to a merchant for the conveyance of goods on a determined voyage to one or more places. Abb. Shipp. (241,) 315. A contract of affreightment in writing, by which the owner of a ship lets the whole or a part of her to a merchant, for the conveyance of goods on a particular voyage, in consideration of the payment of freight. 3 Kent, Comm. 201.

A written agreement, not usually under seal, by which a ship-owner lets an entire ship, or a part of it, to a merchant for the conveyance of goods, binding himself to transport them to a particular place for a sum of money which the merchant undertakes to pay as freight for their carriage. Maude & P. Mer. Shipp. 227.

The contract by which a ship is let is termed a "charter-party." By it the owner may either let the capacity or burden of the ship, continuing the employment of the owner's master, crew, and equipments, or may surrender the entire ship to the charterer, who then provides them himself. The master or part owner may be a charterer. Civil Code Cal. § 1959; Civil Code Dak. § 1127.

CHARTER ROLLS. Ancient English records of royal charters, granted between the years 1199 and 1516.

CHARTERED SHIP. A ship hired or freighted; a ship which is the subject-matter of a charter-party.

CHARTERER. In mercantile law. One who charters (*i. e.*, hires or engages) a vessel for a voyage; a freighter. 2 Steph. Comm. 184; 3 Kent, Comm. 137.

CHARTIS REDDENDIS. (For returning the charters.) An ancient writ which lay against one who had charters of feoffment intrusted to his keeping and refused to deliver them. Reg. Orig. 159.

CHARTOPHYLAX. In old European law. A keeper of records or public instruments; a chartulary; a registrar. Spelman.

CHARUE. In old English law. A plow. *Bestes des charues;* beasts of the plow.

CHASE. The liberty or franchise of hunting, one's self, and keeping protected against all other persons, beasts of the chase within a specified district, without regard to the ownership of the land. 2 Bl. Comm. 414-416.

A privileged place for the preservation of deer and beasts of the forest, of a middle nature between a forest and a park. It is commonly less than a forest, and not endowed with so many liberties, as officers, laws, courts; and yet it is of larger compass than a park, having more officers and game than a park. Every forest is a chase, but every chase is not a forest. It differs from a park in that it is not inclosed, yet it must have certain metes and bounds, but it may be in other men's grounds, as well as in one's own. Manwood, 49.

CHASTITY. Purity; continence. That virtue which prevents the unlawful intercourse of the sexes. Also the state of purity or abstinence from unlawful sexual connection.

CHATTEL. An article of personal property; any species of property not amounting to a freehold or fee in land.

The name given to things which in law are deemed personal property. Chattels are divided into chattels real and chattels personal; chattels real being interests in land which devolve after the manner of personal estate, as leaseholds. As opposed to freeholds, they are regarded as personal estate. But, as being interests in real estate, they are called "chattels real," to distinguish them from movables, which are called "chattels personal." Mozley & Whitley.

Chattels personal are movables only; chattels real are such as savor only of the realty. 19 Johns. 73.

The term "chattels" is a more comprehensive one than "goods," as it includes animate as well as inanimate property. 2 Chit. Bl. Comm. 383, note. In a devise, however, they seem to be of the same import. Shep. Touch. 447; 2 Fonbl. Eq. 335.

CHATTEL INTEREST. An interest in corporeal hereditaments less than a freehold. 2 Kent, Comm. 342.

CHATTEL MORTGAGE. An instrument of sale of personalty conveying the title of the property to the mortgagee with terms of defeasance; and, if the terms of redemption are not complied with, then, at common law, the title becomes absolute in the mortgagee.

A transfer of personal property as security for a debt or obligation in such form that, upon failure of the mortgagor to comply with the terms of the contract, the title to the property will be in the mortgagee. Thomas, Mortg. 427.

An absolute pledge, to become an absolute interest if not redeemed at a fixed time. 2 Caines Cas. 200, per Kent, Ch.

A conditional sale of a chattel as security for the payment of a debt or the performance of some other obligation. Jones, Chat. Mortg. § 1.

A chattel mortgage is a conditional transfer or conveyance of the property itself. The chief distinctions between it and a pledge are that in the latter the title, even after condition broken, does not pass to the pledgee, who has only a lien on the property, but remains in the pledgeor, who has the right to redeem the property at any time before its sale. Besides, the possession of the property must, in all cases, accompany the pledge, and, at a sale thereof by the pledgee to satisfy his demand, he cannot become the purchaser; while by a chattel mortgage the title of the mortgagee becomes absolute at law, on the default of the mortgagor, and it is not essential to the validity of the instrument that possession of the property should be delivered, and, on the foreclosure of the mortgage, the mortgagee is at liberty to become the purchaser. 36 Cal. 414, 428, 441.

The material distinction between a pledge and a mortgage of chattels is that a mortgage is a conveyance of the legal title upon condition, and it becomes absolute in law if not redeemed by a given time; a pledge is a deposit of goods, redeemable on certain terms, either with or without a fixed period for redemption. In pledge, the general property does not pass, as in the case of mortgage, and the pawnee has only a special property in the thing deposited. The pawnee must choose between two remedies,—a bill in chancery for a judicial sale under a decree of foreclosure, or a sale without judicial process, on the refusal of the debtor to redeem, after reasonable notice to do so. 5 Blackf. 320. See, also, 3 Blackf. 309.

In a *conditional sale* the purchaser has merely a right to repurchase, and no debt or obligation exists on the part of the vendor; this distinguishes such a sale from a mortgage. 40 Miss. 462; 4 Daly, 77.

CHAUD-MEDLEY. A homicide committed in the heat of an affray and while under the influence of passion; it is thus distinguished from *chance-medley*, which is the killing of a man in a casual affray in self-defense. 4 Bl. Comm. 184. See 1 Russ. Crimes, 660.

CHAUMPERT. A kind of tenure mentioned in a patent of 35 Edw. III. Cowell; Blount.

CHAUNTRY RENTS. Money paid to the crown by the servants or purchasers of chauntry-lands. See CHANTRY.

CHEAT. Swindling; defrauding. "Deceitful practices in defrauding or *endeavoring* to defraud another of his known right, by some *willful device*, contrary to the plain rules of common honesty." Hawk. P. C. b. 2, c. 23, § 1. "The fraudulent obtaining the property of another by any deceitful and illegal practice or token (short of felony) which affects or may affect the public." Steph. Crim. Law, 93.

Cheats, punishable at common law, are such cheats (not amounting to felony) as are effected by deceitful or illegal symbols or tokens which may affect the public at large, and against which common prudence could not have guarded. 2 Whart. Crim. Law, § 1116; 2 East, P. C. 818.

CHEATERS, or ESCHEATORS, were officers appointed to look after the king's escheats, a duty which gave them great opportunities of fraud and oppression, and in consequence many complaints were made of their misconduct. Hence it seems that a *cheater* came to signify a fraudulent person, and thence the verb to *cheat* was derived. Wharton.

CHECK, *v.* To control or restrain; to hold within bounds. To verify or audit. Particularly used with reference to the control or supervision of one department, bureau, or office over another.

CHECK, *n.* A draft or order upon a bank or banking-house, purporting to be drawn upon a deposit of funds, for the payment at all events of a certain sum of money to a certain person therein named, or to him or his order, or to bearer, and payable instantly on demand. 2 Daniel, Neg. Inst. § 1566.

A check is a bill of exchange drawn upon a bank or banker, or a person described as such upon the face thereof, and payable on demand, without interest. Civil Code Cal. § 3254; Civil Code Dak. § 1933.

A check differs from an ordinary bill of exchange in the following particulars: (1) It is drawn on a bank or bankers, and is payable immediately on presentment, without any days of grace. (2) It is payable immediately on presentment, and no acceptance as distinct from payment is required. (3) By its terms it is supposed to be drawn upon a previous deposit of funds, and is an absolute appropriation of so much money in the hands of the bankers to the holder of the check, to remain there until called for, and cannot after notice be withdrawn by the drawer. 2 Story, 502; 8 Bush, 357.

CHECK-BOOK. A book containing blank checks on a particular bank or banker, with an inner margin, called a "stub," on which to note the number of each check, its amount and date, and the payee's name, and a memorandum of the balance in bank.

CHECK-ROLL. In English law. A list or book, containing the names of such as are attendants on, or in the pay of, the queen or other great personages, as their household servants.

CHECKER. The old Scotch form of exchequer.

CHEFE. In Anglo-Norman law. Were or weregild; the price of the head or person, (*capitis pretium.*)

CHEMERAGE. In old French law. The privilege or perogative of the eldest. A provincial term derived from *chemier,* (*q. v.*) Guyot, Inst.

CHEMIER. In old French law. The eldest born. A term used in Poitou and other places. Guyot, Inst.

CHEMIN. The road wherein every man goes; the king's highway.

CHEMIS. In old Scotch law. A chief dwelling or mansion house.

CHEVAGE. A sum of money paid by villeins to their lords in acknowledgment of their bondage.

Chevage seems also to have been used for a sum of money yearly given to a man of power for his countenance and protection as a chief or leader. Termes de la Ley; Cowell.

CHEVANTIA. In old records. A loan or advance of money upon credit. Cowell.

CHEVISANCE. An agreement or composition; an end or order set down between a creditor or debtor; an indirect gain in point of usury, etc.; also an unlawful bargain or contract. Wharton.

CHEVITIÆ. In old records. Pieces of ground, or *heads* at the end of plowed lands. Cowell.

CHEZÉ. A homestead or homesfall which is accessory to a house.

CHICANE. Swindling; shrewd cunning. The use of tricks and artifice.

CHIEF. Principal; leading; head; eminent in power or importance; the most important or valuable of several.

Declaration in chief is a declaration for the principal cause of action. 1 Tidd, Pr. 419.

Examination in chief is the first examination of a witness by the party who produces him. 1 Greenl. Ev. § 445.

CHIEF BARON. The presiding judge of the English court of exchequer; answering to the chief justice of other courts. 3 Bl. Comm. 44; 3 Steph. Comm. 401.

CHIEF CLERK. The principal clerical officer of a bureau or department, who is generally charged, subject to the direction of his superior officer, with the superintendence of the administration of the business of the office.

CHIEF JUDGE. The judge of the London bankruptcy court is so called.

CHIEF JUSTICE. The presiding, eldest, or principal judge of a court of justice.

CHIEF JUSTICE OF ENGLAND. The presiding judge in the queen's bench division of the high court of justice, and, in the absence of the lord chancellor, president of the high court, and also an *ex officio* judge of the court of appeals. The full title is "Lord Chief Justice of England."

CHIEF JUSTICE OF THE COMMON PLEAS. In England. The presiding judge in the court of common pleas, and afterwards in the common pleas division of the high court of justice, and one of the *ex officio* judges of the high court of appeal.

CHIEF JUSTICIAR. In old English law. A high judicial officer and special magistrate, who presided over the *aula regis* of the Norman kings, and who was also the principal minister of state, the second man in the kingdom, and, by virtue of his office, guardian of the realm in the king's absence. 3 Bl. Comm. 38.

CHIEF LORD. The immediate lord of the fee, to whom the tenants were directly and personally responsible.

CHIEF PLEDGE. The borsholder, or chief of the borough. Spelman.

CHIEF RENTS. In English law. Were the annual payments of freeholders of manors; and were also called "quit-rents," because by paying them the tenant was freed from all other rents or services. 2 Bl. Comm. 42.

CHIEF, TENANT IN. In English feudal law. All the land in the kingdom was supposed to be holden mediately or immediately of the king, who was styled the "Lord Paramount," or "Lord Above All;" and those that held immediately under him, in right of his crown and dignity, were called his tenants "*in capite*" or "in chief," which was the most honorable species of tenure, but at the same time subjected the tenant to greater and more burdensome services than inferior tenures did. Brown.

CHIEFRIE. In feudal law. A small rent paid to the lord paramount.

CHILD. This word has two meanings in law: (1) In the law of the domestic relations, and as to descent and distribution, it is used strictly as the correlative of "parent," and means a son or daughter considered as in relation with the father or mother. (2) In the law of negligence, and in laws for the protection of children, etc., it is used as the opposite of "adult," and means the young of the human species, (generally under the age of puberty,) without any reference to parentage and without distinction of sex.

CHILDREN. Offspring; progeny. Legitimate offspring; children born in wedlock. 7 Ves. 458; 5 Scott, N. R. 990.

The general rule is that "children," in a bequest or devise, means legitimate children. Under a devise or bequest to children, as a class, natural children are not included, unless the testator's intention to include them is manifest, either by express designation or necessary implication. 14 N. J. Eq. 159; 2 Paige, 11.

In deeds, the word "children" signifies the immediate descendants of a person, in the ordinary sense of the word, as contradistinguished from *issue;* unless there be some accompanying expressions, evidencing that the word is used in an enlarged sense. Lewis, Perp. 196.

In wills, where greater latitude of construction is allowed, in order to effect the obvious intention of the testator, the meaning of the word has sometimes been extended, so as to include *grandchildren,* and it has been held to be synonymous with *issue.* Lewis, Perp. 195, 196; 2 Crabb, Real Prop. pp. 38, 39, §§ 988, 989; 4 Kent, Comm. 345, 346, note.

The word "heirs," in its natural signification, is a word of limitation; and it is presumed to be used in that sense, unless a contrary intention appears. But the term "children," in its natural sense, is a word of purchase, and is to be taken to have been used as such, unless there are other expressions in the will showing that the testator intended to use it as a word of limitation only. 4 Paige, 293; 3 Wend. 503.

In the natural and primary sense of the word "children," it implies immediate offspring, and, in its legal acceptation, is not a word of limitation, unless it is absolutely necessary so to construe it in order to give effect to the testator's intention. 39 Ala. 24.

"Children" is ordinarily a word of description, limited to persons standing in the same relation, and has the same effect as if all the names were given; but heirs, in the absence of controlling or explanatory words, includes more remote descendants, and is to be applied *per stirpes.* 14 Allen, 204.

CHILDWIT. In Saxon law. The right which a lord had of taking a fine of his bondwoman gotten with child without his license. Termes de la Ley; Cowell.

CHILTERN HUNDREDS. In English law. The stewardship of the Chiltern Hundreds is a nominal office in the gift of the crown, usually accepted by members of the house of commons desirous of vacating their seats. By law a member once duly elected to parliament is compelled to discharge the duties of the trust conferred upon him, and is not enabled at will to resign it. But by statute, if any member accepts any office of profit from the crown, (except officers in the army or navy accepting a new commission,) his seat is vacated. If, therefore, any member wishes to retire from the representation of the county or borough by which he was sent to parliament, he applies to the lords of the treasury for the stewardship of one of the Chiltern Hundreds, which having received, and thereby accomplished his purpose, he again resigns the office. Brown.

CHIMIN. In old English law. A road, way, highway. It is either the queen's highway (*chiminus reginæ*) or a private way. The first is that over which the subjects of the realm, and all others under the protection of the crown, have free liberty to pass, though the property in the soil itself belong to some private individual; the last is that in which one person or more have liberty to pass over the land of another, by prescription or charter. Wharton.

CHIMINAGE. A toll for passing on a way through a forest; called in the civil law "*pedagium*." Cowell.

CHIMINUS. The way by which the king and all his subjects and all under his protection have a right to pass, though the property of the soil of each side where the way lieth may belong to a private man. Cowell.

CHIMNEY MONEY, or HEARTH MONEY. A tax upon chimneys or hearths; an ancient tax or duty upon houses in England, now repealed.

CHIPPINGAVEL. In old English law. A tax upon trade; a toll imposed upon traffic, or upon goods brought to a place to be sold.

CHIRGEMOT, CHIRCHGEMOT. In Saxon law. An ecclesiastical assembly or court. Spelman. A synod or meeting in a church or vestry. 4 Inst. 321.

CHIROGRAPH. In old English law. A deed or indenture; also the last part of a fine of land.

An instrument of gift or conveyance attested by the subscription and crosses of the witnesses, which was in Saxon times called "*chirographum*," and which, being somewhat changed in form and manner by the Normans, was by them styled "*charta*." Anciently when they made a chirograph or deed which required a counterpart, as we call it, they engrossed it twice upon one piece of parchment contrariwise, leaving a space between, in which they wrote in capital letters the word "chirograph," and then cut the parchment in two through the middle of the word, giving a part to each party. Cowell.

In Scotch law. A written voucher for a debt. Bell.

In civil and canon law. An instrument written out and subscribed by the hand of the party who made it, whether the king or a private person. Cowell.

CHIROGRAPHA. In Roman law. Writings emanating from a single party, the debtor.

CHIROGRAPHER OF FINES. In English law. The title of the officer of the common pleas who engrossed fines in that court so as to be acknowledged into a perpetual record. Cowell.

CHIROGRAPHUM. In Roman law. A handwriting; that which was written with a person's own hand. An obligation which a person wrote or subscribed with his own hand; an acknowledgment of debt, as of money received, with a promise to repay.

An evidence or voucher of debt; a security for debt. Dig. 26, 7, 57, pr.

A right of action for debt.

Chirographum apud debitorem repertum præsumitur solutum. An evidence of debt found in the debtor's possession is presumed to be paid. Halk. Max. 20; Bell, Dict.

Chirographum non extans presumitur solutum. An evidence of debt not existing is presumed to have been discharged. Tray. Lat. Max. 73.

CHIRURGEON. The ancient denomination of a surgeon.

CHIVALRY. In feudal law. Knight-service. Tenure in chivalry was the same as tenure by knight-service. 2 Bl. Comm. 61, 62.

CHIVALRY, COURT OF. In English law. The name of a court anciently held as a court of honor merely, before the earl-marshal, and as a criminal court before the lord high constable, jointly with the earl-marshal. It had jurisdiction as to contracts and other matters touching deeds of arms or war, as well as pleas of life or member. It also corrected encroachments in matters of coat-armor, precedency, and other distinctions of families. It is now grown entirely out of use, on account of the feebleness of its jurisdiction and want of power to enforce its judgments, as it could neither fine nor imprison, not being a court of record. 3 Bl. Comm. 68; 4 Broom. & H. Comm. 360, note.

CHOP-CHURCH. A word mentioned in 9 Hen. VI. c. 65, by the sense of which it was in those days a kind of trade, and by the judges declared to be lawful. But Brooke, in his abridgment, says it was only permissible by law. It was, without doubt, a nickname given to those who used to change benefices, as to "chop and change" is a common expression. Jacob.

CHOPS. The mouth of a harbor. Pub. St. Mass. 1882, p. 1288.

CHORAL. In ancient times a person admitted to sit and worship in the choir; a chorister.

CHOREPISCOPUS. In old European law. A rural bishop, or bishop's vicar. Spelman; Cowell.

CHOSE. A thing; an article of property. A chose is a chattel personal, (Williams, Pers. Prop. 4,) and is either in possession or in action.

CHOSE IN ACTION. A right to personal things of which the owner has not the possession, but merely a right of action for their possession. 2 Bl. Comm. 389, 397; 1 Chit. Pr. 99.

A right to receive or recover a debt, demand, or damages on a cause of action *ex contractu*, or for a tort connected with contract, but which cannot be made available without recourse to an action.

Personalty to which the owner has a right of possession in future, or a right of immediate possession, wrongfully withheld, is termed by the law a "chose in action." Code Ga. 1882, § 2239.

Chose in action is a phrase which is sometimes used to signify a right of bringing an action, and, at others, the thing itself which forms the subject-matter of that right, or with regard to which that right is exercised; but it more properly includes the idea both of the thing itself and of the right of action as annexed to it. Thus, when it is said that a debt is a chose in action, the phrase conveys the idea, not only of the thing itself, *i. e.*, the debt, but also of the right of action or of recovery possessed by the person to whom the debt is due. When it is said that a chose in action cannot be assigned, it means that a thing to which a right of action is annexed cannot be transferred to another, together with such right. Brown.

A chose in action is any right to damages, whether arising from the commission of a tort, the omission of a duty, or the breach of a contract. 4 Ala. 350; 8 Port. 36.

CHOSE IN POSSESSION. A thing in possession, as distinguished from a thing in action. See CHOSE IN ACTION. Taxes and customs, if paid, are a chose in possession; if unpaid, a chose in action. 2 Bl. Comm. 408.

CHOSE LOCAL. A local thing; a thing annexed to a place, as a mill. Kitchin, fol. 18; Cowell; Blount.

CHOSE TRANSITORY. A thing which is movable, and may be taken away or carried from place to place. Cowell; Blount.

CHOSEN FREEHOLDERS. Under the municipal organization of the state of New Jersey, each county has a board of officers, called by this name, composed of representatives from the cities and townships within its limits, and charged with administering the revenues of the county. They correspond to the "county commissioners" or "supervisors" in other states.

CHOUT. In Hindu law. A fourth, a fourth part of the sum in litigation. The "Mahratta chout" is a fourth of the revenues exacted as tribute by the Mahrattas.

CHREMATISTICS. The science of wealth.

CHRENECRUDA. Under the Salic law. This was a ceremony performed by a person who was too poor to pay his debt or fine, whereby he applied to a rich relative to pay it for him. It consisted (after certain preliminaries) in throwing green herbs upon the party, the effect of which was to bind him to pay the whole demand.

CHRISTIAN. Pertaining to Jesus Christ or the religion founded by him; professing Christianity. The adjective is also used in senses more remote from its original meaning. Thus a "court Christian" is an ecclesiastical court; a "Christian name" is that conferred upon a person at baptism into the Christian church. As a noun, it signifies one who accepts and professes to live by the doctrines and principles of the Christian religion.

CHRISTIAN NAME. The baptismal name distinct from the surname. It has been said from the bench that a Christian name may consist of a single letter. Wharton.

CHRISTIANITATIS CURIA. The court Christian. An ecclesiastical court, as opposed to a civil or lay tribunal. Cowell.

CHRISTIANITY. The religion founded and established by Jesus Christ.

Christianity has been judicially declared to be a part of the common law.

CHRISTMAS-DAY. A festival of the Christian church, observed on the 25th of December, in memory of the birth of Jesus Christ.

CHRYSOLOGY. That branch of the science of political economy which relates to the production of wealth.

CHURCH. In its most general sense, the religious society founded and established by Jesus Christ, to receive, preserve, and propagate his doctrines and ordinances.

A body or community of Christians, united under one form of government by the profession of the same faith, and the observance of the same ritual and ceremonies.

The term may denote either a society of persons who, professing Christianity, hold certain doctrines or observances which differentiate them from other like groups, and who use a common discipline, or the building in which such persons habitually assemble for public worship.

The body of communicants gathered into church order, according to established usage in any town, parish, precinct, or religious society, established according to law, and actually connected and associated therewith for religious purposes, for the time being, is to be regarded as the church of such society, as to all questions of property depending upon that relation. 10 Pick. 193. See, also, 3 Me. 247.

A congregational church is a voluntary association of Christians united for discipline and worship, connected with, and forming a part of, some religious society, having a legal existence. 3 Me. 248.

In English ecclesiastical law. An institution established by the law of the land in reference to religion. 3 Steph. Comm. 54. The word "church" is said to mean, in strictness, not the material fabric, but the cure of souls and the right of tithes. 1 Mod. 201.

CHURCH BUILDING ACTS. Statutes passed in England in and since the year 1818, with the object of extending the accommodation afforded by the national church, so as to make it more commensurate with the wants of the people. 3 Steph. Comm. 152–164.

CHURCH DISCIPLINE ACT. The statute 3 & 4 Vict. c. 86, containing regulations for trying clerks in holy orders charged with offenses against ecclesiastical law, and for enforcing sentences pronounced in such cases. Phillim. Ecc. Law, 1314.

CHURCH OF ENGLAND. The Church of England is a distinct branch of Christ's church, and is also an institution of the state, (see the first clause of *Magna Charta*,) of which the sovereign is the supreme head by act of parliament, (26 Hen. VIII. c. 1,) but in what sense is not agreed. The sovereign must be a member of the church, and every subject is in theory a member. Wharton.

CHURCH RATE. In English law. A sum assessed for the repair of parochial churches by the representatives of the parishioners in vestry assembled.

CHURCH REEVE. A church warden; an overseer of a church. Now obsolete. Cowell.

CHURCH-SCOT. In old English law. Customary obligations paid to the parish priest; from which duties the religious sometimes purchased an exemption for themselves and their tenants.

CHURCH WARDENS. A species of ecclesiastical officers who are intrusted with the care and guardianship of the church building and property. These, with the rector and vestry, represent the parish in its corporate capacity.

CHURCHESSET. In old English law. A certain portion or measure of wheat, anciently paid to the church on St. Martin's day; and which, according to Fleta, was paid as well in the time of the Britons as of the English. Fleta, lib. 1, c. 47, § 28.

CHURCHYARD. See CEMETERY.

CHURL. In Saxon law. A freeman of inferior rank, chiefly employed in husbandry. 1 Reeve, Eng. Law, 5. A tenant at will of free condition, who held land from a thane, on condition of rents and services. Cowell. See CEORL.

CI. Fr. So; here. *Ci Dieiu vous eyde*, so help you God. *Ci devant*, heretofore. *Ci bien*, as well.

CIBARIA. Lat. In the civil law. Food; victuals. Dig. 34, 1.

CINQUE PORTS. Five (now seven) ports or havens on the south-east coast of England, towards France, formerly esteemed the most important in the kingdom. They are Dover, Sandwich, Romney, Hastings, and Hythe, to which Winchelsea and Rye have been since added. They had similar franchises, in some respects, with the counties palatine, and particularly an exclusive jurisdiction, (before the mayor and jurats, corresponding to aldermen, of the ports,) in which the king's ordinary writ did not run. 3 Bl. Comm. 79.

The 18 & 19 Vict. c. 48, (amended by 20 & 21 Vict. c. 1,) abolishes all jurisdiction and authority of the lord warden of the Cinque Ports and constable of Dover Castle, in or in relation to the administration of justice in actions, suits, or other civil proceedings at law or in equity.

CIPPI. An old English law term for the stocks, an instrument in which the wrists or ankles of petty offenders were confined.

CIRCADA. A tribute anciently paid to the bishop or archbishop for visiting churches. Du Fresne.

CIRCAR. In Hindu law. Head of affairs; the state or government; a grand division of a province; a headman. A name used by Europeans in Bengal to denote the Hindu writer and accountant employed by themselves, or in the public offices. Wharton.

CIRCUIT. A division of the country, appointed for a particular judge to visit for the trial of causes or for the administration of justice. Bouvier.

Circuits, as the term is used in England, may be otherwise defined to be *the periodical progresses of the judges* of the superior courts of common law, through the several counties of England and Wales, for the purpose of administering civil and criminal justice.

CIRCUIT COURTS. The name of a system of courts of the United States, invested with general original jurisdiction of such matters and causes as are of Federal cognizance, except the matters specially delegated to the district courts.

The United States circuit courts are held by one of the justices of the supreme court appointed for the circuit, (and bearing the name, in that capacity, of *circuit justice*,) together with the circuit judge and the district judge of the district in which they are held. Their business is not only the supervision of trials of issues in fact, but the hearing of causes as a court in *banc;* and they have equity as well as common-law jurisdiction, together with appellate jurisdiction from the decrees and judgments of the district courts. 1 Kent, Comm. 301-303.

In several of the states, *circuit court* is the name given to a tribunal, the territorial jurisdiction of which comprises several counties or districts, and whose sessions are held in such counties or districts alternately. These courts usually have general original jurisdiction.

CIRCUIT COURTS OF APPEALS. A system of courts of the United States (one in each circuit) created by act of congress of March 3, 1891, composed of the circuit justice, the circuit judge, and an additional circuit judge appointed for each such court, and having appellate jurisdiction from the circuit and district courts except in certain specified classes of cases.

CIRCUIT PAPER. In English practice. A paper containing a statement of the time and place at which the several assises will be held, and other statistical information connected with the assises. Holthouse.

Circuitus est evitandus; et boni judicis est lites dirimere, ne lis ex lite oriatur. 5 Coke, 31. Circuity is to be avoided; and it is the duty of a good judge to determine litigations, lest one lawsuit arise out of another.

CIRCUITY OF ACTION. This occurs where a litigant, by a complex, indirect, or roundabout course of legal proceeding, makes two or more actions necessary, in order to effect that adjustment of rights between all the parties concerned in the transaction which, by a more direct course, might have been accomplished in a single suit.

CIRCULAR NOTES. Similar instruments to "letters of credit." They are drawn by resident bankers upon their foreign correspondents, in favor of persons traveling abroad. The correspondents must be satisfied of the identity of the applicant, before payment; and the requisite proof of such identity is usually furnished, upon the applicant's producing a letter with his signature, by a comparison of the signatures. Brown.

CIRCULATING MEDIUM. This term is more comprehensive than the term "money," as it is the medium of exchanges, or purchases and sales, whether it be gold or silver coin or any other article.

CIRCUMDUCTION. In Scotch law. A closing of the period for lodging papers, or doing any other act required in a cause. Paters. Comp.

CIRCUMDUCTION OF THE TERM. In Scotch practice. The sentence of a judge, declaring the time elapsed within which a proof ought to have been led, and precluding the party from bringing forward any further evidence. Bell.

CIRCUMSPECTE AGATIS. The title of a statute passed 13 Edw. I., A. D. 1285, and so called from the initial words of it, the object of which was to ascertain the boundaries of ecclesiastical jurisdiction in some particulars, or, in other words, to regulate the jurisdiction of the ecclesiastical and temporal courts. 2 Reeve, Eng. Law, 215, 216.

CIRCUMSTANCES. A principal fact or event being the object of investigation, the *circumstances* are the related or accessory facts or occurrences which attend upon it, which closely precede or follow it, which surround and accompany it, which depend upon it, or which support or qualify it.

The terms "circumstance" and "fact" are, in many applications, synonymous; but the true distinction of a circumstance is its *relative* character. "Any fact may be a circumstance with reference to any other fact." 1 Benth. Jud. Evid. 42, note; Id. 142.

Thrift, integrity, good repute, business capacity, and stability of character, for example, are "circumstances" which may be very properly considered in determining the question of "adequate security." 5 Redf. Sur. 600.

CIRCUMSTANTIAL EVIDENCE. Evidence directed to the attending circumstances; evidence which inferentially proves the principal fact by establishing a condition of surrounding and limiting circumstances, whose existence is a premise from which the existence of the principal fact may be concluded by necessary laws of reasoning.

When the existence of any fact is attested by witnesses, as having come under the cognizance of their senses, or is stated in documents, the genuineness and veracity of which there seems no reason to question, the evidence of that fact is said to be direct or positive. When, on the contrary, the existence of the principal fact is only inferred from one or more circumstances which have been established directly, the evidence is said to be circumstantial. And when the existence of the principal fact does not follow from the evidentiary facts as a necessary consequence of the law of nature, but is deduced from them by a process of probable reasoning, the evidence and proof are said to be presumptive. Best, Pres. 246; Id. 12.

All presumptive evidence is circumstantial, because necessarily derived from or made up of *circumstances*, but all circumstantial evidence is not presumptive, that is, it does not operate in the way of *presumption*, being sometimes of a higher grade, and leading to necessary conclusions, instead of probable ones. Burrill.

CIRCUMSTANTIBUS, TALES DE. See TALES.

CIRCUMVENTION. In Scotch law. Any act of fraud whereby a person is reduced to a deed by decreet. It has the same sense in the civil law. Dig. 50, 17, 49, 155.

CIRIC-BRYCE. In old English law. Any violation of the privileges of a church.

CIRIC SCEAT. In old English law. Church-scot, or shot; an ecclesiastical due, payable on the day of St. Martin, consisting chiefly of corn.

CIRLISCUS. A ceorl, (*q. v.*)

CISTA. A box or chest for the deposit of charters, deeds, and things of value.

CITACION. In Spanish law. Citation; summons; an order of a court requiring a person against whom a suit has been brought to appear and defend within a given time.

CITATIO. A citation or summons to court.

CITATIO AD REASSUMENDAM CAUSAM. A summons to take up the cause. A process, in the civil law, which issued when one of the parties to a suit died before its determination, for the plaintiff against the defendant's heir, or for the plaintiff's heir against the defendant, as the case might be; analogous to a modern bill of revivor.

Citatio est de juri naturali. A summons is by natural right. Cases in Banco Regis Wm. III. 453.

CITATION. **In practice.** A writ issued out of a court of competent jurisdiction, commanding a person therein named to appear on a day named and do something therein mentioned, or show cause why he should not. Proc. Prac.

The act by which a person is so summoned or cited.

It is used in this sense, in American law, in the practice upon writs of error from the United States supreme court, and in the proceedings of courts of probate in many of the states.

This is also the name of the process used in the English ecclesiastical, probate, and divorce courts to call the defendant or respondent before them. 3 Bl. Comm. 100; 3 Steph. Comm. 720.

In Scotch practice. The calling of a party to an action done by an officer of the court under a proper warrant.

The service of a writ or bill of summons. Paters. Comp.

CITATION OF AUTHORITIES. The reading of, or reference to, legal authorities and precedents, (such as constitutions, statutes, reported cases, and elementary treatises,) in arguments to courts, or in legal text-books, to establish or fortify the propositions advanced.

Citationes non concedantur priusquam exprimatur super qua re fieri debet citatio. Citations should not be granted before it is stated about what matter the citation is to be made. A maxim of ecclesiastical law. 12 Coke, 44.

CITE. L. Fr. City; a city. *Cite de Loundr'*, city of London.

CITE. To summon; to command the presence of a person; to notify a person of legal proceedings against him and require his appearance thereto.

To read or refer to legal authorities, in an argument to a court or elsewhere, in support of propositions of law sought to be established.

CITIZEN. In general. A member of a free city or jural society, (*civitas,*) possessing all the rights and privileges which can be enjoyed by any person under its constitution and government, and subject to the corresponding duties.

In American law. One who, under the constitution and laws of the United States, has a right to vote for civil officers, and himself is qualified to fill elective offices.

One of the sovereign people. A constituent member of the sovereignty, synonymous with the people. 19 How. 404.

A member of the civil state entitled to all its privileges. Cooley, Const. Law, 77.

The term "citizen" has come to us derived from antiquity. It appears to have been used in the Roman government to designate a person who had the freedom of the city, and the right to exercise all political and civil privileges of the government. There was also, at Rome, a partial citizenship, including civil, but not political, rights. Complete citizenship embraced both. 15 Ind. 451.

All persons born or naturalized in the United States, and subject to the jurisdiction thereof, are citizens of the United States and of the state wherein they reside. Amend. XIV. Const. U. S.

There is in our political system a government of each of the several states, and a government of the United States. Each is distinct from the others, and has citizens of its own, who owe it allegiance, and whose rights, within its jurisdiction, it must protect. The same person may be at the same time a citizen of the United States and a citizen of a state; but his rights of citizenship under one of these governments will be different from those he has under the other. The government of the United States, although it is, within the scope of its powers, supreme and beyond the states, can neither grant nor secure to its citizens rights or privileges which are not expressly or by implication placed under its jurisdiction. All that cannot be so granted or secured are left to the exclusive protection of the states. 92 U. S. 542.

"Citizen" and "inhabitant" are not synonymous. One may be a citizen of a state without being an inhabitant, or an inhabitant without being a citizen. 4 Har. (Del.) 383.

"Citizen" is sometimes used as synonymous with "resident;" as in a statute authorizing funds to be distributed among the religious societies of a township, proportionably to the number of their members who are citizens of the township. 11 Ohio, 24.

In English law. An inhabitant of a city. 1 Rolle, 138. The representative of a city, in parliament. 1 Bl. Comm. 174. It will be perceived that, in the English usage, the word adheres closely to its original meaning, as shown by its derivation, (*civis*, a free inhabitant of a city.) When it is designed to designate an inhabitant of the *country*, or one amenable to the laws of the nation, "subject" is the word there employed.

CITIZENSHIP. The *status* of being a citizen, (*q. v.*)

CITY. In England. An incorporated town or borough which is or has been the see of a bishop. Co. Litt. 108; 1 Bl. Comm. 114; Cowell.

A large town incorporated with certain privileges. The inhabitants of a city. The citizens. Worcester.

In America. A city is a municipal corporation of a larger class, the distinctive feature of whose organization is its government by a chief executive (usually called "mayor") and a legislative body, composed of representatives of the citizens, (usually called a "council" or "board of aldermen,") and other officers having special functions.

CITY OF LONDON COURT. A court having a local jurisdiction within the city of London. It is to all intents and purposes a county court, having the same jurisdiction and procedure.

CIVIL. In its original sense, this word means pertaining or appropriate to a member of a *civitas* or free political community; natural or proper to a *citizen*. Also, relating to the community, or to the policy and government of the citizens and subjects of a state.

In the language of the law, it has various significations. In contradistinction to *barbarous* or *savage*, it indicates a state of society reduced to order and regular government; thus, we speak of civil life, civil society, civil government, and civil liberty. In contradistinction to *criminal*, it indicates the private rights and remedies of men, as members of the community, in contrast to those which are public and relate to the government; thus, we speak of civil process and criminal process, civil jurisdiction and criminal jurisdiction.

It is also used in contradistinction to *military* or *ecclesiastical*, to *natural* or *foreign;* thus, we speak of a civil station, as opposed to a military or an ecclesiastical station; a civil death, as opposed to a natural death; a civil war, as opposed to a foreign war. Story, Const. § 791.

CIVIL ACTION. In the civil law. A personal action which is instituted to compel payment, or the doing some other thing which is purely civil.

At common law. As distinguished from a *criminal* action, it is one which seeks the establishment, recovery, or redress of private and civil rights.

Civil suits relate to and affect, as to the parties against whom they are brought, only individual rights which are within their individual control, and which they may part with at their pleasure. The design of such suits is the enforcement of merely private obligations and duties. Criminal prosecutions, on the other hand, involve public wrongs, or a breach and violation of public rights and duties, which affect the whole community, considered as such in its social and aggregate capacity. The end they have in view is the prevention of similar offenses, not atonement or expiation for crime committed. 18 N. Y. 128.

Civil cases are those which involve disputes or contests between man and man, and which only terminate in the adjustment of the rights of plaintiffs and defendants. They include all cases which cannot legally be denominated "criminal cases." T. U. P. Charlt. 175.

In code practice. A civil action is a proceeding in a court of justice in which one party, known as the "plaintiff," demands against another party, known as the "defendant," the enforcement or protection of a private right, or the prevention or redress of a private wrong. It may also be brought for the recovery of a penalty or forfeiture. Rev. Code Iowa 1880, § 2505.

The distinction between actions at law and suits in equity, and the forms of all such actions and suits, heretofore existing, is abolished; and there shall be in this state, hereafter, but one form of action for the enforcement or protection of private rights and the redress of private wrongs, which shall be denominated a "civil action." Code N.Y. § 69.

CIVIL BILL COURT. A tribunal in Ireland with a jurisdiction analogous to that of the county courts in England. The judge of it is also chairman of quarter sessions, (where the jurisdiction is more extensive than in England,) and performs the duty of revising barrister. Wharton.

CIVIL COMMOTION. An insurrection of the people for general purposes, though it may not amount to rebellion where there is a usurped power. 2 Marsh. Ins. 793.

CIVIL CORPORATIONS. An old English term for all lay corporations which are not eleemosynary or charitable.

Civil corporations are those which relate to temporal police; such are the corporations of the cities, the companies for the advancement of commerce and agriculture, literary societies, colleges or universities founded for the instruction of youth, and the like. Religious corporations are those whose establishment relates only to religion; such are the congregations of the different religious persuasions. Civil Code La. art. 431.

CIVIL DAMAGE ACTS. Acts passed in many of the United States which provide an action for damages against a vendor of intoxicating liquors, (and, in some cases, against his lessor,) on behalf of the wife or family of a person who has sustained injuries by reason of his intoxication.

CIVIL DEATH. That change in a person's legal and civil condition which deprives him of civic rights and juridical capacities and qualifications, as natural death extinguishes his natural condition. It follows as a consequence of being attainted of treason or felony, in English law, and anciently of entering a monastery or abjuring the realm. The person in this condition is said to be *civiliter mortuus*, civilly dead, or dead in law.

CIVIL INJURY. Injuries to person or property, resulting from a breach of contract, delict, or criminal offense, which may be redressed by means of a civil action.

CIVIL LAW. The "Roman Law" and the "Civil Law" are convertible phrases, meaning the same system of jurisprudence; it is now frequently denominated the "Roman Civil Law."

The word "civil," as applied to the laws in force in Louisiana, before the adoption of the Civil Code, is not used in contradistinction to the word "criminal," but must be restricted to the Roman law. It is used in contradistinction to the laws of England and those of the respective states. 5 La. 493.

1. The system of jurisprudence held and administered in the Roman empire, particularly as set forth in the compilation of Justinian and his successors,—comprising the Institutes, Code, Digest, and Novels, and collectively denominated the "*Corpus Juris Civilis*,"—as distinguished from the common law of England and the canon law.

2. That rule of action which every particular nation, commonwealth, or city has established peculiarly for itself; more properly called "municipal" law, to distinguish it from the "law of nature," and from international law.

The law which a people enacts is called the "civil law" of that people, but that law which natural reason appoints for all mankind is called the "law of nations," because all nations use it. Bowyer, Mod. Civil Law, 19.

3. That division of municipal law which is occupied with the exposition and enforce-

ment of *civil rights*, as distinguished from *criminal law*.

CIVIL LIBERTY. The liberty of a member of society, being a man's natural liberty, so far restrained by human laws (and no further) as is necessary and expedient for the general advantage of the public. 1 Bl. Comm. 125; 2 Steph. Comm. 487. The power of doing whatever the laws permit. 1 Bl. Comm. 6; Inst. 1, 3, 1. See LIBERTY.

CIVIL LIST. In English public law. An annual sum granted by parliament, at the commencement of each reign, for the expense of the royal household and establishment, as distinguished from the general exigencies of the state, being a provision made for the crown out of the taxes in lieu of its proper patrimony, and in consideration of the assignment of that patrimony to the public use. 2 Steph. Comm. 591; 1 Bl. Comm. 332.

CIVIL OBLIGATION. An obligation binding in law, and enforceable in a court of justice. Poth. Obl. 173, 191.

CIVIL OFFICER. Any officer of the United States who holds his appointment under the national government, whether his duties are executive or judicial, in the highest or the lowest departments of the government, with the exception of officers of the army and navy. 1 Story, Const. § 792.

CIVIL REMEDY. The remedy afforded by law to a private person in the civil courts in so far as his private and individual rights have been injured by a delict or crime; as distinguished from the remedy by criminal prosecution for the injury to the rights of the public.

CIVIL RESPONSIBILITY. The liability to be called upon to respond to an action at law for an injury caused by a delict or crime, as opposed to criminal responsibility, or liability to be proceeded against in a criminal tribunal.

CIVIL RIGHTS. Rights appertaining to a person in virtue of his citizenship in a state or community. Rights capable of being enforced or redressed in a civil action. Also a term applied to certain rights secured to citizens of the United States by the thirteenth and fourteenth amendments to the constitution, and by various acts of congress made in pursuance thereof.

CIVIL SERVICE. This term properly includes all functions under the government, except military functions. In general it is confined to functions in the great administrative departments of state. Wharton.

CIVIL SIDE. When the same court has jurisdiction of both civil and criminal matters, proceedings of the first class are often said to be on the civil side; those of the second, on the criminal side.

CIVIL WAR. An internecine war. A war carried on between opposing masses of citizens of the same country or nation.

Before the declaration of independence, the war between Great Britain and the United Colonies was a civil war; but instantly on that event the war changed its nature, and became a public war between independent governments. 3 Dall. 199, 224.

CIVILIAN. One who is skilled or versed in the civil law. A doctor, professor, or student of the civil law. Also a private citizen, as distinguished from such as belong to the army and navy or (in England) the church.

CIVILIS. Civil, as distinguished from criminal. *Civilis actio*, a civil action. Bract. fol. 101*b*.

CIVILISTA. In old English law. A civil lawyer, or civilian. Dyer, 267.

CIVILITER. Civilly. In a person's civil character or position, or by civil (not criminal) process or procedure. This term is used in distinction or opposition to the word "*criminaliter*,"—criminally,—to distinguish civil actions from criminal prosecutions.

CIVILITER MORTUUS. Civilly dead; dead in the view of the law. The condition of one who has lost his civil rights and capacities, and is accounted dead in law.

CIVILIZATION. In practice. A law; an act of justice, or judgment which renders a criminal process civil; performed by turning an information into an inquest, or the contrary. Wharton.

In public law. This is a term which covers several states of society; it is relative, and has not a fixed sense, but it implies an improved and progressive condition of the people, living under an organized government, with systematized labor, individual ownership of the soil, individual accumulations of property, humane and somewhat cultivated manners and customs, the institution of the family, with well-defined and respected domestic and social relations, institutions of learning, intellectual activity, etc. 19 Ind. 56.

CIVIS. Lat. In the Roman law. A citizen; as distinguished from *incola*, (an inhabitant;) origin or birth constituting the former, domicile the latter. Code, 10, 40, 7.

CIVITAS. Lat. In the Roman law. Any body of people living under the same laws; a state. *Jus civitatis*, the law of a state; civil law. Inst. 1, 2, 1, 2. *Civitates fœderatæ*, towns in alliance with Rome, and considered to be free. Butl. Hor. Jur. 29.

Citizenship; one of the three *status*, conditions, or qualifications of persons. Mackeld. Rom. Law, § 131.

Civitas et urbs in hoc differunt, quod incolæ dicuntur civitas, urbs vero complectitur ædificia. Co. Litt. 409. A city and a town differ, in this: that the inhabitants are called the "city," but town includes the buildings.

CLAIM, *v.* To demand as one's own; to assert a personal right to any property or any right; to demand the possession or enjoyment of something rightfully one's own, and wrongfully withheld.

CLAIM, *n.* 1. A challenge of the property or ownership of a thing which is wrongfully withheld from the possession of the claimant. Plowd. 359.

A claim is a right or title, actual or supposed, to a debt, privilege, or other thing in the possession of another; not the possession, but the means by or through which the claimant obtains the possession or enjoyment. 2 N. Y. 245, 254.

A claim is, in a just, juridical sense, a demand of some matter as of right made by one person upon another, to do or to forbear to do some act or thing as a matter of duty. A more limited, but at the same time an equally expressive, definition was given by Lord Dyer, that "a claim is a challenge by a man of the propriety or ownership of a thing, which he has not in possession, but which is wrongfully detained from him." 16 Pet. 615.

"Claim" has generally been defined as a demand for a thing, the ownership of which, or an interest in which, is in the claimant, but the possession of which is wrongfully withheld by another. But a broader meaning must be accorded to it. A demand for damages for criminal conversation with plaintiff's wife is a claim; but it would be doing violence to language to say that such damages are property of plaintiff which defendant withholds. In common parlance the noun "claim" means an assertion, a pretension; and the verb is often used (not quite correctly) as a synonym for "state," "urge," "insist," or "assert." In a statute authorizing the courts to order a bill of particulars of the "claim" of either party, "claim" is co-extensive with "case," and embraces all causes of action and all grounds of defense, the pleas of both parties, and pleas in confession and avoidance, no less than complaints and counter-claims. It warrants the court in requiring a defendant who justifies in a libel suit to furnish particulars of the facts relied upon in justification. 6 Daly, 446.

2. Under the mechanic's lien law of Pennsylvania, a demand put on record by a mechanic or material-man against a building for work or material contributed to its erection is called a "claim."

3. Under the land laws of the United States, the tract of land taken up by a preemptioner or other settler (and also his possession of the same) is called a "claim."

CLAIM IN EQUITY. In English practice. In simple cases, where there was not any great conflict as to facts, and a discovery from a defendant was not sought, but a reference to chambers was nevertheless necessary before final decree, which would be as of course, all parties being before the court, the summary proceeding by claim was sometimes adopted, thus obviating the recourse to plenary and protracted pleadings. This summary practice was created by orders 22d April, 1850, which came into operation on the 22d May following. See Smith, Ch. Pr. 664. By Consolid. Ord. 1860, viii. r. 4, claims were abolished. Wharton.

CLAIM OF CONUSANCE. In practice. An intervention by a third person in a suit, claiming that he has rightful jurisdiction of the cause which the plaintiff has commenced out of the claimant's court. Now obsolete. 2 Wils. 409; 3 Bl. Comm. 298.

CLAIM OF LIBERTY. In English practice. A suit or petition to the queen, in the court of exchequer, to have liberties and franchises confirmed there by the attorney general.

CLAIMANT. In admiralty practice. The name given to a person who lays claim to property seized on a libel *in rem*, and who is authorized and admitted to defend the action.

CLAM. In the civil law. Covertly; secretly.

Clam delinquentes magis puniuntur quam palam. 8 Coke, 127. Those sinning secretly are punished more severely than those sinning openly.

CLAM, VI, AUT PRECARIO. A technical phrase of the Roman law, meaning by force, stealth, or importunity.

CLAMEA ADMITTENDA IN ITINERE PER ATTORNATUM. An ancient writ by which the king commanded the justices in eyre to admit the claim by attorney of a person who was in the royal service, and could not appear in person. Reg. Orig. 19.

CLAMOR. In old English law. A claim or complaint; an outcry; clamor.

In the civil law. A claimant. A debt; anything claimed from another. A proclamation; an accusation. Du Cange.

CLARE CONSTAT. (It clearly appears.) In Scotch law. The name of a precept for giving seisin of lands to an heir; so called from its initial words. Ersk. Inst. 3, 8, 71.

CLAREMETHEN. In old Scotch law. The warranty of stolen cattle or goods; the law regulating such warranty. Skene.

CLARENDON, CONSTITUTIONS OF. The constitutions of Clarendon were certain statutes made in the reign of Henry II. of England, at a parliament held at Clarendon, (A. D. 1164,) by which the king checked the power of the pope and his clergy, and greatly narrowed the exemption they claimed from secular jurisdiction. 4 Bl. Comm. 422.

CLARIFICATIO. Lat. In old Scotch law. A making clear; the purging or clearing (clenging) of an assise. Skene.

CLASS. The order or rank according to which persons or things are arranged or assorted. Also a group of persons or things, taken collectively, having certain qualities in common, and constituting a unit for certain purposes; *e. g.*, a class of legatees.

CLASSIARIUS. A seaman or soldier serving at sea.

CLASSICI. In the Roman law. Persons employed in servile duties on board of vessels. Cod. 11, 12.

CLASSIFICATION. In the practice of the English chancery division, where there are several parties to an administration action, including those who have been served with notice of the decree or judgment, and it appears to the judge (or chief clerk) that any of them form a class having the same interest, (*e. g.*, residuary legatees,) he may require them to be represented by one solicitor, in order to prevent the expense of each of them attending by separate solicitors. This is termed "classifying the interests of the parties attending," or, shortly, "classifying," or "classification." In practice the term is also applied to the directions given by the chief clerk as to which of the parties are to attend on each of the accounts and inquiries directed by the judgment. Sweet.

CLAUSE. A single paragraph or subdivision of a legal document, such as a contract, deed, will, constitution, or statute. Sometimes a sentence or part of a sentence.

CLAUSE IRRITANT. In Scotch law. By this clause, in a deed or settlement, the acts or deeds of a tenant for life or other proprietor, contrary to the conditions of his right, become null and void; and by the "resolutive" clause such right becomes resolved and extinguished. Bell.

CLAUSE POTESTATIVE. In French law. The name given to the clause whereby one party to a contract reserves to himself the right to annul it.

CLAUSE ROLLS. In English Law. Rolls which contain all such matters of record as were committed to close writs; these rolls are preserved in the Tower.

CLAUSULA. A clause; a sentence or part of a sentence in a written instrument or law.

Clausula generalis de residuo non ea complectitur quæ non ejusdem sint generis cum iis quæ speciatim dicta fuerant. A general clause of remainder does not embrace those things which are not of the same kind with those which had been specially mentioned. Lofft, Appendix, 419.

Clausula generalis non refertur ad expressa. 8 Coke, 154. A general clause does not refer to things expressed.

Clausula quæ abrogationem excludit ab initio non valet. A clause [in a law] which precludes its abrogation is void from the beginning. Bac. Max. 77.

Clausula vel dispositio inutilis per presumptionem remotam, vel causam ex post facto non fulcitur. A useless clause or disposition [one which expresses no more than the law by intendment would have supplied] is not supported by a remote presumption, [or foreign intendment of some purpose, in regard whereof it might be material,] or by a cause arising afterwards, [which may induce an operation of those idle words.] Bac. Max. 82, regula 21.

Clausulæ inconsuetæ semper inducunt suspicionem. Unusual clauses [in an instrument] always induce suspicion. 3 Coke, 81.

CLAUSUM. Close, closed up, sealed. Inclosed, as a parcel of land.

CLAUSUM FREGIT. L. Lat. (He broke the close.) In pleading and practice. Technical words formerly used in certain actions of trespass, and still retained in the phrase *quare clausum fregit*, (*q. v.*)

CLAUSUM PASCHIÆ. In English law. The morrow of the *utas*, or eight days of Easter; the end of Easter; the Sunday after Easter-day. 2 Inst. 157.

CLAUSURA. In old English law. An inclosure. *Clausura heyæ*, the inclosure of a hedge. Cowell.

CLAVES CURIÆ. The keys of the court. They were the officers of the Scotch courts, such as clerk, doomster, and serjeant. Burrill.

CLAVES INSULÆ. In Manx law. The keys of the Island of Man, or twelve persons to whom all ambiguous and weighty causes are referred.

CLAVIA. In old English law. A club or mace; tenure *per serjeantiam claviæ*, by the serjeanty of the club or mace. Cowell.

CLAVIGERATUS. A treasurer of a church.

CLAWA. A close, or small inclosure. Cowell.

CLEAN HANDS. It is a rule of equity that a plaintiff must come with "clean hands," *i. e.*, he must be free from reproach in his conduct. But there is this limitation to the rule: that his conduct can only be excepted to in respect to the subject-matter of his claim; everything else is immaterial.

CLEAR. In a devise of money for the purchase of an annuity, this term means free from taxes. 2 Atk. 376.

In the phrase "clear yearly value," clear means free from all outgoings like a rent-charge, as losses by tenants and management, to which a rent charge is not liable. 2 Ves. 499.

CLEAR DAYS. If a certain number of clear days be given for the doing of any act, the time is to be reckoned exclusively, as well of the first day as the last.

CLEARANCE. In maritime law. A document in the nature of a certificate given by the collector of customs to an outward-bound vessel, to the effect that she has complied with the law, and is duly authorized to depart.

CLEARING. The departure of a vessel from port, after complying with the customs and health laws and like local regulations.

In mercantile law. A method of making exchanges and settling balances, adopted among banks and bankers.

CLEARING-HOUSE. An institution organized by the banks of a city, where their messengers may meet daily, adjust balances of accounts, and receive and pay differences.

CLEMENTINES. In canon law. The collection of decretals or constitutions of Pope Clement V., made by order of John XXII., his successor, who published it in 1317.

CLEMENT'S INN. An inn of chancery. See INNS OF CHANCERY.

CLENGE. In old Scotch law. To clear or acquit of a criminal charge. Literally, to cleanse or clean.

CLEP AND CALL. In old Scotch practice. A solemn form of words prescribed by law, and used in criminal cases, as in pleas of wrong and unlaw.

CLERGY. The whole body of clergymen or ministers of religion. Also an abbreviation for "benefit of clergy."

CLERGYABLE. In old English law. Admitting of clergy, or benefit of clergy. A clergyable felony was one of that class in which clergy was allowable. 4 Bl. Comm. 371-373.

CLERICAL. Pertaining to clergymen; or pertaining to the office or labor of a clerk.

CLERICAL ERROR. A mistake in writing or copying; the mistake of a clerk or writer. 1 Ld. Raym. 183.

CLERICAL TONSURE. The having the head shaven, which was formerly peculiar to clerks, or persons in orders, and which the coifs worn by serjeants at law are supposed to have been introduced to conceal. 1 Bl. Comm. 24, note *t*; 4 Bl. Comm. 367.

CLERICALE PRIVILEGIUM. In old English law. The clerical privilege; the privilege or benefit of clergy.

CLERICI DE CANCELLARIA. Clerks of the chancery.

Clerici non ponantur in officiis. Co. Litt. 96. Clergymen should not be placed in offices; *i. e.*, in secular offices. See Lofft, 508.

CLERICI PRÆNOTARII. The six clerks in chancery. 2 Reeve, Eng. Law, 251.

CLERICO ADMITTENDO. See ADMITTENDO CLERICO.

CLERICO CAPTO PER STATUTUM MERCATORUM. A writ for the delivery of a clerk out of prison, who was taken and incarcerated upon the breach of a statute merchant. Reg. Orig. 147.

CLERICO CONVICTO COMMISSO GAOLÆ IN DEFECTU ORDINARII DELIBERANDO. An ancient writ, that lay for the delivery to his ordinary of a clerk convicted of felony, where the ordinary did not challenge him according to the privilege of clerks. Reg. Orig. 69.

CLERICO INFRA SACROS ORDINES CONSTITUTO, NON ELIGENDO IN OFFICIUM. A writ directed to those who had thrust a bailiwick or other office upon one in holy orders, charging them to release him. Reg. Orig. 143.

CLERICUS. In Roman law. A minister of religion in the Christian church; an ecclesiastic or priest. Cod. 1, 3; Nov. 3, 123, 137. A general term, including bishops, priests, deacons, and others of inferior order. Brissonius.

In old English law. A clerk or priest; a person in holy orders; a secular priest; a clerk of a court.

An officer of the royal household, having charge of the receipt and payment of moneys, etc. Fleta enumerates several of them, with their appropriate duties; as *clericus coquinæ*, clerk of the kitchen; *clericus panetr' et butelr'*, clerk of the pantry and buttery. Lib. 2, cc. 18, 19.

Clericus et agricola et mercator, tempore belli, ut oret, colat, et commutet, pace fruuntur. 2 Inst. 58. Clergymen, husbandmen, and merchants, in order that they may preach, cultivate, and trade, enjoy peace in time of war.

CLERICUS MERCATI. In old English law. Clerk of the market. 2 Inst. 543.

Clericus non connumeretur in duabus ecclesiis. 1 Rolle. A clergyman should not be appointed to two churches.

CLERICUS PAROCHIALIS. In old English law. A parish clerk.

CLERIGOS. In Spanish law. Clergy; men chosen for the service of God. White, New Recop. b. 1, tit. 5, ch. 4.

CLERK. In ecclesiatical law. A person in holy orders; a clergyman; an individual attached to the ecclesiastical state, and who has the clerical tonsure. See 4 Bl. Comm. 366, 367.

In practice. A person employed in a public office, or as an officer of a court, whose duty is to keep records or accounts.

In commercial law. A person employed by a merchant, or in a mercantile establishment, as a salesman, book-keeper, accountant, amanuensis, etc., invested with more or less authority in the administration of some branch or department of the business, while the principal himself superintends the whole.

CLERK OF ARRAIGNS. In English law. An assistant to the clerk of assise. His duties are in the crown court on circuit

CLERK OF ASSISE. In English law. Officers who officiate as associates on the circuits. They record all judicial proceedings done by the judges on the circuit.

CLERK OF COURT. An officer of a court of justice who has charge of the clerical part of its business, who keeps its records and seal, issues process, enters judgments and orders, gives certified copies from the records, etc.

CLERK OF ENROLLMENTS. In English law. The former chief officer of the English enrollment office, (*q. v.*) He now forms part of the staff of the central office.

CLERK OF THE CROWN IN CHANCERY. See CROWN OFFICE IN CHANCERY.

CLERK OF THE HOUSE OF COMMONS. An important officer of the English house of commons. He is appointed by the crown as under-clerk of the parliaments to attend upon the commons. He makes a declaration, on entering upon his office, to make true entries, remembrances, and journals of the things done and passed in the house. He signs all orders of the house, indorses the bills sent or returned to the lords, and reads whatever is required to be read in the house. He has the custody of all records and other documents. May, Parl. Pr. 236.

CLERK OF THE MARKET. The overseer or superintendent of a public market. In old English law, he was a *quasi* judicial officer, having power to settle controversies arising in the market between persons dealing there. Called "*clericus mercati.*" 4 Bl. Comm. 275.

CLERK OF THE PARLIAMENTS. One of the chief officers of the house of lords. He is appointed by the crown, by letters patent. On entering office he makes a declaration to make true entries and records of the things done and passed in the parliaments, and to keep secret all such matters as shall be treated therein. May, Parl. Pr. 238.

CLERK OF THE PEACE. In English aw. An officer whose duties are to officiate it sessions of the peace, to prepare indictments, and to record the proceedings of the justices, and to perform a number of special duties in connection with the affairs of the county.

CLERK OF THE PETTY BAG. See PETTY BAG.

CLERK OF THE PRIVY SEAL. There are four of these officers, who attend the lord privy seal, or, in the absence of the lord privy seal, the principal secretary of state. Their duty is to write and make out all things that are sent by warrant from the signet to the privy seal, and which are to be passed to the great seal; and also to make out privy seals (as they are termed) upon any special occasion of his majesty's affairs, as for the loan of money and such like purposes. Cowell.

CLERK OF THE SIGNET. An officer, in England, whose duty it is to attend on the king's principal secretary, who always has the custody of the privy signet, as well for the purpose of sealing his majesty's private letters, as also grants which pass his majesty's hand by bill signed; there are four of these officers. Cowell.

CLERKS OF INDICTMENTS. Officers attached to the central criminal court in England, and to each circuit. They prepare and settle indictments against offenders, and assist the clerk of arraigns.

CLERKS OF RECORDS AND WRITS. Officers formerly attached to the English court of chancery, whose duties consisted principally in sealing bills of complaint and writs of execution, filing affidavits, keeping a record of suits, and certifying office copies of pleadings and affidavits. They were three in number, and the business was distributed among them according to the letters of the alphabet. By the judicature acts, 1873, 1875, they were transferred to the chancery division of the high court. Now, by the judicature (officers') act, 1879, they have been transferred to the central office of the supreme court, under the title of "Masters of the Supreme Court," and the office of clerk of records and writs has been abolished. Sweet.

CLERKS OF SEATS, in the principal registry of the probate division of the English high court, discharge the duty of preparing and passing the grants of probate and letters of administration, under the supervision of the registrars. There are six seats, the business of which is regulated by an alphabetical arrangement, and each seat has four clerks. They have to take bonds from administrators, and to receive *caveats* against a grant being made in a case where a will is contested. They also draw the "acts," *i. e.*, a short summary of each grant made, containing the name of the deceased, amount of assets, and other particulars. Sweet.

CLERKSHIP. The period which must be spent by a law-student in the office of a practising attorney before admission to the bar. 1 Tidd, Pr. 61, et seq.

In old English practice. The art of drawing pleadings and entering them on record in Latin, in the ancient court hand; otherwise called "skill of pleading in actions at the common law."

CLIENS. Lat. In the Roman law. A client or dependent. One who depended upon another as his patron or protector, adviser or defender, in suits at law and other difficulties; and was bound, in return, to pay him all respect and honor, and to serve him with his life and fortune in any extremity. Dionys. ii. 10; Adams, Rom. Ant. 33.

CLIENT. A person who employs or retains an attorney, or counsellor, to appear for him in courts, advise, assist, and defend him in legal proceedings, and to act for him in any legal business.

CLIENTELA. In old English law. Clientship, the state of a client; and, correlatively, protection, patronage, guardianship.

CLIFFORD'S INN. An inn of chancery. See INNS OF CHANCERY.

CLITO. In Saxon law. The son of a king or emperor. The next heir to the throne; the Saxon adeling. Spelman.

CLOERE. A gaol; a prison or dungeon.

CLOSE, *adj.* In practice. Close or sealed up. A term applied to writs and letters, as distinguished from those that are open or patent.

CLOSE, *n.* A portion of land, as a field, inclosed, as by a hedge, fence, or other visible inclosure. 3 Bl. Comm. 209. The interest of a person in any particular piece of ground, whether actually inclosed or not. 7 East, 207.

The noun "close," in its legal sense, imports a portion of land inclosed, but not necessarily inclosed by actual or visible barriers. The invisible, ideal boundary, founded on limit of title, which surrounds every man's land, constitutes it his close, irrespective of walls, fences, ditches, or the like.

In practice. The word means termination; winding up. Thus the close of the pleadings is where the pleadings are finished, *i. e.*, when issue has been joined.

CLOSE COPIES. Copies of legal documents which might be written closely or loosely at pleasure; as distinguished from *office* copies, which were to contain only a prescribed number of words on each sheet.

CLOSE-HAULED. In admiralty law, this nautical term means the arrangement or trim of a vessel's sails when she endeavors to make a progress in the nearest direction possible towards that point of the compass from which the wind blows. But a vessel may be considered as close-hauled, although she is not quite so near to the wind as she could possibly lie. 6 El. & Bl. 771.

CLOSE ROLLS. Rolls containing the record of the close writs (*literæ clausæ*) and grants of the king, kept with the public records. 2 Bl. Comm. 346.

CLOSE WRITS. In English law. Certain letters of the king, sealed with his great seal, and directed to particular persons and for particular purposes, which, not being proper for public inspection, are closed up and sealed on the outside, and are thence called "writs close." 2 Bl. Comm. 346; Sewell, Sheriffs, 372.

Writs directed to the sheriff, instead of to the lord. 3 Reeve, Eng. Law, 45.

CLOTURE. The procedure in deliberative assemblies whereby debate is closed. Introduced in the English parliament in the session of 1882.

CLOUD ON TITLE. An outstanding claim or incumbrance which, if valid, would affect or impair the title of the owner of a particular estate, and which apparently and on its face has that effect, but which can be shown by extrinsic proof to be invalid or inapplicable to the estate in question. A conveyance, mortgage, judgment, tax-levy, etc., may all, in proper cases, constitute a cloud on title.

CLOUGH. A valley. Also an allowance for the turn of the scale, on buying goods wholesale by weight.

CLUB. A voluntary, unincorporated association of persons for purposes of a social, literary, or political nature, or the like. A club is not a partnership. 2 Mees. & W. 172.

The word "club" has no very definite meaning. Clubs are formed for all sorts of purposes, and there is no uniformity in their constitutions and rules. It is well known that clubs exist which limit the number of the members and select them with great care, which own considerable property in common, and in which the furnishing of food and drink to the members for money is but one of many conveniences which the members enjoy. 137 Mass. 567.

CLUB-LAW. Rule of violence; regulation by force; the law of arms.

CLYPEUS, or CLIPEUS. In old English law. A shield; metaphorically one of a noble family. *Clypei prostrati*, noble families extinct. Mat. Paris, 463.

CO. A prefix to words, meaning "with" or "in conjunction" or "joint;" *e. g.*, co-trustees, co-executors.

COACH. Coach is a generic term. It is a kind of carriage, and is distinguished from other vehicles, chiefly, as being a covered box, hung on leathers, with four wheels. 9 Ohio, 12.

COADJUTOR. An assistant, helper, or ally; particularly a person appointed to assist a bishop who from age or infirmity is unable to perform his duty. Also an overseer, (coadjutor of an executor,) and one who disseises a person of land not to his own use, but to that of another.

CO-ADMINISTRATOR. One who is a joint administrator with one or more others.

COADUNATIO. A uniting or combining together of persons; a conspiracy. 9 Coke, 56.

COAL NOTE. A species of promissory note, formerly in use in the port of London, containing the phrase "value received in coals." By the statute 3 Geo. II. c. 26, §§ 7, 8, these were to be protected and noted as inland bills of exchange. But this was repealed by the statute 47 Geo. III. sess. 2, c. 68, § 28.

COALITION. In French law. An unlawful agreement among several persons not to do a thing except on some conditions agreed upon; particularly, industrial combinations, strikes, etc.; a conspiracy.

CO-ASSIGNEE. One of two or more assignees of the same subject-matter.

COAST. The edge or margin of a country bounding on the sea. It is held that the term includes small islands and reefs naturally connected with the adjacent land, and rising above the surface of the water, although their composition may not be sufficiently firm and stable to admit of their being inhabited or fortified; but not shoals which are perpetually covered by the water. 5 C. Rob. Adm. 385*c*.

This word is particularly appropriate to the edge of the sea, while "shore" may be used of the margins of inland waters.

COAST-GUARD. In English law. A body of officers and men raised and equipped by the commissioners of the admiralty for the defense of the coasts of the realm, and for the more ready manning of the navy in case of war or sudden emergency, as well as for the protection of the revenue against smugglers. Mozley & Whitley.

COASTING TRADE. In maritime law. Commerce and navigation between different places along the coast of the United States, as distinguished from commerce with ports in foreign countries.

Commercial intercourse carried on between different districts in different states, different districts in the same state, or different places in the same district, on the sea-coast or on a navigable river. 3 Cow. 713; 1 Newb. Adm. 241.

COASTWISE. Vessels "plying coastwise" are those which are engaged in the domestic trade, or plying between port and port in the United States, as contradistinguished from those engaged in the foreign trade, or plying between a port of the United States and a port of a foreign country. 10 Cal. 504.

COAT ARMOR. Heraldic ensigns, introduced by Richard I. from the Holy Land, where they were first invented. Originally they were painted on the shields of the Christian knights who went to the Holy Land during the crusades, for the purpose of identifying them, some such contrivance being necessary in order to distinguish knights when clad in armor from one another. Wharton.

COCKBILL. To place the yards of a ship at an angle with the deck. Pub. St. Mass. 1882, p. 1288.

COCKET. In English law. A seal belonging to the custom-house, or rather a scroll of parchment, sealed and delivered by the officers of the custom-house to merchants, as a warrant that their merchandises are entered; likewise a sort of measure. Fleta, lib. 2, c. ix.

COCKPIT. A name which used to be given to the judicial committee of the privy council, the council-room being built on the old cockpit of Whitehall Place.

COCKSETUS. A boatman; a cockswain. Cowell.

CODE. A collection or compendium of laws. A complete system of positive law, scientifically arranged, and promulgated by legislative authority.

The collection of laws and constitutions made by order of the Emperor Justinian is distinguished by the appellation of "The Code," by way of eminence. See CODE OF JUSTINIAN.

A body of law established by the legislative authority, and intended to set forth, in generalized and systematic form, the principles of the entire law, whether written or unwritten, positive or customary, derived from enactment or from precedent. Abbott.

A *code* is to be distinguished from a *digest*. The subject-matter of the latter is usually reported decisions of the courts. But there are also digests of statutes. These consist of an orderly collection and classification of the existing statutes of a state or nation, while a code is promulgated as one new law covering the whole field of jurisprudence.

CODE CIVIL. The code which embodies the civil law of France. Framed in the first instance by a commission of jurists appointed in 1800. This code, after having passed both the tribunate and the legislative body, was promulgated in 1804 as the "Code Civil des Français." When Napoleon became emperor, the name was changed to that of "Code Napoleon," by which it is still often designated, though it is now officially styled by its original name of "Code Civil."

CODE DE COMMERCE. A French code, enacted in 1807, as a supplement to the Code Napoleon, regulating commercial transactions, the laws of business, bankruptcies, and the jurisdiction and procedure of the courts dealing with these subjects.

CODE DE PROCÉDURE CIVIL. That part of the Code Napoleon which regulates the system of courts, their organization, civil procedure, special and extraordinary remedies, and the execution of judgments.

CODE D'INSTRUCTION CRIMINELLE. A French code, enacted in 1808, regulating criminal procedure.

CODE NAPOLEON. See CODE CIVIL.

CODE OF JUSTINIAN. The Code of Justinian (*Codex Justinianeus*) was a collection of imperial constitutions, compiled, by order of that emperor, by a commission of ten jurists, including Tribonian, and promulgated A. D. 529. It comprised twelve books, and was the first of the four compilations of law which make up the *Corpus Juris Civilis*.

This name is often met in a connection indicating that the entire *Corpus Juris Civilis* is intended, or, sometimes, the *Digest;* but its use should be confined to the *Codex*.

CODE PÉNAL. The penal or criminal code of France, enacted in 1810.

CODEX. Lat. A code or collection of laws; particularly the Code of Justinian. Also a roll or volume, and a book written on paper or parchment.

CODEX GREGORIANUS. A collection of imperial constitutions made by Gregorius, a Roman jurist of the fifth century, about the middle of the century. It contained the constitutions from Hadrian down to Constantine. Mackeld. Rom. Law, § 63.

CODEX HERMOGENIANUS. A collection of imperial constitutions made by Hermogenes, a jurist of the fifth century. It was nothing more than a supplement to the Codex Gregorianus, (supra,) containing the constitutions of Diocletian and Maximilian. Mackeld. Rom. Law, § 63.

CODEX JUSTINIANEUS. A collection of imperial constitutions, made by a commission of ten persons appointed by Justinian, A. D. 528.

CODEX REPETITÆ PRÆLECTIONIS. The new code of Justinian; or the new edition of the first or old code, promulgated A. D. 534, being the one now extant. Mackeld. Rom. Law, § 78. Tayl. Civil Law, 22.

CODEX THEODOSIANUS. A code compiled by the emperor Theodosius the younger, A. D. 438, being a methodical collection, in sixteen books, of ali the imperial constitutions then in force. It was the only body of civil law publicly received as authentic in the western part of Europe till the twelfth century, the use and authority of the Code of Justinian being during that interval confined to the East. 1 Bl. Comm. 81.

CODEX VETUS. The old code. The first edition of the Code of Justinian; now lost. Mackeld. Rom. Law, § 70.

CODICIL. A testamentary disposition subsequent to a will, and by which the will is altered, explained, added to, subtracted from, or confirmed by way of republication, but in no case totally revoked. 2 Woodd. Lect. 284.

A codicil is an addition or supplement to a will, either to add to, take from, or alter the provisions of the will. It must be executed with the same formality as a will, and, when admitted to probate, forms a part of the will. Code Ga. 1882, § 2404.

CODICILLUS. In the Roman law. A codicil; an informal and inferior kind of will, in use among the Romans.

CODIFICATION. The process of collecting and arranging the laws of a country or state into a code, *i. e.*, into a complete system of positive law, scientifically ordered, and promulgated by legislative authority.

COEMPTIO. Mutual purchase. One of the modes in which marriage was contracted among the Romans. The man and the woman delivered to each other a small piece of money. The man asked the woman whether she would become to him a *materfamilias*, (mistress of his family,) to which she replied that she would. In her turn she asked the man whether he would become to her a *paterfamilias*, (master of a family.) On his replying in the affirmative, she delivered her piece of money and herself into his hands, and so became his wife. Adams, Rom. Ant. 501.

CO-EMPTION. The act of purchasing the whole quantity of any commodity. Wharton.

COERCION. Compulsion; force; duress. It may be either *actual*, (direct or positive,) where physical force is put upon a man to compel him to do an act against his will, or *implied*, (legal or constructive,) where the relation of the parties is such that one is under subjection to the other, and is thereby constrained to do what his free will would refuse.

CO-EXECUTOR. One who is a joint executor with one or more others.

COFFEE-HOUSE. A house of entertainment where guests are supplied with coffee and other refreshments, and sometimes with lodging. Century Dict. A coffee-house is not an inn. 4 Camp. 76.

COFFERER OF THE QUEEN'S HOUSEHOLD. In English law. A principal officer of the royal establishment, next under the controller, who, in the counting-house and elsewhere, had a special charge and oversight of the other officers, whose wages he paid.

Cogitationis pœnam nemo patitur. No one is punished for his thoughts. Dig. 48, 19, 18.

COGNATES. (Lat. *cognati.*) Relations by the mother's side, or by females. Mackeld. Rom. Law, § 144. A common term in Scotch law. Ersk. Inst. 1, 7, 4.

COGNATI. Lat. In the civil law. Cognates; relations by the mother's side. 2 Bl. Comm. 235. Relations in the line of the mother. Hale, Com. Law, c. xi. Relations by or through females.

COGNATIO. Lat. In the civil law. Cognation. Relationship, or kindred generally. Dig. 38, 10, 4, 2; Inst. 3, 6, pr.

Relationship through females, as distinguished from *agnatio*, or relationship through males. *Agnatio a patre sit, cognatio a matre.* Inst. 3, 5, 4. See AGNATIO.

In canon law. Consanguinity, as distinguished from affinity. 4 Reeve, Eng. Law, 56–58.

Consanguinity, as including affinity. Id.

COGNATION. In the civil law. Signifies generally the kindred which exists between two persons who are united by ties of blood or family, or both.

COGNATUS. Lat. In the civil law. A relation by the mother's side; a cognate.

A relation, or kinsman, generally.

COGNITIO. In old English law. The acknowledgment of a fine; the certificate of such acknowledgment.

In the Roman law. The judicial examination or hearing of a cause.

COGNITIONES. Ensigns and arms, or a military coat painted with arms. Mat. Par. 1250.

COGNITIONIBUS MITTENDIS. In English law. A writ to a justice of the common pleas, or other, who has power to take a fine, who, having taken the fine, defers to certify it, commanding him to certify it. Now abolished. Reg. Orig. 68.

COGNITIONIS CAUSÆ. In Scotch practice. A name given to a judgment or decree pronounced by a court, ascertaining the amount of a debt against the estate of a deceased landed proprietor, on cause shown, or after a due investigation. Bell.

COGNITOR. In the Roman law. An advocate or defender in a private cause; one who defended the cause of a person who was present. Calvin. Lex. Jurid.

COGNIZANCE. In old practice. That part of a fine in which the defendant *acknowledged* that the land in question was the right of the complainant. From this the fine itself derived its name, as being *sur* cognizance *de droit*, etc., and the parties their titles of *cognizor* and *cognizee*.

In modern practice. Judicial notice or knowledge; the judicial hearing of a cause; jurisdiction, or right to try and determine causes; acknowledgment; confession; recognition.

Of pleas. Jurisdiction of causes. A privilege granted by the king to a city or town to hold pleas within the same.

Claim of cognizance (or of conusance) is an intervention by a third person, demanding judicature in the cause against the plaintiff, who has chosen to commence his action out of claimant's court. 2 Wils. 409; 2 Bl. Comm. 350, note.

In pleading. A species of answer in the action of replevin, by which the defendant acknowledges the taking of the goods which are the subject-matter of the action, and also that he has no title to them, but justifies the taking on the ground that it was done by the command of one who was entitled to the property.

In the process of levying a fine, it is an acknowledgment by the deforciant that the lands in question belong to the complainant.

In the language of American jurisprudence, this word is used chiefly in the sense of jurisdiction, or the exercise of jurisdiction; the judicial examination of a matter, or power and authority to make it.

Judicial cognizance is judicial notice, or knowledge upon which a judge is bound to act without having it proved in evidence.

COGNIZEE. The party to whom a fine was levied. 2 Bl. Comm. 351.

COGNIZOR. In old conveyancing. The party levying a fine. 2 Bl. Comm. 350, 351.

COGNOMEN. In Roman law. A man's family name. The first name (*prænomen*) was the proper name of the individual; the second (*nomen*) indicated the *gens* or tribe to which he belonged; while the third (*cognomen*) denoted his family or house.

In English law. A surname. A name added to the *nomen* proper, or name of the individual; a name descriptive of the family.

Cognomen majorum est ex sanguine tractum, hoc intrinsecum est; agnomen extrinsecum ab eventu. 6 Coke, 65. The cognomen is derived from the blood of ancestors, and is intrinsic; an agnomen arises from an event, and is extrinsic.

COGNOVIT ACTIONEM. (He has confessed the action.) A defendant's written confession of an action brought against him, to which he has no available defense. It is usually upon condition that he shall be allowed a certain time for the payment of the debt or damages, and costs. It is supposed to be given in court, and it impliedly authorizes the plaintiff's attorney to sign judgment and issue execution.

COHABIT. To live together as husband and wife; to live together at bed and board. Burrows, Sett. Cas. 26.

To live together, as in the same house. "That his sisters, the Lady Turner and Arabella Clerk, might *cohabit* in the capital house." 2 Vern. 323.

COHABITATION. Living together; living together as husband and wife.

Cohabitation means having the same habitation, not a sojourn, a habit of visiting or remaining for a time; there must be something more than mere meretricious intercourse. 75 Pa. St. 207.

Cohæredes una persona censentur, propter unitatem juris quod habent. Co. Litt. 163. Co-heirs are deemed as one person, on account of the unity of right which they possess.

COHÆRES. In old English law. A coheir, or joint heir.

CO-HEIR. One of several to whom an inheritance descends.

CO-HEIRESS. A joint heiress. A woman who has an equal share of an inheritance with another woman.

COHUAGIUM. A tribute made by those who meet promiscuously in a market or fair. Du Cange.

COIF. A title given to serjeants at law, who are called "serjeants of the coif," from the coif they wear on their heads. The use of this coif at first was to cover the clerical tonsure, many of the practising serjeants being clergymen who had abandoned their profession. It was a thin linen cover, gathered together in the form of a skull or helmet; the material being afterwards changed into white silk, and the form eventually into the black patch at the top of the forensic wig, which is now the distinguishing mark of the degree of serjeant at law. (Cowell; Foss, Judg.; 3 Steph. Comm. 272, note.) Brown.

COIN, *v.* To fashion pieces of metal into a prescribed shape, weight, and degree of fineness, and stamp them with prescribed devices, by authority of government, in order that they may circulate as money. See 2 Duv. 29; 22 Ind. 306; 25 How. Pr. 105.

COIN, *n.* Pieces of gold, silver, or other metal, fashioned into a prescribed shape, weight, and degree of fineness, and stamped, by authority of government, with certain marks and devices, and put into circulation as money at a fixed value.

Strictly speaking, coin differs from money, as the species differs from the genus. Money is any matter, whether metal, paper, beads, shells, etc., which has currency as a medium in commerce. Coin is a particular species, always made of metal, and struck according to a certain process called "coinage." Wharton.

COINAGE. The process or the function of coining metallic money; also the great mass of metallic money in circulation.

COJUDICES. Lat. In old English law. Associate judges having equality of power with others.

COLD WATER ORDEAL. The trial which was anciently used for the common sort of people, who, having a cord tied about them under their arms, were cast into a river; if they sank to the bottom until they were drawn up, which was in a very short time, then were they held guiltless; but such as did remain upon the water were held culpable, being, as they said, of the water rejected and kept up. Wharton.

COLIBERTUS. In feudal law. One who, holding in free socage, was obliged to do certain services for the lord. A middle class of tenants between servile and free, who held their freedom of tenure on condition of performing certain services. Said to be the same as the *conditionales*. Cowell.

COLLATERAL. By the side; at the side; attached upon the side. Not lineal, but upon a parallel or diverging line. Additional or auxiliary; supplementary; co-operating.

COLLATERAL ACT. In old practice. The name "collateral act" was given to any act (except the payment of money) for the performance of which a bond, recognizance, etc., was given as security.

COLLATERAL ANCESTORS A phrase sometimes used to designate uncles and aunts, and other collateral antecessors, who are not strictly ancestors. 3 Barb. Ch. 438, 446.

COLLATERAL ASSURANCE. That which is made over and above the principal assurance or deed itself.

COLLATERAL CONSANGUINITY. That relationship which subsists between persons who have the same ancestors but not the same descendants, who do not descend one from the other. 2 Bl. Comm. 203.

Lineal consanguinity being usually represented by a perpendicular or *right line*, (*linea recta*,) in which the kindred are ranked relatively, one above or below the other, as father, son, grandson, *collateral* consanguinity is properly denoted by one or more *transverse* lines, crossing this, or proceeding *obliquely* from it *on the side* (*a latere*) upon which the kindred are ranked in their order. Burrill.

COLLATERAL DESCENT. Descent in a collateral or oblique line, *i. e.*, up through the common ancestor and then down from him; descent to collaterals.

COLLATERAL ESTOPPEL. The collateral determination of a question by a court having general jurisdiction of the subject. See 26 Vt. 209.

COLLATERAL FACTS. Such as are outside the controversy, or are not directly connected with the principal matter or issue in dispute.

COLLATERAL IMPEACHMENT. A collateral impeachment of a judgment or decree is an attempt made to destroy or evade its effect as an estoppel. by reopening the merits of the cause or by showing reasons why the judgment should not have been rendered or should not have a conclusive effect, in a *collateral* proceeding, *i. e.*, in any action other than that in which the judgment was rendered; for, if this be done upon appeal, error, or *certiorari*, the impeachment is *direct*.

COLLATERAL INHERITANCE TAX. A tax levied upon the collateral devolution of property by will or under the intestate law.

COLLATERAL ISSUE. In practice. An issue taken upon matter *aside* from the intrinsic merits of the action, as upon a plea in abatement; or *aside* from the direct and regular order of the pleadings, as on a demurrer. 2 Archb. Pr. K. B. 1, 6, bk. 2, pts. 1, 2.

The term "collateral" is also applied in England to an issue raised upon a plea of diversity of person, pleaded by a criminal who has been tried and convicted, in bar of execution, viz., that he is not the same person who was attainted, and the like. 4 Bl. Comm. 396.

COLLATERAL KINSMEN. Those who descend from one and the same common ancestor, but not from one another.

COLLATERAL LIMITATION. One which gives an interest in an estate for a specified period, but makes the right of enjoyment to depend on some collateral event, as an estate to A. till B. shall go to Rome. Park, Dower, 163; 4 Kent, Comm. 128.

COLLATERAL SECURITY. A security given in addition to the direct security, and subordinate to it, intended to guaranty its validity or convertibility or insure its performance; so that, if the direct security fails, the creditor may fall back upon the collateral security.

Collateral security, in bank phraseology, means some security additional to the personal obligation of the borrower. 2 Abb. (U. S.) 423.

COLLATERAL UNDERTAKING. "Collateral" and "original" have become the technical terms whereby to distinguish promises that are within, and such as are not within, the statute of frauds. 7 Har. & J. 391.

COLLATERAL WARRANTY, in old conveyancing, was where the heir's title to the land neither was nor could have been derived from the warranting ancestor. Thus where a younger brother released to his father's disseisor, with warranty, this was collateral to the elder brother. The whole doctrine of collateral warranty seems repugnant to plain and unsophisticated reason and justice; and even its technical grounds are so obscure that the ablest legal writers are not agreed upon the subject. Wharton.

COLLATERALIS ET SOCII. The ancient title of masters in chancery.

COLLATIO BONORUM. A joining together or contribution of goods into a common fund. This occurs where a portion of money, advanced by the father to a son or daughter, is brought into *hotchpot*, in order to have an equal distributory share of his personal estate at his death. See COLLATION.

COLLATIO SIGNORUM. In old English law. A comparison of marks or seals. A mode of testing the genuineness of a seal, by comparing it with another known to be genuine. Adams. See Bract. fol. 389*b*.

COLLATION. In the civil law. The collation of goods is the supposed or real return to the mass of the succession which an heir makes of property which he received in advance of his share or otherwise, in order that such property may be divided together with the other effects of the succession. Civil Code La. art. 1227.

The term is sometimes used also in common-law jurisdictions in the sense given above. It is synonymous with "hotchpot."

In practice. The comparison of a copy with its original to ascertain its correctness; or the report of the officer who made the comparison.

COLLATION OF SEALS. When upon the same label one seal was set on the back or reverse of the other. Wharton.

COLLATION TO A BENEFICE. In ecclesiastical law. This occurs where the bishop and patron are one and the same person, in which case the bishop cannot present the clergyman to himself, but does, by the one act of collation or conferring the benefice, the whole that is done in common cases both by presentation and institution. 2 Bl. Comm. 22.

COLLATIONE FACTÂ UNI POST MORTEM ALTERIUS. A writ directed to justices of the common pleas, commanding them to issue their writ to the bishop, for the admission of a clerk in the place of another presented by the crown, where there had been a demise of the crown during a suit; for judgment once passed for the king's clerk, and he dying before admittance, the king may bestow his presentation on another. Reg. Orig. 31.

COLLATIONE HEREMITAGII. In old English law. A writ whereby the king conferred the keeping of an hermitage upon a clerk. Reg. Orig. 303, 308.

COLLECT. To gather together; to bring scattered things (assets, accounts, articles of property) into one mass or fund.

To collect a debt or claim is to obtain payment or liquidation of it, either by personal solicitation or legal proceedings.

COLLECTOR. One authorized to receive taxes or other impositions; as "collector of taxes." A person appointed by a private person to collect the credits due him.

COLLECTOR OF DECEDENT'S ESTATE. A person temporarily appointed by the probate court to collect rents, assets, interest, bills receivable, etc., of a decedent's estate, and act for the estate in all financial matters requiring immediate settlement. Such collector is usually appointed when there is protracted litigation as to the probate of the will, or as to the person to take out administration, and his duties cease as soon as an executor or administrator is qualified.

COLLECTOR OF THE CUSTOMS. An officer of the United States, appointed for the term of four years. Act May 15, 1820, § 1; 3 Story, U. S. Laws, 1790.

COLLEGA. In the civil law. One invested with joint authority. A colleague; an associate.

COLLEGATARIUS. Lat. In the civil law. A co-legatee. Inst. 2, 20, 8.

COLLEGATORY. A co-legatee; a person who has a legacy left to him in common with other persons.

COLLEGE. An organized assembly or collection of persons, established by law, and empowered to co-operate for the performance of some special function or for the promotion of some common object, which may be educational, political, ecclesiastical, or scientific in its character.

The assemblage of the cardinals at Rome is called a "college." So, in the United States, the body of presidential electors is called the "electoral college."

In the most common use of the word, it designates an institution of learning (usually incorporated) which offers instruction in the liberal arts and humanities and in scientific branches, but not in the technical arts or those studies preparatory to admission to the professions.

In England, it is a civil corporation, company, or society of men, having certain privileges, and endowed with certain revenues, founded by royal license. An assemblage of several of these colleges is called a "university." Wharton.

COLLEGIA. In the civil law. The guild of a trade.

COLLEGIALITER. In a corporate capacity. 2 Kent, Comm. 296.

COLLEGIATE CHURCH. In English ecclesiastical law. A church built and endowed for a society or body corporate of a dean or other president, and secular priests, as canons or prebendaries in the said church; such as the churches of Westminster, Windsor, and others. Cowell.

COLLEGIUM. In the civil law. A word having various meanings; *e. g.*, an assembly, society, or company; a body of bishops; an army; a class of men. But the principal idea of the word was that of an association of individuals of the same rank and station, or united for the pursuit of some business or enterprise.

COLLEGIUM AMMIRALITATIS. The college or society of the admiralty.

Collegium est societas plurium corporum simul habitantium. Jenk. Cent. 229. A college is a society of several persons dwelling together.

COLLEGIUM ILLICITUM. One which abused its right, or assembled for any other purpose than that expressed in its charter.

COLLEGIUM LICITUM. An assemblage or society of men united for some useful purpose or business, with power to act like a single individual. 2 Kent, Comm. 269.

COLLIERY. This term is sufficiently wide to include all contiguous and connected veins and seams of coal which are worked as one concern, without regard to the closes or pieces of ground under which they are carried, and apparently also the engines and machinery in such contiguous and connected veins. MacSwin. Mines, 25. See 58 Pa. St. 85.

COLLIGENDUM BONA DEFUNCTI. See AD COLLIGENDUM, etc.

COLLISION. In maritime law. The act of ships or vessels striking together.

In its strict sense, collision means the impact of two vessels both moving, and is distinguished from *allision*, which designates the striking of a moving vessel against one that is stationary. But collision is used in a broad sense, to include allision, and perhaps other species of encounters between vessels.

The term is not inapplicable to cases where a stationary vessel is struck by one under way, strictly termed "allision;" or where one vessel is brought into contact with another by swinging at anchor. And even an injury received by a vessel at her moorings, in consequence of being violently rubbed or pressed against by a second vessel lying along-side of her, in consequence of a collision against such second vessel by a third one under way, may be compensated for, under the general head of "collision," as well as an injury which is the direct result of a "blow," properly so called. Abb. Adm. 73.

COLLISTRIGIUM. The pillory.

COLLITIGANT. One who litigates with another.

COLLOBIUM. A hood or covering for the shoulders, formerly worn by serjeants at law.

COLLOCATION. In French law. The arrangement or marshaling of the creditors of an estate in the order in which they are to be paid according to law. Merl. Repert.

COLLOQUIUM. One of the usual parts of the declaration in an action for slander. It is a general averment that the words complained of were spoken "of and concerning the plaintiff," or concerning the extrinsic matters alleged in the inducement, and its office is to connect the whole publication with the previous statement.

An averment that the words in question are spoken of or concerning some usage, report, or fact which gives to words otherwise indifferent the peculiar defamatory meaning assigned to them. 16 Pick. 6.

COLLUSION. A deceitful agreement or compact between two or more persons, for the one party to bring an action against the other for some evil purpose, as to defraud a third party of his right. Cowell.

A secret arrangement between two or more persons, whose interests are apparently conflicting, to make use of the forms and proceedings of law in order to defraud a third person, or to obtain that which justice would not give them, by deceiving a court or its officers.

In divorce proceedings, collusion is an agreement between husband and wife that one of them shall commit, or appear to have committed, or be represented in court as having committed, acts constituting a cause of divorce, for the purpose of enabling the other to obtain a divorce. Civil Code Cal. § 114. But it also means connivance or conspiracy in initiating or prosecuting the suit, as where there is a compact for mutual aid in carrying it through to a decree.

COLLYBISTA. In the civil law. A money-changer; a dealer in money.

COLLYBUM. In the civil law. Exchange.

COLNE. In Saxon and old English law. An account or calculation.

COLONIAL LAWS. In America, this term designates the body of law in force in the thirteen original colonies before the Declaration of Independence. In England, the term signifies the laws enacted by Canada and the other present British colonies.

COLONIAL OFFICE. In the English government, this is the department of state through which the sovereign appoints colonial governors, etc., and communicates with them. Until the year 1854, the secretary for the colonies was also secretary for war.

COLONUS. In old European law. A husbandman; an inferior tenant employed in cultivating the lord's land. A term of Roman origin, corresponding with the Saxon ceorl. 1 Spence, Ch. 51.

COLONY. A dependent political community, consisting of a number of citizens of the same country who have emigrated therefrom to people another, and remain subject to the mother-country. 3 Wash. C. C. 287.

A settlement in a foreign country possessed and cultivated, either wholly or partially, by immigrants and their descendants, who have a political connection with and subordination to the mother-country, whence they emigrated. In other words, it is a place peopled from some more ancient city or country. Wharton.

COLOR. An appearance, semblance, or *simulacrum*, as distinguished from that which is real. A *prima facie* or apparent right. Hence, a deceptive appearance; a plausible, assumed exterior, concealing a lack of reality; a disguise or pretext.

In pleading. Ground of action admitted to subsist in the opposite party by the pleading of one of the parties to an action, which is so set out as to be apparently valid, but which is in reality legally insufficient.

This was a term of the ancient rhetoricians, and early adopted into the language of pleading. It was an apparent or *prima facie* right; and the meaning of the rule that pleadings in confession and avoidance should give color was that they should confess the matter adversely alleged, to such an extent, at least, as to admit some apparent right in the opposite party, which required to be encountered and avoided by the allegation of new matter. Color was either express, *i. e.*, inserted in the pleading, or implied, which was naturally inherent in the structure of the pleading. Steph. Pl. 233.

The word also means the dark color of the skin showing the presence of negro blood; and hence it is equivalent to African descent or parentage.

COLOR OF OFFICE. An act unjustly done by the countenance of an office, being grounded upon corruption, to which the office is as a shadow and color. Plow. 64.

A claim or assumption of right to do an act by virtue of an office, made by a person who is legally destitute of any such right.

The phrase implies, we think, some official power vested in the actor,—he must be at least officer *de facto*. We do not understand that an act of a mere pretender to an office, or false personator of an officer, is said to be done by color of office. And it implies an illegal claim of authority, by virtue of the office, to do the act or thing in question. 23 Wend. 606.

COLOR OF TITLE. The appearance, semblance, or *simulacrum* of title. Any fact, extraneous to the act or mere will of the claimant, which has the appearance, on its face, of supporting his claim of a present title to land, but which, for some defect, in reality falls short of establishing it.

"Color of title is anything in writing purporting to convey title to the land, which defines the extent of the claim, it being immaterial how defective or imperfect the writing may be, so that it is a sign, semblance, or color of title." 70 Ga. 809.

Color of title is that which the law considers *prima facie* a good title, but which, by reason of some defect, not appearing on its face, does not in fact amount to title. An abolute nullity, as a void deed, judgment, etc., will not constitute color of title. 33 Cal. 668.

"Any instrument having a grantor and grantee, and containing a description of the lands intended to be conveyed, and apt words for their conveyance, gives color of title to the lands described. Such an instrument purports to be a conveyance of the title, and because it does not, for some reason, have that effect, it passes only color or the semblance of a title." 35 Ill. 392.

It is not synonymous with "claim of title." To the former, a paper title is requisite; but the latter may exist wholly in parol. 30 Iowa, 480.

COLORABLE. That which has or gives color. That which is in appearance only, and not in reality, what it purports to be.

COLORABLE ALTERATION. One which makes no real or substantial change, but is introduced only as a subterfuge or means of evading the patent or copyright law.

COLORABLE IMITATION. In the law of trade-marks, this phrase denotes such a close or ingenious imitation as to be calculated to deceive ordinary persons.

COLORABLE PLEADING. The practice of giving *color* in pleading.

COLORE OFFICII. By color of office.

"COLORED MAN." There is no legal, technical signification in this phrase which the courts are bound judicially to know. 31 Tex. 74.

COLORED PERSON. A person of African descent or negro blood.

COLPICES. Young poles, which, being cut down, are made levers or lifters. Blount.

COLPINDACH. In old Scotch law. A young beast or cow, of the age of one or two years; in later times called a "cowdash."

COLT. An animal of the horse species, whether male or female, not more than four years old. Russ. & R. 416.

COMBARONES. In old English law. Fellow-barons; fellow-citizens. The citizens or freemen of the Cinque Ports being anciently called "barons;" the term "*combarones*" is used in this sense in a grant of Henry III. to the barons of the port of Fevresham. Cowell.

COMBAT. A forcible encounter between two or more persons; a battle; a duel. Trial by battel.

COMBATERRÆ. A valley or piece of low ground between two hills. Kennett, Gloss.

COMBE. A small or narrow valley.

COMBINATION. A conspiracy, or confederation of men for unlawful or violent deeds.

A union of different elements. A patent may be taken out for a new combination of existing machines. 2 Mason, 112.

COMBUSTIO. Burning.

In old English law. The punishment inflicted upon apostates.

COMBUSTIO DOMORUM. House-burning; arson. 4 Bl. Comm. 272.

COMBUSTIO PECUNIÆ. Burning of money; the ancient method of testing mixed and corrupt money, paid into the exchequer, by melting it down.

COME. To present oneself; to appear in court. In modern practice, though such presence may be constructive only, the word is still used to indicate participation in the proceedings. Thus, a pleading may begin, "Now *comes* the defendant," etc. In case of a default, the technical language of the record is that the party "*comes* not, but makes default."

COMES, *v*. A word used in a pleading to indicate the defendant's presence in court. See COME.

COMES, *n*. Lat. A follower or attendant; a count or earl.

COMES AND DEFENDS. This phrase, anciently used in the language of pleading, and still surviving in some jurisdictions, occurs at the commencement of a defendant's plea or demurrer; and of its two verbs the former signifies that he appears in court, the latter that he defends the action.

COMINUS. Lat. Immediately; hand-to-hand; in personal contact.

COMITAS. Lat. Comity, courtesy, civility. *Comitas inter communitates;* or *comitas inter gentes;* comity between communities or nations; comity of nations. 2 Kent, Comm. 457.

COMITATU COMMISSO. A writ or commission, whereby a sheriff is authorized to enter upon the charges of a county. Reg. Orig. 295.

COMITATU ET CASTRO COMMISSO. A writ by which the charge of a county, together with the keeping of a castle, is committed to the sheriff.

COMITATUS. In old English law. A county or shire; the body of a county. The territorial jurisdiction of a *comes, i. e.*, count or earl. The county court, a court of great antiquity and of great dignity in early times.

Also, the retinue or train of a prince or high governmental official.

COMITES. Counts or earls. Attendants or followers. Persons composing the retinue of a high functionary. Persons who are attached to the suite of a public minister.

COMITES PALEYS. Counts or earls palatine; those who had the government of a county palatine.

COMITIA. In Roman law. An assembly, either (1) of the Roman curiæ, in which case it was called the "*comitia curiata vel calata;*" or (2) of the Roman centuries, in which case it was called the "*comitia centuriata;*" or (3) of the Roman tribes, in which case it was called the "*comitia tributa.*" Only patricians were members of the first *comitia*, and only plebians of the last; but the *comitia centuriata* comprised the entire populace, patricians and plebians both, and was the great legislative assembly passing the *leges*, properly so called, as the senate passed the *senatus consulta*, and the *comitia tributa* passed the *plebiscita*. Under the *Lex Hortensia*, 287 B. C., the *plebiscitum* acquired the force of a *lex*. Brown.

COMITISSA. In old English law. A countess; an earl's wife.

COMITIVA. In old English law. The dignity and office of a *comes*, (count or earl;) the same with what was afterwards called "*comitatus.*"

Also a companion or fellow-traveler; a troop or company of robbers. Jacob.

COMITY. Courtesy; complaisance; respect; a willingness to grant a privilege, not as a matter of right, but out of deference and good will. See next title.

COMITY OF NATIONS. The most appropriate phrase to express the true foundation and extent of the obligation of the laws of one nation within the territories of another. It is derived altogether from the voluntary consent of the latter; and it is inadmissible when it is contrary to its known policy, or prejudicial to its interests. In the silence of any positive rule affirming or denying or restraining the operation of foreign laws, courts of justice presume the tacit adoption of them by their own government, unless repugnant to its policy, or prejudicial to its interests. It is not the comity of the courts, but the comity of the nation, which is administered and ascertained in the same way, and guided by the same reasoning, by which all other principles of the municipal law are ascertained and guided. Story, Confl. Laws, § 38.

The comity of nations (*comitas gentium*) is that body of rules which states observe towards one another from courtesy or mutual convenience, although they do not form part of international law. Holtz. Enc. *s. v.*

COMMAND. An order, imperative direction, or behest.

COMMANDEMENT. In French law. A writ served by the *huissier* pursuant to a judgment or to an executory notarial deed. Its object is to give notice to the debtor that if he does not pay the sum to which he has been condemned by the judgment, or which he engaged to pay by the notarial deed, his property will be seized and sold. Arg. Fr. Merc. Law, 550.

COMMANDER IN CHIEF. By article 2, § 2, of the constitution it is declared that the president shall be commander in chief of the army and navy of the United States. The term implies supreme control of military operations during the progress of a war, not only on the side of strategy and tactics, but also in reference to the political and international aspects of the war.

COMMANDERY. In old English law. A manor or chief messuage with lands and tenements thereto appertaining, which belonged to the priory of St. John of Jerusalem, in England; he who had the government of such a manor or house was styled the "commander," who could not dispose of it, but to the use of the priory, only taking thence his own sustenance, according to his degree. The manors and lands belonging to the priory of St. John of Jerusalem were given to Henry the Eighth by 32 Hen. VIII. c. 20, about the time of the dissolution of abbeys and monasteries; so that the name only of commanderies remains, the power being long since extinct. Wharton.

COMMANDITAIRES. Special partners; partners *en commandité*. See COMMANDITÉ.

COMMANDITÉ. In French law. A special or limited partnership, where the contract is between one or more persons who are general partners, and jointly and severally responsible, and one or more other persons who merely furnish a particular fund or capital stock, and thence are called "*commandataires*," or "*commendataires*," or "partners *en commandité;*" the business being carried on under the social name or firm of the general partners only, composed of the names of the general or complementary partners, the partners in *commandité* being liable to losses only to the extent of the funds or capital furnished by them. Story, Partn. § 78; 3 Kent, Comm. 34.

COMMANDMENT. **In practice.** An authoritative order of a judge or magisterial officer.

In criminal law. The act or offense of one who commands another to transgress the law, or do anything contrary to law, as theft, murder, or the like. Particularly applied to the act of an accessary before the fact, in inciting, procuring, setting on, or stirring up another to do the fact or act. 2 Inst. 182.

COMMARCHIO. A boundary; the confines of land.

COMMENDA. **In French law.** The delivery of a benefice to one who cannot hold the legal title, to keep and manage it for a time limited and render an account of the proceeds. Guyot, Rép. Univ.

In mercantile law. An association in which the management of the property was intrusted to individuals. Troub. Lim. Partn. c. 3, § 27.

Commenda est facultas recipiendi et retinendi beneficium contra jus positivum à supremâ potestate. Moore, 905. A commendam is the power of receiving and retaining a benefice contrary to positive law, by supreme authority.

COMMENDAM. **In ecclesiastical law.** The appointment of a suitable clerk to hold a void or vacant benefice or church living until a regular pastor be appointed. Hob. 144; Latch, 236.

In commercial law. The limited partnership (or *Société en commandité*) of the French law has been introduced into the Code of Louisiana under the title of "Partnership *in Commendam.*" Civil Code La. art. 2810.

COMMENDATIO. In the civil law. Commendation, praise, or recommendation.

COMMENDATION. In feudal law. This was the act by which an owner of allodial land placed himself and his land under the protection of a lord, so as to constitute himself his vassal or feudal tenant.

COMMENDATORS. Secular persons upon whom ecclesiastical benefices were bestowed in Scotland; called so because the benefices were commended and intrusted to their supervision.

COMMENDATORY. He who holds a church living or preferment *in commendam.*

COMMENDATORY LETTERS. In ecclesiastical law. Such as are written by one bishop to another on behalf of any of the clergy, or others of his diocese traveling thither, that they may be received among the faithful, or that the clerk may be promoted, or necessaries administered to others, etc. Wharton.

COMMENDATUS. In feudal law. One who intrusts himself to the protection of another. Spelman. A person who, by voluntary homage, put himself under the protection of a superior lord. Cowell.

COMMERCE. The various agreements which have for their object facilitating the exchange of the products of the earth or the industry of man, with an intent to realize a profit. Pard. Droit Com. n. 1. A general term including the specific contracts of sale and exchange.

The intercourse of nations in each other's produce and manufactures, in which the superfluities of one are given for those of another, and then re-exchanged with other nations for mutual wants. Wharton.

Commerce is the interchange or mutual change of goods, productions, or property of any kind between nations or individuals. Transportation is the means by which commerce is carried on. 45 Iowa, 338.

Commerce is a term of the largest import. It comprehends intercourse for the purposes of trade in any and all its forms, including the transportation, purchase, sale, and exchange of commodities between the citizens of our country and the citizens or subjects of other countries, and between the citizens of different states. The power to regulate it embraces all the instruments by which such commerce may be conducted. 91 U. S. 275.

Commerce is not limited to an exchange of commodities only, but includes, as well, intercourse with foreign nations and between the states; and includes the transportation of passengers. 3 Cow. 713; 34 Cal. 492.

The words "commerce" and "trade" are synonymous, but not identical. They are often used interchangeably; but, strictly speaking, commerce relates to intercourse or dealings with foreign nations, states, or political communities, while trade denotes business intercourse or mutual traffic within the limits of a state or nation, or the buying, selling, and exchanging of articles between members of the same community. See 4 Denio, 353; Jacob; Wharton.

COMMERCIA BELLI. War contracts. Compacts entered into by belligerent nations to secure a temporary and limited peace. 1 Kent, Comm. 159. Contracts between nations at war, or their subjects.

COMMERCIAL LAW. A phrase used to designate the whole body of substantive jurisprudence applicable to the rights, intercourse, and relations of persons engaged in commerce, trade, or mercantile pursuits. It is not a very scientific or accurate term. As foreign commerce is carried on by means of shipping, the term has come to be used occasionally as synonymous with "maritime law;" but, in strictness, the phrase "commercial law" is wider, and includes many transactions or legal questions which have nothing to do with shipping or its incidents.

COMMERCIAL PAPER. The term "commercial paper" means bills of exchange, promissory notes, bank-checks, and other negotiable instruments for the payment of money, which, by their form and on their face, purport to be such instruments as are, by the law-merchant, recognized as falling under the designation of "commercial paper." 6 N. B. R. 338.

Commercial paper means negotiable paper given in due course of business, whether the element of negotiability be given it by the law-merchant or by statute. A note given by a merchant for money loaned is within the meaning. 5 Biss. 113.

COMMERCIAL TRAVELER. Where an agent simply exhibits samples of goods kept for sale by his principal, and takes orders from purchasers for such goods, which goods are afterwards to be delivered by the principal to the purchasers, and payment for the goods is to be made by the purchasers to the principal on such delivery, such agent is generally called a "drummer" or "commercial traveler." 34 Kan. 434, 8 Pac. Rep. 865; 93 N. C. 511.

COMMERCIUM. Lat. In the civil law. Commerce; business; trade; dealings in the nature of purchase and sale; a contract.

Commercium jure gentium commune esse debet, et non in monopolium et privatum paucorum quæstum convertendum. 3 Inst. 181. Commerce, by the law of nations, ought to be common, and not converted to monopoly and the private gain of a few.

COMMINALTY. The commonalty or the people.

COMMINATORIUM. In old practice. A clause sometimes added at the end of writs, admonishing the sheriff to be faithful in executing them. Bract. fol. 398.

COMMISE. In old French law. Forfeiture; the forfeiture of a fief; the penalty attached to the ingratitude of a vassal. Guyot, Inst. Feod. c. 12.

COMMISSAIRE. In French law. A person who receives from a meeting of shareholders a special authority, viz., that of checking and examining the accounts of a manager or of valuing the *apports en nature*, (*q. v.*) The name is also applied to a judge who receives from a court a special mission, *e. g.*, to institute an inquiry, or to examine certain books, or to supervise the operations of a bankruptcy. Arg. Fr. Merc. Law, 551.

COMMISSAIRES-PRISEURS. In French law. Auctioneers, who possess the exclusive right of selling personal property at public sale in the towns in which they are established; and they possess the same right concurrently with notaries, *greffiers*, and *huissiers*, in the rest of the arrondissement. Arg. Fr. Merc. Law, 551.

COMMISSARIAT. The whole body of officers who make up the commissaries' department of an army.

COMMISSARY. In ecclesiastical law. One who is sent or delegated to execute some office or duty as the representative of his superior; an officer of the bishop, who exercises spiritual jurisdiction in distant parts of the diocese.

In military law. An officer whose principal duties are to supply an army with provisions and stores.

COMMISSARY COURT. A Scotch ecclesiastical court of general jurisdiction, held before four commissioners, members of the Faculty of Advocates, appointed by the crown.

COMMISSION. A warrant or authority or letters patent, issuing from the government, or one of its departments, or a court, empowering a person or persons named to do certain acts, or to exercise jurisdiction, or to perform the duties and exercise the authority of an office, (as in the case of an officer in the army or navy.)

Also, in private affairs, it signifies the authority or instructions under which one person transacts business or negotiates for another.

In a derivative sense, a body of persons to whom a commission is directed. A board or committee officially appointed and empowered to perform certain acts or exercise certain jurisdiction of a public nature or relation; as a "commission of assise."

In the civil law. A species of bailment, being an undertaking, without reward, to do something in respect to an article bailed; equivalent to "mandate."

In commercial law. The recompense or reward of an agent, factor, broker, or bailee, when the same is calculated as a percentage on the amount of his transactions or on the profit to the principal. But in this sense the word occurs more frequently in the plural.

In criminal law. Doing or perpetration; the performance of an act.

In practice. An authority or writ issuing from a court, in relation to a cause before it, directing and authorizing a person or persons named to do some act or exercise some special function; usually to take the depositions of witnesses.

A commission is a process issued under the seal of the court and the signature of the clerk, directed to some person designated as commissioner, authorizing him to examine the witness upon oath on interrogatories annexed thereto, to take and certify the deposition of the witness, and to return it according to the directions given with the commission. Pen. Code Cal. § 1351.

COMMISSION DAY. In English practice. The opening day of the assises.

COMMISSION DEL CREDERE, in commercial law, is where an agent of a seller undertakes to guaranty to his principal the payment of the debt due by the buyer. The phrase "*del credere*" is borrowed from the Italian language, in which its signification is equivalent to our word "guaranty" or "warranty." Story, Ag. 28.

COMMISSION MERCHANT. A term which is synonymous with "factor." It means one who receives goods, chattels, or merchandise for sale, exchange, or other disposition, and who is to receive a compensation for his services, to be paid by the owner, or derived from the sale, etc., of the goods. 50 Ala. 154.

COMMISSION OF ANTICIPATION. In English law. An authority under the great seal to collect a tax or subsidy before the day.

COMMISSION OF APPRAISEMENT AND SALE. Where property has been arrested in an admiralty action *in rem* and ordered by the court to be sold, the order is carried out by a commission of appraisement and sale; in some cases (as where the property is to be released on bail and the value is disputed) a commission of appraisement only is required. Sweet.

COMMISSION OF ARRAY. In English law. A commission issued to send into every county officers to muster or set in military order the inhabitants. The introduction of commissions of lieutenancy, which contained, in substance, the same powers as these commissions, superseded them. 2 Steph. Comm. (7th Ed.) 582.

COMMISSION OF ASSISE. Those issued to judges of the high court or court of appeal, authorizing them to sit at the assises for the trial of civil actions.

COMMISSION OF BANKRUPT. A commission or authority formerly granted by the lord chancellor to such persons as he should think proper, to examine the bankrupt in all matters relating to his trade and effects, and to perform various other important duties connected with bankruptcy matters. But now, under St. 1 & 2 Wm. IV. c. 56, § 12, a fiat issues instead of such commission.

COMMISSION OF CHARITABLE USES. This commission issues out of chancery to the bishop and others, where lands given to charitable uses are misemployed, or there is any fraud or dispute concerning them, to inquire of and redress the same, etc.

COMMISSION OF DELEGATES. When any sentence was given in any ecclesiastical cause by the archbishop, this commission, under the great seal, was directed to certain persons, usually lords, bishops, and judges of the law, to sit and hear an appeal of the same to the king, in the court of chancery. But latterly the judicial committee of the privy council has supplied the place of this commission. Brown.

COMMISSION OF LUNACY. A writ issued out of chancery, or such court as may have jurisdiction of the case, directed to a proper officer, to inquire whether a person named therein is a lunatic or not. 1 Bouv. Inst. n. 382, et seq.

COMMISSION OF PARTITION. In the former English equity practice, this was a commission or authority issued to certain persons, to effect a division of lands held by tenants in common desiring a partition; when the commissioners reported, the parties were ordered to execute mutual conveyances to confirm the division.

COMMISSION OF REBELLION. In English law. An attaching process, formerly issuable out of chancery, to enforce obedience to a process or decree; abolished by order of 26th August, 1841.

COMMISSION OF REVIEW. In English ecclesiastical law. A commission formerly sometimes granted in extraordinary cases, to revise the sentence of the court of delegates. 3 Bl. Comm. 67. Now out of use, the privy council being substituted for the court of delegates, as the great court of appeal in all ecclesiastical causes. 3 Steph. Comm. 432.

COMMISSION OF THE PEACE. In English law. A commission from the crown, appointing certain persons therein named, jointly and severally, to keep the *peace*, etc. Justices of the peace are always appointed by special commission under the great seal, the form of which was settled by all the judges, A. D. 1590, and continues with little alteration to this day. 1 Bl. Comm. 351; 3 Steph. Comm. 39, 40.

COMMISSION OF TREATY WITH FOREIGN PRINCES. Leagues and arrangements made between states and kingdoms, by their ambassadors and ministers, for the mutual advantage of the kingdoms in alliance. Wharton.

COMMISSION OF UNLIVERY. In an action in the English admiralty division, where it is necessary to have the cargo in a ship unladen in order to have it appraised, a commission of unlivery is issued and executed by the marshal. Williams & B. Adm. Jur. 233.

COMMISSION TO EXAMINE WITNESSES. In practice. A commission issued out of the court in which an action is pending, to direct the taking of the depositions of witnesses who are beyond the territorial jurisdiction of the court.

COMMISSION TO TAKE ANSWER IN CHANCERY. In English law. A commission issued when defendant lives abroad to swear him to such answer. 15 & 16 Vict. c. 86, § 21. Obsolete. See Jud. Acts, 1873, 1875.

COMMISSION TO TAKE DEPOSITIONS. A written authority issued by a court of justice, giving power to take the testimony of witnesses who cannot be personally produced in court.

COMMISSIONER. A person to whom a commission is directed by the government or a court.

In the governmental system of the United States, this term denotes an officer who is charged with the administration of the laws relating to some particular subject-matter, or the management of some bureau or agency of the government. Such are the commissioners of education, of patents, of pensions, of fisheries, of the general land-office, of Indian affairs, etc.

In the state governmental systems, also, and in England, the term is quite extensively used as a designation of various officers having a similar authority and similar duties.

COMMISSIONER OF PATENTS. An officer of the United States government, being at the head of the bureau of the patent-office.

COMMISSIONERS OF BAIL. Officers appointed to take recognizances of bail in civil cases.

COMMISSIONERS OF BANKRUPTS. The name given, under the former English practice in bankruptcy, to the persons appointed under the great seal to execute a commission of bankruptcy, (*q. v.*)

COMMISSIONERS OF CIRCUIT COURTS. Officers appointed by and attached to the circuit courts of the United States, performing functions partly ministerial and partly judicial. To a certain extent they represent the judge in his absence. In the examination of persons arrested for violations of the laws of the United States they have the powers of committing magistrates. They also take bail, recognizances, affidavits, etc., and hear preliminary proceedings for foreign extradition.

COMMISSIONERS OF DEEDS. Officers empowered by the government of one state to reside in another state, and there take acknowledgments of deeds and other papers which are to be used as evidence or put on record in the former state.

COMMISSIONERS OF HIGHWAYS. Officers appointed in each county or township, in many of the states, with power to take charge of the altering, opening, repair, and vacating of highways within such county or township.

COMMISSIONERS OF SEWERS. In English law. Commissioners appointed under the great seal, and constituting a court of special jurisdiction; which is to overlook the repairs of the banks and walls of the seacoast and navigable rivers, or, with consent of a certain proportion of the owners and occupiers, to make new ones, and to cleanse such rivers, and the streams communicating therewith. St. 3 & 4 Wm. IV. c. 22, § 10; 3 Steph. Comm. 442.

COMMISSIONS. The compensation or reward paid to a factor, broker, agent, bailee, executor, trustee, receiver, etc., when the same is calculated as a percentage on the amount of his transactions or the amount received or expended.

COMMISSORIA LEX. In Roman law. A clause which might be inserted in an agreement for a sale upon credit, to the effect that the vendor should be freed from his obligation, and might rescind the sale, if the vendee did not pay the purchase price at the appointed time. Also a similar agreement between a debtor and his pledgee that, if the debtor did not pay at the day appointed, the pledge should become the absolute property of the creditor. This, however, was abolished by a law of Constantine. Cod. 8, 35, 3. See Dig. 18, 3; Mackeld. Rom. Law, §§ 447, 461; 2 Kent, Comm. 583.

COMMIT. In practice. To send a person to prison by virtue of a lawful authority, for any crime or contempt. 4 Bl. Comm. 295, 300; 1 Tidd, Pr. 479, 481.

To deliver a defendant to the custody of the sheriff or marshal, on his surrender by his bail. 1 Tidd, Pr. 285, 287.

COMMITMENT. In practice. The warrant or *mittimus* by which a court or magistrate directs an officer to take a person to prison.

The act of sending a person to prison by means of such a warrant or order. 9 N. H. 204.

COMMITTEE. In practice. An assembly or board of persons to whom the consideration or management of any matter is committed or referred by some court.

An individual or body to whom others have delegated or committed a particular duty, or who have taken on themselves to perform it in the expectation of their act being confirmed by the body they profess to represent or act for. 15 Mees. & W. 529.

The term is especially applied to the person or persons who are invested, by order of the proper court, with the guardianship of the person and estate of one who has been adjudged a lunatic.

In parliamentary law. A portion of a legislative body, comprising one or more members, who are charged with the duty of examining some matter specially referred to them by the house, or of deliberating upon it, and reporting to the house the result of their investigations or recommending a course of action. A committee may be appointed for one special occasion, or it may be appointed to deal with all matters which may be referred to it during a whole session or during the life of the body. In the latter case, it is called a "standing committee." It is usually composed of a comparatively small number of members, but may include the whole house.

COMMITTITUR. In practice. An order or minute, setting forth that the person named in it *is committed* to the custody of the sheriff.

COMMITTITUR PIECE. An instrument in writing on paper or parchment, which charges a person, already in prison, in execution at the suit of the person who arrested him. 2 Chit. Archb. Pr. (12th Ed.) 1208.

COMMIXTIO. In the civil law. The mixing together or confusion of things, dry or solid, belonging to different owners, as distinguished from *confusio*, which has relation to liquids.

COMMODATE. In Scotch law. A gratuitous loan for use. Ersk. Inst. 3, 1, 20. Closely formed from the Lat. *commodatum*, (*q. v.*)

COMMODATI ACTIO. Lat. In the civil law. An action of loan; an action for a thing lent. An action given for the recovery of a thing loaned, (*commodatum*,) and not returned to the lender. Inst. 3, 15, 2; Id. 4, 1, 16.

COMMODATO. In Spanish law. A contract by which one person lends gratuitously to another some object not consumable, to be restored to him in kind at a given period; the same contract as *commodatum*, (*q. v.*)

COMMODATUM. In the civil law. He who lends to another a thing for a definite time, to be enjoyed and used under certain conditions, without any pay or reward, is called "*commodans;*" the person who receives the thing is called "*commodatarius,*" and the contract is called "*commodatum.*" It differs from *locatio* and *conductio*, in this: that the use of the thing is gratuitous. Dig. 13, 6; Inst. 3, 2, 14; Story, Bailm. § 221.

COMMODITIES. Goods, wares, and merchandise of any kind; movables; articles of trade or commerce.

Commodum ex injuriâ suâ nemo habere debet. Jenk. Cent. 161. No person ought to have advantage from his own wrong.

COMMON. As an *adjective*, this word denotes usual, ordinary, accustomed; shared among several; owned by several jointly.

COMMON, *n.* An incorporeal hereditament which consists in a profit which one man has in connection with one or more others in the land of another. 12 Serg. & R. 32; 10 Wend. 647; 11 Johns. 498.

Common, in English law, is an incorporeal right which lies in grant, originally commencing on some agreement between lords and tenants, which by time has been formed into prescription, and continues good, although there be no deed or instrument to prove the original contract. 4 Coke, 37; 1 Crabb, Real Prop. p. 258, § 268.

Common, or a right of common, is a right or privilege which several persons have to the produce of the lands or waters of another. Thus, common of pasture is a right of feeding the beasts of one person on the lands of another; common of estovers is the right a tenant has of taking necessary wood and timber from the woods of the lord for fuel, fencing, etc. 10 Wend. 647.

The word "common" also denotes an uninclosed piece of land set apart for public or municipal purposes, in many cities and villages of the United States.

COMMON APPENDANT. A right annexed to the possession of arable land, by which the owner is entitled to feed his beasts on the lands of another, usually of the owner of the manor of which the lands entitled to common are a part. 10 Wend. 648; 2 Bl. Comm. 33.

COMMON APPURTENANT. A right of feeding one's beasts on the land of another, (in common with the owner or with others,) which is founded on a grant, or a prescription which supposes a grant. 1 Crabb, Real Prop. p. 264, § 277. This kind of common arises from no connection of tenure, and is against common right; it may commence by grant within time of memory, or, in other words, may be created at the present day; it may be claimed as annexed to any kind of land, and may be claimed for beasts not commonable, as well as those that are. 2 Bl. Comm. 33.

COMMON ASSURANCES. The several modes or instruments of conveyance established or authorized by the law of England. Called "common" because thereby *every man's* estate is assured to him. 2 Bl. Comm. 294.

The legal evidences of the translation of property, whereby every person's estate is assured to him, and all controversies, doubts, and difficulties are either prevented or removed. Wharton.

COMMON BAIL. In practice. The form of entering merely fictitious bail, in cases where special bail is not required. A species of bail intended only to express the appearance of a defendant.

COMMON BAR. In pleading. (Otherwise called "blank bar.") A plea to compel the plaintiff to assign the particular place where the trespass has been committed. Steph. Pl. 256.

COMMON BARRETOR. In criminal law. One who frequently excites and stirs up groundless suits and quarrels, either at law or otherwise.

COMMON BECAUSE OF VICINAGE is where the inhabitants of two townships which lie contiguous to each other have usually intercommoned with one another, the beasts of the one straying mutually into the other's fields, without any molestation from either. This is, indeed, only a permissive right, intended to excuse what, in strictness, is a trespass in both, and to prevent a multiplicity of suits, and therefore either township may inclose and bar out the other, though they have intercommoned time out of mind. 2 Bl. Comm. 33; Co. Litt. 122*a*.

COMMON BENCH. The English court of common pleas was formerly so called. Its original title appears to have been simply "The Bench," but it was designated "Common Bench" to distinguish it from the "King's Bench," and because in it were tried and determined the causes of *common* persons, *i. e.*, causes between subject and subject, in which the crown had no interest.

COMMON CARRIERS. A common carrier is one whose regular business or calling it is to carry chattels for all persons who may choose to employ and remunerate him. Schouler, Bailm. 297.

Every one who offers to the public to carry persons, property, or messages, excepting only telegraphic messages, is a common carrier of whatever he thus offers to carry. Civil Code Cal. § 2168.

A common carrier is one who holds himself out to the public to carry persons or freight for hire. 24 Conn. 479.

At common law, a common carrier is an insurer of the goods intrusted to him, and he is responsible for all losses of the same, save such as are occasioned by the act of God or the public enemy. 15 Minn. 279, (Gil. 208.)

Common carriers are of two kinds,—by *land*, as owners of stages, stage-wagons, railroad cars, teamsters, cartmen, draymen, and porters; and by *water*, as owners of ships, steam-boats, barges, ferrymen, lightermen, and canal boatmen. 2 Kent, Comm. 597.

COMMON CARRIERS OF PASSENGERS. Commôn carriers of passengers are such as undertake for hire to carry all persons indifferently who may apply for passage. Thomp. Carr. p. 26, n. § 1.

COMMON CHASE. In old English law. A place where all alike were entitled to hunt wild animals.

COMMON COUNCIL. In American law. The lower or more numerous branch of the legislative assembly of a city.

In English law. The councillors of the city of London. The parliament, also, was anciently called the "common council of the realm." Fleta, 2, 13.

COMMON COUNTS. Certain general counts or forms inserted in a declaration in an action to recover a money debt, not founded on the circumstances of the individual case, but intended to guard against a possible variance, and to enable the plaintiff to take advantage of any ground of liability which the proof may disclose, within the general scope of the action. In the action of *assumpsit*, these counts are as follows: For goods sold and delivered, or bargained and sold; for work done; for money lent; for money paid; for money received to the use of the plaintiff; for interest; or for money due on an account stated.

COMMON DAY. In old English practice. An ordinary day in court. Cowell; Termes de la Ley.

COMMON DEBTOR. In Scotch law. A debtor whose effects have been arrested by several creditors. In regard to these creditors, he is their common debtor, and by this term is distinguished in the proceedings that take place in the competition. Bell.

COMMON ERROR. (Lat. *communis error, q. v.*) An error for which there are many precedents. "Common error goeth for a law." Finch, Law, b. 1, c. 3, no. 54.

COMMON FINE. In old English law. A certain sum of money which the residents in a leet paid to the lord of the leet, otherwise called "head silver," "cert money," (*q. v.*,) or "*certum letæ.*" Termes de la Ley; Cowell. A sum of money paid by the inhabitants of a manor to their lord, towards the charge of holding a court leet. Bailey, Dict.

COMMON FISHERY. A fishing ground where all persons have a right to take fish. Not to be confounded with "common of fishery," as to which see COMMON OF PISCARY.

COMMON FORM. A will is said to be proved in common form when the executor proves it on his own oath; as distinguished from "proof by witnesses," which is necessary when the paper propounded as a will is disputed.

COMMON HALL. A court in the city of London, at which all the citizens, or such as are free of the city, have a right to attend.

COMMON HIGHWAY. By this term is meant a road to be used by the community at large for any purpose of transit or traffic. Ham. N. P. 239.

COMMON IN GROSS, OR AT LARGE. A species of common which is neither appendant nor appurtenant to *land*, but is annexed to a man's *person*, being granted to him and his heirs by deed; or it may be claimed by prescriptive right, as by a parson of a church or the like corporation sole. 2 Bl. Comm. 34. It is a separate inheritance, entirely distinct from any other landed property, vested in the person to whom the common right belongs. 2 Steph. Comm. 6.

COMMON INFORMER. A common prosecutor. A person who habitually ferrets out crimes and offenses and lays information thereof before the ministers of justice, in order to set a prosecution on foot, not because of his office or any special duty in the matter, but for the sake of the share of the fine or penalty which the law allots to the informer in certain cases.

COMMON INTENDMENT. The natural and usual sense; the common meaning or understanding; the plain meaning of any writing as apparent on its face without straining or distorting the construction.

COMMON INTENT. The natural sense given to words.

COMMON JURY. In practice. The ordinary kind of jury by which issues of fact are generally tried, as distinguished from a *special jury*, (*q. v.*)

COMMON LAW 1. As distinguished from the Roman law, the modern civil law, the canon law, and other systems, the common law is that body of law and juristic theory which was originated, developed, and formulated and is administered in England, and has obtained among most of the states and peoples of Anglo-Saxon stock.

2. As distinguished from law created by the enactment of legislatures, the common law comprises the body of those principles and rules of action, relating to the government and security of persons and property, which derive their authority solely from usages and customs of immemorial antiquity, or from the judgments and decrees of the courts recognizing, affirming, and enforcing such usages and customs; and, in this sense, particularly the ancient unwritten law of England.

3. As distinguished from equity law, it is a body of rules and principles, written or unwritten, which are of fixed and immutable authority, and which must be applied to controversies rigorously and in their entirety, and cannot be modified to suit the peculiarities of a specific case, or colored by any judicial discretion, and which rests confessedly upon custom or statute, as distinguished from any claim to ethical superiority.

4. As distinguished from ecclesiastical law, it is the system of jurisprudence administered by the purely secular tribunals.

5. As concerns its force and authority in the United States, the phrase designates that portion of the common law of England (including such acts of parliament as were applicable) which had been adopted and was in force here at the time of the Revolution. This, so far as it has not since been expressly abrogated, is recognized as an organic part of the jurisprudence of most of the United States.

6. In a wider sense than any of the foregoing, the "common law" may designate all that part of the positive law, juristic theory, and ancient custom of any state or nation which is of general and universal application, thus marking off special or local rules or customs.

COMMON-LAW PROCEDURE ACTS. Three acts of parliament, passed in the years 1852, 1854, and 1860, respectively, for the amendment of the procedure in the common-law courts. The common-law procedure act of 1852 is St. 15 & 16 Vict. c. 76; that of 1854, St. 17 & 18 Vict. c. 125, and that of 1860, St. 23 & 24 Vict. c. 126. Mozley & Whitley.

COMMON LAWYER. A lawyer learned in the common law.

COMMON LEARNING. Familiar law or doctrine. Dyer, 27*b*, 33.

COMMON NUISANCE. One which affects the public in general, and not merely some particular person. 1 Hawk. P. C. 197. See NUISANCE.

COMMON OF DIGGING. Common of digging, or common in the soil, is the right to take for one's own use part of the soil or minerals in another's land; the most usual subjects of the right are sand, gravel, stones, and clay. It is of a very similar nature to common of estovers and of turbary. Elton, Com. 109.

COMMON OF ESTOVERS. A liberty of taking necessary wood for the use or furniture of a house or farm from off another's estate, in common with the owner or with others. 2 Bl. Comm. 35. It may be claimed, like common of pasture, either by grant or prescription. 2 Steph. Comm. 10.

COMMON OF FOWLING. In some parts of the country a right of taking wild animals (such as conies or wildfowl) from the land of another has been found to exist; in the case of wildfowl, it is called a "common of fowling." Elton, Com, 118.

COMMON OF PASTURE. The right or liberty of pasturing one's cattle upon another man's land. It may be either appendant, appurtenant, in gross, or because of vicinage.

COMMON OF PISCARY, or FISHERY. The right or liberty of fishing in another man's water, in common with the owner or with other persons. 2 Bl. Comm. 34. A liberty or right of fishing in the water covering the soil of another person, or in a river running through another's land. 3 Kent, Comm. 409. It is quite different from a common fishery, with which, however, it is frequently confounded.

COMMON OF SHACK. A species of common by vicinage prevailing in the counties of Norfolk, Lincoln, and Yorkshire, in England; being the right of persons occupying lands lying together in the same common field to turn out their cattle after harvest to feed promiscuously in that field. 2 Steph. Comm. 6, 7; 5 Coke, 65.

COMMON OF TURBARY. Common of turbary, in its modern sense, is the right of taking peat or turf from the waste land of another, for fuel in the commoner's house. Williams, Common, 187.

Common opinion is good authority in law. Co. Litt. 186*a;* 3 Barb. Ch. 528, 577.

COMMON PLACE. Common pleas. The English court of common pleas is sometimes so called in the old books.

COMMON PLEAS. The name of a court of record having general original jurisdiction in civil suits.

Common causes or suits. A term anciently used to denote civil actions, or those depending between subject and subject, as distinguished from *pleas of the crown.*

COMMON PLEAS, THE COURT OF. In English law. (So called because its original jurisdiction was to determine controversies between subject and subject.) One of the three superior courts of common law at Westminster, presided over by a lord chief justice and five (formerly four, until 31 & 32 Vict. c. 125, § 11, subsec. 8) *puisné* judges. It was detached from the king's court (*aula regis*) as early as the reign of Richard I., and the fourteenth clause of *Magna Charta* enacted that it should not follow the king's court, but be held in some certain place. Its jurisdiction was altogether confined to civil matters, having no cognizance in criminal cases, and was concurrent with that of the queen's bench and exchequer in personal actions and ejectment. Wharton.

COMMON PRAYER. The liturgy, or public form of prayer prescribed by the Church of England to be used in all churches and chapels, and which the clergy are enjoined to use under a certain penalty.

COMMON RECOVERY. In conveyancing. A species of common assurance, or mode of conveying lands by matter of record, formerly in frequent use in England. It was in the nature and form of an action at law, carried regularly through, and ending in a *recovery* of the lands against the tenant of the freehold; which recovery, being a supposed adjudication of the right, bound all persons, and vested a free and absolute fee-simple in the recoverer. 2 Bl. Comm. 357. Common recoveries were abolished by the statute 3 & 4 Wm. IV. c. 74.

COMMON SANS NOMBRE. Common without number, that is, without *limit* as to the *number* of cattle which may be turned on; otherwise called "common without stint." Bract. fols. 53*b*, 222*b;* 2 Steph. Comm. 6, 7; 2 Bl. Comm. 34.

COMMON SCHOOLS. Schools maintained at the public expense and administered by a bureau of the state, district, or municipal government, for the gratuitous education of the children of all citizens without distinction.

COMMON SCOLD. One who, by the practice of frequent scolding, disturbs the neighborhood. Bish. Crim. Law, § 147. A quarrelsome, brawling, vituperative person.

COMMON SEAL. A seal adopted and used by a corporation for authenticating its corporate acts and executing legal instruments.

COMMON SENSE. Sound practical judgment; that degree of intelligence and reason, as exercised upon the relations of persons and things and the ordinary affairs of life, which is possessed by the generality of mankind, and which would suffice to direct the conduct and actions of the individual in a manner to agree with the behavior of ordinary persons.

COMMON SERJEANT. A judicial officer attached to the corporation of the city of London, who assists the recorder in disposing of the criminal business at the Old Bailey sessions, or central criminal court. Brown.

COMMON, TENANTS IN. See TENANTS IN COMMON.

COMMON TRAVERSE. See TRAVERSE.

COMMON VOUCHEE. In common recoveries, the person who is vouched to warranty. In this fictitious proceeding the crier of the court usually performs the office of a common vouchee. 2 Bl. Comm. 358; 2 Bouv. Inst. n. 2093.

COMMON WEAL. The public or common good or welfare.

COMMONABLE. Entitled to common. Commonable beasts are either beasts of the plow, as horses and oxen, or such as manure the land, as kine and sheep. Beasts not commonable are swine, goats, and the like. Co. Litt. 122*a;* 2 Bl. Comm. 33.

COMMONAGE. In old deeds. The right of common. See COMMON.

COMMONALTY. In English law. The great body of citizens; the mass of the people, excluding the nobility.

In American law. The body of people composing a municipal corporation, excluding the corporate officers.

COMMONANCE. The commoners, or tenants and inhabitants, who have the right of common or commoning in open field. Cowell.

COMMONERS. In English law. Persons having a right of *common.* So called because they have a right to pasture on the waste, in common with the lord. 2 H. Bl. 389.

COMMONS. 1. The class of subjects in Great Britain exclusive of the royal family and the nobility. They are represented in parliament by the house of commons.

2. Part of the demesne land of a manor, (or land the property of which was in the lord,) which, being uncultivated, was termed the "lord's waste," and served for public roads and for common of pasture to the lord and his tenants. 2 Bl. Comm. 90.

COMMONS HOUSE OF PARLIAMENT. In the English parliament. The lower house, so called because the commons of the realm, that is, the knights, citizens, and burgesses returned to parliament, representing the whole body of the commons, sit there.

COMMONTY. In Scotch law. Land possessed in common by different proprietors, or by those having acquired rights of servitude. Bell.

COMMONWEALTH. The public or common weal or welfare. This cannot be regarded as a technical term of public law, though often used in political science. It generally designates, when so employed, a republican frame of government,—one in which the welfare and rights of the entire mass of people are the main consideration, rather than the privileges of a class or the will of a monarch; or it may designate the body of citizens living under such a government. Sometimes it may denote the corporate entity, or the government, of a jural society (or state) possessing powers of self-government in respect of its immediate concerns, but forming an integral part of a larger government, (or nation.) In this latter sense, it is the official title of several of the United States, (as Pennsylvania and Massachusetts,) and would be appropriate to them all. In the former sense, the word was used to designate the English government during the protectorate of Cromwell. See GOVERNMENT; NATION; STATE.

COMMORANCY. The dwelling in any place as an inhabitant; which consists in usually lying there. 4 Bl. Comm. 273. In American law it is used to denote a mere temporary residence. 19 Pick. 247, 248.

COMMORANT. Staying or abiding; dwelling temporarily in a place.

COMMORIENTES. Several persons who perish at the same time in consequence of the same calamity.

COMMORTH, or COMORTH. A contribution which was gathered at marriages, and when young priests said or sung the first masses. Prohibited by 26 Hen. VIII. c. 6. Cowell.

COMMOTE. Half a cantred or hundred in Wales, containing fifty villages. Also a great seignory or lordship, and may include one or divers manors. Co. Litt. 5.

COMMUNE. A self-governing town or village. The name given to the committee of the people in the French revolution of 1793; and again, in the revolutionary uprising of 1871, it signified the attempt to establish absolute self-government in Paris, or the mass of those concerned in the attempt. In old French law, it signified any municipal corporation. And in old English law, the commonalty or common people.

COMMUNE CONCILIUM REGNI. The common council of the realm. One of the names of the English parliament.

COMMUNE FORUM. The common place of justice. The seat of the principal courts, especially those that are fixed.

COMMUNE PLACITUM. In old English law. A common plea or civil action, such as an action of debt.

COMMUNE VINCULUM. A common or mutual bond. Applied to the common stock of consanguinity, and to the feodal bond of fealty, as the common bond of union between lord and tenant. 2 Bl. Comm. 250; 3 Bl. Comm. 230.

COMMUNI CUSTODIA. In English law. An obsolete writ which anciently lay for the lord, whose tenant, holding by knight's service, died, and left his eldest son under age, against a stranger that entered the land, and obtained the ward of the body. Reg. Orig. 161.

COMMUNI DIVIDUNDO. In the civil law. An action which lies for those who have property in common, to procure a division. It lies where parties hold land in common but not in partnership. Calvin.

COMMUNIA. In old English law. Common things, *res communes*. Such as running water, the air, the sea, and sea shores. Bract. fol. 7*b*.

COMMUNIA PLACITA. In old English law. Common pleas or actions; those between one subject and another, as distinguished from pleas of the crown.

COMMUNIA PLACITA NON TENENDA IN SCACCARIO. An ancient writ directed to the treasurer and barons of the exchequer, forbidding them to hold pleas between common persons (*i. e.*, not debtors to the king, who alone originally sued and were sued there) in that court, where neither of the parties belonged to the same. Reg. Orig. 187.

COMMUNIÆ. In feudal law on the continent of Europe, this name was given to towns enfranchised by the crown, about the twelfth century, and formed into free corporations by grants called "charters of community."

COMMUNIBUS ANNIS. In ordinary years; on the annual average.

COMMUNICATION. Information given; the sharing of knowledge by one with another; conference; consultation or bargaining preparatory to making a contract. Also intercourse; connection.

In French law. The production of a merchant's books, by delivering them either to a person designated by the court, or to his adversary, to be examined in all their parts, and as shall be deemed necessary to the suit. Arg. Fr. Merc. Law, 552.

COMMUNINGS. In Scotch law. The negotiations preliminary to the entering into a contract.

COMMUNIO BONORUM. In the civil law. A term signifying a community (*q. v.*) of goods.

COMMUNION OF GOODS. In Scotch law. The right enjoyed by married persons in the movable goods belonging to them. Bell.

Communis error facit jus. Common error makes law. 4 Inst. 240; Noy, Max. p. 37, max. 27. Common error goeth for a law. Finch, Law, b. 1, c. 3, no. 54. Common error sometimes passes current as law. Broom, Max. 139, 140.

COMMUNIS OPINIO. Common opinion; general professional opinion. According to Lord Coke, (who places it on the footing of observance or usage,) common opinion is good authority in law. Co. Litt. 186*a*.

COMMUNIS PARIES. In the civil law. A common or party wall. Dig. 8, 2, 8, 13.

COMMUNIS RIXATRIX. In old English law. A common scold, (*q. v.*) 4 Bl. Comm. 168.

COMMUNIS SCRIPTURA. In old English law. A common writing; a writing common to both parties; a chirograph. Glan. lib. 8, c. 1.

COMMUNIS STIPES. A common stock of descent; a common ancestor.

COMMUNISM. A name given to proposed systems of life or social organization based upon the fundamental principle of the non-existence of private property and of a community of goods in a society.

An equality of distribution of the physical means of life and enjoyment as a transition to a still higher standard of justice that all should work according to their capacity and receive according to their wants. 1 Mill, Pol. Ec. 248.

COMMUNITAS REGNI ANGLIÆ. The general assembly of the kingdom of England. One of the ancient names of the English parliament. 1 Bl. Comm. 148.

COMMUNITY. A society of people living in the same place, under the same laws and regulations, and who have common rights and privileges.

In the civil law. A corporation or body politic. Dig. 3, 4.

In French law. A species of partnership which a man and a woman contract when they are lawfully married to each other.

COMMUNITY PROPERTY. Community property is property acquired by husband and wife, or either, during marriage, when not acquired as the separate property of either. Civil Code Cal. § 687.

This partnership or community consists of the profits of all the effects of which the husband has the administration and enjoyment, either of right or in fact, of the produce of the reciprocal industry and labor of both husband and wife, and of the estates which they may acquire during the marriage, either by donations made jointly to them both, or by purchase, or in any other similar way, even although the purchase be only in the name of one of the two, and not of both, because in that case the period of time when the purchase is made is alone attended to, and not the person who made the purchase. Civil Code La. art. 2402.

COMMUTATION. In criminal law. Change; substitution. The substitution of one punishment for another, after conviction of the party subject to it. The change of a punishment from a greater to a less; as from hanging to imprisonment.

Commutation of a punishment is not a conditional pardon, but the substitution of a lower for a higher grade of punishment, and is presumed to be for the culprit's benefit. 31 Ohio St. 206; 1 Nev. 321.

In civil matters. The conversion of the right to receive a variable or periodical payment into the right to receive a fixed or gross payment. Commutation may be effected by private agreement, but it is usually done under a statute.

COMMUTATION OF TITHES. Signifies the conversion of tithes into a fixed payment in money.

COMMUTATIVE CONTRACT. In the civil law. One in which each of the contracting parties gives and receives an equivalent.

Commutative contracts are those in which what is done, given, or promised by one party is considered as equivalent to, or a consideration for, what is done, given, or promised by the other. Civil Code La. art. 1768.

COMMUTATIVE JUSTICE. See JUSTICE.

COMPACT. An agreement or contract. Usually applied to conventions between nations or sovereign states.

A compact is a mutual consent of parties concerned respecting some property or right that is the object of the stipulation, or something that is to be done or forborne. 4 Gill & J. 1.

The terms "compact" and "contract" are synonymous. 8 Wheat. 1, 92.

COMPANAGE. All kinds of food, except bread and drink. Spelman.

COMPANIES CLAUSES CONSOLIDATION ACT. An English statute, (8 Vict. c. 16,) passed in 1845, which consolidated the clauses of previous laws still remaining in force on the subject of public companies. It is considered as incorporated into all subsequent acts authorizing the execution of undertakings of a public nature by companies, unless expressly excepted by such later acts. Its purpose is declared by the preamble to be to avoid repeating provisions as to the constitution and management of the companies, and to secure greater uniformity in such provisions. Wharton.

COMPANION OF THE GARTER. One of the knights of the Order of the Garter.

COMPANIONS. In French law. A general term, comprehending all persons who compose the crew of a ship or vessel. Poth. Mar. Cont. no. 163.

COMPANY. A society or association of persons, in considerable number, interested in a common object, and uniting themselves for the prosecution of some commercial or industrial undertaking, or other legitimate business.

The proper signification of the word "company," when applied to persons engaged in trade, denotes those united for the same purpose or in a joint concern., It is so commonly used in this sense, or as indicating a partnership, that few persons accustomed to purchase goods at shops, where they are sold by retail, would misapprehend that such was its meaning. 33 Me. 32.

Joint stock companies. Joint stock companies are those having a joint stock or capital, which is divided into numerous transferable shares, or consists of transferable stock. Lindl. Partn. 6.

The term is not identical with "partnership," although every unincorporated society is, in its legal relations, a partnership. In common use a distinction is made, the name "partnership" being reserved for business associations of a limited number of persons (usually not more than four or five) trading under a name composed of their individual names set out in succession; while "company" is appropriated as the designation of a society comprising a larger number of persons, with greater capital, and engaged in more extensive enterprises, and trading under a title not disclosing the names of the individuals.

Sometimes the word is used to represent those members of a partnership whose names do not appear in the name of the firm. See 12 Toullier, 97.

COMPARATIO LITERARUM. In the civil law. Comparison of writings, or handwritings. A mode of proof allowed in certain cases.

COMPARATIVE JURISPRUDENCE. The study of the principles of legal science by the comparison of various systems of law.

COMPARATIVE NEGLIGENCE. That doctrine in the law of negligence by which the negligence of the parties is compared, in the degrees of "slight," "ordinary," and "gross" negligence, and a recovery permitted, notwithstanding the contributory negligence of the plaintiff, when the negligence of the plaintiff is slight and the negligence of the defendant gross, but refused when the plaintiff has been guilty of a want of ordinary care, thereby contributing to his injury, or when the negligence of the defendant is not gross, but only ordinary or slight, when compared, under the circumstances of the case, with the contributory negligence of the plaintiff. 3 Amer. & Eng. Enc. Law, 367. See 103 Ill. 512; 115 Ill. 358, 3 N. E. Rep. 456; 82 Ill. 198; 1 Shear. & R. Neg. §§ 102, 103; Whart. Neg. § 334.

COMPARISON OF HANDWRITING. A comparison by the juxtaposition of two writings, in order, by such comparison, to ascertain whether both were written by the same person.

A method of proof resorted to where the genuineness of a written document is disputed; it consists in comparing the handwriting of the disputed paper with that of another instrument which is proved or admitted to be in the writing of the party sought to be charged, in order to infer, from their identity or similarity in this respect, that they are the work of the same hand.

COMPASCUUM. Belonging to commonage. *Jus compascuum,* the right of common of pasture.

COMPASS, THE MARINER'S. An instrument used by mariners to point out the course of a ship at sea. It consists of a magnetized steel bar called the "needle," attached to the under side of a card, upon which are drawn the points of the compass, and supported by a fine pin, upon which it turns freely in a horizontal plane.

COMPASSING. Imagining or contriving, or plotting.

COMPATERNITAS. In the canon law. A kind of spiritual relationship contracted by baptism.

COMPATERNITY. Spiritual affinity, contracted by sponsorship in baptism.

COMPATIBILITY. Such relation and consistency between the duties of two offices that they may be held and filled by one person.

COMPEAR. In Scotch law. To appear.

COMPEARANCE. In Scotch practice. Appearance; an appearance made for a defendant; an appearance by counsel. Bell.

COMPELLATIVUS. An adversary or accuser.

Compendia sunt dispendia. Co. Litt. 305. Abbreviations are detriments.

COMPENDIUM. An abridgment, synopsis, or digest.

COMPENSACION. In Spanish law. Compensation; set-off. The extinction of a debt by another debt of equal dignity.

COMPENSATIO. In the civil law. Compensation, or set-off. A proceeding resembling a set-off in the common law, being a claim on the part of the defendant to have an amount due to him from the plaintiff deducted from his demand. Dig. 16, 2; Inst. 4, 6, 30, 39; 3 Bl. Comm. 305.

COMPENSATIO CRIMINIS. (Set-off of crime or guilt.) In practice. The plea of recrimination in a suit for a divorce; that is, that the complainant is guilty of the same kind of offense with which the respondent is charged.

COMPENSATION. Indemnification; payment of damages; making amends; that which is necessary to restore an injured party to his former position. An act which a court orders to be done, or money which a court orders to be paid, by a person whose acts or omissions have caused loss or injury to another, in order that thereby the person damnified may receive equal value for his loss, or be made whole in respect of his injury.

Also that equivalent in money which is paid to the owners and occupiers of lands taken or injuriously affected by the operations of companies exercising the power of eminent domain.

In the constitutional provision for "just compensation" for property taken under the power of eminent domain, this term means a payment in money. Any benefit to the remaining property of the owner, arising from public works for which a part has been taken, cannot be considered as compensation. 42 Ala. 83.

As compared with consideration and damages, compensation, in its most careful use, seems to be between them. Consideration is amends for something given by consent, or by the owner's choice. Damages is amends exacted from a wrong-doer for a tort. Compensation is amends for something which was taken without the owner's choice, yet without commission of a tort. Thus, one should say, consideration for land sold; compensation for land taken for a railway; damages for a trespass. But such distinctions are not uniform. Land damages is a common expression for compensation for lands taken for public use. Abbott.

The word also signifies the remuneration or wages given to an employe or officer. But it is not exactly synonymous with "salary." See 76 Ill. 548.

In the civil, Scotch, and French law. Recoupment; set-off. The meeting of two debts due by two parties, where the debtor in the one debt is the creditor in the other; that is to say, where one person is both debtor and creditor to another, and therefore, to the extent of what is due to him, claims allowance out of the sum that he is due. Bell; 1 Kames, Eq. 395, 396.

Compensation is of three kinds,—legal, or by operation of law; compensation by way of exception; and by reconvention. 16 La. Ann. 181.

COMPERENDINATIO. In the Roman law. The adjournment of a cause, in order to hear the parties or their advocates a second time; a second hearing of the parties to a cause. Calvin.

COMPERTORIUM. In the civil law. A judicial inquest made by delegates or commissioners to find out and relate the truth of a cause.

COMPERUIT AD DIEM. In practice. A plea in an action of debt on a bail bond that the defendant appeared at the day required.

COMPETENCY. **In the law of evidence.** The presence of those characteristics, or the absence of those disabilities, which render a witness legally fit and qualified to give testimony in a court of justice. The term is also applied, in the same sense, to documents or other written evidence.

Competency differs from credibility. The former is a question which arises before considering the evidence given by the witness; the latter concerns the degree of credit to be given to his story. The former denotes the personal qualification of the witness; the latter his veracity. A witness may be competent, and yet give incredible testimony; he may be incompetent, and yet his evidence, if received, be perfectly credible. Competency is for the court; credibility for the jury. Yet in some cases the term "credible" is used as an equivalent for "competent." Thus, in a statute relating to the execution of wills, the term "credible witness" is held to mean one who is entitled to be examined and to give evidence in a court of justice; not necessarily one who is personally worthy of belief, but one who is not disqualified by imbecility, interest, crime, or other cause. 1 Jarm. Wills, 124; 23 Pick. 18.

In French law. Competency, as applied to a court, means its right to exercise jurisdiction in a particular case.

COMPETENT AND OMITTED. In Scotch practice. A term applied to a plea which might have been urged by a party during the dependence of a cause, but which had been omitted. Bell.

COMPETENT EVIDENCE. That which the very nature of the thing to be proven requires, as the production of a writing where its contents are the subject of inquiry. 1 Greenl. Ev. § 2; 1 Lea, 504.

COMPETENT WITNESS. One who is legally qualified to be heard to testify in a cause. See COMPETENCY.

COMPETITION. In Scotch practice. The contest among creditors claiming on their respective diligences, or creditors claiming on their securities. Bell.

COMPILE. To compile is to copy from various authors into one work. Between a compilation and an abridgment there is a clear distinction. A compilation consists of selected extracts from different authors; an abridgment is a condensation of the views of one author. 4 McLean, 306, 314.

COMPILATION. A literary production, composed of the works of others and arranged in a methodical manner.

COMPLAINANT. In practice. One who applies to the courts for legal redress; one who exhibits a bill of complaint. This is the proper designation of one suing in equity, though "plaintiff" is often used in equity proceedings as well as at law.

COMPLAINT. In civil practice. In those states having a Code of Civil Procedure, the complaint is the first or initiatory pleading on the part of the plaintiff in a civil action. It corresponds to the declaration in the common-law practice. Code N. Y. § 141.

The complaint shall contain: (1) The title of the cause, specifying the name of the court in which the action is brought, the name of the county in which the trial is required to be had, and the names of the parties to the action, plaintiff and defendant. (2) A plain and concise statement of the facts constituting a cause of action, without unnecessary repetition; and each material allegation shall be distinctly numbered. (3) A demand of the relief to which the plaintiff supposes himself entitled. If the recovery of money be demanded, the amount thereof must be stated. Code N. C. 1883, § 233.

In criminal law. A charge, preferred before a magistrate having jurisdiction, that a person named (or an unknown person) has committed a specified offense, with an offer to prove the fact, to the end that a prosecution may be instituted. It is a technical term, descriptive of proceedings before a magistrate. 11 Pick. 436.

The complaint is an allegation, made before a proper magistrate, that a person has been guilty of a designated public offense. Code Ala. 1886, § 4255.

COMPLICE. One who is united with others in an ill design; an associate; a confederate; an accomplice.

COMPOS MENTIS. Sound of mind. Having use and control of one's mental faculties.

COMPOS SUI. Having the use of one's limbs, or the power of bodily motion. *Si fuit ita compos sui quod itinerare potuit de loco in locum*, if he had so far the use of his limbs as to be able to travel from place to place. Bract. fol. 14*b*.

COMPOSITIO MENSURARUM. The ordinance of measures. The title of an ancient ordinance, not printed, mentioned in the statute 23 Hen. VIII. c. 4; establishing a standard of measures. 1 Bl. Comm. 275.

COMPOSITIO ULNARUM ET PERTICARUM. The statute of ells and perches. The title of an English statute establishing a standard of measures. 1 Bl. Comm. 275.

COMPOSITION. An agreement, made upon a sufficient consideration, between an insolvent or embarrassed debtor and his creditors, whereby the latter, for the sake of immediate payment, agree to accept a dividend less than the whole amount of their claims, to be distributed *pro rata*, in discharge and satisfaction of the whole.

"Composition" should be distinguished from "accord." The latter properly denotes an arrangement between a debtor and a single creditor for a discharge of the obligation by a part payment or on different terms. The former designates an arrangement between a debtor and the whole body of his creditors (or at least a considerable proportion of them) for the liquidation of their claims by the dividend offered.

In ancient law. Among the Franks, Goths, Burgundians, and other barbarous peoples, this was the name given to a sum of money paid, as satisfaction for a wrong or personal injury, to the person harmed, or to his family if he died, by the aggressor. It was originally made by mutual agreement of the parties, but afterwards established by law, and took the place of private physical vengeance.

COMPOSITION DEED. An agreement embodying the terms of a composition between a debtor and his creditors.

COMPOSITION IN BANKRUPTCY. An arrangement between a bankrupt and his creditors, whereby the amount he can be expected to pay is liquidated, and he is allowed to retain his assets, upon condition of his making the payments agreed upon.

COMPOSITION OF MATTER. A mixture or chemical combination of materials.

COMPOSITION OF TITHES, or REAL COMPOSITION. This arises in English ecclesiastical law, when an agreement is made between the owner of lands and the incumbent of a benefice, with the consent of the ordinary and the patron, that the lands shall, for the future, be discharged from payment of tithes, by reason of some land or other real recompense given in lieu and satisfaction thereof. 2 Bl. Comm. 28; 3 Steph. Comm. 129.

COMPOST. Several sorts of soil or earth and other matters mixed, in order to make a fine kind of mould for fertilizing lands.

COMPOTARIUS. In old English law. A party accounting. Fleta, lib. 2, c. 71, § 17.

COMPOUND. To compromise; to effect a composition with a creditor; to obtain discharge from a debt by the payment of a smaller sum.

COMPOUND INTEREST. Interest upon interest, *i. e.*, when the interest of a sum of money is added to the principal, and then bears interest, which thus becomes a sort of secondary principal.

COMPOUNDER. In Louisiana. The maker of a composition, generally called the "amicable compounder."

COMPOUNDING A FELONY. The offense committed by a person who, having been directly injured by a felony, agrees with the criminal that he will not prosecute him, on condition of the latter's making reparation, or on receipt of a reward or bribe not to prosecute.

The offense of taking a reward for forbearing to prosecute a felony; as where a party robbed takes his goods again, or other amends, upon an agreement not to prosecute. 29 Ark. 301; 4 Steph. Comm. 259.

COMPRA Y VENTA. In Spanish law. Purchase and sale.

COMPRINT. A surreptitious printing of another book-seller's copy of a work, to make gain thereby, which was contrary to common law, and is illegal. Wharton.

COMPRIVIGNI. In the civil law. Children by a former marriage, (individually called "*privigni*," or "*privignæ*,") considered relatively to each other. Thus, the son of a husband by a former wife, and the daughter of a wife by a former husband, are the *comprivigni* of each other. Inst. 1, 10, 8.

COMPROMISE. An arrangement arrived at, either in court or out of court, for settling a dispute upon what appears to the parties to be equitable terms, having regard to the uncertainty they are in regarding the facts, or the law and the facts together. Brown.

An agreement between two or more persons, who, for preventing or putting an end to a lawsuit, adjust their difficulties by mutual consent in the manner which they agree on, and which every one of them prefers to the hope of gaining, balanced by the danger of losing. 4 La. 456.

In the civil law. An agreement whereby two or more persons mutually bind themselves to refer their legal dispute to the decision of a designated third person, who is termed "umpire" or "arbitrator." Dig. 4, 8; Mackeld. Rom. Law, § 471.

Compromissarii sunt judices. Jenk. Cent. 128. Arbitrators are judges.

COMPROMISSARIUS. In the civil law. An arbitrator.

COMPROMISSUM. A submission to arbitration.

Compromissum ad similitudinem judiciorum redigitur. A compromise is brought into affinity with judgments. 9 Cush. 571.

COMPTE ARRÊTÉ. Fr. A *compte arrêté* is an account stated in writing, and acknowledged to be correct on its face by the party against whom it is stated. 9 La. Ann. 484.

COMPTER. In Scotch law. An accounting party.

COMPTROLLER. A public officer of a state or municipal corporation, charged with certain duties in relation to the fiscal affairs of the same, principally to examine and audit the accounts of collectors of the public money, to keep records, and report the financial situation from time to time. There are also officers bearing this name in the treasury department of the United States.

COMPTROLLER IN BANKRUPTCY. An officer in England, whose duty it is to receive from the trustee in each bankruptcy his accounts and periodical statements showing the proceedings in the bankruptcy, and also to call the trustee to account for any misfeasance, neglect, or omission in the discharge of his duties. Robs. Bankr. 13; Bankr. Act 1869, § 55.

COMPTROLLERS OF THE HANAPER. In English law. Officers of the court of chancery; their offices were abolished by 5 & 6 Vict. c. 103.

COMPULSION. Constraint; objective necessity. Forcible inducement to the commission of an act.

COMPULSORY. In ecclesiastical procedure, a compulsory is a kind of writ to compel the attendance of a witness, to undergo examination. Phillim. Ecc. Law, 1258.

COMPURGATOR. One of several neighbors of a person accused of a crime, or charged as a defendant in a civil action, who appeared and swore that they believed him on his oath. 3 Bl. Comm. 341.

COMPUTATION. The act of computing, numbering, reckoning, or estimating.

The account or estimation of time by rule of law, as distinguished from any arbitrary construction of the parties. Cowell.

COMPUTUS. A writ to compel a guardian, bailiff, receiver, or accountant to yield up his accounts. It is founded on the statute Westm. 2, c. 12; Reg. Orig. 135.

COMTE. Fr. A count or earl. In the ancient French law, the *comte* was an officer having jurisdiction over a particular district or territory, with functions partly military and partly judicial.

CON BUENA FE. In Spanish law. With (or in) good faith.

CONACRE. In Irish practice. The payment of wages in land, the rent being worked out in labor at a money valuation. Wharton.

Conatus quid sit, non definitur in jure. 2 Bulst. 277. What an attempt is, is not defined in law.

CONCEAL. To hide; secrete; withhold from the knowledge of others.

The word "conceal," according to the best lexicographers, signifies to withhold or keep secret mental facts from another's knowledge, as well as to hide or secrete physical objects from sight or observation. 57 Me. 339.

CONCEALED. The term "concealed" is not synonymous with "lying in wait." If a person conceals himself for the purpose of shooting another unawares, he is lying in wait; but a person may, while concealed, shoot another without committing the crime of murder. 55 Cal. 207.

The term "concealed weapons" means weapons willfully or knowingly covered or kept from sight. 31 Ala. 387.

CONCEALERS. In old English law. Such as find out concealed lands; that is, lands privily kept from the king by common persons having nothing to show for them. They are called "a troublesome, disturbant sort of men; turbulent persons." Cowell.

CONCEALMENT. The improper suppression or disguising of a fact, circumstance, or qualification which rests within the knowledge of one only of the parties to a contract, but which ought in fairness and good faith to be communicated to the other, whereby the party so concealing draws the other into an engagement which he would not make but for his ignorance of the fact concealed.

A neglect to communicate that which a party knows, and ought to communicate, is called a "concealment." Civil Code Cal. § 2561.

The terms "misrepresentation" and "concealment" have a known and definite meaning in the law of insurance. Misrepresentation is the statement of something as fact which is untrue in fact, and which the assured states, knowing it to be not true, with an intent to deceive the underwriter, or which he states positively as true, without knowing it to be true, and which has a tendency to mislead, such fact in either case being material to the risk. Concealment is the designed and intentional withholding of any fact material to the risk, which the assured, in honesty and good faith, ought to communicate to the underwriter; mere silence on the part of the assured, especially as to some matter of fact which he does not consider it important for the underwriter to know, is not to be considered as such concealment. If the fact so untruly stated or purposely suppressed is not material, that is, if the knowledge or ignorance of it would not naturally influence the judgment of the underwriter in making the contract, or in estimating the degree and character of the risk, or in fixing the rate of the premium, it is not a "misrepresentation" or "concealment," within the clause of the conditions annexed to policies. 12 Cush. 416.

CONCEDO. I grant. A word used in old Anglo-Saxon grants, and in statutes merchant.

CONCEPTUM. In the civil law. A theft (*furtum*) was called "*conceptum,*" when the thing stolen was searched for, and found upon some person in the presence of witnesses. Inst. 4, 1, 4.

CONCESSI. Lat. I have granted. At common law, in a feoffment or estate of inheritance, this word does not imply a warranty; it only creates a covenant in a lease for years. Co. Litt. 384*a;* 2 Caines, 194.

CONCESSIMUS. Lat. We have granted. A term used in conveyances, the effect of which was to create a joint covenant on the part of the grantors.

CONCESSIO. In old English law. A grant. One of the old common assurances, or forms of conveyance.

Concessio per regem fieri debet de certitudine. 9 Coke, 46. A grant by the king ought to be made from certainty.

Concessio versus concedentem latam interpretationem habere debet. A grant ought to have a broad interpretation (to be liberally interpreted) against the grantor. Jenk. Cent. 279.

CONCESSION. A grant; ordinarily applied to the grant of specific privileges by a government; French and Spanish grants in Louisiana.

CONCESSIT SOLVERE. (He granted and agreed to pay.) In English law. An action of debt upon a simple contract. It lies by custom in the mayor's court, London, and Bristol city court.

CONCESSOR. In old English law. A grantor.

CONCESSUM. Accorded; conceded. This term, frequently used in the old reports, signifies that the court admitted or assented to a point or proposition made on the argument.

CONCESSUS. A grantee.

CONCILIABULUM. A council house.

CONCILIATION. In French law. The formality to which intending litigants are subjected in cases brought before the *juge de paix.* The judge convenes the parties and endeavors to reconcile them. Should he not succeed, the case proceeds. In criminal and commercial cases, the preliminary of conciliation does not take place. Arg. Fr. Merc. Law, 552.

CONCILIUM. A council. Also argument in a cause, or the sitting of the court to hear argument; a day allowed to a defendant to present his argument; an imparlance.

CONCILIUM ORDINARIUM. In Anglo-Norman times. An executive and residuary judicial committee of the *Aula Regis,* (*q. v.*)

CONCILIUM REGIS. An ancient English tribunal, existing during the reigns of Edward I. and Edward II., to which was referred cases of extraordinary difficulty. Co. Litt. 304.

CONCIONATOR. In old records. A common council man; a freeman called to a legislative hall or assembly. Cowell.

CONCLUDE. To finish; determine; to estop; to prevent.

CONCLUDED. Ended; determined; estopped; prevented from.

CONCLUSION. The end; the termination; the act of finishing or bringing to a close. The conclusion of a declaration or complaint is all that part which follows the statement of the plaintiff's cause of action. The conclusion of a plea is its final clause, in which the defendant either "puts himself upon the country" (where a material averment of the declaration is traversed and issue tendered) or offers a verification, which is proper where new matter is introduced.

In trial practice. It signifies making the final or concluding address to the jury or the court. This is, in general, the privilege of the party who has to sustain the burden of proof.

Conclusion also denotes a bar or estoppel; the consequence, as respects the individual, of a judgment upon the subject-matter, or of his confession of a matter or thing which the law thenceforth forbids him to deny.

CONCLUSION AGAINST THE FORM OF THE STATUTE. The proper form for the conclusion of an indictment for an offense created by statute is the technical phrase "against the form of the statute in such case made and provided;" or, in Latin, *contra formam statuti.*

CONCLUSION TO THE COUNTRY. In pleading. The tender of an issue to be tried by jury. Steph. Pl. 230.

CONCLUSIVE. Shutting up a matter; shutting out all further evidence; not admitting of explanation or contradiction; putting an end to inquiry; final; decisive.

CONCLUSIVE EVIDENCE. Evidence which, in its nature, does not admit of explanation or contradiction; such as what is called "certain circumstantial" evidence. Burrill, Circ. Ev. 89.

Evidence which, of itself, whether contradicted or uncontradicted, explained or unexplained, is sufficient to determine the matter at issue. 6 Lond. Law Mag. 373.

CONCLUSIVE PRESUMPTION. A rule of law determining the quantity of evidence requisite for the support of a particular averment which is not permitted to be overcome by any proof that the fact is otherwise. 1 Greenl. Ev. § 15.

CONCORD. In the old process of levying a fine of lands, the concord was an agreement between the parties (real or feigned) in which the deforciant (or he who keeps the other out of possession) acknowledges that the lands in question are the right of complainant; and, from the acknowledgment or admission of right thus made, the party who levies the fine is called the "cognizor," and the person to whom it is levied the "cognizee." 2 Bl. Comm. 350.

The term also denotes an agreement between two persons, one of whom has a right of action against the other, settling what amends shall be made for the breach or wrong; a compromise or an accord.

In old practice. An agreement between two or more, upon a trespass committed, by way of amends or satisfaction for it. Plowd. 5, 6, 8.

Concordare leges legibus est optimus interpretandi modus. To make laws agree with laws is the best mode of interpreting them. Halk. Max. 70.

CONCORDAT. **In public law.** A compact or convention between two or more independent governments.

An agreement made by a temporal sovereign with the pope, relative to ecclesiastical matters.

In French law. A compromise effected by a bankrupt with his creditors, by virtue of which he engages to pay within a certain time a certain proportion of his debts, and by which the creditors agree to discharge the whole of their claims in consideration of the same. Arg. Fr. Merc. Law, 553.

CONCORDIA. Lat. In old English law. An agreement, or concord. Fleta, lib. 5, c. 3, § 5. The agreement or unanimity of a jury. *Compellere ad concordiam.* Fleta, lib. 4, c. 9, § 2.

CONCORDIA DISCORDANTIUM CANONUM. The harmony of the discordant canons. A collection of ecclesiastical constitutions made by Gratian, an Italian monk, A. D. 1151; more commonly known by the name of "*Decretum Gratiani.*"

Concordia parvæ res crescunt et opulentia lites. 4 Inst. 74. Small means increase by concord and litigations by opulence.

CONCUBARIA. A fold, pen, or place where cattle lie. Cowell.

CONCUBEANT. Lying together, as cattle.

CONCUBINAGE. A species of loose or informal marriage which took place among the ancients, and which is yet in use in some countries. See CONCUBINATUS.

The act or practice of cohabiting, in sexual commerce, without the authority of law or a legal marriage.

An exception against a woman suing for dower, on the ground that she was the concubine, and not the wife, of the man of whose land she seeks to be endowed. Britt. c. 107.

CONCUBINATUS. In Roman law. An informal, unsanctioned, or "natural" marriage, as contradistinguished from the *justæ nuptiæ*, or *justum matrimonium*, the civil marriage.

CONCUBINE. (1) A woman who cohabits with a man to whom she is not married. (2) A sort of inferior wife, among the Romans, upon whom the husband did not confer his rank or quality.

CONCUR. In Louisiana. To join with other claimants in presenting a demand against an insolvent estate.

CONCURATOR. In the civil law. A joint or co-curator, or guardian.

CONCURRENCE. In French law. The possession, by two or more persons, of equal rights or privileges over the same subject-matter.

CONCURRENT. Having the same authority; acting in conjunction; agreeing in the same act; contributing to the same event; contemporaneous.

CONCURRENT JURISDICTION. The jurisdiction of several different tribunals, both authorized to deal with the same subject-matter at the choice of the suitor.

CONCURRENT WRITS. Duplicate originals, or several writs running at the same time for the same purpose, for service on or arrest of a person, when it is not known where he is to be found; or for service on several persons, as when there are several defendants to an action. Mozley & Whitley.

CONCURSUS. In the civil law. (1) A running together; a collision, as *concursus creditorum*, a conflict among creditors. (2) A concurrence, or meeting, as *concursus actionum*, concurrence of actions.

CONCUSS. In Scotch law. To coerce.

CONCUSSIO. In the civil law. The offense of extortion by threats of violence. Dig. 47, 13.

CONCUSSION. In the civil law. The unlawful forcing of another by threats of violence to give something of value. It differs from robbery, in this: that in robbery the thing is taken by force, while in concussion it is obtained by threatened violence. Heinec. Elem. § 1071.

CONDEDIT. In ecclesiastical law. The name of a plea entered by a party to a libel filed in the ecclesiastical court, in which it is pleaded that the deceased made the will which is the subject of the suit, and that he was of sound mind. 2 Eng. Ecc. R. 438; 6 Eng. Ecc. R. 431.

CONDEMN. To find or adjudge guilty. 3 Leon. 68. To adjudge or sentence. 3 Bl. Comm. 291. To adjudge (as an admiralty court) that a vessel is a prize, or that she is unfit for service. 1 Kent, Comm. 102; 5 Esp. 65. To set apart or expropriate property for public use, in the exercise of the power of eminent domain.

CONDEMNATION. In admiralty law. The judgment or sentence of a court having jurisdiction and acting *in rem*, by which (1) it is declared that a vessel which has been captured at sea as a prize was lawfully so seized and is liable to be treated as prize; or (2) that property which has been seized for an alleged violation of the revenue laws, neutrality laws, navigation laws, etc., was lawfully so seized, and is, for such cause, forfeited to the government; or (3) that the vessel which is the subject of inquiry is unfit and unsafe for navigation.

In the civil law. A sentence or judgment which condemns some one to do, to give, or to pay something, or which declares that his claim or pretensions are unfounded.

CONDEMNATION MONEY. In practice. The damages which the party failing in an action is adjudged or *condemned* to pay; sometimes simply called the "condemnation."

As used in an appeal-bond, this phrase means the damages which should be awarded against the appellant by the judgment of the court. It does not embrace damages not included in the judgment. 6 Blackf. 8.

CONDESCENDENCE. In the Scotch law. A part of the proceedings in a cause, setting forth the facts of the case on the part of the pursuer or plaintiff.

CONDICTIO. In Roman law. A general term for actions of a personal nature, founded upon an obligation to give or do a certain and defined thing or service. It is distinguished from *vindicatio rei*, which is an action to vindicate one's right of property in a thing by regaining (or retaining) possession of it against the adverse claim of the other party.

CONDICTIO CERTI. In the civil law. An action which lies upon a promise to do a thing, where such promise or stipulation is certain, (*si certa sit stipulatio.*) Inst. 3, 16, pr.; Id. 3, 15, pr.; Dig. 12, 1; Bract. fol. 103*b*.

CONDICTIO EX LEGE. In the civil law. An action arising where the law gave a remedy, but provided no appropriate form of action. Calvin.

CONDICTIO INDEBITATI. In the civil law. An action which lay to recover anything which the plaintiff had given or paid to the defendant, by mistake, and which he was not bound to give or pay, either in fact or in law.

CONDICTIO REI FURTIVÆ. In the civil law. An action which lay to recover a thing stolen, against the thief himself, or his heir. Inst. 4, 1, 19.

CONDICTIO SINE CAUSA. In the civil law. An action which lay in favor of a person who had given or promised a thing without consideration, (*causa.*) Dig. 12, 7: Cod. 4, 9.

CONDITIO. Lat. A condition.

Conditio beneficialis, quæ statum construit, benignè secundum verborum intentionem est interpretanda; odiosa autem, quæ statum destruit, stricte secundum verborum proprietatem accipienda. 8 Coke, 90. A beneficial condition, which creates an estate, ought to be construed favorably, according to the intention of the words; but a condition which destroys an estate is odious, and ought to be construed strictly according to the letter of the words.

Conditio dicitur, cum quid in casum incertum qui potest tendere ad esse aut non esse, confertur. Co. Litt. 201. It is called a "condition," when something is given on an uncertain event, which may or may not come into existence.

Conditio illicita habetur pro non adjectâ. An unlawful condition is deemed as not annexed.

Conditio præcedens adimpleri debet prius quam sequatur effectus. Co. Litt. 201. A condition precedent must be fulfilled before the effect can follow.

CONDITION. In the civil law. The rank, situation, or degree of a particular person in some one of the different orders of society.

An agreement or stipulation in regard to some uncertain future event, not of the essential nature of the transaction, but annexed to it by the parties, providing for a change or modification of their legal relations upon its occurrence. Mackeld. Rom. Law, § 184.

In the civil law, conditions are of the following several kinds:

The *casual* condition is that which depends on chance, and is in no way in the power either of the creditor or of the debtor. Civil Code La. art. 2023.

A *mixed* condition is one that depends at the same time on the will of one of the parties and on the will of a third person, or on the will of one of the parties and also on a casual event. Civil Code La. art. 2025.

The *potestative* condition is that which makes the execution of the agreement depend on an event which it is in the power of the one or the other of the contracting parties to bring about or to hinder. Civil Code La. art. 2024.

A *resolutory* condition is one which destroys or releases an obligation already vested, as soon as the condition is fulfilled.

A *suspensive* condition is one which postpones the obligation until the happening of a future and uncertain event, or a present but unknown event.

In French law. In French law, the following peculiar distinctions are made: (1) A condition is *casuelle* when it depends on a chance or hazard; (2) a condition is *potestative* when it depends on the accomplishment of something which is in the power of the party to accomplish; (3) a condition is *mixte* when it depends partly on the will of the party and partly on the will of others; (4) a condition is *suspensive* when it is a future and uncertain event, or present but unknown event, upon which an obligation takes or fails to take effect; (5) a condition is *resolutoire* when it is the event which undoes an obligation which has already had effect as such. Brown.

In common law. The rank, situation, or degree of a particular person in some one of the different orders of society; or his *status* or situation, considered as a juridicial person, arising from positive law or the institutions of society.

A clause in a contract or agreement which has for its object to suspend, rescind, or modify the principal obligation, or, in case of a will, to suspend, revoke, or modify the devise or bequest. 1 Bouv. Inst. no. 730.

A *modus* or quality annexed by him that hath an estate, or interest or right to the same, whereby an estate, etc., may either be defeated, enlarged, or created upon an uncertain event. Co. Litt. 201*a*.

A qualification or restriction annexed to a conveyance of lands, whereby it is provided that in case a particular event does or does not happen, or in case the grantor or grantee does or omits to do a particular act, an estate shall commence, be enlarged, or be defeated. Greenl. Cruise, Dig. tit. xiii. c. i. § 1.

The different kinds of conditions known to the common law are defined under their appropriate names in the following titles. A further classification is, however, here subjoined:

Conditions are either *express* or *implied.* They are express when they appear in the contract; they are implied whenever they result from the operation of law, from the nature of the contract, or from the presumed intent of the parties. Civil Code La. art. 2026.

They are *possible* or *impossible;* the former when they admit of performance in the ordinary course of events; the latter when it is contrary to the course of nature or human limitations that they should ever be performed.

They are *lawful* or *unlawful;* the former when their character is not in violation of any rule, principle, or policy of law; the latter when they are such as the law will not allow to be made.

They are *consistent* or *repugnant;* the former when they are in harmony and concord with the other parts of the transaction; the latter when they contradict, annul, or neutralize the main purpose of the contract. Repugnant conditions are also called "insensible."

They are *independent, dependent,* or *mutual;* the first when each of the two conditions must be performed without any reference to the other; the second when the performance of one is not obligatory until the actual performance of the other; the third when neither party need perform his condition unless the other is ready and willing to perform his.

Synonyms distinguished. A "condition" is to be distinguished from a *limitation,* in that the latter may be to or for the benefit of a stranger, who may then take advantage of its determination, while only the grantor, or those who stand in his place, can take advantage of a condition, (16 Me. 158;) and in that a limitation ends the estate without entry or claim, which is not true of a condition. It also differs from a *conditional limitation;*

for in the latter the estate is limited over to a third person, while in case of a simple condition it reverts to the grantor, or his heirs or devisees. It differs also from a *covenant*, which can be made by either grantor or grantee, while only the grantor can make a condition, (Co. Litt. 70.) A *charge* is a devise of land with a bequest out of the subject-matter, and a charge upon the devisee personally, in respect of the estate devised, gives him an estate on condition. A condition also differs from a *remainder;* for, while the former may operate to defeat the estate before its natural termination, the latter cannot take effect until the completion of the preceding estate.

CONDITION AFFIRMATIVE. A condition which consists in doing a thing; as provided that the lessee shall pay rent, etc. Shep. Touch. 118.

CONDITION COLLATERAL. A condition where the act to be done is a collateral act. Shep. Touch. 118.

CONDITION COMPULSORY. A condition expressly requiring a thing to be done; as that a lessee shall pay £10 such a day, or his lease shall be void. Shep. Touch. 118.

CONDITION COPULATIVE. A condition to do divers things. Shep. Touch. 118.

CONDITION DISJUNCTIVE. A condition requiring one of several things to be done. Shep. Touch. 118.

CONDITION EXPRESSED. A condition expressed in the deed by which it is created, (*conditio expressa.*) 2 Crabb, Real Prop. p. 792, § 2127; Bract. fol. 47. A condition annexed, by express words, to any feoffment, lease, or grant. Termes de la Ley.

CONDITION IMPLIED. One which the law infers or presumes, from the nature of the transaction or the conduct of the parties, to have been tacitly understood between them as a part of the agreement, although not expressly mentioned.

CONDITION IN DEED. Fr. *condition en fait.* A condition expressed in a deed, (as a feoffment, lease, or grant,) in plain words, or legal terms of law. Cowell; Co. Litt. 201*a*. See CONDITION EXPRESSED.

CONDITION IN LAW. A condition tacitly created or annexed to a grant, by law, without any words used by the party. Co. Litt. 201*a*. See CONDITION IMPLIED.

CONDITION INHERENT. A condition annexed to the rent reserved out of the land whereof the estate is made; or rather to the estate in the land, in respect of rent, etc. Shep. Touch. 118.

CONDITION NEGATIVE. A condition which consists in not doing a thing; as provided that the lessee shall not alien, etc. Shep. Touch. 118.

CONDITION POSITIVE. One which requires that an event shall happen or an act be done.

CONDITION PRECEDENT. A condition precedent is one which is to be performed before some right dependent thereon accrues, or some act dependent thereon is performed. Civil Code Cal. § 1436.

A condition which must happen or be performed *before* the estate to which it is annexed can vest or be enlarged.

Conditions may be precedent or subsequent. In the former, the condition must be performed before the contract becomes absolute and obligatory upon the other party. In the latter, the breach of the condition may destroy the party's rights under the contract, or may give a right to damages to the other party, according to a true construction of the intention of the parties. Code Ga. 1882, § 2722.

CONDITION RESTRICTIVE. A condition for not doing a thing; as that the lessee shall not alien or do waste, or the like. Shep. Touch. 118.

CONDITION SINGLE. A condition to do one thing only. Shep. Touch. 118.

CONDITION SUBSEQUENT. A condition subsequent is one referring to a future event, upon the happening of which the obligation becomes no longer binding upon the other party, if he chooses to avail himself of the condition. Civil Code Cal. § 1438.

A condition annexed to an estate already vested, by the performance of which such estate is kept and continued, and by the failure or non-performance of which it is defeated. Co. Litt. 201; 2 Bl. Comm. 154.

CONDITIONAL. That which is dependent upon or granted subject to a condition.

CONDITIONAL CREDITOR. In the civil law. A creditor having a future right of action, or having a right of action in expectancy. Dig. 50, 16, 54.

CONDITIONAL DEVISE. A conditional disposition is one which depends upon the occurrence of some uncertain event, by which it is either to take effect or be defeated. Civil Code Cal. § 1345.

CONDITIONAL FEE. An estate restrained to some particular heirs, exclusive of others, as to the heirs of a man's body, by which only his lineal descendants were admitted, in exclusion of collateral; or to the heirs male of his body, in exclusion of heirs female, whether lineal or collateral. It was called a "conditional fee," by reason of the condition expressed or implied in the donation of it that, if the donee died without such particular heirs, the land should revert to the donor. 2 Bl. Comm. 110.

CONDITIONAL LEGACY. One which is liable to take effect or to be defeated according to the occurrence or non-occurrence of some uncertain event.

CONDITIONAL LIMITATION. A condition followed by a limitation over to a third person in case the condition be not fulfilled or there be a breach of it.

A conditional limitation is where an estate is so expressly defined and limited by the words of its creation that it cannot endure for any longer time than till the contingency happens upon which the estate is to fail. 1 Steph. Comm. 309. Between conditional limitations and estates depending on conditions subsequent there is this difference: that in the former the estate determines as soon as the contingency happens; but in the latter it endures until the grantor or his heirs take advantage of the breach. Id. 310.

CONDITIONAL OBLIGATION. An obligation is conditional when the rights or duties of any party thereto depend upon the occurrence of an uncertain event. Civil Code Cal. § 1434.

The Louisiana Code defines conditional obligations as those which result from the operation of law, from the nature of the contract, or from the presumed intent of the parties. 2 La. Ann. 989.

CONDITIONAL SALE. A sale in which the transfer of title is made to depend upon the performance of a condition.

Conditional sales are distinguishable from mortgages. They are to be taken strictly as independent dealings between strangers. A mortgage is a security for a debt, while a conditional sale is a purchase for a price paid, or to be paid, to become absolute on a particular event; or a purchase accompanied by an agreement to resell upon particular terms. 9 Ala. 24.

CONDITIONAL STIPULATION. In the civil law. A stipulation to do a thing upon condition, as the happening of any event.

Conditiones quælibet odiosæ; maxime autem contra matrimonium et commercium. Any conditions are odious, but especially those which are against [in restraint of] marriage and commerce. Lofft, Appendix, 644.

CONDITIONS CONCURRENT. Conditions concurrent are those which are mutually dependent, and are to be performed at the same time. Civil Code Cal. § 1437.

CONDITIONS OF SALE. The terms upon which sales are made at auction; usually written or printed and exposed in the auction room at the time of sale.

CONDOMINIA. In the civil law. Co-ownerships or limited ownerships, such as *emphyteusis, superficies, pignus, hypotheca, ususfructus, usus,* and *habitatio.* These were more than mere *jura in re alienâ,* being portion of the *dominium* itself, although they are commonly distinguished from the *dominium* strictly so called. Brown.

CONDONACION. In Spanish law. The remission of a debt, either expressly or tacitly.

CONDONATION. The conditional remission or forgiveness, by one of the married parties, of a matrimonial offense committed by the other, and which would constitute a cause of divorce; the condition being that the offense shall not be repeated. See Civil Code Cal. § 115; 3 Hagg. Ecc. 351, 629.

"A blotting out of an offense [against the marital relation] imputed so as to restore the offending party to the same position he or she occupied before the offense was committed." 1 Swab. & T. 334.

Condonation is a conditional forgiveness founded on a full knowledge of all antecedent guilt. 36 Ga. 286.

CONDONE. To make condonation of.

CONDUCT MONEY. In English practice. Money paid to a witness who has been subpœnaed on a trial, sufficient to defray the reasonable expenses of going to, staying at, and returning from the place of trial. Lush, Pr. 460; Archb. New Pr. 639.

CONDUCTI ACTIO. In the civil law. An action which the hirer (*conductor*) of a thing might have against the letter, (*locator.*) Inst. 3, 25, pr. 2.

CONDUCTIO. In the civil law. A hiring. Used generally in connection with the term *locatio,* a letting. *Locatio et conductio,* (sometimes united as a compound word, "*locatio-conductio,*") a letting and hiring.

Inst. 3, 25; Bract. fol. 62, c. 28; Story, Bailm. §§ 8, 368.

CONDUCTOR. In the civil law. A hirer.

CONDUCTOR OPERARUM. In the civil law. A person who engages to perform a piece of work for another, at a stated price.

CONDUCTUS. A thing hired.

CONE AND KEY. In old English law. A woman at fourteen or fifteen years of age may take charge of her house and receive *cone* and *key;* that is, keep the accounts and keys. Cowell. Said by Lord Coke to be *cover* and *keye*, meaning that at that age a woman knew what in her house should be kept under lock and key. 2 Inst. 203.

CONFARREATIO. In Roman law. A sacrificial rite resorted to by marrying persons of high patrician or priestly degree, for the purpose of clothing the husband with the *manus* over his wife; the civil modes of effecting the same thing being *coemptio*, (formal,) and *usus mulieris*, (informal.) Brown.

CONFECTIO. The making and completion of a written instrument. 5 Coke, 1.

CONFEDERACY. In criminal law. The association or banding together of two or more persons for the purpose of committing an act or furthering an enterprise which is forbidden by law, or which, though lawful in itself, becomes unlawful when made the object of the confederacy. *Conspiracy* is a more technical term for this offense.

The act of two or more who combine together to do any damage or injury to another, or to do any unlawful act. Jacob. See 52 How. Pr. 353; 41 Wis. 284.

In equity pleading. An improper combination alleged to have been entered into between the defendants to a bill in equity.

In international law. A league or agreement between two or more independent states whereby they unite for their mutual welfare and the furtherance of their common aims. The term may apply to a union so formed for a temporary or limited purpose, as in the case of an offensive and defensive alliance; but it is more commonly used to denote that species of political connection between two or more independent states by which a central government is created, invested with certain powers of sovereignty, (mostly external,) and acting upon the several component states as its units, which, however, retain their sovereign powers for domestic purposes and some others. See FEDERAL GOVERNMENT.

CONFEDERATION. A league or compact for mutual support, particularly of princes, nations, or states. Such was the colonial government during the Revolution.

CONFERENCE. A meeting of several persons for deliberation, for the interchange of opinion, or for the removal of differences or disputes. Thus, a meeting between a counsel and solicitor to advise on the cause of their client.

In the practice of legislative bodies, when the two houses cannot agree upon a pending measure, each appoints a committee of "conference," and the committees meet and consult together for the purpose of removing differences, harmonizing conflicting views, and arranging a compromise which will be accepted by both houses.

In international law. A personal meeting between the diplomatic agents of two or more powers, for the purpose of making statements and explanations that will obviate the delay and difficulty attending the more formal conduct of negotiations.

In French law. A concordance or identity between two laws or two systems of laws.

CONFESS. To admit the truth of a charge or accusation. Usually spoken of charges of tortious or criminal conduct.

CONFESSING ERROR. A plea to an assignment of error, admitting the same.

CONFESSIO. Lat. A confession. *Confessio in judicio*, a confession made in or before a court.

Confessio facta in judicio omni probatione major est. A confession made in court is of greater effect than any proof. Jenk. Cent. 102.

CONFESSION. In criminal law. A voluntary statement made by a person charged with the commission of a crime or misdemeanor, communicated to another person, wherein he acknowledges himself to be guilty of the offense charged, and discloses the circumstances of the act or the share and participation which he had in it.

Also the act of a prisoner, when arraigned for a crime or misdemeanor, in acknowledging and avowing that he is guilty of the offense charged.

Judicial confessions are those made before

a magistrate or in court in the due course of legal proceedings.

Extra-judicial confessions are those made by the party elsewhere than before a magistrate or in open court. 1 Greenl. Ev. § 216.

CONFESSION AND AVOIDANCE. A plea in confession and avoidance is one which avows and confesses the truth of the averments of fact in the declaration, either expressly or by implication, but then proceeds to allege new matter which tends to deprive the facts admitted of their ordinary legal effect, or to obviate, neutralize, or *avoid* them.

CONFESSION OF DEFENSE. In English practice. Where defendant alleges a ground of defense arising since the commencement of the action, the plaintiff may deliver confession of such defense and sign judgment for his costs up to the time of such pleading, unless it be otherwise ordered. Jud. Act 1875, Ord. XX. r. 3.

CONFESSION OF JUDGMENT. The act of a debtor in permitting judgment to be entered against him by his creditor, for a stipulated sum, by a written statement to that effect or by warrant of attorney, without the institution of legal proceedings of any kind.

CONFESSO, BILL TAKEN PRO. In equity practice. An order which the court of chancery makes when the defendant does not file an answer, that the plaintiff may take such a decree as the case made by his bill warrants.

CONFESSOR An ecclesiastic who receives auricular confessions of sins from persons under his spiritual charge, and pronounces absolution upon them. The secrets of the confessional are not privileged communications at common law, but this has been changed by statute in some states. See 1 Greenl. Ev. §§ 247, 248.

CONFESSORIA ACTIO. Lat. In the civil law. An action for enforcing a servitude. Mackeld. Rom. Law, § 324.

Confessus in judicio pro judicato habetur, et quodammodo sua sententiâ damnatur. 11 Coke, 30. A person confessing his guilt when arraigned is deemed to have been found guilty, and is, as it were, condemned by his own sentence.

CONFIDENCE. Trust; reliance; ground of trust. In the construction of wills, this word is considered peculiarly appropriate to create a trust. "It is as applicable to the subject of a trust, as nearly a synonym, as the English language is capable of. Trust is a confidence which one man reposes in another, and confidence is a trust." 2 Pa. St. 133.

CONFIDENTIAL COMMUNICATIONS. These are certain classes of communications, passing between persons who stand in a confidential or fiduciary relation to each other, (or who, on account of their relative situation, are under a special duty of secrecy and fidelity,) which the law will not permit to be divulged, or allow them to be inquired into in a court of justice, for the sake of public policy and the good order of society. Examples of such privileged relations are those of husband and wife and attorney and client.

CONFIDENTIAL RELATION. A fiduciary relation. These phrases are used as convertible terms. It is a peculiar relation which exists between client and attorney, principal and agent, principal and surety, landlord and tenant, parent and child, guardian and ward, ancestor and heir, husband and wife, trustee and *cestui que trust*, executors or administrators and creditors, legatees, or distributees, appointer and appointee under powers, and partners and part owners. In these and like cases, the law, in order to prevent undue advantage from the unlimited confidence or sense of duty which the relation naturally creates, requires the utmost degree of good faith in all transactions between the parties. 57 Cal. 497; 1 Story, Eq. Jur. 218.

CONFINEMENT. Confinement may be by either a moral or a physical restraint, by threats of violence with a present force, or by physical restraint of the person. 1 Sum. 171.

CONFIRM. To complete or establish that which was imperfect or uncertain; to ratify what has been done without authority or insufficiently.

Confirmare est id firmum facere quod prius infirmum fuit. Co. Litt. 295. To confirm is to make firm that which was before infirm.

Confirmare nemo potest prius quam jus ei acciderit. No one can confirm before the right accrues to him. 10 Coke, 48.

Confirmat usum qui tollit abusum. He confirms the use [of a thing] who removes the abuse, [of it.] Moore, 764.

CONFIRMATIO. The conveyance of an estate, or the communication of a right that one hath in or unto lands or tenements, to another that hath the possession thereof, or some other estate therein, whereby a voidable estate is made sure and unavoidable, or whereby a particular estate is increased or enlarged. Shep. Touch. 311; 2 Bl. Comm. 325.

CONFIRMATIO CHARTARUM. Lat. Confirmation of the charters. A statute passed in the 25 Edw. I., whereby the Great Charter is declared to be allowed as the common law; all judgments contrary to it are declared void; copies of it are ordered to be sent to all cathedral churches and read twice a year to the people; and sentence of excommunication is directed to be as constantly denounced against all those that, by word or deed or counsel, act contrary thereto or in any degree infringe it. 1 Bl. Comm. 128.

CONFIRMATIO CRESCENS. An enlarging confirmation; one which enlarges a rightful estate. Shep. Touch. 311.

CONFIRMATIO DIMINUENS. A diminishing confirmation. A confirmation which tends and serves to diminish and abridge the services whereby a tenant doth hold, operating as a release of part of the services. Shep. Touch. 311.

Confirmatio est nulla ubi donum præcedens est invalidum. Moore, 764; Co. Litt. 295. Confirmation is void where the preceding gift is invalid.

Confirmatio omnes supplet defectus, licet id quod actum est ab initio non valuit. Co. Litt. 295*b*. Confirmation supplies all defects, though that which had been done was not valid at the beginning.

CONFIRMATIO PERFICIENS. A confirmation which makes valid a wrongful and defeasible title, or makes a conditional estate absolute. Shep. Touch. 311.

CONFIRMATION. A contract by which that which was infirm, imperfect, or subject to be avoided is made firm and unavoidable.

A conveyance of an estate or right *in esse*, whereby a voidable estate is made sure and unavoidable, or whereby a particular estate is increased. Co. Litt. 295*b*.

In English ecclesiastical law. The ratification by the archbishop of the election of a bishop by dean and chapter under the king's letter missive prior to the investment and consecration of the bishop by the archbishop. 25 Hen. VIII. c. 20.

CONFIRMAVI. Lat. I have confirmed. The emphatic word in the ancient deeds of confirmation. Fleta, lib. 3, c. 14, § 5.

CONFIRMEE. The grantee in a deed of confirmation.

CONFIRMOR. The grantor in a deed of confirmation.

CONFISCARE. In civil and old English law. To confiscate; to claim for or bring into the fisc, or treasury. Bract. fol. 150.

CONFISCATE. To appropriate property to the use of the state. To adjudge property to be forfeited to the public treasury; to seize and condemn private forfeited property to public use.

Formerly, it appears, this term was used as synonymous with "forfeit," but at present the distinction between the two terms is well marked. Confiscation supervenes upon forfeiture. The person, by his act, forfeits his property; the state thereupon appropriates it, that is, confiscates it. Hence, to confiscate property implies that it has first been forfeited; but to forfeit property does not necessarily imply that it will be confiscated.

"Confiscation" is also to be distinguished from "condemnation" as prize. The former is the act of the sovereign against a rebellious subject; the latter is the act of a belligerent against another belligerent. Confiscation may be effected by such means, summary or arbitrary, as the sovereign, expressing its will through lawful channels, may please to adopt. Condemnation as prize can only be made in accordance with principles of law recognized in the common jurisprudence of the world. Both are proceedings *in rem*, but confiscation recognizes the title of the original owner to the property, while in prize the tenure of the property is qualified, provisional, and destitute of absolute ownership. 14 Ct. Cl. 48.

CONFISCATION. The act of confiscating; or of condemning and adjudging to the public treasury.

CONFISK. An old form of *confiscate*.

CONFITENS REUS. An accused person who admits his guilt.

CONFLICT OF LAWS. 1. An opposition, conflict, or antagonism between different laws of the same state or sovereignty upon the same subject-matter.

2. A similar inconsistency between the municipal laws of different states or countries, arising in the case of persons who have acquired rights or a *status*, or made contracts, or incurred obligations, within the territory of two or more states.

3. That branch of jurisprudence, arising from the diversity of the laws of different na-

tions in their application to rights and remedies, which reconciles the inconsistency, or decides which law or system is to govern in the particular case, or settles the degree of force to be accorded to the law of a foreign country, (the acts or rights in question having arisen under it,) either where it varies from the domestic law, or where the domestic law is silent or not exclusively applicable to the case in point. In this sense, it is more properly called "private international law."

CONFLICT OF PRESUMPTIONS. In this conflict certain rules are applicable, viz.: (1) Special take precedence of general presumptions; (2) constant of casual ones; (3) presume in favor of innocence; (4) of legality; (5) of validity; and, when these rules fail, the matter is said to be at large. Brown.

CONFORMITY. In English ecclesiastical law. Adherence to the doctrines and usages of the Church of England.

CONFORMITY, BILL OF. See BILL OF CONFORMITY.

CONFRAIRIE. Fr. In old English law. A fraternity, brotherhood, or society. Cowell.

CONFRERES. Brethren in a religious house; fellows of one and the same society. Cowell.

CONFRONTATION. In criminal law. The act of setting a witness face to face with the prisoner, in order that the latter may make any objection he has to the witness, or that the witness may identify the accused.

CONFUSIO. In the civil law. The inseparable intermixture of property belonging to different owners; it is properly confined to the pouring together of fluids, but is sometimes also used of a melting together of metals or any compound formed by the irrecoverable commixture of different substances. It is distinguished from *commixtion* by the fact that in the latter case a separation may be made, while in a case of *confusio* there cannot be. 2 Bl. Comm. 405.

CONFUSION. In Roman and French law. A mode of extinguishing a debt, by the concurrence in the same person of two qualities which mutually destroy one another. This may occur in several ways, as where the creditor becomes the heir of the debtor, or the debtor the heir of the creditor, or either accedes to the title of the other by any other mode of transfer.

This term, as used in the civil law, is synonymous with "merger," as used in the common law. It arises where two titles to the same property unite in the same person. 1 Woods, 182.

CONFUSION OF BOUNDARIES. The title of that branch of equity jurisdiction which relates to the discovery and settlement of conflicting, disputed, or uncertain boundaries.

CONFUSION OF GOODS. The inseparable intermixture of property belonging to different owners; properly confined to the pouring together of fluids, but used in a wider sense to designate any indistinguishable compound of elements belonging to different owners.

The term "confusion" is applicable to a mixing of chattels of one and the same general description, differing thus from "accession," which is where various materials are united in one product. Confusion of goods arises wherever the goods of two or more persons are so blended as to have become undistinguishable. 1 Schouler, Pers. Prop. 41.

CONFUSION OF RIGHTS. A union of the qualities of debtor and creditor in the same person. The effect of such a union is, generally, to extinguish the debt. 1 Salk. 306; Cro. Car. 551.

CONFUSION OF TITLES. A civil-law expression, synonymous with "merger," as used in the common law, applying where two titles to the same property unite in the same person. 1 Woods, 179.

CONGÉ. In the French law. Permission, leave, license; a passport or clearance to a vessel; a permission to arm, equip, or navigate a vessel.

CONGÉ D'ACCORDER. Leave to accord. A permission granted by the court, in the old process of levying a fine, to the defendant to agree with the plaintiff.

CONGÉ D'EMPARLER. Fr. Leave to imparl. The privilege of an imparlance, (*licentia loquendi.*) 3 Bl. Comm. 299.

CONGÉ D'ESLIRE. A permission or license from the British sovereign to a dean and chapter to elect a bishop, in time of vacation; or to an abbey or priory which is of royal foundation, to elect an abbot or prior.

CONGEABLE. L. Fr. Lawful; permissible; allowable. "Disseisin is properly where a man entereth into any lands or tenements where his entry is not *congeable*, and putteth out him that hath the freehold." Litt. § 279. See 7 Wheat. 107.

CONGILDONES. In Saxon law. Fellow-members of a guild.

CONGIUS. An ancient measure containing about a gallon and a pint. Cowell.

CONGREGATION. An assembly or society of persons who together constitute the principal supporters of a particular parish, or habitually meet at the same church for religious exercises.

In the ecclesiastical law, this term is used to designate certain bureaus at Rome, where ecclesiastical matters are attended to.

CONGRESS. In international law. An assembly of envoys, commissioners, deputies, etc., from different sovereignties who meet to concert measures for their common good, or to adjust their mutual concerns.

In American law. The name of the legislative assembly of the United States, composed of the senate and house of representatives, (*q. v.*)

CONGRESSUS. The extreme practical test of the truth of a charge of impotence brought against a husband by a wife. It is now disused. Causes Célèbres, 6, 183.

CONJECTIO. In the civil law of evidence. A throwing together. Presumption; the putting of things together, with the inference drawn therefrom.

CONJECTIO CAUSÆ. In the civil law. A statement of the case. A brief synopsis of the case given by the advocate to the judge in opening the trial. Calvin.

CONJECTURE. A slight degree of credence, arising from evidence too weak or too remote to cause belief.

Supposition or surmise. The idea of a fact, suggested by another fact; as a possible cause, concomitant, or result. Burrill, Circ. Ev. 27.

CONJOINTS. Persons married to each other. Story, Confl. Laws, § 71.

CONJUDEX. In old English law. An associate judge. Bract. 403.

CONJUGAL RIGHTS. Matrimonial rights; the right which husband and wife have to each other's society, comfort, and affection.

CONJUGIUM. One of the names of marriage, among the Romans. Tayl. Civil Law, 284.

CONJUNCT. In Scotch law. Joint.

CONJUNCTA. In the civil law. Things joined together or united; as distinguished from *disjuncta*, things disjoined or separated. Dig. 50, 16, 53.

CONJUNCTIM. Lat. In old English law. Jointly. Inst. 2, 20, 8.

CONJUNCTIM ET DIVISIM. L. Lat. In old English law. Jointly and severally.

CONJUNCTIO. In the civil law. Conjunction; connection of words in a sentence. See Dig. 50, 16, 29, 142.

Conjunctio mariti et feminæ est de jure naturæ. The union of husband and wife is of the law of nature.

CONJUNCTIVE. A grammatical term for particles which serve for joining or connecting together. Thus, the conjunction "and" is called a "conjunctive," and "or" a "disjunctive," conjunction.

CONJUNCTIVE OBLIGATION. A conjunctive obligation is one in which the several objects in it are connected by a copulative, or in any other manner which shows that all of them are severally comprised in the contract. This contract creates as many different obligations as there are different objects; and the debtor, when he wishes to discharge himself, may force the creditor to receive them separately. Civil Code La. art. 2063.

CONJURATIO. In old English law. A swearing together; an oath administered to several together; a combination or confederacy under oath. Cowell.

In old European law. A compact of the inhabitants of a commune, or municipality, confirmed by their oaths to each other, and which was the basis of the commune. Steph. Lect. 119.

CONJURATION. In old English law. A plot or compact made by persons combining by oath to do any public harm. Cowell.

The offense of having conference or commerce with evil spirits, in order to discover some secret, or effect some purpose. Id. Classed by Blackstone with witchcraft, enchantment, and sorcery, but distinguished from each of these by other writers. 4 Bl. Comm. 60; Cowell.

CONJURATOR. In old English law. One who swears or is sworn with others; one bound by oath with others; a compurgator; a conspirator.

CONNECTIONS. Relations by blood or marriage, but more commonly the relations of a person with whom one is connected by marriage. In this sense, the relations of a wife are "connections" of her husband. The term is vague and indefinite. See 1 Pa. St. 507.

CONNEXITÉ. In French law. This exists when two actions are pending which, although not identical as in *lis pendens*, are so nearly similar in object that it is expedient to have them both adjudicated upon by the same judges. Arg. Fr. Merc. Law, 553.

CONNIVANCE. The secret or indirect consent or permission of one person to the commission of an unlawful or criminal act by another.

Literally, a winking at; intentional forbearance to see a fault or other act; generally implying consent to it. Webster.

Connivance is the corrupt consent of one party to the commission of the acts of the other, constituting the cause of divorce. Civil Code Cal. § 112.

Connivance differs from condonation, though the same legal consequences may attend it. Connivance necessarily involves criminality on the part of the individual who connives; condonation may take place without imputing the slightest blame to the party who forgives the injury. Connivance must be the act of the mind before the offense has been committed; condonation is the result of a determination to forgive an injury which was not known until after it was inflicted. 3 Hagg. Ecc. 350.

CONNOISSEMENT. In French law. An instrument similar to our bill of lading.

CONNUBIUM. In the civil law. Marriage. Among the Romans, a lawful marriage as distinguished from "concubinage," (*q. v.*,) which was an inferior marriage.

CONOCIAMENTO. In Spanish law. A recognizance. White, New Recop. b. 3, tit. 7, c. 5, § 3.

CONOCIMIENTO. In Spanish law. A bill of lading. In the Mediterranean ports it is called "*poliza de cargamiento.*"

CONPOSSESSIO. In modern civil law. A joint possession. Mackeld. Rom. Law, § 245.

CONQUEREUR. In Norman and old English law. The first purchaser of an estate; he who first brought an estate into his family.

CONQUEROR. In old English and Scotch law. The first purchaser of an estate; he who brought it into the family owning it. 2 Bl. Comm. 242, 243.

CONQUEST. In feudal law. Conquest; acquisition by purchase; any method of acquiring the ownership of an estate other than by descent. Also an estate acquired otherwise than by inheritance.

In international law. The acquisition of the sovereignty of a country by force of arms, exercised by an independent power which reduces the vanquished to the submission of its empire.

In Scotch law. Purchase. Bell.

CONQUESTOR. Conqueror. The title given to William of Normandy.

CONQUÊTS. In French law. The name given to every acquisition which the husband and wife, jointly or severally, make during the conjugal community. Thus, whatever is acquired by the husband and wife, either by his or her industry or good fortune, inures to the extent of one-half for the benefit of the other. Merl. Repert. "*Conquêt.*"

CONQUISITIO. In feudal and old English law. Acquisition. 2 Bl. Comm. 242.

CONQUISITOR. In feudal law. A purchaser, acquirer, or conqueror. 2 Bl. Comm. 242, 243.

CONSANGUINEUS. A person related by blood; a person descended from the same common stock.

Consanguineus est quasi eodem sanguine natus. Co. Litt. 157. A person related by consanguinity is, as it were, sprung from the same blood.

CONSANGUINEUS FRATER. In civil and feudal law. A half-brother by the father's side, as distinguished from *frater uterinus*, a brother by the mother's side.

CONSANGUINITY. The connection or relation of persons descended from the same stock or common ancestor. It is either lineal or collateral. Lineal is that which subsists between persons of whom one is descended in a direct line from the other, as between son, father, grandfather, great-grandfather, and so upwards in the direct ascending line; or between son, grandson, great-grandson, and so downwards in the direct descending line. Collateral agree with the lineal in this, that they descend from the same stock or ancestor; but differ in this, that they do not descend one from the other. 2 Bl. Comm. 202.

CONSCIENCE. This term is not synonymous with "principle." An "objection on principle" is not the same thing as a "conscientious scruple" or opinion. 7 Cal. 140.

CONSCIENCE, COURTS OF. Courts, not of record, constituted by act of parliament in the city of London, and other towns, for the recovery of small debts; otherwise and more commonly called "Courts of Requests." 3 Steph. Comm. 451.

Conscientia dicitur a con et scio, quasi scire cum Deo. 1 Coke, 100. Conscience is called from *con* and *scio*, to know, as it were, with God.

CONSCIENTIA REI ALIENI. In Scotch law. Knowledge of another's property; knowledge that a thing is not one's own, but belongs to another. He who has this knowledge, and retains possession, is chargeable with "violent profits."

CONSCRIPTION. Drafting into the military service of the state; compulsory service falling upon all male subjects evenly, within or under certain specified ages.

CONSECRATE. In ecclesiastical law. To dedicate to sacred purposes, as a bishop by imposition of hands, or a church or churchyard by prayers, etc. Consecration is performed by a bishop or archbishop.

Consecratio est periodus electionis; electio est præambula consecrationis. 2 Rolle, 102. Consecration is the termination of election; election is the preamble of consecration.

CONSEIL DE FAMILLE. In French law. A family council. Certain acts require the sanction of this body. For example, a guardian can neither accept nor reject an inheritance to which the minor has succeeded without its authority, (Code Nap. 461;) nor can he accept for the child a gift *inter vivos* without the like authority, (Id. 463.)

CONSEIL JUDICIAIRE. In French law. When a person has been subjected to an interdiction on the ground of his insane extravagance, but the interdiction is not absolute, but limited only, the court of first instance, which grants the interdiction, appoints a council, called by this name, with whose assistance the party may bring or defend actions, or compromise the same, alienate his estate, make or incur loans, and the like. Brown.

CONSEILS DE PRUDHOMMES. In French law. A species of trade tribunals, charged with settling differences between masters and workmen. They endeavor, in the first instance, to conciliate the parties. In default, they adjudicate upon the questions in dispute. Their decisions are final up to 200*f*. Beyond that amount, appeals lie to the tribunals of commerce. Arg. Fr. Merc. Law, 553.

CONSENSUAL CONTRACT. A term derived from the civil law, denoting a contract founded upon and completed by the mere consent of the contracting parties, without any external formality or symbolic act to fix the obligation.

Consensus est voluntas plurium ad quos res pertinet, simul juncta. Lofft, 514. Consent is the conjoint will of several persons to whom the thing belongs.

Consensus facit legem. Consent makes the law. (A contract is law between the parties agreeing to be bound by it.) Branch. Princ.

Consensus, non concubitus, facit nuptias vel matrimonium, et consentire non possunt ante annos nubiles. 6 Coke, 22. Consent, and not cohabitation, constitutes nuptials or marriage, and persons cannot consent before marriageable years. 1 Bl. Comm. 434.

Consensus tollit errorem. Co. Litt. 126. Consent (acquiescence) removes mistake.

Consensus voluntas multorum ad quos res pertinet, simul juncta. Consent is the united will of several interested in one subject-matter. Davis, 48; Branch, Princ.

CONSENT. A concurrence of wills.

Express consent is that directly given, either *viva voce* or in writing.

Implied consent is that manifested by signs, actions, or facts, or by inaction or silence, which raise a presumption that the consent has been given.

Consent is an act of reason, accompanied with deliberation, the mind weighing as in a balance the good or evil on each side. 1 Story, Eq. Jur. § 222.

There is a difference between consenting and submitting. Every consent involves a submission; but a mere submission does not necessarily involve consent. 9 Car. & P. 722.

CONSENT-RULE. In English practice. A superseded instrument, in which a defendant in an action of ejectment specified for what purpose he intended to defend, and undertook to confess not only the fictitious lease, entry, and ouster, but that he was in possession.

Consentientes et agentes pari pœna plectentur. They who consent to an act, and they who do it, shall be visited with equal punishment. 5 Coke, 80.

Consentire matrimonio non possunt infra [ante] annos nubiles. Parties cannot consent to marriage within the years of marriage, [before the age of consent.] 6 Coke, 22.

Consequentiæ non est consequentia. Bac. Max. The consequence of a consequence exists not.

CONSEQUENTIAL DAMAGE. Such damage, loss, or injury as does not flow directly and immediately from the act of the party, but only from some of the consequences or results of such act.

The term "consequential damage" means sometimes damage which is so remote as not to be actionable; sometimes damage which, though somewhat remote, is actionable; or damage which, though actionable, does not follow immediately, in point of time, upon the doing of the act complained of. 51 N. H. 504.

CONSEQUENTS. In Scotch law. Implied powers or authorities. Things which follow, usually by implication of law. A commission being given to execute any work, every power necessary to carry it on is implied. 1 Kames, Eq. 242.

CONSERVATOR. A guardian; protector; preserver.

"When any person having property shall be found to be incapable of managing his affairs, by the court of probate in the district in which he resides, * * * it shall appoint some person to be his *conservator*, who, upon giving a probate bond, shall have the charge of the person and estate of such incapable person." Gen. St. Conn. 1875, p. 346, § 1.

CONSERVATORS OF RIVERS. Commissioners or trustees in whom the control of a certain river is vested, in England, by act of parliament.

CONSIDERATIO CURIÆ. The judgment of the court.

CONSIDERATION. The inducement to a contract. The cause, motive, price, or impelling influence which induces a contracting party to enter into a contract. The reason or material cause of a contract.

Any benefit conferred, or agreed to be conferred, upon the promisor, by any other person, to which the promisor is not lawfully entitled, or any prejudice suffered, or agreed to be suffered, by such person, other than such as he is at the time of consent lawfully bound to suffer, as an inducement to the promisor, is a good consideration for a promise. Civil Code Cal. § 1605.

Any act of the plaintiff from which the defendant or a stranger derives a benefit or advantage, or any labor, detriment, or inconvenience sustained by the plaintiff, however small, if such act is performed or inconvenience suffered by the plaintiff by the consent, express or implied, of the defendant. 3 Scott, 250.

Considerations are classified and defined as follows:

They are either *express* or *implied;* the former when they are specifically stated in a deed, contract, or other instrument; the latter when inferred or supposed by the law from the acts or situation of the parties.

They are either *executed* or *executory;* the former being acts done or values given before or at the time of making the contract; the latter being promises to give or do something in future.

They are either *good* or *valuable.* A good consideration is such as is founded on natural duty and affection, or on a strong moral obligation. A valuable consideration is founded on money, or something convertible into money, or having a value in money, except marriage, which is a valuable consideration. Code Ga. 1882, § 2741. See Chit. Cont. 7.

A *continuing* consideration is one consisting in acts or performances which must necessarily extend over a considerable period of time.

Concurrent considerations are those which arise at the same time or where the promises are simultaneous.

Equitable or *moral* considerations are devoid of efficacy in point of strict law, but are founded upon a moral duty, and may be made the basis of an express promise.

A *gratuitous* consideration is one which is not founded upon any such loss, injury, or inconvenience to the party to whom it moves as to make it valid in law.

Past consideration is an act done before the contract is made, and is really by itself no consideration for a promise. Anson, Cont. 82.

CONSIDERATUM EST PER CURIAM. (It is considered by the court.) The formal and ordinary commencement of a judgment.

CONSIDERATUR. L. Lat. It is considered. Held to mean the same with *consideratum est.* 2 Strange, 874.

CONSIGN. **In the civil law.** To deposit in the custody of a third person a thing belonging to the debtor, for the benefit of the creditor, under the authority of a court of justice. Poth. Obl. pt. 3, c. 1, art. 8.

In commercial law. To deliver goods to a carrier to be transmitted to a designated factor or agent.

To deliver or transfer as a charge or trust; to commit, intrust, give in trust; to transfer from oneself to the care of another; to send or transmit goods to a merchant or factor for sale. 4 Daly, 320.

CONSIGNATION. **In Scotch law.** The payment of money into the hands of a third party, when the creditor refuses to accept of it. The person to whom the money is given is termed the "consignatory." Bell.

In French law. A deposit which a debtor makes of the thing that he owes into the hands of a third person, and under the authority of a court of justice. 1 Poth. Obl. 536; 1 N. H. 304.

CONSIGNEE. In mercantile law. One to whom a consignment is made. The person to whom goods are shipped for sale.

CONSIGNMENT. The act or process of consigning goods; the transportation of goods consigned; an article or collection of goods sent to a factor to be sold; goods or property sent, by the aid of a common carrier, from one person in one place to another person in another place. See CONSIGN.

CONSIGNOR. One who sends or makes a consignment. A shipper of goods.

Consilia multorum quæruntur in magnis. 4 Inst. 1. The counsels of many are required in great things.

CONSILIARIUS. In the civil law. A counsellor, as distinguished from a pleader or advocate. An assistant judge. One who participates in the decisions. Du Cange.

CONSILIUM. A day appointed to hear the counsel of both parties. A case set down for argument.

It is commonly used for the day appointed for the argument of a demurrer, or errors assigned. 1 Tidd, Pr. 438.

CONSIMILI CASU. In practice. A writ of entry, framed under the provisions of the statute Westminster 2, (13 Edw. I.,) c. 24, which lay for the benefit of the reversioner, where a tenant by the curtesy aliened in fee or for life.

CONSISTING. Being composed or made up of. This word is not synonymous with "including;" for the latter, when used in connection with a number of specified objects, always implies that there may be others which are not mentioned. 6 Mo. App. 331.

CONSISTORIUM. The state council of the Roman emperors. Mackeld. Rom. Law, § 58.

CONSISTORY. In ecclesiastical law. An assembly of cardinals convoked by the pope.

CONSISTORY COURTS. Courts held by diocesan bishops within their several cathedrals, for the trial of ecclesiastical causes arising within their respective dioceses. The bishop's chancellor, or his commissary, is the judge; and from his sentence an appeal lies to the archbishop. Mozley & Whitley.

CONSOBRINI. In the civil law. Cousins-german, in general; brothers' and sisters' children, considered in their relation to each other.

CONSOLATO DEL MARE. The name of a code of sea-laws, said to have been compiled by order of the kings of Arragon (or, according to other authorities, at Pisa or Barcelona) in the fourteenth century, which comprised the maritime ordinances of the Roman emperors, of France and Spain, and of the Italian commercial powers. This compilation exercised a considerable influence in the formation of European maritime law.

CONSOLIDATE. To consolidate means something more than rearrange or redivide. In a general sense, it means to unite into one mass or body, as to consolidate the forces of an army, or various funds. In parliamentary usage, to consolidate two bills is to unite them into one. In law, to consolidate benefices is to combine them into one. 45 Iowa, 56.

CONSOLIDATED FUND. In England. A fund for the payment of the public debt.

CONSOLIDATED ORDERS. The orders regulating the practice of the English court of chancery, which were issued, in 1860, in substitution for the various orders which had previously been promulgated from time to time.

CONSOLIDATION. In the civil law. The union of the usufruct with the estate out of which it issues, in the same person; which happens when the usufructuary acquires the estate, or *vice versa*. In either case the usufruct is extinct. Lec. El. Dr. Rom. 424.

In Scotch law. The junction of the property and superiority of an estate, where they have been disjoined. Bell.

CONSOLIDATION OF ACTIONS. The act or process of uniting several actions into one trial and judgment, by order of a court, where all the actions are between the same parties, pending in the same court, and turning upon the same or similar issues; or the court may order that one of the actions be tried, and the others decided without trial according to the judgment in the one selected.

CONSOLIDATION OF BENEFICES. The act or process of uniting two or more of them into one.

CONSOLIDATION OF CORPORATIONS. The union or merger into one corporate body of two or more corporations which had been separately created for similar or connected purposes. In England this is termed "amalgamation."

When the rights, franchises, and effects of two or more corporations are, by legal authority and agreement of the parties, combined and united into one whole, and committed to a single corporation, the stockholders of which are composed of those (so far as they choose to become such) of the companies thus agreeing, this is in law, and according to common understanding, a consolidation of such companies, whether such single corporation, called the consolidated company, be a new one then created, or one of the original companies, continuing in existence with only larger rights, capacity, and property. 64 Ala. 656.

CONSOLIDATION RULE. In practice. A rule or order of court requiring a plaintiff who has instituted separate suits upon several claims against the same defendant, to consolidate them in one action, where that can be done consistently with the rules of pleading.

CONSOLS. An abbreviation of the expression "consolidated annuities," and used in modern times as a name of various funds united in one for the payment of the British national debt.

Consortio malorum me quoque malum facit. Moore, 817. The company of wicked men makes me also wicked.

CONSORTIUM. In the civil law. A union of fortunes; a lawful Roman marriage. Also, the joining of several persons as parties to one action. In old English law, the term signified company or society. In the language of pleading, (as in the phrase *per quod consortium amisit*) it means the companionship or society of a wife.

CONSPIRACY. In criminal law. A combination or confederacy between two or more persons formed for the purpose of committing, by their joint efforts, some unlawful or criminal act, or some act which is innocent in itself, but becomes unlawful when done by the concerted action of the conspirators, or for the purpose of using criminal or unlawful means to the commission of an act not in itself unlawful.

The agreement or engagement of persons to co-operate in accomplishing some unlawful purpose, or some purpose which may not be unlawful, by unlawful means. 48 Me. 218.

Conspiracy is a consultation or agreement between two or more persons, either falsely to accuse another of a crime punishable by law; or wrongfully to injure or prejudice a third person, or any body of men, in any manner; or to commit any offense punishable by law; or to do any act with intent to prevent the course of justice; or to effect a legal purpose with a corrupt intent, or by improper means. Hawk. P. C. c. 72, § 2; Archb. Crim. Pl. 390, adding also combinations by journeymen to raise wages. 6 Ala. 765.

CONSPIRATIONE. An ancient writ that lay against conspirators. Reg. Orig. 134; Fitzh. Nat. Brev. 114.

CONSPIRATORS. Persons guilty of a conspiracy.

Those who bind themselves by oath, covenant, or other alliance that each of them shall aid the other falsely and maliciously to indict persons; or falsely to move and maintain pleas, etc. 33 Edw. I. St. 2. Besides these, there are conspirators in treasonable purposes; as for plotting against the government. Wharton.

CONSTABLE. In medieval law. The name given to a very high functionary under the French and English kings, the dignity and importance of whose office was only second to that of the monarch. He was in general the leader of the royal armies, and had cognizance of all matters pertaining to war and arms, exercising both civil and military jurisdiction. He was also charged with the conservation of the peace of the nation. Thus there was a "Constable of France" and a "Lord High Constable of England."

In English law. A public civil officer, whose proper and general duty is to keep the peace within his district, though he is frequently charged with additional duties. 1 Bl. Comm. 356.

High constables, in England, are officers appointed in every hundred or franchise, whose proper duty seems to be to keep the king's peace within their respective hundreds. 1 Bl. Comm. 356; 3 Steph. Comm. 47.

Petty constables are inferior officers in every town and parish, subordinate to the high constable of the hundred, whose principal duty is the preservation of the peace, though they also have other particular duties assigned to them by act of parliament, particularly the service of the summonses and the execution of the warrants of justices of the peace. 1 Bl. Comm. 356; 3 Steph. Comm. 47, 48.

Special constables are persons appointed (with or without their consent) by the magistrates to execute warrants on particular occasions, as in the case of riots, etc.

In American law. An officer of a municipal corporation (usually elected) whose duties are similar to those of the sheriff, though his powers are less and his jurisdiction smaller. He is to preserve the public peace, execute the process of magistrates' courts, and of some other tribunals, serve writs, attend the sessions of the criminal courts, have the custody of juries, and discharge other functions sometimes assigned to him by the local law or by statute.

CONSTABLE OF A CASTLE. In English law. An officer having charge of a castle; a warden, or keeper; otherwise called a "castellain."

CONSTABLE OF ENGLAND. (Called, also, "Marshal.") His office consisted in the care of the common peace of the realm in deeds of arms and matters of war. Lamb. Const. 4.

CONSTABLE OF SCOTLAND. An officer who was formerly entitled to command all the king's armies in the absence of the king, and to take cognizance of all crimes committed within four miles of the king's person or of parliament, the privy council, or any general convention of the states of the kingdom. The office was hereditary in the family of Errol, and was abolished by the 20 Geo. III. c. 43. Bell.; Ersk. Inst. 1, 3, 37.

CONSTABLE OF THE EXCHEQUER. An officer mentioned in Fleta, lib. 2, c. 31.

CONSTABLEWICK. In English law. The territorial jurisdiction of a constable; as bailiwick is of a bailiff or sheriff. 5 Nev. & M. 261.

CONSTABULARIUS. An officer of horse; an officer having charge of foot or horse; a naval commander; an officer having charge of military affairs generally. Spelman.

CONSTAT. It is clear or evident; it appears; it is certain; there is no doubt. *Non constat*, it does not appear.

A certificate which the clerk of the pipe and auditors of the exchequer made, at the request of any person who intended to plead or move in that court, for the discharge of anything. The effect of it was the certifying what appears (*constat*) upon record, touching the matter in question. Wharton.

CONSTAT D'HUISSIER. In French law. An affidavit made by a *huissier*, setting forth the appearance, form, quality, color, etc., of any article upon which a suit depends. Arg. Fr. Merc. Law, 554.

CONSTATE. To establish, constitute, or ordain. "Constating instruments" of a corporation are its charter, organic law, or the grant of powers to it. See examples of the use of the term, Green's Brice, Ultra Vires, p. 39; 37 N. J. Eq. 363.

CONSTITUENT. A word used as a correlative to "attorney," to denote one who constitutes another his agent or invests the other with authority to act for him.

It is also used in the language of politics, as a correlative to "representative," the constituents of a legislator being those whom he represents and whose interests he is to care for in public affairs; usually the electors of his district.

CONSTITUERE. To appoint, constitute, establish, ordain, or undertake. Used principally in ancient powers of attorney, and now supplanted by the English word "constitute."

CONSTITUIMUS. A Latin term, signifying *we constitute* or *appoint*.

CONSTITUTED AUTHORITIES. Officers properly appointed under the constitution for the government of the people.

CONSTITUTIO. In the civil law. An imperial ordinance or constitution, distinguished from *Lex*, *Senatus-Consultum*, and other kinds of law, and having its effect from the sole will of the emperor.

An establishment or settlement. Used of controversies settled by the parties without a trial. Calvin.

A sum paid according to agreement. Du Cange.

In old English law. An ordinance or statute. A provision of a statute.

CONSTITUTIO DOTIS. Establishment of dower.

CONSTITUTION. In public law. The organic and fundamental law of a nation or state, which may be written or unwritten, establishing the character and conception of its government, laying the basic principles to which its internal life is to be conformed, organizing the government, and regulating, distributing, and limiting the functions of its different departments, and prescribing the extent and manner of the exercise of sovereign powers.

In a more general sense, any fundamental or important law or edict; as the Novel Constitutions of Justinian; the Constitutions of Clarendon.

In American law. The written instrument agreed upon by the people of the Union or of a particular state, as the absolute rule of action and decision for all departments and officers of the government in respect to all the points covered by it, which must control until it shall be changed by the authority which established it, and in opposition to which any act or ordinance of any such department or officer is null and void. Cooley, Const. Lim. 3.

CONSTITUTIONAL. Consistent with the constitution; authorized by the constitution; not conflicting with any provision of the constitution or fundamental law of the state. Dependent upon a constitution, or secured or regulated by a constitution; as "constitutional monarchy," "constitutional rights."

CONSTITUTIONAL LAW. 1. That branch of the public law of a state which treats of the organization and frame of government, the organs and powers of sovereignty, the distribution of political and governmental authorities and functions, the fundamental principles which are to regulate the relations of government and subject, and which prescribes generally the plan and method according to which the public affairs of the state are to be administered.

2. That department of the science of law which treats of constitutions, their establishment, construction, and interpretation, and of the validity of legal enactments as tested by the criterion of conformity to the fundamental law.

3. A constitutional law is one which is consonant to, and agrees with, the constitution; one which is not in violation of any provision of the constitution of the particular state.

CONSTITUTIONES. Laws promulgated, *i. e.*, enacted, by the Roman Emperor. They were of various kinds, namely, the following: (1) *Edicta;* (2) *decreta;* (3) *rescripta,* called also "*epistolæ.*" Sometimes they were general, and intended to form a precedent for other like cases; at other times they were special, particular, or individual, (*personales,*) and not intended to form a precedent. The emperor had this power of irresponsible enactment by virtue of a certain *lex regia,* whereby he was made the fountain of justice and of mercy. Brown.

Constitutiones tempore posteriores potiores sunt his quæ ipsas præcesserunt. Dig. 1, 4, 4. Later laws prevail over those which preceded them.

CONSTITUTIONS OF CLARENDON. See CLARENDON.

CONSTITUTOR. In the civil law. One who, by a simple agreement, becomes responsible for the payment of another's debt.

CONSTITUTUM. In the civil law. An agreement to pay a subsisting debt which exists without any stipulation, whether of the promisor or another party. It differs from a stipulation in that it must be for an existing debt. Du Cange.

Constitutum esse eam domum unicuique nostrum debere existimari, ubi quisque sedes et tabulas haberet, suarumque rerum constitutionem fecisset. It is settled that that is to be considered the home of each one of us where he may have his habitation and account-books, and where he may have made an establishment of his business. Dig. 50, 16, 203.

CONSTRAINT. This term is held to be exactly equivalent with "restraint." 2 Tenn. Ch. 427.

In Scotch law. Constraint means duress.

CONSTRUCT. To build; erect; put together; make ready for use.

Constructio legis non facit injuriam. The construction of the law (a construction made by the law) works no injury. Co. Litt. 183; Broom, Max. 603. The law will make such a construction of an instrument as not to injure a party.

CONSTRUCTION. The process, or the art, of determining the sense, real meaning, or proper explanation of obscure or ambiguous terms or provisions in a statute, written instrument, or oral agreement, or the application of such subject to the case in question, by reasoning in the light derived from extraneous connected circumstances or laws or writings bearing upon the same or a connected matter, or by seeking and applying the probable aim and purpose of the provision.

It is to be noted that this term is properly distinguished from *interpretation*, although the two are often used synonymously. In strictness, interpretation is limited to exploring the written text, while construction goes beyond and may call in the aid of extrinsic considerations, as above indicated.

CONSTRUCTION, COURT OF. A court of equity or of common law, as the case may be, is called the court of construction with regard to wills, as opposed to the court of probate, whose duty is to decide whether an instrument be a will at all. Now, the court of probate may decide that a given instrument is a will, and yet the court of construction may decide that it has no operation, by reason of perpetuities, illegality, uncertainty, etc. Wharton.

CONSTRUCTIVE. That which is established by the mind of the law in its act of *construing* facts, conduct, circumstances, or instruments; that which has not the character assigned to it in its own essential nature, but acquires such character in consequence of the way in which it is regarded by a rule or policy of law; hence, inferred, implied, made out by legal interpretation.

CONSTRUCTIVE ASSENT. An assent or consent imputed to a party from a construction or interpretation of his conduct; as distinguished from one which he actually expresses.

CONSTRUCTIVE BREAKING INTO A HOUSE. A breaking made out by construction of law. As where a burglar gains an entry into a house by threats, fraud, or conspiracy. 2 Russ. Crimes, 9, 10.

CONSTRUCTIVE FRAUD. Constructive fraud consists (1) in any breach of duty which, without an actually fraudulent intent, gains an advantage to the person in fault, or any one claiming under him, by misleading another to his prejudice, or to the prejudice of any one claiming under him; or (2) in any such act or omission as the law specially declares to be fraudulent, without respect to actual fraud. Civil Code Cal. § 1573.

By *constructive frauds* are meant such acts or contracts as, though not originating in any actual evil design or contrivance to perpetrate a positive fraud or injury upon other persons, are yet, by their tendency to deceive or mislead other persons, or to violate private or public confidence, or to impair or injure the public interests, deemed equally reprehensible with positive fraud; and therefore are prohibited by law, as within the same reason and mischief as acts and contracts done *malo animo*. 1 Story, Eq. Jur. § 258.

CONSTRUCTIVE LARCENY. One where the felonious intent to appropriate the goods to his own use, at the time of the asportation, is made out by construction from the defendant's conduct, although, originally, the taking was not apparently felonious. 2 East, P. C. 685; 1 Leach, 212.

CONSTRUCTIVE MALICE. Implied malice; malice inferred from acts; malice imputed by law; malice which is not shown by direct proof of an intention to do injury, (express malice,) but which is inferentially established by the necessarily injurious results of the acts shown to have been committed.

CONSTRUCTIVE NOTICE. Information or knowledge of a fact imputed by law to a person, (although he may not actually have it,) because he could have discovered the fact by proper diligence, and his situation was such as to cast upon him the duty of inquiring into it.

CONSTRUCTIVE TAKING. A phrase used in the law to characterize an act not amounting to an actual appropriation of chattels, but which shows an intention to convert them to his use; as if a person intrusted with the possession of goods deals with them contrary to the orders of the owner.

CONSTRUCTIVE TOTAL LOSS. In marine insurance. This occurs where the loss or injury to the vessel insured does not amount to its total disappearance or destruction, but where, although the vessel still remains, the cost of repairing or recovering it would amount to more than its value when so repaired, and consequently the insured abandons it to the underwriters. See ACTUAL TOTAL LOSS.

CONSTRUCTIVE TREASON. Treason imputed to a person by law from his conduct or course of actions, though his deeds taken severally do not amount to actual treason. This doctrine is not known in the United States.

CONSTRUCTIVE TRUST. A trust raised by construction of law, or arising by operation of law, as distinguished from an express trust.

Wherever the circumstances of a transaction are such that the person who takes the legal estate in property cannot also enjoy the beneficial interest without necessarily violating some established principle of equity, the court will immediately raise a *constructive trust*, and fasten it upon the conscience of the legal owner, so as to convert him into a trustee for the parties who in equity are entitled to the beneficial enjoyment. Hill, Trustees, 116; 1 Spence, Eq. Jur. 511.

CONSTRUE. To put together; to arrange or marshal the words of an instrument. To ascertain the meaning of language by a process of arrangement and inference.

CONSUETUDINARIUS. In ecclesiastical law. A ritual or book, containing the rites and forms of divine offices, or the customs of abbeys and monasteries.

CONSUETUDINARY LAW. Customary law. Law derived by oral tradition from a remote antiquity. Bell.

CONSUETUDINES. In old English law. Customs. Thus, *consuetudines et assisa forestæ*, the customs and assise of the forest.

CONSUETUDINES FEUDORUM. (Lat. feudal customs.) A compilation of the law of feuds or fiefs in Lombardy, made A. D. 1170.

CONSUETUDINIBUS ET SERVICIIS. In old English law. A writ of right close, which lay against a tenant who deforced his lord of the rent or service due to him. Reg. Orig. 159; Fitzh. Nat. Brev. 151.

CONSUETUDO. Lat. A custom; an established usage or practice. Co. Litt. 58. Tolls; duties; taxes. Id. 58*b*.

CONSUETUDO ANGLICANA. The custom of England; the ancient common law, as distinguished from *lex*, the Roman or civil law.

Consuetudo contra rationem introducta potius usurpatio quam consuetudo appellari debet. A custom introduced against reason ought rather to be called a "usurpation" than a "custom." Co. Litt. 113.

CONSUETUDO CURIÆ. The custom or practice of a court. Hardr. 141.

Consuetudo debet esse certa; nam incerta pro nullâ habetur. Dav. 33. A custom should be certain; for an uncertain custom is considered null.

Consuetudo est altera lex. Custom is another law. 4 Coke, 21.

Consuetudo est optimus interpres legum. 2 Inst. 18. Custom is the best expounder of the laws.

Consuetudo et communis assuetudo vincit legem non scriptam, si sit specialis; et interpretatur legem scriptam, si lex sit generalis. Jenk. Cent. 273. Custom and common usage overcomes the unwritten law, if it be special; and interprets the written law, if the law be general.

Consuetudo ex certa causa rationabili usitata privat communem legem. A custom, grounded on a certain and reasonable cause, supersedes the common law. Litt. § 169; Co. Litt. 113; Broom, Max. 919.

Consuetudo, licet sit magnæ auctoritatis, nunquam tamen præjudicat manifestæ veritati. A custom, though it be of great authority, should never prejudice manifest truth. 4 Coke, 18.

Consuetudo loci observanda est. Litt. § 169. The custom of a place is to be observed.

Consuetudo manerii et loci observanda est. 6 Coke, 67. A custom of a manor and place is to be observed.

CONSUETUDO MERCATORUM. Lat. The custom of merchants, the same with *lex mercatoria*.

Consuetudo neque injuriâ oriri neque tolli potest. Lofft, 340. Custom can neither arise from nor be taken away by injury.

Consuetudo non trahitur in consequentiam. 3 Keb. 499. Custom is not drawn into consequence. 4 Jur. (N. S.) Ex. 139.

Consuetudo præscripta et legitima vincit legem. A prescriptive and lawful custom overcomes the law. Co. Litt. 113; 4 Coke, 21.

Consuetudo regni Angliæ est lex Angliæ. Jenk. Cent. 119. The custom of the kingdom of England is the law of England. See 2 Bl. Comm. 422.

Consuetudo semel reprobata non potest amplius induci. A custom once disallowed cannot be again brought forward, [or relied on.] Dav. 33.

Consuetudo tollit communem legem. Co. Litt. 33*b*. Custom takes away the common law.

Consuetudo volentes ducit, lex nolentes trahit. Custom leads the willing, law compels [drags] the unwilling. Jenk. Cent. 274.

CONSUL. In Roman law. During the republic, the name "consul" was given to the chief executive magistrate, two of whom were chosen annually. The office was continued under the empire, but its powers and prerogatives were greatly reduced. The name is supposed to have been derived from *consulo*, to consult, because these officers consulted with the senate on administrative measures.

In old English law. An ancient title of an earl.

In international law. An officer of a commercial character, appointed by the different states to watch over the mercantile interests of the appointing state and of its subjects in foreign countries. There are usually a number of consuls in every maritime country, and they are usually subject to a chief consul, who is called a "consul general." Brown.

The word "consul" has two meanings: (1) It denotes an officer of a particular grade in the consular service; (2) it has a broader generic sense, embracing all consular officers. 15 Ct. Cl. 64.

The official designations employed throughout this title shall be deemed to have the following meanings, respectively: *First.* "Consul general," "consul," and "commercial agent" shall be deemed to denote full, principal, and permanent consular officers, as distinguished from subordinates and substitutes. *Second.* "Deputy-consul" and "consular agent" shall be deemed to denote consular officers subordinate to such principals, exercising the powers and performing the duties within the limits of their consulates or commercial agencies respectively, the former at the same ports or places and the latter at ports or places different from those at which such principals are located respectively. *Third.* "Vice-consuls" and "vice-commercial agents" shall be deemed to denote consular officers who shall be substituted, temporarily, to fill the places of consuls general, consuls, or commercial agents, when they shall be temporarily absent or relieved from duty. *Fourth.* "Consular officer" shall be deemed to include consuls general, consuls, commercial agents, deputy-consuls, vice-consuls, vice-commercial agents, and consular agents, and none others. *Fifth.* "Diplomatic officer" shall be deemed to include ambassadors, envoys extraordinary, ministers plenipotentiary, ministers resident, commissioners, chargés d'affaires, agents, and secretaries of legation, and none others. Rev. St. U. S. § 1674.

CONSULAR COURTS. Courts held by the consuls of one country, within the territory of another, under authority given by treaty, for the settlement of civil cases between citizens of the country which the consul represents. In some instances they have also a criminal jurisdiction, but in this respect are subject to review by the courts of the home government. See Rev. St. U. S. § 4083.

CONSULTA ECCLESIA. In ecclesiastical law. A church full or provided for. Cowell.

CONSULTARY RESPONSE. The opinion of a court of law on a special case.

CONSULTATION. A writ whereby a cause which has been wrongfully removed by prohibition out of an ecclesiastical court to a temporal court is returned to the ecclesiastical court. Phillim. Ecc. Law, 1439.

A conference between the counsel engaged in a case, to discuss its questions or arrange the method of conducting it.

In French law. The opinion of counsel upon a point of law submitted to them.

CONSULTO. In the civil law. Designedly; intentionally. Dig. 28, 41.

CONSUMMATE. Completed; as distinguished from *initiate*, or that which is merely begun. The husband of a woman seised of an estate of inheritance becomes, by the birth of a child, tenant by the curtesy *initiate*, and may do many acts to charge the lands, but his estate is not *consummate* till the death of the wife. 2 Bl. Comm. 126, 128; Co. Litt. 30*a*.

CONSUMMATION. The completion of a thing; the completion of a marriage between two affianced persons by cohabitation.

CONTAGIOUS DISORDERS. Diseases which are capable of being transmitted by mediate or immediate contact.

CONTANGO. In English law. The commission received for carrying over or putting off the time of execution of a contract to deliver stocks or pay for them at a certain time. Wharton.

CONTEK. L. Fr. A contest, dispute, disturbance, opposition. Britt. c. 42; Kelham. *Conteckours;* brawlers; disturbers of the peace. Britt. c. 29.

CONTEMNER. One who has committed contempt of court.

CONTEMPLATION. The act of the mind in considering with attention. Continued attention of the mind to a particular subject. Consideration of an act or series of acts with the intention of doing or adopting them. The consideration of an event or state of facts with the expectation that it will transpire.

CONTEMPLATION OF BANKRUPTCY. Contemplation of a *state* of bankruptcy or a known insolvency and inability to carry on business, and a stoppage of business. 5 Reporter, 295, 299.

Something more is meant by the phrase than the expectation of insolvency; it includes the making provision against the results of it. 13 How. 150; 8 Bosw. 194.

By contemplation of bankruptcy is meant a contemplation of the breaking up of one's business, or an inability to continue it. Crabbe, 529.

CONTEMPORANEA EXPOSITIO. Lat. Contemporaneous exposition, or construction; a construction drawn from the *time* when, and the circumstances under which, the subject-matter to be construed, as a statute or custom, originated.

Contemporanea expositio est optima et fortissima in lege. Contemporaneous exposition is the best and strongest in the law. 2 Inst. 11. A statute is best explained by following the construction put upon it by judges who lived at the *time* it was made, or soon after. 10 Coke, 70; Broom, Max. 682.

CONTEMPT. Contumacy; a willful disregard of the authority of a court of justice or legislative body or disobedience to its lawful orders.

Contempt of court is committed by a person who does any act in willful contravention of its authority or dignity, or tending to impede or frustrate the administration of justice, or by one who, being under the court's authority as a party to a proceeding therein, willfully disobeys its lawful orders or fails to comply with an undertaking which he has given.

The disobedience of the defendant to the decree of that court, in this instance, is palpable, willful, and utterly inexcusable; and therefore constitutes, beyond a doubt, what is termed a "contempt," which is well described by an eminent jurist as "a disobedience to the court, by acting in opposition to the authority, justice, and dignity thereof," adding that "it commonly consists in a party doing otherwise than he is enjoined to do, or not doing what he is commanded or required by the process, order, or decree of the court; in all which cases the party disobeying is liable to be attached and committed for the contempt." 21 Conn. 199.

Contempts are of two kinds,—criminal and constructive. Criminal contempts are those committed in the immediate view and presence of the court, such as insulting language or acts of violence, which interrupt the regular proceedings in courts. Constructive contempts are those which arise from matters not transpiring in court, but in reference to failures to comply with the orders and decrees issued by the court, and to be performed elsewhere. 49 Me. 392.

Or they may be divided into such as are committed in the face of the court (*in facie curiæ*) which are punishable by commitment and fine, and such as are committed out of court, which are punishable by attachment. 1 Tidd, Pr. 479, 480. 4 Bl. Comm. 285, 286; 4 Steph. Comm. 348–353.

CONTEMPT OF CONGRESS, LEGISLATURE, or PARLIAMENT. Whatever obstructs or tends to obstruct the due course of proceeding of either house, or grossly reflects on the character of a member of either house, or imputes to him what it would be a libel to impute to an ordinary person, is a contempt of the house, and thereby a breach of privilege. Sweet.

CONTEMPTIBILITER. Lat. Contemptuously.

In old English law. Contempt, contempts. Fleta, lib. 2, c. 60, § 35.

CONTENTIOUS. Contested; adversary; litigated between adverse or contending parties; a judicial proceeding not merely *ex parte* in its character, but comprising attack and defense as between opposing parties, is so called. The litigious proceedings in ecclesiastical courts are sometimes said to belong to its "contentious" jurisdiction, in contradistinction to what is called its "voluntary" jurisdiction, which is exercised in the granting of licenses, probates of wills, dispensations, faculties, etc.

CONTENTIOUS JURISDICTION. In English ecclesiastical law. That branch of the jurisdiction of the ecclesiastical courts which is exercised upon adversary or *contentious* proceedings. See CONTENTIOUS.

CONTENTMENT, CONTENEMENT. A man's countenance or credit, which he has together with, and by reason of, his freehold; or that which is necessary for the support and maintenance of men, agreeably to their several qualities or states of life. Wharton; Cowell.

CONTENTS AND NOT-CONTENTS. In parliamentary law. The "contents" are those who, in the house of lords, express assent to a bill; the "not" or "non contents" dissent. May, Parl. Law, cc. 12, 357.

"CONTENTS UNKNOWN." Words sometimes annexed to a bill of lading of goods in cases. Their meaning is that the master only means to acknowledge the shipment, in good order, of the cases, as to their external condition. 12 How. 273.

CONTERMINOUS. Adjacent; adjoining; having a common boundary; coterminous.

CONTEST. To make defense to an adverse claim in a court of law; to oppose, resist, or dispute the case made by a plaintiff.

CONTESTATIO LITIS. In Roman law. Contestation of suit; the framing an issue; joinder in issue. The formal act of both the parties with which the proceedings *in jure* were closed when they led to a judicial investigation, and by which the neighbors whom the parties brought with them were called to testify. Mackeld. Rom. Law, § 219.

In old English law. Coming to an issue; the issue so produced. Crabb, Eng. Law, 216.

Contestatio litis eget terminos contradictarios. An issue requires terms of contradiction. Jenk. Cent. 117. To constitute an issue, there must be an affirmative on one side and a negative on the other

CONTESTATION OF SUIT. In an ecclesiastical cause, that stage of the suit which is reached when the defendant has answered the libel by giving in an allegation.

CONTESTED ELECTION. This phrase has no technical or legally defined meaning. An election may be said to be contested whenever an objection is formally urged against it which, if found to be true in fact, would invalidate it. This is true both as to objections founded upon some constitutional provision and to such as are based on statutes. 109 Ind. 116, 10 N. E. Rep. 600.

CONTEXT. The context of a particular sentence or clause in a statute, contract, will, etc., comprises those parts of the text which immediately precede and follow it. The context may sometimes be scrutinized, to aid in the interpretation of an obscure passage.

CONTIGUOUS. In close proximity; in actual close contact. 69 N. Y. 191. Touching; bounded or traversed by. The term is not synonymous with "vicinal." 32 La. Ann. 435.

CONTINENCIA. In Spanish law. Continency or unity of the proceedings in a cause. White, New Recop. b. 3, tit. 6, c. 1.

CONTINENS. In the Roman law. Continuing; holding together. Adjoining buildings were said to be *continentia*.

CONTINENTIA. In old English practice. Continuance or connection. Applied to the proceedings in a cause. Bract. fol. 362*b*.

CONTINGENCY. An event that may or may not happen, a doubtful or uncertain future event. The quality of being contingent.

A fortuitous event, which comes without design, foresight, or expectation. A contingent expense must be deemed to be an expense depending upon some future uncertain event. 39 Barb. 272.

CONTINGENCY OF A PROCESS. In Scotch law. Where two or more processes are so connected that the circumstances of the one are likely to throw light on the others, the process first enrolled is considered as the leading process, and those subsequently brought into court, if not brought in the same division, may be remitted to it, *ob contingentiam*, on account of their nearness or proximity in character to it. The effect of remitting processes in this manner is merely to bring them before the same division of the court or same lord ordinary. In other respects they remain distinct. Bell.

CONTINGENCY WITH DOUBLE ASPECT. A remainder is said to be "in a contingency with double aspect," when there is another remainder limited on the same estate, not in derogation of the first, but as a substitute for it in case it should fail. Fearne, Rem. 373.

CONTINGENT. Possible, but not assured; doubtful or uncertain; conditioned upon the occurrence of some future event which is itself uncertain or questionable.

This term, when applied to a use, remainder, devise, bequest, or other legal right or interest, implies that no present interest exists, and that whether such interest or right ever will exist depends upon a future uncertain event. 5 Barb. 692.

CONTINGENT DAMAGES. Where a demurrer has been filed to one or more counts in a declaration, and its consideration is postponed, and meanwhile other counts in the same declaration, not demurred to, are taken as issues, and tried, and damages awarded upon them, such damages are called "contingent damages."

CONTINGENT ESTATE. An estate which depends for its effect upon an event which may or may not happen; as an estate limited to a person not *in esse*, or not yet born. 2 Crabb, Real Prop. p. 4, § 946.

CONTINGENT INTEREST IN PERSONAL PROPERTY. It may be defined as a future interest not transmissible to the representatives of the party entitled thereto, in case he dies before it vests in possession. Thus, if a testator leaves the income of a fund to his wife for life, and the capital of the fund to be distributed among such of his children as shall be living at her death, the interest of each child during the widow's life-time is *contingent*, and in case of his death is not transmissible to his representatives. Mozley & Whitley.

CONTINGENT LEGACY. A legacy given to a person at a future uncertain time. that may or may not arrive; as "at his age of twenty-one," or "if" or "when he attains twenty-one." 2 Bl. Comm. 513; 2 Steph. Comm. 259.

A legacy made dependent upon some uncertain event. 1 Rop. Leg. 506.

A legacy which has not vested.

CONTINGENT REMAINDER. An estate in remainder which is limited to take effect either to a dubious and uncertain person, or upon a dubious and uncertain event, by which no present or particular interest passes to the remainder-man, so that the particular estate may chance to be determined and the remainder never take effect. 2 Bl. Comm. 169.

A remainder limited so as to depend upon an event or condition which may never happen or be performed, or which may not happen or be performed till after the determination of the preceding estate. Fearne, Rem. 3.

CONTINGENT USE. A use limited to take effect upon the happening of some future contingent event; as where lands are conveyed to the use of A. and B., after a marriage shall be had between them. 2 Bl. Comm. 334.

CONTINUAL CLAIM. In old English law. A formal claim made by a party entitled to enter upon any lands or tenements, but deterred from such entry by menaces, or bodily fear, for the purpose of preserving or keeping alive his right. It was called "continual," because it was required to be repeated once in the space of every year and day. It had to be made as near to the land as the party could approach with safety, and, when made in due form, had the same effect with, and in all respects amounted to, a legal entry. Litt. §§ 419-423; Co. Litt. 250*a*; 3 Bl. Comm. 175.

CONTINUANCE. The adjournment or postponement of an action pending in a court, to a subsequent day of the same or another term.

Also the entry of a continuance made upon the record of the court, for the purpose of formally evidencing the postponement, or of connecting the parts of the record so as to make one continuous whole.

CONTINUANDO. In pleading. A word which was formerly used in a special declaration of trespass when the plaintiff would recover damages for several trespasses in the same action; and, to avoid multiplicity of actions, a man might in one action of trespass recover damages for many trespasses, laying the first to be done with a *continuando* to the whole time in which the rest of the trespasses were done; which was in this form: *Continuando* (by continuing) the trespasses aforesaid, etc., from the day aforesaid, etc., until such a day, including the last trespass. Termes de la Ley.

CONTINUING CONSIDERATION. See CONSIDERATION.

CONTINUING DAMAGES. See DAMAGES.

CONTINUOUS ADVERSE USE. Is interchangeable with the term "uninterrupted adverse use." 59 Ind. 411.

CONTINUOUS EASEMENT. One the enjoyment of which is or may be continual, without the necessity of any actual interference by man, as a water-spout, or a right of light or air; as distinguished from a *discontinuous* easement, which is one the enjoyment of which can be had only by the interference of man, as a right of way, or a right to draw water. Washb. Easem. 13; Gale, Easem. 16; 21 N. Y 505; 60 Mich. 252, 27 N. W. Rep. 512. This distinction is derived from the French law. See Civil Code, art. 688.

CONTRA. Against, confronting, opposite to; on the other hand; on the contrary. The word is used in many Latin phrases, as appears by the following titles. In the books of reports, *contra*, appended to the name of a judge or counsel, indicates that he held a view of the matter in argument *contrary* to that next before advanced. Also, after citation of cases in support of a position, *contra* is often prefixed to citations of cases opposed to it.

CONTRA BONOS MORES. Against good morals. Contracts *contra bonos mores* are void.

CONTRA FORMAM COLLATIONIS. In old English law. A writ that issued where lands given in perpetual alms to lay houses of religion, or to an abbot and convent, or to the warden or master of an hospital and his convent, to find certain poor men with necessaries, and do divine service, etc., were alienated, to the disherison of the house and church. By means of this writ the donor or his heirs could recover the lands. Reg. Orig. 238; Fitzh. Nat. Brev. 210.

CONTRA FORMAM DONI. Against the form of the grant. See FORMEDON.

CONTRA FORMAM FEOFFAMENTI. In old English law. A writ that lay for the heir of a tenant, enfeoffed of certain lands or tenements, by charter of feoffment from a lord to make certain services and suits to his court, who was afterwards distrained for more services than were mentioned in the charter. Reg. Orig. 176; Old Nat. Brev. 162.

CONTRA FORMAM STATUTI. In criminal pleading. (Contrary to the form of the statute in such case made and provided.) The usual conclusion of every indictment, etc., brought for an offense created by statute.

CONTRA JUS BELLI. Lat. Against the law of war. 1 Kent, Comm. 6.

CONTRA JUS COMMUNE. Against common right or law; contrary to the rule of the common law. Bract. fol. 48*b*.

Contra legem facit qui id facit quod lex prohibit; in fraudem vero qui, salvis verbis legis, sententiam ejus circumvenit. He does contrary to the law who does what the law prohibits; he acts in fraud of the law who, the letter of the law being inviolate, uses the law contrary to its intention. Dig. 1, 3, 29.

CONTRA LEGEM TERRÆ. Against the law of the land.

Contra negantem principia non est disputandum. There is no disputing against one who denies first principles. Co. Litt. 343.

Contra non valentem agere nulla currit præscriptio. No prescription runs against a person unable to bring an action. Broom, Max. 903.

CONTRA OMNES GENTES. Against all people. Formal words in old covenants of warranty. Fleta, lib. 3, c. 14, § 11.

CONTRA PACEM. Lat. Against the peace. A phrase used in the Latin forms of indictments, and also of actions for trespass, to signify that the offense alleged was committed against the public peace, *i. e.*, involved a breach of the peace. The full formula was *contra pacem domini regis*, against the peace of the lord the king. In modern pleading, in this country, the phrase "against the peace of the commonwealth" or "of the people" is used.

CONTRA PROFERENTEM. Against the party who proffers or puts forward a thing.

CONTRA TABULAS. In the civil law. Against the will, (testament.) Dig. 37, 4.

CONTRA VADIUM ET PLEGIUM. In old English law. Against gage and pledge. Bract. fol. 15*b*.

Contra veritatem lex nunquam aliquid permittit. The law never suffers anything contrary to truth. 2 Inst. 252.

CONTRABAND. Against law or treaty; prohibited. Goods exported from or imported into a country against its laws. Brande. Articles, the importation or exportation of which is prohibited by law. P. Enc.

CONTRABAND OF WAR. Certain classes of merchandise, such as arms and ammunition, which, by the rules of international law, cannot lawfully be furnished or carried by a neutral nation to either of two belligerents; if found in transit in neutral vessels, such goods may be seized and condemned for violation of neutrality.

A recent American author on international law says that, "by the term 'contraband of war,' we now understand a class of articles of commerce which *neutrals* are prohibited from furnishing to either one of the belligerents, for the reason that, by so doing, injury is done to the other belligerent;" and he treats of the subject, chiefly, in its relation to commerce upon the high seas. (Hall, Int. Law, 570, 592.) 4 Heisk. 345.

CONTRACAUSATOR. A criminal; one prosecuted for a crime.

CONTRACT. An agreement, upon sufficient consideration, to do or not to do a particular thing. 2 Bl. Comm. 442; 2 Kent, Comm. 449.

A covenant or agreement between two or more persons, with a lawful consideration or cause. Jacob.

A deliberate engagement between competent parties, upon a legal consideration, to do, or abstain from doing, some act. Wharton.

A contract or agreement is either where a promise is made on one side and assented to on the other; or where two or more persons enter into engagement with each other by a promise on either side. 2 Steph. Comm. 54.

A contract is an agreement by which one person obligates himself to another to give, to do, or permit, or not to do, something expressed or implied by such agreement. Civil Code La. art. 1761.

A contract is an agreement to do or not to do a certain thing. Civil Code Cal. § 1549.

A contract is an agreement between two or more parties for the doing or not doing of some specified thing. Code Ga. 1882, § 2714.

A contract is an agreement between two or more persons to do or not to do a particular thing; and the *obligation* of a contract is found in the terms in which the contract is expressed, and is the duty thus assumed by the contracting parties respectively to perform the stipulations of such contract. When that duty is recognized and enforced by the municipal law, it is one of *perfect*, and when not so recognized and enforced, of *imperfect*, obligation. 31 Conn. 265.

The writing which contains the agreement of parties, with the terms and conditions, and which serves as a proof of the obligation.

Contracts may be classified on several different methods, according to the element in them which is brought into prominence. The usual classifications are as follows:

Record, specialty, simple. Contracts are divided into three classes: (1) Contracts of record, such as judgments, recognizances, and statutes staple; (2) specialties, which are under seal, such as deeds and bonds; (3) simple contracts, or contracts by parol. There is no such fourth class as contracts in writing, distinct from verbal and sealed contracts; both verbal and written contracts are included in the class of simple contracts, and the only distinction between them is in regard to the mode of proof. Wharton.

Contracts of record are not really contracts at all, but are transactions which, being entered on the records of certain courts called "courts of record," are conclusive proof of the facts thereby appearing, and could formerly be enforced by action of law as if they had been put in the shape of a contract. They consist of judgments, recognizances, etc. Sweet.

Express and implied. When the agreement of the parties is definite and formal, and is stated either verbally or in writing, the contract is *express;* but when its terms have to be gathered by inference and deduction from facts or conduct, it is *implied*.

Executed and executory. Contracts are also distinguished into executed and executory; *executed,* where nothing remains to be done by either party, and where the transaction is completed at the moment that the arrangement is made, as where an article is sold and delivered, and payment therefor is made on the spot; *executory,* where some future act is to be done, as where an agreement is made to build a house in six months, or to do an act on or before some future day, or to lend money upon a certain interest, payable at a future time. Wharton.

An executed contract is one in which all the parties thereto have performed all the obligation which they have originally assumed. An executory contract is one in which something remains to be done by one or more parties. Code Ga. 1882, § 2715.

An executed contract is one the object of which is fully performed. All others are executory. Civil Code Cal. § 1661.

Entire and severable. An *entire* contract is one the consideration of which is entire on both sides. The entire fulfillment of the promise by either is a condition precedent to the fulfillment of any part of the promise by the other. Whenever, therefore, there is a contract to pay the gross sum for a certain and definite consideration, the contract is entire. A *severable* contract is one the consideration of which is, by its terms, susceptible of apportionment on either side, so as to correspond to the unascertained consideration on the other side, as a contract to pay a person the worth of his services so long as he will do certain work; or to give a certain price for every bushel of so much corn as corresponds to a sample. Wharton.

Principal and accessory. A *principal* contract is one which stands by itself, justifies its own existence, and is not subordinate or auxiliary to any other. *Accessory* contracts are those made for assuring the performance of a prior contract, either by the same parties or by others, such as suretyship, mortgage, and pledges. Civil Code La. art. 1764.

Unilateral and bilateral. A *unilateral* contract is one in which one party makes an express engagement or undertakes a performance, without receiving in return any express engagement or promise of performance from the other. *Bilateral* (or reciprocal) contracts are those by which the parties expressly enter into mutual engagements, such as sale or hire. Civil Code La. art. 1758; Poth. Obl. 1, 1, 1, 2.

Consensual and real. *Consensual* contracts are such as are founded upon and completed by the mere agreement of the contracting parties, without any external formality or symbolic act to fix the obligation. *Real* contracts are those in which it is necessary that there should be something more than mere consent, such as a loan of money, deposit, or pledge, which, from their nature, require a delivery of the thing, (*res.*)

Certain and hazardous. *Certain* contracts are those in which the thing to be done is supposed to depend on the will of the party, or when, in the usual course of events, it must happen in the manner stipulated. *Hazardous* contracts are those in which the performance of that which is one of its objects depends on an uncertain event. Civil Code La. 1769.

Commutative and independent. *Commutative* contracts are those in which what is done, given, or promised by one party is considered as an equivalent to or in consideration of what is done, given, or promised by the other. Civil Code La. 1761. *Independent* contracts are those in which the mutual acts or promises have no relation to each other, either as equivalents or as considerations. Civil Code La. 1762.

Gratuitous and onerous. *Gratuitous* contracts are those of which the object is the benefit of the person with whom it is made, without any profit or advantage received or promised as a consideration for it. It is not, however, the less gratuitous if it proceed either from gratitude for a benefit before received or from the hope of receiving one hereafter, although such benefit be of a pecuniary nature. Civil Code La. 1766. *Onerous* contracts are those in which something is given or promised as a consideration for the engagement or gift, or some service, interest, or condition is imposed on what is given or promised, although unequal to it in value.

Mutual interest, mixed, etc. Contracts of *mutual interest* are such as are entered into for the reciprocal interest and utility of each of the parties; as sales, exchange, partnership, and the like. *Mixed* contracts are those by which one of the parties confers a benefit on the other, receiving something of inferior value in return, such as a donation subject to a charge. Contracts *of beneficence* are those by which only one of the contracting parties is benefited; as, loans, deposit, and mandate. Poth. Obl. 1, 1, 1, 2.

CONTRACT OF BENEVOLENCE. A contract made for the benefit of one of the contracting parties only, as a mandate or deposit.

CONTRACT OF RECORD. A contract of record is one which has been declared and adjudicated by a court having jurisdiction, or which is entered of record in obedience to, or in carrying out, the judgments of a court. Code Ga. 1882, § 2716.

CONTRACT OF SALE. A contract by which one of the contracting parties, called the "seller," enters into an obligation to the other to cause him to have freely, by a title of proprietor, a thing, for the price of a certain sum of money, which the other contracting party, called the "buyer," on his part obliges himself to pay. Poth. Cont.

CONTRACTION. Abbreviation; abridgment or shortening of a word by omitting a letter or letters or a syllable, with a mark over the place where the elision occurs. This was customary in records written in the ancient "court hand," and is frequently found in the books printed in black-letter.

CONTRACTOR. This term is strictly applicable to any person who enters into a contract, but is commonly reserved to designate one who, for a fixed price, undertakes to procure the performance of works on a large scale, or the furnishing of goods in large quantities, whether for the public or a company or individual.

The primary meaning of the word is one who contracts; one of the parties to a bargain. He who agrees to do anything for another is a contractor. 12 N. Y. 628.

CONTRACTUS. Contract; a contract; contracts.

CONTRACTUS BONÆ FIDEI. In Roman law. Contracts of good faith. Those contracts which, when brought into litigation, were not determined by the rules of the strict law alone, but allowed the judge to examine into the *bona fides* of the transaction, and to hear equitable considerations against their enforcement. In this they were opposed to contracts *stricti juris*, against which equitable defenses could not be entertained.

CONTRACTUS CIVILES. In Roman law. Civil contracts. Those contracts which were recognized as actionable by the strict civil law of Rome, or as being founded upon a particular statute, as distinguished from those which could not be enforced in the courts except by the aid of the prætor, who, through his equitable powers, gave an action upon them. The latter were called "*contractus prætorii.*"

Contractus est quasi actus contra actum. 2 Coke, 15. A contract is, as it were, act against act.

Contractus ex turpi causa, vel contra bonos mores, nullus est. A contract founded on a base consideration, or against good morals, is null. Hob. 167.

Contractus legem ex conventione accipiunt. Contracts receive legal sanction from the agreement of the parties. Dig. 16, 3, 1, 6.

CONTRADICT. In practice. To disprove. To prove a fact contrary to what has been asserted by a witness.

CONTRADICTION IN TERMS. A phrase of which the parts are expressly inconsistent, as, *e. g.*, "an innocent murder;" "a fee-simple for life."

CONTRÆSCRITURA. In Spanish law. A counter-writing; counter-letter. A document executed at the same time with an act of sale or other instrument, and operating by way of defeasance or otherwise modifying the apparent effect and purport of the original instrument.

CONTRAFACTIO. Counterfeiting; as *contrafactio sigilli regis*, counterfeiting the king's seal. Cowell.

CONTRAINTE PAR CORPS. In French law. The civil process of arrest of the person, which is imposed upon vendors falsely representing their property to be unincumbered, or upon persons mortgaging property which they are aware does not belong to them, and in other cases of moral heinousness. Brown.

CONTRALIGATIO. In old English law. Counter-obligation. Literally, counter-binding. *Est enim obligatio quasi contraligatio.* Fleta, lib. 2, c. 56, § 1.

CONTRAMANDATIO. A countermanding. *Contramandatio placiti*, in old English law, was the respiting of a defendant, or giving him further time to answer, by countermanding the day fixed for him to plead, and appointing a new day; a sort of imparlance.

CONTRAMANDATUM. A lawful excuse, which a defendant in a suit by attorney alleges for himself to show that the plaintiff has no cause of complaint. Blount.

CONTRAPLACITUM. In old English law. A counter-plea. Townsh. Pl. 61.

CONTRAPOSITIO. In old English law. A plea or answer. Blount. A counter-position.

CONTRARIENTS. This word was used in the time of Edw. II. to signify those who were opposed to the government, but were neither rebels nor traitors. Jacob.

Contrariorum contraria est ratio. Hob. 344. The reason of contrary things is contrary.

CONTRAROTULATOR. A controller. One whose business it was to observe the money which the collectors had gathered for the use of the king or the people. Cowell.

CONTRAROTULATOR PIPÆ. An officer of the exchequer that writeth out summons twice every year, to the sheriffs, to levy the rents and debts of the pipe. Blount.

CONTRAT. In French law. Contracts are of the following varieties: (1) *Bilateral*, or *synallagmatique*, where each party is bound to the other to do what is just and proper; or (2) *unilateral*, where the one side only is bound; or (3) *commutatif*, where one does to the other something which is supposed to be an equivalent for what the other does to him; or (4) *aléatoire*, where the consideration for the act of the one is a mere chance; or (5) *contrat de bienfaisance*, where the one party procures to the other a purely gratuitous benefit; or (6) *contrat à titre onereux*, where each party is bound under some duty to the other. Brown.

CONTRATALLIA. In old English law. A counter-tally. A term used in the exchequer. Mem. in Scacc. M. 26 Edw. I.

CONTRATENERE. To hold against; to withhold. Whishaw.

CONTRAVENING EQUITY. A right or equity, in another person, which is inconsistent with and opposed to the equity sought to be enforced or recognized.

CONTRAVENTION. In French law. An act which violates the law, a treaty, or an agreement which the party has made. That infraction of the law punished by a fine which does not exceed fifteen francs and by an imprisonment not exceeding three days. Pen. Code, 1.

In Scotch law. The act of breaking through any restraint imposed by deed, by covenant, or by a court.

CONTRECTARE. Lat. **In the civil law.** To handle; to take hold of; to meddle with.

In old English law. To treat. *Vel malè contrectet;* or shall ill treat. Fleta, lib. 1, c. 17, § 4.

CONTRECTATIO. In the civil and old English law. Touching; handling; meddling. The act of removing a thing from its place in such a manner that, if the thing be not restored, it will amount to theft.

Contrectatio rei alienæ, animo furandi, est furtum. Jenk. Cent. 132. The touching or removing of another's property, with an intention of stealing, is theft.

CONTREFACON. In French law. The offense of printing or causing to be printed a book, the copyright of which is held by another, without authority from him. Merl. Repert.

CONTRE-MAITRE. In French marine law. The chief officer of a vessel, who, in case of the sickness or absence of the master, commanded in his place. Literally, the counter-master.

CONTRIBUTE. To supply a share or proportional part of money or property towards the prosecution of a common enterprise or the discharge of a joint obligation.

CONTRIBUTION. In common law. The sharing of a loss or payment among several. The act of any one or several of a number of co-debtors, co-sureties, etc., in reimbursing one of their number who has paid the whole debt or suffered the whole liability, each to the extent of his proportionate share.

In maritime law. Where the property of one of several parties interested in a vessel and cargo has been voluntarily sacrificed for the common safety, (as by throwing goods overboard to lighten the vessel,) such loss must be made good by the contribution of the others, which is termed "general average." 3 Kent, Comm. 232-244; 1 Story, Eq. Jur. § 490.

In the civil law. A partition by which the creditors of an insolvent debtor divide among themselves the proceeds of his property proportionably to the amount of their respective credits. Code La. art. 2522, no. 10.

Contribution is the division which is made among the heirs of the succession of the debts with which the succession is charged, according to the proportion which each is bound to bear. Civil Code La. art. 1420.

CONTRIBUTIONE FACIENDA. In old English law. A writ that lay where tenants in common were bound to do some act, and one of them was put to the whole burthen, to compel the rest to make contribution. Reg. Orig. 175; Fitzh. Nat. Brev. 162.

CONTRIBUTORY. A person liable to contribute to the assets of a company which is being wound up, as being a member or (in some cases) a past member thereof. Mozley & Whitley.

CONTRIBUTORY NEGLIGENCE. Contributory negligence, when set up as a defense to an action for injuries alleged to have been caused by the defendant's negligence, means any want of ordinary care on the part of the person injured, (or on the part of another whose negligence is imputable to him,) which combined and concurred with the defendant's negligence, and contributed to the injury as a proximate cause thereof, and as an element without which the injury would not have occurred.

CONTROLLER. A comptroller, which see.

CONTROLMENT. In old English law. The controlling or checking of another officer's account; the keeping of a counter-roll.

CONTROVER. In old English law. An inventer or deviser of false news. 2 Inst. 227.

CONTROVERSY. A litigated question; adversary proceeding in a court of law; a civil action or suit, either at law or in equity.

It differs from "case," which includes all suits, criminal as well as civil; whereas "controversy" is a civil and not a criminal proceeding. 2 Dall. 419, 431, 432.

CONTROVERT. To dispute; to deny; to oppose or contest; to take issue on.

CONTUBERNIUM. In Roman law. The marriage of slaves; a permitted cohabitation.

CONTUMACE CAPIENDO. In English law. Excommunication in all cases of contempt in the spiritual courts is discontinued by 53 Geo. III. c. 127, § 2, and in lieu thereof, where a lawful citation or sentence has not been obeyed, the judge shall have power, after a certain period, to pronounce such person contumacious and in contempt, and to signify the same to the court of chancery, whereupon a writ *de contumace capiendo* shall issue from that court, which shall have the same force and effect as formerly belonged, in case of contempt, to a writ *de excommunicato capiendo*. (2 & 3 Wm. IV. c. 93; 3 & 4 Vict. c. 93.) Wharton.

CONTUMACY. The refusal or intentional omission of a person who has been duly cited before a court to appear and defend the charge laid against him, or, if he is duly before the court, to obey some lawful order or direction made in the cause. In the former case it is called "presumed" contumacy; in the latter, "actual." The term is chiefly used in ecclesiastical law. See 3 Curt. Ecc. 1.

CONTUMAX. One accused of a crime who refuses to appear and answer to the charge. An outlaw.

CONTUSION. In medical jurisprudence. A bruise; a hurt or injury to the flesh or some part of the body by the blow of a blunt instrument, or by a fall, producing no severance of tissue or apparent wound. If the skin is broken, it is called a "contused wound."

CONTUTOR. Lat. In the civil law. A co-tutor, or co-guardian. Inst. 1, 24, 1.

CONUSANCE. In English law. Cognizance or jurisdiction. Conusance of pleas. Termes de la Ley.

CONUSANCE, CLAIM OF. See COGNIZANCE.

CONUSANT. One who knows; as, if a party knowing of an agreement in which he has an interest makes no objection to it, he is said to be conusant. Co. Litt. 157.

CONUSEE. See COGNIZEE.

CONUSOR. See COGNIZOR.

CONVENABLE. In old English law. Suitable; agreeable; convenient; fitting. Litt. § 103.

CONVENE. In the civil law. To bring an action.

CONVENIENT. Proper; just; suitable.

CONVENIT. In civil and old English law. It is agreed; it was agreed.

CONVENT. The fraternity of an abbey or priory, as *societas* is the number of fellows in a college. A religious house, now regarded as a merely voluntary association, not importing civil death. 33 Law J. Ch. 308.

CONVENTICLE. A private assembly or meeting for the exercise of religion. The word was first an appellation of reproach to the religious assemblies of Wycliffe in the reigns of Edward III. and Richard II., and was afterwards applied to a meeting of dissenters from the established church. As this word in strict propriety denotes an unlawful assembly, it cannot be justly applied to the assembling of persons in places of worship licensed according to the requisitions of law. Wharton.

CONVENTIO. In canon law. The act of summoning or calling together the parties by summoning the defendant.

In the civil law. A compact, agreement, or convention. An agreement between two or more persons respecting a legal relation between them. The term is one of very wide scope, and applies to all classes of subjects in which an engagement or business relation may be founded by agreement. It is to be distinguished from the negotiations or preliminary transactions on the object of the convention and fixing its extent, which are not binding so long as the convention is not concluded. Mackeld. Rom. Law, §§ 385, 386.

In contracts. An agreement; a covenant. Cowell.

CONVENTIO IN UNUM. In the civil law. The agreement between the two parties to a contract upon the sense of the contract proposed. It is an essential part of the contract, following the pollicitation or proposal emanating from the one, and followed by the consension or agreement of the other.

Conventio privatorum non potest publico juri derogare. The agreement of private persons cannot derogate from public right, *i. e.*, cannot prevent the application of general rules of law, or render valid any contravention of law. Co. Litt. 166*a;* Wing. Max. p. 746, max. 201.

Conventio vincit legem. The express agreement of parties overcomes [prevails against] the law. Story, Ag. § 368.

CONVENTION. In Roman law. An agreement between parties; a pact. A convention was a mutual engagement between two persons, possessing all the subjective requisites of a contract, but which did not give rise to an action, nor receive the sanction of the law, as bearing an "obligation," until the objective requisite of a solemn ceremonial, (such as *stipulatio*) was supplied. In other words, convention was the informal agreement of the parties, which formed the basis of a contract, and which became a contract when the external formalities were superimposed. See Maine, Anc. Law, 313.

"The division of conventions into contracts and pacts was important in the Roman law. The former were such conventions as already, by the older civil law, founded an obligation and action; all the other conventions were termed 'pacts.' These generally did not produce an actionable obligation. Actionability was subsequently given to several pacts, whereby they received the same power and efficacy that contracts received." Mackeld. Rom. Law, § 395.

In English law. An extraordinary assembly of the houses of lords and commons, without the assent or summons of the sovereign. It can only be justified *ex necessitate rei*, as the parliament which restored Charles II., and that which disposed of the crown and kingdom to William and Mary. Wharton.

Also the name of an old writ that lay for the breach of a covenant.

In legislation. An assembly of delegates or representatives chosen by the people for special and extraordinary legislative purposes, such as the framing or revision of a state constitution. Also an assembly of delegates chosen by a political party, or by the party organization in a larger or smaller territory, to nominate candidates for an approaching election.

CONVENTIONAL. Depending on, or arising from, the mutual agreement of parties; as distinguished from *legal*, which means created by, or arising from, the act of the law.

CONVENTIONAL ESTATES. Those freeholds not of inheritance or estates for life, which are created by the express acts of the parties, in contradistinction to those which are legal and arise from the operation of law.

CONVENTIONAL MORTGAGE. The conventional mortgage is a contract by which a person binds the whole of his property, or a portion of it only, in favor of another, to secure the execution of some engagement, but without divesting himself of possession. Civil Code La. art. 3290.

CONVENTIONE. The name of a writ for the breach of any covenant in writing, whether real or personal. Reg. Orig. 115; Fitzh. Nat. Brev. 145.

CONVENTIONS. This name is sometimes given to compacts or treaties with foreign countries as to the apprehension and extradition of fugitive offenders. See EXTRADITION.

CONVENTUAL CHURCH. In ecclesiastical law. That which consists of regular clerks, professing some order or religion; or of dean and chapter; or other societies of spiritual men.

CONVENTUALS. Religious men united in a convent or religious house. Cowell.

CONVENTUS. A coming together; a convention or assembly. *Conventus magnatum vel procerum* (the assembly of chief men or peers) was one of the names of the English parliament. 1 Bl. Comm. 148.

In the civil law. The term meant a gathering together of people; a crowd assembled for any purpose; also a convention, pact, or bargain.

CONVENTUS JURIDICUS. In the Roman law. A court of sessions held in the Roman provinces, by the president of the province, assisted by a certain number of counsellors and assessors, at fixed periods, to hear and determine suits, and to provide for the civil administration of the province. Schm. Civil Law, Introd. 17.

CONVERSANT. One who is in the habit of being in a particular place is said to be conversant there. Barnes, 162. Acquainted; familiar.

CONVERSANTES. In old English law. Conversant or dwelling; commorant.

CONVERSE. The transposition of the subject and predicate in a proposition, as: "Everything is good in its place." *Converse*, "Nothing is good which is not in its place." Wharton.

CONVERSION. In equity. The transformation of one species of property into another, as money into land or land into money; or, more particularly, a fiction of law, by which equity assumes that such a transformation has taken place (contrary to the fact) when it is rendered necessary by the equities of the case,—as to carry into effect the directions of a will or settlement,—and by which the property so dealt with becomes invested with the prop rties and attributes of that into which it is supposed to have been converted.

At law. An unauthorized assumption and exercise of the right of ownership over goods or personal chattels belonging to another, to the alteration of their condition or the exclusion of the owner's rights. 44 Me. 197; 36 N. H. 311; 45 Wis. 262.

Conversion is defined to be an unauthorized assumption and exercise of the right of ownership over goods belonging to another to the exclusion of the owner's rights. A *constructive* conversion takes place when a person does such acts in reference to the goods of another as amount in law to appropriation of the property to himself. Every unauthorized taking of personal property, and all intermeddling with it, beyond the extent of the authority conferred, in case a limited authority has been given, with intent so to apply and dispose of it as to alter its condition or interfere with the owner's dominion, is a conversion. 68 N. Y. 524.

"Conversion" and "carrying away" are not synonymous nor convertible terms. There may be a conversion without any carrying away. 26 Ala. 101.

CONVEY. To pass or transmit the title to property from one to another; to transfer property or the title to property by deed or instrument under seal.

To convey real estate is, by an appropriate instrument, to transfer the legal title to it from the present owner to another. 29 Conn. 356.

Convey relates properly to the disposition of real property, not to personal. 21 Barb. 551, 561.

CONVEYANCE. In pleading. Introduction or inducement.

In real property law. The transfer of the title of land from one person or class of persons to another. 21 Barb. 551; 29 Conn. 356.

An instrument in writing under seal, (anciently termed an "assurance,") by which some estate or interest in lands is transferred from one person to another; such as a deed, mortgage, etc. 2 Bl. Comm. 293, 295, 309.

Conveyance includes every instrument in writing by which any estate or interest in real estate is created, aliened, mortgaged, or assigned, or by which the title to any real estate may be affected in law or equity, except last wills and testaments, leases for a term not exceeding three years, and executory contracts for the sale or purchase of lands. 1 Rev. St. N. Y. p. 762, § 38; Gen. St. Minn. 1878, c. 40, § 26; How. St. Mich. 1882, § 5689.

The term "conveyance," as used in the California Code, embraces every instrument in writing by which any estate or interest in real property is created, aliened, mortgaged, or incumbered, or by which the title to any real property may be affected, except wills. Civil Code Cal. § 1215.

CONVEYANCE OF VESSELS. The transfer of the title to vessels.

CONVEYANCER. One whose business it is to draw deeds, bonds, mortgages, wills, writs, or other legal papers, or to examine titles to real estate. 14 St. at Large, 118.

He who draws conveyances; especially a barrister who confines himself to drawing conveyances, and other chamber practice. Mozley & Whitley.

CONVEYANCING. A term including both the science and act of transferring titles to real estate from one man to another.

Conveyancing is that part of the lawyer's business which relates to the alienation and transmission of property and other rights from one person to another, and to the framing of legal documents intended to create, define, transfer, or extinguish rights. It therefore includes the investigation of the title to land, and the preparation of agreements, wills, articles of association, private statutes operating as conveyances, and many other instruments in addition to conveyances properly so called. Sweet.

CONVEYANCING COUNSEL TO THE COURT OF CHANCERY. Certain counsel, not less than six in number, appointed by the lord chancellor, for the purpose of assisting the court of chancery, or any judge thereof, with their opinion in matters of title and conveyancing. Mozley & Whitley.

Convicia si irascaris tua divulgas; spreta exolescunt. 3 Inst. 198. If you be moved to anger by insults, you publish them; if despised, they are forgotten.

CONVICIUM. In the civil law. The name of a species of slander or injury uttered in public, and which charged some one with some act *contra bonos mores*.

CONVICT, *v*. To condemn after judidial investigation; to find a man guilty of a criminal charge. The word was formerly used also in the sense of finding against the defendant in a civil case.

CONVICT, *n*. One who has been condemned by a court. One who has been adjudged guilty of a crime or misdemeanor. Usually spoken of condemned felons or the prisoners in penitentiaries.

Formerly a man was said to be convict when he had been found guilty of treason or felony, but before judgment had been passed on him, after which he was said to be attaint, (*q. v.*) Co. Litt. 390*b*.

CONVICTED. This term has a definite signification in law, and means that a judgment of final condemnation has been pronounced against the accused. 10 Tex. App. 469.

CONVICTION. In practice. In a general sense, the result of a criminal trial which ends in a judgment or sentence that the prisoner is guilty as charged.

Finding a person guilty by verdict of a jury. 1 Bish. Crim. Law, § 223.

A record of the summary proceedings upon any penal statute before one or more justices of the peace or other persons duly authorized, in a case where the offender has been *convicted* and sentenced. Holthouse.

Summary conviction is one which takes place before an authorized magistrate without the intervention of a jury.

In ordinary phrase, the meaning of the word "conviction" is the finding by the jury of a verdict that the accused is guilty. But, in legal parlance, it often denotes the final judgment of the court. 69 N. Y. 109.

The ordinary legal meaning of "conviction," when used to designate a particular stage of a criminal prosecution triable by a jury, is the confession of the accused in open court, or the verdict returned against him by the jury, which ascertains and publishes the fact of his guilt; while "judgment" or "sentence" is the appropriate word to denote the action of the court before which the trial is had, declaring the consequences to the convict of the fact thus ascertained. A pardon granted after verdict of guilty, but before sentence, and pending a hearing upon exceptions taken by the accused during the trial, is granted after conviction, within the meaning of a constitutional restriction upon granting pardon before conviction. When, indeed, the word "conviction" is used to describe the effect of the guilt of the accused as judicially proved in one case, when pleaded or given in evidence in another, it is sometimes used in a more comprehensive sense, including the judgment of the court upon the verdict or confession of guilt; as, for instance, in speaking of the plea of *autrefois convict*, or of the effect of guilt, judicially ascertained, as a disqualification of the convict. 109 Mass. 323. See 17 Pick. 380.

CONVIVIUM. A tenure by which a tenant was bound to provide meat and drink for his lord at least once in the year. Cowell.

CONVOCATION. In ecclesiastical law. The general assembly of the clergy to consult upon ecclesiastical matters.

CONVOY. A naval force, under the command of an officer appointed by government, for the protection of merchant-ships and others, during the whole voyage, or such part of it as is known to require such protection. Marsh. Ins. b. 1, c. 9, § 5; Park, Ins. 388; Peake, Add. Cas. 143*n*; 2 H. Bl. 551.

CO-OBLIGOR. A joint obligor; one bound jointly with another or others in a bond or obligation.

COOL BLOOD. In the law of homicide. Calmness or tranquillity; the undisturbed possession of one's faculties and reason; the absence of violent passion, fury, or uncontrollable excitement.

COOLING TIME. Time for the mind to become so calm and sedate as that it is supposed to contemplate, comprehend, and coolly act with reference to the consequences likely to ensue. 10 Tex. App. 447.

CO-OPERATION. The combined action of numbers. It is of two distinct kinds: (1) Such co-operation as takes place when several persons help each other in the same employment; (2) such co-operation as takes place when several persons help each other in different employments. These may be termed "simple co-operation" and "complex co-operation." Mill, Pol. Ec. 142.

COOPERTIO. In old English law. The head or branches of a tree cut down; though *coopertio arborum* is rather the bark of timber trees felled, and the chumps and broken wood. Cowell.

COOPERTUM. In forest law. A covert; a thicket (*dumetum*) or shelter for wild beasts in a forest. Spelman.

COOPERTURA. In forest law. A thicket, or covert of wood.

COOPERTUS. Covert; covered.

CO-OPTATION. A concurring choice; the election, by the members of a close corporation, of a person to fill a vacancy.

CO-ORDINATE and SUBORDINATE are terms often applied as a test to ascertain the doubtful meaning of clauses in an act of parliament. If there be two, one of which is grammatically governed by the other, it is said to be "subordinate" to it; but, if both are equally governed by some third clause, the two are called "co-ordinate." Wharton.

COPARCENARY. A species of estate, or tenancy, which exists where lands of inheritance descend from the ancestor to two or more persons. It arises in England either by common law or particular custom. By common law, as where a person, seised in fee-simple or fee-tail, dies, and his next heirs are two or more females, his daughters, sisters, aunts, cousins, or their representatives; in this case they all inherit, and these coheirs are then called "coparceners," or, for brevity, "parceners" only. Litt. §§ 241, 242; 2 Bl. Comm. 187. By particular custom, as where lands descend, as in gavelkind, to all the males in equal degree, as sons, brothers, uncles, etc. Litt. § 265; 1 Steph. Comm. 319.

While joint tenancies refer to persons, the idea of coparcenary refers to the estate. The title to it is always by descent. The respective shares may be unequal; as, for instance, one daughter and two granddaughters, children of a deceased daughter, may take by the same act of descent. As to strangers, the tenants' seisin is a joint one, but, as between themselves, each is seised of his or her own share, on whose death it goes to the heirs, and not by survivorship. The right of possession of coparceners is in common, and the possession of one is, in general, the possession of the others. 1 Washb. Real Prop. *414.

COPARCENERS. Persons to whom an estate of inheritance descends jointly, and by whom it is held as an entire estate. 2 Bl. Comm. 187.

COPARTICEPS. In old English law. A coparcener.

COPARTNER. One who is a partner with one or more other persons; a member of a partnership.

COPARTNERSHIP. A partnership.

COPARTNERY. In Scotch law. The contract of copartnership. A contract by which the several partners agree concerning the communication of loss or gain, arising from the subject of the contract. Bell.

COPE. A custom or tribute due to the crown or lord of the soil, out of the lead mines in Derbyshire; also a hill, or the roof and covering of a house; a church vestment.

COPEMAN, or COPESMAN. A chapman, (*q. v.*)

COPESMATE. A merchant; a partner in merchandise.

COPIA. Lat. In civil and old English law. Opportunity or means of access.

In old English law. A copy. *Copia libelli*, the copy of a libel. Reg. Orig. 58.

COPIA LIBELLI DELIBERANDA. The name of a writ that lay where a man could not get a copy of a libel at the hands of a spiritual judge, to have the same delivered to him. Reg. Orig. 51.

COPIA VERA. In Scotch practice. A true copy. Words written at the top of copies of instruments.

COPPA. In English law. A crop or cock of grass, hay, or corn, divided into titheable portions, that it may be more fairly and justly tithed.

COPPER AND SCALES. See MANCIPATIO.

COPPICE, or COPSE. A small wood, consisting of underwood, which may be cut at twelve or fifteen years' growth for fuel.

COPULA. The corporal consummation of marriage. *Copula*, (in logic,) the link between subject and predicate contained in the verb.

Copulatio verborum indicat acceptationem in eodem sensu. Coupling of words together shows that they are to be understood in the same sense. 4 Bacon's Works, p. 26; Broom, Max. 588.

COPULATIVE TERM. One which is placed between two or more others to join them together.

COPY. The transcript or double of an original writing; as the copy of a patent, charter, deed, etc.

Exemplifications are copies verified by the

great seal or by the seal of a court. 1 Gilb. Ev. 19.

Examined copies are those which have been compared with the original or with an official record thereof.

Office copies are those made by officers intrusted with the originals and authorized for that purpose.

COPYHOLD. A species of estate at will, or customary estate in England, the only visible title to which consists of the *copies* of the *court rolls*, which are made out by the steward of the manor, on a tenant's being admitted to any parcel of land, or tenement belonging to the manor. It is an estate at the *will* of the lord, yet such a will as is agreeable to the *custom* of the manor, which customs are preserved and evidenced by the *rolls* of the several courts baron, in which they are entered. 2 Bl. Comm. 95. In a larger sense, *copyhold* is said to import every *customary* tenure, (that is, every tenure pending on the particular custom of a manor,) as opposed to free socage, or *freehold*, which may now (since the abolition of knight-service) be considered as the general or common-law tenure of the country. 1 Steph. Comm. 210.

COPYHOLD COMMISSIONERS. Commissioners appointed to carry into effect various acts of parliament, having for their principal objects the compulsory commutation of manorial burdens and restrictions, (fines, heriots, rights to timber and minerals, etc.,) and the compulsory enfranchisement of copyhold lands. 1 Steph. Comm. 643; Elton, Copyh.

COPYHOLDER. A tenant by copyhold tenure, (by copy of court-roll.) 2 Bl. Comm. 95.

COPYRIGHT. The right of literary property as recognized and sanctioned by positive law. A right granted by statute to the author or originator of certain literary or artistic productions, whereby he is invested, for a limited period, with the sole and exclusive privilege of multiplying copies of the same and publishing and selling them.

An incorporeal right, being the exclusive privilege of printing, reprinting, selling, and publishing his own original work, which the law allows an author. Wharton.

Copyright is the exclusive right of the owner of an intellectual production to multiply and dispose of copies; the sole right to the copy, or to copy it. The word is used indifferently to signify the statutory and the common-law right; or one right is sometimes called "copyright" after publication, or statutory copyright; the other copyright before publication, or common-law copyright. The word is also used synonymously with "literary property;" thus, the exclusive right of the owner publicly to read or exhibit a work is often called "copyright." This is not strictly correct. Drone, Copyr. 100.

International copyright is the right of a subject of one country to protection against the republication in another country of a work which he originally published in his own country. Sweet.

CORAAGIUM, or CORAAGE. Measures of corn. An unusual and extraordinary tribute, arising only on special occasions. They are thus distinguished from services. Mentioned in connection with *hidage* and *carvage*. Cowell.

CORAM. Lat. Before; in presence of. Applied to persons only. Townsh. Pl. 22.

CORAM DOMINO REGE. Before our lord the king. *Coram domino rege ubicumque tunc fuerit Angliæ*, before our lord the king wherever he shall then be in England.

CORAM IPSO REGE. Before the king himself. The old name of the court of king's bench, which was originally held before the king in person. 3 Bl. Comm. 41.

CORAM NOBIS. Before us ourselves, (the king, *i. e.*, in the king's or queen's bench.) Applied to writs of error directed to another branch of the same court, *e. g.*, from the full bench to the court at *nisi prius*. 1 Archb. Pr. K. B. 234.

CORAM NON JUDICE. In presence of a person not a judge. When a suit is brought and determined in a court which has no jurisdiction in the matter, then it is said to be *coram non judice*, and the judgment is void.

CORAM PARIBUS. Before the peers or freeholders. The attestation of deeds, like all other solemn transactions, was originally done only *coram paribus*. 2 Bl. Comm. 307. *Coram paribus de vicineto*, before the peers or freeholders of the neighborhood. Id. 315.

CORAM SECTATORIBUS. Before the suitors. Cro. Jac. 582.

CORAM VOBIS. Before you. A writ of error directed by a court of review to the court which tried the cause, to correct an error in fact. 3 Md. 325; 3 Steph. Comm. 642.

CORD. A measure of wood, containing 128 cubic feet.

CO-RESPONDENT. A person summoned to answer a bill, petition, or libel, together with another respondent. Now chiefly used to designate the person charged with adultery with the respondent in a suit for divorce for that cause, and joined as a defendant with such party.

CORIUM FORISFACERE. To forfeit one's skin, applied to a person condemned to be whipped; anciently the punishment of a servant. *Corium perdere*, the same. *Corium redimere*, to compound for a whipping. Wharton.

CORN. In English law, a general term for any sort of grain; but in America it is properly applied only to maize. In the memorandum clause in policies of insurance it includes pease and beans, but not rice. Park, Ins. 112.

CORN LAWS. A species of protective tariff formerly in existence in England, imposing import-duties on various kinds of grain. The corn laws were abolished in 1846.

CORN RENT. A rent in wheat or malt paid on college leases by direction of St. 18 Eliz. c. 6. 2 Bl. Comm. 609.

CORNAGE. A species of tenure in England, by which the tenant was bound to blow a horn for the sake of alarming the country on the approach of an enemy. It was a species of grand serjeanty. Bac. Abr. "Tenure," N.

CORNER. A combination among the dealers in a specific commodity, or outside capitalists, for the purpose of buying up the greater portion of that commodity which is upon the market or may be brought to market, and holding the same back from sale, until the demand shall so far outrun the limited supply as to advance the price abnormally. 72 Pa. St. 158; 101 Mass. 145.

In surveying. An angle made by two boundary lines; the common end of two boundary lines, which run at an angle with each other.

CORNET. A commissioned officer of cavalry, abolished in England in 1871, and not existing in the United States army.

CORODIO HABENDO. The name of a writ to exact a corody of an abbey or religious house.

CORODIUM. In old English law. A corody.

CORODY. In old English law. A sum of money or allowance of meat, drink, and clothing due to the crown from the abbey or other religious house, whereof it was founder, towards the sustentation of such one of its servants as is thought fit to receive it. It differs from a pension, in that it was allowed towards the maintenance of any of the king's servants in an abbey; a pension being given to one of the king's chaplains, for his better maintenance, till he may be provided with a benefice. Fitzh. Nat. Brev. 250. See 1 Bl. Comm. 283.

COROLLARY. In logic. A collateral or secondary consequence, deduction, or inference.

CORONA. The crown. *Placita coronæ;* pleas of the crown; criminal actions or proceedings, in which the crown was the prosecutor.

CORONA MALA. In old English law. The clergy who abuse their character were so called. Blount.

CORONARE. In old records. To give the tonsure, which was done on the crown, or in the form of a crown; to make a man a priest. Cowell.

CORONARE FILIUM. To make one's son a priest. *Homo coronatus* was one who had received the first tonsure, as preparatory to superior orders, and the tonsure was in form of a corona, or crown of thorns. Cowell.

CORONATION OATH. The oath administered to a sovereign at the ceremony of crowning or investing him with the insignia of royalty, in acknowledgment of his right to govern the kingdom, in which he swears to observe the laws, customs, and privileges of the kingdom, and to act and do all things conformably thereto. Wharton.

CORONATOR. A coroner, (*q. v.*) Spelman.

CORONATORE ELIGENDO. The name of a writ issued to the sheriff, commanding him to proceed to the election of a coroner.

CORONATORE EXONERANDO. In English law. The name of a writ for the removal of a coroner, for a cause which is to be therein assigned, as that he is engaged in other business, or incapacitated by years or sickness, or has not a sufficient estate in the county, or lives in an inconvenient part of it.

CORONER. The name of an ancient officer of the common law, whose office and functions are continued in modern English and American administration. The coroner is an officer belonging to each county, and is charged with duties both judicial and ministerial, but chiefly the former. It is his special province and duty to make inquiry into the causes and circumstances of any death happening within his territory which occurs through violence or suddenly and with marks of suspicion. This examination (called the "coroner's inquest") is held with a jury of proper persons upon view of the dead body. See Bract. fol. 121; 1 Bl. Comm. 346-348; 3 Steph. Comm. 33. In England, another branch of his judicial office is to inquire concerning shipwrecks, and certify whether wreck or not, and who is in possession of the goods; and also to inquire concerning treasure trove, who were the finders, and where it is, and whether any one be suspected of having found and concealed a treasure. 1 Bl. Comm. 349. It belongs to the ministerial office of the coroner to serve writs and other process, and generally to discharge the duties of the sheriff, in case of the incapacity of that officer or a vacancy in his office.

CORONER'S COURT. In England. A tribunal of record, where a coroner holds his inquiries.

CORPORAL. Relating to the body; bodily. Should be distinguished from corporeal, (*q. v.*)

A non-commissioned officer of the lowest grade in a company of soldiers in the army.

CORPORAL OATH. An oath, the external solemnity of which consists in laying one's hand upon the Gospels while the oath is administered to him. More generally, a solemn oath.

The terms "corporal oath" and "solemn oath" are, in Indiana, at least, used synonymously; and an oath taken with the uplifted hand may be properly described by either term. 1 Ind. 184.

CORPORAL TOUCH. Bodily touch; actual physical contact; manual apprehension.

CORPORALE SACRAMENTUM. In old English law. A corporal oath.

Corporalis injuria non recipit æstimationem de futuro. A personal injury does not receive satisfaction from a future course of proceeding, [is not left for its satisfaction to a future course of proceeding.] Bac. Max reg. 6; Broom, Max. 278.

CORPORATE. Belonging to a corporation; as a corporate name. Incorporated; as a corporate body.

CORPORATE NAME. When a corporation is erected, a name is always given to it, or, supposing none to be actually given, will attach to it by implication, and by that name alone it must sue and be sued, and do all legal acts, though a very minute variation therein is not material, and the name is capable of being changed (by competent authority) without affecting the identity or capacity of the corporation. Wharton.

CORPORATION. A franchise possessed by one or more individuals, who subsist as a body politic, under a special denomination, and are vested by the policy of the law with the capacity of perpetual succession, and of acting in several respects, however numerous the association may be, as a single individual. 2 Kent, Comm. 267.

An artificial person or being, endowed by law with the capacity of perpetual succession; consisting either of a single individual, (termed a "corporation sole,") or of a collection of several individuals, (which is termed a "corporation aggregate.") 3 Steph. Comm. 166; 1 Bl. Comm. 467, 469.

A corporation is an intellectual body, created by law, composed of individuals united under a common name, the members of which succeed each other, so that the body continues always the same, notwithstanding the change of the individuals who compose it, and which, for certain purposes, is considered a natural person. Civil Code La. art. 427.

A corporation is an artificial person created by law for specific purposes, the limit of whose existence, powers, and liabilities is fixed by the act of incorporation, usually called its "charter." Code Ga. 1882, § 1670.

Classification. According to the accepted classification of corporations, they are first divided into public and private.

A *public* corporation is one having for its object the administration of a portion of the powers of government delegated to it for that purpose; such are municipal corporations. All others are private. Code Ga. 1882, § 1672.

Corporations are either public or private. Public corporations are formed or organized for the government of a portion of the state; all other corporations are private. Civil Code Cal. § 284.

Public corporations are generally esteemed such as exist for political purposes only, such as towns, cities, parishes, and counties; and in many respects they are so, although they involve some private interest; but, strictly speaking, public corporations are such only as are founded by the government for public purposes, where the whole interests belong also to the government. If, therefore, the foundation be private, though under the charter of the government, the corporation is private, however extensive the uses may be to which it is devoted, either by the bounty of the founder or the nature and objects of the institution. The uses may, in a certain sense, be called "public," but the corporations are private, as much so, indeed, as if the franchises were vested in a single person. 4 Wheat. 518, 562; 1 Wall. Jr. 275.

All *private* corporations are divided into *ecclesiastical* and *lay;* the former are such as are composed of religious persons organized for spiritual purposes, or for administering property held for religious uses; the latter are such as exist for secular or business purposes.

Lay corporations are classified as *eleemosynary* or *civil;* the former are such as are created for the distribution of charities or for purposes falling under the head of "charitable" in its widest sense, *e. g.*, hospitals, asylums, colleges; the latter are organized for the facilitating of business transactions and the profit of the members.

Corporations are also classed as *aggregate* or *sole;* as to this division, see CORPORATION AGGREGATE; CORPORATION SOLE.

CORPORATION ACT. In English law. The statute 13 Car. II. St. 2, c. 1; by which it was provided that no person should thereafter be elected to office in any corporate town that should not, within one year previously, have taken the sacrament of the Lord's Supper, according to the rites of the Church of England; and every person so elected was also required to take the oaths of allegiance and supremacy. 3 Steph. Comm. 103, 104; 4 Bl. Comm. 58. This statute is now repealed. 4 Steph. Comm. 511.

CORPORATION AGGREGATE. A collection of several individuals united into one body, under a special denomination, and having perpetual succession under an artificial form, and vested by the policy of the law with the capacity of acting in several respects as an individual. Shelf. Mortm. 22; 1 Kyd, Corp. 13; 2 Kent, Comm. 267.

An aggregate corporation, at common law, is a collection of individuals, united into one collective body, under a special name, and possessing certain immunities, privileges, and capacities, in its collective character, which do not belong to the natural persons composing it. It is an artificial person, existing in contemplation of law, and endowed with certain powers and franchises, which, though they must be exercised through the medium of its natural members, are yet considered as subsisting in the corporation itself, as distinctly as if it were a real personage. 4 Wheat. 518, 561.

CORPORATION COURTS. Certain courts in Virginia described as follows: "For each city of the state, there shall be a court called a 'corporation court,' to be held by a judge, with like qualifications and elected in the same manner as judges of the county court." Code Va. 1887, § 3050.

CORPORATION SOLE. A corporation consisting of one person only, and his successors in some particular station, who are incorporated by law in order to give them some legal capacities and advantages, particularly that of perpetuity, which in their natural persons they could not have had. In this sense, the sovereign in England is a sole corporation, so is a bishop, so are some deans distinct from their several chapters, and so is every parson and vicar. 3 Steph. Comm. 168, 169; 2 Kent, Comm. 273.

A corporation sole consists of a single person, who is made a body corporate and politic, in order to give him some legal capacities and advantages, and especially that of perpetuity; as a bishop, dean, etc. 7 Abb. Pr. 134; 22 Pick. 122.

CORPORATOR. A member of a corporation aggregate. Grant, Corp. 48.

CORPORE ET ANIMO. Lat. By the body and by the mind; by the physical act and by the mental intent. Dig. 41, 2, 3.

CORPOREAL. A term descriptive of such things as have an objective, material existence; perceptible by the senses of sight and touch; possessing a real body. Opposed to incorporeal and spiritual.

There is a distinction between "corporeal" and "corporal." The former term means "possessing a body," that is, tangible, physical, material; the latter means "relating to or affecting a body," that is, bodily, external. Corporeal denotes the nature or physical existence of a body; corporal denotes its exterior or the co-ordination of it with some other body. Hence we speak of "corporeal hereditaments," but of "corporal punishment," "corporal touch," "corporal oath," etc.

CORPOREAL HEREDITAMENTS. Substantial permanent objects which may be inherited. The term "land" will include all such. 2 Bl. Comm. 17.

CORPOREAL PROPERTY. Such as affects the senses, and may be seen and handled by the body, as opposed to incorporeal property, which cannot be seen or handled, and exists only in contemplation. Thus a house is corporeal, but the annual rent payable for its occcupation is incorporeal. Corporeal property is, if movable, capable of manual transfer; if immovable, possession of it may be delivered up. But incorporeal property cannot be so transferred, but some other means must be adopted for its transfer, of which the most usual is an instrument in writing. Mozley & Whitley.

CORPS DIPLOMATIQUE. In international law. Ambassadors and diplomatic persons at any court or capital.

CORPSE. The dead body of a human being.

CORPUS. (Lat.) Body; the body; an aggregate or mass, (of men, laws, or articles;) physical substance, as distinguished from intellectual conception; the principal sum or capital, as distinguished from interest or income.

A substantial or positive fact, as distinguished from what is equivocal and ambiguous. The *corpus delicti* (body of an offense) is the fact of its having been actually committed. Best, Pres. 269–279.

A corporeal act of any kind, (as distinguished from *animus* or mere intention,) on the part of him who wishes to acquire a thing, whereby he obtains the physical ability to exercise his power over it whenever he pleases. The word occurs frequently in this sense in the civil law. Mackeld. Rom. Law, § 248.

CORPUS CHRISTI DAY. In English law. A feast instituted in 1264, in honor of the sacrament. 32 Hen. VIII. c. 21.

CORPUS COMITATUS. The body of a county. The whole county, as distinguished from a part of it, or any particular place in it. 5 Mason, 290.

CORPUS CORPORATUM. A corporation; a corporate body, other than municipal.

CORPUS CUM CAUSA. (The body with the cause.) An English writ which issued out of chancery, to remove both the *body* and the record, touching the *cause* of any man lying in execution upon a judgment for debt, into the king's bench, there to remain until he satisfied the judgment. Cowell; Blount.

CORPUS DELICTI. The body of a crime. The body (material substance) upon which a crime has been committed, *e. g.*, the corpse of a murdered man, the charred remains of a house burned down. In a derivative sense, the substance or foundation of a crime; the substantial fact that a crime has been committed.

Corpus humanum non recipit æstimationem. The human body does not admit of valuation. Hob. 59.

CORPUS JURIS. A body of law. A term used to signify a book comprehending several collections of law. There are two principal collections to which this name is given; the *Corpus Juris Civilis*, and the *Corpus Juris Canonici*, (*q. v.*)

CORPUS JURIS CANONICI. The body of the canon law. A compilation of the canon law, comprising the decrees and canons of the Roman Church, constituting the body of ecclesiastical law of that church.

CORPUS JURIS CIVILIS. The body of the civil law. The system of Roman jurisprudence compiled and codified under the direction of the emperor Justinian, in A. D. 528–534. This collection comprises the Institutes, Digest, (or Pandects,) Code, and Novels. The name is said to have been first applied to this collection early in the seventeenth century.

CORPUS PRO CORPORE. Lat. In old records. Body for body. A phrase expressing the liability of manucaptors. 3 How. State Tr. 110.

CORRECTION. Discipline; chastisement administered by a master or other person in authority to one who has committed an offense, for the purpose of curing his faults or bringing him into proper subjection.

CORRECTION, HOUSE OF. A prison for the reformation of petty or juvenile offenders.

CORRECTOR OF THE STAPLE. In old English law. A clerk belonging to the staple, to write and record the bargains of merchants there made.

CORREGIDOR. In Spanish law. A magistrate who took cognizance of various misdemeanors, and of civil matters. 2 White, New Recop. 53.

CORREI. Lat. In the civil law. Co-stipulators; joint stipulators.

CORREI CREDENDI. Lat. In the civil and Scotch law. Joint creditors; creditors *in solido*. Poth. Obl. pt. 2, c. 4, art. 3, § 11.

CORREI DEBENDI. Lat. In Scotch law. Two or more persons bound as principal debtors to another. Ersk. Inst. 3, 3, 74.

CORRELATIVE. Having a mutual or reciprocal relation, in such sense that the existence of one necessarily implies the existence of the other. *Father* and *son* are correlative terms. *Right* and *duty* are correlative terms.

CORRESPONDENCE. Interchange of written communications. The letters written by a person and the answers written by the one to whom they are addressed.

CORROBORATE. To strengthen; to add weight or credibility to a thing by additional and confirming facts or evidence.

The expression "corroborating circumstances" clearly does not mean facts which, independent of a confession, will warrant a conviction; for then the verdict would stand not on the confession, but upon those independent circumstances. To corroborate is to strengthen, to confirm by additional security, to add strength. The testimony of a witness is said to be corroborated when it is shown to correspond with the representation of some other witness, or to comport with some facts otherwise known or established. Corroborating circumstances, then, used in reference to a confession, are such as serve to strengthen it, to render it more probable; such, in short, as may serve to impress a jury with a belief in its truth. 10 N. J. Law, 163.

Corruptio optimi est pessima. Corruption of the best is worst.

CORRUPTION. Illegality; a vicious and fraudulent intention to evade the prohibitions of the law.

The act of an official or fiduciary person who unlawfully and wrongfully uses his station or character to procure some benefit for himself or for another person, contrary to duty and the rights of others.

CORRUPTION OF BLOOD. In English law. This was the consequence of *attainder.* It meant that the attainted person could neither inherit lands or other hereditaments from his ancestor, nor retain those he already had, nor transmit them by descent to any heir, because his blood was considered in law to be corrupted. This was abolished by St. 3 & 4 Wm. IV. c. 106, and 33 & 34 Vict. c. 23; and is unknown in America. Const. U. S. art. 3, § 3.

CORSELET. Ancient armor which covered the body.

CORSE-PRESENT. A mortuary, thus termed because, when a mortuary became due on the death of a man, the best or second-best beast was, according to custom, offered or presented to the priest, and carried with the corpse. In Wales a corse-present was due upon the death of a clergyman to the bishop of the diocese, till abolished by 12 Anne St. 2, c. 6. 2 Bl. Comm. 426.

CORSNED. In Saxon law. The morsel of execration. A species of ordeal in use among the Saxons, performed by eating a piece of bread over which the priest had pronounced a certain imprecation. If the accused ate it freely, he was pronounced innocent; but, if it stuck in his throat, it was considered as a proof of his guilt. Crabb, Eng. Law, 30; 1 Reeve, Eng. Law, 21; 4 Bl. Comm. 345.

CORTES. The name of the legislative assemblies, the parliament or congress, of Spain and Portugal.

CORTEX. The bark of a tree; the outer covering of anything.

CORTIS. A court or yard before a house. Blount.

CORTULARIUM, or CORTARIUM. In old records. A yard adjoining a country farm.

CORVEE. In French law. Gratuitous labor exacted from the villages or communities, especially for repairing roads, constructing bridges, etc.

COSA JUZGADA. In Spanish law. A cause or matter adjudged, (*res judicata.*) White, New Recop. b. 3, tit. 8, note.

COSDUNA. In feudal law. A custom or tribute.

COSEN, COZEN. In old English law. To cheat. "A cosening knave." 3 Leon. 171.

COSENAGE. In old English law. Kindred; cousinship. Also a writ that lay for the heir where the *tresail, i. e.*, the father of the *besail,* or great-grandfather, was seised of lands in fee at his death, and a stranger entered upon the land and abated. Fitzh. Nat. Brev. 221.

COSENING. In old English law. An offense, mentioned in the old books, where anything was done deceitfully, whether belonging to contracts or not, which could not be properly termed by any special name. The same as the *stellionatus* of the civil law. Cowell.

COSHERING. In old English law. A feudal prerogative or custom for lords to lie and feast themselves at their tenants' houses. Cowell.

COSMUS. Clean. Blount.

COSS. A term used by Europeans in India to denote a road-measure of about two miles, but differing in different parts. Wharton.

COST. The cost of an article purchased for exportation is the price paid, with all incidental charges paid at the place of exportation. 2 Wash. C. C. 493. Cost price is that actually paid for goods. 18 N. Y. 337.

COST-BOOK. A book in which a number of adventurers who have obtained permission to work a lode, and have agreed to share the enterprise in certain proportions, enter the agreement, and from time to time the receipts and expenditures of the mine, the names of the shareholders, their respective accounts with the mine, and transfers of shares. These associations are called "Cost-Book Mining Companies," and are governed by the general law of partnership. Lindl. Partn. *147.

CO-STIPULATOR. A joint promisor.

COSTS. A pecuniary allowance, made to the successful party, (and recoverable from the losing party,) for his expenses in prosecuting or defending a suit or a distinct proceeding within a suit.

Costs and fees were originally altogether different in their nature. The one is an allowance to a *party* for expenses incurred in prosecuting or defending a suit; the other, a compensation to an *officer* for services rendered in the progress of a cause. Therefore, while an executor or administrator was not personally liable to his adversary for costs, yet, if at his instance an officer performed services for him, he had a personal demand for his fees. 11 Serg. & R. 247. There is in our statute a manifest difference between costs and fees in another respect. Costs are an allowance to a party for the expenses incurred in prosecuting or defending a suit,—an incident to the judgment; while fees are compensation to public officers for services rendered individuals not in the course of litigation. 58 Ala. 579.

In England, the term is also used to designate the charges which an attorney or solicitor is entitled to make and recover from his client, as his remuneration for professional services, such as legal advice, attendances, drafting and copying documents, conducting legal proceedings, etc.

COSTS DE INCREMENTO. Increased costs, costs of increase. Costs adjudged by the court in addition to those assessed by the jury. 13 How. 372.

Those extra expenses incurred which do not appear on the face of the proceedings, such as witnesses' expenses, fees to counsel, attendances, court fees, etc. Wharton.

COSTS OF THE DAY. Costs which are incurred in preparing for the trial of a cause on a specified *day*, consisting of witnesses' fees, and other fees of attendance. Archb. N. Prac. 281.

COSTUMBRE. In Spanish law. Custom; an unwritten law established by usage, during a long space of time. Las Partidas, pt. 1, tit. 2, l. 4.

CO-SURETIES. Joint sureties; two or more sureties to the same obligation.

COTA. A cot or hut. Blount.

COTAGIUM. In old English law. A cottage.

COTARIUS. In old English law. A cottager, who held in free socage, and paid a stated fine or rent in provisions or money, with some occasional personal services.

COTERELLI. Anciently, a kind of peasantry who were outlaws; robbers. Blount.

COTERELLUS. In feudal law. A servile tenant, who held in mere villenage; his person, issue, and goods were disposable at the lord's pleasure.

COTERIE. A fashionable association, or a knot of persons forming a particular circle. The origin of the term was purely commercial, signifying an association, in which each member furnished his part, and bore his share in the profit and loss. Wharton.

COTESWOLD. In old records. A place where there is no wood.

COTLAND. In old English law. Land held by a cottager, whether in socage or villenage. Cowell.

COTSETHLA. In old English law. The little seat or mansion belonging to a small farm.

COTSETHLAND. The seat of a cottage with the land belonging to it. Spelman.

COTSETUS. A cottager or cottage-holder who held by servile tenure and was bound to do the work of the lord. Cowell.

COTTAGE. In English law. A small dwelling-house that has no land belonging to it. Shep. Touch. 94; 1 Strange, 405; 2 Ld. Raym. 1015; 15 Ad. & El. (N. S.) 244.

COTTIER TENANCY. A species of tenancy in Ireland, constituted by an agreement in writing, and subject to the following terms: That the tenement consist of a dwelling-house with not more than half an acre of land; at a rental not exceeding £5 a year; the tenancy to be for not more than a month at a time; the landlord to keep the house in good repair. Landlord and Tenant Act, Ireland, (23 & 24 Vict. c. 154, § 81.)

COTUCA. Coat armor.

COTUCHANS. A term used in Dómesday for peasants, boors, husbandmen.

COUCHANT. Lying down; squatting. *Couchant and levant* (lying down and rising up) is a term applied to animals trespassing on the land of one other than their owner, for one night or longer. 3 Bl. Comm. 9.

COUCHER, or COURCHER. A factor who continues abroad for traffic, (37 Edw. III. c. 16;) also the general book wherein any corporation, etc., register their acts, (3 & 4 Edw. VI. c. 10.)

COUNCIL. An assembly of persons for the purpose of concerting measures of state or municipal policy; hence called "councillors."

In American law. The legislative body in the government of cities or boroughs. An advisory body selected to aid the executive.

COUNCIL OF CONCILIATION. By the Act 30 & 31 Vict. c. 105, power is given for the crown to grant licenses for the formation of councils of conciliation and arbitration, consisting of a certain number of masters and workmen in any trade or employment, having power to hear and determine all questions between masters and workmen which may be submitted to them by both parties, arising out of or with respect to the particular trade or manufacture, and incapable of being otherwise settled. They have power to apply to a justice to enforce the performance of their award. The members are elected by persons engaged in the trade. Davis, Bldg. Soc. 232; Sweet.

COUNCIL OF JUDGES. Under the English judicature act, 1873, § 75, an annual council of the judges of the supreme court is to be held, for the purpose of considering the operation of the new practice, offices, etc., introduced by the act, and of reporting to a secretary of state as to any alterations which they consider should be made in the law for the administration of justice. An extraordinary council may also be convened at any time by the lord chancellor. Sweet.

COUNCIL OF THE NORTH. A court instituted by Henry VIII., in 1537, to administer justice in Yorkshire and the four other northern counties. Under the presidency of Stratford, the court showed great rigor, bordering, it is alleged, on harshness. It was abolished by 16 Car. I., the same act which abolished the Star Chamber. Brown.

COUNSEL. 1. In practice. An advocate, counsellor, or pleader. 3 Bl. Comm. 26; 1 Kent, Comm. 307. One who assists his client with advice, and pleads for him in open court. See COUNSELLOR.

Counsellors who are associated with those regularly retained in a cause, either for the purpose of advising as to the points of law involved, or preparing the case on its legal side, or arguing questions of law to the court, or preparing or conducting the case on its appearance before an appellate tribunal, are said to be "of counsel."

2. Knowledge. A grand jury is sworn to keep secret "the commonwealth's *counsel*, their fellows', and their own."

3. Advice given by one person to another in regard to a proposed line of conduct, claim, or contention.

COUNSEL'S SIGNATURE. This is required, in some jurisdictions, to be affixed to pleadings, as affording the court a means of judging whether they are interposed in good faith and upon legal grounds.

COUNSELLOR. An advocate or barrister. A member of the legal profession whose special function is to give counsel or advice as to the legal aspects of judicial controversies, or their preparation and management, and to appear in court for the conduct of trials, or the argument of causes, or presentation of motions, or any other legal business that takes him into the presence of the court.

In some of the states, the two words "counsellor" and "attorney" are used interchangeably to designate all lawyers. In others, the latter term alone is used, "counsellor" not being recognized as a technical name. In still others, the two are associated together as the full legal title of any person who has been admitted to practice in the courts; while in a few they denote different grades, it being prescribed that no one can become a counsellor until he has been an attorney for a specified time and has passed a second examination.

In the practice of the United States supreme court, the term denotes an officer who is employed by a party in a cause to conduct the same on its trial on his behalf. He differs from an attorney at law.

In the supreme court of the United States, the two degrees of attorney and counsel were at first kept separate, and no person was permitted to practice in both capacities, but the present practice is otherwise. Weeks, Attys. at Law, 54. It is the duty of the counsel to draft or review and correct the special pleadings, to manage the cause on trial, and, during the whole course of the suit, to apply established principles of law to the exigencies of the case. 1 Kent, Comm. 307.

COUNT, *v.* In pleading. To declare; to recite; to state a case; to narrate the facts constituting a plaintiff's cause of action. In a special sense, to set out the claim or count of the demandant in a real action.

To plead orally; to plead or argue a case in court; to recite or read in court; to recite a count in court.

COUNT, *n.* In pleading. The different parts of a declaration, each of which, if it stood alone, would constitute a ground for action, are the counts of the declaration. Used also to signify the several parts of an indictment, each charging a distinct offense.

COUNT. (Fr. *comte;* from the Latin *comes.*) An earl.

COUNT AND COUNT-OUT. These words have a technical sense in a count of the house of commons by the speaker.

COUNT-OUT. Forty members form a house of commons; and, though there be ever so many at the beginning of a debate, yet, if during the course of it the house should be deserted by the members, till reduced below the number of forty, any one member may have it adjourned upon its being counted; but a debate may be continued when only one member is left in the house, provided no one choose to move an adjournment. Wharton.

COUNTEE. In old English law. The most eminent dignity of a subject before the Conquest. He was *præfectus* or *præpositus comitatûs,* and had the charge and custody of the county; but this authority is now vested in the sheriff. 9 Coke, 46.

COUNTENANCE. In old English law. Credit; estimation. Wharton.

COUNTER. The name of two prisons formerly standing in London, but now demolished. They were the Poultry Counter and Wood Street Counter.

COUNTER-AFFIDAVIT. An affidavit made and presented in contradiction or opposition to an affidavit which is made the basis or support of a motion or application.

COUNTER-BOND. In old practice. A bond of indemnity. 2 Leon. 90.

COUNTER-CLAIM. A claim presented by a defendant in opposition to or deduction from the claim of the plaintiff. A species of set-off or recoupment introduced by the codes of civil procedure in several of the states, of a broad and liberal character.

A counter-claim must be one "existing in favor of a defendant and against a plaintiff, between whom a several judgment might be had in the action, and arising out of one of the following causes of action: (1) A cause of action arising out of the contract or transaction set forth in the complaint as the foundation of the plaintiff's claim, or connected with the subject of action; (2) in an action arising on contract, any other cause of action arising also on contract, and existing at the commencement of the action." Code Proc. N. Y. § 150.

The term "counter-claim," of itself, imports a claim opposed to, or which qualifies, or at least in some degree affects, the plaintiff's cause of action. 35 Wis. 626.

A counter-claim is an opposition claim, or demand of something due; a demand of something which of right belongs to the defendant, in opposition to the right of the plaintiff. 8 How. Pr. 122.

A counter claim is that which might have arisen out of, or could have had some connection with, the original transaction, in view of the parties, and which, at the time the contract was made, they could have intended might, in some event, give one party a claim against the other for compliance or non-compliance with its provisions. 7 Ind. 523, 524.

COUNTER-DEED. A secret writing, either before a notary or under a private seal, which destroys, invalidates, or alters a public one.

COUNTERFEIT. In criminal law. To forge; to copy or imitate, without authority or right, and with a view to deceive or defraud, by passing the copy or thing forged for that which is original or genuine. Most commonly applied to the fraudulent and criminal imitation of money.

COUNTERFEIT COIN. Coin not genuine, but resembling or apparently intended to resemble or pass for genuine coin, including genuine coin prepared or altered so as to resemble or pass for coin of a higher denomination.

COUNTERFEITER. In criminal law. One who unlawfully makes base coin in imitation of the true metal, or forges false currency, or any instrument of writing, bearing a likeness and similitude to that which is lawful and genuine, with an intention of deceiving and imposing upon mankind. 1 Stew. (Ala.) 384.

COUNTER-FESANCE. The act of forging.

COUNTER-LETTER. A species of instrument of defeasance common in the civil law. It is executed by a party who has taken a deed of property, absolute on its face, but intended as security for a loan of money, and by it he agrees to reconvey the property on payment of a specified sum. The two instruments, taken together, constitute what is known in Louisiana as an "*antichresis,*" (*q. v.*)

COUNTERMAND. A change or revocation of orders, authority, or instructions previously issued. It may be either express or implied; the former where the order or instruction already given is explicitly annulled or recalled; the latter where the party's conduct is incompatible with the further continuance of the order or instruction, as where a new order is given inconsistent with the former order.

COUNTER-MARK. A sign put upon goods already marked; also the several marks put upon goods belonging to several persons, to show that they must not be opened, but in the presence of all the owners or their agents.

COUNTERPART. In conveyancing. The corresponding part of an instrument; a duplicate or copy. Where an instrument of conveyance, as a lease, is executed in parts, that is, by having several copies or duplicates made and interchangeably executed, that which is executed by the grantor is usually called the "original," and the rest are "counterparts;" although, where all the parties execute every part, this renders them all originals. 2 Bl. Comm. 296; Shep. Touch. 50. See DUPLICATE.

COUNTER-PLEA. In pleading. A plea to some matter incidental to the main object of the suit, and out of the direct line of pleadings.

In the more ancient system of pleading, counter-plea was applied to what was, in effect, a replication to aid prayer, (*q. v.;*) that is, where a tenant for life or other limited interest in land, having an action brought against him in respect to the title to such land, prayed in aid of the lord or reversioner for his better defense, that which the demandant alleged against either request was called a "counter-plea." Cowell.

COUNTER-ROLLS. In English law. The rolls which sheriffs have with the coroners, containing particulars of their proceedings, as well of appeals as of inquests, etc. 3 Edw. I. c. 10.

COUNTER-SECURITY. A security given to one who has entered into a bond or become surety for another; a countervailing bond of indemnity.

COUNTERSIGN. The signature of a secretary or other subordinate officer to any writing signed by the principal or superior to vouch for the authenticity of it.

COUNTERVAILING EQUITY. A contrary and balancing equity; an equity or right opposed to that which is sought to be enforced or recognized, and which ought not to be sacrificed or subordinated to the latter, because it is of equal strength and justice, and equally deserving of consideration.

COUNTEZ. L. Fr. Count, or reckon. In old practice. A direction formerly given by the clerk of a court to the crier, after a jury was sworn, to *number* them; and which Blackstone says was given in his time, in good English, "count these." 4 Bl. Comm. 340, note (*u.*)

COUNTORS. Advocates, or serjeants at law, whom a man retains to defend his cause and speak for him in court, for their fees. 1 Inst. 17.

COUNTRY. The portion of the earth's surface occupied by an independent nation or people; or the inhabitants of such territory.

In its primary meaning "country" signifies "place;" and, in a larger sense, the territory or dominions occupied by a community; or even waste and unpeopled sections or regions of the earth. But its metaphorical meaning is no less definite and well understood; and in common parlance, in historical and geographical writings, in diplomacy, legislation, treaties, and international codes, the word is employed to denote the population, the nation, the state, or the government, having possession and dominion over a territory. 1 Blatchf. 218, 225; 5 N. Y. Leg. Obs. 286.

In pleading and practice. The inhabitants of a district from which a jury is to be summoned; pais; a jury. 3 Bl. Comm. 349; Steph. Pl. 73, 78, 230.

COUNTY. The name given to the principal subdivisions of the kingdom of England and of most of the states of the American Union, denoting a distinct portion of territory organized by itself for political and judicial purposes. The etymology of the word shows it to have been the district anciently governed by a *count* or earl. In modern use, the word may denote either the territory marked off to form a county, or the citizens resident within such territory, taken collectively and considered as invested with political rights, or the county regarded as a municipal corporation possessing subordinate governmental powers, or an organized jural society invested with specific rights and duties.

COUNTY BRIDGE. A bridge of the larger class, erected by the county, and which the county is liable to keep in repair. 40 Iowa, 295.

COUNTY COMMISSIONERS. Officers of a county charged with a variety of administrative and executive duties, but principally with the management of the financial affairs of the county, its police regulations, and its corporate business. Sometimes the local laws give them limited judicial powers. In some states they are called "supervisors."

COUNTY CORPORATE. A city or town, with more or less territory annexed, having the privilege to be a county of itself, and not to be comprised in any other county; such as London, York, Bristol, Norwich, and other cities in England. 1 Bl. Comm. 120.

COUNTY COURT. A court of high antiquity in England, incident to the jurisdiction of the sheriff. It is not a court of record, but may hold pleas of debt or damages, under the value of forty shillings. The freeholders of the county (anciently termed the "suitors" of the court) are the real judges in this court, and the sheriff is the ministerial officer. See 3 Bl. Comm. 35, 36; 3 Steph. Comm. 395.

But in modern English law the name is appropriated to a system of tribunals established by the statute 9 & 10 Vict. c. 95, having a limited jurisdiction, principally for the recovery of small debts.

It is also the name of certain tribunals of limited jurisdiction in the county of Middlesex, established under the statute 22 Geo. II. c. 33.

In American law. The name is used in many of the states to designate the ordinary courts of record having jurisdiction for trials at *nisi prius*. Their powers generally comprise ordinary civil jurisdiction, also the charge and care of persons and estates coming within legal guardianship, a limited criminal jurisdiction, appellate jurisdiction over justices of the peace, etc.

COUNTY PALATINE. A term bestowed upon certain counties in England, the lords of which in former times enjoyed especial privileges. They might pardon treasons, murders, and felonies. All writs and indictments ran in their names, as in other counties in the king's; and all offenses were said to be done against their peace, and not, as in other places, *contra pacem domini regis*. But these privileges have in modern times nearly disappeared.

COUNTY RATE. In English law. An imposition levied on the occupiers of lands, and applied to many miscellaneous purposes, among which the most important are those of defraying the expenses connected with prisons, reimbursing to private parties the costs they have incurred in prosecuting public offenders, and defraying the expenses of the county police. See 15 & 16 Vict. c. 81.

COUNTY-SEAT. A county-seat or county-town is the chief town of a county, where the county buildings and courts are located and the county business transacted.

COUNTY SESSIONS. In England, the court of general quarter sessions of the peace held in every county once in every quarter of a year. Mozley & Whitley.

COUPONS. Interest and dividend certificates; also those parts of a commercial instrument which are to be *cut*, and which are evidence of something connected with the contract mentioned in the instrument. They are generally attached to certificates of loan, where the interest is payable at particular periods, and, when the interest is paid, they are cut off and delivered to the payer. Wharton.

COUR DE CASSATION. The supreme judicial tribunal of France, having appellate jurisdiction only. For an account of its composition and powers, see Jones, French Bar, 22; Guyot, Repert. Univ.

COURIER. An express messenger of haste.

COURSE. A term used in surveying, meaning the direction of a line with reference to a meridian.

COURSE OF THE VOYAGE. By this term is understood the regular and customary track, if such there be, which a ship takes in going from one port to another, and the shortest way. Marsh. Ins. 185.

COURSE OF TRADE. What is customarily or ordinarily done in the management of trade or business.

COURT. In legislation. A legislative assembly. Parliament is called in the old books a court of the king, nobility, and commons assembled. Finch, Law, b. 4, c. 1, p. 233; Fleta, lib. 2, c. 2.

This meaning of the word has been retained in the titles of some deliberative bodies, such as the general court of Massachusetts, (the legislature.)

In international law. The person and suite of the sovereign; the place where the sovereign sojourns with his regal retinue, wherever that may be. The English government is spoken of in diplomacy as the court of St. James, because the palace of St. James is the official palace.

In practice. An organ of the government, belonging to the judicial department, whose function is the application of the laws to controversies brought before it and the public administration of justice.

The presence of a sufficient number of the members of such a body regularly convened in an authorized place at an appointed time, engaged in the full and regular performance of its functions. 20 Ala. 446; 20 Ark. 77.

A court may be more particularly described as an organized body with defined powers, meeting at certain times and places for the hearing and decision of causes and other matters brought before it, and aided in this, its proper business, by its proper officers, viz., attorneys and counsel to present and manage the business, clerks to record and attest its acts and decisions, and ministerial officers to execute its commands, and secure due order in its proceedings. Burrill.

The place where justice is judicially administered. Co. Litt. 58*a;* 3 Bl. Comm. 23.

The judge, or the body of judges, presiding over a court.

The words "court" and "judge," or "judges," are frequently used in our statutes as synonymous. When used with reference to orders made by the court or judges, they are to be so understood. 3 Ind. 239.

The term "court" may be construed to mean the judges of the court, or to include the judges and jury, according to the connection and the object of its use. 19 Vt. 478.

Classification. Courts may be classified and divided according to several methods, the following being the more usual:

Courts of record and *courts not of record;* the former being those whose acts and judicial proceedings are enrolled, or recorded, for a perpetual memory and testimony, and which have power to fine or imprison for contempt. Error lies to their judgments, and they generally possess a seal. Courts not of record are those of inferior dignity, which have no power to fine or imprison, and in which the proceedings are not enrolled or recorded.

Superior and *inferior* courts; the former being courts of general original jurisdiction in the first instance, and which exercise a control or supervision over a system of lower courts, either by appeal, error, or *certiorari;* the latter being courts of small or restricted jurisdiction, and subject to the review or correction of higher courts. Sometimes the former term is used to denote a particular group or system of courts of high powers, and all others are called "inferior courts."

To constitute a court a superior court as to any class of actions, within the common-law meaning of that term, its jurisdiction of such actions must be unconditional, so that the only thing requisite to enable the court to take cognizance of them is the acquisition of jurisdiction of the persons of the parties. 4 Bosw. 547.

An inferior court is a court whose judgments or decrees can be reviewed, on appeal or writ of error, by a higher tribunal, whether that tribunal be the circuit or supreme court. 18 Ala. 521.

Civil and *criminal* courts; the former being such as are established for the adjudication of controversies between subject and subject, or the ascertainment, enforcement, and redress of private rights; the latter, such as are charged with the administration of the criminal laws, and the punishment of wrongs to the public.

Equity courts and *law* courts; the former being such as possess the jurisdiction of a chancellor, apply the rules and principles of chancery law, and follow the procedure in equity; the latter, such as have no equitable powers, but administer justice according to the rules and practice of the common law.

As to the division of courts according to their *jurisdiction,* see JURISDICTION.

COURT-BARON. In English law. A court which, although not one of record, is incident to every manor, and cannot be severed therefrom. It was ordained for the maintenance of the services and duties stipulated for by lords of manors, and for the purpose of determining actions of a personal nature, where the debt or damage was under forty shillings. Wharton.

Customary court-baron is one appertaining entirely to copyholders.

Freeholders' court-baron is one held before the freeholders who owe suit and service to the manor. It is the court-baron proper.

COURT CHRISTIAN. The ecclesiastical courts in England are often so called, as distinguished from the civil courts. 1 Bl. Comm. 83; 3 Bl. Comm. 64; 3 Steph. Comm. 430.

COURT, CONSISTORY. See CONSISTORY COURT.

COURT FOR CONSIDERATION OF CROWN CASES RESERVED. A court established by St. 11 & 12 Vict. c. 78, composed of such of the judges of the superior courts of Westminster as were able to attend, for the consideration of questions of law reserved by any judge in a court of oyer and terminer, gaol delivery, or quarter sessions, before which a prisoner had been found guilty by verdict. Such question is stated in the form of a special case. Mozley & Whiteley; 4 Steph. Comm. 442.

COURT FOR DIVORCE AND MATRIMONIAL CAUSES. This court was established by St. 20 & 21 Vict. c. 85, which transferred to it all jurisdiction then exercisable by any ecclesiastical court in England, in matters matrimonial, and also gave it new powers. The court consisted of the lord chancellor, the three chiefs, and three senior puisne judges of the common-law courts, and the judge ordinary, who together constituted, and still constitute, the "full court." The judge ordinary heard almost all matters in the first instance. By the judicature act, 1873, § 3, the jurisdiction of the court was transferred to the supreme court of judicature. Sweet.

COURT FOR THE CORRECTION OF ERRORS. The style of a court having jurisdiction for review, by appeal or writ of error. The name was formerly used in New York and South Carolina.

COURT FOR THE RELIEF OF INSOLVENT DEBTORS. In English law. A local court which has its sittings in London only, which receives the petitions of insolvent debtors, and decides upon the question of granting a discharge.

COURT FOR THE TRIAL OF IMPEACHMENTS. A tribunal empowered to try any officer of government or other person brought to its bar by the process of impeachment. In England, the house of lords constitutes such a court; in the United States, the senate; and in the several states, usually, the upper house of the legislative assembly.

COURT-HAND. In old English practice. The peculiar hand in which the records of courts were written from the earliest period down to the reign of George II. Its characteristics were great strength, compactness, and undeviating uniformity; and its use undoubtedly gave to the ancient record its acknowledged superiority over the modern, in the important quality of durability.

The writing of this hand, with its peculiar abbreviations and contractions, constituted, while it was in use, an art of no little importance, being an indispensable part of the profession of "clerkship," as it was called. Two sizes of it were employed, a large and a small hand; the former, called "great court-hand," being used for initial words or clauses, the *placita* of records, etc. Burrill.

COURT-HOUSE. The building occupied for the public sessions of a court, with its various offices. The term may be used of a place temporarily occupied for the sessions of a court, though not the regular court-house. 55 Mo. 181; 71 Ill. 350.

COURT-LANDS. Domains or lands kept in the lord's hands to serve his family.

COURT-LEET. The name of an English court of record held once in the year, and not oftener, within a particular hundred, lordship, or manor, before the steward of the leet; being the king's court granted by charter to the lords of those hundreds or manors. Its office was to view the frankpledges,—that is, the freemen within the liberty; to present by jury crimes happening within the jurisdiction; and to punish trivial misdemeanors. It has now, however, for the most part, fallen into total desuetude; though in some manors a court-leet is still periodically held for the transaction of the administrative business of the manor. Mozley & Whitley.

COURT-MARTIAL. A military court, convened under authority of government and the articles of war, for trying and punishing military offenses committed by soldiers or sailors in the army or navy.

COURT OF ADMIRALTY. A court having jurisdiction of causes arising under the rules of admiralty law. See ADMIRALTY.

COURT OF ANCIENT DEMESNE. In English law. A court of peculiar constitution, held by a bailiff appointed by the king, in which alone the tenants of the king's demesne could be impleaded. 2 Burrows, 1046; 1 Spence, Eq. Jur. 100; 2 Bl. Comm. 99; 1 Steph. Comm. 224.

COURT OF APPEAL, HER MAJESTY'S. The chief appellate tribunal of England. It was established by the judicature acts of 1873 and 1875, and is invested with the jurisdiction formerly exercised by the court of appeal in chancery, the exchequer chamber, the judicial committee of the privy council in admiralty and lunacy appeals, and with general appellate jurisdiction from the high court of justice.

COURT OF APPEALS. In American law. An appellate tribunal which, in Kentucky, Maryland, and New York, is the court of last resort. In Delaware and New Jersey, it is known as the "court of errors and appeals;" in Virginia and West Virginia, the "supreme court of appeals." In Texas the court of appeals is inferior to the supreme court.

COURT OF APPEALS IN CASES OF CAPTURE. A court erected by act of congress under the articles of confederation which preceded the adoption of the constitution. It had appellate jurisdiction in prize causes.

COURT OF ARBITRATION OF THE CHAMBER OF COMMERCE. A court of arbitrators, created for the convenience of merchants in the city of New York, by act of the legislature of New York. It decides disputes between members of the chamber of commerce, and between members and outside merchants who voluntarily submit themselves to the jurisdiction of the court.

COURT OF ARCHDEACON. The most inferior of the English ecclesiastical courts, from which an appeal generally lies to that of the bishop. 3 Bl. Comm. 64.

COURT OF ARCHES. See ARCHES COURT.

COURTS OF ASSIZE AND NISI PRIUS. Courts in England composed of two or more commissioners, called "judges of assize," (or of "assize and *nisi prius*,") who are twice in every year sent by the queen's special commission, on circuits all round the kingdom, to try, by a jury of the respective counties, the truth of such matters of fact as are there under dispute in the courts of Westminster Hall. 3 Steph. Comm. 421, 422; 3 Bl. Comm. 57.

COURT OF ATTACHMENTS. The lowest of the three courts held in the forests. It has fallen into total disuse.

COURT OF AUDIENCE. Ecclesiastical courts, in which the primates once exercised in person a considerable part of their jurisdiction. They seem to be now obsolete, or at least to be only used on the rare occurrence of the trial of a bishop. Phillim. Ecc. Law, 1201, 1204.

COURT OF AUGMENTATION. An English court created in the time of Henry VIII., with jurisdiction over the property and revenue of certain religious foundations, which had been made over to the king by act of parliament, and over suits relating to the same.

COURT OF BANKRUPTCY. An English court of record, having original and appellate jurisdiction in matters of bankruptcy, and invested with both legal and equitable powers for that purpose.

COURT OF CHANCERY. A court having the jurisdiction of a chancellor; a court administering equity and proceeding according to the forms and principles of equity. In England, prior to the judicature acts, the style of the court possessing the largest equitable powers and jurisdiction was the "high court of chancery." In some of the United States, the title "court of chancery" is applied to a court possessing general equity powers, distinct from the courts of common law.

The terms "equity" and "chancery," "court of equity" and "court of chancery," are constantly used as synonymous in the United States. It is presumed that this custom arises from the circumstance that the equity jurisdiction which is exercised by the courts of the various states is assimilated to that possessed by the English courts of chancery. Indeed, in some of the states it is made identical therewith by statute, so far as conformable to our institutions. Bouvier.

COURT OF CHIVALRY, or COURT MILITARY, was a court not of record, held before the lord high constable and earl marshal of England. It had jurisdiction, both civil and criminal, in deeds of arms and war, armorial bearings, questions of precedence, etc., and as a court of honor. It has long been disused. 3 Bl. Comm. 103; 3 Steph. Comm. 335, note *l*.

COURTS OF CINQUE PORTS. In English law. Courts of limited local jurisdiction formerly held before the mayor and jurats (aldermen) of the Cinque Ports.

COURT OF CLAIMS. One of the courts of the United States, erected by act of congress. It consists of a chief justice and four associates, and holds one annual session. It is located at Washington. Its jurisdiction extends to all claims against the United States arising out of any contract with the government or based on an act of congress or regulation of the executive, and all claims referred to it by either house of congress, as well as to claims for exoneration by a disbursing officer. Its judgments are, in certain cases, reviewable by the United States supreme court. It has no equity powers. Its decisions are reported and published.

COURT OF THE CLERK OF THE MARKET. An English court of inferior jurisdiction held in every fair or market for the punishment of misdemeanors committed therein, and the recognizance of weights and measures.

COURT OF COMMISSIONERS OF SEWERS. The name of certain English courts created by commission under the great seal pursuant to the statute of sewers, (23 Hen. VIII. c. 5.)

COURT OF COMMON PLEAS. The English court of common pleas was one of the four superior courts at Westminster, and existed up to the passing of the judicature acts. It was also styled the "Common Bench." It was one of the courts derived from the breaking up of the *aula regis*, and had exclusive jurisdiction of all real actions and of *communia placita*, or common pleas, *i. e.*, between subject and subject. It was presided over by a chief justice with four puisne judges. Appeals lay anciently to the king's bench, but afterwards to the exchequer chamber. See 3 Bl. Comm. 37, et seq.

In American law. The name sometimes given to a court of original and general jurisdiction for the trial of issues of fact and law according to the principles of the common law.

COURT OF COMMON PLEAS FOR THE CITY AND COUNTY OF NEW YORK. The oldest court in the state of New York. Its jurisdiction is unlimited as respects amount, but restricted to the city and county of New York as respects locality. It has also appellate jurisdiction of cases tried in the marine court and district courts of New York city. Rap. & L.

COURTS OF CONSCIENCE. These were the same as courts of request, (*q. v.*)

COURT OF CONVOCATION. In English ecclesiastical law. A court, or assembly, comprising all the high officials of each province and representatives of the minor clergy. It is in the nature of an ecclesiastical parliament; and, so far as its judicial functions extend, it has jurisdiction of cases of heresy, schism, and other purely ecclesiastical matters. An appeal lies to the queen in council.

COURT OF THE CORONER. In English law. A court of record, to inquire, when any one dies in prison, or comes to a violent or sudden death, by what manner he came to his end. 4 Steph. Comm. 323; 4 Bl. Comm. 274. See CORONER.

COURTS OF THE COUNTIES PALATINE. In English law. A species of private court which formerly appertained to the counties palatine of Lancaster and Durham.

COURT OF COUNTY COMMISSIONERS. There is in each county of Alabama a court of record, styled the "court of county commissioners," composed of the judge of probate, as principal judge, and four commissioners, who are elected at the times prescribed by law, and hold office for four years. Code Ala. 1886, § 819.

COURT OF DELEGATES. A tribunal composed of delegates appointed by royal commission, and formerly the great court of appeal in all ecclesiastical causes. The powers of the court were, by 2 & 3 Wm. IV. c. 92, transferred to the privy council. A commission of review was form·rly granted, in extraordinary cases, to revise a sentence of the court of delegates, when that court had apparently been led into material error. Brown.

COURT OF THE DUCHY OF LANCASTER. A court of special jurisdiction, held before the chancellor of the duchy or his deputy, concerning all matters of equity relating to lands holden of the king in right of the duchy of Lancaster. 3 Bl. Comm. 78.

COURT OF EQUITY. A court which has jurisdiction in equity, which administers justice and decides controversies in accordance with the rules, principles, and precedents of equity, and which follows the forms and procedure of chancery; as distinguished from a court having the jurisdiction, rules, principles, and practice of the common law.

COURT OF ERROR. An expression applied especially to the court of exchequer chamber and the house of lords, as taking cognizance of *error* brought. Mozley & Whitley. It is applied in some of the United States to the court of last resort in the state; and in its most general sense denotes any court having power to review the decisions of lower courts on appeal, error, *certiorari*, or other process.

COURT OF ERRORS AND APPEALS. The court of last resort in the state of New Jersey is so named. Formerly, the same title was given to the highest court of appeal in New York.

COURT OF EXCHEQUER. In English law. A very ancient court of record, set up by William the Conqueror as a part of the *aula regis*, and afterwards one of the four superior courts at Westminster. It was, however, inferior in rank to both the king's bench and the common pleas. It was presided over by a chief baron and four puisne barons. It was originally the king's treasury, and was charged with keeping the king's accounts and collecting the royal revenues. But pleas between subject and subject were anciently heard there, until this was forbidden by the *Articula super Chartas*, (1290,) after which its jurisdiction as a court only extended to revenue cases arising out of the non-payment or withholding of debts to the crown. But the privilege of suing and being sued in this court was extended to the king's accountants, and later, by the use of a convenient fiction to the effect that the plaintiff was the king's debtor or accountant, the court was thrown open to all suitors in personal actions. The exchequer had formerly both an equity side and a common-law side, but its equity jurisdiction was taken away by the statute 5 Vict. c. 5, (1842,) and transferred to the court of chancery. The judicature act (1873) transferred the business and jurisdiction of this court to the "Exchequer Division" of the "High Court of Justice."

In Scotch law. A court which formerly had jurisdiction of matters of revenue, and a limited jurisdiction over cases between the crown and its vassals where no questions of title were involved.

COURT OF EXCHEQUER CHAMBER. The name of a former English court of appeal, intermediate between the superior courts of common law and the house of lords. When sitting as a court of appeal from any one of the three superior courts of common law, it was composed of judges of the other two courts. 3 Bl. Comm. 56, 57; 3 Steph. Comm. 333, 356. By the judicature act (1873) the jurisdiction of this court is transferred to the court of appeal.

COURT OF GENERAL QUARTER SESSIONS OF THE PEACE. In American law. A court of criminal jurisdiction in New Jersey.

In English law. A court of criminal jurisdiction, in England, held in each county once in every quarter of a year, but in the county of Middlesex twice a month. 4 Steph. Comm. 317–320.

COURT OF GENERAL SESSIONS. The name given in some of the states (as New York) to a court of general original jurisdiction in criminal cases.

COURT OF GREAT SESSIONS IN WALES. A court formerly held in Wales; abolished by 11 Geo. IV. and 1 Wm. IV. c. 70, and the Welsh judicature incorporated with that of England. 3 Steph. Comm. 317, note.

COURT OF HUSTINGS. In English law. The county court of London, held before the mayor, recorder, and sheriff, but of which the recorder is, in effect, the sole judge. No actions can be brought in this court that are merely personal. 3 Steph. Comm. 449, note *l*.

In American law. A local court in some parts of the state of Virginia. 6 Grat. 696.

COURT OF INQUIRY. In English law. A court sometimes appointed by the crown to ascertain whether it be proper to resort to extreme measures against a person charged before a court-martial.

In American law. A court constituted by authority of the articles of war, invested with the power to examine into the nature of any transaction, accusation, or imputation against any officer or soldier. The said court shall consist of one or more officers, not exceeding three, and a judge advocate, or other suitable person, as a recorder, to reduce the proceedings and evidence to writing; all of whom shall be sworn to the performance of their duty. Rev. St. § 1342, arts. 115, 116.

COURT OF JUSTICE SEAT. In English law. The principal of the forest courts.

COURT OF JUSTICIARY. A Scotch court of general criminal jurisdiction of all offenses committed in any part of Scotland, both to try causes and to review decisions of inferior criminal courts. It is composed of five lords of session with the lord president or justice-clerk as president. It also has appellate jurisdiction in civil causes involving small amounts. An appeal lies to the house of lords.

COURT OF KING'S BENCH. In English law. The supreme court of common law in the kingdom, now merged in the high court of justice under the judicature act of 1873, § 16.

COURT OF THE LORD HIGH STEWARD. In English law. A court instituted for the trial, during the recess of parliament, of peers indicted for treason or felony, or for misprision of either. This court is not a permanent body, but is created in modern times, when occasion requires, and for the time being, only; and the lord high steward, so constituted, with such of the temporal lords as may take the proper oath, and act, constitute the court.

COURT OF THE LORD HIGH STEWARD OF THE UNIVERSITIES. In English law. A court constituted for the trial of scholars or privileged persons connected with the university at Oxford or Cambridge who are indicted for treason, felony, or mayhem.

COURT OF MAGISTRATES AND FREEHOLDERS. In American law. The name of a court formerly established in South Carolina for the trial of slaves and free persons of color for criminal offenses.

COURT OF MARSHALSEA. A court which had jurisdiction of all trespasses committed within the verge of the king's court, where one of the parties was of the royal household; and of all debts and contracts, when both parties were of that establishment. It was abolished by 12 & 13 Vict. c. 101, § 13. Mozley & Whitley.

COURT OF NISI PRIUS. In American law. Though this term is frequently used as a general designation of any court exercising general, original jurisdiction in civil cases, (being used interchangeably with "trial-court,") it belonged as a legal title only to a court which formerly existed in the city and county of Philadelphia, and which was presided over by one of the judges of the supreme court of Pennsylvania. This court was abolished by the constitution of 1874. See COURTS of ASSIZE AND NISI PRIUS.

COURT OF ORDINARY. In some of the United States (*e. g.*, Georgia) this name is given to the probate or surrogate's court, or the court having the usual jurisdiction in respect to the proving of wills and the administration of decedents' estates.

COURT OF ORPHANS. In English law. The court of the lord mayor and aldermen of London, which has the care of those orphans whose parent died in London and was free of the city.

In Pennsylvania (and perhaps some other states) the name "orphans' court" is applied to that species of tribunal which is elsewhere known as the "probate court" or "surrogate's court."

COURT OF OYER AND TERMINER. In English law. A court for the trial of cases of treason and felony. The commissioners of assise and *nisi prius* are judges selected by the queen and appointed and authorized under the great seal, including usually two of the judges at Westminster, and sent out twice a year into most of the counties of England, for the trial (with a jury of the county) of causes then depending at Westminster, both civil and criminal. They sit by virtue of several commissions, each of which, in reality, constitutes them a separate and distinct court. The commission of *oyer and terminer* gives them authority for the trial of treasons and felonies; that of *general gaol delivery* empowers them to try every prisoner then in gaol for whatever offense; so that, altogether, they possess full criminal jurisdiction.

In American law. This name is generally used (sometimes, with additions) as the title, or part of the title, of a state court of criminal jurisdiction, or of the criminal branch of a court of general jurisdiction, being commonly applied to such courts as may try *felonies*, or the higher grades of crime.

COURT OF OYER AND TERMINER AND GENERAL JAIL DELIVERY. In American law. A court of criminal jurisdiction in the state of Pennsylvania.

It is held at the same time with the court of quarter sessions, as a general rule, and by the same judges. See Brightly's Purd. Dig. Pa. pp. 26, 382, 1201.

COURT OF OYER AND TERMINER, GENERAL JAIL DELIVERY, AND COURT OF QUARTER SESSIONS OF THE PEACE, IN AND FOR THE CITY AND COUNTY OF PHILA-

DELPHIA. In American law. A court of record of general criminal jurisdiction in and for the city and county of Philadelphia, in the state of Pennsylvania.

COURT OF PALACE AT WESTMINSTER. This court had jurisdiction of personal actions arising within twelve miles of the palace at Whitehall. Abolished by 12 & 13 Vict. c. 101, 3 Steph. Comm. 317, note.

COURT OF PASSAGE. An inferior court, possessing a very ancient jurisdiction over causes of action arising within the borough of Liverpool. It appears to have been also called the "Borough Court of Liverpool." It has the same jurisdiction in admiralty matters as the Lancashire county court. Rosc. Adm. 75.

COURT OF PECULIARS. A spiritual court in England, being a branch of, and annexed to, the Court of Arches. It has a jurisdiction over all those parishes dispersed through the province of Canterbury, in the midst of other dioceses, which are exempt from the ordinary's jurisdiction, and subject to the metropolitan only. All ecclesiastical causes arising within these *peculiar* or exempt jurisdictions are originally cognizable by this court, from which an appeal lies to the Court of Arches. 3 Steph. Comm. 431; 4 Reeve, Eng. Law, 104.

COURT OF PIEPOUDRE. The lowest (and most expeditious) of the courts of justice known to the older law of England. It is supposed to have been so called from the dusty feet of the suitors. It was a court of record incident to every fair and market, was held by the steward, and had jurisdiction to administer justice for all commercial injuries and minor offenses done in that same fair or market, (not a preceding one.) An appeal lay to the courts at Westminster. This court long ago fell into disuse. 3 Bl. Comm. 32.

COURT OF PLEAS. A court of the county palatine of Durham, having a local common-law jurisdiction. It was abolished by the judicature act, which transferred its jurisdiction to the high court. Jud. Act 1873, § 16; 3 Bl. Comm. 79.

COURT OF POLICIES OF ASSURANCE. A court established by statute 43 Eliz. c. 12, to determine in a summary way all causes between merchants, concerning policies of insurance. Crabb, Eng. Law, 503.

COURTS OF PRINCIPALITY OF WALES. A species of private courts of a limited though extensive jurisdiction, which, upon the thorough reduction of that principality and the settling of its polity in the reign of Henry VIII., were erected all over the country. These courts, however, have been abolished by 1 Wm. IV. c. 70; the principality being now divided into two circuits, which the judges visit in the same manner as they do the circuits in England, for the purpose of disposing of those causes which are ready for trial. Brown.

COURT OF PROBATE. In English law. The name of a court established in 1857, under the probate act of that year, (20 & 21 Vict. c. 77,) to be held in London, to which court was transferred the testamentary jurisdiction of the ecclesiastical courts. 2 Steph. Comm. 192. By the judicature acts, this court is merged in the high court of justice.

In American law. A court having jurisdiction over the probate of wills, the grant of administration, and the supervision of the management and settlement of the estates of decedents, including the collection of assets, the allowance of claims, and the distribution of the estate. In some states the probate courts also have jurisdiction of the estates of minors, including the appointment of guardians and the settlement of their accounts, and of the estates of lunatics, habitual drunkards, and spendthrifts. And in some states these courts possess a limited jurisdiction in civil and criminal cases. They are also called "orphans' courts" and "surrogate's courts."

COURT OF QUARTER SESSIONS OF THE PEACE. In American law. A court of criminal jurisdiction in the state of Pennsylvania, having power to try misdemeanors, and exercising certain functions of an administrative nature. There is one such court in each county of the state. Its sessions are, in general, held at the same time and by the same judges as the *court of oyer and terminer and general jail delivery.* See Brightly's Purd. Dig. pp. 26, 383, § 35, p. 1198, § 1.

COURT OF QUEEN'S BENCH. See KING'S BENCH.

COURT OF RECORD. A court where the acts and judicial proceedings are enrolled on parchment or paper for a perpetual memorial and testimony; and which has power to fine and imprison for contempt of its authority. 3 Steph. Comm. 383; 3 Bl. Comm. 24.

A court which has jurisdiction to fine and imprison, or one having jurisdiction of civil causes above forty shillings, and proceeding according to the course of the common law. 37 Me. 29.

A judicial organized tribunal having attributes and exercising functions independently of the person of the magistrate designated generally to hold it, and proceeding according to the course of the common law. Bouvier.

Courts *not of record* are those of inferior dignity, which have no power to fine or imprison, and in which the proceedings are not enrolled or recorded. 3 Steph. Comm. 384.

COURT OF REGARD. In English law. One of the forest courts, in England, held every third year, for the lawing or expeditation of dogs, to prevent them from running after deer. It is now obsolete. 3 Steph. Comm. 440; 3 Bl. Comm. 71, 72.

COURTS OF REQUEST. Inferior courts, in England, having local jurisdiction in claims for small debts, established in various parts of the kingdom by special acts of parliament. They were abolished in 1846, and the modern county courts (*q. v.*) took their place. 3 Steph. Comm. 283.

COURT OF SESSION. The name of the highest court of civil jurisdiction in Scotland.

It was composed of fifteen judges, now of thirteen. It sits in two divisions. The lord president and three ordinary lords form the first division; the lord justice clerk and three other ordinary lords form the second division. There are five permanent lords ordinary attached equally to both divisions; the last appointed of whom officiates on the bills, *i. e.*, petitions preferred to the court during the session, and performs the other duties of junior lord ordinary. The chambers of the parliament house in which the first and second divisions hold their sittings are called the "inner house;" those in which the lords ordinary sit as single judges to hear motions and causes are collectively called the "outer house." The nomination and appointment of the judges is in the crown. Wharton.

COURT OF SESSIONS. Courts of criminal jurisdiction existing in California, New York, and one or two other of the United States.

COURT OF STANNARIES. In English law. A court established in Devonshire and Cornwall, for the administration of justice among the miners and tinners, and that they may not be drawn away from their business to attend suits in distant courts. The stannary court is a court of record, with a special jurisdiction. 3 Bl. Comm. 79.

COURT OF STAR CHAMBER. This was an English court of very ancient origin, but new-modeled by St. 3 Hen. VII. c. 1, and 21 Hen. VIII. c. 20, consisting of divers lords, spiritual and temporal, being privy councillors, together with two judges of the courts of common law, without the intervention of any jury. The jurisdiction extended legally over riots, perjury, misbehavior of sheriffs, and other misdemeanors contrary to the laws of the land; yet it was afterwards stretched to the asserting of all proclamations and orders of state, to the vindicating of illegal commissions and grants of monopolies; holding for honorable that which it pleased, and for just that which it profited, and becoming both a court of law to determine civil rights and a court of revenue to enrich the treasury. It was finally abolished by St. 16 Car. I. c. 10, to the general satisfaction of the whole nation. Brown.

COURT OF THE STEWARD AND MARSHAL. A high court, formerly held in England by the steward and marshal of the king's household, having jurisdiction of all actions against the king's peace within the bounds of the household for twelve miles, which circuit was called the "verge." Crabb, Eng. Law, 185. It had also jurisdiction of actions of debt and covenant, where both the parties were of the household. 2 Reeve, Eng. Law, 235, 247.

COURT OF THE STEWARD OF THE KING'S HOUSEHOLD. In English law. A court which had jurisdiction of all cases of treason, misprision of treason, murder, manslaughter, bloodshed, and other malicious strikings whereby blood is shed, occurring in or within the limits of any of the palaces or houses of the king, or any other house where the royal person is abiding.

It was created by statute 33 Hen. VIII. c. 12, but long since fell into disuse. 4 Bl. Comm. 276, 277, and notes.

COURT OF SURVEY. A court for the hearing of appeals by owners or masters of ships, from orders for the detention of unsafe ships, made by the English board of trade, under the merchant shipping act, 1876, § 6.

COURT OF SWEINMOTE. In old English law. One of the forest courts, having a somewhat similar jurisdiction to that of the court of attachments, (*q. v.*)

COURTS OF THE UNITED STATES comprise the following: The senate of the United States, sitting as a court of impeachment; the supreme court; the circuit courts; the circuit courts of appeals; the district courts; the supreme court of the District of Columbia; the territorial courts; and the court of claims. See the several titles.

COURTS OF THE UNIVERSITIES of Oxford and Cambridge have jurisdiction in all personal actions to which any member or servant of the respective university is a party, provided that the cause of action arose within the liberties of the university, and that the member or servant was resident in the university when it arose, and when the action was brought. 3 Steph. Comm. 299: St. 25 & 26 Vict. c. 26, § 12; St. 19 & 20 Vict. c. 17 Each university court also has a criminal jurisdiction in all offenses committed by its members. 4 Steph. Comm. 325.

COURT OF WARDS AND LIVERIES. A court of record, established in England in the reign of Henry VIII. For the survey and management of the valuable fruits of tenure, a court of record was created by St. 32 Hen. VIII. c. 46, called the "Court of the King's Wards." To this was annexed, by St. 33 Hen. VIII. c. 22, the "Court of Liveries;" so that it then became the "Court of Wards and Liveries." 4 Reeve, Eng. Law, 258. This court was not only for the management of "wards," properly so called, but also of idiots and natural fools in the king's custody, and for licenses to be granted to the king's widows to marry, and fines to be made for marrying without his license. Id. 259. It was abolished by statute 12 Car. II. c. 24. Crabb, Eng. Law, 468.

COURTS OF WESTMINSTER HALL. The superior courts, both of law and equity, were for centuries fixed at Westminster, an ancient palace of the monarchs of England. Formerly, all the superior courts were held before the king's capital justiciary of England, in the *aula regis*, or such of his palaces wherein his royal person resided, and removed with his household from one end of the kingdom to another. This was found to occasion great inconvenience to the suitors, to remedy which it was made an article of the great charter of liberties, both of King John and King Henry III., that "common pleas should no longer follow the king's court, but be held in some certain place," in consequence of which they have ever since been held (a few necessary removals in times of the plague excepted) in the palace of Westminster only. The courts of equity also sit at Westminster, nominally, during term-time, although, actually, only during the first day of term, for they generally sit in courts provided for the purpose in, or in the neighborhood of, Lincoln's Inn. Brown.

COURT PREROGATIVE. See PREROGATIVE COURT.

COURT ROLLS. The rolls of a manor, containing all acts relating thereto. While belonging to the lord of the manor, they are not in the nature of public books for the benefit of the tenant.

COURTESY. See CURTESY.

COUSIN. Kindred in the fourth degree, being the issue (male or female) of the brother or sister of one's father or mother.

Those who descend from the brother or sister of the father of the person spoken of are called "paternal cousins;" "maternal cousins" are those who are descended from the brothers or sisters of the mother.

In English writs, commissions, and other formal instruments issued by the crown, the word signifies any peer of the degree of an earl. The appellation is as ancient as the reign of Henry IV., who, being related or allied to every earl then in the kingdom, acknowledged that connection in all his letters and public acts; from which the use has descended to his successors, though the reason has long ago failed. Mozley & Whitley.

COUSINAGE. See COSINAGE.

COUSTOM. Custom; duty; toll; tribute. 1 Bl. Comm. 314.

COUSTOUMIER. (Otherwise spelled "*Coustumier*" or "*Coutumier.*") In old French law. A collection of customs, unwritten laws, and forms of procedure. Two such volumes are of especial importance in juridical history, viz., the *Grand Coustumier de Normandie*, and the *Coutumier de France* or *Grand Coutumier*.

COUTHUTLAUGH. A person who willingly and knowingly received an outlaw, and cherished or concealed him; for which offense he underwent the same punishment as the outlaw himself. Bract. 128*b*; Spelman.

COUVERTURE, in French law, is the deposit ("margin") made by the client in the hands of the broker, either of a sum of money or of securities, in order to guaranty the broker for the payment of the securities which he purchases for the client. Arg. Fr. Merc. Law, 555.

COVENABLE. A French word signifying convenient or suitable; as covenably endowed. It is anciently written "convenable." Termes de la Ley.

COVENANT. In practice. The name of a common-law form of action *ex contractu*, which lies for the recovery of damages for breach of a covenant, or contract under seal.

In the law of contracts. An agreement, convention, or promise of two or more parties, *by deed* in writing, signed, sealed, and delivered, by which either of the parties pledges himself to the other that something is either done or shall be done, or stipulates for the truth of certain facts.

An agreement between two or more parties, reduced to writing and executed by a sealing and delivery thereof, whereby some of the parties named therein engage, or one of them engages, with the other, or others, or some of them, therein also named, that some act hath or hath not already been done, or for the performance or non-performance of some specified duty. 4 Whart. 71.

A promise by deed. 2 Steph. Comm. 108. A species of express contract, contained in a deed, to do a direct act, or to omit one. 3 Bl. Comm. 155.

Covenant is a contract, and is a writing obligatory, or parol promise, according as it is sealed or not. 8 Ala. 320.

Covenants may be classified according to several distinct principles of division. According as one or other of these is adopted, they are:

Express or implied; the former being those which are created by the express words of the parties to the deed declaratory of their intention, (Platt, Cov. 25;) while implied covenants are those which are inferred by the law from certain words in a deed which imply (though they do not express) them. Express covenants are also called covenants "in deed," as distinguished from covenants "in law."

Dependent, concurrent, and independent.

Covenants are either dependent, concurrent, or mutual and independent. The first depends on the prior performance of some act or condition, and, until the condition is performed, the other party is not liable to an action on his covenant. In the second, mutual acts are to be performed at the same time; and if one party is ready, and offers to perform his part, and the other neglects or refuses to perform his, he who is ready and offers has fulfilled his engagement, and may maintain an action for the default of the other, though it is not certain that either is obliged to do the first act. The third sort is where either party may recover damages from the other for the injuries he may have received by a breach of the covenants in his favor; and it is no excuse for the defendant to allege a breach of the covenants on the part of the plaintiff. 3 Ala. 330.

Principal and auxiliary; the former being those which relate directly to the principal matter of the contract entered into between the parties; while auxiliary covenants are those which do not relate directly to the principal matter of contract between the parties, but to something connected with it.

Inherent or collateral; the former being such as affect the particular property immediately, while the latter affect some property collateral thereto.

Joint or several. The former bind both or all the covenantors together; the latter bind each of them separately. A covenant may be both joint and several at the same time, as regards the covenantors; but, as regards the covenantees, they cannot be joint and several for one and the same cause, (5 Coke, 19*a*,) but must be either joint or several only. Covenants are usually joint or several according as the interests of the covenantees are such; but the words of the covenant, where they are unambiguous, will decide, although, where they are ambiguous, the nature of the interests as being joint or several is left to decide. Brown.

General or specific. The former relate to land generally and place the covenantee in the position of a specialty creditor only; the latter relate to particular lands and give the covenantee a lien thereon. Brown.

Executed or executory; the former being such as relate to an act already performed; while the latter are those whose performance is to be future. Shep. Touch. 161.

Affirmative or negative; the former being those in which the party binds himself to the existence of a present state of facts as represented or to the future performance of some act; while the latter are those in which the covenantor obliges himself *not* to do or perform some act.

Declaratory or obligatory; the former being those which serve to limit or direct uses; while the latter are those which are binding on the party himself. 1 Sid. 27; 1 Keb. 337.

Real or personal; the former being such as bind the heirs of the covenantor, and passing to assignees, or to the purchaser; while a personal covenant affects only the covenantor and the assets in the hands of his representatives after his death. 4 Kent, Comm. 470, 471.

Transitive or intransitive; the former being those personal covenants the duty of performing which passes over to the representatives of the covenantor; while the latter are those the duty of performing which is limited to the covenantee himself, and does not pass over to his representative. Bac. Abr. Cov.

Disjunctive covenants. Those which are for the performance of one or more of several things at the election of the covenantor or covenantee, as the case may be. Platt, Cov. 21.

COVENANT AGAINST INCUMBRANCES. A covenant that there are no incumbrances upon the land conveyed.

COVENANT COLLATERAL. A covenant which is conversant about some collateral thing that doth nothing at all, or not so immediately concern the thing granted; as to pay a sum of money in gross, etc. Shep. Touch. 161.

COVENANT FOR FURTHER ASSURANCE. An undertaking, in the form of a covenant, on the part of the vendor of real estate to do such further acts for the purpose of perfecting the purchaser's title as the latter may reasonably require. This covenant is deemed of great importance, since it relates both to the title of the vendor and to the instrument of conveyance to the vendee, and operates as well to secure the performance of all acts necessary for supplying any defect in the former as to remove all objections to the sufficiency and security of the latter. Platt, Cov.; Rawle, Cov. §§ 98, 99.

COVENANT FOR QUIET ENJOYMENT. An assurance against the consequences of a defective title, and of any disturbances thereupon. Platt, Cov. 312; Rawle, Cov. 125.

COVENANT IN DEED. A covenant expressed in words, or inserted in a deed in specific terms.

COVENANT IN LAW. A covenant implied by law from certain words in a deed which do not express it. 1 Archb. N. P. 250.

COVENANT INHERENT. A covenant which is conversant about the land, and knit to the estate in the land; as that the thing demised shall be quietly enjoyed, shall be kept in reparation, shall not be aliened, etc. Shep. Touch. 161.

COVENANT NOT TO SUE. A covenant by one who had a right of action at the time of making it against another person, by which he agrees not to sue to enforce such right of action.

COVENANT OF NON-CLAIM. A covenant sometimes employed, particularly in the New England states, and in deeds of extinguishment of ground rents in Pennsylvania, that neither the vendor, nor his heirs, nor any other person, etc., shall claim any title in the premises conveyed. Rawle, Cov. § 22.

COVENANT OF RIGHT TO CONVEY. An assurance by the covenantor that the grantor has sufficient capacity and title to convey the estate which he by his deed undertakes to convey.

COVENANT OF SEISIN. An assurance to the purchaser that the grantor has the very estate in quantity and quality which he purports to convey. 11 East, 641; Rawle, Cov. § 58. It is said that the covenant of seisin is not now in use in England, being embraced in that of a right to convey; but it is used in several of the United States. 2 Washb. Real Prop. *648.

COVENANT OF WARRANTY. An assurance by the grantor of an estate that the grantee shall enjoy the same without interruption by virtue of paramount title.

COVENANT REAL. A covenant in a deed binding the heirs of the covenantor, and passing to assignees, or to the purchaser.

It is thus distinguished from a *personal* covenant, which affects only the covenantor, and the assets in the hands of his representatives after his death. 4 Kent, Comm. 470.

A covenant real has for its object something annexed to, or inherent in, or connected with, land or other real property, and runs with the land, so that the grantee of the land is invested with it, and may sue upon it for any breach happening in his time. 6 Conn. 249.

In the old books, a covenant real is also defined to be a covenant by which a man binds himself to pass a thing real, as lands or tenements. Termes de la Ley; 3 Bl. Comm. 156.

COVENANT RUNNING WITH LAND. A covenant which goes with the land, as being annexed to the estate, and which cannot be separated from the land, and transferred without it. 4 Kent, Comm. 472, note. A covenant is said to run with the land, when not only the original parties or their representatives, but each successive owner of the land, will be entitled to its benefit, or be liable (as the case may be) to its obligation. 1 Steph. Comm. 455. Or, in other words, it is so called when either the liability to perform it or the right to take advantage of it passes to the assignee of the land.

COVENANT TO CONVEY. A covenant by which the covenantor agrees to convey to the covenantee a certain estate, under certain circumstances.

COVENANT TO STAND SEISED. A conveyance adapted to the case where a person seised of land in possession, reversion, or vested remainder, proposes to convey it to his wife, child, or kinsman. In its terms it consists of a covenant by him, in consideration of his natural love and affection, to stand seised of the land to the use of the intended transferee. Before the statute of uses this would merely have raised a use in favor of the covenantee; but by that act this use is converted into the legal estate, and the covenant therefore operates as a conveyance of the land to the covenantee. It is now almost obsolete. 1 Steph. Comm. 532; Williams, Seis. 145.

COVENANTEE. The party to whom a covenant is made. Shep. Touch. 160.

COVENANTOR. The party who makes a covenant. Shep. Touch. 160.

COVENANTS FOR TITLE. Covenants usually inserted in a conveyance of land, on the part of the grantor, and binding him for the completeness, security, and continuance of the title transferred to the grantee. They comprise "covenants for seisin, for right to convey, against incumbrances, for quiet enjoyment, sometimes for further assurance, and almost always of warranty." Rawle, Cov. § 21.

COVENANTS IN GROSS. Such as do not run with the land.

COVENANTS PERFORMED. In Pennsylvania practice. This is the name of a plea to the action of covenant whereby the defendant, upon informal notice to the plaintiff, may give anything in evidence which he might have pleaded. 4 Dall. 439.

COVENT. A contraction, in the old books, of the word "convent."

COVENTRY ACT. The name given to the statute 22 & 23 Car. II. c. 1, which provided for the punishment of assaults with intent to maim or disfigure a person. It was so named from its being occasioned by an assault on Sir John Coventry in the street. 4 Bl. Comm. 207.

COVERT. Covered, protected, sheltered. A *pound covert* is one that is close or covered over, as distinguished from *pound overt*, which is open overhead. Co. Litt. 47*b*; 3 Bl. Comm. 12. A *feme covert* is so called, as being under the wing, protection, or *cover* of her husband. 1 Bl. Comm. 442.

COVERT BARON, or COVERT DE BARON. Under the protection of a husband; married. 1 Bl. Comm. 442. *La feme que est covert de baron*, the woman which is covert of a husband. Litt. § 670.

COVERTURE. The condition or state of a married woman. Sometimes used elliptically to describe the legal disability arising from a state of coverture.

COVIN. A secret conspiracy or agreement between two or more persons to injure or defraud another.

COVINOUS. Deceitful, fraudulent.

COWARDICE. Pusillanimity; fear; misbehavior through fear in relation to some duty to be performed before an enemy. O'Brien, Ct. M. 142.

CRAFT. A general term, now commonly applied to all kinds of sailing vessels, though formerly restricted to the smaller vessels. Worcester; 21 Grat. 693.

A guild.

CRANAGE. A liberty to use a crane for drawing up goods and wares of burden from ships and vessels, at any creek of the sea, or wharf, unto the land, and to make a profit of doing so. It also signifies the money paid and taken for the service. Tomlins.

CRASSA NEGLIGENTIA. Gross neglect; absence of ordinary care and diligence. 82 N. Y. 72.

CRASSUS. Large; gross; excessive; extreme. *Crassa ignorantia*, gross ignorance. Fleta, lib. 5, c. 22, § 18.

CRASTINO. The morrow, the day after. The return-day of writs; because the first day of the term was always some saint's day, and writs were returnable on the day after. 2 Reeve, Eng. Law, 56.

CRATES. An iron gate before a prison. 1 Vent. 304.

CRAVE. To ask or demand; as to crave oyer. See OYER.

CRAVEN. In old English law. A word of disgrace and obloquy, pronounced on either champion, in the ancient trial by battle, proving recreant, *i. e.*, yielding. Glanville calls it "*infestum et inverecundum verbum.*" His condemnation was *amittere liberam legem*, *i. e.*, to become infamous, and not to be accounted *liber et legalis homo*, being supposed by the event to have been proved forsworn, and not fit to be put upon a jury or admitted as a witness. Wharton.

CREAMER. A foreign merchant, but generally taken for one who has a stall in a fair or market. Blount.

CREAMUS. We create. One of the words by which a corporation in England was formerly created by the king. 1 Bl. Comm. 473.

CREANCE. In French law. A claim; a debt; also belief, credit, faith.

CREANCER. One who trusts or gives credit; a creditor. Britt. cc. 28, 78.

CREANSOR. A creditor. Cowell.

CREATE. To *create* a charter or a corporation is to make one which never existed before, while to *renew* one is to give vitality to one which has been forfeited or has expired; and to *extend* one is to give an existing charter more time than originally limited. 21 Pa. St. 188.

CREDENTIALS. In international law. The instruments which authorize and establish a public minister in his character with the state or prince to whom they are addressed. If the state or prince receive the minister, he can be received only in the quality attributed to him in his credentials. They are, as it were, his letter of attorney, his mandate patent, *mandatum manifestum*. Vattel, liv. 4, c. 6, § 76.

CREDIBILITY. Worthiness of belief; that quality in a witness which renders his evidence worthy of belief. After the competence of a witness is allowed, the consideration of his *credibility* arises, and not before. 1 Burrows, 414, 417; 3 Bl. Comm. 369.

As to the distinction between *competency* and *credibility*, see COMPETENCY.

CREDIBLE. Worthy of belief; entitled to credit. See COMPETENCY.

CREDIBLE WITNESS. One who, being competent to give evidence, is worthy of belief. 5 Mass. 229; 17 Pick. 154; 2 Curt. Ecc. 336.

CREDIT. 1. The ability of a business man to borrow money, or obtain goods on time, in consequence of the favorable opinion held by the community, or by the particular lender, as to his solvency and reliability.

2. Time allowed to the buyer of goods by the seller, in which to make payment for them.

3. The correlative of a *debt;* that is, a debt considered from the creditor's stand-point, or that which is incoming or due *to* one.

4. That which is due to a merchant, as distinguished from debit, that which is due by him.

5. That influence connected with certain social positions. 20 Toullier, n. 19.

The credit of an individual is the trust reposed in him by those who deal with him that he is of ability to meet his engagements; and he is trusted because through the tribunals of the country he may be made to pay. The credit of a government is founded on a belief of its ability to comply with its engagements, and a confidence in its honor, that it will do that voluntarily which it cannot be compelled to do. 3 Ala. 258.

Credit is the capacity of being trusted. 3 N. Y. 344, 356.

CREDIT, BILLS OF. See BILLS OF CREDIT.

CRÉDIT FONCIER. Fr. A company or corporation formed for the purpose of carrying out improvements, by means of loans and advances on real estate security.

CRÉDIT MOBILIER. Fr. A company or association formed for carrying on a banking business, or for the construction of public works, building of railroads, operation of mines, or other such enterprises, by means of loans or advances on the security of personal property.

CREDITOR. A person to whom a debt is owing by another person, called the "debtor." The creditor is called a "simple contract creditor," a "specialty creditor," a "bond creditor," or a "judgment creditor," according to the nature of the obligation giving rise to the debt; and, if he has issued execution to enforce a judgment, he is called an "execution creditor." He may also be a sole or a joint creditor. Sweet.

CREDITOR, JUDGMENT. One who has obtained a judgment against his debtor, under which he can enforce execution.

CREDITORS' BILL. In English practice. A bill in equity, filed by one or more creditors, for an account of the assets of a decedent, and a legal settlement and distribution of his estate among themselves and such other creditors as may come in under the decree.

In American practice. A proceeding to enforce the security of a judgment creditor against the property or interests of his debtor. This action proceeds upon the theory that the judgment is in the nature of a lien, such as may be enforced in equity.

A creditors' bill, strictly, is a bill by which a creditor seeks to satisfy his debt out of some equitable estate of the defendant, which is not liable to levy and sale under an execution at law. But there is another sort of a creditors' bill, very nearly allied to the former, by means of which a party seeks to remove a fraudulent conveyance out of the way of his execution. But a naked bill to set aside a fraudulent deed, which seeks no discovery of any property, chose in action, or other thing alleged to belong to the defendant, and which ought to be subjected to the payment of the judgment, is not a creditors' bill. 52 Ill. 98.

Creditorum appellatione non hi tantum accipiuntur qui pecuniam crediderunt, sed omnes quibus ex qualibet causa debetur. Under the head of "creditors" are included, not alone those who have lent money, but all to whom from any cause a debt is owing. Dig. 50, 16, 11.

CREDITRIX. A female creditor.

CREEK. In maritime law. Such little inlets of the sea, whether within the precinct or extent of a port or without, as are narrow passages, and have shore on either side of them. Call. Sew. 56.

A small stream less than a river. 12 Pick. 184.

The term imports a recess, cove, bay, or inlet in the shore of a river, and not a separate or independent stream; though it is sometimes used in the latter meaning. 38 N. Y. 103.

CREMENTUM COMITATÛS. The increase of a county. The sheriffs of counties anciently answered in their accounts for the improvement of the king's rents, above the *viscontiel* rents, under this title.

CREPARE OCULUM. In Saxon law. To put out an eye; which had a pecuniary punishment of fifty shillings annexed to it.

CREPUSCULUM. Twilight. In the law of burglary, this term means the presence of sufficient light to discern the face of a man; such light as exists immediately before the rising of the sun or directly after its setting.

Crescente malitiâ crescere debet et pœna. 2 Inst. 479. Vice increasing, punishment ought also to increase.

CREST. A term used in heraldry; it signifies the devices set over a coat of arms.

CRETINUS. In old records. A sudden stream or torrent; a rising or inundation.

CRETIO. Lat. In the civil law. A certain number of days allowed an heir to deliberate whether he would take the inheritance or not. Calvin.

CREW. The aggregate of seamen who man a ship or vessel, including the master and officers; or it may mean the ship's company, exclusive of the master, or exclusive of the master and all other officers. See 3 Sum. 209, et seq.

CREW LIST. In maritime law. A list of the crew of a vessel; one of a ship's papers. This instrument is required by act of congress, and sometimes by treaties. Rev. St. U. S. §§ 4374, 4375. It is necessary for the protection of the crews of every vessel, in the course of the voyage, during a war abroad. Jac. Sea Laws, 66, 69, note.

CRIER. An officer of a court, who makes proclamations. His principal duties are to announce the opening of the court and its adjournment and the fact that certain special matters are about to be transacted, to announce the admission of persons to the bar, to call the names of jurors, witnesses, and parties, to announce that a witness has been sworn, to proclaim silence when so directed, and generally to make such proclamations of a public nature as the judges order.

CRIEZ LA PEEZ. Rehearse the concord, or peace. A phrase used in the ancient proceedings for levying fines. It was the form of words by which the justice before whom the parties appeared directed the serjeant or countor in attendance to recite or *read aloud* the *concord* or agreement between the parties, as to the lands intended to be conveyed. 2 Reeve, Eng. Law, 224, 225.

CRIM. CON. An abbreviation for "criminal conversation," of very frequent use, denoting adultery.

CRIME. A crime is an act committed or omitted, in violation of a public law, either forbidding or commanding it; a breach or violation of some public right or duty due to a whole community, considered as a community in its social aggregate capacity, as distinguished from a civil injury. "Crime" and "misdemeanor," properly speaking, are synonymous terms; though in common usage "crime" is made to denote such offenses as are of a deeper and more atrocious dye. 4 Bl. Comm. 5.

Crimes are those wrongs which the government notices as injurious to the public, and punishes in what is called a "criminal proceeding," in its own name. 1 Bish. Crim. Law, § 43.

A crime may be defined to be any act done in violation of those duties which an individual owes to the community, and for the breach of which the law has provided that the offender shall make satisfaction to the public. Bell.

A crime or public offense is an act committed or omitted in violation of a law forbidding or commanding it, and to which is annexed, upon conviction, either of the following punishments: (1) Death; (2) imprisonment; (3) fine; (4) removal from office; or (5) disqualification to hold and enjoy any office of honor, trust, or profit in this state. Pen. Code Cal. § 15.

A crime or misdemeanor shall consist in a violation of a public law, in the commission of which there shall be a union or joint operation of act and intention, or criminal negligence. Code Ga. 1882, § 4292.

According to Blackstone, the word "crime" denotes such offenses as are of a deeper and more atrocious dye, while smaller faults and omissions of less consequence are called "misdemeanors." But the better use appears to be to make *crime* a term of broad and general import, including both felonies and misdemeanors, and hence covering all infractions of the criminal law. In this sense it is not a technical phrase, strictly speaking, (as "felony" and "misdemeanor" are,) but a convenient general term. In this sense, also, "offense" or "public offense" should be used as synonymous with it.

The distinction between a *crime* and a *tort* or civil injury is that the former is a breach and violation of the public right and of duties due to the whole community considered as such, and in its social and aggregate capacity; whereas the latter is an infringement or privation of the civil rights of individuals merely. Brown.

A crime, as opposed to a civil injury, is the violation of a right, considered in reference to the evil tendency of such violation, as regards the community at large. 4 Steph. Comm. 4.

CRIME AGAINST NATURE. The offense of buggery or sodomy.

CRIMEN. Lat. Crime. Also an accusation or charge of crime.

CRIMEN FALSI. **In the civil law.** The crime of falsifying; which might be committed either by writing, as by the forgery of a will or other instrument; by words, as by bearing false witness, or perjury; and by acts, as by counterfeiting or adulterating the public money, dealing with false weights and measures, counterfeiting seals, and other fraudulent and deceitful practices. Dig. 48, 10; Hallifax, Civil Law, b. 3, c. 12, nn. 56–59.

In Scotch law. It has been defined: "A fraudulent imitation or suppression of truth, to the prejudice of another." Ersk. Inst. 4, 4, 66.

At common law. Any crime which may injuriously affect the administration of justice, by the introduction of falsehood and fraud. 1 Greenl. Ev. § 373.

In modern law. This phrase is not used as a designation of any specific crime, but as a general designation of a class of offenses, including all such as involve deceit or falsification; *e. g.*, forgery, counterfeiting, using false weights or measures, perjury, etc.

Includes forgery, perjury, subornation of perjury, and offenses affecting the public administration of justice. 29 Ohio St. 358.

Crimen falsi dicitur, cum quis illicitus, cui non fuerit ad hæc data auctoritas, de sigillo regis, rapto vel invento, brevia, cartasve consignaverit. Fleta, lib. 1, c. 23. The crime of forgery is when any one illicitly, to whom power has not been given for such purposes, has signed writs or charters with the king's seal, either stolen or found.

CRIMEN FURTI. The offense of theft.

CRIMEN INCENDII. In old criminal law. The crime of burning, which included not only the modern crime of arson, (or burning of a house,) but also the burning of a man, beast, or other chattel. Britt. c. 9; Crabb, Eng. Law, 308.

CRIMEN INNOMINATUM. The nameless crime. A term for buggery or sodomy.

CRIMEN LÆSÆ MAJESTATIS. In criminal law. The crime of *lese-majesty,* or injuring majesty or royalty; high treason. The term was used by the older English law-writers to denote any crime affecting the king's person or dignity.

It is borrowed from the civil law, in which it signified the undertaking of any enterprise against the emperor or the republic. Inst. 4, 18, 3.

Crimen læsæ majestatis omnia alia crimina excedit quoad pœnam. 3 Inst. 210. The crime of treason exceeds all other crimes in its punishment.

Crimen omnia ex se nata vitiat. Crime vitiates everything which springs from it. 5 Hill, 523, 531.

CRIMEN RAPTUS. The offense of rape.

CRIMEN ROBERIÆ. The offense of robbery.

Crimen trahit personam. The crime carries the person, (*i. e.*, the commission of a crime gives the courts of the place where it is committed jurisdiction over the person of the offender.) 3 Denio, 190, 210.

Crimina morte extinguuntur. Crimes are extinguished by death.

CRIMINAL. That which pertains to or is connected with the law of crimes, or the administration of penal justice, or which relates to or has the character of crime. Also a person who has committed a crime; one who is guilty of a felony or misdemeanor.

CRIMINAL ACT. A term which is equivalent to crime; or is sometimes used with a slight softening or glossing of the meaning, or as importing a possible question of the legal guilt of the deed.

CRIMINAL ACTION. The proceeding by which a party charged with a public offense is accused and brought to trial and punishment is known as a "criminal action." Pen. Code Cal. § 683.

A criminal action is (1) an action prosecuted by the state as a party, against a person charged with a public offense, for the punishment thereof; (2) an action prosecuted by the state, at the instance of an individual, to prevent an apprehended crime, against his person or property. Code N. C. 1883, § 129.

CRIMINAL CASE. An action, suit, or cause instituted to punish an infraction of the criminal laws.

CRIMINAL CONTEMPT. A contempt of court which consists in openly insulting or resisting the powers of the court or the persons of the judges who preside there. Otherwise called "direct" contempt. 4 Bl. Comm. 283.

CRIMINAL CONVERSATION. Adultery, considered in its aspect of a civil injury to the husband entitling him to damages; the tort of debauching or seducing of a wife. Often abbreviated to *crim. con.*

CRIMINAL INFORMATION. A criminal suit brought, without interposition of a grand jury, by the proper officer of the king or state. Cole, Crim. Inf.; 4 Bl. Comm. 398.

CRIMINAL INTENT. The intent to commit a crime; malice, as evidenced by a criminal act.

CRIMINAL LAW. That branch or division of law which treats of crimes and their punishments.

In the plural—"criminal laws"—the term may denote the laws which define and prohibit the various species of crimes and establish their punishments.

CRIMINAL LAW AMENDMENT ACT. This act was passed in 1871, (34 & 35 Vict. c. 32,) to prevent and punish any violence, threats, or molestation, on the part either of master or workmen, in the various relations arising between them. 4 Steph. Comm. 241.

CRIMINAL LAW CONSOLIDATION ACTS. The statutes 24 & 25 Vict. cc. 94-100, passed in 1861, for the consolidation of the criminal law of England and Ireland. 4 Steph. Comm. 297. These important statutes amount to a codification of the modern criminal law of England.

CRIMINAL LETTERS. In Scotch law. A process used as the commencement of a criminal proceeding, in the nature of a summons issued by the lord advocate or his deputy. It resembles a criminal information at common law.

CRIMINAL LIBEL. A libel which is punishable criminally; one which tends to excite a breach of the peace.

CRIMINAL PROCEDURE. The method pointed out by law for the apprehension, trial, or prosecution, and fixing the punishment, of those persons who have broken or violated, or are supposed to have broken or violated, the laws prescribed for the regulation of the conduct of the people of the community, and who have thereby laid themselves liable to fine or imprisonment or other punishment. 4 Amer. & Eng. Enc. Law, 730.

CRIMINAL PROCESS. Process which issues to compel a person to answer for a crime or misdemeanor. 1 Stew. (Ala.) 27.

CRIMINAL PROSECUTION. An action or proceeding instituted in a proper court on behalf of the public, for the purpose of securing the conviction and punishment of one accused of crime.

CRIMINALITER. Criminally. This term is used, in distinction or opposition to the word "*civiliter*," civilly, to distinguish a criminal liability or prosecution from a civil one.

CRIMINATE. To charge one with crime; to furnish ground for a criminal prosecution; to expose a person to a criminal charge. A witness cannot be compelled to answer any question which has a tendency to *criminate* him.

CRIMP. One who decoys and plunders sailors under cover of harboring them. Wharton.

CRO, CROO. In old Scotch law. A weregild. A composition, satisfaction, or assythment for the slaughter of a man.

CROCIA. The *crosier*, or pastoral staff.

CROCIARIUS. A cross-bearer, who went before the prelate. Wharton.

CROCKARDS, CROCARDS. A foreign coin of base metal, prohibited by statute 27 Edw. I. St. 3, from being brought into the realm. 4 Bl. Comm. 98; Crabb, Eng. Law, 176.

CROFT. A little close adjoining a dwelling-house, and inclosed for pasture and tillage or any particular use. Jacob. A small place fenced off in which to keep farm-cattle. Spelman. The word is now entirely obsolete.

CROISES. Pilgrims; so called as wearing the sign of the *cross* on their upper garments. Britt. c. 122. The knights of the order of St. John of Jerusalem, created for the defense of the pilgrims. Cowell; Blount.

CROITEIR. A crofter; one holding a croft.

CROP. The products of the harvest in corn or grain. Emblements.

CROPPER. One who, having no interest in the land, works it in consideration of receiving a portion of the crop for his labor. 2 Rawle, 11.

The difference between a tenant and a cropper is: A tenant has an estate in the land for the term, and, consequently, he has a right of property in the crops. Until division, the right of property and of possession in the whole is the tenant's. A cropper has no estate in the land; and, although he has in some sense the possession of the crop, it is the possession of a servant only, and is, in law, that of the landlord, who must divide off to the cropper his share. 71 N. C. 7.

CROSS. A mark made by persons who are unable to write, to stand instead of a signature; usually made in the form of a Maltese cross.

As an adjective, the word is applied to various demands and proceedings which are connected in subject-matter, but opposite or contradictory in purpose or object.

CROSS-ACTION. An action brought by one who is defendant in a suit against the party who is plaintiff in such suit, upon a cause of action growing out of the same transaction which is there in controversy, whether it be a contract or tort.

CROSS-APPEAL. Where both parties to a judgment appeal therefrom, the appeal of each is called a "cross-appeal" as regards that of the other. 3 Steph. Comm. 581.

CROSS-BILL. In equity practice. One which is brought by a defendant in a suit against a plaintiff in or against other defendants in the same suit, or against both, touching the matters in question in the original bill. Story, Eq. Pl. § 389; Mitf. Eq. Pl. 80.

A cross-bill is a bill brought by a defendant against a plaintiff, or other parties in a former bill depending, touching the matter in question in that bill. It is usually brought either to obtain a necessary discovery of facts in aid of the defense to the original bill, or to obtain full relief to all parties in reference to the matters of the original bill. It is to be treated as a mere auxiliary suit. 17 How. 591; 35 N. H. 235.

A cross-bill is a species of pleading, used for the purpose of obtaining a discovery necessary to the defense, or to obtain some relief founded on the collateral claims of the party defendant to the original suit. 14 Ga. 167.

Also, if a bill of exchange or promissory note be given in consideration of another bill or note, it is called a "cross" or "counter" bill or note.

CROSS-COMPLAINT. In code practice. Whenever the defendant seeks affirmative relief against any party, relating to or depending upon the contract or transaction upon which the action is brought, or affecting the property to which the action relates, he may, in addition to his answer, file at the same time, or by permission of the court subsequently, a cross-complaint. The cross-complaint must be served upon the parties affected thereby, and such parties may demur or answer thereto as to the original complaint. Code Civil Proc. Cal. § 442.

CROSS-DEMAND. Where a person against whom a demand is made by another, in his turn makes a demand against that other, these mutual demands are called "cross-demands." A *set-off* is a familiar example.

CROSS-ERRORS. Errors being assigned by the respondent in a writ of error, the errors assigned on both sides are called "cross-errors."

CROSS-EXAMINATION. In practice. The examination of a witness upon a trial or hearing, or upon taking a deposition, by the party opposed to the one who produced him, upon his evidence given in chief, to test its truth, to further develop it, or for other purposes.

CROSS-REMAINDER. Where land is devised or conveyed to two or more persons as tenants in common, or where different parts of the same land are given to such persons in severalty, with such limitations that, upon the determination of the particular estate of either, his share is to pass to the other, to the entire exclusion of the ultimate remainder-man or reversioner until all the particular estates shall be exhausted, the remainders so limited are called "cross-remainders." In wills, such remainders may arise by implication; but, in deeds, only by express limitation. See 2 Bl. Comm. 381; 2 Washb. Real Prop. 233; 1 Prest. Est. 94.

CROSS-RULES. These were rules where each of the opposite litigants obtained a rule *nisi*, as the plaintiff to increase the damages, and the defendant to enter a nonsuit. Wharton.

CROSSED CHECK. A check crossed with two lines, between which are either the name of a bank or the words "and company," in full or abbreviated. In the former case, the banker on whom it is drawn must not pay the money for the check to any other than the banker named; in the latter case, he must not pay it to any other than a banker. 2 Steph. Comm. 118, note *c*.

CROWN. The sovereign power in a monarchy, especially in relation to the punishment of crimes. "Felony is an offense of the crown." Finch, Law, b. 1, c. 16.

An ornamental badge of regal power worn on the head by sovereign princes. The word is frequently used when speaking of the sovereign herself, or the rights, duties, and prerogatives belonging to her. Also a silver coin of the value of five shillings. Wharton.

CROWN CASES. In English law. Criminal prosecutions on behalf of the crown, as representing the public; causes in the criminal courts.

CROWN CASES RESERVED. In English law. Questions of law arising in criminal trials at the assizes, (otherwise than by way of demurrer,) and not decided there, but reserved for the consideration of the court of criminal appeal.

CROWN COURT. In English law. The court in which the crown cases, or criminal business, of the assizes is transacted.

CROWN DEBTS. In English law. Debts due to the crown, which are put, by various statutes, upon a different footing from those due to a subject.

CROWN LANDS. The demesne lands of the crown.

CROWN LAW. Criminal law in England is sometimes so termed, the crown being always the prosecutor in criminal proceedings. 4 Bl. Comm. 2.

CROWN OFFICE. The criminal side of the court of king's bench. The king's attorney in this court is called "master of the crown office." 4 Bl. Comm. 308.

CROWN OFFICE IN CHANCERY. One of the offices of the English high court of chancery, now transferred to the high court of justice. The principal official, the clerk of the crown, is an officer of parliament, and of the lord chancellor, in his non-judicial capacity, rather than an officer of the courts of law.

CROWN PAPER. A paper containing the list of criminal cases which await the hearing or decision of the court, and particularly of the court of queen's bench; and it then includes all cases arising from informations *quo warranto*, criminal informations, criminal cases brought up from inferior courts by writ of *certiorari*, and cases from the sessions. Brown.

CROWN SIDE. The criminal department of the court of queen's bench; the civil department or branch being called the "plea side." 4 Bl. Comm. 265.

CROWN SOLICITOR. In England, the solicitor to the treasury acts, in state prosecutions, as solicitor for the crown in preparing the prosecution. In Ireland there are officers called "crown solicitors" attached to each circuit, whose duty it is to get up every case for the crown in criminal prosecutions. They are paid by salaries. There is no such system in England, where prosecutions are conducted by solicitors appointed by the parish, or other persons bound over to prosecute by the magistrates on each committal; but in Scotland the still better plan exists of a crown prosecutor (called the "procurator-fiscal," and being a subordinate of the lord-advocate) in every county, who prepares every criminal prosecution. Wharton.

CROWNER. In old Scotch law. Coroner; a coroner.

CROY. In old English law. Marsh land. Blount.

CRUCE SIGNATI. In old English law. Signed or marked with a cross. Pilgrims to the holy land, or crusaders; so called because they wore the sign of the cross upon their garments. Spelman.

CRUELTY. The intentional and malicious infliction of physical suffering upon living creatures, particularly human beings; or, as applied to the latter, the wanton, malicious, and unnecessary infliction of pain upon the body, or the feelings and emotions; abusive treatment; inhumanity; outrage.

Extreme cruelty is the infliction of grievous bodily injury or grievous mental suffering upon the other by one party to the marriage. Civil Code Cal. § 94.

As between husband and wife. Those acts which affect the life, the health, or even the comfort, of the party aggrieved, and give a reasonable apprehension of bodily hurt, are called "cruelty." What merely wounds the feelings is seldom admitted to be cruelty, unless the act be accompanied with bodily injury, either actual or menaced. Mere austerity of temper, petulance of manners, rudeness of language, a want of civil attention and accommodation, even occasional sallies of passion, will not amount to legal cruelty; *a fortiori*, the denial of little indulgences and particular accommodations, which the delicacy of the world is apt to number among its necessaries, is not cruelty. The negative descriptions of cruelty are perhaps the best, under the infinite variety of cases that may occur, by showing what is not cruelty. 1 Hagg. Const. 35; 4 Eng. Ecc. 238, 311, 312.

Cruelty includes both willfulness and malicious temper of mind with which an act is done, as well as a high degree of pain inflicted. Acts merely accidental, though they inflict great pain, are not "cruel," in the sense of the word as used in statutes against cruelty. 101 Mass. 34.

CRUISE. A voyage undertaken for a given purpose; a voyage for the purpose of making captures *jure belli.* 2 Gall. 538.

A voyage or expedition in quest of vessels or fleets of the enemy which may be expected to sail in any particular track at a certain season of the year. The region in which these cruises are performed is usually termed the "rendezvous," or "cruising latitude." Bouvier.

Imports a definite place, as well as time of commencement and termination, unless such construction is repelled by the context. When not otherwise specially agreed, a cruise begins and ends in the country to which a ship belongs, and from which she derives her commission. 2 Gall. 526.

CRY. To call out aloud; to proclaim; to publish; to sell at auction. "To cry a tract of land." 1 Wash. (Va.) 335, (260.)

CRY DE PAIS, or CRI DE PAIS. The hue and cry raised by the people in ancient times, where a felony had been committed and the constable was absent.

CRYER. An auctioneer. 1 Wash. (Va.) 337, (262.) One who calls out aloud; one who publishes or proclaims. See CRIER.

CRYPTA. A chapel or oratory underground, or under a church or cathedral. Du Cange.

CUCKING-STOOL. An engine of correction for common scolds, which in the Saxon language is said to signify the scolding-stool, though now it is frequently corrupted into *ducking-stool*, because the judgment was that, when the woman was placed therein, she should be plunged in the water for her punishment. It was also variously called a "trebucket," "tumbrel," or "castigatory." 3 Inst. 219; 4 Bl. Comm. 169; Brown.

CUEILLETTE. A term of French maritime law. See A CUEILLETTE.

CUI ANTE DIVORTIUM. (To whom before divorce.) A writ for a woman divorced from her husband to recover her lands and tenements which she had in fee-simple or in tail, or for life, from him to whom her husband alienated them during the marriage, when she could not gainsay it. Reg. Orig. 233.

CUI BONO. For whose good; for whose use or benefit. "*Cui bono* is ever of great weight in all agreements." Parker, C. J.,

10 Mod. 135. Sometimes translated, for what good, for what useful purpose.

Cuicunque aliquis quid concedit concedere videtur et id, sine quo res ipsa esse non potuit. 11 Coke, 52. Whoever grants anything to another is supposed to grant that also without which the thing itself would be of no effect.

CUI IN VITA. (To whom in life.) A writ of entry for a widow against him to whom her husband aliened her lands or tenements in his life-time; which must contain in it that during his life she could not withstand it. Reg. Orig. 232; Fitzh. Nat. Brev. 193.

Cui jurisdictio data est, ea quoque concessa esse videntur, sine quibus jurisdictio explicari non potest. To whomsoever a jurisdiction is given, those things also are supposed to be granted, without which the jurisdiction cannot be exercised. Dig. 2, 1, 2. The grant of jurisdiction implies the grant of all powers necessary to its exercise. 1 Kent, Comm. 339.

Cui jus est donandi, eidem et vendendi et concedendi jus est. He who has the right of giving has also the right of selling and granting. Dig. 50, 17, 163.

Cuilibet in arte sua perito est credendum. Any person skilled in his peculiar art or profession is to be believed, [*i. e.*, when he speaks of matters connected with such art.] Co. Litt. 125*a*; Shelf. Mar. & Div. 206. Credence should be given to one skilled in his peculiar profession. Broom, Max. 932.

Cuilibet licet juri pro se introducto renunciare. Any one may waive or renounce the benefit of a principle or rule of law that exists only for his protection.

Cui licet quod majus, non debet quod minus est non licere. He who is allowed to do the greater ought not to be prohibited from doing the less. He who has authority to do the more important act ought not to be debarred from doing what is of less importance. 4 Coke, 23.

Cui pater est populus non habet ille patrem. He to whom the people is father has not a father. Co. Litt. 123.

Cuique in sua arte credendum est. Every one is to be believed in his own art. 9 Mass. 227.

Cujus est commodum ejus debet esse incommodum. Whose is the advantage, his also should be the disadvantage.

Cujus est dare, ejus est disponere. Wing. Max. 53. Whose it is to give, his it is to dispose; or, as Broom says, "the bestower of a gift has a right to regulate its disposal." Broom, Max. 459, 461, 463, 464.

Cujus est divisio, alterius est electio. Whichever [of two parties] has the division, [of an estate,] the choice [of the shares] is the other's. Co. Litt. 166*b*. In partition between coparceners, where the division is made by the eldest, the rule in English law is that she shall choose her share last. Id.; 2 Bl. Comm. 189; 1 Steph. Comm. 323.

Cujus est dominium ejus est periculum. The risk lies upon the owner of the subject. Tray. Lat. Max. 114.

Cujus est instituere, ejus est abrogare. Whose right it is to institute, his right it is to abrogate. Broom, Max. 878, note.

Cujus est solum ejus est usque ad cœlum. Whose is the soil, his it is up to the sky. Co. Litt. 4*a*. He who owns the soil, or surface of the ground, owns, or has an exclusive right to, everything which is upon or above it to an indefinite height. 9 Coke, 54; Shep. Touch. 90; 2 Bl. Comm. 18; 3 Bl. Comm. 217; Broom, Max. 395.

Cujus est solum, ejus est usque ad cœlum et ad inferos. To whomsoever the soil belongs, he owns also to the sky and to the depths. The owner of a piece of land owns everything above and below it to an indefinite extent. Co. Litt. 4.

Cujus juris (*i. e.*, jurisdictionis) est principale, ejusdem juris erit accessorium. 2 Inst. 493. An accessory matter is subject to the same jurisdiction as its principal.

Cujus per errprem dati repetitio est, ejus consulto dati donatio est. He who gives a thing by mistake has a right to recover it back; but, if he gives designedly, it is a gift. Dig. 50, 17, 53.

Cujusque rei potissima pars est principium. The chiefest part of everything is the beginning. Dig. 1, 2, 1; 10 Coke, 49*a*.

CUL DE SAC. (Fr. the bottom of a sack.) A blind alley; a street which is open at one end only.

CULAGIUM. In old records. The laying up a ship in a dock, in order to be repaired. Cowell; Blount.

CULPA. A term of the civil law, meaning fault, neglect, or negligence. There are three degrees of *culpa,—lata culpa,* gross fault or neglect; *levis culpa,* ordinary fault or neglect; *levissima culpa,* slight fault or neglect,—and the definitions of these degrees are precisely the same as those in our law. Story, Bailm. § 18. This term is to be distinguished from *dolus,* which means fraud, guile, or deceit.

Culpa caret qui scit sed prohibere non potest. He is clear of blame who knows, but cannot prevent. Dig. 50, 17, 50.

Culpa est immiscere se rei ad se non pertinenti. 2 Inst. 208. It is a fault for any one to meddle in a matter not pertaining to him.

Culpa lata dolo æquiparatur. Gross negligence is held equivalent to intentional wrong.

Culpa tenet [teneat] suos auctores. Misconduct binds [should bind] its own authors. It is a never-failing axiom that every one is accountable only for his own delicts. Ersk. Inst. 4, 1, 14.

CULPABILIS. Lat. In old English law. Guilty. *Culpabilis de intrusione,*—guilty of intrusion. Fleta, lib. 4, c. 30, § 11.

CULPABLE. Means not only criminal, but censurable; and, when the term is applied to the omission by a person to preserve the means of enforcing his own rights, censurable is more nearly an equivalent. As he has merely lost a right of action which he might voluntarily relinquish, and has wronged nobody but himself, culpable neglect conveys the idea of neglect which exists where the loss can fairly be ascribed to the party's own carelessness, improvidence, or folly. 8 Allen, 121.

CULPABLE HOMICIDE. Described as a crime varying from the very lowest culpability, up to the very verge of murder. Lord Moncrieff, Arkley, 72.

Culpæ pœna par esto. Pœna ad mensuram delicti statuenda est. Let the punishment be proportioned to the crime. Punishment is to be measured by the extent of the offense.

CULPRIT. A person who is indicted for a criminal offense, but not yet convicted. It is not, however, a techical term of the law; and in its vernacular usage it seems to imply only a light degree of censure or moral reprobation.

Blackstone believes it an abbreviation of the old forms of arraignment, whereby, on the prisoner's pleading not guilty, the clerk would respond, "*culpabilis, prit,*" *i. e.*, he is guilty and the crown is ready. It was (he says) the *viva voce* replication, by the clerk, on behalf of the crown, to the prisoner's plea of *non culpabilis; prit* being a technical word, anciently in use in the formula of joining issue. 4 Bl. Comm. 339.

But a more plausible explanation is that given by Donaldson, (cited Whart. Lex.,) as follows: The clerk asks the prisoner, "Are you guilty, or not guilty?" Prisoner, "Not guilty." Clerk, "*Qu'il paroit,* [may it prove so.] How will you be tried?" Prisoner, "By God and my country." These words being hurried over, came to sound, "Culprit, how will you be tried?" The ordinary derivation is from *culpa.*

CULRACH. In old Scotch law. A species of pledge or cautioner, (Scotticé, *back borgh,*) used in cases of the replevin of persons from one man's court to another's. Skene.

CULTIVATED. A field on which a crop of wheat is growing is a cultivated field, although not a stroke of labor may have been done in it since the seed was put in the ground, and it is a cultivated field after the crop is removed. It is, strictly, a cultivated piece of ground. 13 Ired. 36.

CULTURA. A parcel of arable land. Blount.

CULVERTAGE. In old English law. A base kind of slavery. The confiscation or forfeiture which takes place when a lord seizes his tenant's estate. Blount; Du Cange.

Cum actio fuerit mere criminalis, institui poterit ab initio criminaliter vel civiliter. When an action is merely criminal, it can be instituted from the beginning either criminally or civilly. Bract. 102.

Cum adsunt testimonia rerum, quid opus est verbis? When the proofs of facts are present, what need is there of words? 2 Bulst. 53.

Cum aliquis renunciaverit societati, solvitur societas. When any partner renounces the partnership, the partnership is dissolved. Tray. Lat. Max. 118.

Cum confitente sponte mitius est agendum. 4 Inst. 66. One confessing willingly should be dealt with more leniently.

Cum de lucro duorum quæritur, melior est causa possidentis. When the question is as to the gain of two persons, the cause of him who is in possession is the better. Dig. 50, 17, 126.

Cum duo inter se pugnantia reperiuntur in testamento, ultimum ratum est. Where two things repugnant to each other are found in a will, the last shall stand. Co. Litt. 112*b;* Shep. Touch. 451; Broom, Max. 583.

Cum duo jura concurrunt in una persona æquum est ac si essent in duobus. When two rights meet in one person, it is the same as if they were in two persons.

CUM GRANO SALIS. (With a grain of salt.) With allowance for exaggeration.

Cum in corpore dissentitur, apparet nullam esse acceptionem. When there is a disagreement in the substance, it appears that there is no acceptance. 12 Allen, 44.

Cum in testamento ambigue aut etiam perperam scriptum est benigne interpretari et secundum id quod credibile est cogitatum credendum est. Dig. 34, 5, 24. Where an ambiguous, or even an erroneous, expression occurs in a will, it should be construed liberally, and in accordance with the testator's probable meaning. Broom, Max. 568.

Cum legitimæ nuptiæ factæ sunt, patrem liberi sequuntur. Children born under a legitimate marriage follow the condition of the father.

CUM ONERE. With the burden; subject to an incumbrance or charge. What is taken *cum onere* is taken subject to an existing burden or charge.

Cum par delictum est duorum, semper oneratur petitor et melior habetur possessoris causa. Dig. 50, 17, 154. When both parties are in fault the plaintiff must always fail, and the cause of the person in possession be preferred.

CUM PERA ET LOCULO. With satchel and purse. A phrase in old Scotch law.

CUM PERTINENTIIS. With the appurtenances. Bract. fol. 73*b*.

CUM PRIVILEGIO. The expression of the monopoly of Oxford, Cambridge, and the royal printers to publish the Bible.

Cum quod ago non valet ut ago, valeat quantum valere potest. 4 Kent, Comm. 493. When that which I do is of no effect as I do it, it shall have as much effect as it can; *i. e.*, in some other way.

CUM TESTAMENTO ANNEXO. L. Lat. With the will annexed. A term applied to administration granted where a testator makes an incomplete will, without naming any executors, or where he names incapable persons, or where the executors named refuse to act. 2 Bl. Comm. 503, 504.

CUMULATIVE. Additional; heaping up; increasing; forming an aggregate. The word signifies that two things are to be added together, instead of one being a repetition or in substitution of the other.

CUMULATIVE EVIDENCE. Additional or corroborative evidence to the same point. That which goes to prove what has already been established by other evidence. 20 Conn. 305; 28 Me. 376; 24 Pick. 246.

All evidence material to the issue, after any such evidence has been given, is in a certain sense cumulative; that is, is added to what has been given before. It tends to sustain the issue. But cumulative evidence, in legal phrase, means evidence from the same or a new witness, simply repeating, in substance and effect, or adding to, what has been before testified to. 43 Barb. 212.

Evidence is not cumulative merely because it tends to establish the same ultimate or *principally controverted* fact. Cumulative evidence is additional evidence of the same kind to the same point. 43 Iowa, 177.

CUMULATIVE LEGACIES. These are legacies so called to distinguish them from legacies which are merely *repeated.* In the construction of testamentary instruments, the question often arises whether, where a testator has twice bequeathed a legacy to the same person, the legatee is entitled to both, or only to one of them; in other words, whether the second legacy must be considered as a mere repetition of the first, or as cumulative, *i. e.*, additional. In determining this question, the intention of the testator, if it appears on the face of the instrument, prevails. Wharton.

CUMULATIVE REMEDY. A remedy created by statute in addition to one which still remains in force.

CUMULATIVE SENTENCES. Separate sentences (each additional to the others) imposed upon a defendant who has been convicted upon an indictment containing several counts, each of such counts charging a distinct offense.

CUMULATIVE VOTING. A system of voting, by which the elector, having a number of votes equal to the number of officers to be chosen, is allowed to concentrate the whole number of his votes upon one person, or to distribute them as he may see fit. For example, if ten directors of a corporation are to be elected, then, under this system, the voter may cast ten votes for one person, or five votes for each of two persons, etc. It is intended to secure representation of a minority.

CUNADES. In Spanish law. Affinity; alliance; relation by marriage. Las Partidas, pt. 4, tit. 6, l. 5.

CUNEATOR. A coiner. Du Cange. *Cuneare*, to coin. *Cuneus*, the die with which to coin. *Cuneata*, coined. Du Cange; Spelman.

CUNTEY-CUNTEY. In old English law. A kind of trial, as appears from Bract. lib. 4, tract 3, ca. 18, and tract 4, ca. 2, where it seems to mean, one by the ordinary jury.

CUR. A common abbreviation of *curia*.

CURA. Lat. Care; charge; oversight; guardianship.

In the civil law. A species of guardianship which commenced at the age of puberty, (when the guardianship called "*tutela*" expired,) and continued to the completion of the twenty-fifth year. Inst. 1, 23, pr.; Id. 1, 25, pr.; Hallifax, Civil Law, b. 1, c. 9.

CURAGULOS. One who takes care of a thing.

CURATE. In ecclesiastical law. Properly, an incumbent who has the *cure* of souls, but now generally restricted to signify the spiritual assistant of a rector or vicar in his *cure*. An officiating temporary minister in the English church, who represents the proper incumbent; being regularly employed either to serve in his absence or as his assistant, as the case may be. 1 Bl. Comm. 393; 3 Steph. Comm. 88; Brande.

CURATEUR. In French law. A person charged with supervising the administration of the affairs of an emancipated minor, of giving him advice, and assisting him in the important acts of such administration. Duverger.

CURATIO. In the civil law. The power or duty of managing the property of him who, either on account of infancy or some defect of mind or body, cannot manage his own affairs. The duty of a curator or guardian. Calvin.

CURATOR. In the civil law. A person who is appointed to take care of anything for another. A guardian. One appointed to take care of the estate of a minor above a certain age, a lunatic, a spendthrift, or other person not regarded by the law as competent to administer it for himself. The title was also applied to a variety of public officers in Roman administrative law.

In Scotch law. The term means a guardian.

In Louisiana. A person appointed to take care of the estate of an absentee. Civil Code La. art. 50.

In Missouri. The term "curator" has been adopted from the civil law, and it is applied to the guardian of the estate of the ward as distinguished from the guardian of his person. 49 Mo. 117.

CURATOR AD HOC. In the civil law. A guardian for this purpose; a special guardian.

CURATOR AD LITEM. Guardian for the suit. In English law, the corresponding phrase is "guardian *ad litem*."

CURATOR BONIS. In the civil law. A guardian or trustee appointed to take care of *property* in certain cases; as for the benefit of creditors. Dig. 42, 7.

In Scotch law. The term is applied to guardians for minors, lunatics, etc.

CURATORES VIARUM. Surveyors of the highways.

CURATORSHIP. The office of a curator. Curatorship differs from tutorship, (*q. v.*,) in this; that the latter is instituted for the protection of property in the first place, and, secondly, of the person; while the former is intended to protect, first, the person, and secondly, the property. 1 Lec. El. Dr. Civ. Rom. 241.

CURATRIX. A woman who has been appointed to the office of curator; a female guardian. 4 Grat. 227.

Curatus non habet titulum. A curate has no title, [to tithes.] 3 Bulst. 310.

CURE BY VERDICT. See AIDER BY VERDICT.

CURE OF SOULS. In ecclesiastical law. The ecclesiastical or spiritual charge of a parish, including the usual and regular duties of a minister in charge.

CURFEW. An institution supposed to have been introduced into England by order of William the Conqueror, which consisted in the ringing of a bell or bells at eight o'clock at night, at which signal the people were required to extinguish all lights in their dwellings, and to put out or rake up their fires, and retire to rest, and all companies to disperse. The word is probably derived from the French *couvre feu*, to cover the fire.

CURIA. In old European law. A court. The palace, household, or retinue of a sovereign. A judicial tribunal or court held in the sovereign's palace. A court of justice. The civil power, as distinguished from the ecclesiastical. A manor; a nobleman's house; the hall of a manor. A piece of ground attached to a house; a yard or court-yard. Spelman. A lord's court held in his manor. The tenants who did suit and service at the lord's court. A manse. Cowell.

In Roman law. A division of the Roman people, said to have been made by Romulus. They were divided into three tribes, and each tribe into ten *curiæ*, making thirty *curiæ* in all. Spelman.

The place or building in which each *curia* assembled to offer sacred rites.

The place of meeting of the Roman senate; the senate house.

The senate house of a province; the place where the *decuriones* assembled. Cod. 10, 31, 2. See DECURIO.

CURIA ADMIRALITATIS. The court of admiralty.

CURIA ADVISARI VULT. L. Lat. The court will advise; the court will consider. A phrase frequently found in the reports, signifying the resolution of the court to suspend judgment in a cause, after the argument, until they have deliberated upon the question, as where there is a new or difficult point involved. It is commonly abbreviated to *cur. adv. vult*, or *c. a. v.*

CURIA BARONIS, or BARONUM. In old English law. A court-baron. Fleta, lib. 2, c. 53.

Curia cancellariæ officina justitiæ. 2 Inst. 552. The court of chancery is the workshop of justice.

CURIA CHRISTIANITATIS. The ecclesiastical court.

CURIA CLAUDENDA. The name of a writ to compel another to make a fence or wall, which he was bound to make, between his land and the plaintiff's. Reg. Orig. 155. Now obsolete.

CURIA COMITATUS. The county court, (*q. v.*)

CURIA CURSUS AQUÆ. A court held by the lord of the manor of Gravesend for the better management of barges and boats plying on the river Thames between Gravesend and Windsor, and also at Gravesend bridge, etc. 2 Geo. II. c. 26.

CURIA DOMINI. In old English law. The lord's court, house, or hall, where all the tenants met at the time of keeping court. Cowell.

CURIA LEGITIME AFFIRMATA. A phrase used in old Scotch records to show that the court was opened in due and lawful manner.

CURIA MAGNA. In old English law. The great court; one of the ancient names of parliament.

CURIA MAJORIS. In old English law. The mayor's court. Calth. 144.

CURIA MILITUM. A court so called, anciently held at Carisbrook Castle, in the Isle of Wight. Cowell.

CURIA PALATII. The palace court. It was abolished by 12 & 13 Vict. c. 101.

Curia parliamenti suis propriis legibus subsistit. 4 Inst. 50. The court of parliament is governed by its own laws.

CURIA PEDIS PULVERIZATI. In old English law. The court of *piedpoudre* or *piepouders*, (*q. v.*) 3 Bl. Comm. 32.

CURIA PENTICIARUM. A court held by the sheriff of Chester, in a place there called the "*Pendice*" or "*Pentice*;" probably it was so called from being originally held under a pent-house, or open shed covered with boards. Blount.

CURIA PERSONÆ. In old records. A parsonage-house, or manse. Cowell.

CURIA REGIS. The king's court. A term applied to the *aula regis*, the *bancus*, or *communis bancus*, and the *iter* or *eyre*, as being courts of the king, but especially to the *aula regis*, (which title see.)

CURIÆ CHRISTIANITATIS. Courts of Christianity; ecclesiastical courts.

CURIALITY. In Scotch law. Curtesy. Also the privileges, prerogatives, or, perhaps, retinue, of a court.

Curiosa et captiosa interpretatio in lege reprobatur. A curious [overnice or subtle] and captious interpretation is reprobated in law. 1 Bulst. 6.

CURNOCK. In old English law. A measure containing four bushels or half a quarter of corn. Cowell; Blount.

CURRENCY. Coined money and such bank-notes or other paper money as are authorized by law and do in fact circulate from hand to hand as the medium of exchange.

CURRENT. Running; now in transit; whatever is at present in course of passage; as "the current month." When applied to money, it means "lawful;" current money is equivalent to lawful money. 1 Dall. 124.

CURRENT FUNDS. This phrase means gold or silver, or something equivalent thereto, and convertible at pleasure into coined money. 4 Ala. 90.

CURRENT MONEY. The currency of the country; whatever is intended to and does actually circulate as currency; every species of coin or currency. 5 Lea, 96. In this phrase the adjective "current" is not synonymous with "convertible." It is employed to describe money which passes from hand to hand, from person to person, and circulates through the community, and is generally received. Money is current which is received as money in the common business transactions, and is the common medium in barter and trade. 41 Ala. 321.

CURRICULUM. The year; of the course of a year; the set of studies for a particular period, appointed by a university.

CURRIT QUATUOR PEDIBUS. L. Lat. It runs upon four feet; or, as sometimes expressed, it runs upon all fours. A phrase used in arguments to signify the entire and exact application of a case quoted. "It does not follow that they run *quatuor pedibus.*" 1 W. Bl. 145.

Currit tempus contra desides et sui juris contemptores. Time runs against the slothful and those who neglect their rights. Bract. fols. 100*b*, 101.

CURSITOR BARON. An officer of the court of exchequer, who is appointed by patent under the great seal to be one of the barons of the exchequer. The office was abolished by St. 19 & 20 Vict. c. 86.

CURSITORS. Clerks in the chancery office, whose duties consisted in drawing up those writs which were of course, *de cursu*, whence their name. They were abolished by St. 5 & 6 Wm. IV. c. 82. Spence, Eq. Jur. 238; 4 Inst. 82.

CURSO. In old records. A ridge. *Cursones terræ*, ridges of land. Cowell.

CURSOR. An inferior officer of the papal court.

Cursus curiæ est lex curiæ. 3 Bulst. 53. The practice of the court is the law of the court.

CURTESY. The estate to which by common law a man is entitled, on the death of his wife, in the lands or tenements of which she was seised in possession in fee-simple or in tail during their coverture, provided they have had lawful issue born alive which might have been capable of inheriting the estate. It is a freehold estate for the term of his natural life. 1 Washb. Real Prop. 127; 2 Bl. Comm. 126; Co. Litt. 30*a*.

CURTEYN. The name of King Edward the Confessor's sword. It is said that the point of it was broken, as an emblem of mercy. (Mat. Par. in Hen. III.) Wharton.

CURTILAGE. The inclosed space of ground and buildings immediately surrounding a dwelling-house.

In its most comprehensive and proper legal signification, it includes all that space of ground and buildings thereon which is usually inclosed within the *general fence* immediately surrounding a principal messuage and outbuildings, and yard closely adjoining to a dwelling-house, but it may be large enough for cattle to be levant and couchant therein. 1 Chit. Gen. Pr. 175.

The curtilage of a dwelling-house is a space, necessary and convenient and habitually used for the family purposes, and the carrying on of domestic employments. It includes the garden, if there be one, and it need not be separated from other lands by fence. 31 Me. 522; 10 Cush. 480; 29 N. J. Law, 474.

The curtilage is the court-yard in the front or rear of a house, or at its side, or any piece of ground lying near, inclosed and used with, the house, and necessary for the convenient occupation of the house. 10 Hun, 154.

In Michigan the meaning of curtilage has been extended to include more than an inclosure near the house. 2 Mich. 250.

CURTILES TERRÆ. In old English law. Court lands. Cowell. See COURT LANDS.

CURTILLIUM. A curtilage; the area or space within the inclosure of a dwelling-house. Spelman.

CURTIS. A garden; a space about a house; a house, or manor; a court, or palace; a court of justice; a nobleman's residence. Spelman.

CUSSORE. A term used in Hindostan for the discount or allowance made in the exchange of rupees, in contradistinction to *batta*, which is the sum deducted. Enc. Lond.

CUSTA, CUSTAGIUM, CUSTANTIA. Costs.

CUSTODE ADMITTENDO, CUSTODE AMOVENDO. Writs for the admitting and removing of guardians.

CUSTODES. **In Roman law.** Guardians; observers; inspectors. Persons who acted as inspectors of elections, and who counted the votes given. Tayl. Civil Law, 193.

In old English law. Keepers; guardians; conservators.

Custodes pacis, guardians of the peace. 1 Bl. Comm. 349.

CUSTODES LIBERTATIS ANGLIÆ AUCTORITATE PARLIAMENTI. The style in which writs and all judicial processes were made out during the great revolution, from the execution of King Charles I. till Oliver Cromwell was declared protector.

CUSTODIA LEGIS. In the custody of the law.

CUSTODIAM LEASE. In English law. A grant from the crown under the exchequer seal, by which the custody of lands, etc., seised in the king's hands, is demised or committed to some person as custodee or lessee thereof. Wharton.

CUSTODY. The care and keeping of anything; as when an article is said to be "in the custody of the court." Also the detainer of a man's person by virtue of lawful process or authority; actual imprisonment. 59 Pa. St. 320.

In a sentence that the defendant "be in custody until," etc., this term imports actual imprisonment. The duty of the sheriff under such a sentence is not performed by allowing the defendant to go at large under his general watch and control, but so doing renders him liable for an escape. 59 Pa. St. 320.

CUSTOM. A usage or practice of the people, which, by common adoption and acquiescence, and by long and unvarying habit, has become compulsory, and has acquired the force of a law with respect to the place or subject-matter to which it relates.

A law not written, established by long usage, and the consent of our ancestors. Termes de la Ley; Cowell; Bract. fol. 2. If it be universal, it is common law; if particular to this or that place, it is then properly *custom*. 3 Salk. 112.

Customs result from a long series of actions constantly repeated, which have, by such repetition, and by uninterrupted acquiescence, acquired the force of a tacit and common consent. Civil Code La. art. 3.

It differs from prescription, which is personal and is annexed to the person of the owner of a particular estate; while the other is local, and relates to a particular district. An instance of the latter occurs where the question is upon the manner of conducting a particular branch of trade at a certain place; of the former, where a certain person and his ancestors, or those whose estates he has, have been entitled to a certain advantage or privilege, as to have common of pasture in a certain close, or the like. The distinction has been thus expressed: "While prescription is the making of a right, custom is the making of a law." Lawson, Usages & Cust. 15, note 2.

Customs are either *general* or *particular*. General customs are such as prevail throughout a country and become the law of the country; and their existence is to be determined by the court. Particular customs are such as prevail in some county, city, town, parish, or place. 23 Me. 90.

CUSTOM-HOUSE. In administrative law. The house or office where commodities are entered for importation or exportation; where the duties, bounties, or drawbacks payable or receivable upon such importation or exportation are paid or received; and where ships are cleared out, etc.

CUSTOM-HOUSE BROKER. One whose occupation it is, as the agent of others, to arrange entries and other custom-house papers, or transact business, at any port of entry, relating to the importation or exportation of goods, wares, or merchandise. 14 St. at Large, 117.

A person authorized by the commissioners of customs to act for parties, at their option, in the entry or clearance of ships and the transaction of general business. Wharton.

Custom is the best interpreter of the law. 4 Inst. 75; 2 Eden, 74; 5 Cranch, 32; 1 Serg. & R. 106.

CUSTOM OF MERCHANTS. A system of customs or rules relative to bills of exchange, partnership, and other mercantile matters, and which, under the name of the "*lex mercatoria*," or "law-merchant," has been ingrafted into, and made a part of, the common law. 1 Bl. Comm. 75; 1 Steph. Comm. 54; 2 Burrows, 1226, 1228.

CUSTOM OF YORK. A custom of intestacy in the province of York similar to that of London. Abolished by 19 & 20 Vict. c. 94.

CUSTOMARY COURT-BARON. A court-baron at which copyholders might transfer their estates, and where other matters relating to their tenures were transacted. 3 Bl. Comm. 33.

CUSTOMARY ESTATES. Estates which owe their origin and existence to the custom of the manor in which they are held. 2 Bl. Comm. 149.

CUSTOMARY FREEHOLD. In English law. A variety of copyhold estate, the evidences of the title to which are to be found upon the court rolls; the entries declaring the holding to be according to the custom of the manor, but it is not said to be at the will of the lord. The incidents are similar to those of common or pure copyhold. 1 Steph. Comm. 212, 213, and note.

CUSTOMARY SERVICES. Such as are due by ancient custom or prescription only.

CUSTOMARY TENANTS. Tenants holding by custom of the manor.

Custome serra prise stricte. Custom shall be taken [is to be construed] strictly. Jenk. Cent. 83.

CUSTOMS. This term is usually applied to those taxes which are payable upon goods and merchandise imported or exported. Story, Const. § 949; Bac. Abr. "Smuggling."

The duties, toll, tribute, or tariff payable upon merchandise exported or imported. These are called "customs" from having been paid from time immemorial. Expressed in law Latin by *custuma*, as distinguished from *consuetudines*, which are usages merely. 1 Bl. Comm. 314.

CUSTOMS AND SERVICES annexed to the tenure of lands are those which the tenants thereof owe unto their lords, and which, if withheld, the lord might anciently have resorted to "a writ of customs and services" to compel them. Cowell. But at the present day he would merely proceed to eject the tenant as upon a forfeiture, or claim damages for the subtraction. Brown.

CUSTOMS CONSOLIDATION ACT. The statute 16 & 17 Vict. c. 107, which has been frequently amended. See 2 Steph. Comm. 563.

CUSTOMS OF LONDON. Particular customs within the city of London, with regard to trade, apprentices, widows, orphans, and a variety of other matters. 1 Bl. Comm. 75; 1 Steph. Comm. 54, 55.

CUSTOS. A custodian, guard, keeper, or warden; a magistrate.

CUSTOS BREVIUM. The keeper of the writs. A principal clerk belonging to the courts of queen's bench and common pleas, whose office it was to keep the writs returnable into those courts. The office was abolished by 1 Wm. IV. c. 5.

CUSTOS FERARUM. A gamekeeper. Townsh. Pl. 265.

CUSTOS HORREI REGII. Protector of the royal granary. 2 Bl. Comm. 394.

CUSTOS MARIS. In old English law. Warden of the sea. The title of a high naval officer among the Saxons and after the Conquest, corresponding with *admiral*.

CUSTOS MORUM. The guardian of morals. The court of queen's bench has been so styled. 4 Steph. Comm. 377.

CUSTOS PLACITORUM CORONÆ. In old English law. Keeper of the pleas of the crown. Bract. fol. 14*b*. Cowell supposes this office to have been the same with the *custos rotulorum*. But it seems rather to have been another name for "coroner." Crabb, Eng. Law, 150; Bract. fol. 136*b*.

CUSTOS ROTULORUM. Keeper of the rolls. An officer in England who has the custody of the rolls or records of the sessions of the peace, and also of the commission of the peace itself. He is always a justice of the quorum in the county where appointed, and is the principal civil officer in the county. 1 Bl. Comm. 349; 4 Bl. Comm. 272.

CUSTOS SPIRITUALIUM. In English ecclesiastical law. Keeper of the spiritualities. He who exercises the spiritual jurisdiction of a diocese during the vacancy of the see. Cowell.

Custos statum hæredis in custodia existentis meliorem, non deteriorem, facere potest. 7 Coke, 7. A guardian can make the estate of an existing heir under his guardianship better, not worse.

CUSTOS TEMPORALIUM. In English ecclesiastical law. The person to whom a vacant see or abbey was given by the king, as supreme lord. His office was, as steward of the goods and profits, to give an account to the escheator, who did the like to the exchequer.

CUSTOS TERRÆ. In old English law. Guardian, warden, or keeper of the land.

CUSTUMA ANTIQUA SIVE MAGNA. (Lat. Ancient or great duties.) The duties on wool, sheep-skin, or wool-pelts and leather exported were so called, and were payable by every merchant, stranger as well as native, with the exception that merchant strangers paid one-half as much again as natives. 1 Bl. Comm. 314.

CUSTUMA PARVA ET NOVA. (Small and new customs.) Imposts of 3d. in the pound, due formerly in England from merchant strangers only, for all commodities, as well imported as exported. This was usually called the "aliens duty," and was first granted in 31 Edw. I. 1 Bl. Comm. 314; 4 Inst. 29.

CUT. A wound made with a sharp instrument.

CUTCHERRY. In Hindu law. Corrupted from *Kachari*. A court; a hall; an office; the place where any public business is transacted.

CUTH, COUTH. Sax. Known, knowing. *Uncuth*, unknown. See COUTHUTLAUGH, UNCUTH.

CUTHRED. A knowing or skillful counsellor.

CUTPURSE. One who steals by the method of cutting purses; a common practice when men wore their purses at their girdles, as was once the custom. Wharton.

CUTTER OF THE TALLIES. In old English law. An officer in the exchequer, to whom it belonged to provide wood for the tallies, and to cut the sum paid upon them, etc.

CUTWAL, KATWAL. The chief officer of police or superintendent of markets in a large town or city in India.

CWT. A hundred-weight; one hundred and twelve pounds. 11 B. Mon. 64.

CY. In law French. Here. (*Cy-apres*, hereafter; *cy-devant*, heretofore.) Also as, so.

CYCLE. A measure of time; a space in which the same revolutions begin again; a periodical space of time. Enc. Lond.

CYNE-BOT, or CYNE-GILD. The portion belonging to the nation of the mulct for slaying the king, the other portion or *were* being due to his family. Blount.

CYNEBOTE. A mulct anciently paid by one who killed another, to the kindred of the deceased. Spelman.

CYPHONISM. That kind of punishment used by the ancients, and still used by the Chinese, called by Staunton the "wooden collar," by which the neck of the malefactor is bent or weighed down. Enc. Lond.

CY-PRES. As near as [possible.] The rule of *cy-pres* is a rule for the construction of instruments in equity, by which the intention of the party is carried out *as near as may be*, when it would be impossible or illegal to give it literal effect. Thus, where a testator attempts to create a perpetuity, the court will endeavor, instead of making the devise entirely void, to explain the will in such a way as to carry out the testator's general intention as far as the rule against perpetuities will allow. So in the case of bequests to charitable uses; and particularly where the language used is so vague or uncertain that the testator's design must be sought by construction. See 6 Cruise, Dig. 165; 1 Spence, Eq. Jur. 532; 3 Hare, 12.

CYRCE. In Saxon law. A church.

CYRICBRYCE. In Saxon law. A breaking into a church. Blount.

CYRICSCEAT. (From *cyric*, church, and *sceat*, a tribute.) In Saxon law. A tribute or payment due to the church. Cowell.

CYROGRAPHARIUS. In old English law. A cyrographer; an officer of the *bancus*, or court of common bench. Fleta, lib. 2, c. 36.

CYROGRAPHUM. A chirograph, (which see.)

CZAR. The title of the emperor of Russia, first assumed by Basil, the son of Basilides, under whom the Russian power began to appear, about 1740.

CZARINA. The title of the empress of Russia.

CZAROWITZ. The title of the eldest son of the czar and czarina.

D.

D. The fourth letter of the English alphabet. It is used as an abbreviation for a number of words, the more important and usual of which are as follows:

1. *Digestum*, or *Digesta*, that is, the Digest or Pandects in the Justinian collections of the civil law. Citations to this work are sometimes indicated by this abbreviation, but more commonly by "Dig."

2. *Dictum*. A remark or observation, as in the phrase "*obiter dictum*," (*q. v.*)

3. *Demissione*. "On the demise." An action of ejectment is entitled "Doe *d.* Stiles v. Roe;" that is, "Doe, on the demise of Stiles, against Roe."

4. "*Doctor*." As in the abbreviated forms of certain academical degrees. "M. D.," "doctor of medicine;" "LL.D.," "doctor of laws;" "D. C. L.," "doctor of civil law."

5. "*District*." Thus, "U. S. Cir. Ct. W. *D.* Pa." stands for "United States Circuit Court for the Western *District* of Pennsylvania."

6. "*Dialogue*." Used only in citations to the work called "Doctor and Student."

D. In the Roman system of notation, this letter stands for five hundred; and, when a horizontal dash or stroke is placed above it, it denotes five thousand.

D. B. E. An abbreviation for *de bene esse*, (*q. v.*)

D. B. N. An abbreviation for *de bonis non;* descriptive of a species of administration.

D. C. An abbreviation standing either for "District Court" or "District of Columbia."

D. E. R. I. C. An abbreviation used for *De ea re ita censuere*, (concerning that matter have so decreed,) in recording the decrees of the Roman senate. Tayl. Civil Law, 564, 566.

D. J. An abbreviation for "District Judge."

D. P. An abbreviation for *Domus Procerum*, the house of lords.

D. S. An abbreviation for "Deputy Sheriff."

D. S. B. An abbreviation for *debitum sine brevi*, or *debit sans breve.*

Da tua dum tua sunt, post mortem tunc tua non sunt. 3 Bulst. 18. Give the things which are yours whilst they are yours; after death they are not yours.

DABIS? DABO. Lat. (Will you give? I will give.) In the Roman law. One of the forms of making a verbal stipulation. Inst. 3, 15, 1; Bract. fol. 15*b*.

DACION. In Spanish law. The real and effective delivery of an object in the execution of a contract.

DAGGE. A kind of gun. 1 How. State Tr. 1124, 1125.

DAGUS, or DAIS. The raised floor at the upper end of a hall.

DAILY. Every day; every day in the week; every day in the week except one. A newspaper which is published six days in each week is a "daily" newspaper. 45 Cal. 30.

DAKER, or DIKER. Ten hides. Blount.

DALE and SALE. Fictitious names of places, used in the English books, as examples. "The manor of *Dale* and the manor of *Sale*, lying both in Vale."

DALUS, DAILUS, DAILIA. A certain measure of land; such narrow slips of pasture as are left between the plowed furrows in arable land. Cowell.

DAM. A construction of wood, stone, or other materials, made across a stream for the purpose of penning back the waters.

This word is used in two different senses. It properly means the work or structure, raised to obstruct the flow of the water in a river; but, by a well-settled usage, it is often applied to designate the pond of water created by this obstruction. 19 N. J. Eq. 248. See, also, 44 N. H. 78.

DAMAGE. Loss, injury, or deterioration, caused by the negligence, design, or accident of one person to another, in respect of the latter's person or property. The word is to be distinguished from its plural,—"damages,"—which means a compensation in money for a loss or damage.

An injury produces a right in them who have suffered any damage by it to demand reparation of such damage from the authors of the injury. By damage, we understand every loss or diminution of what is a man's own, occasioned by the fault of another. 1 Ruth. Inst. 399.

DAMAGE-CLEER. A fee assessed of the tenth part in the common pleas, and the twentieth part in the queen's bench and exchequer, out of all damages exceeding five marks recovered in those courts, in actions upon the case, covenant, trespass, etc., wherein the damages were uncertain; which the plaintiff was obliged to pay to the prothonotary or the officer of the court wherein he recovered, before he could have execution for the damages. This was originally a gratuity given to the prothonotaries and their clerks for drawing special writs and pleadings; but it was taken away by statute, since which, if any officer in these courts took any money in the name of damage-cleer, or anything in lieu thereof, he forfeited treble the value. Wharton.

DAMAGE FEASANT or FAISANT. Doing damage. A term applied to a person's cattle or beasts found upon another's land, doing damage by treading down the grass, grain, etc. 3 Bl. Comm. 7, 211; Tomlins. This phrase seems to have been introduced in the reign of Edward III., in place of the older expression "*en son damage,*" (*in damno suo.*) Crabb, Eng. Law, 292.

DAMAGED GOODS. Goods, subject to duties, which have received some injury either in the voyage home or while bonded in warehouse.

DAMAGES. A pecuniary compensation or indemnity, which may be recovered in the courts by any person who has suffered loss, detriment, or injury, whether to his person, property, or rights, through the unlawful act or omission or negligence of another.

A sum of money assessed by a jury, on finding for the plaintiff or successful party in an action, as a compensation for the injury done him by the opposite party. 2 Bl. Comm. 438; Co. Litt. 257*a;* 2 Tidd, Pr. 869, 870.

Every person who suffers detriment from the unlawful act or omission of another may recover from the person in fault a compensation therefor in money, which is called "damages." Civil Code Cal. § 3281; Civil Code Dak. § 1940.

In the ancient usage, the word "damages" was employed in two significations. According to Coke, its proper and general sense included the costs of suit, while its strict or relative sense was exclusive of costs. 10 Coke, 116, 117; Co. Litt. 257*a;* 9 East, 299. The latter meaning has alone survived.

Damages are either *general* or *special.* Damages for losses which necessarily result from the wrong sued for are called "general" damages, and may be shown under the *ad damnum,* or general allegation of damage; for the defendant does not need notice of such consequences to enable him to make his defense; he knows that they must exist, and will be in evidence. But if certain losses do not necessarily result from defendant's wrongful act, but, in fact, follow it as a natural and proximate consequence in the particular case, they are called "special," and must be specially alleged, that the defendant may have notice and be prepared to go into the inquiry. 28 Conn. 201, 212.

"General" damages are such as the law presumes to flow from any tortious act, and may be recovered without proof of any amount. "Special" damages are such as actually flowed from the act, and must be proved in order to be recovered. Code Ga. 1882, § 3070.

Damages may also be classed as *direct* and *consequential.* "Direct" damages are such as follow immediately upon the act done. "Consequential" damages are such as are the necessary and connected effect of the tortious act, though to some extent depending upon other circumstances. Code Ga. 1882, § 3071.

Another division of damages is into *liquidated* and *unliquidated;* the former term being applicable when the amount thereof has been ascertained by the judgment in the action or by the specific agreement of the parties; while the latter denotes such damages as are not yet reduced to a certainty in respect of amount, nothing more being established than the plaintiff's right to recover.

Damages are also either *nominal* or *substantial;* the former being trifling in amount, and not awarded as compensation for any injury, but merely in recognition of plaintiff's right and its technical infraction by defendant; while the latter are considerable in amount, and intended as real compensation for a real injury

Damages are either *compensatory* or *vindictive;* the former when nothing more is allowed than a just and exact equivalent for plaintiff's loss or injury; the latter when a greater sum is given than amounts to mere compensation, in order to punish the defendant for violence, outrage, or other circumstances of aggravation attending the transaction. Vindictive damages are also called "exemplary" or "punitive."

DAMAGES ULTRA. Additional damages claimed by a plaintiff not satisfied with those paid into court by the defendant.

DAMAIOUSE. In old English law. Causing damage or loss, as distinguished from *torcenouse*, wrongful. Britt. c. 61.

DAME. In English law. The legal designation of the wife of a knight or baronet.

DAMNA. Damages, both inclusive and exclusive of costs.

DAMNATUS. In old English law. Condemned; prohibited by law; unlawful. *Damnatus coitus*, an unlawful connection.

DAMNI INJURIÆ ACTIO. An action given by the civil law for the damage done by one who intentionally injured the slave or beast of another. Calvin.

DAMNIFICATION. That which causes damage or loss.

DAMNIFY. To cause damage or injurious loss to a person.

DAMNOSA HÆREDITAS. In the civil law. A losing inheritance; an inheritance that was a charge, instead of a benefit. Dig. 50, 16, 119.

The term has also been applied to that species of property of a bankrupt which, so far from being valuable, would be a charge to the creditors; for example, a term of years where the rent would exceed the revenue. 7 East, 342; 3 Camp. 340; 1 Esp. N. P. 234.

DAMNUM. Lat. In the civil law. Damage; the loss or diminution of what is a man's own, either by fraud, carelessness, or accident.

In pleading and old English law. Damage; loss.

DAMNUM ABSQUE INJURIA. A loss which does not give rise to an action of damages against the person causing it; as where a person blocks up the windows of a new house overlooking his land, or injures a person's trade by setting up an establishment of the same kind in the neighborhood. Broom, Com. Law, 75.

DAMNUM FATALE. In the civil law. Fatal damage; damage from fate; loss happening from a cause beyond human control, (*quod ex fato contingit*,) or an act of God, and for which bailees are not liable; such as shipwreck, lightning, and the like. Dig. 4, 9, 3, 1; Story, Bailm. § 465.

The civilians included in the phrase "*damnum fatale*" all those accidents which are summed up in the common-law expression, "Act of God or public enemies;" though, perhaps, it embraced some which would not now be admitted as occurring from an irresistible force. 8 Blackf. 535.

DAMNUM INFECTUM. In Roman law. Damage not yet committed, but threatened or impending. A preventive interdict might be obtained to prevent such damage from happening; and it was treated as a *quasi-delict*, because of the imminence of the danger.

DAMNUM REI AMISSÆ. In the civil law. A loss arising from a payment made by a party in consequence of an error of law. Mackeld. Rom. Law, § 178.

Damnum sine injuriâ esse potest. Lofft, 112. There may be damage or injury inflicted without any act of injustice.

DAN. Anciently the better sort of men in England had this title; so the Spanish *Don*. The old term of honor for men, as we now say Master or Mister. Wharton.

DANEGELT, DANEGELD. A tribute of 1s. and afterwards of 2s. upon every hide of land through the realm, levied by the Anglo-Saxons, for maintaining such a number of forces as were thought sufficient to clear the British seas of Danish pirates, who greatly annoyed their coasts. It continued a tax until the time of Stephen, and was one of the rights of the crown. Wharton.

DANELAGE. A system of laws introduced by the Danes on their invasion and conquest of England, and which was principally maintained in some of the midland counties, and also on the eastern coast. 1 Bl. Comm. 65; 4 Bl. Comm. 411; 1 Steph. Comm. 42.

DANGERIA. In old English law. A money payment made by forest-tenants, that they might have liberty to plow and sow in time of pannage, or mast feeding.

DANGEROUS WEAPON. One dangerous to life; one by the use of which a fatal wound may probably or possibly be given. As the manner of use enters into the consideration as well as other circumstances, the question is for the jury.

DANGERS OF THE RIVER. This phrase, as used in bills of lading, means only the natural accidents incident to river navigation, and does not embrace such as may be avoided by the exercise of that skill, judgment, or foresight which are demanded from persons in a particular occupation. 35 Mo. 213. It includes dangers arising from unknown reefs which have suddenly formed in the channel, and are not discoverable by care and skill. 17 Fed. Rep. 478.

DANGERS OF THE ROAD. This phrase, in a bill of lading, when it refers to inland transportation, means such dangers as are immediately caused by roads, as the overturning of carriages in rough and precipitous places. 7 Exch. 743.

DANGERS OF THE SEA. The expression "dangers of the sea" means those accidents peculiar to navigation that are of an extraordinary nature, or arise from irresistible force or overwhelming power, which cannot be guarded against by the ordinary exertions of human skill and prudence. 32 J. Law, 320.

The expression is equivocal. It is capable of being interpreted to mean all dangers that arise upon the seas; or may be restricted to perils which arise directly and exclusively from the sea, or of which it is the efficient cause. In insurance policies, it may have the wider meaning; but in charter-parties, an exception, introduced to limit the obligation of the charterer to return the vessel, of dangers of the seas, should be construed, since the charterer has possession, against him, and confined to the limited sense. Thus construed, it does not include destruction of the vessel by fire. 8 Ware, 215. 2 Curt. 8.

DANISM. The act of lending money on usury.

DANO. In Spanish law. Damage; the deterioration, injury, or destruction which a man suffers with respect to his person or his property by the fault (*culpa*) of another. White, New Recop. b. 2, tit. 19, c. 3, § 1.

Dans et retinens, nihil dat. One who gives and yet retains does not give effectually. Tray. Lat. Max. 129. Or, one who gives, yet retains, [possession,] gives nothing.

DAPIFER. A steward either of a king or lord. Spelman.

DARE. In the civil law. To transfer property. When this transfer is made in order to discharge a debt, it is *datio solvendi animo;* when in order to receive an equivalent, to create an obligation, it is *datio contrahendi animo;* lastly, when made *donandi animo*, from mere liberality, it is a gift, *dono datio*.

DARE AD REMANENTIAM. To give away in fee, or forever.

DARRAIGN. To clear a legal account; to answer an accusation; to settle a controversy.

DARREIN. L. Fr. Last.

DARREIN CONTINUANCE. L. Fr. In practice. The last continuance.

DARREIN PRESENTMENT. L. Fr. In old English law. The last presentment. See ASSISE OF DARREIN PRESENTMENT.

DARREIN SEISIN. (L. Fr. Last seisin.) A plea which lay in some cases for the tenant in a writ of right. See 1 Rosc. Real Act. 206.

DATA. In old practice and conveyancing. The date of a deed; the time when it was *given;* that is, executed.

Grounds whereon to proceed; facts from which to draw a conclusion.

DATE. The specification or mention, in a written instrument, of the time (day and year) when it was made. Also the time so specified.

That part of a deed or writing which expresses the day of the month and year in which it was made or *given*. 2 Bl. Comm. 304; Tomlins.

The primary signification of *date* is not time in the abstract, nor time taken absolutely, but time given or specified; time in some way ascertained and fixed. When we speak of the date of a deed, we do not mean the time when it was actually executed, but the time of its execution, as given or stated in the deed itself. The date of an item, or of a charge in a book-account, is not necessarily the time when the article charged was, in fact, furnished, but rather the time given or set down in the account, in connection with such charge. And so the expression "the date of the last work done, or materials furnished," in a mechanic's lien law, may be taken, in the absence of anything in the act indicating a different intention, to mean the time when such work was done or materials furnished, as specified in the plaintiff's written claim. 32 N. J. Law, 513.

DATE CERTAINE. In French law. A deed is said to have a *date certaine* (fixed date) when it has been subjected to the formality of registration; after this formality has been complied with, the parties to the deed cannot by mutual consent change the date thereof. Arg. Fr. Merc. Law, 555.

DATIO. In the civil law. A giving, or act of giving. *Datio in solutum;* a giving in payment; a species of accord and satisfaction. Called, in modern law, "dation."

DATION. In the civil law. A gift; a giving of something. It is not exactly synonymous with "donation," for the latter implies generosity or liberality in making a gift, while dation may mean the giving of something to which the recipient is already entitled.

DATION EN PAIEMENT. In French law. A giving by the debtor and receipt by the creditor of something in payment of a debt, instead of a sum of money.

It is somewhat like the accord and satisfaction of the common law. 16 Toullier, no. 45; Poth. Vente, no. 601.

DATIVE. A word derived from the Roman law, signifying "appointed by public authority." Thus, in Scotland, an executor-dative is an executor appointed by a court of justice, corresponding to an English *administrator*. Mozley & Whitley.

In old English law. In one's gift; that may be given and disposed of at will and pleasure.

DATUM. A first principle; a thing given; a date.

DATUR DIGNIORI. It is given to the more worthy. 2 Vent. 268.

DAUGHTER. An immediate female descendant.

DAUGHTER-IN-LAW. The wife of one's son.

DAUPHIN. In French law. The title of the eldest sons of the kings of France. Disused since 1830.

DAY. A period of time consisting of twenty-four hours, and including the solar day and the night. Co. Litt. 135*a;* Bract. fol. 264.

The space of time which elapses between two successive midnights. 2 Bl. Comm. 141.

That portion of time during which the sun is above the horizon, (called, sometimes, a "solar" day,) and, in addition, that part of the morning or evening during which sufficient of his light is above for the features of a man to be reasonably discerned. 3 Inst. 63; 9 Mass. 154.

The term may also denote an artificial period of time, computed from one fixed point to another twenty-four hours later, without any reference to the prevalence of light or darkness.

The word is sometimes used, in jurisprudence, in its astronomical sense of the space of time in which the earth makes one revolution upon its axis; or of the time between one midnight and the next; sometimes, in the popular sense, of the time between sunrise and sunset; and sometimes, in a conventional sense, of those hours or that recurring time which is by usage or law allotted to and deemed sufficient for the discharge of some duty or performance of some business; as where one speaks of a day's work, the whole of a business day, etc. Abbott.

In practice and pleading. A particular time assigned or given for the appearance of parties in court, the return of writs, etc. See DAYS IN BANK.

The whole of a term of court is considered as one day; and, by a legal fiction, the time between the submission and decision of a cause is also considered as but one day; so that, although a party to an action may die between the time of the decision in the cause by the supreme court of a state and the filing of the mandate of the supreme court of the United States reversing that decision, no change of parties in the state court is necessary before carrying the mandate into effect. 18 Ark. 653.

DAY-BOOK. A tradesman's account book; a book in which all the occurrences of the day are set down. It is usually a book of original entries.

DAYERIA. A dairy. Cowell.

DAYLIGHT. That portion of time before sunrise, and after sunset, which is accounted part of the day, (as distinguished from *night*,) in defining the offense of burglary. 4 Bl. Comm. 224; Cro. Jac. 106.

DAY-RULE, or DAY-WRIT. In English law. A permission granted to a prisoner to go out of prison, for the purpose of transacting his business, as to hear a case in which he is concerned at the assizes, etc. Abolished by 5 & 6 Vict. c. 22, § 12.

DAYS IN BANK. (L. Lat. *dies in banco*.) In practice. Certain stated days in term appointed for the appearance of parties, the return of process, etc., originally peculiar to the court of common bench, or bench, (bank,) as it was anciently called. 3 Bl. Comm. 277.

DAYS OF GRACE. A number of days allowed, as a matter of favor or *grace*, to a person who has to perform some act, or make some payment, after the time originally limited for the purpose has elapsed.

In old practice. Three days allowed to persons summoned in the English courts, beyond the day named in the writ, to make their appearance; the last day being called the "*quarto die post*." 3 Bl. Comm. 278.

In mercantile law. A certain number of days (generally three) allowed to the maker or acceptor of a bill, draft, or note, in which to make payment, after the expiration of the time expressed in the paper itself. Originally these days were granted only as a matter of *grace* or favor, but the allowance of them became an established custom of merchants, and was sanctioned by the courts, (and in some cases prescribed by statute,) so that they are now demandable as of right.

DAYSMAN. An arbitrator, umpire, or elected judge. Cowell.

DAY-TIME. The time during which there is the light of day, as distinguished from night or night-time. That portion of the twenty-four hours during which a man's person and countenance are distinguishable. 9 Mass. 154; 1 Car. & P. 297.

In law, this term is chiefly used in the definition of certain crimes, as to which it is material whether the act was committed by day or by night.

DAYWERE. In old English law. A term applied to land, and signifying as much arable ground as could be plowed up in one day's work. Cowell.

DE. A Latin preposition, signifying of; by; from; out of; affecting; concerning; respecting.

DE ACQUIRENDO RERUM DOMINIO. Of (about) acquiring the ownership of things. Dig. 41, 1; Bract. lib. 2, fol. 8*b*.

DE ADMENSURATIONE. Of admeasurement. Thus, *de admensuratione dotis* was a writ for the admeasurement of dower, and *de admensuratione pasturæ* was a writ for the admeasurement of pasture.

DE ADVISAMENTO CONSILII NOSTRI. L. Lat. With or by the advice of our council. A phrase used in the old writs of summons to parliament. Crabb, Eng. Law, 240.

DE ÆQUITATE. In equity. *De jure stricto, nihil possum vendicare, de œquitate tamen, nullo modo hoc obtinet;* in strict law, I can claim nothing, but in equity this by no means obtains. Fleta, lib. 3, c. 2, § 10.

DE ÆSTIMATO. In Roman law. One of the innominate contracts, and, in effect, a sale of land or goods at a price fixed, (*æstimato,*) and guarantied by some third party, who undertook to find a purchaser.

DE ÆTATE PROBANDA. For proving age. A writ which formerly lay to summon a jury in order to determine the age of the heir of a tenant *in capite* who claimed his estate as being of full age. Fitzh. Nat. Brev. 257; Reg. Orig. 294.

DE ALEATORIBUS. About gamesters. The name of a title in the Pandects. Dig. 11, 5.

DE ALLOCATIONE FACIENDA, *Breve.* Writ for making an allowance. An old writ directed to the lord treasurer and barons of the exchequer, for allowing certain officers (as collectors of customs) in their accounts certain payments made by them. Reg. Orig. 192.

DE ALTO ET BASSO. Of high and low. A phrase anciently used to denote the absolute submission of all differences to arbitration. Cowell.

DE AMBITU. Lat. Concerning bribery. A phrase descriptive of the subject-matter of several of the Roman laws; as the *Lex Aufidia*, the *Lex Pompeia*, the *Lex Tullia*, and others. See AMBITUS.

DE AMPLIORI GRATIA. Of more abundant or especial grace. Townsh. Pl. 18.

DE ANNO BISSEXTILI. Of the bissextile or leap year. The title of a statute passed in the twenty-first year of Henry III., which in fact, however, is nothing more than a sort of writ or direction to the justices of the bench, instructing them how the extraordinary day in the leap year was to be reckoned in cases where persons had a day to appear at the distance of a year, as on the essoin *de malo lecti*, and the like. It was thereby directed that the additional day should, together with that which went before, be reckoned only as one, and so, of course, within the preceding year. 1 Reeve, Eng. Law, 266.

DE ANNUA PENSIONE, *Breve.* Writ of annual pension. An ancient writ by which the king, having a yearly pension due him out of an abbey or priory for any of his chaplains, demanded the same of the abbot or prior, for the person named in the writ. Reg. Orig. 265*b*, 307; Fitzh. Nat. Brev. 231 G.

DE ANNUO REDITU. For a yearly rent. A writ to recover an annuity, no matter how payable, in goods or money. 2 Reeve, Eng. Law, 258.

DE APOSTATA CAPIENDO, *Breve.* Writ for taking an apostate. A writ which anciently lay against one who, having entered and professed some order of religion, left it and wandered up and down the country, contrary to the rules of his order, commanding the sheriff to apprehend him and deliver him again to his abbot or prior. Reg. Orig. 71*b*, 267; Fitzh. Nat. Brev. 233, 234.

DE ARBITRATIONE FACTA. (Lat. Of arbitration had.) A writ formerly used when an action was brought for a cause which had been settled by arbitration. Wats. Arb. 256.

DE ARRESTANDIS BONIS NE DISSIPENTUR. An old writ which lay to seize goods in the hands of a party during the pendency of a suit, to prevent their being made away with. Reg. Orig. 126*b*.

DE ARRESTANDO IPSUM QUI PECUNIAM RECEPIT. A writ which lay for the arrest of one who had taken the king's money to serve in the war, and hid himself to escape going. Reg. Orig. 24*b*.

DE ARTE ET PARTE. Of art and part. A phrase in old Scotch law.

DE ASPORTATIS RELIGIOSORUM. Concerning the property of religious persons carried away. The title of the statute 35 Edward I. passed to check the abuses of clerical possessions, one of which was the waste they suffered by being drained into foreign countries. 2 Reeve, Eng. Law, 157; 2 Inst. 580.

DE ASSISA PROROGANDA. (Lat. For proroguing assise.) A writ to put off an assise, issuing to the justices, where one of the parties is engaged in the service of the king.

DE ATTORNATO RECIPIENDO. A writ which lay to the judges of a court, requiring them to receive and admit an attorney for a party. Reg. Orig. 172; Fitzh. Nat. Brev. 156.

DE AUDIENDO ET TERMINANDO. For hearing and determining; to hear and determine. The name of a writ, or rather commission granted to certain justices to hear and determine cases of heinous misdemeanor, trespass, riotous breach of the peace, etc. Reg. Orig. 123, et seq.; Fitzh. Nat. Brev. 110 B. See OYER AND TERMINER.

DE AVERIIS CAPTIS IN WITHERNAMIUM. Writ for taking cattle in withernam. A writ which lay where the sheriff returned to a *pluries* writ of replevin that the cattle or goods, etc., were eloined, etc.; by which he was commanded to take the cattle of the defendant in withernam, (or reprisal,) and detain them until he could replevy the other cattle. Reg. Orig. 82; Fitzh. Nat. Brev. 73, E. F. See WITHERNAM.

DE AVERIIS REPLEGIANDIS. A writ to replevy beasts. 3 Bl. Comm. 149.

DE AVERIIS RETORNANDIS. For returning the cattle. A term applied to pledges given in the old action of replevin. 2 Reeve, Eng. Law, 177.

DE BANCO. Of the bench. A term formerly applied in England to the justices of the court of common pleas, or "bench," as it was originally styled.

DE BENE ESSE. Conditionally; provisionally; in anticipation of future need. A phrase applied to proceedings which are taken *ex parte* or provisionally, and are allowed to stand as *well done* for the present, but which may be subject to future exception or challenge, and must then stand or fall according to their intrinsic merit and regularity.

Thus, "in certain cases, the courts will allow evidence to be taken out of the regular course, in order to prevent the evidence being lost by the death or the absence of the witness. This is called 'taking evidence *de bene esse*,' and is looked upon as a temporary and conditional examination, to be used only in case the witness cannot afterwards be examined in the suit in the regular way." Hunt, Eq. 75; Haynes, Eq. 183; Mitf. Eq. Pl. 52, 149.

DE BIEN ET DE MAL. L. Fr. For good and evil. A phrase by which a party accused of a crime anciently put himself upon a jury, indicating his entire submission to their verdict.

DE BIENS LE MORT. L. Fr. Of the goods of the deceased. Dyer, 32.

DE BIGAMIS. Concerning men twice married. The title of the statute 4 Edw. I. St. 3; so called from the initial words of the fifth chapter. 2 Inst. 272; 2 Reeve, Eng. Law, 142.

DE BONE MEMORIE. L. Fr. Of good memory; of sound mind. 2 Inst. 510.

DE BONIS ASPORTATIS. For goods taken away; for taking away goods. The action of trespass for taking personal property is technically called "trespass *de bonis asportatis*." 1 Tidd, Pr. 5.

DE BONIS NON. An abbreviation of *De bonis non administratis*, (*q. v.*) 1 Strange, 34.

DE BONIS NON ADMINISTRATIS. Of the goods not administered. When an administrator is appointed to succeed another, who has left the estate partially unsettled, he is said to be granted "administration *de bonis non*;" that is, of the goods not already administered.

DE BONIS NON AMOVENDIS. Writ for not removing goods. A writ anciently directed to the sheriffs of London, commanding them, in cases where a writ of error was brought by a defendant against whom a judgment was recovered, to see that his *goods* and chattels were safely kept *without being removed*, while the error remained undetermined, so that execution might be had of them, etc. Reg. Orig. 131*b;* Termes de la Ley.

DE BONIS PROPRIIS. Of his own goods. The technical name of a judgment against an administrator or executor to be satisfied from his own property, and not from the estate of the deceased, as in cases where he has been guilty of a *devastavit* or of a false plea of *plene administravit.*

DE BONIS TESTATORIS, or INTESTATI. Of the goods of the testator, or intestate. A term applied to a judgment awarding execution against the property of a testator or intestate, as distinguished from the individual property of his executor or administrator. 2 Archb. Pr. K. B. 148, 149.

DE BONIS TESTATORIS AC SI. (Lat. From the goods of the testator, *if he has any*, and, if *not, from those of the executor*.) A judgment rendered where an executor falsely pleads any matter as a release, or, generally, in any case where he is to be charged in case his testator's estate is insufficient. 1 Williams' Saund. 336*b;* Bac. Abr. "Executor," B, 3; 2 Archb. Pr. K. B. 148.

DE BONO ET MALO. "For good and ill." The Latin form of the law French phrase "*De bien et de mal.*" In ancient criminal pleading, this was the expression with which the prisoner put himself upon a jury, indicating his absolute submission to their verdict.

This was also the name of the special writ of jail delivery formerly in use in England, which issued for each particular prisoner, of course. It was superseded by the general commission of jail delivery.

DE BONO GESTU. For good behavior; for good abearance.

DE CÆTERO. Henceforth.

DE CALCETO REPARANDO. Writ for repairing a causeway. An old writ by which the sheriff was commanded to distrain the inhabitants of a place to repair and maintain a causeway, etc. Reg. Orig. 154.

DE CAPITALIBUS DOMINIS FEODI. Of the chief lords of the fee.

DE CAPITE MINUTIS. Of those who have lost their *status*, or civil condition. Dig. 4, 5. The name of a title in the Pandects. See CAPITIS DEMINUTIO.

DE CARTIS REDDENDIS. (For restoring charters.) A writ to secure the delivery of charters or deeds; a writ of detinue. Reg. Orig. 159*b*.

DE CATALLIS REDDENDIS. (For restoring chattels.) A writ to secure the return specifically of chattels detained from the owner. Cowell.

DE CAUTIONE ADMITTENDA. Writ to take caution or security. A writ which anciently lay against a bishop who held an excommunicated person in prison for his contempt, notwithstanding he had offered sufficient security (*idoneam cautionem*) to obey the commands of the church; commanding him to take such security and release the prisoner. Reg. Orig. 66; Fitzh. Nat. Brev. 63, C.

DE CERTIFICANDO. A writ requiring a thing to be certified. A kind of *certiorari*. Reg. Orig. 151, 152.

DE CERTIORANDO. A writ for certifying. A writ directed to the sheriff, requiring him to certify to a particular fact. Reg. Orig. 24.

DE CHAMPERTIA. Writ of champerty. A writ directed to the justices of the bench, commanding the enforcement of the statute of *champertors*. Reg. Orig. 183; Fitzh. Nat. Brev. 172.

DE CHAR ET DE SANK. L. Fr. Of flesh and blood. *Affaire rechat de char et de sank*. Words used in claiming a person to be a villein, in the time of Edward II. Y. B. P. 1 Edw. II. p. 4.

DE CHIMINO. A writ for the enforcement of a right of way. Reg. Orig. 155.

DE CIBARIIS UTENDIS. Of victuals to be used. The title of a sumptuary statute passed 10 Edw. III. St. 3, to restrain the expense of entertainments. Barring. Ob. St. 240.

DE CLAMIA ADMITTENDA IN ITINERE PER ATTORNATUM. See CLAMIA ADMITTENDA, etc.

DE CLARO DIE. By daylight. Fleta, lib. 2, c. 76, § 8.

DE CLAUSO FRACTO. Of close broken; of breach of close. See CLAUSUM FREGIT.

DE CLERICO ADMITTENDO. See ADMITTENDO CLERICO.

DE CLERICO CAPTO PER STATUTUM MERCATORIUM DELIBERANDO. Writ for delivering a clerk arrested on a statute merchant. A writ for the delivery of a clerk out of prison, who had been taken and imprisoned upon the breach of a statute merchant. Reg. Orig. 147*b*.

DE CLERICO CONVICTO DELIBERANDO. See CLERICO CONVICTO, etc.

DE CLERICO INFRA SACROS ORDINES CONSTITUTO NON ELIGENDO IN OFFICIUM. See CLERICO INFRA SACROS, etc.

DE CLERO. Concerning the clergy. The title of the statute 25 Edw. III. St. 3; containing a variety of provisions on the subject of presentations, indictments of spiritual persons, and the like. 2 Reeve, Eng. Law, 378.

DE COMBUSTIONE DOMORUM. Of house burning. One of the kinds of appeal formerly in use in England. Bract. fol. 146*b*; 2 Reeve, Eng. Law, 38.

DE COMMUNI DIVIDUNDO. For dividing a thing held in common. The name of an action given by the civil law. Mackeld. Rom. Law, § 499.

DE COMON DROIT. L. Fr. Of common right; that is, by the common law. Co. Litt. 142*a*.

DE COMPUTO. Writ of account. A writ commanding a defendant to render a reasonable account to the plaintiff, or show cause to the contrary. Reg. Orig. 135–138; Fitzh. Nat. Brev. 117, E. The foundation of the modern action of account.

DE CONCILIO CURIÆ. By the advice (or direction) of the court.

DE CONFLICTU LEGUM. Concerning the conflict of laws. The title of several works written on that subject. 2 Kent, Comm. 455.

DE CONJUNCTIM FEOFFATIS. Concerning persons jointly enfeoffed, or seised. The title of the statute 34 Edw. I., which was passed to prevent the delay occasioned by tenants in novel disseisin, and other writs, pleading that some one else was seised jointly with them. 2 Reeve, Eng. Law, 243.

DE CONSANGUINEO, and DE CONSANGUINITATE. Writs of cosinage, (*q. v.*)

DE CONSILIO. In old criminal law. Of counsel; concerning counsel or advice to commit a crime. Fleta, lib. 1, c. 31, § 8.

DE CONSILIO CURIÆ. By the advice or direction of the court. Bract. fol. 345*b*.

DE CONTINUANDO ASSISAM. Writ to continue an assise. Reg. Orig. 217*b*.

DE CONTUMACE CAPIENDO. Writ for taking a contumacious person. A writ which issues out of the English court of chancery, in cases where a person has been pronounced by an ecclesiastical court to be contumacious, and in contempt. Shelf. Mar. & Div. 494–496, and notes. It is a commitment for contempt. Id.

DE COPIA LIBELLI DELIBERANDA. Writ for delivering the copy of a libel. An ancient writ directed to the judge of a spiritual court, commanding him to *deliver* to a defendant a *copy* of the libel filed against him in such court. Reg. Orig. 58. The writ in the register is directed to the Dean of the Arches, and his commissary. Id.

DE CORONATORE ELIGENDO. Writ for electing a coroner. A writ issued to the sheriff in England, commanding him to proceed to the election of a coroner, which is done in full county court, the freeholders being the electors. Sewell, Sheriffs, 372.

DE CORONATORE EXONERANDO. Writ for discharging or removing a coroner. A writ by which a coroner in England may be removed from office for some cause therein assigned. Fitzh. Nat. Brev. 163, 164; 1 Bl. Comm. 348.

DE CORPORE COMITATUS. From the body of the county at large, as distinguished from a particular neighborhood, (*de vicineto.*) 3 Bl. Comm. 360.

DE CORRODIO HABENDO. Writ for having a corody. A writ to exact a corody from a religious house. Reg. Orig. 264; Fitzh. Nat. Brev. 230. See CORODY.

DE CURIA CLAUDENDA. An obsolete writ, to require a defendant to fence in his court or land about his house, where it was left open to the injury of his neighbor's freehold. 1 Crabb, Real Prop. 314; 6 Mass. 90.

DE CURSU. Of course. The usual, necessary, and formal proceedings in an action are said to be *de cursu;* as distinguished from *summary* proceedings, or such as are incidental and may be taken on summons or motion. Writ *de cursu* are such as are issued of course, as distinguished from prerogative writs.

DE CUSTODE ADMITTENDO. Writ for admitting a guardian. Reg. Orig. 93*b*, 198.

DE CUSTODE AMOVENDO. Writ for removing a guardian. Reg. Orig. 198.

DE CUSTODIA TERRÆ ET HÆREDIS, *Breve.* L. Lat. Writ of ward, or writ of right of ward. A writ which lay for a guardian in knight's service or in socage, to recover the possession and custody of the infant, or the *wardship of the land and heir.* Reg. Orig. 161*b;* Fitzh. Nat. Brev. 139, B; 3 Bl. Comm. 141.

DE DEBITO. A writ of debt. Reg. Orig. 139.

DE DEBITORE IN PARTES SECANDO. In Roman law. "Of cutting a debtor in pieces." This was the name of a law contained in the Twelve Tables, the meaning of which has occasioned much controversy. Some commentators have concluded that it was literally the privilege of the creditors of an insolvent debtor (all other means failing) to cut his body into pieces and distribute it among them. Others contend that the language of this law must be taken figuratively, denoting a cutting up and apportionment of the debtor's *estate.*

The latter view has been adopted by Montesquieu, Bynkershoek, Heineccius, and Taylor. (Esprit des Lois, liv. 29, c. 2; Bynk. Obs. Jur. Rom. l. 1, c. 1; Heinecc. Ant. Rom. lib. 3, tit. 30, § 4; Tayl. Comm. in Leg. Decemv.) The literal meaning, on the other hand, is advocated by Aulus Gellius and other writers of antiquity, and receives support from an expression (*semoto omni cruciatu*) in the Roman code itself. (Aul. Gel. Noctes Atticæ, lib. 20, c. 1; Code, 7, 7, 8.) This is also the opinion of Gibbon, Gravina, Pothier, Hugo, and Niebuhr. (3 Gib. Rom. Emp., Am. Ed., p. 183; Grav. de Jur. Nat. Gent. et XII. Tab. § 72; Poth. Introd. Pand.; Hugo, Hist. du Droit Rom. tom. i., p. 233, § 149; 2 Niehb. Hist. Rom. p. 597; 1 Kent, Comm. 523, note.) Burrill.

DE DECEPTIONE. A writ of deceit which lay against one who acted in the name of another whereby the latter was damnified and deceived. Reg. Orig. 112.

DE DEONERANDA PRO RATA PORTIONIS. A writ that lay where one was distrained for rent that ought to be paid by others proportionably with him. Fitzh. Nat. Brev. 234; Termes de la Ley.

DE DIE IN DIEM. From day to day. Bract. fol. 205*b*.

DE DIVERSIS REGULIS JURIS ANTIQUI. Of divers rules of the ancient law. A celebrated title of the Digests, and the last in that collection. It consists of two hundred and eleven rules or maxims. Dig. 50, 17.

DE DOLO MALO. Of or founded upon fraud. Dig. 4, 3. See ACTIO DE DOLO MALO.

DE DOMO REPARANDA. A writ which lay for one tenant in common to compel his co-tenant to contribute towards the repair of the common property.

DE DONIS. Concerning gifts, (or more fully, *de donis conditionalibus,* concerning conditional gifts.) The name of a celebrated English statute, passed in the thirteenth year of Edw. I., and constituting the first chapter of the statute of Westm. 2, by virtue of which estates in fee-simple conditional (formerly known as "*dona conditionalia*") were converted into estates in fee-tail, and which, by rendering such estates inalienable, introduced perpetuities, and so strengthened the power of the nobles. See 2 Bl. Comm. 112.

DE DOTE ASSIGNANDA. Writ for assigning dower. A writ which lay for the widow of a tenant *in capite,* commanding the king's escheator to cause her dower to be assigned to her. Reg. Orig. 297; Fitzh. Nat. Brev. 263, C.

DE DOTE UNDE NIHIL HABET. A writ of dower which lay for a widow where no part of her dower had been assigned to her. It is now much disused; but a form closely resembling it is still sometimes used in the United States. 4 Kent, Comm. 63; Stearns, Real Act. 302; 1 Washb. Real Prop. 230.

DE EJECTIONE CUSTODIÆ. A writ which lay for a guardian who had been forcibly ejected from his wardship. Reg. Orig. 162.

DE EJECTIONE FIRMÆ. A writ which lay at the suit of the tenant for years against the lessor, reversioner, remainder-man, or stranger who had himself deprived the tenant of the occupation of the land during his term. 3 Bl. Comm. 199.

By a gradual extension of the scope of this form of action its object was made to include not only damages for the unlawful detainer, but also the possession for the remainder of the term, and eventually the possession of land generally. And, as it turned on the right of possession, this involved a determination of the right of property, or the title, and thus arose the modern action of ejectment.

DE ESCÆTA. Writ of escheat. A writ which a lord had, where his tenant died without heir, to recover the land. Reg. Orig. 164*b;* Fitzh. Nat. Brev. 143, 144, E.

DE ESCAMBIO MONETÆ. A writ of exchange of money. An ancient writ to authorize a merchant to make a bill of exchange, (*literas cambitorias facere.*) Reg. Orig. 194.

DE ESSE IN PEREGRINATIONE. Of being on a journey. A species of essoin. 1 Reeve, Eng. Law, 119.

DE ESSENDO QUIETUM DE TOLONIO. A writ which lay for those who were by privilege free from the payment of toll, on their being molested therein. Fitzh. Nat. Brev. 226; Reg. Orig. 258*b*.

DE ESSONIO DE MALO LECTI. A writ which issued upon an essoin of *malum lecti* being cast, to examine whether the party was in fact sick or not. Reg. Orig. 8*b*.

DE ESTOVERIIS HABENDIS. Writ for having estovers. A writ which lay for a wife divorced *a mensa et thoro,* to recover her alimony or estovers. 1 Bl. Comm. 441; 1 Lev. 6.

DE ESTREPAMENTO. A writ which lay to prevent or stay waste by a tenant, during the pendency of a suit against him to recover the lands. Reg. Orig. 76*b*· Fitzh. Nat. Brev. 60.

DE EU ET TRENE. L. Fr. Of water and whip of three cords. A term applied to a neife, that is, a bond woman or female villein, as employed in servile work, and subject to corporal punishment. Co. Litt. 25*b*.

DE EVE ET DE TREVE. A law French phrase, equivalent to the Latin *de avo et de tritavo,* descriptive of the ancestral rights of lords in their villeins. Literally, "from grandfather and from great-grandfather's great-grandfather." It occurs in the Year Books.

DE EXCOMMUNICATO CAPIENDO. A writ commanding the sheriff to arrest one who was excommunicated, and imprison him till he should become reconciled to the church. 3 Bl. Comm. 102.

DE EXCOMMUNICATO DELIBERANDO. A writ to deliver an excommunicated person, who has made satisfaction to the church, from prison. 3 Bl. Comm. 102.

DE EXCOMMUNICATO RECAPIENDO. Writ for retaking an excommunicated person, where he had been liberated from prison without making satisfaction to the church, or giving security for that purpose. Reg. Orig. 67.

DE EXCUSATIONIBUS. "Concerning excuses." This is the title of book 27 of the Pandects, (in the *Corpus Juris Civilis.*) It treats of the circumstances which excuse one from filling the office of tutor or curator. The bulk of the extracts are from Modestinus.

DE EXECUTIONE FACIENDA IN WITHERNAMIUM. Writ for making execution in withernam. Reg. Orig. 82*b*. A species of *capias in withernam.*

DE EXECUTIONE JUDICII. A writ directed to a sheriff or bailiff, commanding him to do execution upon a judgment. Reg. Orig. 18; Fitzh. Nat. Brev. 20.

DE EXEMPLIFICATIONE. Writ of exemplification. A writ granted for the exemplification of an original. Reg. Orig. 290*b*.

DE EXONERATIONE SECTÆ. Writ for exoneration of suit. A writ that lay for the king's ward to be discharged of all suit to the county court, hundred, leet, or court-baron, during the time of his wardship. Fitzh. Nat. Brev. 158; New Nat. Brev. 352.

DE EXPENSIS CIVIUM ET BURGENSIUM. An obsolete writ addressed to the sheriff to levy the expenses of every citizen and burgess of parliament. 4 Inst. 46.

DE EXPENSIS MILITUM LEVANDIS. Writ for levying the expenses of knights. A writ directed to the sheriff for levying the allowance for knights of the shire in parliament. Reg. Orig. 191*b*, 192.

DE FACTO. In fact, in deed, actually. This phrase is used to characterize an officer, a government, a past action, or a state of affairs which exists actually and must be accepted for all practical purposes, but which is illegal or illegitimate. In this sense it is the contrary of *de jure*, which means rightful, legitimate, just, or constitutional. Thus, an officer, king, or government *de facto* is one who is in actual possession of the office or supreme power, but by usurpation, or without respect to lawful title; while an officer, king, or governor *de jure* is one who has just claim and rightful title to the office or power, but who has never had plenary possession of the same, or is not now in actual possession. (4 Bl. Comm. 77, 78.) So a wife *de facto* is one whose marriage is voidable by decree, as distinguished from a wife *de jure*, or lawful wife. (4 Kent, Comm. 36.) (As to the distinction between governments *de facto* and *de jure*, see GOVERNMENT. As to officers *de facto*, see that title.)

But the term is also frequently used independently of any distinction from *de jure;* thus a blockade *de facto* is a blockade which is actually maintained, as distinguished from a mere paper blockade.

In old English law. *De facto* means respecting or concerning the principal act of a murder, which was technically denominated *factum*. See Fleta, lib. 1, c. 27, § 18.

DE FACTO CONTRACT. One which has purported to pass the property from the owner to another. 74 N. Y. 575; L. R. 3 App. Cas. 459.

DE FAIRE ECHELLE. In French law. A clause commonly inserted in policies of marine insurance, equivalent to a license to touch and trade at intermediate ports. 14 Wend. 491.

DE FALSO JUDICIO. Writ of false judgment. Reg. Orig. 15; Fitzh. Nat Brev. 18. See FALSE JUDGMENT.

DE FALSO MONETA. Of false money. The title of the statute 27 Edw. I. ordaining that persons importing certain coins, called "pollards," and "crokards," should forfeit their lives and goods, and everything they could forfeit. 2 Reeve, Eng. Law, 228, 229.

De fide et officio judicis non recipitur quæstio, sed de scientia, sive sit error juris, sive facti. Concerning the fidelity and official conduct of a judge, no question is [will be] entertained; but [only] concerning his knowledge, whether the error [committed] be of law or of fact. Bac. Max. 68, reg. 17. The *bona fides* and honesty of purpose of a judge cannot be questioned, but his decision may be impugned for error either of law or fact. Broom, Max. 85. The law doth so much respect the certainty of judgments, and the credit and authority of judges, that it will not permit any error to be assigned which impeacheth them in their *trust* and *office*, and in willful abuse of the same; but only in ignorance and mistaking either of the law, or of the case and matter of fact. Bac. Max. ubi supra. Thus, it cannot be assigned for error that a judge did that which he ought not to do; as that he entered a verdict for the plaintiff, where the jury gave it for the defendant. Fitzh. Nat. Brev. 20, 21; Bac. Max. ubi supra; Hardr. 127, arg.

DE FIDEI LÆSIONE. Of breach of faith or fidelity. 4 Reeve, Eng. Law, 99.

DE FINE FORCE. L. Fr. Of necessity; of pure necessity. See FINE FORCE.

DE FINE NON CAPIENDO PRO PULCHRE PLACITANDO. A writ prohibiting the taking of fines for beau pleader. Reg. Orig. 179.

DE FINE PRO REDISSEISINA CAPIENDO. A writ which lay for the release of one imprisoned for a re-disseisin, on payment of a reasonable fine. Reg. Orig. 222*b*.

DE FINIBUS LEVATIS. Concerning fines levied. The title of the statute 27 Edw. I., requiring fines thereafter to be levied, to be read openly and solemnly in court. 2 Inst. 521.

DE FORISFACTURA MARITAGII. Writ of forfeiture of marriage. Reg. Orig. 163, 164.

DE FRANGENTIBUS PRISONAM. Concerning those that break prison. The title of the statute 1 Edw. II., ordaining that none from thenceforth who broke prison should have judgment of life or limb for breaking prison only, unless the cause for which he was taken and imprisoned required such a judgment if he was lawfully convicted thereof. 2 Reeve, Eng. Law, 290; 2 Inst. 589.

DE FURTO. Of theft. One of the kinds of criminal appeal formerly in use in England. 2 Reeve, Eng. Law, 40.

DE GESTU ET FAMA. Of behavior and reputation. An old writ which lay in cases where a person's conduct and reputation were impeached.

DE GRATIA. Of grace or favor, by favor. *De speciali gratia*, of special grace or favor.

De gratia speciali certa scientia et mero motu, talis clausula non valet in his in quibus præsumitur principem esse ignorantem. 1 Coke, 53. The clause "of our special grace, certain knowledge, and mere motion," is of no avail in those things in which it is presumed that the prince was ignorant.

De grossis arboribus decimæ non dabuntur sed de sylvia cædua decimæ dabuntur. 2 Rolle, 123. Of whole trees, tithes are not given; but of wood cut to be used, tithes are given.

DE HÆREDE DELIBERANDO ILLI QUI HABET CUSTODIAM TERRÆ. Writ for delivering an heir to him who has wardship of the land. A writ directed to the sheriff, to require one that had the body of him that was ward to another to deliver him to the person whose ward he was by reason of his land. Reg. Orig. 161.

DE HÆREDE RAPTO ET ABDUCTO. Writ concerning an heir ravished and carried away. A writ which anciently lay for a lord who, having by right the wardship of his tenant under age, could not obtain his body, the same being carried away by another person. Reg. Orig. 163; Old Nat. Brev. 93.

DE HÆRETICO COMBURENDO. (Lat. For burning a heretic.) A writ which lay where a heretic had been convicted of heresy, had abjured, and had relapsed into heresy. It is said to be very ancient. Fitzh. Nat. Brev. 269; 4 Bl. Comm. 46.

DE HOMAGIO RESPECTUANDO. A writ for respiting or postponing homage. Fitzh. Nat. Brev. 269, A.

DE HOMINE CAPTO IN WITHERNAM. (Lat. For taking a man in withernam.) A writ to take a man who had carried away a bondman or bondwoman into another country beyond the reach of a writ of replevin.

DE HOMINE REPLEGIANDO. (Lat. For replevying a man.) A writ which lies to replevy a man out of prison, or out of the custody of a private person, upon giving security to the sheriff that the man shall be forthcoming to answer any charge against him. Fitzh. Nat. Brev. 66; 3 Bl. Comm. 129.

This writ has been superseded almost wholly, in modern practice, by that of *habeas corpus;* but it is still used, in some of the states, in an amended and altered form. See 1 Kent, Comm. 404*n;* 34 Me. 136.

DE IDENTITATE NOMINIS. A writ which lay for one arrested in a personal action and committed to prison under a mistake as to his identity, the proper defendant bearing the same name. Reg. Orig. 194.

DE IDIOTA INQUIRENDO. An old common-law writ, long obsolete, to inquire whether a man be an idiot or not. 2 Steph. Comm. 509.

DE IIS QUI PONENDI SUNT IN ASSISIS. Of those who are to be put on assises. The title of a statute passed 21 Edw. I., defining the qualifications of jurors. Crabb, Eng. Law, 167, 189; 2 Reeve, Eng. Law, 184.

DE INCREMENTO. Of increase; in addition. Costs *de incremento,* or costs of increase, are the costs adjudged by the court in civil actions, *in addition* to the damages and nominal costs found by the jury. Gilb. Com. Pl. 260.

DE INFIRMITATE. Of infirmity. The principal essoin in the time of Glanville; afterwards called "*de malo.*" 1 Reeve, Eng. Law, 115. See DE MALO; ESSOIN.

DE INGRESSU. A writ of entry. Reg. Orig. 227*b*, et seq.

DE INJURIA. Of [his own] wrong. In the technical language of pleading, a replication *de injuria* is one that may be made in an action of tort where the defendant has admitted the acts complained of, but alleges, in his plea, certain new matter by way of justification or excuse; by this replication the plaintiff avers that the defendant committed the grievances in question "of his own wrong, and without any such cause," or motive or excuse, as that alleged in the plea, (*de injuria sua propria absque tali causa;*) or, admitting part of the matter pleaded, "without the rest of the cause" alleged, (*absque residuo causæ.*)

In form it is a species of traverse, and it is frequently used when the pleading of the defendant, in answer to which it is directed, consists merely of matter of excuse of the alleged trespass, grievance, breach of contract, or other cause of action. Its comprehensive character in putting in issue all the material facts of the defendant's plea has also obtained for it the title of the general replication. Holthouse.

DE INOFFICIOSO TESTAMENTO. Concerning an inofficious or undutiful will. A title of the civil law. Inst. 2, 18.

DE INTEGRO. Anew; a second time. As it was before.

DE INTRUSIONE. A writ of intrusion; where a stranger entered after the death of the tenant, to the injury of the reversioner. Reg. Orig. 233*b*.

DE JACTURA EVITANDA. For avoiding a loss. A phrase applied to a defendant, as *de lucro captando* is to a plaintiff. 1 Litt. (Ky.) 51.

DE JUDAISMO, STATUTUM. The name of a statute passed in the reign of Edward I., which enacted severe and arbitrary penalties against the Jews.

DE JUDICATO SOLVENDO. For payment of the amount adjudged. A term applied in the Scotch law to bail to the action, or special bail.

DE JUDICIIS. Of judicial proceedings. The title of the second part of the Digests or Pandects, including the fifth, sixth, seventh, eighth, ninth, tenth, and eleventh books. See Dig. procem. § 3.

DE JUDICIO SISTI. For appearing in court. A term applied in the Scotch and admiralty law, to bail for a defendant's appearance.

DE JURE. Of right; legitimate; lawful; by right and just title. In this sense it is the contrary of *de facto*, (which see.) It may also be contrasted with *de gratia*, in which case it means "as a matter of right," as *de gratia* means "by grace or favor." Again it may be contrasted with *de æquitate;* here meaning "by law," as the latter means "by equity." See GOVERNMENT.

De jure decimarum, originem ducens de jure patronatus, tunc cognitio spectat at legem civilem, i. e., communem. Godb. 63. With regard to the right of tithes, deducing its origin from the right of the patron, then the cognizance of them belongs to the civil law; that is, the common law.

DE LA PLUIS BEALE, or BELLE. L. Fr. Of the most fair. A term applied to a species of dower, which was assigned out of the fairest of the husband's tenements. Litt. § 48. This was abolished with the military tenures. 2 Bl. Comm. 132; 1 Steph. Comm. 252.

DE LATERE. From the side; on the side; collaterally; of collaterals. Cod. 5, 5, 6.

DE LEGATIS ET FIDEI COMMISSIS. Of legacies and trusts. The name of a title of the Pandects. Dig. 30.

DE LEPROSO AMOVENDO. Writ for removing a leper. A writ to remove a leper who thrust himself into the company of his neighbors in any parish, in public or private places, to their annoyance. Reg. Orig. 267; Fitzh. Nat. Brev. 234, E; New Nat. Brev. 521.

DE LIBERA FALDA. Writ of free fold. A species of *quod permittat*. Reg. Orig. 155.

DE LIBERA PISCARIA. Writ of free fishery. A species of *quod permittat.* Reg. Orig. 155.

DE LIBERO PASSAGIO. Writ of free passage. A species of *quod permittat*. Reg. Orig. 155.

DE LIBERTATE PROBANDA. Writ for proving liberty. A writ which lay for such as, being demanded for villeins or niefs, offered to prove themselves free. Reg. Orig. 87*b;* Fitzh. Nat. Brev. 77, F.

DE LIBERTATIBUS ALLOCANDIS. A writ of various forms, to enable a citizen to recover the liberties to which he was entitled. Fitzh. Nat. Brev. 229; Reg. Orig. 262.

DE LICENTIA TRANSFRETANDI. Writ of permission to cross the sea. An old writ directed to the wardens of the port of Dover, or other seaport in England, commanding them to permit the persons named in the writ to cross the sea from such port, on certain conditions. Reg. Orig. 193*b*.

DE LUNATICO INQUIRENDO. The name of a writ directed to the sheriff, directing him to inquire by good and lawful men whether the party charged is a lunatic or not.

DE MAGNA ASSISA ELIGENDA. A writ by which the grand assise was chosen and summoned. Reg. Orig. 8; Fitzh. Nat. Brev. 4.

De majori et minori non variant jura. Concerning greater and less laws do not vary. 2 Vern. 552.

DE MALO. Of illness. This phrase was frequently used to designate several species of essoin, (*q. v.*,) such as *de malo lecti*, of illness in bed; *de malo veniendi*, of illness (or misfortune) in coming to the place where the court sat; *de malo villæ*, of illness in the town where the court sat.

DE MANUCAPTIONE. Writ of manucaption, or mainprise. A writ which lay for one who, being taken and imprisoned on a charge of felony, had offered bail, which had been refused; requiring the sheriff to discharge him on his finding sufficient mainpernors or bail. Reg. Orig. 268*b*; Fitzh. Nat. Brev. 249, G.

DE MANUTENENDO. Writ of maintenance. A writ which lay against a person for the offense of maintenance. Reg. Orig. 189, 182*b*.

DE MEDIETATE LINGUÆ. Of the half tongue; half of one tongue and half of another. This phrase describes that species of jury which, at common law, was allowed in both civil and criminal cases where one of the parties was an alien, not speaking or understanding English. It was composed of six English denizens or natives and six of the alien's own countrymen.

DE MEDIO. A writ in the nature of a writ of right, which lay where upon a subinfeudation the *mesne* (or middle) lord suffered his under-tenant or tenant *paravail* to be distrained upon by the lord paramount for the rent due him from the *mesne* lord. Booth, Real Act. 136.

DE MELIORIBUS DAMNIS. Of or for the better damages. A term used in practice to denote the election by a plaintiff against which of several defendants (where the damages have been assessed separately) he will take judgment. 1 Arch. Pr. K. B. 219; 8 Cow. 111.

DE MERCATORIBUS. "Concerning merchants." The name of a statute passed in the eleventh year of Edw. I., (1233,) more commonly called the "Statute of Acton Burnel," authorizing the recognizance by statute merchant. See 2 Reeve, Eng. Law, 160–162; 2 Bl. Comm. 161.

De minimis non curat lex. The law does not care for, or take notice of, very small or trifling matters. The law does not concern itself about trifles. Cro. Eliz. 353. Thus, error in calculation of a fractional part of a penny will not be regarded. Hob. 88. So, the law will not, in general, notice the fraction of a day. Broom, Max. 142.

DE MINIS. Writ of threats. A writ which lay where a person was threatened with personal violence, or the destruction of his property, to compel the offender to keep the peace. Reg. Orig. 88*b*, 89; Fitzh. Nat. Brev. 79, G, 80.

DE MITTENDO TENOREM RECORDI. A writ to send the tenor of a record, or to exemplify it under the great seal. Reg. Orig. 220*b*.

DE MODERATA MISERICORDIA CAPIENDA. Writ for taking a moderate amercement. A writ, founded on *Magna Charta*, (c. 14,) which lay for one who was excessively amerced in a court not of record, directed to the lord of the court, or his bailiff, commanding him *to take a moderate amercement* of the party. Reg. Orig. 86*b*; Fitzh. Nat. Brev. 75, 76.

DE MODO DECIMANDI. Of a *modus* of tithing. A term applied in English ecclesiastical law to a prescription to have a special manner of tithing. 2 Bl. Comm. 29; 3 Steph. Comm. 130.

De molendino de novo erecto non jacet prohibitio. Cro. Jac. 429. A prohibition lies not against a newly-erected mill.

De morte hominis nulla est cunctatio longa. Where the death of a human being is concerned, [in a matter of life and death,] no delay is [considered] long. Co. Litt. 134.

DE NATIVO HABENDO. A writ which lay for a lord directed to the sheriff, commanding him to apprehend a fugitive villein, and restore him, with all his chattels, to the lord. Reg. Orig. 87; Fitzh. Nat. Brev. 77.

De nomine proprio non est curandum cum in substantia non erretur; quia nomina mutabilia sunt, res autem immobiles. 6 Coke, 66. As to the proper name, it is not to be regarded where it errs not in substance, because names are changeable, but things immutable.

De non apparentibus, et non existentibus, eadem est ratio. 5 Coke, 6. As to things not apparent, and those not existing, the rule is the same.

DE NON DECIMANDO. Of not paying tithes. A term applied in English ecclesiastical law to a prescription or claim to be entirely discharged of tithes, and to pay no compensation in lieu of them. 2 Bl. Comm. 31.

DE NON PROCEDENDO AD ASSISAM. A writ forbidding the justices from holding an assise in a particular case. Reg. Orig. 221.

DE NON RESIDENTIA CLERICI REGIS. An ancient writ where a parson was employed in the royal service, etc., to excuse and discharge him of non-residence. 2 Inst. 264.

DE NON SANE MEMORIE. L. Fr. Of unsound memory or mind; a phrase synonymous with *non compos mentis*.

DE NOVI OPERIS NUNCIATIONE. In the civil law. A form of interdict or injunction which lies in some cases where the defendant is about to erect a "new work" (*q. v.*) in derogation or injury of the plaintiff's rights.

DE NOVO. Anew; afresh; a second time. A *venire de novo* is a writ for summoning a jury for the second trial of a case which has been sent back from above for a new trial.

De nullo, quod est sua natura indivisibile, et divisionem non patitur, nullam partem habebit vidua, sed satisfaciat ei ad valentiam. Co. Litt. 32. A widow shall have no part of that which in its own nature is indivisible, and is not susceptible of division, but let the heir satisfy her with an equivalent.

De nullo tenemento, quod tenetur ad terminum, fit homagii, fit tamen inde fidelitatis sacramentum. In no tenement which is held for a term of years is there an avail of homage; but there is the oath of fealty. Co. Litt. 67*b*.

DE ODIO ET ATIA. A writ directed to the sheriff, commanding him to inquire whether a prisoner charged with murder was committed upon just cause of suspicion, or merely *propter odium et atiam*, (through hatred and ill will;) and if, upon the inquisition, due cause of suspicion did not appear, then there issued another writ for the sheriff to admit him to bail. 3 Bl. Comm. 128.

DE OFFICE. L. Fr. Of office; in virtue of office; officially; in the discharge of ordinary duty.

DE ONERANDO PRO RATA PORTIONE. Writ for charging according to a rateable proportion. A writ which lay for a joint tenant, or tenant in common, who was distrained for more rent than his proportion of the land came to. Reg. Orig. 182; Fitzh. Nat. Brev. 234, H.

DE PACE ET LEGALITATE TENENDA. For keeping the peace, and for good behavior.

DE PACE ET PLAGIS. Of peace, (breach of peace,) and wounds. One of the kinds of criminal appeal formerly in use in England, and which lay in cases of assault, wounding, and breach of the peace. Bract. fol. 144; 2 Reeve, Eng. Law, 33.

DE PACE ET ROBERIA. Of peace [breach of peace] and robbery. One of the kinds of criminal appeal formerly in use in England, and which lay in cases of robbery and breach of the peace. Bract. fol. 146; 2 Reeve, Eng. Law, 37.

DE PALABRA. Span. By word; by parol. White, New Recop. b. 2, tit. 19, c. 3, § 2.

DE PARCO FRACTO. A writ or action for damages caused by a pound-breach, (*q. v.*) It has long been obsolete. Co. Litt. 47*b*; 3 Bl. Comm. 146.

DE PARTITIONE FACIENDA. A writ which lay to make partition of lands or tenements held by several as coparceners, tenants in common, etc. Reg. Orig. 76; Fitzh. Nat. Brev. 61, R; Old Nat. Brev. 142.

DE PERAMBULATIONE FACIENDA. A writ which lay where there was a dispute as to the boundaries of two adjacent lordships or towns, directed to the sheriff, commanding him to take with him twelve discreet and lawful knights of his county and make the perambulation and set the bounds and limits in certainty. Fitzh. Nat. Brev. 309, D.

DE PIGNORE SURREPTO FURTI, ACTIO. In the civil law. An action to recover a pledge stolen. Inst. 4, 1, 14.

DE PIPA VINI CARIANDA. A writ of trespass for carrying a pipe of wine so carelessly that it was stove, and the contents lost. Reg. Orig. 110. Alluded to by Sir William Jones in his remarks on the case of Coggs v. Barnard. Jones, Bailm. 59.

DE PLACITO. Of a plea; of or in an action. Formal words used in declarations and other proceedings, as descriptive of the particular action brought.

DE PLAGIS ET MAHEMIO. Of wounds and mayhem. The name of a criminal appeal formerly in use in England, in cases of wounding and maiming. Bract. fol. 144*b;* 2 Reeve, Eng. Law, 34. See APPEAL.

DE PLANO. Lat. On the ground; on a level. A term of the Roman law descriptive of the method of hearing causes, when the prætor stood on the ground with the suitors, instead of the more formal method when he occupied a bench or tribunal; hence informal, or summary.

DE PLEGIIS ACQUIETANDIS. Writ for acquitting or releasing pledges. A writ that lay for a surety, against him for whom he had become surety for the payment of a certain sum of money at a certain day, where the latter had not paid the money at the appointed day, and the surety was compelled to pay it. Reg. Orig. 158; Fitzh. Nat. Brev. 137, C; 3 Reeve, Eng. Law, 65.

DE PONENDO SIGILLUM AD EXCEPTIONEM. Writ for putting a seal to an exception. A writ by which justices were formerly commanded to put their seals to exceptions taken by a party in a suit. Reg. Orig. 182.

DE POST DISSEISINA. Writ of post disseisin. A writ which lay for him who, having recovered lands or tenements by *præcipe quod reddat*, on default, or reddition, was again disseised by the former disseisor. Reg. Orig. 208; Fitzh. Nat. Brev. 190.

DE PRÆROGATIVA REGIS. The statute 17 Edw. I. St. 1, c. 9, defining the prerogatives of the crown on certain subjects, but especially directing that the king shall have ward of the lands of idiots, taking the profits without waste, and finding them necessaries. 2 Steph. Comm. 529.

DE PRÆSENTI. Of the present; in the present tense. See PER VERBA DE PRÆSENTI.

DE PROPRIETATE PROBANDA. Writ for proving property. A writ directed to the sheriff, to inquire of the property or goods distrained, where the defendant in an action of replevin claims the property. 3 Bl. Comm. 148; Reg. Orig. 85*b*.

DE QUIBUS SUR DISSEISIN. An ancient writ of entry.

DE QUO, and DE QUIBUS. Of which. Formal words in the simple writ of entry, from which it was called a writ of entry "in the *quo*," or "in the *quibus*." 3 Reeve, Eng. Law, 33.

DE QUOTA LITIS. In the civil law. A contract by which one who has a claim difficult to recover agrees with another to give a part, for the purpose of obtaining his services to recover the rest. 1 Duval, no. 201.

DE RAPTU VIRGINUM. Of the ravishment of maids. The name of an appeal formerly in use in England in cases of rape. Bract. fol. 147; 2 Reeve, Eng. Law, 38.

DE RATIONABILI PARTE BONORUM. A writ which lay for the wife and children of a deceased person against his executors, to recover their reasonable part or share of his goods. 2 Bl. Comm. 492; Fitzh. Nat. Brev. 122, L.

DE RATIONABILIBUS DIVISIS. Writ for fixing reasonable boundaries. A writ which lay to settle the boundaries between the lands of persons in different towns, where one complained of encroachment. Reg. Orig. 157*b;* Fitzh. Nat. Brev. 128, M; Rosc. Real Act. 31; 3 Reeve, Eng. Law, 48.

DE REBUS. Of things. The title of the third part of the Digests or Pandects, comprising books 12–19, inclusive.

DE REBUS DUBIIS. Of doubtful things or matters. Dig. 34, 5.

DE RECORDO ET PROCESSU MITTENDIS. Writ to send the record and process of a cause to a superior court; a species of writ of error. Reg. Orig. 209.

DE RECTO. Writ of right. Reg. Orig. 1, 2; Bract. fol. 327*b*. See WRIT OF RIGHT.

DE RECTO DE ADVOCATIONE. Writ of right of advowson. Reg. Orig. 29*b*. A writ which lay for one who had an estate in an advowson to him and his heirs in fee-simple, if he were disturbed to present. Fitzh. Nat. Brev. 30, B. Abolished by St. 3 & 4 Wm. IV. c. 27.

DE RECTO DE RATIONABILI PARTE. Writ of right, of reasonable part. A writ which lay between privies in blood, as between brothers in gavelkind, or between sisters or other coparceners for lands in fee-simple, where one was deprived of his or her share by another. Reg. Orig. 3*b;* Fitzh. Nat. Brev. 9, B. Abolished by St. 3 & 4 Wm. IV. c. 27.

DE RECTO PATENS. Writ of right patent. Reg. Orig. 1.

DE REDISSEISINA. Writ of redisseisin. A writ which lay where a man recovered by assise of novel disseisin land, rent, or common, and the like, and was put in possession thereof by verdict, and afterwards was disseised of the same land, rent, or common, by him by whom he was disseised before. Reg. Orig. 206*b*, Fitzh. Nat. Brev. 188, B.

DE REPARATIONE FACIENDA. A writ by which one tenant in common seeks to compel another to aid in repairing the property held in common. 8 Barn. & C. 269.

DE RESCUSSU. Writ of rescue or rescous. A writ which lay where cattle distrained, or persons arrested, were rescued from those taking them. Reg. Orig. 117, 118; Fitzh. Nat. Brev. 101, C, G.

DE RETORNO HABENDO. For having a return; to have a return. A term applied to the judgment for the defendant in an action of replevin, awarding him a return of the goods replevied; and to the writ or execution issued thereon. 2 Tidd, Pr. 993, 1038; 3 Bl. Comm. 149. Applied also to the sureties given by the plaintiff on commencing the action. Id. 147.

DE RIEN CULPABLE. L. Fr. Guilty of nothing; not guilty.

DE SA VIE. L. Fr. Of his or her life; of his own life; as distinguished from *pur autre vie*, for another's life. Litt. §§ 35, 36.

DE SALVA GARDIA. A writ of safeguard allowed to strangers seeking their rights in English courts, and apprehending violence or injury to their persons or property Reg. Orig. 26.

DE SALVO CONDUCTU. A writ of safe conduct. Reg. Orig. 25*b*, 26.

DE SCACCARIO. Of or concerning the exchequer. The title of a statute passed in the fifty-first year of Henry III. 2 Reeve, Eng. Law, 61.

DE SCUTAGIO HABENDO. Writ for having (or to have) escuage or scutage. A writ which anciently lay against tenants by knight-service, to compel them to serve in the king's wars or send substitutes, or to pay escuage; that is, a sum of money. Fitzh. Nat. Brev. 83, C. The same writ lay for one who had already served in the king's army, or paid a fine instead, against those who held of him by knight-service, to recover his escuage or scutage. Reg. Orig. 88; Fitzh. Nat. Brev. 83, D, F.

DE SE BENE GERENDO. For behaving himself well; for his good behavior. Yelv. 90, 154.

DE SECTA AD MOLENDINUM. Of suit to a mill. A writ which lay to compel one to continue his custom (of grinding) at a mill. 3 Bl. Comm. 235; Fitzh. Nat. Brev. 122, M.

De similibus ad similia eadem ratione procedendum est. From like things to like things we are to proceed by the same rule or reason, [*i. e.*, we are allowed to argue from the analogy of cases.] Branch, Princ.

De similibus idem est judicandum. Of [respecting] like things, [in like cases,] the judgment is to be the same. 7 Coke, 18.

DE SON TORT. L. Fr. Of his own wrong. A stranger who takes upon him to act as an executor without any just authority is called an "executor of his own wrong," (*de son tort.*) 2 Bl. Comm. 507; 2 Steph. Comm. 244.

DE SON TORT DEMESNE. Of his own wrong. The law French equivalent of the Latin phrase *de injuria*, (*q. v.*)

DE STATUTO MERCATORIO. The writ of statute merchant. Reg. Orig. 146*b*.

DE STATUTO STAPULÆ. The writ of statute staple. Reg. Orig. 151.

DE SUPERONERATIONE PASTURÆ. Writ of surcharge of pasture. A judicial writ which lay for him who was impleaded in the county court, for surcharging a common with his cattle, in a case where he was formerly impleaded for it in the same court, and the cause was removed into one of the courts at Westminster. Reg. Jud. 36*b*.

DE TABULIS EXHIBENDIS. Of showing the tablets of a will. Dig. 43, 5.

DE TALLAGIO NON CONCEDENDO. Of not allowing talliage. The name given to the statutes 25 and 34 Edw. I., restricting the power of the king to grant talliage. 2 Inst. 532; 2 Reeve, Eng. Law, 104.

DE TEMPORE CUJUS CONTRARIUM MEMORIA HOMINUM NON EXISTIT. From time whereof the memory of man does not exist to the contrary. Litt. § 170.

DE TEMPORE IN TEMPUS ET AD OMNIA TEMPORA. From time to time, and at all times. Townsh. Pl. 17

DE TEMPS DONT MEMORIE NE COURT. L. Fr. From time whereof memory runneth not; time out of memory of man. Litt. §§ 143, 145, 170.

DE TESTAMENTIS. Of testaments. The title of the fifth part of the Digests or Pandects; comprising the twenty-eighth to the thirty-sixth books, both inclusive.

DE THEOLONIO. A writ which lay for a person who was prevented from taking toll. Reg. Orig. 103.

DE TRANSGRESSIONE. A writ of trespass. Reg. Orig. 92.

DE TRANSGRESSIONE, AD AUDIENDUM ET TERMINANDUM. A writ or commission for the hearing and determining any outrage or misdemeanor.

DE UNA PARTE. A deed *de una parte* is one where only one party grants, gives, or binds himself to do a thing to another. It differs from a deed *inter partes*, (*q. v.*) 2 Bouv. Inst. no. 2001.

DE UXORE RAPTA ET ABDUCTA. A writ which lay where a man's wife had been ravished and carried away. A species of writ of trespass. Reg. Orig. 97; Fitzh. Nat. Brev. 89, O; 3 Bl. Comm. 139.

DE VASTO. Writ of waste. A writ which might be brought by him who had the immediate estate of inheritance in reversion or remainder, against the tenant for life, in dower, by curtesy, or for years, where the latter had committed *waste* in lands; calling upon the tenant to appear and show cause why he committed waste and destruction in the place named, to the disinherison (*ad exhæredationem*) of the plaintiff. Fitzh. Nat. Brev. 55, C; 3 Bl. Comm. 227, 228. Abolished by St. 3 & 4 Wm. IV. c. 27. 3 Steph. Comm. 506.

DE VENTRE INSPICIENDO. A writ to inspect the body, where a woman feigns to be pregnant, to see whether she is with child. It lies for the heir presumptive to examine a widow suspected to be feigning pregnancy in order to enable a supposititious heir to obtain the estate. 1 Bl. Comm. 456; 2 Steph. Comm. 287.

It lay also where a woman sentenced to death pleaded pregnancy. 4 Bl. Comm. 495. This writ has been recognized in America. 2 Chand. Crim. Tr. 38‥.

DE VERBO IN VERBUM. Word for word. Bract. fol. 138*b*. Literally, from word to word.

DE VERBORUM SIGNIFICATIONE. Of the signification of words. An important title of the Digests or Pandects, (Dig. 50, 16,) consisting entirely of definitions of words and phrases used in the Roman law.

DE VI LAICA AMOVENDA. Writ of (or for) removing lay force. A writ which lay where two parsons contended for a church, and one of them entered into it with a great number of *laymen*, and held out the other *vi et armis;* then he that was holden out had this writ directed to the sheriff, that he remove the force. Reg. Orig. 59; Fitzh. Nat. Brev. 54, D.

DE VICINETO. From the neighborhood, or vicinage. 3 Bl. Comm. 360. A term applied to a jury.

DE WARRANTIA CHARTÆ. Writ of warranty of charter. A writ which lay for him who was enfeoffed, with clause of warranty, [in the charter of feoffment,] and was afterwards impleaded in an assise or other action, in which he could not *vouch* or call to warranty; in which case he might have this writ against the feoffor, or his heir, to compel him to warrant the land unto him. Reg. Orig. 157*b;* Fitzh. Nat. Brev. 134, D. Abolished by St. 3 & 4 Wm. IV. c. 27.

DE WARRANTIA DIEI. A writ that lay where a man had a day in any action to appear in proper person, and the king at that day, or before, employed him in some service, so that he could not appear at the day in court. It was directed to the justices, that they should not record him to be in default for his not appearing. Fitzh. Nat. Brev. 17, A; Termes de la Ley.

DEACON. In ecclesiastical law. A minister or servant in the church, whose office is to assist the priest in divine service and the distribution of the sacrament. It is the lowest order in the Church of England.

DEAD BODY. A corpse.

DEAD FREIGHT. When a merchant who has chartered a vessel puts on board a part only of the intended cargo, but yet, having chartered the whole vessel, is bound to pay freight for the unoccupied capacity, the freight thus due is called "dead freight." L. R. 6 Q. B. 528; 15 East, 547.

DEAD LETTERS. Letters which the postal department has not been able to deliver to the persons for whom they were intended. They are sent to the "dead-letter office," where they are opened, and returned to the writer if his address can be ascertained.

DEAD MAN'S PART. In English law. That portion of the effects of a deceased person which, by the custom of London and York, is allowed to the administrator; being, where the deceased leaves a widow and children, one-third; where he leaves only a widow or only children, one-half; and, where he leaves neither, the whole. This portion the administrator was wont to apply to his own use, till the statute 1 Jac. II. c. 17, declared that the same should be subject to the statute of distributions. 2 Bl. Comm. 518; 2 Steph. Comm. 254; 4 Reeve, Eng. Law, 83. A similar portion in Scotch law is called "dead's part," (*q. v.*)

DEAD-PLEDGE. A mortgage; *mortuum vadium.*

DEAD RENT. In English law. A rent payable on a mining lease in addition to a royalty, so called because it is payable although the mine may not be worked.

DEAD USE. A future use.

DEADHEAD. This term is applied to persons other than the officers, agents, or employes of a railroad company who are permitted by the company to travel on the road without paying any fare therefor. Phillips, 21.

DEADLY FEUD. In old European law. A profession of irreconcilable hatred till a person is revenged even by the death of his enemy.

DEADLY WEAPON. Such weapons or instruments as are made and designed for offensive or defensive purposes, or for the destruction of life or the infliction of injury. 8 Bush, 387.

A deadly weapon is one likely to produce death or great bodily harm. 58 Cal. 245.

A deadly weapon is one which in the manner used is capable of producing death, or of inflicting great bodily injury, or seriously wounding. 4 Tex. App. 327.

DEAD'S PART. In Scotch law. The part remaining over beyond the shares secured to the widow and children by law. Of this the testator had the unqualified disposal. Bell.

DEAF AND DUMB. A man that is born deaf, dumb, and blind is looked upon by the law as in the same state with an idiot, he being supposed incapable of any understanding. 1 Bl. Comm. 304. Nevertheless, a deaf and dumb person may be tried for felony if the prisoner can be made to understand by means of signs. 1 Leach, C. L. 102.

DEAFFOREST. In old English law. To discharge from being forest. To free from forest laws.

DEAFFORESTED. Discharged from being a forest, or freed and exempted from the forest laws.

DEAL. To traffic; to transact business; to trade. Makers of an accommodation note are deemed dealers with whoever discounts it. 17 Wend. 524.

DEALER. A dealer, in the popular, and therefore in the statutory, sense of the word, is not one who buys to keep, or makes to sell, but one who buys to sell again. 27 Pa. St. 494; 33 Pa. St. 380.

DEALINGS. Transactions in the course of trade or business. Held to include payments to a bankrupt. Moody & M. 137; 3 Car. & P. 85.

DEAN. In English ecclesiastical law. An ecclesiastical dignitary who presides over the chapter of a cathedral, and is next in rank to the bishop. So called from having been originally appointed to superintend *ten* canons or prebendaries. 1 Bl. Comm. 382; Co. Litt. 95; Spelman.

There are several kinds of deans, namely: Deans of chapters; deans of peculiars; rural deans; deans in the colleges; honorary deans; deans of provinces.

DEAN AND CHAPTER. In ecclesiastical law. The council of a bishop, to assist him with their advice in the religious and also in the temporal affairs of the see. 3 Coke, 75; 1 Bl. Comm. 382; Co. Litt. 103, 300.

DEAN OF THE ARCHES. The presiding judge of the Court of Arches. He is also an assistant judge in the court of admiralty. 1 Kent, Comm. 371; 3 Steph. Comm. 727.

DEATH. The extinction of life; the departure of the soul from the body; defined by physicians as a total stoppage of the circulation of the blood, and a cessation of the animal and vital functions consequent thereon, such as respiration, pulsation, etc.

In legal contemplation, it is of two kinds: (1) *Natural, i. e.*, the extinction of life; (2) *civil*, where a person is not actually dead, but is adjudged so by the law, as when a person is banished or abjures the realm, or enters into a monastery. Civil death also occurs where a man, by act of parliament or judgment of law, is attainted of treason or felony; for immediately upon such attainder he loses (subject, indeed, to some exceptions) his civil rights and capacities, and becomes, as it were, *civiliter mortuus*. But now, by the 33 & 34 Vict. c. 23, forfeiture for treason or felony has been abolished, but the person convicted is disqualified for offices, etc. Wharton.

Natural death is also used to denote a death which occurs by the unassisted operation of natural causes, as distinguished from a *violent* death, or one caused or accelerated by the interference of human agency.

DEATH-BED. In Scotch law. A state of sickness which ends in death. Ersk. Inst. 3, 8, 95.

DEATH-BED DEED. In Scotch law. A deed made by a person while laboring under a distemper of which he afterwards died. Ersk. Inst. 3, 8, 96. A deed is understood to be in death-bed, if, before signing and delivery thereof, the grantor was sick, and never convalesced thereafter. 1 Forbes, Inst. pt. 3, b. 2, c. 4, tit. 1, § 1. But it is not necessary that he should be actually confined to his bed at the time of making the deed. Bell.

DEATH'S PART. See DEAD'S PART; DEAD MAN'S PART.

DEATHSMAN. The executioner; hangman; he that executes the extreme penalty of the law

DEBAUCH. To entice, to corrupt, and, when used of a woman, to seduce. Originally, the term had a limited signification, meaning to entice or draw one away from his work, employment, or duty; and from this sense its application has enlarged to include the corruption of manners and violation of the person. In its modern legal sense, the word carries with it the idea of "carnal knowledge," aggravated by assault, violent seduction, ravishment. 2 Hilt. 323.

DEBENTURE. A certificate given by the collector of a port, under the United States customs laws, to the effect that an importer of merchandise therein named is entitled to a drawback, (*q. v.*,) specifying the amount and time when payable. See Act Cong. March 2, 1799, § 80.

In English law. A security for a loan of money issued by a public company, usually creating a charge on the whole or a part of the company's stock and property, though not necessarily in the form of a mortgage. They are subject to certain regulations as to the mode of transfer, and ordinarily have coupons attached to facilitate the payment of interest. They are generally issued in a series, with provision that they shall rank *pari passu* in proportion to their amounts.

An instrument in use in some government departments, by which government is charged to pay to a creditor or his assigns the sum found due on auditing his accounts. Brande; Blount.

DEBENTURE STOCK. A stock or fund representing money borrowed by a company or public body, in England, and charged on the whole or part of its property.

Debet esse finis litium. There ought to be an end of suits; there should be some period put to litigation. Jenk. Cent. 61.

DEBET ET DETINET. He owes and detains. Words anciently used in the original writ, (and now, in English, in the plaintiff's declaration,) in an action of debt, where it was brought by one of the original contracting parties who personally gave the credit, against the other who personally incurred the debt, or against his heirs, if they were bound to the payment; as by the obligee against the obligor, by the landlord against the tenant, etc. The declaration, in such cases, states that the defendant "*owes* to," as well as "*detains* from," the plaintiff the debt or thing in question; and hence the action is said to be "in the *debet et detinet*." Where the declaration merely states that the defendant *detains* the debt, (as in actions by and against an executor for a debt due to or from the testator,) the action is said to be "in the *detinet*" alone. Fitzh. Nat. Brev. 119, G.; 3 Bl. Comm. 155.

DEBET ET SOLET. (Lat. He owes and is used to.) Where a man sues in a writ of right or to recover any right of which he is for the first time disseised, as of a suit at a mill or in case of a writ of *quod permittat*, he brings his writ in the *debet et solet*. Reg. Orig. 144*a*; Fitzh. Nat. Brev. 122, M.

Debet quis juri subjacere ubi delinquit. One [every one] ought to be subject to the law [of the place] where he offends. 3 Inst. 34. This maxim is taken from Bracton. Bract. fol. 154*b*.

Debet sua cuique domus esse perfugium tutissimum. Every man's house should be a perfectly safe refuge. 12 Johns. 31, 54.

Debile fundamentum fallit opus. A weak foundation frustrates [or renders vain] the work [built upon it.] Shep. Touch. 60; Noy, Max. 5, max. 12; Finch, Law, b. 1, ch. 3. When the foundation fails, all goes to the ground; as, where the cause of action fails, the action itself must of necessity fail. Wing, Max., 113, 114, max. 40; Broom, Max. 180.

DEBIT. A sum charged as due or owing. The term is used in book-keeping to denote the charging of a person or an account with all that is supplied to or paid out for him or for the subject of the account.

DEBITA FUNDI. L. Lat. In Scotch law. Debts secured upon land. Ersk. Inst. 4, 1, 11.

DEBITA LAICORUM. L. Lat. In old English law. Debts of the laity, or of lay persons. Debts recoverable in the civil courts were anciently so called. Crabb, Eng. Law, 107.

Debita sequuntur personam debitoris. Debts follow the person of the debtor; that is, they have no locality, and may be collected wherever the debtor can be found. 2 Kent, Comm. 429; Story, Confl. Laws, § 362.

DEBITOR. In the civil and old English law. A debtor.

Debitor non præsumitur donare. A debtor is not presumed to make a gift. Whatever disposition he makes of his property is supposed to be in satisfaction of his debts. 1 Kames, Eq. 212. Where a debtor gives money or goods, or grants land to his creditor, the natural presumption is that he means to get free from his obligation, and not to make a present, unless donation be expressed. Ersk. Inst. 3, 3, 93.

Debitorum pactionibus creditorum petitio nec tolli nec minui potest. 1 Poth. Obl. 108; Broom, Max. 697. The rights of creditors can neither be taken away nor diminished by agreements among the debtors.

DEBITRIX. A female debtor.

DEBITUM. Something due, or owing; a debt.

Debitum et contractus sunt nullius loci. Debt and contract are of [belong to] no place; have no particular locality. The obligation in these cases is purely personal, and actions to enforce it may be brought anywhere. 2 Inst. 231; Story, Confl. Laws, § 362; 1 Smith, Lead. Cas. 340, 363.

DEBITUM IN PRÆSENTI SOLVENDUM IN FUTURO. A debt or obligation complete when contracted, but of which the performance cannot be required till some future period.

DEBITUM SINE BREVI. L. Lat. Debt without writ; debt without a declaration. In old practice, this term denoted an action begun by original bill, instead of by writ. In modern usage, it is sometimes applied to a debt evidenced by confession of judgment without suit. The equivalent Norman-French phrase was "*debit sans breve.*" Both are abbreviated to *d. s. b.*

DEBT. A sum of money due by certain and express agreement; as by bond for a determinate sum, a bill or note, a special bargain, or a rent reserved on a lease, where the amount is fixed and specific, and does not depend upon any subsequent valuation to settle it. 3 Bl. Comm. 154.

A debt is a sum of money due by contract. It is most frequently due by a certain and express agreement, which fixes the amount, independent of extrinsic circumstances. But it is not essential that the contract should be express, or that it should fix the precise amount to be paid. 1 Pet. 145.

Standing alone, the word "debt" is as applicable to a sum of money which has been promised at a future day, as to a sum of money now due and payable. To distinguish between the two, it may be said of the former that it is a debt owing, and of the latter that it is a debt due. Whether a claim or demand is a debt or not is in no respect determined by a reference to the time of payment. A sum of money which is certainly and in all events payable is a debt, without regard to the fact whether it be payable now or at a future time. A sum payable upon a contingency, however, is not a debt, or does not become a debt until the contingency has happened. 37 Cal. 524.

The word "debt" is of large import, including not only debts of record, or judgments, and debts by specialty, but also obligations arising under simple contract, to a very wide extent; and in its popular sense includes all that is due to a man under any form of obligation or promise. 3 Metc. (Mass.) 522, 526.

"Debt" has been differently defined, owing to the different subject-matter of the statutes in which it has been used. Ordinarily, it imports a

sum of money arising upon a contract, express or implied. In its more general sense, it is defined to be that which is due from one person to another, whether money, goods, or services; that which one person is bound to pay or perform to another. Under the legal-tender statutes, it seems to import any obligation by contract, express or implied, which may be discharged by money through the voluntary action of the party bound. Wherever he may be at liberty to perform his obligation by the payment of a specific sum of money, the party owing the obligation is subject to what, in these statutes, is termed "debt." 45 Barb. 618.

The word is sometimes used to denote an aggregate of separate debts, or the total sum of the existing claims against a person or company. Thus we speak of the "national debt," the "bonded debt" of a corporation, etc.

Synonyms. The term "demand" is of much broader import than "debt," and embraces rights of action belonging to the debtor beyond those which could appropriately be called "debts." In this respect the term "demand" is one of very extensive import. 2 Hill, 223.

The words "debt" and "liability" are not synonymous. As applied to the pecuniary relations of parties, liability is a term of broader significance than debt. The legal acceptation of debt is a sum of money due by certain and express agreement. Liability is responsibility; the state of one who is bound in law and justice to do something which may be enforced by action. This liability may arise from contracts either express or implied, or in consequence of torts committed. 36 Iowa, 226.

"Debt" is not exactly synonymous with "duty." A debt is a legal liability to pay a specific sum of money; a duty is a legal obligation to perform some act. 1 Minor, 120.

In practice. The name of a common-law action, which lies to recover a certain specific sum of money, or a sum that can readily be reduced to a certainty. 3 Bl. Comm. 154; 3 Steph. Comm. 461; 1 Tidd. Pr. 3.

It is said to lie in the *debet* and *detinet*, (when it is stated that the defendant owes and detains,) or in the *detinet*, (when it is stated merely that he detains.) Debt in the *detinet* for goods differs from detinue, because it is not essential in this action, as in detinue, that the specific property in the goods should have been vested in the plaintiff at the time the action is brought. Dyer, 24*b*.

DEBT BY SIMPLE CONTRACT. A debt or demand founded upon a verbal or implied contract, or upon any written agreement that is not under seal.

DEBT BY SPECIALTY. A debt due, or acknowledged to be due, by some deed or instrument under seal; as a deed of covenant or sale, a lease reserving rent, or a bond or obligation. 2 Bl. Comm. 465. See SPECIALTY.

DEBT EX MUTUO. A species of debt or obligation mentioned by Glanville and Bracton, and which arose *ex mutuo*, out of a certain kind of loan. Glan. lib. 10, c. 3; Bract. fol. 99. See MUTUUM; EX MUTUO.

DEBT OF RECORD. A debt which appears to be due by the evidence of a court of record, as by a judgment or recognizance. 2 Bl. Comm. 465.

DEBTEE. A person to whom a debt is due; a creditor. 3 Bl. Comm. 18; Plowd. 543. Not used.

DEBTOR. One who owes a debt; he who may be compelled to pay a claim or demand.

DEBTOR'S ACT 1869. The statute 32 & 33 Vict. c. 62, abolishing imprisonment for debt in England, and for the punishment of fraudulent debtors. 2 Steph. Comm. 159–164. Not to be confounded with the Bankruptcy Act of 1869. Mozley & Whitley.

DEBTOR'S SUMMONS. In English law. A summons issuing from a court having jurisdiction in bankruptcy, upon the creditor proving a liquidated debt of not less than £50, which he has failed to collect after reasonable effort, stating that if the debtor fail, within one week if a trader, and within three weeks if a non-trader, to pay or compound for the sum specified, a petition may be presented against him praying that he may be adjudged a bankrupt. Bankruptcy Act 1869, § 7; Robs. Bankr.; Mozley & Whitley.

DECALOGUE. The ten commandments given by God to Moses. The Jews called them the "Ten Words," hence the name.

DECANATUS. A deanery. Spelman. A company of ten persons. Calvin.

DECANIA. The office, jurisdiction, territory, or command of a *decanus*, or dean. Spelman.

DECANUS. In ecclesiastical and old European law. An officer having supervision over *ten;* a dean. A term applied not only to ecclesiastical, but to civil and military, officers. *Decanus monasticus;* a monastic dean, or dean of a monastery; an officer over ten monks. *Decanus in majori ecclesiæ;* dean of a cathedral church, presiding over ten prebendaries. *Decanus episcopi;* a bishop's or rural dean, presiding over ten clerks or parishes. *Decanus friborgi;* dean of a friborg. An officer among the Saxons who presided over a friborg, tithing, decennary, or association of ten inhabitants; otherwise called a "tithing man," or "borshold r." *Decanus militaris;* a military officer, having command of ten soldiers. Spelman.

In Roman law. An officer having the command of a company or "mess" of ten soldiers. Also an officer at Constantinople having charge of the burial of the dead.

DECAPITATION. The act of beheading. A mode of capital punishment by cutting off the head.

DECEASE, *n.* Death; departure from life.

DECEASE, *v.* To die; to depart life, or from life. This has always been a common term in Scotch law. "Gif ane man *deceasis.*" Skene.

DECEDENT. A deceased person; one who has lately died. Etymologically the word denotes a person who is *dying,* but it has come to be used in law as signifying any defunct person, (testate or intestate,) but always with reference to the settlement of his estate or the execution of his will.

DECEIT. A fraudulent and cheating misrepresentation, artifice, or device, used by one or more persons to deceive and trick another, who is ignorant of the true facts, to the prejudice and damage of the party imposed upon.

A subtle trick or device, whereunto may be referred all manner of craft and collusion used to deceive and defraud another by any means whatsoever, which hath no other or more proper name than *deceit* to distinguish the offense. [West Symb. § 68;] Jacob.

The word "deceit," as well as "fraud," excludes the idea of mistake, and imports knowledge that the artifice or device used to deceive or defraud is untrue. 61 Ill. 373.

In old English law. The name of an original writ, and the action founded on it, which lay to recover damages for any injury committed *deceitfully,* either in the name of another, (as by bringing an action in another's name, and then suffering a nonsuit, whereby the plaintiff became liable to costs,) or by a fraudulent warranty of goods, or other personal injury committed contrary to good faith and honesty. Reg. Orig. 112–116; Fitzh. Nat. Brev. 95, E, 98.

Also the name of a judicial writ which formerly lay to recover lands which had been lost by default by the tenant in a real action, in consequence of his not having been summoned by the sheriff, or by the collusion of his attorney. Rosc. Real Act. 136; 3 Bl. Comm. 166.

DECEM TALES. (Ten such; or ten tales, jurors.) In practice. The name of a writ which issues in England, where, on a trial at bar, *ten* jurors are necessary to make up a full panel, commanding the sheriff to summon the requisite number. 3 Bl. Comm. 364; Reg. Jud. 30*b;* 3 Steph. Comm. 602.

DECEMVIRI LITIBUS JUDICANDIS. Lat. In the Roman law. Ten persons (five senators and five *equites*) who acted as the council or assistants of the prætor, when he decided on matters of law. Hallifax, Civil Law, b. 3, c. 8. According to others, they were themselves judges. Calvin.

DECENNA. In old English law. A tithing or decennary; the precinct of a frankpledge; consisting of ten freeholders with their families. Spelman.

DECENNARIUS. Lat. One who held one-half a virgate of land. Du Cange. One of the ten freeholders in a *decennary.* Id.; Calvin. *Decennier.* One of the *decennarii,* or ten freeholders making up a tithing. Spelman.

DECENNARY. A tithing, composed of ten neighboring families. 1 Reeve, Eng. Law, 13; 1 Bl. Comm. 114.

Deceptis non decipientibus, jura subveniunt. The laws help persons who are deceived, not those deceiving. Tray. Lat. Max. 149.

DECERN. In Scotch law. To decree. "Decernit and ordainit." 1 How. State Tr. 927. "Decerns." Shaw, 16.

DECESSUS. In the civil and old English law. Death; departure.

Decet tamen principem servare leges, quibus ipse servatus est. It behoves, indeed, the prince to keep the laws by which he himself is preserved.

DECIDE. To decide includes the power and right to deliberate, to weigh the reasons for and against, to see which preponderate, and to be governed by that preponderance. 5 Gray, 253.

DECIES TANTUM. (Ten times as much.) The name of an ancient writ that was used against a juror who had taken a bribe in money for his verdict. The injured party could thus recover ten times the amount of the bribe.

DECIMÆ. In ecclesiastical law. Tenths, or tithes. The tenth part of the annual profit of each living, payable formerly to the pope. There were several valuations made of these livings at different times. The *decimæ* (tenths) were appropriated to the crown, and a new valuation established, by 26 Hen. VIII. c. 3. 1 Bl. Comm. 284. See TITHES.

Decimæ debentur parocho. Tithes are due to the parish priest.

Decimæ de decimatis solvi non debent. Tithes are not to be paid from that which is given for tithes.

Decimæ de jure divino et canonica institutione pertinent ad personam. Dal. 50. Tithes belong to the parson by divine right and canonical institution.

Decimæ non debent solvi, ubi non est annua renovatio; et ex annuatis renovantibus simul semel. Cro. Jac. 42. Tithes ought not to be paid where there is not an annual renovation, and from annual renovations once only.

DECIMATION. The punishing every tenth soldier by lot, for mutiny or other failure of duty, was termed "*decimatio legionis*" by the Romans. Sometimes only the twentieth man was punished, (*vicesimatio,*) or the hundredth, (*centesimatio.*)

DECIME. A French coin of the value of the tenth part of a franc, or nearly two cents.

Decipi quam fallere est tutius. It is safer to be deceived than to deceive. Lofft, 396.

DECISION. In practice. A judgment or decree pronounced by a court in settlement of a controversy submitted to it and by way of authoritative answer to the questions raised before it.

"Decision" is not synonymous with "opinion." A decision of the court is its judgment; the opinion is the reasons given for that judgment. 13 Cal. 27.

DECISIVE OATH. In the civil law. Where one of the parties to a suit, not being able to prove his charge, offered to refer the decision of the cause to the oath of his adversary, which the adversary was bound to accept, or tender the same proposal back again, otherwise the whole was taken as confessed by him. Cod. 4, 1, 12.

DECLARANT. A person who makes a declaration.

DECLARATION. In pleading. The first of the pleadings on the part of the plaintiff in an action at law, being a formal and methodical specification of the facts and circumstances constituting his cause of action. It commonly comprises several sections or divisions, called "counts," and its formal parts follow each other in this order: Title, venue, commencement, cause of action, counts, conclusion. The declaration, at common law, answers to the "libel" in ecclesiastical and admiralty law, the "bill" in equity, the "petition" in civil law, the "complaint" in code pleading, and the "count" in real actions.

In evidence. An unsworn statement or narration of facts made by a party to the transaction, or by one who has an interest in the existence of the facts recounted. Or a similar statement made by a person since deceased, which is admissible in evidence in some cases, contrary to the general rule, *e. g.*, a "dying declaration."

In practice. The declaration or declaratory part of a judgment, decree, or order is that part which gives the decision or opinion of the court on the question of law in the case. Thus, in an action raising a question as to the construction of a will, the judgment or order declares that, according to the true construction of the will, the plaintiff has become entitled to the residue of the testator's estate, or the like. Sweet.

In Scotch practice. The statement of a criminal or prisoner, taken before a magistrate. 2 Alis. Crim. Pr. 555.

DECLARATION OF INDEPENDENCE. A formal declaration or announcement, promulgated July 4, 1776, by the congress of the United States of America, in the name and behalf of the people of the colonies, asserting and proclaiming their independence of the British crown, vindicating their pretensions to political autonomy, and announcing themselves to the world as a free and independent nation.

DECLARATION OF INTENTION. A declaration made by an alien, as a preliminary to naturalization, before a court of record, to the effect that it is *bona fide* his intention to become a citizen of the United

States, and to renounce forever all allegiance and fidelity to any foreign prince, potentate, state, or sovereignty whereof at the time he may be a citizen or subject. Rev. St. § 2165.

DECLARATION OF PARIS. The name given to an agreement announcing four important rules of international law effected between the principal European powers at the Congress of Paris in 1856. These rules are: (1) Privateering is and remains abolished; (2) the neutral flag covers enemy's goods, except contraband of war; (3) neutral goods, except contraband of war, are not liable to confiscation under a hostile flag; (4) blockades, to be binding, must be effective.

DECLARATION OF RIGHT. See BILL OF RIGHTS.

DECLARATION OF TRUST. The act by which the person who holds the legal title to property or an estate acknowledges and declares that he holds the same in trust to the use of another person or for certain specified purposes. The name is also used to designate the deed or other writing embodying such a declaration.

DECLARATION OF WAR. A public and formal proclamation by a nation, through its executive or legislative department, that a state of war exists between itself and another nation, and forbidding all persons to aid or assist the enemy.

DECLARATOR. In Scotch law. An action whereby it is sought to have some right of property, or of *status*, or other right judicially ascertained and declared. Bell.

DECLARATOR OF TRUST. In Scotch law. An action resorted to against a trustee who holds property upon titles *ex facie* for his own benefit. Bell.

DECLARATORY. Explanatory; designed to fix or elucidate what before was uncertain or doubtful; as a declaratory statute, which is one passed to put an end to a doubt as to what the law is, and which declares what it is and what it has been. 1 Bl. Comm. 86.

DECLARATORY ACTION. In Scotch law. An action in which the right of the pursuer (or plaintiff) is craved to be *declared*, but nothing claimed to be done by the defender, (defendant.) Ersk. Inst. 5, 1, 46. Otherwise called an "action of declarator."

DECLARATORY DECREE. In practice. A binding declaration of right in equity without consequential relief.

DECLARATORY JUDGMENT. A declaratory judgment is one which simply declares the rights of the parties, or expresses the opinion of the court on a question of law, without ordering anything to be done.

DECLARATORY PART OF A LAW. That which clearly defines rights to be observed and wrongs to be eschewed.

DECLARE. To solemnly assert a fact before witnesses, *e. g.*, where a testator *declares* a paper signed by him to be his last will and testament.

This also is one of the words customarily used in the promise given by a person who is *affirmed* as a witness,—"sincerely and truly declare and affirm." Hence, to make a positive and solemn asseveration.

With reference to pleadings, it means to draw up, serve, and file a declaration; *e. g.*, a "rule to declare." Also to allege in a declaration as a ground or cause of action; as "he declares upon a promissory note."

DECLINATION. In Scotch law. A plea to the jurisdiction, on the ground that the judge is interested in the suit.

DÉCLINATOIRES. In French law. Pleas to the jurisdiction of the court; also of *lis pendens*, and of *connexité*, (*q. v.*)

DECLINATORY PLEA. In English practice. The plea of sanctuary, or of benefit of clergy, before trial or conviction. 2 Hale, P. C. 236; 4 Bl. Comm. 333. Now abolished. 4 Steph. Comm. 400, note; Id. 436, note.

DECLINATURE. In Scotch practice. An objection to the jurisdiction of a judge. Bell.

DECOCTION. The act of boiling a substance in water, for extracting its virtues. Also the liquor in which a substance has been boiled; water impregnated with the principles of any animal or vegetable substance boiled in it. Webster.

In an indictment "decoction" and "infusion" are *ejusdem generis;* and if one is alleged to have been administered, instead of the other, the variance is immaterial. 3 Camp. 74.

DECOCTOR. In the Roman law. A bankrupt; a spendthrift; a squanderer of public funds. Calvin.

DECOLLATIO. In old English and Scotch law. Decollation; the punishment of beheading. Fleta, lib. 1, c. 21, § 6.

DECONFES. In French law. A name formerly given to those persons who died without confession, whether they refused to confess or whether they were criminals to whom the sacrament was refused.

DECOY. A pond used for the breeding and maintenance of water-fowl. 11 Mod. 74, 130; 3 Salk. 9.

DECOY LETTER. A letter prepared and mailed for the purpose of detecting a criminal, particularly one who is perpetrating frauds upon the postal or revenue laws. 5 Dill. 39.

DECREE. **In practice.** The judgment of a court of equity or admiralty, answering to the judgment of a court of common law. A decree in equity is a sentence or order of the court, pronounced on hearing and understanding all the points in issue, and determining the right of all the parties to the suit, according to equity and good conscience. 2 Daniell, Ch. Pr. 986.

Decree is the judgment of a court of equity, and is, to most intents and purposes, the same as a judgment of a court of common law. A decree, as distinguished from an order, is final, and is made at the hearing of the cause, whereas an order is interlocutory, and is made on motion or petition. Wherever an order may, in a certain event resulting from the direction contained in the order, lead to the termination of the suit in like manner as a decree made at the hearing, it is called a "decretal order." Brown.

It is either interlocutory or final; the former where it passes upon some plea or issue arising in the cause, but not involving a definitive adjudication of the main question; the latter where it finally determines the whole matter in dispute.

In French law. Certain acts of the legislature or of the sovereign which have the force of law are called "*decrees;*" as the Berlin and Milan decrees.

In Scotch law. A final judgment or sentence of court by which the question at issue between the parties is decided.

DECREE DATIVE. In Scotch law. An order of a probate court appointing an administrator.

DECREE NISI. A provisional decree, which will be made absolute on motion unless cause be shown against it. In English practice, it is the order made by the court for divorce, on satisfactory proof being given in support of a petition for dissolution of marriage; it remains imperfect for at least six months, (which period may be shortened by the court down to three,) and then, unless sufficient cause be shown, it is made absolute on motion, and the dissolution takes effect, subject to appeal. Wharton.

DECREE OF CONSTITUTION. In Scotch practice. A decree by which a debt is ascertained. Bell.

In technical language, a decree which is requisite to found a title in the person of the creditor, whether that necessity arises from the death of the debtor or of the creditor. Id.

DECREE OF FORTHCOMING. In Scotch law. A decree made after an arrestment (*q. v.*) ordering the debt to be paid or the effects of the debtor to be delivered to the arresting creditor. Bell.

DECREE OF LOCALITY. In Scotch law. The decree of a teind court allocating stipend upon different heritors. It is equivalent to the apportionment of a tithe rent-charge.

DECREE OF MODIFICATION. In Scotch law. A decree of the teind court modifying or fixing a stipend.

DECREE OF REGISTRATION. In Scotch law. A proceeding giving immediate execution to the creditor; similar to a warrant of attorney to confess judgment.

DECREET. In Scotch law. The final judgment or sentence of a court.

DECREET ABSOLVITOR. In Scotch law. A decree dismissing a claim, or acquitting a defendant. 2 Kames, Eq. 367.

DECREET ARBITRAL. In Scotch law. An award of arbitrators. 1 Kames, Eq. 312, 313; 2 Kames, Eq. 367.

DECREET COGNITIONIS CAUSÂ. In Scotch law. When a creditor brings his action against the heir of his debtor in order to constitute the debt against him and attach the lands, and the heir appears and renounces the succession, the court then pronounces a decree *cognitionis causâ.* Bell.

DECREET CONDEMNATOR. In Scotch law. One where the decision is in favor of the plaintiff. Ersk. Inst. 4, 3, 5.

DECREET OF VALUATION OF TEINDS. In Scotch law. A sentence of the court of sessions, (who are now in the place of the commissioners for the valuation of teinds,) determining the extent and value of teinds. Bell.

DECREMENTUM MARIS. Lat. In old English law. Decrease of the sea; the receding of the sea from the land. Callis, Sewers, (53,) 65. See RELICTION.

DECREPIT. This term designates a person who is disabled, incapable, or incompetent, either from physical or mental weakness or defects, whether produced by age or other causes, to such an extent as to render the individual comparatively helpless in a personal conflict with one possessed of ordinary health and strength. 16 Tex. App. 11.

DECRETA. In the Roman law. Judicial sentences given by the emperor as supreme judge.

Decreta conciliorum non ligant reges nostros. Moore, 906. The decrees of councils bind not our kings.

DECRETAL ORDER. In chancery practice. An order made by the court of chancery, in the nature of a decree, upon a motion or petition.

An order in a chancery suit made on motion or otherwise not at the regular hearing of a cause, and yet not of an interlocutory nature, but finally disposing of the cause, so far as a decree could then have disposed of it. Mozley & Whitley.

DECRETALES BONIFACII OCTAVI. A supplemental collection of the canon law, published by Boniface VIII. in 1298, called, also, "*Liber Sextus Decretalium*," (Sixth Book of the Decretals.)

DECRETALES GREGORII NONI. The decretals of Gregory the Ninth. A collection of the laws of the church, published by order of Gregory IX. in 1227. It is composed of five books, subdivided into titles, and each title is divided into chapters. They are cited by using an X, (or *extra;*) thus "*Cap.* 8 X *de Regulis Juris*," etc.

DECRETALS. In ecclesiastical law. Letters of the pope, written at the suit or instance of one or more persons, determining some point or question in ecclesiastical law, and possessing the force of law. The decretals form the second part of the body of canon law.

This is also the title of the second of the two great divisions of the canon law, the first being called the "*Decree*," (*decretum.*)

DECRETO. In Spanish colonial law. An order emanating from some superior tribunal, promulgated in the name and by the authority of the sovereign, in relation to ecclesiastical matters. Schm. Civil Law, 93, note.

DECRETUM. In the civil law. A species of imperial constitution, being a judgment or sentence given by the emperor upon hearing of a cause, (*quod imperator cognoscens decrevit.*) Inst. 1, 2, 6.

In canon law. An ecclesiastical law, in contradistinction to a secular law, (*lex.*) 1 Mackeld. Civil Law, p. 81, § 93, (Kaufmann's note.)

DECRETUM GRATIANI. Gratian's decree, or *decretum*. A collection of ecclesiastical law in three books or parts, made in the year 1151, by Gratian, a Benedictine monk of Bologna, being the oldest as well as the first in order of the collections which together form the body of the Roman canon law. 1 Bl. Comm. 82; 1 Reeve, Eng. Law, 67.

DECROWNING. The act of depriving of a crown.

DECRY. To cry down; to deprive of credit. "The king may at any time *decry* or cry down any coin of the kingdom, and make it no longer current." 1 Bl. Comm. 278.

DECURIO. In the provincial administration of the Roman empire, the decurions were the chief men or official personages of the large towns. Taken as a body, the decurions of a city were charged with the entire control and administration of its internal affairs; having powers both magisterial and legislative. See 1 Spence, Eq. Jur. 54.

DEDBANA. In Saxon law. An actual homicide or manslaughter.

DEDI. (Lat. I have given.) A word used in deeds and other instruments of conveyance when such instruments were made in Latin, and anciently held to imply a warranty of title.

DEDI ET CONCESSI. I have given and granted. The operative words of conveyance in ancient charters of feoffment, and deeds of gift and grant; the English "*given and granted*" being still the most proper, though not the essential, words by which such conveyances are made. 2 Bl. Comm. 53, 316, 317; 1 Steph. Comm. 164, 177, 473, 474.

DEDICATE. To appropriate and set apart one's private property to some public use; as to make a private way public by acts evincing an intention to do so.

DEDICATION. **In real property law.** An appropriation of land to some public use, made by the owner, and accepted for such use by or on behalf of the public. 23 Wis. 416; 33 N. J. Law, 13.

A deliberate appropriation of land by its owner for any general and public uses, reserving to himself no other rights than such as are perfectly compatible with the full exercise and enjoyment of the public uses to which he has devoted his property. 22 Wend. 472.

In copyright law. The first publication of a work, without having secured a copyright, is a dedication of it to the public; that having been done, any one may republish it. 5 McLean, 32; 7 West. Law J. 49; 5 McLean, 328.

DEDICATION-DAY. The feast of dedication of churches, or rather the feast day of the saint and patron of a church, which was celebrated not only by the inhabitants of the place, but by those of all the neighboring villages, who usually came thither; and such assemblies were allowed as lawful. It was usual for the people to feast and to drink on those days. Cowell.

DEDIMUS ET CONCESSIMUS. (Lat. We have given and granted.) Words used by the king, or where there were more grantors than one, instead of *dedi et concessi.*

DEDIMUS POTESTATEM. (We have given power.) In English practice. A writ or commission issuing out of chancery, empowering the persons named therein to perform certain acts, as to administer oaths to defendants in chancery and take their answers, to administer oaths of office to justices of the peace, etc. 3 Bl. Comm. 447. It was anciently allowed for many purposes not now in use, as to make an attorney, to take the acknowledgment of a fine, etc.

In the United States, a commission to take testimony is sometimes termed a "*dedimus potestatem.*" 3 Cranch, 293; 4 Wheat. 508.

DEDIMUS POTESTATEM DE ATTORNO FACIENDO. In old English practice. A writ, issued by royal authority, empowering an attorney to appear for a defendant. Prior to the statute of Westminster 2, a party could not appear in court by attorney without this writ.

DEDITION. The act of yielding up anything; surrender.

DEDITITII. In Roman law. Criminals who had been marked in the face or on the body with fire or an iron, so that the mark could not be erased, and subsequently manumitted. Calvin.

DEDUCTION. By "deduction" is understood a portion or thing which an heir has a right to take from the mass of the succession before any partition takes place. Civil Code La. art. 1358.

DEDUCTION FOR NEW. In marine insurance. An allowance or drawback credited to the insurers on the cost of repairing a vessel for damage arising from the perils of the sea insured against. This allowance is usually one-third, and is made on the theory that the parts restored with new materials are better, in that proportion, than they were before the damage.

DEED. A sealed instrument, containing a contract or covenant, delivered by the party to be bound thereby, and accepted by the party to whom the contract or covenant runs.

A writing containing a contract sealed and delivered to the party thereto. 3 Washb. Real Prop. 239.

In its legal sense, a "deed" is an instrument in writing, upon paper or parchment, between parties able to contract, subscribed, sealed, and delivered. 60 Ind. 572; 4 Kent, Comm. 452.

In a more restricted sense, a written agreement, signed, sealed, and delivered, by which one person conveys land, tenements, or hereditaments to another. This is its ordinary modern meaning.

The term is also used as synonymous with "fact," "actuality," or "act of parties." Thus a thing "in deed" is one that has been really or expressly done; as opposed to "in law," which means that it is merely implied or presumed to have been done.

DEED INDENTED, or INDENTURE. In conveyancing. A deed executed or purporting to be executed in parts, between two or more parties, and distinguished by having the edge of the paper or parchment on which it is written indented or cut at the top in a particular manner. This was formerly done at the top or side, in a line resembling the teeth of a saw; a formality derived from the ancient practice of dividing chirographs; but the cutting is now made either in a waving line, or more commonly by notching or nicking the paper at the edge. 2 Bl. Comm. 295, 296; Litt. § 370; Smith, Cont. 12.

DEED OF COVENANT. Covenants are sometimes entered into by a separate deed, for title, or for the indemnity of a purchaser or mortgagee, or for the production of title-deeds. A covenant with a penalty is sometimes taken for the payment of a debt, instead of a bond with a condition, but the legal remedy is the same in either case.

DEED POLL. In conveyancing. A deed of one part or made by one party only; and originally so called because the edge of the paper or parchment was *polled* or cut in a straight line, wherein it was distinguished from a deed indented or indenture.

DEED TO DECLARE USES. A deed made after a fine or common recovery, to show the object thereof.

DEED TO LEAD USES. A deed made before a fine or common recovery, to show the object thereof.

DEEM. To hold; consider; adjudge; condemn. When, by statute, certain acts are "deemed" to be a crime of a particular nature, they are such crime, and not a semblance of it, nor a mere fanciful approximation to or designation of the offense. 132 Mass. 247.

DEEMSTERS. Judges in the Isle of Man, who decide all controversies without process, writings, or any charges. These judges are chosen by the people, and are said by Spelman to be two in number. Spelman.

DEER-FALD. A park or fold for deer.

DEER-HAYES. Engines or great nets made of cord to catch deer. 19 Hen. VIII. c. 11.

DEFALCATION. The act of a defaulter; misappropriation of trust funds or money held in any fiduciary capacity; failure to properly account for such funds. Usually spoken of officers of corporations or public officials.

Also set-off. The diminution of a debt or claim by deducting from it a smaller claim held by the debtor or payor.

DEFAMATION. The taking from one's reputation. The offense of injuring a person's character, fame, or reputation by false and malicious statements. The term seems to be comprehensive of both libel and slander.

DEFAMES. L. Fr. Infamous. Britt. c. 15.

DEFAULT. The omission or failure to fulfill a duty, observe a promise, discharge an obligation, or perform an agreement.

In practice. Omission; neglect or failure. When a defendant in an action at law omits to plead within the time allowed him for that purpose, or fails to appear on the trial, he is said to *make default*, and the judgment entered in the former case is technically called a "judgment by default." 3 Bl. Comm. 396; 1 Tidd, Pr. 562.

DEFAULTER. One who makes default. One who misappropriates money held by him in an official or fiduciary character, or fails to account for such money.

DEFEASANCE. An instrument which defeats the force or operation of some other deed or estate. That which is in the same deed is called a "condition;" and that which is in another deed is a "defeasance." Com. Dig. "Defeasance."

In conveyancing. A collateral deed made at the same time with a feoffment or other conveyance, containing certain conditions, upon the performance of which the estate then created may be *defeated* or totally undone. 2 Bl. Comm. 327; Co. Litt. 236, 237.

An instrument accompanying a bond, recognizance, or judgment, containing a condition which, when performed, *defeats* or undoes it. 2 Bl. Comm. 342; Co. Litt. 236, 237.

DEFEASIBLE. Subject to be defeated, annulled, revoked, or undone upon the happening of a future event or the performance of a condition subsequent, or by a conditional limitation. Usually spoken of estates and interests in land. For instance, a mortgagee's estate is defeasible (liable to be defeated) by the mortgagor's equity of redemption.

DEFEAT. See DEFEASANCE.

DEFECT. The want or absence of some legal requisite; deficiency; imperfection; insufficiency.

DEFECTUM. Challenge *propter*. See CHALLENGE.

DEFECTUS SANGUINIS. Lat. Failure of issue.

DEFEND. To prohibit or forbid. To deny. To contest and endeavor to defeat a claim or demand made against one in a court of justice. To oppose, repel, or resist.

In covenants of warranty in deeds, it means to protect, to maintain or keep secure, to guaranty, to agree to indemnify.

DEFENDANT. The person defending or denying; the party against whom relief or recovery is sought in an action or suit.

In common usage, this term is applied to the party put upon his defense, or summoned to answer a charge or complaint, in any species of action, civil or criminal, at law or in equity. Strictly, however, it does not apply to the person against whom a real action is brought, for in that proceeding the technical usage is to call the parties respectively the "demandant" and the "tenant."

DEFENDANT IN ERROR. The distinctive term appropriate to the party against whom a writ of error is sued out.

DEFENDEMUS. Lat. A word used in grants and donations, which binds the donor and his heirs to defend the donee, if any one go about to lay any incumbrance on the thing given other than what is contained in the deed of donation. Bract. l. 2, c. 16.

DEFENDER. (Fr.) To deny; to defend; to conduct a suit for a defendant; to forbid; to prevent; to protect.

DEFENDER. In Scotch and canon law. A defendant.

DEFENDER OF THE FAITH. A peculiar title belonging to the sovereign of England, as that of "Catholic" to the king of Spain, and that of "Most Christian" to the king of France. These titles were originally given by the popes of Rome; and that of *Defensor Fidei* was first conferred by Pope Leo X. on King Henry VIII., as a reward for writing against Martin Luther; and the bull for it bears date *quinto Idus Octob.*, 1521. Enc. Lond.

DEFENDERE SE PER CORPUS SUUM. To offer duel or combat as a legal trial and appeal. Abolished by 59 Geo. III. § 46. See BATTEL.

DEFENDERE UNICÂ MANU. To wage law; a denial of an accusation upon oath. See WAGER OF LAW.

DEFENDIT VIM ET INJURIAM. He defends the force and injury. Fleta, lib. 5, c. 39, § 1.

DEFENDOUR. L. Fr. A defender or defendant; the party accused in an appeal. Britt. c. 22.

DEFENERATION. The act of lending money on usury.

DEFENSA. In old English law. A park or place fenced in for deer, and defended as a property and peculiar for that use and service. Cowell.

DEFENSE. That which is offered and alleged by the party proceeded against in an action or suit, as a reason in law or fact why the plaintiff should not recover or establish what he seeks; what is put forward to defeat an action. More properly what is *sufficient* when offered for this purpose. In either of these senses it may be either a denial, justification, or confession and avoidance of the facts averred as a ground of action, or an exception to their sufficiency in point of law.

In a stricter sense, defense is used to denote the answer made by the defendant to the plaintiff's action, by demurrer or plea at law or answer in equity. This is the meaning of the term in Scotch law. Ersk. Inst. 4, 1, 66.

Half defense was that which was made by the form "defends the force and injury, and says," (*defendit vim et injuriam, et dicit.*)

Full defense was that which was made by the form "defends the force and injury when and where it shall behoove him, and the damages, and whatever else he ought to defend," (*defendit vim et injuriam quando et ubi curia consideravit, et damna et quicquid quod ipse defendere debet, et dicit,*) commonly shortened into "defends the force and injury when," etc. Gilb. Com. Pl. 188; 8 Term. 632; 3 Bos. & P. 9, note; Co. Litt. 127*b*.

In matrimonial suits, in England, defenses are divided into *absolute*, *i. e.*, such as, being established to the satisfaction of the court, are a complete answer to the petition, so that the court can exercise no discretion, but is bound to dismiss the petition; and *discretionary*, or such as, being established, leave to the court a discretion whether it will pronounce a decree or dismiss the petition. Thus, in a suit for dissolution, condonation is an absolute, adultery by the petitioner a discretionary, defense. Browne, Div. 30.

Defense also means the forcible repelling of an attack made unlawfully with force and violence.

In old statutes and records, the term means prohibition; denial or refusal. *Encounter le defense et le commandement de roy;* against the prohibition and commandment of the king. St. Westm. 1, c. 1. Also a state of severalty, or of several or exclusive occupancy; a state of inclosure.

DEFENSE AU FOND EN DROIT. In French and Canadian law. A demurrer.

DEFENSE AU FOND EN FAIT. In French and Canadian law. The general issue. 3 Low. Can. 421.

DEFENSIVA. In old English law. A lord or earl of the marches, who was the warden and defender of his country. Cowell.

DEFENSIVE ALLEGATION. In English ecclesiastical law. A species of pleading, where the defendant, instead of denying the plaintiff's charge upon oath, has any circumstances to offer in his defense. This entitles him, in his turn, to the plaintiff's answer upon oath, upon which he may proceed to proofs as well as his antagonist. 3 Bl. Comm. 100; 3 Steph. Comm. 720.

DEFENSIVE WAR. A war in defense of, or for the protection of, national rights. It may be *defensive* in its principles, though *offensive* in its operations. 1 Kent, Comm. 50, note.

DEFENSO. That part of any open field or place that was allotted for corn or hay, and upon which there was no common or feeding, was anciently said to be *in defenso;* so of any meadow ground that was laid in for hay only. The same term was applied to a wood where part was inclosed or fenced, to secure the growth of the underwood from the injury of cattle. Cowell.

DEFENSOR. In the civil law. A defender; one who assumed the defense of another's case in court. Also an advocate. A tutor or curator.

In canon law. The advocate or patron of a church. An officer who had charge of the temporalities of the church.

In old English law. A guardian, defender, or protector. The defendant in an action. A person vouched in to warranty.

DEFENSOR CIVITATIS. Lat. Defender or protector of a city or municipality. An officer under the Roman empire, whose duty it was to protect the people against the injustice of the magistrates, the insolence of the subaltern officers, and the rapacity of the money-lenders. Schm. Civil Law, Introd. 16; Cod. 1, 55, 4. He had the powers of a judge, with jurisdiction of pecuniary causes to a limited amount, and the lighter species of offenses. Cod. 1, 55, 1; Nov. 15, c. 3, § 2; Id. c. 6, § 1. He had also the care of the public records, and powers similar to those of a notary in regard to the execution of wills and conveyances.

DEFENSUM. An inclosure of land; any fenced ground. See DEFENSO.

DEFERRED LIFE ANNUITIES. In English law. Annuities for the life of the purchaser, but not commencing until a date subsequent to the date of buying them, so that, if the purchaser die before that date, the purchase money is lost. Granted by the commissioners for reduction of the national debt. See 16 & 17 Vict. c. 45, § 2. Wharton.

DEFERRED STOCK. Stock in a corporation is sometimes divided into "preferred," the holders of which are entitled to a fixed dividend payable out of the net earnings of the whole stock, and "deferred," the holders of which are entitled to all the residue of the net earnings after such fixed dividend has been paid to the holders of the preferred stock. Wharton.

Deficiente uno sanguine non potest esse hæres. 3 Coke, 41. One blood being wanting, he cannot be heir. But see 3 & 4 Wm. IV. c. 106, § 9, and 33 & 34 Vict. c. 23, § 1.

DEFICIT. Someting wanting, generally in the accounts of one intrusted with money, or in the money received by him.

DEFINE. To explain or state the exact meaning of words and phrases; to settle, make clear, establish boundaries.

"An examination of our Session Laws will show that acts have frequently been passed, the constitutionality of which has never been questioned, where the powers and duties conferred could not be considered as merely explaining or making more clear those previously conferred or attempted to be, although the word 'define' was used in the title. In legislation it is frequently used in the creation, enlarging, and extending the powers and duties of boards and officers, in defining certain offenses and providing punishment for the same, and thus enlarging and extending the scope of the criminal law. And it is properly used in the title where the object of the act is to determine or fix boundaries, more especially where a dispute has arisen concerning them. It is used between different governments, as to define the extent of a kingdom or country." 36 Mich. 452.

DEFINITION. A description of a thing by its properties; an explanation of the meaning of a word or term. Webster. The process of stating the exact meaning of a word by means of other words. Worcester.

DEFINITIVE. That which finally and completely ends and settles a controversy. A definitive sentence or judgment is put in opposition to an interlocutory judgment.

A distinction may be taken between a *final* and a *definitive* judgment. The former term is applicable when the judgment exhausts the powers of the particular court in which it is rendered; while the latter word designates a judgment that is above any review or contingency of reversal. 1 Cranch, 103.

DEFINITIVE SENTENCE. The final judgment, decree, or sentence of an ecclesiastical court. 3 Bl. Comm. 101.

DEFLORATION. Seduction or debauching. The act by which a woman is deprived of her virginity.

DEFORCE. **In English law.** To withhold wrongfully; to withhold the possession of lands from one who is lawfully entitled to them. 3 Bl. Comm. 172.

In Scotch law. To resist the execution of the law; to oppose by force a public officer in the execution of his duty. Bell.

DEFORCEMENT. Deforcement is where a man wrongfully holds lands to which another person is entitled. It therefore includes disseisin, abatement, discontinuance, and intrusion. Co. Litt. 277*b*, 331*b*. But it is applied especially to cases, not falling under those heads, where the person entitled to the freehold has never had possession; thus, where a lord has a seignory, and lands escheat to him *propter defectum sanguinis*, but the seisin is withheld from him, this is a deforcement, and the person who withholds the seisin is called a "deforceor." 3 Bl. Comm. 172.

In Scotch law. The opposition or resistance made to messengers or other public officers while they are actually engaged in the exercise of their offices. Ersk. Inst. 4, 4, 32.

DEFORCIANT. One who wrongfully keeps the owner of lands and tenements out of the possession of them. 2 Bl. Comm. 350.

DEFORCIARE. To withhold lands or tenements from the rightful owner. This is a word of art which cannot be supplied by any other word. Co. Litt. 331*b*.

DEFORCIATIO. In old English law. A distress, distraint, or seizure of goods for satisfaction of a lawful debt. Cowell.

DEFOSSION. The punishment of being buried alive.

DEFRAUD. To practice fraud; to cheat or trick; to deprive a person of property or any interest, estate, or right by fraud, deceit, or artifice.

DEFRAUDACION. In Spanish law. The crime committed by a person who fraudulently avoids the payment of some public tax.

DEFRAUDATION. Privation by fraud.

DEFUNCT. Deceased; a deceased person. A common term in Scotch law.

DEGASTER. L. Fr. To waste.

DEGRADATION. A deprivation of dignity; dismission from office. An ecclesiastical censure, whereby a clergyman is divested of his holy orders. There are two sorts by the canon law,—one *summary*, by word only; the other *solemn*, by stripping the party degraded of those ornaments and rights which are the ensigns of his degree. Degradation is otherwise called "deposition," but the canonists have distinguished between these two terms, deeming the former as the greater punishment of the two. There is likewise a degradation of a lord or knight at common law, and also by act of parliament. Wharton.

DEGRADATIONS. A term for waste in the French law.

DEGRADING. Reviling; holding one up to public obloquy; lowering a person in the estimation of the public.

DEGREE. **In the law of descent and family relations.** A step or grade, *i. e.*, the distance, or number of removes, which separates two persons who are related by consanguinity. Thus we speak of cousins in the "second degree."

In criminal law. The term "degree" denotes a division or classification of one specific crime into several grades or *stadia* of guilt, according to the circumstances attending its commission. Thus, in some states, there may be "murder in the second degree."

DEHORS. L. Fr. Out of; without; beyond; foreign to; unconnected with. *Dehors* the record; foreign to the record. 3 Bl. Comm. 387.

DEI GRATIA. Lat. By the grace of God. A phrase used in the formal title of a king or queen, importing a claim of sovereignty by the favor or commission of God. In ancient times it was incorporated in the titles of inferior officers, (especially ecclesiastical,) but in later use was reserved as an assertion of "the divine right of kings."

DEI JUDICIUM. The judgment of God. The old Saxon trial by ordeal, so called because it was thought to be an appeal to God for the justice of a cause, and it was believed that the decision was according to the will and pleasure of Divine Providence. Wharton.

DEJACION. In Spanish law. Surrender; release; abandonment; *e. g.*, the act of an insolvent in surrendering his property for the benefit of his creditors, of an heir in renouncing the succession, the abandonment of insured property to the underwriters.

DEJERATION. A taking of a solemn oath.

DEL BIEN ESTRE. L. Fr. In old English practice. Of well being; of form. The same as *de bene esse*. Britt. c. 39.

DEL CREDERE. In mercantile law. A phrase borrowed from the Italians, equivalent to our word "guaranty" or "warranty," or the Scotch term "warrandice;" an agreement by which a factor, when he sells goods on credit, for an additional commission, (called a "*del credere* commission,") guaranties the solvency of the purchaser and his performance of the contract. Such a factor is called a "*del credere* agent." He is a mere surety, liable only to his principal in case the purchaser makes default. Story, Ag. 28.

DELAISSEMENT. In French marine law. Abandonment. Emerig. Tr. des Ass. ch. 17.

DELATE. In Scotch law. To accuse. Delated, accused. *Delatit off arte and parte*, accused of being accessary to. 3 How. St. Tr. 425, 440.

DELATIO. In the civil law. An accusation or information.

DELATOR. An accuser; an informer; a sycophant.

DELATURA. In old English law. The reward of an informer. Whishaw.

DELECTUS PERSONÆ. Lat. Choice of the person. By this term is understood the right of a partner to exercise his choice and preference as to the admission of any new members to the firm, and as to the persons to be so admitted, if any.

In Scotch law. The personal preference which is supposed to have been exercised by a landlord in selecting his tenant, by the members of a firm in making choice of partners, in the appointment of persons to office, and other cases. Nearly equivalent to personal trust, as a doctrine in law. Bell.

Delegata potestas non potest delegari. 2 Inst. 597. A delegated power cannot be delegated.

DELEGATE. A person who is delegated or commissioned to act in the stead of another; a person to whom affairs are committed by another; an attorney.

A person elected or appointed to be a member of a representative assembly. Usually spoken of one sent to a special or occasional assembly or convention.

The representative in congress of one of the organized territories of the United States.

DELEGATES, THE HIGH COURT OF. In English law. Formerly the court of appeal from the ecclesiastical and admiralty courts. Abolished, upon the judicial committee of the privy council being constituted the court of appeal in such cases.

DELEGATION. A sending away; a putting into commission; the assignment of a debt to another; the intrusting another with a general power to act for the good of those who depute him.

At common law. The transfer of authority by one person to another; the act of making or commissioning a delegate.

The whole body of delegates or representatives sent to a convention or assembly from one district, place, or political unit are collectively spoken of as a "delegation."

In the civil law. A species of novation which consists in the change of one debtor for another, when he who is indebted substitutes a third person who obligates himself in his stead to the creditor, so that the first debtor is acquitted and his obligation extinguished, and the creditor contents himself with the obligation of the second debtor. Delegation is essentially distinguished from any other species of novation, in this: that the former demands the consent of all three parties, but the latter that only of the two parties to the new debt. 1 Domat, § 2318; 48 Miss. 454.

Delegation is novation effected by the intervention of another person whom the debtor, in order to be liberated from his creditor, gives to such creditor, or to him whom the creditor appoints; and such person so given becomes obliged to the creditor in the place of the original debtor. Burge, Sur. 173.

Delegatus non potest delegare. A delegate cannot delegate; an agent cannot delegate his functions to a subagent without the knowledge or consent of the principal; the person to whom an office or duty is delegated cannot lawfully devolve the duty on another, unless he be expressly authorized so to do. 9 Coke, 77; Broom, Max. 840; 2 Kent, Comm. 633; 2 Steph. Comm. 119.

DELESTAGE. In French marine law. A discharging of ballast (*lest*) from a vessel.

DELETE. In Scotch law. To erase; to strike out.

DELF. A quarry or mine. 31 Eliz. c. 7.

Deliberandum est diu quod statuendum est semel. 12 Coke, 74. That which is to be resolved once for all should be long deliberated upon.

DELIBERATE, *v.* To weigh, ponder, discuss. To examine, to consult, in order to form an opinion.

DELIBERATE, *adj.* By the use of this word, in describing a crime, the idea is conveyed that the perpetrator weighs the motives for the act and its consequences, the nature of the crime, or other things connected with his intentions, with a view to a decision thereon; that he carefully considers all these; and that the act is not suddenly committed. It implies that the perpetrator must be capable of the exercise of such mental powers as are called into use by deliberation and the consideration and weighing of motives and consequences. 28 Iowa, 524.

"Deliberation" and "premeditation" are of the same character of mental operations, differing only in degree. Deliberation is but prolonged premeditation. In other words, in law, deliberation is premeditation in a cool state of the blood, or, where there has been heat of passion, it is premeditation continued beyond the period within which there has been time for the blood to cool, in the given case. Deliberation is not only to think of beforehand, which may be but for an instant, but the inclination to do the act is considered, weighed, pondered upon, for such a length of time after a provocation is given as the jury may find was sufficient for the blood to cool. One in a heat of passion may premeditate without deliberating. Deliberation is only exercised in a cool state of the blood, while premeditation may be either in that state of the blood or in the heat of passion. 74 Mo. 249. See, also, 20 Tex. 522; 15 Nev. 178; 5 Mo. 364; 66 Mo. 13.

DELIBERATION. The act or process of deliberating. The act of weighing and examining the reasons for and against a contemplated act or course of conduct, or a choice of acts or means. See DELIBERATE.

Delicatus debitor est odiosus in lege. A luxurious debtor is odious in law. 2 Bulst. 148. Imprisonment for debt has now, however, been generally abolished.

DELICT. In the civil law. A wrong or injury; an offense; a violation of public or private duty. It will be observed that this word, taken in its most general sense, is wider in both directions than our English term "tort." On the one hand, it includes those wrongful acts which, while directly affecting some individual or his property, yet extend in their injurious consequences to the peace or security of the community at large, and hence rise to the grade of crimes or misdemeanors. These acts were termed in the Roman law "public delicts;" while those for which the only penalty exacted was compensation to the person primarily injured were denominated "private delicts." On the other hand, the term appears to have included injurious actions which transpired without any malicious intention on the part of the doer. Thus Pothier gives the name "*quasi* delicts" to the acts of a person who, without malignity, but by an inexcusable imprudence, causes an injury to another. Poth. Obl. 116. But the term is used in modern jurisprudence as a convenient synonym of "tort;" that is, a wrongful and injurious violation of a *jus in rem* or right available against all the world. This appears in the two contrasted phrases, "actions *ex contractu*" and "actions *ex delicto*."

DELICTUM. Lat. A delict, tort, wrong, injury, or offense. Actions *ex delicto* are such as are founded on a tort, as distinguished from actions on contract.

Culpability, blameworthiness, or legal delinquency. The word occurs in this sense in the maxim, "*In pari delicto melior est conditio defendentis*," (which see.)

A challenge of a juror *propter delictum* is for some crime or misdemeanor that affects his credit and renders him infamous. 3 Bl. Comm. 363; 2 Kent, Comm. 241.

DELIMIT. To mark or lay out the limits or boundary line of a territory or country.

DELIMITATION. The act of fixing, marking off, or describing the limits or boundary line of a territory or country.

Dilinquens per iram provocatus puniri debet mitius. 3 Inst. 55. A delinquent provoked by anger ought to be punished more mildly.

DELINQUENT. In the civil law. He who has been guilty of some crime, offense, or failure of duty.

DELIRIUM. In medical jurisprudence. Delirium is that state of the mind in which it acts without being directed by the power of volition, which is wholly or partially suspended. This happens most perfectly in dreams. But what is commonly called "delirium" is always preceded or attended by a feverish and highly diseased state of the body. The patient in delirium is wholly unconscious of surrounding objects, or conceives them to be different from what they really are. His thoughts seem to drift about, wildering and tossing amidst distracted dreams. And his observations, when he makes any, as often happens, are wild and incoherent; or, from excess of pain, he sinks into a low muttering, or silent and death-like stupor. Rush, Mind, 9, 298.

The law contemplates this species of mental derangement as an intellectual eclipse; as a darkness occasioned by a cloud of disease passing over the mind; and which must soon terminate in health or in death. 1 Bland. 386.

DELIRIUM FEBRILE. In medical jurisprudence. A form of mental aberration incident to fevers, and sometimes to the last stages of chronic diseases.

DELIRIUM TREMENS. A species of mental aberration or temporary insanity which is induced by the excessive and protracted use of intoxicating liquors.

DELITO. In Spanish law. Crime; a crime, offense, or delict. White, New Recop. b. 2, tit. 19, c. 1, § 4.

DELIVERANCE. In practice. The verdict rendered by a jury.

DELIVERY. In conveyancing. The final and absolute transfer of a deed, properly executed, to the grantee, or to some person for his use, in such manner that it cannot be recalled by the grantor. 13 N. J. Eq. 455; 1 Dev. Eq. 14.

In the law of sales. The tradition or transfer of the possession of personal property from one person to another.

Delivery is either actual or constructive. Thus, if goods cannot conveniently be actually handed from one person to another, as if they are in a warehouse or a ship, the delivery of the key of the warehouse, a delivery order, bill of lading, etc., is a constructive or symbolical delivery of the goods themselves. Williams, Pers. Prop. 37; Benj. Sales, 573.

In medical jurisprudence. The act of a woman giving birth to her offspring.

DELIVERY BOND. A bond given upon the seizure of goods (as under the revenue laws) conditioned for their restoration to the defendant, or the payment of their value, if so adjudged.

DELIVERY ORDER. An order addressed, in England, by the owner of goods to a person holding them on his behalf, requesting him to deliver them to a person named in the order. Delivery orders are chiefly used in the case of goods held by dock companies, wharfingers, etc.

DELUSION. In medical jurisprudence. An insane delusion is an unreasoning and incorrigible belief in the existence of facts which are either impossible absolutely, or, at least, impossible under the circumstances of the individual. It is never the result of reasoning and reflection; it is not generated by them, and it cannot be dispelled by them; and hence it is not to be confounded with an *opinion*, however fantastic the latter may be. 10 Fed. Rep. 170.

DEM. An abbreviation for "demise;" *e. g., Doe dem. Smith*, Doe, on the demise of Smith.

DEMAIN. See DEMESNE.

DEMAND, *v.* In practice. To claim as one's due; to require; to ask relief. To summon; to call in court. "Although solemnly *demanded*, comes not, but makes default."

DEMAND, *n.* A claim: the assertion of a legal right; a legal obligation asserted in the courts. "Demand" is a word of art of an extent greater in its signification than any other word except "claim." Co. Litt. 291; 2 Hill, 220.

Demand embraces all sorts of actions, rights, and titles, conditions before or after breach, executions, appeals, rents of all kinds, covenants, annuities, contracts, recognizances, statutes, commons, etc. A release of all demands to date bars an action for damages accruing after the date from a nuisance previously erected. 1 Denio, 257.

Demand is more comprehensive in import than "debt" or "duty." 4 Johns. 536; 2 Hill, 220.

Demand, or claim, is properly used in reference to a cause of action. 32 How. Pr. 280.

An imperative request preferred by one person to another, under a claim of right, requiring the latter to do or yield something or to abstain from some act.

DEMAND IN RECONVENTION. A demand which the defendant institutes in consequence of that which the plaintiff has brought against him. Used in Louisiana.

DEMANDA. In Spanish law. The petition of a plaintiff, setting forth his demand. Las Partidas, pt. 3, tit. 10, l. 3.

DEMANDANT. The plaintiff or party suing in a real action. Co. Litt. 127.

DEMANDRESS. A female demandant.

DEMEASE. In old English law. Death.

DEMEMBRATION. In Scotch law. Maliciously cutting off or otherwise separating one limb from another. 1 Hume, 323; Bell.

DEMENS. One whose mental faculties are enfeebled; one who has lost his mind; distinguishable from *amens*, one totally insane. 4 Coke, 128.

DEMENTED. Of unsound mind.

DEMENTENANT EN AVANT. L. Fr. From this time forward. Kelham.

DEMENTIA. In medical jurisprudence. That form of insanity where the mental derangement is accompanied with a general derangement of the faculties. It is characterized by forgetfulness, inability to follow any train of thought, and indifference to passing events. 4 Sawy. 677, per Field, J.

Senile dementia is that peculiar decay of the mental faculties which occurs in extreme old age, and in many cases much earlier, whereby the person is reduced to second childhood, and becomes sometimes wholly incompetent to enter into any binding contract, or even to execute a will. It is the recurrence of second childhood by mere decay. 1 Redf. Wills, 63.

Dementia denotes an impaired state of the mental powers, a feebleness of mind caused by disease, and not accompanied by delusion or uncontrollable impulse, without defining the degree of incapacity. *Dementia* may exist without complete prostration of the mental powers. 44 N. H. 531.

DEMESNE. Domain; dominical; held in one's own right, and not of a superior; not allotted to tenants. See DEMESNE LANDS.

In the language of pleading, own; proper; original. Thus, *son assault demesne*, his own assault, his assault originally or in the first place.

DEMESNE AS OF FEE. A man is said to be seised *in his demesne as of fee* of a corporeal inheritance, because he has a property, *dominicum* or *demesne*, in the *thing* itself. But when he has no dominion in the thing itself, as in the case of an incorporeal hereditament, he is said to be *seised* as of fee, and not in his *demesne* as of fee. 2 Bl. Comm. 106; Littleton, § 10; 17 Serg. & R. 196.

DEMESNE LANDS. In English law. Those lands of a manor not granted out in tenancy, but reserved by the lord for his own use and occupation. Lands set apart and appropriated by the lord for his own private use, as for the supply of his table, and the maintenance of his family; the opposite of *tenemental* lands. Tenancy and demesne, however, were not in every sense the opposites of each other; lands held for years or at will being included among demesne lands, as well as those in the lord's actual possession. Spelman; 2 Bl. Comm. 90.

DEMESNE LANDS OF THE CROWN. That share of lands reserved to the crown at the original distribution of landed property, or which came to it afterwards by forfeiture or otherwise. 1 Bl. Comm. 286; 2 Steph. Comm. 550.

DEMESNIAL. Pertaining to a *demesne*.

DEMI. French. Half; the half. Used chiefly in composition.

DEMI-MARK. Half a mark; a sum of money which was anciently required to be tendered in a writ of right, the effect of such tender being to put the demandant, in the first instance, upon proof of the seisin as stated in his count; that is, to prove that the seisin was in the king's reign there stated. Rosc. Real Act. 216.

DEMI-OFFICIAL. Partly official or authorized. Having color of official right.

DEMI-SANGUE, or DEMY-SANGUE. Half-blood.

DEMI-VILL. A town consisting of five freemen, or frank-pledges. Spelman.

DEMIDIETAS. In old records. A half or moiety.

DEMIES. In some universities and colleges this term is synonymous with "scholars."

DEMINUTIO. In the civil law. A taking away; loss or deprivation. See CAPITIS DEMINUTIO.

DEMISE, *v.* In conveyancing. To convey or create an estate for years or life; to lease. The usual and operative word in leases: "Have granted, *demised*, and to farm let, and by these presents do grant, *demise*, and to farm let." 2 Bl. Comm. 317; 1 Steph. Comm. 476; Co. Litt. 45*a*.

DEMISE, *n.* In conveyancing. A conveyance of an estate to another for life, for years, or at will; most commonly for years; a lease. 1 Steph. Comm. 475.

Originally a posthumous grant; commonly a lease or conveyance for a term of years; sometimes applied to any conveyance, in fee, for life, or for years. Pub. St. Mass. 1882, p. 1289.

"Demise" is synonymous with "lease" or "let," except that demise *ex vi termini* implies a covenant for title, and also a covenant for quiet enjoyment, whereas lease or let implies neither of these covenants. Brown.

The word is also used as a synonym for "decease" or "death." It England it is especially employed to denote the death of the sovereign.

DEMISE AND REDEMISE. In conveyancing. Mutual leases made from one party to another on each side, of the same land, or something out of it; as when A. grants a lease to B. at a nominal rent, (as of a pepper corn,) and B. redemises the same property to A. for a shorter time at a real, substantial rent. Jacob; Whishaw.

DEMISE OF THE CROWN. The natural dissolution of the king is generally so called; an expression which signifies merely a transfer of property. By demise of the crown we mean only that, in consequence of the disunion of the king's natural body from his body politic, the kingdom is transferred or demised to his successor, and so the royal dign ty remains perpetual. 1 Bl. Comm. 249; Plowd. 234.

DEMISI. I have demised or leased. *Demisi, concessi, et ad firmam tradidi;* have demised, granted, and to farm let. The usual operative words in ancient leases, as the corresponding English words are in the modern forms. 2 Bl. Comm. 317, 318.

DEMOBILIZATION. In military law. The dismissal of an army or body of troops from active service.

DEMOCRACY. That form of government in which the sovereign power resides in and is exercised by the whole body of free citizens; as distinguished from a monarchy, aristocracy, or oligarchy. According to the theory of a pure democracy, every citizen should participate directly in the business of governing, and the legislative assembly should comprise the whole people. But the ultimate lodgment of the sovereignty being the distinguishing feature, the introduction of the representative system does not remove a government from this type. However, a government of the latter kind is sometimes specifically described as a "representative democracy."

DEMOCRATIC. Of or pertaining to democracy, or to the party of the democrats.

DEMONETIZATION. The disuse of a particular metal for purposes of coinage. The withdrawal of the value of a metal as money.

DEMONSTRATIO. Description; addition; denomination. Occurring often in the phrase, "*Falsa demonstratio non nocet,*" (a false description does not harm.)

DEMONSTRATION. Description; pointing out. That which is said or written to designate a thing or person.

In evidence. Absolutely convincing proof. That proof which excludes all possibility of error.

DEMONSTRATIVE LEGACY. A bequest of a certain sum of money, with a direction that it shall be paid out of a particular fund. It differs from a specific legacy in this respect: that, it the fund out of which it is payable fails for any cause, it is nevertheless entitled to come on the estate as a general legacy. And it differs from a general legacy in this: that it does not abate in that class, but in the class of specific legacies. 63 Pa. St. 316. See, also, 17 Ohio St. 413; 42 Ala. 9.

A legacy of quantity is ordinarily a general legacy; but there are legacies of quantity in the nature of specific legacies, as of so much money, with reference to a particular fund for payment. This kind of legacy is called by the civilians a "demonstrative legacy," and it is so far general and differs so much in effect from one properly specific that, if the fund be called in or fail, the legatee will not be deprived of his legacy, but be permitted to receive it out of the general assets; yet the legacy is so far specific that it will not be liable to abate with general legacies upon a deficiency of assets. 2 Williams, Ex'rs, 1078.

DEMPSTER. In Scotch law. A doomsman. One who pronounced the sentence of court. 1 How. State Tr. 937.

DEMUR. To present a demurrer; to take an exception to the sufficiency in point of law of a pleading or state of facts alleged.

DEMURRABLE. A pleading, petition, or the like, is said to be demurrable when it does not state such facts as support the claim, prayer, or defense put forward. 5 Ch. Div. 979.

DEMURRAGE. In maritime law. The sum which is fixed by the contract of carriage, or which is allowed, as remuneration to the owner of a ship for the detention of his vessel beyond the number of days allowed by the charter-party for loading and unloading or for sailing. Also the detention of the vessel by the freighter beyond such time. See 3 Kent, Comm. 203; 2 Steph. Comm. 185.

Demurrage is only an extended freight or reward to the vessel, in compensation for the earnings she is improperly caused to lose. Every improper detention of a vessel may be considered a demurrage, and compensation under that name be obtained for it. 1 Holmes, 290.

Demurrage is the allowance or compensation due to the master or owners of a ship, by the freighter, for the time the vessel may have been detained beyond the time specified or implied in the contract of affreightment or the charter-party. Bell.

DEMURRANT. One who demurs; the party who, in pleading, interposes a demurrer.

DEMURRER. In pleading. The formal mode of disputing the sufficiency in law of the pleading of the other side. In effect it is an allegation that, even if the facts as stated in the pleading to which objection is taken be true, yet their legal consequences are not such as to put the demurring party to the necessity of answering them or proceeding further with the cause.

An objection made by one party to his opponent's pleading, alleging that he ought not to answer it, for some defect in law in the pleading. It admits the facts, and refers the law arising thereon to the court. 7 How. 581.

It imports that the objecting party will not proceed, but will wait the judgment of the court whether he is bound so to do. Co. Litt. 71*b*; Steph. Pl. 61.

A *general* demurrer is one which excepts to the sufficiency of a previous pleading in general terms, without showing specifically the nature of the objection; and such demurrer is sufficient when the objection is on matter of substance.

A *special* demurrer is one which excepts to the sufficiency of the pleadings of the other party, and shows specifically the nature of the objection and the particular ground of exception. Steph. Pl. 158.

In equity. An allegation of a defendant, which, admitting the matters of fact alleged by the bill to be true, shows that as they are therein set forth they are insufficient for the plaintiff to proceed upon or to oblige the defendant to answer; or that, for some reason apparent on the face of the bill, or on account of the omission of some matter which ought to be contained therein, or for want of some circumstances which ought to be attendant thereon, the defendant ought not to be compelled to answer to the whole bill, or to some certain part thereof. Mitf. Eq. Pl. 107.

Demurrer to interrogatories is the reason which a witness tenders for not answering a particular question in interrogatories. 2 Swanst. 194. It is not, strictly speaking, a demurrer, except in the popular sense of the word. Gres. Eq. Ev. 61.

DEMURRER BOOK. In practice. A record of the issue on a demurrer at law, containing a transcript of the pleadings, with proper entries; and intended for the use of the court and counsel on the argument. 3 Bl. Comm. 317; 3 Steph. Comm. 581.

DEMURRER TO EVIDENCE. This proceeding (now practically obsolete) was analogous to a demurrer to a pleading. It was an objection or exception by one of the parties in an action at law, to the effect that the evidence which his adversary had produced was insufficient in point of law (whether true or not) to make out his case or sustain the issue. Upon joinder in demurrer, the jury was discharged, and the case was argued to the court *in banc*, who gave judgment upon the facts as shown in evidence. See 3 Bl. Comm. 372.

DEMY SANKE, DEMY SANGUE. Half-blood. A corruption of *demi-sang*.

DEN. A valley. Blount. A hollow place among woods. Cowell.

DEN AND STROND. In old English law. Liberty for ships or vessels to run aground, or come ashore. Cowell.

DENARIATE. In old English law. As much land as is worth one penny *per annum*.

DENARII. An ancient general term for any sort of *pecunia numerata*, or ready money. The French use the word "*denier*" in the same sense,—*payer de ses propres deniers*.

DENARII DE CARITATE. In English law. Customary oblations made to a cathedral church at Pentecost.

DENARII S. PETRI. (Commonly called "Peter's Pence.") An annual payment on St. Peter's feast of a penny from every family to the pope, during the time that the Roman Catholic religion was established in England.

DENARIUS. The chief silver coin among the Romans, worth 8d.; it was the seventh part of a Roman ounce. Also an English penny. The denarius was first coined five years before the first Punic war, B. C. 269. In later times a copper coin was called "*denarius.*" Smith, Dict. Antiq.

DENARIUS DEI. (Lat. "God's penny.") Earnest money; money given as a token of the completion of a bargain. It differs from *arrhæ*, in this: that *arrhæ* is a part of the consideration, while the *denarius Dei* is no part of it. The latter was given away in charity; whence the name.

DENARIUS TERTIUS COMITATÛS. In old English law. A third part or penny of the county paid to its earl, the other two parts being reserved to the crown.

DENIAL. A traverse in the pleading of one party of an allegation of fact set up by the other; a defense.

DENIER. L. Fr. In old English law. Denial; refusal. *Denier* is when the rent (being demanded upon the land) is not paid. Finch, Law, b. 3, c. 5.

DENIER A DIEU In French law. Earnest money; a sum of money given in token of the completion of a bargain. The phrase is a translation of the Latin *Denarius Dei*, (*q. v.*)

DENIZATION. The act of making one a denizen; the conferring of the privileges of citizenship upon an alien born. Cro. Jac. 540. See DENIZEN.

DENIZE. To make a man a denizen or citizen.

DENIZEN. In English law. A person who, being an alien born, has obtained, *ex donatione regis*, letters patent to make him an English subject,—a high and incommunicable branch of the royal prerogative. A denizen is in a kind of middle state between an alien and a natural-born subject, and partakes of the *status* of both of these. 1 Bl. Comm. 374; 7 Coke, 6.

The term is used to signify a person who, being an alien by birth, has obtained letters patent making him an English subject. The king may denize, but not naturalize, a man; the latter requiring the consent of parliament, as under the naturalization act, 1870, (33 & 34 Vict. c. 14.) A denizen holds a position midway between an alien and a natural-born or naturalized subject, being able to take lands by purchase or devise, (which an alien could not until 1870 do,) but not able to take lands by descent, (which a natural-born or naturalized subject may do.) Brown.

The word is also used in this sense in South Carolina. See 1 McCord, Eq. 352.

A denizen, in the primary, but obsolete, sense of the word, is a natural-born subject of a country. Co. Litt. 129*a*.

DENMAN'S (LORD) ACT. An English statute, for the amendment of the law of evidence, (6 & 7 Vict. c. 85,) which provides that no person offered as a witness shall thereafter be excluded by reason of incapacity, from crime or interest, from giving evidence.

DENMAN'S (MR.) ACT. An English statute, for the amendment of procedure in criminal trials, (28 & 29 Vict. c. 18,) allowing counsel to sum up the evidence in criminal as in civil trials, provided the prisoner be defended by counsel.

DENOMBREMENT. In French feudal law. A minute or act drawn up, on the creation of a fief, containing a description of the fief, and all the rights and incidents belonging to it. Guyot, Inst. Feud. c. 3.

Denominatio fieri debet a dignioribus. Denomination should be made from the more worthy.

DENOUNCEMENT. In Mexican law. A denouncement was a judicial proceeding, and, though real property might be acquired by an alien in fraud of the law,—that is, without observing its requirements,—he nevertheless retained his right and title to it, but was liable to be deprived of it by the proper proceeding of denouncement, which in its substantive characteristics was equivalent to the inquest of office found, at common law. 26 Cal. 477.

DENSHIRING OF LAND. (Otherwise called "burn-beating.") A method of improving land by casting parings of earth, turf, and stubble into heaps, which when dried are burned into ashes for a compost. Cowell.

DENUMERATION. The act of present payment.

DENUNCIA DE OBRA NUEVA. In Spanish law. The denouncement of a new work; being a proceeding to restrain the erection of some new work, as, for instance, a building which may, if completed, injuriously affect the property of the complainant; it is of a character similar to the interdicts of possession. Escriche; 1 Cal. 63.

DENUNCIATION. In the civil law. The act by which an individual informs a public officer, whose duty it is to prosecute offenders, that a crime has been committed.

In Scotch practice. The act by which a person is declared to be a rebel, who has disobeyed the charge given on letters of horning. Bell.

DENUNTIATIO. In old English law. A public notice or summons. Bract. 202*b*.

DEODAND. (L. Lat. *Deo dandum*, a thing to be given to God.) In English law. Any personal chattel which was the immediate occasion of the death of any reasonable creature, and which was forfeited to the crown to be applied to *pious* uses, and distributed in alms by the high almoner. 1 Hale, P. C. 419; Fleta, lib. 1, c. 25; 1 Bl. Comm. 300; 2 Steph. Comm. 365.

DEOR HEDGE. In old English law. The hedge inclosing a deer park.

DEPART. In pleading. To forsake or abandon the ground assumed in a former pleading, and assume a new one. See DEPARTURE.

In maritime law. To leave a port; to be out of a port. To *depart* imports more than to *sail*, or set sail. A warranty in a policy that a vessel shall *depart* on or before a particular day is a warranty not only that she shall sail, but that she shall be *out of the port* on or before that day. 3 Maule & S. 461; 3 Kent, Comm. 307, note. "To depart" does not mean merely to break ground, but fairly to set forward upon the voyage. 6 Taunt. 241.

DEPARTMENT. 1. One of the territorial divisions of a country. The term is chiefly used in this sense in France, where the division of the country into departments is somewhat analogous, both territorially and for governmental purposes, to the division of an American state into counties.

2. One of the divisions of the executive branch of government. Used in this sense in the United States, where each department is charged with a specific class of duties, and comprises an organized staff of officials; *e. g.*, the department of state, department of war, etc.

DEPARTURE. In maritime law. A deviation from the course prescribed in the policy of insurance.

In pleading. The statement of matter in a replication, rejoinder, or subsequent pleading, as a cause of action or defense, which is not pursuant to the previous pleading of the same party, and which does not support and fortify it. 2 Williams, Saund. 84*a*, note 1; 2 Wils. 98; Co. Litt. 304*a*.

A departure, in pleading, is when a party quits or departs from the case or defense which he has first made, and has recourse to another. 49 Ind. 111; 16 Johns. 205; 13 N. Y. 83, 89.

A departure takes place when, in any pleading, the party deserts the ground that he took in his last antecedent pleading, and resorts to another. Steph. Pl. 410. Or, in other words, when the second pleading contains matter not pursuant to the former, and which does not support and fortify it. Co. Litt. 304*a*. Hence a departure obviously can never take place till the replication. Steph. Pl. 410. Each subsequent pleading must pursue or support the former one; *i. e.*, the replication must support the declaration, and the rejoinder the plea, without departing out of it. 3 Bl. Comm. 310.

DEPARTURE IN DESPITE OF COURT. In old English practice. The tenant in a real action, having once appeared, was considered as constructively present in court until again called upon. Hence if, upon being demanded, he failed to appear, he was said to have "departed in despite [*i. e.*, contempt] of the court."

DEPASTURE. In old English law. To pasture. "If a man *depastures* unprofitable cattle in his ground." Bunb. 1, case 1.

DEPECULATION. A robbing of the prince or commonwealth; an embezzling of the public treasure.

DEPENDENCY. A territory distinct from the country in which the supreme sovereign power resides, but belonging rightfully to it, and subject to the laws and regulations which the sovereign may think proper to prescribe. 3 Wash. C. C. 286.

It differs from a *colony*, because it is not settled by the citizens of the sovereign or mother state; and from *possession*, because it is held by other title than that of mere conquest.

DEPENDENT CONTRACT. One which depends or is conditioned upon another. One which it is not the duty of the contractor to perform until some obligation contained in the same agreement has been performed by the other party. Ham. Parties, 17, 29, 30, 109.

DEPENDENT COVENANTS are those in which the performance of one depends on the performance of the other.

DEPENDING. In practice. Pending or undetermined; in progress. See 5 Coke, 47.

DEPESAS. In Spanish-American law. Spaces of ground in towns reserved for commons or public pasturage. 12 Pet. 443, note.

DEPONE. In Scotch practice. To depose; to make oath in writing.

DEPONENT. In practice. One who *deposes* (that is, testifies or makes oath in *writing*) to the truth of certain facts; one who gives under oath testimony which is reduced to writing; one who makes oath to a written statement. The party making an affidavit is generally so called.

The word "depone," from which is derived "deponent," has relation to the mode in which the oath is administered, (by the witness placing his hand upon the book of the holy evangelists,) and not as to whether the testimony is delivered orally or reduced to writing. "Deponent" is included in the term "witness," but "witness" is more general. 47 Me. 248.

DEPONER. In old Scotch practice. A deponent. 3 How. State Tr. 695.

DEPOPULATIO AGRORUM. In old English law. The crime of destroying, ravaging, or laying waste a country. 2 Hale, P. C. 333; 4 Bl. Comm. 373.

DEPOPULATION. In old English law. A species of waste by which the population of the kingdom was diminished. Depopulation of houses was a public offense. 12 Coke, 30, 31.

DEPORTATIO. Lat. In the civil law. A kind of banishment, where a condemned person was sent or carried away to some foreign country, usually to an island, (*in insulam deportatur,*) and thus taken out of the number of Roman citizens.

DEPORTATION. Banishment to a foreign country, attended with confiscation of property and deprivation of civil rights. A punishment derived from the *deportatio* (*q. v.*) of the Roman law, and still in use in France.

In Roman law. A perpetual banishment, depriving the banished of his rights as a citizen; it differed from relegation (*q. v.*) and exile, (*q. v.*) 1 Brown, Civil & Adm. Law, 125, note; Inst. 1, 12, 1, and 2; Dig. 48, 22, 14, 1.

DEPOSE. **In practice.** In ancient usage, to testify as a witness; to give evidence under oath.

In modern usage. To make a deposition; to give evidence in the shape of a deposition; to make statements which are written down and sworn to; to give testimony which is reduced to writing by a duly-qualified officer and sworn to by the deponent.

To deprive an individual of a public employment or office against his will. Wolffius, Inst. § 1063. The term is usually applied to the deprivation of all authority of a sovereign.

DEPOSIT. A naked bailment of goods to be kept for the depositor without reward, and to be returned when he shall require it. Jones, Bailm. 36, 117; 9 Mass. 470.

A bailment of goods to be kept by the bailee without reward, and delivered according to the object or purpose of the original trust. Story, Bailm. § 41.

A *deposit*, in general, is an act by which a person receives the property of another, binding himself to preserve it and return it in kind. Civil Code La. art. 2926.

When chattels are delivered by one person to another to keep for the use of the bailor, it is called a "deposit." The depositary may undertake to keep it without reward, or gratuitously; it is then a naked deposit. If he receives or expects a reward or hire, he is then a depositary for hire. Very variant consequences follow the differences in the contract. Code Ga. 1882, § 2103.

According to the classification of the civil law, deposits are of the following several sorts: (1) *Necessary*, made upon some sudden emergency, and from some pressing necessity; as, for instance, in case of a fire, a shipwreck, or other overwhelming calamity, when property is confided to any person whom the depositor may meet without proper opportunity for reflection or choice, and thence it is called "*miserabile depositum.*" (2) *Voluntary*, which arises from the mere consent and agreement of the parties. The common law has made no such division. There is another class of deposits called "involuntary," which may be without the assent or even knowledge of the depositor: as lumber, etc., left upon another's land by the subsidence of a flood.

The civilians again divide deposits into "simple deposits," made by one or more persons having a common interest, and "sequestrations," made by one or more persons, each of whom has a different and adverse interest in controversy touching it; and these last are of two sorts,—"conventional," or such as are made by the mere agreement of the parties without any judicial act; and "judicial," or such as are made by order of a court in the course of some proceeding.

There is another class of deposits called "irregular," as when a person, having a sum of money which he does not think safe in his own hands, confides it to another, who is to return to him, not the same money, but a like sum when he shall demand it. There is also a "*quasi* deposit," as where a person comes lawfully to the possession of another person's property by finding it; and a "special deposit" of money or bills in a bank, where the specific money, the very silver or gold, coin or bills, deposited, are to be restored, and not an equivalent. Story, Bailm. § 44, et seq.

The difference between a deposit and a mandate is that while the object of a deposit is that the thing bailed be kept, simply, the object of a mandate is that the thing may be transported from point to point, or that something be done about it. 8 Ga. 178.

Deposits made with bankers may be divided into two classes,—those in which the bank becomes bailee of the depositor, the title to the thing deposited remaining with the latter; and that kind peculiar to banking business, in which the depositor, for his own convenience, parts with the title to his money, and loans it to the banker, and the latter, in consideration of the loan of the money, and the right to use it for his own profit, agrees to refund the same amount, or any part thereof, on demand. Money collected by one bank for another, placed by the collecting bank with the bulk of its ordinary banking funds, and credited to the transmitting bank in account, becomes the money of the former. It is a deposit of the latter class. 2 Wall. 252.

Deposit, in respect to dealings of banks, includes not only a bailment of money to be returned in the same identical specie, but also all that class of contracts where money is placed in the hands of bankers to be returned, in other money, on call. 15 N. Y. 9, 166, 168.

The word is also sometimes used to designate money lodged with a person as an earnest or security for the performance of some contract, to be forfeited if the depositor fails in his undertaking.

DEPOSIT ACCOUNT. An account of sums lodged with a bank not to be drawn upon by checks, and usually not to be withdrawn except after a fixed notice.

DEPOSIT COMPANY. A company whose business is the safe-keeping of securities or other valuables deposited in boxes or safes in its building which are leased to the depositors.

DEPOSIT, GRATUITOUS. Gratuitous deposit is a deposit for which the depositary receives no consideration beyond the mere possession of the thing deposited. Civil Code Cal. § 1844.

DEPOSIT OF TITLE-DEEDS. A method of pledging real property as security for a loan, by placing the title-deeds of the land in the keeping of the lender as pledgee.

DEPOSITARY. The party receiving a deposit; one with whom anything is lodged in trust, as "depository" is the place where it is put. The obligation on the part of the depositary is that he keep the thing with reasonable care, and, upon request, restore it to the depositor, or otherwise deliver it, according to the original trust.

DEPOSITATION. In Scotch law. Deposit or *depositum*, the species of bailment so called. Bell.

DEPOSITION. The testimony of a witness taken upon interrogatories, not in open court, but in pursuance of a commission to take testimony issued by a court, or under a general law on the subject, and reduced to writing and duly authenticated, and intended to be used upon the trial of an action in court.

A deposition is a written declaration under oath, made upon notice to the adverse party for the purpose of enabling him to attend and cross-examine; or upon written interrogatories. Code Civil Proc. Cal. § 2004; Code Civil Proc. Dak. § 465.

A deposition is evidence given by a witness under interrogatories, oral or written, and usually written down by an official person. In its generic sense, it embraces all written evidence verified by oath, and includes affidavits; but, in legal language, a distinction is maintained between depositions and affidavits. 3 Blatchf. 456.

The term sometimes is used in a special sense to denote a statement made orally by a person on oath before an examiner, commissioner, or officer of the court, (but not in open court,) and taken down in writing by the examiner or under his direction. Sweet.

In ecclesiastical law. The act of depriving a clergyman, by a competent tribunal, of his clerical orders, to punish him for some offense and to prevent his acting in future in his clerical character. Ayl. Par. 206.

DEPOSITO. In Spanish law Deposit; the species of bailment so called. Schm. Civil Law, 193.

DEPOSITOR. One who makes a deposit.

DEPOSITORY. The place where a deposit (*q. v.*) is placed and kept.

DEPOSITUM. One of the four real contracts specified by Justinian, and having the following characteristics: (1) The depositary or depositee is not liable for negligence, however extreme, but only for fraud, *dolus;* (2) the property remains in the depositor, the depositary having only the possession.

Precarium and *sequestre* were two varieties of the *depositum*.

DÉPÔT. In the French law, is the *depositum* of the Roman and the deposit of the English law. It is of two kinds, being either (1) *dépôt* simply so called, and which may be either voluntary or necessary, and (2) *séquestre*, which is a deposit made either under an agreement of the parties, and to abide the event of pending litigation regarding it, or by virtue of the direction of the court or a judge, pending litigation regarding it. Brown; Civil Code La. 2897.

DEPRAVE. To defame; vilify; exhibit contempt for. In England it is a criminal offense to "deprave" the Lord's supper or the Book of Common Prayer. Steph. Crim. Dig. 99.

DEPREDATION. In French law. The pillage which is made of the goods of a decedent.

DEPRIVATION. In English ecclesiastical law. The taking away from a clergyman his benefice or other spiritual promotion or dignity, either by sentence declaratory in the proper court for fit and sufficient causes or in pursuance of divers penal statutes which declare the benefice void for some non-feasance or neglect, or some malfeasance or crime. 3 Steph. Comm. 87, 88; Burn, Ecc. Law, tit. "Deprivation."

DEPRIVE. In a constitutional provision that no person shall be "*deprived* of his property" without due process of law, this word is equivalent to the term "take," and denotes a taking altogether, a seizure, a direct appropriation, dispossession of the owner. 21 Pa. St. 147.

DEPUTIZE. To appoint a deputy; to appoint or commission one to act as deputy to an officer. In a general sense, the term is descriptive of empowering one person to act for another in any capacity or relation, but in law it is almost always restricted to the substitution of a person appointed to act for an officer of the law.

DEPUTY. A substitute; a person duly authorized by an officer to exercise some or all of the functions pertaining to the office, in the place and stead of the latter.

A deputy differs from an assignee, in that an assignee has an interest in the office itself, and does all things in his own name, for whom his grantor shall not answer, except in special cases; but a deputy has not any interest in the office, and is only the shadow of the officer in whose name he acts. And there is a distinction in doing an act by an agent and by a deputy. An agent can only bind his principal when he does the act in the name of the principal. But a deputy may do the act and sign his own name, and it binds his principal; for a deputy has, in law, the whole power of his principal. Wharton.

DEPUTY LIEUTENANT. The deputy of a lord lieutenant of a county in England.

DEPUTY STEWARD. A steward of a manor may depute or authorize another to hold a court; and the acts done in a court so holden will be as legal as if the court had been holden by the chief steward in person. So an under steward or deputy may authorize another as subdeputy, *pro hac vice*, to hold a court for him; such limited authority not being inconsistent with the rule *delegatus non potest delegare*. Wharton.

DERAIGN. Seems to mean, literally, to confound and disorder, or to turn out of course, or displace; as deraignment or departure out of religion, in St. 31 Hen. VIII. c. 6. In the common law, the word is used generally in the sense of to prove; viz., to deraign a right, deraign the warranty, etc. Glanv. lib. 2, c. 6; Fitzh. Nat. Brev. 146. Perhaps this word "deraign," and the word "deraignment," derived from it, may be used in the sense of to prove and a proving, by disproving of what is asserted in opposition to truth and fact. Jacob.

DERECHO. In Spanish law. Law or right. *Derecho comun*, common law. The civil law is so called. A right. *Derechos*, rights.

DERELICT. Forsaken; abandoned; deserted; cast away.

Personal property abandoned or thrown away by the owner in such manner as to indicate that he intends to make no further claim thereto. 2 Bl. Comm. 9; 2 Reeve, Eng. Law, 9.

Land left uncovered by the receding of water from its former bed. 2 Rolle, Abr. 170; 2 Bl. Comm. 262; 1 Crabb, Real Prop. 109.

DERELICTION. The gaining of land from the water, in consequence of the sea shrinking back below the usual water mark; the opposite of *alluvion*, (*q. v.*) Dyer, 326*b*; 2 Bl. Comm. 262; 1 Steph. Comm. 419.

In the civil law. The voluntary abandonment of goods by the owner, without the hope or the purpose of returning to the possession. 12 Ga. 473; 2 Bl. Comm. 9.

Derivativa potestas non potest esse major primitiva. Noy, Max.; Wing. Max. 66. The derivative power cannot be greater than the primitive.

DERIVATIVE. Coming from another; taken from something preceding; secondary; that which has not its origin in itself, but owes its existence to something foregoing.

DERIVATIVE CONVEYANCES. Conveyances which presuppose some other conveyance precedent, and only serve to enlarge, confirm, alter, restrain, restore, or transfer the interest granted by such original conveyance. They are releases, confirmations, surrenders, assignments, and defeasances. 2 Bl. Comm. 324.

DEROGATION. The partial repeal or abolishing of a law, as by a subsequent act which limits its scope or impairs its utility and force. Distinguished from *abrogation*, which means the entire repeal and annulment of a law. Dig. 50, 17, 102.

DEROGATORY CLAUSE. In a will, this is a sentence or secret character inserted by the testator, of which he reserves the knowledge to himself, with a condition that no will he may make thereafter should be valid, unless this clause be inserted word for word. This is done as a precaution to guard against later wills being extorted by violence, or otherwise improperly obtained. By the law of England such a clause would be void, as tending to make the will irrevocable. Wharton.

Derogatur legi, cum pars detrahitur; abrogatur legi, cum prorsus tollitur. To derogate from a law is to take away part of it; to abrogate a law is to abolish it entirely. Dig. 50, 17, 102.

DESAFUERO. In Spanish law. An irregular action committed with violence against law, custom, or reason.

DESAMORTIZACION. In Mexican law. The *desamortizacion* of property is to take it out of mortmain, (dead hands;) that is, to unloose it from the grasp, as it were, of ecclesiastical or civil corporations. The term has no equivalent in English. Hall, Mex. Law. § 749.

DESCENDANT. One who is descended from another; a person who proceeds from the body of another, such as a child, grandchild, etc., to the remotest degree. The term is the opposite of "ascendant," (*q. v.*)

Descendants is a good term of description in a will, and includes all who proceed from the body of the person named; as grandchildren and great-grandchildren. Amb. 397; 2 Hil. Real. Prop. 242.

DESCENDER. Descent; in the descent. See FORMEDON.

DESCENT. Hereditary succession. Succession to the ownership of an estate by inheritance, or by any act of law, as distinguished from "purchase." Title by descent is the title by which one person, upon the death of another, acquires the real estate of the latter as his heir at law. 2 Bl. Comm. 201; Com. Dig. "Descent," A.

Descents are of two sorts,—lineal, as from father or grandfather to son or grandson; or collateral, as from brother to brother, or cousin to cousin. They are also distinguished into mediate and immediate descents. But these terms are used in different senses. A descent may be said to be a mediate or immediate descent of the estate or right; or it may be said to be mediate or immediate, in regard to the mediateness or immediateness of the pedigree or consanguinity. Thus, a descent from the grandfather, who dies in possession, to the grandchild, the father being then dead, or from the uncle to the nephew, the brother being dead, is, in the former sense, in law, immediate descent, although the one is collateral and the other lineal; for the heir is in the *per*, and not in the *per* and *cui*. On the other hand, with reference to the line of pedigree or consanguinity, a descent is often said to be immediate, when the ancestor from whom the party derives his blood is immediate, and without any intervening link or degrees; and mediate, when the kindred is derived from him *mediante altero*, another ancestor intervening between them. Thus a descent in lineals from father to son is in this sense immediate; but a descent from grandfather to grandson, the father being dead, or from uncle to nephew, the brother being dead, is deemed mediate; the father and the brother being, in these latter cases, the *medium deferens*, as it is called, of the descent or consanguinity. 6 Pet. 102.

Descent was denoted, in the Roman law, by the term "*successio*," which is also used by Bracton, and from which has been derived the *succession* of the Scotch and French jurisprudence.

DESCENT CAST. The devolving of realty upon the heir on the death of his ancestor intestate.

DESCRIPTIO PERSONÆ. Lat. Description of the person. By this is meant a word or phrase used merely for the purpose of identifying or pointing out the person intended, and not as an intimation that the language in connection with which it occurs is to apply to him only in the official or technical character which might appear to be indicated by the word.

DESCRIPTION. 1. A delineation or account of a particular subject by the recital of its characteristic accidents and qualities.

2. A written enumeration of items composing an estate, or of its condition, or of titles or documents; like an inventory, but with more particularity, and without involving the idea of an appraisement.

3. An exact written account of an article, mechanical device, or process which is the subject of an application for a patent.

4. A method of pointing out a particular person by referring to his relationship to some other person or his character as an officer, trustee, executor, etc.

5. That part of a conveyance, advertisement of sale, etc., which identifies the land intended to be affected.

DESERT. To leave or quit with an intention to cause a permanent separation; to forsake utterly; to abandon.

DESERTION. The act by which a person abandons and forsakes, without justification, or unauthorized, a station or condition of public or social life, renouncing its responsibilities and evading its duties.

The act of forsaking, deserting, or abandoning a *person* with whom one is legally bound to live, or for whom one is legally bound to provide, as a wife or husband.

The act by which a man quits the society of his wife and children, or either of them, and renounces his duties towards them.

"For the purposes of this case it is sufficient to say that the offense of desertion consists in the cessation of cohabitation, coupled with a determination in the mind of the offending person not to renew it." 43 Conn. 318.

An offense which consists in the abandonment of his duties by a person employed in the public service, in the army or navy, without leave, and with the intention not to return.

In respect to the military service, there is a distinction between desertion and simple absence without leave. In order to constitute desertion, there must be both an absence and an intention not to return to the service. 115 Mass. 336.

DESERTION OF A SEAMAN. The act by which a seaman deserts and abandons a ship or vessel, in which he had engaged to perform a voyage, before the expiration of his time, and without leave.

By desertion, in the maritime law, is meant, not a mere unauthorized absence from the ship without leave, but an unauthorized absence from the ship, with an intention not to return to her service, or, as it is often expressed, *animo non revertendi;* that is, with an intention to desert. 3 Story, 108.

DESHONORA. In Spanish law. Dishonor; injury; slander. Las Partidas, pt. 7, tit. 9, l. 1, 6.

DESIGN. In the law of evidence. Purpose or intention, combined with plan, or implying a plan in the mind. Burrill, Circ. Ev. 331.

As a term of art, the giving of a visible form to the conceptions of the mind, or invention. 4 Wash. C. C. 48.

Designatio justiciariorum est a rege; jurisdictio vero ordinaria a lege. 4 Inst. 74. The appointment of justices is by the king, but their ordinary jurisdiction by the law.

DESIGNATIO PERSONÆ. The description of a person or a party to a deed or contract.

Designatio unius est exclusio alterius, et expressum facit cessare tacitum. Co. Litt. 210. The specifying of one is the exclusion of another, and that which is expressed makes that which is understood to cease.

DESIGNATION. A description or descriptive expression by which a person or thing is denoted in a will without using the name.

DESIRE. This term, used in a will in relation to the management and distribution of property, is sufficient to create a trust, although it is precatory rather than imperative. 78 Ky. 123.

DESLINDE. A term used in the Spanish law, denoting the act by which the boundaries of an estate or portion of a country are determined.

DESMEMORIADOS. In Spanish law. Persons deprived of memory. White, New Recop. b. 1, tit. 2, c. 1, § 4.

DESPACHEURS. In maritime law. Persons appointed to settle cases of average.

DESPATCHES. Official communications of official persons on the affairs of government.

DESPERATE. Hopeless; worthless. This term is used in inventories and schedules of assets, particularly by executors, etc., to describe debts or claims which are considered impossible or hopeless of collection. See 11 Wend. 365.

DESPERATE DEBT. A hopeless debt; an irrecoverable obligation.

DESPITE. Contempt. *Despitz*, contempts. Kelham.

DESPITUS. Contempt. See DESPITE. A contemptible person. Fleta, lib. 4, c. 5.

DESPOJAR. A possessory action of the Mexican law. It is brought to recover possession of immovable property, of which one has been despoiled (*despojado*) by another. The word "despoil" (*despojar*) involves, in its signification, violence or clandestine means by which one is deprived of that which he possesses. 1 Cal. 268.

DESPOIL. This word involves, in its signification, violence or clandestine means by which one is deprived of that which he possesses. Its Spanish equivalent, *despojar*, is a term used in Mexican law. 1 Cal. 268.

DESPONSATION. The act of betrothing persons to each other.

DESPOSORIO. In Spanish law. Espousals; mutual promises of future marriage. White, New Recop. b. 1, tit. 6, c. 1, § 1.

DESPOT. This word, in its original and most simple acceptation, signifies *master and supreme lord;* it is synonymous with monarch; but taken in bad part, as it is usually employed, it signifies a tyrant. In some states, despot is the title given to the sovereign, as king is given in others. Enc. Lond.

DESPOTISM. That abuse of government where the sovereign power is not divided, but united in the hands of a single man, whatever may be his official title. It is not, properly, a form of government. Toullier, Dr. Civ. Fr. tit. prél. n. 32.

"Despotism" is not exactly synonymous with "autocracy," for the former involves the idea of tyrrany or abuse of power, which is not necessarily implied by the latter. Every despotism is autocratic; but an autocracy is not necessarily despotic.

DESPOTIZE. To act as a despot. Webster.

DESRENABLE. L. Fr. Unreasonable. Britt. c. 121.

DESSAISISSEMENT. In French law. When a person is declared bankrupt, he is immediately deprived of the enjoyment and administration of all his property; this deprivation, which extends to all his rights, is called "*dessaisissement.*" Arg. Fr. Merc. Law, 556.

DESTINATION. The purpose to which it is intended an article or a fund shall be applied. A testator gives a destination to a legacy when he prescribes the specific use to which it shall be put.

The port at which a ship is to end her voyage is called her "port of destination." Pardessus, no. 600.

DESTRUCTION. A term used in old English law, generally in connection with *waste*, and having, according to some, the same meaning. 1 Reeve, Eng. Law, 385; 3 Bl. Comm. 223. Britton, however, makes a distinction between waste of woods and destruction of houses. Britt. c. 66.

DESUBITO. To weary a person with continual barkings, and then to bite; spoken of dogs. Leg Alured. 26, cited in Cunningham's Dict.

DESUETUDE. Disuse; cessation or discontinuance of use. Applied to obsolete statutes.

DETACHIARE. To seize or take into custody another's goods or person.

DETAINER. The act (or the juridical fact) of withholding from a person lawfully entitled the possession of land or goods; or the restraint of a man's personal liberty against his will.

The wrongful keeping of a person's goods is called an "unlawful detainer" although the original taking may have been lawful. As, if one distrains another's cattle, *damage feasant*, and before they are impounded the owner tenders sufficient amends; now, though the original taking was lawful, the subsequent detention of them after tender of amends is not lawful, and the owner has an action of replevin to recover them, in which he will recover damages for the *detention*, and not for the *caption*, because the original taking was lawful. 3 Steph. Comm. 548.

In practice. A writ or instrument, issued or made by a competent officer, authorizing the keeper of a prison to keep in his custody a person therein named. A detainer may be lodged against one within the walls of a prison, on what account soever he is there. Com. Dig. "Process," E, (3 B.) This writ was superseded by 1 & 2 Vict. c. 110, §§ 1, 2.

DETAINMENT. This term is used in policies of marine insurance, in the clause relating to "arrests, restraints, and detainments." The last two words are construed as equivalents, each meaning the effect of superior force operating directly on the vessel. 6 Mass. 109.

DETENTIO. In the civil law. That condition of fact under which one can exercise his power over a corporeal thing at his pleasure, to the exclusion of all others. It forms the substance of possession in all its varieties. Mackeld. Rom. Law, § 238.

DETENTION. The act of keeping back or withholding, either accidentally or by design, a person or thing. See DETAINER.

DETENTION IN A REFORMATORY, as a punishment or measure of prevention, is where a juvenile offender is sentenced to be sent to a reformatory school, to be there detained for a certain period of time. 1 Russ. Crimes, 82.

DETERMINABLE. That which may cease or determine upon the happening of a certain contingency. 2 Bl. Comm. 121.

DETERMINABLE FEE. (Also called a "qualified" or "base" fee.) One which has a qualification subjoined to it, and which must be determined whenever the qualification annexed to it is at an end. 2 Bl. Comm. 109.

An estate in fee which is liable to be determined by some act or event expressed on its limitation to circumscribe its continuance, or inferred by law as bounding its extent. 1 Washb. Real Prop. 62; 35 Wis. 36.

DETERMINABLE FREEHOLDS. Estates for life, which may determine upon future contingencies before the life for which they are created expires. As if an estate be granted to a woman during her widowhood, or to a man until he be promoted to a benefice; in these and similar cases, whenever the contingency happens,—when the widow marries, or when the grantee obtains the benefice,—the respective estates are absolutely determined and gone. Yet, while they subsist, they are reckoned estates for life; because they may by possibility last for life, if the contingencies upon which they are to determine do not sooner happen. 2 Bl. Comm. 121.

DETERMINATE. That which is ascertained; what is particularly designated.

DETERMINATION. The decision of a court of justice. The ending or expiration of an estate or interest in property, or of a right, power, or authority.

DETERMINE. To come to an end. To bring to an end. 2 Bl. Comm. 121; 1 Washb. Real Prop. 380.

DETESTATIO. Lat. In the civil law. A summoning made, or notice given, in the presence of witnesses, (*denuntiatio facta cum testatione.*) Dig. 50, 16, 40.

DETINET. Lat. He detains. In old English law. A species of action of debt, which lay for the specific recovery of goods, under a contract to deliver them. 1 Reeves, Eng. Law, 159.

In pleading. An action of *debt* is said to be in the *detinet* when it is alleged merely that the defendant withholds or unjustly detains from the plaintiff the thing or amount demanded.

An action of *replevin* is said to be in the *detinet* when the defendant retains possession of the property until after judgment in the action. Bull. N. P. 52; Chit. Pl. 145.

DETINUE. In practice. A form of action which lies for the recovery, *in specie,* of personal chattels from one who acquired possession of them lawfully, but retains it without right, together with damages for the detention. 3 Bl. Comm. 152.

The action of *detinue* is defined in the old books as a remedy founded upon the delivery of goods by the owner to another to keep, who afterwards refuses to redeliver them to the bailor; and it is said that, to authorize the maintenance of the action, it is necessary that the defendant should have come lawfully into the possession of the chattel, either by delivery to him or by finding it. In fact, it was once understood to be the law that *detinue* does not lie where the property had been tortiously taken. But it is, upon principle, very unimportant in what manner the defendant's possession commenced, since the gist of the action is the wrongful detainer, and not the original taking. It is only incumbent upon the plaintiff to prove property in himself, and possession in the defendant. At present, the action of *detinue* is proper in every case where the owner prefers recovering the specific property to damages for its conversion, and no regard is had to the manner in which the defendant acquired the possession. 9 Port. (Ala.) 151.

DETINUE OF GOODS IN FRANK MARRIAGE. A writ formerly available to a wife after a divorce, for the recovery of the goods given with her in marriage. Mozley & Whitley.

DETINUIT. In pleading. An action of replevin is said to be in the *detinuit* when the plaintiff acquires possession of the property claimed by means of the writ. The right to retain is, of course, subject in such case to the judgment of the court upon his title to the property claimed. Bull. N. P. 521.

DETRACTARI. To be torn in pieces by horses. Fleta, l. 1, c. 37.

DETUNICARI. To discover or lay open to the world. Matt. Westm. 1240.

DEUNX, pl. **DEUNCES.** Lat. In the Roman law. A division of the *as*, containing eleven *unciæ* or duodecimal parts; the proportion of eleven-twelfths. 2 Bl. Comm. 462, note. See As.

Deus solus hæredem facere potest, non homo. God alone, and not man, can make an heir. Co. Litt. 7*b;* Broom. Max. 516.

DEUTEROGAMY. The act, or condition, of one who marries a wife after the death of a former wife.

DEVADIATUS, or DIVADIATUS. An offender without sureties or pledges. Cowell.

DEVASTATION. Wasteful use of the property of a deceased person, as for extravagant funeral or other unnecessary expenses. 2 Bl. Comm. 508.

DEVASTAVERUNT. They have wasted. A term applied in old English law to waste by executors and administrators, and to the process issued against them therefor. Cowell. See DEVASTAVIT.

DEVASTAVIT. Lat. He has wasted. The act of an executor or administrator in wasting the goods of the deceased; mismanagement of the estate by which a loss occurs; a breach of trust or misappropriation of assets held in a fiduciary character; any violation or neglect of duty by an executor or administrator, involving loss to the decedent's estate, which makes him personally responsible to heirs, creditors, or legatees.

Also, if plaintiff, in an action against an executor or administrator, has obtained judgment, the usual execution runs *de bonis testatoris;* but, if the sheriff returns to such a writ *nulla bona testatoris nec propria*, the plaintiff may, forthwith, upon this return, sue out an execution against the property or person of the executor or administrator, in as full a manner as in an action against him, sued in his own right. Such a return is called a "*devastavit.*" Brown.

DEVENERUNT. A writ, now obsolete, directed to the king's escheators when any of the king's tenants *in capite* dies, and when his son and heir dies within age and in the king's custody, commanding the escheat, or that by the oaths of twelve good and lawful men they shall inquire what lands or tenements by the death of the tenant have come to the king. Dyer, 360; Termes de la Ley.

DEVEST. To deprive; to take away; to withdraw. Usually spoken of an authority, power, property, or title; as the estate is devested.

Devest is opposite to invest. As to invest signifies to deliver the possession of anything to another, so to devest signifies to take it away. Jacob.

It is sometimes written "*di*vest" but "devest" has the support of the best authority. Burrill.

DEVIATION. **In insurance.** Varying from the risks insured against, as described in the policy, without necessity or just cause, after the risk has begun. 1 Phil. Ins. § 977, et seq.; 1 Arn. Ins. 415, et seq.

Any unnecessary or unexcused departure from the usual or general mode of carrying on the voyage insured. 15 Amer. Law Rev. 108.

Deviation is a departure from the course of the voyage insured, or an unreasonable delay in pursuing the voyage, or the commencement of an entirely different voyage. Civil Code Cal. § 2694.

A deviation is a voluntary departure from or delay in the usual and regular course of a voyage insured, without necessity or reasonable cause. This discharges the insurer, from the time of the deviation. 9 Mass. 436.

In contracts. A change made in the progress of a work from the original terms or design or method agreed upon.

DEVICE. In a statute against gaming devices, this term is to be understood as meaning something formed by design, a contrivance, an invention. It is to be distinguished from "substitute," which means something put in the place of another thing, or used instead of something else. 59 Ala. 91.

DEVIL ON THE NECK. An instrument of torture, formerly used to extort confessions, etc. It was made of several irons, which were fastened to the neck and legs, and wrenched together so as to break the back. Cowell.

DEVISABLE. Capable of being devised. 1 Pow. Dev. 165; 2 Bl. Comm. 373.

DEVISAVIT VEL NON. In practice. The name of an issue sent out of a court of chancery, or one which exercises chancery jurisdiction, to a court of law, to try the validity of a paper asserted and denied to be a will, to ascertain whether or not the testator did devise, or whether or not that paper was his will. 7 Brown, Parl. Cas. 437; 2 Atk. 424; 5 Pa. St. 21.

DEVISE. A gift of real property by will.

Devise properly relates to the disposal of real property, not of personal. 21 Barb. 551, 561.

Devise is properly applied to gifts of real property by will, but may be extended to embrace personal property, to execute the intention of the testator. 6 Ired. Eq. 173.

The words "devise," "legacy," and "bequest" may be applied indifferently to real or personal property, if such appears by the context of a will to have been the testator's intention. 21 N. H. 514.

Devises are *contingent* or *vested;* that is, after the death of the testator. Contingent, when the vesting of any estate in the devisee is made to depend upon some future event, in which case, if the event never occur, or until it does occur, no estate vests under the devise. But, when the future event is referred to merely to determine the time at which the devisee shall come into the use of the estate, this does not hinder the vesting of the estate at the death of the testator. 1 Jarm. Wills, c. 26.

An *executory* devise of lands is such a disposition of them by will that thereby no estate vests at the death of the devisor, but only on some future contingency. It differs from a remainder in three very material points: (1) That it needs not any particular estate to support it; (2) that by it a fee-simple or other less estate may be limited after a fee-simple; (3) that by this means a remainder may be limited of a chattel interest, after a particular estate for life created in the same. 2 Bl. Comm. 172.

DEVISEE. The person to whom lands or other real property are devised or given by will. 1 Pow. Dev. c. 7.

DEVISOR. A giver of lands or real estate by will; the maker of a will of lands; a testator.

DEVOIR. Fr. Duty. It is used in the statute of 2 Rich. II. c. 3, in the sense of duties or customs.

DEVOLUTION. In ecclesiastical law. The forfeiture of a right or power (as the right of presentation to a living) in consequence of its non-user by the person holding it, or of some other act or omission on his part, and its resulting transfer to the person next entitled.

DEVOLVE. "To devolve means to pass from a person dying to a person living; the etymology of the word shows its meaning." 1 Mylne & K. 648.

DEVY. L. Fr. Dies; deceases. Bendloe, 5.

DEXTANS. Lat. In Roman law. A division of the *as*, consisting of ten *unciæ;* ten-twelfths, or five-sixths. 2 Bl. Comm. 462, note *m*.

DEXTRARIUS. One at the right hand of another.

DEXTRAS DARE. To shake hands in token of friendship; or to give up oneself to the power of another person.

DI COLONNA. In maritime law. The contract which takes place between the owner of a ship, the captain, and the mariners, who agree that the voyage shall be for the benefit of all. The term is used in the Italian law. Emerig. Mar. Loans, § 5.

DI. ET FI. L. Lat. In old writs. An abbreviation of *dilecto et fideli*, (to his beloved and faithful.)

DIACONATE. The office of a deacon.

DIACONUS. A deacon.

DIAGNOSIS. A medical term, meaning the discovery of the source of a patient's illness.

DIALECTICS. That branch of logic which teaches the rules and modes of reasoning.

DIALLAGE. A rhetorical figure in which arguments are placed in various points of view, and then turned to one point. Enc. Lond.

DIALOGUS DE SCACCARIO. Dialogue of or about the exchequer. An ancient treatise on the court of exchequer, attributed by some to Gervase of Tilbury, by others to Richard Fitz Nigel, bishop of London in the reign of Richard I. It is quoted by Lord Coke under the name of Ockham. Crabb, Eng. Law, 71.

DIANATIC. A logical reasoning in a progressive manner, proceeding from one subject to another. Enc. Lond.

DIARIUM. Daily food, or as much as will suffice for the day. Du Cange.

DIATIM. In old records. Daily; every day; from day to day. Spelman.

DICA. In old English law. A tally for accounts, by number of cuts, (*taillees*,) marks, or notches. Cowell. See TALLIA, TALLY.

DICAST. An officer in ancient Greece answering in some respects to our juryman, but combining, on trials had before them, the functions of both judge and jury. The dicasts sat together in numbers varying, according to the importance of the case, from one to five hundred.

DICE. Small cubes of bone or ivory, marked with figures or devices on their several sides, used in playing certain games of chance. See 55 Ala. 198.

DICTATE. To order or instruct what is to be said or written. To pronounce, word by word, what is meant to be written by another. 6 Mart. (N. S.) 143.

DICTATION. In Louisiana, this term is used in a technical sense, and means to pronounce orally what is destined to be written at the same time by another. It is used in reference to nuncupative wills. 16 La. Ann. 220.

DICTATOR. A magistrate invested with unlimited power, and created in times of national distress and peril. Among the Romans, he continued in office for six months only, and had unlimited power and authority over both the property and lives of the citizens.

DICTORES. Arbitrators.

DICTUM. In general. A statement, remark, or observation. *Gratis dictum;* a gratuitous or voluntary representation; one which a party is not bound to make. 2 Kent, Comm. 486. *Simplex dictum;* a mere assertion; an assertion without proof. Bract. fol. 320.

The word is generally used as an abbreviated form of *obiter dictum,* "a remark by the way;" that is, an observation or remark made by a judge in pronouncing an opinion upon a cause, concerning some rule, principle, or application of law, or the solution of a question suggested by the case at bar, but not necessarily involved in the case or essential to its determination; any statement of the law enunciated by the court merely by way of illustration, argument, analogy, or suggestion.

Dicta are opinions of a judge which do not embody the resolution or determination of the court, and made without argument, or full consideration of the point, are not the professed deliberate determinations of the judge himself. *Obiter dicta* are such opinions uttered by the way, not upon the point or question pending, as if turning aside for the time from the main topic of the case to collateral subjects. 62 N. Y. 47, 58.

In old English law. *Dictum* meant an arbitrament, or the award of arbitrators.

In French law. The report of a judgment made by one of the judges who has given it. Poth. Proc. Civil, pt. 1, c. 5, art. 2.

DICTUM DE KENILWORTH. The edict or declaration of Kenilworth. An edict or award between King Henry III. and all the barons and others who had been in arms against him; and so called because it was made at Kenilworth Castle, in Warwickshire, in the fifty-first year of his reign. containing a composition of five years' rent for the lands and estates of those who had forfeited them in that rebellion. Blount; 2 Reeve, Eng. Law, 62.

DIE WITHOUT ISSUE. See DYING WITHOUT ISSUE.

DIEI DICTIO. Lat. In Roman law. This name was given to a notice promulgated by a magistrate of his intention to present an impeachment against a citizen before the people, specifying the day appointed, the name of the accused, and the crime charged.

DIEM CLAUSIT EXTREMUM. (Lat. He has closed his last day,—died.) A writ which formerly lay on the death of a tenant *in capite,* to ascertain the lands of which he died seised, and reclaim them into the king's hands. It was directed to the king's escheators. Fitzh. Nat. Brev. 251, K; 2 Reeve, Eng. Law, 327.

A writ awarded out of the exchequer after the death of a crown debtor, the sheriff being commanded by it to inquire by a jury when and where the crown debtor died, and what chattels, debts, and lands he had at the time of his decease, and to take and seize them into the crown's hands. 4 Steph. Comm. 47, 48.

DIES. Lat. A day; days. Days for appearance in court. Provisions or maintenance for a day. The king's rents were anciently reserved by so many days' provisions. Spelman; Cowell; Blount.

DIES A QUO. (The day from which.) In the civil law. The day from which a transaction begins; the commencement of it; the conclusion being the *dies ad quem.* Mackeld. Rom. Law, § 185.

DIES AMORIS. A day of favor. The name given to the appearance day of the term on the fourth day, or *quarto die post.* It was the day given by the favor and indulgence of the court to the defendant for his appearance, when all parties appeared in court, and had their appearance recorded by the proper officer. Wharton.

DIES CEDIT. The day begins; *dies venit*, the day has come. Two expressions in Roman law which signify the vesting or fixing of an interest, and the interest becoming a present one. Sandars' Just. Inst. (5th Ed.) 225, 232.

DIES COMMUNES IN BANCO. Regular days for appearance in court; called, also, "common return-days." 2 Reeve, Eng. Law, 57.

DIES DATUS. A day given or allowed, (to a defendant in an action;) amounting to a continuance. But the name was appropriate only to a continuance before a declaration filed; if afterwards allowed, it was called an "imparlance."

DIES DATUS IN BANCO. A day given in the *bench*, (or court of common pleas.) Bract. fols. 257*b*, 361. A day given in bank, as distinguished from a day at *nisi prius*. Co. Litt. 135.

DIES DATUS PARTIBUS. A day given to the parties to an action; an adjournment or continuance. Crabb, Eng. Law, 217.

DIES DATUS PRECE PARTIUM. A day given on the prayer of the parties. Bract. fol. 358; Gilb. Comm. Pl. 41; 2 Reeve, Eng. Law, 60.

DIES DOMINICUS. The Lord's day; Sunday.

Dies dominicus non est juridicus. Sunday is not a court day, or day for judicial proceedings, or legal purposes. Co. Litt. 135*a;* Noy, Max. 2; Wing. Max. 7, max. 5; Broom, Max. 21.

DIES EXCRESCENS. In old English law. The added or increasing day in leap year. Bract. fols. 359, 359*b*.

DIES FASTI. In Roman law. Days on which the courts were open, and justice could be legally administered; days on which it was lawful for the prætor to pronounce (*fari*) the *three* words, "*do*," "*dico*," "*addico*." Mackeld. Rom. Law, § 39, and note; 3 Bl. Comm. 424, note; Calvin. Hence called "*triverbial* days," answering to the *dies juridici* of the English law.

DIES FERIATI. Lat. In the civil law. Holidays. Dig. 2, 12, 2, 9.

DIES GRATIÆ. In old English practice. A day of grace, courtesy, or favor. Co. Litt. 134*b*. The *quarto die post* was sometimes so called. Id. 135*a*.

Dies inceptus pro completo habetur. A day begun is held as complete.

Dies incertus pro conditione habetur. An uncertain day is held as a condition.

DIES INTERCISI. In Roman law. Divided days; days on which the courts were open for a part of the day. Calvin.

DIES LEGITIMUS. In the civil and old English law. A lawful or law day; a term day; a day of appearance.

DIES MARCHIÆ. In old English law. The day of meeting of English and Scotch, which was annually held on the marches or borders to adjust their differences and preserve peace.

DIES NEFASTI. In Roman law. Days on which the courts were closed, and it was unlawful to administer justice; answering to the *dies non juridici* of the English law. Mackeld. Rom. Law, § 39, note.

DIES NON. An abbreviation of *Dies non juridicus*, (*q. v.*)

DIES NON JURIDICUS. In practice. A day not juridical; not a court day. A day on which courts are not open for business, such as Sundays and some holidays.

DIES PACIS. (Lat. Day of peace.) The year was formerly divided into the days of the peace of the church and the days of the peace of the king, including in the two divisions all the days of the year. Crabb, Eng. Law, 35.

DIES SOLARIS. In old English law. A solar day, as distinguished from what was called "*dies lunaris*," (a lunar day;) both composing an artificial day. Bract. fol. 264. See DAY.

DIES SOLIS. In the civil and old English law. Sunday, (literally, the day of the sun.) See Cod. 3, 12, 7.

DIES UTILES. Juridical days; useful or available days. A term of the Roman law, used to designate those especial days occurring within the limits of a prescribed period of time upon which it was lawful, or possible, to do a specific act.

DIET. A general legislative assembly is sometimes so called on the continent of Europe.

In Scotch practice. The sitting of a court. An appearance day. A day fixed for the trial of a criminal cause. A criminal cause as prepared for trial.

DIETA. A day's journey; a day's work; a day's expenses.

DIETS OF COMPEARANCE. In Scotch law. The days within which parties in civil and criminal prosecutions are cited to appear. Bell.

DIEU ET MON DROIT. Fr. God and my right. The motto of the royal arms of England, first assumed by Richard I.

DIEU SON ACTE. L. Fr. In old law. God his act; God's act. An event beyond human foresight or control. Termes de la Ley.

DIFFACERE. To destroy; to disfigure or deface.

Difficile est ut unus homo vicem duorum sustineat. 4 Coke, 118. It is difficult that one man should sustain the place of two.

DIFFORCIARE. In old English law. To deny, or keep from one. *Difforciare rectum*, to deny justice to any one, after having been required to do it.

DIGAMA, or DIGAMY. Second marriage; marriage to a second wife after the death of the first, as "bigamy," in law, is having two wives at once. Originally, a man who married a widow, or married again after the death of his wife, was said to be guilty of bigamy. Co. Litt. 40*b*, note.

DIGEST. A collection or compilation, embodying the chief matter of numerous books in one, disposed under proper heads or titles, and usually by an alphabetical arrangement, for facility in reference.

As a legal term, "digest" is to be distinguished from "abridgment." The latter is a summary or epitome of the contents of a single work, in which, as a rule, the original order or sequence of parts is preserved, and in which the principal labor of the compiler is in the matter of consolidation. A digest is wider in its scope; is made up of quotations or paraphrased passages; and has its own system of classification and arrangement. An "index" merely points out the places where particular matters may be found, without purporting to give such matters *in extenso*. A "treatise" or "commentary" is not a compilation, but an original composition, though it may include quotations and excerpts.

A reference to the "Digest," or "Dig.," is always understood to designate the Digest (or Pandects) of the Justinian collection; that being the digest *par eminence*, and the authoritative compilation of the Roman law.

DIGESTA. Digests. One of the titles of the Pandects of Justinan. Inst. *prooem*, § 4. Bracton uses the singular, "*Digestum*." Bract. fol. 19.

DIGESTS. The ordinary name of the Pandects of Justinian, which are now usually cited by the abbreviation "Dig." instead of "Ff.," as formerly. Sometimes called "Digest," in the singular.

DIGGING. Has been held as synonymous with "excavating," and not confined to the removal of earth. 1 N. Y. 316.

DIGNITARY. In canon law. A person holding an ecclesiastical benefice or dignity, which gave him some pre-eminence above mere priests and canons. To this class exclusively belonged all bishops, deans, archdeacons, etc.; but it now includes all the prebendaries and canons of the church. Brande.

DIGNITY. In English law. An honor; a title, station, or distinction of honor. Dignities are a species of incorporeal hereditaments, in which a person may have a property or estate. 2 Bl. Comm. 37; 1 Bl. Comm. 396; 1 Crabb, Real Prop. 468, et seq.

DIJUDICATION. Judicial decision or determination.

DILACION. In Spanish law. A space of time granted to a party to a suit in which to answer a demand or produce evidence of a disputed fact.

DILAPIDATION. A species of ecclesiastical waste which occurs whenever the incumbent suffers any edifices of his ecclesiastical living to go to ruin or decay. It is either voluntary, by pulling down, or permissive, by suffering the church, parsonage-houses, and other buildings thereunto belonging, to decay. And the remedy for either lies either in the spiritual court, where the canon law prevails, or in the courts of common law. It is also held to be good cause of deprivation if the bishop, parson, or other ecclesiastical person dilapidates buildings or cuts down timber growing on the patrimony of the church, unless for necessary repairs; and that a writ of prohibition will also lie against him in the common-law courts. 3 Bl. Comm. 91.

The term is also used, in the law of landlord and tenant, to signify the neglect of necessary repairs to a building, or suffering it to fall into a state of decay, or the pulling down of the building or any part of it.

Dilationes in lege sunt odiosæ. Delays in law are odious. Branch, Princ.

DILATORY DEFENSE. In chancery practice. One the object of which is to dismiss, suspend, or obstruct the suit, without touching the merits, until the impediment or obstacle insisted on shall be removed. 3 Bl. Comm. 301, 302.

DILATORY PLEAS. A class of defenses at common law, founded on some matter of fact not connected with the merits of the case, but such as might exist without impeaching the right of action itself. They were either pleas to the *jurisdiction*, showing that, by reason of some matter therein stated, the case was not within the jurisdiction of the court; or pleas in *suspension*, showing some matter of temporary incapacity to proceed with the suit; or pleas in *abatement*, showing some matter for abatement or quashing the declaration. 3 Steph. Comm. 576.

DILIGENCE. Prudence; vigilant activity; attentiveness; or care, of which there are infinite shades, from the slightest momentary thought to the most vigilant anxiety; but the law recognizes only three degrees of diligence: (1) Common or ordinary, which men, in general, exert in respect of their own concerns; the standard is necessarily variable with respect to the facts, although it may be uniform with respect to the principle. (2) High or great, which is extraordinary diligence, or that which very prudent persons take of their own concerns. (3) Low or slight, which is that which persons of less than common prudence, or indeed of no prudence at all, take of their own concerns.

The civil law is in perfect conformity with the common law. It lays down three degrees of diligence,—ordinary, (*diligentia;*) extraordinary, (*exactissima diligentia;*) slight, (*levissima diligentia.*) Story, Bailm. 19.

There may be a high degree of diligence, a common degree of diligence, and a slight degree of diligence, with their corresponding degrees of negligence, and these can be clearly enough defined for all practical purposes, and, with a view to the business of life, seem to be all that are really necessary. Common or ordinary diligence is that degree of diligence which men in general exercise in respect to their own concerns; high or great diligence is of course extraordinary diligence, or that which very prudent persons take of their own concerns; and low or slight diligence is that which persons of less than common prudence, or indeed of any prudence at all, take of their own concerns. Ordinary negligence is the want of ordinary diligence; slight, or less than ordinary, negligence is the want of great diligence; and gross or more than ordinary negligence is the want of slight diligence. 5 Kan. 180.

In Scotch law and practice. Process of law, by which persons, lands, or effects are seized in execution or in security for debt. Ersk. Inst. 2, 11, 1. Brande. Process for enforcing the attendance of witnesses, or the production of writings. Ersk. Inst. 4, 1, 71.

DILIGIATUS. (Fr. *De lege ejectus*, Lat.) Outlawed.

DILLIGROUT. In old English law. Pottage formerly made for the king's table on the coronation day. There was a tenure in serjeantry, by which lands were held of the king by the service of finding this pottage at that solemnity.

DIME. A silver coin of the United States, of the value of ten cents, or one-tenth of the dollar.

DIMIDIA, DIMIDIUM, DIMIDIUS. Half; a half; the half.

DIMIDIETAS. The moiety or half of a thing.

DIMINUTIO. In the civil law. Diminution; a taking away; loss or deprivation. *Diminutio capitis*, loss of *status* or condition. See CAPITIS DIMINUTIO.

DIMINUTION. Incompleteness. A word signifying that the record sent up from an inferior to a superior court for review is incomplete, or not fully certified. In such case the party may suggest a "diminution of the record," which may be rectified by a *certiorari*. 2 Tidd, Pr. 1109.

DIMISI. In old conveyancing. I have demised. *Dimisi, concessi, et ad firmam tradidi*, have demised, granted, and to farm let. The usual words of operation in a lease. 2 Bl. Comm. 317, 318.

DIMISIT. In old conveyancing. [He] has demised. See DIMISI.

DIMISSORIÆ LITTERÆ. In the civil law. Letters dimissory or dismissory, commonly called "apostles," (*quæ vulgo apostoli dicuntur.*) Dig. 50, 16, 106. See APOSTOLI, APOSTLES.

DIMISSORY LETTERS. Where a candidate for holy orders has a title of ordination in one diocese in England, and is to be ordained in another, the bishop of the former diocese gives letters dimissory to the bishop of the latter to enable him to ordain the candidate. Holthouse.

DINARCHY. A government of two persons.

DINERO. In Spanish law. Money. *Dinero contado*, money counted. White, New Recop. b. 2, tit. 13, c. 1, § 1.

In Roman law. A civil division of the Roman empire, embracing several provinces. Calvin.

DIOCESAN. Belonging to a diocese; a bishop, as he stands related to his own clergy or flock.

DIOCESAN COURTS. In English law. The consistorial courts of each diocese, exercising general jurisdiction of all matters arising locally within their respective limits, with the exception of places subject to *peculiar* jurisdiction; deciding all matters of spiritual discipline,—suspending or depriving clergymen,—and administering the other branches of the ecclesiastical law. 2 Steph. Comm. 672.

DIOCESE. The territorial extent of a bishop's jurisdiction. The circuit of every bishop's jurisdiction. Co. Litt. 94; 1 Bl. Comm. 111.

DIOICHIA. The district over which a bishop exercised his spiritual functions.

DIPLOMA. In the civil law. A royal charter; letters patent granted by a prince or sovereign. Calvin.

An instrument given by colleges and societies on the conferring of any degrees.

A license granted to a physician, etc., to practice his art or profession. See 25 Wend. 469.

DIPLOMACY. The science which treats of the relations and interests of nations with nations.

Negotiation or intercourse between nations through their representatives. The rules, customs, and privileges of representatives at foreign courts.

DIPLOMATIC AGENT. In international law. A general name for all classes of persons charged with the negotiation, transaction, or superintendence of the diplomatic business of one nation at the court of another. See Rev. St. U. S. § 1674.

DIPLOMATICS. The science of diplomas, or of ancient writings and documents; the art of judging of ancient charters, public documents, diplomas, etc., and discriminating the true from the false. Webster.

DIPSOMANIA. In medical jurisprudence. An irresistible impulse to indulge in intoxication, either by the use of alcohol or of drugs such as opium. This mania or disease is classed as one of the minor forms of insanity. 19 Neb. 614, 28 N. W. Rep. 273; 1 Bish. Crim. Law, § 304.

DIPSOMANIAC. A person subject to dipsomania. One who has an irresistible desire for alcoholic liquors.

DIPTYCHA. Diptychs; tablets of wood, metal, or other substance, used among the Romans for the purpose of writing, and folded like a book of two leaves. The diptychs of antiquity were especially employed for public registers. They were used in the Greek, and afterwards in the Roman, church, as registers of the names of those for whom supplication was to be made, and are ranked among the earliest monastic records. Burrill.

DIRECT. Immediate; by the shortest course; without circuity; operating by an immediate connection or relation, instead of operating through a medium; the opposite of *indirect*.

In the usual or natural course or line; immediately upwards or downwards; as distinguished from that which is out of the line, or on the side of it; the opposite of *collateral*.

In the usual or regular course or order, as distinguished from that which diverts, interrupts, or opposes; the opposite of *cross* or contrary.

DIRECT EVIDENCE. Evidence directly proving any matter, as opposed to circumstantial evidence, which is often called "indirect." It is usually conclusive, but, like other evidence, it is fallible, and that on various accounts. It is not to be confounded with primary evidence, as opposed to secondary, although in point of fact it usually is primary. Brown.

DIRECT EXAMINATION. In practice. The first interrogation or examination of a witness, on the merits, by the party on whose behalf he is called. This is to be distinguished from an examination *in pais*, or on the *voir dire*, which is merely preliminary, and is had when the competency of the witness is challenged; from the cross-examination, which is conducted by the adverse party; and from the redirect examination, which follows the cross-examination, and is had by the party who first examined the witness.

DIRECT INTEREST. A direct interest, such as would render the interested party incompetent to testify in regard to the matter, is an interest which is certain, and not contingent or doubtful. A matter which is dependent alone on the successful prosecution of an execution cannot be considered as uncertain, or otherwise than direct, in this sense. 1 Ala. 65.

DIRECT INTERROGATORIES. On the taking of a deposition, where written interrogatories are framed, those put by the party calling the witness are named "direct interrogatories," (corresponding to the questions asked on a direct examination,) while those put by the adverse party are called "cross-interrogatories."

DIRECT LINE. Property is said to descend or be inherited in the direct line when it passes in lineal succession; from ancestor to son, grandson, great-grandson, and so on.

DIRECT TAX. A direct tax is one which is demanded from the very persons who, it is intended or desired, should pay it. Indirect taxes are those which are demanded from one person, in the expectation and intention that he shall indemnify himself at the expense of another. Mill, Pol. Econ.

Taxes are divided into "direct," under which designation would be included those which are assessed upon the property, person, business, income, etc., of those who are to pay them, and "indirect," or those which are levied on commodities before they reach the consumer, and are paid by those upon whom they ultimately fall, not as taxes, but as part of the market price of the commodity. Cooley, Tax'n, 6.

Historical evidence shows that personal property, contracts, occupations, and the like, have never been regarded as the subjects of direct tax. The phrase is understood to be limited to taxes on land and its appurtenances, and on polls. 8 Wall. 533.

DIRECTION. 1. The act of governing; management; superintendence. Also the body of persons (called "directors") who are charged with the management and administration of a corporation or institution.

2. The charge or instruction given by the court to a jury upon a point of law arising or involved in the case, to be by them applied to the facts in evidence.

3. The clause of a bill in equity containing the address of the bill to the court.

DIRECTOR OF THE MINT. An officer having the control, management, and superintendence of the United States mint and its branches. He is appointed by the president, by and with the advice and consent of the senate.

DIRECTORS. Persons appointed or elected according to law, authorized to manage and direct the affairs of a corporation or company. The whole of the directors collectively form the board of directors. Wharton.

DIRECTORY. A provision in a statute, rule of procedure, or the like, is said to be directory when it is to be considered as a mere direction or instruction of no obligatory force, and involving no invalidating consequence for its disregard, as opposed to an imperative or mandatory provision, which must be followed. The general rule is that the prescriptions of a statute relating to the performance of a public duty are so far directory that, though neglect of them may be punishable, yet it does not affect the validity of the acts done under them, as in the case of a statute requiring an officer to prepare and deliver a document to another officer on or before a certain day. Maxw. Interp. St. 330, et seq.

DIRECTORY TRUST. Where, by the terms of a trust, the fund is directed to be vested in a particular manner till the period arrives at which it is to be appropriated, this is called a "directory trust." It is distinguished from a discretionary trust, in which the trustee has a discretion as to the management of the fund. 10 Yerg. 272.

DIRIBITORES. In Roman law. Officers who distributed ballots to the people, to be used in voting. Tayl. Civil Law, 192.

DIRIMENT IMPEDIMENTS. In canon law. Absolute bars to marriage, which would make it null *ab initio.*

DISABILITY. The want of legal ability or capacity to exercise legal rights, either special or ordinary, or to do certain acts with proper legal effect, or to enjoy certain privileges or powers of free action.

At the present day, disability is generally used to indicate an incapacity for the full enjoyment of ordinary legal rights; thus married women, persons under age, insane persons, and felons convict are said to be under disability. Sometimes the term is used in a more limited sense, as when it signifies an impediment to marriage, or the restraints placed upon clergymen by reason of their spiritual avocations. Mozley & Whitley.

Disability is either *general* or *special;* the former when it incapacitates the person for the performance of all legal acts of a general class, or giving to them their ordinary legal effect; the latter when it debars him from one specific act.

Disability is also either *personal* or *absolute;* the former where it attaches to the particular person, and arises out of his *status*, his previous act, or his natural or juridical incapacity; the latter where it originates with a particular person, but extends also to his descendants or successors.

Considered with special reference to the capacity to contract a marriage, disability is either *canonical* or *civil;* a disability of the former class makes the marriage voidable only, while the latter, in general, avoids it entirely.

DISABLE. In its ordinary sense, to disable is to cause a disability, (*q. v.*)

In the old language of pleading, to disable is to take advantage of one's own or another's disability. Thus, it is "an express maxim of the common law that the party shall not disable himself;" but "this disability to disable himself * * * is personal." 4 Coke, 123*b*.

DISABLING STATUTES. These are acts of parliament, restraining and regulating the exercise of a right or the power of alienation; the term is specially applied to 1 Eliz. c. 19, and similar acts restraining the power of ecclesiastical corporations to make leases.

DISADVOCARE. To deny a thing.

DISAFFIRM. To repudiate; to revoke a consent once given; to recall an affirmance. To refuse one's subsequent sanction to a former act; to disclaim the intention of being bound by an antecedent transaction.

DISAFFIRMANCE. The repudiation of a former transaction. The refusal by one who has the right to refuse, (as in the case of a voidable contract,) to abide by his former acts, or accept the legal consequences of the same. It may either be "express" (in words) or "implied" from acts expressing the intention of the party to disregard the obligations of the contract.

DISAFFOREST. To restore to their former condition lands which have been turned into forests. To remove from the operation of the forest laws. 2 Bl. Comm. 416.

DISAGREEMENT. The refusal by a grantee, lessee, etc., to accept an estate, lease, etc., made to him; the annulling of a thing that had essence before. No estate can be vested in a person against his will. Consequently no one can become a grantee, etc., without his *agreement*. The law implies such an agreement until the contrary is shown, but his disagreement renders the grant, etc., inoperative. Wharton.

DISALT. To disable a person.

DISAPPROPRIATION. This is where the appropriation of a benefice is severed, either by the patron presenting a clerk or by the corporation which has the appropriation being dissolved. 1 Bl. Comm. 385.

DISAVOW. To repudiate the unauthorized acts of an agent; to deny the authority by which he assumed to act.

DISBAR. In England, to deprive a barrister permanently of the privileges of his position; it is analogous to striking an attorney off the rolls. In America, the word describes the act of a court in withdrawing from an attorney the right to practise at its bar.

DISBOCATIO. In old English law. A conversion of wood grounds into arable or pasture; an assarting. Cowell. See ASSART.

DISBURSEMENTS. Money expended by an executor, guardian, trustee, etc., for the benefit of the estate in his hands, or in connection with its administration.

The term is also used under the codes of civil procedure, to designate the expenditures necessarily made by a party in the progress of an action, aside from the fees of officers and court costs, which are allowed, *eo nomine*, together with costs.

DISCARCARE. In old English law. To discharge, to unload; as a vessel. *Carcare et discarcare;* to charge and discharge; to load and unload. Cowell.

DISCARGARE. In old European law. To discharge or unload, as a wagon. Spelman.

DISCEPTIO CAUSÆ. In Roman law. The argument of a cause by the counsel on both sides. Calvin.

DISCHARGE. The opposite of *charge;* hence to release; liberate; annul; unburden; disincumber.

In the law of contracts. To cancel or unloose the obligation of a contract; to make an agreement or contract null and inoperative. As a noun, the word means the act or instrument by which the binding force of a contract is terminated, irrespective of whether the contract is carried out to the full extent contemplated (in which case the discharge is the result of *performance*) or is broken off before complete execution.

Discharge is a generic term; its principal species are rescission, release, accord and satisfaction, performance, judgment, composition, bankruptcy, merger, (*q. v.*) Leake, Cont. 413.

As applied to demands, claims, rights of action, incumbrances, etc., to discharge the debt or claim is to extinguish it, to annul its obligatory force, to satisfy it. And here also the term is generic; thus a debt, a mortgage, a legacy, may be discharged by payment or performance, or by any act short of that, lawful in itself, which the creditor accepts as sufficient. To discharge a person is to liberate him from the binding force of an obligation, debt, or claim.

Discharge by operation of law is where the discharge takes place, whether it was intended by the parties or not; thus, if a creditor appoints his debtor his executor, the debt is discharged by operation of law, because the executor cannot have an action against himself. Co. Litt. 264*b*, note 1; Williams, Ex'rs, 1216; Chit. Cont. 714.

In civil practice. To discharge a rule, an order, an injunction, a certificate, process of execution, or in general any proceeding in a court, is to cancel or annul it, or to revoke it, or to refuse to confirm its original provisional force.

To discharge a jury is to relieve them from any further consideration of a cause. This is done when the continuance of the trial is, by any cause, rendered impossible; also when the jury, after deliberation, cannot agree on a verdict.

In equity practice. In the process of accounting before a master in chancery, the *discharge* is a statement of expenses and counter-claims brought in and filed, by way of set-off, by the accounting defendant; which follows the *charge* in order.

In criminal practice. The act by which a person in confinement, held on an accusation of some crime or misdemeanor, is set at liberty. The writing containing the order for his being so set at liberty is also called a "discharge."

In bankruptcy practice. The discharge of the bankrupt is the step which regularly follows the adjudication of bankruptcy and the administration of his estate. By it he is released from the obligation of all his debts which were or might be proved in the proceedings, so that they are no longer a charge upon him, and so that he may thereafter engage in business and acquire property without its being liable for the satisfaction of such former debts.

In maritime law. The unlading or unlivery of a cargo from a vessel. Story, J., 2 Sum. 589, 600.

DISCLAIMER. The repudiation or renunciation of a right or claim vested in a person or which he had formerly alleged to be his. The refusal, waiver, or denial of an estate or right offered to a person. The disavowal, denial, or renunciation of an interest, right, or property imputed to a person or alleged to be his. Also the declaration, or the instrument, by which such disclaimer is published.

Of estates. The act by which a party refuses to accept an estate which has been conveyed to him. Thus, a trustee is said to disclaim who releases to his fellow-trustees his estate, and relieves himself of the trust. 1 Hil. Real Prop. 354; 13 Conn. 83.

A renunciation or a denial by a tenant of his landlord's title, either by refusing to pay rent, denying any obligation to pay, or by setting up a title in himself or a third person, and this is a distinct ground of forfeiture of the lease or other tenancy, whether of land or tithe. See 16 Ch. Div. 730.

In pleading. A renunciation by the defendant of all claim to the subject of the demand made by the plaintiff's bill. Coop. Eq. Pl. 309; Mitf. Eq. Pl. 318.

In patent law. When the title and specifications of a patent do not agree, or when part of that which it covers is not strictly patentable, because neither new nor useful, the patentee is empowered, with leave of the court, to enter a disclaimer of any part of either the title or the specification, and the disclaimer is then deemed to be part of the letters patent or specification, so as to render them valid for the future. Johns. Pat. 151.

DISCLAMATION. In Scotch law. Disavowal of tenure; denial that one holds lands of another. Bell.

DISCOMMON. To deprive commonable lands of their commonable quality, by inclosing and appropriating or improving them.

DISCONTINUANCE. In practice. The termination of an action, in consequence of the plaintiff's omitting to continue the process or proceedings by proper entries on the record. 3 Bl. Comm. 296; 1 Tidd, Pr. 678; 2 Arch. Pr. K. B. 233.

In practice, a discontinuance is a chasm or gap left by neglecting to enter a continuance. By our practice, a neglect to enter a continuance, even in a defaulted action, by no means puts an end to it;

and such actions may always be brought forward. 56 N. H. 416.

The cessation of the proceedings in an action where the plaintiff voluntarily puts an end to it, either by giving notice in writing to the defendant before any step has been taken in the action subsequent to the answer, or at any other time by order of the court or a judge.

In practice, discontinuance and dismissal import the same thing, viz., that the cause is sent out of court. 48 Mo. 235.

In pleading. That technical interruption of the proceedings in an action which follows where a defendant does not answer the whole of the plaintiff's declaration, and the plaintiff omits to take judgment for the part unanswered. Steph. Pl. 216, 217.

DISCONTINUANCE OF AN ESTATE. The termination or suspension of an estate-tail, in consequence of the act of the tenant in tail, in conveying a larger estate in the land than he was by law entitled to do. 2 Bl. Comm. 275; 3 Bl. Comm. 171. An alienation made or suffered by tenant in tail, or by any that is seised in *auter droit*, whereby the issue in tail, or the heir or successor, or those in reversion or remainder, are driven to their action, and cannot enter. Co. Litt. 325*a*. The cesser of a seisin under an estate, and the acquisition of a seisin under a new and necessarily a wrongful title. Prest. Merg. c. ii.

Discontinuare nihil aliud significat quam intermittere, desuescere, interrumpere. Co. Litt. 325. To discontinue signifies nothing else than to intermit, to disuse, to interrupt.

DISCONTINUOUS EASEMENT. One the enjoyment of which can be had only by the interference of man, as rights of way, or a right to draw water; as distinguished from a *continuous* easement, which is one the enjoyment of which is or may be continual, without the necessity of any actual interference by man, as a water-spout, or a right of light or air. Washb. Easem. 13; Gale, Easem. 16; 21 N. Y. 505; 60 Mich. 252, 27 N. W. Rep. 509. This distinction is derived from the French law. See Code Civil, art. 688.

DISCONTINUOUS SERVITUDE. See DISCONTINUOUS EASEMENT.

DISCONVENABLE. L. Fr. Improper; unfit. Kelham.

DISCOUNT. In a general sense. An allowance or deduction made from a gross sum on any account whatever. In a more limited and technical sense. The taking of interest in advance.

By the language of the commercial world and the settled practice of banks, a discount by a bank means a drawback or deduction made upon its advances or loans of money, upon negotiable paper or other evidences of debt payable at a future day, which are transferred to the bank. 8 Wheat. 338; 15 Ohio St. 87.

Although the discounting of notes or bills, in its most comprehensive sense, may mean lending money and taking notes in payment, yet, in its more ordinary sense, the discounting of notes or bills means advancing a consideration for a bill or note, deducting or discounting the interest which will accrue for the time the note has to run. 13 Conn. 248.

Discounting by a bank means lending money upon a note, and deducting the interest or premium in advance. 17 N. Y. 507, 515; 48 Mo. 189.

The ordinary meaning of the term "to discount" is to take interest in advance, and in banking is a mode of loaning money. It is the advance of money not due till some future period, less the interest which would be due thereon when payable. 42 Md. 592.

Discount, as we have seen, is the difference between the price and the amount of the debt, the evidence of which is transferred. That difference represents interest charged, being at the same rate, according to which the price paid, if invested until the maturity of the debt, will just produce its amount. 104 U. S. 276.

Discounting a note and buying it are not identical in meaning, the latter expression being used to denote the transaction when the seller does not indorse the note, and is not accountable for it. 23 Minn. 206.

In practice. A set-off or defalcation in an action. Vin. Abr. "Discount." But see 1 Metc. (Ky.) 597.

DISCOUNT BROKER. A bill broker; one who discounts bills of exchange and promissory notes, and advances money on securities.

DISCOVERT. Not married; not subject to the disabilities of coverture. It applies equally to a maid and a widow.

DISCOVERY. Invention; finding out. The finding of an island or country not previously known to geographers.

In patent law. The finding out some substance, mechanical device, improvement, or application, not previously known.

Discovery, as used in the patent laws, depends upon invention. Every invention may, in a certain sense, embrace more or less of discovery, for it must always include something that is new; but it by no means follows that every discovery is an invention. 5 Blatchf. 121.

Also used of the disclosure by a bankrupt of his property for the benefit of creditors.

In practice. The disclosure by the defendant of facts, titles, documents, or other things which are in his exclusive knowledge or possession, and which are necessary to the party seeking the discovery as a part of a cause or action pending or to be brought in another court, or as evidence of his rights or title in such proceeding.

DISCOVERY, BILL OF. In equity pleading. A bill for the discovery of facts resting in the knowledge of the defendant, or of deeds or writings, or other things in his custody or power; but seeking no relief in consequence of the discovery, though it may pray for a stay of proceedings at law till the discovery is made. Story, Eq. Pl. §§ 311, 312, and notes; Mitf. Eq. Pl. 53.

DISCREDIT. To destroy or impair the credibility of a person; to impeach; to lessen the degree of credit to be accorded to a witness or document, as by impugning the veracity of the one or the genuineness of the other; to disparage or weaken the reliance upon the testimony of a witness, or upon documentary evidence, by any means whatever.

DISCREPANCY. A difference between two things which ought to be identical, as between one writing and another; a variance, (*q. v.*)

Discretio est discernere per legem quid sit justum. 10 Coke, 140. Discretion is to know through law what is just.

DISCRETION. A liberty or privilege allowed to a judge, within the confines of right and justice, but independent of narrow and unbending rules of positive law, to decide and act in accordance with what is fair, equitable, and wholesome, as determined upon the peculiar circumstances of the case, and as discerned by his personal wisdom and experience, guided by the spirit, principles, and analogies of the law.

When applied to public functionaries, discretion means a power or right conferred upon them by law of acting officially in certain circumstances, according to the dictates of their own judgment and conscience, uncontrolled by the judgment or conscience of others. This discretion undoubtedly is to some extent regulated by usage, or, if the term is preferred, by fixed principles. But by this is to be understood nothing more than that the same court cannot, consistently with its own dignity, and with its character and duty of administering impartial justice, decide in different ways two cases in every respect exactly alike. The question of fact whether the two cases are alike in every color, circumstance, and feature is of necessity to be submitted to the judgment of some tribunal. 18 Wend. 79, 99.

Lord Coke defines judicial discretion to be "*discernere per legem quid sit justum*," to see what would be just according to the laws in the premises. It does not mean a wild self-willfulness, which may prompt to any and every act; but this judicial discretion is guided by the law, (see what the law declares upon a certain statement of facts, and then decide in accordance with the law,) so as to do substantial equity and justice. 13 Mo. 543.

True, it is a matter of discretion; but then the discretion is not willful or arbitrary, but legal. And, although its exercise be not purely a matter of law, yet it "*involves* a matter of law or legal inference," in the language of the Code, and an appeal will lie. 70 N. C. 171.

In criminal law and the law of torts, it means the capacity to distinguish between what is right and wrong, lawful or unlawful, wise or foolish, sufficiently to render one amenable and responsible for his acts.

DISCRETIONARY TRUSTS. Such as are not marked out on fixed lines, but allow a certain amount of discretion in their exercise. Those which cannot be duly administered without the application of a certain degree of prudence and judgment.

DISCUSSION. In the civil law A proceeding, at the instance of a surety, by which the creditor is obliged to exhaust the property of the principal debtor, towards the satisfaction of the debt, before having recourse to the surety; and this right of the surety is termed the "benefit of discussion." Civil Code La. art. 3045, et seq.

In Scotch law. The ranking of the proper order in which heirs are liable to satisfy the debts of the deceased. Bell.

DISEASE. In construing a policy of life insurance, it is generally true that, before any temporary ailment can be called a "disease," it must be such as to indicate a vice in the constitution, or be so serious as to have some bearing upon general health and the continuance of life, or such as, according to common understanding, would be called a "disease." 70 N. Y. 77.

DISENTAILING DEED. In English law. An enrolled assurance barring an entail, pursuant to 3 & 4 Wm. IV. c. 74.

DISFRANCHISE. To deprive of the rights and privileges of a free citizen; to deprive of chartered rights and immunities; to deprive of any franchise, as of the right of voting in elections, etc. Webster.

DISFRANCHISEMENT. The act of disfranchising. The act of depriving a member of a corporation of his right as such, by expulsion. 1 Bouv. Inst. no. 192.

It differs from amotion, (*q. v.*) which is applicable to the removal of an officer from office, leaving him his rights as a member. Willcock, Mun. Corp. no. 708; Ang. & A. Corp. 237.

DISGAVEL. In English law. To deprive lands of that principal quality of gavelkind tenure by which they descend equally among all the sons of the tenant. 2 Wood. Lect. 76; 2 Bl. Comm. 85.

DISGRACE. Ignominy; shame; dishonor. No witness is required to disgrace himself. 13 How. State Tr. 17, 334.

DISGRADING. In old English law. The depriving of an order or dignity.

DISGUISE. A counterfeit habit; a dress intended to conceal the person who wears it. Webster.

Anything worn upon the person with the intention of so altering the wearer's appearance that he shall not be recognized by those familiar with him, or that he shall be taken for another person.

A person lying in ambush, or concealed behind bushes, is not in "disguise," within the meaning of a statute declaring the county liable in damages to the next of kin of any one murdered by persons in disguise. 46 Ala. 118, 142.

DISHERISON. Disinheritance; depriving one of an inheritance. Obsolete.

DISHONOR. In mercantile law and usage. To refuse or decline to accept a bill of exchange, or to refuse or neglect to pay a bill or note at maturity.

A negotiable instrument is dishonored when it is either not paid or not accepted, according to its tenor, on presentment for that purpose, or without presentment, where that is excused. Civil Code Cal. § 3141.

DISINCARCERATE. To set at liberty, to free from prison.

DISINHERISON. In the civil law. The act of depriving a forced heir of the inheritance which the law gives him.

DISINHERITANCE. The act by which the owner of an estate deprives a person of the right to inherit the same, who would otherwise be his heir.

DISINTERESTED. Not concerned, in respect to possible gain or loss, in the result of the pending proceeding.

DISINTERESTED WITNESS. One who has no interest in the cause or matter in issue, and who is lawfully competent to testify.

DISJUNCTIM. Lat. In the civil law. Separately; severally. The opposite of *conjunctim*, (*q. v.*) Inst. 2, 20, 8.

DISJUNCTIVE ALLEGATION. A statement in a pleading or indictment which expresses or charges a thing alternatively, with the conjunction "or;" for instance, an averment that defendant "murdered, or caused to be murdered," etc., would be of this character.

DISJUNCTIVE TERM. One which is placed between two contraries, by the affirming of one of which the other is taken away; it is usually expressed by the word "or."

DISMES. Tenths; tithes, (*q. v.*) The original form of "dime," the name of the American coin.

DISMISS. To send away; to discharge; to cause to be removed. To dismiss an action or suit is to send it out of court without any further consideration or hearing.

DISMORTGAGE. To redeem from mortgage.

DISORDER. Turbulent or riotous behavior; immoral or indecent conduct. The breach of the public decorum and morality.

DISORDERLY HOUSE. In criminal law. A house the inmates of which behave so badly as to become a nuisance to the neighborhood. It has a wide meaning, and includes bawdy houses, common gaming houses, and places of a like character. 1 Bish. Crim. Law, § 1106; 2 Cranch, C. C. 675.

DISORDERLY PERSONS. Such as are dangerous or hurtful to the public peace and welfare by reason of their misconduct or vicious habits, and are therefore amenable to police regulation. The phrase is chiefly used in statutes, and the scope of the term depends on local regulations. See 4 Bl. Comm. 169.

DISPARAGARE. In old English law. To bring together those that are unequal, (*dispares conferre;*) to connect in an indecorous and unworthy manner; to connect in marriage those that are unequal in blood and parentage.

DISPARAGATIO. In old English law. Disparagement. *Hæredes maritentur absque* *disparagatione*, heirs shall be married without disparagement. *Magna Charta*, (9 Hen. III.) c. 6.

DISPARAGATION. L. Fr. Disparagement; the matching an heir, etc., in marriage, under his or her degree or condition, or against the rules of decency. Kelham.

DISPARAGE. To connect unequally; to match unsuitably.

DISPARAGEMENT. In old English law. An injury by union or comparison with some person or thing of inferior rank or excellence.

Marriage without *disparagement* was marriage to one of suitable rank and character. 2 Bl. Comm. 70; Co. Litt. 82*b*.

DISPARAGIUM. In old Scotch law. Inequality in blood, honor, dignity, or otherwise. Skene de Verb. Sign.

Disparata non debent jungi. Things unlike ought not to be joined. Jenk. Cent. 24, marg.

DISPARK. To dissolve a park. Cro. Car. 59. To convert it into ordinary ground.

DISPATCH or DESPATCH. A message, letter, or order sent with speed on affairs of state; a telegraphic message.

DISPAUPER. When a person, by reason of his poverty, is admitted to sue *in formâ pauperis*, and afterwards, before the suit be ended, acquires any lands, or personal estate, or is guilty of anything whereby he is liable to have this privilege taken from him, then he loses the right to sue *in formâ pauperis*, and is said to be dispaupered. Wharton.

Dispensatio est mali prohibiti provida relaxatio, utilitate seu necessitate pensata; et est de jure domino regi concessa, propter impossibilitatem prævidendi de omnibus particularibus. A dispensation is the provident relaxation of a *malum prohibitum* weighed from utility or necessity; and it is conceded by law to the king on account of the impossibility of foreknowledge concerning all particulars. 10 Coke, 88.

Dispensatio est vulnus, quod vulnerat jus commune. A dispensation is a wound, which wounds common law. Dav. Ir. K. B. 69.

DISPENSATION. An exemption from some laws; a permission to do something forbidden; an allowance to omit something commanded; the canonistic name for a license. Wharton.

A relaxation of law for the benefit or advantage of an individual. In the United States, no power exists, except in the legislature, to dispense with law; and then it is not so much a dispensation as a change of the law. Bouvier.

DISPERSONARE. To scandalize or disparage. Blount.

DISPLACE. This term, as used in shipping articles, means "disrate," and does not import authority of the master to discharge a second mate, notwithstanding a usage in the whaling trade never to disrate an officer to a seaman. 103 Mass. 68.

DISPONE. In Scotch law. To grant or convey. A technical word essential to the conveyance of heritable property, and for which no equivalent is accepted, however clear may be the meaning of the party. Paters. Comp.

DISPOSE. To alienate or direct the ownership of property, as disposition by will. 42 N. Y. 79. Used also of the determination of suits. 13 Wall. 664. Called a word of large extent. Freem. 177.

DISPOSING CAPACITY OR MIND. These are alternative or synonymous phrases in the law of wills for "sound mind," and "testamentary capacity," (*q. v.*)

DISPOSITION. In Scotch law. A deed of alienation by which a right to property is conveyed. Bell.

DISPOSITIVE FACTS. Such as produce or bring about the origination, transfer, or extinction of rights. They are either *investitive*, those by means of which a right comes into existence, *divestitive*, those through which it terminates, or *translative*, those through which it passes from one person to another.

DISPOSSESSION. Ouster; a wrong that carries with it the amotion of possession. An act whereby the wrong-doer gets the actual occupation of the land or hereditament. It includes abatement, intrusion, disseisin, discontinuance, deforcement. 3 Bl. Comm. 167.

DISPUNISHABLE. In old English law. Not answerable. Co. Litt. 27*b*. 53. 1 Steph. Comm. 245. Not punishable. "This murder is dispunishable." 1 Leon. 270.

DISPUTABLE PRESUMPTION. A presumption of law, which may be rebutted or disproved. Best, Pres. § 25.

DISPUTATIO FORI. In the civil law. Discussion or argument before a court. Mackeld. Rom. Law, § 38; Dig. 1, 2, 2, 5.

DISRATIONARE, or DIRATIONARE. To justify; to clear one's self of a fault; to traverse an indictment; to disprove. Enc. Lond.

DISSASINA. In old Scotch law. Disseisin; dispossession. Skene.

DISSECTION. The anatomical examination of a dead body.

DISSEISE. To dispossess; to deprive.

DISSEISEE. One who is wrongfully put out of possession of his lands; one who is disseised.

DISSEISIN. Dispossession; a deprivation of possession; a privation of seisin; a usurpation of the right of seisin and possession, and an exercise of such powers and privileges of ownership as to keep out or displace him to whom these rightfully belong. 3 Washb. Real Prop. 125.

It is a wrongful putting out of him that is seised of the freehold, not, as in *abatement* or *intrusion*, a wrongful entry, where the possession was vacant, but an attack upon him who is in actual possession, and turning him out. It is an ouster from a freehold in deed, as abatement and intrusion are ousters in law. 3 Steph. Comm. 386.

When one man invades the possession of another, and by force or surprise turns him out of the occupation of his lands, this is termed a "disseisin," being a deprivation of that actual seisin or corporal possession of the freehold which the tenant before enjoyed. In other words, a disseisin is said to be when one enters intending to usurp the possession, and to oust another from the freehold. To constitute an entry a disseisin, there must be an ouster of the freehold, either by taking the profits or by claiming the inheritance. Brown.

According to the modern authorities, there seems to be no legal difference between the words "seisin" and "possession," although there is a difference between the words "disseisin" and "dispossession;" the former meaning an estate gained by wrong and injury, whereas the latter may be by right or by wrong; the former denoting an ouster of the disseisee, or some act equivalent to it, whereas by the latter no such act is implied. 6 Metc. (Mass.) 439.

Equitable disseisin is where a person is wrongfully deprived of the equitable seisin of land, *e. g.*, of the rents and profits. 2 Meriv. 171; 2 Jac. & W. 166.

Disseisin by election is where a person alleges or admits himself to be disseised when he has not really been so.

Disseisinam satis facit, qui uti non permittit possessorem, vel minus commode, licet omnino non expellat. Co. Litt. 331. He makes disseisin enough who does not permit the possessor to enjoy, or makes his enjoyment less beneficial, although he does not expel him altogether.

DISSEISITRIX. A female disseisor; a disseisoress. Fleta, lib. 4, c. 12, § 4.

DISSEISOR. One who puts another out of the possession of his lands wrongfully.

DISSEISORESS. A woman who unlawfully puts another out of his land.

DISSENT. Contrariety of opinion; refusal to agree with something already stated or adjudged or to an act previously performed.

The term is most commonly used in American law to denote the explicit disagreement of one or more judges of a court with the decision passed by the majority upon a case before them. In such event, the non-concurring judge is reported as "dissenting," and sometimes files a "dissenting opinion."

DISSENTERS. Protestant seceders from the established church of England. They are of many denominations, principally Presbyterians, Independents, Methodists, and Baptists; but, as to church government, the Baptists are Independents.

DISSENTING OPINION. The opinion in which a judge announces his dissent from the conclusions held by the majority of the court, and expounds his own views.

DISSIGNARE. In old law. To break open a seal. Whishaw.

Dissimilium dissimilis est ratio. Co. Litt. 191. Of dissimilars the rule is dissimilar.

Dissimulatione tollitur injuria. An injury is extinguished by the forgiveness or reconcilement of the party injured. Ersk. Inst. 4, 4, 108.

DISSOLUTION. **In contracts.** The dissolution of a contract is the cancellation or abrogation of it by the parties themselves, with the effect of annulling the binding force of the agreement, and restoring each party to his original rights. In this sense it is frequently used in the phrase "dissolution of a partnership."

Of corporations. The dissolution of a corporation is the termination of its existence as a body politic. This may take place in several ways; as by act of the legislature, where that is constitutional; by surrender or forfeiture of its charter; by expiration of its charter by lapse of time; by proceedings for winding it up under the law; by loss of all its members or their reduction below the statutory limit.

In practice. The act of rendering a legal proceeding null, abrogating or revoking it; unloosing its constraining force; as when an injunction is dissolved by the court.

DISSOLUTION OF PARLIAMENT. The crown may dissolve parliament either in person or by proclamation; the dissolution is usually by proclamation, after a prorogation. No parliament may last for a longer period than seven years. Septennial Act, 1 Geo. I. c. 38. Under 6 Anne, c. 37, upon a demise of the crown, parliament became *ipso facto* dissolved six months afterwards, but under the Reform Act, 1867, its continuance is now nowise affected by such demise. May, Parl. Pr. (6th Ed.) 48. Brown.

DISSOLVE. To terminate; abrogate; cancel; annul; disintegrate. To release or unloose the binding force of anything. As to "dissolve a corporation," to "dissolve an injunction."

The phrase "dissolving a corporation" is sometimes used as synonymous with annulling the charter or terminating the existence of the corporation, and sometimes as meaning merely a judicial act which alienates the property and suspends the business of the corporation, without terminating its existence. A corporation may, for certain purposes, be considered as dissolved so far as to be incapable of doing injury to the public, while it yet retains vitality so far as essential for the protection of the rights of others. 1 Holmes, 104.

DISSUADE. In criminal law. To advise and procure a person not to do an act.

To dissuade a witness from giving evidence against a person indicted is an indictable offense at common law. Hawk. P. C. b. 1, c. 21, § 15.

DISTILLER. Every person who produces distilled spirits, or who brews or makes mash, wort, or wash, fit for distillation or for the production of spirits, or who, by any process of evaporization, separates alcoholic spirit from any fermented substance, or who, making or keeping mash, wort, or wash, has also in his possession or use a still, shall be regarded as a distiller. Rev. St. U. S. § 3247. See 16 Blatchf. 547; 2 Ben. 438.

DISTILLERY. The strict meaning of "distillery" is a place or building where alcoholic liquors are distilled or manufactured; not every building where the process of distillation is used. 45 N. Y. 499.

DISTINCTE ET APERTE. In old English practice. Distinctly and openly. Formal words in writs of error, referring to the return required to be made to them. Reg. Orig. 17.

Distinguenda sunt tempora. The time is to be considered. 1 Coke, 16*a;* 2 Pick. 327; 14 N. Y. 380, 393.

Distinguenda sunt tempora; aliud est facere, aliud perficere. Times must be distinguished; it is one thing to do, another to perfect. 3 Leon. 243; Branch, Princ.

Distinguenda sunt tempora; distingue tempora et concordabis leges. Times are to be distinguished; distinguish times, and you will harmonize laws. 1 Coke, 24. A maxim applied to the construction of statutes.

DISTINGUISH. To point out an essential difference; to prove a case cited as applicable, inapplicable.

DISTRACTED PERSON. A term used in the statutes of Illinois (Rev. Laws Ill. 1833, p. 332) and New Hampshire (Dig. N. H. Laws, 1830, p. 339) to express a state of insanity.

DISTRACTIO. In the civil law. The sale of a pledge by a debtor. The appropriation of the property of a ward by a guardian. Calvin.

DISTRAHERE. To sell; to draw apart; to dissolve a contract; to divorce. Calvin.

DISTRAIN. To take as a pledge property of another, and keep the same until he performs his obligation or until the property is replevied by the sheriff. It was used to secure an appearance in court, payment of rent, performance of services, etc. 3 Bl. Comm. 231; Fitzh. Nat. Brev. 32, B, C, 223.

Distress is now generally resorted to for the purpose of enforcing the payment of rent, taxes, or other duties.

DISTRAINER, or DISTRAINOR. He who seizes a distress.

DISTRAINT. Seizure.

DISTRESS. The taking a personal chattel out of the possession of a wrong-doer into the custody of the party injured, to procure a satisfaction for a wrong committed; as for non-payment of rent, or injury done by cattle. 3 Bl. Comm. 6, 7; Co. Litt. 47. The taking of beasts or other personal property by way of pledge, to enforce the performance of something due from the party distrained upon. 3 Bl. Comm. 231. The taking of a defendant's goods, in order to compel an appearance in court. Id. 280; 3 Steph. Comm. 361, 363.

DISTRESS INFINITE. One that has no bounds with regard to its quantity, and may be repeated from time to time, until the stubbornness of the party is conquered. Such are distresses for fealty or suit of court, and for compelling jurors to attend. 3 Bl. Comm. 231.

DISTRIBUTEE. Distributee is admissible to denote one of the persons who are entitled, under the statute of distributions, to the personal estate of one who is dead intestate. 9 Ired. 278.

DISTRIBUTION. In practice. The apportionment and division, under authority of a court, of the remainder of the estate of an intestate, after payment of the debts and charges, among those who are legally entitled to share in the same.

DISTRIBUTIVE FINDING OF THE ISSUE. The jury are bound to give their verdict for that party who, upon the evidence, appears to them to have succeeded in establishing his side of the issue. But there are cases in which an issue may be found distributively, *i. e.*, in part for plaintiff, and in part for defendant. Thus, in an action for goods sold and work done, if the defendant pleaded that he never was indebted, on which issue was joined, a verdict might be found for the plaintiff as to the goods, and for the defendant as to the work. Steph. Pl. (7th Ed.) 77*d*.

DISTRIBUTIVE JUSTICE. See JUSTICE.

DISTRICT. One of the portions into which an entire state or country may be divided, for judicial, political, or administrative purposes.

The United States are divided into judicial districts, in each of which is established a district court. They are also divided into election districts, collection districts, etc.

The circuit or territory within which a person may be compelled to appear. Cowell. Circuit of authority; province. Enc. Lond.

DISTRICT ATTORNEY. The prosecuting officer of the United States government in each of the federal judicial districts. Also, under the state governments, the prosecuting officer who represents the state in each of its judicial districts. In some states, where the territory is divided, for judicial purposes, into sections called by some other name than "districts," the same officer is denominated "county attorney" or "state's attorney."

DISTRICT CLERK. The clerk of a district court of either a state or the United States.

DISTRICT COURTS. Courts of the United States, each having territorial jurisdiction over a *district*, which may include a whole state or only part of it. Each of these courts is presided over by one judge, who must reside within the district. These courts have original jurisdiction over all admiralty and maritime causes and all proceedings in bankruptcy, and over all penal and criminal matters cognizable under the laws of the United States, exclusive jurisdiction over which is not vested either in the supreme or circuit courts.

Inferior courts of record in California, Connecticut, Iowa, Kansas, Louisiana, Minnesota, Nebraska, Nevada, Ohio, and Texas are also called "district courts." Their jurisdiction is for the most part similar to that of county courts, (*q. v.*)

DISTRICT JUDGE. The judge of a United States district court; also, in some states, the judge of a district court of the state.

DISTRICT OF COLUMBIA. A territory situated on the Potomac river, and being the seat of government of the United States. It was originally ten miles square, and was composed of portions of Maryland and Virginia ceded by those states to the United States; but in 1846 the tract coming from Virginia was retroceded. Legally it is neither a state nor a territory, but is made subject, by the constitution, to the exclusive jurisdiction of congress.

DISTRICT PARISHES. Ecclesiastical divisions of parishes in England, for all purposes of worship, and for the celebration of marriages, christenings, churchings, and burials, formed at the instance of the queen's commissioners for building new churches. See 3 Steph. Comm. 744.

DISTRICT REGISTRY. By the English judicature act, 1873, § 60, it is provided that to facilitate proceedings in country districts the crown may, from time to time, by order in council, create district registries, and appoint district registrars for the purpose of issuing writs of summons, and for other purposes. Documents sealed in any such district registry shall be received in evidence without further proof, (section 61;) and the district registrars may administer oaths or do other things as provided by rules or a special order of the court, (section 62.) Power, however, is given to a judge to remove proceedings from a district registry to the office of the high court. Section 65. By order in council of 12th of August, 1875, a number of district registries have been established in the places mentioned in that order; and the prothonotaries in Liverpool, Manchester, and Preston, the district registrar of the court of admiralty at Liverpool, and the county court registrars in the other places named, have been appointed district registrars. Wharton.

DISTRICTIO. A distress; a distraint. Cowell.

DISTRINGAS. In English practice. A writ directed to the sheriff of the county in which a defendant resides, or has any goods or chattels, commanding him to *distrain* upon the goods and chattels of the defendant for forty shillings, in order to compel his appearance. 3 Steph. Comm. 567. This writ issues in cases where it is found impracticable to get at the defendant personally, so as to serve a summons upon him. Id.

A *distringas* is also used in equity, as the first process to compel the appearance of a corporation aggregate. St. 11 Geo. IV. and 1 Wm. IV. c. 36.

A form of execution in the actions of detinue and assise of nuisance. Brooke, Abr. pl. 26; 1 Rawle, 44.

DISTRINGAS JURATORES. A writ commanding the sheriff to have the bodies of the jurors, or to *distrain* them by their lands and goods, that they may appear upon the day appointed. 3 Bl. Comm. 354. It issues at the same time with the *venire*, though in theory afterwards, founded on the supposed neglect of the juror to attend. 3 Steph. Comm. 590.

DISTRINGAS NUPER VICE COMITEM. A writ to distrain the goods of one who lately filled the office of sheriff, to compel him to do some act which he ought to have done before leaving the office; as to bring in the body of a defendant, or to sell goods attached under a *fi. fa.*

DISTRINGAS VICECOMITEM. A writ of *distringas*, directed to the coroner, may be issued against a sheriff if he neglects to execute a writ of *venditioni exponas*. Arch. Pr. 584.

DISTRINGERE. In feudal and old English law. To distrain; to coerce or compel. Spelman; Calvin.

DISTURBANCE. A wrong done to an incorporeal hereditament by hindering or disquieting the owner in the enjoyment of it. Finch, 187; 3 Bl. Comm. 235.

DISTURBANCE OF COMMON. The doing any act by which the right of another to his common is incommoded or diminished; as where one who has no right of common puts his cattle into the land, or where one who has a right of common puts in cattle which are not commonable, or surcharges the common; or where the owner of the land, or other person, incloses or otherwise obstructs it. 3 Bl. Comm. 237–241; 3 Steph. Comm. 511, 512.

DISTURBANCE OF FRANCHISE. The disturbing or incommoding a man in the lawful exercise of his franchise, whereby the profits arising from it are diminished. 3 Bl. Comm. 236; 3 Steph. Comm. 510; 2 Crabb, Real Prop. p. 1074, § 2472*a*.

DISTURBANCE OF PATRONAGE. The hindrance or obstruction of a patron from presenting his clerk to a benefice. 3 Bl. Comm. 242; 3 Steph. Comm. 514.

DISTURBANCE OF PUBLIC WORSHIP. Any acts or conduct which interfere with the peace and good order of an assembly of persons lawfully met together for religious exercises.

DISTURBANCE OF TENURE. In the law of tenure, disturbance is where a stranger, by menaces, force, persuasion, or otherwise, causes a tenant to leave his tenancy; this disturbance of tenure is an injury to the lord for which an action will lie. 3 Steph. Comm. 414.

DISTURBANCE OF WAYS. This happens where a person who has a right of way over another's ground by grant or prescription is obstructed by inclosures or other obstacles, or by plowing across it, by which means he cannot enjoy his right of way, or at least in so commodious a manner as he might have done. 3 Bl. Comm. 241.

DISTURBER. If a bishop refuse or neglect to examine or admit a patron's clerk, without reason assigned or notice given, he is styled a "disturber" by the law, and shall not have any title to present by lapse; for no man shall take advantage of his own wrong. 2 Bl. Comm. 278.

DITCH. The words "ditch" and "drain" have no technical or exact meaning. They both may mean a hollow space in the ground, natural or artificial, where water is collected or passes off. 5 Gray, 64.

DITES OUSTER. L. Fr. Say over. The form of awarding a *respondeas ouster*, in the Year Books. M. 6 Edw. III. 49.

DITTAY. In Scotch law. A technical term in civil law, signifying the matter of charge or ground of indictment against a person accused of crime. *Taking up dittay* is obtaining informations and presentments of crime in order to trial. Skene, de Verb. Sign.; Bell.

DIVERSION. A turning aside or altering the natural course of a thing. The term is chiefly applied to the unauthorized changing the course of a water-course to the prejudice of a lower proprietor.

DIVERSITE DES COURTS. A treatise on courts and their jurisdiction, written in French in the reign of Edward III. as is supposed, and by some attributed to Fitzherbert. It was first printed in 1525, and again in 1534. Crabb, Eng. Law, 330, 483.

DIVERSITY. In criminal pleading. A plea by the prisoner in bar of execution, alleging that he is not the same who was attainted, upon which a jury is immediately impaneled to try the collateral issue thus raised, viz., the identity of the person, and not whether he is guilty or innocent, for that has been already decided. 4 Bl. Comm. 396.

DIVERSO INTUITU. Lat. With a different view, purpose, or design; in a different view or point of view; by a different course or process. 1 W. Bl. 89; 4 Kent, Comm. 211, note.

DIVERSORIUM. In old English law. A lodging or inn. Townsh. Pl. 38.

DIVERT. To turn aside; to turn out of the way; to alter the course of things. Usually applied to water-courses. Ang. Water-Courses, § 97, et seq. Sometimes to roads. 8 East, 394.

DIVES. In the practice of the English chancery division, "dives costs" are costs on the ordinary scale, as opposed to the costs formerly allowed to a successful pauper suing or defending *in formâ pauperis*, and which consisted only of his costs out of pocket. Daniell, Ch. Pr. 43.

DIVEST. Equivalent to devest, (*q. v.*)

DIVESTITIVE FACT. A fact by means of which a right is divested, terminated, or extinguished; as the right of a tenant terminates with the expiration of his lease, and the right of a creditor is at an end when his debt has been paid. Holl. Jur. 132.

Divide et impera, cum radix et vertex imperii in obedientium consensu rata sunt. 4 Inst. 35. Divide and govern, since the foundation and crown of empire are established in the consent of the obedient.

DIVIDEND. A fund to be divided. The share allotted to each of several persons entitled to share in a division of profits or property. Thus, dividend may denote a fund set apart by a corporation out of its profits, to be apportioned among the shareholders, or the proportional amount falling to each. In bankruptcy or insolvency practice, a dividend is a proportional payment to the creditors out of the insolvent estate.

In old English law. The term denotes one part of an indenture, (*q. v.*)

DIVIDENDA. In old records. An indenture; one counterpart of an indenture.

DIVINARE. Lat. To divine; to conjecture or guess; to foretell. *Divinatio*, a conjecturing or guessing.

Divinatio, non interpretatio est, quæ omnino recedit a litera. That is guessing, not interpretation, which altogether departs from the letter. Bac. Max. 18, (in reg. 3,) citing Yearb. 3 Hen. VI. 20.

DIVINE SERVICE. Divine service was the name of a feudal tenure, by which the tenants were obliged to do some special divine services in certain; as to sing so many masses, to distribute such a sum in alms, and the like. (2 Bl. Comm. 102; 1 Steph. Comm. 227.) It differed from tenure in *frankalmoign*, in this: that, in case of the tenure by divine service, the lord of whom the lands were holden might distrain for its non-performance, whereas, in case of *frankalmoign*, the lord has no remedy by distraint for neglect of the service, but merely a right of complaint to the visitor to correct it. Mozley & Whitley.

DIVISA. In old English law. A device, award, or decree; also a devise; also bounds or limits of division of a parish or farm, etc. Cowell. Also a court held on the boundary, in order to settle disputes of the tenants.

Divisibilis est semper divisibilis. A thing divisible may be forever divided.

DIVISIBLE. That which is susceptible of being divided.

A contract cannot, in general, be divided in such a manner that an action may be brought, or a right accrue, on a part of it. 2 Pa. St. 454.

DIVISIM. In old English law. Severally; separately. Bract. fol. 47.

DIVISION. In English law. One of the smaller subdivisions of a county. Used in Lincolnshire as synonymous with "riding" in Yorkshire.

DIVISION OF OPINION. In the practice of appellate courts, this term denotes such a disagreement among the judges that there is not a majority in favor of any one view, and hence no decision can be rendered on the case. But it sometimes also denotes a division into two classes, one of which may comprise a majority of the judges; as when we speak of a decision having proceeded from a "divided court."

DIVISIONAL COURTS. Courts in England, consisting of two or (in special cases) more judges of the high court of justice, sitting to transact certain kinds of business which cannot be disposed of by one judge.

DIVISUM IMPERIUM. Lat. A divided jurisdiction. Applied, *e. g.*, to the jurisdiction of courts of common law and equity over the same subject. 1 Kent, Comm. 366; 4 Steph. Comm. 9.

DIVORCE. The legal separation of man and wife, effected, for cause, by the judgment of a court, and either totally dissolving the marriage relation, or suspending its effects so far as concerns the cohabitation of the parties.

The dissolution is termed "divorce from the bond of matrimony," or, in the Latin form of the expression, "*a vinculo matrimonii;*" the suspension, "divorce from bed and board," "*a mensa et thoro.*" The former divorce puts an end to the marriage; the latter leaves it in full force. 2 Bish. Mar. & Div. § 225.

The term "divorce" is now applied, in England, both to decrees of nullity and decrees of dissolution of marriage, while in America it is used only in cases of divorce *a mensa* or *a vinculo*, a decree of nullity of marriage being granted for the causes for which a divorce *a vinculo* was formerly obtainable in England.

DIVORCE A MENSA ET THORO. A divorce from table and bed, or from bed and board. A partial or qualified divorce, by which the parties are separated and forbidden to live or cohabit together, without affecting the marriage itself. 1 Bl. Comm. 440; 3 Bl. Comm. 94; 2 Steph. Comm. 311; 2 Bish. Mar. & Div. § 225.

DIVORCE A VINCULO MATRIMONII. A divorce from the bond of marriage. A total divorce of husband and wife, dissolving the marriage tie, and releasing the parties wholly from their matrimonial obligations. 1 Bl. Comm. 440; 2 Steph. Comm. 310, 311; 2 Bish. Mar. & Div. § 225.

Divortium dicitur a divertendo, quia vir divertitur ab uxore. Co. Litt. 235. Divorce is called from *divertendo*, because a man is diverted from his wife.

DIXIEME. Fr. Tenth; the tenth part. Ord. Mar. liv. 1, tit. 1, art. 9.

In old French law. An income tax payable to the crown. Steph. Lect. 359.

DO. Lat. I give. The ancient and aptest word of feoffment and of gift. 2 Bl. Comm. 310, 316; Co. Litt. 9.

DO, DICO, ADDICO. Lat. I give, I say, I adjudge. Three words used in the Roman law, to express the extent of the civil jurisdiction of the prætor. *Do* denoted that he *gave* or granted actions, exceptions, and judices; *dico*, that he pronounced judgment; *addico*, that he adjudged the controverted property, or the goods of the debtor, etc., to the plaintiff. Mackeld. Rom. Law, § 39.

DO, LEGO. Lat. I give, I bequeath; or I give and bequeath. The formal words of making a bequest or legacy, in the Roman law. *Titio et Seio hominem Stichum do, lego*, I give and bequeath to Titius and Seius my man Stichus. Inst. 2, 20, 8, 30, 31. The expression is literally retained in modern wills.

DO UT DES. Lat. I give that you may give; I give [you] that you may give [me.] A formula in the civil law, constituting a general division under which those contracts (termed "innominate") were classed in which something was *given* by one party as a consideration for something *given* by the other. Dig. 19, 4; Id. 19, 5, 5; 2 Bl. Comm. 444.

DO UT FACIAS. Lat. I give that you may do; I give [you] that you may do or make [for me.] A formula in the civil law, under which those contracts were classed in which one party *gave* or agreed to give money, in consideration the other party *did* or performed certain work. Dig. 19, 5, 5; 2 Bl. Comm. 444.

In this and the foregoing phrase, the conjunction "*ut*" is not to be taken as the technical means of expressing a consideration. In the Roman usage, this word imported a *modus*, that is, a qualification; while a consideration (*causa*) was more aptly expressed by the word "*quia.*"

DOCK, *v.* To curtail or diminish, as to dock an entail.

DOCK, *n.* The cage or inclosed space in a criminal court where prisoners stand when brought in for trial.

The space, in a river or harbor, inclosed between two wharves. 17 How. 434.

DOCK-MASTER. An officer invested with powers within the docks, and a certain distance therefrom, to direct the mooring and removing of ships, so as to prevent obstruction to the dock entrances. Mozley & Whitley.

DOCK WARRANT. In English law. A warrant given by dock-owners to the owner of merchandise imported and warehoused on the dock, upon the faith of the bills of lading, as a recognition of his title to the goods. It is a negotiable instrument. Pull. Port of London, p. 375.

DOCKAGE. The sum charged for the use of a dock. In the case of a dry-dock, it has been held in the nature of rent. 1 Newb. Adm. 69.

DOCKET, *v.* To abstract and enter in a book. 3 Bl. Comm. 397, 398. To make a brief entry of any proceeding in a court of justice in the docket.

DOCKET, *n.* A minute, abstract, or brief entry; or the book containing such entries. A small piece of paper or parchment having the effect of a larger. Blount.

In practice. A formal record, entered in brief, of the proceedings in a court of justice.

A book containing an entry in brief of all the important acts done in court in the conduct of each case, from its inception to its conclusion. Pub. St. Mass. 1882, p. 1290.

The docket of judgments is a brief writing or statement of a judgment made from the record or roll, generally kept in books, alphabetically arranged, by the clerk of the court or county clerk. 1 Bradf. Sur. 343.

The name of "docket" or "trial docket" is sometimes given to the list or calendar of causes set to be tried at a specified term, prepared by the clerks for the use of the court and bar.

In the practice of some of the states there are several species of dockets, such as the "appearance docket," "judgment docket," "execution docket," etc., each containing a brief record of the class of proceedings indicated by its name.

DOCKET, STRIKING A. A phrase formerly used in English bankruptcy practice. It referred to the entry of certain papers at the bankruptcy office, preliminary to the prosecution of the fiat against a trader who had become bankrupt. These papers consisted of the affidavit, the bond, and the petition of the creditor, and their object was to obtain from the lord chancellor his fiat, authorizing the petitioner to prosecute his complaint against the bankrupt in the bankruptcy courts. Brown.

DOCTOR. This term means, simply, practitioner of physic, without respect to system pursued. A certificate of a homœpathic physician is a "doctor's certificate." 4 E. D. Smith, 1.

DOCTOR AND STUDENT. The title of a work written by St. Germain in the reign of Henry VIII. in which many principles of the common law are discussed in a popular manner. It is in the form of a dialogue between a doctor of divinity and a student in law, and has always been considered a book of merit and authority. 1 Kent, Comm. 504; Crabb, Eng. Law, 482.

DOCTORS' COMMONS. An institution near St. Paul's Churchyard, in London, where, for a long time previous to 1857, the ecclesiastical and admiralty courts used to be held.

DOCTRINE. A rule, principle, theory, or tenet of the law; as, the doctrine of merger, the doctrine of relation, etc.

DOCUMENT. An instrument on which is recorded, by means of letters, figures, or marks, matter which may be evidentially used. In this sense the term "document" applies to writings; to words printed, lithographed, or photographed; to seals, plates, or stones on which inscriptions are cut or engraved; to photographs and pictures; to maps and plans. The inscription may be on stone or gems, or on wood, as well as on paper or parchment. 1 Whart. Ev. § 614.

DOCUMENTS. The deeds, agreements, title-papers, letters, receipts, and other written instruments used to prove a fact.

In the civil law. Evidence delivered in the forms established by law, of whatever nature such evidence may be. The term is, however, applied principally to the testimony of witnesses. Sav. Dr. Rom. § 165.

DODRANS. Lat. In Roman law. A subdivision of the *as*, containing nine *unciæ;* the proportion of nine-twelfths, or three-fourths. 2 Bl. Comm. 462, note.

DOE, JOHN. The name of the fictitious plaintiff in the action of ejectment. 3 Steph. Comm. 618.

DŒD-BANA. In Saxon law. The actual perpetrator of a homicide.

DOER. In Scotch law. An agent or attorney. 1 Kames, Eq. 325.

DOG-DRAW. In old forest law. The manifest deprehension of an offender against venison in a forest, when he was found drawing after a deer by the scent of a hound led in his hand; or where a person had wounded a deer or wild beast, by shooting at him, or otherwise, and was caught with a dog drawing after him to receive the same. Manwood, Forest Law, 2, c. 8.

DOG-LATIN. The Latin of illiterate persons; Latin words put together on the English grammatical system.

DOGGER. In maritime law. A light ship or vessel; *dogger-fish,* fish brought in ships. Cowell.

DOGGER-MEN. Fishermen that belong to dogger-ships.

DOGMA. In the civil law. A word occasionally used as descriptive of an ordinance of the senate. See Nov. 2, 1, 1; Dig. 27, 1, 6.

DOING. The formal word by which *services* were reserved and expressed in old conveyances; as "rendering" (*reddendo*) was expressive of *rent.* Perk. c. 10, §§ 625, 635, 638.

DOITKIN, or DOIT. A base coin of small value, prohibited by St. 3 Hen. V. c. 1. We still retain the phrase, in the common saying, when we would undervalue a man, that he is not worth a doit. Jacob.

DOLE. A part or portion of a meadow is so called; and the word has the general signification of share, portion, or the like; as "to dole out" anything among so many poor persons, meaning to deal or distribute in portions to them. Holthouse.

In Scotch law. Criminal intent; evil design. Bell, Dict. voc. "Crime."

DOLES, or DOOLS. Slips of pasture left between the furrows of plowed land.

DOLG. Sax. A wound. Spelman.

DOLG-BOTE. A recompense for a scar or wound. Cowell.

DOLI CAPAX. Lat. Capable of malice or criminal intention; having sufficient discretion and intelligence to distinguish between right and wrong, and so to become amenable to the criminal laws.

DOLI INCAPAX. Incapable of criminal intention or malice; not of the age of discretion; not possessed of sufficient discretion and intelligence to distinguish between right and wrong to the extent of being criminally responsible for his actions.

DOLLAR. The unit employed in the United States in calculating money values. It is coined both in gold and silver, and is of the value of one hundred cents.

DOLO. In Spanish law. Bad or mischievous design. White, New Recop. b. 1, tit. 1, c. 1, § 3.

Dolo facit qui petit quod redditurus est. He acts with guile who demands that which he will have to return. Broom, Max. 346.

Dolo malo pactum se non servaturum. Dig. 2, 14, 7, § 9. An agreement induced by fraud cannot stand.

Dolosus versatur in generalibus. A person intending to deceive deals in general terms. Wing. Max. 636; 2 Coke, 34*a;* 6 Clark & F. 699; Broom. Max. 289.

Dolum ex indiciis perspicuis probari convenit. Fraud should be proved by clear tokens. Code, 2, 21, 6; 1 Story, Cont. § 625.

DOLUS. In the civil law. Guile; deceitfulness; malicious fraud. A fraudulent address or trick used to deceive some one; a fraud. Dig. 4, 3, 1. Any subtle contrivance by words or acts with a design to circumvent. 2 Kent, Comm. 560; Code, 2, 21.

Such acts or omissions as operate as a deception upon the other party, or violate the just confidence reposed by him, whether there be a deceitful intent (*malus animus*) or not. Poth. Traité de Dépôt, nn. 23, 27; Story, Bailm. § 20*a;* 2 Kent, Comm. 506, note.

Fraud, willfulness, or intentionality. In that use it is opposed to *culpa*, which is negligence merely, in greater or less degree. The policy of the law may sometimes treat extreme *culpa* as if it were *dolus*, upon the maxim *culpa dolo comparatur*. A person is always liable for *dolus* producing damage, but not always for *culpa* producing damage, even though extreme, *e. g.*, a depositary is only liable for *dolus*, and not for negligence. Brown.

Dolus auctoris non nocet successori. The fraud of a predecessor prejudices not his successor.

Dolus circuitu non purgatur. Fraud is not purged by circuity. Bac. Max. 4; Broom, Max. 228.

DOLUS DANS LOCUM CONTRACTUI. Fraud (or deceit) giving rise to the contract; that is, a fraudulent misrepresentation made by one of the parties to the contract, and relied upon by the other, and which was actually instrumental in inducing the latter to enter into the contract.

Dolus est machinatio, cum aliud dissimulat aliud agit. Lane, 47. Deceit is an artifice, since it pretends one thing and does another.

Dolus et fraus nemini patrocinentur, (patrocinari debent.) Deceit and fraud shall excuse or benefit no man. Yearb. 14 Hen. VIII. 8; Best, Ev. p. 469, § 428; 1 Story, Eq. Jur. § 395.

Dolus latet in generalibus. Fraud lurks in generalities. Tray. Lat. Max. 162.

DOLUS MALUS. Fraud; deceit with an evil intention. Distinguished from *dolus bonus*, justifiable or allowable deceit. Calvin.; Broom, Max. 349; Mackeld. Rom. Law, § 179. Misconduct. *Magna negligentia culpa est; magna culpa dolus est*, (great negligence is a fault; a great fault is fraud.) 2 Kent, Comm. 560, note.

Dolus versatur in generalibus. Fraud deals in generalities. 2 Coke, 34*a;* 3 Coke, 81*a*.

DOM. PROC. An abbreviation of *Domus Procerum* or *Domo Procerum;* the house of lords in England. Sometimes expressed by the letters D. P.

DOMAIN. The complete and absolute ownership of land; a paramount and individual right of property in land. Also the real estate so owned. The inherent sovereign power claimed by the legislature of a state, of controlling private property for public uses, is termed the "right of eminent domain." 2 Kent, Comm. 339.

The public lands of a state are frequently termed the "public domain," or "domain of the state." 1 Kent, Comm. 166, 259; 2 Kent, Comm. 339, note.

A distinction has been made between "property" and "domain." The former is said to be that quality which is conceived to be in the thing itself, considered as belonging to such or such person, exclusively of all others. By the latter is understood that right which the owner has of disposing of the thing. Hence "domain" and "property" are said to be correlative terms. The one is the active right to dispose of; the other a passive quality which follows the thing and places it at the disposition of the owner. 3 Toullier, no. 83.

DOMBEC, DOMBOC. (Sax. From *dom*, judgment, and *bec, boc*, a book.) Dome-book or doom-book. A name given among the Saxons to a code of laws. Several of the Saxon kings published *dombocs*, but the most important one was that attributed to Alfred. Crabb, Com. Law, 7. This is sometimes confounded with the celebrated *Domesday-Book*. See DOME-BOOK, DOMESDAY.

DOME. (Sax.) Doom; sentence; judgment. An oath. The homager's oath in the black book of Hereford. Blount.

DOME-BOOK. A book or code said to have been compiled under the direction of Alfred, for the general use of the whole kingdom of England; containing, as is supposed, the principal maxims of the common law, the penalties for misdemeanors, and the forms of judicial proceedings. It is said to have been extant so late as the reign of Edward IV., but is now lost. 1 Bl. Comm. 64, 65.

DOMESDAY, DOMESDAY-BOOK. (Sax.) An ancient record made in the time of William the Conqueror, and now remaining in the English exchequer, consisting of two volumes of unequal size, containing minute and accurate surveys of the lands in England. 2 Bl. Comm. 49, 50. The work was begun by five justices in each county in 1081, and finished in 1086.

DOMESMEN. (Sax.) An inferior kind of judges. Men appointed to doom (judge) in matters in controversy. Cowell. Suitors in a court of a manor in ancient demesne, who are judges there. Blount; Whishaw; Termes de la Ley.

DOMESTIC, *n.* Domestics, or, in full, domestic servants, are servants who reside in the same house with the master they serve. The term does not extend to workmen or laborers employed out of doors. 5 Bin. 167.

The Louisiana Civil Code enumerates as domestics those who receive wages and stay in the house of the person paying and employing them, for his own service or that of his family; such as valets, footmen, cooks, butlers, and others who reside in the house. Persons employed in public houses are not included. 6 La. Ann. 276.

DOMESTIC, *adj.* Pertaining, belonging, or relating to a home, a domicile, or to the place of birth, origin, creation, or transaction. See the following titles.

DOMESTIC ADMINISTRATOR. One appointed at the place of the domicile of the decedent; distinguished from a foreign or an ancillary administrator.

DOMESTIC ANIMALS. Horses are embraced within this description. 2 Allen, 209. But dogs are not. 75 Me. 562.

DOMESTIC ATTACHMENT. A species of attachment against resident debtors who absent or conceal themselves, as foreign attachment (*q. v.*) is against non-residents. 20 Pa. St. 144.

DOMESTIC BILL OF EXCHANGE. A bill of exchange drawn on a person residing in the same state with the drawer; or dated at a place in the state, and drawn on a person living within the state. It is the residence of the drawer and drawee which must determine whether a bill is domestic or foreign. 25 Miss. 143.

DOMESTIC COMMERCE. Commerce carried on wholly within the limits of the United States, as distinguished from foreign commerce. Also, commerce carried on within the limits of a single state, as distinguished from interstate commerce.

DOMESTIC CORPORATIONS. Such as were created by the laws of the same state wherein they transact business.

DOMESTIC COURTS. Those existing and having jurisdiction at the place of the party's residence or domicile.

DOMESTIC FACTOR. One who resides and does business in the same state or country with his principal.

DOMESTIC JUDGMENT. A judgment or decree is *domestic* in the courts of the same state or country where it was originally rendered; in other states or countries it is called *foreign.*

DOMESTIC MANUFACTURES. This term in a state statute is used, generally, of manufactures within its jurisdiction. 64 Pa. St. 100.

DOMESTICUS. In old European law. A *seneschal,* steward, or *major domo;* a judge's assistant; an assessor, (*q. v.*) Spelman.

DOMICELLA. In old English law. A damsel. Fleta, lib. 1, c. 20, § 80.

DOMICELLUS. In old English law. A better sort of servant in monasteries; also an appellation of a king's bastard.

DOMICILE. That place in which a man has voluntarily fixed the habitation of himself and family, not for a mere special or temporary purpose, but with the present intention of making a permanent home, until some unexpected event shall occur to induce him to adopt some other permanent home.

In its ordinary acceptation, a person's domicile is the place where he lives or has his home. In a strict and legal sense, that is properly the domicile of a person where he has his true, fixed, permanent home and principal establishment, and to which, whenever he is absent, he has the intention of returning. 42 Vt. 350; 9 Ired. 99.

Domicile is but the established, fixed, permanent, or ordinary dwelling-place or place of residence of a person, as distinguished from his temporary and transient, though actual, place of residence. It is his legal residence, as distinguished from his temporary place of abode; or his home, as distinguished from a place to which business or pleasure may temporarily call him. 29 Conn. 74.

Domicile is the place where a person has fixed his habitation and has a permanent residence, without any present intention of removing therefrom. 4 Barb. 504, 520.

One's domicile is the place where one's family permanently resides. 46 Ga. 277.

In international law, "domicile" means a residence at a particular place, accompanied with positive or presumptive proof of intending to continue there for an unlimited time. 32 N. J. Law, 192.

"Domicile" and "residence" are not synonymous. The domicile is the home, the fixed place of habitation; while residence is a transient place of dwelling. 5 Sandf. 44.

The domicile is the habitation fixed in any place with an intention of always staying there, while simple residence is much more temporary in its character. 4 Hun, 489.

Domicile is of three sorts,—domicile by birth, domicile by choice, and domicile by operation of law. The first is the common case of the place of birth, *domicilium originis;* the second is that which is voluntarily acquired by a party, *proprio motu;* the last is consequential, as that of the wife arising from marriage. Story, Confl. Laws, § 46.

The term "domicile of succession," as contradistinguished from a commercial, a political, or a forensic domicile, may be defined to be the actual residence of a man within some particular jurisdiction, of such character as shall, in accordance with certain well-established principles of the public law, give direction to the succession of his personal estate. 7 Fla. 81.

DOMICILE OF ORIGIN. The home of the parents. Phillim. Dom. 25, 101. That which arises from a man's birth and connections. 5 Ves. 750. The domicile of the parents at the time of birth, or what is termed the "domicile of origin," constitutes the domicile of an infant, and continues until abandoned, or until the acquisition of a new domicile in a different place. 1 Brock. 389, 393.

DOMICILED. Established in a given domicile; belonging to a given state or jurisdiction by right of domicile.

DOMICILIARY. Pertaining to domicile; relating to one's domicile. Existing or created at, or connected with, the domicile of a suitor or of a decedent.

DOMICILIATE. To establish one's domicile; to take up one's fixed residence in a given place. To establish the domicile of another person whose legal residence follows one's own.

DOMICILIUM. Domicile, (*q. v.*)

DOMIGERIUM. In old English law. Power over another; also danger. Bract. l. 4, t. 1, c. 10.

DOMINA, (DAME.) A title given to honorable women, who anciently, in their own right of inheritance, held a barony. Cowell.

DOMINANT. The tenement whose owner, as such, enjoys an easement over an adjoining tenement is called the "dominant tenement;" while that which is subject to the easement is called the "servient" one.

DOMINANT TENEMENT. A term used in the civil and Scotch law, and thence in ours, relating to servitudes, meaning the tenement or subject in favor of which the service is constituted; as the tenement over which the servitude extends is called the "servient tenement." Wharton.

DOMINATIO. In old English law. Lordship.

DOMINICA PALMARUM. (*Dominica in ramis palmarum.*) L. Lat. Palm Sunday. Townsh. Pl. 131; Cowell; Blount.

DOMINICAL. That which denotes the Lord's day, or Sunday.

DOMINICIDE. The act of killing one's lord or master.

DOMINICUM. Lat. Domain; demain; demesne. A lordship. That of which one has the lordship or ownership. That which remains under the lord's immediate charge and control. Spelman.

Property; domain; anything pertaining to a lord. Cowell.

In ecclesiastical law. A church, or any other building consecrated to God. Du Cange.

DOMINICUM ANTIQUUM. In old English law. Ancient demesne. Bract. fol. 369*b*.

DOMINION. Ownership, or right to property. 2 Bl. Comm. 1. "The holder has the dominion of the bill." 8 East, 579.

Sovereignty or lordship; as the dominion of the seas. Moll. de Jure Mar. 91, 92.

DOMINIUM. In the civil and old English law. Ownership; property in the largest sense, including both the right of property and the right of possession or use.

The mere right of property, as distinguished from the possession or usufruct. Dig. 41, 2, 17, 1; Calvin. The right which a lord had in the fee of his tenant. In this sense the word is very clearly distinguished by Bracton from *dominicum*.

The estate of a feoffee to uses. "The feoffees to use shall have the *dominium*, and the *cestui que use* the disposition." Latch, 137.

Sovereignty or dominion. *Dominium maris*, the sovereignty of the sea.

DOMINIUM DIRECTUM. In the civil law. Strict ownership; that which was founded on strict law, as distinguished from equity.

In later law. Property without use; the right of a landlord. Tayl. Civil Law, 478.

In feudal law. Right or proper ownership; the right of a superior or lord, as distinguished from that of his vassal or tenant.

The title or property which the sovereign in England is considered as possessing in all the lands of the kingdom, they being holden either immediately or mediately of him as lord paramount.

DOMINIUM DIRECTUM ET UTILE. The complete and absolute dominion in property; the union of the title and the exclusive use. 7 Cranch, 603.

DOMINIUM EMINENS. Eminent domain.

Dominium non potest esse in pendenti. Lordship cannot be in suspense, *i. e.*, property cannot remain in abeyance. Halk. Law Max. 39.

DOMINIUM PLENUM. Full ownership; the union of the *dominium directum* with the *dominium utile.* Tayl. Civil Law, 478.

DOMINIUM UTILE. In the civil law. Equitable or prætorian ownership; that which was founded on equity. Mackeld. Rom. Law, § 327, note.

In later law. Use without property; the right of a tenant. Tayl. Civil Law, 478.

In feudal law. Useful or beneficial ownership; the usufruct, or right to the use and profits of the soil, as distinguished from the *dominium directum,* (*q. v.*,) or ownership of the soil itself; the right of a vassal or tenant. 2 Bl. Comm. 105.

DOMINO VOLENTE. Lat. The owner being willing; with the consent of the owner.

DOMINUS. In feudal and ecclesiastical law. A lord, or feudal superior. *Dominus rex,* the lord the king; the king's title as lord paramount. 1 Bl. Comm. 367. *Dominus capitalis,* a chief lord. *Dominus medius,* a mesne or intermediate lord. *Dominus ligius,* liege lord or sovereign. Id.

Lord or sir; a title of distinction. It usually denoted a knight or clergyman; and, according to Cowell, was sometimes given to a gentleman of quality, though not a knight, especially if he were lord of a manor.

The owner or proprietor of a thing, as distinguished from him who uses it merely. Calvin. A master or principal, as distinguished from an agent or attorney. Story, Ag. § 3.

In the civil law. A husband. A family. Vicat.

Dominus capitalis loco hæredis habetur, quoties per defectum vel delictum extinguitur sanguis sui tenentis. Co. Litt. 18. The supreme lord takes the place of the heir, as often as the blood of the tenant is extinct through deficiency or crime.

DOMINUS LITIS. Lat. The master of the suit; *i. e.*, the person who was really and directly interested in the suit as a party, as distinguished from his attorney or advocate. But the term is also applied to one who, though not originally a party, has made himself such, by intervention or otherwise, and has assumed entire control and responsibility for one side, and is treated by the court as liable for costs. See 1 Curt. 201.

DOMINUS NAVIS. In the civil law. The owner of a vessel. Dig. 39, 4, 11, 2.

Dominus non maritabit pupillum nisi semel. Co. Litt. 9. A lord cannot give a ward in marriage but once.

Dominus rex nullum habere potest parem, multo minus superiorem. The king cannot have an equal, much less a superior. 1 Reeves, Eng. Law, 115.

DOMITÆ. Lat. Tame; domesticated; not wild. Applied to domestic animals, in which a man may have an absolute property. 2 Bl. Comm. 391.

DOMMAGES INTERETS. In French law. Damages.

DOMO REPARANDÂ. A writ that lay for one against his neighbor, by the anticipated fall of whose house he feared a damage and injury to his own. Reg. Orig. 153.

DOMUS. Lat. In the civil and old English law. A house or dwelling; a habitation. Inst. 4,4, 8; Townsh. Pl. 183-185.

DOMUS CAPITULARIS. In old records. A chapter-house; the chapter-house. Dyer, 26*b*.

DOMUS CONVERSORUM. An ancient house built or appointed by King Henry III. for such Jews as were converted to the Christian faith; but King Edward III., who expelled the Jews from the kingdom, deputed the place for the custody of the rolls and records of the chancery. Jacob.

DOMUS DEI. The house of God; a name applied to many hospitals and religious houses.

DOMUS PROCERUM. The house of lords, abbreviated into *Dom. Proc.*, or *D. P.*

Domus sua cuique est tutissimum refugium. To every man his own house is his safest refuge. 5 Coke, 91*b;* 11 Coke, 82; 3 Inst. 162. The house of every one is to him as his castle and fortress, as well for his defense against injury and violence as for his repose. 5 Coke, 91*b;* Say. 227; Broom, Max. 432. A man's dwelling-house is his castle, not for his own personal protection merely, but also for the protection of his family and his property therein. 4 Hill, 437.

Domus tutissimum cuique refugium atque receptaculum sit. A man's house should be his safest refuge and shelter. A maxim of the Roman law. Dig. 2, 4, 18.

Dona clandestina sunt semper suspiciosa. 3 Coke, 81. Clandestine gifts are always suspicious.

Donari videtur, quod nullo jure cogente conceditur. Dig. 50, 17, 82. A thing is said to be given when it is yielded otherwise than by virtue of right.

DONATARIUS. A donee; one to whom something is given.

DONATIO. Lat. A gift. A transfer of the title to property to one who receives it without paying for it. Vicat. The act by which the owner of a thing voluntarily transfers the title and possession of the same from himself to another person, without any consideration.

Its literal translation, "gift," has acquired in real law a more limited meaning, being applied to the conveyance of estates tail. 2 Bl. Comm. 316; Littleton, § 59; West. Symb. § 254; 4 Cruise, Dig. 51. There are several kinds of *donatio*, as: *Donatio simplex et pura*, (simple and pure gift without compulsion or consideration;) *donatio absoluta et larga*, (an absolute gift;) *donatio conditionalis*, (a conditional gift;) *donatio stricta et coarctura*, (a restricted gift, as an estate tail.)

DONATIO INTER VIVOS. A gift between the living. The ordinary kind of gift by one person to another. 2 Kent, Comm. 438; 2 Steph. Comm. 102. A term derived from the civil law. Inst. 2, 7, 2.

A donation *inter vivos* (between living persons) is an act by which the donee divests himself at present and irrevocably of the thing given in favor of the donee who accepts it. Civil Code La. art. 1468.

DONATIO MORTIS CAUSA. (Lat. A gift in prospect of death.) A gift made by a person in sickness, who, apprehending his dissolution near, delivers, or causes to be delivered, to another the possession of any personal goods, to keep as his own in case of the donor's decease. 2 Bl. Comm. 514.

The civil law defines it to be a gift under apprehension of death; as when anything is given upon condition that, if the donor dies, the donee shall possess it absolutely, or return it if the donor should survive or should repent of having made the gift, or if the donee should die before the donor. 1 Miles, 109–117.

A gift in view of death is one which is made in contemplation, fear, or peril of death, and with intent that it shall take effect only in case of the death of the giver. Civil Code Cal. § 1149.

A donation *mortis causa* (in prospect of death) is an act to take effect when the donor shall no longer exist, by which he disposes of the whole or a part of his property, and which is irrevocable. Civil Code La. art. 1469.

Donatio non præsumitur. A gift is not presumed. Jenk. Cent. 109.

Donatio perficitur possessione accipientis. A gift is perfected [made complete] by the possession of the receiver. Jenk. Cent. 109, case 9. A gift is incomplete until possession is delivered. 2 Kent, Comm. 438.

Donatio principis intelligitur sine præjudicio tertii. Dav. Ir. K. B. 75. A gift of the prince is understood without prejudice to a third party.

DONATIO PROPTER NUPTIAS. A gift on account of marriage. In Roman law, the bridegroom's gift to the bride in anticipation of marriage and to secure her *dos* was called "*donatio ante nuptias;*" but by an ordinance of Justinian such gift might be made after as well as before marriage, and in that case it was called "*donatio propter nuptias.*" Mackeld. Rom. Law, § 572.

DONATION. In ecclesiastical law. A mode of acquiring a benefice by deed of gift alone, without presentation, institution, or induction. 3 Steph. Comm. 81.

In general. A gift. See DONATIO.

DONATIVE ADVOWSON. In ecclesiastical law. A species of advowson, where the benefice is conferred on the clerk by the patron's deed of donation, without presentation, institution, or induction. 2 Bl. Comm. 23; Termes de la Ley.

DONATOR. A donor; one who makes a gift, (*donatio.*)

Donator nunquam desinit possidere, antequam donatorius incipiat possidere. The donor never ceases to possess, until the donee begins to possess. Bract. fol. 41b

DONATORIUS. A donee; a person to whom a gift is made; a purchaser. Bract. fol. 13, et seq.

DONATORY. The person on whom the king bestows his right to any forfeiture that has fallen to the crown.

DONE. Distinguished from "made." "A 'deed made' may no doubt mean an 'instrument made;' but a 'deed done' is not an 'instrument done,'—it is an 'act done;' and therefore these words, 'made and done,' apply to acts, as well as deeds." Lord Brougham, 4 Bell, App. Cas. 38.

DONEE. In old English law. He to whom lands were given; the party to whom a *donatio* was made.

In later law. He to whom lands or tenements are given in tail. Litt. § 57.

In modern and American law. The party executing a power; otherwise called the "appointer." 4 Kent, Comm. 316.

DONIS, STATUTE DE. See DE DONIS, THE STATUTE.

DONNEUR D'AVAL. In French law. Guarantor of negotiable paper other than by indorsement.

DONOR. In old English law. He by whom lands were given to another; the party making a *donatio*.

In later law. He who gives lands or tenements to another in tail. Litt. § 57; Termes de la Ley.

In modern and American law. The party conferring a power. 4 Kent, Comm. 316.

DONUM. Lat. In the civil law. A gift; a free gift. Calvin. Distinguished from *munus*. Dig. 50, 16, 194.

DOOM. In Scotch law. Judicial sentence, or judgment. The decision or sentence of a court orally pronounced by an officer called a "dempster" or "deemster." In modern usage, criminal sentences still end with the words "which is pronounced for doom."

DOOMSDAY-BOOK. See DOMESDAY-BOOK.

DOOR. The place of usual entrance in a house, or into a room in the house.

DORMANT. Literally, sleeping; hence inactive; in abeyance; unknown; concealed.

DORMANT CLAIM. One which is in abeyance.

DORMANT EXECUTION. One which a creditor delivers to the sheriff with directions to levy only, and not to sell, until further orders, or until a junior execution is received.

DORMANT JUDGMENT. One which has not been satisfied, nor extinguished by lapse of time, but which has remained so long unexecuted that execution cannot now be issued upon it without first reviving the judgment.

DORMANT PARTNERS. Those whose names are not known or do not appear as partners, but who nevertheless are silent partners, and partake of the profits, and thereby become partners, either absolutely to all intents and purposes, or at all events in respect to third parties. Dormant partners, in strictness of language, mean those who are merely passive in the firm, whether known or unknown, in contradistinction to those who are active and conduct the business of the firm, as principals. See Story, Partn. § 80.

A dormant partner is one who takes no part in the business, and whose connection with the business is unknown. Both secrecy and inactivity are implied by the word. 47 N. Y. 15.

Dormiunt aliquando leges, nunquam moriuntur. 2 Inst. 161. The laws sometimes sleep, never die.

DORSUM. Lat. The back. *In dorso recordi*, on the back of the record. 5 Coke, 44*b*.

DORTURE. (Contracted from *dormiture*.) A dormitory of a convent; a place to sleep in.

DOS. In Roman law. Dowry; a wife's marriage portion; all that property which on marriage is transferred by the wife herself or by another to the husband with a view of diminishing the burden which the marriage will entail upon him. It is of three kinds. *Profectitia dos* is that which is derived from the property of the wife's father or paternal grandfather. That *dos* is termed *adventitia* which is not *profectitia* in respect to its source, whether it is given by the wife from her own estate or by the wife's mother or a third person. It is termed *receptitia dos* when accompanied by a stipulation for its reclamation by the constitutor on the termination of the marriage. See Mackeld. Rom. Law, §§ 561, 563.

In old English law. The portion given to the wife by the husband at the church door, in consideration of the marriage; dower; the wife's portion out of her deceased husband's estate in case he had not endowed her.

Dos de dote peti non debet. Dower ought not to be demanded of dower. Co. Litt. 31; 4 Coke, 122*b*. A widow is not dowable of lands assigned to another woman in dower. 1 Hil. Real Prop. 135.

DOS RATIONABILIS. A reasonable marriage portion. A reasonable part of her husband's estate, to which every widow is entitled, of lands of which her husband may have endowed her on the day of marriage. Co. Litt. 336. Dower, at common law. 2 Bl. Comm. 134.

Dos rationabilis vel legitima est cujuslibet mulieris de quocunque tenemento tertia pars omnium terrarum et tenementorum, quæ vir suus tenuit in dominio suo ut de feodo, etc. Co. Litt. 336. Reasonable or legitimate dower belongs to every woman of a third part of all the lands and tenements of which her husband was seised in his demesne, as of fee, etc.

DOT. (A French word, adopted in Louisiana.) The fortune, portion, or dowry which a woman brings to her husband by the marriage. 6 Mart. (N. S.) 460.

DOTAGE. Dotage is that feebleness of the mental faculties which proceeds from old age. It is a diminution or decay of that intellectual power which was once possessed. It is the slow approach of death; of that irrevocable cessation, without hurt or disease, of all the functions which once belonged to the living animal. The external functions gradually cease; the senses waste away by degrees; and the mind is imperceptibly visited by decay. 1 Bland, 389.

DOTAL. Relating to the *dos* or portion of a woman; constituting her portion; comprised in her portion.

DOTAL PROPERTY. In the civil law in Louisiana, by this term is understood that property which the wife brings to the husband to assist him in bearing the expenses of the marriage establishment. Extradotal property, otherwise called "paraphernal property," is that which forms no part of the dowry. Civil Code La. art. 2335.

DOTALITIUM. In canon and feudal law. Dower. Spelman, voc. "Doarium;" Calvin. 2 Bl. Comm. 129. Used as early as A. D. 841.

DOTATION. The act of giving a dowry or portion; endowment in general, including the endowment of a hospital or other charitable institution.

DOTE, *n*. In Spanish law. The marriage portion of a wife. White, New Recop. b. 1, tit. 6, c. 1. The property which the wife gives to the husband on account of marriage, or for the purpose of supporting the matrimonial expenses. Id. b. 1, tit. 7, c. 1, § 1; Schm. Civil Law, 75.

DOTE, *v*. "To besot" is to stupefy, to make dull or senseless, to make to dote; and "to dote" is to be delirious, silly, or insane. These are some of the meanings. 7 Ind. 441.

DOTE ASSIGNANDA. A writ which lay for a widow, when it was judicially ascertained that a tenant to the king was seised of tenements in fee or fee-tail at the day of his death, and that he held of the king in chief. In such case the widow might come into chancery, and then make oath that she would not marry without the king's leave, and then she might have this writ. These widows were called the "king's widows." Jacob; Holthouse.

DOTE UNDE NIHIL HABET. A writ which lies for a widow to whom no dower has been assigned. 3 Bl. Comm. 182. By 23 & 24 Vict. c. 126, an ordinary action commenced by writ of summons has taken its place; but it remains in force in the United States. Dower *unde nihil habet* (which title see.)

Doti lex favet; præmium pudoris est; ideo parcatur. Co. Litt. 31. The law favors dower; it is the reward of chastity; therefore let it be preserved.

DOTIS ADMINISTRATIO. Admeasurement of dower, where the widow holds more than her share, etc.

DOTISSA. A dowager.

DOUBLE AVAIL OF MARRIAGE. In Scotch law. Double the ordinary or single value of a marriage. Bell. See DUPLEX VALOR MARITAGII.

DOUBLE BOND. In Scotch law. A bond with a penalty, as distinguished from a single bond. 2 Kames, Eq. 359.

DOUBLE COMPLAINT, or DOUBLE QUARREL. A grievance made known by a clerk or other person, to the archbishop of the province, against the ordinary, for delaying or refusing to do justice in some cause ecclesiastical, as to give sentence, institute a clerk, etc. It is termed a "double complaint," because it is most commonly made against both the judge and him at whose suit justice is denied or delayed; the effect whereof is that the archbishop, taking notice of the delay, directs his letters, under his authentical seal, to all clerks of his province, commanding them to admonish the ordinary, within a certain number of days, to do the justice required, or otherwise to appear before him or his official, and there allege the cause of his delay; and to signify to the ordinary that if he neither perform the thing enjoined, nor appear nor show cause against it, he himself, in his court of audience, will forthwith proceed to do the justice that is due. Cowell.

DOUBLE COSTS. In practice. The ordinary single costs of suit, and one-half of that amount in addition. 2 Tidd, Pr. 987. "Double" is not used here in its ordinary sense of "twice" the amount. These costs are now abolished in England by St. 5 & 6 Vict. c. 97. Wharton.

DOUBLE DAMAGES. Twice the amount of actual damages as found by the verdict of a jury.

DOUBLE EAGLE. A gold coin of the United States of the value of twenty dollars.

DOUBLE ENTRY. A system of mercantile book-keeping, in which the entries in the day-book, etc., are posted *twice* into the ledger. *First*, to a *personal* account, that is, to the account of the *person* with whom the dealing to which any given entry refers has taken place; *secondly*, to an impersonal account, as "goods." Mozley & Whitley.

DOUBLE FINE. In old English law. A fine *sur done grant et render* was called a "double fine," because it comprehended the fine *sur cognizance de droit come ceo*, etc., and the fine *sur concessit*. 2 Bl. Comm. 353.

DOUBLE INSURANCE is where divers insurances are made upon the same interest in the same subject against the same risks in favor of the same assured, in proportions exceeding the value. 1 Phill. Ins. §§ 359, 366.

A double insurance exists where the same person is insured by several insurers separately in respect to the same subject and interest. Civil Code Cal. § 2641.

DOUBLE PLEADING. This is not allowed either in the declaration or subsequent pleadings. Its meaning with respect to the former is that the declaration must not, in support of a single demand, allege several distinct matters, by any one of which that demand is sufficiently supported. With respect to the subsequent pleadings, the meaning is that none of them is to contain several distinct answers to that which preceded it; and the reason of the rule in each case is that such pleading tends to several issues in respect of a single claim. Wharton.

DOUBLE POSSIBILITY. A possibility upon a possibility. 2 Bl. Comm. 170.

DOUBLE RENT. In English law. Rent payable by a tenant who continues in possession after the time for which he has given notice to quit, until the time of his quitting possession. St. 11 Geo. II. c. 19.

DOUBLE VALUE. This is a penalty on a tenant holding over after his landlord's notice to quit. By 4 Geo. II. c. 28, § 1, it is enacted that if any tenant for life or years hold over any lands, etc., after the determination of his estate, after demand made, and notice in writing given, for delivering the possession thereof, by the landlord, or the person having the reversion or remainder therein, or his agent thereunto lawfully authorized, such tenant so holding over shall pay to the person so kept out of possession at the rate of *double* the yearly value of the lands, etc., so detained, for so long a time as the same are detained. See Woodf. Landl. & Ten. (12th Ed.) 717, et seq.

DOUBLE VOUCHER. This was when a common recovery was had, and an estate of freehold was first conveyed to any indifferent person against whom the *præcipe* was brought, and then he vouched the tenant in tail, who vouched over the common vouchee. For, if a recovery were had immediately against a tenant in tail, it barred only the estate in the premises of which he was then actually seised, whereas, if the recovery were had against another person, and the tenant in tail were vouchee, it barred every latent right and interest which he might have in the lands recovered. 2 Bl. Comm. 359.

DOUBLE WASTE. When a tenant bound to repair suffers a house to be wasted, and then unlawfully fells timber to repair it, he is said to commit double waste. Co. Litt. 53.

DOUBLES. Letters-patent. Cowell.

DOUBT. The uncertainty which exists in relation to a fact, a proposition, or other thing; an equipoise of the mind arising from an equality of contrary reasons. Ayl. Pand. 121.

The term "reasonable doubt" is often used, but not easily defined. It is not mere possible doubt; because everything relating to human affairs and depending on moral evidence is open to some possible or imaginary doubt. It is that state of the case which, after the entire comparison and consideration of all the evidence, leaves the minds of jurors in such a condition that they cannot say they feel an abiding conviction, to a moral certainty, of the truth of the charge. The burden of proof is upon the prosecutor. All the presumptions of law independent of evidence are in favor of innocence; and every person is presumed to be innocent until he is proved guilty. If upon such proof there is reasonable doubt remaining, the accused is entitled to the benefit of it by an acquittal; for it is not sufficient to establish a probability, though a strong one, arising from the doctrine of chances, that the fact charged is more likely to be true than the contrary, but the evidence must establish the truth of the fact to a reasonable and moral certainty,—a certainty that convinces and directs the understanding and satisfies the reason and judgment of those who are bound to act conscientiously upon it. This is proof beyond reasonable doubt; because if the law, which mostly depends upon considerations of a moral nature, should go further than this, and require absolute certainty, it would exclude circumstantial evidence altogether. Per Shaw, C. J., in 5 Cush. 320.

DOUN. L. Fr. A gift. Otherwise written "*don*" and "*done.*" The thirty-fourth chapter of Britton is entitled "*De Douns.*"

DOVE. Doves are animals *feræ naturæ*, and not the subject of larceny unless they are in the owner's custody; as, for example, in a dove-house, or when in the nest before they can fly. 9 Pick. 15.

DOWABLE. Subject to be charged with dower; as dowable lands.

Entitled or entitling to dower. Thus, a dowable interest in lands is such as entitles the owner to have such lands charged with dower.

DOWAGER. A widow who is endowed, or who has a jointure in lieu of dower. In England, this is a title or addition given to the widows of princes, dukes, earls, and other noblemen, to distinguish them from the wives of the heirs, who have right to bear the title. 1 Bl. Comm. 224.

DOWAGER-QUEEN. The widow of the king. As such she enjoys most of the privileges belonging to her as queen consort. It is not treason to conspire her death or violate her chastity, because the succession to the crown is not thereby endangered. No man, however, can marry her without a special license from the sovereign, on pain of forfeiting his lands or goods. 1 Bl. Comm. 233.

DOWER. The provision which the law makes for a widow out of the lands or tenements of her husband, for her support and the nurture of her children. Co. Litt. 30*a;* 2 Bl. Comm. 130; 4 Kent, Comm. 35; 1 Washb. Real Prop. 146.

Dower is an estate for the life of the widow in a certain portion of the following real estate of her husband, to which she has not relinquished her right during the marriage: (1) Of all lands of which the husband was seised in fee during the marriage; (2) of all lands to which another was seised in fee to his use; (3) of all lands to which, at the time of his death, he had a perfect equity, having paid all the purchase money therefor. Code Ala. 1886, § 1892.

The term, both technically and in popular acceptation, has reference to real estate exclusively.

"Dower," in modern use, is and should be distinguished from "dowry." The former is a provision for a widow on her husband's death; the latter is a bride's portion on her marriage.

DOWER AD OSTIUM ECCLESIÆ. Dower at the church door or porch. An ancient kind of dower in England, where a man, (being tenant in fee-simple, of full age,) openly *at the church door*, where all marriages were formerly celebrated, after affiance made and troth plighted between them, *endowed* his wife with the whole of his lands, or such quantity as he pleased, at the same time specifying and ascertaining the same. Litt. § 39; 2 Bl. Comm. 133.

DOWER BY THE COMMON LAW. The ordinary kind of dower in English and American law, consisting of one-third of the lands of which the husband was seised in fee at any time during the coverture. Litt. § 36; 2 Bl. Comm. 132; 2 Steph. Comm. 302; 4 Kent, Comm. 35.

DOWER BY CUSTOM. A kind of dower in England, regulated by custom, where the quantity allowed the wife differed from the proportion of the common law; as that the wife should have half the husband's lands; or, in some places, the whole; and, in some, only a quarter. 2 Bl. Comm. 132; Litt. § 37.

DOWER DE LA PLUIS BELLE. L. Fr. Dower of the fairest [part.] A species of ancient English dower, incident to the old tenures, where there was a guardian in chivalry, and the wife occupied lands of the heir as guardian in socage. If the wife brought a writ of dower against such guardian in chivalry, he might show this matter, and pray that the wife might be endowed *de la pluis belle* of the tenement in socage. Litt. § 48. This kind of dower was abolished with the military tenures. 2 Bl. Comm. 132.

DOWER EX ASSENSU PATRIS. Dower by the father's assent. A species of dower *ad ostium ecclesiæ*, made when the husband's father was alive, and the son, by his consent expressly given, endowed his wife with parcel of his father's lands. Litt. § 40; 2 Bl. Comm. 133.

DOWER UNDE NIHIL HABET. A writ of right which lay for a widow to whom no dower had been assigned.

DOWLE STONES. Stones dividing lands, etc. Cowell.

DOWMENT. In old English law. Endowment; dower.

DOWRESS. A woman entitled to dower; a tenant in dower. 2 P. Wms. 707.

DOWRY. The property which a woman brings to her husband in marriage; now more commonly called a "portion."

By dowry is meant the effects which the wife brings to the husband to support the expenses of marriage. Civil Code La. art. 2337.

This word expresses the proper meaning of the "*dos*" of the Roman, the "*dot*" of the French, and the "*dote*" of the Spanish, law, but is a very different thing from "dower," with which it has sometimes been confounded.

By dowry, in the Louisiana Civil Code, is meant the effects which the wife brings to the husband to support the expenses of marriage. It is given to the husband, to be enjoyed by him so long as the marriage shall last, and the income of it belongs to him. He alone has the administration of it during marriage, and his wife cannot deprive him of it. The real estate settled as dowry is inalienable during marriage, unless the marriage contract contains a stipulation to the contrary. 6 La. Ann. 786.

DOZEIN. L. Fr. Twelve; a person twelve years of age. St. 18 Edw. II.; Barring. Ob. St. 208.

DOZEN PEERS. Twelve peers assembled at the instance of the barons, in the reign of Henry III., to be privy counselors, or rather conservators of the kingdom.

DRACHMA. A term employed in old pleadings and records, to denote a groat. Townsh. Pl. 180.

An Athenian silver coin, of the value of about $7\frac{3}{4}$d. sterling.

DRACO REGIS. The standard, ensign, or military colors borne in war by the ancient kings of England, having the figure of a dragon painted thereon.

DRACONIAN LAWS. A code of laws prepared by Draco, the celebrated lawgiver of Athens. These laws were exceedingly severe, and the term is now sometimes applied to any laws of unusual harshness.

DRAFT. The common term for a bill of exchange; as being *drawn* by one person on another. 2 Bl. Comm. 467.

An order for the payment of money drawn by one person on another. It is said to be a *nomen generalissimum*, and to include all such orders. 1 Story, 30.

Draft also signifies a tentative, provisional, or preparatory writing out of any document (as a will, contract, lease, etc.) for purposes of discussion and correction, and which is afterwards to be copied out in its final shape.

DRAFTSMAN. Any one who draws or frames a legal document, *e. g.*, a will, conveyance, pleading, etc.

DRAGOMAN. An interpreter employed in the east, and particularly at the Turkish court.

DRAIN, *v.* To make dry; to draw off water; to rid land of its superfluous moisture by adapting or improving natural watercourses and supplementing them, when necessary, by artificial ditches. 58 Cal. 639.

DRAIN, *n.* A trench or ditch to convey water from wet land; a channel through which water may flow off.

The word has no technical legal meaning. Any hollow space in the ground, natural or artificial, where water is collected and passes off, is a ditch or drain. 5 Gray, 61.

The word "drain" also sometimes denotes the easement or servitude (acquired by grant or prescription) which consists in the right to drain water through another's land. See 3 Kent, Comm. 436.

DRAM. In common parlance, this term means a drink of some substance containing alcohol, something which can produce intoxication. 32 Tex. 228.

DRAM-SHOP. A drinking saloon, where liquors are sold to be drunk on the premises.

DRAMATIC COMPOSITION. A mere exhibition, spectacle, or scene is not a "dramatic composition," within the meaning of the copyright laws. 1 Abb. (U. S.) 356.

DRAW. **In old criminal practice.** To drag (on a hurdle) to the place of execution. Anciently no hurdle was allowed, but the criminal was actually dragged along the road to the place of execution. A part of the ancient punishment of traitors was the being thus drawn. 4 Bl. Comm. 92, 377.

In mercantile law. To draw a bill of exchange is to write (or cause it to be written) and sign it.

DRAWBACK. In the customs laws, this term denotes an allowance made by the government upon the duties due on imported merchandise when the importer, instead of selling it here, re-exports it; or the refunding of such duties if already paid. This allowance amounts, in some cases, to the whole of the original duties; in others, to a part only.

A drawback is a device resorted to for enabling a commodity affected by taxes to be exported and sold in the foreign market on the same terms as if it had not been taxed at all. It differs in this from a bounty, that the latter enables a commodity to be sold for *less* than its natural cost, whereas a drawback enables it to be sold exactly at its natural cost.

DRAWEE. A person to whom a bill of exchange is addressed, and who is requested to pay the amount of money therein mentioned.

DRAWER. The person making a bill of exchange and addressing it to the drawee.

DRAWING. In patent law. A representation of the appearance of material objects by means of lines and marks upon paper, card-board, or other substance.

DRAWING TO EXECUTION. In English criminal law. The act of drawing a condemned criminal on a hurdle from the place of prison to the place of execution. 4 Bl. Comm. 377. Where a man was hanged on an appeal of death, the wife of the person killed and all his kindred drew the felon to execution.

DRAWLATCHES. Thieves; robbers. Cowell.

DREIT-DREIT. Droit-droit. Double right. A union of the right of possession and the right of property. 2 Bl. Comm. 199.

DRENCHES, or DRENGES. In Saxon law. Tenants *in capite.* They are said to be such as, at the coming of William the Conqueror, being put out of their estates, were afterwards restored to them, on their making it appear that they were the true owners thereof, and neither *in auxilio* or *consilio* against him. Spelman.

DRENGAGE. The tenure by which the drenches, or drenges, held their lands.

DRIFT. In old English law. A driving, especially of cattle.

DRIFT-STUFF. This term signifies, not goods which are the subject of salvage, but matters floating at random, without any known or discoverable ownership, which, if cast ashore, will probably never be reclaimed, but will, as a matter of course, accrue to the riparian proprietor. 13 R. I. 641.

DRIFTLAND, DROFLAND, or DRYFLAND. A Saxon word, signifying a tribute or yearly payment made by some tenants to the king, or their landlords, for driving their cattle through a manor to fairs or markets. Cowell.

DRIFTS OF THE FOREST. A view or examination of what cattle are in a forest, chase, etc., that it may be known whether it be surcharged or not; and whose the beasts are, and whether they are commonable. These drifts are made at certain times in the year by the officers of the forest, when all cattle are driven into some pound or place inclosed, for the before-mentioned purposes, and also to discover whether any cattle of strangers be there, which ought not to common. Manwood, p. 2, c. 15.

DRIFTWAY. A road or way over which cattle are driven. 1 Taunt. 279.

DRINCLEAN. Sax. A contribution of tenants, in the time of the Saxons, towards a potation, or ale, provided to entertain the lord, or his steward. Cowell. See CERVISARII.

DRIP. A species of easement or servitude obligating one man to permit the water falling from another man's house to fall upon his own land. 3 Kent, Comm. 436.

DRIVER. One employed in conducting a coach, carriage, wagon, or other vehicle, with horses, mules, or other animals.

DROFDEN, or DROFDENNE. A grove or woody place where cattle are kept. Jacob.

DROFLAND. Sax. A quit rent, or yearly payment, formerly made by some tenants to the king, or their landlords, for *driving* their cattle through a manor to fairs or markets. Cowell; Blount.

DROIT. In French law. Right, justice, equity, law, the whole body of law; also a right.

This term exhibits the same ambiguity which is discoverable in the German equivalent, "*recht*" and the English word "*right.*" On the one hand, these terms answer to the Roman "*jus*," and thus indicate law in the abstract, considered as the foundation of all rights, or the complex of underlying moral principles which impart the character of justice to all positive law, or give it an ethical content. Taken in this abstract sense, the terms may be adjectives, in which case they are equivalent to "just," or nouns, in which case they may be paraphrased by the expressions "justice," "morality," or "equity." On the other hand, they serve to point out *a* right; that is, a power, privilege, faculty, or demand, inherent in one person, and incident upon another. In the latter signification, *droit* (or *recht* or *right*) is the correlative of "duty" or "obligation." In the former sense, it may be considered as opposed to wrong, injustice, or the absence of law. *Droit* has the further ambiguity that it is sometimes used to denote the existing body of law considered as one whole, or the sum total of a number of individual laws taken together. See JUS; RECHT; RIGHT.

In old English law. A writ of right, so called in the old books. Co. Litt. 158*b*.

Law. The common law is sometimes termed "*common droit.*" Litt. § 213; Co. Litt. 142*a*.

DROIT-CLOSE. An ancient writ, directed to the lord of ancient demesne on behalf of those of his tenants who held their lands and tenements by charter in fee-simple, in fee-tail, for life, or in dower. Fitzh. Nat. Brev. 23.

DROIT D'ACCESSION. In French law. That property which is acquired by making a new species out of the material of another. It is equivalent to the Roman "*specificatio.*"

DROIT D'AUBAINE. In French law. A rule by which all the property of a deceased foreigner, whether movable or immovable, was confiscated to the use of the state, to the exclusion of his heirs, whether claiming *ab intestato* or under a will of the deceased. Finally abolished in 1819.

DROIT D'EXECUTION. In French law. The right of a stockbroker to sell the securities bought by him for account of a client, if the latter does not accept delivery thereof. The same expression is also applied to the sale by a stockbroker of securities deposited with him by his client, in order to guaranty the payment of operations for which the latter has given instructions. Arg. Fr. Merc. Law, 557.

DROIT DE BRIS. A right formerly claimed by the lords of the coasts of certain parts of France, to shipwrecks, by which not only the property, but the persons of those who were cast away, were confiscated for the prince who was lord of the coast. Otherwise called "*droit de bris sur le naufrage.*" This right prevailed chiefly in Bretagne, and was solemnly abrogated by Henry III., as duke of Normandy, Aquitaine, and Guienne, in a charter granted A. D. 1226, preserved among the rolls at Bordeaux.

DROIT DE GARDE. In French feudal law. Right of ward. The guardianship of the estate and person of a noble vassal, to which the king, during his minority, was entitled. Steph. Lect. 250.

DROIT DE GITE. In French feudal law. The duty incumbent on a *roturier*, holding lands within the royal domain, of supplying board and lodging to the king and to his suite while on a royal progress. Steph. Lect. 351.

DROIT DE GREFFE. In old French law. The right of selling various offices connected with the custody of judicial records or notarial acts. Steph. Lect. 354. A privilege of the French kings.

DROIT DE MAITRISE. In old French law. A charge payable to the crown by any one who, after having served his apprenticeship in any commercial guild or brotherhood, sought to become a master workman in it on his own account. Steph. Lect. 354.

DROIT DE PRISE. In French feudal law. The duty (incumbent on a *roturier*) of supplying to the king on credit, during a certain period, such articles of domestic consumption as might be required for the royal household. Steph. Lect. 351.

DROIT DE QUINT. In French feudal law. A relief payable by a noble vassal to the king as his *seigneur*, on every change in the ownership of his fief. Steph. Lect. 350.

DROIT DE SUITE. In French law. The right of a creditor to pursue the debtor's property into the hands of third persons for the enforcement of his claim.

DROIT-DROIT. A double right; that is, the right of possession and the right of property. These two rights were, by the theory of our ancient law, distinct; and the above phrase was used to indicate the concurrence of both in one person, which concurrence was necessary to constitute a complete title to land. Mozley & Whitley.

DROIT ÉCRIT. In French law. (The written law.) The Roman civil law, or *Corpus Juris Civilis*. Steph. Lect. 130.

Droit ne done pluis que soit demaunde. The law gives not more than is demanded. 2 Inst. 286.

Droit ne poet pas morier. Right cannot die. Jenk. Cent. 100, case 95.

DROITS CIVILS. This phrase in French law denotes private rights, the exercise of which is independent of the *status* (*qualité*) of citizen. Foreigners enjoy them; and the extent of that enjoyment is determined by the principle of reciprocity. Conversely, foreigners may be sued on contracts made by them in France. Brown.

DROITS OF ADMIRALTY. Rights or perquisites of the admiralty. A term applied to goods found derelict at sea. Applied also to property captured in time of war by non-commissioned vessels of a belligerent nation. 1 Kent, Comm. 96.

DROITURAL. What belongs of right; relating to right; as real actions are either droitural or possessory,—*droitural* when the plaintiff seeks to recover the property. Finch, Law, 257.

DROMONES, DROMOS, DROMUNDA. These were at first high ships of great burden, but afterwards those which we now call "men-of-war." Jacob.

DROP. In English practice. When the members of a court are equally divided on the argument showing cause against a rule *nisi*, no order is made, *i. e.*, the rule is neither discharged nor made absolute, and the rule is said to *drop*. In practice, there being a right to appeal, it has been usual to make an order in one way, the junior judge withdrawing his judgment. Wharton.

DROP-LETTER. A letter addressed for delivery in the same city or district in which it is posted.

DROVE-ROAD. In Scotch law. A road for driving cattle. 7 Bell, App. Cas. 43, 53, 57. A drift-road. Lord Brougham, Id.

DROVE-STANCE. In Scotch law. A place adjoining a drove-road, for resting and refreshing sheep and cattle on their journey. 7 Bell, App. Cas. 53, 57.

DROWN. To merge or sink. "In some cases a right of freehold shall *drown* in a chattel." Co. Litt. 266*a*, 321*a*.

DRU. A thicket of wood in a valley. Domesday.

DRUG. The general name of substances used in medicine; any substance, vegetable, animal, or mineral, used in the composition or preparation of medicines. The term is also applied to materials used in dyeing and in chemistry. See 79 N. C. 281; 53 Vt. 426.

DRUGGIST. A dealer in drugs; one whose business is to sell drugs and medicines. In strict usage, this term is to be distinguished from "apothecary." A druggist deals in the uncompounded medicinal substances; the business of an apothecary is to mix and compound them. But in America the two words are used interchangeably, as the same persons usually discharge both functions.

DRUMMER. A term applied to commercial agents who travel for wholesale merchants and supply the retail trade with goods, or take orders for goods to be shipped to the retail dealer. 4 Lea, 96; 34 Ark. 557.

DRUNGARIUS. In old European law. The commander of a *drungus*, or band of soldiers. Applied also to a naval commander. Spelman.

DRUNGUS. In old European law. A band of soldiers, (*globus militum.*) Spelman.

DRUNKARD. He is a drunkard whose habit it is to get drunk; whose ebriety has become habitual. The terms "drunkard" and "habitual drunkard" mean the same thing. 5 Gray, 85.

DRUNKENNESS. In medical jurisprudence. The condition of a man whose mind is affected by the immediate use of intoxicating drinks.

DRY-CRÆFT. Witchcraft; magic. Anc. Inst. Eng.

DRY EXCHANGE. In English law. A term formerly in use, said to have been invented for the purpose of disguising and covering usury; something being pretended to pass on both sides, whereas, in truth, nothing passed but on one side, in which respect it was called "dry." Cowell; Blount.

DRY-MULTURES. In Scotch law. Corn paid to the owner of a mill, whether the payers grind or not.

DRY RENT. Rent-seck; a rent reserved without a clause of distress.

DRY TRUST. A passive trust; one which requires no action on the part of the trustee beyond turning over money or property to the *cestui que trust.*

DUARCHY. A form of government where two reign jointly.

Duas uxores eodem tempore habere non licet. It is not lawful to have two wives at the same time. Inst. 1, 10, 6; 1 Bl. Comm. 436.

DUBITANS. Doubting. Dobbin, J., *dubitans.* 1 Show. 364.

DUBITANTE. Doubting. Is affixed to the name of a judge, in the reports, to signify that he doubted the decision rendered.

DUBITATUR. It is doubted. A word frequently used in the reports to indicate that a point is considered doubtful.

DUBITAVIT. Doubted. Vaughan, C. J., *dubitavit.* Freem. 150.

DUCAT. A foreign coin, varying in value in different countries, but usually worth about $2.26 of our money.

DUCATUS. In feudal and old English law. A duchy, the dignity or territory of a duke.

DUCES TECUM. (Lat. Bring with you.) The name of certain species of writs, of which the *subpœna duces tecum* is the most usual, requiring a party who is summoned to appear in court to bring with him some document, piece of evidence, or other thing to be used or inspected by the court.

DUCES TECUM LICET LANGUIDUS. (Bring with you, although sick.) In practice. An ancient writ, now obsolete, directed to the sheriff, upon a return that he could not bring his prisoner without danger of death, he being *adeo languidus,* (so sick;) whereupon the court granted a *habeas corpus* in the nature of a *duces tecum licet languidus.* Cowell; Blount.

DUCHY COURT OF LANCASTER. A tribunal of special jurisdiction, held before the chancellor of the duchy, or his deputy, concerning all matters of equity relating to lands holden of the crown in right of the duchy of Lancaster; which is a thing very distinct from the county palatine, (which has also its separate chancery, for sealing of writs, and the like,) and comprises much territory which lies at a vast distance from it; as particularly a very large district surrounded by the city of Westminster. The proceedings in this court are the same as were those on the equity side of the court of chancery, so that it seems not to be a court of record; and, indeed, it has been holden that the court of chancery has a concurrent jurisdiction with the duchy court, and may take cognizance of the same causes. The appeal from this court lies to the court of appeal. Jud. Act 1873, § 18; 3 Bl. Comm. 78.

DUCHY OF LANCASTER. Those lands which formerly belonged to the dukes of Lancaster, and now belong to the crown in right of the duchy. The duchy is distinct from the county palatine of Lancaster, and includes not only the county, but also much territory at a distance from it, especially the Savoy in London and some land near Westminster. 3 Bl. Comm. 78.

DUCKING-STOOL. See CASTIGATORY.

DUCROIRE. In French law. Guaranty; equivalent to *del credere,* (which see.)

DUE. 1. Just; proper; regular; lawful; sufficient; as in the phrases "due care," "due process of law," "due notice."

2. Owing; payable; justly owed. That which one contracts to pay or perform to another; that which law or justice requires to be paid or done.

3. Owed, or owing, as distinguished from payable. A debt is often said to be *due* from a person where he is the party owing it, or primarily bound to pay, whether the time for payment has or has not arrived.

4. Payable. A bill or note is commonly said to be *due* when the time for payment of it has arrived. 6 Pet. 29, 36.

DUE-BILL. A brief written acknowledgment of a debt. It is not made payable to order, like a promissory note. See I. O. U.

DUE CARE. Just, proper, and sufficient care, so far as the circumstances demand it; the absence of negligence.

This term, as usually understood in cases where the gist of the action is the defendant's negligence, implies not only that a party has not been negligent or careless, but that he has been guilty of no violation of law in relation to the subject-matter or transaction which constitutes the cause of action. Evidence that a party is guilty of a violation of law supports the issue of a want of proper care; nor can it be doubted that in these and similar actions the averment in the declaration of the use of due care, and the denial of it in the answer, properly and distinctly put in issue the legality of the conduct of the party as contributing to the accident or injury which forms the groundwork of the action. No specific averment of the particular unlawful act which caused or contributed to produce the result complained of should, in such cases, be deemed necessary. 10 Allen, 18. See, also, Id. 532.

DUE COURSE OF LAW. This phrase is synonymous with "due process of law," or "the law of the land," and the general definition thereof is "law in its regular course of administration through courts of justice;" and, while not always necessarily confined to judicial proceedings, yet these words have such a signification, when used to designate the kind of an eviction, or ouster, from real estate by which a party is dispossessed, as to preclude thereunder proof of a constructive eviction resulting from the purchase of a paramount title when hostilely asserted by the party holding it. 19 Kan. 542. See, also, 34 Ala. 236; 11 Wend. 635; 63 Ala. 436; 38 Miss. 424; 3 Stew. 108; 4 Dill. 266.

DUE NOTICE. No fixed rule can be established as to what shall constitute "due notice." "Due" is a relative term, and must be applied to each case in the exercise of the discretion of the court in view of the particular circumstances. 1 McAll. 420.

DUE PROCESS OF LAW. Law in its regular course of administration through courts of justice. 3 Story, Const. 264, 661.

"Due process of law in each particular case means such an exercise of the powers of the government as the settled maxims of law permit and sanction, and under such safeguards for the protection of individual rights as those maxims prescribe for the class of cases to which the one in question belongs." Cooley, Const. Lim. 441. See, also, 12 N. Y. 209; 5 Mich. 251; 6 Cold. 233; 49 Cal. 403.

Whatever difficulty may be experienced in giving to those terms a definition which will embrace every permissible exertion of power affecting private rights, and exclude such as is forbidden, there can be no doubt of their meaning when applied to judicial proceedings. They then mean a course of legal proceedings according to those rules and principles which have been established in our systems of jurisprudence for the enforcement and protection of private rights. To give such proceedings any validity, there must be a tribunal competent by its constitution—that is, by the law of its creation—to pass upon the subject-matter of the suit; and, if that involves merely a determination of the personal liability of the defendant, he must be brought within its jurisdiction by service of process within the state, or his voluntary appearance. 95 U. S. 733.

Due process of law implies the right of the person affected thereby to be present before the tribunal which pronounces judgment upon the question of life, liberty, or property, in its most comprehensive sense; to be heard, by testimony or otherwise, and to have the right of controverting, by proof, every material fact which bears on the question of right in the matter involved. If any question of fact or liability be conclusively presumed against him, this is not due process of law. 58 Ala. 599.

These phrases in the constitution do not mean the general body of the law, common and statute, as it was at the time the constitution took effect; for that would seem to deny the right of the legislature to amend or repeal the law. They refer to certain fundamental rights, which that system of jurisprudence, of which ours is a derivative, has always recognized. 50 Miss. 468.

"Due process of law," as used in the constitution, cannot mean less than a prosecution or suit instituted and conducted according to the prescribed forms and solemnities for ascertaining guilt, or determining the title to property. 3 N. Y. 511, 517; 4 Hill, 140; 10 N. Y. 374, 397.

DUEL. A duel is any combat with deadly weapons, fought between two or more persons, by previous agreement or upon a previous quarrel. Pen. Code Cal. § 225.

DUELLUM. The trial by battel or judicial combat. See BATTEL.

DUES. Certain payments; rates or taxes.

DUKE, in English law, is a title of nobility, ranking immediately next to the Prince of Wales. It is only a title of dignity. Conferring it does not give any domain, territory, or jurisdiction over the place whence the title is taken. *Duchess,* the consort of a duke. Wharton.

DUKE OF EXETER'S DAUGHTER. The name of a rack in the Tower, so called after a minister of Henry VI., who sought to introduce it into England.

DULOCRACY. A government where servants and slaves have so much license and privilege that they domineer. Wharton.

DULY. In due or proper form or manner.

Regularly; upon a proper foundation, as distinguished from mere form.

DUM. Lat. While; as long as; until; upon condition that; provided that.

DUM BENE SE GESSERIT. While he shall conduct himself well; during good behavior. Expressive of a tenure of office not dependent upon the pleasure of the appointing power, nor for a limited period, but terminable only upon the death or misconduct of the incumbent.

DUM FERVET OPUS. While the work glows; in the heat of action. 1 Kent, Comm. 120.

DUM FUIT IN PRISONA. In English law. A writ which lay for a man who had aliened lands under duress by imprisonment, to restore to him his proper estates. 2 Inst. 482. Abolished by St. 3 & 4 Wm. IV. c. 27.

DUM FUIT INFRA ÆTATEM. (While he was within age.) In old English practice. A writ of entry which formerly lay for an infant after he had attained his full age, to recover lands which he had aliened in fee, in tail, or for life, during his infancy; and, after his death, his heir had the same remedy. Reg. Orig. 228*b*; Fitzh. Nat. Brev. 192, G; Litt. § 406; Co. Litt. 247*b*.

DUM NON FUIT COMPOS MENTIS. The name of a writ which the heirs of a person who was *non compos mentis*, and who aliened his lands, might have sued out to restore him to his rights. Abolished by 3 & 4 Wm. IV. c. 27.

DUM RECENS FUIT MALEFICIUM. While the offense was fresh. A term employed in the old law of appeal of rape. Bract. fol. 147.

DUM SOLA. While sole, or single. *Dum sola fuerit*, while she shall remain sole. *Dum sola et casta vixerit*, while she lives single and chaste. Words of limitation in old conveyances. Co. Litt. 235*a*. Also applied generally to an unmarried woman in connection with something that was or might be done during that condition.

DUMB. One who cannot speak; a person who is mute.

DUMB-BIDDING. In sales at auction, when the minimum amount which the owner will take for the article is written on a piece of paper, and placed by the owner under a candlestick, or other thing, and it is agreed that no bidding shall avail unless equal to that, this is called "dumb-bidding." Bab. Auct. 44.

DUMMODO. Provided; provided that. A word of limitation in the Latin forms of conveyances, of frequent use in introducing a reservation; as in reserving a rent.

DUN. A mountain or high open place. The names of places ending in *dun* or *don* were either built on hills or near them in open places.

DUNA. In old records. A bank of earth cast up; the side of a ditch. Cowell.

DUNGEON. Such an under-ground prison or cell as was formerly placed in the strongest part of a fortress; a dark or subterraneous prison.

DUNIO. A double; a kind of base coin less than a farthing.

DUNNAGE. Pieces of wood placed against the sides and bottom of the hold of a vessel, to preserve the cargo from the effect of leakage, according to its nature and quality. Abb. Shipp. 227.

There is considerable resemblance between dunnage and ballast. The latter is used for trimming the ship, and bringing it down to a draft of water proper and safe for sailing. Dunnage is placed under the cargo to keep it from being wetted by water getting into the hold, or between the different parcels to keep them from bruising and injuring each other. 13 Wall. 674.

DUNSETS. People that dwell on hilly places or mountains. Jacob.

Duo non possunt in solido unam rem possidere. Two cannot possess one thing in entirety. Co. Litt. 368.

Duo sunt instrumenta ad omnes res aut confirmandas aut impugnandas, ratio et authoritas. There are two instruments for confirming or impugning all things,—reason and authority. 8 Coke, 16.

DUODECEMVIRALE JUDICIUM. The trial by twelve men, or by jury. Applied to juries *de medietate linguæ*. Mol. de Jure Mar. 448.

DUODECIMA MANUS. Twelve hands. The oaths of twelve men, including himself, by whom the defendant was allowed to make his law. 3 Bl. Comm. 343.

DUODENA. In old records. A jury of twelve men. Cowell.

DUODENA MANU. A dozen hands, *i. e.*, twelve witnesses to purge a criminal of an offense.

Duorum in solidum dominium vel possessio esse non potest. Ownership or possession in entirety cannot be in two persons of the same thing. Dig. 13, 6, 5, 15; Mackeld. Rom. Law, § 245. Bract. fol. 28*b*.

DUPLA. In the civil law. Double the price of a thing. Dig. 21, 2, 2.

DUPLEX QUERELA. Double complaint. An ecclesiastical proceeding, which is in the nature of an appeal from an ordinary's refusal to institute, to his next immediate superior; as from a bishop to the archbishop. If the superior adjudges the cause of refusal to be insufficient, he will grant institution to the appellant. Phillim. Ecc. Law, 440.

DUPLEX VALOR MARITAGII. In old English law. Double the value of the marriage. While an infant was in ward, the guardian had the power of tendering him or her a suitable match, without disparagement, which if the infants refused, they forfeited the value of the marriage to their guardian, that is, so much as a jury would assess or any one would give to the guardian for such an alliance; and, if the infants married themselves without the guardian's consent, they forfeited double the value of the marriage. 2 Bl. Comm. 70; Litt. § 110; Co. Litt. 82*b*.

DUPLICATE. When two written documents are substantially alike, so that each might be a copy or transcript from the other, while both stand on the same footing as original instruments, they are called "duplicates." Agreements, deeds, and other documents are frequently executed in duplicate, in order that each party may have an original in his possession.

A duplicate is sometimes defined to be the "copy" of a thing; but, though generally a copy, a duplicate differs from a mere copy, in having all the validity of an original. Nor, it seems, need it be an exact copy. Defined also to be the "counterpart" of an instrument; but in indentures there is a distinction between *counterparts* executed by the several parties respectively, each party affixing his or her seal to only one counterpart, and *duplicate originals*, each executed by all the parties. 7 Man. & G. 91, note. The old indentures, charters, or chirographs seem to have had the character of duplicates. Burrill.

In English law. The certificate of discharge given to an insolvent debtor who takes the benefit of the act for the relief of insolvent debtors.

The ticket given by a pawnbroker to the pawner of a chattel.

DUPLICATE WILL. A term used in England, where a testator executes two copies of his will, one to keep himself, and the other to be deposited with another person. Upon application for probate of a duplicate will, both copies must be deposited in the registry of the court of probate.

DUPLICATIO. In the civil law. The defendant's answer to the plaintiff's replication; corresponding to the rejoinder of the common law.

Duplicationem possibilitatis lex non patitur. The law does not allow the doubling of a possibility. 1 Rolle, 321.

DUPLICATUM JUS. Double right. Bract. fol. 283*b*. See DROIT-DROIT.

DUPLICITY. The technical fault, in pleading, of uniting two or more causes of action in one count in a writ, or two or more grounds of defense in one plea, or two or more breaches in a replication.

DUPLY, *n.* (From Lat. *duplicatio, q. v.*) In Scotch pleading. The defendant's answer to the plaintiff's replication.

DUPLY, *v.* In Scotch pleading. To rejoin. "It is *duplyed* by the panel." 3 State Trials, 471.

DURANTE. Lat. During. A word of limitation in old conveyances. Co. Litt. 234*b*. *Durante viduitate*, during widowhood. *Durante virginitate*, during virginity. *Durante vita*, during life.

DURANTE ABSENTIA. During absence. In some jurisdictions, administration of a decedent's estate is said to be granted *durante absentia* in cases where the absence of the proper proponents of the will, or of an executor, delays or imperils the settlement of the estate.

DURANTE BENE PLACITO. During good pleasure. The ancient tenure of English judges was *durante bene placito*. 1 Bl. Comm. 267, 342.

DURANTE MINORE ÆTATE. During minority. 2 Bl. Comm. 503; 5 Coke, 29, 30. Words taken from the old form of letters of administration. 5 Coke, ubi supra.

DURANTE VIDUITATE. During widowhood. 2 Bl. Comm. 124. *Durante casta viduitate*, during chaste widowhood. 10 East, 520.

DURBAR. In India. A court, audience, or levee. Mozley & Whitley.

DURESS, v. To subject to duress. A word used by Lord Bacon. "If the party *duressed* do make any motion," etc. Bac. Max. 89, reg. 22.

DURESS, n. Unlawful constraint exercised upon a man whereby he is forced to do some act against his will. It may be either "duress of imprisonment," where the person is deprived of his liberty in order to force him to compliance, or by violence, beating, or other actual injury, or duress *per minas*, consisting in threats of imprisonment or great physical injury or death. Duress may also include the same injuries, threats, or restraint exercised upon the man's wife, child, or parent.

Duress consists in any illegal imprisonment, or legal imprisonment used for an illegal purpose, or threats of bodily or other harm, or other means amounting to or tending to coerce the will of another, and actually inducing him to do an act contrary to his free will. Code Ga. 1882, § 2637.

By duress, in its more extended sense, is meant that degree of severity, either threatened or impending or actually inflicted, which is sufficient to overcome the mind and will of a person of ordinary firmness. Duress *per minas* is restricted to fear of loss of life, or of mayhem, or loss of limb, or other remediless harm to the person. 39 Me. 559.

DURESS OF IMPRISONMENT. The wrongful imprisonment of a person, or the illegal restraint of his liberty, in order to compel him to do some act. 1 Bl. Comm. 130, 131, 136, 137; 1 Steph. Comm. 137; 2 Kent, Comm. 453.

DURESS PER MINAS. Duress by threats. The use of threats and menaces to compel a person, by the fear of death, or grievous bodily harm, as mayhem or loss of limb, to do some lawful act, or to commit a misdemeanor. 1 Bl. Comm. 130; 4 Bl. Comm. 30; 4 Steph. Comm. 83. See METUS.

DURESSOR. One who subjects another to duress; one who compels another to do a thing, as by menace. Bac. Max. 90, reg. 22.

DURHAM. A county palatine in England, the jurisdiction of which was vested in the Bishop of Durham until the statute 6 & 7 Wm. IV. c. 19, vested it as a separate franchise and royalty in the crown. The jurisdiction of the Durham court of pleas was transferred to the supreme court of judicature by the judicature act of 1873.

DURSLEY. In old English law. Blows without wounding or bloodshed; dry blows. Blount.

DUSTUCK. A term used in Hindostan for a passport, permit, or order from the English East Indian Company. It generally meant a permit under their seal, exempting goods from the payment of duties. Enc. Lond.

DUTCH AUCTION. A method of sale by auction which consists in the public offer of the property at a price beyond its value, and then gradually lowering the price until some one becomes the purchaser. 28 Ohio St. 482.

DUTIES. In its most usual signification this word is the synonym of imposts or customs; but it is sometimes used in a broader sense, as including all manner of taxes, charges, or governmental impositions.

DUTY. In its use in jurisprudence, this word is the correlative of *right*. Thus, wherever there exists a right in any person, there also rests a corresponding duty upon some other person or upon all persons generally. But it is also used, in a wider sense, to designate that class of moral obligations which lie outside the jural sphere; such, namely, as rest upon an imperative ethical basis, but have not been recognized by the law as within its proper province for purposes of enforcement or redress. Thus, gratitude towards a benefactor is a *duty*, but its refusal will not ground an action. In this meaning "duty" is the equivalent of "moral obligation," as distinguished from a "legal obligation."

As a technical term of the law, "duty" signifies a thing due; that which is due from a person; that which a person owes to another. An obligation to do a thing. A word of more extensive signification than "debt," although both are expressed by the same Latin word "*debitum*." 26 Vt. 725, 733.

But in practice it is commonly reserved as the designation of those obligations of performance, care, or observance which rest upon a person in an official or fiduciary capacity; as the *duty* of an executor, trustee, manager, etc.

It also denotes a tax or impost due to the

government upon the importation or exportation of goods.

DUUMVIRI. (From *duo*, two, and *viri*, men.) A general appellation among the ancient Romans, given to any magistrates elected in pairs to fill any office, or perform any function. Brande.

Duumviri municipales were two annual magistrates in the towns and colonies, having judicial powers. Calvin.

Duumviri navales were officers appointed to man, equip, and refit the navy. Id.

DUX. In Roman law. A leader or military commander. The commander of an army. Dig. 3, 2, 2, pr.

In feudal and old European law. Duke; a title of honor, or order of nobility. 1 Bl. Comm. 397; Crabb, Eng. Law, 236.

In later law. A military governor of a province. See Cod. 1, 27, 2. A military officer having charge of the borders or frontiers of the empire, called "*dux limitis*." Cod. 1, 49, 1, pr. At this period, the word began to be used as a title of honor or dignity.

DWELL. To have an abode; to inhabit; to live in a place.

DWELLING-HOUSE. The house in which a man lives with his family; a residence; the apartment or building, or group of buildings, occupied by a family as a place of residence.

In conveyancing. Includes all buildings attached to or connected with the house. 2 Hil. Real Prop. 338, and note.

In the law of burglary. A house in which the occupier and his family usually reside, or, in other words, dwell and lie in. Whart. Crim. Law, 357.

DWELLING-PLACE. This term is not synonymous with a "place of pauper settlement." 49 N. H. 553.

Dwelling-place, or home, means some permanent abode or residence, with intention to remain; and is not synonymous with "domicile," as used in international law, but has a more limited and restricted meaning. 19 Me. 293.

DYING DECLARATIONS. Statements made by a person who is lying at the point of death, and is conscious of his approaching dissolution, in reference to the manner in which he received the injuries of which he is dying, or other immediate cause of his death, and in reference to the person who inflicted such injuries or the connection with such injuries of a person who is charged or suspected of having committed them; which statements are admissible in evidence in a trial for homicide where the killing of the declarant is the crime charged to the defendant.

DYING WITHOUT ISSUE. At common law this phrase imports an indefinite failure of issue, and not a dying without issue surviving at the time of the death of the first taker. But this rule has been changed in some of the states, by statute or decisions, and in England by St. 7 Wm. IV., and 1 Vict. c. 26, § 29.

The words "die without issue," and "die without leaving issue," in a devise of real estate, import an indefinite failure of issue, and not the failure of issue at the death of the first taker. And no distinction is to be made between the words "without issue" and "without leaving issue." 32 Barb. 328; 20 How. Pr 41; 3 Port. 69; 6 Port. 319.

In Connecticut, it has been repeatedly held that the expression "dying without issue," and like expressions, have reference to the time of the death of the party, and not to an indefinite failure of issue. 34 Me. 176.

Dying without children imports not a failure of issue at any indefinite future period, but a leaving no children at the death of the legatee. 13 N. J. Eq. 105.

DYKE-REED, or DYKE-REEVE. An officer who has the care and oversight of the *dykes* and *drains* in fenny counties.

DYSNOMY. Bad legislation; the enactment of bad laws.

DYSPEPSIA. A state of the stomach in which its functions are disturbed, without the presence of other diseases, or when, if other diseases are present, they are of minor importance. Dungl. Med. Dict.

DYVOUR. In Scotch law. A bankrupt.

DYVOUR'S HABIT. In Scotch law. A habit which debtors who are set free on a *cessio bonorum* are obliged to wear, unless in the summons and process of *cessio* it be libeled, sustained, and proved that the bankruptcy proceeds from misfortune. And bankrupts are condemned to submit to the habit, even where no suspicion of fraud lies against them, if they have been dealers in an illicit trade. Ersk. Prin. 4, 3, 13.

E.

E. As an abbreviation, this letter may stand for "Exchequer," "English," "Edward," "Equity," "East," "Eastern," "Easter," or "Ecclesiastical."

E. A Latin preposition, meaning from, out of, after, or according. It occurs in many Latin phrases; but (in this form) only before a consonant. When the initial of the following word is a vowel, *ex* is used.

E CONTRA. From the opposite; on the contrary.

E CONVERSO. Conversely. On the other hand; on the contrary. Equivalent to *e contra.*

E. G. An abbreviation of *exempli gratia.* For the sake of an example.

E MERA GRATIA. Out of mere grace or favor.

E PLURIBUS UNUM. One out of many. The motto of the United States of America.

EA. Sax. The water or river; also the mouth of a river on the shore between high and low water-mark.

Ea est accipienda interpretatio, quæ vitio caret. That interpretation is to be received [or adopted] which is free from fault [or wrong.] The law will not intend a wrong. Bac. Max. 17, (in reg. 3.)

EA INTENTIONE. With that intent. Held not to make a condition, but a confidence and trust. Dyer, 138*b*.

Ea quæ, commendandi causa, in venditionibus dicuntur, si palam appareant, venditorem non obligant. Those things which are said on sales, in the way of commendation, if [the qualities of the thing sold] appear openly, do not bind the seller. Dig. 18, 1, 43, pr.

Ea quæ dari impossibilia sunt, vel quæ in rerum natura non sunt, pro non adjectis habentur. Those things which are impossible to be given, or which are not in the nature of things, are regarded as not added, [as no part of an agreement.] Dig. 50, 17, 135.

Ea quæ in curia nostra rite acta sunt debitæ executioni demandari debent. Co. Litt. 289. Those things which are properly transacted in our court ought to be committed to a due execution.

Ea quæ raro accidunt non temere in agendis negotiis computantur. Those things which rarely happen are not to be taken into account in the transaction of business, without sufficient reason. Dig. 50, 17, 64.

EACH. The effect of this word, used in the covenants of a bond, is to create a several obligation. 3 Dowl. & R. 112; 5 Term 522; 2 Day, 442; 104 Mass. 217.

Eadem causa diversis rationibus coram judicibus ecclesiasticis et secularibus ventilatur. 2 Inst. 622. The same cause is argued upon different principles before ecclesiastical and secular judges.

Eadem est ratio, eadem est lex. The same reason, the same law. 7 Pick. 493.

Eadem mens præsumitur regis quæ est juris et quæ esse debet, præsertim in dubiis. Hob. 154. The mind of the sovereign is presumed to be coincident with that of the law, and with that which it ought to be, especially in ambiguous matters.

EAGLE. A gold coin of the United States of the value of ten dollars.

EALDER, or EALDING. In old Saxon law. An elder or chief.

EALDERMAN, or EALDORMAN. The name of a Saxon magistrate; alderman; analogous to *earl* among the Danes, and *senator* among the Romans. See ALDERMAN.

EALDOR-BISCOP. An archbishop.

EALDORBURG. Sax. The metropolis; the chief city. Obsolete.

EALEHUS. (Fr. *eale*, Sax., ale, and *hus*, house.) An ale-house.

EALHORDA. Sax. The privilege of assising and selling beer. Obsolete.

EAR GRASS. In English law. Such grass which is upon the land after the mowing, until the feast of the Annunciation after. 3 Leon. 213.

EAR-MARK. A mark put upon a thing to distinguish it from another. Originally and literally, a mark upon the ear; a mode of marking sheep and other animals.

Property is said to be *ear-marked* when it can be identified or distinguished from other property of the same nature.

Money has no ear-mark, but it is an ordinary term for a privy mark made by any one on a coin.

EAR-WITNESS. In the law of evidence. One who attests or can attest anything as heard by himself.

EARL. A title of nobility, formerly the highest in England, now the third, ranking between a marquis and a viscount, and corresponding with the French "*comte*" and the German "*graf.*" The title originated with the Saxons, and is the most ancient of the English peerage. William the Conqueror first made this title hereditary, giving it in fee to his nobles; and allotting them for the support of their state the third penny out of the sheriff's court, issuing out of all pleas of the shire, whence they had their ancient title "shiremen." At present the title is accompanied by no territory, private or judicial rights, but merely confers nobility and an hereditary seat in the house of lords. Wharton.

EARL MARSHAL OF ENGLAND. A great officer of state who had anciently several courts under his jurisdiction, as the court of chivalry and the court of honor. Under him is the herald's office, or college of arms. He was also a judge of the Marshalsea court, now abolished. This office is of great antiquity, and has been for several ages hereditary in the family of the Howards. 3 Bl. Comm. 68, 103; 3 Steph. Comm. 335, note.

EARLDOM. The dignity or jurisdiction of an earl. The dignity only remains now, as the jurisdiction has been given over to the sheriff. 1 Bl. Comm. 339.

EARLES-PENNY. Money given in part payment. See EARNEST.

EARNEST. The payment of a part of the price of goods sold, or the delivery of part of such goods, for the purpose of binding the contract. 108 Mass. 54.

A token or pledge passing between the parties, by way of evidence, or ratification of the sale. 2 Kent, Comm. 495, note.

EARNINGS. This term is used to denote a larger class of credits than would be included in the term "wages." 102 Mass. 235; 115 Mass. 165.

The gains of the person derived from his services or labor without the aid of capital. 20 Wis. 330. See, also, 46 N. H. 48.

"Gross" earnings are the total receipts before deducting expenditures. "As a general proposition, net earnings are the excess of the gross earnings over the expenditures defrayed in producing them, aside from, and exclusive of, the expenditure of capital laid out in constructing and equipping the works themselves." 99 U. S. 420. See, also, 44 Ohio St. 315, 7 N. E. Rep. 139; 54 Conn. 168, 5 Atl. Rep. 851.

"Surplus" earnings of a company or corporation means the amount owned by the company over and above its capital and actual liabilities. 76 N. Y. 74.

EARTH. Soil of all kinds, including gravel, clay, loam, and the like, in distinction from the firm rock. 75 N. Y. 76.

EASEMENT. A right in the owner of one parcel of land, by reason of such ownership, to use the land of another for a special purpose not inconsistent with a general property in the owner. 2 Washb. Real Prop. 25.

A privilege which the owner of one adjacent tenement hath of another, existing in respect of their several tenements, by which that owner against whose tenement the privilege exists is obliged to suffer or not to do something on or in regard to his own land for the advantage of him in whose land the privilege exists. Termes de la Ley.

A private easement is a privilege, service, or convenience which one neighbor has of another, by prescription, grant, or necessary implication, and without profit; as a way over his land, a gate-way, water-course, and the like. Kitch. 105; 3 Cruise, Dig. 484.

The land against which the easement or privilege exists is called the "servient" tenement, and the estate to which it is annexed the "dominant" tenement; and their owners are called respectively the "servient" and "dominant" owner. These terms are taken from the civil law.

At the present day, the distinction between an "easement" and a "license" is well settled and fully recognized, although it becomes difficult in some of the cases to discover a substantial difference between them. An easement, it has appeared, is a liberty, privilege, or advantage in land, without profit, and existing distinct from the ownership of the soil; and it has appeared, also, that a claim for an easement must be founded upon a deed or writing, or upon prescription, which supposes one. It is a permanent interest in another's land, with a right to enjoy it fully and without obstruction. A license, on the other hand, is a bare authority to do a certain act or series of acts upon another's land, without possessing any estate therein; and, it being founded in personal confidence, it is not assignable, and it is gone if the owner of the land who gives the license transfers his title to another, or if either party die. 3 Pin. 415.

Classification. Easements are classified as *affirmative* or *negative;* the former being those where the servient estate must permit something to be done thereon, (as to pass over it, or to discharge water upon it;) the latter being those where the owner of the servient estate is prohibited from doing something otherwise lawful upon his estate, because it will affect the dominant estate, (as interrupting the light and air from the latter by building on the former.) 2 Washb. Real Prop. 301.

They are also either *continuous* or *discontinuous;* the former depending on some natural conformation of the servient tenement, or artificial structure upon it, which constistutes the easement or the means of enjoying it; the latter being such as have no means specially constructed or appropriated for their enjoyment, and are enjoyed at intervals, leaving in the mean time no visible signs of their existence. 18 N. J. Eq. 262.

Easements are also classified as *private* or *public,* according as their enjoyment belongs to an individual or to the community.

They may also be either *of necessity* or *of convenience.* The former is the case where the easement is indispensable to the enjoyment of the dominant estate; the latter, where the easement increases the facility, comfort, or convenience of the enjoyment of the dominant estate, or of some right connected with it.

An *appurtenant* (or appendant) easement is one which is attached to and passes with the dominant tenement as an appurtenance thereof.

EAST. In the customs laws of the United States, the term "countries *east* of the Cape of Good Hope" means countries with which, formerly, the United States ordinarily carried on commercial intercourse by passing around that cape. 101 U. S. 790.

EAST GREENWICH. The name of a royal manor in the county of Kent, England; mentioned in royal grants or patents, as descriptive of the tenure of free socage.

EAST INDIA COMPANY. The East India Company was originally established for prosecuting the trade between England and India, which they acquired a right to carry on exclusively. Since the middle of the last century, however, the company's political affairs had become of more importance than their commerce. In 1858, by 21 & 22 Vict. c. 106, the government of the territories of the company was transferred to the crown. Wharton.

EASTER. A feast of the Christian church held in memory of our Saviour's resurrection. The Greeks and Latins call it "*pascha,*" (passover,) to which Jewish feast our Easter answers. This feast has been annually celebrated since the time of the apostles, and is one of the most important festivals in the Christian calendar, being that which regulates and determines the times of all the other movable feasts. Enc. Lond.

EASTER-OFFERINGS, or EASTER-DUES. In English law. Small sums of money paid to the parochial clergy by the parishioners at Easter as a compensation for personal tithes, or the tithe for personal labor; recoverable under 7 & 8 Wm. III. c. 6, before justices of the peace.

EASTER TERM. In English law. One of the four terms of the courts. It is now a fixed term, beginning on the 15th of April and ending on the 8th of May in every year, though sometimes prolonged so late as the 13th of May, under St. 11 Geo. IV. and 1 Wm. IV. c. 70. From November 2, 1875, the division of the legal year into terms is abolished so far as concerns the administration of justice. 3 Steph. Comm. 482–486; Mozley & Whitley.

EASTERLING. A coin struck by Richard II., which is supposed to have given rise to the name of "sterling," as applied to English money.

EASTERLY. This word, when used alone, will be construed to mean "due east." But that is a rule of necessity growing out of the indefiniteness of the term, and has no application where other words are used for the purpose of qualifying its meaning. Where such is the case, instead of meaning "due east," it means precisely what the qualifying word makes it mean. 32 Cal. 227.

EASTINUS. An easterly coast or country.

EAT INDE SINE DIE. In criminal practice. Words used on the acquittal of a defendant, *that he may go thence without a day, i. e.*, be dismissed without any further continuance or adjournment.

EATING-HOUSE. Any place where food or refreshments of any kind, not including spirits, wines, ale, beer, or other malt liquors, are provided for casual visitors, and sold for consumption therein. Act Cong. July 13, 1866, § 9, (14 St. at Large, 118.)

EAVES. The edge of a roof, built so as to project over the walls of a house, in order that the rain may drop therefrom to the ground instead of running down the wall.

EAVESDROPPING. In English criminal law. The offense of listening under walls or windows, or the *eaves* of a house, to hearken after discourse, and thereupon to frame slanderous and mischievous tales. 4 Bl. Comm. 168. It is a misdemeanor at common law, indictable at sessions, and punishable by fine and finding sureties for good behavior. Id.; Steph. Crim. Law, 109. See 3 Head, 300.

EBB AND FLOW. An expression used formerly in this country to denote the limits of admiralty jurisdiction. See 3 Mason, 127; 2 Story, 176; 2 Gall. 398; 4 Wall. 562; 8 Wall. 15.

EBBA. In old English law. Ebb. *Ebba et fluctus;* ebb and flow of tide; ebb and flood. Bract. fols. 255, 338. The time occupied by one ebb and flood was anciently granted to persons essoined as being beyond sea, in addition to the period of forty days. See Fleta, lib. 6, c. 8, § 2.

EBDOMADARIUS. In ecclesiastical law. An officer in cathedral churches who supervised the regular performance of divine service, and prescribed the particular duties of each person in the choir.

EBEREMORTH, EBEREMORS, EBERE-MURDER. See ABEREMURDER.

Ecce modo mirum, quod fœmina fert breve regis, non nominando virum, conjunctum robore legis. Co. Litt. 132*b*. Behold, indeed, a wonder! that a woman has the king's writ without naming her husband, who by law is united to her.

ECCHYMOSIS. In medical jurisprudence. Blackness. It is an extravasation of blood by rupture of capillary vessels, and hence it follows contusion; but it may exist, as in cases of scurvy and other morbid conditions, without the latter. Ry. Med. Jur. 172.

ECCLESIA. Lat. An assembly. A Christian assembly; a church. A place of religious worship. Spelman.

Ecclesia ecclesiæ decimas solvere non debet. Cro. Eliz. 479. A church ought not to pay tithes to a church.

Ecclesia est domus mansionalis Omnipotentis Dei. 2 Inst. 164. The church is the mansion-house of the Omnipotent God.

Ecclesia est infra ætatem et in custodia domini regis, qui tenetur jura et hæreditates ejusdem manu tenere et defendere. 11 Coke, 49. The church is under age, and in the custody of the king, who is bound to uphold and defend its rights and inheritances.

Ecclesia fungitur vice minoris; meliorem conditionem suam facere potest, deteriorem nequaquam. Co. Litt. 341. The church enjoys the privilege of a minor; it can make its own condition better, but not worse.

Ecclesia non moritur. 2 Inst. 3. The church does not die.

Ecclesiæ magis favendum est quam personæ. Godol. Ecc. Law, 172. The church is to be more favored than the parson.

ECCLESIÆ SCULPTURA. The image or sculpture of a church in ancient times was often cut out or cast in plate or other metal, and preserved as a religious treasure or relic, and to perpetuate the memory of some famous churches. Jacob.

ECCLESIARCH. The ruler of a church.

ECCLESIASTIC, *n.* A clergyman; a priest; a man consecrated to the service of the church.

ECCESIASTICAL. Something belonging to or set apart for the church, as distinguished from "civil" or "secular," with regard to the world. Wharton.

ECCLESIASTICAL AUTHORITIES. In England, the clergy, under the sovereign, as temporal head of the church, set apart from the rest of the people or laity, in order to superintend the public worship of God and the other ceremonies of religion, and to administer spiritual counsel and instruction. The several orders of the clergy are: (1) Archbishops and bishops; (2) deans and chapters; (3) archdeacons; (4) rural deans; (5) parsons (under whom are included appropriators) and vicars; (6) curates. Church-wardens or sidesmen, and parish clerks and sextons, inasmuch as their duties are connected with the church, may be considered to be a species of ecclesiastical authorities. Wharton.

ECCLESIASTICAL COMMISSIONERS. In English law. A body corporate, erected by St. 6 & 7 Wm. IV. c. 77, empowered to suggest measures conducive to the efficiency of the established church, to be ratified by orders in council. Wharton. See 3 Steph. Comm. 156, 157.

ECCLESIASTICAL CORPORATIONS. Such corporations as are composed of persons who take a lively interest in the advancement of religion, and who are associated and incorporated for that purpose. Ang. & A. Corp. § 36.

Corporations whose members are spiritual persons are distinguished from *lay* corporations. 1 Bl. Comm. 470.

ECCLESIASTICAL COURTS. A system of courts in England, held by authority of the sovereign, and having jurisdiction over matters pertaining to the religion and ritual of the established church, and the rights, duties, and discipline of ecclesiastical persons as such. They are as follows: The archdeacon's court, consistory court, court of arches, court of peculiars, prerogative court, court of delegates, court of convocation, court of audience, court of faculties, and court of commissioners of review. See those several titles; and see 3 Bl. Comm. 64-68.

ECCLESIASTICAL DIVISION OF ENGLAND. This is a division into provinces, dioceses, archdeaconries, rural deaneries, and parishes.

ECCLESIASTICAL LAW. The body of jurisprudence administered by the ecclesiastical courts of England; derived, in large measure, from the canon and civil law. As now restricted, it applies mainly to the affairs, and the doctrine, discipline, and worship, of the established church.

ECDICUS. The attorney, proctor, or advocate of a corporation. *Episcoporum ecdici;* bishops' proctors; church lawyers. 1 Reeve, Eng. Law, 65.

ECHANTILLON. In French law. One of the two parts or pieces of a wooden tally. That in possession of the debtor is properly called the "tally," the other "*echantillon.*" Poth. Obl. pt. 4, c. 1, art. 2, § 8.

ECHEVIN. In French law. A municipal officer corresponding with alderman or burgess, and having in some instances a civil jurisdiction in certain causes of trifling importance.

ECHOUEMENT. In French marine law. Stranding. Emerig. Tr. des Ass. c. 12, s. 13, no. 1.

ECLAMPSIA PARTURIENTIUM. In medical jurisprudence. The name of a disease accompanied by apoplectic convulsions, and which produces aberration of mind at childbirth.

ECLECTIC PRACTICE. In medicine. That system followed by physicians who select their modes of practice and medicines from various schools. Webster.

"Without professing to understand much of medical phraseology, we suppose that the terms 'allopathic practice' and 'legitimate business' mean the ordinary method commonly adopted by the great body of learned and eminent physicians, which is taught in their institutions, established by their highest authorities, and accepted by the larger and more respectable portion of the community. By 'eclectic practice,' without imputing to it, as the counsel for the plaintiff seem inclined to, an odor of illegality, we presume is intended another and different system, unusual and eccentric, not countenanced by the classes before referred tó, but characterized by them as spurious and denounced as dangerous. It is sufficient to say that the two modes of treating human maladies are essentially distinct, and based upon different views of the nature and causes of diseases, their appropriate remedies, and the modes of applying them." 34 Conn. 453.

ECRIVAIN. In French marine law. The clerk of a ship. Emerig. Tr. des Ass. c. 11, s. 3, no. 2.

ECUMENICAL. General; universal; as an ecumenical council.

EDDERBRECHE. In Saxon law. The offense of hedge-breaking. Obsolete.

EDESTIA. In old records. Buildings.

EDICT. A positive law promulgated by the sovereign of a country, and having reference either to the whole land or some of its divisions, but usually relating to affairs of state. It differs from a "public proclamation," in that it enacts a new statute, and carries with it the authority of law.

EDICTAL CITATION. In Scotch law. A citation published at the market-cross of Edinburgh, and pier and shore of Leith. Used against foreigners not within the kingdom, but having a landed estate there, and against natives out of the kingdom. Bell.

EDICTS OF JUSTINIAN. Thirteen constitutions or laws of this prince, found in most editions of the *Corpus Juris Civilis*, after the Novels. Being confined to matters of police in the provinces of the empire, they are of little use.

EDICTUM. In the Roman law. An edict; a mandate, or ordinance. An ordinance, or law, enacted by the emperor without the senate; belonging to the class of *constitutiones principis*. Inst. 1, 2, 6. An edict was a mere voluntary constitution of the emperor; differing from a rescript, in not being returned in the way of answer; and from a decree, in not being given in judgment; and from both, in not being founded upon solicitation. Tayl. Civil Law, 233.

A general order published by the prætor, on entering upon his office, containing the system of rules by which he would administer justice during the year of his office. Dig. 1, 2, 2, 10; Mackeld. Rom. Law, § 35. Tayl. Civil Law, 214. See Calvin.

EDICTUM PERPETUUM. In Roman law. The perpetual edict. A compilation or system of law in fifty books, digested by Julian, a lawyer of great eminence under the reign of Adrian, from the Prætor's edicts and other parts of the *Jus Honorarium*. All the remains of it which have come down to us are the extracts of it in the Digests. Butl. Hor. Jur. 52.

EDICTUM THEODORICI. This is the first collection of law that was made after the downfall of the Roman power in Italy. It was promulgated by Theodoric, king of the Ostrogoths, at Rome in A. D. 500. It consists of 154 chapters, in which we recognize parts taken from the Code and Novellæ of Theodosius, from the Codices Gregorianus and Hermogenianus, and the Sententiæ of Paulus. The edict was doubtless drawn up by Roman writers, but the original sources are more disfigured and altered than in any other compilation. This collection of law was intended to apply both to the Goths and the Romans, so far as its provisions went; but, when it made no alteration in the Gothic law, that law was still to be in force. Savigny, Geschichte des R. R.

EDITUS. In old English law. Put forth or promulgated, when speaking of the passage of a statute; and brought forth, or born, when speaking of the birth of a child.

EDUCATE. Includes proper moral, as well as intellectual and physical, instruction. Code Tenn. § 2521; 6 Heisk. 395.

EDUCATION. Within the meaning of a statute relative to the powers and duties of guardians, this term comprehends not merely the instruction received at school or college, but the whole course of training, moral, intellectual, and physical. 6 Heisk. 400.

Education may be particularly directed to either the mental, moral, or physical powers and faculties, but in its broadest and best sense it relates to them all. 145 Mass. 146, 13 N. E. Rep. 354.

EFFECT. The result which an instrument between parties will produce in their relative rights, or which a statute will produce upon the existing law, as discovered from the language used, the forms employed, or other materials for construing it.

The phrases "take effect," "be in force," "go into operation," etc., have been used interchangeably ever since the organization of the state. 4 Ind. 342.

EFFECTS. Personal estate or property. This word has been held to be more comprehensive than the word "goods," as including fixtures, which "goods" will not include. 7 Taunt. 188; 4 J. B. Moore, 73; 4 Barn. & A. 206.

In wills. The word "effects" is equivalent to "property," or "worldly substance," and, if used *simpliciter*, as in a gift of "all my effects," will carry the whole personal estate. Ves. Jr. 507; Ward, Leg. 209. The addition of the words "real and personal" will extend it so as to embrace the whole of the testator's real and personal estate. Cowp. 299; 3 Brown, Parl. Cas. 388.

This is a word often found in wills, and, being equivalent to "property," or "worldly substance," its force depends greatly upon the association of the adjectives "real" and "personal." "Real and personal effects" would embrace the whole estate; but the word "effects" alone must be confined to personal estate simply, unless an intention appears to the contrary. Schouler, Wills, § 509. See 1 Cowp. 304.

Effectus sequitur causam. Wing. 226. The effect follows the cause.

EFFENDI. In Turkish language. Master; a title of respect.

EFFIGY. The corporeal representation of a person.

To make the effigy of a person with an intent to make him the object of ridicule is a libel. 2 Chit. Crim. Law, 866.

EFFLUX. The running of a prescribed period of time to its end; expiration by lapse of time. Particularly applied to the termination of a lease by the expiration of the term for which it was made.

EFFLUXION OF TIME. When this phrase is used in leases, conveyances, and other like deeds, or in agreements expressed in simple writing, it indicates the conclusion or expiration of an agreed term of years specified in the deed or writing, such conclusion or expiration arising in the natural course of events, in contradistinction to the determination of the term by the acts of the parties or by some unexpected or unusual incident or other sudden event. Brown.

EFFORCIALITER. Forcibly; applied to military force.

EFFRACTION. A breach made by the use of force.

EFFRACTOR. One who breaks through; one who commits a burglary.

EFFUSIO SANGUINIS. In old English law. The shedding of blood; the mulct, fine, *wite*, or penalty imposed for the shedding of blood, which the king granted to many lords of manors. Cowell; Tomlins. See BLOODWIT.

EFTERS. In Saxon law. Ways, walks, or hedges. Blount.

EGALITY. Owelty, (*q. v.*) Co. Litt. 169*a*.

EGO. I; myself. This term is used in forming genealogical tables, to represent the person who is the object of inquiry.

EGO, TALIS. I, such a one. Words used in describing the forms of old deeds. Fleta, lib. 3, c. 14, § 5.

EGREDIENS ET EXEUNS. In old pleading. Going forth and issuing out of (land.) Townsh. Pl. 17.

EGYPTIANS, commonly called "Gypsies," are counterfeit rogues, Welsh or English, that disguise themselves in speech and apparel, and wander up and down the country, pretending to have skill in telling fortunes, and to deceive the common people, but live chiefly by filching and stealing, and, therefore, the statutes of 1 & 2 Mar. c. 4, and 5 Eliz. c. 20, were made to punish such as felons if they departed not the realm or continued to a month. Termes de la Ley.

Ei incumbit probatio, qui dicit, non qui negat; cum per rerum naturam factum negantis probatio nulla sit. The proof lies upon him who affirms, not upon him who denies; since, by the nature of things, he who denies a fact cannot produce any proof.

Ei nihil turpe, cui nihil satis. To him to whom nothing is enough, nothing is base. 4 Inst. 53.

EIA, or EY. An island. Cowell.

EIGNE. L. Fr. Eldest; eldest-born. The term is of common occurrence in the old books. Thus, *bastard eigne* means an illegitimate son whose parents afterwards marry and have a second son for lawful issue, the latter being called *mulier puisne*, (after-born.) *Eigne* is probably a corrupt form of the French "*ainé*." 2 Bl. Comm. 248; Litt. § 399.

EIK. In Scotch law. An addition; as, *eik* to a reversion, *eik* to a confirmation. Bell.

EINECIA. Eldership. See ESNECY.

EINETIUS. In English law. The oldest; the first-born. Spelman.

EIRE, or EYRE. In old English law. A journey, route, or circuit. Justices *in eire* were judges who were sent by commission, every seven years, into various counties to hold the assizes and hear pleas of the crown. 3 Bl. Comm. 58.

EIRENARCHA. A name formerly given to a justice of the peace. In the Digests, the word is written "*irenarcha.*"

Eisdem modis dissolvitur obligatio quæ nascitur ex contractu, vel quasi, quibus contrahitur. An obligation which arises from contract, or *quasi* contract, is dissolved in the same ways in which it is contracted. Fleta, lib. 2, c. 60, § 19.

EISNE. The senior; the oldest son. Spelled, also, "*eigne*," "*einsne*," "*aisne*," "*eign.*" Termes de la Ley; Kelham.

EISNETIA, EINETIA. The share of the oldest son. The portion acquired by primogeniture. Termes de la Ley; Co. Litt. 166*b;* Cowell.

EITHER. May be used in the sense of "each." 59 Ill. 87.

This word does not mean "all;" but does mean one or the other of two or more specified things. (Tex.) 4 S. W. Rep. 538.

EJECT. To cast, or throw out; to oust, or dispossess; to put or turn out of possession. 3 Bl. Comm. 198, 199, 200.

EJECTA. In old English law. A woman ravished or deflowered, or cast forth from the virtuous. Blount.

EJECTION. A turning out of possession. 3 Bl. Comm. 199.

EJECTIONE CUSTODIÆ. In old English law. Ejectment of ward. This phrase, which is the Latin equivalent for the French "*ejectment de garde*," was the title of a writ which lay for a guardian when turned out of any land of his ward during the minority of the latter. Brown.

EJECTIONE FIRMÆ. Ejection, or ejectment of farm. The name of a writ or action of trespass, which lay at common law where lands or tenements were let for a term of years, and afterwards the lessor, reversioner, remainder-man, or any stranger *ejected* or ousted the lessee of his term, *ferme*, or *farm*, (*ipsum a firma ejecit.*) In this case the latter might have his writ of *ejection*, by which he recovered at first *damages* for the trespass only, but it was afterwards made a remedy to recover back the *term* itself, or the remainder of it, with damages. Reg. Orig. 227*b;* Fitzh. Nat. Brev. 220, F, G; 3 Bl. Comm. 199; Litt. § 322; Crabb, Eng. Law, 290, 448. It is the foundation of the modern action of ejectment.

EJECTMENT. At common law, this was the name of a mixed action (springing from the earlier personal action of *ejectione firmæ*) which lay for the recovery of the possession of land, and for damages for the unlawful detention of its possession. The action was highly fictitious, being in theory only for the recovery of a term for years, and brought by a purely fictitious person, as lessee in a supposed lease from the real party in interest. The latter's title, however, must be established in order to warrant a recovery, and the establishment of such title, though nominally a mere incident, is in reality the object of the action. Hence this convenient form of suit came to be adopted as the usual method of trying titles to land. See 3 Bl. Comm. 199.

It was the only mixed action at common law, the whole method of proceeding in which was anomalous, and depended on fictions invented and upheld by the court for the convenience of justice, in order to escape from the inconveniences which were found to attend the ancient forms of real and mixed actions.

It is also a form of action by which possessory titles to corporeal hereditaments may be tried and possession obtained.

EJECTUM. That which is thrown up by the sea. Also jetsam, wreck, etc.

EJECTUS. In old English law. A whoremonger. Blount.

EJERCITORIA. In Spanish law. The name of an action lying against a ship's owner, upon the contracts or obligations made by the master for repairs or supplies. It corresponds to the *actio exercitoria* of the Roman law. Mackeld. Rom. Law, § 512.

EJIDOS. In Spanish law. Commons; lands used in common by the inhabitants of a city, pueblo, or town, for pasture, wood, threshing-ground, etc. 15 Cal. 554.

EJURATION. Renouncing or resigning one's place.

Ejus est interpretari cujus est condere. It is his to interpret whose it is to enact. Tayl. Civil Law, 96.

Ejus est nolle, qui potest velle. He who can will, [exercise volition,] has a right to refuse to will, [to withhold consent.] Dig. 50, 7, 3.

Ejus est periculum cujus est dominium aut commodum. He who has the dominion or advantage has the risk.

Ejus nulla culpa est, cui parere necesse sit. No guilt attaches to him who is compelled to obey. Dig. 50, 17, 169, pr. Obedience to existing laws is a sufficient extenuation of guilt before a civil tribunal. Broom, Max. 12, note.

EJUSDEM GENERIS. Of the same kind, class, or nature.

ELABORARE. In old European law. To gain, acquire, or purchase, as by labor and industry.

ELABORATUS. Property which is the acquisition of labor. Spelman.

ELDER BRETHREN. A distinguished body of men, elected as masters of Trinity House, an institution incorporated in the reign of Henry VIII., charged with numerous important duties relating to the marine, such as the superintendence of light-houses. Mozley & Whitley; 2 Steph. Comm. 502.

ELDER TITLE. A title of earlier date, but coming simultaneously into operation with a title of younger origin, is called the "elder title," and prevails.

ELDEST. He or she who has the greatest age.

The "eldest son" is the first-born son. If there is only one son, he may still be described as the "eldest." L. R. 7 H. L. 644.

Electa una via, non datur recursus ad alteram. He who has chosen one way cannot have recourse to another. 10 Toull. no. 170.

ELECTED. The word "elected," in its ordinary signification, carries with it the idea of a vote, generally popular, sometimes more restricted, and cannot be held the synonym of any other mode of filling a position. 5 Nev. 121.

Electio est interna libera et spontanea separatio unius rei ab alia, sine compulsione, consistens in animo et voluntate. Dyer, 281. Election is an internal, free, and spontaneous separation of one thing from another, without compulsion, consisting in intention and will.

Electio semel facta, et placitum testatum non patitur regressum. Co. Litt. 146. Election once made, and plea witnessed, suffers not a recall.

ELECTION. The act of choosing or selecting one or more from a greater number of persons, things, courses, or rights. The choice of an alternative.

The internal, free, and spontaneous separation of one thing from another, without compulsion, consisting in intention and will. Dyer, 281.

The selection of one man from among several candidates to discharge certain duties in a state, corporation, or society.

The choice which is open to a debtor who is bound in an alternative obligation to select either one of the alternatives.

In equity. The obligation imposed upon a party to choose between two inconsistent or alternative rights or claims, in cases where there is clear intention of the person from whom he derives one that he should not enjoy both. 2 Story, Eq. Jur. § 1075.

The doctrine of election presupposes a plurality of gifts or rights, with an intention, express or implied, of the party who has a right to control one or both, that one should be a substitute for the other. 1 Swanst. 394, note *b;* 3 Wood. Lect. 491; 2 Rop. Leg. 480-578.

In practice. The liberty of choosing (or the act of choosing) one out of several means afforded by law for the redress of an injury, or one out of several available forms of action.

In criminal law. The choice, by the prosecution, upon which of several counts in an indictment (charging distinct offenses of the same degree, but not parts of a continuous series of acts) it will proceed.

ELECTION AUDITORS. In English law. Officers annually appointed, to whom was committed the duty of taking and publishing the account of all expenses incurred at parliamentary elections. See 17 & 18 Vict. c. 102, §§ 18, 26-28. But these sections have been repealed by the 26 Vict. c. 29, which throws the duty of preparing the accounts on the declared agent of the candidate, and the duty of publishing an abstract of it on the returning officer. Wharton.

ELECTION DISTRICT. A subdivision of territory, whether of state, county, or city, the boundaries of which are fixed by law, for convenience in local or general elections. 41 Pa. St. 403.

ELECTION JUDGES. In English law. Judges of the high court selected in pursuance of the 31 & 32 Vict. c. 125, § 11, and Jud. Act 1873, § 38, for the trial of election petitions.

ELECTION PETITIONS. Petitions for inquiry into the validity of elections of members of parliament, when it is alleged that the return of a member is invalid for bribery or any other reason. These petitions are heard by a judge of one of the common-law divisions of the high court.

Electiones fiant rite et libere sine interruptione aliqua. Elections should be made in due form, and freely, without any interruption. 2 Inst. 169.

ELECTIVE. Dependent upon choice; bestowed or passing by election. Also pertaining or relating to elections; conferring the right or power to vote at elections.

ELECTOR. He that has a vote in the choice of any officer; a constituent; also the title of certain German princes who formerly had a voice in the election of the German emperors.

ELECTORAL. Pertaining to electors or elections; composed or consisting of electors.

ELECTORAL COLLEGE. The body of princes formerly entitled to elect the emperor of Germany. Also a name sometimes given, in the United States, to the body of electors chosen by the people to elect the president and vice-president. Webster.

ELECTORS OF PRESIDENT. Persons chosen by the people at a so-called "presidential election," to elect a president and vice-president of the United States.

ELEEMOSYNA REGIS, and ELEEMOSYNA ARATRI, or CARUCARUM. A penny which King Ethelred ordered to be paid for every plow in England towards the support of the poor. Leg. Ethel. c. 1.

ELEEMOSYNÆ. Possessions belonging to the church. Blount.

ELEEMOSYNARIA. The place in a religious house where the common alms were deposited, and thence by the almoner distributed to the poor.

In old English law. The *aumerie, aumbry*, or *ambry;* words still used in common speech in the north of England, to denote a pantry or cupboard. Cowell.

The office of almoner. Cowell.

ELEEMOSYNARIUS. In old English law. An almoner, or chief officer, who received the eleemosynary rents and gifts, and in due method distributed them to pious and charitable uses. Cowell; Wharton.

The name of an officer (lord almoner) of the English kings, in former times, who distributed the royal alms or bounty. Fleta, lib. 2, c. 23.

ELEEMOSYNARY. Relating to the distribution of alms, bounty, or charity; charitable.

ELEEMOSYNARY CORPORATIONS. Such as are constituted for the perpetual distribution of the free alms and bounty of the founder, in such manner as he has directed; and in this class are ranked hospitals for the relief of poor and impotent p rsons, and colleges for the promotion of learning and piety, and the support of persons engaged in literary pursuits. These corporations are lay, and not ecclesiastical, even though composed of ecclesiastical persons, and although they in some things partake of the nature, privileges, and restrictions of ecclesiastical bodies. 1 Bl. Comm. 471.

Eleemosynary corporations are for the management of private property according to the will of the donors. They are private lay corporations, such as colleges, hospitals, etc. They differ from civil corporations in that the former are the mere creatures of public institution, created exclusively for the public advantage, and subject to governmental control and visitation; whereas a private corporation, especially one organized for charitable purposes, is the creature of private benefaction, endowed and founded by private individuals, and subject to their control, laws, and visitation, and not to those of the government. 4 Wheat. 518, 660.

ELEGANTER. In the civil law. Accurately; with discrimination. 3 Story, 611, 636.

ELEGIT. (Lat. He has chosen.) This is the name, in English practice, of a writ of execution first given by the statute of Westm. 2 (13 Edw. I. c. 18) either upon a judgment for a debt or damages or upon the forfeiture of a recognizance taken in the king's court. It is so called because it is in the choice or election of the plaintiff whether he will sue out this writ or a *fi. fa.* By it the defendant's goods and chattels are appraised, and all of them (except oxen and beasts of the plow) are delivered to the plaintiff, at such reasonable appraisement and price, in part satisfaction of his debt. If the goods are not sufficient, then the moiety of his freehold lands, which he had at the time of the judgment given, are also to be delivered to the plaintiff, to hold till out of the rents and profits thereof the debt be levied, or till the defendant's interest be expired. During this period the plaintiff is called "tenant by *elegit,*" and his estate, an "estate by *elegit.*" This writ, or its analogue, is in use in some of the United States, as Virginia and Kentucky. See 3 Bl. Comm. 418; 4 Kent, Comm. 431, 436, and notes; 10 Grat. 580.

ELEMENTS. The forces of nature. The elements are the means through which God acts, and "damages by the elements" means the same thing as "damages by the act of God." 35 Cal. 416.

ELIGIBLE. As applied to a candidate for an elective office, this term means capable of being chosen; the subject of selection or choice; and also implies competency to hold the office if chosen. 15 Ind. 331; 15 Cal. 121; 14 Wis. 497.

ELIMINATION. In old English law. The act of banishing or turning out of doors; rejection.

ELINGUATION. The punishment of cutting out the tongue.

ELISORS. In practice. Electors or choosers. Persons appointed by the court to execute writs of *venire*, in cases where both the sheriff and coroner are disqualified from acting, and whose duty is to *choose*—that is, name and return—the jury. 3 Bl. Comm. 355; Co. Litt. 158; 3 Steph. Comm. 597, note.

Persons appointed to execute *any* writ, in default of the sheriff and coroner, are also called "elisors."

ELL. A measure of length, answering to the modern yard. 1 Bl. Comm. 275.

ELOGIUM. In the civil law. A will or testament.

ELOIGNE. In practice. (Fr. *éloigner*, to remove to a distance; to remove afar off.) A return to a writ of replevin, when the chattels have been removed out of the way of the sheriff.

ELOIGNMENT. The getting a thing or person out of the way; or removing it to a distance, so as to be out of reach.

ELONGATA. In practice. Eloigned; carried away to a distance. The old form of the return made by a sheriff to a writ of replevin, stating that the goods or beasts had been *eloigned;* that is, carried to a distance, to places to him unknown. 3 Bl. Comm. 148; 3 Steph. Comm. 522; Fitzh. Nat. Brev. 73, 74; Archb. N. Pract. 552.

ELONGATUS. Eloigned. A return made by a sheriff to a writ *de homine replegiando*, stating that the party to be replevied has been eloigned, or conveyed out of his jurisdiction. 3 Bl. Comm. 129.

ELONGAVIT. In England, where in a proceeding by foreign attachment the plaintiff has obtained judgment of appraisement, but by reason of some act of the garnishee the goods cannot be appraised, (as where he has removed them from the city, or has sold them, etc.,) the serjeant-at-mace returns that the garnishee has eloigned them, *i. e.*, removed them out of the jurisdiction, and on this return (called an "elongavit") judgment is given for the plaintiff that an inquiry be made of the goods eloigned. This inquiry is set down for trial, and the assessment is made by a jury after the manner of ordinary issues. Sweet.

ELOPEMENT. The act of a wife who voluntarily deserts her husband to cohabit with another man. 2 Bl. Comm. 130. To constitute an elopement, the wife must not only leave the husband, but go beyond his actual control; for if she abandons the husband, and goes and lives in adultery in a house belonging to him, it is said not to be an elopement. 3 N. H. 42.

"ELSEWHERE." In another place; in any other place. See 1 Vern. 4, and note.

In shipping articles, this term, following the designation of the port of destination, must be construed either as void for uncertainty or as subordinate to the principal voyage stated in the preceding words. 2 Gall. 477.

ELUVIONES. In old pleading. Spring tides. Townsh. Pl. 197.

EMANCIPATION. The act by which one who was unfree, or under the power and control of another, is set at liberty and made his own master.

In Roman law. The enfranchisement of a son by his father, which was anciently done by the formality of an imaginary *sale.* This was abolished by Justinian, who substituted the simpler proceeding of a manumission before a magistrate. Inst. 1, 12, 6.

In Louisiana. The emancipation of minors is especially recognized and regulated by law.

In England. The term "emancipation" has been borrowed from the Roman law, and is constantly used in the law of parochial settlements. 7 Adol. & E. (N. S.) 574, note.

EMANCIPATION PROCLAMATION. An executive proclamation, declaring that all persons held in slavery in certain designated states and districts were and should remain free. It was issued January 1, 1863, by Abraham Lincoln, as president of the United States and commander in chief.

EMBARGO. A proclamation or order of state, usually issued in time of war or threatened hostilities, prohibiting the departure of ships or goods from some or all the ports of such state until further order. 2 Wheat. 148.

Embargo is the hindering or detention by any government of ships of commerce in its ports. If the embargo is laid upon ships belonging to citizens of the state imposing it, it is called a "civil embargo;" if, as more commonly happens, it is laid upon ships belonging to the enemy, it is called a "hostile embargo." The effect of this latter embargo is that the vessels detained are restored to the rightful owners if no war follows, but are forfeited to the embargoing government if war does follow, the declaration of war being held to relate back to the original seizure and detention. Brown.

The temporary or permanent sequestration of the property of individuals for the purposes of a government, *e. g.*, to obtain vessels for the transport of troops, the owners being reimbursed for this forced service. Man. Int. Law, 143.

EMBASSADOR. See AMBASSADOR.

EMBASSAGE, or EMBASSY. The message or commission given by a sovereign or state to a minister, called an "ambassador," empowered to treat or communicate with another sovereign or state; also the establishment of an ambassador.

EMBER DAYS. In ecclesiastical law. Those days which the ancient fathers called "*quatuor tempora jejunii*" are of great antiquity in the church. They are observed on Wednesday, Friday, and Saturday next after Quadragesima Sunday, or the first Sunday in Lent, after Whitsuntide, Holyrood Day, in September, and St. Lucy's Day, about the middle of December. Brit. c. 53. Our almanacs call the weeks in which they fall the "Ember Weeks," and they are now chiefly noticed on account of the ordination of priests and deacons; because the canon appoints the Sundays next after the Ember weeks for the solemn times of ordination, though the bishops, if they please, may ordain on any Sunday or holiday. Enc. Lond.

EMBEZZLEMENT. The fraudulent appropriation to his own use or benefit of property or money intrusted to him by another, by a clerk, agent, trustee, public officer, or other person acting in a fiduciary character. See 4 Bl. Comm. 230, 231; 3 Kent, Comm. 194; 4 Steph. Comm. 168, 169, 219; 40 N. Y. Super. Ct. 41.

Embezzlement is the fraudulent appropriation of property by a person to whom it has been intrusted. Pen. Code Cal. § 503; Pen. Code Dak. § 596.

Embezzlement is a species of larceny, and the term is applicable to cases of furtive and fraudulent appropriation by clerks, servants, or carriers of property coming into their possession by virtue of their employment. It is distinguished from "larceny," properly so called, as being committed in respect of property which is not at the time in the actual or legal possession of the owner. 41 How. Pr. 294; 4 Steph. Comm. 168.

Embezzlement is not an offense at common law, but was created by statute. "Embezzle" includes in its meaning appropriation to one's own use, and therefore the use of the single word "embezzle," in the indictment or information, contains within itself the charge that the defendant appropriated the money or property to his own use. 34 La. Ann. 1153.

EMBLEMENTS. The vegetable chattels called "emblements" are the corn and other growth of the earth which are produced annually, not spontaneously, but by labor and industry, and thence are called "*fructus industriales.*" 64 Pa. St. 137.

The growing crops of those vegetable productions of the soil which are annually produced by the labor of the cultivator. They are deemed personal property, and pass as such to the executor or administrator of the occupier, whether he were the owner in fee, or for life, or for years, if he die before he has actually cut, reaped, or gathered the same; and this, although, being affixed to the soil, they might for some purposes be considered, while growing, as part of the realty. Wharton.

The term also denotes the right of a tenant to take and carry away, after his tenancy has ended, such annual products of the land as have resulted from his own care and labor.

Emblements are the away-going crop; in other words, the crop which is upon the ground and unreaped when the tenant goes away, his lease having determined; and the right to emblements is the right in the tenant to take away the away-going crop, and for that purpose to come upon the land, and do all other necessary things thereon. Brown.

EMBLERS DE GENTZ. L. Fr. A stealing from the people. The phrase occurs in the old rolls of parliament: "Whereas divers murders, *emblers de gentz*, and robberies are committed," etc.

EMBRACEOR. A person guilty of the offense of embracery, (*q. v.*) See Co. Litt. 369.

EMBRACERY. In criminal law. This offense consists in the attempt to influence a jury corruptly to one side or the other, by promises, persuasions, entreaties, entertainments, *douceurs*, and the like. The person guilty of it is called an "embraceor." Brown.

EMENDA. Amends; something given in reparation for a trespass; or, in old Saxon times, in compensation for an injury or crime. Spelman.

EMENDALS. An old word still made use of in the accounts of the society of the Inner Temple, where so much in *emendals* at the foot of an account on the balance thereof signifies so much money in the bank or stock of the houses, for reparation of losses, or other emergent occasions. Spelman.

EMENDARE. In Saxon law. To make amends or satisfaction for any crime or trespass committed; to pay a fine; to be fined. Spelman. *Emendare se*, to redeem, or ransom one's life, by payment of a weregild.

EMENDATIO. In old English law. Amendment, or correction. The power of amending and correcting abuses, according to certain rules and measures. Cowell.

In Saxon law. A pecuniary satisfaction for an injury; the same as *emenda*, (*q. v.*) Spelman.

EMENDATIO PANIS ET CEREVISIÆ. In old English law. The power of supervising and correcting the weights and measures of bread and ale, (assising bread and beer.) Cowell.

EMERGE. To arise; to come to light. "Unless a matter happen to *emerge* after issue joined." Hale, Anal. § 1.

EMERGENT YEAR. The epoch or date whence any people begin to compute their time.

EMIGRANT. One who quits his country for any lawful reason, with a design to settle elsewhere, and who takes his family and property, if he has any, with him. Vattel, b. 1, c. 19, § 224.

EMIGRATION. The act of changing one's domicile from one country or state to another.

It is to be distinguished from "expatriation." The latter means the abandonment of one's country and renunciation of one's citizenship in it, while emigration denotes merely the removal of person and property to a foreign state. The former is usually the consequence of the latter. Emigration is also used of the removal from one section to another of the same country.

EMINENCE. An honorary title given to cardinals. They were called "*illustrissimi*" and "*reverendissimi*" until the pontificate of Urban VIII.

EMINENT DOMAIN. Eminent domain is the right of the people or government to take private property for public use. Code Civil Proc. Cal. § 1237.

The right of eminent domain is the right of the state, through its regular organization, to reassert, either temporarily or permanently, its dominion over any portion of the soil of the state on account of public exigency and for the public good. Thus, in time of war or insurrection, the proper authorities may possess and hold any part of the territory of the state for the common safety; and in time of peace the legislature may authorize the appropriation of the same to public purposes, such as the opening of roads, construction of defenses, or providing channels for trade or travel. Code Ga. 1882, § 2222.

Eminent domain is the right which a government retains over the estates of individuals to resume them for public use. Wharton.

The right of society, or of the sovereign, to dispose, in case of necessity, and for the public safety, of all the wealth contained in the state, is called "eminent domain." 2 Paine, 688.

Eminent domain is the highest and most exact idea of property remaining in the government, or in the aggregate body of the people in their sovereign capacity. It gives a right to resume the possession of the property in the manner directed by the constitution and the laws of the state, whenever the public interest requires it. 3 Paige, 45, 73.

"The exaction of money from individuals under the right of taxation, and the appropriation of private property for public use by virtue of the power of eminent domain, must not be confused. In paying taxes the citizen contributes his just and ascertained share to the expenses of the government under which he lives. But when his property is taken under the power of eminent domain, he is compelled to surrender to the public something above and beyond his due proportion for the public benefit. The matter is special. It is in the nature of a compulsory sale to the state." Black, Tax-Titles, § 3.

The term "eminent domain" is sometimes (but inaccurately) applied to the land, buildings, etc., owned directly by the government, and which have not yet passed into any private ownership. This species of property is much better designated as the "public domain," or "national domain."

EMISSARY. A person sent upon a mission as the agent of another; also a secret agent sent to ascertain the sentiments and designs of others, and to propagate opinions favorable to his employer.

EMISSION. In medical jurisprudence. The ejection or throwing out of any secretion or other matter from the body; the expulsion of urine, semen, etc.

EMIT. **In American law.** To put forth or send out; to issue. "No state shall *emit* bills of credit." Const. U. S. art. 1, § 10.

To issue; to give forth with authority; to put into circulation. See BILL OF CREDIT.

The word "emit" is never employed in describing those contracts by which a state binds itself to pay money at a future day for services actually received, or for money borrowed for present use. Nor are instruments executed for such purposes, in common language, denominated "bills of credit." "To emit bills of credit" conveys to the mind the idea of issuing paper intended to circulate through the community, for its ordinary purposes, as money, which paper is redeemable at a future day. 4 Pet. 410; 11 Pet. 257; 28 Ark. 369; 1 Scam. 87.

In Scotch practice. To speak out; to state in words. A prisoner is said to *emit* a declaration. 2 Alis. Crim. Pr. 560.

EMMENAGOGUES. In medical jurisprudence. The name of a class of medicines supposed to have the property of promoting the menstrual discharge, and sometimes used for the purpose of procuring abortion.

EMOLUMENT. The profit arising from office or employment; that which is received as a compensation for services, or which is annexed to the possession of office as salary, fees, and perquisites; advantage; gain, public or private. Webster. Any perquisite, advantage, profit, or gain arising from the possession of an office. 105 Pa. St. 303.

EMOTIONAL INSANITY. The species of mental aberration produced by a violent excitement of the emotions or passions, though the reasoning faculties may remain unimpaired.

EMPALEMENT. In ancient law. A mode of inflicting punishment, by thrusting a sharp pole up the fundament. Enc. Lond.

EMPANNEL. The writing or entering by the sheriff, on a parchment schedule or roll of paper, the names of a jury summoned by him. Cowell.

EMPARLANCE. See IMPARLANCE.

EMPARNOURS. L. Fr. Undertakers of suits. Kelham.

EMPEROR. The title of the sovereign ruler of an empire. This designation was adopted by the rulers of the Roman world after the decay of the republic, and was assumed by those who claimed to be their successors in the "Holy Roman Empire," as also by Napoleon. It is now used as the title of the monarch of some single countries, as lately in Brazil, and some composite states, as Germany and Austria-Hungary, and by the queen of England as "Empress of India."

The title "emperor" seems to denote a power and dignity superior to that of a "king." It appears to be the appropriate style of the executive head of a federal government, constructed on the monarchical principle, and comprising in its organization several distinct kingdoms or other *quasi* sovereign states; as is the case with the German empire at the present day.

EMPHYTEUSIS. In the Roman and civil law. A contract by which a landed estate was leased to a tenant, either in perpetuity or for a long term of years, upon the reservation of an annual rent or *canon*, and upon the condition that the lessee should improve the property, by building, cultivating, or otherwise, and with a right in the lessee to alien the estate at pleasure or pass it to his heirs by descent, and free from any revocation, re-entry, or claim of forfeiture on the part of the grantor, except for non-payment of the rent. Inst. 3, 25, 3; 3 Bl. Comm. 232; Maine, Anc. Law, 289.

The right granted by such a contract, (*jus emphyteuticum*, or *emphyteuticarium*.) The real right by which a person is entitled to enjoy another's estate as if it were his own, and to dispose of its substance, as far as can be done without deteriorating it. Mackeld. Rom. Law, § 326.

EMPHYTEUTA. In the civil law. The person to whom an *emphyteusis* is granted; the lessee or tenant under a contract of *emphyteusis*.

EMPHYTEUTICUS. In the civil law. Founded on, growing out of, or having the character of, an *emphyteusis;* held under an *emphyteusis*. 3 Bl. Comm. 232.

EMPIRE. The dominion or jurisdiction of an emperor; the region over which the dominion of an emperor extends; imperial power; supreme dominion; sovereign command.

EMPIRIC. A practitioner in medicine or surgery, who proceeds on *experience only*, without science or legal qualification; a quack.

EMPLAZAMIENTO. In Spanish law. A summons or citation, issued by authority of a judge, requiring the person to whom it is addressed to appear before the tribunal at a designated day and hour.

EMPLEAD. To indict; to prefer a charge against; to accuse.

EMPLOI. In French law. Equitable conversion. When property covered by the *régime dotal* is sold, the proceeds of the sale must be reinvested for the benefit of the wife. It is the duty of the purchaser to see that the price is so reinvested. Arg. Fr. Merc. Law, 557.

EMPLOY. To engage in one's service; to use as an agent or substitute in transacting business; to commission and intrust with the management of one's affairs; and, when used in respect to a servant or hired laborer, the term is equivalent to hiring, which implies a request and a contract for a compensation, and has but this one meaning when used in the ordinary affairs and business of life. 11 N. Y. 599; 58 N. Y. 371.

EMPLOYED. This signifies both the act of doing a thing and the being under contract or orders to do it. 14 Pet. 464, 475; 2 Paine, 721, 745.

EMPLOYEE. This word "is from the French, but has become somewhat naturalized in our language. Strictly and etymologically, it means 'a person employed,' but, in practice in the French language, it ordinarily is used to signify a person in some official employment, and as generally used with us, though perhaps not confined to any official employment, it is understood to mean some permanent employment or position." 2 Lans. 453. See, also, 75 N. Y. 41; 111 Ind. 324, 12 N. E. Rep. 501.

The word is more extensive than "clerk" or "officer." It signifies any one in place, or having charge or using a function, as well as one in office. 3 Ct. Cl. 260.

EMPLOYMENT. This word does not necessarily import an engagement or rendering services for another. A person may as well be "employed" about his own business as in the transaction of the same for a principal. 43 Mo. 51; 56 Law J. Q. B. Div. 251.

EMPORIUM. A place for wholesale trade in commodities carried by sea. The name is sometimes applied to a seaport town, but it properly signifies only a particular place in such a town. Smith, Dict. Antiq.

EMPRESTITO. In Spanish law. A loan. Something lent to the borrower at his request. Las Partidas, pt. 3, tit. 18, l. 70.

EMPTIO, EMPTION. The act of buying; a purchase.

EMPTIO BONORUM. Lat. In Roman law. A species of forced assignment for the benefit of creditors; being a public sale of an insolvent debtor's estate, whereby the purchaser succeeded to all his property, rights, and claims, and became responsible for his debts and liabilities to the extent of a quota fixed before the transfer. See Mackeld. Rom. Law, § 521.

EMPTIO ET VENDITIO. Lat. Purchase and sale; sometimes translated "emption and vendition." The name of the contract of sale in the Roman law. Inst. 3, 23; Bract. fol. 61*b*. Sometimes made a compound word,—*emptio-venditio*.

A consensual contract to deliver a thing for a certain price.

An agreement for the seller to part with a thing for money given to him by the buyer. 3 Salk. 61.

EMPTOR. A buyer or purchaser.

Emptor emit quam minimo potest, venditor vendit quam maximo potest. The buyer purchases for the lowest price he can; the seller sells for the highest price he can. 2 Kent, Comm. 486.

EMTIO. In the civil law. Purchase. This form of the word is used in the Digests and Code. Dig. 18, 1; Cod. 4, 49.

EMTOR. In the civil law. A buyer or purchaser; the buyer. Dig. 18, 1; Cod. 4, 49.

EMTRIX. In the civil law. A female purchaser; the purchaser. Cod. 4, 54, 1.

EN ARERE. L. Fr. In time past. 2 Inst. 506.

EN AUTRE DROIT. In the right of another. See AUTER DROIT.

EN BANKE. L. Fr. In the bench. 1 Anders. 51.

EN BREVET. In French law. An *acte* is said to be *en brevet* when a copy of it has not been recorded by the notary who drew it.

EN DECLARATION DE SIMULATION. A form of action used in Louisiana. Its object is to have a contract declared judicially a simulation and a nullity, to remove a cloud from the title, and to bring back, for any legal purpose, the thing sold to the estate of the true owner. 20 La. Ann. 169.

EN DEMEURE. In default. Used in Louisiana of a debtor who fails to pay on demand according to the terms of his obligation. See 3 Mart. (N. S.) 574.

En eschange il covient que les estates soient egales. Co. Litt. 50. In an exchange it is desirable that the estates be equal.

EN FAIT. Fr. In fact; in deed; actually.

EN GROS. Fr. In gross. Total; by wholesale.

EN JUICIO. Span. Judicially; in a court of law; in a suit at law. White, New Recop. b. 2, tit. 8, c. 1.

EN MASSE. Fr. In a mass; in a lump; at wholesale.

EN MORT MEYNE. L. Fr. In a dead hand; in mortmain. Britt. c. 43.

EN OWEL MAIN. L. Fr. In equal hand. The word "*owel*" occurs also in the phrase "*owelty* of partition."

EN RECOUVREMENT. Fr. In French law. An expression employed to denote that an indorsement made in favor of a person does not transfer to him the property in the bill of exchange, but merely constitutes an authority to such person to recover the amount of the bill. Arg. Fr. Merc. Law, 558.

EN ROUTE. Fr. On the way; in the course of a voyage or journey; in course of transportation.

EN VENTRE SA MERE. L. Fr. In its mother's womb. A term descriptive of an unborn child. For some purposes the law regards an infant *en ventre* as in being. It may take a legacy; have a guardian; an estate may be limited to its use, etc. 1 Bl. Comm. 130.

EN VIE. L. Fr. In life; alive. Britt. c. 50.

ENABLING POWER. When the donor of a power, who is the owner of the estate, confers upon persons not seised of the fee the right of creating interests to take effect out of it, which could not be done by the donee of the power unless by such authority, this is called an "enabling power." 2 Bouv. Inst. no. 1928.

ENABLING STATUTE. The act of 32 Henry VIII. c. 28, by which tenants in tail, husbands seised in right of their wives, and others, were empowered to make leases for their lives or for twenty-one years, which they could not do before. 2 Bl. Comm. 319; Co. Litt. 44*a*. The phrase is also applied to any statute enabling persons or corporations to do what before they could not.

ENACH. In Saxon law. The satisfaction for a crime; the recompense for a fault. Skene.

ENACT. To establish by law; to perform or effect; to decree. The usual introductory formula in making laws is, "*Be it enacted.*"

ENAJENACION. In Spanish and Mexican law. Alienation; transfer of property. The act by which the property in a thing, by lucrative title, is transferred, as a donation; or by onerous title, as by sale or barter. In a more extended sense, the term comprises also the contracts of emphyteusis, pledge, and mortgage, and even the creation of a servitude upon an estate. Escriche; 26 Cal. 88.

ENBREVER. L. Fr. To write down in short; to abbreviate, or, in old language, *imbreviate;* to put into a schedule. Britt. c. 1.

ENCAUSTUM. In the civil law. A kind of ink or writing fluid appropriate to the use of the emperor. Cod. 1, 23, 6.

ENCEINTE. Pregnant. See PREGNANCY.

ENCHESON. The occasion, cause, or reason for which anything is done. Termes de la Ley.

ENCLOSE. In the Scotch law. To shut up a jury after the case has been submitted to them. 2 Alis. Crim. Pr. 634. See INCLOSE.

ENCLOSURE. See INCLOSURE.

ENCOMIENDA. In Spanish law. A grant from the crown to a private person of a certain portion of territory in the Spanish colonies, together with the concession of a certain number of the native inhabitants, on the feudal principle of commendation. 2 Wools. Pol. Science, 161, 162. Also a royal grant of privileges to the military orders of Spain.

ENCOURAGE. In criminal law. To instigate; to incite to action; to give courage to; to inspirit; to embolden; to raise confidence; to make confident. 7 Q. B. Div. 258; 4 Burr. 2073. See AID.

ENCROACH. To gain unlawfully upon the lands, property, or authority of another; as if one man presses upon the grounds of another too far, or if a tenant owe two shillings rent-service, and the lord exact three. So, too, the Spencers were said to encroach the king's authority. Blount; Plowd. 94*a*.

In the law of easements. Where the owner of an easement alters the dominant tenement, so as to impose an additional restriction or burden on the servient tenement, he is said to commit an encroachment. Sweet.

ENCUMBER. See INCUMBER.

ENCUMBRANCE. See INCUMBRANCE.

END. Object; intent. Things are construed according to the end. Finch, Law, b. 1, c. 3, no. 10.

ENDENZIE, or ENDENIZEN. To make free; to enfranchise.

ENDORSE. See INDORSE.

ENDOWED SCHOOLS. In England, certain schools having endowments are distinctively known as "endowed schools;" and a series of acts of parliament regulating them are known as the "endowed schools acts." Mozley & Whitley.

ENDOWMENT. 1. The assignment of dower; the setting off a woman's dower. 2 Bl. Comm. 135.

2. In appropriations of churches, (in English law,) the setting off a sufficient maintenance for the vicar in perpetuity. 1 Bl. Comm. 387.

3. The act of settling a fund, or permanent pecuniary provision, for the maintenance of a public institution, charity, college, etc.

4. A fund settled upon a public institution, etc., for its maintenance or use.

The words "endowment" and "fund," in a statute exempting from taxation the real estate, the furniture and personal property, and the "endowment or fund" of religious and educational corporations, are *ejusdem generis*, and intended to comprehend a class of property different from the other two, not real estate or chattels. The difference between the words is that "fund" is a general term, including the endowment, while "endowment" means that particular fund, or part of the fund, of the institution, bestowed for its more permanent uses, and usually kept sacred for the purposes intended. The word "endowment" does not, in such an enactment, include real estate. 32 N. J. Law, 360.

ENDOWMENT POLICY In life insurance. A policy which is payable when the insured reaches a given age, or upon his decease, if that occurs earlier.

ENEMY, in public law, signifies either the nation which is at war with another, or a citizen or subject of such nation.

ENFEOFF. To invest with an estate by feoffment. To make a gift of any corporeal hereditaments to another. See FEOFFMENT.

ENFEOFFMENT. The act of investing with any dignity or possession; also the instrument or deed by which a person is invested with possessions.

ENFRANCHISE. To make free; to incorporate a man in a society or body politic.

ENFRANCHISEMENT. The act of making free; giving a franchise or freedom to; investiture with privileges or capacities of freedom, or municipal or political liberty. Admission to the freedom of a city; admission to political rights, and particularly the right of suffrage. Anciently, the acquisition of freedom by a villein from his lord.

The word is now used principally either of the manumission of slaves, (*q. v.*,) of giving to a borough or other constituency a right to return a member or members to parliament, or of the conversion of copyhold into freehold. Mozley & Whitley.

ENFRANCHISEMENT OF COPYHOLDS. In English law. The conversion of copyhold into freehold tenure, by a conveyance of the fee-simple of the property from the lord of the manor to the copyholder, or by a release from the lord of all seigniorial rights, etc., which destroys the customary descent, and also all rights and privileges annexed to the copyholder's estate. 1 Watk. Copyh. 362; 2 Steph. Comm. 51.

ENGAGEMENT. In French law. A contract. The obligation arising from a *quasi* contract.

The terms "obligation" and "engagement" are said to be synonymous, (17 Toullier, no. 1;) but the Code seems specially to apply the term "engagement" to those obligations which the law imposes on a man without the intervention of any contract, either on the part of the obligor or the obligee, (article 1370.) An engagement to do or omit to do something amounts to a promise. 21 N. J. Law, 369.

In English Practice. The term has been appropriated to denote a contract entered into by a married woman with the intention of binding or charging her separate estate, or, with stricter accuracy, a promise which in the case of a person *sui juris* would be a contract, but in the case of a married woman is not a contract, because she cannot bind herself personally, even in equity. Her engagements, therefore, merely operate as dispositions or appointments *pro tanto* of her separate estate. Sweet.

"ENGINE." This is said to be a word of very general signification: and, when used in an act, its meaning must be sought out from the act itself, and the language which surrounds it, and also from other acts *in pari materia*, in which it occurs. Abbott, J., 6 Maule & S. 192. In a large sense, it applies to all utensils and tools which afford the means of carrying on a trade. But in a more limited sense it means a thing of considerable dimensions, of a fixed or permanent nature, analogous to an erection or building. Id. 182.

ENGLESHIRE. A law was made by Canute, for the preservation of his Danes, that, when a man was killed, the hundred or town should be liable to be amerced, unless it could be proved that the person killed was an Englishman. This proof was called "*Engleshire.*" 1 Hale, P. C. 447; 4 Bl. Comm. 195; Spelman.

ENGLETERRE. England.

ENGLISH INFORMATION. In English law. A proceeding in the court of exchequer in matters of revenue.

"ENGLISH MARRIAGE." This phrase may refer to the place where the marriage is solemnized, or it may refer to the nationality and domicile of the parties between whom it is solemnized, the place where the union so created is to be enjoyed. 6 Prob. Div. 51.

ENGRAVE does not include the process of reproducing pictures by means of photography. 5 Blatchf. 325.

ENGROSS. To copy the rude draft of an instrument in a fair, large hand. To write out, in a large, fair hand, on parchment.

In old criminal law. To buy up so much of a commodity on the market as to obtain a monopoly and sell again at a forced price.

ENGROSSER. One who engrosses or writes on parchment in a large, fair hand.

One who purchases large quantities of any commodity in order to acquire a monopoly, and to sell them again at high prices.

ENGROSSING. In English law. The getting into one's possession, or buying up, large quantities of corn, or other dead victuals, with intent to sell them again. The total engrossing of any other commodity, with intent to sell it at an unreasonable price. 4 Bl. Comm. 158, 159. This was a misdemeanor, punishable by fine and imprisonment. Steph. Crim. Law, 95. Now repealed by 7 & 8 Vict. c. 24. 4 Steph. Comm. 291, note.

ENHANCED. This word, taken in an unqualified sense, is synonymous with "increased," and comprehends any increase of value, however caused or arising. 32 Fed. Rep. 812.

ENITIA PARS. The share of the eldest. A term of the English law descriptive of the lot or share chosen by the eldest of coparceners when they make a voluntary partition. The first choice (*primer election*) belongs to the eldest. Co. Litt. 166.

Enitia pars semper præferenda est propter privilegium ætatis. Co. Litt. 166. The part of the elder sister is always to be preferred on account of the privilege of age.

ENJOIN. To require; command; positively direct. To require a person, by writ of injunction from a court of equity, to perform, or to abstain or desist from, some act.

ENJOYMENT. The exercise of a right; the possession and fruition of a right, privilege, or incorporeal hereditament.

ENLARGE. To make larger; to increase; to extend a time limit; to grant further time. Also to set at liberty one who has been imprisoned or in custody.

ENLARGER L'ESTATE. A species of release which inures by way of enlarging an estate, and consists of a conveyance of the ulterior interest to the particular tenant; as if there be tenant for life or years, remainder to another in fee, and he in remainder releases all his right to the particular tenant and his heirs, this gives him the estate in fee. 1 Steph. Comm. 518.

ENLARGING. Extending, or making more comprehensive; as an enlarging statute, which is one extending the common law.

ENLARGING STATUTE. A remedial statute which enlarges or extends the common law. 1 Bl. Comm. 86, 87.

ENLISTMENT. The act of one who voluntarily enters the military or naval service of the government, contracting to serve in a subordinate capacity.

The words "enlist" and "enlistment," in law, as in common usage, may signify either the complete fact of entering into the military service, or the first step taken by the recruit towards that end. When used in the former sense, as in statutes conferring a right to compel the military service of enlisted men, the enlistment is not deemed completed until the man has been mustered into the service. 8 Allen, 480.

Enlistment does not include the entry of a person into the military service under a commission as an officer. 48 N. H. 280.

Enlisted applies to a drafted man as well as a volunteer, whose name is duly entered on the military rolls. 107 Mass. 282.

ENORMIA. In old practice and pleading. Unlawful or wrongful acts; wrongs. *Et alia enormia*, and other wrongs. This phrase constantly occurs in the old writs and declarations of trespass.

ENORMOUS. Aggravated. "So enormous a trespass." Vaughan, 115. Written "enormious," in some of the old books. *Enormious* is where a thing is made without a rule or against law. Brownl. pt. 2, p. 19.

ENPLEET. Anciently used for implead. Cowell.

ENQUÊTE, or ENQUEST. In canon law. An examination of witnesses, taken down in writing, by or before an authorized judge, for the purpose of gathering testimony to be used on a trial.

ENRÉGISTREMENT. In French law. Registration. A formality which consists in inscribing on a register, specially kept for the purpose by the government, a summary analysis of certain deeds and documents. At the same time that such analysis is inscribed upon the register, the clerk places upon the deed a memorandum indicating the date upon which it was registered, and at the side of such memorandum an impression is made with a stamp. Arg. Fr. Merc. Law, 558.

ENROLL. To register; to make a record; to enter on the rolls of a court; to transcribe.

ENROLLMENT. In English law. The registering or entering on the rolls of chancery, king's bench, common pleas, or exchequer, or by the clerk of the peace in the records of the quarter sessions, of any lawful act; as a recognizance, a deed of bargain and sale, and the like. Jacob.

ENROLLMENT OF VESSELS. In the laws of the United States on the subject of merchant shipping, the recording and certification of vessels employed in coastwise or inland navigation; as distinguished from the "registration" of vessels employed in foreign commerce. 3 Wall. 566.

ENS LEGIS. L. Lat. A creature of the law; an artificial being, as contrasted with a natural person. Applied to corporations, considered as deriving their existence entirely from the law.

ENSCHEDULE. To insert in a list, account, or writing.

ENSEAL. To seal. *Ensealing* is still used as a formal word in conveyancing

ENSERVER. L. Fr. To make subject to a service or servitude. Britt. c. 54.

ENTAIL, *v.* To settle or limit the succession to real property; to create an estate tail.

ENTAIL, *n.* A fee abridged or limited to the issue, or certain classes of issue, instead of descending to all the heirs. 1 Washb. Real Prop. 66; Cowell; 2 Bl. Comm. 112, note.

Entail, in legal treatises, is used to signify an estate tail, especially with reference to the restraint which such an estate imposes upon its owner, or, in other words, the points wherein such an estate differs from an estate in fee-simple. And this is often its popular sense; but sometimes it is, in popular language, used differently, so as to signify a succession of life-estates, as when it is said that "an entail ends with A.," meaning that A. is the first person who is entitled to bar or cut off the entail, being in law the first tenant in tail. Mozley & Whitley.

ENTAILED. Settled or limited to specified heirs, or in tail.

ENTAILED MONEY. Money directed to be invested in realty to be entailed. 3 & 4 Wm. IV. c. 74, §§ 70, 71, 72.

ENTENCION. In old English law. The plaintiff's count or declaration.

ENTENDMENT. The old form of *intendment*, (*q. v.*,) derived directly from the French, and used to denote the true meaning or signification of a word or sentence; that is, the understanding or construction of law. Cowell.

ENTER. In the law of real property. To go upon land for the purpose of taking possession of it. In strict usage, the entering is preliminary to the taking possession, but in common parlance the entry is now merged in the taking possession.

In practice. To place anything before a court, or upon or among the records, in a formal and regular manner, and usually in writing; as to "enter an appearance," to "enter a judgment." In this sense the word is nearly equivalent to setting down formally in writing, in either a full or abridged form.

ENTERCEUR. L. Fr. A party challenging (claiming) goods; he who has placed them in the hands of a third person. Kelham.

ENTERING JUDGMENTS. The formal entry of the judgment on the rolls of the court, which is necessary before bringing an appeal or an action on the judgment.

ENTERING SHORT. When bills not due are paid into a bank by a customer, it is the custom of some bankers not to carry the amount of the bills directly to his credit, but to "enter them short," as it is called, *i. e.*, to note down the receipt of the bills, their amounts, and the times when they become due in a previous column of the page, and the amounts when received are carried forward into the usual cash column. Sometimes, instead of entering such bills short, bankers credit the customer directly with the amount of the bills as cash, charging interest on any advances they may make on their account, and allow him at once to draw upon them to that amount. If the banker becomes bankrupt, the property in bills entered short does not pass to his assignees, but the customer is entitled to them if they remain in his hands, or to their proceeds, if received, subject to any lien the banker may have upon them. Wharton.

ENTERTAINMENT. This word is synonymous with "board," and includes the ordinary necessaries of life. 2 Miles, 323.

ENTICE. To solicit, persuade, or procure. 12 Abb. Pr. (N. S.) 187.

ENTIRE. Whole; without division, separation, or diminution.

ENTIRE CONTRACT. Where a contract consists of many parts, which may be considered as parts of one whole, the contract is entire. When the parts may be considered as so many distinct contracts, entered into at one time, and expressed in the same instrument, but not thereby made one contract, the contract is a separable contract. But, if the consideration of the contract is single and entire, the contract must be held to be entire, although the subject of the contract may consist of several distinct and wholly independent items. 2 Pars. Cont. 517.

ENTIRE DAY. This phrase signifies an undivided day, not parts of two days. An entire day must have a legal, fixed, precise time to begin, and a fixed, precise time to end. A day, in contemplation of law, comprises all the twenty-four hours, beginning and ending at twelve o'clock at night. 43 Ala. 325.

In a statute requiring the closing of all liquor saloons during "the entire day of any election," etc., this phrase means the natural day of twenty-four hours, commencing and terminating at midnight. 7 Tex. App. 30; Id. 192.

ENTIRE INTEREST. The whole interest or right, without diminution. Where a person in selling his tract of land sells also his entire interest in all improvements upon public land adjacent thereto, this vests in the purchaser only a quitclaim of his interest in the improvements. 13 La. Ann. 410.

ENTIRE TENANCY. A sole possession by one person, called "severalty," which is contrary to several tenancy, where a joint or common possession is in one or more.

ENTIRE USE, BENEFIT, ETC. These words in the *habendum* of a trust-deed for the benefit of a married woman are equivalent to the words "sole use," or "sole and separate use," and consequently her husband takes nothing under such deed. 3 Ired. Eq. 414.

ENTIRETY. The whole, in contradistinction to a moiety or part only. When land is conveyed to husband and wife, they do not take by moieties, but both are seised of the *entirety*. 2 Kent, Comm. 132; 4 Kent, Comm. 362. Parceners, on the other hand, have not an *entirety* of interest, but each is properly entitled to the whole of a distinct moiety. 2 Bl. Comm. 188.

The word is also used to designate that which the law considers as one whole, and not capable of being divided into parts. Thus, a judgment, it is held, is an *entirety*, and, if void as to one of the two defendants, cannot be valid as to the other. So, if a contract is an *entirety*, no part of the consideration is due until the whole has been performed.

ENTITLE. In its usual sense, to entitle is to give a right or title. Therefore a person is said to be entitled to property when he has a right to it.

In ecclesiastical law. To entitle is to give a title or ordination as a minister.

ENTREBAT. L. Fr. An intruder or interloper. Britt. c. 114.

ENTREGA. Span. Delivery. Las Partidas, pt. 6, tit. 14, l. 1.

ENTREPOT. A warehouse or magazine for the deposit of goods. In France, a building or place where goods from abroad may be deposited, and from whence they may be withdrawn for exportation to another country, without paying a duty. Brande; Webster.

ENTRY. 1. **In real property law.** Entry is the act of going peaceably upon a piece of land which is claimed as one's own, but which is held by another person, with the intention and for the purpose of taking possession of the same.

Entry is a remedy which the law affords to an injured party ousted of his lands by another person who has taken possession thereof without right. This remedy (which must in all cases be pursued peaceably) takes place in three only out of the five species of ouster, viz., abatement, intrusion, and disseisin; for, as in these three cases the original entry of the wrong-doer is unlawful, so the wrong may be remedied by the mere entry of the former possessor. But it is otherwise upon a discontinuance or deforcement, for in these latter two cases the former possessor cannot remedy the wrong by entry, but must do so by action, inasmuch as the original entry being in these cases lawful, and therefore conferring an apparent right of possession, the law will not suffer such apparent right to be overthrown by the mere act or entry of the claimant. Brown.

An entry at common law is nothing more than an assertion of title by going on the land; or, if that was hazardous, by making continual claim. Anciently, an actual entry was required to be made and a lease executed on the land to sustain the action of ejectment; but now nothing of that kind is necessary. The entry and the lease, as well as the ouster, are fictions, and nothing is required but that the lessor should have the right to enter. A proceeding precisely analogous obtained in the civil law. 1 Ala. 660.

2. **In criminal law.** Entry is the unlawful making one's way into a dwelling or other house, for the purpose of committing a crime therein.

In cases of burglary, the least entry with the whole or any part of the body, hand, or foot, or with any instrument or weapon, introduced for the purpose of committing a felony, is sufficient to complete the offense. 3 Inst. 64.

Without reference to burglary, a breaking into a house or going upon lands with violence and circumstances of aggression is termed "forcible entry," and was a breach of the peace at common law. "Forcible entry and detainer" is made an offense by statute in many of the states.

3. **In practice.** Entry denotes the formal inscription upon the rolls or records of a court of a note or minute of any of the proceedings in an action; and it is frequently applied to the filing of a proceeding in writing, such as a notice of appearance by a defendant, and, very generally, to the filing of the judgment roll as a record in the office of the court.

4. **In commercial law.** Entry denotes the act of a merchant, trader, or other business man in recording in his account-books the facts and circumstances of a sale, loan, or other transaction. Also the note or record so made. The books in which such memoranda are first (or originally) inscribed are called "books of original entry," and are *prima facie* evidence for certain purposes.

5. **In revenue law.** The entry of imported goods at the custom house consists in submitting them to the inspection of the revenue officers, together with a statement or description of such goods, and the original invoices of the same, for the purpose of estimating the duties to be paid thereon.

6. Under the provisions of the land laws of the United States, the term "entry" denotes the filing at the land-office, or inscription upon its records, of the documents required to found a claim for a homestead or pre-emption right, and as preliminary to the issuing of a patent for the land.

7. **In Scotch law.** The term refers to the acknowledgment of the title of the heir, etc., to be admitted by the superior.

ENTRY AD COMMUNEM LEGEM. Entry at common law. The name of a writ of entry which lay for a reversioner after the alienation and death of the particular tenant for life, against him who was in possession of the land. Brown.

ENTRY AD TERMINUM QUI PRÆTERIIT. The writ of entry *ad terminum qui præteriit* lies where a man leases land to another for a term of years, and the tenant holds over his term. And if lands be leased to a man for the term of another's life, and he for whose life the lands are leased dies, and the lessee holds over, then the lessor shall have this writ. Termes de la Ley.

ENTRY FOR MARRIAGE IN SPEECH. A writ of entry *causa matrimonii præloquuti* lies where lands or tenements are given to a man upon condition that he shall take the donor to be his wife within a certain time, and he does not espouse her within the said term, or espouses another woman, or makes himself priest. Termes de la Ley.

ENTRY IN CASU CONSIMILI. A writ of entry *in casu consimili* lies where a tenant for life or by the curtesy aliens in fee. Termes de la Ley.

ENTRY IN THE CASE PROVIDED. A writ of entry *in casu proviso* lies if a tenant in dower alien in fee, or for life, or for another's life, living the tenant in dower. Termes de la Ley.

ENTRY OF CAUSE FOR TRIAL. In English practice. The proceeding by a plaintiff in an action who had given notice of trial, depositing with the proper officer of the court the *nisi prius* record, with the panel of jurors annexed, and thus bringing the issue before the court for trial.

ENTRY ON THE ROLL. In former times, the parties to an action, personally or by their counsel, used to appear in open court and make their mutual statements *vivâ voce*, instead of as at the present day delivering their mutual pleadings, until they arrived at the issue or precise point in dispute between them. During the progress of this oral statement, a minute of the various proceedings was made on parchment by an officer of the court appointed for that purpose. The parchment then became the record; in other words, the official history of the suit. Long after the practice of oral pleading had fallen into disuse, it continued necessary to enter the proceedings in like manner upon the parchment roll, and this was called "entry on the roll," or making up the "issue roll." But by a rule of H. T. 4 Wm. IV., the practice of making up the issue roll was abolished; and it was only necessary to make up the issue in the form prescribed for the purpose by a rule of H. T. 1853, and to deliver the same to the court and to the opposite party. The issue which was delivered to the court was called the "*nisi prius record;*" and that was regarded as the official history of the suit, in like manner as the issue roll formerly was. Under the present practice, the issue roll or *nisi prius record* consists of the papers delivered to the court, to facilitate the trial of the action, these papers consisting of the pleadings simply, with the notice of trial. Brown.

ENTRY WITHOUT ASSENT OF THE CHAPTER. A writ of entry *sine assensu capituli* lies where an abbot, prior, or such as hath covent or common seal, aliens lands or tenements of the right of his church, without the assent of the covent or chapter, and dies. Termes de la Ley.

ENTRY, WRIT OF. In old English practice. This was a writ made use of in a form of real action brought to recover the possession of lands from one who wrongfully withheld the same from the demandant.

Its object was to regain the *possession* of lands of which the demandant, or his ancestors, had been unjustly deprived by the tenant of the freehold, or those under whom he claimed, and hence it belonged to the *possessory* division of real actions. It decided nothing with respect to the *right of property*, but only restored the demandant to that situation in which he was (or by law ought to have been) before the dispossession committed. 3 Bl. Comm. 180.

It was usual to specify in such writs the degree or degrees within which the writ was brought, and it was said to be "in the *per*" or "in the *per and cui*," according as there had been one or two descents or alienations from the original wrongdoer. If more than two such transfers had intervened, the writ was said to be "in the *post*." See 3 Bl. Comm. 181.

Enumeratio infirmat regulam in casibus non enumeratis. Enumeration disaffirms the rule in cases not enumerated. Bac. Aph. 17.

Enumeratio unius est exclusio alterius. The specification of one thing is the exclusion of a different thing. A maxim more generally expressed in the form "*expressio unius est exclusio alterius*," (*q. v.*)

ENUMERATORS. Persons appointed to collect census papers or schedules. 33 & 34 Vict. c. 108, § 4.

ENURE. To operate or take effect. To serve to the use, benefit, or advantage of a person. A release to the tenant for life *enures* to him in reversion; that is, it has the same effect for him as for the tenant for life. Often written "inure."

ENVOY. In international law. A public minister of the second class, ranking next after an ambassador.

Envoys are either ordinary or extraordinary; by custom the latter is held in greater consideration.

EO INSTANTE. At that instant; at the very or same instant; immediately. 1 Bl. Comm. 196, 249; 2 Bl. Comm. 168; Co. Litt. 298*a;* 1 Coke, 138.

EO INTUITU. With or in that view; with that intent or object. Hale, Anal. § 2.

EO LOCI. In the civil law. In that state or condition; in that place, (*eo loco.*) Calvin.

EO NOMINE. Under that name; by that appellation. *Perinde ac si eo nomine tibi tradita fuisset*, just as if it had been delivered to you by that name. Inst. 2, 1, 43. A common phrase in the books.

Eodem ligamine quo ligatum est dissolvitur. A bond is released by the same formalities with which it is contracted. Co. Litt. 212*b;* Broom, Max. 891.

Eodem modo quo quid constituitur, dissolvitur. In the manner in which [by the same means by which] a thing is constituted, is it dissolved. 6 Coke, 53*b*.

EORLE. In Saxon law. An earl.

EOTH. In Saxon law. An oath.

EPIDEMIC. This term, in its ordinary and popular meaning, applies to *any* disease which is widely spread or generally prevailing at a given place and time. 36 N. Y. Super. Ct. 234.

EPILEPSY. In medical jurisprudence. A disease of the brain, which occurs in paroxysms with uncertain intervals between them.

EPIMENIA. Expenses or gifts. Blount.

EPIPHANY. A Christian festival, otherwise called the "Manifestation of Christ to the Gentiles," observed on the 6th of January, in honor of the appearance of the star to the three *magi*, or wise men, who came to adore the Messiah, and bring him presents. It is commonly called "Twelfth Day." Enc. Lond.

EPIQUEYA. In Spanish law. A term synonymous with "equity" in one of its senses, and defined as "the benignant and prudent interpretation of the law according to the circumstances of the time, place, and person."

EPISCOPACY. The office of overlooking or overseeing; the office of a bishop, who is to overlook and oversee the concerns of the church. A form of church government by diocesan bishops.

EPISCOPALIA. In ecclesiastical law. Synodals, pentecostals, and other customary payments from the clergy to their diocesan bishop, formerly collected by the rural deans. Cowell.

EPISCOPALIAN. Of or pertaining to episcopacy, or to the Episcopal Church.

EPISCOPATE. A bishopric. The dignity or office of a bishop.

EPISCOPUS. In the civil law. An overseer; an inspector. A municipal officer who had the charge and oversight of the bread and other provisions which served the citizens for their daily food. Vicat.

In medieval history. A bishop; a bishop of the Christian church.

Episcopus alterius mandato quam regis non tenetur obtemperare. Co. Litt. 134. A bishop needs not obey any mandate save the king's.

EPISCOPUS PUERORUM. It was an old custom that upon certain feasts some lay person should plait his hair, and put on the garments of a bishop, and in them pretend to exercise episcopal jurisdiction, and do several ludicrous actions, for which reason he was called "bishop of the boys;" and this custom obtained in England long after several constitutions were made to abolish it. Blount.

Episcopus teneat placitum, in curia christianitatis, de iis quæ mere sunt spiritualia. 12 Coke, 44. A bishop may hold plea in a Court Christian of things merely spiritual.

EPISTOLA. A letter; a charter; an instrument in writing for conveyance of lands or assurance of contracts. Calvin; Spelman.

EPISTOLÆ. In the civil law. Rescripts; opinions given by the emperors in cases submitted to them for decision.

Answers of the emperors to petitions.

The answers of counsellors, (*juris-consulti,*) as Ulpian and others, to questions of law proposed to them, were also called "*epistolæ.*"

Opinions written out. The term originally signified the same as *literæ*. Vicat.

EPOCH. The time at which a new computation is begun; the time whence dates are numbered. Enc. Lond.

EQUALITY. The condition of possessing the same rights, privileges, and immunities, and being liable to the same duties.

Equality is equity. Fran. Max. 9, max. 3. Thus, where an heir buys in an incumbrance for less than is due upon it, (except it be to protect an incumbrance to which he himself is entitled,) he shall be allowed no more than what he really paid for it, as against other incumbrancers upon the estate. 2 Vent. 353; 1 Vern. 49; 1 Salk. 155.

EQUERRY. An officer of state under the master of the horse.

EQUES. Lat. In Roman and old English law. A knight.

EQUILOCUS. An equal. It is mentioned in Simeon Dunelm, A. D. 882. Jacob.

EQUINOXES. The two periods of the year (vernal equinox about March 21st, and autumnal equinox about September 22d) when the time from the rising of the sun to its setting is equal to the time from its setting to its rising. See Dig. 43, 13, 1, 8.

EQUITABLE. Just; conformable to the principles of natural justice and right.

Just, fair, and right, in consideration of the facts and circumstances of the individual case.

Existing in equity; available or sustainable only in equity, or only upon the rules and principles of equity.

EQUITABLE ASSETS. Equitable assets are all assets which are chargeable with the payment of debts or legacies in equity, and which do not fall under the description of legal assets. 1 Story, Eq. Jur. § 552.

Those portions of the property which by the ordinary rules of law are exempt from debts, but which the testator has voluntarily charged as assets, or which, being non-existent at law, have been created in equity. Adams, Eq. 254, et seq.

They are so called because they can be reached only by the aid and instrumentality of a court of equity, and because their distribution is governed by a different rule from that which governs the distribution of legal assets. 2 Fonbl. Eq. b. 4, pt. 2, c. 2, § 1, and notes; Story, Eq. Jur. § 552.

EQUITABLE ASSIGNMENT. An assignment which, though invalid at law, will be recognized and enforced in equity; *e. g.*, an assignment of a chose in action, or of future acquisitions of the assignor.

EQUITABLE CONSTRUCTION. A construction of a law, rule, or remedy which has regard more to the equities of the particular transaction or state of affairs involved than to the strict application of the rule or remedy; that is, a liberal and extensive construction, as opposed to a literal and restrictive.

EQUITABLE CONVERSION. The transformation, by a doctrine of equity, of personalty into realty, in respect to its qualities and disposition, and of real estate into personalty. By this doctrine, money which, by will or agreement, is to be invested in land, is considered and treated as realty, and land which is to be turned into money is considered and treated as money. 8 Wall. 214; 45 Pa. St. 87; 61 Wis. 477, 21 N. W. Rep. 615.

EQUITABLE DEFENSE. In English practice. A defense to an action on grounds which, prior to the passing of the common-law procedure act, (17 & 18 Vict. c. 125,) would have been cognizable only in a court of equity. Mozley & Whitley.

In American practice. A defense which is available only in equity, except under the reformed codes of practice, where it may be interposed in a legal action.

EQUITABLE ESTATE. An equitable estate is an estate an interest in which can only be enforced in a court of chancery. 9 Ohio, 145.

That is properly an equitable estate or interest for which a court of equity affords the only remedy; and of this nature, especially, is the benefit of every trust, express or implied, which is not converted into a legal estate by the statute of uses. The rest are equities of redemption, constructive trusts, and all equitable charges. Burt. Comp. c. 8.

EQUITABLE MORTGAGE. A mortgage arising in equity, out of the transactions of the parties, without any deed or express contract for that special purpose. 4 Kent, Comm. 150.

A lien upon realty, which is of such a character that a court of equity will recognize it as a security for the payment of money loaned or due. 2 Story, Eq. Jur. § 1018.

A mortgage upon a purely equitable estate or interest.

In English law. The following mortgages are equitable: (1) Where the subject of a mortgage is trust property, which security is effected either by a formal deed or a written memorandum, notice being given to the trustees in order to preserve the priority. (2) Where it is an equity of redemption, which is merely a right to bring an action in the chancery division to redeem the estate. (3) Where there is a written agreement only to make a mortgage, which creates an equitable lien on the land. (4) Where a debtor deposits the title-deeds of his estate with his creditor or some person on his behalf, without even a verbal communication. The deposit itself is deemed evidence of an executed agreement or contract for a mortgage for such estate. Wharton.

EQUITABLE WASTE. Injury to a reversion or remainder in real estate, which is not recognized by the courts of law as waste, but which equity will interpose to prevent or remedy.

EQUITATURA. In old English law. Traveling furniture, or riding equipments, including horses, horse harness, etc. Reg. Orig. 100*b*; St. Westm. 2, c. 39.

EQUITY. 1. In its broadest and most general signification, this term denotes the spirit and the habit of fairness, justness, and right dealing which should regulate the intercourse of men with men,—the rule of doing to all others as we desire them to do to us; or, as it is expressed by Justinian, "to live honestly, to harm nobody, to render to every man his due." Inst. 1, 1, 3. It is therefore the synonym of natural right or justice. But in this sense its obligation is ethical rather than jural, and its discussion belongs to the sphere of morals. It is grounded in the precepts of the conscience, not in any sanction of positive law.

2. In a more restricted sense, the word denotes equal and impartial justice as between two persons whose rights or claims are in conflict; justice, that is, as ascertained by natural reason or ethical insight, but independent of the formulated body of law. This is not a technical meaning of the term, except in so far as courts which administer equity seek to discover it by the agencies above mentioned, or apply it beyond the strict lines of positive law.

3. In one of its technical meanings, equity is a body of jurisprudence, or field of jurisdiction, differing in its origin, theory, and methods from the common law.

It is a body of rules existing by the side of the original civil law, founded on distinct principles, and claiming incidentally to supersede the civil law in virtue of a superior sanctity inherent in those principles. Maine, Anc. Law, 27.

"As old rules become too narrow, or are felt to be out of harmony with advancing civilization, a machinery is needed for their gradual enlargement and adaptation to new views of society. One mode of accomplishing this object on a large scale, without appearing to disregard existing law, is the introduction, by the prerogative of some high functionary, of a more perfect body of rules, discoverable in his judicial conscience, which is to stand side by side with the law of the land, overriding it in case of conflict, as on some title of inherent superiority, but not purporting to repeal it. Such a body of rules has been called 'Equity.'" Holl. Jur. 59.

"Equity," in its technical sense, contradistinguished from natural and universal equity or justice, may well be described as a "portion of justice" or natural equity, not embodied in legislative enactments, or in the rules of common law, yet modified by a due regard thereto and to the complex relations and conveniences of an artificial state of society, and administered in regard to cases where the particular rights, in respect of which relief is sought, come within some general class of rights enforced at law, or may be enforced without detriment or inconvenience to the community; but where, as to such particular rights, the ordinary courts of law cannot, or originally did not, clearly afford relief. Rob. Eq.

4. In a still more restricted sense, it is a system of jurisprudence, or branch of remedial justice, administered by certain tribunals, distinct from the common-law courts, and empowered to decree "equity" in the sense last above given. Here it becomes a complex of well-settled and well-understood rules, principles, and precedents.

"The meaning of the word 'equity,' as used in its technical sense in English jurisprudence, comes back to this: that it is simply a term descriptive of a certain field of jurisdiction exercised, in the English system, by certain courts, and of which the extent and boundaries are not marked by lines founded upon principle so much as by the features of the original constitution of the English scheme of remedial law, and the accidents of its development." Bisp. Eq. § 11.

A system of jurisprudence collateral to, and in some respects independent of, "law," properly so called; the object of which is to render the administration of justice more complete, by affording relief where the courts of law are incompetent to give it, or to give it with effect, or by exercising certain branches of jurisdiction independently of them. This is equity in its proper modern sense; an elaborate system of rules and process, administered in many cases by distinct tribunals, (termed "courts of chancery,") and with exclusive jurisdiction over certain subjects. It is "still distinguished by its original and animating principle that no right should be without an adequate remedy," and its doctrines are founded upon the same basis of natural justice; but its action has become systematized, deprived of any loose and arbitrary character which might once have belonged to it, and as carefully regulated by fixed rules and precedents as the law itself. Burrill.

Equity, in its technical and scientific legal use, means neither natural justice nor even all that portion of natural justice which is susceptible of being judicially enforced. It has a precise, limited, and definite signification, and is used to denote a system of justice which was administered in a particular court,—the English high court of chancery,—which system can only be understood and explained by studying the history of that court, and how it came to exercise what is known as its extraordinary jurisdiction. Bisp. Eq. § 1.

That part of the law which, having power to enforce discovery, (1) administers trusts, mortgages, and other fiduciary obligations; (2) administers and adjusts common-law rights where the courts of common law have no machinery; (3) supplies a specific and preventive remedy for common-law wrongs where courts of common law only give subsequent damages. Chute, Eq. 4.

Equity is not the chancellor's sense of moral right, or his sense of what is equal and just, but is a complex system of established law; and an equitable maxim—as equality is equity—can only be applied according to established rules. 23 Me. 360.

5. Equity also signifies an equitable right, *i. e.*, a right enforceable in a court of equity; hence, a bill of complaint which did not show that the plaintiff had a right entitling him to relief was said to be demurrable for want of equity; and certain rights now recognized in all the courts are still known as "equities," from having been originally recognized only in the court of chancery. Sweet.

EQUITY, COURTS OF. Courts which administer justice according to the system of equity, and according to a peculiar course of procedure or practice. See EQUITY. Frequently termed "courts of chancery." See 1 Bl. Comm. 92.

Equity delights to do justice, and that not by halves. 5 Barb. 277, 280; Story, Eq. Pl. § 72.

Equity follows the law. Talb. 52. Equity adopts and follows the rules of law in all cases to which those rules may, in terms, be applicable. Equity, in dealing with cases of an equitable nature, adopts and follows the analogies furnished by the rules of law. A leading maxim of equity jurisprudence, which, however, is not of universal application, but liable to many exceptions. Story, Eq. Jur. § 64.

Equity looks upon that as done which ought to have been done. 1 Story, Eq. Jur. § 64*g*. Equity will treat the subject-matter, as to collateral consequences and incidents, in the same manner as if the final acts contemplated by the parties had been executed exactly as they ought to have been; not as the parties might have executed them. Id.

EQUITY OF A STATUTE. By this phrase is intended the rule of statutory construction which admits within the operation of a statute a class of cases which are neither expressly named nor excluded, but which, from their analogy to the cases that are named, are clearly and justly within the spirit and general meaning of the law; such cases are said to be "within the equity of the statute."

EQUITY OF REDEMPTION. The right of the mortgagor of an estate to redeem the same after it has been forfeited, at law, by a breach of the condition of the mortgage, upon paying the amount of debt, interest, and costs.

Equity suffers not a right without a remedy. 4 Bouv. Inst. no. 3726.

EQUITY TO A SETTLEMENT. The equitable right of a wife, when her husband sues in equity for the reduction of her equitable estate to his own possession, to have the whole or a portion of such estate settled upon herself and her children. Also a similar right now recognized by the equity courts as directly to be asserted against the husband. Also called the "wife's equity."

EQUIVALENT. In patent law. The term "equivalent," when used of machines, has a certain definite meaning; but, when used with regard to the chemical actions of such fluids as can be discovered only by experiment, it means equally good. 7 Wall. 327.

EQUIVOCAL. Having a double or several meanings or senses. See AMBIGUITY.

EQUULEUS. A kind of rack for extorting confessions.

EQUUS COOPERTUS. A horse equipped with saddle and furniture.

ERABILIS. A maple tree. Not to be confounded with *arabilis*, (arable land.)

ERASTIANS. The followers of Erastus. The sect obtained much influence in England, particularly among common lawyers in the time of Selden. They held that offenses against religion and morality should be punished by the civil power, and not by the censures of the church or by excommunication. Wharton.

ERASURE. The obliteration of words or marks from a written instrument by rubbing, scraping, or scratching them out. Also the place in a document where a word or words have been so removed. The term is sometimes used for the removal of parts of a writing by any means whatever, as by cancellation; but this is not an accurate use.

ERCISCUNDUS. In the civil law. To be divided. *Judicium familiæ erciscundæ*, a suit for the partition of an inheritance. Inst. 4, 17, 4. An ancient phrase derived from the Twelve Tables. Calvin.

"ERECT." One of the formal words of incorporation in royal charters. "We do, incorporate, *erect*, ordain, name, constitute, and establish."

ERECTION. Raising up; building; a completed building. In a statute on the "erection" of wooden buildings, this term does not include repairing, alteration, enlarging, or removal. See 45 N. Y. 153; 27 Conn. 332; 2 Rawle, 262; 119 Mass. 254; 51 Ill. 422.

ERGO. Lat. Therefore; hence; because.

ERGOLABI. In the civil law. Undertakers of work; contractors. Cod. 4, 59.

ERIACH. A term of the Irish Brehon law, denoting a pecuniary mulct or recompense which a murderer was judicially condemned to pay to the family or relatives of his victim. It corresponded to the Saxon "weregild." See 4 Bl. Comm. 313.

ERIGIMUS. We erect. One of the words by which a corporation may be created in England by the king's charter. 1 Bl. Comm. 473.

ERMINE. By metonymy, this term is used to describe the office or functions of a judge, whose state robe, lined with ermine, is emblematical of purity and honor without stain. Webster.

ERNES. In old English law. The loose scattered ears of corn that are left on the ground after the binding.

EROSION. The gradual eating away of the soil by the operation of currents or tides. Distinguished from *submergence*, which is the disappearance of the soil under the water and the formation of a navigable body over it. 100 N. Y. 433, 3 N. E. Rep. 584.

EROTOMANIA. Sometimes also called "*Erotico-Mania*," a disease of the brain on sexual subjects. The distinction between it and *nymphomania* is that in the latter, although the condition of mind is similar, the disease is caused by a local disorder of the sexual organs reacting on the brain. Wharton.

ERRANT. Wandering; itinerant; applied to justices on circuit, and bailiffs at large, etc.

ERRATICUM. In old law. A waif or stray; a wandering beast. Cowell.

ERRONEOUS. Involving error; deviating from the law. This term is never used by courts or law-writers as designating a corrupt or evil act. 72 Ind. 338.

ERRONICE. Lat. Erroneously; through error or mistake.

ERROR. A mistaken judgment or incorrect belief as to the existence or effect of matters of fact, or a false or mistaken conception or application of the law.

Such a mistaken or false conception or application of the law to the facts of a cause as will furnish ground for a review of the proceedings upon a writ of error; a mistake of law, or false or irregular application of it, such as vitiates the proceedings and warrants the reversal of the judgment.

Error is also used as an elliptical expression for "writ of error;" as in saying that *error* lies; that a judgment may be reversed *on error*.

ERROR, WRIT OF. See WRIT OF ERROR.

Error fucatus nuda veritate in multis est probabilior; et sæpenumero rationibus vincit veritatem error. Error artfully disguised [or colored] is, in many instances, more probable than naked truth; and frequently error overwhelms truth by [its show of] reasons. 2 Coke, 73.

Error juris nocet. Error of law injures. A mistake of the law has an injurious effect; that is, the party committing it must suffer the consequences. Mackeld. Rom. Law, § 178; 1 Story, Eq. Jur. § 139, note.

ERROR NOMINIS. Error of name. A mistake of detail in the name of a person; used in contradistinction to error *de personâ*, a mistake as to identity.

Error nominis nunquam nocet, si de identitate rei constat. A mistake in the name of a thing is never prejudicial, if it be clear as to the identity of the thing itself, [where the thing intended is certainly known.] 1 Duer, Ins. 171. This maxim is applicable only where the means of correcting the mistake are apparent on the face of the instrument to be construed. Id.

ERROR OF FACT. That is called "error of fact" which proceeds either from ignorance of that which really exists or from a mistaken belief in the existence of that which has none. Civil Code La. art. 1821.

ERROR OF LAW. He is under an error of law who is truly informed of the existence of facts, but who draws from them erroneous conclusions of law. Civil Code La. art. 1822.

Error qui non resistitur approbatur. An error which is not resisted or opposed is approved. Doct. & Stud. c. 40.

Errores ad sua principia referre, est refellere. To refer errors to their sources is to refute them. 3 Inst. 15. To bring errors to their beginning is to see their last.

Errores scribentis nocere non debent. The mistakes of the writer ought not to harm. Jenk. Cent. 324.

ERRORS EXCEPTED. A phrase appended to an account stated, in order to excuse slight mistakes or oversights.

ERTHMIOTUM. In old English law. A meeting of the neighborhood to compromise differences among themselves; a court held on the boundary of two lands.

Erubescit lex filios castigare parentes. 8 Coke, 116. The law blushes when children correct their parents.

ESBRANCATURA. In old law. A cutting off the branches or boughs of trees. Cowell; Spelman.

ESCALDARE. To scald. It is said that to *scald hogs* was one of the ancient tenures in serjeanty. Wharton.

ESCAMBIO. In old English law. A writ of exchange. A license in the shape of a writ, formerly granted to an English merchant to draw a bill of exchange on another in foreign parts. Reg. Orig. 194.

ESCAMBIUM. An old English law term, signifying exchange.

ESCAPE. The departure or deliverance out of custody of a person who was lawfully imprisoned, before he is entitled to his liberty by the process of law.

The voluntarily or negligently allowing any person lawfully in confinement to leave the place. 2 Bish. Crim. Law, § 917.

Escapes are either *voluntary* or *negligent*. The former is the case when the keeper voluntarily concedes to the prisoner any liberty not authorized by law. The latter is the case when the prisoner contrives to leave his prison by forcing his way out, or any other means, without the knowledge or against the will of the keeper, but through the latter's carelessness or the insecurity of the building.

ESCAPE WARRANT. In English practice. This was a warrant granted to retake a prisoner committed to the custody of the queen's prison who had escaped therefrom. It was obtained on affidavit from the judge of the court in which the action had been brought, and was directed to all the sheriffs throughout England, commanding them to retake the prisoner and commit him to gaol when and where taken, there to remain until the debt was satisfied. Jacob; Brown.

ESCAPIO QUIETUS. In old English law. Delivered from that punishment which by the laws of the forest lay upon those whose beasts were found upon forbidden land. Jacob.

ESCAPIUM. That which comes by chance or accident. Cowell.

ESCEPPA. A measure of corn. Cowell.

Eschæta derivatur a verbo Gallico eschoir, quod est accidere, quia accidit domino ex eventu et ex insperato. Co. Litt. 93. Escheat is derived from the French word "*eschoir,*" which signifies to happen, because it falls to the lord from an event and from an unforeseen circumstance.

Eschætæ vulgo dicuntur quæ decidentibus iis quæ de rege tenent, cum non existit ratione sanguinis hæres, ad fiscum relabuntur. Co. Litt. 13. Those things are commonly called "escheats" which revert to the exchequer from a failure of issue in those who hold of the king, when there does not exist any heir by consanguinity.

ESCHEAT. In feudal law. Escheat is an obstruction of the course of descent, and consequent determination of the tenure, by some unforeseen contingency, in which case the land naturally results back, by a kind of reversion, to the original grantor, or lord of the fee. 2 Bl. Comm. 15.

It is the casual descent, in the nature of forfeiture, of lands and tenements within his manor, to a lord, either on failure of issue of the tenant dying seised or on account of the felony of such tenant. Jacob.

Also the land or fee itself, which thus fell back to the lord. Such lands were called "*excadentiæ,*" or "*terræ excadentiales.*" Fleta, lib. 6, c. 1; Co. Litt. 13*a*.

In American law. Escheat signifies a reversion of property to the state in consequence of a want of any individual competent to inherit. The state is deemed to occupy the place and hold the rights of the feudal lord. See 4 Kent, Comm. 423, 424.

"Escheat at feudal law was the right of the lord of a fee to re-enter upon the same when it became vacant by the extinction of the blood of the tenant. This extinction might either be *per defectum sanguinis* or else *per delictum tenentis*, where the course of descent was broken by the corruption of the blood of the tenant. As a fee might be holden either of the crown or from some inferior lord, the escheat was not always to the crown. The word 'escheat,' in this country, at the present time, merely indicates the preferable right of the state to an estate left vacant, and without there being any one in existence able to make claim thereto." 29 Amer. Dec. 232, note.

ESCHEAT, WRIT OF. A writ which anciently lay for a lord, to recover possession of lands that had escheated to him. Reg. Orig. 164*b;* Fitzh. Nat. Brev. 143.

ESCHEATOR. In English law. The name of an officer who was appointed in every county to look after the escheats which fell due to the king in that particular county, and to certify the same into the exchequer. An escheator could continue in office for one year only, and was not re-eligible until three years. There does not appear to exist any such officer at the present day. Brown. See 10 Vin. Abr. 158; Co. Litt. 13*b*.

ESCHECCUM. In old English law. A jury or inquisition.

ESCHIPARE. To build or equip. Du Cange.

ESCOT. A tax formerly paid in boroughs and corporations towards the support of the community, which is called "scot and lot."

ESCRIBANO. In Spanish law. An officer, resembling a notary in French law, who has authority to set down in writing, and verify by his attestation, transactions and contracts between private persons, and also judicial acts and proceedings.

ESCRITURA. In Spanish law. A written instrument. Every deed that is made by the hand of a public *escribano*, or notary of a corporation or council (*concejo*,) or sealed with the seal of the king or other authorized persons. White, New Recop. b. 3, tit. 7, c. 5.

ESCROQUERIE. Fr. Fraud, swindling, cheating.

ESCROW. A scroll; a writing; a deed. Particularly a deed delivered by the grantor into the hands of a third person, to be held by the latter until the happening of a contingency or performance of a condition, and then by him delivered to the grantee.

A grant may be deposited by the grantor with a third person, to be delivered on the performance of a condition, and on delivery by the depositary it will take effect. While in the possession of the third person, and subject to condition, it is called an "escrow." Civil Code Cal. § 1057; Civil Code Dak. § 609.

The state or condition of a deed which is conditionally held by a third person, or the possession and retention of a deed by a third person pending a condition; as when an instrument is said to be delivered "in escrow." This use of the term, however, is a perversion of its meaning.

ESCROWL. In old English law. An escrow; a scroll. "And deliver the deed to a stranger, as an escrowl." Perk. c. 1, § 9; Id. c. 2, §§ 137, 138.

ESCUAGE. Service of the shield. One of the varieties of tenure in knight's service, the duty imposed being that of accompanying the king to the wars for forty days, at the tenant's own charge, or sending a substitute. In later times, this service was commuted for a certain payment in money, which was then called "escuage certain." See 2 Bl. Comm. 74, 75.

ESCURARE. To scour or cleanse. Cowell.

ESGLISE, or EGLISE. A church. Jacob.

ESKETORES. Robbers, or destroyers of other men's lands and fortunes. Cowell.

ESKIPPAMENTUM. Tackle or furniture; outfit. Certain towns in England were bound to furnish certain ships at their own expense and with double *skippage* or tackle. Cowell.

ESKIPPER, ESKIPPARE. To ship.

ESKIPPESON. Shippage, or passage by sea. Spelled, also, "*skippeson.*" Cowell.

ESLISORS. See ELISORS.

ESNE. In old law. A hireling of servile condition.

ESNECY. Seniority; the condition or right of the eldest; the privilege of the eldest-born. Particularly used of the privilege of the eldest among coparceners to make a first choice of purparts upon a voluntary partition.

ESPERA. A period of time fixed by law or by a court within which certain acts are to be performed, *e. g.*, the production of papers, payment of debts, etc.

ESPERONS. L. Fr. Spurs.

ESPLEES. An old term for the products which the ground or land yields; as the hay of the meadows, the herbage of the pasture, corn of arable fields, rent and services, etc. The word has been anciently applied to the land itself. Jacob.

ESPOUSALS. A mutual promise between a man and a woman to marry each other at some other time. It differs from a marriage, because then the contract is completed. Wood, Inst. 57.

ESPURIO. Span. In Spanish law. A spurious child; one begotten on a woman who has promiscuous intercourse with many men. White, New Recop. b. 1, tit. 5, c. 2, § 1.

ESQUIRE. In English law. A title of dignity next above gentleman, and below knight. Also a title of office given to sheriffs, serjeants, and barristers at law, justices of the peace, and others. 1 Bl. Comm. 406; 3 Steph. Comm. 15, note; Tomlins.

ESSARTER. L. Fr. To cut down woods, to clear land of trees and underwood; properly to thin woods, by cutting trees, etc., at intervals. Spelman.

ESSARTUM. Woodlands turned into tillage by uprooting the trees and removing the underwood.

ESSENCE. That which is indispensable to that of which it is the essence.

ESSENCE OF THE CONTRACT. Any condition or stipulation in a contract which is mutually understood and agreed by the parties to be of such vital importance that a sufficient performance of the contract cannot be had without exact compliance with it is said to be "of the essence of the contract."

ESSENDI QUIETUM DE TOLONIO. A writ to be quit of toll; it lies for citizens and burgesses of any city or town who, by charter or prescription, ought to be exempted from toll, where the same is exacted of them. Reg. Orig. 258.

ESSOIN, *v.* In old English practice. To present or offer an excuse for not appearing in court on an appointed day in obedience to a summons; to cast an essoin. Spelman. This was anciently done by a person whom the party sent for that purpose, called an "essoiner."

ESSOIN, *n.* In old English law. An excuse for not appearing in court at the return of the process. Presentation of such excuse. Spelman; 1 Sel. Pr. 4; Com. Dig. "Exoine," B 1. Essoin is not now allowed at all in personal actions. 2 Term 16; 16 East, 7*a;* 3 Bl. Comm. 278, note.

ESSOIN DAY. Formerly the first general return-day of the term, on which the courts sat to receive essoins, *i. e.*, excuses for parties who did not appear in court, according to the summons of writs. 3 Bl. Comm. 278; Boote, Suit at Law, 130; Gilb. Com. Pl. 13; 1 Tidd, Pr. 107. But, by St. 11 Geo. IV. and 1 Wm. IV. c. 70, § 6, these days were done away with, as a part of the term.

ESSOIN DE MALO VILLÆ is when the defendant is in court the first day; but gone without pleading, and being afterwards surprised by sickness, etc., cannot attend, but sends two essoiners, who openly protest in court that he is detained by sickness in such a village, that he cannot come *pro lucrari* and *pro perdere;* and this will be admitted, for it lieth on the plaintiff to prove whether the essoin is true or not. Jacob.

ESSOIN ROLL. A roll upon which essoins were formerly entered, together with the day to which they were adjourned. Boote, Suit at Law, 130; Rosc. Real Act. 162, 163; Gilb. Com. Pl. 13.

ESSOINIATOR. A person who made an essoin.

Est aliquid quod non oportet etiam si licet; quicquid vero non licet certe non oportet. Hob. 159. There is that which is not proper, even though permitted; but whatever is not permitted is certainly not proper.

EST ASCAVOIR. It is to be understood or known; "it is to-wit." Litt. §§ 9, 45, 46, 57, 59. A very common expression in Littleton, especially at the commencement of a section; and, according to Lord Coke, "it ever teacheth us some rule of law, or general or sure leading point." Co. Litt. 16.

Est autem jus publicum et privatum, quod ex naturalibus præceptis aut gentium, aut civilibus est collectum; et quod in jure scripto jus appellatur, id in lege Angliæ rectum esse dicitur. Public and private law is that which is collected from natural precepts, on the one hand of nations, on the other of citizens; and that which in the civil law is called "*jus,*" that, in the law of England, is said to be right. Co. Litt. 558.

Est autem vis legem simulans. Violence may also put on the mask of law.

Est ipsorum legislatorum tanquam viva vox. The voice of the legislators themselves is like the living voice; that is, the language of a statute is to be understood and interpreted like ordinary spoken language. 10 Coke, 101*b*.

Est quiddam perfectius in rebus licitis. Hob. 159. There is something more perfect in things allowed.

ESTABLISH. This word occurs frequently in the constitution of the United

States, and it is there used in different meanings: (1) To settle firmly, to fix unalterably; as to establish justice, which is the avowed object of the constitution. (2) To make or form; as to establish a uniform rule of naturalization, and uniform laws on the subject of bankruptcies, which evidently does not mean that these laws shall be unalterably established as justice. (3) To found, to create, to regulate; as: "Congress shall have power to establish post-roads and post-offices." (4) To found, recognize, confirm, or admit; as: "Congress shall make no law respecting an establishment of religion." (5) To create, to ratify, or confirm; as: "We, the people," etc., "do ordain and establish this constitution." 1 Story, Const. § 454.

Establish ordinarily means to settle certainly, or fix permanently, what was before uncertain, doubtful, or disputed. 49 N. H. 230.

ESTABLISHMENT. An ordinance or statute. Especially used of those ordinances or statutes passed in the reign of Edw. I. 2 Inst. 156; Britt. c. 21.

ESTABLISHMENT OF DOWER. The assurance of dower made by the husband, or his friends, before or at the time of the marriage. Britt. cc. 102, 103.

ESTACHE. A bridge or stank of stone or timber. Cowell.

ESTADAL. In Spanish law. In Spanish America this was a measure of land of sixteen square varas, or yards. 2 White, Recop. 139.

ESTADIA. In Spanish law. Delay in a voyage, or in the delivery of cargo, caused by the charterer or consignee, for which demurrage is payable.

ESTANDARD. L. Fr. A standard, (of weights and measures.) So called because it stands constant and immovable, and hath all other measures coming towards it for their conformity. Termes de la Ley.

ESTANQUES. Wears or kiddles in rivers.

ESTATE. 1. The interest which any one has in lands, or in any other subject of property. 1 Prest. Est. 20. An estate in lands, tenements, and hereditaments signifies such interest as the tenant has therein. 2 Bl. Comm. 103. The condition or circumstance in which the owner *stands* with regard to his property. 2 Crabb, Real Prop. p. 2, § 942. In this sense, "estate" is constantly used in conveyances in connection with the words "right," "title," and "interest," and is, in a great degree, synonymous with all of them. See Co. Litt. 345.

"Estate in land" means the kind and quantum of one's interest therein. The term is susceptible of every possible variation in which man can be related to the soil. 2 Mass. 284.

"Estate" is a very comprehensive word, and signifies the quantity of interest which a person has, from absolute ownership down to naked possession; and the quantity of interest is determined by the duration and extent of the right of possession. 9 Cow. 73, 81.

2. In another sense, the term denotes the property (real or personal) in which one has a right or interest; the subject-matter of ownership; the *corpus* of property. Thus, we speak of a "valuable estate," "all my estate," "separate estate," "trust estate," etc. This, also, is its meaning in the classification of property into "real estate" and "personal estate."

The word "estate" is a word of the greatest extension, and comprehends every species of property, real and personal. It describes both the *corpus* and the extent of interest. 55 Me. 284.

"Estate" comprehends everything a man owns, real and personal, and ought not to be limited in its construction, unless connected with some other word which must necessarily have that effect. Cam. & N. 202.

It means, ordinarily, the whole of the property owned by any one, the realty as well as the personalty. Busb. Eq. 141.

3. In a wider sense, the term "estate" denotes a man's whole financial *status* or condition,—the aggregate of his interests and concerns, so far as regards his situation with reference to wealth or its objects, including debts and obligations, as well as possessions and rights.

Here not only property, but indebtedness, is part of the idea. The estate does not consist of the assets only. If it did, such expressions as "insolvent estate" would be misnomers. Debts and assets, taken together, constitute the estate. It is only by regarding the demands against the original proprietor as constituting, together with his resources available to defray them, one entirety, that the phraseology of the law governing what is called "settlement of estates" can be justified. Abbott.

4. The word is also used to denote the aggregate of a man's financial concerns (as above) *personified.* Thus, we speak of "debts due the estate," or say that "A.'s estate is a stockholder in the bank." In this sense it is a fictitious or juridical person, the idea being that a man's business *status* continues his existence, for its special purposes, until its final settlement and dissolution.

5. In its broadest sense, "estate" signifies the social, civic, or political condition or standing of a person; or a class of persons

considered as grouped for social, civic, or political purposes; as in the phrases, "the third estate," "the estates of the realm." See 1 Bl. Comm. 153.

"Estate" and "degree," when used in the sense of an individual's personal *status*, are synonymous, and indicate the individual's rank in life. 15 Me. 122.

ESTATE AD REMANENTIAM. An estate in fee-simple. Glan. l. 7, c. 1.

ESTATE AT SUFFERANCE. The interest of a tenant who has come rightfully into possession of lands by permission of the owner, and continues to occupy the same after the period for which he is entitled to hold by such permission. 1 Washb. Real Prop. 392; 2 Bl. Comm. 150; Co. Litt. 57*b*.

ESTATE AT WILL. A species of estate less than freehold, where lands and tenements are let by one man to another, to have and to hold at the will of the lessor; and the tenant by force of this lease obtains possession. 2 Bl. Comm. 145; 4 Kent, Comm. 110; Litt. § 68. Or it is where lands are let without limiting any certain and determinate estate. 2 Crabb, Real Prop. p. 403, § 1543.

ESTATE BY ELEGIT. See ELEGIT.

ESTATE BY STATUTE MERCHANT. An estate whereby the creditor, under the custom of London, retained the possession of all his debtor's lands until his debts were paid. 1 Greenl. Cruise, Dig. 515. See STATUTE MERCHANT.

ESTATE BY THE CURTESY. Tenant by the curtesy of England is where a man survives a wife who was seised in fee-simple or fee-tail of lands or tenements, and has had issue male or female by her born alive and capable of inheriting the wife's estate as heir to her; in which case he will, on the decease of his wife, hold the estate during his life as tenant by the curtesy of England. 2 Crabb, Real Prop. § 1074.

ESTATE FOR LIFE. A freehold estate, not of inheritance, but which is held by the tenant for his own life or the life or lives of one or more other persons, or for an indefinite period, which may endure for the life or lives of persons in being, and not beyond the period of a life. 1 Washb. Real Prop. 88.

ESTATE FOR YEARS. A species of estate less than freehold, where a man has an interest in lands and tenements, and a possession thereof, by virtue of such interest, for some fixed and determinate period of time; as in the case where lands are let for the term of a certain number of years, agreed upon between the lessor and the lessee, and the lessee enters thereon. 1 Steph. Comm. 263, 264. Blackstone calls this estate a "contract" for the possession of lands or tenements for some determinate period. 2 Bl. Comm. 140.

ESTATE IN COMMON. An estate in lands held by two or more persons, with interests accruing under different titles; or accruing under the same title, but at different periods; or conferred by words of limitation importing that the grantees are to take in distinct shares. 1 Steph. Comm. 323. See TENANCY IN COMMON.

ESTATE IN COPARCENARY. An estate which several persons hold as one heir, whether male or female. This estate has the three unities of time, title, and possession; but the interests of the coparceners may be unequal. 1 Washb. Real Prop. 414; 2 Bl. Comm. 188. See COPARCENARY.

ESTATE IN DOWER. A species of life-estate which a woman is, by law, entitled to claim on the death of her husband, in the lands and tenements of which he was seised in fee during the marriage, and which her issue, if any, might by possibility have inherited. 1 Steph. Comm. 249; 2 Bl. Comm. 129; Cruise, Dig. tit. 6; 2 Crabb, Real Prop. p. 124, § 1117; 4 Kent, Comm. 35. See DOWER.

ESTATE IN EXPECTANCY. One which is not yet in possession, but the enjoyment of which is to begin at a future time; a present or vested contingent right of future enjoyment. These are remainders and reversions.

ESTATE IN FEE-SIMPLE. The estate which a man has where lands are given to him and to his heirs absolutely without any end or limit put to his estate. 2 Bl. Comm. 106; Plowd. 557; 1 Prest. Est. 425; Litt. § 1.

The word "fee," used alone, is a sufficient designation of this species of estate, and hence "simple" is not a necessary part of the title, but it is added as a means of clearly distinguishing this estate from a fee-tail or from any variety of conditional estates.

ESTATE IN FEE-TAIL, generally termed an "estate tail." An estate of inheritance which a man has, to hold to him and the heirs of his body, or to him and particular heirs of his body. 1 Steph. Comm. 228. An estate of inheritance by force of the statute *De Donis*, limited and restrained to some particular heirs of the donee, in exclusion of others. 2 Crabb, Real Prop. pp. 22, 23, § 971; Cruise, Dig. tit. 2, c. 1, § 12. See TAIL; FEE-TAIL.

ESTATE IN JOINT TENANCY. An estate in lands or tenements granted to two or more persons, to hold in fee-simple, fee-tail, for life, for years, or at will. 2 Bl. Comm. 180; 2 Crabb, Real Prop. 937. An estate acquired by two or more persons in the same land, by the same title, (not being a title by descent,) and at the same period; and without any limitation by words importing that they are to take in distinct shares. 1 Steph. Comm. 312. The most remarkable incident or consequence of this kind of estate is that it is subject to survivorship.

ESTATE IN POSSESSION. An estate whereby a present interest passes to and resides in the tenant, not depending on any subsequent circumstance or contingency. 2 Bl. Comm. 163. An estate where the tenant is in actual pernancy, or receipt of the rents and other advantages arising therefrom. 2 Crabb, Real Prop. p. 958, § 2322.

ESTATE IN REMAINDER. An estate limited to take effect in possession, or in enjoyment, or in both, subject only to any term of years or contingent interest that may intervene, immediately after the regular expiration of a particular estate of freehold previously created together with it, by the same instrument, out of the same subject of property. 2 Fearne, Rem. § 159; 2 Bl. Comm. 163; 1 Greenl. Cruise, Dig. 701.

ESTATE IN REVERSION. A species of estate in expectancy, created by operation of law, being the residue of an estate left in the grantor, to commence in possession after the determination of some particular estate granted out by him. 2 Bl. Comm. 175; 2 Crabb, Real Prop. p. 978, § 2345. The residue of an estate left in the grantor or his heirs, or in the heirs of a testator, commencing in possession on the determination of a particular estate granted or devised. 1 Rev. St. N. Y. p. 718, (723,) § 12. An estate in reversion is where any estate is derived, by grant or otherwise, out of a larger one, leaving in the original owner an ulterior estate immediately expectant on that which is so derived; the latter interest being called the "particular estate," (as being only a small part or *particula* of the original one,) and the ulterior interest, the "reversion." 1 Steph. Comm. 290. See REVERSION.

ESTATE IN SEVERALTY. An estate held by a person in his own right only, without any other person being joined or connected with him in point of interest, during his estate. This is the most common and usual way of holding an estate. 2 Bl Comm. 179; Cruise, Dig. tit. 18, c. 1, § 1.

ESTATE IN VADIO. An estate in gage or pledge. 2 Bl. Comm. 157; 1 Steph. Comm. 282.

ESTATE OF FREEHOLD. An estate in land or other real property, of uncertain duration; that is, either of inheritance or which may possibly last for the life of the tenant at the least, (as distinguished from a leasehold;) and held by a free tenure, (as distinguished from copyhold or villeinage.)

ESTATE OF INHERITANCE. A species of freehold estate in lands, otherwise called a "fee," where the tenant is not only entitled to enjoy the land for his own life, but where, after his death, it is cast by the law upon the persons who successively represent him *in perpetuum*, in right of blood, according to a certain established order of descent. 1 Steph. Comm. 218; Litt. § 1; 1 Rev. St. N. Y. p. 717, (722,) § 2.

ESTATE PUR AUTRE VIE. Estate for another's life. An estate in lands which a man holds for the life of another person. 2 Bl. Comm. 120; Litt. § 56.

ESTATE TAIL. See ESTATE IN FEE-TAIL.

ESTATE TAIL, QUASI. When a tenant for life grants his estate to a man and his heirs, as these words, though apt and proper to create an estate tail, cannot do so, because the grantor, being only tenant for life, cannot grant *in perpetuum*, therefore they are said to create an estate tail *quasi*, or improper. Brown.

ESTATE UPON CONDITION. An estate in lands, the existence of which depends upon the happening or not happening of some uncertain event, whereby the estate may be either originally created, or enlarged, or finally defeated. 2 Bl. Comm. 151; 1 Steph. Comm. 276; Co. Litt. 201*a*.

An estate having a qualification annexed to it, by which it may, upon the happening of a particular event, be created, or enlarged, or destroyed. 4 Kent, Comm. 121.

ESTATE UPON CONDITION EXPRESSED. An estate granted, either in fee-simple or otherwise, with an express qualification annexed, whereby the estate granted shall either commence, be enlarged, or be defeated upon performance or breach of such qualification or condition. 2 Bl. Comm. 154.

An estate which is so expressly defined and limited by the words of its creation that it cannot endure for any longer time than till the contingency happens upon which the estate is to fail. 1 Steph. Comm. 278.

ESTATE UPON CONDITION IMPLIED. An estate having a condition annexed to it inseparably from its essence and constitution, although no condition be expressed in words. 2 Bl. Comm. 152; 4 Kent, Comm. 121.

ESTATES OF THE REALM. The lords spiritual, the lords temporal, and the commons of Great Britain. 1 Bl. Comm. 153. Sometimes called the "three estates."

ESTENDARD, ESTENDART, or STANDARD. An ensign for horsemen in war.

ESTER IN JUDGMENT. To appear before a tribunal either as plaintiff or defendant. Kelham.

ESTIMATE. This word is used to express the mind or judgment of the speaker or writer on the particular subject under consideration. It implies a calculation or computation, as to *estimate* the gain or loss of an enterprise. 37 Hun, 203.

ESTOP. To stop, bar, or impede; to prevent; to preclude. Co. Litt. 352*a*. See ESTOPPEL.

ESTOPPEL. A bar or impediment raised by the law, which precludes a man from alleging or from denying a certain fact or state of facts, in consequence of his previous allegation or denial or conduct or admission, or in consequence of a final adjudication of the matter in a court of law.

A preclusion, in law, which prevents a man from alleging or denying a fact, in consequence of his own previous act, allegation, or denial of a contrary tenor. Steph. Pl. 239.

An admission of so conclusive a nature that the party whom it affects is not permitted to aver against it or offer evidence to controvert it. 2 Smith, Lead. Cas. 778.

Estoppel is that which concludes and "shuts a man's mouth from speaking the truth." When a fact has been agreed on, or decided in a court of record, neither of the parties shall be allowed to call it in question, and have it tried over again at any time thereafter, so long as the judgment or decree stands unreversed; and when parties, by deed or solemn act *in pais*, agree on a state of facts, and act on it, neither shall ever afterwards be allowed to gainsay a fact so agreed on, or be heard to dispute it; in other words, his mouth is shut, and he shall not say that is not true which he had before in a solemn manner asserted to be true. Busb. 157.

Equitable estoppel (or estoppel by conduct, or *in pais*) is the species of estoppel which equity puts upon a person who has made a false representation or a concealment of material facts, with knowledge of the facts, to a party ignorant of the truth of the matter, with the intention that the other party should act upon it, and with the result that such party is actually induced to act upon it, to his damage. Bigelow, Estop. 484.

In pleading. A plea, replication, or other pleading, which, without confessing or denying the matter of fact adversely alleged, relies merely on some matter of estoppel as a ground for excluding the opposite party from the allegation of the fact. Steph. Pl. 219; 3 Bl. Comm. 308.

A plea which neither admits nor denies the facts alleged by the plaintiff, but denies his right to allege them. Gould, Pl. c. 2, § 39.

A special plea in bar, which happens where a man has done some act or executed some deed which precludes him from averring anything to the contrary. 3 Bl. Comm. 308.

ESTOPPEL BY DEED is where a party has executed a deed, that is, a writing under seal (as a bond) reciting a certain fact, and is thereby precluded from afterwards denying, in any action brought upon that instrument, the fact so recited. Steph. Pl. 197. A man shall always be *estopped* by his own deed, or not permitted to aver or prove anything in contradiction to what he has once so solemnly and deliberately avowed. 2 Bl. Comm. 295; Plowd. 434.

ESTOPPEL BY MATTER IN PAIS. An estoppel by the conduct or admissions of the party; an estoppel not arising from deed or matter of record. Thus, where one man has accepted rent of another, he will be estopped from afterwards denying, in any action with that person, that he was, at the time of such acceptance, his tenant. Steph. Pl. 197.

The doctrine of *estoppels in pais* is one which, so far at least as that term is concerned, has grown up chiefly within the last few years. But it is, and always was, a familiar principle in the law of contracts. It lies at the foundation of morals, and is a cardinal point in the exposition of promises, that one shall be bound by the state of facts which he has induced another to act upon. Redfield, C. J., 26 Vt. 366, 373.

ESTOPPEL BY MATTER OF RECORD. An estoppel founded upon matter of record; as a confession or admission made in pleading in a court of record, which precludes the party from afterwards contesting the same fact in the same suit. Steph. Pl. 197.

ESTOPPEL, COLLATERAL. The collateral determination of a question by a court having general jurisdiction of the subject.

Estoveria sunt ardendi, arandi, construendi et claudendi. 13 Coke, 68. Estovers are of fire-bote, plow-bote, house-bote, and hedge-bote.

ESTOVERIIS HABENDIS. A writ for a wife judicially separated to recover her alimony or estovers. Obsolete.

ESTOVERS. An allowance made to a person out of an estate or other thing for his or her support, as for food and raiment.

An allowance (more commonly called "alimony") granted to a woman divorced *a mensa et thoro*, for her support out of her husband's estate. 1 Bl. Comm. 441.

The right or privilege which a tenant has to furnish himself with so much wood from the demised premises as may be sufficient or necessary for his fuel, fences, and other agricultural operations. 2 Bl. Comm. 35; Woodf. Landl. & Ten. 232; 10 Wend. 639.

ESTRAY. Cattle whose owner is unknown. 2 Kent, Comm. 359; Spelman; 29 Iowa, 437. Any beast, not wild, found within any lordship, and not owned by any man. Cowell; 1 Bl. Comm. 297.

Estray must be understood as denoting a wandering beast whose owner is unknown to the person who takes it up. 27 Wis. 422; 29 Iowa, 437.

An estray is an animal that has escaped from its owner, and wanders or strays about; usually defined, at common law, as a wandering animal whose owner is unknown. An animal cannot be an estray when on the range where it was raised, and permitted by its owner to run, and especially when the owner is known to the party who takes it up. The fact of its being breachy or vicious does not make it an estray. 4 Or. 206.

ESTREAT, *v.* To take out a forfeited recognizance from the records of a court, and return it to the court of exchequer, to be prosecuted. See ESTREAT, *n.*

ESTREAT, *n.* (From Lat. *extractum.*) In English law. A copy or extract from the book of estreats, that is, the rolls of any court, in which the amercements or fines, recognizances, etc., imposed or taken by that court upon or from the accused, are set down, and which are to be levied by the bailiff or other officer of the court. Cowell; Brown.

A forfeited recognizance taken out from among the other records for the purpose of being sent up to the exchequer, that the parties might be sued thereon, was said to be estreated. 4 Bl. Comm. 253.

ESTRECIATUS. Straightened, as applied to roads. Cowell.

ESTREPE. To strip; to despoil; to lay waste; to commit waste upon an estate, as by cutting down trees, removing buildings, etc. To injure the value of a reversionary interest by stripping or spoiling the estate.

ESTREPEMENT. A species of aggravated waste, by stripping or devastating the land, to the injury of the reversioner, and especially pending a suit for possession.

ESTREPEMENT, WRIT OF. This was a common-law writ of waste, which lay in particular for the reversioner against the tenant for life, in respect of damage or injury to the land committed by the latter. As it was only auxiliary to a real action for recovery of the land, and as equity afforded the same relief by injunction, the writ fell into disuse.

ET. And. The introductory word of several Latin and law French phrases formerly in common use.

ET ADJOURNATUR. And it is adjourned. A phrase used in the old reports, where the argument of a cause was adjourned to another day, or where a second argument was had. 1 Keb. 692, 754, 773.

ET AL. An abbreviation for *et alii*, "and others."

ET ALII È CONTRA. And others on the other side. A phrase constantly used in the Year Books, in describing a joinder in issue. P. 1 Edw. II. *Prist; et alii è contra, et sic ad patriam:* ready; and others, *è contra*, and so to the country. T. 3 Edw. III. 4.

ET ALIUS. And another. The abbreviation *et al.* (sometimes in the plural written *et als.*) is affixed to the name of the person first mentioned, where there are several plaintiffs, grantors, persons addressed, etc.

ET ALLOCATUR. And it is allowed.

ET CÆTERA. And others; and other things; and so on. In its abbreviated form (*etc.*) this phrase is frequently affixed to one of a series of articles or names to show that others are intended to follow or understood to be included. So, after reciting the initiatory words of a set formula, or a clause already given in full, *etc.* is added, as an abbreviation, for the sake of convenience.

ET DE CEO SE METTENT EN LE PAYS. L. Fr. And of this they put themselves upon the country.

ET DE HOC PONIT SE SUPER PATRIAM. And of this he puts himself upon the country. The formal conclusion of a common-law plea in bar by way of traverse. The literal translation is retained in the modern form.

ET EI LEGITUR IN HÆC VERBA. L. Lat. And it is read to him in these words. Words formerly used in entering the prayer of oyer on record.

ET HABEAS IBI TUNC HOC BREVE. And have you then there this writ. The formal words directing the return of a writ. The literal translation is retained in the modern form of a considerable number of writs.

ET HABUIT. And he had it. A common phrase in the Year Books, expressive of the allowance of an application or demand by a party. Parn. *demanda la view. Et habuit,* etc. M. 6 Edw. III. 49.

ET HOC PARATUS EST VERIFICARE. And this he is prepared to verify. The Latin form of concluding a plea in confession and avoidance.

These words were used, when the pleadings were in Latin, at the conclusion of any pleading which contained new affirmative matter. They expressed the willingness or readiness of the party so pleading to establish by proof the matter alleged in his pleading. A pleading which concluded in that manner was technically said to "conclude with a verification," in contradistinction to a pleading which simply denied matter alleged by the opposite party, and which for that reason was said to "conclude to the country," because the party merely put himself upon the country, or left the matter to the jury. Brown.

ET HOC PETIT QUOD INQUIRATUR PER PATRIAM. And this he prays may be inquired of by the country. The conclusion of a plaintiff's pleading, tendering an issue to the country. 1 Salk. 6. Literally translated in the modern forms.

ET INDE PETIT JUDICIUM. And thereupon [or thereof] he prays judgment. A clause at the end of pleadings, praying the judgment of the court in favor of the party pleading. It occurs as early as the time of Bracton, and is literally translated in the modern forms. Bract. fol. 57*b;* Crabb, Eng. Law, 217.

ET INDE PRODUCIT SECTAM. And thereupon he brings suit. The Latin conclusion of a declaration, except against attorneys and other officers of the court. 3 Bl. Comm. 295.

ET MODO AD HUNC DIEM. Lat. And now at this day. This phrase was the formal beginning of an entry of appearance or of a continuance. The equivalent English words are still used in this connection.

ET NON. Lat. And not. A technical phrase in pleading, which introduces the negative averments of a special traverse. It has the same force and effect as the words "*absque hoc,*" and is occasionally used instead of the latter.

ET SEQ. An abbreviation for *et sequentia,* "and the following." Thus a reference to "p. 1, et seq." means "page first and the following pages."

ET SIC. And so. In the Latin forms of pleading these were the introductory words of a special conclusion to a plea in bar, the object being to render it positive and not argumentative; as *et sic nil debet.*

ET SIC AD JUDICIUM. And so to judgment. Yearb. T. 1 Edw. II. 10.

ET SIC AD PATRIAM. And so to the country. A phrase used in the Year Books, to record an issue to the country.

ET SIC FECIT. And he did so. Yearb. P. 9 Hen. VI. 17.

ET SIC PENDET. And so it hangs. A term used in the old reports to signify that a point was left undetermined. T. Raym. 168.

ET SIC ULTERIUS. And so on; and so further; and so forth. Fleta, lib. 2, c. 50, § 27.

ET UX. An abbreviation for *et uxor,*—"and wife." Where a grantor's wife joins him in the conveyance, it is sometimes expressed (in abstracts, etc.) to be by "A. B. *et ux.*"

ETIQUETTE OF THE PROFESSION. The code of honor agreed on by mutual understanding and tacitly accepted by members of the legal profession, especially by the bar. Wharton.

Eum qui nocentem infamat, non est æquum et bonum ob eam rem condemnari; delicta enim nocentium nota esse oportet et expedit. It is not just and proper that he who speaks ill of a bad man should be condemned on that account; for it is fitting and expedient that the crimes of bad men should be known. Dig. 47, 10, 17; 1 Bl. Comm. 125.

EUNDO ET REDEUNDO. Lat. In going and returning. Applied to vessels. 3 C. Rob. Adm. 141.

EUNDO, MORANDO, ET REDEUNDO. Lat. Going, remaining, and returning. A person who is privileged from arrest (as a witness, legislator, etc.) is generally so privileged *eundo, morando, et redeundo;* that is, on his way to the place where his duties are to be performed, while he remains there, and on his return journey.

EUNOMY. Equal laws and a well-adjusted constitution of government.

EUNUCH. A male of the human species who has been castrated. See Domat, liv. prél. tit. 2, § 1, n. 10.

EVASIO. Lat. In old practice. An escape from prison or custody. Reg. Orig. 312.

EVASION. A subtle endeavoring to set aside truth or to escape the punishment of the law. This will not be allowed. If one person says to another that he will not strike him, but will give him a pot of ale to strike first, and, accordingly, the latter strikes, the returning the blow is punishable; and, if the person first striking is killed, it is murder, for no man shall evade the justice of the law by such a pretense. 1 Hawk. P. C. 81. So no one may plead ignorance of the law to evade it. Jacob.

EVASIVE. Tending or seeking to evade; elusive; shifting; as an *evasive* argument or plea.

EVENINGS. In old English law. The delivery at even or night of a certain portion of grass, or corn, etc., to a customary tenant, who performs the service of cutting, mowing, or reaping for his lord, given him as a gratuity or encouragement. Kennett, Gloss.

Eventus est qui ex causâ sequitur; et dicitur eventus quia ex causis evenit. 9 Coke, 81. An event is that which follows from the cause, and is called an "event" because it eventuates from causes.

Eventus varios res nova semper habet. Co. Litt. 379. A new matter always produces various events.

Every man must be taken to contemplate the probable consequences of the act he does. Lord Ellenborough, 9 East, 277. A fundamental maxim in the law of evidence. Best, Pres. § 16; 1 Phil. Ev. 444.

EVES-DROPPERS. See EAVES-DROPPERS.

EVICT. In the civil law. To recover anything from a person by virtue of the judgment of a court or judicial sentence.

At common law. To dispossess, or turn out of the possession of lands by process of law. Also to recover land by judgment at law. "If the land is *evicted*, no rent shall be paid." 10 Coke, 128*a*.

EVICTION. Dispossession by process of law; the act of depriving a person of the possession of lands which he has held, in pursuance of the judgment of a court.

Technically, the dispossession must be by judgment of law; if otherwise, it is an *ouster*.

Eviction implies an entry under paramount title, so as to interfere with the rights of the grantee. The object of the party making the entry is immaterial, whether it be to take all or a part of the land itself or merely an incorporeal right. Phrases equivalent in meaning are "ouster by paramount title," "entry and disturbance," "possession under an elder title," and the like. 5 Conn. 497.

Eviction is an actual expulsion of the lessee out of all or some part of the demised premises. 4 Cow. 581, 585.

In a more popular sense, the term denotes turning a tenant of land out of possession, either by re-entry or by legal proceedings, such as an action of ejectment. Sweet.

By a loose extension, the term is sometimes applied to the ousting of a person from the possession of chattels; but, properly, it applies only to realty.

In the civil law. The abandonment which one is obliged to make of a thing, in pursuance of a sentence by which he is condemned to do so. Poth. Contr. Sale, pt. 2, c. 1, § 2, art. 1, no. 83. The abandonment which a buyer is compelled to make of a thing purchased, in pursuance of a judicial sentence.

Eviction is the loss suffered by the buyer of the totality of the thing sold, or of a part thereof, occasioned by the right or claims of a third person. Civil Code La. art. 2500.

EVIDENCE. Any species of proof, or probative matter, legally presented at the trial of an issue, by the act of the parties and through the medium of witnesses, records, documents, concrete objects, etc., for the purpose of inducing belief in the minds of the court or jury as to their contention.

The word "evidence," in legal acceptation, includes all the means by which any alleged matter of fact, the truth of which is submitted to investigation, is established or disproved. 1 Greenl. Ev. c. 1, § 1.

That which is legally submitted to a jury, to enable them to decide upon the questions in dispute or issue, as pointed out by the pleadings, and distinguished from all comment and argument, is termed "evidence." 1 Starkie, Ev. pt. 1, § 3.

Synonyms distinguished. The term "evidence" is to be carefully distinguished from its synonyms "proof" and "testimony." "Proof" is the logically sufficient reason for assenting to the truth of a proposition advanced. In its juridical sense it is a term of wide import, and comprehends everything that may be adduced at a trial, within the legal rules, for the purpose of producing conviction in the mind of judge or jury, aside from mere argument; that is, everything that has a probative force intrinsically, and not merely as a deduction from, or combination of, original probative facts. But "evidence" is a narrower term, and includes only such kinds of proof as may be legally presented at a trial, by the act of the parties, and through the aid of such concrete facts as witnesses, records, or other documents. Thus, to urge a presumption of law in support of one's case is adducing proof, but it is not offering evidence. "Testimony," again, is a still more restricted term. It properly means only such evidence as is delivered by a witness on the trial of a cause, either orally or in the form of affidavits or depositions. Thus, an ancient deed, when offered under proper circumstances, is evidence, but it could not strictly be called "testimony." "Belief" is a subjective condition resulting from proof. It is a conviction of the truth of a proposition, existing in the mind, and induced by persuasion, proof, or argument addressed to the judgment.

The bill of exceptions states that all the "testimony" is in the record; but this is not equivalent to a statement that all the "evidence" is in the record. Testimony is one species of evidence. But the word "evidence" is a generic term which includes every species of it. And, in a bill of exceptions, the general term covering all species should be used in the statement as to its embracing the evidence, not the term "testimony," which is satisfied if the bill only contains all of that species of evidence. The statement that all the testimony is in the record may, with reference to judicial records, properly be termed an "affirmative pregnant." 60 Ind. 157.

The word "proof" seems properly to mean anything which serves, either immediately or mediately, to convince the mind of the truth or falsehood of a fact or proposition. It is also applied to the conviction generated in the mind by proof properly so called. The word "evidence" signifies, in its original sense, the state of being evident, *i. e.*, plain, apparent, or notorious. But by an almost peculiar inflection of our language, it is applied to that which tends to render evident or to generate proof. Best, Ev. §§ 10, 11.

Classification. There are many species of evidence, and it is susceptible of being classified on several different principles. The more usual divisions are here subjoined.

Evidence is either *judicial* or *extrajudicial*. Judicial evidence is the means, sanctioned by law, of ascertaining in a judicial proceeding the truth respecting a question of fact, (Code Civil Proc. Cal. § 1823;) while extrajudicial evidence is that which is used to satisfy private persons as to facts requiring proof.

Evidence is either *primary* or *secondary*. Primary evidence is that kind of evidence which, under every possible circumstance, affords the greatest certainty of the fact in question. Thus, a written instrument is itself the best possible evidence of its existence and contents. Secondary evidence is that which is inferior to primary. Thus, a copy of an instrument, or oral evidence of its contents, is secondary evidence of the instrument and contents. Code Civil Proc. Cal. §§ 1829, 1830.

Primary evidence is such as in itself does not indicate the existence of other and better proof. *Secondary* evidence is such as from necessity in some cases is substituted for stronger and better proof. Code Ga. 1882, § 3761.

Primary evidence is that particular means of proof which is indicated by the nature of the fact under investigation, as the most natural and satisfactory; the best evidence the nature of the case admits; such evidence as may be called for in the first instance, upon the principle that its non-production gives rise to a reasonable suspicion that if produced it would tend against the fact alleged. Abbott.

Evidence is either *direct* or *indirect*. Direct evidence is that which proves the fact in dispute directly, without an inference or presumption, and which in itself, if true, conclusively establishes that fact; for example, if the fact in dispute be an agreement, the evidence of a witness who was present and witnessed the making of it is direct. Indirect evidence is that which tends to establish the fact in dispute by proving another, and which, though true, does not of itself conclusively establish that fact, but which affords an inference or presumption of its existence; for example, a witness proves an admission of the party to the fact in dispute. This proves a fact, from which the fact in dispute is inferred. Code Civil Proc. Cal. §§ 1831, 1832.

Evidence is either *intrinsic* or *extrinsic*. Intrinsic evidence is that which is derived from a document without anything to explain it. Extrinsic evidence is external evidence, or that which is not contained in the body of an agreement, contract, and the like.

In respect to its *nature*, evidence is also of the following several kinds:

Circumstantial evidence. This is proof of various facts or circumstances which usually attend the main fact in dispute, and therefore tend to prove its existence, or to sustain, by their consistency, the hypothesis claimed.

Circumstantial evidence consists in reasoning from facts which are known or proved, to establish such as are conjectured to exist. 32 N. Y. 141.

Presumptive evidence. This consists of inferences drawn by human experience from the connection of cause and effect, and observations of human conduct. Code Ga. 1882, § 3748.

Prima facie evidence. It is that which suffices for the proof of a particular fact, until contradicted and overcome by other evidence; for example, the certificate of a recording officer is *prima facie* evidence of a record, but it may afterwards be rejected upon proof that there is no such record. Code Civil Proc. Cal. § 1833.

Prima facie evidence is evidence which, standing alone and unexplained, would maintain the proposition and warrant the conclusion to support which it is introduced. 97 Mass. 230.

Partial evidence, is that which goes to establish a detached fact, in a series tending to the fact in dispute. It may be received, subject to be rejected as incompetent, unless connected with the fact in dispute by proof of other facts; for example, on an issue of title to real property, evidence of the continued possession of a remote occupant is partial, for it is of a detached fact, which may or may not be afterwards connected with the fact in dispute. Code Civil Proc. Cal. § 1834.

Satisfactory evidence. That evidence is deemed satisfactory which ordinarily produces moral certainty or conviction in an unprejudiced mind. Such evidence alone will justify a verdict. Evidence less than this is denominated "slight evidence." Code Civil Proc. Cal. § 1835.

Conclusive evidence. Conclusive or unanswerable evidence is that which the law does not permit to be contradicted; for example, the record of a court of competent jurisdiction cannot be contradicted by the parties to it. Code Civil Proc. Cal. § 1837.

Indispensable evidence is that without which a particular fact cannot be proved. Code Civil Proc. Cal. § 1836.

Documentary evidence is that derived from conventional symbols (such as letters) by which ideas are represented on material substances.

Hearsay evidence is the evidence, not of what the witness knows himself, but of what he has heard from others.

In respect to its *object*, evidence is of the following several kinds:

Substantive evidence is that adduced for the purpose of proving a fact in issue, as opposed to evidence given for the purpose of discrediting a witness, (*i. e.*, showing that he is unworthy of belief,) or of corroborating his testimony. Best, Ev. 246, 773, 803.

Corroborative evidence is additional evidence of a different character to the same point. Code Civil Proc. Cal. § 1839.

Cumulative evidence is additional evidence of the same character to the same point. Civil Code Proc. Cal. § 1838.

EVIDENCE OF DEBT. A term applied to written instruments or securities for the payment of money, importing on their face the existence of a debt. 1 Rev. St. N. Y. p. 599, § 55.

EVIDENCE OF TITLE. A deed or other document establishing the title to property, especially real estate.

EVIDENTIARY. Having the quality of evidence; constituting evidence; evidencing. A term introduced by Bentham, and, from its convenience, adopted by other writers.

EVOCATION. In French law. The withdrawal of a cause from the cognizance of an inferior court, and bringing it before another court or judge. In some respects this process resembles the proceedings upon *certiorari*.

EWAGE. (L. Fr. *Ewe*, water.) In old English law. Toll paid for water passage. The same as *aquage*. Tomlins.

EWBRICE. Adultery; spouse breach; marriage breach. Cowell; Tomlins.

EWRY. An office in the royal household where the table linen, etc., is taken care of. Wharton.

EX. 1. A Latin preposition meaning from, out of, by, on, on account of, or according to.

2. A prefix, denoting removal or cessation. Prefixed to the name of an office, relation, *status*, etc., it denotes that the person spoken of once occupied that office or relation, but does so no longer, or that he is now *out* of it. Thus, *ex*-mayor, *ex*-partner, *ex*-judge.

3. A prefix which is equivalent to "without," "reserving," or "excepting." In this use, probably an abbreviation of "except." Thus, *ex*-interest, *ex*-coupons.

"A sale of bonds 'ex. July coupons' means a sale reserving the coupons; that is, a sale in which the seller receives, in addition to the purchase price, the benefit of the coupons, which benefit he may realize either by detaching them or receiving from the buyer an equivalent consideration." 94 N. Y. 445.

EX ABUNDANTI. Out of abundance; abundantly; superfluously; more than sufficient. Calvin.

EX ABUNDANTI CAUTELA. Lat. Out of abundant caution. "The practice has arisen *abundanti cautela.*" 8 East, 326; Lord Ellenborough, 4 Maule & S. 544.

EX ADVERSO. On the other side. 2 Show. 461. Applied to counsel.

EX ÆQUITATE. According to equity; in equity. Fleta, lib. 3, c. 10, § 3.

EX ÆQUO ET BONO. A phrase derived from the civil law, meaning, in justice and fairness; according to what is just and good; according to equity and conscience. 3 Bl. Comm. 163.

EX ALTERA PARTE. Of the other part.

Ex antecedentibus et consequentibus fit optima interpretatio. The best interpretation [of a part of an instrument] is made from the antecedents and the consequents, [from the preceding and following parts.] 2 Inst. 317. The law will judge of a deed or other instrument, consisting of divers parts or clauses, by looking at the whole; and will give to each part its proper office, so as to ascertain and carry out the intention of the parties. Broom, Max. *577. The whole instrument is to be viewed and compared in all its parts, so that every part of it may be made consistent and effectual. 2 Kent, Comm. 555.

EX ARBITRIO JUDICIS. At, in, or upon the discretion of the judge. 4 Bl. Comm. 394. A term of the civil law. Inst. 4, 6, 31.

EX ASSENSU CURIÆ. By or with the consent of the court.

EX ASSENSU PATRIS. By or with the consent of the father. A species of dower *ad ostium ecclesiæ*, during the life of the father of the husband; the son, by the father's consent expressly given, endowing his wife with parcel of his father's lands. Abolished by 3 & 4 Wm. IV. c. 105, § 13.

EX ASSENSU SUO. With his assent. Formal words in judgments for damages by default. Comb. 220.

EX BONIS. Of the goods or property. A term of the civil law; distinguished from *in bonis*, as being descriptive of or applicable to property not in actual possession. Calvin.

EX CATHEDRA. From the chair. Originally applied to the decisions of the popes from their *cathedra*, or chair. Hence, authoritative; having the weight of authority.

EX CAUSA. L. Lat. By title.

EX CERTA SCIENTIA. Of certain or sure knowledge. These words were anciently used in patents, and imported full knowledge of the subject-matter on the part of the king. See 1 Coke, 40*b*.

EX COLORE. By color; under color of; under pretense, show, or protection of. Thus, *ex colore officii*, under color of office.

EX COMITATE. Out of comity or courtesy.

EX COMMODATO. From or out of loan. A term applied in the old law of England to a right of action arising out of a loan, (*commodatum.*) Glanv. lib. 10, c. 13; 1 Reeve, Eng. Law, 166.

EX COMPARATIONE SCRIPTORUM. By a comparison of writings or handwritings. A term in the law of evidence. Best, Pres. 218.

EX CONCESSIS. From the premises granted. According to what has been already allowed.

EX CONSULTO. With consultation or deliberation.

EX CONTINENTI. Immediately; without any interval or delay: incontinently. A term of the civil law. Calvin.

EX CONTRACTU. From or out of a contract. In both the civil and the common law, rights and causes of action are divided into two classes,—those arising *ex contractu,* (from a contract,) and those arising *ex delicto,* (from a delict or tort.) See 3 Bl. Comm. 117; Mackeld. Rom. Law, § 384.

EX CURIA. Out of court; away from the court.

EX DEBITO JUSTITIÆ. From or as a debt of justice; in accordance with the requirement of justice; of right; as a matter of right. The opposite of *ex gratia,* (*q. v.*) 3 Bl. Comm. 48, 67.

EX DEFECTU SANGUINIS. From failure of blood; for want of issue.

EX DELICTO. From a delict, tort, fault, crime, or malfeasance. In both the civil and the common law, obligations and causes of action are divided into two great classes, —those arising *ex contractu,* (out of a contract,) and those *ex delicto.* The latter are such as grow out of or are founded upon a wrong or tort, *e. g.*, trespass, trover, replevin. These terms were known in English law at a very early period. See Inst. 4, 1, pr.; Mackeld. Rom. Law, § 384; 3 Bl. Comm. 117; Bract. fol. 101*b*.

Ex delicto non ex supplicio emergit infamia. Infamy arises from the crime, not from the punishment.

EX DEMISSIONE, (commonly abbreviated *ex dem.*) Upon the demise. A phrase forming part of the title of the old action of ejectment.

EX DIRECTO. Directly; immediately. Story, Bills, § 199.

Ex diuturnitate temporis, omnia præsumuntur solemniter esse acta. From length of time [after lapse of time] all things are presumed to have been done in due form. Co. Litt. 6*b;* Best, Ev. Introd. § 43; 1 Greenl. Ev. § 20.

EX DOLO MALO. Out of fraud; out of deceitful or tortious conduct. A phrase applied to obligations and causes of action vitiated by fraud or deceit.

Ex dolo malo non oritur actio. Out of fraud no action arises; fraud never gives a right of action. No court will lend its aid to a man who founds his cause of action upon an immoral or illegal act. Cowp. 343; Broom, Max. 729.

Ex donationibus autem feoda militaria vel magnum serjeantium non continentibus oritur nobis quoddam nomen generale, quod est socagium. Co. Litt. 86. From grants not containing military fees or grand serjeanty, a kind of general name is used by us, which is "socage."

EX EMPTO. Out of purchase; founded on purchase. A term of the civil law, adopted by Bracton. Inst. 4, 6, 28; Bract. fol. 102. See ACTIO EX EMPTO.

EX FACIE. From the face; apparently; evidently. A term applied to what appears on the face of a writing.

EX FACTO. From or in consequence of a fact or action; actually. Usually applied to an unlawful or tortious act as the foundation of a title, etc. Sometimes used as equivalent to "*de facto.*" Bract. fol. 172.

Ex facto jus oritur. The law arises out of the fact. Broom, Max. 102. A rule of law continues in abstraction and theory, until an act is done on which it can attach and assume as it were a body and shape. Best, Ev. Introd. § 1.

EX FICTIONE JURIS. By a fiction of law.

Ex frequenti delicto augetur pœna. 2 Inst. 479. Punishment increases with increasing crime.

EX GRATIA. Out of grace; as a matter of grace, favor, or indulgence; gratuitous. A term applied to anything accorded as a favor; as distinguished from that which may be demanded *ex debito,* as a matter of right.

EX GRAVI QUERELA. (From or on the grievous complaint.) In old English practice. The name of a writ (so called from its initial words) which lay for a person to whom any lands or tenements in fee were devised by will, (within any city, town, or borough wherein lands were devisable by custom,) and the heir of the devisor entered and detained them from him. Fitzh. Nat. Brev. 198, L, et seq.; 3 Reeve, Eng. Law, 49. Abolished by St. 3 & 4 Wm. IV. c. 27, § 36.

EX HYPOTHESI. By the hypothesis; upon the supposition; upon the theory or facts assumed.

EX INDUSTRIA. With contrivance or deliberation; designedly; on purpose. See 1 Kent, Comm. 318; 1 Wheat. 304.

EX INTEGRO. Anew; afresh.

EX JUSTA CAUSA. From a just or lawful cause; by a just or legal title.

EX LEGE. By the law; by force of law; as a matter of law.

EX LEGIBUS. According to the laws. A phrase of the civil law, which means according to the intent or spirit of the law, as well as according to the words or letter. Dig. 50, 16, 6. See Calvin.

EX LICENTIA REGIS. By the king's license. 1 Bl. Comm. 168, note.

EX LOCATO. From or out of lease or letting. A term of the civil law, applied to actions or rights of action arising out of the contract of *locatum*, (*q. v.*) Inst. 4, 6, 28. Adopted at an early period in the law of England. Bract. fol. 102; 1 Reeve, Eng. Law, 168.

EX MALEFICIO. Growing out of, or founded upon, misdoing or tort. This term is frequently used in the civil law as the synonym of "*ex delicto*," (*q. v.*,) and is thus contrasted with "*ex contractu*." In this sense it is of more rare occurrence in the common law, though found in Bracton, (fols. 99, 101, 102.)

Ex maleficio non oritur contractus. A contract cannot arise out of an act radically vicious and illegal. 1 Term 734; 3 Term 422; Broom, Max. 734.

Ex malis moribus bonæ leges natæ sunt. 2 Inst. 161. Good laws arise from evil morals, *i. e.*, are necessitated by the evil behavior of men.

EX MERO MOTU. Of his own mere motion; of his own accord; voluntarily and without prompting or request. Royal letters patent which are granted at the crown's own instance, and without request made, are said to be granted *ex mero motu*. When a court interferes, of its own motion, to object to an irregularity, or to do something which the parties are not strictly entitled to, but which will prevent injustice, it is said to act *ex mero motu*, or *ex proprio motu*, or *sua sponte*, all these terms being here equivalent.

EX MORA. From or in consequence of delay. Interest is allowed *ex mora;* that is, where there has been delay in returning a sum borrowed. A term of the civil law. Story, Bailm. § 84.

EX MORE. According to custom. Calvin.

Ex multitudine signorum, colligitur identitas vera. From a great number of signs or marks, true identity is gathered or made up. Bac. Max. 103, in regula 25. A thing described by a great number of marks is easily identified, though, as to some, the description may not be strictly correct. Id.

EX MUTUO. From or out of loan. In the old law of England, a debt was said to arise *ex mutuo* when one lent another anything which consisted in number, weight, or measure. 1 Reeve, Eng. Law, 159; Bract. fol. 99.

EX NECESSITATE. Of necessity. 3 Rep. Ch. 123.

EX NECESSITATE LEGIS. From or by necessity of law. 4 Bl. Comm. 394.

EX NECESSITATE REI. From the necessity or urgency of the thing or case. 2 Pow. Dev. (by Jarman,) 308.

Ex nihilo nihil fit. From nothing nothing comes. 13 Wend. 178, 221; 18 Wend. 257, 301.

Ex nudo pacto non oritur [nascitur] actio. Out of a nude or naked pact [that is, a bare parol agreement without consideration] no action arises. Bract. fol. 99; Fleta, lib. 2, c. 56, § 3; Plowd. 305. Out of a promise neither attended with particular solemnity (such as belongs to a specialty) nor with any consideration no legal liability can arise. 2 Steph. Comm. 113. A parol agreement, without a valid consideration, cannot be made the foundation of an action. A leading maxim both of the civil and common law. Cod. 2, 3, 10; Id. 5, 14, 1; 2 Bl. Comm. 445; Smith, Cont. 85, 86.

EX OFFICIO. From office; by virtue of the office; without any other warrant or appointment than that resulting from the holding of a particular office. Powers may be exercised by an officer which are not specifically conferred upon him, but are necessarily implied in his office; these are *ex officio*. Thus, a judge has *ex officio* the powers of a conservator of the peace. Courts are bound to notice public statutes judicially and *ex officio*.

EX OFFICIO INFORMATION. In English law. A criminal information filed by the attorney general *ex officio* on behalf of the crown, in the court of queen's bench, for offenses more immediately affecting the government, and to be distinguished from informations in which the crown is the nominal prosecutor. Mozley & Whitley; 4 Steph. Comm. 372-378.

EX OFFICIO OATH. An oath taken by offending priests; abolished by 13 Car. II. St. 1, c. 12.

Ex pacto illicito non oritur actio. From an illegal contract an action does not arise. Broom, Max. 742. See 7 Clark & F. 729.

EX PARTE. On one side only; by or for one party; done for, in behalf of, or on the application of, one party only. A judicial proceeding, order, injunction, etc., is said to be *ex parte* when it is taken or granted at the instance and for the benefit of one party only, and without notice to, or contestation by, any person adversely interested.

"*Ex parte*," in the heading of a reported case, signifies that the name following is that of the party upon whose application the case is heard.

In its primary sense, *ex parte*, as applied to an application in a judicial proceeding, means that it is made by a person who is not a party to the proceeding, but who has an interest in the matter which entitles him to make the application. Thus, in a bankruptcy proceeding or an administration action, an application by A. B., a creditor, or the like, would be described as made "*ex parte* A. B.," *i. e.*, on the part of A. B.

In its more usual sense, *ex parte* means that an application is made by one party to a proceeding in the absence of the other. Thus, an *ex parte* injunction is one granted without the opposite party having had notice of the application. It would not be called "*ex parte*" if he had proper notice of it, and chose not to appear to oppose it. Sweet.

EX PARTE MATERNA. On the mother's side; of the maternal line.

EX PARTE PATERNA. On the father's side; of the paternal line.

The phrases "*ex parte materna*" and "*ex parte paterna*" denote the line or blood of the mother or father, and have no such restricted or limited sense as from the mother or father exclusively. 24 N. J. Law, 431.

EX PARTE TALIS. A writ that lay for a bailiff or receiver, who, having auditors appointed to take his accounts, cannot obtain of them reasonable allowance, but is cast into prison. Fitzh. Nat. Brev. 129.

Ex paucis dictis intendere plurima possis. Litt. § 384. You can imply many things from few expressions.

Ex paucis plurima concipit ingenium. Litt. § 550. From a few words or hints the understanding conceives many things.

EX POST FACTO. After the fact; by an act or fact occurring after some previous act or fact, and relating thereto; by subsequent matter; the opposite of *ab initio*. Thus, a deed may be good *ab initio*, or, if invalid at its inception, may be confirmed by matter *ex post facto*.

EX POST FACTO LAW. A law passed after the occurrence of a fact or commission of an act, which retrospectively changes the legal consequences or relations of such fact or deed. By Const. U. S. art. 1, § 10, the states are forbidden to pass "any *ex post facto* law." In this connection the phrase has a much narrower meaning than its literal translation would justify, as will appear from the extracts given below.

The phrase "*ex post facto*," in the constitution, extends to criminal and not to civil cases. And under this head is included: (1) Every law that makes an action, done before the passing of the law, and which was innocent when done, criminal, and punishes such action. (2) Every law that aggravates a crime, or makes it greater than it was when committed. (3) Every law that changes the punishment, and inflicts a greater punishment than the law annexed to the crime when committed. (4) Every law that alters the legal rules of evidence, and receives less or different testimony than the law required at the time of the commission of the offense, in order to convict the offender. All these, and similar laws, are prohibited by the constitution. But a law may be *ex post facto*, and still not amenable to this constitutional inhibition; that is, provided it mollifies, instead of aggravating, the rigor of the criminal law. 16 Ga. 102; 4 Wall. 277; 2 Wash. C. C. 366; 3 N. H. 473; 3 Dall. 390; 3 Story, Const. 212.

An *ex post facto* law is one which renders an act punishable, in a manner in which it was not punishable when committed. Such a law may inflict penalties on the person, or pecuniary penalties which swell the public treasury. The legislature is therefore prohibited from passing a law by which a man's estate, or any part of it, shall be seized for a crime, which was not declared, by some previous law, to render him liable to such punishment. 6 Cranch, 87, 138.

The plain and obvious meaning of this prohibition is that the legislature shall not pass any law, after a fact done by any citizen, which shall have relation to that fact, so as to punish that which was innocent when done; or to add to the punishment of that which was criminal; or to increase the malignity of a crime; or to retrench the rules of evidence, so as to make conviction more easy. This definition of an *ex post facto* law is sanctioned by long usage. 1 Blackf. 196.

The term "*ex post facto* law," in the United States constitution, cannot be construed to include and to prohibit the enacting any law after a fact, nor even to prohibit the depriving a citizen of a vested right to property. 3 Dall. 386.

"*Ex post facto*" and "retrospective" are not convertible terms. The latter is a term of wider signification than the former and includes it. All *ex post facto* laws are necessarily retrospective, but not *e converso*. A curative or confirmatory stat-

ute is retrospective, but not *ex post facto*. Constitutions of nearly all the states contain prohibitions against *ex post facto* laws, but only a few forbid retrospective legislation in specific terms. Black, Const. Prohib. §§ 170, 172, 222.

Retrospective laws divesting vested rights are impolitic and unjust; but they are not "*ex post facto* laws," within the meaning of the constitution of the United States, nor repugnant to any other of its provisions; and, if not repugnant to the state constitution, a court cannot pronounce them to be void, merely because in their judgment they are contrary to the principles of natural justice. 2 Paine, 74.

Every retrospective act is not necessarily an *ex post facto* law. That phrase embraces only such laws as impose or affect penalties or forfeitures. 4 Wall. 172.

Retrospective laws which do not impair the obligation of contracts, or affect vested rights, or partake of the character of *ex post facto* laws, are not prohibited by the constitution. 36 Barb. 447.

Ex præcedentibus et consequentibus optima fit interpretatio. 1 Roll. 374. The best interpretation is made from the context.

EX PRÆCOGITATA MALICIA. Of malice aforethought. Reg. Orig. 102.

EX PROPRIO MOTU. Of his own accord.

EX PROPRIO VIGORE. By their or its own force. 2 Kent, Comm. 457.

EX PROVISIONE HOMINIS. By the provision of man. By the limitation of the party, as distinguished from the disposition of the law. 11 Coke, 80*b*.

EX PROVISIONE MARITI. From the provision of the husband.

EX QUASI CONTRACTU. From *quasi* contract. Fleta, lib. 2, c. 60.

EX RELATIONE. Upon relation or information. Legal proceedings which are instituted by the attorney general (or other proper person) in the name and behalf of the state, but on the information and at the instigation of an individual who has a private interest in the matter, are said to be taken "on the relation" (*ex relatione*) of such person, who is called the "relator." Such a cause is usually entitled thus: "State *ex rel.* Doe *v.* Roe."

In the books of reports, when a case is said to be reported *ex relatione*, it is meant that the reporter derives his account of it, not from personal knowledge, but from the relation or narrative of some person who was present at the argument.

EX RIGORE JURIS. According to the rigor or strictness of law; in strictness of law. Fleta, lib 3. c. 10, § 2.

EX SCRIPTIS OLIM VISIS. From writings formerly seen. A term used as descriptive of that kind of proof of handwriting where the knowledge has been acquired by the witness having seen letters or other documents professing to be the handwriting of the party, and having afterwards communicated personally with the party upon the contents of those letters or documents, or having otherwise acted upon them by written answers, producing further correspondence or acquiescence by the party in some matter to which they relate, or by the witness transacting with the party some business to which they relate, or by any other mode of communication between the party and the witness which, in the ordinary course of the transactions of life, induces a reasonable presumption that the letters or documents were the handwriting of the party. 5 Adol. & E. 730.

EX STATUTO. According to the statute. Fleta, lib. 5, c. 11, § 1.

EX STIPULATU ACTIO. In the civil law. An action of stipulation. An action given to recover marriage portions. Inst. 4, 6, 29.

EX TEMPORE. From or in consequence of time; by lapse of time. Bract. fols. 51, 52. *Ex diuturno tempore*, from length of time. Id. fol. 51*b*.

Without preparation or premeditation.

EX TESTAMENTO. From, by, or under a will. The opposite of *ab intestato*, (*q. v.*)

Ex tota materia emergat resolutio. The explanation should arise out of the whole subject-matter; the exposition of a statute should be made from all its parts together. Wing. Max. 238.

Ex turpi causa non oritur actio. Out of a base [illegal, or immoral] consideration, an action does [can] not arise. 1 Selw. N. P. 63; Broom, Max. 730, 732; Story, Ag. § 195.

Ex turpi contractu actio non oritur. From an immoral or iniquitous contract an action does not arise. A contract founded upon an illegal or immoral consideration cannot be enforced by action. 2 Kent, Comm. 466; Dig. 2, 14, 27, 4.

EX UNA PARTE. Of one part or side; on one side.

Ex uno disces omnes. From one thing you can discern all.

EX UTRAQUE PARTE. On both sides. Dyer, 126*b*.

EX UTRISQUE PARENTIBUS CONJUNCTI. Related on the side of both parents; of the whole blood. Hale, Com. Law, c. 11.

EX VI TERMINI. From or by the force of the term. From the very meaning of the expression used. 2 Bl. Comm. 109, 115.

EX VISCERIBUS. From the bowels. From the vital part, the very essence of the thing. 10 Coke, 24*b*; 2 Metc. (Mass.) 213. *Ex visceribus verborum*, from the mere words and nothing else. 10 Johns. 494; 1 Story, Eq. Jur. § 980.

EX VISITATIONE DEI. By the dispensation of God; by reason of physical incapacity. Anciently, when a prisoner, being arraigned, stood silent instead of pleading, a jury was impaneled to inquire whether he obstinately stood mute or was dumb *ex visitatione Dei*. 4 Steph. Comm. 394.

Also by natural, as distinguished from violent, causes. When a coroner's inquest finds that the death was due to disease or other natural cause, it is frequently phrased "*ex visitatione Dei.*"

EX VISU SCRIPTIONIS. From sight of the writing; from having seen a person write. A term employed to describe one of the modes of proof of handwriting. Best, Pres. 218.

EX VOLUNTATE. Voluntarily; from free-will or choice.

EXACTION. The wrongful act of an officer or other person in compelling payment of a fee or reward for his services, under color of his official authority, where no payment is due.

Between "extortion" and "exaction" there is this difference: that in the former case the officer extorts more than his due, when something is due to him; in the latter, he exacts what is not his due, when there is nothing due to him. Co. Litt. 368.

EXACTOR. In the civil law. A gatherer or receiver of money; a collector of taxes. Cod. 10, 19.

In old English law. A collector of the public moneys; a tax gatherer. Thus, *exactor regis* was the name of the king's tax collector, who took up the taxes and other debts due the treasury.

EXACTOR REGIS. The king's collector of taxes; also a sheriff.

EXALTARE. In old English law. To raise; to elevate. Frequently spoken of water, *i. e.*, to raise the surface of a pond or pool.

EXAMEN. L. Lat. A trial. *Examen computi*, the balance of an account. Townsh. Pl. 223.

EXAMINATION. An investigation; search; interrogating.

In trial practice. The examination of a witness consists of the series of questions put to him by a party to the action, or his counsel, for the purpose of bringing before the court and jury in legal form the knowledge which the witness has of the facts and matters in dispute, or of probing and sifting his evidence previously given.

The examination of a witness by the party producing him is denominated the "direct examination;" the examination of the same witness, upon the same matter, by the adverse party, the "cross-examination." The direct examination must be completed before the cross-examination begins, unless the court otherwise direct. Code Civil Proc. Cal. § 2045.

In criminal practice. An investigation by a magistrate of a person who has been charged with crime and arrested, or of the facts and circumstances which are alleged to have attended the crime and to fasten suspicion upon the party so charged, in order to ascertain whether there is sufficient ground to hold him to bail for his trial by the proper court.

EXAMINATION DE BENE ESSE. A provisional examination of a witness; an examination of a witness whose testimony is important and might otherwise be lost, held out of court and before the trial, with the proviso that the deposition so taken may be used on the trial in case the witness is unable to attend in person at that time or cannot be produced.

EXAMINATION OF A LONG ACCOUNT. This phrase does not mean the examination of the account to ascertain the result or effect of it, but the proof by testimony of the correctness of the items composing it. 5 Daly, 63.

EXAMINATION OF BANKRUPT. This is the interrogation of a bankrupt, in the course of proceedings in bankruptcy, touching the state of his property. This is authorized in the United States by Rev. St.

§ 5086; and § 5087 authorizes the examination of a bankrupt's wife.

EXAMINATION OF INVENTION. An inquiry made at the patent-office, upon application for a patent, into the novelty and utility of the alleged invention, and as to its interfering with any other patented invention. Rev. St. U. S. § 4893.

EXAMINATION OF TITLE. An investigation made by or for a person who intends to purchase real estate, in the offices where the public records are kept, to ascertain the history and present condition of the title to such land, and its *status* with reference to liens, incumbrances, clouds, etc.

EXAMINED COPY. A copy of a record, public book, or register, and which has been compared with the original. 1 Campb. 469.

EXAMINER. In English law. A person appointed by a court to take the examination of witnesses in an action, *i. e.*, to take down the result of their interrogation by the parties or their counsel, either by written interrogatories or *vivâ voce*. An examiner is generally appointed where a witness is in a foreign country, or is too ill or infirm to attend before the court, and is either an officer of the court, or a person specially appointed for the purpose. Sweet.

In New Jersey. An examiner is an officer appointed by the court of chancery to take testimony in causes depending in that court. His powers are similar to those of the English examiner in chancery.

In the patent-office. An officer in the patent-office charged with the duty of examining the patentability of inventions for which patents are asked.

EXAMINER IN CHANCERY. An officer of the court of chancery, before whom witnesses are examined, and their testimony reduced to writing, for the purpose of being read on the hearing of the cause. Cowell.

EXAMINERS. Persons appointed to question students of law in order to ascertain their qualifications before they are admitted to practice.

EXANNUAL ROLL. In old English practice. A roll into which (in the old way of exhibiting sheriffs' accounts) the illeviable fines and desperate debts were transcribed, and which was *annually* read to the sheriff upon his accounting, to see what might be gotten. Cowell.

EXCAMB. In Scotch law. To exchange. 6 Bell, App. Cas. 19, 22.

EXCAMBIATOR. An exchanger of lands; a broker. Obsolete.

EXCAMBION. In Scotch law. Exchange. 1 Forb. Inst. pt. 2, p. 173.

EXCAMBIUM. An exchange; a place where merchants meet to transact their business; also an equivalent in recompense; a recompense in lieu of dower *ad ostium ecclesiæ*.

EXCELLENCY. In English law. The title of a viceroy, governor general, ambassador, or commander in chief.

In America. The title is sometimes given to the chief executive of a state or of the nation.

EXCEPTANT. One who excepts; one who makes or files exceptions; one who objects to a ruling, instruction, or anything proposed or ordered.

EXCEPTIO. In Roman law. An exception. In a general sense, a judicial allegation opposed by a defendant to the plaintiff's action. Calvin.

A stop or stay to an action opposed by the defendant. Cowell.

Answering to the "defense" or "plea" of the common law. An allegation and defense of a defendant by which the plaintiff's claim or complaint is defeated, either according to strict law or upon grounds of equity.

In a stricter sense, the exclusion of an action that lay in strict law, on grounds of equity, (*actionis jure stricto competentis ob æquitatem exclusio.*) Heinecc. A kind of limitation of an action, by which it was shown that the action, though otherwise just, did not lie in the particular case. Calvin. A species of defense allowed in cases where, though the action as brought by the plaintiff was in itself just, yet it was unjust as against the particular party sued. Inst. 4, 13, pr.

In modern civil law. A plea by which the defendant admits the cause of action, but alleges new facts which, provided they be true, totally or partially answer the allegations put forward on the other side; thus distinguished from a mere traverse of the plaintiff's averments. Tomkins & J. Mod. Rom. Law, 90. In this use, the term corresponds to the common-law plea in confession and avoidance.

EXCEPTIO DILATORIA. In the civil law. A dilatory exception; called also "*tem-*

poralis," (temporary;) one which defeated the action for a time, (*quæ ad tempus nocet,*) and created delay, (*et temporis dilationem tribuit;*) such as an agreement not to sue within a certain time, as five years. Inst. 4, 13, 10. See Dig. 44, 1, 3.

EXCEPTIO DOLI MALI. In the civil law. An exception or plea of fraud. Inst. 4, 13, 1, 9; Bract. fol. 100*b*.

Exceptio ejus rei cujus petitur dissolutio nulla est. A plea of that matter the dissolution of which is sought [by the action] is null, [or of no effect.] Jenk. Cent. 37, case 71.

Exceptio falsi omnium ultima. A plea denying a fact is the last of all.

EXCEPTIO IN FACTUM. In the civil law. An exception on the fact. An exception or plea founded on the peculiar circumstances of the case. Inst. 4, 13, 1.

EXCEPTIO JURISJURANDI. In the civil law. An exception of oath; an exception or plea that the matter had been sworn to. Inst. 4, 13, 4. This kind of exception was allowed where a debtor, at the instance of his creditor, (*creditore deferente,*) had sworn that nothing was due the latter, and had notwithstanding been sued by him. Id.

EXCEPTIO METUS. In the civil law. An exception or plea of fear or compulsion. Inst. 4, 13, 1, 9; Bract. fol. 100*b*. Answering to the modern plea of duress.

Exceptio nulla est versus actionem quæ exceptionem perimit. There is [can be] no plea against an action which destroys [the matter of] the plea. Jenk. Cent. 106, case 2.

EXCEPTIO PACTI CONVENTI. In the civil law. An exception of compact; an exception or plea that the plaintiff had agreed not to sue. Inst. 4, 13, 3.

EXCEPTIO PECUNIÆ NON NUMERATÆ. An exception or plea of money not paid; a defense which might be set up by a party who was sued on a promise to repay money which he had never received. Inst. 4, 13, 2.

EXCEPTIO PEREMPTORIA. In the civil law. A peremptory exception; called also "*perpetua,*" (perpetual;) one which forever destroyed the subject-matter or ground of the action, (*quæ semper rem de qua agitur perimit;*) such as the *exceptio doli mali,* the *exceptio metus,* etc. Inst. 4, 13, 9. See Dig. 44, 1, 3.

In common law. A peremptory plea; a plea in bar. Bract. fols. 240, 399*b*.

Exceptio probat regulam. The exception proves the rule. 11 Coke, 41; 3 Term, 722. Sometimes quoted with the addition "*de rebus non exceptis,*" ("so far as concerns the matters not excepted.")

Exceptio quæ firmat legem, exponit legem. An exception which confirms the law explains the law. 2 Bulst. 189.

EXCEPTIO REI JUDICATÆ. In the civil law. An exception or plea of matter adjudged; a plea that the subject-matter of the action had been determined in a previous action. Inst. 4, 13, 5.

This term is adopted by Bracton, and is constantly used in modern law to denote a defense founded upon a previous adjudication of the same matter. Bract. fols. 100*b*, 177; 2 Kent, Comm. 120. A plea of a former recovery or judgment.

EXCEPTIO REI VENDITÆ ET TRADITÆ. In the civil law. An exception or plea of the sale and delivery of the thing. This exception presumes that there was a valid sale and a proper tradition; but though, in consequence of the rule that no one can transfer to another a greater right than he himself has, no property was transferred, yet because of some particular circumstance the real owner is estopped from contesting it. Mackeld. Rom. Law, § 299.

Exceptio semper ultimo ponenda est. An exception should always be put last. 9 Coke, 53.

EXCEPTIO TEMPORIS. In the civil law. An exception or plea analogous to that of the statute of limitations in our law; viz., that the time prescribed by law for bringing such actions has expired. Mackeld. Rom. Law, § 213.

EXCEPTION. In practice. A formal objection to the action of the court, during the trial of a cause, in refusing a request or overruling an objection; implying that the party excepting does not acquiesce in the decision of the court, but will seek to procure its reversal, and that he means to save the benefit of his request or objection in some future proceeding.

It is also somewhat used to signify other objections in the course of a suit; for example, exception to bail is a formal objection that special bail offered by defendant are insufficient. 1 Tidd, Pr. 255.

An exception is an objection upon a matter of law to a decision made, either before or after judgment, by a court, tribunal, judge, or other judicial officer, in an action or proceeding. The exception must be taken at the time the decision is made. Code Civil Proc. Cal. § 646; 32 Cal. 307.

In admiralty and equity practice. An exception is a formal allegation tendered by a party that some previous pleading or proceeding taken by the adverse party is insufficient.

In statutory law. An exception in a statute is a clause designed to reserve or exempt some individuals from the general class of persons or things to which the language of the act in general attaches.

An exception differs from an explanation, which, by the use of a *videlicet*, *proviso*, etc., is allowed only to explain doubtful clauses precedent, or to separate and distribute generals into particulars. 3 Pick. 272.

In contracts. A clause in a deed or other conveyance by which the grantor excepts something out of that which he granted before by the deed.

The distinction between an exception and a reservation is that an *exception* is always of part of the thing granted, and of a thing *in esse;* a *reservation* is always of a thing not *in esse*, but newly created or reserved out of the land or tenement demised. Co. Litt. 47*a;* 4 Kent, Comm. 468. It has been also said that there is a diversity between an exception and a saving, for an exception exempts clearly, but a saving goes to the matters touched, and does not exempt. Plowd. 361.

In the civil law. An *exceptio* or plea. Used in this sense in Louisiana.

Declinatory exceptions are such dilatory exceptions as merely decline the jurisdiction of the judge before whom the action is brought. Code Proc. La. 334.

Dilatory exceptions are such as do not tend to defeat the action, but only to retard its progress.

Peremptory exceptions are those which tend to the dismissal of the action.

EXCEPTION TO BAIL. An objection to the special bail put in by the defendant to an action at law made by the plaintiff on grounds of the insufficiency of the bail. 1 Tidd, Pr. 255.

EXCEPTIS EXCIPIENDIS. With all necessary exceptions.

EXCEPTOR. In old English law. A party who entered an exception or plea.

EXCERPTA, or EXCERPTS. Extracts.

EXCESS. When a defendant pleaded to an action of assault that the plaintiff trespassed on his land, and he would not depart when ordered, whereupon he, *molliter manus imposuit*, gently laid hands on him, the replication of *excess* was to the effect that the defendant used more force than necessary. Wharton.

EXCESSIVE. In order that bail required (or punishment inflicted) should be described as "excessive," it must be, *per se*, unreasonably great and clearly disproportionate to the offense involved, or the peculiar circumstances appearing must show it to be so in the particular case. 44 Cal. 558; 53 Cal. 410; 39 Conn. 484.

EXCESSIVE DAMAGES. Damages awarded by a jury which are grossly in excess of the amount warranted by law on the facts and circumstances of the case; unreasonable or outrageous damages. A verdict giving excessive damages is ground for a new trial.

Excessivum in jure reprobatur. Excessus in re qualibet jure reprobatur communi. Co. Litt. 44. Excess in law is reprehended. Excess in anything is reprehended at common law.

EXCHANGE. In conveyancing. A mutual grant of equal interests, (in lands or tenements,) the one in consideration of the other. 2 Bl. Comm. 323. In the United States, it appears, exchange does not differ from bargain and sale. See 2 Bouv. Inst. 2055.

In commercial law. A negotiation by which one person transfers to another funds which he has in a certain place, either at a price agreed upon or which is fixed by commercial usage.

The profit which arises from a maritime loan, when such profit is a percentage on the money lent, considering it in the light of money lent in one place to be returned in another, with a difference in amount in the sum borrowed and that paid, arising from the difference of time and place. The term is commonly used in this sense by French writers. Hall, Emerig. Mar. Loans, 56*n*.

A public place where merchants, brokers, factors, etc., meet to transact their business.

EXCHANGE, BILL OF. See BILL OF EXCHANGE.

EXCHANGE OF GOODS. A commutation, transmutation, or transfer of goods for other goods, as distinguished from *sale*, which is a transfer of goods for money. 2 Bl. Comm. 446; 2 Steph. Comm. 120.

Exchange is a contract by which the parties mutually give, or agree to give, one thing for another, neither thing, or both things, being money only. Civil Code Cal. § 1804; Civil Code Dak. § 1029; Civil Code La. art. 2660.

The distinction between a sale and exchange of property is rather one of shadow than of substance. In both cases the title to property is absolutely transferred; and the same rules of law are applicable to the transaction, whether the consideration of the contract is money or by way of barter. It can make no essential difference in the rights and obligations of parties that goods and merchandise are transferred and paid for by other goods and merchandise instead of by money, which is but the representative of value or property. 14 Gray, 367.

EXCHANGE OF LIVINGS. In ecclesiastical law. This is effected by resigning them into the bishop's hands, and each party being inducted into the other's benefice. If either die before both are inducted, the exchange is void.

EXCHEQUER. That department of the English government which has charge of the collection of the national revenue; the treasury department.

It is said to have been so named from the chequered cloth, resembling a chess-board, which anciently covered the table there, and on which, when certain of the king's accounts were made up, the sums were marked and scored with counters. 3 Bl. Comm. 44.

EXCHEQUER BILLS. Bills of credit issued in England by authority of parliament. Brande. Instruments issued at the exchequer, under the authority, for the most part, of acts of parliament passed for the purpose, and containing an engagement on the part of the government for repayment of the principal sums advanced with interest. 2 Steph. Comm. 586.

EXCHEQUER CHAMBER, COURT OF. In English law. A tribunal of error and appeal.

First, it existed in former times as a court of mere debate, such causes from the other courts being sometimes adjourned into it as the judges, upon argument, found to be of great weight and difficulty, before any judgment was given upon them in the court below. It then consisted of all the judges of the three superior courts of common law, and at times the lord chancellor also.

Second, it existed as a court of error, where the judgments of each of the superior courts of common law, in all actions whatever, were subject to revision by the judges of the other two sitting collectively. The composition of this court consequently admitted of three different combinations, consisting of any two of the courts below which were not parties to the judgment appealed against. There was no given number required to constitute the exchequer chamber, but the court never consisted of less than five. One counsel only was heard on each side. Error lay from this court to the house of lords. The court is abolished, and its jurisdiction in appeals (proceedings in error in civil cases and bills of exceptions being abolished) is transferred to the court of appeal. Jud. Act 1875, § 18. Wharton.

EXCHEQUER, COURT OF. See COURT OF EXCHEQUER.

EXCHEQUER DIVISION. A division of the English high court of justice, to which the special business of the court of exchequer was specially assigned by section 34 of the judicature act of 1873. Merged in the queen's bench division from and after 1881, by order in council under section 31 of that act. Wharton.

EXCISE. An inland imposition, paid sometimes upon the consumption of the commodity, and frequently upon the retail sale. 1 Bl. Comm. 318; Story, Const. § 950.

The words "tax" and "excise," although often used as synonymous, are to be considered as having entirely distinct and separate significations, under Const. Mass. c. 1, § 1, art. 4. The former is a charge apportioned either among the whole people of the state or those residing within certain districts, municipalities, or sections. It is required to be imposed, so that, if levied for the public charges of government, it shall be shared according to the estate, real and personal, which each person may possess; or, if raised to defray the cost of some local improvement of a public nature, it shall be borne by those who will receive some special and peculiar benefit or advantage which an expenditure of money for a public object may cause to those on whom the tax is assessed. An excise, on the other hand, is of a different character. It is based on no rule of apportionment or equality whatever. It is a fixed, absolute, and direct charge laid on merchandise, products, or commodities, without any regard to the amount of property belonging to those on whom it may fall, or to any supposed relation between money expended for a public object and a special benefit occasioned to those by whom the charge is to be paid. 11 Allen, 268.

In English law. The name given to the duties or taxes laid on certain articles produced and consumed at home, among which spirits have always been the most important; but, exclusive of these, the duties on the licenses of auctioneers, brewers, etc., and on the licenses to keep dogs, kill game, etc., are included in the excise duties. Wharton.

EXCISE LAW. A law imposing excise duties on specified commodities, and providing for the collection of revenue therefrom.

In a more restricted and more popular sense, a law regulating, restricting, or taxing the manufacture or sale of intoxicating liquors.

EXCLUSA. In old English law. A sluice to carry off water; the payment to the lord for the benefit of such a sluice. Cowell.

EXCLUSIVE. Shutting out; debarring from interference or participation; vested in one person alone. An exclusive right is one which only the grantee thereof can exercise, and from which all others are prohibited or shut out.

A statute does not grant an "exclusive" privilege or franchise, unless it shuts out or excludes others from enjoying a similar privilege or franchise. 98 N. Y. 151.

EXCOMMENGEMENT. Excommunication, (*q. v.*) Co. Litt. 134*a*.

EXCOMMUNICATION. A sentence of censure pronounced by one of the spiritual courts for offenses falling under ecclesiastical cognizance. It is described in the books as twofold: (1) The *lesser* excommunication, which is an ecclesiastical censure, excluding the party from the sacraments; (2) the *greater*, which excludes him from the company of all Christians. Formerly, too, an excommunicated man was under various civil disabilities. He could not serve upon juries, or be a witness in any court; neither could he bring an action to recover lands or money due to him. These penalties are abolished by St. 53 Geo. III. c. 127. 3 Steph. Comm. 721.

EXCOMMUNICATO CAPIENDO. In ecclesiastical law. A writ issuing out of chancery, founded on a bishop's certificate that the defendant had been excommunicated, and requiring the sheriff to arrest and imprison him, returnable to the king's bench. 4 Bl. Comm. 415; Bac. Abr. "Excommunication," E.

EXCOMMUNICATO DELIBERANDO. A writ to the sheriff for delivery of an excommunicated person out of prison, upon certificate from the ordinary of his conformity to the ecclesiastical jurisdiction. Fitzh. Nat. Brev. 63.

Excommunicato interdicitur omnis actus legitimus, ita quod agere non potest, nec aliquem convenire, licet ipse ab aliis possit conveniri. Co. Litt. 133. Every legal act is forbidden an excommunicated person, so that he cannot act, nor sue any person, but he may be sued by others.

EXCOMMUNICATO RECAPIENDO. A writ commanding that persons excommunicated, who for their obstinacy had been committed to prison, but were unlawfully set free before they had given caution to obey the authority of the church, should be sought after, retaken, and imprisoned again. Reg. Orig. 67.

EXCULPATION, LETTERS OF. In Scotch law. A warrant granted at the suit of a prisoner for citing witnesses in his own defense.

EXCUSABLE HOMICIDE. In criminal law. The killing of a human being, either by misadventure or in self-defense. The name itself imports some fault, error, or omission, so trivial, however, that the law excuses it from the guilt of felony, though in strictness it judges it deserving of some little degree of punishment. 4 Bl. Comm. 182.

It is of two sorts,—either *per infortunium*, by misadventure, or *se defendendo*, upon a sudden affray. Homicide *per infortunium* is where a man, doing a lawful act, without any intention of hurt, unfortunately kills another; but, if death ensue from any unlawful act, the offense is manslaughter, and not misadventure. Homicide *se defendendo* is where a man kills another upon a sudden affray, merely in his own defense, or in defense of his wife, child, parent, or servant, and not from any vindictive feeling. 4 Bl. Comm. 182.

Excusat aut extenuat delictum in capitalibus quod non operatur idem in civilibus. Bac. Max. r. 15. That may excuse or palliate a wrongful act in capital cases which would not have the same effect in civil injuries. See Broom, Max. 324.

EXCUSATIO. In the civil law. An excuse or reason which exempts from some duty or obligation.

EXCUSATOR. In English law. An excuser.

In old German law. A defendant; he who utterly denies the plaintiff's claim. Du Cange.

Excusatur quis quod clameum non opposuerit, ut si toto tempore litigii fuit ultra mare quacunque occasione. Co. Litt. 260. He is excused who does not bring his claim, if, during the whole period in which it ought to have been brought, he has been beyond sea for any reason.

EXCUSE. A reason alleged for doing or not doing a thing. Worcester.

A matter alleged as a reason for relief or exemption from some duty or obligation.

EXCUSS. To seize and detain by law.

EXCUSSIO. In the civil law. A diligent prosecution of a remedy against a debtor; the exhausting of a remedy against a principal debtor, before resorting to his sureties. Translated "discussion," (*q. v.*)

In old English law. Rescue or rescous. Spelman.

EXEAT. A permission which a bishop grants to a priest to go out of his diocese; also leave to go out generally.

EXECUTE. To finish, accomplish, make complete, fulfill. To perform; obey the injunctions of.

To make; as to execute a deed, which includes signing, sealing, and delivery.

To perform; carry out according to its terms; as to execute a contract.

To fulfill the purpose of; to obey; to perform the commands of; as to execute a writ.

To fulfill the sentence of the law upon a person judicially condemned to suffer death.

A statute is said to *execute* a use where it transmutes the equitable interest of the *cestui que use* into a legal estate of the same nature, and makes him tenant of the land accordingly, in lieu of the feoffee to uses or trustee, whose estate, on the other hand, is at the same moment annihilated. 1 Steph. Comm. 339.

EXECUTED. Completed; carried into full effect; already done or performed; taking effect immediately; now in existence or in possession; conveying an immediate right or possession. The opposite of *executory.*

EXECUTED CONSIDERATION. A consideration which is wholly past. 1 Pars. Cont. 391. An act done or value given before the making of the agreement.

EXECUTED CONTRACT. One where nothing remains to be done by either party, and where the transaction is completed at the moment that the agreement is made, as where an article is sold and delivered, and payment therefor is made on the spot. A contract is said to be *executory* where some future act is to be done, as where an agreement is made to build a house in six months, or to do an act on or before some future day, or to lend money upon a certain interest, payable at a future time. Story, Cont. 8.

EXECUTED ESTATE. An estate whereby a present interest passes to and resides in the tenant, not dependent upon any subsequent circumstance or contingency. They are more commonly called "estates in possession." 2 Bl. Comm. 162.

An estate where there is vested in the grantee a present and immediate right of present or future enjoyment.

EXECUTED FINE. The fine *sur cognizance de droit, come ceo que il ad de son done;* or a fine upon acknowledgment of the right of the cognizee, as that which he has of the gift of the cognizor. Abolished by 3 & 4 Wm. IV. c. 74.

EXECUTED REMAINDER. A remainder which vests a present interest in the tenant, though the enjoyment is postponed to the future. 2 Bl. Comm. 168; Fearne, Rem. 31.

EXECUTED TRUST. A trust of which the scheme has in the outset been completely declared. Adams, Eq. 151. A trust in which the estates and interest in the subject-matter of the trust are completely limited and defined by the instrument creating the trust, and require no further instruments to complete them. Bisp. Eq. 20.

As all trusts are executory in this sense, that the trustee is bound to dispose of the estate according to the tenure of his trust, whether active or passive, it would be more accurate and precise to substitute the terms, "perfect" and "imperfect" for "executed" and "executory" trusts. 1 Hayes, Conv. 85.

EXECUTED USE. The first use in a conveyance upon which the statute of uses operates by bringing the possession to it, the combination of which, *i. e.*, the use and the possession, form the legal estate, and thus the statute is said to execute the use. Wharton.

EXECUTED WRIT. In practice. A writ carried into effect by the officer to whom it is directed. The term "executed," applied to a writ, has been held to mean "used." Amb. 61.

EXECUTIO. Lat. The doing or following up of a thing; the doing a thing completely or thoroughly; management or administration.

In old practice. Execution; the final process in an action.

EXECUTIO BONORUM. In old English law. Management or administration of goods. *Ad ecclesiam et ad amicos pertinebit executio bonorum,* the execution of the goods shall belong to the church and to the friends of the deceased. Bract. foi. 60*b*.

Executio est executio juris secundum judicium. 3 Inst. 212. Execution is the execution of the law according to the judgment.

Executio est finis et fructus legis. Co. Litt. 289. Execution is the end and fruit of the law.

Executio juris non habet injuriam. 2 Roll. 301. The execution of law does no injury.

EXECUTION. The completion, fulfillment, or perfecting of anything, or carrying it into operation and effect. The signing, sealing, and delivery of a deed. The signing and publication of a will. The performance of a contract according to its terms.

In practice. The last stage of a suit, whereby possession is obtained of anything recovered. It is styled "final process," and consists in putting the sentence of the law in force. 3 Bl. Comm. 412. The carrying into effect of the sentence or judgment of a court.

Also the name of a writ issued to a sheriff, constable, or marshal, authorizing and requiring him to execute the judgment of the court.

At common law, executions are said to be either *final* or *quousque;* the former, where complete satisfaction of the debt is intended to be procured by this process; the latter, where the execution is only a means to an end, as where the defendant is arrested on *ca. sa.*

In criminal law. The carrying into effect the sentence of the law by the infliction of capital punishment. 4 Bl. Comm. 403; 4 Steph. Comm. 470.

EXECUTION OF DECREE. Sometimes from the neglect of parties, or some other cause, it became impossible to carry a decree into execution without the further decree of the court upon a bill filed for that purpose. This happened generally in cases where, parties having neglected to proceed upon the decree, their rights under it became so embarrassed by a variety of subsequent events that it was necessary to have the decree of the court to settle and ascertain them. Such a bill might also be brought to carry into execution the judgment of an inferior court of equity, if the jurisdiction of that court was not equal to the purpose; as in the case of a decree in Wales, which the defendant avoided by fleeing into England.

This species of bill was generally partly an original bill, and partly a bill in the nature of an original bill, though not strictly original. Story, Eq. Pl. 342; Daniell, Ch. Pr. 1429.

EXECUTION OF DEEDS. The signing, sealing, and delivery of them by the parties, as their own acts and deeds, in the presence of witnesses.

EXECUTION PAREE. In French law. A right founded on an act passed before a notary, by which the creditor may immediately, without citation or summons, seize and cause to be sold the property of his debtor, out of the proceeds of which to receive his payment. It imports a confession of judgment, and is not unlike a warrant of attorney. Code Proc. La. art. 732; 6 Toullier, no. 208; 7 Toullier, no. 99.

EXECUTIONE FACIENDÂ. A writ commanding execution of a judgment. Obsolete. Cowell.

EXECUTIONE FACIENDÂ IN WITHERNAMIUM. A writ that lay for taking cattle of one who has conveyed the cattle of another out of the county, so that the sheriff cannot replevy them. Reg. Orig. 82.

EXECUTIONE JUDICII. A writ directed to the judge of an inferior court to do execution upon a judgment therein, or to return some reasonable cause wherefore he delays the execution. Fitzh. Nat. Brev. 20.

EXECUTIONER. The name given to him who puts criminals to death, according to their sentence; a hangman.

EXECUTIVE. As distinguished from the legislative and judicial departments of government, the executive department is that which is charged with the detail of carrying the laws into effect and securing their due observance. The word "executive" is also used as an impersonal designation of the chief executive officer of a state or nation.

Executive officer means an officer in whom resides the power to execute the laws. 4 Cal. 127, 146.

EXECUTIVE ADMINISTRATION, or MINISTRY. A political term in England, applicable to the higher and responsible class of public officials by whom the chief departments of the government of the kingdom are administered. The number of these amounts to fifty or sixty persons. Their tenure of office depends on the confidence of a majority of the house of commons, and they are supposed to be agreed on all matters of general policy except such as are specifically left open questions. Cab. Lawy.

EXECUTOR. A person appointed by a testator to carry out the directions and requests in his will, and to dispose of the property according to his testamentary provisions after his decease.

One to whom another man commits by his last will the execution of that will and testament. 2 Bl. Comm. 503.

A person to whom a testator by his will commits the *execution*, or putting in force, of that instrument and its codicils. Fonbl. 307.

Executors are classified according to the following several methods:

They are either *general* or *special*. The former term denotes an executor who is to have charge of the whole estate, wherever found, and administer it to a final settlement; while a special executor is only empowered by the will to take charge of a limited portion of the estate, or such part as may lie in one place, or to carry on the administration only to a prescribed point.

They are either *instituted* or *substituted*. An instituted executor is one who is appointed by the testator without any condition; while a substituted executor is one named to fill the office in case the person first nominated should refuse to act.

In the phraseology of ecclesiastical law, they are of the following kinds:

Executor à lege constitutus, an executor appointed by law; the ordinary of the diocese.

Executor ab episcopo constitutus, or *executor dativus*, an executor appointed by the bishop; an administrator to an intestate.

Executor à testatore constitutus, an executor appointed by a tes ator. Otherwise termed "*executor testamentarius;*" a testamentary executor.

An *executor to the tenor* is one who, though not directly constituted executor by the will, is therein charged with duties in relation to the estate which can only be performed by the executor.

In the civil law. A ministerial officer who executed or carried into effect the judgment or sentence in a cause. Calvin.

EXECUTOR DE SON TORT. Executor of his own wrong. A person who assumes to act as executor of an estate without any lawful warrant or authority, but who, by his intermeddling, makes himself liable as an executor to a certain extent.

If a stranger takes upon him to act as executor without any just authority, (as by intermeddling with the goods of the deceased, and many other transactions,) he is called in law an "executor of his own wrong," *de son tort*. 2 Bl. Comm. 507.

EXECUTOR LUCRATUS. An executor who has assets of his testator who in his life-time made himself liable by a wrongful interference with the property of another. 6 Jur. (N. S.) 543.

EXECUTORY. That which is yet to be executed or performed; that which remains to be carried into operation or effect; incomplete; depending upon a future performance or event. The opposite of *executed*.

EXECUTORY BEQUEST. See BEQUEST.

EXECUTORY CONSIDERATION. A consideration which is to be performed after the contract for which it is a consideration is made.

EXECUTORY CONTRACT. A contract which is to be executed at some future time, and which conveys only a *chose in action*. 2 Bl. Comm. 443; 2 Kent, Comm. 511, 512, note. See EXECUTED CONTRACT.

EXECUTORY DEVISE. In a general sense, a devise of a future interest in lands, not to take effect at the testator's death, but limited to arise and vest upon some future contingency. 1 Fearne, Rem. 382. A disposition of lands by will, by which no estate vests at the death of the devisor, but only on some future contingency. 2 Bl. Comm. 172.

In a stricter sense, a limitation by will of a future contingent interest in lands, contrary to the rules of the common law. 4 Kent, Comm. 263; 1 Steph. Comm. 564. A limitation by will of a future estate or interest in land, which cannot, consistently with the rules of law, take effect as a remainder. 2 Pow. Dev. (by Jarman,) 237.

By the executory devise no estate vests at the death of the devisor or testator, but only on the future contingency. It is only an indulgence to the last will and testament which is supposed to be made by one *inops consilii*. When the limitation by devise is such that the future interest falls within the rules of contingent remainders, it is a contingent remainder, and not an executory devise. 2 Bl. Comm. 173; 4 Kent, 257; 3 Term, 763.

EXECUTORY ESTATE. An estate or interest in lands, the vesting or enjoyment of which depends upon some future contingency. Such estate may be an *executory devise*, or an *executory remainder*, which is the same as a contingent remainder, because no present interest passes.

EXECUTORY FINES. These are the fines *sur cognizance de droit tantum; sur concessit;* and *sur done, grant et render*. Abolished by 3 & 4 Wm. IV. c. 74.

EXECUTORY INTERESTS. A general term, comprising all future estates and interests in land or personalty, other than reversions and remainders.

EXECUTORY LIMITATION. A limitation of a future interest by deed or will; if by will, it is also called an "executory devise."

EXECUTORY PROCESS. A process which can be resorted to in the following cases, namely: (1) When the right of the creditor arises from an act importing confession of judgment, and which contains a privilege or mortgage in his favor; (2) when the creditor demands the execution of a judgment which has been rendered by a tribunal different from that within whose jurisdiction the execution is sought. Code Prac. La. art. 732.

EXECUTORY TRUST. One which requires the execution of some further instrument, or the doing of some further act, on the part of the creator of the trust or of the trustee, towards its complete creation or full effect. An *executed* trust is one fully created and of immediate effect. These terms do not relate to the execution of the trust as regards the beneficiary.

EXECUTORY USES. These are springing uses, which confer a legal title answering to an executory devise; as when a limitation to the use of A. in fee is defeasible by a limitation to the use of B., to arise at a future period, or on a given event.

EXECUTRESS. A female executor. Hardr. 165, 473. See EXECUTRIX.

EXECUTRIX. A woman who has been appointed by will to execute such will or testament.

EXECUTRY. In Scotch law. The movable estate of a person dying, which goes to his nearest of kin. So called as falling under the distribution of an executor. Bell.

Exempla illustrant non restringunt legem. Co. Litt. 240. Examples illustrate, but do not restrain, the law.

EXEMPLARY DAMAGES. Damages on a punitive scale, given in respect of tortious acts, committed through malice or other circumstances of aggravation; damages designed not only as a compensation to the injured party, but also as a punishment to the wrong-doer for his violence, oppression, malice, or fraud.

EXEMPLI GRATIÂ. For the purpose of example, or for instance. Often abbreviated "*ex. gr.*" or "*e. g.*"

EXEMPLIFICATION. An official transcript of a document from public records, made in form to be used as evidence, and authenticated as a true copy.

EXEMPLIFICATIONE. A writ granted for the exemplification or transcript of an original record. Reg. Orig. 290.

EXEMPLUM. In the civil law. Copy; a written authorized copy. This word is also used in the modern sense of "example,"—*ad exemplum constituti singulares non trahi*, exceptional things must not be taken for examples. Calvin.

EXEMPT, *v*. To relieve, excuse, or set free from a duty or service imposed upon the general class to which the individual exempted belongs; as to exempt from militia service. See 1 St. at Large, 272.

To relieve certain classes of property from liability to sale on execution.

EXEMPT, *n*. One who is free from liability to military service; as distinguished from a *detail*, who is one belonging to the army, but detached or set apart for the time to some particular duty or service, and liable, at any time, to be recalled to his place in the ranks. 39 Ala. 379.

EXEMPTION. Freedom from a general duty or service; immunity from a general burden, tax, or charge.

A privilege allowed by law to a judgment

debtor, by which he may hold property to a certain amount, or certain classes of property, free from all liability to levy and sale on execution or attachment.

EXEMPTION LAWS. Laws which provide that a certain amount or proportion of a debtor's property shall be exempt from execution.

EXEMPTION, WORDS OF. It is a maxim of law that words of exemption are not to be construed to import any liability; the maxim *expressio unius exclusio alterius*, or its converse, *exclusio unius inclusio alterius*, not applying to such a case. For example, an exemption of the crown from the bankruptcy act 1869, in one specified particular, would not inferentially subject the crown to that act in any other particular. Brown.

EXEMPTS. Persons who are not bound by law, but excused from the performance of duties imposed upon others.

EXENNIUM. In old English law. A gift; a new year's gift. Cowell.

EXEQUATUR. Lat. Let it be executed. In French practice, this term is subscribed by judicial authority upon a transcript of a judgment from a foreign country, or from another part of France, and authorizes the execution of the judgment within the jurisdiction where it is so indorsed.

In international law. A certificate issued by the foreign department of a state to a consul or commercial agent of another state, recognizing his official character, and authorizing him to fulfill his duties.

EXERCISE. To make use of. Thus, to exercise a right or power is to do something which it enables the holder to do.

EXERCITALIS. A soldier; vassal. Spelman.

EXERCITOR NAVIS. The temporary owner or charterer of a ship.

EXERCITORIA ACTIO. In the civil law An action which lay against the employer of a vessel (*exercitor navis*) for the contracts made by the master. Inst. 4, 7, 2; 3 Kent, Comm. 161.

EXERCITORIAL POWER. The trust given to a ship-master.

EXERCITUAL. In old English law. A heriot paid only in arms, horses, or military accouterments.

EXERCITUS. In old European law. An army; an armed force. A collection of thirty-five men and upwards.

A gathering of forty-two armed men.

A meeting of four men. Spelman.

EXETER DOMESDAY. The name given to a record preserved among the muniments and charters belonging to the dean and chapter of Exeter Cathedral, which contains a description of the western parts of the kingdom, comprising the counties of Wilts, Dorset, Somerset, Devon, and Cornwall. The Exeter Domesday was published with several other surveys nearly contemporary, by order of the commissioners of the public records, under the direction of Sir Henry Ellis, in a volume supplementary to the Great Domesday, folio, London, 1816. Wharton.

EXFESTUCARE. To abdicate or resign; to resign or surrender an estate, office, or dignity, by the symbolical delivery of a staff or rod to the alienee.

EXFREDIARE. To break the peace; to commit open violence. Jacob.

EXHÆREDATIO. In the civil law. Disinheriting; disherison. The formal method of excluding an indefeasible (or forced) heir from the entire inheritance, by the testator's express declaration in the will that such person shall be *exhæres*. Mackeld. Rom. Law, § 711.

EXHÆRES. In the civil law. One disinherited. Vicat; Du Cange.

EXHEREDATE. In Scotch law. To disinherit; to exclude from an inheritance.

EXHIBERE. To present a thing corporeally, so that it may be handled. Vicat. To appear personally to conduct the defense of an action at law.

EXHIBIT, *v.* To show or display; to offer or present for inspection. To produce anything in public, so that it may be taken into possession. Dig. 10, 4, 2.

To present; to offer publicly or officially; to file of record. Thus we speak of *exhibiting* a charge of treason, *exhibiting* a bill against an officer of the king's bench by way of proceeding against him in that court.

To administer; to cause to be taken; as medicines.

EXHIBIT, *n.* A paper or document produced and exhibited to a court during a trial or hearing, or to a commissioner taking depositions, or to auditors, arbitrators, etc., as a voucher, or in proof of facts, or as otherwise connected with the subject-matter, and which, on being accepted, is marked for identification and annexed to the deposition, report, or other principal document, or filed of record, or otherwise made a part of the case.

A paper referred to in and filed with the bill, answer, or petition in a suit in equity, or with a deposition. 16 Ga. 68.

EXHIBITANT. A complainant in articles of the peace. 12 Adol. & E. 599.

EXHIBITIO BILLÆ. Lat. Exhibition of a bill. In old English practice, actions were instituted by presenting or exhibiting a bill to the court, in cases where the proceedings were by bill; hence this phrase is equivalent to "commencement of the suit."

EXHIBITION. In Scotch law. An action for compelling the production of writings.

In ecclesiastical law. An allowance for meat and drink, usually made by religious appropriators of churches to the vicar. Also the benefaction settled for the maintaining of scholars in the universities, not depending on the foundation. Paroch. Antiq. 304.

EXIGENCE. Demand, want, need, imperativeness.

EXIGENCY OF A BOND. That which the bond demands or exacts, *i. e.*, the act, performance, or event upon which it is conditioned.

EXIGENCY OF A WRIT. The command or imperativeness of a writ; the directing part of a writ; the act or performance which it commands.

EXIGENDARY. In English law. An officer who makes out exigents.

EXIGENT, or EXIGI FACIAS. L. Lat. In English practice. A judicial writ made use of in the process of outlawry, commanding the sheriff to *demand* the defendant, (or *cause him to be demanded, exigi faciat,*) from county court to county court, until he be outlawed; or, if he appear, then to take and have him before the court on a day certain in term, to answer to the plaintiff's action. 1 Tidd, Pr. 132; 3 Bl. Comm. 283, 284; Archb. N. Pr. 485. Now regulated by St. 2 Wm. IV. c. 39.

EXIGENTER. An officer of the English court of common pleas, whose duty it was to make out the *exigents* and proclamations in the process of outlawry. Cowell. Abolished by St. 7 Wm. IV. and 1 Vict. c. 30. Holthouse.

EXIGI FACIAS. That you cause to be demanded. The emphatic words of the Latin form of the writ of *exigent.* They are sometimes used as the name of that writ.

EXIGIBLE. Demandable; requirable.

EXILE. Banishment; the person banished.

EXILIUM. Lat. In old English law. 1. Exile; banishment from one's country.

2. Driving away; despoiling. The name of a species of waste, which consisted in driving away tenants or vassals from the estate; as by demolishing buildings, and so compelling the tenants to leave, or by enfranchising the bond-servants, and unlawfully turning them out of their tenements. Fleta, l. 1, c. 9.

Exilium est patriæ privatio, natalis soli mutatio, legum nativarum amissio. 7 Coke, 20. Exile is a privation of country, a change of natal soil, a loss of native laws.

EXISTIMATIO. In the civil law. The civil reputation which belonged to the Roman citizen, as such. Mackeld. Rom. Law, § 135. Called a state or condition of unimpeached dignity or character, (*dignitatis illæsæ status;*) the highest standing of a Roman citizen. Dig. 50, 13, 5, 1.

Also the decision or award of an arbiter.

EXIT. Lat. It goes forth. This word is used in docket entries as a brief mention of the issue of process. Thus, "*exit fi. fa.*" denotes that a writ of *fieri facias* has been issued in the particular case. The "*exit* of a writ" is the fact of its issuance.

EXIT WOUND. A term used in medical jurisprudence to denote the wound made by a weapon on the side where it *emerges,* after it has passed completely through the body, or through any part of it.

EXITUS. Children; offspring. The rents, issues, and profits of lands and tenements. An export duty. The conclusion of the pleadings.

EXLEGALITAS. In old English law. Outlawry. Spelman.

EXLEGALITUS. He who is prosecuted as an outlaw. Jacob.

EXLEGARE. In old English law. To outlaw; to deprive one of the benefit and protection of the law, (*exuere aliquem beneficio legis.*) Spelman.

EXLEX. In old English law. An outlaw; *qui est extra legem*, one who is *out* of the *law's* protection. Bract. fol. 125. *Qui beneficio legis privatur.* Spelman.

EXOINE. In French law. An act or instrument in writing which contains the reasons why a party in a civil suit, or a person accused, who has been summoned, agreeably to the requisitions of a decree, does not appear. Poth. Proc. Crim. § 3, art. 3. The same as "Essoin," (*q. v.*)

EXONERATION. The removal of a burden, charge, or duty. Particularly, the act of relieving a person or estate from a charge or liability by casting the same upon another person or estate.

A right or equity which exists between those who are successively liable for the same debt. "A surety who discharges an obligation is entitled to look to the principal for reimbursement, and to invoke the aid of a court of equity for this purpose, and a subsequent surety who, by the terms of the contract, is responsible only in case of the default of the principal and a prior surety, may claim *exoneration* at the hands of either." Bisp. Eq. § 331.

In Scotch law. A discharge; or the act of being legally disburdened of, or liberated from, the performance of a duty or obligation. Bell.

EXONERATIONE SECTÆ. A writ that lay for the crown's ward, to be free from all suit to the county court, hundred court, leet, etc., during wardship. Fitzh. Nat. Brev. 158.

EXONERATIONE SECTÆ AD CURIAM BARON. A writ of the same nature as that last above described, issued by the guardian of the crown's ward, and addressed to the sheriffs or stewards of the court, forbidding them to distrain him, etc., for not doing suit of court, etc. New Nat. Brev. 352.

EXONERETUR. Lat. Let him be relieved or discharged. An entry made on a bail-piece, whereby the surety is relieved or discharged from further obligation, when the condition is fulfilled by the surrender of the principal or otherwise.

EXORDIUM. The beginning or introductory part of a speech.

EXPATRIATION. The voluntary act of abandoning one's country, and becoming the citizen or subject of another. See EMIGRATION.

EXPECT. To await; to look forward to something intended, promised, or likely to happen.

EXPECTANCY. The condition of being deferred to a future time, or of dependence upon an expected event; contingency as to possession or enjoyment.

With respect to the time of their enjoyment, estates may either be in possession or in expectancy; and of expectancies there are two sorts,—one created by the act of the parties, called a "remainder;" the other by act of law, called a "reversion." 2 Bl. Comm. 163.

EXPECTANT. Having relation to, or dependent upon, a contingency.

EXPECTANT ESTATES. Interests to come into possession and be enjoyed *in futuro*. They are of two sorts at common law,—reversions and remainders. 2 Bl. Comm. 163.

EXPECTANT HEIR. A person who has the expectation of inheriting property or an estate, but small present means. The term is chiefly used in equity, where relief is afforded to such persons against the enforcement of "catching bargains," (*q. v.*)

EXPECTATION OF LIFE, in the doctrine of life annuities, is the share or number of years of life which a person of a given age may, upon an equality of chance, expect to enjoy. Wharton.

EXPEDIMENT. The whole of a person's goods and chattels, bag and baggage. Wharton.

Expedit reipublicæ ne sua re quis male utatur. It is for the interest of the state that a man should not enjoy his own property improperly, (to the injury of others.) Inst. 1, 8, 2.

Expedit reipublicæ ut sit finis litium. It is for the advantage of the state that there be an end of suits; it is for the public good that actions be brought to a close. Co. Litt. 303*b*.

EXPEDITATÆ ARBORES. Trees rooted up or cut down to the roots. Fleta, l. 2, c. 41.

EXPEDITATE. In forest law. To cut out the ball of a dog's forefeet, for the preservation of the royal game.

EXPEDITATION. A cutting off the claws or ball of the forefeet of mastiffs, to prevent their running after deer. Spelman; Cowell.

EXPEDITIO. An expedition; an irregular kind of army. Spelman.

EXPEDITIO BREVIS. In old practice. The service of a writ. Townsh. Pl. 43.

EXPENDITORS. Paymasters. Those who expend or disburse certain taxes. Especially the sworn officer who supervised the repairs of the banks of the canals in Romney Marsh. Cowell.

EXPENSÆ LITIS. Costs or expenses of the suit, which are generally allowed to the successful party.

EXPENSIS MILITUM NON LEVANDIS. An ancient writ to prohibit the sheriff from levying any allowance for knights of the shire upon those who held lands in ancient demesne. Reg. Orig. 261.

Experientia per varios actus legem facit. Magistra rerum experientia. Co. Litt. 60. Experience by various acts makes law. Experience is the mistress of things.

EXPERTS. Persons examined as witnesses in a cause, who testify in regard to some professional or technical matter arising in the case, and who are permitted to give their opinions as to such matter on account of their special training, skill, or familiarity with it.

Persons selected by the court or parties in a cause, on account of their knowledge or skill, to examine, estimate, and ascertain things and make a report of their opinions. Merl. Repert.

Persons professionally acquainted with the science or practice in question. Strick. Ev. 408. Persons conversant with the subject-matter on questions of science, skill, trade, and others of like kind. Best, Ev. § 346.

An expert is a person who possesses peculiar skill and knowledge upon the subject-matter that he is required to give an opinion upon. 48 Vt. 366.

An expert is a skillful or experienced person; a person having skill or experience, or peculiar knowledge on certain subjects, or in certain professions; a scientific witness. 45 Me. 392; 52 Me. 68.

EXPILARE. In the civil law. To spoil; to rob or plunder. Applied to inheritances. Dig. 47, 19; Cod. 9, 32.

EXPILATIO. In the civil law. The offense of unlawfully appropriating goods belonging to a succession. It is not technically theft (*furtum*) because such property no longer belongs to the decedent, nor to the heir, since the latter has not yet taken possession.

EXPILATOR. In the civil law. A robber; a spoiler or plunderer. *Expilatores sunt atrociores fures.* Dig. 47, 18, 1, 1.

EXPIRATION. Cessation; termination from mere lapse of time; as the expiration of a lease, or statute, and the like.

EXPIRY OF THE LEGAL. In Scotch law and practice. Expiration of the period within which an adjudication may be redeemed, by paying the debt in the decree of adjudication. Bell.

EXPLEES. See ESPLEES.

EXPLETA, EXPLETIA, or EXPLECIA. In old records. The rents and profits of an estate.

EXPLICATIO. In the civil law. The fourth pleading; equivalent to the surrejoinder of the common law. Calvin.

EXPLORATOR. A scout, huntsman, or chaser.

EXPLOSION. A sudden and rapid combustion, causing violent expansion of the air, and accompanied by a report.

The word "explosion" is variously used in ordinary speech, and is not one that admits of exact definition. Every combustion of an explosive substance, whereby other property is ignited and consumed, would not be an "explosion," within the ordinary meaning of the term. It is not used as a synonym of "combustion." An explosion may be described generally as a sudden and rapid combustion, causing violent expansion of the air, and accompanied by a report. But the rapidity of the combustion, the violence of the expansion, and the vehemence of the report vary in intensity as often as the occurrences multiply. Hence an explosion is an idea of degrees; and the true meaning of the word, in each particular case, must be settled, not by any fixed standard or accurate measurement, but by the common experience and notions of men in matters of that sort. 22 Ohio St. 340.

EXPORT, *v.* To send, take, or carry an article of trade or commerce out of the country. To transport merchandise from one country to another in the course of trade. To carry out or convey goods by sea. Vaughn, 171, 172; 5 Harr. 501.

EXPORT, *n.* A thing or commodity exported. More commonly used in the plural.

EXPORTATION. The act of sending or carrying goods and merchandise from one country to another.

EXPOSE, *v.* To show publicly; to exhibit.

EXPOSÉ, *n.* Fr. A statement; account; recital; explanation. The term is used in diplomatic language as descriptive of a written explanation of the reasons for a certain act or course of conduct.

EXPOSITIO. Explanation; exposition; interpretation.

Expositio quæ ex visceribus causæ nascitur, est aptissima et fortissima in lege. That kind of interpretation which is born [or drawn] from the bowels of a cause is the aptest and most forcible in the law. 10 Coke, 24*b*.

EXPOSITION. Explanation; interpretation.

EXPOSITION DE PART. In French law. The abandonment of a child, unable to take care of itself, either in a public or private place.

EXPOSURE OF PERSON. In criminal law. Such an intentional exposure, in a public place, of the naked body or the private parts as is calculated to shock the feelings of chastity or to corrupt the morals of the community.

EXPRESS. Made known distinctly and explicitly, and not left to inference or implication. Declared in terms; set forth in words. Manifested by direct and appropriate language, as distinguished from that which is inferred from conduct. The word is usually contrasted with "implied."

EXPRESS ABROGATION. Abrogation by express provision or enactment; the repeal of a law or provision by a subsequent one, referring directly to it.

EXPRESS ASSUMPSIT. An undertaking to do some act, or to pay a sum of money to another, manifested by express terms.

EXPRESS COLOR. An evasive form of special pleading in a case where the defendant ought to plead the general issue. Abolished by the common-law procedure act, 1852, (15 & 16 Vict. c. 76, § 64.)

EXPRESS COMPANY. A firm or corporation engaged in the business of transporting parcels or other movable property, in the capacity of common carriers.

EXPRESS CONSIDERATION. A consideration which is distinctly and specifically named in the written contract or in the oral agreement of the parties.

EXPRESS CONTRACT. A contract the terms of which are openly uttered or declared at the time of making it. 2 Bl. Comm. 443; 2 Steph. Comm. 110. A contract made in distinct and explicit language, or by writing; as distinguished from an implied contract. 2 Kent, Comm. 450.

EXPRESS MALICE. Actual malice; malice in fact; a deliberate intention to commit an injury, evidenced by external circumstances.

EXPRESS TRUST. A trust created or declared in express terms, and usually in writing, as distinguished from one inferred by the law from the conduct or dealings of the parties.

Express trusts are those which are created in express terms in the deed, writing, or will, while implied trusts are those which, without being expressed, are deducible from the nature of the transaction, as matters of intent, or which are superinduced upon the transactions by operation of law, as matters of equity, independently of the particular intention of the parties. 56 Barb. 635.

EXPRESS WARRANTY. One expressed by particular words. 2 Bl. Comm. 300.

In the law of insurance. An agreement expressed in a policy, whereby the assured stipulates that certain facts relating to the risk are or shall be true, or certain acts relating to the same subject have been or shall be done. 1 Phil. Ins. (4th Ed.) p. 425.

Expressa nocent, non expressa non nocent. Things expressed are [may be] prejudicial; things not expressed are not. Express words are sometimes prejudicial, which, if omitted, had done no harm. Dig. 35, 1, 52; Id. 50, 17, 195. See Calvin.

Expressa non prosunt quæ non expressa proderunt. 4 Coke, 73. The expression of things of which, if unexpressed, one would have the benefit, is useless.

Expressio eorum quæ tacite insunt nihil operatur. The expression or express mention of those things which are tacitly implied avails nothing. 2 Inst. 365. A man's own words are void, when the law speaketh as much. Finch, Law. b. 1, c. 3, no. 26. Words used to express what the law will imply without them are mere words of abundance. 5 Coke, 11.

Expressio unius est exclusio alterius. The expression of one thing is the exclusion of another. Co. Litt. 210*a*. The express mention of one thing [person or place] implies the exclusion of another.

Expressio unius personæ est exclusio alterius. Co. Litt. 210. The mention of one person is the exclusion of another. See Broom, Max. 651.

Expressum facit cessare tacitum. That which is expressed makes that which is implied to cease, [that is, supersedes it, or controls its effect.] Thus, an implied covenant in a deed is in all cases controlled by an express covenant. 4 Coke, 80; Broom, Max. 651.

Expressum servitium regat vel declaret tacitum. Let service expressed rule or declare what is silent.

EXPROMISSIO. In the civil law. The species of novation by which a creditor accepts a new debtor, who becomes bound instead of the old, the latter being released. 1 Bouv. Inst. no. 802.

EXPROMISSOR. In the civil law. A person who assumes the debt of another, and becomes solely liable for it, by a stipulation with the creditor. He differs from a surety, inasmuch as this contract is one of novation, while a surety is jointly liable with his principal. Mackeld. Rom. Law, § 538.

EXPROMITTERE. In the civil law. To undertake for another, with the view of becoming liable in his place. Calvin.

EXPROPRIATION. This word properly denotes a voluntary surrender of rights or claims; the act of divesting oneself of that which was previously claimed as one's own, or renouncing it. In this sense it is the opposite of "appropriation." But a meaning has been attached to the term, imported from its use in foreign jurisprudence, which makes it synonymous with the exercise of the power of eminent domain, *i. e.*, the compulsory taking from a person, on compensation made, of his private property for the use of a railroad, canal, or other public work.

In French law. Expropriation is the compulsory realization of a debt by the creditor out of the lands of his debtor, or the usufruct thereof. When the debtor is co-tenant with others, it is necessary that a partition should first be made. It is confined, in the first place, to the lands (if any) that are in *hypothèque*, but afterwards extends to the lands not in *hypothèque*. Moreover, the debt must be of a liquidated amount. Brown.

EXPULSION. A putting or driving out. The act of depriving a member of a corporation, legislative body, assembly, society, commercial organization, etc., of his membership in the same, by a legal vote of the body itself, for breach of duty, improper conduct, or other sufficient cause.

EXPUNGE. To blot out; to efface designedly; to obliterate; to strike out wholly. Webster.

EXPURGATION. The act of purging or cleansing, as where a book is published without its obscene passages.

EXPURGATOR. One who corrects by expurging.

EXQUÆSTOR. In Roman law. One who had filled the office of *quæstor*. A title given to Tribonian. Inst. proœm. § 3. Used only in the ablative case, (*exquæstore.*)

EXROGARE. (From *ex*, from, and *rogare*, to pass a law.) In Roman law. To take something from an old law by a new law. Tayl. Civil Law, 155.

EXTEND. In English practice. To value the lands or tenements of a person bound by a statute or recognizance which has become forfeited, to their full *extended* value. 3 Bl. Comm. 420; Fitzh. Nat. Brev. 131. To execute the writ of *extent* or *extendi facias*, (*q. v.*) 2 Tidd, Pr. 1043, 1044.

In taxation. Extending a tax consists in adding to the assessment roll the precise amount due from each person whose name appears thereon. "The subjects for taxation having been properly listed, and a basis for apportionment established, nothing will remain to fix a definite liability but to *extend* upon the list or roll the several proportionate amounts, as a charge against the several taxables." Cooley, Tax'n, (2d Ed.) 423.

EXTENDI FACIAS. Lat. You cause to be extended. In English practice. The name of a writ of execution, (derived from its two emphatic words;) more commonly called an "extent." 2 Tidd, Pr. 1043; 4 Steph. Comm. 43.

EXTENSION. In mercantile law. An allowance of additional time for the payment of debts. An agreement between a debtor and his creditors, by which they allow him further time for the payment of his liabilities.

EXTENSION OF PATENT. An extension of the life of a patent for an additional period of seven years, formerly allowed by law in the United States, upon proof being made that the inventor had not succeeded in obtaining a reasonable remuneration from his patent-right. This is no longer allowed, except as to designs. See Rev. St. U. S. § 4924.

EXTENSORES. In old English law. Extenders or appraisers. The name of certain officers appointed to appraise and divide or apportion lands. It was their duty to make a survey, schedule, or inventory of the lands, to lay them out under certain heads, and then to ascertain the value of each, as preparatory to the division or partition. Bract. fols. 72*b*, 75; Britt. c. 71.

EXTENT. **In English practice.** A writ of execution issuing from the exchequer upon a debt due the crown, or upon a debt due a private person, if upon recognizance or statute merchant or staple, by which the sheriff is directed to appraise the debtor's lands, and, instead of selling them, to set them off to the creditor for a term during which the rental will satisfy the judgment.

In Scotch practice. The value or valuation of lands. Bell.

The rents, profits, and issues of lands. Skene.

EXTENT IN AID. In English practice. That kind of extent which issues at the instance and for the benefit of a debtor to the crown, for the recovery of a debt due to himself. 2 Tidd, Pr. 1045; 4 Steph. Comm. 47.

EXTENT IN CHIEF. In English practice. The principal kind of extent, issuing at the suit of the crown, for the recovery of the crown's debt. 4 Steph. Comm. 47. An adverse proceeding by the king, for the recovery of his own debt. 2 Tidd, Pr. 1045.

EXTENTA MANERII. (The extent or survey of a manor.) The title of a statute passed 4 Edw. I. St. 1; being a sort of direction for making a *survey* or terrier of a *manor*, and all its appendages. 2 Reeve, Eng. Law, 140.

EXTENUATE. To lessen; to palliate; to mitigate.

EXTENUATING CIRCUMSTANCES. Such as render a delict or crime less aggravated, heinous, or reprehensible than it would otherwise be, or tend to palliate or lessen its guilt. Such circumstances may ordinarily be shown in order to reduce the punishment or damages.

EXTERRITORIALITY. The privilege of those persons (such as foreign ministers) who, though temporarily resident within a state, are not subject to the operation of its laws.

EXTERUS. Lat. A foreigner or alien; one born abroad. The opposite of *civis*.

Exterus non habet terras. An alien holds no lands. Tray. Lat. Max. 203.

EXTINCT. Extinguished. A rent is said to be extinguished when it is destroyed and put out. Co. Litt. 147*b*. See EXTINGUISHMENT.

Extincto subjecto, tollitur adjunctum. When the subject is extinguished, the incident ceases. Thus, when the business for which a partnership has been formed is completed, or brought to an end, the partnership itself ceases. Inst. 3, 26, 6; 3 Kent, Comm. 52, note.

EXTINGUISHMENT. The destruction or cancellation of a right, power, contract, or estate. The annihilation of a collateral thing or subject in the subject itself out of which it is derived. Prest. Merg. 9. For the distinction between an extinguishment and passing a right, see 2 Shars. Bl. Comm. 325, note.

"Extinguishment" is sometimes confounded with "merger," though there is a clear distinction between them. "Merger" is only a mode of extinguishment, and applies to estates only under particular circumstances; but "extinguishment" is a term of general application to rights, as well as estates. 2 Crabb, Real Prop. p. 367, § 1487.

EXTINGUISHMENT OF COMMON. Loss of the right to have common. This may happen from various causes.

EXTINGUISHMENT OF COPYHOLD. In English law. A copyhold is said to be *extinguished* when the freehold and copyhold interests unite in the same person and in the same right, which may be either by the copyhold interest coming to the freehold or by the freehold interest coming to the copyhold. 1 Crabb, Real Prop. p. 670, § 864.

EXTINGUISHMENT OF DEBTS. This takes place by payment; by accord and satisfaction; by novation, or the substitution of a new debtor; by merger, when the creditor recovers a judgment or accepts a security of a higher nature than the original obligation; by a release; by the marriage of a *feme sole* creditor with the debtor, or of an obligee with one of two joint obligors; and where one of the parties, debtor or creditor, makes the other his executor.

EXTINGUISHMENT OF RENT. If a person have a yearly rent of lands, and afterwards purchase those lands, so that he has as good an estate in the land as in the rent, the rent is *extinguished*. Termes de la Ley; Cowell; Co. Litt. 147. Rent may also be extinguished by conjunction of estates, by confirmation, by grant, by release, and by surrender. 1 Crabb, Real Prop. pp. 210–213, § 209.

EXTINGUISHMENT OF WAYS. This is usually effected by unity of possession. As if a man have a way over the close of another, and he purchase that close, the way is *extinguished*. 1 Crabb, Real Prop. p. 341, § 384.

EXTIRPATION. In English law. A species of destruction or waste, analogous to estrepement. See ESTREPEMENT.

EXTIRPATIONE. A judicial writ, either before or after judgment, that lay against a person who, when a verdict was found against him for land, etc., maliciously overthrew any house or extirpated any trees upon it. Reg. Jud. 13, 56.

EXTOCARE. In old records. To grub woodland, and reduce it to arable or meadow; "to stock up." Cowell.

EXTORSIVELY. A technical word used in indictments for extortion.

It is a sufficient averment of a corrupt intent, in an indictment for extortion, to allege that the defendant "extorsively" took the unlawful fee. 35 Ark. 438.

EXTORT. The natural meaning of the word "extort" is to obtain money or other valuable thing either by compulsion, by actual force, or by the force of motives applied to the will, and often more overpowering and irresistible than physical force. 12 Cush. 90.

Extortio est crimen quando quis colore officii extorquet quod non est debitum, vel supra debitum, vel ante tempus quod est debitum. 10 Coke, 102. Extortion is a crime when, by color of office, any person extorts that which is not due, or more than is due, or before the time when it is due.

EXTORTION. Any oppression by color or pretense of right, and particularly the exaction by an officer of money, by color of his office, either when none at all is due, or not so much is due, or when it is not yet due. 4 Conn. 480.

Extortion consists in any public officer unlawfully taking, by color of his office, from any person any money or thing of value that is not due to him, or more than his due. Code Ga. 1882, § 4507.

Extortion is the obtaining of property from another, with his consent, induced by wrongful use of force or fear, or under color of official right. Pen. Code Cal. § 518; Pen. Code Dak. § 608.

Extortion is an abuse of public justice, which consists in any officer unlawfully taking, by color of his office, from any man any money or thing of value that is not due to him, or before it is due. 4 Bl. Comm. 141.

Extortion is any oppression under color of right. In a stricter sense, the taking of money by any officer, by color of his office, when none, or not so much, is due, or it is not yet due. 1 Hawk. P. C. (Curw. Ed.) 418.

It is the corrupt demanding or receiving by a person in office of a fee for services which should be performed gratuitously; or, where compensation is permissible, of a larger fee than the law justifies, or a fee not due. 2 Bish. Crim. Law, § 390.

The distinction between "bribery" and "extortion" seems to be this: the former offense consists in the offering a present, or receiving one, if offered; the latter, in demanding a fee or present, by color of office. Jacob.

For the distinction between "extortion" and "exaction," see EXACTION.

EXTRA. A Latin preposition, occurring in many legal phrases; it means beyond, except, without, out of, outside.

EXTRA COSTS. In English practice. Those charges which do not appear upon the face of the proceedings, such as witnesses' expenses, fees to counsel, attendances, court fees, etc., an affidavit of which must be made, to warrant the master in allowing them upon taxation of costs. Wharton.

EXTRA-DOTAL PROPERTY. In Louisiana this term is used to designate that property which forms no part of the dowry of a woman, and which is also called "paraphernal property." Civil Code La. art. 2315.

EXTRA FEODUM. Out of his fee; out of the seigniory, or not holden of him that claims it. Co. Litt. 1*b*; Reg. Orig. 97*b*.

EXTRA-JUDICIUM. Extrajudicial; out of the proper cause; out of court; beyond the jurisdiction. See EXTRAJUDICIAL.

EXTRA JUS. Beyond the law; more than the law requires. *In jure, vel extra jus.* Bract. fol. 169*b*.

EXTRA LEGEM. Out of the law; out of the protection of the law.

Extra legem positus est civiliter mortuus. Co. Litt. 130. He who is placed out of the law is civilly dead.

EXTRA PRÆSENTIAM MARITI. Out of her husband's presence.

EXTRA QUATUOR MARIA. Beyond the four seas; out of the kingdom of England. 1 Bl. Comm. 457.

EXTRA REGNUM. Out of the realm. 7 Coke, 16*a;* 2 Kent, Comm. 42, note.

EXTRA SERVICES, when used with reference to officers, means services incident to the office in question, but for which compensation has not been provided by law. 21 Ind. 32.

EXTRA-TERRITORIALITY. The extra-territorial operation of laws; that is, their operation upon persons, rights, or jural relations, existing beyond the limits of the enacting state, but still amenable to its laws.

EXTRA TERRITORIUM. Beyond or without the territory. 6 Bin. 353; 2 Kent, Comm. 407.

Extra territorium jus dicenti impune non paretur. One who exercises jurisdiction out of his territory is not obeyed with impunity. Dig. 2, 1, 20; Branch, Princ.; 10 Coke, 77. He who exercises judicial authority beyond his proper limits cannot be obeyed with safety.

EXTRA VIAM. Outside the way. Where the defendant in trespass pleaded a right of way in justification, and the replication alleged that the trespass was committed outside the limits of the way claimed, these were the technical words to be used.

EXTRA VIRES. Beyond powers. See ULTRA VIRES.

EXTRACT. A portion or fragment of a writing. In Scotch law, the certified copy, by a clerk of a court, of the proceedings in an action carried on before the court, and of the judgment pronounced; containing also an order for execution or proceedings thereupon. Jacob; Whishaw.

EXTRACTA CURIÆ. In old English law. The issues or profits of holding a court, arising from the customary fees, etc.

EXTRADITION. The surrender of a criminal by a foreign state to which he has fled for refuge from prosecution to the state within whose jurisdiction the crime was committed, upon the demand of the latter state, in order that he may be dealt with according to its laws. Extradition may be accorded as a mere matter of comity, or may take place under treaty stipulations between the two nations. It also obtains as between the different states of the American Union.

Extradition between the states must be considered and defined to be a political duty of imperfect obligation, founded upon compact, and requiring each state to surrender one who, having violated the criminal laws of another state, has fled from its justice, and is found in the state from which he is demanded, on demand of the executive authority of the state from which he fled. Abbott.

EXTRAHURA. In old English law. An animal wandering or straying about, without an owner; an estray. Spelman.

EXTRAJUDICIAL. That which is done, given, or effected outside the course of regular judicial proceedings; not founded upon, or unconnected with, the action of a court of law; as extrajudicial evidence, an extrajudicial oath.

That which, though done in the course of regular judicial proceedings, is unnecessary to such proceedings, or interpolated, or beyond their scope; as an extrajudicial opinion, (*dictum.*)

That which does not belong to the judge or his jurisdiction, notwithstanding which he takes cognizance of it.

EXTRANEUS. In old English law. One foreign born; a foreigner. 7 Coke, 16.

In Roman law. An heir not born in the family of the testator. Those of a foreign state. The same as *alienus*. Vicat; Du Cange.

Extraneus est subditus qui extra terram, i. e., potestatem regis natus est. 7 Coke, 16. A foreigner is a subject who is born out of the territory, *i. e.*, government of the king.

EXTRAORDINARY. The writs of *mandamus, quo warranto, habeas corpus,* and some others are sometimes called "extraordinary remedies," in contradistinction to the ordinary remedy by action.

EXTRAORDINARY CARE is synonymous with greatest care, utmost care, highest degree of care. 54 Ill. 19. See CARE; DILIGENCE; NEGLIGENCE.

EXTRAPAROCHIAL. Out of a parish; not within the bounds or limits of any parish. 1 Bl. Comm. 113, 284.

EXTRAVAGANTES. In canon law. Those decretal epistles which were published after the Clementines. They were so called because at first they were not digested or arranged with the other papal constitutions, but seemed to be, as it were, detached from the canon law. They continued to be called by the same name when they were afterwards inserted in the body of the canon law. The first extravagantes are those of Pope John XXII., successor of Clement V. The last collection was brought down to the year 1483, and was called the "Common Extravagantes," notwithstanding that they were likewise incorporated with the rest of the canon law. Enc. Lond.

EXTREME HAZARD. To constitute extreme hazard, the situation of a vessel must be such that there is imminent danger of her being lost, notwithstanding all the means that can be applied to get her off. 1 Conn. 421.

EXTREMIS. When a person is sick beyond the hope of recovery, and near death, he is said to be *in extremis.*

Extremis probatis, præsumuntur media. Extremes being proved, intermediate things are presumed. Tray. Lat. Max. 207.

EXTRINSIC. Foreign; from outside sources; *dehors.*

EXTUMÆ. In old records. Relics. Cowell.

EXUERE PATRIAM. To throw off or renounce one's country or native allegiance; to *expatriate* one's self. Phillim. Dom. 18.

EXULARE. In old English law. To exile or banish. *Nullus liber homo, exuletur, nisi,* etc., no freeman shall be exiled, unless, etc. Magna Charta, c. 29; 2 Inst. 47.

EXUPERARE. To overcome; to apprehend or take. Leg. Edm. c. 2.

EY. A watery place; water. Co. Litt. 6.

EYDE. Aid; assistance; relief. A subsidy.

EYE-WITNESS. One who saw the act, fact, or transaction to which he testifies. Distinguished from an ear-witness, (*auritus.*)

EYOTT. A small island arising in a river. Fleta, l. 3, c. 2, § b; Bract. l. 2, c. 2.

EYRE. Justices in eyre were judges commissioned in Anglo-Norman times in England to travel systematically through the kingdom, once in seven years, holding courts in specified places for the trial of certain descriptions of causes.

EYRER. L. Fr. To travel or journey; to go about or itinerate. Britt. c. 2.

EZARDAR. In Hindu law. A farmer or renter of land in the districts of Hindoostan.

F.

F. In old English criminal law, this letter was branded upon felons upon their being admitted to clergy; as also upon those convicted of fights or frays, or of falsity. Jacob; Cowell; 2 Reeve, Eng. Law, 392; 4 Reeve, Eng. Law, 485.

F. O. B. Free on board. A term frequently inserted, in England, in contracts for the sale of goods to be conveyed by ship, meaning that the cost of shipping will be paid by the buyer. When goods are so sold in London the buyer is considered as the shipper, and the goods when shipped are at his risk. Wharton.

FABRIC LANDS. In English law. Lands given towards the maintenance, rebuilding, or repairing of cathedral and other churches. Cowell; Blount.

FABRICA. In old English law. The making or coining of money.

FABRICARE. Lat. To make. Used in old English law of a lawful coining, and also of an unlawful making or counterfeiting of coin. See 1 Salk. 342.

FABRICATE. To fabricate evidence is to arrange or manufacture circumstances or *indicia*, after the fact committed, with the purpose of using them as evidence, and of deceitfully making them appear as if accidental or undesigned; to devise falsely or contrive by artifice with the intention to deceive. Such evidence may be wholly forged and artificial, or it may consist in so warping and distorting real facts as to create an erroneous impression in the minds of those who observe them and then presenting such impression as true and genuine.

FABRICATED EVIDENCE. Evidence manufactured or arranged after the fact, and either wholly false or else warped and discolored by artifice and contrivance with a deceitful intent. See FABRICATE.

FABRICATED FACT. In the law of evidence. A fact existing only in statement, without any foundation in truth. An actual or genuine fact to which a false appearance has been designedly given; a physical object placed in a false connection with another, or with a person on whom it is designed to cast suspicion. See FABRICATE.

FABULA. In old European law. A contract or formal agreement; but particularly used in the Lombardic and Visigothic laws to denote a marriage contract or a will.

FAC SIMILE. An exact copy, preserving all the marks of the original.

FAC SIMILE PROBATE. In England, where the construction of a will may be affected by the appearance of the original paper, the court will order the probate to pass in *fac simile*, as it may possibly help to show the meaning of the testator. 1 Williams, Ex'rs, (7th Ed.) 331, 386, 566.

FACE. The face of an instrument is that which is shown by the mere language employed, without any explanation, modification, or addition from extrinsic facts or evidence. Thus, if the express terms of the paper disclose a fatal legal defect, it is said to be "void on its face."

Regarded as an evidence of debt, the face of an instrument is the principal sum which it expresses to be due or payable, without any additions in the way of interest or costs. Thus, the expression "the face of a judgment" means the sum for which the judgment was rendered, excluding the interest accrued thereon. 32 Iowa, 265.

FACERE. Lat. To do; to make. Thus, *facere defaltam*, to make default; *facere duellum*, to make the duel, or make or do battle; *facere finem*, to make or pay a fine; *facere legem*, to make one's law; *facere sacramentum*, to make oath.

FACIAS. That you cause. Occurring in the phrases "*scire facias*," (that you cause to know,) "*fieri facias*," (that you cause to be made,) etc.

FACIENDO. In doing or paying; in some activity.

FACIES. Lat. The face or countenance; the exterior appearance or view; hence, contemplation or study of a thing on its external or apparent side. Thus, *prima facie* means at the first inspection, on a preliminary or exterior scrutiny. When we speak of a "*prima facie* case." we mean one which, on its own showing, on a first examination, or without investigating any alleged defenses, is apparently good and maintainable.

FACILE. In Scotch law. Easily persuaded; easily imposed upon. Bell.

FACILITIES. This name was formerly given to certain notes of some of the banks in the state of Connecticut, which were made payable in two years after the close of the war of 1812. 14 Mass. 322.

FACILITY. In Scotch law. Pliancy of disposition. Bell.

Facinus quos inquinat æquat. Guilt makes equal those whom it stains.

FACIO UT DES. (Lat. I do that you may give.) A species of contract in the civil law (being one of the *innominate* contracts) which occurs when a man agrees to perform anything for a price either specifically mentioned or left to the determination of the law to set a value on it; as when a servant hires himself to his master for certain wages or an agreed sum of money. 2 Bl. Comm. 445.

FACIO UT FACIAS. (Lat. I do that you may do.) A species of contract in the civil law (being one of the *innominate* contracts) which occurs when I agree with a man to do his work for him if he will do mine for me; or if two persons agree to marry together, or to do any other positive acts on both sides; or it may be to forbear on one side in consideration of something done on the other. 2 Bl. Comm. 444.

FACT. A thing done; an action performed or an incident transpiring; an event or circumstance; an actual occurrence.

In the earlier days of the law "fact" was used almost exclusively in the sense of "action" or "deed;" but, although this usage survives, in some such phrases as "accessary before the fact," it has now acquired the broader meaning given above.

A fact is either a state of things, that is, an existence, or a motion, that is, an event. 1 Benth. Jud. Ev. 48.

In the law of evidence. A circumstance, event, or occurrence as it actually takes or took place; a physical object or appearance, as it actually exists or existed. An actual and absolute reality, as distinguished from mere supposition or opinion; a truth, as distinguished from fiction or error. Burrill, Circ. Ev. 218.

"Fact" is very frequently used in opposition or contrast to "law." Thus, questions of *fact* are for the jury; questions of *law* for the court. So an attorney *at law* is an officer of the courts of justice; an attorney *in fact* is appointed by the written authorization of a principal to manage business affairs usually not professional. Fraud *in fact* consists in an actual intention to defraud, carried into effect; while fraud imputed by *law* arises from the man's conduct in its necessary relations and consequences.

The word is much used in phrases which contrast it with law. Law is a principle; fact is an event. Law is conceived; fact is actual. Law is a rule of duty; fact is that which has been according to or in contravention of the rule. The distinction is well illustrated in the rule that the existence of foreign laws is matter of fact. Within the territory of its jurisdiction, law operates as an obligatory rule which judges must recognize and enforce; but, in a tribunal outside that jurisdiction, it loses its obligatory force and its claim to judicial notice. The fact that it exists, if important to the rights of parties, must be alleged and proved the same as the actual existence of any other institution. Abbott.

The terms "fact" and "truth" are often used in common parlance as synonymous, but, as employed in reference to pleading, they are widely different. A fact in pleading is a circumstance, act, event, or incident; a truth is the legal principle which declares or governs the facts and their operative effect. Admitting the facts stated in a complaint, the truth may be that the plaintiff is not entitled, upon the face of his complaint, to what he claims. The mode in which a defendant sets up that truth for his protection is a demurrer. 4 E. D. Smith, 37.

As to the classification of facts, see DISPOSITIVE FACTS.

FACTA. In old English law. Deeds. *Facta armorum*, deeds or feats of arms; that is, jousts or tournaments. Cowell.

Facts. *Facta et casus*, facts and cases. Bract. fol. 1*b*.

Facta sunt potentiora verbis. Deeds are more powerful than words.

Facta tenent multa quæ fieri prohibentur. 12 Coke, 124. Deeds contain many things which are prohibited to be done.

FACTIO TESTAMENTI. In the civil law. The right, power, or capacity of making a will; called "*factio activa*." Inst. 2, 10, 6.

The right or capacity of taking by will; called "*factio passiva*." Inst. 2, 10, 6.

FACTO. In fact; by an act; by the act or fact. *Ipso facto*, by the act itself; by the mere effect of a fact, without anything superadded, or any proceeding upon it to give it effect. 3 Kent, Comm. 55, 58.

FACTOR. A commercial agent, employed by a principal to sell merchandise consigned to him for that purpose, for and in behalf of the principal, but usually in his own name, being intrusted with the possession and control of the goods, and being remunerated by a commission, commonly called "factorage."

A factor is an agent who, in the pursuit of an independent calling, is employed by another to sell property for him, and is vested by the latter with the possession or control of the property, or authorized to receive payment therefor from the purchaser. Civil Code Cal. § 2026; Civil Code Dak. § 1168.

When the agent accompanies the ship, taking a cargo aboard, and it is consigned to him for sale, and he is to purchase a return cargo out of the proceeds, such agent is properly called a "factor." He is, however, usually known by the name of a "supercargo." Beaw. Lex. Merc. 44, 47; Liverm. Ag. 69, 70; 1 Domat, b. 1, t. 16, § 3, art. 2.

Factors are called "domestic" or "foreign," according as they reside in the same country with the principal or in a different country.

A "factor" is distinguished from a "broker" by being intrusted with the possession, management, and control of the goods, and by being authorized to buy and sell in his own name, as well as in that of his principal. Russ. Fact. 4; Story, Ag. § 33; 2 Steph. Comm. 127; 2 Barn. & Ald. 137, 143; 2 Kent, Comm. 622, note.

The term is used in some of the states to denote the person who is elsewhere called "garnishee" or "trustee." See FACTORIZING PROCESS.

FACTORAGE. The allowance or commission paid to a factor by his principal. Russ. Fact. 1; Tomlins.

FACTORIZING PROCESS. In American law. A process by which the effects of a debtor are attached in the hands of a third person. A term peculiar to the practice in Vermont and Connecticut. Otherwise termed "trustee process" and "garnishment." Drake, Attachm. § 451.

FACTORS' ACTS. The name given to several English statutes (6 Geo. IV. c. 94; 5 & 6 Vict. c. 39; 40 & 41 Vict. c. 39) by which a factor is enabled to make a valid pledge of the goods, or of any part thereof, to one who believes him to be the *bona fide* owner of the goods.

FACTORY. In English law. The term includes all buildings and premises wherein, or within the close or curtilage of which, steam, water, or any mechanical power is used to move or work any machinery employed in preparing, manufacturing, or finishing cotton, wool, hair, silk, flax, hemp, jute, or tow. So defined by the statute 7 Vict. c. 15, § 73. By later acts this definition has been extended to various other manufacturing places. Mozley & Whitley.

Also a place where a considerable number of factors reside, in order to negotiate for their masters or employers. Enc. Brit.

In American law. The word "factory" does not necessarily mean a single building or edifice, but may apply to several, where they are used in connection with each other, for a common purpose, and stand together in the same inclosure. 45 Ill. 303.

In Scotch law. This name is given to a species of contract or employment which falls under the general designation of "agency," but which partakes both of the nature of a mandate and of a bailment of the kind called "*locatio ad operandum.*" 1 Bell, Comm. 259.

"FACTORY PRICES." The prices at which goods may be bought at the factories, as distinguished from the prices of goods bought in the market after they have passed into the hands of third persons or shop-keepers. 2 Mason, 90.

Facts cannot lie. 18 How. State Tr. 1187; 17 How. State Tr. 1430.

FACTUM. Lat. In old English law. A deed; a person's act and deed; anything stated or made certain; a sealed instrument; a deed of conveyance.

A fact; a circumstance; particularly a fact in evidence. Bract. fol. 1*b*.

In testamentary law. The execution or due execution of a will. The *factum* of an instrument means not barely the signing of it, and the formal publication or delivery, but proof that the party well knew and understood the contents thereof, and did give, will, dispose, and do, in all things, as in the said will is contained. 11 How. 354.

In the civil law. Fact; a fact; a matter of fact, as distinguished from a matter of law. Dig. 41, 2, 1, 3.

In French law. A memoir which contains concisely set down the fact on which a contest has happened, the means on which a party founds his pretensions, with the refutation of the means of the adverse party. Vicat.

In old European law. A portion or allotment of land. Spelman.

Factum a judice quod ad ejus officium non spectat non ratum est. An action of a judge which relates not to his office is of no force. Dig. 50, 17, 170; 10 Coke, 76.

Factum cuique suum non adversario, nocere debet. Dig. 50, 17, 155. A party's own act should prejudice himself, not his adversary.

Factum infectum fieri nequit. A thing done cannot be undone. 1 Kames, Eq. 96, 259.

FACTUM JURIDICUM. A juridical fact. Denotes one of the factors or elements constituting an obligation.

Factum negantis nulla probatio sit. Cod. 4, 19, 23. There is no proof incumbent upon him who denies a fact.

"Factum" non dicitur quod non perseverat. 5 Coke, 96. That is not called a "deed" which does not continue operative.

FACTUM PROBANDUM. Lat. In the law of evidence. The fact to be proved; a fact which is in issue, and to which evidence is to be directed. 1 Greenl. Ev. § 13.

FACTUM PROBANS. A probative or evidentiary fact; a subsidiary or connected fact tending to prove the principal fact in issue; a piece of circumstantial evidence.

Factum unius alteri noceri non debet. Co. Litt. 152. The deed of one should not hurt another.

Facultas probationum non est angustanda. The power of proofs [right of offering or giving testimony] is not to be narrowed. 4 Inst. 279.

FACULTIES, COURT OF. In English ecclesiastical law. A jurisdiction or tribunal belonging to the archbishop. It does not hold pleas in any suits, but creates rights to pews, monuments, and particular places, and modes of burial. It has also various powers under 25 Hen. VIII. c. 21, in granting licenses of different descriptions, as a license to marry, a faculty to erect an organ in a parish church, to level a church-yard, to remove bodies previously buried. 4 Inst. 337.

FACULTY. In ecclesiastical law. A license or authority; a privilege granted by the ordinary to a man by favor and indulgence to do that which by law he may not do; *e. g.*, to marry without banns, to erect a monument in a church, etc. Termes de la Ley.

In Scotch law. A power founded on consent, as distinguished from a power founded on property. 2 Kames, Eq. 265.

FACULTY OF A COLLEGE. The corps of professors, instructors, tutors, and lecturers. To be distinguished from the board of trustees, who constitute the corporation.

FACULTY OF ADVOCATES. The college or society of advocates in Scotland.

FADERFIUM. In old English law. A marriage gift coming from the father or brother of the bride.

FÆDER-FEOH. In old English law. The portion brought by a wife to her husband, and which reverted to a widow, in case the heir of her deceased husband refused his consent to her second marriage; *i. e.*, it reverted to her family in case she returned to them. Wharton.

FÆSTING-MEN. Approved men who were strong-armed; *habentes homines* or rich men, men of substance; pledges or bondsmen, who, by Saxon custom, were bound to answer for each other's good behavior. Cowell; Du Cange.

FAGGOT. A badge worn in popish times by persons who had recanted and abjured what was then adjudged to be heresy, as an emblem of what they had merited. Cowell.

FAGGOT VOTES. A faggot vote is where a man is formally possessed of a right to vote for members of parliament, without possessing the substance which the vote should represent; as if he is enabled to buy a property, and at the same moment mortgage it to its full value for the mere sake of the vote. Such a vote is called a "faggot vote." See 7 & 8 Wm. III. c. 25, § 7. Wharton.

FAIDA. In Saxon law. Malice; open and deadly hostility; deadly feud. The word designated the enmity between the family of a murdered man and that of his murderer, which was recognized, among the Teutonic peoples, as justification for vengeance taken by any one of the former upon any one of the latter.

FAIL. The difference between "fail" and "refuse" is that the latter involves an act of the will, while the former may be an act of inevitable necessity. 9 Wheat. 344.

FAILING OF RECORD. When an action is brought against a person who alleges in his plea matter of record in bar of the action, and avers to prove it by the record, but the plaintiff saith *nul tiel record*, viz., denies there is any such record, upon which the defendant has a day given him by the court to bring it in, if he fail to do it, then he is said to fail of his record, and the plaintiff is entitled to sign judgment. Termes de la Ley.

FAILLITE. In French law. Bankruptcy; failure; the situation of a debtor who finds himself unable to fulfill his engagements. Code de Com. arts. 442, 580; Civil Code La. art. 3522.

FAILURE. In legal parlance, the neglect of any duty may be described as a "failure." But in the language of the business world this term, applied to a merchant or mercantile concern, means an inability to pay his or their debts, from insolvency, and the word must be regarded as synonymous with "insolvency." 1 Rice, 140.

According to other authorities, "failure," in this sense, means a failure to meet current obligations at maturity. Insolvency looks to the ability to pay; failure to the fact of payment. Failure is the outward act which stands for evidence of insolvency. 13 S. C. 226. See, also, 10 Blatchf. 256; 24 Conn. 310.

FAILURE OF CONSIDERATION. The want or failure of a consideration sufficient to support a note, contract, or conveyance. It may be either partial or entire.

FAILURE OF EVIDENCE. Judicially speaking, a total "failure of evidence" means not only the utter absence of all evidence, but it also means a failure to offer proof, either positive or inferential, to establish one or more of the many facts, the establishment of *all* of which is indispensable to the finding of the issue for the plaintiff. 7 Gill & J. 28.

FAILURE OF ISSUE. The failure at a fixed time, or the total extinction, of issue to take an estate limited over by an executory devise.

A definite failure of issue is when a precise time is fixed by the will for the failure of issue, as in the case where there is a devise to one, but if he dies without issue or lawful issue living at the time of his death, etc. An indefinite failure of issue is the period when the issue or descendants of the first taker shall become extinct, and when there is no longer any issue of the issue of the grantee, without reference to any particular time or any particular event. 50 Ind. 546.

An executory devise to take effect on an indefinite failure of issue is void for remoteness, and hence courts are astute to devise some construction which shall restrain the failure of issue to the term of limitation allowed. 40 Pa. St. 18; 2 Redf. Wills, 276, note.

FAILURE OF JUSTICE. The defeat of a particular right, or the failure of reparation for a particular wrong, from the lack of a legal remedy for the enforcement of the one or the redress of the other.

FAILURE OF RECORD. Failure of the defendant to produce a record which he has alleged and relied on in his plea.

FAILURE OF TITLE. The inability or failure of a vendor to make good title to the whole or a part of the property which he has contracted to sell.

FAILURE OF TRUST. The lapsing or non-efficiency of a proposed trust, by reason of the defect or insufficiency of the deed or instrument creating it, or on account of illegality, indefiniteness, or other legal impediment.

FAINT (or FEIGNED) ACTION. In old English practice. An action was so called where the party bringing it had no title to recover, although the words of the writ were true; a *false* action was properly where the words of the writ were false. Litt. § 689; Co. Litt. 361.

FAINT PLEADER. A fraudulent, false, or collusive manner of pleading to the deception of a third person.

FAIR, *n.* In English law. A greater species of market; a privileged market. It is an incorporeal hereditament, granted by royal patent, or established by prescription presupposing a grant from the crown.

In the earlier English law, the franchise to hold a fair conferred certain important privileges; and fairs, as legally recognized institutions, possessed distinctive legal characteristics. Most of these privileges and characteristics, however, are now obsolete. In America, fairs, in the ancient technical sense, are unknown, and, in the modern and popular sense, they are entirely voluntary and non-legal, and transactions arising in or in connection with them are subject to the ordinary rules governing sales, etc.

FAIR, *adj.* Just; equitable; even-handed; equal, as between conflicting interests.

FAIR-PLAY MEN. A local irregular tribunal which existed in Pennsylvania about the year 1769, as to which see Serg. Land Laws Pa. 77; 2 Smith, Laws Pa. 195.

FAIR PLEADER. See BEAUPLEADER.

FAIRLY. Justly; rightly; equitably. With substantial correctness.

"Fairly" is not synonymous with "truly," and "truly" should not be substituted for it in a commissioner's oath to take testimony fairly. Language may be truly, yet unfairly, reported; that is, an answer may be truly written down, yet in a manner conveying a different meaning from that intended and conveyed. And language may be fairly reported, yet not in accordance with strict truth. 17 N. J. Eq. 234.

FAIT. L. Fr. Anything done. A deed; act; fact.

A deed lawfully executed. Com. Dig.

Feme de fait. A wife *de facto.*

FAIT ENROLLE. A deed enrolled, as a bargain and sale of freeholds. 1 Keb. 568.

FAIT JURIDIQUE. In French law. A juridical fact. One of the factors or elements constitutive of an obligation.

FAITH. 1. Confidence; credit; reliance. Thus, an act may be said to be done "on the faith" of certain representations.

2. Belief; credence; trust. Thus, the constitution provides that "full faith and credit" shall be given to the judgments of each state in the courts of the others.

3. Purpose; intent; sincerity; state of knowledge or design. This is the meaning of the word in the phrases "good faith" and "bad faith."

In Scotch law. A solemn pledge; an oath. "To make faith" is to swear, with the right hand uplifted, that one will declare the truth. 1 Forb. Inst. pt. 4, p. 235.

FAITOURS. Idle persons; idle livers; vagabonds. Cowell; Blount.

FALANG. In old English law. A jacket or close coat. Blount.

FALCARE. In old English law. To mow. *Falcare prata,* to mow or cut grass in meadows laid in for hay. A customary service to the lord by his inferior tenants.

Jus falcandi, the right of cutting wood. Bract. fol. 231.

Falcata, grass fresh mown, and laid in swaths.

Falcatio, a mowing. Bract. fols. 35*b*, 230.

Falcator, a mower; a servile tenant who performed the labor of mowing.

Falcatura, a day's mowing.

FALCIDIA. In Spanish law. The Falcidian portion; the portion of an inheritance which could not be legally bequeathed away from the heir, viz., one-fourth.

FALCIDIAN LAW. In Roman law. A law on the subject of testamentary disposition, enacted by the people in the year of Rome 714, on the proposition of the tribune Falcidius. By this law, the testator's right to burden his estate with legacies was subjected to an important restriction. It prescribed that no one could bequeath more than three-fourths of his property in legacies, and that the heir should have at least one-fourth of the estate, and that, should the testator violate this prescript, the heir may have the right to make a proportional deduction from each legatee, so far as necessary. Mackeld. Rom. Law, § 771; Inst. 2, 22.

FALCIDIAN PORTION. That portion of a testator's estate which, by the Falcidian law, was required to be left to the heir, amounting to at least one-fourth.

FALD, or FALDA. A sheep-fold. Cowell.

FALDA. Span. In Spanish law. The slope or skirt of a hill. 2 Wall. 673.

FALDÆ CURSUS. In old English law. A fold-course; the course (going or taking about) of a fold. Spelman.

A sheep walk, or feed for sheep. 2 Vent. 139.

FALDAGE. The privilege which anciently several lords reserved to themselves of setting up folds for sheep in any fields within their manors, the better to manure them, and this not only with their own but their tenants' sheep. Called, variously, "*secta faldare,*" "fold-course," "free-fold," "*faldagii.*" Cowell; Spelman.

FALDATA. In old English law. A flock or fold of sheep. Cowell.

FALDFEY. Sax. A fee or rent paid by a tenant to his lord for leave to fold his sheep on his own ground. Blount.

FALDISDORY. In ecclesiastical law. The bishop's seat or throne within the chancel.

FALDSOCA. Sax. The liberty or privilege of foldage.

FALDSTOOL. A place at the south side of the altar at which the sovereign kneels at his coronation. Wharton.

FALDWORTH. In Saxon law. A person of age that he may be reckoned of some decennary. Du Fresne.

FALERÆ. In old English law. The tackle and furniture of a cart or wain. Blount.

FALESIA. In old English law. A hill or down by the sea-side. Co. Litt. 5*b*; Domesday.

FALK-LAND. See FOLC-LAND.

FALL. In Scotch law. To lose. To fall from a right is to lose or forfeit it. 1 Kames, Eq. 228.

FALL OF LAND. In English law. A quantity of land six ells square superficial measure.

FALLO. In Spanish law. The final decree or judgment given in a controversy at law.

FALLOW-LAND. Land plowed, but not sown, and left uncultivated for a time after successive crops.

FALLUM. In old English law. An unexplained term for some particular kind of land. Cowell.

FALSA DEMONSTRATIO. In the civil law. False designation; erroneous description of a person or thing in a written instrument. Inst. 2, 20, 30.

Falsa demonstratio non nocet, cum de corpore (persona) constat. False description does not injure or vitiate, provided the thing or person intended has once been sufficiently described. Mere false description does not make an instrument inoperative. Broom, Max. 629; 6 Term, 676; 11 Mees. & W. 189; 2 Story, 291.

Falsa demonstratione legatum non perimi. A bequest is not rendered void by an erroneous description. Inst. 2, 20, 30; Broom, Max. 645.

Falsa grammatica non vitiat concessionem. False or bad grammar does not vitiate a grant. Shep. Touch. 55; 9 Coke, 48*a*. Neither false Latin nor false English will make a deed void when the intent of the parties doth plainly appear. Shep. Touch. 87.

FALSA MONETA. In the civil law. False or counterfeit money. Cod. 9, 24.

Falsa orthographia non vitiat chartam, [concessionem.] False spelling does not vitiate a deed. Shep. Touch. 55, 87; 9 Coke, 48*a;* Wing. Max. 19.

FALSARE. In old English law. To counterfeit. *Quia falsavit sigillum*, because he counterfeited the seal. Bract. fol. 276*b*.

FALSARIUS. A counterfeiter. Townsh. Pl. 260.

FALSE. Untrue; erroneous; deceitful; contrived or calculated to deceive and injure. Unlawful.

In law, this word means something more than untrue; it means something designedly untrue and deceitful, and implies an intention to perpetrate some treachery or fraud. 18 U. C. C. P. 19; 7 Amer. & Eng. Enc. Law, 661.

FALSE ACTION. See FEIGNED ACTION.

FALSE CHARACTER. Personating the master or mistress of a servant, or any representative of such master or mistress, and giving a false character to the servant, is an offense punishable in England with a fine of £20. St. 32 Geo. III. c. 56.

FALSE CLAIM, in the forest law, was where a man claimed more than his due, and was amerced and punished for the same. Manw. c. 25; Tomlins.

FALSE FACT. In the law of evidence. A feigned, simulated, or fabricated fact; a fact not founded in truth, but existing only in assertion; the deceitful semblance of a fact.

FALSE IMPRISONMENT. The unlawful arrest or detention of a person without warrant, or by an illegal warrant, or a warrant illegally executed, and either in a prison or a place used temporarily for that purpose, or by force and constraint without confinement.

False imprisonment consists in the unlawful detention of the person of another, for any length of time, whereby he is deprived of his personal liberty. Code Ga. 1882, § 2990; Pen. Code Cal. § 236.

The term is also used as the name of the action which lies for this species of injury. 3 Bl. Comm. 138.

FALSE JUDGMENT. In old English law. A writ which lay when a false judgment had been pronounced in a court not of record, as a county court, court baron, etc. Fitzh. Nat. Brev. 17, 18.

In old French law. The defeated party in a suit had the privilege of accusing the judges of pronouncing a false or corrupt judgment, whereupon the issue was determined by his challenging them to the combat or *duellum*. This was called the "appeal of false judgment." Montesq. Esprit des Lois, liv. 28, c. 27.

FALSE LATIN. When law proceedings were written in Latin, if a word were significant though not good Latin, yet an indictment, declaration, or fine should not be made void by it; but if the word were not Latin, nor allowed by the law, and it were in a material point, it made the whole vicious. (5 Coke, 121; 2 Nels. 830.) Wharton.

FALSE LIGHTS AND SIGNALS. Lights and signals falsely and maliciously displayed for the purpose of bringing a vessel into danger.

FALSE NEWS. Spreading false news, whereby discord may grow between the queen of England and her people, or the great men of the realm, or which may produce other mischiefs, still seems to be a misdemeanor, under St. 3 Edw. I. c. 34. Steph. Cr. Dig. § 95.

FALSE OATH. See PERJURY.

FALSE PERSONATION. The criminal offense of falsely representing some other person and acting in the character thus unlawfully assumed, in order to deceive others, and thereby gain some profit or advantage, or enjoy some right or privilege belonging to the one so personated, or subject him to some expense, charge, or liability. See 4 Steph. Comm. 181, 290.

FALSE PLEA. See SHAM PLEA.

FALSE PRETENSES. In criminal law. False representations and statements, made with a fraudulent design to obtain money, goods, wares, or merchandise, with intent to cheat. 2 Bouv. Inst. no. 2308.

A representation of some fact or circumstance, calculated to mislead, which is not true. 19 Pick. 184.

False statements or representations made with intent to defraud, for the purpose of obtaining money or property.

A pretense is the holding out or offering to others something false and feigned. This may be done either by words or actions, which amount to false representations. In fact, false representations are inseparable from the idea of a pretense. Without a representation which is false there can be no pretense. 43 Iowa, 132.

FALSE REPRESENTATION. See FRAUD; DECEIT.

FALSE RETURN. A return to a writ, in which the officer charged with it falsely reports that he served it, when he did not, or makes some other false or incorrect statement, whereby injury results to a person interested.

FALSE SWEARING. The misdemeanor committed in English law by a person who swears falsely before any person authorized to administer an oath upon a matter of public concern, under such circumstances that the false swearing would have amounted to perjury if committed in a judicial proceeding; as where a person makes a false affidavit under the bills of sale acts. Steph. Cr. Dig. p. 84.

FALSE TOKEN. In criminal law. A false document or sign of the existence of a fact, used with intent to defraud, for the purpose of obtaining money or property.

FALSE VERDICT. An untrue verdict. Formerly, if a jury gave a false verdict, the party injured by it might sue out and prosecute a writ of attaint against them, either at common law or on the statute 11 Hen. VII. c. 24, at his election, for the purpose of reversing the judgment and punishing the jury for their verdict; but not where the jury erred merely in point of law, if they found according to the judge's direction. The practice of setting aside verdicts and granting new trials, however, so superseded the use of attaints that there is no instance of one to be found in the books of reports later than in the time of Elizabeth, and it was altogether abolished by 6 Geo. IV. c. 50, § 60. Wharton.

FALSE WEIGHTS. False weights and measures are such as do not comply with the standard prescribed by the state or government, or with the custom prevailing in the place and business in which they are used. 7 Amer. & Eng. Enc. Law, 796.

FALSEDAD. In Spanish law. Falsity; an alteration of the truth. Las Partidas, pt. 3, tit. 26, l. 1.

Deception; fraud. Id. pt. 3, tit. 32, l. 21.

FALSEHOOD. A statement or assertion known to be untrue, and intended to deceive. A willful act or declaration contrary to the truth. 51 N. H. 207.

In Scotch law. A fraudulent imitation or suppression of truth, to the prejudice of another. Bell. "Something used and published falsely." An old Scottish *nomen juris*. "Falsehood is undoubtedly a nominate crime, so much so that Sir George Mackenzie and our older lawyers used no other term for the falsification of writs, and the name 'forgery' has been of modern introduction." "If there is any distinction to be made between 'forgery' and 'falsehood,' I would consider the latter to be more comprehensive than the former." 2 Broun, 77, 78.

FALSI CRIMEN. Fraudulent subornation or concealment, with design to darken or hide the truth, and make things appear otherwise than they are. It is committed (1) by words, as when a witness swears falsely; (2) by writing, as when a person antedates a contract; (3) by deed, as selling by false weights and measures. Wharton. See CRIMEN FALSI.

FALSIFICATION. In equity practice. The showing an item in the debit of an account to be either wholly false or in some part erroneous. 1 Story, Eq. Jur. § 525.

FALSIFY. To disprove; to prove to be false or erroneous; to avoid or defeat; spoken of verdicts, appeals, etc.

To counterfeit or forge; to make something false; to give a false appearance to anything.

In equity practice. To show, in accounting before a master in chancery, that a charge has been inserted which is wrong; that is, either wholly false or in some part erroneous. Pull. Accts. 162; 1 Story, Eq. Jur. § 525.

FALSIFYING A RECORD. A high offense against public justice, punishable in England by 24 & 25 Vict. c. 98, §§ 27, 28, and in the United States, generally, by statute.

FALSING. In Scotch law. False making; forgery. "Falsing of *evidentis*." 1 Pitc. Crim. Tr. pt. 1, p. 85.

Making or proving false.

FALSING OF DOOMS. In Scotch law. The proving the injustice, *falsity*, or error of the *doom* or sentence of a court. Tomlins; Jacob. The reversal of a sentence or judgment. Skene. An appeal. Bell.

FALSO RETORNO BREVIUM. A writ which formerly lay against the sheriff who had execution of process for false returning of writs. Reg. Jud. 43*b*.

FALSONARIUS. A forger; a counterfeiter. Hov. 424.

FALSUM. Lat. In the civil law. A false or forged thing; a fraudulent simulation; a fraudulent counterfeit or imitation, such as a forged signature or instrument. Also falsification, which may be either by falsehood, concealment of the truth, or fraudulent alteration, as by cutting out or erasing part of a writing.

FALSUS. False; fraudulent; erroneous. Deceitful; mistaken.

Falsus in uno, falsus in omnibus. False in one thing, false in everything. Where a party is clearly shown to have embezzled one article of property, it is a ground of presumption that he may have embezzled others also. 1 Sumn. 329, 356; 7 Wheat. 338.

FAMA. Fame; character; reputation; report of common opinion.

Fama, fides et oculus non patiuntur ludum. 3 Bulst. 226. Fame, faith, and eyesight do not suffer a cheat.

Fama, quæ suspicionem inducit, oriri debet apud bonos et graves, non quidem malevolos et maledicos, sed providas et fide dignas personas, non semel sed sæpius, quia clamor minuit et defamatio manifestat. 2 Inst. 52. Report, which induces suspicion, ought to arise from good and grave men; not, indeed, from malevolent and malicious men, but from cautious and credible persons; not only once, but frequently; for clamor diminishes, and defamation manifests.

FAMACIDE. A killer of reputation; a slanderer.

FAMILIA. **In Roman law.** A household; a family. On the composition of the Roman family, see AGNATI; COGNATI; and see Mackeld. Rom. Law, § 144.

Family right; the right or *status* of being the head of a family, or of exercising the *patria potestas* over others. This could belong only to a Roman citizen who was a "man in his own right," (*homo sui juris*.) Mackeld. Rom. Law, §§ 133, 144.

In old English law. A household; the body of household servants; a quantity of land, otherwise called "*mansa*," sufficient to maintain one family.

In Spanish law. A family, which might consist of domestics or servants. It seems that a single person owning negroes was the "head of a family," within the meaning of the colonization laws of Coahuila and Texas. 9 Tex. 156.

FAMILIÆ EMPTOR. In Roman law. An intermediate person who purchased the aggregate inheritance when sold *per æs et* *libram*, in the process of making a will under the Twelve Tables. This purchaser was merely a man of straw, transmitting the inheritance to the *hæres* proper. Brown.

FAMILIÆ ERCISCUNDÆ. In Roman law. An action for the partition of the aggregate succession of a *familia*, where that devolved upon *co-hæredes*. It was also applicable to enforce a contribution towards the necessary expenses incurred on the *familia*. See Mackeld. Rom. Law, § 499.

FAMILIARES REGIS. Persons of the king's household. The ancient title of the "six clerks" of chancery in England. Crabb, Com. Law, 184; 2 Reeve, Eng. Law, 249, 251.

FAMILY. A family comprises a father, mother, and children. In a wider sense, it may include domestic servants; all who live in one house under one head. In a still broader sense, a group of blood-relatives; all the relations who descend from a common ancestor, or who spring from a common root. See Civil Code La. art. 3522, no. 16; 9 Ves. 323.

A husband and wife living together may constitute a "family," within the meaning of that word as used in a homestead law. (Fla.) 7 South. Rep. 140.

"Family," in its origin, meant "servants;" but, in its more modern and comprehensive meaning, it signifies a collective body of persons living together in one house, or within the curtilage, in legal phrase. 31 Tex. 677.

"Family" may mean children, wife and children, blood-relatives, or the members of the domestic circle, according to the connection in which the word is used. 11 Paige, 159.

"Family," in popular acceptation, includes parents, children, and servants,—all whose domicile or home is ordinarily in the same house and under the same management and head. In a statute providing that to gain a settlement in a town one must have "supported himself and his family therein" for six years, it includes the individuals whom it was the right of the head to control, and his duty to support. The wife is a member of the family, within such an enactment. 31 Conn. 326.

FAMILY ARRANGEMENT. A term denoting an agreement between a father and his children, or between the heirs of a deceased father, to dispose of property, or to partition it in a different manner than that which would result if the law alone directed it, or to divide up property without administration.

In these cases, frequently, the mere relation of the parties will give effect to bargains otherwise without adequate consideration. 1 Chit. Pr. 67; 1 Turn. & R. 13.

FAMILY BIBLE. A Bible containing a record of the births, marriages, and deaths of the members of a family.

FAMILY MEETING. An institution of the laws of Louisiana, being a council of the relatives (or, if there are no relatives, of the friends) of a minor, for the purpose of advising as to his affairs and the administration of his property. The family meeting is called by order of a judge, and presided over by a justice or notary, and must consist of at least five persons, who are put under oath.

FAMOSUS. In the civil and old English law. Relating to or affecting character or reputation; defamatory; slanderous.

FAMOSUS LIBELLUS. A libelous writing. A term of the civil law denoting that species of *injuria* which corresponds nearly to libel or slander.

FANAL. Fr. In French marine law. A large lantern, fixed upon the highest part of a vessel's stern.

FANATICS. Persons pretending to be inspired, and being a general name for Quakers, Anabaptists, and all other sectaries, and factious dissenters from the Church of England. (St. 13 Car. II. c. 6.) Jacob.

FANEGA. In Spanish law. A measure of land varying in different provinces, but in the Spanish settlements in America consisting of 6,400 square varas or yards.

FAQUEER, or FAKIR. A Hindu term for a poor man, mendicant; a religious beggar.

FARANDMAN. In Scotch law. A traveler or merchant stranger. Skene.

FARDEL OF LAND. In old English law. The fourth part of a yard-land. Noy says an eighth only, because, according to him, two fardels make a nook, and four nooks a yard-land. Wharton.

FARDELLA. In old English law. A bundle or pack; a fardel. Fleta, lib. 1, c. 22, § 10.

FARDING-DEAL. The fourth part of an acre of land. Spelman.

FARE. A voyage or passage by water; also the money paid for a passage either by land or by water. Cowell.

The price of passage, or the sum paid or to be paid for carrying a passenger. 26 N. Y. 526.

FARINAGIUM. A mill; a toll of meal or flour. Jacob; Spelman.

FARLEU. Money paid by tenants in lieu of a heriot. It was often applied to the best chattel, as distinguished from *heriot*, the best beast. Cowell.

FARLINGARII. Whoremongers and adulterers.

FARM. A certain amount of provision reserved as the rent of a messuage. Spelman.

Rent generally which is reserved on a lease; when it was to be paid in money, it was called "*blanche firme*." Spelman; 2 Bl. Comm. 42.

A term, a lease of lands; a leasehold interest. 2 Bl. Comm. 17; 1 Reeve, Eng. Law, 301, note. The land itself, let to farm or rent. 2 Bl. Comm. 368.

A portion of land used for agricultural purposes, either wholly or in part. 18 Pick. 553; 2 Bin. 238.

The original meaning of the word was "rent," and by a natural transition it came to mean the land out of which the rent issued.

In old English law. A lease of other things than land, as of imposts. There were several of these, such as "the sugar farm," "the silk farm," and farms of wines and currants, called "petty farms." See 2 How. State Tr. 1197–1206.

In American law. "Farm" denotes a tract of land devoted in part, at least, to cultivation, for agricultural purposes, without reference to its extent, or to the tenure by which it is held. 2 Bin. 238.

FARM LET. Operative words in a lease, which strictly mean to let upon payment of a certain rent in farm; *i. e.*, in agricultural produce.

FARM OUT. To let for a term at a stated rental. Among the Romans the collection of revenue was farmed out, and in England taxes and tolls sometimes are.

FARMER. 1. The lessee of a farm. It is said that every lessee for life or years, although it be but of a small house and land, is called "farmer." This word implies no mystery, except it be that of husbandman. Cunningham; Cowell.

2. A husbandman or agriculturist; one who cultivates a farm, whether the land be his own or another's.

3. One who assumes the collection of the public revenues, taxes, excise, etc., for a certain commission or percentage; as a *farmer* of the revenues.

FARO. An unlawful game of cards, in which all the other players play against the banker or dealer, staking their money upon the order in which the cards will lie and be dealt from the pack. Webster.

FARRAGO LIBELLI. Lat. An ill-composed book containing a collection of miscellaneous subjects not properly associated nor scientifically arranged. Wharton.

FARRIER. One whose business is to shoe horses for all such as apply to him.

FARTHING. The fourth part of an English penny.

FARTHING OF GOLD. An ancient English coin, containing in value the fourth part of a noble.

FARYNDON INN. The ancient appellation of Serjeants' Inn, Chancery lane.

FAS. Lat. Right; justice; the divine law. 3 Bl. Comm. 2; Calvin.

FASIUS. A faggot of wood.

FAST. In Georgia, a "fast" bill of exceptions is one which may be taken in injunction suits and similar cases, at such time and in such manner as to bring the case up for review with great expedition. It must be certified within twenty days from the rendering of the decision. 66 Ga. 353.

FAST-DAY. A day of fasting and penitence, or of mortification by religious abstinence. See 1 Chit. Archb. Pr. (12th Ed.) 160, et seq.

FAST ESTATE. Real property. A term sometimes used in wills. 6 Johns. 185; 9 N. Y. 502.

FASTERMANS, or FASTING-MEN. Men in repute and substance; pledges, sureties, or bondsmen, who, according to the Saxon polity, were *fast* bound to answer for each other's peaceable behavior. Enc. Lond.

FASTI. In Roman law. Lawful. *Dies fasti*, lawful days; days on which justice could lawfully be administered by the prætor. See DIES FASTI.

Fatetur facinus qui judicium fugit. 3 Inst. 14. He who flees judgment confesses his guilt.

FATHER. The male parent. He by whom a child is begotten.

FATHER-IN-LAW. The father of one's wife or husband.

FATHOM. A nautical measure of six feet in length.

FATUA MULIER. A whore. Du Fresne.

FATUITAS. In old English law. Fatuity; idiocy. Reg. Orig. 266.

FATUITY. Mental weakness; foolishness; imbecility; idiocy.

FATUM. Lat. Fate; a superhuman power; an event or cause of loss, beyond human foresight or means of prevention.

FATUOUS PERSON. One entirely destitute of reason; *is qui omnino desipit.* Ersk. Inst. 1, 7, 48.

FATUUS. An idiot or fool. Bract. fol. 420*b*.

Foolish; absurd; indiscreet; or ill considered. *Fatuum judicium,* a foolish judgment or verdict. Applied to the verdict of a jury which, though false, was not criminally so, or did not amount to perjury. Bract. fol. 289.

Fatuus, apud jurisconsultos nostros, accipitur pro non compos mentis; et fatuus dicitur, qui omnino desipit. 4 Coke, 128. Fatuous, among our jurisconsults, is understood for a man not of right mind; and he is called "*fatuus*" who is altogether foolish.

Fatuus præsumitur qui in proprio nomine errat. A man is presumed to be simple who makes a mistake in his own name. Code, 6, 24, 14; 5 Johns. Ch. 148, 161.

FAUBOURG. In French law, and in Louisiana. A district or part of a town adjoining the principal city; a suburb. See 18 La. 286.

FAUCES TERRÆ. (Jaws of the land.) Narrow headlands and promontories, inclosing a portion or arm of the sea within them. 1 Kent, Comm. 367, and note; Hale, De Jure Mar. 10; 1 Story, 251, 259.

FAULT. In the civil law. Negligence; want of care. An improper act or omission, injurious to another, and transpiring through negligence, rashness, or ignorance.

There are in law three degrees of faults,—the gross, the slight, and the very slight fault. The *gross* fault is that which proceeds from inexcusable negligence or ignorance; it is considered as nearly equal to fraud. The *slight* fault is that want of care which a prudent man usually takes of his business. The *very slight* fault is that which is excusable, and for which no responsibility is incurred. Civil Code La. art. 3556, par. 13.

FAUTOR. In old English law. A favorer or supporter of others; an abettor. Cowell; Jacob. A partisan. One who encouraged resistance to the execution of process.

In Spanish law. Accomplice; the person who aids or assists another in the commission of a crime.

FAUX. In old English law. False; counterfeit. *Faux action,* a false action. Litt. § 688. *Faux money,* counterfeit money. St. Westm. 1, c. 15. *Faux peys,* false weights. Britt. c. 20. *Faux serement,* a false oath. St. Westm. 1, c. 38.

In French law. A falsification or fraudulent alteration or suppression of a thing by words, by writings, or by acts without either. Biret.

"*Faux* may be understood in three ways. In its most extended sense it is the alteration of truth, with or without intention; it is nearly synonymous with 'lying.' In a less extended sense, it is the alteration of truth, accompanied with fraud, *mutatio veritatis cum dolo facta.* And lastly, in a narrow, or rather the legal, sense of the word, when it is a question to know if the *faux* be a crime, it is the fraudulent alteration of the truth in those cases ascertained and punished by the law." Toullier, t. 9, n. 188.

In the civil law. The fraudulent alteration of the truth. The same with the Latin *falsum* or *crimen falsi.*

FAVOR. Bias; partiality; lenity; prejudice. See CHALLENGE.

Favorabilia in lege sunt fiscus, dos, vita, libertas. Jenk. Cent. 94. Things favorably considered in law are the treasury, dower, life, liberty.

Favorabiliores rei, potius quam actores, habentur. The condition of the defendant must be favored, rather than that of the plaintiff. In other words, *melior est conditio defendentis.* Dig. 50, 17, 125; Broom, Max. 715.

Favorabiliores sunt executiones aliis processibus quibuscunque. Co. Litt. 289. Executions are preferred to all other processes whatever.

Favores ampliandi sunt; odia restringenda. Jenk. Cent. 186. Favors are to be enlarged; things hateful restrained.

FEAL. Faithful. Tenants by knight service swore to their lords to be *feal* and *leal; i. e.*, faithful and loyal.

FEAL AND DIVOT. A right in Scotland, similar to the right of turbary in England, for fuel, etc.

FEALTY. In feudal law. Fidelity; allegiance to the feudal lord of the manor; the feudal obligation resting upon the tenant or vassal by which he was bound to be faithful and true to his lord, and render him obedience and service.

Fealty signifies fidelity, the phrase "feal and leal" meaning simply "faithful and loyal." Tenants by knights' service and also tenants in socage were required to take an oath of fealty to the king or others, their immediate lords; and fealty was one of the conditions of their tenure, the breach of which operated a forfeiture of their estates. Brown.

Although foreign jurists consider fealty and homage as convertible terms, because in some continental countries they are blended so as to form one engagement, yet they are not to be confounded in our country, for they do not imply the same thing, *homage* being the acknowledgment of tenure, and *fealty*, the vassal oath of fidelity, being the essential feudal bond, and the animating principle of a feud, without which it could not subsist. Wharton.

FEAR. Apprehension of harm.

Apprehension of harm or punishment, as exhibited by outward and visible marks of emotion. An evidence of guilt in certain cases. See Burril, Circ. Ev. 476.

FEASANCE. A doing; the doing of an act.

A making; the making of an indenture, release, or obligation. Litt. § 371; Dyer, (Fr. Ed.) 56*b*. The making of a statute. Keilw. 1*b*.

FEASANT. Doing, or making.

FEASOR. Doer; maker. *Feasors del estatute*, makers of the statute. Dyer, 3*b*.

FEASTS. Certain established festivals or holidays in the ecclesiastical calendar. These days were anciently used as the dates of legal instruments, and in England the quarter-days, for paying rent, are four feast-days. The terms of the courts, in England, before 1875, were fixed to begin on certain days determined with reference to the occurrence of four of the chief feasts.

FECIAL LAW. The nearest approach to a system of international law known to the ancient world. It was a branch of Roman jurisprudence, concerned with embassies, declarations of war, and treaties of peace. It received this name from the *feciales*, (*q. v.*,) who were charged with its administration.

FECIALES. Among the ancient Romans, that order of priests who discharged the duties of ambassadors. Subsequently their duties appear to have related more particularly to the declaring war and peace. Calvin.; 1 Kent, Comm. 6.

FEDERAL. In constitutional law. A term commonly used to express a league or compact between two or more states.

In American law. Belonging to the general government or union of the states. Founded on or organized under the constitution or laws of the United States.

The United States has been generally styled, in American political and judicial writings, a "federal government." The term has not been imposed by any specific constitutional authority, but only expresses the general sense and opinion upon the nature of the form of government. In recent years, there is observable a disposition to employ the term "national" in speaking of the government of the Union. Neither word settles anything as to the nature or powers of the government. "Federal" is somewhat more appropriate if the government is considered a union of the states; "national" is preferable if the view is adopted that the state governments and the Union are two distinct systems, each established by the people directly, one for local and the other for national purposes. See 92 U. S. 542; Abbott.

FEDERAL GOVERNMENT. The system of government administered in a state formed by the union or confederation of several independent or *quasi* independent states; also the composite state so formed.

In strict usage, there is a distinction between a *confederation* and a *federal government*. The former term denotes a league or permanent alliance between several states, each of which is fully sovereign and independent, and each of which retains its full dignity, organization, and sovereignty, though yielding to the central authority a controlling power for a few limited purposes, such as external and diplomatic relations. In this case, the component states are the units, with respect to the confederation, and the central government acts upon them, not upon the individual citizens. In a *federal government*, on the other hand, the allied states form a union,—not, indeed, to such an extent as to destroy their separate organization or deprive them of *quasi* sovereignty with respect to the administration of their purely local concerns, but so that the central power is erected into a true state or nation, possessing sovereignty both external and internal,—while the administration of national affairs is directed, and its effects felt, not by the separate states deliberating as units, but by the people of all, in their collective capacity, as citizens of the nation. The distinction is expressed, by the German writers, by the use of the two words "*Staatenbund*" and "*Bundesstaat;*" the former denoting a league or confederation of states, and the latter a federal government, or state formed by means of a league or confederation.

FEE. 1. A freehold estate in lands, held of a superior lord, as a reward for services, and on condition of rendering some service in return for it. The true meaning of the word "fee" is the same as that of "feud" or "fief," and in its original sense it is taken in contradistinction to "allodium," which latter is defined as a man's own land, which he possesses merely in his own right, without owing any rent or service to any superior. 2 Bl. Comm. 105. See 1 N. Y. 491.

In modern English tenures, "fee" signifies an estate of inheritance, being the highest and most extensive interest which a man can have in a feud; and when the term is used simply, without any adjunct, or in the form "fee-simple," it imports an absolute inheritance clear of any condition, limitation, or restriction to particuliar heirs, but descendible to the heirs general, male or female, lineal or collateral. 2 Bl. Comm. 106.

In modern English tenures, a fee signifies an estate of inheritance, and a fee-simple imports an absolute inheritance, clear of any condition or limitation whatever, and, when not disposed of by will, descends to the heirs generally. There are also limited fees: (1) Qualified or base fees; and (2) fees conditional at the common law. A base fee was confined to a person as tenant of a particular place. A conditional fee was restrained to particular heirs, as to the heirs of a man's body. 11 Wend. 259, 277.

A *determinable* fee is one which may possibly continue indefinitely, but which is liable to be determined. Plowd. 557.

A *qualified* (or base) fee is one which has a qualification subjoined thereto, and which must be determined whenever the qualification annexed to it is at an end. 2 Bl. Comm. 109.

A *conditional* fee, at the common law, was a fee restrained to some particular heirs exclusive of others. These afterwards became estates tail. 2 Bl. Comm. 110.

2. The word "fee" is also frequently used to denote the land which is held in fee.

3. The compass or circuit of a manor or lordship. Cowell.

4. **In American law.** A fee is an estate of inheritance without condition, belonging to the owner, and alienable by him, or transmissible to his heirs absolutely and simply. It is an absolute estate in perpetuity, and the largest possible estate a man can have, being, in fact, allodial in its nature.

5. A reward or wages given to one for the execution of his office, or for professional services, as those of a counsellor or physician. Cowell.

FEE-BILL. A schedule of the fees to be charged by clerks of courts, sheriffs, or other officers, for each particular service in the line of their duties.

FEE EXPECTANT. An estate where lands are given to a man and his wife, and the heirs of their bodies.

FEE-FARM. This is a species of tenure, where land is held of another in perpetuity at a yearly rent, without fealty, homage, or other services than such as are specially comprised in the feoffment. It corresponds very nearly to the "*emphyteusis*" of the Roman law.

Fee-farm is where an estate in fee is granted subject to a rent in fee of at least one-fourth of the value of the lands at the time of its reservation. Such rent appears to be called "fee-farm" because a grant of lands reserving so considerable a rent is indeed only letting lands to farm in fee-simple, instead of the usual method of life or years. 2 Bl. Comm. 43; 1 Steph. Comm. 676.

Fee-farms are lands held in fee to render for them annually the true value, or more or less; so called because a farm rent is reserved upon a grant in fee. Such estates are estates of inheritance. They are classed among estates in fee-simple. No reversionary interest remains in the lessor, and they are therefore subject to the operation of the legal principles which forbid restraints upon alienation in all cases where no feudal relation exists between grantor and grantee. 6 N. Y. 467, 497.

FEE-FARM RENT. The rent reserved on granting a fee-farm. It might be one-fourth the value of the land, according to Cowell; one-third, according to other authors. Spelman; Termes de la Ley; 2 Bl. Comm. 43.

Fee-farm rent is a rent-charge issuing out of an estate in fee; a perpetual rent reserved on a conveyance in fee-simple. 6 N. Y. 467, 495.

FEE-SIMPLE. **In English law.** A freehold estate of inheritance, absolute and unqualified. It stands at the head of estates as the highest in dignity and the most ample in extent; since every other kind of estate is derivable thereout, and mergeable therein, for *omne majus continet in se minus.* It may be enjoyed not only in land, but also in advowsons, commons, estovers, and other hereditaments, as well as in personalty, as an annuity or dignity, and also in an upper chamber, though the lower buildings and soil belong to another. Wharton.

In American law. An absolute or fee-simple estate is one in which the owner is entitled to the entire property, with unconditional power of disposition during his life, and descending to his heirs and legal representatives upon his death intestate. Code Ga. 1882, § 2246.

Fee-simple signifies a pure fee; an absolute estate of inheritance; that which a person holds inheritable to him and his heirs general forever. It is called "fee-simple," that is, "pure," because clear of any condition or restriction to particular heirs, being descendible to the heirs general, whether male or female, lineal or collateral. It is the largest estate and most extensive interest that can be enjoyed in land, being the entire property therein, and it confers an unlimited power of alienation. 42 Vt. 686.

A fee-simple is the largest estate known to the law, and, where no words of qualification or limitation are added, it means an estate in possession, and owned in severalty. It is undoubtedly true that a person may own a remainder or reversion in fee. But such an estate is not a fee-simple; it is a fee qualified or limited. So, when a person owns in common with another, he does not own the entire fee,—a fee-simple; it is a fee divided or shared with another. 54 Me. 426.

FEE-SIMPLE CONDITIONAL. This estate, at the common law, was a fee restrained to some particular heirs, exclusive of others. But the statute *De Donis* converted all such into estates tail. 2 Bl. Comm. 110.

FEE-TAIL. An estate tail; an estate of inheritance given to a man and the heirs of his body, or limited to certain classes of particular heirs. It corresponds to the *feudum talliatum* of the feudal law, and the idea is believed to have been borrowed from the Roman law, where, by way of *fidei commissa*, lands might be entailed upon children and freedmen and their descendants, with restrictions as to alienation. 1 Washb. Real Prop. *66.

FEED. To lend additional support; to strengthen *ex post facto*. "The interest when it accrues *feeds* the estoppel." 5 Mood. & R. 202.

FEGANGI. In old English law. A thief caught while escaping with the stolen goods in his possession. Spelman.

FEHMGERICHTE. The name given to certain secret tribunals which flourished in Germany from the end of the twelfth century to the middle of the sixteenth, usurping many of the functions of the governments which were too weak to maintain law and order, and inspiring dread in all who came within their jurisdiction. Enc. Brit. Such a court existed in Westphalia (though with greatly diminished powers) until finally suppressed in 1811.

FEIGNED ACTION. In practice. An action brought on a pretended right, when the plaintiff has no true cause of action, for some illegal purpose. In a feigned action the words of the writ are true. It differs from *false action*, in which case the words of the writ are false. Co. Litt. 361.

FEIGNED DISEASES. Simulated maladies. Diseases are generally feigned from one of three causes,—fear, shame, or the hope of gain.

FEIGNED ISSUE. An issue made up by the direction of a court of equity, (or by consent of parties,) and sent to a common-law court, for the purpose of obtaining the verdict of a jury on some disputed matter of fact which the court has not jurisdiction, or is unwilling, to decide. It rests upon a supposititious wager between the parties. See 3 Bl. Comm. 452.

FELAGUS. In Saxon law. One bound for another by oath; a sworn brother. A friend bound in the decennary for the good behavior of another. One who took the place of the deceased. Thus, if a person was murdered, the recompense due from the murderer went to the *felagus* of the slain, in default of parents or lord. Cunningham.

FELD. A field; in composition, wild. Blount.

FELE, FEAL. L. Fr. Faithful. See FEAL.

FELLOW. A companion; one with whom we consort; one joined with another in some legal *status* or relation; a member of a college or corporate body.

FELLOW-HEIR. A co-heir; partner of the same inheritance.

FELLOW-SERVANTS. "The decided weight of authority is to the effect that all who serve the same master, work under the same control, derive authority and compensation from the same common source, and are engaged in the same general business, though it may be in different grades or departments of it, are fellow-servants, who take the risk of each other's negligence." 2 Thomp. Neg. p. 1026, § 31.

Persons who are employed under the same master, derive authority and compensation from the same common source, and are engaged in the same general business, although one is a foreman of the work and the other a common laborer, are fellow-servants. 76 Me. 143.

Where two servants are employed by the same master, labor under the same control, derive their authority and receive their compensation from a common source, and are engaged in the same business, though in different departments of the common service, they are fellow-servants. 62 Tex. 597.

FELO DE SE. A felon of himself; a suicide or murderer of himself. One who deliberately and intentionally puts an end to his own life, or who commits some unlawful or malicious act which results in his own death.

FELON. One who has committed felony; one convicted of felony.

FELONIA. Felony. The act or offense by which a vassal forfeited his fee. Spelman; Calvin. *Per feloniam*, with a criminal intention. Co. Litt. 391.

Felonia, ex vi termini significat quodlibet capitale crimen felleo animo perpetratum. Co. Litt. 391. Felony, by force of the term, signifies any capital crime perpetrated with a malignant mind.

Felonia implicatur in qualibet proditione. 3 Inst. 15. Felony is implied in every treason.

FELONICE. Feloniously. Anciently an indispensable word in indictments for felony, and classed by Lord Coke among those *voces artis* (words of art) which cannot be expressed by any periphrasis or circumlocution. 4 Coke, 39; Co. Litt. 391*a*; 4 Bl. Comm. 307.

FELONIOUS HOMICIDE. In criminal law. The offense of killing a human creature, of any age or sex, without justification or excuse. There are two degrees of this offense, manslaughter and murder. 4 Bl. Comm. 188, 190; 4 Steph. Comm. 108, 111.

FELONIOUSLY. An indispensable word in modern indictments for felony, as *felonice* was in the Latin forms. 4 Bl. Comm. 307.

FELONY. **In English law.** This term meant originally the state of having forfeited lands and goods to the crown upon conviction for certain offenses, and then, by transition, any offense upon conviction for which such forfeiture followed, in addition to any other punishment prescribed by law; as distinguished from a "misdemeanor," upon conviction for which no forfeiture followed. All indictable offenses are either felonies or misdemeanors, but a material part of the distinction is taken away by St. 33 & 34 Vict. c. 23, which abolishes forfeiture for felony. Wharton.

In American law. The term has no very definite or precise meaning, except in some cases where it is defined by statute. For the most part, the state laws, in describing any particular offense, declare whether or not it shall be considered a felony. Apart from this, the word seems merely to imply a crime of a graver or more atrocious nature than those designated as "misdemeanors."

The statutes or codes of several of the states define felony as any public offense on conviction of which the offender is liable to be sentenced to death or to imprisonment in a penitentiary or state prison. Pub. St. Mass. 1882, p. 1290; Code Ala. 1886, § 3701; Code Ga. 1882, § 3404; 34 Ohio St. 301; 1 Wis. 188; 2 Rev. St. N. Y. p. 587, § 30; 1 Park. Crim. R. 39.

In feudal law. An act or offense on the part of the vassal, which cost him his fee, or in consequence of which his fee fell into the hands of his lord; that is, became forfeited. (See FELONIA.) Perfidy, ingratitude, or disloyalty to a lord.

FELONY ACT. The statute 33 & 34 Vict. c. 23, abolishing forfeitures for felony, and sanctioning the appointment of *interim curators* and *administrators* of the property of felons. Mozley & Whitley; 4 Steph. Comm. 10, 459.

FELONY, COMPOUNDING OF. See COMPOUNDING FELONY.

FEMALE. The sex which conceives and gives birth to young. Also a member of such sex.

FEME. L. Fr. A woman. In the phrase "*baron et feme*" (*q. v.*) the word has the sense of "wife."

FEME COVERT. A married woman. Generally used in reference to the legal disabilities of a married woman, as compared with the condition of a *feme sole*.

FEME SOLE. A single woman, including those who have been married, but whose marriage has been dissolved by death or divorce, and, for most purposes, those women who are judicially separated from their husbands. Mozley & Whitley; 2 Steph. Comm. 250.

FEME SOLE TRADER. In English law. A married woman, who, by the custom of London, trades on her own account, independently of her husband; so called because, with respect to her trading, she is the same as a *feme sole*. Jacob; Cro. Car. 68.

The term is applied also to women deserted by their husbands, who do business as *femes sole*. 1 Pet. 105.

FEMICIDE. The killing of a woman. Wharton.

FEMININE. Of or pertaining to females, or the female sex.

FENATIO. In forest law. The fawning of deer; the fawning season. Spelman.

FENCE, *v*. In old Scotch law. To defend or protect by formalities. To "fence a court" was to open it in due form, and interdict all manner of persons from disturbing their proceedings. This was called "fencing," *q. d.*, defending or protecting the court.

FENCE, *n*. A hedge, structure, or partition, erected for the purpose of inclosing a piece of land, or to divide a piece of land into distinct portions, or to separate two contiguous estates. See 63 Me. 308; 77 Ill. 169.

FENCE-MONTH, or DEFENSE-MONTH. In old English law. A period of time, occurring in the middle of summer, during which it was unlawful to hunt deer in the forest, that being their fawning season. Probably so called because the deer were then *defended* from pursuit or hunting. Manwood; Cowell.

FENERATION. Usury; the gain of interest; the practice of increasing money by lending.

FENGELD. In Saxon law. A tax or imposition, exacted for the repelling of enemies.

FENIAN. A champion, hero, giant. This word, in the plural, is generally used to signify invaders or foreign spoilers. The modern meaning of "fenian" is a member of an organization of persons of Irish birth, resident in the United States, Canada, and elsewhere, having for its aim the overthrow of English rule in Ireland. Webster, (Supp.)

FEOD. The same as *feud* or *fief*, being the right which the vassal had in land, or some immovable property of his lord, to use the same and take the profits thereof, rendering unto the lord such duties and services as belonged to the particular tenure; the actual property in the soil always remaining in the lord. Spel. Feuds & Tenures.

FEODAL. Belonging to a fee or feud; feudal. More commonly used by the old writers than *feudal*.

FEODAL ACTIONS. Real actions; so called in the old books, as originally relating to *feoda*, fees, or estates in land. Mirr. c. 2, § 6; 3 Bl. Comm. 117.

FEODAL SYSTEM. See FEUDAL SYSTEM.

FEODALITY. Fidelity or fealty. Cowell. See FEALTY.

FEODARUM CONSUETUDINES. The customs of feuds. The name of a compilation of feudal laws and customs made at Milan in the twelfth century. It is the most ancient work on the subject, and was always regarded, on the continent of Europe, as possessing the highest authority.

FEODARY. An officer of the court of wards, appointed by the master of that court, under 32 Hen. VIII. c. 26, whose business it was to be present with the escheator in every county at the finding of offices of lands, and to give evidence for the king, as well concerning the value as the tenure; and his office was also to survey the land of the ward, after the office found, and to rate it. He also assigned the king's widows their dower; and received all the rents, etc. Abolished by 12 Car. II. c. 24. Wharton.

FEODATORY. In feudal law. The grantee of a *feod*, *feud*, or fee; the vassal or tenant who held his estate by feudal service. Termes de la Ley. Blackstone uses "*feudatory*." 2 Bl. Comm. 46.

FEODI FIRMA. In old English law. Fee-farm, (*q. v.*)

FEODI FIRMARIUS. The lessee of a fee-farm.

FEODUM. This word (meaning a feud or fee) is the one most commonly used by the older English law-writers, though its equivalent, "*feudum*," is used generally by the more modern writers and by the *feudal* law-writers. Litt. § 1; Spelman. There were various classes of *feoda*, among which may be enumerated the following: *Feodum laicum*, a lay fee. *Feodum militare*, a knight's fee. *Feodum improprium*, an improper or derivative fee. *Feodum proprium*, a proper and original fee, regulated by the strict rules of feudal succession and tenure. *Feodum simplex*, a simple or pure fee; fee-simple. *Feodum talliatum*, a fee-tail. See 2 Bl. Comm. 58, 62; Litt. §§ 1, 13; Bract. fol. 175; Glan. 13, 23.

In old English law. A seigniory or jurisdiction. Fleta, lib. 2, c. 63, § 4.

A fee; a perquisite or compensation for a service. Fleta, lib. 2, c. 7.

FEODUM ANTIQUUM. A feud which devolved upon a vassal from his intestate ancestor.

Feodum est quod quis tenet ex quacunque causa sive sit tenementum sive reditus. Co. Litt. 1. A fee is that which any one holds from whatever cause, whether tenement or rent.

FEODUM NOBILE. A fief for which the tenant did guard and owed homage. Spelman.

FEODUM NOVUM. A feud acquired by a vassal himself.

Feodum simplex quia feodum idem est quod hæreditas, et simplex idem est quod legitimum vel purum; et sic feodum simplex idem est quod hæreditas legitima vel hæreditas pura. Litt. § 1. A fee-simple, so called because fee is the same as inheritance, and simple is the same as lawful or pure; and thus fee-simple is the same as a lawful inheritance, or pure inheritance.

Feodum talliatum, i. e., hæreditas in quandam certitudinem limitata. Litt. § 13. Fee-tail, *i. e.*, an inheritance limited in a definite descent.

FEOFFAMENTUM. A feoffment. 2 Bl. Comm. 310.

FEOFFARE. To enfeoff; to bestow a fee. The bestower was called "*feoffator*," and the grantee or feoffee, "*feoffatus*."

FEOFFATOR. In old English law. A feoffor; one who gives or bestows a fee; one who makes a feoffment. Bract. fols. 12*b*, 81.

FEOFFATUS. In old English law. A feoffee; one to whom a fee is given, or a feoffment made. Bract. fols. 17*b*, 44*b*.

FEOFFEE. He to whom a fee is conveyed. Litt. § 1; 2 Bl. Comm. 20.

FEOFFEE TO USES. A person to whom land was conveyed for the use of a third party. The latter was called "*cestui que use.*"

FEOFFMENT. The gift of any corporeal hereditament to another, (2 Bl. Comm. 310,) operating by transmutation of possession, and requiring, as essential to its completion, that the seisin be passed, (Watk. Conv. 183,) which might be accomplished either by investiture or by livery of seisin. 1 Washb. Real Prop. 33.

Also the deed or conveyance by which such corporeal hereditament is passed.

A feoffment originally meant the grant of a *feud* or *fee;* that is, a barony or knight's fee, for which certain services were due from the feoffee to the feoffor. This was the proper sense of the word; but by custom it came afterwards to signify also a grant (with livery of seisin) of a free inheritance to a man and his heirs, referring rather to the perpetuity of the estate than to the feudal tenure. 1 Reeve, Eng. Law, 90, 91. It was for ages the only method (in ordinary use) for conveying the freehold of land in possession, but has now fallen in great measure into disuse, even in England, having been almost entirely supplanted by some of that class of conveyances founded on the statute law of the realm. 1 Steph. Comm. 467, 468.

FEOFFMENT TO USES. A feoffment of lands to one person to the use of another.

FEOFFOR. The person making a feoffment, or enfeoffing another in fee. 2 Bl. Comm. 310; Litt. §§ 1, 57.

FEOH. This Saxon word meant originally cattle, and thence property or money, and, by a second transition, wages, reward, or fee. It was probably the original form from which the words "feod," "feudum," "fief," "feu," and "fee" (all meaning a feudal grant of land) have been derived.

FEONATIO. In forest law. The fawning season of deer.

FEORME. A certain portion of the produce of the land due by the grantee to the lord according to the terms of the charter. Spel. Feuds, c. 7.

FERÆ BESTIÆ. Wild beasts.

FERÆ NATURÆ. Lat. Of a wild nature or disposition. Animals which are by nature wild are so designated, by way of distinction from such as are naturally tame, the latter being called "*domitæ naturæ.*"

FERCOSTA. Ital. A kind of small vessel or boat. Mentioned in old Scotch law, and called "*fercost.*" Skene.

FERDELLA TERRÆ. A fardel-land; ten acres; or perhaps a yard-land. Cowell.

FERDFARE. Sax. A summons to serve in the army. An acquittance from going into the army. Fleta, lib. 1, c. 47, § 23.

FERDINGUS. A term denoting, apparently, a freeman of the lowest class, being named after the *cotseti*.

FERDWITE. In Saxon law. An acquittance of manslaughter committed in the army; also a fine imposed on persons for not going forth on a military expedition. Cowell.

FERIA. In old English law. A week-day; a holiday; a day on which process could not be served; a fair; a ferry. Cowell; Du Cange; Spelman.

FERIÆ. In Roman law. Holidays; generally speaking, days or seasons during which free-born Romans suspended their political transactions and their lawsuits, and during which slaves enjoyed a cessation from labor. All *feriæ* were thus *dies nefasti*. All *feriæ* were divided into two classes,—"*feriæ publicæ*" and "*feriæ privatæ.*" The latter were only observed by single families or individuals, in commemoration of some particular event which had been of importance to them or their ancestors. Smith, Dict. Antiq.

FERIAL DAYS. Holidays; also week-days, as distinguished from Sunday. Cowell.

FERITA. In old European law. A wound; a stroke. Spelman.

FERLING. In old records. The fourth part of a penny; also the quarter of a ward in a borough.

FERLINGATA. A fourth part of a yard-land.

FERLINGUS. A furlong. Co. Litt. 5*b*.

FERM, or FEARM. A house or land, or both, let by lease. Cowell.

FERME. A farm; a rent; a lease; a house or land, or both, taken by indenture or lease. Plowd. 195; Vicat. See FARM.

FERMER, FERMOR. A lessee; a farmer. One who holds a term, whether of lands or an incorporeal right, such as customs or revenue.

FERMIER. In French law. One who farms any public revenue.

FERMISONA. In old English law. The winter season for killing deer.

FERMORY. In old records. A place in monasteries, where they received the poor, (*hospicio excipiebant,*) and gave them provisions, (*ferm, firma.*) Spelman. Hence the modern *infirmary*, used in the sense of a hospital.

FERNIGO. In old English law. A waste ground, or place where fern grows. Cowell.

FERRATOR. A farrier, (*q. v.*)

FERRI. In the civil law. To be borne; that is on or about the person. This was distinguished from *portari*, (to be carried,) which signified to be carried on an animal. Dig. 50, 16, 235.

FERRIAGE. The toll or fare paid for the transportation of persons and property across a ferry.

Literally speaking, it is the price or fare fixed by law for the transportation of the traveling public, with such goods and chattels as they may have with them, across a river, bay, or lake. 85 Cal. 606.

FERRIFODINA. In old pleading. An iron mine. Townsh. Pl. 273.

FERRUM. Iron. In old English law. A horse-shoe. *Ferrura*, shoeing of horses.

FERRY. A liberty to have a boat upon a river for the transportation of men, horses, and carriages with their contents, for a reasonable toll. The term is also used to designate the place where such liberty is exercised. See 42 Me. 9; 4 Mart. (N. S.) 426.

"Ferry" properly means a place of transit across a river or arm of the sea; but in law it is treated as a franchise, and defined as the exclusive right to carry passengers across a river, or arm of the sea, from one vill to another, or to connect a continuous line of road leading from one township or vill to another. It is not a servitude or easement. It is wholly unconnected with the ownership or occupation of land, so much so that the owner of the ferry need not have any property in the soil adjacent on either side. (12 C. B., N. S., 32.) Brown.

FERRYMAN. One employed in taking persons across a river or other stream, in boats or other contrivances, at a ferry. 3 Ala. 160; 8 Dana, 158.

FESTA IN CAPPIS. In old English law. Grand holidays, on which choirs wore caps. Jacob.

Festinatio justitiæ est noverca infortunii. Hob. 97. Hasty justice is the step-mother of misfortune.

FESTING-MAN. In old English law. A frank-pledge, or one who was surety for the good behavior of another. Monasteries enjoyed the privilege of being "free from festing-men," which means that they were "not bound for any man's forthcoming who should transgress the law." Cowell. See FRANK-PLEDGE.

FESTING-PENNY. Earnest given to servants when hired or retained. The same as *aries-penny*. Cowell.

FESTINUM REMEDIUM. Lat. A speedy remedy. The writ of assise was thus characterized (in comparison with the less expeditious remedies previously available) by the statute of Westminster 2, (13 Edw. I. c. 24.)

FESTUM. A feast or festival. *Festum stultorum*, the feast of fools.

FETTERS. Chains or shackles for the feet; irons used to secure the legs of convicts, unruly prisoners, etc. Similar chains securing the wrists are called "handcuffs."

FEU. In Scotch law. A holding or tenure where the vassal, in place of military service, makes his return in grain or money. Distinguished from "wardholding," which is the military tenure of the country. Bell.

FEU ANNUALS. In Scotch law. The *reddendo*, or annual return from the vassal to a superior in a feu holding.

FEU ET LIEU. Fr. In old French and Canadian law. Hearth and home. A term importing actual settlement upon land by a tenant.

FEU HOLDING. In Scotch law. A holding by tenure of rendering grain or money in place of military service. Bell.

FEUAR. In Scotch law. The tenant of a feu; a feu-vassal. Bell.

FEUD. In feudal law. An estate in land held of a superior on condition of rendering him services. 2 Bl. Comm. 105.

An inheritable right to the use and occupation of lands, held on condition of rendering services to the lord or proprietor, who himself retains the property in the lands. See Spel. Feuds, c. 1.

In this sense the word is the same as "feod," "feodum," "feudum," "fief," or "fee."

In Saxon and old German law. An enmity, or species of private war, existing between the family of a murdered man and the family of his slayer; a combination of the former to take vengeance upon the latter. See DEADLY FEUD; FAIDA.

FEUDA. Feuds or fees.

FEUDAL. Pertaining to feuds or fees; relating to or growing out of the feudal system or feudal law; having the quality of a feud, as distinguished from "allodial."

FEUDAL ACTIONS. An ancient name for *real* actions, or such as concern real property only. 3 Bl. Comm. 117.

FEUDAL LAW. The body of jurisprudence relating to feuds; the real-property law of the feudal system; the law anciently regulating the property relations of lord and vassal, and the creation, incidents, and transmission of feudal estates.

The body of laws and usages constituting the "feudal law" was originally customary and unwritten, but a compilation was made in the twelfth century, called "Feodarum Consuetudines," which has formed the basis of later digests. The feudal law prevailed over Europe from the twelfth to the fourteenth century, and was introduced into England at the Norman Conquest, where it formed the entire basis of the law of real property until comparatively modern times. Survivals of the feudal law, to the present day, so affect and color that branch of jurisprudence as to require a certain knowledge of the feudal law in order to the perfect comprehension of modern tenures and rules of real-property law.

FEUDAL POSSESSION. The equivalent of "seisin" under the feudal system.

FEUDAL SYSTEM. The system of feuds. A political and social system which prevailed throughout Europe during the eleventh, twelfth, and thirteenth centuries, and is supposed to have grown out of the peculiar usages and policy of the Teutonic nations who overran the continent after the fall of the Western Roman Empire, as developed by the exigencies of their military domination, and possibly furthered by notions taken from the Roman jurisprudence. It was introduced into England, in its completeness, by William I., A. D. 1085, though it may have existed in a rudimentary form among the Saxons before the Conquest. It formed the entire basis of the real-property law of England in medieval times; and survivals of the system, in modern days, so modify and color that branch of jurisprudence, both in England and America, that many of its principles require for their complete understanding a knowledge of the feudal system. The feudal system originated in the relations of a military chieftain and his followers, or king and nobles, or lord and vassals, and especially their relations as determined by the bond established by a grant of *land* from the former to the latter. From this it grew into a complete and intricate complex of rules for the tenure and transmission of real estate, and of correlated duties and services; while, by tying men to the land and to those holding above and below them, it created a close-knit hierarchy of persons, and developed an aggregate of social and political institutions.

For an account of the feudal system in its juristic relations, see 2 Bl. Comm. 44; 1 Steph. Comm. 160; 3 Kent, Comm. 487; Spel. Feuds; Litt. Ten.; Sull. Lect.; Spence, Eq. Jur.; 1 Washb. Real Prop. 15; Dalr. Feu. Prop. For its political and social relations, see Hall. Middle Ages; Maine, Anc. Law; Rob. Car. V.; Montesq. Esprit des Lois, bk. 30; Guizot, Hist. Civilization.

FEUDAL TENURES. The tenures of real estate under the feudal system, such as knight-service, socage, villenage, etc.

FEUDALISM. The feudal system; the aggregate of feudal principles and usages.

FEUDALIZE. To reduce to a feudal tenure; to conform to feudalism. Webster.

FEUDARY. A tenant who holds by feudal tenure. Held by feudal service. Relating to feuds or feudal tenures.

FEUDATORY. See FEODATORY.

FEUDBOTE. A recompense for engaging in a feud, and the damages consequent, it having been the custom in ancient times for all the kindred to engage in their kinsman's quarrel. Jacob.

FEUDE, or DEADLY FEUDE. A German word, signifying implacable hatred, not to be satisfied but with the death of the enemy. Such was that among the people in Scotland and in the northern parts of England, which was a combination of all the kindred to revenge the death of any of the blood upon the slayer and all his race. Termes de la Ley.

FEUDIST. A writer on feuds, as Cujacius, Spelman, etc.

FEUDO. In Spanish law. Feud or fee. White, New Recop. b. 2, tit. 2, c. 2.

FEUDUM. A feud, fief, or fee. A right of using and enjoying forever the lands of another, which the lord grants on condition that the tenant shall render fealty, military duty, and other services. Spelman. See FEODUM; FEUD.

FEUDUM ANTIQUUM. An ancient feud or fief; a fief descended to the vassal from his ancestors. 2 Bl. Comm. 212, 221. A fief which ancestors had possessed for more than four generations. Spelman.

FEUDUM APERTUM. An open feud or fief; a fief resulting back to the lord, where the blood of the person last seised was utterly extinct and gone. 2 Bl. Comm. 245.

FEUDUM FRANCUM. A free feud. One which was noble and free from talliage and other subsidies to which the *plebeia feuda* (vulgar feuds) were subject. Spelman.

FEUDUM HAUBERTICUM. A fee held on the military service of appearing fully armed at the *ban* and *arriere ban.* Spelman.

FEUDUM IMPROPRIUM. An improper or derivative feud or fief. 2 Bl. Comm. 58.

FEUDUM INDIVIDUUM. An indivisible or impartible feud or fief; descendible to the eldest son alone. 2 Bl. Comm. 215.

FEUDUM LIGIUM. A liege feud or fief; a fief held immediately of the sovereign; one for which the vassal owed fealty to his lord against all persons. 1 Bl. Comm. 367; Spelman.

FEUDUM MATERNUM. A maternal fief; a fief descended to the feudatory from his mother. 2 Bl. Comm. 212.

FEUDUM NOBILE. A fee for which the tenant did guard and owed fealty and homage. Spelman.

FEUDUM NOVUM. A new feud or fief; a fief which began in the person of the feudatory, and did not come to him by succession. Spelman; 2 Bl. Comm. 212.

FEUDUM NOVUM UT ANTIQUUM. A new fee held with the qualities and incidents of an ancient one. 2 Bl. Comm. 212.

FEUDUM PATERNUM. A fee which the paternal ancestors had held for four generations. Calvin. One descendible to heirs on the paternal side only. 2 Bl. Comm. 223. One which might be held by males only. Du Cange.

FEUDUM PROPRIUM. A proper, genuine, and original feud or fief; being of a purely military character, and held by military service. 2 Bl. Comm. 57, 58.

FEUDUM TALLIATUM. A restricted fee. One limited to descend to certain classes of heirs. 2 Bl. Comm. 112, note; 1 Washb. Real Prop. 66.

FEW. An indefinite expression for a small or limited number. In cases where exact description is required, the use of this word will not answer. 53 Vt. 600; 2 Car. & P. 300.

FI. FA An abbreviation for *fieri facias*, (which see.)

FIANCER. L. Fr. To pledge one's faith. Kelham.

FIANZA. In Spanish law. A surety or guarantor; the contract or engagement of a surety.

FIAR. In Scotch law. He that has the fee or *feu*. The proprietor is termed "fiar," in contradistinction to the life-renter. 1 Kames, Eq. Pref. One whose property is charged with a life-rent.

FIARS PRICES. The value of grain in the different counties of Scotland, fixed yearly by the respective sheriffs, in the month of February, with the assistance of juries. These regulate the prices of grain stipulated to be sold at the fiar prices, or when no price has been stipulated. Ersk. 1, 4, 6.

FIAT. In English practice. A short order or warrant of a judge or magistrate directing some act to be done; an authority issuing from some competent source for the doing of some legal act.

One of the proceedings in the English bankrupt practice, being a power, signed by the lord chancellor, addressed to the court of bankruptcy, authorizing the petitioning creditor to prosecute his complaint before it. 2 Steph. Comm. 199. By the statute 12 & 13 Vict. c. 116, fiats were abolished.

Fiat jus, ruat justitia. Let law prevail, though justice fail.

FIAT JUSTITIA. Let justice be done. On a petition to the king for his warrant to bring a writ of error in parliament, he writes on the top of the petition, "*Fiat justitia*," and then the writ of error is made out, etc. Jacob.

Fiat justitia, ruat cœlum. Let right be done, though the heavens should fall.

Fiat prout fieri consuevit, (nil temere novandum.) Let it be done as it hath used to be done, (nothing must be rashly innovated.) Jenk. Cent. 116, case 39; Branch, Princ.

FIAT UT PETITUR. Let it be done as it is asked. A form of granting a petition.

FICTIO. In Roman law. A fiction; an assumption or supposition of the law.

"*Fictio*" in the old Roman law was properly a term of pleading, and signified a false averment on the part of the plaintiff which the defendant was not allowed to traverse; as that the plaintiff was a Roman citizen, when in truth he was a foreigner. The object of the fiction was to give the court jurisdiction. Maine, Anc. Law, 25.

Fictio cedit veritati. Fictio juris non est ubi veritas. Fiction yields to truth. Where there is truth, fiction of law exists not.

Fictio est contra veritatem, sed pro veritate habetur. Fiction is against the truth, but it is to be esteemed truth.

Fictio juris non est ubi veritas. Where truth is, fiction of law does not exist.

Fictio legis inique operatur alicui damnum vel injuriam. A legal fiction does not properly work loss or injury. 3 Coke, 36; Broom, Max. 129.

Fictio legis neminem lædit. A fiction of law injures no one. 2 Rolle, 502; 3 Bl. Comm. 43; 17 Johns. 348.

FICTION. An assumption or supposition of law that something which is or may be false is true, or that a state of facts exists which has never really taken place.

A fiction is a rule of law which assumes as true, and will not allow to be disproved, something which is false, but not impossible. Best, Ev. 419.

These assumptions are of an innocent or even beneficial character, and are made for the advancement of the ends of justice. They secure this end chiefly by the extension of procedure from cases to which it is applicable to other cases to which it is not strictly applicable, the ground of inapplicability being some difference of an immaterial character. Brown.

Fictions are to be distinguished from presumptions of law. By the former, something known to be false or unreal is assumed as true; by the latter, an inference is set up, which may be and probably is true, but which, at any rate, the law will not permit to be controverted.

Mr. Best distinguishes legal fictions from presumptions *juris et de jure*, and divides them into three kinds,—affirmative or positive fictions, negative fictions, and fictions by relation. Best, Pres. p. 27, § 24.

FICTITIOUS ACTION. An action brought for the sole purpose of obtaining the opinion of the court on a point of law, not for the settlement of any actual controversy between the parties.

Courts of justice were constituted for the purpose of deciding really existing questions of right between parties; and they are not bound to answer impertinent questions which persons think proper to ask them in the form of an action on a wager. 12 East, 248.

FICTITIOUS PLAINTIFF. A person appearing in the writ or record as the plaintiff in a suit, but who in reality does not exist, or who is ignorant of the suit and of the use of his name in it. It is a contempt of court to sue in the name of a fictitious party. See 4 Bl. Comm. 134.

FIDEI-COMMISSARIUS. In the civil law this term corresponds nearly to our "*cestui que trust.*" It designates a person who has the real or beneficial interest in an estate or fund, the title or administration of which is temporarily confided to another. See Story, Eq. Jur. § 966.

FIDEI-COMMISSUM. In the civil law. A species of trust; being a gift of property (usually by will) to a person, accompanied by a request or direction of the donor that the recipient will transfer the property to another, the latter being a person not capable of taking directly under the will or gift.

FIDE-JUBERE. In the civil law. To order a thing upon one's faith; to pledge one's self; to become surety for another. *Fide-jubes? Fide-jubeo:* Do you pledge yourself? I do pledge myself. Inst. 3, 16, 1. One of the forms of stipulation.

FIDE-JUSSOR. In Roman law. A guarantor; one who becomes responsible for the payment of another's debt, by a stipulation which binds him to discharge it if the principal debtor fails to do so. Mackeld. Rom. Law, § 452; 3 Bl. Comm. 108.

The sureties taken on the arrest of a defendant, in the court of admiralty, were formerly denominated "fide-jussors." 3 Bl. Comm. 108.

FIDELIS. Faithful; trustworthy.

FIDELITAS. Fealty; fidelity.

Fidelitas. De nullo tenemento, quod tenetur ad terminum, fit homagii; fit tamen inde fidelitatis sacramentum. Co. Litt. 676. Fealty. For no tenement which is held for a term is there the oath of homage, but there is the oath of fealty.

FIDEM MENTIRI. When a tenant does not keep that fealty which he has sworn to the lord. Leg. Hen. I. c. 53.

FIDE-PROMISSOR. See FIDE-JUSSOR.

FIDES. Faith; honesty; confidence; trust; veracity; honor. Occurring in the phrase "*bona fides;*" so, also, "*mala fides.*"

Fides est obligatio conscientiæ alicujus ad intentionem alterius. Bacon. A trust is an obligation of conscience of one to the will of another.

Fides servanda est. Faith must be observed. An agent must not violate the confidence reposed in him. Story, Ag. § 192.

Fides servanda est; simplicitas juris gentium prævaleat. Faith must be kept; the simplicity of the law of nations must prevail. A rule applied to bills of exchange as a sort of sacred instruments. 3 Burrows, 1672; Story, Bills, § 15.

FIDUCIA. In the civil law. A contract by which we sell a thing to some one—that is, transmit to him the property of the thing, with the solemn forms of emancipation—on condition that he will sell it back to us. This species of contract took place in the emancipation of children, in testaments, and in pledges. Poth. Pand. h. t.

FIDUCIARIUS TUTOR. In Roman law. The elder brother of an emancipated *pupillus*, whose father had died leaving him still under fourteen years of age.

FIDUCIARY. The term is derived from the Roman law, and means (as a noun) a person holding the character of a trustee, or a character analogous to that of a trustee, in respect to the trust and confidence involved in it and the scrupulous good faith and candor which it requires. Thus, a person is a fiduciary who is invested with rights and powers to be exercised for the benefit of another person.

As an adjective it means of the nature of a trust; having the characteristics of a trust; analogous to a trust; relating to or founded upon a trust or confidence.

FIDUCIARY CONTRACT. An agreement by which a person delivers a thing to another on the condition that he will restore it to him.

FIEF. A fee, feod, or feud.

FIEF D'HAUBERT. Fr. In Norman feudal law. A fief or fee held by the tenure of knight-service; a knight's fee. 2 Bl. Comm. 62.

FIEF-TENANT. In old English law. The holder of a fief or fee; a feeholder or freeholder.

FIEL. In Spanish law. A sequestrator; a person in whose hands a thing in dispute is judicially deposited; a receiver. Las Partidas, pt. 3, tit. 9, l. 1.

FIELD. This term might well be considered as definite and certain a description as "close," and might be used in law; but it is not a usual description in legal proceedings. 1 Chit. Gen. Pr. 160.

FIELD-ALE. An ancient custom in England, by which officers of the forest and bailiffs of hundreds had the right to compel the hundred to furnish them with ale. Tomlins.

FIELD REEVE. An officer elected, in England, by the owners of a regulated pasture to keep in order the fences, ditches, etc., on the land, to regulate the times during which animals are to be admitted to the pasture, and generally to maintain and manage the pasture subject to the instructions of the owners. (General Inclosure Act, 1845, § 118.) Sweet.

FIELDAD. In Spanish law. Sequestration. This is allowed in six cases by the Spanish law where the title to property is in dispute. Las Partidas, pt. 3, tit. 3, l. 1.

FIERDING COURTS. Ancient Gothic courts of an inferior jurisdiction, so called because *four* were instituted within every inferior district or hundred. 3 Bl. Comm. 34.

FIERI. Lat. To be made; to be done. See IN FIERI.

FIERI FACIAS. (That you cause to be made.) In practice. A writ of execution commanding the sheriff to levy and make the amount of a judgment from the goods and chattels of the judgment debtor.

FIERI FACIAS DE BONIS ECCLESIASTICIS. When a sheriff to a common *fi. fa.* returns *nulla bona*, and that the defendant is a beneficed clerk, not having any lay fee, a plaintiff may issue a *fi. fa. de bonis ecclesiasticis*, addressed to the bishop of the diocese or to the archbishop, (during the vacancy of the bishop's see,) commanding him to make of the ecclesiastical goods and chattels belonging to the defendant within his diocese the sum therein mentioned. 2 Chit Archb. Pr. (12th Ed.) 1062.

FIERI FACIAS DE BONIS TESTATORIS. The writ issued on an ordinary judgment against an executor when sued for a debt due by his testator. If the sheriff returns to this writ *nulla bona*, and a *devastavit*, (*q. v.*,) the plaintiff may sue out a *fieri facias de bonis propriis*, under which the goods of the executor himself are seized. Sweet.

FIERI FECI. (I have caused to be made.) In practice. The name given to the return made by a sheriff or other officer to a writ of *fieri facias*, where he has collected the whole, or a part, of the sum directed to be levied. 2 Tidd, Pr. 1018. The return, as actually made, is expressed by the word "Satisfied" indorsed on the writ.

Fieri non debet, (debuit,) sed factum valet. It ought not to be done, but [if] done, it is valid. Shep. Touch, 6; 5 Coke, 39; T. Raym. 58; 1 Strange, 526. A maxim frequently applied in practice. 19 Johns. 84, 92.

FIFTEENTHS. In English law. This was originally a tax or tribute, levied at intervals by act of parliament, consisting of one-fifteenth of all the movable property of the subject or personalty in every city, township, and borough. Under Edward III., the taxable property was assessed, and the value of its fifteenth part (then about £29,000) was recorded in the exchequer, whence the tax, levied on that valuation, continued to be called a "fifteenth," although, as the wealth of the kingdom increased, the name ceased to be an accurate designation of the proportion of the tax to the value taxed. See 1 Bl. Comm. 309.

FIGHT. An encounter, with blows or other personal violence, between two persons. See 73 N. C. 155.

FIGHTWITE. Sax. A mulct or fine for making a quarrel to the disturbance of the peace. Called also by Cowell "*forisfactura pugnæ.*" The amount was one hundred and twenty shillings. Cowell.

FIGURES. The numerical characters by which numbers are expressed or written.

FILACER. An officer of the superior courts at Westminster, whose duty it was to file the writs on which he made process. There were fourteen filacers, and it was their duty to make out all original process.

Cowell; Blount. The office was abolished in 1837.

FILARE. In old English practice. To file. Townsh. Pl. 67.

FILE, *v.* In practice. To put upon the *files*, or deposit in the custody or among the records of a court.

"Filing a bill" in equity is an equivalent expression to "commencing a suit."

"To file" a paper, on the part of a party, is to place it in the official custody of the clerk. "To file," on the part of the clerk, is to indorse upon the paper the date of its reception, and retain it in his office, subject to inspection by whomsoever it may concern. 14 Tex. 339.

The expressions "filing" and "entering of record" are not synonymous. They are nowhere so used, but always convey distinct ideas. "Filing" originally signified placing papers in order on a thread or wire for safe-keeping. In this country and at this day it means, agreeably to our practice, depositing them in due order in the proper office. Entering of record uniformly implies writing. 2 Blackf. 247.

FILE, *n.* A thread, string, or wire upon which writs and other exhibits in courts and offices are fastened or filed for the more safe-keeping and ready turning to the same. Spelman; Cowell; Tomlins. Papers put together and tied in bundles. A paper is said also to be filed when it is delivered to the proper officer, and by him received to be kept on file. 13 Vin. Abr. 211; 1 Litt. 113; 1 Hawk. P. C. 7, 207. But, in general, "file," or "the files," is used loosely to denote the official custody of the court or the place in the offices of a court where the records and papers are kept.

FILEINJAID. Brit. A name given to villeins in the laws of Hoel Dda. Barring. Obs. St. 302.

FILIATE. To fix a bastard child on some one, as its father. To declare whose child it is. 2 W Bl. 1017.

Filiatio non potest probari. Co. Litt. 126. Filiation cannot be proved.

FILIATION. The relation of a child to its parent; correlative to "paternity."

The judicial assignment of an illegitimate child to a designated man as its father.

In the civil law. The descent of son or daughter, with regard to his or her father, mother, and their ancestors.

FILICETUM. In old English law. A ferny or bracky ground; a place where fern grows. Co. Litt. 4*b*; Shep. Touch. 95.

FILIOLUS. In old records. A godson; Spelman.

FILIUS. Lat. A son; a child.

A distinction was sometimes made, in the civil law, between "*filii*" and "*liberi*;" the latter word including grandchildren, (*nepotes*,) the former not. Inst. 1, 14, 5. But, according to Paulus and Julianus, they were of equally extensive import. Dig. 50, 16, 84; Id. 50, 16, 201.

Filius est nomen naturæ, sed hæres nomen juris. 1 Sid. 193. Son is a name of nature, but heir is a name of law.

FILIUS FAMILIAS. In the civil law. The son of a family; an unemancipated son. Inst. 2, 12, pr.; Id. 4, 5, 2; Story, Confl. Laws, § 61.

Filius in utero matris est pars viscerum matris. 7 Coke, 8. A son in the mother's womb is part of the mother's vitals.

FILIUS MULIERATUS. In old English law. The eldest legitimate son of a woman, who previously had an illegitimate son by his father. Glanv. lib. 7, c. 1. Otherwise called "*mulier*." 2 Bl. Comm. 248.

FILIUS NULLIUS. The son of nobody; *i. e.*, a bastard.

FILIUS POPULI. A son of the people; a natural child.

FILL. To make full; to complete; to satisfy or fulfill; to possess and perform the duties of.

The election of a person to an office constitutes the essence of his appointment; but the office cannot be considered as actually *filled* until his acceptance, either express or implied. 2 N. H. 202.

Where one subscribes for shares in a corporation, agreeing to "take and *fill*" a certain number of shares, *assumpsit* will lie against him to recover an assessment on his shares; the word "fill," in this connection, amounting to a promise to pay assessments. 10 Me. 478.

To *fill* a prescription is to furnish, prepare, and combine the requisite materials in due proportion as prescribed. 61 Ga. 505.

FILLY. A young mare; a female colt. An indictment charging the theft of a "filly" is not sustained by proof of the larceny of a "mare." 1 Tex. App. 448.

FILUM. In old practice. A file; *i. e.*, a thread or wire on which papers were strung, that being the ancient method of filing.

An imaginary thread or line passing through the middle of a stream or road, as in the phrases "*filum aquæ*," "*filum viæ*;" or along the edge or border, as in "*filum forestæ*."

FILUM AQUÆ. A thread of water; a line of water; the middle line of a stream of water, supposed to divide it into two equal parts, and constituting in many cases the boundary between the riparian proprietors on each side.

FILUM FORESTÆ. Lat. The border of the forest. 2 Bl. Comm. 419; 4 Inst. 303.

FILUM VIÆ. The thread or middle line of a road. An imaginary line drawn through the middle of a road, and constituting the boundary between the owners of the land on each side. 2 Smith, Lead. Cas. (Am. Ed.) 98, note.

FIN. An end, or limit; a limitation, or period of limitation.

FIN DE NON RECEVOIR. In French law. An exception or plea founded on law, which, without entering into the merits of the action, shows that the plaintiff has no right to bring it, either because the time during which it ought to have been brought has elapsed, which is called "prescription," or that there has been a compromise, accord and satisfaction, or any other cause which has destroyed the right of action which once subsisted. Poth. Proc. Civile, pt. 1, c. 2, § 2, art. 2.

FINAL. Definitive; terminating; completed; last. In its use in jurisprudence, this word is generally contrasted with "interlocutory."

FINAL COSTS. Such costs as are to be paid at the end of the suit; costs, the liability for which depends upon the final result of the litigation.

FINAL DECISION. One from which no appeal or writ of error can be taken. 47 Ill. 167; 6 El. & Bl. 408.

FINAL DECREE. A decree in equity which fully and finally disposes of the whole litigation, determining all questions raised by the case, and leaving nothing that requires further judicial action.

FINAL DISPOSITION. When it is said to be essential to the validity of an award that it should make a "final disposition" of the matters embraced in the submission, this term means such a disposition that nothing further remains to fix the rights and obligations of the parties, and no further controversy or litigation is required or can arise on the matter. It is such an award that the party against whom it is made can perform or pay it without any further ascertainment of rights or duties. 50 Me. 401.

FINAL HEARING. This term designates the trial of an equity case upon the merits, as distinguished from the hearing of any preliminary questions arising in the cause, which are termed "interlocutory." 24 Wis. 165.

FINAL JUDGMENT. In practice. A judgment which puts an *end* to an action at law by declaring that the plaintiff either has or has not entitled himself to recover the remedy he sues for. 3 Bl. Comm. 398. So distinguished from *interlocutory* judgments, which merely establish the right of the plaintiff to recover, in general terms. Id. 397. A judgment which determines a particular cause.

A judgment which cannot be appealed from, which is perfectly conclusive upon the matter adjudicated. 24 Pick. 300. A judgment which terminates all litigation on the same right. The term "final judgment," in the judiciary act of 1789, § 25, includes both species of judgments as just defined. 2 Pet. 494; 1 Kent, Comm. 316; 6 How. 201, 209.

A judgment is final and conclusive between the parties, when rendered on a verdict on the merits, not only as to the facts actually litigated and decided, but also as to all facts necessarily involved in the issue. 26 Ala. 504.

FINAL PASSAGE. In parliamentary law. The final passage of a bill is the vote on its passage in either house of the legislature, after it has received the prescribed number of readings on as many different days in that house. 54 Ala. 613.

FINAL PROCESS. The last process in a suit; that is, writs of execution. Thus distinguished from *mesne* process, which includes all writs issued during the progress of a cause and before final judgment.

FINAL RECOVERY. The final judgment in an action. Also the final verdict in an action, as distinguished from the judgment entered upon it. 6 Allen, 243.

FINAL SENTENCE. One which puts an end to a case. Distinguished from interlocutory.

FINAL SETTLEMENT. This term, as applied to the administration of an estate, is usually understood to have reference to the order of court approving the account which closes the business of the estate, and which finally discharges the executor or administrator from the duties of his trust. 13 N. E. Rep. 131. See, also, 65 Ala. 442.

FINALIS CONCORDIA. A final or conclusive agreement. In the process of "levying a fine," this was a final agreement entered by the litigating parties upon the record, by permission of court, settling the title to the land, and which was binding upon them like any judgment of the court. 1 Washb. Real Prop. *70.

FINANCES. The public wealth of a state or government, considered either statically (as the property or money which a state now owns) or dynamically, (as its income, revenue, or public resources.) Also the revenue or wealth of an individual.

FINANCIER. A person employed in the economical management and application of public money; one skilled in the management of financial affairs.

FIND. To discover; to determine; to ascertain and declare. To announce a conclusion, as the result of judicial investigation, upon a disputed fact or state of facts; as a jury are said to "find a will." To determine a controversy in favor of one of the parties; as a jury "find for the plaintiff."

FINDER. One who discovers and takes possession of another's personal property, which was then lost.

A searcher employed to discover goods imported or exported without paying custom. Jacob.

FINDING. A decision upon a question of fact reached as the result of a judicial examination or investigation by a court, jury, referee, coroner, etc.

FINE, *v.* To impose a pecuniary punishment or mulct. To sentence a person convicted of an offense to pay a penalty in money.

FINE, *n.* **In conveyancing.** An amicable composition or agreement of a suit, either actual or fictitious, by leave of the court, by which the lands in question become, or are acknowledged to be, the right of one of the parties. 2 Bl. Comm. 349. Fines were abolished in England by St. 3 & 4 Wm. IV. c. 74, substituting a disentailing deed, (*q. v.*)

The party who parted with the land, by acknowledging the right of the other, was said to *levy* the fine, and was called the "cognizor" or "conusor," while the party who recovered or received the estate was termed the "cognizee" or "conusee," and the fine was said to be levied to him.

In the law of tenure. A fine is a money payment made by a feudal tenant to his lord. The most usual fine is that payable on the admittance of a new tenant, but there are also due in some manors fines upon alienation, on a license to demise the lands, or on the death of the lord, or other events. Elton, Copyh. 159.

In criminal law. Pecuniary punishment imposed by a lawful tribunal upon a person convicted of crime or misdemeanor.

It means, among other things, "a sum of money paid at the *end*, to make an *end* of a transaction, suit, or prosecution; mulct; penalty." In ordinary legal language, however, it means a sum of money imposed by a court according to law, as a punishment for the breach of some penal statute. 22 Kan. 15.

It is not confined to a pecuniary punishment of an offense, inflicted by a court in the exercise of criminal jurisdiction. It has other meanings, and may include a forfeiture, or a penalty recoverable by civil action. 11 Gray, 373.

FINE AND RECOVERY ACT. The English statutes 3 & 4 Wm. IV. c. 74, for abolishing fines and recoveries. 1 Steph. Comm. 514, et seq.

FINE ANULLANDO LEVATO DE TENEMENTO QUOD FUIT DE ANTIQUO DOMINICO. An abolished writ for disannulling a fine levied of lands in ancient demesne to the prejudice of the lord. Reg. Orig. 15.

FINE CAPIENDO PRO TERRIS. An obsolete writ which lay for a person who, upon conviction by jury, had his lands and goods taken, and his body imprisoned, to be remitted his imprisonment, and have his lands and goods redelivered to him, on obtaining favor of a sum of money, etc. Reg. Orig. 142.

FINE FOR ALIENATION. A fine anciently payable upon the alienation of a feudal estate and substitution of a new tenant. It was payable to the lord by all tenants holding by knight's service or tenants *in capite* by socage tenure. Abolished by 12 Car. II. c. 24. See 2 Bl. Comm. 71, 89.

FINE FOR ENDOWMENT. A fine anciently payable to the lord by the widow of a tenant, without which she could not be endowed of her husband's lands. Abolished under Henry I., and by *Magna Charta.* 2 Bl. Comm. 135; Mozley & Whitley.

FINE NON CAPIENDO PRO PULCHRE PLACITANDO. An obsolete writ to inhibit officers of courts to take fines for fair pleading.

FINE PRO REDISSEISINÂ CAPIENDO. An old writ that lay for the release of one imprisoned for a redisseisin, on payment of a reasonable fine. Reg. Orig. 222.

FINE SUR COGNIZANCE DE DROIT COME CEO QUE IL AD DE SON DONE. A fine upon acknowledgment of the right of the cognizee as that which he hath of the gift of the cognizor. By this the deforciant acknowledged in court a former foeffment or gift in possession to have been made by him to the plaintiff. 2 Bl. Comm. 352.

FINE SUR COGNIZANCE DE DROIT TANTUM. A fine upon acknowledgment of the right merely, and not with the circumstance of a *preceding gift* from the cognizor. This was commonly used to pass a *reversionary* interest which was in the cognizor, of which there could be no foeffment supposed. 2 Bl. Comm. 353; 1 Steph. Comm. 519.

FINE SUR CONCESSIT. A fine upon *concessit*, (he hath granted.) A species of fine, where the cognizor, in order to make an end of disputes, though he acknowledged no precedent right, yet *granted* to the cognizee an estate *de novo*, usually for life or years, by way of supposed composition. 2 Bl. Comm. 353; 1 Steph. Comm. 519.

FINE SUR DONE GRANT ET RENDER. A double fine, comprehending the fine *sur cognizance de droit come ceo* and the fine *sur concessit*. It might be used to convey particular limitations of estates, whereas the fine *sur cognizance de droit come ceo*, etc., conveyed nothing but an absolute estate, either of inheritance, or at least freehold. In this last species of fines, the cognizee, after the right was acknowledged to be in him, granted back again or rendered to the cognizor, or perhaps to a stranger, some other estate in the premises. 2 Bl. Comm. 353.

FINE-FORCE. An absolute necessity or inevitable constraint. Plowd. 94; 6 Coke, 11; Cowell.

FINEM FACERE. To make or pay a fine. Bract. 106.

FINES LE ROY. In old English law. The king's fines. Fines formerly payable to the king for any contempt or offense, as where one committed any trespass, or falsely denied his own deed, or did anything in contempt of law. Termes de la Ley.

FINIRE. In old English law. To fine, or pay a fine. Cowell. To end or finish a matter.

FINIS. An end; a fine; a boundary or terminus; a limit.

Finis est amicabilis compositio et finalis concordia ex consensu et concordia domini regis vel justiciarum. Glan. lib. 8, c. 1. A fine is an amicable settlement and decisive agreement by consent and agreement of our lord, the king, or his justices.

Finis finem litibus imponit. A fine puts an end to litigation. 3 Inst. 78.

Finis rei attendendus est. 3 Inst. 51. The end of a thing is to be attended to.

Finis unius diei est principium alterius. 2 Bulst. 305. The end of one day is the beginning of another.

FINITIO. An ending; death, as the end of life. Blount; Cowell.

FINIUM REGUNDORUM ACTIO. In the civil law. Action for regulating boundaries. The name of an action which lay between those who had lands bordering on each other, to settle disputed boundaries. Mackeld. Rom. Law, § 499.

FINORS. Those that purify gold and silver, and part them by fire and water from coarser metals; and therefore, in the statute of 4 Hen. VII. c. 2, they are also called "parters." Termes de la Ley.

FIRDFARE. Sax. In old English law. A summoning forth to a military expedition, (*indictio ad profectionem militarem*.) Spelman.

FIRDIRINGA. Sax. A preparation to go into the army. Leg. Hen. I.

FIRDSOCNE. Sax. In old English law. Exemption from military service. Spelman.

FIRDWITE. In old English law. A fine for refusing military service, (*mulcta detrectantis militiam*.) Spelman.

A fine imposed for murder committed in the army; an acquittance of such fine. Fleta, lib. 1, c. 47.

FIRE. The effect of combustion. The juridical meaning of the word does not differ from the vernacular. 1 Pars. Mar. Law, 231, et seq.

FIRE AND SWORD, LETTERS OF. In old Scotch law. Letters issued from the privy council in Scotland, addressed to the sheriff of the county, authorizing him to call for the assistance of the county to dispossess a tenant retaining possession, contrary to the order of a judge or the sentence of a court. Wharton.

FIRE-ARMS. This word comprises all sorts of guns, fowling-pieces, blunderbusses, pistols, etc.

FIREBARE. A beacon or high tower by the seaside, wherein are continual lights, either to direct sailors in the night, or to give warning of the approach of an enemy. Cowell.

FIRE-BOTE. An allowance of wood or *estovers* to maintain competent firing for the tenant. A sufficient allowance of wood to burn in a house. 1 Washb. Real Prop. 99.

FIRE INSURANCE. A contract of insurance by which the underwriter, in consideration of the premium, undertakes to indemnify the insured against all losses in his houses, buildings, furniture, ships in port, or merchandise, by means of accidental fire happening within a prescribed period. 3 Kent, Comm. 370.

FIRE ORDEAL. In Saxon and old English law. The ordeal by fire or red-hot iron, which was performed either by taking up in the hand a piece of red-hot iron, of one, two, or three pounds weight, or by walking barefoot and blindfolded over nine red-hot plowshares, laid lengthwise at unequal distances. 4 Bl. Comm. 343; Cowell.

FIRE POLICY. A contract of insurance, by which, in consideration of a single or periodical payment of premium, (as the case may be,) the company engages to pay to the assured such loss as may occur by fire to his property therein described, within the period or periods therein specified, to an amount not exceeding a particular sum fixed for that purpose by the policy. 2 Steph. Comm. 180.

FIRE-PROOF. To say of any article that it is "fire-proof" conveys no other idea than that the material out of which it is formed is incombustible. To say of a building that it is fire-proof excludes the idea that it is of wood, and necessarily implies that it is of some substance fitted for the erection of fire-proof buildings. To say of a certain portion of a building that it is fire-proof suggests a comparison between that portion and other parts of the building not so characterized, and warrants the conclusion that it is of a different material. 102 N. Y. 459, 7 N. E. Rep. 321.

FIRKIN. A measure containing nine gallons; also a weight of fifty-six pounds avoirdupois, used in weighing butter and cheese.

FIRLOT. A Scotch measure of capacity, containing two gallons and a pint. Spelman.

FIRM. A partnership; the group of persons constituting a partnership.

The name or title under which the members of a partnership transact business.

FIRMA. In old English law. The contract of lease or letting; also the rent (or farm) reserved upon a lease of lands, which was frequently payable in provisions, but sometimes in money, in which latter case it was called "*alba firma*," white rent. A messuage, with the house and garden belonging thereto. Also provision for the table; a banquet; a tribute towards the entertainment of the king for one night.

FIRMA FEODI. In old English law. A farm or lease of a fee; a fee-farm.

FIRMAN. An Asiatic word denoting a decree or grant of privileges, or passport to a traveler.

FIRMARATIO. The right of a tenant to his lands and tenements. Cowell.

FIRMARIUM. In old records. A place in monasteries, and elsewhere, where the poor were received and supplied with food. Spelman. Hence the word "infirmary."

FIRMARIUS. L. Lat. A fermor. A lessee of a term. *Firmarii* comprehend all such as hold by lease for life or lives or for year, by deed or without deed. 2 Inst. 144, 145; 1 Washb. Real Prop. 107.

FIRMATIO. The doe season. Also a supplying with food. Cowell.

FIRME. In old records. A farm.

Firmior et potentior est operatio legis quam dispositio hominis. The operation of the law is firmer and more powerful [or efficacious] than the disposition of man. Co. Litt. 102*a*.

FIRMITAS. In old English law. An assurance of some privilege, by deed or charter.

FIRMURA. In old English law. Liberty to scour and repair a mill-dam, and carry away the soil, etc. Blount.

FIRST-CLASS MISDEMEANANT. In English law. Under the prisons act (28 & 29 Vict. c. 126, § 67) prisoners in the county, city, and borough prisons convicted of misdemeanor, and not sentenced to hard labor, are divided into two classes, one of which is called the "first division;" and it is in the discretion of the court to order that such a prisoner be treated as a *misdemeanant of the first division*, usually called "first-class misdemeanant," and as such not to be deemed a criminal prisoner, *i. e.*, a prisoner convicted of a crime. Bouvier.

FIRST FRUITS. In English ecclesiastical law. The first year's whole profits of every benefice or spiritual living, anciently paid by the incumbent to the pope, but afterwards transferred to the fund called "Queen Anne's Bounty," for increasing the revenue from poor livings.

In feudal law. One year's profits of land which belonged to the king on the death of a tenant *in capite;* otherwise called "*primer seisin.*" One of the incidents to the old feudal tenures. 2 Bl. Comm. 66, 67.

FIRST IMPRESSION. A case is said to be "of the first impression" when it presents an entirely novel question of law for the decision of the court, and cannot be governed by any existing precedent.

FIRST PURCHASER. In the law of descent, this term signifies the ancestor who first acquired (in any other manner than by inheritance) the estate which still remains in his family or descendants.

FISC. An Anglicized form of the Latin "*fiscus*," (which see.)

FISCAL. Belonging to the fisc, or public treasury. Relating to accounts or the management of revenue.

FISCAL AGENT. This term does not necessarily mean depositary of the public funds, so as, by the simple use of it in a statute, without any directions in this respect, to make it the duty of the state treasurer to deposit with him any moneys in the treasury. 27 La. Ann. 29.

FISCAL JUDGE. A public officer named in the laws of the Ripuarians and some other Germanic peoples, apparently the same as the "*Graf*," "*reeve*," "*comes*," or "*count*," and so called because charged with the collection of public revenues, either directly or by the imposition of fines. See Spelman, voc. "Grafio."

FISCUS. In Roman law. The treasury of the prince or emperor, as distinguished from "*ærarium*," which was the treasury of the state. Spelman.

The treasury or property of the state, as distinguished from the private property of the sovereign.

In English law. The king's treasury, as the repository of forfeited property.

The treasury of a noble, or of any private person. Spelman.

FISH. An animal which inhabits the water, breathes by means of gills, swims by the aid of fins, and is oviparous.

FISH COMMISSIONER. A public officer of the United States, created by act of congress of February 9, 1871, whose duties principally concern the preservation and increase throughout the country of fish suitable for food. Rev. St. § 4395.

FISH ROYAL. These were the whale and the sturgeon, which, when thrown ashore or caught near the coast of England, became the property of the king by virtue of his prerogative and in recompense for his protecting the shore from pirates and robbers. Brown; 1 Bl. Comm. 290.

FISHERY. A place prepared for catching fish with nets or hooks. This is commonly applied to the place of drawing a seine or net. 1 Whart. 131, 132.

A right or liberty of taking fish; a species of incorporeal hereditament, anciently termed "piscary," of which there are several kinds. 2 Bl. Comm. 34, 39; 3 Kent, Comm. 409-418.

A free fishery is said to be a franchise in the hands of a subject, existing by grant or prescription, distinct from an ownership in the soil. It is an exclusive right, and applies to a public navigable river, without any right in the soil. 3 Kent, Comm. 329.

A common of fishery is not an exclusive right, but one enjoyed in common with certain other persons. 3 Kent, Comm. 329.

A several fishery is one by which the party claiming it has the right of fishing, independently of all others, so that no person can have a co-extensive right with him in the object claimed; but a partial and independent right in another, or a limited liberty, does not derogate from the right of the owner. 5 Burrows, 2814.

FISHERY LAWS. A series of statutes passed in England for the regulation of fishing, especially to prevent the destruction of fish during the breeding season, and of small fish, spawn, etc., and the employment of improper modes of taking fish. 3 Steph. Comm. 165.

FISHGARTH. A dam or wear in a river for taking fish. Cowell.

FISHING BILL. A term descriptive of a bill in equity which seeks a discovery upon general, loose, and vague allegations. Story, Eq. Pl. § 325; 32 Fed. Rep. 263.

FISK. In Scotch law. The *fiscus* or fisc. The revenue of the crown. Generally used of the personal estate of a rebel which has been forfeited to the crown. Bell.

FISTUCA, or FESTUCA. In old English law. The rod or wand, by the delivery of which the property in land was formerly transferred in making a feoffment. Called, also, "*baculum,*" "*virga,*" and "*fustis.*" Spelman.

FISTULA. In the civil law. A pipe for conveying water. Dig. 8, 2, 18.

FITZ. A Norman word, meaning "son." It is used in law and genealogy; as *Fitzherbert,* the son of Herbert; *Fitzjames,* the son of James; *Fitzroy,* the son of the king. It was originally applied to illegitimate children.

FIVE-MILE ACT. An act of parliament, passed in 1665, against non-conformists, whereby ministers of that body were prohibited from coming within five miles of any corporate town, or place where they had preached or lectured. Brown.

FIX. To liquidate or render certain. To fasten a liability upon one. To transform a possible or contingent liability into a present and definite liability.

FIXING BAIL. In practice. Rendering absolute the liability of special bail.

FIXTURE. A fixture is a personal chattel substantially affixed to the land, but which may afterwards be lawfully removed therefrom by the party affixing it, or his representative, without the consent of the owner of the freehold. 3 Nev. 82; 18 Ind. 231; 8 Iowa, 544.

Personal chattels which have been annexed to land, and which may be afterwards severed and removed by the party who has annexed them, or his personal representative, against the will of the owner of the freehold. Ferard, Fixt. 2; Bouvier.

The word "fixtures" has acquired the peculiar meaning of chattels which have been annexed to the freehold, but which are removable at the will of the person who annexed them. 1 Cromp., M. & R. 266.

"Fixtures" does not necessarily import things affixed to the freehold. The word is a modern one, and is generally understood to comprehend any article which a tenant has the power to remove. 5 Mees. & W. 174; 30 Pa. St. 185, 189.

Chattels which, by being physically annexed or affixed to real estate, become a part of and accessory to the freehold, and the property of the owner of the land. Hill.

Things fixed or affixed to other things. The rule of law regarding them is that which is expressed in the maxim, "*accessio cedit principali,*" "the accessory goes with, and as part of, the principal subject-matter." Brown.

A thing is deemed to be affixed to land when it is attached to it by roots, as in the case of trees, vines, or shrubs; or imbedded in it, as in the case of walls; or permanently resting upon it, as in the case of buildings; or permanently attached to what is thus permanent, as by means of cement, plaster, nails, bolts, or screws. Civil Code Cal. § 660.

That which is fixed or attached to something permanently as an appendage, and not removable. Webster.

That which is fixed; a piece of furniture fixed to a house, as distinguished from movable; something fixed or immovable. Worcester.

The general result seems to be that three views have been taken. One is that "fixture" means something which has been affixed to the realty, so as to become a part of it; it is fixed, irremovable. An opposite view is that "fixture" means something which appears to be a part of the realty, but is not fully so; it is only a chattel fixed to it, but removable. An intermediate view is that "fixture" means a chattel annexed, affixed, to the realty, but imports nothing as to whether it is removable; that is to be determined by considering its circumstances and the relation of the parties. Abbott.

FLACO. A place covered with standing water.

FLAG. A national standard on which are certain emblems; an ensign; a banner. It is carried by soldiers, ships, etc., and commonly displayed at forts and many other suitable places.

FLAG, DUTY OF THE. This was an ancient ceremony in acknowledgment of British sovereignty over the British seas, by which a foreign vessel struck her flag and lowered her top-sail on meeting the British flag.

FLAG OF THE UNITED STATES. By the act entitled "An act to establish the flag of the United States," (Rev. St. §§ 1791, 1792,) it is provided "that, from and after the fourth day of July next, the flag of the United States be thirteen horizontal stripes, alternate red and white; that the union be twenty stars, white in a blue field; that, on the admission of every new state into the Union, one star be added to the union of the flag; and that such addition shall take effect on the fourth day of July then next succeeding such admission."

FLAGELLAT. Whipped; scourged. An entry on old Scotch records. 1 Pitc. Crim. Tr. pt. 1, p. 7.

FLAGRANS. Burning; raging; in actual perpetration. *Flagrans bellum*, a war actually going on.

FLAGRANS CRIMEN. In Roman law. A fresh or recent crime. This term designated a crime in the very act of its commission, or while it was of recent occurrence.

FLAGRANT DÉLIT. In French law. A crime which is in actual process of perpetration or which has just been committed. Code d'Instr. Crim. art. 41.

FLAGRANT NECESSITY. A case of urgency rendering lawful an otherwise illegal act, as an assault to remove a man from impending danger.

FLAGRANTE BELLO. During an actual state of war.

FLAGRANTE DELICTO. In the very act of committing the crime. 4 Bl. Comm. 307.

FLASH CHECK. A check drawn upon a banker by a person who has no funds at the banker's, and knows that such is the case.

FLAT. A place covered with water too shallow for navigation with vessels ordinarily used for commercial purposes. 34 Conn. 370; 7 Cush. 195.

FLAVIANUM JUS. In Roman law. The title of a book containing the forms of actions, published by Cneius Flavius, A. U. C. 449. Mackeld. Rom. Law, § 39. Calvin.

FLECTA. A feathered or fleet arrow. Cowell.

FLEDWITE. A discharge or freedom from amercements where one, having been an outlawed fugitive, cometh to the place of our lord of his own accord. Termes de la Ley.

The liberty to hold court and take up the amercements for beating and striking. Cowell.

The fine set on a fugitive as the price of obtaining the king's freedom. Spelman.

FLEE FROM JUSTICE. To leave one's home, residence, or known place of abode, or to conceal one's self therein, with intent, in either case, to avoid detection or punishment for some public offense. 3 Dill. 381; 48 Mo. 240.

"FLEE TO THE WALL." A metaphorical expression, used in connection with homicide done in self-defense, signifying the exhaustion of every possible means of escape, or of averting the assault, before killing the assailant.

FLEET. A place where the tide flows; a creek, or inlet of water; a company of ships or navy; a prison in London, (so called from a river or ditch formerly in its vicinity,) now abolished by 5 & 6 Vict. c. 22.

FLEM. In Saxon and old English law. A fugitive bondman or villein. Spelman.

The privilege of having the goods and fines of fugitives.

FLEMENE FRIT, FLEMENES FRINTHE—FLYMENA FRYNTHE. The reception or relief of a fugitive or outlaw. Jacob.

FLEMESWITE. The possession of the goods of fugitives. Fleta, lib. 1, c. 147.

FLET. In Saxon law. Land; a house; home.

FLETA. The name given to an ancient treatise on the laws of England, founded mainly upon the writings of Bracton and Glanville, and supposed to have been written in the time of Edw. I. The author is unknown, but it is surmised that he was a judge or learned lawyer who was at that time confined in the Fleet prison, whence the name of the book.

FLICHWITE. In Saxon law. A fine on account of brawls and quarrels. Spelman.

FLIGHT. In criminal law. The act of one under accusation, who evades the law by voluntarily withdrawing himself. It is presumptive evidence of guilt.

FLOAT. In American land law, especially in the western states. A certificate authorizing the entry, by the holder, of a certain quantity of land. 20 How. 501, 504.

FLOATABLE. Used for floating. A floatable stream is a stream used for floating logs, rafts, etc. 2 Mich. 519.

FLOATING CAPITAL, (or circulating capital.) The capital which is consumed at each operation of production and reappears transformed into new products. At each sale of these products the capital is represented in cash, and it is from its transformations that profit is derived. Floating capital includes raw materials destined for fabrication, such as wool and flax, products in the warehouses of manufacturers or merchants, such as cloth and linen, and money for wages, and stores. De Laveleye, Pol. Ec.

Capital retained for the purpose of meeting current expenditure.

FLOATING DEBT. By this term is meant that mass of lawful and valid claims against the corporation for the payment of which there is no money in the corporate treasury specifically designed, nor any taxation nor other means of providing money to pay particularly provided. 71 N. Y. 374.

Debt not in the form of bonds or stocks bearing regular interest. Pub. St. Mass. 1882, p. 1290.

FLODE-MARK. Flood-mark, high-water mark. The mark which the sea, at flowing water and highest tide, makes on the shore. Blount.

FLOOR. A section of a building between horizontal planes. 145 Mass. 1, 12 N. E. Rep. 401.

A term used metaphorically, in parliamentary practice, to denote the exclusive right to address the body in session. A member who has been recognized by the chairman, and who is in order, is said to "have the floor," until his remarks are concluded. Similarly, the "floor of the house" means the main part of the hall where the members sit, as distinguished from the galleries, or from the corridors or lobbies.

In England, the floor of a court is that part between the judge's bench and the front row of counsel. Litigants appearing in person, in the high court or court of appeal, are supposed to address the court from the floor.

FLORENTINE PANDECTS. A copy of the Pandects discovered accidentally about the year 1137, at Amalphi, a town in Italy, near Salerno. From Amalphi, the copy found its way to Pisa, and, Pisa having submitted to the Florentines in 1406, the copy was removed in great triumph to Florence. By direction of the magistrates of the town, it was immediately bound in a superb manner, and deposited in a costly chest. Formerly, these Pandects were shown only by torch-light, in the presence of two magistrates, and two Cistercian monks, with their heads uncovered. They have been successively collated by Politian, Bolognini, and Antonius Augustinus. An exact copy of them was published in 1553 by Franciscus Taurellus. For its accuracy and beauty, this edition ranks high among the ornaments of the press. Brenchman, who collated the manuscript about 1710, refers it to the sixth century. Butl. Hor. Jur. 90, 91.

FLORIN. A coin originally made at Florence, now of the value of about two English shillings.

FLOTAGES. 1. Such things as by accident swim on the top of great rivers or the sea. Cowell.

2. A commission paid to water bailiffs. Cun. Dict.

FLOTSAM, FLOTSAN. A name for the goods which float upon the sea when cast overboard for the safety of the ship, or when a ship is sunk. Distinguished from "jetsam" and "ligan." Bract. lib. 2, c. 5; 5 Coke, 106; 1 Bl. Comm. 292.

FLOUD-MARKE. In old English law. High-water mark; flood-mark. 1 And. 88, 89.

FLOWING LANDS. This term has acquired a definite and specific meaning in law. It commonly imports raising and setting back water on another's land, by a dam placed across a stream or water-course which is the natural drain and outlet for surplus water on such land. 2 Gray, 235.

FLUCTUS. Flood; flood-tide. Bract. fol. 255.

FLUMEN. In Roman law. A servitude which consists in the right to conduct the rain-water, collected from the roof and carried off by the gutters, onto the house or ground of one's neighbor. Mackeld. Rom. Law, § 317; Ersk. Inst. 2, 9, 9. Also a river or stream.

In old English law. Flood; flood-tide.

Flumina et portus publica sunt, ideoque jus piscandi omnibus commune est. Rivers and ports are public. Therefore the right of fishing there is common to all. Day. Ir. K. B. 55; Branch, Princ.

FLUMINÆ VOLUCRES. Wild fowl; water-fowl. 11 East, 571, note.

FLUVIUS. A river; a public river; flood; flood-tide.

FLUXUS. In old English law. Flow. *Per fluxum et refluxum maris*, by the flow and reflow of the sea. Dal. pl. 10.

FLY FOR IT. On a criminal trial in former times, it was usual after a verdict of not guilty to inquire also, "Did he fly for it?" This practice was abolished by the 7 & 8 Geo. IV. c. 28, § 5. Wharton.

FLYING SWITCH. In railroading, a flying switch is made by uncoupling the cars from the engine while in motion, and throwing the cars onto the side track, by turning the switch, after the engine has passed it upon the main track. 29 Iowa, 39. See, also, 32 N. Y. 597, note.

FLYMA. In old English law. A runaway; fugitive; one escaped from justice, or who has no "hlaford."

FLYMAN-FRYMTH. In old English law. The offense of harboring a fugitive, the penalty attached to which was one of the rights of the crown.

FOCAGE. House-bote; fire-bote. Cowell.

FOCALE. In old English law. Fire-wood. The right of taking wood for the fire. Fire-bote. Cunningham.

FODDER. Food for horses or cattle. In feudal law, the term also denoted a prerogative of the prince to be provided with corn, etc., for his horses by his subjects in his wars.

FODERTORIUM. Provisions to be paid by custom to the royal purveyors. Cowell.

FODERUM. See FODDER.

FODINA. A mine. Co. Litt. 6*a*.

FŒDUS. In international law. A treaty; a league; a compact.

FŒMINA VIRO CO-OPERTA. A married woman; a *feme covert*.

Fœminæ ab omnibus officiis civilibus vel publicis remotæ sunt. Women are excluded from all civil and public charges or offices. Dig. 50, 17, 2; 1 Exch. 645; 6 Mees. & W. 216.

Fœminæ non sunt capaces de publicis officiis. Jenk. Cent. 237. Women are not admissible to public offices.

FŒNERATION. Lending money at interest; the act of putting out money to usury.

FŒNUS NAUTICUM. In the civil law. Nautical or maritime interest. An extraordinary rate of interest agreed to be paid for the loan of money on the hazard of a voyage; sometimes called "*usura maritima.*" Dig. 22, 2; Code, 4, 33; 2 Bl. Comm. 458.

The extraordinary rate of interest, proportioned to the risk, demanded by a person lending money on a ship, or on "bottomry," as it is termed. The agreement for such a rate of interest is also called "*fœnus nauticum.*" (2 Bl. Comm. 458; 2 Steph. Comm. 93.) Mozley & Whitley.

FŒSA. In old records. Grass; herbage. 2 Mon. Angl. 906*b*; Cowell.

FŒTICIDE. In medical jurisprudence. Destruction of the *fœtus;* the act by which criminal abortion is produced. 1 Beck, Med. Jur. 288; Guy, Med. Jur. 133.

FŒTURA. In the civil law. The produce of animals, and the fruit of other property, which are acquired to the owner of such animals and property by virtue of his right. Bowyer, Mod. Civil Law, c. 14, p. 81.

FŒTUS. In medical jurisprudence. An unborn child. An infant *in ventre sa mère*.

FOGAGIUM. In old English law. Fogage or fog; a kind of rank grass of late growth, and not eaten in summer. Spelman; Cowell.

FOI. In French feudal law. Faith; fealty. Guyot, Inst. Feod. c. 2.

FOINESUN. In old English law. The fawning of deer. Spelman.

FOIRFAULT. In old Scotch law. To forfeit. 1 How. State Tr. 927.

FOIRTHOCHT. In old Scotch law. Forethought; premeditated. 1 Pitc. Crim. Tr. pt. 1, p. 90.

FOITERERS. Vagabonds. Blount.

FOLC-GEMOTE. In Saxon law. A general assembly of the people in a town or shire. It appears to have had judicial functions of a limited nature, and also to have discharged political offices, such as deliberating upon the affairs of the commonwealth or complaining of misgovernment, and probably possessed considerable powers of local self-government. The name was also given to any sort of a popular assembly. See Spelman; Manwood; Cunningham.

FOLC-LAND. In Saxon law. Land of the folk or people. Land belonging to the people or the public.

Folc-land was the property of the community. It might be occupied in common, or possessed in severalty; and, in the latter case, it was probably parceled out to individuals in the folc-gemote or court of the district, and the grant sanctioned by the freemen who were there present. But, while it continued to be folc-land, it could not be alienated in perpetuity; and therefore, on the expiration of the term for which it had been granted, it reverted to the community, and was again distributed by the same authority. It was subject to many burdens and exactions from which boc-land was exempt. Wharton.

FOLC-MOTE. A general assembly of the people, under the Saxons. See FOLC-GEMOTE.

FOLC-RIGHT. The common right of all the people. 1 Bl. Comm. 65, 67.

The *jus commune*, or common law, mentioned in the laws of King Edward the Elder, declaring the same equal right, law, or justice to be due to persons of all degrees. Wharton.

FOLD-COURSE. In English law. Land to which the sole right of folding the cattle of others is appurtenant. Sometimes it means merely such right of folding. The right of folding on another's land, which is called "common foldage." Co. Litt. 6*a*, note 1.

FOLDAGE. A privilege possessed in some places by the lord of a manor, which consists in the right of having his tenant's sheep to feed on his fields, so as to manure the land. The name of foldage is also given in parts of Norfolk to the customary fee paid to the lord for exemption at certain times from this duty. Elton, Com. 45, 46.

FOLGARII. Menial servants; followers. Bract.

FOLGERE. In old English law. A freeman, who has no house or dwelling of his own, but is the follower or retainer of another, (*heorthfæst,*) for whom he performs certain predial services.

FOLGOTH. Official dignity.

FOLIO. 1. A leaf. In the ancient law-books it was the custom to number the leaves, instead of the pages; hence a folio would include both sides of the leaf, or two pages. The references to these books are made by the number of the folio, the letters "*a*" and "*b*" being added to show which of the two pages is intended; thus "Bracton, fol. 100*a*."

2. A large size of book, the page being obtained by folding the sheet of paper once only in the binding. Many of the ancient law-books are folios.

3. In computing the length of written legal documents, the term "folio" denotes a certain number of words, fixed by statute in some states at one hundred.

The term "folio," when used as a measure for computing fees or compensation, or in any legal proceedings, means one hundred words, counting every figure necessarily used as a word; and any portion of a folio, when in the whole draft or figure there is not a complete folio, and when there is any excess over the last folio, shall be computed as a folio. Gen. St. Minn. 1878, c. 4, § 1, par. 4.

FOLK-LAND; FOLK-MOTE. See FOLC-LAND; FOLC-GEMOTE.

FONDS PERDUS. In French law. A capital is said to be invested *à fonds perdus* when it is stipulated that in consideration of the payment of an amount as interest, higher than the normal rate, the lender shall be repaid his capital in this manner. The borrower, after having paid the interest during the period determined, is free as regards the capital itself. Arg. Fr. Merc. Law, 560.

FONSADERA. In Spanish law. Any tribute or loan granted to the king for the purpose of enabling him to defray the expenses of a war.

FONTANA. A fountain or spring. Bract. fol. 233.

FOOT. 1. A measure of length containing twelve inches or one-third of a yard.

2. The base, bottom, or foundation of anything; and, by metonomy, the end or termination; as the foot of a fine.

FOOT OF THE FINE. The fifth part of the conclusion of a fine. It includes the whole matter, reciting the names of the parties, day, year, and place, and before whom it was acknowledged or levied. 2 Bl. Comm. 351.

FOOTGELD. In the forest law. An amercement for not cutting out the ball or cutting off the claws of a dog's feet, (expeditating him.) To be quit of *footgeld* is to have the privilege of keeping dogs in the forest *unlawed* without punishment or control. Manwood.

FOOT-PRINTS. In the law of evidence. Impressions made upon earth, snow, or other surface by the feet of persons, or by the shoes, boots, or other covering of the feet. Burrill, Circ. Ev. 264.

FOR. In French law. A tribunal. *Le for interieur*, the interior forum; the tribunal of conscience. Poth. Obl. pt. 1, c. 1, § 1, art. 3, § 4.

FOR THAT. In pleading. Words used to introduce the allegations of a declaration. "For that" is a positive allegation; "For that whereas" is a recital. Ham. N. P. 9.

FOR THAT WHEREAS. In pleading. Formal words introducing the statement of the plaintiff's case, by way of recital, in his declaration, in all actions except trespass. 1 Instr. Cler. 170; 1 Burrill, Pr. 127. In trespass, where there was no recital, the expression used was, "For that." Id.; 1 Instr. Cler. 202.

FOR USE. 1. For the benefit or advantage of another. Thus, where an assignee is obliged to sue in the name of his assignor, the suit is entitled "A. *for use* of B. v. C."

2. For enjoyment or employment without destruction. A loan "for use" is one in which the bailee has the right to use and enjoy the article, but without consuming or destroying it, in which respect it differs from a loan "for consumption."

"FOR WHOM IT MAY CONCERN." In a policy of marine or fire insurance, this phrase indicates that the insurance is taken for the benefit of all persons (besides those named) who may have an insurable interest in the subject.

FORAGE. Hay and straw for horses, particularly in the army. Jacob.

FORAGIUM. Straw when the corn is threshed out. Cowell.

FORANEUS. One from without; a foreigner; a stranger. Calvin.

FORATHE. In forest law. One who could make oath, *i. e.*, bear witness for another. Cowell; Spelman.

FORBALCA. In old records. A forebalk; a balk (that is, an unplowed piece of land) lying forward or next the highway. Cowell.

FORBANNITUS. A pirate; an outlaw; one banished.

FORBARRER. L. Fr. To bar out; to preclude; hence, to estop.

FORBATUDUS. In old English law. The aggressor slain in combat. Jacob.

FORBEARANCE. The act of abstaining from proceeding against a delinquent debtor; delay in exacting the enforcement of a right; indulgence granted to a debtor.

Refraining from action. The term is used in this sense, in general jurisprudence, in contradistinction to "act."

FORCE. Power dynamically considered, that is, in motion or in action; constraining power; compulsion; strength directed to an end. Usually the word occurs in such connections as to show that unlawful or wrongful action is meant.

Unlawful violence. It is either *simple*, as entering upon another's possession, without doing any other unlawful act; *compound*, when some other violence is committed, which of itself alone is criminal; or *implied*, as in every trespass, rescous, or disseisin.

Power statically considered; that is, at rest, or latent, but capable of being called into activity upon occasion for its exercise. Efficacy; legal validity. This is the meaning when we say that a statute or a contract is "in force."

In old English law. A technical term applied to a species of accessary before the fact.

In Scotch law. Coercion; duress. Bell.

FORCE AND ARMS. A phrase used in declarations of trespass and in indictments, but now unnecessary in declarations, to denote that the act complained of was done with violence. 2 Chit. Pl. 846, 850.

FORCE AND FEAR, called also "*vi metuque,*" means that any contract or act extorted under the pressure of force (*vis*) or under the influence of fear (*metus*) is voidable on that ground, provided, of course, that the force or the fear was such as influenced the party. Brown.

FORCE MAJEURE. Fr. In the law of insurance. Superior or irresistible force. Emerig. Tr. des Ass. c. 12.

FORCED HEIRS. In Louisiana. Those persons whom the testator or donor cannot deprive of the portion of his estate reserved for them by law, except in cases where he has a just cause to disinherit them. Civil Code La. art. 1495.

FORCED SALE. In practice. A sale made at the time and in the manner prescribed by law, in virtue of execution issued on a judgment already rendered by a court of competent jurisdiction; a sale made under the process of the court, and in the mode prescribed by law. 6 Tex. 110.

A forced sale is a sale against the consent of the owner. The term should not be deemed to embrace a sale under a power in a mortgage. 15 Fla. 336.

FORCES. The military and naval power of the country.

FORCHEAPUM. Pre-emption; forestalling the market. Jacob.

FORCIBLE DETAINER. The offense of violently keeping possession of lands and tenements, with menaces, force, and arms, and without the authority of law. 4 Bl. Comm. 148; 4 Steph. Comm. 280.

Forcible detainer may ensue upon a peaceable entry, as well as upon a forcible entry; but it is most commonly spoken of in the phrase "forcible entry and detainer."

FORCIBLE ENTRY. An offense against the public peace, or private wrong, committed by violently taking possession of lands and tenements with menaces, force, and arms, against the will of those entitled to the possession, and without the authority of law. 4 Bl. Comm. 148; 4 Steph. Comm. 280; Code Ga. 1882, § 4524.

Every person is guilty of forcible entry who either (1) by breaking open doors, windows, or other parts of a house, or by any kind of violence or circumstance of terror, enters upon or into any real property; or (2) who, after entering peaceably upon real property, turns out by force, threats, or menacing conduct the party in possession. Code Civil Proc. Cal. § 1159.

FORDA. In old records. A ford or shallow, made by damming or penning up the water. Cowell.

FORDAL. A butt or headland, jutting out upon other land. Cowell.

FORDANNO. In old European law. He who first assaulted another. Spelman.

FORDIKA. In old records. Grass or herbage growing on the edge or bank of dykes or ditches. Cowell.

FORE. Sax. Before. Fr. Out. Kelham.

FORECLOSE. To shut out; to bar. Used of the process of destroying an equity of redemption existing in a mortgagor.

FORECLOSURE. A process in chancery by which all further right existing in a mortgagor to redeem the estate is defeated and lost to him, and the estate becomes the absolute property of the mortgagee; being applicable when the mortgagor has forfeited his estate by non-payment of the money due on the mortgage at the time appointed, but still retains the equity of redemption. 2 Washb. Real Prop. 237.

The term is also loosely applied to any of the various methods, statutory or otherwise, known in different jurisdictions, of enforcing payment of the debt secured by a mortgage, by taking and selling the mortgaged estate.

Foreclosure is also applied to proceedings founded upon some other liens; thus there are proceedings to foreclose a mechanic's lien.

FOREFAULT. In Scotch law. To forfeit; to lose.

FOREGIFT. A premium for a lease.

FOREGOERS. Royal purveyors. 26 Edw. III. c. 5.

FOREHAND RENT. In English law. Rent payable in advance; or, more properly, a species of premium or bonus paid by the tenant on the making of the lease, and particularly on the renewal of leases by ecclesiastical corporations.

FOREIGN. Belonging to another nation or country; belonging or attached to another jurisdiction; made, done, or rendered in another state or jurisdiction; subject to another jurisdiction; operating or solvable in another territory; extrinsic; outside; extraordinary.

FOREIGN ADMINISTRATOR. One appointed or qualified under the laws of a foreign state or country, where the decedent was domiciled.

FOREIGN ANSWER. In old English practice. An answer which was not triable in the county where it was made. (St. 15 Hen. VI. c. 5.) Blount.

FOREIGN APPOSER. An officer in the exchequer who examines the sheriff's *estreats*, comparing them with the records, and apposeth (interrogates) the sheriff what he says to each particular sum therein. 4 Inst. 107; Blount; Cowell.

FOREIGN ASSIGNMENT. An assignment made in a foreign country, or in another state. 2 Kent, Comm. 405, et seq.

FOREIGN ATTACHMENT. In American law. A process by which the property (lying within the jurisdiction of the court) of an absent or non-resident debtor is seized, in order to compel his appearance, or to satisfy the judgment that may be rendered, so far as the property goes.

In English law. A custom which prevails in the city of London, whereby a debt owing to a defendant sued in the court of the mayor or sheriff may be attached in the hands of the debtor.

FOREIGN BILL OF EXCHANGE. A bill of exchange drawn in one state or country, upon a foreign state or country.

A bill of exchange drawn in one country upon another country not governed by the same homogeneous laws, or not governed throughout by the same municipal laws.

A bill of exchange drawn in one of the United States upon a person residing in another state is a foreign bill. See Story, Bills, § 22; 2 Pet. 586; 3 Kent, Comm. 94, note.

FOREIGN BOUGHT AND SOLD. A custom in London which, being found prejudicial to sellers of cattle in Smithfield, was abolished. Wharton.

FOREIGN CHARITY. One created or endowed in a state or country foreign to that of the domicile of the benefactor. 34 N. J. Eq. 101.

FOREIGN COINS. Coins issued as money under the authority of a foreign government. As to their valuation in the United States, see Rev. St. U. S. §§ 3564, 3565.

FOREIGN COMMERCE. Commerce or trade between the United States and foreign countries. The term is sometimes applied to commerce between ports of two sister states not lying on the same coast, *e. g.*, New York and San Francisco.

FOREIGN CORPORATION. A corporation created by or under the laws of another state, government, or country.

FOREIGN COUNTY. Any county having a judicial and municipal organization separate from that of the county where matters arising in the former county are called in question, though both may lie within the same state or country.

FOREIGN COURTS. The courts of a foreign state or nation. In the United States, this term is frequently applied to the courts of one of the states when their judgments or records are introduced in the courts of another.

FOREIGN CREDITOR. One who resides in a state or country foreign to that where the debtor has his domicile or his property.

FOREIGN DIVORCE. A divorce obtained out of the state or country where the marriage was solemnized. 2 Kent, Comm. 106, et seq.

FOREIGN DOCUMENT. One which was prepared or executed in, or which comes from, a foreign state or country.

FOREIGN DOMICILE. A domicile established by a citizen or subject of one sovereignty within the territory of another.

FOREIGN DOMINION. In English law this means a country which at one time formed part of the dominions of a foreign state or potentate, but which by conquest or cession has become a part of the dominions of the British crown. 5 Best & S. 290.

FOREIGN ENLISTMENT ACT. The statute 59 Geo. III. c. 69, prohibiting the enlistment, as a soldier or sailor, in any foreign service. 4 Steph. Comm. 226. A later and more stringent act is that of 33 & 34 Vict. c. 90.

FOREIGN EXCHANGE. Drafts drawn on a foreign state or country.

FOREIGN FACTOR. A factor who resides in a country foreign to that where his principal resides.

FOREIGN-GOING SHIP. By the English merchant shipping act, 1854, (17 & 18 Vict. c. 104,) § 2, any ship employed in trading, going between some place or places in the United Kingdom and some place or places situate beyond the following limits, that is to say: The coasts of the United Kingdom, the islands of Guernsey, Jersey, Sark, Alderney, and Man, and the continent of Europe, between the river Elbe and Brest, inclusive. Home-trade ship includes every ship employed in trading and going between places within the last-mentioned limits.

FOREIGN JUDGMENT OR DECREE. A judgment rendered by the courts of a state or country politically and judicially distinct from that where the judgment or its effect is brought in question. One pronounced by a tribunal of a foreign country, or of a sister state.

FOREIGN JURISDICTION. Any jurisdiction foreign to that of the forum. Also the exercise by a state or nation of jurisdiction beyond its own territory, the right being acquired by treaty or otherwise.

FOREIGN JURY. A jury obtained from a county other than that in which issue was joined.

FOREIGN LAWS. The laws of a foreign country, or of a sister state. Foreign laws are often the suggesting occasions of changes in, or additions to, our own laws, and in that respect are called "*jus receptum.*" Brown.

FOREIGN MATTER. In old practice. Matter triable or done in another county. Cowell.

FOREIGN MINISTER. An ambassador, minister, or envoy from a foreign government.

FOREIGN OFFICE. The department of state through which the English sovereign communicates with foreign powers. A secretary of state is at its head. Till the middle of the last century, the functions of a secretary of state as to foreign and home questions were not disunited.

FOREIGN PLEA. A plea objecting to the jurisdiction of a judge, on the ground that he had not cognizance of the subject-matter of the suit. Cowell.

FOREIGN PORT. A port exclusively within the sovereignty of a foreign nation. A foreign port or place is a port or place without the United States. 19 Johns. 375.

FOREIGN SERVICE, in feudal law, was that whereby a mesne lord held of another, without the compass of his own fee, or that which the tenant performed either to his own lord or to the lord paramount out of the fee. (Kitch. 299.) Foreign service seems also to be used for knight's service, or escuage uncertain. (Perk. 650.) Jacob.

FOREIGN STATE. A foreign country or nation. The several United States are considered "foreign" to each other except as regards their relations as common members of the Union.

FOREIGN VESSEL. A vessel owned by residents in, or sailing under the flag of, a foreign nation.

"Foreign vessel," under the embargo act of January, 1808, means a vessel under the flag of a foreign power, and not a vessel in which foreigners domiciled in the United States have an interest. 1 Gall. 58.

FOREIGN VOYAGE. A voyage to some port or place within the territory of a foreign nation. The *terminus* of a voyage determines its character. If it be within the limits of a foreign jurisdiction, it is a foreign voyage, and not otherwise. 1 Story, 1. See 3 Kent, Comm. 177, note; 1 Gall. 55.

FOREIGNER. In old English law, this term, when used with reference to a particular city, designated any person who was not an inhabitant of that city. According to later usage, it denotes a person who is not a citizen or subject of the state or country of which mention is made, or any one owing allegiance to a foreign state or sovereign.

FOREIN. An old form of *foreign*, (*q. v.*) Blount.

FOREJUDGE. In old English law and practice. To expel from court for some offense or misconduct. When an officer or attorney of a court was expelled for any offense, or for not appearing to an action by bill filed against him, he was said to be *forejudged the court.* Cowell.

To deprive or put out of a thing by the judgment of a court. To condemn to lose a thing.

To expel or banish.

FOREJUDGER. In English practice. A judgment by which a man is deprived or *put out* of a thing; a judgment of expulsion or banishment. See FOREJUDGE.

FOREMAN. The presiding member of a grand or petit jury, who speaks or answers for the jury.

FORENSIC. Belonging to courts of justice.

FORENSIC MEDICINE, or medical jurisprudence, as it is also called, is "that science which teaches the application of every branch of medical knowledge to the purposes of the law; hence its limits are, on the one hand, the requirements of the law, and, on the other, the whole range of medicine. Anatomy, physiology, medicine, surgery, chemistry, physics, and botany lend their aid as necessity arises; and in some cases all these branches of science are required to enable a court of law to arrive at a proper conclusion on a contested question affecting life or property." Tayl. Med. Jur. 1.

FORENSIS. In the civil law. Belonging to or connected with a court; forensic. *Forensis homo,* an advocate; a pleader of causes; one who practices in court. Calvin.

In old Scotch law. A strange man or stranger; an out-dwelling man; an "unfreeman," who dwells not within burgh.

FORESAID is used in Scotch law as *aforesaid* is in English, and sometimes, in a plural form, *foresaids.* 2 How. State Tr. 715. *Forsaidis* occurs in old Scotch records. "The Loirdis assesouris forsaidis." 1 Pitc. Crim. Tr. pt. 1, p. 107.

FORESCHOKE. Forsaken; disavowed. 10 Edw. II. c. 1.

FORESHORE. That part of the land adjacent to the sea which is alternately covered and left dry by the ordinary flow of the tides; *i. e.*, by the medium line between the greatest and least range of tide, (spring tides and neap tides.) Sweet.

FOREST. In old English law. A certain territory of wooded ground and fruitful pastures, privileged for wild beasts and fowls of forest, chase, and warren, to rest and abide in the safe protection of the prince for his princely delight and pleasure, having a peculiar court and officers. Manw. For. Laws, c. 1, no. 1; Termes de la Ley; 1 Bl. Comm. 289.

A royal hunting-ground which lost its peculiar character with the extinction of its courts, or when the franchise passed into the hands of a subject. Spelman; Cowell.

The word is also used to signify a franchise or right, being the right of keeping, for the purpose of hunting, the wild beasts and fowls of forest, chase, park, and warren, in a territory or precinct of woody ground or pasture set apart for the purpose. 1 Steph. Comm. 665.

FOREST COURTS. In English law. Courts instituted for the government of the king's forest in different parts of the kingdom, and for the punishment of all injuries done to the king's deer or *venison*, to the *vert* or greensward, and to the *covert* in which such deer were lodged. They consisted of the courts of attachments, of regard, of sweinmote, and of justice-seat; but in later times these courts are no longer held. 3 Bl. Comm. 71.

FOREST LAW. The system or body of old law relating to the royal forests.

FORESTAGE. A duty or tribute payable to the king's foresters. Cowell.

FORESTAGIUM. A duty or tribute payable to the king's foresters. Cowell.

FORESTALL. To intercept or obstruct a passenger on the king's highway. Cowell. To beset the way of a tenant so as to prevent his coming on the premises. 3 Bl. Comm. 170. To intercept a deer on his way to the forest before he can regain it. Cowell.

FORESTALLER. In old English law. Obstruction; hindrance; the offense of stopping the highway; the hindering a tenant from coming to his land; intercepting a deer before it can regain the forest. Also one who forestalls; one who commits the offense of forestalling. 3 Bl. Comm. 170; Cowell.

FORESTALLING. Obstructing the highway. Intercepting a person on the highway.

FORESTALLING THE MARKET. The act of the buying or contracting for any merchandise or provision on its way to the market, with the intention of selling it again at a higher price; or the dissuading persons from bringing their goods or provisions there; or persuading them to enhance the price when there. 4 Bl. Comm. 158. This was formerly an indictable offense in England, but is now abolished by St. 7 & 8 Vict. c. 24. 4 Steph. Comm. 291, note.

FORESTARIUS. In English law. A forester. An officer who takes care of the woods and forests. *De forestario apponendo*, a writ which lay to appoint a forester to prevent further commission of waste when a tenant in dower had committed waste. Bract. 316; Du Cange.

In Scotch law. A forester or keeper of woods, to whom, by reason of his office, pertains the bark and the hewn branches. And, when he rides through the forest, he may take a tree as high as his own head. Skene de Verb. Sign.

FORESTER. A sworn officer of the *forest*, appointed by the king's letters patent to walk the forest, watching both the vert and the venison, attaching and presenting all trespassers against them within their own bailiwick or walk. These letters patent were generally granted during good behavior; but sometimes they held the office in fee. Blount.

FORETHOUGHT FELONY. In Scotch law. Murder committed in consequence of a previous design. Ersk. Inst. 4, 4, 50; Bell.

FORFANG. In old English law. The taking of provisions from any person in fairs or markets before the royal purveyors were served with necessaries for the sovereign. Cowell. Also the seizing and rescuing of stolen or strayed cattle from the hands of a thief, or of those having illegal possession of them; also the reward fixed for such rescue.

FORFEIT. To lose an estate, a franchise, or other property belonging to one, by the act of the law, and as a consequence of some misfeasance, negligence, or omission. The further ideas connoted by this term are that it is a deprivation, (that is, against the will of the losing party,) and that the property is either transferred to another or resumed by the original grantor.

To incur a penalty; to become liable to the payment of a sum of money, as the consequence of a certain act.

FORFEITABLE. Liable to be forfeited; subject to forfeiture for non-user, neglect, crime, etc.

FORFEITURE. 1. A punishment annexed by law to some illegal act or negligence in the owner of lands, tenements, or hereditaments, whereby he loses all his interest therein, and they go to the party injured as a recompense for the wrong which he alone, or the public together with himself, hath sustained. 2 Bl. Comm. 267.

2. The loss of land by a tenant to his lord, as the consequence of some breach of fidelity. 1 Steph. Comm. 166.

3. The loss of lands and goods to the state, as the consequence of crime. 4 Bl. Comm. 381, 387; 4 Steph. Comm. 447, 452; 2 Kent, Comm. 385; 4 Kent, Comm. 426.

4. The loss of goods or chattels, as a punishment for some crime or misdemeanor in the party forfeiting, and as a compensation for the offense and injury committed against him to whom they are forfeited. 2 Bl. Comm. 420.

It should be noted that "forfeiture" is not an identical or convertible term with "confiscation." The latter is the consequence of the former. Forfeiture is the result which the law attaches as an immediate and necessary consequence to the illegal acts of the individual; but confiscation implies the action of the state; and property, although it may be forfeited, cannot be said to be confiscated until the government has formally claimed or taken possession of it.

5. The loss of office by abuser, non-user, or refusal to exercise it.

6. The loss of a corporate franchise or charter in consequence of some illegal act, or of malfeasance or non-feasance.

7. The loss of the right to life, as the consequence of the commission of some crime to which the law has affixed a capital penalty.

8. The incurring a liability to pay a definite sum of money as the consequence of violating the provisions of some statute, or refusal to comply with some requirement of law.

9. A thing or sum of money forfeited. Something imposed as a punishment for an offense or delinquency. The word in this sense is frequently associated with the word "penalty."

FORFEITURE OF A BOND. A failure to perform the condition on which the obligor was to be excused from the penalty in the bond.

FORFEITURE OF MARRIAGE. A penalty incurred by a ward in chivalry who married without the consent or against the will of the guardian. See DUPLEX VALOR MARITAGII.

FORFEITURE OF SILK, supposed to lie in the docks, used, in times when its importation was prohibited, to be proclaimed each term in the exchequer.

FORFEITURES ABOLITION ACT. Another name for the felony act of 1870, abolishing forfeitures for felony in England.

FORGABULUM, or FORGAVEL. A quit-rent; a small reserved rent in money. Jacob.

FORGE. To fabricate, construct, or prepare one thing in imitation of another thing, with the intention of substituting the false for the genuine, or otherwise deceiving and defrauding by the use of the spurious article. To counterfeit or make falsely. Especially, to make a spurious written instrument with the intention of fraudulently substituting it for another, or of passing it off as genuine; or to fraudulently alter a genuine instrument to another's prejudice; or to sign another person's name to a document, with a deceitful and fraudulent intent.

To forge (a metaphorical expression, borrowed from the occupation of the smith) means, properly speaking, no more than *to make* or *form*, but in our law it is always taken in an evil sense. 2 East, P. C. p. 852, c. 19, § 1.

To forge is to make in the likeness of something else; to counterfeit is to make in imitation of something else, with a view to defraud by passing the false copy for genuine or original. Both words, "forged" and "counterfeited," convey the idea of similitude. 42 Me. 392.

In common usage, however, *forgery* is almost always predicated of some private instrument or writing, as a deed, note, will, or a signature; and *counterfeiting* denotes the fraudulent imitation of coined or paper money or some substitute therefor.

FORGERY. In criminal law. The falsely making or materially altering, with intent to defraud, any writing which, if genuine, might apparently be of legal efficacy or the foundation of a legal liability. 2 Bish. Crim. Law, § 523.

The fraudulent making and alteration of a writing to the prejudice of another man's right. 4 Bl. Comm. 247. See FORGE.

Forgery, at common law, denotes a false making, (which includes every alteration or addition to a true instrument;) a making, *malo animo*, of any written instrument for the purpose of fraud and deceit. 2 East, P. C. 852.

The false making an instrument which purports on its face to be good and valid for the purposes for which it was created, with a design to defraud any person or persons. 1 Leach, 366.

The thing itself, so falsely made, imitated, or forged; especially a forged writing. A forged signature is frequently said to be "a *forgery.*"

In the law of evidence. The fabrication or counterfeiting of evidence. The artful and fraudulent manipulation of physical objects, or the deceitful arrangement of genuine facts or things, in such a manner as to create an erroneous impression or a false inference in the minds of those who may observe them. See Burrill, Circ. Ev. 131, 420.

FORGERY ACT, 1870. The statute 33 & 34 Vict. c. 58, was passed for the punishment of forgers of stock certificates, and for extending to Scotland certain provisions of the forgery act of 1861. Mozley & Whitley.

FORHERDA. In old records. A herdland, headland, or foreland. Cowell.

FORI DISPUTATIONES. In the civil law. Discussions or arguments before a court. 1 Kent, Comm. 530.

FORINSECUM MANERIUM. That part of a manor which lies without the town, and is not included within the liberties of it. Paroch. Antiq. 351.

FORINSECUM SERVITIUM. The payment of extraordinary aid. Kennett, Gloss.

FORINSECUS. Lat. Foreign; exterior; outside; extraordinary. *Servitium forinsecum,* the payment of aid, scutage, and other extraordinary military services. *Forinsecum manerium,* the manor, or that part of it which lies outside the bars or town, and is not included within the liberties of it. Cowell; Blount; Jacob; 1 Reeve, Eng. Law, 273.

FORINSIC. In old English law. Exterior; foreign; extraordinary In feudal law, the term "forinsic services" comprehended the payment of extraordinary aids or the rendition of extraordinary military services, and in this sense was opposed to "intrinsic services." 1 Reeve, Eng. Law, 273.

FORIS. Abroad; out of doors; on the outside of a place; without; extrinsic.

FORISBANITUS. In old English law. Banished.

FORISFACERE. Lat. To forfeit; to lose an estate or other property on account of some criminal or illegal act. To confiscate.

To act beyond the law, *i. e.,* to transgress or infringe the law; to commit an offense or wrong; to do any act against or beyond the law. See Co. Litt. 59*a;* Du Cange; Spelman.

Forisfacere, i. e., extra legem seu consuetudinem facere. Co. Litt. 59. *Forisfacere, i. e.,* to do something beyond law or custom.

FORISFACTUM. Forfeited. *Bona forisfacta,* forfeited goods. 1 Bl. Comm. 299. A crime. Du Cange; Spelman.

FORISFACTURA. A crime or offense through which property is forfeited.

A fine or punishment in money.

Forfeiture. The loss of property or life in consequence of crime.

Forisfactura plena. A forfeiture of all a man's property. Things which were forfeited. Du Cange; Spelman.

FORISFACTUS. A criminal. One who has forfeited his life by commission of a capital offense. Spelman.

Forisfactus servus. A slave who has been a free man, but has forfeited his freedom by crime. Du Cange.

FORISFAMILIARE. In old English and Scotch law. Literally, to put out of a family, (*foris familiam ponere.*) To portion off a son, so that he could have no further claim upon his father. Glanv. lib. 7, c. 3.

To emancipate, or free from paternal authority.

FORISFAMILIATED. In old English law. Portioned off. A son was said to be forisfamiliated (*forisfamiliari*) if his father assigned him part of his land, and gave him seisin thereof, and did this at the request or with the free consent of the son himself, who expressed himself satisfied with such portion. 1 Reeve, Eng. Law, 42, 110.

FORISFAMILIATUS. In old English law. Put out of a family; portioned off; emancipated; forisfamiliated. Bract. fol. 64.

FORISJUDICATIO. In old English law. Forejudger. A forejudgment. A judgment of court whereby a man is put out of possession of a thing. Co. Litt. 100*b*.

FORISJUDICATUS. Forejudged; sent from court; banished. Deprived of a thing by judgment of court. Bract. fol. 250*b;* Co. Litt. 100*b;* Du Cange.

FORISJURARE. To forswear; to abjure; to abandon. *Forisjurare parentilam.* To remove oneself from parental authority. The person who did this lost his rights as heir. Du Cange.

Provinciam forisjurare. To forswear the country. Spelman.

FORJUDGE. See FOREJUDGE.

FORJURER. L. Fr. In old English law. To forswear; to abjure. *Forjurer royalme,* to abjure the realm. Britt. cc. 1, 16.

FORLER-LAND. Land in the diocese of Hereford, which had a peculiar custom attached to it, but which has been long since disused, although the name is retained. But. Surv. 56.

FORM. 1. A model or skeleton of an instrument to be used in a judicial proceeding, containing the principal necessary matters, the proper technical terms or phrases, and whatever else is necessary to make it formally correct, arranged in proper and methodical order, and capable of being adapted to the circumstances of the specific case.

2. As distinguished from "substance," "form" means the legal or technical manner or order to be observed in legal instruments or juridical proceedings, or in the construction of legal documents or processes.

The distinction between "form" and "substance" is often important in reference to the validity or amendment of pleadings. If the matter of the plea is bad or insufficient, irrespective of the manner of setting it forth, the defect is one of substance. If the matter of the plea is good and sufficient, but is inartificially or defectively pleaded, the defect is one of form.

FORMA. Form; the prescribed form of judicial proceedings. *Forma et figura judicii,* the form and shape of judgment or judicial action. 3 Bl. Comm. 271.

Forma dat esse. Form gives being. Called "the old physical maxim." Lord Henley, Ch., 2 Eden, 99.

Forma legalis forma essentialis. Legal form is essential form. 10 Coke, 100.

Forma non observata, infertur adnullatio actus. Where form is not observed, a nullity of the act is inferred. 12 Coke, 7. Where the law prescribes a form, the non-observance of it is fatal to the proceeding, and the whole becomes a nullity. Best, Ev. Introd. § 59.

FORMA PAUPERIS. See IN FORMA PAUPERIS.

FORMALITIES. In England, robes worn by the magistrates of a city or corporation, etc., on solemn occasions. Enc. Lond.

FORMALITY. The conditions, in regard to method, order, arrangement, use of technical expressions, performance of specific acts, etc., which are required by the law in the making of contracts or conveyances, or in the taking of legal proceedings, to insure their validity and regularity.

FORMATA. In canon law. Canonical letters. Spelman.

FORMATA BREVIA. Formed writs; writs of form. See BREVIA FORMATA.

FORMED ACTION. An action for which a set form of words is prescribed, which must be strictly adhered to. 10 Mod. 140, 141.

FORMEDON. An ancient writ in English law which was available for one who had a right to lands or tenements by virtue of a gift in tail. It was in the nature of a writ of right, and was the highest action that a tenant in tail could have; for he could not have an absolute writ of right, that being confined to such as claimed in fee-simple, and for that reason this writ of formedon was granted to him by the statute *de donis,* Westm. 2, (13 Edw. I. c. 1,) and was emphatically called "his" writ of right. The writ was distinguished into three species, viz.: Formedon in the descender, in the remainder, and in the reverter. It was abolished in England by St. 3 & 4 Wm. IV. c. 27. See 3 Bl. Comm. 191; Co. Litt. 316; Fitzh. Nat. Brev. 255.

FORMEDON IN THE DESCENDER. A writ of formedon which lay where a gift was made in tail, and the tenant in tail aliened the lands or was disseised of them and died, for the heir in tail to recover them, against the actual tenant of the freehold. 3 Bl. Comm. 192.

FORMEDON IN THE REMAINDER. A writ of formedon which lay where a man gave lands to another for life or in tail, with remainder to a third person in tail or in fee, and he who had the particular estate died without issue inheritable, and a stranger intruded upon him in remainder, and kept him out of possession. In this case he in *remainder,* or his heir, was entitled to this writ. 3 Bl. Comm. 192.

FORMEDON IN THE REVERTER. A writ of formedon which lay where there was a gift in tail, and afterwards, by the death of the donee or his heirs without issue of his body, the reversion fell in upon the donor, his heirs or assigns. In such case, the *reversioner* had this writ to recover the lands. 3 Bl. Comm. 192.

FORMELLA. A certain weight of above 70 lbs., mentioned in 51 Hen. III. Cowell.

FORMER ADJUDICATION, or FORMER RECOVERY. An adjudication or recovery in a former action. See RES JUDICATA.

FORMIDO PERICULI. Lat. Fear of danger. 1 Kent, Comm. 23.

FORMS OF ACTION. The general designation of the various species or kinds of personal actions known to the common law, such as trover, trespass, debt, *assumpsit*, etc. These differ in their pleadings and evidence, as well as in the circumstances to which they are respectively applicable.

FORMULA. In common-law practice, a set form of words used in judicial proceedings. In the civil law, an action. Calvin.

FORMULÆ. In Roman law. When the *legis actiones* were proved to be inconvenient, a mode of procedure called "*per formulas*," (*i. e.*, by means of *formulæ*,) was gradually introduced, and eventually the *legis actiones* were abolished by the *Lex Æbutia*, B. C. 164, excepting in a very few exceptional matters. The *formulæ* were four in number, namely: (1) The *Demonstratio*, wherein the plaintiff stated, *i. e.*, showed, the facts out of which his claim arose; (2) the *Intentio*, where he made his claim against the defendant; (3) the *Adjudicatio*, wherein the judex was directed to assign or adjudicate the property or any portion or portions thereof according to the rights of the parties; and (4) the *Condemnatio*, in which the judex was authorized and directed to condemn or to acquit according as the facts were or were not proved. These *formulæ* were obtained from the magistrate, (*in jure*,) and were thereafter proceeded with before the judex, (*in judicio*.) Brown. See Mackeld. Rom. Law, § 204.

FORMULARIES. Collections of *formulæ*, or forms of forensic proceedings and instruments used among the Franks, and other early continental nations of Europe. Among these the formulary of Marculphus may be mentioned as of considerable interest. Butl. Co. Litt. note 77, lib. 3.

FORNAGIUM. The fee taken by a lord of his tenant, who was bound to bake in the lord's common oven, (*in furno domini*,) or for a commission to use his own.

FORNICATION. Unlawful sexual intercourse between two unmarried persons. Further, if one of the persons be married and the other not, it is fornication on the part of the latter, though adultery for the former. In some jurisdictions, however, by statute, it is adultery on the part of both persons if the woman is married, whether the man is married or not.

FORNIX. Lat. A brothel; fornication.

FORNO. In Spanish law. An oven. Las Partidas, pt. 3, tit. 32, l. 18.

FORO. In Spanish law. The place where tribunals hear and determine causes,—*exercendarum litium locus*.

FOROS. In Spanish law. Emphyteutic rents. Schm. Civil Law, 309.

FORPRISE. An exception; reservation; excepted; reserved. Anciently, a term of frequent use in leases and conveyances. Cowell; Blount.

In another sense, the word is taken for any exaction.

FORSCHEL. A strip of land lying next to the highway.

FORSES. Waterfalls. Camden, Brit.

FORSPEAKER. An attorney or advocate in a cause. Blount; Whishaw.

FORSPECA. In old English law. Prolocutor; paranymphus.

FORSTAL. See FORESTALL.

Forstellarius est pauperum depressor et totius communitatis et patriæ publicus inimicus. 3 Inst. 196. A forestaller is an oppressor of the poor, and a public enemy of the whole community and country.

FORSWEAR. In criminal law. To make oath to that which the deponent knows to be untrue.

This term is wider in its scope than "perjury," for the latter, as a technical term, includes the idea of the oath being taken before a competent court or officer, and relating to a material issue, which is not implied by the word "forswear."

FORT. This term means "something more than a mere military camp, post, or station. The term implies a fortification, or a place protected from attack by some such means as a moat, wall, or parapet." 12 Fed. Rep. 424.

FORTALICE. A fortress or place of strength, which anciently did not pass without a special grant. 11 Hen. VII. c. 18.

FORTALITIUM. In old Scotch law. A fortalice; a castle. Properly a house or tower which has a battlement or a ditch or moat about it.

FORTHCOMING. In Scotch law. The action by which an arrestment (garnishment) is made effectual. It is a decree or process by which the creditor is given the right to demand that the sum arrested be applied for payment of his claim. 2 Kames, Eq. 288, 289; Bell.

FORTHCOMING BOND. A bond given to a sheriff who has levied on property, conditioned that the property shall be forthcoming, *i. e.*, produced, when required. On the giving of such bond, the goods are allowed to remain in the possession of the debtor. 2 Wash. (Va.) 189; 11 Grat. 522; 61 Ga. 520.

The sheriff or other officer levying a writ of *fieri facias*, or distress warrant, may take from the debtor a bond, with sufficient surety, payable to the creditor, reciting the service of such writ or warrant, and the amount due thereon, (including his fee for taking the bond, commissions, and other lawful charges, if any,) with condition that the property shall be forthcoming at the day and place of sale; whereupon such property may be permitted to remain in the possession and at the risk of the debtor. Code Va. 1887, § 3617.

FORTHWITH. As soon as, by reasonable exertion, confined to the object, a thing may be done. Thus, when a defendant is ordered to plead forthwith, he must plead within twenty-four hours. When a statute enacts that an act is to be done "forthwith," it means that the act is to be done within a reasonable time. 1 Chit. Archb. Pr. (12th Ed.) 164.

FORTIA. Force. In old English law. Force used by an accessary, to enable the principal to commit a crime, as by binding or holding a person while another killed him, or by aiding or counseling in any way, or commanding the act to be done. Bract. fols. 138, 138*b*. According to Lord Coke, *fortia* was a word of art, and properly signified the furnishing of a weapon of force to do the fact, and by force whereof the fact was committed, and he that furnished it was not present when the fact was done. 2 Inst. 182.

FORTIA FRISCA. Fresh force, (*q. v.*)

FORTILITY. In old English law. A fortified place; a castle; a bulwark. Cowell; 11 Hen. VII. c. 18.

FORTIOR. Lat. Stronger. A term applied, in the law of evidence, to that species of presumption, arising from facts shown in evidence, which is strong enough to shift the burden of proof to the opposite party. Burrill, Circ. Ev. 64, 66.

Fortior est custodia legis quam hominis. 2 Rolle, 325. The custody of the law is stronger than that of man.

Fortior et potentior est dispositio legis quam hominis. The disposition of the law is of greater force and effect than that of man. Co. Litt. 234*a;* Shep. Touch. 302; 15 East, 178. The law in some cases overrides the will of the individual, and renders ineffective or futile his expressed intention or contract. Broom, Max. 697.

FORTIORI. See A FORTIORI.

FORTIS. Strong. *Fortis et sana*, strong and sound; staunch and strong; as a vessel. Townsh. Pl. 227.

FORTLETT. A place or port of some strength; a little fort. Old Nat. Brev. 45.

FORTUIT. In French law. Accidental; fortuitous. *Cas fortuit*, a fortuitous event. *Fortuitment*, accidentally; by chance.

FORTUITOUS. Accidental; undesigned; adventitious. Resulting from unavoidable physical causes.

FORTUITOUS COLLISION. In maritime law. The accidental running foul of vessels. 14 Pet. 112.

FORTUITOUS EVENT. In the civil law. That which happens by a cause which cannot be resisted. An unforseen occurrence, not caused by either of the parties, nor such as they could prevent. In French it is called "*cas fortuit.*" Civil Code La. art. 3556, no. 15.

There is a difference between a fortuitous event, or inevitable accident, and irresistible force. By the former, commonly called the "act of God," is meant any accident produced by physical causes which are irresistible; such as a loss by lightning or storms, by the perils of the seas, by inundations and earthquakes, or by sudden death or illness. By the latter is meant such an interposition of human agency as is, from its nature and power, absolutely uncontrollable. Of this nature are losses occasioned by the inroads of a hostile army, or by public enemies. Story, Bailm. § 25.

FORTUNA. Lat. Fortune; also treasure-trove. Jacob.

Fortunam faciunt judicem. They make fortune the judge. Co. Litt. 167. Spoken of the process of making partition among coparceners by drawing lots for the several purparts.

FORTUNE-TELLERS. Persons pretending or professing to tell fortunes, and punishable as rogues and vagabonds or disorderly persons.

FORTUNIUM. In old English law. A tournament or fighting with spears, and an appeal to fortune therein.

FORTY-DAYS COURT. The court of attachment in forests, or wood-mote court.

FORUM. Lat. A court of justice, or judicial tribunal; a place of jurisdiction; a place where a remedy is sought; a place of litigation. 3 Story, 347.

In Roman law. The market place, or public paved court, in the city of Rome, where such public business was transacted as the assemblies of the people and the judicial trial of causes, and where also elections, markets, and the public exchange were held.

FORUM ACTUS. The forum of the act. The forum of the place where the act was done which is now called in question.

FORUM CONSCIENTIÆ. The forum or tribunal of conscience.

FORUM CONTENTIOSUM. A contentious forum or court; a place of litigation; the ordinary court of justice, as distinguished from the tribunal of conscience. 3 Bl. Comm. 211.

FORUM CONTRACTUS. The forum of the contract; the court of the place where a contract is made; the place where a contract is made, considered as a place of jurisdiction. 2 Kent, Comm. 463.

FORUM DOMESTICUM. A domestic forum or tribunal. The visitatorial power is called a "*forum domesticum,*" calculated to determine, *sine strepitu,* all disputes that arise within themselves. 1 W. Bl. 82.

FORUM DOMICILII. The forum or court of the domicile; the domicile of a defendant, considered as a place of jurisdiction. 2 Kent, Comm. 463.

FORUM ECCLESIASTICUM. An ecclesiastical court. The spiritual jurisdiction, as distinguished from the secular.

FORUM LIGEANTIÆ REI. The forum of defendant's allegiance. The court or jurisdiction of the country to which he owes allegiance.

FORUM ORIGINIS. The court of one's nativity. The place of a person's birth, considered as a place of jurisdiction.

FORUM REGIUM. The king's court. St. Westm. 2, c. 43.

FORUM REI. This term may mean either (1) the forum of the defendant, that is, of his residence or domicile; or (2) the forum of the *res* or thing in controversy, that is, of the place where the property is situated. The ambiguity springs from the fact that *rei* may be the genitive of either *reus* or *res.*

FORUM REI GESTÆ. The forum or court of a *res gesta,* (thing done;) the place where an act is done, considered as a place of jurisdiction and remedy. 2 Kent, Comm. 463.

FORUM REI SITÆ. The court where the thing in controversy is situated. The place where the subject-matter in controversy is situated, considered as a place of jurisdiction. 2 Kent, Comm. 463.

FORUM SECULARE. A secular, as distinguished from an ecclesiastical or spiritual, court.

FORURTH. In old records. A long slip of ground. Cowell.

FORWARDING MERCHANT, or FORWARDER. One who receives and forwards goods, taking upon himself the expenses of transportation, for which he receives a compensation from the owners, having no concern in the vessels or wagons by which they are transported, and no interest in the freight, and not being deemed a common carrier, but a mere warehouseman and agent. Story, Bailm. §§ 502, 509.

FOSSA. In the civil law. A ditch; a receptacle of water, made by hand. Dig. 43, 14, 1, 5.

In old English law. A ditch. A pit full of water, in which women committing felony were drowned. A grave or sepulcher. Spelman.

FOSSAGIUM. In old English law. The duty levied on the inhabitants for repairing the moat or ditch round a fortified town.

FOSSATORUM OPERATIO. In old English law. Fosse-work; or the service of laboring, done by inhabitants and adjoining tenants, for the repair and maintenance of the *ditches* round a city or town, for which some paid a contribution, called "*fossagium.*" Cowell.

FOSSATUM. A dyke, ditch, or trench; a place inclosed by a ditch; a moat; a canal.

FOSSE-WAY, or FOSSE. One of the four ancient Roman ways through England. Spelman.

FOSSELLUM. A small ditch. Cowell.

FOSTERING. An ancient custom in Ireland, in which persons put away their children to fosterers. Fostering was held to be a stronger alliance than blood, and the foster children participated in the fortunes of their foster fathers. Mozley & Whitley.

FOSTERLAND. Land given, assigned, or allotted to the finding of food or victuals for any person or persons; as in monasteries for the monks, etc. Cowell; Blount.

FOSTERLEAN. The remuneration fixed for the rearing of a foster child; also the jointure of a wife. Jacob.

FOUJDAR. In Hindu law. Under the Mogul government a magistrate of the police over a large district, who took cognizance of all criminal matters within his jurisdiction, and sometimes was employed as receiver general of the revenues. Wharton.

FOUJDARRY COURT. In Hindu law. A tribunal for administering criminal law.

FOUNDATION. The founding or building of a college or hospital. The incorporation or endowment of a college or hospital is the foundation; and he who endows it with land or other property is the founder.

FOUNDER. The person who endows an eleemosynary corporation or institution, or supplies the funds for its establishment.

FOUNDEROSA. Founderous; out of repair, as a road. Cro. Car. 366.

FOUNDLING. A deserted or exposed infant; a child found without a parent or guardian, its relatives being unknown. It has a settlement in the district where found.

FOUNDLING HOSPITALS. Charitable institutions which exist in most countries for taking care of infants forsaken by their parents, such being generally the offspring of illegal connections. The foundling hospital act in England is the 13 Geo. II. c. 29.

FOUR. In old French law. An oven or bake-house. *Four banal,* an oven, owned by the seignior of the estate, to which the tenants were obliged to bring their bread for baking. Also the proprietary right to maintain such an oven.

FOUR CORNERS. The face of a written instrument. That which is contained on the face of a deed (without any aid from the knowledge of the circumstances under which it is made) is said to be within its four corners, because every deed is still supposed to be written on one entire skin, and so to have but four corners.

To look at the *four corners* of an instrument is to examine the whole of it, so as to construe it as a whole, without reference to any one part more than another. 2 Smith, Lead. Cas. 295.

FOUR SEAS. The seas surrounding England. These were divided into the Western, including the Scotch and Irish; the Northern, or North sea; the Eastern, being the German ocean; the Southern, being the British channel.

FOURCHER. Fr. To fork. This was a method of delaying an action anciently resorted to by defendants when two of them were joined in the suit. Instead of appearing together, each would appear in turn and cast an essoin for the other, thus postponing the trial.

FOURCHING. The act of delaying legal proceedings. Termes de la Ley.

FOURIERISM. A form of socialism. See 1 Mill, Pol. Ec. 260.

FOWLS OF WARREN. Such fowls as are preserved under the game laws in warrens. According to Manwood, these are partridges and pheasants. According to Coke, they are partridges, rails, quails, woodcocks, pheasants, mallards, and herons. Co. Litt. 233.

FOX'S LIBEL ACT. In English law. This was the statute 52 Geo. III. c. 60, which secured to juries, upon the trial of indictments for libel, the right of pronouncing a general verdict of guilty or not guilty upon the whole matter in issue, and no longer bound them to find a verdict of guilty on proof of the publication of the paper charged to be a libel, and of the sense ascribed to it in the indictment. Wharton.

FOY. L. Fr. Faith; allegiance; fidelity.

FRACTIO. A breaking; division; fraction; a portion of a thing less than the whole.

FRACTION. A breaking, or breaking up; a fragment or broken part; a portion of a thing, less than the whole.

FRACTION OF A DAY. A portion of a day. The dividing a day. Generally, the law does not allow the fraction of a day. 2 Bl. Comm. 141.

Fractionem diei non recipit lex. Lofft, 572. The law does not take notice of a portion of a day.

FRACTITIUM. Arable land. Mon. Angl.

FRACTURA NAVIUM. The breaking or wreck of ships; the same as *naufragium*, (*q. v.*)

FRAIS. Fr. Expense; charges; costs. *Frais d'un procès*, costs of a suit.

FRAIS DE JUSTICE. In French and Canadian law. Costs incurred incidentally to the action.

FRAIS JUSQU'A BORD. Fr. In French commercial law. Expenses to the board; expenses incurred on a shipment of goods, in packing, cartage, commissions, etc., up to the point where they are actually put on board the vessel. 16 Fed. Rep. 336.

FRANC. A French coin of the value of a little over eighteen cents.

FRANC ALEU. In French feudal law. An allod; a free inheritance; or an estate held free of any services except such as were due to the sovereign.

FRANCHILANUS. A freeman. Chart. Hen. IV. A free tenant. Spelman.

FRANCHISE. A special privilege conferred by government upon an individual, and which does not belong to the citizens of the country generally, of common right. It is essential to the character of a franchise that it should be a grant from the sovereign authority, and in this country no franchise can be held which is not derived from a law of the state. See Ang. & A. Corp. § 104: 3 Kent, Comm. 458; 2 Bl. Comm. 37.

In England, a franchise is defined to be a royal privilege in the hands of a subject. In this country, it is a privilege of a public nature, which cannot be exercised without a legislative grant. 45 Mo. 17.

A franchise is a privilege or immunity of a public nature, which cannot be legally exercised without legislative grant. To be a corporation is a franchise. The various powers conferred on corporations are franchises. The execution of a policy of insurance by an insurance company, and the issuing a bank-note by an incorporated bank, are franchises. 15 Johns. 387.

The word "franchise" has various significations, both in a legal and popular sense. A corporation is itself a franchise belonging to the members of the corporation, and the corporation, itself a franchise, may hold other franchises. So, also, the different powers of a corporation, such as the right to hold and dispose of property, are its franchises. In a popular sense, the political rights of subjects and citizens are franchises, such as the right of suffrage, etc. 32 N. H. 484.

The term "franchise" has several significations, and there is some confusion in its use. When used with reference to corporations, the better opinion, deduced from the authorities, seems to be that it consists of the entire privileges embraced in and constituting the grant. It does not embrace the property acquired by the exercise of the franchise. 36 Conn. 255.

The term is also used, in a popular sense, to denote a political right or privilege belonging to a free citizen; as the "elective franchise."

FRANCIA. France. Bract. fol. 427*b*.

FRANCIGENA. A man born in France. A designation formerly given to aliens in England.

FRANCUS. Free; a freeman; a Frank. Spelman.

FRANCUS BANCUS. Free bench, (*q. v.*)

FRANCUS HOMO. In old European law. A free man. Domesday.

FRANCUS PLEGIUS. In old English law. A frank pledge, or free pledge. See FRANK-PLEDGE.

FRANCUS TENENS. A freeholder. See FRANK-TENEMENT.

FRANK, *v.* To send matter through the public mails free of postage, by a personal or official privilege.

FRANK, *adj.* In old English law. Free. Occurring in several compounds.

FRANK-ALMOIGNE. In English law. Free alms. A spiritual tenure whereby religious corporations, aggregate or sole, held lands of the donor to them and their successors forever. They were discharged of all other except religious services, and the *trinoda necessitas*. It differs from tenure by divine service, in that the latter required the performance of certain divine services, whereas the former, as its name imports, is free. This tenure is expressly excepted in the 12 Car. II. c. 24, § 7, and therefore still subsists in some few instances. 2 Broom & H. Comm. 203.

FRANK BANK. In old English law. Free bench. Litt. § 166; Co. Litt. 110*b*. See FREE-BENCH.

FRANK-CHASE. A liberty of free chase enjoyed by any one, whereby all other persons having ground within that compass are forbidden to cut down wood, etc., even in their own demesnes, to the prejudice of the owner of the liberty. Cowell. See CHASE.

FRANK-FEE. Freehold lands exempted from all services, but not from homage; lands held otherwise than in ancient demesne.

That which a man holds to himself and his heirs, and not by such service as is required in ancient demesne, according to the custom of the manor. Cowell.

FRANK FERM. In English law. A species of estate held in socage, said by Britton to be "lands and tenements whereof the nature of the fee is changed by feoffment out of chivalry for certain yearly services, and in respect whereof neither homage, ward, marriage, nor relief can be demanded." Britt. c. 66; 2 Bl. Comm. 80.

FRANK-FOLD. In old English law. Free-fold; a privilege for the lord to have all the sheep of his tenants and the inhabitants within his seigniory, in his fold, in his demesnes, to manure his land. Keilw. 198.

FRANK-LAW. An obsolete expression signifying the rights and privileges of a citizen, or the liberties and civic rights of a freeman.

FRANK-MARRIAGE. A species of entailed estates, in English law, now grown out of use, but still capable of subsisting. When tenements are given by one to another, together with a wife, who is a daughter or cousin of the donor, to hold in frank-marriage, the donees shall have the tenements to them and the heirs of their two bodies begotten, *i. e.*, in special tail. For the word "frank-marriage," *ex vi termini*, both creates and limits an inheritance, not only supplying words of descent, but also terms of procreation. The donees are liable to no service except fealty, and a reserved rent would be void, until the fourth degree of consanguinity be passed between the issues of the donor and donee, when they were capable by the law of the church of intermarrying. Litt. § 19; 2 Bl. Comm. 115.

FRANK-PLEDGE. In old English law. A pledge or surety for freemen; that is, the pledge, or corporate responsibility, of all the inhabitants of a tithing for the general good behavior of each free-born citizen above the age of fourteen, and for his being forthcoming to answer any infraction of the law. Termes de la Ley; Cowell.

FRANK-TENANT. A freeholder. Litt. § 91.

FRANK-TENEMENT. In English law. A free tenement, freeholding, or freehold. 2 Bl. Comm. 61, 62, 104; 1 Steph. Comm. 217; Bract. fol. 207. Used to denote both the tenure and the estate.

FRANKING PRIVILEGE. The privilege of sending certain matter through the public mails without payment of postage, in pursuance of a personal or official privilege.

FRANKLEYN, (spelled, also, "Francling" and "Franklin.") A freeman; a freeholder; a gentleman. Blount; Cowell.

FRASSETUM. In old English law. A wood or wood-ground where ash-trees grow. Co. Litt. 4*b*.

FRATER. In the civil law. A brother. *Frater consanguineus*, a brother having the same father, but born of a different mother. *Frater uterinus*, a brother born of the same mother, but by a different father. *Frater nutricius*, a bastard brother.

Frater fratri uterino non succedet in hæreditate paterna. A brother shall not succeed a uterine brother in the paternal inheritance. 2 Bl. Comm. 223; Fortes. de Laud. c. 5. A maxim of the common law of England, now superseded by the statute 3 & 4 Wm. IV. c. 106, § 9. See Broom, Max. 530.

FRATERIA. In old records. A fraternity, brotherhood, or society of religious persons, who were mutually bound to pray for the good health and life, etc., of their living brethren, and the souls of those that were dead. Cowell.

FRATERNIA. A fraternity or brotherhood.

FRATERNITY. "Some people of a place united together, in respect of a mystery and business, into a company." 1 Salk. 193.

FRATRES CONJURATI. Sworn brothers or companions for the defense of their sovereign, or for other purposes. Hoved. 445.

FRATRES PYES. In old English law. Certain friars who wore white and black garments. Walsingham, 124.

FRATRIAGE. A younger brother's inheritance.

FRATRICIDE. One who has killed a brother or sister; also the killing of a brother or sister.

FRAUD. Fraud consists of some deceitful practice or willful device, resorted to with intent to deprive another of his right, or in some manner to do him an injury. As distinguished from negligence, it is always positive, intentional. 3 Denio, 232.

Fraud, as applied to contracts, is the cause of an error bearing on a material part of the contract, created or continued by artifice, with design to obtain some unjust advantage to the one party, or to cause an inconvenience or loss to the other. Civil Code La. art. 1847.

Fraud, in the sense of a court of equity, properly includes all acts, omissions, and concealments which involve a breach of legal or equitable duty, trust, or confidence justly reposed, and are injurious to another, or by which an undue and unconscientious advantage is taken of another. 1 Story, Eq. Jur. § 187.

The unlawful appropriation of another's property, with knowledge, by design and without criminal intent. Bac. Abr.

Fraud may be *actual* or *constructive*. Actual fraud consists in any kind of artifice by which another is deceived. Constructive fraud consists in any act of omission or commission contrary to legal or equitable duty, trust, or confidence justly reposed, which is contrary to good conscience and operates to the injury of another. The former implies moral guilt; the latter may be consistent with innocence. Code Ga. 1882, § 3173. Actual fraud is otherwise called "fraud in fact." Constructive fraud is also called "fraud in law."

Actual or *positive fraud* includes cases of the intentional and successful employment of any cunning, deception, or artifice, used to circumvent, cheat, or deceive another. 1 Story, Eq. Jur. § 186.

Actual fraud or fraud in fact consists in the intention to prevent creditors from recovering their just debts by an act which withdraws the property of a debtor from their reach. Fraud in law consists in acts which, though not fraudulently intended, yet, as their tendency is to defraud creditors if they vest the property of the debtor in his grantee, are void for legal fraud, and fraudulent in themselves, the policy of the law making the acts illegal. Actual fraud is always a question for the jury; legal fraud, where the facts are undisputed or are ascertained, is for the court. 64 Pa. St. 356.

The modes of fraud are infinite, and it has been said that courts of equity have never laid down what shall constitute fraud, or any general rule, beyond which they will not go, on the ground of fraud. Fraud is, however, usually divided into two large classes,—actual fraud and constructive fraud. An actual fraud may be defined to be something said, done, or omitted by a person with the design of perpetrating what he must have known to be a positive fraud. Constructive frauds are acts, statements, or omissions which operate as virtual frauds on individuals, or which, if generally permitted, would be prejudicial to the public welfare, and yet may have been unconnected with any selfish or evil design; as, for instance, bonds and agreements entered into as a reward for using influence over another, to induce him to make a will for the benefit of the obligor. For such contracts encourage a spirit of artifice and scheming, and tend to deceive and injure others. Smith, Man. Eq.

Synonyms. The term "fraud" is sometimes used as synonymous with "covin," "collusion," or "deceit." But distinctions are properly taken in the meanings of these words, for which reference may be had to the titles COVIN; COLLUSION; DECEIT.

FRAUD IN FACT. Actual, positive, intentional fraud. Fraud disclosed by matters of fact, as distinguished from constructive fraud or fraud in law.

FRAUD IN LAW. Fraud in contemplation of law; fraud implied or inferred by law; fraud made out by construction of law, as distinguished from fraud found by a jury from matter of fact; constructive fraud, (*q. v.*) See 2 Kent, Comm. 512-532.

FRAUDARE. In the civil law. To deceive, cheat, or impose upon; to defraud.

FRAUDS, STATUTE OF. This is the common designation of a very celebrated English statute, (29 Car. II. c. 3,) passed in 1677, and which has been adopted, in a more or less modified form, in nearly all of the United States. Its chief characteristic is the provision that no suit or action shall be maintained on certain classes of contracts or engagements unless there shall be a note or memorandum thereof in writing signed by the party to be charged or by his authorized agent. Its object was to close the door to the numerous frauds which were believed to be perpetrated, and the perjuries which were believed to be committed, when such obligations could be enforced upon no other evidence than the mere recollection of witnesses. It is more fully named as the "statute of frauds and perjuries."

FRAUDULENT CONVEYANCE. A conveyance or transfer of property, the object of which is to defraud a creditor, or hinder or delay him, or to put such property beyond his reach.

Every transfer of property or charge thereon made, every obligation incurred, and every judicial proceeding taken with intent to delay or defraud any creditor or other person of his demands, is void against all creditors of the debtor, and their successors in interest, and against any person upon whom the estate of the debtor devolves in trust for the benefit of others than the debtor. Civil Code Cal. § 3439.

A transfer made by a person indebted or in embarrassed circumstances, which was intended or will necessarily operate to defeat the right of his creditors to have the property applied to the payment of their demands. Abbott.

FRAUDULENT CONVEYANCES, STATUTES OF, OR AGAINST. The name given to two celebrated English statutes,—the statute 13 Eliz. c. 5, made perpetual by 29 Eliz. c. 5; and the statute 27 Eliz. c. 4, made perpetual by 29 Eliz. c. 18.

FRAUDULENT PREFERENCES. In English law. Every conveyance or transfer of property or charge thereon made, every judgment made, every obligation incurred, and every judicial proceeding taken or suffered by any person unable to pay his debts as they become due from his own moneys, in favor of any creditor, with a view of giving such creditor a preference over other creditors, shall be deemed fraudulent and void if the debtor become bankrupt within three months. 32 & 33 Vict. c. 71, § 92.

FRAUNC, FRAUNCHE, FRAUNKE. See FRANK.

FRAUNCHISE. L. Fr. A franchise.

FRAUS. Lat. Fraud. More commonly called, in the civil law, "*dolus*" and "*dolus malus*," (*q. v.*) A distinction, however, was sometimes made between "*fraus*" and "*dolus;*" the former being held to be of the most extensive import. Calvin.

FRAUS DANS LOCUM CONTRACTUI. Lat. A misrepresentation or concealment of some fact that is material to the contract, and had the truth regarding which been known the contract would not have been made as made, is called a "fraud *dans locum contractui;*" *i. e.*, a fraud occasioning the contract, or giving place or occasion for the contract.

Fraus est celare fraudem. It is a fraud to conceal a fraud. 1 Vern. 240; 1 Story, Eq. Jur. §§ 389, 390.

Fraus est odiosa et non præsumenda. Fraud is odious, and not to be presumed. Cro. Car. 550.

Fraus et dolus nemini patrocinari debent. Fraud and deceit should defend or excuse no man. 3 Coke, 78; Fleta, lib. 1, c. 13, § 15; Id. lib. 6, c. 6, § 5.

Fraus et jus nunquam cohabitant. Wing. 680. Fraud and justice never dwell together.

Fraus latet in generalibus. Fraud lies hid in general expressions.

FRAUS LEGIS. Lat. In the civil law. Fraud of law; fraud upon law. See IN FRAUDEM LEGIS.

Fraus meretur fraudem. Plowd. 100. Fraud merits fraud.

FRAXINETUM. In old English law. A wood of ashes; a place where ashes grow. Co. Litt. 4*b;* Shep. Touch. 95.

FRAY. See AFFRAY.

FRECTUM. In old English law. Freight. *Quoad frectum navium suarum*, as to the freight of his vessels. Blount.

FREDNITE. In old English law. A liberty to hold courts and take up the fines for beating and wounding. To be free from fines. Cowell.

FREDSTOLE. Sanctuaries; seats of peace.

FREDUM. A fine paid for obtaining pardon when the peace had been broken. Spelman; Blount. A sum paid the magistrate for protection against the right of revenge.

FREE. 1. Unconstrained; having power to follow the dictates of his own will. Not subject to the dominion of another. Not compelled to involuntary servitude. Used in this sense as opposed to "slave."

2. Not bound to service for a fixed term of

years; in distinction to being bound as an apprentice.

3. Enjoying full civic rights.

4. Available to all citizens alike without charge; as a free school.

5. Available for public use without charge or toll; as a free bridge.

6. Not despotic; assuring liberty; defending individual rights against encroachment by any person or class; instituted by a free people; said of governments, institutions, etc. Webster.

7. Certain, and also consistent with an honorable degree in life; as free services, in the feudal law.

8. Confined to the person possessing, instead of being shared with others; as a free fishery.

9. Not engaged in a war as belligerent or ally; neutral; as in the maxim, "Free ships make free goods."

FREE ALMS. The name of a species of tenure. See FRANK-ALMOIGNE.

FREE-BENCH. A widow's dower out of copyholds to which she is entitled by the custom of some manors. It is regarded as an excrescence growing out of the husband's interest, and is indeed a continuance of his estate. Wharton.

FREE-BORD. In old records. An allowance of land over and above a certain limit or boundary, as so much beyond or without a fence. Cowell; Blount.

The right of claiming that quantity. Termes de la Ley.

FREE BOROUGH MEN. Such great men as did not engage, like the frank-pledge men, for their decennier. Jacob.

FREE CHAPEL. In English ecclesiastical law. A place of worship, so called because not liable to the visitation of the ordinary. It is always of royal foundation, or founded at least by private persons to whom the crown has granted the privilege. 1 Burn, Ecc. Law, 298.

FREE COURSE. In admiralty law. A vessel having the wind from a favorable quarter is said to sail on a "free course."

FREE ENTRY, EGRESS, AND REGRESS. An expression used to denote that a person has the right to go on land again and again as often as may be reasonably necessary. Thus, in the case of a tenant entitled to emblements.

FREE FISHERY. A franchise in the hands of a subject, existing by grant or prescription, distinct from an ownership in the soil. It is an exclusive right, and applies to a public navigable river, without any right in the soil. 3 Kent, Comm. 410.

FREE ON BOARD. A sale of goods "free on board" imports that they are to be delivered on board the cars, vessel, etc., without expense to the buyer for packing, cartage, or other such charges.

In a contract for sale and delivery of goods "free on board" vessel, the seller is under no obligation to act until the buyer names the ship to which the delivery is to be made. 117 Pa. St. 508, 12 Atl. Rep. 32.

FREE SERVICES. In feudal and old English law. Such feudal services as were not unbecoming the character of a soldier or a freeman to perform; as to serve under his lord in the wars, to pay a sum of money, and the like. 2 Bl. Comm. 60, 61.

FREE SHIPS. In international law. Ships of a neutral nation. The phrase "free ships shall make free goods" is often inserted in treaties, meaning that goods, even though belonging to an enemy, shall not be seized or confiscated, if found in neutral ships. Wheat. Int. Law, 507, et seq.

FREE SOCAGE. In English law. A tenure of lands by certain free and honorable services, (such as fealty and rent,) and which are liquidated and reduced to a certainty. It was called "*free* socage" because the services were not only free, but honorable; whereas in *villein* socage the services, though certain, were of a baser nature. 2 Bl. Comm. 78, 79.

FREE SOCMEN. In old English law. Tenants in free socage. Glanv. lib. 3, c. 7; 2 Bl. Comm. 79.

FREE TENURE. Tenure by free services; freehold tenure.

FREE WARREN. A franchise for the preserving and custody of beasts and fowls of warren. 2 Bl. Comm. 39, 417; Co. Litt. 233. This franchise gave the grantee sole right of killing, so far as his warren extended, on condition of excluding other persons. 2 Bl. Comm. 39.

FREEDMAN. In Roman law. One who was set free from a state of bondage; an emancipated slave. The word is used in the same sense in the United States, respecting negroes who were formerly slaves.

FREEDOM. The state of being free; liberty; self-determination; absence of restraint; the opposite of slavery.

The power of acting, in the character of a moral personality, according to the dictates of the will, without other check, hindrance, or prohibition than such as may be imposed by just and necessary laws and the duties of social life.

The prevalence, in the government and constitution of a country, of such a system of laws and institutions as secure civil liberty to the individual citizen.

FREEHOLD. An estate in land or other real property, of uncertain duration; that is, either of inheritance or which may possibly last for the life of the tenant at the least, (as distinguished from a leasehold;) and held by a free tenure, (as distinguished from copyhold or villeinage.)

Such an interest in lands of frank-tenement as may endure not only during the owner's life, but which is cast after his death upon the persons who successively represent him, according to certain rules elsewhere explained. Such persons are called "heirs," and he whom they thus represent, the "ancestor." When the interest extends beyond the ancestor's life, it is called a "freehold of inheritance," and, when it only endures for the ancestor's life, it is a freehold not of inheritance.

An estate to be a freehold must possess these two qualities: (1) Immobility, that is, the property must be either land or some interest issuing out of or annexed to land; and (2) indeterminate duration, for, if the utmost period of time to which an estate can endure be fixed and determined, it cannot be a freehold. Wharton.

FREEHOLD IN LAW. A freehold which has descended to a man, upon which he may enter at pleasure, but which he has not entered on. Termes de la Ley.

FREEHOLD LAND SOCIETIES. Societies in England designed for the purpose of enabling mechanics, artisans, and other working-men to purchase at the least possible price a piece of freehold land of a sufficient yearly value to entitle the owner to the elective franchise for the county in which the land is situated. Wharton.

FREEHOLDER. A person who possesses a freehold estate.

FREEMAN. This word has had various meanings at different stages of history. In the Roman law, it denoted one who was either born free or emancipated, and was the opposite of "slave." In feudal law, it designated an allodial proprietor, as distinguished from a vassal or feudal tenant. In old English law, the word described a freeholder or tenant by free services; one who was not a villein. In modern legal phraseology, it is the appellation of a member of a city or borough having the right of suffrage, or a member of any municipal corporation invested with full civic rights.

A person in the possession and enjoyment of all the civil and political rights accorded to the people under a free government.

FREEMAN'S ROLL. A list of persons admitted as burgesses or freemen for the purposes of the rights reserved by the municipal corporation act, (5 & 6 Wm. IV. c. 76.) Distinguished from the Burgess Roll. 3 Steph. Comm. 197. The term was used, in early colonial history, in some of the American colonies.

FREIGHT. Freight is properly the price or compensation paid for the transportation of goods by a carrier, at sea, from port to port. But the term is also used to denote the hire paid for the carriage of goods on land from place to place, (usually by a railroad company, not an express company,) or on inland streams or lakes. The name is also applied to the goods or merchandise transported by any of the above means.

Property carried is called "freight;" the reward, if any, to be paid for its carriage is called "freightage;" the person who delivers the freight to the carrier is called the "consignor;" and the person to whom it is to be delivered is called the "consignee." Civil Code Cal. § 2110; Civil Code Dak. § 1220.

The term "freight" has several different meanings, as the price to be paid for the carriage of goods, or for the hire of a vessel under a charter-party or otherwise; and sometimes it designates goods carried, as "a freight of lime," or the like. But, as a subject of insurance, it is used in one of the two former senses. 10 Gray, 109.

The sum agreed on for the hire of a ship, entirely or in part, for the carriage of goods from one port to another. 13 East, 300. All rewards or compensation paid for the use of ships. 1 Pet. Adm. 206.

Freight is a compensation received for the transportation of goods and merchandise from port to port; and is never claimable by the owner of the vessel until the voyage has been performed and terminated. 7 Gill & J. 300.

"Dead freight" is money payable by a person who has chartered a ship and only partly loaded her, in respect of the loss of freight caused to the ship-owner by the deficiency of cargo. L. R. 2 H. L. Sc. 128.

Freight is the mother of wages. 2 Show. 283; 3 Kent, Comm. 196. Where a voyage is broken up by *vis major*, and no freight earned, no wages, *eo nomine*, are due.

FREIGHTER. In maritime law. The party by whom a vessel is engaged or chartered; otherwise called the "charterer." 2 Steph. Comm. 148. In French law, the owner of a vessel is called the "freighter," (*freteur;*) the merchant who hires it is called the "affreighter," (*affreteur.*) Emerig. Tr. des Ass. ch. 11, § 3.

FRENCHMAN. In early times, in English law, this term was applied to every stranger or "outlandish" man. Bract. lib. 3, tr. 2, c. 15.

FRENDLESMAN. Sax. An outlaw. So called because on his outlawry he was denied all help of friends after certain days. Cowell; Blount.

FRENDWITE. In old English law. A mulct or fine exacted from him who harbored an outlawed friend. Cowell; Tomlins.

FRENETICUS. In old English law. A madman, or person in a frenzy. Fleta, lib. 1, c. 36.

FREOBORGH. A free-surety, or free-pledge. Spelman. See FRANK-PLEDGE.

FREQUENT, *v.* To visit often; to resort to often or habitually. 109 Ind. 176, 9 N. E. Rep. 781.

Frequentia actus multum operatur. The frequency of an act effects much. 4 Coke, 78; Wing. Max. p. 719, max. 192. A continual usage is of great effect to establish a right.

FRERE. A brother. *Frere eyne*, elder brother. *Frere puisne*, younger brother. Britt. c. 75.

FRESCA. In old records. Fresh water, or rain and land flood.

FRESH DISSEISIN. By the ancient common law, where a man had been disseised, he was allowed to right himself by force, by ejecting the disseisor from the premises, without resort to law, provided this was done forthwith, while the disseisin was *fresh*, (*flagrante disseisina.*) Bract. fol. 162*b*. No particular time was limited for doing this, but Bracton suggested it should be fifteen days. Id. fol. 163. See Britt. cc. 32, 43, 44, 65.

FRESH FINE. In old English law. A fine that had been levied within a year past. St. Westm. 2, c. 45; Cowell.

FRESH FORCE. Force done within forty days. Fitzh. Nat. Brev. 7; Old Nat. Brev. 4. The heir or reversioner in a case of disseisin by *fresh force* was allowed a remedy in chancery by bill before the mayor. Cowell.

FRESH PURSUIT. A pursuit instituted immediately, and with intent to reclaim or recapture, after an animal escaped, a thief flying with stolen goods, etc.

FRESH SUIT. In old English law. Immediate and unremitting pursuit of an escaping thief. "Such a present and earnest following of a robber as never ceases from the time of the robbery until apprehension. The party pursuing then had back again his goods, which otherwise were forfeited to the crown." Staundef. P. C. lib. 3, cc. 10, 12; 1 Bl. Comm. 297.

FRESHET. A flood, or overflowing of a river, by means of rains or melted snow; an inundation. 3 Phila. 42.

FRET. Fr. In French marine law. Freight. Ord. Mar. liv. 3, tit. 3.

FRETER. Fr. In French marine law. To freight a ship; to let it. Emerig. Tr. des Ass. c. 11, § 3.

FRETEUR. Fr. In French marine law. Freighter. The owner of a ship, who lets it to the merchant. Emerig. Tr. des Ass. c. 11, § 3.

FRETTUM, FRECTUM. In old English law. The freight of a ship; freight money. Cowell.

FRETUM. A strait.

FRETUM BRITANNICUM. The strait between Dover and Calais.

FRIARS. An order of religious persons, of whom there were four principal branches, viz.: (1) Minors, Grey Friars, or Franciscans; (2) Augustines; (3) Dominicans, or Black Friars; (4) White Friars, or Carmelites, from whom the rest descend. Wharton.

FRIBUSCULUM. In the civil law. A temporary separation between husband and wife, caused by a quarrel or estrangement, but not amounting to a divorce, because not accompanied with an intention to dissolve the marriage.

FRIDBORG, FRITHBORG. Frank-pledge. Cowell. Security for the peace. Spelman.

FRIDHBURGUS. In old English law. A kind of frank-pledge, by which the lords or principal men were made responsible for their dependents or servants. Bract. fol. 124*b*.

FRIEND OF THE COURT. See AMICUS CURIÆ.

FRIENDLESS MAN. In old English law. An outlaw; so called because he was denied all help of friends. Bract. lib. 3, tr. 2, c. 12.

FRIENDLY SOCIETIES. In English law. Associations supported by subscription, for the relief and maintenance of the members, or their wives, children, relatives, and nominees, in sickness, infancy, advanced age, widowhood, etc. The statutes regulating these societies were consolidated and amended by St. 38 & 39 Vict. c. 60. Wharton.

FRIENDLY SUIT. A suit brought by a creditor in chancery against an executor or administrator, being really a suit by the executor or administrator, in the name of a creditor, against himself, in order to compel the creditors to take an equal distribution of the assets. 2 Williams, Ex'rs, 1915.

Also any suit instituted by agreement between the parties to obtain the opinion of the court upon some doubtful question in which they are interested.

FRIGIDITY. Impotence. Johnson.

FRILINGI. Persons of free descent, or freemen born; the middle class of persons among the Saxons. Spelman.

FRISCUS. Fresh uncultivated ground. Mon. Angl. t. 2, p. 56. Fresh; not salt. Reg. Orig. 97. Recent or new. See FRESH, and subsequent titles.

FRITHBORG. Frank-pledge. Cowell.

FRITHBOTE. A satisfaction or fine for a breach of the peace.

FRITHBREACH. The breaking of the peace. Cowell.

FRITHGAR. The year of jubilee, or of meeting for peace and friendship. Jacob.

FRITHGILDA. Guildhall; a company or fraternity for the maintenance of peace and security; also a fine for breach of the peace. Jacob.

FRITHMAN. A member of a company or fraternity. Blount.

FRITHSOCNE. Surety of defense. Jurisdiction of the peace. The franchise of preserving the peace. Cowell; Spelman.

FRITHSPLOT. A spot or plot of land, encircling some stone, tree, or well, considered sacred, and therefore affording sanctuary to criminals.

FRIVOLOUS. An answer or plea is called "frivolous" when it is clearly insufficient on its face, and does not controvert the material points of the opposite pleading, and is presumably interposed for mere purposes of delay or to embarrass the plaintiff.

A frivolous demurrer has been defined to be one which is so clearly untenable, or its insufficiency so manifest upon a bare inspection of the pleadings, that its character may be determined without argument or research. 40 Wis. 558.

FRODMORTEL, or FREOMORTEL. An immunity for committing manslaughter. Mon. Angl. t. 1, p. 173.

FRONTAGE—FRONTAGER. In English law a frontager is a person owning or occupying land which abuts on a highway, river, sea-shore, or the like. The term is generally used with reference to the liability of frontagers on streets to contribute towards the expense of paving, draining, or other works on the highway carried out by a local authority, in proportion to the frontage of their respective tenements. Sweet.

FRUCTUARIUS. Lat. In the civil law. One who had the usufruct of a thing; *i. e.*, the use of the fruits, profits, or increase, as of land or animals. Inst. 2, 1, 36, 38. Bracton applies it to a lessee, fermor, or farmer of land, or one who held lands *ad firmam*, for a farm or term. Bract. fol. 261.

FRUCTUS. Lat. In the civil law. Fruit, fruits; produce; profit or increase; the organic productions of a thing. *Fructus fundi*, the fruits of land. *Fructus pecudum*, the produce of flocks.

The right to the fruits of a thing belonging to another.

The compensation which a man receives from another for the use or enjoyment of a thing, such as interest or rent. See Mackeld. Rom. Law, § 167; Inst. 2, 1, 35, 37; Dig. 7, 1, 33; Id. 5, 3, 29; Id. 22, 1, 34.

Fructus augent hæreditatem. The yearly increase goes to enchance the inheritance. Dig. 5, 3, 20, 3.

FRUCTUS CIVILES. (Lat. Civil fruits.) All revenues and recompenses which, though not *fruits*, properly speaking, are recognized as such by the law.

FRUCTUS INDUSTRIALES. Industrial fruits, or fruits of industry. Those fruits of a thing, as of land, which are produced by the labor and industry of the occupant, as crops of grain; as distinguished from such as are produced solely by the powers of nature. Emblements are so called in the common law. 2 Steph. Comm. 258; 1 Chit. Gen. Pr. 92.

FRUCTUS NATURALES. Those products which are produced by the powers of nature alone; as wool, metals, milk, the young of animals.

FRUCTUS PENDENTES. Hanging fruits; those not severed. The fruits united with the thing which produces them. These form a part of the principal thing.

Fructus pendentes pars fundi videntur. Hanging fruits make part of the land. Dig. 6, 1, 44; 2 Bouv. Inst. no. 1578.

Fructus perceptos villæ non esse constat. Gathered fruits do not make a part of the farm. Dig. 19, 1, 17, 1; 2 Bouv. Inst. no. 1578.

FRUCTUS REI ALIENÆ. The fruits of another's property; fruits taken from another's estate.

FRUCTUS SEPARATI. In the civil law. Separate fruits; the fruits of a thing when they are separated from it. Dig. 7, 4, 13.

FRUGES. In the civil law. Anything produced from vines, underwood, chalk-pits, stone-quarries. Dig. 50, 16, 77.

Grains and leguminous vegetables. In a more restricted sense, any esculent growing in pods. Vicat, Voc. Jur.; Calvin.

FRUIT. The produce of a tree or plant which contains the seed or is used for food.

This term, in legal acceptation, is not confined to the produce of those trees which in popular language are called "fruit trees," but applies also to the produce of oak, elm, and walnut trees. 5 Barn. & C. 847.

FRUIT FALLEN. The produce of any possession detached therefrom, and capable of being enjoyed by itself. Thus, a next presentation, when a vacancy has occurred, is a fruit fallen from the advowson. Wharton.

FRUITS OF CRIME. In the law of evidence. Material objects acquired by means and in consequence of the commission of crime, and sometimes constituting the subject-matter of the crime. Burrill, Circ. Ev. 445; 3 Benth. Jud. Ev. 31.

Frumenta quæ sata sunt solo cedere intelliguntur. Grain which is sown is understood to form a part of the soil. Inst. 2, 1, 32.

FRUMENTUM. In the civil law. Grain. That which grows in an ear. Dig. 50, 16, 77.

FRUMGYLD. Sax. The first payment made to the kindred of a slain person in recompense for his murder. Blount.

FRUMSTOLL. Sax. In Saxon law. A chief seat, or mansion house. Cowell.

FRUSCA TERRA. In old records. Uncultivated and desert ground. 2 Mon. Angl. 327; Cowell.

FRUSSURA. A breaking; plowing. Cowell.

Frustra agit qui judicium prosequi nequit cum effectu. He sues to no purpose who cannot prosecute his judgment with effect, [who cannot have the fruits of his judgment.] Fleta, lib. 6, c. 37, § 9.

Frustra [vana] est potentia quæ nunquam venit in actum. That power is to no purpose which never comes into act, or which is never exercised. 2 Coke, 51.

Frustra expectatur eventùs cujus effectus nullus sequitur. An event is vainly expected from which no effect follows.

Frustra feruntur leges nisi subditis et obedientibus. Laws are made to no purpose, except for those that are subject and obedient. Branch, Princ.

Frustra fit per plura, quod fieri potest per pauciora. That is done to no purpose by many things which can be done by fewer. Jenk. Cent. p. 68, case 28. The employment of more means or instruments for effecting a thing than are necessary is to no purpose.

Frustra legis auxilium invocat [quærit] qui in legem committit. He vainly invokes the aid of the law who transgresses the law. Fleta, lib. 4, c. 2, § 3; 2 Hale, P. C. 386; Broom, Max. 279, 297.

Frustra petis quod mox es restiturus. In vain you ask that which you will have immediately to restore. 2 Kames, Eq. 104; 5 Man. & G. 757.

Frustra petis quod statim alteri reddere cogeris. Jenk. Cent. 256. You ask in vain that which you might immediately be compelled to restore to another.

Frustra probatur, quod probatum non relevat. That is proved to no purpose which, when proved, does not help. Halk. Lat. Max. 50.

FRUSTRUM TERRÆ. A piece or parcel of land lying by itself. Co. Litt. 5*b*.

FRUTECTUM. In old records. A place overgrown with shrubs and bushes. Spelman; Blount.

FRUTOS. In Spanish law. Fruits; products; produce; grains; profits. White, New Recop. b. 1, tit. 7, c. 5, § 2

FRYMITH. In old English law. The affording harbor and entertainment to any one.

FRYTHE. Sax. In old English law. A plain between woods. Co. Litt. 5*b*.

An arm of the sea, or a strait between two lands. Cowell.

FUAGE, FOCAGE. Hearth money. A tax laid upon each fire-place or hearth. An imposition of a shilling for every hearth, levied by Edward III. in the dukedom of Aquitaine. Spelman; 1 Bl. Comm. 324.

FUER. In old English law. Flight. It is of two kinds: (1) *Fuer in fait*, or *in facto*, where a person does apparently and corporally flee; (2) *fuer in ley*, or *in lege*, when, being called in the county court, he does not appear, which legal interpretation makes flight. Wharton.

FUERO. In Spanish law. A law; a code.

A general usage or custom of a province, having the force of law. *Ir contra fuero*, to violate a received custom.

A grant of privileges and immunities. *Conceder fueros*, to grant exemptions.

A charter granted to a city or town. Also designated as "*cartas pueblas*."

An act of donation made to an individual, a church, or convent, on certain conditions.

A declaration of a magistrate, in relation to taxation, fines, etc.

A charter granted by the sovereign, or those having authority from him, establishing the franchises of towns, cities, etc.

A place where justice is administered.

A peculiar *forum*, before which a party is amenable.

The jurisdiction of a tribunal, which is entitled to take cognizance of a cause; as *fuero ecclesiastico*, *fuero militar*. See Schm. Civil Law, Introd. 64.

FUERO DE CASTILLA. In Spanish law. The body of laws and customs which formerly governed the Castilians.

FUERO DE CORREOS Y CAMINOS. In Spanish law. A special tribunal taking cognizance of all matters relating to the post-office and roads.

FUERO DE GUERRA. In Spanish law. A special tribunal taking cognizance of all matters in relation to persons serving in the army.

FUERO DE MARINA. In Spanish law. A special tribunal taking cognizance of all matters relating to the navy and to the persons employed therein.

FUERO JUZGO. Span. The *Forum Judicium;* a code of laws established in the seventh century for the Visigothic kingdom in Spain. Some of its principles and rules are found surviving in the modern jurisprudence of that country. Schm. Civil Law, Introd. 28.

FUERO MUNICIPAL. In Spanish law. The body of laws granted to a city or town for its government and the administration of justice.

FUERO REAL. The title of a code of Spanish law promulgated by Alphonso the Learned, (*el Sabio*,) A. D. 1255. It was the precursor of the Partidas. Schm. Civil Law, Introd. 67.

FUERO VIEJO. The title of a compilation of Spanish law, published about A. D. 992. Schm. Civil Law, Introd. 65.

FUGA CATALLORUM. In old English law. A drove of cattle. Blount.

FUGACIA. A chase. Blount.

FUGAM FECIT. Lat. He has made flight; he fled. A clause inserted in an inquisition, in old English law, meaning that a person indicted for treason or felony had fled. The effect of this is to make the party forfeit his goods absolutely, and the profits of his lands until he has been pardoned or acquitted.

FUGATOR. In old English law. A privilege to hunt. Blount.

A driver. *Fugatores carrucarum*, drivers of wagons. Fleta, lib. 2, c. 78.

FUGITATE. In Scotch practice. To outlaw, by the sentence of a court; to outlaw for non-appearance in a criminal case. 2 Alis. Crim. Pr. 350.

FUGITATION. In Scotch law. When a criminal does not obey the citation to answer, the court pronounces sentence of fugitation against him, which induces a forfeiture of goods and chattels to the crown.

FUGITIVE FROM JUSTICE. A person who, having committed a crime, flies from the state or country where it transpired, in order to evade arrest and escape justice.

FUGITIVE OFFENDERS. In English law. Where a person accused of any offense punishable by imprisonment, with hard labor for twelve months or more, has left that part of her majesty's dominions where the offense is alleged to have been committed, he is liable, if found in any other part of her majesty's dominions, to be apprehended and returned in manner provided by the fugitive offenders' act, 1881, to the part from which he is a fugitive. Wharton.

FUGITIVE SLAVE. One who, held in bondage, flees from his master's power.

FUGITIVUS. In the civil law. A fugitive; a runaway slave. Dig. 11, 4; Cod. 6, 1. See the various definitions of this word in Dig. 21, 1, 17.

FULL. Complete; exhaustive; detailed. A "full" answer is as extensive a term, in describing one which is ample and sufficient, as though the term "complete" had been superadded. 22 Ala. 817

FULL AGE. In common law. The age of twenty-one years, in males and females. Litt. § 259; 1 Bl. Comm. 463.

In the civil law. The age of twenty-five years, in males and females. Inst. 1, 23, pr.

FULL BLOOD. A term of relation, denoting descent from the same couple. Brothers and sisters of *full blood* are those who are born of the same father and mother, or, as Justinian calls them, "*ex utroque parente conjuncti.*" Nov. 118, cc. 2, 3; Mackeld. Rom. Law, § 145. The more usual term in modern law is "whole blood," (*q. v.*)

FULL COURT. In practice. A court *in banc*. A court duly organized with all the judges present.

FULL DEFENSE. In pleading. The formula of defense in a plea, stated at length and without abbreviation, thus: "And the said C. D., by E. F., his attorney, comes and defends the force (or wrong) and injury when and where it shall behoove him, and the damages, and whatsoever else he ought to defend, and says," etc. Steph. Pl. p. 481.

FULL LIFE. Life in fact and in law. See In Full Life.

FULL PROOF. In the civil law. Proof by two witnesses, or a public instrument. Hallifax, Civil Law, b. 3, c. 9, nn. 25, 30; 3 Bl. Comm. 370.

Evidence which satisfies the minds of the jury of the truth of the fact in dispute, to the entire exclusion of every reasonable doubt. 38 N. J. Law, 450.

FULL RIGHT. The union of a good title with actual possession.

FULLUM AQUÆ. A fleam, or stream of water. Blount.

FUMAGE. In old English law. The same as *fuage*, or smoke farthings. 1 Bl. Comm. 324. See Fuage.

FUNCTION. Office; duty; fulfillment of a definite end or set of ends by the correct adjustment of means. The occupation of an office. By the performance of its duties, the officer is said to fill his function. Dig. 32, 65, 1.

FUNCTIONARY. A public officer or employe. An officer of a private corporation is also sometimes so called.

FUNCTUS OFFICIO. Lat. Having fulfilled the function, discharged the office, or accomplished the purpose, and therefore of no further force or authority. Applied to an officer whose term has expired, and who has consequently no further official authority; and also to an instrument, power, agency, etc., which has fulfilled the purpose of its creation, and is therefore of no further virtue or effect.

FUND, *v.* To capitalize, with a view to the production of interest. 24 N. J. Eq. 376.

To fund a debt is to pledge a specific fund to keep down interest and reduce the principal. When extinguishment of the debt is the object prominently contemplated, the provision is called a "sinking fund." The term "fund" was originally applied to a portion of the national revenue set apart or pledged to the payment of a particular debt. Hence a funded debt was a debt for the payment of the principal or interest of which some fund was appropriated. 14 N. Y. 356, 367, 377; 21 Barb. 294.

FUND, *n.* A sum of money set apart for a specific purpose, or available for the payment of debts or claims.

In its narrower and more usual sense, "fund" signifies "capital," as opposed to "interest" or "income;" as where we speak of a corporation funding the arrears of interest due on its bonds, or the like, meaning that the interest is capitalized and made to bear interest in its turn until it is repaid. Sweet.

FUNDAMENTAL LAW. The law which determines the constitution of government in a state, and prescribes and regulates the manner of its exercise; the organic law of a state; the constitution.

FUNDAMUS. We found. One of the words by which a corporation may be created in England. 1 Bl. Comm. 473; 3 Steph. Comm. 173.

FUNDATIO. A founding or foundation.

FUNDATOR. A founder, (*q. v.*)

FUNDI PATRIMONIALES. Lands of inheritance.

FUNDING SYSTEM. The practice of borrowing money to defray the expenses of government, and creating a "sinking fund," designed to keep down interest, and to effect the gradual reduction of the principal debt.

FUNDITORES. Pioneers. Jacob.

FUNDS. 1. Money in hand; cash; money available for the payment of a debt, legacy, etc.

2. The proceeds of sales of real and personal estate, or the proceeds of any other assets converted into money. 43 N. J. Eq. 533.

3. Corporate stocks or government securities; in this sense usually spoken of as the "funds."

4. Assets, securities, bonds, or revenue of a state or government appropriated for the discharge of its debts.

FUNDUS. In the civil and old English law. Land; land or ground generally; land, without considering its specific use; land, including buildings generally; a farm.

FUNERAL EXPENSES. Money expended in procuring the interment of a corpse.

FUNGIBILES RES. Lat. A term applied in the civil law to things of such a nature as that they could be replaced by equal quantities and qualities, because, *mutua vice funguntur*, they replace and represent each other; thus, a bushel of wheat. A particular horse would not be *fungibilis res.* Sandars, Just. Inst. (5th Ed.) 322.

FUNGIBLE THINGS. Movable goods which may be estimated and replaced according to weight, measure, and number. Things belonging to a class, which do not have to be dealt with *in specie.*

Those things one specimen of which is as good as another, as is the case with half-crowns, or pounds of rice of the same quality. Horses, slaves, and so forth, are non-fungible things, because they differ individually in value, and cannot be exchanged indifferently one for another. Holl. Jur. 88.

Where a thing which is the subject of an obligation (which one man is bound to deliver to another) must be delivered *in specie*, the thing is not fungible; that very individual thing, and not another thing of the same or another class, in lieu of it, must be delivered. Where the subject of the obligation is a thing of a given class, the thing is said to be fungible; *i. e.*, the delivery of any object which answers to the generic description will satisfy the terms of the obligation. Aust. Jur. 483, 484.

FUR. Lat. A thief. One who stole secretly or without force or weapons, as opposed to robber.

FUR MANIFESTUS. Lat. In the civil law. A manifest thief. A thief who is taken in the very act of stealing.

FURANDI ANIMUS. An intention of stealing.

FURCA. A fork. A gallows or gibbet. Bract. fol. 56.

FURCA ET FLAGELLUM. In old English law. Gallows and whip. *Tenure ad furcam et flagellum*, tenure by gallows and whip. The meanest of servile tenures, where the bondman was at the disposal of his lord for life and limb. Cowell.

FURCA ET FOSSA. In old English law. Gallows and pit, or pit and gallows. A term used in ancient charters to signify a jurisdiction of punishing thieves, viz., men by hanging, women by drowning. Spelman; Cowell.

FURIGELDUM. A fine or mulct paid for theft.

Furiosi nulla voluntas est. A madman has no will. Dig. 50, 17, 40; Broom, Max. 314.

FURIOSITY. In Scotch law. Madness, as distinguished from fatuity or idiocy.

FURIOSUS. An insane man; a madman; a lunatic.

Furiosus absentis loco est. A madman is the same with an absent person, [that is, his presence is of no effect.] Dig. 50, 17, 24, 1.

Furiosus nullum negotium contrahere potest. A madman can contract nothing, [can make no contract.] Dig. 50, 17, 5.

Furiosus solo furore punitur. A madman is punished by his madness alone; that is, he is not answerable or punishable for his actions. Co. Litt. 247*b;* 4 Bl. Comm. 24, 396; Broom, Max. 15.

Furiosus stipulare non potest nec aliquid negotium agere, qui non intelligit quid agit. 4 Coke, 126. A madman who knows not what he does cannot make a bargain, nor transact any business.

FURLINGUS. A furlong, or a furrow one-eighth part of a mile long. Co. Litt. 5*b*.

FURLONG. A measure of length, being forty poles, or one-eighth of a mile.

FURLOUGH. Leave of absence; especially, leave given to a military or naval officer, or soldier or seaman, to be absent from service for a certain time. Also the document granting leave of absence.

FURNAGE. See FORNAGIUM; FOUR.

FURNITURE. This term includes that which furnishes, or with which anything is furnished or supplied; whatever must be supplied to a house, a room, or the like, to make it habitable, convenient, or agreeable; goods, vessels, utensils, and other appendages necessary or convenient for housekeeping; whatever is added to the interior of a house or apartment, for use or convenience. 27 Ind. 173.

The term "furniture" embraces everything about the house that has been usually enjoyed therewith, including plate, linen, china, and pictures. 41 N. J. Eq. 96.

The word "furniture" made use of in the disposition of the law, or in the conventions or acts of persons, comprehends only such furniture as is intended for use and ornament of apartments, but not libraries which happen to be there, nor plate. Civil Code La. art. 477.

FURNITURE OF A SHIP. This term includes everything with which a ship requires to be furnished or equipped to make her seaworthy; it comprehends all articles furnished by ship-chandlers, which are almost innumerable. 1 Wall. Jr. 369.

FURNIVAL'S INN. Formerly an inn of chancery. See INNS OF CHANCERY.

Furor contrahi matrimonium non sinit, quia consensu opus est. Insanity prevents marriage from being contracted, because consent is needed. Dig. 23, 2, 16, 2; 1 Ves. & B. 140; 1 Bl. Comm. 439; 4 Johns. Ch. 343, 345.

FURST AND FONDUNG. In old English law. Time to advise or take counsel. Jacob.

FURTHER ADVANCE. A second or subsequent loan of money to a mortgagor by a mortgagee, either upon the same security as the original loan was advanced upon, or an additional security. Equity considers the arrears of interest on a mortgage security converted into principal, by agreement between the parties, as a further advance. Wharton.

FURTHER ASSURANCE, COVENANT FOR. One of the usual agreements entered into by a vendor for the protection of the vendee's interest in the subject of purchase. It seems to be confined to an agreement that the grantor will execute any further instruments of conveyance that may be lawfully required, and not to extend to further obligations to be imposed on the covenantor by way of covenant. Sugd. Vend. 500.

FURTHER CONSIDERATION. In English practice, upon a motion for judgment or application for a new trial, the court may, if it shall be of opinion that it has not sufficient materials before it to enable it to give judgment, direct the motion to stand over for *further consideration*, and direct such issues or questions to be tried or determined, and such accounts and inquiries to be taken and made, as it may think fit. Rules Sup. Ct. xl., 10.

FURTHER DIRECTIONS. When a master ordinary in chancery made a report in pursuance of a decree or decretal order, the cause was again set down before the judge who made the decree or order, to be proceeded with. Where a master made a separate report, or one not in pursuance of a decree or decretal order, a petition for consequential directions had to be presented, since the cause could not be set down for further directions under such circumstances. See 2 Daniell, Ch. Pr. (5th Ed.) 1233, note.

FURTHER HEARING. In practice. Hearing at another time.

FURTHER MAINTENANCE OF ACTION, PLEA TO. A plea grounded upon some fact or facts which have arisen since the commencement of the suit, and which the defendant puts forward for the purpose of showing that the plaintiff should not further maintain his action. Brown.

FURTIVE. In old English law. Stealthily; by stealth. Fleta, lib. 1, c. 38, § 3.

FURTUM. Lat. Theft. The fraudulent appropriation to one's self of the property of another, with an intention to commit theft without the consent of the owner. Fleta, l. 1, c. 36; Bract. fol. 150; 3 Inst. 107.

The thing which has been stolen. Bract. fol. 151.

FURTUM CONCEPTUM. In Roman law. The theft which was disclosed where, upon searching any one in the presence of witnesses in due form, the thing stolen was discovered in his possession.

Furtum est contrectatio rei alienæ fraudulenta, cum animo furandi, invito illo domino cujus res illa fuerat. 3 Inst. 107. Theft is the fraudulent handling of another's property, with an intention of stealing, against the will of the proprietor, whose property it was.

FURTUM GRAVE. In Scotch law. An aggravated degree of theft, anciently punished with death. It still remains an open point what amount of value raises the theft to this serious denomination. 1 Broun, 352, note. See 1 Swint. 467.

FURTUM MANIFESTUM. Open theft. Theft where a thief is caught with the property in his possession. Bract. fol. 150*b*.

Furtum non est ubi initium habet detentionis per dominium rei. 3 Inst. 107. There is no theft where the foundation of the detention is based upon ownership of the thing.

FURTUM OBLATUM. In the civil law. Offered theft. *Oblatum furtum dicitur cum res furtiva ab aliquo tibi oblata sit, eaque apud te concepta sit.* Theft is called "*oblatum*" when a thing stolen is offered to you by any one, and found upon you. Inst. 4, 1, 4.

FUSTIGATIO. In old English law. A beating with sticks or clubs; one of the ancient kinds of punishment of malefactors. Bract. fol. 104*b*, lib. 3, tr. 1, c. 6.

FUSTIS. In old English law. A staff, used in making livery of seisin. Bract. fol. 40.

A baton, club, or cudgel.

FUTURE DEBT. In Scotch law. A debt which is created, but which will not become due till a future day. 1 Bell, Comm. 315.

FUTURE ESTATE. An estate which is not now vested in the grantee, but is to commence in possession at some future time. It includes remainders, reversions, and estates limited to commence *in futuro* without a particular estate to support them, which last are not good at common law, except in the case of chattel interests. See 2 Bl. Comm. 165.

An estate limited to commence in possession at a future day, either without the intervention of a precedent estate, or on the determination by lapse of time, or otherwise, of a precedent estate created at the same time. 11 Rev. St. N. Y. (3d Ed.) § 10.

"FUTURES." This term has grown out of those purely speculative transactions, in which there is a nominal contract of sale for future delivery, but where in fact none is ever intended or executed. The nominal seller does not have or expect to have the stock or merchandise he purports to sell, nor does the nominal buyer expect to receive it or to pay the price. Instead of that, a percentage or margin is paid, which is increased or diminished as the market rates go up or down, and accounted for to the buyer. 14 R. I. 138.

FUTURI. Those who are to be. Part of the commencement of old deeds. "*Sciant præsentes et futuri, quod ego talis, dedi et concessi,*" etc., (Let all men now living and to come know that I, A. B., have, etc.) Bract. fol. 34*b*.

FUZ, or FUST. A Celtic word, meaning a wood or forest.

FYHTWITE. One of the fines incurred for homicide.

FYKE. A bow-net for catching fish. Pub. St. Mass. 1882, p. 1291.

FYLE. In old Scotch law. To defile; to declare foul or defiled. Hence, to find a prisoner guilty.

FYLIT. In old Scotch practice. Fyled; found guilty. See FYLE.

FYNDERINGA. Sax. An offense or trespass for which the fine or compensation was reserved to the king's pleasure. Its nature is not known.

FYRD. The military array or land force of the whole country. Contribution to the fyrd was one of the imposts forming the *trinoda necessitas*.

FYRD-WITE. The fine incurred by neglecting to join the fyrd; one of the rights of the crown.

G.

G. In the Law French orthography, this letter is often substituted for the English W, particularly as an initial. Thus, "gage" for "wage," "garranty" for "warranty," "gast" for "waste."

GABEL. An excise; a tax on movables; a rent, custom, or service. Co. Litt. 213.

GABELLA. A tax or duty on personalty. Cowell; Spelman.

GABLATORES. Persons who paid *gabel*, rent, or tribute. Domesday; Cowell.

GABLUM. A rent; a tax. Domesday; Du Cange. The gable-end of a house. Cowell.

GABULUS DENARIORUM. Rent paid in money. Seld. Tit. Hon. 321.

GAFFOLDGILD. The payment of custom or tribute. Scott.

GAFFOLDLAND. Property subject to the gaffoldgild, or liable to be taxed. Scott.

GAFOL. The same word as "gabel" or "gavel." Rent; tax; interest of money.

GAGE, *v*. In old English law. To pawn or pledge; to give as security for a payment or performance; to wage or wager.

GAGE, *n*. In old English law. A pawn or pledge; something deposited as security for the performance of some act or the payment of money, and to be forfeited on failure or non-performance. Glanv. lib. 10, c. 6; Britt. c. 27.

A mortgage is a *dead-gage* or pledge; for, whatsoever profit it yields, it redeems not itself, unless the whole amount secured is paid at the appointed time. Cowell.

In French law. The contract of pledge or pawn; also the article pawned.

GAGE, ESTATES IN. Those held *in vadio*, or pledge. They are of two kinds: (1) *Vivum vadium*, or living pledge, or vifgage; (2) *mortuum vadium*, or dead pledge, better known as "mortgage."

GAGER DE DELIVERANCE. In old English law. When he who has distrained, being sued, has not delivered the cattle distrained, then he shall not only avow the distress, but *gager deliverance, i. e.*, put in surety or pledge that he will deliver them. Fitzh. Nat. Brev.

GAGER DEL LEY. Wager of law, (*q. v.*)

GAIN. Profits; winnings; increment of value.

GAINAGE. The gain or profit of tilled or planted land, raised by cultivating it; and the draught, plow, and furniture for carrying on the work of tillage by the baser kind of *sokemen* or *villeins*. Bract. l. i. c. 9.

GAINERY. Tillage, or the profit arising from it, or from the beasts employed therein.

GAINOR. In old English law. A sokeman; one who occupied or cultivated arable land. Old Nat. Brev. fol. 12.

GAJUM. A thick wood. Spelman.

GALE. The payment of a rent, tax, duty, or annuity.

A gale is the right to open and work a mine within the Hundred of St. Briavel's, or a stone quarry within the open lands of the Forest of Dean. The right is a license or interest in the nature of real estate, conditional on the due payment of rent and observance of the obligations imposed on the galee. It follows the ordinary rules as to the devolution and conveyance of real estate. The galee pays the crown a rent known as a "galeage rent," "royalty," or some similar name, proportionate to the quantity of minerals got from the mine or quarry. Sweet.

GALEA. In old records. A piratical vessel; a galley.

GALENES. In old Scotch law. Amends or compensation for slaughter. Bell.

GALLI-HALFPENCE. A kind of coin which, with suskins and doitkins, was forbidden by St. 3 Hen. V. c. 1.

GALLIVOLATIUM. A cock-shoot, or cock-glade.

GALLON. A liquid measure, containing 231 cubic inches, or four quarts. The *imperial* gallon contains about 277, and the ale gallon 282, cubic inches.

GALLOWS. A scaffold; a beam laid over either one or two posts, from which malefactors are hanged.

GAMACTA. In old European law. A stroke or blow. Spelman.

GAMALIS. A child born in lawful wedlock; also one born to betrothed but unmarried parents. Spelman.

GAMBLE. The word "gamble" is perhaps the most apt and substantial to convey the idea of unlawful play that our language affords. It is inclusive of hazarding and betting as well as playing. 2 Yerg. 474.

GAMBLER. One who follows or practices games of chance or skill, with the expectation and purpose of thereby winning money or other property. 113 Mass. 193.

GAMBLING. See GAMING.

GAMBLING DEVICE. A machine or contrivance of any kind for the playing of an unlawful game of chance or hazard.

GAMBLING POLICY. In life insurance. One issued to a person, as beneficiary, who has no pecuniary interest in the life insured. Otherwise called a "wager policy." 50 Mo. 47.

GAME. Birds and beasts of a wild nature, obtained by fowling and hunting. Bacon, Abr. See 11 Metc. (Mass.) 79. The term is said to include (in England) hares, pheasants, partridges, grouse, heath or moor game, black game, and bustards. Brown. See 1 & 2 Wm. IV. c. 32.

A sport or pastime played with cards, dice, or other contrivance. See GAMING.

GAME-KEEPER. One who has the care of keeping and preserving the game on an estate, being appointed thereto by a lord of a manor.

GAME-LAWS. Laws passed for the preservation of game. They usually forbid the killing of specified game during certain seasons or by certain described means. As to English game-laws, see 2 Steph. Comm. 82; 1 & 2 Wm. IV. c. 32.

GAMING. The act or practice of playing games for stakes or wagers; gambling; the playing at any game of hazard. An agreement between two or more persons to play together at a game of chance for a stake or wager which is to become the property of the winner, and to which all contribute.

Gaming is an agreement between two or more to risk money on a contest or chance of any kind, where one must be loser and the other gainer. 5 Sneed, 507.

In general, the words "gaming" and "gambling," in statutes, are similar in meaning, and either one comprehends the idea that, by a bet, by chance, by some exercise of skill, or by the transpiring of some event unknown until it occurs, something of value is, as the conclusion of premises agreed, to be transferred from a loser to a winner, without which latter element there is no gaming or gambling. Bish. St. Crimes, § 858.

"Gaming" implies, when used as describing a condition, an element of illegality; and, when people are said to be "gaming," this generally supposes that the "games" have been games in which money comes to the victor or his backers. When the terms "game" or "gaming" are used in statutes, it is almost always in connection with words giving them the latter sense, and in such case it is only by averring and proving the *differentia* that the prosecution can be sustained. But when "gaming" is spoken of in a statute as indictable, it is to be regarded as convertible with "gambling." 2 Whart. Crim. Law, § 1465*b*.

"Gaming" is properly the act or engagement of the players. If by-standers or other third persons put up a stake or wager among themselves, to go to one or the other according to the result of the game, this is more correctly termed "betting."

GAMING CONTRACTS. See WAGER.

GAMING-HOUSES. In criminal law. Houses in which gambling is carried on as the business of the occupants, and which are frequented by persons for that purpose. They are nuisances, in the eyes of the law, being detrimental to the public, as they promote cheating and other corrupt practices. 1 Russ. Crimes, 299; Rosc. Crim. Ev. 663; 3 Denio, 101.

GANANCIAL PROPERTY. In Spanish law. A species of community in property enjoyed by husband and wife, the property being divisible between them equally on a dissolution of the marriage. 1 Burge, Confl. Law, 418. See 18 Tex. 634; 22 Mo. 254.

GANANCIAS. In Spanish law. Gains or profits resulting from the employment of property held by husband and wife in common. White, New Recop. b. 1, tit. 7, c. 5.

GANG-WEEK. The time when the bounds of the parish are lustrated or gone over by the parish officers,—rogation week. Enc. Lond.

GANGIATORI. Officers in ancient times whose business it was to examine weights and measures. Skene.

GANTELOPE, (pronounced "gauntlett.") A military punishment, in which the criminal running between the ranks receives a lash from each man. Enc. Lond. This was called "running the gauntlett."

GAOL. A prison for temporary confinement; a jail; a place for the confinement of offenders against the law.

There is said to be a distinction between "gaol" and "prison;" the former being a place for temporary or provisional confinement, or for the punishment of the lighter offenses and misdemeanors, while the latter is a place for permanent or long-continued confinement, or for the punishment of graver crimes. In modern usage, this distinction is commonly taken between the words "gaol" and "penitentiary," (or state's prison,) but the name "prison" is indiscriminately applied to either.

GAOL DELIVERY. In criminal law. The delivery or clearing of a gaol of the prisoners confined therein, by trying them. A commission of general gaol delivery is one of the four commissions under which the judges in England sit at the assizes; and it empowers them to try and *deliver* every prisoner who shall be in the *gaol*, (that is, either in actual custody, or out on bail,) when the judges arrive at the circuit town. 4 Chit. Bl. 270, and notes; 4 Steph. Comm. 333; 1 Chit. Crim. Law, 145, 146.

GAOL LIBERTIES, GAOL LIMITS. A district around a gaol, defined by limits, within which prisoners are allowed to go at large on giving security to return. It is considered a part of the gaol.

GAOLER. The master or keeper of a prison; one who has the custody of a place where prisoners are confined.

GARANDIA, or GARANTIA. A warranty. Spelman.

GARANTIE. In French law. This word corresponds to warranty or covenants for title in English law. In the case of a sale this *garantie* extends to two things: (1) Peaceful possession of the thing sold; and (2) absence of undisclosed defects, (*défauts cachés*.) Brown.

GARATHINX. In old Lombardic law. A gift; a free or absolute gift; a gift of the whole of a thing. Spelman.

GARAUNTOR. L. Fr. In old English law. A warrantor of land; a vouchee; one bound by a warranty to defend the title and seisin of his alienee, or, on default thereof, and on eviction of the tenant, to give him other lands of equal value. Britt. c. 75.

GARBA. In old English law. A bundle or sheaf. *Blada in garbis*, corn or grain in sheaves. Reg. Orig. 96; Bract. fol. 209.

GARBA SAGITTARUM. A sheaf of arrows, containing twenty-four. Otherwise called "*schaffa sagittarum*." Skene.

GARBALES DECIMÆ. In Scotch law. Tithes of corn, (grain.) Bell.

GARBLE. In English statutes. To sort or cull out the good from the bad in spices, drugs, etc. Cowell.

GARBLER OF SPICES. An ancient officer in the city of London, who might enter into any shop, warehouse, etc., to view and search drugs and spices, and garble and make clean the same, or see that it be done. Mozley & Whitley.

GARCIO STOLÆ. Groom of the stole.

GARCIONES. Servants who follow a camp. Wals. 242.

GARD, or GARDE. Wardship; care; custody; also the ward of a city.

GARDEIN. A keeper; a guardian.

GARDEN. A small piece of land, appropriated to the cultivation of herbs, fruits, flowers, or vegetables.

GARDIA. Custody; wardship.

GARDIANUS. In old English law. A guardian, defender, or protector. In feudal law, *gardio*. Spelman.

A warden. *Gardianus ecclesiæ*, a church-warden. *Gardianus quinque portuum*, warden of the Cinque Ports. Spelman.

GARDINUM. In old English law. A garden. Reg. Orig. 1*b*, 2.

GARENE. L. Fr. A warren; a privileged place for keeping animals.

GARNESTURA. In old English law. Victuals, arms, and other implements of war, necessary for the defense of a town or castle. Mat. Par. 1250.

GARNISH, *n.* In English law. Money paid by a prisoner to his fellow-prisoners on his entrance into prison.

GARNISH, *v.* To warn or summon.

To issue process of garnishment against a person.

GARNISHEE. One garnished; a person against whom process of garnishment is issued; one who has money or property in his possession belonging to a defendant, or who owes the defendant a debt, which money, property, or debt is attached in his hands, with notice to him not to deliver or pay it over until the result of the suit be ascertained.

GARNISHMENT. In the process of attachment. A warning to a person in whose hands the effects of another are attached not to pay the money or deliver the property of the defendant in his hands to him, but to appear and answer the plaintiff's suit. Drake, Attachm. § 451.

A "garnishment," as the word is employed in this Code, is process to reach and subject money or effects of a defendant in attachment, or in a judgment or decree, or in a pending suit commenced in the ordinary form, in the possession or under the control of a third person, or debts owing such defendant, or liabilities to him on contracts for the delivery of personal property, or on contracts for the payment of money which may be discharged by the delivery of personal property, or on a contract payable in personal property; and such third person is called the "garnishee." Code Ala. 1886, § 2994.

Garnishment is a proceeding to apply the debt due by a third person to a judgment defendant, to the extinguishment of that judgment, or to appropriate effects belonging to a defendant, in the hands of a third person, to its payment. 4 Ga. 393.

Also a warning to any one for his appearance, in a cause in which he is not a party, for the information of the court and explaining a cause. Cowell.

GARNISTURA. In old English law. Garniture; whatever is necessary for the fortification of a city or camp, or for the ornament of a thing. 8 Rymer, 328; Du Cange; Cowell; Blount.

GARSUMME. In old English law. An amerciament or fine. Cowell.

GARTER. A string or ribbon by which the stocking is held upon the leg. The mark of the highest order of English knighthood, ranking next after the nobility. This military order of knighthood is said to have been first instituted by Richard I., at the siege of Acre, where he caused twenty-six knights who firmly stood by him to wear thongs of blue leather about their legs. It is also said to have been perfected by Edward III., and to have received some alterations, which were afterwards laid aside, from Edward VI. The badge of the order is the image of St. George, called the "George," and the motto is "*Honi soit qui mal y pense.*" Wharton.

GARTH. In English law. A yard; a little close or homestead in the north of England. Cowell; Blount.

A dam or wear in a river, for the catching of fish.

GARYTOUR. In old Scotch law. Warder. 1 Pitc. Crim. Tr. pt. 1, p. 8.

GASTALDUS. A temporary governor of the country. Blount. A bailiff or steward. Spelman.

GASTEL. L. Fr. Wastel; wastel bread; the finest sort of wheat bread. Britt. c. 30; Kelham.

GASTINE. L. Fr. Waste or uncultivated ground. Britt. c. 57.

GAUDIES. A term used in the English universities to denote double commons.

GAUGE. The measure of width of a railway, fixed, with some exceptions, at 4 feet 8½ inches in Great Britain and America, and 5 feet 3 inches in Ireland.

GAUGEATOR. A gauger. Lowell.

GAUGER. A surveying officer under the customs, excise, and internal revenue laws, appointed to examine all tuns, pipes, hogsheads, barrels and tierces of wine, oil, and other liquids, and to give them a mark of allowance, as containing lawful measure. There are also private gaugers in large seaport towns, who are licensed by government to perform the same duties. Rapal. & L.

GAUGETUM. A gauge or gauging; a measure of the contents of any vessel.

GAVEL. In English law. Custom; tribute; toll; yearly rent; payment of revenue; of which there were anciently several sorts; as *gavel-corn*, *gavel-malt*, *oat-gavel*, *gavel-fodder*, etc. Termes de la Ley; Cowell; Co. Litt. 142*a*.

GAVELBRED. In English law. Rent reserved in bread, corn, or provision; rent payable in kind. Cowell.

GAVELCESTER. A certain measure of rent-ale. Cowell.

GAVELET. An ancient and special kind of *cessavit*, used in Kent and London for the recovery of rent. Obsolete. The statute of gavelet is 10 Edw. II. 2 Reeve, Eng. Law, c. 12, p. 298.

GAVELGELD. That which yields annual profit or toll. The tribute or toll itself. Cowell; Du Cange.

GAVELHERTE. A service of plowing performed by a customary tenant. Cowell; Du Cange.

GAVELING MEN. Tenants who paid a reserved rent, besides some customary duties to be done by them. Cowell.

GAVELKIND. A species of socage tenure common in Kent, in England, where the lands descend to all the sons, or heirs of the nearest degree, together; may be disposed of by will; do not escheat for felony; may be aliened by the heir at the age of fifteen; and dower and curtesy is given of half the land. Stim. Law Gloss.

GAVELLER. An officer of the English crown having the general management of the mines, pits, and quarries in the Forest of Dean and Hundred of St. Briavel's, subject, in some respects, to the control of the commissioners of woods and forests. He grants gales to free miners in their proper order, accepts surrenders of gales, and keeps the registers required by the acts. There is a deputy-gaveller, who appears to exercise most of the gaveller's functions. Sweet.

GAVEL-MAN. In old English law. A tenant liable to the payment of gavel or tribute. Somn. Gavelkind, 23.

GAVELMED. A customary service of mowing meadow-land or cutting grass, (*consuetudo falcandi.*) Blount.

GAVELREP. In old English law. Bedreap or bidreap; the duty of reaping at the bid or command of the lord. Somn. Gavelkind, 19, 21; Cowell.

GAVELWERK. A customary service, either *manuopera*, by the person of the tenant, or *carropera*, by his carts or carriages. Blount; Somn. Gavelkind, 24; Du Cange.

GAZETTE. The official publication of the English government, also called the "London Gazette." It is evidence of acts of state, and of everything done by the queen in her political capacity. Orders of adjudication in bankruptcy are required to be published therein; and the production of a copy of the "Gazette," containing a copy of the order of adjudication, is evidence of the fact. Mozley & Whitley.

GEBOCCED. An Anglo-Saxon term, meaning "conveyed."

GEBOCIAN. In Saxon law. To convey; to transfer *boc* land, (book-land or land held by charter.) The grantor was said to *gebocian* the alienee. See 1 Reeve, Eng. Law, 10.

GEBURSCRIPT. Neighborhood or adjoining district. Cowell.

GEBURUS. In old English law. A country neighbor; an inhabitant of the same *geburscript*, or village. Cowell.

GELD. In Saxon law. Money or tribute. A mulct, compensation, value, price. *Angeld* was the single value of a thing; *twigeld*, double value, etc. So, *weregeld* was the value of a man slain; *orfgeld*, that of a beast. Brown.

GELDABILIS. In old English law. Taxable; geldable.

GELDABLE. Liable to pay geld; liable to be taxed. Kelham.

GELDING. A horse that has been castrated, and which is thus distinguished from the horse in his natural and unaltered condition. A "ridgling" (a half-castrated horse) is not a gelding, but a horse, within the denomination of animals in the statutes. 4 Tex. App. 219.

GEMMA. Lat. In the civil law. A gem; a precious stone. Gems were distinguished by their transparency; such as emeralds, chrysolites, amethysts. Dig. 34, 2, 19, 17.

GEMOT. In Saxon law. A meeting or moot; a convention; a public assemblage. These were of several sorts, such as the *witena-gemot*, or meeting of the wise men; the *folc-gemot*, or general assembly of the people; the *shire-gemot*, or county court; the *burg-gemot*, or borough court; the *hundred-gemot*, or hundred court; the *hali-gemot*, or court-baron; the *hal-mote*, a convention of citizens in their public hall; the *holy-mote*, or holy court; the *swein-gemote*, or forest court; the *ward-mote*, or ward court. Wharton; Cunningham.

GENEALOGY. An account or history of the descent of a person or family from an ancestor; enumeration of ancestors and their children in the natural order of succession. Webst.

GENEARCH. The head of a family.

GENEATH. In Saxon law. A villein, or agricultural tenant, (*villanus villicus;*) a hind or farmer, (*firmarius rusticus.*) Spelman.

GENER. Lat. In the civil law. A son-in-law; a daughter's husband. (*Filiæ vir.*) Dig. 38, 10, 4, 6.

GENERAL. Pertaining to, or designating, the *genus* or class, as distinguished from that which characterizes the *species* or individual. Universal, not particularized; as opposed to special. Principal or central; as opposed to local. Open or available to all;

as opposed to select. Obtaining commonly, or recognized universally; as opposed to particular. Universal or unbounded; as opposed to limited. Comprehending the whole, or directed to the whole; as distinguished from anything applying to or designed for a portion only.

As a noun, the word is the title of a principal officer in the army, usually one who commands a whole army, division, corps, or brigade. In the United States army, the rank of "general" is the highest possible, next to the commander in chief, and is only occasionally created. The officers next in rank are lieutenant general, major general, and brigadier general.

GENERAL AGENT. A person who is authorized by his principal to execute all deeds, sign all contracts, or purchase all goods, required in a particular trade, business, or employment. Story, Ag. § 17.

In another sense, a person who has a general authority in regard to a particular object or thing. Id. § 18.

A general agent is one appointed to act in the affairs of his principal generally; a special agent is one appointed to act concerning some particular object. 7 Ala. 800, 804.

GENERAL APPEARANCE. An unqualified or unrestricted submission to the jurisdiction of the court. See APPEARANCE.

GENERAL ASSEMBLY. A name given in some of the United States to the senate and house of representatives, which compose the legislative body.

GENERAL ASSIGNMENT. An assignment made for the benefit of *all* the assignor's creditors, instead of a few only; or one which transfers the *whole* of his estate to the assignee, instead of a part only.

GENERAL AVERAGE. In commercial law. A contribution made by the proprietors in general of a ship or cargo, towards the loss sustained by any individual of their number, whose property has been voluntarily sacrificed for the common safety; as where, in a storm, jettison is made of any goods, or sails or masts are cut away *levandæ navis causâ*, (to lighten the vessel.) 2 Steph. Comm. 179.

The term expresses that contribution to a loss or expense voluntarily incurred for the preservation of the whole, in which all who are concerned in ship, freight, and cargo are to bear an equal part, proportionable to their respective interests. And for the loss incurred by this contribution, however small in amount, the respective owners are to be indemnified by their insurers. 4 Mass. 548.

GENERAL CHALLENGE. A species of challenge for cause, being an objection to a particular juror, to the effect that the juror is disqualified from serving in any case. Pen. Code Cal. § 1071.

GENERAL CHARACTER. See CHARACTER.

GENERAL CHARGE. A charge or instruction by the court to the jury upon the case as a whole, or upon its general features or characteristics.

GENERAL COUNCIL. (1) A council consisting of members of the Roman Catholic Church from most parts of the world, but not from every part, as an ecumenical council. (2) One of the names of the English parliament.

GENERAL COVENANT. One which relates to lands generally, and places the covenantee in the position of a specialty creditor. Brown.

GENERAL CREDIT. The character of a witness as one generally worthy of credit. According to Bouvier, there is a distinction between this and "particular credit," which may be affected by proof of particular facts relating to the particular action.

GENERAL CUSTOM. General customs are such as prevail throughout a country and become the law of that country, and their existence is to be determined by the court. Particular customs are such as prevail in some county, city, town, parish, or place; their existence is to be determined by a jury upon proof. 23 Me. 95.

GENERAL DAMAGES. In pleading and practice. Such damages as necessarily result from the injury complained of, and which may be shown under the *ad damnum*, or general allegation of damages at the end of the declaration. 2 Greenl. Ev. § 254.

GENERAL DEMURRER. In pleading. A demurrer framed in general terms, without showing specifically the nature of the objection, and which is usually resorted to where the objection is to matter of substance. Steph. Pl. 140–142; 1 Chit. Pl. 663. See DEMURRER.

GENERAL DEPOSIT. A general deposit is where the money deposited is not itself to be returned, but an equivalent in money (that is, a like sum) is to be returned. It is equivalent to a loan, and the money deposited becomes the property of the depositary. 43 Ala. 138.

GENERAL ELECTION. 1. One at which the officers to be elected are such as belong to the *general* government,—that is, the general and central political organization of the whole state; as distinguished from an election of officers for a particular locality only.

2. One held for the selection of an officer after the expiration of the full term of the former officer; thus distinguished from a *special* election, which is one held to supply a vacancy in office occurring before the expiration of the full term for which the incumbent was elected. 52 Cal. 164.

GENERAL EXECUTOR. One whose power is not limited either territorially or as to the duration or subject of his trust.

GENERAL FIELD. Several distinct lots or pieces of land inclosed and fenced in as one common field. 14 Mass. 440.

GENERAL FUND. This phrase, in New York, is a collective designation of all the assets of the state which furnish the means for the support of government and for defraying the discretionary appropriations of the legislature. 27 Barb. 575, 588.

GENERAL GAOL DELIVERY. In English law. At the assizes (*q. v.*) the judges sit by virtue of five several authorities, one of which is the commission of "general gaol delivery." This empowers them to try and deliverance make of every prisoner who shall be in the gaol when the judges arrive at the circuit town, whether an indictment has been preferred at any previous assize or not. 4 Bl. Comm. 270.

GENERAL GUARDIAN. One who has the general care and control of the person and estate of his ward.

GENERAL IMPARLANCE. In pleading. One granted upon a prayer in which the defendant reserves to himself no exceptions.

GENERAL INCLOSURE ACT. The statute 41 Geo. III. c. 109, which consolidates a number of regulations as to the inclosure of common fields and waste lands.

GENERAL INTENT. An intention, purpose, or design, either without specific plan or particular object, or without reference to such plan or object.

GENERAL INTEREST. In speaking of matters of public and general interest, the terms "public" and "general" are sometimes used as synonyms. But in regard to the admissibility of hearsay evidence, a distinction has been taken between them, the term "public" being strictly applied to that which concerns every member of the state, and the term "general" being confined to a lesser, though still a considerable, portion of the community. Tayl. Ev. § 609.

GENERAL ISSUE. In pleading. A plea which traverses and denies, briefly and in general and summary terms, the whole declaration, indictment, or complaint, without tendering new or special matter. See Steph. Pl. 155. Examples of the general issue are "not guilty," "*non assumpsit,*" "*nil debet,*" "*non est factum.*"

GENERAL JURISDICTION. Such as extends to all controversies that may be brought before a court within the legal bounds of rights and remedies; as opposed to *special* or *limited* jurisdiction, which covers only a particular class of cases, or cases where the amount in controversy is below a prescribed sum, or which is subject to specific exceptions.

The terms "general" and "special," applied to jurisdiction, indicate the difference between a legal authority extending to the whole of a particular subject and one limited to a part; and, when applied to the terms of court, the occasion upon which these powers can be respectively exercised. 1 N. Y. 232.

GENERAL LAND-OFFICE. In the United States, one of the bureaus of the interior department, which has charge of the survey, sale, granting of patents, and other matters relating to the public lands.

GENERAL LAW. A general law, as contradistinguished from one that is special or local, is a law that embraces a class of subjects or places, and does not omit any subject or place naturally belonging to such class. 40 N. J. Law, 1.

A law, framed in general terms, restricted to no locality, and operating equally upon all of a group of objects, which, having regard to the purposes of the legislation, are distinguished by characteristics sufficiently marked and important to make them a class by themselves, is not a special or local law, but a general law. 40 N. J. Law, 123.

GENERAL LEGACY. A pecuniary legacy, payable out of the general assets of a testator. 2 Bl. Comm. 512; Ward, Leg. 1, 16.

GENERAL LIEN. A right to detain a chattel, etc., until payment be made, not only of any debt due in respect of the particular chattel, but of any balance that may be due on general account in the same line of business. A general lien, being against the ordinary rule of law, depends entirely upon contract, express or implied, from the special usage of dealing between the parties. Wharton.

GENERAL MALICE. General malice is wickedness, a disposition to do wrong, a "black and diabolical heart, regardless of social duty and fatally bent on mischief." 11 Ired. 261.

GENERAL MEETING. A meeting of all the stockholders of a corporation, all the creditors of a bankrupt, etc.

GENERAL MONITION. In civil law and admiralty practice. A monition or summons to all parties in interest to appear and show cause against the decree prayed for.

GENERAL OCCUPANT. At common law where a man was tenant *pur auter vie*, or had an estate granted to himself only (without mentioning his heirs) for the life of another man, and died without alienation during the life of *cestui que vie*, or him by whose life it was holden, he that could first enter on the land might lawfully retain the possession, so long as *cestui que vie* lived, by right of occupancy, and was hence termed a "general" or common "occupant." 1 Steph. Comm. 415.

GENERAL ORDERS. Orders or rules of court, promulgated for the guidance of practitioners and the regulation of procedure in general, or in some general branch of its jurisdiction; as opposed to a rule or an order made in an individual case; the rules of court.

GENERAL OWNER. The general owner of a thing is he who has the primary or residuary title to it; as distinguished from a *special* owner, who has a special interest in the same thing, amounting to a qualified ownership, such, for example, as a bailee's lien.

GENERAL PARTNERSHIP. A partnership in which the parties carry on all their trade and business, whatever it may be, for the joint benefit and profit of all the parties concerned, whether the capital stock be limited or not, or the contributions thereto be equal or unequal. Story, Partn. § 74.

GENERAL PROPERTY. The right and property in a thing enjoyed by the *general owner*, (*q. v.*)

GENERAL RESTRAINT OF TRADE. One which forbids the person to employ his talents, industry, or capital in any undertaking within the limits of the state or country. 9 How. Pr. 337.

GENERAL RETAINER. A general retainer of an attorney or solicitor "merely gives a right to expect professional service when requested, but none which is not requested. It binds the person retained not to take a fee from another against his retainer, but to do nothing except what he is asked to do, and for this he is to be distinctly paid." 6 R. I. 206.

GENERAL RETURN-DAY. The day for the general return of all writs of summons, subpœna, etc., running to a particular term of the court.

GENERAL RULES. General or standing orders of a court, in relation to practice, etc. See GENERAL ORDERS.

GENERAL SESSIONS. A court of record, in England, held by two or more justices of the peace, for the execution of the authority given them by the commission of the peace and certain statutes. General sessions held at certain times in the four quarters of the year pursuant to St. 2 Hen. V. are properly called "quarter sessions," (*q. v.*,) but intermediate general sessions may also be held. Sweet.

GENERAL SHIP. Where a ship is not chartered wholly to one person, but the owner offers her generally to carry the goods of all comers, or where, if chartered to one person, he offers her to several subfreighters for the conveyance of their goods, she is called a "general" ship, as opposed to a "chartered" one. Brown.

A vessel in which the master or owners engage separately with a number of persons unconnected with each other to convey their respective goods to the place of the ship's destination. 6 Cow. 173.

GENERAL SPECIAL IMPARLANCE. An imparlance (*q. v.*) granted upon a prayer in which the defendant reserves to himself "all advantages and exceptions whatsoever." 2 Chit. Pl. 408.

GENERAL STATUTE. A statute relating to the whole community, or concerning all persons generally, as distinguished from a private or special statute. 4 Coke, 75*a;* 1 Bl. Comm. 85, 86.

GENERAL TAIL. An estate tail where one parent only is specified, whence the issue must be derived, as to A. and the heirs of his body.

GENERAL TENANCY. A tenancy which is not fixed and made certain in point of duration by the agreement of the parties. 22 Ind. 122.

GENERAL TERM. A phrase used in some jurisdictions to denote the ordinary session of a court, for the trial and determination of causes, as distinguished from a *special* term, for the hearing of motions or arguments or the despatch of various kinds of formal business, or the trial of a special list or class of cases. Or it may denote a sitting of the court *in banc.*

GENERAL TRAVERSE. One preceded by a general inducement, and denying in general terms all that is last before alleged on the opposite side, instead of pursuing the words of the allegations which it denies. Gould, Pl. vii. 5.

GENERAL USAGE. One which prevails generally throughout the country, or is followed generally by a given profession or trade, and is not local in its nature or observance.

GENERAL VERDICT. A verdict whereby the jury find either for the plaintiff or for the defendant in general terms; the ordinary form of a verdict; distinguished from a *special* verdict, (*q. v.*)

GENERAL WARRANT. A process which formerly issued from the state secretary's office in England to take up (without naming any persons) the author, printer, and publisher of such obscene and seditious libels as were specified in it. It was declared illegal and void for uncertainty by a vote of the house of commons on the 22d April, 1766. Wharton.

GENERAL WARRANTY. The name of a covenant of warranty inserted in deeds, by which the grantor binds himself, his heirs, etc., to "warrant and forever defend" to the grantee, his heirs, etc., the title thereby conveyed, against the lawful claims of all persons whatsoever. Where the warranty is only against the claims of persons claiming "by, through, or under" the grantor or his heirs, it is called a "special warranty."

GENERALE. The usual commons in a religious house, distinguished from *pietantiæ,* which on extraordinary occasions were allowed beyond the commons. Cowell.

Generale dictum generaliter est interpretandum. A general expression is to be interpreted generally. 8 Coke, 116*a.*

Generale nihil certum implicat. A general expression implies nothing certain. 2 Coke, 34*b.* A general recital in a deed has not the effect of an estoppel. Best, Ev. p. 408, § 370.

Generale tantum valet in generalibus, quantum singulare in singulis. What is general is of as much force among general things as what is particular is among things particular. 11 Coke, 59*b.*

Generalia præcedunt, specialia sequuntur. Things general precede, things special follow. Reg. Brev.; Branch, Princ.

Generalia specialibus non derogant. Jenk. Cent. 120, cited L. R. 4 Exch. 226. General words do not derogate from special.

Generalia s[illegible] præponenda singularibus. Branch, [illegible]rinc. General things are to precede particular things.

Generalia verba sunt generaliter intelligenda. General words are to be understood generally, or in a general sense. 3 Inst. 76; Broom, Max. 647.

Generalibus specialia derogant. Special things take from generals. Halk. Lat. Max. 51.

Generalis clausula non porrigitur ad ea quæ antea specialiter sunt comprehensa. A general clause does not extend to those things which are previously provided for specially. 8 Coke, 154*b.* Therefore, where a deed at the first contains special words, and afterwards concludes in general words, both words, as well general as special, shall stand.

Generalis regula generaliter est intelligenda. A general rule is to be understood generally. 6 Coke, 65.

GENERALS OF ORDERS. Chiefs of the several orders of monks, friars, and other religious societies.

GENERATIO. The issue or offspring of a mother-monastery. Cowell.

GENEROSA. Gentlewoman. Cowell; 2 Inst. 668.

GENEROSI FILIUS. The son of a gentleman. Generally abbreviated "*gen. fil.*"

GENEROSUS. Gentleman; a gentleman. Spelman.

GENICULUM. A degree of consanguinity. Spelman.

GENS. In Roman law. A tribe or clan; a group of families, connected by common descent and bearing the same name, being all free-born and of free ancestors, and in possession of full civic rights.

GENTES. People. *Contra omnes gentes,* against all people. Bract. fol. 37*b*. Words used in the clause of warranty in old deeds.

GENTILES. In Roman law. The members of a *gens* or common tribe.

GENTLEMAN. In English law. A person of superior birth.

Under the denomination of "gentlemen" are comprised all above yeoman; whereby noblemen are truly called "gentlemen." Smith de Rep. Ang. lib. 1, cc. 20, 21.

A "gentleman" is defined to be one who, without any title, bears a coat of arms, or whose ancestors have been freemen; and, by the coat that a gentleman giveth, he is known to be, or not to be, descended from those of his name that lived many hundred years since. Jacob.

GENTLEMAN USHER. One who holds a post at court to usher others to the presence, etc.

GENTLEWOMAN. A woman of birth above the common, or equal to that of a gentleman; an addition of a woman's state or degree.

GENTOO LAW. See HINDU LAW.

GENUINE. This term, when used with reference to a note, imports nothing in regard to the collectibility of the note, or in regard to its legal effect or operation, other than that the note is not false, fictitious, simulated, spurious, counterfeit, or, in short, that the apparent maker did make and deliver the note offered for sale. 37 N. Y. 487.

GENUS. In the civil law. A general class or division, comprising several species. *In toto jure generi per speciem derogatur, et illud potissimum habetur quod ad speciem directum est,* throughout the law, the species takes from the genus, and that is most particularly regarded which refers to the species. Dig. 50, 17, 80.

A man's lineage, or direct descendants.

In logic, it is the first of the universal ideas, and is when the idea is so common that it extends to other ideas which are also universal; *e. g.*, incorporeal hereditament is *genus* with respect to a *rent*, which is *species*. Woolley, Introd. Log. 45; 1 Mill, Log. 133.

GEOPONICS. The science of cultivating the ground; agriculture.

GEORGE-NOBLE. A gold coin, value 6s. 8d.

GERECHTSBODE. In old New York law. A court messenger or constable. O'Callaghan, New Neth. 322.

GEREFA. In Saxon law. Greve, reve, or reeve; a ministerial officer of high antiquity in England; answering to the *grave* or *graf* (*grafio*) of the early continental nations. The term was applied to various grades of officers, from the *scyre-gerefa, shire-grefe,* or *shire-reve,* who had charge of the county, (and whose title and office have been perpetuated in the modern "sheriff,") down to the *tun-gerefa,* or town-reeve, and lower. Burrill.

GERENS. Bearing. *Gerens datum,* bearing date. 1 Ld. Raym. 336; Hob. 19.

GERMAN. Whole, full, or own, in respect to relationship or descent. Brothers-german, as opposed to half-brothers, are those who have both the same father and mother. Cousins-german are "first" cousins; that is, children of brothers or sisters.

GERMANUS. Descended of the same stock, or from the same couple of ancestors; of the whole or full blood. Mackeld. Rom. Law, § 145.

GERMEN TERRÆ. A sprout of the earth. A young tree, so called.

GERONTOCOMI. In the civil law. Officers appointed to manage hospitals for the aged poor.

GERONTOCOMIUM. In the civil law. An institution or hospital for taking care of the old. Cod. 1, 3, 46, 1; Calvin.

GERSUMARIUS. Finable; liable to be amerced at the discretion of the lord of a manor. Cowell.

GERSUME. In old English law. Expense; reward; compensation; wealth. It is also used for a fine or compensation for an offense. 2 Mon. Angl. 973.

GEST. In Saxon law. A guest. A name given to a stranger on the *second night* of his entertainment in another's house. *Twa-night gest.*

GESTATION, UTERO-GESTATION. In medical jurisprudence. The time during which a female, who has conceived, carries the embryo or *fœtus* in her *uterus.*

GESTIO. In the civil law. Behavior or conduct.

Management or transaction. *Negotiorum gestio,* the doing of another's business; an interference in the affairs of another in his absence, from benevolence or friendship, and without authority. Dig. 3, 5, 45; Id. 46, 3, 12, 4; 2 Kent, Comm. 616, note.

GESTIO PRO HÆREDE. Behavior as heir. This expression was used in the Roman law, and adopted in the civil law and Scotch law, to denote conduct on the part of a person appointed heir to a deceased person, or otherwise entitled to succeed as heir, which indicates an intention to enter upon the inheritance, and to hold himself out as heir to creditors of the deceased; as by receiving the rents due to the deceased, or by taking possession of his title-deeds, etc. Such acts will render the heir liable to the debts of his ancestor. Mozley & Whitley.

GESTOR. In the civil law. One who acts for another, or transacts another's business. Calvin.

GESTU ET FAMA. An ancient and obsolete writ resorted to when a person's good behavior was impeached. Lamb. Eir. l. 4, c. 14.

GESTUM. Lat. In Roman law. A deed or act; a thing done. Some writers affected to make a distinction between "*gestum*" and "*factum.*" But the best authorities pronounced this subtile and indefensible. Dig. 50, 16, 58.

GEVILLOURIS. In old Scotch law. Gaolers. 1 Pitc. Crim. Tr. pt. 2, p. 234.

GEWINEDA. In Saxon law. The ancient convention of the people to decide a cause.

GEWITNESSA. In Saxon and old English law. The giving of evidence.

GEWRITE. In Saxon law. Deeds or charters; writings. 1 Reeve, Eng. Law, 10.

GIBBET. A gallows; the post on which malefactors are hanged, or on which their bodies are exposed. It differs from a common gallows, in that it consists of one perpendicular post, from the top of which proceeds one arm, except it be a double gibbet, which is formed in the shape of the Roman capital T. Enc. Lond.

GIFT. A voluntary conveyance of land, or transfer of goods, from one person to another, made gratuitously, and not upon any consideration of blood or money. 2 Bl. Comm. 440; 2 Steph. Comm. 102; 2 Kent, Comm. 437.

A gift is a transfer of personal property, made voluntarily and without consideration. Civil Code Cal. § 1146.

In popular language, a voluntary conveyance or assignment is called a "deed of gift."

"Gift" and "advancement" are sometimes used interchangeably as expressive of the same operation. But, while an advancement is always a gift, a gift is very frequently not an advancement. 3 Brewst. 314.

In English law. A conveyance of lands in tail; a conveyance of an estate tail in which the operative words are "I give," or "I have given." 2 Bl. Comm. 316; 1 Steph. Comm. 473.

GIFT ENTERPRISE. A scheme for the division or distribution of certain articles of property, to be determined by chance, among those who have taken shares in the scheme. The phrase has attained such a notoriety as to justify a court in taking judicial notice of what is meant and understood by it. 81 Ind. 17; 106 Mass. 422.

GIFTA AQUÆ. The stream of water to a mill. Mon. Angl. tom. 3.

GIFTOMAN. In Swedish law. The right to dispose of a woman in marriage; or the person possessing such right,—her father, if living, or, if he be dead, the mother.

GILD. In Saxon law. A tax or tribute. Spelman.

A fine, mulct, or amerciament; a satisfaction or compensation for an injury.

A fraternity, society, or company of persons combined together, under certain regulations, and with the king's license, and so called because its expenses were defrayed by the *contributions* (*geld, gild*) of its members. Spelman. In other words, a corporation; called, in Latin, "*societas,*" "*collegium,*" "*fratria,*" "*fraternitas,*" "*sodalitium,*" "*adunatio;*" and, in foreign law, "*gildonia.*" Spelman. There were various kinds of these *gilds,* as merchant or commercial *gilds,* religious *gilds,* and others. 3 Turn. Anglo

Sax. 98; 3 Steph. Comm. 173, note *u*. See GILDA MERCATORIA.

A friborg, or decennary; called, by the Saxons, "*gyldscipes*," and its members, "*gildones*" and "*congildones*." Spelman.

GILD-HALL. See GUILDHALL.

GILD-RENT. Certain payments to the crown from any gild or fraternity.

GILDA MERCATORIA. A gild merchant, or merchant gild; a gild, corporation, or company of merchants. 10 Coke, 30.

GILDABLE. In old English law. Taxable, tributary, or contributory; liable to pay tax or tribute. Cowell; Blount.

GILDO. In Saxon law. Members of a *gild* or decennary. Oftener spelled "*congildo*." Du Cange; Spelman.

GILL. A liquid measure, containing one-fourth of a pint.

GILOUR. L. Fr. A cheat or deceiver. Applied in Britton to those who sold false or spurious things for good, as pewter for silver or laten for gold. Britt. c. 15.

GIRANTE. An Italian word, which signifies the drawer of a bill. It is derived from "*girare*," to draw.

GIRTH. In Saxon and old English law. A measure of length, equal to one yard, derived from the girth or circumference of a man's body.

GIRTH AND SANCTUARY. In old Scotch law. An asylum given to murderers, where the murder was committed without any previous design, and in *chaude mella*, or heat of passion. Bell.

GISEMENT. Agistment; cattle taken in to graze at a certain price; also the money received for grazing cattle.

GISER. L. Fr. To lie. *Gist en le bouche*, it lies in the mouth. *Le action bien gist*, the action well lies. *Gisant*, lying.

GISETAKER. An agister; a person who takes cattle to graze.

GISLE. A pledge. *Fredgisle*, a pledge of peace. *Gislebert*, an illustrious pledge.

GIST. In pleading. The essential ground or object of the action in point of law, without which there would be no cause of action. Gould, Pl. c. 4, § 12; 19 Vt. 102.

The gist of an action is the cause for which an action will lie; the ground or foundation of a suit, without which it would not be maintainable; the essential ground or object of a suit, and without which there is not a cause of action. 101 Ill. 394.

GIVE. A term used in deeds of conveyance. At common law, it implied a covenant for quiet enjoyment. 2 Hil. Real Prop. 366.

In their ordinary and familiar signification, the words "sell" and "give" have not the same meaning, but are commonly used to express different modes of transferring the right to property from one person to another. "To sell" means to transfer for a valuable consideration, while "to give" signifies to transfer gratuitously, without any equivalent. 14 Md. 184.

"GIVE AND BEQUEATH." These words, in a will, import a benefit in point of right, to take effect upon the decease of the testator and proof of the will, unless it is made in terms to depend upon some contingency or condition precedent. 9 Cush. 519; 33 Conn. 297; 8 Wheat. 538.

GIVE BAIL. To furnish or put in bail or security for one's appearance.

GIVE COLOR. To admit an apparent or colorable right in the opposite party. See COLOR.

GIVER. A donor; he who makes a gift.

GIVING IN PAYMENT. In Louisiana law. A phrase (translating the Fr. "*dation en payement*") which signifies the delivery and acceptance of real or personal property in satisfaction of a debt, instead of a payment in money. See Civil Code La. art. 2655.

GIVING RINGS. A ceremony anciently performed in England by serjeants at law at the time of their appointment. The rings were inscribed with a motto, generally in Latin.

GIVING TIME. The act of a creditor in extending the time for the payment or satisfaction of a claim beyond the time stipulated in the original contract. If done without the consent of the surety, indorser, or guarantor, it discharges him.

GLADIOLUS. A little sword or dagger; a kind of sedge. Mat. Paris.

GLADIUS. Lat. A sword. An ancient emblem of defense. Hence the ancient earls or *comites* (the king's attendants, advisers, and associates in his government) were made by being girt with swords, (*gladio succincti.*)

The emblem of the executory power of the law in punishing crimes. 4 Bl. Comm. 177.

In old Latin authors, and in the Norman laws, this word was used to signify supreme jurisdiction, (*jus gladii.*)

GLAIVE. A sword, lance, or horseman's staff. One of the weapons allowed in a trial by combat.

GLANS. In the civil law. Acorns or nuts of the oak or other trees. In a larger sense, all fruits of trees.

GLASS-MEN. A term used in St. 1 Jac. I. c. 7, for wandering rogues or vagrants.

GLAVEA. A hand dart. Cowell.

GLEANING. The gathering of grain after reapers, or of grain left ungathered by reapers. Held not to be a right at common law. 1 H. Bl. 51.

GLEBA. A turf, sod, or clod of earth. The soil or ground; cultivated land in general. Church land, (*solum et dos ecclesiæ.*) Spelman. See GLEBE.

GLEBÆ ASCRIPTITII. Villein-socmen, who could not be removed from the land while they did the service due. Bract. c. 7; 1 Reeve, Eng. Law, 269.

GLEBARIÆ. Turfs dug out of the ground. Cowell.

GLEBE. **In ecclesiastical law.** The land possessed as part of the endowment or revenue of a church or ecclesiastical benefice.

In Roman law. A clod; turf; soil. Hence, the soil of an inheritance; an agrarian estate. *Servi addicti glebæ* were serfs attached to and passing with the estate. Cod. 11, 47, 7, 21; Nov. 54, 1.

GLISCYWA. In Saxon law. A fraternity.

GLOMERELLS. Commissioners appointed to determine differences between scholars in a school or university and the townsmen of the place. Jacob.

GLOS. Lat. In the civil law. A husband's sister. Dig. 38, 10, 4, 6.

GLOSS. An interpretation, consisting of one or more words, interlinear or marginal; an annotation, explanation, or comment on any passage in the text of a work, for purposes of elucidation or amplification. Particularly applied to the comments on the *Corpus Juris.*

GLOSSA. A gloss, explanation, or interpretation. The *glossæ* of the Roman law are brief illustrative comments or annotations on the text of Justinian's collections, made by the professors who taught or lectured on them about the twelfth century, (especially at the law school of Bologna,) and were hence called "*glossators.*" These glosses were at first inserted in the text with the words to which they referred, and were called "*glossæ interlineares;*" but afterwards they were placed in the margin, partly at the side, and partly under the text, and called "*glossæ marginales.*" A selection of them was made by Accursius, between A. D. 1220 and 1260, under the title of "*Glossa Ordinaria,*" which is of the greatest authority. Mackeld. Rom. Law, § 90.

Glossa viperina est quæ corrodit viscera textus. 11 Coke, 34. It is a poisonous gloss which corrupts the essence of the text.

GLOSSATOR. In the civil law. A commentator or annotator. A term applied to the professors and teachers of the Roman law in the twelfth century, at the head of whom was Irnerius. Mackeld. Rom. Law, § 90.

GLOUCESTER, STATUTE OF. The statute is the 6 Edw. I. c. 1, A. D. 1278. It takes its name from the place of its enactment, and was the first statute giving costs in actions.

GLOVE SILVER. Extraordinary rewards formerly given to officers of courts, etc.; money formerly given by the sheriff of a county in which no offenders are left for execution to the clerk of assize and judges' officers. Jacob.

GLOVES. It was an ancient custom on a maiden assize, when there was no offender to be tried, for the sheriff to present the judge with a pair of white gloves. It is an immemorial custom to remove the glove from the right hand on taking oath. Wharton.

GLYN. A hollow between two mountains; a valley or glen. Co. Litt. 5*b*.

GO. To be dismissed from a court. To issue from a court. "The court said a *mandamus* must *go.*" 1 W. Bl. 50. "Let a *supersedeas go.*" 5 Mod. 421. "The writ may *go.*" 18 C. B. 35.

This word, in a statutory provision that property "shall *go* to the survivor," etc., is to be construed as equivalent to *vest.*

GO BAIL. To assume the responsibility of a surety on a bail-bond.

GO TO PROTEST. Commercial paper is said to "go to protest" when it is dishonored by non-payment or non-acceptance and is handed to a notary for protest.

GO WITHOUT DAY. Words used to denote that a party is dismissed the court. He is said to go without day, because there is no day appointed for him to appear again.

GOAT, GOTE. In old English law. A contrivance or structure for draining waters out of the land into the sea. Callis describes *goats* as "usual engines erected and built with portcullises and doors of timber and stone or brick, invented first in Lower Germany." Callis, Sewers, (91,) 112, 113. Cowell defines "gote," a ditch, sewer, or gutter.

GOD AND MY COUNTRY. The answer made by a prisoner, when arraigned, in answer to the question, "How will you be tried?" In the ancient practice he had the choice (as appears by the question) whether to submit to the trial by ordeal (by God) or to be tried by a jury, (by the country;) and it is probable that the original form of the answer was, "By God *or* my country," whereby the prisoner averred his innocence by declining neither of the modes of trial.

GOD-BOTE. An ecclesiastical or church fine paid for crimes and offenses committed against God. Cowell.

GOD-GILD. That which is offered to God or his service. Jacob.

GOD'S ACRE. A churchyard.

GOD'S PENNY. In old English law. Earnest-money; money given as evidence of the completion of a bargain. This name is probably derived from the fact that such money was given to the church or distributed in alms.

GOGING-STOLE. An old form of the word "cucking-stool," (*q. v.*) Cowell.

GOING CONCERN. A firm or corporation which, though embarrassed or even insolvent, continues to transact its ordinary business. 30 Fed. Rep. 865.

GOING OFF LARGE. This is a nautical phrase, and signifies having the wind free on either tack. 1 Newb. Adm. 8, 26; 6 McLean, 152, 170.

A vessel, in nautical technicality, "is going off large" when the wind blows from some point "abaft the beam;" is going "before the wind" when the wind is "free," comes over the stern, and the yards of the ship are braced square across. 1 Newb. Adm. 115.

GOING THROUGH THE BAR. The act of the chief of an English common-law court in demanding of every member of the bar, in order of seniority, if he has anything to move. This was done at the sitting of the court each day in term, except special paper days, crown paper days in the queen's bench, and revenue paper days in the exchequer. On the last day of term this order is reversed, the first and second time round. In the exchequer the postman and tubman are first called on. Wharton.

GOING TO THE COUNTRY. When a party, under the common-law system of pleading, finished his pleading by the words "and of this he puts himself upon the country," this was called "going to the country." It was the essential termination to a pleading which took issue upon a material fact in the preceding pleading. Wharton.

GOING WITNESS. One who is about to take his departure from the jurisdiction of the court, although only into a state or country under the general sovereignty; as from one to another of the United States, or from England to Scotland.

GOLDA. A mine. Blount. A sink or passage for water. Cowell.

GOLDSMITHS' NOTES. Bankers' cash notes (*i. e.*, promissory notes given by a banker to his customers as acknowledgments of the receipt of money) were originally called in London "goldsmiths' notes," from the circumstance that all the banking business in England was originally transacted by goldsmiths. Wharton.

GOLDWIT. A mulct or fine in gold.

GOLIARDUS. L. Lat. A jester, buffoon, or juggler. Spelman, voc. "Goliardensis."

GOMASHTAH. In Hindu law. An agent; a steward; a confidential factor; a representative.

GOOD. 1. Valid; sufficient in law; effectual; unobjectionable.

2. Responsible; solvent; able to pay an amount specified.

3. Of a value corresponding with its terms; collectible. A note is said to be "good" when the payment of it at maturity may be relied on.

Writing the word "Good" across the face of a check is the customary mode in which bankers at the present day certify that the drawer has funds to meet it, and that it will be paid on presentation for that purpose.

GOOD ABEARING. See ABEARANCE.

GOOD AND LAWFUL MEN. Those who are not disqualified for service on juries by non-age, alienage, infamy, or lunacy, and who reside in the county of the venue.

GOOD AND VALID. Reliable, sufficient, and unimpeachable in law; adequate; responsible. See GOOD.

GOOD BEHAVIOR. Orderly and lawful conduct; behavior such as is proper for a peaceable and law-abiding citizen. Surety of good behavior may be exacted from any one who manifests an intention to commit crime or is otherwise reasonably suspected of a criminal design.

GOOD CONSIDERATION. As distinguished from *valuable* consideration, a consideration founded on motives of generosity, prudence, and natural duty; such as natural love and affection.

GOOD COUNTRY. In Scotch law. Good men of the country. A name given to a jury.

GOOD FAITH. Good faith consists in an honest intention to abstain from taking any unconscientious advantage of another, even through the forms or technicalities of law, together with an absence of all information or belief of facts which would render the transaction unconscientious. Civil Code Dak. § 2105; 1 Dak. 399, 46 N. W. Rep. 1132.

As to a purchaser in good faith, see BONA FIDE PURCHASER.

GOOD JURY. A jury of which the members are selected from the list of special jurors. See L. R. 5 C. P. 155.

GOOD TITLE. This means such a title as a court of chancery would adopt as a sufficient ground for compelling specific performance, and such a title as would be a good answer to an action of ejectment by any claimant. 6 Exch. 873. See, also, 23 Barb. 370.

GOOD-WILL. The custom or patronage of any established trade or business; the benefit or advantage of having established a business and secured its patronage by the public.

The advantage or benefit which is acquired by an establishment, beyond the mere value of the capital, stocks, funds, or property employed therein, in consequence of the general public patronage and encouragement which it receives from constant or habitual customers, on account of its local position, or common celebrity, or reputation for skill or affluence or punctuality, or from other accidental circumstances or necessities, or even from ancient partialities or prejudices. Story, Partn. § 99; 33 Cal. 624.

The good-will of a business is the expectation of continued public patronage, but it does not include a right to use the name of any person from whom it was acquired. Civil Code Cal. § 992; Civil Code Dak. § 577.

The term "good-will" does not mean simply the advantage of occupying particular premises which have been occupied by a manufacturer, etc. It means every advantage, every positive advantage, that has been acquired by a proprietor in carrying on his business, whether connected with the premises in which the business is conducted, or with the name under which it is managed, or with any other matter carrying with it the benefit of the business. 61 N. Y. 226.

GOODRIGHT, GOODTITLE. The fictitious plaintiff in the old action of ejectment, most frequently called "John Doe," was sometimes called "Goodright" or "Goodtitle."

GOODS. In contracts. The term "goods" is not so wide as "chattels," for it applies to inanimate objects, and does not include animals or chattels real, as a lease for years of house or land, which "chattels" does include. Co. Litt. 118; 1 Russ. 376.

In wills. In wills "goods" is *nomen generalissimum*, and, if there is nothing to limit it, will comprehend all the personal estate of the testator, as stocks, bonds, notes, money, plate, furniture, etc. 1 Atk. 180-182.

GOODS AND CHATTELS. This phrase is a general denomination of personal property, as distinguished from real property; the term "chattels" having the effect of extending its scope to any objects of that nature which would not properly be included by the term "goods" alone, *e. g.*, living animals, emblements, and fruits, and terms under leases for years. The general phrase also embraces choses in action, as well as personalty in possession.

In wills. The term "goods and chattels" will, unless restrained by the context, pass all the personal estate, including leases for years, cattle, corn, debts, and the like. Ward, Leg. 208, 211.

GOODS SOLD AND DELIVERED. A phrase frequently used in the action of *as-*

sumpsit, when the sale and delivery of goods furnish the cause.

"GOODS, WARES, AND MERCHANDISE." A general and comprehensive designation of such chattels as are ordinarily the subject of traffic and sale. The phrase is used in the statute of frauds, and is frequently found in pleadings and other instruments. As to its scope, see 20 Pick. 9; 118 Mass. 285; 2 Mason, 407; 2 Sum. 362; 4 Blatchf. 136; 20 Mich. 357; 6 Wend. 355; 40 Ind. 593; Dudley, 28; 55 Iowa, 520, 8 N. W. Rep. 334; 2 Pars. Cont. 330; Benj. Sales, 111; 2 Kent, Comm. 510, note.

GOOLE. In old English law. A breach in a bank or sea wall, or a passage worn by the flux and reflux of the sea. St. 16 & 17 Car. II. c. 11.

GORCE, or GORS. A wear, pool, or pit of water. Termes de la Ley.

GORE. A small, narrow slip of ground. Cowell.

GOSSIPRED. In canon law. Compaternity; spiritual affinity.

GOUT. In medical jurisprudence. An inflammation of the fibrous and ligamentous parts of the joints.

GOVERNMENT. 1. The regulation, restraint, supervision, or control which is exercised upon the individual members of an organized jural society by those invested with the supreme political authority, for the good and welfare of the body politic; or the *act* of exercising supreme political power or control.

2. The system of polity in a state; that form of fundamental rules and principles by which a nation or state is governed, or by which individual members of a body politic are to regulate their social actions; a constitution, either written or unwritten, by which the rights and duties of citizens and public officers are prescribed and defined, as a monarchical government, a republican government, etc. Webster.

3. An empire, kingdom, state, or independent political community; as in the phrase, "Compacts between independent governments."

4. The sovereign or supreme power in a state or nation.

5. The machinery by which the sovereign power in a state expresses its will and exercises its functions; or the framework of political institutions, departments, and offices, by means of which the executive, judicial, legislative, and administrative business of the state is carried on.

6. The whole class or body of office-holders or functionaries considered in the aggregate, upon whom devolves the executive, judicial, legislative, and administrative business of the state.

7. In a colloquial sense, the United States, or its representatives, considered as the prosecutor in a criminal action; as in the phrase, "the government objects to the witness."

We understand, in modern political science, by "state," in its widest sense, an independent society, acknowledging no superior, and by the term "government," that institution or aggregate of institutions by which that society makes and carries out those rules of action which are necessary to enable men to live in a social state, or which are imposed upon the people forming that society by those who possess the power or authority of prescribing them. "Government" is the aggregate of authorities which rule a society. By "administration," again, we understand in modern times, and especially in more or less free countries, the aggregate of those persons in whose hands the reins of government are for the time being, (the chief ministers or heads of departments.) But the terms "state," "government," and "administration" are not always used in their strictness. The government of a state being its most prominent feature, which is most readily perceived, "government" has frequently been used for "state;" and the publicists of the last century almost always used the term "government," or "form of government," when they discussed the different political societies or states On the other hand, "government" is often used, to this day, for "administration," in the sense in which it has been explained. Bouvier.

GOVERNMENT ANNUITIES SOCIETIES. These societies are formed in England under 3 & 4 Wm. IV. c. 14, to enable the industrious classes to make provisions for themselves by purchasing, on advantageous terms, a government annuity for life or term of years. By 16 & 17 Vict. c. 45, this act, as well as 7 & 8 Vict. c. 83, amending it, were repealed, and the whole law in relation to the purchase of government annuities, through the medium of savings banks, was consolidated. And by 27 & 28 Vict. c. 43, additional facilities were afforded for the purchase of such annuities, and for assuring payments of money on death. Wharton.

GOVERNMENT DE FACTO. A government of fact. A government actually exercising power and control in the state, as opposed to the true and lawful government; a government not established according to the constitution of the state, or not lawfully entitled to recognition or supremacy, but which has nevertheless supplanted or displaced the government *de jure*.

A government deemed unlawful, or deemed wrongful or unjust, which, nevertheless, receives presently habitual obedience from the bulk of the community. Aust. Jur. 324.

There are several degrees of what is called "*de facto* government."

Such a government, in its highest degree, assumes a character very closely resembling that of a lawful government. This is when the usurping government expels the regular authorities from their customary seats and functions, and establishes itself in their place, and so becomes the actual government of a country. The distinguishing characteristic of such a government is that adherents to it in war against the government *de jure* do not incur the penalties of treason; and, under certain limitations, obligations assumed by it in behalf of the country or otherwise will, in general, be respected by the government *de jure* when restored.

But there is another description of government, called also by publicists a "government *de facto*," but which might, perhaps, be more aptly denominated a "government of paramount force." Its distinguishing characteristics are (1) that its existence is maintained by active military power, within the territories, and against the rightful authority, of an established and lawful government; and (2) that, while it exists, it must necessarily be obeyed in civil matters by private citizens who, by acts of obedience, rendered in submission to such force, do not become responsible, as wrong-doers, for those acts, though not warranted by the laws of the rightful government. Actual governments of this sort are established over districts differing greatly in extent and conditions. They are usually administered directly by military authority, but they may be administered, also, by civil authority, supported more or less by military force. 8 Wall. 8, 9.

The term "*de facto*," as descriptive of a government, has no well-fixed and definite sense. It is, perhaps, most correctly used as signifying a government completely, though only temporarily, established in the place of the lawful or regular government, occupying its capitol, and exercising its power, and which is ultimately overthrown, and the authority of the government *de jure* re-established. 42 Miss. 651, 703.

A government *de facto* is a government that unlawfully gets the possession and control of the rightful legal government, and maintains itself there, by force and arms, against the will of such legal government, and claims to exercise the powers thereof. 43 Ala. 204.

GOVERNMENT DE JURE. A government of right; the true and lawful government; a government established according to the constitution of the state, and lawfully entitled to recognition and supremacy and the administration of the state, but which is actually cut off from power or control.

A government deemed lawful, or deemed rightful or just, which, nevertheless, has been supplanted or displaced; that is to say, which receives not presently (although it received formerly) habitual obedience from the bulk of the community. Aust. Jur. 324.

GOVERNOR. The title of the chief executive in each of the states and territories of the United States; and also of the chief magistrate of some colonies, provinces, and dependencies of other nations.

GRACE. This word is commonly used in contradistinction to "right." Thus, in St. 22 Edw. III., the lord chancellor was instructed to take cognizance of matters of grace, being such subjects of equity jurisdiction as were exclusively matters of equity. Brown.

A faculty, license, or dispensation; also general and free pardon by act of parliament. See ACT OF GRACE.

GRACE, DAYS OF. Time of indulgence granted to an acceptor or maker for the payment of his bill of exchange or note. It was originally a gratuitous favor, (hence the name,) but custom has rendered it a legal right.

GRADATIM. In old English law. By degrees or steps; step by step; from one degree to another. Bract. fol. 64.

GRADIENT. Moving step by step; a grade; the deviation of railways from a level surface to an inclined plane.

GRADUATES. Scholars who have taken a degree in a college or university.

GRADUS. In the civil and old English law. A measure of space. A degree of relationship.

A step or degree generally; *e. g.*, *gradus honorum*, degrees of honor. Vicat. A pulpit; a year; a generation. Du Cange.

A port; any place where a vessel can be brought to land. Du Cange.

GRADUS PARENTELÆ. A pedigree; a table of relationship.

GRAFFARIUS. In old English law. A graffer, notary, or scrivener. St. 5 Hen. VIII. c. 1.

GRAFFER. A notary or scrivener. See St. 5 Hen. VIII. c. 1. The word is a corruption of the French "*greffier*," (*q. v.*)

GRAFFIUM. A writing-book, register, or cartulary of deeds and evidences. Cowell.

GRAFIO. A baron, inferior to a count. A fiscal judge. An advocate. Spelman; Cowell.

GRAFT. A term used in equity to denote the confirmation, by relation back, of the right of a mortgagee in premises to which, at the making of the mortgage, the mortgagor had only an imperfect title, but to which the latter has since acquired a good title.

GRAIL. A gradual, or book containing some of the offices of the Romish Church.

A chalice; a broad dish or vessel. The holy grail was the vessel out of which our Lord was believed to have eaten at the Last Supper. Cowell.

GRAIN. In Troy weight, the twenty-fourth part of a pennyweight. Any kind of corn sown in the ground.

GRAINAGE. An ancient duty in London under which the twentieth part of salt imported by aliens was taken.

GRAMMAR SCHOOL. In England, this term designates a school in which such instruction is given as will prepare the student to enter a college or university, and in this sense the phrase was used in the Massachusetts colonial act of 1647, requiring every town containing a hundred householders to set up a "grammar school." See 103 Mass. 97. But in modern American usage the term denotes a school, intermediate between the primary school and the high school, in which English grammar and other studies of that grade are taught.

Grammatica falsa non vitiat chartam. 9 Coke, 48. False grammar does not vitiate a deed.

GRAMMATOPHYLACIUM. (Græco-Lat.) In the civil law. A place for keeping writings or records. Dig. 48, 19, 9, 6.

GRAMME. The unit of weight in the metric system. The gramme is the weight of a cubic centimeter of distilled water at the temperature of 4° C. It is equal to 15.4341 grains troy, or 5.6481 drachms avoirdupois.

GRANATARIUS. In old English law. An officer having charge of a granary. Fleta, lib. 2, c. 82, § 1; Id. c. 84.

GRAND ASSIZE. A peculiar species of trial by jury, introduced in the time of Henry II., giving the tenant or defendant in a writ of right the alternative of a trial by battel, or by his peers. Abolished by 3 & 4 Wm. IV. c. 42, § 13. See 3 Bl. Comm. 341.

GRAND BILL OF SALE. In English law. The name of an instrument used for the transfer of a ship while she is at sea. An expression which is understood to refer to the instrument whereby a ship was originally transferred from the builder to the owner, or first purchaser. 3 Kent, Comm. 133.

GRAND CAPE. In practice. A judicial writ in the old real actions, which issued for the demandant where the tenant, after being duly summoned, neglected to appear on the return of the writ, or to cast an essoin, or, in case of an essoin being cast, neglected to appear on the adjournment day of the essoin; its object being to compel an appearance. Rosc. Real Act. 165, et seq. It was called a "cape," from the word with which it commenced, and a "grand cape" (or *cape magnum*) to distinguish it from the *petit cape*, which lay after appearance.

GRAND COUTUMIER. A collection of customs, laws, and forms of procedure in use in early times in France. See COUTUMIER.

GRAND DAYS. In English practice. Certain days in the terms, which are solemnly kept in the inns of court and chancery, viz., Candlemas day in Hilary term, Ascension day in Easter, St. John the Baptist's day in Trinity, and All Saints in Michaelmas; which are *dies non juridici*. Termes de la Ley; Cowell; Blount. They are days set apart for peculiar festivity; the members of the respective inns being on such occasions regaled at their dinner in the hall, with more than usual sumptuousness. Holthouse.

GRAND DISTRESS, WRIT OF. A writ formerly issued in the real action of *quare impedit*, when no appearance had been entered after the attachment; it commanded the sheriff to distrain the defendant's lands and chattels in order to compel appearance. It is no longer used, 23 & 24 Vict. c. 126, § 26, having abolished the action of *quare impedit*, and substituted for it the procedure in an ordinary action. Wharton.

GRAND JURY. A jury of inquiry, consisting of from twelve to twenty-three men, who are summoned and returned by the sheriff to each session of the criminal courts, and whose duty is to receive complaints and accusations in criminal cases, hear the evidence adduced on the part of the state, and find bills of indictment in cases where they are satisfied a trial ought to be had. They are first sworn, and instructed by the court. This is called a "grand jury" because it comprises a greater number of jurors than the ordinary trial jury or "petit jury."

GRAND LARCENY. In criminal law. In England, simple larceny was originally divided into two sorts,—*grand* larceny, where the value of the goods stolen was above twelve pence, and *petit* larceny, where their value was equal to or below that sum. 4 Bl. Comm. 229. The distinction was abolished in England by St. 7 & 8 Geo. IV. c. 29, and is not generally recognized in the United States.

GRAND SERJEANTY. A species of tenure *in capite*, resembling knight-service, as the service or render was of a free and honorable nature and military in its character. But the tenant by grand serjeanty was bound, instead of attending the king generally in his wars, to do some special honorary service to the king in person, as to carry his banner or sword, or to be his butler or champion at his coronation. Litt. § 153; 2 Bl. Comm. 73; 1 Steph. Comm. 188.

GRANDCHILD. The child of one's child.

GRANDFATHER. The father of either of one's parents.

GRANDMOTHER. The mother of either of one's parents.

GRANGE. A farm furnished with barns, granaries, stables, and all conveniences for husbandry. Co. Litt. 5*a*.

GRANGEARIUS. A keeper of a grange or farm.

GRANGIA. A grange. Co. Litt. 5*a*.

GRANT. A generic term applicable to all transfers of real property. 3 Washb. Real Prop. 181, 353.

A transfer by deed of that which cannot be passed by livery. Williams, Real Prop. 147, 149.

An act evidenced by letters patent under the great seal, granting something from the king to a subject. Cruise, Dig. tit. 33, 34.

A technical term made use of in deeds of conveyance of lands to import a transfer. 3 Washb. Real Prop. 378–380.

Though the word "grant" was originally made use of, in treating of conveyances of interests in lands, to denote a transfer by deed of that which could not be passed by livery, and, of course, was applied only to incorporeal hereditaments, it has now become a generic term, applicable to the transfer of all classes of real property. 3 Washb. Real Prop. 181.

As distinguished from a mere license, a grant passes some estate or interest, corporeal or incorporeal, in the lands which it embraces; can only be made by an instrument in writing, under seal; and is irrevocable, when made, unless an express power of revocation is reserved. A license is a mere authority; passes no estate or interest whatever; may be made by parol; is revocable at will; and, when revoked, the protection which it gave ceases to exist. 3 Duer, 255, 258.

The term "grant," in Scotland, is used in reference (1) to original dispositions of land, as when a lord makes grants of land among tenants; (2) to gratuitous deeds. Paterson. In such case, the superior or donor is said to to grant the deed; an expression totally unknown in English law. Mozley & Whitley.

By the word "grant," in a treaty, is meant not only a formal grant, but any concession, warrant, order, or permission to survey, possess, or settle, whether written or parol, express, or presumed from possession. Such a grant may be made by law, as well as by a patent pursuant to a law. 12 Pet. 410. See 9 Adol. & E. 532; 5 Mass. 472; 9 Pick. 80.

"GRANT, BARGAIN, AND SELL." Operative words in conveyances of real estate.

GRANT OF PERSONAL PROPERTY. A method of transferring personal property, distinguished from a gift by being always founded on some consideration or equivalent. 2 Bl. Comm. 440, 441. Its proper legal designation is an "assignment," or "bargain and sale." 2 Steph. Comm. 102.

GRANT TO USES. The common grant with uses superadded, which has become the favorite mode of transferring realty in England. Wharton.

GRANTEE. The person to whom a grant is made.

GRANTOR. The person by whom a grant is made.

GRANTZ. In old English law. Noblemen or grandees. Jacob.

GRASS HEARTH. In old records. The grazing or turning up the earth with a plow. The name of a customary service for inferior tenants to bring their plows, and do one day's work for their lords. Cowell.

GRASS WEEK. Rogation week, so called anciently in the inns of court and chancery.

GRASS WIDOW. A slang term for a woman separated from her husband by abandonment or prolonged absence; a woman living apart from her husband. Webster.

GRASSON, or GRASSUM. A fine paid upon the transfer of a copyhold estate.

GRATIFICATION. A gratuity; a recompense or reward for services or benefits, given voluntarily, without solicitation or promise.

GRATIS. Freely; gratuitously; without reward or consideration.

GRATIS DICTUM. A voluntary assertion; a statement which a party is not legally bound to make, or in which he is not held to precise accuracy. 2 Kent, Comm. 486; 6 Metc. (Mass.) 260.

GRATUITOUS. Without valuable or legal consideration. A term applied to deeds of conveyance.

In old English law. Voluntary; without force, fear, or favor. Bract. fols. 11, 17.

GRATUITOUS CONTRACT. In the civil law. One which tends wholly to the benefit or advantage of one of the parties, without any compensation, profit, or gain moving to the other.

GRATUITOUS DEEDS. Instruments made without binding consideration.

GRAVA. In old English law. A grove; a small wood; a coppice or thicket. Co. Litt. 4*b*.

A thick wood of high trees. Blount.

GRAVAMEN. The burden or gist of a charge; the grievance or injury specially complained of.

In English ecclesiastical law. A grievance complained of by the clergy before the bishops in convocation.

GRAVATIO. An accusation or impeachment. Leg. Ethel. c. 19.

GRAVE. A sepulcher. A place where a dead body is interred.

GRAVIS. Grievous; great. *Ad grave damnum*, to the grievous damage. 11 Coke, 40.

GRAVIUS. A graf; a chief magistrate or officer. A term derived from the more ancient "*grafio*," and used in combination with various other words, as an official title in Germany; as *Margravius*, *Rheingravius*, *Landgravius*, etc. Spelman.

Gravius est divinam quam temporalem lædere majestatem. It is more serious to hurt divine than temporal majesty. 11 Coke, 29.

GRAY'S INN. An inn of court. See INNS OF COURT.

GREAT CATTLE. All manner of beasts except sheep and yearlings. 2 Rolle, 173.

GREAT CHARTER. *Magna Charta*, (*q. v.*)

GREAT LAW, THE, or "The Body of Laws of the Province of Pennsylvania and Territories thereunto belonging, Past at an Assembly held at Chester, *alias* Upland, the 7th day of the tenth month, called 'December,' 1682." This was the first code of laws established in Pennsylvania, and is justly celebrated for the provision in its first chapter for liberty of conscience. Bouvier.

GREAT SEAL. In English law. A seal by virtue of which a great part of the royal authority is exercised. The office of the lord chancellor, or lord keeper, is created by the delivery of the great seal into his custody. There is one great seal for all public acts of state which concern the United Kingdom. Mozley & Whitley.

GREAT TITHES. In English ecclesiastical law. Tithes of corn, pease and beans, hay and wood. 2 Chit. Bl. Comm. 24, note; 3 Steph. Comm. 127.

GREE. Satisfaction for an offense committed or injury done. Cowell.

GREEK KALENDS. A colloquial expression to signify a time indefinitely remote, there being no such division of time known to the Greeks.

GREEN CLOTH. In English law. A board or court of justice held in the counting-house of the king's (or queen's) household, and composed of the lord steward and inferior officers. It takes its name from the green cloth spread over the board at which it is held. Wharton; Cowell.

GREEN SILVER. A feudal custom in the manor of Writtel, in Essex, where every tenant whose front door opens to Greenbury shall pay a half-penny yearly to the lord, by the name of "green silver" or "rent." Cowell.

GREEN WAX. In English law. The name of the estreats in the exchequer, delivered to the sheriff under the seal of that court, which was impressed upon green wax.

GREENBACK. The popular and almost exclusive name applied to all United States treasury issues. It is not applied to any other species of paper currency; and, when employed in testimony by way of description, is as certain as the phrase "treasury notes." 23 Ind. 21.

GREENHEW. In forest law. The same as *vert*, (*q. v.*) Termes de la Ley.

GREFFIERS. In French law. Registrars, or clerks of the courts. They are officials attached to the courts to assist the judges in their duties. They keep the minutes, write out the judgments, orders, and other decisions given by the tribunals, and deliver copies thereof to applicants.

GREGORIAN CODE. The code or collection of constitutions made by the Roman jurist Gregorius. See CODEX GREGORIANUS.

GREGORIAN EPOCH. The time from which the Gregorian calendar or computation dates; *i. e.*, from the year 1582.

GREMIO. In Spanish law. A guild; an association of workmen, artificers, or merchants following the same trade or business; designed to protect and further the interests of their craft.

GREMIUM. Lat. The bosom or breast; hence, derivatively, safeguard or protection. In English law, an estate which is in abeyance is said to be *in gremio legis;* that is, in the protection or keeping of the law.

GRENVILLE ACT. The statute 10 Geo. III. c. 16, by which the jurisdiction over parliamentary election petitions was transferred from the whole house of commons to select committees. Repealed by 9 Geo. IV. c. 22, § 1.

GRESSUME. In English law. A customary fine due from a copyhold tenant on the death of the lord. 1 Strange, 654; 1 Crabb, Real Prop. p. 615, § 778. Called also "*grassum*," and "*grossome*."

GRETNA GREEN MARRIAGE. A marriage celebrated at Gretna, in Dumfries, (bordering on the county of Cumberland,) in Scotland. By the law of Scotland a valid marriage may be contracted by consent alone, without any other formality. When the marriage act (26 Geo. II. c. 33) rendered the publication of banns, or a license, necessary in England, it became usual for persons who wished to marry clandestinely to go to Gretna Green, the nearest part of Scotland, and marry according to the Scotch law; so a sort of chapel was built at Gretna Green, in which the English marriage service was performed by the village blacksmith. Wharton.

GREVA. In old records. The sea shore, sand, or beach. 2 Mon. Angl. 625; Cowell.

GRIEVED. Aggrieved. 3 East, 22.

GRITH. Peace; protection. Termes de la Ley.

GRITHBRECH. Sax. Breach of the king's peace, as opposed to *frithbrech*, a breach of the nation's peace with other nations.

GRITHSTOLE. Sax. In Saxon law. A seat, chair, or place of peace; a sanctuary; a stone within a church-gate, to which an offender might flee.

GROCER. In old English law. A merchant or trader who *engrossed* all vendible merchandise; an engrosser. St. 37 Edw. III. c. 5. See ENGROSSER.

GRONNA. In old records. A deep hollow or pit; a bog or miry place. Cowell.

GROOM OF THE STOLE. In England. An officer of the royal household, who has charge of the king's wardrobe.

GROOM PORTER. Formerly an officer belonging to the royal household. Jacob.

GROSS. Great; culpable. General. Absolute or entire. A thing *in gross* exists in its own right, and not as an appendage to another thing.

GROSS ADVENTURE. In maritime law. A loan on bottomry. So named because the lender, in case of a loss, or expense incurred for the common safety, must contribute to the *gross* or general average.

GROSS AVERAGE. In maritime law. A contribution made by the owners of a ship, its cargo, and the freight, towards the loss sustained by the voluntary and necessary sacrifice of property for the common safety, in proportion to their respective interests. More commonly called "general average," (*q. v.*) See 3 Kent, Comm. 232; 2 Steph. Comm. 179.

GROSS NEGLIGENCE. In the law of bailment. The want of slight diligence. The want of that care which every man of common sense, how inattentive soever, takes of his own property. The omission of that care which even inattentive and thoughtless men never fail to take of their own property.

GROSS WEIGHT. The whole weight of goods and merchandise, including the dust and dross, and also the chest or bag, etc., upon which tare and tret are allowed.

GROSSE AVANTURE. Fr. In French marine law. The contract of bottomry. Ord. Mar. liv. 3, tit. 5.

GROSSE BOIS. Timber. Cowell.

GROSSEMENT. L. Fr. Largely, greatly. *Grossement enseint*, big with child. Plowd. 76.

GROSSOME. In old English law. A fine, or sum of money paid for a lease. Plowd. 270, 271. Supposed to be a corruption of *gersuma*, (*q. v.*) See GRESSUME.

GROUND ANNUAL. In Scotch law. An annual rent of two kinds: *First*, the feu duties payable to the lords of erection and their successors; *second*, the rents reserved for building lots in a city, where *sub-feus* are prohibited. This rent is in the nature of a perpetual annuity. Bell.; Ersk. Inst. 11, 3, 52.

GROUND LANDLORD. The grantor of an estate on which a ground-rent is reserved.

GROUND-RENT. A perpetual rent reserved to himself and his heirs, by the grantor of land in fee-simple, out of the land conveyed. It is in the nature of an emphyteutic rent. Also, in English law, rent paid on a building lease.

GROUND WRIT. By the English common-law procedure act, 1852, c. 121, "it shall not be necessary to issue any writ directed to the sheriff of the county in which the venue is laid, but writs of execution may issue at once into any county, and be directed to and executed by the sheriff of any county, whether a county palatine or not, without reference to the county in which the venue is laid, and without any suggestion of the issuing of a prior writ into such county." Before this enactment, a *ca. sa.* or *fi. fa.* could not be issued into a county different from that in which the venue in the action was laid, without first issuing a writ, called a "ground writ," into the latter county, and then another writ, which was called a "*testatum* writ," into the former. The above enactment abolished this useless process. Wharton.

GROUNDAGE. A custom or tribute paid for the standing of shipping in port. Jacob.

GROWING CROP. A crop must be considered and treated as a *growing* crop from the time the seed is deposited in the ground, as at that time the seed loses the qualities of a chattel, and becomes a part of the freehold, and passes with a sale of it. 69 Ala. 435.

Growing crops of grain, and other annual productions raised by cultivation of the earth and industry of man, are personal chattels. Growing trees, fruit, or grass, and other natural products of the earth, are parcel of the land. 1 Denio, 550.

GROWTH HALF-PENNY. A rate paid in some places for the tithe of every fat beast, ox, or other unfruitful cattle. Clayt. 92.

GRUARII. The principal officers of a forest.

GUADIA. In old European law. A pledge. Spelman; Calvin. A custom. Spelman. Spelled also "wadia."

GUARANTEE. He to whom a guaranty is made. This word is also used, as a noun, to denote the contract of guaranty or the obligation of a guarantor, and, as a verb, to denote the action of assuming the responsibilities of a guarantor. But on the general principle of legal orthography,—that the title of the person to whom the action passes over should end in "ee," as "donee," "grantee," "payee," "bailee," "drawee," etc.,—it seems better to use this word only as the correlative of "guarantor," and to spell the verb, and also the name of the contract, "guaranty."

GUARENTIGIO. In Spanish law. A written authorization to a court to enforce the performance of an agreement in the same manner as if it had been decreed upon regular legal proceedings.

GUARANTOR. He who makes a guaranty.

GUARANTY, *v.* To undertake collaterally to answer for the payment of another's debt or the performance of another's duty, liability, or obligation; to assume the responsibility of a guarantor; to warrant. See GUARANTY, *n.*

GUARANTY, *n.* A promise to answer for the payment of some debt, or the performance of some duty, in case of the failure of another person, who, in the first instance, is liable to such payment or performance. Fell, Guar. 1; 3 Kent, Comm. 121; 60 N. Y. 438; 1 Miles, 277.

A guaranty is an undertaking by one person to be answerable for the payment of some debt, or the due performance of some contract or duty, by another person, who himself remains liable to pay or perform the same. Story, Prom. Notes, § 457.

A guaranty is a promise to answer for the debt, default, or miscarriage of another person. Civil Code Cal. § 2787.

A guaranty is a contract that some particular thing shall be done exactly as it is agreed to be done, whether it is to be done by one person or another, and whether there be a prior or principal contractor or not. 27 Conn. 31.

The definition of a "guaranty," by text-writers, is an undertaking by one person that another shall perform his contract or fulfill his obligation, or that, if he does not, the guarantor will do it for him. A guarantor of a bill or note is said to be one who engages that the note shall be paid, but is not an indorser or surety. 72 Ill. 13.

The terms "guaranty" and "suretyship" are sometimes used interchangeably; but they should not be confounded. The contract of a surety corresponds with that of a guarantor in many respects; yet important differences exist. The surety is bound with his principal as an original promisor. He is a debtor from the beginning, and must see that the debt is paid, and is held ordinarily to know every default of his principal, and cannot protect himself by the mere indulgence of the creditor, nor by want of notice of the default of the principal, however such indulgence or want of notice may in fact injure him. On the other hand, the contract of a guarantor is his own separate contract. It is in the nature of a warranty by him that the thing guarantied to be done by the principal shall be done, not merely an engagement jointly with the principal to do the thing. The original contract of the principal is not his contract, and he is not bound to take notice of its non-performance. Therefore the creditor should give him notice; and it is universally held that, if the guarantor can prove that he has suffered damage by the failure to give such notice, he will be discharged to the extent of the damage thus sustained. It is not so with a surety. 32 Ind. 11; 2 N. Y. 533.

A guaranty relating to a future liability of the principal, under successive transactions, which either continue his liability, or from time to time renew it after it has been satisfied, is called a "continuing guaranty." Civil Code Cal. § 2814.

GUARANTY INSURANCE. A guaranty or insurance against loss in case a person named shall make a designated default or be guilty of specified conduct. It is usually against the misconduct or dishonesty of an employee or officer, though sometimes against the breach of a contract. 9 Amer. & Eng. Enc. Law, 65.

GUARDAGE. A state of wardship.

GUARDIAN. A guardian is a person lawfully invested with the power, and charged with the duty, of taking care of the person and managing the property and rights of another person, who, for some peculiarity of *status*, or defect of age, understanding, or self-control, is considered incapable of administering his own affairs.

A guardian is a person appointed to take care of the person or property of another. Civil Code Cal. § 236.

One who legally has the care and management of the person, or the estate, or both, of a child during its minority. Reeve, Dom. Rel. 311.

This term might be appropriately used to designate the person charged with the care and control of idiots, lunatics, habitual drunkards, spendthrifts, and the like; but such person is, under many of the statutory systems authorizing the appointment, styled "committee," and in common usage the name "guardian" is applied only to one having the care and management of a minor.

The name "curator" is given in some of the states to a person having the control of a minor's estate, without that of his person; and this is also the usage of the civil law.

A *testamentary* guardian is one appointed by the deed or last will of the child's father; while a guardian *by election* is one chosen by the infant himself, in a case where he would otherwise be without one.

GUARDIAN AD LITEM. A guardian appointed by a court of justice to prosecute or defend for an infant in any suit to which he may be a party. 2 Steph. Comm. 342. Most commonly appointed for infant *defendants;* infant plaintiffs generally suing by *next friend*. This kind of guardian has no right to interfere with the infant's person or property. 2 Steph. Comm. 343.

GUARDIAN BY APPOINTMENT OF COURT. The most important species of guardian in modern law, having custody of the infant until the attainment of full age. It has in England in a manner superseded the guardian in socage, and in the United States the guardian by nature also. The appointment is made by a court of chancery, or probate or orphans' court. 2 Steph. Comm. 341; 2 Kent, Comm. 226.

GUARDIAN BY NATURE. The father, and, on his death, the mother, of a child. 1 Bl. Comm. 461; 2 Kent, Comm. 219. This guardianship extends only to the custody of the person of the child to the age of twenty-one years. Sometimes called "natural guardian," but this is rather a popular than a technical mode of expression. 2 Steph. Comm. 337.

GUARDIAN BY STATUTE. A guardian appointed for a child by the deed or last will of the father, and who has the custody both of his person and estate until the attainment of full age. This kind of guardianship is founded on the statute of 12 Car. II. c. 24, and has been pretty extensively adopted in this country. 1 Bl. Comm. 462; 2 Steph. Comm. 339, 340; 2 Kent, Comm. 224–226.

GUARDIAN DE L'EGLISE. A church-warden.

GUARDIAN DE L'ESTEMARY. The warden of the stannaries or mines in Cornwall, etc.

GUARDIAN FOR NURTURE. The father, or, at his decease, the mother, of a child. This kind of guardianship extends only to the person, and determines when the infant arrives at the age of fourteen. 2 Kent, Comm. 221; 1 Bl. Comm. 461; 2 Steph. Comm. 338.

GUARDIAN IN CHIVALRY. In the tenure by knight's service, in the feudal law, if the heir of the feud was under the age of twenty-one, being a male, or fourteen, being a female, the lord was entitled to the wardship (and marriage) of the heir, and was called the "guardian in chivalry." This wardship consisted in having the custody of the body and lands of such heir, without any account of the profits. 2 Bl. Comm. 67.

GUARDIAN IN SOCAGE. At the common law, this was a species of guardian who had the custody of lands coming to the infant by descent, as also of the infant's person, until the latter reached the age of fourteen Such guardian was always "the next of kin to whom the inheritance cannot possibly descend." 1 Bl. Comm. 461; 2 Steph. Comm. 338.

GUARDIAN OF THE PEACE. A warden or conservator of the peace.

GUARDIAN OF THE POOR. In English law. A person elected by the ratepayers of a parish to have the charge and management of the parish work-house or union. See 3 Steph. Comm. 203, 215.

GUARDIAN OF THE SPIRITUALITIES. The person to whom the spiritual jurisdiction of any diocese is committed during the vacancy of the see.

GUARDIAN OF THE TEMPORALITIES. The person to whose custody a vacant see or abbey was committed by the crown.

GUARDIAN, or WARDEN, OF THE CINQUE PORTS. A magistrate who has the jurisdiction of the ports or havens which are called the "Cinque Ports," (*q. v.*) This office was first created in England, in imitation of the Roman policy, to strengthen the sea-coasts against enemies, etc.

GUARDIANSHIP. The office, duty, or authority of a guardian. Also the relation subsisting between guardian and ward.

GUARDIANUS. A guardian, warden, or keeper. Spelman.

GUARNIMENTUM. In old European law. A provision of necessary things. Spelman. A furnishing or garnishment.

GUASTALD. One who had the custody of the royal mansions.

GUBERNATOR. Lat. In Roman law. The pilot or steersman of a ship.

GUERPI, GUERPY. L. Fr. Abandoned; left; deserted. Britt. c. 33.

GUERRA, GUERRE. War. Spelman.

GUERILLA PARTY. In military law. An independent body of marauders or armed men, not regularly or organically connected with the armies of either belligerent, who carry on a species of irregular war, chiefly by depredation and massacre.

GUEST. A traveler who lodges at an inn or tavern with the consent of the keeper. Bac. Abr. "Inns," C, 5; 8 Coke, 32.

A guest, as distinguished from a boarder, is bound for no stipulated time. He stops at the inn for as short or as long time as he pleases, paying, while he remains, the customary charge. 24 How. Pr. 62.

GUEST-TAKER. An agister; one who took cattle in to feed in the royal forests. Cowell.

GUET. In old French law. Watch. Ord. Mar. liv. 4, tit. 6.

GUIA. In Spanish law. A right of way for narrow carts. White, New Recop. l. 2, c. 6, § 1.

GUIDAGE. In old English law. That which was given for safe conduct through a strange territory, or another's territory. Cowell.

The office of guiding of travelers through dangerous and unknown ways. 2 Inst. 526.

GUIDE-PLATE. An iron or steel plate to be attached to a rail for the purpose of guiding to their place on the rail wheels thrown off the track. Pub. St. Mass. 1882, p. 1291.

GUIDON DE LA MER. The name of a treatise on maritime law, by an unknown author, supposed to have been written about 1671 at Rouen, and considered, in continental Europe, as a work of high authority.

GUILD. A voluntary association of persons pursuing the same trade, art, profession, or business, such as printers, goldsmiths, wool merchants, etc., united under a distinct organization of their own, analogous to that of a corporation, regulating the affairs of their trade or business by their own laws and rules, and aiming, by co-operation and organization, to protect and promote the interests of their common vocation. In medieval history these fraternities or guilds played an important part in the government of some states; as at Florence, in the thirteenth and following centuries, where they chose the council of government of the city. But with the growth of cities and the advance in the organization of municipal government, their importance and prestige has declined. The place of meeting of a guild, or association of guilds, was called the "Guildhall." The word is said to be derived from the Anglo-Saxon "*gild*" or "*geld*," a tax or tribute, because each member of the society was required to pay a tax towards its support.

GUILD RENTS. Rents payable to the crown by any guild, or such as formerly belonged to religious guilds, and came to the crown at the general dissolution of the monasteries. Tomlins.

GUILDHALL. The *hall* or place of meeting of a *guild*, or gild.

The place of meeting of a municipal corporation. 3 Steph. Comm. 173, note. The mercantile or commercial *gilds* of the Saxons are supposed to have given rise to the present municipal corporations of England, whose place of meeting is still called the "Guildhall."

GUILDHALL SITTINGS. The sittings held in the Guildhall of the city of London for city of London causes.

GUILT. In criminal law. That quality which imparts criminality to a motive or act, and renders the person amenable to punishment by the law.

That disposition to violate the law which has manifested itself by some act already done. The opposite of innocence. See Ruth. Inst. b. 1, c. 18, § 10.

GUILTY. Having committed a crime or tort; the word used by a prisoner in pleading to an indictment when he confesses the crime of which he is charged, and by the jury in convicting.

GUINEA. A coin formerly issued by the English mint, but all these coins were called in in the time of Wm. IV. The word now means only the sum of £1. 1s., in which denomination the fees of counsel are always given.

GULE OF AUGUST. The first of August, being the day of *St. Peter ad Vincula.*

GULES. The heraldic name of the color usually called "red." The word is derived from the Arabic word "*gule,*" a rose, and was probably introduced by the Crusaders. Gules is denoted in engravings by numerous perpendicular lines. Heralds who blazoned by planets and jewels called it "Mars," and "ruby." Wharton.

GURGITES. Wears. Jacob.

GUTI. Jutes; one of the three nations who migrated from Germany to Britain at an early period. According to Spelman, they established themselves chiefly in Kent and the Isle of Wight.

GUTTER. The diminutive of a sewer. Callis, Sew. (80,) 100.

GWABR MERCHED. Maid's fee. A British word signifying a customary fine payable to lords of some manors on marriage of the tenant's daughters, or otherwise on their committing incontinence. Cowell.

GWALSTOW. A place of execution. Jacob.

GWAYF. Waif, or waived; that which has been stolen and afterwards dropped in the highway for fear of a discovery. Cowell.

GYLPUT. The name of a court which was held every three weeks in the liberty or hundred of Pathbew in Warwick. Jacob.

GYLTWITE. Sax. Compensation for fraud or trespass. Cowell.

GYNARCY, or GYNÆCOCRACY. Government by a woman; a state in which women are legally capable of the supreme command; *e. g.*, in Great Britain and Spain.

GYROVAGI. Wandering monks.

GYVES. Fetters or shackles for the legs.

H.

H. This letter, as an abbreviation, stands for Henry (a king of that name) in the citation of English statutes. In the Year Books, it is used as an abbreviation for Hilary term.

H. A. An abbreviation for *hoc anno*, this year, in this year.

H. B. An abbreviation for house bill, *i. e.*, a bill in the house of representatives, as distinguished from a senate bill.

H. C. An abbreviation for house of commons, or for *habeas corpus*.

H. L. An abbreviation for house of lords.

H. R. An abbreviation for house of representatives.

H. T. An abbreviation for *hoc titulo*, this title, under this title; used in references to books.

H. V. An abbreviation for *hoc verbo* or *hac voce*, this word, under this word; used in references to dictionaries and other works alphabetically arranged.

HABE, or HAVE. Lat. A form of the salutatory expression "*Ave*," (hail,) in the titles of the constitutions of the Theodosian and Justinianean Codes. Calvin.; Spelman.

HABEAS CORPORA JURATORUM. A writ commanding the sheriff to bring up the persons of jurors, and, if need were, to distrain them of their lands and goods, in order to insure or compel their attendance in court on the day of trial of a cause. It issued from the Common Pleas, and served the same purpose as a *distringas juratores* in the King's Bench. It was abolished by the C. L. P. Act, 1852, § 104. Brown.

HABEAS CORPUS. (You have the body.) The name given to a variety of writs, (of which these were anciently the emphatic words,) having for their object to bring a party before a court or judge. In common usage, and whenever these words are used alone, they are understood to mean the *habeas corpus ad subjiciendum*, (*q. v.*)

HABEAS CORPUS ACT. The English statute of 31 Car. II. c. 2, is the original and prominent *habeas corpus* act. It was amended and supplemented by St. 56 Geo. III. c. 100. And similar statutes have been enacted in all the United States. This act is justly regarded as the great constitutional guaranty of personal liberty.

HABEAS CORPUS AD DELIBERANDUM ET RECIPIENDUM. A writ which is issued to remove, for trial, a person confined in one county to the county or place where the offense of which he is accused was committed. Bac. Abr. "*Habeas Corpus*," A; 1 Chit. Crim. Law, 132. Thus, it has been granted to remove a person in custody for contempt to take his trial for perjury in another county. 1 Tyrw. 185.

HABEAS CORPUS AD FACIENDUM ET RECIPIENDUM. A writ issuing in civil cases, to remove the cause, as also the body of the defendant, from an inferior court to a superior court having jurisdiction, there to be disposed of. It is also called "*habeas corpus cum causa*."

HABEAS CORPUS AD PROSEQUENDUM. A writ which issues when it is necessary to remove a prisoner in order to *prosecute* in the proper jurisdiction wherein the fact was committed. 3 Bl. Comm. 130.

HABEAS CORPUS AD RESPONDENDUM. A writ which is usually employed in civil cases to remove a person out of the custody of one court into that of another, in order that he may be sued and answer the action in the latter. 2 Sell. Pr. 259; 2 Mod. 198; 3 Bl. Comm. 129; 1 Tidd, Pr. 300.

HABEAS CORPUS AD SATISFACIENDUM. In English practice. A writ which issues when a prisoner has had judgment against him in an action, and the plaintiff is desirous to bring him up to some superior court, to charge him with process of execution. 3 Bl. Comm. 129, 130; 3 Steph. Comm. 693; 1 Tidd, Pr. 350.

HABEAS CORPUS AD SUBJICIENDUM. In practice. A writ directed to the person detaining another, and commanding him to produce the body of the prisoner, (or person detained,) with the day and cause of his caption and detention, *ad faciendum, subjiciendum et recipiendum*, to do, submit to, and receive whatsoever the judge or court awarding the writ shall consider in that behalf. 3 Bl. Comm. 131; 3 Steph. Comm. 695. This is the well-known remedy for deliverance from illegal confinement, called by

Sir William Blackstone the most celebrated writ in the English law, and the great and efficacious writ in all manner of illegal confinement. 3 Bl. Comm. 129.

HABEAS CORPUS AD TESTIFICANDUM. In practice. A writ to bring a witness into court, when he is in custody at the time of a trial, commanding the sheriff to have his body before the court, to testify in the cause. 3 Bl. Comm. 130; 2 Tidd, Pr. 809.

HABEAS CORPUS CUM CAUSA. (You have the body, with the cause.) In practice. Another name for the writ of *habeas corpus ad faciendum et recipiendum,* (*q. v.*) 1 Tidd, Pr. 348, 349.

Habemus optimum testem, confitentem reum. 1 Phil. Ev. 397. We have the best witness, — a confessing defendant. "What is taken *pro confesso* is taken as indubitable truth. The plea of guilty by the party accused shuts out all further inquiry. *Habemus confitentem reum* is demonstration, unless indirect motives can be assigned to it." 2 Hagg. Eccl. 315.

HABENDUM. In conveyancing. The clause usually following the granting part of the premises of a deed, which defines the extent of the ownership in the thing granted to be held and enjoyed by the grantee. 3 Washb. Real Prop. 437.

HABENDUM ET TENENDUM. In old conveyancing. To have and to hold. Formal words in deeds of land from a very early period. Bract. fol. 17*b*.

HABENTES HOMINES. In old English law. Rich men; literally, having men. The same with *fæsting-men,* (*q. v.*) Cowell.

HABENTIA. Riches. Mon. Angl. t. 1, 100.

HABERE. Lat. In the civil law. To have. Sometimes distinguished from *tenere,* (to hold,) and *possidere,* (to possess;) *habere* referring to the right, *tenere* to the fact, and *possidere* to both. Calvin.

HABERE FACIAS POSSESSIONEM. That you cause to have possession. The name of the process commonly resorted to by the successful party in an action of ejectment, for the purpose of being placed by the sheriff in the actual possession of the land recovered. It is commonly termed simply "*habere facias,*" or "*hab. fa.*"

HABERE FACIAS SEISINAM. That you cause to have seisin. The writ of execution in real actions, directing the sheriff to cause the demandant to have seisin of the lands recovered. It was the proper process for giving seisin of a freehold, as distinguished from a chattel interest in lands.

HABERE FACIAS VISUM. That you cause to have a view. A writ to cause the sheriff to take a view of lands or tenements.

HABERE LICERE. Lat. In Roman law. To allow [one] to have [possession.] This phrase denoted the duty of the seller of property to allow the purchaser to have the possession and enjoyment. For a breach of this duty, an *actio ex empto* might be maintained.

HABERGEON. A diminutive of hauberk, a short coat of mail without sleeves. Blount.

HABERJECTS. A cloth of a mixed color. Magna Charta, c. 26.

HABETO TIBI RES TUAS. Have or take your effects to yourself. One of the old Roman forms of divorcing a wife. Calvin.

HABILIS. Lat. Fit; suitable; active; useful, (of a servant.) Proved; authentic, (of Book of Saints.) Fixed; stable, (of authority of the king.) Du Cange.

HABIT. A disposition or condition of the body or mind acquired by custom or a usual repetition of the same act or function.

HABIT AND REPUTE. By the law of Scotland, marriage may be established by "habit and repute" where the parties cohabit and are at the same time held and reputed as man and wife. See Bell. The same rule obtains in some of the United States.

HABITABLE REPAIR. A covenant by a lessee to "put the premises into habitable repair" binds him to put them into such a state that they may be occupied, not only with safety, but with reasonable comfort, for the purposes for which they are taken. 2 Moody & R. 186.

HABITANCY. It is difficult to give an exact definition of "habitancy." In general terms, one may be designated as an "inhabitant" of that place which constitutes the principal seat of his residence, of his business, pursuits, connections, attachments, and of his political and municipal relations. The term, therefore, embraces the fact of residence at a place, together with the intent to regard it and make it a home. The act and intent must concur. 17 Pick. 231.

HABITANT. Fr. In French and Canadian law. A resident tenant; a settler; a tenant who kept hearth and home on the seigniory.

HABITATIO. In the civil law. The right of dwelling; the right of free residence in another's house. Inst. 2, 5; Dig. 7, 8.

HABITATION. In the civil law. The right of a person to live in the house of another without prejudice to the property. It differed from a usufruct, in this: that the usufructuary might apply the house to any purpose, as of a store or manufactory; whereas the party having the right of habitation could only use it for the residence of himself and family. 1 Browne, Civil Law, 184.

In estates. A dwelling-house; a homestall. 2 Bl. Comm. 4; 4 Bl. Comm. 220.

HABITUAL CRIMINALS ACT. The statute 32 & 33 Vict. c. 99. By this act power was given to apprehend on suspicion convicted persons holding license under the penal servitude acts, 1853, 1857, and 1864. The act was repealed and replaced by the prevention of crimes act, 1871, (34 & 35 Vict. c. 112.)

HABITUAL DRUNKARD. A person given to ebriety or the excessive use of intoxicating drink, who has lost the power or the will, by frequent indulgence, to control his appetite for it. 18 Pa. St. 172.

One who has the habit of indulging in intoxicating liquors so firmly fixed that he becomes intoxicated as often as the temptation is presented by his being in the vicinity where liquors are sold is an "habitual drunkard," within the meaning of the divorce law. 35 Mich. 210.

In England, it is defined by the habitual drunkards' act, 1879, (42 & 43 Vict. c. 19,) which authorizes confinement in a retreat, upon the party's own application, as "a person who, not being amenable to any jurisdiction in lunacy, is, notwithstanding, by reason of habitual intemperate drinking of intoxicating liquor, at times dangerous to himself, or herself, or others, or incapable of managing himself or herself, or his or her affairs."

HABLE. L. Fr. In old English law. A port or harbor; a station for ships. St. 27 Hen. VI. c. 3.

HACIENDA. In Spanish law. The public domain; the royal estate; the aggregate wealth of the state. The science of administering the national wealth; public economy. Also an estate or farm belonging to a private person.

HACKNEY CARRIAGES. Carriages plying for hire in the street. The driver is liable for negligently losing baggage.

HADBOTE. In Saxon law. A recompense or satisfaction for the violation of holy orders, or violence offered to persons in holy orders. Cowell; Blount.

HADD. In Hindu law. A boundary or limit. A statutory punishment defined by law, and not arbitrary. Mozley & Whitley.

HADERUNGA. Hatred; ill will; prejudice, or partiality. Spelman; Cowell.

HADGONEL. A tax or mulct. Jacob.

HÆC EST CONVENTIO. Lat. This is an agreement. Words with which agreements anciently commenced. Yearb. H. 6 Edw. II. 191.

HÆC EST FINALIS CONCORDIA. L. Lat. This is the final agreement. The words with which the foot of a fine commenced. 2 Bl. Comm. 351.

HÆREDA. In Gothic law. A tribunal answering to the English court-leet.

HÆREDE ABDUCTO. An ancient writ that lay for the lord, who, having by right the wardship of his tenant under age, could not obtain his person, the same being carried away by another person. Old Nat. Brev. 93.

HÆREDE DELIBERANDO ALTERI QUI HABET CUSTODIUM TERRÆ. An ancient writ, directed to the sheriff, to require one that had the body of an heir, being in ward, to deliver him to the person whose ward he was by reason of his land. Reg. Orig. 161.

HÆREDE RAPTO. An ancient writ that lay for the ravishment of the lord's ward. Reg. Orig. 163.

Hæredem Deus facit, non homo. God makes the heir, not man. Co. Litt. 7*b*.

HÆREDES. Lat. In the civil law. Heirs. The plural of *hæres*, (*q. v.*)

HÆREDES EXTRANEI. In the civil law. Extraneous, strange, or foreign heirs; those who were not subject to the power of the testator. Inst. 2, 19, 3.

HÆREDES NECESSARII. In Roman law. Necessary heirs; those who, being named heirs in the will, had no election whether to accept or decline the inheritance, but were compelled to take it. This was the case with a slave who was made heir. Upon the testator's death, he at once became free, but was also obliged to take the succession.

HÆREDES PROXIMI. Nearest or next heirs. The children or descendants of the deceased.

HÆREDES REMOTIORES. More remote heirs. The kinsmen other than children or descendants.

HÆREDES SUI ET NECESSARII. In Roman law. Own and necessary heirs; *i. e.*, the lineal descendants of the estate-leaver. They were called "necessary" heirs, because it was the law that made them heirs, and not the choice of either the decedent or themselves. But since this was also true of slaves (when named "heirs" in the will) the former class were designated "*sui et necessarii,*" by way of distinction, the word "*sui*" denoting that the necessity arose from their relationship to the decedent. Mackeld. Rom. Law, § 733.

HÆREDIPETA. Lat. In old English law. A seeker of an inheritance; hence, the next heir to lands.

Hæredipetæ suo propinquo vel extraneo periculoso sane custodi nullus committatur. To the next heir, whether a relation or a stranger, certainly a dangerous guardian, let no one be committed. Co. Litt. 88*b*.

HÆREDITAS. In Roman law. The *hæreditas* was a universal succession by law to any deceased person, whether such person had died testate or intestate, and whether in trust (*ex fideicommisso*) for another or not. The like succession according to Prætorian law was *bonorum possessio*. The *hæreditas* was called "*jacens*," until the *hæres* took it up, *i. e.*, made his *aditio hæreditatis;* and such *hæres*, if a *suus hæres*, had the right to abstain, (*potestas abstinendi,*) and, if an *extraneus hæres*, had the right to consider whether he would accept or decline, (*potestas deliberandi,*) the reason for this precaution being that (prior to Justinian's enactment to the contrary) a *hæres* after his *aditio* was liable to the full extent of the debts of the deceased person, and could have no relief therefrom, except in the case of a *damnum emergens* or *damnosa hæreditas*, *i. e.*, an *hæreditas* which disclosed (after the *aditio*) some enormous unsuspected liability. Brown.

In old English law. An estate transmissible by descent; an inheritance. Co. Litt. 9.

Hæreditas, alia corporalis, alia incorporalis; corporalis est, quæ tangi potest et videri; incorporalis quæ tangi non potest nec videri. Co. Litt. 9. An inheritance is either corporeal or incorporeal. Corporeal is that which can be touched and seen; incorporeal, that which can neither be touched nor seen.

HÆREDITAS DAMNOSA. A burdensome inheritance. See DAMNOSA HÆREDITAS.

Hæreditas est successio in universum jus quod defunctus habuerit. Co. Litt. 237. Inheritance is the succession to every right which the deceased had.

HÆREDITAS JACENS. In the civil law. A vacant inheritance. So long as no one had acquired the inheritance, it was termed "*hæreditas jacens;*" and this, by a legal fiction, represented the person of the decedent. Mackeld. Rom. Law, § 737.

The estate of a person deceased, where the owner left no heirs or legatee to take it, called also "*caduca;*" an escheated estate. Cod. 10, 10, 1; 4 Kent, Comm. 425.

In English law. An estate in abeyance; that is, after the ancestor's death, and before assumption of heir. Co. Litt. 342*b*. An inheritance without legal owner, and therefore open to the first occupant. 2 Bl. Comm. 259.

HÆREDITAS LUCTUOSA. In the civil law. A sad or mournful inheritance or succession; as that of a parent to the estate of a child, which was regarded as disturbing the natural order of mortality, (*turbato ordine mortalitatis.*) Cod. 6, 25, 9; 4 Kent, Comm. 397.

Hæreditas nihil aliud est, quam successio in universum jus, quod defunctus habuerit. The right of inheritance is nothing else than the faculty of succeeding to all the rights of the deceased. Dig. 50, 17, 62.

Hæreditas nunquam ascendit. An inheritance never ascends. Glanv. lib. 7, c. 1; 2 Bl. Comm. 211. A maxim of feudal origin, and which invariably prevailed in the law of England down to the passage of the statute 3 & 4 Wm. IV. c. 106, § 6, by which it was abrogated. 1 Steph. Comm. 378. See Broom, Max. 527, 528.

Hæredum appellatione veniunt hæredes hæredum in infinitum. By the title of heirs, come the heirs of heirs to infinity. Co. Litt. 9.

HÆRES. In Roman law. The heir, or universal successor in the event of death. The heir is he who actively or passively succeeds to the entire property of the estate-leaver. He is not only the successor to the rights and claims, but also to the estate-leaver's debts, and in relation to his estate is to be regarded as the identical person of the estate-leaver, inasmuch as he represents him in all his active and passive relations to his estate. Mackeld. Rom. Law, § 651.

It should be remarked that the office, powers, and duties of the *hæres*, in Roman law, were much more closely assimilated to those of a modern *executor* than to those of an heir at law. Hence "heir" is not at all an accurate translation of "*hæres*," unless it be understood in a special, technical sense.

In common law. An heir; he to whom lands, tenements, or hereditaments by the act of God and right of blood do descend, of some estate of inheritance. Co. Litt. 7*b*.

HÆRES ASTRARIUS. In old English law. An heir in actual possession.

HÆRES DE FACTO. In old English law. Heir from fact; that is, from the deed or act of his ancestor, without or against right. An heir in fact, as distinguished from an heir *de jure*, or by law.

Hæres est alter ipse, et filius est pars patris. An heir is another self, and a son is part of the father. 3 Coke, 12*b*.

Hæres est aut jure proprietatis aut jure representationis. An heir is either by right of property, or right of representation. 3 Coke, 40*b*.

Hæres est eadem persona cum antecessore. An heir is the same person with his ancestor. Co. Litt. 22; Branch, Princ. See Nov. 48, c. 1, § 1.

Hæres est nomen collectivum. "Heir" is a collective name or noun. 1 Vent. 215.

Hæres est nomen juris; filius est nomen naturæ. "Heir" is a name or term of law; "son" is a name of nature. Bac. Max. 52, in reg. 11.

Hæres est pars antecessoris. An heir is a part of the ancestor. So said because the ancestor, during his life, bears in his body (in judgment of law) all his heirs.

HÆRES EX ASSE. In the civil law. An heir to the whole estate; a sole heir. Inst. 2, 23, 9.

HÆRES EXTRANEUS. In the civil law. A strange or foreign heir; one who was not subject to the power of the testator, or person who made him heir. *Qui testatoris juri subjecti non sunt, extranei hæredes appellantur.* Inst. 2, 19, 3.

HÆRES FACTUS. In the civil law. An heir made by will; a testamentary heir; the person created universal successor by will. Story, Confl. Laws, § 507; 3 Bl. Comm. 224. Otherwise called "*hæres ex testamento*," and "*hæres institutus.*" Inst. 2, 9, 7; Id. 2, 14.

HÆRES FIDEICOMMISSARIUS. In the civil law. The person for whose benefit an estate was given to another (termed "*hæres fiduciarius*," (*q. v.*) by will. Inst. 2, 23, 6, 7, 9. Answering nearly to the *cestui que trust* of the English law.

HÆRES FIDUCIARIUS. A fiduciary heir, or heir in trust; a person constituted heir by will, in trust for the benefit of another, called the "*fideicommissarius.*"

Hæres hæredis mei est meus hæres. The heir of my heir is my heir.

HÆRES LEGITIMUS. A lawful heir; one pointed out as such by the marriage of his parents.

Hæres legitimus est quem nuptiæ demonstrant. He is a lawful heir whom marriage points out as such; who is born in wedlock. Co. Litt. 7*b*; Bract. fol. 88; Fleta, lib. 6, c. 1; Broom, Max. 515.

Hæres minor uno et viginti annis non respondebit, nisi in casu dotis. Moore, 348. An heir under twenty-one years of age is not answerable, except in the matter of dower.

HÆRES NATUS. In the civil law. An heir born; one born heir, as distinguished from one made heir, (*hæres factus, q. v.*;) an heir at law, or by intestacy, (*ab intestato*;) the next of kin by blood, in cases of intestacy. Story, Confl. Laws, § 507; 3 Bl. Comm. 224.

HÆRES NECESSARIUS. In the civil law. A necessary or compulsory heir. This name was given to the heir when, being a slave, he was named "heir" in the testament, because on the death of the testator, whether he would or not, he at once became free, and was compelled to assume the heirship. Inst. 2, 19, 1.

Hæres non tenetur in Anglia ad debita antecessoris reddenda, nisi per antecessorem ad hoc fuerit obligatus, præterquam debita regis tantum. Co. Litt.

386. In England, the heir is not bound to pay his ancestor's debts, unless he be bound to it by the ancestor, except debts due to the king. But now, by 3 & 4 Wm. IV. c. 104, he is liable.

HÆRES RECTUS. In old English law. A right heir. Fleta, lib. 6, c. 1, § 11.

HÆRES SUUS. In the civil law. A man's *own* heir; a decedent's proper or natural heir. This name was given to the lineal descendants of the deceased. Inst. 3, 1, 4-5.

HÆRETARE. In old English law. To give a right of inheritance, or make the donation hereditary to the grantee and his heirs. Cowell.

HÆRETICO COMBURENDO. The statute 2 Hen. IV. c. 15, *de hæretico comburendo*, was the first penal law enacted against heresy, and imposed the penalty of death by burning against all heretics who relapsed or who refused to abjure their opinions. It was repealed by the statute 29 Car. II. c. 9. Brown. This was also the name of a writ for the purpose indicated.

HAFNE. A haven or port. Cowell.

HAFNE COURTS. Haven courts; courts anciently held in certain ports in England. Spelman.

HAGA. A house in a city or borough. Scott.

HAGIA. A hedge. Mon. Angl. tom. 2, p. 273.

HAGNE. A little hand-gun. St. 33 Hen. VIII. c. 6.

HAGNEBUT. A hand-gun of a larger description than the hagne. St. 2 & 3 Edw. VI. c. 14; 4 & 5 P. & M. c. 2.

HAIA. A park inclosed. Cowell.

HAIEBOTE. In old English law. A permission or liberty to take thorns, etc., to make or repair hedges. Blount.

HAILL. In Scotch law. Whole; the whole. "All and haill" are common words in conveyances. 1 Bell, App. Cas. 499.

HAILWORKFOLK, (*i. e.*, holywork-folk.) Those who formerly held lands by the service of defending or repairing a church or monument.

HAIMHALDARE. In old Scotch law. To seek restitution of one's own goods and gear, and bring the same *home* again. Skene de Verb. Sign.

HAIMSUCKEN. In Scotch law. The crime of assaulting a person in his own house. Bell.

HAKETON. A military coat of defense.

HALF-BLOOD. A term denoting the degree of relationship which exists between those who have the same father or the same mother, but not both parents in common. See BROTHER.

HALF-BROTHER, HALF-SISTER. Persons who have the same father, but different mothers; or the same mother, but different fathers.

HALF-CENT. A copper coin of the United States, of the value of five mills, and of the weight of ninety-four grains. The coinage of these was discontinued in 1857.

HALF-DEFENSE. In common-law pleading. The technical name of the common clause at the commencement of a defendant's plea: "And the said defendant, by ———, his attorney, *comes and defends the wrong*, (or force,) *and injury, when*," etc. Called "*half*-defense" from its abbreviated form.

HALF-DIME. A silver (now nickel) coin of the United States, of the value of five cents.

HALF-DOLLAR. A silver coin of the United States, of the value of fifty cents, or one-half the value of a dollar.

HALF-EAGLE. A gold coin of the United States, of the value of five dollars.

HALF-ENDEAL. A moiety, or half of a thing.

HALF-KINEG. In Saxon law. Half-king, (*semi-rex.*) A title given to the aldermen of all England. Crabb, Eng. Law, 28; Spelman.

HALF-MARK. A noble, or six shillings and eight pence in English money.

HALF-PROOF. In the civil law. Proof by one witness, or a private instrument. Hallifax, Civil Law, b. 3, c. 9, no. 25; 3 Bl. Comm. 370. Or *prima facie* proof, which yet was not sufficient to found a sentence or decree.

HALF-SEAL. That which was formerly used in the English chancery for sealing of commissions to delegates, upon any appeal to the court of delegates, either in ecclesiastical or marine causes.

HALF-TIMER. A child who, by the operation of the English factory and education acts, is employed for less than the full time in a factory or workshop, in order that he may attend some "recognized efficient school." See factory and workshop act, 1878, § 23; elementary education act, 1876, § 11.

HALF-TONGUE. A jury half of one *tongue* or nationality and half of another. See DE MEDIETATE LINGUÆ.

HALF-YEAR. In legal computation. The period of one hundred and eighty-two days; the odd hours being rejected. Co. Litt. 135*b;* Cro. Jac. 166; Yel. 100; 1 Steph. Comm. 265.

HALIGEMOT. In Saxon law. The meeting of a hall, (*conventus aulæ,*) that is, a lord's court; a court of a manor, or court-baron. Spelman. So called from the *hall,* where the tenants or freemen met, and justice was administered. Crabb, Eng. Law, 26.

HALIMAS. In English law. The feast of All Saints, on the 1st of November; one of the cross-quarters of the year, was computed from Halimas to Candlemas. Wharton.

HALL. A building or room of considerable size, used as a place for the meeting of public assemblies, conventions, courts, etc.

In English law. A name given to many manor-houses because the magistrate's court was held in the hall of his mansion; a chief mansion-house. Cowell.

HALLAGE. In old English law. A fee or toll due for goods or merchandise vended in a hall. Jacob.

A toll due to the lord of a fair or market, for such commodities as were vended in the common hall of the place. Cowell; Blount.

HALLAZCO. In Spanish law. The finding and taking possession of something which previously had no owner, and which thus becomes the property of the first occupant. Las Partidas, 3, 5, 28; 5, 48, 49; 5, 20, 50.

HALLE-GEMOTE. Hall assembly. A species of court-baron.

HALLUCINATION. In medical jurisprudence. A species of mania; the perception of objects which have no reality, or of sensations which have no corresponding external cause, arising from disorder of the nervous system; delusion. Webster.

HALMOTE. See HALLE-GEMOTE.

HALYMOTE. A holy or ecclesiastical court.

A court held in London before the lord mayor and sheriffs, for regulating the bakers.

It was anciently held on Sunday next before St. Thomas' day, and therefore called the "*holymote,*" or holy court. Cowell.

HALYWERCFOLK. Sax. In old English law. Tenants who held land by the service of repairing or defending a church or monument, whereby they were exempted from feudal and military services.

HAMA. In old English law. A hook; an engine with which a house on fire is pulled down. Yel. 60.

A piece of land.

HAMBLING. In forest law. The hoxing or hock-sinewing of dogs; an old mode of laming or disabling dogs. Termes de la Ley.

HAMESECKEN. In Scotch law. The violent entering into a man's house without license or against the peace, and the seeking and assaulting him there. Skene de Verb. Sign.; 2 Forb. Inst. 139.

The crime of housebreaking or burglary. 4 Bl. Comm. 223.

HAMFARE. (Sax. From *ham,* a house.) In Saxon law. An assault made in a house; a breach of the peace in a private house.

HAMLET. A small village; a part or member of a vill. It is the diminutive of "*ham,*" a village. Cowell.

HAMMA. A close joining to a house; a croft; a little meadow. Cowell.

HAMMER. Metaphorically, a forced sale or sale at public auction. "To bring to the hammer," to put up for sale at auction. "Sold under the hammer," sold by an officer of the law or by an auctioneer.

HAMSOCNE. The right of security and privacy in a man's house. Du Cange. The breach of this privilege by a forcible entry of a house is breach of the peace. Du Cange.

HANAPER. A hamper or basket in which were kept the writs of the court of chancery relating to the business of a subject, and their returns. 3 Bl. Comm. 49. According to others, the fees accruing on writs, etc., were there kept. Spelman; Du Cange.

HANAPER-OFFICE. An office belonging to the common-law jurisdiction of the court of chancery, so called because all writs relating to the business of a subject, and their returns, were formerly kept in a hamper, *in hanaperio.* 5 & 6 Vict. c. 103.

HAND. A measure of length equal to four inches, used in measuring the height of horses. A person's signature.

In old English law. An oath.

HAND DOWN. An appellate court is said to "hand down" its decision in a case, when the opinion is prepared and filed for transmission to the court below.

HAND-FASTING. Betrothment.

HAND-GRITH. Peace or protection given by the king with his own hand.

HAND MONEY. Money paid in hand to bind a bargain; earnest money.

HANDBILL. A written or printed notice displayed to inform those concerned of something to be done.

HANDBOROW. In Saxon law. A hand pledge; a name given to the nine pledges in a decennary or friborg; the tenth or chief, being called "*headborow,*" (*q. v.*) So called as being an inferior pledge to the chief. Spelman.

HANDHABEND. In Saxon law. One having a thing in his hand; that is, a thief found having the stolen goods in his possession. Jurisdiction to try such thief.

HANDSALE. Anciently, among all the northern nations, shaking of hands was held necessary to bind a bargain,—a custom still retained in verbal contracts. A sale thus made was called "handsale," (*venditio per mutuam manum complexionem.*) In process of time the same word was used to signify the price or earnest which was given immediately after the shaking of hands, or instead thereof. 2 Bl. Comm. 448.

HANDSEL. Handsale, or earnest money.

HANDWRITING. The chirography of a person; the cast or form of writing peculiar to a person, including the size, shape, and style of letters, tricks of penmanship, and whatever gives individuality to his writing, distinguishing it from that of other persons.

Anything written by hand; an instrument written by the hand of a person, or a specimen of his writing.

Handwriting, considered under the law of evidence, includes not only the ordinary writing of one able to write, but also writing done in a disguised hand, or in cipher, and a mark made by one able or unable to write. 9 Amer. & Eng. Enc. Law, 264.

HANG. In old practice. To remain undetermined. "It has *hung* long enough; it is time it were made an end of." Holt, C. J., 1 Show. 77.

Thus, the present participle means pending; during the pendency. "If the tenant alien, *hanging* the *præcipe.*" Co. Litt. 266*a*.

HANGING. In criminal law. Suspension by the neck; the mode of capital punishment used in England from time immemorial, and generally adopted in the United States. 4 Bl. Comm. 403.

HANGING IN CHAINS. In atrocious cases it was at one time usual, in England, for the court to direct a murderer, after execution, to be hanged upon a gibbet in chains near the place where the murder was committed, a practice quite contrary to the Mosaic law. (Deut. xxi. 23.) Abolished by 4 & 5 Wm. IV. c. 26. Wharton.

HANGMAN. An executioner. One who executes condemned criminals by hanging.

HANGWITE. In Saxon law. A fine for illegal hanging of a thief, or for allowing him to escape. Immunity from such fine. Du Cange.

HANIG. Customary labor.

HANSE. An alliance or confederation among merchants or cities, for the good ordering and protection of the commerce of its members. An imposition upon merchandise. Du Cange.

HANSE TOWNS, LAWS OF THE. The maritime ordinances of the Hanseatic towns, first published in German at Lubeck, in 1597, and in May, 1614, revised and enlarged.

HANSE TOWNS. The collective name of certain German cities, including Lubeck, Hamburg, and Bremen, which formed an alliance for the mutual protection and furtherance of their commercial interests, in the twelfth century. The powerful confederacy thus formed was called the "Hanseatic League." The league framed and promulgated a code of maritime law, which was known as the "Laws of the Hanse Towns," or *Jus Hanseaticum Maritimum.*

HANSEATIC. Pertaining to a hanse or commercial alliance; but, generally, the union of the Hanse towns is the one referred to, as in the expression the "Hanseatic League."

HANSGRAVE. The chief of a company; the head man of a corporation.

HANTELOD. In old European law. An arrest, or attachment. Spelman.

HAP. To catch. Thus, "hap the rent," "hap the deed-poll," were formerly used.

HAPPINESS. The constitutional right of men to pursue their "happiness" means the right to pursue any lawful business or vocation, in any manner not inconsistent with the equal rights of others, which may increase their prosperity, or develop their faculties, so as to give to them their highest enjoyment. 111 U. S. 757, 4 Sup. Ct. Rep. 652; 1 Bl. Comm. 41.

HAQUE. In old statutes. A hand-gun, about three-quarters of a yard long.

HARACIUM. In old English law. A race of horses and mares kept for breed; a stud. Spelman.

HARBINGER. In England, an officer of the royal household.

HARBOR, *v.* To receive clandestinely and without lawful authority a person for the purpose of so concealing him that another having a right to the lawful custody of such person shall be deprived of the same. 5 How. 215, 227. A distinction has been taken, in some decisions, between "harbor" and "conceal." A person may be convicted of harboring a slave, although he may not have concealed her. 24 Ala. 71.

HARBOR, *n.* A haven, or a space of deep water so sheltered by the adjacent land as to afford a safe anchorage for ships.

"Port" is a word of larger import than "harbor," since it implies the presence of wharves, or at any rate the means and opportunity of receiving and discharging cargo.

HARBOR AUTHORITY. In England a harbor authority is a body of persons, corporate or unincorporate, being proprietors of, or intrusted with the duty of constructing, improving, managing, or lighting, any harbor. St. 24 & 25 Vict. c. 47.

HARD LABOR. A punishment, additional to mere imprisonment, sometimes imposed upon convicts sentenced to a penitentiary. But the labor is not, as a rule, any harder than ordinary mechanical labor.

HARDHEIDIS. In old Scotch law. Lions; coins formerly of the value of three half-pence. 1 Pitc. Crim. Tr. pt. 1, p. 64, note.

HARDSHIP. The severity with which a proposed construction of the law would bear upon a particular case, founding, sometimes, an argument against such construction, which is otherwise termed the "argument *ab inconvenienti.*"

HARNASCA. In old European law. The defensive armor of a man; harness. Spelman.

HARNESS. All warlike instruments; also the tackle or furniture of a ship.

HARO, HARRON. Fr. In Norman and early English law. An outcry, or hue and cry after felons and malefactors. Cowell.

HARRIOTT. The old form of "heriot," (*q. v.*) Williams, Seis. 203.

HART. A stag or male deer of the forest five years old complete.

HASP AND STAPLE. In old Scotch law. The form of entering an heir in a subject situated within a royal borough. It consisted of the heir's taking hold of the hasp and staple of the door, (which was the symbol of possession,) with other formalities. Bell; Burrill.

HASPA. In old English law. The hasp of a door; by which livery of seisin might anciently be made, where there was a house on the premises.

HASTA. Lat. A spear. In the Roman law, a spear was the sign of a public sale of goods or sale by auction. Hence the phrase "*hastæ subjicere*" (to put under the spear) meant to put up at auction. Calvin.

In feudal law. A spear. The symbol used in making investiture of a fief. Feud. lib. 2, tit. 2.

HAT MONEY. In maritime law. Primage; a small duty paid to the captain and mariners of a ship.

HAUBER. O. Fr. A high lord; a great baron. Spelman.

HAUGH, or HOWGH. A green plot in a valley.

HAUL. The use of this word, instead of the statutory word "carry," in an indictment charging that the defendant "did feloniously steal, take, and *haul* away" certain personalty, will not render the indictment bad, the words being in one sense equivalent. 108 Ind. 171, 8 N. E. Rep. 911.

HAUR. In old English law. Hatred. Leg. Wm. I. c. 16; Blount.

HAUSTUS. Lat. In the civil law. A species of servitude, consisting in the right to draw water from another's well or spring, in which the *iter*, (right of way to the well or spring,) so far as it is necessary, is tacitly included. Dig. 8, 3, 1; Mackeld. Rom. Law, § 318.

HAUT CHEMIN. L. Fr. Highway. Yearb. M. 4 Hen. VI. 4.

HAUT ESTRET. L. Fr. High street; highway. Yearb. P. 11 Hen. VI. 2.

HAUTHONER. A man armed with a coat of mail. Jacob.

HAVE. Lat. A form of the salutatory expression "*Ave*," used in the titles of some of the constitutions of the Theodosian and Justinianean codes. See Cod. 7, 62, 9; Id. 9, 2, 11.

HAVE. To possess corporally. "No one, at common law, was said to *have* or to be in possession of land, unless it were conveyed to him by the livery of seisin, which gave him the corporal investiture and bodily occupation thereof." Bl. Law Tracts, 113.

HAVE AND HOLD. A common phrase in conveyancing, derived from the *habendum et tenendum* of the old common law. See HABENDUM ET TENENDUM.

HAVEN. A place of a large receipt and safe riding of ships, so situate and secured by the land circumjacent that the vessels thereby ride and anchor safely, and are protected by the adjacent land from dangerous or violent winds; as Milford Haven, Plymouth Haven, and the like. Hale de Jure Mar. par. 2, c. 2.

HAW. A small parcel of land so called in Kent; houses. Co. Litt. 5.

HAWBERK. He who held land in France, by finding a coat or shirt of mail, with which he was to be ready when called upon. Wharton.

HAWGH, HOWGH. In old English law. A valley. Co. Litt. 5*b*.

HAWKER. A trader who goes from place to place, or along the streets of a town, selling the goods which he carries with him.

It is perhaps not essential to the idea, but is generally understood from the word, that a hawker is to be one who not only carries goods for sale, but seeks for purchasers, either by outcry, which some lexicographers conceive as intimated by the derivation of the word, or by attracting notice and attention to them, as goods for sale, by an actual exhibition or exposure of them, by placards or labels, or by a conventional signal, like the sound of a horn for the sale of fish. 12 Cush. 495.

HAWKING. The business of one who sells or offers goods for sale on the streets, by outcry, or by attracting the attention of persons by exposing his goods in a public place, or by placards, labels, or signals. 107 Ind. 505, 8 N. E. Rep. 609.

HAY-BOTE. Another name for "hedge-bote," being one of the estovers allowed to a tenant for life or years, namely, material for repairing the necessary hedges or fences of his grounds. 2 Bl. Comm. 35; 1 Washb. Real Prop. 129.

HAYWARD. In old English law. An officer appointed in the lord's court to keep a common herd of cattle of a town; so called because he was to see that they did not break or injure the hedges of inclosed grounds. His duty was also to impound trespassing cattle, and to guard against pound-breaches. Kitch. 46; Cowell.

HAZARD. An unlawful game at dice; and those who play at it are called "hazardors." Jacob.

HAZARDOUS. Exposed to or involving danger; perilous; risky.

The terms "hazardous," "extra-hazardous," "specially hazardous," and "not hazardous" are well-understood technical terms in the business of insurance, having distinct and separate meanings. Although what goods are included in each designation may not be so known as to dispense with actual proof, the terms themselves are distinct and known to be so. 38 N. Y. 364; 47 N. Y. 597.

HAZARDOUS CONTRACT. A contract in which the performance of that which is one of its objects depends on an uncertain event. Civil Code La. art. 1769. See 1 J. J. Marsh. 596.

HE. The use of this pronoun in a written instrument, in referring to a person whose Christian name is designated therein by a mere initial, is not conclusive that the person referred to is a male; it may be shown by parol that the person intended is a female. 71 Cal. 38, 11 Pac. Rep. 802.

He who has committed iniquity shall not have equity. Francis, Max.

He who seeks equity must do equity. It is in pursuance of this maxim that equity enforces the right of the wife's equity to a settlement. Snell, Eq. (5th Ed.) 374.

HEAD. Chief; leading; principal; the upper part or principal source of a stream.

HEAD OF A CREEK. This term means the source of the longest branch, unless general reputation has given the appellation to another. 2 Bibb, 110.

HEAD OF A FAMILY. A term used in homestead and exemption laws to designate a person who maintains a family; a householder.

HEADBOROUGH. In Saxon law. The head or chief officer of a borough; chief of the frankpledge tithing or decennary. This office was afterwards, when the petty constableship was created, united with that office.

HEAD-COURTS. Certain tribunals in Scotland, abolished by 20 Geo. II. c. 50. Ersk. 1, 4, 5.

HEADLAND. In old English law. A narrow piece of unplowed land left at the end of a plowed field for the turning of the plow. Called, also, "butt."

HEAD-NOTE. A syllabus to a reported case; a summary of the points decided in the case, which is placed at the *head* or beginning of the report.

HEAD-PENCE. An exaction of 40d. or more, collected by the sheriff of Northumberland from the people of that county twice in every seven years, without account to the king. Abolished in 1444. Cowell.

HEAFODWEARD. In old English law. One of the services to be rendered by a thane, but in what it consisted seems uncertain.

HEALGEMOTE. In Saxon law. A court-baron; an ecclesiastical court.

HEALSFANG. In Saxon law. A sort of pillory, by which the head of the culprit was caught between two boards, as feet are caught in a pair of stocks. Cowell.

HEALTH. Freedom from sickness or suffering. The right to the enjoyment of *health* is a subdivision of the right of personal security, one of the absolute rights of persons. 1 Bl. Comm. 129, 134. As to injuries affecting health, see 3 Bl. Comm. 122.

HEALTH LAWS. Laws prescribing sanitary measures, and designed to promote or preserve the health of the community.

HEALTH OFFICER. The officer charged with the execution and enforcement of health laws. The powers and duties of health officers are regulated by local laws.

HEALTHY. Free from disease or bodily ailment, or any state of the system peculiarly susceptible or liable to disease or bodily ailment. 13 Ired. Law, 356.

HEARING. **In equity practice.** The hearing of the arguments of the counsel for the parties upon the pleadings, or pleadings and proofs; corresponding to the trial of an action at law.

The word "hearing" has an established meaning as applicable to equity cases. It means the same thing in those cases that the word "trial" does in cases at law. And the words "final hearing" have long been used to designate the trial of an equity case upon the merits, as distinguished from the hearing of any preliminary questions arising in the cause, and which are termed "interlocutory." 24 Wis. 171.

In criminal law. The examination of a prisoner charged with a crime or misdemeanor, and of the witnesses for the accused.

HEARSAY. A term applied to that species of testimony given by a witness who relates, not what he knows personally, but what others have told him, or what he has heard said by others.

Hearsay evidence is that which does not derive its value solely from the credit of the witness, but rests mainly on the veracity and competency of other persons. The very nature of the evidence shows its weakness, and it is admitted only in specified cases from necessity. Code Ga. 1882, § 3770; 1 Phil. Ev. 185.

Hearsay evidence is second-hand evidence, as distinguished from original evidence; it is the repetition at second-hand of what would be original evidence if given by the person who originally made the statement.

HEARTH MONEY. A tax levied in England by St. 14 Car. II. c. 10, consisting of two shillings on every hearth or stove in the kingdom. It was extremely unpopular, and was abolished by 1 W. & M. St. 1, c. 10. This tax was otherwise called "chimney money."

HEARTH SILVER. In English law. A species of *modus* or composition for tithes. Anstr. 323, 326.

HEAT OF PASSION. In criminal law. A state of violent and uncontrollable rage engendered by a blow or certain other provocation given, which will reduce a homicide from the grade of murder to that of manslaughter. A state of mind contradistinguished from a cool state of the blood. 66 Mo. 13; 74 Mo. 250.

HEBBERMAN. An unlawful fisher in the Thames below London bridge; so called because they generally fished at *ebbing* tide or water. 4 Hen. VII. c. 15; Jacob.

HEBBERTHEF. In Saxon law. The privilege of having the goods of a thief, and the trial of him, within a certain liberty. Cowell.

HEBBING-WEARS. A device for catching fish in ebbing water. St. 23 Hen. VIII. c. 5.

HEBDOMAD. A week; a space of seven days.

HEBDOMADIUS. A week's man; the canon or prebendary in a cathedral church, who had the peculiar care of the choir and the offices of it for his own week. Cowell.

HECCAGIUM. In feudal law. Rent paid to a lord of the fee for a liberty to use the engines called "hecks."

HECK. An engine to take fish in the river Ouse. 23 Hen. VIII. c. 18.

HEDA. A small haven, wharf, or landing place.

HEDAGIUM. Toll or customary dues at the hithe or wharf, for landing goods, etc., from which exemption was granted by the crown to some particular persons and societies. Wharton.

HEDGE-BOTE. An allowance of wood for repairing hedges or fences, which a tenant or lessee has a right to take off the land let or demised to him. 2 Bl. Comm. 35.

HEDGE-PRIEST. A vagabond priest in olden time.

HEGEMONY. The leadership of one among several independent confederate states.

HEGIRA. The epoch or account of time used by the Arabians and the Turks, who begin their computation from the day that Mahomet was compelled to escape from Mecca, which happened on Friday, July 16, A. D. 622, under the reign of the Emperor Heraclius. Wharton.

HEGUMENOS. The leader of the monks in the Greek Church.

HEIFER. A young cow which has not had a calf. 2 East, P. C. 616.

HEIR. **At common law.** A person who succeeds, by the rules of law, to an estate in lands, tenements, or hereditaments, upon the death of his ancestor, by descent and right of relationship.

The term "heir" has a very different signification at common law from what it has in those states and countries which have adopted the civil law. In the latter, the term is indiscriminately applied to all persons who are called to the succession, whether by the act of the party or by operation of law. The person who is created universal successor by a will is called the "testamentary heir;" and the next of kin by blood is, in cases of intestacy, called the "heir at law," or "heir by intestacy." The executor of the common law in many respects corresponds to the testamentary heir of the civil law. Again, the administrator in many respects corresponds with the heir by intestacy. By the common law, executors and administrators have no right except to the personal estate of the deceased; whereas the heir by the civil law is authorized to administer both the personal and real estate. Story, Confl. Laws, §§ 507, 508.

In the civil law. A universal successor in the event of death. He who actively or passively succeeds to the entire property or estate, rights and obligations, of a decedent, and occupies his place.

The term "heir" has several significations. Sometimes it refers to one who has formally accepted a succession and taken possession thereof; sometimes to one who is called to succeed, but still retains the faculty of accepting or renouncing, and it is frequently used as applied to one who has formally renounced. 26 La. Ann. 417.

In Scotch law. The person who succeeds to the heritage or heritable rights of one deceased. 1 Forb. Inst. pt. 3, p. 75. The word has a more extended signification than in English law, comprehending not only those who succeed to lands, but successors to personal property also. Wharton.

HEIR APPARENT. An heir whose right of inheritance is indefeasible, provided he outlive the ancestor; as in England the eldest son, or his issue, who must, by the course of the common law, be heir to the father whenever he happens to die. 2 Bl. Comm. 208; 1 Steph. Comm. 358.

HEIR AT LAW. He who, after his ancestor's death intestate, has a right to inherit all lands, tenements, and hereditaments which belonged to him or of which he was seised. The same as "heir general."

HEIR BENEFICIARY. In the civil law. One who has accepted the succession under the benefit of an inventory regularly made.

Heirs are divided into two classes, according to the manner in which they accept the successions left to them, to-wit, unconditional and beneficiary heirs. Unconditional heirs are those who inherit without any reservation, or without making an inventory, whether their acceptance be express or tacit. Beneficiary heirs are those who have accepted the succession under the benefit of an inventory regularly made. Civil Code La. art. 881.

HEIR BY CUSTOM. In English law. One whose right of inheritance depends upon a particular and local custom, such as *gavelkind*, or *borough English*. Co. Litt. 140.

HEIR BY DEVISE. One to whom lands are devised by will; a devisee of lands. Answering to the *hæres factus* (*q. v.*) of the civil law.

HEIR COLLATERAL. One who is not lineally related to the decedent, but is of collateral kin; *e. g.*, his uncle, cousin, brother, nephew.

HEIR CONVENTIONAL. In the civil law. One who takes a succession by virtue of a contract or settlement entitling him thereto.

HEIR, FORCED. One who cannot be disinherited. See FORCED HEIRS.

HEIR GENERAL. An heir at law. The ordinary heir by blood, succeeding to all the lands.

HEIR INSTITUTE. In Scotch law. One to whom the right of succession is ascertained by disposition or express deed of the deceased. 1 Forb. Inst. pt. 3, p. 75.

HEIR, IRREGULAR. In Louisiana. Irregular heirs are those who are neither testamentary nor legal, and who have been established by law to take the succession. See Civil Code La. art. 874. When there are no direct or collateral relatives surviving the decedent, and the succession consequently devolves upon the surviving husband or wife, or illegitimate children, or the state, it is called an "irregular succession."

HEIR, LEGAL. In the civil law. A legal heir is one who takes the succession by relationship to the decedent and by force of law. This is different from a testamentary or conventional heir, who takes the succession in virtue of the disposition of man. See Civil Code La. arts. 873, 875.

HEIR-LOOMS. Such goods and chattels as, contrary to the nature of chattels, shall go by special custom to the heir along with the inheritance, and not to the executor. The termination "*loom*" (Sax.) signifies a limb or member; so that an heir-loom is nothing else but a limb or member of the inheritance. They are generally such things as cannot be taken away without damaging or dismembering the freehold; such as deer in a park, doves in a cote, deeds and charters, etc. 2 Bl. Comm. 427.

HEIR MALE. In Scotch law. An heir institute, who, though not next in blood to the deceased, is his nearest male relation that can succeed to him. 1 Forb. Inst. pt. 3, p. 76.

HEIR OF CONQUEST. In Scotch law. One who succeeds to the deceased in *conquest, i. e.*, lands or other heritable rights to which the deceased neither did nor could succeed as heir to his predecessor.

HEIR OF LINE. In Scotch law. One who succeeds lineally by right of blood; one who succeeds to the deceased in his heritage; *i. e.*, lands and other heritable rights derived to him by succession as heir to his predecessor. 1 Forb. Inst. pt. 3, p. 77.

HEIR OF PROVISION. In Scotch law. One who succeeds as heir by virtue of a particular provision in a deed or instrument.

HEIR OF TAILZIE. In Scotch law. He on whom an estate is settled that would not have fallen to him by legal succession. 1 Forb. Inst. pt. 3, p. 75.

HEIR PRESUMPTIVE. The person who, if the ancestor should die immediately, would, in the present circumstances of things, be his heir, but whose right of inheritance may be defeated by the contingency of some nearer heir being born; as a brother or nephew, whose presumptive succession may be destroyed by the birth of a child. 2 Bl. Comm. 208; 1 Steph. Comm. 358.

HEIR SPECIAL. In English law. The issue in tail, who claims *per formam doni*; by the form of the gift.

HEIR SUBSTITUTE, IN A BOND. In Scotch law. He to whom a bond is payable expressly in case of the creditor's decease, or after his death. 1 Forb. Inst. pt. 3, p. 76.

HEIR TESTAMENTARY. In the civil law. One who is named and appointed heir in the testament of the decedent. This name distinguishes him from a *legal* heir, (one upon whom the law casts the succession,) and from a *conventional* heir, (one who takes it by virtue of a previous contract or settlement.)

HEIR UNCONDITIONAL. In the civil law. One who inherits without any reservation, or without making an inventory, whether his acceptance be express or tacit. Distinguished from *heir beneficiary*, (*q. v.*)

HEIRDOM. Succession by inheritance.

HEIRESS. A female heir to a person having an estate of inheritance. When there are more than one, they are called "co-heiresses," or "co-heirs."

HEIRS. A word used in deeds of conveyance, (either solely, or in connection with others,) where it is intended to pass a fee.

HEIRS OF THE BODY. An heir begotten or borne by the person referred to; a lineal descendant. The terms "natural heirs" and "heirs of the body," in a will, and by way of executory devise, are considered as of the same legal import. 19 Conn. 112.

HEIRSHIP. The quality or condition of being heir, or the relation between the heir and his ancestor.

HEIRSHIP MOVABLES. In Scotch law. The movables which go to the heir, and not to the executor, that the land may not go to the heir completely dismantled, such as the best of furniture, horses, cows, etc., but not fungibles. Bell.

HELL. The name given to a place under the exchequer chamber, where the king's debtors were confined. Rich. Dict.

HELM. Thatch or straw; a covering for the head in war; a coat of arms bearing a crest; the tiller or handle of the rudder of a ship.

HELOWE-WALL. The end-wall covering and defending the rest of the building. Paroch. Antiq. 573.

HELSING. A Saxon brass coin, of the value of a half-penny.

HEMOLDBORH, or HELMELBORCH. A title to possession. The admission of this old Norse term into the laws of the Conqueror is difficult to be accounted for; it is not found in any Anglo-Saxon law extant. Wharton.

HENCHMAN. A page; an attendant; a herald.

HENEDPENNY. A customary payment of money instead of hens at Christmas; a composition for eggs. Cowell.

HENFARE. A fine for flight on account of murder. Domesday Book.

HENGHEN. In Saxon law. A prison, a gaol, or house of correction.

HENGWYTE. Sax. In old English law. An acquittance from a fine for hanging a thief. Fleta, lib. 1, c. 47, § 17.

HENRICUS VETUS. Henry the Old, or Elder. King Henry I. is so called in ancient English chronicles and charters, to distinguish him from the subsequent kings of that name. Spelman.

HEORDFÆTE, or HUDEFÆST. In Saxon law. A master of a family, keeping house, distinguished from a lower class of freemen, viz., *folgeras*, (*folgarii*,) who had no habitations of their own, but were house-retainers of their lords.

HEORDPENNY. Peter-pence, (*q. v.*)

HEORDWERCH. In Saxon law. The service of herdsmen, done at the will of their lord.

HEPTARCHY. A government exercised by seven persons, or a nation divided into seven governments. In the year 560, seven different monarchies had been formed in England by the German tribes, namely, that of Kent by the Jutes; those of Sussex, Wessex, and Essex by the Saxons; and those of East Anglia, Bernicia, and Deira by the Angles. To these were added, about the year 586, an eighth, called the "Kingdom of Mercia," also founded by the Angles, and comprehending nearly the whole of the heart of the kingdom. These states formed what has been designated the "Anglo-Saxon Octarchy," or more commonly, though not so correctly, the "Anglo-Saxon Heptarchy," from the custom of speaking of Deira and Bernicia under the single appellation of the "Kingdom of Northumberland." Wharton.

HERALD. In ancient law, a herald was a diplomatic messenger who carried messages between kings or states, and especially proclamations of war, peace, or truce. In English law, a herald is an officer whose duty is to keep genealogical lists and tables, adjust armorial bearings, and regulate the ceremonies at royal coronations and funerals.

HERALDRY. The art, office, or science of heralds. Also an old and obsolete abuse of buying and selling precedence in the paper of causes for hearing.

HERALDS' COLLEGE. In England. An ancient royal corporation, first instituted by Richard III. in 1483. It comprises three kings of arms, six heralds, and four marshals or pursuivants of arms, together with the earl marshal and a secretary. The heralds' books, compiled when progresses were solemnly and regularly made into every part of the kingdom, to inquire into the state of families, and to register such marriages and descents as were verified to them upon oath, are allowed to be good evidence of pedigrees. The heralds' office is still allowed to make grants of arms and to permit change of names. 3 Starkie, Ev. 843; Wharton.

HERBAGE. In English law. An easement or liberty, which consists in the right to pasture cattle on another's ground.

Feed for cattle in fields and pastures. Bract. fol. 222; Co. Litt. 46; Shep. Touch. 97. A right to herbage does not include a right to cut grass, or dig potatoes, or pick apples. 4 N. H. 303.

HERBAGIUM ANTERIUS. The first crop of grass or hay, in opposition to aftermath or second cutting. Paroch. Antiq. 459.

HERBENGER, or HARBINGER. An officer in the royal house, who goes before and allots the noblemen and those of the household their lodgings; also an innkeeper.

HERBERGAGIUM. Lodgings to receive guests in the way of hospitality. Cowell.

HERBERGARE. To harbor; to entertain.

HERBERGATUS. Harbored or entertained in an inn. Cowell.

HERBERY, or HERBURY. An inn. Cowell.

HERCIA. A harrow. Fleta, lib. 2, c. 77.

HERCIARE. To harrow. 4 Inst. 270.

HERCIATURA. In old English law. Harrowing; work with a harrow. Fleta, lib. 2, c. 82, § 2.

HERCISCUNDA. In the civil law. To be divided. *Familia herciscunda*, an inheritance to be divided. *Actio familiæ herciscundæ*, an action for dividing an inheritance. *Erciscunda* is more commonly used in the civil law. Dig. 10, 2; Inst. 3, 28, 4; Id. 4, 6, 20.

HERDEWICH. A grange or place for cattle or husbandry. Mon. Angl. pt. 3.

HERDWERCH, HEORDWERCH. Herdsmen's work, or customary labor, done by shepherds and inferior tenants, at the will of the lord. Cowell.

HEREBANNUM. In old English law. A proclamation summoning the army into the field.

A mulct or fine for not joining the army when summoned. Spelman.

A tax or tribute for the support of the army. Du Cange.

HEREBOTE. The royal edict summoning the people to the field. Cowell.

HEREDAD. In Spanish law. A piece of land under cultivation; a cultivated farm; real estate.

HEREDAD YACENTE. From Lat. "*hæreditas jacens*," (*q. v.*) In Spanish law. An inheritance not yet entered upon or appropriated. White, New Recop. b. 2, tit. 19, c. 2, § 8.

HEREDERO. In Spanish law. Heir; he who, by legal or testamentary disposition, succeeds to the property of a deceased person. "*Hæres censeatur cum defuncto una eademque persona.*" Las Partidas, 7, 9, 13.

HEREDITAGIUM. In Sicilian and Neapolitan law. That which is held by hereditary right; the same with *hereditamentum* (*hereditament*) in English law. Spelman.

HEREDITAMENTS. Things capable of being inherited, be it corporeal or incorporeal, real, personal, or mixed, and including not only lands and everything thereon, but also heir-looms, and certain furniture which, by custom, may descend to the heir together with the land. Co. Litt. 5*b;* 2 Bl. Comm. 17.

The two kinds of hereditaments are *corporeal*, which are tangible, (in fact, they mean the same thing as land,) and *incorporeal*, which are not tangible, and are the rights and profits annexed to or issuing out of land. Wharton.

The term includes a few rights unconnected with land, but it is generally used as the widest expression for real property of all kinds, and is therefore employed in conveyances after the words "lands" and "tenements," to include everything of the nature of realty which they do not cover. Sweet.

HEREDITARY. That which is the subject of inheritance.

HEREDITARY RIGHT TO THE CROWN. The crown of England, by the positive constitution of the kingdom, has ever been descendible, and so continues, in a course peculiar to itself, yet subject to limitation by parliament; but, notwithstanding such limitation, the crown retains its descendible quality, and becomes hereditary in the prince to whom it is limited. 1 Bl. Comm. 191.

HEREFARE. Sax. A going into or with an army; a going out to war, (*profectio militaris;*) an expedition. Spelman.

HEREGEAT. A heriot, (*q. v.*)

HEREGELD. Sax. In old English law. A tribute or tax levied for the maintenance of an army. Spelman.

HEREMITORIUM. A place of retirement for hermits. Mon. Angl. tom. 3, p. 18.

HEREMONES. Followers of an army.

HERENACH. An archdeacon. Cowell.

HERES. Heir; an heir. A form of *hœres*, very common in the civil law. See HÆRES.

HERESCHIP. In old Scotch law. Theft or robbery. 1 Pitc. Crim. Tr. pt. 2, pp. 26, 89.

HERESLITA, HERESSA, HERESSIZ. A hired soldier who departs without license. 4 Inst. 128.

HERESY. In English law. An offense against religion, consisting not in a total denial of Christianity, but of some of its essential doctrines, publicly and obstinately avowed. 4 Bl. Comm. 44, 45. An opinion on divine subjects devised by human reason, openly taught, and obstinately maintained. 1 Hale, P. C. 384. This offense is now subject only to ecclesiastical correction, and is no longer punishable by the secular law. 4 Steph. Comm. 233.

HERETOCH. A general, leader, or commander; also a baron of the realm. Du Fresne.

HERETOFORE. This word simply denotes time past, in distinction from time present or time future, and has no definite and precise signification beyond this. 40 Conn. 157.

HERETUM. In old records. A court or yard for drawing up guards or military retinue. Cowell.

HEREZELD. In Scotch law. A gift or present made or left by a tenant to his lord as a token of reverence. Skene.

HERGE. In Saxon law. Offenders who joined in a body of more than thirty-five to commit depredations.

HERIGALDS. In old English law. A sort of garment. Cowell.

HERIOT. In English law. A customary tribute of goods and chattels, payable to the lord of the fee on the decease of the owner of the land.

Heriots are divided into heriot *service* and heriot *custom*. The former expression denotes such as are due upon a special reservation in a grant or lease of lands, and therefore amount to little more than a mere rent; the latter arise upon no special reservation whatever, but depend solely upon immemorial usage and custom. 2 Bl. Comm. 422.

HERISCHILD. A species of military service, or knight's fee. Cowell.

HERISCHULDA. In old Scotch law. A fine or penalty for not obeying the proclamation made for warfare. Skene.

HERISCINDIUM. A division of household goods. Blount.

HERISLIT. Laying down of arms. Blount. Desertion from the army. Spelman.

HERISTAL. The station of an army; the place where a camp is pitched. Spelman.

HERITABLE. Capable of being taken by descent. A term chiefly used in Scotch law, where it enters into several phrases.

HERITABLE BOND. In Scotch law. A bond for a sum of money to which is added, for further security of the creditor, a conveyance of land or heritage to be held by the creditor as pledge. 1 Ross, Conv. 76; 2 Ross, Conv. 324.

HERITABLE JURISDICTIONS. In Scotch law. Grants of criminal jurisdiction formerly bestowed on great families in Scotland, to facilitate the administration of justice. Whishaw. Abolished in effect by St. 20 Geo. II. c. 50. Tomlins.

HERITABLE OBLIGATION. In Louisiana. An obligation is heritable when the heirs and assigns of one party may enforce the performance against the heirs of the other. Civil Code La. art. 1997.

HERITABLE RIGHTS. In Scotch law. Rights of the heir; all rights to land or whatever is connected with land, as mills, fishings, tithes, etc.

HERITAGE. In the civil law. Every species of immovable which can be the subject of property; such as lands, houses, orchards, woods, marshes, ponds, etc., in whatever mode they may have been acquired, either by descent or purchase. 3 Toullier, no. 472.

In Scotch law. Land, and all property connected with land; real estate, as distinguished from movables, or personal estate. Bell.

HERITOR. In Scotch law. A proprietor of land. 1 Kames, Eq. Pref.

HERMANDAD. In Spanish law. A fraternity formed among different towns and villages to prevent the commission of crimes, and to prevent the abuses and vexations to which they were subjected by men in power. Bouvier.

HERMAPHRODITE. An animal or human being so malformed as to have the organs of generation of both sexes.

Hermaphroditus tam masculo quam fœminæ comparatur, secundum prævalentiam sexus incalescentis. An hermaphrodite is to be considered male or female according to the predominance of the exciting sex. Co. Litt. 8; Bract. fol. 5.

HERMENEUTICS. The science or art of construction and interpretation. By the phrase "legal hermeneutics" is understood the systematic body of rules which are recognized as applicable to the construction and interpretation of legal writings.

HERMER. A great lord. Jacob.

HERMOGENIAN CODE. See CODEX HERMOGENIANUS.

HERNESCUS. A heron. Cowell.

HERNESIUM, or HERNASIUM. Household goods; implements of trade or husbandry; the rigging or tackle of a ship. Cowell.

HEROUD, HERAUD. L. Fr. A herald.

HERPEX. A harrow. Spelman.

HERPICATIO. In old English law. A day's work with a harrow. Spelman.

HERRING SILVER. This was a composition in money for the custom of supplying herrings for the provision of a religious house. Wharton.

HERUS. A master. *Servus facit ut herus det*, the servant does [the work] in order that the master may give [him the wages agreed on.] *Herus dat ut servus facit*, the master gives [or agrees to give, the wages,] in consideration of, or with a view to, the servant's doing [the work.] 2 Bl. Comm. 445.

HESIA. An easement. Du Cange.

HEST CORN. In old records. Corn or grain given or devoted to religious persons or purposes. 2 Mon. Angl. 367*b;* Cowell.

HESTA, or HESTHÀ. A little loaf of bread.

HETÆRARCHA. The head of a religious house; the head of a college; the warden of a corporation.

HETÆRIA. In Roman law. A company, society, or college.

HEUVELBORH. Sax. In old English law. A surety, (*warrantus.*)

HEYLODE. In old records. A customary burden upon inferior tenants, for mending or repairing hays or hedges.

HEYMECTUS. A hay-net; a net for catching conies. Cowell.

HIBERNAGIUM. The season for sowing winter corn. Cowell.

HIDAGE. An extraordinary tax formerly payable to the crown for every hide of land. This taxation was levied, not in money, but provision of armor, etc. Cowell.

HIDALGO. In Spanish law. A noble; a person entitled to the rights of nobility. By *hidalgos* are understood men chosen from good situations in life, (*de buenos lugares,*) and possessed of property, (*algo.*) White, New Recop. b. 1, tit. 5, c. 1.

HIDALGUIA. In Spanish law. Nobility by descent or lineage. White, New Recop. b. 1, tit. 5, c 3, § 4.

HIDE. In old English law. A measure of land, being as much as could be worked with one plow. It is variously estimated at from 60 to 100 acres, but was probably determined by local usage. Another meaning was as much land as would support one family or the dwellers in a mansion-house. Also a house; a dwelling-house.

HIDE AND GAIN. In English law. A term anciently applied to arable land. Co. Litt. 85*b*.

HIDE LANDS. In Saxon law. Lands belonging to a hide; that is, a house or mansion. Spelman.

HIDEL. In old English law. A place of protection; a sanctuary. St. 1 Hen. VII. cc. 5, 6; Cowell.

HIDGILD. A sum of money paid by a villein or servant to save himself from a whipping. Fleta, l. 1, c. 47, § 20.

HIERARCHY. Originally, government by a body of priests. Now, the body of officers in any church or ecclesiastical institution, considered as forming an ascending series of ranks or degrees of power and authority, with the correlative subjection, each to the one next above. Derivatively, any body of men, taken in their public capacity, and considered as forming a chain of powers, as above described.

HIGH BAILIFF. An officer attached to an English county court. His duties are to attend the court when sitting; to serve summonses; and to execute orders, warrants, writs, etc. St. 9 & 10 Vict. c. 95, § 33; Poll. C. C. Pr. 16. He also has similar duties under the bankruptcy jurisdiction of the county courts.

HIGH COMMISSION COURT. In English law. An ecclesiastical court of very formidable jurisdiction, for the vindication of the peace and dignity of the church, by reforming, ordering, and correcting the ecclesiastical state and persons, and all manner of errors, heresies, schisms, abuses, offenses, contempts, and enormities. 3 Bl. Comm. 67. It was erected by St. 1 Eliz. c. 1, and abolished by 16 Car. I. c. 11.

HIGH CONSTABLE. In English law. An officer of public justice, otherwise called "chief constable" and "constable of the hundred," whose proper duty is to keep the king's peace within the hundred, as the petty constable does within the parish or township. 3 Steph. Comm. 46, 47. See CONSTABLE.

An officer appointed in some cities with powers generally limited to matters of police.

HIGH CONSTABLE OF ENGLAND, LORD. His office has been disused (except only upon great and solemn occasions, as the coronation, or the like) since the attainder of Stafford, Duke of Buckingham, in the reign of Henry VII.

HIGH COURT OF ADMIRALTY. In English law. This was a court which exercised jurisdiction in prize cases, and had general jurisdiction in maritime causes, on the instance side. Its proceedings were usually *in rem*, and its practice and principles derived in large measure from the civil law. The judicature acts of 1873 transferred all the powers and jurisdiction of this tribunal to the probate, divorce, and admiralty division of the high court of justice.

HIGH COURT OF DELEGATES. In English law. A tribunal which formerly exercised appellate jurisdiction over cases brought from the ecclesiastical and admiralty courts. 3 Bl. Comm. 66.

It was a court of great dignity, erected by the statute 25 Hen. VII. c. 19. It was abolished, and its jurisdiction transferred to the judicial committee of the privy council.

HIGH COURT OF ERRORS AND APPEALS. The court of last resort in the state of Mississippi.

HIGH COURT OF JUSTICE. That branch of the English supreme court of judicature (*q. v.*) which exercises (1) the original jurisdiction formerly exercised by the court of chancery, the courts of queen's bench, common pleas, and exchequer, the courts of probate, divorce, and admiralty, the court of common pleas at Lancaster, the court of pleas at Durham, and the courts of the judges or commissioners of assize; and (2) the appellate jurisdiction of such of those courts as heard appeals from inferior courts. Judicature act, 1873, § 16.

HIGH COURT OF JUSTICIARY. See COURT OF JUSTICIARY.

HIGH COURT OF PARLIAMENT. In English law. The English parliament, as composed of the house of peers and house of commons; or the house of lords sitting in its judicial capacity.

HIGH CRIMES. High crimes and misdemeanors are such immoral and unlawful acts as are nearly allied and equal in guilt to felony, yet, owing to some technical circumstance, do not fall within the definition of "felony." 6 Conn. 417.

HIGH JUSTICE. In feudal law. The jurisdiction or right of trying crimes of every kind, even the highest. This was a privilege claimed and exercised by the great lords or barons of the middle ages. 1 Robertson's Car. V., appendix, note 23.

HIGH JUSTICIER. In old French and Canadian law. A feudal lord who exercised the right called "high justice." Guyot, Inst. Feod. c. 26.

HIGH MISDEMEANORS. See MISPRISION; HIGH CRIMES.

HIGH SCHOOL. A school in which higher branches of learning are taught than in the common schools. 123 Mass. 306. A school in which such instruction is given as will prepare the students to enter a college or university.

HIGH SEAS. The ocean; public waters. According to the English doctrine, the high sea begins at the distance of three miles from the coast of any country; according to the American view, at low-water mark, except in the case of small harbors and roadsteads inclosed within the *fauces terræ*.

The open ocean outside of the *fauces terræ*, as distinguished from arms of the sea; the waters of the ocean without the boundary of any county.

Any waters on the sea-coast which are without the boundaries of low-water mark.

HIGH STEWARD, COURT OF THE LORD. In English law. A tribunal instituted for the trial of peers indicted for treason or felony, or for misprision of either, but not for any other offense. The office is very ancient, and was formerly hereditary, or held for life, or *dum benè se gesserit;* but it has been for many centuries granted *pro hâc vice* only, and always to a lord of parliament. When, therefore, such an indictment is found by a grand jury of freeholders in the queen's bench, or at the assizes before a judge of *oyer and terminer*, it is removed by a writ of *certiorari* into the court of the lord high steward, which alone has power to determine it. A peer may plead a pardon before the queen's bench, in order to prevent the trouble of appointing a high steward, merely to receive the plea, but he cannot plead any other plea, because it is possible that, in consequence of such plea, judgment of death might be pronounced upon him. Wharton.

HIGH TREASON. In English law. Treason against the king or sovereign, as distinguished from petit or petty treason, which might formerly be committed against a subject. 4 Bl. Comm. 74, 75; 4 Steph. Comm. 183, 184, note.

HIGH-WATER MARK. This term is properly applicable only to tidal waters, and designates the line on the shore reached by the water at the high or flood tide. But it is sometimes also used with reference to the waters of artificial ponds or lakes, created by dams in unnavigable streams, and then denotes the highest point on the shores to which the dams can raise the water in ordinary circumstances.

HIGH WOOD. Timber.

HIGHER AND LOWER SCALE. In the practice of the English supreme court of judicature there are two scales regulating the fees of the court and the fees which solicitors are entitled to charge. The lower scale applies (unless the court otherwise orders) to the following cases: All causes and matters assigned by the judicature acts to the queen's bench, or the probate, divorce, and admiralty divisions; all actions of debt, contract, or tort; and in almost all causes and matters assigned by the acts to the chancery division in which the amount in litigation is under £1,000. The higher scale applies in all other causes and matters, and also in actions falling under one of the above classes, but in which the principal relief sought to be obtained is an injunction. Sweet.

HIGHNESS. A title of honor given to princes. The kings of England, before the time of James I., were not usually saluted with the title of "Majesty," but with that of "Highness." The children of crowned heads generally receive the style of "Highness." Wharton.

HIGHWAY. A free and public road, way, or street; one which every person has the right to use.

"In all counties of this state, public highways are roads, streets, alleys, lanes, courts, places, trails, and bridges, laid out or erected as such by the public, or, if laid out and erected by others, dedicated or abandoned to the public, or made such in actions for the partition of real property." Pol. Code Cal. § 2618.

There is a difference in the shade of meaning conveyed by two uses of the word. Sometimes it signifies right of free passage, in the abstract, not importing anything about the character or construction of the way. Thus, a river is called a "highway;" and it has been not unusual for congress, in granting a privilege of building a bridge, to declare that it shall be a public highway. Again, it has reference to some system of law authorizing the taking a strip of land, and preparing and devoting it to the use of travelers. In this use it imports a road-way upon the soil, constructed under the authority of these laws. Abbott.

HIGHWAY ACTS, or LAWS. The body or system of laws governing the laying out, repair, and use of highways.

HIGHWAY CROSSING. A place where the track of a railroad crosses the line of a highway.

HIGHWAY-RATE. In English law. A tax for the maintenance and repair of highways, chargeable upon the same property that is liable to the poor-rate.

HIGHWAY ROBBERY. In criminal law. The crime of robbery committed upon or near a public highway. In England, by St. 23 Hen. VIII. c. 1, this was made felony without benefit of clergy, while robbery committed elsewhere was less severely punished. The distinction was abolished by St. 3 & 4 W. & M. c. 9, and in this country it has never prevailed generally.

HIGHWAY TAX. A tax for and applicable to the making and repair of highways.

HIGHWAYMAN. A bandit; one who robs travelers upon the highway.

HIGLER. In English law. A hawker or peddler. A person who carries from door to door, and sells by retail, small articles of provisions, and the like.

HIGUELA. In Spanish law. A receipt given by an heir of a decedent, setting forth what property he has received from the estate.

HIKENILD STREET. One of the four great Roman roads of Britain. More commonly called "Ikenild Street."

HILARY RULES. A collection of orders and forms extensively modifying the pleading and practice in the English superior courts of common law, established in Hilary term, 1834. Stimson.

HILARY TERM. In English law. A term of court, beginning on the 11th and ending on the 31st of January in each year. Superseded (1875) by Hilary sittings, which begin January 11th, and end on the Wednesday before Easter.

HINDENI HOMINES. A society of men. The Saxons ranked men into three classes, and valued them, as to satisfaction for injuries, etc., according to their class. The highest class were valued at 1,200s., and were called "*twelf hindmen;*" the middle class at 600s., and called "*sexhindmen;*" the lowest at 200s., called "*twyhindmen.*" Their wives were termed "*hindas.*" Brompt. Leg. Alfred. c. 12.

HINDER AND DELAY. To hinder and delay is to do something which is an attempt to defraud, rather than a successful fraud; to put some obstacle in the path, or interpose some time, unjustifiably, before the creditor can realize what is owed out of his debtor's property. 42 N. Y. Super. Ct. 63.

HINDU LAW. The system of native law prevailing among the Gentoos, and administered by the government of British India.

HINE, or HIND. A husbandry servant.

HINEFARE. The loss or departure of a servant from his master. Domesday.

HIPOTECA. In Spanish law. A mortgage of real property.

HIRCISCUNDA. See HERCISCUNDA.

HIRE, *v.* To purchase the temporary use of a thing, or to stipulate for the labor or services of another. See HIRING.

To engage in service for a stipulated reward, as to hire a servant for a year, or laborers by the day or month; to engage a man to temporary service for wages. To "employ" is a word of more enlarged signification. A man hired to labor is employed, but a man may be employed in a work who is not hired. 11 N. Y. 605.

For definitions of the various species of this class of contracts, under their Latin names, see LOCATIO and following titles.

HIRE, *n.* Compensation for the use of a thing, or for labor or services.

HIREMAN. A subject. Du Cange.

HIRER. One who hires a thing, or the labor or services of another person.

HIRING. Hiring is a contract by which one person grants to another either the enjoyment of a thing or the use of the labor and industry, either of himself or his servant, during a certain time, for a stipulated compensation, or where one contracts for the labor or services of another about a thing bailed to him for a specified purpose. Code Ga. 1882, § 2085.

Hiring is a contract by which one gives to another the temporary possession and use of property, other than money, for reward, and the latter agrees to return the same to the former at a future time. Civil Code Cal. § 1925; Civil Code Dak. § 1103.

HIRST, HURST. In old English law. A wood. Co. Litt. 4*b*.

HIS. The use of this pronoun in a written instrument, in referring to a person whose Christian name is designated therein by a mere initial, is not conclusive that the person referred to is a male; it may be shown by parol that the person intended is a female. 71 Cal. 38, 11 Pac. Rep. 802.

HIS EXCELLENCY. In English law. The title of a viceroy, governor general, ambassador, or commander in chief.

In American law. This title is given to the governor of Massachusetts by the constitution of that state; and it is commonly given, as a title of honor and courtesy, to the governors of the other states and to the president of the United States. It is also customarily used by foreign ministers in addressing the secretary of state in written communications.

HIS HONOR. A title given by the constitution of Massachusetts to the lieutenant-governor of that commonwealth. Const. Mass. pt. 2, c. 2, § 2, art. 1.

HIS TESTIBUS. Lat. These being witnesses. The attestation clause in old deeds and charters.

HIWISC. A hide of land.

HLAF ÆTA. Sax. A servant fed at his master's cost.

HLAFORD. Sax. A lord. 1 Spence, Ch. 36.

HLAFORDSOCNA. Sax. A lord's protection. Du Cange.

HLAFORDSWICE. Sax. In Saxon law. The crime of betraying one's lord, (*proditio domini;*) treason. Crabb, Eng. Law, 59, 301.

HLASOCNA. Sax. The benefit of the law. Du Cange.

HLOTHBOTE. In Saxon law. A fine for being present at an unlawful assembly. Spelman.

HLOTHE. In Saxon law. An unlawful assembly from eight to thirty-five, inclusive. Cowell.

HOASTMEN. In English law. An ancient gild or fraternity at Newcastle-upon-Tyne, who dealt in sea coal. St. 21 Jac. I. c. 3.

HOBBLERS. In old English law. Light horsemen or bowmen; also certain tenants, bound by their tenure to maintain a little light horse for giving notice of any invasion, or such like peril, towards the seaside. Camden, Brit.

HOC. Lat. This. *Hoc intuitu*, with this expectation. *Hoc loco*, in this place. *Hoc nomine*, in this name. *Hoc titulo*, under this title. *Hoc voce*, under this word.

HOC QUIDEM PERQUAM DURUM EST, SED ITA LEX SCRIPTA EST. Lat. (This indeed is exceedingly hard, but so the law is written; such is the written or positive law.) An observation quoted by Blackstone as used by Ulpian in the civil law; and applied to cases where courts of equity have no power to abate the rigor of the law. Dig. 40, 9, 12, 1; 3 Bl. Comm. 430.

HOC PARATUS EST VERIFICARE. Lat. This he is ready to verify.

Hoc servabitur quod initio convenit. This shall be preserved which is useful in the beginning. Dig. 50, 17, 23; Bract. 73*b*.

HOCCUS SALTIS. A hoke, hole, or lesser pit of salt. Cowell.

HOCK-TUESDAY MONEY. This was a duty given to the landlord that his tenants and bondmen might solemnize the day on which the English conquered the Danes, being the second Tuesday after Easter week. Cowell.

HOCKETTOR, or HOCQUETEUR. A knight of the post; a decayed man; a basket carrier. Cowell.

HODGE-PODGE ACT. A name applied to a statute which comprises a medley of incongruous subjects.

HOGA. In old English law. A hill or mountain. In old English, a *how*. *Grene hoga*, Grenehow. Domesday; Spelman.

HOGASTER. In old English law. A sheep of the second year. Fleta, lib. 2, c. 79, §§ 4, 12. A young hog. Cowell.

HOGGUS, or HOGIETUS. A hog or swine. Cowell.

HOGHENHYNE. In Saxon law. A house-servant. Any stranger who lodged three nights or more at a man's house in a decennary was called "*hoghenhyne*," and his host became responsible for his acts as for those of his servant.

HOGSHEAD. A measure of a capacity containing the fourth part of a tun, or sixty-three gallons. Cowell. A large cask, of indefinite contents, but usually containing from one hundred to one hundred and forty gallons. Webster.

HOLD, *v.* 1. To possess in virtue of a lawful title; as in the expression, common in grants, "to have and to hold," or in that applied to notes, "the owner and holder."

2. To be the grantee or tenant of another; to take or have an estate from another. Properly, to have an estate on condition of paying rent, or performing service.

3. To adjudge or decide, spoken of a court, particularly to declare the conclusion of law reached by the court as to the legal effect of the facts disclosed.

4. To maintain or sustain; to be under the necessity or duty of sustaining or proving; as when it is said that a party "holds the affirmative" or negative of an issue in a cause.

5. To bind or obligate; to restrain or constrain; to keep in custody or under an obligation; as in the phrases "hold to bail," "hold for court," "held and firmly bound," etc.

6. To administer; to conduct or preside at; to convoke, open, and direct the operations of; as to hold a court, hold pleas, etc.

7. To prosecute; to direct and bring about officially; to conduct according to law; as to hold an election.

8. To possess; to occupy; to be in possession and administration of; as to hold office.

HOLD, *n.* In old law. Tenure. A word constantly occurring in conjunction with others, as *freehold, leasehold, copyhold,* etc., but rarely met with in the separate form.

HOLD OVER. To hold possession after the expiration of a term or lease. To retain possession of property leased, after the end of the term. To continue in possession of an office, and continue to exercise its functions, after the end of the officer's lawful term.

HOLD PLEAS. To hear or try causes. 3 Bl. Comm. 35, 298.

HOLDER. The holder of a bill of exchange, promissory note, or check is the person who has legally acquired the possession of the same, from a person capable of transferring it, by indorsement or delivery, and who is entitled to receive payment of the instrument from the party or parties liable to meet it.

HOLDER IN DUE COURSE, in English law, is "a holder who has taken a bill of exchange (check or note) complete and regular on the face of it, under the following conditions, namely: (*a*) That he became the holder of it before it was overdue, and without notice that it had been previously dishonored, if such was the fact. (*b*) That he took the bill (check or note) in good faith and for value, and that at the time it was negotiated to him he had no notice of any defect in the title of the person who negotiated it." Bills of exchange act, 1882, (45 & 46 Vict. c. 61, § 29.)

HOLDES. Sax. In Saxon law. A military commander. Spelman.

HOLDING. In English law. A piece of land held under a lease or similar tenancy for agricultural, pastoral, or similar purposes.

In Scotch law. The tenure or nature of the right given by the superior to the vassal. Bell.

HOLDING OVER. A holding beyond a term; a continuing in possession after the expiration of a term. The act of keeping possession of premises leased, after the expiration of the term of the lease, without the consent of the landlord; or of an office after the expiration of the incumbent's legal term.

HOLDING UP THE HAND. In criminal practice. A formality observed in the arraignment of prisoners. Held to be not absolutely necessary. 1 W. Bl. 3, 4.

HOLIDAY. A religious festival; a day set apart for commemorating some important event in history; a day of exemption from labor. Webster. A day upon which the usual operations of business are suspended and the courts closed, and, generally, no legal process is served.

HOLM. An island in a river or the sea. Spelman.

Plain grassy ground upon water sides or in the water. Blount. Low ground intersected with streams. Spelman.

HOLOGRAFO. In Spanish law. A holograph. An instrument (particularly a will) wholly in the handwriting of the person executing it; or which, to be valid, must be so written by his own hand.

HOLOGRAPH. A will or deed written entirely by the testator or grantor with his own hand.

HOLT. Sax. In old English law. A wood or grove. Spelman; Cowell; Co. Litt. 4*b*.

HOLY ORDERS. In ecclesiastical law. The orders of bishops, (including archbishops,) priests, and deacons in the Church of England. The Roman canonists had the orders of bishop, (in which the pope and archbishops were included,) priest, deacon, subdeacon, psalmist, acolyte, exorcist, reader, ostiarius. 3 Steph. Comm. 55, and note *a*.

HOMAGE. In feudal law. A service (or the ceremony of rendering it) which a tenant was bound to perform to his lord on receiving investiture of a fee, or succeeding to it as heir, in acknowledgment of the tenure. It is described by Littleton as the most honorable service of reverence that a free tenant might do to his lord. The ceremony was as follows: The tenant, being ungirt and with bare head, knelt before the lord, the latter sitting, and held his hands extended and joined between the hands of the lord, and said: "I become your man [*homo*] from this day forward, of life and limb and earthly honor, and to you will be faithful and loyal, and bear you faith, for the tenements that I claim to hold of you, saving the faith that I owe unto our sovereign lord the king, so help me God." The tenant then received a kiss from the lord. Homage could be done only to the lord himself. Litt. § 85; Glanv. lib. 9, c. 1; Bract. fols. 77*b*, 78-80; Wharton.

"Homage" is to be distinguished from "fealty," another incident of feudalism, and which consisted in the solemn oath of fidelity made by the vassal to the lord, whereas homage was merely an acknowledgment of tenure. If the homage was intended to include fealty, it was called "liege homage;" but otherwise it was called "simple homage." Brown.

HOMAGE ANCESTRAL. In feudal law. Homage was called by this name where a man and his ancestors had immemorially held of another and his ancestors by the service of homage, which bound the lord to warrant the title, and also to hold the tenant clear of all services to superior lords. If the tenant aliened in fee, his alienee was a tenant by homage, but not by homage ancestral. Litt. § 143; 2 Bl. Comm. 300.

HOMAGE JURY. A jury in a court-baron, consisting of tenants that do homage, who are to inquire and make presentments of the death of tenants, surrenders, admittances, and the like.

HOMAGE LIEGE. That kind of homage which was due to the sovereign alone as supreme lord, and which was done without any saving or exception of the rights of other lords. Spelman.

HOMAGER. One who does or is bound to do homage. Cowell.

HOMAGIO RESPECTUANDO. A writ to the escheator commanding him to deliver seisin of lands to the heir of the king's tenant, notwithstanding his homage not done. Fitzh. Nat. Brev. 269.

HOMAGIUM. Homage, (*q. v.*)

HOMAGIUM LIGIUM. Liege homage; that kind of homage which was due to the sovereign alone as supreme lord, and which was done without any saving or exception of the rights of other lords. Spelman. So called from *ligando*, (binding,) because it could not be renounced like other kinds of homage.

Homagium, non per procuratores nec per literas fieri potuit, sed in propria persona tam domini quam tenentis capi debet et fieri. Co. Litt. 68. Homage cannot be done by proxy, nor by letters, but must be paid and received in the proper person, as well of the lord as the tenant.

HOMAGIUM PLANUM. In feudal law. Plain homage; a species of homage which bound him who did it to nothing more than fidelity, without any obligation either of military service or attendance in the courts of his superior. 1 Robertson's Car. V., Appendix, note 8.

HOMAGIUM REDDERE. To renounce homage. This was when a vassal made a solemn declaration of disowning and defying his lord; for which there was a set form and method prescribed by the feudal laws. Bract. l. 2, c. 35, § 35.

HOMAGIUM SIMPLEX. In feudal law. Simple homage; that kind of homage which was merely an acknowledgment of tenure, with a saving of the rights of other lords. Harg. Co. Litt. note 18, lib. 2.

HOMBRE BUENO. In Spanish law. The judge of a district. Also an arbitrator chosen by the parties to a suit. Also a man in good standing; one who is competent to testify in a suit.

HOME. When a person voluntarily takes up his abode in a given place, with intention to remain permanently, or for an indefinite period of time, or without any present intention to remove therefrom, such place of abode becomes his residence or *home*. 43 Me. 418. This word has not the same technical meaning as "domicile." 19 Me. 301.

HOME, or HOMME. L. Fr. Man; a man.

Home ne sera puny pur suer des briefes en court le roy, soit il a droit ou a tort. A man shall not be punished for suing out writs in the king's court, whether he be right or wrong. 2 Inst. 228.

HOME OFFICE. The department of state through which the English sovereign administers most of the internal affairs of the kingdom, especially the police, and communicates with the judicial functionaries.

HOME PORT. A port in a state in which the owner of a vessel resides.

HOMESOKEN, HOMSOKEN. See HAMESOKEN.

HOMESTALL. A mansion-house.

HOMESTEAD. The home place; the place where the home is. It is the home, the house and the adjoining land, where the head of the family dwells; the home farm. 36 N. H. 166.

The fixed residence of the head of a family, with the land and buildings surrounding the main house.

HOMESTEAD CORPORATIONS. Corporations organized for the purpose of acquiring lands in large tracts, paying off incumbrances thereon, improving and subdividing them into homestead lots or parcels, and distributing them among the shareholders, and for the accumulation of a fund for such purposes, are known as "homestead corporations," and must not have a corporate existence for a longer period than ten years. Civil Code Cal. § 557.

HOMESTEAD EXEMPTION LAWS. Laws passed in most of the states allowing a householder or head of a family to designate a house and land as his homestead, and exempting the same homestead from execution for his general debts.

HOMICIDAL. Pertaining to homicide; relating to homicide; impelling to homicide; as a homicidal mania.

HOMICIDE. The killing any human creature. 4 Bl. Comm. 177. The act of a human being in killing another human being.

"Homicide," as a term, does not import crime. It includes crimes, such, for instance, as murder and manslaughter. But a homicide may be innocent; may even be in the performance of a duty. The execution of the sentence of death upon a criminal by the officer of the law is a homicide. The term "homicide" embraces all man-killing. 1 Park. Crim. R. 182, 186.

Justifiable homicide is such as is committed intentionally, but without any evil design, and under such circumstances of necessity or duty as render the act proper, and relieve the party from any shadow of blame; as where a sheriff lawfully executes a sentence of death upon a malefactor, or where the killing takes place in the endeavor to prevent the commission of a felony which could not be otherwise avoided.

Excusable homicide is such as is committed through misadventure or accident, without any willful or malicious intention; or by necessity, in self-defense.

Felonious homicide (which may be either murder or manslaughter) is that committed without justification or excuse in law, *i. e.*, with malice and intention, and under such circumstances as to make it punishable.

HOMICIDE PER INFORTUNIUM. In criminal law. Homicide by misfortune, or accidental homicide; as where a man doing a lawful act, without any intention of hurt, unfortunately kills another; a species of excusable homicide. 4 Bl. Comm. 182; 4 Steph. Comm. 101.

HOMICIDE PER MISADVENTURE. See HOMICIDE PER INFORTUNIUM.

HOMICIDE SE DEFENDENDO. In criminal law. Homicide in self-defense; the killing of a person in self-defense upon a sudden affray, where the slayer had no other possible (or, at least, probable) means of escaping from his assailant. 4 Bl. Comm. 183–186; 4 Steph. Comm. 103–105. A species of excusable homicide. Id.; 1 Russ. Crimes, 660.

HOMICIDIUM. Lat. Homicide, (*q. v.*) *Homicidium ex justitia*, homicide in the administration of justice, or in the execution of the sentence of the law.

Homicidium ex necessitate, homicide from inevitable necessity, as for the protection of one's person or property.

Homicidium ex casu, homicide by accident.

Homicidium ex voluntate, voluntary or willful homicide. Bract. fols. 120*b*, 121.

HOMINATIO. The mustering of men; the doing of homage.

HOMINE CAPTO IN WITHERNAMIUM. A writ to take him that had taken any bond man or woman, and led him or her out of the country, so that he or she could not be replevied according to law. Reg. Orig. 79.

HOMINE ELIGENDO. In old English law. A writ directed to a corporation, requiring the members to make choice of a man to keep one part of the seal appointed for statutes merchant, when a former is dead, according to the statute of Acton Burnell. Reg. Orig. 178; Wharton.

HOMINE REPLEGIANDO. In English law. A writ which lay to replevy a man out of prison, or out of the custody of any private person, in the same manner that chattels taken in distress may be replevied. Brown.

HOMINES. Lat. In feudal law. Men; feudatory tenants who claimed a privilege of having their causes, etc., tried only in their lord's court. Paroch. Antiq. 15.

HOMINES LIGII. In feudal law. Liege men; feudal tenants or vassals, especially those who held immediately of the sovereign. 1 Bl. Comm. 367.

Hominum causa jus constitutum est. Law is established for the benefit of man.

HOMIPLAGIUM. In old English law. The maiming of a man. Blount.

HOMME. Fr. Man; a man. This term is defined by the Civil Code of Louisiana to include a woman. Article 3522, nn. 1, 2.

HOMMES DE FIEF. Fr. In feudal law. Men of the fief; feudal tenants; the peers in the lords' courts. Montesq., Esprit des Lois, liv. 28, c. 27.

HOMMES FEODAUX. Fr. In feudal law. Feudal tenants; the same with *hommes de fief*, (*q. v.*) Montesq., Esprit des Lois, liv. 28, c. 36.

HOMO. Lat. A man; a human being, male or female; a vassal, or feudal tenant; a retainer, dependent, or servant.

HOMO CHARTULARIUS. A slave manumitted by charter.

HOMO COMMENDATUS. In feudal law. One who surrendered himself into the power of another for the sake of protection or support. See COMMENDATION.

HOMO ECCLESIASTICUS. A church vassal; one who was bound to serve a church, especially to do service of an agricultural character. Spelman.

HOMO EXERCITALIS. A man of the army, (*exercitus;*) a soldier.

HOMO FEODALIS. A vassal or tenant; one who held a fee, (*feodum,*) or part of a fee. Spelman.

HOMO FISCALIS, or FISCALINUS. A servant or vassal belonging to the treasury or *fiscus.*

HOMO FRANCUS. In old English law. A freeman. A Frenchman.

HOMO INGENUUS. A free man. A free and lawful man. A yeoman.

HOMO LIBER. A freeman.

HOMO LIGIUS. A liege man; a subject; a king's vassal. The vassal of a subject.

HOMO NOVUS. In feudal law. A new tenant or vassal; one who was invested with a new fee. Spelman.

HOMO PERTINENS. In feudal law. A feudal bondman or vassal; one who *belonged* to the soil, (*qui glebæ adscribitur.*)

Homo potest esse habilis et inhabilis diversis temporibus. 5 Coke, 98. A man may be capable and incapable at different times.

HOMO REGIUS. A king's vassal.

HOMO ROMANUS. A Roman. An appellation given to the old inhabitants of Gaul and other Roman provinces, and retained in the laws of the barbarous nations. Spelman.

HOMO TRIUM LITTERARUM. A man of the three letters; that is, the three letters, "f," "u," "r;" the Latin word *fur* meaning "thief."

Homo vocabulum est naturæ; persona juris civilis. Man (*homo*) is a term of nature; person (*persona*) of civil law. Calvin.

HOMOLOGACION. In Spanish law. The tacit consent and approval inferred by law from the omission of the parties, for the space of ten days, to complain of the sentences of arbitrators, appointment of syndics, or assignees of insolvents, settlements of successions, etc. Also the approval given by the judge of certain acts and agreements for the purpose of rendering them more binding and executory. Escriche.

HOMOLOGARE. In the civil law. To confirm or approve; to consent or assent; to confess. Calvin.

HOMOLOGATE. In modern civil law. To approve; to confirm; as a court *homologates* a proceeding. See HOMOLOGATION. Literally, to use the *same words* with another; to say the like. 9 Mart. (La.) 324. To assent to what another says or writes.

HOMOLOGATION. In the civil law. Approbation; confirmation by a court of justice; a judgment which orders the execution of some act. Merl. Répert. The term is also used in Louisiana.

In English law. An estoppel *in pais.* L. R. 3 App. Cas. 1026.

In Scotch law. An act by which a person approves of a deed, the effect of which is to render that deed, though in itself defective, binding upon the person by whom it is homologated. Bell. Confirmation of a voidable deed.

HOMONYMIÆ. A term applied in the civil law to cases where a law was repeated, or laid down in the same terms or to the same effect, more than once. Cases of iteration and repetition. 2 Kent, Comm. 489, note.

HONDHABEND. Sax. Having in hand. See HANDHABEND.

HONESTE VIVERE. Lat. To live honorably, creditably, or virtuously. One of the three general precepts to which Justinian reduced the whole doctrine of the law, (Inst. 1, 1, 3; Bract. fols. 3, 3b,) the others being *alterum non lædere,* (not to injure others,) and *suum cuique tribuere,* (to render to every man his due.)

HONESTUS. Of good character or standing. *Coram duobus vel pluribus viris legalibus et honestis,* before two or more lawful and good men. Bract. fol. 61.

HONOR, *v.* To accept a bill of exchange, or to pay a note, check, or accepted bill, at maturity and according to its tenor.

HONOR, *n.* In English law. A seigniory of several manors held under one baron or lord paramount. Also those dignities or privileges, degrees of nobility, knighthood, and other titles, which flow from the crown as the fountain of honor. Wharton.

In American law. The customary title of courtesy given to judges of the higher courts, and occasionally to some other officers; as "his honor," "your honor."

HONOR COURTS. Tribunals held within honors or seigniories.

HONORABLE. A title of courtesy given in England to the younger children of earls, and the children of viscounts and barons; and, collectively, to the house of commons. In America, the word is used as a title of courtesy for various classes of officials, but without any clear lines of distinction.

HONORARIUM. In the civil law. An honorary or free gift; a gratuitous payment, as distinguished from hire or compensation for service; a lawyer's or counsellor's fee. Dig. 50, 13, 1, 10–12.

An *honorarium* is a voluntary donation, in consideration of services which admit of no compensation in money; in particular, to advocates at law, deemed to practice for honor or influence, and not for fees. 14 Ga. 89.

HONORARIUM JUS. In Roman law. The law of the prætors and the edicts of the ædiles.

HONORARY CANONS. Those without emolument. 3 & 4 Vict. c. 113, § 23.

HONORARY FEUDS. Titles of nobility, descendible to the eldest son, in exclusion of all the rest. 2 Bl. Comm. 56.

HONORARY SERVICES. In feudal law. Special services to be rendered to the king in person, characteristic of the tenure by grand serjeanty; such as to carry his banner, his sword, or the like, or to be his butler, champion, or other officer, at his coronation. Litt. § 153; 2 Bl. Comm. 73.

HONORARY TRUSTEES. Trustees to preserve contingent remainders, so called because they are bound, in honor only, to decide on the most proper and prudential course. Lewin, Trusts, 408.

HONORIS RESPECTUM. By reason of honor or privilege. See CHALLENGE.

HONTFONGENETHEF. In Saxon law. A thief taken with *hondhabend; i. e.,* having the thing stolen in his hand. Cowell.

HONY. L. Fr. Shame; evil; disgrace. *Hony soit qui mal y pense*, evil be to him who evil thinks.

HOO. A hill. Co. Litt. 5*b*.

HOOKLAND. Land plowed and sown every year.

HOPCON. A valley. Cowell.

HOPE. In old English law. A valley. Co. Litt. 4*b*.

HOPPO. A Chinese term for a collector; an overseer of commerce.

HORA AURORÆ. In old English law. The morning bell, as *ignitegium* or *coverfeu* (curfew) was the evening bell.

Hora non est multum de substantia negotii, licet in appello de ea aliquando fiat mentio. The hour is not of much consequence as to the substance of business, although in appeal it is sometimes mentioned. 1 Bulst. 82.

HORÆ JURIDICÆ, or JUDICIÆ. Hours during which the judges sat in court to attend to judicial business.

HORCA. In Spanish law. A gallows; the punishment of hanging. White, New Recop. b. 2, tit. 19, c. 4, § 1.

HORDA. In old records. A cow in calf.

HORDERA. A treasurer. Du Cange.

HORDERIUM. In old English law. A hoard; a treasure, or repository. Cowell.

HORDEUM. In old records. Barley. *Hordeum palmale*, beer barley, as distinguished from common barley, which was called "*hordeum quadragesimale.*" Blount.

HORN. In old Scotch practice. A kind of trumpet used in denouncing contumacious persons rebels and outlaws, which was done with three blasts of the horn by the king's sergeant. This was called "putting to the horn;" and the party so denounced was said to be "at the horn." Bell.

HORN-BOOK. A primer; a book explaining the rudiments of any science or branch of knowledge. The phrase "horn-book law" is a colloquial designation of the rudiments or most familiar principles of law.

HORN TENURE. In old English law. Tenure by cornage; that is, by the service of winding a horn when the Scots or other enemies entered the land, in order to warn the king's subjects. This was a species of grand serjeanty. Litt. § 156; 2 Bl. Comm. 74.

HORN WITH HORN, or HORN UNDER HORN. The promiscuous feeding of bulls and cows or all horned beasts that are allowed to run together upon the same common. Spelman.

HORNGELD. Sax. In old English law. A tax within a forest, paid for horned beasts. Cowell; Blount.

HORNING. In Scotch law. "Letters of horning" is the name given to a judicial process issuing on the decree of a court, by which the debtor is summoned to perform his obligation in terms of the decree, the consequence of his failure to do so being liability to arrest and imprisonment. It was anciently the custom to proclaim a debtor who had failed to obey such process a rebel or outlaw, which was done by three blasts of the horn by the king's sergeant in a public place. This was called "putting to the horn," whence the name.

HORREUM. Lat. A place for keeping grain; a granary. A place for keeping fruits, wines, and goods generally; a store-house. Calvin.; Bract. fol. 48.

HORS. L. Fr. Out; out of; without.

HORS DE SON FEE. L. Fr. Out of his fee. In old pleading, this was the name of a plea in an action for rent or services, by which the defendant alleged that the land in question was out of the compass of the plaintiff's fee.

HORS PRIS. L. Fr. Except. Literally translated by the Scotch "out taken."

HORS WEALH. In old English law. The wealh, or Briton who had care of the king's horses.

HORS WEARD. In old English law. A service or *corvée*, consisting in watching the horses of the lord. Anc. Inst. Eng.

HORSE. Until a horse has attained the age of four years, he is called a colt. 1 Russ. & R. 416.

The word "horse" is used in a *quasi* generic sense, to include every description of the male, in contradistinction to the female or mare, whether stallion or gelding. 38 Tex. 555.

HORSE GUARDS. The directing power of the military forces of the kingdom of Great Britain. The commander in chief, or general commanding the forces, is at the head of this department. It is subordinate to the war office, but the relations between them are complicated. Wharton.

HORTUS. Lat. In the civil law. A garden. Dig. 32, 91, 5.

HOSPES. Lat. A guest. 8 Coke, 32.

HOSPES GENERALIS. A great chamberlain.

HOSPITAL. An institution for the reception and care of sick, wounded, infirm, or aged persons: generally incorporated, and then of the class of corporations called "eleemosynary" or "charitable."

HOSPITALLERS. The knights of a religious order, so called because they built a hospital at Jerusalem, wherein pilgrims were received. All their lands and goods in England were given to the sovereign by 32 Hen. VIII. c. 24.

HOSPITATOR. A host or entertainer. *Hospitator communis.* An innkeeper. 8 Coke, 32.

Hospitator magnus. The marshal of a camp.

HOSPITIA. Inns. *Hospitia communia,* common inns. Reg. Orig. 105. *Hospitia curiæ,* inns of court. *Hospitia cancellariæ,* inns of chancery. Crabb, Eng. Law, 428, 429; 4 Reeve, Eng. Law, 120.

HOSPITICIDE. One that kills his guest or host.

HOSPITIUM. An inn; a household.

HOSPODAR. A Turkish governor in Moldavia or Wallachia.

HOST. L. Fr. An army. Britt. c. 22. A military expedition; war. Kelham.

HOSTAGE. A person who is given into the possession of the enemy, in a public war, his freedom (or life) to stand as security for the performance of some contract or promise made by the belligerent power giving the hostage with the other.

HOSTELAGIUM. In old records. A right to receive lodging and entertainment, anciently reserved by lords in the houses of their tenants. Cowell.

HOSTELER. An innkeeper. Now applied, under the form "ostler," to those who look to a guest's horses. Cowell.

HOSTES. Enemies. *Hostes humani generis,* enemies of the human race; *i. e.,* pirates.

Hostes sunt qui nobis vel quibus nos bellum decernimus; cæteri proditores vel prædones sunt. 7 Coke, 24. Enemies are those with whom we declare war, or who declare it against us; all others are traitors or pirates.

HOSTIA. In old records. The host-bread, or consecrated wafer, in the eucharist. Cowell.

HOSTICIDE. One who kills an enemy.

HOSTILARIA, HOSPITALARIA. A place or room in religious houses used for the reception of guests and strangers.

HOSTILE. Having the character of an enemy; standing in the relation of an enemy. See 1 Kent, Comm. c. 4.

HOSTILE EMBARGO. One laid upon the vessels of an actual or prospective enemy.

HOSTILE WITNESS. A witness who manifests so much hostility or prejudice under examination in chief that the party who has called him, or his representative, is allowed to cross-examine him, *i. e.,* to treat him as though he had been called by the opposite party. Wharton.

HOSTILITY. In the law of nations. A state of open war. "At the breaking out of hostility." 1 Kent, Comm. 60.

An act of open war. "When *hostilities* have commenced." Id. 56.

A hostile character. "Hostility may attach only to the person." Id.

HOT-WATER ORDEAL. In old English law. This was a test, in cases of accusation, by hot water; the party accused and suspected being appointed by the judge to put his arms up to the elbows in seething hot water, which, after sundry prayers and invocations, he did, and was, by the effect which followed, judged guilty or innocent. Wharton.

HOTCHPOT. The blending and mixing property belonging to different persons, in order to divide it equally. 2 Bl. Comm. 190.

Anciently applied to the mixing and blending of lands given to one daughter in frank marriage, with those descending to her and her sisters in fee-simple, for the purpose of dividing the whole equally among them; without which the daughter who held in frank marriage could have no share in the lands in fee-simple. Litt. §§ 267, 268; Co. Litt. 177*a;* 2 Bl. Comm. 190.

Hotchpot, or the *putting in hotchpot,* is applied in modern law to the throwing the amount of an advancement made to a particular child, in real or personal estate, into the common stock, for the purpose of a more equal division, or of equalizing the shares of all the children. 2 Kent, Comm. 421, 422. This answers to or resembles the *collatio bonorum*, or *collation* of the civil law.

HOTEL. An inn; a public house or tavern; a house for entertaining strangers or travelers. 54 Barb. 316; 2 Daly, 15; 46 Mo. 594.

HOUR. The twenty-fourth part of a natural day; sixty minutes of time.

HOUR OF CAUSE. In Scotch practice. The hour when a court is met. 3 How. State Tr. 603.

HOUSE. 1. A dwelling; a building designed for the habitation and residence of men.

"House" means, presumptively, a dwelling-house; a building divided into floors and apartments, with four walls, a roof, and doors and chimneys; but it does not necessarily mean precisely this. 14 Mees. & W. 181; 7 Man. & G. 122.

"House" is not synonymous with "dwelling-house." While the former is used in a broader and more comprehensive sense than the latter, it has a narrower and more restricted meaning than the word "building." 46 N. H. 61.

In the devise of a house, the word "house" is synonymous with "messuage," and conveys all that comes within the curtilage. 4 Pa. St. 93.

2. A legislative assembly, or (where the bicameral system obtains) one of the two branches of the legislature; as the "house of lords," "house of representatives." Also a quorum of a legislative body. See 2 Mich. 287.

3. The name "house" is also given to some collections of men other than legislative bodies, to some public institutions, and (colloquially) to mercantile firms or joint-stock companies.

HOUSE-BOTE. A species of estovers, belonging to a tenant for life or years, consisting in the right to take from the woods of the lessor or owner such timber as may be necessary for making repairs upon the house. See Co. Litt. 41*b*.

HOUSE-BURNING. See ARSON.

HOUSE-DUTY. A tax on inhabited houses imposed by 14 & 15 Vict. c. 36, in lieu of window-duty, which was abolished.

HOUSE OF COMMONS. One of the constituent houses of the British parliament, composed of representatives of the counties, cities, and boroughs.

HOUSE OF CORRECTION. A reformatory. A place for the imprisonment of juvenile offenders, or those who have committed crimes of lesser magnitude.

HOUSE OF ILL FAME. A bawdy-house; a brothel; a dwelling allowed by its chief occupant to be used as a resort of persons desiring unlawful sexual intercourse. 33 Conn. 91.

HOUSE OF LORDS. The upper chamber of the British parliament. It comprises the archbishops and bishops, (called "Lords Spiritual,") the English peers sitting by virtue of hereditary right, sixteen Scotch peers elected to represent the Scotch peerage under the act of union, and twenty-eight Irish peers elected under similar provisions. The house of lords, as a judicial body, has ultimate appellate jurisdiction, and may sit as a court for the trial of impeachments.

HOUSE OF REFUGE. A prison for juvenile delinquents. A house of correction or reformatory.

HOUSE OF REPRESENTATIVES. The name of the body forming the more popular and numerous branch of the congress of the United States; also of the similar branch in many of the state legislatures.

HOUSEAGE. A fee paid for housing goods by a carrier, or at a wharf, etc.

HOUSEBREAKING. In criminal law. Breaking and entering a dwelling-house with intent to commit any felony therein. If done by night, it comes under the definition of "burglary."

HOUSEHOLD. A family living together. 18 Johns. 400, 402. Those who dwell under the same roof and compose a family. Webster. A man's family living together constitutes his household, though he may have gone to another state.

Belonging to the house and family; domestic. Webster.

HOUSEHOLD FURNITURE. This term, in a will, includes all personal chattels that may contribute to the use or convenience of the householder, or the ornament of the house; as plate, linen, china, both useful and ornamental, and pictures. But goods in trade, books, and wines will not pass by a bequest of household furniture. 1 Rop. Leg. 203.

HOUSEHOLD GOODS. These words, in a will, include everything of a permanent nature (*i. e.*, articles of household which are not consumed in their enjoyment) that are used in or purchased or otherwise acquired by a testator for his house. 1 Rop. Leg. 191.

HOUSEHOLD STUFF. This phrase, in a will, includes everything which may be used for the convenience of the house, as tables, chairs, bedding, and the like. But apparel, books, weapons, tools for artificers, cattle, victuals, and choses in action will not pass by those words, unless the context of the will clearly show a contrary intention. 1 Rop. Leg. 206.

HOUSEHOLDER. The occupier of a house. Brande. More correctly, one who keeps house with his family; the head or master of a family. Webster; 18 Johns. 302. One who has a household; the head of a household.

HOUSEKEEPER. One who is in actual possession of and who occupies a house, as distinguished from a "boarder," "lodger," or "guest."

HOVEL. A place used by husbandmen to set their plows, carts, and other farming utensils out of the rain and sun. A shed; a cottage; a mean house.

HOWE. In old English law. A hill. Co. Litt. 5*b*.

HOY. A small coasting vessel, usually sloop-rigged, used in conveying passengers and goods from place to place, or as a tender to larger vessels in port. Webster.

HOYMAN. The master or captain of a hoy.

HUCUSQUE. In old pleading. Hitherto. 2 Mod. 24.

HUDE-GELD. In old English law. An acquittance for an assault upon a trespassing servant. Supposed to be a mistake or misprint in Fleta for "*hinegeld.*" Fleta, lib. 1, c. 47, § 20. Also the price of one's skin, or the money paid by a servant to save himself from a whipping. Du Cange.

HUE AND CRY. In old English law. A loud outcry with which felons (such as robbers, burglars, and murderers) were anciently pursued, and which all who heard it were bound to take up, and join in the pursuit, until the malefactor was taken. Bract. fols. 115*b*, 124; 4 Bl. Comm. 293.

A written proclamation issued on the escape of a felon from prison, requiring all officers and people to assist in retaking him. 3 How. State Tr. 386.

HUEBRAS. In Spanish law. A measure of land equal to as much as a yoke of oxen can plow in one day. 2 White, Recop. (38,) 49; 12 Pet. 443.

HUISSERIUM. A ship used to transport horses. Also termed "*uffer.*"

HUISSIERS. In French law. Marshals; ushers; process-servers; sheriffs' officers. Ministerial officers attached to the courts, to effect legal service of process required by law in actions, to issue executions, etc., and to maintain order during the sitting of the courts.

HULKA. In old records. A hulk or small vessel. Cowell.

HULLUS. In old records. A hill. 2 Mon. Angl. 292; Cowell.

HUMAGIUM. A moist place. Mon. Angl.

HUNDRED. Under the Saxon organization of England, each county or shire comprised an indefinite number of *hundreds*, each hundred containing ten *tithings*, or groups of ten families of freeholders or frank-pledges. The hundred was governed by a high constable, and had its own court; but its most remarkable feature was the corporate responsibility of the whole for the crimes or defaults of the individual members. The introduction of this plan of organization into England is commonly ascribed to Alfred, but the idea, as well of the collective liability as of the division, was probably known to the ancient German peoples, as we find the same thing established in the Frankish kingdom under Clothaire, and in Denmark. See 1 Bl. Comm. 115; 4 Bl. Comm. 411.

HUNDRED COURT. In English law. A larger court-baron, being held for all the inhabitants of a particular *hundred*, instead of a manor. The free suitors are the judges, and the steward the registrar, as in the case of a court-baron. It is not a court of record, and resembles a court-baron in all respects except that in point of territory it is of greater jurisdiction. These courts have long since fallen into desuetude. 3 Bl. Comm. 34, 35; 3 Steph. Comm. 394, 395.

HUNDRED GEMOTE. Among the Saxons, a meeting or court of the freeholders of a hundred, which assembled, originally, twelve times a year, and possessed civil and criminal jurisdiction and ecclesiastical powers. 1 Reeve, Eng. Law, 7.

HUNDRED LAGH. The law of the hundred, or hundred court; liability to attend the hundred court. Spelman.

HUNDRED PENNY. In old English law. A tax collected from the hundred, by the sheriff or lord of the hundred. Spel. voc. "*Hundredus.*"

HUNDRED SECTA. The performance of suit and service at the hundred court.

HUNDRED SETENA. In Saxon law. The dwellers or inhabitants of a hundred. Cowell; Blount. Spelman suggests the reading of *sceatena* from Sax. "*sceat,*" a tax.

HUNDRED-WEIGHT. A denomination of weight containing, according to the English system, 112 pounds; but in this country, generally, it consists of 100 pounds avoirdupois.

HUNDREDARIUS. In old English law. A hundredary or hundredor. A name given to the chief officer of a hundred, as well as to the freeholders who composed it. Spel. voc. "*Hundredus.*"

HUNDREDARY. The chief or presiding officer of a hundred.

HUNDREDES EARLDOR, or HUNDREDES MAN. The presiding officer in the hundred court. Anc. Inst. Eng.

HUNDREDORS. In English law. The inhabitants or freeholders of a hundred, anciently the suitors or judges of the hundred court. Persons impaneled or fit to be impaneled upon juries, dwelling within the hundred where the cause of action arose. Cromp. Jur. 217. It was formerly necessary to have some of these upon every panel of jurors. 3 Bl. Comm. 359, 360; 4 Steph. Comm. 370.

The term "hundredor" was also used to signify the officer who had the jurisdiction of a hundred, and held the hundred court, and sometimes the bailiff of a hundred. Termes de la Ley; Cowell.

HURDEREFERST. A domestic; one of a family.

HURDLE. In English criminal law. A kind of sledge, on which convicted felons were drawn to the place of execution.

HURST, HYRST, HERST, or HIRST. A wood or grove of trees. Co. Litt. 4*b*.

HURTARDUS, or HURTUS. A ram or wether.

HURTO. In Spanish law. Theft. White, New Recop. b. 2, tit. 20.

HUSBAND. A married man; one who has a lawful wife living. The correlative of "wife."

Etymologically, the word signified the "house bond;" the man who, according to Saxon ideas and institutions, held around him the family, for whom he was in law responsible.

HUSBAND AND WIFE. One of the great domestic relationships; being that of a man and woman lawfully joined in marriage, by which, at common law, the legal existence of a wife is incorporated with that of her husband.

HUSBAND LAND. In old Scotch law. A quantity of land containing commonly six acres. Skene.

HUSBAND OF A SHIP. See SHIP'S HUSBAND.

HUSBANDMAN. A farmer; a cultivator or tiller of the ground. The word "farmer" is colloquially used as synonymous with "husbandman," but originally meant a tenant who cultivates *leased* ground.

HUSBANDRIA. In old English law. Husbandry. Dyer, (Fr. Ed.) 35*b*.

HUSBANDRY. Agriculture; cultivation of the soil for food; farming, in the sense of operating land to raise provisions.

HUSBREC. In Saxon law. The crime of housebreaking or burglary. Crabb, Eng. Law, 59, 308.

HUSCARLE. In old English law. A house servant or domestic; a man of the household. Spelman.

A king's vassal, thane, or baron; an earl's man or vassal. A term of frequent occurrence in Domesday Book.

HUSFASTNE. He who holds house and land. Bract. l. 3, t. 2, c. 10.

HUSGABLUM. In old records. House rent; or a tax or tribute laid upon a house. Cowell; Blount.

HUSH-MONEY. A colloquial expression to designate a bribe to hinder information; pay to secure silence.

HUSTINGS. Council; court; tribunal. Apparently so called from being held within a building, at a time when other courts were held in the open air. It was a local court. The county court in the city of London bore this name. There were hustings at York,

Winchester, Lincoln, and in other places similar to the London hustings. Also the raised place from which candidates for seats in parliament address the constituency, on the occasion of their nomination. Wharton.

In Virginia, some of the local courts are called "hustings," as in the city of Richmond. 6 Grat. 696.

HUTESIUM ET CLAMOR. Hue and cry. See HUE AND CRY.

HUTILAN. Taxes. Mon. Angl. i. 586.

HWATA, HWATUNG. In old English law. Augury; divination.

HYBERNAGIUM. In old English law. The season for sowing winter grain, between Michaelmas and Christmas. The land on which such grain was sown. The grain itself; winter grain or winter corn. Cowell.

HYBRID. A mongrel; an animal formed of the union of different species, or different genera; also (metaphorically) a human being born of the union of persons of different races.

HYD. In old English law. Hide; skin. A measure of land, containing, according to some, a hundred acres, which quantity is also assigned to it in the *Dialogus de Scaccario*. It seems, however, that the hide varied in different parts of the kingdom.

HYDAGE. See HIDAGE.

HYDROMETER. An instrument for measuring the density of fluids. Being immersed in fluids, as in water, brine, beer, brandy, etc., it determines the proportion of their density, or their specific gravity, and thence their quality. See 3 Story, U. S. Laws, 1976.

HYEMS, HIEMS. Lat. In the civil law. Winter. Dig. 43, 20, 4, 34. Written, in some of the old books, "*yems*." Fleta, lib. 2, c. 73, §§ 16, 18.

HYPOBOLUM. In the civil law. The name of the bequest or legacy given by the husband to his wife, at his death, above her dowry.

HYPOTHEC. In Scotland, the term "hypothec" is used to signify the landlord's right which, independently of any stipulation, he has over the crop and stocking of his tenant. It gives a security to the landlord over the crop of each year for the rent of that year, and over the cattle and stocking on the farm for the current year's rent, which last continues for three months after the last conventional term for the payment of the rent. Bell.

HYPOTHECA. "Hypotheca" was a term of the Roman law, and denoted a pledge or mortgage. As distinguished from the term "*pignus*," in the same law, it denoted a mortgage, whether of lands or of goods, in which the subject in pledge remained in the possession of the mortgagor or debtor; whereas in the *pignus* the mortgagee or creditor was in the possession. Such an hypotheca might be either express or implied; express, where the parties upon the occasion of a loan entered into express agreement to that effect; or implied, as, *e. g.*, in the case of the stock and utensils of a farmer, which were subject to the landlord's right as a creditor for rent; whence the Scotch law of hypothec.

The word has suggested the term "hypothecate," as used in the mercantile and maritime law of England. Thus, under the factor's act, goods are frequently said to be "hypothecated;" and a captain is said to have a right to hypothecate his vessel for necessary repairs. Brown. See Mackeld. Rom. Law, §§ 334–359.

HYPOTHECARIA ACTIO. In the civil law. An hypothecary action; an action for the enforcement of an *hypotheca*, or right of mortgage; or to obtain the surrender of the thing mortgaged. Inst. 4, 6, 7; Mackeld. Rom. Law, § 356. Adopted in the Civil Code of Louisiana, under the name of "*l'action hypothècarie*," (translated, "action of mortgage.") Article 3361.

HYPOTHECARII CREDITORES. In the civil law. Hypothecary creditors; those who loaned money on the security of an *hypotheca*, (*q. v.*) Calvin.

HYPOTHECARY ACTION. The name of an action allowed under the civil law for the enforcement of the claims of a creditor by the contract of hypotheca.

HYPOTHECATE. To pledge a thing without delivering the possession of it to the pledgee. "The master, when abroad, and in the absence of the owner, may *hypothecate* the ship, freight, and cargo, to raise money requisite for the completion of the voyage." 3 Kent, Comm. 171.

HYPOTHECATION. A term borrowed from the civil law. In so far as it is naturalized in English and American law, it means a contract of mortgage or pledge in which the subject-matter is not delivered into the possession of the pledgee or pawnee; or, conversely, a conventional right existing in one person over specific property of another, which consists in the power to cause a sale of the same, though it be not in his possession, in order that a specific claim of the creditor may be satisfied out of the proceeds.

The term is frequently used in our text-books and reports, particularly upon the law of bottomry and maritime liens; thus a vessel is said to be hypothecated for the demand of one who has advanced money for supplies.

In the common law, there are but few, if any, cases of hypothecation, in the strict sense of the civil law; that is, a pledge without possession by the pledgee. The nearest approaches, perhaps, are cases of bottomry bonds and claims of materialmen, and of seamen for wages; but these are liens and privileges, rather than hypothecations. Story, Bailm. § 288.

"Hypothecation" is a term of the civil law, and is that kind of pledge in which the possession of the thing pledged remains with the debtor, (the obligation resting in mere contract without delivery;) and in this respect distinguished from "*pignus*," in which possession is delivered to the creditor or pawnee. 24 Ark. 27. See 2 Bell, Comm. 25.

HYPOTHECATION BOND. A bond given in the contract of bottomry or *respondentia*.

HYPOTHÈQUE. In French law. Hypothecation; a mortgage on real property; the right vested in a creditor by the assignment to him of real estate as security for the payment of his debt, whether or not it be accompanied by possession. See Civil Code La. art. 3360.

It corresponds to the mortgage of real property in English law, and is a real charge, following the property into whosesoever hands it comes. It may be *légale*, as in the case of the charge which the state has over the lands of its accountants, or which a married woman has over those of her husband; *judiciaire*, when it is the result of a judgment of a court of justice; and *conventionelle*, when it is the result of an agreement of the parties. Brown.

HYPOTHESIS. A supposition, assumption, or theory; a theory set up by the prosecution, on a criminal trial, or by the defense, as an explanation of the facts in evidence, and a ground for inferring guilt or innocence, as the case may be, or as indicating a probable or possible motive for the crime.

HYPOTHETICAL CASE. A combination of assumed or proved facts and circumstances, stated in such form as to constitute a coherent and specific situation or state of facts, upon which the opinion of an expert is asked, by way of evidence on a trial.

HYPOTHETICAL YEARLY TENANCY. The basis, in England, of rating lands and hereditaments to the poor-rate, and to other rates and taxes that are expressed to be leviable or assessable in like manner as the poor-rate.

HYRNES. In old English law. A parish.

HYSTEROPOTMOI. Those who, having been thought dead, had, after a long absence in foreign countries, returned safely home; or those who, having been thought dead in battle, had afterwards unexpectedly escaped from their enemies and returned home. These, among the Romans, were not permitted to enter their own houses at the door, but were received at a passage opened in the roof. Enc. Lond.

HYSTEROTOMY. The Cæsarian operation.

HYTHE. In English law. A port, wharf, or small haven to embark or land merchandise at. Cowell; Blount.

I.

I. The initial letter of the word "*Instituta,*" used by some civilians in citing the Institutes of Justinian. Tayl. Civil Law, 24.

I—CTUS. An abbreviation for "*jurisconsultus,*" one learned in the law; a jurisconsult.

I. E. An abbreviation for "*id est,*" that is; that is to say.

I O U. A memorandum of debt, consisting of these letters, ("I owe you,") a sum of money, and the debtor's signature, is termed an "I O U."

IBERNAGIUM. The season for sowing winter corn.

Ibi semper debet fieri triatio ubi juratores meliorem possunt habere notitiam. 7 Coke, 1*b*. A trial should always be had where the jurors can be the best informed.

IBIDEM. Lat. In the same place; in the same book; on the same page, etc. Abbreviated to "*ibid.*" or "*ib.*"

ICENI. The ancient name for the people of Suffolk, Norfolk, Cambridgeshire, and Huntingdonshire, in England.

ICONA. An image, figure, or representation of a thing. Du Cange.

ICTUS. In old English law. A stroke or blow from a club or stone; a bruise, contusion, or swelling produced by a blow from a club or stone, as distinguished from "*plaga,*" (a wound.) Fleta, lib. 1, c. 41, § 3.

ICTUS ORBIS. In medical jurisprudence. A maim, a bruise, or swelling; any hurt without cutting the skin.

When the skin is cut, the injury is called a "wound." Bract. lib. 2, tr. 2, cc. 5, 24.

Id certum est quod certum reddi potest. That is certain which can be made certain. 2 Bl. Comm. 143; 1 Bl. Comm. 78; 4 Kent, Comm. 462; Broom, Max. 624.

Id certum est quod certum reddi potest, sed id magis certum est quod de semetipso est certum. That is certain which can be made certain, but that is more certain which is certain of itself. 9 Coke, 47*a*.

ID EST. Lat. That is. Commonly abbreviated "*i. e.*"

Id perfectum est quod ex omnibus suis partibus constat. That is perfect which consists of all its parts. 9 Coke, 9.

Id possumus quod de jure possumus. Lane, 116. We may do only that which by law we are allowed to do.

Id quod est magis remotum, non trahit ad se quod est magis junctum, sed e contrario in omni casu. That which is more remote does not draw to itself that which is nearer, but the contrary in every case. Co. Litt. 164.

Id quod nostrum est sine facto nostro ad alium transferri non potest. That which is ours cannot be transferred to another without our act. Dig. 50, 17, 11.

Id solum nostrum quod debitis deductis nostrum est. That only is ours which remains to us after deduction of debts. Tray. Lat. Max. 227.

IDEM. Lat. The same. According to Lord Coke, "*idem*" has two significations, *sc., idem syllabis seu verbis,* (the same in syllables or words,) and *idem re et sensu,* (the same in substance and in sense.) 10 Coke, 124*a*.

In old practice. The said, or aforesaid; said, aforesaid. Distinguished from "*prædictus*" in old entries, though having the same general signification. Townsh. Pl. 15, 16.

Idem agens et patiens esse non potest. Jenk. Cent. 40. The same person cannot be both agent and patient; *i. e.*, the doer and person to whom the thing is done.

Idem est facere, et non prohibere cum possis; et qui non prohibit, cum prohibere possit, in culpâ est, (aut jubet.) 3 Inst. 158. To commit, and not to prohibit when in your power, is the same thing; and he who does not prohibit when he can prohibit is in fault, or does the same as ordering it to be done.

Idem est nihil dicere, et insufficienter dicere. It is the same thing to say nothing, and to say a thing insufficiently. 2 Inst. 178. To say a thing in an insufficient manner is the same as not to say it at all. Applied to the plea of a prisoner. Id.

Idem est non esse, et non apparere. It is the same thing not to be as not to appear. Jenk. Cent. 207. Not to appear is the same thing as not to be. Broom, Max. 165.

Idem est non probari et non esse; non deficit jus, sed probatio. What is not proved and what does not exist are the same; it is not a defect of the law, but of proof.

Idem est scire aut scire debere aut potuisse. To be bound to know or to be able to know is the same as to know.

IDEM PER IDEM. The same for the same. An illustration of a kind that really adds no additional element to the consideration of the question.

Idem semper antecedenti proximo refertur. Co. Litt. 685. "The same" is always referred to its next antecedent.

IDEM SONANS. Sounding the same or alike; having the same sound. A term applied to names which are substantially the same, though slightly varied in the spelling, as "Lawr*e*nce" and "Lawr*a*nce," and the like. 1 Cromp. & M. 806; 3 Chit. Gen. Pr. 171.

IDENTIFICATION. Proof of identity; the proving that a person, subject, or article before the court is the very same that he or it is alleged, charged, or reputed to be; as where a witness recognizes the prisoner at the bar as the same person whom he saw committing the crime; or where handwriting, stolen goods, counterfeit coin, etc., are recognized as the same which once passed under the observation of the person identifying them.

Identitas vera colligitur ex multitudine signorum. True identity is collected from a multitude of signs. Bac. Max.

IDENTITATE NOMINIS. In English law. An ancient writ (now obsolete) which lay for one taken and arrested in any personal action, and committed to prison, by mistake for another man of the same name. Fitzh. Nat. Brev. 267.

IDENTITY. In the law of evidence. Sameness; the fact that a subject, person, or thing before a court is *the same* as it is represented, claimed, or charged to be. See Burrill, Circ. Ev. 382, 453, 631, 644.

IDEO. Lat. Therefore. Calvin.

IDEO CONSIDERATUM EST. Therefore it is considered. These were the words used at the beginning of the entry of judgment in an action, when the forms were in Latin. They are also used as a name for that portion of the record.

IDES. A division of time among the Romans. In March, May, July, and October, the Ides were on the 15th of the month; in the remaining months, on the 13th. This method of reckoning is still retained in the chancery of Rome, and in the calendar of the breviary. Wharton.

IDIOCHIRA. Græco-Lat. In the civil law. An instrument privately executed, as distinguished from such as were executed before a public officer. Cod. 8, 18, 11; Calvin.

IDIOCY. In medical jurisprudence. That condition of mind in which the reflective, and all or a part of the affective, powers are either entirely wanting, or are manifested to the slightest possible extent. Ray, Insan. § 58; Whart. & S. Med. Jur. § 222.

There is a distinction between "idiocy" and "*dementia;*" the first being due to the fact that there are original structural defects in the brain; the second resulting from the supervention of organic changes in a brain originally of normal power. Ham. Nervous System, 338.

Idiocy is that condition in which the human creature has never had, from birth, any, the least, glimmering of reason; and is utterly destitute of all those intellectual faculties by which man, in general, is so eminently and peculiarly distinguished. It is not the condition of a deranged mind, but that of a total absence of all mind. Hence this state of fatuity can rarely ever be mistaken by any, the most superficial, observer. The medical profession seem to regard it as a natural defect, not as a disease in itself, or as the result of any disorder. In law, it is also considered as a defect, and as a permanent and hopeless incapacity. 1 Bland. Ch. 386.

IDIOT. A person who has been without understanding from his nativity, and whom the law, therefore, presumes never likely to attain any. Shelf. Lun. 2. See IDIOCY.

IDIOTA. In the civil law. An unlearned, illiterate, or simple person. Calvin. A private man; one not in office.

In common law. An idiot or fool.

IDIOTA INQUIRENDO, WRIT DE. This is the name of an old writ which directs the sheriff to inquire whether a man be an idiot or not. The inquisition is to be made by a jury of twelve men. Fitzh. Nat. Brev.

232. And, if the man were found an idiot, the profits of his lands and the custody of his person might be granted by the king to any subject who had interest enough to obtain them. 1 Bl. Comm. 303.

IDONEUM SE FACERE; IDONEARE SE. To purge one's self by oath of a crime of which one is accused.

IDONEUS. Lat. In the civil and common law. Sufficient; competent; fit or proper; responsible; unimpeachable. *Idoneus homo*, a responsible or solvent person; a good and lawful man. Sufficient; adequate; satisfactory. *Idonea cautio*, sufficient security.

IDONIETAS. In old English law. Ability or fitness, (of a parson.) Artic. Cleri, c. 13.

IF. In deeds and wills, this word, as a rule, implies a condition precedent, unless it be controlled by other words. 2 Crabb, Real Prop. p. 309, § 2152; 77 N. C. 431.

IFUNGIA. The finest white bread, formerly called "cocked bread." Blount.

IGLISE. L. Fr. A church. Kelham. Another form of "*eglise.*"

IGNIS JUDICIUM. The old judicial trial by fire. Blount.

IGNITEGIUM. In old English law. The curfew, or evening bell. Cowell. See CURFEW.

IGNOMINY. Public disgrace; infamy; reproach; dishonor. Ignominy is the opposite of esteem. Wolff, § 145. See 38 Iowa, 220.

IGNORAMUS. Lat. "We are ignorant;" "We ignore it." Formerly the grand jury used to write this word on bills of indictment when, after having heard the evidence, they thought the accusation against the prisoner was groundless, intimating that, though the facts might possibly be true, the truth did not appear to them; but now they usually write in English the words "Not a true bill," or "Not found," if that is their verdict; but they are still said to *ignore* the bill. Brown.

IGNORANCE. The want or absence of knowledge.

Ignorance *of law* is want of knowledge or acquaintance with the laws of the land in so far as they apply to the act, relation, duty, or matter under consideration. Ignorance *of fact* is want of knowledge of some fact or facts constituting or relating to the subject-matter in hand.

Ignorance is not a state of the mind in the sense in which sanity and insanity are. When the mind is ignorant of a fact, its condition still remains sound; the power of thinking, of judging, of willing, is just as complete before communication of the fact as after; the essence or texture, so to speak, of the mind, is not, as in the case of insanity, affected or impaired. Ignorance of a particular fact consists in this: that the mind, although sound and capable of healthy action, has never acted upon the fact in question, because the subject has never been brought to the notice of the perceptive faculties. 28 N. J. Law, 274.

"Ignorance" and "error" are not convertible terms. The former is a lack of information or absence of knowledge; the latter, a misapprehension or confusion of information, or a mistaken supposition of the possession of knowledge. Error as to a fact may imply ignorance of the truth; but ignorance does not necessarily imply error.

Essential ignorance is ignorance in relation to some essential circumstance so intimately connected with the matter in question, and which so influences the parties, that it induces them to act in the business. Poth. Vente, nn. 3, 4; 2 Kent, Comm. 367.

Non-essential or accidental ignorance is that which has not of itself any necessary connection with the business in question, and which is not the true consideration for entering into the contract.

Involuntary ignorance is that which does not proceed from choice, and which cannot be overcome by the use of any means of knowledge known to a person and within his power; as the ignorance of a law which has not yet been promulgated.

Voluntary ignorance exists when a party might, by taking reasonable pains, have acquired the necessary knowledge. For example, every man might acquire a knowledge of the laws which have been promulgated. Doct. & Stud. 1, 46; Plowd. 343.

IGNORANTIA. Ignorance; want of knowledge. Distinguished from mistake, (error,) or wrong conception. Mackeld, Rom. Law, § 178; Dig. 22, 6. Divided by Lord Coke into *ignorantia facti* (ignorance of fact) and *ignorantia juris*, (ignorance of law.) And the former, he adds, is twofold,—*lectionis et linguæ*, (ignorance of reading and ignorance of language.) 2 Coke, 3*b*.

Ignorantia eorum quæ quis scire tenetur non excusat. Ignorance of those things which one is bound to know excuses not. Hale, P. C. 42; Broom, Max. 267.

Ignorantia facti excusat. Ignorance of fact excuses or is a ground of relief. 2 Coke, 3*b*. Acts done and contracts made under mistake or ignorance of a material fact are voidable and relievable in law and equity. 2 Kent, Comm. 491, and notes.

Ignorantia facti excusat, ignorantia juris non excusat. Ignorance of the fact excuses; ignorance of the law excuses not. Every man must be taken to be cognizant of the law; otherwise there is no saying to what extent the excuse of ignorance may not be carried. 1 Coke, 177; Broom, Max. 253.

Ignorantia juris quod quisque tenetur scire, neminem excusat. Ignorance of the [or a] law, which every one is bound to know, excuses no man. A mistake in point of law is, in criminal cases, no sort of defense. 4 Bl. Comm. 27; 4 Steph. Comm. 81; Broom, Max. 253; 7 Car. & P. 456. And, in civil cases, ignorance of the law, with a full knowledge of the facts, furnishes no ground, either in law or equity, to rescind agreements, or reclaim money paid, or set aside solemn acts of the parties. 2 Kent, Comm. 491, and note.

Ignorantia juris sui non præjudicat juri. Ignorance of one's right does not prejudice the right. Lofft, 552.

Ignorantia legis neminem excusat. Ignorance of law excuses no one. 4 Bouv. Inst. no. 3828; 1 Story, Eq. Jur. § 111; 7 Watts, 374.

IGNORATIO ELENCHI. Lat. In logic. An overlooking of the adversary's counter-position in an argument.

Ignoratis terminis artis, ignoratur et ars. Where the terms of an art are unknown, the art itself is unknown also. Co. Litt. 2*a*.

IGNORE. 1. To be ignorant of, or unacquainted with.

2. To disregard willfully; to refuse to recognize; to decline to take notice of.

3. To reject as groundless, false, or unsupported by evidence; as when a grand jury *ignores* a bill of indictment.

Ignoscitur ei qui sanguinem suum qualiter redemptum voluit. The law holds him excused from obligation who chose to redeem his blood (or life) upon any terms. Whatever a man may do under the fear of losing his life or limbs will not be held binding upon him in law. 1 Bl. Comm. 131.

IKENILD STREET. One of the four great Roman roads in Britain; supposed to be so called from the *Iceni*.

ILET. A little island.

ILL. In old pleading. Bad; defective in law; null; naught; the opposite of good or valid.

ILL FAME. Evil repute; notorious bad character. Houses of prostitution, gaming houses, and other such disorderly places are called "houses of ill fame," and a person who frequents them is a person of ill fame.

ILLATA ET INVECTA. Things brought into the house for use by the tenant were so called, and were liable to the *jus hypothecæ* of Roman law, just as they are to the landlord's right of distress at common law.

ILLEGAL. Not authorized by law; illicit; unlawful; contrary to law.

Sometimes this term means merely that which lacks authority of or support from law; but more frequently it imports a violation. Etymologically, the word seems to convey the negative meaning only. But in ordinary use it has a severer, stronger signification; the idea of censure or condemnation for breaking law is usually presented. But the law implied in illegal is not necessarily an express statute. Things are called "illegal" for a violation of common-law principles. And the term does not imply that the act spoken of is immoral or wicked; it implies only a breach of the law. 1 Abb. Pr. (N. S.) 432; 48 N. H. 196; Id. 211; 3 Sneed, 64.

ILLEGAL CONDITIONS. All those that are impossible, or contrary to law, immoral, or repugnant to the nature of the transaction.

ILLEGAL CONTRACT. An agreement to do any act forbidden by the law, or to omit to do any act enjoined by the law.

ILLEGAL TRADE. Such traffic or commerce as is carried on in violation of the municipal law, or contrary to the law of nations. See ILLICIT TRADE.

ILLEGITIMACY. The condition before the law, or the social *status*, of a bastard; the state or condition of one whose parents were not intermarried at the time of his birth.

ILLEGITIMATE. That which is contrary to law; it is usually applied to bastards, or children born out of lawful wedlock.

The Louisiana Code divided illegitimate children into two classes: (1) Those born from two persons who, at the moment when such children were conceived, could have lawfully intermarried; and (2) those who are born from persons to whose marriage there existed at the time some legal impediment. Both classes, however, could be acknowledged and take by devise. 12 Rob. (La.) 56.

ILLEVIABLE. Not leviable; that cannot or ought not to be levied. Cowell.

ILLICENCIATUS. In old English law. Without license. Fleta, lib. 3, c. 5, § 12.

ILLICIT. Not permitted or allowed; prohibited; unlawful; as an *illicit* trade; *illicit* intercourse.

ILLICIT TRADE. Policies of marine insurance usually contain a covenant of warranty against "illicit trade," meaning thereby trade which is forbidden, or declared unlawful, by the laws of the country where the cargo is to be delivered.

"It is not the same with 'contraband trade,' although the words are sometimes used as synonymous. Illicit or prohibited trade is one which cannot be carried on without a distinct violation of some positive law of the country where the transaction is to take place." 1 Pars. Mar. Ins. 614.

ILLICITE. Unlawfully. This word has a technical meaning, and is requisite in an indictment where the act charged is unlawful; as in the case of a riot. 2 Hawk. P. C. c. 25, § 96.

ILLICITUM COLLEGIUM. An illegal corporation.

ILLITERATE. Unlettered; ignorant; unlearned. Generally used of one who cannot read and write.

ILLOCABLE. Incapable of being placed out or hired.

ILLUD. Lat. That.

Illud, quod alias licitum non est, necessitas facit licitum; et necessitas inducit privilegium quoad jura privata. Bac. Max. That which is otherwise not permitted, necessity permits; and necessity makes a privilege as to private rights.

Illud, quod alteri unitur, extinguitur, neque amplius per se vacare licet. Godol. Ecc. Law, 169. That which is united to another is extinguished, nor can it be any more independent.

ILLUSION. In medical jurisprudence. An image or impression in the mind, excited by some external object addressing itself to the senses, but which, instead of corresponding with the reality, is perverted, distorted, or wholly mistaken.

ILLUSORY. Deceiving by false appearances; nominal, as distinguished from substantial.

ILLUSORY APPOINTMENT. Formerly the appointment of a merely nominal share of the property to one of the objects of a power, in order to escape the rule that an exclusive appointment could not be made unless it was authorized by the instrument creating the power, was considered illusory and void in equity. But this rule has been abolished in England. (1 Wm. IV. c. 46; 37 & 38 Vict. c. 37.) Sweet.

ILLUSORY APPOINTMENT ACT. The statute 1 Wm. IV. c. 46. This statute enacts that no appointment made after its passing, (July 16, 1830,) in exercise of a power to appoint property, real or personal, among several objects, shall be invalid, or impeached in equity, on the ground that an unsubstantial, illusory, or nominal share only was thereby appointed, or left unappointed, to devolve upon any one or more of the objects of such power; but that the appointment shall be valid in equity, as at law. See, too, 37 & 38 Vict. c. 37. Wharton.

ILLUSTRIOUS. The prefix to the title of a prince of the blood in England.

IMAGINE. In English law. In cases of treason the law makes it a crime to imagine the death of the king. But, in order to complete the crime, this act of the mind must be demonstrated by some overt act. The terms "imagining" and "compassing" are in this connection synonymous. 4 Bl. Comm. 78.

IMAN, IMAM, or IMAUM. A Mohammedan prince having supreme spiritual as well as temporal power; a regular priest of the mosque.

IMBARGO. An old form of "embargo," (*q. v.*) St. 18 Car. II. c. 5.

IMBASING OF MONEY. The act of mixing the species with an alloy below the standard of sterling. 1 Hale, P. C. 102.

IMBECILITY. Weakness, or feebleness of intellect, either congenital, or resulting from an obstacle to the development of the faculties, supervening in infancy. See Whart. & S. Med. Jur. §§ 229-233.

IMBEZZLE. See EMBEZZLE.

IMBLADARE. In old English law. To plant or sow grain. Bract. fol. 176*b*.

IMBRACERY. See EMBRACERY.

IMBROCUS. A brook, gutter, or water-passage. Cowell.

IMMATERIAL. Not material, essential, or necessary; not important or pertinent; not decisive.

IMMATERIAL AVERMENT. An averment alleging with needless particularity or unnecessary circumstances what is material and necessary, and which might properly have been stated more generally, and without such circumstances and particulars; or, in other words, a statement of unnecessary particulars in connection with and as descriptive of what is material. Gould, Pl. c. 3, § 188; 3 Ala. 237, 245.

IMMATERIAL ISSUE. In pleading. An issue taken on an immaterial point; that is, a point not proper to decide the action. Steph. Pl. 99, 130; 2 Tidd, Pr. 921.

IMMEDIATE. 1. Present; at once; without delay; not deferred by any interval of time. In this sense, the word, without any very precise signification, denotes that action is or must be taken either instantly or without any considerable loss of time.

Immediately does not, in legal proceedings, necessarily import the exclusion of any interval of time. It is a word of no very definite signification, and is much in subjection to its grammatical connections. 31 N. J. Law, 313.

2. Not separated in respect to place; not separated by the intervention of any intermediate object, cause, relation, or right. Thus we speak of an action as prosecuted for the "immediate benefit" of A., of a devise as made to the "immediate issue" of B., etc.

IMMEDIATE DESCENT. "A descent may be said to be mediate or immediate in regard to the mediate or immediate descent of the estate or right: or it may be said to be mediate or immediate in regard to the mediateness or immediateness of the pedigree or degrees of consanguinity." Story, J., 6 Pet. 112.

IMMEDIATELY. "It is impossible to lay down any hard and fast rule as to what is the meaning of the word 'immediately' in all cases. The words 'forthwith' and 'immediately' have the same meaning. They are stronger than the expression 'within a reasonable time,' and imply prompt, vigorous action, without any delay, and whether there has been such action is a question of fact, having regard to the circumstances of the particular case." Cockburn, C. J., 4 Q. B. Div. 471.

IMMEMORIAL. Beyond human memory; time out of mind.

IMMEMORIAL POSSESSION. In Louisiana. Possession of which no man living has seen the beginning, and the existence of which he has learned from his elders. Civil Code La. art. 762; 2 Mart. (La.) 214.

IMMEMORIAL USAGE. A practice which has existed time out of mind; custom; prescription.

IMMEUBLES. These are, in French law, the immovables of English law. Things are *immeubles* from any one of three causes: (1) From their own nature, *e. g.*, lands and houses; (2) from their destination, *e. g.*, animals and instruments of agriculture when supplied by the landlord; or (3) by the object to which they are annexed, *e. g.*, easements. Brown.

IMMIGRATION. The coming into a country of foreigners for purposes of permanent residence. The correlative term "emigration" denotes the act of such persons in leaving their former country.

IMMISCERE. Lat. In the civil law. To mix or mingle with; to meddle with; to join with. Calvin.

IMMITTERE. **In the civil law.** To put or let into, as a beam into a wall. Calvin.; Dig. 50, 17, 242, 1.

In old English law. To put cattle on a common. Fleta, lib. 4, c. 20, § 7.

Immobilia situm sequuntur. Immovable things follow their site or position; are governed by the law of the place where they are fixed. 2 Kent, Comm. 67.

IMMOBILIS. Immovable. *Immobilia*, or *res immobiles*, immovable things, such as lands and buildings. Mackeld. Rom. Law, § 160.

IMMORAL. Contrary to good morals; inconsistent with the rules and principles of morality which regard men as living in a community, and which are necessary for the public welfare, order, and decency.

IMMORAL CONSIDERATION. One contrary to good morals, and therefore invalid. Contracts based upon an immoral consideration are generally void.

IMMORAL CONTRACTS. Contracts founded upon considerations *contra bonos mores* are void.

IMMORALITY. That which is *contra bonos mores*. See IMMORAL.

IMMOVABLES. In the civil law. Property which, from its nature, destination, or the object to which it is applied, cannot move itself, or be removed.

Immovable things are, in general, such as cannot either move themselves or be removed from one place to another. But this definition, strictly speaking, is applicable only to such things as are immovable by their own nature, and not to such as are so only by the disposition of the law. Civil Code La. art. 462.

IMMUNITY. An exemption from serving in an office, or performing duties which the law generally requires other citizens to perform.

IMPAIR. To weaken, diminish, or relax, or otherwise affect in an injurious manner.

"IMPAIRING THE OBLIGATION OF CONTRACTS." For the meaning of this phrase in the constitution of the United States, see 2 Story, Const. §§ 1374–1399; 1 Kent, Comm. 413–422; Pom. Const. Law; Black, Const. Prohib. pt. 1.

IMPANEL. In English practice. To impanel a jury signifies the entering by the sheriff upon a piece of parchment, termed a "panel," the names of the jurors who have been summoned to appear in court on a certain day to form a jury of the country to hear such matters as may be brought before them. Brown.

In American practice. Besides the meaning above given, "impanel" signifies the act of the clerk of the court in making up a list of the jurors who have been selected for the trial of a particular cause.

Impaneling has nothing to do with drawing, selecting, or swearing jurors, but means simply making the list of those who have been selected. 7 How. Pr. 441.

IMPARCARE. In old English law. To impound. Reg. Orig. 92*b*.

To shut up, or confine in prison. *Inducti sunt in carcerem et imparcati*, they were carried to prison and shut up. Bract. fol. 124.

IMPARGAMENTUM. The right of impounding cattle.

IMPARL. To have license to settle a litigation amicably; to obtain delay for adjustment.

IMPARLANCE. In early practice, imparlance meant time given to either of the parties to an action to answer the pleading of the other. It thus amounted to a continuance of the action to a further day. Literally the term signified leave given to the parties to *talk together; i. e.*, with a view to settling their differences amicably. But in modern practice it denotes a time given to the defendant to plead.

A general imparlance is the entry of a general prayer and allowance of time to plead till the next term, without reserving to the defendant the benefit of any exception; so that after such an imparlance the defendant cannot object to the jurisdiction of the court, or plead any matter in abatement. This kind of imparlance is always from one term to another.

A general special imparlance contains a saving of all exceptions whatsoever, so that the defendant after this may plead not only in abatement, but he may also plead a plea which affects the jurisdiction of the court, as privilege. He cannot, however, plead a tender, and that he was always ready to pay, because by craving time he admits that he is not ready, and so falsifies his plea.

A special imparlance reserves to the defendant all exceptions to the writ, bill, or count; and therefore after it the defendant may plead in abatement, though not to the jurisdiction of the court. 1 Tidd, Pr. 462, 463.

IMPARSONEE. L. Fr. In ecclesiastical law. One who is inducted and in possession of a benefice. Parson imparsonee, (*persona impersonata.*) Cowell; Dyer, 40.

IMPATRONIZATION. The act of putting into full possession of a benefice.

IMPEACH. To accuse; to charge a liability upon; to sue.

To proceed against a public officer for crime or misfeasance, before a proper court, by the presentation of a written accusation called "articles of impeachment."

In the law of evidence. To call in question the veracity of a witness, by means of evidence adduced for that purpose.

IMPEACHMENT. A criminal proceeding against a public officer, before a *quasi* political court, instituted by a written accusation called "articles of impeachment;" for example, a written accusation by the house of representatives of the United States to the senate of the United States against an officer.

In England, a prosecution by the house of commons before the house of lords of a commoner for treason, or other high crimes and misdemeanors, or of a peer for any crime.

In evidence. An allegation, supported by proof, that a witness who has been examined is unworthy of credit.

IMPEACHMENT OF WASTE. Liability for waste committed; or a demand or suit for compensation for waste committed upon lands or tenements by a tenant thereof who, having only a leasehold or particular estate, had no right to commit waste. See 2 Bl. Comm. 283.

IMPEACHMENT OF WITNESS. Proof that a witness who has testified in a cause is unworthy of credit.

IMPECHIARE. To impeach, to accuse, or prosecute for felony or treason.

IMPEDIENS. In old practice. One who hinders; an impedient. The defendant or deforciant in a fine was sometimes so called. Cowell; Blount.

IMPEDIMENTO. In Spanish law. A prohibition to contract marriage, established by law between certain persons.

IMPEDIMENTS. Disabilities, or hindrances to the making of contracts, such as coverture, infancy, want of reason, etc.

In the civil law. Bars to marriage.

Absolute impediments are those which prevent the person subject to them from marrying at all, without either the nullity of marriage or its being punishable. *Dirimant impediments* are those which render a marriage void; as where one of the contracting parties is unable to marry by reason of a prior undissolved marriage. *Prohibitive impediments* are those which do not render the marriage null, but subject the parties to a punishment. *Relative impediments* are those which regard only certain persons with respect to each other; as between two particular persons who are related within the prohibited degrees. Bowyer, Mod. Civil Law, 44, 45.

IMPEDITOR. In old English law. A disturber in the action of *quare impedit.* St. Marlb. c. 12.

IMPENSÆ. Lat. In the civil law. Expenses; outlays. Mackeld. Rom. Law, § 168; Calvin. Divided into necessary, (*necessariæ,*) useful, (*utiles,*) and tasteful or ornamental, (*voluptuariæ.*) Dig. 50, 16, 79. See Id. 25, 1.

IMPERATIVE. See DIRECTORY.

IMPERATOR. Emperor. The title of the Roman emperors, and also of the kings of England before the Norman conquest. Cod. 1, 14, 12; 1 Bl. Comm. 242. See EMPEROR.

IMPERFECT OBLIGATIONS. Moral duties, such as charity, gratitude, etc., which cannot be enforced by law.

IMPERFECT RIGHTS. See RIGHTS.

IMPERFECT TRUST. An executory trust, (which see;) and see EXECUTED TRUST.

Imperii majestas est tutelæ salus. Co. Litt. 64. The majesty of the empire is the safety of its protection.

IMPERITIA. Unskillfulness; want of skill.

Imperitia culpæ adnumeratur. Want of skill is reckoned as *culpa;* that is, as blamable conduct or neglect. Dig. 50, 17, 132.

Imperitia est maxima mechanicorum pœna. Unskillfulness is the greatest punishment of mechanics; [that is, from its effect in making them liable to those by whom they are employed.] 11 Coke, 54*a*. The word "*pœna*" in some translations is erroneously rendered "fault."

IMPERIUM. The right to command, which includes the right to employ the force of the state to enforce the laws. This is one of the principal attributes of the power of the executive. 1 Toullier, no. 58.

IMPERSONALITAS. Impersonality. A mode of expression where no reference is made to any person, such as the expression "*ut dicitur,*" (as is said.) Co. Litt. 352*b*.

Impersonalitas non concludit nec ligat. Co. Litt. 352*b*. Impersonality neither concludes nor binds.

IMPERTINENCE. Irrelevancy; the fault of not properly pertaining to the issue or proceeding. The introduction of any matters into a bill, answer, or other pleading or proceeding in a suit, which are not properly before the court for decision, at any particular stage of the suit. Story, Eq. Pl. § 266.

In practice. A question propounded to a witness, or evidence offered or sought to be elicited, is called "impertinent" when it has no logical bearing upon the issue, is not necessarily connected with it, or does not belong to the matter in hand. On the distinction between pertinency and relevancy, we may quote the following remark of Dr. Wharton: "*Relevancy* is that which conduces to the proof of a *pertinent* hypothesis; a pertinent hypothesis being one which, if sustained, would logically influence the issue." 1 Whart. Ev. § 20.

IMPERTINENT. In equity pleading. That which does not belong to a pleading, interrogatory, or other proceeding; out of place; superfluous; irrelevant.

At law. A term applied to matter not necessary to constitute the cause of action or ground of defense. Cowp. 683; 5 East, 275; 2 Mass. 283. It constitutes surplusage, (which see.)

IMPESCARE. In old records. To impeach or accuse. *Impescatus*, impeached. Blount.

IMPETITIO VASTI. Impeachment of waste, (*q. v.*)

IMPETRARE. In old English practice. To obtain by request, as a writ or privilege. Bract. fols. 57, 172*b*. This application of the word seems to be derived from the civil law. Calvin.

IMPETRATION. In old English law. The obtaining anything by petition or entreaty. Particularly, the obtaining of a benefice from Rome by solicitation, which benefice belonged to the disposal of the king or other lay patron. Webster; Cowell.

IMPIER. Umpire, (*q. v.*)

IMPIERMENT. Impairing or prejudicing. Jacob.

IMPIGNORATA. Pledged; given in pledge, (*pignori data;*) mortgaged. A term applied in Bracton to land. Bract. fol. 20.

IMPIGNORATION. The act of pawning or putting to pledge.

Impius et crudelis judicandus est qui libertati non favet. He is to be judged impious and cruel who does not favor liberty. Co. Litt. 124.

IMPLACITARE. Lat. To implead; to sue.

IMPLEAD. In practice. To sue or prosecute by due course of law. 9 Watts, 47.

IMPLEADED. Sued or prosecuted; used particularly in the titles of causes where there are several defendants; as "A. B., impleaded with C. D."

IMPLEMENTS. Such things as are used or *employed* for a trade, or furniture of a house. 11 Metc. (Mass.) 82.

Whatever may supply wants; particularly applied to tools, utensils, vessels, instruments of labor; as, the *implements* of trade or of husbandry. 23 Iowa, 359; 6 Gray, 298.

IMPLICATA. A term used in mercantile law, derived from the Italian. In order to avoid the risk of making fruitless voyages, merchants have been in the habit of receiving small adventures, on freight, at so much per cent., to which they are entitled at all events, even if the adventure be lost; and this is called "*implicata.*" Wharton.

IMPLICATION. Intendment or inference, as distinguished from the actual expression of a thing in words. In a will, an estate may pass by mere *implication*, without any express words to direct its course. 2 Bl. Comm. 381.

An inference of something not directly declared, but arising from what is admitted or expressed.

In construing a will conjecture must not be taken for implication; but necessary implication means, not natural necessity, but so strong a probability of intention that an intention contrary to that which is imputed to the testator cannot be supposed. 1 Ves. & B. 466.

"Implication" is also used in the sense of "inference;" *i. e.*, where the existence of an intention is inferred from acts not done for the sole purpose of communicating it, but for some other purpose. Sweet.

IMPLIED. This word is used in law as contrasted with "express;" *i. e.*, where the intention in regard to the subject-matter is not manifested by explicit and direct words, but is gathered by implication or necessary deduction from the circumstances, the general language, or the conduct of the parties.

IMPLIED ABROGATION. A statute is said to work an "implied abrogation" of an earlier one, when the later statute contains provisions which are inconsistent with the further continuance of the earlier law; or a statute is impliedly abrogated when the reason of it, or the object for which it was passed, no longer exists.

IMPLIED ASSUMPSIT. An undertaking or promise not formally made, but presumed or implied from the conduct of a party. See ASSUMPSIT.

IMPLIED CONDITION. See CONDITION IMPLIED.

IMPLIED CONSIDERATION. A consideration implied or presumed by law, as distinguished from an *express* consideration, (*q. v.*)

IMPLIED CONTRACT. One not created or evidenced by the explicit agreement of the parties, but inferred by the law, as a matter of reason and justice, from their acts or conduct. For example, if A. hires B. to do any business or perform any work for him, the law implies a contract or undertaking on A.'s part to pay B. as much as his labor or service deserves. 2 Bl. Comm. 443.

IMPLIED COVENANT. One which is not set forth explicitly, but is raised by implication of law from the use of certain terms ("grant," "give," "demise," etc.) in the conveyance, contract, or lease. See COVENANT.

IMPLIED MALICE. Malice inferred by legal reasoning and necessary deduction from the *res gestæ* or the conduct of the party. Malice inferred from any deliberate cruel act committed by one person against another, however sudden. Whart. Hom. 38. What is called "general malice" is often thus inferred.

IMPLIED TRUST. A trust raised or created by implication of law; a trust implied or presumed from circumstances.

IMPLIED USE. See RESULTING USE.

IMPLIED WARRANTY. A warranty raised by the law as an inference from the acts of the parties or the circumstances of the transaction. Thus, if the seller of a chattel have possession of it and sell it as his own, and not as agent for another, and for a fair price, he is understood to *warrant the title*. 2 Kent, Comm. 478.

A warranty implied from the general tenor of an instrument, or from particular words used in it, although no express warranty is mentioned. Thus, in every policy of insurance there is an *implied* warranty that the ship is seaworthy when the policy attaches. 3 Kent, Comm. 287; 1 Phil. Ins. 308.

IMPORTATION. The act of bringing goods and merchandise into a country from a foreign country.

IMPORTS. Importations; goods or other property imported or brought into the country from a foreign country.

IMPORTUNITY. Pressing solicitation; urgent request; application for a claim or favor which is urged with troublesome frequency or pertinacity. Webster.

IMPOSITION. An impost; tax; contribution.

IMPOSSIBILITY. That which, in the constitution and course of nature or the law, no man can do or perform.

Impossibility is of the following several sorts:

An act is *physically* impossible when it is contrary to the course of nature. Such an impossibility may be either *absolute*, *i. e.*, impossible in any case, (*e. g.*, for A. to reach the moon,) or *relative*, (sometimes called "impossibility in fact,") *i. e.*, arising from the circumstances of the case, (*e. g.*, for A. to make a payment to B., he being a deceased person.) To the latter class belongs what is sometimes called "*practical* impossibility," which exists when the act *can* be done, but only at an excessive or unreasonable cost. An act is *legally* or juridically impossible when a rule of law makes it impossible to do it; *e. g.*, for A. to make a valid will before his majority. This class of acts must not be confounded with those which are possible, although forbidden by law, as to commit a theft. An act is *logically* impossible when it is contrary to the nature of the transaction, as where A. gives property to B. expressly for his own benefit, on condition that he transfers it to C. Sweet.

Impossibilium nulla obligatio est. There is no obligation to do impossible things. Dig. 50, 17, 185; Broom, Max. 249.

IMPOSSIBLE CONTRACTS. An impossible contract is one which the law will not hold binding upon the parties, because of the natural or legal impossibility of the performance by one party of that which is the consideration for the promise of the other. 7 Wait, Act. & Def. 124.

Impossible contracts, which will be deemed void in the eye of the law, or of which the performance will be excused, are such contracts as cannot be performed, either because of the nature of the obligation undertaken, or because of some supervening event which renders the performance of the obligation either physically or legally impossible. 10 Amer. & Eng. Enc. Law, 176.

IMPOSTS. Taxes, duties, or impositions. A duty on imported goods or merchandise. Story, Const. § 949.

Impost is a tax received by the prince for such merchandises as are brought into any haven within his dominions from foreign nations. It may in some sort be distinguished from customs, because customs are rather that profit the prince maketh of wares shipped out; yet they are frequently confounded. Cowell.

IMPOTENCE. In medical jurisprudence. The incapacity for copulation or propagating the species. Properly used of the male; but it has also been used synonymously with "sterility."

Impotentia excusat legem. Co. Litt. 29. The impossibility of doing what is required by the law excuses from the performance.

IMPOTENTIAM, PROPERTY PROPTER. A qualified property, which may subsist in animals *feræ naturæ* on account of their inability, as where hawks, herons, or other birds build in a person's trees, or conies, etc., make their nests or burrows in a person's land, and have young there, such person has a qualified property in them till they can fly or run away, and then such property expires. 2 Steph. Comm. (7th Ed.) 8.

IMPOUND. To shut up stray animals or distrained goods in a pound.

To take into the custody of the law or of a court. Thus, a court will sometimes *impound* a suspicious document produced at a trial.

IMPRESCRIPTIBILITY. The state or quality of being incapable of prescription; not of such a character that a right to it can be gained by prescription.

IMPRESCRIPTIBLE RIGHTS. Such rights as a person may use or not, at pleasure, since they cannot be lost to him by the claims of another founded on prescription.

IMPRESSION. A "case of the first impression" is one without a precedent; one presenting a wholly new state of facts; one involving a question never before determined.

IMPRESSMENT. A power possessed by the English crown of taking persons or property to aid in the defense of the country, with or without the consent of the persons concerned. It is usually exercised to obtain hands for the queen's ships in time of war, by taking seamen engaged in merchant vessels, (1 Bl. Comm. 420; Maud & P. Shipp. 123;) but in former times impressment of merchant ships was also practiced. The admiralty issues protections against impressment in certain cases, either under statutes passed in favor of certain callings (*e. g.*, persons employed in the Greenland fisheries) or voluntarily. Sweet.

IMPREST MONEY. Money paid on enlisting or impressing soldiers or sailors.

IMPRETIABILIS. Lat. Beyond price; invaluable.

IMPRIMATUR. Lat. Let it be printed. A license or allowance, granted by the constituted authorities, giving permission to print and publish a book. This allowance was formerly necessary, in England, before any book could lawfully be printed, and in some other countries is still required.

IMPRIMERE. To press upon; to impress or press; to imprint or print.

IMPRIMERY. In some of the ancient English statutes this word is used to signify a printing-office, the art of printing, a print or impression.

IMPRIMIS. Lat. In the first place; first of all.

IMPRISON. To put in a prison; to put in a place of confinement.

To confine a person, or restrain his liberty, in any way.

IMPRISONMENT. The act of putting or confining a man in prison; the restraint of a man's personal liberty; coercion exercised upon a person to prevent the free exercise of his powers of locomotion.

It is not a necessary part of the definition that the confinement should be in a place usually appropriated to that purpose; it may be in a locality used only for the specific occasion; or it may take place without the actual application of any physical agencies of restraint, (such as locks or bars,) but by verbal compulsion and the display of available force. See 9 N. H. 491.

Any forcible detention of a man's person, or control over his movements, is imprisonment. 3 Har. (Del.) 416.

IMPRISTI. Adherents; followers. Those who side with or take the part of another, either in his defense or otherwise.

IMPROBATION. In Scotch law. An action brought for the purpose of having some instrument declared false and forged. 1 Forb. Inst. pt. 4, p. 161. The verb "improve" (*q. v.*) was used in the same sense.

IMPROPER. Not suitable; unfit; not suited to the character, time, and place. 48 N. H. 199. Wrongful. 53 Law J. P. D. 65.

IMPROPER FEUDS. These were derivative feuds; as, for instance, those that were originally bartered and sold to the feudatory for a price, or were held upon base or less honorable services, or upon a rent in lieu of military service, or were themselves alienable, without mutual license, or descended indifferently to males or females. Wharton.

IMPROPER NAVIGATION. Anything improperly done with the ship or part of the ship in the course of the voyage. L. R. 6 C. P. 563. See, also, 53 Law J. P. D. 65.

IMPROPRIATE RECTOR. In ecclesiastical law. Commonly signifies a lay rector as opposed to a spiritual rector; just as impropriate tithes are tithes in the hands of a lay owner, as opposed to appropriate tithes, which are tithes in the hands of a spiritual owner. Brown.

IMPROPRIATION. In ecclesiastical law. The annexing an ecclesiastical benefice to the use of a lay person, whether individual or corporate, in the same way as *appropriation* is the annexing of any such benefice to the proper and perpetual use of some spiritual corporation, whether sole or aggregate, to enjoy forever. Brown.

IMPROVE. In Scotch law. To disprove; to invalidate or impeach; to prove false or forged. 1 Forb. Inst. pt. 4, p. 162.

To improve a lease means to grant a lease of unusual duration to encourage a tenant, when the soil is exhausted, etc. Bell; Stair, Inst. p. 676, § 23.

IMPROVED. Improved land is such as has been reclaimed, is used for the purpose of husbandry, and is cultivated as such, whether the appropriation is for tillage, meadow, or pasture. "Improve" is synonymous with "cultivate." 4 Cow. 190.

IMPROVEMENT. A valuable addition made to property (usually real estate) or an amelioration in its condition, amounting to more than mere repairs or replacement of waste, costing labor or capital, and intended to enhance its value and utility or to adapt it for new or further purposes.

In American land law. An act by which a locator or settler expresses his intention to cultivate or clear certain land; an act expressive of the actual possession of land; as by erecting a cabin, planting a corn-field, deadening trees in a forest; or by merely marking trees, or even by piling up a brush-heap. Burrill.

An "improvement," under our land system, does not mean a general enhancement of the value of the tract from the occupant's operations. It has a more limited meaning, which has in view the population of our forests, and the increase of agricultural products. All works which are directed to the creation of homes for families, or are substantial steps towards bringing lands into cultivation, have in their results the special character of "improvements," and, under the land laws of the United States and of the several states, are encouraged. Sometimes their minimum extent is defined as requisite to convey rights. In other cases not. But the test which runs through all the cases is always this: Are they real, and made *bona fide*, in accordance with the policy of the law, or are they only colorable, and made for the purpose of fraud and speculation? 37 Ark. 137.

In the law of patents. An addition to, or modification of, a previous invention or discovery, intended or claimed to increase its utility or value. See 2 Kent, Comm. 366–372.

IMPROVEMENTS. A term used in leases, of doubtful meaning. It would seem to apply principally to buildings, though generally it extends to the amelioration of every description of property, whether real or personal; but, when contained in any document, its meaning is generally explained by other words. 1 Chit. Gen. Pr. 174.

IMPROVIDENCE, as used in a statute excluding one found incompetent to execute the duties of an administrator by reason of improvidence, means that want of care and foresight in the management of property which would be likely to render the estate and effects of the intestate unsafe, and liable to be lost or diminished in value, in case the administration should be committed to the improvident person. 1 Barb. Ch. 45.

IMPRUIARE. In old records. To improve land. *Impruiamentum*, the improvement so made of it. Cowell.

IMPUBES. Lat. In the civil law. A minor under the age of puberty; a male under fourteen years of age; a female under twelve. Calvin.; Mackeld. Rom. Law, § 138.

Impunitas continuum affectum tribuit delinquendi. 4 Coke, 45. Impunity confirms the disposition to commit crime.

Impunities semper ad deteriora invitat. 5 Coke, 109. Impunity always invites to greater crimes.

IMPUNITY. Exemption or protection from penalty or punishment. 36 Tex. 153.

IMPUTATIO. In the civil law. Legal liability.

IMPUTATION OF PAYMENT. In the civil law. The application of a payment made by a debtor to his creditor.

IMPUTED NEGLIGENCE. Negligence which is not directly attributable to the person himself, but which is the negligence of a person who is in privity with him, and with whose fault he is chargeable.

IN. In the law of real estate, this preposition has always been used to denote the fact of seisin, title, or possession, and apparently serves as an elliptical expression for some such phrase as "in possession," or as an abbreviation for "*in*titled" or "*in*vested with title." Thus, in the old books, a tenant is said to be "*in* by lease of his lessor." Litt. § 82.

IN ACTION. Attainable or recoverable by action; not in possession. A term applied to property of which a party has not the possession, but only a right to recover it by action. Things in action are rights of personal things, which nevertheless are not in possession. See CHOSE IN ACTION.

IN ADVERSUM. Against an adverse, unwilling, or resisting party. "A decree not by consent, but *in adversum*." 3 Story, 318.

In ædificiis lapis male positus non est removendus. 11 Coke, 69. A stone badly placed in buildings is not to be removed.

IN ÆQUA MANU. In equal hand. Fleta, lib. 3, c. 14, § 2.

IN ÆQUALI JURE. In equal right; on an equality in point of right.

In æquali jure melior est conditio possidentis. In [a case of] equal right the condition of the party in possession is the better. Plowd. 296; Broom, Max. 713.

IN ÆQUALI MANU. In equal hand; held equally or indifferently between two parties. Where an instrument was deposited by the parties to it in the hands of a third person, to keep on certain conditions, it was said to be held *in æquali manu.* Reg. Orig. 28.

IN ALIENO SOLO. In another's land. 2 Steph. Comm. 20.

IN ALIO LOCO. In another place.

In alta proditione nullus potest esse accessorius sed principalis solummodo. 3 Inst. 138. In high treason no one can be an accessary, but only principal.

In alternativis electio est debitoris. In alternatives the debtor has the election.

In ambigua voce legis ea potius accipienda est significatio quæ vitio caret, præsertim cum etiam voluntas legis ex hoc colligi possit. In an ambiguous expression of law, that signification is to be preferred which is consonant with equity, especially when the spirit of the law can be collected from that. Dig. 1, 3, 19; Broom, Max. 576.

In ambiguis casibus semper præsumitur pro rege. In doubtful cases the presumption is always in favor of the king.

In ambiguis orationibus maxime sententia spectanda est ejus qui eas protulisset. In ambiguous expressions, the intention of the person using them is chiefly to be regarded. Dig. 50, 17, 96; Broom, Max. 567.

In Anglia non est interregnum. In England there is no interregnum. Jenk. Cent. 205; Broom, Max. 50.

IN APERTA LUCE. In open daylight; in the day-time. 9 Coke, 65*b*.

IN APICIBUS JURIS. Among the subtleties or extreme doctrines of the law. 1 Kames, Eq. 190. See APEX JURIS.

IN ARBITRIUM JUDICIS. At the pleasure of the judge.

IN ARCTA ET SALVA CUSTODIA. In close and safe custody. 3 Bl. Comm. 415.

IN ARTICULO. In a moment; immediately. Cod. 1, 34, 2.

IN ARTICULO MORTIS. In the article of death; at the point of death. 1 Johns. 159.

In atrocioribus delictis punitur affectus licet non sequatur effectus. 2 Rolle R. 82. In more atrocious crimes the intent is punished, though an effect does not follow.

IN AUTRE DROIT. L. Fr. In another's right. As representing another. An executor, administrator, or trustee sues *in autre droit.*

IN BANCO. In bank; in the bench. A term applied to proceedings in the court in bank, as distinguished from proceedings at *nisi prius.* Also, in the English court of common bench.

IN BLANK. A term applied to the indorsement of a bill or note, where it consists merely of the indorser's name, without restriction to any particular indorsee. 2 Steph. Comm. 164.

IN BONIS. Among the goods or property; in actual possession. Inst. 4, 2, 2. *In bonis defuncti*, among the goods of the deceased.

IN CAMERA. In chambers; in private. A cause is said to be heard *in camera* either when the hearing is had before the judge in his private room, or when all spectators are excluded from the court-room.

IN CAPITA. To the heads; by heads or polls. Persons succeed to an inheritance *in capita* when they individually take equal shares. So challenges to individual jurors are challenges *in capita,* as distinguished from challenges to the array.

IN CAPITE. In chief. 2 Bl. Comm. 60. Tenure *in capite* was a holding directly from the king.

In casu extremæ necessitatis omnia sunt communia. Hale, P. C. 54. In cases of extreme necessity, everything is in common.

IN CASU PROVISO. In a (or the) case provided. *In tali casu editum et provisum,* in such case made and provided. Townsh. Pl. 164, 165.

IN CAUSA. In the cause, as distinguished from *in initialibus,* (*q. v.*) A term in Scotch practice. 1 Brown, Ch. 252.

IN CHIEF. Principal; primary; directly obtained. A term applied to the evidence obtained from a witness upon his examination in court by the party producing him.

Tenure in chief, or *in capite,* is a holding directly of the king or chief lord.

In civilibus ministerium excusat, in criminalibus non item. In civil matters agency (or service) excuses, but not so in criminal matters. Lofft, 228; Tray. Lat. Max. 243.

In claris non est locus conjecturis. In things obvious there is no room for conjecture.

IN COMMENDAM. In commendation; as a commended living. 1 Bl. Comm. 393. See COMMENDA.

A term applied in Louisiana to a limited partnership, answering to the French "*en commandite.*" Civil Code La. art. 2810.

In commodato hæc pactio, ne dolus præstetur, rata non est. In the contract of loan, a stipulation not to be liable for fraud is not valid. Dig. 13, 7, 17, pr.

IN COMMUNI. In common. Fleta, lib. 3, c. 4, § 2.

In conjunctivis, oportet utramque partem esse veram. In conjunctives, it is necessary that each part be true. Wing. Max. 13, max. 9. In a condition consisting of divers parts in the copulative, both parts must be performed.

IN CONSIDERATIONE INDE. In consideration thereof. 3 Salk. 64, pl. 5.

IN CONSIDERATIONE LEGIS. In consideration or contemplation of law; in abeyance. Dyer, 102*b*.

IN CONSIDERATIONE PRÆMISSORUM. In consideration of the premises. 1 Strange, 535.

In consimili casu, consimile debet esse remedium. Hardr. 65. In similar cases the remedy should be similar.

IN CONSPECTU EJUS. In his sight or view. 12 Mod. 95.

In consuetudinibus, non diuturnitas temporis sed soliditas rationis est consideranda. In customs, not length of time, but solidity of reason, is to be considered. Co. Litt. 141*a*. The antiquity of a custom is to be less regarded than its reasonableness.

IN CONTINENTI. Immediately; without any interval or intermission. Calvin. Sometimes written as one word, "*incontinenti.*"

In contractibus, benigna; in testamentis, benignior; in restitutionibus, benignissima interpretatio facienda est. Co. Litt. 112. In contracts, the interpretation is to be liberal; in wills, more liberal; in restitutions, most liberal.

In contractibus, rei veritas potius quam scriptura perspici debet. In contracts, the truth of the matter ought to be regarded rather than the writing. Cod. 4, 22, 1.

In contractibus, tacite insunt [veniunt] quæ sunt moris et consuetudinis. In contracts, matters of custom and usage are tacitly implied. A contract is understood to contain the customary clauses, although they are not expressed. Story, Bills, § 143; 3 Kent, Comm. 260, note; Broom, Max. 842.

In contrahenda venditione, ambiguum pactum contra venditorem interpretandum est. In the contract of sale, an ambiguous agreement is to be interpreted against the seller. Dig. 50, 17, 172. See Id. 18, 1, 21.

**In conventionibus, contrahentium voluntas potius quam verba spectari placuit. In agreements, the intention of the contracting parties, rather than the words used, should be regarded. 17 Johns. 150; Broom, Max. 551.

IN CORPORE. In body or substance; in a material thing or object.

IN CRASTINO. On the morrow. *In crastino Animarum*, on the morrow of All Souls. 1 Bl. Comm. 342.

In criminalibus, probationes debent esse luce clariores. In criminal cases, the proofs ought to be clearer than light. 3 Inst. 210.

In criminalibus, sufficit generalis malitia intentionis, cum facto paris gradus. In criminal matters or cases, a general malice of intention is sufficient, [if united] with an act of equal or corresponding degree. Bac. Max. p. 65, reg. 15; Broom, Max. 323.

In criminalibus, voluntas reputabitur pro facto. In criminal acts, the will will be taken for the deed. 3 Inst. 106.

IN CUJUS REI TESTIMONIUM. In testimony whereof. The initial words of the concluding clause of ancient deeds in Latin, literally translated in the English forms.

IN CUSTODIA LEGIS. In the custody or keeping of the law. 2 Steph. Comm. 74.

IN DELICTO. In fault. See IN PARI DELICTO, etc.

IN DIEM. For a day; for the space of a day. Calvin.

In disjunctivis sufficit alteram partem esse veram. In disjunctives it is sufficient that either part be true. Where a condition is in the disjunctive, it is sufficient if either part be performed. Wing. Max. 13, max. 9; 7 East, 272; Broom, Max. 592.

IN DOMINICO. In demesne. *In dominico suo ut de feodo*, in his demesne as of fee.

IN DORSO. On the back. 2 Bl. Comm. 468; 2 Steph. Comm. 164. *In dorso recordi*, on the back of the record. 5 Coke, 45. Hence the English *indorse, indorsement*, etc.

In dubiis, benigniora præferenda sunt. In doubtful cases, the more favorable views are to be preferred; the more liberal interpretation is to be followed. Dig. 50, 17, 56; 2 Kent, Comm. 557.

In dubiis, magis dignum est accipiendum. Branch, Princ. In doubtful cases, the more worthy is to be accepted.

In dubiis, non præsumitur pro testamento. In cases of doubt, the presumption is not in favor of a will. Branch, Princ. But see Cro. Car. 51.

IN DUBIO. In doubt; in a state of uncertainty, or in a doubtful case.

In dubio, hæc legis constructio quam verba ostendunt. In a case of doubt, that is the construction of the law which the words indicate. Branch, Princ.

In dubio, pars mitior est sequenda. In doubt, the milder course is to be followed.

In dubio, sequendum quod tutius est. In doubt, the safer course is to be adopted.

IN DUPLO. In double. *Damna in duplo*, double damages. Fleta, lib. 4, c. 10, § 1.

IN EADEM CAUSA. In the same state or condition. Calvin.

IN EMULATIONEM VICINI. In envy or hatred of a neighbor. Where an act is done, or action brought, solely to hurt or distress another, it is said to be *in emulationem vicini*. 1 Kames, Eq. 56.

In eo quod plus sit, semper inest et minus. In the greater is always included the less also. Dig. 50, 17, 110.

IN EQUITY. In a court of equity, as distinguished from a court of law; in the purview, consideration, or contemplation of equity; according to the doctrines of equity.

IN ESSE. In being. Actually existing. Distinguished from *in posse*, which means "that which is not, but may be." A child before birth is *in posse;* after birth, *in esse*.

IN EVIDENCE. Included in the evidence already adduced. The "facts in evidence" are such as have already been proved in the cause.

IN EXCAMBIO. In exchange. Formal words in old deeds of exchange.

IN EXITU. In issue. *De materia in exitu*, of the matter in issue. 12 Mod. 372.

In expositione instrumentorum, mala grammatica, quod fieri potest, vitanda est. In the construction of instruments, bad grammar is to be avoided as much as possible. 6 Coke, 39; 2 Pars. Cont. 26.

IN EXTENSO. In extension; at full length; from beginning to end, leaving out nothing.

IN EXTREMIS. In extremity; in the last extremity; in the last illness. 20 Johns. 502; 2 Bl. Comm. 375, 500. *Agens in extremis*, being in extremity. Bract. fol. 373*b*. Declarations *in extremis*, dying declarations. 15 Johns. 286; 1 Greenl. Ev. § 156.

IN FACIE CURIÆ. In the face of the court. Dyer, 28.

IN FACIE ECCLESIÆ. In the face of the church. A term applied in the law of England to marriages, which are required to be solemnized in a parish church or public chapel, unless by dispensation or license. 1 Bl. Comm. 439; 2 Steph. Comm. 288, 289. Applied in Bracton to the old mode of conferring dower. Bract. fol. 92; 2 Bl. Comm. 133.

IN FACIENDO. In doing; in feasance; in the performance of an act. 2 Story, Eq. Jur. § 1308.

IN FACT. Actual, real; as distinguished from implied or inferred. Resulting from the acts of parties, instead of from the act or intendment of law.

IN FACTO. In fact; in deed. *In facto dicit*, in fact says. 1 Salk. 22, pl. 1.

In facto quod se habet ad bonum et malum, magis de bono quam de malo lex intendit. In an act or deed which admits of being considered as both good and bad, the law intends more from the good than from the bad; the law makes the more favorable construction. Co. Litt. 78*b*.

In favorabilibus magis attenditur quod prodest quam quod nocet. In things favored, what profits is more regarded than what prejudices. Bac. Max. p. 57, in reg. 12.

IN FAVOREM LIBERTATIS. In favor of liberty.

IN FAVOREM VITÆ. In favor of life.

In favorem vitæ, libertatis, et innocentiæ, omnia præsumuntur. In favor of life, liberty, and innocence, every presumption is made. Lofft. 125.

IN FEODO. In fee. Bract. fol. 207; Fleta, lib. 2, c. 64, § 15. *Seisitus in feodo*, seised in fee. Fleta, lib. 3, c. 7, § 1.

In fictione juris semper æquitas existit. In the fiction of law there is always equity; a legal fiction is always consistent with equity. 11 Coke, 51*a*; Broom, Max. 127, 130.

IN FIERI. In being made; in process of formation or development; hence, incomplete or inchoate. Legal proceedings are described as *in fieri* until judgment is entered.

IN FINE. Lat. At the end. Used, in references, to indicate that the passage cited is at the *end* of a book, chapter, section, etc.

IN FORMA PAUPERIS. In the character or manner of a pauper. Describes permission given to a poor person to sue without liability for costs.

IN FORO. In a (or the) forum, court, or tribunal.

IN FORO CONSCIENTIÆ. In the tribunal of conscience; conscientiously; considered from a moral, rather than a legal, point of view.

IN FORO CONTENTIOSO. In the forum of contention or litigation.

IN FORO ECCLESIASTICO. In an ecclesiastical forum; in the ecclesiastical court. Fleta, lib. 2, c. 57, § 13.

IN FORO SÆCULARI. In a secular forum or court. Fleta, lib. 2, c. 57, § 14; 1 Bl. Comm. 20.

IN FRAUDEM CREDITORUM. In fraud of creditors; with intent to defraud creditors. Inst. 1, 6, pr., 3.

IN FRAUDEM LEGIS. In fraud of the law. 3 Bl. Comm. 94. With the intent or view of evading the law. 1 Johns. 424, 432.

IN FULL. Relating to the whole or *full* amount; as a receipt in full. Complete; giving all details.

IN FULL LIFE. Continuing in both physical and civil existence; that is, neither actually dead nor *civiliter mortuus*.

IN FUTURO. In future; at a future time; the opposite of *in præsenti*. 2 Bl. Comm. 166, 175.

IN GENERALI PASSAGIO. In the general passage; that is, on the journey to Palestine with the general company or body of Crusaders. This term was of frequent occurrence in the old law of essoins, as a means of accounting for the absence of the party, and was distinguished from *simplex passagium*, which meant that he was performing a pilgrimage to the Holy Land alone.

In generalibus versatur error. Error dwells in general expressions. 3 Sum. 290; 1 Cush. 292.

IN GENERE. In kind; in the same *genus* or class; the same in quantity and quality, but not individually the same. In the Roman law, things which may be given or restored *in genere* are distinguished from such as must be given or restored *in specie;* that is, identically. Mackeld. Rom. Law, § 161.

IN GREMIO LEGIS. In the bosom of the law; in the protection of the law; in abeyance. 1 Coke, 131*a;* T. Raym. 319.

IN GROSS. In a large quantity or sum; without division or particulars; by wholesale.

At large; not annexed to or dependent upon another thing. Common in gross is such as is neither appendant nor appurtenant to land, but is annexed to a man's person. 2 Bl. Comm. 34.

IN HAC PARTE. In this behalf; on this side.

IN HÆC VERBA. In these words; in the same words.

In hæredes non solent transire actiones quæ pœnales ex maleficio sunt. 2 Inst. 442. Penal actions arising from anything of a criminal nature do not pass to heirs.

In his enim quæ sunt favorabilia animæ, quamvis sunt damnosa rebus, fiat aliquando extentio statuti. In things that are favorable to the spirit, though injurious to property, an extension of the statute should sometimes be made. 10 Coke, 101.

In his quæ de jure communi omnibus conceduntur, consuetudo alicujus patriæ vel loci non est allegenda. 11 Coke, 85. In those things which by common right are conceded to all, the custom of a particular district or place is not to be alleged.

IN HOC. In this; in respect to this.

IN IISDEM TERMINIS. In the same terms. 9 East, 487.

IN INDIVIDUO. In the distinct, identical, or individual form; *in specie.* Story, Bailm. § 97.

IN INFINITUM. Infinitely; indefinitely. Imports indefinite succession or continuance.

IN INITIALIBUS. In the preliminaries. A term in Scotch practice, applied to the preliminary examination of a witness as to the following points: Whether he knows the parties, or bears ill will to either of them, or has received any reward or promise of reward for what he may say, or can lose or gain by the cause, or has been told by any person what to say. If the witness answer these questions satisfactorily, he is then examined *in causa,* in the cause. Bell, Dict. "Evidence."

IN INITIO. In or at the beginning. *In initio litis,* at the beginning, or in the first stage of the suit. Bract. fol. 400.

IN INTEGRUM. To the original or former state. Calvin.

IN INVIDIAM. To excite a prejudice.

IN INVITUM. Against an unwilling party; against one not assenting. A term applied to proceedings against an adverse party, to which he does not consent.

IN IPSIS FAUCIBUS. In the very throat or entrance. *In ipsis faucibus* of a port, actually entering a port. 1 C. Rob. Adm. 233, 234.

IN ITINERE. In eyre; on a journey or circuit. In old English law, the justices *in itinere* (or in eyre) were those who made a circuit through the kingdom once in seven years for the purposes of trying causes. 3 Bl. Comm. 58.

In course of transportation; on the way; not delivered to the vendee. In this sense the phrase is equivalent to "*in transitu.*"

IN JUDGMENT. In a court of justice; in a seat of judgment. Lord Hale is called "one of the greatest and best men who ever sat in judgment." 1 East, 306.

In judiciis, minori ætati succurritur. In courts or judicial proceedings, infancy is aided or favored. Jenk. Cent. 46, case 89.

IN JUDICIO. In Roman law. In the course of an actual trial; before a judge, (*judex.*) A cause, during its preparatory stages, conducted before the prætor, was said to be *in jure;* in its second stage, after it had been sent to a *judex* for trial, it was said to be *in judicio.*

In judicio non creditur nisi juratis. Cro. Car. 64. In a trial, credence is given only to those who are sworn.

IN JURE. In law; according to law. In the Roman practice, the procedure in an action was divided into two stages. The first was said to be *in jure;* it took place before the prætor, and included the formal and introductory part and the settlement of questions of law. The second stage was committed to the *judex*, and comprised the investigation and trial of the facts; this was said to be *in judicio.*

IN JURE ALTERIUS. In another's right. Hale, Anal. § 26.

In jure, non remota causa sed proxima spectatur. Bac. Max. reg. 1. In law, the proximate, and not the remote, cause is regarded.

IN JURE PROPRIO. In one's own right. Hale, Anal. § 26.

IN JUS VOCARE. To call, cite, or summon to court. Inst. 4, 16, 3; Calvin. *In jus vocando*, summoning to court. 3 Bl. Comm. 279.

IN KIND. In the same kind, class, or genus. A loan is returned "in kind" when not the identical article, but one corresponding and equivalent to it, is given to the lender. See IN GENERE.

IN LAW. In the intendment, contemplation, or inference of the law; implied or inferred by law; existing in law or by force of law. See IN FACT.

IN LECTO MORTALI. On the deathbed. Fleta, lib. 5, c. 28, § 12.

IN LIMINE. On or at the threshold; at the very beginning; preliminarily.

IN LITEM. For a suit; to the suit. Greenl. Ev. § 348.

IN LOCO. In place; in lieu; instead; in the place or stead. Townsh. Pl. 38.

IN LOCO PARENTIS. In the place of a parent; instead of a parent; charged, factitiously, with a parent's rights, duties, and responsibilities.

In majore summa continetur minor. 5 Coke, 115. In the greater sum is contained the less.

IN MAJOREM CAUTELAM. For greater security. 1 Strange, 105, arg.

IN MALAM PARTEM. In a bad sense, so as to wear an evil appearance.

In maleficiis voluntas spectatur, non exitus. In evil deeds regard must be had to the intention, and not to the result. Dig. 48, 8, 14; Broom, Max. 324.

In maleficio, ratihabitio mandato comparatur. In a case of malfeasance, ratification is equivalent to command. Dig. 50, 17, 152, 2.

In maxima potentia minima licentia. In the greatest power there is the least freedom. Hob. 159.

IN MEDIAS RES. Into the heart of the subject, without preface or introduction.

IN MEDIO. Intermediate. A term applied, in Scotch practice, to a fund held between parties litigant.

In mercibus illicitis non sit commercium. There should be no commerce in illicit or prohibited goods. 3 Kent, Comm. 262, note.

IN MERCY. To be in mercy is to be at the discretion of the king, lord, or judge in respect to the imposition of a fine or other punishment.

IN MISERICORDIA. The entry on the record where a party was in mercy was, "*Ideo in misericordia,*" etc. Sometimes "*misericordia*" means the being quit of all amercements.

IN MITIORI SENSU. In the milder sense; in the less aggravated acceptation. In actions of slander, it was formerly the rule that, if the words alleged would admit of two constructions, they should be taken in the less injurious and defamatory sense, or *in mitiori sensu.*

IN MODUM ASSISÆ. In the manner or form of an assize. Bract. fol. 183*b*. *In modum juratæ*, in manner of a jury. Id. fol. 181*b*.

IN MORA. In default; literally, in delay. In the civil law, a borrower who omits or refuses to return the thing loaned at the proper time is said to be *in mora.* Story, Bailm. §§ 254, 259.

In Scotch law. A creditor who has begun without completing diligence necessary for attaching the property of his debtor is said to be *in mora.* Bell.

IN MORTUA MANU. Property owned by religious societies was said to be held *in mortua manu*, or in mortmain, since religious men were *civiliter mortui.* 1 Bl. Comm. 479; Tayl. Gloss.

IN NOMINE DEI, AMEN. In the name of God, Amen. A solemn introduction, anciently used in wills and many other instruments. The translation is often used in wills at the present day.

IN NOTIS. In the notes.

In novo casu, novum remedium apponendum est. 2 Inst. 3. A new remedy is to be applied to a new case.

IN NUBIBUS. In the clouds; in abeyance; in custody of law. *In nubibus, in mare, in terrâ, vel in custodiâ legis,* in the air, sea, or earth, or in the custody of the law. Tayl. Gloss. In case of abeyance, the inheritance is figuratively said to rest *in nubibus,* or *in gremio legis.*

IN NULLIUS BONIS. Among the goods or property of no person; belonging to no person, as treasure-trove and wreck were anciently considered.

IN NULLO EST ERRATUM. In nothing is there error. The name of the common plea or joinder in error, denying the existence of error in the record or proceedings; which is in the nature of a demurrer, and at once refers the matter of law arising thereon to the judgment of the court. 2 Tidd, Pr. 1173; 7 Metc. (Mass.) 285, 287.

In obscura voluntate manumittentis, favendum est libertati. Where the expression of the will of one who seeks to manumit a slave is ambiguous, liberty is to be favored. Dig. 50, 17, 179.

In obscuris, inspici solere quod verisimilius est, aut quod plerumque fieri solet. In obscure cases, we usually look at what is most probable, or what most commonly happens. Dig. 50, 17, 114.

In obscuris, quod minimum est sequimur. In obscure or doubtful cases, we follow that which is the least. Dig. 50, 17, 9; 2 Kent, Comm. 557.

IN ODIUM SPOLIATORIS. In hatred of a despoiler, robber, or wrong-doer. 1 Gall. 174; 2 Story, 99; 1 Greenl. Ev. § 348.

In odium spoliatoris omnia præsumuntur. To the prejudice (in condemnation) of a despoiler all things are presumed; every presumption is made against a wrongdoer. 1 Vern. 452.

In omni actione ubi duæ concurrunt districtiones, videlicet, in rem et in personam, illa districtio tenenda est quæ magis timetur et magis ligat. In every action where two distresses concur, that is, *in rem* and *in personam,* that is to be chosen which is most dreaded, and which binds most firmly. Bract. fol. 372; Fleta, l. 6, c. 14, § 28.

In omni re nascitur rẹs quæ ipsam rem exterminat. In everything there arises a thing which destroys the thing itself. Everything contains the element of its own destruction. 2 Inst. 15.

IN OMNIBUS. In all things; on all points. "A case parallel *in omnibus.*" 10 Mod. 104.

In omnibus contractibus, sive nominatis sive innominatis, permutatio continetur. In all contracts, whether nominate or innominate, an exchange [of value, *i. e.,* a consideration] is implied. Gravin. lib. 2, § 12; 2 Bl. Comm. 444, note.

In omnibus obligationibus in quibus dies non ponitur, præsenti die debetur. In all obligations in which a date is not put, the debt is due on the present day; the liability accrues immediately. Dig. 50, 17, 14.

In omnibus [fere] pœnalibus judiciis, et ætati et imprudentiæ succurritur. In nearly all penal judgments, immaturity of age and imbecility of mind are favored. Dig. 50, 17, 108; Broom, Max. 314.

In omnibus quidem, maxime tamen in jure, æquitas spectanda sit. In all things, but especially in law, equity is to be regarded. Dig. 50, 17, 90; Story, Bailm. § 257.

IN PACATO SOLO. In a country which is at peace.

IN PACE DEI ET REGIS. In the peace of God and the king. Fleta, lib. 1, c. 31, § 6. Formal words in old appeals of murder.

IN PAIS. This phrase, as applied to a legal transaction, primarily means that it has taken place without legal proceedings. Thus a widow was said to make a request *in pais* for her dower when she simply applied to the heir without issuing a writ. (Co. Litt. 32*b*.) So conveyances are divided into those by matter of record and those by matter *in pais.* In some cases, however, "matters *in pais*" are opposed not only to "matters of record," but also to "matters in writing," *i. e.,* deeds, as where estoppel by deed is distinguished from estoppel by matter *in pais.* (Id. 352*a*.) Sweet.

IN PAPER. A term formerly applied to the proceedings in a cause before the record was made up. 3 Bl. Comm. 406; 2 Burrows, 1098. Probably from the circumstance of the record being always on parchment. The opposite of "on record." 1 Burrows, 322.

IN PARI CAUSA. In an equal cause. In a cause where the parties on each side have equal rights.

In pari causa possessor potior haberi debet. In an equal cause he who has the possession should be preferred. Dig. 50, 17, 128, 1.

IN PARI DELICTO. In equal fault; equally culpable or criminal; in a case of equal fault or guilt.

In pari delicto potior est conditio possidentis, [defendentis.] In a case of equal or mutual fault [between two parties] the condition of the party in possession [or defending] is the better one. 2 Burrows, 926. Where each party is equally in fault, the law favors him who is actually in possession. Broom, Max. 290, 729. Where the fault is mutual, the law will leave the case as it finds it. Story, Ag. § 195.

IN PARI MATERIA. Upon the same matter or subject. Statutes *in pari materia* are to be construed together. 7 Conn. 456.

IN PATIENDO. In suffering, permitting, or allowing.

IN PECTORE JUDICIS. In the breast of the judge. Latch, 180. A phrase applied to a judgment.

IN PEJOREM PARTEM. In the worst part; on the worst side. Latch, 159, 160.

IN PERPETUAM REI MEMORIAM. In perpetual memory of a matter; for preserving a record of a matter. Applied to depositions taken in order to preserve the testimony of the deponent.

IN PERPETUUM REI TESTIMONIUM. In perpetual testimony of a matter; for the purpose of declaring and settling a thing forever. 1 Bl. Comm. 86.

IN PERSON. A party, plaintiff or defendant, who sues out a writ or other process, or appears to conduct his case in court himself, instead of through a solicitor or counsel, is said to act and appear *in person.*

IN PERSONAM, IN REM. In the Roman law, from which they are taken, the expressions "*in rem*" and "*in personam*" were always opposed to one another, an act or proceeding *in personam* being one done or directed against or with reference to a specific person, while an act or proceeding *in rem* was one done or directed with reference to no specific person, and consequently against or with reference to all whom it might concern, or "all the world." The phrases were especially applied to actions; an *actio in personam* being the remedy where a claim against a specific person arose out of an obligation, whether *ex contractu* or *ex maleficio,* while an *actio in rem* was one brought for the assertion of a right of property, easement, *status,* etc., against one who denied or infringed it. See Inst. 4, 6, 1; Gaius, 4, 1, 1–10; 5 Sav. Syst. 13, et seq.; Dig. 2, 14, 7, 8; Id. 4, 2, 9, 1.

From this use of the terms, they have come to be applied to signify the antithesis of "available against a particular person," and "available against the world at large." Thus, *jura in personam* are rights primarily available against specific persons; *jura in rem,* rights only available against the world at large.

So a judgment or decree is said to be *in rem* when it binds third persons. Such is the sentence of a court of admiralty on a question of prize, or a decree of nullity or dissolution of marriage, or a decree of a court in a foreign country as to the *status* of a person domiciled there.

Lastly, the terms are sometimes used to signify that a judicial proceeding operates on a thing or a person. Thus, it is said of the court of chancery that it acts *in personam,* and not *in rem,* meaning that its decrees operate by compelling defendants to do what they are ordered to do, and not by producing the effect directly. Sweet.

In personam actio est, qua cum eo agimus qui obligatus est nobis ad faciendum aliquid vel dandum. The action *in personam* is that by which we sue him who is under obligation to us to do something or give something. Dig. 44, 7, 25; Bract. 101*b*.

IN PIOS USUS. For pious uses; for religious purposes. 2 Bl. Comm. 505.

IN PLENA VITA. In full life. Yearb. P. 18 Hen. VI. 2.

IN PLENO COMITATU. In full county court. 3 Bl. Comm. 36.

IN PLENO LUMINE. In public; in common knowledge; in the light of day.

In pœnalibus causis benignius interpretandum est. In penal causes or cases, the more favorable interpretation should be adopted. Dig. 50, 17, (197,) 155, 2; Plowd. 86*b*, 124; 2 Hale, P. C. 365.

IN POSSE. In possibility; not in actual existence. See IN ESSE.

IN POTESTATE PARENTIS. In the power of a parent. Inst. 1, 8, pr.; Id. 1, 9; 2 Bl. Comm. 498.

IN PRÆMISSORUM FIDEM. In confirmation or attestation of the premises. A notarial phrase.

In præparatoriis ad judicium favetur actori. 2 Inst. 57. In things preceding judgment the plaintiff is favored.

IN PRÆSENTI. At the present time. 2 Bl. Comm. 166. Used in opposition to *in futuro.*

In præsentia majoris potestatis, minor potestas cessat. In the presence of the superior power, the inferior power ceases. Jenk. Cent. 214, c. 53. The less authority is merged in the greater. Broom, Max. 111.

IN PRENDER. L. Fr. In taking. A term applied to such incorporeal hereditaments as a party entitled to them was to *take* for himself; such as common. 2 Steph. Comm. 23; 3 Bl. Comm. 15.

In pretio emptionis et venditionis, naturaliter licet contrahentibus se circumvenire. In the price of buying and selling, it is naturally allowed to the contracting parties to overreach each other. 1 Story, Cont. 606.

IN PRIMIS. In the first place. A phrase used in argument.

IN PRINCIPIO. At the beginning.

IN PROMPTU. In readiness; at hand.

In propria causa nemo judex. No one can be judge in his own cause. 12 Coke, 13.

IN PROPRIA PERSONA. In one's own proper person.

In quo quis delinquit, in eo de jure est puniendus. In whatever thing one offends, in that is he rightfully to be punished. Co. Litt. 233*b;* Wing. Max. 204, max. 58. The punishment shall have relation to the nature of the offense.

IN RE. In the affair; in the matter of. This is the usual method of entitling a judicial proceeding in which there are not adversary parties, but merely some *res* concerning which judicial action is to be taken, such as a bankrupt's estate, an estate in the probate court, a proposed public highway, etc. It is also sometimes used as a designation of a proceeding where one party makes an application on his own behalf, but such proceedings are more usually entitled "*Ex parte* ———."

In re communi neminem dominorum jure facere quicquam, invito altero, posse. One co-proprietor can exercise no authority over the common property against the will of the other. Dig. 10, 3, 28.

In re communi potior est conditio prohibentis. In a partnership the condition of one who forbids is the more favorable.

In re dubia, benigniorem interpretationem sequi, non minus justius est quam tutius. In a doubtful matter, to follow the more liberal interpretation is not less the juster than the safer course. Dig. 50, 17, 192, 1.

In re dubia, magis inficiatio quam affirmatio intelligenda. In a doubtful matter, the denial or negative is to be understood, [or regarded,] rather than the affirmative. Godb. 37.

In re lupanari, testes lupanares admittentur. In a matter concerning a brothel, prostitutes are admitted as witnesses. 6 Barb. 320, 324.

In re pari potiorem causam esse prohibentis constat. In a thing equally shared [by several] it is clear that the party refusing [to permit the use of it] has the better cause. Dig. 10, 3, 28. A maxim applied to partnerships, where one partner has a right to withhold his assent to the acts of his copartner. 3 Kent, Comm. 45.

In re propria iniquum admodum est alicui licentiam tribuere sententiæ. It is extremely unjust that any one should be judge in his own cause.

In rebus manifestis, errat qui authoritates legum allegat; quia perspicue vera non sunt probanda. In clear cases, he mistakes who cites legal authorities; for obvious truths are not to be proved. 5 Coke, 67*a*. Applied to cases too plain to require the support of authority; "because," says the report, "he who endeavors to prove them obscures them."

In rebus quæ sunt favorabilia animæ, quamvis sunt damnosa rebus, fiat aliquando extensio statuti. 10 Coke, 101.

In things that are favorable to the spirit, though injurious to things, an extension of a statute should sometimes be made.

IN REM. A technical term used to designate proceedings or actions instituted *against the thing*, in contradistinction to personal actions, which are said to be *in personam*. See IN PERSONAM.

It is true that, in a strict sense, a proceeding *in rem* is one taken directly against property, and has for its object the disposition of property, without reference to the title of individual claimants; but, in a larger and more general sense, the terms are applied to actions between parties, where the direct object is to reach and dispose of property owned by them, or of some interest therein. Such are cases commenced by attachment against the property of debtors, or instituted to partition real estate, foreclose a mortgage, or enforce a lien. So far as they affect property in this state, they are substantially proceedings *in rem* in the broader sense which we have mentioned. 95 U. S. 734.

In rem actio est per quam rem nostram quæ ab alio possidetur petimus, et semper adversus eum est qui rem possidet. The action *in rem* is that by which we seek our property which is possessed by another, and is always against him who possesses the property. Dig. 44, 7, 25; Bract. fol. 102.

IN RENDER. A thing is said to lie *in render* when it must be rendered or given by the tenant; as rent. It is said to lie *in prender* when it consists in the right in the lord or other person to *take* something.

In republica maxime conservanda sunt jura belli. In a state the laws of war are to be especially upheld. 2 Inst. 58.

IN RERUM NATURA. In the nature of things; in the realm of actuality; in existence. In a dilatory plea, an allegation that the plaintiff is not *in rerum natura* is equivalent to averring that the person named is fictitious. 3 Bl. Comm. 301. In the civil law the phrase is applied to things. Inst. 2, 20, 7.

In restitutionem, non in pœnam hæres succedit. The heir succeeds to the restitution, not to the penalty. An heir may be compelled to make restitution of a sum unlawfully appropriated by the ancestor, but is not answerable criminally, as for a penalty. 2 Inst. 198.

In restitutionibus benignissima interpretatio facienda est. Co. Litt. 112. The most benignant interpretation is to be made in restitutions.

In satisfactionibus non permittitur amplius fieri quam semel factum est. In payments, more must not be received than has been received once for all. 9 Coke, 53.

IN SCRINIO JUDICIS. In the writing-case of the judge; among the judge's papers. "That is a thing that rests *in scrinio judicis*, and does not appear in the body of the decree." Hardr. 51.

IN SEPARALI. In several; in severalty. Fleta, lib. 2, c. 54, § 20.

IN SIMILI MATERIA. Dealing with the same or a kindred subject-matter.

IN SIMPLICI PEREGRINATIONE. In simple pilgrimage. Bract. fol. 338. A phrase in the old law of essoins. See IN GENERALI PASSAGIO.

IN SOLIDO. In the civil law. For the whole; as a whole. An obligation *in solido* is one where each of the several obligors is liable for the whole; that is, it is joint and several. Possession *in solidum* is exclusive possession.

When several persons obligate themselves to the obligee by the terms "*in solido*," or use any other expressions which clearly show that they intend that each one shall be separately bound to perform the whole of the obligation, it is called an "obligation *in solido*" on the part of the obligors. Civil Code La. art. 2082.

IN SOLIDUM. For the whole. *Si plures sint fidejussores, quotquot erunt numero, singuli in solidum tenentur*, if there be several sureties, however numerous they may be, they are individually bound for the whole debt. Inst. 3, 21, 4. *In parte sive in solidum*, for a part or for the whole. Id. 4, 1, 16. See Id. 4, 6, 20; Id. 4, 7, 2.

IN SOLO. In the soil or ground. *In solo alieno*, in another's ground. *In solo proprio*, in one's own ground. 2 Steph. Comm. 20.

IN SPECIE. Specific; specifically. Thus, to decree performance *in specie* is to decree specific performance.

In kind; in the same or like form. A thing is said to exist *in specie* when it retains its existence as a distinct individual of a particular class.

IN STATU QUO. In the condition in which it was. See STATUS QUO.

In stipulationibus cum quæritur quid actum sit verba contra stipulatorem in-

terpretanda sunt. In the construction of agreements words are interpreted against the person using them. Thus, the construction of the *stipulatio* is against the stipulator, and the construction of the *promissio* against the promissor. Dig. 45, 1, 38, 18; Broom, Max. 599.

In stipulationibus, id tempus spectatur quo contrahimus. In stipulations, the time when we contract is regarded. Dig. 50, 17, 144, 1.

IN STIRPES. In the law of intestate succession. According to the roots or stocks; by representation; as distinguished from succession *per capita*. See PER STIRPES; PER CAPITA.

IN SUBSIDIUM. In aid.

In suo quisque negotio hebetior est quam in alieno. Every one is more dull in his own business than in another's.

IN TANTUM. In so much; so much; so far; so greatly. Reg. Orig. 97, 106.

IN TERMINIS TERMINANTIBUS. In terms of determination; exactly in point. 11 Coke, 40*b*. In express or determinate terms. 1 Leon. 93.

IN TERROREM. In terror or warning; by way of threat. Applied to legacies given upon condition that the recipient shall not dispute the validity or the dispositions of the will; such a condition being usually regarded as a mere threat.

IN TERROREM POPULI. Lat. To the terror of the people. A technical phrase necessary in indictments for riots. 4 Car. & P. 373.

In testamentis plenius testatoris intentionem scrutamur. In wills we more especially seek out the intention of the testator. 3 Bulst. 103; Broom, Max. 555.

In testamentis plenius voluntates testantium interpretantur. Dig. 50, 17, 12. In wills the intention of testators is more especially regarded. "That is to say," says Mr. Broom, (Max., 568,) "a will will receive a more liberal construction than its strict meaning, if alone considered, would permit."

In testamentis ratio tacita non debet considerari, sed verba solum spectari debent; adeo per divinationem mentis a verbis recedere durum est. In wills an unexpressed meaning ought not to be considered, but the words alone ought to be looked to; so hard is it to recede from the words by guessing at the intention.

IN TESTIMONIUM. Lat. In witness; in evidence whereof.

IN TOTIDEM VERBIS. In so many words; in precisely the same words; word for word.

IN TOTO. In the whole; wholly; completely; as the award is void *in toto*.

In toto et pars continetur. In the whole the part also is contained. Dig. 50, 17, 113.

In traditionibus scriptorum, non quod dictum est, sed quod gestum est, inspicitur. In the delivery of writings, not what is said, but what is done, is looked to. 9 Coke, 137*a*.

IN TRAJECTU. In the passage over; on the voyage over. See Sir William Scott, 3 C. Rob. Adm. 141.

IN TRANSITU. In transit; on the way or passage; while passing from one person or place to another. 2 Kent, Comm. 540–552. On the voyage. 1 C. Rob. Adm. 338.

IN VACUO. Without object; without concomitants or coherence.

IN VADIO. In gage or pledge. 2 Bl. Comm. 157.

IN VENTRE SA MERE. L. Fr. In his mother's womb; spoken of an unborn child.

In veram quantitatem fidejussor teneatur, nisi pro certa quantitate accessit. Let the surety be holden for the true quantity, unless he agree for a certain quantity. 17 Mass. 597.

In verbis, non verba, sed res et ratio, quærenda est. Jenk. Cent. 132. In the construction of words, not the mere words, but the thing and the meaning, are to be inquired after.

IN VINCULIS. In chains; in actual custody. Gilb. Forum Rom. 97.

Applied also, figuratively, to the condition of a person who is compelled to submit to terms which oppression and his necessities impose on him. 1 Story, Eq. Jur. § 302.

IN VIRIDI OBSERVANTIA. Present to the minds of men, and in full force and operation.

IN WITNESS WHEREOF. The initial words of the concluding clause in deeds: "In witness whereof the said parties have hereunto set their hands," etc. A translation of the Latin phrase "*in cujus rei testimonium.*"

INADEQUATE PRICE. A term applied to indicate the want of a sufficient consideration for a thing sold, or such a price as would ordinarily be entirely incommensurate with its intrinsic value.

INADMISSIBLE. That which, under the established rules of law, cannot be admitted or received; *e. g.*, parol evidence to contradict a written contract.

INÆDIFICATIO. In the civil law. Building on another's land with one's own materials, or on one's own land with another's materials.

INALIENABLE. Not subject to alienation; the characteristic of those things which cannot be bought or sold or transferred from one person to another, such as rivers and public highways, and certain personal rights; *e. g.*, liberty.

INAUGURATION. The act of installing or inducting into office with formal ceremonies, as the coronation of a sovereign, the inauguration of a president or governor, or the consecration of a prelate.

INBLAURA. In old records. Profit or product of ground. Cowell.

INBORH. In Saxon law. A security, pledge, or *hypotheca*, consisting of the chattels of a person unable to obtain a personal "borg," or surety.

INBOUND COMMON. An uninclosed common, marked out, however, by boundaries.

INCAPACITY. Want of capacity; want of power or ability to take or dispose; want of legal ability to act.

INCASTELLARE. To make a building serve as a castle. Jacob.

INCAUSTUM, or ENCAUSTUM. Ink. Fleta, l. 2, c. 27, § 5.

Incaute factum pro non facto habetur. A thing done unwarily (or unadvisedly) will be taken as not done. Dig. 28, 4, 1.

INCENDIARY. A house-burner; one guilty of arson; one who maliciously and willfully sets another person's building on fire.

Incendium ære alieno non exuit debitorem. Cod. 4, 2, 11. A fire does not release a debtor from his debt.

INCEPTION. Commencement; opening; initiation. The beginning of the operation of a contract or will.

Incerta pro nullis habentur. Uncertain things are held for nothing. Dav. Ir. K. B. 33.

Incerta quantitas vitiat actum. 1 Rolle R. 465. An uncertain quantity vitiates the act.

INCEST. The crime of sexual intercourse or cohabitation between a man and woman who are related to each other within the degrees wherein marriage is prohibited by law.

INCESTUOUS ADULTERY. The elements of this offense are that defendant, being married to one person, has had sexual intercourse with another related to the defendant within the prohibited degrees. 11 Ga. 53.

INCESTUOUS BASTARDY. Incestuous bastards are those who are produced by the illegal connection of two persons who are relations within the degrees prohibited by law. Civil Code La. art. 183.

INCH. A measure of length, containing one-twelfth part of a foot; originally supposed equal to three barleycorns.

INCH OF CANDLE. A mode of sale at one time in use among merchants. A notice is first given upon the exchange, or other public place, as to the time of sale. The goods to be sold are divided into lots, printed papers of which, and the conditions of sale, are published. When the sale takes place, a small piece of candle, about an inch long, is kept burning, and the last bidder, when the candle goes out, is entitled to the lot or parcel for which he bids. Wharton.

INCHARTARE. To give, or grant, and assure anything by a written instrument.

INCHOATE. Imperfect; unfinished; begun, but not completed; as a contract not executed by all the parties.

INCHOATE DOWER. A wife's interest in the lands of her husband during his life, which may become a right of dower upon his death.

INCIDENT. This word, used as a noun, denotes anything which inseparably belongs to, or is connected with, or inherent in, another thing, called the "principal." In this sense a court-baron is incident to a manor. Also, less strictly, it denotes anything which is usually connected with another, or connected for some purposes, though not inseparably. Thus, the right of alienation is incident to an estate in fee-simple, though separable in equity.

INCIDERE. Lat. In the civil and old English law. To fall into. Calvin.

To fall out; to happen; to come to pass. Calvin.

To fall upon or under; to become subject or liable to. *Incidere in legem*, to incur the penalty of a law. Brissonius.

INCILE. Lat. In the civil law. A trench. A place sunk by the side of a stream, so called because it is *cut* (*incidatur*) into or through the stone or earth. Dig. 43, 21, 1, 5. The term seems to have included ditches (*fossæ*) and wells, (*putei.*)

INCIPITUR. Lat. It is begun; it begins. In old practice, when the pleadings in an action at law, instead of being recited at large on the issue-roll, were set out merely by their commencements, this was described as entering the *incipitur; i. e.*, the beginning.

INCISED WOUND. In medical jurisprudence. A cut or incision on a human body; a wound made by a cutting instrument, such as a razor. Burrill, Circ. Ev. 693; Whart. & S. Med. Jur. § 808.

INCIVILE. Irregular; improper; out of the due course of law.

Incivile est, nisi tota lege perspecta, una aliqua particula ejus proposita, judicare, vel respondere. It is improper, without looking at the whole of a law, to give judgment or advice, upon a view of any one clause of it. Dig. 1, 3, 24.

Incivile est, nisi tota sententia inspecta, de aliqua parte judicare. It is irregular, or legally improper, to pass an opinion upon any part of a sentence, without examining the whole. Hob. 171*a*.

INCIVISM. Unfriendliness to the state or government of which one is a citizen.

INCLAUSA. In old records. A home close or inclosure near the house. Paroch. Antiq. 31; Cowell.

INCLOSE. To shut up. "To inclose a jury," in Scotch practice, is to shut them up in a room by themselves. Bell.

INCLOSED LANDS. Lands which are actually inclosed and surrounded with fences. 7 Mees. & W. 441.

INCLOSURE. In English law. Inclosure is the act of freeing land from rights of common, commonable rights, and generally all rights which obstruct cultivation and the productive employment of labor on the soil.

Also, an artificial fence around one's estate. 39 Vt. 34, 326; 36 Wis. 42. See CLOSE.

Inclusio unius est exclusio alterius. The inclusion of one is the exclusion of another. The certain designation of one person is an absolute exclusion of all others. 11 Coke, 58*b*.

INCLUSIVE. Embraced; comprehended; comprehending the stated limits or extremes. Opposed to "exclusive."

INCOLA. Lat. In the civil law. An inhabitant; a dweller or resident. Properly, one who has transferred his domicile to any country.

Incolas domicilium facit. Residence creates domicile. 1 Johns. Cas. 363, 366.

INCOME. The return in money from one's business, labor, or capital invested; gains, profit, or private revenue.

"Income" means that which comes in or is received from any business or investment of capital, without reference to the outgoing expenditures; while "profits" generally means the gain which is made upon any business or investment when both receipts and payments are taken into account. "Income," when applied to the affairs of individuals, expresses the same idea that "revenue" does when applied to the affairs of a state or nation. 4 Hill, 20; 7 Hill, 504.

INCOME TAX. A tax on the yearly profits arising from property, professions, trades, and offices. 2 Steph. Comm. 573.

Incommodum non solvit argumentum. An inconvenience does not destroy an argument.

INCOMMUNICATION. In Spanish law. The condition of a prisoner who is not permitted to see or to speak with any person visiting him during his confinement. A person accused cannot be subjected to this treatment unless it be expressly ordered by the judge, for some grave offense, and it cannot be continued for a longer period than is absolutely necessary. This precaution is resorted to for the purpose of preventing the accused from knowing beforehand the testimony of the witnesses, or from attempting to corrupt them and concert such measures as will efface the traces of his guilt. As soon, therefore, as the danger of his doing so has ceased, the interdiction ceases likewise. Escriche.

INCOMPATIBLE. Two or more relations, offices, functions, or rights which cannot naturally, or may not legally, exist in or be exercised by the same person at the same time, are said to be incompatible. Thus, the relations of lessor and lessee of the same land, in one person at the same time, are incompatible. So of trustee and beneficiary of the same property.

INCOMPETENCY. Lack of ability, legal qualification, or fitness to discharge the required duty.

As applied to evidence, the word "incompetent" means not proper to be received; inadmissible, as distinguished from that which the court should admit for the consideration of the jury, though they may not find it worthy of credence.

In French law. Inability or insufficiency of a judge to try a cause brought before him, proceeding from lack of jurisdiction.

INCONCLUSIVE. That which may be disproved or rebutted; not shutting out further proof or consideration. Applied to evidence and presumptions.

INCONSULTO. In the civil law. Unadvisedly; unintentionally. Dig. 28, 4, 1.

INCONTINENCE. Want of chastity; indulgence in unlawful carnal connection.

INCOPOLITUS. A proctor or vicar.

Incorporalia bello non adquiruntur. Incorporeal things are not acquired by war. 6 Maule & S. 104.

INCORPORAMUS. We incorporate. One of the words by which a corporation may be created in England. 1 Bl. Comm. 473; 3 Steph. Comm 173.

INCORPORATE. 1. To create a corporation; to confer a corporate franchise upon determinate persons.

2. To declare that another document shall be taken as part of the document in which the declaration is made as much as if it were set out at length therein.

INCORPORATION. 1. The act or process of forming or creating a corporation; the formation of a legal or political body, with the quality of perpetual existence and succession, unless limited by the act of incorporation.

2. The method of making one document of any kind become a part of another separate document by referring to the former in the latter, and declaring that the former shall be taken and considered as a part of the latter the same as if it were fully set out therein. This is more fully described as "incorporation by reference." If the one document is copied at length in the other, it is called "actual incorporation."

3. **In the civil law.** The union of one domain to another.

INCORPOREAL. Without body; not of material nature; the opposite of "corporeal," (*q. v.*)

INCORPOREAL CHATTELS. A class of incorporeal rights growing out of or incident to things *personal;* such as patent-rights and copyrights. 2 Steph. Comm. 72.

INCORPOREAL HEREDITAMENT. Anything, the subject of property, which is inheritable and not tangible or visible. 2 Woodd. Lect. 4. A right issuing out of a thing corporate (whether real or personal) or concerning or annexed to or exercisable within the same. 2 Bl. Comm. 20; 1 Washb. Real Prop. 10.

INCORPOREAL PROPERTY. In the civil law. That which consists in legal right merely. The same as choses in action at common law.

INCORRIGIBLE ROGUE. A species of rogue or offender, described in the statutes 5 Geo. IV. c. 83, and 1 & 2 Vict. c. 38. 4 Steph. Comm. 309.

INCREASE. (1) The produce of land; (2) the offspring of animals.

INCREASE, AFFIDAVIT OF. Affidavit of payment of increased costs, produced on taxation.

INCREASE, COSTS OF. In English law. It was formerly a practice with the jury to award to the successful party in an action the nominal sum of 40s. only for his costs; and the court assessed by their own officer the actual amount of the successful party's costs; and the amount so assessed, over and above the nominal sum awarded by the jury, was thence called "costs of increase." Lush, Com. Law Pr. 775. The practice has now wholly ceased. Rapal. & Law.

INCREMENTUM. Increase or improvement, opposed to *decrementum* or abatement.

INCROACHMENT. An unlawful gaining upon the right or possession of another. See ENCROACHMENT.

INCULPATE. To impute blame or guilt; to accuse; to involve in guilt or crime.

INCULPATORY. In the law of evidence. Going or tending to establish guilt; intended to establish guilt; criminative. Burrill, Circ. Ev. 251, 252.

INCUMBENT. A person who is in present possession of an office; one who is legally authorized to discharge the duties of an office. 11 Ohio, 50.

In ecclesiastical law, the term signifies a clergyman who is in possession of a benefice.

INCUMBER. To incumber land is to make it subject to a charge or liability; *e. g.*, by mortgaging it. Incumbrances include not only mortgages and other voluntary charges, but also liens, *lites pendentes*, registered judgments, and writs of execution, etc. Sweet.

INCUMBRANCE. Any right to, or interest in, land which may subsist in third persons, to the diminution of the value of the estate of the tenant, but consistently with the passing of the fee. 8 Neb. 8; 2 Greenl. Ev. § 242.

A claim, lien, or liability attached to property; as a mortgage, a registered judgment, etc.

INCUMBRANCER. The holder of an incumbrance, *e. g.*, a mortgage, on the estate of another.

INCUR. Men contract debts; they incur liabilities. In the one case, they act affirmatively; in the other, the liability is incurred or cast upon them by act or operation of law. "Incur" means something beyond contracts, —something not embraced in the word "debts." 15 How. Pr. 48; 5 Abb. Pr. 162.

INCURRAMENTUM. The liability to a fine, penalty, or amercement. Cowell.

INDE. Lat. Thence; thenceforth; thereof; thereupon; for that cause.

Inde datæ leges ne fortior omnia posset. Laws are made to prevent the stronger from having the power to do everything. Dav. Ir. K. B. 36.

INDEBITATUS. Lat. Indebted. *Nunquam indebitatus*, never indebted. The title of the plea substituted in England for *nil debet*.

INDEBITATUS ASSUMPSIT. Lat. Being indebted, he promised or undertook. This is the name of that form of the action of *assumpsit* in which the declaration alleges a debt or obligation to be due from the defendant, and then avers that, in consideration thereof, he promised to pay or discharge the same.

INDEBITI SOLUTIO. Lat. In the civil and Scotch law. A payment of what is not due. When made through ignorance or by mistake, the amount paid might be recovered back by an action termed "*condictio indebiti.*" (Dig. 12, 6.) Bell.

INDEBITUM. In the civil law. Not due or owing. (Dig. 12, 6.) Calvin.

INDEBTEDNESS. The state of being in debt, without regard to the ability or inability of the party to pay the same. See 1 Story, Eq. Jur. 343; 2 Hill, Abr. 421.

The word implies an absolute or complete liability. A contingent liability, such as that of a surety before the principal has made default, does not constitute indebtedness. On the other hand, the money need not be immediately payable. Obligations yet to become due constitute indebtedness, as well as those already due. 9 Mo. 149.

INDECENCY. An act against good behavior and a just delicacy. 2 Serg. & R. 91.

This is scarcely a technical term of the law, and is not susceptible of exact definition or description in its juridical uses. The question whether or not a given act, publication, etc., is indecent is for the court and jury in the particular case.

INDECENT EXPOSURE. Exposure to sight of the private parts of the body in a lewd or indecent manner in a public place. It is an indictable offense at common law, and by statute in many of the states.

INDECIMABLE. In old English law. That which is not titheable, or liable to pay tithe. 2 Inst. 490.

INDEFEASIBLE. That which cannot be defeated, revoked, or made void. This term is usually applied to an estate or right which cannot be defeated.

INDEFENSUS. In old English practice. Undefended; undenied by pleading.

A defendant who makes no defense or plea. Blount.

INDEFINITE FAILURE OF ISSUE. A failure of issue not merely at the death of the party whose issue are referred to, but at any subsequent period, however remote. 1 Steph. Comm. 562. A failure of issue whenever it shall happen, sooner or later, without any fixed, certain, or definite period within which it must happen. 4 Kent, Comm. 274.

INDEFINITE NUMBER. An uncertain or indeterminate number. A number which may be increased or diminished at pleasure.

INDEFINITE PAYMENT. In Scotch law. Payment without specification. Indefinite payment is where a debtor, owing several debts to one creditor, makes a payment to the creditor, without specifying to which of the debts he means the payment to be applied. See Bell.

Indefinitum æquipollet universali. The undefined is equivalent to the whole. 1 Vent. 368.

Indefinitum supplet locum universalis. The undefined or general supplies the place of the whole. Branch, Princ.

INDEMNIFICATUS. Lat. Indemnified. See INDEMNIFY.

INDEMNIFY. To save harmless; to secure against loss or damage; to give security for the reimbursement of a person in case of an anticipated loss falling upon him.

Also to make good; to compensate; to make reimbursement to one of a loss already incurred by him.

INDEMNIS. Lat. Without hurt, harm, or damage; harmless.

INDEMNITEE. The person who, in a contract of indemnity, is to be indemnified or protected by the other.

INDEMNITOR. The person who is bound, by an indemnity contract, to indemnify or protect the other.

INDEMNITY. An indemnity is a collateral contract or assurance, by which one person engages to secure another against an anticipated loss, or to prevent him from being damnified by the legal consequences of an act or forbearance on the part of one of the parties or of some third person. See Civil Code Cal. § 2772. Thus, insurance is a contract of indemnity. So an indemnifying bond is given to a sheriff who fears to proceed under an execution where the property is claimed by a stranger.

The term is also used to denote a compensation given to make the person whole from a loss already sustained; as where the government gives indemnity for private property taken by it for public use.

A legislative act, assuring a general dispensation from punishment or exemption from prosecution to persons involved in offenses, omissions of official duty, or acts in excess of authority, is called an indemnity; strictly it is an act of indemnity.

INDEMNITY CONTRACT. An agreement between two parties, whereby the one party, the indemnitor, either agrees to indemnify and save harmless the other party, the indemnitee, from loss or damage, or binds himself to do some particular act or thing, or to protect the indemnitee against liability to, or the claim of, a third party. 10 Amer. & Eng. Enc. Law, 402.

INDEMPNIS. The old form of writing *indemnis*. Townsh. Pl. 19. So, *indempnificatus* for *indemnificatus*.

INDENIZATION. The act of making a denizen, or of naturalizing.

INDENT, *n.* In American law. A certificate or indented certificate issued by the government of the United States at the close of the Revolution, for the principal or interest of the public debt. Webster.

INDENT, *v.* To cut in a serrated or waving line. In old conveyancing, if a deed was made by more parties than one, it was usual to make as many copies of it as there were parties, and each was cut or indented (either in acute angles, like the teeth of a saw, or in a waving line) at the top or side, to tally or correspond with the others, and the deed so made was called an "indenture." Anciently, both parts were written on the same piece of parchment, with some word or letters written between them through which the parchment was cut, but afterwards, the word or letters being omitted, indenting came into use, the idea of which was that the genuineness of each part might be proved by its fitting into the angles cut in the other. But at length even this was discontinued, and at present the term serves only to give name to the species of deed executed by two or more parties, as opposed to a deed-poll, (*q. v.*) 2 Bl. Comm. 295.

To bind by indentures; to apprentice; as to indent a young man to a shoe-maker. Webster.

INDENTURE. A deed to which two or more persons are parties, and in which these enter into reciprocal and corresponding grants or obligations towards each other; whereas a deed-poll is properly one in which only the party making it executes it, or binds himself by it as a deed, though the grantors or grantees therein may be several in number. 3 Washb. Real Prop. 311. See INDENT, *v.*

INDENTURE OF APPRENTICESHIP. A contract in two parts, by which a person, generally a minor, is bound to serve another in his trade, art, or occupation for a stated time, on condition of being instructed in the same.

INDEPENDENCE. The state or condition of being free from dependence, subjection, or control. Political independence is the attribute of a nation or state which is entirely autonomous, and not subject to the government, control, or dictation of any exterior power.

INDEPENDENT CONTRACT. One in which the mutual acts or promises have no relation to each other, either as equivalents or considerations. Civil Code La. art. 1769; 1 Bouv. Inst. no. 699.

INDEPENDENT COVENANTS. Covenants in an instrument which are independent of each other, or where the performance of one, or the right to require its performance, or to obtain damages for its non-performance, does not depend upon the performance of the other.

Independenter se habet assecuratio a viaggio navis. The voyage insured is an independent or distinct thing from the voyage of the ship. 3 Kent, Comm. 318, note.

INDETERMINATE. That which is uncertain, or not particularly designated; as if I sell you one hundred bushels of wheat, without stating what wheat. 1 Bouv. Inst. no. 950.

INDEX. A book containing references, alphabetically arranged, to the contents of a series or collection of volumes; or an addition to a single volume or set of volumes containing such references to its contents.

Index animi sermo. Language is the exponent of the intention. The language of a statute or instrument is the best guide to the intention. Broom, Max. 622.

INDIAN COUNTRY. This term does not necessarily import territory owned and occupied by Indians, but it means all those portions of the United States designated by this name in the legislation of congress. 4 Sawy. 121.

INDIAN TRIBE. A separate and distinct community or body of the aboriginal Indian race of men found in the United States.

INDIANS. The aboriginal inhabitants of North America.

INDICARE. In the civil law. To show or discover. To fix or tell the price of a thing. Calvin. To inform against; to accuse.

INDICATIF. An abolished writ by which a prosecution was in some cases removed from a court-christian to the queen's bench. Enc. Lond.

INDICATION. In the law of evidence. A sign or token; a fact pointing to some inference or conclusion. Burrill, Circ. Ev. 251, 252, 263, 275.

INDICATIVE EVIDENCE. This is not evidence properly so called, but the mere suggestion of evidence proper, which may possibly be procured if the suggestion is followed up. Brown.

INDICAVIT. In English practice. A writ of prohibition that lies for a patron of a church, whose clerk is sued in the spiritual court by the clerk of another patron, for tithes amounting to a fourth part of the value of the living. 3 Bl. Comm. 91; 3 Steph. Comm. 711. So termed from the emphatic word of the Latin form. Reg. Orig. 35*b*, 36.

INDICIA. Signs; indications. Circumstances which point to the existence of a given fact as probable, but not certain. For example, "*indicia* of partnership" are any circumstances which would induce the belief that a given person was in reality, though not ostensibly, a member of a given firm.

INDICIUM. In the civil law. A sign or mark. A species of proof, answering very nearly to the *circumstantial evidence* of the common law. Best, Pres. p. 13, § 11, note; Wills, Circ. Ev. 34.

INDICT. See INDICTMENT.

INDICTABLE. Proper or necessary to be prosecuted by process of indictment.

INDICTED. Charged in an indictment with a criminal offense. See INDICTMENT.

INDICTEE. A person indicted.

INDICTIO. In old public law. A declaration; a proclamation. *Indictio belli*, a declaration or indiction of war. An indictment.

INDICTION, CYCLE OF. A mode of computing time by the space of fifteen years, instituted by Constantine the Great; originally the period for the payment of certain taxes. Some of the charters of King Edgar and Henry III. are dated by indictions. Wharton.

INDICTMENT. An indictment is an accusation in writing found and presented by a grand jury, legally convoked and sworn, to the court in which it is impaneled, charging that a person therein named has done some act, or been guilty of some omission, which, by law, is a public offense, punishable on indictment. Code Iowa 1880, § 4295; Pen. Code Cal. § 917; Code Ala. 1886, § 4364.

A presentment differs from an indictment in that it is an accusation made by a grand jury of their own motion, either upon their own observation and knowledge, or upon evidence before them; while an indictment is preferred at the suit of the government, and is usually framed in the first instance by the prosecuting officer of the government, and by him laid before the grand jury, to be found or ignored. An information resembles in its form and substance an indictment, but is filed at the mere discretion of the proper law officer of the government, without the intervention or approval of a grand jury. 2 Story, Const. §§ 1784, 1786.

In Scotch law. An indictment is the form of process by which a criminal is brought to trial at the instance of the lord advocate. Where a private party is a principal prosecutor, he brings his charge in what is termed the "form of criminal letters."

Indictment de felony est contra pacem domini regis, coronam et dignitatem suam, in genere et non in individuo; quia in Angliâ non est interregnum. Jenk. Cent. 205. Indictment for felony is against the peace of our lord the king, his crown and dignity in general, and not against his individual person; because in England there is no interregnum.

INDICTOR. He who causes another to be indicted. The latter is sometimes called the "indictee."

INDIFFERENT. Impartial; unbiased; disinterested.

INDIGENA. In old English law. A subject born; one born within the realm, or naturalized by act of parliament. Co. Litt. 8*a*. The opposite of "*alienigena*," (*q. v.*)

INDIRECT EVIDENCE. Evidence which does not tend directly to prove the controverted fact, but to establish a state of facts, or the existence of other facts, from which it will follow as a logical inference.

Inferential evidence as to the truth of a disputed fact, not by testimony of any witness to the fact, but by collateral circumstances ascertained by competent means. 1 Starkie, Ev. 15.

INDISTANTER. Forthwith; without delay.

INDITEE. L. Fr. In old English law. A person indicted. Mirr. c. 1, § 3; 9 Coke, pref.

INDIVIDUUM. Lat. In the civil law. That cannot be divided. Calvin.

INDIVISIBLE. Not susceptible of division or apportionment; inseparable; entire. Thus, a contract, covenant, consideration, etc., may be divisible or indivisible; *i. e.*, separable or entire.

INDIVISUM. That which two or more persons hold in common without partition; undivided.

INDORSAT. In old Scotch law. Indorsed. 2 Pitc. Crim. Tr. 41.

INDORSE. To write a name on the back of a paper or document. Bills of exchange and promissory notes are indorsed by a party's writing his name on the back. 7 Pick. 117.

"Indorse" is a technical term, having sufficient legal certainty without words of more particular description. 7 Vt. 351.

INDORSEE. The person to whom a bill of exchange, promissory note, bill of lading, etc., is assigned by indorsement, giving him a right to sue thereon.

INDORSEE IN DUE COURSE. An indorsee in due course is one who, in good faith, in the ordinary course of business, and for value, before its apparent maturity or presumptive dishonor, and without knowledge of its actual dishonor, acquires a negotiable instrument duly indorsed to him, or indorsed generally, or payable to the bearer. Civil Code Cal. § 3123.

INDORSEMENT. The act of a payee, drawee, accommodation indorser, or holder of a bill, note, check, or other negotiable instrument, in writing his name upon the back of the same, with or without further or qualifying words, whereby the property in the same is assigned and transferred to another.

That which is so written upon the back of a negotiable instrument.

One who writes his name upon a negotiable instrument, otherwise than as a maker or acceptor, and delivers it, with his name thereon, to another person, is called an "indorser," and his act is called "indorsement." Civil Code Cal. § 3108; Civil Code Dak. § 1836.

An indorsement in full is one in which mention is made of the name of the indorsee. Chit. Bills, 170.

A blank indorsement is one which does not mention the name of the indorsee, and consists, generally, simply of the name of the indorser written on the back of the instrument. 1 Daniel, Neg. Inst. § 693.

A conditional indorsement is one by which the indorser annexes some condition (other than the failure of prior parties to pay) to his liability. The condition may be either precedent or subsequent. 1 Daniel, Neg. Inst. § 697.

A restrictive indorsement is one which is so worded as to restrict the further negotiability of the instrument.

A qualified indorsement is one which restrains or limits or qualifies or enlarges the liability of the indorser, in any manner different from what the law generally imports as his true liability, deducible from the nature of the instrument. Chit. Bills, (8th Ed.) 261; 7 Taunt. 160.

In criminal law. An entry made upon the back of a writ or warrant.

INDORSER. He who indorses; *i. e.*, being the payee or holder, writes his name on the back of a bill of exchange, etc.

INDUCEMENT. In contracts. The benefit or advantage which the promisor is to receive from a contract is the inducement for making it.

In criminal evidence. Motive; that which leads or tempts to the commission of crime. Burrill, Circ. Ev. 283.

In pleading. That portion of a declaration or of any subsequent pleading in an action which is brought forward by way of explanatory introduction to the main allegations. Brown.

INDUCIÆ. In international law. A truce; a suspension of hostilities; an agreement during war to abstain for a time from warlike acts.

In old maritime law. A period of twenty days after the safe arrival of a vessel under bottomry, to dispose of the cargo, and raise the money to pay the creditor, with interest.

In old English practice. Delay or indulgence allowed a party to an action; further time to appear in a cause. Bract. fol. 352*b;* Fleta, lib. 4, c. 5, § 8.

In Scotch practice. Time allowed for the performance of an act. Time to appear to a citation. Time to collect evidence or prepare a defense.

INDUCIÆ LEGALES. In Scotch law. The days between the citation of the defendant and the day of appearance; the days between the test day and day of return of the writ.

INDUCTIO. In the civil law. Obliteration, by drawing the pen or *stylus* over the writing. Dig. 28, 4; Calvin.

INDUCTION. In ecclesiastical law. Induction is the ceremony by which an incumbent who has been instituted to a benefice is vested with full possession of all the profits belonging to the church, so that he becomes seised of the temporalities of the church, and is then complete incumbent. It is performed by virtue of a mandate of induction directed by the bishop to the archdeacon, who either performs it in person, or directs his precept to one or more other clergymen to do it. Phillim. Ecc. Law, 477.

INDULGENCE. In the Roman Catholic Church. A remission of the punishment due to sins, granted by the pope or church, and supposed to save the sinner from purgatory. Its abuse led to the Reformation in Germany. Wharton. • Forbearance, (*q. v.*)

INDULTO. In ecclesiastical law. A dispensation granted by the pope to do or obtain something contrary to the common law.

In Spanish law. The condonation or remission of the punishment imposed on a criminal for his offense. This power is exclusively vested in the king.

INDUMENT. Endowment, (*q. v.*)

INDUSTRIAL AND PROVIDENT SOCIETIES. Societies formed in England for carrying on any labor, trade, or handicraft, whether wholesale or retail, including the buying and selling of land and also (but subject to certain restrictions) the business of banking.

INDUSTRIAL SCHOOLS. Schools (established by voluntary contribution) in which industrial training is provided, and in which children are lodged, clothed, and fed, as well as taught.

INDUSTRIAM, PER. Lat. A qualified property in animals *feræ naturæ* may be acquired *per industriam, i. e.*, by a man's reclaiming and making them tame by art, industry, and education; or by so confining them within his own immediate power that they cannot escape and use their natural liberty. 2 Steph. Comm. 5.

INEBRIATE. A person addicted to the use of intoxicating liquors; an habitual drunkard.

Any person who habitually, whether continuously or periodically, indulges in the use of intoxicating liquors to such an extent as to stupefy his mind, and to render him incompetent to transact ordinary business with safety to his estate, shall be deemed an inebriate, within the meaning of this chapter: provided, the habit of so indulging in such use shall have been at the time of inquisition of at least one year's standing. Code N. C. 1883, § 1671.

INELIGIBILITY. Disqualification or legal incapacity to be elected to an office. Thus, an alien or naturalized citizen is ineligible to be elected president of the United States.

INELIGIBLE. Disqualified to be elected to an office; also disqualified to hold an office if elected or appointed to it. 28 Wis. 99.

Inesse potest donationi, modus, conditio sive causa; ut modus est; si conditio; quia causa. In a gift there may be manner, condition, and cause; as [*ut*] introduces a manner; if, [*si*,] a condition; because, [*quia*,] a cause. Dyer, 138.

INEST DE JURE. Lat. It is implied of right; it is implied by law.

INEVITABLE. Incapable of being avoided; fortuitous; transcending the power of human care, foresight, or exertion to avoid or prevent, and therefore suspending legal relations so far as to excuse from the performance of contract obligations, or from liability for consequent loss.

INEVITABLE ACCIDENT. An inevitable accident is one produced by an irresistible physical cause; an accident which cannot be prevented by human skill or foresight, but results from natural causes, such as lightning or storms, perils of the sea, inundations or earthquakes, or sudden death or illness. By irresistible force is meant an interposition of human agency, from its nature and power absolutely uncontrollable. 11 La. Ann. 427. As used in the civil law, this term is nearly synonymous with "fortuitous event."

Inevitable accident is where a vessel is pursuing a lawful avocation in a lawful manner, using the proper precautions against danger, and an accident occurs. The highest degree of caution that can be used is not required. It is enough that it is reasonable under the circumstances; such as is usual in similar cases, and has been found by long experience to be sufficient to answer the end in view,—the safety of life and property. 7 Wall. 196.

Inevitable accident is only when the disaster happens from natural causes, without negligence or fault on either side, and when both parties have endeavored, by every means in their power, with due care and caution, and with a proper display of nautical skill, to prevent the occurrence of the accident. 12 Ct. Cl. 491.

INEWARDUS. A guard; a watchman. Domesday.

INFALISTATUS. In old English law. Exposed upon the sands, or sea-shore. A species of punishment mentioned in Hengham. Cowell.

INFAMIA. Lat. Infamy; ignominy or disgrace.

By *infamia juris* is meant infamy established by law as the consequence of crime; *infamia facti* is where the party is supposed to be guilty of such crime, but it has not been judicially proved. 17 Mass. 515, 541.

INFAMIS. Lat. In Roman law. A person whose right of reputation was diminished (involving the loss of some of the rights of citizenship) either on account of his infamous avocation or because of conviction for crime. Mackeld. Rom. Law, § 135.

INFAMOUS CRIME. A crime which entails infamy upon one who has committed it. See INFAMY.

The term "infamous"—*i. e.*, without fame or good report—was applied at common law to certain crimes, upon the conviction of which a person became incompetent to testify as a witness, upon the theory that a person would not commit so heinous a crime unless he was so depraved as to be unworthy of credit. These crimes are treason, felony, and the *crimen falsi*. Abbott.

A crime punishable by imprisonment in the state prison or penitentiary, with or without hard labor, is an infamous crime, within the provision of the fifth amendment of the constitution that "no person shall be held to answer for a capital or otherwise infamous crime unless on a presentment or indictment of a grand jury." 117 U. S. 348, 6 Sup. Ct. Rep. 777.

"Infamous," as used in the fifth amendment to the United States constitution, in reference to crimes, includes those only of the class called "*crimen falsi*," which both involve the charge of falsehood, and may also injuriously affect the public administration of justice by introducing falsehood and fraud. 15 N. B. R. 325.

By the Revised Statutes of New York the term "infamous crime," when used in any statute, is directed to be construed as including every offense punishable with death or by imprisonment in a state-prison, and no other. 2 Rev. St. (p. 702, § 31,) p. 587, § 32.

INFAMY. A qualification of a man's legal *status* produced by his conviction of an infamous crime and the consequent loss of honor and credit, which, at common law, rendered him incompetent as a witness, and by statute in some jurisdictions entails other disabilities.

INFANCY. Minority; the state of a person who is under the age of legal majority, —at common law, twenty-one years. According to the sense in which this term is used, it may denote the condition of the person merely with reference to his years, or the contractual disabilities which non-age entails, or his *status* with regard to other powers or relations.

INFANGENTHEF. In old English law. A privilege of lords of certain manors to judge any thief taken within their fee.

INFANS. In the civil law. A child under the age of seven years; so called "*quasi impos fandi*," (as not having the faculty of speech.) Cod. Theodos. 8, 18, 8.

Infans non multum a furioso distat. An infant does not differ much from a lunatic. Bract. l. 3, c. 2, § 8; Dig. 50, 17, 5, 40; 1 Story, Eq. Jur. §§ 223, 224, 242.

INFANT. A person within age, not of age, or not of full age; a person under the age of twenty-one years; a minor. Co. Litt. 171*b;* 1 Bl. Comm. 463-466; 2 Kent, Comm. 233.

INFANTIA. In the civil law. The period of infancy between birth and the age of seven years. Calvin.

INFANTICIDE. The murder or killing of an infant soon after its birth. The fact of the birth distinguishes this act from "fœticide" or "procuring abortion," which terms denote the destruction of the *fœtus* in the womb.

INFANTS' MARRIAGE ACT. The statute 18 & 19 Vict. c. 43. By virtue of this act every infant, (if a male, of twenty, or, if a female, of seventeen, years,—section 4,) upon or in contemplation of marriage, may, with the sanction of the chancery division of the high court, make a valid settlement or contract for a settlement of property. Wharton.

INFANZON. In Spanish law. A person of noble birth, who exercises within his domains and inheritance no other rights and privileges than those conceded to him. Escriche.

INFEFT. In Scotch law. To give seisin or possession of lands; to invest or enfeoff. 1 Kames, Eq. 215.

INFEFTMENT. In old Scotch law. Investiture or infeudation, including both charter and seisin. 1 Forb. Inst. pt. 2, p. 110.

In later law. *Saisine*, or the instrument of possession. Bell.

INFENSARE CURIAM. An expression applied to a court when it suggested to an advocate something which he had omitted through mistake or ignorance. Spelman.

INFEOFFMENT. The act or instrument of feoffment. In Scotland it is synonymous with "*saisine*," meaning the instrument of possession. Formerly it was synonymous with "investiture." Bell.

INFERENCE. In the law of evidence. A truth or proposition drawn from another which is supposed or admitted to be true. A process of reasoning by which a fact or proposition sought to be established is deduced as a logical consequence from other facts, or a state of facts, already proved or admitted.

An inference is a deduction which the reason of the jury makes from the facts proved, without an express direction of law to that effect. Code Civil Proc. Cal. § 1958.

INFERENTIAL. In the law of evidence. Operating in the way of inference; argumentative. Presumptive evidence is sometimes termed "inferential." 4 Pa. St. 272.

INFERIOR. One who, in relation to another, has less power and is below him; one who is bound to obey another. He who makes the law is the superior; he who is bound to obey it, the inferior. 1 Bouv. Inst. no. 8.

INFERIOR COURT. This term may denote any court subordinate to the chief appellate tribunal in the particular judicial system; but it is commonly used as the designation of a court of special, limited, or statutory jurisdiction, whose record must show the existence and attaching of jurisdiction in any given case, in order to give presumptive validity to its judgment. See Cooley, Const. Lim. 508.

The English courts of judicature are classed generally under two heads,—the superior courts and the inferior courts; the former division comprising the courts at Westminster, the latter comprising all the other courts in general, many of which, however, are far from being of inferior importance in the common acceptation of the word. Brown.

INFEUDATION. The placing in possession of a freehold estate; also the granting of tithes to laymen.

INFICIARI. Lat. In the civil law. To deny; to deny one's liability; to refuse to pay a debt or restore a pledge; to deny the allegation of a plaintiff; to deny the charge of an accuser. Calvin.

INFICIATIO. Lat. In the civil law. Denial; the denial of a debt or liability; the denial of the claim or allegation of a party plaintiff. Calvin.

INFIDEL. One who does not believe in the existence of a God who will reward or punish in this world or that which is to come. Willes, 550. One who professes no religion that can bind his conscience to speak the truth. 1 Greenl. Ev. § 368.

INFIDELIS. In old English law. An infidel or heathen.

In feudal law. One who violated fealty.

INFIDELITAS. In feudal law. Infidelity; faithlessness to one's feudal oath. Spelman.

INFIDUCIARE. In old European law. To pledge property. Spelman.

INFIHT. Sax. An assault made on a person inhabiting the same dwelling.

Infinitum in jure reprobatur. That which is endless is reprobated in law. 12 Coke, 24. Applied to litigation.

INFIRM. Weak, feeble. The testimony of an "infirm" witness may be taken *de bene esse* in some circumstances. See 1 P. Wms. 117.

INFIRMATIVE. In the law of evidence. Having the quality of diminishing force; having a tendency to weaken or render infirm. 3 Benth. Jud. Ev. 14; Best. Pres. § 217.

INFIRMATIVE CONSIDERATION. In the law of evidence. A consideration, supposition, or hypothesis of which the criminative facts of a case admit, and which tends to weaken the inference or presumption of guilt deducible from them. Burrill, Circ. Ev. 153–155.

INFIRMATIVE FACT. In the law of evidence. A fact set up, proved, or even supposed, in opposition to the criminative facts of a case, the tendency of which is to weaken the force of the inference of guilt deducible from them. 3 Benth. Jud. Ev. 14; Best, Pres. § 217, et seq.

INFIRMATIVE HYPOTHESIS. A term sometimes used in criminal evidence to denote an hypothesis or theory of the case which assumes the defendant's innocence, and explains the criminative evidence in a manner consistent with that assumption.

INFORMAL. Deficient in legal form; inartificially drawn up.

INFORMALITY. Want of legal form.

INFORMATION. In practice. An accusation exhibited against a person for some criminal offense, without an indictment. 4 Bl. Comm. 308.

An accusation in the nature of an indictment, from which it differs only in being presented by a competent public officer on his oath of office, instead of a grand jury on their oath. 1 Bish. Crim. Proc. § 141.

The word is also frequently used in the law in its sense of communicated knowledge, and affidavits are frequently made, and pleadings and other documents verified, on "information and belief."

In French law. The act or instrument which contains the depositions of witnesses against the accused. Poth. Proc. Civil, § 2, art. 5.

INFORMATION IN THE NATURE OF A QUO WARRANTO. A proceeding against the usurper of a franchise or office. See QUO WARRANTO.

INFORMATION OF INTRUSION. A proceeding instituted by the state prosecuting officer against intruders upon the public domain. See Gen. St. Mass. c. 141; 3 Pick. 224; 6 Leigh, 588.

INFORMATUS NON SUM. In practice. I am not informed. A formal answer made by the defendant's attorney in court to the effect that he has not been advised of any defense to be made to the action. Thereupon judgment by default passes.

INFORMER. A person who informs or prefers an accusation against another, whom he suspects of the violation of some penal statute.

A common informer is a person who sues for a penalty which is given to any person who will sue for it, as opposed to a penalty which is only given to a person specially aggrieved by the act complained of. 3 Bl. Comm. 161.

INFORTIATUM. The name given by the glossators to the second of the three parts or volumes into which the Pandects were divided. The glossators at Bologna had at first only two parts, the first called "*Digestum Vetus*," (the Old Digest,) and the last called "*Digestum Novum*," (the New Digest.) When they afterwards received the middle or second part, they separated from the *Digestum Novum* the beginning it had then, and added it to the second part, from which *enlargement* the latter received the name "*Infortiatum*." Mackeld. Rom. Law, § 110.

INFORTUNIUM, HOMICIDE PER. Where a man doing a lawful act, without intention of hurt, unfortunately kills another.

INFRA. Lat. Below; underneath; within. This word occurring by itself in a book refers the reader to a subsequent part of the book, like "*post*." It is the opposite of "*ante*" and "*supra*," (*q. v.*)

INFRA ÆTATEM. Under age; not of age. Applied to minors.

INFRA ANNOS NUBILES. Under marriageable years; not yet of marriageable age.

INFRA ANNUM. Under or within a year. Bract. fol. 7.

INFRA ANNUM LUCTÛS. (Within the year of mourning.) The phrase is used in reference to the marriage of a widow within a year after her husband's death, which was prohibited by the civil law.

INFRA BRACHIA. Within her arms. Used of a husband *de jure*, as well as *de facto*. 2 Inst. 317. Also *inter brachia*. Bract. fol. 148*b*. It was in this sense that a woman could only have an appeal for murder of her husband *inter brachia sua*.

INFRA CIVITATEM. Within the state. 1 Camp. 23, 24.

INFRA CORPUS COMITATUS. Within the body (territorial limits) of a county. In English law, waters which are *infra corpus comitatus* are exempt from the jurisdiction of the admiralty.

INFRA DIGNITATEM CURIÆ. Beneath the dignity of the court; unworthy of the consideration of the court. Where a bill in equity is brought upon a matter too trifling to deserve the attention of the court, it is demurrable, as being *infra dignitatem curiæ*.

INFRA FUROREM. During madness; while in a state of insanity. Bract. fol. 19*b*.

INFRA HOSPITIUM. Within the inn. When a traveler's baggage comes *infra hospitium, i. e.*, in the care and under the custody of the innkeeper, the latter's liability attaches.

INFRA JURISDICTIONEM. Within the jurisdiction. 2 Strange, 827.

INFRA LIGEANTIAM REGIS. Within the king's ligeance. Comb. 212.

INFRA METAS. Within the bounds or limits. *Infra metas forestæ*, within the bounds of the forest. Fleta, lib. 2. c. 41, § 12. *Infra metas hospitii*, within the limits of the household; within the verge. Id. lib. 2, c. 2, § 2.

INFRA PRÆSIDIA. Within the protection; within the defenses. In international law, when a prize, or other captured property, is brought into a port of the captors, or within their lines, or otherwise under their complete custody, so that the chance of rescue is lost, it is said to be *infra præsidia*.

INFRA QUATUOR MARIA. Within the four seas; within the kingdom of England; within the jurisdiction.

INFRA QUATUOR PARIETES. Within four walls. 2 Crabb, Real Prop. p. 106, § 1089.

INFRA REGNUM. Within the realm.

INFRA SEX ANNOS. Within six years.

INFRA TRIDUUM. Within three days. Formal words in old appeals. Fleta, lib. 1, c. 31, § 6; Id. c. 35, § 3.

INFRACTION. A breach, violation, or infringement; as of a law, a contract, a right or duty.

In French law, this term is used as a general designation of all punishable actions.

INFRINGEMENT. A breaking into; a trespass or encroachment upon; a violation of a law, regulation, contract, or right. Used especially of invasions of the rights secured by patents, copyrights, and trademarks.

INFUGARE. To put to flight.

INFULA. A coif, or a cassock. Jacob.

INFUSION. In medical jurisprudence. The process of steeping in liquor; an operation by which the medicinal qualities of a substance may be extracted by a liquor without boiling. Also the product of this operation. "Infusion" and "decoction," though not identical, are *ejusdem generis* in law. 3 Camp. 74. See DECOCTION.

INGE. Meadow, or pasture. Jacob.

INGENIUM. (1) Artifice, trick, fraud; (2) an engine, machine, or device. Spelman.

INGENUITAS. Liberty given to a servant by manumission.

INGENUITAS REGNI. In old English law. The freemen, yeomanry, or commonalty of the kingdom. Cowell. Applied sometimes also to the barons.

INGENUUS. In Roman law. A person who, immediately that he was born, was a free person. He was opposed to *libertinus*, or *libertus*, who, having been born a slave, was afterwards manumitted or made free. It is not the same as the English law term "*generosus*," which denoted a person not merely free, but of good family. There were no distinctions among *ingenui;* but among *libertini* there were (prior to Justinian's abolition of the distinctions) three varieties, namely: Those of the highest rank, called "*Cives Romani;*" those of the second rank, called "*Latini Juniani;*" and those of the lowest rank, called "*Dediticii.*" Brown.

INGRATITUDE. In Roman law, ingratitude was accounted a sufficient cause for revoking a gift or recalling the liberty of a freedman. Such is also the law of France, with respect to the first case. But the English law has left the matter entirely to the moral sense.

INGRESS, EGRESS, AND REGRESS. These words express the right of a lessee to enter, go upon, and return from the lands in question.

INGRESSU. In English law. An ancient writ of entry, by which the plaintiff or complainant sought an entry into his lands. Abolished in 1833.

INGRESSUS. In old English law. Ingress; entry. The relief paid by an heir to the lord was sometimes so called. Cowell.

INGROSSATOR. An engrosser. *Ingrossator magni rotuli*, engrosser of the great roll; afterwards called "clerk of the pipe." Spelman; Cowell.

INGROSSING. The act of making a fair and perfect copy of any document from a rough draft of it, in order that it may be executed or put to its final purpose.

INHABITANT. One who resides actually and permanently in a given place, and has his domicile there.

"The words 'inhabitant,' 'citizen,' and 'resident,' as employed in different constitutions to define the qualifications of electors, mean substantially the same thing; and one is an inhabitant, resident, or citizen at the place where he has his domicile or home." Cooley, Const. Lim. *600. But the terms "resident" and "inhabitant" have also been held not synonymous, the latter implying a more fixed and permanent abode than the former, and importing privileges and duties to which a mere resident would not be subject. 40 Ill. 197.

INHABITED HOUSE DUTY. A tax assessed in England on inhabited dwelling-houses, according to their annual value, (St. 14 & 15 Vict. c. 36; 32 & 33 Vict. c. 14, § 11,) which is payable by the occupier, the landlord being deemed the occupier where the house is let to several persons, (St. 48 Geo. III. c. 55, Schedule B.) Houses occupied solely for business purposes are exempt from duty, although a care-taker may dwell therein, and houses partially occupied for business purposes are to that extent exempt. Sweet.

INHERENT POWER. An authority possessed without its being derived from another. A right, ability, or faculty of doing a thing, without receiving that right, ability, or faculty from another.

INHERETRIX. The old term for "heiress." Co. Litt. 13*a*.

INHERIT. To take by inheritance; to take as heir on the death of the ancestor. "To inherit *to*" a person is a common expression in the books. 3 Coke, 41; 2 Bl. Comm. 254, 255.

INHERITABLE BLOOD. Blood which has the purity (freedom from attainder) and legitimacy necessary to give its possessor the character of a lawful heir; that which is capable of being the medium for the transmission of an inheritance.

INHERITANCE. An estate in things real, descending to the heir. 2 Bl. Comm. 201.

Such an estate in lands or tenements or other things as may be inherited by the heir. Termes de la Ley.

An estate or property which a man has by descent, as heir to another, or which he may transmit to another, as his heir. Litt. § 9.

A perpetuity in lands or tenements to a man and his heirs. Cowell; Blount.

"Inheritance" is also used in the old books where "hereditament" is now commonly employed. Thus, Coke divides inheritances into corporeal and incorporeal, into real, personal, and mixed, and into entire and several.

In the civil law. The succession of the heir to all the rights and property of the estate-leaver. It is either testamentary, where the heir is created by will, or *ab intestato*, where it arises merely by operation of law. Heinec. § 484.

INHERITANCE ACT. The English statute of 3 & 4 Wm. IV. c. 106, by which the law of inheritance or descent has been considerably modified. 1 Steph. Comm. 359, 500.

INHIBITION. **In ecclesiastical law.** A writ issuing from a superior ecclesiastical court, forbidding an inferior judge to proceed further in a cause pending before him. In this sense it is closely analogous to the writ of *prohibition* at common law.

Also the command of a bishop or ecclesiastical judge that a clergyman shall cease from taking any duty.

In Scotch law. A species of diligence or process by which a debtor is prohibited from contracting any debt which may become a burden on his heritable property, in competition with the creditor at whose instance the inhibition is taken out; and from granting any deed of alienation, etc., to the prejudice of the creditor. Brande.

In the civil law. A prohibition which the law makes or a judge ordains to an individual. Hallifax, Civil Law, p. 126.

INHIBITION AGAINST A WIFE. In Scotch law. A writ in the sovereign's name, passing the signet, which prohibits all and sundry from having transactions with a wife or giving her credit. Bell; Ersk. Inst. 1, 6, 26.

INHOC. In old records. A nook or corner of a common or fallow field, inclosed and cultivated. Kennett, Par. Antiq. 297, 298; Cowell.

INHONESTUS. In old English law. Unseemly; not in due order. Fleta, lib. 1, c. 31, § 8.

Iniquissima pax est anteponenda justissimo bello. The most unjust peace is to be preferred to the justest war. 18 Wend. 257, 305.

INIQUITY. In Scotch practice. A technical expression applied to the decision of an inferior judge who has decided contrary to law; he is said to have committed iniquity. Bell.

Iniquum est alios permittere, alios inhibere mercaturam. It is inequitable to permit some to trade and to prohibit others. 3 Inst. 181.

Iniquum est aliquem rei sui esse judicem. It is wrong for a man to be a judge in his own cause. Branch, Princ.; 12 Coke, 113.

Iniquum est ingenuis hominibus non esse liberam rerum suarum alienationem. It is unjust that freemen should not have the free disposal of their own property. Co. Litt. 223*a*; Hob. 87; 4 Kent, Comm. 131.

INITIAL. That which *begins* or stands at the *beginning*. The first letter of a man's name.

INITIALIA TESTIMONII. In Scotch law. Preliminaries of testimony. The preliminary examination of a witness, before examining him in chief, answering to the *voir dire* of the English law, though taking a somewhat wider range. Wharton.

INITIATE. Commenced; inchoate. *Curtesy initiate* is the interest which a husband has in the wife's lands after a child is born who may inherit, but before the wife dies.

INITIATIVE. In French law. The name given to the important prerogative conferred by the *charte constitutionnelle*, article 16, on the late king to propose through his ministers projects of laws. 1 Toullier, no. 39.

INJUNCTION. A prohibitive writ issued by a court of equity, at the suit of a party complainant, directed to a party defendant in the action, or to a party made a defendant for that purpose, forbidding the latter to do some act, or to permit his servants or agents to do some act, which he is threatening or attempting to commit, or restraining him in the continuance thereof, such act being unjust and inequitable, injurious to the plaintiff, and not such as can be adequately redressed by an action at law.

An injunction is a writ or order requiring a person to refrain from a particular act. It may be granted by the court in which the action is brought, or by a judge thereof, and when made by a judge it may be enforced as an order of the court. Code Civil Proc. Cal. § 525.

Mandatory injunctions command defendant to do a particular thing. *Preventive*, command him to refrain from an act.

An injunction is called "preliminary" or "provisional," or an "injunction *pendente lite*," when it is granted at the outset of a suit brought for the purpose of restraining the defendant from doing the act threatened, until the suit has been heard and the rights of the parties determined. It is called "final" or "perpetual" when granted upon a bearing and adjudication of the rights in question, and as a measure of permanent relief.

INJURIA. Injury; wrong; the privation or violation of right. 3 Bl. Comm. 2.

INJURIA ABSQUE DAMNO. Injury or wrong without damage. A wrong done, but from which no loss or damage results, and which, therefore, will not sustain an action.

Injuria fit ei cui convicium dictum est, vel de eo factum carmen famosum. An injury is done to him of whom a reproachful thing is said, or concerning whom an infamous song is made. 9 Coke, 60.

Injuria illata judici, seu locum tenenti regis, videtur ipsi regi illata maxime si fiat in exercentem officium. 3 Inst. 1. An injury offered to a judge, or person representing the king, is considered as offered to the king himself, especially if it be done in the exercise of his office.

Injuria non excusat injuriam. One wrong does not justify another. Broom, Max. 395. See 6 El. & Bl. 47.

Injuria non præsumitur. Injury is not presumed. Co. Litt. 232. Cruel, oppressive, or tortuous conduct will not be presumed. Best. Ev. p. 336, § 298.

Injuria propria non cadet in beneficium facientis. One's own wrong shall not fall to the advantage of him that does it. A man will not be allowed to derive benefit from his own wrongful act. Branch, Princ.

Injuria servi dominum pertingit. The master is liable for injury done by his servant. Lofft, 229.

INJURIOUS WORDS. In Louisiana. Slander, or libelous words. Civil Code La. art. 3501.

INJURY. Any wrong or damage done to another, either in his person, rights, reputation, or property.

In the civil law. A delict committed in contempt or outrage of any one, whereby his body, his dignity, or his reputation is maliciously injured. Voet, Com. ad Pand. 47, t. 10, no. 1.

Injustum est, nisi tota lege inspecta, de una aliqua ejus particula proposita judicare vel respondere. 8 Coke, 117*b*. It is unjust to decide or respond as to any particular part of a law without examining the whole of the law.

INLAGARE. In old English law. To restore to protection of law. To restore a man from the condition of outlawry. Opposed to *utlagare*. Bract. lib. 3, tr. 2, c. 14, § 1; Du Cange.

INLAGATION. Restoration to the protection of law. Restoration from a condition of outlawry.

INLAGH. A person within the law's protection; contrary to *utlagh*, an outlaw. Cowell.

INLAND. Within a country, state, or territory; within the same country.

In old English law, inland was used for the demesne (*q. v.*) of a manor; that part which lay next or most convenient for the lord's mansion-house, as within the view thereof, and which, therefore, he kept in his own hands for support of his family and for hospitality; in distinction from outland or utland, which was the portion let out to tenants. Cowell; Kennett; Spelman.

INLAND BILL OF EXCHANGE. A bill of which both the drawer and drawee reside within the same state or country. Otherwise called a "domestic bill," and distinguished from a "foreign bill."

INLAND NAVIGATION. Within the meaning of the legislation of congress upon the subject, this phrase means navigation upon the rivers of the country, but not upon the great lakes. 24 How. 1; 6 Biss. 364.

INLAND TRADE. Trade wholly carried on at home; as distinguished from commerce, (which see.)

INLANTAL, INLANTALE. Demesne or inland, opposed to *delantal*, or land tenanted. Cowell.

INLAUGHE. Sax. In old English law. Under the law, (*sub lege,*) in a frank-pledge, or decennary. Bract. fol. 125*b*.

INLAW. To place under the protection of the law. "Swearing obedience to the king in a leet, which doth *inlaw* the subject." Bacon.

INLEASED. In old English law. Entangled, or ensnared. 2 Inst. 247; Cowell; Blount.

INLIGARE. In old European law. To confederate; to join in a league, (*in ligam coire.*) Spelman.

INMATE. A person who lodges or dwells in the same house with another, occupying different rooms, but using the same door for passing in and out of the house. Webster; Jacob.

INN. An inn is a house where a traveler is furnished with everything which he has occasion for while on his way. 3 Barn. & Ald. 283. See 5 Sandf. 242; 35 Conn. 183.

Under the term "inn" the law includes all taverns, hotels, and houses of public general entertainment for guests. Code Ga. 1882, § 2114.

The words "inn," "tavern," and "hotel" are used synonymously to designate what is ordinarily and popularly known as an "inn" or "tavern," or place for the entertainment of travelers, and where all their wants can be supplied. A restaurant where meals only are furnished is not an inn or tavern. 54 Barb. 311; 1 Hilt. 193.

An inn is distinguished from a private boarding-house mainly in this: that the keeper of the latter is at liberty to choose his guests, while the innkeeper is obliged to entertain and furnish all travelers of good conduct and means of payment with what they may have occasion for, as such travelers, while on their way. 33 Cal. 557.

The distinction between a boarding-house and an inn is that in the former the guest is under an express contract for a certain time at a certain rate; in the latter the guest is entertained from day to day upon an implied contract. 2 E. D. Smith, 148.

INNAMIUM. A pledge.

INNAVIGABILITY. In insurance law. The condition of being *innavigable*, (*q. v.*) The foreign writers distinguish "innavigability" from "shipwreck." 3 Kent, Comm. 323, and note. The term is also applied to the condition of streams which are not large enough or deep enough, or are otherwise unsuited, for navigation.

INNAVIGABLE. As applied to streams, not capable of or suitable for navigation; impassable by ships or vessels.

As applied to vessels in the law of marine insurance, it means unfit for navigation; so damaged by misadventures at sea as to be no longer capable of making a voyage. See 3 Kent, Comm. 323, note.

INNER BARRISTER. A serjeant or queen's counsel, in England, who is admitted to plead within the bar.

INNER HOUSE. The name given to the chambers in which the first and second divisions of the court of session in Scotland hold their sittings. See OUTER HOUSE.

INNINGS. In old records. Lands recovered from the sea by draining and banking. Cowell.

INNKEEPER. One who keeps an *inn*, or house for the lodging and entertainment of travelers. The keeper of a common inn for the lodging and entertainment of travelers and passengers, their horses and attendants, for a reasonable compensation. Story, Bailm. § 475. One who keeps a tavern or coffee-house in which lodging is provided. 2 Steph. Comm. 133.

One who receives as guests all who choose to visit his house, without any previous agreement as to the time of their stay, or the terms. His liability as innkeeper ceases when his guest pays his bill, and leaves the house with the declared intention of not returning, notwithstanding the guest leaves his baggage behind him. 5 Sandf. 242.

INNOCENCE. The absence of guilt. The law presumes in favor of innocence.

INNOCENT CONVEYANCES. A technical term of the English law of conveyancing, used to designate such conveyances as may be made by a leasehold tenant without working a forfeiture. These are said to be lease and re-lease, bargain and sale, and, in case of a life-tenant, a covenant to stand seised. See 1 Chit. Pr. 243.

INNOMINATE. In the civil law. Not named or classed; belonging to no specific class; ranking under a general head. A term applied to those contracts for which no certain or precise remedy was appointed, but a general action on the case only. Dig. 2, 1, 4, 7, 2; Id. 19, 4, 5.

INNOMINATE CONTRACTS, literally, are the "unclassified" contracts of Roman law. They are contracts which are neither *re, verbis, literis,* nor *consensu* simply, but some mixture of or variation upon two or more of such contracts. They are principally the contracts of *permutatio, de æstimato, precarium,* and *transactio.* Brown.

INNONIA. In old English law. A close or inclosure, (*clausum, inclausura.*) Spelman.

INNOTESCIMUS. Lat. We make known. A term formerly applied to letters patent, derived from the emphatic word at the conclusion of the Latin forms. It was a species of exemplification of charters of feoffment or other instruments not of record. 5 Coke, 54*a*.

INNOVATION. In Scotch law. The exchange of one obligation for another, so as to make the second obligation come in the place of the first, and be the only subsisting obligation against the debtor. Bell. The same with "novation," (*q. v.*)

INNOXIARE. In old English law. To purge one of a fault and make him innocent.

INNS OF CHANCERY. So called because anciently inhabited by such clerks as chiefly studied the framing of writs, which regularly belonged to the cursitors, who were officers of the court of chancery. There are nine of them,—Clement's, Clifford's, and Lyon's Inn; Furnival's, Thavies, and Symond's Inn; New Inn; and Barnard's and Staples' Inn. These were formerly preparatory colleges for students, and many entered them before they were admitted into the inns of court. They consist chiefly of solicitors, and possess corporate property, hall, chambers, etc., but perform no public functions like the inns of court. Wharton.

INNS OF COURT. These are certain private unincorporated associations, in the nature of collegiate houses, located in London, and invested with the exclusive privilege of calling men to the bar; that is, conferring the rank or degree of a barrister. They were founded probably about the beginning of the fourteenth century. The principal inns of court are the Inner Temple, Middle Temple, Lincoln's Inn, and Gray's Inn. (The two former originally belonged to the Knights Templar; the two latter to the earls of Lincoln and Gray respectively.) These bodies now have a "common council of legal education," for giving lectures and holding examinations. The inns of chancery, distinguishable from the foregoing, but generally classed with them under the general name, are the buildings known as "Clifford's Inn," "Clement's Inn," "New Inn," "Staples' Inn," and "Barnard's Inn." They were formerly a sort of collegiate houses in which law students learned the elements of law before being admitted into the inns of court, but they have long ceased to occupy that position.

INNUENDO. This Latin word (commonly translated "meaning") was the technical beginning of that clause in a declaration or indictment for slander or libel in which the application of the language charged to the plaintiff was pointed out. Hence it gave its name to the whole clause; and this usage is still retained, although an equivalent English word is now substituted. Thus, it may be charged that the defendant said "he (*meaning* the said plaintiff) is a perjurer."

The word is also used, (though more rarely,) in other species of pleadings, to introduce an explanation of a preceding word, charge, or averment.

It is said to mean no more than the words "*id est,*" "*scilicet,*" or "meaning," or "aforesaid," as explanatory of a subject-matter sufficiently expressed before; as "such a one, *meaning* the defendant," or "such a subject, *meaning* the subject in question." Cowp. 683. It is only explanatory of some matter already expressed. It serves to point out where there is precedent matter, but never for a new charge. It may *apply* what is *already expressed,* but cannot add to or enlarge or change the sense of the previous words. 1 Chit. Pl. 422.

INOFFICIOSUM. In the civil law. Inofficious; contrary to natural duty or affection. Used of a will of a parent which disinherited a child without just cause, or that of a child which disinherited a parent, and which could be contested by *querela inofficiosi testamenti.* Dig. 2, 5, 3, 13; Paulus, lib. 4, tit. 5, § 1.

INOFFICIOUS TESTAMENT. A will not in accordance with the testator's natural affection and moral duties. Williams, Ex'rs, (7th Ed.) 38.

INOFICIOCIDAD. In Spanish law. Everything done contrary to a duty or obligation assumed, as well as in opposition to the piety and affection dictated by nature. Escriche.

INOPS CONSILII. Lat. Destitute of counsel; without legal counsel. A term applied to the acts or condition of one acting without legal advice, as a testator drafting his own will.

INORDINATUS. An intestate.

INPENY and OUTPENY. In old English law. A customary payment of a penny on entering into and going out of a tenancy, (*pro exitu de tenura, et pro ingressu.*) Spelman.

INQUEST. 1. A body of men appointed by law to inquire into certain matters. The grand jury is sometimes called the "grand inquest."

2. The judicial inquiry made by a jury summoned for the purpose is called an "inquest." The finding of such men, upon an investigation, is also called an "inquest."

3. The inquiry by a coroner, termed a "coroner's inquest," into the manner of the death of any one who has been slain, or has died suddenly or in prison.

4. This name is also given to a species of proceeding under the New York practice, allowable where the defendant in a civil action has not filed an affidavit of merits nor verified his answer. In such case the issue may be taken up, out of its regular order, on plaintiff's motion, and tried without the admission of any affirmative defense.

An inquest is a trial of an issue of fact where the plaintiff alone introduces testimony. The defendant is entitled to appear at the taking of the inquest, and to cross-examine the plaintiff's witnesses; and, if he do appear, the inquest must be taken before a jury, unless a jury be expressly waived by him. 6 How. Pr. 118.

INQUEST OF OFFICE. In English practice. An inquiry made by the king's (or queen's) officer, his sheriff, coroner, or escheator, *virtute officii*, or by writ sent to them for that purpose, or by commissioners specially appointed, concerning any matter that entitles the king to the possession of lands or tenements, goods or chattels; as to inquire whether the king's tenant for life died seised, whereby the reversion accrues to the king: whether A., who held immediately of the crown, died without heir, in which case the lands belong to the king by escheat; whether B. be attainted of treason, whereby his estate is forfeited to the crown; whether C., who has purchased land, be an alien, which is another cause of forfeiture, etc. 3 Bl. Comm. 258. These *inquests of office* were more frequent in practice during the continuance of the military tenures than at present; and were devised by law as an authentic means to give the king his right by solemn matter of record. Id. 258, 259; 4 Steph. Comm. 40, 41. Sometimes simply termed "*office*," as in the phrase "office found," (*q. v.*) See 7 Cranch, 603.

INQUILINUS. In Roman law. A tenant; one who hires and occupies another's house; but particularly, a tenant of a hired house in a city, as distinguished from *colonus*, the hirer of a house or estate in the country. Calvin.

INQUIRENDO. An authority given to some official person to institute an inquiry concerning the crown's interests.

INQUIRY. The writ of inquiry is a judicial process addressed to the sheriff of the county in which the venue is laid, stating the former proceedings in the action, and, "because it is unknown what damages the plaintiff has sustained," commanding the sheriff that, by the oath of twelve men of his county, he diligently inquire into the same, and return the inquisition into court. This writ is necessary after an interlocutory judgment, the defendant having let judgment go by default, to ascertain the *quantum* of damages. Wharton.

INQUISITIO. In old English law. An inquisition or inquest. *Inquisitio post mortem*, an inquisition after death. An inquest of office held, during the continuance of the military tenures, upon the death of every one of the king's tenants, to inquire of what lands he died seised, who was his heir, and of what age, in order to entitle the king to his marriage, wardship, relief, primer seisin, or other advantages, as the circumstances of the case might turn out. 3 Bl. Comm. 258. *Inquisitio patriæ*, the inquisition of the country; the ordinary jury, as distinguished from the grand assise. Bract. fol. 15*b*.

INQUISITION. In practice. An inquiry or inquest; particularly, an investigation of certain facts made by a sheriff, together with a jury impaneled by him for the purpose.

INQUISITOR. A designation of sheriffs, coroners *super visum corporis*, and the like, who have power to inquire into certain matters.

INROLL. A form of "enroll," used in the old books. 3 Rep. Ch. 63, 73; 3 East, 410.

INROLLMENT. See ENROLLMENT.

INSANE. Unsound in mind; of unsound mind; deranged, disordered, or diseased in mind. Violently deranged; mad.

INSANITY. A manifestation of disease of the brain, characterized by a general or partial derangement of one or more faculties of the mind, and in which, while consciousness is not abolished, mental freedom is perverted, weakened, or destroyed. Ham. Nervous System, 332.

The prolonged departure, without any adequate cause, from the states of feeling and modes of thinking usual to the individual in health. Bouvier.

This is not, strictly speaking, a legal term, but it is commonly used to denote that state of mind which prevents a person from knowing right from wrong, and, therefore, from being responsible for acts which in a sane person would be criminal. Pope, Lun. 6, 19, 356.

By insanity is not meant a total deprivation of reason, but only an inability, from defect of perception, memory, and judgment, to do the act in question. So, by a lucid interval is not meant a perfect restoration to reason, but a restoration so far as to be able, beyond doubt, to comprehend and to do the act with such reason, memory, and judgment as to make it a legal act. 2 Del. Ch. 263.

Insanus est qui, abjecta ratione, omnia cum impetu et furore facit. He is insane who, reason being thrown away, does everything with violence and rage. 4 Coke, 128.

INSCRIBERE. Lat. In the civil law. To subscribe an accusation. To bind one's self, in case of failure to prove an accusation, to suffer the same punishment which the accused would have suffered had he been proved guilty. Calvin.

INSCRIPTIO. Lat. In the civil law. A written accusation in which the accuser undertakes to suffer the punishment appropriate to the offense charged, if the accused is able to clear himself of the accusation. Calvin.; Cod. 9, 1, 10; Id. 9, 2, 16, 17.

INSCRIPTION. In evidence. Anything written or engraved upon a metallic or other solid substance, intended for great durability; as upon a tombstone, pillar, tablet, medal, ring, etc.

INSCRIPTIONES. The name given by the old English law to any written instrument by which anything was granted. Blount.

INSENSIBLE. In pleading. Unintelligible; without sense or meaning, from the omission of material words, etc. Steph. Pl. 377.

INSETENA. In old records. An inditch; an interior ditch; one made within another, for greater security. Spelman.

INSIDIATORES VIARUM. Lat. Highwaymen; persons who lie in wait in order to commit some felony or other misdemeanor.

INSIGNIA. Ensigns or arms; distinctive marks; badges; *indicia;* characteristics.

INSILIARIUS. An evil counsellor. Cowell.

INSILIUM. Evil advice or counsel. Cowell.

INSIMUL. Lat. Together; jointly. Townsh. Pl. 44.

INSIMUL COMPUTASSENT. They accounted together. The name of the count in *assumpsit* upon an account stated; it being averred that the parties had settled their accounts together, and defendant engaged to pay plaintiff the balance.

INSIMUL TENUIT. One species of the writ of *formedon* brought against a stranger by a coparcener on the possession of the ancestor, etc. Jacob.

INSINUACION. In Spanish law. The presentation of a public document to a competent judge, in order to obtain his approbation and sanction of the same, and thereby give it judicial authenticity. Escriche.

INSINUARE. Lat. In the [illegible]ivil law. To put into; to deposit a [illegible]g in court, answering nearly to [illegible]n expression "to file." *Si non [illegible]n actis insinuatum est*, if the po[illegible]er or authority be not deposited among the records of the court. Inst. 4, 11, 3.

To declare or acknowledge before a judicial officer; to give an act an official form.

INSINUATIO. Lat. In old English law. Information or suggestion. *Ex insinuatione*, on the information. Reg. Jud. 25, 50.

INSINUATION. In the civil law. The transcription of an act on the public registers, like our recording of deeds. It was not necessary in any other alienation but that appropriated to the purpose of donation. Inst. 2, 7, 2.

INSINUATION OF A WILL. In the civil law. The first production of a will, or the leaving it with the registrar, in order to its probate. Cowell; Blount.

INSOLVENCY. The condition of a person who is insolvent; inability to pay one's debts; lack of means to pay one's debts. Such a relative condition of a man's assets and liabilities that the former, if all made immediately available, would not be sufficient to discharge the latter. Or the condition of a person who is unable to pay his debts as they fall due, or in the usual course of trade and business. See 2 Kent, Comm. 389; 4 Hill, 652; 15 N. Y. 141, 200; 3 Gray, 600; 2 Bell, Comm. 162.

As to the distinction between bankruptcy and insolvency, see BANKRUPTCY.

INSOLVENCY FUND. In English law. A fund, consisting of moneys and securities, which, at the time of the passing of the bankruptcy act, 1861, stood, in the Bank of England, to the credit of the commissioners of the insolvent debtors' court, and was, by the twenty-sixth section of that act, directed to be carried by the bank to the account of the accountant in bankruptcy. Provision has now been made for its transfer to the commissioners for the reduction of the national debt. Robs. Bankr. 20, 56.

INSOLVENT. One who cannot or does not pay; one who is unable to pay his debts; one who is not solvent; one who has not means or property sufficient to pay his debts.

A debtor is "insolvent," within the meaning of the bankrupt act, when he is unable to pay his debts and meet his engagements in the ordinary course of business, as persons in trade usually do. 3 Ben. 153; Id. 520; 1 Abb. (U. S.) 440; 1 Dill. 186.

A trader is insolvent when he is not in a condition to meet his engagements or pay his debts in the usual and ordinary course of business. His solvency or insolvency does not depend upon the simple question whether his assets at the date alleged will or will not satisfy all the demands against him, due and to become due. 33 Cal. 625.

INSOLVENT LAW. A term applied to a law, usually of one of the states, regulating the settlement of insolvent estates, and according a certain measure of relief to insolvent debtors.

INSPECTATOR. A prosecutor or adversary.

INSPECTION. The examination or testing of food, fluids, or other articles made subject by law to such examination, to ascertain their fitness for use or commerce.

Also the examination by a private person of public records and documents; or of the books and papers of his opponent in an action, for the purpose of better preparing his own case for trial.

INSPECTION LAWS. Laws authorizing and directing the inspection and examination of various kinds of merchandise intended for sale, especially food, with a view to ascertaining its fitness for use, and excluding unwholesome or unmarketable goods from sale, and directing the appointment of official inspectors for that purpose. See Const. U. S. art. 1, § 10, cl. 2; Story, Const. § 1017, et seq.

INSPECTION OF DOCUMENTS. This phrase refers to the right of a party, in a civil action, to inspect and make copies of documents which are essential or material to the maintenance of his cause, and which are either in the custody of an officer of the law or in the possession of the adverse party.

INSPECTION, TRIAL BY. A mode of trial formerly in use in England, by which the judges of a court decided a point in dispute, upon the testimony of their own senses, without the intervention of a jury. This took place in cases where the fact upon which issue was taken must, from its nature, be evident to the court from ocular demonstration, or other irrefragable proof; and was adopted for the greater expedition of a cause. 3 Bl. Comm. 331.

INSPECTORS. Officers whose duty it is to examine the quality of certain articles of merchandise, food, weights and measures, etc.

INSPECTORSHIP, DEED OF. In English law. An instrument entered into between an insolvent debtor and his creditors, appointing one or more persons to inspect and oversee the winding up of such insolvent's affairs on behalf of the creditors.

INSPEXIMUS. Lat. In old English law. We have inspected. An exemplification of letters patent, so called from the emphatic word of the old forms. 5 Coke, 53*b*.

INSTALLATION. The ceremony of inducting or investing with any charge, office, or rank, as the placing a bishop into his see, a dean or prebendary into his stall or seat, or a knight into his order. Wharton.

INSTALLMENTS. Different portions of the same debt payable at different successive periods as agreed. Brown.

INSTANCE. **In pleading and practice.** Solicitation, properly of an earnest or urgent kind. An act is often said to be done at a party's "special *instance* and request."

In the civil and French law. A general term, designating all sorts of actions and judicial demands. Dig. 44, 7, 58.

In ecclesiastical law. Causes of *instance* are those proceeded in at the solicitation of some party, as opposed to causes of office, which run in the name of the judge. Hallifax, Civil Law, p. 156.

In Scotch law. That which may be insisted on at one diet or course of probation. Wharton.

INSTANCE COURT. In English law. That division or department of the court of admiralty which exercises all the ordinary admiralty jurisdiction, with the single exception of prize cases, the latter belonging to the branch called the "Prize Court."

The term is sometimes used in American law for purposes of explanation, but has no proper application to admiralty courts in the United States, where the powers of both instance and prize courts are conferred without any distinction. 3 Dall. 6; 1 Gall. 563; 3 Kent, Comm. 355, 378.

INSTANCIA. In Spanish law. The institution and prosecution of a suit from its commencement until definitive judgment. The first instance, "*primera instancia*," is the prosecution of the suit before the judge competent to take cognizance of it at its inception; the second instance, "*secunda instancia*," is the exercise of the same action before the court of appellate jurisdiction; and the third instance, "*tercera instancia*," is the prosecution of the same suit, either by an application of revision before the appellate tribunal that has already decided the cause, or before some higher tribunal, having jurisdiction of the same. Escriche.

INSTANTER. Immediately; instantly; forthwith; without delay. Trial *instanter* was had where a prisoner between attainder and execution pleaded that he was not the same who was attainted.

When a party is ordered to plead *instanter*, he must plead the same day. The term is usually understood to mean within twenty-four hours.

INSTAR. Lat. Likeness; the likeness, size, or equivalent of a thing. *Instar dentium*, like teeth. 2 Bl. Comm. 295. *Instar omnium*, equivalent or tantamount to all. Id. 146; 3 Bl. Comm. 231.

INSTAURUM. In old English deeds. A stock or store of cattle, and other things; the whole stock upon a farm, including cattle, wagons, plows, and all other implements of husbandry. 1 Mon. Angl. 548*b*; Fleta, lib. 2, c. 72, § 7. *Terra instaurata*, land ready stocked.

INSTIGATION. Incitation; urging; solicitation. The act by which one incites another to do something, as to commit some crime or to commence a suit.

INSTIRPARE. To plant or establish.

INSTITOR. Lat. In the civil law. A clerk in a store; an agent.

INSTITORIA ACTIO. Lat. In the civil law. The name of an action given to those who had contracted with an *institor* (*q. v.*) to compel the principal to performance. Inst. 4, 7, 2; Dig. 14, 3, 1; Story, Ag. § 426.

INSTITORIAL POWER. The charge given to a clerk to manage a shop or store. 1 Bell, Comm. 506, 507.

INSTITUTE, *v.* To inaugurate or commence; as to institute an action.

To nominate, constitute, or appoint; as to institute an heir by testament. Dig. 28, 5, 65.

INSTITUTE, *n.* **In the civil law.** A person named in the will as heir, but with a direction that he shall pass over the estate to another designated person, called the "substitute."

In Scotch law. The person to whom an estate is first given by destination or limitation; the others, or the heirs of tailzie, are called "substitutes."

INSTITUTES. A name sometimes given to text-books containing the elementary principles of jurisprudence, arranged in an orderly and systematic manner. For example, the Institutes of Justinian, of Gaius, of Lord Coke.

INSTITUTES OF GAIUS. An elementary work of the Roman jurist Gaius; important as having formed the foundation of the Institutes of Justinian, (*q. v.*) These Institutes were discovered by Niebuhr in 1816, in a *codex rescriptus* of the library of the cathedral chapter at Verona, and were first published at Berlin in 1820. Two editions have since appeared. Mackeld. Rom. Law, § 54.

INSTITUTES OF JUSTINIAN. One of the four component parts or principal divisions of the *Corpus Juris Civilis*, being an elementary treatise on the Roman law, in four books. This work was compiled from earlier sources, (resting principally on the Institutes of Gaius,) by a commission composed of Tribonian and two others, by command and under direction of the emperor Justinian, and was first published November 21, A. D. 533.

INSTITUTES OF LORD COKE. The name of four volumes by Lord Coke, published A. D. 1628. The first is an extensive comment upon a treatise on tenures, compiled by Littleton, a judge of the common pleas, *temp.* Edward IV. This comment is a rich mine of valuable common-law learning, collected and heaped together from the ancient reports and Year Books, but greatly defective in method. It is usually cited by the name of "Co. Litt.," or as "1 Inst." The second volume is a comment upon old acts of parliament, without systematic order; the third a more methodical treatise on the pleas of the crown; and the fourth an account of the several species of courts. These are cited as 2, 3, or 4 "Inst.," without any author's name. Wharton.

INSTITUTIO HÆREDIS. Lat. In Roman law. The appointment of the *hæres* in the will. It corresponds very nearly to the nomination of an executor in English law. Without such an appointment the will was void at law, but the *prætor* (*i. e.*, equity) would, under certain circumstances, carry out the intentions of the testator. Brown.

INSTITUTION. The commencement or inauguration of anything. The first establishment of a law, rule, rite, etc. Any custom, system, organization, etc., firmly established. An elementary rule or principle.

In practice. The commencement of an action or prosecution; as, A. B. has instituted a suit against C. D. to recover damages for trespass.

In political law. A law, rite, or ceremony enjoined by authority as a permanent rule of conduct or of government. Webster.

A system or body of usages, laws, or regulations, of extensive and recurring operation, containing within itself an organism by which it effects its own independent action, continuance, and generally its own further development. Its object is to generate, effect, regulate, or sanction a succession of acts, transactions, or productions of a peculiar kind or class. We are likewise in the habit of calling single laws or usages "institutions," if their operation is of vital importance and vast scope, and if their continuance is in a high degree independent of any interfering power. Lieb. Civil Lib. 300.

In corporation law. An organization or foundation, for the exercise of some public purpose or function; as an asylum or a university. By the term "institution" in this sense is to be understood an establishment or organization which is permanent in its nature, as distinguished from an enterprise or undertaking which is transient and temporary. 29 Ohio St. 206; 24 Ind. 391.

In ecclesiastical law. A kind of investiture of the spiritual part of the benefice, as induction is of the temporal; for by institution the care of the souls of the parish is committed to the charge of the clerk. Brown.

In the civil law. The designation by a testator of a person to be his heir.

In jurisprudence. The plural form of this word ("institutions") is sometimes used as the equivalent of "institutes," to denote an elementary text-book of the law.

INSTITUTIONES. Works containing the elements of any science; institutions or institutes. One of Justinian's principal law collections, and a similar work of the Roman jurist Gaius, are so entitled. See INSTITUTES.

INSTRUCT. To convey information as a client to an attorney, or as an attorney to a counsel; to authorize one to appear as advocate; to give a case in charge to the jury.

INSTRUCTION. In French criminal law. The first process of a criminal prosecution. It includes the examination of the accused, the preliminary interrogation of witnesses, collateral investigations, the gathering of evidence, the reduction of the whole to order, and the preparation of a document containing a detailed statement of the case, to serve as a brief for the prosecuting officers, and to furnish material for the indictment.

INSTRUCTIONS. In common law. Orders given by a principal to his agent in relation to the business of his agency.

In practice. A detailed statement of the facts and circumstances constituting a cause of action made by a client to his attorney for the purpose of enabling the latter to draw a proper declaration or procure it to be done by a pleader.

INSTRUMENT. A written document; a formal or legal document in writing, such as a contract, deed, will, bond, or lease.

In the law of evidence. Anything which may be presented as evidence to the senses of the adjudicating tribunal. The term "instruments of evidence" includes not merely documents, but witnesses and living things which may be presented for inspection. 1 Whart. Ev. § 615.

INSTRUMENT OF APPEAL. The document by which an appeal is brought in an English matrimonial cause from the president of the probate, divorce, and admiralty division to the full court. It is analogous to a petition. Browne, Div. 322.

INSTRUMENT OF EVIDENCE. Instruments of evidence are the *media* through which the evidence of facts, either disputed or required to be proved, is conveyed to the mind of a judicial tribunal; and they comprise persons, as well as writings. Best, Ev. § 123.

INSTRUMENT OF SAISINE. An instrument in Scotland by which the delivery of "saisine" (*i. e.*, seisin, or the feudal possession of land) is attested. It is subscribed by a notary, in the presence of witnesses, and is executed in pursuance of a "precept of saisine," whereby the "grantor of the deed" desires "any notary public to whom these presents may be presented" to give saisine to the intended grantee or grantees. It must be entered and recorded in the registers of saisines. Mozley & Whitley.

INSTRUMENTA. That kind of evidence which consists of writings not under seal; as court-rolls, accounts, and the like. 3 Co. Litt. 487.

INSUCKEN MULTURES. A quantity of corn paid by those who are thirled to a mill. See THIRLAGE.

INSUFFICIENCY. In equity pleading. The legal inadequacy of an answer in equity which does not fully and specifically reply to some one or more of the material allegations, charges, or interrogatories set forth in the bill.

INSULA. An island; a house not connected with other houses, but separated by a surrounding space of ground. Calvin.

INSUPER. Moreover; over and above. An old exchequer term, applied to a charge made *upon* a person in his account. Blount.

INSURABLE INTEREST. Such a real and substantial interest in specific property as will sustain a contract to indemnify the person interested against its loss. If the assured had no real interest, the contract would be a mere wager policy.

Every interest in property, or any relation thereto, or liability in respect thereof, of such a nature that a contemplated peril might directly damnify the insured, is an insurable interest. Civil Code Cal. § 2546.

INSURANCE. A contract whereby, for a stipulated consideration, one party undertakes to compensate the other for loss on a specified subject by specified perils. The party agreeing to make the compensation is usually called the "insurer" or "underwriter;" the other, the "insured" or "assured;" the agreed consideration, the "premium;" the written contract, a "policy;" the events insured against, "risks" or "perils;" and the subject, right, or interest to be protected, the "insurable interest." 1 Phil. Ins. §§ 1-5.

Insurance is a contract whereby one undertakes to indemnify another against loss, damage, or liability arising from an unknown or contingent event. Civil Code Cal. § 2527; Civil Code Dak. § 1474.

Various classes or kinds of insurance are in use. *Marine* insurance applies to vessels, cargoes, and property exposed to maritime risks. *Fire* insurance covers buildings, merchandise, and other property on land exposed to injury by fire. *Life* insurance means the engagement to pay a stipulated sum upon the death of the insured, or of a third person in whose life the insured has an interest, either whenever it occurs, or in case it occurs within a prescribed term. *Accident* and *health* insurance include insurances of persons against injury from accident, or expense and loss of time from disease. Many other forms might exist, and several others have been to a limited extent introduced in recent times; such as insurance of valuables against theft, insurance of the lives and good condition of domestic animals, insurance of valuable plate-glass windows against breakage. Abbott.

INSURANCE AGENT. An agent employed by an insurance company to solicit risks and effect insurances.

Agents of insurance companies are called "general agents" when clothed with the general oversight of the companies' business in a state or large section of country, and "local agents" when their functions are limited and confined to some particular locality.

INSURANCE BROKER. A broker through whose agency insurances are effected. 3 Kent, Comm. 260. See BROKER.

INSURANCE COMPANY. A corporation or association whose business is to make contracts of insurance. They are either mutual companies or stock companies.

INSURANCE POLICY. See POLICY.

INSURE. To engage to indemnify a person against pecuniary loss from specified perils. To act as an insurer.

INSURED. The person who obtains insurance on his property, or upon whose life an insurance is effected.

INSURER. The underwriter or insurance company with whom a contract of insurance is made.

The person who undertakes to indemnify another by a contract of insurance is called the "insurer," and the person indemnified is called the "insured." Civil Code Cal. § 2538.

INSURGENT. One who participates in an insurrection; one who opposes the execution of law by force of arms, or who rises in revolt against the constituted authorities.

A distinction is often taken between "insurgent" and "rebel," in this: that the former term is not necessarily to be taken in a bad sense, inasmuch as an insurrection, though extralegal, may be just and timely in itself; as where it is undertaken for the overthrow of tyranny or the reform of gross abuses. According to Webster, an insurrection is an incipient or early stage of a rebellion.

INSURRECTION. A rebellion, or rising of citizens or subjects in resistance to their government. See INSURGENT.

Insurrection shall consist in any combined resistance to the lawful authority of the state, with intent to the denial thereof, when the same is manifested, or intended to be manifested, by acts of violence. Code Ga. 1882, § 4315.

INTAKERS. In old English law. A kind of thieves inhabiting Redesdale, on the extreme northern border of England; so called because they *took in* or received such booties of cattle and other things as their accomplices, who were called "outparters," brought in to them from the borders of Scotland. Spelman; Cowell.

INTAKES. Temporary inclosures made by customary tenants of a manor under a special custom authorizing them to inclose part of the waste until one or more crops have been raised on it. Elton, Common, 277.

INTEGER. Whole; untouched. *Res integra* means a question which is new and undecided. 2 Kent, Comm. 177.

INTEMPERANCE. Habitual intemperance is that degree of intemperance from the use of intoxicating drinks which disqualifies the person a great portion of the time from properly attending to business, or which would reasonably inflict a course of great mental anguish upon an innocent party. Civil Code Cal. § 106.

INTEND. To design, resolve, purpose. To apply a rule of law in the nature of presumption; to discern and follow the probabilities of like cases.

INTENDANT. One who has the charge, management, or direction of some office, department, or public business.

INTENDED TO BE RECORDED. This phrase is frequently used in conveyances, when reciting some other conveyance which has not yet been recorded, but which forms a link in the chain of title. In Pennsylvania, it has been construed to be a covenant, on the part of the grantor, to procure the deed to be recorded in a reasonable time. 2 Rawle, 14.

INTENDENTE. In Spanish law. The immediate agent of the minister of finance, or the chief and principal director of the different branches of the revenue, appointed in the various departments in each of the provinces into which the Spanish monarchy is divided. Escriche.

INTENDMENT OF LAW. The true meaning, the correct understanding or intention of the law; a presumption or inference made by the courts. Co. Litt. 78.

INTENT. In criminal law and the law of evidence. Purpose; formulated design; a resolve to do or forbear a particular act; aim; determination. In its literal sense, the stretching of the mind or will towards a particular object.

"Intent" expresses mental action at its most advanced point, or as it actually accompanies an outward, corporal act which has been determined on. *Intent* shows the presence of *will* in the act which consummates a crime. It is the exercise of intelligent will, the mind being fully aware of the nature and consequences of the act which is about to be done, and with such knowledge, and with full liberty of action, willing and electing to do it. Burrill, Circ. Ev. 284, and notes.

INTENTIO. Lat. In the civil law. The formal complaint or claim of a plaintiff before the prætor.

In old English law. A count or declaration in a real action, (*narratio*.) Bract. lib. 4, tr. 2, c. 2; Fleta, lib. 4, c. 7; Du Cange.

Intentio cæca mala. A blind or obscure meaning is bad or ineffectual. 2 Bulst. 179. Said of a testator's intention.

Intentio inservire debet legibus, non leges intentioni. The intention [of a party] ought to be subservient to [or in accordance with] the laws, not the laws to the intention. Co. Litt. 314*a*, 314*b*.

Intentio mea imponit nomen operi meo. Hob. 123. My intent gives a name to my act.

INTENTION. Meaning; will; purpose; design. "The *intention* of the testator, to be collected from the whole will, is to govern, provided it be not unlawful or inconsistent with the rules of law." 4 Kent, Comm. 534.

"Intention," when used with reference to the construction of wills and other documents, means the sense and meaning of it, as gathered from the words used therein. Parol evidence is not ordinarily admissible to explain this. When used with reference to civil and criminal responsibility, a person who contemplates any result, as not unlikely to follow from a deliberate act of his own, may be said to intend that result, whether he desire it or not. Thus, if a man should, for a wager, discharge a gun among a multitude of people, and any should be killed, he would be deemed guilty of intending the death of such person; for every man is presumed to intend the natural consequence of his own actions. Intention is often confounded with motive, as when we speak of a man's "good intentions." Mozley & Whitley.

INTENTIONE. A writ that lay against him who entered into lands after the death of a tenant in dower, or for life, etc., and held out to him in reversion or remainder. Fitzh. Nat. Brev. 203.

INTER. Lat. Among; between.

INTER ALIA. Among other things. A term anciently used in pleading, especially in reciting statutes, where the whole statute was not set forth at length. *Inter alia enactatum fuit*, among other things it was enacted. See Plowd. 65.

Inter alias causas acquisitionis, magna, celebris, et famosa est causa donationis. Among other methods of acquiring property, a great, much-used, and celebrated method is that of gift. Bract. fol. 11.

INTER ALIOS. Between other persons; between those who are strangers to a matter in question.

INTER APICES JURIS. Among the subtleties of the law. See APEX JURIS.

INTER BRACHIA. Between her arms. Fleta, lib. 1, c. 35, §§ 1, 2.

INTER CÆTEROS. Among others; in a general clause; not by name, (*nominatim.*) A term applied in the civil law to clauses of disinheritance in a will. Inst. 2, 13, 1; Id. 2, 13, 3.

INTER CANEM ET LUPUM. (Lat. Between the dog and the wolf.) The twilight; because then the dog seeks his rest, and the wolf his prey. 3 Inst. 63.

INTER CONJUGES. Between husband and wife.

INTER CONJUNCTAS PERSONAS. Between conjunct persons. By the act 1621, c. 18, all conveyances or alienations between conjunct persons, unless granted for onerous causes, are declared, as in a question with creditors, to be null and of no avail. Conjunct persons are those standing in a certain degree of relationship to each other; such, for example, as brothers, sisters, sons, uncles, etc. These were formerly excluded as witnesses, on account of their relationship; but this, as a ground of exclusion, has been abolished. Tray. Lat. Max.

INTER PARTES. Between parties. Instruments in which two persons unite, each making conveyance to, or engagement with, the other, are called "papers *inter partes*."

INTER QUATUOR PARIETES. Between four walls. Fleta, lib. 6, c. 55, § 4.

INTER REGALIA. In English law. Among the things belonging to the sovereign. Among these are rights of salmon fishing, mines of gold and silver, forests, forfeitures, casualties of superiority, etc., which are called "*regalia minora*," and may be conveyed to a subject. The *regalia majora* include the several branches of the royal prerogative, which are inseparable from the person of the sovereign. Tray. Lat. Max.

INTER RUSTICOS. Among the illiterate or unlearned.

INTER SE, INTER SESE. Among themselves. Story, Partn. § 405.

INTER VIRUM ET UXOREM. Between husband and wife.

INTER VIVOS. Between the living; from one living person to another. Where property passes by conveyance, the transaction is said to be *inter vivos*, to distinguish it from a case of succession or devise. So an ordinary gift from one person to another is called a "gift *inter vivos*," to distinguish it from a donation made in contemplation of death, (*mortis causa*.)

INTERCALARE. In the civil law. To introduce or insert among or between others; to introduce a day or month into the calendar; to intercalate. Dig. 50, 16, 98, pr.

INTERCEDERE. In the civil law. To become bound for another's debt.

INTERCHANGEABLY. By way of exchange or interchange. This term properly denotes the method of signing deeds, leases, contracts, etc., executed in duplicate, where each party signs the copy which he delivers to the other.

INTERCOMMON. To enjoy a common mutually or promiscuously with the inhabitants or tenants of a contiguous township, vill, or manor. 2 Bl. Comm. 33; 1 Crabb, Real Prop. p. 271, § 290.

INTERCOMMONING. When the commons of two adjacent manors join, and the inhabitants of both have immemorially fed their cattle promiscuously on each other's common, this is called "intercommoning." Termes de la Ley.

INTERCOMMUNING. Letters of intercommuning were letters from the Scotch privy council passing (on their act) in the king's name, charging the lieges not to reset, supply, or intercommune with the persons thereby denounced; or to furnish them with meat, drink, house, harbor, or any other thing useful or comfortable; or to have any intercourse with them whatever,—under pain of being reputed art and part in their crimes, and dealt with accordingly; and desiring all sheriffs, bailies, etc., to apprehend and commit such rebels to prison. Bell.

INTERCOURSE. Communication; literally, a *running* or passing *between* persons or places; commerce.

INTERDICT. **In Roman law.** A decree of the prætor by means of which, in certain cases determined by the edict, he himself directly commanded what should be done or omitted, particularly in causes involving the right of possession or a *quasi* possession. In the modern civil law, interdicts are regarded precisely the same as actions, though they give rise to a summary proceeding. Mackeld. Rom. Law, § 258.

Interdicts are either prohibitory, restorative, or exhibitory; the first being a prohibition, the second a decree for restoring possession lost by force, the third a decree for the exhibiting of accounts, etc. Heinec. § 1206.

An interdict was distinguished from an "action," (*actio*,) properly so called, by the circumstance that the prætor himself decided in the first instance, (*principaliter*,) on the application of the plaintiff, without previously appointing a *judex*, by issuing a decree commanding what should be done, or left undone. Gaius, 4, 139. It might be adopted as a remedy in various cases where a regular action could not be maintained, and hence interdicts were at one time more extensively used by the prætor than the *actiones* themselves. Afterwards, however, they fell into disuse, and in the time of Justinian were generally dispensed with. Mackeld. Rom. Law, § 258; Inst. 4, 15, 8.

In ecclesiastical law. An ecclesiastical censure, by which divine services are prohibited to be administered either to particular persons or in particular places.

In Scotch law. An order of the court of session or of an inferior court, pronounced, on cause shown, for stopping any act or proceedings complained of as illegal or wrongful. It may be resorted to as a remedy against any encroachment either on property or possession, and is a protection against any unlawful proceeding. Bell.

INTERDICTION. **In French law.** Every person who, on account of insanity, has become incapable of controlling his own interests, can be put under the control of a guardian, who shall administer his affairs with the same effect as he might himself. Such a person is said to be "*interdit*," and his *status* is described as "interdiction." Arg. Fr. Merc. Law, 562.

In the civil law. A judicial decree, by which a person is deprived of the *exercise* of his civil rights.

INTERDICTION OF FIRE AND WATER. Banishment by an order that no man should supply the person banished with fire or water, the two necessaries of life.

INTERDICTUM SALVIANUM. Lat. In Roman law. The Salvian interdict. A process which lay for the owner of a farm to obtain possession of the goods of his tenant who had pledged them to him for the rent of the land. Inst. 4, 15, 3.

Interdum evenit ut exceptio quæ prima facie justa videtur, tamen inique noceat. It sometimes happens that a plea which seems *prima facie* just, nevertheless is injurious and unequal. Inst. 4, 14, 1, 2.

INTERESSE. Lat. Interest. The interest of money; also an interest in lands.

INTERESSE TERMINI. An interest in a term. That species of interest or property which a lessee for years acquires in the lands demised to him, before he has actually become possessed of those lands; as distinguished from that property or interest vested in him by the demise, and also reduced into possession by an actual entry upon the lands and the assumption of ownership therein, and which is then termed an "estate for years." Brown.

INTEREST. In property. The most general term that can be employed to denote a property in lands or chattels. In its application to lands or things real, it is frequently used in connection with the terms "estate," "right," and "title," and, according to Lord Coke, it properly includes them all. Co. Litt. 345*b*.

More particularly it means a right to have the advantage accruing from anything; any right in the nature of property, but less than title; a partial or undivided right; a title to a share.

The terms "interest" and "title" are not synonymous. A mortgagor in possession, and a purchaser holding under a deed defectively executed, have, both of them, absolute as well as insurable interests in the property, though neither of them has the legal title. 29 Conn. 20.

In the law of evidence. "Interest," in a statute that no witness shall be excluded by interest in the event of the suit, means "concern," "advantage," "good," "share, "portion," "part," or "participation." 11 Barb. 471; 11 Metc. (Mass.) 390.

A relation to the matter in controversy, or to the issue of the suit, in the nature of a prospective gain or loss, which actually does, or presumably might, create a bias or prejudice in the mind, inclining the person to favor one side or the other.

For money. Interest is the compensation allowed by law or fixed by the parties for the use or forbearance or detention of money. Civil Code Cal. § 1915.

Legal interest is the rate of interest established by the law of the country, and which will prevail in the absence of express stipulation; *conventional* interest is a certain rate agreed upon by the parties. 2 Cal. 568.

Simple interest is that which is paid for the principal or sum lent, at a certain rate or allowance, made by law or agreement of parties. *Compound* interest is interest upon interest, where accrued interest is added to the principal sum, and the whole treated as a new principal, for the calculation of the interest for the next period.

INTEREST, MARITIME. See MARITIME INTEREST.

INTEREST OR NO INTEREST. These words, inserted in an insurance policy, mean that the question whether the insured has or has not an insurable interest in the subject-matter is waived, and the policy is to be good irrespective of such interest. The effect of such a clause is to make it a *wager* policy.

INTEREST POLICY. In insurance. One which actually, or *prima facie*, covers a substantial and insurable interest; as opposed to a *wager* policy.

Interest reipublicæ ne maleficia remaneant impunita. It concerns the state that crimes remain not unpunished. Jenk. Cent. pp. 30, 31, case 59; Wing. Max. 501.

Interest reipublicæ ne sua quis male utatur. It concerns the state that persons do not misuse their property. 6 Coke, 36*a*.

Interest reipublicæ quod homines conserventur. It concerns the state that [the lives of] men be preserved. 12 Coke, 62.

Interest reipublicæ res judicatas non rescindi. It concerns the state that things adjudicated be not rescinded. 2 Inst. 360. It is matter of public concern that solemn adjudications of the courts should not be disturbed. See Best, Ev. p. 41, § 44.

Interest reipublicæ suprema hominum testamenta rata haberi. It concerns the state that men's last wills be held valid, [or allowed to stand.] Co. Litt. 236*b*.

Interest reipublicæ ut carceres sint in tuto. It concerns the state that prisons be safe places of confinement. 2 Inst. 589.

Interest (imprimis) reipublicæ ut pax in regno conservetur, et quæcunque paci adversentur provide declinentur. It especially concerns the state that peace be preserved in the kingdom, and that whatever things are against peace be prudently avoided. 2 Inst. 158.

Interest reipublicæ ut quilibet re sua bene utatur. It is the concern of the state that every one uses his property properly.

Interest reipublicæ ut sit finis litium. It concerns the state that there be an end of lawsuits. Co. Litt. 303. It is for the general welfare that a period be put to litigation. Broom, Max. 331, 343.

INTEREST SUIT. In English law. An action in the probate branch of the high court of justice, in which the question in dispute is as to which party is entitled to a grant of letters of administration of the estate of a deceased person. Wharton.

INTEREST UPON INTEREST. Compound interest, (*q. v.*)

INTERFERENCE. In patent law, this term designates a collision between rights claimed or granted; that is, where a person claims a patent for the whole or any integral part of the ground already covered by an existing patent or by a pending application.

INTERIM. In the mean time; meanwhile. An assignee *ad interim* is one appointed between the time of bankruptcy and appointment of the regular assignee. 2 Bell, Comm. 355.

INTERIM COMMITTITUR. Lat. "In the mean time, let him be committed." An order of court (or the docket-entry noting it) by which a prisoner is committed to prison and directed to be kept there until some further action can be taken, or until the time arrives for the execution of his sentence.

INTERIM CURATOR. A person appointed by justices of the peace to take care of the property of a felon convict, until the appointment by the crown of an administrator or administrators for the same purpose. Mozley & Whitley.

INTERIM FACTOR. In Scotch law. A judicial officer elected or appointed under the bankruptcy law to take charge of and preserve the estate until a fit person shall be elected trustee. 2 Bell, Comm. 357.

INTERIM OFFICER. One appointed to fill the office during a temporary vacancy, or during an interval caused by the absence or incapacity of the regular incumbent.

INTERIM ORDER. One made in the mean time, and until something is done.

INTERIM RECEIPT. A receipt for money paid by way of premium for a contract of insurance for which application is made. If the risk is rejected, the money is refunded, less the *pro rata* premium.

INTERLAQUEARE. In old practice. To link together, or interchangeably. Writs were called "*interlaqueata*" where several were issued against several parties residing in different counties, each party being summoned by a separate writ to warrant the tenant, together with the other warrantors. Fleta, lib. 5, c. 4, § 2.

INTERLINEATION. The act of writing between the lines of an instrument; also what is written between lines.

INTERLOCUTOR. In Scotch practice. An order or decree of court; an order made in open court. 2 Swint. 362; Arkley, 32.

INTERLOCUTOR OF RELEVANCY. In Scotch practice. A decree as to the relevancy of a libel or indictment in a criminal case. 2 Alis. Crim. Pr. 373.

INTERLOCUTORY. Provisional; temporary; not final. Something intervening between the commencement and the end of a suit which decides some point or matter, but is not a final decision of the whole controversy.

INTERLOCUTORY COSTS. In practice. Costs accruing upon proceedings in the intermediate stages of a cause, as distinguished from final costs; such as the costs of motions. 3 Chit. Gen. Pr. 597.

INTERLOCUTORY DECREE. In equity practice. A provisional or preliminary decree, which is not final and does not determine the suit, but directs some further proceedings preparatory to the final decree. A decree pronounced for the purpose of ascertaining matter of law or fact preparatory to a final decree. 1 Barb. Ch. Pr. 326, 327.

INTERLOCUTORY JUDGMENT. A judgment which is not final is called "interlocutory;" that is, an interlocutory judgment is one which determines some preliminary or subordinate point or plea, or settles some step, question, or default arising in the progress of the cause, but does not adjudicate the ultimate rights of the parties, or finally put the case out of court. Thus, a judgment or order passed upon any provisional or accessory claim or contention is, in general, merely interlocutory, although it may finally dispose of that particular matter. 1 Black, Judgm. § 21.

INTERLOCUTORY ORDER. "An order which decides not the cause, but only settles some intervening matter relating to it; as when an order is made, on a motion in chancery, for the plaintiff to have an injunction to quiet his possession till the hearing of the cause. This or any such order, not being final, is interlocutory." Termes de la Ley.

INTERLOCUTORY SENTENCE. In the civil law. A sentence on some indirect question arising from the principal cause. Hallifax, Civil Law, b. 3, ch. 9, no. 40.

INTERLOPERS. Persons who run into business to which they have no right, or who interfere wrongfully; persons who enter a country or place to trade without license. Webster.

INTERN. To restrict or shut up a person, as a political prisoner, within a limited territory.

INTERNATIONAL LAW. The law which regulates the intercourse of nations; the law of nations. 1 Kent, Comm. 1, 4. The customary law which determines the rights and regulates the intercourse of independent states in peace and war. 1 Wildm. Int. Law, 1.

The system of rules and principles, founded on treaty, custom, precedent, and the consensus of opinion as to justice and moral obligation, which civilized nations recognize as binding upon them in their mutual dealings and relations.

Public international law is the body of rules which control the conduct of independent states in their relations with each other.

Private international law is that branch of municipal law which determines before the courts of what nation a particular action or suit should be brought, and by the law of what nation it should be determined; in other words, it regulates private rights as dependent on a diversity of municipal laws and jurisdictions applicable to the persons, facts, or things in dispute, and the subject of it is hence sometimes called the "conflict of laws." Thus, questions whether a given person owes allegiance to a particular state where he is domiciled, whether his *status*, property, rights, and duties are governed by the *lex sitûs*, the *lex loci*, the *lex fori*, or the *lex domicilii*, are questions with which private international law has to deal. Sweet.

INTERNUNCIO. A minister of a second order, charged with the affairs of the papal court in countries where that court has no nuncio.

INTERNUNCIUS. A messenger between two parties; a go-between. Applied to a broker, as the agent of both parties. 4 C. Rob. Adm. 204.

INTERPELATION. In the civil law. The act by which, in consequence of an agreement, the party bound declares that he will not be bound beyond a certain time. Wolff, Inst. Nat. § 752.

INTERPLEADER. When two or more persons claim the same thing (or fund) of a third, and he, laying no claim to it himself, is ignorant which of them has a right to it, and fears he may be prejudiced by their proceeding against him to recover it, he may file a bill in equity against them, the object of which is to make them litigate their title between themselves, instead of litigating it with him, and such a bill is called a "bill of interpleader." Brown.

By the statute 1 & 2 Wm. IV. c. 58, summary proceedings at *law* were provided for the same purpose, in actions of *assumpsit*, debt, detinue, and trover. And the same remedy is known, in one form or the other, in most or all of the United States.

Under the Pennsylvania practice, when goods levied upon by the sheriff are claimed by a third party, the sheriff takes a rule of interpleader on the parties, upon which, when made absolute, a feigned issue is framed, and the title to the goods is tested. The goods, pending the proceedings, remain in the custody of the defendant upon the execution of a forthcoming bond. Bouvier.

INTERPOLATE. To insert words in a complete document.

INTERPOLATION. The act of interpolating; the words interpolated.

INTERPRET. To construe; to seek out the meaning of language; to translate orally from one tongue to another.

Interpretare et concordare leges legibus, est optimus interpretandi modus. To interpret, and [in such a way as] to harmonize laws with laws, is the best mode of interpretation. 8 Coke, 169*a*.

Interpretatio chartarum benigne facienda est, ut res magis valeat quam pereat. The interpretation of deeds is to be liberal, that the thing may rather have effect than fail. Broom, Max. 543.

Interpretatio fienda est ut res magis valeat quam pereat. Jenk. Cent. 198. Such an interpretation is to be adopted that the thing may rather stand than fall.

Interpretatio talis in ambiguis semper fienda est ut evitetur inconveniens et absurdum. In cases of ambiguity, such an interpretation should always be made that what is inconvenient and absurd may be avoided. 4 Inst. 328.

INTERPRETATION. The discovery and representation of the true meaning of any signs used to convey ideas. Lieb. Herm.

"Construction" is a term of wider scope than "interpretation;" for, while the latter is concerned only with ascertaining the sense and meaning of the subject-matter, the former may also be directed to explaining the legal effects and consequences of the instrument in question. Hence interpretation precedes construction, but stops at the written text.

Close interpretation (*interpretatio restricta*) is adopted if just reasons, connected with the formation and character of the text, induce us to take the words in their narrowest meaning. This species of interpretation has generally been called "literal," but the term is inadmissible. Lieb. Herm. 54.

Extensive interpretation (*interpretatio extensiva*, called, also, "liberal interpretation") adopts a more comprehensive signification of the word. Id. 58.

Extravagant interpretation (*interpretatio excedens*) is that which substitutes a meaning evidently beyond the true one. It is therefore not genuine interpretation. Id. 59.

Free or unrestricted interpretation (*interpretatio soluta*) proceeds simply on the general principles of interpretation in good faith, not bound by any specific or superior principle. Id. 59.

Limited or restricted interpretation (*interpretatio limitata*) is when we are influenced by other principles than the strictly hermeneutic ones. Id. 60.

Predestined interpretation (*interpretatio predestinata*) takes place if the interpreter, laboring under a strong bias of mind, makes the text subservient to his preconceived views or desires. This includes artful interpretation, (*interpretatio vafer*,) by which the interpreter seeks to give a meaning to the text other than the one he knows to have been intended. Id. 60.

It is said to be either "legal," which rests on the same authority as the law itself, or "doctrinal," which rests upon its intrinsic reasonableness. Legal interpretation may be either "authentic," when it is expressly provided by the legislator, or "usual," when it is derived from unwritten practice. Doctrinal interpretation may turn on the meaning of words and sentences, when it is called "grammatical," or on the intention of the legislator, when it is described as "logical." When logical interpretation stretches the words of a statute to cover its obvious meaning, it is called "extensive;" when, on the other hand, it avoids giving full meaning to the words, in order not to go beyond the intention of the legislator, it is called "restrictive." Holl. Jur. 344.

INTERPRETATION CLAUSE. A section of a statute which defines the meaning of certain words occurring frequently in the other sections.

INTERPRETER. A person sworn at a trial to interpret the evidence of a foreigner or a deaf and dumb person to the court.

INTERREGNUM. An interval between reigns. The period which elapses between the death of a sovereign and the election of another. The vacancy which occurs when there is no government.

INTERROGATOIRE. In French law. An act which contains the interrogatories made by the judge to the person accused, on the facts which are the object of the accusation, and the answers of the accused. Poth. Proc. Crim. c. 4, art. 2, § 1.

INTERROGATORIES. A set or series of written questions drawn up for the purpose of being propounded to a party in equity, a garnishee, or a witness whose testimony is taken on deposition; a series of formal written questions used in the judicial examination of a party or a witness. In taking evidence on depositions, the interrogatories are usually prepared and settled by counsel, and reduced to writing in advance of the examination.

Interrogatories are either *direct* or *cross*, the former being those which are put on behalf of the party calling a witness; the latter are those which are interposed by the adverse party.

INTERRUPTIO. Lat. Interruption. A term used both in the civil and common law of prescription. Calvin.

Interruptio multiplex non tollit præscriptionem semel obtentam. 2 Inst. 654. Frequent interruption does not take away a prescription once secured.

INTERRUPTION. The occurrence of some act or fact, during the period of prescription, which is sufficient to arrest the running of the statute of limitations. It is said to be either "natural" or "civil," the former being caused by the act of the party; the latter by the legal effect or operation of some fact or circumstance.

Interruption of the possession is where the right is not enjoyed or exercised continuously; interruption of the right is where the person having or claiming the right ceases the exercise of it in such a manner as to show that he does not claim to be entitled to exercise it.

In Scotch law. The true proprietor's claiming his right during the course of prescription. Bell.

INTERSECTION. The point of intersection of two roads is the point where their middle lines intersect. 73 Pa. St. 127.

INTERSTATE COMMERCE. Traffic, intercourse, commercial trading, or the transportation of persons or property between or among the several states of the Union, or from or between points in one state and points in another state; commerce between two states, or between places lying in different states.

INTERSTATE COMMERCE ACT. The act of congress of February 4, 1887, designed to regulate commerce between the states, and particularly the transportation of persons and property, by carriers, between interstate points, prescribing that charges for such transportation shall be reasonable and just, prohibiting unjust discrimination, rebates, draw-backs, preferences, pooling of freights, etc., requiring schedules of rates to be published, establishing a commission to carry out the measures enacted, and prescribing the powers and duties of such commission and the procedure before it.

INTERSTATE COMMERCE COMMISSION. A commission created by the interstate commerce act (*q. v.*) to carry out the measures therein enacted, composed of five persons, appointed by the President, empowered to inquire into the business of the carriers affected, to enforce the law, to receive, investigate, and determine complaints made to them of any violation of the act, make annual reports, hold stated sessions, etc.

INTERVENER. An intervener is a person who voluntarily interposes in an action or other proceeding with the leave of the court.

INTERVENING DAMAGES. Such damages to an appellee as result from the delay caused by the appeal. 1 Tyler, 267.

INTERVENTION. In international law. Intervention is such an interference between two or more states as may (according to the event) result in a resort to force; while mediation always is, and is intended to be and to continue, peaceful only. Intervention between a sovereign and his own subjects is not justified by anything in international law; but a remonstrance may be addressed to the sovereign in a proper case. Brown.

In English ecclesiastical law. The proceeding of a third person, who, not being originally a party to the suit or proceeding, but claiming an interest in the subject-matter in dispute, in order the better to protect such interest, interposes his claim. 2 Chit. Pr. 492; 3 Chit. Commer. Law, 633; 2 Hagg. Const. 137; 3 Phillim. Ecc. Law, 586.

In the civil law. The act by which a third party demands to be received as a party in a suit pending between other persons.

The intervention is made either for the purpose of being joined to the plaintiff, and to claim the same thing he does, or some other thing connected with it; or to join the defendant, and with him to oppose the claim of the plaintiff, which it is his interest to defeat. Poth. Proc. Civile, pt. 1, c. 2, § 7, no. 3.

INTESTABILIS. A witness incompetent to testify. Calvin.

INTESTABLE. One who has not testamentary capacity; *e. g.*, an infant, lunatic, or person civilly dead.

INTESTACY. The state or condition of dying without having made a valid will.

INTESTATE. Without making a will. A person is said to die intestate when he dies without making a will, or dies without leaving anything to testify what his wishes were with respect to the disposal of his property after his death. The word is also often used to signify the person himself. Thus, in speaking of the property of a person who died intestate, it is common to say "the intestate's property;" *i. e.*, the property of the person dying in an intestate condition. Brown.

Besides the strict meaning of the word as above given, there is also a sense in which intestacy may be partial; that is, where a man leaves a will which does not dispose of his whole estate, he is said to "die intestate" as to the property so omitted.

INTESTATE SUCCESSION. A succession is called "intestate" when the deceased has left no will, or when his will has been revoked or annulled as irregular. Therefore the heirs to whom a succession has fallen by the effects of law only are called "heirs *ab intestato*." Civil Code La. art. 1096.

INTESTATO. In the civil law. Intestate; without a will. Calvin.

INTESTATUS. In the civil and old English law. An intestate; one who dies without a will. Dig. 50, 17, 7.

Intestatus decedit, qui aut omnino testamentum non fecit; aut non jure fecit; aut id quod fecerat ruptum irritumve factum est; aut nemo ex eo hæres exstitit. A person dies intestate who either has made no testament at all or has made one not legally valid; or if the testament he has made be revoked, or made useless; or if no one becomes heir under it. Inst. 3, 1, pr.

INTIMATION. In the civil law. A notification to a party that some step in a legal proceeding is asked or will be taken. Particularly, a notice given by the party taking an appeal, to the other party, that the court above will hear the appeal.

In Scotch law. A formal written notice, drawn by a notary, to be served on a party against whom a stranger has acquired a right or claim; *e. g.*, the assignee of a debt must serve such a notice on the debtor, otherwise a payment to the original creditor will be good.

INTIMIDATION. In English law. Every person commits a misdemeanor, punishable with a fine or imprisonment, who wrongfully uses violence to or *intimidates* any other person, or his wife or children, with a view to compel him to abstain from doing, or to do, any act which he has a legal right to do, or abstain from doing. (St. 38 & 39 Vict. c. 86, § 7.) This enactment is chiefly directed against outrages by trades-unions. Sweet. There are similar statutes in many of the United States.

INTIMIDATION OF VOTERS. This, by statute in several of the states, is made a criminal offense. Under an early Pennsylvania act, it was held that, to constitute the offense of intimidation of voters, there must be a preconceived intention for the purpose of intimidating the officers or interrupting the election. 3 Yeates, 429.

INTITLE. An old form of "*entitle.*" 6 Mod. 304.

INTOL AND UTTOL. In old records. Toll or custom paid for things imported and exported, or bought in and sold out. Cowell.

INTOXICATE. Generally relates to the use of strong drink. "Intoxicated," used without words of qualification, signifies a condition produced by drinking intoxicating spirituous liquor, and is equivalent to "drunk." No additional word is needed to convey this idea. It is sometimes said that a person is intoxicated with opium, or with ether, or with laughing-gas; but this is an unusual or forced use of the word. A complaint, under a statute authorizing proceedings against persons found intoxicated, which avers that defendant was found intoxicated, is in this respect sufficient, and need not allege upon what he became so. 47 Vt. 294.

INTOXICATING LIQUORS. Those the use of which is ordinarily or commonly attended with entire or partial intoxication. 6 Park. Crim. R. 355.

The terms "intoxicating liquor" and "spirituous liquor" are not synonymous. All spirituous liquor is intoxicating, but all intoxicating liquor is not spirituous. Fermented liquor, though intoxicating, is not spirituous, because not distilled. 2 Gray, 501; 4 Gray, 18.

INTRA. Lat. In; near; within. "*Infra*" or "*inter*" has taken the place of "*intra*" in many of the more modern Latin phrases.

INTRA ANNI SPATIUM. Within the space of a year. Cod. 5, 9, 2. *Intra annale tempus.* Id. 6, 30, 19.

INTRA FIDEM. Within belief; credible. Calvin.

INTRA LUCTUS TEMPUS. Within the time of mourning. Cod. 9, 1, auth.

INTRA MŒNIA. Within the walls (of a house.) A term applied to domestic or *menial* servants. 1 Bl. Comm. 425.

INTRA PARIETES. Between walls; among friends; out of court; without litigation. Calvin.

INTRA PRÆSIDIA. Within the defenses. See INFRA PRÆSIDIA.

INTRA QUATUOR MARIA. Within the four seas. Shep. Touch. 378.

INTRA VIRES. An act to said to be *intra vires* ("within the power") of a person or corporation when it is within the scope of his or its powers or authority. It is the opposite of *ultra vires*, (*q. v.*)

INTRARE MARISCUM. To drain a marsh or low ground, and convert it into herbage or pasture.

INTRINSECUM SERVITIUM. Common and ordinary duties with the lord's court.

INTRINSIC VALUE. The intrinsic value of a thing is its true, inherent, and essential value, not depending upon accident, place, or person, but the same everywhere and to every one. 5 Ired. 698.

INTRODUCTION. The part of a writing which sets forth preliminary matter, or facts tending to explain the subject.

INTROMISSION. In Scotch law. The assumption of authority over another's property, either legally or illegally. The irregular intermeddling with the effects of a deceased person, which subjects the party to the whole debts of the deceased, is called "*vitious intromission.*" Kames, Eq. b. 3, c. 8, § 2.

INTROMISSIONS. Dealings in stock, goods, or cash of a principal coming into the hands of his agent, to be accounted for by the agent to his principal. 29 Eng. Law & Eq. 391.

INTRONISATION. In French ecclesiastical law. Enthronement. The installation of a bishop in his episcopal see.

INTRUDER. A stranger who, on the death of the ancestor, enters on the land, unlawfully, before the heir can enter.

INTRUSION. A species of injury by ouster or amotion of possession from the freehold, being an entry of a stranger, after a particular estate of freehold is determined, before him in remainder or reversion.

The name of a writ brought by the owner of a fee-simple, etc., against an intruder. New Nat. Brev. 453. Abolished by 3 & 4 Wm. IV. c. 57.

INTUITUS. A view; regard; contemplation. *Diverso intuitu*, (*q. v.*,) with a different view.

INUNDATION. The overflow of waters by coming out of their bed.

INURE. To take effect; to result.

INUREMENT. Use; user; service to the use or benefit of a person. 100 U. S. 583.

Inutilis labor et sine fructu non est effectus legis. Useless and fruitless labor is not the effect of law. Co. Litt. 127*b*. The law forbids such recoveries whose ends are vain, chargeable, and unprofitable. Id; Wing. Max. p. 110, max. 38.

INVADIARE. To pledge or mortgage lands.

INVADIATIO. A pledge or mortgage.

INVADIATUS. One who is under pledge; one who has had sureties or pledges given for him. Spelman.

INVALID. Vain; inadequate to its purpose; not of binding force or legal efficacy; lacking in authority or obligation.

INVASION. An encroachment upon the rights of another; the incursion of an army for conquest or plunder. Webster.

INVASIONES. The inquisition of serjeanties and knights' fees. Cowell.

INVECTA ET ILLATA. Lat. In the civil law. Things carried in and brought in. Articles brought into a hired tenement by the hirer or tenant, and which became or were pledged to the lessor as security for the rent. Dig. 2, 14, 4, pr. The phrase is adopted in Scotch law. See Bell.

Inveniens libellum famosum et non corrumpens punitur. He who finds a libel and does not destroy it is punished. Moore, 813.

INVENT. To find out something new; to devise, contrive, and produce something not previously known or existing, by the exercise of independent investigation and experiment; particularly applied to machines, mechanical appliances, compositions, and patentable inventions of every sort.

INVENTIO. In the civil law. Finding; one of the modes of acquiring title to property by occupancy. Heinecc. lib. 2, tit. 1, § 350.

In old English law. A thing found; as goods, or treasure-trove. Cowell. The plural, "*inventiones,*" is also used.

INVENTION. In patent law. The act or operation of finding out something new; the process of contriving and producing something not previously known or existing, by the exercise of independent investigation and experiment. Also the article or contrivance or composition so invented.

An "invention" differs from a "discovery." The former term is properly applicable to the contrivance and production of something that did not before exist; while discovery denotes the bringing into knowledge and use of something which, although it existed, was before unknown. Thus, we speak of the "discovery" of the properties of light, electricity, etc., while the telescope and the electric motor are the results of the process of "invention."

INVENTOR. One who finds out or contrives some new thing; one who devises some new art, manufacture, mechanical appliance, or process; one who invents a patentable contrivance.

INVENTORY. A detailed list of articles of property; a list or schedule of property, containing a designation or description of each specific article; an itemized list of the various articles constituting a collection, estate, stock in trade, etc., with their estimated or actual values. In law, the term is particularly applied to such a list made by an executor, administrator, or assignee in bankruptcy.

INVENTUS. Lat. Found. *Thesaurus inventus*, treasure-trove. *Non est inventus*, [he] is not found.

INVERITARE. To make proof of a thing. Jacob.

INVEST. To loan money upon securities of a more or less permanent nature, or to place it in business ventures or real estate, or otherwise lay it out, so that it may produce a revenue or income.

To clothe one with the possession of a fief or benefice. See INVESTITURE.

INVESTITIVE FACT. The fact by means of which a right comes into existence; *e. g.*, a grant of a monopoly, the death of one's ancestor. Holl. Jur. 132.

INVESTITURE. A ceremony which accompanied the grant of lands in the feudal ages, and consisted in the open and notorious delivery of possession in the presence of the other vassals, which perpetuated among them the *æra* of their new acquisition at the time when the art of writing was very little known: and thus the evidence of the property was reposed in the memory of the neighborhood, who, in case of disputed title, were afterwards called upon to decide upon it. Brown.

In ecclesiastical law. Investiture is one of the formalities by which the election of a bishop is confirmed by the archbishop. See Phillim. Ecc. Law, 42, et seq.

INVESTMENT. Money invested.

INVIOLABILITY. The attribute of being secured against violation. The persons of ambassadors are inviolable.

INVITO. Lat. Being unwilling. Against or without the assent or consent.

Invito beneficium non datur. A benefit is not conferred on one who is unwilling to receive it; that is to say, no one can be compelled to accept a benefit. Dig. 50, 17, 69; Broom, Max. 699, note.

INVITO DEBITORE. Against the will of the debtor.

INVITO DOMINO. The owner being unwilling; against the will of the owner; without the owner's consent. In order to constitute larceny, the property must be taken *invito domino*.

INVOICE. In commercial law. An account of goods or merchandise sent by merchants to their correspondents at home or abroad, in which the marks of each package, with other particulars, are set forth. Marsh. Ins. 408; Dane, Abr. Index.

A list or account of goods or merchandise sent or shipped by a merchant to his correspondent, factor, or consignee, containing the particular marks of each description of goods, the value, charges, and other particulars. Jac. Sea Laws, 302.

A writing made on behalf of an importer, specifying the merchandise imported, and its true cost or value. And. Rev. Law, § 294.

INVOICE BOOK. A book in which invoices are copied.

INVOICE PRICE of goods means the prime cost. 7 Johns. 343.

INVOLUNTARY. An involuntary act is that which is performed with constraint (*q. v.*) or with repugnance, or without the will to do it. An action is involuntary, then, which is performed under duress. Wolff. Inst. Nat. § 5.

INVOLUNTARY MANSLAUGHTER. The unintentional killing of a person by one engaged in an unlawful, but not felonious, act. 4 Steph. Comm. 52.

IOTA. The minutest quantity possible. Iota is the smallest Greek letter. The word "jot" is derived therefrom.

Ipsæ leges cupiunt ut jure regantur. Co. Litt. 174. The laws themselves require that they should be governed by right.

IPSE. Lat. He himself; the same; the very person.

IPSE DIXIT. He himself said it; a bare assertion resting on the authority of an individual.

IPSISSIMIS VERBIS. In the identical words; opposed to "substantially." 7 How. 719; 5 Ohio St. 346.

IPSO FACTO. By the fact itself; by the mere fact. By the mere effect of an act or a fact.

In English ecclesiastical law. A censure of excommunication in the ecclesiastical court, immediately incurred for divers offenses, after lawful trial.

IPSO JURE. By the law itself; by the mere operation of law. Calvin.

Ira furor brevis est. Anger is a short insanity. 4 Wend. 336, 355.

IRA MOTUS. Moved or excited by anger or passion. A term sometimes formerly used in the plea of *son assault demesne.* 1 Tidd, Pr. 645.

IRE AD LARGUM. To go at large; to escape; to be set at liberty.

IRENARCHA. In Roman law. An officer whose duties are described in Dig. 5, 4, 18, 7. See Id. 48, 3, 6; Cod. 10, 75. Literally, a peace-officer or magistrate.

IRREGULAR. Not according to rule; improper or insufficient, by reason of departure from the prescribed course.

IRREGULAR DEPOSIT. A species of deposit which arises when a party, having a sum of money which he does not think safe in his own hands, confides it to another, (*e. g.*, a bank,) who is to return to him not the same money, but a like sum, when he shall demand it. An irregular deposit differs from a *mutuum* simply in this respect: that the latter has principally in view the benefit of the borrower, and the former the benefit of the bailor. Story, Bailm. § 84; Poth. du Depot. 82, 83.

IRREGULAR PROCESS. Sometimes the term "irregular process" has been defined to mean process absolutely void, and not merely erroneous and voidable; but usually it has been applied to all process not issued in strict conformity with the law, whether the defect appears upon the face of the process, or by reference to extrinsic facts, and whether such defects render the process absolutely void or only voidable. 2 Ind. 252.

IRREGULARITY. Violation or nonobservance of established rules and practices. The want of adherence to some prescribed rule or mode of proceeding; consisting either in omitting to do something that is necessary for the due and orderly conducting of a suit, or doing it in an unseasonable time or improper manner. 1 Tidd, Pr. 512. "Irregularity" is the technical term for every defect in practical proceedings, or the mode of conducting an action or defense, as distinguishable from defects in pleadings. 3 Chit. Gen. Pr. 509.

The doing or not doing that, in the conduct of a suit at law, which, conformably with the practice of the court, ought or ought not to be done. 2 Ind. 252.

In canon law. Any impediment which prevents a man from taking holy orders.

IRRELEVANCY. The absence of the quality of relevancy in evidence or pleadings.

Irrelevancy, in an answer, consists in statements which are not material to the decision of the case; such as do not form or tender any material issue. 18 N. Y. 315, 321.

IRRELEVANT. In the law of evidence. Not relevant; not relating or applicable to the matter in issue; not supporting the issue.

IRREMOVABILITY. The *status* of a pauper in England, who cannot be legally removed from the parish or union in which he is receiving relief, notwithstanding that he has not acquired a settlement there. 3 Steph. Comm. 60.

IRREPARABLE INJURY. This phrase does not mean such an injury as is beyond the possibility of repair, or beyond possible compensation in damages, or necessarily great damage, but includes an injury, whether great or small, which ought not to be submitted to, on the one hand, or inflicted, on the other; and which, because it is so large or so small, or is of such constant and frequent occurrence, cannot receive reasonable redress in a court of law. 76 Ill. 322.

Wrongs of a repeated and continuing character, or which occasion damages that are estimated only by conjecture, and not by any accurate standard, are included. 3 Pittsb. R. 204.

IRREPLEVIABLE. That cannot be replevied or delivered on sureties. Spelled, also, "irreplevisable." Co. Litt. 145.

IRRESISTIBLE FORCE. A term applied to such an interposition of human agency as is, from its nature and power, absolutely uncontrollable; as the inroads of a hostile army. Story, Bailm. § 25.

IRREVOCABLE. Which cannot be revoked or recalled.

IRRIGATION. The operation of watering lands for agricultural purposes by artificial means.

IRRITANCY. In Scotch law. The happening of a condition or event by which a charter, contract, or other deed, to which a clause irritant is annexed, becomes void.

IRRITANT. In Scotch law. Avoiding or making void; as an irritant clause. See IRRITANCY.

IRRITANT CLAUSE. In Scotch law. A provision by which certain prohibited acts specified in a deed are, if committed, declared to be null and void. A *resolutive* clause dissolves and puts an end to the right of a proprietor on his committing the acts so declared void.

IRROGARE. In the civil law. To impose or set upon, as a fine. Calvin. To inflict, as a punishment. To make or ordain, as a law.

IRROTULATIO. An enrolling; a record.

IS QUI COGNOSCIT. Lat. The cognizor in a fine. *Is cui cognoscitur*, the cognizee.

ISH. In Scotch law. The period of the termination of a tack or lease. 1 Bligh, 522.

ISLAND. A piece of land surrounded by water.

ISSINT. A law French term, meaning "thus," "so," giving its name to part of a plea in debt.

ISSUABLE. In practice. Leading to or producing an issue; relating to an issue or issues.

ISSUABLE PLEA. A plea to the merits; a traversable plea. A plea such that the adverse party can join issue upon it and go to trial.

It is true a plea in abatement is a plea, and, if it be properly pleaded, issues may be found on it. In the ordinary meaning of the word "plea," and of the word "issuable," such pleas may be called "issuable pleas," but, when these two words are used together, "issuable plea," or "issuable defense," they have a technical meaning, to-wit, pleas to the merits. 44 Ga. 434.

ISSUABLE TERMS. In the former practice of the English courts, Hilary term and Trinity term were called "issuable terms," because the issues to be tried at the assizes were made up at those terms. 3 Bl. Comm. 353. But the distinction is superseded by the provisions of the judicature acts of 1873 and 1875.

ISSUE, *v.* To send forth; to emit; to promulgate; as, an officer *issues* orders, process *issues* from a court. To put into circulation; as, the treasury *issues* notes.

ISSUE, *n.* The act of issuing, sending forth, emitting, or promulgating; the giving a thing its first inception; as the issue of an order or a writ.

In pleading. The disputed point or question to which the parties in an action have narrowed their several allegations, and upon which they are desirous of obtaining the decision of the proper tribunal. When the plaintiff and defendant have arrived at some specific point or matter affirmed on the one side, and denied on the other, they are said to be at issue. The question so set apart is called the "issue," and is designated, according to its nature, as an "issue in fact" or an "issue in law." Brown.

Issues arise upon the pleadings, when a fact or conclusion of law is maintained by the one party and controverted by the other. They are of two kinds: (1) Of law; and (2) of fact. Code N. Y. § 248; Rev. Code Iowa 1880, § 2737; Code Civil Proc. Cal. § 588.

Issues are classified and distinguished as follows:

General and *special*. The former is raised by a plea which briefly and directly traverses the whole declaration, such as "not guilty" or "*non assumpsit.*" The latter is formed when the defendant chooses one single material point, which he traverses, and rests his whole case upon its determination.

Material and *immaterial*. They are so described according as they do or do not bring up some material point or question which, when determined by the verdict, will dispose of the whole merits of the case, and leave no uncertainty as to the judgment.

Formal and *informal*. The former species of issue is one framed in strict accordance with the technical rules of pleading. The latter arises when the material allegations of the declaration are traversed, but in an inartificial or untechnical mode.

Real or *feigned*. A real issue is one formed in a regular manner in a regular suit for the purpose of determining an actual controversy. A feigned issue is one made up by direction of the court, upon a supposed case, for the purpose of obtaining the verdict of a jury upon some question of fact collaterally involved in the cause.

Common issue is the name given to the issue raised by the plea of *non est factum* to an action for breach of covenant.

In real law. Descendants. All persons who have descended from a common ancestor.

3 Ves. 257; 17 Ves. 481; 19 Ves. 547; 1 Rop. Leg. 90.

In this sense, the word includes not only a child or children, but all other descendants in whatever degree; and it is so construed generally in deeds. But, when used in wills, it is, of course, subject to the rule of construction that the intention of the testator, as ascertained from the will, is to have effect, rather than the technical meaning of the language used by him; and hence issue may, in such a connection, be restricted to children, or to descendants living at the death of the testator, where such an intention clearly appears. Abbott.

In business law. A class or series of bonds, debentures, etc., comprising all that are emitted at one and the same time.

ISSUE IN FACT. In pleading. An issue taken upon or consisting of matter of *fact*, the fact only, and not the law being disputed, and which is to be tried by a jury. 3 Bl. Comm. 314, 315; Co. Litt. 126*a;* 3 Steph. Comm. 572. See Code Civil Proc. Cal. § 590.

ISSUE IN LAW. In pleading. An issue upon matter of law, or consisting of matter of law, being produced by a demurrer on the one side, and a joinder in demurrer on the other. 3 Bl. Comm. 314; 3 Steph. Comm. 572, 580. See Code Civil Proc. Cal. § 589.

ISSUE ROLL. In English practice. A roll upon which the issue in actions at law was formerly required to be entered, the roll being entitled of the term in which the issue was joined. 2 Tidd, Pr. 733. It was not, however, the practice to enter the issue at full length, if triable by the country, until after the trial, but only to make an *incipitur* on the roll. Id. 734.

ISSUES. In English law. The goods and profits of the lands of a defendant against whom a writ of *distringas* or *distress infinite* has been issued, taken by virtue of such writ, are called "issues." 3 Bl. Comm. 280; 1 Chit. Crim. Law, 351.

ITA EST. Lat. So it is; so it stands. In modern civil law, this phrase is a form of attestation added to exemplifications from a notary's register when the same are made by the successor in office of the notary who made the original entries.

ITA LEX SCRIPTA EST. Lat. So the law is written. Dig. 40, 9, 12. The law must be obeyed notwithstanding the apparent rigor of its application. 3 Bl. Comm. 430. We must be content with the law as it stands, without inquiring into its reasons. 1 Bl. Comm. 32.

ITA QUOD. **In old practice.** So that. Formal words in writs. *Ita quod habeas corpus*, so that you have the body. 2 Mod. 180.

The name of the stipulation in a submission to arbitration which begins with the words "so as [*ita quod*] the award be made of and upon the premises."

In old conveyancing. So that. An expression which, when used in a deed, formerly made an estate upon condition. Litt. § 329. Sheppard enumerates it among the three words that are most proper to make an estate conditional. Shep. Touch. 121, 122.

Ita semper fiat relatio ut valeat dispositio. 6 Coke, 76. Let the interpretation be always such that the disposition may prevail.

ITA TE DEUS ADJUVET. Lat. So help you God. The old form of administering an oath in England, generally in connection with other words, thus: *Ita te Deus adjuvet, et sacrosancta Dei Evangelia*, So help you God, and God's holy Evangelists. *Ita te Deus adjuvet et omnes sancti*, So help you God and all the saints. Willes, 338.

Ita utere tuo ut alienum non lædas. Use your own property and your own rights in such a way that you will not hurt your neighbor, or prevent him from enjoying his. Frequently written, "*Sic utere tuo*," etc., (*q. v.*)

ITEM. Also; likewise; again. This word was formerly used to mark the beginning of a new paragraph or division after the first, whence is derived the common application of it to denote a separate or distinct particular of an account or bill.

The word is sometimes used as a verb. "The whole [costs] in this case that was thus *itemed* to counsel." Bunb. p. 164, case 233.

ITER. **In the civil law.** A way; a right of way belonging as a servitude to an estate in the country, (*prædium rusticum*.) The right of way was of three kinds: (1) *iter*, a right to walk, or ride on horseback, or in a litter; (2) *actus*, a right to drive a beast or vehicle; (3) *via*, a full right of way, comprising right to walk or ride, or drive beast or carriage. Heinec. § 408. Or, as some think, they were distinguished by the width of the objects which could be rightfully carried over the way; *e. g.*, *via*, 8 feet; *actus*, 4 feet, etc. Mackeld. Rom. Law, § 290; Bract. fol. 232; 4 Bell, H. L. Sc. 390.

In old English law. A journey, especially a circuit made by a justice in eyre, or itinerant justice, to try causes according to his own mission. Du Cange; Bract. lib. 3, cc. 11, 12, 13.

In maritime law. A way or route. The route or direction of a voyage; the route or way that is taken to make the voyage assured. Distinguished from the voyage itself.

Iter est jus eundi, ambulandi hominis; non etiam jumentum agendi vel vehiculum. A way is the right of going or walking, and does not include the right of driving a beast of burden or a carriage. Co. Litt. 56*a;* Inst. 2, 3, pr.; Mackeld. Rom. Law, § 318.

ITERATIO. Repetition. In the Roman law, a bonitary owner might liberate a slave, and the quiritary owner's repetition (*iteratio*) of the process effected a complete manumission. Brown.

ITINERA. Eyres, or circuits. 1 Reeve, Eng. Law, 52.

ITINERANT. Wandering; traveling; applied to justices who make circuits.

IULE. In old English law. Christmas.

J.

J. The initial letter of the words "judge" and "justice," for which it frequently stands as an abbreviation. Thus, "J. A.," judge advocate; "J. J.," junior judge; "L. J.," law judge; "P. J.," president judge; "F. J.," first judge; "A. J.," associate judge; "C. J.," chief justice or judge; "J. P.," justice of the peace; "JJ.," judges or justices; "J. C. P.," justice of the common pleas; "J. K. B.," justice of the king's bench; "J. Q. B.," justice of the queen's bench; "J. U. B.," justice of the upper bench.

This letter is sometimes used for "I," as the initial letter of "Institutiones," in references to the Institutes of Justinian.

JAC. An abbreviation for "*Jacobus*," the Latin form of the name James; used principally in citing statutes enacted in the reigns of the English kings of that name; *e. g.*, "St. 1 Jac. II." Used also in citing the second part of Croke's reports; thus, "Cro. Jac." denotes "Croke's reports of cases in the time of James I."

JACENS. Lat. Lying in abeyance.

JACENS HÆREDITAS. An inheritance in abeyance. See HÆREDITAS JACENS.

JACET IN ORE. In old English law. It lies in the mouth. Fleta, lib. 5, c. 5, § 49.

JACK. A kind of defensive coat-armor worn by horsemen in war; not made of solid iron, but of many plates fastened together. Some tenants were bound by their tenure to find it upon invasion. Cowell.

JACOBUS. A gold coin worth 24s., so called from James I., who was king when it was struck. Enc. Lond.

JACTITATION. A false boasting; a false claim; assertions repeated to the prejudice of another's right. The species of defamation or disparagement of another's title to real estate known at common law as "slander of title" comes under the head of jactitation, and in some jurisdictions (as in Louisiana) a remedy for this injury is provided under the name of an "action of jactitation."

JACTITATION OF A RIGHT TO A CHURCH SITTING appears to be the boasting by a man that he has a right or title to a pew or sitting in a church to which he has legally no title.

JACTITATION OF MARRIAGE. In English ecclesiastical law. The boasting or giving out by a party that he or she is married to some other, whereby a common reputation of their matrimony may ensue. To defeat that result, the person may be put to a proof of the actual marriage, failing which proof, he or she is put to silence about it. 3 Bl. Comm. 93.

JACTITATION OF TITHES is the boasting by a man that he is entitled to certain tithes to which he has legally no title.

JACTIVUS. Lost by default; tossed away. Cowell.

JACTURA. In the civil law. A throwing of goods overboard in a storm; jettison. Loss from such a cause. Calvin.

JACTUS. A throwing goods overboard to lighten or save the vessel, in which case the goods so sacrificed are a proper subject for general average. Dig. 14, 2, "*de lege Rhodia de Jactu.*"

JACTUS LAPILLI. The throwing down of a stone. One of the modes, under the civil law, of interrupting prescription. Where one person was building on another's ground, and in this way acquiring a right by *usucapio*, the true owner challenged the intrusion and interrupted the prescriptive right by throwing down one of the stones of the building before witnesses called for the purpose. Tray. Lat. Max.

JAIL. A gaol; a prison; a building designated by law, or regularly used, for the confinement of persons held in lawful custody. See GAOL.

JAIL DELIVERY. See GAOL DELIVERY.

JAIL LIBERTIES. See GAOL LIBERTIES.

JAILER. A keeper or warden of a prison or jail.

JAMBEAUX. Leg-armor. Blount.

JAMMA, JUMMA. In Hindu law. Total amount; collection; assembly. The total of a territorial assignment.

JAMMABUNDY, JUMMABUNDY. In Hindu law. A written schedule of the whole of an assessment.

JAMPNUM. Furze, or grass, or ground where furze grows; as distinguished from "arable," "pasture," or the like. Co. Litt. 5*a*.

JAMUNLINGI, JAMUNDILINGI. Freemen who delivered themselves and property to the protection of a more powerful person, in order to avoid military service and other burdens. Spelman. Also a species of serfs among the Germans. Du Cange. The same as *commendati*.

JANITOR. In old English law. A door-keeper. Fleta, lib. 2, c. 24.

In modern law. A janitor is understood to be a person employed to take charge of rooms or buildings, to see that they are kept clean and in order, to lock and unlock them, and generally to care for them. 84 N. Y. 352.

JAQUES. In old English law. Small money.

JAVELIN-MEN. Yeomen retained by the sheriff to escort the judge of assize.

JAVELOUR. In Scotch law. Jailer or gaoler. 1 Pitc. Crim. Tr. pt. 1, p. 33.

JEDBURGH JUSTICE. Lynch law.

JEMAN. In old records. Yeoman. Cowell; Blount.

JEOFAILE. L. Fr. I have failed; I am in error. An error or oversight in pleading.

Certain statutes are called "statutes of amendments and jeofailes" because, where a pleader perceives any slip in the form of his proceedings, and acknowledges the error, (jeofaile,) he is at liberty, by those statutes, to amend it. The amendment, however, is seldom made; but the benefit is attained by the court's overlooking the exception. 3 Bl. Comm. 407; 1 Saund. p. 228, no. 1.

Jeofaile is when the parties to any suit in pleading have proceeded so far that they have joined issue which shall be tried or is tried by a jury or inquest, and this pleading or issue is so badly pleaded or joined that it will be error if they proceed. Then some of the said parties may, by their counsel, show it to the court, as well after verdict given and before judgment as before the jury is charged. And the counsel shall say: "This inquest ye ought not to take." And if it be after verdict, then he may say: "To judgment you ought not to go." And, because such niceties occasioned many delays in suits, divers statutes are made to redress them. Termes de la Ley.

JEOPARDY. Danger; hazard; peril.

Jeopardy is the danger of conviction and punishment which the defendant in a criminal action incurs when a valid indictment has been found, and a petit jury has been impaneled and sworn to try the case and give a verdict.

JERGUER. In English law. An officer of the custom-house who oversees the waiters. Techn. Dict.

JESSE. A large brass candlestick, usually hung in the middle of a church or choir. Cowell.

JET. Fr. In French law. Jettison. Ord. Mar. liv. 3, tit. 8; Emerig. Traité des Assur. c. 12, § 40.

JETSAM. A term descriptive of goods which, by the act of the owner, have been voluntarily cast overboard from a vessel, in a storm or other emergency, to lighten the ship. 1 C. B. 113.

Jetsam is where goods are cast into the sea, and there sink and remain under water. 1 Bl. Comm. 292.

Jetsam differs from "flotsam," in this: that in the latter the goods float, while in the former they sink, and remain under water. It differs also from "ligan."

JETTISON. The act of throwing overboard from a vessel part of the cargo, in case of extreme danger, to lighten the ship. The same name is also given to the thing or things so cast out.

A carrier by water may, when in case of extreme peril it is necessary for the safety of the ship or cargo, throw overboard, or otherwise sacrifice, any or all of the cargo or appurtenances of the ship. Throwing property overboard for such purpose is called "jettison," and the loss incurred thereby is called a "general average loss." Civil Code Cal. § 2148; Civil Code Dak. § 1245.

JEUX DE BOURSE. In French law. Speculation in the public funds or in stocks; gambling speculations on the stock exchange; dealings in "options" and "futures."

JEWEL. By "jewels" are meant ornaments of the person, such as ear-rings, pearls, diamonds, etc., which are prepared to be worn. Brown, Ch. 467. See, further, 43 N. Y. 539; 36 Barb. 70; 14 Pick. 370; 33 Fed. Rep. 709.

JOB. The whole of a thing which is to be done. "To build by plot, or to work by the job, is to undertake a building for a certain stipulated price." Civil Code La. art. 2727.

JOBBER. One who buys and sells goods for others; one who buys or sells on the stock exchange; a dealer in stocks, shares, or securities.

JOCALIA. In old English law. Jewels. This term was formerly more properly applied to those ornaments which women, although married, call their own. When these *jocalia* are not suitable to her degree, they are assets for the payment of debts. 1 Rolle, Abr. 911.

JOCELET. A little manor or farm. Cowell.

JOCUS. In old English law. A game of hazard. Reg. Orig. 290.

JOCUS PARTITUS. In old English practice. A divided game, risk, or hazard. An arrangement which the parties to a suit were anciently sometimes allowed to make by mutual agreement upon a certain hazard, (*sub periculo;*) as that one should lose if the case turned out in a certain way, and, if it did not, that the other should gain, (*quod unus amittat si ita sit, et si non sit, quod alius lucretur.*) Bract. fols. 211*b*, 379*b*, 432, 434, 200*b*.

JOHN DOE. The name which was usually given to the fictitious lessee of the plaintiff in the mixed action of ejectment. He was sometimes called "Goodtitle." So the Romans had their fictitious personages in law proceedings, as *Titius, Seius.*

JOINDER. Joining or coupling together; uniting two or more constituents or elements in one; uniting with another person in some legal step or proceeding.

JOINDER IN DEMURRER. When a defendant in an action tenders an issue of law, (called a "demurrer,") the plaintiff, if he means to maintain his action, must accept it, and this acceptance of the defendant's tender, signified by the plaintiff in a set form of words, is called a "joinder in demurrer." Brown.

JOINDER IN ISSUE. In pleading. A formula by which one of the parties to a suit joins in or accepts an issue in fact tendered by the opposite party. Steph. Pl. 57, 236. More commonly termed a "*similiter.*" (*q. v.*)

JOINDER IN PLEADING. Accepting the issue, and mode of trial tendered, either by demurrer, error, or issue in fact, by the opposite party.

JOINDER OF ACTIONS. This expression signifies the uniting of two or more demands or rights of action in one action; the statement of more than one cause of action in a declaration.

JOINDER OF ERROR. In proceedings on a writ of error in criminal cases, the joinder of error is a written denial of the errors alleged in the assignment of errors. It answers to a joinder of issue in an action.

JOINDER OF OFFENSES. The uniting of several distinct charges of crime in the same indictment or prosecution.

JOINDER OF PARTIES. The uniting of two or more persons as co-plaintiffs or as co-defendants in one suit.

JOINT. United; combined; undivided; done by or against two or more unitedly; shared by or between two or more.

JOINT ACTION. An action in which there are two or more plaintiffs, or two or more defendants.

JOINT ADVENTURE. A commercial or maritime enterprise undertaken by several persons jointly. See ADVENTURE.

JOINT AND SEVERAL BOND. A bond in which the obligors bind themselves both jointly and individually to the obligee, and which may be enforced either by a joint action against all or separate actions against each.

JOINT BOND. One in which the obligors (two or more in number) bind themselves jointly, but not severally, and which must therefore be prosecuted in a joint action against all the obligors.

JOINT COMMITTEE. A joint committee of a legislative body comprising two chambers is a committee consisting of representatives of each of the two houses, meeting and acting together as one committee.

JOINT CONTRACT. One made by two or more promisors, who are jointly bound to fulfill its obligations, or made to two or more promisees, who are jointly entitled to require performance of the same.

JOINT CREDITORS. Persons jointly entitled to require satisfaction of the same debt or demand.

JOINT DEBTOR ACTS. Statutes enacted in many of the states, which provide that judgment may be given for or against one or more of several plaintiffs, and for or against one or more of several defendants, and that, "in an action against several defendants, the court may, in its discretion, render judgment against one or more of them, leaving the action to proceed against the others, whenever a several judgment is proper." The name is also given to statutes providing that where an action is instituted against two or more defendants upon an alleged joint liability, and some of them are served with process, but jurisdiction is not obtained over the others, the plaintiff may still proceed to trial against those who are before the court, and, if he recovers, may have judgment against all of the defendants whom he shows to be jointly liable. 1 Black, Judgm. §§ 208, 235.

JOINT DEBTORS. Persons united in a joint liability or indebtedness.

JOINT EXECUTORS. Co-executors; two or more who are joined in the execution of a will.

JOINT FIAT. In English law. A fiat in bankruptcy, issued against two or more trading partners.

JOINT FINE. In old English law. "If a whole vill is to be fined, a joint fine may be laid, and it will be good for the necessity of it; but, in other cases, fines for offenses are to be severally imposed on each particular offender, and not jointly upon all of them." Jacob.

JOINT HEIR. A co-heir.

JOINT INDICTMENT. When several offenders are joined in the same indictment, such an indictment is called a "joint indictment;" as when principals in the first and second degree, and accessaries before and after the fact, are all joined in the same indictment. 2 Hale, P. C. 173; Brown.

JOINT LIVES. This expression is used to designate the duration of an estate or right which is granted to two or more persons to be enjoyed so long as they both (or all) shall live. As soon as one dies, the interest determines.

JOINT-STOCK BANKS. In English law. Joint-stock companies for the purpose of banking. They are regulated, according to the date of their incorporation, by charter, or by 7 Geo. IV. c. 46; 7 & 8 Vict. cc. 32, 113; 9 & 10 Vict. c. 45, (in Scotland and Ireland;) 20 & 21 Vict. c. 49; and 27 & 28 Vict. c. 32; or by the "Joint-Stock Companies Act, 1862," (25 & 26 Vict. c. 89.) Wharton.

JOINT-STOCK COMPANY. An unincorporated association of individuals for business purposes, resembling a partnership in many respects, but possessing a common fund or capital stock, divided into shares, which are apportioned among the members according to their respective contributions, and which are assignable by the owner without the consent of the other members.

An association of a large number of persons united together for the common purpose of carrying on a trade or some useful enterprise capable of yielding profit. The common property of the members, applicable to the purposes of the company, is called its "joint stock." Wharton.

The words "joint-stock company" have never been used as descriptive of a corporation created by special act of the legislature, and authorized to issue certificates of stock to its shareholders. They describe a partnership made up of many persons acting under articles of association, for the purpose of carrying on a particular business, and having a capital stock, divided into shares transferable at the pleasure of the holder. 121 Mass. 526.

JOINT-STOCK CORPORATION. This differs from a joint-stock *company* in being regularly incorporated, instead of being a mere partnership, but resembles it in having a capital divided into shares of stock. Most business corporations (as distinguished from eleemosynary corporations) are of this character.

JOINT TENANCY. An estate in joint tenancy is an estate in fee-simple, fee-tail, for life, for years, or at will, arising by purchase or grant to two or more persons. Joint tenants have one and the same interest, accruing by one and the same conveyance, commencing at one and the same time, and held by one and the same undivided possession. The grand incident of joint tenancy is survivorship, by which the entire tenancy on the decease of any joint tenant remains to the survivors, and at length to the last survivor. Pub. St. Mass. 1882, p. 1292.

A joint interest is one owned by several persons in equal shares, by a title created by a single will or transfer, when expressly declared in the will or transfer to be a joint tenancy, or when granted or devised to executors or trustees as joint tenants. Civil Code Cal. § 683.

JOINT TENANTS. Two or more persons to whom are granted lands or tenements to hold in fee-simple, fee-tail, for life, for years, or at will. 2 Bl. Comm. 179.

Persons who own lands by a joint title created expressly by one and the same deed or will. 4 Kent, Comm. 357. Joint tenants have one and the same interest, accruing by one and the same conveyance, commencing at one and the same time, and held by one and the same undivided possession. 2 Bl. Comm. 180.

JOINT TRESPASSERS. Two or more who unite in committing a trespass.

JOINT TRUSTEES. Two or more persons who are intrusted with property for the benefit of one or more others.

JOINTRESS, JOINTURESS. A woman who has an estate settled on her by her husband, to hold during her life, if she survive him. Co. Litt. 46.

JOINTURE. A freehold estate in lands or tenements secured to the wife, and to take effect on the decease of the husband, and to continue during her life at the least, unless she be herself the cause of its determination. 21 Me. 369.

A competent livelihood of freehold for the wife of lands and tenements to take effect presently in possession or profit, after the decease of the husband, for the life of the wife at least. Co. Litt. 36*b;* 2 Bl. Comm. 137.

A jointure strictly signifies a joint estate limited to both husband and wife, and such was its original form; but, in its more usual form, it is a sole estate limited to the wife only, expectant upon a life-estate in the husband. 2 Bl. Comm. 137; 1 Steph. Comm. 255.

JONCARIA, or JUNCARIA. Land where rushes grow. Co. Litt. 5*a*.

JORNALE. As much land as could be plowed in one day. Spelman.

JOUR. A French word, signifying "day." It is used in our old law-books; as "*tout jours,*" forever.

JOUR EN BANC. A day *in banc.* Distinguished from "*jour en pays,*" (a day in the country,) otherwise called "*jour en nisi prius.*"

JOUR IN COURT. In old practice. Day in court; day to appear in court; appearance day. "Every process gives the defendant a day in court." Hale, Anal. § 8.

JOURNAL. A daily book; a book in which entries are made or events recorded from day to day. In maritime law, the journal (otherwise called "log" or "log-book") is a book kept on every vessel, which contains a brief record of the events and occurrences of each day of a voyage, with the nautical observations, course of the ship, account of the weather, etc. In the system of double-entry book-keeping, the journal is an account-book into which are transcribed, daily or at other intervals, the items entered upon the day-book, for more convenient posting into the ledger. In the usage of legislative bodies, the journal is a daily record of the proceedings of either house. It is kept by the clerk, and in it are entered the appointments and actions of committees, introduction of bills, motions, votes, resolutions, etc., in the order of their occurrence.

JOURNEY. The original signification of this word was a day's travel. It is now applied to a travel by land from place to place, without restriction of time. But, when thus applied, it is employed to designate a travel which is without the ordinary habits, business, or duties of the person, to a distance from his home, and beyond the circle of his friends or acquaintances. 53 Ala. 521.

JOURNEY-HOPPERS. In English law. Regrators of yarn. 8 Hen. VI. c. 5.

JOURNEYMAN. A workman hired by the day, or other given time.

JOURNEYS ACCOUNTS. In English practice. The name of a writ (now obsolete) which might be sued out where a former writ had abated without the plaintiff's fault. The length of time allowed for taking it out depended on the length of the *journey* the party must make to reach the court; whence the name.

JUBERE. Lat. In the civil law. To order, direct, or command. Calvin. The word *jubeo,* (I order,) in a will, was called a "word of direction," as distinguished from "precatory words." Cod. 6, 43, 2.

To assure or promise.

To decree or pass a law.

JUBILACION. In Spanish law. The privilege of a public officer to be retired, on account of infirmity or disability, retaining the rank and pay of his office (or part of the same) after twenty years of public service, and on reaching the age of fifty.

JUDÆUS, JUDEUS. Lat. A Jew.

JUDAISMUS. The religion and rites of the Jews. Du Cange. A quarter set apart for residence of Jews. A usurious rate of interest. 1 Mon. Angl. 839; 2 Mon. Angl. 10, 665. *Sex marcus sterlingorum ad acquietandam terram prædictum de Judaismo, in quo fuit impignorata.* Du Cange. An income anciently accruing to the king from the Jews. Blount.

JUDEX. Lat. **In Roman law.** A private person appointed by the prætor, with the consent of the parties, to try and decide a cause or action commenced before him. He received from the prætor a written formula instructing him as to the legal principles according to which the action was to be judged. Calvin. Hence the proceedings before him were said to be *in judicio*, as those before the prætor were said to be *in jure*.

In later and modern civil law. A judge, in the modern sense of the term.

In old English law. A juror. A judge, in modern sense, especially—as opposed to *justiciarius, i. e.*, a common-law judge—to denote an ecclesiastical judge. Bract. fols. 401, 402.

JUDEX A QUO. In modern civil law. The judge *from* whom, as *judex ad quem* is the judge *to* whom, an appeal is made or taken. Hallifax, Civil Law, b. 3, c. 11, no. 34.

JUDEX AD QUEM. A judge to whom an appeal is taken.

Judex æquitatem semper spectare debet. A judge ought always to regard equity. Jenk. Cent. p. 45, case 85.

Judex ante oculos æquitatem semper habere debet. A judge ought always to have equity before his eyes.

Judex bonus nihil ex arbitrio suo faciat, nec proposito domesticæ voluntatis, sed juxta leges et jura pronunciet. A good judge should do nothing of his own arbitrary will, nor on the dictate of his personal inclination, but should decide according to law and justice. 7 Coke, 27*a*.

Judex damnatur cum nocens absolvitur. The judge is condemned when a guilty person escapes punishment.

JUDEX DATUS. In Roman law. A judge given, that is, assigned or appointed, by the prætor to try a cause.

Judex debet judicare secundum allegata et probata. The judge ought to decide according to the allegations and the proofs.

JUDEX DELEGATUS. A delegated judge; a special judge.

Judex est lex loquens. A judge is the law speaking, [the mouth of the law.] 7 Coke, 4*a*.

JUDEX FISCALIS. A fiscal judge; one having cognizance of matters relating to the *fiscus*, (*q. v.*)

Judex habere debet duos sales,—salem sapientiæ, ne sit insipidus; et salem conscientiæ, ne sit diabolus. A judge should have two salts,—the salt of wisdom, lest he be insipid; and the salt of conscience, lest he be devilish.

Judex non potest esse testis in propria causa. A judge cannot be a witness in his own cause. 4 Inst. 279.

Judex non potest injuriam sibi datam punire. A judge cannot punish a wrong done to himself. See 12 Coke, 114.

Judex non reddit plus quam quod petens ipse requirit. A judge does not give more than what the complaining party himself demands. 2 Inst. 286.

JUDEX ORDINARIUS. In the civil law. An ordinary judge; one who had the right of hearing and determining causes as a matter of his own proper jurisdiction, (*ex propria jurisdictione*,) and not by virtue of a delegated authority. Calvin.

JUDEX PEDANEUS. In Roman law. The judge who was commissioned by the prætor to hear a cause was so called, from the low seat which he anciently occupied at the foot of the prætor's tribunal.

JUDGE. A public officer, appointed to preside and to administer the law in a court of justice; the chief member of a court, and charged with the control of proceedings and the decision of questions of law or discretion. "Judge" and "justice" (*q. v.*) are often used in substantially the same sense.

JUDGE ADVOCATE. An officer of a court-martial, whose duty is to swear in the other members of the court, to advise the court, and to act as the public prosecutor; but he is also so far the counsel for the prisoner as to be bound to protect him from the necessity of answering criminating questions, and to object to leading questions when propounded to other witnesses.

JUDGE ADVOCATE GENERAL. The adviser of the government in reference to courts-martial and other matters of military law. In England, he is generally a member of the house of commons and of the government for the time being.

JUDGE-MADE LAW. A phrase used to indicate judicial decisions which construe away the meaning of statutes, or find meanings in them the legislature never intended. It is sometimes used as meaning, simply, the law established by judicial precedent. Cooley, Const. Lim. 70, note.

JUDGE ORDINARY. By St. 20 & 21 Vict. c. 85, § 9, the judge of the court of probate was made judge of the court for divorce and matrimonial causes created by that act, under the name of the "judge ordinary."

In Scotland, the title "judge ordinary" is applied to all those judges, whether supreme or inferior, who, by the nature of their office, have a fixed and determinate jurisdiction in all actions of the same general nature, as contradistinguished from the old Scotch privy council, or from those judges to whom some special matter is committed; such as commissioners for taking proofs, and messengers at arms. Bell.

JUDGE'S CERTIFICATE. In English practice. A certificate, signed by the judge who presided at the trial of a cause, that the party applying is entitled to costs. In some cases, this is a necessary preliminary to the taxing of costs for such party.

A statement of the opinion of the court, signed by the judges, upon a question of law submitted to them by the chancellor for their decision. See 3 Bl. Comm. 453.

JUDGE'S MINUTES, or NOTES. Memoranda usually taken by a judge, while a trial is proceeding, of the testimony of witnesses, of documents offered or admitted in evidence, of offers of evidence, and whether it has been received or rejected, and the like matters.

JUDGE'S ORDER. An order made by a judge at chambers, or out of court.

JUDGER. A Cheshire juryman. Jacob.

JUDGMENT. The official and authentic decision of a court of justice upon the respective rights and claims of the parties to an action or suit therein litigated and submitted to its determination.

The conclusion of law upon facts found, or admitted by the parties, or upon their default in the course of the suit. Tidd, Pr. 930; 32 Md. 147.

The decision or sentence of the law, given by a court of justice or other competent tribunal, as the result of proceedings instituted therein for the redress of an injury. 3 Bl. Comm. 395; 12 Minn. 437, (Gil. 326.)

A judgment is the final determination of the rights of the parties in the action. Code N. Y. § 245; Code Civil Proc. Cal. § 577; Code Civil Proc. Dak. § 228.

A judgment is the final consideration and determination of a court of competent jurisdiction upon the matter submitted to it, and it is only evidenced by a record, or that which is by law, as the files and journal entries of this state, substituted in its stead. An order for a judgment is not the judgment, nor does the entry of such order partake of the nature and qualities of a judgment record. This must clearly ascertain not only the determination of the court upon the subject submitted, but the parties in favor of and against whom it operates. 3 Mich. 88.

The term "judgment" is also used to denote the reason which the court gives for its decision; but this is more properly denominated an "opinion."

Classification. Judgments are either *in rem* or *in personam;* as to which see JUDGMENT IN REM, JUDGMENT IN PERSONAM.

Judgments are either *final* or *interlocutory.* See Code N. C. § 384.

A *final* judgment is one which puts an end to the action, or disposes of the whole case, finally and completely, by declaring either that the plaintiff is entitled to recover a specific sum or that he cannot recover, and leaving nothing to be done but the execution of the judgment.

A final judgment is one that disposes of the case, either by dismissing it before a hearing is had upon the merits, or, after the trial, by rendering judgment either in favor of the plaintiff or defendant; but no judgment or order which does not determine the rights of the parties in the cause, and preclude further inquiry as to their rights in the premises, is a final judgment. 7 Neb. 398.

An *interlocutory* judgment is one given in the progress of a cause upon some plea, proceeding, or default which is only intermediate, and does not finally determine or complete the suit. 3 Bl. Comm. 396.

A judgment may be *upon the merits*, or it may not. A judgment on the merits is one which is rendered after the substance and matter of the case have been judicially investigated, and the court has decided which party is in the right; as distinguished from a judgment which turns upon some preliminary matter or technical point, or which, in consequence of the act or default of one of the parties, is given without a contest or trial.

Of judgments rendered without a regular

trial, or without a complete trial, the several species are enumerated below. And *first:*

Judgment *by default* is a judgment obtained by one party when the other party neglects to take a certain necessary step in the action (as, to enter an appearance, or to plead) within the proper time. In Louisiana, the term "*contradictory* judgment" is used to distinguish a judgment given after the parties have been heard, either in support of their claims or in their defense, from a judgment by default. 11 La. 366.

Judgment *by confession* is where a defendant gives the plaintiff a *cognovit* or written confession of the action (or "confession of judgment," as it is frequently called) by virtue of which the plaintiff enters judgment.

Judgment *nil dicit* is a judgment rendered for the plaintiff when the defendant "says nothing;" that is, when he neglects to plead to the plaintiff's declaration within the proper time.

Judgment by *non sum informatus* is one which is rendered when, instead of entering a plea, the defendant's attorney says he is not informed of any answer to be given to the action. Steph. Pl. 130.

Judgment of *nonsuit* is of two kinds,—voluntary and involuntary. When plaintiff abandons his case, and consents that judgment go against him for costs, it is voluntary. But when he, being called, neglects to appear, or when he has given no evidence on which a jury could find a verdict, it is involuntary. Freem. Judgm. § 6.

Judgment of *retraxit.* A judgment rendered where, after appearance and before verdict, the plaintiff voluntarily goes into court and enters on the record that he "withdraws his suit." It differs from a nonsuit. In the latter case the plaintiff may sue again, upon payment of costs; but a *retraxit* is an open, voluntary renunciation of his claim in court, and by it he forever loses his action.

Judgment of *nolle prosequi.* This judgment is entered when plaintiff declares that he will not further prosecute his suit, or entry of a *stet processus*, by which plaintiff agrees that all further proceedings shall be stayed.

Judgment of *non pros.* (*non prosequitur*) is one given against the plaintiff for a neglect to take any of those steps which it is incumbent on him to take in due time.

Judgment of *cassetur breve* or *billa* (that the writ or bill be quashed) is a judgment rendered in favor of a party pleading in abatement to a writ or action. Steph. Pl. 130, 131.

Judgment of *nil capiat per breve* or *per billam* is a judgment in favor of the defendant upon an issue raised upon a declaration or peremptory plea.

Judgment *quod partes replacitent.* This is a judgment of repleader, and is given if an issue is formed on so immaterial a point that the court cannot know for whom to give judgment. The parties must then reconstruct their pleadings.

Judgment of *respondeat ouster* is a judgment given against the defendant, requiring him to "answer over," after he has failed to establish a dilatory plea upon which an issue in law has been raised.

Judgment *quod recuperet* is a judgment in favor of the plaintiff, (that he do recover,) rendered when he has prevailed upon an issue in fact or an issue in law other than one arising on a dilatory plea. Steph. Pl. 126.

Judgment *non obstante veredicto* is a judgment entered for the plaintiff "notwithstanding the verdict" which has been given for defendant; which may be done where, after verdict and before judgment, it appears by the record that the matters pleaded or replied to, although verified by the verdict, are insufficient to constitute a defense or bar to the action.

Special, technical names are given to the judgments rendered in certain actions. These are explained as follows:

Judgment *quod computet* is a judgment in an action of account-render that the defendant do account.

Judgment *quod partitio fiat* is the interlocutory judgment in a writ of partition, that partition be made.

Judgment *quando acciderint.* If on the plea of *plene administravit* in an action against an executor or administrator, or on the plea of *riens per descent* in an action against an heir, the plaintiff, instead of taking issue on the plea, take judgment of assets *quando acciderint*, in this case, if assets afterwards come to the hands of the executor or heir, the plaintiff must first sue out a *scire facias*, before he can have execution. If, upon this *scire facias*, assets be found for part, the plaintiff may have judgment to recover so much immediately, and the residue of the assets *in futuro.* 1 Sid. 448.

Judgment *de melioribus damnis.* Where, in an action against several persons for a joint tort, the jury by mistake sever the damages by giving heavier damages against one defendant than against the others, the plaintiff may cure the defect by taking judgment for the greater damages (*de melioribus damnis*) against that defendant, and entering a *nolle prosequi* (*q. v.*) against the others. Sweet.

Judgment *in error* is a judgment rendered by a court of error on a record sent up from an inferior court.

JUDGMENT-BOOK. A book required to be kept by the clerk, among the records of the court, for the entry of judgments. Code N. Y. § 279.

JUDGMENT CREDITOR. One who is entitled to enforce a judgment by execution, (*q. v.*) The owner of an unsatisfied judgment.

JUDGMENT DEBTOR. A person against whom judgment has been recovered, and which remains unsatisfied.

JUDGMENT DEBTOR SUMMONS. Under the English bankruptcy act, 1861, §§ 76–85, these summonses might be issued against both traders and non-traders, and, in default of payment of, or security or agreed composition for, the debt, the debtors might be adjudicated bankrupt. This act was repealed by 32 & 33 Vict. c. 83, § 20. The 32 & 33 Vict. c. 71, however, (bankruptcy act, 1869,) provides (section 7) for the granting of a "debtor's summons," at the instance of creditors, and, in the event of failure to pay or compound, a petition for adjudication may be presented, unless in the events provided for by that section. Wharton.

JUDGMENT DEBTS. Debts, whether on simple contract or by specialty, for the recovery of which judgment has been entered up, either upon a *cognovit* or upon a warrant of attorney or as the result of a successful action. Brown.

JUDGMENT DOCKET. A list or docket of the judgments entered in a given court, methodically kept by the clerk or other proper officer, open to public inspection, and intended to afford official notice to interested parties of the existence or lien of judgments.

JUDGMENT IN PERSONAM. A judgment against a particular person, as distinguished from a judgment against a thing or a right or *status*. The former class of judgments are conclusive only upon parties and privies; the latter upon all the world. See next title.

JUDGMENT IN REM. A judgment *in rem* is an adjudication, pronounced upon the *status* of some particular subject-matter, by a tribunal having competent authority for that purpose. It differs from a judgment *in personam*, in this: that the latter judgment is in form, as well as substance, between the parties claiming the right; and that it is so *inter partes* appears by the record itself. It is binding only upon the parties appearing to be such by the record, and those claiming by them. A judgment *in rem* is founded on a proceeding instituted, not against the person, as such, but against or upon the thing or subject-matter itself, whose state or condition is to be determined. It is a proceeding to determine the state or condition of the thing itself; and the judgment is a solemn declaration upon the *status* of the thing, and it *ipso facto* renders it what it declares it to be. 2 Vt. 73.

Various definitions have been given of a judgment *in rem*, but all are criticised as either incomplete or comprehending too much. It is generally said to be a judgment declaratory of the *status* of some subject-matter, whether this be a person or a thing. Thus, the probate of a will fixes the *status* of the document as a will. The personal rights and interests which follow are mere incidental results of the *status* or character of the paper, and do not appear on the face of the judgment. So, a decree establishing or dissolving a marriage is a judgment *in rem*, because it fixes the *status* of the person. A judgment of forfeiture, by the proper tribunal, against specific articles or goods, for a violation of the revenue laws, is a judgment *in rem*. But it is objected that the customary definition does not fit such a case, because there is no fixing of the *status* of anything, the whole effect being a seizure, whatever the thing may be. In the foregoing instances, and many others, the judgment is conclusive against all the world, without reference to actual presence or participation in the proceedings. If the expression "strictly *in rem*" may be applied to any class of cases, it should be confined to such as these. "A very able writer says: 'The distinguishing characteristic of judgments *in rem* is that, wherever their obligation is recognized and enforced as against *any* person, it is equally recognized and enforced as against *all* persons.' It seems to us that the true definition of a 'judgment *in rem*' is 'an adjudication' against some person or thing, or upon the *status* of some subject-matter; which, wherever and whenever binding upon *any* person, is equally binding upon *all* persons." 10 Mo. App. 78.

JUDGMENT NISI. At common law, this was a judgment entered on the return of the *nisi prius* record, which, according to the terms of the *postea*, was to become absolute *unless* otherwise ordered by the court within the first four days of the next succeeding term.

JUDGMENT NOTE. A promissory note, embodying an authorization to any attorney, or to a designated attorney, or to the holder, or the clerk of the court, to enter an appearance for the maker and confess a judgment against him for a sum therein named, upon default of payment of the note.

JUDGMENT PAPER. In English practice. A sheet of paper containing an *incipitur* of the pleadings in an action at law, upon which final judgment is signed by the master. 2 Tidd, Pr. 930.

JUDGMENT RECORD. In English practice. A parchment roll, on which are transcribed the whole proceedings in the cause, deposited and filed of record in the treasury of the court, after signing of judgment. 3 Steph. Comm. 632. In American practice, the record is signed, filed, and docketed by the clerk.

JUDGMENT ROLL. In English practice. A roll of parchment containing the entries of the proceedings in an action at law to the entry of judgment inclusive, and which is filed in the treasury of the court. 1 Arch. Pr. K. B. 227, 228; 2 Tidd, Pr. 931. See ROLL.

Judicandum est legibus, non exemplis. Judgment is to be given according to the laws, not according to examples or precedents. 4 Coke, 33*b*; 4 Bl. Comm. 405.

JUDICARE. In the civil and old English law. To judge; to decide or determine judicially; to give judgment or sentence.

JUDICATIO. In the civil law. Judging; the pronouncing of sentence, after hearing a cause. Hallifax, Civil Law, b. 3, c. 8, no. 7.

JUDICATORES TERRARUM. Persons in the county palatine of Chester, who, on a writ of error, were to consider of the judgment given there, and reform it; otherwise they forfeited £100 to the crown by custom. Jenk. Cent. 71.

JUDICATURE. 1. The state or profession of those officers who are employed in administering justice; the judiciary.

2. A judicatory, tribunal, or court of justice.

3. Jurisdiction; the right of judicial action; the scope or extent of jurisdiction.

JUDICATURE ACTS. The statutes of 36 & 37 Vict. c. 66, and 38 & 39 Vict. c. 77, which went into force November 1, 1875, with amendments in 1877, c. 9; 1879, c. 78; and 1881, c. 68,—made most important changes in the organization of, and methods of procedure in, the superior courts of England, consolidating them together so as to constitute one supreme court of judicature, consisting of two divisions,—her majesty's high court of justice, having chiefly original jurisdiction; and her majesty's court of appeal, whose jurisdiction is chiefly appellate.

Judices non tenentur exprimere causam sententiæ suæ. Jenk. Cent. 75. Judges are not bound to explain the reason of their sentence.

JUDICES ORDINARII. In the civil law. Ordinary *judices;* the common *judices* appointed to try causes, and who, according to Blackstone, determined only questions of fact. 3 Bl. Comm. 315.

JUDICES PEDANEI. In the civil law. The ordinary *judices* appointed by the prætor to try causes.

JUDICES SELECTI. In the civil law. Select or selected *judices* or judges; those who were used in criminal causes, and between whom and modern *jurors* many points of resemblance have been noticed. 3 Bl. Comm. 366.

Judici officium suum excedenti non paretur. A judge exceeding his office is not to be obeyed. Jenk. Cent. p. 139, case 84. Said of void judgments.

Judici satis pœna est, quod Deum habet ultorem. It is punishment enough for a judge that he has God as his avenger. 1 Leon. 295.

JUDICIA. Lat. In Roman law. Judicial proceedings; trials. *Judicia publica,* criminal trials. Dig. 48, 1.

Judicia in curia regis non adnihilentur, sed stent in robore suo quousque per errorem aut attinctum adnullentur. Judgments in the king's courts are not to be annihilated, but to remain in force until annulled by error or attaint. 2 Inst. 539.

Judicia in deliberationibus crebro maturescunt, in accelerato processu nunquam. Judgments frequently become matured by deliberations, never by hurried process or precipitation. 3 Inst. 210.

Judicia posteriora sunt in lege fortiora. 8 Coke, 97. The later decisions are the stronger in law.

Judicia sunt tanquam juris dicta, et pro veritate accipiuntur. Judgments are, as it were, the sayings of the law, and are received as truth. 2 Inst. 537.

JUDICIAL. Belonging to the office of a judge; as *judicial* authority.

Relating to or connected with the administration of justice; as a *judicial* officer.

Having the character of judgment or formal legal procedure; as a *judicial* act.

Proceeding from a court of justice; as a *judicial* writ, a *judicial* determination.

JUDICIAL ACTION. Action of a court upon a cause, by hearing it, and determining what shall be adjudged or decreed between the parties, and with which is the right of the case. 12 Pet. 718.

JUDICIAL ACTS. Acts requiring the exercise of some judicial discretion, as distinguished from ministerial acts, which require none.

JUDICIAL ADMISSIONS. Admissions made voluntarily by a party which appear of record in the proceedings of the court.

JUDICIAL AUTHORITY. The power and authority appertaining to the office of a judge; jurisdiction; the official right to hear and determine questions in controversy.

JUDICIAL COMMITTEE OF THE PRIVY COUNCIL. In English law. A tribunal composed of members of the privy council, being judges or retired judges, which acts as the queen's adviser in matters of law referred to it, and exercises a certain appellate jurisdiction, chiefly in ecclesiastical causes, though its power in this respect was curtailed by the judicature act of 1873.

JUDICIAL CONFESSION. In the law of evidence. A confession of guilt, made by a prisoner before a magistrate, or in court, in the due course of legal proceedings. 1 Greenl. Ev. § 216.

JUDICIAL CONVENTIONS. Agreements entered into in consequence of an order of court; as, for example, entering into a bond on taking out a writ of sequestration. 6 Mart. (N. S.) 494.

JUDICIAL DECISIONS. The opinions or determinations of the judges in causes before them, particularly in appellate courts.

JUDICIAL DISCRETION. The power confided to a judge to exercise his individual discrimination and opinion in deciding certain minor or collateral matters. This power is not arbitrary, but is confined within narrow limits, within which, however, its exercise is not subject to review.

"Judicial discretion" means a discretion to be exercised in discerning the course prescribed by law. 26 Wend. 143.

JUDICIAL DOCUMENTS. Proceedings relating to litigation. They are divided into (1) judgments, decrees, and verdicts; (2) depositions, examinations, and inquisitions taken in the course of a legal process; (3) writs, warrants, pleadings, etc., which are incident to any judicial proceedings. See 1 Starkie, Ev. 252.

JUDICIAL MORTGAGE. In the law of Louisiana. The lien resulting from judgments, whether rendered on contested cases or by default, whether final or provisional, in favor of the person obtaining them. Civil Code La. art. 3321.

JUDICIAL NOTICE. The act by which a court, in conducting a trial, or framing its decision, will, of its own motion, and without the production of evidence, recognize the existence and truth of certain facts, having a bearing on the controversy at bar, and which, from their nature, are not properly the subject of testimony, or which are universally regarded as established by common notoriety, *e. g.*, the laws of the state, international law, historical events, the constitution and course of nature, main geographical features, etc.

JUDICIAL OFFICER. A person in whom is vested authority to decide causes or exercise powers appropriate to a court.

JUDICIAL POWER. The authority vested in courts and judges, as distinguished from the executive and legislative power.

JUDICIAL PROCEEDINGS. A general term for proceedings relating to, practiced in, or proceeding from, a court of justice; or the course prescribed to be taken in various cases for the determination of a controversy or for legal redress or relief.

JUDICIAL SALE. A judicial sale is one made under the process of a court having competent authority to order it, by an officer duly appointed and commissioned to sell, as distinguished from a sale by an owner in virtue of his right of property. 8 How. 495.

JUDICIAL SEPARATION. A separation of man and wife by decree of court, less complete than an absolute divorce; otherwise called a "limited divorce."

JUDICIAL STATISTICS. In English law. Statistics, published by authority, of the civil and criminal business of the United Kingdom, and matters appertaining thereto. Annual reports are published separately for England and Wales, for Ireland, and for Scotland.

JUDICIAL WRITS. In English practice. Such writs as issue under the private seal of the courts, and not under the great seal of England, and are tested or witnessed, not in the king's name, but in the name of the chief judge of the court out of which they issue. The word "judicial" is used in contradistinction to "original;" original writs being such as issue out of chancery under the great seal, and are witnessed in the king's name. See 3 Bl. Comm. 282.

JUDICIARY, *adj.* Pertaining or relating to the courts of justice, to the judicial department of government, or to the administration of justice.

JUDICIARY, *n.* That branch of government invested with the judicial power; the system of courts in a country; the body of judges; the bench.

JUDICIARY ACT. The name commonly given to the act of congress of September 24, 1789, (1 St. at Large, 73,) by which the system of federal courts was organized, and their powers and jurisdiction defined.

Judiciis posterioribus fides est adhibenda. Faith or credit is to be given to the later judgments. 13 Coke, 14.

JUDICIO SISTI. A caution, or security, given in Scotch courts for the defendant to abide judgment within the jurisdiction. Stim. Law Gloss.

Judicis est in pronuntiando sequi regulam, exceptione non probata. The judge in his decision ought to follow the rule, when the exception is not proved.

Judicis est judicare secundum allegata et probata. Dyer, 12. It is the duty of a judge to decide according to facts alleged and proved.

Judicis est jus dicere, non dare. It is the province of a judge to declare the law, not to give it. Lofft, Append. 42.

Judicis officium est opus diei in die suo perficere. It is the duty of a judge to finish the work of each day within that day. Dyer, 12.

Judicis officium est ut res, ita tempora rerum, quærere. It is the duty of a judge to inquire into the times of things, as well as into things themselves. Co. Litt. 171.

JUDICIUM. Lat. Judicial authority or jurisdiction; a court or tribunal; a judicial hearing or other proceeding; a verdict or judgment.

Judicium a non suo judice datum nullius est momenti. 10 Coke, 70. A judgment given by one who is not the proper judge is of no force.

JUDICIUM CAPITALE. In old English law. Judgment of death; capital judgment. Fleta, lib. 1, c. 39, § 2. Called, also, "*judicium vitæ amissionis,*" judgment of loss of life. Id. lib. 2, c. 1, § 5.

JUDICIUM DEI. Lat. In old English and European law. The judgment of God; otherwise called "*divinum judicium,*" the "divine judgment." A term particularly applied to the ordeals by fire or hot iron and water, and also to the trials by the cross, the eucharist, and the corsned, and the *duellum* or trial by battle, (*q. v.*,) it being supposed that the interposition of heaven was directly manifest, in these cases, in behalf of the innocent. Spelman; Burrill.

Judicium est quasi juris dictum. Judgment is, as it were, a declaration of law.

Judicium non debet esse illusorium; suum effectum habere debet. A judgment ought not to be illusory; it ought to have its proper effect. 2 Inst. 341.

JUDICIUM PARIUM. In old English law. Judgment of the peers; judgment of one's peers; trial by jury. Magna Charta, c. 29.

Judicium redditur in invitum. Co. Litt. 248*b*. Judgment is given against one, whether he will or not.

Judicium (semper) pro veritate accipitur. A judgment is always taken for truth, [that is, as long as it stands in force it cannot be contradicted.] 2 Inst. 380; Co. Litt. 39*a*, 168*a*.

JUG. In old English law. A watery place. Domesday; Cowell.

JUGE. In French law. A judge.

JUGE DE PAIX. In French law. An inferior judicial functionary, appointed to decide summarily controversies of minor importance, especially such as turn mainly on questions of fact. He has also the functions of a police magistrate. Ferrière.

JUGERUM. An acre. Co. Litt. 5*b*. As much as a yoke (*jugum*) of oxen could plow in one day.

JUGES D'INSTRUCTION. In French law. Officers subject to the *procureur impérial* or *général*, who receive in cases of criminal offenses the complaints of the parties injured, and who summon and examine witnesses upon oath, and, after communication with the *procureur impérial*, draw up the forms of accusation. They have also the right, subject to the approval of the same superior officer, to admit the accused to bail. They are appointed for three years, but are re-eligible for a further period of office. They are usually chosen from among the regular judges. Brown.

JUGULATOR. In old records. A cutthroat or murderer. Cowell.

JUGUM. In the civil law. A yoke; a measure of land; as much land as a yoke of oxen could plow in a day. Nov. 17, c. 8.

JUGUM TERRÆ. In old English law. A yoke of land; half a plow-land. Domesday; Co. Litt. 5*a;* Cowell.

JUICIO. In Spanish law. A trial or suit. White, New Recop. b. 3, tit. 4, c. 1.

JUICIO DE APEO. In Spanish law. The decree of a competent tribunal directing the determining and marking the boundaries of lands or estates.

JUICIO DE CONCURSO DE ACREEDORES. In Spanish law. The judgment granted for a debtor who has various creditors, or for such creditors, to the effect that their claims be satisfied according to their respective form and rank, when the debtor's estate is not sufficient to discharge them all in full. Escriche.

JUMENT. In old Scotch law. An ox used for tillage. 1 Pitc. Crim. Tr. pt. 2, p. 89.

JUMENTA. In the civil law. Beasts of burden; animals used for carrying burdens. This word did not include "oxen." Dig. 32, 65, 5.

JUMP BAIL. To abscond, withdraw, or secrete one's self, in violation of the obligation of a bail-bond. The expression is colloquial, and is applied only to the act of the principal.

JUNCARIA. In old English law. The soil where rushes grow. Co. Litt. 5*a;* Cowell.

Juncta juvant. United they aid. A portion of the maxim, "*Quæ non valeant singula juncta juvant,*" (*q. v.*,) frequently cited. 3 Man. & G. 99.

JUNGERE DUELLUM. In old English law. To join the *duellum;* to engage in the combat. Fleta, lib. 1, c. 21, § 10.

JUNIOR. Younger. This has been held to be no part of a man's name, but an addition by use, and a convenient distinction between a father and son of the same name. 10 Paige, 170; 7 Johns. 549; 2 Caines, 164.

JUNIOR BARRISTER. A barrister under the rank of queen's counsel. Also the junior of two counsel employed on the same side in a case. Mozley & Whitley.

JUNIOR COUNSEL. The younger of the counsel employed on the same side of a case, or the one lower in standing or rank, or who is intrusted with the less important parts of the preparation or trial of the cause.

JUNIOR CREDITOR. One whose claim or demand accrued at a date posterior to that of a claim or demand held by another creditor.

JUNIOR EXECUTION. One which was issued after the issuance of another execution, on a different judgment, against the same defendant.

JUNIOR JUDGMENT. One which was rendered or entered after the rendition or entry of another judgment, on a different claim, against the same defendant.

JUNIOR WRIT. One which is issued, or comes to the officer's hands, at a later time than a similar writ, at the suit of another party, or on a different claim, against the same defendant.

JUNIPERUS SABINA. In medical jurisprudence. This plant is commonly called "savin."

JUNK-SHOP. A shop where old cordage and ships' tackle, old iron, rags, bottles, paper, etc., are kept and sold. A place where odds and ends are purchased and sold. 12 Rich. Law, 470.

JUNTA, or JUNTO. A select council for taking cognizance of affairs of great consequence requiring secrecy; a cabal or faction. This was a popular nickname applied to the Whig ministry in England, between 1693–1696. They clung to each other for mutual protection against the attacks of the so-called "Reactionist Stuart Party."

JURA. Rights; laws. 1 Bl. Comm. 123. See Jus.

Jura ecclesiastica limitata sunt infra limites separatos. Ecclesiastical laws are limited within separate bounds. 3 Bulst. 53.

Jura eodem modo destituuntur quo constituuntur. Laws are abrogated by the same means [authority] by which they are made. Broom, Max. 878.

JURA FISCALIA. In English law. Fiscal rights; rights of the exchequer. 3 Bl. Comm. 45.

JURA IN RE. In the civil law. Rights in a thing; rights which, being separated from the *dominium*, or right of property, exist independently of it, and are enjoyed by some other person than him who has the *dominium*. Mackeld. Rom. Law, § 237.

JURA MIXTI DOMINII. In old English law. Rights of mixed dominion. The king's right or power of jurisdiction was so termed. Hale, Anal. § 6.

Jura naturæ sunt immutabilia. The laws of nature are unchangeable. Branch, Princ.

JURA PERSONARUM. Rights of persons; the rights of persons. Rights which concern and are annexed to the persons of men. 1 Bl. Comm. 122.

JURA PRÆDIORUM. In the civil law. The rights of estates. Dig. 50, 16, 86.

Jura publica anteferenda privatis. Public rights are to be preferred to private. Co. Litt. 130*a*. Applied to protections.

Jura publica ex privato [privatis] promiscue decidi non debent. Public rights ought not to be decided promiscuously with private. Co. Litt. 130*a*, 181*b*.

JURA REGALIA. In English law. Royal rights or privileges. 1 Bl. Comm. 117, 119; 3 Bl. Comm. 44.

JURA REGIA. In English law. Royal rights; the prerogatives of the crown. Crabb, Com. Law, 174.

Jura regis specialia non conceduntur per generalia verba. The special rights of the king are not granted by general words. Jenk. Cent. p. 103.

JURA RERUM. Rights of things; the rights of things; rights which a man may acquire over external objects or things unconnected with his person. 1 Bl. Comm. 122; 2 Bl. Comm. 1.

Jura sanguinis nullo jure civili dirimi possunt. The right of blood and kindred cannot be destroyed by any civil law. Dig. 50, 17, 9; Bac. Max. reg. 11; Broom, Max. 533; 14 Allen, 562.

JURA SUMMI IMPERII. Rights of supreme dominion; rights of sovereignty. 1 Bl. Comm. 49; 1 Kent, Comm. 211.

JURAL. 1. Pertaining to natural or positive right, or to the doctrines of rights and obligations; as "jural relations."

2. Of or pertaining to jurisprudence; juristic; juridical.

3. Recognized or sanctioned by positive law; embraced within, or covered by, the rules and enactments of positive law. Thus, the "jural sphere" is to be distinguished from the "moral sphere;" the latter denoting the whole scope or range of ethics or the science of conduct, the former embracing only such portions of the same as have been made the subject of legal sanction or recognition.

4. Founded in law; organized upon the basis of a fundamental law, and existing for the recognition and protection of rights. Thus, the term "jural society" is used as the synonym of "state" or "organized political community."

JURAMENTÆ CORPORALES. Corporal oaths, (*q. v.*)

JURAMENTUM. Lat. In the civil law. An oath.

JURAMENTUM CALUMNIÆ. In the civil and canon law. The oath of calumny. An oath imposed upon both parties to a suit, as a preliminary to its trial, to the effect that they are not influenced by malice or any sinister motives in prosecuting or defending the same, but by a belief in the justice of their cause. It was also required of the attorneys and proctors.

Juramentum est indivisibile; et non est admittendum in parte verum et in parte falsum. An oath is indivisible; it is not to be held partly true and partly false. 4 Inst. 274.

JURAMENTUM IN LITEM. In the civil law. An assessment oath; an oath taken by the plaintiff in an action, that the extent of the damages he has suffered, estimated in money, amounts to a certain sum, which oath, in certain cases, is accepted in lieu of other proof. Mackeld. Rom. Law, § 376.

JURAMENTUM JUDICIALE. In the civil law. An oath which the judge, of his own accord, defers to either of the parties.

It is of two kinds: *First*, that which the judge defers for the decision of the cause, and which is understood by the general name "*juramentum judiciale*," and is sometimes called "suppletory oath," *juramentum suppletorium; second*, that which the judge defers in order to fix and determine the amount of the condemnation which he ought to pronounce, and which is called "*juramentum in litem*." Poth. Obl. p. 4, c. 3, § 3, art. 3.

JURAMENTUM NECESSARIUM. In Roman law. A compulsory oath. A disclosure under oath, which the prætor compelled one of the parties to a suit to make, when the other, applying for such an appeal, agreed to abide by what his adversary should swear. 1 Whart. Ev. § 458; Dig. 12, 2, 5, 2.

JURAMENTUM VOLUNTARIUM. In Roman law. A voluntary oath. A species of appeal to conscience, by which one of the parties to a suit, instead of proving his case, offered to abide by what his adversary should answer under oath. 1 Whart. Ev. § 458; Dig. 12, 2, 34, 6.

JURARE. To swear; to take an oath.

Jurare est Deum in testem vocare, et est actus divini cultus. 3 Inst. 165. To swear is to call God to witness, and is an act of religion.

JURAT. The clause written at the foot of an affidavit, stating when, where, and before whom such affidavit was sworn.

JURATA. In old English law. A jury of twelve men sworn. Especially, a jury of the common law, as distinguished from the *assisa*.

The jury clause in a *nisi prius* record, so called from the emphatic words of the old forms: "*Jurata ponitur in respectum*," the jury is put in respite. Townsh. Pl. 487.

Also a jurat, (which see.)

JURATION. The act of swearing; the administration of an oath.

Jurato creditur in judicio. He who makes oath is to be believed in judgment. 3 Inst. 79.

JURATOR. A juror; a compurgator, (*q. v.*)

Juratores debent esse vicini, sufficientes, et minus suspecti. Jurors ought to be neighbors, of sufficient estate, and free from suspicion. Jenk. Cent. 141.

Juratores sunt judices facti. Jenk. Cent. 61. Juries are the judges of fact.

JURATORY CAUTION. In Scotch law. A description of caution (security) sometimes offered in a suspension or advocation where the complainer is not in circumstances to offer any better. Bell.

JURATS. In English law. Officers in the nature of aldermen, sworn for the government of many corporations. The twelve assistants of the bailiff in Jersey are called "jurats."

JURE. Lat. By right; in right; by the law.

JURE BELLI. By the right or law of war. 1 Kent, Comm. 126; 1 C. Rob. Adm. 289.

JURE CIVILI. By the civil law. Inst. 1, 3, 4; 1 Bl. Comm. 423.

JURE CORONÆ. In right of the crown.

JURE DIVINO. By divine right. 1 Bl. Comm. 191.

JURE ECCLESIÆ. In right of the church. 1 Bl. Comm. 401.

JURE EMPHYTEUTICO. By the right or law of *emphyteusis*. 3 Bl. Comm. 232. See EMPHYTEUSIS.

JURE GENTIUM. By the law of nations. Inst. 1, 3, 4; 1 Bl. Comm. 423.

Jure naturæ æquum est neminem cum alterius detrimento et injuria fieri locupletiorem. By the law of nature it is not just that any one should be enriched by the detriment or injury of another. Dig. 50, 17, 206.

JURE PROPINQUITATIS. By right of propinquity or nearness. 2 Crabb, Real Prop. p. 1019, § 2398.

JURE REPRESENTATIONIS. By right of representation; in the right of another person. 2 Bl. Comm. 224, 517; 2 Crabb, Real Prop. p. 1019, § 2398.

JURE UXORIS. In right of a wife. 3 Bl. Comm. 210.

Juri non est consonum quod aliquis accessorius in curia regis convincatur antequam aliquis de facto fuerit attinctus. It is not consonant to justice that any accessary should be convicted in the king's court before any one has been attainted of the fact. 2 Inst. 183.

JURIDICAL. Relating to administration of justice, or office of a judge.

Regular; done in conformity to the laws of the country and the practice which is there observed.

JURIDICAL DAYS. Days in court on which the laws are administered.

JURIDICUS. Lat. Relating to the courts or to the administration of justice; juridical; lawful. *Dies juridicus*, a lawful day for the transaction of business in court; a day on which the courts are open.

JURIS. Lat. Of right; of law.

Juris affectus in executione consistit. The effect of the law consists in the execution. Co. Litt. 289*b*.

JURIS ET DE JURE. Of law and of right. A presumption *juris et de jure*, or an irrebuttable presumption, is one which the law will not suffer to be rebutted by any counter-evidence, but establishes as conclusive; while a presumption *juris tantum* is one which holds good in the absence of evidence to the contrary, but may be rebutted.

JURIS ET SEISINÆ CONJUNCTIO. The union of seisin or possession and the right of possession, forming a complete title. 2 Bl. Comm. 199, 311.

Juris ignorantia est cum jus nostrum ignoramus. It is ignorance of the law when we do not know our own rights. 9 Pick. 130.

JURIS POSITIVI. Of positive law; a regulation or requirement of positive law, as distinguished from natural or divine law. 1 Bl. Comm. 439; 2 Steph. Comm. 286.

Juris præcepta sunt hæc: Honeste vivere; alterum non lædere; suum cuique tribuere. These are the precepts of the law: To live honorably; to hurt nobody; to render to every one his due. Inst. 1, 1, 3; 1 Bl. Comm. 40.

JURIS PRIVATI. Of private right; subjects of private property. Hale, Anal. § 23.

JURIS PUBLICI. Of common right; of common or public use; such things as, at least in their own use, are common to all the king's subjects; as common highways, common bridges, common rivers, and common ports. Hale, Anal. § 23.

JURIS UTRUM. In English law. An abolished writ which lay for the parson of a church whose predecessor had alienated the lands and tenements thereof. Fitzh. Nat. Brev. 48.

JURISCONSULT. A jurist; a person skilled in the science of law, particularly of international or public law.

JURISCONSULTUS. Lat. In Roman law. An expert in juridical science; a person thoroughly versed in the laws, who was habitually resorted to, for information and advice, both by private persons as his clients, and also by the magistrates, advocates, and others employed in administering justice.

Jurisdictio est potestas de publico introducta, cum necessitate juris dicendi. Jurisdiction is a power introduced for the public good, on account of the necessity of dispensing justice. 10 Coke, 73*a*.

JURISDICTION. The power and authority constitutionally conferred upon (or constitutionally recognized as existing in) a court or judge to pronounce the sentence of the law, or to award the remedies provided by law, upon a state of facts, proved or admitted, referred to the tribunal for decision, and authorized by law to be the subject of investigation or action by that tribunal, and in favor of or against persons (or a *res*) who present themselves, or who are brought, before the court in some manner sanctioned by law as proper and sufficient. 1 Black, Judgm. § 215.

Jurisdiction is a power constitutionally conferred upon a judge or magistrate to take cognizance of and determine causes according to law, and to carry his sentence into execution. 6 Pet. 591; 9 Johns. 239; 2 Neb. 135.

The authority of a court as distinguished from the other departments; judicial power considered with reference to its scope and extent as respects the questions and persons subject to it; power given by law to hear and decide controversies. Abbott.

Jurisdiction is the power to hear and determine the subject-matter in controversy between parties to the suit; to adjudicate or exercise any judicial power over them. 12 Pet. 657, 717.

Jurisdiction is the power to hear and determine a cause; the authority by which judicial officers take cognizance of and decide causes. 43 Tex. 440.

JURISDICTION CLAUSE. In equity practice. That part of a bill which is intended to give jurisdiction of the suit to the court, by a general averment that the acts complained of are contrary to equity, and tend to the injury of the complainant, and that he has no remedy, or not a complete remedy, without the assistance of a court of equity, is called the "jurisdiction clause." Mitf. Eq. Pl. 43.

JURISDICTIONAL. Pertaining or relating to jurisdiction; conferring jurisdiction; showing or disclosing jurisdiction; defining or limiting jurisdiction; essential to jurisdiction.

JURISINCEPTOR. A student of the civil law.

JURISPERITUS. Skilled or learned in the law.

JURISPRUDENCE. The philosophy of law, or the science which treats of the principles of positive law and legal relations.

"The term is wrongly applied to actual systems of law, or to current views of law, or to suggestions for its amendment, but is the name of a science. This science is a formal, or analytical, rather than a material, one. It is the science of actual or positive law. It is wrongly divided into 'general' and 'particular,' or into 'philosophical' and 'historical.' It may therefore be defined as the formal science of positive law." Holl. Jur. 12.

In the proper sense of the word, "jurisprudence" is the science of law, namely, that science which has for its function to ascertain the principles on which legal rules are based, so as not only to classify those rules in their proper order, and show the relation in which they stand to one another, but also to settle the manner in which new or doubtful cases should be brought under the appropriate rules. Jurisprudence is more a formal than a material science. It has no direct concern with questions of moral or political policy, for they fall under the province of ethics and legislation; but, when a new or doubtful case arises to which two different rules seem, when taken literally, to be equally applicable, it may be, and often is, the function of jurisprudence to consider the ultimate effect which would be produced if each rule were applied to an indefinite number of similar cases, and to choose that rule which, when so applied, will produce the greatest advantage to the community. Sweet.

JURISPRUDENTIA. In the civil and common law. Jurisprudence, or legal science.

Jurisprudentia est divinarum atque humanarum rerum notitia, justi atque injusti scientia. "Jurisprudence" is the knowledge of things divine and human, the science of what is right and what is wrong. Dig. 1, 1, 10, 2; Inst. 1, 1, 1. This definition is adopted by Bracton, word for word. Bract. fol. 3.

Jurisprudentia legis communis Angliæ est scientia socialis et copiosa. The jurisprudence of the common law of England is a science social and comprehensive. 7 Coke, 28*a*.

JURIST. One who is versed or skilled in law; answering to the Latin "*jurisperitus*," (*q. v.*)

One who is skilled in the civil law, or law of nations. The term is now usually applied to those who have distinguished themselves by their *writings* on legal subjects.

JURISTIC. Pertaining or belonging to, or characteristic of, jurisprudence, or a jurist, or the legal profession.

JURISTIC ACT. One designed to have a legal effect, and capable thereof.

JURNEDUM. In old English law. A journey; a day's traveling. Cowell.

JURO. In Spanish law. A certain perpetual pension, granted by the king on the public revenues, and more especially on the salt-works, by favor, either in consideration of meritorious services, or in return for money loaned the government, or obtained by it through forced loans. Escriche.

JUROR. One member of a jury. Sometimes, one who takes an oath; as in the term "non-juror," a person who refuses certain oaths.

JUROR'S BOOK. A list of persons qualified to serve on juries.

JURY In practice. A certain number of men, selected according to law, and *sworn* (*jurati*) to inquire of certain matters of fact, and declare the truth upon evidence to be laid before them. This definition embraces the various subdivisions of juries; as *grand jury, petit jury, common jury, special jury, coroner's jury, sheriff's jury*, (*q. v.*)

A jury is a body of men temporarily selected from the citizens of a particular district, and invested with power to present or indict a person for a public offense, or to try a question of fact. Code Civil Proc. Cal. § 190.

The terms "jury" and "trial by jury," as used in the constitution, mean twelve competent men, disinterested and impartial, not of kin, nor personal dependents of either of the parties, having their homes within the jurisdictional limits of the court, drawn and selected by officers free from all bias in favor of or against either party, duly impaneled and sworn to render a true verdict according to the law and the evidence. 11 Nev. 39.

A *grand* jury is a body of men, (twelve to twenty-three in number,) returned in pursuance of law, from the citizens of a county, or city and county, before a court of competent jurisdiction, and sworn to inquire of public offenses committed or triable within the county, or city and county. Code Civil Proc. Cal. § 192.

A *trial* jury is a body of men returned from the citizens of a particular district before a court or officer of competent jurisdiction, and sworn to try and determine, by verdict, a question of fact. Code Civil Proc. Cal. § 193.

JURY-BOX. In practice. The place in court (strictly an inclosed place) where the jury sit during the trial of a cause. 1 Archb. Pr. K. B. 208; 1 Burrill, Pr. 455.

JURY COMMISSIONER. An officer charged with the duty of selecting the names to be put into the jury wheel, or of drawing the panel of jurors for a particular term of court.

JURY-LIST. A paper containing the names of jurors impaneled to try a cause, or it contains the names of all the jurors summoned to attend court.

JURY OF MATRONS. In common-law practice. A jury of twelve matrons or discreet women, impaneled upon a writ *de ventre inspiciendo*, or where a female prisoner, being under sentence of death, pleaded her pregnancy as a ground for staying execution. In the latter case, such jury inquired into the truth of the plea.

JURY PROCESS. The process by which a jury is summoned in a cause, and by which their attendance is enforced.

JURY WHEEL. A machine containing the names of persons qualified to serve as grand and petit jurors, from which, in an order determined by the hazard of its revolutions, are drawn a sufficient number of such names to make up the panels for a given term of court.

JURYMAN. A juror; one who is impaneled on a jury.

JURYWOMAN. One member of a jury of matrons, (*q. v.*)

JUS. Lat. In Roman law. Right; justice; law; the whole body of law; also a right. The term is used in two meanings:

1. "*Jus*" means "law," considered in the abstract; that is, as distinguished from any specific enactment, the science or department of learning, or *quasi* personified factor in human history or conduct or social development, which we call, in a general sense, "the law." Or it means the law taken as a system, an aggregate, a whole; "the sum total of a number of individual laws taken together." Or it may designate some one particular system or body of particular laws; as in the phrases "*jus civile*," "*jus gentium*," "*jus prætorium*."

2. In a second sense, "*jus*" signifies "a right;" that is, a power, privilege, faculty, or demand inherent in one person and incident upon another; or a capacity residing in one person of controlling, with the assent and assistance of the state, the actions of another. This is its meaning in the expressions "*jus in rem*," "*jus accrescendi*," "*jus possessionis*."

It is thus seen to possess the same ambiguity as the words "*droit*," "*recht*," and "right," (which see.)

The continental jurists seek to avoid this ambiguity in the use of the word "*jus*," by calling its former signification "objective," and the latter meaning "subjective." Thus Mackeldey (Rom. Law, § 2) says: "The laws of the first kind [compulsory or positive laws] form law [*jus*] in its objective sense, [*jus est norma agendi*, law is a rule of conduct.] The possibility resulting from law in this sense to do or require another to do is law in its subjective sense, [*jus est facultas agendi*, law is a license to act.] The voluntary action of man in conformity with the precepts of law is called 'justice,' [*justitia*.]"

Some further meanings of the word are:

An action. Bract. fol. 3. Or, rather, those proceedings in the Roman action which were conducted before the prætor.

Power or authority. *Sui juris*, in one's own power; independent. Inst. 1, 8, pr.; Bract. fol. 3. *Alieni juris*, under another's power. Inst. 1, 8, pr.

The profession (*ars*) or practice of the law. *Jus ponitur pro ipsa arte.* Bract. fol. 2*b*.

A court or judicial tribunal, (*locus in quo redditur jus*.) Id. fol. 3.

JUS ABUTENDI. The right to abuse. By this phrase is understood the right to do exactly as one likes with property, or having full dominion over property. 3 Toullier, no. 86.

JUS ACCRESCENDI. The right of survivorship. The right of the survivor or survivors of two or more joint tenants to the tenancy or estate, upon the death of one or more of the joint tenants.

Jus accrescendi inter mercatores, pro beneficio commercii, locum non habet. The right of survivorship has no place between merchants, for the benefit of commerce. Co. Litt. 182*a;* 2 Story, Eq. Jur. § 1207; Broom, Max. 455. There is no survivorship in cases of partnership, as there is in joint-tenancy. Story, Partn. § 90.

Jus accrescendi præfertur oneribus. The right of survivorship is preferred to incumbrances. Co. Litt. 185*a*. Hence no dower or curtesy can be claimed out of a joint estate. 1 Steph. Comm. 316.

Jus accrescendi præfertur ultimæ voluntati. The right of survivorship is preferred to the last will. Co. Litt. 185*b*. A devise of one's share of a joint estate, by will, is no severance of the jointure; for no testament takes effect till after the death of the testator, and by such death the right of the survivor (which accrued at the original creation of the estate, and has therefore a priority to the other) is already vested. 2 Bl. Comm. 186; 3 Steph. Comm. 316.

JUS AD REM. A term of the civil law, meaning "a right to a thing;" that is, a right exercisable by one person over a particular article of property in virtue of a contract or obligation incurred by another person in respect to it, and which is enforceable only against or through such other person. It is thus distinguished from *jus in re*, which is a complete and absolute dominion over a thing available against all persons.

The disposition of modern writers is to use the term "*jus ad rem*" as descriptive of a right without possession, and "*jus in re*" as descriptive of a right accompanied by possession. Or, in a somewhat wider sense, the former denotes an inchoate or incomplete right to a thing; the latter, a complete and perfect right to a thing.

In canon law. A right to a thing. An inchoate and imperfect right, such as is gained by nomination and institution; as distinguished from *jus in re*, or complete and full right, such as is acquired by corporal possession. 2 Bl. Comm. 312.

JUS ÆLIANUM. A body of laws drawn up by Sextus Ælius, and consisting of three parts, wherein were explained, respectively: (1) The laws of the Twelve Tables; (2) the interpretation of and decisions upon such laws; and (3) the forms of procedure. In date, it was subsequent to the *jus Flavianum*, (*q. v.*) Brown.

JUS ÆSNECIÆ. The right of primogeniture, (*q. v.*)

JUS ALBINATUS. The *droit d'aubaine,* (*q. v.*) See ALBINATUS JUS.

JUS ANGLORUM. The laws and customs of the West Saxons, in the time of the Heptarchy, by which the people were for a long time governed, and which were preferred before all others. Wharton.

JUS AQUÆDUCTUS. In the civil law. The name of a servitude which gives to the owner of land the right to bring down water through or from the land of another.

JUS BANCI. In old English law. The right of bench. The right or privilege of having an elevated and separate *seat of judgment,* anciently allowed only to the king's judges, who hence were said to administer *high* justice, (*summam administrant justitiam.*) Blount.

JUS BELLI. The law of war. The law of nations as applied to a state of war, defining in particular the rights and duties of the belligerent powers themselves, and of neutral nations.

The right of war; that which may be done without injustice with regard to an enemy. Gro. de Jure B. lib. 1, c. 1, § 3.

JUS BELLUM DICENDI. The right of proclaiming war.

JUS CANONICUM. The canon law.

JUS CIVILE. Civil law. The system of law peculiar to one state or people. Inst. 1, 2, 1. Particularly, in Roman law, the civil law of the Roman people, as distinguished from the *jus gentium*. The term is also applied to the body of law called, emphatically, the "civil law."

The *jus civile* and the *jus gentium* are distinguished in this way. All people ruled by statutes and customs use a law partly peculiar to themselves, partly common to all men. The law each people has settled for itself is peculiar to the state itself, and is called "*jus civile,*" as being peculiar to that very state. The law, again, that natural reason has settled among all men,—the law that is guarded among all peoples quite alike,—is called the "*jus gentium,*" and all nations use it as if law. The Roman people, therefore, use a law that is partly peculiar to itself, partly common to all men. Hunter, Rom. Law, 38.

But this is not the only, or even the general, use of the words. What the Roman jurists had chiefly in view, when they spoke of "*jus civile,*" was not local as opposed to cosmopolitan law, but the old law of the city as contrasted with the newer law introduced by the prætor, (*jus prætorium, jus honorarium.*) Largely, no doubt, the *jus gentium* corresponds with the *jus prætorium;* but the correspondence is not perfect. Id. 39.

Jus civile est quod sibi populus constituit. The civil law is what a people establishes for itself. Inst. 1, 2, 1; 1 Johns. 424, 426.

JUS CIVITATUS. The right of citizenship; the freedom of the city of Rome. It differs from *jus quiritium*, which comprehended all the privileges of a free native of Rome. The difference is much the same as between "denization" and "naturalization" with us. Wharton.

JUS CLOACÆ. In the civil law. The right of sewerage or drainage. An easement consisting in the right of having a sewer, or of conducting surface water, through the house or over the ground of one's neighbor. Mackeld. Rom. Law, § 317.

JUS COMMUNE. In the civil law. Common right; the common and natural rule of right, as opposed to *jus singulare*, (*q. v.*) Mackeld. Rom. Law, § 196.

In English law. The common law, answering to the Saxon "*folcright.*" 1 Bl. Comm. 67.

Jus constitui oportet in his quæ ut plurimum accidunt non quæ ex inopinato. Laws ought to be made with a view to those cases which happen most frequently, and not to those which are of rare or accidental occurrence. Dig. 1, 3, 3; Broom, Max. 43.

JUS CORONÆ. In English law. The right of the crown, or to the crown; the right of succession to the throne. 1 Bl. Comm. 191; 2 Steph. Comm. 434.

JUS CUDENDÆ MONETÆ. In old English law. The right of coining money. 2 How. State Tr. 118.

JUS CURIALITATIS. In English law. The right of curtesy. Spelman.

JUS DARE. To give or to make the law; the function and prerogative of the legislative department.

JUS DELIBERANDI. In the civil law. The right of deliberating. A term granted by the proper officer at the request of him who is called to the inheritance, (the heir,) within which he has the right to investigate its condition and to consider whether he will accept or reject it. Mackeld. Rom. Law, § 742; Civil Code La. art. 1028.

Jus descendit, et non terra. A right descends, not the land. Co. Litt. 345.

JUS DEVOLUTUM. The right of the church of presenting a minister to a vacant parish, in case the patron shall neglect to exercise his right within the time limited by law.

JUS DICERE. To declare the law; to say what the law is. The province of a court or judge. 2 Eden, 29; 3 P. Wms. 485.

JUS DISPONENDI. The right of disposing. An expression used either generally to signify the right of alienation, as when we speak of depriving a married woman of the *jus disponendi* over her separate estate, or specially in the law relating to sales of goods, where it is often a question whether the vendor of goods has the intention of reserving to himself the *jus disponendi; i. e.*, of preventing the ownership from passing to the purchaser, notwithstanding that he (the vendor) has parted with the possession of the goods. Sweet.

JUS DIVIDENDI. The right of disposing of realty by will. Du Cange.

JUS DUPLICATUM. A double right; the right of possession united with the right of property; otherwise called "*droit-droit.*" 2 Bl. Comm. 199.

Jus est ars boni et æqui. Law is the science of what is good and just. Dig. 1, 1, 1, 1; Bract. fol. 2*b*.

Jus est norma recti; et quicquid est contra normam recti est injuria. Law is a rule of right; and whatever is contrary to the rule of right is an injury. 3 Bulst. 313.

Jus et fraus nunquam cohabitant. Right and fraud never dwell together. 10 Coke, 45*a*. Applied to the title of a statute. Id.; Best, Ev. p. 250, § 205.

Jus ex injuria non oritur. A right does (or can) not arise out of a wrong. 4 Bing. 639; Broom, Max. 738, note.

JUS FALCANDI. In old English law. The right of mowing or cutting. Fleta, lib. 4, c. 27, § 1.

JUS FECIALE. In Roman law. The law of arms, or of heralds. A rudimentary species of international law founded on the rites and religious ceremonies of the different peoples.

JUS FIDUCIARIUM. In the civil law. A right in trust; as distinguished from *jus legitimum*, a legal right. 2 Bl. Comm. 328.

JUS FLAVIANUM. In old Roman law. A body of laws drawn up by Cneius Flavius, a clerk of Appius Claudius, from the materials to which he had access. It was a popularization of the laws. Mackeld. Rom. Law, § 39.

JUS FLUMINUM. In the civil law. The right to the use of rivers. Locc. de Jure Mar. lib. 1, c. 6.

JUS FODIENDI. In the civil and old English law. A right of digging on another's land. Inst. 2, 3, 2; Bract. fol. 222.

JUS GENTIUM. The law of nations. That law which natural reason has established among all men is equally observed among all nations, and is called the "law of nations," as being the law which all nations use. Inst. 1, 2, 1; Dig. 1, 1, 9; 1 Bl. Comm. 43; 1 Kent, Comm. 7; Mackeld. Rom. Law, § 125.

Although this phrase had a meaning in the Roman law which may be rendered by our expression "law of nations," it must not be understood as equivalent to what we now call "international law," its scope being much wider. It was originally a system of law, or more properly equity, gathered by the early Roman lawyers and magistrates from the common ingredients in the customs of the old Italian tribes,—those being the nations, *gentes*, whom they had opportunities of observing, —to be used in cases where the *jus civile* did not apply; that is, in cases between foreigners or between a Roman citizen and a foreigner. The principle upon which they proceeded was that any rule of law which was common to all the nations they knew of must be intrinsically consonant to right reason, and therefore fundamentally valid and just. From this it was an easy transition to the converse principle, viz., that any rule which instinctively commended itself to their sense of justice and reason must be a part of the *jus gentium*. And so the latter term came eventually to be about synonymous with "equity," (as the Romans understood it,) or the system of prætorian law.

Modern jurists frequently employ the term "*jus gentium privatum*" to denote private international law, or that subject which is otherwise styled the "conflict of laws;" and "*jus gentium publicum*" for public international law, or the system of rules governing the intercourse of nations with each other as persons.

JUS GLADII. The right of the sword; the executory power of the law; the right, power, or prerogative of punishing for crime. 4 Bl. Comm. 177.

JUS HABENDI. The right to have a thing. The right to be put in actual possession of property. Lewin, Trusts, 585.

JUS HABENDI ET RETINENDI. A right to have and to retain the profits, tithes, and offerings, etc., of a rectory or parsonage.

JUS HÆREDITATIS. The right of inheritance.

JUS HAURIENDI. In the civil and old English law. The right of drawing water. Fleta, lib. 4, c. 27, § 1.

JUS HONORARIUM. The body of Roman law, which was made up of edicts of the supreme magistrates, particularly the prætors.

JUS IMAGINIS. In Roman law. The right to use or display pictures or statues of ancestors; somewhat analogous to the right, in English law, to bear a coat of arms.

JUS IMMUNITATIS. In the civil law. The law of immunity or exemption from the burden of public office. Dig. 50, 6.

JUS IN PERSONAM. A right against a person; a right which gives its possessor a power to oblige another person to give or procure, to do or not to do, something.

JUS IN RE. In the civil law. A right in a thing. A right existing in a person with respect to an article or subject of property, inherent in his relation to it, implying complete ownership with possession, and available against all the world. See JUS AD REM.

Jus in re inhærit ossibus usufructuarii. A right in the thing cleaves to the person of the usufructuary.

JUS IN RE PROPRIA. The right of enjoyment which is incident to full ownership or property, and is often used to denote the full ownership or property itself. It is distinguished from *jus in re alienâ*, which is a mere easement or right in or over the property of another.

JUS INCOGNITUM. An unknown law. This term is applied by the civilians to obsolete laws. Bowyer, Mod. Civil Law, 33.

JUS INDIVIDUUM. An individual or indivisible right; a right incapable of division. 36 Eng. Law & Eq. 25.

Jus jurandi forma verbis differt, re convenit; hunc enim sensum habere debet: ut Deus invocetur. Grot. de Jur. B., l. 2, c. 13, § 10. The form of taking an oath differs in language, agrees in meaning; for it ought to have this sense: that the Deity is invoked.

JUS LATII. In Roman law. The right of Latium or of the Latins. The principal privilege of the Latins seems to have been the use of their own laws, and their not being subject to the edicts of the prætor, and that they had occasional access to the freedom of Rome, and a participation in her sacred rites. Butl. Hor. Jur. 41.

JUS LATIUM. In Roman law. A rule of law applicable to magistrates in Latium. It was either *majus Latium* or *minus Latium*,—the *majus Latium* raising to the dignity of Roman citizen not only the magistrate himself, but also his wife and children; the *minus Latium* raising to that dignity only the magistrate himself. Brown.

JUS LEGITIMUM. A legal right. In the civil law. A right which was enforceable in the ordinary course of law. 2 Bl. Comm. 328.

JUS MARITI. The right of a husband; especially the right which a husband acquires to his wife's movable estate by virtue of the marriage. 1 Forb. Inst. pt. 1, p. 63.

JUS MERUM. In old English law. Mere or bare right; the mere right of property in lands, without either possession or even the right of possession. 2 Bl. Comm. 197; Bract fol. 23.

JUS NATURÆ. The law of nature. See JUS NATURALE.

JUS NATURALE. The natural law, or law of nature; law, or legal principles, supposed to be discoverable by the light of nature or abstract reasoning, or to be taught by nature to all nations and men alike; or law supposed to govern men and peoples in a state of nature, *i. e.*, in advance of organized governments or enacted laws. This conceit originated with the philosophical jurists of Rome, and was gradually extended until the phrase came to denote a supposed basis or substratum common to all systems of positive law, and hence to be found, in greater or less purity, in the laws of all nations. And, conversely, they held that if any rule or principle of law was observed in common by all peoples with whose systems they were acquainted, it must be a part of the *jus naturale*, or derived from it. Thus the phrases "*jus naturale*" and "*jus gentium*" came to be used interchangeably.

Jus naturale est quod apud homines eandem habet potentiam. Natural right is that which has the same force among all mankind. 7 Coke, 12.

JUS NAVIGANDI. The right of navigating or navigation; the right of commerce by ships or by sea. Locc. de Jure Mar. lib. 1, c. 3.

JUS NECIS. In Roman law. The right of death, or of putting to death. A right which a father anciently had over his children.

Jus non habenti tute non paretur. One who has no right cannot be safely obeyed. Hob. 146.

Jus non patitur ut idem bis solvatur. Law does not suffer that the same thing be twice paid.

JUS NON SCRIPTUM. The unwritten law. 1 Bl. Comm. 64.

JUS PAPIRIANUM. The civil law of Papirius. The title of the earliest collection of Roman *leges curiatæ*, said to have been made in the time of Tarquin, the last of the kings, by a *pontifex maximus* of the name of Sextus or Publius Papirius. Very few fragments of this collection now remain, and the authenticity of these has been doubted. Mackeld. Rom. Law, § 21.

JUS PASCENDI. In the civil and old English law. The right of pasturing cattle. Inst. 2, 3, 2; Bract. fols. 53*b*, 222.

JUS PATRONATUS. In English ecclesiastical law. The right of patronage; the right of presenting a clerk to a benefice. Blount.

A commission from the bishop, where two presentations are offered upon the same avoidance, directed usually to his chancellor and others of competent learning, who are to summon a jury of six clergymen and six laymen to inquire into and examine who is the rightful patron. 3 Bl. Comm. 246; 3 Steph. Comm. 517.

JUS PERSONARUM. Rights of persons. Those rights which, in the civil law, belong to persons as such, or in their different characters and relations; as parents and children, masters and servants, etc.

JUS PORTUS. In maritime law. The right of port or harbor.

JUS POSSESSIONIS. The right of possession.

JUS POSTLIMINII. In the civil law. The right of postliminy; the right or claim of a person who had been restored to the possession of a thing, or to a former condition, to be considered as though he had never been deprived of it. Dig. 49, 15, 5; 3 Bl. Comm. 107, 210.

In international law. The right by which property taken by an enemy, and recaptured or rescued from him by the fellow-subjects or allies of the original owner, is restored to the latter upon certain terms. 1 Kent, Comm. 108.

JUS PRÆSENS. In the civil law. A present or vested right; a right already completely acquired. Mackeld. Rom. Law, § 191.

JUS PRÆTORIUM. In the civil law. The discretion of the prætor, as distinct from the *leges*, or standing laws. 3 Bl. Comm. 49. That kind of law which the prætors introduced for the purpose of aiding, supplying, or correcting the civil law for the public benefit. Dig. 1, 1, 7. Called, also, "*jus honorarium*," (*q. v.*)

JUS PRECARIUM. In the civil law. A right to a thing held for another, for which there was no remedy. 2 Bl. Comm. 328.

JUS PRESENTATIONIS. The right of presentation.

JUS PRIVATUM. The civil or municipal law of Rome.

JUS PROJICIENDI. In the civil law. The name of a servitude which consists in the right to build a projection, such as a balcony or gallery, from one's house in the open space belonging to one's neighbor, but without resting on his house. Dig. 50, 16, 242; Id. 8, 2, 2; Mackeld. Rom. Law, § 317.

JUS PROPRIETATIS. The right of property, as distinguished from the *jus possessionis*, or right of possession. Bract. fol. 3. Called by Bracton "*jus merum*," the mere right. Id.; 2 Bl. Comm. 197; 3 Bl. Comm. 19, 176.

JUS PROTEGENDI. In the civil law, The name of a servitude. It is a right by which a part of the roof or tiling of one house is made to extend over the adjoining house. Dig. 50, 16, 242, 1; Id. 8, 2, 25; Id. 8, 5, 8, 5.

Jus publicum et privatum quod ex naturalibus præceptis aut gentium aut civilibus est collectum; et quod in jure scripto jus appellatur, id in lege Angliæ rectum esse dicitur. Co. Litt. 185. Public and private law is that which is collected from natural principles, either of nations or in states; and that which in the civil law is called "*jus*," in the law of England is said to be "right."

Jus publicum privatorum pactis mutari non potest. A public law or right cannot be altered by the agreements of private persons.

JUS QUÆSITUM. A right to ask or recover; for example, in an obligation there is a binding of the obligor, and a *jus quæsitum* in the obligee. 1 Bell, Comm. 323.

JUS QUIRITIUM. The old law of Rome, that was applicable originally to patricians only, and, under the Twelve Tables, to the entire Roman people, was so called, in contradistinction to the *jus prætorium*, (*q. v.*,) or equity. Brown.

Jus quo universitates utuntur est idem quod habent privati. The law which governs corporations is the same which governs individuals. 16 Mass. 44.

JUS RECUPERANDI. The right of recovering [lands.]

JUS RELICTÆ. In Scotch law. The right of a relict; the right or claim of a relict or widow to her share of her husband's estate, particularly the movables. 2 Kames, Eq. 340; 1 Forb. Inst. pt. 1, p. 67.

JUS REPRESENTATIONIS. The right of representing or standing in the place of another, or of being represented by another.

JUS RERUM. The law of things. The law regulating the rights and powers of persons over things; how property is acquired, enjoyed, and transferred.

Jus respicit æquitatem. Law regards equity. Co. Litt. 24*b*; Broom, Max. 151.

JUS SCRIPTUM. In Roman law. Written law. Inst. 1, 2, 3. All law that was actually committed to writing, whether it had originated by enactment or by custom, in contradistinction to such parts of the law of custom as were not committed to writing. Mackeld. Rom. Law, § 126.

In English law. Written law, or statute law, otherwise called "*lex scripta*," as distinguished from the common law, "*lex non scripta*." 1 Bl. Comm. 62.

JUS SINGULARE. In the civil law. A peculiar or individual rule, differing from the *jus commune*, or common rule of right, and established for some special reason. Mackeld. Rom. Law, § 196.

JUS STAPULÆ. In old European law. The law of staple; the right of staple. A right or privilege of certain towns of stopping imported merchandise, and compelling it to be offered for sale in their own markets. Locc. de Jure Mar. lib. 1, c. 10.

JUS STRICTUM. Strict law; law interpreted without any modification, and in its utmost rigor.

Jus superveniens auctori accrescit successori. A right growing to a possessor accrues to the successor. Halk. Lat. Max. 76.

JUS TERTII. The right of a third party. A tenant, bailee, etc., who pleads that the title is in some person other than his landlord, bailor, etc., is said to set up a *jus tertii.*

Jus testamentorum pertinet ordinario. Yearb. 4 Hen. VII., 13*b*. The right of testaments belongs to the ordinary.

JUS TRIPERTITUM. In Roman law. A name applied to the Roman law of wills, in the time of Justinian, on account of its threefold derivation, viz., from the prætorian edict, from the civil law, and from the imperial constitutions. Maine, Anc. Law, 207.

Jus triplex est,—proprietatis, possessionis, et possibilitatis. Right is threefold,—of property, of possession, and of possibility.

JUS TRIUM LIBERORUM. In Roman law. A right or privilege allowed to the parent of *three* or more *children.* 2 Kent, Comm. 85; 2 Bl. Comm. 247. These privileges were an exemption from the trouble of guardianship, priority in bearing offices, and a treble proportion of corn. Adams, Rom. Ant. (Amer. Ed.) 227.

JUS UTENDI. The right to use property without destroying its substance. It is employed in contradistinction to the *jus abutendi.* 3 Toullier, no. 86.

JUS VENANDI ET PISCANDI. The right of hunting and fishing.

Jus vendit quod usus approbavit. Ellesm. Postn. 35. The law dispenses what use has approved.

JUSJURANDUM. Lat. An oath.

Jusjurandum inter alios factum nec nocere nec prodesse debet. An oath made between others ought neither to hurt nor profit. 4 Inst. 279.

JUST. Right; in accordance with law and justice.

"The words 'just' and 'justly' do not always mean 'just' and 'justly' in a moral sense, but they not unfrequently, in their connection with other words in a sentence, bear a very different signification. It is evident, however, that the word 'just' in the statute [requiring an affidavit for an attachment to state that plaintiff's claim is *just*] means 'just' in a moral sense; and from its isolation, being made a separate subdivision of the section, it is intended to mean 'morally just' in the most emphatic terms. The claim must be *morally* just, as well as *legally* just, in order to entitle a party to an attachment." 5 Kan. 300.

JUST COMPENSATION. As used in the constitutional provision that private property shall not be taken for public use without "just compensation," this phrase means a full and fair equivalent for the loss sustained by the taking for public use. It may be more or it may be less than the mere money value of the property actually taken. The exercise of the power being necessary for the public good, and all property being held subject to its exercise when and as the public good requires it, it would be unjust to the public that it should be required to pay the owner more than a fair indemnity for the loss he sustains by the appropriation of his property for the general good. On the other hand, it would be equally unjust to the owner if he should receive less than a fair indemnity for such loss. To arrive at this fair indemnity, the interests of the public and of the owner, and all the circumstances of the particular appropriation, should be taken into consideration. Lewis, Em. Dom. § 462.

JUST TITLE. By the term "just title," in cases of prescription, we do not understand that which the possessor may have derived from the true owner, for then no true prescription would be necessary, but a title which the possessor may have received from any person whom he honestly believed to be the real owner, provided the title were such as to transfer the ownership of the property. Civil Code La. art. 3484.

JUSTA. In old English law. A certain measure of liquor, being as much as was sufficient to drink at once. Mon. Angl. t. 1, c. 149.

JUSTA CAUSA. In the civil law. A just cause; a lawful ground; a legal transaction of some kind. Mackeld. Rom. Law, § 283.

JUSTICE, *v.* In old English practice. To do justice; to see justice done; to summon one to do justice.

JUSTICE, *n.* **In jurisprudence.** The constant and perpetual disposition to render every man his due. Inst. 1, 1, pr.; 2 Inst. 56. The conformity of our actions and our will to the law. Toull. Droit Civil Fr. tit. prél. no. 5.

In the most extensive sense of the word, it differs little from "virtue;" for it includes within itself the whole circle of virtues. Yet the common distinction between them is that that which, considered positively and in itself, is called "virtue," when considered relatively and with respect to others has the name of "justice." But "justice," being in itself a part of "virtue," is confined to things simply good or evil, and consists in a man's taking such a proportion of them as he ought. Bouvier.

Commutative justice is that which should govern contracts. It consists in rendering to every man the exact measure of his dues, without regard to his personal worth or merits, *i. e.*, placing all men on an equality. *Distributive* justice is that which should govern the distribution of rewards and punishments. It assigns to each the rewards which his personal merit or services deserve, or the proper punishment for his crimes. It does not consider all men as equally deserving or equally blameworthy, but discriminates between them, observing a just proportion and comparison. This distinction originated with Aristotle. (Eth. Nic. V.) See Fonbl. Eq. 3; Toull. Droit Civil Fr. tit. prél. no. 7.

In Norman French. Amenable to justice. Kelham.

In feudal law. Jurisdiction; judicial cognizance of causes or offenses.

In common law. The title given in England to the judges of the king's bench and the common pleas, and in America to the judges of the supreme court of the United States and of the appellate courts of many of the states. It is said that this word in its Latin form (*justitia*) was properly applicable only to the judges of common-law courts, while the term "*judex*" designated the judges of ecclesiastical and other courts. See Leg. Hen. I. §§ 24, 63; Co. Litt. 71*b*.

The same title is also applied to some of the judicial officers of the lowest rank and jurisdiction, such as police justices and justices of the peace.

JUSTICE AYRES, (or AIRES.) In Scotch law. Circuits made by the judges of the justiciary courts through the country, for the distribution of justice. Bell.

JUSTICE IN EYRE. From the old French word "*eire*," *i. e.*, a journey. Those justices who in ancient times were sent by commission into various counties, to hear more especially such causes as were termed "pleas of the crown," were called "justices in eyre." They differed from justices in oyer and terminer, inasmuch as the latter were sent to one place, and for the purpose of trying only a limited number of special causes; whereas the justices in eyre were sent through the various counties, with a more indefinite and general commission. In some respects they resembled our present justices of assize, although their authority and manner of proceeding differed much from them. Brown.

JUSTICE OF THE PEACE. In American law. A judicial officer of inferior rank, holding a court not of record, and having (usually) civil jurisdiction of a limited nature, for the trial of minor cases, to an extent prescribed by statute, and for the conservation of the peace and the preliminary hearing of criminal complaints and the commitment of offenders.

In English law. Judges of record appointed by the crown to be justices within a certain district, (*e. g.*, a county or borough,) for the conservation of the peace, and for the execution of divers things, comprehended within their commission and within divers statutes, committed to their charge. Stone, J. Pr. 2.

JUSTICE SEAT. In English law. The principal court of the forest, held before the chief justice in eyre, or chief itinerant judge, or his deputy; to hear and determine all trespasses within the forest, and all claims of franchises, liberties, and privileges, and all pleas and causes whatsoever therein arising. 3 Bl. Comm. 72; 4 Inst. 291; 3 Steph. Comm. 440.

JUSTICEMENTS. An old general term for all things appertaining to justice.

JUSTICER. The old form of *justice*. Blount.

JUSTICES' COURTS. Inferior tribunals, not of record, with limited jurisdiction, both civil and criminal, held by justices of the peace. There are courts so called in many of the states.

JUSTICES OF APPEAL. The title given to the ordinary judges of the English court of appeal. The first of such ordinary judges are the two former lords justices of appeal in chancery, and one other judge appointed by the crown by letters patent. Jud. Act 1875, § 4.

JUSTICES OF ASSIZE. These justices, or, as they are sometimes called, "justices of *nisi prius*," are judges of the superior English courts, who go on circuit into the various counties of England and Wales for the purpose of disposing of such causes as are ready for trial at the assizes. See ASSIZE.

JUSTICES OF GAOL DELIVERY. Those justices who are sent with a commission to hear and determine all causes appertaining to persons, who, for any offense, have been cast into gaol. Part of their authority was to punish those who let to mainprise those prisoners who were not bailable by law, and they seem formerly to have been sent into the country upon this exclusive occasion, but afterwards had the same authority given them as the justices of assize. Brown.

JUSTICES OF LABORERS. In old English law. Justices appointed to redress the frowardness of laboring men, who would either be idle or have unreasonable wages. Blount.

JUSTICES OF NISI PRIUS. In English law. This title is now usually coupled with that of *justices of assize;* the judges of the superior courts acting on their circuits in both these capacities. 3 Bl. Comm. 58, 59.

JUSTICES OF OYER AND TERMINER. Certain persons appointed by the king's commission, among whom were usually two judges of the courts at Westminster, and who went twice in every year to every county of the kingdom, (except London and Middlesex,) and, at what was usually called the "assizes," heard and determined all treasons, felonies, and misdemeanors. Brown.

JUSTICES OF THE BENCH. The justices of the court of common bench or common pleas.

JUSTICES OF THE FOREST. In old English law. Officers who had jurisdiction over all offenses committed within the forest against vert or venison. The court wherein these justices sat and determined such causes was called the "justice seat of the forest." They were also sometimes called the "justices in eyre of the forest." Brown.

JUSTICES OF THE HUNDRED. Hundredors; lords of the hundreds; they who had the jurisdiction of hundreds and held the hundred courts.

JUSTICES OF THE JEWS. Justices appointed by Richard I. to carry into effect the laws and orders which he had made for regulating the money contracts of the Jews. Brown.

JUSTICES OF THE PAVILION. In old English law. Judges of a pyepowder court, of a most transcendent jurisdiction, anciently authorized by the bishop of Winchester, at a fair held on St. Giles' hills near that city. Cowell; Blount.

JUSTICES OF TRAIL-BASTON. In old English law. A kind of justices appointed by King Edward I. upon occasion of great disorders in the realm, during his absence in the Scotch and French wars. They were a kind of justices in eyre, with great powers adapted to the emergency, and which they exercised in a summary manner. Cowell; Blount.

JUSTICESHIP. Rank or office of a justice.

JUSTICIABLE. Proper to be examined in courts of justice.

JUSTICIAR. In old English law. A judge or justice. One of several persons learned in the law, who sat in the *aula regis,* and formed a kind of court of appeal in cases of difficulty.

JUSTICIARII ITINERANTES. In English law. Justices in eyre, who formerly went from county to county to administer justice. They were so called to distinguish them from justices residing at Westminister, who were called "*justicii residentes.*" Co. Litt. 293.

JUSTICIARII RESIDENTES. In English law. Justices or judges who usually resided in Westminister. They were so called to distinguish them from justices in eyre. Co. Litt. 293.

JUSTICIARY. An old name for a judge or justice. The word is formed on the analogy of the Latin "*justiciarius*" and French "*justicier.*"

JUSTICIARY COURT. The chief criminal court of Scotland, consisting of five lords of session, added to the justice general and justice clerk; of whom the justice general, and, in his absence, the justice clerk, is president. This court has a jurisdiction over all crimes, and over the whole of Scotland. Bell.

JUSTICIATUS. Judicature; prerogative.

JUSTICIES. In English law. A writ directed to the sheriff, empowering him, for the sake of dispatch, to try an action in his county court for a larger amount than he has the ordinary power to do. It is so called because it is a commission to the sheriff to do the party justice, the word itself meaning, "You may do justice to ———." 3 Bl. Comm. 36; 4 Inst. 266.

JUSTIFIABLE. Rightful; warranted or sanctioned by law; that which can be shown to be sustained by law; as justifiable homicide.

JUSTIFIABLE HOMICIDE. Such as is committed intentionally, but without any evil design, and under such circumstances of necessity or duty as render the act proper, and relieve the party from any shadow of blame; as where a sheriff lawfully executes a sentence of death upon a malefactor, or where the killing takes place in the endeavor to prevent the commission of a felony which could not be otherwise avoided.

JUSTIFICATION. A maintaining or showing a sufficient reason in court why the defendant did what he is called upon to answer, particularly in an action of libel. A defense of justification is a defense showing the libel to be true, or in an action of assault showing the violence to have been necessary. See Steph. Pl. 184.

In practice. The proceeding by which bail establish their ability to perform the undertaking of the bond or recognizance.

JUSTIFICATORS. A kind of compurgators, (*q. v.*,) or those who by oath justified the innocence or oaths of others; as in the case of wager of law.

JUSTIFYING BAIL consists in proving the sufficiency of bail or sureties in point of property, etc.

The production of bail in court, who there justify themselves against the exception of the plaintiff.

JUSTINIANIST. A civilian; one who studies the civil law.

JUSTITIA. Lat. Justice. A jurisdiction, or the office of a judge.

Justitia debet esse libera, quia nihil iniquius venali justitia; plena, quia justitia non debet claudicare; et celeris, quia dilatio est quædam negatio. Justice ought to be free, because nothing is more iniquitous than venal justice; full, because justice ought not to halt; and speedy, because delay is a kind of denial. 2 Inst. 56.

Justitia est constans et perpetua voluntas jus suum cuique tribuendi. Justice is a steady and unceasing disposition to render to every man his due. Inst. 1, 1, pr.; Dig. 1, 1, 10.

Justitia est duplex, viz., severe puniens et vere præveniens. 3 Inst. Epil. Justice is double; punishing severely, and truly preventing.

Justitia est virtus excellens et Altissimo complacens. 4 Inst. 58. Justice is excellent virtue and pleasing to the Most High.

Justitia firmatur solium. 3 Inst. 140. By justice the throne is established.

Justitia nemini neganda est. Jenk. Cent. 178. Justice is to be denied to none.

Justitia non est neganda non differenda. Jenk. Cent. 93. Justice is neither to be denied nor delayed.

Justitia non novit patrem nec matrem; solam veritatem spectat justitia. Justice knows not father nor mother; justice looks at truth alone. 1 Bulst. 199.

JUSTITIA PIEPOUDROUS. Speedy justice. Bract. 333*b*.

JUSTITIUM. In the civil law. A suspension or intermission of the administration of justice in courts; vacation time. Calvin.

JUSTITIUM FACERE. To hold a plea of anything.

JUSTIZA. In Spanish law. The name anciently given to a high judicial magistrate, or supreme judge, who was the ultimate interpreter of the laws, and possessed other high powers.

JUSTS, or JOUSTS. Exercises between martial men and persons of honor, with spears, on horseback; different from *tournaments*, which were military exercises between many men in troops. 24 Hen. VIII. c. 13.

Justum non est aliquem antenatum mortuum facere bastardum, qui pro tota vita sua pro legitimo habetur. It is not just to make a bastard after his death one elder born who all his life has been accounted legitimate. 8 Coke, 101.

JUXTA. Lat. Near; following; according to.

JUXTA CONVENTIONEM. According to the covenant. Fleta, lib. 4, c. 16, § 6.

JUXTA FORMAM STATUTI. According to the form of the statute.

JUXTA RATAM. At or after the rate. Dyer, 82.

JUXTA TENOREM SEQUENTEM. According to the tenor following. 2 Salk. 417. A phrase used in the old books when the very words themselves referred to were set forth. Id.; 1 Ld. Raym. 415.

JUZGADO. In Spanish law. The judiciary; the body of judges; the judges who concur in a decree.

K.

K. B. An abbreviation for "King's Bench," (*q. v.*)

KABANI. A person who, in oriental states, supplies the place of our notary public. All obligations, to be valid, are drawn by him; and he is also the public weigh-master, and everything of consequence ought to be weighed before him. Enc. Lond.

KABOOLEAT. In Hindu law. A written agreement, especially one signifying assent, as the counterpart of a revenue lease, or the document in which a payer of revenue, whether to the government, the zamindar, or the farmer, expresses his consent to pay the amount assessed upon his land. Wils. Ind. Gloss.

KAIA. A key, kay, or quay. Spelman.

KAIAGE, or KAIAGIUM. A wharfage-due.

KAIN. In Scotch law. Poultry renderable by a vassal to his superior, reserved in the lease as the whole or a part of the rent. Bell.

KALALCONNA. A duty paid by shopkeepers in Hindostan, who retail spirituous liquors; also the place where spirituous liquors are sold. Wharton.

KALENDÆ. In English ecclesiastical law. Rural chapters, or conventions of the rural deans and parochial clergy, which were formerly held on the calends of every month; hence the name. Paroch. Antiq. 604.

KALENDAR. An account of time, exhibiting the days of the week and month, the seasons, etc. More commonly spelled "calendar."

KALENDARIUM. In the civil law. A calendar; a book of accounts, memorandum-book, or debt-book; a book in which accounts were kept of moneys loaned out on interest. Dig. 32, 64. So called because the Romans used to let out their money and receive the interest on the calends of each month. Calvin.

KALENDS. See CALENDS.

KARL. In Saxon and old English law. A man; a serving man. *Buskarl*, a seaman. *Huskarl*, a house servant. Spelman.

KARRATA. In old records. A cart-load. Cowell; Blount.

KAST. In Swedish law. Jettison; a literal translation of the Latin "*jactus.*"

KAST-GELD. In Swedish law. Contribution for a jettison; average.

KAY. A quay, or key.

KAZY. A Mohammedan judge or magistrate in the East Indies, appointed originally by the court at Delhi, to administer justice according to their written law. Under the British authorities their judicial functions ceased, and their duties were confined to the preparation and attestation of deeds, and the superintendence and legalization of marriage and other ceremonies among the Mohammedans. Wharton.

KEELAGE. The right to demand money for the privilege of anchoring a vessel in a harbor; also the money so paid.

KEELHALE, KEELHAUL. To drag a person under the keel of a ship by means of ropes from the yard-arms, a punishment formerly practiced in the British navy. Enc. Lond.

KEELS. This word is applied, in England, to vessels employed in the carriage of coals. Jacob.

KEEP. A strong tower or hold in the middle of any castle or fortification, wherein the besieged make their last efforts of defense, was formerly, in England, called a "keep;" and the inner pile within the castle of Dover, erected by King Henry II. about the year 1153, was termed the "King's Keep;" so at Windsor, etc. It seems to be something of the same nature with what is called abroad a "citadel." Jacob.

KEEP DOWN INTEREST. The expression "keeping down interest" is familiar in legal instruments, and means the payment of interest periodically as it becomes due; but it does not include the payment of all arrears of interest which may have become due on any security from the time when it was executed. 4 El. & Bl. 211.

KEEP IN REPAIR. When a lessee is bound to *keep* the premises in repair, he must have them in repair at all times during the term; and, if they are at any time out of repair, he is guilty of a breach of the covenant. 1 Barn. & Ald. 585.

KEEPER OF THE FOREST. In old English law. An officer (called also chief warden of the forest) who had the principal government of all things relating to the forest, and the control of all officers belonging to the same. Cowell; Blount.

KEEPER OF THE GREAT SEAL. In English law. A high officer of state, through whose hands pass all charters, grants, and commissions of the king under the great seal. He is styled "lord keeper of the great seal," and this office and that of lord chancellor are united under one person: for the authority of the lord keeper and that of the lord chancellor were, by St. 5 Eliz. c. 18, declared to be exactly the same; and, like the lord chancellor, the lord keeper at the present day is created by the mere delivery of the king's great seal into his custody. Brown.

KEEPER OF THE PRIVY SEAL. In English law. An officer through whose hands pass all charters signed by the king before they come to the great seal. He is a privy councillor, and was anciently called "clerk of the privy seal," but is now generally called the "lord privy seal." Brown.

KEEPER OF THE TOUCH. The master of the assay in the English mint. 12 Hen. VI. c. 14.

KEEPING HOUSE. The English bankrupt laws use the phrase "keeping house" to denote an act of bankruptcy. It is committed when a trader absents himself from his place of business and retires to his private residence to evade the importunity of creditors. The usual evidence of "keeping house" is refusal to see a creditor who has called on the debtor at his house for money. Robs. Bankr. 119.

KEEPING OPEN. To allow general access to one's shop, for purposes of traffic, is a violation of a statute forbidding him to "keep open" his shop on the Lord's day, although the outer entrances are closed. 11 Gray, 308.

To "keep open," in the sense of such a law, implies a readiness to carry on the usual business in the store, shop, saloon, etc. 16 Mich. 472.

KEEPING TERM. In English law. A duty performed by students of law, consisting in eating a sufficient number of dinners in hall to make the term count for the purpose of being called to the bar. Mozley & Whitley.

KEEPING THE PEACE. Avoiding a breach of the peace; dissuading or preventing others from breaking the peace.

KENILWORTH EDICT. An edict or award between Henry III. and those who had been in arms against him; so called because made at Kenilworth Castle, in Warwickshire, *anno* 51 Hen. III., A. D. 1266. It contained a composition of those who had forfeited their estates in that rebellion, which composition was five years' rent of the estates forfeited. Wharton.

KENNING TO A TERCE. In Scotch law. The act of the sheriff in ascertaining the just proportion of the husband's lands which belong to the widow in right of her *terce* or dower. Bell.

KENTLAGE. In maritime law. A permanent ballast, consisting usually of pigs of iron, cast in a particular form, or other weighty material, which, on account of its superior cleanliness, and the small space occupied by it, is frequently preferred to ordinary ballast. Abb. Shipp. 5.

KENTREF. The division of a county; a hundred in Wales. See CANTRED.

KENTUCKY RESOLUTIONS. A series of resolutions drawn up by Jefferson, and adopted by the legislature of Kentucky in 1799, protesting against the "alien and sedition laws," declaring their illegality, announcing the strict constructionist theory of the federal government, and declaring "nullification" to be "the rightful remedy."

KERF. The jagged end of a stick of wood made by the cutting. Pub. St. Mass. 1882, p. 1292.

KERHERE. A customary cart-way; also a commutation for a customary carriage-duty. Cowell.

KERNELLATUS. Fortified or embattled. Co. Litt. 5*a*.

KERNES. Idlers; vagabonds.

KEY. A wharf for the lading and unlading of merchandise from vessels. More commonly spelled "quay."

An instrument for fastening and opening a lock.

This appears as an English word as early as the time of Bracton, in the phrase "*cone et keye*," being applied to women at a certain age, to denote the capacity of having charge of household affairs. Bract. fol. 86*b*. See CONE AND KEY.

KEYAGE. A toll paid for loading and unloading merchandise at a key or wharf.

KEYS, in the Isle of Man, are the twenty-four chief commoners, who form the local legislature. 1 Steph. Comm. 99.

In old English law. A guardian, warden, or keeper.

KEYS OF COURT. In old Scotch law. Certain officers of courts. See CLAVES CURIÆ.

KEYUS. A guardian, warden, or keeper. Mon. Angl. tom. 2, p. 71.

KHALSA. In Hindu law. An office of government in which the business of the revenue department was transacted under the Mohammedan government, and during the early period of British rule. Khalsa lands are lands, the revenue of which is paid into the exchequer. Wharton.

KIDDER. An engrosser of corn to enhance its price.

KIDDLE. In old English law. A dam or open wear in a river, with a loop or narrow cut in it, accommodated for the laying of engines to catch fish. 2 Inst. 38; Blount.

KIDNAPPING. The forcible abduction or stealing away of a man, woman, or child from their own country, and sending them into another. It is an offense punishable at the common law by fine and imprisonment. 4 Bl. Comm. 219.

In American law, this word is seldom, if at all, applied to the abduction of other persons than children, and the intent to send them out of the country does not seem to constitute a necessary part of the offense. The term is said to include false imprisonment. 2 Bish. Crim. Law, § 671.

KILDERKIN. A measure of eighteen gallons.

KILKETH. An ancient servile payment made by tenants in husbandry. Cowell.

KILL, *v.* To deprive of life; to destroy the life of an animal. The word "homicide" expresses the killing of a human being.

KILL, *n.* A Dutch word, signifying a channel or bed of the river, and hence the river or stream itself. It is found used in this sense in descriptions of land in old conveyances. 1 N. Y. 96.

KILLYTH-STALLION. A custom by which lords of manors were bound to provide a stallion for the use of their tenants' mares. Spelman.

KIN. Relation or relationship by blood or consanguinity. "The nearness of *kin* is computed according to the civil law." 2 Kent, Comm. 413.

KIND. Genus; generic class; description. See IN KIND.

KINDRED. Relatives by blood. "Kindred of the whole blood, preferred to kindred of the half blood." 4 Kent, Comm. 404, notes.

KING. The sovereign, ruler, or chief executive magistrate of a state or nation whose constitution is of the kind called "monarchical" is thus named if a man; if it be a woman, she is called "queen." The word expresses the idea of one who rules singly over a whole people or has the highest executive power; but the office may be either hereditary or elective, and the sovereignty of the king may or may not be absolute, according to the constitution of the country.

KING-CRAFT. The art of governing.

KING-GELD. A royal aid; an escuage, (*q. v.*)

KING'S BENCH. The supreme court of common law in England, being so called because the king used formerly to sit there in person, the style of the court being "*coram ipso rege.*" It was called the "queen's bench" in the reign of a queen, and during the protectorate of Cromwell it was styled the "upper bench." It consisted of a chief justice and three puisne justices, who were by their office the sovereign conservators of the peace and supreme coroners of the land. It was a remnant of the *aula regis*, and was not originally fixed to any certain place, but might follow the king's person, though for some centuries past it usually sat at Westminster. It had a very extended jurisdiction both in criminal and civil causes; the former in what was called the "crown side" or "crown office," the latter in the "plea side," of the court. Its civil jurisdiction was gradually enlarged until it embraced all species of personal actions. Since the judicature acts, this court constitutes the "queen's bench division" of the "high court of justice." See 3 Bl. Comm. 41-43.

KING'S CHAMBERS. Those portions of the seas, adjacent to the coasts of Great Britain, which are inclosed within headlands so as to be cut off from the open sea by imaginary straight lines drawn from one promontory to another.

KING'S (or QUEEN'S) COUNSEL. Barristers or serjeants who have been called within the bar and selected to be the king's counsel. They answer in some measure to the *advocati fisci*, or advocates of the revenue, among the Romans. They must not be employed against the crown without special leave, which is, however, always granted, at a cost of about nine pounds. 3 Bl. Comm. 27.

KING'S EVIDENCE. An accomplice in a felony, who, on an implied promise of pardon if he fully and fairly discloses the truth, is admitted as evidence for the crown against his accomplices. 1 Phil. Ev. 31.

KING'S SILVER. In old English practice. A fine due the king *pro licentia concordandi*, (for leave to agree,) in the process of levying a fine. 5 Coke, 39, 43; 2 Inst. 511; 2 Bl. Comm. 350.

KING'S WIDOW. In feudal law. A widow of the king's tenant in chief, who was obliged to take oath in chancery that she would not marry without the king's leave.

KINGDOM. A country where an officer called a "king" exercises the powers of government, whether the same be absolute or limited. Wolff, Inst. Nat. § 994. In some kingdoms, the executive officer may be a woman, who is called a "queen."

KINGS-AT-ARMS. The principal herald of England was of old designated "king of the heralds," a title which seems to have been exchanged for "king-at-arms" about the reign of Henry IV. The kings-at-arms at present existing in England are three,—Garter, Clarenceux, and Norroy, besides Bath, who is not a member of the college. Scotland is placed under an officer called "Lyon King-at-Arms," and Ireland is the province of one named "Ulster." Wharton.

KINSBOTE. In Saxon law. A composition or satisfaction paid for killing a kinsman. Spelman.

KINSFOLK. Relations; those who are of the same family.

KINSMAN. A man of the same race or family.

KINSWOMAN. A female relation.

KINTAL, or KINTLE. A hundred pounds in weight. See QUINTAL.

KINTLIDGE. A ship's ballast. See KENTLAGE.

KIPPER-TIME. In old English law. The space of time between the 3d of May and the Epiphany, in which fishing for salmon in the Thames, between Gravesend and Henley-on-Thames, was forbidden. Rot. Parl. 50 Edw. III.

KIRBY'S QUEST. In English law. An ancient record remaining with the remembrancer of the exchequer, being an inquisition or survey of all the lands in England, taken in the reign of Edward I. by John de Kirby, his treasurer. Blount; Cowell.

KIRK-MOTE. In Scotch law. A meeting of parishioners on church affairs.

KIRK-OFFICER. The beadle of a church in Scotland.

KIRK-SESSION. A parochial church court in Scotland, consisting of the ministers and elders of each parish.

KISSING THE BOOK. The ceremony of touching the lips to a copy of the Bible, used in administering oaths. It is the external symbol of the witness' acknowledgment of the obligation of the oath.

KIST. In Hindu law. A stated payment; installment of rent.

KLEPTOMANIA. A species (or symptom) of mania, consisting in an irresistible propensity to steal. See 10 Tex. App. 520.

KNAVE. A rascal; a false, tricky, or deceitful person. The word originally meant a boy, attendant, or servant, but long-continued usage has given it its present signification.

KNAVESHIP. A portion of grain given to a mill-servant from tenants who were bound to grind their grain at such mill.

KNIGHT. In English law. The next personal dignity after the nobility. Of knights there are several orders and degrees. The first in rank are knights of the Garter, instituted by Richard I. and improved by Edward III. in 1344; next follows a knight banneret; then come knights of the Bath, instituted by Henry IV., and revived by George I.; and they were so called from a ceremony of bathing the night before their creation. The last order are knights bachelors, who, though the lowest, are yet the most ancient, order of knighthood; for we find that King Alfred conferred this order upon his son Athelstan. 1 Bl. Comm. 403.

KNIGHT-MARSHAL. In English law. An officer in the royal household who has jurisdiction and cognizance of offenses committed within the household and verge, and of all contracts made therein, a member of the household being one of the parties. Wharton.

KNIGHT-SERVICE. A species of feudal tenure, which differed very slightly from a pure and perfect feud, being entirely of a military nature; and it was the first, most universal, and most honorable of the feudal tenures. To make a tenure by knight-service, a determinate quantity of land was necessary, which was called a "knight's fee," (*feodum militare,*) the measure of which was estimated at 680 acres. Co. Litt. 69*a;* Brown.

KNIGHT'S FEE. The determinate quantity of land, (held by an estate of inheritance,) or of annual income therefrom, which was sufficient to maintain a knight. Every man holding such a fee was obliged to be knighted, and attend the king in his wars for the space of forty days in the year, or pay a fine (called "escuage") for his non-compliance. The estate was estimated at £20 a year, or, according to Coke, 680 acres. See 1 Bl. Comm. 404, 410; 2 Bl. Comm. 62; Co. Litt. 69*a*.

KNIGHTENCOURT. A court which used to be held twice a year by the bishop of Hereford, in England.

KNIGHTENGUILD. An ancient guild or society formed by King Edgar.

KNIGHTHOOD. The rank, order, character, or dignity of a knight.

KNIGHTS BACHELORS. In English law. The most ancient, though lowest, order of knighthood. 1 Bl. Comm. 404.

KNIGHTS BANNERET. In English law. Those created by the sovereign in person on the field of battle. They rank, generally, after knights of the Garter. 1 Bl. Comm. 403.

KNIGHTS OF ST. MICHAEL AND ST. GEORGE. An English order of knighthood, instituted in 1818.

KNIGHTS OF ST. PATRICK. Instituted in Ireland by George III., A. D. 1763. They have no rank in England.

KNIGHTS OF THE BATH. An order instituted by Henry IV., and revived by George I. They are so called from the ceremony formerly observed of bathing the night before their creation.

KNIGHTS OF THE CHAMBER. Those created in the sovereign's chamber in time of peace, not in the field. 2 Inst. 666.

KNIGHTS OF THE GARTER. Otherwise called "Knights of the Order of St. George." This order was founded by Richard I., and improved by Edward III., A. D. 1344. They form the highest order of knights.

KNIGHTS OF THE POST. A term for hireling witnesses.

KNIGHTS OF THE SHIRE. In English law. Members of parliament representing counties or shires, in contradistinction to citizens or burgesses, who represent boroughs or corporations. A knight of the shire is so called, because, as the terms of the writ for election still require, it was formerly necessary that he should be a knight. This restriction was coeval with the tenure of knight-service, when every man who received a knight's fee immediately of the crown was constrained to be a knight; but at present any person may be chosen to fill the office who is not an alien. The money qualification is abolished by 21 Vict. c. 26. Wharton.

KNIGHTS OF THE THISTLE. A Scottish order of knighthood. This order is said to have been instituted by Achaius, king of Scotland, A. D. 819. The better opinion, however, is that it was instituted by James V. in 1534, was revived by James VII. (James II. of England) in 1687, and re-established by Queen Anne in 1703. They have no rank in England. Wharton.

KNOCK DOWN. To assign to a bidder at an auction by a knock or blow of the hammer. Property is said to be "knocked down" when the auctioneer, by the fall of his hammer, or by any other audible or visible announcement, signifies to the bidder that he is entitled to the property on paying the amount of his bid, according to the terms of the sale. "Knocked down" and "struck off" are synonymous terms. 7 Hill, 439.

KNOT. In seamen's language, a "knot" is a division of the log-line serving to measure the rate of the vessel's motion. The number of knots which run off from the reel in half a minute shows the number of miles the vessel sails in an hour. Hence when a ship goes eight miles an hour she is said to go "eight knots." Webster.

KNOW ALL MEN. In conveyancing. A form of public address, of great antiquity, and with which many written instruments, such as bonds, letters of attorney, etc., still commence.

KNOWINGLY. With knowledge; consciously; intelligently. The use of this word in an indictment is equivalent to an averment that the defendant knew what he was about to do, and, with such knowledge, proceeded to do the act charged. 14 Fed. Rep. 128.

KNOWLEDGE. The difference between "knowledge" and "belief" is nothing more than in the degree of certainty. With regard to things which make not a very deep impression on the memory, it may be called "belief." "Knowledge" is nothing more than a man's firm belief. The difference is ordinarily merely in the degree, to be judged of by the court, when addressed to the court; by the jury, when addressed to the jury. 9 Gray, 271.

Knowledge may be classified, in a legal sense, as positive and imputed,—imputed, when the means of knowledge exists, known and accessible to the party, and capable of communicating positive information. When there is knowledge, notice, as legally and technically understood, becomes immaterial. It is only material when, in the absence of knowledge, it produces the same results. However closely actual notice may, in many instances, approximate knowledge, and constructive notice may be its equivalent in effect, there may be actual notice without knowledge; and, when constructive notice is made the test to determine priorities of right, it may fall far short of knowledge, and be sufficient. 81 Ala. 140, 1 South. Rep. 773.

Personal knowledge of an allegation in a pleading is a personal knowledge of its truth or falsity; and, if the allegation is a negative one, this necessarily includes a knowledge of the truth or falsity of the allegation denied. 18 Fed. Rep. 622.

KNOWN-MEN. A title formerly given to the Lollards. Cowell.

KORAN. The Mohammedan book of faith. It contains both ecclesiastical and secular laws.

KUT-KUBALA. In Hindu law. A mortgage-deed or deed of conditional sale, being one of the customary deeds or instruments of security in India as declared by regulation of 1806, which regulates the legal proceedings to be taken to enforce such a security. It is also called "*Byebil-Wuffa.*" Wharton.

KYMORTHA. A Welsh term for a waster, rhymer, minstrel, or other vagabond who makes assemblies and collections. Barring. Ob. St. 360.

KYTH. Kin or kindred.

L.

L. This letter, as a Roman numeral, stands for the number "fifty." It is also used as an abbreviation for "law," "*liber*," (a book,) "lord," and some other words of which it is the initial.

L. 5. An abbreviation of "*Long Quinto*," one of the parts of the Year Books.

L. C. An abbreviation which may stand either for "Lord Chancellor," "Lower Canada," or "Leading Cases."

L. J. An abbreviation for "Law Judge;" also for "Law Journal."

L. L. (also L. Lat.) and **L. F.** (also L. Fr.) are used as abbreviations of the terms "Law Latin" and "Law French."

L. R. An abbreviation for "Law Reports."

L. S. An abbreviation for "*Locus sigilli*," the place of the seal, *i. e.*, the place where a seal is to be affixed, or a scroll which stands instead of a seal.

LL. The reduplicated form of the abbreviation "L," for "law," used as a plural. It is generally used in citing old collections of statute law; as "LL. Hen. I."

LL.B., LL.M., and LL.D. Abbreviations used to denote, respectively, the three academic degrees in law,—bachelor, master, and doctor of laws.

LA. Fr. The. The definite article in the feminine gender. Occurs in some legal terms and phrases; as "*Termes de la Ley*," terms of the law.

LA. Fr. There. An adverb of time and place; whereas.

LA CHAMBRE DES ESTEILLES. The star-chamber.

La conscience est la plus changeante des régles. Conscience is the most changeable of rules. Bouv. Dict.

La ley favour la vie d'un home. The law favors the life of a man. Yearb. M. 10 Hen. VI. 51.

La ley favour l'enheritance d'un home. The law favors the inheritance of a man. Yearb. M. 10 Hen. VI. 51.

La ley voct plus tost suffer un mischeife que un inconvenience. The law will sooner suffer a mischief than an inconvenience. Litt. § 231. It is holden for an inconvenience that any of the maxims of the law should be broken, though a private man suffer loss. Co. Litt. 152*b*.

LAAS. A net, gin, or snare.

LABEL. Anything appended to a larger writing, as a codicil; a narrow slip of paper or parchment affixed to a deed or writ, in order to hold the appending seal.

In the vernacular, the word denotes a printed or written slip of paper affixed to a manufactured article, giving information as to its nature or quality, or the contents of a package, name of the maker, etc.

A copy of a writ in the exchequer. 1 Tidd, Pr. 156.

LABINA. In old records. Watery land.

LABOR. Work; toil; service. Continued exertion, of the more onerous and inferior kind, usually and chiefly consisting in the protracted expenditure of muscular force, adapted to the accomplishment of specific useful ends. It is used in this sense in several legal phrases, such as "a count for work and labor," "wages of labor," etc.

"Labor," "business," and "work" are not synonyms. Labor may be business, but it is not necessarily so; and business is not always labor. Labor implies toil; exertion producing weariness; manual exertion of a toilsome nature. Making an agreement for the sale of a chattel is not within a prohibition of common labor upon Sunday, though it is (if by a merchant in his calling) within a prohibition upon business. 2 Ohio St. 387.

LABOR A JURY. In old practice. To tamper with a jury; to endeavor to influence them in their verdict, or their verdict generally.

LABORARIIS. An ancient writ against persons who refused to serve and do labor, and who had no means of living; or against such as, having served in the winter, refused to serve in the summer. Reg. Orig. 189.

LABORER. One who, as a means of livelihood, performs work and labor for those who employ him. In English statutes, this term is generally understood to designate a servant employed in husbandry or manufactures, and not dwelling in the home of his employer. Wharton; Mozley & Whitley.

A laborer, as the word is used in the Pennsylvania act of 1872, giving a certain preference of lien, is one who performs, with his own hands, the contract which he makes with his employer. 82 Pa. St. 469.

LABORERS, STATUTES OF. In English law. These are the statutes 23 Edw. III., 12 Rich. II., 5 Eliz. c. 4, and 26 & 27 Vict. c. 125, making various regulations as to laborers, servants, apprentices, etc.

LAC, LAK. In Indian computation, 100,000. The value of a lac of rupees is about £10,000 sterling. Wharton.

LACE. A measure of land equal to one pole. This term is widely used in Cornwall.

LACERTA. In old English law. A fathom. Co. Litt. 4*b*.

LACHES. Negligence, consisting in the omission of something which a party might do, and might reasonably be expected to do, towards the vindication or enforcement of his rights. The word is generally the synonym of "remissness," "dilatoriness," "unreasonable or unexcused delay," the opposite of "vigilance," and means a want of activity and diligence in making a claim or moving for the enforcement of a right (particularly in equity) which will afford ground for presuming against it, or for refusing relief, where that is discretionary with the court.

LACTA. L. Lat. In old English law. Defect in the weight of money; *lack* of weight. This word and the verb "*lactare*" are used in an assise or statute of the sixth year of King John. Spelman.

LACUNA. In old records. A ditch or dyke; a furrow for a drain; a gap or blank in writing.

LACUS. In the civil law. A lake; a receptacle of water which is never dry. Dig. 43, 14, 1, 3.

In old English law. Allay or alloy of silver with base metal. Fleta, lib. 1, c. 22, § 6.

LADA. In Saxon law. A purgation, or mode of trial by which one purged himself of an accusation; as by oath or ordeal. Spelman.

A water-course; a trench or canal for draining marshy grounds. In old English, a *lade* or *load*. Spelman.

In old English law. A court of justice; a lade or lath. Cowell.

LADE, or LODE. The mouth of a river.

LADEN IN BULK. A term of maritime law, applied to a vessel which is freighted with a cargo which is neither in casks, boxes, bales, nor cases, but lies loose in the hold, being defended from wet or moisture by a number of mats and a quantity of dunnage. Cargoes of corn, salt, etc., are usually so shipped.

LADY. In English law. The title belonging to the wife of a peer, and (by courtesy) the wife of a baronet or knight, and also to any woman, married or sole, whose father was a nobleman of a rank not lower than that of earl.

LADY-COURT. In English law. The court of a lady of the manor.

LADY DAY. The 25th of March, the feast of the Annunication of the Blessed Virgin Mary. In parts of Ireland, however, they so designate the 15th of August, the festival of the Assumption of the Virgin.

LADY'S FRIEND. The style of an officer of the English house of commons, whose duty was to secure a suitable provision for the wife, when her husband sought a divorce by special act of parliament. The act of 1857 abolished parliamentary divorces, and this office with them.

LÆSA MAJESTAS. Lat. Leze-majesty, or injured majesty; high treason. It is a phrase taken from the civil law, and anciently meant any offense against the king's person or dignity.

LÆSIO ULTRA DIMIDIUM VEL ENORMIS. In Roman law. The injury sustained by one of the parties to an onerous contract when he had been overreached by the other to the extent of more than one-half of the value of the subject-matter; *e. g.*, when a vendor had not received half the value of property sold, or the purchaser had paid more than double value. Colq. Rom. Civil Law, § 2094.

LÆSIONE FIDEI, SUITS PRO. Suits in the ecclesiastical courts for spiritual offenses against conscience, for non-payment of debts, or breaches of civil contracts. This attempt to turn the ecclesiastical courts into courts of equity was checked by the constitutions of Clarendon, A. D. 1164. 3 Bl. Comm. 52.

LÆSIWERP. A thing surrendered into the hands or power of another; a thing given or delivered. Spelman.

LÆT. In old English law. One of a class between servile and free. Palgrave, i. 354.

LÆTERE JERUSALEM. Easter offerings, so called from these words in the hymn of the day. They are also denominated "*quadragesimalia.*" Wharton.

LÆTHE, or LATHE. A division or district peculiar to the county of Kent. Spelman.

LAFORDSWIC. In Saxon law. A betraying of one's lord or master.

LAGA. L. Lat., from the Saxon "*lag.*" Law; a law.

LAGAN. See LIGAN.

LAGE DAY. In old English law. A law day; a time of open court; the day of the county court; a juridical day.

LAGE-MAN. A lawful man; a good and lawful man. A juror. Cowell.

LAGENA. L. Lat. In old English law. A measure of ale. Fleta, lib. 2, c. 11. Said to consist of six sextaries. Cowell.

LAGU. In old English law. Law; also used to express the territory or district in which a particular law was in force, as *Dena lagu, Mercna lagu,* etc.

LAHLSLIT. A breach of law. Cowell. A mulct for an offense, viz., twelve "ores."

LAHMAN, or LAGEMANNUS. An old word for a lawyer. Domesday, I. 189.

LAIA. A roadway in a wood. Mon. Angl. t. 1, p. 483.

LAICUS. A layman. One who is not in holy orders, or not engaged in the ministry of religion.

LAIRWITE, or LAIRESITE. A fine for adultery or fornication, anciently paid to the lords of some manors. 4 Inst. 206.

LAIS GENTS. L. Fr. Lay people; a jury.

LAITY. In English law. Those persons who do not make a part of the clergy. They are divided into three states: (1) *Civil,* including all the nation, except the clergy, the army, and navy, and subdivided into the *nobility* and the *commonalty;* (2) *military;* (3) *maritime,* consisting of the navy. Wharton.

LAKE. A large body of water, contained in a depression of the earth's surface, and supplied from the drainage of a more or less extended area. Webster.

The fact that there is a current from a higher to a lower level does not make that a river which would otherwise be a lake; and the fact that a river swells out into broad, pond-like sheets, with a current, does not make that a lake which would otherwise be a river. 14 N. H. 477.

LAMANEUR. Fr. In French marine law. A pilot. Ord. Mar. liv. 4, tit. 3.

LAMB. A sheep, ram, or ewe under the age of one year. 4 Car. & P. 216.

LAMBARD'S ARCHAIONOMIA. A work printed in 1568, containing the Anglo-Saxon laws, those of William the Conqueror, and of Henry I.

LAMBARD'S EIRENARCHA. A work upon the office of a justice of the peace, which, having gone through two editions, one in 1579, the other in 1581, was reprinted in English in 1599.

LAMBETH DEGREE. In English law. A degree conferred by the Archbishop of Canterbury, in prejudice of the universities. 3 Steph. Comm. 65; 1 Bl. Comm. 381.

LAME DUCK. A cant term on the stock exchange for a person unable to meet his engagements.

LAMMAS DAY. The 1st of August. It is one of the Scotch quarter days, and is what is called a "conventional term."

LAMMAS LANDS. Lands over which there is a right of pasturage by persons other than the owner from about Lammas, or reaping time, until sowing time. Wharton.

LANA. Lat. In the civil law. Wool. See Dig. 32, 60, 70, 88.

LANCASTER. A county of England, erected into a county palatine in the reign of Edward III., but now vested in the crown.

LANCETI. In feudal law. Vassals who were obliged to work for their lord one day in the week, from Michaelmas to autumn, either with fork, spade, or flail, at the lord's option. Spelman.

LAND, in the most general sense, comprehends any ground, soil, or earth whatsoever; as meadows, pastures, woods, moors, waters, marshes, furzes, and heath. Co. Litt. 4*a*.

The word "land" includes not only the soil, but everything attached to it, whether attached by the course of nature, as trees, herbage, and water, or by the hand of man, as buildings and fences. 1 N. Y. 572; 2 Bl. Comm. 16, 17.

Land is the solid material of the earth, whatever may be the ingredients of which it is composed, whether soil, rock, or other substance. Civil Code Cal. § 659.

Philosophically, it seems more correct to say that the word "land" means, in law, as in the vernacular, the soil, or portion of the earth's crust; and to explain or justify such expressions as that "whoever owns the land owns the buildings above and the minerals below," upon the view, not that these are within the extension of the term "land," but that they are so connected with it that by rules of law they pass by a conveyance of the land. This view makes "land," as a term, narrower in signification than "realty;" though it would allow an instrument speaking of land to operate co-extensively with one granting realty or real property by either of those terms. But many of the authorities use the expression "land" as including these incidents to the soil. Abbott.

LAND CERTIFICATE. Upon the registration of freehold land under the English land transfer act, 1875, a certificate is given to the registered proprietor, and similarly upon every transfer of registered land. This registration supersedes the necessity of any further registration in the register counties. Sweet.

LAND COURT. In American law. A court formerly existing in St. Louis, Mo., having a limited territorial jurisdiction over actions concerning real property, and suits for dower, partition, etc.

LAND-GABEL. A tax or rent issuing out of land. Spelman says it was originally a penny for every house. This *land-gabel*, or *land-gavel*, in the register of Domesday, was a quit-rent for the site of a house, or the land whereon it stood; the same with what we now call "ground-rent." Wharton.

"LAND-POOR." By this term is generally understood that a man has a great deal of unproductive land, and perhaps is obliged to borrow money to pay taxes; but a man "land-poor" may be largely responsible. 46 Mich. 397, 9 N. W. Rep. 445.

LAND-REEVE. A person whose business it is to overlook certain parts of a farm or estate; to attend not only to the woods and hedge-timber, but also to the state of the fences, gates, buildings, private roads, drift-ways, and water-courses; and likewise to the stocking of commons, and encroachments of every kind, as well as to prevent or detect waste and spoil in general, whether by the tenants or others; and to report the same to the manager or land steward. Enc. Lond.

LAND STEWARD. A person who overlooks or has the management of a farm or estate.

LAND TAX. A tax laid upon the legal or beneficial owner of real property, and apportioned upon the assessed value of his land.

LAND TENANT. The person actually in possession of land; otherwise styled the "terre-tenant."

LAND TITLES AND TRANSFER ACT. An English statute (38 & 39 Vict. c. 87) providing for the establishment of a registry for titles to real property, and making sundry provisions for the transfer of lands and the recording of the evidences therof. It presents some analogies to the recording laws of the American states.

LAND WAITER. In English law. An officer of the custom-house, whose duty is, upon landing any merchandise, to examine, taste, weigh, or measure it, and to take an account thereof. In some ports they also execute the office of a coast waiter. They are likewise occasionally styled "searchers," and are to attend and join with the patent searcher in the execution of all cockets for the shipping of goods to be exported to foreign parts; and, in cases where drawbacks on bounties are to be paid to the merchant on the exportation of any goods, they, as well as the patent searchers, are to certify the shipping thereof on the debentures. Enc. Lond.

LAND-WARRANT. The evidence which the state, on good consideration, gives that the person therein named is entitled to the quantity of land therein specified, the bounds and description of which the owner of the warrant may fix by entry and survey, in the section of country set apart for its location and satisfaction. 6 Yerg. 205.

LANDA. An open field without wood; a lawnd or lawn. Cowell; Blount.

LANDAGENDE, LANDHLAFORD, or LANDRICA. In Saxon law. A proprietor of land; lord of the soil. Anc. Inst. Eng.

LANDBOC. In Saxon law. A charter or deed by which lands or tenements were given or held. Spelman; Cowell; 1 Reeve, Eng. Law, 10.

LANDCHEAP. In old English law. An ancient customary fine, paid either in money or cattle, at every alienation of land lying within some manor, or within the liberty of some borough. Cowell; Blount.

LANDEA. In old English law. A ditch or trench for conveying water from marshy grounds. Spelman.

LANDED. Consisting in real estate or land; having an estate in land.

LANDED ESTATES COURT. The court which deals with the transfer of land and the creation of title thereto in Ireland.

LANDED PROPRIETOR. Any person having an estate in lands, whether highly improved or not. 10 La. Ann. 677.

LANDEFRICUS. A landlord; a lord of the soil.

LANDEGANDMAN. Sax. In old English law. A kind of customary tenant or inferior tenant of a manor. Spelman.

LANDGRAVE. A name formerly given to those who executed justice on behalf of the German emperors, with regard to the internal policy of the country. It was applied, by way of eminence, to those sovereign princes of the empire who possessed by inheritance certain estates called "*land-gravates*," of which they received investiture from the emperor. Enc. Lond.

LANDIMER. In old Scotch law. A measurer of land. Skene.

LANDING. A place on a river or other navigable water for lading and unlading goods, or for the reception and delivery of passengers; the terminus of a road on a river or other navigable water, for the use of travelers, and the loading and unloading of goods. 1 Strob. 111.

A place for loading or unloading boats, but not a harbor for them. 74 Pa. St. 373.

LANDIRECTA. In Saxon law. Services and duties laid upon all that held land, including the three obligations called "*trinoda necessitas*," (*q. v.*;) *quasi* land rights. Cowell.

LANDLOCKED. An expression sometimes applied to a piece of land belonging to one person and surrounded by land belonging to other persons, so that it cannot be approached except over their land. L. R. 13 Ch. Div. 798; Sweet.

LANDLORD. He of whom lands or tenements are holden. He who, being the owner of an estate in land, has leased the same for a term of years, on a rent reserved, to another person, called the "tenant."

When the absolute property in or fee-simple of the land belongs to a landlord, he is then sometimes denominated the "ground landlord," in contradistinction to such a one as is possessed only of a limited or particular interest in land, and who himself holds under a superior landlord. Brown.

LANDLORD AND TENANT. A phrase used to denote the familiar legal relation existing between lessor and lessee of real estate. The relation is contractual, and is constituted by a lease (or agreement therefor) of lands for a term of years, from year to year, for life, or at will.

LANDLORD'S WARRANT. A distress warrant; a warrant from a landlord to levy upon the tenant's goods and chattels, and sell the same at public sale, to compel payment of the rent or the observance of some other stipulation in the lease.

LANDMARK. A monument or erection set up on the boundary line of two adjoining estates, to fix such boundary. The removing of a landmark is a wrong for which an action lies.

LANDS. This term, the plural of "land," is said, at common law, to be a word of less extensive signification than either "tenements" or "hereditaments." But in some of the states it has been provided by statute that it shall include both those terms.

LANDS CLAUSES CONSOLIDATION ACTS. The name given to certain English statutes, (8 Vict. c. 8, amended by 23 & 24 Vict. c. 106, and 32 & 33 Vict. c. 18,) the object of which was to provide legislative clauses in a convenient form for incorporation by reference in future special acts of parliament for taking lands, with or without the consent of their owners, for the promotion of railways, and other public undertakings. Mozley & Whitley.

LANDS, TENEMENTS, AND HEREDITAMENTS. The technical and most comprehensive description of real property, as "goods and chattels" is of personalty. Williams, Real Prop. 5.

LANDSLAGH. In Swedish law. A body of common law, compiled about the thirteenth century, out of the particular customs of every province; being analogous to the *common law* of England. 1 Bl. Comm. 66.

LANDWARD. In Scotch law. Rural. 7 Bell, App. Cas. 2.

LANGEMAN. A lord of a manor. 1 Inst. 5.

LANGEOLUM. An undergarment made of wool, formerly worn by the monks, which reached to their knees. Mon. Angl. 419.

LANGUAGE. Any means of conveying or communicating ideas; specifically, human speech, or the expression of ideas by written characters. The letter, or grammatical import, of a document or instrument, as distinguished from its spirit; as "the language of the statute."

LANGUIDUS. In practice. The name of a return made by the sheriff when a defendant, whom he has taken by virtue of process, is so dangerously sick that to remove him would endanger his life or health. 3 Chit. Pr. 249, 358.

LANIS DE CRESCENTIA WALLIÆ TRADUCENDIS ABSQUE CUSTUMA, etc. An ancient writ that lay to the customer of a port to permit one to pass wool without paying custom, he having paid it before in Wales. Reg. Orig. 279.

LANO NIGER. A sort of base coin, formerly current in England. Cowell.

LANZAS. In Spanish law. A commutation in money, paid by the nobles and high officers, in lieu of the quota of soldiers they might be required to furnish in war.

LAPIDATION. The act of stoning a person to death.

LAPIDICINA. Lat. In the civil law. A stone-quarry. Dig. 7, 1, 9, 2.

LAPILLI. Lat. In the civil law. Precious stones. Dig. 34, 2, 19, 17. Distinguished from "gems," (*gemmæ.*) Id.

LAPIS MARMORIUS. A marble stone about twelve feet long and three feet broad, placed at the upper end of Westminster Hall, where was likewise a marble chair erected on the middle thereof, in which the English sovereigns anciently sat at their coronation dinner, and at other times the lord chancellor. Wharton.

LAPSE, *v.* To glide; to pass slowly, silently, or by degrees. To slip; to deviate from the proper path. Webster. To fall or fail.

LAPSE, *n.* **In ecclesiastical law.** The transfer, by forfeiture, of a right to present or collate to a vacant benefice from a person vested with such right to another, in consequence of some act of negligence by the former. Ayl. Par. 331.

In the law of wills. The failure of a testamentary gift in consequence of the death of the devisee or legatee during the life of the testator.

In criminal proceedings, "lapse" is used, in England, in the same sense as "abate" in ordinary procedure; *i. e.*, to signify that the proceedings came to an end by the death of one of the parties or some other event.

LAPSE PATENT. A patent for land issued in substitution for an earlier patent to the same land, which was issued to another party, but has lapsed in consequence of his neglect to avail himself of it. 1 Wash. (Va.) 39.

LAPSED DEVISE. A devise which fails, or takes no effect, in consequence of the death of the devisee before the testator; the subject-matter of it being considered as not disposed of by the will. 1 Steph. Comm. 559; 4 Kent, Comm. 541.

LAPSED LEGACY. Where the legatee dies before the testator, or before the legacy is payable, the bequest is said to *lapse*, as it then falls into the residuary fund of the estate.

LARCENOUS. Having the character of larceny; as a "larcenous taking." Contemplating or intending larceny; as a "larcenous purpose."

LARCENY. In criminal law. The wrongful and fraudulent taking and carrying away by one person of the mere personal goods of another from any place, with a felonious intent to convert them to his (the taker's) use, and make them his property, without the consent of the owner. 2 East, P. C. 553; 4 Wash. C. C. 700.

The felonious taking and carrying away of the personal goods of another. 4 Bl. Comm. 229. The unlawful taking and carrying away of things personal, with intent to deprive the right owner of the same. 4 Steph. Comm. 152. The felonious taking the property of another, without his consent and against his will, with intent to convert it to the use of the taker. 2 Leach, 1089.

The taking and removing, by trespass, of personal property which the trespasser knows to belong either generally or specially to another, with the intent to deprive such owner of his ownership therein; and, perhaps it should be added, for the sake of some advantage to the trespasser,—a proposition on which the decisions are not harmonious. 2 Bish. Crim. Law, §§ 757, 758.

Larceny is the taking of personal property, accomplished by fraud or stealth, and with intent to deprive another thereof. Pen. Code Dak. § 580.

Larceny is the felonious stealing, taking, carrying, leading, or driving away the personal property of another. Pen. Code Cal. § 484.

Larceny is sometimes divided into "simple" and "compound" or "mixed" larceny; the former term applying to cases of simple theft; the latter to cases of stealing attended with some recognized circumstances of aggravation, such as larceny from a ship or wharf, or from a dwelling-house in the day-time, or from the person.

Larceny was also divided into "grand" and "petit" larceny, the distinction turning on an arbitrary division of the value of the goods stolen. This division is now abolished in England (7 & 8 Geo. IV. c. 29, § 2) and in many of the United States, but still subsists in some jurisdictions.

For the distinction between "larceny" and "burglary," "extortion," "false pretenses," and "robbery," see those titles.

LARCENY BY BAILEE. In Pennsylvania law. The crime of larceny committed where "any person, being a bailee of any property, shall fraudulently take or convert the same to his own use, or to the use of any other person except the owner thereof, although he shall not break bulk or otherwise determine the bailment." Brightly's Purd. Dig. p. 436, § 177.

LARDARIUS REGIS. The king's larderer, or clerk of the kitchen. Cowell.

LARDING MONEY. In the manor of Bradford, in Wilts, the tenants pay to their lord a small yearly rent by this name, which is said to be for liberty to feed their hogs with the masts of the lord's wood, the fat of a hog being called "lard;" or it may be a commutation for some customary service of carrying salt or meat to the lord's larder. Mon. Angl. t. 1, p. 321.

LARGE. L. Fr. Broad; the opposite of "*estreyte*," strait or strict. *Pures et larges*. Britt. c. 34.

LARONS. In old English law. Thieves.

LAS PARTIDAS. In Spanish law. The name of a code of laws, more fully described as "*Las Siete Partidas*," ("the seven parts," from the number of its divisions,) which was compiled under the direction of Alphonso X., about the year 1250. Its sources were the customary law of all the provinces, the canon law as there administered, and (chiefly) the Roman law. This work has always been regarded as of the highest authority in Spain and in those countries and states which have derived their jurisprudence from Spain.

LASCAR. A native Indian sailor; the term is also applied to tent pitchers, inferior artillery-men, and others.

LASCIVIOUS CARRIAGE. In Connecticut. A term including those wanton acts between persons of different sexes that flow from the exercise of lustful passions, and which are not otherwise punished as crimes against chastity and public decency. 2 Swift. Dig. 343. It includes, also, indecent acts by one against the will of another. 5 Day, 81.

LASHITE, or LASHLITE. A kind of forfeiture during the government of the Danes in England. Enc. Lond.

LAST, in old English law, signifies a burden; also a measure of weight used for certain commodities of the bulkier sort.

LAST COURT. A court held by the twenty-four jurats in the marshes of Kent, and summoned by the bailiffs, whereby orders were made to lay and levy taxes, impose penalties, etc., for the preservation of the said marshes. Enc. Lond.

LAST HEIR. In English law. He to whom lands come by escheat for want of lawful heirs; that is, in some cases, the lord of whom the lands were held; in others, the sovereign. Cowell.

LAST RESORT. A court from which there is no appeal is called the "court of last resort."

LAST SICKNESS. That illness of which a person dies is so called.

LAST WILL. This term, according to Lord Coke, is most commonly used where lands and tenements are devised, and "testament" where it concerns chattels. Co. Litt. 111*a*. Both terms, however, are now generally employed in drawing a will either of lands or chattels.

LASTAGE. A custom exacted in some fairs and markets to carry things bought whither one will. But it is more accurately taken for the ballast or lading of a ship. Also custom paid for wares sold by the last, as herrings, pitch, etc. Wharton.

LATA CULPA. Lat. In the law of bailment. Gross fault or neglect; extreme negligence or carelessness, (*nimia negligentia.*) Dig. 50, 16, 213, 2.

Lata culpa dolo æquiparatur. Gross negligence is equivalent to fraud.

LATCHING. An under-ground survey.

LATE. Defunct; existing recently, but now dead. 17 Ala. 190. Formerly; recently; lately.

"LATELY." This word has been held to have "a very large retrospect, as we say '*lately* deceased' of one dead ten or twenty years." Per Cur. 2 Show. 294.

LATENS. Lat. Latent; hidden; not apparent. See AMBIGUITAS.

LATENT. Hidden; concealed; that does not appear upon the face of a thing.

LATENT AMBIGUITY. An ambiguity which arises not upon the words of the will, deed, or other instrument, as looked at in themselves, but upon those words when applied to the object or to the subject which they describe. The term is opposed to the phrase "patent ambiguity." The rule of law is that extrinsic or parol evidence is admissible in all cases to remove a latent ambiguity, but in no case to remove a patent one. Brown.

LATENT DEED. A deed kept for twenty years or more in a man's scrutoire or strong-box. 7 N. J. Law, 177.

LATENT DEFECT. A defect in an article sold, which is known to the seller, but not to the purchaser, and is not discoverable by mere observation. See 21 N. Y. 552.

LATERA. In old records. Sidesmen; companions; assistants. Cowell..

LATERAL RAILROAD. A lateral road is one which proceeds from some point on the main trunk between its termini; it is but another name for a branch road, both being a part of the main road. 14 Ill. 273.

LATERAL SUPPORT. The right of lateral and subjacent support is that right which the owner of land has to have his land supported by the adjoining land or the soil beneath. 27 Grat. 77; 19 Barb. 380; 2 Allen, 131; 12 Amer. & Eng. Enc. Law, 933.

LATERARE. To lie sideways, in opposition to lying endways; used in descriptions of lands.

LATH, LATHE. The name of an ancient civil division in England, intermediate between the county or shire and the hundred. Said to be the same as what, in other parts of the kingdom, was termed a "rape." 1 Bl. Comm. 116; Cowell; Spelman.

LATHREVE. An officer under the Saxon government, who had authority over a lathe. Cowell; 1 Bl. Comm. 116.

LATIFUNDIUM. In the civil law. Great or large possessions; a great or large field; a common. A great estate made up of smaller ones, (*fundis,*) which began to be common in the latter times of the empire.

LATIFUNDUS. A possessor of a large estate made up of smaller ones. Du Cange.

LATIMER. A word used by Lord Coke in the sense of an interpreter. 2 Inst. 515. Supposed to be a corruption of the French "*latinier,*" or "*latiner.*" Cowell; Blount.

LATIN. The language of the ancient Romans. There are three sorts of law Latin: (1) Good Latin, allowed by the grammarians and lawyers; (2) false or incongruous Latin, which in times past would abate original writs, though it would not make void any judicial writ, declaration, or plea, etc.; (3) words of art, known only to the sages of the law, and not to grammarians, called "Lawyers' Latin." Wharton.

LATINARIUS. An interpreter of Latin.

LATINI JUNIANI. Lat. In Roman law. A class of freedmen (*libertini*) intermediate between the two other classes of freedmen called, respectively, "*Cives Romani*" and "*Dediticii.*" Slaves under thirty years of age at the date of their manumission, or manumitted otherwise than by *vindicta*, *census*, or *testamentum*, or not the quiritary property of their manumissors at the time of manumission, were called "*Latini.*" By reason of one or other of these three defects, they remained slaves by strict law even after their manumission, but were protected in their liberties first by equity, and eventually by the *Lex Junia Norbana*, A. D. 19, from which law they took the name of "*Juniani*" in addition to that of "*Latini.*" Brown.

LATITAT. In old English practice. A writ which issued in personal actions, on the return of *non est inventus* to a bill of Middlesex; so called from the emphatic word in its recital, in which it was "testified that the defendant *lurks* [*latitat*] and wanders about" in the county. 3 Bl. Comm. 286. Abolished by St. 2 Wm. IV. c. 39.

LATITATIO. In the civil law and old English practice. A lying hid; lurking, or concealment of the person. Dig. 42, 4, 7, 5; Bract. fol. 126.

LATOR. A bearer; a messenger.

LATRO. In the civil and old English law. A robber. Dig. 50, 16, 118; Fleta, lib. 1, c. 38, § 1. A thief.

LATROCINATION. The act of robbing; a depredation.

LATROCINIUM. The prerogative of adjudging and executing thieves; also larceny; theft; a thing stolen.

LATROCINY. Larceny.

LATTER-MATH. A second mowing; the aftermath.

LAUDARE. In the civil law. To name; to cite or quote; to show one's title or authority. Calvin.

In feudal law. To determine or pass upon judicially. *Laudamentum*, the finding or award of a jury. 2 Bl. Comm. 285.

LAUDATIO. In Roman law. Testimony delivered in court concerning an accused person's good behavior and integrity of life. It resembled the practice which prevails in our trials of calling persons to speak to a prisoner's character. The least number of the *laudatores* among the Romans was ten. Wharton.

LAUDATOR. An arbitrator; a witness to character.

LAUDEMEO. In Spanish law. The tax paid by the possessor of land held by quit-rent or *emphyteusis* to the owner of the estate, when the tenant alienates his right in the property. Escriche.

LAUDEMIUM. In the civil law. A sum paid by a new *emphyteuta* (*q. v.*) who acquires the *emphyteusis*, not as heir, but as a singular successor, whether by gift, devise, exchange, or sale. It was a sum equal to the fiftieth part of the purchase money, paid to the *dominus* or proprietor for his acceptance of the new *emphyteuta*. Mackeld. Rom. Law, § 328. Called, in old English law, "acknowledgment money." Cowell.

LAUDUM. An arbitrament or award.

In old Scotch law. Sentence or judgment; dome or doom. 1 Pitc. Crim. Tr. pt. 2, p. 8.

LAUGHE. Frank-pledge. 2 Reeve, Eng. Law, 17.

LAUNCEGAY. A kind of offensive weapon, now disused, and prohibited by 7 Rich. II. c. 13.

LAUNCH. 1. The act of launching a vessel; the movement of a vessel from the land into the water, especially the sliding on ways from the stocks on which it is built.

2. A boat of the largest size belonging to a ship of war; an open boat of large size used in any service; a lighter.

LAUREATE. In English law. An officer of the household of the sovereign, whose business formerly consisted only in composing an ode annually, on the sovereign's birthday, and on the new year; sometimes also, though rarely, on occasion of any remarkable victory.

LAURELS. Pieces of gold, coined in 1619, with the king's head laureated; hence the name.

LAUS DEO. Lat. Praise be to God. An old heading to bills of exchange.

LAVATORIUM. A laundry or place to wash in; a place in the porch or entrance of cathedral churches, where the priest and other officiating ministers were obliged to wash their hands before they proceeded to divine service.

LAVOR NUEVA. In Spanish law. A new work. Las Partidas, pt. 3, tit. 32, l. 1.

LAW. 1. That which is laid down, ordained, or established. A rule or method according to which phenomena or actions coexist or follow each other.

2. A system of principles and rules of human conduct, being the aggregate of those commandments and principles which are either prescribed or recognized by the governing power in an organized jural society as its will in relation to the conduct of the members of such society, and which it undertakes to maintain and sanction and to use as the *criteria* of the actions of such members.

"Law" is a solemn expression of legislative will. It orders and permits and forbids. It announces rewards and punishments. Its provisions generally relate not to solitary or singular cases, but to what passes in the ordinary course of affairs. Civil Code La. arts. 1, 2.

"Law," without an article, properly implies a *science* or *system* of principles or rules of human conduct, answering to the Latin "*jus;*" as when it is spoken of as a subject of study or practice. In this sense, it includes the decisions of courts of justice, as well as acts of the legislature. The judgment of a competent court, until reversed or otherwise superseded, is *law*, as much as any statute. Indeed, it may happen that a statute may be passed in violation of *law*, that is, of the fundamental *law* or constitution of a state; and it is the prerogative of courts in such cases to declare it void, or, in other words, to declare it not to be *law*. Burrill.

3. A rule of civil conduct prescribed by the supreme power in a state. 1 Steph. Comm. 25; Civil Code Dak. § 2; Pol. Code Cal. § 4466.

A "law," in the proper sense of the term, is a general rule of human action, taking cognizance only of external acts, enforced by a determinate authority, which authority is human, and among human authorities is that which is paramount in a political society. Holl. Jur. 36.

A "law," properly so called, is a command which obliges a person or persons; and, as distinguished from a particular or occasional command, obliges generally to acts or forbearances of a class. Aust. Jur.

A rule or enactment promulgated by the legislative authority of a state; a long-established local custom which has the force of such an enactment. 10 Pet. 18.

4. In another sense the word signifies an enactment; a distinct and complete act of positive law; a statute, as opposed to rules of civil conduct deduced from the customs of the people or judicial precedents.

When the term "law" is used to denote enactments of the legislative power, it is frequently confined, especially by English writers, to permanent rules of civil conduct, as distinguished from other acts, such as a divorce act, an appropriation bill, an estates act. Rep. Eng. St. L. Com. Mar. 1856.

Historically considered. With reference to its origin, "law" is derived either from judicial precedents, from legislation, or from custom. That part of the law which is derived from judicial precedents is called "common law," "equity," or "admiralty," "probate," or "ecclesiastical law," according to the nature of the courts by which it was originally enforced. (See the respective titles.) That part of the law which is derived from legislation is called the "statute law." Many statutes are classed under one of the divisions above mentioned because they have merely modified or extended portions of it, while others have created altogether new rules. That part of the law which is derived from custom is sometimes called the "customary law," as to which, see CUSTOM. Sweet.

The earliest notion of law was not an enumeration of a principle, but a judgment in a particular case. When pronounced in the early ages, by a king, it was assumed to be the result of direct divine inspiration. Afterwards came the notion of a custom which a judgment affirms, or punishes its breach. In the outset, however, the only authoritative statement of right and wrong is a judicial sentence rendered after the fact has occurred. It does not presuppose a law to have been violated, but is enacted for the first time by a higher form into the judge's mind at the moment of adjudication. Maine, Anc. Law, (Dwight's Ed.) pp. xv, 5.

Synonyms and distinctions. According to the usage in the United States, the name "constitution" is commonly given to the organic or fundamental law of a state, and the term "law" is used in contradistinction to the former, to denote a statute or enactment of the legislative body.

"Law," as distinguished from "equity," denotes the doctrine and procedure of the common law of England and America, from which equity is a departure.

The term is also used in opposition to "fact." Thus questions of law are to be decided by the court, while it is the province of the jury to solve questions of fact.

Classification. With reference to its subject-matter, law is either *public* or *private*. Public law is that part of the law which deals with the state, either by itself or in its relations with individuals, and is divided into (1) constitutional law; (2) administrative law; (3) criminal law; (4) criminal procedure; (5) the law of the state considered in its *quasi* private personality; (6) the procedure relating to the state as so considered. Holl. Jur. 300.

Law is also divided into *substantive* and *adjective*. Substantive law is that part of the law which creates rights and obligations, while adjective law provides a method of enforcing and protecting them. In other words, adjective law is the law of procedure. Holl. Jur. 61, 238.

The ordinary, but not very useful, division of law into *written* and *unwritten* rests on the same principle. The written law is the statute law; the unwritten law is the common law, (*q. v.*) 1 Steph. Comm. 40, following Blackstone.

Kinds of statutes. Statutes are called "general" or "public" when they affect the community at large; and *local* or *special* when their operation is confined to a limited region, or particular class or interest.

Statutes are also either *prospective* or *retrospective;* the former, when they are intended to operate upon future cases only; the latter, when they may also embrace transactions occurring before their passage.

Statutes are called "enabling" when they

confer new powers; "remedial" when their effect is to provide relief or reform abuses; "penal" when they impose punishment, pecuniary or corporal, for a violation of their provisions.

5. In old English jurisprudence, "law" is used to signify an oath, or the privilege of being sworn; as in the phrases "to wage one's law," "to lose one's law."

As to the different kinds of law, or law regarded in its different aspects, see ADJECTIVE LAW; ADMINISTRATIVE LAW; CONSTITUTIONAL LAW; CRIMINAL LAW; INTERNATIONAL LAW; LAW OF NATIONS; LAW OF NATURE; LAW-MERCHANT; MUNICIPAL LAW; POSITIVE LAW; PRIVATE LAW; PUBLIC LAW; RETROSPECTIVE LAW; SUBSTANTIVE LAW.

LAW AGENTS. Solicitors practicing in the Scotch courts.

Law always construeth things to the best. Wing. Max. p. 720, max. 193.

LAW ARBITRARY. Opposed to *immutable*, a law not founded in the nature of things, but imposed by the mere will of the legislature.

LAW BURROWS. In Scotch law. Security for the peaceable behavior of a party; security to keep the peace. Properly, a process for obtaining such security. 1 Forb. Inst. pt. 2, p. 198.

LAW CHARGES. This phrase is used, under the Louisiana Civil Code, to signify costs incurred in court in the prosecution of a suit, to be paid by the party cast. 17 La. 206; 11 Rob. (La.) 28.

Law construeth every act to be lawful, when it standeth indifferent whether it should be lawful or not. Wing. Max. p. 722, max. 194; Finch, Law, b. 1, c. 3, n. 76.

Law construeth things according to common possibility or intendment. Wing. Max. p. 705, max. 189.

Law [the law] construeth things with equity and moderation. Wing. Max. p. 685, max. 183; Finch, Law, b. 1, c. 3, n. 74.

LAW COURT OF APPEALS. In American law. An appellate tribunal, formerly existing in the state of South Carolina, for hearing appeals from the courts of law.

LAW DAY. The day prescribed in a bond, mortgage, or defeasible deed for payment of the debt secured thereby, or, in default of payment, the forfeiture of the property mortgaged. But this does not now occur until foreclosure.

In old English law. Law day or lage day denoted a day of open court; especially the courts of a county or hundred.

Law disfavoreth impossibilities. Wing. Max. p. 606, max. 155.

Law disfavoreth improbabilities. Wing. Max. p. 620, max. 161.

Law [the law] favoreth charity. Wing. Max. p. 497, max. 135.

Law favoreth common right. Wing. Max. p. 547, max. 144.

Law favoreth diligence, and therefore hateth folly and negligence. Wing. Max. p. 665, max. 172; Finch, Law, b. 1, c. 3, no. 70.

Law favoreth honor and order. Wing. Max. p. 739, max. 199.

Law favoreth justice and right. Wing. Max. p. 502, max. 141.

Law favoreth life, liberty, and dower. 4 Bacon's Works, 345.

Law favoreth mutual recompense. Wing. Max. p. 411, max. 108; Finch, Law, b. 1, c. 3, no. 42.

Law [the law] favoreth possession, where the right is equal. Wing. Max. p. 375, max. 98; Finch, Law, b. 1, c. 3, no. 36.

Law favoreth public commerce. Wing. Max. p. 738, max. 198.

Law favoreth public quiet. Wing. Max. p. 742, max. 200; Finch, Law, b. 1, c. 3, no. 54.

Law favoreth speeding of men's causes. Wing. Max. p. 673, max. 175.

Law [the law] favoreth things for the commonwealth, [common weal.] Wing. Max. p. 729, max. 197; Finch, Law, b. 1, c. 3, no. 53.

Law favoreth truth, faith, and certainty. Wing. Max. p. 604, max. 154.

LAW FRENCH. The Norman French language, introduced into England by William the Conqueror, and which, for several centuries, was, in an emphatic sense, the language of the English *law*, being that in which the proceedings of the courts and of parliament were carried on, and in which many of the ancient statutes, reports, abridgments, and treatises were written and printed. It is called by Blackstone a "barbarous dialect," and the later specimens of it fully warrant the appellation, but at the time of its introduction it was, as has been observed, the best form of the language spoken in Normandy. Burrill.

Law hateth delays. Wing. Max. p. 674, max. 176; Finch, Law, b. 1, ch. 3, no. 71.

Law hateth new inventions and innovations. Wing. Max. p. 756, max. 204.

Law hateth wrong. Wing. Max. p. 563, max. 146; Finch, Law, b. 1, ch. 3, no. 62.

LAW LATIN. The corrupt form of the Latin language employed in the old English law-books and legal proceedings. It contained many barbarous words and combinations.

LAW LIST. An annual English publication of a *quasi* official character, comprising various statistics of interest in connection with the legal profession. It includes (among other information) the following matters: A list of judges, queen's counsel, and serjeants at law; the judges of the county courts; benchers of the inns of court; barristers, in alphabetical order; the names of counsel practicing in the several circuits of England and Wales; London attorneys; country attorneys; officers of the courts of chancery and common law; the magistrates and law officers of the city of London; the metropolitan magistrates and police; recorders; county court officers and circuits; lord lieutenants and sheriffs; colonial judges and officers; public notaries. Mozley & Whitley.

LAW LORDS. Peers in the British parliament who have held high judicial office, or have been distinguished in the legal profession. Mozley & Whitley.

LAW-MARTIAL. The military law; a code of law established for the government of the army and navy.

LAW-MERCHANT. The general system of usages and customs, in relation to commercial transactions, mercantile paper, etc., commonly observed alike among all commercial nations.

Since, however, its character is not local, nor its obligation confined to a particular district, it cannot with propriety be considered as a *custom* in the technical sense. 1 Steph. Comm. 54. It is a system of law which does not rest essentially on the positive institutions and local customs of any particular country, but consists of certain principles of equity and usages of trade which general convenience and a common sense of justice have established, to regulate the dealings of merchants and mariners in all the commercial countries of the civilized world. 3 Kent, Comm. 2.

LAW OF ARMS. That law which gives precepts and rules concerning war; how to make and observe leagues and truce, to punish offenders in the camp, and such like. Cowell; Blount. Now more commonly called the "law of war," (*q. v.*)

LAW OF CITATIONS. In Roman law. An act of Valentinian, passed A. D. 426, providing that the writings of only five jurists, viz., Papinian, Paul, Gaius, Ulpian, and Modestinus, should be quoted as authorities. The majority was binding on the judge. If they were equally divided, the opinion of Papinian was to prevail; and in such a case, if Papinian was silent upon the matter, then the judge was free to follow his own view of the matter. Brown.

Law of itself prejudiceth no man. Wing. Max. p. 575, max. 148; Finch, Law, b. 1, c. 3, no. 63.

LAW OF MARQUE. A sort of law of reprisal, which entitles him who has received any wrong from another and cannot get ordinary justice to take the shipping or goods of the wrong-doer, where he can find them within his own bounds or precincts, in satisfaction of the wrong. Cowell; Brown.

LAW OF NATIONS. A system of rules and principles established among nations, and intended for the regulation of their mutual intercourse; otherwise called "international law," (*q. v.*) A code of public instruction which defines the rights and prescribes the duties of nations in their intercourse with each other. 1 Kent, Comm. 1. It is founded for the most part on usage, consent, and agreement, but in an important degree, also, on the principles of natural law. Id. 2.

LAW OF NATURE. A rule of conduct arising out of the natural relations of human beings, established by the Creator, and existing prior to any positive precept. Webster. The foundation of this law is placed by the best writers in the will of God, discovered by right reason, and aided by divine revelation; and its principles, when applicable, apply with equal obligation to individuals and to nations. 1 Kent, Comm. 2, note; Id. 4, note. See JUS NATURALE.

We understand all laws to be either human or divine, according as they have man or God for their author; and divine laws are of two kinds, that is to say: (1) Natural laws; (2) positive or revealed laws. A natural law is defined by Burlamaqui to be "a rule which so necessarily agrees with the nature and state of man that, without observing its maxims, the peace and happiness of society can never be preserved." And he says that these are called "natural laws" because a knowledge of them may be attained merely by the light of reason, from the fact of their essential agreeableness with the constitution of human nature; while, on the contrary, positive or revealed laws are not founded upon the general constitution of human nature, but only upon the will of God; though in other respects such law is established upon very good reason, and procures the advantage of those to whom it is sent. The ceremonial or political laws of the Jews are of this latter class. 11 Ark. 527.

LAW OF THE LAND. Due process of law, (*q. v.*)

By the law of the land is most clearly intended the general law which hears before it condemns, which proceeds upon inquiry, and renders judgment only after trial. The meaning is that every citizen shall hold his life, liberty, property, and immunities under the protection of general rules which govern society. Everything which may pass under the form of an enactment is not the law of the land. Sedg. St. & Const. Law, (2d Ed.) 475.

When first used in *Magna Charta*, the phrase "the law of the land" probably meant the established law of the kingdom, in opposition to the civil or Roman law, which was about being introduced. It is now generally regarded as meaning general public laws binding on all members of the community, in contradistinction from partial or private laws. 2 Tex. 251; 2 Yerg. 270; 6 Heisk. 186.

It means due process of law warranted by the constitution, by the common law adopted by the constitution, or by statutes passed in pursuance of the constitution. 1 N. H. 53.

It means the law as established in a fair, open trial, or after opportunity given for such trial, by due course and process of law; not a bill of attainder. 6 Pa. St. 87.

LAW OF THE STAPLE. Law administered in the court of the mayor of the staple; the law-merchant. 4 Inst. 235. See STAPLE.

LAW REPORTS. Published volumes containing the reports of cases argued and adjudged in the courts of law.

Law respecteth matter of substance more than matter of circumstance. Wing. Max. p. 382, max. 101; Finch, Law, b. 1, c. 3, no. 39.

Law respecteth possibility of things. Wing. Max. p. 403, max. 104; Finch, Law, b. 1, c. 3, no. 40.

Law [the law] respecteth the bonds of nature. Wing. Max. p. 268, max. 78; Finch, Law, b. 1, c. 3, no. 29.

LAW SPIRITUAL. The ecclesiastical law, or law Christian. Co. Litt. 344.

LAW TERMS. See TERMS.

LAW WORTHY. Being entitled to, or having the benefit and protection of, the law.

LAWFUL. Legal; warranted or authorized by the law; having the qualifications prescribed by law; not contrary to nor forbidden by the law.

The principal distinction between the terms "lawful" and "legal" is that the former contemplates the substance of law, the latter the form of law. To say of an act that it is "lawful" implies that it is authorized, sanctioned, or at any rate not forbidden, by law. To say that it is "legal" implies that it is done or performed in accordance with the forms and usages of law, or in a technical manner. In this sense "illegal" approaches the meaning of "invalid." For example, a contract or will, executed without the required formalities, might be said to be invalid or illegal, but could not be described as unlawful. Further, the word "lawful" more clearly implies an ethical content than does "legal." The latter goes no further than to denote compliance with positive, technical, or formal rules; while the former usually imports a moral substance or ethical permissibility. A further distinction is that the word "legal" is used as the synonym of "constructive," which "lawful" is not. Thus "legal fraud" is fraud implied or inferred by law, or made out by construction. "Lawful fraud" would be a contradiction of terms. Again, "legal" is used as the antithesis of "equitable." Thus, we speak of "legal assets," "legal estate," etc., but not of "lawful assets" or "lawful estate." But there are some connections in which the two words are used as exact equivalents. Thus, a "lawful" writ, warrant, or process is the same as a "legal" writ, warrant, or process.

LAWFUL AGE. Full age; majority; generally the age of twenty-one years.

LAWFUL AUTHORITIES. The expression "lawful authorities," used in our treaty with Spain, refers to persons who exercised the power of making grants by authority of the crown. 9 Pet. 711.

LAWFUL DISCHARGE. Such a discharge in insolvency as exonerates the debtor from his debts. 12 Wheat. 370.

LAWFUL GOODS. Whatever is not prohibited to be exported by the positive law of the country, even though it be contraband of war; for a neutral has a right to carry such goods at his own risk. 1 Johns. Cas. 1; 2 Johns. Cas. 77; Id. 120.

LAWFUL MAN. A freeman, unattainted, and capable of bearing oath; a *legalis homo*.

LAWFUL MONEY. Money which is a legal tender in payment of debts; *e. g.*, gold and silver coined at the mint.

LAWING OF DOGS. The cutting several claws of the forefeet of dogs in the forest, to prevent their running at deer.

LAWLESS COURT. An ancient local English court, said to have been held in Essex once a year, at cock-crowing, without a light or pen and ink, and conducted in a whisper. Jacob.

LAWLESS MAN. An outlaw.

LAWNDE, LOWNDE. In old English law. A plain between woods. Co. Litt. 5*b*.

LAWS OF OLERON. A maritime code said to have been drawn up by Richard I. at the Isle of Oleron, whence its name. These laws are constantly quoted in proceedings before the admiralty courts, as are also the Rhodian laws. Co. Litt. 11.

LAWS OF WAR. This term denotes a branch of public international law, and comprises the body of rules and principles observed by civilized nations for the regulation of matters inherent in, or incidental to, the conduct of a public war; such, for example, as the relations of neutrals and belligerents, blockades, captures, prizes, truces and armistices, capitulations, prisoners, and declarations of war and peace.

LAWSUIT. A vernacular term for a suit, action, or cause instituted or depending between two private persons in the courts of law.

LAWYER. A person learned in the law; as an attorney, counsel, or solicitor.

Any person who, for fee or reward, prosecutes or defends causes in courts of record or other judicial tribunals of the United States, or of any of the states, or whose business it is to give legal advice in relation to any cause or matter whatever. Act of July 13, 1866, § 9, (14 St. at Large, 121.)

LAY, *v.* To state or allege in pleading.

LAY, *adj.* Relating to persons or things not clerical or ecclesiastical; a person not in ecclesiastical orders. Also non-professional.

LAY, *n.* A share of the profits of a fishing or whaling voyage, allotted to the officers and seamen, in the nature of wages. 3 Story, 108.

LAY CORPORATION. A corporation composed of lay persons or for lay purposes. They are either civil or eleemosynary. Ang. & A. Corp. 28-30; 1 Bl. Comm. 470.

LAY DAMAGES. To state at the conclusion of the declaration the amount of damages which the plaintiff claims.

LAY DAYS. In the law of shipping. Days allowed in charter-parties for loading and unloading the cargo. 3 Kent, Comm. 202, 203.

LAY FEE. A fee held by ordinary feudal tenure, as distinguished from the ecclesiastical tenure of *frankalmoign*, by which an ecclesiastical corporation held of the donor. The tenure of *frankalmoign* is reserved by St. 12 Car. II., which abolished military tenures. 2 Bl. Comm. 101.

LAY IMPROPRIATOR. In English ecclesiastical law. A lay person holding a spiritual appropriation. 3 Steph. Comm. 72.

LAY INVESTITURE. In ecclesiastical law. The ceremony of putting a bishop in possession of the temporalities of his diocese.

LAY OUT. This term has come to be used technically in highway laws as embracing all the series of acts necessary to the complete establishment of a highway. 28 Conn. 375.

LAY PEOPLE. Jurymen.

LAYE. Law.

LAYING THE VENUE. Stating in the margin of a declaration the county in which the plaintiff proposes that the trial of the action shall take place.

LAYMAN. One of the people, and not one of the clergy; one who is not of the legal profession; one who is not of a particular profession.

LAYSTALL. A place for dung or soil.

LAZARET, or LAZARETTO. A pesthouse, or public hospital for persons affected with the more dangerous forms of contagious diseases; a quarantine station for vessels coming from countries where such diseases are prevalent.

LAZZI. A Saxon term for persons of a servile condition.

LE CONGRÈS. A species of proof on charges of impotency in France, *coitus coram testibus.* Abolished A. D. 1677.

Le contrat fait la loi. The contract makes the law.

LE GUIDON DE LA MER. The title of a French work on marine insurance, by an unknown author, dating back, probably, to the sixteenth century, and said to have been prepared for the merchants of Rouen. It is noteworthy as being the earliest treatise on that subject now extant.

Le ley de Dieu et ley de terre sont tout un; et l'un et l'autre preferre et favour le common et publique bien del terre. The law of God and the law of the land are all one; and both preserve and favor the common and public good of the land. Keilw. 191.

Le ley est le plus haut enheritance que le roy ad, car per le ley il mesme et touts ses sujets sont rules; et, si le ley ne fuit, nul roy ne nul enheritance serra. 1 J. H. 6, 63. The law is the highest inheritance that the king possesses, for by the law both he and all his subjects are ruled; and, if there were no law, there would be neither king nor inheritance.

LE ROI, or ROY. The old law-French words for "the king."

LE ROI VEUT EN DELIBERER. The king will deliberate on it. This is the formula which the king of the French used when he intended to veto an act of the legislative assembly. 1 Toullier, no. 42.

LE ROY (or LA REINE) LE VEUT. The king (or the queen) wills it. The form of the royal assent to public bills in parliament.

LE ROY (or LA REINE) REMERCIE SES LOYAL SUJETS, ACCEPTE LEUR BENEVOLENCE, ET AINSI LE VEUT. The king (or the queen) thanks his (or her) loyal subjects, accepts their benevolence, and therefore wills it to be so. The form of the royal assent to a bill of supply.

LE ROY (or LA REINE) S'AVISERA. L. Fr. The king (or queen) will advise upon it. The form of words used to express the refusal of the royal assent to public bills in parliament. 1 Bl. Comm. 184. This is supposed to correspond to the judicial phrase "*curia advisari vult,*" (*q. v.*) 1 Chit. Bl. Comm. 184, note.

Le salut du peuple est la supreme loi. Montesq. Esprit des Lois, l. xxvii. c. 23. The safety of the people is the highest law.

LEA, or LEY. A pasture. Co. Litt. 4*b*.

LEAD. The counsel on either side of a litigated action who is charged with the principal management and direction of the party's case, as distinguished from his juniors or subordinates, is said to "lead in the cause," and is termed the "leading counsel" on that side.

LEADING A USE. Where a deed was executed before the levy of a fine of land, for the purpose of specifying to whose use the fine should inure, it was said to "lead" the use. If executed after the fine, it was said to "declare" the use. 2 Bl. Comm. 363.

LEADING CASE. Among the various cases that are argued and determined in the courts, some, from their important character, have demanded more than usual attention from the judges, and from this circumstance are frequently looked upon as having settled or determined the law upon all points involved in such cases, and as guides for subsequent decisions, and from the importance they thus acquire are familiarly termed "leading cases." Brown.

LEADING COUNSEL. That one of two or more counsel employed on the same side in a cause who has the principal management of the cause.

LEADING QUESTION. A question put or framed in such a form as to suggest the answer sought to be obtained by the person interrogating.

Questions are leading which suggest to the witness the answer desired, or which embody a material fact, and may be answered by a mere negative or affirmative, or which involve an answer bearing immediately upon the merits of the cause, and indicating to the witness a representation which will best accord with the interests of the party propounding them. 8 Smedes & M. 104.

A question is leading which puts into a witness' mouth the words that are to be echoed back, or plainly suggests the answer which the party wishes to get from him. 4 Wend. 229, 247.

LEAGUE. 1. A treaty of alliance between different states or parties. It may be offensive or defensive, or both. It is *offensive* when the contracting parties agree to unite in attacking a common enemy; *defensive* when the parties agree to act in concert in defending each other against an enemy. Wharton.

2. A measure of distance, varying in different countries. The marine league, marking the limit of national jurisdiction on the high seas, is equal to three geographical (or marine) miles of 6,075 feet each.

LEAKAGE. The waste or diminution of a liquid caused by its leaking from the cask, barrel, or other vessel in which it was placed.

Also an allowance made to an importer of liquids, at the custom-house, in the collection of duties, for his loss sustained by the leaking of the liquid from its cask or vessel.

LEAL. Loyal; that which belongs to the law.

LEALTE. Legality; the condition of a *legalis homo*, or lawful man.

LEAN. To incline in opinion or preference. A court is sometimes said to "lean against" a doctrine, construction, or view contended for, whereby it is meant that the court regards it with disfavor or repugnance, because of its inexpedience, injustice, or inconsistency.

LEAP-YEAR. See BISSEXTILE.

LEARNED. Possessing learning; erudite; versed in the law. In statutes prescribing the qualifications of judges, "learned in the law" designates one who has received a regular legal education, the almost invariable evidence of which is the fact of his admission to the bar.

LEARNING. Legal doctrine. 1 Leon. 77.

LEASE. A conveyance of lands or tenements to a person for life, for a term of years, or at will, in consideration of a return of rent or some other recompense. The person who so conveys such lands or tenements is termed the "lessor," and the person to whom they are conveyed, the "lessee;" and when the lessor so conveys lands or tenements to a lessee, he is said to lease, demise, or let them. 4 Cruise, Dig. 58.

A conveyance of any lands or tenements, (usually in consideration of rent or other annual recompense,) made for life, for years, or at will, but always for a less time than the lessor has in the premises; for, if it be for the whole interest, it is more properly an assignment than a lease. 2 Bl. Comm. 317; Shep. Touch. 266; Watk. Conv. 220.

A contract in writing, under seal, whereby a person having a legal estate in hereditaments, corporeal or incorporeal, conveys a portion of his interest to another, in consideration of a certain annual rent or render, or other recompense. Archb. Landl. & Ten. 2.

"Lease" or "hire" is a synallagmatic contract, to which consent alone is sufficient, and by which one party gives to the other the enjoyment of a thing, or his labor, at a fixed price. Civil Code La. art. 2669.

When the contract is bipartite, the one part is called the "lease," the other the "counterpart." In the United States, it is usual that both papers should be executed by both parties; but in England the lease is executed by the lessor alone, and given to the lessee, while the counterpart is executed by the lessee alone, and given to the lessor.

A *concurrent* lease, or lease of a reversion, is one granted for a term which is to commence before the determination of a previous lease of the same land to another person.

An *underlease* or *sublease* is one executed by the lessee of an estate to a third person, conveying the same estate for a shorter term than that for which the lessee holds it.

LEASE AND RELEASE. A species of conveyance much used in England, said to have been invented by Serjeant Moore, soon after the enactment of the statute of uses. It is thus contrived: A lease, or rather bargain and sale upon some pecuniary consideration for one year, is made by the tenant of the freehold to the lessee or bargainee. This, without any enrolment, makes the bargainor stand seised to the use of the bargainee, and vests in the bargainee the use of the term for one year, and then the statute immediately annexes the *possession*. Being thus in possession, he is capable of receiving a release of the freehold and reversion, which must be made to the tenant in possession, and accordingly the next day a release is granted to him. The lease and release, when used as a conveyance of the fee, have the joint operation of a single conveyance. 2 Bl. Comm. 339; 4 Kent, Comm. 482; Co. Litt. 207; Cruise, Dig. tit. 32, c. 11.

LEASEHOLD. An estate in realty held under a lease; an estate for a fixed term of years.

LEASING, or LESING. Gleaning.

LEASING-MAKING. In old Scotch criminal law. An offense consisting in slanderous and untrue speeches, to the disdain, reproach, and contempt of the king, his council and proceedings, etc. Bell.

LEAUTE. L. Fr. Legality; sufficiency in law. Britt. c. 109.

LEAVE. To give or dispose of by will. "The word 'leave,' as applied to the subject-matter, *prima facie* means a disposition by will." 10 East, 438.

LEAVE AND LICENSE. A defense to an action in trespass setting up the consent of the plaintiff to the trespass complained of.

LEAVE OF COURT. Permission obtained from a court to take some action which, without such permission, would not be allowable.

LECCATOR. A debauched person. Cowell.

LECHERWITE, LAIRWITE, or LEGERWITE. A fine for adultery or fornication, anciently paid to the lords of certain manors. 4 Inst. 206.

LECTOR DE LETRA ANTIQUA. In Spanish law. A person appointed by competent authority to read and decipher ancient writings, to the end that they may be presented on the trial of causes as documents entitled to legal credit. Escriche.

LECTRINUM. A pulpit. Mon. Angl. tom. iii. p. 243.

LECTURER. An instructor; a reader of lectures; also a clergyman who assists rectors, etc., in preaching, etc.

LEDGER. A book of accounts in which a trader enters the names of all persons with whom he has dealings; there being two parallel columns in each account, one for the entries to the debit of the person charged, the other for his credits. Into this book are posted the items from the day-book or journal.

LEDGER-BOOK. In ecclesiastical law. The name of a book kept in the prerogative courts in England. It is considered as a roll of the court, but, it seems, it cannot be read in evidence. Bac. Abr.

LEDGREVIUS. In old English law. A lathe-reeve, or chief officer of a lathe. Spelman.

LEDO. The rising water or increase of the sea.

LEET. In English law. The name of a court of criminal jurisdiction, formerly of much importance, but latterly fallen into disuse. See COURT-LEET.

LEETS. Meetings which were appointed for the nomination or election of ecclesiastical officers in Scotland. Cowell.

LEGA, or LACTA. The alloy of money. Spelman.

LEGABILIS. In old English law. That which may be bequeathed. Cowell.

LEGACY. A bequest or gift of personal property by last will and testament.

The word "legacy" properly imports a gift of *personal*, as "devise" does a gift of *real*, property; but it may, by reference and construction, be descriptive of real estate. 1 Burrows, 268, 272; 3 Term, 716.

Legacies are distinguished and designated, according to their nature, as follows: (1) A legacy of a particular thing, specified, and distinguished from all others of the same kind belonging to the testator, is specific. If such legacy fails, resort cannot be had to the other property of the testator. (2) A legacy is demonstrative when the particular fund or personal property is pointed out, from which it is to be taken or paid. If such fund or property fails, in whole or in part, resort may be had to the general assets, as in case of a general legacy. (3) An annuity is a bequest of certain specified sums periodically. If the fund or property out of which they are payable fails, resort may be had to the general assets, as in case of a general legacy. (4) A residuary legacy embraces only that which remains after all the bequests of the will are discharged. (5) All other legacies are general legacies. Civil Code Dak. § 755.

An *absolute* legacy is one given without condition, to vest immediately. 1 Vern. 254; 2 Vern. 181; 5 Ves. 461; 19 Ves. 86.

An *additional* legacy is one given to the same legatee in addition to (not in lieu of) another legacy given before by the same will or in a codicil thereto.

An *alternate* legacy is one by which the testator gives one of two or more things without designating which.

A *conditional* legacy is a bequest whose existence depends upon the happening or not happening of some uncertain event. 1 Rop. Leg. 500.

A *cumulative* legacy is an additional legacy, this being its more proper technical name.

A *demonstrative* legacy is a gift of money or other fungible substance in quantity, expressed to be made payable out of a specified sum of money or other specified fungible substance.

A *general* legacy is one so given as not to amount to a bequest of a particular thing or money of the testator, distinguished from all others of the same kind. 1 Rop. Leg. 170.

An *indefinite* legacy is one which passes property by a general or collective term, without enumeration of number or quantity; as a bequest of all the testator's "goods," or his "bank-stock." Lown. Leg. 84.

A *lapsed* legacy is one which, in consequence of the death of the legatee before the testator or before the period for vesting, has never vested.

A *modal* legacy is a bequest accompanied with directions as to the mode in which it should be applied for the legatee's benefit; for example, a legacy to A., to put him an apprentice. Lown. Leg. 151.

A *pecuniary* legacy is a bequest of a sum of money. It may or may not specify the fund from which it is to be drawn. It is not the less a pecuniary legacy if it comprises the specific pieces of money in a designated receptacle, as a purse or chest.

A *residuary* legacy is a bequest of all the testator's personal estate not otherwise effectually disposed of by his will. Lown. Leg. 10; Bac. Abr. "Legacies," I; 6 H. L. Cas. 217.

A *specific* legacy is a gift of a particular portion of the testator's personal estate, specified and distinguished from the rest; or a bequest of ear-marked money or of other ear-marked fungible substance, in mass, or of any non-fungible substance by description.

A *trust* legacy is a bequest of personal property to trustees to be held upon trust; as to pay the annual income to a beneficiary for life.

LEGACY DUTY. A duty imposed in England upon personal property (other than leaseholds) devolving under any will or intestacy. Brown.

LEGAL. 1. Conforming to the law; according to law; required or permitted by law; not forbidden or discountenanced by law; good and effectual in law.

2. Proper or sufficient to be recognized by the law; cognizable in the courts; competent or adequate to fulfill the requirements of the law.

3. Cognizable in courts of law, as distinguished from courts of equity; construed or governed by the rules and principles of law, in contradistinction to rules of equity.

4. Posited by the courts as the inference or imputation of the law, as a matter of construction, rather than established by actual proof; *e. g.*, legal malice. See LAWFUL.

LEGAL ASSETS. That portion of the assets of a deceased party which by law is directly liable, in the hands of his executor or administrator, to the payment of debts and legacies. 1 Story, Eq. Jur. § 551. Such assets as can be reached in the hands of an executor or administrator, by a suit at law against him.

LEGAL CONSIDERATION. One recognized or permitted by the law as valid and lawful; as distinguished from such as are illegal or immoral.

LEGAL CRUELTY. Such as will warrant the granting of a divorce to the injured party; as distinguished from such kinds or degrees of cruelty as do not, under the statutes and decisions, amount to sufficient cause for a decree.

Legal cruelty may be defined to be such conduct on the part of the husband as will endanger the life, limb, or health of the wife, or create a reasonable apprehension of bodily hurt; such acts as render cohabitation unsafe, or are likely to be attended with injury to the person or to the health of the wife. 36 Ga. 286.

LEGAL DEBTS. Those that are recoverable in a court of common law, as debt on a bill of exchange, a bond, or a simple contract.

LEGAL DEFENSE. 1. A defense which is complete and adequate in point of law.

2. A defense which may be set up in a court of law; as distinguished from an "equitable defense," which is cognizable only in a court of equity or court possessing equitable powers.

LEGAL DISCRETION. The discretion to be exercised by a judge in interpreting the law, or in applying equitable principles to the determination of causes or the granting of relief.

LEGAL ESTATE. That kind of estate which is properly cognizable in the courts of common law, though noticed, also, in the courts of equity. 1 Steph. Comm. 217.

LEGAL HEIRS. This phrase, used in a devise or a policy of life insurance, will be held to mean those to whom the law would give the person's property, real and personal, if he should die intestate. 88 Ill. 251; (Tex.) 8 S. W. Rep. 203.

LEGAL HOLIDAY. A day designated by law as exempt from judicial proceedings, service of process, demand and protest of commercial paper, etc.

LEGAL INCAPACITY. This expression implies that the person in view has the right vested in him, but is prevented by some impediment from exercising it; as in the case of minors, *femes covert*, lunatics, etc.

An administrator has no right until letters are issued to him. Therefore he cannot benefit (as respects the time before obtaining letters) by a saving clause in a statute of limitations in favor of persons under a legal incapacity to sue. 1 Root, 187.

LEGAL INTEREST. That rate of interest prescribed by the laws of the particular state or country as the highest which may be lawfully contracted for or exacted, and which must be paid in all cases where the law allows interest without the assent of the debtor.

LEGAL IRREGULARITY. An irregularity occurring in the course of some legal proceeding. A defect or informality which, in the technical view of the law, is to be accounted an irregularity.

LEGAL MALICE. An expression used as the equivalent of "constructive malice," or "malice in law." 52 Me. 502.

LEGAL MEMORY. See MEMORY.

LEGAL MORTGAGE. A term used in Louisiana. The law alone in certain cases gives to the creditor a mortgage on the property of his debtor, without it being requisite that the parties should stipulate it. This is called "legal mortgage." Civil Code La. art. 3311.

LEGAL NOTICE. Such notice as is adequate in point of law; such notice as the law requires to be given for the specific purpose or in the particular case.

LEGAL REPRESENTATIVE. A person who, in the law, represents the person and controls the rights of another. The phrase is commonly used as the equivalent of "executor" or "administrator."

The term imports a higher authority than "agent," for an agent acts for his principal, who retains the beneficial right; but the legal representative succeeds to the place of the former owner, and is vested with his title.

LEGAL REVERSION. In Scotch law. The period within which a proprietor is at liberty to redeem land adjudged from him for debt.

LEGAL TENDER. That kind of coin, money, or circulating medium which the law compels a creditor to accept in payment of his debt, when tendered by the debtor in the right amount.

LEGALIS HOMO. Lat. A lawful man; a person who stands *rectus in curia;* a person not outlawed, excommunicated, or infamous. It occurs in the phrase, "*probi et legales homines,*" (good and lawful men, competent jurors,) and "legality" designates the condition of such a man. Jacob.

LEGALIS MONETA ANGLIÆ. Lawful money of England. 1 Inst. 207.

LEGALITY, or LEGALNESS. Lawfulness.

LEGALIZATION. The act of legalizing or making legal or lawful. See LEGALIZE.

LEGALIZE. To make legal or lawful; to confirm or validate what was before void or unlawful; to add the sanction and authority of law to that which before was without or against law.

LEGALLY. Lawfully; according to law.

LEGANTINE CONSTITUTIONS. The name of a code of ecclesiastical laws, enacted in national synods, held under legates from Pope Gregory IX. and Clement IV., in the reign of Henry III., about the years 1220 and 1268. 1 Bl. Comm. 83.

LEGARE. Lat. In the civil and old English law. To bequeath; to leave or give by will; to give in anticipation of death. In Scotch phrase, to *legate*.

LEGATARIUS. Lat. In the civil law. One to whom a thing is bequeathed; a legatee or legatary. Inst. 2, 20, 2, 4, 5, 10; Bract. fol. 40.

In old European law. A legate, messenger, or envoy. Spelman.

LEGATEE. The person to whom a legacy is given.

LEGATES. Nuncios, deputies, or extraordinary ambassadors sent by the pope to be his representatives and to exercise his jurisdiction in countries where the Roman Catholic Church is established by law.

LEGATION. An embassy; a diplomatic minister and his suite; the persons commissioned by one government to exercise diplomatic functions at the court of another, including the minister, secretaries, *attachés*, interpreters, etc., are collectively styled the "legation" of their government. The word also denotes the official residence of a foreign minister.

LEGATOR. One who makes a will, and leaves legacies.

LEGATORY. The third part of a freeman's personal estate, which by the custom of London, in case he had a wife and children, the freeman might always have disposed of by will. Bac. Abr. "Customs of London," D. 4.

Legatos violare contra jus gentium est. 4 Coke, pref. It is contrary to the law of nations to injure ambassadors.

LEGATUM. Lat. In the civil law. A legacy; a gift left by a deceased person, to be executed by the heir. Inst. 2, 20, 1.

In old English law. A legacy given to the church, or an accustomed mortuary. Cowell.

Legatum morte testatoris tantum confirmatur, sicut donatio inter vivos traditione sola. Dyer, 143. A legacy is confirmed by the death of a testator, in the same manner as a gift from a living person is by delivery alone.

LEGATUM OPTIONIS. In Roman law. A legacy to A. B. of any article or articles that A. B. liked to choose or select out of the testator's estate. If A. B. died after the testator, but before making the choice or selection, his representative (*hæres*) could not, prior to Justinian, make the selection for him, but the legacy failed altogether. Justinian, however, made the legacy good, and enabled the representative to choose. Brown.

Legatus regis vice fungitur a quo destinatur et honorandus est sicut ille cujus vicem gerit. 12 Coke, 17. An ambassador fills the place of the king by whom he is sent, and is to be honored as he is whose place he fills.

LEGEM AMITTERE. Lat. To lose one's law; that is, to lose one's privilege of being admitted to take an oath.

LEGEM FACERE. L. Lat. In old English law. To make law or oath.

LEGEM FERRE. Lat. In Roman law. To propose a law to the people for their adoption. Heinecc. Ant. Rom. lib. 1, tit. 2.

LEGEM HABERE. Lat. To be capable of giving evidence upon oath. Witnesses who had been convicted of crime were incapable of giving evidence, until 6 & 7 Vict. c. 85.

LEGEM JUBERE. Lat. In Roman law. To give consent and authority to a proposed law; to make or pass it. Tayl. Civil Law, 9.

LEGEM SCISCERE. Lat. To give consent and authority to a proposed law; applied to the consent of the people.

Legem terræ amittentes, perpetuam infamiæ notam inde merito incurrunt. Those who lose the law of the land, then justly incur the ineffaceable brand of infamy. 3 Inst. 221.

LEGEM VADIARE. In old English law. To wage law; to offer or to give pledge to make defense, by oath, with compurgators.

LEGES. Lat. Laws. At Rome, the *leges* (the decrees of the people in a strict sense) were laws which were proposed by a magistrate presiding in the senate, and adopted by the Roman people in the *comitia centuriata*. Mackeld. Rom. Law, § 31.

LEGES ANGLIÆ. Lat. The laws of England, as distinguished from the civil law and other foreign systems.

Leges Angliæ sunt tripartitæ,—jus commune, consuetudines, ac decreta comitiorum. The laws of England are threefold,—common law, customs, and decrees of parliament.

Leges figendi et refigendi consuetudo est periculosissima. The practice of fixing and refixing [making and remaking] the laws is a most dangerous one. 4 Coke, pref.

Leges humanæ nascuntur, vivunt, et moriuntur. Human laws are born, live, and die. 7 Coke, 25; 2 Atk. 674; 11 C. B. 767; 1 Bl. Comm. 89.

Leges naturæ perfectissimæ sunt et immutabiles; humani vero juris conditio semper in infinitum decurrit, et nihil est in eo quod perpetuo stare possit. Leges humanæ nascuntur, vivunt, moriuntur. The laws of nature are most perfect and immutable; but the condition of human law is an unending succession, and there is nothing in it which can continue perpetually. Human laws are born, live, and die. 7 Coke, 25.

LEGES NON SCRIPTÆ. Lat. In English law. Unwritten or customary laws, including those ancient acts of parliament which were made before time of memory. Hale, Com. Law, 5. See 1 Bl. Comm. 63, 64.

Leges non verbis, sed rebus, sunt impositæ. Laws are imposed, not on words, but things. 10 Coke, 101; Branch, Princ.

Leges posteriores priores contrarias abrogant. Later laws abrogate prior laws that are contrary to them. Broom, Max. 27, 29.

LEGES SCRIPTÆ. Lat. In English law. Written laws; statute laws, or acts of parliament which are originally reduced into writing before they are enacted, or receive any binding power. Hale, Com. Law, 1, 2.

LEGES SUB GRAVIORI LEGE. Laws under a weightier law. Hale, Com. Law, 46, 44.

Leges suum ligent latorem. Laws should bind their own maker. Fleta, lib. 1, c. 17, § 11.

LEGES TABELLARIÆ. Lat. Roman laws regulating the mode of voting by ballot, (*tabella.*) 1 Kent, Comm. 232, note.

Leges vigilantibus, non dormientibus, subveniunt. The laws aid the vigilant, not the negligent. 5 Johns. Ch. 122, 145; 16 How. Pr. 142, 144.

LEGIBUS SOLUTUS. Lat. Released from the laws; not bound by the laws. An expression applied in the Roman civil law to the emperor. Calvin.

Legibus sumptis desinentibus, lege naturæ utendum est. When laws imposed by the state fail, we must act by the law of nature. 2 Rolle, 298.

LEGIOSUS. In old records. Litigious, and so subjected to a course of law. Cowell.

Legis constructio non facit injuriam. Co. Litt. 183. The construction of law does no injury.

Legis interpretatio legis vim obtinet. Ellesm. Postn. 55. The interpretation of law obtains the force of law.

Legis minister non tenetur in executione officii sui, fugere aut retrocedere. The minister of the law is bound, in the execution of his office, not to fly nor to retreat. Branch, Princ.

LEGISLATION. The act of giving or enacting laws.

LEGISLATIVE POWER. The law-making power; the department of government whose function is the framing and enactment of laws.

LEGISLATOR. One who makes laws.

Legislatorum est viva vox, rebus et non verbis legem imponere. The voice of legislators is a living voice, to impose laws on things, and not on words. 10 Coke, 101.

LEGISLATURE. The department, assembly, or body of men that makes laws for a state or nation; a legislative body.

LEGISPERITUS. A person skilled or learned in the law; a lawyer or advocate. Feud. lib. 2, tit. 1.

LEGIT VEL NON? In old English practice, this was the formal question propounded to the ordinary when a prisoner claimed the benefit of clergy,—does he read or not? If the ordinary found that the prisoner was entitled to clergy, his formal answer was, "*Legit ut clericus,*" he reads like a clerk.

LEGITIM. In Scotch law. The children's share in the father's movables.

LEGITIMACY. Lawful birth; the condition of being born in wedlock; the opposite of illegitimacy or bastardy.

LEGITIMATE, *v.* To make lawful; to confer legitimacy; to place a child born before marriage on the footing of those born in lawful wedlock. 26 Vt. 653, 657, 658.

LEGITIMATE, *adj.* That which is lawful, legal, recognized by law, or according to law; as legitimate children, legitimate authority, or lawful power.

LEGITIMATION. The making legitimate or lawful that which was not originally so; especially the act of legalizing the *status* of a bastard.

LEGITIMATION PER SUBSEQUENS MATRIMONIUM. The legitimation of a bastard by the subsequent marriage of his parents. Bell.

LEGITIME. Lat. In the civil law. That portion of a parent's estate of which he cannot disinherit his children without a legal cause.

Legitime imperanti parere necesse est. Jenk. Cent. 120. One lawfully commanding must be obeyed.

LEGITIMI HÆREDES. Lat. In Roman law. Legitimate heirs; the agnate relations of the estate-leaver; so called because the inheritance was given to them by a law of the Twelve Tables.

LEGITIMUS. Lawful; legitimate. *Legitimus hæres et filius est quem nuptiæ* *demonstrant*, a lawful son and heir is he whom the marriage points out to be lawful. Bract. fol. 63.

LEGO. Lat. In Roman law. I bequeath. A common term in wills. Dig. 30, 36, 81, et seq.

LEGRUITA. In old records. A fine for criminal conversation with a woman.

LEGULEIUS. A person skilled in law, (*in legibus versatus;*) one versed in the forms of law. Calvin.

LEIDGRAVE. An officer under the Saxon government, who had jurisdiction over a lath. Enc. Lond. See LATH.

LEIPA. In old English law. A fugitive or runaway.

LENDER. He from whom a thing is borrowed. The bailor of an article loaned.

LENT. The quadragesimal fast; a time of abstinence; the time from Ash-Wednesday to Easter.

LEOD. People; a people; a nation. Spelman.

LEODES. In old European law. A vassal, or liege man; service; a *were* or *weregild*. Spelman.

LEOHT-GESCEOT. A tax for supplying the church with lights. Anc. Inst. Eng.

LEONINA SOCIETAS. Lat. An attempted partnership, in which one party was to bear all the losses, and have no share in the profits. This was a void partnership in Roman law; and, apparently, it would also be void as a partnership in English law, as being inherently inconsistent with the notion of partnership. (Dig. 17, 2, 29, 2.) Brown.

LEP AND LACE. A custom in the manor of Writtle, in Essex, that every cart which goes over Greenbury within that manor (except it be the cart of a nobleman) shall pay 4d. to the lord. Blount.

LEPORARIUS. A greyhound. Cowell.

LEPORIUM. A place where hares are kept. Mon. Angl. t. 2, p. 1035.

LEPROSO AMOVENDO. An ancient writ that lay to remove a leper or lazar, who thrust himself into the company of his neighbors in any parish, either in the church or at other public meetings, to their annoyance. Reg. Orig. 237.

LESCHEWES. Trees fallen by chance or wind-falls. Brooke, Abr. 341.

LESE MAJESTY. The old English and Scotch translation of "*læsa majestas*," or high treason. 2 Reeve, Eng. Law, 6.

LESION. Fr. Damage; injury; detriment. Kelham. A term of the Scotch law.

In the civil law. The injury suffered by one who does not receive a full equivalent for what he gives in a commutative contract. Civil Code La. art. 1860.

Inequality in contracts. Poth. Obl., no. 33.

LESPEGEND. An inferior officer in forests to take care of the vert and venison therein, etc. Wharton.

LESSEE. He to whom a lease is made. He who holds an estate by virtue of a lease.

LESSOR. He who grants a lease.

LESSOR OF THE PLAINTIFF. In the action of ejectment, this was the party who really and in effect prosecuted the action and was interested in its result. The reason of his having been so called arose from the circumstance of the action having been carried on in the name of a nominal plaintiff, (John Doe,) to whom the real plaintiff had granted a fictitious lease, and thus had become his lessor.

LEST. Fr. In French maritime law. Ballast. Ord. Mar. liv. 4, tit. 4, art. 1.

LESTAGE, LASTAGE. A custom for carrying things in fairs and markets. Fleta, l. 1, c. 47; Termes de la Ley.

LESTAGEFRY. Lestage free, or exempt from the duty of paying ballast money. Cowell.

LESTAGIUM. Lastage or lestage; a duty laid on the cargo of a ship. Cowell.

LESWES. Pastures. Domesday; Co. Litt. 4*b*. A term often inserted in old deeds and conveyances. Cowell.

LET, *v.* **In conveyancing.** To demise or lease. "To *let* and set" is an old expression.

In practice. To deliver. "To *let* to bail" is to deliver to bail on arrest.

In contracts. To award to one of several persons, who have submitted proposals therefor, the contract for erecting public works or doing some part of the work connected therewith, or rendering some other service to government for a stipulated compensation.

Letting the contract is the choosing one from among the number of bidders, and the formal making of the contract with him. The letting, or putting out, is a different thing from the invitation to make proposals; the letting is subsequent to the invitation. It is the act of awarding the contract to the proposer, after the proposals have been received and considered. See 35 Ala. 33, 55.

LET, *n.* In old conveyancing. Hindrance; obstruction; interruption. Still occasionally used in the phrase "without any *let*, suit, trouble," etc.

LET IN. In practice. To admit a party as a matter of favor; as to open a judgment and "let the defendant in" to a defense.

LETHAL WEAPON. In Scotch law. A deadly weapon.

LETRADO. In Spanish law. An advocate. White, New Recop. b. 1, tit. 1, c. 1, § 3, note.

LETTER. 1. One of the arbitrary marks or characters constituting the alphabet, and used in written language as the representatives of sounds or articulations of the human organs of speech. Several of the letters of the English alphabet have a special significance in jurisprudence, as abbreviations and otherwise, or are employed as numerals.

2. A dispatch or epistle; a written or printed message; a communication in writing from one person to another at a distance.

3. In the imperial law of Rome, "letter" or "epistle" was the name of the answer returned by the emperor to a question of law submitted to him by the magistrates.

4. A commission, patent, or written instrument containing or attesting the grant of some power, authority, or right. The word appears in this generic sense in many compound phrases known to commercial law and jurisprudence; *e. g.*, letter of attorney, letter missive, letter of credit, letters patent. The plural is frequently used.

5. Metaphorically, the verbal expression; the strict literal meaning. The *letter* of a statute, as distinguished from its *spirit*, means the strict and exact force of the language employed, as distinguished from the general purpose and policy of the law.

6. He who, being the owner of a thing, lets it out to another for hire or compensation. Story, Bailm. § 369.

LETTER-BOOK. A book in which a merchant or trader keeps copies of letters sent by him to his correspondents.

LETTER-CARRIER. An employe of the post-office, whose duty it is to carry letters from the post-office to the persons to whom they are addressed.

LETTER MISSIVE. In English law. A letter from the king or queen to a dean and chapter, containing the name of the person whom he would have them elect as bishop. 1 Steph. Comm. 666. A request addressed to a peer, peeress, or lord of parliament against whom a bill has been filed desiring the defendant to appear and answer to the bill.

In civil-law practice. The phrase "letters missive," or "letters dimissory," is sometimes used to denote the papers sent up on an appeal by the judge or court below to the superior tribunal, otherwise called the "apostles," (*q. v.*)

LETTER OF ADVICE. A communication from one person to another, advising or warning the latter of something which he ought to know, and commonly apprising him beforehand of some act done by the writer which will ultimately affect the recipient.

It is usual and perfectly proper for the drawer of a bill of exchange to write a letter of advice to the drawee, as well to prevent fraud or alteration of the bill, as to let the drawee know what provision has been made for the payment of the bill. Chit. Bills, 162.

LETTER OF ADVOCATION. In Scotch law. The process or warrant by which, on appeal to the supreme court or court of session, that tribunal assumes to itself jurisdiction of the cause, and discharges the lower court from all further proceedings in the action. Ersk. Inst. 732.

LETTER OF ATTORNEY. A power of attorney; a written instrument by which one person constitutes another his true and lawful attorney, in order that the latter may do for the former, and in his place and stead, some lawful act.

LETTER OF CREDENCE. In international law. The document which accredits an ambassador, minister, or envoy to the court or government to which he is sent; *i. e.*, certifies to his appointment and qualification, and bespeaks credit for his official actions and representations.

LETTER OF CREDIT. An open or sealed letter, from a merchant in one place, directed to another, in another place or country, requiring him, if a person therein named, or the bearer of the letter, shall have occasion to buy commodities, or to want money to any particular or unlimited amount, either to procure the same or to pass his promise, bill, or bond for it, the writer of the letter undertaking to provide him the money for the goods, or to repay him by exchange, or to give him such satisfaction as he shall require, either for himself, or the bearer of the letter. 3 Chit. Com. Law, 336.

A letter of credit is a written instrument, addressed by one person to another, requesting the latter to give credit to the person in whose favor it is drawn. Civil Code Cal. § 2858.

LETTER OF EXCHANGE. A bill of exchange, (*q. v.*)

LETTER OF LICENSE. A letter or written instrument given by creditors to their debtor, who has failed in trade, etc., allowing him longer time for the payment of his debts, and protecting him from arrest in the mean time. Tomlins; Holthouse.

LETTER OF MARQUE. A commission given to a private ship by a government to make reprisals on the ships of another state; hence, also, the ship thus commissioned.

LETTER OF RECALL. A document addressed by the executive of one nation to that of another, informing the latter that a minister sent by the former has been recalled.

LETTER OF RECOMMENDATION. A writing whereby one person certifies concerning another that he is of good character, solvent, possessed of commercial credit, skilled in his trade or profession, or otherwise worthy of trust, aid, or employment. It may be addressed to an individual or to whom it may concern, and is designed to aid the person commended in obtaining credit, employment, etc. See 13 How. 198.

LETTER OF RECREDENTIALS. A document embodying the formal action of a government upon a letter of recall of a foreign minister. It, in effect, accredits him back to his own government. It is addressed to the latter government, and is delivered to the minister by the diplomatic secretary of the state from which he is recalled.

LETTERS AD COLLIGENDUM BONA DEFUNCTI. In practice. In default of the representatives and creditors to administer to the estate of an intestate, the officer entitled to grant letters of administration may grant, to such persons as he approves, *letters to collect the goods of the deceased*, which neither make him executor nor administrator; his only business being to collect the goods and keep them in his safe custody. 2 Bl. Comm. 505.

LETTERS CLOSE. In English law. Close letters are grants of the king, and, being of private concern, they are thus distinguished from letters patent.

LETTERS OF ABSOLUTION. Absolvatory letters, used in former times, when an abbot released any of his brethren *ab omnia subjectione et obedientia*, etc., and made them capable of entering into some other order of religion. Jacob.

LETTERS OF ADMINISTRATION. The instrument by which an administrator or administratrix is authorized by the probate court, surrogate, or other proper officer, to have the charge and administration of the goods and chattels of an intestate.

LETTERS OF CORRESPONDENCE. In Scotch law. Letters are admissible in evidence against the panel, *i. e.*, the prisoner at the bar, in criminal trials. A letter written by the panel is evidence against him; not so one from a third party found in his possession. Bell.

LETTERS OF FIRE AND SWORD. See FIRE AND SWORD.

LETTERS OF HORNING, in the law Scotland, are letters running in the sovereign's name and passing the signet. They are directed to messengers at arms, as sheriffs in that part, (*i. e.*, persons specially appointed to perform particular duties appertaining to the office of sheriff,) to charge the person against whom the letters are directed to pay or perform in terms of the "will" of the letters, which must be consistent with the warrant on which the letters proceed. The warrant on which the letters proceed is a decree either of the court of session or of some inferior court. Bell.

LETTERS OF REQUEST. A formal instrument by which an inferior judge of ecclesiastical jurisdiction requests the judge of a superior court to take and determine any matter which has come before him, thereby waiving or remitting his own jurisdiction. This is a mode of beginning a suit originally in the court of arches, instead of the consistory court.

LETTERS OF SAFE CONDUCT. No subject of a nation at war with England can, by the law of nations, come into the realm, nor can travel himself upon the high seas, or send his goods and merchandise from one place to another, without danger of being seized, unless he has *letters of safe conduct*, which, by divers old statutes, must be granted under the great seal, and enrolled in chancery, or else are of no effect; the sovereign being the best judge of such emergencies as may deserve exemption from the general law of arms. But passports or licenses from the ambassadors abroad are now more usually obtained, and are allowed to be of equal validity. Wharton.

LETTERS OF SLAINS, or SLANES. Letters subscribed by the relatives of a person who had been slain, declaring that they had received an assythment, and concurring in an application to the crown for a pardon to the offender. These or other evidences of their concurrence were necessary to found the application. Bell.

LETTERS PATENT. Open letters, as distinguished from letters close. An instrument proceeding from the government, and conveying a right, authority, or grant to an individual, as a patent for a tract of land, or for the exclusive right to make and sell a new invention. Familiarly termed a "patent."

LETTERS ROGATORY. A formal communication in writing, sent by a court in which an action is pending to a court or judge of a foreign country, requesting that the testimony of a witness resident within the jurisdiction of the latter court may be there formally taken under its direction and transmitted to the first court for use in the pending action. This process was also in use, at an early period, between the several states of the Union. The request rests entirely upon the comity of courts towards each other.

LETTERS TESTAMENTARY. The formal instrument of authority and appointment given to an executor by the proper court, empowering him to enter upon the discharge of his office as executor. It corresponds to letters of administration granted to an administrator.

LETTING OUT. The act of awarding a contract; *e. g.*, a construction contract, or contract for carrying the mails.

LETTRE. In French law. A letter. It is used, like our English "letter," for a formal instrument giving authority.

LETTRES DE CACHET. Letters issued and signed by the kings of France, and countersigned by a secretary of state, authorizing the imprisonment of a person. It is said that they were devised by Père Joseph, under the administration of Richelieu. They were at first made use of occasionally as a means of delaying the course of justice; but during the reign of Louis XIV. they were obtained by any person of sufficient influence with the king or his ministers. Under them, persons were imprisoned for life or for a long period on the most frivolous pretexts, for the gratification of private pique or revenge, and without any reason being assigned for such punishment. They were also granted by the king for the purpose of shielding his favorites or their friends from the consequences of their crimes; and thus were as pernicious in their operation as the protection afforded by the church to criminals in a former age. Abolished during the Revolution of 1789. Wharton.

LEUCA. In old French law. A league, consisting of fifteen hundred paces. Spelman.

In old English law. A league or mile of a thousand paces. Domesday; Spelman.

A privileged space around a monastery of a league or mile in circuit. Spelman.

LEVANDÆ NAVIS CAUSA. Lat. For the sake of lightening the ship; denotes a purpose of throwing overboard goods, which renders them subjects of general average.

LEVANT ET COUCHANT. L. Fr. Rising up and lying down. A term applied to trespassing cattle which have remained long enough upon land to have lain down to rest and risen up to feed; generally the space of a night and a day, or, at least, one night.

LEVANTES ET CUBANTES. Rising up and lying down. A term applied to cattle. 3 Bl. Comm. 9.

LEVARI FACIAS. Lat. In English practice. A writ of execution directing the sheriff to cause to be made of the lands and chattels of the judgment debtor the sum recovered by the judgment.

Also a writ to the bishop of the diocese, commanding him to enter into the benefice of a judgment debtor, and take and sequester the same into his possession, and hold the same until he shall have levied the amount of the judgment out of the rents, tithes, and profits thereof.

In American law. A writ used to sell lands mortgaged, after a judgment has been obtained by the mortgagee, or his assignee, against the mortgagor, under a peculiar proceeding authorized by statute. 3 Bouv. Inst. no. 3396.

LEVARI FACIAS DAMNA DE DISSEISITORIBUS. A writ formerly directed to the sheriff for the levying of damages, which a disseisor had been condemned to pay to the disseisee. Cowell.

LEVARI FACIAS QUANDO VICECOMES RETURNAVIT QUOD NON HABUIT EMPTORES. An old writ commanding the sheriff to sell the goods of a debtor which he had already taken, and had returned that he could not sell them; and as much more of the debtor's goods as would satisfy the whole debt. Cowell.

LEVARI FACIAS RESIDUUM DEBITI. An old writ directed to the sheriff for levying the remnant of a partly-satisfied debt upon the lands and tenements or chattels of the debtor. Cowell.

LEVATO VELO. Lat. An expression used in the Roman law, and applied to the trial of wreck and salvage. Commentators disagree about the origin of the expression; but all agree that its general meaning is that these causes shall be heard summarily. The most probable solution is that it refers to the place where causes were heard. A sail was spread before the door and officers employed to keep strangers from the tribunal. When these causes were heard, this sail was raised, and suitors came directly to the court, and their causes were heard immediately. As applied to maritime courts, its meaning is that causes should be heard without delay. These causes require dispatch, and a delay amounts practically to a denial of justice. (See Cod. 11, 4, 5.) Bouvier.

LEVIABLE. That which may be levied.

LEVIR. In Roman law. A husband's brother; a wife's brother-in-law. Calvin.

LEVIS. Lat. Light; slight; trifling. *Levis culpa*, slight fault or neglect. *Levissima culpa*, the slightest neglect. *Levis nota*, a slight mark or brand.

LEVITICAL DEGREES. Degrees of kindred within which persons are prohibited to marry. They are set forth in the eighteenth chapter of Leviticus.

LEVY, *v.* To raise; execute; exact; collect; gather; take up; seize. Thus, to levy (raise or collect) a tax; to levy (raise or set up) a nuisance; to levy (acknowledge) a fine; to levy (inaugurate) war; to levy an execution, *i. e.*, to levy or collect a sum of money on an execution.

LEVY, *n.* In practice. A seizure; the raising of the money for which an execution has been issued.

LEVY COURT. A court formerly existing in the District of Columbia. It was a body charged with the administration of the ministerial and financial duties of Washington county. It was charged with the duty of laying out and repairing roads, building bridges, providing poor-houses, laying and collecting the taxes necessary to enable it to discharge these and other duties, and to pay the other expenses of the county. It had capacity to make contracts in reference to any of these matters, and to raise money to meet such contracts. It had perpetual succession, and its functions were those which, in the several states, are performed by "county commissioners," "overseers of the poor," "county supervisors," and similar bodies with other designations. 2 Wall. 507.

LEVYING WAR. In criminal law. The assembling of a body of men for the purpose of effecting by force a treasonable object; and all who perform any part, however minute, or however remote from the scene of action, and who are leagued in the general conspiracy, are considered as engaged in levying war, within the meaning of the constitution. 4 Cranch, 473, 474; Const. art. 3, § 3.

LEWDNESS. Licentiousness; an offense against the public economy, when of an open and notorious character; as by frequenting houses of ill fame, which is an indictable offense, or by some grossly scandalous and public indecency, for which the punishment at common law is fine and imprisonment. Wharton.

LEX. Lat. Law; a law; the law. In the Roman jurisprudence this term was often used as the synonym of "*jus*," in the sense of a rule of civil conduct authoritatively prescribed for the government of the actions of the members of an organized jural society.

In a more limited and particular sense, it was a resolution adopted by the whole Roman "*populus*" (patricians and plebians) in the *comitia*, on the motion of a magistrate of senatorial rank, as a consul, a prætor, or a dictator. Such a statute frequently took the name of the proposer; as the *lex Falcidia*, *lex Cornelia* etc.

Other specific meanings of the word in Roman jurisprudence were as follows:

Positive law, as opposed to natural.

That system of law which descended from the Twelve Tables, and formed the basis of all the Roman law.

The terms of a private covenant; the condition of an obligation.

A form of words prescribed to be used upon particular occasions.

In the language of the middle ages, "*lex*" meant a body or collection of law; not a "code," in the proper sense of that term. Mackeld. Rom. Law, § 98.

In old English law. A body or collection of law; particularly, the Roman or civil law. Also the oath of a party with compurgators; as *legem facere, legem vadiare*, etc. Sometimes in the sense of legal rights; civil rights; the protection of the law; as in the phrase "*legem amittere.*"

LEX ÆLIA SENTIA. In Roman law. The Ælian Sentian law, respecting wills, proposed by the consuls Ælius and Sentius, and passed A. U. C. 756, restraining a master from manumitting his slaves in certain cases. Calvin.

Lex æquitate gaudet. Law delights in equity. Jenk. Cent. p. 36, case 69.

LEX AGRARIA. In Roman law. The agrarian law. A law proposed by Tiberius Gracchus, A. U. C. 620, that no one should possess more than five hundred acres of land; and that three commissioners should be appointed to divide among the poorer people what any one had above that extent.

LEX ALAMANNORUM. The law of the Alemanni; first reduced to writing from the customs of the country, by Theodoric, king of the Franks, A. D. 512. Amended and re-enacted by Clotaire II. Spelman.

Lex aliquando sequitur æquitatem. Law sometimes follows equity. 3 Wils. 119.

LEX AMISSA. One who is an infamous, perjured, or outlawed person. Bract. lib. 4, c. 19.

LEX ANGLIÆ. The law of England. The common law. Or, the curtesy of England.

Lex Angliæ est lex misericordiæ. 2 Inst. 315. The law of England is a law of mercy.

Lex Angliæ non patitur absurdum. 9 Coke, 22*a*. The law of England does not suffer an absurdity.

Lex Angliæ nunquam matris sed semper patris conditionem imitari partum judicat. Co. Litt. 123. The law of England rules that the offspring shall always follow the condition of the father, never that of the mother.

Lex Angliæ nunquam sine parliamento mutari potest. 2 Inst. 218. The law of England cannot be changed but by parliament.

LEX APOSTATA. A thing contrary to law. Jacob.

LEX APPARENS. In old English and Norman law. Apparent or manifest law. A term used to denote the trial by battel or duel, and the trial by ordeal, "*lex*" having the sense of process of law. Called "apparent" because the plaintiff was obliged to make his right *clear* by the testimony of witnesses, before he could obtain an order from the court to summon the defendant. Spelman.

LEX AQUILIA. In Roman law. The Aquilian law; a celebrated law passed on the proposition of the tribune C. Aquilius Gallus, A. U. C. 672, regulating the compensation to be made for that kind of damage called "injurious," in the cases of killing or wounding the slave or beast of another. Inst. 4, 3; Calvin.

LEX ATILIA. The Atilian law; a law of Rome proposed by the tribune L. Atilius Regulus, A. U. C. 443, regulating the appointment of guardians.

LEX ATINIA. In Roman law. The Atinian law; a law declaring that the property in things stolen should not be acquired by prescription, (*usucapione.*) Inst. 2, 6, 2; Adams, Rom. Ant. 207.

LEX BAIUVARIORUM, (BAIORIORUM, or BOIORUM.) The law of the Bavarians, a barbarous nation of Europe, first collected (together with the law of the Franks and Alemanni) by Theodoric I., and finally completed and promulgated by Dagobert. Spelman.

LEX BARBARA. The barbarian law. The laws of those nations that were not subject to the Roman empire were so called. Spelman.

Lex beneficialis rei consimili remedium præstat. 2 Inst. 689. A beneficial law affords a remedy for a similar case.

LEX BREHONIA. The Brehon or Irish law, overthrown by King John. See BREHON LAW.

LEX BRETOISE. The law of the ancient Britons, or Marches of Wales. Cowell.

LEX BURGUNDIONUM. The law of the Burgundians, a barbarous nation of Europe, first compiled and published by Gundebald, one of the last of their kings, about A. D. 500. Spelman.

Lex citius tolerare vult privatum damnum quam publicum malum. The law will more readily tolerate a private loss than a public evil. Co. Litt. 152.

LEX COMITATUS. The law of the county, or that administered in the county court before the earl or his deputy. Spelman.

LEX COMMISSORIA. In Roman law. A law by which a debtor and creditor might agree (where a thing had been pledged to the latter to secure the debt) that, if the debtor did not pay at the day, the pledge should become the absolute property of the creditor. 2 Kent, Comm. 583. This was abolished by a law of Constantine.

A law according to which a seller might stipulate that, if the price of the thing sold were not paid within a certain time, the sale should be void. Dig. 18, 3.

LEX COMMUNIS. The common law. See JUS COMMUNE.

Lex contra id quod præsumit, probationem non recipit. The law admits no proof against that which it presumes. Lofft, 573.

LEX CORNELIA. In Roman law. The Cornelian law; a law passed by the dictator L. Cornelius Sylla, providing remedies for certain injuries, as for battery, forcible entry of another's house, etc. Calvin.

LEX CORNELIA DE FALSO. In Roman law. The Cornelian law respecting forgery or counterfeiting. Passed by the dictator Sylla. Dig. 48, 10; Calvin.

LEX CORNELIA DE SICARIIS ET VENEFICIS. In Roman law. The Cornelian law respecting assassins and poisoners. Passed by the dictator Sylla. Dig. 48, 8; Calvin.

LEX DANORUM. The law of the Danes; Dane-law or Dane-lage. Spelman.

Lex de futuro, judex de præterito. The law provides for the future, the judge for the past.

Lex deficere non potest in justitia exhibenda. Co. Litt. 197. The law cannot be defective in dispensing justice.

LEX DERAISNIA. The proof of a thing which one denies to be done by him, where another affirms it; defeating the assertion of his adversary, and showing it be against reason or probability. This was used among the old Romans, as well as the Normans. Cowell.

Lex dilationes semper exhorret. 2 Inst. 240. The law always abhors delays.

LEX DOMICILII. The law of the domicile. 2 Kent, Comm. 112, 433.

Lex est ab æterno. Law is from everlasting. A strong expression to denote the remote antiquity of the law. Jenk. Cent. p. 34, case 66.

Lex est dictamen rationis. Law is the dictate of reason. Jenk. Cent. p. 117, case 33. The common law will judge according to the law of nature and the public good.

Lex est norma recti. Law is a rule of right. Branch, Princ.

Lex est ratio summa, quæ jubet quæ sunt utilia et necessaria, et contraria prohibet. Law is the perfection of reason, which commands what is useful and necessary, and forbids the contrary. Co. Litt. 319*b*; Id. 97*b*.

Lex est sanctio sancta, jubens honesta, et prohibens contraria. Law is a sacred sanction, commanding what is right, and prohibiting the contrary. 2 Inst. 587.

Lex est tutissima cassis; sub clypeo legis nemo decipitur. Law is the safest helmet; under the shield of the law no one is deceived. 2 Inst. 56.

LEX ET CONSUETUDO PARLIAMENTI. The law and custom (or usage) of parliament. The houses of parliament constitute a court not only of legislation, but also of justice, and have their own rules, by which the court itself and the suitors therein are governed. May, Parl. Pr. (6th Ed.) 38-61.

LEX ET CONSUETUDO REGNI. The law and custom of the realm. One of the names of the common law. Hale, Com. Law, 52.

LEX FALCIDIA. In Roman law. The Falcidian law; a law passed on the motion of the tribune P. Falcidius, A. U. C. 713, forbidding a testator to give more in legacies than three-fourths of all his estate, or, in other words, requiring him to leave at least one-fourth to the heir. Inst. 2, 22; Heinecc. Elem. lib. 2, tit. 22.

Lex favet doti. Jenk. Cent. 50. The law favors dower.

Lex fingit ubi subsistit æquitas. 11 Coke, 90. The law makes use of a fiction where equity subsists.

LEX FORI. The law of the forum, or court; that is, the positive law of the state, country, or jurisdiction of whose judicial system the court where the suit is brought or remedy sought is an integral part.

"Remedies upon contracts and their incidents are regulated and pursued according to the law of the place where the action is instituted, and the *lex loci* has no application." 2 Kent, Comm. 462. "The remedies are to be governed by the laws of the country where the suit is brought; or, as it is compendiously expressed, by the *lex fori.*" 8 Pet. 361, 372. "So far as the law affects the remedy, the *lex fori*, the law of the place where that remedy is sought, must govern. But, so far as the law of the construction, the legal operation and effect, of the contract, is concerned, it is governed by the *law of the place* where the *contract* is made." 4 Metc. (Mass.) 594, 597. See LEX LOCI CONTRACTUS.

LEX FRANCORUM. The law of the Franks; promulgated by Theodoric I., son of Clovis I., at the same time with the law of the Alemanni and Bavarians. Spelman. This was a different collection from the Salic law.

LEX FRISIONUM. The law of the Frisians, promulgated about the middle of the eighth century. Spelman.

LEX FURIA CANINIA. In Roman law. The Furian Caninian law; a law passed in the consulship of P. Furius Camillus and C. Caninius Gallus, A. U. C. 752, prohibiting masters from manumitting by will more than a certain number or proportion of their slaves. This law was abrogated by Justinian. Inst. 1, 7; Heinecc. Elem. lib. 1, tit. 7.

LEX GOTHICA. The Gothic law, or law of the Goths. First promulgated in writing, A. D. 466. Spelman.

LEX HOSTILIA DE FURTIS. A Roman law, which provided that a prosecution for theft might be carried on without the owner's intervention. 4 Steph. Comm. (7th Ed.) 118.

LEX IMPERATORIA. The Imperial or Roman law. Quoted under this name, by Fleta, lib. 1, c. 38, § 15; Id. lib. 3, c. 10, § 3.

Lex intendit vicinum vicini facta scire. The law intends [or presumes] that one neighbor knows what another neighbor does. Co. Litt. 78*b*.

Lex judicat de rebus necessario faciendis quasi re ipsa factis. The law judges of things which must necessarily be done as if actually done. Branch, Princ.

LEX JUDICIALIS. An ordeal.

LEX JULIA MAJESTATIS. In Roman law. The Julian law of majesty; a law promulgated by Julius Cæsar, and again published with additions by Augustus, comprehending all the laws before enacted to punish transgressors against the state. Calvin.

LEX LOCI. The law of the place. This may be of the following several descriptions: *Lex loci contractus*, the law of the place where the contract was made or to be performed; *lex loci actus*, the law of the place where the act was done; *lex loci rei sitæ*, the law of the place where the subject-matter is situated; *lex loci domicilii*, the law of the place of domicile.

LEX LOCI CONTRACTUS. The law of the place of the contract. The local law which governs as to the nature, construction, and validity of a contract.

LEX LOCI DELICTUS. The law of the place where the crime took place.

LEX LOCI REI SITÆ. The law of the place where a thing is situated. "It is equally settled in the law of all civilized countries that real property, as to its tenure, mode of enjoyment, transfer, and descent, is to be regulated by the *lex loci rei sitæ.*" 2 Kent, Comm. 429.

LEX LOCI SOLUTIONIS. The law of the place of solution; the law of the place where payment or performance of a contract is to be made.

LEX LONGOBARDORUM. The law of the Lombards. The name of an ancient code of laws among that people, framed, probably, between the fifth and eighth centuries. It continued in force after the incorporation of Lombardy into the empire of Charlemagne, and traces of its laws and institutions are said to be still discoverable in some parts of Italy.

LEX MANIFESTA. Manifest or open law; the trial by duel or ordeal. The same with *lex apparens*, (*q. v.*) In King John's charter (chapter 38) and the articles of that charter (chapter 28) the word "*manifestam*" is omitted.

LEX MERCATORIA. The law-merchant. That system of laws which is adopted by all commercial nations, and constitutes a part of the law of the land.

Lex necessitatis est lex temporis; i. e., instantis. The law of necessity is the law of the time; that is, of the instant, or present moment. Hob. 159.

Lex neminem cogit ad vana seu inutilia peragenda. The law compels no one to do vain or useless things. 5 Coke, 21*a;* Co. Litt. 197*b;* Broom, Max. 252.

Lex neminem cogit ostendere quod nescire præsumitur. Lofft, 569. The law compels no one to show that which he is presumed not to know.

Lex nemini facit injuriam. The law does injury to no one. Branch, Princ.

Lex nemini operatur iniquum. The law works injustice to no one. Jenk. Cent. p. 18, case 33.

Lex nil facit frustra. The law does nothing in vain. 1 Ventr. 417; Jenk. Cent. p. 12, case 19; Broom, Max. 252.

Lex nil frustra jubet. The law commands nothing vainly. 3 Bulst. 280.

Lex non a rege est violanda. Jenk. Cent. 7. The law is not to be violated by the king.

Lex non cogit ad impossibilia. The law does not compel the doing of impossibilities. Hob. 96; Broom, Max. 242.

Lex non curat de minimis. Hob. 88. The law cares not about trifles.

Lex non deficit in justitia exhibenda. The law does not fail in showing justice. Jenk. Cent. p. 31, case 61.

Lex non exacte definit, sed arbitrio boni viri permittit. The law does not define exactly, but trusts in the judgment of a good man. 9 Mass. 475.

Lex non favet delicatorum votis. The law favors not the wishes of the dainty. 9 Coke, 58; Broom, Max. 379.

Lex non intendit aliquid impossibile. The law does not intend anything impossible. 12 Coke, 89*a*. For otherwise the law should not be of any effect.

Lex non patitur fractiones et divisiones statuum. The law does not suffer fractions and divisions of estates. Branch, Princ.; 1 Coke, 87*a*.

Lex non præcipit inutilia, quia inutilis labor stultus. Co. Litt. 197. The law commands not useless things, because useless labor is foolish.

Lex non requirit verificari quod apparet curiæ. The law does not require that to be verified [or proved] which is apparent to the court. 9 Coke, 54*b*.

LEX NON SCRIPTA. The unwritten or common law, which includes general and particular customs, and particular local laws.

LEX ORDINANDI. The same as *lex fori*, (*q. v.*)

LEX PAPIA POPPÆA. In Roman law. The Papian Poppæan law; a law proposed by the consuls Papius and Poppæus at the desire of Augustus, A. U. C. 762, enlarging the *Lex Prætoria*, (*q. v.*) Inst. 3, 8, 2.

Lex plus laudatur quando ratione probatur. The law is the more praised when it is approved by reason. Broom, Max. 159.

Lex posterior derogat priori. A later statute takes away the effect of a prior one. But the later statute must either expressly repeal, or be manifestly repugnant to, the earlier one. Broom, Max. 29; Mackeld. Rom. Law, § 7.

LEX PRÆTORIA. In Roman law. The Prætorian law. A law by which every freedman who made a will was commanded to leave a moiety to his patron. Inst. 3, 8, 1.

The term has been applied to the rules that govern in a court of equity. Gilb. Ch. pt. 2.

Lex prospicit, non respicit. Jenk. Cent. 284. The law looks forward, not backward.

Lex punit mendacium. The law punishes falsehood. Jenk. Cent. p. 15, case 26.

LEX REGIA. In Roman law. The royal or imperial law. A law enacted (or supposed or claimed to have been enacted) by the Roman people, constituting the emperor a source of law, conferring the legislative power upon him, and according the force and obligation of law to the expression of his mere will or pleasure. See Inst. 1, 2, 6; Gaius, 1, 5; Mackeld. Rom. Law, § 46; Heinecc. Rom. Ant. l. 1, tit. 2, §§ 62-67; 1 Kent, Comm. 544, note.

LEX REI SITÆ. The law of the place of situation of the thing.

Lex rejicit superflua, pugnantia, incongrua. Jenk. Cent. 133. The law rejects superfluous, contradictory, and incongruous things.

Lex reprobat moram. Jenk. Cent. 35. The law dislikes delay.

Lex respicit æquitatem. Co. Litt. 24*b*. The law pays regard to equity.

LEX RHODIA. The Rhodian law, particularly the fragment of it on the subject of jettison, (*de jactu*,) preserved in the Pandects. Dig. 14, 2, 1; 3 Kent, Comm. 232, 233.

LEX SACRAMENTALIS. Purgation by oath.

LEX SALICA. The Salic law, or law of the Salian Franks, a Teutonic race who settled in Gaul in the fifth century. This ancient code, said to have been compiled about the year 420, embraced the laws and customs of that people, and is of great historical value, in connection with the origins of feudalism and similar subjects. Its most celebrated provision was one which excluded women from the inheritance of landed estates, by an extension of which law females were always excluded from succession to the crown of France. Hence this provision, by itself, is often referred to as the "Salic Law."

LEX SCRIPTA. Written law; law deriving its force, not from usage, but from express legislative enactment; statute law. 1 Bl. Comm. 62, 85.

Lex scripta si cesset, id custodiri oportet quod moribus et consuetudine inductum est; et, si qua in re hoc defecerit, tunc id quod proximum et consequens ei est; et, si id non appareat, tunc jus quo urbs Romana utitur servari oportet. 7 Coke, 19. If the written law be silent, that which is drawn from manners and custom ought to be observed; and, if that is in any manner defective, then that which is next and analogous to it; and, if that does not appear, then the law which Rome uses should be followed. This maxim of Lord Coke is so far followed at the present day that, in cases where there is no precedent of the English courts, the civil law is always heard with respect, and often, though not necessarily, followed. Wharton.

Lex semper dabit remedium. The law will always give a remedy. Branch, Princ; Broom, Max. 192.

Lex semper intendit quod convenit rationi. Co. Litt. 78*b*. The law always intends what is agreeable to reason.

LEX SITUS. Modern law Latin for "the law of the place where property is situated." The general rule is that lands and other immovables are governed by the *lex situs*; *i. e.*, by the law of the country in which they are situated. Westl. Priv. Int. Law, 62.

Lex spectat naturæ ordinem. The law regards the order of nature. Co. Litt. 197*b*.

Lex succurrit ignoranti. Jenk. Cent. 15. The law assists the ignorant.

Lex succurrit minoribus. The law aids minors. Jenk. Cent. p. 51, case 97.

LEX TALIONIS. The law of retaliation; which requires the infliction upon a wrongdoer of the same injury which he has caused to another. Expressed in the Mosaic law by the formula, "an eye for an eye; a tooth for a tooth," etc. In modern international law, the term describes the rule by which one state may inflict upon the citizens of another state death, imprisonment, or other hardship, in retaliation for similar injuries imposed upon its own citizens.

LEX TERRÆ. The law of the land. The common law, or the due course of the common law; the general law of the land. Bract. fol. 17*b*. Equivalent to "due process of law."

In the strictest sense, trial by oath; the privilege of making oath. Bracton uses the phrase to denote a freeman's privilege of being sworn in court as a juror or witness, which jurors convicted of perjury forfeited, (*legem terræ amittant*.) Bract. fol. 292*b*.

Lex uno ore omnes alloquitur. The law addresses all with one [the same] mouth or voice. 2 Inst. 184.

Lex vigilantibus, non dormientibus, subvenit. Law assists the wakeful, not the sleeping. 1 Story, Cont. § 529.

LEX WALLENSICA. The Welsh law; the law of Wales. Blount.

LEX WISIGOTHORUM. The law of the Visigoths, or Western Goths who settled in Spain; first reduced to writing A. D. 466. A revision of these laws was made by Egigas. Spelman.

LEY. In Spanish law. A law; the law; law in the abstract.

LEY CIVILE. In old English law. The civil or Roman law. Yearb. H. 8 Edw. III. 42. Otherwise termed "*ley escripte*," the written law. Yearb. 10 Edw. III. 24.

LEY GAGER. L. Fr. Law wager; wager of law; the giving of gage or security by a defendant that he would make or perfect his law at a certain day. Litt. § 514; Co. Litt. 294*b*, 295*a*.

LEYES DE ESTILO. In Spanish law. A collection of laws, usually published as an appendix to the Fuero Real; treating of the mode of conducting suits, prosecuting them to judgment, and entering appeals. Schm. Civil Law, Introd. 74.

LEZE-MAJESTY. An offense against sovereign power; treason; rebellion.

LIABILITY. The state of being bound or obliged in law or justice to do, pay, or make good something; legal responsibility. 36 Iowa, 226; 36 N. J. Law, 145; 57 Cal. 209.

LIABLE. 1. Bound or obliged in law or equity; responsible; chargeable; answerable; compellable to make satisfaction, compensation, or restitution.

2. Exposed or subject to a given contingency, risk, or casualty, which is more or less probable.

LIARD. A farthing.

LIBEL, *v.* In admiralty practice. To proceed against, by filing a libel; to seize under admiralty process, at the commencement of a suit. Also to defame or injure a person's reputation by a published writing.

LIBEL, *n.* **In practice.** The initiatory pleading on the part of the plaintiff or complainant in an admiralty or ecclesiastical cause, corresponding to the declaration, bill, or complaint.

In the Scotch law it is the form of the complaint or ground of the charge on which either a civil action or criminal prosecution takes place. Bell.

In torts. That which is written or printed, and published, calculated to injure the character of another by bringing him into ridicule, hatred, or contempt. 15 Mees. & W. 344.

Libel is a false and unprivileged publication by writing, printing, picture, effigy, or other fixed representation to the eye which exposes any person to hatred, contempt, ridicule, or obloquy, or which causes him to be shunned or avoided, or which has a tendency to injure him in his occupation. Civil Code Cal. § 45.

A libel is a false and malicious defamation of another, expressed in print or writing or pictures or signs, tending to injure the reputation of an individual, and exposing him to public hatred, contempt, or ridicule. The publication of the libelous matter is essential to recovery. Code Ga. 1882, § 2974.

A libel is a malicious defamation, expressed either by writing, printing, or by signs or pictures, or the like, tending to blacken the memory of one who is dead, or to impeach the honesty, integrity, virtue, or reputation, or publish the natural or alleged defects, of one who is alive, and thereby to expose him to public hatred, contempt, or ridicule. Pen. Code Cal. § 248; Rev. Code Iowa 1880, § 4097; Bac. Abr. tit. "Libel;" 1 Hawk. P. C. 1, 73, § 1; 4 Mass. 163; 2 Pick. 113; 25 Wend. 198; 7 Cow. 613.

A libel is a censorious or ridiculing writing, picture, or sign made with a mischievous intent. 4 McCord, 317; 3 Johns. Cas. 354; 9 Johns. 215; 5 Bin. 340; 68 Me. 295.

Any publication the tendency of which is to degrade or injure another person, or to bring him into contempt, ridicule, or hatred, or which accuses him of a crime punishable by law, or of an act odious and disgraceful in society, is a libel. 4 Mason, 115; 3 How. 266, 291.

A libel is a publication, without justification or lawful excuse, of words calculated to injure the reputation of another, and expose him to hatred or contempt. 5 Biss. 330.

Everything, written or printed, which reflects on the character of another, and is published without lawful justification or excuse, is a libel, whatever the intention may have been. 15 Mees. & W. 435.

LIBEL OF ACCUSATION. In Scotch law. The instrument which contains the charge against a person accused of a crime. Libels are of two kinds, namely, indictments and criminal letters.

LIBELANT. The complainant or party who files a libel in an ecclesiastical or admiralty case, corresponding to the plaintiff in actions at law.

LIBELEE. A party against whom a libel has been filed in an ecclesiastical court or in admiralty.

LIBELLUS. Lat. In the civil law. A little book. *Libellus supplex,* a petition, especially to the emperor, all petitions to whom must be in writing. *Libellum rescribere,* to mark on such petition the answer to it. *Libellum agere,* to assist or counsel the emperor in regard to such petitions. *Libellus accusatorius,* an information and accusation of a crime. *Libellus divortii,* a writing of divorcement. *Libellus rerum,* an inventory. Calvin. *Libellus* or *oratio consultoria,* a message by which emperors laid matters before the senate. Id.

A writing in which are contained the names of the plaintiff (*actor*) and defendant, (*reus,*) the thing sought, the right relied upon, and name of the tribunal before which the action is brought. Calvin.

In feudal law. An instrument of alienation or conveyance, as of a fief, or a part of it.

LIBELLUS CONVENTIONIS. In the civil law. The statement of a plaintiff's claim in a petition presented to the magistrate, who directed an officer to deliver it to the defendant.

LIBELLUS FAMOSUS. In the civil law. A defamatory publication; a publication injuriously affecting character; a libel. Inst. 4, 4, 1; Dig. 47, 10; Cod. 9, 36.

LIBELOUS. Defamatory; of the nature of a libel; constituting or involving libel.

LIBER. Lat. A book, of whatever material composed; a main division of a literary work. Also, as an adjective, free or exempt.

LIBER ASSISARUM. The Book of Assizes. A collection of cases that arose on assizes and other trials in the country. It was the fourth volume of the reports of the reign of Edward III. 3 Reeve, Eng. Law, 148.

LIBER BANCUS. In old English law. Free bench. Bract. fol. 97*b*.

LIBER ET LEGALIS HOMO. In old English law. A free and lawful man. A term applied to a juror, from the earliest period.

LIBER FEUDORUM. The book of feuds. This was a compilation of feudal law, prepared by order of the emperor Frederick I., and published at Milan in 1170. It comprised five books, of which only the first two are now extant with fragmentary portions of the others.

LIBER HOMO. A free man; a freeman lawfully competent to act as juror. Ld. Raym. 417; Kebl. 563.

An allodial proprietor, as distinguished from a vassal or feudatory. This was the sense of the term in the laws of the barbarous nations of Europe.

LIBER JUDICIALIS OF ALFRED. Alfred's dome-book. See DOMESDAY.

LIBER JUDICIARUM. The book of judgment, or doom-book. The Saxon Dom-boc. Conjectured to be a book of statutes of ancient Saxon kings.

LIBER NIGER. Black book. A name given to several ancient records.

LIBER NIGER DOMÛS REGIS, (the black book of the king's household.) The title of a book in which there is an account of the household establishment of King Edward IV., and of the several musicians retained in his service, as well for his private amusement as for the service in his chapel. Enc. Lond.

LIBER NIGER SCACCARII. The black book of the exchequer, attributed to Gervase of Tilbury. 1 Reeve, Eng. Law, 220, note.

LIBER RUBER SCACCARII. The red book of the exchequer. 1 Reeve, Eng. Law, 220, note.

LIBERA. A livery or delivery of so much corn or grass to a customary tenant, who cut down or prepared the said grass or corn, and received some part or small portion of it as a reward or gratuity. Cowell.

LIBERA BATELLA. In old records. A free boat; the right of having a boat to fish in a certain water; a species of free fishery.

LIBERA CHASEA HABENDA. A judicial writ granted to a person for a free chase belonging to his manor after proof made by inquiry of a jury that the same of right belongs to him. Wharton.

LIBERA ELEEMOSYNA. In old English law. Free alms; frankalmoigne. Bract. fol. 27*b*.

LIBERA FALDA. In old English law. Frank fold; free fold; free foldage. 1 Leon. 11.

LIBERA LEX. In old English law. Free law; frank law; the law of the land. The law enjoyed by free and lawful men, as distinguished from such men as have lost the benefit and protection of the law in consequence of crime. Hence this term denoted the *status* of a man who stood guiltless before the law, and was *free*, in the sense of being entitled to its full protection and benefit. *Amittere liberam legem* (to lose one's free law) was to fall from that *status* by crime or infamy. See Co. Litt. 94*b*.

LIBERA PISCARIA. In old English law. A free fishery. Co. Litt. 122*a*.

LIBERA WARRENA. In old English law. Free warren, (*q. v.*)

LIBERAM LEGEM AMITTERE. To lose one's free law, (called the villainous judgment,) to become discredited or disabled as juror and witness, to forfeit goods and chattels and lands for life, to have those lands wasted, houses razed, trees rooted up, and one's body committed to prison. It was anciently pronounced against conspirators, but is now disused, the punishment substituted being fine and imprisonment. Hawk. P. C. 61, c. lxxii., s. 9; 3 Inst. 221.

LIBERARE. In the civil law. To free or set free; to liberate; to give one his liberty. Calvin.

In old English law. To deliver, transfer, or hand over. Applied to writs, panels of jurors, etc. Bract. fols. 116, 176*b*.

Liberata pecunia non liberat offerentem. Co. Litt. 207. Money being restored does not set free the party offering.

LIBERATE. In old English practice. An original writ issuing out of chancery to the treasurer, chamberlains, and barons of the exchequer, for the payment of any annual pension, or other sum. Reg. Orig. 193; Cowell.

A writ issued to a sheriff, for the delivery of any lands or goods taken upon forfeits of recognizance. 4 Coke, 64*b*.

A writ issued to a gaoler, for the delivery of a prisoner that had put in bail for his appearance. Cowell.

LIBERATIO. In old English law. Livery; money paid for the delivery or use of a thing.

In old Scotch law. Livery; a fee given to a servant or officer. Skene.

Money, meat, drink, clothes, etc., yearly given and delivered by the lord to his domestic servants. Blount.

LIBERATION. In the civil law. The extinguishment of a contract, by which he who was bound becomes free or liberated. Wolff, Inst. Nat. § 749. Synonymous with "payment." Dig. 50, 16, 47.

LIBERI. In Saxon law. Freemen; the possessors of allodial lands. 1 Reeve, Eng. Law, 5.

In the civil law. Children. The term included "grandchildren."

LIBERTAS. Liberty; freedom; a privilege; a franchise.

LIBERTAS ECCLESIASTICA. Church liberty, or ecclesiastical immunity.

Libertas est naturalis facultas ejus quod cuique facere libet, nisi quod de jure aut vi prohibetur. Co. Litt. 116. Liberty is that natural faculty which permits every one to do anything he pleases except that which is restrained by law or force.

Libertas inestimabilis res est. Liberty is an inestimable thing; a thing above price. Dig. 50, 17, 106.

Libertas non recipit æstimationem. Freedom does not admit of valuation. Bract. fol. 14.

Libertas omnibus rebus favorabilior est. Liberty is more favored than all things, [anything.] Dig. 50, 17, 122.

Libertates regales ad coronam spectantes ex concessione regum à coronâ exierunt. 2 Inst. 496. Royal franchises relating to the crown have emanated from the crown by grant of kings.

LIBERTATIBUS ALLOCANDIS. A writ lying for a citizen or burgess, impleaded contrary to his liberty, to have his privilege allowed. Reg. Orig. 262.

LIBERTATIBUS EXIGENDIS IN ITINERE. An ancient writ whereby the king commanded the justices in eyre to admit of an attorney for the defense of another's liberty. Reg. Orig. 19.

LIBERTI, LIBERTINI. In Roman law. Freedmen. There seems to have been some difference in the use of these two words; the former denoting the manumitted slaves considered in their relations with their former master, who was now called their "patron;" the latter term describing the *status* of the same persons in the general social economy of Rome.

LIBERTICIDE. A destroyer of liberty.

LIBERTIES. Privileged districts exempt from the sheriff's jurisdiction.

Libertinum ingratum leges civiles in pristinam servitutem redigunt; sed leges Angliæ semel manumissum semper liberum judicant. Co. Litt. 137. The civil laws reduce an ungrateful freedman to his original slavery; but the laws of England regard a man once manumitted as ever after free.

LIBERTY. 1. Freedom; exemption from extraneous control. The power of the will, in its moral freedom, to follow the dictates of its unrestricted choice, and to direct the external acts of the individual without restraint, coercion, or control from other persons.

Civil liberty is the greatest amount of absolute liberty which can, in the nature of things, be equally possessed by every citizen in a state. Bouvier.

The term is frequently used to denote the amount of absolute liberty which is actually enjoyed by the various citizens under the government and laws of the state as administered. 1 Bl. Comm. 125.

Civil liberty is guarantied protection against interference with the interests and rights held dear and important by large classes of civilized men, or by all the members of a state, together with an effectual share in the making and administration of the laws, as the best apparatus to secure that protection. Lieb. Civil Lib. 24.

Natural liberty is the right which nature gives to all mankind of disposing of their persons and property after the manner they judge most consistent with their happiness, on condition of their acting within the limits of the law of nature, and so as not to interfere with an equal exercise of the same rights by other men. Burlamaqui, c. 3, § 15; 1 Bl. Comm. 125.

Personal liberty consists in the power of locomotion, of changing situation, of removing one's person to whatever place one's inclination may direct, without imprisonment or restraint unless by due course of law. 1 Bl. Comm. 134.

Political liberty is an effectual share in the making and administration of the laws. Lieb. Civil Lib.

2. The word also means a franchise or personal privilege, being some part of the sovereign power, vested in an individual, either by grant or prescription.

3. In a derivative sense, the term denotes the place, district, or boundaries within which a special franchise is enjoyed, an immunity claimed, or a jurisdiction exercised. In this sense, the term is commonly used in the plural; as "the liberties of the city," "the northern liberties of Philadelphia."

LIBERTY OF SPEECH. Freedom accorded by the constitution or laws of a state to express opinions and facts by word of mouth, uncontrolled by any censorship or restrictions of government.

LIBERTY OF THE PRESS. The right to print and publish the truth, from good motives and for justifiable ends. 3 Johns. Cas. 394. The right freely to publish whatever the citizen may please, and to be protected against any responsibility for so doing, except so far as such publications, from their blasphemy, obscenity, or scandalous character, may be a public offense, or as by their falsehood and malice they may injuriously affect the standing, reputation, or pecuniary interests of individuals. Cooley, Const. Lim. p. 422. It is said to consist in this: "That neither courts of justice, nor any judges whatever, are authorized to take notice of writings *intended* for the press, but are confined to those which are actually printed." De Lolme, Eng. Const. 254.

LIBERTY OF THE RULES. A privilege to go out of the Fleet and Marshalsea prisons within certain limits, and there reside. Abolished by 5 & 6 Vict. c. 22.

LIBERTY TO HOLD PLEAS. The liberty of having a court of one's own. Thus, certain lords had the privilege of holding pleas within their own manors.

Liberum corpus nullam recipit æstimationem. Dig. 9, 3, 7. The body of a freeman does not admit of valuation.

Liberum est cuique apud se explorare an expediat sibi consilium. Every one is free to ascertain for himself whether a recommendation is advantageous to his interests. 6 Johns. 181, 184.

LIBERUM MARITAGIUM. In old English law. Frank-marriage. Bract. fol. 21.

LIBERUM SERVITIUM. Free service. Service of a warlike sort by a feudatory tenant; sometimes called "*servitium liberum armorum.*" Jacob.

Service not unbecoming the character of a freeman and a soldier to perform; as to serve under the lord in his wars, to pay a sum of money, and the like. 2 Bl. Comm. 60.

LIBERUM SOCAGIUM. In old English law. Free socage. Bract. fol. 207; 2 Bl. Comm. 61, 62.

LIBERUM TENEMENTUM. In real law. Freehold. Frank-tenement.

In pleading. A plea of freehold. A plea by the defendant in an action of trespass to real property that the *locus in quo* is his freehold, or that of a third person, under whom he acted. 1 Tidd, Pr. 645.

LIBLAC. In Saxon law. Witchcraft, particularly that kind which consisted in the compounding and administering of drugs and philters.

LIBLACUM. In Saxon law. Bewitching any person; also a barbarous sacrifice.

LIBRA. In old English law. A pound; also a sum of money equal to a pound sterling.

LIBRA ARSA. In old English law. A pound burned; that is, melted, or assayed by melting, to test its purity. *Libræ arsæ et pensatæ,* pounds burned and weighed. A frequent expression in Domesday, to denote the purer coin in which rents were paid. Spelman; Cowell.

LIBRA NUMERATA. A pound of money counted instead of being weighed. Spelman.

LIBRA PENSA. A pound of money by weight. It was usual in former days not only to sell the money, but to weigh it; because many cities, lords, and bishops, having their mints, coined money, and often very bad money, too, for which reason, though the pound consisted of 20 shillings, they weighed it. Enc. Lond.

LIBRARIUS. In Roman law. A writer or amanuensis; a copyist. Dig. 50, 17, 92.

LIBRATA TERRÆ. A portion of ground containing four oxgangs, and every oxgang fourteen acres. Cowell. This is the same with what in Scotland was called "poundland" of old extent. Wharton.

LIBRIPENS. In Roman law. A weigher or balance-holder. The person who held a brazen balance in the ceremony of emancipation *per æs et libram.* Inst. 2, 10, 1.

Librorum appellatione continentur omnia volumina, sive in charta, sive in membrana sint, sive in quavis alia materia. Under the name of books are contained all volumes, whether upon paper, or parchment, or any other material. Dig. 32, 52, *pr.*

LICENCIADO. In Spanish law. An attorney or advocate; particularly, a person admitted to the degree of "Licentiate in Jurisprudence" by any of the literary universities of Spain, and who is thereby authorized to practice in all the courts. Escriche.

LICENSE. In the law of contracts. A permission, accorded by a competent authority, conferring the right to do some act which without such authorization would be illegal, or would be a trespass or a tort. Also the written evidence of such permission.

In real property law. An authority to do a particular act or series of acts upon another's land without possessing any estate therein. Also the written evidence of authority so accorded.

It is distinguished from an "easement," which implies an interest in the land to be affected, and a "lease," or right to take the profits of land. It may be, however, and often is, coupled with a grant of some interest in the land itself, or right to take the profits. 1 Washb. Real Prop. *398.

In pleading. A plea of justification to an action of trespass that the defendant was authorized by the owner of the freehold to commit the trespass complained of.

In the law of patents. A written authority granted by the owner of a patent to another person empowering the latter to make or use the patented article for a limited period or in a limited territory.

In international law. Permission granted by a belligerent state to its own subjects, or to the subjects of the enemy, to carry on a trade interdicted by war. Wheat. Int. Law, 447.

Marriage license. A marriage license is an authority enabling two persons to be married.

LICENSED VICTUALLER. A term applied, in England, to all persons selling any kind of intoxicating liquor under a license from the justices of the peace. Wharton.

LICENSEE. A person to whom a license has been granted.

In patent law. One who has had transferred to him, either in writing or orally, a less or different interest than either the interest in the whole patent, or an undivided part of such whole interest, or an exclusive sectional interest. 4 Blatchf. 211.

LICENSING ACTS. This expression is applied by Hallam (Const. Hist. c. 13) to acts of parliament for the restraint of printing, except by license. It may also be applied to any act of parliament passed for the purpose of requiring a license for doing any act whatever. But, generally, when we speak of the licensing acts, we mean the acts regulating the sale of intoxicating liquors. Mozley & Whitley.

LICENSOR. The person who gives or grants a license.

LICENTIA CONCORDANDI. Lat. In old practice and conveyancing. License or leave to agree; one of the proceedings on levying a fine of lands. 2 Bl. Comm. 350.

LICENTIA LOQUENDI. Lat. In old practice. Leave to speak, (*i. e.*, with the plaintiff;) an imparlance; or rather leave to imparl. 3 Bl. Comm. 299.

LICENTIA SURGENDI. Lat. In old English practice. License to arise; permission given by the court to a tenant in a real action, who had cast an essoin *de malo lecti*, to *arise* out of his bed, which he could not do without such permission, and after being viewed by four knights appointed for the purpose. Bract. fol. 355.

LICENTIA TRANSFRETANDI. Lat. A writ or warrant directed to the keeper of the port of Dover, or other seaport, commanding him to let such persons pass over sea as have obtained the royal license thereunto. Reg. Orig. 193.

LICENTIATE. One who has license to practice any art or faculty.

LICENTIOUSNESS. The indulgence of the arbitrary will of the individual, without regard to ethics or law, or respect for the rights of others. In this it differs from "liberty;" for the latter term may properly be used only of the exercise of the will in its *moral* freedom, with justice to all men and obedience to the laws.

In a narrower and more technical sense, the word is equivalent to lewdness or lasciviousness.

LICERE. Lat. To be lawful; to be allowed or permitted by law. Calvin.

LICERE, LICERI. Lat. In Roman law. To offer a price for a thing; to bid for it.

LICET. Lat. From the verb "*licere,*" (*q. v.*) Although; notwithstanding. Importing, in this sense, a direct affirmation.

Also, it is allowed, it is permissible.

Licet dispositio de interesse futuro sit inutilis, tamen potest fieri declaratio præcedens quæ sortiatur effectum, interveniente novo actu. Although the grant of a future interest be inoperative, yet a declaration precedent may be made, which may take effect provided a new act intervene. Bac. Max. pp. 60, 61. reg. 14; Broom, Max. 498.

LICET SÆPIUS REQUISITUS. (Although often requested.) In pleading. A phrase used in the old Latin forms of declarations, and literally translated in the modern precedents. Yel. 66; 2 Chit. Pl. 90; 1 Chit. Pl. 331. The clause in a declaration which contains the general averment of a request by the plaintiff of the defendant to pay the sums claimed is still called the "*licet sæpius requisitus.*"

Licita bene miscentur, formula nisi juris obstet. Lawful acts [done by several authorities] are well mingled, [*i. e.*, become united or consolidated into one good act,] unless some form of law forbid. Bac. Max. p. 94, reg. 24.

LICITACION. In Spanish law. The offering for sale at public auction of an estate or property held by co-heirs or joint proprietors, which cannot be divided up without detriment to the whole.

LICITARE. Lat. In Roman law. To offer a price at a sale; to bid; to bid often; to make several bids, one above another. Calvin.

LICITATION. In the civil law. An offering for sale to the highest bidder, or to him who will give most for a thing. An act by which co-heirs or other co-proprietors of a thing in common and undivided between them put it to bid between them, to be adjudged and to belong to the highest and last bidder, upon condition that he pay to each of his co-proprietors a part in the price equal to the undivided part which each of the said co-proprietors had in the estate *licited*, before the adjudication. Poth. Cont. Sale, nn. 516, 638.

LICITATOR. In Roman law. A bidder at a sale.

LICKING OF THUMBS. An ancient formality by which bargains were complete

LIDFORD LAW. A sort of lynch law, whereby a person was first punished and then tried. Wharton.

LIE. To subsist; to exist; to be sustainable; to be proper or available. Thus the phrase "an action will not *lie*" means that an action cannot be sustained, or that there is no ground upon which to found the action.

LIE IN FRANCHISE. Property is said to "lie in franchise" when it is of such a nature that the persons entitled thereto may seize it without the aid of a court; *e. g.*, wrecks, waifs, estrays.

LIE IN GRANT. Incorporeal hereditaments are said to "lie in grant;" that is, they pass by force of the grant (deed or charter) without livery.

LIE IN LIVERY. A term applied to corporeal hereditaments, freeholds, etc., signifying that they pass by livery, not by the mere force of the grant.

LIE IN WAIT. See LYING IN WAIT.

LIE TO. To adjoin. A cottage must have had four acres of land *laid to* it. See 2 Show. 279.

LIEFTENANT. An old form of "lieutenant," and still retained as the vulgar pronunciation of the word.

LIEGE. In feudal law. Bound by a feudal tenure; bound in allegiance to the lord paramount, who owned no superior.

In old records. Full; absolute; perfect; pure. *Liege* widowhood was pure widowhood. Cowell.

LIEGE HOMAGE. Homage which, when performed by one sovereign prince to another, included fealty and services, as opposed to *simple homage*, which was a mere acknowledgment of tenure. (1 Bl. Comm. 367; 2 Steph. Comm. 400.) Mozley & Whitley.

LIEGE LORD. A sovereign; a superior lord.

LIEGE POUSTIE. In Scotch law. That state of health which gives a person full power to dispose of, *mortis causâ* or otherwise, his heritable property. Bell.

A deed executed at the time of such a state of health, as opposed to a death-bed conveyance.

The term seems to be derived from the Latin "*legitima potestas.*"

LIEGEMAN. He that oweth allegiance. Cowell.

LIEGER, or LEGER. A resident ambassador.

LIEGES, or LIEGE PEOPLE. Subjects.

LIEN. A qualified right of property which a creditor has in or over specific property of his debtor, as security for the debt or charge or for performance of some act.

In every case in which property, either real or personal, is charged with the payment of a debt or duty, every such charge may be denominated a lien on the property. Whitak. Liens, p. 1.

A lien is a charge imposed upon specific property, by which it is made security for the performance of an act. Code Civil Proc. Cal. § 1180.

Lien is the right of one man to retain property in his possession belonging to another, until certain demands of the party in possession are satisfied. 26 Wend. 467. And see 1 Hilt. 292.

Lien is familiarly understood to be a binding or attachment of the thing spoken of, for the benefit of him who is entitled thereto. 2 Hawks, 309.

In the Scottish law, the doctrine of lien is known by the name of "retention," and that of set-off by the name of "compensation."

Liens are either *particular*, as a right to retain a thing for some charge or claim growing out of, or connected with, the identical thing; or *general*, as a right to retain a thing not only for such charges and claims, but also for a general balance of accounts between the parties in respect to other dealings of the like nature.

Liens are also either *conventional* or *by operation of law*. The former is the case where the lien is raised by the express agreement and stipulation of the parties, in circumstances where the law alone would not create a lien from the mere relation of the parties or the details of their transaction. The latter is the case where the law itself, without the stipulation of the parties, raises a lien, as an implication or legal consequence from the relation of the parties or the circumstances of their dealings. Liens of this species may arise either under the rules of common law or of equity or under a statute. In the first case they are called "common-law liens;" in the second, "equitable liens;" in the third, "statutory liens."

Liens are either *possessory* or *charging*; the former, where the creditor has the right to hold possession of the specific property until satisfaction of the debt; the latter, where the debt is a charge upon the specific property although it remains in the debtor's possession.

Equitable liens are such as exist in equity, and of which courts of equity alone take cognizance.

A lien is neither a *jus in re* nor a *jus ad rem.* It is not property in the thing, nor does it constitute a right of action for the thing. It more properly constitutes a charge upon the thing. Equitable liens most commonly grow out of constructive trusts. Story, Eq. Jur. § 1215.

Maritime liens. Maritime liens do not include or require possession. The word "lien" is used in maritime law not in the strict legal sense in which we understand it in courts of common law, in which case there could be no lien where there was no possession, actual or constructive, but to express, as if by analogy, the nature of claims which neither presuppose nor originate in possession. 22 Eng. Law & Eq. 62.

The civil law lien. The civil law embraces, under the head of "mortgage and privilege," the peculiar securities which, in the common and maritime law and equity, are termed "liens."

As to BAILEE'S LIEN, MECHANIC'S LIEN, and VENDOR'S LIEN, see those titles.

LIEN OF A COVENANT. The commencement of a covenant stating the names of the covenantors and covenantees, and the character of the covenant, whether joint or several. Wharton.

LIENOR. The person having or owning a lien; one who has a right of lien upon property of another.

LIEU. Fr. Place; room. It is only used with "in;" *in lieu,* instead of. Enc. Lond.

LIEU CONUS. L. Fr. In old pleading. A known place; a place well known and generally taken notice of by those who dwell about it, as a castle, a manor, etc. Whishaw; 1 Ld. Raym. 259.

LIEUTENANCY, COMMISSION OF. See COMMISSION OF ARRAY.

LIEUTENANT. 1. A deputy; substitute; an officer who supplies the place of another; one acting by vicarious authority. Etymologically, one who holds the post or office of another, in the place and stead of the latter.

2. The word is used in composition as part of the title of several civil and military officers, who are subordinate to others, and especially where the duties and powers of the higher officer may, in certain contingencies, devolve upon the lower; as lieutenant governor, lieutenant colonel, etc. See the following titles.

3. In the army, a lieutenant is a commissioned officer, ranking next below a captain. In the United States navy, he is an officer whose rank is intermediate between that of an ensign and that of a lieutenant commander. In the British navy, his rank is next below that of a commander.

LIEUTENANT COLONEL. An officer of the army whose rank is above that of a major and below that of a colonel.

LIEUTENANT COMMANDER. A commissioned officer of the United States navy, whose rank is above that of lieutenant and below that of commander.

LIEUTENANT GENERAL. An officer in the army, whose rank is above that of major general and below that of "general of the army." In the United States, this rank is not permanent, being usually created for special persons or in times of war.

LIEUTENANT GOVERNOR. In English law. A deputy-governor, acting as the chief civil officer of one of several colonies under a governor general. Webster.

In American law. An officer of a state, sometimes charged with special duties, but chiefly important as the deputy or substitute of the governor, acting in the place of the governor upon the latter's death, resignation, or disability.

LIFE. That state of animals and plants, or of an organized being, in which its natural functions and motions are performed, or in which its organs are capable of performing their functions. Webster.

The sum of the forces by which death is resisted. Bichat.

LIFE-ANNUITY. An engagement to pay an income yearly during the life of some person; also the sum thus promised.

LIFE-ESTATE. An estate whose duration is limited to the life of the party holding it, or of some other person; a freehold estate, not of inheritance.

LIFE INSURANCE. That kind of insurance in which the risk contemplated is the death of a particular person; upon which event (if it occurs within a prescribed term, or, according to the contract, whenever it occurs) the insurer engages to pay a stipulated sum to the legal representatives of such person, or to a third person having an insurable interest in the life of such person.

LIFE-INTEREST. A claim or interest, not amounting to ownership, and limited by a term of life, either that of the person in whom the right is vested or that of another.

LIFE-LAND, or LIFE-HOLD. Land held on a lease for lives.

LIFE PEERAGE. Letters patent, conferring the dignity of baron for life only, do not enable the grantee to sit and vote in the house of lords, not even with the usual writ of summons to the house. Wharton.

LIFE POLICY. A policy of life insurance; a policy of insurance upon the life of an individual.

LIFE-RENT. In Scotch law. An estate for life; a right to the use and enjoyment of an estate or thing for one's life, but without destruction of its substance. They are either *legal*, such as terce and curtesy, (*q. v.*,) or *conventional*, *i. e.*, created by act of the parties. Conventional life-rents are either *simple*, where the owner of an estate grants a life-interest to another, or *by reservation*, where the owner, in conveying away the fee, reserves a life-estate to himself.

LIFE-RENTER. In Scotch law. A tenant for life without waste. Bell.

LIFT. To raise; to take up. To "lift" a promissory note is to discharge its obligation by paying its amount or substituting another evidence of debt. To "lift the bar" of the statute of limitations, or of an estoppel, is to remove the obstruction which it interposes, by some sufficient act or acknowledgment.

LIGA. In old European law. A league or confederation. Spelman.

LIGAN, LAGAN. Goods cast into the sea tied to a buoy, so that they may be found again by the owners, are so denominated. When goods are cast into the sea in storms or shipwrecks, and remain there, without coming to land, they are distinguished by the barbarous names of "jetsam," "flotsam," and "ligan." 5 Coke, 108; Harg. State Tr. 48; 1 Bl. Comm. 292.

LIGARE. To tie or bind. Bract. fol. 369*b*.

To enter into a league or treaty. Spelman.

LIGEA. In old English law. A liege-woman; a female subject. Reg. Orig. 312*b*.

LIGEANCE. Allegiance; the faithful obedience of a subject to his sovereign, of a citizen to his government. Also, derivatively, the territory of a state or sovereignty.

LIGEANTIA. Lat. Ligeance; allegiance.

Ligeantia est quasi legis essentia; est vinculum fidei. Co. Litt. 129. Allegiance is, as it were, the essence of law; it is the chain of faith.

Ligeantia naturalis nullis claustris coercetur, nullis metis refrænatur, nullis finibus premitur. 7 Coke, 10. Natural allegiance is restrained by no barriers, reined by no bounds, compressed by no limits.

LIGEAS. In old records. A liege.

LIGHT. A window, or opening in the wall for the admission of light. Also a privilege or easement to have light admitted into one's building by the openings made for that purpose, without obstruction or obscuration by the walls of adjacent or neighboring structures.

LIGHT-HOUSE. A structure, usually in the form of a tower, containing signal-lights for the guidance of vessels at night, at dangerous points of a coast, shoals, etc. They are usually erected by government, and subject to governmental regulation.

LIGHT-HOUSE BOARD. A commission authorized by congress, consisting of two officers of the navy, two officers of the corps of engineers of the army, and two civilians, together with an officer of the navy and an officer of engineers of the army as secretaries, attached to the office of the secretary of the treasury, at Washington, and charged with superintending the construction and management of light-houses, light-ships, and other maritime signals for protection of commerce. Abbott.

LIGHT-SHIP, LIGHT-VESSEL. A vessel serving the purpose of a light-house, usually at a place where the latter could not well be built.

LIGHTER. A small vessel used in loading and unloading ships and steamers.

LIGHTERAGE. The business of transferring merchandise to and from vessels by means of lighters; also the compensation or price demanded for such service.

LIGHTERMAN. The master or owner of a lighter. He is liable as a common carrier.

LIGHTS. 1. Windows; openings in the wall of a house for the admission of light.

2. Signal-lamps on board a vessel or at particular points on the coast, required by the navigation laws to be displayed at night.

LIGIUS. A person bound to another by a solemn tie or engagement. Now used to express the relation of a subject to his sovereign.

Ligna et lapides sub "armorum" appellatione non continentur. Sticks and stones are not contained under the name of "arms." Bract. fol. 144*b*.

LIGNAGIUM. A right of cutting fuel in woods; also a tribute or payment due for the same. Jacob.

LIGNAMINA. Timber fit for building. Du Fresne.

LIGULA. In old English law. A copy, exemplification, or transcript of a court roll or deed. Cowell.

LIMB. A member of the human body. In the phrase "life and limb," the latter term appears to denote bodily integrity in general; but in the definition of "mayhem" it refers only to those members or parts of the body which may be useful to a man in fighting. 1 Bl. Comm. 130.

LIMENARCHA. In Roman law. An officer who had charge of a harbor or port. Dig. 50, 4, 18, 10; Cod. 7, 16, 38.

LIMIT, *v.* To mark out; to define; to fix the extent of. Thus, to limit an estate means to mark out or to define the period of its duration, and the words employed in deeds for this purpose are thence termed "words of limitation," and the act itself is termed "limiting the estate." Brown.

LIMIT, *n.* A bound; a restraint; a circumscription; a boundary. 22 N. Y. 429.

LIMITATION. Restriction or circumspection; settling an estate or property; a certain time allowed by a statute for litigation.

In estates. A limitation, whether made by the express words of the party or existing in intendment of law, circumscribes the continuance of time for which the property is to be enjoyed, and by positive and certain terms, or by reference to some event which possibly may happen, marks the period at which the time of enjoyment shall end. Prest. Estates, 25.

LIMITATION IN LAW. A limitation in law, or an estate limited, is an estate to be holden only during the continuance of the condition under which it was granted, upon the determination of which the estate vests immediately in him in expectancy. 2 Bl. Comm. 155.

LIMITATION OF ACTIONS. The restriction by statute of the right of action to certain periods of time, after the accruing of the cause of action, beyond which, except in certain specified cases, it will not be allowed.

Also the period of time so limited by law for the bringing of actions.

LIMITATION OF ASSIZE. In old practice. A certain time prescribed by statute, within which a man was required to allege himself or his ancestor to have been seised of lands sued for by a writ of assize. Cowell.

LIMITATION OF ESTATE. The restriction or circumscription of an estate, in the conveyance by which it is granted, in respect to the interest of the grantee or its duration; the specific curtailment or confinement of an estate, by the terms of the grant, so that it cannot endure beyond a certain period or a designated contingency.

A conditional limitation (in the generic sense of the term) is where one estate is limited to end and another to commence on the doing of some act or the happening of some event.

A collateral limitation is one which marks the extreme duration of an estate, and at the same time indicates an uncertain event, the happening of which will put an end to it before the expiration of that period. Sweet.

LIMITATION, WORDS OF. Those which operate by reference to, or in connection with, other words, and extend or modify an estate given by such other words, as "heirs," "heirs of the body."

LIMITED. Restricted; bounded; prescribed. Confined within positive bounds; restricted in duration, extent, or scope.

LIMITED ADMINISTRATION. An administration of a temporary character, granted for a particular period, or for a special or particular purpose. Holthouse.

LIMITED COMPANY. A company in which the liability of each shareholder is limited by the number of shares he has taken, so that he cannot be called on to contribute beyond the amount of his shares. In England, the memorandum of association of such company may provide that the liability of the directors, manager, or managing director thereof shall be unlimited. 30 & 31 Vict. c. 131; 1 Lindl. Partn. 383. Mozley & Whitley.

LIMITED DIVORCE. A divorce from bed and board; or a judicial separation of husband and wife not dissolving the marriage tie.

LIMITED EXECUTOR. An executor whose appointment is qualified by limitations as to the time or place wherein, or the subject-matter whereon, the office is to be exercised; as distinguished from one whose appointment is absolute, *i. e.*, certain and immediate, without any restriction in regard to the testator's effects or limitation in point of time. 1 Williams, Ex'rs, 249, et seq.

LIMITED FEE. An estate of inheritance in lands, which is clogged or confined with some sort of condition or qualification. Such estates are *base* or qualified fees, *conditional* fees, and fees-*tail*. The term is opposed to "fee-simple." 2 Bl. Comm. 109.

LIMITED JURISDICTION. This term is ambiguous, and the books sometimes use it without due precision. It is sometimes carelessly employed instead of "special." The true distinction between courts is between such as possess a general and such as have only a special jurisdiction for a particular purpose, or are clothed with special powers for the performance. 18 N. J. Law, 73.

LIMITED LIABILITY. The liability of the members of a joint-stock company may be either unlimited or limited; and, if the latter, then the limitation of liability is either the amount, if any, unpaid on the shares, (in which case the limit is said to be "by shares,") or such an amount as the members guaranty in the event of the company being wound up, (in which case the limit is said to be "by guaranty.") Brown.

LIMITED OWNER. A tenant for life, in tail, or by the curtesy, or other person not having a fee-simple in his absolute disposition.

LIMITED PARTNERSHIP. A partnership consisting of one or more general partners, jointly and severally responsible as ordinary partners, and by whom the business is conducted, and one or more special partners, contributing in cash payments a specific sum as capital to the common stock, and who are not liable for the debts of the partnership beyond the fund so contributed. 1 Rev. St. N. Y. 764.

LIMOGIA. Enamel. Du Cange.

LINARIUM. In old English law. A flax plat, where flax is grown. Du Cange.

LINCOLN'S INN. An inn of court. See INNS OF COURT.

LINE. In descents. The order or series of persons who have descended one from the other or all from a common ancestor, considered as placed in a line of succession in the order of their birth, the line showing the connection of all the blood-relatives.

Measures. A line is a lineal measure, containing the one-twelfth part of an inch.

In estates. The boundary or line of division between two estates.

LINEA. Lat. A line; line of descent. See LINE.

LINEA OBLIQUA. In the civil law. The oblique line. More commonly termed "*linea transversalis*," (*q. v.*)

LINEA RECTA. The direct line; the vertical line. In computing degrees of kindred and the succession to estates, this term denotes the direct line of ascendants and descendants.

Where a person springs from another immediately, or mediately through a third person, they are said to be in the direct line, (*linea recta*,) and are called "ascendants" and "descendants." Mackeld. Rom. Law, § 129.

Linea recta est index sui et obliqui; lex est linea recti. Co. Litt. 158. A right line is a test of itself, and of an oblique; law is a line of right.

Linea recta semper præfertur transversali. The right line is always preferred to the collateral. Co. Litt. 10; Broom, Max. 529.

LINEA TRANSVERSALIS. A collateral, transverse, or oblique line. Where two persons are descended from a third, they are called "collaterals," and are said to be related in the collateral line, (*linea transversa* or *obliqua*.)

LINEAGE. Race; progeny; family, ascending or descending.

LINEAL. That which comes in a line; especially a direct line, as from father to son. Collateral relationship is not called "lineal," though the expression "collateral line," is not unusual.

LINEAL CONSANGUINITY. That kind of consanguinity which subsists between persons of whom one is descended in a *direct line* from the other; as between a particular person and his father, grandfather, great-grandfather, and so upward, in the direct ascending line; or between the same person and his son, grandson, great-grandson, and so downwards in the direct descending line. 2 Bl. Comm. 203.

LINEAL DESCENT. Descent in a right line, as where an estate descends from ancestor to heir in one line of succession, as opposed to collateral descent.

LINEAL WARRANTY. A warranty by an ancestor from whom the title did or might have come to the heir. 2 Bl. Comm. 301; Rawle, Cov. 30.

LINES AND CORNERS. In surveying and conveyancing. Boundary lines and their terminating points, where an angle is formed by the next boundary line.

LINK. A unit in a connected series; anything which serves to connect or bind together the things which precede and follow it. Thus, we speak of a "link in the chain of title."

LIQUERE. Lat. In the civil law. To be clear, evident, or satisfactory. When a *judex* was in doubt how to decide a case, he represented to the prætor, under oath, *sibi non liquere*, (that it was not clear to him,) and was thereupon discharged. Calvin.

LIQUET. It is clear or apparent; it appears. *Satis liquet*, it sufficiently appears. 1 Strange, 412.

LIQUIDATE. To adjust or settle an indebtedness; to determine an amount to be paid; to clear up an account and ascertain the balance; to fix the amount required to satisfy a judgment.

To clear away; to lessen; to pay. "To *liquidate* a balance means to *pay* it." 8 Wheat. 338, 362.

LIQUIDATED. Ascertained; determined; fixed; settled; made clear or manifest. Cleared away; paid; discharged.

LIQUIDATED ACCOUNT. An account whereof the amount is certain and fixed, either by the act and agreement of the parties or by operation of law; a sum which cannot be changed by the proof; it is so much or nothing; but the term does not necessarily refer to a writing. 1 Ga. 287.

LIQUIDATED DAMAGES. Agreed or settled damages; a specific sum of money expressly stipulated by the parties to a bond or other contract, as the amount of damages to be recovered by either party for a breach of the agreement by the other. It is generally distinguished from a penalty.

LIQUIDATED DEBT. A debt is liquidated when it is certain what is due and how much is due. 20 Ga. 562.

LIQUIDATED DEMAND. A demand is a liquidated one if the amount of it has been ascertained—settled—by the agreement of the parties to it, or otherwise. 20 Ga. 53.

LIQUIDATING PARTNER. The partner who upon the dissolution or insolvency of the firm, is appointed to settle its accounts, collect assets, adjust claims, and pay debts.

LIQUIDATION. The act or process of settling or making clear, fixed, and determinate that which before was uncertain or unascertained.

As applied to a company, (or sometimes to the affairs of an individual,) liquidation is used in a broad sense as equivalent to "winding up;" that is, the comprehensive process of settling accounts, ascertaining and adjusting debts, collecting assets, and paying off claims.

LIQUIDATOR. A person appointed to carry out the winding up of a company.

LIQUOR. This term, when used in statutes forbidding the sale of liquors, refers only to spirituous or intoxicating liquors. 18 N. J. Law, 311; 20 Barb. 246; 3 Denio, 407.

LIQUOR-SHOP. A house where spirituous liquors are kept and sold. 6 Baxt. 534.

LIRA. The name of an Italian coin, of the value of about eighteen cents.

LIS. Lat. A controversy or dispute; a suit or action at law.

LIS ALIBI PENDENS. A suit pending elsewhere. The fact that proceedings are pending between a plaintiff and defendant in one court in respect to a given matter is frequently a ground for preventing the plaintiff from taking proceedings in another court against the same defendant for the same object and arising out of the same cause of action. Sweet.

LIS MOTA. A controversy moved or begun. By this term is meant a dispute which has arisen upon a point or question which *afterwards* forms the issue upon which legal proceedings are instituted. After such controversy has arisen, (*post litem motam,*) it is held, declarations as to pedigree, made by members of the family since deceased, are not admissible. See 4 Camp. 417; 6 Car. & P. 560.

LIS PENDENS. A suit pending; that legal process, in a suit regarding land, which amounts to legal notice to all the world that there is a dispute as to the title. In equity the filing of the bill and serving a subpœna creates a *lis pendens,* except when statutes require some record. Stim. Law Gloss.

In the civil law. A suit pending. A suit was not said to be pending before that stage of it called "*litis contestatio,*" (*q. v.*) Mackeld. Rom. Law, § 219. Calvin.

LIST. A docket or calendar of causes ready for trial or argument, or of motions ready for hearing.

LISTED. Included in a list; put on a list, particularly on a list of taxable persons or property.

LISTERS. This word is used in some of the states to designate the persons appointed to make lists of taxables. See Rev. St. Vt. 538.

LITE PENDENTE. Lat. Pending the suit. Fleta, lib. 2, c. 54, § 23.

LITEM SUAM FACERE. Lat. To make a suit his own. Where a *judex,* from partiality or enmity, evidently favored either of the parties, he was said *litem suam facere.* Calvin.

LITERA. Lat. A letter. The letter of a law, as distinguished from its spirit. See Letter.

LITERA PISANA. The Pisan letter. A term applied to the old character in which the copy of the Pandects formerly kept at Pisa, in Italy, was written. Spelman.

LITERÆ. Letters. A term applied in old English law to various instruments in writing, public and private.

LITERÆ DIMISSORIÆ. Dimissory letters, (*q. v.*)

LITERÆ HUMANIORES. A term including Greek, Latin, general philology, logic, moral philosophy, metaphysics; the name of the principal course of study in the University of Oxford. Wharton.

LITERÆ MORTUÆ. Dead letters; fulfilling words of a statute. Lord Bacon observes that "there are in every statute certain words which are as veins, where the life and blood of the statute cometh, and where all doubts do arise, and the rest are *literæ mortuæ,* fulfilling words." Bac. St. Uses, (Works, iv. 189.)

LITERÆ PATENTES. Letters patent; literally, open letters.

Literæ patentes regis non erunt vacuæ. 1 Bulst. 6. The king's letters patent shall not be void.

LITERÆ PROCURATORIÆ. In old English law. Letters procuratory; letters of procuration; letters of attorney. Bract. fols. 40, 43.

LITERÆ RECOGNITIONIS. In maritime law. A bill of lading. Jac. Sea Laws, 172.

Literæ scriptæ manent. Written words last.

LITERÆ SIGILLATÆ. In old English law. Sealed letters. The return of a sheriff was so called. Fleta, lib. 2, c. 64, § 19.

LITERAL. According to language; following expression in words. A literal construction of a document adheres closely to its words, without making differences for extrinsic circumstances; a literal performance of a condition is one which complies exactly with its terms.

LITERAL CONTRACT. In Roman law. A species of written contract, in which the formal act by which an obligation was superinduced on the convention was an entry of the sum due, where it should be specifically ascertained, on the debit side of a ledger. Maine, Anc. Law, 320.

A contract, the whole of the evidence of which is reduced to writing, and binds the party who subscribed it, although he has received no consideration. Lec. El. Dr. Rom. § 887.

LITERAL PROOF. In the civil law. Written evidence.

LITERARY. Pertaining to polite learning; connected with the study or use of books and writings.

The word "literary," having no legal signification, is to be taken in its ordinary and usual meaning. We speak of literary persons as learned, erudite; of literary property, as the productions of ripe scholars, or, at least, of professional writers; of literary institutions, as those where the positive sciences are taught, or persons eminent for learning associate, for purposes connected with their professions. This we think the popular meaning of the word; and that it would not be properly used as descriptive of a school for the instruction of youth. 8 Ind. 332.

LITERARY PROPERTY may be described as the right which entitles an author and his assigns to all the use and profit of his composition, to which no independent right is, through any act or omission on his or their part, vested in another person. 9 Amer. Law Reg. 44.

A distinction is to be taken between "literary property" (which is the natural, common-law right which a person has in the form of written expression to which he has, by labor and skill, reduced his thoughts) and "copyright," (which is a statutory monopoly, above and beyond natural property, conferred upon an author to encourage and reward a dedication of his literary property to the public.) Abbott.

LITERATE. In English ecclesiastical law. One who qualifies himself for holy orders by presenting himself as a person accomplished in classical learning, etc., not as a graduate of Oxford, Cambridge, etc.

LITERATURA. "*Ad literaturam ponere*" means to put children to school. This liberty was anciently denied to those parents who were servile tenants, without the lord's consent. The prohibition against the education of sons arose from the fear that the son, being bred to letters, might enter into holy orders, and so stop or divert the services which he might otherwise do as heir to his father. Paroch. Antiq. 401.

LITERIS OBLIGATIO. In Roman law. The contract of *nomen*, which was constituted by writing, (*scripturâ*.) It was of two kinds, viz.: (1) *A re in personam*, when a transaction was transferred from the day-book (*adversaria*) into the ledger (*codex*) in the form of a debt under the name or heading of the purchaser or debtor, (*nomen*;) and (2) *a personâ in personam*, where a debt already standing under one *nomen* or heading was transferred in the usual course of *novatio* from that *nomen* to another and substituted *nomen*. By reason of this transferring, these obligations were called "*nomina transcriptitia*." No money was, in fact, paid to constitute the contract. If ever money was paid, then the *nomen* was *arcarium*, (*i. e.*, a real contract, *re contractus*,) and not a *nomen proprium*. Brown.

LITIGANT. A party to a lawsuit; one engaged in litigation; usually spoken of active parties, not of nominal ones.

LITIGARE. Lat. To litigate; to carry on a suit, (*litem agere*,) either as plaintiff or defendant; to claim or dispute by action; to test or try the validity of a claim by action.

LITIGATE. To dispute or contend in form of law; to carry on a suit.

LITIGATION. A judicial controversy. A contest in a court of justice, for the purpose of enforcing a right.

LITIGIOSITY. In Scotch law. The pendency of a suit; it is a tacit legal prohibition of alienation, to the disappointment of an action, or of diligence, the direct object of which is to obtain possession, or to acquire the property of a particular subject. The effect of it is analogous to that of inhibition. Bell.

LITIGIOUS. That which is the subject of a suit or action; that which is contested in a court of justice. In another sense, "litigious" signifies fond of litigation; prone to engage in suits.

LITIGIOUS CHURCH. In ecclesiastical law, a church is said to be litigious where two presentations are offered to the bishop upon the same avoidance. Jenk. Cent. 11.

LITIGIOUS RIGHT. In the civil law. A right which cannot be exercised without undergoing a lawsuit. Civil Code La. arts. 918, 3556.

LITIS ÆSTIMATIO. The measure of damages.

LITIS CONTESTATIO. In the civil and canon law. Contestation of suit; the process of contesting a suit by the opposing statements of the respective parties; the process of coming to an issue; the attainment of an issue; the issue itself.

In the practice of the ecclesiastical courts. The general answer made by the defendant, in which he denies the matter charged against him in the libel. Hallifax, Civil Law, b. 3, c. 11, no. 9.

In admiralty practice. The general issue. 2 Browne, Civil & Adm. Law, 358, and note.

LITIS DOMINIUM. In the civil law. Ownership, control, or direction of a suit. A fiction of law by which the employment of an attorney or proctor (*procurator*) in a suit was authorized or justified, he being supposed to become, by the appointment of his principal (*dominus*) or client, the *dominus litis*. Heinecc. Elem. lib. 4, tit. 10, §§ 1246, 1247.

Litis nomen omnem actionem significat, sive in rem, sive in personam sit. Co. Litt. 292. A lawsuit signifies every action, whether it be *in rem* or *in personam*.

LITISPENDENCE. An obsolete term for the time during which a lawsuit is going on.

LITISPENDENCIA. In Spanish law. Litispendency. The condition of a suit pending in a court of justice.

LITRE. Fr. A measure of capacity in the metric system, being a cubic decimetre, equal to 61.022 cubic inches, or 2.113 American pints, or 1.76 English pints. Webster.

LITTORAL. Belonging to the shore; as of seas and great lakes. Webster. Corresponding to riparian proprietors on a stream or small pond are littoral proprietors on a sea or lake. But "riparian" is also used co-extensively with "littoral." 7 Cush. 94. See 17 How. 426.

LITURA. In the civil law. An obliteration or blot in a will or other instrument. Dig. 28, 4, 1, 1.

LITUS. In old European law. A kind of servant; one who surrendered himself into another's power. Spelman.

In the civil law. The bank of a stream or shore of the sea; the coast.

Litus est quousque maximus fluctus a mari pervenit. The shore is where the highest wave from the sea has reached. Dig. 50, 16, 96. Ang. Tide-Waters, 67.

LITUS MARIS. The sea-shore. "It is certain that that which the sea overflows, either at high spring tides or at extraordinary tides, comes not, as to this purpose, under the denomination of '*litus maris*,' and consequently the king's title is not of that large extent, but only to land that is usually overflowed at ordinary tides. That, therefore, I call the '*shore*' that is between the common high-water and low-water mark, and no more." Hale de Jure Mar. c. 4.

LIVELODE. Maintenance; support.

LIVERY. 1. In English law. Delivery of possession of their lands to the king's tenants *in capite* or tenants by knight's service.

2. A writ which may be sued out by a ward in chivalry, on reaching his majority, to obtain delivery of the possession of his lands out of the hands of the guardian. 2 Bl. Comm. 68.

3. A particular dress or garb appropriate or peculiar to certain persons, as the members of a guild, or, more particularly, the servants of a nobleman or gentleman.

4. The privilege of a particular guild or company of persons, the members thereof being called "livery-men."

5. A contract of hiring of work-beasts, particularly horses, to the use of the hirer. It is seldom used alone in this sense, but appears in the compound, "livery-stable."

LIVERY IN CHIVALRY. In feudal law. The delivery of the lands of a ward in chivalry out of the guardian's hands, upon the heir's attaining the requisite age,—twenty-one for males, sixteen for females. 2 Bl. Comm. 68.

LIVERY-MAN. A member of some company in the city of London; also called a "freeman."

LIVERY OF SEISIN. The appropriate ceremony, at common law, for transferring the corporal possession of lands or tenements by a grantor to his grantee. It was livery *in deed* where the parties went together upon the land, and there a twig, clod, key, or other symbol was delivered in the name of the whole. Livery *in law* was where the same ceremony was performed, not upon the land itself, but in sight of it. 2 Bl. Comm. 315, 316.

LIVERY-OFFICE. An office appointed for the delivery of lands.

LIVERY STABLE KEEPER. One whose business it is to keep horses for hire or to let, or to keep, feed, or board horses for others.

LIVRE TOURNOIS. In common law. A coin used in France before the Revolution. It is to be computed in the *ad valorem* duty on goods, etc., at eighteen and a half cents. Act March 2, 1798, § 61; 1 Story, Laws, 629.

LLOYD'S. An association in the city of London, the members of which underwrite each other's policies.

LLOYD'S BONDS. The name of a class of evidences of debt, used in England; being acknowledgments, by a borrowing company made under its seal, of a debt incurred and actually due by the company to a contractor or other person for work done, goods supplied, or otherwise, as the case may be, with a covenant for payment of the principal and interest at a future time. Brown.

LOADMANAGE. The pay to loadsmen; that is, persons who sail or row before ships, in barks or small vessels, with instruments for towing the ship and directing her course, in order that she may escape the dangers in her way. Poth. Des Avaries, no. 137.

LOAN. A bailment without reward; consisting of the delivery of an article by the owner to another person, to be used by the latter gratuitously, and returned either *in specie* or in kind. A sum of money confided to another.

A loan of money is a contract by which one delivers a sum of money to another, and the latter agrees to return at a future time a sum equivalent to that which he borrowed. Civil Code Cal. § 1912.

LOAN CERTIFICATES. Certificates issued by a clearing-house to the associated banks to the amount of seventy-five per cent. of the value of the collaterals deposited by the borrowing banks with the loan committee of the clearing-house. Anderson.

LOAN FOR CONSUMPTION. The loan for consumption is an agreement by which one person delivers to another a certain quantity of things which are consumed by the use, under the obligation, by the borrower, to return to him as much of the same kind and quality. Civil Code La. art. 2910.

Loans are of two kinds,—for consumption or for use. A loan for consumption is where the article is not to be returned *in specie*, but in kind. This is a sale, and not a bailment. Code Ga. 1882, § 2125.

LOAN FOR EXCHANGE. A loan for exchange is a contract by which one delivers personal property to another, and the latter agrees to return to the lender a similar thing at a future time, without reward for its use. Civil Code Cal. § 1902.

LOAN FOR USE. The loan for use is an agreement by which a person delivers a thing to another, to use it according to its natural destination, or according to the agreement, under the obligation on the part of the borrower to return it after he shall have done using it. Civil Code La. art. 2893.

A loan for use is a contract by which one gives to another the temporary possession and use of personal property, and the latter agrees to return the same thing to him at a future time, without reward for its use. Civil Code Cal. § 1884.

A loan for use is the gratuitous grant of an article to another for use, to be returned *in specie*, and may be either for a certain time or indefinitely, and at the will of the grantor. Code Ga. 1882, § 2126.

Loan for use (called "*commodatum*" in the civil law) differs from a loan for consumption, (called "*mutuum*" in the civil law,) in this: that the *commodatum* must be specifically returned; the *mutuum* is to be returned in kind. In the case of a *commodatum*, the property in the thing remains in the lender; in a *mutuum*, the property passes to the borrower. Bouvier.

LOAN, GRATUITOUS, (or COMMODATE.) A class of bailment which is called "*commodatum*" in the Roman law, and is denominated by Sir William Jones a "loan for use," (*prêt à usage,*) to distinguish it from "*mutuum*," a loan for consumption. It is the gratuitous lending of an article to the borrower for his own use. Wharton.

LOAN SOCIETIES. In English law. A kind of club formed for the purpose of advancing money on loan to the industrial classes.

LOBBYING. "Lobbying" is defined to be any personal solicitation of a member of a legislative body during a session thereof, by private interview, or letter or message, or other means and appliances not addressed solely to the judgment, to favor or oppose, or to vote for or against, any bill, resolution, report, or claim pending, or to be introduced by either branch thereof, by any person who misrepresents the nature of his interest in the matter to such member, or who is employed for a consideration by a person or corporation interested in the passage or defeat of such bill, resolution, report, or claim, for the purpose of procuring the passage or defeat thereof. But this does not include such services as drafting petitions, bills, or resolutions, attending to the taking of testimony, collecting facts, preparing arguments and memorials, and submitting them orally or in writing to a committee or member of the legislature, and other services of like character, intended to reach the reason of legislators. Code Ga. 1882, § 4486

L'obligation sans cause, ou sur une fausse cause, ou sur cause illicite, ne peut avoir aucun effet. An obligation without consideration, or upon a false consideration, (which fails,) or upon unlawful consideration, cannot have any effect. Code Civil, 3, 3, 4; Chit. Cont. (11th Amer. Ed.) 25, note.

LOCAL. Relating to place; expressive of place; belonging or confined to a particular place. Distinguished from "general," "personal," and "transitory."

LOCAL ACT OF PARLIAMENT. An act which has for its object the interest of some particular locality, as the formation of a road, the alteration of the course of a river, the formation of a public market in a particular district, etc. Brown.

LOCAL ACTION. An action is so termed when all the principal facts on which it is founded are of a local nature; as where possession of land is to be recovered, or damages for an actual trespass, or for waste affecting land, because in such case the cause of action relates to some particular locality, which usually also constitutes the venue of the action.

LOCAL ALLEGIANCE. That measure of obedience which is due from a subject of one government to another government, within whose territory he is temporarily resident.

LOCAL CHATTEL. A thing is local that is fixed to the freehold. Kitchin, 180.

LOCAL COURTS. Courts whose jurisdiction is limited to a particular territory or district. The expression often signifies the courts of the state, in opposition to the United States courts.

LOCAL CUSTOM. A particular or special custom; one not general in its nature or observance, but confined to a particular district or locality.

LOCAL FREIGHT. Freight shipped from either terminus of a railroad to a way station, or *vice versa*, or from one way station to another; that is, over a part of the road only. 61 Ala. 579.

LOCAL GOVERNMENT. The government or administration of a particular locality; especially, the governmental authority of a municipal corporation, as a city or county, over its local and individual affairs, exercised in virtue of power delegated to it for that purpose by the general government of the state or nation.

LOCAL IMPROVEMENT. By common usage, especially as evidenced by the practice of courts and text-writers, the term "local improvements" is employed as signifying improvements made in a particular locality, by which the real property adjoining or near such locality is specially benefited. 22 Minn. 507.

LOCAL LAW. A law which, instead of relating to and binding all persons, corporations, or institutions to which it may be applicable, within the whole territorial jurisdiction of the law-making power, is limited in its operation to certain districts of such territory or to certain individual persons or corporations. See GENERAL LAW.

LOCAL OPTION. A privilege accorded by the legislature of a state to the several counties or other districts of the state to determine, each for itself, by popular vote, whether or not licenses should be issued for the sale of intoxicating liquors within such districts.

LOCAL PREJUDICE. The "prejudice or local influence" which will warrant the removal of a cause from a state court to a federal court may be either prejudice and influence existing against the party seeking such removal or existing in favor of his adversary. 31 Fed. Rep. 53.

LOCAL STATUTE. Such a statute as has for its object the interest of some particular locality, as the formation of a road, the alteration of the course of a river, the formation of a public market in a particular district, etc.

LOCAL TAXES. Those assessments which are limited to certain districts, as poor-rates, parochial taxes, county rates, municipal taxes, etc.

LOCAL VENUE. In pleading. A venue which must be laid in a particular county. When the action could have arisen only in a particular county, it is local, and the venue must be laid in that county. 1 Tidd, Pr. 427.

LOCALITY. In Scotch law. This name is given to a life-rent created in marriage contracts in favor of the wife, instead of leaving her to her legal life-rent of tierce. 1 Bell, Comm. 55.

LOCARE. To let for hire; to deliver or bail a thing for a certain reward or compensation. Bract. fol. 62.

LOCARIUM. In old European law. The price of letting; money paid for the hire of a thing; rent. Spelman.

LOCATAIRE. In French law. A lessee, tenant, or renter.

LOCATARIUS. A depositee.

LOCATE. To ascertain and fix the position of something, the place of which was before uncertain or not manifest; as to locate the calls in a deed.

To decide upon the place or direction to be occupied by something not yet in being; as to locate a road.

LOCATIO. Lat. In the civil law. Letting for hire. The term is also used by text-writers upon the law of bailment at common law. In Scotch law it is translated "location." Bell.

LOCATIO-CONDUCTIO. In the civil law. A compound word used to denote the contract of bailment for hire, expressing the action of *both* parties, viz., a letting by the one, and a hiring by the other. 2 Kent, Comm. 586, note; Story, Bailm. § 368.

LOCATIO CUSTODIÆ. A letting to keep; a bailment or deposit of goods for hire. Story, Bailm. § 442.

LOCATIO OPERIS. In the civil law. The contract of hiring work, *i. e.*, labor and services.

It is a contract by which one of the parties gives a certain work to be performed by the other, who binds himself to do it for the price agreed between them, which he who gives the work to be done promises to pay to the other for doing it. Poth. Louage, no. 392.

LOCATIO OPERIS FACIENDI. A letting out of work to be done; a bailment of a thing for the purpose of having some work and labor or care and pains bestowed on it for a pecuniary recompense. 2 Kent, Comm. 586, 588; Story, Bailm. §§ 370, 421, 422.

LOCATIO OPERIS MERCIUM VEHENDARUM. A letting of work to be done in the carrying of goods; a contract of bailment by which goods are delivered to a person to carry for hire. 2 Kent, Comm. 597; Story, Bailm. §§ 370, 457.

LOCATIO REI. A letting of a thing to hire. 2 Kent, Comm. 586. The bailment or letting of a thing to be used by the bailee for a compensation to be paid by him. Story, Bailm. § 370.

LOCATION. **In American land law.** The designation of the boundaries of a particular piece of land, either upon record or on the land itself. 1 Bibb, 84.

The finding and marking out the bounds of a particular tract of land, upon the land itself, in conformity to a certain description contained in an entry, grant, map, etc.; such description consisting in what are termed "locative calls."

In mining law. The act of appropriating a "mining claim" (parcel of land containing precious metal in its soil or rock) according to certain established rules. It usually consists in placing on the ground, in a conspicuous position, a notice setting forth the name of the locator, the fact that it is thus taken or located, with the requisite description of the extent and boundaries of the parcel. 104 U. S. 649.

In a secondary sense, the mining claim covered by a single act of appropriation or location. Id.

In Scotch law. A contract by which the temporary use of a subject, or the work or service of a person, is given for an ascertained hire. 1 Bell, Comm. 255.

LOCATIVE CALLS. In a deed, patent, or other instrument containing a description of land, locative calls are specific calls, descriptions, or marks of location, referring to landmarks, physical objects, or other points by which the land can be exactly located and identified.

LOCATOR. **In the civil and Scotch law.** A letter; one who lets; he who, being the owner of a thing, lets it out to another for hire or compensation.

In American land law. One who locates land, or intends or is entitled to locate. See LOCATION.

LOCK-UP HOUSE. A place used temporarily as a prison.

LOCKMAN. An officer in the Isle of Man, to execute the orders of the governor, much like our under-sheriff. Wharton.

LOCMAN. Fr. In French marine law. A pilot.

LOCO PARENTIS. See IN LOCO PARENTIS.

LOCOCESSION. The act of giving place.

LOCULUS. In old records. A coffin; a purse.

LOCUM TENENS. Lat. Holding the place. A deputy, substitute, lieutenant, or representative.

LOCUPLES. Lat. In the civil law. Able to respond in an action; good for the amount which the plaintiff might recover. Dig. 50, 16, 234, 1.

LOCUS. Lat. A place; the place where a thing is done.

LOCUS CONTRACTUS. The place of a contract; the place where a contract is made.

LOCUS CRIMINIS. The locality of a crime; the place where a crime was committed.

LOCUS DELICTI. The place of the offense; the place where an offense was committed. 2 Kent, Comm. 109.

LOCUS IN QUO. The place in which. The place in which the cause of action arose, or where anything is alleged, in pleadings, to have been done. The phrase is most frequently used in actions of trespass *quare clausum fregit.*

LOCUS PARTITUS. In old English law. A place divided. A division made between two towns or counties to make out in which the land or place in question lies. Fleta, lib. 4, c. 15, § 1; Cowell.

LOCUS PŒNITENTIÆ. A place for repentance; an opportunity for changing one's mind; a chance to withdraw from a contemplated bargain or contract before it results in a definite contractual liability. Also used of a chance afforded to a person, by the circumstances, of relinquishing the intention which he has formed to commit a crime, before the perpetration thereof.

Locus pro solutione reditus aut pecuniæ secundum conditionem dimissionis aut obligationis est stricte observandus. 4 Coke, 73. The place for the payment of rent or money, according to the condition of a lease or bond, is to be strictly observed.

LOCUS PUBLICUS. In the civil law. A public place. Dig. 43, 8, 1; Id. 43, 8, 2, 3.

LOCUS REGIT ACTUM. In private international law. The rule that, when a legal transaction complies with the formalities required by the law of the country where it is done, it is also valid in the country where it is to be given effect, although by the law of that country other formalities are required. 8 Sav. Syst. § 381; Westl. Priv. Int. Law, 159.

LOCUS REI SITÆ. The place where a thing is situated. In proceedings *in rem*, or the real actions of the civil law, the proper forum is the *locus rei sitæ.* 2 Gall. 191, 197.

LOCUS SIGILLI. The place of the seal; the place occupied by the seal of written instruments. Usually abbreviated to "L. S."

LOCUS STANDI. A place of standing; standing in court. A right of appearance in a court of justice, or before a legislative body, on a given question.

LODE. This term, as used in the legislation of congress, is applicable to any zone or belt of mineralized rock lying within boundaries clearly separating it from the neighboring rock. It includes all deposits of mineral matter found through a mineralized zone or belt coming from the same source, impressed with the same forms, and appearing to have been created by the same processes. 4 Sawy. 312.

LODEMAN, or LOADSMAN. The pilot conducts the ship up the river or into port; but the loadsman is he that undertakes to bring a ship through the haven, after being brought thither by the pilot, to the quay or place of discharge. Jacob.

LODEMANAGE. The hire of a pilot for conducting a vessel from one place to another. Cowell.

LODGER. One who occupies hired apartments in another's house; a tenant of part of another's house.

A tenant, with the right of exclusive possession of a part of a house, the landlord, by himself or an agent, retaining general dominion over the house itself.

LODGINGS. Habitation in another's house; apartments in another's house, furnished or unfurnished, occupied for habitation; the occupier being termed a "lodger."

LODS ET VENTES. In old French and Canadian law. A fine payable by a *roturier* on every change of ownership of his land; a mutation or alienation fine. Steph. Lect. 351.

LOG-BOOK. A ship's journal. It contains a minute account of the ship's course, with a short history of every occurrence during the voyage. 1 Marsh. Ins. 312.

The part of the log-book relating to transactions in the harbor is termed the "harbor log;" that relating to what happens at sea, the "sea log." Young, Naut. Dict.

LOG-ROLLING. A mischievous legislative practice, of embracing in one bill several distinct matters, none of which, perhaps, could singly obtain the assent of the legislature, and then procuring its passage by a combination of the minorities in favor of each of the measures into a majority that will adopt them all. 60 Ala. 369.

LOGATING. An unlawful game mentioned in St. 33 Hen. VIII. c. 9.

LOGIA. A small house, lodge, or cottage. Mon. Angl. tom. 1, p. 400.

LOGIC. The science of reasoning, or of the operations of the understanding which are subservient to the estimation of evidence. The term includes both the process itself of proceeding from known truths to unknown, and all other intellectual operations, in so far as auxiliary to this.

LOGIUM. In old records. A lodge, hovel, or outhouse.

LOGOGRAPHUS. In Roman law. A public clerk, register, or book-keeper; one who wrote or kept books of accounts. Dig. 50, 4, 18, 10; Cod. 10, 69.

LOGS. Stems or trunks of trees cut into convenient lengths for the purpose of being afterwards manufactured into lumber of various kinds; not including manufactured lumber of any sort, nor timber which is squared or otherwise shaped for use without further change in form. 52 Wis. 398, 9 N. W. Rep. 67.

LOLLARDS. A body of primitive Wesleyans, who assumed importance about the time of John Wycliffe, (1360,) and were very successful in disseminating evangelical truth; but, being implicated (apparently against their will) in the insurrection of the villeins in 1381, the statute *De Hæretico Comburendo* (2 Hen. IV. c. 15) was passed against them, for their suppression. However, they were not suppressed, and their representatives survive to the present day under various names and disguises. Brown.

LOMBARDS. A name given to the merchants of Italy, numbers of whom, during the twelfth and thirteenth centuries, were established as merchants and bankers in the principal cities of Europe.

LONDRES. L. Fr. London. Yearb. P. 1 Edw. II. p. 4.

LONG PARLIAMENT. The name usually given to the parliament which met in November, 1640, under Charles I., and was dissolved by Cromwell on the 10th of April, 1653. The name "Long Parliament" is, however, also given to the parliament which met in 1661, after the restoration of the monarchy, and was dissolved on the 30th of December, 1678. This latter parliament is sometimes called, by way of distinction, the "long parliament of Charles II." Mozley & Whitley.

LONG QUINTO, THE. An expression used to denote part second of the year-book which gives reports of cases in 5 Edw. IV.

LONG VACATION. The recess of the English courts from August 10th to October 24th.

Longa possessio est pacis jus. Long possession is the law of peace. Branch, Princ.; Co. Litt. 6.

Longa possessio jus parit. Long possession begets right. Fleta, lib. 3, c. 15, § 6.

Longa possessio parit jus possidendi, et tollit actionem vero domino. Long possession produces the right of possession, and takes away from the true owner his action. Co. Litt. 110*b*.

Longum tempus et longus usus qui excedit memoria hominum sufficit pro jure. Co. Litt. 115*a*. Long time and long use, exceeding the memory of men, suffices for right.

LOOKOUT. A proper lookout on a vessel is some one in a favorable position to see, stationed near enough to the helmsman to communicate with him, and to receive communications from him, and exclusively employed in watching the movements of vessels which they are meeting or about to pass. 12 How. 462.

LOPWOOD. A right in the inhabitants of a parish within a manor, in England, to lop for fuel, at certain periods of the year, the branches of trees growing upon the waste lands of the manor. Sweet.

LOQUELA. Lat. A colloquy; talk. In old English law, this term denoted the oral altercations of the parties to a suit, which led to the issue now called the "pleadings." It also designated an "imparlance," (*q. v.*,) both names evidently referring to the talking together of the parties. *Loquela sine die*, a postponement to an indefinite time.

Loquendum ut vulgus; sentiendum ut docti. We must speak as the common people; we must think as the learned. 7 Coke, 11*b*. This maxim expresses the rule that, when words are used in a technical sense, they must be understood technically; otherwise, when they may be supposed to be used in their ordinary acceptation.

LORD. In English law. A title of honor or nobility belonging properly to the degree of baron, but applied also to the whole peerage, as in the expression "the house of lords." 1 Bl. Comm. 396-400.

A title of office, as lord mayor, lord commissioner, etc.

In feudal law. A feudal superior or proprietor; one of whom a fee or estate is held.

LORD ADVOCATE. The chief public prosecutor of Scotland. 2 Alis. Crim. Pr. 84.

LORD AND VASSAL. In the feudal system, the grantor, who retained the dominion or ultimate property, was called the "lord," and the grantee, who had only the use or possession, was called the "vassal" or "feudatory."

LORD CHIEF BARON. The chief judge of the English court of exchequer, prior to the judicature acts.

LORD CHIEF JUSTICE. See JUSTICE.

LORD HIGH CHANCELLOR. See CHANCELLOR, THE LORD HIGH.

LORD HIGH STEWARD. In England, when a person is impeached, or when a peer is tried on indictment for treason or felony before the house of lords, one of the lords is appointed lord high steward, and acts as speaker *pro tempore*. Sweet.

LORD HIGH TREASURER. An officer formerly existing in England, who had the charge of the royal revenues and customs duties, and of leasing the crown lands. His functions are now vested in the lords commissioners of the treasury. Mozley & Whitley.

LORD IN GROSS. In feudal law. He who is lord, not by reason of any manor, but as the king in respect of his crown, etc. "Very lord" is he who is immediate lord to his tenant; and "very tenant," he who holds immediately of that lord. So that, where there is lord paramount, lord mesne, and tenant, the lord paramount is not very lord to the tenant. Wharton.

LORD JUSTICE CLERK. The second judicial officer in Scotland.

LORD KEEPER, or keeper of the great seal, was originally another name for the lord chancellor. After Henry II.'s reign they were sometimes divided, but now there cannot be a lord chancellor and lord keeper at the same time, for by St. 5 Eliz. c. 18, they are declared to be the same office. Com. Dig. "Chancery," B. 1.

LORD LIEUTENANT. In English law. The viceroy of the crown in Ireland.

The principal military officer of a county, originally appointed for the purpose of mustering the inhabitants for the defense of the country.

LORD MAYOR. The chief officer of the corporation of the city of London is so called. The origin of the appellation of "lord," which the mayor of London enjoys, is attributed to the fourth charter of Edward III., which conferred on that officer the honor of having maces, the same as royal, carried before him by the serjeants. Pull. Laws & Cust. Lond.

LORD MAYOR'S COURT. In English law. This is a court of record, of law and equity, and is the chief court of justice within the corporation of London. Theoretically the lord mayor and aldermen are supposed to preside, but the recorder is in fact the acting judge. It has jurisdiction of all personal and mixed actions arising within the city and liberties without regard to the amount in controversy. See 3 Steph. Comm. 449, note *l*.

LORD OF A MANOR. The grantee or owner of a manor.

LORD ORDINARY is the judge of the court of session in Scotland, who officiates for the time being as the judge of first instance. Darl. Pr. Ct. Sess.

LORD PRIVY SEAL, before the 30 Hen. VIII., was generally an ecclesiastic. The office has since been usually conferred on temporal peers above the degree of barons. He is appointed by letters patent. The lord privy seal, receiving a warrant from the signet office, issues the privy seal, which is an authority to the lord chancellor to pass the great seal where the nature of the grant requires it. But the privy seals for money begin in the treasury, whence the first warrant issues, countersigned by the lord treasurer. The lord privy seal is a member of the cabinet council. Enc. Lond.

LORD WARDEN OF CINQUE PORTS. See CINQUE PORTS.

LORDS APPELLANTS. Five peers who for a time superseded Richard II. in his government, and whom, after a brief control of the government, he in turn superseded in 1397, and put the survivors of them to death. Richard II.'s eighteen commissioners (twelve peers and six commoners) took their place, as an embryo privy council acting with full powers, during the parliamentary recess. Brown.

LORDS COMMISSIONERS. In English law. When a high public office in the state, formerly executed by an individual, is put into commission, the persons charged with the commission are called "lords commissioners," or sometimes "lords" or "commissioners" simply. Thus, we have, in lieu of the lord treasurer and lord high admiral of former times, the lords commissioners of the treasury, and the lords commissioners of the admiralty; and, whenever the great seal is put into commission, the persons charged with it are called "commissioners" or "lords commissioners" of the great seal. Mozley & Whitley.

LORD'S DAY. A name sometimes given to Sunday. Co. Litt. 135.

LORDS JUSTICES OF APPEAL. In English law. The title of the ordinary judges of the court of appeal, by Jud. Act 1877, § 4. Prior to the judicature acts, there were two "lords justices of appeal in chancery," to whom an appeal lay from a vice-chancellor, by 14 & 15 Vict. c. 83.

LORDS MARCHERS. Those noblemen who lived on the marches of Wales or Scotland, who in times past had their laws and power of life and death, like petty kings. Abolished by 27 Hen. VIII. c. 26, and 6 Edw. VI. c. 10. Wharton.

LORDS OF APPEAL. Those members of the house of lords of whom at least three must be present for the hearing and determination of appeals. They are the lord chancellor, the lords of appeal in ordinary, and such peers of parliament as hold, or have held, high judicial offices, such as ex-chancellors and judges of the superior courts in Great Britain and Ireland. App. Jur. Act 1876, §§ 5, 25.

LORDS OF APPEAL IN ORDINARY. These are appointed, with a salary of £6,000 a year, to aid the house of lords in the hearing of appeals. They rank as barons for life, but sit and vote in the house of lords during the tenure of their office only. App. Jur. Act 1876, § 6.

LORDS OF ERECTION. On the Reformation in Scotland, the king, as proprietor of benefices formerly held by abbots and priors, gave them out in temporal lordships to favorites, who were termed "lords of erection." Wharton.

LORDS OF PARLIAMENT. Those who have seats in the house of lords. During bankruptcy, peers are disqualified from sitting or voting in the house of lords. 34 & 35 Vict. c. 50.

LORDS OF REGALITY. In Scotch law. Persons to whom rights of civil and criminal jurisdiction were given by the crown.

LORDS ORDAINERS. Lords appointed in 1312, in the reign of Edward II., for the control of the sovereign and the court party, and for the general reform and better government of the country. Brown.

LORDS SPIRITUAL. The archbishops and bishops who have seats in the house of lords.

LORDS TEMPORAL. Those lay peers who have seats in the house of lords.

LORDSHIP. In English law. Dominion, manor, seigniory, domain; also a title of honor used to a nobleman not being a duke. It is also the customary titulary appellation of the judges and some other persons in authority and office.

LOSS. In insurance. The injury or damage sustained by the insured in consequence of the happening of one or more of the accidents or misfortunes against which the insurer, in consideration of the premium, has undertaken to indemnify the insured. 1 Bouv. Inst. no. 1215.

A loss is *total* when the subject insured is wholly destroyed or reduced to an entirely worthless condition. It is *partial* when the subject is injured, but not destroyed, or when it still retains some value, or some part of it escapes. It is *actual* when the destruction of the thing is real and substantial. It it *constructive* when the injury, without entire destruction, is such as to entitle the assured to abandon the property to the underwriter and claim as for an actual loss. See ACTUAL TOTAL LOSS.

LOST OR NOT LOST. A phrase sometimes inserted in policies of marine insurance to signify that the contract is meant to relate back to the beginning of a voyage now in progress, or to some other antecedent time, and to be valid and effectual even if, at the moment of executing the policy, the vessel should have already perished by some of the perils insured against, provided that neither party has knowledge of that fact or any advantage over the other in the way of superior means of information.

LOST PAPERS. Papers which have been so mislaid that they cannot be found after diligent search.

LOT. The arbitrament of chance; hazard. That which fortuitously determines what course shall be taken or what disposition be made of property or rights.

A share; one of several parcels into which property is divided. Used particularly of land.

The thirteenth dish of lead in the mines of Derbyshire, which belonged to the crown.

LOT AND SCOT. In English law. Certain duties which must be paid by those who claim to exercise the elective franchise within certain cities and boroughs, before they are entitled to vote. It is said that the practice became uniform to refer to the poor-rate as a register of "scot and lot" voters; so that the term, when employed to define a right of election, meant only the payment by a parishioner of the sum to which he was assessed on the poor-rate. Brown.

LOT OF LAND. A small tract or parcel of land in a village, town, or city, suitable for building, or for a garden, or other similar uses. See 28 N. J. Law, 44; 37 N. J. Eq. 486; 28 Minn. 17, 8 N. W. Rep. 830.

LOTHERWITE, or LEYERWIT. In old English law. A liberty or privilege to take amends for lying with a bondwoman without license.

LOTTERY. A lottery is any scheme for the disposal or distribution of property by chance among persons who have paid, or promised or agreed to pay, any valuable consideration for the chance of obtaining such property, or a portion of it, or for any share of or interest in such property, upon any agreement, understanding, or expectation that it is to be distributed or disposed of by lot or chance, whether called a "lottery," a "raffle," or a "gift enterprise," or by whatever name the same may be known. Pen. Code Cal. § 319; Pen. Code Dak. § 373.

A lottery is a distribution of prizes by chance or lot, where a valuable consideration is given for the chance of drawing a prize. 1 Abb. (U. S.) 275; 42 Tex. 580; 8 Phila. 457.

Lou le ley done chose, la ceo done remedie a vener a ceo. 2 Rolle, 17. Where the law gives a right, it gives a remedy to recover.

LOUAGE. Fr. This is the contract of hiring and letting in French law, and may be either of things or of labor. The varieties of each are the following:

1. Letting of things,—*Bail à loyer* being the letting of houses; *bail à ferme* being the letting of lands.

2. Letting of labor,—*loyer* being the letting of personal service; *bail à cheptel* being the letting of animals. Brown.

LOURCURDUS. A ram or bell-wether. Cowell.

LOVE-DAY. In old English law. The day on which any dispute was amicably settled between neighbors; or a day on which one neighbor helps another without hire. Wharton.

LOW JUSTICE. In old European law. Jurisdiction of petty offenses, as distinguished from "high justice," (*q. v.*)

LOW WATER. The furthest receding point of ebb-tide. 13 How. 417.

LOW-WATER MARK. That line on the shore of the sea which marks the edge of the waters at the lowest point of the ordinary ebb tide. See 60 Pa. St. 339; 26 Me. 384.

LOWBOTE. A recompense for the death of a man killed in a tumult. Cowell.

LOWERS. Fr. In French maritime law. Wages. Ord. Mar. liv. 1, tit. 14, art. 16.

LOYAL. Legal; authorized by or conforming to law. Also faithful in one's political relations; giving faithful support to one's prince or sovereign or to the existing government.

LOYALTY. Adherence to law. Faithfulness to one's prince or sovereign or to the existing government.

Lubricum linguæ non facile trahendum est in pœnam. Cro. Car. 117. A slip of the tongue ought not lightly to be subjected to punishment.

LUCID INTERVALS. In medical jurisprudence. Intervals occurring in the mental life of an insane person during which he is completely restored to the use of his reason, or so far restored that he has sufficient intelligence, judgment, and will to enter into contractual relations, or perform other legal acts, without disqualification by reason of his disease.

LUCRATIVA CAUSA. Lat. In Roman law. A consideration which is voluntary; that is to say, a gratuitous gift, or such like. It was opposed to *onerosa causa*, which denoted a valuable consideration. It was a principle of the Roman law that two lucrative causes could not concur in the same person as regarded the same thing; that is to say, that, when the same thing was bequeathed to a person by two different testators, he could not have the thing (or its value) twice over. Brown.

LUCRATIVA USUCAPIO. Lat. This species of *usucapio* was permitted in Roman law only in the case of persons taking possession of property upon the decease of its late owner, and in exclusion or deforcement of the heir, whence it was called "*usucapio pro hærede.*" The adjective "*lucrativa*" denoted that property was acquired by this *usucapio* without any consideration or payment for it by way of purchase; and, as the possessor who so acquired the property was a *malâ fide* possessor, his acquisition, or *usucapio*, was called also "*improba*," (*i. e.*, dishonest;) but this dishonesty was tolerated (until abolished by Hadrian) as an incentive to force the *hæres* to take possession, in order that the debts might be paid and the sacrifices performed; and, as a further incentive to the *hæres*, this *usucapio* was complete in one year. Brown.

LUCRATIVE SUCCESSION. In Scotch law. A kind of passive title by which a person accepting from another, without any onerous cause, (or without paying value,) a disposition of any part of his heritage, to which the receiver would have succeeded as heir, is liable to all the grantor's debts contracted before the said disposition. 1 Forb. Inst. pt. 3, p. 102.

LUCRATUS. In Scotch law. A gainer.

LUCRE. Gain in money or goods; profit; usually in an ill sense, or with the sense of something base or unworthy. Webster.

LUCRI CAUSA. Lat. In criminal law. A term descriptive of the intent with which property is taken in cases of larceny, the phrase meaning "for the sake of lucre" or gain.

LUCRUM CESSANS. Lat. In Scotch law. A ceasing gain, as distinguished from *damnum datum*, an actual loss.

Lucrum facere ex pupilli tutela tutor non debet. A guardian ought not to make money out of the guardianship of his ward. 1 Johns. Ch. 527, 535.

LUCTUOSA HÆREDITAS. A mournful inheritance. See HÆREDITAS LUCTUOSA.

LUCTUS. In Roman law. Mourning. See ANNUS LUCTUS.

LUGGAGE. Luggage may consist of any articles intended for the use of a passenger while traveling, or for his personal equipment. Civil Code Cal. § 2181.

This term is synonymous with "baggage," but is more commonly used in England than in America.

LUMEN. In the civil law. Light; the light of the sun or sky; the privilege of receiving light into a house.

A light or window.

LUMINA. In the civil law. Lights; windows; openings to obtain light for one's building.

LUMINARE. A lamp or candle set burning on the altar of any church or chapel, for the maintenance whereof lands and rent-charges were frequently given to parish churches, etc. Kennett, Gloss.

LUNACY. Lunacy is that condition or habit in which the mind is directed by the will, but is wholly or partially misguided or erroneously governed by it; or it is the impairment of any one or more of the faculties of the mind, accompanied with or inducing a defect in the comparing faculty. 1 Bland, 386.

"Lunacy" means either (1) the condition or *status* of a lunatic, (*q. v.*,) or (2) judicial proceedings taken before the proper court or officer for the purpose of making inquiry into the state of mind of persons alleged to be lunatics, of taking charge of them and their property if they are found to be lunatics, and for removing the restraint on their restoration to sanity. Sweet.

Lunacy includes both the forms of mental alienation known, respectively, as "mania" and "dementia." 10 N. J. Eq. 186.

LUNACY, COMMISSION OF. A commission issuing from a court of competent jurisdiction, authorizing an inquiry to be made into the mental condition of a person who is alleged to be a lunatic.

LUNAR. Belonging to or measured by the revolutions of the moon.

LUNAR MONTH. See MONTH.

LUNATIC. A person of deranged or unsound mind; a person whose mental faculties are in the condition called "lunacy," (*q. v.*)

Lunaticus, qui gaudet in lucidis intervallis. He is a lunatic who enjoys lucid intervals. 1 Story, Cont. § 73.

LUNDRESS. In old English law. A silver penny, so called because it was to be coined only at London, (*a Londres,*) and not at the country mints. Lown. Essay Coins, 17; Cowell.

LUPANATRIX. A bawd or strumpet. 3 Inst. 206.

LUPINUM CAPUT GERERE. Lat. To be outlawed, and have one's head exposed, like a wolf's, with a reward to him who should take it. Cowell.

LURGULARY. Casting any corrupt or poisonous thing into the water. Wharton.

LUSHBOROW. In old English law. A base sort of money, coined beyond sea in the likeness of English coin, and introduced into England in the reign of Edward III. Prohibited by St. 25 Edw. III. c. 4. Spelman; Cowell.

LUXURY. Excess and extravagance, which was formerly an offense against the public economy, but is not now punishable. Wharton.

LYCH-GATE. The gate into a churchyard, with a roof or awning hung on posts over it to cover the body brought for burial, when it rests underneath. Wharton.

LYEF-GELD. Sax. In old records. Lief silver or money; a small fine paid by the customary tenant to the lord for *leave* to plow or sow, etc. Somn. Gavelkind, 27.

LYING BY. A person who, by his presence and silence at a transaction which affects his interests, may be fairly supposed to acquiesce in it, if he afterwards propose to disturb the arrangement, is said to be prevented from doing so by reason that he has been *lying by.*

LYING IN FRANCHISE. A term descriptive of waifs, wrecks, estrays, and the like, which may be seized without suit or action.

LYING IN GRANT. A phrase applied to incorporeal rights, incapable of manual tradition, and which must pass by mere delivery of a deed.

LYING IN WAIT. Lying in ambush; lying hid or concealed for the purpose of making a sudden and unexpected attack upon a person when he shall arrive at the scene. In some jurisdictions, where there are several degrees of murder, lying in wait is made evidence of that deliberation and premeditated intent which is necessary to characterize murder in the first degree.

This term is not synonymous with "concealed." If a person conceals himself for the purpose of shooting another unawares, he is lying in wait; but a person may, while concealed, shoot another without committing the crime of murder. 55 Cal. 207.

LYNCH LAW. A term descriptive of the action of unofficial persons, organized bands, or mobs, who seize persons charged with or suspected of crimes, or take them out of the custody of the law, and inflict summary punishment upon them, without legal trial, and without the warrant or authority of law.

LYNDHURST'S (LORD) ACT. This statute (5 & 6 Wm. IV. c. 54) renders marriages within the prohibited degrees absolutely null and void. Theretofore such marriages were voidable merely.

LYON KING OF ARMS. In Scotch law. The ancient duty of this officer was to carry public messages to foreign states, and it is still the practice of the heralds to make all royal proclamations at the Cross of Edinburgh. The officers serving under him are heralds, pursuivants, and messengers. Bell.

LYTÆ. In old Roman law. A name given to students of the civil law in the fourth year of their course, from their being supposed capable of *solving* any difficulty in law. Tayl. Civil Law, 39.

M.

M. This letter, used as a Roman numeral, stands for one thousand.

It was also, in old English law, a brand or stigma impressed upon the brawn of the thumb of a person convicted of manslaughter and admitted to the benefit of clergy.

This letter was sometimes put on the face of treasury notes of the United States, and signifies that the treasury note bears interest at the rate of one mill per centum, and not one per centum interest. 13 Pet. 176.

M. also stands as an abbreviation for several words of which it is the initial letter; as "Mary," (the English queen of that name,) "Michaelmas," "master," "middle."

M. D. An abbreviation for "Middle District," in reference to the division of the United States into judicial districts. Also an abbreviation for "Doctor of Medicine."

M. R. An abbreviation for "Master of the Rolls."

M. T. An abbreviation for "Michaelmas Term."

MACE. A large staff, made of the precious metals, and highly ornamented. It is used as an emblem of authority, and carried before certain public functionaries by a mace-bearer.

MACE-BEARER. In English law. One who carries the mace before certain functionaries. In Scotland, an officer attending the court of session, and usually called a "macer."

MACE-GREFF. In old English law. One who buys stolen goods, particularly food, knowing it to have been stolen.

MACE-PROOF. Secure against arrest.

MACEDONIAN DECREE. In Roman law. This was the *Senatus-consultum Macedonianum,* a decree of the Roman senate, first given under Claudius, and renewed under Vespasian, by which it was declared that no action should be maintained to recover a loan of money made to a child who was under the *patria potestas.* It was intended to strike at the practice of usurers in making loans, on unconscionable terms, to family heirs who would mortgage their future expectations from the paternal estate. The law is said to have derived its name from that of a notorious usurer. See Mackeld. Rom. Law, § 432; Inst. 4, 7, 1; Dig. 14, 6.

MACER. A mace-bearer; an officer attending the court of session in Scotland.

MACHECOLLARE. To make a warlike device over a gate or other passage like to a grate, through which scalding water or ponderous or offensive things may be cast upon the assailants. Co. Litt. 5*a*.

MACHINATION. Contriving a plot or conspiracy. The act of planning or contriving a scheme for executing some purpose, particularly an evil purpose; an artful design formed with deliberation.

MACHINE. In patent law. Any contrivance used to regulate or augment force or motion; more properly, a complex structure, consisting of a combination, or peculiar modification, of the mechanical powers.

The term "machine," in patent law, includes every mechanical device, or combination of mechanical powers and devices, to perform some function and produce a certain effect or result. But where the result or effect is produced by chemical action, by the operation or application of some element or power of nature, or of one substance to another, such modes, methods, or operations are called "processes." A new process is usually the result of discovery; a machine, of invention. 15 How. 252, 267.

MACHINERY. A more comprehensive term than "machine;" including the appurtenances necessary to the working of a machine. 111 Mass. 540; 108 Mass. 78.

MACHOLUM. A barn or granary open at the top; a rick or stack of corn. Spelman.

MACTATOR. A murderer.

MACULARE. In old European law. To wound. Spelman.

MADE KNOWN. Where a writ of *scire facias* has been actually served upon a defendant, the proper return is that its contents have been "made known" to him.

MADRAS REGULATIONS. Certain regulations prescribed for the government of the Madras presidency. Mozley & Whitley.

MÆC-BURGH. Kindred; family.

MÆGBOTE. In Saxon law. A recompense or satisfaction for the slaying or murder of a kinsman. Spelman.

MÆRE. Famous; great; noted; as *Ælmere,* all famous. Gibs. Camd.

MÆREMIUM. Timber; wood suitable for building purposes.

MAGIC. In English statutes. Witchcraft and sorcery.

MAGIS. Lat. More; more fully; more in number; rather.

Magis de bono quam de malo lex intendit. Co. Litt. 78*b*. The law favors a good rather than a bad construction. Where the words used in an agreement are susceptible of two meanings, the one agreeable to, the other against, the law, the former is adopted. Thus, a bond conditioned "to assign all offices" will be construed to apply to such offices only as are assignable. Chit. Cont. 78.

Magis dignum trahit ad se minus dignum. The more worthy draws to itself the less worthy. Yearb. 20 Hen. VI. 2, arg.

MAGISTER. **In English law.** A master or ruler; a person who has attained to some eminent degree in science. Cowell.

In the civil law. A title of several offices under the Roman Empire.

MAGISTER AD FACULTATES. In English ecclesiastical law. The title of an officer who grants dispensations; as to marry, to eat flesh on days prohibited, and the like. Bac. Abr. "Ecclesiastical Courts," A, 5.

MAGISTER CANCELLARIÆ. In old English law. Master of the chancery; master in chancery. These officers were said to be called "*magistri,*" because they were priests. Latch, 133.

MAGISTER EQUITUM. Master of the horse. A title of office under the Roman Empire.

MAGISTER LIBELLORUM. Master of requests. A title of office under the Roman Empire.

MAGISTER LITIS. Master of the suit; the person who controls the suit or its prosecution, or has the right so to do.

MAGISTER NAVIS. In the civil law. The master of a ship or vessel. He to whom the care of the whole vessel is committed. Dig. 14, 1, 1, 1, 5.

MAGISTER PALATII. Master of the palace or of the offices. An officer under the Roman Empire bearing some resemblance to the modern lord chamberlain. Tayl. Civil Law, 37.

Magister rerum usus. Use is the master of things. Co. Litt. 229*b*. Usage is a principal guide in practice.

Magister rerum usus; magistra rerum experientia. Use is the master of things; experience is the mistress of things. Co. Litt. 69, 229; Wing. Max. 752.

MAGISTER SOCIETATIS. In the civil law. The master or manager of a partnership; a managing partner or general agent; a manager specially chosen by a firm to administer the affairs of the partnership. Story, Partn. § 95.

MAGISTERIAL. Relating or pertaining to the character, office, powers, or duties of a magistrate or of the magistracy.

MAGISTRACY. This term may have a more or less extensive signification according to the use and connection in which it occurs. In its widest sense it includes the whole body of public functionaries, whether their offices be legislative, judicial, executive, or administrative. In a more restricted (and more usual) meaning, it denotes the class of officers who are charged with the application and execution of the laws. In a still more confined use, it designates the body of judicial officers of the lowest rank, and more especially those who have jurisdiction for the trial and punishment of petty misdemeanors or the preliminary steps of a criminal prosecution, such as police judges and justices of the peace. The term also denotes the office of a magistrate.

MAGISTRALIA BREVIA. In old English practice. Magisterial writs; writs adapted to special cases, and so called from being framed by the *masters* or principal clerks of the chancery. Bract. fol. 413*b;* Crabb, Com. Law, 547, 548.

MAGISTRATE. A public officer belonging to the civil organization of the state, and invested with powers and functions which may be either judicial, legislative, or executive.

But the term is commonly used in a narrower sense, designating, in England, a person intrusted with the commission of the peace, and, in America, one of the class of inferior judicial officers, such as justices of the peace and police justices.

A magistrate is an officer having power to issue a warrant for the arrest of a person charged with a public offense. Pen. Code Cal. § 807.

The word "magistrate" does not necessarily imply an officer exercising any judicial functions, and might very well be held to embrace notaries and commissioners of deeds. 57 Mo. 336.

MAGISTRATE'S COURT. In American law. Courts in the state of South Carolina, having exclusive jurisdiction in matters of contract of and under twenty dollars.

A local court in the city of Philadelphia, possessing the criminal jurisdiction of a police court and civil jurisdiction in actions involving not more than one hundred dollars. It is not a court of record. See Const. Pa. art. 4, § 12.

MAGISTRATUS. In the civil law. A magistrate. Calvin. A judicial officer who had the power of hearing and determining causes, but whose office properly was to inquire into matters of law, as distinguished from fact. Hallifax, Civil Law, b. 3, c. 8.

MAGNA ASSISA. In old English law. The grand assize. Glanv. lib. 2, cc. 11, 12.

MAGNA ASSISA ELIGENDA. An ancient writ to summon four lawful knights before the justices of assize, there to choose twelve others, with themselves to constitute the *grand assize* or great jury, to try the matter of right. The trial by grand assize was instituted by Henry II. in parliament, as an alternative to the duel in a writ of right. Abolished by 3 & 4 Wm. IV. c. 27. Wharton.

MAGNA AVERIA. In old pleading. Great beasts, as horses, oxen, etc. Cro. Jac. 580.

MAGNA CENTUM. The great hundred, or six score. Wharton.

MAGNA CHARTA. The great charter. The name of a charter (or constitutional enactment) granted by King John of England to the barons, at Runnymede, on June 15, 1215, and afterwards, with some alterations, confirmed in parliament by Henry III. and Edward I. This charter is justly regarded as the foundation of English constitutional liberty. Among its thirty-eight chapters are found provisions for regulating the administration of justice, defining the temporal and ecclesiastical jurisdictions, securing the personal liberty of the subject and his rights of property, and the limits of taxation, and for preserving the liberties and privileges of the church. *Magna Charta* is so called, partly to distinguish it from the *Charta de Foresta*, which was granted about the same time, and partly by reason of its own transcendent importance.

Magna Charta et Charta de Foresta sont appelès les "deux grandes charters." 2 Inst. 570. *Magna Charta* and the Charter of the Forest are called the "two great charters."

MAGNA COMPONERE PARVIS. To compare great things with small things.

MAGNA CULPA. Great fault; gross negligence.

MAGNA NEGLIGENTIA. In the civil law. Great or gross negligence.

Magna negligentia culpa est; magna culpa dolus est. Gross negligence is fault; gross fault is fraud. Dig. 50, 16, 226.

MAGNA PRECARIA. In old English law. A great or general reap-day. Cowell; Blount.

MAGNA SERJEANTIA. In old English law. Grand serjeanty. Fleta, lib. 2, c. 4, § 1.

MAGNUM CAPE. In old practice. Great or grand *cape*. 1 Reeve, Eng. Law, 418. See GRAND CAPE.

MAGNUM CONCILIUM. In old English law. The great council; the general council of the realm; afterwards called "parliament." 1 Bl. Comm. 148; 1 Reeve, Eng. Law, 62; Spelman.

The king's great council of barons and prelates. Spelman; Crabb, Com. Law, 228.

MAGNUS ROTULUS STATUTORUM. The great statute roll. The first of the English statute rolls, beginning with *Magna Charta*, and ending with Edward III. Hale, Com. Law, 16, 17.

MAHA-GEN. In Hindu law. A banker or any great shop-keeper.

MAHAL. In Hindu law. Any land or public fund producing a revenue to the government of Hindostan. "*Mahalaat*" is the plural.

MAHLBRIEF. In maritime law. The German name for the contract for the building of a vessel. This contract contains a specification of the kind of vessel intended, her dimensions, the time within which she is to be completed, the price and times of payment, etc. Jac. Sea Laws, 2-8.

MAIDEN. In Scotch law. An instrument formerly used in beheading criminals.

It resembled the French guillotine, of which it is said to have been the prototype. Wharton.

MAIDEN ASSIZE. In English law. Originally an assize at which no person was condemned to die. Now it is a session of a criminal court at which there are no prisoners to be tried.

MAIDEN RENTS. A fine paid by the tenants of some manors to the lord for a license to marry a daughter. Cowell. Or, perhaps, for the lord's omitting the custom of *marcheta*, (*q. v.*)

MAIGNAGIUM. A brasier's shop, or, perhaps, a house. Cowell.

MAIHEM. See MAYHEM; MAIM.

MAIHEMATUS. Maimed or wounded.

MAIHEMIUM. In old English law. Mayhem, (*q. v.*)

Maihemium est homicidium inchoatum. 3 Inst. 118. Mayhem is incipient homicide.

Maihemium est inter crimina majora minimum, et inter minora maximum. Co. Litt. 127. Mayhem is the least of great crimes, and the greatest of small.

Maihemium est membri mutilatio, et dici poterit, ubi aliquis in aliqua parte sui corporis effectus sit inutilis ad pugnandum. Co. Litt. 126. Mayhem is the mutilation of a member, and can be said to take place when a man is injured in any part of his body so as to be useless in fight.

MAIL. As applied to the post-office, this term means the carriage of letters, whether applied to the bag into which they are put, the coach or vehicle by means of which they are transported, or any other means employed for their carriage and delivery by public authority. 6 Daly, 560. It may also denote the letters or other matter so carried.

The term "mail," as used in Rev. St. U. S. § 5469, relative to robbing the mails, may mean either the whole body of matter transported by the postal agents, or any letter or package forming a component part of it. 41 Fed. Rep. 130.

Mail also denotes armor, as in the phrase a "coat of mail."

In Scotch law. Rent; a rent or tribute. A tenant who pays a rent is called a "mail-payer," "mailer," or "mail-man." Skene.

MAIL MATTER. This term includes letters, packets, etc., received for transmission, and to be transmitted by post to the person to whom such matter is directed. 30 Fed. Rep. 820.

MAILABLE. Suitable or admissible for transmission by the mail; belonging to the classes of articles which, by the laws and postal regulations, may be sent by post.

MAILE. In old English law. A kind of ancient money, or silver half-pence; a small rent.

MAILED. This word, as applied to a letter, means that the letter was properly prepared for transmission by the servants of the postal department, and that it was put in the custody of the officer charged with the duty of forwarding the mail. 67 Mo. 163.

MAILLS AND DUTIES. In Scotch law. The rents of an estate. Bell.

MAIM. To deprive a person of a member or part of the body, the loss of which renders him less capable of fighting; to commit mayhem, (*q. v.*)

In this respect, "to wound" is distinguishable from "to maim;" for the latter implies a permanent injury, whereas a wound is any mutilation or laceration which breaks the continuity of the outer skin. 11 Cox, Crim. Cas. 125.

MAIMING. Depriving of any necessary part. See MAYHEM.

MAIN. L. Fr. A hand. More commonly written "*meyn.*"

MAIN-A-MAIN. L. Fr. Immediately. Kelham.

MAIN CHANNEL. The main channel of a river is that bed over which the principal volume of water flows. 31 Fed. Rep. 755.

MAIN-RENT. Vassalage.

MAIN SEA. The open, uninclosed ocean; or that portion of the sea which is without the *fauces terræ* on the sea-coast, in contradistinction to that which is surrounded or inclosed between narrow headlands or promontories. 5 Mason, 298; 73 N. Y. 396; 2 East, P. C. c. 17, § 9; 7 N. Y. 555; 3 Barb. 203.

MAINAD. A false oath; perjury. Cowell.

MAINE-PORT. A small tribute, commonly of loaves of bread, which in some places the parishioners paid to the rector in lieu of small tithes. Cowell.

MAINOUR. In criminal law. An article stolen, when found in the hands of the thief. A thief caught with the stolen goods in his possession is said to be taken "with the mainour," that is, with the property *in manu*, in his hands. 4 Bl. Comm. 307.

The word seems to have corresponded with the Saxon "*handhabend*," (*q. v.*) In modern law it has sometimes been written as an English word "manner," and the expression "taken in the manner" occurs in the books. Crabb, Eng. Law, 154.

MAINOVRE, or MAINŒUVRE. A trespass committed by hand. See 7 Rich. II. c. 4.

MAINPERNABLE. Capable of being bailed; bailable; admissible to bail on giving surety by mainpernors.

MAINPERNOR. In old practice. A surety for the appearance of a person under arrest, who is delivered out of custody into the hands of his bail. "Mainpernors" differ from "bail" in that a man's bail may imprison or surrender him up before the stipulated day of appearance; mainpernors can do neither, but are barely sureties for his appearance at the day. Bail are only sureties that the party be answerable for the special matter for which they stipulate; mainpernors are bound to produce him to answer all charges whatsoever. 3 Bl. Comm. 128. Other distinctions are made in the old books. See Cowell.

MAINPRISE. The delivery of a person into the custody of *mainpernors*, (*q. v.*) Also the name of a writ (now obsolete) commanding the sheriff to take the security of mainpernors and set the party at liberty.

MAINSWORN. Forsworn, by making false oath with *hand* (*main*) on book. Used in the north of England. Brownl. 4; Hob. 125.

MAINTAIN. To maintain an action or suit is to commence or institute it; the term imports the existence of a cause of action. 8 Minn. 105, (Gil. 80, 81.)

MAINTAINED. In pleading. A technical word indispensable in an indictment for maintenance. 1 Wils. 325.

MAINTAINOR. In criminal law. One that maintains or seconds a cause depending in suit between others, either by disbursing money or making friends for either party towards his help. Blount. One who is guilty of *maintenance* (*q. v.*)

MAINTENANCE. Sustenance; support; assistance. The furnishing by one person to another, for his support, of the means of living, or food, clothing, shelter, etc., particularly where the legal relation of the parties is such that one is bound to support the other, as between father and child, or husband and wife.

In criminal law. An unauthorized and officious interference in a suit in which the offender has no interest, to assist one of the parties to it, against the other, with money or advice to prosecute or defend the action. 1 Russ. Crimes, 254.

Maintenance, in general, signifies an unlawful taking in hand or upholding of quarrels and sides, to the hindrance of common right. Co. Litt. 368*b*; Hawk. P. C. 393.

The intermeddling of a stranger in a suit, for the purpose of stirring up strife and continuing litigation. 35 Vt. 69.

Maintenance is the assisting another person in a lawsuit, without having any concern in the subject. 8 Johns. 220.

Maintenance is where one officiously intermeddles in a suit which in no way belongs to him. The term does not include all kinds of aid in the prosecution or defense of another's cause. It does not extend to persons having an interest in the thing in controversy, nor to persons of kin or affinity to either party, nor to counsel or attorneys, for their acts are not officious, nor unlawful. The distinction between "champerty" and "maintenance" is that maintenance is the promoting, or undertaking to promote, a suit by one who has no lawful cause to do so, and champerty is an agreement for a division of the thing in controversy, in the event of success, as a reward for the unlawful assistance. 3 Har. (Del.) 208.

"Maintenance," at common law, signifies an unlawful taking in hand or upholding of quarrels or sides, to the disturbance or hindrance of common right. The maintaining of one side, in consideration of some bargain to have part of the thing in dispute, is called "champerty." Champerty, therefore, is a species of maintenance. 40 Conn. 570.

MAIOR. An old form of "mayor."

MAIRE. In old Scotch law. An officer to whom process was directed. Otherwise called "mair of fie," (fee,) and classed with the "serjand." Skene.

MAIRIE. In French law. The government building of each commune. It contains the record office of all civil acts and the list of voters; and it is there that political and municipal elections take place. Arg. Fr. Merc. Law, 566.

MAISON DE DIEU. Fr. A hospital; an almshouse; a monastery. St. 39 Eliz. c. 5. Literally, "house of God."

MAISTER. An old form of "master."

MAISURA. A house, mansion, or farm. Cowell.

MAITRE. Fr. In French maritime law. Master; the master or captain of a vessel. Ord. Mar. liv. 2, tit. 1, art. 1.

MAJESTAS. Lat. In Roman law. The majesty, sovereign authority, or supreme prerogative of the state or prince. Also a shorter form of the expression "*crimen majestatis*," or "*crimen læsæ majestatis*," an offense against sovereignty, or against the safety or organic life of the Roman people; *i. e.*, high treason.

MAJESTY. Royal dignity. A term used of kings and emperors as a title of honor.

MAJOR. A person of full age; one who is no longer a minor; one who has attained the management of his own concerns and the enjoyment of his civic rights.

In military law. The officer next in rank above a captain.

MAJOR ANNUS. The greater year; the bissextile year, consisting of 366 days. Bract. fol. 359*b*.

MAJOR GENERAL. In military law. An officer next in rank above a brigadier general, and next below a lieutenant general, and who usually commands a division or an army corps.

Major hæreditas venit unicuique nostrum a jure et legibus quam a parentibus. 2 Inst. 56. A greater inheritance comes to every one of us from right and the laws than from parents.

Major numerus in se continet minorem. Bract. fol. 16. The greater number contains in itself the less.

MAJORA REGALIA. The king's dignity, power, and royal prerogative, as opposed to his revenue, which is comprised in the *minora* regalia. 2 Steph. Comm. 475; 1 Bl. Comm. 240.

Majore pœna affectus quam legibus statuta est, non est infamis. One affected with a greater punishment than is provided by law is not infamous. 4 Inst. 66.

MAJORES. In Roman law and genealogical tables. The male ascendants beyond the sixth degree.

In old English law. Greater persons; persons of higher condition or estate.

Majori summæ minor inest. In the greater sum the less is included. 2 Kent, Comm. 618; Story, Ag. § 172.

MAJORITY. Full age; the age at which, by law, a person is entitled to the management of his own affairs and to the enjoyment of civic rights. The opposite of minority. Also the *status* of a person who is a major in age.

In the law of elections, majority signifies the greater number of votes. When there are only two candidates, he who receives the greater number of the votes cast is said to have a majority; when there are more than two competitors for the same office, the person who receives the greatest number of votes has a *plurality*, but he has not a majority unless he receives a greater number of votes than those cast for all his competitors combined.

In military affairs, majority denotes the rank and commission of a major.

Majus dignum trahit ad se minus dignum. The more worthy draws to itself the less worthy. Co. Litt. 43, 355*b*; Bract. fol. 175; Noy, Max. p. 6, max. 18.

MAJUS JUS. In old practice. Greater right or more right. A plea in the old real actions. 1 Reeve, Eng. Law, 476. *Majus jus merum*, more mere right. Bract. fol. 31.

MAKE. 1. To cause to exist; to form, fashion, or produce; to do, perform, or execute; as to make an issue, to make oath, to make a presentment.

2. To do in form of law; to perform with due formalities; to execute in legal form; as to make answer, to make a return.

3. To execute as one's act or obligation; to prepare and sign; to sign, execute, and deliver; as to make a conveyance, to make a note.

4. To conclude, determine upon, agree to, or execute; as to make a contract.

5. To cause to happen by one's neglect or omission; as to make default.

6. To make acquisition of; to procure; to collect; as to make the money on an execution.

7. To have authority or influence; to support or sustain; as in the phrase, "This precedent makes for the plaintiff."

MAKE AN ASSIGNMENT. To transfer one's property to an assignee for the benefit of one's creditors.

MAKE A CONTRACT. To agree upon, and conclude or adopt, a contract. In case of a written contract, to reduce it to writing, execute it in due form, and deliver it as binding.

MAKE DEFAULT. To fail or be wanting in some legal duty; particularly, to omit the entering of an appearance when duly summoned in an action at law or other judicial proceeding, to neglect to obey the command of a subpœna, etc.

MAKE ONE'S FAITH. A Scotch phrase, equivalent to the old English phrase, "to make one's law."

MAKER. One who makes, frames, or ordains; as a "law-maker." One who makes or executes; as the maker of a promissory note.

MAKING LAW. In old practice. The formality of denying a plaintiff's charge under oath, in open court, with compurgators. One of the ancient methods of trial, frequently, though inaccurately, termed "waging law," or "wager of law." 3 Bl. Comm. 341.

MAL. A prefix meaning bad, wrong, fraudulent; as maladministration, malpractice, malversation, etc.

MAL GREE. L. Fr. Against the will; without the consent. Hence the single word "*malgre*," and more modern "*maugre*," (*q. v.*)

MAL-TOLTE. Fr. In old French law. A term said to have arisen from the usurious gains of the Jews and Lombards in their management of the public revenue. Steph. Lect. 372.

MALA. Lat. Bad; evil; wrongful.

MALA FIDES. Bad faith. The opposite of *bona fides*, (*q. v.*) *Malâ fide*, in bad faith. *Malæ fidei possessor*, a possessor in bad faith. Mackeld. Rom. Law, § 297.

Mala grammatica non vitiat chartam. Sed in expositione instrumentorum mala grammatica quoad fieri possit evitanda est. Bad grammar does not vitiate a deed. But in the exposition of instruments, bad grammar, as far as it can be done, is to be avoided. 6 Coke, 39; Broom, Max. 686.

MALA IN SE. Wrongs in themselves; acts morally wrong; offenses against conscience. 1 Bl. Comm. 57, 58; 4 Bl. Comm. 8.

MALA PRAXIS. Malpractice; unskillful management or treatment. Particularly applied to the neglect or unskillful management of a physician, surgeon, or apothecary. 3 Bl. Comm. 122.

MALA PROHIBITA. Prohibited wrongs or offenses; acts which are made *offenses* by positive laws, and *prohibited* as such. 1 Bl. Comm. 57, 58; 4 Bl. Comm. 8.

MALADMINISTRATION. This term is used, in the law-books, interchangeably with *mis*-administration, and both words mean "wrong administration." 14 Neb. 183, 15 N. W. Rep. 331.

MALANDRINUS. In old English law. A thief or pirate. Wals. 338.

MALARY. In Hindu law. Judicial; belonging to a judge or magistrate.

MALBERGE. A hill where the people assembled at a court, like the English assizes; which by the Scotch and Irish were called "parley hills." Du Cange.

MALCONNA. In Hindu law. A treasury or store-house.

MALE. Of the masculine sex; of the sex that begets young.

MALE CREDITUS. In old English law. Unfavorably thought of; in bad repute or credit. Bract. fols. 116, 154.

Maledicta est expositio quæ corrumpit textum. That is a cursed interpretation which corrupts the text. 4 Coke, 35*a;* Broom, Max. 622.

MALEDICTION. A curse, which was anciently annexed to donations of lands made to churches or religious houses, against those who should violate their rights. Cowell.

MALEFACTION. A crime; an offense.

MALEFACTOR. He who is guilty, or has been convicted, of some crime or offense.

Maleficia non debent remanere impunita; et impunitas continuum affectum tribuit delinquenti. 4 Coke, 45. Evil deeds ought not to remain unpunished; and impunity affords continual incitement to the delinquent.

Maleficia propositis distinguuntur. Jenk. Cent. 290. Evil deeds are distinguished from evil purposes, or *by* their purposes.

MALEFICIUM. In the civil law. Waste; damage; tort; injury. Dig. 5, 18, 1.

MALESON, or MALISON. A curse.

MALESWORN, or MALSWORN. Forsworn. Cowell.

MALFEASANCE. The wrongful or unjust doing of some act which the doer has no right to perform, or which he has stipulated by contract not to do. It differs from "misfeasance" and "non-feasance," (which titles see.) See 1 Chit. Pr. 9; 1 Chit. Pl. 134.

MALFETRIA. In Spanish law. Offense. White, New Recop. b. 2, tit. 19, c. 1, § 1.

MALICE. In criminal law. In its legal sense, this word does not simply mean ill will against a person, but signifies a wrongful act done intentionally, without just cause or excuse. 4 Barn. & C. 255.

A conscious violation of the law (or the prompting of the mind to commit it) which operates to the prejudice of another person.

About as clear, comprehensive, and correct a definition as the authorities afford is that "malice is a condition of the mind which shows a heart regardless of social duty and fatally bent on mischief, the existence of which is inferred from acts committed or words spoken." 8 Tex. App. 109.

"Malice," in its common acceptation, means ill will towards some person. In its legal sense, it applies to a wrongful act done intentionally, without legal justification or excuse. 1 Ind. 344.

A man may do an act willfully, and yet be free of malice. But he cannot do an act maliciously without at the same time doing it willfully. The malicious doing of an act includes the willful doing of it. Malice includes intent and will. 66 Me. 328.

Malice is either *express* or *implied*. The former is the case where the party declares or manifests a positive intention to commit the crime; while implied malice is gathered, as an inference of law, from the facts and circumstances proved.

In the definition of "murder," *malice aforethought* exists where the person doing the act which causes death has an intention to cause death or grievous bodily harm to any person, (whether the person is actually killed or not,) or to commit any felony whatever, or has the knowledge that the act will probably cause the death of or grievous bodily harm to some person, although he does not desire it, or even wishes that it may not be caused. Steph. Crim. Dig. 144; 1 Russ. Crimes, 641.

The words "malice aforethought" long ago acquired in law a settled meaning, somewhat different from the popular one. In their legal sense they do not import an actual intention to kill the deceased. The idea is not spite or malevolence to the deceased in particular, but evil design in general, the dictate of a wicked, depraved, and malignant heart; not premeditated personal hatred or revenge towards the person killed, but that kind of unlawful purpose which, if persevered in, must produce mischief. 49 N. H. 399.

MALICE PREPENSE. Malice aforethought; deliberate, predetermined malice. 2 Rolle, 461.

MALICIOUS. Evincing malice; done with malice and an evil design; willful.

MALICIOUS ABANDONMENT. In criminal law. The desertion of a wife or husband without just cause.

MALICIOUS ARREST. An arrest made willfully and without probable cause, but in the course of a regular proceeding.

MALICIOUS INJURY. An injury committed against a person at the prompting of malice or hatred towards him, or done spitefully or wantonly.

MALICIOUS MISCHIEF. A term applied to the willful destruction of personal property, from actual ill will or resentment towards its owner or possessor. 3 Dev. & B. 130.

Malicious mischief or damage is a species of injury to private property, which the law considers as a public crime. This is such as is done, not *animo furandi*, or with an intent of gaining by another's loss, but either out of a spirit of wanton cruelty or wicked revenge. In this latter light it bears a near relation to the crime of arson, for, as that affects the habitation, so does this the property, of individuals; and therefore any damage arising from this mischevious disposition, though only a trespass at the common law, is now, by several statutes, made severely penal. Jacob.

MALICIOUS PROSECUTION. A judicial proceeding instituted against a person out of the prosecutor's malice and ill will, with the intention of injuring him, without probable cause to sustain it, the process and proceedings being regular and formal, but not justified by the facts. For this injury an action on the case lies, called the "action of malicious prosecution."

MALIGNARE. To malign or slander; also to maim.

MALITIA. Lat. Actual evil design; express malice.

Malitia est acida; est mali animi affectus. Malice is sour; it is the quality of a bad mind. 2 Bulst. 49.

MALITIA PRÆCOGITATA. Malice aforethought.

Malitia supplet ætatem. Malice supplies [the want of] age. Dyer, 104*b;* Broom, Max. 316.

Malitiis hominum est obviandum. The wicked or malicious designs of men must be thwarted. 4 Coke, 15*b*.

MALLUM. In old European law. A court of the higher kind in which the more important business of the county was dispatched by the count or earl. Spelman. A public national assembly.

MALO ANIMO. Lat. With an evil mind; with a bad purpose or wrongful intention; with malice.

MALO GRATO. In spite; unwillingly.

MALO SENSU. In an evil sense or meaning; with an evil signification.

MALPRACTICE. See MALA PRAXIS.

MALT MULNA. A quern or malt-mill.

MALT-SHOT or MALT-SCOT. A certain payment for making malt. Somner.

MALT-TAX. An excise duty upon malt in England. 1 Bl. Comm. 313; 2 Steph. Comm. 581.

MALTREATMENT. In reference to the treatment of his patient by a surgeon, this term signifies improper or unskillful treatment; it may result either from ignorance, neglect, or willfulness; but the word does not necessarily imply that the conduct of the surgeon, in his treatment of the patient, is either willfully or grossly careless. 2 Allen, 142.

MALUM. Lat. In Roman law. A mast; the mast of a ship. Dig. 50, 17, 242, pr. Held to be part of the ship. Id.

MALUM IN SE. A wrong in itself; an act or case involving illegality from the very nature of the transaction, upon principles of natural, moral, and public law. Story, Ag. § 346.

An act is said to be *malum in se* when it is inherently and essentially evil, that is, immoral in its nature and injurious in its consequences, without any regard to the fact of its being noticed or punished by the law of the state. Such are most or all of the offenses cognizable at common law, (without the denouncement of a statute;) as murder, larceny, etc. An act is said to be *malum prohibitum* when it is wrong only because prohibited; that is, it is not inherently immoral, but becomes illegal because its commission is expressly forbidden by positive law. Many acts contrary to excise or revenue laws are considered by moralists to be of this character.

Malum non habet efficientem, sed deficientem, causam. 3 Inst. Proem. Evil has not an efficient, but a deficient, cause.

Malum non præsumitur. Wickedness is not presumed. Branch, Princ.; 4 Coke, 72*a*.

MALUM PROHIBITUM. A wrong prohibited; a thing which is wrong *because* prohibited; an act which is not inherently immoral, but becomes so because its commission is expressly forbidden by positive law; an act involving an illegality resulting from positive law. Contrasted with *malum in se*. Story, Ag. § 346.

Malum quo communius eo pejus. The more common an evil is, the worse it is. Branch, Princ.

Malus usus abolendus est. A bad or invalid custom is [ought] to be abolished. Litt. § 212; Co. Litt. 141; 1 Bl. Comm. 76; Broom, Max. 921.

MALVEILLES. In old English law. Ill will; crimes and misdemeanors; malicious practices. Cowell.

MALVEIS PROCURORS. Such as used to pack juries, by the nomination of either party in a cause, or other practice. Cowell.

MALVEISA. A warlike engine to batter and beat down walls.

MALVERSATION. In French law. This word is applied to all grave and punishable faults committed in the exercise of a charge or commission, (office,) such as corruption, exaction, concussion, larceny. Merl. Repert.

MAN. A human being. A person of the male sex. A male of the human species above the age of puberty.

In feudal law. A vassal; a tenant or feudatory. The Anglo-Saxon relation of *lord and man* was originally purely personal, and founded on mutual contract. 1 Spence, Ch. 37.

MAN OF STRAW. See MEN OF STRAW.

MANACLES. Chains for the hands; shackles.

MANAGE. To conduct; to carry on; to direct the concerns of a business or establishment. Generally applied to affairs that are somewhat complicated and that involve skill and judgment.

MANAGER. A person chosen or appointed to manage, direct, or administer the affairs of another person or of a corporation or company.

MANAGERS OF A CONFERENCE. Members of the houses of parliament appointed to represent each house at a conference between the two houses. It is an ancient rule that the number of commons named for a conference should be double those of the lords. May, Parl. Pr. c. 16.

MANAGING AGENT. A person who is invested with general power, involving the exercise of judgment and discretion, as distinguished from an ordinary agent or employe, who acts in an inferior capacity, and under the direction and control of superior authority, both in regard to the extent of the work and the manner of executing the same. 19 Hun, 408.

MANAGING OWNER OF SHIP. The managing owner of a ship is one of several co-owners, to whom the others, or those of them who join in the adventure, have delegated the management of the ship. He has authority to do all things usual and necessary in the management of the ship and the delivery of the cargo, to enable her to prosecute her voyage and earn freight, with the right to appoint an agent for the purpose. 6 Q. B. Div. 93; Sweet.

MANAGIUM. A mansion-house or dwelling-place. Cowell.

MANAS MEDIÆ. Men of a mean condition, or of the lowest degree.

MANBOTE. In Saxon law. A compensation or recompense for homicide, particularly due to the lord for killing his man or vassal, the amount of which was regulated by that of the *were.*

MANCA, MANCUS, or MANCUSA. A square piece of gold coin, commonly valued at thirty pence. Cowell.

MANCEPS. In Roman law. A purchaser; one who took the article sold in his hand; a formality observed in certain sales. Calvin. A farmer of the public taxes.

MANCHE-PRESENT. A bribe; a present from the donor's own hand.

MANCIPARE. In Roman law. To sell, alienate, or make over to another; to sell with certain formalities; to sell a person; one of the forms observed in the process of emancipation.

MANCIPATE. To enslave; to bind; to tie.

MANCIPATIO. In Roman law. A certain ceremony or formal process anciently required to be performed, to perfect the sale or conveyance of *res mancipi,* (land, houses, slaves, horses, or cattle.) The parties were present, (vendor and vendee,) with five witnesses and a person called "*libripens,*" who held a balance or scales. A set form of words was repeated on either side, indicative of transfer of ownership, and certain prescribed gestures performed, and the vendee then struck the scales with a piece of copper, thereby symbolizing the payment, or weighing out, of the stipulated price.

The ceremony of *mancipatio* was used, in later times, in one of the forms of making a will. The testator acted as vendor, and the heir (or *familiæ emptor*) as purchaser, the latter symbolically *buying* the whole estate, or succession, of the former. The ceremony was also used by a father in making a fictitious sale of his son, which sale, when three times repeated, effectuated the emancipation of the son.

MANCIPI RES. In Roman law. Certain classes of things which could not be aliened or transferred except by means of a certain formal ceremony of conveyance called "*mancipatio,*" (*q. v.*) These included land, houses, slaves, horses, and cattle. All other things were called "*res nec mancipi.*" The distinction was abolished by Justinian. The distinction corresponded as nearly as may be to the early distinction of English law into real and personal property; *res mancipi* being objects of a military or agricultural character, and *res nec mancipi* being all other subjects of property. Like personal estate, *res nec mancipi* were not originally either valuable *in se* or valued. Brown.

MANCIPIUM. In Roman law. The momentary condition in which a *filius,* etc., might be when in course of emancipation from the *potestas,* and before that emancipation was absolutely complete. The condition was not like the *dominica potestas* over slaves, but slaves are frequently called "*mancipia*" in the non-legal Roman authors. Brown.

MANCIPLE. A clerk of the kitchen, or caterer, especially in colleges. Cowell.

MANCOMUNAL. In Spanish law. An obligation is said to be *mancomunal* when one person assumes the contract or debt of another, and makes himself liable to pay or fulfill it. Schm. Civil Law, 120.

MANDAMIENTO. In Spanish law. Commission; authority or power of attorney. A contract of good faith, by which one person commits to the gratuitous charge of another his affairs, and the latter accepts the charge. White, New Recop. b. 2, tit. 12, c. 1.

MANDAMUS. Lat. We command. This is the name of a writ (formerly a high prerogative writ) which issues from a court of superior jurisdiction, and is directed to a private or municipal corporation, or any of its officers, or to an executive, administrative, or judicial officer, or to an inferior court, commanding the performance of a particular act therein specified, and belonging to his or their public, official, or ministerial duty, or directing the restoration of the complainant to rights or privileges of which he has been illegally deprived.

The action of *mandamus* is one, brought in a court of competent jurisdiction, to obtain an order of such court commanding an inferior tribunal, board, corporation, or person to do or not to do an act the performance or omission of which the law enjoins as a duty resulting from an office, trust, or station. Where discretion is left to the inferior tribunal or person, the *mandamus* can only compel it to act, but cannot control such discretion. Rev. Code Iowa, 1880, § 3373.

The writ of *mandamus* is either *peremptory* or *alternative*, according as it requires the defendant absolutely to obey its behest, or gives him an opportunity to show cause to the contrary. It is the usual practice to issue the alternative writ first. This commands the defendant to do the particular act, or else to appear and show cause against it at a day named. If he neglects to obey the writ, and either makes default in his appearance or fails to show good cause against the application, the peremptory *mandamus* issues, which commands him absolutely and without qualification to do the act.

MANDANS. In the civil law. The employing party in a contract of mandate. One who gives a thing in charge to another; one who requires, requests, or employs another to do some act for him. Inst. 3, 27, 1, et seq.

MANDANT. In French and Scotch law. The employing party in the contract of *mandatum*, or mandate. Story, Bailm. § 138.

Mandata licita recipiunt strictam interpretationem, sed illicita latam et extensam. Lawful commands receive a strict interpretation, but unlawful commands a broad and extended one. Bac. Max. reg. 16.

MANDATAIRE. Fr. In French law. A person employed by another to do some act for him; a mandatary.

Mandatarius terminos sibi positos transgredi non potest. A mandatary cannot exceed the limits assigned him. Jenk. Cent. 53.

MANDATARY. He to whom a mandate, charge, or commandment is given; also, he that obtains a benefice by *mandamus*.

MANDATE. In practice. A judicial command or precept proceeding from a court or judicial officer, directing the proper officer to enforce a judgment, sentence, or decree. Jones, Bailm. 52.

In the practice of the supreme court of the United States, the mandate is a precept or order, issued upon the decision of an appeal or writ of error, directing the action to be taken, or disposition to be made of the case, by the inferior court.

In some of the state jurisdictions, the name "mandate" has been substituted for "*mandamus*" as the formal title of that writ.

In contracts. A bailment of property in regard to which the bailee engages to do some act without reward. Story, Bailm. § 137.

A mandate is a contract by which a lawful business is committed to the management of another, and by him undertaken to be performed gratuitously. The mandatary is bound to the exercise of slight diligence, and is responsible for gross neglect. The fact that the mandator derives no benefit from the acts of the mandatary is not of itself evidence of gross negligence. 42 Miss. 525.

A mandate, procuration, or letter of attorney is an act by which one person gives power to another to transact for him and in his name one or several affairs. The mandate may take place in five different manners, —for the interest of the person granting it only; for the joint interest of both parties; for the interest of a third person; for the interest of a third person and that of the party granting it; and, finally, for the interest of the mandatary and a third person. Civil Code La. arts. 2985, 2986.

Mandates and deposits closely resemble each other; the distinction being that in mandates the care and service are the principal, and the custody the accessory, while in deposits the custody is the principal thing, and the care and service are merely accessory. Story, Bailm. § 140.

The word may also denote a request or direction. Thus, a check is a *mandate* by the drawer to his banker to pay the amount to the transferee or holder of the check. 1 Q. B. Div. 33.

In the civil law. The instructions which the emperor addressed to a public functionary, and which were rules for his conduct. These mandates resembled those of the proconsuls, the *mandata jurisdictio*, and were ordinarily binding on the legates or lieutenants of the empéror in the imperial provinces, and there they had the authority of the principal edicts. Sav. Dr. Rom. c. 3, § 24, no. 4.

MANDATO. In Spanish law. The contract of mandate. Escriche.

MANDATO, PANES DE. Loaves of bread given to the poor upon Maundy Thursday.

MANDATOR. The person employing another to perform a mandate.

MANDATORY. Containing a command; preceptive; imperative; peremptory. A provision in a statute is *mandatory* when disobedience to it will make the act done under the statute absolutely void; if the provision is such that disregard of it will constitute an irregularity, but one not necessarily fatal, it is said to be *directory*. So, the mandatory part of a writ is that which commands the person to do the act specified.

MANDATORY INJUNCTION. In equity practice. An order compelling a defendant to restore things to the condition in which they were at the time when the plaintiff's complaint was made. 33 Law J Eq. (N. S.) 393.

MANDATUM. In the civil law. The contract of mandate, (*q. v.*)

MANDAVI BALLIVO. (I have commanded or made my mandate to the bailiff.) In English practice. The return made by a sheriff, where the bailiff of a liberty has the execution of a writ, that he has commanded the bailiff to execute it. 1 Tidd, Pr. 309; 2 Tidd, Pr. 1025.

MANENTES. Tenants. Obsolete. Cowell.

MANERA. In Spanish law. Manner or mode. Las Partidas, pt. 4, tit. 4, l. 2.

MANERIUM. In old English law. A manor.

Manerium dicitur a manendo, secundum excellentiam, sedes magna, fixa, et stabilis. Co. Litt. 58. A manor is so called from *manendo*, according to its excellence, a seat, great, fixed, and firm.

MANGONARE. In old English law. To buy in a market.

MANGONELLUS. A warlike instrument for casting stones against the walls of a castle. Cowell.

MANHOOD. In feudal law. A term denoting the ceremony of doing homage by the vassal to his lord. The formula used was, "*Devenio vester homo*," I become your man. 2 Bl. Comm. 54.

To arrive at manhood means to arrive at twenty-one years of age. 1 Dev. & B. Eq. 585.

MANIA. "Mania is that form of insanity where the mental derangement is accompanied with more or less of excitement. Sometimes the excitement amounts to a fury. The individual in such cases is subject to hallucinations and illusions. He is impressed with the reality of events which have never occurred, and of things which do not exist, and acts more or less in conformity with his belief in these particulars. The mania may be general, and affect all or most of the operations of the mind; or it may be partial, and be confined to particular subjects. In the latter case it is generally termed 'monomania.'" Per Field, J., 2 Abb. (U. S.) 510.

MANIA A POTU. A disease induced from the intemperate use of spirituous liquors; the same as *delirium tremens*.

MANIFEST. In maritime law. A sea-letter; a written document required to be carried by merchant vessels, containing an account of the cargo, with other particulars, for the facility of the customs officers.

In evidence. That which is clear and requires no proof; that which is notorious.

Manifesta probatione non indigent. 7 Coke, 40. Things manifest do not require proof.

MANIFESTO. A formal written declaration, promulgated by a prince, or by the executive authority of a state or nation, proclaiming its reasons and motives for declaring a war, or for any other important international action.

MANIPULUS. In canon law. A handkerchief, which the priest always had in his left hand. Blount.

MANKIND. The race or species of human beings. In law, females, as well as males, may be included under this term. Fortesc. 91.

MANNER. This is a word of large signification, but cannot exceed the subject to which it belongs. The incident cannot be extended beyond its principal. 75 Pa. St. 39, 54.

Manner does not necessarily include time. Thus, a statutory requirement that a mining tax shall be "enforced in the same manner" as certain annual taxes need not imply an annual collection. 8 Nev. 15, 29.

Also a thing stolen, in the hand of the thief; a corruption of "*mainour*," (*q. v.*)

MANNER AND FORM; MODO ET FORMA. Formal words introduced at the conclusion of a traverse. Their object is to put the party whose pleading is traversed not only to the proof that the matter of fact denied is, in its general effect, true as alleged, but also that the manner and form in which the fact or facts are set forth are also capable of proof. Brown.

MANNING. A day's work of a man. Cowell. A summoning to court. Spelman.

MANNIRE. To cite any person to appear in court and stand in judgment there. It is different from *bannire;* for, though both of them are citations, this is by the adverse party, and that is by the judge. Du Cange.

MANNOPUS. In old English law. Goods taken in the hands of an apprehended thief. The same as "*mainour*," (*q. v.*)

MANNUS. A horse. Cowell.

MANOR. A house, dwelling, seat, or residence.

In English law, the manor was originally a tract of land granted out by the king to a lord or other great person, in fee. It was otherwise called a "barony" or "lordship," and appendant to it was the right to hold a court, called the "court-baron." The lands comprised in the manor were divided into *terræ tenementales* (tenemental lands or bocland) and *terræ dominicales*, or demesne lands. The former were given by the lord of the manor to his followers or retainers in freehold. The latter were such as he reserved for his own use; but of these part were held by tenants in copyhold, *i. e.*, those holding by a copy of the record in the lord's court; and part, under the name of the "lord's waste," served for public roads and commons of pasture for the lord and tenants. The tenants, considered in their relation to the court-baron and to each other, were called "*pares curiæ.*" The word also signified the franchise of having a manor, with jurisdiction for a court-baron and the right to the rents and services of copyholders.

In American law. A manor is a tract held of a proprietor by a fee-farm rent in money or in kind, and descending to the oldest son of the proprietor, who in New York is called a "patroon." 13 N. Y. 291.

MANQUELLER. In Saxon law. A murderer.

MANRENT. In Scotch law. The service of a man or vassal. A bond of manrent was an instrument by which a person, in order to secure the protection of some powerful lord, bound himself to such lord for the performance of certain services.

MANSE. In old English law. A habitation or dwelling, generally with land attached. Spelman.

A residence or dwelling-house for the parish priest; a parsonage or vicarage house. Cowell. Still used in Scotch law in this sense.

MANSER. A bastard. Cowell.

MANSION. A dwelling-house.

In old English law. Residence; dwelling.

MANSION-HOUSE. In the law of burglary, etc., any species of dwelling-house. 3 Inst. 64.

MANSLAUGHTER. In criminal law. The unlawful killing of another without malice, either express or implied; which may be either voluntarily, upon a sudden heat, or involuntarily, but in the commission of some unlawful act. 1 Hale, P. C. 466; 4 Bl. Comm. 191.

Manslaughter is the unlawful killing of a human creature without malice, either express or implied, and without any mixture of deliberation whatever; which may be voluntary, upon a sudden heat of passion, or involuntary, in the commission of an unlawful act, or a lawful act without due caution and circumspection. Code Ga. 1882, § 4324; Pen. Code Cal. § 192.

The distinction between "manslaughter" and "murder" consists in the following: In the former, though the act which occasions the death be unlawful or likely to be attended with bodily mischief, yet the malice, either express or implied, which is the very essence of murder, is presumed to be wanting in manslaughter. 1 East, P. C. 218; 5 Cush. 304.

It also differs from "murder" in this: that there can be no accessaries before the fact, there having been no time for premeditation. 1 Hale, P. C. 437; 1 Russ. Crimes, 485; 1 Bish. Crim. Law, 678.

MANSO, or MANSUM. A mansion or house. Spelman.

MANSTEALING. A word sometimes used synonymously with "kidnapping," (*q. v.*)

MANSUETUS. Tame; as though accustomed to come to the hand. 2 Bl. Comm. 391.

MANSUM CAPITALE. The manor-house or lord's court. Paroch. Antiq. 150.

MANTEA. In old records. A long robe or mantle.

MANTHEOFF. In Saxon law. A horse-stealer.

MANTICULATE. To pick pockets.

MAN-TRAPS. Engines to catch trespassers, now unlawful unless set in a dwelling-house for defense between sunset and sunrise. 24 & 25 Vict. c. 100, § 31.

MANU BREVI. Lat. With a short hand. A term used in the civil law, signifying shortly; directly; by the shortest course; without circuity.

MANU FORTI. With strong hand. A term used in old writs of trespass. *Manu forti et cum multitudine gentium*, with strong hand and multitude of people. Reg. Orig. 183.

MANU LONGA. With a long hand. A term used in the civil law, signifying indirectly or circuitously. Calvin.

MANU OPERA. Cattle or implements of husbandry; also stolen goods taken from a thief caught in the fact. Cowell.

MANUAL. Performed by the hand; used or employed by the hand; held in the hand. Thus, a distress cannot be made of tools in the "manual occupation" of the debtor.

MANUAL GIFT. The manual gift, that is, the giving of corporeal movable effects, accompanied by a real delivery, is not subject to any formality. Civil Code La. art. 1539.

MANUALIA BENEFICIA. The daily distributions of meat and drink to the canons and other members of cathedral churches for their present subsistence. Cowell.

MANUALIS OBEDIENTIA. Sworn obedience or submission upon oath. Cowell.

MANUCAPTIO. In old English practice. A writ which lay for a man taken on suspicion of felony, and the like, who could not be admitted to bail by the sheriff, or others having power to let to mainprise. Fitzh. Nat. Brev. 249.

MANUCAPTORS. The same as mainpernors.

MANUFACTORY. A building, the main or principal design or use of which is to be a place for producing articles as products of labor; not merely a place where something may be made by hand or machinery, but what in common understanding is known as a "factory." 57 Pa. St. 82.

MANUFACTURE, *v*. The primary meaning of this word is "making with the hand," but this definition is too narrow for its present use. Its meaning has expanded as workmanship and art have advanced, so that now nearly all artificial products of human industry, nearly all such materials as have acquired changed conditions or new and specific combinations, whether from the direct action of the human hand, from chemical processes devised and directed by human skill, or by the employment of machinery, are now commonly designated as "manufactured." 57 Md. 526. See, also, 5 Blatchf. 215; 59 Mich. 163, 26 N. W. Rep. 311.

MANUFACTURE, *n*. In patent law. Any useful product made directly by human labor, or by the aid of machinery directed and controlled by human power, and either from raw materials, or from materials worked up into a new form. Also the process by which such products are made or fashioned.

MANUFACTURER. One who is engaged in the business of working raw materials into wares suitable for use. 63 How. Pr. 453. See MANUFACTURE.

MANUFACTURING CORPORATION. A corporation engaged in the production of some article, thing, or object, by skill or labor, out of raw material, or from matter which has already been subjected to artificial forces, or to which something has been added to change its natural condition. 99 N. Y. 181, 1 N. E. Rep. 669. The term does not include a mining corporation. 106 Mass. 135.

MANUMISSION. The act of liberating a slave from bondage and giving him freedom. In a wider sense, releasing or delivering one person from the power or control of another.

Manumittere idem est quod extra manum vel potestatem ponere. Co. Litt. 137. To manumit is the same as to place beyond hand and power.

MANUNG, or MONUNG. In old English law. The district within the jurisdiction of a reeve, apparently so called from his power to exercise therein one of his chief functions, viz., to exact (*amanian*) all fines.

MANUPES. A foot of full and legal measure.

MANURABLE. In old English law. Capable of being had or held in hand; capable of manual occupation; capable of being cultivated; capable of being touched; tangible; corporeal. Hale, Anal. § 24.

MANURE. In old English law. To occupy; to use or cultivate; to have in manual occupation; to bestow manual labor upon. Cowell.

MANUS. Lat. A hand.

In the civil law, this word signified power, control, authority, the right of physical coercion, and was often used as synonymous with "*potestas.*"

In old English law, it signified an oath or the person taking an oath; a compurgator.

MANUS MORTUA. A dead hand; mortmain. Spelman.

MANUSCRIPT. A writing; a paper written with the hand; a writing that has not been printed.

MANUTENENTIA. The old writ of maintenance. Reg. Orig. 182.

MANWORTH. In old English law. The price or value of a man's life or head. Cowell.

MANY. This term denotes a multitude, not merely a number greater than that denoted by the word "few." (Ala.) 6 South. Rep. 282.

MANZIE. In old Scotch law. Mayhem; mutilation of the body of a person. Skene.

MAP. A representation of the earth's surface, or of some portion of it, showing the relative position of the parts represented, usually on a flat surface. Webster. "A map is but a transcript of the region which it portrays, narrowed in compass so as to facilitate an understanding of the original." 3 Minn. 103, (Gil. 55.)

MARA. In old records. A mere or moor; a lake, pool, or pond; a bog or marsh that cannot be drained. Cowell; Blount; Spelman.

MARAUDER. "A marauder is defined in the law to be 'one who, while employed in the army as a soldier, commits larceny or robbery in the neighborhood of the camp, or while wandering away from the army.' But in the modern and metaphorical sense of the word, as now sometimes used in common speech, it seems to be applied to a class of persons who are not a part of any regular army, and are not answerable to any military discipline, but who are mere lawless banditti, engaged in plundering, robbery, murder, and all conceivable crimes." 37 Mo. 328.

MARC-BANCO. The name of a piece of money coined at Hamburg. Its value is thirty-five cents.

MARCA. A mark; a coin of the value of 13s. 4d. Spelman.

MARCATUS. The rent of a mark by the year anciently reserved in leases, etc.

MARCH. In Scotch law. A boundary line or border. Bell. The word is also used in composition; as *march-dike, march-stone.*

MARCHANDISES AVARIÉES. In French mercantile law. Damaged goods.

MARCHERS. In old English law. Noblemen who lived on the marshes of Wales or Scotland, and who, according to Camden, had their private laws, as if they had been petty kings; which were abolished by the statute 27 Hen. VIII. c. 26. Called also "lords marchers." Cowell.

MARCHES. An old English term for boundaries or frontiers, particularly the boundaries and limits between England and Wales, or between England and Scotland, or the borders of the dominions of the crown, or the boundaries of properties in Scotland. Mozley & Whitley.

MARCHES, COURT OF. An abolished tribunal in Wales, where pleas of debt or damages, not above the value of £50, were tried and determined. Cro. Car. 384.

MARCHETA. In old Scotch law. A custom for the lord of a fee to lie the first night with the bride of his tenant. Abolished by Malcolm III. Spelman; 2 Bl. Comm. 83.

A fine paid by the tenant for the remission of such right, originally a mark or half a mark of silver. Spelman.

In old English law. A fine paid for leave to marry, or to bestow a daughter in marriage. Cowell.

MARCHIONESS. A dignity in a woman answerable to that of marquis in a man, conferred either by creation or by marriage with a marquis. Wharton.

MARE. Lat. The sea.

MARE CLAUSUM. The sea closed; that is, not open or free. The title of Selden's great work, intended as an answer to the *Mare Liberum* of Grotius; in which he undertakes to prove the sea to be capable of private dominion. 1 Kent, Comm. 27.

MARE LIBERUM. The sea free. The title of a work written by Grotius against the Portuguese claim to an exclusive trade to the Indies, through the South Atlantic and Indian oceans; showing that the sea was not capable of private dominion. 1 Kent, Comm. 27.

MARESCALLUS. In old English law. A marshal; a master of the stables; an officer of the exchequer; a military officer of high rank, having powers and duties similar to those of a constable. Du Cange. See MARSHAL.

MARESCHAL. L. Fr. Marshal; a high officer of the royal household. Britt. fol. 1*b*.

MARETTUM. Marshy ground overflowed by the sea or great rivers. Co. Litt. 5.

MARGIN. A sum of money, or its equivalent, placed in the hands of a stockbroker by the principal or person on whose account the purchase is to be made, as a security to the former against losses to which he may be exposed by a subsequent depression in the market value of the stock. 49 Barb. 468.

MARGINAL NOTE. In Scotch law. A note inserted on the margin of a deed, embodying either some clause which was omitted in transcribing or some change in the agreement of the parties. Bell.

An abstract of a reported case, a summary of the facts, or brief statement of the principle decided, which is prefixed to the report of the case, sometimes in the margin, is also spoken of by this name.

MARINARIUS. An ancient word which signified a mariner or seaman. In England, *marinarius capitaneus* was the admiral or warden of the ports.

MARINE. Naval; relating or pertaining to the sea; transacted at sea; doing duty or service on the sea.

This is also a general name for the navy of a kingdom or state; as also the whole economy of naval affairs, or whatever respects the building, rigging, arming, equipping, navigating, and fighting ships. It comprehends also the government of naval armaments, and the state of all the persons employed therein, whether civil or military. Also one of the marines. Wharton.

MARINE CONTRACT. One relating to maritime affairs, shipping, navigation, marine insurance, affreightment, maritime loans, or other business to be done upon the sea or in connection with navigation.

MARINE CORPS. A body of soldiers enlisted and equipped for service on board vessels of war; also the naval forces of the nation.

MARINE COURT IN THE CITY OF NEW YORK. A local court of New York having original jurisdiction of civil causes, where the action is for personal injuries or defamation, and of other civil actions where the damages claimed do not exceed $2,000. It is a court of record. It was originally created as a tribunal for the settlement of causes between seamen.

MARINE INSURANCE. A contract whereby, for a consideration stipulated to be paid by one interested in a ship, freight, or cargo, subject to the risks of marine navigation, another undertakes to indemnify him against some or all of those risks during a certain period or voyage. 1 Phil. Ins. 1.

A contract whereby one party, for a stipulated premium, undertakes to indemnify the other against certain perils or sea-risks to which his ship, freight, and cargo, or some of them, may be exposed during a certain voyage, or a fixed period of time. 3 Kent, Comm. 253.

Marine insurance is an insurance against risks connected with navigation, to which a ship, cargo, freightage, profits, or other insurable interest in movable property may be exposed during a certain voyage or a fixed period of time. Civil Code Cal. § 2655.

A contract of marine insurance is one by which a person or corporation, for a stipulated premium, insures another against losses occurring by the casualties of the sea. Code Ga. 1882, § 2824.

MARINE INTEREST. Interest, allowed to be stipulated for at an extraordinary rate, for the use and risk of money loaned on *respondentia* and bottomry bonds.

MARINE LEAGUE. A measure of distance commonly employed at sea, being equal to one-twentieth part of a degree of latitude.

MARINE RISK. The perils of the sea; the perils necessarily incident to navigation.

MARINE SOCIETY. In English law. A charitable institution for the purpose of apprenticing boys to the naval service, etc., incorporated by 12 Geo. III. c. 67.

MARINER. A seaman or sailor; one engaged in navigating vessels upon the sea.

MARINES. A body of infantry soldiers, trained to serve on board of vessels of war when in commission and to fight in naval engagements.

Maris et fœminæ conjunctio est de jure naturæ. 7 Coke, 13. The connection of male and female is by the law of nature.

MARISCHAL. An officer in Scotland, who, with the lord high constable, possessed a supreme itinerant jurisdiction in all crimes committed within a certain space of the court, wherever it might happen to be. Wharton.

MARISCUS. A marshy or fenny ground. Co. Litt. 5*a*.

MARITAGIO AMISSO PER DEFALTAM. An obsolete writ for the tenant in frank-marriage to recover lands, etc., of which he was deforced.

MARITAGIUM. The portion which is given with a daughter in marriage. Also the power which the lord or guardian in chivalry had of disposing of his infant ward in matrimony.

Maritagium est aut liberum aut servitio obligatum; liberum maritagium dicitur ubi donator vult quod terra sic data quieta sit et libera ab omni seculari servitio. Co. Litt. 21. A marriage portion is either free or bound to service; it is called "frank-marriage" when the giver wills that land thus given be exempt from all secular service.

MARITAGIUM HABERE. To have the free disposal of an heiress in marriage.

MARITAL. Relating to, or connected with, the *status* of marriage; pertaining to a husband; incident to a husband.

MARITAL COERCION. Coercion of the wife by the husband.

MARITAL PORTION. In Louisiana. The name given to that part of a deceased husband's estate to which the widow is entitled. Civil Code La. art. 55; 3 Mart. (N. S.) 1.

MARITAL RIGHTS. The rights of a husband. The expression is chiefly used to denote the right of a husband to property which his wife was entitled to during the continuance of the marriage.

MARITIMA ANGLIÆ. In old English law. The emolument or revenue coming to the king from the sea, which the sheriffs anciently collected, but which was afterwards granted to the admiral. Spelman.

MARITIMA INCREMENTA. In old English law. Marine increases. Lands gained from the sea. Hale, de Jure Mar. pt. 1, c. 4.

MARITIME. Pertaining to the sea or ocean or the navigation thereof; or to commerce conducted by navigation of the sea or (in America) of the great lakes and rivers.

It is nearly equivalent to "marine" in many connections and uses; in others, the two words are used as quite distinct.

MARITIME CAUSE. A cause of action originating on the high seas, or growing out of a maritime contract. 1 Kent, Comm. 367, et seq.

MARITIME CONTRACT. A contract whose subject-matter has relation to the navigation of the seas or to trade or commerce to be conducted by navigation or to be done upon the sea or in ports. Over such contracts the admiralty has concurrent jurisdiction with the common-law courts.

MARITIME COURT. A court exercising jurisdiction in maritime causes; one which possesses the powers and jurisdiction of a court of admiralty.

MARITIME INTEREST. An expression equivalent to marine interest, (*q. v.*)

MARITIME JURISDICTION. Jurisdiction in maritime causes; such jurisdiction as belongs to a court of admiralty on the instance side.

MARITIME LAW. That system of law which particularly relates to commerce and navigation, to business transacted at sea or relating to navigation, to ships and shipping, to seamen, to the transportation of persons and property by sea, and to marine affairs generally.

The law relating to harbors, ships, and seamen. An important branch of the commercial law of maritime nations; divided into a variety of departments, such as those about harbors, property of ships, duties and rights of masters and seamen, contracts of affreightment, average, salvage, etc. Wharton.

MARITIME LIEN. A lien arising out of damage done by a ship in the course of navigation, as by collision, which attaches to the vessel and freight, and is to be enforced by an action *in rem* in the admiralty courts.

MARITIME LOAN. A contract or agreement by which one, who is the lender, lends to another, who is the borrower, a certain sum of money, upon condition that if the thing upon which the loan has been made should be lost by any peril of the sea, or *vis major*, the lender shall not be repaid unless what remains shall be equal to the sum borrowed; and if the thing arrive in safety, or in case it shall not have been injured but by its own defects or the fault of the master or mariners, the borrower shall be bound to return the sum borrowed, together with a certain sum agreed upon as the price of the hazard incurred. Emerig. Mar. Loans, c. 1, s. 2.

MARITIME PROFIT. A term used by French writers to signify any profit derived from a maritime loan.

MARITIME SERVICE. In admiralty law. A service rendered upon the high seas or a navigable river, and which has some relation to commerce or navigation,—some connection with a vessel employed in trade, with her equipment, her preservation, or the preservation of her cargo or crew. 4 Woods, 267, 16 Fed. Rep. 924.

MARITIME STATE, in English law, consists of the officers and mariners of the British navy, who are governed by express and permanent laws, or the articles of the navy, established by act of parliament.

MARITIME TORT. A tort committed upon the high seas, or upon a navigable river or other navigable water, and hence falling within the jurisdiction of a court of admiralty. The term is never applied to a tort committed upon land, though relating to maritime matters. See 3 Wall. 33; 17 Fed. Rep. 387.

MARITUS. Lat. A husband; a married man. Calvin.

MARK. 1. A character, usually in the form of a cross, made as a substitute for his signature by a person who cannot write, in executing a conveyance or other legal document. It is commonly made as follows: A third person writes the name of the marksman, leaving a blank space between the Christian name and surname; in this space the latter traces the mark, or crossed lines, and above the mark is written "his," (or "her,") and below it, "mark."

2. The sign, writing, or ticket put upon manufactured goods to distinguish them from others, appearing thus in the compound, "trade-mark."

3. A token, evidence, or proof; as in the phrase "a mark of fraud."

4. A weight used in several parts of Europe, and for several commodities, especially gold and silver. When gold and silver are sold by the *mark*, it is divided into twenty-four carats.

5. A money of accounts in England, and in some other countries a coin. The English mark is two-thirds of a pound sterling, or 13s. 4d.; and the Scotch mark is of equal value in Scotch money of account. Enc. Amer.

6. In early Teutonic and English law. A species of village community, being the lowest unit in the political system; one of the forms of the *gens* or clan, variously known as the "*mark*," "*gemeinde*," "*commune*," or "*parish*." Also the land held in common by such a community. The union of several such village communities and their *marks*, or common lands, forms the next higher political union, the hundred. Freem. Compar. Politics, 116, 117.

7. The word is sometimes used as another form of "*marque*," a license of reprisals.

MARKEPENNY. A penny anciently paid at the town of Maldon by those who had gutters laid or made out of their houses into the streets. Wharton.

MARKET. A public time and appointed place of buying and selling; also purchase and sale. It differs from the *forum*, or market of antiquity, which was a public market-place on one side only, or during one part of the day only, the other sides being occupied by temples, theaters, courts of justice, and other public buildings. Wharton.

The liberty, privilege, or franchise by which a town holds a market, which can only be by royal grant or immemorial usage.

By the term "market" is also understood the demand there is for any particular article; as, "the cotton market in Europe is dull."

MARKET GELD. The toll of a market.

MARKET OVERT. In English law. An open and public market. The market-place or spot of ground set apart by custom for the sale of particular goods is, in the country, the only market *overt;* but in London every shop in which goods are exposed publicly to sale is market overt, for such things only as the owner professes to trade in. Godb. 131; 5 Coke, 83; 2 Bl. Comm. 449.

MARKET PRICE means, when price at the place of exportation is in view, the price at which articles are sold and purchased, clear of every charge but such as is laid upon it at the time of sale. 2 Wash. C. C. 493.

MARKET TOWNS. Those towns which are entitled to hold markets. 1 Steph. Comm. (7th Ed.) 130.

MARKET VALUE signifies a price established by public sales, or sales in the way of ordinary business. 99 Mass. 345.

MARKET ZELD, (properly *market geld.*) In old records. The toll of a market. Cowell.

MARKETABLE. Such things as may be sold in the market; those for which a buyer may be found.

MARKETABLE TITLE. A "marketable title" to land is such a title as a court of equity, when asked to decree specific performance of the contract of sale, will compel the vendee to accept as sufficient. It is said to be not merely a defensible title, but a title which is free from plausible or reasonable objections.

MARKSMAN. In practice and conveyancing. One who makes his mark; a person who cannot write, and only makes his mark in executing instruments. Arch. N. Pr. 13; 2 Chit. 92.

MARLBRIDGE, STATUTE OF. An English statute enacted in 1267 (52 Hen. III.) at Marlbridge, (now called "Marlborough,") where parliament was then sitting. It related to land tenures, and to procedure, and to unlawful and excessive distresses.

MARQUE AND REPRISAL, LETTERS OF. These words, "marque" and "reprisal," are frequently used as synonymous, but, taken in their strict etymological sense, the latter signifies a "taking in return;" the former, the passing the frontiers (*marches*) in order to such taking. Letters of marque and reprisal are grantable, by the law of nations, whenever the subjects of one state are oppressed and injured by those of another, and justice is denied by that state to which the oppressor belongs; and the party to whom these letters are granted may then seize the bodies or the goods of the subjects of the state to which the offender belongs, until satisfaction be made, wherever they happen to be found. Reprisals are to be granted only in case of a clear and open denial of justice. At the present day, in consequence partly of treaties and partly of the practice of nations, the making of reprisals is confined to the seizure of commercial property on the high seas by public cruisers, or by private cruisers specially authorized thereto. Brown.

MARQUIS, or MARQUESS. In English law. One of the second order of nobility; next in order to a duke.

MARQUISATE. The seigniory of a marquis.

MARRIAGE. Marriage, as distinguished from the agreement to marry and from the act of becoming married, is the civil *status* of one man and one woman united in law for life, for the discharge to each other and the community of the duties legally incumbent on those whose association is founded on the distinction of sex. 1 Bish. Mar. & Div. § 3.

A contract, according to the form prescribed by law, by which a man and woman, capable of entering into such contract, mutually engage with each other to live their whole lives together in the state of union which ought to exist between a husband and wife. Shelf. Mar. & Div. 1.

Marriage is a personal relation arising out of a civil contract, to which the consent of parties capable of making it is necessary. Consent alone will not constitute marriage; it must be followed by a solemnization, or by a mutual assumption of marital rights, duties, or obligations. Civil Code Cal. § 55.

Marriage is the union of one man and one woman, "so long as they both shall live," to the exclusion of all others, by an obligation which, during that time, the parties cannot of their own voli-

tion and act dissolve, but which can be dissolved only by authority of the state. 19 Ind. 53.

The word also signifies the act, ceremony, or formal proceeding by which persons take each other for husband and wife.

In old English law, marriage is used in the sense of "*maritagium*," (*q. v.*,) or the feudal right enjoyed by the lord or guardian in chivalry of disposing of his ward in marriage.

MARRIAGE ARTICLES. Articles of agreement between parties contemplating marriage, intended as preliminary to a formal marriage settlement, to be drawn after marriage. Ath. Mar. Sett. 92.

MARRIAGE BROKAGE. The act by which a third person, for a consideration, negotiates a marriage between a man and woman. The money paid for such services is also known by this name.

MARRIAGE CEREMONY. The form, religious or civil, for the solemnization of a marriage.

MARRIAGE CONSIDERATION. The consideration furnished by an intended marriage of two persons. It is the highest consideration known to the law.

MARRIAGE LICENSE. A license or permission granted by public authority to persons who intend to intermarry. By statute, in some jurisdictions, it is made an essential prerequisite to the lawful solemnization of the marriage.

MARRIAGE-NOTICE BOOK. A book kept, in England, by the registrar, in which applications for and issue of registrar's licenses to marry are recorded.

MARRIAGE PORTION. Dowry; a sum of money or other property which is given to or settled on a woman on her marriage.

MARRIAGE PROMISE. Betrothal; engagement to intermarry with another.

MARRIAGE SETTLEMENT. A written agreement in the nature of a conveyance, called a "settlement," which is made in contemplation of a proposed marriage and in consideration thereof, either by the parties about to intermarry, or one of them, or by a parent or relation on their behalf, by which the title to certain property is settled, *i. e.*, fixed or limited to a prescribed course of succession; the object being, usually, to provide for the wife and children. Thus, the estate might be limited to the husband and issue, or to the wife and issue, or to husband and wife for their joint lives, remainder to the survivor for life, remainder over to the issue, or otherwise. Such settlements may also be made after marriage, in which case they are called "post-nuptial."

MARRIED WOMAN. A woman who has a husband living and not divorced; a *feme covert.*

MARSHAL. In old English law. The title borne by several officers of state and of the law, of whom the most important were the following: (1) The earl-marshal, who presided in the court of chivalry; (2) the marshal of the king's house, or knight-marshal, whose special authority was in the king's palace, to hear causes between members of the household, and punish faults committed within the verge; (3) the marshal of the king's bench prison, who had the custody of that jail; (4) the marshal of the exchequer, who had the custody of the king's debtors; (5) the marshal of the judge of assize, whose duty was to swear in the grand jury.

In American law. An officer pertaining to the organization of the federal judicial system, whose duties are similar to those of a sheriff. He is to execute the process of the United States courts within the district for which he is appointed, etc.

Also, in some of the states, this is the name of an officer of police, in a city or borough, having powers and duties corresponding generally to those of a constable or sheriff.

MARSHAL OF THE QUEEN'S BENCH. An officer who had the custody of the queen's bench prison. The St. 5 & 6 Vict. c. 22, abolished this office, and substituted an officer called "keeper of the queen's prison."

MARSHALING ASSETS. In equity. The arranging or ranking of assets in the due order of administration. Such an arrangement of the different funds under administration as shall enable all the parties having equities thereon to receive their due proportions, notwithstanding any intervening interests, liens, or other claims of particular persons to prior satisfaction out of a portion of these funds. The arrangement or ranking of assets in a certain order towards the payment of debts. 1 Story, Eq. Jur. § 558; 4 Kent, Comm. 421.

The arrangement of assets or claims so as to secure the proper application of the assets to the various claims; especially when there are two classes of assets, and some creditors can enforce their claims against both, and others against only one, and the creditors of the former class are compelled to exhaust the assets against which they alone have a claim before having recourse to other assets, thus providing for the settlement of as many claims as possible. Pub. St. Mass. p. 1292.

MARSHALING LIENS. The ranking or ordering of several estates or parcels of land, for the satisfaction of a judgment or mortgage to which they are all liable, though successively conveyed away by the debtor. The rule is that, where lands subject to the lien of a judgment or mortgage have been sold or incumbered by the owner at different times to different purchasers, the various tracts are liable to the satisfaction of the lien in the inverse order of their alienation or incumbrance, the land last sold being first chargeable. 1 Black, Judgm. § 440.

MARSHALING SECURITIES. An equitable practice, which consists in so ranking or arranging classes of creditors, with respect to the assets of the common debtor, as to provide for satisfaction of the greatest number of claims. The process is this: Where one class of creditors have liens or securities on *two* funds, while another class of creditors can resort to only *one* of those funds, equity will compel the doubly-secured creditors to first exhaust that fund which will leave the single security of the other creditors intact. See 1 Story, Eq. Jur. § 633.

MARSHALSEA. In English law. A prison belonging to the king's bench. It has now been consolidated with others, under the name of the "Queen's Prison."

MARSHALSEA, COURT OF. The court of the Marshalsea had jurisdiction in actions of debt or torts, the cause of which arose within the verge of the royal court. It was abolished by St. 12 & 13 Vict. c. 101. 4 Steph. Comm. 317, note *d*.

MART. A place of public traffic or sale.

MARTE SUO DECURRERE. Lat. To run by its own force. A term applied in the civil law to a suit when it ran its course to the end without any impediment. Calvin.

MARTIAL LAW. A system of law, obtaining only in time of actual war and growing out of the exigencies thereof, arbitrary in its character, and depending only on the will of the commander of an army, which is established and administered in a place or district of hostile territory held in belligerent possession, or, sometimes, in places occupied or pervaded by insurgents or mobs, and which suspends all existing civil laws, as well as the civil authority and the ordinary administration of justice. See, also, MILITARY LAW.

"Martial law, which is built upon no settled principles, but is entirely arbitrary in its decisions, is in truth and reality no law, but something indulged rather than allowed as a law. The necessity of order and discipline in an army is the only thing which can give it countenance, and therefore it ought not to be permitted in time of peace, when the king's courts are open for all persons to receive justice according to the laws of the land." 1 Bl. Comm. 413.

Martial law is neither more nor less than the will of the general who commands the army. It overrides and suppresses all existing civil laws, civil officers, and civil authorities, by the arbitrary exercise of military power; and every citizen or subject—in other words, the entire population of the country, within the confines of its power—is subjected to the mere will or caprice of the commander. He holds the lives, liberty, and property of all in the palm of his hand. Martial law is regulated by no known or established system or code of laws, as it is over and above all of them. The commander is the legislator, judge, and executioner. 5 Blatchf. 321.

Martial law is not the same thing as *military* law. The latter applies only to persons connected with the military forces of the country or to affairs connected with the army or with war, but is permanent in its nature, specific in its rules, and a recognized part of the law of the land. The former applies, when in existence, to all persons alike who are within the territory covered, but is transient in its nature, existing only in time of war or insurrection, is not specific or always the same, as it depends on the will and discretion of the military commander, and is no part of the law of the land.

MARTINMAS. The feast of St. Martin of Tours, on the 11th of November; sometimes corrupted into "Martilmas" or "Martlemas." It is the third of the four cross quarter-days of the year. Wharton.

MARUS. In old Scotch law. A maire; an officer or executor of summons. Otherwise called "*præco regis.*" Skene.

MASAGIUM. A messuage.

MASCULINE. Of the male sex.

MASSA. In the civil law. A mass; an unwrought substance, such as gold or silver, before it is wrought into cups or other articles. Dig. 47, 2, 52, 14; Fleta, lib. 2, c. 60, §§ 17, 22.

MAST. To fatten with mast, (acorns, etc.) 1 Leon. 186.

MAST-SELLING. In old English law. The practice of selling the goods of dead seamen at the mast. Held void. 7 Mod. 141.

MASTER. One having authority; one who rules, directs, instructs, or superintends; a head or chief; an instructor; an employer. Applied to several judicial officers. See *infra.*

MASTER AND SERVANT. The relation of master and servant exists where one person, for pay or other valuable consideration, enters into the service of another and devotes to him his personal labor for an agreed period. Sweet.

MASTER AT COMMON LAW. The title of officers of the English superior courts of common law appointed to record the proceedings of the court to which they belong; to superintend the issue of writs and the formal proceedings in an action; to receive and account for the fees charged on legal proceedings, and moneys paid into court. There are five to each court. They are appointed under St. 7 Wm. IV. and 1 Vict. c. 30, passed in 1837. Mozley & Whitley.

MASTER IN CHANCERY. An officer of a court of chancery who acts as an assistant to the judge or chancellor. His office is to inquire into such matters as may be referred to him by the court, examine causes, take testimony, take accounts, compute damages, etc., reporting his findings to the court in such shape that a decree may be made; also to take oaths and affidavits and acknowledgments of deeds. In modern practice, many of the functions of a master are performed by clerks, commissioners, auditors, and referees, and in some jurisdictions the office has been superseded.

MASTER IN LUNACY. In English law. The masters in lunacy are judicial officers appointed by the lord chancellor for the purpose of conducting inquiries into the state of mind of persons alleged to be lunatics. Such inquiries usually take place before a jury. 2 Steph. Comm. 511-513.

MASTER OF A SHIP. In maritime law. The commander of a merchant vessel, who has the chief charge of her government and navigation and the command of the crew, as well as the general care and control of the vessel and cargo, as the representative and confidential agent of the owner. He is commonly called the "captain."

MASTER OF THE CROWN OFFICE. The queen's coroner and attorney in the criminal department of the court of queen's bench, who prosecutes at the relation of some private person or common informer, the crown being the nominal prosecutor. St. 6 & 7 Vict. c. 20; Wharton.

MASTER OF THE FACULTIES. In English law. An officer under the archbishop, who grants licenses and dispensations, etc.

MASTER OF THE HORSE. In English law. The third great officer of the royal household, being next to the lord steward and lord chamberlain. He has the privilege of making use of any horses, footmen, or pages belonging to the royal stables.

MASTER OF THE MINT. In English law. An officer who receives bullion for coinage, and pays for it, and superintends everything belonging to the mint. He is usually called the "warden of the mint." It is provided by St. 33 Vict. c. 10, § 14, that the chancellor of the exchequer for the time being shall be the master of the mint.

MASTER OF THE ORDNANCE. In English law. A great officer, to whose care all the royal ordnance and artillery were committed.

MASTER OF THE ROLLS. In English law. An assistant judge of the court of chancery, who holds a separate court ranking next to that of the lord chancellor, and has the keeping of the rolls and grants which pass the great seal, and the records of the chancery. He was originally appointed only for the superintendence of the writs and records appertaining to the common-law department of the court, and is still properly the chief of the masters in chancery. 3 Steph. Comm. 417.

Under the act constituting the supreme court of judicature, the master of the rolls becomes a judge of the high court of justice and *ex officio* a member of the court of appeal. The same act, however, provides for the abolition of this office, under certain conditions, when the next vacancy occurs. See 36 & 37 Vict. c. 66, §§ 5, 31, 32.

MASTERS OF THE SUPREME COURT. In English law. Officials deriving their title from Jud. (Officers') Act 1879, and being, or filling the places of, the sixteen masters of the common-law courts, the queen's coroner and attorney, the master of the crown office, the two record and writ clerks, and the three associates. Wharton.

MASTER OF THE TEMPLE. The chief ecclesiastical functionary of the Temple Church.

MASTER'S REPORT. The formal report or statement made by a master in chancery of his decision on any question referred to him, or of any facts or action he has been directed to ascertain or take.

MASURA. In old records. A decayed house; a wall; the ruins of a building; a certain quantity of land, about four oxgangs.

MATE. The officer second in command on a merchant vessel.

MATELOTAGE. In French law. The hire of a ship or boat.

MATER-FAMILIAS. Lat. In the civil law. The mother or mistress of a family. A chaste woman, married or single. Calvin.

MATERIA. Lat. In the civil law. Materials; as distinguished from *species*, or the *form* given by labor and skill. Dig. 41, 1, 7, 7-12; Fleta, lib. 3, c. 2, § 14.

Materials (wood) for building, as distinguished from "*lignum*." Dig. 32, 55, pr.

In English law. Matter; substance; subject-matter. 3 Bl. Comm. 322.

MATERIAL. Important; more or less necessary; having influence or effect; going to the merits; having to do with matter, as distinguished from form. An allegation is said to be material when it forms a substantive part of the case presented by the pleading. Evidence offered in a cause, or a question propounded, is material when it is relevant and goes to the substantial matters in dispute, or has a legitimate and effective influence or bearing on the decision of the case.

MATERIAL-MAN. A person who has furnished materials used in the construction or repair of a building, structure, or vessel.

MATERIALITY. The property or character of being material. See MATERIAL.

MATERIALS. The substance or matter of which anything is made; matter furnished for the erection of a house, ship, or other structure; matter used or intended to be used in the construction of any mechanical product. See 71 Pa. St. 293.

MATERNA MATERNIS. Lat. A maxim of the French law, signifying that property of a decedent acquired by him through his mother descends to the relations on the mother's side.

MATERNAL. That which belongs to, or comes from, the mother; as maternal authority, maternal relation, maternal estate, maternal line.

MATERNAL PROPERTY. That which comes from the mother of the party, and other ascendants of the maternal stock. Dom. Liv. Prél. t. 3, s. 2, no. 12.

MATERNITY. The character, relation, state, or condition of a mother.

MATERTERA. Lat. In the civil law. A maternal aunt; a mother's sister. Inst. 3, 6, 1; Bract. fol. 68*b*.

MATERTERA MAGNA. In the civil law. A great aunt; a grandmother's sister, (*aviæ soror*.) Dig. 38, 10, 10, 15.

MATERTERA MAJOR. In the civil law. A greater aunt; a great-grandmother's sister, (*proaviæ soror;*) a father's or mother's great-aunt, (*patris vel matris matertera magna.*) Dig. 38, 10, 10, 16.

MATERTERA MAXIMA. In the civil law. A greatest aunt; a great-great-grandmother's sister, (*abaviæ soror;*) a father's or mother's greater aunt, (*patris vel matris matertera major.*) Dig. 38, 10, 10, 17.

MATH. A mowing.

MATHEMATICAL EVIDENCE. Demonstrative evidence; such as establishes its conclusions with absolute necessity and certainty. It is used in contradistinction to *moral* evidence.

MATIMA. A godmother.

MATRICIDE. The murder of a mother; or one who has slain his mother.

MATRICULA. In the civil and old English law. A register of the admission of officers and persons entered into any body or society, whereof a list was made. Hence those who are admitted to a college or university are said to be "matriculated." Also a kind of almshouse, which had revenues appropriated to it, and was usually built near the church, whence the name was given to the church itself. Wharton.

MATRICULATE. To enter as a student in a university.

Matrimonia debent esse libera. Marriages ought to be free. A maxim of the civil law. 2 Kent, Comm. 102.

MATRIMONIAL CAUSES. In English ecclesiastical law. Causes of action or injuries respecting the rights of marriage. One of the three divisions of causes or injuries cognizable by the ecclesiastical courts, comprising suits for jactitation of marriage, and for restitution of conjugal rights, divorces, and suits for alimony. 3 Bl. Comm. 92–94; 3 Steph. Comm. 712–714.

MATRIMONIUM. Lat. In Roman law. A legal marriage, contracted in strict accordance with the forms of the older Roman law, *i. e.*, either with the *farreum*, the *co-emptio*, or by *usus*. This was allowed only to Roman citizens and to those neighboring peoples to whom the right of *connubium* had been conceded. The effect of such a marriage was to bring the wife into the *manus*, or marital power, of the husband, and to create the *patria potestas* over the children.

Matrimonium subsequens tollit peccatum præcedens. Subsequent marriage cures preceding criminality.

MATRIMONY. Marriage, (*q. v.*,) in the sense of the relation or *status*, not of the ceremony.

MATRIX. In the civil law. The protocol or first draft of a legal instrument, from which all copies must be taken. See (Tex.) 16 S. W. Rep. 53.

MATRIX ECCLESIA. Lat. A mother church. This term was anciently applied to a cathedral, in relation to the other churches in the same see, or to a parochial church, in relation to the chapels or minor churches attached to it or depending on it. Blount.

MATRON. A married woman; an elderly woman. The female superintendent of an establishment or institution, such as a hospital, an orphan asylum, etc., is often so called.

MATRONS, JURY OF. Such a jury is impaneled to try if a woman condemned to death be with child.

MATTER. Facts; substance as distinguished from form; the merits of a case.

MATTER IN CONTROVERSY, OR IN DISPUTE. The subject of litigation; the matter for which a suit is brought and upon which issue is joined. 1 Wall. 337.

MATTER IN DEED. Such matter as may be proved or established by a deed or specialty. Matter of fact, in contradistinction to matter of law. Co. Litt. 320; Steph. Pl. 197.

MATTER IN ISSUE. That upon which the plaintiff proceeds in his action, and which the defendant controverts by his pleadings, not including facts offered in evidence to establish the matters in issue. 15 N. H. 9. That ultimate fact or state of facts in dispute upon which the verdict or finding is predicated. 4 Fed. Rep. 386. See 2 Black, Judgm. § 614, and cases cited.

Matter in ley ne serra mise in boutche del jurors. Jenk. Cent. 180. Matter of law shall not be put into the mouth of the jurors.

MATTER IN PAIS. Matter of fact that is not in writing; thus distinguished from matter in deed and matter of record; matter that must be proved by parol evidence.

MATTER OF COURSE. Anything done or taken in the course of routine or usual procedure, which is permissible and valid without being specially applied for and allowed.

MATTER OF FACT. That which is to be ascertained by the senses, or by the testimony of witnesses describing what they have perceived. Distinguished from matter of law.

MATTER OF FORM. Whatever belongs or relates merely to the *form* of a pleading or other instrument, or to its language, arrangement, or technicality, without affecting its *substance*, (*i. e.*, its substantial validity or sufficiency,) is called "matter of form," as distinguished from "matter of substance."

MATTER OF LAW. Whatever is to be ascertained or decided by the application of statutory rules or the principles and determinations of the law, as distinguished from the investigation of particular facts, is called "matter of law."

MATTER OF RECORD. Any judicial matter or proceeding entered on the records of a court, and to be proved by the production of such record. It differs from matter in deed, which consists of facts which may be proved by specialty.

MATTER OF SUBSTANCE. That which goes to the merits. The opposite of matter of form.

MATTERS OF SUBSISTENCE FOR MAN. This phrase comprehends all articles or things, whether animal or vegetable, living or dead, which are used for food, and whether they are consumed in the form in which they are bought from the producer or are only consumed after undergoing a process of preparation, which is greater or less, according to the character of the article. 19 Grat. 813.

Maturiora sunt vota mulierum quam virorum. 6 Coke, 71. The desires of women are more mature than those of men; *i. e.*, women arrive at maturity earlier than men.

MATURITY. In mercantile law. The time when a bill of exchange or promissory note becomes due. Story, Bills, § 329.

MAUGRE. L. Fr. In spite of; against the will of. Litt. § 672.

MAUNDY THURSDAY. The day preceding Good Friday, on which princes gave alms.

MAXIM. An established principle or proposition. A principle of law universally admitted, as being a correct statement of the law, or as agreeable to natural reason.

Coke defines a maxim to be "conclusion of reason," and says that it is so called "*quia maxima ejus dignitas et certissima auctoritas, et quod maxime omnibus probetur.*" Co. Litt. 11*a*. He says in another place: "A maxime is a proposition to be of all men confessed and granted without proofe, argument, or discourse." Id. 67*a*.

The maxims of the law, in Latin, French, and English, will be found distributed through this book in their proper alphabetical order.

Maxime paci sunt contraria vis et injuria. The greatest enemies to peace are force and wrong. Co. Litt. 161*b*.

Maximus erroris populus magister. Bacon. The people is the greatest master of error.

"MAY," in the construction of public statutes, is to be construed "must" in all cases where the legislature mean to impose a positive and absolute duty, and not merely to give a discretionary power. 1 Pet. 46, 64; 3 Hill, 612, 615.

MAYHEM. In criminal law. The act of unlawfully and violently depriving another of the use of such of his members as may render him less able, in fighting, either to defend himself or annoy his adversary. 4 Bl. Comm. 205.

Every person who unlawfully and maliciously deprives a human being of a member of his body, or disables, disfigures, or renders it useless, or cuts or disables the tongue, or puts out an eye, or slits the nose, ear, or lip, is guilty of mayhem. Pen. Code Cal. § 203.

MAYHEMAVIT. Maimed. This is a term of art which cannot be supplied in pleading by any other word, as *mutilavit*, *truncavit*, etc. 3 Thom. Co. Litt. 548; 7 Mass. 247.

MAYN. L. Fr. A hand; handwriting. Britt. c. 28.

MAYNOVER. L. Fr. A work of the hand; a thing produced by manual labor. Yearb. M. 4 Edw. III. 38.

MAYOR. The executive head of a municipal corporation; the governor or chief magistrate of a city.

MAYOR'S COURT. A court established in some cities, in which the mayor sits with the powers of a police judge or committing magistrate in respect to offenses committed within the city, and sometimes with civil jurisdiction in small causes, or other special statutory powers.

MAYOR'S COURT OF LONDON. An inferior court having jurisdiction in civil cases where the whole cause of action arises within the city of London.

MAYORALTY. The office or dignity of a mayor.

MAYORAZGO. In Spanish law. The right to the enjoyment of certain aggregate property, left with the condition thereon imposed that they are to pass in their integrity, perpetually, successively to the eldest son. Schm. Civil Law, 62.

MAYORESS. The wife of a mayor.

MEAD. Ground somewhat watery, not plowed, but covered with grass and flowers. Enc. Lond.

MEADOW. A tract of low or level land producing grass which is mown for hay. Webster.

A tract which lies above the shore, and is overflowed by spring and extraordinary tides only, and yields grasses which are good for hay. 34 Conn. 429.

MEAL-RENT. A rent formerly paid in meal.

MEAN, or MESNE. A middle between two extremes, whether applied to persons, things, or time.

MEANDER. To meander means to follow a winding or flexuous course; and when it is said, in a description of land, "thence with the meander of the river," it must mean a meandered line,—a line which follows the sinuosities of the river,—or, in other words, that the river is the boundary between the points indicated. 14 Or. 341, 12 Pac. Rep. 495; 10 Minn. 100, (Gil. 75.)

This term is used in some jurisdictions with the meaning of surveying and mapping a stream according to its meanderings, or windings and turnings. See 2 Wis. 317.

MEANS. 1. The instrument or agency through which an end or purpose is accomplished.

2. Resources; available property; money or property, as an available instrumentality for effecting a purpose, furnishing a livelihood, paying a debt, or the like.

MEANS OF SUPPORT. This term embraces all those resources from which the necessaries and comforts of life are or may be supplied, such as lands, goods, salaries, wages, or other sources of income. 71 Ill. 241.

MEASE, or MESE. Norman-French for a house. Litt. §§ 74, 251.

MEASON-DUE. (Corruption of *maison de Dieu.*) A house of God; a monastery; religious house or hospital. See 39 Eliz. c. 5.

MEASURE. That by which extent or dimension is ascertained, either length, breadth, thickness, capacity, or amount. Webster. The rule by which anything is adjusted or proportioned.

MEASURE OF DAMAGES. The rule, or rather the system of rules, governing the adjustment or apportionment of damages as a compensation for injuries in actions at law.

MEASURE OF VALUE. In the ordinary sense of the word, "measure" would mean something by comparison with which we may ascertain what is the value of anything. When we consider, further, that value itself is relative, and that two things are necessary to constitute it, independently of the third thing, which is to measure it, we may define a "measure of value" to be something by comparing with which any two other things we may infer their value in relation to one another. 2 Mill, Pol. Econ. 101.

MEASURER, or METER. An officer in the city of London, who measured woolen clothes, coals, etc.

MEASURING MONEY. In old English law. A duty which some persons exacted, by letters patent, for every piece of cloth made, besides alnage. Now abolished.

MECHANIC. A workman employed in shaping and uniting materials, such as wood, metal, etc., into some kind of structure, machine, or other object, requiring the use of tools. 11 Lea, 517; 13 Pa. St. 525.

MECHANIC'S LIEN. A species of lien created by statute in most of the states, which exists in favor of persons who have performed work or furnished material in and for the erection of a building. Their lien attaches to the land as well as the building, and is intended to secure for them a priority of payment.

The lien of a mechanic is created by law, and is intended to be a security for the price and value of work performed and materials furnished, and as such it attaches to and exists on the land and the building erected thereon, from the commencement of the time that the labor is being performed and the materials furnished; and the mechanic has an actual and positive interest in the building anterior to the time of its recognition by the court, or the reducing of the amount due to a judgment. 12 Iowa, 292.

MEDERIA. In old records. A house or place where metheglin, or mead, was made.

MEDFEE. In old English law. A bribe or reward; a compensation given in exchange, where the things exchanged were not of equal value. Cowell.

MEDIA ANNATA. In Spanish law. Half-yearly profits of land. 5 Tex. 34, 79.

MEDIA NOX. In old English law. Midnight. *Ad mediam noctem,* at midnight. Fleta, lib. 5, c. 5, § 31.

MEDIÆ ET INFIRMÆ MANUS HOMINES. Men of a middle and base condition. Blount.

MEDIANUS HOMO. A man of middle fortune.

MEDIATE POWERS. Those incident to primary powers given by a principal to his agent. For example, the general authority given to collect, receive, and pay debts due by or to the principal is a primary power. In order to accomplish this, it is frequently required to settle accounts, adjust disputed claims, resist those which are unjust, and answer and defend suits. These subordinate powers are sometimes called "mediate powers." Story, Ag. § 58.

MEDIATE TESTIMONY. Secondary evidence, (*q. v.*)

MEDIATION. Intervention; interposition; the act of a third person who interferes between two contending parties with a view to reconcile them or persuade them to adjust or settle their dispute. In international law and diplomacy, the word denotes the friendly interference of a state in the controversies of others, for the purpose, by its influence and by adjusting their difficulties, of keeping the peace in the family of nations.

MEDIATOR. One who interposes between parties at variance for the purpose of reconciling them.

MEDIATORS OF QUESTIONS. In English law. Six persons authorized by statute, (27 Edw. III. St. 2, c. 24,) who, upon any question arising among merchants relating to unmerchantable wool, or undue packing, etc., might, before the mayor and officers of the staple, upon their oath certify and settle the same; to whose determination therein the parties concerned were to submit. Cowell.

MEDICAL EVIDENCE. Evidence furnished by medical men, testifying in their professional capacity as experts, or by standard treatises on medicine or surgery.

MEDICAL JURISPRUDENCE. The science which applies the principles and practice of the different branches of medicine to the elucidation of doubtful questions in a court of justice. Otherwise called "forensic medicine," (*q. v.*) A sort of mixed science, which may be considered as common ground to the practitioners both of law and physic. 1 Steph. Comm. 8.

MEDICINE. "The practice of medicine is a pursuit very generally known and understood, and so also is that of surgery. The former includes the application and use of medicines and drugs for the purpose of curing, mitigating, or alleviating bodily diseases, while the functions of the latter are limited to manual operations usually performed by surgical instruments or appliances." 24 Hun, 633.

MEDICINE-CHEST. A box containing an assortment of medicines, required by statute to be carried by all vessels above a certain tonnage.

MEDICO-LEGAL. Relating to the law concerning medical questions.

MEDIETAS LINGUÆ. In old practice. Moiety of tongue; half-tongue. Applied to a jury impaneled in a cause consisting the one half of natives, and the other half of foreigners. See DE MEDIETATE LINGUÆ.

MEDIO ACQUIETANDO. A judicial writ to distrain a lord for the acquitting of a mesne lord from a rent, which he had acknowledged in court not to belong to him. Reg. Jur. 129.

MEDITATIO FUGÆ. In Scotch law. Contemplation of flight; intention to abscond. 2 Kames, Eq. 14, 15.

MEDIUM TEMPUS. In old English law. Meantime; mesne profits. Cowell.

MEDLETUM. In old English law. A mixing together; a medley or *mêlée;* an affray or sudden encounter. An offense suddenly committed in an affray. The English word "medley" is preserved in the term "chance-medley." An intermeddling, without violence, in any matter of business. Spelman.

MEDLEY. An affray; a sudden or casual fighting; a hand to hand battle; a *mêlée*. See CHANCE-MEDLEY; CHAUD-MEDLEY.

MEDSCEAT. In old English law. A bribe; hush money.

MEDSYPP. A harvest supper or entertainment given to laborers at harvest-home. Cowell.

MEETING. A coming together of persons; an assembly.

In the law of corporations, meetings are of two kinds,—ordinary and extraordinary; or, as they are also called, general and special. Ordinary or general meetings are usually held at stated times and for the transaction of business generally. Extraordinary or special meetings are held as occasion may require for the transaction of some particular business, which ought to be specified in the notice convening the meeting. One meeting may be both ordinary and extraordinary. Lind. Comp. 572.

MEGBOTE. In Saxon law. A recompense for the murder of a relation.

MEIGNE, or MAISNADER. In old English law. A family.

MEINDRE AGE. L. Fr. Minority; lesser age. Kelham.

MEINY, MEINE, or MEINIE. The royal household; a retinue.

MEJORADO. In Spanish law. Preferred; advanced. White, New Recop. l. 3, tit. 10, c. 1, § 4.

MELANCHOLIA. In medical jurisprudence. A kind of mental unsoundness characterized by extreme depression of spirits, ill-grounded fears, delusions, and brooding over one particular subject or train of ideas. Webster.

MELDFEOH. In Saxon law. The recompense due and given to him who made discovery of any breach of penal laws committed by another person, called the "promoter's [*i. e.*, informer's] fee." Wharton.

MELIOR. Lat. Better; the better. *Melior res*, the better (best) thing or chattel. Bract. fol. 60.

Melior est conditio defendentis. The condition of the party in possession is the better one, *i. e.*, where the right of the parties is equal. Broom, Max. 715, 719.

Melior est conditio possidentis, et rei quam actoris. The condition of the possessor is the better, and the condition of the defendant is better than that of the plaintiff. 4 Inst. 180; Broom, Max. 714, 719.

Melior est conditio possidentis ubi neuter jus habet. Jenk. Cent. 118. The condition of the possessor is the better where neither of the two has a right.

Melior est justitia vere præveniens quam severe puniens. That justice which absolutely prevents [a crime] is better than that which severely punishes it. 3 Inst. Epil.

MELIORATIONS. In Scotch law. Improvements of an estate, other than mere repairs; betterments. 1 Bell, Comm. 73.

Meliorem conditionem ecclesiæ suæ facere potest prælatus, deteriorem nequaquam. Co. Litt. 101. A bishop can make the condition of his own church better, but by no means worse.

Meliorem conditionem suam facere potest minor, deteriorem nequaquam. Co. Litt. 337. A minor can make his own condition better, but by no means worse.

Melius est in tempore occurrere, quam post causam vulneratum remedium quærere. 2 Inst. 299. It is better to meet a thing in time than after an injury inflicted to seek a remedy.

Melius est jus deficiens quam jus incertum. Law that is deficient is better than law that is uncertain. Lofft, 395.

Melius est omnia mala pati quam malo consentire. 3 Inst. 23. It is better to suffer every ill than to consent to ill.

Melius est petere fontes quam sectari rivulos. It is better to go to the fountain head than to follow little streamlets.

Melius est recurrere quam male currere. It is better to run back than to run badly; it is better to retrace one's steps than to proceed improperly. 4 Inst. 176.

MELIUS INQUIRENDUM. To be better inquired into.

In old English law. The name of a writ commanding a further inquiry respecting a matter; as, after an imperfect inquisition in proceedings in outlawry, to have a new inquest as to the value of lands.

MEMBER. One of the persons constituting a partnership, association, corporation, guild, etc.

One of the persons constituting a court, a legislative assembly, etc.

One of the limbs or portions of the body capable of being used in fighting in self-defense.

MEMBER OF CONGRESS. A member of the senate or house of representatives of the United States. In popular usage, particularly the latter.

MEMBER OF PARLIAMENT. One having the right to sit in either house of the British parliament.

MEMBERS. In English law. Places where a custom-house has been kept of old time, with officers or deputies in attendance; and they are lawful places of exportation or importation. 1 Chit. Com. Law, 726.

MEMBRANA. Lat. In the civil law. Parchment. Dig. 32, 52.

In old English law. A skin of parchment. The ancient rolls usually consist of several of these skins, and the word "*membrana*" is used, in citations to them, in the same way as "page" or "folio," to distinguish the particular skin referred to.

MEMBRUM. A slip or small piece of land.

MÉMOIRE. In French law. A document in the form of a petition, by which appeals to the court of cassation are initiated.

MEMORANDUM. Lat. To be remembered; be it remembered. A formal word with which the body of a record in the court of king's bench anciently commenced. Townsh. Pl. 486; 2 Tidd, Pr. 719. The whole clause is now, in practice, termed, from this initial word, the "memorandum," and its use is supposed to have originated from the circumstance that proceedings "by bill" (in which alone it has been employed) were formerly considered as the by-business of the court. Gilb. Com. Pl. 47, 48.

Also an informal note or instrument embodying something that the parties desire to fix in memory by the aid of written evidence, or that is to serve as the basis of a future formal contract or deed.

This word is used in the statute of frauds as the designation of the written agreement, or note or evidence thereof, which must exist in order to bind the parties in the cases provided. The memorandum must be such as to disclose the parties, the nature and substance of the contract, the consideration and promise, and be signed by the party to be bound or his authorized agent. See 2 Kent, Comm. 510.

MEMORANDUM ARTICLES. In the law of marine insurance, this phrase designates the articles of merchandise which are usually mentioned in the memorandum clause, (*q. v.*,) and for which the underwriter's liability is thereby limited.

MEMORANDUM CHECK. A check given by a borrower to a lender, for the amount of a short loan, with the understanding that it is not to be presented at the bank, but will be redeemed by the maker himself when the loan falls due. This understanding is evidenced by writing the word "*Mem.*" on the check. This is not unusual among merchants.

MEMORANDUM CLAUSE. In a policy of marine insurance the memorandum clause is a clause inserted to prevent the underwriters from being liable for injury to goods of a peculiarly perishable nature, and for minor damages. It begins as follows: "N. B. Corn, fish, salt, fruit, flour, and seed are warranted free from average, unless general, or the ship be stranded,"—meaning that the underwriters are not to be liable for damage to these articles caused by sea-water or the like. Maude & P. Shipp. 371; Sweet.

MEMORANDUM IN ERROR. A document alleging error in fact, accompanied by an affidavit of such matter of fact.

MEMORANDUM OF ALTERATION. Formerly, in England, where a patent was granted for two inventions, one of which was not new or not useful, the whole patent was bad, and the same rule applied when a material part of a patent for a single invention had either of those defects. To remedy this the statute 5 & 6 Wm. IV. c. 83, empowers a patentee (with the fiat of the attorney general) to enter a disclaimer (*q. v.*) or a memorandum of an alteration in the title or specification of the patent, not being of such a nature as to extend the exclusive right granted by the patent, and thereupon the memorandum is deemed to be part of the letters patent or the specification. Sweet.

MEMORANDUM OF ASSOCIATION. A document to be subscribed by seven or more persons associated for a lawful purpose, by subscribing which, and otherwise complying with the requisitions of the companies' acts in respect of registration, they may form themselves into an incorporated company, with or without limited liability. 3 Steph. Comm. 20.

MEMORIAL. A document presented to a legislative body, or to the executive, by one or more individuals, containing a petition or a representation of facts.

In English law. That which contains the particulars of a deed, etc., and is the instrument registered, as in the case of an annuity which must be registered. Wharton.

MEMORITER. Lat. From memory; by or from recollection. Thus, *memoriter* proof of a written instrument is such as is furnished by the recollection of a witness who had seen and known it.

MEMORIZATION. Committing anything to memory. Used to describe the act of one who listens to a public representation of a play or drama, and then, from his recollection of its scenes, incidents, or language, reproduces it, substantially or in part, in derogation of the rights of the author. See 5 Term R. 245; 14 Amer. Law Reg. (N. S.) 207.

MEMORY. Mental capacity; the mental power to review and recognize the successive states of consciousness in their consecutive order. This word, as used in jurisprudence to denote one of the psychological elements necessary in the making of a valid will or contract or the commission of a crime, implies the mental power to conduct a consecutive train of thought, or an orderly planning of affairs, by recalling correctly the past states of the mind and past events, and arranging them in their due order of sequence and in their logical relations with the events and mental states of the present.

The phrase "sound and disposing mind and memory" means not merely distinct recollection of the items of one's property and the persons among whom it may be given, but entire power of mind to dispose of property by will. Abbott.

Also the reputation and name, good or bad, which a man leaves at his death.

MEMORY, TIME OF. According to the English common law, which has been altered by 2 & 3 Wm. IV. c. 71, the time of memory commenced from the reign of Richard I., A. D. 1189. 2 Bl. Comm. 31.

MEN OF STRAW. Men who used in former days to ply about courts of law, so called from their manner of making known their occupation, (*i. e.*, by a straw in one of their shoes,) recognized by the name of "straw-shoes." An advocate or lawyer who wanted a convenient witness knew by these signs where to meet with one, and the colloquy between the parties was brief. "Don't you remember?" said the advocate; to which the ready answer was, "To be sure I do." "Then come into court and swear it." And straw-shoes went into court and swore it. Athens abounded in straw-shoes. Quart. Rev. vol. 33, p. 344.

MENACE. A threat; the declaration or show of a disposition or determination to inflict an evil or injury upon another.

MENETUM. In old Scotch law. A stock-horn; a horn made of wood, "with circles and girds of the same." Skene.

MENIAL. A servant of the lowest order; more strictly, a domestic servant living under his master's roof.

MENS. Lat. Mind; intention; meaning; understanding; will.

MENS LEGISLATORIS. The intention of the law-maker.

MENS REA. Lat. A guilty mind; a guilty or wrongful purpose; a criminal intent.

Mens testatoris in testamentis spectanda est. Jenk. Cent. 277. The intention of the testator is to be regarded in wills.

MENSA. Patrimony or goods and necessary things for livelihood. Jacob. A table; the table of a money-changer. Dig. 2, 14, 47.

MENSA ET THORO. From bed and board. See DIVORCE.

MENSALIA. Parsonages or spiritual livings united to the tables of religious houses, and called "mensal benefices" amongst the canonists. Cowell.

MENSIS. Lat. In the civil and old English law. A month. *Mensis vetitus*, the prohibited month; fence-month, (*q. v.*)

MENSOR. In the civil law. A measurer of land; a surveyor. Dig. 11, 6; Id. 50, 6, 6; Cod. 12, 28.

MENSULARIUS. In the civil law. A money-changer or dealer in money. Dig. 2, 14, 47, 1.

MENSURA. In old English law. A measure.

MENSURA DOMINI REGIS. "The measure of our lord the king," being the weights and measures established under King Richard I. in his parliament at Westminster, 1197. 1 Bl. Comm. 275; Mozley & Whitley.

MENTAL ALIENATION. A phrase sometimes used to describe insanity, (*q. v.*)

MENTAL RESERVATION. A silent exception to the general words of a promise or agreement not expressed, on account of a general understanding on the subject. But the word has been applied to an exception existing in the mind of the one party only, and has been degraded to signify a dishonest excuse for evading or infringing a promise. Wharton.

MENTIRI. Lat. To lie; to assert a falsehood. Calvin.; 3 Bulst. 260.

MENTITION. The act of lying; a falsehood.

MENU, LAWS OF. A collection or institute of the earliest laws of ancient India. The work is of very remote antiquity.

MER, or MERE. A fenny place. Cowell.

MERA NOCTIS. Midnight. Cowell.

MERANNUM. In old records. Timbers; wood for building.

MERCABLE. Merchantable; to be sold or bought.

MERCANTANT. A foreign trader.

MERCANTILE AGENCIES. Establishments which make a business of collecting information relating to the credit, character, responsibility, and reputation of merchants, for the purpose of furnishing the information to subscribers. 15 Amer. & Eng. Enc. Law, 280.

MERCANTILE LAW. An expression substantially equivalent to the law-merchant or commercial law. It designates the system of rules, customs, and usages generally recognized and adopted by merchants and traders, and which, either in its simplicity or as modified by common law or statutes, constitutes the law for the regulation of their transactions and the solution of their controversies.

MERCANTILE LAW AMENDMENT ACTS. The statutes 19 & 20 Vict. cc. 60, 97, passed mainly for the purpose of assimilating the mercantile law of England, Scotland, and Ireland.

MERCANTILE PAPER. Commercial paper; such negotiable paper (bills, notes, checks, etc.) as is made or transferred by and between merchants or traders, and is governed by the usages of the business world and the law-merchant.

MERCANTILE PARTNERSHIP. One which habitually buys and sells; one which buys for the purpose of afterwards selling. 32 Pittsb. Leg. J. (O. S.) 310.

MERCAT. A market. An old form of the latter word common in Scotch law, formed from the Latin "*mercatum.*"

MERCATIVE. Belonging to trade.

MERCATUM. Lat. A market. A contract of sale. Supplies for an army, (*commeatus.*)

MERCATURE. The practice of buying and selling.

MERCEDARY. A hirer; one that hires.

MERCEN-LAGE. The law of the Mercians. One of the three principal systems of laws which prevailed in England about the beginning of the eleventh century. It was observed in many of the midland counties, and those bordering on the principality of Wales. 1 Bl. Comm. 65.

MERCENARIUS. A hireling or servant. Jacob.

MERCES. In the civil law. Reward of labor in money or other things. As distinguished from "*pensio,*" it means the rent of farms, (*prædia rustici.*) Calvin.

MERCHANDISE. All commodities which merchants usually buy and sell, whether at wholesale or retail; wares and commodities such as are ordinarily the objects of trade and commerce. But the term is never understood as including real estate, and is rarely applied to provisions such as are purchased day by day, or to such other articles as are required for immediate consumption.

MERCHANDISE MARKS ACT, 1862. The statute 25 & 26 Vict. c. 88, designed to prevent the fraudulent marking of merchandise and the fraudulent sale of merchandise falsely marked.

MERCHANT. A man who traffics or carries on trade with foreign countries, or who exports and imports goods and sells them by wholesale. Webster. Merchants of this description are commonly known by the name of "shipping merchants."

A trader; one who, as a business, buys and sells wares and merchandise.

MERCHANT APPRAISERS. Where the appraisement of an invoice of imported goods made by the revenue officers at the custom-house is not satisfactory to the importer, persons may be selected (under this name) to make a definitive valuation. They must be merchants engaged in trade.

MERCHANT SHIPPING ACTS. Certain English statutes, beginning with the St. 16 & 17 Vict. c. 131, whereby a general superintendence of merchant shipping is vested in the board of trade.

MERCHANTABLE. Fit for sale; vendible in market; of a quality such as will bring the ordinary market price.

MERCHANTMAN. A ship or vessel employed in foreign or domestic commerce or in the merchant service.

MERCHANTS' ACCOUNTS. Accounts between merchant and merchant, which must be current, mutual, and unsettled, consisting of debts and credits for merchandise. 6 How. (Miss.) 328.

MERCHANTS, STATUTE OF. The English statute 13 Edw. I. St. 3, repealed by 26 & 27 Vict. c. 125.

MERCHET. In feudal law. A fine or composition paid by inferior tenants to the lord for liberty to dispose of their daughters in marriage. Cowell. The same as *marcheta* (*q. v.*)

MERCIAMENT. An amerciament, penalty, or fine, (*q. v.*)

MERCIMONIA. In old writs. Wares. *Mercimonia et merchandizas,* wares and merchandises. Reg. Brev. Append. 10.

MERCIMONIATUS ANGLIÆ. In old records. The impost of England upon merchandise. Cowell.

Mercis appellatio ad res mobiles tantum pertinet. The term "merchandise" belongs to movable things only. Dig. 50, 16, 66.

Mercis appellatione homines non contineri. Men are not included under the denomination of "merchandise." Dig. 50, 16, 207.

MERCY. In practice. The arbitrament of the king or judge in punishing offenses not directly censured by law. Jacob. So, "to be in mercy" signifies to be amerced or fined for bringing or defending an unjust suit, or to be liable to punishment in the discretion of the court.

In criminal law. The discretion of a judge, within the limits prescribed by positive law, to remit altogether the punishment to which a convicted person is liable, or to mitigate the severity of his sentence; as when a jury recommends the prisoner to the *mercy* of the court.

MERE. Sax. A marsh. Spelman.

MERE. L. Fr. Mother. *Æle, mere, fille,* grandmother, mother, daughter. Britt. c. 89. *En ventre sa mere,* in its mother's womb.

MERE MOTION. The free and voluntary act of a party himself, done without the suggestion or influence of another person, is said to be done of his mere motion, *ex mero motu,* (*q. v.*) Brown.

The phrase is used of an interference of the courts of law, who will, under some circumstances, of their own motion, object to an irregularity in the proceedings, though no objection has been taken to the informality by the plaintiff or defendant in the suit. 3 Chit. Gen. Pr. 430.

MERE RIGHT. The mere right of property in land; the *jus proprietatis,* without either possession or even the right of possession. 2 Bl. Comm. 197. The abstract right of property.

MERE-STONE. In old English law. A stone for bounding or dividing lands. Yearb. P. 18 Hen. VI. 5.

MERENNIUM. In old records. Timber. Cowell.

MERETRICIOUS. Of the nature of unlawful sexual connection. The term is descriptive of the relation sustained by persons who contract a marriage that is void by reason of legal incapacity. 1 Bl. Comm. 436.

MERGER. The fusion or absorption of one thing or right into another; generally spoken of a case where one of the subjects is of less dignity or importance than the other. Here the less important ceases to have an independent existence.

In real-property law. It is a general principle of law that where a greater estate and a less coincide and meet in one and the same person, without any intermediate estate, the less is immediately annihilated, or, in the law phrase, is said to be *merged,* that is, sunk or drowned, in the greater. Thus, if there be tenant for years, and the reversion in fee-simple descends to or is purchased by him, the term of years is *merged* in the inheritance, and shall never exist any more. 2 Bl. Comm. 177; 1 Steph. Comm. 293; 4 Kent, Comm. 99.

Of rights. This term, as applied to rights, is equivalent to "*confusio*" in the Roman law, and indicates that where the qualities of debtor and creditor become united in the same individual, there arises a confusion of rights which extinguishes both qualities; whence, also, merger is often called "extinguishment." Brown.

Rights of action. In the law relating to rights of action, when a person takes or acquires a remedy or security of a higher nature, in legal estimation, than the one which he already possesses for the same right, then his remedies in respect of the minor right or security merge in those attaching to the higher one. Leake, Cont. 506; 10 C. B. 561. As where a claim is merged in the judgment recovered upon it.

In criminal law. When a man commits a great crime which includes a lesser, or commits a felony which includes a tort against a private person, the latter is merged in the former. 1 East, P. C. 411.

MERIDIES. In old English law. Noon. Fleta, lib. 5, c. 5, § 31.

MERITORIOUS CAUSE OF ACTION. This description is sometimes applied to a person with whom the ground of action, or the consideration, originated or from whom it moved. For example, where a cause of action accrues to a woman while sole, and is sued for, after her marriage, by her husband and herself jointly, she is called the "meritorious cause of action."

MERITORIOUS CONSIDERATION. One founded upon some moral obligation; a valuable consideration in the second degree.

MERITS. In practice. Matter of substance in law, as distinguished from matter of mere form; a substantial ground of defense in law. A defendant is said "to swear to *merits*" or "to make affidavit of *merits*" when he makes affidavit that he has a good and sufficient or substantial defense to the action on the merits. 3 Chit. Gen. Pr. 543, 544. "Merits," in this application of it, has the technical sense of merits *in law*, and is not confined to a strictly moral and conscientious defense. Id. 545; 1 Burrill, Pr. 214.

As used in the New York Code of Procedure, § 349, it has been held to mean "the strict legal rights of the parties, as contradistinguished from those mere questions of practice which every court regulates for itself, and from all matters which depend upon the *discretion* or *favor* of the court." 4 How. Pr. 332.

A "defense upon the merits" is one which depends upon the inherent justice of the defendant's contention, as shown by the substantial facts of the case, as distinguished from one which rests upon technical objections or some collateral matter. Thus there may be a *good* defense growing out of an error in the plaintiff's pleadings, but there is not a defense upon the merits unless the real nature of the transaction in controversy shows the defendant to be in the right.

MERO MOTU. See EX MERO MOTU; MERE MOTION.

MERSCUM. A lake; also a marsh or fen-land.

MERTLAGE. A church calendar or rubric. Cowell.

MERTON, STATUTE OF. An old English statute, relating to dower, legitimacy, wardships, procedure, inclosure of common, and usury. It was passed in 1235, (20 Hen. III.,) and was named from Merton, in Surrey, where parliament sat that year. See Barring. St. 41, 46.

MERUM. In old English law. Mere; naked or abstract. *Merum jus*, mere right. Bract. fol. 31.

MERX. Lat. Merchandise; movable articles that are bought and sold; articles of trade.

Merx est quicquid vendi potest. Merchandise is whatever can be sold. Com. 355; 3 Wood. Lect. 263.

MESCREAUNTES. L. Fr. Apostates; unbelievers.

MESCROYANT. A term used in the ancient books to designate an infidel or unbeliever.

MESE. A house and its appurtenance. Cowell.

MESNE. Intermediate; intervening; the middle between two extremes, especially of rank or time.

An intermediate lord; a lord who stood between a tenant and the chief lord; a lord who was also a tenant. "Lord, *mesne*, and tenant; the tenant holdeth by four pence, and the mesne by twelve pence." Co. Litt. 23*a*.

MESNE ASSIGNMENT. If A. grant a lease of land to B., and B. assign his interest to C., and C. in his turn assign his interest therein to D., in this case the assignments so made by B. and C. would be termed "mesne assignments;" that is, they would be assignments intervening between A.'s original grant and the vesting of D.'s interest in the land under the last assignment. Brown.

MESNE INCUMBRANCE. An intermediate charge, burden, or liability; an incumbrance which has been created or has attached to property between two given periods.

MESNE LORD. In old English law. A middle or intermediate lord; a lord who held of a superior lord. 2 Bl. Comm. 59. More commonly termed a "mesne," (*q. v.*)

MESNE PROCESS. As distinguished from *final* process, this signifies any writ or process issued between the commencement of the action and the suing out of execution. It includes the writ of summons, (although that is now the usual commencement of actions,) because anciently that was preceded by the original writ.

The writ of *capias ad respondendum* was called "mesne" to distinguish it, on the one hand, from the original process by which a suit was formerly commenced; and, on the other, from the final process of execution.

MESNE PROFITS. Intermediate profits; that is, profits which have been accruing between two given periods. Thus, after a party has recovered the land itself in an action of ejectment, he frequently brings another action for the purpose of recovering the profits which have been accruing or arising out of the land between the time when his title to the possession accrued or was raised and the time of his recovery in the action of ejectment, and such an action is thence termed an "action for mesne profits." Brown.

MESNE PROFITS, ACTION OF. An action of trespass brought to recover profits derived from land, while the possession of it has been improperly withheld; that is, the yearly value of the premises.

MESNE, WRIT OF. An ancient and abolished writ, which lay when the lord paramount distrained on the tenant paravail. The latter had a writ of mesne against the mesne lord.

MESNALTY, or MESNALITY. A manor held under a superior lord. The estate of a mesne.

MESS BRIEF. In Danish sea law. One of a ship's papers; a certificate of admeasurement granted at the home port of a vessel by the government or by some other competent authority. Jac. Sea Laws, 51.

MESSAGE FROM THE CROWN. In English law. The method of communicating between the sovereign and the house of parliament. A written message under the royal sign-manual is brought by a member of the house, being a minister of the crown or one of the royal household. Verbal messages are also sometimes delivered. May, Parl. Pr. c. 17.

MESSAGE, PRESIDENT'S. An annual communication from the president of the United States to congress, made at or near the beginning of each session, embodying his views on the state and exigencies of national affairs, suggestions and recommendations for legislation, and other matters. Const. U. S. art. 2, § 3.

MESSARIUS. In old English law. A chief servant in husbandry; a bailiff.

MESSE THANE. One who said mass; a priest. Cowell.

MESSENGER. One who bears messages or errands; a ministerial officer employed by executive officers, legislative bodies, and courts of justice, whose service consists principally in carrying verbal or written communications or executing other orders. In Scotland there are officers attached to the courts, called "messengers at arms."

An officer attached to a bankruptcy court, whose duty consists, among other things, in seizing and taking possession of the bankrupt's estate during the proceedings in bankruptcy.

The messenger of the English court of chancery has the duty of attending on the great seal, either in person or by deputy, and must be ready to execute all such orders as he shall receive from the lord chancellor, lord keeper, or lords commissioners. Brown.

Messis sementem sequitur. The crop belongs to [follows] the sower. A maxim in Scotch law. Where a person is in possession of land which he has reason to believe is his own, and sows that land, he will have a right to the crops, although before it is cut down it should be discovered that another has a preferable title to the land. Bell.

MESSUAGE. This term is now synonymous with "dwelling-house," but had once a more extended signification. It is frequently used in deeds, in describing the premises.

Although the word "messuage" may, there is no necessity that it must, import more than the word "dwelling-house," with which word it is frequently put in apposition and used synonymously. 2 Bing. N. C. 617.

In Scotland. The principal dwelling-house within a barony. Bell.

META. Lat. A goal, bound, or turning-point. In old English law, the term was used to denote a bound or boundary line of land; a landmark; a material object, as a tree or a pillar, marking the position or beginning of a boundary line.

METACHRONISM. An error in computation of time.

METALLUM. In Roman law. Metal; a mine. Labor in mines, as a punishment for crime. Dig. 40, 5, 24, 5; Calvin.

METATUS. In old European law. A dwelling; a seat; a station; quarters; the place where one lives or stays. Spelman.

METAYER SYSTEM. A system of agricultural holdings, under which the land is divided, in small farms, among single families, the landlord generally supplying the stock which the agricultural system of the country is considered to require, and receiving, in lieu of rent and profit, a fixed proportion of the produce. This proportion, which is generally paid in kind, is usually one-half. 1 Mill, Pol. Econ. 296, 363; and 2 Smith, Wealth Nat. 3, c. ii. The system prevails in some parts of France and Italy.

METECORN. A measure or portion of corn, given by a lord to customary tenants as a reward and encouragement for labor. Cowell.

METEGAVEL. A tribute or rent paid in victuals. Cowell.

METER. An instrument of measurement; as a coal-meter, a gas-meter, a land-meter.

METES AND BOUNDS. In conveyancing. The boundary lines of lands, with their terminating points or angles.

METEWAND, or METEYARD. A staff of a certain length wherewith measures are taken.

METHEL. Sax. Speech; discourse. *Mathlian*, to speak; to harangue. Anc. Inst. Eng.

METHOD. In patent law. "Engine" and "method" mean the same thing, and may be the subject of a patent. Method, properly speaking, is only placing several things, or performing several operations, in the most convenient order, but it may signify a contrivance or device. Fessen. Pat. 127; 8 Term R. 106.

METRE. The unit of measure in the "metric system" of weights and measures. It is a measure of length, being the ten-millionth part of the distance from the equator to the north pole, and equivalent to 39.37 inches. From this unit all the other denominations of measure, as well as of weight, are derived. The metric system was first adopted in France in 1795.

METRIC SYSTEM. A system of measures for length, surface, weight, and capacity, founded on the *metre* as a unit. It originated in France, has been established by law there and in some other countries, and is recommended for general use by other governments.

METROPOLIS. A mother city; one from which a colony was sent out. The capital of a province. Calvin.

METROPOLITAN. In English law. One of the titles of an archbishop. Derived from the circumstance that archbishops were consecrated at first in the metropolis of a province. 4 Inst. 94.

In England, the word is frequently used to designate a statute, institution, governmental agency, etc., relating exclusively or especially to the city of London; *e. g.*, the metropolitan board of works, metropolitan buildings act, etc.

METROPOLITAN BOARD OF WORKS. A board constituted in 1855 by St. 18 & 19 Vict. c. 120, for the better sewering, draining, paving, cleansing, lighting, and improving the metropolis (London.) The board is elected by vestries and district boards, who in their turn are elected by the rate-payers. Wharton.

METROPOLITAN POLICE DISTRICT. A region composed of New York city and some adjacent territory, which was, for police purposes, organized as one district, and provided with a police force common to the whole.

METTESHEP, or METTENSCHEP. In old records. An acknowledgment paid in a certain measure of corn; or a fine or penalty imposed on tenants for default in not doing their customary service in cutting the lord's corn.

METUS. Lat. Fear; terror. In a technical sense, a reasonable and well-grounded apprehension of some great evil, such as death or mayhem, and not arising out of mere timidity, but such as might fall upon a man of courage. Fear must be of this description in order to amount to duress avoiding a contract. See Bract. lib. 2, c. 5; 1 Bl. Comm. 131; Calvin.

MEUBLES. In French law. The movables of English law. Things are *meubles* from either of two causes: (1) From their own nature, *e. g.*, tables, chairs; or (2) from the determination of the law, *e. g.*, obligations.

MEUBLES MEUBLANS. In French law. The utensils and articles of ornament usual in a dwelling-house. Brown.

Meum est promittere, non dimittere. It is mine to promise, not to discharge. 2 Rolle, 39.

MICHAELMAS. The feast of the Archangel Michael, celebrated in England on the 29th of September, and one of the usual quarter days.

MICHAELMAS HEAD COURT. A meeting of the heritors of Scotland, at which the roll of freeholders used to be revised. See Bell.

MICHAELMAS TERM. One of the four terms of the English courts of common law, beginning on the 2d day of November and ending on the 25th. 3 Steph. Comm. 562.

MICHE, or MICH. O. Eng. To practice crimes requiring concealment or secrecy; to pilfer articles secretly. *Micher,* one who practices secret crime. Webster.

MICHEL-GEMOT. One of the names of the general council immemorially held in England. The *Witenagemote.*

One of the great councils of king and noblemen in Saxon times. Jacob.

MICHEL-SYNOTH. Great council. One of the names of the general council of the kingdom in the times of the Saxons. 1 Bl. Comm. 147.

MICHERY. Theft; cheating.

MIDDLE TERM. A phrase used in logic to denote the term which occurs in both of the premises in the syllogism, being the means of bringing together the two terms in the conclusion.

MIDDLE THREAD. The middle thread of a stream is an imaginary line drawn lengthwise through the middle of its current.

MIDDLEMAN. An agent between two parties; an intermediary who performs the office of a broker or factor between seller and buyer, producer and consumer, land-owner and tenant, etc.

A middleman, in Ireland, is a person who takes land in large tracts from the proprietors, and then rents it out to the peasantry in small portions at a greatly enhanced price. Wharton.

MIDDLESEX, BILL OF. See BILL OF MIDDLESEX.

MIDSHIPMAN. In ships of war, a kind of naval cadet, whose business is to second or transmit the orders of the superior officers and assist in the necessary business of the vessel, but understood to be in training for a commission. A *passed* midshipman is one who has passed an examination and is a candidate for promotion to the rank of lieutenant.

MIDSUMMER-DAY. The summer solstice, which is on the 24th day of June, and the feast of St. John the Baptist, a festival first mentioned by Maximus Tauricensis, A. D. 400. It is generally a quarter-day for the payment of rents, etc. Wharton.

MIDWIFE. In medical jurisprudence. A woman who practices midwifery; an *accoucheuse.*

MIESES. In Spanish law. Crops of grain. White, New Recop. b. 1, tit. 7, c. 5, § 2.

Migrans jura amittat ac privilegia et immunitates domicilii prioris. One who emigrates will lose the rights, privileges, and immunities of his former domicile. Voet, Com. ad Pand. tom. i. 347; 1 Kent, Comm. 76.

MILE. A measure of length or distance, containing 8 furlongs, or 1,760 yards, or 5,280 feet.

MILEAGE. A payment or charge, at a fixed rate per mile, allowed as a compensation for traveling expenses to members of legislative bodies, witnesses, sheriffs, and bailiffs.

MILES. In the civil law. A soldier.

In old English law. A knight, because military service was part of the feudal tenure. Also a tenant by military service, not a knight. 1 Bl. Comm. 404; Seld. Tit. Hon. 334.

MILITARE. To be knighted.

MILITARY. Pertaining to war or to the army; concerned with war. Also the whole body of soldiers; an army.

MILITARY BOUNTY LAND. Land granted by various laws of the United States, by way of bounty, to soldiers for services rendered in the army; being given in lieu of a money payment.

MILITARY CAUSES. In English law. Causes of action or injuries cognizable in the court military, or court of chivalry. 3 Bl. Comm. 103.

MILITARY COMMISSIONS. Courts whose procedure and composition are modeled upon courts-martial, being the tribunals by which alleged violations of martial law are tried and determined. The membership of such commissions is commonly made up of civilians and army officers. They are probably not known outside of the United States, and were first used by General Scott during the Mexican war. 15 Amer. & Eng. Enc. Law, 473.

MILITARY COURTS. In England the court of chivalry and courts-martial, in America courts-martial and courts of inquiry, are called by this general name.

MILITARY FEUDS. The genuine or original feuds which were in the hands of military men, who performed military duty for their tenures.

MILITARY JURISDICTION. "There are, under the constitution, three kinds of military jurisdiction,—one to be exercised both in peace and war; another to be exercised in time of foreign war without the boundaries of the United States, or in time of rebellion and civil war within states or districts occupied by rebels treated as belligerents; and a third to be exercised in time of invasion or insurrection within the limits of the United States, or during rebellion within the limits of states maintaining adhesion to the national government, when the public danger requires its exercise. The first of these may be called 'jurisdiction under military law,' and is found in acts of congress prescribing rules and articles of war, or otherwise providing for the government of the national forces; the second may be distinguished as 'military government,' superseding, as far as may be deemed expedient, the local law, and exercised by the military commander under the direction of the president, with the express or implied sanction of congress; while the third may be denominated 'martial law proper,' and is called into action by congress, or temporarily, when the action of congress cannot be invited, and in the case of justifying or excusing peril, by the president, in times of insurrection or invasion, or of civil or foreign war, within districts or localities where ordinary law no longer adequately secures public safety and private rights." Per Chase, C. J., 4 Wall. 141.

MILITARY LAW. A system of regulations for the government of an army. 1 Kent, Comm. 341, note.

That branch of the laws which respects military discipline and the government of persons employed in the military service. De Hart, Mil. Law, 16. See MARTIAL LAW.

MILITARY OFFENSES. Those offenses which are cognizable by the courts military, as insubordination, sleeping on guard, desertion, etc.

MILITARY STATE. The soldiery of the kingdom of Great Britain.

MILITARY TENURES. The various tenures by knight-service, grand-serjeanty, cornage, etc., are frequently called "military tenures," from the nature of the services which they involved. 1 Steph. Comm. 204.

MILITARY TESTAMENT. In English law. A nuncupative will, that is, one made by word of mouth, by which a soldier may dispose of his goods, pay, and other personal chattels, without the forms and solemnities which the law requires in other cases. St. 1 Vict. c. 26, § 11.

MILITES. Knights; and, in Scotch law, freeholders.

MILITIA. The body of soldiers in a state enrolled for discipline, but not engaged in actual service except in emergencies, as distinguished from regular troops or a standing army.

MILL. A machine or engine for grinding, sawing, manufacturing, etc.; also the building containing such machinery.

An American money of account, of the value of the tenth part of a cent.

MILL-HOLMS. Low meadows and other fields in the vicinity of mills, or watery places about mill-dams. Enc. Lond.

MILLBANK PRISON. Formerly called the "Penitentiary at Millbank." A prison at Westminster, for convicts under sentence of transportation, until the sentence or order shall be executed, or the convict be entitled to freedom, or be removed to some other place of confinement. This prison is placed under the inspectors of prisons appointed by the secretary of state, who are a body corporate, "The Inspectors of the Millbank Prison." The inspectors make regulations for the government thereof, subject to the approbation of the secretary of state, and yearly reports to him, to be laid before parliament. The secretary also appoints a governor, chaplain, medical officer, matron, etc. Wharton.

MILLEATE, or MILL-LEAT. A trench to convey water to or from a mill. St. 7 Jac. I. c. 19.

MILLED MONEY. This term means merely coined money; and it is not necessary that it should be marked or rolled on the edges. Leach, 708.

MIL-REIS. The name of a piece of money in the coinage of Portugal, and the Azores and Madeira islands. Its value at the custom-house, according as it is coined in the first, second, or third of the places named, is $1.12, or 83⅓ cents, or $1.

MINA. In old English law. A measure of corn or grain. Cowell; Spelman.

MINAGE. A toll or duty paid for selling corn by the mina. Cowell.

MINARE. In old records. To mine or dig mines. *Minator,* a miner. Cowell.

MINATOR CARUCÆ. A plowman. Cowell.

Minatur innocentibus qui parcit nocentibus. 4 Coke, 45. He threatens the innocent who spares the guilty.

MIND. In its legal sense, "mind" means only the ability to will, to direct, to permit, or to assent. In this sense, a corporation has a mind, and exerts its mind each time that it assents to the terms of a contract. 43 N. J. Law, 492.

MIND AND MEMORY. A phrase applied to testators, denoting the possession of mental capacity to make a will. In order to make a valid will, the testator must have a sound and disposing *mind and memory.* In other words, he ought to be capable of making his will, with an understanding of the nature of the business in which he is engaged, a recollection of the property he means to dispose of, of the persons who are the objects of his bounty, and the manner in which it is to be distributed between them. 3 Wash. C. C. 585.

MINE. A pit or excavation in the earth, from which metallic ores or other mineral substances are taken by digging. Webster.

MINER. One who mines; a digger for metals and other minerals. While men of scientific attainments, or of experience in the use of machinery, are to be found in this class, yet the word by which the class is designated imports neither learning nor skill. (Colo.) 19 Pac. Rep. 604.

MINERALS. All fossil bodies or matters dug out of mines or quarries, whence anything may be dug; such as beds of stone which may be quarried. 14 Mees. & W. 859.

Any natural production, formed by the action of chemical affinities, and organized when becoming solid by the powers of crystalization. Webster.

MINERATOR. In old records. A miner.

Minima pœna corporalis est major qualibet pecuniaria. The smallest corporal punishment is greater than any pecuniary one. 2 Inst. 220.

Minime mutanda sunt quæ certam habuerunt interpretationem. Things which have had a certain interpretation [whose interpretation has been settled, as by common opinion] are not to be altered. Co. Litt. 365; Wing. Max. p. 748, max. 202.

MINIMENT. An old form of *muniment,* (*q. v.*) Blount.

Minimum est nihilo proximum. The smallest is next to nothing.

MINING CLAIM. A parcel of land, containing precious metal in its soil or rock, and appropriated by an individual, according to established rules, by the process of "location." 104 U. S. 649.

MINING COMPANIES. This designation was formerly applied in England to the associations formed in London in 1825 for working mines in Mexico and South America; but at present it comprises, both in England and America, all mining projects carried on by joint-stock associations or corporations. Rapalje & Lawrence.

MINING PARTNERSHIP. An association of several owners of a mine for cooperation in working the mine. A mining partnership is governed by many of the rules relating to ordinary partnerships, but also by some rules peculiar to itself, one of which is that one person may convey his interest in the mine and business without dissolving the partnership. 102 U. S. 645; 23 Cal. 203; 9 Colo. 46, 10 Pac. Rep. 232.

MINISTER. In public law. One of the highest functionaries in the organization of civil government, standing next to the sovereign or executive head, acting as his immediate auxiliary, and being generally charged with the administration of one of the great bureaus or departments of the executive branch of government. Otherwise called a "cabinet minister," "secretary of state," or "secretary of a department."

In international law. An officer appointed by the government of one nation as a mediator or arbitrator between two other nations who are engaged in a controversy, with their consent, with a view to effecting an amicable adjustment of the dispute.

A general name given to the diplomatic representatives sent by one state to another, including ambassadors, envoys, and residents.

In ecclesiastical law. A person ordained according to the usages of some church or associated body of Christians for the preaching of the gospel and filling the pastoral office.

In practice. An officer of justice, charged with the execution of the law, and hence termed a "ministerial officer;" such as a sheriff, bailiff, coroner, sheriff's officer. Britt. c. 21.

An agent; one who acts not by any inherent authority, but under another.

MINISTERIAL. That which is done under the authority of a superior; opposed to *judicial;* that which involves obedience to instructions, but demands no special discretion, judgment, or skill.

MINISTERIAL ACT. A ministerial act may be defined to be one which a person performs in a given state of facts, in a prescribed manner, in obedience to the mandate of legal authority, without regard to or the exercise of his own judgment, upon the propriety of the act being done. Acts done out of court in bringing parties into court are, as a general proposition, ministerial acts. 54 Ind. 376.

MINISTERIAL POWERS. A phrase used in English conveyancing to denote powers given for the good, not of the donee himself exclusively, or of the donee himself necessarily at all, but for the good of several persons, including or not including the donee also. They are so called because the donee of them is as a minister or servant in his exercise of them. Brown.

MINISTERIAL TRUSTS. (Also called "instrumental trusts.") Those which demand no further exercise of reason or understanding than every intelligent agent must necessarily employ; as to convey an estate. They are a species of special trusts, distinguished from discretionary trusts, which necessarily require much exercise of the understanding. 2 Bouv. Inst. no. 1896.

MINISTRANT. The party cross-examining a witness was so called, under the old system of the ecclesiastical courts.

MINISTRI REGIS. Lat. In old English law. Ministers of the king, applied to the judges of the realm, and to all those who hold ministerial offices in the government. 2 Inst. 208.

MINISTRY. Office; service. Those members of the government who are in the cabinet.

MINOR. An infant or person who is under the age of legal competence. A term derived from the civil law, which described a person under a certain age as *less than* so many years. *Minor viginti quinque annis,* one less than twenty-five years of age. Inst. 1, 14, 2.

Also, less; of less consideration; lower; a person of inferior condition. Fleta, 2, 47, 13, 15; Calvin.

MINOR ÆTAS. Lat. Minority or infancy. Cro. Car. 516. Literally, lesser age.

Minor ante tempus agere non potest in casu proprietatis nec etiam convenire; differetur usque ætatem; sed non cadit breve. 2 Inst. 291. A minor before majority cannot act in a case of property, nor even agree; it should be deferred until majority; but the writ does not fail.

MINOR FACT. In the law of evidence. A relative, collateral, or subordinate fact; a circumstance. Wills, Circ. Ev. 27; Burrill, Circ. Ev. p. 121, note, 582.

Minor jurare non potest. A minor cannot make oath. Co. Litt. 172*b*. An infant cannot be sworn on a jury. Litt. 289.

Minor minorem custodire non debet, alios enim præsumitur male regere qui seipsum regere nescit. A minor ought not to be guardian to a minor, for he who knows not how to govern himself is presumed to be unfit to govern others. Fleta, lib. 1, c. 10; Co. Litt. 88*b*.

Minor non tenetur respondere durante minori ætate, nisi in causa dotis, propter favorem. 3 Bulst. 143. A minor is not bound to reply during his minority, except as a matter of favor in a cause of dower.

Minor qui infra ætatem 12 annorum fuerit ultagari non potest, nec extra legem poni, quia ante talem ætatem, non est sub lege aliqua, nec in decenna. Co. Litt. 128. A minor who is under twelve years of age cannot be outlawed, nor placed without the law, because before such age he is not under any law, nor in a decennary.

Minor septemdecim annis non admittitur fore executorem. A person under seventeen years is not admitted to be an executor. 6 Coke, 67. A rule of ecclesiastical law.

MINORA REGALIA. In English law. The lesser prerogatives of the crown, including the rights of the revenue. 1 Bl. Comm. 241.

MINORITY. The state or condition of a minor; infancy.

The smaller number of votes of a deliberative assembly; opposed to majority, (which see.)

MINT. The place designated by law where bullion is coined into money under authority of the government.

Also a place of privilege in Southwark, near the queen's prison, where persons formerly sheltered themselves from justice under the pretext that it was an ancient palace of the crown. The privilege is now abolished. Wharton.

MINT-MARK. The masters and workers of the English mint, in the indentures made with them, agree "to make a privy mark in the money they make, of gold and silver, so that they may know which moneys were of their own making." After every trial of the pix, having proved their moneys to be lawful, they are entitled to their *quietus* under the great seal, and to be discharged from all suits or actions. Wharton.

MINT-MASTER. One who manages the coinage. See MASTER OF THE MINT.

MINTAGE. The charge or commission taken by the mint as a consideration for coining into money the bullion which is brought to it for that purpose; the same as "seigniorage."

Also that which is coined or stamped as money; the product of the mint.

MINUS. Lat. In the civil law. Less; less than. The word had also, in some connections, the sense of "not at all." For example, a debt remaining wholly unpaid was described as "*minus solutum.*"

Minus solvit, qui tardius solvit. He does not pay who pays too late. Dig. 50, 16, 12, 1.

MINUTE. In measures of time or circumference, a minute is the sixtieth part of an hour or degree.

In practice. A memorandum of what takes place in court, made by authority of the court.

MINUTE-BOOK. A book kept by the clerk or prothonotary of a court for entering memoranda of its proceedings.

MINUTE TITHES. Small tithes, such as usually belong to a vicar, as of wool, lambs, pigs, butter, cheese, herbs, seeds, eggs, honey, wax, etc.

MINUTES. **In Scotch practice.** A pleading put into writing before the lord ordinary, as the ground of his judgment. Bell.

In business law. Memoranda or notes of a transaction or proceeding. Thus, the record of the proceedings at a meeting of directors or shareholders of a company is called the "minutes."

MINUTIO. In the civil law. A lessening; diminution or reduction. Dig. 4, 5, 1.

MIRROR. The Mirror of Justice, or of the Justices, commonly spoken of as the "Mirror," is an ancient treatise on the laws of England, written during the reign of Edward II., and attributed to one Andrew Horne.

MIS. An inseparable particle used in composition, to mark an ill sense or depravation of the meaning; as "miscomputation" or "misaccompting," *i. e.*, false reckoning. Several of the words following are illustrations of the force of this monosyllable.

MISA. **In old English law.** The mise or issue in a writ of right. Spelman.

In old records. A compact or agreement; a form of compromise. Cowell.

MISADVENTURE. A mischance or accident; a casualty caused by the act of one person and inflicting injury upon another. Homicide "by misadventure" is where a man, doing a lawful act, without any intention of hurt, unfortunately kills another. 4 Bl. Comm. 182.

MISALLEGE. To cite falsely as a proof or argument.

MISAPPLICATION. Improper, illegal, wrongful, or corrupt use or application of funds, property, etc.

MISAPPROPRIATION. This is not a technical term of law, but it is sometimes applied to the misdemeanor which is committed by a banker, factor, agent, trustee, etc., who fraudulently deals with money, goods, securities, etc., intrusted to him, or by a director or public officer of a corporation or company who fraudulently misapplies any of its property. Steph. Crim. Dig. 257, et seq. Sweet.

MISBEHAVIOR. Ill conduct; improper or unlawful behavior. Verdicts are sometimes set aside on the ground of misbehavior of jurors.

MISCARRIAGE. In medical jurisprudence. The expulsion of the *ovum* or embryo from the *uterus* within the first six weeks after conception. Between that time, and before the expiration of the sixth month, when the child may possibly live, it is termed "abortion." When the delivery takes place soon after the sixth month, it is denominated "premature labor." But the criminal act of destroying the *fœtus* at any time before birth is termed, in law, "procuring miscarriage." Chit. Med. Jur. 410.

In practice. As used in the statute of frauds, ("debt, default, or miscarriage of another,") this term means any species of unlawful conduct or wrongful act for which the doer could be held liable in a civil action.

MISCEGENATION. Mixture of races; marriage between persons of different races; as between a white person and a negro.

MISCHARGE. An erroneous charge; a charge, given by a court to a jury, which involves errors for which the judgment may be reversed.

MISCHIEF. In legislative parlance, the word is often used to signify the evil or danger which a statute is intended to cure or avoid.

In the phrase "malicious mischief," (which see,) it imports a wanton or reckless injury to persons or property.

MISCOGNISANT. Ignorant; uninformed. The word is obsolete.

MISCONDUCT. Any unlawful conduct on the part of a person concerned in the administration of justice which is prejudicial to the rights of parties or to the right determination of the cause; as "misconduct of jurors," "misconduct of an arbitrator." The term is also used to express a dereliction from duty, injurious to another, on the part of one employed in a professional capacity, as an attorney at law, (1 Denio, 267,) or a public officer, (60 Me. 58.)

MISCONTINUANCE. In practice. An improper continuance; want of proper form in a continuance; the same with "discontinuance." Cowell.

MISCREANT. In old English law. An apostate; an unbeliever; one who totally renounced Christianity. 4 Bl. Comm. 44.

MISDATE. A false or erroneous date affixed to a paper or document.

MISDELIVERY. The delivery of property by a carrier or warehouseman to a person not authorized by the owner or person to whom the carrier or warehouseman is bound by his contract to deliver it. 133 Mass. 156.

MISDEMEANANT. A person guilty of a misdemeanor; one sentenced to punishment upon conviction of a misdemeanor. See FIRST-CLASS MISDEMEANANT.

MISDEMEANOR. In criminal law. A general name for criminal offenses of every sort, punishable by indictment or special proceedings, which do not in law amount to the grade of felony.

A misdemeanor is an act committed or omitted in violation of a public law either forbidding or commanding it. This general definition, however, comprehends both "crimes" and "misdemeanors," which, properly speaking, are mere synonymous terms; though, in common usage, the word "crimes" is made to denote such offenses as are of a deeper and more atrocious dye; while smaller faults and omissions of less consequence are comprised under the milder term of "misdemeanors" only. In the English law, "misdemeanor" is generally used in contradistinction to "felony;" and misdemeanors comprehend all indictable offenses which do not amount to felony, as libels, conspiracies, attempts, and solicitations to commit felonies, etc. Brown.

MISDESCRIPTION. An error or falsity in the description of the subject-matter of a contract which deceives one of the parties to his injury, or is misleading in a material or substantial point.

MISDIRECTION. In practice. An error made by a judge in instructing the jury upon the trial of a cause.

MISE. The issue in a writ of right. When the tenant in a writ of right pleads that his title is better than the demandant's, he is said to join the *mise* on the mere right.

Also expenses; costs; disbursements in an action.

MISE-MONEY. Money paid by way of contract or composition to purchase any liberty, etc. Blount.

Misera est servitus, ubi jus est vagum aut incertum. It is a wretched state of slavery which subsists where the law is vague or uncertain. 4 Inst. 245; Broom, Max. 150.

MISERABILE DEPOSITUM. Lat. In the civil law. The name of an involuntary deposit, made under pressing necessity; as, for instance, shipwreck, fire, or other inevitable calamity. Poth. Proc. Civile, pt. 5, c. 1, § 1; Code La. 2935.

MISERERE. The name and first word of one of the penitential psalms, being that which was commonly used to be given by the ordinary to such condemned malefactors as were allowed the benefit of clergy; whence it is also called the "psalm of mercy." Wharton.

MISERICORDIA. Mercy; a fine or amerciament; an arbitrary or discretionary amercement.

MISERICORDIA COMMUNIS. In old English law. A fine set on a whole county or hundred.

MISFEASANCE. A misdeed or trespass. The doing what a party ought to do improperly. 1 Tidd, Pr. 4. The improper performance of some act which a man may lawfully do. 3 Steph. Comm. 460.

Misfeasance, strictly, is not doing a lawful act in a proper manner, omitting to do it as it should be done; while malfeasance is the doing an act wholly wrongful; and non-feasance is an omission to perform a duty, or a total neglect of duty. But "misfeasance" is often carelessly used in the sense of "malfeasance." 33 Conn. 109.

MISFEAZANCE. See MISFEASANCE.

MISFORTUNE. An adverse event, calamity, or evil fortune, arising by accident, (or without the will or concurrence of him who suffers from it,) and not to be foreseen or guarded against by care or prudence. See 20 Q. B. Div. 816. In its application to the law of homicide, this term always involves the further idea that the person causing the death is not at the time engaged in any unlawful act. 4 Bl. Comm. 182.

MISJOINDER. The improper joining together of parties to a suit, as plaintiffs or defendants, or of different causes of action.

MISKENNING. In Saxon and old English law. An unjust or irregular summoning to court; to speak unsteadily in court; to vary in one's plea. Cowell; Blount; Spelman.

MISLAY. To deposit in a place not afterwards recollected; to lose anything by forgetfulness of the place where it was laid.

MISLEADING. Delusive; calculated to lead astray or to lead into error. Instructions which are of such a nature as to be misunderstood by the jury, or to give them a wrong impression, are said to be "misleading."

MISNOMER. Mistake in name; the giving an incorrect name to a person in a pleading, deed, or other instrument.

MISPLEADING. Pleading incorrectly, or omitting anything in pleading which is essential to the support or defense of an action, is so called; as in the case of a plaintiff not merely stating his title in a defective manner, but setting forth a title which is essentially defective in itself; or if, to an action of debt, the defendant pleads "not guilty" instead of *nil debet*. Brown.

MISPRISION. In criminal law. A term used to signify every considerable misdemeanor which has not a certain name given to it by law. 3 Inst. 36.

Neglect or light account made of a crime; omission to reveal it. "Misprision of treason" is the bare knowledge and concealment of treason, without any degree of assent thereto, for any assent makes the party a principal traitor. 4 Bl. Comm. 120; 4 Steph. Comm. 200. "Misprision of felony" is the concealment of a felony committed by another, without such previous concert with or subsequent assistance of the latter as will make the party concealing an accessary before or after the fact. 4 Steph. Comm. 260. These are "misprisions," in the proper sense of the term. Contempts and high misdemeanors were formerly termed "positive misprisions." 4 Bl. Comm. 121.

Misprisions of clerks are mistakes made by clerks, etc., in writing or keeping records.

MISPRISION OF TREASON. Misprision of treason is the knowledge and concealment of treason, without otherwise assenting to or participating in the crime. Pen. Code Cal. § 38.

MISREADING. Reading a deed or other instrument to an illiterate or blind man (who is a party to it) in a false or deceitful manner, so that he conceives a wrong idea of its tenor or contents. See 5 Coke, 19; 6 East, 309; 2 Johns. 404.

MISRECITAL. The erroneous or incorrect recital of a matter of fact, either in an agreement, deed, or pleading.

MISREPRESENTATION. An intentional false statement respecting a matter of fact, made by one of the parties to a contract, which is material to the contract and influential in producing it. 29 N. J. Eq. 262.

False or *fraudulent* misrepresentation is a representation contrary to the fact, made by a person with a knowledge of its falsehood, and being the cause of the other party's entering into the contract. 6 Clark & F. 232.

Negligent misrepresentation is a false representation made by a person who has no reasonable grounds for believing it to be true, though he does not know that it is untrue, or even believes it to be true. L. R. 4 H. L. 79.

Innocent misrepresentation is where the person making the representation had reasonable grounds for believing it to be true. L. R. 2 Q. B. 580.

MISSA. The mass.

MISSÆ PRESBYTER. A priest in orders. Blount.

MISSAL. The mass-book.

MISSILIA. In Roman law. Gifts or liberalities, which the prætors and consuls were in the habit of throwing among the people. Inst. 2, 1, 45.

MISSING SHIP. In maritime law. A vessel is so called when, computed from her known day of sailing, the time that has elapsed exceeds the average duration of similar voyages at the same season of the year. 2 Duer, Ins. 469.

MISSIO. Lat. In the civil law. A sending or putting. *Missio in bona*, a putting the creditor in possession of the debtor's property. Mackeld. Rom. Law, § 521. *Missio judicum in consilium*, a sending out of the *judices* (or jury) to make up their sentence. Hallifax, Civil Law, b. 3, c. 13, no. 31.

MISSIVES. In Scotch law. Writings passed between parties as evidence of a transaction. Bell.

MISSTAICUS. In old records. A messenger.

MISTAKE. Some unintentional act, omission, or error arising from ignorance, surprise, imposition, or misplaced confidence. Code Ga. § 3117; 1 Story, Eq. Jur. § 110.

That result of ignorance of law or fact which has misled a person to commit that which, if he had not been in error, he would not have done. Jeremy, Eq. Jur. 358.

A mistake exists when a person, under some erroneous conviction of law or fact, does, or omits to do, some act which, but for the erroneous conviction, he would not have done or omitted. It may arise either from unconsciousness, ignorance, forgetfulness, imposition, or misplaced confidence. Bisph. Eq. § 185.

Mistake of fact is a mistake not caused by the neglect of a legal duty on the part of the person making the mistake, and consisting in (1) an unconscious ignorance or forgetfulness of a fact, past or present, material to the contract; or (2) belief in the present existence of a thing material to the contract which does not exist, or in the past existence of such a thing which has not existed. Civil Code Cal. § 1577.

A *mistake of law* happens when a party, having full knowledge of the facts, comes to an erroneous conclusion as to their legal effect. It is a mistaken opinion or inference, arising from an imperfect or incorrect exercise of the judgment, upon facts as they really are; and, like a correct opinion, which is law, necessarily presupposes that the person forming it is in full possession of them. The facts precede the law, and the true and false opinion alike imply an acquaintance with them. Neither can exist without it. The one is the result of a correct application to them of legal principles, which every man is presumed to know, and is called "law;" the other, the result of a faulty application, and is called a "mistake of law." 12 Wis. 124.

Mutual mistake is where the parties have a common intention, but it is induced by a common or mutual mistake.

MISTERY. A trade or calling. Cowell.

MISTRESS. The proper style of the wife of an esquire or a gentleman in England.

MISTRIAL. An erroneous, invalid, or nugatory trial; a trial of an action which cannot stand in law because of want of jurisdiction, or a wrong drawing of jurors, or disregard of some other fundamental requisite.

MISUSER. Abuse of an office or franchise. 2 Bl. Comm. 153.

MITIGATION. Alleviation; abatement or diminution of a penalty or punishment imposed by law. "Mitigating circumstances" are such as do not constitute a justification or excuse of the offense in question, but which, in fairness and mercy, may be considered as extenuating or reducing the degree of moral culpability.

MITIGATION OF DAMAGES. A reduction of the amount of damages, not by proof of facts which are a bar to a part of the plaintiff's cause of action, or a justification, nor yet of facts which constitute a cause of action in favor of the defendant, but rather facts which show that the plaintiff's conceded cause of action does not entitle him to so large an amount as the showing on his side would otherwise justify the jury in allowing him. 1 Suth. Dam. 226.

MITIOR SENSUS. Lat. The more favorable acceptation.

Mitius imperanti melius paretur. The more mildly one commands, the better is he obeyed. 3 Inst. 24.

MITOYENNETÉ. In French law. The joint ownership of two neighbors' in a wall, ditch, or hedge which separates their estates.

MITTENDO MANUSCRIPTUM PEDIS FINIS. An abolished judicial writ addressed to the treasurer and chamberlain of the exchequer to search for and transmit the foot of a fine acknowledged before justices in eyre into the common pleas. Reg. Orig. 14.

MITTER. L. Fr. To put, to send, or to pass; as, *mitter l'estate*, to pass the estate; *mitter le droit*, to pass a right. These words are used to distinguish different kinds of releases.

MITTER AVANT. L. Fr. In old practice. To put before; to present before a court; to produce in court.

MITTIMUS. In English law. A writ used in sending a record or its tenor from one court to another. Thus, where a *nul tiel record* is pleaded in one court to the record of another court of equal or superior jurisdiction, the tenor of the record is brought into chancery by a *certiorari*, (*q. v.*,) and thence sent by *mittimus* into the court where the action is. Tidd, Pr. 745.

In criminal practice. The name of a precept in writing, issuing from a court or magistrate, directed to the sheriff or other officer, commanding him to convey to the prison the person named therein, and to the jailer, commanding him to receive and safely keep such person until he shall be delivered by due course of law. Pub. St. Mass. 1882, p. 1293.

MIXED ACTION. An action partaking of the twofold nature of real and personal actions, having for its object the demand and restitution of real property and also personal damages for a wrong sustained. 3 Bl. Comm. 118.

Mixed actions are those which are brought for the specific recovery of lands, like real actions, but comprise, joined with this claim, one for damages in respect of such property; such as the action of waste, where, in addition to the recovery of the place wasted, the demandant claims damages; the writ of entry, in which, by statute, a demand of mesne profits may be joined; and dower, in which a claim for detention may be included. 48 Me. 255.

In the civil law. An action in which some specific thing was demanded, and also some personal obligation claimed to be performed; or, in other words, an action which proceeded both *in rem* and *in personam*. Inst. 4, 6, 20.

MIXED CONTRACT. In the civil law. A contract in which one of the parties confers a benefit on the other, and requires of the latter something of less value than what he has given; as a donation subject to a charge. Poth. Obl. no. 12.

MIXED GOVERNMENT. A form of government combining some of the features of two or all of the three primary forms, viz., monarchy, aristocracy, and democracy.

MIXED JURY. A bilingual jury; a jury of the half-tongue. See DE MEDIETATE LINGUÆ.

Also a jury composed partly of negroes and partly of white men.

MIXED LARCENY. Otherwise called "compound" or "complicated larceny;" that which is attended with circumstances of aggravation or violence to the person, or taking from a house.

MIXED LAWS. A name sometimes given to those which concern both persons and property.

MIXED MARRIAGE. A marriage between persons of different nationalities; or, more particularly, between persons of different racial origin; as between a white person and a negro or an Indian.

MIXED PERSONALTY. Impure personalty.

MIXED POLICY. A policy of marine insurance in which not only the time is specified for which the risk is limited, but the voyage also is described by its local termini;

as opposed to policies of insurance for a particular voyage, without any limits as to time, and also to purely time policies, in which there is no designation of local termini at all. Mozley & Whitley.

MIXED PRESUMPTIONS. Presumptions partaking of the nature both of presumptions of law and presumptions of fact; *i. e.*, presumptions of fact recognized by law.

MIXED PROPERTY. Property which is personal in its essential nature, but is invested by the law with certain of the characteristics and features of real property. Heirlooms, tombstones, monuments in a church, and title-deeds to an estate are of this nature. 2 Bl. Comm. 428; 3 Barn. & Adol. 174; 4 Bing. 106.

MIXED QUESTIONS. This phrase may mean either those which arise from the conflict of foreign and domestic laws, or questions arising on a trial involving both law and fact.

MIXED SUBJECTS OF PROPERTY. Such as fall within the definition of things real, but which are attended, nevertheless, with some of the legal qualities of things personal, as emblements, fixtures, and shares in public undertakings, connected with land. Besides these, there are others which, though things personal in point of definition, are, in respect of some of their legal qualities, of the nature of things real; such are animals *feræ naturæ*, charters and deeds, court rolls, and other evidences of the land, together with the chests in which they are contained, ancient family pictures, ornaments, tombstones, coats of armor, with pennons and other ensigns, and especially heir-looms. Wharton.

MIXED TITHES. In ecclesiastical law. Those which arise not immediately from the ground, but from those things which are nourished by the ground, *e. g.*, colts, chickens, calves, milk, eggs, etc. 3 Burn, Ecc. Law, 380; 2 Bl. Comm. 24.

MIXED WAR. A mixed war is one which is made on one side by public authority, and on the other by mere private persons. 1 Hill, 377, 415.

MIXTION. The mixture or confusion of goods or chattels belonging severally to different owners, in such a way that they can no longer be separated or distinguished; as where two measures of wine belonging to different persons are poured together into the same cask.

MIXTUM IMPERIUM. Lat. In old English law. Mixed authority; a kind of civil power. A term applied by Lord Hale to the "power" of certain subordinate civil magistrates as distinct from "jurisdiction." Hale, Anal. § 11.

MOB. An assemblage of many people, acting in a violent and disorderly manner, defying the law, and committing, or threatening to commit, depredations upon property or violence to persons.

The word, in legal use, is practically synonymous with "riot," but the latter is the more correct term.

MOBBING AND RIOTING. In Scotch law. A general term including all those convocations of the lieges for violent and unlawful purposes, which are attended with injury to the persons or property of the lieges, or terror and alarm to the neighborhood in which it takes place. The two phrases are usually placed together; but, nevertheless, they have distinct meanings, and are sometimes used separately in legal language, the word "mobbing" being peculiarly applicable to the unlawful assemblage and violence of a number of persons, and that of "rioting" to the outrageous behavior of a single individual. Alis. Crim. Law, c. 23, p. 509.

MOBILIA. Lat. Movables; movable things; otherwise called "*res mobiles.*"

Mobilia non habent situm. Movables have no *situs* or local habitation. 4 Johns. Ch. 472.

Mobilia sequuntur personam. Movables follow the [law of the] person. Story, Confl. Law, § 378; Broom, Max. 522.

MOCKADOES. A kind of cloth made in England, mentioned in St. 23 Eliz. c. 9.

MODEL. A pattern or representation of something to be made. A *fac simile* of something invented, made on a reduced scale, in compliance with the patent laws.

MODERAMEN INCULPATÆ TUTELÆ. Lat. In Roman law. The regulation of justifiable defense. A term used to express that degree of force in defense of the person or property which a person might safely use, although it should occasion the death of the aggressor. Calvin.; Bell.

MODERATA MISERICORDIA. A writ founded on *Magna Charta*, which lies for him who is amerced in a court, not of record, for any transgression beyond the quality or quantity of the offense. It is addressed to the lord of the court, or his bailiff, commanding him to take a moderate amerciament of the parties. New Nat. Brev. 167; Fitzh. Nat. Brev. 76.

MODERATE CASTIGAVIT. Lat. In pleading. He moderately chastised. The name of a plea in trespass which justifies an alleged battery on the ground that it consisted in a moderate chastisement of the plaintiff by the defendant, which, from their relations, the latter had a legal right to inflict.

MODERATE SPEED. In admiralty law. As applied to a steam-vessel, "such speed only is moderate as will permit the steamer reasonably and effectually to avoid a collision by slackening speed, or by stopping and reversing, within the distance at which an approaching vessel can be seen." 35 Fed. Rep. 609; 39 Fed. Rep. 480.

MODERATOR. A chairman or president of an assembly. A person appointed to preside at a popular meeting. The presiding officer of town-meetings in New England is so called.

MODIATIO. In old English law. A certain duty paid for every tierce of wine.

Modica circumstantia facti jus mutat. A small circumstance attending an act may change the law.

MODIFICATION. A change; an alteration which introduces new elements into the details, or cancels some of them, but leaves the general purpose and effect of the subject-matter intact.

"Modification" is not exactly synonymous with "amendment," for the former term denotes some minor change in the substance of the thing, without reference to its improvement or deterioration thereby, while the latter word imports an amelioration of the thing (as by changing the phraseology of an instrument, so as to make it more distinct or specific) without involving the idea of any change in substance or essence.

In Scotch law. The term usually applied to the decree of the teind court, awarding a suitable stipend to the minister of a parish. Bell.

MODIFY. To alter; to change in incidental or subordinate features.

MODIUS. A measure, usually a bushel.

MODIUS TERRÆ VEL AGRI. In old English law. A quantity of ground containing in length and breadth 100 feet.

MODO ET FORMA. In manner and form. Words used in the old Latin forms of pleadings by way of traverse, and literally translated in the modern precedents, importing that the party traversing denies the allegation of the other party, not only in its general effect, but in the exact *manner and form* in which it is made. Steph. Pl. 189, 190.

MODUS. Lat. In the civil law. Manner; means; way.

In old conveyancing. Mode; manner; the arrangement or expression of the terms of a contract or conveyance.

Also a consideration; the consideration of a conveyance, technically expressed by the word "*ut.*"

A qualification, involving the idea of variance or departure from some general rule or form, either by way of restriction or enlargement, according to the circumstances of a particular case, the will of a donor, the particular agreement of parties, and the like. Burrill.

In criminal pleading. The *modus* of an indictment is that part of it which contains the narrative of the commission of the crime; the statement of the mode or manner in which the offense was committed. Tray. Lat. Max.

In ecclesiastical law. A peculiar manner of tithing, growing out of custom.

MODUS DE NON DECIMANDO. In ecclesiastical law. A custom or prescription of entire exemption from the payment of tithes; this is not valid, unless in the case of abbey-lands.

Modus de non decimando non valet. A *modus* (prescription) not to pay tithes is void. Lofft, 427; Cro. Eliz. 511; 2 Shars. Bl. Comm. 31.

MODUS DECIMANDI. In ecclesiastical law. A manner of tithing; a partial exemption from tithes, or a pecuniary composition prescribed by immemorial usage, and of reasonable amount; for it will be invalid as a *rank modus* if greater than the value of the tithes in the time of Richard I. Stim. Law Gloss.

Modus et conventio vincunt legem. Custom and agreement overrule law. This maxim forms one of the first principles relative to the law of contracts. The exceptions to the rule here laid down are in cases against public policy, morality, etc. 2 Coke, 73; Broom, Max. 689, 691-695.

MODUS HABILIS. A valid manner.

Modus legem dat donationi. Custom gives law to the gift. Co. Litt. 19; Broom, Max. 459.

MODUS LEVANDI FINES. The manner of levying fines. The title of a short statute in French passed in the eighteenth year of Edward I. 2 Inst. 510; 2 Bl. Comm. 349.

MODUS TENENDI. The manner of holding; *i. e.*, the different species of tenures by which estates are held.

MODUS TRANSFERRENDI. The manner of transferring.

MODUS VACANDI. The manner of vacating. How and why an estate has been relinquished or surrendered by a vassal to his lord might well be referred to by this phrase. See Tray. Lat. Max. *s. v.*

MOEBLE. L. Fr. Movable. *Biens moebles*, movable goods. Britt. c. 11.

MOERDA. The secret killing of another; murder. 4 Bl. Comm. 194.

MOFUSSIL. In Hindu law. Separated; particularized; the subordinate divisions of a district in contradistinction to *Sadder* or *Sudder*, which implies the chief seat of government. Wharton.

MOHAMMEDAN LAW. A system of native law prevailing among the Mohammedans in India, and administered there by the British government.

MOHATRA. In French law. A transaction covering a fraudulent device to evade the laws against usury.

It takes place where an individual buys merchandise from another on a credit at a high price, to sell it immediately to the first seller, or to a third person who acts as his agent, at a much less price for cash. 16 Toullier, no. 44.

MOIDORE. A gold coin of Portugal, valued at twenty-seven English shillings.

MOIETY. The half of anything. Joint tenants are said to hold by moieties. Litt. 125; 3 C. B. 274, 283.

MOLENDINUM. In old records. A mill.

MOLENDUM. A grist; a certain quantity of corn sent to a mill to be ground.

MOLESTATION. In Scotch law. A possessory action calculated for continuing proprietors of landed estates in the lawful possession of them till the point of right be determined against all who shall attempt to disturb their possession. It is chiefly used in questions of commonty or of controverted marches. Ersk. Inst. 4, 1, 48.

MOLITURA. The toll or multure paid for grinding corn at a mill. Jacob.

MOLITURA LIBERA. Free grinding; a liberty to have a mill without paying tolls to the lord. Jacob.

MOLLITER MANUS IMPOSUIT. Lat. He gently laid hands upon. Formal words in the old Latin pleas in actions of trespass and assault where a defendant justified laying hands upon the plaintiff, as where it was done to keep the peace, etc. The phrase is literally translated in the modern precedents, and the original is retained as the name of the plea in such cases. 3 Bl. Comm. 21; 1 Chit. Pl. 501, 502; Id. 1071.

MOLMUTIAN LAWS. The laws of Dunvallo Molmutius, a legendary or mythical king of the Britons, who is supposed to have begun his reign about 400 B. C. These laws were famous in the land till the Conquest. Tomlins; Mozley & Whitley.

MOMENTUM. In the civil law. An instant; an indivisible portion of time. Calvin.

A portion of time that might be measured; a division or subdivision of an hour; answering in some degree to the modern *minute*, but of longer duration. Calvin.

MONACHISM. The state of monks.

MONARCHY. A government in which the supreme power is vested in a single person. Where a monarch is invested with absolute power, the monarchy is termed "despotic;" where the supreme power is virtually in the laws, though the majesty of government and the administration are vested in a single person, it is a "limited" or "constitutional" monarchy. It is hereditary where the regal power descends immediately from the possessor to the next heir by blood, as in England; or elective, as was formerly the case in Poland. Wharton.

MONASTERIUM. A monastery; a church. Spelman.

MONASTICON. A book giving an account of monasteries, convents, and religious houses.

MONETA. Money, (*q. v.*)

Moneta est justum medium et mensura rerum commutabilium, nam per medium monetæ fit omnium rerum conveniens et justa æstimatio. Dav. Ir. K. B. 18. Money is the just medium and measure of commutable things, for by the medium of money a convenient and just estimation of all things is made.

MONETAGIUM. Mintage, or the right of coining money. Cowell. Hence, anciently, a tribute payable to a lord who had the prerogative of coining money, by his tenants, in consideration of his refraining from changing the coinage.

Monetandi jus comprehenditur in regalibus quæ nunquam a regio sceptro abdicantur. The right of coining money is comprehended among those royal prerogatives which are never relinquished by the royal scepter. Dav. Ir. K. B. 18.

MONEY. A general, indefinite term for the measure and representative of value; currency; the circulating medium; cash.

"Money" is a generic term, and embraces every description of coin or bank-notes recognized by common consent as a representative of value in effecting exchanges of property or payment of debts. 5 Humph. 140.

Money is used in a specific and also in a general and more comprehensive sense. In its specific sense, it means what is coined or stamped by public authority, and has its determinate value fixed by governments. In its more comprehensive and general sense, it means wealth,—the representative of commodities of all kinds, of lands, and of everything that can be transferred in commerce. 31 Tex. 10.

In its strict technical sense, "money" means coined metal, usually gold or silver, upon which the government stamp has been impressed to indicate its value. In its more popular sense, "money" means any currency, tokens, bank-notes, or other circulating medium in general use as the representative of value. 45 Tex. 305.

The term "moneys" is not of more extensive signification than "money," and means only cash, and not things in action. 14 Johns. 1; 1 Johns. Ch. 231.

MONEY-BILL. In parliamentary language, an act by which revenue is directed to be raised, for any purpose or in any shape whatsoever, either for governmental purposes, and collected from the whole people generally, or for the benefit of a particular district, and collected in that district, or for making appropriations.

MONEY-BROKER. A money-changer; a scrivener or jobber; one who lends or raises money to or for others.

MONEY CLAIMS. In English practice. Under the judicature act of 1875, claims for the price of goods sold, for money lent, for arrears of rent, etc., and other claims where money is directly payable on a contract express or implied, as opposed to the cases where money is claimed by way of damages for some independent wrong, whether by breach of contract or otherwise. These "money claims" correspond very nearly to the "money counts" hitherto in use. Mozley & Whitley.

MONEY COUNTS. In pleading. A species of common counts, so called from the subject-matter of them; embracing the *indebitatus assumpsit* count for money lent and advanced, for money paid and expended, and for money had and received, together with the *insimul computassent* count, or count for money due on an account stated. 1 Burrill, Pr. 132.

MONEY DEMAND. A claim for a fixed and liquidated amount of money, or for a sum which can be ascertained by mere calculation; in this sense, distinguished from a claim which must be passed upon and liquidated by a jury, called "damages."

MONEY HAD AND RECEIVED. In pleading. The technical designation of a form of declaration in *assumpsit*, wherein the plaintiff declares that the defendant *had and received* certain money, etc.

MONEY JUDGMENT. One which adjudges the payment of a sum of money, as distinguished from one directing an act to be done or property to be restored or transferred.

MONEY LAND. A phrase descriptive of money which is held upon a trust to convert it into land.

MONEY LENT. In pleading. The technical name of a declaration in an action of *assumpsit* for that the defendant promised to pay the plaintiff for money lent.

MONEY MADE. The return made by a sheriff to a writ of execution, signifying that he has collected the sum of money required by the writ.

MONEY OF ADIEU. In French law. Earnest money; so called because given at parting in completion of the bargain. *Arrhes* is the usual French word for earnest money; "money of adieu" is a provincialism found in the province of Orleans. Poth. Cont. 507;

MONEY ORDER. Under the postal regulations of the United States, a money order is a species of draft drawn by one post-office upon another for an amount of money deposited at the first office by the person purchasing the money order, and payable at the second office to a payee named in the order.

MONEY-ORDER OFFICE. One of the post-offices authorized to draw or pay money orders.

MONEY PAID. In pleading. The technical name of a declaration in *assumpsit*, in which the plaintiff declares for money paid for the use of the defendant.

MONEYED CAPITAL. This term has a more limited meaning than the term "personal property," and applies to such capital as is readily solvable in money. 28 Fed. Rep. 776.

MONEYED CORPORATION. A corporation having the power to make loans upon pledges or deposits, or authorized by law to make insurance. 2 Rev. St. N. Y. (7th Ed.) 1371.

MONGER. A dealer or seller. It is seldom or never used alone, or otherwise than after the name of any commodity, to express a seller of such commodity.

MONIERS, or MONEYEERS. Ministers of the mint; also bankers. Cowell.

MONIMENT. A memorial, superscription, or record.

MONITION. **In practice.** A monition is a formal order of the court commanding something to be done by the person to whom it is directed, and who is called the "person monished." Thus, when money is decreed to be paid, a monition may be obtained commanding its payment. In ecclesiastical procedure, a monition is an order monishing or warning the party complained against to do or not to do a certain act "under pain of the law and contempt thereof." A monition may also be appended to a sentence inflicting a punishment for a past offense; in that case the monition forbids the repetition of the offense. Sweet.

In admiralty practice. The summons to appear and answer, issued on filing the libel; which is either a simple monition *in personam* or an attachment and monition *in rem*. Ben. Adm. 228, 239. It is sometimes termed "monition *viis et modis*," and has been supposed to be derived from the old Roman practice of summoning a defendant. 10 Wheat. 490.

The monition, in American admiralty practice, is, in effect, a summons, citation, or notice, though in form a command to the marshal to cite and admonish the defendant to appear and answer, and not a summons addressed to the party. 2 Conk. Adm. (2d Ed.) 147.

MONITORY LETTERS. Communications of warning and admonition sent from an ecclesiastical judge, upon information of scandal and abuses within the cognizance of his court.

MONOCRACY. A government by one person.

MONOCRAT. A monarch who governs alone; an absolute governor.

MONOGAMY. The marriage of one wife only, or the state of such as are restrained to a single wife. Webster.

A marriage contracted between one man and one woman, in exclusion of all the rest of mankind. The term is used in opposition to "bigamy" and "polygamy." Wolff, Dr. de la Nat. § 857.

MONOGRAM. A character or cipher composed of one or more letters interwoven, being an abbreviation of a name.

MONOGRAPH. A special treatise upon a particular subject of limited range; a treatise or commentary upon a particular branch or division of a general subject.

MONOMACHY. A duel; a single combat.

It was anciently allowed by law for the trial or proof of crimes. It was even permitted in pecuniary causes, but it is now forbidden both by the civil law and canon laws.

MONOMANIA. In medical jurisprudence. Derangement of a single faculty of the mind, or with regard to a particular subject, the other faculties being in regular exercise.

Monopolia dicitur, cum unus solus aliquod genus mercaturæ universum emit, pretium ad suum libitum statuens. 11 Coke, 86. It is said to be a monopoly when one person alone buys up the whole of one kind of commodity, fixing a price at his own pleasure.

MONOPOLIUM. The sole power, right, or privilege of sale; monopoly; a monopoly. Calvin.

MONOPOLY. In commercial law. A privilege or peculiar advantage vested in one or more persons or companies, consisting in the exclusive right (or power) to carry on a particular business or trade, manufacture a particular article, or control the sale of the whole supply of a particular commodity.

Defined in English law to be "a license or privilege allowed by the king for the sole buying and selling, making, working, or using, of anything whatsoever; whereby the subject in general is restrained from that liberty of manufacturing or trading which he had before." 4 Bl. Comm. 159; 4 Steph. Comm. 291.

MONSTER. A prodigious birth; a human birth or offspring not having the shape of mankind; which cannot be heir to any land, albeit it be brought forth in marriage. Bract. fol. 5; Co. Litt. 7, 8; 2 Bl. Comm. 246.

MONSTRANS DE DROIT. L. Fr. In English law. A showing or manifestation of right; one of the common law methods of obtaining possession or restitution from the crown, of either real or personal property. It is the proper proceeding when the right of the party, as well as the right of the crown, appears upon record, and consists in putting in a claim of right grounded on facts already acknowledged and established, and praying the judgment of the court whether upon these facts the king or the subject has the right. 3 Bl. Comm. 256; 4 Coke, 54*b*.

MONSTRANS DE FAITS. L. Fr. In old English practice. A showing of deeds; a species of profert. Cowell.

MONSTRAVERUNT, WRIT OF. In English law. A writ which lies for the tenants of ancient demesne who hold by free charter, and not for those tenants who hold by copy of court roll, or by the rod, according to the custom of the manor. Fitzh. Nat. Brev. 14.

MONSTRUM. A box in which relics are kept; also a muster of soldiers. Cowell.

MONTES. In Spanish law. Forests or woods. White, New Recop. b. 2, tit. 1, c. 6, § 1.

MONTES PIETATIS. Public pawnbroking establishments; institutions established by government, in some European countries, for lending small sums of money on pledges of personal property. In France they are called "*monts de piété.*"

MONTH. One of the divisions of a year. The space of time denoted by this term varies according as one or another of the following varieties of months is intended:

Astronomical, containing one-twelfth of the time occupied by the sun in passing through the entire zodiac.

Calendar, civil, or *solar,* which is one of the months in the Gregorian calendar,—January, February, March, etc.,—which are of unequal length.

Lunar, being the period of one revolution of the moon, or twenty-eight days.

MONUMENT. Anything by which the memory of a person or an event is preserved or perpetuated. A tomb where a dead body has been deposited.

Monumenta quæ nos recorda vocamus sunt veritatis et vetustatis vestigia. Co. Litt. 118. Monuments, which we call "records," are the vestiges of truth and antiquity.

MONUMENTS. Permanent landmarks established for the purpose of indicating boundaries.

MONYA. In Norman law. Moneyage. A tax or tribute of one shilling on every hearth, payable to the duke every three years, in consideration that he should not alter the coin. Hale, Com. Law, 148, and note.

MOOKTAR. In Hindu law. An agent or attorney.

MOOKTARNAMA. In Hindu law. A written authority constituting an agent; a power of attorney.

MOOR. An officer in the Isle of Man, who summons the courts for the several sheadings. The office is similar to the English bailiff of a hundred.

MOORAGE. A sum due by law or usage for mooring or fastening of ships to trees or posts at the shore, or to a wharf. 3 Bland, 373.

MOORING. In maritime law. Anchoring or making fast to the shore or dock; the securing or confining a vessel in a particular station, as by cables and anchors or by a line or chain run to the wharf. A vessel is "moored in safety," within the meaning of a policy of marine insurance, when she is thus moored to a wharf or dock, free from any immediate danger from any of the perils insured against. See 1 Phil. Ins. 968.

MOOT, *adj.* A subject for argument; unsettled; undecided. As a *moot* case, a *moot* point.

MOOT, *n.* In English law. Moots are exercises in pleading, and in arguing doubtful cases and questions, by the students of an inn of court before the benchers of the inn. Sweet.

MOOT COURT. A court held for the arguing of moot cases or questions.

MOOT HALL. The place where moot cases were argued. Also a council-chamber, hall of judgment, or town-hall.

MOOT HILL. Hill of meeting, (*gemot,*) on which the Britons used to hold their courts, the judge sitting on the eminence; the parties, etc., on an elevated platform below. Enc. Lond.

MOOT MAN. One of those who used to argue the reader's cases in the inns of court.

MOOTA CANUM. A pack of dogs. Cowell.

MOOTING. The exercise of arguing questions of law or equity, raised for the purpose. See MOOT.

MORA. Lat. In the civil law. Delay; default; neglect; culpable delay or default. Calvin.

MORA. Sax. A moor; barren or unprofitable ground; marsh; a heath; a watery bog or moor. Co. Litt. 5; Fleta, l. 2, c. 71.

MORA MUSSA. A watery or boggy moor; a morass.

Mora reprobatur in lege. Delay is reprobated in law. Jenk. Cent. p. 51, case 97.

MORAL ACTIONS. Those only in which men have knowledge to guide them, and a will to choose for themselves. Ruth. Inst. lib. l. c. i.

MORAL CERTAINTY. In the law of criminal evidence. That degree of assurance which induces a man of sound mind to act, without doubt, upon the conclusions to which it leads. Wills, Circ. Ev. 7.

A certainty that convinces and directs the understanding and satisfies the reason and judgment of those who are bound to act conscientiously upon it.

A high degree of impression of the truth of a fact, falling short of absolute certainty, but sufficient to justify a verdict of guilty, even in a capital case. See Burrill, Circ. Ev. 198-200.

The phrase "moral certainty" has been introduced into our jurisprudence from the publicists and metaphysicians, and signifies only a very high degree of probability. It was observed by Pufendorf that, "when we declare such a thing to be morally certain, because it has been confirmed by credible witnesses, this moral certitude is nothing else but a strong presumption grounded on probable reasons, and which very seldom fails and deceives us." "Probable evidence," says Bishop Butler, in the opening sentence of his Analogy, "is essentially distinguished from demonstrative by this: that it admits of degrees, and of all variety of them, from the highest moral certainty to the very lowest presumption." 118 Mass. 23.

MORAL EVIDENCE. As opposed to "mathematical" or "demonstrative" evidence, this term denotes that kind of evidence which, without developing an absolute and necessary certainty, generates a high degree of probability or persuasive force. It is founded upon analogy or induction, experience of the ordinary course of nature or the sequence of events, and the testimony of men.

MORAL FRAUD. This phrase is one of the less usual designations of "actual" or "positive" fraud or "fraud in fact," as distinguished from "constructive" fraud or "fraud in law." It means fraud which involves actual guilt, a wrongful purpose, or moral obliquity.

MORAL INSANITY. In medical jurisprudence. A derangement of the moral system; a morbid condition, in which the passions, appetites, inclinations, and moral dispositions have escaped from the control of the will and the conscience, and are perverted to immoral acts or uses, although the faculties of perception, reason, and judgment remain normal, or nearly so, and there is no especial hallucination or illusion. Kleptomania is an example of this condition.

Incapacity, from disease, to control one's conduct according to one's knowledge; uncontrollable morbid impulse; disability of the will to refrain from what one knows is wrong and punishable; a morbid perversion of the affections, inclinations, and temper, independent of any disease or delusion operating directly on the intellect. Abbott.

MORAL OBLIGATION. A duty which is valid and binding in the forum of the conscience, but is not recognized by the law as adequate to set in motion the machinery of justice; that is, one which rests upon ethical considerations alone, and is not imposed or enforced by positive law.

MORANDÆ SOLUTIONIS CAUSA. Lat. For the purpose of delaying or postponing payment or performance.

MORATUR IN LEGE. Lat. He delays in law. The phrase describes the action of one who demurs, because the party does not proceed in pleading, but rests or abides upon the judgment of the court on a certain point, as to the legal sufficiency of his opponent's pleading. The court deliberate and determine thereupon.

MORAVIANS. Otherwise called "Herrnhutters" or "United Brethren." A sect of Christians whose social polity is particular and conspicuous. It sprung up in Moravia and Bohemia, on the opening of that reformation which stripped the chair of St. Peter of so many votaries, and gave birth to so many denominations of Christians. They give evidence on their solemn affirmation. 2 Steph. Comm. 338*n*.

MORBUS SONTICUS. Lat. In the civil law. A sickness which rendered a man incapable of attending to business.

MORE COLONICO. Lat. In old pleading. In husband-like manner. Townsh. Pl. 198.

MORE OR LESS. This phrase, inserted in a conveyance of land immediately after the statement of the quantity of land conveyed, means that such statement is not to be taken as a warranty of the quantity, but only an approximate estimate, and that the tract or parcel described is to pass, without regard to an excess or deficiency in the quantity it actually contains.

MORGANATIC MARRIAGE. The lawful and inseparable conjunction of a man, of noble or illustrious birth, with a woman of inferior station, upon condition that neither the wife nor her children shall partake of the titles, arms, or dignity of the husband, or succeed to his inheritance, but be contented with a certain allowed rank assigned to them by the morganatic contract. But since these restrictions relate only to the rank of the parties and succession to property, without affecting the nature of a matrimonial engagement, it must be considered as a just marriage. The marriage ceremony was regularly performed; the union was indissoluble; the children legitimate. Wharton.

MORGANGINA, or MORGANGIVA. A gift on the morning after the wedding; dowry; the husband's gift to his wife on the day after the wedding. Du Cange; Cowell.

MORGEN. Anglo-Dutch. In old New York law. A measure of land, equal to about two acres.

MORGUE. A place where the bodies of persons found dead are kept for a limited time and exposed to view, to the end that their friends may identify them.

MORMONISM. A social and religious system prevailing in the territory of Utah, a distinctive feature of which is the practice of polygamy. These plural marriages are not recognized by law, but are indictable offenses under the statutes of the United States and of Utah.

MORS. Lat. Death.

Mors dicitur ultimum supplicium. Death is called the "last punishment," the "extremity of punishment." 3 Inst. 212.

Mors omnia solvit. Death dissolves all things. Jenk. Cent. p. 160, case 2. Applied to the case of the death of a party to an action.

MORSELLUM, or MORSELLUS, TERRÆ. In old English law. A small parcel or bit of land.

MORT CIVILE. In French law. Civil death, as upon conviction for felony. It was nominally abolished by a law of the 31st of May, 1854, but something very similar to it, in effect at least, still remains. Thus, the property of the condemned, possessed by him at the date of his conviction, goes and belongs to his successors, (*héritiers*,) as in case of an intestacy; and his future acquired property goes to the state by right of its prerogative, (*par droit de déshérence*,) but the state may, as a matter of grace, make it over in whole or in part to the widow and children. Brown.

MORT D'ANCESTOR. An ancient and now almost obsolete remedy in the English law. An assize of *mort d'ancestor* was a writ which lay for a person whose ancestor died seised of lands in fee-simple, and after his death a stranger abated; and this writ directed the sheriff to summon a jury or assize, who should view the land in question and recognize whether such ancestor were seised thereof on the day of his death, and whether the demandant were the next heir.

MORTALITY. This word, in its ordinary sense, never means violent death, but death arising from natural causes. 5 Barn. & Ald. 110; 3 Barn. & C. 793.

MORTGAGE. An estate created by a conveyance absolute in its form, but intended to secure the performance of some act, such as the payment of money, and the like, by the grantor or some other person, and to become void if the act is performed agreeably to the terms prescribed at the time of making such conveyance. 1 Washb. Real Prop. *475.

A conditional conveyance of land, designed as a security for the payment of money, the fulfillment of some contract, or the performance of some act, and to be void upon such payment, fulfillment, or performance. 44 Me. 299.

A debt by specialty, secured by a pledge of lands, of which the legal ownership is vested in the creditor, but of which, in equity, the debtor and those claiming under him remain the actual owners, until debarred by judicial sentence or their own laches. Coote, Mortg. 1.

Mortgage is a right granted to the creditor over the property of the debtor for the security of his debt, and gives him the power of having the property seized and sold in default of payment. Civil Code La. art. 3278.

Mortgage is a contract by which specific property is hypothecated for the performance of an act, without the necessity of a change of possession. Civil Code Cal. § 2920.

In the law of Louisiana. The *conventional* mortgage is a contract by which a person binds the whole of his property, or a portion of it only, in favor of another, to secure the execution of some engagement, but without divesting himself of the possession. Civil Code La. art. 3290.

The *judicial* mortgage is that resulting from judgments (whether these be rendered on contested cases or by default, or whether they be final or provisional) in favor of the person obtaining them. Civil Code La. art. 3321.

The law alone in certain cases gives to the creditor a mortgage on the property of his debtor, without it being requisite that the parties should stipulate it. This is called "legal mortgage." It is called also "tacit mortgage," because it is established by the law without the aid of any agreement. Civil Code La. art. 3311.

MORTGAGE OF GOODS. A conveyance of goods in gage or mortgage by which the whole legal title passes conditionally to the mortgagee; and, if the goods are not redeemed at the time stipulated, the title becomes absolute in law, although equity will interfere to compel a redemption. It is distinguished from a "pledge" by the circumstance that possession by the mortgagee is not or may not be essential to create or to support the title. Story, Bailm. § 287.

MORTGAGEE. He that takes or receives a mortgage.

MORTGAGOR. He that gives a mortgage.

MORTH. Sax. Murder, answering exactly to the French "*assassinat*" or "*muertre de guet-apens.*"

MORTHLAGA. A murderer. Cowell.

MORTHLAGE. Murder. Cowell.

MORTIFICATION. In Scotch law. A term nearly synonymous with "mortmain." Bell. Lands are said to be *mortified* for a charitable purpose.

MORTIS CAUSA. Lat. By reason of death; in contemplation of death. Thus used in the phrase "*Donatio mortis causa,*" (*q. v.*)

Mortis momentum est ultimum vitæ momentum. The last moment of life is the moment of death. 4 Bradf. 245, 250.

MORTMAIN. A term applied to denote the alienation of lands or tenements to any corporation, sole or aggregate, ecclesiastical or temporal. These purchases having been chiefly made by religious houses, in consequence of which lands became perpetually inherent in one dead hand, this has occasioned the general appellation of "mortmain" to be applied to such alienations. 2 Bl. Comm. 268; Co. Litt. 2*b*.

MORTMAIN ACTS. These acts had for their object to prevent lands getting into the possession or control of religious corporations, or, as the name indicates, *in mortua manu.* After numerous prior acts dating from the reign of Edward I., it was enacted by the statute 9 Geo. II. c. 36, (called the "Mortmain Act" *par excellence,*) that no lands should be given to charities unless certain requisites should be observed. Brown.

MORTUARY. In ecclesiastical law. A burial-place. A kind of ecclesiastical heriot, being a customary gift of the second best living animal belonging to the deceased, claimed by and due to the minister in many parishes, on the death of his parishioners, whether buried in the church-yard or not. 2 Bl. Comm. 425.

It has been sometimes used in a civil as well as in an ecclesiastical sense, and applied to a payment to the lord of the fee. Paroch. Antiq. 470.

MORTUARY TABLES. Tables for estimating the probable duration of the life of a party at a given age. 67 Cal. 16, 6 Pac. Rep. 871.

MORTUUM VADIUM. A dead pledge; a mortgage, (*q. v.*;) a pledge where the profits or rents of the thing pledged are not applied to the payment of the debt.

MORTUUS. Dead. So in sheriff's return, *mortuus est*, he is dead.

Mortuus exitus non est exitus. A dead issue is no issue. Co. Litt. 29. A child born dead is not considered as issue.

Mos retinendus est fidelissimæ vetustatis. 4 Coke, 78. A custom of the truest antiquity is to be retained.

MOSTRENCOS. In Spanish law. Strayed goods; estrays. White, New Recop. b. 2, tit. 2, c. 6.

MOTE. Sax. A meeting; an assembly. Used in composition, as *burgmote*, *folkmote*, etc.

MOTE-BELL. The bell which was used by the Saxons to summon people to the court. Cowell.

MOTEER. A customary service or payment at the mote or court of the lord, from which some were exempted by charter or privilege. Cowell.

MOTHER. A woman who has borne a child; a female parent; correlative to "son" or "daughter."

MOTHER-IN-LAW. The mother of one's wife or of one's husband.

MOTION. In practice. An occasional application to a court by the parties or their counsel, in order to obtain some rule or order, which becomes necessary either in the progress of a cause, or summarily and wholly unconnected with plenary proceedings.

A motion is a written application for an order addressed to the court or to a judge in vacation by any party to a suit or proceeding, or by any one interested therein. Rev. Code Iowa 1880, § 2911; Code N. Y. § 401.

In parliamentary law. The formal mode in which a member submits a proposed measure or resolve for the consideration and action of the meeting.

MOTION FOR DECREE. Under the chancery practice, the most usual mode of bringing on a suit for hearing when the defendant has answered is by motion for decree. To do this the plaintiff serves on the defendant a notice of his intention to move for a decree. Hunter, Suit Eq. 59; Daniell, Ch. Pr. 722.

MOTION FOR JUDGMENT. In English practice. A proceeding whereby a party to an action moves for the judgment of the court in his favor. See Sup. Ct. Rules 1883, ord. 40.

MOTION TO SET ASIDE JUDGMENT. This is a step taken by a party in an action who is dissatisfied with the judgment directed to be entered at the trial of the action.

MOTIVE. The inducement, cause, or reason why a thing is done. An act legal in itself, and which violates no right, is not actionable on account of the motive which actuated it. 5 Amer. Law Reg. (O. S.) 528.

MOTU PROPRIO. Lat. Of his own motion. The commencing words of a certain kind of papal rescript.

MOURNING. The dress or apparel worn by mourners at a funeral and for a time afterwards. Also the expenses paid for such apparel.

MOVABLE. That which can be changed in place, as movable property; or in time, as movable feasts or terms of court.

MOVABLES. Things movable; movable or personal chattels, which may be annexed to or attendant on the person of the owner, and carried about with him from one part of the world to another. 2 Bl. Comm. 387. *Movables* consist—*First*, of inanimate things, as goods, plate, money, jewels, implements of war, garments, and the like, or vegetable productions, as the fruit or other parts of a plant when severed from the body of it, or the whole plant itself when severed from the ground; *secondly*, of animals, which have in themselves a principle and power of motion. 2 Steph. Comm. 67.

In the civil law. Movables (*mobilia*,) properly denoted inanimate things; animals being distinguished as *moventia*, things moving. Calvin.

In Scotch law. "Movables" are opposed to "heritage." So that every species of property, and every right a man can hold, is by that law either heritable or movable. Bell.

MOVE. 1. To make an application to a court for a rule or order.

2. To propose a resolution, or recommend action in a deliberative body.

3. To pass over; to be transferred; as when the consideration of a contract is said to "move" from one party to the other.

4. To occasion; to contribute to; to tend or

lead to. The forewheel of a wagon was said "to *move* to the death of a man." Sayer, 249.

MOVENT. One who moves; one who makes a motion before a court; the applicant for a rule or order.

MOVING FOR AN ARGUMENT. Making a motion on a day which is not motion day, in virtue of having argued a special case; used in the exchequer after it became obsolete in the queen's bench. Wharton.

MUEBLES. In Spanish law. Movables; all sorts of personal property. White, New Recop. b. 1, tit. 3, c. 1, § 2.

MUIRBURN. In Scotch law. The offense of setting fire to a muir or moor. 1 Brown, Ch. 78, 116.

MULATTO. A mulatto is defined to be "a person that is the offspring of a negress by a white man, or of a white woman by a negro." 18 Ala. 276.

MULCT. A penalty or punishment imposed on a person guilty of some offense, tort, or misdemeanor, usually a pecuniary fine or condemnation in damages.

Mulcta damnum famæ non irrogat. Cod. 1, 54. A fine does not involve loss of character.

MULIER. Lat. (1) A woman; (2) a virgin; (3) a wife; (4) a legitimate child. 1 Inst. 243.

MULIER PUISNÉ. L. Fr. When a man has a bastard son, and afterwards marries the mother, and by her has also a legitimate son, the elder son is *bastard eigné*, and the younger son is *mulier puisné*.

MULIERATUS. A legitimate son. Glanvil.

MULIERTY. In old English law. The state or condition of a *mulier*, or lawful issue. Co. Litt. 352*b*. The opposite of bastardy. Blount.

Multa conceduntur per obliquum quæ non conceduntur de directo. Many things are allowed indirectly which are not allowed directly. 6 Coke, 47.

MULTA, or MULTURA EPISCOPI. A fine or final satisfaction, anciently given to the king by the bishops, that they might have power to make their wills, and that they might have the probate of other men's wills, and the granting of administration. 2 Inst. 291.

Multa fidem promissa levant. Many promises lessen confidence. 11 Cush. 350.

Multa ignoramus quæ nobis non laterent si veterum lectio nobis fuit familiaris. 10 Coke, 73. We are ignorant of many things which would not be hidden from us if the reading of old authors was familiar to us.

Multa in jure communi contra rationem disputandi, pro communi utilitate introducta sunt. Many things have been introduced into the common law, with a view to the public good, which are inconsistent with sound reason. Co. Litt. 70*b*; Broom, Max. 158.

Multa multo exercitatione facilius quam regulis percipies. 4 Inst. 50. You will perceive many things much more easily by practice than by rules.

Multa non vetat lex, quæ tamen tacite damnavit. The law forbids not many things which yet it has silently condemned.

Multa transeunt cum universitate quæ non per se transeunt. Many things pass with the whole which do not pass separately. Co. Litt. 12*a*.

Multi multa, nemo omnia novit. 4 Inst. 348. Many men have known many things; no one has known everything.

MULTIFARIOUSNESS. In equity pleading. The fault of improperly joining in one bill distinct and independent matters, and thereby confounding them; as, for example, the uniting in one bill of several matters perfectly distinct and unconnected against one defendant, or the demand of several matters of a distinct and independent nature against several defendants, in the same bill. Story, Eq. Pl. § 271.

MULTIPARTITE. Divided into many or several parts.

MULTIPLE POINDING. In Scotch law. Double distress; a name given to an action, corresponding to proceedings by way of interpleader, which may be brought by a person in possession of goods claimed by different persons pretending a right thereto, calling the claimants and all others to settle their claims, so that the party who sues may be liable only "in once and single payment." Bell.

Multiplex et indistinctum parit confusionem; et quæstiones, quo simpliciores, eo lucidiores. Hob. 335. Multiplicity and indistinctness produce confusion; and questions, the more simple they are, the more lucid.

Multiplicata transgressione crescat pœnæ inflictio. As transgression is multiplied, the infliction of punishment should increase. 2 Inst. 479.

MULTIPLICITY. A state of being many. That quality of a pleading which involves a variety of matters or particulars; undue variety. 2 Saund. 410. A multiplying or increasing. Story, Eq. Pl. § 287.

MULTIPLICITY OF ACTIONS. A phrase descriptive of the state of affairs where several different suits or actions are brought upon the same issue. It is obviated in equity by a bill of peace; in courts of law, by a rule of court for the consolidation of different actions.

MULTITUDE. An assemblage of many people. According to Coke it is not a word of very precise meaning; for some authorities hold that there must be at least ten persons to make a multitude, while others maintain that no definite number is fixed by law. Co. Litt. 257.

Multitudinem decem faciunt. Co. Litt. 257. Ten make a multitude.

Multitudo errantium non parit errori patrocinum. The multitude of those who err furnishes no countenance or excuse for error. 11 Coke, 75*a*. It is no excuse for error that it is entertained by numbers.

Multitudo imperitorum perdit curiam. The great number of unskillful practitioners ruins a court. 2 Inst. 219.

MULTO. In old records. A wether sheep.

Multo utilius est pauca idonea effundere quam multis inutilibus homines gravari. 4 Coke, 20. It is more useful to pour forth a few useful things than to oppress men with many useless things.

MULTURE. In Scotch law. The quantity of grain or meal payable to the proprietor of a mill, or to the multurer, his tacksman, for manufacturing the corns. Ersk. Inst. 2, 9, 19.

MUMMIFICATION. In medical jurisprudence. A term applied to the complete drying up of the body. It is the result of burial in a dry, hot soil, or the exposure of the body to a continuously cold and dry atmosphere. 15 Amer. & Eng. Enc. Law, 261.

MUMMING. Antic diversions in the Christmas holidays, suppressed in Queen Anne's time.

MUND. In old English law. Peace; whence *mundbryc*, a breach of the peace.

MUNDBYRD, MUNDEBURDE. A receiving into favor and protection. Cowell.

MUNDIUM. In old French law. A tribute paid by a church or monastery to their seignorial *avoués* and *vidames*, as the price of protecting them. Steph. Lect. 236.

MUNERA. In the early ages of the feudal law, this was the name given to the grants of land made by a king or chieftain to his followers, which were held by no certain tenure, but merely at the will of the lord. Afterwards they became life-estates, and then hereditary, and were called first "benefices," and then "feuds." See Wright, Ten. 19.

MUNICEPS. In Roman law. A provincial person; a countryman. This was the designation of one born in the provinces or in a city politically connected with Rome, and who, having become a Roman citizen, was entitled to hold any offices at Rome except some of the highest. In the provinces the term seems to have been applied to the freemen of any city who were eligible to the municipal offices. Calvin.

MUNICIPAL. "Municipal" signifies that which belongs to a corporation or a city. The term includes the rules or laws by which a particular district, community, or nation is governed. It may also mean local, particular, independent. 43 Ala. 598.

"Municipal," in one of its meanings, is used in opposition to "international," and denotes that which pertains or belongs properly to an individual state or separate community, as distinguished from that which is common to, or observed between, all nations. Thus, piracy is an "international offense," and is denounced by "international law," but smuggling is a "municipal offense," and cognizable by "municipal law."

MUNICIPAL AID. A contribution or assistance granted by a municipal corporation towards the execution or progress of some enterprise, undertaken by private parties, but likely to be of benefit to the municipality; *e. g.*, a railroad.

MUNICIPAL BONDS. Negotiable bonds issued by a municipal corporation, to secure its indebtedness.

MUNICIPAL CLAIMS. In Pennsylvania law. Claims filed by a city against property owners therein, for taxes, rates, levies, or assessments for local improvements, such as the cost of grading, paving, or curbing the streets, or removing nuisances.

MUNICIPAL CORPORATION. A public corporation, created by government for political purposes, and having subordinate and local powers of legislation; *e. g.*, a county, town, city, etc. 2 Kent, Comm. 275.

An incorporation of persons, inhabitants of a particular place, or connected with a particular district, enabling them to conduct its local civil government. Glov. Mun. Corp. 1.

In English law. A body of persons in a town having the powers of acting as one person, of holding and transmitting property, and of regulating the government of the town. Such corporations existed in the chief towns of England (as of other countries) from very early times, deriving their authority from "incorporating" charters granted by the crown. Wharton.

MUNICIPAL CORPORATIONS ACT. In English law. A general statute, (5 & 6 Wm. IV. c. 76,) passed in 1835, prescribing general regulations for the incorporation and government of boroughs.

MUNICIPAL COURTS. In the judicial organization of several states, courts are established under this name, whose territorial authority is confined to the city or community in which they are erected. Such courts usually have a criminal jurisdiction corresponding to that of a police court, and, in some cases, possess civil jurisdiction in small causes.

MUNICIPAL LAW, in contradistinction to international law, is the law of an individual state or nation. It is the rule or law by which a particular district, community, or nation is governed. 1 Bl. Comm. 44.

That which pertains solely to the citizens and inhabitants of a state, and is thus distinguished from political law, commercial law, and the law of nations. Wharton.

MUNICIPAL LIEN. A lien or claim existing in favor of a municipal corporation against a property owner for his proportionate share of a public improvement, made by the municipality, whereby his property is specially and individually benefited.

MUNICIPAL OFFICER. An officer belonging to a municipality; that is, a city, town, or borough.

MUNICIPAL ORDINANCE. A law, rule, or ordinance enacted or adopted by a municipal corporation.

MUNICIPAL SECURITIES. The evidences of indebtedness issued by cities, towns, counties, townships, school-districts, and other such territorial divisions of a state. They are of two general classes: (1) Municipal warrants, orders, or certificates; (2) municipal negotiable bonds. 15 Amer. & Eng. Enc. Law, 1206.

MUNICIPAL WARRANTS. A municipal warrant or order is an instrument, generally in the form of a bill of exchange, drawn by an officer of a municipality upon its treasurer, directing him to pay an amount of money specified therein to the person named or his order, or to bearer. 15 Amer. & Eng. Enc. Law, 1206.

MUNICIPALITY. A municipal corporation; a city, town, borough, or incorporated village. Also the body of officers, taken collectively, belonging to a city.

MUNICIPIUM. In Roman law. A foreign town to which the freedom of the city of Rome was granted, and whose inhabitants had the privilege of enjoying offices and honors there; a free town. Adams, Rom. Ant. 47, 77.

MUNIMENTS. The instruments of writing and written evidences which the owner of lands, possessions, or inheritances has, by which he is enabled to defend the title of his estate. Termes de la Ley; 3 Inst. 170.

MUNIMENT-HOUSE, or MUNIMENT-ROOM. A house or room of strength, in cathedrals, collegiate churches, castles, colleges, public buildings, etc., purposely made for keeping deeds, charters, writings, etc. 3 Inst. 170.

MUNUS. Lat. A gift; an office; a benefice or feud. A gladiatorial show or spectacle. Calvin.; Du Cange.

MURAGE. A toll formerly levied in England for repairing or building public walls.

MURDER. In criminal law. The willful killing of any subject whatever, with malice aforethought, whether the person slain shall be an Englishman or a foreigner. Hawk. P. C. b. 1, c. 13, § 3. The killing of any person under the king's peace, with malice prepense or aforethought, either express, or implied by law. 1 Russ. Crimes, 421; 5 Cush. 304. When a person of sound mind and discretion unlawfully killeth any reasonable creature in being, and under the king's peace, with malice aforethought, either express or implied. 3 Inst. 47.

Murder is the unlawful killing of a human being, with malice aforethought. Pen. Code Cal. § 187.

Whoever kills any human being with malice aforethought, either express or implied, is guilty of murder. Rev. Code Iowa 1880, § 3848.

Murder is the unlawful killing of a human being, in the peace of the state, by a person of sound memory and discretion, with malice aforethought, either express or implied. Code Ga. 1882, § 4320.

The killing of a human being, without the authority of law, by any means, or in any manner, shall be murder in the following cases: When done with deliberate design to effect the death of the person killed, or of any human being; when done in the commission of an act eminently dangerous to others, and evincing a depraved heart, regardless of human life, although without any premeditated design to effect the death of any particular individual; when done without any design to effect death, by any person engaged in the commission of the crime of rape, burglary, arson, or robbery, or in any attempt to commit such felonies. Rev. Code Miss. 1880, § 2875.

Every homicide, perpetrated by poison, lying in wait, or any other kind of willful, deliberate, malicious, and premeditated killing; or committed in the perpetration of, or the attempt to perpetrate, any arson, rape, robbery, or burglary; or perpetrated from a premeditated design unlawfully and maliciously to effect the death of any human being other than him who is killed; or perpetrated by any act greatly dangerous to the lives of others, and evidencing a depraved mind, regardless of human life, although without any preconceived purpose to deprive any particular person of life,—is murder in the first degree; and every other homicide committed under such circumstances as would have constituted murder at common law is murder in the second degree. Code Ala. 1886, § 3725.

MURDRUM. In old English law. The killing of a man in a secret manner.

MURORUM OPERATIO. The service of work and labor done by inhabitants and adjoining tenants in building or repairing the walls of a city or castle; their personal service was commuted into *murage*, (*q. v.*) Cowell.

MURTHRUM. In old Scotch law. Murther or murder. Skene.

MUSEUM. A building or institution for the cultivation of science or the exhibition of curiosities or works of art.

The term "museum" embraces not only collections of curiosities for the entertainment of the sight, but also such as would interest, amuse, and instruct the mind. 5 Stew. & P. 109.

MUSSA. In old English law. A moss or marsh ground, or a place where sedges grow; a place overrun with moss. Cowell.

MUSTER. To assemble together troops and their arms, whether for inspection, drill, or service in the field. To take recruits into the service in the army and inscribe their names on the muster-roll or official record. See 8 Allen, 498.

MUSTER-BOOK. A book in which the forces are registered. Termes de la Ley.

MUSTER-MASTER. One who superintended the muster to prevent frauds. St. 35 Eliz. c. 4.

MUSTER-ROLL. In maritime law. A list or account of a ship's company, required to be kept by the master or other person having care of the ship, containing the name, age, national character, and quality of every person employed in the ship. Abb. Shipp. 191, 192; Jac. Sea Laws, 161.

MUSTIZO. A name given to the issue of an Indian and a negro. Dud. (S. C.) 174.

MUTA-CANUM. A kennel of hounds; one of the mortuaries to which the crown was entitled at a bishop's or abbot's decease. 2 Bl. Comm. 426.

MUTATIO NOMINIS. Lat. In the civil law. Change of name. Cod. 9, 25.

MUTATION. In French law. This term is synonymous with "change," and is especially applied to designate the change which takes place in the property of a thing in its transmission from one person to another. Mutation, therefore, happens when the owner of the thing sells, exchanges, or gives it. Merl. Répert.

MUTATION OF LIBEL. In practice. An amendment allowed to a libel, by which there is an alteration of the substance of the libel, as by propounding a new cause of action, or asking one thing instead of another. Dunl. Adm. Pr. 213.

MUTATIS MUTANDIS. Lat. With the necessary changes in points of detail.

MUTE. Speechless; dumb; that cannot or will not speak. In English criminal law, a prisoner is said to *stand mute* when, being arraigned for treason or felony, he either makes no answer at all, or answers foreign to the purpose or with such matter as is not allowable, and will not answer otherwise, or, upon having pleaded not guilty, refuses to put himself upon the country. 4 Bl. Comm. 324.

MUTILATION. In criminal law. The depriving a man of the use of any of those limbs which may be useful to him in fight, the loss of which amounts to *mayhem.* 1 Bl. Comm. 130.

MUTINOUS. Insubordinate; disposed to mutiny; tending to incite or encourage mutiny.

MUTINY. In criminal law. An insurrection of soldiers or seamen against the authority of their commanders; a sedition or revolt in the army or navy.

MUTINY ACT. In English law. An act of parliament annually passed to punish mutiny and desertion. 1 Bl. Comm. 415.

MUTUAL. Interchangeable; reciprocal; each acting in return or correspondence to the other; given and received; spoken of an engagement or relation in which like duties and obligations are exchanged.

"Mutual" is not synonymous with "common." The latter word, in one of its meanings, denotes that which is shared, in the same or different degrees, by two or more persons; but the former implies reciprocal action or interdependent connection.

MUTUAL ACCOUNTS. Accounts comprising mutual credits between the parties; or an existing credit on one side which constitutes a ground for credit on the other, or where there is an understanding that mutual debts shall be a satisfaction or set-off *pro tanto* between the parties. 27 Ark. 343.

MUTUAL CREDITS. In bankrupt law. Credits which must, from their nature, terminate in debts; as where a debt is due from one party, and credit given by him to the other for a sum of money payable at a future day, and which will then become a debt; or where there is a debt on one side, and a delivery of property with directions to turn it into money on the other. 8 Taunt. 499; 2 Smith, Lead. Cas. 179.

By this phrase, in the rule under which courts of equity allow set-off in cases of mutual credit, we are to understand a knowledge on both sides of an existing debt due to one party, and a credit by the other party, founded on and trusting to such debt, as a means of discharging it. 9 N. J. Eq. 44.

Credits given by two persons mutually; *i. e.*, each giving credit to the other. It is a more extensive phrase than "mutual debts." Thus, the sum credited by one may be due at once, that by the other payable *in futuro;* yet the credits are mutual, though the transaction would not come within the meaning of "mutual debts." 1 Atk. 230; 7 Term R. 378.

MUTUAL DEBTS. Money due on both sides between two persons.

MUTUAL INSURANCE. That form of insurance in which each person insured becomes a member of the company, and the members reciprocally engage to indemnify each other against losses, any loss being met by an assessment laid upon all the members.

MUTUAL MISTAKE. See MISTAKE.

MUTUAL PROMISES. Promises simultaneously made by and between two parties; each being the consideration for the other.

MUTUAL TESTAMENTS. Wills made by two persons who leave their effects reciprocally to the survivor.

MUTUALITY. Reciprocation; interchange. An acting by each of two parties; an acting in return.

In every agreement the parties must, as regards the principal or essential part of the transaction, intend the same thing; *i. e.*, each must know what the other is to do. This is called "mutuality of assent." Chit. Cont. 13.

In a simple contract arising from agreement, it is sometimes the essence of the transaction that each party should be bound to do something under it. This requirement is called "mutuality." Sweet.

Mutuality of a contract means an obligation on each to do, or permit to be done, something in consideration of the act or promise of the other. 26 Md. 37.

MUTUANT. The person who lends chattels in the contract of *mutuum,* (*q. v.*)

MUTUARI. To borrow; *mutuatus,* a borrowing. 2 Arch. Pr. 25.

MUTUARY. A person who borrows personal chattels to be consumed by him and returned to the lender in kind and quantity; the borrower in a contract of *mutuum*.

MUTUS ET SURDUS. Lat. In civil and old English law. Dumb and deaf.

MUTUUM. Lat. In the law of bailments. A loan for consumption; a loan of chattels, upon an agreement that the borrower may consume them, returning to the lender an equivalent in kind and quantity. Story, Bailm. § 228.

MYNSTER-HAM. Monastic habitation; perhaps the part of a monastery set apart for purposes of hospitality, or as a sanctuary for criminals. Anc. Inst. Eng.

MYSTERY. A trade, art, or occupation. 2 Inst. 668. Masters frequently bind themselves in the indentures with their apprentices to teach them their art, trade, and *mystery*.

MYSTIC TESTAMENT. In the law of Louisiana. A sealed testament.

The mystic or secret testament, otherwise called the "closed testament," is made in the following manner: The testator must sign his dispositions, whether he has written them himself or has caused them to be written by another person. The paper containing those dispositions, or the paper serving as their envelope, must be closed and sealed. The testator shall present it thus closed and sealed to the notary and to seven witnesses, or he shall cause it to be closed and sealed in their presence. Then he shall declare to the notary, in presence of the witnesses, that that paper contains his testament written by himself, or by another by his direction, and signed by him, the testator. The notary shall then draw up the act of superscription, which shall be written on that paper, or on the sheet that serves as its envelope, and that act shall be signed by the testator, and by the notary and the witnesses. Civil Code La. art. 1584.

N.

N. An abbreviation of "*Novellæ*," the Novels of Justinian, used in citing them. Tayl. Civil Law, 24.

N. A. An abbreviation for "*non allocatur*," it is not allowed.

N. B. An abbreviation for "*nota bene*," mark well, observe; also "*nulla bona*," no goods.

N. D. An abbreviation for "Northern District."

N. E. I. An abbreviation for "*non est inventus*," he is not found.

N. L. An abbreviation of "*non liquet*," (which see.)

N. P. An abbreviation for "notary public;" also for "*nisi prius*," (*q. v.*)

N. R. An abbreviation for "New Reports;" also for "not reported," and for "nonresident."

N. S. An abbreviation for "New Series;" also for "New Style."

NAAM. The attaching or taking of movable goods and chattels, called "*vif*" or "*mort*" according as the chattels were living or dead. Termes de la Ley.

NABOB. Originally the governor of a province under the Mogul government of Hindostan, whence it became a mere title of any man of high rank, upon whom it was conferred without any office being attached to it. Wils. Indian Gloss.

NAIF. L. Fr. A villein; a born slave; a bondwoman.

NAIL. A lineal measure of two inches and a quarter.

NAKED. As a term of jurisprudence, this word is equivalent to bare, wanting in necessary conditions, incomplete, as a naked contract, (*nudum pactum*,) *i. e.*, a contract devoid of consideration, and therefore invalid; or simple, unilateral, comprising but a single element, as a naked authority, *i. e.* one which is not coupled with any interest in the agent, but subsists for the benefit of the principal alone.

NAKED CONFESSION. A confession of crime which is unsupported by any evidence of the commission of the offense.

NAKED DEPOSIT. A bailment of goods to be kept for the depositor, without hire or reward on either side.

NAKED POWER. One which is simply collateral and without interest in the donee, which arises when, to a mere stranger, authority is given of disposing of an interest, in which he had not before, nor has by the instrument creating the power, any estate whatsoever. Caines, Cas. 15.

NAKED TRUST. A dry or passive trust; one which requires no action on the part of the trustee, beyond turning over money or property to the *cestui que trust*.

NAM. In old English law. A distress or seizure of chattels.

As a Latin conjunction, for; because. Often used by the old writers in introducing the quotation of a Latin maxim.

NAMARE. L. Lat. In old records. To take, seize, or distrain.

NAMATIO. L. Lat. In old English and Scotch law. A distraining or taking of a distress; an impounding. Spelman.

NAME. The designation of an individual person, or of a firm or corporation. In law a man cannot have more than one Christian name. 1 Ld. Raym. 562.

NAME AND ARMS CLAUSE. The popular name in English law for the clause, sometimes inserted in a will or settlement by which property is given to a person, for the purpose of imposing on him the condition that he shall assume the surname and arms of the testator or settlor, with a direction that, if he neglects to assume or discontinues the use of them, the estate shall devolve on the next person in remainder, and a provision for preserving contingent remainders. 3 Dav. Prec. Conv. 277; Sweet.

NAMIUM. L. Lat. In old English law. A taking; a distress. Spelman. Things, goods, or animals taken by way of distress. *Simplex namium*, a simple taking or pledge. Bract. fol. 205*b*.

NAMIUM VETITUM. An unjust taking of the cattle of another and driving them to an unlawful place, pretending damage done by them. 3 Bl. Comm. 149.

NANTES, EDICT OF. A celebrated law for the security of Protestants, made by Henry IV. of France, and revoked by Louis XIV., October 2, 1685.

NANTISSEMENT, in French law, is the contract of pledge; if of a movable, it is called "*gage;*" and if of an immovable, it is called "*antichrèse.*" Brown.

NARR. A common abbrevation of "*narratio,*" (*q. v.*) A declaration in an action. Jacob.

NARRATIO. One of the common law names for a plaintiff's count or declaration, as being a narrative of the facts on which he relies.

NARRATIVE. In Scotch conveyancing. That part of a deed which describes the grantor, and person in whose favor the deed is granted, and states the cause (consideration) of granting. Bell.

NARRATOR. A countor; a pleader who draws *narrs. Serviens narrator,* a serjeant at law. Fleta, l. 2, c. 37.

NARROW SEAS. Those seas which run between two coasts not far apart. The term is sometimes applied to the English channel. Wharton.

NASCITURUS. Lat. That shall hereafter be born. A term used in marriage settlements to designate the future issue of the marriage, as distinguished from "*natus,*" a child already born.

NATALE. The state and condition of a man acquired by birth.

NATI ET NASCITURI. Born and to be born. All heirs, near and remote.

NATIO. In old records. A native place. Cowell.

NATION. A people, or aggregation of men, existing in the form of an organized jural society, inhabiting a distinct portion of the earth, speaking the same language, using the same customs, possessing historic continuity, and distinguished from other like groups by their racial origin and characteristics, and generally, but not necessarily, living under the same government and sovereignty.

Besides the element of autonomy or self-government, that is, the independence of the community as a whole from the interference of any foreign power in its affairs or any subjection to such power, it is further necessary to the constitution of a nation that it should be an organized jural society, that is, both governing its own members by regular laws, and defining and protecting their rights, and respecting the rights and duties which attach to it as a constituent member of the family of nations. Such a society, says Vattel, has her affairs and her interests; she deliberates and takes resolutions in common; thus becoming a moral person, who possesses an understanding and will peculiar to herself, and is susceptible of obligations and rights. Vattel, §§ 1, 2.

The words "nation" and "people" are frequently used as synonyms, but there is a great difference between them. A nation is an aggregation of men speaking the same language, having the same customs, and endowed with certain moral qualities which distinguish them from other groups of a like nature. It would follow from this definition that a nation is destined to form only one *state*, and that it constitutes one indivisible whole. Nevertheless, the history of every age presents us with nations divided into several states. Thus, Italy was for centuries divided among several different governments. The *people* is the collection of all citizens without distinction of rank or order. All men living under the same *government* compose the *people* of the *state*. In relation to the state, the citizens constitute the people; in relation to the human race, they constitute the nation. A free nation is one not subject to a foreign government, whatever be the constitution of the state; a *people* is free when all the citizens can participate in a certain measure in the direction and in the examination of public affairs. The people is the political body brought into existence by community of laws, and the people may perish with these laws. The nation is the moral body, independent of political revolutions, because it is constituted by inborn qualities which render it indissoluble. The *state* is the people organized into a political body. Lalor, Pol. Enc. *s. v.*

In American constitutional law the word "state" is applied to the several members of the American Union, while the word "nation" is applied to the whole body of the people embraced within the jurisdiction of the federal government. Cooley, Const. Lim. 1. See 7 Wall. 720.

NATIONAL BANK. A bank incorporated and doing business under the laws of the United States, as distinguished from a *state* bank, which derives its powers from the authority of a particular state.

NATIONAL CURRENCY. Notes issued by national banks, and by the United States government.

NATIONAL DEBT. The money owing by government to some of the public, the interest of which is paid out of the taxes raised by the whole of the public.

NATIONAL DOMAIN. A term sometimes applied to the aggregate of the property owned directly by a nation.

NATIONAL DOMICILE. The domicile of a person, considered as being within the territory of a particular nation, and not with reference to a particular locality or subdivision of a nation.

NATIONAL GOVERNMENT. The government of a whole nation, as distinguished from that of a local or territorial division of the nation, and also as distinguished from that of a league or confederation.

"A *national* government is a government of the people of a single state or nation, united as a community by what is termed the 'social compact,' and possessing complete and perfect supremacy over persons and things, so far as they can be made the lawful objects of civil government. A *federal* government is distinguished from a national government, by its being the government of a community of independent and sovereign states, united by compact." 6 Ohio St. 393.

NATIONALITY. That quality or character which arises from the fact of a person's belonging to a nation or state. Nationality determines the political *status* of the individual, especially with reference to allegiance; while domicile determines his civil *status*. Nationality arises either by birth or by naturalization. According to Savigny, "nationality" is also used as opposed to "territoriality," for the purpose of distinguishing the case of a nation having no national territory; *e. g.*, the Jews. 8 Sav. Syst. § 346; Westl. Priv. Int. Law, 5.

NATIONALIZACION. In Spanish and Mexican law. Nationalization. "The nationalization of property is an act which denotes that it has become that of the nation by some process of law, whereby private individuals or corporations have been for specified reasons deprived thereof." Hall, Mex. Law, § 749.

NATIONS, LAW OF. See INTERNATIONAL LAW.

NATIVA. In old English law. A niefe or female villein. So called because for the most part bond by nativity. Co. Litt. 122*b*.

NATIVE. A natural-born subject or citizen; a denizen by birth; one who owes his domicile or citizenship to the fact of his birth within the country referred to. The term may also include one born abroad, if his parents were then citizens of the country, and not permanently residing in foreign parts.

NATIVI CONVENTIONARII. Villeins or bondmen by contract or agreement.

NATIVI DE STIPITE. Villeins or bondmen by birth or stock. Cowell.

NATIVITAS. In old English law. Villenage; that state in which men were born slaves. 2 Mon. Angl. 643.

NATIVO HABENDO. In old English law. A writ which lay for a lord when his villein had run away from him. It was directed to the sheriff, and commanded him to apprehend the villein, and to restore him together with his goods to the lord. Brown.

NATIVUS. A servant born. Spelman.

Natura appetit perfectum; ita et lex. Nature covets perfection; so does law also. Hob. 144.

NATURA BREVIUM. The name of an ancient collection of original writs, accompanied with brief comments and explanations, compiled in the time of Edward III. This is commonly called "*Old* Natura Brevium," (or "O. N. B.,") to distinguish it from Fitzherbert's Natura Brevium, a later work, cited as "F. N. B," or "Fitzh. Nat. Brev."

Natura fide jussionis sit strictissimi juris et non durat vel extendatur de re ad rem, de persona ad personam, de tempore ad tempus. The nature of the contract of suretyship is *strictissimi juris*, and cannot endure nor be extended from thing to thing, from person to person, or from time to time. Burge, Sur. 40.

Natura non facit saltum; ita nec lex. Nature makes no leap, [no sudden or irregular movement;] so neither does law. Co. Litt. 238. Applied in old practice to the regular observance of the degrees in writs of entry, which could not be passed over *per saltum*.

Natura non facit vacuum, nec lex supervacuum. Nature makes no vacuum, the law nothing purposeless. Co. Litt. 79.

Naturæ vis maxima; natura bis maxima. The force of nature is greatest; nature is doubly great. 2 Inst. 564.

NATURAL AFFECTION. Such as naturally subsists between near relatives, as a father and child, brother and sister, husband and wife. This is regarded in law as a good consideration.

NATURAL ALLEGIANCE. In English law. That kind of allegiance which is due from all men born within the king's dominions, immediately upon their birth, which is intrinsic and perpetual, and cannot be divested by any act of their own. 1 Bl. Comm. 369; 2 Kent, Comm. 42.

In American law. The allegiance due from citizens of the United States to their native country, and also from naturalized citizens, and which cannot be renounced without the permission of government, to be declared by law. 2 Kent, Comm. 43-49.

It differs from *local* allegiance, which is temporary only, being due from an alien or stranger born for so long a time as he continues within the sovereign's dominions and protection. Fost. Cr. Law, 184.

NATURAL-BORN SUBJECT. In English law. One born within the dominions, or rather within the allegiance, of the king of England.

NATURAL CHILD. A bastard; a child born out of lawful wedlock. But in a statute declaring that adopted shall have all the rights of "natural" children, the word "natural" was used in the sense of "legitimate." 9 Amer. Law Reg. (O. S.) 747.

In Louisiana. Illegitimate children who have been adopted by the father. Civil Code La. art. 220.

In the civil law. A child by natural relation or procreation; a child by birth, as distinguished from a child by adoption. Inst. 1, 11, pr.; Id. 3, 1, 2; Id. 3, 8, pr.

A child by concubinage, in contradistinction to a child by marriage. Cod. 5, 27.

NATURAL DAY. That space of time included between the rising and the setting of the sun. See DAY.

NATURAL DEATH. 1. Death resulting from disease, or from natural forces without the concurrence of man's agency; as distinguished from "violent" death

2. Physical death; the separation of soul and body; as distinguished from "civil" death, which is the loss of rights and juristic personality as a legal consequence of certain acts.

NATURAL EQUITY. A term sometimes employed in works on jurisprudence, possessing no very precise meaning, but used as equivalent to justice, honesty, or morality in business relations, or man's innate sense of right dealing and fair play.

Inasmuch as equity, as now administered, is a complex system of rules, doctrines, and precedents, and possesses, within the range of its own fixed principles, but little more elasticity than the law, the term "natural equity" may be understood to denote, in a general way, that which strikes the ordinary conscience and sense of justice as being fair, right, and equitable, in advance of the question whether the technical jurisprudence of the chancery courts would so regard it.

NATURAL FOOL. A person born without understanding; a born fool or idiot. Sometimes called, in the old books, a "natural."

NATURAL FRUITS. The produce of the soil, or of fruit-trees, bushes, vines, etc., which are edible or otherwise useful or serve for the reproduction of their species. The term is used in contradistinction to "artificial fruits," *i. e.*, such as by metaphor or analogy are likened to the fruits of the earth. Of the latter, interest on money is an example.

NATURAL HEIRS. In a statute of distributions, this term may be understood and interpreted as meaning "legitimate heirs," and hence may include an adopted child. 9 Amer. Law Reg. (O. S.) 747.

NATURAL INFANCY. A period of non-responsible life, which ends with the seventh year. Wharton.

NATURAL LAW. The rule and dictate of right reason, showing the moral deformity or moral necessity there is in any act, according to its suitableness or unsuitableness to a reasonable nature. Tayl. Civil Law, 99.

This expression, "natural law," or *jus naturale,* was largely used in the philosophical speculations of the Roman jurists of the Antonine age, and was intended to denote a system of rules and principles for the guidance of human conduct which, independently of enacted law or of the systems peculiar to any one people, might be discovered by the rational intelligence of man, and would be found to grow out of and conform to his *nature,* meaning by that word his whole mental, moral, and physical constitution. The point of departure for this conception was the Stoic doctrine of a life ordered "according to nature," which in its turn rested upon the purely supposititious existence, in primitive times, of a "state of nature;" that is, a condition of society in which men universally were governed solely by a rational and consistent obedience to the needs, impulses, and promptings of their true nature, such nature being as yet undefaced by dishonesty, falsehood, or indulgence of the baser passions. See Maine, Anc. Law, 50, et seq.

NATURAL LIBERTY. The power of acting as one thinks fit, without any restraint or control, unless by the law of nature. 1 Bl. Comm. 125.

NATURAL LIFE. The period between birth and natural death, as distinguished from civil death, (*q. v.*)

NATURAL OBLIGATION. One which lacks legal sanction, and therefore cannot be enforced in a court of justice, but which imposes a moral duty upon the person bound.

NATURAL PERSONS. Such as are formed by nature, as distinguished from *artificial* persons, or corporations, formed by human laws for purposes of society and government. Wharton.

NATURAL PRESUMPTION. In the law of evidence. That species of presumption, or process of probable reasoning, which is exercised by persons of ordinary intelligence, in inferring one fact from another, without reference to any technical rules. Otherwise called "*præsumptio hominis.*" Burrill, Circ. Ev. 11, 12, 22, 24.

NATURAL RIGHTS. Those rights which are plainly assured by natural law; such as the right to life, to personal liberty, etc.

NATURAL YEAR. In old English law. That period of time in which the sun was supposed to revolve in its orbit, consisting of 365 days and one-fourth of a day, or six hours. Bract. fol. 359*b*.

Naturale est quidlibet dissolvi eo modo quo ligatur. It is natural for a thing to be unbound in the same way in which it was bound. Jenk. Cent. 66; Broom, Max. 877.

NATURALEZA. In Spanish law. The state of a natural-born subject. White, New Recop. b. 1, tit. 5, c. 2.

NATURALIZATION. The act of adopting an alien into a nation, and clothing him with all the rights possessed by a natural-born citizen.

NATURALIZE. To confer citizenship upon an alien; to make a foreigner the same, in respect to rights and privileges, as if he were a native citizen or subject.

NATURALIZED CITIZEN. One who, being an alien by birth, has received citizenship under the laws of the state or nation.

NATURALLY. Damages which "naturally" arise from a breach of contract are such as arise in the usual course of things, from the breach itself, or such as may reasonably be supposed to have been contemplated by the parties when making the contract as the probable result of the breach. 71 Cal. 164, 11 Pac. Rep. 882.

NATUS. Lat. Born, as distinguished from *nasciturus*, about to be born.

NAUCLERUS. Lat. In the civil law. The master or owner of a merchant vessel. Calvin.

NAUFRAGE. In French maritime law. Shipwreck. "The violent agitation of the waves, the impetuous force of the winds, storm, or lightning, may swallow up the vessel, or shatter it, in such a manner that nothing remains of it but the wreck; this is called 'making shipwreck,' (*faire naufrage.*) The vessel may also strike or run aground upon a bank, where it remains grounded, which is called '*échouement;*' it may be dashed against the coast or a rock, which is called '*bris;*' an accident of any kind may sink it in the sea, where it is swallowed up, which is called '*sombrer.*'" 3 Pard. Droit Commer. § 643.

NAUFRAGIUM. Lat. Shipwreck.

NAUGHT. In old practice. Bad; defective. "The bar is *naught.*" 1 Leon. 77. "The avowry is *naught.*" 5 Mod. 73. "The plea is undoubtedly *naught.*" 10 Mod. 329. See 11 Mod. 179.

NAULAGE. The freight of passengers in a ship. Johnson; Webster.

NAULUM. In the civil law. The freight or fare paid for the transportation of cargo or passengers over the sea in a vessel. This is a Latinized form of a Greek word.

NAUTA. Lat. In the civil and maritime law. A sailor; one who works a ship. Calvin.

Any one who is on board a ship for the purpose of navigating her.

The employer of a ship. Dig. 4, 9, 1, 2.

NAUTICAL ASSESSORS. Experienced shipmasters, or other persons having special knowledge of navigation and nautical affairs, who are called to the assistance of a court of admiralty, in difficult cases involving questions of negligence, and who sit with the judge during the argument, and give their advice upon questions of seamanship or the weight of testimony. 19 Fed. Rep. 559; 2 Curt. 369.

NAVAGIUM. In old English law. A duty on certain tenants to carry their lord's goods in a ship.

NAVAL. Appertaining to the navy, (*q. v.*)

NAVAL COURTS. Courts held abroad in certain cases to inquire into complaints by the master or seamen of a British ship, or as to the wreck or abandonment of a British ship. A naval court consists of three, four, or five members, being officers in her majesty's navy, consular officers, masters of British merchant ships, or British merchants. It has power to supersede the master of the ship with reference to which the inquiry is held, to discharge any of the seamen, to decide questions as to wages, send home offenders for trial, or try certain offenses in a summary manner. Sweet.

NAVAL COURTS-MARTIAL. Tribunals for the trial of offenses arising in the management of public war vessels.

NAVAL LAW. The system of regulations and principles for the government of the navy.

NAVAL OFFICER. An officer in the navy. Also an important functionary in the United States custom-houses, who estimates duties, signs permits and clearances, certifies the collectors' returns, etc.

NAVARCHUS. In the civil law. The master or commander of a ship; the captain of a man-of-war.

NAVICULARIUS. In the civil law. The master or captain of a ship. Calvin.

NAVIGABLE. Capable of being navigated; that may be navigated or passed over in ships or vessels. But the term is generally understood in a more restricted sense, viz., subject to the ebb and flow of the tide.

"The doctrine of the common law as to the navigability of waters has no application in this country. Here the ebb and flow of the tide do not constitute the usual test, as in England, or any test at all, of the navigability of waters. There no waters are navigable in fact, or at least to any considerable extent, which are not subject to the tide, and from this circumstance tide-water and navigable water there signify substantially the same thing. But in this country the case is widely different. Some of our rivers are as navigable for many hundreds of miles above as they are below the limits of tide-water, and some of them are navigable for great distances by large vessels, which are not even affected by the tide at any point during their entire length. A different test must therefore be applied to determine the navigability of our rivers, and that is found in their navigable capacity. Those rivers must be regarded as public navigable rivers, in law, which are navigable in fact. And they are navigable in fact when they are used, or are susceptible of being used, in their ordinary condition, as highways for commerce, over which trade and travel are or may be conducted in the customary modes of trade and travel on water. And they constitute navigable waters of the United States, within the meaning of the acts of congress, in contradistinction from the navigable waters of the states, when they form, in their ordinary condition, by themselves, or by uniting with other waters, a continued highway over which commerce is or may be carried on with other states or foreign countries in the customary modes in which such commerce is conducted by water." Field, J., 10 Wall. 563.

It is true that the flow and ebb of the tide is not regarded, in this country, as the usual, or any real, test of navigability; and it only operates to impress, *prima facie*, the character of being public and navigable, and to place the *onus* of proof on the party affirming the contrary. But the navigability of tide-waters does not materially depend upon past or present actual public use. Such use may establish navigability, but it is not essential to give the character. Otherwise, streams in new and unsettled sections of the country, or where the increase, growth, and development have not been sufficient to call them into public use, would be excluded, though navigable in fact, thus making the character of being a navigable stream dependent on the occurrence of the necessity of public use. Capability of being used for useful purposes of navigation, of trade and travel, in the usual and ordinary modes, and not the extent and manner of the use, is the test of navigability. 82 Ala. 166, 2 South. Rep. 716.

NAVIGABLE RIVER or STREAM. A river or stream in which the tide ebbs and flows, or as far as the tide ebbs and flows. 3 Kent, Comm. 412, 414, 417, 418; 2 Hil. Real Prop. 90, 91.

NAVIGABLE WATERS. Those waters which afford a channel for useful commerce. 20 Wall. 430.

NAVIGATE. To conduct vessels through navigable waters; to use the waters as a means of communication.

NAVIGATION. The act or the science or the business of traversing the sea or other waters in ships or vessels.

NAVIGATION ACTS, in English law, were various enactments passed for the protection of British shipping and commerce as against foreign countries. For a sketch of their history and operation, see 3 Steph. Comm. They are now repealed. See 16 & 17 Vict. c. 107, and 17 & 18 Vict. cc. 5, 120. Wharton.

NAVIGATION, RULES OF. Rules and regulations adopted by commercial nations to govern the steering and management of vessels approaching each other at sea so as to avoid the danger of collision or fouling.

NAVIRE. Fr. In French law. A ship. Emerig. Traité des Assur. c. 6, § 1.

NAVIS. Lat. A ship; a vessel.

NAVIS BONA. Lat. A good ship; one that was staunch and strong, well caulked, and stiffened to bear the sea, obedient to her helm, swift, and not unduly affected by the wind. Calvin.

NAVY. A fleet of ships; the aggregate of vessels of war belonging to an independent nation.

NAVY BILLS. Bills drawn by officers of the English navy for their pay, etc.

NAVY DEPARTMENT. One of the executive departments of the United States, presided over by the secretary of the navy, and having in charge the defense of the country by sea, by means of ships of war and other naval appliances.

NAVY PENSION. A pecuniary allowance made in consideration of past services of some one in the navy.

NAZERANNA. A sum paid to government as an acknowledgment for a grant of lands, or any public office. Enc. Lond.

NAZIM. In Hindu law. Composer, arranger, adjuster. The first officer of a province, and minister of the department of criminal justice.

NE ADMITTAS. Lat. In ecclesiastical law. The name of a prohibitory writ, directed to the bishop, at the request of the plaintiff or defendant, where a *quare impedit* is pending, when either party fears that the bishop will admit the other's clerk pending the suit between them. Fitzh. Nat. Brev. 37.

NE BAILA PAS. L. Fr. He did not deliver. A plea in detinue, denying the delivery to the defendant of the thing sued for.

NE DISTURBA PAS. L. Fr. (Does or did not disturb.) In English practice. The general issue or general plea in *quare impedit*. 3 Steph. Comm. 663.

NE DONA PAS, or NON DEDIT. The general issue in a formedon, now abolished. It denied the gift in tail to have been made in manner and form as alleged; and was therefore the proper plea, if the tenant meant to dispute the fact of the gift, but did not apply to any other case. 5 East, 289.

NE EXEAT REGNO. Lat. In English practice. A writ which issues to restrain a person from leaving the kingdom. It was formerly used for political purposes, but is now only resorted to in equity when the defendant is about to leave the kingdom; it is only in cases where the intention of the party to leave can be shown that the writ is granted.

NE EXEAT REPUBLICA. Lat. In American practice. A writ similar to that of *ne exeat regno*, (*q. v.*,) available to the plaintiff in a civil suit, under some circumstances, when the defendant is about to leave the state.

NE GIST PAS EN BOUCHE. L. Fr. It does not lie in the mouth. A common phrase in the old books. Yearb. M. 3 Edw. II. 50.

NE INJUSTE VEXES. Lat. In old English practice. A prohibitory writ, commanding a lord not to demand from the tenant more services than were justly due by the tenure under which his ancestors held.

NE LUMINIBUS OFFICIATUR. Lat. In the civil law. The name of a servitude which restrains the owner of a house from making such erections as obstruct the light of the adjoining house. Dig. 8, 4, 15, 17.

NE QUID IN LOCO PUBLICO VEL ITINERE FIAT. Lat. That nothing shall be done (put or erected) in a public place or way. The title of an interdict in the Roman law. Dig. 43, 8.

NE RECIPIATUR. Lat. That it be not received. A *caveat* or warning given to a law officer, by a party in a cause, not to receive the next proceedings of his opponent. 1 Sell. Pr. 8.

NE RECTOR PROSTERNET ARBORES. L. Lat. The statute 35 Edw. I. § 2, prohibiting rectors, *i. e.*, parsons, from cutting down the trees in church-yards. In Rutland v. Green, 1 Keb. 557, it was extended to prohibit them from opening new mines and working the minerals therein. Brown.

NE RELESSA PAS. L. Fr. Did not release. Where the defendant had pleaded a release, this was the proper replication by way of traverse.

NE UNQUES ACCOUPLE. L. Fr. Never married. More fully, *ne unques accouple en loiall matrimonie*, never joined in lawful marriage. The name of a plea in the action of dower *unde nihil habet*, by which the tenant denied that the dowress was ever lawfully married to the decedent.

NE UNQUES EXECUTOR. L. Fr. Never executor. The name of a plea by which the defendant denies that he is an executor, as he is alleged to be; or that the plaintiff is an executor, as he claims to be.

NE UNQUES SEISE QUE DOWER. L. Fr. (Never seised of a dowable estate.) In pleading. The general issue in the action of dower *unde nil habet*, by which the tenant denies that the demandant's husband was *ever seised* of an estate of which dower might be had. Rosc. Real Act. 219, 220.

NE UNQUES SON RECEIVER. L. Fr. In pleading. The name of a plea in an action of account-render, by which the defendant denies that he ever was receiver of the plaintiff. 12 Vin. Abr. 183.

NE VARIETUR. Lat. It must not be altered. A phrase sometimes written by a notary upon a bill or note, for the purpose of establishing its identity, which, however, does not affect its negotiability. 8 Wheat. 338.

NEAP TIDES. Those tides which happen between the full and change of the moon, twice in every twenty-four hours. 18 Cal. 21.

NEAR. This word, as applied to space, can have no positive or precise meaning. It is a relative term, depending for its signification on the subject-matter in relation to which it is used and the circumstances under which it becomes necessary to apply it to surrounding objects. 5 Allen, 227. See, also, 44 Mo. 202; 31 Fed. Rep. 872.

NEAT, NET. The clear weight or quantity of an article, without the bag, box, keg, or other thing in which it may be enveloped.

NEAT CATTLE. Oxen or heifers. "Beeves" may include neat stock, but all neat stock are not beeves. 36 Tex. 324; 32 Tex. 479.

NEAT-LAND. Land let out to the yeomanry. Cowell.

NEATNESS. In pleading. The statement in apt and appropriate words of all the necessary facts, and no more. Lawes, Pl. 62.

Nec curia deficeret in justitia exhibenda. Nor should the court be deficient in showing justice. 4 Inst. 63.

Nec tempus nec locus occurrit regi. Jenk. Cent. 190. Neither time nor place affects the king.

Nec veniam effuso sanguine casus habet. Where blood is spilled, the case is unpardonable. 3 Inst. 57.

Nec veniam, læso numine, casus habet. Where the Divinity is insulted, the case is unpardonable. Jenk. Cent. 167.

NECATION. The act of killing.

NECESSARIES. Things indispensable, or things proper and useful, for the sustenance of human life. This is a relative term, and its meaning will contract or expand according to the situation and social condition of the person referred to.

In reference to the contracts of infants, this term is not used in its strictest sense, nor limited to that which is required to sustain life. Those things which are proper and suitable to each individual, according to his circumstances and condition in life, are necessaries, if not supplied from some other source. 12 Cush. 513. See, also, 133 Mass. 504; 114 Mass. 424; 3 C. P. Div. 401; 31 Conn. 306.

In the case of ships the term "necessaries" means such things as are fit and proper for the service in which the ship is engaged, and such as the owner, being a prudent man, would have ordered if present; *e. g.*, anchors, rigging, repairs, victuals. Maude & P. Shipp. 71, 113. The master may hypothecate the ship for necessaries supplied abroad so as to bind the owner. Sweet.

Necessarium est quod non potest aliter se habere. That is necessary which cannot be otherwise.

NECESSARIUS. Lat. Necessary; unavoidable; indispensable; not admitting of choice or the action of the will; needful.

NECESSARY. As used in jurisprudence, the word "necessary" does not always import an absolute physical necessity, so strong that one thing, to which another may be termed "necessary," cannot exist without that other. It frequently imports no more than that one thing is convenient or useful or essential to another. To employ the means *necessary* to an end is generally understood as employing any means calculated to produce the end, and not as being confined to those single means without which the end would be entirely unattainable. 4 Wheat. 316, 413.

NECESSARY DEPOSIT. The *necessary* deposit is that which has been compelled by some accident; such as fire, falling down of a house, pillage, shipwreck, or other casualty. Civil Code La. art. 2964.

NECESSARY DOMICILE. That kind of domicile which exists by operation of law, as distinguished from voluntary domicile or domicile of choice. Phillim. Dom. 27-97.

NECESSARY IMPLICATION. In construing a will, necessary implication means not natural necessity, but so strong a probability of intention that an intention contrary to that which is imputed to the testator cannot be supposed. 1 Ves. & B. 466.

NECESSARY INTROMISSION. In Scotch law. That kind of intromission or interference where a husband or wife continues in possession of the other's goods after their decease, for preservation. Wharton.

NECESSARY REPAIRS. Necessary repairs (for which the master of a ship may lawfully bind the owner) are such as are reasonably fit and proper for the ship under the circumstances, and not merely such as are absolutely indispensable for the safety of the ship or the accomplishment of the voyage. 3 Sum. 237.

NECESSITAS. Lat. Necessity; a force, power, or influence which compels one to act against his will. Calvin.

NECESSITAS CULPABILIS. Culpable necessity; unfortunate necessity; necessity which, while it excuses the act done under its compulsion, does not leave the doer entirely free from blame. The necessity which compels a man to kill another in self-defense is thus distinguished from that which requires the killing of a felon. See 4 Bl. Comm. 187.

Necessitas est lex temporis et loci. Necessity is the law of time and of place. 1 Hale, P. C. 54.

Necessitas excusat aut extenuat delictum in capitalibus, quod non operatur idem in civilibus. Necessity excuses or extenuates a delinquency in capital cases, which has not the same operation in civil cases. Bac. Max.

Necessitas facit licitum quod alias non est licitum. 10 Coke, 61. Necessity makes that lawful which otherwise is not lawful.

Necessitas inducit privilegium quoad jura privata. Bac. Max. 25. Necessity gives a privilege with reference to private rights. The necessity involved in this maxim is of three kinds, viz.: (1) Necessity of self-preservation; (2) of obedience; and (3) necessity resulting from the act of God, or of a stranger. Noy, Max. 32.

Necessitas non habet legem. Necessity has no law. Plowd. 18*a*. "Necessity shall be a good excuse in our law, and in every other law." Id.

Necessitas publica major est quam privata. Public necessity is greater than private. "Death," it has been observed, "is the last and furthest point of particular necessity, and the law imposes it upon every subject that he prefer the urgent service of his king and country before the safety of his life." Noy, Max. 34; Broom, Max. 18.

Necessitas quod cogit, defendit. Necessity defends or justifies what it compels. 1 Hale, P. C. 54. Applied to the acts of a sheriff, or ministerial officer, in the execution of his office. Broom, Max. 14.

Necessitas sub lege non continetur, quia quod alias non est licitum necessitas facit licitum. 2 Inst. 326. Necessity is not restrained by law; since what otherwise is not lawful necessity makes lawful.

Necessitas vincit legem. Necessity overrules the law. Hob. 144; Cooley, Const. Lim. (4th Ed.) 747.

Necessitas vincit legem; legum vincula irridet. Hob. 144. Necessity overcomes law; it derides the fetters of laws.

NECESSITUDO. In the civil law. An obligation; a close connection; relationship by blood. Calvin.

NECESSITY. Controlling force; irresistible compulsion; a power or impulse so great that it admits no choice of conduct. When it is said that an act is done "under necessity," it may be, in law, either of three kinds of necessity: (1) The necessity of preserving one's own life, which will excuse a homicide; (2) the necessity of obedience, as to the laws, or the obedience of one not *sui juris* to his superior; (3) the necessity caused by the act of God or a stranger. See Jacob; Mozley & Whitley.

A constraint upon the will whereby a person is urged to do that which his judgment disapproves, and which, it is to be presumed, his will (if left to itself) would reject. A man, therefore, is excused for those actions which are done through unavoidable force and compulsion. Wharton.

NECESSITY, HOMICIDE BY. A species of justifiable homicide, because it arises from some unavoidable necessity, without any will, intention, or desire, and without any inadvertence or negligence in the party killing, and therefore without any shadow of blame. As, for instance, by virtue of such an office as obliges one, in the execution of public justice, to put a malefactor to death who has forfeited his life to the laws of his country. But the law must require it, otherwise it is not justifiable. 4 Bl. Comm. 178.

NECK-VERSE. The Latin sentence, "*Miserere mei, Deus,*" was so called, because the reading of it was made a test for those who claimed benefit of clergy.

NEEDLESS. In a statute against "needless" killing or mutilation of any animal, this term denotes an act done without any useful motive, in a spirit of wanton cruelty, or for the mere pleasure of destruction. 37 Ark. 460; 4 Mo. App. 215.

NEFAS. Lat. That which is against right or the divine law. A wicked or impious thing or act. Calvin.

NEFASTUS. Lat. Inauspicious. Applied, in the Roman law, to a day on which it was unlawful to open the courts or administer justice.

Negatio conclusionis est error in lege. Wing. 268. The denial of a conclusion is error in law.

Negatio destruit negationem, et ambæ faciunt affirmationem. A negative destroys a negative, and both make an affirmative. Co. Litt. 146*b*. Lord Coke cites this as a rule of grammatical construction, not always applying in law.

Negatio duplex est affirmatio. A double negative is an affirmative.

NEGATIVE. A denial; a proposition by which something is denied; a statement in the form of denial. Two negatives do not make a good issue. Steph. Pl. 386, 387.

NEGATIVE AVERMENT. As opposed to the traverse or simple denial of an affirmative allegation, a negative averment is an allegation of some substantive fact, *e. g.*, that premises are not in repair, which, although negative in form, is really affirmative in substance, and the party alleging the fact of non-repair must prove it. Brown.

NEGATIVE CONDITION. One by which it is stipulated that a given thing shall not happen.

NEGATIVE COVENANT. One in which the covenantor binds himself *not* to do or perform a specified act or thing.

NEGATIVE EASEMENT. One by which the owner of the servient estate is prohibited from doing something otherwise lawful upon his estate, because it will affect the dominant estate, (as interrupting the light and air from the latter by building on the former.) 2 Washb. Real Prop. 301; 70 N. Y. 447.

NEGATIVE PREGNANT. In pleading. A negative implying also an affirmative. Cowell. Such a form of negative expression as may imply or carry within it an affirmative. Steph. Pl. 381. As if a man be said to have aliened land *in fee*, and he says *he has not aliened in fee*, this is a negative pregnant; for, though it be true that he has not aliened in fee, yet it may be that he has made an estate *in tail.* Cowell.

NEGATIVE STATUTE. A statute expressed in negative terms; a statute which prohibits a thing from being done, or declares what shall *not* be done.

NEGLECT. Omission; failure to do something that one is bound to do; carelessness.

The term is used in the law of bailment as synonymous with "negligence." But the latter word is the closer translation of the Latin "*negligentia.*"

As used in respect to the payment of money, refusal is the failure to pay money when demanded; neglect is the failure to pay money which the party is bound to pay without demand. 6 Gray, 224.

The term means to omit, as to neglect business or payment or duty or work, and is generally used in this sense. It does not generally imply carelessness or imprudence, but simply an omission to do or perform some work, duty, or act. 54 N. Y. 262.

NEGLIGENCE. The omission to do something which a reasonable man, guided by those considerations which ordinarily regulate the conduct of human affairs, would do, or doing something which a prudent and reasonable man would not do. It must be determined in all cases by reference to the situation and knowledge of the parties and all the attendant circumstances. 15 Wall. 536; 11 Exch. 784.

Negligence, in its civil relation, is such an inadvertent imperfection, by a responsible human agent, in the discharge of a legal duty, as immediately produces, in an ordinary and natural sequence, a damage to another. Whart. Neg. § 3.

It is conceded by all the authorities that the standard by which to determine whether a person has been guilty of negligence is the conduct of the prudent or careful or diligent man. Bigelow, Torts, 261.

The failure to observe, for the protection of the interests of another person, that degree of care, precaution, and vigilance which the circumstances justly demand, whereby such other person suffers injury. Cooley, Torts, 630.

The failure to do what a reasonable and prudent person would ordinarily have done under the circumstances of the situation, or the doing what such a person under the existing circumstances would not have done. 95 U. S. 441.

The opposite of care and prudence; the omission to use the means reasonably necessary to avoid injury to others. 39 Ill. 353.

Negligence or carelessness signifies want of care, caution, attention, diligence, or discretion in one having no positive intention to injure the person complaining thereof. The words "reckless," "indifferent," "careless," and "wanton" are never understood to signify positive will or intention, unless when joined with other words which show that they are to receive an artificial or unusual, if not an unnatural, interpretation. 10 Bush, 677.

Negligence is any culpable omission of a positive duty. It differs from heedlessness, in that heedlessness is the doing of an act in violation of a negative duty, without adverting to its possible consequences. In both cases there is inadvertence, and there is breach of duty. Aust. Jur. § 630.

Negligence is commonly classed under three degrees,—slight, ordinary, and gross. Slight negligence consists in the want of great care and diligence; ordinary negligence, in the want of ordinary care and diligence; and gross negligence, in the want of slight care and diligence. Civil Code Dak. § 2102. See, further, CARE; GROSS NEGLIGENCE; SLIGHT NEGLIGENCE.

Negligence cannot be considered "gross" unless evidenced by an entire failure to exercise care, or by the exercise of so slight a degree of care as to justify the belief that the person on whom care was incumbent was indifferent to the interest and welfare of others. 64 Tex. 156.

NEGLIGENT ESCAPE. An escape from confinement effected by the prisoner without the knowledge or connivance of the keeper of the prison, but which was made possible or practicable by the latter's negligence, or by his omission of such care and vigilance as he was legally bound to exercise in the safe-keeping of the prisoner.

NEGLIGENTIA. Lat. In the civil law. Carelessness; inattention; the omission of proper care or forethought. The term is not exactly equivalent to our "negligence," inasmuch as it was not any *negligentia*, but only a high or gross degree of it, that amounted to *culpa*, (actionable or punishable fault.)

Negligentia semper habet infortunium comitem. Negligence always has misfortune for a companion. Co. Litt. 246*b;* Shep. Touch. 476.

NEGOCE. Fr. Business; trade; management of affairs.

NEGOTIABILITY. In mercantile law. Transferable quality. That quality of bills of exchange and promissory notes which renders them transferable from one person to another, and from possessing which they are emphatically termed "negotiable paper." 3 Kent, Comm. 74, 77, 89, et seq. See Story, Bills, § 60.

NEGOTIABLE. The word "negotiation," as used by writers upon mercantile law, means the act by which a bill of exchange or promissory note is put into circulation, by being passed by one of the original parties to another person. "Negotiable" means that which is capable of being transferred by assignment; a thing which may be transferred by a sale and indorsement or delivery. This negotiable quality transfers the debt from the party to whom it was originally owing, to the holder, when the instrument is properly indorsed, so as to enable the latter to sue, in his own name, either the maker of a promissory note or the acceptor of a bill of exchange, and the other parties to such instruments, such as the drawer of a bill, or the indorser of a bill or note, unless the holder has been guilty of laches in giving the required notice. It must, however, be payable to order or bearer, and, at all events, in money only, and not out of any particular fund. 60 Ind. 250.

NEGOTIABLE INSTRUMENTS. A general name for bills, notes, checks, transferable bonds or coupons, letters of credit, and other negotiable written securities.

Any written securities which may be transferred by indorsement and delivery or by delivery merely, so as to vest in the indorsee the legal title, and thus enable him to sue thereon in his own name. Or, more technically, those instruments which not only carry the legal title with them by indorsement or delivery, but carry as well, when transferred before maturity, the right of the transferee to demand the full amounts which their faces call for. Daniel, Neg. Inst. § 1*a*.

A negotiable instrument is a written promise or request for the payment of a certain sum of money to order or bearer. Civil Code Cal. § 3087.

NEGOTIABLE WORDS. Words and phrases which impart the character of negotiability to bills, notes, checks, etc., in which they are inserted; for instance, a direction to pay to A. "or order" or "bearer."

NEGOTIATE. To discuss or arrange a sale or bargain; to arrange the preliminaries of a business transaction. Also to sell or discount negotiable paper, or assign or transfer it by indorsement and delivery.

NEGOTIATION. The deliberation, discussion, or conference upon the terms of a proposed agreement; the act of settling or arranging the terms and conditions of a bargain, sale, or other business transaction. Also the transfer of, or act of putting into circulation, a negotiable instrument.

NEGOTIORUM GESTIO. Lat. In the civil law. Literally, a doing of business or businesses. A species of spontaneous agency, or an interference by one in the affairs of another, in his absence, from benevolence or friendship, and without authority. 2 Kent, Comm. 616, note; Inst. 3, 28, 1.

NEGOTIORUM GESTOR. Lat. In the civil law. A transacter or manager of business; a person voluntarily constituting himself agent for another; one who, without any mandate or authority, assumes to take charge of an affair or concern for another person, in the latter's absence, but for his interest.

One who spontaneously, and without the knowledge or consent of the owner, intermeddles with his property, as to do work on it, or to carry it to another place, etc. Story, Bailm. § 189.

NEGRO. The word "negro" means a black man, one descended from the African race, and does not commonly include a mulatto. 18 Ala. 720.

NEIF. In old English law. A woman who was born a villein, or a bondwoman.

NEIGHBORHOOD. A place near; an adjoining or surrounding district; a more immediate vicinity; vicinage. See 63 N. H. 247; 3 N. Y. 502; 38 Iowa, 484.

NEMBDA. In Swedish and Gothic law. A jury. 3 Bl. Comm. 349, 359.

NEMINE CONTRADICENTE. Lat. No one dissenting; no one voting in the negative. A phrase used to indicate the unanimous consent of a court or legislative body to a judgment, resolution, vote, or motion. Commonly abbreviated "*nem. con.*"

Neminem oportet esse sapientiorem legibus. Co. Litt. 97*b*. No man ought to be wiser than the laws.

NEMO. Lat. No one; no man. The initial word of many Latin phrases and maxims, among which are the following:

Nemo admittendus est inhabilitare seipsum. Jenk. Cent. 40. No man is to be admitted to incapacitate himself.

Nemo agit in seipsum. No man acts against himself. Jenk. Cent. p. 40, case 76. A man cannot be a judge and a party in his own cause. Id.; Broom, Max. 216*n*.

Nemo alienæ rei, sine satisdatione, defensor idoneus intelligitur. No man is considered a competent defender of another's property, without security. A rule of the Roman law, applied in part in admiralty cases. 1 Curt. 202.

Nemo alieno nomine lege agere potest. No one can sue in the name of another. Dig. 50, 17, 123.

Nemo allegans suam turpitudinem est audiendus. No one alleging his own baseness is to be heard. The courts of law have properly rejected this as a rule of evidence. 7 Term R. 601.

Nemo bis punitur pro eodem delicto. No man is punished twice for the same offense. 4 Bl. Comm. 315; 2 Hawk. P. C. 377.

Nemo cogitationis pœnam patitur. No one suffers punishment on account of his thoughts. Tray. Lat. Max. 362.

Nemo cogitur rem suam vendere, etiam justo pretio. No man is compelled to sell his own property, even for a just price. 4 Inst. 275.

Nemo contra factum suum venire potest. No man can contravene or contradict his own deed. 2 Inst. 66. The principle of estoppel by deed. Best, Ev. p. 408, § 370.

Nemo dare potest quod non habet. No man can give that which he has not. Fleta, lib. 3, c. 15, § 8.

Nemo dat qui non habet. He who hath not cannot give. Jenk. Cent. 250; Broom, Max. 499*n;* 6 C. B. (N. S.) 478.

Nemo de domo sua extrahi potest. No one can be dragged out of his own house. In other words, every man's house is his castle. Dig. 50, 17, 103.

Nemo debet bis puniri pro uno delicto. No man ought to be punished twice for one offense. 4 Coke, 43*a*; 11 Coke, 59*b*. No man shall be placed in peril of legal penalties more than once upon the same accusation. Broom, Max. 348.

Nemo debet bis vexari [si constet curiæ quod sit] pro una et eadem causa. No man ought to be twice troubled or harassed [if it appear to the court that it is] for one and the same cause. 5 Coke, 61*a*. No man can be sued a second time for the same cause of action, if once judgment has been rendered. See Broom, Max. 327, 348. No man can be held to bail a second time at the suit of the same plaintiff for the same cause of action. 1 Chit. Archb. Pr. 476.

Nemo debet esse judex in propria causa. No man ought to be a judge in his own cause. 12 Coke, 114*a*. A maxim derived from the civil law. Cod. 3, 5. Called a "fundamental rule of reason and of natural justice." Burrows, Sett. Cas. 194, 197.

Nemo debet immiscere se rei ad se nihil pertinenti. No one should intermeddle with a thing that in no respect concerns him. Jenk. Cent. p. 18, case 32.

Nemo debet in communione invitus teneri. No one should be retained in a partnership against his will. 2 Sandf. 568, 593; 1 Johns. 106, 114.

Nemo debet locupletari aliena jactura. No one ought to be enriched by another's loss. Dig. 6, 1, 48, 65; 2 Kent, Comm. 336; 1 Kames, Eq. 331.

Nemo debet locupletari ex alterius incommodo. No one ought to be made rich out of another's loss. Jenk. Cent. 4; 10 Barb. 626, 633.

Nemo debet rem suam sine facto aut defectu suo amittere. No man ought to lose his property without his own act or default. Co. Litt. 263*a*.

Nemo duobus utatur officiis. 4 Inst. 100. No one should hold two offices, *i. e.*, at the same time.

Nemo ejusdem tenementi simul potest esse hæres et dominus. No one can at the same time be the heir and the owner of the same tenement. See 1 Reeve, Eng. Law, 106.

Nemo enim aliquam partem recte intelligere possit antequam totum iterum atque iterum perlegerit. No one is able rightly to understand one part before he has again and again read through the whole. Broom, Max. 593.

Nemo est hæres viventis. No one is the heir of a living person. Co. Litt. 8*a*, 22*b*. No one can be heir during the life of his ancestor. Broom, Max. 522, 523. No person can be the actual complete heir of another till the ancestor is previously dead. 2 Bl. Comm. 208.

Nemo est supra leges. No one is above the law. Lofft, 142.

Nemo ex alterius facto prægravari debet. No man ought to be burdened in consequence of another's act. 2 Kent, Comm. 646.

Nemo ex consilio obligatur. No man is bound in consequence of his advice. Mere advice will not create the obligation of a mandate. Story, Bailm. § 155.

Nemo ex dolo suo proprio relevetur, aut auxilium capiat. Let no one be relieved or gain an advantage by his own fraud. A civil law maxim.

Nemo ex proprio dolo consequitur actionem. No one maintains an action arising out of his own wrong. Broom, Max. 297.

Nemo ex suo delicto meliorem suam conditionem facere potest. No one can make his condition better by his own misdeed. Dig. 50, 17, 134, 1.

Nemo in propria causa testis esse debet. No one ought to be a witness in his own cause. 3 Bl. Comm. 371.

Nemo inauditus condemnari debet si non sit contumax. No man ought to be condemned without being heard unless he be contumacious. Jenk. Cent. p. 18, case 12, in marg.

Nemo jus sibi dicere potest. No one can declare the law for himself. No one is entitled to take the law into his own hands. Tray. Lat. Max. 366.

Nemo militans Deo implicetur secularibus negotiis. No man who is warring for [in the service of] God should be involved in secular matters. Co. Litt. 70*b*. A principle of the old law that men of religion were not bound to go in person with the king to war.

Nemo nascitur artifex. Co. Litt. 97. No one is born an artificer.

Nemo patriam in qua natus est exuere, nec ligeantiæ debitum ejurare possit. No man can renounce the country in which he was born, nor abjure the obligation of his allegiance. Co. Litt. 129*a;* Broom, Max. 75; Fost. Cr. Law, 184.

Nemo plus commodi heredi suo relinquit quam ipse habuit. No one leaves a greater benefit to his heir than he had himself. Dig. 50, 17, 120.

Nemo plus juris ad alium transferre potest quam ipse habet. No one can transfer more right to another than he has himself. Dig. 50, 17, 54; Broom, Max. 467, 469.

Nemo potest contra recordum verificare per patriam. No one can verify by the country against a record. 2 Inst. 380. The issue upon matter of record cannot be to the jury. A maxim of old practice.

Nemo potest esse dominus et hæres. No man can be both owner and heir. Hale, Com. Law, c. 7.

Nemo potest esse simul actor et judex. No one can be at once suitor and judge. Broom, Max. 117.

Nemo potest esse tenens et dominus. No man can be both tenant and lord [of the same tenement.] Gilb. Ten. 142.

Nemo potest facere per alium quod per se non potest. No one can do that by another which he cannot do of himself. Jenk. Cent. p. 237, case 14. A rule said to hold in original grants, but not in descents; as where an office descended to a woman, in which case, though she could not exercise the office in person, she might by deputy. Id.

Nemo potest facere per obliquum quod non potest facere per directum. No man can do that indirectly which he cannot do directly. 1 Eden, 512.

Nemo potest mutare consilium suum in alterius injuriam. No man can change his purpose to another's injury. Dig. 50, 17, 75; Broom, Max. 34.

Nemo potest plus juris ad alium transferre quam ipse habet. Co. Litt. 309; Wing. Max. 56. No one can transfer a greater right to another than he himself has.

Nemo potest sibi debere. No one can owe to himself.

Nemo præsens nisi intelligat. One is not present unless he understands.

Nemo præsumitur alienam posteritatem suæ prætulisse. No man is presumed to have preferred another's posterity to his own. Wing. Max. p. 285, max. 79.

Nemo præsumitur donare. No one is presumed to give. 9 Pick. 128.

Nemo præsumitur esse immemor suæ æternæ salutis, et maxime in articulo mortis. 6 Coke, 76. No one is presumed to be forgetful of his own eternal welfare, and particularly at the point of death.

Nemo præsumitur ludere in extremis. No one is presumed to trifle at the point of death.

Nemo præsumitur malus. No one is presumed to be bad.

Nemo prohibetur plures negotiationes sive artes exercere. No one is prohibited from following several kinds of business or several arts. 11 Coke, 54*a*. The common law doth not prohibit any person from using several arts or mysteries at his pleasure. Id.

Nemo prohibetur pluribus defensionibus uti. Co. Litt. 304*a*. No one is prohibited from making use of several defenses.

Nemo prudens punit ut præterita revocentur, sed ut futura præveniantur. No wise man punishes in order that past things may be recalled, but that future wrongs may be prevented. 2 Bulst. 173.

Nemo punitur pro alieno delicto. Wing. Max. 336. No one is punished for another's wrong.

Nemo punitur sine injuria, facto, seu defalta. No one is punished unless for some wrong, act, or default. 2 Inst. 287.

Nemo qui condemnare potest, absolvere non potest. No one who may condemn is unable to acquit. Dig. 50, 17, 37.

Nemo sibi esse judex vel suis jus dicere debet. No one ought to be his own judge, or the tribunal in his own affairs. Broom, Max. 116, 121. See L. R. 1 C. P. 722, 747.

Nemo sine actione experitur, et hoc non sine breve sive libello conventionali. No one goes to law without an action, and no one can bring an action without a writ or bill. Bract. fol. 112.

Nemo tenetur ad impossibile. No one is bound to an impossibility. Jenk. Cent. 7; Broom, Max. 244.

Nemo tenetur armare adversarium contra se. Wing. Max. 665. No one is bound to arm his adversary against himself.

Nemo tenetur divinare. No man is bound to divine, or to have foreknowledge of, a future event. 10 Coke, 55*a*.

Nemo tenetur edere instrumenta contra se. No man is bound to produce writings against himself. A rule of the Roman law, adhered to in criminal prosecutions, but departed from in civil questions. Bell.

Nemo tenetur informare qui nescit, sed quisquis scire quod informat. Branch, Princ. No one is bound to give information about things he is ignorant of, but every one is bound to know that which he gives information about.

Nemo tenetur jurare in suam turpitudinem. No one is bound to swear to the fact of his own criminality; no one can be forced to give his own oath in evidence of his guilt. Bell; Halk. 100.

Nemo tenetur prodere seipsum. No one is bound to betray himself. In other words, no one can be compelled to criminate himself. Broom, Max. 968.

Nemo tenetur seipsum accusare. Wing. Max. 486. No one is bound to accuse himself.

Nemo tenetur seipsum infortuniis et periculis exponere. No one is bound to expose himself to misfortunes and dangers. Co. Litt. 253*b*.

Nemo unquam judicet in se. No one can ever be a judge in his own cause.

Nemo unquam vir magnus fuit, sine aliquo divino afflatu. No one was ever a great man without some divine inspiration. Cicero.

Nemo videtur fraudare eos qui sciunt et consentiunt. No one seems [is supposed] to defraud those who know and assent [to his acts.] Dig. 50, 17, 145.

NEMY. L. Fr. Not. Litt. § 3.

NEPHEW. The son of a brother or sister. Nephew and uncle are related in the third degree according to the civil law, but by the canon law, in the second degree.

NEPOS. Lat. A grandson.

NEPTIS. Lat. A granddaughter.

NEPUOY. In Scotch law. A grandson. Skene.

NET BALANCE. The proceeds of sale, after deducting expenses. 71 Pa. St. 69.

NET PRICE. The lowest price, after deducting all discounts.

NET PROFITS. This term does not mean what is made over the losses, expenses, and interest on the amount invested. It includes the gain that accrues on the investment, after deducting simply the losses and expenses of the business. 50 Ga. 350.

NET WEIGHT. The weight of an article or collection of articles, after deducting from the gross weight the weight of the boxes, coverings, casks, etc., containing the same. The weight of an animal dressed for sale, after rejecting hide, offal, etc.

NETHER HOUSE OF PARLIAMENT. A name given to the English house of commons in the time of Henry VIII.

NEUTRAL. In international law. Indifferent; impartial; not engaged on either side; not taking an active part with either of the contending states. In an international war, the principal hostile powers are called "belligerents;" those actively co-operating with and assisting them, their "allies;" and those taking no part whatever, "neutrals."

NEUTRAL PROPERTY. Property which belongs to citizens of neutral powers, and is used, treated, and accompanied by proper *insignia* as such.

NEUTRALITY. The state of a nation which takes no part between two or more other nations at war.

NEVER INDEBTED, PLEA OF. A species of traverse which occurs in actions of debt on simple contract, and is resorted to when the defendant means to deny in point of fact the existence of any express contract to the effect alleged in the declaration, or to deny the matters of fact from which such contract would by law be implied. Steph. Pl. 153, 156; Wharton.

NEW AND USEFUL INVENTION. This phrase is used in the United States patent laws to designate the kind of invention which is patentable. The word "useful" does not import that the invention should invariably be superior to the modes previously in use for the same purpose, but means that it must have real utility, in contradistinction to frivolous or mischievous inventions. 1 Mason, 182.

NEW ASSIGNMENT. Under the common law practice, where the declaration in an action is ambiguous, and the defendant pleads facts which are literally an answer to it, but not to the real claim set up by the plaintiff, the plaintiff's course is to reply by way of new assignment; *i. e.*, allege that he brought his action not for the cause supposed by the defendant, but for some other cause to which the plea has no application. 3 Steph. Comm. 507; Sweet.

NEW FOR OLD. In making an adjustment of a partial loss under a policy of marine insurance, the rule is to apply the old materials towards the payment of the new, by deducting the value of them from the gross amount of the expenses for repairs, and to allow the deduction of one-third *new for old* upon the balance. 3 Kent, Comm. 339.

NEW INN. An inn of chancery. See INNS OF CHANCERY.

NEW MATTER. In pleading. Matter of fact not previously alleged by either party in the pleadings.

NEW PROMISE. An undertaking or promise, based upon and having relation to a former promise which, for some reason, can no longer be enforced, whereby the promisor recognizes and revives such former promise and engages to fulfill it.

NEW STYLE. The modern system of computing time was introduced into Great Britain A. D. 1752, the 3d of September of that year being reckoned as the 14th.

NEW TRIAL. A new trial is a re-examination of an issue of fact in the same court after a trial and decision by a jury or court or by referees. Code Civil Proc. Cal. § 656.

A new trial is a re-examination of the issue in the same court, before another jury, after a verdict has been given. Pen. Code Cal. § 1179.

A new trial is a re-examination in the same court of an issue of fact, or some part or portions thereof, after the verdict by a jury, report of a referee, or a decision by the court. Rev. Code Iowa 1880, § 2837.

NEW TRIAL PAPER. In English practice. A paper containing a list of causes in which rules *nisi* have been obtained for a new trial, or for entering a verdict in place of a nonsuit, or for entering judgment *non obstante veredicto*, or for otherwise varying or setting aside proceedings which have taken place at *nisi prius*. These are called on for argument in the order in which they stand in the paper, on days appointed by the judges for the purpose. Brown.

NEW WORKS. In the civil law. By a new work is understood every sort of edifice or other work which is newly commenced on any ground whatever. When the ancient form of work is changed, either by an addition being made to it or by some part of the ancient work being taken away, it is styled also a "new work." Civil Code La. art. 856.

NEW YEAR'S DAY. The first day of January. The 25th of March was the civil and legal New Year's Day, till the alteration of the style in 1752, when it was permanently fixed at the 1st of January. In Scotland the year was, by a proclamation, which bears date 27th of November, 1599, ordered thenceforth to commence in that kingdom on the 1st of January instead of the 25th of March. Enc. Lond.

NEWGATE. The name of a prison in London, said to have existed as early as 1207. It was three times destroyed and rebuilt. For centuries the condition of the place was horrible, but it has been greatly improved since 1808. Since 1815, debtors have not been committed to this prison.

NEWLY-DISCOVERED EVIDENCE. Evidence of a new and material fact, or new evidence in relation to a fact in issue, discovered by a party to a cause after the rendition of a verdict or judgment therein.

NEWSPAPER. According to the usage of the commercial world, a newspaper is defined to be a publication in numbers, consisting commonly of single sheets, and published at short and stated intervals, conveying intelligence of passing events. 4 Op. Attys. Gen. 10.

NEXI. Lat. In Roman law. Bound; bound persons. A term applied to such insolvent debtors as were delivered up to their creditors, by whom they might be held in bondage until their debts were discharged. Calvin.; Adams, Rom. Ant. 49.

NEXT FRIEND. A person, usually a relative, not appointed by the court, in whose name suit is brought by an infant, married woman, or other person not *sui juris*.

NEXT OF KIN. In the law of descent and distribution. This term properly denotes the persons nearest of kindred to the decedent, that is, those who are most nearly related to him by blood; but it is sometimes construed to mean only those who are entitled to take under the statute of distributions, and sometimes to include other persons. 2 Story, Eq. Jur. § 1065*b*.

The words "next of kin," used *simpliciter* in a deed or will, mean, not nearest of kindred, but those relatives who share in the estate according to the statute of distributions, including those claiming *per stirpes* or by representation. 28 How. Pr. 417; 43 Barb. 147.

NEXT PRESENTATION. In the law of advowsons. The right of next presentation is the right to present to the first vacancy of a benefice.

NEXUM. Lat. In Roman law. In ancient times the *nexum* seems to have been a species of formal contract, involving a loan of money, and attended with peculiar consequences, solemnized with the "copper and balance." Later, it appears to have been used as a general term for any contract struck with those ceremonies, and hence to have included the special form of conveyance called "*mancipatio*." In a general sense it means the obligation or *bond* between contracting parties. See Maine, Anc. Law, 305, et seq.; Hadl. Rom. Law, 247.

In Roman law, this word expressed the tie or obligation involved in the old conveyance by *mancipatio;* and came latterly to be used interchangeably with (but less frequently than) the word "*obligatio*" itself. Brown.

NICHILLS. In English practice. Debts due to the exchequer which the sheriff could not levy, and as to which he returned *nil*. These sums were transcribed once a year by the clerk of the nichills, and sent to the treasurer's remembrancer's office, whence process was issued to recover the "nichill" debts. Both of these offices were abolished in 1833. Mozley & Whitley.

NICKNAME. A short name; one *nicked* or cut off for the sake of brevity, without conveying any idea of opprobrium, and frequently evincing the strongest affection or the most perfect familiarity. Busb. Eq. 74.

NIDERLING, NIDERING, or NITHING. A vile, base person, or sluggard; chicken-hearted. Spelman.

NIECE. The daughter of one's brother or sister. Ambl. 514.

NIEFE. In old English law. A woman born in vassalage; a bondwoman.

NIENT. L. Fr. Nothing; not.

NIENT COMPRISE. Not comprised; not included. An exception taken to a petition because the thing desired is not contained in that deed or proceeding whereon the petition is founded. Tomlins.

NIENT CULPABLE. Not guilty. The name in law French of the general issue in tort or in a criminal action.

NIENT DEDIRE. To say nothing; to deny nothing; to suffer judgment by default.

NIENT LE FAIT. In pleading. Not the deed; not his deed. The same as the plea of *non est factum.*

NIENT SEISI. In old pleading. Not seised. The general plea in the writ of annuity. Crabb, Eng. Law, 424.

NIGER LIBER. The black book or register in the exchequer; chartularies of abbeys, cathedrals, etc.

NIGHT. As to what, by the common law, is reckoned night and what day, it seems to be the general opinion that, if there be daylight, or *crepusculum*, enough begun or left to discern a man's face, that is considered day; and night is when it is so dark that the countenance of a man cannot be discerned. 1 Hale, P. C. 350. However, the limit of 9 P. M. to 6 A. M. has been fixed by statute, in England, as the period of night, in prosecutions for burglary and larceny. St. 24 & 25 Vict. c. 96, § 1; Brown.

NIGHT MAGISTRATE. A constable of the night; the head of a watch-house.

NIGHT WALKERS. Described in the statute 5 Edw. III. c. 14, as persons who sleep by day and walk by night. Persons who prowl about at night, and are of a suspicious appearance and behavior.

Nigrum nunquam excedere debet rubrum. The black should never go beyond the red, [*i. e.* the text of a statute should never be read in a sense more comprehensive than the rubric, or title.] Tray. Lat. Max. 373.

NIHIL. Nothing. Also the name of a return made by a sheriff, etc., when the circumstances warrant it.

Nihil aliud potest rex quam quod de jure potest. 11 Coke, 74. The king can do nothing except what he can by law do.

NIHIL CAPIAT PER BREVE. In practice. That he take nothing by his writ. The form of judgment against the plaintiff in an action, either in bar or in abatement. When the plaintiff has commenced his proceedings by bill, the judgment is *nihil capiat per billam.* Co. Litt. 363.

Nihil consensui tam contrarium est quam vis atque metus. Nothing is so opposed to consent as force and fear. Dig. 50, 17, 116.

Nihil de re accrescit ei qui nihil in re quando jus accresceret habet. Co. Litt. 188. Nothing of a matter accrues to him who, when the right accrues, has nothing in that matter.

NIHIL DICIT. He says nothing. This is the name of the judgment which may be taken as of course against a defendant who omits to plead or answer the plaintiff's declaration or complaint within the time limited. In some jurisdictions it is otherwise known as judgment "for want of a plea."

Nihil dictum quod non dictum prius. Nothing is said which was not said before. Said of a case where former arguments were repeated. Hardr. 464.

NIHIL EST. Lat. There is nothing. A form of return made by a sheriff when he has been unable to serve the writ. "Although *non est inventus* is the more frequent return in such a case, yet it is by no means as full an answer to the command of the writ as is the return of *nihil.* That amounts to an averment that the defendant has nothing in the bailiwick, no dwelling-house, no family, no residence, and no personal presence to enable the officer to make the service required by the act of assembly. It is therefore a full answer to the exigency of the writ." 33 Pa. St. 139.

Nihil est enim liberale quod non idem justum. For there is nothing generous which is not at the same time just. 2 Kent, Comm. 441, note *a.*

Nihil est magis rationi consentaneum quam eodem modo quodque dissolvere quo conflatum est. Nothing is more consonant to reason than that a thing should be dissolved or discharged in the same way in which it was created. Shep. Touch. 323.

Nihil facit error nominis cum de corpore constat. 11 Coke, 21. An error as to a name is nothing when there is certainty as to the person.

NIHIL HABET. He has nothing. The name of a return made by a sheriff to a *scire facias* or other writ which he has been unable to serve on the defendant.

Nihil habet forum ex scena. The court has nothing to do with what is not before it. Bac. Max.

Nihil in lege intolerabilius est [quam] eandem rem diverso jure censeri. Nothing is more intolerable in law than that the same matter, thing, or case should be subject to different views of law. 4 Coke, 93*a.* Applied to the difference of opinion entertained by different courts, as to the law of a particular case. Id.

Nihil infra regnum subditos magis conservat in tranquilitate et concordia quam debita legum administratio. Nothing preserves in tranquility and concord those who are subjected to the same government better than a due administration of the laws. 2 Inst. 158.

Nihil iniquius quam æquitatem nimis intendere. Nothing is more unjust than to extend equity too far. Halk. 103.

Nihil magis justum est quam quod necessarium est. Nothing is more just than that which is necessary. Dav. Ir. K. B. 12; Branch, Princ.

Nihil nequam est præsumendum Nothing wicked is to be presumed. 2 P. Wms. 583.

Nihil perfectum est dum aliquid restat agendum. Nothing is perfect while anything remains to be done. 9 Coke, 9*b.*

Nihil peti potest ante id tempus quo per rerum naturam persolvi possit. Nothing can be demanded before the time when, by the nature of things, it can be paid. Dig. 50, 17, 186.

Nihil possumus contra veritatem. We can do nothing against truth. Doct. & Stud. dial. 2, c. 6.

Nihil præscribitur nisi quod possidetur. There is no prescription for that which is not possessed. 5 Barn. & Ald. 277.

Nihil quod est contra rationem est licitum. Nothing that is against reason is lawful. Co. Litt. 97*b.*

Nihil quod est inconveniens est licitum. Nothing that is inconvenient is lawful. Co. Litt. 66*a*, 97*b*. A maxim very frequently quoted by Lord Coke, but to be taken in modern law with some qualification. Broom, Max. 186, 366.

Nihil simul inventum est et perfectum. Co. Litt. 230. Nothing is invented and perfected at the same moment.

Nihil tam conveniens est naturali æquitati quam unumquodque dissolvi eo ligamine quo ligatum est. Nothing is so consonant to natural equity as that a thing should be dissolved by the same means by which it was bound. 2 Inst. 359; Broom, Max. 877.

Nihil tam conveniens est naturali æquitati quam voluntatem domini rem suam in alium transferre ratam habere. 1 Coke, 100. Nothing is so consonant to natural equity as to regard the intention of the owner in transferring his own property to another.

Nihil tam naturale est, quam eo genere quidque dissolvere, quo colligatum est; ideo verborum obligatio verbis tollitur; nudi consensus obligatio contrario consensu dissolvitur. Nothing is so natural as to dissolve anything in the way in which it was bound together; therefore the obligation of words is taken away by words; the obligation of mere consent is dissolved by the contrary consent. Dig. 50, 17, 35; Broom, Max. 887.

Nihil tam proprium imperio quam legibus vivere. Nothing is so becoming to authority as to live in accordance with the laws. Fleta, lib. 1, c. 17, § 11.

NIHILIST. A member of a secret association, (especially in Russia,) which is devoted to the destruction of the present political, religious, and social institutions. Webster.

Nil agit exemplum litem quod lite resolvit. An example does no good which settles one question by another. 15 Wend. 44, 49.

Nil consensui tam contrarium est quam vis atque metus. Nothing is so opposed to consent as force and fear. Dig. 50, 17, 116.

NIL DEBET. He owes nothing. The form of the general issue in all actions of debt on simple contract.

Nil facit error nominis cum de corpore vel persona constat. A mistake in the name does not matter when the body or person is manifest. 11 Coke, 21; Broom, Max. 634.

NIL HABUIT IN TENEMENTIS. He had nothing [no interest] in the tenements. A plea in debt on a lease indented, by which the defendant sets up that the person claiming to be landlord had no title or interest.

NIL LIGATUM. Nothing bound; that is, no obligation has been incurred. Tray. Lat. Max.

Nil sine prudenti fecit ratione vetustas. Antiquity did nothing without a good reason. Co. Litt. 65.

Nil temere novandum. Nothing should be rashly changed. Jenk. Cent. 163.

Nimia certitudo certitudinem ipsam destruit. Too great certainty destroys certainty itself. Lofft, 244.

Nimia subtilitas in jure reprobatur. Wing. Max. 26. Too much subtlety in law is discountenanced.

Nimium altercando veritas amittitur. Hob. 344. By too much altercation truth is lost.

NIMMER. A thief; a pilferer.

NISI. Lat. Unless. The word is often affixed, as a kind of elliptical expression, to the words "rule," "order," "decree," "judgment," or "confirmation," to indicate that the adjudication spoken of is one which is to stand as valid and operative *unless* the party affected by it shall appear and show cause against it, or take some other appropriate step to avoid it or procure its revocation. Thus a "decree *nisi*" is one which will definitely conclude the defendant's rights unless, within the prescribed time, he shows cause to set it aside or successfully appeals. The word, in this sense, is opposed to "absolute." And when a rule *nisi* is finally confirmed, for the defendant's failure to show cause against it, it is said to be "made absolute."

NISI FECERIS. Lat. The name of a clause commonly occurring in the old manorial writs, commanding that, if the lords failed to do justice, the king's court or officer should do it. By virtue of this clause, the king's court usurped the jurisdiction of the private, manorial, or local courts. Stim. Law Gloss.

NISI PRIUS. Lat. The *nisi prius* courts are such as are held for the trial of issues of fact before a jury and one presiding judge. In America the phrase is familiarly used to denote the forum (whatever may be its statutory name) in which the cause was tried to a jury, as distinguished from the appellate court. See 3 Bl. Comm. 58.

NISI PRIUS CLAUSE. In practice. A clause entered on the record in an action at law, authorizing the trial of the cause at *nisi prius* in the particular county designated. It was first used by way of continuance.

NISI PRIUS ROLL. In practice. The roll or record containing the pleadings, issue, and jury process of an action, made up for use in the *nisi prius* court.

NISI PRIUS WRIT. The old name of the writ of *venire*, which originally, in pursuance of the statute of Westminster 2, contained the *nisi prius* clause. Reg. Jud. 28, 75; Cowell.

NIVICOLLINI BRITONES. In old English law. Welshmen, because they live near high mountains covered with snow. Du Cange.

NO AWARD. The name of a plea in an action on an award, by which the defendant traverses the allegation that an award was made.

NO BILL. This phrase, when indorsed by a grand jury on an indictment, is equivalent to "not found," "not a true bill," or "*ignoramus*."

NO FUNDS. This term denotes a lack of assets or money for a specific use. It is the return made by a bank to a check drawn upon it by a person who has no deposit to his credit there; also by an executor, trustee, etc., who has no assets for the specific purpose.

NO GOODS. This is the English equivalent of the Latin term "*nulla bona*," being the form of the return made by a sheriff or constable, charged with an execution, when he has found no property of the debtor on which to levy.

No man can hold the same land immediately of two several landlords. Co. Litt. 152.

No man is presumed to do anything against nature. 22 Vin. Abr. 154.

No man shall set up his infamy as a defense. 2 W. Bl. 364.

No one can grant or convey what he does not own. 25 Barb. 284, 301. See 20 Wend. 267; 23 N. Y. 252; 13 N. Y. 121; 6 Duer, 232.

NOBILE OFFICIUM. In Scotch law. An equitable power of the court of session, to give relief when none is possible at law. Ersk. Inst. 1, 3, 22; Bell.

Nobiles magis plectuntur pecunia; plebes vero in corpore. 3 Inst. 220. The higher classes are more punished in money; but the lower in person.

Nobiles sunt, qui arma gentilitia antecessorum suorum proferre possunt. 2 Inst. 595. The gentry are those who are able to produce armorial bearings derived by descent from their own ancestors.

Nobiliores et benigniores præsumptiones in dubiis sunt præferendæ. In cases of doubt, the more generous and more benign presumptions are to be preferred. A civil-law maxim.

Nobilitas est duplex, superior et inferior. 2 Inst. 583. There are two sorts of nobility, the higher and the lower.

NOBILITY. In English law. A division of the people, comprehending dukes, marquises, earls, viscounts, and barons. These had anciently duties annexed to their respective honors. They are created either by writ, *i. e.*, by royal summons to attend the house of peers, or by letters patent, *i. e.*, by royal grant of any dignity and degree of peerage; and they enjoy many privileges, exclusive of their senatorial capacity. 1 Bl. Comm. 396.

NOCENT. From Latin "*nocere.*" Guilty. "The *nocent* person." 1 Vern. 429.

NOCTANTER. By night. An abolished writ which issued out of chancery, and returned to the queen's bench, for the prostration of inclosures, etc.

NOCTES and NOCTEM DE FIRMA. Entertainment of meat and drink for so many nights. Domesday.

NOCUMENTUM. Lat. In old English law. A nuisance. *Nocumentum damnosum*, a nuisance occasioning loss or damage. *Nocumentum injuriosum*, an injurious nuisance. For the latter only a remedy was given. Bract. fol. 221.

NOLENS VOLENS. Lat. Whether willing or unwilling; consenting or not.

NOLIS. Fr. In French law. Freight. The same with "*fret.*" Ord. Mar. liv. 3, tit. 3.

NOLISSEMENT. Fr. In French marine law. Affreightment. Ord. Mar. liv. 3, tit. 1.

NOLLE PROSEQUI. Lat. In practice. A formal entry upon the record, by the plaintiff in a civil suit or the prosecuting officer in a criminal action, by which he declares that he "will no further prosecute" the case, either as to some of the counts, or some of the defendants, or altogether.

A *nolle prosequi* is in the nature of an acknowledgment or undertaking by the plaintiff in an action to forbear to proceed any further either in the action altogether, or as to some part of it, or as to some of the defendants; and is different from a *non pros.*, by which the plaintiff is put out of court with respect to all the defendants. Brown.

NOLO CONTENDERE. Lat. I will not contest it. This is the name of a plea in a criminal action, upon which the defendant may be sentenced.

NOMEN. In the civil law. A name; the name, style, or designation of a person. Properly, the name showing to what *gens* or tribe he belonged, as distinguished from his own individual name, (the *prænomen*,) from his surname or family name, (*cognomen*,) and from any name added by way of a descriptive title, (*agnomen.*)

The name or style of a class or genus of persons or objects.

A debt or a debtor. Ainsworth; Calvin.

NOMEN COLLECTIVUM. A collective name or term; a term expressive of a class; a term including several of the same kind; a term expressive of the plural, as well as singular, number.

Nomen est quasi rei notamen. A name is, as it were, the note of a thing. 11 Coke, 20.

NOMEN GENERALE. A general name; the name of a *genus*. Fleta, lib. 4, c. 19, § 1.

NOMEN GENERALISSIMUM. A name of the most general kind; a name or term of the most general meaning. By the name of "land," which is *nomen generalissimum*, everything terrestrial will pass. 2 Bl. Comm. 19; 3 Bl. Comm. 172.

NOMEN JURIS. A name of the law; a technical legal term.

Nomen non sufficit, si res non sit de jure aut de facto. A name is not sufficient if there be not a thing [or subject for it] *de jure* or *de facto*. 4 Coke, 107*b*.

Nomina mutabilia sunt, res autem immobiles. Names are mutable, but things are immovable, [immutable.] A name may be true or false, or may change, but the thing itself always maintains its identity. 6 Coke, 66.

Nomina si nescis perit cognitio rerum; et nomina si perdas, certe distinctio rerum perditur. Co. Litt. 86. If you know not the names of things, the knowledge of things themselves perishes; and, if you lose the names, the distinction of the things is certainly lost.

Nomina sunt notæ rerum. 11 Coke, 20. Names are the notes of things.

Nomina sunt symbola rerum. Godb. Names are the symbols of things.

NOMINA TRANSCRIPTITIA. In Roman law. Obligations contracted by *literæ* (*i. e., literis obligationes*) were so called because they arose from a peculiar *transfer* (*transcriptio*) from the creditor's day-book (*adversaria*) into his ledger, (*codex.*)

NOMINA VILLARUM. In English law. An account of the names of all the villages and the possessors thereof, in each county, drawn up by several sheriffs, (9 Edw. II.,) and returned by them into the exchequer, where it is still preserved. Wharton.

NOMINAL. Titular; existing in name only; not real or substantial; connected with the transaction or proceeding in name only, not in interest.

NOMINAL DAMAGES. In practice. A trifling sum awarded to a plaintiff in an action, where there is no substantial loss or injury to be compensated, but still the law recognizes a technical invasion of his rights or a breach of the defendant's duty.

NOMINAL DEFENDANT. A person who is joined as defendant in an action, not because he is immediately liable in damages or because any specific relief is demanded as against him, but because his connection with the subject-matter is such that the plaintiff's action would be defective, under the technical rules of practice, if he were not joined.

NOMINAL PARTNER. A person who appears to be a partner in a firm, or is so represented to persons dealing with the firm, or who allows his name to appear in the style of the firm or to be used in its business, in the character of a partner, but who has no actual interest in the firm or business. Story, Partn. § 80.

NOMINAL PLAINTIFF. One who has no interest in the subject-matter of the action, having assigned the same to another, (the real plaintiff in interest, or "use plaintiff,") but who must be joined as plaintiff, because, under technical rules of practice, the suit cannot be brought directly in the name of the assignee.

NOMINATE. To propose for an appointment; to designate for an office, a privilege, a living, etc.

NOMINATE CONTRACTS. In the civil law. Contracts having a proper or peculiar name and form, and which were divided into four kinds, expressive of the ways in which they were formed, viz.: (1) Real, which arose *ex re*, from something done; (2) verbal, *ex verbis*, from something said; (3) literal, *ex literis*, from something written; and (4) consensual, *ex consensu*, from something agreed to. Calvin.

NOMINATIM. By name; expressed one by one.

NOMINATING AND REDUCING. A mode of obtaining a panel of special jurors in England, from which to select the jury to try a particular action. The proceeding takes place before the under-sheriff or secondary, and in the presence of the parties' solicitors. Numbers denoting the persons on the sheriff's list are put into a box and drawn until forty-eight unchallenged persons have been nominated. Each party strikes off twelve, and the remaining twenty-four are returned as the "panel," (*q. v.*) This practice is now only employed by order of the court or judge. (Sm. Ac. 130; Juries Act 1870, § 17.) Sweet.

NOMINATION. An appointment or designation of a person to fill an office or discharge a duty. The act of suggesting or proposing a person by name as a candidate for an office.

NOMINATION TO A LIVING. In English ecclesiastical law. The rights of nominating and of presenting to a living are distinct, and may reside in different persons. Presentation is the offering a clerk to the bishop. Nomination is the offering a clerk to the person who has the right of presentation. Brown.

NOMINATIVUS PENDENS. Lat. A nominative case grammatically unconnected with the rest of the sentence in which it stands. The opening words in the ordinary form of a deed *inter partes*, "This indenture," etc., down to "whereas," though an intelligible and convenient part of the deed, are of this kind. Wharton.

NOMINE. Lat. By name; by the name of; under the name or designation of.

NOMINE PŒNÆ. In the name of a penalty. In the civil law, a legacy was said to be left *nomine pœnæ* where it was left for the purpose of coercing the heir to do or not to do something. Inst. 2, 20, 36.

The term has also been applied, in English law, to some kinds of covenants, such as a covenant inserted in a lease that the lessee shall forfeit a certain sum on non-payment of rent, or on doing certain things, as plowing up ancient meadow, and the like. 1 Crabb, Real Prop. p. 171, § 155.

NOMINEE. One who has been nominated or proposed for an office.

NOMOCANON. (1) A collection of canons and imperial laws relative or conformable thereto. The first nomocanon was made by Johannes Scholasticus in 554. Photius, patriarch of Constantinople, in 883, compiled another nomocanon, or collation of the civil laws with the canons; this is the most celebrated. Balsamon wrote a commentary upon it in 1180. (2) A collection of the ancient canons of the apostles, councils, and fathers, without any regard to imperial constitutions. Such is the nomocanon by M. Cotelier. Enc. Lond.

NOMOGRAPHER. One who writes on the subject of laws.

NOMOGRAPHY. A treatise or description of laws.

NOMOTHETA. A lawgiver; such as Solon and Lycurgus among the Greeks, and Cæsar, Pompey, and Sylla among the Romans. Calvin.

NON. Lat. Not. The common particle of negation.

NON-ABILITY. Want of ability to do an act in law, as to sue. A plea founded upon such cause. Cowell.

NON-ACCEPTANCE. The refusal to accept anything.

NON ACCEPTAVIT. In pleading. The name of a plea to an action of *assumpsit* brought against the drawee of a bill of exchange by which he denies that he *accepted* the same.

NON-ACCESS. In legal parlance this term denotes the absence of opportunities for sexual intercourse between husband and wife; or the absence of such intercourse.

Non accipi debent verba in demonstrationem falsam, quæ competunt in limitationem veram. Words ought not to be taken to import a false demonstration which may have effect by way of true limitation. Bac. Max. p. 59, reg. 13; Broom, Max. 642.

NON ACCREVIT INFRA SEX ANNOS. It did not accrue within six years. The name of a plea by which the defendant sets up the statute of limitations against a cause of action which is barred after six years.

NON-ACT. A forbearance from action; the contrary to act.

NON-ADMISSION. The refusal of admission.

NON-AGE. Lack of requisite legal age. The condition of a person who is under twenty-one years of age, in some cases, and under fourteen or twelve in others; minority.

Non alio modo puniatur aliquis quam secundum quod se habet condemnatio. 3 Inst. 217. A person may not be punished differently than according to what the sentence enjoins.

Non aliter a significatione verborum recedi oportet quam cum manifestum est, aliud sensisse testatorem. We must never depart from the signification of words, unless it is evident that they are not conformable to the will of the testator. Dig. 32, 69, pr.; Broom, Max. 568.

NON-APPARENT EASEMENT. A non-continous or discontinuous easement. 18 N. J. Eq. 262. See EASEMENT.

NON-APPEARANCE. A failure of appearance; the omission of the defendant to appear within the time limited.

NON-ASSESSABLE. This word, placed upon a certificate of stock, does not cancel or impair the obligation to pay the amount due upon the shares created by the acceptance and holding of such certificate. At most its legal effect is a stipulation against liability from further assessment or taxation after the entire subscription of one hundred per cent. shall have been paid. 91 U. S. 45.

NON-ASSUMPSIT. The general issue in the action of *assumpsit;* being a plea by which the defendant avers that "he did not undertake" or promise as alleged.

NON-ASSUMPSIT INFRA SEX ANNOS. He did not undertake within six years. The name of the plea of the statute of limitations, in the action of *assumpsit.*

Non auditur perire volens. He who is desirous to perish is not heard. Best, Ev. 423, § 385. He who confesses himself guilty of a crime, with the view of meeting death, will not be heard. A maxim of the foreign law of evidence. Id.

NON-BAILABLE. Not admitting of bail; not requiring bail.

NON BIS IN IDEM. Not twice for the same; that is, a man shall not be twice tried for the same crime. This maxim of the civil law (Code, 9, 2, 9, 11) expresses the same principle as the familiar rule of our law that a man shall not be twice "put in jeopardy" for the same offense.

NON CEPIT. He did not take. The general issue in replevin, where the action is for the wrongful *taking* of the property; putting in issue not only the taking, but the *place* in which the taking is stated to have been made. Steph. Pl. 157, 167.

NON-CLAIM. The omission or neglect of him who ought to claim his right within the time limited by law; as within a year and a day where a continual claim was required, or within five years after a fine had been levied. Termes de la Ley.

NON-COMBATANT. A person connected with an army or navy, but for purposes other than fighting; such as the surgeons and chaplains. Also a neutral.

NON-COMMISSIONED. A non-commissioned officer of the army or militia is a subordinate officer who holds his rank, not by commission from the executive authority of the state or nation, but by appointment by a superior officer.

NON COMPOS MENTIS. Lat. Not sound of mind; insane. This is a very general term, embracing all varieties of mental derangement.

Coke has enumerated four different classes of persons who are deemed in law to be *non compotes mentis: First,* an idiot, or fool natural; *second,* he who was of good and sound mind and memory, but by the act of God has lost it; *third*, a lunatic, *lunaticus qui gaudet lucidis intervallis*, who sometimes is of good sound mind and memory, and sometimes *non compos mentis; fourth*, one who is *non compos mentis* by his own act, as a drunkard. Co. Litt., 247*a;* 4 Coke, 124; 6 Neb. 404.

Non concedantur citationes priusquam exprimatur super qua re fieri debet citatio. 12 Coke, 47. Summonses should not be granted before it is expressed on what matter the summons ought to be made.

NON CONCESSIT. Lat. He did not grant. The name of a plea denying a grant, which could be made only by a stranger.

NON-CONFORMIST. In English law. One who refuses to comply with others; one who refuses to join in the established forms of worship.

Non-conformists are of two sorts: (1) Such as absent themselves from divine worship in the Established Church through total irreligion, and attend the service of no other persuasion; (2) such as attend the religious service of another persuasion. Wharton.

Non consentit qui errat. Bract. fol. 44. He who mistakes does not consent.

NON CONSTAT. Lat. It does not appear; it is not clear or evident. A phrase used in general to state some conclusion as not necessarily following although it may appear on its face to follow.

NON-CONTINUOUS EASEMENT. A non-apparent or discontinuous easement. 18 N. J. Eq. 262. See EASEMENT.

NON CULPABILIS. Lat. In pleading. Not guilty. It is usually abbreviated "*non cul.*"

NON DAMNIFICATUS. Lat. Not injured. This is a plea in an action of debt on an indemnity bond, or bond conditioned "to keep the plaintiff harmless and indemnified," etc. It is in the nature of a plea of performance, being used where the defendant means to allege that the plaintiff has been kept harmless and indemnified, according to the tenor of the condition. Steph. Pl. (7th Ed.) 300, 301.

Non dat qui non habet. He who has not does not give. Lofft, 258; Broom, Max. 467.

Non debeo melioris conditionis esse, quam auctor meus a quo jus in me transit. I ought not to be in better condition than he to whose rights I succeed. Dig. 50, 17, 175, 1.

Non debet actori licere quod reo non permittitur. A plaintiff ought not to be allowed what is not permitted to a defendant. A rule of the civil law. Dig. 50, 17, 41.

Non debet adduci exceptio ejus rei cujus petitur dissolutio. A plea of the same matter the dissolution of which is sought [by the action] ought not to be brought forward. Broom, Max. 166.

Non debet alii nocere, quod inter alios actum est. A person ought not to be prejudiced by what has been done between others. Dig. 12, 2, 10.

Non debet alteri per alterum iniqua conditio inferri. A burdensome condition ought not to be brought upon one man by the act of another. Dig. 50, 17, 74.

Non debet cui plus licet, quod minus est non licere. He to whom the greater is lawful ought not to be debarred from the less as unlawful. Dig. 50, 17, 21; Broom, Max. 176.

Non debet dici tendere in præjudicium ecclesiasticæ liberatatis quod pro rege et republica necessarium videtur. 2 Inst. 625. That which seems necessary for the king and the state ought not to be said to tend to the prejudice of spiritual liberty.

Non decet homines dedere causa non cognita. It is unbecoming to surrender men when no cause is shown. 4 Johns. Ch. 106, 114; 3 Wheel. Crim. Cas. 473, 482.

NON DECIMANDO. See DE NON DECIMANDO.

Non decipitur qui scit se decipi. 5 Coke, 60. He is not deceived who knows himself to be deceived.

NON DEDIT. Lat. In pleading. He did not grant. The general issue in formedon.

NON-DELIVERY. Neglect, failure, or refusal to deliver goods, on the part of a carrier, vendor, bailee, etc.

NON DETINET. Lat. He does not detain. The name of the general issue in the action of detinue. 1 Tidd, Pr. 645.

The general issue in the action of replevin, where the action is for the wrongful detention only. 2 Burrill, Pr. 14.

Non differunt quæ concordant re, tametsi non in verbis iisdem. Those things do not differ which agree in substance, though not in the same words. Jenk. Cent. p. 70, case 32.

NON DIMISIT. L. Lat. He did not demise. A plea resorted to where a plaintiff declared upon a demise without stating the indenture in an action of debt for rent. Also, a plea in bar, in replevin, to an avowry for arrears of rent, that the avowant did not demise.

NON-DIRECTION. Omission on the part of a judge to properly instruct the jury upon a necessary conclusion of law.

NON DISTRINGENDO. A writ not to distrain.

Non dubitatur, etsi specialiter venditor evictionem non promiserit, re evicta, ex empto competere actionem. It is certain that, although the vendor has not given a special guaranty, an action *ex empto* lies against him, if the purchaser is evicted. Code, 8, 45, 6; Broom, Max. 768.

Non efficit affectus nisi sequatur effectus. The intention amounts to nothing unless the effect follow. 1 Rolle, 226.

Non erit alia lex Romæ, alia Athænis; alia nunc, alia posthac; sed et omnes gentes, et omni tempore, una lex, et sempiterna, et immortalis continebit. There will not be one law at Rome, another at Athens; one law now, another hereafter; but one eternal and immortal law shall bind together all nations throughout all time. Cic. Frag. de Repub. lib. 3; 3 Kent, Comm. 1.

Non est arctius vinculum inter homines quam jusjurandum. There is no closer [or firmer] bond between men than an oath. Jenk. Cent. p. 126, case 54.

Non est certandum de regulis juris. There is no disputing about rules of law.

Non est consonum rationi, quod cognitio accessorii in curia christianitatis impediatur, ubi cognitio causæ principalis ad forum ecclesiasticum noscitur pertinere. 12 Coke, 65. It is unreasonable that the cognizance of an accessory matter should be impeded in an ecclesiastical court, when the cognizance of the principal cause is admitted to appertain to an ecclesiastical court.

Non est disputandum contra principia negantem. Co. Litt. 343. We cannot dispute against a man who denies first principles.

NON EST FACTUM. Lat. A plea by way of traverse, which occurs in debt on bond or other specialty, and also in covenant. It denies that the deed mentioned in the declaration is the defendant's deed. Under this, the defendant may contend at the trial that the deed was never executed in point of fact; but he cannot deny its validity in point of law. Wharton.

The plea of *non est factum* is a denial of the execution of the instrument sued upon, and applies to notes or other instruments, as well as deeds, and applies only when the execution of the instrument is alleged to be the act of the party filing the plea, or adopted by him. Code Ga. 1882, § 3472.

NON EST INVENTUS. Lat. He is not found. The sheriff's return to process requiring him to arrest the body of the defendant, when the latter is not found within his jurisdiction. It is often abbreviated "*n. e. i.*," or written, in English, "not found."

Non est justum aliquem antenatum post mortem facere bastardum qui toto tempore vitæ suæ pro legitimo habebatur. It is not just to make an elder-born a bastard after his death, who during his lifetime was accounted legitimate. 12 Coke, 44.

Non est novum ut priores leges ad posteriores trahantur. It is no new thing that prior statutes should give place to later ones. Dig. 1, 3, 36; Broom, Max. 28.

Non est regula quin fallet. There is no rule but what may fail. Off. Exec. 212.

Non est singulis concedendum, quod per magistratum publice possit fieri, ne occasio sit majoris tumultus faciendi. That is not to be conceded to private persons which can be publicly done by the magistrate, lest it be the occasion of greater tumults. Dig. 50, 17, 176.

Non ex opinionibus singulorum, sed ex communi usi, nomina exaudiri debent. The names of things ought to be understood, not according to the opinions of individuals, but according to common usage. Dig. 33, 10, 7, 2.

Non facias malum, ut inde fiat bonum. You are not to do evil, that good may be or result therefrom. 11 Coke, 74*a;* 5 Coke, 30*b*.

NON FECIT. Lat. He did not make it. A plea in an action of *assumpsit* on a promissory note. 3 Man. & G. 446.

NON FECIT VASTUM CONTRA PROHIBITIONEM. He did not commit waste against the prohibition. A plea to an action founded on a writ of estrepement for waste. 3 Bl. Comm. 226, 227.

NON HÆC IN FŒDERA VENI. I did not agree to these terms.

Non impedit clausula derogatoria quo minus ad eadem potestate res dissolvantur a qua constituuntur. A derogatory clause does not impede things from being dissolved by the same power by which they are created. Broom, Max. 27.

NON IMPEDIVIT. Lat. He did not impede. The plea of the general issue in *quare impedit*. The Latin form of the law French "*ne disturba pas.*"

NON IMPLACITANDO ALIQUEM DE LIBERO TENEMENTO SINE BREVI. A writ to prohibit bailiffs, etc., from distraining or impleading any man touching his freehold without the king's writ. Reg. Orig. 171.

Non in legendo sed in intelligendo legis consistunt. The laws consist not in being read, but in being understood. 8 Coke, 167*a*.

NON INFREGIT CONVENTIONEM. Lat. He did not break the contract. The name of a plea sometimes pleaded in the action of covenant, and intended as a general issue, but held to be a bad plea; there being, properly speaking, no general issue in that action. 1 Tidd, Pr. 356.

NON-INTERCOURSE. 1. The refusal of one state or nation to have commercial dealings with another; similar to an embargo, (*q. v.*)

2. The absence of access, communication, or sexual relations between husband and wife.

NON INTERFUI. I was not present. A reporter's note. T. Jones, 10.

NON INTROMITTANT CLAUSE. In English law. A clause of a charter of a municipal borough, whereby the borough is exempted from the jurisdiction of the justices of the peace for the county.

NON INTROMITTENDO, QUANDO BREVE PRÆCIPE IN CAPITE SUBDOLE IMPETRATUR. A writ addressed to the justices of the bench, or in eyre, commanding them not to give one who, under color of entitling the king to land, etc., as holding of him *in capite*, had deceitfully obtained the writ called "*præcipe in capite*," any benefit thereof, but to put him to his writ of right. Reg. Orig. 4.

NON-ISSUABLE PLEAS. Those upon which a decision would not determine the action upon the merits, as a plea in abatement. 1 Chit. Archb. Pr. (12th Ed.) 249.

NON-JOINDER. The omission to join some person as party to a suit, whether as plaintiff or defendant, who ought to have been so joined, according to the rules of pleading and practice.

NON JURIDICUS. Not judicial; not legal. *Dies non juridicus* is a day on which legal proceedings cannot be had.

NON-JURORS. In English law. Persons who refuse to take the oaths, required by law, to support the government.

Non jus ex regula, sed regula ex jure. The law does not arise from the rule, (or maxim,) but the rule from the law. Tray. Lat. Max. 384.

Non jus, sed seisina, facit stipitem. Not right, but seisin, makes a stock. Fleta, lib. 6, c. 2, § 2. It is not a mere *right* to enter on lands, but actual *seisin*, which makes a person the root or *stock* from which all future inheritance by right of blood must be derived. 2 Bl. Comm. 209, 312. See Broom, Max. 525, 527.

Non licet quod dispendio licet. That which may be [done only] at a loss is not allowed [to be done.] The law does not permit or require the doing of an act which will result only in loss. The law forbids such recoveries whose ends are vain, chargeable, and unprofitable. Co. Litt. 127*b*.

NON LIQUET. Lat. It is not clear. In the Roman courts, when any of the judges, after the hearing of a cause, were not satisfied that the case was made clear enough for them to pronounce a verdict, they were privileged to signify this opinion by casting a ballot inscribed with the letters "N. L.," the abbreviated form of the phrase "*non liquet.*"

NON MERCHANDIZANDA VICTUALIA. An ancient writ addressed to justices of assize, to inquire whether the magistrates of a town sold victuals in gross or by retail during the time of their being in office, which was contrary to an obsolete statute; and to punish them if they did. Reg. Orig. 184.

NON MOLESTANDO. A writ that lay for a person who was molested contrary to the king's protection granted to him. Reg. Orig. 184.

Non nasci, et natum mori, paria sunt. Not to be born, and to be dead-born, are the same.

NON-NEGOTIABLE. Not negotiable; not capable of passing title or property by indorsement and delivery.

Non obligat lex nisi promulgata. A law is not obligatory unless it be promulgated.

Non observata forma, infertur adnullatio actus. Where form is not observed, an annulling of the act is inferred or follows. 12 Coke, 7.

NON OBSTANTE. Lat. Notwithstanding. Words anciently used in public and private instruments, intended to preclude, in advance, any interpretation contrary to certain declared objects or purposes. Burrill.

A clause frequent in old English statutes and letters patent, (so termed from its initial words,) importing a license from the crown to do a thing which otherwise a person would be restrained by act of parliament from doing. Crabb, Com. Law, 570; Plowd. 501; Cowell.

A power in the crown to dispense with the laws in any particular case. This was abolished by the bill of rights at the Revolution. 1 Bl. Comm. 342.

NON OBSTANTE VEREDICTO. Notwithstanding the verdict. A judgment entered by order of court for the plaintiff, although there has been a verdict for the defendant, is so called.

Non officit conatus nisi sequatur effectus. An attempt does not harm unless a consequence follow. 11 Coke, 98.

NON OMITTAS. A clause usually inserted in writs of execution, in England, directing the sheriff "not to omit" to execute the writ by reason of any liberty, because there are many liberties or districts in which the sheriff has no power to execute process unless he has special authority. 2 Steph. Comm. 630.

Non omne damnum inducit injuriam. It is not every loss that produces an injury. Bract. fol. 45*b*.

Non omne quod licet honestum est. It is not everything which is permitted that is honorable. Dig. 50, 17, 144; 4 Johns. Ch. 121.

Non omnium quæ a majoribus nostris constituta sunt ratio reddi potest. There cannot be given a reason for all the things which have been established by our ancestors. Branch, Princ.; 4 Coke, 78; Broom, Max. 157.

NON-PAYMENT. The neglect, failure, or refusal of payment of a debt or evidence of debt when due.

NON-PERFORMANCE. Neglect, failure, or refusal to do or perform an act stipulated to be done. Failure to keep the terms of a contract or covenant, in respect to acts or doings agreed upon.

Non pertinet ad judicem secularem cognoscere de iis quæ sunt mere spiritualia annexa. 2 Inst. 488. It belongs not to the secular judge to take cognizance of things which are merely spiritual.

NON-PLEVIN. In old English law. Default in not replevying land in due time, when the same was taken by the king upon a default. The consequence thereof (loss of seisin) was abrogated by St. 9 Edw. III. c. 2.

NON PONENDIS IN ASSISIS ET JURATIS. A writ formerly granted for freeing and discharging persons from serving on assizes and juries. Fitzh. Nat. Brev. 165.

Non possessori incumbit necessitas probandi possessiones ad se pertinere. A person in possession is not bound to prove that the possessions belong to him. Broom, Max. 714.

Non potest adduci exceptio ejus rei cujus petitur dissolutio. An exception of the same thing whose avoidance is sought cannot be made. Broom, Max. 166.

Non potest probari quod probatum non relevat. 1 Exch. 91, 92. That cannot be proved which, if proved, is immaterial.

Non potest quis sine brevi agere. No one can sue without a writ. Fleta, lib. 2, c. 13, § 4. A fundamental rule of old practice.

Non potest rex gratiam facere cum injuria et damno aliorum. The king cannot confer a favor on one subject which occasions injury and loss to others. 3 Inst. 236; Broom, Max. 63.

Non potest rex subditum renitentem onerare impositionibus. The king cannot load a subject with imposition against his consent. 2 Inst. 61.

Non potest videri desisse habere qui nunquam habuit. He cannot be considered as having ceased to have a thing who never had it. Dig. 50, 17, 208.

NON PROSEQUITUR. Lat. If, in the proceedings in an action at law, the plaintiff neglects to take any of those steps which he ought to take within the time prescribed by the practice of the court for that purpose, the defendant may enter judgment of *non pros.* against him, whereby it is adjudged that the plaintiff does not follow up (*non prosequitur*) his suit as he ought to do, and therefore the defendant ought to have judgment against him. Smith, Act. 96.

NON QUIETA MOVERE. Lat. Not to disturb what is settled. A rule expressing the same principle as that of *stare decisis*, (*q. v.*)

Non quod dictum est, sed quod factum est inspicitur. Not what is said, but what is done, is regarded. Co. Litt. 36*a*.

Non refert an quis assensum suum præfert verbis, aut rebus ipsis et factis. 10 Coke, 52. It matters not whether a man gives his assent by his words or by his acts and deeds.

Non refert quid ex æquipollentibus fiat. 5 Coke, 122. It matters not which of [two] equivalents happen.

Non refert quid notum sit judici, si notum non sit in forma judicii. It matters not what is known to a judge, if it be not known in judicial form. 3 Bulst. 115. A leading maxim of modern law and practice. Best, Ev. Introd. 31, § 38.

Non refert verbis an factis fit revocatio. Cro. Car. 49. It matters not whether a revocation is made by words or deeds.

NON-RESIDENCE. Residence beyond the limits of the particular jurisdiction.

In ecclesiastical law. The absence of spiritual persons from their benefices.

NON-RESIDENT. One who is not a dweller within some jurisdiction in question; not an inhabitant of the state of the forum.

NON-RESIDENTIO PRO CLERICO REGIS. A writ, addressed to a bishop, charging him not to molest a clerk employed in the royal service, by reason of his non-residence; in which case he is to be discharged. Reg. Orig. 58.

Non respondebit minor nisi in causa dotis, et hoc pro favore doti. 4 Coke, 71. A minor shall not answer unless in a case of dower, and this in favor of dower.

NON SANÆ MENTIS. Lat. Of unsound mind. Fleta, lib. 6, c. 40, § 1.

NON-SANE. As "sane," when applied to the mind, means whole, sound, in a healthful state, "non-sane" must mean not whole, not sound, not in a healthful state; that is, broken, impaired, shattered, infirm, weak, diseased, unable, either from nature or accident, to perform the rational functions common to man upon the objects presented to it. 5 N. J. Law, 589, 661.

NON-SANE MEMORY. Unsound memory; unsound mind.

NON SEQUITUR. Lat. It does not follow.

Non solent quæ abundant vitiare scripturas. Superfluities [things which abound] do not usually vitiate writings. Dig. 50, 17, 94.

Non solum quid licet, sed quid est conveniens, est considerandum; quia nihil quod est inconveniens est licitum. Not only what is lawful, but what is proper or convenient, is to be considered; because nothing that is inconvenient is lawful. Co Litt. 66*a*.

NON SOLVENDO PECUNIAM AD QUAM CLERICUS MULCTATUR PRO NON-RESIDENTIA. A writ prohibiting an ordinary to take a pecuniary mulct imposed on a clerk of the sovereign for non-residence. Reg. Writ. 59.

NON SUBMISSIT. Lat. He did not submit. A plea to an action of debt, on a bond to perform an award, to the effect that the defendant did not submit to the arbitration.

NON SUI JURIS. Lat. Not his own master. The opposite of *sui juris*, (*q. v.*)

NON SUM INFORMATUS. Lat. I am not informed; I have not been instructed. The name of a species of judgment by default, which is entered when the defendant's attorney announces that he is not informed of any answer to be given by him; usually in pursuance of a previous arrangement between the parties.

NON-SUMMONS, WAGER OF LAW OF. The mode in which a tenant or defendant in a real action pleaded, when the summons which followed the original was not served within the proper time.

Non temere credere est nervus sapientiæ. 5 Coke, 114. Not to believe rashly is the nerve of wisdom.

NON TENENT INSIMUL. Lat. In pleading. A plea to an action in partition, by which the defendant denies that he and the plaintiff are joint tenants of the estate in question.

NON TENUIT. Lat. He did not hold. This is the name of a plea in bar in replevin, by which the plaintiff alleges that he did not hold in manner and form as averred, being given in answer to an avowry for rent in arrear. See Rosc. Real Act. 638.

NON-TENURE. A plea in a real action, by which the defendant asserts, either as to the whole or as to some part of the land mentioned in the plaintiff's declaration, that he does not hold it. Pub. St. Mass. 1882, p. 1293.

NON-TERM. The vacation between two terms of a court.

NON-TERMINUS. The vacation between term and term, formerly called the time or days of the king's peace.

NON-USER. Neglect to use. Neglect to use a franchise; neglect to exercise an office. 2 Bl. Comm. 153. Neglect or omission to use an easement or other right. 3 Kent, Comm. 448. A right acquired by use may be lost by *non-user*.

NON USURPAVIT. Lat. He has not usurped. A form of traverse, in an action or proceeding against one alleged to have usurped an office or franchise, denying the usurpation charged. See 53 Pa. St. 62.

Non valebit felonis generatio, nec ad hæreditatem paternam vel maternam; si autem ante feloniam generationem fecerit, talis generatio succedit in hæreditate patris vel matris a quo non fuerit felonia perpetrata. 3 Coke, 41. The offspring of a felon cannot succeed either to a maternal or paternal inheritance; but, if he had offspring before the felony, such offspring may succeed as to the inheritance of the father or mother by whom the felony was not committed.

NON VALENTIA AGERE. Inability to sue. 5 Bell, App. Cas. 172.

Non valet confirmatio, nisi ille, qui confirmat, sit in possessione rei vel juris unde fieri debet confirmatio; et eodem modo, nisi ille cui confirmatio fit sit in possessione. Co. Litt. 295. Confirmation is not valid unless he who confirms is either in possession of the thing itself or of the right of which confirmation is to be made, and, in like manner, unless he to whom confirmation is made is in possession.

Non valet exceptio ejusdem rei cujus petitur dissolutio. A plea of the same matter the dissolution of which is sought, is not valid. Called a "maxim of law and common sense." 2 Eden, 134.

Non valet impedimentum quod de jure non sortitur effectum. 4 Coke, 31*a*. An impediment which does not derive its effect from law is of no force.

Non verbis, sed ipsis rebus, leges imponimus. Cod. 6, 43, 2. We impose laws, not upon words, but upon things themselves.

Non videntur qui errant consentire. They are not considered to consent who commit a mistake. Dig. 50, 17, 116, § 2; Broom, Max. 262.

Non videtur consensum retinuisse si quis ex præscripto minantis aliquid immutavit. He does not appear to have retained consent, who has changed anything through menaces. Broom, Max. 278.

Non videtur perfecte cujusque id esse, quod ex casu auferri potest. That does not seem to be completely one's own which can be taken from him on occasion. Dig. 50, 17, 139, 1.

Non videtur quisquam id capere quod ei necesse est alii restitutere. Dig. 50, 17, 51. No one is considered entitled to recover that which he must give up to another.

Non videtur vim facere, qui jure suo utitur et ordinaria actione experitur. He is not deemed to use force who exercises his own right, and proceeds by ordinary action. Dig. 50, 17, 155, 1.

NONÆ ET DECIMÆ. Payments made to the church, by those who were tenants of church-farms. The first was a rent or duty for things belonging to husbandry; the second was claimed in right of the church. Wharton.

NONAGIUM, or NONAGE. A ninth part of movables which was paid to the clergy on the death of persons in their parish, and claimed on pretense of being distributed to pious uses. Blount.

NONES. In the Roman calendar. The fifth and, in March, May, July, and October, the seventh day of the month. So called because, counting inclusively, they were *nine* days from the ides. Adams, Rom. Ant. 355, 357.

NONFEASANCE. The neglect or failure of a person to do some act which he ought to do. The term is not generally used to denote a breach of contract, but rather the failure to perform a duty towards the public whereby some individual sustains special damage, as where a sheriff fails to execute a writ. Sweet.

NONNA. In old ecclesiastical law. A nun. *Nonnus,* a monk. Spelman.

NONSENSE. Unintelligible matter in a written agreement or will.

NONSUIT. Not following up the cause; failure on the part of a plaintiff to continue the prosecution of his suit. An abandonment or renunciation of his suit, by a plaintiff, either by omitting to take the next necessary steps, or voluntarily relinquishing the action, or pursuant to an order of the court. An order or judgment, granted upon the trial of a cause, that the plaintiff has abandoned, or shall abandon, the further prosecution of his suit.

A *voluntary* nonsuit is one incurred by the plaintiff's own act or omission, and is a judgment entered against him as a consequence of his abandoning or not following up his cause, or being absent when his presence is required.

An *involuntary* nonsuit is a judgment entered against the plaintiff by direction of the court when, upon trial, he has not adduced any evidence on which the jury could find a verdict under the rules of law.

NOOK OF LAND. Twelve acres and a half.

NORMAL. Opposed to exceptional; that state wherein any body most exactly comports in all its parts with the abstract idea thereof, and is most exactly fitted to perform its proper functions, is entitled "normal."

NORMAL LAW. A term employed by modern writers on jurisprudence to denote the law as it affects persons who are in a normal condition; *i. e., sui juris* and sound in mind.

NORMAN FRENCH. The tongue in which several formal proceedings of state are still carried on. The language, having remained the same since the date of the Conquest, at which it was introduced into England, is very different from the French of this day, retaining all the peculiarities which at that time distinguished every province from the rest. A peculiar mode of pronunciation (considered authentic) is handed down and preserved by the officials who have, on particular occasions, to speak the tongue. Norman French was the language of our legal procedure till the 36 Edw. III. Wharton.

NORROY. In English law. The title of the third of the three kings-at-arms, or provincial heralds.

NORTHAMPTON TABLES. Longevity and annuity tables compiled from bills of mortality kept in All Saints parish, England, in 1735–1780.

Noscitur a sociis. It is known from its associates. 1 Vent. 225. The meaning of a word is or may be known from the accompanying words. 3 Term R. 87; Broom, Max. 588.

Noscitur ex socio, qui non cognoscitur ex se. Moore, 817. He who cannot be known from himself may be known from his associate.

NOSOCOMI. In the civil law. Persons who have the management and care of hospitals for paupers.

NOT FOUND. These words, indorsed on a bill of indictment by a grand jury, have the same effect as the indorsement "Not a true bill" or "*Ignoramus.*"

NOT GUILTY. A plea of the general issue in the actions of trespass and case and in criminal prosecutions.

The form of the verdict in criminal cases, where the jury acquit the prisoner. 4 Bl. Comm. 361.

NOT GUILTY BY STATUTE. In English practice. A plea of the general issue by a defendant in a civil action, when he intends to give special matter in evidence by virtue of some act or acts of parliament, in which case he must add the reference to such act or acts, and state whether such acts are public or otherwise. But, if a defendant so plead, he will not be allowed to plead any other defense, without the leave of the court or a judge. Mozley & Whitley.

NOT POSSESSED. A special traverse used in an action of trover, alleging that defendant was not possessed, at the time of action brought, of the chattels alleged to have been converted by him.

NOT PROVEN. A verdict in a Scotch criminal trial, to the effect that the guilt of the accused is not made out, though his innocence is not clear.

NOTA. In the civil law. A mark or brand put upon a person by the law. Mackeld. Rom. Law, § 135.

NOTÆ. In civil and old European law. Short-hand characters or marks of contraction, in which the emperors' secretaries took down what they dictated. Spelman; Calvin.

NOTARIAL. Taken by a notary.

NOTARIUS. Lat. In Roman law. A draughtsman; an amanuensis; a short-hand writer; one who took notes of the proceedings in the senate or a court, or of what was dictated to him by another; one who prepared draughts of wills, conveyances, etc.

In old English law. A scribe or scrivener who made short draughts of writings and other instruments; a notary. Cowell.

NOTARY PUBLIC. A public officer whose function is to attest and certify, by his hand and official seal, certain classes of documents, in order to give them credit and authenticity in foreign jurisdictions; to take acknowledgments of deeds and other conveyances, and certify the same; and to perform certain official acts, chiefly in commercial matters, such as the protesting of notes and bills, the noting of foreign drafts, and marine protests in cases of loss or damage.

NOTATION. In English probate practice, notation is the act of making a memorandum of some special circumstance on a probate or letters of administration. Thus, where a grant is made for the whole personal estate of the deceased within the United Kingdom, which can only be done in the case of a person dying domiciled in England, the fact of his having been so domiciled is noted on the grant. Coote, Prob. Pr. 36; Sweet.

NOTE, *v.* To make a brief written statement; to enter a memorandum; as to note an exception.

NOTE, *n.* An abstract, a memorandum; an informal statement in writing. Also a negotiable promissory note. See BOUGHT NOTE; NOTES; JUDGMENT NOTE; PROMISSORY NOTE; SOLD NOTE.

NOTE A BILL. When a foreign bill has been dishonored, it is usual for a notary public to present it again on the same day, and, if it be not then paid, to make a minute, consisting of his initials, the day, month, and year, and reason, if assigned, of non-payment. The making of this minute is called "noting the bill." Wharton.

NOTE OF A FINE. In old conveyancing. One of the parts of a fine of lands, being an abstract of the writ of covenant, and the concord; naming the parties, the parcels of land, and the agreement. 2 Bl. Comm. 351.

NOTE OF ALLOWANCE. In English practice. This was a note delivered by a master to a party to a cause, who alleged that there was error in law in the record and proceedings, allowing him to bring error.

NOTE OF HAND. A popular name for a promissory note.

NOTE OF PROTEST. A memorandum of the fact of protest, indorsed by the notary upon the bill, at the time, to be afterwards written out at length.

NOTE OR MEMORANDUM. The statute of frauds requires a "note or memorandum" of the particular transaction to be made in writing and signed, etc. By this is generally understood an informal minute or memorandum made on the spot. See 14 Johns. 492.

NOTES. In practice. Memoranda made by a judge on a trial, as to the evidence adduced, and the points reserved, etc. A copy of the judge's notes may be obtained from his clerk.

NOTHUS. Lat. In Roman law. A natural child or a person of spurious birth.

NOTICE. Knowledge; information; the result of observation, whether by the senses or the mind; knowledge of the existence of a fact or state of affairs; the means of knowledge. Used in this sense in such phrases as "A. had notice of the conversion," "a purchaser without notice of fraud," etc.

Notice is either (1) statutory, *i. e.*, made so by legislative enactment; (2) actual, which brings the knowledge of a fact directly home to the party; or (3) constructive or implied, which is no more than evidence of facts which raise such a strong presumption of notice that equity will not allow the presumption to be rebutted. Constructive notice may be subdivided into: (a) Where there exists actual notice of matter, to which equity has added constructive notice of facts, which an inquiry after such matter would have elicited; and (b) where there has been a designed abstinence from inquiry for the very purpose of escaping notice. Wharton.

Notice is actual when it is directly and personally given to the party to be notified; and constructive when the party, by circumstances, is put upon inquiry, and must be presumed to have had notice, or, by judgment of law, is held to have had notice. 14 Ga. 145.

Every person who has actual notice of circumstances sufficient to put a prudent man upon inquiry as to a particular fact has constructive notice of the fact itself in all cases in which, by prosecuting such inquiry, he might have learned such fact. Civil Code Cal. § 19.

Actual notice consists in express information of a fact. Constructive notice is notice imputed by the law to a person not having actual notice; and every person who has actual notice of circumstances sufficient to put a prudent man upon inquiry as to a particular fact, and who omits to make such inquiry with reasonable diligence, is deemed to have constructive notice of the fact itself. 1 Dak. T. 399, 400, 46 N. W. Rep. 1134.

In another sense, "notice" means information of an act *to be done* or *required to be* done; as of a motion to be made, a trial to be had, a plea or answer to be put in, costs to be taxed, etc.

In this sense, "notice" means an advice, or written warning, in more or less formal shape, intended to apprise a person of some proceeding in which his interests are involved, or informing him of some fact which it is his right to know and the duty of the notifying party to communicate.

NOTICE, AVERMENT OF. In pleading. The allegation in a pleading that notice has been given.

NOTICE IN LIEU OF SERVICE. In lieu of personally serving a writ of summons (or other legal process,) in English practice, the court occasionally allows the plaintiff (or other party) to give notice in lieu of service, such notice being such as will in all probability reach the party. This notice is peculiarly appropriate in the case of a foreigner out of the jurisdiction, whom it is desired to serve with a writ of summons. Sweet.

NOTICE OF ACTION. When it is intended to sue certain particular individuals, as in the case of actions against justices of the peace, it is necessary in some jurisdictions to give them notice of the action some time before.

NOTICE OF APPEARANCE. A notice given by defendant to a plaintiff that he appears in the action in person or by attorney.

NOTICE OF DISHONOR. When a negotiable bill or note is dishonored by non-acceptance on presentment for acceptance, or by non-payment at its maturity, it is the duty of the holder to give immediate notice of such dishonor to the drawer, if it be a bill, and to the indorser, whether it be a bill or note. 2 Daniel, Neg. Inst. § 970.

NOTICE OF JUDGMENT. It is required by statute in several of the states that the party for whom the verdict in an action has been given shall serve upon the other party or his attorney a written notice of the time when judgment is entered. The time allowed for taking an appeal runs from such notice.

NOTICE OF LIS PENDENS. A notice filed for the purpose of warning all persons that the title to certain property is in litigation, and that, if they purchase the defendant's claim to the same, they are in danger of being bound by an adverse judgment.

NOTICE OF MOTION. A notice in writing, entitled in a cause, stating that, on a certain day designated, a motion will be made to the court for the purpose or object stated.

NOTICE OF PROTEST. A notice given by the holder of a bill or note to the drawer or indorser that the bill has been protested for refusal of payment or acceptance.

NOTICE OF TRIAL. A notice given by one of the parties in an action to the other, after an issue has been reached, that he intends to bring the cause forward for trial at the next term of the court.

NOTICE TO ADMIT. In the practice of the English high court, either party to an action may call on the other party by notice to admit the existence and execution of any document, in order to save the expense of proving it at the trial; and the party refusing to admit must bear the costs of proving it unless the judge certifies that the refusal to admit was reasonable. No costs of proving a document will in general be allowed, unless such a notice is given. Rules of Court, xxxii. 2; Sweet.

NOTICE TO PLEAD. This is a notice which, in the practice of some states, is prerequisite to the taking judgment by default. It proceeds from the plaintiff, and warns the defendant that he must plead to the declaration or complaint within a prescribed time.

NOTICE TO PRODUCE. In practice. A notice in writing, given in an action at law, requiring the opposite party to produce a certain described paper or document at the trial. Chit. Archb. Pr. 230; 3 Chit. Gen. Pr. 834.

NOTICE TO QUIT. A written notice given by a landlord to his tenant, stating that the former desires to repossess himself of the demised premises, and that the latter is required to quit and remove from the same at a time designated, either at the expiration of the term, if the tenant is in under a lease, or immediately, if the tenancy is at will or by sufferance. The term is also sometimes applied to a written notice given by the tenant to the landlord, to the effect that he intends to quit the demised premises and deliver possession of the same on a day named.

NOTIFY. In legal proceedings, and in respect to public matters, this word is generally, if not universally, used as importing a notice *given* by some person, whose duty it was to give it, in some manner prescribed, and to some person entitled to receive it, or be notified. 31 Conn. 384.

NOTING. As soon as a notary has made presentment and demand of a bill of exchange, or at some seasonable hour of the same day, he makes a minute on the bill, or on a ticket attached thereto, or in his book of registry, consisting of his initials, the month, day, and year, the refusal of acceptance or payment, the reason, if any, assigned for such refusal, and his charges of protest. This is the preliminary step towards the protest, and is called "noting." 2 Daniel, Neg. Inst. § 939.

NOTIO. Lat. In the civil law. The power of hearing and trying a matter of fact; the power or authority of a *judex;* the power of hearing causes and of pronouncing sentence, without any degree of jurisdiction. Calvin.

NOTITIA. Knowledge; information; intelligence; notice.

Notitia dicitur a noscendo; et notitia non debet claudicare. Notice is named from a knowledge being had; and notice ought not to halt, [*i. e.*, be imperfect.] 6 Coke, 29.

NOTORIAL. The Scotch form of "notarial," (*q. v.*) Bell.

NOTORIETY. The state of being notorious or universally well known.

NOTORIOUS. In the law of evidence, matters deemed notorious do not require to be proved. There does not seem to be any recognized rule as to what matters are deemed notorious. Cases have occurred in which the state of society or public feeling has been treated as notorious; *e. g.*, during times of sedition. Best, Ev. 354; Sweet.

NOTOUR. In Scotch law. Open; notorious. A *notour* bankrupt is a debtor who, being under diligence by horning and caption of his creditor, retires to sanctuary or absconds or defends by force, and is afterwards found insolvent by the court of session. Bell.

Nova constitutio futuris formam imponere debet non præteritis. A new state of the law ought to affect the future, not the past. 2 Inst. 292; Broom, Max. 34, 37.

NOVA CUSTUMA. The name of an imposition or duty. See ANTIQUA CUSTUMA.

NOVA STATUTA. New statutes. An appellation sometimes given to the statutes which have been passed since the beginning of the reign of Edward III. 1 Steph. Comm. 68.

NOVÆ NARRATIONES. New counts. The collection called "*Novæ Narrationes*" contains pleadings in actions during the reign of Edward III. It consists principally of declarations, as the title imports; but there are sometimes pleas and subsequent pleadings. The *Articuli ad Novas Narrationes* is usually subjoined to this little book, and is a small treatise on the method of pleading. It first treats of actions and courts, and then goes through each particular writ, and the declaration upon it, accompanied with directions, and illustrated by precedents. 3 Reeves, Eng. Law, 152; Wharton.

NOVALE. Land newly plowed and converted into tillage, and which has not been tilled before within the memory of man; also fallow land.

NOVALIS. In the civil law. Land that rested a year after the first plowing. Dig. 50, 16, 30, 2.

Novatio non præsumitur. Novation is not presumed. Halk. Lat. Max. 109.

NOVATION. Novation is the substitution of a new debt or obligation for an existing one. Civil Code Cal. § 1530; Civil Code Dak. § 863.

Novation is a contract, consisting of two stipulations,—one to extinguish an existing obligation; the other to substitute a new one in its place. Civil Code La. art. 2185.

The term was originally a technical term of the civil law, but is now in very general use in English and American jurisprudence.

In the civil law, there are three kinds of novation: (1) Where the debtor and creditor remain the same, but a new debt takes the place of the old one; (2) where the debt remains the same, but a new debtor is substituted; (3) Where the debt and debtor remain, but a new creditor is substituted. 48 Miss. 451.

NOVEL ASSIGNMENT. See NEW ASSIGNMENT.

NOVEL DISSEISIN. See ASSISE OF NOVEL DISSEISIN.

NOVELLÆ, (or NOVELLÆ CONSTITUTIONES.) New constitutions; generally translated in English, "Novels." The Latin name of those constitutions which were issued by Justinian after the publication of his Code; most of them being originally written in Greek. After his death, a collection of 168 Novels was made, 154 of which had been issued by Justinian, and the rest by his successors. These were afterwards included in the *Corpus Juris Civilis*, (*q. v.*,) and now constitute one of its four principal divisions. Mackeld. Rom. Law, § 80; 1 Kent, Comm. 541.

NOVELLÆ LEONIS. The ordinances of the Emperor Leo, which were made from the year 887 till the year 893, are so called. These Novels changed many rules of the Justinian law. This collection contains 113 Novels, written originally in Greek, and afterwards, in 1560, translated into Latin by Agilæus. Mackeld. Rom. Law, § 84.

NOVELS. The title given in English to the New Constitutions (*Novellæ Constitutiones*) of Justinian and his successors, now forming a part of the *Corpus Juris Civilis*. See NOVELLÆ.

NOVELTY. An objection to a patent or claim for a patent on the ground that the invention is not new or original is called an objection "for want of novelty."

NOVERCA. Lat. In the civil law. A step-mother.

NOVERINT UNIVERSI PER PRÆSENTES. Know all men by these presents. Formal words used at the commencement of deeds of release in the Latin forms.

NOVI OPERIS NUNCIATIO. Lat. Denunciation of, or protest against, a new work. This was a species of remedy in the civil law, available to a person who thought his rights or his property were threatened with injury by the act of his neighbor in erecting or demolishing any structure, (which was called a "new work.") In such case, he might go upon the ground, while the work was in progress, and publicly protest against or forbid its completion, in the presence of the workmen or of the owner or his representative.

NOVIGILD. In Saxon law. A pecuniary satisfaction for an injury, amounting to nine times the value of the thing for which it was paid. Spelman.

NOVISSIMA RECOPILACION. (Latest Compilation.) The title of a collection of Spanish law compiled by order of Don Carlos IV. in 1805. 1 White, Recop. 355.

NOVITAS. Lat. Novelty; newness; a new thing.

Novitas non tam utilitate prodest quam novitate perturbat. A novelty does not benefit so much by its utility as it disturbs by its novelty. Jenk. Cent. p. 167, case 23.

NOVITER PERVENTA, or NOVITER AD NOTITIAM PERVENTA. In ecclesiastical procedure. Facts "newly come" to the knowledge of a party to a cause. Leave to plead facts *noviter perventa* is generally given, in a proper case, even after the pleadings are closed. Phillim. Ecc. Law, 1257; Rog. Ecc. Law, 723.

NOVODAMUS. In old Scotch law. (We give anew.) The name given to a charter, or clause in a charter, granting a renewal of a right. Bell.

Novum judicium non dat novum jus, sed declarat antiquum; quia judicium est juris dictum et per judicium jus est noviter revelatum quod diu fuit velatum. A new adjudication does not make a new law, but declares the old; because adjudication is the utterance of the law, and by adjudication the law is newly revealed which was for a long time hidden. 10 Coke, 42.

NOVUM OPUS. In the civil law. A new work. See NOVI OPERIS NUNCIATIO.

NOVUS HOMO. Lat. A new man. This term is applied to a man who has been pardoned of a crime, and so made, as it were, a "new man."

NOXA. Lat. In the civil law. This term denoted any damage or injury done to persons or property by an unlawful act committed by a man's slave or animal. An action for damages lay against the master or owner, who, however, might escape further responsibility by delivering up the offending agent to the party injured. "*Noxa*" was also used as the designation of the offense committed, and of its punishment, and sometimes of the slave or animal doing the damage.

Noxa sequitur caput. The injury [*i. e.*, liability to make good an injury caused by a slave] follows the head or person, [*i. e.*, attaches to his master.] Heinecc. Elem. l. 4, t. 8, § 1231.

NOXAL ACTION. An action for damage done by slaves or irrational animals. Sandars, Just. Inst. (5th Ed.) 457.

NOXALIS ACTIO. Lat. In the civil law. An action which lay against the master of a slave, for some offense (as theft or robbery) committed or damage or injury done by the slave, which was called "*noxa*." Usually translated "noxal action."

NOXIA. Lat. In the civil law. An offense committed or damage done by a slave. Inst. 4, 8, 1.

NOXIOUS. Hurtful; offensive; offensive to the smell. 1 Burrows, 337. The word "noxious" includes the complex idea both of insalubrity and offensiveness. Id.

NUBILIS. In the civil law. Marriageable; one who is of a proper age to be married.

NUCES COLLIGERE. To collect nuts. This was formerly one of the works or services imposed by lords upon their inferior tenants. Paroch. Antiq. 495.

Nuda pactio obligationem non parit. A naked agreement [*i. e.*, without consideration] does not beget an obligation. Dig. 2, 14, 7, 4; Broom, Max. 746.

NUDA PATIENTIA. Lat. Mere sufferance.

NUDA POSSESSIO. Lat. Bare or mere possession.

Nuda ratio et nuda pactio non ligant aliquem debitorem. Naked reason and naked promise do not bind any debtor. Fleta, l. 2, c. 60, § 25.

NUDE. Naked. This word is applied metaphorically to a variety of subjects to indicate that they are lacking in some essential legal requisite.

NUDE CONTRACT. One made without any consideration; upon which no action will lie, in conformity with the maxim "*ex nudo pacto non oritur actio.*" 2 Bl. Comm. 445.

NUDE MATTER. A bare allegation of a thing done, unsupported by evidence.

NUDUM PACTUM. Lat. A naked pact; a bare agreement; a promise or undertaking made without any consideration for it.

Nudum pactum est ubi nulla subest causa præter conventionem; sed ubi subest causa, fit obligatio, et parit actionem. A naked contract is where there is no consideration except the agreement; but, where there is a consideration, it becomes an obligation and gives a right of action. Plowd. 309; Broom, Max. 745, 750.

Nudum pactum ex quo non oritur actio. *Nudum pactum* is that upon which no action arises. Cod. 2, 3, 10; Id. 5, 14, 1; Broom, Max. 676.

NUEVA RECOPILACION. (New Compilation.) The title of a code of Spanish law, promulgated in the year 1567. Schm. Civil Law, Introd. 79–81.

NUGATORY. Futile; ineffectual; invalid; destitute of constraining force or vitality. A legislative act may be "nugatory" because unconstitutional.

NUISANCE. Anything that unlawfully worketh hurt, inconvenience, or damage. 3 Bl. Comm. 216.

That class of wrongs that arise from the unreasonable, unwarrantable, or unlawful use by a person of his own property, either real or personal, or from his own improper, indecent, or unlawful personal conduct, working an obstruction of or injury to the right of another or of the public, and producing such material annoyance, inconvenience, discomfort, or hurt that the law will presume a consequent damage. Wood, Nuis. § 1.

Anything which is injurious to health, or is indecent or offensive to the senses, or an obstruction to the free use of property, so as to interfere with the comfortable enjoyment of life or property, or unlawfully obstructs the free passage or use, in the customary manner, of any navigable lake or river, bay, stream, canal, or basin, or any public park, square, street, or highway, is a nuisance. Civil Code Cal. § 3479.

Nuisances are either *public* or *private*. A public nuisance is one which damages all persons who come within the sphere of its operation, though it may vary in its effects on individuals. A private nuisance is one limited in its injurious effects to one or few individuals. Generally, a public nuisance gives no right of action to any individual, but must be abated by a process instituted in the name of the state. A private nuisance gives a right of action to the person injured. Code Ga. 1882, § 2997.

A *public* nuisance is one which affects at the same time an entire community or neighborhood, or any considerable number of persons, although the extent of the annoyance or damage inflicted upon individuals may be unequal. Civil Code Cal. § 3480.

A *private* nuisance is anything done to the hurt or annoyance of the lands, tenements, or hereditaments of another. It produces damage to but one or a few persons, and cannot be said to be public. 3 Bl. Comm. 216; 80 N. Y. 582.

A *mixed* nuisance is one which, while producing injury to the public at large, does some special damage to some individual or class of individuals. Wood, Nuis. § 16.

NUISANCE, ASSISE OF. In old practice. A judicial writ directed to the sheriff of the county in which a nuisance existed, in which it was stated that the party injured complained of some particular fact done *ad nocumentum liberi tenementi sui*, (to the nuisance of his freehold,) and commanding the sheriff to summon an assize (that is, a jury) to view the premises, and have them at the next commission of assizes, that justice might be done, etc. 3 Bl. Comm. 221.

NUL. No; none. A law French negative particle, commencing many phrases.

NUL AGARD. No award. The name of a plea in an action on an arbitration bond, by which the defendant traverses the making of any legal award

Nul charter, nul vente, ne nul done vault perpetualment, si le donor n'est seise al temps de contracts de deux droits, sc. del droit de possession et del droit de propertie. Co. Litt. 266. No grant, no sale, no gift, is valid forever, unless the donor, at the time of the contract, is seised of two rights, namely, the right of possession, and the right of property.

NUL DISSEISIN. In pleading. No disseisin. A plea of the general issue in a real action, by which the defendant denies that there was any disseisin.

Nul ne doit s'enrichir aux depens des autres. No one ought to enrich himself at the expense of others.

Nul prendra advantage de son tort demesne. No one shall take advantage of his own wrong. 2 Inst. 713; Broom, Max. 290.

Nul sans damage avera error ou attaint. Jenk. Cent. 323. No one shall have error or attaint unless he has sustained damage.

NUL TIEL CORPORATION. No such corporation [exists.] The form of a plea denying the existence of an alleged corporation.

NUL TIEL RECORD. No such record. A plea denying the existence of any such record as that alleged by the plaintiff. It is the general plea in an action of debt on a judgment.

NUL TORT. In pleading. A plea of the general issue to a real action, by which the defendant denies that he committed any wrong.

NUL WASTE. No waste. The name of a plea in an action of waste, denying the committing of waste, and forming the general issue.

NULL. Naught; of no validity or effect. Usually coupled with the word "void;" as "null and void."

NULLA BONA. Lat. No goods. The name of the return made by the sheriff to a writ of execution, when he has not found any goods of the defendant within his jurisdiction on which he could levy.

Nulla curia quæ recordum non habet potest imponere finem neque aliquem mandare carceri; quia ista spectant tantummodo ad curias de recordo. 8 Coke, 60. No court which has not a record can impose a fine or commit any person to prison; because those powers belong only to courts of record.

Nulla emptio sine pretio esse potest. There can be no sale without a price. 4 Pick. 189.

Nulla impossibilia aut inhonesta sunt præsumenda; vera autem et honesta et possibilia. No things that are impossible or dishonorable are to be presumed; but things that are true and honorable and possible. Co. Litt. 78*b*.

Nulla pactione effici potest ut dolus præstetur. By no agreement can it be effected that a fraud shall be practiced. Fraud will not be upheld, though it may seem to be authorized by express agreement. 5 Maule & S. 466; Broom, Max. 696.

Nulla virtus, nulla scientia, locum suum et dignitatem conservare potest sine modestia. Co. Litt. 394. Without modesty, no virtue, no knowledge, can preserve its place and dignity.

Nulle terre sans seigneur. No land without a lord. A maxim of feudal law. Guyot, Inst. Feod. c. 28.

Nulli enim res sua servit jure servitutis. No one can have a servitude over his own property. Dig. 8, 2, 26; 17 Mass. 443; 2 Bouv. Inst. no. 1600.

NULLITY. Nothing; no proceeding; an act or proceeding in a cause which the opposite party may treat as though it had not taken place, or which has absolutely no legal force or effect.

NULLITY OF MARRIAGE. The entire invalidity of a supposed, pretended, or attempted marriage, by reason of relationship or incapacity of the parties or other diriment impediments. An action seeking a decree declaring such an assumed marriage to be null and void is called a suit of "nullity of marriage." It differs from an action for divorce, because the latter supposes the existence of a valid and lawful marriage. See 2 Bish. Mar. & Div. §§ 289-294.

NULLIUS FILIUS. The son of nobody; a bastard.

Nullius hominis auctoritas apud nos valere debet, ut meliora non sequeremur si quis attulerit. The authority of no man ought to prevail with us, so far as to prevent our following better [opinions] if any one should present them. Co. Litt. 383*b*.

NULLIUS IN BONIS. Among the property of no person.

NULLIUS JURIS. In old English law. Of no legal force. Fleta, lib. 2, c. 60, § 24.

NULLUM ARBITRIUM. L. Lat. No award. The name of a plea in an action on an arbitration bond, for not fulfilling the award, by which the defendant traverses the allegation that there was an award made.

Nullum crimen majus est inobedientia. No crime is greater than disobedience. Jenk. Cent. p. 77, case 48. Applied to the refusal of an officer to return a writ.

Nullum exemplum est idem omnibus. No example is the same for all purposes. Co. Litt. 212*a*. No one precedent is adapted to all cases. A maxim in conveyancing.

NULLUM FECERUNT ARBITRIUM. L. Lat. In pleading. The name of a plea to an action of debt upon an obligation for the performance of an award, by which the defendant denies that he submitted to arbitration, etc. Bac. Abr. "*Arbitr.*" etc., G.

Nullum iniquum est præsumendum in jure. 7 Coke, 71. No iniquity is to be presumed in law.

Nullum matrimonium, ibi nulla dos. No marriage, no dower. 4 Barb. 192, 194.

Nullum simile est idem nisi quatuor pedibus currit. Co. Litt. 3. No like is identical, unless it run on all fours.

Nullum simile quatuor pedibus currit. No simile runs upon four feet, (or *all fours*, as it is otherwise expressed.) No simile holds in everything. Co. Litt. 3*a*; 2 Story, 143.

NULLUM TEMPUS ACT. In English law. A name given to the statute 3 Geo. III. c. 16, because that act, in contravention of the maxim "*Nullum tempus occurrit regi*," (no lapse of time bars the king,) limited the crown's right to sue, etc., to the period of sixty years.

Nullum tempus aut locus occurrit regi. No time or place affects the king. 2 Inst. 273; Jenk. Cent. 83; Broom, Max. 65.

Nullum tempus occurrit reipublicæ. No time runs [time does not run] against the commonwealth or state. 11 Grat. 572.

Nullus alius quam rex possit episcopo demandare inquisitionem faciendam. Co. Litt. 134. No other than the king can command the bishop to make an inquisition.

Nullus commodum capere potest de injuria sua propria. No one can obtain an advantage by his own wrong. Co. Litt. 148; Broom, Max. 279.

Nullus debet agere de dolo, ubi alia actio subest. Where another form of action is given, no one ought to sue in the action *de dolo*. 7 Coke, 92.

Nullus dicitur accessorius post feloniam, sed ille qui novit principalem feloniam fecisse, et illum receptavit et

comfortavit. 3 Inst. 138. No one is called an "accessary" after the fact but he who knew the principal to have committed a felony, and received and comforted him.

Nullus dicitur felo principalis nisi actor, aut qui præsens est, abettans aut auxilians ad feloniam faciendam. No one is called a "principal felon" except the party actually committing the felony, or the party present aiding and abetting in its commission.

Nullus idoneus testis in re sua intelligitur. No person is understood to be a competent witness in his own cause. Dig. 22, 5, 10.

Nullus jus alienum forisfacere potest. No man can forfeit another's right. Fleta, lib. 1, c. 28, § 11.

Nullus recedat e curia cancellaria sine remedio. No person should depart from the court of chancery without a remedy. 4 Hen. VII. 4; Branch, Princ.

Nullus simile est idem, nisi quatuor pedibus currit. No like is exactly identical unless it runs on all fours.

Nullus videtur dolo facere qui suo jure utitur. No one is considered to act with guile who uses his own right. Dig. 50, 17, 55; Broom, Max. 130.

NUMERATA PECUNIA. In the civil law Money told or counted; money paid by tale. Inst. 3, 24, 2; Bract. fol. 35.

NUMMATA. The price of anything in money, as *denariata* is the price of a thing by computation of pence, and *librata* of pounds.

NUMMATA TERRÆ. An acre of land. Spelman.

NUNC PRO TUNC. Lat. Now for then. A phrase applied to acts allowed to be done after the time when they should be done, with a retroactive effect, *i. e.*, with the same effect as if regularly done.

NUNCIATIO. In the civil law. A solemn declaration, usually in prohibition of a thing; a protest.

NUNCIO. The permanent official representative of the pope at a foreign court or seat of government. Webster. They are called "ordinary" or "extraordinary," according as they are sent for general purposes or on a special mission.

NUNCIUS. In international law. A messenger; a minister; the pope's legate, commonly called a "nuncio."

NUNCUPARE. Lat. In the civil law. To name; to pronounce orally or in words without writing.

NUNCUPATE. To declare publicly and solemnly.

NUNCUPATIVE WILL. A will which depends merely upon oral evidence, having been declared or dictated by the testator in his last sickness before a sufficient number of witnesses, and afterwards reduced to writing.

NUNDINÆ. Lat. In the civil and old English law. A fair. *In nundinis et mercatis*, in fairs and markets. Bract. fol. 56.

NUNDINATION. Traffic at fairs and markets; any buying and selling.

Nunquam crescit ex postfacto præteriti delicti æstimatio. The character of a past offense is never aggravated by a subsequent act or matter. Dig. 50, 17, 139, 1; Bac. Max. p. 38, reg. 8; Broom, Max. 42.

Nunquam decurritur ad extraordinarium sed ubi deficit ordinarium. We are never to resort to what is extraordinary, but [until] what is ordinary fails. 4 Inst. 84.

Nunquam fictio sine lege. There is no fiction without law.

NUNQUAM INDEBITATUS. Lat. Never indebted. The name of a plea in an action of *indebitatus assumpsit*, by which the defendant alleges that he is not indebted to the plaintiff.

Nunquam nimis dicitur quod nunquam satis dicitur. What is never sufficiently said is never said too much. Co. Litt. 375.

Nunquam præscribitur in falso. There is never a prescription in case of falsehood or forgery. A maxim in Scotch law. Bell.

Nunquam res humanæ prospere succedunt ubi negliguntur divinæ. Co. Litt. 15. Human things never prosper where divine things are neglected.

NUNTIUS. In old English practice. A messenger. One who was sent to make an excuse for a party summoned, or one who explained as for a friend the reason of a party's absence. Bract. fol. 345. An officer of a court; a summoner, apparitor, or beadle. Cowell.

NUPER OBIIT. Lat. In practice. The name of a writ (now abolished) which, in the English law, lay for a sister co-heiress dispossessed by her coparcener of lands and tenements whereof their father, brother, or any common ancestor died seised of an estate in fee-simple. Fitzh. Nat. Brev. 197.

NUPTIÆ SECUNDÆ. Lat. A second marriage. In the canon law, this term included any marriage subsequent to the first.

NUPTIAL. Pertaining to marriage; constituting marriage; used or done in marriage.

Nuptias non concubitus sed consensus facit. Co. Litt. 33. Not cohabitation but consent makes the marriage.

NURTURE. The act of taking care of children, bringing them up, and educating them.

NURUS. Lat. In the civil law. A son's wife; a daughter-in-law. Calvin.

NYCTHEMERON. The whole natural day, or day and night, consisting of twenty-four hours. Enc. Lond.

O.

O. C. An abbreviation, in the civil law, for "*ope consilio*," (*q. v.*) In American law, these letters are used as an abbreviation for "Orphans' Court."

O. N. B. An abbreviation for "Old Natura Brevium." See NATURA BREVIUM.

O. Ni. It was the course of the English exchequer, as soon as the sheriff entered into and made up his account for issues, amerciaments, etc., to mark upon each head "*O. Ni.*," which denoted *oneratur, nisi habeat sufficientem exonerationem*, and presently he became the king's debtor, and a *debet* was set upon his head; whereupon the parties *paravaile* became debtors to the sheriff, and were discharged against the king, etc. 4 Inst. 116; Wharton.

O. S. An abbreviation for "Old Style," or "Old Series."

OATH. An external pledge or asseveration, made in verification of statements made or to be made, coupled with an appeal to a sacred or venerated object, in evidence of the serious and reverent state of mind of the party, or with an invocation to a supreme being to witness the words of the party and to visit him with punishment if they be false.

A religious asseveration, by which a person renounces the mercy and imprecates the vengeance of heaven, if he do not speak the truth 1 Leach, 430.

The calling upon God to witness that what is said by the person sworn is true, and invoking the divine vengeance upon his head, if what he says is false. 10 Ohio, 123.

Oaths are either *judicial* or *extrajudicial;* the former, when taken in some judicial proceeding or in relation to some matter connected with judicial proceedings; the latter, when not taken in any judicial proceeding, or without any authority of law, though taken formally before a proper person.

An *official* oath is one taken by an officer when he assumes charge of his office, whereby he declares that he will faithfully discharge the duties of the same, or whatever else may be required by statute in the particular case.

An *assertory* oath is one required by law other than in judicial proceedings and upon induction to office; such, for example, as an oath to be made at the custom-house relative to goods imported.

A *corporal* oath is one taken by the form of laying the hand on or kissing a copy of the gospels.

The terms "corporal oath" and "solemn oath" are synonymous; and an oath taken with the uplifted hand is properly described by either term in an indictment for perjury. 1 Ind. 184.

OATH AGAINST BRIBERY. One which could have have administered to a voter at an election for members of parliament. Abolished in 1854. Wharton.

OATH DECISORY. In the civil law. An oath which one of the parties defers or refers back to the other for the decision of the cause.

OATH EX OFFICIO. The oath by which a clergyman charged with a criminal offense was formerly allowed to swear himself to be innocent; also the oath by which the compurgators swore that they believed in his innocence. 3 Bl. Comm. 101, 447; Mozley & Whitley.

OATH IN LITEM. In the civil law. An oath permitted to be taken by the plaintiff, for the purpose of proving the value of the subject-matter in controversy, when there was no other evidence on that point, or when the defendant fraudulently suppressed evidence which might have been available.

OATH OF CALUMNY. In the civil law. An oath which a plaintiff was obliged to take that he was not prompted by malice or trickery in commencing his action, but that he had *bona fide* a good cause of action. Poth. Pand. lib. 5, tt. 16, 17, s. 124.

OATH PURGATORY. An oath by which a person *purges* or clears himself from presumptions, charges, or suspicions standing against him, or from a contempt.

OATH-RITE. The form used at the taking of an oath.

OATH SUPPLETORY. In the civil and ecclesiastical law. The testimony of a single witness to a fact is called "half-proof," on which no sentence can be founded; in order to supply the other half of proof, the party himself (plaintiff or defendant) is admitted to be examined in his own behalf, and the oath administered to him for that purpose is called the "suppletory oath," because it supplies the necessary *quantum* of proof on which to found the sentence. 3 Bl. Comm. 370.

OB. On account of; for. Several Latin phrases and maxims, commencing with this word, are more commonly introduced by "*in*" (*q. v.*)

OB CAUSAM ALIQUAM A RE MARITIMA ORTAM. For some cause arising out of a maritime matter. 1 Pet. Adm. 92. Said to be Selden's translation of the French definition of admiralty jurisdiction, "*pour le fait de la mer.*" Id.

OB CONTINENTIAM DELICTI. On account of contiguity to the offense, *i. e.*, being contaminated by conjunction with something illegal. For example, the cargo of a vessel, though not contraband or unlawful, may be condemned in admiralty, along with the vessel, when the vessel has been engaged in some service which renders her liable to seizure and confiscation. The cargo is then said to be condemned *ob continentiam delicti*, because found in company with an unlawful service. See 1 Kent, Comm. 152.

OB CONTINGENTIAM. On account of connection; by reason of similarity. In Scotch law, this phrase expresses a ground for the consolidation of actions.

OB FAVOREM MERCATORUM. In favor of merchants. Fleta, lib. 2, c. 63, § 12.

Ob infamiam non solet juxta legem terræ aliquis per legem apparentem se purgare, nisi prius convictus fuerit vel confessus in curia. Glan. lib. 14, c. ii. On account of evil report, it is not usual, according to the law of the land, for any person to purge himself, unless he have been previously convicted, or confessed in court.

OB TURPEM CAUSAM. For an immoral consideration. Dig. 12, 5.

OBÆRATUS. In Roman law. A debtor who was obliged to serve his creditor till his debt was discharged. Adams, Rom. Ant. 49.

OBEDIENCE. Compliance with a command, prohibition, or known law and rule of duty prescribed; the performance of what is required or enjoined by authority, or the abstaining from what is prohibited, in compliance with the command or prohibition. Webster.

OBEDIENTIA. An office, or the administration of it; a kind of rent; submission; obedience.

Obedientia est legis essentia. 11 Coke, 100. Obedience is the essence of law.

OBEDIENTIARIUS. A monastic officer. Du Cange.

OBIIT SINE PROLE. Lat. [He] died without issue. Yearb. M. 1 Edw. II. 1.

OBIT. In old English law. A funeral solemnity, or office for the dead. Cowell. The anniversary of a person's death; the anniversary office. Cro. Jac. 51.

OBITER. Lat. By the way; in passing; incidentally; collaterally.

OBITER DICTUM. Lat. A remark made, or opinion expressed, by a judge, in his decision upon a cause, "by the way," that is, incidentally or collaterally, and not directly upon the question before him, or upon a point not necessarily involved in the determination of the cause, or introduced by way of illustration, or analogy or argument.

OBJECT, *v.* In legal proceedings, to object (*e. g.*, to the admission of evidence) is to interpose a declaration to the effect that the particular matter or thing under consideration is not done or admitted with the consent of the party objecting, but is by him considered improper or illegal, and referring the question of its propriety or legality to the court.

OBJECT, *n.* This term "includes whatever is presented to the mind, as well as what may be presented to the senses; whatever, also, is acted upon, or operated upon, affirmatively, or intentionally influenced by anything done, moved, or applied thereto." Woodruff, J., 8 Blatchf. 257.

OBJECTION. The act of a party who objects to some matter or proceeding in the course of a trial, (see OBJECT, *v.*;) or an argument or reason urged by him in support of his contention that the matter or proceeding objected to is improper or illegal.

OBJECTS OF A POWER. Where property is settled subject to a power given to any person or persons to appoint the same among a limited class, the members of the class are called the "objects" of the power. Thus, if a parent has a power to appoint a fund among his children, the children are called the "objects" of the power. Mozley & Whitley.

OBJURGATRICES. In old English law. Scolds or unquiet women, punished with the cucking-stool.

OBLATA. Gifts or offerings made to the king by any of his subjects; old debts, brought, as it were, together from preceding years, and put on the present sheriff's charge. Wharton.

OBLATA TERRÆ. Half an acre, or, as some say, half a perch, of land. Spelman.

OBLATI. In old European law. Voluntary slaves of churches or monasteries.

OBLATI ACTIO. In the civil law. An action given to a party against another who had *offered* to him a stolen thing, which was found in his possession. Inst. 3, 1, 4.

OBLATIO. In the civil law. A tender of money in payment of a debt made by debtor to creditor. Whatever is offered to the church by the pious. Calvin.

Oblationes dicuntur quæcunque a piis fidelibusque Christianis offeruntur Deo et ecclesiæ, sive res solidæ sive mobiles. 2 Inst. 389. Those things are called "oblations" which are offered to God and to the church by pious and faithful Christians, whether they are movable or immovable.

OBLATIONS, or obventions, are offerings or customary payments made, in England, to the minister of a church, including fees on marriages, burials, mortuaries, etc., (*q. v.*,) and Easter offerings. 2 Steph. Comm. 740; Phillim. Ecc. Law, 1596. They may be commuted by agreement.

OBLIGATE. To bind or constrain; to bind to the observance or performance of a duty; to place under an obligation. To bind one's self by an obligation or promise; to assume a duty; to execute a written promise or covenant; to make a writing obligatory.

OBLIGATIO. Lat. In Roman law. The legal relation existing between two certain persons whereby one (the creditor) is authorized to demand of the other (the debtor) a certain performance which has a money value. In this sense *obligatio* signifies not only the duty of the debtor, but also the right of the creditor. The fact establishing such claim and debt, as also the instrument evidencing it, is termed "obligation." Mackeld. Rom. Law, § 360.

That legal relation subsisting between two persons by which one is bound to the other for a certain performance. The passive relation sustained by the debtor to the creditor is likewise called an "obligation." Sometimes, also, the term "*obligatio*" is used for the *causa obligationis*, and the contract itself is designated an "obligation." There are passages in which even the document which affords the proof of a contract is called an "obligation." Such applications, however, are but a loose extension of the term, which, according to its true idea, is only properly employed when it is used to denote the debt, relationship, in its totality, active and passive, substituting between the creditor and the debtor. Tomk. & J. Mod. Rom. Law, 301.

Obligations, in the civil law, are of the several descriptions enumerated below.

Obligatio civilis is an obligation enforceable by action, whether it derives its origin from *jus civile*, as the obligation engendered by formal contracts or the obligation enforceable by bilaterally penal suits, or from such portion of the *jus gentium* as had been completely naturalized in the civil law and protected by all its remedies, such as the obligation engendered by formless contracts.

Obligatio naturalis is an obligation not immediately enforceable by action, or an obligation imposed by that portion of the *jus gentium* which is only imperfectly recognized by civil law.

Obligatio ex contractu, an obligation arising from contract, or an antecedent *jus in personam*. In this there are two stages,—first, a primary or sanctioned personal right antecedent to wrong, and, afterwards, a secondary or sanctioning personal right consequent on a wrong. Poste's Gaius' Inst. 359.

Obligatio ex delicto, an obligation founded on wrong or tort, or arising from the invasion of a *jus in rem*. In this there is the second stage, a secondary or sanctioning personal right consequent on a wrong, but the first stage is not a personal right, (*jus in personam*,) but a real right, (*jus in rem*,) whether a primordial right, right of *status*, or of property. Poste's Gaius' Inst. 359.

Oligationes ex delicto are obligations arising from the commission of a wrongful injury to the person or property of another. "*Delictum*" is not exactly synonymous with "tort," for, while it includes most of the wrongs known to the common law as torts, it is also wide enough to cover some offenses (such as theft and robbery) primarily injurious to the individual, but now only punished as crimes. Such acts gave rise to an *obligatio*, which consisted in the liability to pay damages.

Obligationes quasi ex contractu. Often persons who have not contracted with each other, under a certain state of facts, are regarded by the Roman law as if they had actually concluded a convention between themselves. The legal relation which then takes place between these persons, which has always a similarity to a contract obligation, is therefore termed "*obligatio quasi ex contractu.*" Such a relation arises from the conducting of affairs without authority, (*negotiorum gestio*:) from the management of property that is in common, when the community arose from casualty, (*communis incidens*;) from the payment of what was not due, (*solutio indebiti*;) from tutorship and curatorship; and from taking possession of an inheritance. Mackeld. Rom. Law, § 491.

Obligationes quasi ex delicto. This class embraces all torts not coming under the denomination of "*delicta*," and not having a special form of action provided for them by law. They differed widely in character, and at common law would in some cases give rise to an action on the case; in others to an action on an implied contract. Ort. Inst. §§ 1781–1792.

OBLIGATION. An obligation is a legal duty, by which a person is bound to do or not to do a certain thing. Civil Code Cal. § 1427; Civil Code Dak. § 798.

The binding power of a vow, promise, oath, or contract, or of law, civil, political, or moral, independent of a promise; that which constitutes legal or moral duty, and which renders a person liable to coercion and punishment for neglecting it. Webster.

"Obligation" is the correlative of "right." Taking the latter word in its politico-ethical sense, as a power of free action lodged in a person, "obligation" is the corresponding duty, constraint, or binding force which should prevent all other persons from denying, abridging, or obstructing such right, or interfering with its exercise. And the same is its meaning as the correlative of a "*jus in rem.*" Taking "right" as meaning a "*jus in personam,*" (a power, demand, claim, or privilege inherent in one person, and incident upon another,) the "obligation" is the coercive force or control imposed upon the person of incidence by the moral law and the positive law, (or the moral law as recognized and sanctioned by the positive law,) constraining him to accede to the demand, render up the thing claimed, pay the money due, or otherwise perform what is expected of him with respect to the subject-matter of the right.

In a limited and arbitrary sense, it means a penal bond or "writing obligatory," that is, a bond containing a penalty, with a condition annexed for the payment of money or performance of covenants. Co. Litt. 172.

Obligation is (1) legal or moral duty, as opposed to physical compulsion; (2) a duty incumbent upon an individual, or a specific and limited number of individuals, as opposed to a duty imposed upon the world at large; (3) the right to enforce such a duty, (*jus in personam,*) as opposed to such a right as that of property, (*jus in rem,*) which avails against the world at large; (4) a bond containing a penalty, with a condition annexed, for the payment of money, performance of covenants, or the like. Mozley & Whitley.

In English expositions of the Roman law, and works upon general jurisprudence, "obligation" is used to translate the Latin "*obligatio.*" In this sense its meaning is much wider than as a technical term of English law. See OBLIGATIO.

Classification. The various sorts of obligations may be classified and defined as follows:

They are either *perfect* or *imperfect.* A perfect obligation is one recognized and sanctioned by positive law; one of which the fulfillment can be enforced by the aid of the law. But if the duty created by the obligation operates only on the moral sense, without being enforced by any positive law, it is called an "imperfect obligation," and creates no right of action, nor has it any legal operation. The duty of exercising gratitude, charity, and the other merely moral duties is an example of this kind of obligation. Civil Code La. art. 1757.

They are either *natural* or *civil.* A natural obligation is one which cannot be enforced by action, but which is binding on the party who makes it in conscience and according to natural justice. A civil obligation is a legal tie, which gives the party with whom it is contracted the right of enforcing its performance by law. Civil Code La. art. 1757.

They are either *express* or *implied;* the former being those by which the obligor binds himself in express terms to perform his obligation; while the latter are such as are raised by the implication or inference of the law from the nature of the transaction.

They are *determinate* or *indeterminate;* the former being the case where the thing contracted to be delivered is specified as an individual; the latter, where it may be any one of a particular class or species.

They are *divisible* or *indivisible,* according as the obligation may or may not be lawfully broken into several distinct obligations without the consent of the obligor.

They are *joint* or *several;* the former, where there are two or more obligors binding themselves jointly for the performance of the obligation; the latter, where the obligors promise, each for himself, to fulfill the engagement.

They are *personal* or *real;* the former being the case when the obligor himself is personally liable for the performance of the engagement, but does not directly bind his property; the latter, where real estate, not the person of the obligor, is primarily liable for performance.

They are *heritable* or *personal.* The former is the case when the heirs and assigns of one party may enforce the performance against the heirs of the other; the latter, when the obligor binds himself only, not his heirs or representatives.

They are either *principal* or *accessory*. A principal obligation is one which is the most important object of the engagement of the contracting parties; while an accessory obligation depends upon or is collateral to the principal.

They may be either *conjunctive* or *alternative*. The former is one in which the several objects in it are connected by a copulative, or in any other manner which shows that all of them are severally comprised in the contract. This contract creates as many different obligations as there are different objects; and the debtor, when he wishes to discharge himself, may force the creditor to receive them separately. But where the things which form the object of the contract are separated by a disjunctive, then the obligation is *alternative*. A promise to deliver a certain thing or to pay a specified sum of money is an example of this kind of obligation. Civil Code La. art. 2063.

They are either *simple* or *conditional*. Simple obligations are such as are not dependent for their execution on any event provided for by the parties, and which are not agreed to become void on the happening of any such event. Conditional obligations are such as are made to depend on an uncertain event. If the obligation is not to take effect until the event happens, it is a suspensive condition; if the obligation takes effect immediately, but is liable to be defeated when the event happens, it is then a resolutory condition. Civil Code La. arts. 2020, 2021.

They may be either *single* or *penal;* the latter, when a penal clause is attached to the undertaking, to be enforced in case the obligor fails to perform; the former, when no such penalty is added.

OBLIGATION OF A CONTRACT. As used in Const. U. S. art. 1, § 10, the term means the binding and coercive force which constrains every man to perform the agreements he has made; a force grounded in the ethical principle of fidelity to one's promises, but deriving its legal efficacy from its recognition by positive law, and sanctioned by the law's providing a remedy for the infraction of the duty or for the enforcement of the correlative right. See Story, Const. § 1378; Black, Const. Prohib. § 139.

The obligation of a contract is that which obliges a party to perform his contract, or repair the injury done by a failure to perform. 4 Gilman, 277.

OBLIGATION SOLIDAIRE. This, in French law, corresponds to joint and several liability in English law, but is applied also to the joint and several rights of the creditors parties to the obligation.

OBLIGATORY. The term "writing obligatory" is a technical term of the law, and means a written contract under seal. 7 Yerg. 350.

OBLIGEE. The person in favor of whom some obligation is contracted, whether such obligation be to pay money or to do or not to do something. Code La. art. 3522, no. 11. The party to whom a bond is given.

OBLIGOR. The person who has engaged to perform some obligation. Code La. art. 3522, no. 12. One who makes a bond.

OBLIQUUS. Lat. **In the old law of descents.** Oblique; cross; transverse; collateral. The opposite of *rectus*, right, or upright.

In the law of evidence. Indirect; circumstantial.

OBLITERATION. Erasure or blotting out of written words.

Obliteration is not limited to effacing the letters of a will or scratching them out or blotting them so completely that they cannot be read. A line drawn through the writing is obliteration, though it may leave it as legible as it was before. 58 Pa. St. 244.

OBLOQUY. To expose one to "obloquy" is to expose him to censure and reproach, as the latter terms are synonymous with "obloquy." 70 Cal. 275, 11 Pac. Rep. 716.

OBRA. In Spanish law. Work. *Obras*, works or trades; those which men carry on in houses or covered places. White, New Recop. b. 1, tit. 5, c. 3, § 6.

OBREPTIO. Lat. The obtaining a thing by fraud or surprise. Calvin. Called, in Scotch law, "*obreption.*"

OBREPTION. Obtaining anything by fraud or surprise. Acquisition of escheats, etc., from the sovereign, by making false representations. Bell.

OBROGARE. Lat. In the civil law. To pass a law contrary to a former law, or to some clause of it; to change a former law in some part of it. Calvin.

OBROGATION. In the civil law. The alteration of a law by the passage of one inconsistent with it. Calvin.

OBSCENE. Lewd; impure; indecent: calculated to shock the moral sense of man by a disregard of chastity or modesty.

OBSCENITY. The character or quality of being obscene; conduct tending to corrupt the public morals by its indecency or lewdness.

OBSERVE. In the civil law. To perform that which has been prescribed by some law or usage. Dig. 1, 3, 32.

OBSES. In the law of war. A hostage. *Obsides*, hostages.

OBSIGNARE. In the civil law. To seal up: as money that had been tendered and refuse

OBSIGNATORY. Ratifying and confirming.

OBSOLESCENT. Becoming obsolete; going out of use; not entirely disused, but gradually becoming so.

OBSOLETE. Disused; neglected; not observed. The term is applied to statutes which have become inoperative by lapse of time, either because the reason for their enactment has passed away, or their subject-matter no longer exists, or they are not applicable to changed circumstances, or are tacitly disregarded by all men, yet without being expressly abrogated or repealed.

OBSTA PRINCIPIIS. Lat. Withstand beginnings; resist the first approaches or encroachments. "It is the duty of courts to be watchful for the constitutional rights of the citizen, and against any stealthy encroachments thereon. Their motto should be '*Obsta principiis*.'" Bradley, J., 116 U. S. 635, 6 Sup. Ct. Rep. 535.

OBSTANTE. Withstanding; hindering. See NON OBSTANTE.

OBSTRICTION. Obligation; bond.

OBSTRUCT. 1. To block up; to interpose obstacles; to render impassable; to fill with barriers or impediments; as to obstruct a road or way.

2. To impede or hinder; to interpose obstacles or impediments, to the hindrance or frustration of some act or service; as to obstruct an officer in the execution of his duty.

OBSTRUCTING PROCESS. In criminal law. The act by which one or more persons attempt to prevent or do prevent the execution of lawful process.

OBSTRUCTION. This is the word properly descriptive of an injury to any one's incorporeal hereditament, *e. g.*, his right to an easement, or *profit à prendre;* an alternative word being "disturbance." On the other hand, "infringement" is the word properly descriptive of an injury to any one's patent-rights or to his copyright. But "obstruction" is also a very general word in law, being applicable to every hindrance of a man in the discharge of his duty, (whether official, public, or private.) Brown.

Obtemperandum est consuetudini rationabili tanquam legi. 4 Coke, 38. A reasonable custom is to be obeyed as a law.

OBTEMPERARE. Lat. To obey. Hence the Scotch "*obtemper,*" to obey or comply with a judgment of a court.

OBTEST. To protest.

OBTORTO COLLO. In Roman law. Taking by the neck or collar; as a plaintiff was allowed to drag a reluctant defendant to court. Adams, Rom. Ant. 242.

OBTULIT SE. (Offered himself.) In old practice. The emphatic words of entry on the record where one party *offered himself* in court against the other, and the latter did not appear. 1 Reeve, Eng. Law, 417.

OBVENTIO. Lat. In the civil law. Rent; profits; income; the return from an investment or thing owned; as the earnings of a vessel.

In old English law. The revenue of a spiritual living, so called. Also, in the plural, "offerings."

OCASION. In Spanish law. Accident. Las Partidas, pt. 3, tit. 32, l. 21; White, New Recop. b. 2, tit. 9, c. 2.

OCCASIO. A tribute which the lord imposed on his vassals or tenants for his necessity. Hindrance; trouble; vexation by suit.

OCCASIONARI. To be charged or loaded with payments or occasional penalties.

OCCASIONES. In old English law. Assarts. Spelman.

Occultatio thesauri inventi fraudulosa. 3 Inst. 133. The concealment of discovered treasure is fraudulent.

OCCUPANCY. Occupancy is a mode of acquiring property by which a thing which belongs to nobody becomes the property of the person who took possession of it, with the intention of acquiring a right of ownership in it. Civil Code La. art. 3412.

The taking possession of things which before belonged to nobody, with an intention of appropriating them to one's own use.

"Possession" and "occupancy," when applied to land, are nearly synonymous terms, and may exist through a tenancy. Thus, occupancy of a homestead, such as will satisfy the statute, may be by means other than that of actual residence on the premises by the widow or child. 21 Ill. 178.

There is a use of the word in public-land laws, homestead laws, "occupying-claimant" laws, cases of landlord and tenant, and like connections, which seems to require the broader sense of possession, although there is, in most of these uses, a shade of meaning discarding any prior title as a foundation of right. Perhaps both uses or views may be harmonized, by saying that in jurisprudence occupancy or occupation is possession, presented independent of the idea of a chain of title, of any earlier owner. Or "occupancy" and "occupant" might be used for assuming property which has no owner, and "occupation" and "occupier" for the more general idea of possession. Judge Bouvier's definitions seem partly founded on such a distinction, and there are indications of it in English usage. It does not appear generally drawn in American books. Abbott.

In international law. The taking possession of a newly discovered or conquered country with the intention of holding and ruling it.

OCCUPANT. **In a general sense.** One who takes possession of a thing, of which there is no owner; one who has the actual possession or control of a thing.

In a special sense. One who takes possession of lands held *pur autre vie*, after the death of the tenant, and during the life of the *cestui que vie*.

Occupantis fiunt derelicta. Things abandoned become the property of the (first) occupant. 1 Pet. Adm. 53.

OCCUPARE. In the civil law. To seize or take possession of; to enter upon a vacant possession; to take possession before another. Calvin.

OCCUPATILE. That which has been left by the right owner, and is now possessed by another.

OCCUPATION. Possession; control; tenure; use.

In its usual sense "occupation" is where a person exercises physical control over land. Thus, the lessee of a house is in occupation of it so long as he has the power of entering into and staying there at pleasure, and of excluding all other persons (or all except one or more specified persons) from the use of it. Occupation is therefore the same thing as actual possession. Sweet.

The word "occupation," applied to real property, is, ordinarily, equivalent to "possession." In connection with other expressions, it may mean that the party should be living upon the premises; but, standing alone, it is satisfied by actual possession. 19 Cal. 683; 11 Abb. Pr. 97; 1 El. & El. 533.

A trade; employment; profession; business; means of livelihood.

OCCUPATIVE. Possessed; used; employed.

OCCUPAVIT. Lat. In old English law. A writ that lay for one who was ejected out of his land or tenement in time of war. Cowell.

OCCUPIER. An occupant; one who is in the enjoyment of a thing.

OCCUPY. To hold in possession; to hold or keep for use. 107 U. S. 343, 2 Sup. Ct. Rep. 677; 11 Johns. 214.

OCHIERN. In old Scotch law. A name of dignity; a freeholder. Skene de Verb. Sign.

OCHLOCRACY. Government by the multitude. A form of government wherein the populace has the whole power and administration in its own hands.

OCTAVE. In old English law. The eighth day inclusive after a feast; one of the return days of writs. 3 Bl. Comm. 278.

OCTO TALES. Eight such; eight such men; eight such jurors. The name of a writ, at common law, which issues when upon a trial at bar, *eight* more jurors are necessary to fill the panel, commanding the sheriff to summon the requisite number. 3 Bl. Comm. 364. See DECEM TALES.

OCTROI. Fr. In old French law. Originally, a duty, which, by the permission of the *seigneur*, any city was accustomed to collect on liquors and some other goods, brought within its precincts, for the consumption of the inhabitants. Afterwards appropriated to the use of the king. Steph. Lect. p. 361.

Oderunt peccare boni, virtutis amore; oderunt peccare mali, formidine pœnæ. Good men hate sin through love of virtue; bad men, through fear of punishment.

ODHAL. Complete property, as opposed to feudal tenure. The transposition of the syllables of "*odhal*" makes it "*allodh*," and hence, according to Blackstone, arises the word "*allod*" or "*allodial*," (*q. v.*) "*All-*

odh" is thus put in contradistinction to "*fee-odh*." Mozley & Whitley.

ODIO ET ATIA. A writ anciently called "*breve de bono et malo*," addressed to the sheriff to inquire whether a man committed to prison upon suspicion of murder were committed on just cause of suspicion, or only upon malice and ill will; and if, upon the inquisition, it were found that he was not guilty, then there issued another writ to the sheriff to bail him. Reg. Orig. 133.

Odiosa et inhonesta non sunt in lege præsumanda. Odious and dishonest acts are not presumed in law. Co. Litt. 78; 6 Wend. 228, 231; 18 N. Y. 295, 300.

Odiosa non præsumuntur. Odious things are not presumed. Burrows, Sett. Cas. 190.

ŒCONOMICUS. L. Lat. In old English law. The executor of a last will and testament. Cowell.

ŒCONOMUS. Lat. In the civil law. A manager or administrator. Calvin.

OF COUNSEL. A phrase commonly applied in practice to the counsel employed by a party in a cause.

OF COURSE. Any action or step taken in the course of judicial proceedings which will be allowed by the court upon mere application, without any inquiry or contest, or which may be effectually taken without even applying to the court for leave, is said to be "of course."

OF FORCE. In force; extant; not obsolete; existing as a binding or obligatory power.

OF NEW. A Scotch expression, closely translated from the Latin "*de novo*," (*q. v.*)

OF RECORD. Recorded; entered on the records; existing and remaining in or upon the appropriate records.

OFFA EXECRATA. In old English law. The morsel of execration; the corsned, (*q. v.*) 1 Reeve, Eng. Law, 21.

OFFENSE. A crime or misdemeanor; a breach of the criminal laws.

It is used as a *genus*, comprehending every crime and misdemeanor, or as a *species*, signifying a crime not indictable, but punishable summarily or by the forfeiture of a penalty.

OFFER. A proposal to do a thing. A proposal to make a contract. Also an attempt.

OFFERINGS. In English ecclesiastical law. Personal tithes, payable by custom to the parson or vicar of a parish, either occasionally, as at sacraments, marriages, churching of women, burials, etc., or at constant times, as at Easter, Christmas, etc.

OFFERTORIUM. In English ecclesiastical law. The offerings of the faithful, or the place where they are made or kept; the service at the time of the Communion.

OFFICE. "Office" is defined to be a right to exercise a public or private employment, and to take the fees and emoluments thereunto belonging, whether public, as those of magistrates, or private, as of bailiffs, receivers, or the like. 2 Bl. Comm. 36.

That function by virtue whereof a person has some employment in the affairs of another, whether judicial, ministerial, legislative, municipal, ecclesiastical, etc. Cowell.

An employment on behalf of the government in any station or public trust, not merely transient, occasional, or incidental. 20 Johns. 493.

The most frequent occasions to use the word arise with reference to a duty and power conferred on an individual by the government; and, when this is the connection, "public office" is a usual and more discriminating expression. But a power and duty may exist without immediate grant from government, and may be properly called an "office;" as the office of executor, the office of steward. Here the individual acts towards legatees or towards tenants in performance of a duty, and in exercise of a power not derived from their consent, but devolved on him by an authority which *quoad hoc* is superior. Abbott.

Offices may be classed as civil and military; and civil offices may be classed as political, judicial, and ministerial. Political offices are such as are not connected immediately with the administration of justice, or the execution of the mandates of a superior officer. Judicial are those which relate to the administration of justice. Ministerial are those which give the officer no power to judge of the matter to be done, and require him to obey the mandates of a superior. It is a general rule that a judicial office cannot be exercised by deputy, while a ministerial one may. 12 Ind. 569.

"Office" is frequently used in the old books as an abbreviation for "inquest of office," (*q. v.*)

OFFICE-BOOK. Any book for the record of official or other transactions, kept under authority of the state, in public offices not connected with the courts.

OFFICE-COPY. A copy or transcript of a deed or record or any filed document made by the officer having it in custody or under his sanction, and by him sealed or certified.

OFFICE FOUND. In English law. Inquest of office found; the finding of certain facts by a jury on an inquest or inquisition of office. 3 Bl. Comm. 258, 259. This phrase has been adopted in American law. 2 Kent, Comm. 61.

OFFICE GRANT. A designation of a conveyance made by some officer of the law to effect certain purposes, where the owner is either unwilling or unable to execute the requisite deeds to pass the title; such, for example, as a tax-deed. 3 Washb. Real Prop. *537

OFFICE HOURS. That portion of the day during which public offices are usually open for the transaction of business.

OFFICE OF JUDGE. A criminal suit in an ecclesiastical court, not being directed to the reparation of a private injury, is regarded as a proceeding emanating from the office of the judge, and may be instituted by the mere motion of the judge. But, in practice, these suits are instituted by private individuals, with the permission of the judge or his surrogate; and the private prosecutor in any such case is, accordingly, said to "promote the office of the judge." Mozley & Whitley.

OFFICER. The incumbent of an office; one who is lawfully invested with an office. One who is charged by a superior power (and particularly by government) with the power and duty of exercising certain functions.

OFFICER DE FACTO. As distinguished from an officer *de jure*, this is the designation of one who is in the actual possession and administration of the office, under some colorable or apparent authority, although his title to the same, whether by election or appointment, is in reality invalid or at least formally questioned.

An officer *de facto* is one who exercises the duties of an office under color of right, by virtue of an appointment or election to that office; being distinguished, on the one hand, from a mere usurper of an office, and, on the other, from an officer *de jure*. 17 Conn. 585; 3 Bush, 14; 37 Me. 423; 48 Id. 79; 55 Pa. St. 468; 7 Jones, (N. C.) 107.

The true doctrine seems to be that it is sufficient if the officer holds the office under some power having color of authority to appoint; and that a statute, though it should be found repugnant to the constitution, will give such color. 21 Ohio St. 618.

An officer *de facto* is one whose acts, though he was not a lawful officer, the law, upon principles of policy and justice, will hold valid so far as they involve the public and third persons. 38 Conn. 449.

A *de facto* officer is one who goes in under color of authority, or who exercises the duties of the office so long or under such circumstances as to raise a presumption of his right. 73 N. C. 546.

OFFICERS OF JUSTICE. A general name applicable to all persons connected with the administration of the judicial department of government, but commonly used only of the class of officers whose duty is to serve the process of the courts, such as sheriffs, constables, bailiffs, marshals, sequestrators, etc.

Officia judicialia non concedantur antequam vacent. 11 Coke, 4. Judicial offices should not be granted before they are vacant.

Officia magistratus non debent esse venalia. Co. Litt. 234. The offices of magistrates ought not to be sold.

OFFICIAL, *adj.* Pertaining to an office; invested with the character of an officer; proceeding from, sanctioned by, or done by, an officer.

OFFICIAL, *n.* An officer; a person invested with the authority of an office.

In the civil law. The minister or apparitor of a magistrate or judge.

In canon law. A person to whom a bishop commits the charge of his spiritual jurisdiction.

In common and statute law. The person whom the archdeacon substitutes in the execution of his jurisdiction. Cowell.

OFFICIAL ASSIGNEE. In English practice. An assignee in bankruptcy appointed by the lord chancellor to co-operate with the other assignees in administering a bankrupt's estate.

OFFICIAL BOND. A bond given by a public officer, conditioned that he shall well and faithfully perform all the duties of the office. The term is sometimes made to include the bonds of executors, guardians, trustees, etc.

OFFICIAL LIQUIDATOR. In English law. A person appointed by the judge in chancery, in whose court a joint-stock company is being wound up, to bring and defend suits and actions in the name of the company, and generally to do all things necessary for winding up the affairs of the company, and distributing its assets. 3 Steph. Comm. 24.

OFFICIAL LOG-BOOK. A log-book in a certain form, and containing certain specified entries required by 17 & 18 Vict. c. 104, §§ 280-282, to be kept by all British merchant ships, except those exclusively engaged in the coasting trade.

OFFICIAL MANAGERS. Persons formerly appointed, under English statutes now repealed, to superintend the winding up of insolvent companies under the control of the court of chancery. Wharton.

OFFICIAL OATH. One taken by an officer when he assumes charge of his office, whereby he declares that he will faithfully discharge the duties of the same, or whatever else may be required by statute in the particular case.

OFFICIAL PRINCIPAL. An ecclesiastical officer whose duty it is to hear causes between party and party as the delegate of the bishop or archbishop by whom he is appointed. He generally also holds the office of vicar general and (if appointed by a bishop) that of chancellor. The official principal of the province of Canterbury is called the "dean of arches." Phillim. Ecc. Law, 1203, et seq.; Sweet.

OFFICIAL SOLICITOR TO THE COURT OF CHANCERY. An officer in England whose functions are to protect the suitors' fund, and to administer, under the direction of the court, so much of it as now comes under the spending power of the court. He acts for persons suing or defending *in forma pauperis*, when so directed by the judge, and for those who, through ignorance or forgetfulness, have been guilty of contempt of court by not obeying process. He also acts generally as solicitor in all cases in which the chancery division requires such services. The office is transferred to the high court by the judicature acts, but no alteration in its name appears to have been made. Sweet.

OFFICIAL TRUSTEE OF CHARITY LANDS. The secretary of the English charity commissioners. He is a corporation sole for the purpose of taking and holding real property and leaseholds upon trust for an endowed charity in cases where it appears to the court desirable to vest them in him. He is a bare trustee, the possession and management of the land remaining in the persons acting in the administration of the charity. Sweet.

OFFICIAL USE. An active use before the statute of uses, which imposed some duty on the legal owner or feofee to uses; as a conveyance to A. with directions for him to sell the estate and distribute the proceeds among B., C., and D. To enable A. to perform this duty, he had the legal possession of the estate to be sold. Wharton.

OFFICIALTY. The court or jurisdiction of which an official is head.

OFFICIARIIS NON FACIENDIS VEL AMOVENDIS. A writ addressed to the magistrates of a corporation, requiring them not to make such a man an officer, or to put one out of the office he has, until inquiry is made of his manners, etc. Reg. Orig. 126.

OFFICINA JUSTITIÆ. The workshop or office of justice. The chancery was formerly so called.

OFFICIO, EX, OATH. An oath whereby a person may be obliged to make any presentment of any crime or offense, or to confess or accuse himself of any criminal matter or thing whereby he may be liable to any censure, penalty, or punishment. 3 Bl. Comm. 447.

OFFICIOUS WILL. A testament by which a testator leaves his property to his family. Sandars, Just. Inst. 207. See IN-OFFICIOUS TESTAMENT.

Officit conatus si effectus sequatur. The attempt becomes of consequence, if the effect follows. Jenk. Cent. 55.

Officium nemini debet esse damnosum. Office ought not to be an occasion of loss to any one. A maxim in Scotch law. Bell.

OIR. In Spanish law. To hear; to take cognizance. White, New Recop. b. 3, tit. 1, c. 7.

OKER. In Scotch law. Usury; the taking of interest for money, contrary to law. Bell.

OLD NATURA BREVIUM. The title of a treatise written in the reign of Edward III. containing the writs which were then most in use, annexing to each a short comment concerning their nature and the application of them, with their various properties and effects. 3 Reeve, Eng. Law, 152.

It is so called by way of distinction from the *New* Natura Brevium of Fitzherbert, and is generally cited as "O. N. B.," or as "Vet. Na. B.," using the abbreviated form of the Latin title.

OLD STYLE. The ancient calendar or method of reckoning time, whereby the year commenced on March 25th. It was superseded by the new style (that now in use) in most countries of Europe in 1582 and in England in 1752.

OLD TENURES. A treatise, so called to distinguish it from Littleton's book on the same subject, which gives an account of the various tenures by which land was holden, the nature of estates, and some other incidents to landed property in the reign of Edward III. It is a very scanty tract, but has the merit of having led the way to Littleton's famous work. 3 Reeve, Eng. Law, 151.

OLEOMARGARINE. An artificial imitation of butter, made chiefly from animal fats. Its sale is prohibited by statute in several states. See 114 Pa. St. 265, 7 Atl. Rep. 913; 127 U. S. 678, 8 Sup. Ct. Rep. 992, 1257; 63 Md. 596; 36 Minn. 69, 30 N. W. Rep. 308; 77 Mo. 110; 105 N. Y. 123, 11 N. E. Rep. 277; 64 N. H. 549, 15 Atl. Rep. 210.

OLERON, LAWS OF. A code of maritime laws published at the island of Oleron in the twelfth century by Eleanor of Guienne. They were adopted in England successively under Richard I., Henry III., and Edward III., and are often cited before the admiralty courts.

OLIGARCHY. A form of government wherein the administration of affairs is lodged in the hands of a few persons.

OLOGRAPH. An instrument (*e. g.*, a will) wholly written by the person from whom it emanates.

OLOGRAPHIC TESTAMENT. The olographic testament is that which is written by the testator himself. In order to be valid it must be entirely written, dated, and signed by the hand of the testator. It is subject to no other form, and may be made anywhere, even out of the state. Civil Code La. art. 1588; Civil Code Cal. § 1277.

OLYMPIAD. A Grecian epoch; the space of four years.

OME BUENO. In Spanish law. A good man; a substantial person. Las Partidas, pt. 5, tit. 13, l. 38.

Omissio eorum quæ tacite insunt nihil operatur. The omission of those things which are tacitly implied is of no consequence. 2 Bulst. 131.

OMISSIS OMNIBUS ALIIS NEGOTIIS. Lat. Laying aside all other businesses. 9 East, 347.

OMITTANCE. Forbearance; omission.

Omne actum ab intentione agentis est judicandum. Every act is to be judged by the intention of the doer. Branch, Princ.

Omne crimen ebrietas et incendit et detegit. Drunkenness both inflames (or aggravates) and reveals every crime. Co. Litt. 247*a;* 4 Bl. Comm. 26; Broom, Max. 17.

Omne jus aut consensus fecit, aut necessitas constituit aut firmavit consuetudo. Every right is either made by consent, or is constituted by necessity, or is established by custom. Dig. 1, 3, 40.

Omne magis dignum trahit ad se minus dignum, quamvis minus dignum sit antiquius. Every worthier thing draws to it the less worthy, though the less worthy be the more ancient. Co. Litt. 355*b*.

Omne magnum exemplum habet aliquid ex iniquo, quod publica utilitate compensatur. Hob. 279. Every great example has some portion of evil, which is compensated by the public utility.

Omne majus continet in se minus. Every greater contains in itself the less. 5 Coke, 115*a*. The greater always contains the less. Broom, Max. 174.

Omne majus dignum continet in se minus dignum. Co. Litt. 43. The more worthy contains in itself the less worthy.

Omne majus minus in se complectitur. Every greater embraces in itself the less. Jenk. Cent. 208.

Omne principale trahit ad se accessorium. Every principal thing draws to itself the accessory. 17 Mass. 425; 1 Johns. 580.

Omne quod solo inædificatur solo cedit. Everything which is built upon the soil belongs to the soil. Dig. 47, 3, 1; Broom, Max. 401.

Omne sacramentum debet esse de certa scientia. Every oath ought to be of certain knowledge. 4 Inst. 279.

Omne testamentum morte consummatum est. 3 Coke, 29. Every will is completed by death.

Omnes actiones in mundo infra certa tempora habent limitationem. All actions in the world are limited within certain periods. Bract. fol. 52.

Omnes homines aut liberi sunt aut servi. All men are freemen or slaves. Inst. 1, 3, pr.; Fleta, l. 1, c. 1, § 2.

Omnes licentiam habere his quæ pro se indulta sunt, renunciare. [It is a rule of the ancient law that] all persons shall have liberty to renounce those privileges which have been conferred for their benefit. Cod. 1, 3, 51; Id. 2, 3, 29; Broom, Max. 699.

Omnes prudentes illa admittere solent quæ probantur iis qui in arte sua bene versati sunt. All prudent men are accustomed to admit those things which are approved by those who are well versed in the art. 7 Coke, 19.

Omnes sorores sunt quasi unus hæres de una hæreditate. Co. Litt. 67. All sisters are, as it were, one heir to one inheritance.

OMNI EXCEPTIONE MAJUS. 4 Inst. 262. Above all exception.

Omnia delicta in aperto leviora sunt. All crimes that are committed openly are lighter, [or have a less odious appearance than those committed secretly.] 8 Coke, 127*a*.

OMNIA PERFORMAVIT. He has done all. In pleading. A good plea in bar where all the covenants are in the affirmative. 1 Me. 189.

Omnia præsumuntur contra spoliatorem. All things are presumed against a despoiler or wrong-doer. A leading maxim in the law of evidence. Best, Ev. p. 340, § 303; Broom, Max. 938.

Omnia præsumuntur legitime facta donec probetur in contrarium. All things are presumed to be lawfully done, until proof be made to the contrary. Co. Litt. 232*b*; Best, Ev. p. 337, § 300.

Omnia præsumuntur rite et solemniter esse acta donec probetur in contrarium. All things are presumed to have been rightly and duly performed until it is proved to the contrary. Co. Litt. 232; Broom, Max. 944.

Omnia præsumuntur solemniter esse acta. Co. Litt. 6. All things are presumed to have been done rightly.

Omnia quæ jure contrahuntur contrario jure pereunt. Dig. 50, 17, 100. All things which are contracted by law perish by a contrary law.

Omnia quæ sunt uxoris sunt ipsius viri. All things which are the wife's are the husband's. Bract. fol. 32; Co. Litt. 112*a*. See 2 Kent, Comm. 130–143.

Omnia rite acta præsumuntur. All things are presumed to have been rightly done. Broom, Max. 944.

OMNIBUS AD QUOS PRÆSENTES LITERÆ PERVENERINT, SALUTEM. To all to whom the present letters shall come, greeting. A form of address with which charters and deeds were anciently commenced.

Omnis actio est loquela. Every action is a plaint or complaint. Co. Litt. 292*a*.

Omnis conclusio boni et veri judicii sequitur ex bonis et veris præmissis et dictis juratorum. Every conclusion of a good and true judgment follows from good and true premises, and the verdicts of jurors. Co. Litt. 226*b*.

Omnis consensus tollit errorem. Every consent removes error. Consent always removes the effect of error. 2 Inst. 123.

Omnis definitio in jure civili periculosa est, parum est enim ut non subverti possit. Dig. 50, 17, 202. All definition in the civil law is hazardous, for there is little that cannot be subverted.

Omnis definitio in lege periculosa. All definition in law is hazardous. 2 Wood. Lect. 196.

Omnis exceptio est ipsa quoque regula. Every exception is itself also a rule.

Omnis indemnatus pro innoxis legibus habetur. Every uncondemned person is held by the law as innocent. Lofft, 121.

Omnis innovatio plus novitate perturbat quam ultilitate prodest. Every innovation occasions more harm by its novelty than benefit by its utility. 2 Bulst. 338; Broom, Max. 147.

Omnis interpretatio si fieri potest ita fienda est in instrumentis, ut omnes contrarietates amoveantur. Jenk. Cent. 96. Every interpretation, if it can be done, is to be so made in instruments that all contradictions may be removed.

Omnis interpretatio vel declarat, vel extendit, vel restringit. Every interpretation either declares, extends, or restrains.

Omnis nova constitutio futuris formam imponere debet, non præteritis. Every new statute ought to prescribe a form to future, not to past, acts. Bract. fol. 228; 2 Inst. 95.

Omnis persona est homo, sed non vicissim. Every person is a man, but not every man a person. Calvin.

Omnis privatio præsupponit habitum. Every privation presupposes a former enjoyment. Co. Litt. 339*a*. A "rule of philosophie" quoted by Lord Coke, and applied to the discontinuance of an estate.

Omnis querela et omnis actio injuriarum limita est infra certa tempora. Co. Litt. 114*b*. Every plaint and every action for injuries is limited within certain times.

Omnis ratihabitio retrotrahitur et mandato priori æquiparatur. Every ratification relates back and is equivalent to a prior authority. Broom, Max. 757, 871; Chit. Cont. 196.

Omnis regula suas patitur exceptiones. Every rule is liable to its own exceptions.

OMNIUM. In mercantile law. A term used to express the aggregate value of the different stock in which a loan is usually funded. Tomlins.

Omnium contributione sarciatur quod pro omnibus datum est. 4 Bing. 121. That which is given for all is recompensed by the contribution of all. A principle of the law of general average.

Omnium rerum quarum usus est, potest esse abusus, virtute solo excepta. There may be an abuse of everything of which there is a use, virtue only excepted. Dav. Ir. K. B. 79.

ON ACCOUNT. In part payment; in partial satisfaction of an account. The phrase is usually contrasted with "in full."

ON ACCOUNT OF WHOM IT MAY CONCERN. When a policy of insurance expresses that the insurance is made "on account of whom it may concern," it will cover all persons having an insurable interest in the subject-matter at the date of the policy and who were then contemplated by the party procuring the insurance. 2 Pars. Mar. Law, 30.

ON CALL. There is no legal difference between an obligation payable "when demanded" or "on demand" and one payable "on call" or "at any time called for." In each case the debt is payable immediately. 22 Grat. 609.

ON CONDITION. These words may be construed to mean "on the terms," in order to effectuate the intention of parties. 4 Watts & S. 302.

ON DEFAULT. In case of default; upon failure of stipulated action or performance; upon the occurrence of a failure, omission, or neglect of duty.

ON DEMAND. A promissory note payable "on demand" is a present debt, and is payable without any demand. 2 Mees. & W. 461; 39 Me. 494.

ON FILE. Filed; entered or placed upon the files; existing and remaining upon or among the proper files.

ON OR ABOUT. A phrase used in reciting the date of an occurrence or conveyance, to escape the necessity of being bound by the statement of an exact date.

ON OR BEFORE. These words, inserted in a stipulation to do an act or pay money, entitle the party stipulating to perform at any time before the day; and upon performance, or tender and refusal, he is immediately vested with all the rights which would have attached if performance were made on the day. 6 J. J. Marsh. 156.

Once a fraud, always a fraud. 13 Vin. Abr. 539.

ONCE A MORTGAGE, ALWAYS A MORTGAGE. This rule signifies that an instrument originally intended as a mortgage, and not a deed, cannot be converted into anything else than a mortgage by any subsequent clause or agreement.

Once a recompense, always a recompense. 19 Vin. Abr. 277.

ONCE IN JEOPARDY. A phrase used to express the condition of a person charged with crime, who has once already, by legal proceedings, been put in danger of conviction and punishment for the same offense.

Once quit and cleared, ever quit and cleared. (Scotch, anis quit and clenged, ay quit and clenged.) Skene, de Verb. Sign. voc. "Iter.," ad fin.

ONCUNNE. Accused. Du Cange.

ONE HUNDRED THOUSAND POUNDS CLAUSE. A precautionary stipulation inserted in a deed making a good tenant to the *præcipe* in a common recovery. See 1 Prest. Conv. 110.

ONE-THIRD NEW FOR OLD. See NEW FOR OLD.

ONERANDO PRO RATA PORTIONIS. A writ that lay for a joint tenant or tenant in common who was distrained for more rent than his proportion of the land comes to. Reg. Orig. 182.

ONERARI NON. In pleading. The name of a plea, in an action of debt, by which the defendant says that he ought not to be charged.

ONERATIO. A lading; a cargo.

ONERATUR NISI. See O. NI.

ONERIS FERENDI. Lat. In the civil law. The servitude of support; a servitude by which the wall of a house is required to sustain the wall or beams of the adjoining house.

ONEROUS. A contract, lease, share, or other right is said to be "onerous" when the obligations attaching to it counter-balance or exceed the advantage to be derived from it, either absolutely or with reference to the particular possessor. Sweet.

ONEROUS CAUSE. In Scotch law. A good and legal consideration.

ONEROUS CONTRACT. In the civil law this term designates a contract based upon any consideration given or promised, however trifling or inconsiderable such consideration may be. Civil Code La. art. 1767.

ONEROUS DEED. In Scotch law. A deed given for a valuable consideration. Bell.

ONEROUS GIFT. A gift made subject to certain charges imposed by the donor on the donee.

ONOMASTIC. A term applied to the signature of an instrument, the body of which is in a different handwriting from that of the signature. Best, Ev. 315.

ONUS. Lat. A burden or load; a weight. The lading, burden, or cargo of a vessel. A charge; an incumbrance. *Cum onere*, (*q.v.*,) with the incumbrance.

ONUS EPISCOPALE. Ancient customary payments from the clergy to their diocesan bishop, of synodals, pentecostals, etc.

ONUS IMPORTANDI. The charge of importing merchandise, mentioned in St. 12 Car. II. c. 28.

ONUS PROBANDI. Lat. Burden of proving; the burden of proof. The strict meaning of the term "*onus probandi*" is that, if no evidence is adduced by the party on whom the burden is cast, the issue must be found against him. 1 Houst. 44.

OPE CONSILIO. Lat. By aid and counsel. A civil law term applied to accessaries, similar in import to the "aiding and abetting" of the common law. Often written "*ope et consilio.*" Burrill.

OPEN. 1. To open a case is to begin it; to make an initiatory explanation of its features to the court, jury, referee, etc., by outlining the nature of the transaction on which it is founded, the questions involved, and the character and general course of the evidence to be adduced.

2. To open a court is to make a formal announcement, usually by the crier, that its session has now begun, and that the business before the court will be proceeded with.

3. To open a legal document, *e. g.*, a deposition, is to break the seals by which it was secured, and lay it open to view, or to bring it into court ready for use.

4. To open a judgment, decree, or similar act of a court is to lift the bar of finality which it imposes, so as to allow a party who is entitled to such relief to proceed to a re-examination of the merits.

5. To open a street or highway is to establish it and make it available to public travel.

6. To open a rule or order is to revoke the action by which it was made final or absolute, and give an opportunity to show cause against it.

7. To open bids received on a judicial sale of property is to reject or cancel them for fraud or other cause, and direct a resale.

OPEN ACCOUNT. An account which has not been finally settled or closed, but is still running or open to future adjustment or liquidation.

Open account, in legal as well as in ordinary language, means an indebtedness subject to future adjustment, and which may be reduced or modified by proof. 1 Ga. 275.

OPEN A CREDIT. To accept or pay the draft of a correspondent who has not furnished funds. Pardessus, no. 296.

OPEN CORPORATION. One in which all the citizens or corporators have a vote in the election of the officers of the corporation. 3 Bland, 416, note.

OPEN COURT. This term may mean either a court which has been formally convened and declared open for the transaction of its proper judicial business, or a court which is freely open to the approach of all decent and orderly persons in the character of spectators.

OPEN DOORS. In Scotch law. "Letters of open doors" are process which empowers the messenger, or officer of the law, to break open doors of houses or rooms in which the debtor has placed his goods. Bell.

OPEN FIELDS, or MEADOWS. In English law. Fields which are undivided, but belong to separate owners; the part of each owner is marked off by boundaries until the crop has been carried off, when the pasture is shared promiscuously by the joint herd of all the owners. Elton, Commons, 31; Sweet.

OPEN INSOLVENCY. The condition of one who has no property, within the reach of the law, applicable to the payment of any debt. 8 Blackf. 305.

OPEN LAW. The making or waging of law. Magna Charta, c. 21.

OPEN POLICY. In marine insurance. One in which the value of the subject insured is not fixed or agreed upon in the policy, as between the assured and the underwriter, but is left to be estimated in case of loss. The term is opposed to "valued policy," in which the value of the subject insured is fixed for the purpose of the insurance, and expressed on the face of the policy. Mozley & Whitley.

OPEN THEFT. In Saxon law. The same with the Latin "*furtum manifestum,*" (*q. v.*)

OPENING. In American practice. The beginning; the commencement; the first address of the counsel.

OPENING A COMMISSION. An entering upon the duties under a commission, or commencing to act under a commission, is so termed. Thus, the judges of assize and *nisi prius* derive their authority to act under or by virtue of commissions directed to them for that purpose; and, when they commence acting under the powers so committed to them, they are said to open the commissions; and the day on which they so commence their proceedings is thence termed the "commission day of the assizes." Brown.

OPENING A JUDGMENT. The act of the court in so far relaxing the finality and conclusiveness of a judgment as to allow a re-examination of the case on which it was rendered. This is done at the instance of a party showing good cause why the execution of the judgment would be inequitable. It so far annuls the judgment as to prevent its enforcement until the final determination upon it, but does not in the mean time release its lien upon real estate.

OPENING A RULE. The act of restoring or recalling a rule which has been made absolute to its conditional state, as a rule *nisi,* so as to readmit of cause being shown against the rule. Thus, when a rule to show cause has been made absolute under a mistaken impression that no counsel had been instructed to show cause against it, it is usual for the party at whose instance the rule was obtained to consent to have the rule opened, by which all the proceedings subsequent to the day when cause ought to have been shown against it are in effect nullified, and the rule is then argued in the ordinary way. Brown.

OPENING BIDDINGS. In equity practice. The allowance by a court, on sufficient cause shown, of a resale of property once sold under a decree.

OPENING THE PLEADINGS. Stating briefly at a trial before a jury the substance of the pleadings. This is done by the junior counsel for the plaintiff at the commencement of the trial.

OPENTIDE. The time after corn is carried out of the fields.

OPERA. A composition of a dramatic kind, set to music and sung, accompanied with musical instruments, and enriched with appropriate costumes, scenery, etc. The house in which operas are represented is termed an "opera-house." 1 Pittsb. R. 71.

OPERARII. Such tenants, under feudal tenures, as held some little portions of land by the duty of performing bodily labor and servile works for their lord.

OPERATIO. One day's work performed by a tenant for his lord.

OPERATION OF LAW. This term expresses the manner in which rights, and sometimes liabilities, devolve upon a person by the mere application to the particular transaction of the established rules of law, without the act or co-operation of the party himself.

OPERATIVE. A workman; a laboring man; an artisan; particularly one employed in factories.

OPERATIVE PART. That part of a conveyance, or of any instrument intended for the creation or transference of rights, by which the main object of the instrument is carried into effect. It is distinguished from introductory matter, recitals, formal conclusion, etc.

OPERATIVE WORDS, in a deed or lease, are the words which effect the transaction intended to be consummated by the instrument.

OPERIS NOVI NUNTIATIO. In the civil law. A protest or warning against [of] a new work. Dig. 39, 1.

OPETIDE. The ancient time of marriage, from Epiphany to Ash-Wednesday.

Opinio est duplex, scilicet, opinio vulgaris, orta inter graves et discretos, et quæ vultum veritatis habet; et opinio tantum orta inter leves et vulgares homines, absque specie veritatis. 4 Coke, 107. Opinion is of two kinds, namely, common opinion, which springs up among grave and discreet men, and which has the appearance of truth, and opinion which springs up only among light and foolish men, without the semblance of truth.

Opinio quæ favet testamento est tenenda. The opinion which favors a will is to be followed. 1 W. Bl. 13, arg.

OPINION. 1. In the law of evidence, opinion is an inference or conclusion drawn by a witness from facts some of which are known to him and others assumed, or drawn from facts which, though lending probability to the inference, do not evolve it by a process of absolutely necessary reasoning.

An inference necessarily involving certain facts may be stated without the facts, the inference being an equivalent to a specification of the facts; but, when the facts are not necessarily involved in the inference (*e. g.*, when the inference may be sustained upon either of several distinct phases of fact, neither of which it necessarily involves,) then the facts must be stated. Whart. Ev. § 510.

2. A document prepared by an attorney for his client, embodying his understanding of the law as applicable to a state of facts submitted to him for that purpose.

3. The statement by a judge or court of the decision reached in regard to a cause tried or argued before them, expounding the law as applied to the case, and detailing the reasons upon which the judgment is based.

Oportet quod certa res deducatur in donationem. It is necessary that a certain thing be brought into the gift, or made the subject of the conveyance. Bract. fol. 15*b*.

Oportet quod certa res deducatur in judicium. Jenk. Cent. 84. A thing certain must be brought to judgment.

Oportet quod certa sit res quæ venditur. It is necessary that there should be a certain thing which is sold. To make a valid sale, there must be certainty as to the thing which is sold. Bract. fol. 61*b*.

Oportet quod certæ personæ, terræ, et certi status comprehendantur in declaratione usuum. 9 Coke, 9. It is necessary that given persons, lands, and estates should be comprehended in a declaration of uses.

OPPIGNERARE. Lat. In the civil law. To pledge. Calvin.

OPPOSER. An officer formerly belonging to the green-wax in the exchequer.

OPPOSITE. An old word for "opponent."

OPPOSITION. **In bankruptcy practice.** Opposition is the refusal of a creditor to assent to the debtor's discharge under the bankrupt law.

In French law. A motion to open a judgment by default and let the defendant in to a defense.

OPPRESSION. The misdemeanor committed by a public officer, who, under color of his office, wrongfully inflicts upon any person any bodily harm, imprisonment, or other injury. 1 Russ. Crimes, 297; Steph. Dig. Crim. Law, 71.

OPPRESSOR. A public officer who unlawfully uses his authority by way of oppression, (*q. v.*)

OPPROBRIUM. In the civil law. Ignominy; infamy; shame.

Optima est legis interpres consuetudo. Custom is the best interpreter of the law. Dig. 1, 3, 37; Lofft, 237; Broom, Max. 931.

Optima est lex quæ minimum relinquit arbitrio judicis; optimus judex qui minimum sibi. That law is the best which leaves least to the discretion of the judge; that judge is the best who leaves least to his own. Bac. Aphorisms, 46; 2 Dwar. St. 782. That system of law is best which confides as little as possible to the discretion of the judge; that judge the best who relies as little as possible on his own opinion. Broom, Max. 84; 1 Kent, Comm. 478.

Optima statuti interpretatrix est (omnibus particulis ejusdem inspectis) ipsum statutum. The best interpreter of a statute is (all its parts being considered) the statute itself. 8 Coke, 117*b*; Wing. Max. p. 239, max. 68.

OPTIMACY. Nobility; men of the highest rank.

Optimam esse legem, quæ minimum relinquit arbitrio judicis; id quod certitudo ejus præstat. That law is the best which leaves the least discretion to the judge; and this is an advantage which results from its certainty. Bac. Aphorisms, 8.

Optimus interpres rerum usus. Use or usage is the best interpreter of things. 2 Inst. 282; Broom, Max. 917, 930, 931.

Optimus interpretandi modus est sic leges interpretari ut leges legibus concordant. 8 Coke, 169. The best mode of interpretation is so to interpret laws that they may accord with each other.

Optimus legum interpres consuetudo. 4 Inst. 75. Custom is the best interpreter of the laws.

OPTION. **In English ecclesiastical law.** A customary prerogative of an archbishop, when a bishop is consecrated by him, to name a clerk or chaplain of his own to be provided for by such suffragan bishop; in lieu of which it is now usual for the bishop to make over by deed to the archbishop, his executors and assigns, the next presentation of such dignity or benefice in the bishop's disposal within that see, as the archbishop himself shall *choose*, which is therefore called his "option." 1 Bl. Comm. 381; 3 Steph. Comm. 63, 64; Cowell.

In contracts. An option is a privilege existing in one person, for which he has paid money, which gives him the right to *buy* certain merchandise or certain specified securities from another person, if he chooses, at any time within an agreed period, at a fixed price, or to *sell* such property to such other person at an agreed price and time. If the option gives the choice of buying or not buying, it is denominated a "call." If it gives the choice of selling or not, it is called a "put." If it is a combination of both these, and gives the privilege of *either* buying or selling or not, it is called a "straddle" or a "spread eagle." These terms are used on the stock-exchange.

OPTIONAL WRIT. In old English practice. That species of original writ, otherwise called a "*præcipe*," which was framed in the alternative, commanding the defendant to do the thing required, *or* show the reason wherefore he had not done it. 3 Bl. Comm. 274.

OPUS. Lat. Work; labor; the product of work or labor.

OPUS LOCATUM. The product of work let for use to another; or the hiring out of work or labor to be done upon a thing.

OPUS MANIFICUM. In old English law. Labor done by the hands; manual labor; such as making a hedge, digging a ditch. Fleta, lib. 2, c. 48, § 3.

OPUS NOVUM. In the civil law. A new work. By this term was meant something newly built upon land, or taken from a work already erected. He was said *opus novum facere* (to make a new work) who, either by building or by taking anything away, changed the former appearance of a work. Dig. 39, 1, 1, 11.

OR. A term used in heraldry, and signifying gold; called "sol" by some heralds when it occurs in the arms of princes, and "topaz" or "carbuncle" when borne by peers. Engravers represent it by an indefinite number of small points. Wharton.

ORA. A Saxon coin, valued at sixteen pence, and sometimes at twenty pence.

ORACULUM. In the civil law. The name of a kind of response or sentence given by the Roman emperors.

ORAL. Uttered by the mouth or in words; spoken, not written.

ORAL PLEADING. Pleading by word of mouth, in the actual presence of the court. This was the ancient mode of pleading in England, and continued to the reign of Edward III. Steph. Pl. 23-26.

ORANDO PRO REGE ET REGNO. An ancient writ which issued, while there was no standing collect for a sitting parliament, to pray for the peace and good government of the realm.

ORANGEMEN. A party in Ireland who keep alive the views of William of Orange. Wharton.

ORATOR. The plaintiff in a cause or matter in chancery, when addressing or petitioning the court, used to style himself "orator," and, when a woman, "oratrix." But these terms have long gone into disuse, and the customary phrases now are "plaintiff" or "petitioner."

In Roman law, the term denoted an advocate.

ORATRIX. A female petitioner; a female plaintiff in a bill in chancery was formerly so called.

ORBATION. Deprivation of one's parents or children, or privation in general. Little used.

ORCINUS LIBERTUS. Lat. In Roman law. A freedman who obtained his liberty by the direct operation of the will or testament of his deceased master was so called, being the freedman of the deceased, (*orcinus*,) not of the *hæres*. Brown.

ORDAIN. To institute or establish; to make an ordinance; to enact a constitution or law.

ORDEAL. The most ancient species of trial, in Saxon and old English law, being peculiarly distinguished by the appellation of "*judicium Dei*," or judgment of God, it being supposed that supernatural intervention would rescue an innocent person from the danger of physical harm to which he was exposed in this species of trial. The ordeal was of two sorts,—either fire ordeal or water ordeal; the former being confined to persons of higher rank, the latter to the common people. 4 Bl. Comm. 342.

ORDEFFE, or ORDELFE. A liberty whereby a man claims the ore found in his own land; also, the ore lying under land. Cowell.

ORDELS. In old English law. The right of administering oaths and adjudging trials by ordeal within a precinct or liberty. Cowell.

ORDENAMIENTO. In Spanish law. An order emanating from the sovereign, and differing from a *cedula* only in form and in the mode of its promulgation. Schm. Civil Law, Introd. 93, note.

ORDENAMIENTO DE ALCALA. A collection of Spanish law promulgated by the Cortes in the year 1348. Schm. Civil Law, Introd. 75.

ORDER. In a general sense. A mandate, precept; a command or direction authoritatively given; a rule or regulation.

The distinction between "order" and "requisition" is that the first is a mandatory act, the latter a request. 19 Johns. 7.

In practice. Every direction of a court or judge made or entered in writing, and not included in a judgment, is denominated an "order." An application for an order is a motion. Code Civil Proc. Cal. § 1003; Code N. Y. § 400.

Orders are also issued by subordinate legislative authorities. Such are the English orders in council, or orders issued by the privy council in the name of the queen, either in exercise of the royal prerogative or in pursuance of an act of parliament. The rules of court under the judicature act are grouped together in the form of orders, each order dealing with a particular subject-matter. Sweet.

An order is also an informal bill of exchange or letter of request whereby the party to whom it is addressed is directed to pay or deliver to a person therein named the whole or part of a fund or other property of the person making the order, and which is in the possession of the drawee.

It is further a designation of the person to whom a bill of exchange or negotiable promissory note is to be paid.

It is also used to designate a rank, class, or division of men; as the order of nobles, order of knights, order of priests, etc.

In French law. The name order (*ordre*) is given to the operation which has for its object to fix the rank of the preferences claimed by the creditors in the distribution of the price [arising from the sale] of an immovable affected by their liens. Dalloz, *mot* "Ordre."

ORDER AND DISPOSITION of goods and chattels. When goods are in the "order and disposition" of a bankrupt, they go to his trustee, and have gone so since the time of James I. Wharton.

ORDER NISI. A provisional or conditional order, allowing a certain time within which to do some required act, on failure of which the order will be made absolute.

ORDER OF DISCHARGE. In England. An order made under the bankruptcy act of 1869, by a court of bankruptcy, the effect of which is to discharge a bankrupt from all debts, claims, or demands provable under the bankruptcy.

ORDER OF FILIATION. An order made by a court or judge having jurisdiction, fixing the paternity of a bastard child upon a given man, and requiring him to provide for its support.

ORDER OF REVIVOR. In English practice. An order as of course for the continuance of an abated suit. It superseded the bill of revivor.

ORDERS. The directions as to the course and purpose of a voyage given by the owner of the vessel to the captain or master. For other meanings, see ORDER.

ORDERS OF THE DAY. Any member of the English house of commons who wishes to propose any question, or to "move the house," as it is termed, must, in order to give the house due notice of his intention, state the form or nature of his motion on a previous day, and have it entered in a book termed the "order-book;" and the motions so entered, the house arranges, shall be considered on particular days, and such motions or matters, when the day arrives for their being considered, are then termed the "orders of the day." Brown. A similar practice obtains in the legislative bodies of this country.

ORDINANCE. A rule established by authority; a permanent rule of action; a law or statute. In a more limited sense, the term is used to designate the enactments of the legislative body of a municipal corporation.

Strictly, a bill or law which might stand with the old law, and did not alter any statute in force at the time, and which became complete by the royal assent on the *parliament roll*, without any entry on the *statute roll*. A bill or law which might at any time be amended by the parliament, without any statute. Hale, Com. Law. An ordinance was otherwise distinguished from a statute by the circumstance that the latter required the threefold assent of king, lords, and commons, while an ordinance might be ordained by one or two of these constituent bodies. See 4 Inst. 25.

The name has also been given to certain enactments, more general in their character than ordinary statutes, and serving as organic laws, yet not exactly to be called "constitutions." Such was the "Ordinance for the government of the North-West Territory," enacted by congress in 1787.

ORDINANCE OF THE FOREST. In English law. A statute made touching matters and causes of the forest. 33 & 34 Edw. I.

ORDINANDI LEX. The law of procedure, as distinguished from the substantial part of the law.

Ordinarius ita dicitur quia habet ordinariam jurisdictionem, in jure proprio, et non propter deputationem. Co. Litt. 96. The ordinary is so called because he has an ordinary jurisdiction in his own right, and not a deputed one.

ORDINARY. **At common law.** One who has exempt and immediate jurisdiction in causes ecclesiastical. Also a bishop; and an archbishop is the ordinary of the whole province, to visit and receive appeals from inferior jurisdictions. Also a commissary or official of a bishop or other ecclesiastical judge having judicial power; an archdeacon; officer of the royal household. Wharton.

In American law. A judicial officer, in several of the states, clothed by statute with powers in regard to wills, probate, administration, guardianship, etc.

In Scotch law. A single judge of the court of session, who decides with or without a jury, as the case may be. Brande.

In the civil law. A judge who has authority to take cognizance of causes in his own right, and not by deputation.

ORDINARY CARE. That degree of care which persons of ordinary care and prudence are accustomed to use and employ, under the same or similar circumstances, in order to conduct the enterprise in which they are engaged to a safe and successful termination, having due regard to the rights of others and the objects to be accomplished. 8 Ohio St. 581.

The phrase "ordinary care" is equivalent to reasonable care, and necessarily involves the idea that such care was to be used as a reasonable person, under like circumstances, would adopt to avoid an accident. 3 Allen, 39. See, also, 25 Ind. 185; 6 Duer, 633; 28 Vt. 458; 23 Conn. 443.

ORDINARY CONVEYANCES. Those deeds of transfer which are entered into between two or more persons, without an assurance in a superior court of justice. Wharton.

ORDINARY DILIGENCE is that degree of care which men of common prudence generally exercise in their affairs, in the country and the age in which they live. 3 Brewst. 9.

ORDINARY NEGLECT or NEGLIGENCE. The omission of that care which a man of common prudence usually takes of his own concerns. 1 Edw. Ch. 513, 543. See 24 N. Y. 181.

ORDINARY OF ASSIZE AND SESSIONS. In old English law. A deputy of the bishop of the diocese, anciently appointed to give malefactors their neck-verses, and judge whether they read or not; also to perform divine services for them, and assist in preparing them for death. Wharton.

ORDINARY OF NEWGATE. The clergyman who is attendant upon condemned malefactors in that prison to prepare them for death; he records the behavior of such persons. Formerly it was the custom of the ordinary to publish a small pamphlet upon the execution of any remarkable criminal. Wharton.

ORDINARY SKILL in an art, means that degree of skill which men engaged in that particular art usually employ; not that which belongs to a few men only, of extraordinary endowments and capacities. 20 Pa. St. 130; 11 Mees. & W. 113; 20 Mart. (La.) 75.

ORDINATION is the ceremony by which a bishop confers on a person the privileges and powers necessary for the execution of sacerdotal functions in the church. Phillim. Ecc. Law, 110.

ORDINATIONE CONTRA SERVIENTES. A writ that lay against a servant for leaving his master contrary to the ordinance of St. 23 & 24 Edw. III. Reg. Orig. 189.

ORDINATUM EST. In old practice. It is ordered. The initial words of rules of court when entered in Latin.

Ordine placitandi servato, servatur et jus. When the order of pleading is observed, the law also is observed. Co. Litt. 303*a*; Broom, Max. 188.

ORDINES. A general chapter or other solemn convention of the religious of a particular order.

ORDINES MAJORES ET MINORES. In ecclesiastical law. The holy orders of priest, deacon, and subdeacon, any of which qualified for presentation and admission to an ecclesiastical dignity or cure were called "*ordines majores;*" and the inferior orders of chanters, psalmists, ostiary, reader, exorcist, and acolyte were called "*ordines minores.*" Persons ordained to the *ordines minores* had their *prima tonsura*, different from the *tonsura clericalis*. Cowell.

ORDINIS BENEFICIUM. Lat. In the civil law. The benefit or privilege of order; the privilege which a surety for a debtor had of requiring that his principal should be discussed, or thoroughly prosecuted, before the creditor could resort to him. Nov. 4, c. 1; Heinecc. Elem. lib. 3, tit. 21, § 883.

ORDINUM FUGITIVI. In old English law. Those of the religious who deserted their houses, and, throwing off the habits, renounced their particular order in contempt of their oath and other obligations. Paroch. Antiq. 388.

ORDO. Lat. That rule which monks were obliged to observe. Order; regular succession. An order of a court.

ORDO ALBUS. The white friars or Augustines. Du Cange.

ORDO ATTACHIAMENTORUM. In old practice. The order of attachments. Fleta, lib. 2, c. 51, § 12.

ORDO GRISEUS. The gray friars, or order of Cistercians. Du Cange.

ORDO JUDICIORUM. In the canon law. The order of judgments; the rule by which the due course of hearing each cause was prescribed. 4 Reeve, Eng. Law, 17.

ORDO NIGER. The black friars, or Benedictines. The Cluniacs likewise wore black. Du Cange.

ORE-LEAVE. A license or right to dig and take ore from land. 84 Pa. St. 340.

ORE TENUS. By word of mouth; orally. Pleading was anciently carried on *ore tenus*, at the bar of the court. 3 Bl. Comm. 293.

ORFGILD. In Saxon law. The price or value of a beast. A payment for a beast. The payment or forfeiture of a beast. A penalty for taking away cattle. Spelman.

ORGANIC LAW. The fundamental law, or constitution, of a state or nation, written or unwritten; that law or system of laws or principles which defines and establishes the organization of its government.

ORGANIZE. To establish or furnish with organs; to systematize; to put into working order; to arrange in order for the normal exercise of its appropriate functions.

The word "organize," as used in railroad and other charters, ordinarily signifies the choice and qualification of all necessary officers for the transaction of the business of the corporation. This is usually done after all the capital stock has been subscribed for. 38 Conn. 66.

ORGILD. In Saxon law. Without recompense; as where no satisfaction was to be made for the death of a man killed, so that he was judged lawfully slain. Spelman.

ORIGINAL. Primitive; first in order; bearing its own authority, and not deriving authority from an outside source; as *original* jurisdiction, *original* writ, etc. As applied to documents, the original is the first copy or archetype; that from which another instrument is transcribed, copied, or imitated.

ORIGINAL AND DERIVATIVE ESTATES. An original is the first of several estates, bearing to each other the relation of a particular estate and a reversion. An original estate is contrasted with a derivative estate; and a derivative estate is a particular interest carved out of another estate of larger extent. Prest. Est. 125.

ORIGINAL BILL. In equity pleading. A bill which relates to some matter not before litigated in the court by the same persons standing in the same interests. Mitf. Eq. Pl. 33.

In old practice. The ancient mode of commencing actions in the English court of king's bench. See BILL.

ORIGINAL CHARTER. In Scotch law. One by which the first grant of land is made. On the other hand, a charter by progress is one renewing the grant in favor of the heir or singular successor of the first or succeeding vassals. Bell.

ORIGINAL CONVEYANCES. Those conveyances at common law, otherwise termed "primary," by which a benefit or estate is created or first arises; comprising feoffments, gifts, grants, leases, exchanges, and partitions. 2 Bl. Comm. 309.

ORIGINAL ENTRY. The first entry of an item of an account made by a trader or other person in his account-books, as distinguished from entries posted into the ledger or copied from other books.

ORIGINAL JURISDICTION. Jurisdiction in the first instance; jurisdiction to take cognizance of a cause at its inception, try it, and pass judgment upon the law and facts. Distinguished from *appellate* jurisdiction.

ORIGINAL PROCESS. That by which a judicial proceeding is instituted; process to compel the appearance of the defendant. Distinguished from "mesne" process, which issues, during the progress of a suit, for some subordinate or collateral purpose; and from "final" process, which is process of execution.

ORIGINAL WRIT. In English practice. An original writ was the process formerly in use for the commencement of personal actions. It was a mandatory letter from the king, issuing out of chancery, sealed with the great seal, and directed to the sheriff of the county wherein the injury was committed, or was supposed to have been committed, requiring him to command the wrong-doer or accused party either to do justice to the plaintiff or else to appear in court and answer the accusation against him. This writ is now disused, the writ of summons being the process prescribed by the uniformity of process act for commencing personal actions; and under the judicature act, 1873, all suits, even in the court of chancery, are to be commenced by such writs of summons. Brown.

ORIGINALIA. In English law. Transcripts sent to the remembrancer's office in the exchequer out of the chancery, distinguished from *recorda*, which contain the judgments and pleadings in actions tried before the barons.

Origine propria neminem posse voluntate sua eximi manifestum est. It is evident that no one is able of his own pleasure, to do away with his proper origin. Code 10, 38, 4; Broom, Max. 77.

Origo rei inspici debet. The origin of a thing ought to be regarded. Co. Litt. 248*b*.

ORNEST. In old English law. The trial by battle, which does not seem to have been usual in England before the time of the Conqueror, though originating in the kingdoms of the north, where it was practiced under the name of "*holmgang,*" from the custom of fighting duels on a small island or *holm*. Wharton.

ORPHAN. A minor or infant who has lost both (or one) of his or her parents. More particularly, a fatherless child. 33 Pa. St. 9.

ORPHANAGE PART. That portion of an intestate's effects which his children were entitled to by the custom of London. This custom appears to have been a remnant of what was once a general law all over England, namely, that a father should not by his will bequeath the entirety of his personal estate away from his family, but should leave them a third part at least, called the "children's part," corresponding to the "bairns' part" or *legitim* of Scotch law, and also (although not in amount) to the *legitima quarta* of Roman law. (Inst. 2, 18.) This custom of London was abolished by St. 19 & 20 Vict. c. 94. Brown.

ORPHANOTROPHI. In the civil law. Managers of houses for orphans.

ORPHANS' COURT. In American law. Courts of probate jurisdiction, in Delaware, Maryland, New Jersey, and Pennsylvania.

ORTELLI. The claws of a dog's foot. Kitch.

ORTOLAGIUM. A garden plot or hortilage.

ORWIGE, SINE WITÂ. In old English law. Without war or feud, such security being provided by the laws, for homicides under certain circumstances, against the *fæhth*, or deadly feud, on the part of the family of the slain. Anc. Inst. Eng.

OSTENDIT VOBIS. Lat. In old pleading. Shows to you. Formal words with which a demandant began his count. Fleta, lib. 5, c.38, § 2.

OSTENSIBLE PARTNER. A partner whose name is made known and appears to the world as a partner, and who is in reality such. Story, Partn. § 80.

OSTENSIO. A tax anciently paid by merchants, etc., for leave to show or expose their goods for sale in markets. Du Cange.

OSTENTUM. In the civil law. A monstrous or prodigious birth. Dig. 50, 16, 38.

OSTIA REGNI. Gates of the kingdom. The ports of the kingdom of England are so called by Sir Matthew Hale. De Jure Mar. pt. 2, c. 3.

OSTIUM ECCLESIÆ. In old English law. The door or porch of the church, where dower was anciently conferred.

OSWALD'S LAW. The law by which was effected the ejection of married priests, and the introduction of monks into churches, by Oswald, bishop of Worcester, about A. D. 964. Wharton.

OSWALD'S LAW HUNDRED. An ancient hundred in Worcestershire, so called from Bishop Oswald, who obtained it from King Edgar, to be given to St. Mary's Church in Worcester. It was exempt from the sheriff's jurisdiction, and comprehends 300 hides of land. Camd. Brit.

OTER LA TOUAILLE. In the laws of Oleron. To deny a seaman his mess. Literally, to deny the table-cloth or victuals for three meals.

OTHESWORTHE. In Saxon law. Oathsworth; oathworthy; worthy or entitled to make oath. Bract. fols. 185, 292*b*.

OUGHT. This word, though generally directory only, will be taken as mandatory if the context requires it. 49 Mo. 518.

OUNCE. The twelfth part; the twelfth part of a pound.

OURLOP. The lierwite or fine paid to the lord by the inferior tenant when his daughter was debauched. Cowell.

OUST. To put out; to eject; to remove or deprive; to deprive of the possession or enjoyment of an estate or franchise.

OUSTER. In practice. A putting out; dispossession; amotion of possession. A species of injury to things real, by which the wrong-doer gains actual occupation of the land, and compels the rightful owner to seek his legal remedy in order to gain possession. 2 Crabb, Real Prop. p. 1063, § 2454*a*.

OUSTER LE MAIN. L. Fr. Literally, out of the hand.

1. A delivery of lands out of the king's hands by judgment given in favor of the petitioner in a *monstrans de droit*.

2. A delivery of the ward's lands out of the hands of the guardian, on the former arriving at the proper age, which was twenty-one in males, and sixteen in females. Abolished by 12 Car. II. c. 24. Mozley & Whitley.

OUSTER LE MER. L. Fr. Beyond the sea; a cause of excuse if a person, being summoned, did not appear in court. Cowell.

OUT OF COURT. He who has no legal *status* in court is said to be "out of court," *i. e.*, he is not before the court. Thus, when the plaintiff in an action, by some act of omission or commission, shows that he is unable to maintain his action, he is frequently said to put himself "out of court." Brown.

OUT OF THE STATE. Beyond sea, (which title see.)

OUT OF TIME. A mercantile phrase applied to a ship or vessel that has been so long at sea as to justify the belief of her total loss.

In another sense, a vessel is said to be *out of time* when, computed from her known day of sailing, the time that has elapsed exceeds the average duration of similar voyages at the same season of the year. The phrase is identical with "missing ship." 2 Duer, Ins. 469.

OUTER BAR. In the English courts, barristers at law have been divided into two classes, viz., queen's counsel, who are admitted within the bar of the courts, in seats specially reserved for themselves, and junior counsel, who sit without the bar; and the latter are thence frequently termed barristers of the "outer bar," or "utter bar," in contradistinction to the former class. Brown.

OUTER HOUSE. The name given to the great hall of the parliament house in Edinburgh, in which the lords ordinary of the court of session sit as single judges to hear causes. The term is used colloquially as expressive of the business done there in contradistinction to the "Inner House," the name given to the chambers in which the first and second divisions of the court of session hold their sittings. Bell.

OUTFANGTHEF. A liberty or privilege in the ancient common law, whereby a lord was enabled to call any man dwelling in his manor, and taken for felony in another place out of his fee, to judgment in his own court. Du Cange.

OUTFIT. 1. An allowance made by the United States government to one of its diplomatic representatives going abroad, for the expense of his equipment.

2. This term, in its original use, as applying to ships, embraced those objects connected with a ship which were necessary for the sailing of her, and without which she would not in fact be navigable. But in ships engaged in whaling voyages the word has acquired a much more extended signification. 9 Metc. (Mass.) 364.

OUTHEST, or OUTHOM. A calling men out to the army by sound of horn. Jacob.

OUTHOUSE. Any house necessary for the purposes of life, in which the owner does not make his constant or principal residence, is an outhouse. 2 Root, 516.

A smaller or subordinate building connected with a dwelling, usually detached from it and standing at a little distance from it, not intended for persons to live in, but to serve some purpose of convenience or necessity; as a barn, a dairy, a tool-house, and the like.

OUTLAND. The Saxon thanes divided their hereditary lands into inland, such as lay nearest their dwelling, which they kept to their own use, and outland, which lay beyond the demesnes, and was granted out to tenants, at the will of the lord, like copyhold estates. This outland they subdivided into two parts. One part they disposed among those who attended their persons, called "theodans," or lesser thanes; the other part they allotted to their husbandmen, or churls. Jacob.

OUTLAW. In English law. One who is put out of the protection or aid of the law.

OUTLAWED, when applied to a promissory note, means barred by the statute of limitations. 37 Me. 389.

OUTLAWRY. In English law. A process by which a defendant or person in contempt on a civil or criminal process was declared an outlaw. If for treason or felony, it amounted to conviction and attainder. Stim. Law Gloss.

OUTPARTERS. Stealers of cattle. Cowell.

OUTPUTERS. Such as set watches for the robbing any manor-house. Cowell.

OUTRAGE. Injurious violence, or, in general, any species of serious wrong offered to the person, feelings, or rights of another. See 44 Iowa, 314.

OUTRIDERS. In English law. Bailiffs-errant employed by sheriffs or their deputies to ride to the extremities of their counties or hundreds to summon men to the county or hundred court. Wharton.

OUTROPER. A person to whom the business of selling by auction was confined by statute. 2 H. Bl. 557.

OUTSETTER. In Scotch law. Publisher. 3 How. State Tr. 603.

OUTSTANDING. 1. Remaining undischarged; unpaid; uncollected; as an outstanding debt.

2. Existing as an adverse claim or pretension; not united with, or merged in, the title or claim of the party; as an outstanding title.

OUTSTANDING TERM. A term in gross at law, which, in equity, may be made attendant upon the inheritance, either by express declaration or by implication.

OUTSUCKEN MULTURES. In Scotch law. Out-town multures; multures, duties, or tolls paid by persons voluntarily grinding corn at any mill to which they are not *thirled*, or bound by tenure. 1 Forb. Inst. pt. 2, p. 140.

OUVERTURE DES SUCCESSIONS. In French law. The right of succession which arises to one upon the death, whether natural or civil, of another.

OVELTY. In old English law. Equality.

OVER. In conveyancing, the word "over" is used to denote a contingent limitation intended to take effect on the failure of a prior estate. Thus, in what is commonly called the "name and arms clause" in a will or settlement there is generally a proviso that if the devisee fails to comply with the condition the estate is to go to some one else. This is a limitation or gift over. Wats. Comp. Eq. 1110; Sweet.

OVERCYTED, or OVERCYHSED. Proved guilty or convicted. Blount.

OVERDRAW. To draw upon a person or a bank, by bills or checks, to an amount in excess of the funds remaining to the drawer's credit with the drawee, or to an amount greater than what is due.

The term "overdraw" has a definite and well-understood meaning. Money is drawn from the bank by him who draws the check, not by him who receives the money; and it is drawn upon the account of the individual by whose check it is drawn, though it be paid to and for the benefit of another. No one can draw money from bank upon his own account, except by means of his own check or draft, nor can he overdraw his account with the bank in any other manner. 24 N. J. Law, 478, 484.

OVERDUE. A negotiable instrument or other evidence of debt is overdue when the day of its maturity is past and it remains unpaid. A vessel is said to be overdue when she has not reached her destination at the time when she might ordinarily have been expected to arrive.

OVERHAUL. To inquire into; to review; to disturb. "The merits of a judgment can never be *overhauled* by an original suit." 2 H. Bl. 414.

OVERHERNISSA. In Saxon law. Contumacy or contempt of court. Leg. Æthel. c. 25.

OVERLIVE. To survive; to live longer than another. Finch, Law, b. 1, c. 3, no. 58; 1 Leon. 1.

OVERPLUS. What is left beyond a certain amount; the residue; the remainder of a thing.

OVERREACHING CLAUSE. In a resettlement, a clause which saves the powers of sale and leasing annexed to the estate for life created by the original settlement, when it is desired to give the tenant for life the same estate and powers under the resettlement. The clause is so called because it provides that the resettlement shall be overreached by the exercise of the old powers. If the resettlement were executed without a provision to this effect, the estate of the tenant for life and the annexed powers would be subject to any charges for portions, etc., created under the original settlement. 3 Dav. Conv. 489; Sweet.

OVERRULE. To supersede; annul; reject by subsequent action or decision. A judicial decision is said to be overruled when a later decision, rendered by the same court or by a superior court in the same system, expresses a judgment upon the same question of law directly opposite to that which was before given, thereby depriving the earlier opinion of all authority as a precedent. The term is not properly applied to conflicting decisions on the same point by co-ordinate or independent tribunals.

In another sense, "overrule" is spoken of the action of a court in refusing to sustain, or recognize as sufficient, an objection made in the course of a trial, as to the introduction of particular evidence, etc.

OVERSAMESSA. In old English law. A forfeiture for contempt or neglect in not pursuing a malefactor. 3 Inst. 116.

OVERSEER. A superintendent or supervisor; a public officer whose duties involve general superintendence of routine affairs.

OVERSEERS OF HIGHWAYS. The name given, in some of the states, to a board of officers of a city, township, or county, whose special function is the construction and repair of the public roads or highways.

OVERSEERS OF THE POOR. Persons appointed or elected to take care of the poor with moneys furnished to them by the public authority.

OVERSMAN. In Scotch law. An umpire appointed by a submission to decide where two arbiters have differed in opinion, or he is named by the arbiters themselves, under powers given them by the submission. Bell.

OVERT. Open; manifest; public; issuing in action, as distinguished from that which rests merely in intention or design.

OVERT ACT. In criminal law. An open, manifest act from which criminality may be implied. An open act, which must be manifestly proved. 3 Inst. 12.

OVERT WORD. An open, plain word, not to be misunderstood. Cowell.

OVERTURE. An opening; a proposal.

OWELTY. Equality. This word is used in law in several compound phrases, as follows:

1. *Owelty of partition* is a sum of money paid by one of two coparceners or co-tenants to the other, when a partition has been effected between them, but, the land not being susceptible of division into exactly equal shares, such payment is required to make the portions respectively assigned to them of equal value.

2. In the feudal law, when there is lord, mesne, and tenant, and the tenant holds the mesne by the same service that the mesne holds over the lord above him, this was called "owelty of services." Tomlins.

3. *Owelty of exchange* is a sum of money given, when two persons have exchanged lands, by the owner of the less valuable estate to the owner of the more valuable, to equalize the exchange.

OWING. Something unpaid. A debt, for example, is owing while it is unpaid, and whether it be due or not.

OWLERS. In English law. Persons who carried wool, etc., to the sea-side by night, in order that it might be shipped off contrary to law. Jacob.

OWLING. In English law. The offense of transporting wool or sheep out of the kingdom; so called from its being usually carried on in the night. 4 Bl. Comm. 154.

OWNER. The person in whom is vested the ownership, dominion, or title of property; proprietor.

He who has dominion of a thing, real or personal, corporeal or incorporeal, which he has a right to enjoy and do with as he pleases, even to spoil or destroy it, as far as the law permits, unless he be prevented by some agreement or covenant which restrains his right. Bouvier.

OWNERSHIP. The complete dominion, title, or proprietary right in a thing or claim. See PROPERTY.

The ownership of a thing is the right of one or more persons to possess and use it to the exclusion of others. In this Code, the thing of which there may be ownership is called "property." Civil Code Cal. § 654.

Ownership is the right by which a thing belongs to some one in particular, to the exclusion of all other persons. Civil Code La. art. 488.

Ownership is divided into *perfect* and *imperfect*. Ownership is perfect when it is perpetual, and when the thing is unincumbered with any real right towards any other person than the owner. On the contrary, ownership is imperfect when it is to terminate at a certain time or on a condition, or if the thing which is the object of it, being an immovable, is charged with any real right towards a third person; as a usufruct, use, or servitude. When an immovable is subject to a usufruct, the owner of it is said to possess the naked ownership. Civil Code La. art. 490.

OXFILD. A restitution anciently made by a hundred or county for any wrong done by one that was within the same. Lamb. Arch. 125.

OXGANG In old English law. As much land as an ox could till. Co. Litt. 5*a*. A measure of land of uncertain quantity. In Scotland, it consisted of thirteen acres. Spelman.

OYER. In old practice. Hearing; the hearing a deed read, which a party sued on a bond, etc., might pray or demand, and it was then *read* to him by the other party; the entry on the record being, "*et ei legitur in hæc verba*," (and it is read to him in these words.) Steph. Pl. 67, 68; 3 Bl. Comm. 299; 3 Salk. 119.

In modern practice. A *copy* of a bond or specialty sued upon, given to the opposite party, in lieu of the old practice of *reading* it.

OYER AND TERMINER. A half French phrase applied in England to the assizes, which are so called from the commission of *oyer and terminer* directed to the judges, empowering them to "inquire, *hear, and determine*" all treasons, felonies, and misdemeanors. This commission is now issued regularly, but was formerly used only on particular occasions, as upon sudden outrage or insurrection in any place. In the United States, the higher criminal courts are called "courts of oyer and terminer." Burrill.

OYER DE RECORD. A petition made in court that the judges, for better proof's sake, will hear or look upon any record. Cowell.

OYEZ. Hear ye. A word used in courts by the public crier to command attention when a proclamation is about to be made. Commonly corrupted into "O yes."

P.

P. An abbreviation for "page;" also for "Paschalis," (Easter term,) in the Year Books, and for numerous other words of which it is the initial.

P. C. An abbreviation for "Pleas of the Crown;" sometimes also for "Privy Council," "Parliamentary Cases," "Patent Cases," "Practice Cases," "Penal Code," or "Political Code."

P. H. V. An abbreviation for "*pro hac vice*," for this turn, for this purpose or occasion.

P. J. An abbreviation for "president" (or presiding) "judge," (or justice.)

P. L. An abbreviation for "Pamphlet Laws" or "Public Laws."

P. M. An abbreviation for "postmaster;" also for "post-meridian," afternoon.

P. O. An abbreviation of "public officer;" also of "post-office."

P. P. An abbreviation for "*propria persona*," in his proper person, in his own person.

P. S. An abbreviation for "Public Statutes;" also for "postscript."

PAAGE. A toll for passage through another's land.

PACARE. To pay.

PACATIO. Payment. Mat. Par. A. D. 1248.

PACE. A measure of length containing two feet and a half, being the ordinary length of a step.

PACEATUR. Lat. Let him be freed or discharged.

Paci sunt maxime contraria vis et injuria. Co. Litt. 161. Violence and injury are the things chiefly hostile to peace.

PACIFICATION. The act of making peace between two hostile or belligerent states; re-establishment of public tranquility.

PACK. To put together in sorts with a fraudulent design. To pack a jury is to use unlawful, improper, or deceitful means to have the jury made up of persons favorably disposed to the party so contriving, or who have been or can be improperly influenced to give the verdict he seeks. The term imports the improper and corrupt selection of a jury sworn and impaneled for the trial of a cause. 12 Conn. 289.

PACK OF WOOL. A horse load, which consists of seventeen stone and two pounds, or two hundred and forty pounds weight. Fleta, l. 2, c. 12; Cowell.

PACKAGE. A package means a bundle put up for transportation or commercial handling; a thing in form to become, as such, an article of merchandise or delivery from hand to hand. A parcel is a small package; "parcel" being the diminutive of "package." Each of the words denotes a thing in form suitable for transportation or handling, or sale from hand to hand. 1 Hughes, 529.

"Package," in old English law, signifies one of various duties charged in the port of London on the goods imported and exported by aliens, or by denizens the sons of aliens. Tomlins.

PACKED PARCELS. The name for a consignment of goods, consisting of one large parcel made up of several small ones, (each bearing a different address,) collected from different persons by the immediate consignor, (a carrier,) who unites them into one for his own profit, at the expense of the railway by which they are sent, since the railway company would have been paid more for the carriage of the parcels singly than together. Wharton.

PACT. A bargain; compact; agreement. This word is used in writings on Roman law and on general jurisprudence as the English form of the Latin "*pactum*," (which see.)

Pacta conventa quæ neque contra leges neque dolo malo inita sunt omni modo observanda sunt. Agreements which are not contrary to the laws nor entered into with a fraudulent design are in all respects to be observed. Cod. 2, 3, 39; Broom, Max. 698, 732.

Pacta dant legem contractui. Hob. 118. The stipulations of parties constitute the law of the contract.

Pacta privata juri publico derogare non possunt. 7 Coke, 23. Private compacts cannot derogate from public right.

Pacta quæ contra leges constitutionesque, vel contra bonos mores fiunt, nullam vim habere, indubitati juris est. That contracts which are made against law or against good morals have no force is a principle of undoubted law Cod. 2, 3, 6.

Pacta quæ turpem causam continent non sunt observanda. Agreements founded upon an immoral consideration are not to be observed. Dig. 2, 14, 27, 4; Broom, Max. 732.

PACTIO. Lat. In the civil law. A bargaining or agreeing of which *pactum* (the agreement itself) was the result. Calvin. It is used, however, as the synonym of "*pactum.*"

PACTIONAL. Relating to or generating an agreement; by way of bargain or covenant.

PACTIONS. In international law. Contracts between nations which are to be performed by a single act, and of which execution is at an end at once. 1 Bouv. Inst. no. 100.

Pactis privatorum juri publico non derogatur. Private contracts do not derogate from public law. Broom, Max. 695.

PACTITIOUS. Settled by covenant.

Pacto aliquod licitum est, quod sine pacto non admittitur. Co. Litt. 166. By special agreement things are allowed which are not otherwise permitted.

PACTUM. Lat. **In the civil law.** A pact. An agreement or convention without specific name, and without consideration, which, however, might, in its nature, produce a civil obligation. Heinecc. Elem. lib. 3, tit. 14, § 775.

In Roman law. With some exceptions, those agreements that the law does not directly enforce, but which it recognizes only as a valid ground of defense, were called "*pacta.*" Those agreements that are enforced, in other words, are supported by actions, are called "*contractus.*" The exceptions are few, and belong to a late period. Hunter, Rom. Law, 546.

PACTUM CONSTITUTÆ PECUNIÆ. In the civil law. An agreement by which a person appointed to his creditor a certain day or a certain time at which he promised to pay; or an agreement by which a person promises to pay a creditor. Wharton.

PACTUM DE NON PETENDO. In the civil law. An agreement not to sue. A simple convention whereby a creditor promises the debtor that he will not enforce his claim. Mackeld. Rom. Law, § 542.

PACTUM DE QUOTA LITIS. In the civil law. An agreement by which a creditor promised to pay a portion of a debt difficult to recover to a person who undertook to recover it. Wharton.

PADDER. A robber; a foot highwayman.

PADDOCK. A small inclosure for deer or other animals.

PAGA. In Spanish law. Payment. Las Partidas, pt. 5, tit. 14, l. 1. *Pagamento*, satisfaction.

PAGARCHUS. A petty magistrate of a *pagus* or little district in the country.

PAGODA. A gold or silver coin, of several kinds and values, formerly current in India. It was valued, at the United States custom-house, at $1.94.

PAGUS. A county. Jacob.

PAINE FORTE ET DURE. See PEINE FORTE ET DURE.

PAINS AND PENALTIES, BILLS OF. The name given to acts of parliament to attaint particular persons of treason or felony, or to inflict pains and penalties beyond or contrary to the common law, to serve a special purpose. They are in fact new laws, made *pro re nata.*

PAINTINGS. It is held that colored imitations of rugs and carpets and colored working designs, each of them valuable and designed by skilled persons and hand painted, but having no value as works of art, are not "paintings," within the meaning of that term as used in a statute on the liability of carriers. 3 Ex. Div. 121.

PAIRING-OFF. In the practice of legislative bodies, this is the name given to a species of negative proxies, by which two members, who belong to opposite parties or are on opposite sides with regard to a given question, mutually agree that they will both be absent from voting, either for a specified period or when a division is had on the particular question. By this mutual agreement a vote is neutralized on each side of the question, and the relative numbers on the division are precisely the same as if both members were present. May, Parl. Pr. 370.

PAIS, PAYS. Fr. The country; the neighborhood. A trial *per pais* signifies a trial by the country; that is, by jury. An assurance by matter *in pais* is an assurance transacted between two or more private persons "in the country;" that is, upon the very spot to be transferred. Matter *in pais* signifies matter of fact, probably because matters of fact are triable by the country; *i. e.*, by jury; estoppels *in pais* are estoppels by conduct, as distinguished from estoppels by deed or by record.

PAIS, CONVEYANCES IN. Ordinary conveyances between two or more persons *in the country; i. e.*, upon the land to be transferred.

PALACE COURT. A court formerly existing in England. It was created by Charles I., and abolished in 1849. It was held in the borough of Southwark, and had jurisdiction of all personal actions arising within twelve miles of the royal palace of Whitehall, exclusive of London.

PALAGIUM. A duty to lords of manors for exporting and importing vessels of wine at any of their ports. Jacob.

PALAM. Lat. In the civil law. Openly; in the presence of many. Dig. 50, 16, 33.

PALATINE. Possessing royal privileges. See COUNTY PALATINE.

PALATINE COURTS formerly were the court of common pleas at Lancaster, the chancery court of Lancaster, and the court of pleas at Durham, the second of which alone now exists. (See the respective titles.) Sweet.

PALATIUM. Lat. A palace. The emperor's house in Rome was so called from the *Mons Palatinus* on which it was built. Adams, Rom. Ant. 613.

PALFRIDUS. A palfrey; a horse to travel on.

PALINGMAN. In old English law. A merchant denizen; one born within the English *pale*. Blount.

PALLIO COOPERIRE. In old English law. An ancient custom, where children were born out of wedlock, and their parents afterwards intermarried. The children, together with the father and mother, stood under a cloth extended while the marriage was solemnized. It was in the nature of adoption. The children were legitimate by the civil, but not by the common, law. Jacob.

PALMER ACT. A name given to the English statute 19 & 20 Vict. c. 16, enabling a person accused of a crime committed out of the jurisdiction of the central criminal court, to be tried in that court.

PAMPHLET. A small book, bound in paper covers, usually printed in the octavo form, and stitched.

PAMPHLET LAWS. The name given in Pennsylvania to the publication, in pamphlet or book form, containing the acts passed by the state legislature at each of its biennial sessions.

PANDECTS. A compilation of Roman law, consisting of selected passages from the writings of the most authoritative of the older jurists, methodically arranged, prepared by Tribonian with the assistance of sixteen associates, under a commission from the emperor Justinian. This work, which is otherwise called the "Digest," comprises fifty books, and is one of the four great works composing the *Corpus Juris Civilis*. It was first published in A. D. 533.

PANDOXATOR. In old records. A brewer.

PANDOXATRIX. An ale-wife; a woman that both brewed and sold ale and beer.

PANEL. The roll or slip of parchment returned by the sheriff in obedience to a *venire facias*, containing the names of the persons whom he has summoned to attend the court as jurymen.

The panel is a list of jurors returned by a sheriff, to serve at a particular court or for the trial of a particular action. Pen. Code Cal. § 1057.

The word is also used to denote the whole body of persons summoned as jurors for a particular term of court.

In Scotch law. The prisoner at the bar, or person who takes his trial before the court of justiciary for any crime. This name is given to him after his appearance. Bell.

PANIER, in the parlance of the English bar societies, is an attendant or domestic who waits at table and gives bread, (*panis*,) wine, and other necessary things to those who are dining. The phrase was in familiar use among the knights templar, and from them has been handed down to the learned societies of the inner and middle temples, who at the present day occupy the halls and buildings once belonging to that distinguished order, and who have retained a few of their customs and phrases. Brown.

PANIS. Lat. In old English law. Bread; loaf; a loaf. Fleta, lib. 2, c. 9.

PANNAGE. A common of pannage is the right of feeding swine on mast and acorns at certain seasons in a commonable wood or forest. Elton, Commons, 25; Williams, Common, 168.

Pannagium est pastus porcorum, in nemoribus et in silvis, ut puta, de glandibus, etc. 1 Bulst. 7. A pannagium is a pasture of hogs, in woods and forests, upon acorns, and so forth.

PANNELLATION. The act of impaneling a jury.

PANTOMIME. A dramatic performance in which gestures take the place of words. See 3 C. B. 871.

PAPER. In English practice. The list of causes or cases intended for argument, called "the paper of causes." 1 Tidd, Pr. 504.

PAPER BLOCKADE. The state of a line of coast proclaimed to be under blockade in time of war, when the naval force on watch is not sufficient to repel a real attempt to enter.

PAPER BOOK. In practice. A printed collection or abstract, in methodical order, of the pleadings, evidence, exhibits, and proceedings in a cause, or whatever else may be necessary to a full understanding of it, prepared for the use of the judges upon a hearing or argument on appeal.

Copies of the proceedings on an issue in law or demurrer, of cases, and of the proceedings on error, prepared for the use of the judges, and delivered to them previous to bringing the cause to argument. 3 Bl. Comm. 317; Archb. New Pr. 353; 5 Man. & G. 98.

In proceedings on appeal or error in a criminal case, copies of the proceedings with a note of the points intended to be argued, delivered to the judges by the parties before the argument. Archb. Crim. Pl. 205; Sweet.

PAPER CREDIT. Credit given on the security of any written obligation purporting to represent property.

PAPER DAYS. In English law. Certain days in term-time appointed by the courts for hearings or arguments in the cases set down in the various special papers.

PAPER MONEY. Bills drawn by a government against its own credit, engaging to pay money, but which do not profess to be immediately convertible into specie, and which are put into compulsory circulation as a substitute for coined money.

PAPER OFFICE. In English law. An ancient office in the palace of Whitehall, where all the public writings, matters of state and council, proclamations, letters, intelligences, negotiations of the queen's ministers abroad, and generally all the papers and dispatches that pass through the offices of the secretaries of state, are deposited. Also an office or room in the court of queen's bench where the records belonging to that court are deposited; sometimes called "paper-mill." Wharton.

PAPER TITLE. A title to land evidenced by a conveyance or chain of conveyances; the term generally implying that such title, while it has color or plausibility, is without substantial validity.

PAPIST. One who adheres to the communion of the Church of Rome. The word seems to be considered by the Roman Catholics themselves as a nickname of reproach, originating in their maintaining the supreme ecclesiastical power of the pope. Wharton.

PAR. In commercial law. Equal; equality. An equality subsisting between the nominal or face value of a bill of exchange, share of stock, etc., and its actual selling value. When the values are thus equal, the instrument or share is said to be "at par;" if it can be sold for more than its nominal worth, it is "above par;" if for less, it is "below par."

PAR DELICTUM. Lat. Equal guilt. "This is not a case of *par delictum*. It is oppression on one side and submission on the other. It never can be predicated as *par delictum* when one holds the rod and the other bows to it." 6 Maule & S. 165.

Par in parem imperium non habet. Jenk. Cent. 174. An equal has no dominion over an equal.

PAR OF EXCHANGE. In mercantile law. The precise equality or equivalency of any given sum or quantity of money in the coin of one country, and the like sum or quantity of money in the coin of any other foreign country into which it is to be exchanged, supposing the money of such country to be of the precise weight and purity fixed by the mint standard of the respective countries. Story, Bills, § 30.

The par of the currencies of any two countries means the equivalence of a certain amount of the currency of the one in the currency of the other, supposing the currency of both to be of the precise weight and purity fixed by their respective mints. The exchange between the two countries is said to be at par when bills are negotiated on this footing; *i. e.*, when a bill for £100 drawn on London sells in Paris for 2,520 frs., and *vice versa*. Bowen, Pol. Econ. 284.

PAR ONERI. Lat. Equal to the burden or charge; equal to the detriment or damage.

PARACHRONISM. Error in the computation of time.

PARACIUM. The tenure between parceners, viz., that which the youngest owes to the eldest without homage or service. Domesday.

PARAGE, or PARAGIUM. An equality of blood or dignity, but more especially of land, in the partition of an inheritance between co-heirs; more properly, however, an equality of condition among nobles, or persons holding by a noble tenure. Thus, when a fief is divided among brothers, the younger hold their part of the elder by parage; *i. e.*, without any homage or service. Also the portion which a woman may obtain on her marriage. Cowell.

PARAGRAPH. A part or section of a statute, pleading, affidavit, etc., which contains one article, the sense of which is complete.

PARALLEL. For two lines of street railway to be "parallel," within the meaning of a statute, it may not be necessary that the two lines should be parallel for the whole length of each or either route. Exact parallelism is not contemplated. 144 Mass. 254, 10 N. E. Rep. 835, 836.

PARAMOUNT. Above; upwards. That which is superior; usually applied to the highest lord of the fee of lands, tenements, or hereditaments, as distinguished from the *mesne* (or intermediate) lord. Fitzh. Nat. Brev. 135.

In the law of real property, the term "paramount title" properly denotes one which is superior to the title with which it is compared, in the sense that the former is the source or origin of the latter. It is, however, frequently used to denote a title which is simply better or stronger than another, or will prevail over it. But this use is scarcely correct, unless the superiority consists in the seniority of the title spoken of as "paramount."

PARAMOUNT EQUITY. An equitable right or claim which is prior, superior, or preferable to that with which it is compared.

PARAPHERNA. In the civil law. Goods brought by wife to husband over and above her dowry.

PARAPHERNAL PROPERTY. See PARAPHERNALIA.

PARAPHERNALIA. In the civil law. The separate property of a married woman, other than that which is included in her dowry, or *dos*.

The separate property of the wife is divided into dotal and extradotal. Dotal property is that which the wife brings to the husband to assist him in bearing the expenses of the marriage establishment. Extradotal property, otherwise called "paraphernal property," is that which forms no part of the dowry. Civil Code La. art. 2335.

The wife's paraphernalia shall not be subject to the debts or contracts of the husband, and shall consist of the apparel of herself and her children, her watch, and ornaments suitable to her condition in life, and all such articles of personalty as have been given to her for her own use and comfort. Code Ga. 1882, § 1773.

In English law. Those goods which a woman is allowed to have, after the death of her husband, *besides* her *dower*, consisting of her apparel and ornaments, suitable to her rank and degree. 2 Bl. Comm. 436.

PARAPHERNAUX, BIENS. Fr. In French law. All the wife's property which is not subject to the *régime dotal* is called by this name; and of these articles the wife has the entire administration; but she may allow the husband to enjoy them, and in that case he is not liable to account. Brown.

PARASCEVE. The sixth day of the last week in Lent, particularly called "Good Friday." In English law, it is a *dies non juridicus*.

PARASYNEXIS. In the civil law. A conventicle, or unlawful meeting.

PARATITLA. In the civil law. Notes or abstracts prefixed to titles of law, giving a summary of their contents. Cod. 1, 17, 1, 12.

PARATUM HABEO. Lat. I have him in readiness. The return by the sheriff to a *capias ad respondendum*, signifying that he has the defendant in readiness to be brought into court.

PARATUS EST VERIFICARE. Lat. He is ready to verify. The Latin form for concluding a pleading with a *verification*, (*q. v.*)

PARAVAIL. Inferior; subordinate. Tenant paravail signified the lowest tenant of land, being the tenant of a mesne lord. He was so called because he was supposed to make "avail" or profit of the land for another. Cowell; 2 Bl. Comm. 60.

PARCEL. In the law of real property, parcel signifies a part or portion of land. As used of chattels, it signifies a small package or bundle.

PARCEL MAKERS. Two officers in the exchequer who formerly made the parcels or items of the escheators' accounts, wherein they charged them with everything they had levied for the king during the term of their office. Cowell.

PARCELLA TERRÆ. A parcel of land.

PARCELS. A description of property, formerly set forth in a conveyance, together with the boundaries thereof, in order to its easy identification.

PARCELS, BILL OF. An account of the items composing a parcel or package of goods, transmitted with them to the purchaser.

PARCENARY. The state or condition of holding title to lands jointly by parceners or co-parceners, before a division of the joint estate.

PARCENER. A joint heir; one who, with others, holds an estate in co-parcenary, (*q. v.*)

PARCHMENT. Sheep-skins dressed for writing, so called from *Pergamus*, Asia Minor, where they were invented. Used for deeds, and used for writs of summons in England previous to the judicature act, 1875. Wharton.

PARCO FRACTO. Pound-breach; also the name of an old English writ against one chargeable with pound-breach.

PARCUS. A park, (*q. v.*) A pound for stray cattle. Spelman.

PARDON. An act of grace, proceeding from the power intrusted with the execution of the laws, which exempts the individual on whom it is bestowed from the punishment the law inflicts for a crime he has committed. 7 Pet. 160.

"Pardon" is to be distinguished from "amnesty." The former applies only to the individual, releases him from the punishment fixed by law for his specific offense, but does not affect the criminality of the same or similar acts when performed by other persons or repeated by the same person. The latter term denotes an act of grace, extended by the government to all persons who may come within its terms, and which obliterates the criminality of past acts done, and declares that they shall not be treated as punishable.

PARDONERS. In old English law. Persons who carried about the pope's indulgences, and sold them to any who would buy them.

PARENS. Lat. In Roman law. A parent; originally and properly only the father or mother of the person spoken of; but also, by an extension of its meaning, any relative, male or female, in the line of direct ascent.

"Parens" est nomen generale ad omne genus cognationis. Co. Litt. 80. "Parent" is a name general for every kind of relationship.

PARENS PATRIÆ. Parent of the country. In England, the king. In the United States, the state, as a sovereign, is the *parens patriæ*.

PARENT. The lawful father or the mother of a person. This word is distinguished from "ancestors" in including only the immediate progenitors of the person, while the latter embraces his more remote relatives in the ascending line.

PARENTELA, or *de parentela se tollere*, in old English law, signified a renunciation of one's kindred and family. This was, according to ancient custom, done in open court, before the judge, and in the presence of twelve men, who made oath that they believed it was done for a just cause. We read of it in the laws of Henry I. After such abjuration, the person was incapable of inheriting anything from any of his relations, etc. Enc. Lond.

PARENTHESIS. Part of a sentence occurring in the middle thereof, and inclosed between marks like ( ), the omission of which part would not injure the *grammatical* construction of the rest of the sentence. Wharton.

PARENTICIDE. One who murders a parent; also the crime so committed.

Parentum est liberos alere etiam nothos. It is the duty of parents to support their children even when illegitimate. Lofft, 222.

PARERGON. One work executed in the intervals of another; a subordinate task. Particularly, the name of a work on the Canons, in great repute, by Ayliffe.

PARES. A person's peers or equals; as the jury for the trial of causes, who were originally the vassals or tenants of the lord, being the equals or peers of the parties litigant; and, as the lord's vassals judged each other in the lord's courts, so the sovereign's vassals, or the lords themselves, judged each other in the sovereign's courts. 3 Bl. Comm. 349.

PARES CURIÆ. Peers of the court. Vassals who were bound to attend the lord's court.

PARES REGNI. Peers of the realm. Spelman.

PARI CAUSA. Lat. With equal right; upon an equal footing; equivalent in rights or claims.

PARI DELICTO. Lat. In equal fault. See IN PARI DELICTO.

PARI MATERIA. Lat. Of the same matter; on the same subject; as, laws *pari materia* must be construed with reference to each other. Bac. Abr. "Statute," I, 3.

PARI PASSU. Lat. By an equal progress; equably; ratably; without preference. Coote, Mortg. 56.

PARI RATIONE. Lat. For the like reason; by like mode of reasoning.

Paria copulantur paribus. Like things unite with like. Bac. Max.

Paribus sententiis reus absolvitur. Where the opinions are equal, [where the court is equally divided,] the defendant is acquitted. 4 Inst. 64.

PARIENTES. In Spanish law. Relations. White, New Recop. b. 1, tit. 7, c. 5, § 2.

PARIES. In the civil law. A wall. *Paries est, sive murus, sive maceria est.* Dig. 50, 16, 157.

PARIES COMMUNIS. In the civil law. A common wall; a party-wall. Dig. 29, 2, 39.

PARISH. In English law. A circuit of ground, committed to the charge of one parson or vicar, or other minister having cure of souls therein. 1 Bl. Comm. 111. The precinct of a parish church, and the particular charge of a secular priest. Cowell. An ecclesiastical division of a town or district, subject to the ministry of one pastor. Brande.

In New England. A corporation established for the maintenance of public worship, which may be coterminous with a town, or include only part of it.

A precinct or parish is a corporation established solely for the purpose of maintaining public worship, and its powers are limited to that object. It may raise money for building and keeping in repair its meeting-house and supporting its minister, but for no other purpose. A town is a civil and political corporation, established for municipal purposes. They may both subsist together in the same territory, and be composed of the same persons. 1 Pick. 91.

In Louisiana. A territorial division of the state corresponding to what is elsewhere called a "county."

PARISH APPRENTICE. In English law. The children of parents unable to maintain them may, by law, be apprenticed, by the guardians or overseers of their parish, to such persons as may be willing to receive them as apprentices. Such children are called "parish apprentices." 2 Steph. Comm. 230.

PARISH CHURCH. This expression has various significations. It is applied sometimes to a select body of Christians, forming a local spiritual association, and sometimes to the building in which the public worship of the inhabitants of a parish is celebrated; but the true legal notion of a parochial church is a consecrated place, having attached to it the rights of burial and the administration of the sacraments. Story, J., 9 Cranch, 326.

PARISH CLERK. In English law. An officer, in former times often in holy orders, and appointed to officiate at the altar; now his duty consists chiefly in making responses in church to the minister. By common law he has a freehold in his office, but it seems now to be falling into desuetude. 2 Steph. Comm. 700; Mozley & Whitley.

PARISH CONSTABLE. A petty constable exercising his functions within a given parish. Mozley & Whitley.

PARISH COURT. The name of a court established in each parish in Louisiana, and corresponding to the county courts or common pleas courts in the other states. It has a limited civil jurisdiction, besides general probate powers.

PARISH OFFICERS. Church-wardens, overseers, and constables.

PARISH PRIEST. In English law. The parson; a minister who holds a parish as a benefice. If the predial tithes are appropriated, he is called "rector;" if impropriated, "vicar." Wharton.

PARISHIONERS. Members of a parish. In England, for many purposes they form a body politic.

PARITOR. A beadle; a summoner to the courts of civil law

Parium eadem est ratio, idem jus. Of things equal, the reason is the same, and the same is the law.

PARIUM JUDICIUM. The judgment of peers; trial by a jury of one's peers or equals.

PARK. In English law. A tract of inclosed ground privileged for keeping wild beasts of the chase, particularly deer; an inclosed chase extending only over a man's own grounds. 2 Bl. Comm. 38.

In American law. An inclosed pleasure-ground in or near a city, set apart for the recreation of the public.

PARK-BOTE. To be quit of inclosing a park or any part thereof.

PARKER. A park-keeper.

PARLE HILL or PARLING HILL. A hill where courts were anciently held. Cowell.

PARLIAMENT. The supreme legislative assembly of Great Britain and Ireland, consisting of the king or queen and the three estates of the realm, viz., the lords spiritual, the lords temporal, and the commons. 1 Bl. Comm. 153.

PARLIAMENTARY AGENTS. Persons who act as solicitors in promoting and carrying private bills through parliament. They are usually attorneys or solicitors, but they do not usually confine their practice to this particular department. Brown.

PARLIAMENTARY COMMITTEE. A committee of members of the house of peers or of the house of commons, appointed by either house for the purpose of making inquiries, by the examination of witnesses or otherwise, into matters which could not be conveniently inquired into by the whole house. Wharton.

PARLIAMENTARY TAXES. Such taxes as are imposed directly by act of parliament, *i. e.*, by the legislature itself, as distinguished from those which are imposed by private individuals or bodies under the authority of an act of parliament. Thus, a sewers rate, not being imposed directly by act of parliament, but by certain persons termed "commissioners of sewers," is not a parliamentary tax; whereas the income tax, which is directly imposed, and the amount also fixed, by act of parliament, is a parliamentary tax. Brown.

PARLIAMENTUM DIABOLICUM. A parliament held at Coventry, 38 Hen. VI., wherein Edward, Earl of March, (afterwards King Edward IV.,) and many of the chief nobility were attainted, was so called; but the acts then made were annulled by the succeeding parliament. Jacob.

PARLIAMENTUM INDOCTUM. Unlearned or lack-learning parliament. A name given to a parliament held at Coventry in the sixth year of Henry IV. under an ordinance requiring that no lawyer should be chosen knight, citizen, or burgess; "by reason whereof," says Sir Edward Coke, "this parliament was fruitless, and never a good law made thereat." 4 Inst. 48; 1 Bl. Comm. 177.

PARLIAMENTUM INSANUM. A parliament assembled at Oxford, 41 Hen. III., so styled from the madness of their proceedings, and because the lords came with armed men to it, and contentions grew very high between the king, lords, and commons, whereby many extraordinary things were done. Jacob.

PARLIAMENTUM RELIGIOSORUM. In most convents there has been a common room into which the brethren withdrew for conversation; conferences there being termed "*parliamentum.*" Likewise, the societies of the two temples, or inns of court, call that assembly of the benchers or governors wherein they confer upon the common affairs of their several houses a "parliament." Jacob.

Parochia est locus quo degit populus alicujus ecclesiæ. 5 Coke, 67. A parish is a place in which the population of a certain church resides.

PAROCHIAL. Relating or belonging to a parish.

PAROCHIAL CHAPELS. Places of public worship in which the rites of sacrament and sepulture are performed.

PAROL. A word; speech; hence, oral or verbal; expressed or evidenced by speech only; not expressed by writing; not expressed by sealed instrument.

The pleadings in an action are also, in old law French, denominated the "parol," because they were formerly actual *viva voce* pleadings in court, and not mere written allegations, as at present. Brown.

PAROL AGREEMENTS. Such as are either by word of mouth or are committed to writing, but are not under seal. The common law draws only one great line, between things under seal and not under seal. Wharton.

PAROL ARREST. One ordered by a judge or magistrate from the bench, without written complaint or other proceedings, of a person who is present before him, and which is executed on the spot; as in case of breach of the peace in open court.

PAROL DEMURRER. In practice. A staying of the pleadings; a suspension of the proceedings in an action during the nonage of an infant, especially in a real action. Now abolished. 3 Bl. Comm. 300.

PAROL EVIDENCE. Oral or verbal evidence; that which is given by word of mouth; the ordinary kind of evidence, given by witnesses in court. 3 Bl. Comm. 369.

PAROL LEASE. A lease of real estate not evidenced by writing, but resting in an oral agreement.

PAROL PROMISE. A simple contract; a verbal promise. 2 Steph. Comm. 109.

PAROLE. In military law. A promise given by a prisoner of war, when he has leave to depart from custody, that he will return at the time appointed, unless discharged. Webster.

An engagement by a prisoner of war, upon being set at liberty, that he will not again take up arms against the government by whose forces he was captured, either for a limited period or while hostilities continue.

PAROLS DE LEY. L. Fr. Words of law; technical words.

Parols font plea. Words make the plea. 5 Mod. 458.

PARQUET. In French law. 1. The magistrates who are charged with the conduct of proceedings in criminal cases and misdemeanors.

2. That part of the *bourse* which is reserved for stock-brokers.

PARRICIDE. The crime of killing one's father; also a person guilty of killing his father.

PARRICIDIUM. In the civil law. Parricide; the murder of a parent. Dig. 48, 9, 9.

PARS. Lat. A part; a party to a deed, action, or legal proceeding.

PARS ENITIA. In old English law. The privilege or portion of the eldest daughter in the partition of lands by lot.

PARS GRAVATA. In old practice. A party aggrieved; the party aggrieved. Hardr. 50; 3 Leon. 237.

PARS PRO TOTO. Part for the whole; the name of a part used to represent the whole; as the roof for the house, ten spears for ten armed men, etc.

PARS RATIONABILIS. That part of a man's goods which the law gave to his widow and children. 2 Bl. Comm. 492.

PARS REA. A party defendant. St. Marlbr. c. 13.

PARS VISCERUM MATRIS. Part of the bowels of the mother; *i. e.*, an unborn child.

PARSON. The rector of a church; one that has full possession of all the rights of a parochial church. The appellation of "parson," however it may be depreciated by familiar, clownish, and indiscriminate use, is the most legal, most beneficial, and most honorable title that a parish priest can enjoy, because such a one, Sir Edward Coke observes, and he only, is said *vicem seu personam ecclesiæ gerere*, (to represent and bear the person of the church.) 1 Bl. Comm. 384.

PARSON IMPARSONEE. In English law A clerk or parson in full possession of a benefice. Cowell.

PARSON MORTAL. A rector instituted and inducted for his own life. But any collegiate or conventional body, to whom a church was forever appropriated, was termed "*persona immortalis.*" Wharton.

PARSONAGE. A certain portion of lands, tithes, and offerings, established by law, for the maintenance of the minister who has the cure of souls. Tomlins.

The word is more generally used for the house set apart for the residence of the minister. Mozley & Whitley.

PART. A portion, share, or purpart. One of two duplicate originals of a conveyance or covenant, the other being called "counterpart." Also, in composition, partial or incomplete; as part payment, part performance.

PART AND PERTINENT. In the Scotch law of conveyancing. Formal words equivalent to the English "appurtenances." Bell.

PART OWNERS. Joint owners; co-owners; those who have shares of ownership in the same thing, particularly a vessel.

PART PAYMENT. The reduction of any debt or demand by the payment of a sum less than the whole amount originally due.

PART PERFORMANCE. The doing some portion, yet not the whole, of what either party to a contract has agreed to do.

PARTAGE. In French law. A division made between co-proprietors of a particular estate held by them in common. It is the operation by means of which the goods of a succession are divided among the co-heirs; while licitation (*q. v.*) is an adjudication to the highest bidder of objects which are not divisible. Duverger.

PARTE INAUDITA. Lat. One side being unheard. Spoken of any action which is taken *ex parte*.

PARTE NON COMPARENTE. Lat. The party not having appeared. The condition of a cause called "default."

Parte quacumque integrante sublata, tollitur totum. An integral part being taken away, the whole is taken away 8 Coke, 41.

Partem aliquam recte intelligere nemo potest, antequam totum, iterum atque iterum, perlegerit. 3 Coke, 52. No one can rightly understand any part until he has read the whole again and again.

PARTES FINIS NIHIL HABUERUNT. In old pleading. The parties to the fine had nothing; that is, had no estate which could be conveyed by it. A plea to a fine which had been levied by a stranger. 2 Bl. Comm. 357; 1 P. Wms. 520.

PARTIAL INSANITY. Mental unsoundness always existing, although only occasionally manifest; monomania. 3 Add. 79.

PARTIAL LOSS. A loss of a part of a thing or of its value, or any damage not amounting (actually or constructively) to its entire destruction; as contrasted with *total* loss.

Partial loss is one in which the damage done to the thing insured is not so complete as to amount to a total loss, either actual or constructive. In every such case the underwriter is liable to pay such proportion of the sum which would be payable on total loss as the damage sustained by the subject of insurance bears to the whole value at the time of insurance. 2 Steph. Comm. 132, 133; Crump, Ins. § 331; Mozley & Whitley.

Partial loss implies a damage sustained by the ship or cargo, which falls upon the respective owners of the property so damaged; and, when happening from any peril insured against by the policy, the owners are to be indemnified by the underwriters, unless in cases excepted by the express terms of the policy. 4 Mass. 548.

The terms "partial loss" and "average" are understood, in this country, to mean the same thing. "Partial loss" includes both general and particular average. 4 Wend. 33, 39.

PARTICEPS. Lat. A participant; a sharer; anciently, a part owner, or parcener.

PARTICEPS CRIMINIS. A participant in a crime; an accomplice. One who shares or co-operates in a criminal offense, tort, or fraud.

Participes plures sunt quasi unum corpus in eo quod unum jus habent, et oportet quod corpus sit integrum, et quod in nulla parte sit defectus. Co. Litt. 4. Many parceners are as one body, inasmuch as they have one right, and it is necessary that the body be perfect, and that there be a defect in no part.

PARTICULA. A small piece of land.

PARTICULAR AVERAGE. In the law of insurance. Every kind of expense or damage short of a total loss which regards a particular concern, and which is to be borne by the proprietors of that concern alone. A loss borne wholly by the party upon whose property it takes place; so called in distinction from a *general* average, for which different parties contribute. 2 Phil. Ins. 191.

Particular average is the damage or loss, short of total, falling directly upon specific property; while general average is the liability of property to contribute to the loss of or damage to something else. 3 Bosw. 385, 395.

PARTICULAR CUSTOM. A custom which only affects the inhabitants of some particular district. 1 Bl. Comm. 74.

PARTICULAR ESTATE. A limited estate which is taken out of the fee, and which precedes a remainder; as an estate for years to A., remainder to B. for life; or an estate for life to A., remainder to B. in tail. This precedent estate is called the "particular estate," and the tenant of such estate is called the "particular tenant." 2 Bl. Comm. 165.

PARTICULAR LIEN. A specific lien on the particular goods in a tradesman's hands, for the value of work done upon them. Cross, Liens, 24. A right to retain a certain chattel from the owner, until a certain claim upon it (generally a bailee's claim for work done upon or in relation to the property) be satisfied. 2 Steph. Comm. 132.

PARTICULAR MALICE. Malice directed against a particular individual; ill will; a grudge; a desire to be revenged on a particular person. 11 Ired. 261.

PARTICULAR STATEMENT. This term, in use in Pennsylvania, denotes a statement which a plaintiff may be required to file, exhibiting in detail the items of his claim, (or its nature, if single,) with the dates and sums. It is a species of declaration, but is informal and not required to be methodical. 6 Serg. & R. 28.

PARTICULAR TENANT. The tenant of a particular estate. 2 Bl. Comm. 274. See PARTICULAR ESTATE.

PARTICULARITY, in a pleading, affidavit, or the like, is the detailed statement of particulars.

PARTICULARS. The details of a claim, or the separate items of an account. When these are stated in an orderly form, for the information of a defendant, the statement is called a "bill of particulars," (*q. v.*)

PARTICULARS OF BREACHES AND OBJECTIONS. In an action brought, in England, for the infringement of letters patent, the plaintiff is bound to deliver with his declaration (now with his statement of claim) particulars (*i. e.*, details) of the breaches which he complains of. Sweet.

PARTICULARS OF CRIMINAL CHARGES. A prosecutor, when a charge is general, is frequently ordered to give the defendant a statement of the acts charged, which is called, in England, the "particulars" of the charges.

PARTICULARS OF SALE. When property such as land, houses, shares, reversions, etc., is to be sold by auction, it is usually described in a document called the "particulars," copies of which are distributed among intending bidders. They should fairly and accurately describe the property. Dart, Vend. 113; 1 Dav. Conv. 511.

PARTIDA. Span. Part; a part. See LAS PARTIDAS.

PARTIES. The persons who take part in the performance of any act, or who are directly interested in any affair, contract, or conveyance, or who are actively concerned in the prosecution and defense of any legal proceeding.

In the Roman civil law, the parties were designated as "*actor*" and "*reus*." In the common law, they are called "plaintiff" and "defendant;" in real actions, "demandant" and "tenant;" in equity, "complainant" or "plaintiff" and "defendant;" in Scotch law, "pursuer" and "defender;" in admiralty practice, "libelant" and "respondent;" in appeals, "appellant" and "respondent," sometimes, "plaintiff in error" and "defendant in error;" in criminal proceedings, "prosecutor" and "prisoner."

PARTIES AND PRIVIES. Parties to a deed or contract are those with whom the deed or contract is actually made or entered into. By the term "privies," as applied to contracts, is frequently meant those between whom the contract is mutually binding, although not literally parties to such contract. Thus, in the case of a lease, the lessor and lessee are both parties and privies, the contract being literally made between the two, and also being mutually binding; but, if the lessee assign his interest to a third party, then a privity arises between the assignee and the original lessor, although such assignee is not literally a party to the original lease. Brown.

PARTITIO. In the civil law. Partition; division. This word did not always signify *dimidium*, a dividing into halves. Dig. 50, 16, 164, 1.

PARTITION. The dividing of lands held by joint tenants, coparceners, or tenants in common, into distinct portions, so that they may hold them in severalty. And, in a less technical sense, any division of real or personal property between co-owners or co-proprietors.

PARTITION, DEED OF. In conveyancing. A species of primary or original conveyance between two or more joint tenants, coparceners, or tenants in common, by which they divide the lands so held among them in severalty, each taking a distinct part. 2 Bl. Comm. 323, 324.

PARTITION OF A SUCCESSION. The partition of a succession is the division of the effects of which the succession is composed, among all the co-heirs, according to their respective rights. Partition is voluntary or judicial. It is voluntary when it is made among all the co-heirs present and of age, and by their mutual consent. It is judicial when it is made by the authority of the court, and according to the formalities prescribed by law. Every partition is either definitive or provisional. Definitive partition is that which is made in a permanent and irrevocable manner. Provisional partition is that which is made provisionally, either of certain things before the rest can be divided, or even of everything that is to be divided, when the parties are not in a situation to make an irrevocable partition. Civil Code La. art. 1293, et seq.

PARTNERS. Persons who have united to form a partnership in business; members of a firm.

An *ostensible* partner is one whose name appears to the world as such, and he is bound, though he have no interest in the firm. A *dormant* or *secret* partner is one whose connection with the firm is really or professedly concealed from the world. Code Ga. 1882, § 1889.

A dormant partner is one whose name is not mentioned in the title of the firm, or embraced in some general term, as company, sons, etc. 4 Phila. 1.

A *nominal* partner is one whose name appears in connection with the business as a member of the firm, but who has no real interest in it.

A *special* partner is one whose liability for the debts and losses of the firm is limited, under statutory provisions, to the amount of the capital he has invested.

PARTNERSHIP. A voluntary contract between two or more competent persons to place their money, effects, labor, and skill, or some or all of them, in lawful commerce or business, with the understanding that there shall be a proportional sharing of the profits and losses between them. Story, Partn. § 2; Colly. Partn. § 2; 24 How. 541; 3 Kent, Comm. 23.

Partnership is the association of two or more persons for the purpose of carrying on business together, and dividing its profits between them. Civil Code Cal. § 2395.

Partnership is a synallagmatic and commutative contract made between two or more persons for the mutual participation in the profits which may accrue from property, credit, skill, or industry, furnished in determined proportions by the parties. Civil Code La. art. 2801.

Partnership is where two or more persons agree to carry on any business or adventure together, upon the terms of mutual participation in its profits and losses. Mozley & Whitley.

Partnership and community are not to be confounded. The first is based on the contract of the parties, which creates the community. The last may exist independently of any contract whatsoever. It is founded on the voluntary contract of the parties, as contradistinguished from the relations that may arise between them by mere operation of law, independent of such contract. 11 La. Ann. 277.

A *general* partnership is one which includes all the dealings of the parties in one particular branch of business, as that of bankers, publishers, etc.

To constitute a general partnership, it is enough that the parties agree to conduct a business, and to share its profit and loss. Whether the business is of a general nature, or is confined to particular transactions, the partnership is general. 3 Abb. Pr. (N. S.) 20.

A *special* partnership is properly one formed for a special or particular enterprise or transaction. But the term is also used to denote what is more technically called a "limited" partnership.

A *limited* partnership is one where the firm comprises one or more general partners and one or several special partners, the latter being liable for the debts or losses of the firm only to the extent of their contributions in cash to the firm's capital.

A partnership *at will* is one designed to continue for no fixed period of time, but only during the pleasure of the parties; and it may be dissolved by any partner without previous notice.

A *subpartnership* is formed when one partner in a firm makes a stranger a partner with him in his share of the profits of that firm.

PARTNERSHIP IN COMMENDAM. Partnership *in commendam* is formed by a contract by which one person or partnership agrees to furnish another person or partnership a certain amount, either in property or money, to be employed by the person or partnership to whom it is furnished, in his or their own name or firm, on condition of receiving a share in the profits, in the proportion determined by the contract, and of being liable to losses and expenses to the amount furnished and no more. Civil Code La. art. 2839.

PARTURITION. The act of giving birth to a child.

PARTUS. Lat. Child; offspring; the child just before it is born, or immediately after its birth.

Partus ex legitimo thoro non certius noscit matrem quam genitorem suum. Fortes. 42. The offspring of a legitimate bed knows not his mother more certainly than his father.

Partus sequitur ventrem. The offspring follows the mother; the brood of an animal belongs to the owner of the dam; the offspring of a slave belongs to the owner of the mother, or follow the condition of the mother. A maxim of the civil law, which has been adopted in the law of England in regard to animals, though never allowed in the case of human beings. 2 Bl. Comm. 390, 94; Fortes. 42.

PARTY. A person concerned or having or taking part in any affair, matter, transaction, or proceeding, considered individually.

The term "parties" includes all persons who are directly interested in the subject-matter in issue, who have a right to make defense, control the proceedings, or appeal from the judgment. Strangers are persons who do not possess these rights. 52 N. H. 162.

"Party" is a technical word, and has a precise meaning in legal parlance. By it is understood he or they by or against whom a suit is brought, whether in law or equity; the party plaintiff or defendant, whether composed of one or more individuals, and whether natural or legal persons, (they are parties in the writ, and parties on the record;) and all others who may be affected by the suit, indirectly or consequentially, are persons interested, but not parties. 4 Pick. 405; 21 Me. 481.

PARTY AND PARTY. This phrase signifies the contending parties in an action; *i. e.*, the plaintiff and defendant, as distinguished from the attorney and his client. It is used in connection with the subject of costs, which are differently taxed between party and party and between attorney and client. Brown.

PARTY JURY. A jury *de medietate linguæ*, (which title see.)

PARTY STRUCTURE is a structure separating buildings, stories, or rooms which belong to different owners, or which are approached by distinct staircases or separate entrances from without, whether the same be a partition, arch, floor, or other structure. (St. 18 & 19 Vict. c. 122, § 3.) Mozley & Whitley.

PARTY-WALL. A wall built partly on the land of one owner, and partly on the land of another, for the common benefit of both in supporting timbers used in the construction of contiguous buildings. 40 Md. 19.

In the primary and most ordinary meaning of the term, a party-wall is (1) a wall of which the two adjoining owners are tenants in common. But it may also mean (2) a wall divided longitudinally into two strips, one belonging to each of the neighboring owners; (3) a wall which belongs entirely to one of the adjoining owners, but is subject to an easement or right in the other to have it maintained as a dividing wall between the two tenements, (the term is so used in some of the English building acts;) or (4) a wall divided longitudinally into two moieties, each moiety being subject to a cross-easement in favor of the owner of the other moiety. Sweet.

PARUM. Lat. Little; but little.

Parum cavet natura. Nature takes little heed. 2 Johns. Cas. 127, 166.

PARUM CAVISSE VIDETUR. Lat. In Roman law. He seems to have taken too little care; he seems to have been incautious, or not sufficiently upon his guard. A form of expression used by the judge or magistrate in pronouncing sentence of death upon a criminal. Festus, 325; Tayl. Civil Law, 81; 4 Bl. Comm. 362, note.

Parum differunt quæ re concordant. 2 Bulst. 86. Things which agree in substance differ but little.

Parum est latam esse sententiam nisi mandetur executioni. It is little [or to little purpose] that judgment be given unless it be committed to execution. Co. Litt. 289.

Parum proficit scire quid fieri debet, si non cognoscas quomodo sit facturum. 2 Inst. 503. It profits little to know what ought to be done, if you do not know how it is to be done.

PARVA SERJEANTIA. Petty serjeanty, (*q. v.*)

PARVISE. An afternoon's exercise or moot for the instruction of young students, bearing the same name originally with the *Parvisiæ* (little-go) of Oxford. Wharton.

PARVUM CAPE. See PETIT CAPE.

PAS. In French. Precedence; right of going foremost.

PASCH. The passover; Easter.

PASCHA. In old English law and practice. Easter. *De termino Paschæ*, of the term of Easter. Bract. fol. 246*b*.

PASCHA CLAUSUM. The octave of Easter, or Low-Sunday, which closes that solemnity.

PASCHA FLORIDUM. The Sunday before Easter, called "Palm-Sunday."

PASCHA RENTS. In English ecclesiastical law. Yearly tributes paid by the clergy to the bishop or archdeacon at their Easter visitations.

PASCUA. A particular meadow or pasture land set apart to feed cattle.

PASCUA SILVA. In the civil law. A feeding wood; a wood devoted to the feeding of cattle. Dig. 50, 16, 30, 5.

PASCUAGE. The grazing or pasturage of cattle.

PASS, *v*. 1. In practice. To utter or pronounce; as when the court *passes* sentence upon a prisoner. Also to proceed; to be rendered or given; as when judgment is said to *pass* for the plaintiff in a suit.

2. In legislative parlance, a bill or resolution is said to *pass* when it is agreed to or enacted by the house, or when the body has sanctioned its adoption by the requisite majority of votes; in the same circumstances, the body is said to *pass* the bill or motion.

3. When an auditor appointed to examine into any accounts certifies to their correctness, he is said to *pass* them; *i. e.*, they pass through the examination without being detained or sent back for inaccuracy or imperfection. Brown.

4. The term also means to examine into anything and then authoritatively determine the disputed questions which it involves. In this sense a jury is said to *pass upon* the rights or issues in litigation before them.

5. In the language of conveyancing, the term means to move from one person to another; to be transferred or conveyed from one owner to another; as in the phrase "the word 'heirs' will *pass* the fee."

6. To publish; utter; transfer; circulate; impose fraudulently. This is the meaning of the word when the offense of *passing* counterfeit money or a forged paper is spoken of.

"Pass," "utter," "publish," and "sell" are in some respects convertible terms, and, in a given case, "pass" may include utter, publish, and sell. The words "uttering" and "passing," used of notes, do not necessarily import that they are transferred as genuine. The words include any delivery of a note to another for value, with intent that it shall be put into circulation as money. 1 Abb. (U. S.) 135.

Passing a paper is putting it off in payment or exchange. Uttering it is a declaration that it is good, with an intention to pass, or an offer to pass it.

PASS, *n*. Permission to pass; a license to go or come; a certificate, emanating from authority, wherein it is declared that a designated person is permitted to go beyond certain boundaries which, without such authority, he could not lawfully pass. Also a ticket issued by a railroad or other transportation company, authorizing a designated person to travel free on its lines, between certain points or for a limited time.

PASS-BOOK. A book in which a bank or banker enters the deposits made by a customer, and which is retained by the latter. Also a book in which a merchant enters the items of sales on credit to a customer, and which the latter carries or keeps with him.

PASSAGE. A way over water; an easement giving the right to pass over a piece of private water.

Travel by sea; a voyage over water; the carriage of passengers by water; money paid for such carriage.

Enactment; the act of carrying a bill or resolution through a legislative or deliberative body in accordance with the prescribed forms and requisites; the emergence of the bill in the form of a law, or the motion in the form of a resolution.

PASSAGE COURT. An ancient court of record in Liverpool, once called the "mayor's court of *pays sage*," but now usually called the "court of the passage of the borough of Liverpool." This court was formerly held before the mayor and two bailiffs of the borough, and had jurisdiction in actions where the amount in question exceeded forty shillings. Mozley & Whitley.

PASSAGE MONEY. The fare of a passenger by sea; money paid for the transportation of persons in a ship or vessel; as distinguished from "freight" or "freight-money," which is paid for the transportation of goods and merchandise.

PASSAGIO. An ancient writ addressed to the keepers of the ports to permit a man who had the king's leave to pass over sea. Reg. Orig. 193.

PASSAGIUM REGIS. A voyage or expedition to the Holy Land made by the kings of England in person. Cowell.

PASSATOR. He who has the interest or command of the passage of a river; or a lord to whom a duty is paid for passage. Wharton.

PASSENGER. A person whom a common carrier has contracted to carry from one place to another, and has, in the course of the performance of that contract, received under his care either upon the means of conveyance, or at the point of departure of that means of conveyance. 96 Pa. St. 267.

PASSIAGIARIUS. A ferryman. Jacob.

PASSING-TICKET. In English law. A kind of permit, being a note or check which the toll-clerks on some canals give to the boatmen, specifying the lading for which they have paid toll. Wharton.

PASSIO. Pannage; a liberty for hogs to run in forests or woods to feed upon mast. Mon. Angl. 1, 682.

PASSIVE DEBT. A debt upon which, by agreement between the debtor and creditor, no interest is payable, as distinguished from *active* debt; *i. e.*, a debt upon which interest is payable. In this sense, the terms "active" and "passive" are applied to certain debts due from the Spanish government to Great Britain. Wharton.

In another sense of the words, a debt is "active" or "passive" according as the person of the creditor or debtor is regarded; a passive debt being that which a man owes; an active debt that which is owing to him. In this meaning every debt is both active and passive,—active as regards the creditor, passive as regards the debtor.

PASSIVE TRUST. A trust as to which the trustee has no active duty to perform.

PASSIVE USE. A permissive use, (*q. v.*)

PASSPORT. In international law. A document issued to a neutral merchant vessel, by her own government, during the progress of a war, and to be carried on the voyage, containing a sufficient description of the vessel, master, voyage, and cargo to evidence her nationality and protect her against the cruisers of the belligerent powers. This paper is otherwise called a "pass," "sea-pass," "sea-letter, or "sea-brief."

A license or safe-conduct, issued during the progress of a war, authorizing a person to remove himself or his effects from the territory of one of the belligerent nations to another country, or to travel from country to country without arrest or detention on account of the war.

In American law. A special instrument intended for the protection of American vessels against the Barbary powers, usually called a "Mediterranean pass." Jac. Sea Laws, 69.

In modern European law. A warrant of protection and authority to travel, granted to persons moving from place to place, by the competent officer. Brande.

PASTO. In Spanish law. Feeding; pasture; a right of pasture. White, New Recop. b. 2, tit. 1, c. 6, § 4.

PASTOR. Lat. A shepherd. Applied to a minister of the Christian religion, who has charge of a congregation, hence called his "flock."

PASTURE. Land on which cattle are fed; also the right of pasture. Co. Litt. 4*b*.

PASTUS. In feudal law. The procuration or provision which tenants were bound to make for their lords at certain times, or as often as they made a progress to their lands. It was often converted into money.

PATEAT UNIVERSIS PER PRÆSENTES. Know all men by these presents. Words with which letters of attorney anciently commenced. Reg. Orig. 305*b*, 306.

PATENT, *adj.* Open; manifest; evident; unsealed. Used in this sense in such phrases as "patent ambiguity," "patent writ," "letters patent."

PATENT, *n.* A grant of some privilege, property, or authority, made by the government or sovereign of a country to one or more individuals. Phil. Pat. 1.

In English law. A grant by the sovereign to a subject or subjects, under the great seal, conferring some authority, title, franchise, or property; termed "letters patent" from being delivered open, and not closed up from inspection.

In American law. The instrument by which a state or government grants public lands to an individual.

A grant made by the government to an inventor, conveying and securing to him the exclusive right to make and sell his invention for a term of years.

PATENT AMBIGUITY. An ambiguity which arises upon the words of the will, deed, or other instrument, as looked at in themselves, and before they are attempted to be applied to the object or to the subject which they describe. The term is opposed to "latent ambiguity," (*q. v.*)

PATENT BILL OFFICE. The attorney general's patent bill office is the office in which were formerly prepared the drafts of all letters patent issued in England, other than those for inventions. The draft patent was called a "bill," and the officer who prepared it was called the "clerk of the patents to the queen's attorney and solicitor general." Sweet.

PATENT OF PRECEDENCE. Letters patent granted, in England, to such barristers as the crown thinks fit to honor with that mark of distinction, whereby they are entitled to such rank and preaudience as are assigned in their respective patents, which is sometimes next after the attorney general, but more usually next after her majesty's counsel then being. These rank promiscuously with the king's (or queen's) counsel, but are not the sworn servants of the crown. 3 Bl. Comm. 28; 3 Steph. Comm. 274.

PATENT-OFFICE. In the administrative system of the United States, this is one of the bureaus of the department of the interior. It has charge of the issuing of patents to inventors and of such business as is connected therewith.

PATENT-RIGHT. A right secured by patent; usually meaning a right to the exclusive manufacture and sale of an invention or patented article.

PATENT-RIGHT DEALER. Any one whose business it is to sell, or offer for sale, patent-rights. 14 St. at Large, 118.

PATENT ROLLS. The official records of royal charters and grants; covering from the reign of King John to recent times. They contain grants of offices and lands, restitutions of temporalities to ecclesiastical persons, confirmations of grants made to bodies corporate, patents of creation of peers, and licenses of all kinds. Hubb. Succ. 617; 32 Phila. Law Lib. 429.

PATENT WRIT. In old practice. An open writ; one not closed or sealed up. See CLOSE WRITS.

PATENTABLE. Suitable to be patented; entitled by law to be protected by the issuance of a patent.

PATENTEE. He to whom a patent has been granted. The term is usually applied to one who has obtained letters patent for a new invention.

PATER. Lat. A father; the father. In the civil law, this word sometimes included *avus*, (grandfather.) Dig. 50, 16, 201.

Pater is est quem nuptiæ demonstrant. The father is he whom the marriage points out. 1 Bl. Comm. 446; 7 Mart. (N. S.) 548, 553; Dig. 2, 4, 5; Broom, Max. 516.

PATER PATRIÆ. Father of the country. See PARENS PATRIÆ.

PATERFAMILIAS. The father of a family.

In Roman law. The head or master of a family.

This word is sometimes employed, in a wide sense, as equivalent to *sui juris*. A person *sui juris* is called "*paterfamilias*" even when under the age of puberty. In the narrower and more common use, a *paterfamilias* is any one invested with *potestas* over any person. It is thus as applicable to a grandfather as to a father. Hunter, Rom. Law, 49.

PATERNA PATERNIS. Lat. Paternal estates to paternal heirs. A rule of the French law, signifying that such portion of a decedent's estate as came to him from his father must descend to his heirs on the father's side.

PATERNAL. That which belongs to the father or comes from him.

PATERNAL POWER. The authority lawfully exercised by parents over their children. This phrase is also used to translate the Latin "*patria potestas*," (*q. v.*)

PATERNAL PROPERTY. That which descends or comes to one from his father, grandfather, or other ascendant or collateral on the paternal side of the house.

PATERNITY. The fact of being a father; the relationship of a father.

The Latin "*paternitas*" is used in the canon law to denote a kind of spiritual relationship contracted by baptism. Heinecc. Elem. lib. 1, tit. 10, § 161, note.

PATHOLOGY. In medical jurisprudence. The science or doctrine of diseases. That part of medicine which explains the nature of diseases, their causes, and their symptoms.

PATIBULARY. Belonging to the gallows.

PATIBULATED. Hanged on a gibbet.

PATIBULUM. In old English law. A gallows or gibbet. Fleta, lib. 2, c. 3, § 9.

PATIENS. Lat. One who suffers or permits; one to whom an act is done; the passive party in a transaction.

PATRIA. Lat. The country, neighborhood, or vicinage; the men of the neighborhood; a jury of the vicinage. Synonymous, in this sense, with "*pais.*"

Patria laboribus et expensis non debet fatigari. A jury ought not to be harassed by labors and expenses. Jenk. Cent. 6.

PATRIA POTESTAS. Lat. In Roman law. Paternal authority; the paternal power. This term denotes the aggregate of those peculiar powers and rights which, by the civil law of Rome, belonged to the head of a family in respect to his wife, children, (natural or adopted,) and any more remote descendants who sprang from him through males only. Anciently, it was of very extensive reach, embracing even the power of life and death, but was gradually curtailed, until finally it amounted to little more than a right in the *paterfamilias* to hold as his own any property or acquisitions of one under his power. Mackeld. Rom. Law, § 589.

Patria potestas in pietate debet, non in atrocitate, consistere. Paternal power should consist [or be exercised] in affection, not in atrocity.

PATRIARCH. The chief bishop over several countries or provinces, as an archbishop is of several dioceses. Godb. 20.

PATRICIDE. One who has killed his father. As to the punishment of that offense by the Roman law, see Sandars' Just. Inst. (5th Ed.) 496.

PATRICIUS. In the civil law. A title of the highest honor, conferred on those who enjoyed the chief place in the emperor's esteem.

PATRIMONIAL. Pertaining to a patrimony; inherited from ancestors, but strictly from the direct male ancestors.

PATRIMONIUM. In the civil law. The private and exclusive ownership or dominion of an individual. Things capable of being possessed by a single person to the exclusion of all others (or which are actually so possessed) are said to be *in patrimonio;* if not capable of being so possessed, (or not actually so possessed,) they are said to be *extra patrimonium.* See Gaius, bk. 2, § 1.

PATRIMONY. A right or estate inherited from one's ancestors, particularly from direct male ancestors.

PATRINUS. In old ecclesiastical law. A godfather. Spelman.

PATRITIUS. An honor conferred on men of the first quality in the time of the English Saxon kings.

PATROCINIUM. In Roman law. Patronage; protection; defense. The business or duty of a patron or advocate.

PATRON. In ecclesiastical law. He who has the right, title, power, or privilege of presenting to an ecclesiastical benefice.

In Roman law. The former master of an emancipated slave.

In French marine law. The captain or master of a vessel.

PATRONAGE. In English ecclesiastical law. The right of presentation to a church or ecclesiastical benefice; the same with advowson, (*q. v.*) 2 Bl. Comm. 21.

The right of appointing to office, considered as a perquisite, or personal right; not in the aspect of a public trust.

PATRONATUS. In Roman law. The condition, relation, right, or duty of a patron.

In ecclesiastical law. Patronage, (*q. v.*)

Patronum faciunt dos, ædificatio, fundus. Dod. Adv. 7. Endowment, building, and land make a patron.

PATRONUS. In Roman law. A person who stood in the relation of protector to another who was called his "client." One who advised his client in matters of law, and advocated his causes in court. Gilb. Forum Rom. 25.

PATROON. The proprietors of certain manors created in New York in colonial times were so called.

PATRUELIS. In the civil law. A cousin-german by the father's side; the son or daughter of a father's brother. Wharton.

PATRUUS. An uncle by the father's side; a father's brother.

PATRUUS MAGNUS. A grandfather's brother; granduncle.

PATRUUS MAJOR. A great-grandfather's brother.

PATRUUS MAXIMUS. A great-grandfather's father's brother.

PAUPER. A person so poor that he must be supported at public expense; also a suitor who, on account of poverty, is allowed to sue or defend without being chargeable with costs.

PAUPERIES. Lat. In Roman law. Damage or injury done by an irrational animal, without active fault on the part of the owner, but for which the latter was bound to make compensation. Inst. 4, 9; Mackeld. Rom. Law, § 510.

PAVAGE. Money paid towards paving the streets or highways.

PAVE. To pave is to cover with stones or brick, or other suitable material, so as to make a level or convenient surface for horses, carriages, or foot-passengers, and a sidewalk is paved when it is laid or flagged with flat stones, as well as when paved with brick, as is frequently done. 60 N. Y. 22.

PAWN, *v.* To deliver personal property to another in pledge, or as security for a debt or sum borrowed.

PAWN, *n.* A bailment of goods to a creditor, as security for some debt or engagement; a pledge. Story, Bailm. § 7.

Pawn, or pledge, is a bailment of goods by a debtor to his creditor, to be kept till the debt is discharged. Wharton.

Also the specific chattel delivered to the creditor in this contract.

In the law of Louisiana, *pawn* is known as one species of the contract of *pledge*, the other being *antichresis;* but the word "pawn" is sometimes used as synonymous with "pledge," thus including both species. Civil Code La. art. 3101.

PAWNBROKER. A person whose business is to lend money, usually in small sums, on security of personal property deposited with him or left in pawn.

Whoever loans money on deposit or pledges of personal property, or who purchases personal property or choses in action, on condition of selling the same back again at a stipulated price, is hereby defined and declared to be a pawnbroker. Rev. St. Ohio 1880, § 4387. See, also, 14 U. S. St. at Large, 116.

PAWNEE. The person receiving a pawn, or to whom a pawn is made; the person to whom goods are delivered by another in pledge.

PAWNOR. The person pawning goods or delivering goods to another in pledge.

PAX ECCLESIÆ. Lat. In old English law. The peace of the church. A particular privilege attached to a church; sanctuary, (*q. v.*) Crabb, Eng. Law, 41; Cowell.

PAX REGIS. Lat. The peace of the king; that is, the peace, good order, and security for life and property which it is one of the objects of government to maintain, and which the king, as the personification of the power of the state, is supposed to guaranty to all persons within the protection of the law.

This name was also given, in ancient times, to a certain privileged district or sanctuary. The *pax regis*, or verge of the court, as it was afterwards called, extended from the palace-gate to the distance of three miles, three furlongs, three acres, nine feet, nine palms, and nine barleycorns. Crabb, Eng. Law, 41.

PAY. To pay is to deliver to a creditor the value of a debt, either in money or in goods, for his acceptance, by which the debt is discharged. 36 N. Y. 522.

PAYABLE. A sum of money is said to be payable when a person is under an obligation to pay it. "Payable" may therefore signify an obligation to pay at a future time, but, when used without qualification, "payable" means that the debt is payable at once, as opposed to "owing." Sweet.

PAYEE. In mercantile law. The person in whose favor a bill of exchange, promissory note, or check is made or drawn; the person to whom or to whose order a bill, note, or check is made payable. 3 Kent, Comm. 75.

PAYER, or PAYOR. One who pays, or who is to make a payment; particularly the person who is to make payment of a bill or note. Correlative to "payee."

PAYMASTER. An officer of the army or navy whose duty is to keep the pay-accounts and pay the wages of the officers and men. Any official charged with the disbursement of public money.

PAYMASTER GENERAL. In English law. The officer who makes the various payments out of the public money required for the different departments of the state by issuing drafts on the Bank of England. Sweet.

PAYMENT. The performance of a duty, promise, or obligation, or discharge of a debt or liability, by the delivery of money or other value. Also the money or other thing so delivered.

By "payment" is meant not only the delivery of a sum of money, when such is the obligation of the contract, but the performance of that which the parties respectively undertook, whether it be to give or to do. Civil Code La. art. 2131.

Performance of an obligation for the delivery of money only is called "payment." Civil Code Cal. § 1478.

In pleading. When the defendant alleges that he has paid the debt or claim laid in the declaration, this is called a "plea of payment."

PAYMENT INTO COURT. In practice. The act of a defendant in depositing the amount which he admits to be due, with the proper officer of the court, for the benefit of the plaintiff and in answer to his claim.

PAYS. Fr. Country. Trial *per pays*, trial by jury, (the country.) See PAIS.

PEACE. As applied to the affairs of a state or nation peace may be either external or internal. In the former case, the term denotes the prevalence of amicable relations and mutual good will between the particular society and all foreign powers. In the latter case, it means the tranquillity, security, and freedom from commotion or disturbance which is the sign of good order and harmony and obedience to the laws among all the members of the society. In a somewhat technical sense, peace denotes the quiet, security, good order, and decorum which is guarantied by the constitution of civil society and by the laws.

The concord or final agreement in a fine of lands. 18 Edw. I. "*Modus Levandi Finis.*"

PEACE, BILL OF. See BILL OF PEACE.

PEACE OF GOD AND THE CHURCH. In old English law. That rest and cessation which the king's subjects had from trouble and suit of law between the terms and on Sundays and holidays. Cowell; Spelman.

Peccata contra naturam sunt gravissima. 3 Inst. 20. Crimes against nature are the most heinous.

Peccatum peccato addit qui culpæ quam facit patrocinia defensionis adjungit. 5 Coke, 49. He adds fault to fault who sets up a defense of a wrong committed by him.

PECIA. A piece or small quantity of ground. Paroch. Antiq. 240.

PECK. A measure of two gallons; a dry measure.

PECORA. Lat. In Roman law. Cattle; beasts. The term included all quadrupeds that fed in flocks. Dig. 32, 65, 4.

PECULATION. In the civil law. The unlawful appropriation, by a depositary of public funds, of the property of the government intrusted to his care, to his own use, or that of others. Domat. Supp. au Droit Public, l. 3, tit. 5.

PECULATUS. In the civil law. The offense of stealing or embezzling the public money. Hence the common English word "peculation," but "embezzlement" is the proper legal term. 4 Bl. Comm. 121, 122.

PECULIAR. In ecclesiastical law. A parish or church in England which has jurisdiction of ecclesiastical matters within itself, and independent of the ordinary, and is subject only to the metropolitan.

PECULIARS, COURT OF. In English law. A branch of and annexed to the court of arches. It has a jurisdiction over all those parishes dispersed through the province of Canterbury, in the midst of other dioceses, which are exempt from the ordinary's jurisdiction, and subject to the metropolitan only.

PECULIUM. In Roman law. Such private property as might be held by a slave, wife, or son who was under the *patria potestas*, separate from the property of the father or master, and in the personal disposal of the owner.

PECULIUM CASTRENSE. In Roman law. That kind of *peculium* which a son acquired in war, or from his connection with the camp, (*castrum*.) Heinecc. Elem. lib. 2, tit. 9, § 474.

PECUNIA. Lat. Originally and radically, property in cattle, or cattle themselves. So called because the wealth of the ancients consisted in cattle. Co. Litt. 207*b*.

In the civil law. Property in general, real or personal; anything that is actually the subject of private property. In a narrower sense, personal property; fungible things. In the strictest sense, money. This has become the prevalent, and almost the exclusive, meaning of the word.

In old English law. Goods and chattels. Spelman.

PECUNIA CONSTITUTA. In Roman law. Money owing (even upon a moral obligation) upon a day being fixed (*constituta*) for its payment, became recoverable upon the implied promise to pay on that day, in an action called "*de pecunia constituta,*" the implied promise not amounting (of course) to a *stipulatio*. Brown.

Pecunia dicitur a pecus, omnes enim veterum divitiæ in animalibus consistebant. Co. Litt. 207. Money (*pecunia*) is so called from cattle, (*pecus,*) because all the wealth of our ancestors consisted in cattle.

PECUNIA NON NUMERATA. Lat. In the civil law. Money not paid. The subject of an exception or plea in certain cases. Inst. 4, 13, 2.

PECUNIA NUMERATA. Money numbered or counted out; *i. e.*, given in payment of a debt.

PECUNIA SEPULCHRALIS. Money anciently paid to the priest at the opening of a grave for the good of the deceased's soul.

PECUNIA TRAJECTITIA. In the civil law. A loan in money, or in wares which the debtor purchases with the money to be sent by sea, and whereby the creditor, according to the contract, assumes the risk of the loss from the day of the departure of the vessel till the day of her arrival at her port of destination. Interest does not necessarily arise from this loan, but when it is stipulated for it is termed "*nauticum fœnus,*" (maritime interest,) and, because of the risk which the creditor assumes, he is permitted to receive a higher interest than usual. Mackeld. Rom. Law, § 433.

PECUNIARY. Monetary; relating to money; consisting of money.

PECUNIARY CAUSES. In English ecclesiastical practice. Causes arising from the withholding of ecclesiastical dues, or the doing or neglecting some act relating to the church, whereby some damage accrues to the plaintiff. 3 Bl. Comm. 88.

PECUNIARY LEGACY. A legacy of a sum of money; a gift of a sum of money by will. Otherwise called a "general legacy." 2 Bl. Comm. 512.

PECUNIARY LOSS. A pecuniary loss is a loss of money, or of something by which money, or something of money value, may be acquired. 32 Barb. 33.

PECUS. In Roman law. Cattle; a beast. Under a bequest of *pecudes* were included oxen and other beasts of burden. Dig. 32, 81, 2.

PEDAGE. In old English law. A toll or tax paid by travelers for the privilege of passing, on foot or mounted, through a forest or other protected place. Spelman.

PEDAGIUM. L. Lat. Pedage, (*q. v.*)

PEDANEUS. Lat. In Roman law. At the foot; in a lower position; on the ground. See JUDEX PEDANEUS.

PEDDLERS. Itinerant traders; persons who sell small wares, which they carry with them in traveling about from place to place.

Persons, except those peddling newspapers, Bibles, or religious tracts, who sell, or offer to sell, at retail, goods, wares, or other commodities, traveling from place to place, in the street, or through different parts of the country. 12 U. S. St. at Large, p. 458, § 27.

PEDE PULVEROSUS. In old English and Scotch law. Dusty-foot. A term applied to itinerant merchants, chapmen, or peddlers who attended fairs.

PEDIGREE. Lineage; line of ancestors from which a person descends; genealogy. An account or register of a line of ancestors. Family relationship.

PEDIS ABSCISSIO. In old criminal law. The cutting off a foot; a punishment anciently inflicted instead of death. Fleta, lib. 1, c. 38.

PEDIS POSITIO. In the civil and old English law. A putting or placing of the foot. A term used to denote the possession of lands by actual corporal entry upon them. 15 Johns. 7; 5 Pa. St. 303.

PEDIS POSSESSIO. A foothold; an actual possession. To constitute adverse possession there must be *pedis possessio*, or a substantial inclosure. 2 Bouv. Inst. no. 2193; 2 Nott & McC. 343.

PEDONES. Foot-soldiers.

PEERAGE. The rank or dignity of a peer or nobleman. Also the body of nobles taken collectively.

PEERESS. A woman who belongs to the nobility, which may be either in her own right or by right of marriage.

PEERS. In feudal law. The vassals of a lord who sat in his court as judges of their co-vassals, and were called "peers," as being each other's equals, or of the same condition.

The nobility of Great Britain, being the lords temporal having seats in parliament, and including dukes, marquises, earls, viscounts, and barons.

Equals; those who are a man's equals in rank and station; this being the meaning in the phrase "trial by a jury of his peers."

PEERS OF FEES. Vassals or tenants of the same lord, who were obliged to serve and attend him in his courts, being equal in function. These were termed "peers of fees," because holding fees of the lord, or because their business in court was to sit and judge, under their lords, of disputes arising upon fees; but, if there were too many in one lordship, the lord usually chose twelve, who had the title of peers, by way of distinction; whence, it is said, we derive our common juries and other peers. Cowell.

PEINE FORTE ET DURE. L. Fr. In old English law. A special form of punishment for those who, being arraigned for felony, obstinately "stood mute;" that is, refused to plead or to put themselves upon trial. It is described as a combination of solitary confinement, slow starvation, and crushing the naked body with a great load of iron. This atrocious punishment was vulgarly called "pressing to death." See 4 Bl. Comm. 324-328; Britt. cc. 4, 22; 2 Reeve, Eng. Law, 134; Cowell.

PELA. A peal, pile, or fort. Cowell.

PELES. Issues arising from or out of a thing. Jacob.

PELFE, or PELFRE. Booty; also the personal effects of a felon convict. Cowell.

PELLAGE. The custom or duty paid for skins of leather.

PELLEX. Lat. In Roman law. A concubine. Dig. 50, 16, 144.

PELLICIA. A pilch or surplice. Spelman.

PELLIPARIUS. A leather-seller or skinner. Jacob.

PELLOTA. The ball of a foot. 4 Inst. 308.

PELLS, CLERK OF THE. An officer in the English exchequer, who entered every seller's bill on the parchment rolls, the roll of receipts, and the roll of disbursements.

PELT-WOOL. The wool pulled off the skin or pelt of dead sheep. 8 Hen. VI. c. 22.

PENAL. Punishable; inflicting a punishment; containing a penalty, or relating to a penalty.

PENAL ACTION. In practice. An action upon a penal statute; an action for the recovery of a penalty given by statute. 3 Steph. Comm. 535, 536.

Distinguished from a popular or *qui tam* action, in which the action is brought by the informer, to whom part of the penalty goes. A penal action or information is brought by an officer, and the penalty goes to the king. 1 Chit. Gen. Pr. 25, note; 2 Archb. Pr. 188.

PENAL BILL. An instrument formerly in use, by which a party bound himself to pay a certain sum or sums of money, or to do certain acts, or, in default thereof, to pay a certain specified sum by way of penalty; thence termed a "penal sum." These instruments have been superseded by the use of a bond in a penal sum, with conditions. Brown.

PENAL CLAUSE. A penal clause is a secondary obligation, entered into for the purpose of enforcing the performance of a primary obligation. Civil Code La. art. 2117.

Also a clause in a statute declaring a penalty for a violation of the preceding clauses.

PENAL LAWS. Those laws which prohibit an act and impose a penalty for the commission of it. They are of three kinds, —*pœna pecuniaria, pœna corporalis,* and *pœna exilii.* 2 Cro. Jac. 415.

PENAL SERVITUDE, in English criminal law, is a punishment which consists in keeping an offender in confinement, and compelling him to labor. Steph. Crim. Dig. 2.

PENAL STATUTES. Statutes imposing certain penalties on the commission of certain offenses; and actions brought for the recovery of such penalties are denominated "penal actions."

PENAL SUM. A sum agreed upon in a bond, to be forfeited if the condition of the bond is not fulfilled.

PENALTY. 1. The sum of money which the obligor of a bond undertakes to pay by way of penalty, in the event of his omitting to perform or carry out the terms imposed upon him by the conditions of the bond. Brown.

A penalty is an agreement to pay a greater sum, to secure the payment of a less sum. It is conditional, and can be avoided by the payment of the less sum before the contingency agreed upon shall happen. By what name it is called is immaterial. Minor, (Ala.) 209, 227.

2. A punishment; a punishment imposed by statute as a consequence of the commission of a certain specified offense.

The terms "fine," "forfeiture," and "penalty" are often used loosely, and even confusedly; but, when a discrimination is made, the word "penalty" is found to be generic in its character, including both fine and forfeiture. A "fine" is a pecuniary penalty, and is commonly (perhaps always) to be collected by suit in some form. A "forfeiture" is a penalty by which one loses his rights and interest in his property. 4 Iowa, 300.

3. The term also denotes money recoverable by virtue of a statute imposing a payment by way of punishment.

PENANCE. In ecclesiastical law. An ecclesiastical punishment inflicted by an ecclesiastical court for some spiritual offense. Ayl. Par. 420.

PENDENCY. Suspense; the state of being pendent or undecided; the state of an action, etc., after it has been begun, and before the final disposition of it.

PENDENS. Lat. Pending; as *lis pendens*, a pending suit.

PENDENTE LITE. Lat. Pending the suit; during the actual progress of a suit; during litigation.

Pendente lite nihil innovetur. Co. Litt. 344. During a litigation nothing new should be introduced.

PENDENTES. In the civil law. The fruits of the earth not yet separated from the ground; the fruits hanging by the roots. Ersk. Inst. 2, 2, 4.

PENDICLE. In Scotch law. A piece or parcel of ground.

PENDING. Begun, but not yet completed; unsettled; undetermined; in process of settlement or adjustment. Thus, an action or suit is said to be "pending" from its inception until the rendition of final judgment.

PENETRATION. A term used in criminal law, and denoting (in cases of alleged rape) the insertion of the male part into the female parts to however slight an extent; and by which insertion the offense is complete without proof of emission. Brown.

PENITENTIARY. A prison or place of punishment; the place of punishment in which convicts sentenced to confinement and hard labor are confined by the authority of the law. 2 Kan. 175.

PENNON. A standard, banner, or ensign carried in war.

PENNY. An English coin, being the twelfth part of a shilling. It was also used in America during the colonial period.

PENNYWEIGHT. A Troy weight, equal to twenty-four grains, or one-twentieth part of an ounce.

PENSAM. The full weight of twenty ounces.

PENSIO. Lat. In the civil law. A payment, properly, for the use of a thing. A rent; a payment for the use and occupation of another's house.

PENSION. A stated allowance out of the public treasury granted by government to an individual, or to his representatives, for his valuable services to the country, or in compensation for loss or damage sustained by him in the public service.

In English practice. An annual payment made by each member of the inns of court. Cowell; Holthouse.

Also an assembly of the members of the society of Gray's Inn, to consult of their affairs.

In the civil, Scotch, and Spanish law. A rent; an annual rent.

PENSION OF CHURCHES. In English ecclesiastical law. Certain sums of money paid to clergymen in lieu of tithes. A spiritual person may sue in the spiritual court for a pension originally granted and confirmed by the ordinary, but, where it is granted by a temporal person to a clerk, he cannot; as, if one grant an annuity to a parson, he must sue for it in the temporal courts. Cro. Eliz. 675.

PENSION WRIT. A peremptory order against a member of an inn of court who is in arrear for his pensions, (that is, for his periodical dues,) or for other duties. Cowell.

PENSIONER. One who is supported by an allowance at the will of another; a dependent. It is usually applied (in a public sense) to those who receive pensions or annuities from government, who are chiefly such as have retired from places of honor and emolument. Jacob.

Persons making periodical payments are sometimes so called. Thus, resident undergraduates of the university of Cambridge, who are not on the foundation of any college, are spoken of as "pensioners." Mozley & Whitley.

PENT-ROAD. A road shut up or closed at its terminal points. 40 Vt. 41.

PENTECOSTALS. In ecclesiastical law. Pious oblations made at the feast of Pentecost by parishioners to their priests, and sometimes by inferior churches or parishes to the principal mother churches. They are also called "Whitsun farthings." Wharton

PEON. In Mexico. A debtor held by his creditor in a qualified servitude to work out the debt; a serf. Webster.

In India. A footman; a soldier; an inferior officer; a servant employed in the business of the revenue, police, or judicature.

PEONIA. In Spanish-American law. A lot of land of fifty feet front, and one hundred feet deep. Originally the portion granted to foot-soldiers of spoils taken or lands conquered in war.

PEOPLE. A state; as the people of the state of New York. A nation in its collective and political capacity. 4 Term R. 783.

PEPPERCORN. A dried berry of the black pepper. In English law, the reservation of a merely nominal rent, on a lease, is sometimes expressed by a stipulation for the payment of a peppercorn.

PER. Lat. By. When a writ of entry is sued out against the alienee of the original intruder or disseisor, or against his heir to whom the land has descended, it is said to be brought "in the *per*," because the writ then states that the tenant had not entry but by (*per*) the original wrong-doer. 3 Bl. Comm. 181.

PER ÆS ET LIBRAM. In Roman law. The sale *per æs et libram* (with copper and scales) was a ceremony used in transferring *res mancipi*, in the emancipation of a son or slave, and in one of the forms of making a will. The parties having assembled, with a number of witnesses, and one who held a balance or scales, the purchaser struck the scales with a copper coin, repeating a formula by which he claimed the subject-matter of the transaction as his property, and handed the coin to the vendor.

PER ALLUVIONEM. In the civil law. By alluvion, or the gradual and imperceptible increase arising from deposit by water.

Per alluvionem id videtur adjici quod ita paulatim adjicitur ut intelligere non possumus quantum quoquo momento temporis adjiciatur. That is said to be added by alluvion which is so added little by little that we cannot tell how much is added at any one moment of time. Dig. 41, 1, 7, 1; Fleta, l. 3, c. 2, § 6.

PER AND CUI. When a writ of entry is brought against a second alienee or descendant from the disseisor, it is said to be in the *per* and *cui*, because the form of the writ is that the tenant had not entry but *by* and *under* a prior alienee, *to* whom the intruder himself demised it. 3 Bl. Comm. 181.

PER AND POST. To come in in the *per* is to claim by or through the person last entitled to an estate; as the heirs or assigns of the grantee. To come in in the *post* is to claim by a paramount and prior title; as the lord by escheat.

PER ANNULUM ET BACULUM. In old English law. By ring and staff, or crozier. The symbolical mode of conferring an ecclesiastical investure. 1 Bl. Comm. 378, 379.

PER ANNUM. By the year. A phrase still in common use.

PER AUTRE VIE. L. Fr. For or during another's life; for such period as another person shall live.

PER AVERSIONEM. In the civil law. By turning away. A term applied to that kind of sale where the goods are taken in bulk, and not by weight or measure, and for a single price; or where a piece of land is sold as containing in gross, by estimation, a certain number of acres. Poth. Cont. Sale, nn. 256, 309. So called because the buyer acts without particular examination or discrimination, *turning* his face, as it were, *away*. Calvin.

PER BOUCHE. L. Fr. By the mouth; orally. 3 How. State Tr. 1024.

PER CAPITA. By the heads or polls; according to the number of individuals; share and share alike. This term, derived from the civil law, is much used in the law of descent and distribution, and denotes that method of dividing an intestate estate by which an equal share is given to each of a number of persons, all of whom stand in equal degree to the decedent, without reference to their stocks or the right of representation. It is the antithesis of *per stirpes*, (*q. v.*)

PER CONSEQUENS. By consequence; consequently. Yearb. M. 9 Edw. III. 8.

PER CONSIDERATIONEM CURIÆ. In old practice. By the consideration (judgment) of the court. Yearb. M. 1 Edw. II. 2.

PER CURIAM. By the court. A phrase used in the reports to distinguish an opinion of the whole court from an opinion written by any one judge. Sometimes it denotes an opinion written by the chief justice or presiding judge.

PER EUNDEM. By the same. This phrase is commonly used to express "by, or from the mouth of, the same judge." So "*per eundem in eadem*" means "by the same judge in the same case."

PER EXTENSUM. In old practice. At length.

PER FORMAM DONI. In English law. By the form of the gift; by the designation of the giver, and not by the operation of law. 2 Bl. Comm. 113, 191.

PER FRAUDEM. By fraud. Where a plea alleges matter of discharge, and the replication avers that the discharge was fraudulently obtained and is therefore invalid, it is called a "replication *per fraudem.*"

PER INCURIAM. Through inadvertence. 35 Eng. Law & Eq. 302.

PER INDUSTRIAM HOMINIS. In old English law. By human industry. A term applied to the reclaiming or taming of wild animals by art, industry, and education. 2 Bl. Comm. 391.

PER INFORTUNIUM. By misadventure. In criminal law, homicide *per infortunium* is committed where a man, doing a lawful act, without any intention of hurt, unfortunately kills another. 4 Bl. Comm. 182.

PER LEGEM ANGLIÆ. By the law of England; by the curtesy. Fleta, lib. 2, c. 54, § 18.

PER LEGEM TERRÆ. By the law of the land.

PER METAS ET BUNDAS. In old English law. By metes and bounds.

PER MINAS. By threats. See DURESS.

PER MISADVENTURE. In old English law. By mischance. 4 Bl. Comm. 182. The same with *per infortunium*, (*q. v.*)

PER MY ET PER TOUT. L. Fr. By the half and by the whole. A phrase descriptive of the mode in which joint tenants hold the joint estate, the effect of which, technically considered, is that for purposes of tenure and survivorship each is the holder of the whole, but for purposes of alienation each has only his own share, which is presumed in law to be equal. 1 Washb. Real Prop. 406.

PER PAIS, TRIAL. Trial by the country; *i. e.*, by jury.

PER PROCURATION. By proxy; by one acting as an agent with special powers; as under a letter of attorney. These words "give notice to all persons that the agent is acting under a special and limited authority." 10 C. B. 689. The phrase is commonly abbreviated to "per proc.," or "p. p.," and is more used in the civil law and in England than in American law.

PER QUÆ SERVITIA. A real action by which the grantee of a seigniory could compel the tenants of the grantor to attorn to himself. It was abolished by St. 3 & 4 Wm. IV. c. 27, § 35.

PER QUOD. Whereby. When the declaration in an action of tort, after stating the acts complained of, goes on to allege the consequences of those acts as a ground of special damage to the plaintiff, the recital of such consequences is prefaced by these words, "*per quod,*" whereby; and sometimes the phrase is used as the name of that clause of the declaration.

PER QUOD CONSORTIUM AMISIT. In old pleading. Whereby he lost the company [of his wife.] A phrase used in the old declarations in actions of trespass by a husband, for beating or ill using his wife, descriptive of the special damage he had sustained. 3 Bl. Comm. 140; Cro. Jac. 501, 538.

PER QUOD SERVITIUM AMISIT. In old pleading. Whereby he lost the service [of his servant.] A phrase used in the old declarations in actions of trespass by a master, for beating or ill using his servant, descriptive of the special damage he had himself sustained. 3 Bl. Comm. 142; 9 Coke, 113*a*.

Per rationes pervenitur ad legitimam rationem. Litt. § 386. By reasoning we come to true reason.

Per rerum naturam factum negantis nulla probatio est. It is in the nature of things that he who denies a fact is not bound to give proof.

PER SALTUM. By a leap or bound; by a sudden movement; passing over certain proceedings. 8 East, 511.

PER SE. By himself or itself; in itself; taken alone; inherently; in isolation; unconnected with other matters.

PER STIRPES. By roots or stocks; by representation. This term, derived from the civil law, is much used in the law of descents and distribution, and denotes that method of dividing an intestate estate where a class or group of distributees take the share which their stock (a deceased ancestor) would have been entitled to, taking thus by their right of representing such ancestor, and not as so many individuals; while other heirs, who stand in equal degree with such ancestor to the decedent, take each a share equal to his.

PER TOTAM CURIAM. By the whole court. A common phrase in the old reports.

PER TOUT ET NON PER MY. L. Fr. By the whole, and not by the moiety. Where an estate in fee is given to a man and his wife, they cannot take the estate by moieties, but both are seised of the entirety, *per tout et non per my*. 2 Bl. Comm. 182.

PER UNIVERSITATEM. Lat. In the civil law. By an aggregate or whole; as an entirety. The term described the acquisition of an entire estate by one act or fact, as distinguished from the acquisition of single or detached things.

PER VADIUM. In old practice. By gage. Words in the old writs of attachment or *pone*. 3 Bl. Comm. 280.

Per varios actus legem experientia facit. By various acts experience frames the law. 4 Inst. 50.

PER VERBA DE FUTURO. By words of the future [tense.] A phrase applied to contracts of marriage. 1 Bl. Comm. 439; 2 Kent, Comm. 87.

PER VERBA DE PRÆSENTI. By words of the present [tense.] A phrase applied to contracts of marriage. 1 Bl. Comm. 439.

PER VISUM ECCLESIÆ. In old English law. By view of the church; under the supervision of the church. The disposition of intestates' goods *per visum ecclesiæ* was one of the articles confirmed to the prelates by King John's *Magna Charta*. 3 Bl. Comm. 96.

PER VIVAM VOCEM. In old English law. By the living voice; the same with *viva voce*. Bract. fol. 95.

PER YEAR, in a contract, is equivalent to the word "annually." 39 N. Y. 211.

PERAMBULATION. The act of walking over the boundaries of a district or piece of land, either for the purpose of determining them or of preserving evidence of them. Thus, in many parishes in England, it is the custom for the parishioners to perambulate the boundaries of the parish in rogation week in every year. Such a custom entitles them to enter any man's land and abate nuisances in their way. Phillim. Ecc. Law, 1867; Hunt, Bound. 103; Sweet.

PERAMBULATIONE FACIENDA, WRIT DE. In English law. The name of a writ which is sued by consent of *both* parties when they are in doubt as to the bounds of their respective estates. It is directed to the sheriff to make perambulation, and to set the bounds and limits between them in certainty. Fitzh. Nat. Brev. 133.

PERCA. A perch of land; sixteen and one-half feet. See PERCH.

PERCEPTION. Taking into possession. Thus, perception of crops or of profits is reducing them to possession.

PERCEPTURA. In old records. A wear; a place in a river made up with banks, dams, etc., for the better convenience of preserving and taking fish. Cowell.

PERCH. A measure of land containing five yards and a half, or sixteen feet and a half in length; otherwise called a "rod" or "pole." Cowell.

PERCOLATE, as used in the cases relating to the right of land-owners to use water on their premises, designates any flowage of sub-surface water other than that of a running stream, open, visible, clearly to be traced. 7 Nev. 363.

PERDONATIO UTLAGARIÆ. A pardon for a man who, for contempt in not yielding obedience to the process of a court, is outlawed, and afterwards of his own accord surrenders. Reg. Orig. 28.

PERDUELLIO. In Roman law. Hostility or enmity towards the Roman republic; traitorous conduct on the part of a citizen, subversive of the authority of the laws or tending to overthrow the government. Calvin.; Vicat.

PERDURABLE. As applied to an estate, perdurable signifies lasting long or forever. Thus, a disseisor or tenant in fee upon condition has as high and great an estate as the rightful owner or tenant in fee-simple absolute, but not so perdurable. The term is chiefly used with reference to the extinguishment of rights by unity of seisin, which does not take place unless both the right and the land out of which it issues are held for equally high and perdurable estates. Co. Litt. 313*a*, 313*b*; Gale, Easem. 582; Sweet.

PEREGRINI. In Roman law. The class of *peregrini* embraced at the same time both those who had no capacity in law, (capacity for rights or jural relations,) namely, the slaves, and the members of those nations which had not established amicable relations with the Roman people. Sav. Dr. Rom. § 66.

PEREMPT. In ecclesiastical procedure an appeal is said to be perempted when the appellant has by his own act waived or barred his right of appeal; as where he partially complies with or acquiesces in the sentence of the court. Phillim. Ecc. Law, 1275.

PEREMPTION. A nonsuit; also a quashing or killing.

PEREMPTORIUS. In the civil law. That which takes away or destroys forever; hence, *exceptio peremptoria*, a plea which is a perpetual bar. Calvin.

PEREMPTORY. Imperative; absolute; not admitting of question, delay, or reconsideration. Positive; final; decisive; not admitting of any alternative. Self-determined; arbitrary; not requiring any cause to be shown.

PEREMPTORY CHALLENGE. In criminal practice. A species of challenge which a prisoner is allowed to have against a certain number of jurors, without assigning any cause.

PEREMPTORY DAY. A day assigned for trial or hearing in court, absolutely and without further opportunity for postponement.

PEREMPTORY DEFENSE. A defense which insists that the plaintiff never had the right to institute the suit, or that, if he had, the original right is extinguished or determined. 4 Bouv. Inst. no. 4206.

PEREMPTORY EXCEPTION. In the civil law. Any defense which denies entirely the ground of action.

PEREMPTORY INSTRUCTION. An instruction given by a court to a jury which the latter must obey implicitly; as an instruction to return a verdict for the defendant, or for the plaintiff, as the case may be.

PEREMPTORY MANDAMUS. When a *mandamus* has issued commanding a party either to do a certain thing or to signify some reason to the contrary, and the party to whom such writ is directed returns or signifies an insufficient reason, then there issues in the second place another writ, termed a "peremptory *mandamus*," commanding the party to do the thing absolutely, and to which no other return will be admitted but a certificate of perfect obedience and due execution of the writ. 3 Steph. Comm. 683; Brown.

PEREMPTORY NONSUIT. A compulsory or involuntary nonsuit; one which is ordered by the court, as distinguished from one which the plaintiff takes voluntarily.

PEREMPTORY PAPER. A list of the causes which were enlarged at the request of the parties, or which stood over from press of business in court.

PEREMPTORY PLEAS. "Pleas in bar" are so termed in contradistinction to that class of pleas called "dilatory pleas." The former, viz., peremptory pleas, are usually pleaded to the merits of the action, with the view of raising a material issue between the parties; while the latter class, viz., dilatory pleas, are generally pleaded with a view of retarding the plaintiff's proceedings, and not for the purpose of raising an issue upon which the parties may go to trial and settle the point in dispute. Peremptory pleas are also called "pleas in bar," while dilatory pleas are said to be in abatement only. Brown.

PEREMPTORY RULE. In practice. An absolute rule; a rule without any condition or alternative of showing cause.

PEREMPTORY UNDERTAKING. An undertaking by a plaintiff to bring on a cause for trial at the next sittings or assizes. Lush, Pr. 649.

PEREMPTORY WRIT. An original writ, called from the words of the writ a "*si te fecerit securum*," and which directed the sheriff to cause the defendant to appear in court without any option given him, provided the plaintiff gave the sheriff security effectually to prosecute his claim. The writ was very occasionally in use, and only where nothing was specifically demanded, but only a satisfaction in general; as in the case of writs of trespass on the case, wherein no debt or other specific thing was sued for, but only damages to be assessed by a jury. Brown.

PERFECT. Complete; finished; executed; enforceable.

PERFECT MACHINE. In patent law. A perfected invention; not a perfectly constructed machine, but a machine so constructed as to embody all the essential elements of the invention, in a form that would make them practical and operative so as to accomplish the result. But it is not necessary that it should accomplish that result in the most perfect manner, and be in a condition where it was not susceptible of a higher degree of perfection in its mere mechanical construction. 4 Fish. Pat. Cas. 299.

PERFECT OBLIGATION. A perfect obligation is one which gives to the opposite party the right of compulsion. 37 Ga. 128.

PERFECT TITLE. This term "can mean nothing less than a title which is good both at law and in equity." 21 Conn. 449.

PERFECT TRUST. An executed trust, (*q. v.*)

PERFECTING BAIL. Certain qualifications of a property character being required of persons who tender themselves as bail, when such persons have justified, *i. e.*, established their sufficiency by satisfying the court that they possess the requisite qualifications, a rule or order of court is made for their allowance, and the bail is then said to be perfected, *i. e.*, the process of giving bail is finished or completed. Brown.

Perfectum est cui nihil deest secundum suæ perfectionis vel naturæ modum. That is perfect to which nothing is wanting, according to the measure of its perfection or nature. Hob. 151.

PERFIDY. The act of one who has engaged his faith to do a thing, and does not do it, but does the contrary. Wolff, Inst. § 390.

PERFORM. To perform an obligation or contract is to execute, fulfill, or accomplish it according to its terms. This may consist either in action on the part of the person bound by the contract or in omission to act, according to the nature of the subject-matter; but the term is usually applied to any action in discharge of a contract other than payment.

PERGAMENUM. In old practice. Parchment. *In pergameno scribi fecit.* 1 And. 54.

PERICULOSUS. Dangerous; perilous.

Periculosum est res novas et inusitatas inducere. Co. Litt. 379*a*. It is perilous to introduce new and untried things.

Periculosum existimo quod bonorum virorum non comprobatur exemplo. 9 Coke, 97*b*. I consider that dangerous which is not approved by the example of good men.

PERICULUM. Lat. In the civil law. Peril; danger; hazard; risk.

Periculum rei venditæ, nondum traditæ, est emptoris. The risk of a thing sold, and not yet delivered, is the purchaser's. 2 Kent, Comm. 498, 499.

PERIL. The risk, hazard, or contingency insured against by a policy of insurance.

PERILS OF THE SEA. In maritime and insurance law. Natural accidents peculiar to the sea, which do not happen by the intervention of man, nor are to be prevented by human prudence. 3 Kent, Comm. 216.

Perils of the sea are from (1) storms and waves; (2) rocks, shoals, and rapids; (3) other obstacles, though of human origin; (4) changes of climate; (5) the confinement necessary at sea; (6) animals peculiar to the sea; (7) all other dangers peculiar to the sea. Civil Code Cal. § 2199.

All losses caused by the action of wind and water acting on the property insured under extraordinary circumstances, either directly or mediately, without the intervention of other independent active external causes, are losses by "perils of the sea or other perils and dangers," within the meaning of the usual clause in a policy of marine insurance. Baily, Perils of Sea, 6.

In an enlarged sense, all losses which occur from maritime adventure may be said to arise from the perils of the sea; but underwriters are not bound to this extent. They insure against losses from extraordinary occurrences only; such as stress of weather, winds and waves, lightning, tempests, etc. These are understood to be meant by the phrase "the perils of the sea," in a marine policy, and not those ordinary perils which every vessel must encounter. 8 Pet. 557.

PERINDE VALERE. A dispensation granted to a clerk, who, being defective in capacity for a benefice or other ecclesiastical function, is *de facto* admitted to it. Cowell.

PERIOD. Any point, space, or division of time. "The word 'period' has its etymological meaning, but it also has a distinctive signification, according to the subject with which it may be used in connection. It may mean any portion of complete time, from a thousand years or less to the period of a day; and when used to designate an act to be done or to be begun, though its completion may take an uncertain time, as, for instance, the act of exportation, it must mean the day on which the exportation commences, or it would be an unmeaning and useless word in its connection in the statute." 20 How. 579.

PERIODICAL. Recurring at fixed intervals; to be made or done, or to happen, at successive periods separated by determined intervals of time; as periodical payments of interest on a bond.

PERIPHRASIS. Circumlocution; use of many words to express the sense of one.

PERISH. To come to an end; to cease to be; to die.

PERISHABLE ordinarily means subject to speedy and natural decay. But, where the time contemplated is necessarily long, the term may embrace property liable merely to material depreciation in value from other causes than such decay. 31 Conn. 495.

PERISHABLE GOODS. Goods which decay and lose their value if not speedily put to their intended use.

Perjuri sunt qui servatis verbis juramenti decipiunt aures eorum qui accipiunt. 3 Inst. 166. They are perjured, who, preserving the words of an oath, deceive the ears of those who receive it.

PERJURY. In criminal law. The willful assertion as to a matter of fact, opinion, belief, or knowledge, made by a witness in a judicial proceeding as part of his evidence, either upon oath or in any form allowed by law to be substituted for an oath, whether such evidence is given in open court, or in an affidavit, or otherwise, such assertion being known to such witness to be false, and being intended by him to mislead the court, jury, or person holding the proceeding. 2 Whart. Crim. Law, § 1244.

Perjury shall consist in willfully, knowingly, absolutely, and falsely swearing, either with or without laying the hand on the Holy Evangelist of Almighty God, or affirming, in a matter material to the issue or point in question, in some judicial proceeding, by a person to whom a lawful oath or affirmation is administered. Code Ga. 1882, § 4460.

Every person who, having taken an oath that he will testify, declare, depose, or certify truly before any competent tribunal, officer, or person, in any of the cases in which such an oath may by law be administered, willfully, and contrary to such oath, states as truth any material matter which he knows to be false, is guilty of perjury. Pen. Code Cal. § 118.

The willful giving, under oath, in a judicial proceeding or course of justice, of false testimony material to the issue or point of inquiry. 2 Bish. Crim. Law, § 1015.

Perjury, at common law, is the "taking of a willful false oath by one who, being lawfully sworn by a competent court to depose the truth in any judicial proceeding, swears absolutely and falsely in a matter material to the point in issue, whether he believed or not." 2 Metc. (Ky.) 10; 39 Miss. 541.

PERMANENT TRESPASS. One which consists of a series of acts, done on successive days, which are of the same nature, and are renewed or continued from day to day, so that, in the aggregate, they make up one indivisible wrong. 3 Bl. Comm. 212.

PERMISSION. A license to do a thing; an authority to do an act which, without such authority, would have been unlawful.

PERMISSIONS. Negations of law, arising either from the law's silence or its express declaration. Ruth. Inst. b. 1, c. 1.

PERMISSIVE. Allowed; allowable; that which may be done.

PERMISSIVE USE. A passive use which was resorted to before the statute of uses, in order to avoid a harsh law; as that of mortmain or a feudal forfeiture. It was a mere invention in order to evade the law by secrecy; as a conveyance to A. to the use of B. A. simply held the possession, and B. enjoyed the profits of the estate. Wharton.

PERMISSIVE WASTE. That kind of waste which is a matter of omission only; as by suffering a house to fall for want of necessary reparations. 2 Bl. Comm. 281.

PERMIT. A license or instrument granted by the officers of excise, (or customs,) certifying that the duties on certain goods have been paid, or secured, and permitting their removal from some specified place to another. Wharton.

A written license or warrant, issued by a person in authority, empowering the grantee to do some act not forbidden by law, but not allowable without such authority.

PERMUTATIO. Lat. In the civil law. Exchange; barter. Dig. 19, 4.

PERMUTATION. The exchange of one movable subject for another; barter.

PERMUTATIONE. A writ to an ordinary, commanding him to admit a clerk to a benefice upon exchange made with another. Reg. Orig. 307.

PERNANCY. Taking; a taking or receiving; as of the profits of an estate. Actual pernancy of the profits of an estate is the taking, perception, or receipt of the rents and other advantages arising therefrom. 2 Bl. Comm. 163.

PERNOR OF PROFITS. He who receives the profits of lands, etc.; he who has the actual pernancy of the profits.

PERNOUR. L. Fr. A taker. *Le pernour ou le detenour*, the taker or the detainer. Britt. c. 27.

PERPARS. L. Lat. A purpart; a part of the inheritance.

PERPETRATOR. Generally, this term denotes the person who actually commits a crime or delict, or by whose immediate agency it occurs. But, where a servant of a railroad company is killed through the negligence of a co-employe, the company itself may be regarded as the "perpetrator" of the act, within the meaning of a statute giving an action against the perpetrator. 33 Iowa, 47.

Perpetua lex est nullam legem humanam ac positivam perpetuam esse, et clausula quæ abrogationem excludit ab initio non valet. It is a perpetual law that no human and positive law can be perpetual, and a clause [in a law] which precludes the power of abrogation is void *ab initio*. Bac. Max. p. 77, in reg. 19.

PERPETUAL. Never ceasing; continuous; enduring; lasting; unlimited in respect of time.

PERPETUAL CURACY. The office of a curate in a parish where there is no spiritual rector or vicar, but where a clerk (curate) is appointed to officiate there by the impropriator. 2 Burn, Ecc. Law, 55.

The church or benefice filled by a curate under these circumstances is also so called.

PERPETUAL EDICT. In Roman law. Originally the term "perpetual" was merely opposed to "occasional," and was used to distinguish the general edicts of the prætors from the special edicts or orders which they issued in their judicial capacity. But under Hadrian the edict was revised by the jurist Julianus, and was republished as a permanent act of legislation. It was then styled "perpetual," in the sense of being calculated to endure *in perpetuum*, or until abrogated by competent authority. Aust. Jur. 855.

PERPETUAL INJUNCTION. Opposed to an injuction *ad interim;* an injunction which finally disposes of the suit, and is indefinite in point of time.

PERPETUAL LEASE. A lease of lands which may last without limitation as to time; a grant of lands in fee with the reservation of a rent in fee; a fee-farm.

PERPETUAL STATUTE. One which is to remain in force without limitation as to time; one which contains no provision for its repeal, abrogation, or expiration at any future time.

PERPETUAL SUCCESSION. That continuous existence which enables a corporation to manage its affairs, and hold property without the necessity of perpetual conveyances, for the purpose of transmitting it. By reason of this quality, this ideal and artificial person remains, in its legal entity and personality, the same, though frequent changes may be made of its members. Field, Corp. § 58; 5 Mo. App. 340.

PERPETUATING TESTIMONY. A proceeding for taking and preserving the testimony of witnesses, which otherwise might be lost before the trial in which it is intended to be used. It is usually allowed where the witnesses are aged and infirm or are about to remove from the state. 3 Bl. Comm. 450.

PERPETUITY. A future limitation, whether executory or by way of remainder, and of either real or personal property, which is not to vest until after the expiration of or will not necessarily vest within the period fixed and prescribed by law for the creation of future estates and interests, and which is not destructible by the persons for the time being entitled to the property subject to the future limitation, except with the concurrence of the individual interested under that limitation. Lewis, Perp. 164; 52 Law Lib. 139.

Any limitation tending to take the subject of it out of commerce for a longer period than a life or lives in being, and twenty-one years beyond, and, in case of a posthumous child, a few months more, allowing for the term of gestation. Rand. Perp. 48.

Such a limitation of property as renders it unalienable beyond the period allowed by law. Gilb. Uses, (Sugd. Ed.) 260.

PERPETUITY OF THE KING. That fiction of the English law which for certain political purposes ascribes to the king in his political capacity the attribute of immortality; for, though the reigning monarch may die, yet by this fiction the king never dies, *i. e.*, the office is supposed to be reoccupied for all political purposes immediately on his death. Brown.

PERQUISITES. In its most extensive sense, "perquisites" signifies anything obtained by industry or purchased with money, different from that which descends from a father or ancestor. Bract. l. 2, c. 30, n. 3.

Profits accruing to a lord of a manor by virtue of his court-baron, over and above the yearly profits of his land; also other things that come casually and not yearly. Mozley & Whitley.

In modern use. Emoluments or incidental profits attaching to an office or official position, beyond the salary or regular fees.

PERQUISITIO. Purchase. Acquisition by one's own act or agreement, and not by descent.

PERQUISITOR. In old English law. A purchaser; one who first acquired an estate to his family; one who acquired an estate by sale, by gift, or by any other method, except only that of descent. 2 Bl. Comm. 220.

PERSECUTIO. Lat. In the civil law. A following after; a pursuing at law; a suit or prosecution. Properly that kind of judicial proceeding before the prætor which was called "extraordinary." In a general sense, any judicial proceeding, including not only "actions," (*actiones,*) properly so called, but other proceedings also. Calvin.

PERSEQUI. Lat. In the civil law. To follow after; to pursue or claim in form of law. An action is called a "*jus persequendi.*"

PERSON. A man considered according to the rank he holds in society, with all the rights to which the place he holds entitles him, and the duties which it imposes. 1 Bouv. Inst. no. 137.

A human being considered as capable of having rights and of being charged with duties; while a "thing" is the object over which rights may be exercised.

Persons are divided by law into *natural* and *artificial.* Natural persons are such as the God of nature formed us; artificial are such as are created and devised by human laws, for the purposes of society and government, which are called "corporations" or "bodies politic." 1 Bl. Comm. 123.

PERSONA. Lat. **In the civil law.** Character, in virtue of which certain rights belong to a man and certain duties are imposed upon him. Thus one man may unite many characters, (*personæ,*) as, for example, the characters of father and son, of master and servant. Mackel l. Rom. Law, § 129.

In ecclesiastical law. The rector of a church instituted and inducted, for his own life, was called "*persona mortalis;*" and any collegiate or conventual body, to whom the church was forever appropriated, was termed "*persona immortalis.*" Jacob.

Persona conjuncta æquiparatur interesse proprio. A personal connection [literally, a united person, union with a person] is equivalent to one's own interest; nearness of blood is as good a consideration as one's own interest. Bac. Max. 72, reg.

PERSONA DESIGNATA. A person pointed out or described as an individual, as opposed to a person ascertained as a member of a class, or as filling a particular character.

PERSONA ECCLESIÆ. The parson or personation of the church.

Persona est homo cum statu quodam consideratus. A person is a man considered with reference to a certain *status.* Heinecc. Elem. l. 1, tit. 3, § 75.

Persona regis mergitur persona ducis. Jenk. Cent. 160. The person of duke merges in that of king.

PERSONA STANDI IN JUDICIO. Capacity of standing in court or in judgment; capacity to be a party to an action; capacity or ability to sue.

PERSONABLE. Having the rights and powers of a person; able to hold or maintain a plea in court; also capacity to take anything granted or given.

Personæ vice fungitur municipium et decuria. Towns and boroughs act as if persons. 23 Wend. 103, 144.

PERSONAL. Appertaining to the person; belonging to an individual; limited to the person; having the nature or partaking of the qualities of human beings, or of movable property.

PERSONAL ACTION. In the civil law. An action *in personam.* A personal action seeks to enforce an obligation imposed on the defendant by his contract or delict; that is, it is the contention that he is bound to transfer some dominion or to perform some service or to repair some loss. Gaius, bk. 4, § 2.

In common law. An action brought for the recovery of some debt or for damages for some personal injury, in contradistinction to the old real actions, which related to real property only. See 3 Bl. Comm. 117.

An action which can be brought only by

the person himself who is injured, and not by his representatives.

PERSONAL ASSETS. Chattels, money, and other personal property belonging to a bankrupt, insolvent, or decedent estate, which go to the assignee or executor.

PERSONAL CHATTELS. Things movable which may be annexed to or attendant on the person of the owner, and carried about with him from one part of the world to another. 2 Bl. Comm. 387.

PERSONAL CONTRACT. A contract relating to personal property.

PERSONAL COVENANT. A covenant which, instead of being a charge upon real estate of the covenantor, only binds himself and his personal representatives in respect to assets.

The phrase may also mean a covenant which is personal to the covenantor, *i. e.*, one which he must perform in person, and cannot procure another to perform for him.

PERSONAL CREDIT. That credit which a person possesses as an individual, and which is founded on the opinion entertained of his character and business standing.

PERSONAL DEMAND. A demand for payment of a bill or note, made upon the drawer, acceptor, or maker, in person. See 1 Daniel, Neg. Inst. § 589.

PERSONAL DISABILITY. A disability or incapacity for legal action resulting from the *status* or condition of the particular person, such as coverture, infancy, or lunacy.

PERSONAL ESTATE. Personal property, (*q. v.*)

PERSONAL INJURY. A hurt or damage done to a man's *person*, such as a cut or bruise, a broken limb, or the like, as distinguished from an injury to his property or his reputation. The phrase is chiefly used in connection with actions of tort for negligence.

PERSONAL KNOWLEDGE. Knowledge of the truth in regard to a particular fact or allegation, which is original, and does not depend on information or hearsay.

Personal knowledge of an allegation in an answer is personal knowledge of its truth or falsity; and if the allegation is a negative one, this necessarily includes a knowledge of the truth or falsity of the allegation denied. 18 Fed. Rep. 622.

PERSONAL LAW, as opposed to territorial law, is the law applicable to persons not subject to the law of the territory in which they reside. It is only by permission of the territorial law that personal law can exist at the present day; *e. g.*, it applies to British subjects resident in the Levant and in other Mohammedan and barbarous countries. Under the Roman Empire, it had a very wide application. Brown.

PERSONAL LIABILITY. The liability of the stockholders in corporations, under certain statutes, by which they may be held individually responsible for the debts of the corporation, either to the extent of the par value of their respective holdings of stock, or to twice that amount, or without limit, or otherwise, as the particular statute directs.

PERSONAL LIBERTY. The right or power of locomotion; of changing situation, or moving one's person to whatsoever place one's own inclination may direct, without imprisonment or restraint, unless by due course of law. 1 Bl. Comm. 134. See LIBERTY.

PERSONAL PROPERTY. Property of a personal or movable nature, as opposed to property of a local or immovable character, (such as land or houses,) the latter being called "real property." This term is also applied to the right or interest less than a freehold which a man has in realty.

That kind of property which usually consists of things temporary and movable, but includes all subjects of property not of a freehold nature, nor descendible to the heirs at law. 2 Kent, Comm. 340.

Personal property is divisible into (1) corporeal personal property, which includes movable and tangible things, such as animals, ships, furniture, merchandise, etc.; and (2) incorporeal personal property, which consists of such rights as personal annuities, stocks, shares, patents, and copyrights. Sweet.

PERSONAL REPLEVIN. A species of action to replevy a man out of prison or out of the custody of any private person. It took the place of the old writ *de homine replegiando;* but, as a means of examining into the legality of an imprisonment, it is now superseded by the writ of *habeas corpus*.

PERSONAL REPRESENTATIVES. Executors or administrators.

PERSONAL RIGHTS. The right of personal security, comprising those of life, limb, body, health, reputation, and the right of personal liberty.

PERSONAL SECURITY. A person's legal and uninterrupted enjoyment of his life, his limbs, his body, his health, and his reputation. 1 Bl. Comm. 129.

Evidences of debt which bind the person of the debtor, not real property, are distinguished from such as are liens on land by the name of "personal securities."

PERSONAL SERVICE. Personal service of a writ or notice is made by delivering it to the person named, in person, or handing him a copy and informing him of the nature and terms of the original. Leaving a copy at his place of abode is not personal service. 12 Wis. 336.

PERSONAL SERVITUDES. In the civil law. Such servitudes as are established merely for the advantage of a certain determined person, so that they relate to such person alone, and are extinguished at his death; as distinguished from *real* servitudes, or such as are established for the benefit of land, and which pass with the land to every new owner of it. Mackeld. Rom. Law, § 304.

PERSONAL STATUTES. In foreign and modern civil law. Those statutes which have principally for their object the *person*, and treat of property only incidentally. Story, Confl. Laws, § 13.

A personal statute, in this sense of the term, is a law, ordinance, regulation, or custom, the disposition of which affects the person and clothes him with a capacity or incapacity, which he does not change with every change of abode, but which, upon principles of justice and policy, he is assumed to carry with him wherever he goes. 2 Kent, Comm. 456.

The term is also applied to statutes which, instead of being general, are confined in their operation to one person or group of persons.

Personal things cannot be done by another. Finch, Law, b. 1, c. 3, n. 14.

Personal things cannot be granted over. Finch, Law, b. 1, c. 3, n. 15.

Personal things die with the person. Finch, Law, b. 1, c. 3, n. 16.

PERSONAL TITHES are tithes paid of such profits as come by the labor of a man's person; as by buying and selling, gains of merchandise, and handicrafts, etc. Tomlins.

Personalia personam sequuntur. Personal things follow the person. 10 Cush. 516.

PERSONALIS ACTIO. Lat. In the civil law. A personal action; an action against the person, (*in personam.*) Dig. 50, 16, 178, 2.

In old English law. A personal action. In this sense, the term was borrowed from the civil law by Bracton. The English form is constantly used as the designation of one of the chief divisions of civil actions.

PERSONALITER. In old English law. Personally; in person.

PERSONALITY. In modern civil law. The incidence of a law or statute upon persons, or that quality which makes it a *personal* law rather than a *real* law. "By the personality of laws, foreign jurists generally mean all laws which concern the condition, state, and capacity of persons." Story, Confl. Laws, § 16.

PERSONALTY. Personal property; movable property; chattels.

An abstract of *personal*. In old practice, an action was said to be in the personalty, where it was brought against the right person or the person against whom in law it lay. Old Nat. Brev. 92; Cowell.

PERSONATE. In criminal law. To assume the person (character) of another, without his consent or knowledge, in order to deceive others, and, in such feigned character, to fraudulently do some act or gain some advantage, to the harm or prejudice of the person counterfeited. See 2 East, P. C. 1010.

PERSONERO. In Spanish law. An attorney. So called because he represents the *person* of another, either in or out of court. Las Partidas, pt. 3, tit. 5, l. 1.

PERSONNE. Fr. A person. This term is applicable to men and women, or to either. Civil Code Lat. art. 3522, § 25.

Perspicua vera non sunt probanda. Co. Litt. 16. Plain truths need not be proved.

PERSUADE, PERSUADING. To persuade is to induce to act. Persuading is inducing others to act.

PERSUASION. The act of persuading; the act of influencing the mind by arguments or reasons offered, or by anything that moves the mind or passions, or inclines the will to a determination. Webster.

PERTENENCIA. In Spanish law. The claim or right which one has to the property in anything; the territory which belongs to any one by way of jurisdiction or property; that which is accessory or consequent to a principal thing, and goes with the ownership of it, as when it is said that such an one buys such an estate with all its appurtenances, (*pertenencias.*) Escriche. See 2 Black, 17.

PERTICATA TERRÆ. The fourth part of an acre. Cowell.

PERTICULAS. A pittance; a small portion of alms or victuals. Also certain poor scholars of the Isle of Man. Cowell.

PERTINENT. Applicable; relevant. Evidence is called "pertinent" when it is directed to the issue or matters in dispute, and legitimately tends to prove the allegations of the party offering it; otherwise it is called "impertinent."

PERTINENTS. In Scotch law. Appurtenances. "Parts and pertinents" are formal words in old deeds and charters. 1 Forb. Inst. pt. 2, pp. 112, 118.

PERTURBATION. In the English ecclesiastical courts, a "suit for perturbation of seat" is the technical name for an action growing out of a disturbance or infringement of one's right to a pew or seat in a church. 2 Phillim. Ecc. Law, 1813.

PERTURBATRIX. A woman who breaks the peace.

PERVERSE VERDICT. A verdict whereby the jury refuse to follow the direction of the judge on a point of law.

PERVISE, PARVISE. In old English law. The court or yard of the king's palace at Westminster. Also an afternoon exercise or moot for the instruction of students. Cowell; Blount.

PESA. A weight of two hundred and fifty-six pounds. Cowell.

PESAGE. In England. A toll charged for weighing avoirdupois goods other than wool. 2 Chit. Com. Law, 16,

PESQUISIDOR. In Spanish law. Coroner. White, New Recop. b. 1, tit. 1, § 3.

PESSIMI EXEMPLI. Of the worst example.

PESSONA. Mast of oaks, etc., or money taken for mast, or feeding hogs. Cowell.

PESSURABLE WARES. Merchandise which takes up a good deal of room in a ship. Cowell.

PETENS. Lat. In old English law. A demandant; the plaintiff in a real action. Bract. fols. 102, 106*b*.

PETER-PENCE. An ancient levy or tax of a penny on each house throughout England, paid to the pope. It was called "Peter-pence," because collected on the day of St. Peter, *ad vincula;* by the Saxons it was called "Rome-feoh," "Rome-scot," and "Rome-pennying," because collected and sent to Rome; and, lastly, it was called "hearth money," because every dwelling-house was liable to it, and every religious house, the abbey of St. Albans alone excepted. Wharton.

PETIT. Fr. Small; minor; inconsiderable. Used in several compounds, and sometimes written "petty."

PETIT CAPE. A judicial writ, issued in the old actions for the recovery of land, requiring the sheriff to take possession of the estate, where the tenant, after having appeared in answer to the summons, made default in a subsequent stage of the proceedings.

PETIT JURY. The ordinary jury of twelve men for the trial of a civil or criminal action. So called to distinguish it from the grand jury.

A petit jury is a body of twelve men impaneled and sworn in a district court, to try and determine, by a true and unanimous verdict, any question or issue of fact, in any civil or criminal action or proceeding, according to law and the evidence as given them in the court. Gen. St. Minn. 1878, c. 71, § 1.

PETIT LARCENY. The larceny of things whose value was below a certain arbitrary standard, at common law twelve pence. See LARCENY.

PETIT SERJEANTY. A tenure by which lands were held of the crown by the service of rendering yearly some small implement of war; as a lance, an arrow, etc. 2 Bl. Comm. 82.

PETIT TREASON. In English law. The crime committed by a wife in killing her husband, or a servant his lord or master, or an ecclesiastic his lord or ordinary. 4 Bl. Comm. 75.

PETITE ASSIZE. Used in contradistinction from the *grand assize*, which was a jury to decide on questions of property. *Petite assize*, a jury to decide on questions of possession. Britt. c. 42; Glan. lib. 2, cc. 6, 7.

PETITIO. Lat. In the civil law. The plaintiff's statement of his cause of action in an action *in rem*. Calvin.

In old English law. Petition or demand; the count in a real action; the form of words in which a title to land was stated by the demandant, and which commenced with the word "*peto.*" 1 Reeve, Eng. Law, 176.

PETITIO PRINCIPII. In logic. Begging the question, which is the taking of a thing for true or for granted, and drawing conclusions from it as such, when it is really dubious, perhaps false, or at least wants to be proved, before any inferences ought to be drawn from it.

PETITION. A written address, embodying an application or prayer from the person or persons preferring it, to the power, body, or person to whom it is presented, for the exercise of his or their authority in the redress of some wrong, or the grant of some favor, privilege, or license.

In practice. An application made to a court *ex parte*, or where there are no parties in opposition, praying for the exercise of the judicial powers of the court in relation to some matter which is not the subject for a suit or action, or for authority to do some act which requires the sanction of the court; as for the appointment of a guardian, for leave to sell trust property, etc.

The word "petition" is generally used in judicial proceedings to describe an application in writing, in contradistinction to a motion, which may be *viva voce*. 4 Metc. (Mass.) 371.

In the practice of some of the states, the word "petition" is adopted as the name of that initiatory pleading in an action which is elsewhere called a "declaration" or "complaint." See Code Ga. 1882, § 3332.

In equity practice. An application in writing for an order of the court, stating the circumstances upon which it is founded; a proceeding resorted to whenever the nature of the application to the court requires a fuller statement than can be conveniently made in a notice of motion. 1 Barb. Ch. Pr. 578.

PETITION DE DROIT. L. Fr. In English practice. A petition of right; a form of proceeding to obtain restitution from the crown of either real or personal property, being of use where the crown is in possession of any hereditaments or chattels, and the petitioner suggests such a right as controverts the title of the crown, grounded on facts disclosed in the petition itself. 3 Bl. Comm. 256.

PETITION OF RIGHT. In English law. A proceeding in chancery by which a subject may recover property in the possession of the king. See PETITION DE DROIT.

PETITION OF RIGHTS. A parliamentary declaration of the liberties of the people, assented to by King Charles I. in 1629. It is to be distinguished from the bill of rights, (1689,) which has passed into a permanent constitutional statute. Brown.

PETITIONER. One who presents a petition to a court, officer, or legislative body. In legal proceedings begun by petition, the person against whom action or relief is prayed, or who opposes the prayer of the petition, is called the "respondent."

PETITIONING CREDITOR. The creditor at whose instance an adjudication of bankruptcy is made against a bankrupt.

PETITORY ACTION. A droitural action; that is, one in which the plaintiff seeks to establish and enforce, by an appropriate legal proceeding, his right of property, or his title, to the subject-matter in dispute; as distinguished from a *possessory* action, where the right to the possession is the point in litigation, and not the mere right of property. The term is chiefly used in admiralty. 1 Kent, Comm. 371; 5 Mason, 465.

In Scotch law. Actions in which damages are sought.

PETO. Lat. In Roman law. I request. A common word by which a *fideicommissum*, or trust, was created in a will. Inst. 2, 24, 3.

PETRA. A stone weight. Cowell.

PETTIFOGGER. A lawyer who is employed in a small or mean business, or who carries on a disreputable business by unprincipled or dishonorable means.

"We think that the term 'pettifogging shyster' needed no definition by witnesses before the jury. This combination of epithets, every lawyer and citizen knows, belongs to none but unscrupulous practitioners who disgrace their profession by doing mean work, and resort to sharp practice to do it." 40 Mich. 256.

PETTY AVERAGE. In maritime law. A term used to denote such charges and disbursements as, according to occurrences and the custom of every place, the master necessarily furnishes for the benefit of the ship and cargo, either at the place of loading or unloading, or on the voyage; such as the hire of a pilot for conducting a vessel from one place to another, towage, light money, beaconage, anchorage, bridge toll, quarantine and such like. Park, Ins. 100. The particulars belonging to this head depend, however, entirely upon usage. Abb. Ship. 404.

PETTY BAG OFFICE. In English law. An office in the court of chancery, for suits against attorneys and officers of the court, and for process and proceedings by extent on statutes, recognizances, *ad quod damnum*, and the like. Termes de la Ley.

PETTY CONSTABLE. In English law. The ordinary kind of constable in towns and parishes, as distinguished from the high constable of the hundred.

PETTY SESSIONS. In English law. A special or petty session is sometimes kept in corporations and counties at large by a few justices, for dispatching smaller business in the neighborhood between the times of the general sessions; as for licensing alehouses, passing the accounts of the parish officers, etc. Brown.

PEW. An inclosed seat in a church.

PHAROS. A watch-tower, light-house, or sea-mark.

PHOTOGRAPHER. Any person who makes for sale photographs, ambrotypes, daguerrotypes, or pictures, by the action of light. Act Cong. July 13, 1866, § 9; 14 St. at Large, 120.

PHYLASIST. A jailer.

PHYSICAL DISABILITY. A disability or incapacity caused by physical defect or infirmity, or bodily imperfection, or mental weakness or alienation; as distinguished from *civil* disability, which relates to the civil *status* or condition of the person, and is imposed by the law.

PHYSICAL FACT. In the law of evidence. A fact having a physical existence, as distinguished from a mere conception of the mind; one which is visible, audible, or palpable; such as the sound of a pistol shot, a man running, impressions of human feet on the ground. Burrill, Circ. Ev. 130. A fact considered to have its seat in some inanimate being, or, if in an animate being, by virtue, not of the qualities by which it is constituted animate, but of those which it has in common with the class of inanimate beings. 1 Benth. Jud. Ev. 45.

PHYSICAL NECESSITY. A condition in which a person is absolutely compelled to act in a particular way by overwhelming superior force; as distinguished from *moral* necessity, which arises where there is a duty incumbent upon a rational being to perform, which he ought at the time to perform. 3 Sum. 248.

PHYSICIAN. A practitioner of medicine; a person duly authorized or licensed to treat diseases; one lawfully engaged in the practice of medicine, without reference to any particular school. 62 Wis. 289, 22 N. W. Rep. 430.

PIA FRAUS. Lat. A pious fraud; a subterfuge or evasion considered morally justifiable on account of the ends sought to be promoted. Particularly applied to an evasion or disregard of the laws in the interests of religion or religious institutions, such as circumventing the statutes of mortmain.

PIACLE. An obsolete term for an enormous crime.

PICAROON. A robber; a plunderer.

PICK-LOCK. An instrument by which locks are opened without a key.

PICK OF LAND. A narrow slip of land running into a corner.

PICKAGE. Money paid at fairs for breaking ground for booths.

PICKERY. In Scotch law. Petty theft; stealing of trifles, punishable arbitrarily. Bell.

PICKETING, by members of a trade union on strike, consists in posting members at all the approaches to the works struck against, for the purpose of observing and reporting the workmen going to or coming from the works, and of using such influence as may be in their power to prevent the workmen from accepting work there. Dav. Friend. Soc. 212.

PICKLE, PYCLE, or PIGHTEL. A small parcel of land inclosed with a hedge, which, in some countries, is called a "pingle." Enc. Lond.

PICKPOCKET. A thief who secretly steals money or other property from the person of another.

PIEDPOUDRE. See COURT OF PIEDPOUDRE.

PIERAGE. The duty for maintaining piers and harbors.

PIGNORATIO. In the civil law. The contract of pledge; and also the obligation of such contract.

PIGNORATITIA ACTIO. In the civil law. An action of pledge, or founded on a pledge, which was either *directa*, for the debtor, after payment of the debt, or *con-*

traria, for the creditor. Heinecc. Elem. lib. 3, tit. 13, §§ 824–826.

PIGNORATIVE CONTRACT. In the civil law. A contract of pledge, hypothecation, or mortgage of realty.

PIGNORIS CAPIO. In Roman law. This was the name of one of the *legis actiones*. It was employed only in certain particular kinds of pecuniary cases, and consisted in that the creditor, without preliminary suit and without the co-operation of the magistrate, by reciting a prescribed formula, took an article of property from the debtor to be treated as a pledge or security. The proceeding bears a marked analogy to distress at common law. Mackeld. Rom. Law, § 203; Gaius, bk. 4, §§ 26–29.

PIGNUS. In the civil law. A pledge or pawn; a delivery of a thing to a creditor, as security for a debt. Also a thing delivered to a creditor as security for a debt.

PILA. In old English law. That side of coined money which was called "pile," because it was the side on which there was an impression of a church built on piles. Fleta, lib. 1, c. 39.

PILETTUS. In the ancient forest laws. An arrow which had a round knob a little above the head, to hinder it from going far into the mark. Cowell.

PILFER. To pilfer, in the plain and popular sense, means to steal. To charge another with pilfering is to charge him with stealing, and is slander. 4 Blackf. 499.

PILFERER. One who steals petty things.

PILLAGE. Plunder; the forcible taking of private property by an invading or conquering army from the enemy's subjects.

PILLORY. A frame erected on a pillar, and made with holes and movable boards, through which the heads and hands of criminals were put.

PILOT. A particular officer serving on board a ship during the course of a voyage, and having the charge of the helm and the ship's route; or a person taken on board at any particular place for the purpose of conducting a ship through a river, road, or channel, or from or into a port. Wharton.

PILOTAGE. The navigation of a vessel by a pilot; the duty of a pilot. The charge or compensation allowed for piloting a vessel.

PILOTAGE AUTHORITIES. In English law. Boards of commissioners appointed and authorized for the regulation and appointment of pilots, each board having jurisdiction within a prescribed district.

PIMP-TENURE. A very singular and odious kind of tenure mentioned by the old writers, "*Wilhelmus Hoppeshort tenet dimidiam virgatam terræ per servitium custodiendi sex damisellas, scil. meretrices ad usum domini regis.*" Wharton.

PIN-MONEY. An allowance set apart by a husband for the personal expenses of his wife, for her dress and pocket money.

PINCERNA. In old English law. Butler; the king's butler, whose office it was to select out of the cargo of every vessel laden with wine, one cask at the prow and another at the stern, for the king's use. Fleta, lib. 2, c. 22.

PINNAGE. Poundage of cattle.

PINNER. A pounder of cattle; a pound-keeper.

PINT. A liquid measure of half a quart, or the eighth part of a gallon.

PIOUS USES. See CHARITABLE USES.

PIPE. A roll in the exchequer; otherwise called the "great roll." A liquid measure containing two hogsheads.

PIRACY. In criminal law. A robbery or forcible depredation on the high seas, without lawful authority, done *animo furandi*, in the spirit and intention of universal hostility. 3 Wheat. 610. This is the definition of this offense by the law of nations. 1 Kent, Comm. 183.

There is a distinction between the offense of piracy, as known to the law of nations, which is justiciable everywhere, and offenses created by statutes of particular nations, cognizable only before the municipal tribunals of such nations. 2 Cliff. 394, 418.

The term is also applied to the illicit reprinting or reproduction of a copyrighted book or print or to unlawful plagiarism from it.

Pirata est hostis humani generis. 3 Inst. 113. A pirate is an enemy of the human race.

PIRATE. A person who lives by piracy; one guilty of the crime of piracy. A sea-robber, who, to enrich himself, by subtlety or open force, setteth upon merchants and others trading by sea, despoiling them of their loading, and sometimes bereaving them of life and sinking their ships. Ridley, Civil & Ecc. Law, pt. 2, c. 1, § 3.

A pirate is one who acts solely on his own authority, without any commission or authority from a sovereign state, seizing by force, and appropriating to himself without discrimination, every vessel he meets with. Robbery on the high seas is piracy; but to constitute the offense the taking must be felonious. Consequently the *quo animo* may be inquired into. 2 Paine, 324.

Pirates are common sea-rovers, without any fixed place of residence, who acknowledge no sovereign and no law, and support themselves by pillage and depredations at sea; but there are instances wherein the word "*pirata*" has been formerly taken for a sea-captain. Spelman.

PIRATICAL. "Where the act uses the word 'piratical,' it does so in a general sense; importing that the aggression is unauthorized by the law of nations, hostile in its character, wanton and criminal in its commission, and utterly without any sanction from any public authority or sovereign power. In short, it means that the act belongs to the class of offenses which pirates are in the habit of perpetrating, whether they do it for purposes of plunder, or for purposes of hatred, revenge, or wanton abuse of power." 2 How. 232.

PIRATICALLY. A technical word which must always be used in an indictment for piracy. 3 Inst. 112.

PISCARY. The right or privilege of fishing. Thus, common of piscary is the right of fishing in waters belonging to another person.

PISTAREEN. A small Spanish coin. It is not made current by the laws of the United States. 10 Pet. 618.

PIT. In old Scotch law. An excavation or cavity in the earth in which women who were under sentence of death were drowned.

PIT AND GALLOWS. In Scotch law. A privilege of inflicting capital punishment for theft, given by King Malcolm, by which a woman could be drowned in a pit, (*fossa*,) or a man hanged on a gallows, (*furca*.) Bell.

PITCHING-PENCE. In old English law. Money, commonly a penny, paid for pitching or setting down every bag of corn or pack of goods in a fair or market. Cowell.

PITTANCE. A slight repast or refection of fish or flesh more than the common allowance; and the pittancer was the officer who distributed this at certain appointed festivals. Cowell.

PIX. A mode of testing coin. The ascertaining whether coin is of the proper standard is in England called "pixing" it; and there are occasions on which resort is had for this purpose to an ancient mode of inquisition called the "trial of the pix," before a jury of members of the Goldsmiths' Company. 2 Steph. Comm. 540, note.

PIX JURY. A jury consisting of the members of the corporation of the goldsmiths of the city of London, assembled upon an inquisition of very ancient date, called the "trial of the pix." See PIX.

PLACARD. An edict; a declaration; a manifesto. Also an advertisement or public notification.

PLACE. An old form of the word "pleas." Thus the "Court of Common Pleas" was sometimes called the "Court of Common Place."

PLACE. This word is a very indefinite term. It is applied to any locality, limited by boundaries, however large or however small. It may be used to designate a country, state, county, town, or a very small portion of a town. The extent of the locality designated by it must generally be determined by the connection in which it is used. 46 Vt. 432.

PLACE OF CONTRACT. The place (country or state) in which a contract is made, and whose law must determine questions affecting the execution, validity, and construction of the contract. 91 U. S. 412.

PLACE OF DELIVERY. The place where delivery is to be made of goods sold. If no place is specified in the contract, the articles sold must, in general, be delivered at the place where they are at the time of the sale. 100 U. S. 134.

PLACE WHERE. A phrase used in the older reports, being a literal translation of *locus in quo*, (*q. v.*)

PLACEMAN. One who exercises a public employment, or fills a public station.

PLACIT, or PLACITUM. Decree; determination.

PLACITA. In old English law. The public assemblies of all degrees of men where the sovereign presided, who usually consulted upon the great affairs of the kingdom. Also pleas, pleadings, or debates, and trials at law; sometimes penalties, fines, mulcts, or emendations; also the style of the court at the beginning of the record at *nisi prius*, but this is now omitted. Cowell.

In the civil law. The decrees or constitutions of the emperor; being the expressions of his will and pleasure. Calvin.

PLACITA COMMUNIA. Common pleas. All civil actions between subject and subject. 3 Bl. Comm. 38, 40.

PLACITA CORONÆ. Pleas of the crown. All trials for crimes and misdemeanors, wherein the king is plaintiff, on behalf of the people. 3 Bl. Comm. 40.

Placita de transgressione contra pacem regis, in regno Angliæ vi et armis facta, secundum legem et consuetudinem Angliæ sine brevi regis placitari non debent. 2 Inst. 311. Pleas of trespass against the peace of the king in the kingdom of England, made with force and arms, ought not, by the law and custom of England, to be pleaded without the king's writ.

PLACITA JURIS. Pleas or rules of law; "particular and positive learnings of laws;" "grounds and positive learnings received with the law and set down;" as distinguished from maxims or the formulated conclusions of legal reason. Bac. Max. pref., and reg. 12.

Placita negativa duo exitum non faciunt. Two negative pleas do not form an issue. Lofft, 415.

PLACITABILE. In old English law. Pleadable. Spelman.

PLACITAMENTUM. In old records. The pleading of a cause. Spelman.

PLACITARE. To plead.

PLACITATOR. In old records. A pleader. Cowell; Spelman.

PLACITORY. Relating to pleas or pleading.

PLACITUM. In old English law. A public assembly at which the king presided, and which comprised men of all degrees, met for consultation about the great affairs of the kingdom. Cowell.

A court; a judicial tribunal; a lord's court. *Placita* was the style or title of the courts at the beginning of the old *nisi prius* record.

A suit or cause in court; a judicial proceeding; a trial. *Placita* were divided into *placita coronæ* (crown cases or pleas of the crown, *i. e.*, criminal actions) and *placita communia*, (common cases or common pleas, *i. e.*, private civil actions.)

A fine, mulct, or pecuniary punishment.

A pleading or plea. In this sense, the term was not confined to the defendant's answer to the declaration, but included all the pleadings in the cause, being *nomen generalissimum*. 1 Saund. 388, n. 6.

In the old reports and abridgments, "*placitum*" was the name of a paragraph or subdivision of a title or page where the point decided in a cause was set out separately. It is commonly abbreviated "pl."

In the civil law. An agreement of parties; that which is their *pleasure* to arrange between them.

An imperial ordinance or constitution; literally, the prince's pleasure. Inst. 1, 2, 6.

A judicial decision; the judgment, decree, or sentence of a court. Calvin.

Placitum aliud personale, aliud reale, aliud mixtum. Co. Litt. 284. Pleas [*i. e.*, actions] are personal, real, and mixed.

PLACITUM FRACTUM. A day past or lost to the defendant. 1 Hen. I. c. 59.

PLACITUM NOMINATUM. The day appointed for a criminal to appear and plead and make his defense. Cowell.

PLAGIARISM. The act of appropriating the literary composition of another, or parts or passages of his writings, or the ideas or language of the same, and passing them off as the product of one's own mind.

PLAGIARIST, or PLAGIARY. One who publishes the thoughts and writings of another as his own.

PLAGIARIUS. Lat. In the civil law. A man-stealer; a kidnapper. Dig. 48, 15, 1; 4 Bl. Comm. 219.

PLAGIUM. Lat. In the civil law. Man-stealing; kidnapping. The offense of enticing away and stealing men, children, and slaves. Calvin. The persuading a slave to escape from his master, or the concealing or harboring him without the knowledge of his master. Dig. 48, 15, 6.

PLAGUE. Pestilence; a contagious and malignant fever.

PLAIDEUR. Fr. An obsolete term for an attorney who pleaded the cause of his client; an advocate.

PLAIN STATEMENT is one that may be readily understood, not merely by lawyers, but by all who are sufficiently acquainted with the language in which it is written. 5 Sandf. 557, 564.

PLAINT. In English practice. A private memorial tendered in open court to the judge, wherein the party injured sets forth his cause of action. A proceeding in inferior courts by which an action is commenced without original writ. 3 Bl. Comm. 373. This mode of proceeding is commonly adopted in cases of replevin. 3 Steph. Comm. 666.

PLAINTIFF. A person who brings an action; the party who complains or sues in a personal action and is so named on the record.

PLAINTIFF IN ERROR. The party who sues out a writ of error to review a judgment or other proceeding at law.

PLAN. A map, chart, or design; being a delineation or projection on a plane surface of the ground lines of a house, farm, street, city, etc., reduced in absolute length, but preserving their relative positions and proportion.

PLANT. The fixtures, tools, machinery, and apparatus which are necessary to carry on a trade or business. Wharton.

PLANTATION. In English law. A colony; an original settlement in a new country. See 1 Bl. Comm. 107.

In American law. A farm; a large cultivated estate. Used chiefly in the southern states.

In North Carolina, "plantation" signifies the land a man owns which he is cultivating more or less in annual crops. Strictly, it designates the place planted; but in wills it is generally used to denote more than the inclosed and cultivated fields, and to take in the necessary woodland, and, indeed, commonly all the land forming the parcel or parcels under culture as one farm, or even what is worked by one set of hands. 10 Ired. 431.

PLAT, or PLOT. A map, or representation on paper, of a piece of land subdivided into lots, with streets, alleys, etc., usually drawn to a scale.

PLAY-DEBT. Debt contracted by gaming.

PLAZA. A Spanish word, meaning a public square in a city or town.

PLEA. In old English law. A suit or action. Thus, the power to "hold pleas" is the power to take cognizance of actions or suits; so "common pleas" are actions or suits between private persons. And this meaning of the word still appears in the modern declarations, where it is stated, *e. g.*, that the defendant "has been summoned to answer the plaintiff in a *plea* of debt."

In common-law practice. A pleading; any one in the series of pleadings. More particularly, the first pleading on the part of the defendant. In the strictest sense, the answer which the defendant in an action at law makes to the plaintiff's declaration, and in which he sets up matter of *fact* as defense, thus distinguished from a demurrer, which interposes objections on grounds of *law*.

In equity. A special answer showing or relying upon one or more things as a cause why the suit should be either dismissed or delayed or barred. Mitf. Eq. Pl. 219; Coop. Eq. Pl. 223.

A short statement, in response to a bill in equity, of facts which, if inserted in the bill, would render it demurrable; while an answer is a complete statement of the defendant's case, and contains answers to any interrogatories the plaintiff may have administered. Hunt, Eq. pt. 1, c. 3.

PLEA IN ABATEMENT. In practice. A plea which goes to *abate* the plaintiff's action; that is, to suspend or put it off for the present. 3 Bl. Comm. 301.

PLEA IN BAR. In practice. A plea which goes to *bar* the plaintiff's action; that is, to defeat it absolutely and entirely. 1 Burrill, Pr. 162; 3 Bl. Comm. 303.

PLEA SIDE. The plea side of a court is that branch or department of the court which entertains or takes cognizance of civil actions and suits, as distinguished from its criminal or crown department. Thus the court of queen's bench is said to have a plea side and a crown or criminal side; the one branch or department of it being devoted to the cognizance of civil actions, the other to criminal proceedings and matters peculiarly concerning the crown. So the court of exchequer is said to have a plea side and a crown side; the one being appropriated to civil actions, the other to matters of revenue. Brown.

PLEAD. To make, deliver, or file any pleading; to conduct the pleadings in a cause. To interpose any pleading in a suit which contains allegations of fact; in this sense the word is the antithesis of "demur." More particularly, to deliver in a formal manner the defendant's answer to the plaintiff's declaration, or to the indictment, as the case may be.

To appear as a pleader or advocate in a cause; to argue a cause in a court of justice. But this meaning of the word is not technical, but colloquial.

PLEAD ISSUABLY. This means to interpose such a plea as is calculated to raise a material issue, either of law or of fact.

PLEAD OVER. To pass over, or omit to notice, a material allegation in the last pleading of the opposite party; to pass by a defect in the pleading of the other party without taking advantage of it.

In another sense, to plead the general issue, after one has interposed a demurrer or special plea which has been dismissed by a judgment of *respondeat ouster*.

PLEADED. Alleged or averred, in form, in a judicial proceeding.

It more often refers to matter of defense, but not invariably. To say that matter in a declaration or replication is not well pleaded would not be deemed erroneous. Abbott.

PLEADER. A person whose business it is to draw pleadings. Formerly, when pleading at common law was a highly technical and difficult art, there was a class of men known as "special pleaders not at the bar," who held a position intermediate between counsel and attorneys. The class is now almost extinct, and the term "pleaders" is generally applied, in England, to junior members of the common-law bar. Sweet.

PLEADING. The peculiar science or system of rules and principles, established in the common law, according to which the pleadings or responsive allegations of litigating parties are framed, with a view to preserve technical propriety and to produce a proper issue.

The process performed by the parties to a suit or action, in alternately presenting written statements of their contention, each responsive to that which precedes, and each serving to narrow the field of controversy, until there evolves a single point, affirmed on one side and denied on the other, called the "issue," upon which they then go to trial.

The act or step of interposing any one of the pleadings in a cause, but particularly one on the part of the defendant; and, in the strictest sense, one which sets up allegations of fact in defense to the action.

The name "a pleading" is also given to any one of the formal written statements of accusation or defense presented by the parties alternately in an action at law; the aggregate of such statements filed in any one cause are termed "the pleadings."

The oral advocacy of a client's cause in court, by his barrister or counsel, is sometimes called "pleading;" but this is a popular, rather than technical, use.

In chancery practice. Consists in making the formal written allegations or statements of the respective parties on the record to maintain the suit, or to defeat it, of which, when contested in matters of fact, they propose to offer proofs, and in matters of law to offer arguments to the court. Story, Eq. Pl. § 4, note.

PLEADING, SPECIAL. By special pleading is meant the allegation of special or new matter, as distinguished from a direct denial of matter previously alleged on the opposite side. Gould, Pl. c. 1, § 18.

PLEADINGS. The pleadings are the formal allegations by the parties of their respective claims and defenses, for the judgment of the court. Code Civil Proc. Cal. § 420.

The individual allegations of the respective parties to an action at common law, proceeding from them alternately, in the order and under the distinctive names following: The plaintiff's *declaration*, the defendant's *plea*, the plaintiff's *replication*, the defendant's *rejoinder*, the plaintiff's *surrejoinder*, the defendant's *rebutter*, the plaintiff's *surrebutter;* after which they have no distinctive names. Burrill.

The term "pleadings" has a technical and well-defined meaning. Pleadings are written allegations of what is affirmed on the one side, or denied on the other, disclosing to the court or jury having to try the cause the real matter in dispute between the parties. 1 Minn. 17, (Gil. 1.)

PLEAS OF THE CROWN. In English law. A phrase now employed to signify criminal causes, in which the king is a party. Formerly it signified royal causes for offenses of a greater magnitude than mere misdemeanors.

PLEAS ROLL. In English practice. A record upon which are entered all the pleadings in a cause, in their regular order, and the issue.

PLEBANUS. A rural dean. Cowell.

PLEBEIAN. One who is classed among the common people, as distinguished from the nobles.

PLEBEITY, or PLEBITY. The common or meaner sort of people; the plebeians.

PLEBEYOS. In Spanish law. Commons; those who exercise any trade, or who cultivate the soil. White, New Recop. b. 1, tit. 5, c. 3, § 6, and note.

PLEBIANA. In old records. A mother church.

PLEBISCITE. In modern constitutional law, the name "*plebiscite*" has been given to a vote of the entire people, (that is, the aggregate of the enfranchised individuals composing a state or nation,) expressing their choice for or against a proposed law or enactment, submitted to them, and which, if adopted, will work a radical change in the constitution, or which is beyond the powers of the regular legislative body. The proceeding is extraordinary, and is generally revolutionary in its character; an example of which may be seen in the *plebiscites* submitted to the French people by Louis Napoleon, whereby the Second Empire was established. But the principle of the *plebiscite* has been incorporated in the modern Swiss constitution, (under the name of "*referendum*,") by which a revision of the constitution must be undertaken when demanded by the vote of fifty thousand Swiss citizens. Maine, Popular Govt. 40, 96.

PLEBISCITUM. Lat. In Roman law. A law enacted by the *plebs* or commonalty, (that is, the citizens, with the exception of the patricians and senators,) at the request or on the proposition of a plebeian magistrate, such as a "tribune." Inst. 1, 2, 4.

PLEBS. In Roman law. The commonalty or citizens, exclusive of the patricians and senators. Inst. 1, 2, 4.

PLEDABLE. L. Fr. That may be brought or conducted; as an action or "plea," as it was formerly called. Britt. c. 32.

PLEDGE. In the law of bailment. A bailment of goods to a creditor as security for some debt or engagement. A bailment or delivery of goods by a debtor to his creditor, to be kept till the debt be discharged. Story, Bailm. § 7; Civil Code La. art. 3133; 2 Kent, Comm. 577.

Pledge is a deposit of personal property by way of security for the performance of another act. Civil Code Cal. § 2986.

The specific article delivered to the creditor in security is also called a "pledge" or "pawn."

There is a clear distinction between mortgages and pledges. In a pledge the legal title remains in the pledgor; in a mortgage it passes to the mortgagee. In a mortgage the mortgagee need not have possession; in a pledge the pledgee must have possession, though it be only constructive. In a mortgage, at common law, the property on non-payment of the debt passes wholly to the mortgagee; in a pledge the property is sold, and only so much of the proceeds as will pay his debt passes to the pledgee. A mortgage is a conditional conveyance of property, which becomes absolute unless redeemed at a specified time. A pledge is not strictly a conveyance at all, nor need any day of redemption be appointed for it. A mortgagee can sell and deliver the thing mortgaged, subject only to the right of redemption. A pledgee cannot sell and deliver his pawn until the debt is due and payment denied. Bouvier.

There are two varieties of the contract of pledge known to the law of Louisiana, viz., *pawn* and *antichresis;* the former relating to chattel securities, the latter to landed securities. See Civil Code La. art. 3101; and see those titles.

PLEDGEE. The party to whom goods are pledged, or delivered in pledge. Story, Bailm. § 287.

PLEDGERY. Suretyship, or an undertaking or answering for another.

PLEDGES. In old English law. No person could prosecute a civil action without having in the first stage of it two or more persons as pledges of prosecution; and if judgment was given against the plaintiff, or he deserted his suit, both he and his pledges were liable to amercement to the king *pro falso clamore.* In the course of time, however, these pledges were disused, and the names of fictitious persons substituted for them, two ideal persons, John Doe and Richard Roe, having become the common pledges of every suitor; and now the use of such pledges is altogether discontinued. Brown.

PLEDGES TO RESTORE. In England, before the plaintiff in foreign attachment can issue execution against the property in the hands of the garnishee, he must find "pledges to restore," consisting of two householders, who enter into a recognizance for the restoration of the property, as a security for the protection of the defendant; for, as the plaintiff's debt is not proved in any stage of the proceedings, the court guards the rights of the absent defendant by taking security on his behalf, so that if he should afterwards disprove the plaintiff's claim he may obtain restitution of the property attached. Brand. For. Attachm. 93; Sweet.

PLEDGOR. The party delivering goods in pledge; the party pledging. Story, Bailm. § 287.

PLEGIABILIS. In old English law. That may be pledged; the subject of pledge or security. Fleta, lib. 1, c. 20, § 98.

PLEGII DE PROSEQUENDO. Pledges to prosecute with effect an action of replevin.

PLEGII DE RETORNO HABENDO. Pledges to return the subject of distress, should the right be determined against the party bringing the action of replevin. 3 Steph. Comm. (7th Ed.) 422*n*.

PLEGIIS ACQUIETANDIS. A writ that anciently lay for a surety against him for whom he was surety, if he paid not the money at the day. Fitzh. Nat. Brev. 137.

PLENA ÆTAS. In old English law. Full age.

Plena et celeris justitia fiat partibus. 4 Inst. 67. Let full and speedy justice be done to the parties.

PLENA FORISFACTURA. A forfeiture of all that one possesses.

PLENA PROBATIO. In the civil law. A term used to signify full proof, (that is, proof by two witnesses,) in contradistinction to *semi-plena probatio*, which is only a presumption. Cod. 4, 19, 5.

PLENARTY. In English law. Fullness; a state of being full. A term applied to a benefice when full, or possessed by an incumbent. The opposite state to a *vacation*, or vacancy. Cowell.

PLENARY. Full; entire; complete; unabridged.

In the ecclesiastical courts, (and in admiralty practice,) causes are divided into plenary and summary. The former are those in whose proceedings the order and solemnity of the law is required to be exactly observed, so that if there is the least departure from that order, or disregard of that solemnity, the whole proceedings are annulled. Summary causes are those in which it is unnecessary to pursue that order and solemnity. Brown.

PLENARY CONFESSION. A full and complete confession. An admission or confession, whether in civil or criminal law, is said to be "plenary" when it is, if believed, conclusive against the person making it. Best, Ev. 664; Rosc. Crim. Ev. 39.

PLENE. Completely; fully; sufficiently.

PLENE ADMINISTRAVIT. In practice. A plea by an executor or administrator that he has fully administered all the assets that have come to his hands, and that no assets remain out of which the plaintiff's claim could be satisfied.

PLENE ADMINISTRAVIT PRÆTER. In practice. A plea by an executor or administrator that he has fully administered all the assets that have come to his hands, except assets to a certain amount, which are not sufficient to satisfy the plaintiff. 1 Tidd, Pr. 644.

PLENE COMPUTAVIT. He has fully accounted. A plea in an action of account-render, alleging that the defendant has fully accounted.

PLENIPOTENTIARY. One who has full power to do a thing; a person fully commissioned to act for another. A term applied in international law to ministers and envoys of the second rank of public ministers. Wheat. Hist. Law Nat. 266.

PLENUM DOMINIUM. Lat. In the civil law. Full ownership; the property in a thing united with the usufruct. Calvin.

PLEYTO. In Spanish law. The pleadings in a cause. White, New Recop. b. 3, tit. 7.

PLIGHT. In old English law. An estate, with the habit and quality of the land; extending to a rent charge and to a possibility of dower. Co. Litt. 221*b*; Cowell.

PLOK-PENNIN. A kind of earnest used in public sales at Amsterdam. Wharton.

PLOW-ALMS. The ancient payment of a penny to the church from every plow-land. 1 Mon. Angl. 256.

PLOW-BOTE. An allowance of wood which tenants are entitled to, for repairing their plows and other implements of husbandry.

PLOW-LAND. A quantity of land "not of any certain content, but as much as a plow can, by course of husbandry, plow in a year." Co. Litt. 69*a*.

PLOW-MONDAY. The Monday after twelfth-day.

PLOW-SILVER. Money formerly paid by some tenants, in lieu of service to plow the lord's lands.

PLUMBATURA. Lat. In the civil law. Soldering. Dig. 6, 1, 23, 5.

PLUMBUM. Lat. In the civil law. Lead. Dig. 50, 16, 242, 2.

PLUNDER, *v.* The most common meaning of the term "to plunder" is to take property from persons or places by open force, and this may be in course of a lawful war, or by unlawful hostility, as in the case of pirates or banditti. But in another and very common meaning, though in some degree figurative, it is used to express the idea of taking property from a person or place, without just right, but not expressing the nature or quality of the wrong done. 16 Pick. 9.

PLUNDER, *n.* Personal property belonging to an enemy, captured and appropriated on land; booty. Also the act of seizing such property. See BOOTY; PRIZE.

PLUNDERAGE. In maritime law. The embezzlement of goods on board of a ship is so called.

PLURAL. Containing more than one; consisting of or designating two or more. Webster.

Pluralis numerus est duobus contentus. 1 Rolle, 476. The plural number is satisfied by two.

PLURALIST. One that holds more than one ecclesiastical benefice, with cure of souls.

PLURALITER. In the plural. 10 East, 158, arg.

PLURALITY. In the law of elections. The excess of the votes cast for one candidate over those cast for any other. Where there are only two candidates, he who receives the greater number of the votes cast is said to have a *majority;* when there are more than two competitors for the same office, the person who receives the greatest number of votes has a *plurality,* but he has not a majority unless he receives a greater number of votes than those cast for all his competitors combined.

In ecclesiastical law, "plurality" means the holding two, three, or more benefices by the same incumbent; and he is called a "pluralist." Pluralities are now abolished, except in certain cases. 2 Steph. Comm. 691, 692.

Plures cohæredes sunt quasi unum corpus propter unitatem juris quod habent. Co. Litt. 163. Several co-heirs are, as it were, one body, by reason of the unity of right which they possess.

Plures participes sunt quasi unum corpus, in eo quod unum jus habent. Co. Litt. 164. Several parceners are as one body, in that they have one right.

PLURIES. When an original and *alias* writ have been issued and proved ineffectual, a third writ, called a "*pluries* writ," may frequently be issued. It is to the same effect as the two former, except that it contains the words, "as we have often commanded you," ("*sicut pluries præcepimus,*") after the usual commencement, "We command you." 3 Bl. Comm. 283; Archb. Pr. 585.

PLURIS PETITIO. Lat. In Scotch practice. A *demand of more* than is due. Bell.

Plus exempla quam peccata nocent. Examples hurt more than crimes.

Plus peccat author quam actor. The originator or instigator of a crime is a worse offender than the actual perpetrator of it. 5 Coke, 99*a*. Applied to the crime of subornation of perjury. Id.

PLUS PETITIO. In Roman law. A phrase denoting the offense of *claiming more* than was just in one's pleadings. This *more* might be claimed in four different respects, viz.: (1) *Re, i. e.,* in amount, (*e. g.,* £50 for £5;) (2) *loco, i. e.,* in place, (*e. g.,* delivery at some place more difficult to effect than the place specified;) (3) *tempore, i. e.,* in time, (*e. g.,* claiming payment on the 1st of August of what is not due till the 1st of September;) and (4) *causa, i. e.,* in quality, (*e. g.,* claiming a dozen of champagne, when the contract was only for a dozen of wine generally.) Prior to Justinian's time, this offense was in general fatal to the action; but, under the legislation of the emperors Zeno and Justinian, the offense (if *re, loco,* or *causa*) exposed the party to the payment of three times the damage, if any, sustained by the other side, and (if *tempore*) obliged him to postpone his action for double the time, and to pay the costs of his first action before commencing a second. Brown.

Plus valet consuetudo quam concessio. Custom is more powerful than grant.

Plus valet unus oculatus testis quam auriti decem. One eye-witness is of more weight than ten ear-witnesses, [or those who speak from hearsay.] 4 Inst. 279.

Plus vident oculi quam oculus. Several eyes see more than one. 4 Inst. 160.

PO. LO. SUO. An old abbreviation for the words "*ponit loco suo,*" used in warrants of attorney. Townsh. Pl. 431.

POACH. To steal game on a man's land.

POACHING. In English criminal law. The unlawful entry upon land for the purpose of taking or destroying game; the taking or destruction of game upon another's land, usually committed at night. Steph. Crim. Law, 119, et seq.; 2 Steph. Comm. 82.

POBLADOR. In Spanish law. A colonizer; he who peoples; the founder of a colony.

POCKET JUDGMENT. A statute-merchant which was enforceable at any time after non-payment on the day assigned, without further proceedings. Wharton.

POCKET RECORD. A statute so called. Brownl. pt. 2, p. 81.

POCKET SHERIFF. In English law. A sheriff appointed by the sole authority of the crown, without the usual form of nomination by the judges in the exchequer. 1 Bl. Comm. 342; 3 Steph. Comm. 23.

PŒNA. Lat. Punishment; a penalty. Inst. 4, 6, 18, 19.

Pœna ad paucos, metus ad omnes perveniat. If punishment be inflicted on a few, a dread comes to all.

PŒNA CORPORALIS. Corporal punishment.

Pœna ex delicto defuncti hæres teneri non debet. The heir ought not to be bound by a penalty arising out of the wrongful act of the deceased. 2 Inst. 198.

Pœna non potest, culpa perennis erit. Punishment cannot be, crime will be, perpetual. 21 Vin. Abr. 271.

PŒNA PILLORALIS. In old English law. Punishment of the pillory. Fleta, lib. 1, c. 38, § 11.

Pœna suos tenere debet actores et non alios. Punishment ought to bind the guilty, and not others. Bract. fol. 380*b*.

Pœnæ potius molliendæ quam exasparandæ sunt. 3 Inst. 220. Punishments should rather be softened than aggravated.

Pœnæ sint restringendæ. Punishments should be restrained. Jenk. Cent. 29.

PŒNALIS. In the civil law. Penal; imposing a penalty; claiming or enforcing a penalty. *Actiones pœnales*, penal actions. Inst. 4, 6, 12.

PŒNITENTIA. Lat. In the civil law. Repentance; reconsideration; changing one's mind; drawing back from an agreement already made, or rescinding it.

POINDING. The process of the law of Scotland which answers to the distress of the English law. Poinding is of three kinds:

Real poinding, or poinding of the ground. This is the action by which a creditor, having a security on the land of his debtor, is enabled to appropriate the rents of the land, and the goods of the debtor or his tenants found thereon, to the satisfaction of the debt.

Personal poinding. This consists in the seizure of the goods of the debtor, which are sold under the direction of a court of justice, and the net amount of the sales paid over to the creditor in satisfaction of his debt; or, if no purchaser appears, the goods themselves are delivered.

Poinding of *stray cattle*, committing depredations on corn, grass, or plantations, until satisfaction is made for the damage. Bell.

POINT. A distinct proposition or question of law arising or propounded in a case.

POINT RESERVED. When, in the progress of the trial of a cause, an important or difficult point of law is presented to the court, and the court is not certain of the decision that should be given, it may *reserve* the point, that is, decide it provisionally as it is asked by the party, but reserve its more mature consideration for the hearing on a motion for a new trial, when, if it shall appear that the first ruling was wrong, the verdict will be set aside. The point thus treated is technically called a "point reserved."

POINTS. The distinct propositions of law, or chief heads of argument, presented by a party in his paper-book, and relied upon on the argument of the cause. Also the marks used in punctuation.

POISON. In medical jurisprudence. A substance having an inherent deleterious property which renders it, when taken into the system, capable of destroying life. 2 Whart. & S. Med. Jur. § 1.

A substance which, on being applied to the human body, internally or externally, is capable of destroying the action of the vital functions, or of placing the solids and fluids in such a state as to prevent the continuance of life. Wharton.

POLE. A measure of length, equal to five yards and a half.

POLICE. Police is the function of that branch of the administrative machinery of government which is charged with the preservation of public order and tranquillity, the promotion of the public health, safety, and morals, and the prevention, detection, and punishment of crimes.

The police of a state, in a comprehensive sense, embraces its whole system of internal regulation, by which the state seeks not only to preserve the public order and to prevent offenses against the state, but also to establish for the intercourse of citizen with citizen those rules of good manners and good neighborhood which are calculated to prevent a conflict of rights, and to insure to each the uninterrupted enjoyment of his own, so far as is reasonably consistent with a like enjoyment of rights by others. Cooley, Const. Lim. *572.

It is defined by Jeremy Bentham in his works: "Police is in general a system of precaution, either for the prevention of crime or of calamities. Its business may be distributed into eight distinct branches: (1) Police for the prevention of offenses; (2) police for the prevention of calamities; (3) police for the prevention of epidemic diseases; (4) police of charity; (5) police of interior communications; (6) police of public amusements; (7) police for recent intelligence; (8) police for registration." 6 Or. 222.

POLICE COURT. The name of a kind of inferior court in several of the states, which has a summary jurisdiction over minor offenses and misdemeanors of small consequence, and the powers of a committing magistrate in respect to more serious crimes, and, in some states, a limited jurisdiction for the trial of civil causes.

In English law. Courts in which stipendiary magistrates, chosen from barristers of a certain standing, sit for the dispatch of business. Their general duties and powers are the same as those of the unpaid magistracy, except that one of them may usually act in cases which would require to be heard before two other justices. Wharton.

POLICE DE CHARGEMENT. Fr. In French law. A bill of lading. Ord. Mar. liv. 3, tit. 2.

POLICE JURY, in Louisiana, is the designation of the board of officers in a parish corresponding to the commissioners or supervisors of a county in other states.

POLICE JUSTICE. A magistrate charged exclusively with the duties incident to the common-law office of a conservator or justice of the peace; the prefix "police" serving merely to distinguish them from justices having also civil jurisdiction. 58 N. Y. 530.

POLICE OFFICER. One of the staff of men employed in cities and towns to enforce the municipal police, *i. e.*, the laws and ordinances for preserving the peace and good order of the community. Otherwise called "policeman."

POLICE POWER. The power vested in a state to establish laws and ordinances for the regulation and enforcement of its *police*. See that title.

The power vested in the legislature to make, ordain, and establish all manner of wholesome and reasonable laws, statutes, and ordinances, either with penalties or without, not repugnant to the constitution, as they shall judge to be for the good and welfare of the commonwealth, and of the subjects of the same. 7 Cush. 85.

The police power of the state is an authority conferred by the American constitutional system upon the individual states, through which they are enabled to establish a special department of police; adopt such regulations as tend to prevent the commission of fraud, violence, or other offenses against the state; aid in the arrest of criminals; and secure generally the comfort, health, and prosperity of the state, by preserving the public order, preventing a conflict of rights in the common intercourse of the citizens, and insuring to each an uninterrupted enjoyment of all the privileges conferred upon him by the laws of his country. Lalor, Pol. Enc. *s. v.*

It is true that the legislation which secures to all protection in their rights, and the equal use and enjoyment of their property, embraces an almost infinite variety of subjects. Whatever affects the peace, good order, morals, and health of the community comes within its scope; and every one must use and enjoy his property subject to the restrictions which such legislation imposes. What is termed the "police power" of the state, which, from the language often used respecting it, one would suppose to be an undefined and irresponsible element in government, can only interfere with the conduct of individuals in their intercourse with each other, and in the use of their property, so far as may be required to secure these objects. 94 U. S. 145.

POLICE REGULATIONS. Laws of a state, or ordinances of a municipality, which have for their object the preservation and protection of public peace and good order, and of the health, morals, and security of the people.

POLICE SUPERVISION. In England, subjection to police supervision is where a criminal offender is subjected to the obligation of notifying the place of his residence and every change of his residence to the chief officer of police of the district, and of reporting himself once a month to the chief officer or his substitute. Offenders subject to police supervision are popularly called "habitual criminals." Sweet.

POLICIES OF INSURANCE, COURT OF. A court established in pursuance of the statutes 43 Eliz. c. 12, and 13 & 14 Car. II. c. 23. Composed of the judge of the admiralty, the recorder of London, two doctors of the civil law, two common lawyers, and eight merchants; any three of whom, one being a civilian or a barrister, could determine in a summary way causes concerning policies of assurance in London, with an appeal to chancery. No longer in existence. 3 Bl. Comm. 74.

POLICY. The general principles by which a government is guided in its management of public affairs, or the legislature in its measures.

This term, as applied to a law, ordinance, or rule of law, denotes its general purpose or tendency considered as directed to the welfare or prosperity of the state or community.

POLICY OF INSURANCE. A mercantile instrument in writing, by which one party, in consideration of a premium, engages to indemnify another against a contingent loss, by making him a payment in compensation, whenever the event shall happen by which the loss is to accrue. 2 Steph. Comm. 172.

The written instrument in which a contract of insurance is set forth is called a "policy of insurance." Civil Code Cal. § 2586.

An *interest* policy is one where the insured has a real, substantial, assignable interest in the thing insured.

A *wager* policy is a pretended insurance, founded on an ideal risk, where the insured has no interest in the thing insured, and can therefore sustain no loss by the happening of any of the misfortunes insured against. These policies are strongly reprobated. 3 Kent. Comm. 225.

An *open* policy is where the amount of the interest of the assured (or value of the thing covered) is not fixed by the policy, but is left to be adjusted in case of loss. Such policies may issue in blank to be filled by the insured as new risks may be desired. Code Ga. 1882, § 2833.

When a fire insurance is made for a limited period (*e. g.*, a year,) it is called a "*time* policy." L. R. 5 Exch. 296. When it is made to insure not any specific goods, but the goods which may at the time of the fire be in a certain building, it is called a "*floating* policy." 5 Ch. Div. 560.

A *valued* policy is where the value of the thing is settled by agreement between the parties and inserted in the policy. Smith, Merc. Law, 344.

An insurance may be effected either for a voyage or for a number of voyages, in either of which cases the policy is called a "*voyage* policy;" or the insurance may be for a particular period, irrespective of the voyage or voyages upon which the vessel may be engaged during that period, and the policy is then called a "*time* policy." Sweet.

POLICY OF A STATUTE. The "policy of a statute," or "of the legislature," as applied to a penal or prohibitive statute, means the intention of discouraging conduct of a mischievous tendency. See L. R. 6 P. C. 134; 5 Barn. & Ald. 335; Pol. Cont. 235.

POLICY OF THE LAW. By this phrase is understood the disposition of the law to discountenance certain classes of acts, transactions, or agreements, or to refuse them its sanction, because it considers them immoral, detrimental to the public welfare, subversive of good order, or otherwise contrary to the plan and purpose of civil regulations.

Politiæ legibus non leges politiis adaptandæ. Politics are to be adapted to the laws, and not the laws to politics. Hob. 154.

POLITICAL. Pertaining to policy or the administration of the government.

A *political corporation* is one which has principally for its object the administration of the government, or to which the powers of government, or a part of such powers, have been delegated. 1 Bouv. Inst. no. 182.

POLITICAL ARITHMETIC. An expression sometimes used to signify the art of making calculations on matters relating to a nation; the revenues, the value of land and effects; the produce of lands and manufactures; the population, and the general statistics of a country. Wharton.

POLITICAL ECONOMY. The science which describes the methods and laws of the production, distribution, and consumption of wealth, and treats of economic and industrial conditions and laws, and the rules and principles of rent, wages, capital, labor, exchanges, money, population, etc.

The science which determines what laws men ought to adopt in order that they may, with the least possible exertion, procure the greatest abundance of things useful for the satisfaction of their wants, may distribute them justly, and consume them rationally. De Laveleye, Pol. Econ.

The science which treats of the administration of the revenues of a nation, or the management and regulation of its resources, and productive property and labor. Wharton.

POLITICAL LAW. That branch of jurisprudence which treats of the science of politics, or the organization and administration of government.

POLITICAL (OR CIVIL) LIBERTY. Natural liberty, restrained by human law so far as is necessary and expedient for the public advantage. See 2 Steph. Comm. (7th Ed.) 466. See LIBERTY.

POLITICAL OFFENSES. As a designation of a class of crimes usually excepted from extradition treaties, this term denotes crimes which are incidental to and form a part of political disturbances; but it might also be understood to include offenses consisting in an attack upon the political order of things established in the country where committed, and even to include offenses committed to obtain any political object. 2 Steph. Crim. Law, 70.

POLITICAL OFFICE. Civil offices are usually divided into three classes,—political, judicial, and ministerial. Political offices are such as are not immediately connected with the administration of justice, or with the execution of the mandates of a superior, such as the president, or the head of a department. 13 Wall. 575.

POLITICAL QUESTIONS. Questions of which the courts of justice will refuse to take cognizance, or to decide, on account of their purely political character, or because their determination would involve an encroachment upon the executive or legislative powers; *e. g.*, what sort of government exists in a state, whether peace or war exists, whether a foreign country has become an independent state, etc. 7 How. 1; 14 How. 38; 11 Amer. Law Reg. 419.

POLITICAL RIGHTS. Those which may be exercised in the formation or administration of the government. 90 Ill. 563.

POLITICS. The science of government; the art or practice of administering public affairs.

POLITY. The form of government; civil constitution.

POLL, *v.* In practice. To single out, one by one, of a number of persons. To examine each juror separately, after a verdict has been given, as to his concurrence in the verdict. 1 Burrill, Pr. 238.

POLL, *n.* A head; an individual person; a register of persons.

POLL, *adj.* Cut or shaved smooth or even; cut in a straight line without indentation. A term anciently applied to a deed, and still used, though with little of its former significance. 2 Bl. Comm. 296.

POLL-MONEY. A tax ordained by act of parliament, (18 Car. II., c. 1,) by which every subject in the kingdom was assessed by the head or poll, according to his degree. Cowell. A similar personal tribute was more anciently termed "poll-silver."

POLL-TAX. A capitation tax; a tax assessed on every head, *i. e.*, on every male of a certain age, etc., according to statute.

POLLARDS. A foreign coin of base metal, prohibited by St. 27 Edw. I. c. 3, from being brought into the realm, on pain of forfeiture of life and goods. 4 Bl. Comm. 98. It was computed at two pollards for a sterling or penny. Dyer, 82*b*.

POLLENGERS. Trees which have been lopped; distinguished from timber-trees. Plowd. 649.

POLLICITATION. In the civil law. An offer not yet accepted by the person to whom it is made. Langd. Cont. § 1.

POLLIGAR, POLYGAR. In Hindu law. The head of a village or district; also a military chieftain in the peninsula, answering to a hill *zemindar* in the northern *circars*. Wharton.

POLLING THE JURY. To *poll* a jury is to require that each juror shall himself declare what is his verdict.

POLLS. The place where electors cast in their votes.

Heads; individuals; persons singly considered. A challenge to the *polls* (*in capita*) is a challenge to the individual jurors composing the panel, or an exception to one or more particular jurors. 3 Bl. Comm. 358, 361.

POLYANDRY. The civil condition of having more husbands than one to the same woman; a social order permitting plurality of husbands.

Polygamia est plurium simul virorum uxorumve connubium. 3 Inst. 88. Polygamy is the marriage with many husbands or wives at one time.

POLYGAMY. In criminal law. The offense of having several wives or husbands at the same time, or more than one wife or husband at the same time. 3 Inst. 88.

The offense committed by a layman in marrying while any previous wife is living and undivorced; as distinguished from bigamy in the sense of a breach of ecclesiastical law involved in any second marriage by a clerk.

Polygamy, or bigamy, shall consist in knowingly having a plurality of husbands or wives at the same time. Code Ga. 1882, § 4530.

A bigamist or polygamist, in the sense of the eighth section of the act of congress of March 22, 1882, is a man who, having contracted a bigamous or polygamous marriage, and become the husband at one time, of two or more wives, maintains that relation and *status* at the time when he offers to be registered as a voter; and this without reference to the question whether he was at any time guilty of the offense of bigamy or polygamy, or whether any prosecution for such offense was barred by the lapse of time; neither is it necessary that he should be guilty of polygamy under the first section of the act of March 22, 1882. 114 U. S. 16, 5 Sup. Ct. Rep. 747.

Bigamy literally means a second marriage distinguished from a third or other; while polygamy means many marriages,—implies more than two.

POLYGARCHY. A term sometimes used to denote a government of many or several; a government where the sovereignty is shared by several persons; a collegiate or divided executive.

POMARIUM. In old pleading. An apple-tree; an orchard.

POND. A body of stagnant water without an outlet, larger than a puddle and smaller than a lake; or a like body of water with a small outlet. Webster.

A standing ditch cast by labor of man's hand, in his private grounds, for his private use, to serve his house and household with necessary waters; but a *pool* is a low plat of ground by nature, and is not cast by man's hand. Call. Sew. 103.

Ponderantur testes, non numerantur. Witnesses are weighed, not counted. 1 Starkie, Ev. 554; Best, Ev. p. 426, § 389; 14 Wend. 105, 109.

PONDUS. In old English law. Poundage; *i. e.*, a duty paid to the crown according to the weight of merchandise.

PONDUS REGIS. In old English law. The king's weight; the standard weight appointed by the king. Cowell.

PONE. In English practice. An original writ formerly used for the purpose of removing suits from the court-baron or county court into the superior courts of common law. It was also the proper writ to remove all suits which were before the sheriff by writ of justices. But this writ is now in disuse, the writ of *certiorari* being the ordinary process by which at the present day a cause is removed from a county court into any superior court. Brown.

PONE PER VADIUM. In English practice. An obsolete writ to the sheriff to summon the defendant to appear and answer the plaintiff's suit, on his putting in sureties to prosecute. It was so called from the words of the writ, "*pone per vadium et salvos plegios,*" "put by gage and safe pledges, A. B., the defendant."

PONENDIS IN ASSISIS. An old writ directing a sheriff to impanel a jury for an assize or real action.

PONENDUM IN BALLIUM. A writ commanding that a prisoner be bailed in cases bailable. Reg. Orig. 133.

PONENDUM SIGILLUM AD EXCEPTIONEM. A writ by which justices were required to put their seals to exceptions exhibited by a defendant against a plaintiff's evidence, verdict, or other proceedings, before them, according to the statute Westm. 2, (13 Edw. I. St. 1, c. 31.)

PONERE. Lat. To put, place, lay, or set. Often used in the Latin terms and phrases of the old law.

PONIT SE SUPER PATRIAM. Lat. He puts himself upon the country. The defendant's plea of not guilty in a criminal action is recorded, in English practice, in these words, or in the abbreviated form "*po. se.*"

PONTAGE. In old English law. Duty paid for the reparation of bridges; also a due to the lord of the fee for persons or merchandises that pass over rivers, bridges, etc. Cowell.

PONTIBUS REPARANDIS. An old writ directed to the sheriff, commanding him to charge one or more to repair a bridge.

POOL. A combination of persons contributing money to be used for the purpose of increasing or depressing the market price of stocks, grain, or other commodities; also the aggregate of the sums so contributed. Webster. See 103 U. S. 168.

A mutual arrangement between competing railways, by which the receipts of all are aggregated, and then distributed *pro rata* according to agreement.

A standing water, without any current or issue. Call. Sew. 102. See POND.

POOLING CONTRACTS. Agreements between competing railways for a division of the traffic, or for a *pro rata* distribution of their earnings united into a "pool" or common fund. 15 Fed. Rep. 667, note. See POOL.

POOR, in a statute providing for the relief of the poor, means persons so completely destitute of property as to require assistance from the public. 14 Kan. 418, 422.

POOR DEBTOR'S OATH. An oath allowed, in some jurisdictions, to a person who is arrested for debt. On swearing that he has not property enough to pay the debt, he is set at liberty.

POOR LAW. That part of the law which relates to the public or compulsory relief of paupers.

POOR-LAW BOARD. The English official body appointed under St. 10 & 11 Vict. c. 109, passed in 1847, to take the place of the poor-law commissioners, under whose control the general management of the poor, and the funds for their relief throughout the country, had been for some years previously administered. The poor-law board is now superseded by the local government board, which was established in 1871 by St. 34 & 35 Vict. c. 70. 3 Steph. Comm. 49.

POOR-LAW GUARDIANS. See GUARDIANS OF THE POOR.

POOR RATE. In English law. A tax levied by parochial authorities for the relief of the poor.

POPE. The bishop of Rome, and supreme head of the Roman Catholic Church. 4 Steph. Comm. (7th Ed.) 168–185.

POPE NICHOLAS' TAXATION. The first fruits (*primitiæ* or *annates*) were the first year's profits of all the spiritual preferments in the kingdom, according to a rate made by Walter, bishop of Norwich, in the time of Pope Innocent II., and afterwards advanced in value in the time of Pope Nicholas IV. This last valuation was begun A. D. 1288, and finished 1292, and is still preserved in the exchequer. The taxes were regulated by it till the survey made in the twenty-sixth year of Henry VIII. 2 Steph. Comm. 567.

POPERY. The religion of the Roman Catholic Church, comprehending doctrines and practices.

POPULACE, or POPULACY. The vulgar; the multitude.

POPULAR ACTION. An action for a statutory penalty or forfeiture, given to any such person or persons as will sue for it; an action given to the *people* in general. 3 Bl. Comm. 160.

POPULAR SENSE. In reference to the construction of a statute, this term means that sense which people conversant with the subject-matter with which the statute is dealing would attribute to it. 1 Exch. Div. 248.

POPULISCITUM. Lat. In Roman law. A law enacted by the people; a law passed by an assembly of the Roman people, in the *comitia centuriata*, on the motion of a senator; differing from a *plebiscitum*, in that the latter was always proposed by one of the tribunes.

POPULUS. Lat. In Roman law. The people; the whole body of Roman citizens, including as well the patricians as the plebeians.

PORCION. In Spanish law. A part or portion; a lot or parcel; an allotment of land. See (Tex.) 16 S. W. Rep. 49.

PORRECTING. Producing for examination or taxation, as porrecting a bill of costs, by a proctor.

PORT. A place for the lading and unlading of the cargoes of vessels, and the collection of duties or customs upon imports and exports. A place, either on the seacoast or on a river, where ships stop for the purpose of loading and unloading, from whence they depart, and where they finish their voyages. 7 Mart. (N. S.) 81.

In French maritime law. Burden, (of a vessel;) size and capacity.

PORT CHARGES, DUES, or TOLLS. Pecuniary exactions upon vessels availing themselves of the commercial conveniences and privileges of a port.

PORT-GREVE. The chief magistrate of a sea-port town is sometimes so called.

PORT OF DELIVERY. In maritime law. The port which is to be the terminus of any particular voyage, and where the vessel is to unlade or deliver her cargo, as distinguished from any port at which she may touch, during the voyage, for other purposes.

PORT OF DESTINATION. In maritime law and marine insurance, the term includes both ports which constitute the termini of the voyage, the home-port and the foreign port to which the vessel is consigned, as well as any usual stopping places for the receipt or discharge of cargo. 12 Gray, 501.

PORT OF DISCHARGE, in a policy of marine insurance, means the place where the substantial part of the cargo is discharged, although there is an intent to complete the discharge at another basin. 104 Mass. 510.

PORT OF ENTRY. One of the ports designated by law, at which a custom-house or revenue office is established for the execution of the laws imposing duties on vessels and importations of goods.

PORT-REEVE, or PORT-WARDEN. An officer maintained in some ports to oversee the administration of the local regulations; a sort of harbor-master.

PORT-RISK. In marine insurance. A risk upon a vessel while lying in port, and before she has taken her departure upon another voyage. 71 N. Y. 459.

PORTATICA. In English law. The generic name for port duties charged to ships. Harg. Law Tract, 64.

PORTEOUS. In old Scotch practice. A roll or catalogue containing the names of indicted persons, delivered by the justice-clerk to the coroner, to be attached and arrested by him. Otherwise called the "Porteous Roll." Bell.

PORTER. 1. In old English law, this title was given to an officer of the courts who carried a rod or staff before the justices.

2. A person who keeps a gate or door; as the door-keeper of the houses of parliament.

3. One who carries or conveys parcels, luggage, etc., particularly from one place to another in the same town.

PORTERAGE. A kind of duty formerly paid at the English custom-house to those who attended the water-side, and belonged to the package-office; but it is now abolished. Also the charge made for sending parcels.

PORTION. The share falling to a child from a parent's estate or the estate of any one bearing a similar relation.

Portion is especially applied to payments made to younger children out of the funds comprised in their parents' marriage settlement, and in pursuance of the trusts thereof. Mozley & Whitley.

PORTION DISPONIBLE. In French law. That part of a man's estate which he may bequeath to other persons than his natural heirs. A parent leaving one legitimate child may dispose of one-half only of his property; one leaving two, one-third only; and one leaving three or more, one-fourth only; and it matters not whether the disposition is *inter vivos* or by will.

PORTIONER. In old English law. A minister who serves a benefice, together with others; so called because he has only a portion of the tithes or profits of the living; also an allowance which a vicar commonly has out of a rectory or impropriation. Cowell.

In Scotch law. The proprietor of a small feu or portion of land. Bell.

PORTIONIST. One who receives a portion; the allotee of a portion. One of two or more incumbents of the same ecclesiastical benefice.

PORTMEN. The burgesses of Ipswich and of the Cinque Ports were so called.

PORTMOTE. In old English law. A court held in ports or haven towns, and sometimes in inland towns also. Cowell; Blount.

PORTORIA. In the civil law. Duties paid in ports on merchandise. Taxes levied in old times at city gates. Tolls for passing over bridges.

PORTSALE. In old English law. An auction; a public sale of goods to the highest bidder; also a sale of fish as soon as it is brought into the haven. Cowell.

PORTSOKA, or PORTSOKEN. The suburbs of a city, or any place within its jurisdiction. Somner; Cowell.

Portus est locus in quo exportantur et importantur merces. 2 Inst. 148. A port is a place where goods are exported or imported.

POSITIVE. Laid down, enacted, or prescribed. Express or affirmative. Direct, absolute, explicit.

POSITIVE CONDITION. One which contemplates the performance of a positive act; as distinguished from a negative condition, which contemplates abstention from acting.

POSITIVE EVIDENCE is that which, if believed, establishes the truth or falsehood of a fact in issue, and does not arise from any presumption. It is distinguished from circumstantial evidence. 3 Bouv. Inst. no. 3057.

POSITIVE FRAUD is the intentional and successful employment of any cunning, deception, or artifice, to circumvent, cheat, or deceive another. 1 Story, Eq. Jur. 186. The term is used in opposition to "constructive fraud."

POSITIVE LAW. Law actually and specifically enacted or adopted by proper authority for the government of an organized jural society.

"A 'law,' in the sense in which that term is employed in jurisprudence, is enforced by a sovereign political authority. It is thus distinguished not only from all rules which, like the principles of morality and the so-called laws of honor and of fashion, are enforced by an indeterminate authority, but also from all rules enforced by a determinate authority which is either, on the one hand, superhuman, or, on the other hand, politically subordinate. In order to emphasize the fact that 'laws,' in the strict sense of the term, are thus authoritatively imposed, they are described as *positive* laws." Holl. Jur. 37.

POSITIVE PROOF. Direct or affirmative proof; that which directly establishes the fact in question; as opposed to *negative* proof, which establishes the fact by showing that its opposite is not or cannot be true.

POSTIVI JURIS. Lat. Of positive law. "That was a rule *positivi juris;* I do not mean to say an unjust one." Lord Ellenborough, 12 East, 639.

Posito uno oppositorum, negatur alterum. One of two opposite positions being affirmed, the other is denied. 3 Rolle, 422.

POSSE. Lat. A possibility. A thing is said to be *in posse* when it may possibly be; *in esse* when it actually is.

POSSE COMITATUS. The power or force of the county. The entire population of a county above the age of fifteen, which a sheriff may summon to his assistance in certain cases; as to aid him in keeping the peace, in pursuing and arresting felons, etc. 1 Bl. Comm. 343.

POSSESSED. This word is applied to the right and enjoyment of a termor, or a person having a term, who is said to be possessed, and not seised. Bac. Tr. 335; Poph. 76; Dyer, 369.

POSSESSIO. Lat. In the civil law. That condition of fact under which one can exercise his power over a corporeal thing at his pleasure, to the exclusion of all others. This condition of fact is called "detention," and it forms the substance of possession in all its varieties. Mackeld. Rom. Law, § 238.

"Possession," in the sense of "detention," is the actual exercise of such a power as the owner has a right to exercise. The term "*possessio*" occurs in the Roman jurists in various senses. There is *possessio* simply, and *possessio civilis*, and *possessio naturalis*. *Possessio* denoted, originally, bare detention. But this detention, under certain conditions, becomes a legal state, inasmuch as it leads to ownership, through *usucapio*. Accordingly, the word "*possessio*," which required no qualification so long as there was no other notion attached to *possessio*, requires such qualification when detention becomes a legal state. This detention, then, when it has the conditions necessary to *usucapio*, is called "*possessio civilis;*" and all other *possessio* as opposed to *civilis* is *naturalis*. Sandars, Just. Inst. 274. Wharton.

In old English law. Possession; seisin. The detention of a corporeal thing by means of a physical act and mental intent, aided by some support of right. Bract. fol. 38*b*.

POSSESSIO BONA FIDE. In the civil law. Possession in good faith. *Possessio mala fide*, possession in bad faith. A possessor *bona fide* is one who believes that no other person has a better right to the possession than himself. A possessor *mala fide* is one who knows that he is not entitled to the possession. Mackeld. Rom. Law, § 243.

POSSESSIO BONORUM. In the civil law. The possession of goods. More commonly termed "*bonorum possessio*," (*q. v.*)

POSSESSIO CIVILIS. In Roman law. A legal possession, *i. e.*, a possessing accompanied with the intention to be or to thereby become owner; and, as so understood, it was distinguished from "*possessio naturalis*," otherwise called "*nuda detentio*," which was a possessing without any such intention. *Possessio civilis* was the basis of *usucapio* or of *longi temporis possessio*, and was usually (but not necessarily) adverse possession. Brown.

POSSESSIO FRATRIS. Lat. The possession or seisin of a brother; that is, such possession of an estate by a brother as would entitle his sister of the whole blood to succeed him as heir, to the exclusion of a half-brother. Hence, derivatively, that doctrine of the older English law of descent which shut out the half-blood from the succession to estates; a doctrine which was abolished by the descent act, 3 & 4 Wm. IV. c. 106. See 1 Steph. Comm. 385; Broom, Max. 532.

Possessio fratris de feodo simplici facit sororem esse hæredem. The brother's possession of an estate in fee-simple makes the sister to be heir. 3 Coke, 41; Broom, Max. 532.

POSSESSIO LONGI TEMPORIS. See USUCAPIO.

POSSESSIO NATURALIS. See POSSESSIO CIVILIS.

Possessio pacifica pour anns 60 facit jus. Peaceable possession for sixty years gives a right. Jenk. Cent. 26.

POSSESSION. The detention and control, or the manual or ideal custody, of anything which may be the subject of property, for one's use and enjoyment, either as owner or as the proprietor of a qualified right in it, and either held personally or by another who exercises it in one's place and name. That condition of facts under which one can exercise his power over a corporeal thing at his pleasure to the exclusion of all other persons.

There are two kinds of possession of real property known to the law,—*actual* and *constructive*. It is actual when in the immediate occupancy of the party. It is actual where the party goes upon the land to take possession and exercises acts of ownership over it. It is actual also where one having the title is in possession of lands by his tenant, agent, or steward. *Constructive* possession is where one claims to hold by virtue of some title, without having the actual occupancy, as when the owner of a tract of land, regularly laid out, is in possession of a part, he is constructively in possession of the whole. 30 Iowa, 241.

It is either *actual*, where a person enters into lands or tenements descended or conveyed to him; *apparent*, which is a species of presumptive title where land descended to the heir of an abator, intruder, or disseisor, who died seised; *in law*, when lands, etc., have descended to a man, and he has not actually entered into them; or *naked*, that is, mere possession, without color of right. Wharton.

In the law of Louisiana, (as in the civil law,) possession is divided into two kinds,—natural and civil. *Natural* possession is that by which a man detains a thing corporeal; as, by occupying a house, cultivating ground, or retaining a movable in his possession. Natural possession is also defined to be the corporeal detention of a thing which we possess as belonging to us, without any title to that possession, or with a title which is void. *Civil* possession exists when a person ceases to reside in a house or on the land which he occupied, or to detain the movable which he possessed, but without intending to abandon the possession. It is the detention of a thing by virtue of a just title and under the conviction of possessing as owner. Civil Code La. art. 3391, et seq.

Adverse possession is a possession inconsistent with the right of the true owner. In other words, where a person possesses property in a manner in which he is not entitled to possess it, and without anything to show that he possesses it otherwise than as owner, *i. e.*, with the intention of excluding all persons from it, including the rightful owner, he is in adverse possession of it. Thus, if A. is in possession of a field of B.'s, he is in adverse possession of it, unless there is something to show that his possession is consistent with a recognition of B.'s title. Sweet.

In jurisprudence, the possession of a lessee, bailee, licensee, etc., is called "*derivative* possession," while in law the possessory interest of such a person, considered with reference to his rights against third persons who interfere with his possession, is usually called a "special" or "qualified property," meaning a limited right of ownership. Holl. Jur. 160-163.

In the older books, "possession" is sometimes used as the synonym of "seisin;" but, strictly speaking, they are entirely different terms. "The difference between possession and seisin is: Lessee for years is possessed, and yet the lessor is still seised; and therefore the terms of law are that of chattels a man is possessed, whereas in feoffments, gifts in tail, and leases for life he is described as 'seised.'" Noy, Max. 64.

"Possession" is used in some of the books in the sense of property. "A possession is an hereditament or chattel." Finch, Law, b. 2, c. 3.

Possession is a good title where no better title appears. 20 Vin. Abr. 278.

Possession is nine-tenths of the law. This adage is not to be taken as true to the full extent, so as to mean that the person in possession can only be ousted by one whose title is nine times better than his, but it places in a strong light the legal truth that every claimant must succeed by the strength of his own title, and not by the weakness of his antagonist's. Wharton.

POSSESSION MONEY. In English law. The man whom the sheriff puts in possession of goods taken under a writ of *fieri facias* is entitled, while he continues so in possession, to a certain sum of money *per diem*, which is thence termed "possession money." The amount is 3s. 6d. per day if he is boarded, or 5s. per day if he is not boarded. Brown.

POSSESSION VAUT TITRE. Fr. In English law, as in most systems of jurisprudence, the fact of possession raises a *prima facie* title or a presumption of the right of property in the thing possessed. In other words, the possession is as good as the title (about.) Brown.

POSSESSION, WRIT OF. Where the judgment in an action of ejectment is for the delivery of the land claimed, or its possession, this writ is used to put the plaintiff in possession. It is in the nature of execution.

POSSESSOR. One who possesses; one who has possession.

POSSESSOR BONA FIDE. He is a *bona fide* possessor who possesses as owner by virtue of an act sufficient in terms to transfer property, the defects of which he was ignorant of. He ceases to be a *bona fide* possessor from the moment these defects are made known to him, or are declared to him by a suit instituted for the recovery of the thing by the owner. Civil Code La. art. 503.

POSSESSOR MALA FIDE. The possessor in bad faith is he who possesses as master, but who assumes this quality, when he well knows that he has no title to the thing, or that his title is vicious and defective. Civil Code La. art. 3452.

POSSESSORY. Relating to possession; founded on possession; contemplating or claiming possession.

POSSESSORY ACTION. An action which has for its immediate object to obtain or recover the actual *possession* of the subject-matter; as distinguished from an action which merely seeks to vindicate the plaintiff's *title*, or which involves the bare right only; the latter being called a "petitory" action.

An action founded on possession. Trespass for injuries to personal property is called a "possessory" action, because it lies only for a plaintiff who, at the moment of the injury complained of, was in actual or constructive, immediate, and exclusive possession. 1 Chit. Pl. 168, 169.

In admiralty practice. A possessory suit is one which is brought to recover the possession of a vessel, had under a claim of title. 5 Mason, 465; 1 Kent, Comm. 371.

In old English law. A real action which had for its object the regaining possession of the freehold, of which the demandant or his ancestors had been unjustly deprived by the present tenant or possessor thereof.

In Scotch law. An action for the vindication and recovery of the possession of heritable or movable goods; *e. g.*, the action of molestation. Paters. Comp.

In Louisiana. An action by which one claims to be maintained in the possession of an immovable property, or of a right upon or growing out of it, when he has been disturbed, or to be reinstated to that possession, when he has been divested or evicted. Code Proc. La. § 6.

POSSESSORY JUDGMENT. In Scotch practice. A judgment which entitles a person who has uninterruptedly been in possession for seven years to continue his possession until the question of right be decided in due course of law. Bell.

POSSIBILITAS. Lat. Possibility; a possibility. *Possibilitas post dissolutionem executionis nunquam reviviscatur*, a possibility will never be revived after the dissolution of its execution. 1 Rolle, 321. *Post executionem status, lex non patitur possibilitatem*, after the execution of an estate the law does not suffer a possibility. 3 Bulst. 108.

POSSIBILITY. An uncertain thing which may happen. A contingent interest in real or personal estate.

It is either *near*, (or *ordinary*,) as where an estate is limited to one after the death of another, or *remote*, (or *extraordinary*,) as where it is limited to a man, provided he marries a certain woman, and that she shall die and he shall marry another.

A possibility "coupled with an interest" is an expectation recognized in law as an estate or interest, such as occurs in executory devises or shifting or springing uses. Such a possibility may be sold or assigned. A *bare* possibility is the expectation or hope of succeeding entertained by an heir apparent.

POSSIBILITY ON A POSSIBILITY. A remote possibility, as if a remainder be limited in particular to A.'s son John, or Edward, it is bad if he have no son of that name, for it is too remote a possibility that he should not only have a son, but a son of that particular name. 2 Coke, 51.

POSSIBLE. Capable of existing or happening; feasible. In another sense, the word denotes extreme improbability, without excluding the idea of feasibility. It is also sometimes equivalent to "practicable" or "reasonable," as in some cases where action is required to be taken "as soon as possible." See 44 Wis. 208.

POST. Lat. After; occurring in a report or a text-book, is used to send the reader to a subsequent part of the book.

POST. A conveyance for letters or dispatches. The word is derived from "*positi,*" the horses carrying the letters or dispatches being kept or placed at fixed stations. The word is also applied to the person who conveys the letters to the houses where he takes up and lays down his charge, and to the stages or distances between house and house. Hence the phrases, post-boy, post-horse, post-house, etc. Wharton.

POST-ACT. An after-act; an act done afterwards.

POST CONQUESTUM. After the Conquest. Words inserted in the king's title by King Edward I., and constantly used in the time of Edward III. Tomlins.

POST-DATE. To date an instrument as of a time later than that at which it is really made.

POST DIEM. After the day; as, a plea of payment *post diem*, after the day when the money became due. Com. Dig. "Pleader," 2.

In old practice. The return of a writ after the day assigned. A fee paid in such case. Cowell.

POST DISSEISIN. In English law. The name of a writ which lies for him who, having recovered lands and tenements by force of a novel disseisin, is again disseised by a former disseisor. Jacob.

POST ENTRY. When goods are weighed or measured, and the merchant has got an account thereof at the custom-house, and finds his entry already made too small, he must make a post or additional entry for the surplusage, in the same manner as the first was done. As a merchant is always in time, prior to the clearing of the vessel, to make his post, he should take care not to over-enter, to avoid as well the advance as the trouble of getting back the overplus. McCul. Dict.

Post executionem status lex non patitur possibilitatem. 3 Bulst. 108. After the execution of the estate the law suffers not a possibility.

POST FACTO. After the fact. See Ex post Facto.

POST-FACTUM, or POSTFACTUM. An after-act; an act done afterwards; a post-act.

POST-FINE. In old conveyancing. A fine or sum of money, (otherwise called the "king's silver") formerly due on granting the *licentia concordandi*, or leave to agree, in levying a fine of lands. It amounted to three-twentieths of the supposed annual value of the land, or ten shillings for every five marks of land. 2 Bl. Comm. 350.

POST HAC. Lat. After this; after this time; hereafter.

POST LITEM MOTAM. Lat. After suit moved or commenced. Depositions in relation to the subject of a suit, made after litigation has commenced, are sometimes so termed. 1 Starkie, Ev. 319.

POST-MARK. A stamp or mark put on letters received at the post-office for transmission through the mails.

POST-MORTEM. After death. A term generally applied to an autopsy or examination of a dead body, to ascertain the cause of death, or to the inquisition for that purpose by the coroner.

POST NATUS. Born afterwards. A term applied by old writers to a second or younger son. It is used in private international law to designate a person who was born *after* some historic event, (such as the American Revolution or the act of union between England and Scotland,) and whose rights or *status* will be governed or affected by the question of his birth before or after such event.

POST-NOTES. A species of bank-notes payable at a distant period, and not on demand.

They are a species of obligation resorted to by banks when the exchanges of the country, and especially of the banks, have become embarrassed by excessive speculations. Much concern is then felt for the country, and through the newspapers it is urged that post-notes be issued by the banks "for aiding domestic and foreign exchanges," as a "mode of relief," or a "remedy for the distress," and "to take the place of the southern and foreign exchanges." And so presently this is done. Post-notes are therefore intended to enter into the circulation of the country as a part of its medium of exchanges; the smaller ones for ordinary business, and the larger ones for heavier operations. They are intended to supply the place of demand notes, which the banks cannot afford to issue or reissue, to relieve the necessities of commerce or of the banks, or to avoid a compulsory suspension. They are under seal, or without seal, and at long or short dates, at more or less interest, or without interest, as the necessities of the bank may require. 22 Pa. St. 488.

POST-NUPTIAL. After marriage. Thus, an agreement entered into by a father after the marriage of his daughter, by which he engages to make a provision for her, would be termed a "post-nuptial agreement" Brown.

POST-NUPTIAL SETTLEMENT. A settlement made after marriage upon a wife or children; otherwise called a "voluntary" settlement. 2 Kent, Comm. 173.

POST OBIT BOND. A bond given by an expectant, to become due on the death of a person from whom he will have property. A bond or agreement given by a borrower of money, by which he undertakes to pay a larger sum, exceeding the legal rate of interest, on or *after the death* of a person from whom he has expectations, in case of surviving him. 2 Ves. Sr., 125.

POST-OFFICE. A bureau or department of government, or under governmental superintendence, whose office is to receive, transmit, and deliver letters, papers, and other mail-matter sent by post. Also the office established by government in any city or town for the local operations of the postal system, for the receipt and distribution of mail from other places, the forwarding of mail there deposited, the sale of postage stamps, etc.

POST-OFFICE DEPARTMENT. The name of one of the departments of the executive branch of the government of the United States, which has charge of the transmission of the mails and the general postal business of the country.

POST-OFFICE ORDER. A letter of credit furnished by the government, at a small charge, to facilitate the transmission of money.

POST PROLEM SUSCITATAM. After issue born, (raised.) Co. Litt. 19*b*.

POST ROAD, or ROUTE. A road, route, or line of travel, designated by law to be pursued by contractors and conveyances in the transportation of the mails.

POST-TERMINAL SITTINGS. Sittings after term. See SITTINGS.

POST TERMINUM. After term, or post-term. The return of a writ not only after the day assigned for its return, but after the term also, for which a fee was due. Cowell.

POST, WRIT OF ENTRY IN. In English law. An abolished writ given by statute of Marlbridge, 52 Hen. III. c. 30, which provided that when the number of alienations or descents exceeded the usual degrees, a new writ should be allowed, without any mention of degrees at all.

POSTAGE. The fee charged by law for carrying letters, packets, and documents by the public mails.

POSTAGE STAMP. A ticket issued by government, to be attached to mail-matter, and representing the postage or fee paid for the transmission of such matter through the public mails.

POSTAL. Relating to the mails; pertaining to the post-office.

POSTAL CURRENCY. During a brief period following soon after the commencement of the civil war in the United States, when specie change was scarce, postage stamps were popularly used as a substitute; and the first issues of paper representatives of parts of a dollar, issued by authority of congress, were called "postal currency." This issue was soon merged in others of a more permanent character, for which the later and more appropriate name is "fractional currency." Abbott.

POSTEA. In the common-law practice, a formal statement, indorsed on the *nisi prius* record, which gives an account of the proceedings at the trial of the action. Smith, Act. 167.

POSTERIORES. This term was used by the Romans to denote the descendants in a direct line beyond the sixth degree.

POSTERIORITY. This is a word of comparison and relation in tenure, the correlative of which is the word "priority." Thus, a man who held lands or tenements of two lords was said to hold of his more ancient lord by priority, and of his less ancient lord by posteriority. Old Nat. Brev. 94. It has also a general application in law consistent with its etymological meaning, and, as so used, it is likewise opposed to priority. Brown.

POSTERITY. All the descendants of a person in a direct line to the remotest generation. 8 Bush, 527.

POSTHUMOUS CHILD. One born after the death of its father; or, when the Cæsarean operation is performed, after that of the mother.

Posthumus pro nato habetur. A posthumous child is considered as though born, [at the parent's death.] 15 Pick. 258.

POSTLIMINIUM. In the civil law. A doctrine or fiction of the law by which the restoration of a person to any *status* or right formerly possessed by him was considered as relating back to the time of his original loss or deprivation; particularly in the case of one who, having been taken prisoner in war, and having escaped and returned to Rome, was regarded, by the aid of this fiction, as having never been abroad, and was thereby reinstated in all his rights. Inst. 1, 12, 5.

The term is also applied, in international law, to the recapture of property taken by an enemy, and its consequent restoration to its original owner.

Postliminium fingit eum qui captus est in civitate semper fuisse. Postliminy feigns that he who has been captured has never left the state. Inst. 1, 12, 5; Dig. 49, 51.

POSTLIMINY. See POSTLIMINIUM.

POSTMAN. A senior barrister in the court of exchequer, who has precedence in motions; so called from the place where he sits. 2 Bl. Comm. 28. A letter-carrier.

POSTMASTER. An officer of the United States, appointed to take charge of a local post-office and transact the business of receiving and forwarding the mails at that point, and such other business as is committed to him under the postal laws.

POSTMASTER GENERAL. The head of the post-office department. He is one of the president's cabinet.

POSTNATI. Those born after. See POST NATUS.

POSTPONE. To put off; defer; delay; continue; adjourn; as when a hearing is *postponed*. Also to place after; to set below something else; as when an earlier lien is for some reason *postponed* to a later lien.

POSTREMO-GENITURE. Borough-English, (*q. v.*)

POSTULATIO. Lat. In Roman law. A request or petition. This was the name of the first step in a criminal prosecution, corresponding somewhat to "swearing out a warrant" in modern criminal law. The accuser appeared before the prætor, and stated his desire to institute criminal proceedings against a designated person, and prayed the authority of the magistrate therefor.

In old English ecclesiastical law. A species of petition for transfer of a bishop.

POSTULATIO ACTIONIS. In Roman law. The demand of an action; the request made to the prætor by an *actor* or plaintiff for an action or formula of suit; corresponding with the application for a writ in old English practice. Or, as otherwise explained, the *actor's* asking of leave to institute his action, on appearance of the parties before the prætor. Hallifax, Civil Law, b. 3, c. 9, no. 12.

POT-DE-VIN. In French law. A sum of money frequently paid, at the moment of entering into a contract, beyond the price agreed upon. It differs from *arrha*, in this: that it is no part of the price of the thing sold, and that the person who has received it cannot, by returning double the amount, or the other party by losing what he has paid, rescind the contract. 18 Toullier, no. 52.

POTENTATE. A person who possesses great power or sway; a prince, sovereign, or monarch.

By the naturalization law of the United States, an alien is required to renounce all allegiance to any foreign "prince, potentate, or sovereign whatever."

POTENTIA. Lat. Possibility; power.

Potentia debet sequi justitiam, non antecedere. 3 Bulst. 199. Power ought to follow justice, not go before it.

Potentia est duplex, remota et propinqua; et potentia remotissima et vana est quæ nunquam venit in actum. 11 Coke, 51. Possibility is of two kinds, remote and near; that which never comes into action is a power the most remote and vain.

Potentia inutilis frustra est. Useless power is to no purpose. Branch, Princ.

POTENTIA PROPINQUA. Common possibility. See POSSIBILITY.

Potest quis renunciare pro se et suis juri quod pro se introductum est. Bract. 20. One may relinquish for himself and his heirs a right which was introduced for his own benefit.

POTESTAS. Lat. In the civil law. Power; authority; domination; empire. *Imperium*, or the jurisdiction of magistrates. The power of the father over his children, *patria potestas*. The authority of masters over their slaves. See Inst. 1, 9, 12; Dig. 2, 1, 13, 1; Id. 14, 1; Id. 14, 4, 1, 4.

Potestas stricte interpretatur. A power is strictly interpreted. Jenk. Cent. p. 17, case 29, in marg.

Potestas suprema seipsum dissolvere potest, ligare non potest. Supreme power can dissolve [unloose] but cannot bind itself. Branch, Princ.; Bacon.

Potior est conditio defendentis. Better is the condition of the defendant, [than that of the plaintiff.] Broom, Max. 740; Cowp. 343; 15 Pet. 471; 21 Pick. 289; 22 Pick. 186, 187; 107 Mass. 440.

POTWALLOPER. A term formerly applied to voters in certain boroughs of England, where all who boil (*wallop*) a *pot* were entitled to vote. Webster.

POULTRY COUNTER. The name of a prison formerly existing in London. See COUNTER.

POUND. 1. A place, inclosed by public authority, for the temporary detention of stray animals. 4 Pick. 258.

A pound-*overt* is said to be one that is open overhead; a pound-*covert* is one that is close, or covered over, such as a stable or other building.

2. A measure of weight. The pound avoirdupois contains 7,000 grains; the pound troy 5,760 grains.

In New York, the unit or standard of weight, from which all other weights shall be derived and ascertained, is declared to be the *pound*, of such magnitude that the weight of a cubic foot of distilled water, at its maximum density, weighed in a vacuum with brass weights, shall be equal to sixty-two and a half such pounds. 1 Rev. St. N. Y. p. 617, § 8.

3. "Pound" is also the name of a denomination of English money, containing twenty shillings. It was also used in the United States, in computing money, before the introduction of the federal coinage.

POUND BREACH. The act or offense of breaking a pound, for the purpose of taking out the cattle or goods impounded. 3 Bl. Comm. 12, 146.

POUND-KEEPER. An officer charged with the care of a pound, and of animals confined there.

POUND OF LAND. An uncertain quantity of land, said to be about fifty-two acres.

POUNDAGE. In practice. An allowance to the sheriff of so much in the pound upon the amount levied under an execution.

The money which an owner of animals impounded must pay to obtain their release.

In old English law. A subsidy to the value of twelve pence in the *pound*, granted to the king, of all manner of merchandise of every merchant, as well denizen as alien, either exported or imported. Cowell.

POUR ACQUIT. Fr. In French law. The formula which a creditor prefixes to his signature when he gives a receipt.

POUR COMPTE DE QUI IL APPARTIENT. Fr. For account of whom it may concern.

POUR FAIRE PROCLAIMER. L. Fr. An ancient writ addressed to the mayor or bailiff of a city or town, requiring him to make proclamation concerning nuisances, etc. Fitzh. Nat. Brev. 176.

POUR SEISIR TERRES. L. Fr. An ancient writ whereby the crown seized the land which the wife of its deceased tenant, who held *in capite*, had for her dower, if she married without leave. It was grounded on the statute *De Prærogativa Regis*, 7, (17 Edw. II. St. 1, c. 4.) It is abolished by 12 Car. II. c. 24.

POURPARLER. Fr. In French law. The preliminary negotiations or bargainings which lead to a contract between the parties. As in English law, these form no part of the contract when completed.

POURPARTY. To make *pourparty* is to divide and sever the lands that fall to parceners, which, before partition, they held jointly and *pro indiviso*. Cowell.

POURPRESTURE. An inclosure. Anything done to the nuisance or hurt of the public demesnes, or the highways, etc., by inclosure or building, endeavoring to make that private which ought to be public. The difference between a *pourpresture* and a public nuisance is that *pourpresture* is an invasion of the *jus privatum* of the crown; but where the *jus publicum* is violated it is a nuisance. Skene makes three sorts of this offense: (1) Against the crown; (2) against the lord of the fee; (3) against a neighbor. 2 Inst. 38; 1 Reeve, Eng. Law, 156.

POURSUIVANT. The king's messenger; a royal or state messenger. In the heralds' college, a functionary of lower rank than a herald, but discharging similar duties, called also "poursuivant at arms."

POURVEYANCE. In old English law. The providing corn, fuel, victual, and other necessaries for the king's house. Cowell.

POURVEYOR, or PURVEYOR. A buyer; one who provided for the royal household.

POUSTIE. In Scotch law. Power. See LIEGE POUSTIE. A word formed from the Latin "*potestas.*"

POVERTY AFFIDAVIT. An affidavit, made and filed by one of the parties to a suit, that he is not able to furnish security for the final costs. The use of the term is confined to a few states. 36 Kan. 263, 13 Pac. Rep. 275.

POWER. A power is an authority to do some act in relation to real property, or to the creation or revocation of an estate therein, or a charge thereon, which the owner granting or reserving such power might himself perform for any purpose. Civil Code Dak. § 298; How. St. Mich. § 5591.

"Power" is sometimes used in the same sense as "right," as when we speak of the powers of user and disposition which the owner of property has over it, but, strictly speaking, a power is that which creates a special or exceptional right, or enables a person to do something which he could not otherwise do. Sweet.

Technically, an authority by which one person enables another to do some act for him. 2 Lil. Abr. 339.

An authority enabling a person to dispose, through the medium of the statute of uses, of an interest, vested either in himself or in another person. Sugd. Powers, 82. An authority expressly reserved to a grantor, or expressly given to another, to be exercised over lands, etc., granted or conveyed at the time of the creation of such power. Watk. Conv. 157. A proviso, in a conveyance under the statute of uses, giving to the grantor or grantee, or a stranger, authority to revoke or alter by a subsequent act the estate first granted. 1 Steph. Comm. 505. See POWER OF APPOINTMENT.

POWER COUPLED WITH AN INTEREST. By this phrase is meant a right or power to do some act, together with an interest in the subject-matter on which the power is to be exercised. It is distinguished from a *naked* power, which is a mere authority to act, not accompanied by any interest of the donee in the subject-matter of the power.

Is it an interest in the subject on which the power is to be exercised, or is it an interest in that which is produced by the exercise of the power? We hold it to be clear that the interest which can protect a power after the death of a person who creates it must be an interest in the thing itself. In other words, the power must be engrafted on an estate in the thing. The words themselves would seem to import this meaning. "A power coupled with an interest" is a power which accompanies or is connected with an interest. The power and the interest are united in the same person. But, if we are to understand by the word "interest" an interest in that which is to be produced by the exercise of the power, then they are never united. The power to produce the interest must be exercised, and by its exercise is extinguished. The power ceases when the interest commences, and therefore cannot, in accurate law language, be said to be "coupled" with it. 8 Wheat. 204.

POWER OF APPOINTMENT. A power or authority conferred by one person by deed or will upon another (called the "donee") to appoint, that is, to select and nominate, the person or persons who are to receive and enjoy an estate or an income therefrom or from a fund, after the testator's death, or the donee's death, or after the termination of an existing right or interest.

Powers are either: *Collateral*, which are given to strangers; *i. e.*, to persons who have neither a present nor future estate or interest in the land. These are also called simply "collateral," or powers not coupled with an interest, or powers not being interests. These terms have been adopted to obviate the confusion arising from the circumstance that powers in gross have been by many called powers collateral. Or relating to the land. These are called "appendant" or "appurtenant," because they strictly depend upon the estate limited to the person to whom they are given. Thus, where an estate for life is limited to a man, with a power to grant leases in possession, a lease granted under the power may operate wholly out of the life-estate of the party executing it, and must in every case have its operation out of his estate during his life. Such an estate must be created, which will attach on an interest actually vested in himself. Or they are called "in gross," if given to a person who had an interest in the estate at the execution of the deed creating the power, or to whom an estate is given by the deed, but which enabled him to create such estates only as will not attach on the interest limited to him. Of necessity, therefore, where a man seised in fee settles his estate on others, reserving to himself only a particular power, the power is in gross. A power to a tenant for life to appoint the estate after his death among his children, a power to jointure a wife after his death, a power to raise a term of years to commence from his death, for securing younger children's portions, are all powers in gross. An important distinction is established between *general* and *particular* powers. By a general power we understand a right to appoint to whomsoever the donee pleases. By a particular power it is meant that the donee is restricted to some objects designated in the deed creating the power, as to his own children. Wharton.

We have seen that a general power is *beneficial*

when no person other than the grantee has, by the terms of its creation, any interest in its execution. A general power is *in trust* when any person or class of persons, other than the grantee of such power, is designated as entitled to the proceeds, or any portion of the proceeds, or other benefits to result from the alienation. 20 Hun, 364.

When a power of appointment among a class requires that each shall have a share, it is called a "distributive" or "non-exclusive" power; when it authorizes, but does not direct, a selection of one or more to the exclusion of the others, it is called an "exclusive" power, and is also distributive; when it gives the power of appointing to a certain number of the class, but not to all, it is exclusive only, and not distributive. Leake, 389. A power authorizing the donee either to give the whole to one of a class or to give it equally among such of them as he may select (but not to give one a larger share than the others) is called a "mixed" power. Sugd. Powers, 448. Sweet.

POWER OF ATTORNEY. An instrument authorizing a person to act as the agent or attorney of the person granting it. See LETTER OF ATTORNEY.

POWER OF DISPOSITION. Every power of disposition is deemed absolute, by means of which the donee of such power is enabled in his life-time to dispose of the entire fee for his own benefit; and, where a general and beneficial power to devise the inheritance is given to a tenant for life or years, it is absolute, within the meaning of the statutes of some of the states. Code Ala. 1886, § 1853. See POWER OF APPOINTMENT.

POYNDING. See POINDING.

POYNINGS' ACT. An act of parliament, made in Ireland, (10 Hen. VII. c. 22, A. D. 1495;) so called because Sir Edward Poynings was lieutenant there when it was made, whereby all general statutes before then made in England were declared of force in Ireland, which, before that time, they were not. 1 Broom & H. Comm. 112.

PRACTICAL. A practical construction of a constitution or statute is one determined, not by judicial decision, but practice sanctioned by general consent. 3 Serg. & R. 69.

PRACTICE. The form or mode of proceeding in courts of justice for the enforcement of rights or the redress of wrongs, as distinguished from the substantive law which gives the right or denounces the wrong. The form, manner, or order of instituting and conducting a suit or other judicial proceeding, through its successive stages to its end, in accordance with the rules and principles laid down by law or by the regulations and precedents of the courts. The term applies as well to the conduct of criminal actions as to civil suits, to proceedings in equity as well as at law, and to the defense as well as the prosecution of any proceeding.

It may include pleading, but is usually employed as excluding both pleading and evidence, and to designate all the incidental acts and steps in the course of bringing matters pleaded to trial and proof, and procuring and enforcing judgment on them.

PRACTICE COURT. In English law. A court attached to the court of king's bench, which heard and determined common matters of business and ordinary motions for writs of *mandamus*, prohibition, etc. It was usually called the "bail court." It was held by one of the puisne justices of the king's bench.

PRACTICES. A succession of acts of a similar kind or in a like employment.

PRACTICKS. In Scotch law. The decisions of the court of session, as evidence of the *practice* or custom of the country. Bell.

PRACTITIONER. He who is engaged in the exercise or employment of any art or profession.

PRÆCEPTORES. Masters. The chief clerks in chancery were formerly so called, because they had the direction of making out remedial writs. 2 Reeve, Eng. Law, 251.

PRÆCEPTORIES. In feudal law. A kind of benefices, so called because they were possessed by the more eminent templars, whom the chief master by his authority created and called "*Præceptores Templi.*"

PRÆCIPE. Lat. In practice. An original writ, drawn up in the alternative, commanding the defendant to do the thing required, or show the reason why he had not done it. 3 Bl. Comm. 274.

Also an order, written out and signed, addressed to the clerk of a court, and requesting him to issue a particular writ.

PRÆCIPE IN CAPITE. When one of the king's immediate tenants *in capite* was deforced, his writ of right was called a writ of "*præcipe in capite.*"

PRÆCIPE QUOD REDDAT. Command that he render. A writ directing the defendant to restore the possession of land, employed at the beginning of a common recovery.

PRÆCIPE QUOD TENEAT CONVENTIONEM. The writ which commenced the action of covenant in fines, which are abolished by 3 & 4 Wm. IV. c. 74.

PRÆCIPE, TENANT TO THE. A person having an estate of freehold in possession, against whom the *præcipe* was brought by a tenant in tail, seeking to bar his estate by a recovery.

PRÆCIPITIUM. The punishment of casting headlong from some high place.

PRÆCIPUT CONVENTIONNEL. In French law. Under the *régime en communauté*, when that is of the conventional kind, if the surviving husband or wife is entitled to take any portion of the common property by a paramount title and before partition thereof, this right is called by the somewhat barbarous title of the conventional "*præciput*," from "*præ*," before, and "*capere*," to take. Brown.

PRÆCO. Lat. In Roman law. A herald or crier.

PRÆCOGNITA. Things to be previously known in order to the understanding of something which follows. Wharton.

PRÆDIA. In the civil law. Lands; estates; tenements; properties. See PRÆDIUM, and following titles.

PRÆDIA BELLICA. Booty. Property seized in war.

PRÆDIA STIPENDIARIA. In the civil law. Provincial lands belonging to the people.

PRÆDIA TRIBUTARIA. In the civil law. Provincial lands belonging to the emperor.

PRÆDIA VOLANTIA. In the duchy of Brabant, certain things movable, such as beds, tables, and other heavy articles of furniture, were ranked among immovables, and were called "*prædia volantia*," or "volatile estates." 2 Bl. Comm. 428.

PRÆDIAL SERVITUDE. A right which is granted for the advantage of one piece of land over another, and which may be exercised by every possessor of the land entitled against every possessor of the servient land. It always presupposes two pieces of land (*prædia*) belonging to different proprietors; one burdened with the servitude, called "*prædium serviens*," and one for the advantage of which the servitude is conferred, called "*prædium dominans*." Mackeld. Rom. Law, § 314.

PRÆDIAL TITHES. Such as arise merely and immediately from the ground; as grain of all sorts, hops, hay, wood, fruit, herbs. 2 Bl. Comm. 23; 2 Steph. Comm. 722.

PRÆDICTUS. Lat. Aforesaid. Hob. 6.

Of the three words, "*idem*," "*prædictus*," and "*præfatus*," "*idem*" was most usually applied to plaintiffs or demandants; "*prædictus*," to defendants or tenants, places, towns, or lands; and "*præfatus*," to persons named, not being *actors* or parties. Townsh. Pl. 15. These words may all be rendered in English by "said" or "aforesaid."

PRÆDIUM. Lat. In the civil law. Land; an estate; a tenement; a piece of landed property. See Dig. 50, 16, 115.

PRÆDIUM DOMINANS. Lat. In the civil law. The name given to an estate to which a servitude is due; the dominant tenement.

PRÆDIUM RUSTICUM. Lat. In Roman law. A rustic or rural estate. Primarily, this term denoted an estate lying in the country, *i. e.*, beyond the limits of the city, but it was applied to any landed estate or heritage other than a dwelling-house, whether in or out of the town. Thus, it included gardens, orchards, pastures, meadows, etc. Mackeld. Rom. Law, § 316.

A rural or country estate; an estate or piece of land principally destined or devoted to agriculture; an empty or vacant space of ground without buildings.

PRÆDIUM SERVIENS. Lat. In the civil law. The name of an estate which suffers a servitude or easement to another estate; the servient tenement.

Prædium servit prædio. Land is under servitude to land, [*i. e.*, servitudes are not personal rights, but attach to the dominant tenement.] Tray. Lat. Max. 455.

PRÆDIUM URBANUM. Lat. In the civil law. A building or edifice intended for the habitation and use of man, whether built in cities or in the country. Colq. Rom. Civil Law, § 937.

PRÆDO. Lat. In Roman law. A robber. See Dig. 50, 17, 126.

PRÆFATUS. Aforesaid. Sometimes abbreviated to "*præfat.*" and "*p. fat.*"

PRÆFECTURÆ. In Roman law. Conquered towns, governed by an officer called a "prefect," who was chosen in some instances by the people, in others by the prætors. Butl. Hor. Jur. 29.

PRÆFECTUS URBI. Lat. In Roman law. The name of an officer who, from the time of Augustus, had the superintendence of the city and its police, with jurisdiction extending one hundred miles from the city, and power to decide both civil and criminal cases. As he was considered the direct representative of the emperor, much that previously belonged to the *prætor urbanus* fell gradually into his hands. Colq. Rom. Civil Law, § 2395.

PRÆFECTUS VIGILUM. Lat. In Roman law. The chief officer of the night watch. His jurisdiction extended to certain offenses affecting the public peace, and even to larcenies; but he could inflict only slight punishments. Colq. Rom. Civil Law, § 2395.

PRÆFECTUS VILLÆ. The mayor of a town.

PRÆFINE. The fee paid on suing out the writ of covenant, on levying fines, before the fine was passed. 2 Bl. Comm. 350.

PRÆJURAMENTUM. In old English law. A preparatory oath.

PRÆMIUM. Lat. Reward; compensation. *Præmium assecurationis*, compensation for insurance; premium of insurance. Locc. de Jur. Mar. lib. 2, c. 5, § 6.

PRÆMIUM PUDICITIÆ. The price of chastity; or compensation for loss of chastity. A term applied to bonds and other engagements given for the benefit of a seduced female. Sometimes called "*præmium pudoris.*" 2 Wils. 339, 340.

PRÆMUNIRE. In English law. The name of an offense against the king and his government, though not subject to capital punishment. So called from the words of the writ which issued preparatory to the prosecution: "*Præmunire facias A. B. quod sit coram nobis,*" etc.; "Cause A. B. to be forewarned that he appear before us to answer the contempt with which he stands charged." The statutes establishing this offense, the first of which was made in the thirty-first year of the reign of Edward I., were framed to encounter the papal usurpations in England; the original meaning of the offense called "*præmunire*" being the introduction of a foreign power into the kingdom, and creating *imperium in imperio*, by paying that obedience to papal process which constitutionally belonged to the king alone. The penalties of *præmunire* were afterwards applied to other heinous offenses. 4 Bl. Comm. 103-117; 4 Steph. Comm. 215-217.

PRÆNOMEN. Lat. Forename, or first name. The first of the three names by which the Romans were commonly distinguished. It marked the individual, and was commonly written with one letter; as "A." for "Aulus;" "C." for "Caius," etc. Adams, Rom. Ant. 35.

PRÆPOSITUS. In old English law. An officer next in authority to the alderman of a hundred, called "*præpositus regius;*" or a steward or bailiff of an estate, answering to the "*wicnere.*"

Also the person from whom descents are traced under the old canons.

PRÆPOSITUS ECCLESIÆ. A church-reeve, or warden. Spelman.

PRÆPOSITUS VILLÆ. A constable of a town, or petty constable.

Præpropera consilia raro sunt prospera. 4 Inst. 57. Hasty counsels are rarely prosperous.

PRÆSCRIPTIO. Lat. In the civil law. That mode of acquisition whereby one becomes proprietor of a thing on the ground that he has for a long time possessed it as his own; prescription. Dig. 41, 3. It was anciently distinguished from "*usucapio,*" (*q. v.*,) but was blended with it by Justinian.

Præscriptio est titulus ex usu et tempore substantiam capiens ab auctoritate legis. Co. Litt. 113. Prescription is a title by authority of law, deriving its force from use and time.

Præscriptio et executio non pertinent ad valorem contractus, sed ad tempus et modum actionis instituendæ. Prescription and execution do not affect the validity of the contract, but the time and manner of bringing an action. 3 Mass. 84; 3 Johns. Ch. 190, 219.

PRÆSCRIPTIONES. In Roman law. Forms of words (of a qualifying character) inserted in the *formulæ* in which the claims in actions were expressed; and, as they occupied an early place in the *formulæ*, they were called by this name, *i. e.*, qualifications *preceding* the claim. For example, in an action to recover the arrears of an annuity, the claim was preceded by the words "so far as the annuity is due and unpaid," or words to the like effect, ("*cujus rei dies fuit.*") Brown.

Præsentare nihil aliud est quam præsto dare seu offere. To present is no more than to give or offer on the spot. Co. Litt. 120.

Præsentia corporis tollit errorem nominis; et veritas nominis tollit errorem demonstrationis. The presence of the body cures error in the name; the truth of the name cures an error of description. Broom, Max. 637, 639, 640.

PRÆSES. Lat. In Roman law. A president or governor. Called a "*nomen generale,*" including pro-consuls, legates, and all who governed provinces.

PRÆSTARE. Lat. In Roman law. "*Præstare*" meant to make good, and, when used in conjunction with the words "*dare,*" "*facere,*" "*oportere,*" denoted obligations of a personal character, as opposed to real rights.

Præstat cautela quam medela. Prevention is better than cure. Co. Litt. 304*b*.

Præsumatur pro justitia sententiæ. The presumption should be in favor of the justice of a sentence. Best, Ev. Introd. 42.

Præsumitur pro legitimatione. The presumption is in favor of legitimacy. 1 Bl. Comm. 457; 5 Coke, 98*b*.

Præsumitur pro negante. It is presumed for the negative. The rule of the house of lords when the numbers are equal on a motion. Wharton.

PRÆSUMPTIO. Lat. Presumption; a presumption. Also intrusion, or the unlawful taking of anything.

Præsumptio, ex eo quod plerumque fit. Presumptions arise from what generally happens. 22 Wend. 425, 475.

PRÆSUMPTIO FORTIOR. Lat. A strong presumption; a presumption of fact entitled to great weight. One which determines the tribunal in its belief of an alleged fact, without, however, excluding the belief of the possibility of its being otherwise; the effect of which is to shift the burden of proof to the opposite party, and, if this proof be not made, the presumption is held for truth. Hub. Præl. J. C. lib. 22, tit. 3, n. 16; Burrill, Circ. Ev. 66.

PRÆSUMPTIO HOMINIS. Lat. The presumption of the man or individual; that is, natural presumption unfettered by strict rule.

PRÆSUMPTIO JURIS. Lat. A legal presumption or presumption of law; that is, one in which the law assumes the existence of something until it is disproved by evidence; a conditional, inconclusive, or rebuttable presumption. Best, Ev. § 43.

PRÆSUMPTIO JURIS ET DE JURE. Lat. A presumption of law and of right; a presumption which the law will not suffer to be contradicted; a conclusive or irrebuttable presumption.

Præsumptio violenta plena probatio. Co. Litt. 6*b*. Strong presumption is full proof.

Præsumptio violenta valet in lege. Strong presumption is of weight in law. Jenk. Cent. p. 56, case 3.

Præsumptiones sunt conjecturæ ex signo verisimili ad probandum assumptæ. Presumptions are conjectures from probable proof, assumed for purposes of evidence. J. Voet, Com. ad Pand. l. 22, tit. 3, n. 14.

Prætextu liciti non debet admitti illicitum. Under pretext of legality, what is illegal ought not to be admitted. Wing. Max. p. 728, max. 196.

PRÆTEXTUS. Lat. A pretext; a pretense or color. *Prætextu cujus*, by pretense, or under pretext whereof. 1 Ld. Raym 412.

PRÆTOR. In Roman law. A municipal officer of the city of Rome, being the chief judicial magistrate, and possessing an extensive equitable jurisdiction.

PRÆTOR FIDEI-COMMISSARIUS. In the civil law. A special prætor created to pronounce judgment in cases of trusts or *fidei-commissa*. Inst. 2, 23, 1.

PRÆVARICATOR. In the civil law. One who betrays his trust, or is unfaithful to his trust. An advocate who aids the opposite party by betraying his client's cause. Dig. 47, 15, 1.

PRÆVENTO TERMINO. In old Scotch practice. A form of action known in the forms of the court of session, by which a delay to discuss a suspension or advocation was got the better of. Bell.

PRAGMATIC SANCTION. In French law. An expression used to designate those ordinances which concern the most important objects of the civil or ecclesiastical administration. Merl. Répert.

In the civil law. The answer given by the emperors on questions of law, when consulted by a corporation or the citizens of a province or of a municipality, was called a "pragmatic sanction." Lec. El. Dr. Rom. § 53.

PRAGMATICA. In Spanish colonial law. An order emanating from the sovereign, and differing from a *cedula* only in form and in the mode of promulgation. Schm. Civil Law, Introd. 93, note.

PRAIRIE. An extensive tract of level or rolling land, destitute of trees, covered with coarse grass, and usually characterized by a deep, fertile soil. Webster. See 58 Mo. 45; 42 Iowa, 429.

PRATIQUE. A license for the master of a ship to traffic in the ports of Italy upon a certificate that the place whence he came is not annoyed with any infectious disease. Enc. Lond.

PRAXIS. Lat. Use; practice.

Praxis judicum est interpres legum. Hob. 96. The practice of the judges is the interpreter of the laws.

PRAY IN AID. In old English practice. To call upon for assistance. In real actions, the tenant might *pray in aid* or call for assistance of another, to help him to plead, because of the feebleness or imbecility of his own estate. 3 Bl. Comm. 300.

PRAYER. The request contained in a bill in equity that the court will grant the process, aid, or relief which the complainant desires. Also, by extension, the term is applied to that part of the bill which contains this request.

PRAYER OF PROCESS is a petition with which a bill in equity used to conclude, to the effect that a writ of subpœna might issue against the defendant to compel him to answer upon oath all the matters charged against him in the bill.

PREAPPOINTED EVIDENCE. The kind and degree of evidence prescribed in advance (as, by statute) as requisite for the proof of certain facts or the establishment of certain instruments. It is opposed to *casual* evidence, which is left to grow naturally out of the surrounding circumstances.

PREAUDIENCE. The right of being heard before another. A privilege belonging to the English bar, the members of which are entitled to be heard in their order, according to rank, beginning with the queen's attorney general, and ending with barristers at large. 3 Steph. Comm. 387, note.

PRE-EMPTION. In international law. The right of pre-emption is the right of a nation to detain the merchandise of strangers passing through her territories or seas, in order to afford to her subjects the preference of purchase. 1 Chit. Com. Law, 103.

In English law. The first buying of a thing. A privilege formerly enjoyed by the crown, of buying up provisions and other necessaries, by the intervention of the king's purveyors, for the use of his royal household, at an appraised valuation, in preference to all others, and even without consent of the owner. 1 Bl. Comm. 287.

In the United States, the right of pre-emption is a privilege accorded by the government to the actual settler upon a certain limited portion of the public domain, to purchase such tract at a fixed price to the exclusion of all other applicants.

PRE-EMPTION CLAIMANT. One who has settled upon land subject to pre-emption, with the intention to acquire title to it, and has complied, or is proceeding to comply, in good faith, with the requirements of the law to perfect his right to it. 97 U. S. 575, 581.

PRE-EMPTION RIGHT. The right given to settlers upon the public lands of the United States to purchase them at a limited price in preference to others.

PRE-EMPTIONER. One who, by settlement upon the public land, or by cultivation of a portion of it, has obtained the right to purchase a portion of the land thus settled upon or cultivated, to the exclusion of all other persons. 5 Wis. 480.

PREAMBLE. The introductory clause or section of a statute is so termed. It usually recites the objects and intentions of the legislature in passing the statute, and frequently points out the evils or grievances intended to be remedied.

PREBEND. In English ecclesiastical law. A stipend granted in cathedral churches; also, but improperly, a prebendary. A simple prebend is merely a revenue; a prebend with dignity has some jurisdiction attached to it. The term "prebend" is generally confounded with "canonicate;" but there is a difference between them. The former is the stipend granted to an ecclesiastic in consideration of his officiating and serving in the church; whereas the canonicate is a mere title or spiritual quality which may exist independently of any stipend. 2 Steph. Comm. 674, note.

PREBENDARY. An ecclesiastical person serving on the staff of a cathedral, and receiving a stated allowance or stipend from the income or endowment of the cathedral, in compensation for his services.

PRECARIÆ, or PRECES. Day-works which the tenants of certain manors were bound to give their lords in harvest time. *Magna precaria* was a great or general reaping day. Cowell.

PRECARIOUS. The circumstances of an executor are *precarious,* within the meaning and intent of a statute, only when his character and conduct present such evidence of improvidence or recklessness in the management of the trust-estate, or of his own, as in the opinion of prudent and discreet men endangers its security. 60 Barb. 56.

PRECARIOUS LOAN. A bailment by way of loan which is not to continue for any fixed time, but may be recalled at the mere will and pleasure of the lender.

PRECARIOUS RIGHT. The right which the owner of a thing transfers to another, to enjoy the same until it shall please the owner to revoke it.

PRECARIOUS TRADE. In international law. Such trade as may be carried on by a neutral between two belligerent powers by the mere sufferance of the latter.

PRECARIUM. Lat. In the civil law. A convention whereby one allows another the use of a thing or the exercise of a right gratuitously till revocation. The bailee acquires thereby the lawful possession of the thing, except in certain cases. The bailor can redemand the thing at any time, even should he have allowed it to the bailee for a designated period. Mackeld. Rom. Law, § 447.

PRECATORY TRUST. A trust created by certain words, which are more like words of entreaty and permission than of command or certainty. Examples of such words, which the courts have held sufficient to constitute a trust, are "wish and request," "have fullest confidence," "heartily beseech," and the like. Rapalje & Lawrence.

PRECATORY WORDS. Words of entreaty, request, desire, wish, or recommendation, employed in wills, as distinguished from direct and imperative terms. 1 Williams, Ex'rs, 88, 89, and note.

PRECEDENCE, or PRECEDENCY. The act or state of going before; adjustment of place.

PRECEDENCE, PATENT OF. In English law. A grant from the crown to such barristers as it thinks proper to honor with that mark of distinction, whereby they are entitled to such rank and preaudience as are assigned in their respective patents. 3 Steph. Comm. 274.

PRECEDENT. An adjudged case or decision of a court of justice, considered as furnishing an example or authority for an identical or similar case afterwards arising or a similar question of law.

A draught of a conveyance, settlement, will, pleading, bill, or other legal instrument, which is considered worthy to serve as a pattern for future instruments of the same nature.

PRECEDENT CONDITION. Such as must happen or be performed before an estate can vest or be enlarged. See CONDITION PRECEDENT.

PRECEDENTS SUB SILENTIO. Silent uniform course of practice, uninterrupted though not supported by legal decisions.

Precedents that pass sub silentio are of little or no authority. 16 Vin. Abr. 499.

PRECEPARTIUM. The continuance of a suit by consent of both parties. Cowell.

PRECEPT. In English and American law. An order or direction, emanating from authority, to an officer or body of officers, commanding him or them to do some act within the scope of their powers.

Precept is not to be confined to civil proceedings, and is not of a more restricted meaning than "process." It includes warrants and processes in criminal as well as civil proceedings. 1 Gray, 51, 58.

"Precept" means a commandment in writing, sent out by a justice of the peace or other like officer, for the bringing of a person or record before him. Cowell.

The direction formerly issued by a sheriff to the proper returning officers of cities and boroughs within his jurisdiction for the election of members to serve in parliament. 1 Bl. Comm. 178.

The direction by the judges or commissioners of assize to the sheriff for the summoning a sufficient number of jurors. 3 Steph. Comm. 516.

The direction issued by the clerk of the peace to the overseers of parishes for making out the jury lists. 3 Steph. Comm. 516, note.

In old English criminal law. Instigation to commit a crime. Bract. fol. 138*b*; Cowell.

In Scotch law. An order, mandate, or warrant to do some act. The precept of seisin was the order of a superior to his bailie, to give infeftment of certain lands to his vassal. Bell.

In old French law. A kind of letters issued by the king in subversion of the laws, being orders to the judges to do or tolerate things contrary to law.

PRECEPT OF CLARE CONSTAT. A deed in the Scotch law by which a superior acknowledges the title of the heir of a deceased vassal to succeed to the lands.

PRECES. Lat. In Roman law. Prayers. One of the names of an application to the emperor. Tayl. Civil Law, 230.

PRECES PRIMARIÆ. In English ecclesiastical law. A right of the crown to name to the first prebend that becomes vacant after the accession of the sovereign, in every church of the empire. This right was exercised by the crown of England in the reign of Edward I. 2 Steph. Comm. 670, note.

PRECINCT. A constable's or police district. The immediate neighborhood of a palace or court. A poll-district.

PRECIPE. Another form of the name of the written instructions to the clerk of court; also spelled "*præcipe*," (*q. v.*)

PRÉCIPUT. In French law. A portion of an estate or inheritance which falls to one of the co-heirs over and above his equal share with the rest, and which is to be taken out before partition is made.

PRECLUDI NON. In pleading. The commencement of a replication to a plea in bar, by which the plaintiff "says that, by reason of anything in the said plea alleged, he *ought not to be barred* from having and maintaining his aforesaid action against him, the said defendant, because he says," etc. Steph. Pl. 440.

PRECOGNITION. In Scotch practice. Preliminary examination. The investigation of a criminal case, preliminary to committing the accused for trial. 2 Alis. Crim. Pr. 134.

PRECOGNOSCE. In Scotch practice. To examine beforehand. Arkley, 232.

PRECONIZATION. Proclamation.

PRECONTRACT. A contract or engagement made by a person, which is of such a nature as to preclude him from lawfully entering into another contract of the same nature. See 1 Bish. Mar. & Div. §§ 112, 272.

PREDECESSOR. One who goes or has gone before; the correlative of "successor." Applied to a body politic or corporate, in the same sense as "ancestor" is applied to a natural person.

In Scotch law. An ancestor. 1 Kames, Eq. 371.

PREDIAL SERVITUDE. A real or predial servitude is a charge laid on an estate for the use and utility of another estate belonging to another owner. Civil Code La. art. 647. See PRÆDIAL SERVITUDE.

PREDICATE. In logic. That which is said concerning the subject in a logical proposition; as, "The law is the perfection of common sense." "Perfection of common sense," being affirmed concerning the law, (the subject,) is the predicate or thing predicated. Wharton.

PREDOMINANT. This term, in its natural and ordinary signification, is understood to be something greater or superior in power and influence to others, with which it is connected or compared. So understood, a "predominant motive," when several motives may have operated, is one of greater force and effect, in producing the given result, than any other motive. 22 Pick. 53.

PREFECT. In French law. The name given to the public functionary who is charged in chief with the administration of the laws, in each department of the country. Merl. Répert.

PREFER. To bring before; to prosecute; to try; to proceed with. Thus, preferring an indictment signifies prosecuting or trying an indictment.

To give advantage, priority, or privilege; to select for first payment, as to prefer one creditor over others.

PREFERENCE. The act of an insolvent debtor who, in distributing his property or in assigning it for the benefit of his creditors, pays or secures to one or more creditors the full amount of their claims or a larger amount than they would be entitled to receive on a *pro rata* distribution.

Also the right held by a creditor, in virtue of some lien or security, to be preferred above others (*i. e.*, paid first) out of the debtor's assets constituting the fund for creditors.

PREFERENCE SHARES. A term used in English law to designate a new issue of shares of stock in a company, which, to facilitate the disposal of them, are accorded a priority or preference over the original shares.

Such shares entitle their holders to a preferential dividend, so that a holder of them is entitled to have the whole of his dividend (or so much thereof as represents the extent to which his shares are, by the constitution of the company, to be deemed preference shares) paid before any dividend is paid to the ordinary shareholders. Mozley & Whitley.

PREFERENTIAL ASSIGNMENT. An assignment of property for the benefit of creditors, made by an insolvent debtor, in which it is directed that a preference (right to be paid first in full) shall be given to a creditor or creditors therein named.

PREFERRED CREDITOR. A creditor whom the debtor has directed shall be paid before other creditors.

PREFERRED DEBT. A demand which has priority; which is payable in full before others are paid at all.

PREGNANCY. In medical jurisprudence. The state of a female who has within her ovary or womb a fecundated germ, which gradually becomes developed in the latter receptacle. Dungl. Med. Dict.

PREGNANCY, PLEA OF. A plea which a woman capitally convicted may plead in stay of execution; for this, though it is no stay of judgment, yet operates as a respite of execution until she is delivered. Brown.

PREGNANT NEGATIVE. See NEGATIVE PREGNANT.

PREJUDICE. A forejudgment; bias; preconceived opinion. A leaning towards one side of a cause for some reason other than a conviction of its justice.

The word "prejudice" seemed to imply nearly the same thing as "opinion," a *prejudgment* of the case, and not necessarily an enmity or ill will against either party. 5 Cush. 297.

"Prejudice" also means injury, loss, or damnification. Thus, where an offer or admission is made "without prejudice," or a motion is denied "without prejudice," it is meant as a declaration that no rights or privileges of the party concerned are to be considered as thereby waived or lost, except in so far as may be expressly conceded or decided.

PRELATE. A clergyman of a superior order, as an archbishop or a bishop, having authority over the lower clergy; a dignitary of the church. Webster.

PRÉLÈVEMENT. Fr. In French law. A preliminary deduction; particularly, the portion or share which one member of a firm is entitled to take out of the partnership assets before a division of the property is made between the partners.

PRELIMINARY. Introductory; initiatory; preceding; temporary and provisional; as preliminary examination, injunction, articles of peace, etc.

PRELIMINARY ACT. In English admiralty practice. A document stating the time and place of a collision between vessels, the names of the vessels, and other particulars, required to be filed by each solicitor in actions for damage by such collision, unless the court or a judge shall otherwise order. Wharton.

PRELIMINARY INJUNCTION. An injunction granted at the institution of a suit, to restrain the defendant from doing or continuing some act, the right to which is in dispute, and which may either be discharged or made perpetual, according to the result of the controversy, as soon as the rights of the parties are determined.

PRELIMINARY PROOF. In insurance. The first proof offered of a loss occurring under the policy, usually sent in to the underwriters with the notification of claim.

PREMEDITATE. To think of an act beforehand; to contrive and design; to plot or lay plans for the execution of a purpose. See DELIBERATE.

PREMEDITATION. The act of meditating in advance; deliberation upon a contemplated act; plotting or contriving; a design formed to do something before it is done.

PREMIER. A principal minister of state; the prime minister.

PREMIER SERJEANT, THE QUEEN'S. This officer, so constituted by letters patent, has preaudience over the bar after the attorney and solicitor general and queen's advocate. 3 Steph. Comm. (7th Ed.) 274, note.

PREMISES. That which is put before; that which precedes; the foregoing statements. Thus, in logic, the two introductory propositions of the syllogism are called the "premises," and from them the conclusion is deduced. So, in pleading, the expression "in consideration of the premises" frequently occurs, the meaning being "in consideration of the matters herein before stated."

In conveyancing. That part of a deed which precedes the *habendum*, in which are set forth the names of the parties with their titles and additions, and in which are recited such deeds, agreements, or matters of fact as are necessary to explain the reasons upon which the present transaction is founded; and it is here, also, the consideration on which it is made is set down and the certainty of the thing granted. 2 Bl. Comm. 298.

In estates. Lands and tenements; an estate; the subject-matter of a conveyance.

The term "premises" is used in common parlance to signify land, with its appurtenances; but its usual and appropriate meaning in a conveyance is the thing demised or granted by the deed. 13 N. J. Eq. 322.

The word is also used to denote the subject-matter insured in a policy. 4 Campb. 89.

In equity pleading. The stating part of a bill. It contains a narrative of the facts and circumstances of the plaintiff's case, and the wrongs of which he complains, and the names of the persons by whom done and against whom he seeks redress. Story, Eq. Pl. § 27.

PREMIUM. The sum paid or agreed to be paid by an assured to the underwriter as the consideration for the insurance; being a certain rate per cent. on the amount insured. 1 Phil. Ins. 205.

A bounty or bonus; a consideration given to invite a loan or a bargain; as the consideration paid to the assignor by the assignee of a lease, or to the transferrer by the transferee of shares of stock, etc. So stock is said to be "at a premium" when its market price exceeds its nominal or face value. See PAR.

In granting a lease, part of the rent is sometimes capitalized and paid in a lump sum at the time the lease is granted. This is called a "premium."

PREMIUM NOTE. A promissory note given by the insured for part or all of the amount of the premium.

PREMIUM PUDICITIÆ. The price of chastity. A compensation for the loss of chastity, paid or promised to, or for the benefit of, a seduced female.

PREMUNIRE. See PRÆMUNIRE.

PRENDA. In Spanish law. Pledge. White, New Recop. b. 2, tit. 7.

PRENDER, PRENDRE. L. Fr. To take. The power or right of taking a thing without waiting for it to be offered. See A PRENDER.

PRENDER DE BARON. L. Fr. In old English law. A taking of husband; marriage. An exception or plea which might be used to disable a woman from pursuing an appeal of murder against the killer of her former husband. Staundef. P. C. lib. 3, c. 59.

PREPENSE. Forethought; preconceived; premeditated.

PREPONDERANCE. This word means something more than "weight;" it denotes a superiority of weight, or outweighing. The words are not synonymous, but substantially different. There is generally a "weight" of evidence on each side in case of contested facts. But juries cannot properly act upon the weight of evidence, in favor of the one having the *onus*, unless it overbear, in some degree, the weight upon the other side. 37 Ark. 588.

PREROGATIVE. An exclusive or peculiar privilege. The special power, privilege, immunity, or advantage vested in an official person, either generally, or in respect to the things of his office, or in an official body, as a court or legislature.

In English law. That special pre-eminence which the king (or queen) has over and above all other persons, in right of his (or her) regal dignity. A term used to denote those rights and capacities which the sovereign enjoys alone, in contradistinction to others. 1 Bl. Comm. 239.

PREROGATIVE COURT. In English law. A court established for the trial of all testamentary causes, where the deceased left *bona notabilia* within two different dioceses; in which case the probate of wills belonged to the archbishop of the province, by way of special prerogative. And all causes relating to the wills, administrations, or legacies of such persons were originally cognizable herein, before a judge appointed by the archbishop, called the "judge of the prerogative court," from whom an appeal lay to the privy council. 3 Bl. Comm. 66; 3 Steph. Comm. 432.

In New Jersey the prerogative court is the court of appeal from decrees of the orphans' courts in the several counties of the state. The court is held before the chancellor, under the title of the "ordinary."

PREROGATIVE LAW. That part of the common law of England which is more particularly applicable to the king. Com. Dig. tit. "Ley," A.

PREROGATIVE WRITS. Process issued by an exercise of the extraordinary power of the crown on proper cause shown. They are the writs of *procedendo*, *mandamus*, prohibition, *quo warranto*, *habeas corpus*, and *certiorari*. 3 Steph. Comm. 629.

PRES. L. Fr. Near. *Cy pres*, so near; as near. See CY PRES.

PRESBYTER. Lat. In civil and ecclesiastical law. An elder; a presbyter; a priest. Cod. 1, 3, 6, 20; Nov. 6.

PRESBYTERIUM. That part of the church where divine offices are performed; formerly applied to the choir or chancel, because it was the place appropriated to the bishop, priest, and other clergy, while the laity were confined to the body of the church. Jacob.

PRESCRIBABLE. That to which a right may be acquired by prescription.

PRESCRIBE. To assert a right or title to the enjoyment of a thing, on the ground of having hitherto had the uninterrupted and immemorial enjoyment of it.

To direct; define; mark out. In modern statutes relating to matters of an administrative nature, such as procedure, registration, etc., it is usual to indicate in general terms the nature of the proceedings to be adopted, and to leave the details to be *prescribed* or regulated by rules or orders to be made for that purpose in pursuance of an authority contained in the act. Sweet.

PRESCRIPTION. A mode of acquiring title to incorporeal hereditaments grounded on the fact of immemorial or long-continued enjoyment.

Title by prescription is the right which a possessor acquires to property by reason of the continuance of his possession for a period of time fixed by the laws. Code Ga. 1882, § 2678.

In Louisiana, prescription is defined as a manner of acquiring the ownership of property, or discharging debts, by the effect of time, and under the conditions regulated by law. Each of these prescriptions has its special and particular definition. The prescription by which the ownership of property is acquired, is a right by which a mere possessor acquires the ownership of a thing which he possesses by the continuance of his possession during the time fixed by law. The prescription by which debts are released, is a peremptory and perpetual bar to every species of action, real or personal, when the creditor has been silent for a certain time without urging his claim. Civil Code La. arts. 3457-3459.

"Prescription" and "custom" are frequently confounded in common parlance, arising perhaps from the fact that immemorial usage was essential to both of them; but, strictly, they materially differ from one another, in that custom is properly a local impersonal usage, such as borough-English, or postremogeniture, which is annexed to a given estate, while prescription is simply personal, as that a certain man and his ancestors, or those whose estate he enjoys, have immemorially exercised a right of pasture-common in a certain parish. Again, prescription has its origin in a grant, evidenced by usage, and is allowed on account of its loss, either actual or supposed, and therefore only those things can be prescribed for which could be raised by a grant previously to 8 & 9 Vict. c. 106, § 2; but this principle does not necessarily hold in the case of a custom. Wharton.

The difference between "prescription," "custom," and "usage" is also thus stated: "Prescription hath respect to a certain person who, by intendment, may have continuance forever, as, for instance, he and all they whose estate he hath in such a thing,—this is a prescription; while custom is local, and always applied to a certain place, and is common to all; while usage differs from both, for it may be either to persons or places." Jacob.

PRESCRIPTION ACT. The statute 2 & 3 Wm. IV. c. 71, passed to limit the period of prescription in certain cases.

PRESCRIPTION, CORPORATIONS BY. In English law. Those which have existed beyond the memory of man, and therefore are looked upon in law to be well created, such as the city of London.

PRESCRIPTION, TIME OF. The length of time necessary to establish a right claimed by prescription or a title by prescription. Before the act of 2 & 3 Wm. IV. c. 71, the possession required to constitute a prescription must have existed "time out of mind" or "beyond the memory of man," that is, before the reign of Richard I.; but the time of prescription, in certain cases, was much shortened by that act. 2 Steph. Comm. 35.

PRESENCE. The existence of a person in a particular place at a given time, particularly with reference to some act done there and then. Besides actual presence, the law recognizes *constructive* presence, which latter may be predicated of a person who, though not on the very spot, was near enough to be accounted present by the law, or who was actively co-operating with another who was actually present.

PRESENT, *v.* **In English ecclesiastical law.** To offer a clerk to the bishop of the diocese, to be instituted. 1 Bl. Comm. 389.

In criminal law. To find or represent judicially; used of the official act of a grand jury when they take notice of a crime or offense from their own knowledge or observation, without any bill of indictment laid before them.

In the law of negotiable instruments. Primarily, to present is to tender or offer. Thus, to present a bill of exchange for acceptance or payment is to exhibit it to the drawee or acceptor, (or his authorized agent,) with an express or implied demand for acceptance or payment. Byles, Bills, 183, 201.

PRESENT, *n.* A gift; a gratuity; anything presented or given.

PRESENT ENJOYMENT. The immediate or present possession and use of an estate or property, as distinguished from such as is postponed to a future time.

PRESENT ESTATE. An estate in immediate possession; one now existing, or vested at the present time; as distinguished from a *future* estate, the enjoyment of which is postponed to a future time.

PRESENT USE. One which has an immediate existence, and is at once operated upon by the statute of uses.

PRESENTATION. In ecclesiastical law. The act of a patron or proprietor of a living in offering or presenting a clerk to the ordinary to be instituted in the benefice.

PRESENTATION OFFICE. The office of the lord chancellor's official, the secretary of presentations, who conducts all correspondence having reference to the twelve canonries and six hundred and fifty livings in the gift of the lord chancellor, and draws and issues the fiats of appointment. Sweet.

PRESENTATIVE ADVOWSON. See ADVOWSON.

PRESENTEE. In ecclesiastical law. A clerk who has been presented by his patron to a bishop in order to be instituted in a church.

PRESENTER. One that presents.

PRESENTLY. Immediately; now; at once. A right which may be exercised "presently" is opposed to one in reversion or remainder.

PRESENTMENT. **In criminal practice.** The written notice taken by a grand jury of any offense, from their own knowledge or observation, without any bill of indictment laid before them at the suit of the government. 4 Bl. Comm. 301.

A presentment is an informal statement in writing, by the grand jury, representing to the court that a public offense has been committed which is triable in the county, and that there is reasonable ground for believing that a particular individual named or described therein has committed it. Pen. Code Cal. § 916.

In its limited sense, a presentment is a statement by the grand jury of an offense from their own knowledge, without any bill of indictment laid before them, setting forth the name of the party, place of abode. and the offense committed, informally, upon which the officer of the court afterwards frames an indictment. 13 Fla. 651, 663.

The difference between a presentment and an inquisition is this: that the former is found by a grand jury authorized to inquire of offenses generally, whereas the latter is an accusation found by a jury specially returned to inquire concerning the particular offense. 2 Hawk. P. C. c. 25, § 6.

The writing which contains the accusation so presented by a grand jury is also called a "presentment."

Presentments are also made in courts-leet and courts-baron, before the stewards. Steph. Comm. 644.

In contracts. The production of a bill of exchange to the drawee for his acceptance, or to the drawer or acceptor for payment; or of a promissory note to the party liable, for payment of the same.

PRESENTS. The present instrument. The phrase "these presents" is used in any legal document to designate the instrument in which the phrase itself occurs.

PRESERVATION. Keeping safe from harm; avoiding injury, destruction, or decay. This term always presupposes a real or existing danger.

PRESIDE. To preside over a court is to "hold" it,—to direct, control, and govern it as the chief officer. A judge may "preside" whether sitting as a sole judge or as one of several judges. 47 N. Y. 334.

PRESIDENT. One placed in authority over others; a chief officer; a presiding or managing officer; a governor, ruler, or director.

The chairman, moderator, or presiding officer of a legislative or deliberative body, appointed to keep order, manage the proceedings, and govern the administrative details of their business.

The chief officer of a corporation, company, board, committee, etc., generally having the main direction and administration of their concerns.

The chief executive magistrate of a state or nation, particularly under a democratic form of government; or of a province, colony, or dependency.

In English law. A title formerly given to the king's lieutenant in a province; as the president of Wales. Cowell.

This word is also an old though corrupted form of "precedent," (*q. v.*,) used both as a French and English word. *Le president est rare.* Dyer, 136.

PRESIDENT OF THE COUNCIL. In English law. A great officer of state; a member of the cabinet. He attends on the sovereign, proposes business at the council-table, and reports to the sovereign the transactions there. 1 Bl. Comm. 230.

PRESIDENT OF THE UNITED STATES. The official title of the chief executive officer of the federal government in the United States.

PRESIDENTIAL ELECTORS. A body of electors chosen in the different states, whose sole duty it is to elect a president and vice-president of the United States. Each state appoints, in such manner as the legislature thereof may direct, a number of electors equal to the whole number of senators and representatives to which the state is entitled in congress. Const. U. S. art. 2, § 1.

PRESS. In old practice. A piece or skin of parchment, several of which used to be sewed together in making up a roll or record of proceedings. See 1 Bl. Comm. 183; Townsh. Pl. 486.

Metaphorically, the aggregate of publications issuing from the press, or the giving publicity to one's sentiments and opinions though the medium of printing; as in the phrase "liberty of the press."

PRESSING SEAMEN. See IMPRESSMENT.

PRESSING TO DEATH. See PEINE FORTE ET DURE.

PREST. In old English law. A duty in money to be paid by the sheriff upon his account in the exchequer, or for money left or remaining in his hands. Cowell.

PREST-MONEY. A payment which binds those who receive it to be ready at all times appointed, being meant especially of soldiers. Cowell.

PRESTATION. In old English law. A payment or performance; the rendering of a service.

PRESTATION-MONEY. A sum of money paid by archdeacons yearly to their bishop; also purveyance. Cowell.

PRESTIMONY, or PRÆSTIMONIA. In canon law. A fund or revenue appropriated by the founder for the subsistence of a priest, without being erected into any title or benefice, chapel, prebend, or priory. It is not subject to the ordinary; but of it the patron, and those who have a right from him, are the collators. Wharton.

PRESUMPTIO. See PRÆSUMPTIO; PRESUMPTION.

PRESUMPTION. An inference affirmative or disaffirmative of the truth or falsehood of any proposition or fact drawn by a process of probable reasoning in the absence of actual certainty of its truth or falsehood, or until such certainty can be ascertained. Best, Pres. § 3.

A rule of law that courts and judges shall draw a particular inference from a particular fact, or from particular evidence, unless and until the truth of such inference is disproved. Steph. Ev. 4.

A presumption is a deduction which the law expressly directs to be made from particular facts. Code Civil Proc. Cal. § 1959.

Presumptions are consequences which the law or the judge draws from a known fact to a fact unknown. Civil Code La. art. 2284.

An inference affirmative or disaffirmative of the existence of a disputed fact, drawn by a judicial tribunal, by a process of probable reasoning, from some one or more matters of fact, either admitted in the cause or otherwise satisfactorily established. Best, Pres. § 12.

A presumption is an inference as to the existence of a fact not known, arising from its connection with the facts that are known, and founded upon a knowledge of human nature and the motives which are known to influence human conduct. 7 Wend. 62.

Presumptions are either presumptions *of law* or presumptions *of fact*. "A presumption of law is a juridical postulate that a particular predicate is universally assignable to a particular subject. A presumption of fact is a logical argument from a fact to a fact; or, as the distinction is sometimes put, it is an argument which infers a fact otherwise doubtful from a fact which is proved." 2 Whart. Ev. § 1226. See Code Ga. § 2752.

Presumptions of law are rules which, in certain cases, either forbid or dispense with any ulterior inquiry. 1 Greenl. Ev. § 14. Inferences or positions established, for the most part, by the common, but occasionally by the statute, law, which are obligatory alike on judges and juries. Best, Pres. § 15.

Presumptions of fact are inferences as to the existence of some fact drawn from the existence of some other fact; inferences which common sense draws from circumstances usually occurring in such cases. 1 Phil. Ev. 436.

Presumptions are divided into *præsumptiones juris et de jure*, otherwise called "irrebuttable presumptions," (often, but not necessarily, fictitious,) which the law will not suffer to be rebutted by any counter-evidence; as, that an infant under seven years is not responsible for his actions; *præsumptiones juris tantum*, which hold good in the absence of counter-evidence, but against which counter-evidence may be admitted; and *præsumptiones hominis*, which are not necessarily conclusive, though no proof to the contrary be adduced. Mozley & Whitley.

There are also certain *mixed* presumptions, or presumptions of fact recognized by law, or presumptions of mixed law and fact. These are certain presumptive inferences, which, from their strength, importance, or frequent occurrence, attract, as it were, the observation of the law. The presumption of a "lost grant" falls within this class. Best, Ev. 436.

Presumptions of law are divided into *conclusive* presumptions and *disputable* presumptions. The former are inferences which the law makes so peremptorily that it will not allow them to be overturned by any contrary proof, however strong. Best, Pres. § 17. They are called, also, "absolute" and "irrebuttable" presumptions. The latter are inferences of law which hold good until they are invalidated by proof or a stronger presumption. Best, Pres. § 25.

Legitimate presumptions have been denominated "violent" or "probable," according to the amount of weight which attaches to them. Such presumptions as are drawn from inadequate grounds are termed "light" or "rash" presumptions. Brown.

PRESUMPTION OF SURVIVORSHIP. A presumption of fact, to the effect that one person survived another, applied for the purpose of determining a question of succession or similar matter, in a case where the two persons perished in the same catastrophe, and there are no circumstances extant to show which of them actually died first, except those on which the presumption is founded, viz., differences of age, sex, strength, or physical condition.

PRESUMPTIVE EVIDENCE. Any evidence which is not direct and positive. 1 Starkie, Ev. 558. The proof of facts from which, with more or less certainty, according to the experience of mankind of their more or less universal connection, the existence of other facts can be deduced. 2 Saund. Pl. & Ev. 673. The evidence afforded by circumstances, from which, if unexplained, the jury may or may not infer or presume other circumstances or facts. 1 Greenl. Ev. § 13.

When the conclusion of the existence of a principal fact does not follow necessarily from the facts proved, but is deduced from them by probable inference, the evidence is said to be presumptive, and the inference drawn, a presumption. Best, Pres. § 11.

Evidence of facts, admitting of explanation or contradiction, as distinguished from *conclusive* evidence. Burrill, Circ. Ev. 89.

PRESUMPTIVE HEIR. One who, if the ancestor should die immediately, would, under existing circumstances of things, be his heir, but whose right of inheritance may be defeated by the contingency of some nearer heir being born; as, a brother, who is the presumptive heir, may be defeated in the succession by the birth of a child to the ancestor. 2 Bl. Comm. 208.

PRESUMPTIVE TITLE. A barely presumptive title, which is of the very lowest order, arises out of the mere occupation or simple possession of property, (*jus possessionis*,) without any apparent right, or any pretense of right, to hold and continue such possession.

PRÊT. In French law. Loan. A contract by which one of the parties delivers an article to the other, to be used by the latter, on condition of his returning, after having used it, the same article in nature or an equivalent of the same species and quality. Duverger.

PRÊT A INTÉRÊT. In French law. Loan at interest. A contract by which one of the parties delivers to the other a sum of money, or commodities, or other movable or fungible things, to receive for their use a profit determined in favor of the lender. Duverger.

PRÊT À USAGE. In French law. Loan for use. A contract by which one of the parties delivers an article to the other, to be used by the latter, the borrower agreeing to return the specific article after having used it. Duverger. A contract identical with the *commodatum* (*q. v.*) of the civil law.

PRÊT DE CONSOMMATION. In French law. Loan for consumption. A contract by which one party delivers to the other a certain quantity of things, such as are consumed in the use, on the undertaking of the borrower to return to him an equal quantity of the same species and quality. Duverger. A contract identical with the *mutuum* (*q. v.*) of the civil law.

PRETENSE. See FALSE PRETENSE.

PRETENSED RIGHT. Where one is in possession of land, and another, who is out of possession, claims and sues for it. Here the pretensed right or title is said to be in him who so claims and sues for the same. Mod. Cas. 302.

PRETENSED TITLE STATUTE. The English statute 32 Hen. VIII. c. 9, § 2. It enacts that no one shall sell or purchase any pretended right or title to land, unless the vendor has received the profits thereof for one whole year before such grant, or has been in actual possession of the land, or of the reversion or remainder, on pain that both purchaser and vendor shall each forfeit the value of such land to the king and the prosecutor. See 4 Broom & H. Comm. 150.

PRETENSES. Allegations sometimes made in a bill in chancery for the purpose of negativing an anticipated defense. Hunt, Eq. pt. I. c. 1.

PRETENSION. In French law. The claim made to a thing which a party believes himself entitled to demand, but which is not admitted or adjudged to be his.

PRETER LEGAL. Not agreeable to law; exceeding the limits of law; not legal.

PRETERITION. In the civil law. The omission by a testator of some one of his heirs who is legally entitled to a portion of the inheritance.

PRETEXTS. In international law. Reasons alleged as justificatory, but which are so only in appearance, or which are even absolutely destitute of all foundation. The name of "pretexts" may likewise be applied to reasons which are in themselves true and well-founded, but, not being of sufficient importance for undertaking a war, [or other international act,] are made use of only to cover ambitious views. Vatt. Law Nat. bk. 3, c. 3, § 32.

PRETIUM. Lat. Price; cost; value; the price of an article sold.

PRETIUM AFFECTIONIS. An imaginary value put upon a thing by the fancy of the owner, and growing out of his attachment for the specific article, its associations, his sentiment for the donor, etc. Bell.

PRETIUM PERICULI. The price of the risk, *e. g.*, the premium paid on a policy of insurance; also the interest paid on money advanced on bottomry or respondentia.

PRETIUM SEPULCHRI. A mortuary, (*q. v.*)

Pretium succedit in locum rei. The price stands in the place of the thing sold. 1 Bouv. Inst. no. 939; 2 Bulst. 312.

PRETORIUM. In Scotch law. A courthouse, or hall of justice. 3 How. State Tr. 425.

PREVARICATION. In the civil law. Deceitful, crafty, or unfaithful conduct; particularly, such as is manifested in concealing a crime. Dig. 47, 15, 6.

In English law. A collusion between an informer and a defendant, in order to a feigned prosecution. Cowell. Also any secret abuse committed in a public office or private commission; also the willful concealment or misrepresentation of truth, by giving evasive or equivocating evidence.

PREVENT. To hinder or preclude. To stop or intercept the approach, access, or performance of a thing. Webster.

PREVENTION. In the civil law. The right of a judge to take cognizance of an action over which he has concurrent jurisdiction with another judge.

In canon law. The right which a superior person or officer has to lay hold of, claim, or transact an affair prior to an inferior one, to whom otherwise it more immediately belongs. Wharton.

PREVENTION OF CRIMES ACT. The statute 34 & 35 Vict. c. 112, passed for the purpose of securing a better supervision over habitual criminals. This act provides that a person who is for a second time convicted of crime may, on his second conviction, be subjected to police supervision for a period of seven years after the expiration of the punishment awarded him. Penalties are imposed on lodging-house keepers, etc., for harboring thieves or reputed thieves. There are also provisions relating to receivers of stolen property, and dealers in old metals who purchase the same in small quantities. This act repeals the habitual criminals act of 1869, (32 & 33 Vict. c. 99.) Brown.

PREVENTIVE JUSTICE. The system of measures taken by government with reference to the direct prevention of crime. It generally consists in obliging those persons whom there is probable ground to suspect of future misbehavior to give full assurance to the public that such offense as is apprehended shall not happen, by finding pledges or securities to keep the peace, or for their good behavior. See 4 Bl. Comm. 251; 4 Steph. Comm. 290.

PREVENTIVE SERVICE. The name given in England to the coast-guard, or armed police, forming a part of the customs service, and employed in the prevention and detection of smuggling.

Previous intentions are judged by subsequent acts. 4 Denio, 319, 320.

PREVIOUS QUESTION. In the procedure of parliamentary bodies, moving the "previous question" is a method of avoiding a direct vote on the main subject of discussion. It is described in May, Parl. Prac. 277.

PREVIOUSLY. An adverb of time, used in comparing an act or state named with another act or state, subsequent in order of time, for the purpose of asserting the priority of the first. 40 Iowa, 94.

PRICE. The consideration (usually in money) given for the purchase of a thing.

It is true that "price" generally means the sum of money which an article is sold for; but this is simply because property is generally sold for money, not because the word has necessarily such a restricted meaning. Among writers on political economy, who use terms with philosophical accuracy, the word "price" is not always or even generally used as denoting the moneyed equivalent of property sold. They generally treat and regard price as the equivalent or compensation, in whatever form received, for property sold. The Latin word from which "price" is derived sometimes means "reward," "value," "estimation," "equivalent." 54 N. Y. 177.

PRICE CURRENT. A list or enumeration of various articles of merchandise, with their prices, the duties, if any, payable thereon, when imported or exported, with the drawbacks occasionally allowed upon their exportation, etc. Wharton.

PRICKING FOR SHERIFFS. In England, when the yearly list of persons nominated for the office of sheriff is submitted to the queen, she takes a pin, and to insure impartiality, as it is said, she lets the point of it fall upon one of the three names nominated for each county, etc., and the person upon whose name it chances to fall is sheriff for the ensuing year. This is called "pricking for sheriffs." Atk. Sher. 18.

PRICKING NOTE. Where goods intended to be exported are put direct from the station of the warehouse into a ship alongside, the exporter fills up a document to authorize the receiving the goods on board. This document is called a "pricking note," from a practice of pricking holes in the paper corresponding with the number of packages counted into the ship. Hamel, Cust. 181.

PRIEST. A minister of a church. A person in the second order of the ministry, as distinguished from bishops and deacons.

PRIMA FACIE. Lat. At first sight; on the first appearance; on the face of it; so far as can be judged from the first disclosure; presumably.

A litigating party is said to have a *prima facie* case when the evidence in his favor is sufficiently strong for his opponent to be called on to answer it. A *prima facie* case, then, is one which is established by sufficient evidence, and can be overthrown only by rebutting evidence adduced on the other side. In some cases the only question to be considered is whether there is a *prima facie* case or no. Thus a grand jury are bound to find a true bill of indictment, if the evidence before them creates a *prima facie* case against the accused; and for this purpose, therefore, it is not necessary for them to hear the evidence for the defense. Mozley & Whitley.

PRIMA FACIE EVIDENCE. Such evidence as, in judgment of law, is sufficient to establish the fact, and, if not rebutted, remains sufficient for the purpose. 6 Pet. 632.

That which, not being inconsistent with the falsity of the hypothesis, nevertheless raises such a degree of probability in its favor that it must prevail if it be credited by the jury, unless it be rebutted, or the contrary proved. *Conclusive* evidence, on the other hand, is that which excludes, or at least tends to exclude, the possibility of the truth of any other hypothesis than the one attempted to be established. 1 Starkie, Ev. 544.

PRIMA TONSURA. The first mowing; a grant of a right to have the first crop of grass. 1 Chit. Pr. 181.

PRIMÆ IMPRESSIONIS. A case *primæ impressionis* (of the first impression) is a case of a new kind, to which no established principle of law or precedent directly applies, and which must be decided entirely by reason as distinguished from authority.

PRIMÆ PRECES. Lat. In the civil law. An imperial prerogative by which the emperor exercised the right of naming to the first prebend that became vacant after his accession, in every church of the empire. 1 Bl. Comm. 381.

PRIMAGE. In mercantile law. A small allowance or compensation payable to the master and mariners of a ship or vessel; to the former for the use of his cables and ropes to discharge the goods of the merchant; to the latter for lading and unlading in any port or haven. Abb. Shipp. 404.

PRIMARIA ECCLESIA. The mother church. 1 Steph. Comm. (7th Ed.) 118.

PRIMARY. First; principal; chief; leading.

PRIMARY ALLEGATION. The opening pleading in a suit in the ecclesiastical court. It is also called a "primary plea."

PRIMARY CONVEYANCES. Those by means whereof the benefit or estate is created or first arises; as distinguished from those whereby it may be enlarged, restrained, transferred, or extinguished. The term includes feoffment, gift, grant, lease, exchange, and partition, and is opposed to *derivative* conveyances, such as release, surrender, confirmation, etc. 2 Bl. Comm. 309.

PRIMARY ELECTION. An election by the voters of a ward, precinct, or other small district, belonging to a particular party, of representatives or delegates to a convention which is to meet and nominate the candidates of their party to stand at an approaching municipal or general election.

PRIMARY EVIDENCE. As opposed to secondary evidence, this means original or first-hand evidence; the best evidence that the nature of the case admits of; the evidence which is required in the first instance, and which must fail before secondary evidence can be admitted. Thus, an original document is primary evidence; a copy of it would be secondary.

That evidence which the nature of the case or question suggests as the proper means of ascertaining the truth.

PRIMARY OBLIGATION. An obligation which is the principal object of the contract. For example, the primary obligation of the seller is to deliver the thing sold, and to transfer the title to it. It is distinguished from the accessory or secondary obligation to pay damages for not doing so. 1 Bouv. Inst. no. 702.

PRIMARY POWERS. The principal authority given by a principal to his agent. It differs from "mediate powers." Story, Ag. § 58.

PRIMATE. A chief ecclesiastic; part of the style and title of an archbishop. Thus, the archbishop of Canterbury is styled "Primate of all England;" the archbishop of York is "Primate of England." Wharton.

PRIME. Fr. In French law. The price of the risk assumed by an insurer; premium of insurance. Emerig. Traite des Assur. c. 3, § 1, nn. 1, 2.

PRIME SERJEANT. The queen's first serjeant at law.

PRIMER. A law French word, signifying first; primary.

PRIMER ELECTION. A term used to signify first choice; *e. g.*, the right of the eldest coparcener to first choose a purpart.

PRIMER FINE. On suing out the writ or *præcipe* called a "writ of covenant," there was due to the crown, by ancient prerogative, a *primer fine*, or a noble for every five marks of land sued for. That was one-tenth of the annual value. 1 Steph. Comm. (7th Ed.) 560.

PRIMER SEISIN. In English law. The right which the king had, when any of his tenants died seised of a knight's fee, to receive of the heir, provided he were of full age, one whole year's profits of the lands, if they were in immediate possession; and half a year's profits, if the lands were in reversion, expectant on an estate for life. 2 Bl. Comm. 66.

PRIMICERIUS. In old English law. The first of any degree of men. 1 Mon. Angl. 838.

PRIMITIÆ. In English law. First fruits; the first year's whole profits of a spiritual preferment. 1 Bl. Comm. 284.

PRIMO BENEFICIO. Lat. A writ directing a grant of the first benefice in the sovereign's gift. Cowell.

Primo excutienda est verbi vis, ne sermonis vitio obstruatur oratio, sive lex sine argumentis. Co. Litt. 68. The full meaning of a word should be ascertained at the outset, in order that the sense may not be lost by defect of expression, and that the law be not without reasons.

PRIMO VENIENTI. Lat. To the one first coming. An executor anciently paid debts as they were presented, whether the assets were sufficient to meet all debts or not. Stim. Law Gloss.

PRIMOGENITURE. 1. The state of being the first-born among several children of the same parents; seniority by birth in the same family.

2. The superior or exclusive right possessed by the eldest son, and particularly, his right to succeed to the estate of his ancestor, in right of his seniority by birth, to the exclusion of younger sons.

PRIMOGENITUS. Lat. In old English law. A first-born or eldest son. Bract. fol. 33.

PRIMUM DECRETUM. Lat. In the canon law. The first decree; a preliminary decree granted on the non-appearance of a defendant, by which the plaintiff was put in possession of his goods, or of the thing itself which was demanded. Gilb. Forum Rom. 32, 33.

PRINCE. In a general sense, a sovereign; the ruler of a nation or state. More particularly, the son of a king or emperor, or the issue of a royal family; as princes of the blood. The chief of any body of men. Webster.

PRINCE OF WALES. The eldest son of the English sovereign. He is the heir-apparent to the crown.

PRINCEPS. In the civil law. The prince; the emperor.

Princeps et respublica ex justa causa possunt rem meam auferre. 12 Coke, 13. The prince and the republic, for a just cause, can take away my property.

Princeps legibus solutus est. The emperor is released from the laws; is not bound by the laws. Dig. 1, 3, 31.

Princeps mavult domesticos milites quam stipendiarios bellicis opponere casibus. Co. Litt. 69. A prince, in the chances of war, had better employ domestic than stipendiary troops.

PRINCES OF THE ROYAL BLOOD. In English law. The younger sons and daughters of the sovereign, and other branches of the royal family who are not in the immediate line of succession.

PRINCESS ROYAL. In English law. The eldest daughter of the sovereign. 3 Steph. Comm. 450.

PRINCIPAL. Chief; leading; highest in rank or degree; most important or considerable; primary; original; the source of authority or right.

In the law relating to real and personal property, "principal" is used as the correlative of "accessory," and denotes the more important or valuable subject, with which others are connected in a relation of dependence or subservience, or to which they are incident or appurtenant.

In criminal law. A chief actor or perpetrator, as distinguished from an "accessary." A principal in the first degree is he that is the actor or absolute perpetrator of the crime; and, in the second degree, he who is present, aiding and abetting the fact to be done. 4 Bl. Comm. 34.

All persons concerned in the commission of crime, whether it be felony or misdemeanor, and whether they directly commit the act constituting the offense, or aid and abet in its commission, though not present, are principals. Pen. Code Dak. § 27.

A criminal offender is either a principal or an accessary. A principal is either the actor (*i. e.*, the actual perpetrator of the crime) or else is present, aiding and abetting the fact to be done; an accessary is he who is not the chief actor in the offense, nor yet present at its performance, but is some way concerned therein, either before or after the fact committed. 1 Hale, P. C. 613, 618.

In the law of guaranty and suretyship. The principal is the person primarily liable, and for whose performance of his obligation the guarantor or surety has become bound.

In the law of agency. The employer or constitutor of an agent; the person who gives authority to an agent or attorney to do some act for him.

One who, being competent *sui juris* to do any act for his own benefit or on his own account, confides it to another person to do for him. 1 Domat, b. 1., tit. 15.

The term also denotes the capital sum of a debt or obligation, as distinguished from interest or other additions to it.

An heir-loom, mortuary, or corse-present. Wharton.

PRINCIPAL CHALLENGE. In practice. A challenge of a juror for a cause which carries with it, *prima facie*, evident marks of suspicion either of malice or favor; as that a juror is of kin to either party within the ninth degree; that he has an interest in the cause, etc. 3 Bl. Comm. 363.

A species of challenge to the array made on account of partiality or some default in the sheriff or his under-officer who arrayed the panel.

PRINCIPAL CONTRACT. One which contains the principal subject-matter of an agreement; one to which another engagement is accessory.

PRINCIPAL FACT. In the law of evidence. A fact sought and proposed to be proved by evidence of other facts (termed "evidentiary facts") from which it is to be deduced by inference. A fact which is the principal and ultimate object of an inquiry, and respecting the existence of which a definite belief is required to be formed. 3 Benth. Jud. Ev. 3; Burrill, Circ. Ev. 3, 119.

PRINCIPAL OBLIGATION. That obligation which arises from the principal object of the engagement which has been contracted between the parties. Poth. Obl. no. 182. One to which is appended an accessory or subsidiary obligation.

PRINCIPALIS. Lat. Principal; a principal debtor; a principal in a crime.

Principalis debet semper excuti antequam perveniatur ad fideijussores. The principal should always be exhausted before coming upon the sureties. 2 Inst. 19.

Principia data sequuntur concomitantia. Given principles are followed by their concomitants.

Principia probant, non probantur. Principles prove; they are not proved. 3 Coke, 50*a*. Fundamental principles require no proof; or, in Lord Coke's words, "they ought to be approved, because they cannot be proved." Id.

Principiis obsta. Withstand beginnings; oppose a thing in its early stages, if you would do so with success.

Principiorum non est ratio. There is no reasoning of principles; no argument is required to prove fundamental rules. 2 Bulst. 239.

Principium est potissima pars cujusque rei. 10 Coke, 49. The principle of anything is its most powerful part.

PRINCIPLE. In patent law, the principle of a machine is the particular means of producing a given result by a mechanical contrivance. 5 McLean, 44, 63.

The *principle* of a machine means the *modus operandi*, or that which applies, modifies, or combines mechanical powers to produce a certain result; and, so far, a principle, if new in its application to a useful purpose, may be patentable. See 1 Mason, 470.

PRINCIPLES. Fundamental truths or doctrines of law; comprehensive rules or doctrines which furnish a basis or origin for others; settled rules of action, procedure, or legal determination.

PRINTING. The art of impressing letters; the art of making books or papers by impressing legible characters.

PRIOR. The chief of a convent; next in dignity to an abbot.

PRIOR PETENS. The person first applying.

Prior tempore potior jure. He who is first in time is preferred in right. Co. Litt. 14*a*; Broom, Max. 354, 358.

PRIORI PETENTI. To the person first applying. In probate practice, where there are several persons equally entitled to a grant of administration, (*e. g.*, next of kin of the same degree,) the rule of the court is to make the grant *priori petenti*, to the first applicant. Browne, Prob. Pr. 174; Coote, Prob. Pr. 173, 180.

PRIORITY. A legal preference or precedence. When two persons have similar rights in respect of the same subject-matter, but one is entitled to exercise his right to the exclusion of the other, he is said to have priority.

In old English law. An antiquity of tenure, in comparison with one not so ancient. Cowell.

PRISAGE. An ancient hereditary revenue of the crown, consisting in the right to take a certain quantity from cargoes of wine imported into England. In Edward I.'s reign it was converted into a pecuniary duty called "butlerage." 2 Steph. Comm. 561.

PRISE. Fr. In French law. Prize; captured property. Ord. Mar. liv. 3, tit. 9.

PRISEL EN AUTER LIEU. L. Fr. A taking in another place. A plea in abatement in the action of replevin. 2 Ld. Raym. 1016, 1017.

PRISO. A prisoner taken in war.

PRISON. A public building for the confinement or safe custody of persons, whether as a punishment imposed by the law or otherwise in the course of the administration of justice.

PRISON BOUNDS. The limits of the territory surrounding a prison, within which an imprisoned debtor, who is out on bonds, may go at will. See GAOL LIBERTIES.

PRISON-BREAKING. The common-law offense of one who, being lawfully in custody, escapes from the place where he is confined, by the employment of force and violence. This offense is to be distinguished from "rescue," (*q. v.*,) which is a deliverance of a prisoner from lawful custody by a third person. 2 Bish. Crim. Law, § 1065.

PRISONAM FRANGENTIBUS, STATUTE DE. The English statute 1 Edw. II. St. 2, (in Rev. St. 23 Edw. I.,) a still unrepealed statute, whereby it is felony for a felon to break prison, but misdemeanor only for a misdemeanant to do so. 1 Hale, P. C. 612.

PRISONER. One who is deprived of his liberty; one who is against his will kept in confinement or custody.

A person restrained of his liberty upon any action, civil or criminal, or upon commandment. Cowell.

A person on trial for crime. "The *prisoner* at the bar." The jurors are told to "look upon the *prisoner*." The court, after passing sentence, gives orders to "remove the *prisoner*."

PRISONER AT THE BAR. An accused person, while on trial before the court, is so called.

PRISONER OF WAR. One who has been captured in war while fighting in the army of the public enemy.

PRIST. L. Fr. Ready. In the old forms of oral pleading, this term expressed a tender or joinder of issue.

Prius vitiis laboravimus, nunc legibus. 4 Inst. 76. We labored first with vices, now with laws.

PRIVATE. Affecting or belonging to private individuals, as distinct from the public generally. Not official.

PRIVATE ACT. A statute operating only upon particular persons and private concerns, and of which the courts are not bound to take notice.

PRIVATE AGENT. An agent acting for an individual in his private affairs; as distinguished from a *public* agent, who represents the government in some administrative capacity.

PRIVATE BILL. All legislative bills which have for their object some particular or private interest are so termed, as distinguished from such as are for the benefit of the whole community, which are thence termed "public bills."

PRIVATE BILL OFFICE. An office of the English parliament where the business of obtaining private acts of parliament is conducted.

PRIVATE BOUNDARY. An artificial boundary, consisting of some monument or landmark set up by the hand of man to mark the beginning or direction of a boundary line of lands.

PRIVATE BRIDGE. One which is not open to the use of the public generally, and does not form part of the highway, but is reserved for the use of those who erected it, or their successors, and their licensees.

PRIVATE CARRIER. The distinction between a *common* carrier and a *private* or special carrier is that the former holds himself out in common, that is, to all persons who choose to employ him, as ready to carry for hire; while the latter agrees, in some special case, with some private individual, to carry for hire. 37 N. Y. 342.

PRIVATE CHAPEL. Chapels owned by private persons, and used by themselves and their families, are called "private," as opposed to chapels of ease, which are built for the accommodation of particular districts within a parish, in ease of the original parish church. 2 Steph. Comm. 745.

PRIVATE CORPORATION. One which is founded by and composed of private persons, or in which private persons own all the stock; *e. g.*, a college, hospital, bank, railroad, manufacturing company, etc.

PRIVATE EASEMENT. An easement, the enjoyment of which is restricted to one or more individuals; as distinguished from a *public* easement, the enjoyment of which belongs to the community generally.

PRIVATE EXAMINATION. An examination or interrogation, by a magistrate, of a married woman who is grantor in a deed or other conveyance, held out of the presence of her husband, for the purpose of ascertaining whether her will in the matter is free and unconstrained.

PRIVATE LAW. As used in contradistinction to public law, the term means all that part of the law which is administered between citizen and citizen, or which is concerned with the definition, regulation, and enforcement of rights in cases where both the person in whom the right inheres and the person upon whom the obligation is incident are private individuals. See PUBLIC LAW.

PRIVATE NUISANCE. Anything done to the injury or annoyance of the lands, tenements, or hereditaments of another. 3 Bl. Comm. 216.

PRIVATE PERSON. An individual who is not the incumbent of an office.

PRIVATE PROPERTY, as protected from being taken for public uses, is such property as belongs absolutely to an individual, and of which he has the exclusive right of disposition; property of a specific, fixed, and tangible nature, capable of being had in possession and transmitted to another, such as houses, lands, and chattels. 29 Miss. 21, 32.

PRIVATE RIGHTS. Those rights which appertain to a particular individual or individuals, and relate either to the person, or to personal or real property. 1 Chit. Gen. Pr. 3.

PRIVATE STATUTE. A statute which operates only upon particular persons, and private concerns. 1 Bl. Comm. 86. An act which relates to certain individuals, or to particular classes of men. Dwar. St. 629.

PRIVATE WAY. A right which a person has of passing over the land of another.

PRIVATE WRONGS. The violation of public or private rights, when considered in reference to the injury sustained by the individual, and consequently as subjects for civil redress or compensation. 3 Steph. Comm. 356.

PRIVATEER. A vessel owned, equipped, and armed by one or more private individuals, and duly commissioned by a belligerent power to go on cruises and make war upon the enemy, usually by preying on his commerce.

Privatio præsupponit habitum. 2 Rolle, 419. A deprivation presupposes a possession.

PRIVATION. A taking away or withdrawing. Co. Litt. 239.

Privatis pactionibus non dubium est non lædi jus cæterorum. There is no doubt that the rights of others [third parties] cannot be prejudiced by private agreements. Dig. 2, 15, 3, pr.; Broom, Max. 697.

Privatorum conventio juri publico non derogat. The agreement of private individuals does not derogate from the public right, [law.] Dig. 50, 17, 45, 1; 9 Coke, 141; Broom, Max. 695.

PRIVATUM. Lat. Private. *Privatum jus*, private law. Inst. 1, 1, 4.

Privatum commodum publico cedit. Private good yields to public. Jenk. Cent. p. 223, case 80. The interest of an individual should give place to the public good. Id.

Privatum incommodum publico bono pensatur. Private inconvenience is made up for by public benefit. Jenk. Cent. p. 85, case 65; Broom, Max. 7.

PRIVEMENT ENCEINTE. Fr. Pregnant privately. The term is applied to a woman who is pregnant, but not yet quick with child.

PRIVIES. Persons connected together, or having a mutual interest in the same action or thing, by some relation other than that of actual contract between them; persons whose interest in an estate is derived from the contract or conveyance of others.

Those who are partakers or have an interest in any action or thing, or any relation to another. They are of six kinds:

(1) Privies of blood; such as the heir to his ancestor.

(2) Privies in representation; as executors or administrators to their deceased testator or intestate.

(3) Privies in estate; as grantor and grantee, lessor and lessee, assignor and assignee, etc.

(4) Privities, in respect of contract, are person-

a. privities, and extend only to the persons of the lessor and lessee.

(5) Privies in respect of estate and contract: as where the lessee assigns his interest, but the contract between lessor and lessee continues, the lessor not having accepted of the assignee.

(6) Privies in law; as the lord by escheat, a tenant by the curtesy, or in dower, the incumbent of a benefice, a husband suing or defending in right of his wife, etc. Wharton.

PRIVIGNA. Lat. In the civil law. A step-daughter.

PRIVIGNUS. Lat. In the civil law. A son of a husband or wife by a former marriage; a step-son. Calvin.

PRIVILEGE. A particular and peculiar benefit or advantage enjoyed by a person, company, or class, beyond the common advantages of other citizens. An exceptional or extraordinary power or exemption. A right, power, franchise, or immunity held by a person or class, against or beyond the course of the law.

Privilege is an exemption from some burden or attendance, with which certain persons are indulged, from a supposition of law that the stations they fill, or the offices they are engaged in, are such as require all their time and care, and that, therefore, without this indulgence, it would be impracticable to execute such offices to that advantage which the public good requires. 1 Pin. 118.

In the civil law. A right which the nature of a debt gives to a creditor, and which entitles him to be preferred before other creditors. Civil Code La. art. 3186.

In maritime law. An allowance to the master of a ship of the same general nature with primage, being compensation, or rather a gratuity, customary in certain trades, and which the law assumes to be a fair and equitable allowance, because the contract on both sides is made under the knowledge of such usage by the parties. 3 Chit. Commer. Law, 431.

PRIVILEGE FROM ARREST. A privilege extended to certain classes of persons, either by the rules of international law, the policy of the law, or the necessities of justice or of the administration of government, whereby they are exempted from arrest on civil process, and, in some cases, on criminal charges, either permanently, as in the case of a foreign minister and his suite, or temporarily, as in the case of members of the legislature, parties and witnesses engaged in a particular suit, etc.

PRIVILEGE, WRIT OF. A process to enforce or maintain a privilege. Cowell.

PRIVILEGED COMMUNICATION. **In the law of evidence.** A communication made to a counsel, solicitor, or attorney, in professional confidence, and which he is not permitted to divulge; otherwise called a "confidential communication." 1 Starkie, Ev. 185.

In the law of libel and slander. A defamatory statement made to another in pursuance of a duty, political, judicial, social, or personal, so that an action for libel or slander will not lie, though the statement be false, unless in the last two cases actual malice be proved in addition. Stim. Law Gloss.

PRIVILEGED COPYHOLDS. In English law. Those copyhold estates which are said to be held according to the custom of the manor, and not *at the will of the lord*, as common copyholds are. They include customary freeholds and ancient demesnes. 1 Crabb, Real Prop. p. 709, § 919.

PRIVILEGED DEBTS. Those which an executor or administrator may pay in preference to others; such as funeral expenses, servants' wages, and doctors' bills during last sickness, etc.

PRIVILEGED DEED. In Scotch law. An instrument, for example, a testament, in the execution of which certain statutory formalities usually required are dispensed with, either from necessity or expediency. Ersk. Inst. 3, 2, 22; Bell.

PRIVILEGED VILLENAGE. In old English law. A species of villenage in which the tenants held by certain and determinate services; otherwise called "villein-socage." Bract. fol. 209. Now called "privileged copyhold," including the tenure in ancient demesne. 2 Bl. Comm. 99, 100.

Privilegia quæ re vera sunt in præjudicium reipublicæ, magis tamen habent speciosa frontispicia, et boni publici prætextum, quam bonæ et legales concessiones; sed prætextu liciti non debet admitti illictum. 11 Coke, 88. Privileges which are truly in prejudice of public good have, however, a more specious front and pretext of public good than good and legal grants; but, under pretext of legality, that which is illegal ought not to be admitted.

PRIVILEGIUM. In Roman law. A special constitution by which the Roman emperor conferred on some single person some anomalous or irregular right, or imposed upon some single person some anomalous or irregular obligation, or inflicted on some single person some anomalous or irregular punishment. When such *privilegia* conferred anomalous rights, they were styled "favorable." When they imposed anomalous obligations, or inflicted anomalous punishments, they were styled "odious." Aust. Jur. § 748.

In modern civil law, "*privilegium*" is said to denote, in its general sense, every peculiar right or favor granted by the law, contrary to the common rule. Mackeld. Rom. Law, § 197.

A species of lien or claim upon an article of property, not dependent upon possession, but continuing until either satisfied or released. Such is the lien, recognized by modern maritime law, of seamen upon the ship for their wages. 2 Pars. Mar. Law, 561.

PRIVILEGIUM CLERICALE. The benefit of clergy, (*q. v.*)

Privilegium est beneficium personale, et extinguitur cum persona. 3 Bulst. 8. A privilege is a personal benefit, and dies with the person.

Privilegium est quasi privata lex. 2 Bulst. 189. Privilege is, as it were, a private law.

Privilegium non valet contra rempublicam. Privilege is of no force against the commonwealth. Even necessity does not excuse, where the act to be done is against the commonwealth. Bac. Max. p. 32, in reg. 5.

PRIVILEGIUM, PROPERTY PROPTER. A qualified property in animals *feræ naturæ; i. e.*, a privilege of hunting, taking, and killing them, in exclusion of others. 2 Bl. Comm. 394; 2 Steph. Comm. 9.

PRIVITY. The term "privity" means mutual or successive relationship to the same rights of property. The executor is in privity with the testator, the heir with the ancestor, the assignee with the assignor, the donee with the donor, and the lessee with the lessor. 41 Iowa, 516.

Privity of *contract* is that connection or relationship which exists between two or more contracting parties. It is essential to the maintenance of an action on any contract that there should subsist a privity between the plaintiff and defendant in respect of the matter sued on. Brown.

Privity of *estate* is that which exists between lessor and lessee, tenant for life and remainder-man or reversioner, etc., and their respective assignees, and between joint tenants and coparceners. Privity of estate is required for a release by enlargement. Sweet.

Privity of *blood* exists between an heir and his ancestor, (privity in blood inheritable,) and between coparceners. This privity was formerly of importance in the law of descent cast. Co. Litt. 271*a*, 242*a*; 2 Inst. 516; 8 Coke, 42*b*.

PRIVY. A person who is in privity with another. See PRIVIES; PRIVITY.

PRIVY COUNCIL. In English law. The principal council of the sovereign, composed of the cabinet ministers, and other persons chosen by the king or queen as privy councillors. 2 Steph. Comm. 479, 480. The judicial committee of the privy council acts as a court of ultimate appeal in various cases.

PRIVY COUNCILLOR. A member of the privy council.

PRIVY PURSE. In English law. The income set apart for the sovereign's personal use.

PRIVY SEAL. In English law. A seal used in making out grants or letters patent, preparatory to their passing under the great seal. 2 Bl. Comm. 347.

PRIVY SIGNET. In English law. The signet or seal which is first used in making out grants and letters patent, and which is always in the custody of the principal secretary of state. 2 Bl. Comm. 347.

PRIVY TOKEN. A false mark or sign, forged object, counterfeited letter, key, ring, etc., used to deceive persons, and thereby fraudulently get possession of property. St. 33 Hen. VIII. c. 1.

A false privy token is a false private document or sign, not such as is calculated to deceive men generally, but designed to defraud one or more individuals. Cheating by such false token was not indictable at common law. Pub. St. Mass. 1882, p. 1294.

PRIVY VERDICT. In practice. A verdict given privily to the judge out of court, but which was of no force unless afterwards affirmed by a public verdict given openly in court. 3 Bl. Comm. 377. Now disused.

PRIZE. In admiralty law. A vessel or cargo, belonging to one of two belligerent powers, apprehended or forcibly captured at sea by a war-vessel or privateer of the other belligerent, and claimed as enemy's property, and therefore liable to appropriation and condemnation under the laws of war. See 1 C. Rob. Adm. 228.

Captured property regularly condemned by the sentence of a competent prize court. 1 Kent, Comm. 102.

In contracts. Anything offered as a reward of contest; a reward offered to the person who, among several persons or among the public at large, shall first (or best) perform a certain undertaking or accomplish certain conditions.

PRIZE COURTS. Courts having jurisdiction to adjudicate upon captures made at sea in time of war, and to condemn the captured property as prize if lawfully subject to that sentence. In England, the admiralty courts have jurisdiction as prize courts, distinct from the jurisdiction on the instance side. In America, the federal district courts have jurisdiction in cases of prize. 1 Kent, Comm. 101-103, 353-360.

PRIZE GOODS. Goods which are taken on the high seas, *jure belli*, out of the hands of the enemy. 9 Cranch, 244, 284.

PRIZE LAW. The system of laws and rules applicable to the capture of prize at sea; its condemnation, rights of the captors, distribution of the proceeds, etc.

PRIZE MONEY. A dividend from the proceeds of a captured vessel, etc., paid to the captors.

PRO. For; in respect of; on account of; in behalf of. The introductory word of many Latin phrases.

PRO AND CON. For and against. A phrase descriptive of the presentation of arguments or evidence on both sides of a disputed question.

PRO BONO ET MALO. For good and ill; for advantage and detriment.

PRO BONO PUBLICO. For the public good; for the welfare of the whole.

PRO CONFESSO. For confessed; as confessed. A term applied to a bill in equity, and the decree founded upon it, where no answer is made to it by the defendant. 1 Barb. Ch. Pr. 96.

PRO CONSILIO. For counsel given. An annuity *pro consilio* amounts to a condition, but in a feoffment or lease for life, etc., it is the consideration, and does not amount to a condition; for the state of the land by the feoffment is executed, and the grant of the annuity is executory. Plowd. 412.

PRO CORPORE REGNI. In behalf of the body of the realm. Hale, Com. Law, 32.

PRO DEFECTU EMPTORUM. For want (failure) of purchasers.

PRO DEFECTU EXITUS. For, or in case of, default of issue. 2 Salk. 620.

PRO DEFECTU HÆREDIS. For want of an heir.

PRO DEFECTU JUSTITIÆ. For defect or want of justice. Fleta, lib. 2, c. 62, § 2.

PRO DEFENDENTE. For the defendant. Commonly abbreviated "*pro def.*"

PRO DERELICTO. As derelict or abandoned. A species of usucaption in the civil law. Dig. 41, 7.

PRO DIGNITATE REGALI. In consideration of the royal dignity. 1 Bl. Comm. 223.

PRO DIVISO. As divided; *i. e.*, in severalty.

PRO DOMINO. As master or owner; in the character of master. Calvin.

PRO DONATO. As a gift; as in case of gift; by title of gift. A species of usucaption in the civil law. Dig. 41, 6. See Id. 5, 3, 13, 1.

PRO DOTE. As a dowry; by title of dowry. A species of usucaption. Dig. 41, 9. See Id. 5, 3, 13, 1.

PRO EMTORE. As a purchaser; by the title of a purchaser. A species of usucaption. Dig. 41, 4. See Id. 5, 3, 13, 1.

PRO EO QUOD. In pleading. For this that. This is a phrase of affirmation, and is sufficiently direct and positive for introducing a material averment. 1 Saund. 117, no. 4; 2 Chit. Pl. 369-393.

PRO FACTI. For the fact; as a fact; considered or held as a fact.

PRO FALSO CLAMORE SUO. A nominal amercement of a plaintiff for *his false claim*, which used to be inserted in a judgment for the defendant. Obsolete.

PRO FORMA. As a matter of form. 3 East, 232; 2 Kent, Comm. 245.

PRO HAC VICE. For this turn; for this one particular occasion.

PRO ILLA VICE. For that turn. 3 Wils. 233, arg.

PRO INDEFENSO. As undefended; as making no defense. A phrase in old practice. Fleta, lib. 1, c. 41, § 7.

PRO INDIVISO. As undivided; in common. The joint occupation or possession of lands. Thus, lands held by coparceners are held *pro indiviso;* that is, they are held undividedly, neither party being entitled to any specific portions of the land so held, but both or all having a joint interest in the undivided whole. Cowell.

PRO INTERESSE SUO. According to his interest; to the extent of his interest. Thus, a third party may be allowed to intervene in a suit *pro interesse suo.*

PRO LÆSIONE FIDEI. For breach of faith. 3 Bl. Comm. 52.

PRO LEGATO. As a legacy; by the title of a legacy. A species of usucaption. Dig. 41, 8.

PRO MAJORI CAUTELA. For greater caution; by way of additional security. Usually applied to some act done, or some clause inserted in an instrument, which may not be really necessary, but which will serve to put the matter beyond any question.

PRO NON SCRIPTO. As not written; as though it had not been written; as never written. Ambl. 139.

PRO OPERE ET LABORE. For work and labor. 1 Comyns, 18.

PRO PARTIBUS LIBERANDIS. An ancient writ for partition of lands between co-heirs. Reg. Orig. 316.

PRO POSSE SUO. To the extent of his power or ability. Bract. fol. 109.

PRO POSSESSORE. As a possessor; by title of a possessor. Dig. 41, 5. See Id. 5, 3, 13.

Pro possessore habetur qui dolo injuriave desiit possidere. He is esteemed a possessor whose possession has been disturbed by fraud or injury. Off. Exec. 166.

PRO QUERENTE. For the plaintiff.

PRO RATA. Proportionately; according to a certain rate, percentage, or proportion. Thus, the creditors (of the same class) of an insolvent estate are to be paid *pro rata;* that is, each is to receive a dividend bearing the same ratio to the whole amount of his claim that the aggregate of assets bears to the aggregate of debts.

PRO RE NATA. For the affair immediately in hand; adapted to meet the particular occasion. Thus, a course of judicial action adopted under pressure of the exigencies of the affair in hand, rather than in conformity to established precedents, is said to be taken *pro re nata.*

PRO SALUTE ANIMÆ. For the good of his soul. All prosecutions in the ecclesiastical courts are *pro salute animæ;* hence it will not be a temporal damage founding an action for slander that the words spoken put any one in danger of such a suit. 3 Steph. Comm. (7th. Ed.) 309*n*, 437; 4 Steph. Comm. 207.

PRO SE. For himself; in his own behalf; in person.

PRO SOCIO. For a partner; the name of an action in behalf of a partner. A title of the civil law. Dig. 17, 2; Cod. 4, 37.

PRO SOLIDO. For the whole; as one; jointly; without division. Dig. 50, 17, 141, 1.

PRO TANTO. For so much; for as much as may be; as far as it goes.

PRO TEMPORE. For the time being; temporarily; provisionally.

PROAMITA. Lat. In the civil law. A great paternal aunt; the sister of one's grandfather.

PROAMITA MAGNA. Lat. In the civil law. A great-great-aunt.

PROAVIA. Lat. In the civil law. A great-grandmother. Inst. 3, 6, 3; Dig. 38, 10, 1, 5.

PROAVUNCULUS. Lat. In the civil law. A great-grandfather's brother. Inst. 3, 6, 3; Bract. fol. 68*b*.

PROAVUS. Lat. In the civil law. A great-grandfather. Inst. 3, 6, 1; Bract. fols. 67, 68.

PROBABILITY. Likelihood; appearance of truth; verisimilitude. The likelihood of a proposition or hypothesis being true, from its conformity to reason or experience, or from superior evidence or arguments adduced in its favor.

PROBABLE. Having the appearance of truth; having the character of probability; appearing to be founded in reason or experience.

PROBABLE CAUSE. "Probable cause" may be defined to be an apparent state of facts found to exist upon reasonable inquiry, (that is, such inquiry as the given case renders convenient and proper,) which would induce a reasonably intelligent and prudent man to believe, in a criminal case, that the accused person had committed the crime charged, or, in a civil case, that a cause of action existed. 23 Ind. 67. See, also, 111 Mass. 497; 44 Vt. 124; 9 Hun, 178.

"Probable cause," in malicious prosecution, means the existence of such facts and circumstances as would excite the belief in a reasonable mind, acting on the facts within the knowledge of the prosecutor, that the person charged was guilty of the crime for which he was prosecuted. 24 How. 544.

PROBABLE EVIDENCE. Presumptive evidence is so called, from its foundation in probability.

PROBABLE REASONING. In the law of evidence. Reasoning founded on the probability of the fact or proposition sought to be proved or shown; reasoning in which the mind exercises a discretion in deducing a conclusion from premises. Burrill.

Probandi necessitas incumbit illi qui agit. The necessity of proving lies with him who sues. Inst. 2, 20, 4. In other words, the burden of proof of a proposition is upon him who advances it affirmatively.

PROBARE. In Saxon law. To claim a thing as one's own. Jacob.

In modern law language. To make proof, as in the term "*onus probandi,*" the burden or duty of making proof.

PROBATE. The act or process of proving a will. The proof before an ordinary, surrogate, register, or other duly authorized person that a document produced before him for official recognition and registration, and alleged to be the last will and testament of a certain deceased person, is such in reality.

The copy of the will, made out in parchment or due form, under the seal of the ordinary or court of probate, and usually delivered to the executor or administrator of the deceased, together with a certificate of the will's having been proved, is also commonly called the "probate."

In the canon law, "probate" consisted of *probatio,* the proof of the will by the executor, and *approbatio,* the approbation given by the ecclesiastical judge to the proof. 4 Reeve, Eng. Law, 77.

The term is used, particularly in Pennsylvania, but not in a strictly technical sense, to designate the proof of his claim made by a non-resident plaintiff (when the same is on book-account, promissory note, etc.) who swears to the correctness and justness of the same, and that it is due, before a notary or other officer in his own state; also of the copy or statement of such claim filed in court, with the jurat of such notary attached.

PROBATE, DIVORCE, AND ADMIRALTY DIVISION. That division of the English high court of justice which exercises jurisdiction in matters formerly within the exclusive cognizance of the court of probate, the court for divorce and matrimonial causes, and the high court of admiralty. (Judicature Act 1873, § 34.) It consists of two judges, one of whom is called the "President." The existing judges are the judge of the old probate and divorce courts, who is president of the division, and the judge of the old admiralty court, and of a number of registrars. Sweet.

PROBATE DUTY. A tax laid by government on every will admitted to probate, and payable out of the decedent's estate.

PROBATIO. Lat. Proof; more particularly direct, as distinguished from indirect or circumstantial, evidence.

PROBATIO MORTUA. Dead proof; that is proof by inanimate objects, such as deeds or other written evidence.

PROBATIO PLENA. In the civil law. Full proof; proof by two witnesses, or a public instrument. Hallifax, Civil Law, b. 3, c. 9, no. 25; 3 Bl. Comm. 370.

PROBATIO SEMI-PLENA. In the civil law. Half-full proof; half-proof. Proof by one witness, or a private instrument. Hallifax, Civil Law, b. 3, c. 9, no. 25; 3 Bl. Comm. 370.

PROBATIO VIVA. Living proof; that is, proof by the mouth of living witnesses.

PROBATION. The act of proving; evidence; proof. Also trial; test; the time of novitiate. Used in the latter sense in the monastic orders.

PROBATIONER. One who is upon trial.

Probationes debent esse evidentes, scil. perspicuæ et faciles intelligi. Co. Litt. 283. Proofs ought to be evident, to-wit, perspicuous and easily understood.

Probatis extremis, præsumuntur media. The extremes being proved, the intermediate proceedings are presumed. 1 Greenl. Ev. § 20.

PROBATIVE. In the law of evidence. Having the effect of proof; tending to prove, or actually proving.

PROBATIVE FACT. In the law of evidence. A fact which actually has the effect of proving a fact sought; an evidentiary fact. 1 Benth. Ev. 18.

PROBATOR. In old English law. Strictly, an accomplice in felony who to save himself confessed the fact, and charged or accused any other as principal or accessary, against whom he was bound to make good his charge. It also signified an approver, or one who undertakes to prove a crime charged upon another. Jacob.

PROBATORY TERM. This name is given, in the practice of the English admiralty courts, to the space of time allowed for the taking of testimony in an action, after issue formed.

PROBATUM EST. It is tried or proved.

PROBUS ET LEGALIS HOMO. A good and lawful man. A phrase particularly applied to a juror or witness who was free from all exception. 3 Bl. Comm. 102.

PROCEDENDO. In practice. A writ by which a cause which has been removed from an inferior to a superior court by *certiorari* or otherwise is sent down again to the same court, *to be proceeded in* there, where it appears to the superior court that it was removed on insufficient grounds. Cowell; 1 Tidd, Pr. 408, 410.

A writ which issued out of the common-law jurisdiction of the court of chancery, when judges of any subordinate court delayed the parties, for that they would not give judgment either on the one side or on the other, when they ought so to do. In such a case, a writ of *procedendo ad judicium* was awarded, commanding the inferior court in the sovereign's name to proceed to give judgment, but without specifying any particular judgment. Wharton.

A writ by which the commission of a justice of the peace is revived, after having been suspended. 1 Bl. Comm. 353.

PROCEDENDO ON AID PRAYER. If one pray in aid of the crown in real action, and aid be granted, it shall be awarded that he sue to the sovereign in chancery, and the justices in the common pleas shall stay until this writ of *procedendo de loquela* come to them. So, also, on a personal action. New Nat. Brev. 154.

PROCEDURE. This word is commonly opposed to the sum of legal principles constituting the substance of the law, and denotes the body of rules, whether of practice or of pleading, whereby rights are effectuated through the successful application of the proper remedies. It is also generally distinguished from the law of evidence. Brown.

The law of procedure is what is now commonly termed by jurists "adjective law," (*q. v.*)

PROCEED. A stipulation not to proceed against a party is an agreement not to sue. To sue a man is to proceed against him. 57 Ga. 140.

PROCEEDING. In a general sense, the form and manner of conducting juridical business before a court or judicial officer; regular and orderly progress in form of law; including all possible steps in an action from its commencement to the execution of judgment. In a more particular sense, any application to a court of justice, however made, for aid in the enforcement of rights, for relief, for redress of injuries, for damages, or for any remedial object.

Proceedings are commonly classed as "ordinary" or "summary." The former term denotes the regular and formal method of carrying on an action or suit according to the course of the common law. The latter designates a method of disposing of a suit or prosecution off-hand, and without the intervention of a jury, or otherwise contrary to the course of the common law.

In New York the Code of Practice divides remedies into "actions" and "special proceedings." An action is an ordinary proceeding in a court of justice, by which one party prosecutes another party for the enforcement or protection of a right, the redress or prevention of a wrong, or the punishment of a public offense. Every other remedy is a special proceeding. Code N. Y. § 2.

In Louisiana there is a third kind of proceeding, known by the name of "executory proceeding," which is resorted to in the following cases: When the creditor's right arises from an act importing a confession of judgment, and which contains a privilege or mortgage in his favor; or when the creditor demands the execution of a judgment which has been rendered by a tribunal different from that within whose jurisdiction the execution is sought. Code Prac. La. art. 732.

PROCEEDINGS. In practice. The steps or measures taken in the course of an action, including *all* that are taken. The proceedings of a suit embrace *all* matters that occur in its progress judicially. 6 N. Y. 320.

PROCEEDS. Issues; produce; money obtained by the sale of property; the sum, amount, or value of property sold or converted into money or into other property. See 35 N. Y. Super. Ct. 208.

PROCERES. Nobles; lords. The house of lords in England is called, in Latin, "*Domus Procerum.*"

PROCÈS VERBAL. In French law. A written report, which is signed, setting forth a statement of facts. This term is applied to the report proving the meeting and the resolutions passed at a meeting of shareholders, or to the report of a commission to take testimony. It can also be applied to the statement drawn up by a *huissier* in relation to any facts which one of the parties to a suit can be interested in proving; for instance, the sale of a counterfeited object. Statements, drawn up by other competent authorities, of misdemeanors or other criminal acts, are also called by this name. Arg. Fr. Merc. Law, 570.

PROCESS. In practice. This word is generally defined to be the means of compelling the defendant in an action to appear in court. And when actions were commenced by original writ, instead of, as at present, by writ of summons, the method of compelling the defendant to appear was by what was termed "original process," being founded on the original writ, and so called also to distinguish it from "mesne" or "intermediate" process, which was some writ or process which issued during the progress of the suit. The word "process," however, as now commonly understood, signifies those formal instruments called "writs." The word "process" is in common-law practice frequently applied to the writ of summons, which is the instrument now in use for commencing personal actions. But in its more comprehensive signification it includes not only the writ of summons, but all other writs which may be issued during the progress of an action. Those writs which are used to carry the judgments of the courts into effect, and which are termed "writs of execution," are also commonly denominated "final process," because they usually issue at the end of a suit. Brown.

In the practice of the English privy council in ecclesiastical appeals, "process" means an official copy of the whole proceedings and proofs of the court below, which is transmitted to the registry of the court of appeal by the registrar of the court below in obedience to an order or requisition requiring him so to do, called a "monition for process," issued by the court of appeal. Macph. Jud. Com. 173.

In patent law. A means or method employed to produce a certain result or effect, either by chemical action, by the operation or application of some element or power of nature, or of one substance to another, irrespective of any machine or mechanical device. In this sense, a "process" is patentable. 15 How. 267; 94 U. S. 788.

PROCESS OF INTERPLEADER. A means of determining the right to property claimed by each of two or more persons, which is in the possession of a third.

PROCESS OF LAW. See DUE PROCESS OF LAW.

PROCESS ROLL. In practice. A roll used for the entry of process to save the statute of limitations. 1 Tidd, Pr. 161, 162.

PROCESSIONING. A proceeding to determine boundaries, in use in some of the United States, similar in all respects to the English perambulation, (*q. v.*)

PROCESSUM CONTINUANDO. In English practice. A writ for the continuance of process after the death of the chief justice or other justices in the commission of *oyer* and *terminer*. Reg. Orig. 128.

Processus legis est gravis vexatio; executio legis coronat opus. The process of the law is a grievous vexation; the execution of the law crowns the work. Co. Litt. 289*b*. The proceedings in an action while in progress are burdensome and vexatious; the execution, being the end and object of the action, crowns the labor, or rewards it with success.

PROCHEIN. L. Fr. Next. A term somewhat used in modern law, and more frequently in the old law; as *prochein ami*, *prochein cousin*. Co. Litt. 10.

PROCHEIN AMI. L. Fr. Next friend. As an infant cannot legally sue in his own name, the action must be brought by his *pro-*

chein ami; that is, some friend (not being his guardian) who will appear as plaintiff in his name.

PROCHEIN AVOIDANCE. L. Fr. Next vacancy. A power to appoint a minister to a church when it shall next become void.

PROCHRONISM. An error in chronology; dating a thing before it happened.

PROCINCTUS. Lat. In the Roman law. A girding or preparing for battle. *Testamentum in procinctu,* a will made by a soldier, while girding himself, or preparing to engage in battle. Adams, Rom. Ant. 62; Calvin.

PROCLAIM. To promulgate; to announce; to publish, by governmental authority, intelligence of public acts or transactions or other matters important to be known by the people.

PROCLAMATION. The act of causing some state matters to be published or made generally known. A written or printed document in which are contained such matters, issued by proper authority. 3 Inst. 162; 1 Bl. Comm. 170.

The word "proclamation" is also used to express the public nomination made of any one to a high office; as, such a prince was *proclaimed* emperor.

In practice. The declaration made by the crier, by authority of the court, that something is about to be done.

In equity practice. Proclamation made by a sheriff upon a writ of attachment, summoning a defendant who has failed to appear personally to appear and answer the plaintiff's bill. 3 Bl. Comm. 444.

PROCLAMATION BY LORD OF MANOR. A proclamation made by the lord of a manor (thrice repeated) requiring the heir or devisee of a deceased copyholder to present himself, pay the fine, and be admitted to the estate; failing which appearance, the lord might seize the lands *quousque* (provisionally.)

PROCLAMATION OF EXIGENTS. In old English law. When an *exigent* was awarded, a writ of proclamation issued, at the same time, commanding the sheriff of the county wherein the defendant dwelt to make three proclamations thereof in places the most notorious, and most likely to come to his knowledge, a month before the outlawry should take place. 3 Bl. Comm. 284.

PROCLAMATION OF A FINE. The notice or proclamation which was made after the engrossment of a fine of lands, and which consisted in its being openly read in court sixteen times, viz., four times in the term in which it was made, and four times in each of the three succeeding terms, which, however, was afterwards reduced to one reading in each term. Cowell. See 2 Bl. Comm. 352.

PROCLAMATION OF REBELLION. In old English law. A proclamation to be made by the sheriff commanding the attendance of a person who had neglected to obey a subpœna or attachment in chancery. If he did not surrender himself after this proclamation, a commission of rebellion issued. 3 Bl. Comm. 444.

PROCLAMATION OF RECUSANTS. A proclamation whereby recusants were formerly convicted, on non-appearance at the assizes. Jacob.

PROCLAMATOR. An officer of the English court of common pleas.

PRO-CONSUL. Lat. In the Roman law. Originally a consul whose command was prolonged after his office had expired. An officer with consular authority, but without the title of "consul." The governor of a province. Calvin.

PROCREATION. The generation of children. One of the principal ends of marriage is the procreation of children. Inst. tit. 2, in pr.

PROCTOR. A procurator, proxy, or attorney. More particularly, an officer of the admiralty and ecclesiastical courts whose duties and business correspond exactly to those of an attorney at law or solicitor in chancery.

An ecclesiastical person sent to the lower house of convocation as the representative of a cathedral, a collegiate church, or the clergy of a diocese. Also certain administrative or magisterial officers in the universities.

PROCTORS OF THE CLERGY. They who are chosen and appointed to appear for cathedral or other collegiate churches; as also for the common clergy of every diocese, to sit in the convocation house in the time of parliament. Wharton.

PROCURACY. The writing or instrument which authorizes a procurator to act. Cowell; Termes de la Ley.

PROCURARE. Lat. To take care of another's affairs for him, or in his behalf; to manage; to take care of or superintend.

PROCURATIO. Lat. Management of another's affairs by his direction and in his behalf; procuration; agency.

Procuratio est exhibitio sumptuum necessariorum facta prælatis, qui diœceses peragrando, ecclesias subjectas visitant. Dav. Ir. K. B. 1. Procuration is the providing necessaries for the bishops, who, in traveling through their dioceses, visit the churches subject to them.

PROCURATION. Agency; proxy; the act of constituting another one's attorney in fact; action under a power of attorney or other constitution of agency. Indorsing a bill or note "by procuration" (or *per proc.*) is doing it as proxy for another or by his authority.

PROCURATION FEE, (or MONEY.) In English law. Brokerage or commission allowed to scriveners and solicitors for obtaining loans of money. 4 Bl. Comm. 157.

Procurationem adversus nulla est præscriptio. Dav. Ir. K. B. 6. There is no prescription against procuration.

PROCURATIONS. In ecclesiastical law. Certain sums of money which parish priests pay yearly to the bishops or archdeacons *ratione visitationis*. Dig. 3, 39, 25; Ayl. Par. 429.

PROCURATOR. In the civil law. A proctor; a person who acts for another by virtue of a procuration. Dig. 3, 3, 1.

In old English law. An agent or attorney; a bailiff or servant. A proxy of a lord in parliament.

In ecclesiastical law. One who collected the fruits of a benefice for another. An advocate of a religious house, who was to solicit the interest and plead the causes of the society. A proxy or representative of a parish church.

PROCURATOR FISCAL. In Scotch law, this is the title of the public prosecutor for each district, who institutes the preliminary inquiry into crime within his district. The office is analogous, in some respects, to that of "prosecuting attorney," "district attorney," or "state's attorney" in America.

PROCURATOR IN REM SUAM. Proctor (attorney) in his own affair, or with reference to his own property. This term is used in Scotch law to denote that a person is acting under a procuration (power of attorney) with reference to a thing which has become his own property. See Ersk. Inst. 3, 5, 2.

PROCURATOR LITIS. In the civil law. One who by command of another institutes and carries on for him a suit. Vicat, Voc. Jur.

PROCURATOR NEGOTIORUM. In the civil law. An attorney in fact; a manager of business affairs for another person.

PROCURATOR PROVINCIÆ. In Roman law. A provincial officer who managed the affairs of the revenue, and had a judicial power in matters that concerned the revenue. Adams, Rom. Ant. 178.

PROCURATORES ECCLESIÆ PAROCHIALIS. The old name for churchwardens. Paroch. Antiq. 562.

PROCURATORIUM. In old English law. The procuratory or instrument by which any person or community constituted or delegated their *procurator* or proctors to represent them in any judicial court or cause. Cowell.

PROCURATORY OF RESIGNATION. In Scotch law. A form of proceeding by which a vassal authorizes the feu to be returned to his superior. Bell. It is analogous to the surrender of copyholds in England.

PROCURATRIX. In old English law. A female agent or attorney in fact. Fleta, lib. 3, c. 4, § 4.

PROCURER. A pimp; one that procures the seduction or prostitution of girls. They are punishable by statute in England and America.

PROCUREUR. In French law. An attorney; one who has received a commission from another to act on his behalf. There were in France two classes of *procureurs: Procureurs ad negotia*, appointed by an individual to act for him in the administration of his affairs; persons invested with a power of attorney; corresponding to "attorneys in fact." *Procureurs ad lites* were persons appointed and authorized to act for a party in a court of justice. These corresponded to attorneys at law, (now called, in England, "solicitors of the supreme court.") The order of *procureurs* was abolished in 1791, and that of *avoués* established in their place. Mozley & Whitley.

PROCUREUR DU ROI, in French law, is a public prosecutor, with whom rests the initiation of all criminal proceedings. In the exercise of his office (which appears to include the apprehension of offenders) he is entitled to call to his assistance the public force, (*posse comitatus;*) and the officers of police are auxiliary to him.

PROCUREUR GENERAL, or IMPERIAL. In French law. An officer of the imperial court, who either personally or by his deputy prosecutes every one who is accused of a crime according to the forms of French law. His functions appear to be confined to preparing the case for trial at the assizes, assisting in that trial, demanding the sentence in case of a conviction, and being present at the delivery of the sentence. He has a general superintendence over the officers of police and of the *juges d'instruction*, and he requires from the *procureur du roi* a general report once in every three months. Brown.

PRODES HOMINES. The barons of the realm.

PRODIGUS. In Roman law. A prodigal; a spendthrift; a person whose extravagant habits manifested an inability to administer his own affairs, and for whom a guardian might therefore be appointed.

PRODITION. Treason; treachery.

PRODITOR. A traitor.

PRODITORIE. Treasonably. This is a technical word formerly used in indictments for treason, when they were written in Latin. Tomlins.

PRODUCE. To bring forward; to show or exhibit; to bring into view or notice; as, to produce books or writings at a trial in obedience to a *subpœna duces tecum*.

PRODUCE BROKER. A person whose occupation it is to buy or sell agricultural or farm products. 14 U. S. St. at Large, 117; 1 Abb. (U. S.) 470.

PRODUCENT. The party calling a witness under the old system of the English ecclesiastical courts.

PRODUCTIO SECTÆ. In old English law. Production of suit; the production by a plaintiff of his *secta* or witnesses to prove the allegations of his count. See 3 Bl. Comm. 295.

PRODUCTION. In political economy. The creation of objects which constitute wealth. The requisites of production are labor, capital, and the materials and motive forces afforded by nature. Of these, labor and the raw material of the globe are primary and indispensable. Natural motive powers may be called in to the assistance of labor, and are a help, but not an essential, of production. The remaining requisite, capital, is itself the product of labor. Its instrumentality in production is therefore, in reality, that of labor in an indirect shape. Mill, Pol. Econ.; Wharton.

PRODUCTION OF SUIT. In pleading. The formula, "and therefore he brings his suit," etc., with which declarations always conclude. Steph. Pl. 428, 429.

PROFANE. That which has not been consecrated. By a profane place is understood one which is neither sacred nor sanctified nor religious. Dig. 11, 7, 2, 4.

PROFANELY. In a profane manner. A technical word in indictments for the statutory offense of profanity. See 11 Serg. & R. 394.

PROFANITY. Irreverence towards sacred things; particularly, an irreverent or blasphemous use of the name of God; punishable by statute in some jurisdictions.

PROFECTITIUS. In the civil law. That which descends to us from our ascendants. Dig. 23, 3, 5.

PROFER. In old English law. An offer or proffer; an offer or endeavor to proceed in an action, by any man concerned to do so. Cowell.

A return made by a sheriff of his accounts into the exchequer; a payment made on such return. Id.

PROFERT IN CURIA. L. Lat. He produces in court. In old practice, these words were inserted in a declaration, as an allegation that the plaintiff was ready to produce, or did actually produce, in court, the deed or other written instrument on which his suit was founded, in order that the court might inspect the same and the defendant hear it read. The same formula was used where the defendant pleaded a written instrument.

In modern practice. An allegation formally made in a pleading, where a party alleges a deed, that he shows it in court, it being in fact retained in his own custody. Steph. Pl. 67.

PROFESSION. A public declaration respecting something. Cod. 10, 41, 6.

In ecclesiastical law. The act of entering into a religious order. See 17 Vin. Abr. 545.

Also a calling, vocation, known employment; divinity, medicine, and law are called the "learned professions."

PROFILE. In civil engineering, a drawing representing the elevation of the various points on the plan of a road, or the like, above some fixed elevation. Pub. St. Mass. 1882, p. 1294.

PROFIT AND LOSS. The gain or loss arising from goods bought or sold, or from carrying on any other business, the former of which, in book-keeping, is placed on the creditor's side; the latter on the debtor's side. *Net profit* is the gain made by selling goods at a price beyond what they cost the seller, and beyond all costs and charges. Wharton.

PROFITS. 1. The advance in the price of goods sold beyond the cost of purchase. The gain made by the sale of produce or manufactures, after deducting the value of the labor, materials, rents, and all expenses, together with the interest of the capital employed. Webster.

The usual, ordinary, and correct meaning of the word "profits" is the excess of receipts over expenditures; that is, net earnings. 15 Minn. 519, (Gil. 428.)

2. The benefit, advantage, or pecuniary gain accruing to the owner or occupant of land from its actual use; as in the familiar phrase "rents, issues, and profits," or in the expression "mesne profits."

3. A division sometimes made of incorporeal hereditaments; as distinguished from "easements," which tend rather to the convenience than the profit of the claimant. 2 Steph. Comm. 2.

PROFITS À PRENDRE. These, which are also called "rights of common," are rights exercised by one man in the soil of another, accompanied with participation in the profits of the soil thereof; as rights of pasture, or of digging sand. *Profits à prendre* differ from easements, in that the former are rights of profit, and the latter are mere rights of convenience without profit. Gale, Easem. 1; Hall, Profits à Prendre, 1.

PROGENER. Lat. In the civil law. A grandson-in-law. Dig. 38, 10, 4, 6.

PROGRESSION. That state of a business which is neither the commencement nor the end. Some act done after the matter has commenced, and before it is completed. Plowd. 343.

Prohibetur ne quis faciat in suo quod nocere possit alieno. It is forbidden for any one to do or make on his own [land] what may injure another's. 9 Coke, 59*a*.

PROHIBITIO DE VASTO, DIRECTA PARTI. A judicial writ which used to be addressed to a tenant, prohibiting him from waste, pending suit. Reg. Jud. 21; Moore, 917.

PROHIBITION. In practice. The name of a writ issued by a superior court, directed to the judge and parties of a suit in an inferior court, commanding them to cease from the prosecution of the same, upon a suggestion that the cause originally, or some collateral matter arising therein, does not belong to that jurisdiction, but to the cognizance of some other court. 3 Bl. Comm. 112.

The writ of prohibition is the counterpart of the writ of mandate. It arrests the proceedings of any tribunal, corporation, board, or person, when such proceedings are without or in excess of the jurisdiction of such tribunal, corporation, board, or person. Code Civil Proc. Cal. § 1102.

PROHIBITIVE IMPEDIMENTS. Those impediments to a marriage which are only followed by a punishment, but do not render the marriage null. Bowyer, Mod. Civil Law, 44.

PROJECTIO. Lat. In old English law. A throwing up of earth by the sea.

PROJET. Fr. In international law. The draft of a proposed treaty or convention.

Prolem ante matrimonium natam, ita ut post legitimam, lex civilis succedere facit in hæreditate parentum; sed prolem, quam matrimonium non parit, succedere non sinit lex Anglorum. Fortesc. c. 39. The civil law permits the offspring born before marriage [provided such offspring be afterwards legitimized] to be the heirs of their parents; but the law of the English does not suffer the offspring not produced by the marriage to succeed.

PROLES. Lat. Offspring; progeny; the issue of a lawful marriage.

Proles sequitur sortem paternam. The offspring follows the condition of the father. 1 Sandf. 583, 660.

PROLETARIATE. The class of *proletarii;* the lowest stratum of the people of a country, consisting mainly of the waste of other classes, or of those fractions of the population who, by their isolation and their poverty, have no place in the established order of society.

PROLETARIUS. Lat. In Roman law. A person of poor or mean condition; those among the common people whose fortunes were below a certain valuation; those who were so poor that they could not serve the state with money, but only with their children, (*proles.*) Calvin.; Vicat.

PROLICIDE. In medical jurisprudence. A word used to designate the destruction of the human offspring. Jurists divide the subject into *fœticide,* or the destruction of the *fœtus in utero,* and *infanticide,* or the destruction of the new-born infant. Ry. Med. Jur. 280.

PROLIXITY. The unnecessary and superfluous statement of facts in pleading or in evidence. This will be rejected as impertinent. 7 Price, 278, note.

PROLOCUTOR. In ecclesiastical law. The president or chairman of a convocation.

PROLONGATION. Time added to the duration of something; an extension of the time limited for the performance of an agreement. A prolongation of time accorded to the principal debtor will discharge the surety.

PROLYTÆ. Lat. In Roman law. A name given to students of law in the fifth year of their course; as being in advance of the Lytæ, or students of the fourth year. Calvin.

PROMATERTERA. Lat. In the civil law. A great maternal aunt; the sister of one's grandmother.

PROMATERTERA MAGNA. Lat. In the civil law. A great-great-aunt.

PROMISE. A declaration, verbal or written, made by one person to another for a good or valuable consideration in the nature of a covenant by which the promisor binds himself to do or forbear some act, and gives to the promisee a legal right to demand and enforce a fulfillment.

"Promise" is to be distinguished, on the one hand, from a mere declaration of intention involving no engagement or assurance as to the future; and, on the other, from "agreement," which is an obligation arising upon reciprocal promises, or upon a promise founded on a consideration. Abbott.

"Fictitious promises," sometimes called "implied promises," or "promises implied in law," occur in the case of those contracts which were invented to enable persons in certain cases to take advantage of the old rules of pleading peculiar to contracts, and which are not now of practical importance. Sweet.

PROMISE OF MARRIAGE. A contract mutually entered into by a man and a woman that they will marry each other.

PROMISEE. One to whom a promise has been made.

PROMISOR. One who makes a promise.

PROMISSOR. Lat. In the civil law. A promiser; properly the party who undertook to do a thing in answer to the interrogation of the other party, who was called the "stipulator."

PROMISSORY NOTE. A promise or engagement, in writing, to pay a specified sum at a time therein limited, or on demand, or at sight, to a person therein named, or to his order, or bearer. Byles, Bills, 1, 4; 5 Denio, 484.

A promissory note is a written promise made by one or more to pay another, or order, or bearer, at a specified time, a specific amount of money, or other articles of value. Code Ga. 1882, § 2774.

A promissory note is an instrument negotiable in form, whereby the signer promises to pay a specified sum of money. Civil Code Cal. § 3244.

An unconditional written promise, signed by the maker, to pay absolutely and at all events a sum certain in money, either to the bearer or to a person therein designated or his order. Benj. Chalm. Bills & N. art. 271.

PROMISSORY OATHS. Oaths which bind the party to observe a certain course of conduct, or to fulfill certain duties, in the future, or to demean himself thereafter in a stated manner with reference to specified objects or obligations; such, for example, as the oath taken by a high executive officer, a legislator, a judge, a person seeking naturalization, an attorney at law.

PROMOTERS. In the law relating to corporations, those persons are called the "promoters" of a company who first associate themselves together for the purpose of organizing the company, issuing its prospectus, procuring subscriptions to the stock, securing a charter, etc.

In English practice. Those persons who, in popular and penal actions, prosecute offenders in their own names and that of the king, and are thereby entitled to part of the fines and penalties for their pains, are called "promoters." Brown.

The term is also applied to a party who puts in motion an ecclesiastical tribunal, for the purpose of correcting the manners of any person who has violated the laws ecclesiastical; and one who takes such a course is said to "promote the office of the judge." See Mozley & Whitley.

PROMOVENT. A plaintiff in a suit of *duplex querela*, (*q. v.*) 2 Prob. Div. 192.

PROMULGARE. Lat. In Roman law. To make public; to make publicly known; to promulgate. To publish or make known a law, after its enactment.

PROMULGATE. To publish; to announce officially; to make public as important or obligatory.

PROMULGATION. The order given to cause a law to be executed, and to make it public; it differs from publication. 1 Bl. Comm. 45.

PROMUTUUM. Lat. In the civil law. A *quasi* contract, by which he who receives a certain sum of money, or a certain quantity of fungible things, which have been paid to him through mistake, contracts towards the payer the obligation of returning him as much. Poth. de l'Usure, pt. 3, s. 1, a. 1.

PRONEPOS. Lat. In the civil law. A great-grandson. Inst. 3, 6, 1; Bract. fol. 67.

PRONEPTIS. Lat. In the civil law. A great-granddaughter. Inst. 3, 6, 1; Bract. fol. 67.

PRONOTARY. First notary. See PROTHONOTARY.

PRONUNCIATION. L. Fr. A sentence or decree. Kelham.

PRONURUS. Lat. In the civil law. The wife of a grandson or great-grandson. Dig. 38, 10, 4, 6.

PROOF. Proof, in civil process, is a sufficient reason for the truth of a juridical proposition by which a party seeks either to maintain his own claim or to defeat the claim of another. Whart. Ev. § 1.

Proof is the effect of evidence; the establishment of a fact by evidence. Code Civil Proc. Cal. § 1824.

Ayliffe defines "judicial proof" to be a clear and evident declaration or demonstration of a matter which was before doubtful, conveyed in a judicial manner by fit and proper arguments, and likewise by all other legal methods—*First*, by fit and proper arguments, such as conjectures, presumptions, *indicia*, and other adminicular ways and means; *secondly*, by legal methods, or methods according to law, such as witnesses, public instruments, and the like. Ayl. Par. 442.

For the distinction between "proof," "evidence," "belief," and "testimony," see EVIDENCE.

PROOF OF DEBT. The formal establishment by a creditor of his debt or claim, in some prescribed manner, (as, by his affidavit or otherwise,) as a preliminary to its allowance, along with others, against an estate or property to be divided, such as the estate of a bankrupt or insolvent, a deceased person, or a firm or company in liquidation.

PROOF OF WILL. A term having the same meaning as "probate," (*q. v.*,) and used interchangeably with it.

PROPATRUUS. Lat. In the civil law. A great-grandfather's brother. Inst. 3, 6, 3; Bract. fol. 68*b*.

PROPATRUUS MAGNUS. Lat. In the civil law. A great-great-uncle.

PROPER. That which is fit, suitable, adapted, and correct.

Peculiar; naturally or essentially belonging to a person or thing; not common; appropriate; one's own.

PROPER FEUDS. The original and genuine feuds held by pure military service.

PROPERTY. Rightful dominion over external objects; ownership; the unrestricted and exclusive right to a thing; the right to dispose of the substance of a thing in every legal way, to possess it, to use it, and to exclude every one else from interfering with it. Mackeld. Rom. Law, § 265.

Property is the highest right a man can have to anything; being used for that right which one has to lands or tenements, goods or chattels, which no way depends on another man's courtesy. 17 Johns. 281, 283.

A right imparting to the owner a power of indefinite user, capable of being transmitted to universal successors by way of descent, and imparting to the owner the power of disposition, from himself and his successors *per universitatem*, and from all other persons who have a *spes successionis* under any existing concession or disposition, in favor of such person or series of persons as he may choose, with the like capacities and powers as he had himself, and under such conditions as the municipal or particular law allows to be annexed to the dispositions of private persons. Aust. Jur. (Campbell's Ed.) § 1103.

The right of property is that sole and despotic dominion which one man claims and exercises over the external things of the world, in total exclusion of the right of any other individual in the universe. It consists in the free use, enjoyment, and disposal of all a person's acquisitions, without any control or diminution save only by the laws of the land. 1 Bl. Comm. 138; 2 Bl. Comm. 2, 15.

The word is also commonly used to denote any external object over which the right of property is exercised. In this sense it is a very wide term, and includes every class of acquisitions which a man can own or have an interest in.

Taking the word in the latter signification property is broadly divided into *real* and *personal* property; as to which, see those titles.

Personal property is further divided into property in possession, and property or choses in action. See CHOSE IN ACTION.

Property in chattels personal may be either *absolute* or *qualified*. It is called "absolute" where a man has, solely and exclusively, the right and also the occupation of any movable chattels, so that they cannot be transferred from him, or cease to be his, without his own act or default. Qualified property is such as is not in its nature permanent, but may at some times subsist, and at other times not subsist; such, for example, is the property a man may have in wild animals which he has caught and keeps, and which are his only so long as he retains possession of them. 2 Bl. Comm. 389, et seq.

PROPERTY TAX. An income tax payable in respect of landed property.

PROPINQUI ET CONSANGUINEI. Lat. The nearest of kin to a deceased person.

Propinquior excludit propinquum; propinquus remotum; et remotus remotiorem. Co. Litt. 10. He who is nearer excludes him who is near; he who is near, him who is remote; he who is remote, him who is remoter.

PROPINQUITY. Kindred; parentage.

PROPIOR SOBRINO, PROPIOR SOBRINA. Lat. In the civil law. The son or daughter of a great-uncle or great-aunt, paternal or maternal. Inst. 3, 6, 3.

PROPIOS, PROPRIOS. In Spanish law. Certain portions of ground laid off and reserved when a town was founded in Spanish America as the unalienable property of the town, for the purpose of erecting public buildings, markets, etc., or to be used in any other way, under the direction of the municipality, for the advancement of the revenues or the prosperity of the place. 12 Pet. 442, note.

Thus, there are *solares*, or house lots of a small size, upon which dwellings, shops, stores, etc., are to be built. There are *suertes*, or sowing grounds of a larger size, for cultivating or planting; as gardens, vineyards, orchards, etc. There are *ejidos*, which are quite well described by our word "commons," and are lands used in common by the inhabitants of the place for pasture, wood, threshing ground, etc.; and particular names are assigned to each, according to its particular use. Sometimes additional *ejidos* were allowed to be taken outside of the town limits. There are also *propios* or municipal lands, from which revenues are derived to defray the expenses of the municipal administration. 15 Cal. 554.

PROPONE. In Scotch law. To state. To *propone* a defense is to state or move it. 1 Kames, Eq. pref.

In ecclesiastical and probate law. To bring forward for adjudication; to exhibit as basis of a claim; to proffer for judicial action.

PROPONENT. The propounder of a thing. Thus, the proponent of a will is the party who offers it for probate, (*q. v.*)

PROPORTUM. In old records. Purport; intention or meaning. Cowell.

PROPOSAL. An offer; something proffered. An offer, by one person to another, of terms and conditions with reference to some work or undertaking, or for the transfer of property, the acceptance whereof will make a contract between them. 35 Ala. 33.

In English practice. A statement in writing of some special matter submitted to the consideration of a chief clerk in the court of chancery, pursuant to an order made upon an application *ex parte*, or a decretal order of the court. It is either for maintenance of an infant, appointment of a guardian, placing a ward of the court at the university or in the army, or apprentice to a trade; for the appointment of a receiver, the establishment of a charity, etc. Wharton.

Propositio indefinita æquipollet universali. An indefinite proposition is equivalent to a general one.

PROPOSITION. A single logical sentence; also an offer to do a thing.

PROPOSITUS. The person proposed; the person from whom a descent is traced.

PROPOUND. An executor or other person is said to propound a will or other testamentary paper when he takes proceedings for obtaining probate in solemn form. The term is also technically used, in England, to denote the allegations in the statement of claim, in an action for probate, by which the plaintiff alleges that the testator executed the will with proper formalities, and that he was of sound mind at the time. Sweet.

PROPRES. In French law. The term "*propres*" or "*biens propres*" (as distinguished from "*acquets*") denotes all property inherited by a person, whether by devise or *ab intestato,* from his direct or collateral relatives, whether in the ascending or descending line; that is, in terms of the common law, property acquired by "descent" as distinguished from that acquired by "purchase."

PROPRIA PERSONA. See IN PROPRIA PERSONA.

PROPRIEDAD. In Spanish law. Property. White, New Recop. b. 1, tit. 7, c. 5, § 2.

PROPRIETARY. A proprietor or owner; one who has the exclusive title to a thing; one who possesses or holds the title to a thing in his own right. The grantees of Pennsylvania and Maryland and their heirs were called the proprietaries of those provinces. Webster.

PROPRIETARY ARTICLES. Goods manufactured under some exclusive individual right to make and sell them. The term is chiefly used in the internal revenue laws of the United States.

PROPRIETARY CHAPELS. In English law. Those belonging to private persons who have purchased or erected them with a view to profit or otherwise.

PROPRIETARY GOVERNMENTS. This expression is used by Blackstone to denote governments granted out by the crown to individuals, in the nature of feudatory principalities, with inferior regalities and subordinate powers of legislation such as formerly belonged to the owners of counties palatine. 1 Bl. Comm. 108.

PROPRIETARY RIGHTS. Those rights which an owner of property has by virtue of his ownership. When proprietary rights are opposed to acquired rights, such as easements, franchises, etc., they are more often called "natural rights." Sweet.

PROPRIETAS. Lat. In the civil and old English law. Property; that which is one's own; ownership.

Proprietas plena, full property, including not only the title, but the usufruct, or exclusive right to the use. Calvin.

Proprietas nuda, naked or mere property or ownership; the mere title, separate from the usufruct.

Proprietas totius navis carinæ causam sequitur. The property of the whole ship follows the condition of the keel. Dig. 6, 1, 61. If a man builds a vessel from the very keel with the materials of another, the vessel belongs to the owner of the materials. 2 Kent, Comm. 362.

Proprietas verborum est salus propietatum. Jenk. Cent. 16. Propriety of words is the salvation of property.

PROPRIETATE PROBANDA, DE. A writ addressed to a sheriff to try by an inquest in whom certain property, previous to distress, subsisted. Finch, Law, 316.

Proprietates verborum servandæ sunt. The proprieties of words [proper meanings of words] are to be preserved or adhered to. Jenk. Cent. p. 136, case 78.

PROPRIÉTÉ. The French law term corresponding to our "property," or the right of enjoying and of disposing of things in the most absolute manner, subject only to the laws. Brown.

PROPRIETOR. This term is almost synonymous with "owner," (*q. v.,*) as in the phrase "riparian proprietor." A person entitled to a trade-mark or a design under the acts for the registration or patenting of trade-marks and designs (*q. v.*) is called "proprietor" of the trade-mark or design. Sweet.

PROPRIETY. In Massachusetts colonial ordinance of 1741 is nearly, if not precisely, equivalent to property. 7 Cush. 53, 70.

In old English law. Property. "Propriety in action; propriety in possession; mixed propriety." Hale, Anal. § 26.

PROPRIO VIGORE. Lat. By its own force; by its intrinsic meaning.

PROPTER. For; on account of. The initial word of several Latin phrases.

PROPTER AFFECTUM. For or on account of some affection or prejudice. The name of a species of *challenge*, (*q. v.*)

PROPTER DEFECTUM. On account of or for some defect. The name of a species of *challenge*, (*q. v.*)

PROPTER DEFECTUM SANGUINIS. On account of failure of blood.

PROPTER DELICTUM. For or on account of crime. The name of a species of *challenge*, (*q. v.*)

PROPTER HONORIS RESPECTUM. On account of respect of honor or rank. See CHALLENGE.

PROPTER IMPOTENTIAM. On account of helplessness. The term describes one of the grounds of a qualified property in wild animals, consisting in the fact of their inability to escape; as is the case with the young of such animals before they can fly or run. 2 Bl. Comm. 394.

PROPTER PRIVILEGIUM. On account of privilege. The term describes one of the grounds of a qualified property in wild animals, consisting in the special privilege of hunting, taking, and killing them, in a given park or preserve, to the exclusion of other persons. 2 Bl. Comm. 394.

PROROGATED JURISDICTION. In Scotch law. A power conferred by consent of the parties upon a judge who would not otherwise be competent.

PROROGATION. Prolonging or putting off to another day. In English law, a prorogation is the continuance of the parliament from one session to another, as an adjournment is a continuation of the session from day to day. Wharton.

In the civil law. The giving time to do a thing beyond the term previously fixed. Dig. 2, 14, 27, 1.

PROROGUE. To direct suspension of proceedings of parliament; to terminate a session.

PROSCRIBED. In the civil law. Among the Romans, a man was said to be "proscribed" when a reward was offered for his head; but the term was more usually applied to those who were sentenced to some punishment which carried with it the consequences of civil death. Cod. 9, 49.

PROSECUTE. To follow up; to carry on an action or other judicial proceeding; to proceed against a person criminally.

PROSECUTION. In criminal law. A criminal action; a proceeding instituted and carried on by due course of law, before a competent tribunal, for the purpose of determining the guilt or innocence of a person charged with crime.

By an easy extension of its meaning "prosecution" is sometimes used to designate the state as the party proceeding in a criminal action, or the prosecutor, or counsel; as when we speak of "the evidence adduced by the prosecution."

PROSECUTOR. In practice. He who prosecutes another for a crime in the name of the government.

PROSECUTOR OF THE PLEAS. This name is given, in New Jersey, to the county officer who is charged with the prosecution of criminal actions, corresponding to the "district attorney" or "county attorney" in other states.

PROSECUTRIX. In criminal law. A female prosecutor.

PROSEQUI. Lat. To follow up or pursue; to sue or prosecute. See NOLLE PROSEQUI.

PROSEQUITUR. Lat. He follows up or pursues; he prosecutes. See NON PROS.

PROSOCER. Lat. In the civil law. A father-in-law's father; grandfather of wife.

PROSOCERUS. Lat. In the civil law. A wife's grandmother.

PROSPECTIVE. Looking forward; contemplating the future. A law is said to be prospective (as opposed to retrospective) when it is applicable only to cases which shall arise after its enactment.

PROSPECTIVE DAMAGES. Damages which are expected to follow from the act or state of facts made the basis of a plaintiff's suit; damages which have not yet accrued, at the time of the trial, but which, in the nature of things, must necessarily, or most probably, result from the acts or facts complained of.

PROSPECTUS. A document published by a company or corporation, or by persons acting as its agents or assignees, setting forth the nature and objects of an issue of shares, debentures, or other securities created by the company or corporation, and inviting the public to subscribe to the issue. A prospectus is also usually published on the issue, in

England, of bonds or other securities by a foreign state or corporation. Sweet.

In the civil law. Prospect; the view of external objects. Dig. 8, 2, 3, 15.

PROSTITUTE. A woman who indiscriminately consorts with men for hire.

PROSTITUTION. Common lewdness; whoredom; the act or practice of a woman who permits any man who will pay her price to have sexual intercourse with her. See 12 Metc. (Mass.) 97.

Protectio trahit subjectionem, et subjectio protectionem. Protection draws with it subjection, and subjection protection. 7 Coke, 5*a*. The protection of an individual by government is on condition of his submission to the laws, and such submission on the other hand entitles the individual to the protection of the government. Broom, Max. 78.

PROTECTION. In English law. A writ by which the king might, by a special prerogative, privilege a defendant from all personal and many real suits for one year at a time, and no longer, in respect of his being engaged in his service out of the realm. 3 Bl. Comm. 289.

In former times the name "protection" was also given to a certificate given to a sailor to show that he was exempt from impressment into the royal navy.

In mercantile law. The name of a document generally given by notaries public to sailors and other persons going abroad, in which it is certified that the bearer therein named is a citizen of the United States.

In public commercial law. A system by which a government imposes customs duties upon commodities of foreign origin or manufacture when imported into the country, with the purpose and effect of stimulating and developing the home production of the same or equivalent articles, by discouraging the importation of foreign goods, or by raising the price of foreign commodities to a point at which the home producers can successfully compete with them.

PROTECTION OF INVENTIONS ACT. The statute 33 & 34 Vict. c. 27. By this act it is provided that the exhibition of new inventions shall not prejudice patent rights, and that the exhibition of designs shall not prejudice the right to registration of such designs.

PROTECTION ORDER. In English practice. An order for the protection of the wife's property, when the husband has willfully deserted her, issuable by the divorce court under statutes on that subject.

PROTECTIONIBUS DE. The English statute 33 Edw. I. St. 1, allowing a challenge to be entered against a protection, etc.

PROTECTIVE TARIFF. A law imposing duties on imports, with the purpose and the effect of discouraging the use of products of foreign origin, and consequently of stimulating the home production of the same or equivalent articles. R. E. Thompson, in Enc. Brit.

PROTECTOR OF SETTLEMENT. In English law. By the statute 3 & 4 Wm. IV. c. 74, § 32, power is given to any settlor to appoint any person or persons, not exceeding three, the "protector of the settlement." The object of such appointment is to prevent the tenant in tail from barring any subsequent estate, the consent of the protector being made necessary for that purpose.

PROTECTORATE. (1) The period during which Oliver Cromwell ruled in England. (2) Also the office of protector. (3) The relation of the English sovereign, till the year 1864, to the Ionian Islands. Wharton.

PROTEST. 1. A formal declaration made by a person interested or concerned in some act about to be done, or already performed, and in relation thereto, whereby he expresses his dissent or disapproval, or affirms the act to be done against his will or convictions, the object being generally to save some right which would be lost to him if his implied assent could be made out, or to exonerate himself from some responsibility which would attach to him unless he expressly negatived his assent to or voluntary participation in the act.

2. A notarial act, being a formal statement in writing made by a notary under his seal of office, at the request of the holder of a bill or note, in which such bill or note is described, and it is declared that the same was on a certain day presented for payment, (or acceptance, as the case may be,) and that such payment or acceptance was refused, and stating the reasons, if any, given for such refusal, whereupon the notary *protests* against all parties to such instrument, and declares that they will be held responsible for all loss or damage arising from its dishonor.

A formal notarial certificate attesting the dishonor of a bill of exchange or promissory note. Benj. Chalm. Bills & N. art. 176.

A solemn declaration written by the notary, under a fair copy of the bill, stating that the payment or acceptance has been demanded and refused, the reason, if any, assigned, and that the bill is therefore protested. 17 How. 607.

"Protest," in a technical sense, means only the formal declaration drawn up and signed by the notary; yet, as used by commercial men, the word includes all the steps necessary to charge an indorser. 2 Ohio St. 345.

3. A formal declaration made by a minority (or by certain individuals) in a legislative body that they dissent from some act or resolution of the body, usually adding the grounds of their dissent. The term, in this sense, seems to be particularly appropriate to such a proceeding in the English house of lords.

4. The name "protest" is also given to the formal statement, usually in writing, made by a person who is called upon by public authority to pay a sum of money, in which he declares that he does not concede the legality or justice of the claim or his duty to pay it, or that he disputes the amount demanded; the object being to save his right to recover or reclaim the amount, which right would be lost by his acquiescence. Thus, taxes may be paid under "protest."

5. "Protest" is also the name of a paper served on a collector of customs by an importer of merchandise, stating that he believes the sum charged as duty to be excessive, and that, although he pays such sum for the purpose of getting his goods out of the custom-house, he reserves the right to bring an action against the collector to recover the excess.

6. In maritime law, a protest is a written statement by the master of a vessel, attested by a proper judicial officer or a notary, to the effect that damage suffered by the ship on her voyage was caused by storms or other perils of the sea, without any negligence or misconduct on his own part. Marsh. Ins. 715.

PROTESTANDO. L. Lat. Protesting. The emphatic word formerly used in pleading by way of protestation. 3 Bl. Comm. 311. See PROTESTATION.

PROTESTANTS. Those who adhered to the doctrine of Luther; so called because, in 1529, they protested against a decree of the emperor Charles V. and of the diet of Spires, and declared that they appealed to a general council. The name is now applied indiscriminately to all the sects, of whatever denomination, who have seceded from the Church of Rome. Enc. Lond.

PROTESTATION. In pleading. The indirect affirmation or denial of the truth of some matter which cannot with propriety or safety be positively affirmed, denied, or entirely passed over. See 3 Bl. Comm. 311.

The exclusion of a conclusion. Co. Litt. 124.

In practice. An asseveration made by taking God to witness. A protestation is a form of asseveration which approaches very nearly to an oath. Wolff. Inst. Nat. § 375.

PROTHONOTARY. The title given to an officer who officiates as principal clerk of some courts. Vin. Abr.

PROTOCOL. The first draft or rough minutes of an instrument or transaction; the original copy of a dispatch, treaty, or other document. Brande.

A document serving as the preliminary to, or opening of, any diplomatic transaction.

In old Scotch practice. A book, marked by the clerk-register, and delivered to a notary on his admission, in which he was directed to insert all the instruments he had occasion to execute; to be preserved as a record. Bell.

In France, the minutes of notarial acts were formerly transcribed on registers, which were called "protocols." Toullier, Droit Civil Fr. liv. 3, t. 3, c. 6, s. 1, no. 413.

PROTOCOLO. In Spanish law. The original draft or writing of an instrument which remains in the possession of the *escribano*, or notary. White, New Recop. lib. 3, tit. 7, c. 5, § 2.

The term "*protocolo*," when applied to a single paper, means the first draft of an instrument duly executed before a notary,—the matrix,—because it is the source from which must be taken copies to be delivered to interested parties as their evidence of right; and it also means a bound book in which the notary places and keeps in their order instruments executed before him, from which copies are taken for the use of parties interested. (Tex.) 16 S. W. Rep. 53.

PROTUTOR. In the civil law. He who, not being the tutor of a minor, has administered his property or affairs as if he had been, whether he thought himself legally invested with the authority of a tutor or not. Mackeld. Rom. Law, § 630.

PROUT PATET PER RECORDUM. As appears by the record. In the Latin phraseology of pleading, this was the proper formula for making reference to a record.

PROVABLE. L. Fr. Provable; justifiable; manifest. Kelham.

PROVE. To establish a fact or hypothesis as true by satisfactory and sufficient evidence.

To present a claim or demand against a bankrupt or insolvent estate, and establish by evidence or affidavit that the same is correct and due, for the purpose of receiving a dividend on it.

To establish the genuineness and due execution of a paper, propounded to the proper court or officer, as the last will and testament of a deceased person. See PROBATE.

PROVER. In old English law. A person who, on being indicted of treason or felony, and arraigned for the same, confessed the fact before plea pleaded, and appealed or accused others, his accomplices in the same crime, in order to obtain his pardon. 4 Bl. Comm. 329, 330.

PROVINCE. Sometimes this signifies the district into which a country has been divided; as, the province of Canterbury, in England; the province of Languedoc, in France. Sometimes it means a dependency or colony; as, the province of New Brunswick. It is sometimes used figuratively to signify power or authority; as, it is the province of the court to judge of the law; that of the jury to decide on the facts. 1 Bl. Comm. 111; Tomlins.

PROVINCIAL CONSTITUTIONS. The decrees of provincial synods held under divers archbishops of Canterbury, from Stephen Langton, in the reign of Henry III., to Henry Chichele, in the reign of Henry V., and adopted also by the province of York in the reign of Henry VI. Wharton.

PROVINCIAL COURTS. In English law. The several archi-episcopal courts in the two ecclesiastical provinces of England.

PROVINCIALE. A work on ecclesiastical law, by William Lyndwode, official principal to Archbishop Chichele in the reign of Edward IV. 4 Reeve, Eng. Law, c. 25, p. 117.

PROVINCIALIS. Lat. In the civil law. One who has his domicile in a province. Dig. 50, 16, 190.

PROVING OF THE TENOR. In Scotch practice. An action for proving the tenor of a lost deed. Bell.

PROVISION. In commercial law. Funds remitted by the drawer of a bill of exchange to the drawee in order to meet the bill, or property remaining in the drawee's hands or due from him to the drawer, and appropriated to that purpose.

In ecclesiastical law. A provision was a nomination by the pope to an English benefice before it became void, though the term was afterwards indiscriminately applied to any right of patronage exerted or usurped by the pope.

In French law. Provision is an allowance or alimony granted by a judge to one of the parties in a cause for his or her maintenance until a definite judgment is rendered. Dalloz.

PROVISIONAL ASSIGNEES. In the former practice in bankruptcy in England. Assignees to whom the property of a bankrupt was assigned until the regular or permanent assignees were appointed by the creditors.

PROVISIONAL COMMITTEE. A committee appointed for a temporary occasion.

PROVISIONAL ORDER. In English law. Under various acts of parliament, certain public bodies and departments of the government are authorized to inquire into matters which, in the ordinary course, could only be dealt with by a private act of parliament, and to make orders for their regulation. These orders have no effect unless they are confirmed by an act of parliament, and are hence called "provisional orders." Several orders may be confirmed by one act. The object of this mode of proceeding is to save the trouble and expense of promoting a number of private bills. Sweet.

PROVISIONAL REMEDY. A remedy provided for present need or for the immediate occasion; one adapted to meet a particular exigency. Particularly, a temporary process available to a plaintiff in a civil action, which secures him against loss, irreparable injury, dissipation of the property, etc., while the action is pending. Such are the remedies by injunction, appointment of a receiver, attachment, or arrest. The term is chiefly used in the codes of practice. See 54 How. Pr. 100.

PROVISIONAL SEIZURE. A remedy known under the law of Louisiana, and substantially the same in general nature as attachment of property in other states. Code Proc. La. 284, et seq.

PROVISIONES. Those acts of parliament which were passed to curb the arbitrary power of the crown.

PROVISIONS. Food; victuals. Also the nominations to benefices by the pope were so called, and those who were so nominated were termed "provisors."

PROVISIONS OF OXFORD. Certain provisions made in the Parliament of Oxford, 1258, for the purpose of securing the execution of the provisions of *Magna Charta*, against the invasions thereof by Henry III. The government of the country was in effect committed by these provisions to a standing committee of twenty-four, whose chief merit consisted in their representative character, and their real desire to effect an improvement in the king's government. Brown.

PROVISO. A condition or provision which is inserted in a deed, lease, mortgage, or contract, and on the performance or non-performance of which the validity of the deed, etc., frequently depends; it usually begins with the word "provided."

A proviso in deeds or laws is a limitation or exception to a grant made or authority conferred, the effect of which is to declare that the one shall not operate, or the other be exercised, unless in the case provided. 10 Pet. 449.

The word "proviso" is generally taken for a condition, but it differs from it in several respects; for a condition is usually created by the grantor or lessor, but a proviso by the grantee or lessee. Jacob.

A proviso differs from an exception. 1 Barn. & Ald. 99. An exception *exempts*, absolutely, from the operation of an engagement or an enactment; a proviso defeats their operation, *conditionally*. An exception takes out of an engagement or enactment something which would otherwise be part of the subject-matter of it; a proviso avoids them by way of defeasance or excuse. 8 Amer. Jur. 242.

A clause or part of a clause in a statute, the office of which is either to except something from the enacting clause, or to qualify or restrain its generality, or to exclude some possible ground of misinterpretation of its extent. 15 Pet. 445.

Proviso est providere præsentia et futura, non præterita. Coke, 72. A proviso is to provide for the present or future, not the past.

PROVISO, TRIAL BY. In English practice. A trial brought on by the defendant, in cases where the plaintiff, after issue joined, neglects to proceed to trial; so called from a clause in the writ to the sheriff, which directs him, in case two writs come to his hands, to execute but one of them. 3 Bl. Comm. 357.

PROVISOR. In old English law. A provider, or purveyor. Spelman.

PROVOCATION. The act of inciting another to do a particular deed. Such conduct or actions on the part of one person towards another as tend to arouse rage, resentment, or fury in the latter against the former, and thereby cause him to do some illegal act against or in relation to the person offering the provocation.

PROVOST. The principal magistrate of a royal burgh in Scotland; also a governing officer of a university or college.

PROVOST-MARSHAL. In English law. An officer of the royal navy who had the charge of prisoners taken at sea, and sometimes also on land.

PROXENETA. Lat. In the civil law. A broker; one who negotiated or arranged the terms of a contract between two parties, as between buyer and seller; one who negotiated a marriage; a match-maker. Calvin.

PROXIMATE. Immediate; nearest; next in order.

PROXIMATE CAUSE. The proximate cause is the efficient cause, the one that necessarily sets the other causes in operation. The causes that are merely incidental or instruments of a superior or controlling agency are not the proximate causes and the responsible ones, though they may be nearer in time to the result. It is only when the causes are independent of each other that the nearest is, of course, to be charged with the disaster. 95 U. S. 130.

PROXIMITY. Kindred between two persons. Dig. 38, 16, 8.

Proximus est cui nemo antecedit; supremus est quem nemo sequitur. He is next whom no one precedes; he is last whom no one follows. Dig. 50, 16, 92.

PROXY. A person who is substituted or deputed by another to represent him and act for him, particularly in some meeting or public body. Also the instrument containing the appointment of such person. The word is said to be contracted from "procuracy," (*q. v.*)

One who is appointed or deputed by another to vote for him. Members of the house of lords in England have the privilege of voting by proxy. 1 Bl. Comm. 168.

In ecclesiastical law. A person who is appointed to manage another man's affairs in the ecclesiastical courts; a proctor.

Also an annual payment made by the paro hial clergy to the bishop, on visitations. Tomlins.

Prudenter agit qui præcepto legis obtemperat. 5 Coke, 49. He acts prudently who obeys the command of the law.

PRYK. A kind of service of tenure. Blount says it signifies an old-fashioned spur with one point only, which the tenant, holding land by this tenure, was to find for the king. Wharton.

PSYCHOLOGICAL FACT. In the law of evidence. A fact which can only be perceived mentally; such as the motive by which a person is actuated. Burrill, Circ. Ev. 130, 131.

PUBERTY. The age of fourteen in males and twelve in females, when they are held fit for, and capable of contracting, marriage. Otherwise called the "age of consent to marriage." 1 Bl. Comm. 436; 2 Kent, Comm. 78.

PUBLIC. Pertaining to a state, nation, or whole community; proceeding from, relating to, or affecting the whole body of people or an entire community. Open to all; notorious. Common to all or many; general; open to common use.

A distinction has been made between the terms "public" and "general." They are sometimes used as synonymous. The former term is applied strictly to that which concerns all the citizens and every member of the state; while the latter includes a lesser, though still a large, portion of the community. 1 Greenl. Ev. § 128.

As a noun, the word "public" denotes the whole body politic, or the aggregate of the citizens of a state, district, or municipality.

PUBLIC ACCOUNTS. The accounts kept by officers of the nation, state, or kingdom, of the receipt and expenditure of the revenues of the government.

PUBLIC ACT, or STATUTE. A universal rule or law that regards the whole community, and of which the courts of law are bound to take notice judicially and *ex officio*, without its being particularly pleaded. 1 Bl. Comm. 86.

PUBLIC ADMINISTRATOR. A person appointed by the probate court, to administer the estate of a decedent, when there is no relative living or competent to take the administration. Such appointment is authorized by statute in several of the states.

PUBLIC AGENT. An agent of the public, the state, or the government; a person appointed to act for the public in some matter pertaining to the administration of government or the public business. See Story, Ag. § 302; 93 U. S. 254.

PUBLIC APPOINTMENTS. Public offices or stations which are to be filled by the appointment of individuals, under authority of law, instead of by election.

PUBLIC ATTORNEY. This name is sometimes given to an attorney at law, as distinguished from a *private* attorney, or attorney in fact.

PUBLIC AUCTION. A sale of property at auction, where any and all persons who choose are perm tted to attend and offer bids.

Though this phrase is frequently used, it is doubtful whether the word "public" adds anything to the force of the expression, since "auction" itself imports publicity. If there can be such a thing as a private auction, it must be one where the property is sold to the highest bidder, but only certain persons, or a certain class of persons, are permitted to be present or to offer bids.

PUBLIC BLOCKADE. A blockade which is not only established in fact, but is notified, by the government directing it, to other governments; as distinguished from a *simple* blockade, which may be established by a naval officer acting upon his own discretion or under direction of superiors, without governmental notification. 2 Wall. 150.

PUBLIC BOUNDARY. A natural boundary; a natural object or land-mark, used as a boundary of a tract of land, or as a beginning point for a boundary line.

PUBLIC BRIDGE. One which forms a part of the highway, or which is open to the public generally, or to all who choose to use it, whether toll is required or not; as distinguished from a *private* bridge, which is for the use only of those who own it and their licensees.

PUBLIC BUILDING. One of which the possession and use, as well as the property in it, are in the public. 34 N. J. Law, 383.

PUBLIC CARRIER. A common carrier; one who offers to transport persons or goods for all such as choose to employ him. Distinguished from a *private* carrier, (*q. v.*)

PUBLIC CHAPELS, in English law, are chapels founded at some period later than the church itself. They were designed for the accommodation of such of the parishioners as in course of time had begun to fix their residence at a distance from its site; and chapels so circumstanced were described as "chapels of ease," because built in aid of the original church. 3 Steph. Comm. (7th Ed.) 745.

PUBLIC CHARITY. In this phrase the word "public" is used, not in the sense that it must be executed openly and in public, but in the sense of being so general and indefinite in its objects as to be deemed of common and public benefit. Each individual immediately benefited may be private, and the charity may be distributed in private and by a private hand. It is public and general in its scope and purpose, and becomes definite and private only after the individual objects have been selected. 11 Allen, 456.

PUBLIC COMPANY. In English law. A business corporation; a society of persons joined together for carrying on some commercial or industrial undertaking.

PUBLIC CORPORATION. This term includes the *quasi* corporations created for political purposes, or to exercise some of the functions and powers of government within a particular territory, such as cities, towns, counties, parishes, and villages; also some others founded for public, though not for political or municipal, purposes, if the whole interest in them belongs to the government, not if there are other and private owners of stock in them. 4 Wheat. 518, 668.

PUBLIC DEBT. That which is due or owing by the government of a state or nation.

The terms "public debt" and "public securities," used in legislation, are terms generally applied to national or state obligations and dues, and would rarely, if ever, be construed to include town debts or obligations; nor would the term "public revenue" ordinarily be applied to funds arising from town taxes. 46 Vt. 773.

PUBLIC DOCUMENT. A state paper, or other instrument of public importance or interest, issued or published by authority of congress or a state legislature. Also any document or record, evidencing or connected with the public business or the administration of public affairs, preserved in or issued by any department of the government.

PUBLIC DOMAIN. This term embraces all lands, the title to which is in the United States, including as well land occupied for the purposes of federal buildings, arsenals, dock-yards, etc., as land of an agricultural or mineral character not yet granted to private owners.

PUBLIC EASEMENT. An easement, the right to the enjoyment of which is vested in the public generally, or the whole community.

PUBLIC ENEMY. A nation at war with the United States; also every citizen or subject of such nation.

PUBLIC FUNDS. The funded public debt of a state or nation. Also the funds (money) belonging to a state or nation as such, and in the possession of its government.

PUBLIC GRANT. A grant from the public; a grant of a power, license, privilege, or property, from the state or government to one or more individuals, contained in or shown by a record, conveyance, patent, charter, etc.

PUBLIC HEALTH. As one of the objects of the police power of the state, the "public health" means the prevailingly healthful or sanitary condition of the general body of people or the community in mass, and the absence of any general or wide-spread disease or cause of mortality.

PUBLIC HOLIDAY. A legal holiday, (*q. v.*)

PUBLIC HOUSE. An inn or tavern; a house for the entertainment of the public, or for the entertainment of all who come lawfully and pay regularly. 3 Brewst. 344. A place of public resort, particularly for purposes of drinking or gaming.

PUBLIC INDECENCY. This phrase has no fixed legal meaning, is vague and indefinite, and cannot, in itself, imply a definite offense. The courts, by a kind of judicial legislation, in England and the United States, have usually limited the operation of the term to public displays of the naked person, the publication, sale, or exhibition of obscene books and prints, or the exhibition of a monster,—acts which have a direct bearing on public morals, and affect the body of society. The Indiana statute punishing public indecency, without defining it, can be construed only as that term is used at common law, where it is limited to indecencies in conduct, and does not extend to indecent words. 10 Ind. 140.

PUBLIC LANDS. Such lands as are subject to sale or other disposition by the United States, under general laws. 92 U. S. 761.

PUBLIC LAW. That branch or department of law which is concerned with the state in its political or sovereign capacity, including constitutional and administrative law, and with the definition, regulation, and enforcement of rights in cases where the state is regarded as the subject of the right or object of the duty,—including criminal law and criminal procedure,—and the law of the state, considered in its *quasi* private personality, *i. e.*, as capable of holding or exercising rights, or acquiring and dealing with property, in the character of an individual. See Holl. Jur. 106, 300.

That portion of law which is concerned with political conditions; that is to say, with the powers, rights, duties, capacities, and incapacities which are peculiar to political superiors, supreme and subordinate. Aust. Jur.

"Public law," in one sense, is a designation given to "international law," as distinguished from the laws of a particular nation or state. In another sense, a law or statute that applies to the people generally of the nation or state adopting or enacting it, is denominated a public law, as contradistinguished from a private law, affecting only an individual or a small number of persons. 46 Vt. 773.

PUBLIC MINISTER. In international law. A general term comprehending all the higher classes of diplomatic representatives,—as ambassadors, envoys, residents,—but not including the commercial representatives, such as consuls.

PUBLIC MONEY. This term, as used in the laws of the United States, includes all the funds of the general government derived from the public revenues, or intrusted to the fiscal officers. See 12 Ct. Cl. 281.

PUBLIC NOTICE. Notice given to the public generally, or to the entire community, or to all whom it may concern.

PUBLIC NUISANCE. One affecting an indefinite number of persons, or all the residents of the particular locality, or all people coming within the range of its extent or operation; as distinguished from one which harms or annoys only a particular individual, the latter species being called a "private nuisance."

PUBLIC OFFENSE. A public offense is an act or omission forbidden by law, and punishable as by law provided. Code Ala. 1886, § 3699.

PUBLIC OFFICER. An officer of a public corporation; that is, one holding office under the government of a municipality, state, or nation.

In English law, an officer appointed by a joint-stock banking company, under the statutes regulating such companies, to prosecute and defend suits in its behalf.

PUBLIC PASSAGE. A right, subsisting in the public, to pass over a body of water, whether the land under it be public or owned by a private person.

PUBLIC PEACE. The peace or tranquillity of the community in general; the good order and repose of the people composing a state or municipality.

PUBLIC PLACE. See PUBLIC HOUSE. And see 22 Ala. 15.

PUBLIC POLICY. The principles under which the freedom of contract or private dealings is restricted by law for the good of the community. Wharton.

The term "policy," as applied to a statute, regulation, rule of law, course of action, or the like, refers to its probable effect, tendency, or object, considered with reference to the social or political well-being of the state. Thus, certain classes of acts are said to be "against public policy," when the law refuses to enforce or recognize them, on the ground that they have a mischievous tendency, so as to be injurious to the interests of the state, apart from illegality or immorality. Sweet.

PUBLIC PRINTING means such as is directly ordered by the legislature, or performed by the agents of the government authorized to procure it to be done. 4 Ind. 1.

PUBLIC PROPERTY. This term is commonly used as a designation of those things which are *publici juris*, (*q. v.*,) and therefore considered as being owned by "the public," the entire state or community, and not restricted to the dominion of a private person. It may also apply to any subject of property owned by a state, nation, or municipal corporation as such.

PUBLIC PROSECUTOR. An officer of government (such as a state's attorney or district attorney) whose function is the prosecution of criminal actions, or suits partaking of the nature of criminal actions.

PUBLIC RECORD. A record, memorial of some act or transaction, written evidence of something done, or document, considered as either concerning or interesting the public, affording notice or information to the public, or open to public inspection.

PUBLIC REVENUE. The revenue of the government of the state or nation; sometimes, perhaps, that of a municipality.

PUBLIC RIVER. A river where there is a common navigation exercised; otherwise called a "navigable river." 1 Crabb, Real Prop. p. 111, § 106.

PUBLIC SALE. A sale made in pursuance of a notice, by auction or public outcry. 4 Watts, 258.

PUBLIC SCHOOLS. Schools established under the laws of the state, (and usually regulated in matters of detail by the local authorities,) in the various districts, counties, or towns, maintained at the public expense by taxation, and open without charge to the children of all the residents of the town or other district.

PUBLIC SEAL. A seal belonging to and used by one of the bureaus or departments of government, for authenticating or attesting documents, process, or records.

An impression made of some device, by means of a piece of metal or other hard substance, kept and used by public authority. 7 Port. (Ala.) 534.

PUBLIC STATUTE. See PUBLIC ACT.

PUBLIC STOCKS. The funded or bonded debt of a government or state.

PUBLIC STORE. A government warehouse, maintained for certain administrative purposes, such as the keeping of military supplies, the storing of imported goods under bonds to pay duty, etc.

PUBLIC TRIAL. A trial held in public, in the presence of the public, or in a place accessible and open to the attendance of the public at large, or of persons who may properly be admitted.

"By this [public trial] is not meant that every person who sees fit shall in all cases be permitted to attend criminal trials, because there are many cases where, from the character of the charge and the nature of the evidence by which it is to be supported, the motives to attend the trial, on the part of portions of the community, would be of the worst character, and where a regard to public morals and public decency would require that at least the young be excluded from hearing and witnessing the evidences of human depravity which the trial must necessarily bring to light. The requirement of a public trial is for the benefit of the accused; that the public may see he is fairly dealt with and not unjustly condemned, and that the presence of interested spectators may keep his triers keenly alive to a sense of their responsibility and to the importance of their functions; and the requirement is fairly observed if, without partiality or favoritism, a reasonable proportion of the public is suffered to attend, notwithstanding that those persons whose presence could be of no service to the accused, and who would only be drawn thither by a prurient curiosity, are excluded altogether." Cooley, Const. Lim. *312.

PUBLIC, TRUE, AND NOTORIOUS. The old form by which charges in the *allegations* in the ecclesiastical courts were described at the end of each particular.

PUBLIC USE, in constitutional provisions restricting the exercise of the right to take private property in virtue of eminent domain, means a use concerning the whole community as distinguished from particular individuals. But each and every member of society need not be equally interested in such use, or be personally and directly affected by it; if the object is to satisfy a great public want or exigency, that is sufficient. 18 Cal. 229.

PUBLIC VERDICT. A verdict openly delivered by the jury in court. See PRIVY VERDICT.

PUBLIC VESSEL. One owned and used by a nation or government for its public service, whether in its navy, its revenue service, or otherwise.

PUBLIC WAR. This term includes every contention by force, between two nations, in external matters, under the authority of their respective governments. 4 Dall. 40.

PUBLIC WAYS. Highways, (*q. v.*)

PUBLIC WELFARE. The prosperity, well-being, or convenience of the public at large, or of a whole community, as distinguished from the advantage of an individual or limited class. See 4 Ohio St. 499.

PUBLIC WORKS. Works, whether of construction or adaptation, undertaken and carried out by the national, state, or municipal authorities, and designed to subserve some purpose of public necessity, use, or convenience; such as public buildings, roads, aqueducts, parks, etc.

PUBLIC WORSHIP. This term may mean the worship of God, conducted and observed under public authority; or it may mean worship in an open or public place, without privacy or concealment; or it may mean the performance of religious exercises, under a provision for an equal right in the whole public to participate in its benefits; or it may be used in contradistinction to worship in the family or the closet. In this country, what is called "public worship" is commonly conducted by voluntary societies, constituted according to their own notions of ecclesiastical authority and ritual propriety, opening their places of worship, and admitting to their religious services such persons, and upon such terms, and subject to such regulations, as they may choose to designate and establish. A church absolutely belonging to the public, and in which all persons without restriction have equal rights, such as the public enjoy in highways or public landings, is certainly a very rare institution. 14 Gray, 586.

PUBLIC WRONGS. Violations of public rights and duties which affect the whole community, considered as a community; crimes and misdemeanors. 3 Bl. Comm. 2; 4 Bl. Comm. 1.

PUBLICAN. In the civil law. A farmer of the public revenue; one who held a lease of some property from the public treasury. Dig. 39, 4, 1, 1; Id. 39, 4, 12, 3; Id. 39, 4, 13.

In English law. Persons authorized by license to keep a public house, and retail therein, for consumption on or off the premises where sold, all intoxicating liquors; also termed "licensed victuallers." Wharton.

PUBLICANUS. Lat. In Roman law. A farmer of the customs; a publican. Calvin.

PUBLICATION. 1. The act of publishing anything or making it public; offering it to public notice, or rendering it accessible to public scrutiny.

2. As descriptive of the publishing of laws and ordinances, "publication" means printing or otherwise reproducing copies of them and distributing them in such a manner as to make their contents easily accessible to the public; it forms no part of the enactment of the law. "Promulgation," on the other hand, seems to denote the proclamation or announcement of the edict or statute as a preliminary to its acquiring the force and operation of law. But the two terms are often used interchangeably.

3. The formal declaration made by a testator at the time of signing his will that it is his last will and testament. 4 Kent, Comm. 515, and note.

4. In the law of libel, publication denotes the act of making the defamatory matter known publicly, of disseminating it, or communicating it to one or more persons.

5. In the practice of the states adopting the reformed procedure, and in some others, publication of a summons is the process of giving it currency as an advertisement in a newspaper, under the conditions prescribed by law, as a means of giving notice of the suit to a defendant upon whom personal service cannot be made.

6. In equity practice. The making public the depositions taken in a suit, which have previously been kept private in the office of the examiner. *Publication* is said *to pass* when the depositions are so made public, or openly shown, and copies of them given out, in order to the hearing of the cause. 3 Bl. Comm. 450.

7. In copyright law. The act of making public a book, writing, chart, map, etc.; that is, offering or communicating it to the public by the sale or distribution of copies.

PUBLICI JURIS. Lat. Of public right. This term, as applied to a thing or right, means that it is open to or exercisable by all persons.

When a thing is common property, so that any one can make use of it who likes, it is said to be "*publici juris;*" as in the case of light, air, and public water. Sweet.

Or it designates things which are owned by "the public;" that is, the entire state or community, and not by any private person.

PUBLICIANA. In the civil law. The name of an action introduced by the prætor Publicius, the object of which was to recover a thing which had been lost. Its effects were similar to those of our action of trover. Mackeld. Rom. Law, § 298. See Inst. 4, 6, 4; Dig. 6, 2, 1, 16.

PUBLICIST. One versed in, or writing upon, public law, the science and principles of government, or international law.

PUBLICUM JUS. Lat. In the civil law. Public law; that law which regards the state of the commonwealth. Inst. 1, 1, 4.

PUBLISHER. One whose business is the manufacture, promulgation, and sale of books, pamphlets, magazines, newspapers, or other literary productions.

PUDICITY. Chastity: purity; continence.

PUDZELD. In old English law. Supposed to be a corruption of the Saxon "*wudgeld,*" (woodgeld,) a freedom from payment of money for taking *wood* in any forest. Co. Litt. 233*a*.

PUEBLO. In Spanish law. People; all the inhabitants of any country or place, without distinction. A town, township, or municipality. White, New Recop. b. 2, tit. 1, c. 6, § 4.

This term "*pueblo*," in its original signification, means "people" or "population," but is used in the sense of the English word "town." It has the indefiniteness of that term, and, like it, is sometimes applied to a mere collection of individuals residing at a particular place, a settlement or village, as well as to a regularly organized municipality. 100 U. S. 251.

PUER. Lat. In the civil law. A child; one of the age from seven to fourteen, including, in this sense, a girl. But it also meant a "boy," as distinguished from a "girl;" or a servant.

Pueri sunt de sanguine parentum, sed pater et mater non sunt de sanguine puerorum. 3 Coke, 40. Children are of the blood of their parents, but the father and mother are not of the blood of the children.

PUERILITY. In the civil law. A condition intermediate between infancy and puberty, continuing in boys from the seventh to the fourteenth year of their age, and in girls from seven to twelve.

PUERITIA. Lat. In the civil law. Childhood; the age from seven to fourteen. 4 Bl. Comm. 22.

PUFFER. A person employed by the owner of property which is sold at auction to attend the sale and run up the price by making spurious bids.

PUIS. In law French. Afterwards; since.

PUIS DARREIN CONTINUANCE. L. Fr. Since the last continuance. The name of a plea which a defendant is allowed to put in, after having already pleaded, where some *new* matter of defense arises after issue joined; such as payment, a release by the plaintiff, the discharge of the defendant under an insolvent or bankrupt law, and the like. 3 Bl. Comm. 316; 2 Tidd, Pr. 847.

PUISNE. L. Fr. Younger; subordinate; associate.

The title by which the justices and barons of the several common-law courts at Westminster are distinguished from the *chief* justice and *chief* baron.

PUISSANCE PATERNELLE. Fr. Paternal power. In the French law, the male parent has the following rights over the person of his child: (1) If child is under sixteen years of age, he may procure him to be imprisoned for one month or under. (2) If child is over sixteen and under twenty-one he may procure an imprisonment for six months or under, with power in each case to procure a second period of imprisonment. The female parent, being a widow, may, with the approval of the two nearest relations on the father's side, do the like. The parent enjoys also the following rights over the property of his child, viz., a right to take the income until the child attains the age of eighteen years, subject to maintaining the child and educating him in a suitable manner. Brown.

PULSARE. In the civil law. To beat; to accuse or charge; to proceed against at law. Calvin.

PULSATOR. The plaintiff, or actor.

PUNCTUATION. The division of a written or printed document into sentences by means of periods; and of sentences into smaller divisions by means of commas, semicolons, colons, etc.

PUNCTUM TEMPORIS. Lat. A point of time; an indivisible period of time; the shortest space of time; an instant. Calvin.

PUNCTURED WOUND. In medical jurisprudence. A wound made by the insertion into the body of any instrument having a sharp point. The term is practically synonymous with "stab."

PUNDBRECH. In old English law. Pound-breach; the offense of breaking a pound. The illegal taking of cattle out of a pound by any means whatsoever. Cowell.

PUNDIT. An interpreter of the Hindu law; a learned Brahmin.

PUNISHABLE. Liable to punishment, whether absolutely or in the exercise of a judicial discretion.

PUNISHMENT. In criminal law. Any pain, penalty, suffering, or confinement inflicted upon a person by the authority of the law and the judgment and sentence of a court, for some crime or offense committed by him, or for his omission of a duty enjoined by law.

PUNITIVE DAMAGES. In practice. Damages given by way of punishment; exemplary or vindictive damages. 13 How 371; 2 Metc. (Ky.) 146.

PUNITIVE POWER. The power and authority of a state. or organized jural society, to inflict punishments upon those persons who have committed actions inherently evil and injurious to the public, or actions declared by the laws of that state to be sanctioned with punishments.

PUPIL. In the civil law. One who is in his or her minority. Particularly, one who is in ward or guardianship.

PUPILLARIS SUBSTITUTIO. Lat. In the civil law. Pupillar substitution; the substitution of an heir to a pupil or infant under puberty. The substitution by a father of an heir to his children under his power, disposing of his own estate and theirs, in case the child refused to accept the inheritance, or died before the age of puberty. Hallifax, Civil Law, b. 2, c. 6, no. 64.

PUPILLARITY. In Scotch law. That period of minority from the birth to the age of fourteen in males, and twelve in females. Bell.

PUPILLUS. Lat. In the civil law. A ward or infant under the age of puberty; a person under the authority of a *tutor*, (*q. v.*)

Pupillus pati posse non intelligitur. A pupil or infant is not supposed to be able to suffer, *i. e.*, to do an act to his own prejudice. Dig. 50, 17, 110, 2.

PUR. L. Fr. By or for. Used both as a separable particle, and in the composition of such words as "purparty," "purlieu."

PUR AUTRE VIE. L. Fr. For (or during) the life of another. An estate *pur autre vie* is an estate which endures only for the life of some particular person other than the grantee.

PUR CAUSE DE VICINAGE. L. Fr. By reason of neighborhood. See COMMON.

PUR TANT QUE. L. Fr. Forasmuch as; because; to the intent that. Kelham.

PURCHASE. The word "purchase" is used in law in contradistinction to "descent," and means any other mode of acquiring real property than by the common course of inheritance. But it is also much used in its more restricted vernacular sense, (that of buying for a sum of money,) especially in modern law literature; and this is universally its application to the case of chattels.

PURCHASE MONEY. The consideration in money paid or agreed to be paid by the buyer to the seller of property, particularly of land.

Purchase money means money stipulated to be paid by a purchaser to his vendor, and does not include money the purchaser may have borrowed to complete his purchase. Purchase money, as between vendor and vendee only, is contemplated; as between purchaser and lender, the money is "borrowed money." 38 Md. 270.

PURCHASE-MONEY MORTGAGE. A mortgage given, concurrently with a conveyance of land, by the vendee to the vendor, on the same land, to secure the unpaid balance of the purchase price.

PURCHASE, WORDS OF. Those by which, taken absolutely, without reference to or connection with any other words, an estate first attaches, or is considered as commencing in point of title, in the person described by them; such as the words "son," "daughter." Wharton.

PURCHASER. One who acquires real property in any other mode than by descent. One who acquires either real or personal property by buying it for a price in money; a buyer; vendee.

In the construction of registry acts, the term "purchaser" is usually taken in its technical legal sense. It means a complete purchaser, or, in other words, one clothed with the legal title. 1 Pet. 552, 559.

PURCHASER OF A NOTE OR BILL. The person who buys a promissory note or bill of exchange from the holder without his indorsement.

Purchaser without notice is not obliged to discover to his own hurt. See 4 Bouv. Inst. no. 4336.

PURE DEBT. In Scotch law. A debt due now and unconditionally is so called. It is thus distinguished from a *future* debt,—payable at a fixed day in the future,—and a *contingent* debt, which will only become due upon the happening of a certain contingency.

PURE OBLIGATION. One which is not suspended by any condition, whether it has been contracted without any condition, or, when thus contracted, the condition has been accomplished. Poth. Obl. no. 176.

PURE PLEA. In equity pleading. One which relies wholly on some matter outside those referred to in the bill; as a plea of a release on a settled account.

PURE VILLENAGE. A base tenure, where a man holds upon terms of doing whatsoever is commanded of him, nor knows in the evening what is to be done in the morning, and is always bound to an uncertain service. 1 Steph. Comm. (7th Ed.) 188.

PURGATION. The act of cleansing or exonerating one's self of a crime, accusation, or suspicion of guilt, by denying the charge on oath or by ordeal.

Canonical purgation was made by the party's taking his own oath that he was innocent of the charge, which was supported by the oath of twelve compurgators, who swore they believed he spoke the truth. To this succeeded the mode of purgation by the single oath of the party himself, called the "oath *ex officio*," of which the modern defendant's oath in chancery is a modification. 3 Bl. Comm. 447; 4 Bl. Comm. 368.

Vulgar purgation consisted in ordeals or trials by hot and cold water, by fire, by hot irons, by battel, by corsned, etc.

PURGE. To cleanse; to clear; to clear or exonerate from some charge or imputation of guilt, or from a contempt.

PURGE DES HYPOTHÈQUES. In French law. An expression used to describe the act of freeing an estate from the mortgages and privileges with which it is charged, observing the formalities prescribed by law. Duverger.

PURGED OF PARTIAL COUNSEL. In Scotch practice. Cleared of having been partially advised. A term applied to the preliminary examination of a witness, in which he is sworn and examined whether he has received any bribe or promise of reward, or has been told what to say, or whether he bears malice or ill will to any of the parties. Bell.

PURGING A TORT is like the ratification of a wrongful act by a person who has power of himself to lawfully do the act. But, unlike ratification, the purging of the tort may take place even after commencement of the action. 1 Brod. & B. 282.

PURGING CONTEMPT. Atoning for, or clearing one's self from, contempt of court, (*q. v.*) It is generally done by apologizing and paying fees, and is generally admitted after a moderate time in proportion to the magnitude of the offense.

PURLIEU. In English law. A space of land near a royal forest, which, being severed from it, was made *purlieu;* that is, pure or free from the forest laws.

PURLIEU-MEN. Those who have ground within the purlieu to the yearly value of 40s. a year freehold are licensed to hunt in their own purlieus. Manw. c. 20, § 8.

PURPARTY. A part in a division; a share.

The part or share of an estate held by coparceners, which is by partition allotted to them. Cowell.

PURPORT. Meaning; import; substantial meaning; substance. The "purport" of an instrument means the substance of it as it appears on the face of the instrument, and is distinguished from "tenor," which means an exact copy. 2 East, P. C. 983; Whart. Crim. Law, 83.

PURPRESTURE. A purpresture may be defined as an inclosure by a private party of a part of that which belongs to and ought to be open and free to the enjoyment of the public at large. It is not necessarily a public nuisance. A public nuisance must be something which subjects the public to some degree of inconvenience or annoyance; but a purpresture may exist without putting the public to any inconvenience whatever. 34 Mich. 462.

PURPRISE. A close or inclosure; as also the whole compass of a manor.

PURPURE, or PORPRIN. A term used in heraldry; the color commonly called "purple," expressed in engravings by lines in bend sinister. In the arms of princes it was formerly called "mercury," and in those of peers "amethyst."

PURSE. A purse, prize, or premium is ordinarily some valuable thing, offered by a person for the doing of something by others, into strife for which he does not enter. He has not a chance of gaining the thing offered; and, if he abide by his offer, that he must lose it and give it over to some of those contending for it is reasonably certain. 81 N. Y. 539.

PURSER. The person appointed by the master of a ship or vessel, whose duty it is to take care of the ship's books, in which every thing on board is inserted, as well the names of mariners as the articles of merchandise shipped. Roccius, Ins. note.

PURSUE. To follow a matter judicially, as a complaining party.

To pursue a warrant or authority, in the old books, is to execute it or carry it out. Co. Litt. 52*a*.

PURSUER. The name by which the complainant or plaintiff is known in the ecclesiastical courts, and in the Scotch law.

PURUS IDIOTA. Lat. A congenital idiot.

PURVEYANCE. In old English law. A providing of necessaries for the king's house. Cowell.

PURVEYOR. In old English law. An officer who procured or purchased articles needed for the king's use at an arbitrary price. In the statute 36 Edw. III. c. 2, this is called a "*heignous nome,*" (heinous or hateful name,) and changed to that of "*achator.*" Barring. Ob. St. 289.

PURVIEW. That part of a statute commencing with the words "Be it enacted," and continuing as far as the repealing clause; and hence, the design, contemplation, purpose, or scope of the act.

PUT. In pleading. To confide to; to rely upon; to submit to. As in the phrase, "the said defendant puts himself upon the country;" that is, he trusts his case to the arbitrament of a jury.

PUT IN. In practice. To place in due form before a court; to place among the records of a court.

PUT OUT. To open. To put out lights; to open or cut windows. 11 East, 372.

Putagium hæreditatem non adimit. 1 Reeve, Eng. Law, c. 3, p. 117. Incontinence does not take away an inheritance.

PUTATIVE. Reputed; supposed; commonly esteemed. Applied in Scotch law to creditors and proprietors. 2 Kames, Eq. 105, 107, 109.

PUTATIVE FATHER. The alleged or reputed father of an illegitimate child.

PUTATIVE MARRIAGE. A marriage contracted in good faith and in ignorance (on one or both sides) that impediments exist which render it unlawful. See Mackeld. Rom. Law, § 556.

PUTS AND CALLS. A "put" in the language of the grain or stock market is a privilege of delivering or not delivering the subject-matter of the sale; and a "call" is a privilege of calling or not calling for it. 79 Ill. 351.

PUTS AND REFUSALS. In English law. Time-bargains, or contracts for the sale of supposed stock on a future day.

PUTTING IN FEAR. These words are used in the definition of a robbery from the person. The offense must have been committed by *putting in fear* the person robbed. 3 Inst. 68; 4 Bl. Comm. 243.

PUTTING IN SUIT, as applied to a bond, or any other legal instrument, signifies bringing an action upon it, or making it the subject of an action.

PUTURE. In old English law. A custom claimed by keepers in forests, and sometimes by bailiffs of hundreds, to take man's meat, horse's meat, and dog's meat of the tenants and inhabitants within the perambulation of the forest, hundred, etc. The land subject to this custom was called "*terra putura.*" Others, who call it "*pulture,*" explain it as a demand in general; and derive it from the monks, who, before they were admitted, *pulsabant,* knocked at the gates for several days together. 4 Inst. 307; Cowell.

PYKE, PAIK. In Hindu law. A foot-passenger; a person employed as a night-watch in a village, and as a runner or messenger on the business of the revenue. Wharton.

PYKERIE. In old Scotch law. Petty theft. 2 Pitc. Crim. Tr. 43.

Q.

Q. B. An abbreviation of "Queen's Bench."

Q. B. D. An abbreviation of "Queen's Bench Division."

Q. C. An abbreviation of "Queen's Counsel."

Q. C. F. An abbreviation of "*quare clausum fregit,*" (*q. v.*)

Q. E. N. An abbreviation of "*quare executionem non,*" wherefore execution [should] not [be issued.]

Q. S. An abbreviation for "Quarter Sessions."

Q. T. An abbreviation of "*qui tam,*" (*q. v.*)

Q. V. An abbreviation of "*quod vide,*" used to refer a reader to the word, chapter, etc., the name of which it immediately follows.

QUA. Lat Considered as; in the character or capacity of. For example, "the trustee *qua* trustee [that is, in his character as trustee] is not liable," etc.

QUACK. A pretender to medical skill which he does not possess; one who practices as a physician or surgeon without adequate preparation or due qualification.

QUACUNQUE VIA DATA. Lat. Whichever way you take it.

QUADRAGESIMA. Lat. The fortieth. The first Sunday in Lent is so called because it is about the fortieth day before Easter. Cowell.

QUADRAGESIMALS. Offerings formerly made, on Mid-Lent Sunday, to the mother church.

QUADRAGESMS. The third volume of the year books of the reign of Edward III. So called because beginning with the *fortieth* year of that sovereign's reign. Crabb, Eng. Law, 327.

QUADRANS. In Roman law. The fourth part; the quarter of any number, measure, or quantity. Hence an heir to the fourth part of the inheritance was called "*hæres ex quadrante.*" Also a Roman coin, being the fourth part of an *as*, equal in value to an English half-penny.

In old English law. A farthing; a fourth part or quarter of a penny.

QUADRANT. An angular measure of ninety degrees.

QUADRANTATA TERRÆ. In old English law. A measure of land, variously described as a quarter of an acre or the fourth part of a yard-land.

QUADRARIUM. In old records. A stone-pit or quarry. Cowell.

QUADRIENNIUM. In the civil law. The four-years course of study required to be pursued by law-students before they were qualified to study the Code or collection of imperial constitutions. See Inst. proem.

QUADRIENNIUM UTILE. In Scotch law. The term of four years allowed to a minor, after his majority, in which he may by suit or action endeavor to annul any deed to his prejudice, granted during his minority. Bell.

QUADRIPARTITE. Divided into four parts. A term applied in conveyancing to an indenture executed in four parts.

QUADROON. A person who is descended from a white person and another person who has an equal mixture of the European and African blood. 2 Bailey, 558.

QUADRUPLATORES. Lat. In Roman law. Informers who, if their information were followed by conviction, had the fourth part of the confiscated goods for their trouble.

QUADRUPLICATIO. Lat. In the civil law. A pleading on the part of a defendant, corresponding to the *rebutter* at common law. The third pleading on the part of the defendant. Inst. 4, 14, 3; 3 Bl. Comm. 310.

Quæ ab hostibus capiuntur, statim capientium fiunt. 2 Burrows, 693. Things which are taken from enemies immediately become the property of the captors.

Quæ ab initio inutilis fuit institutio, ex post facto convalescere non potest. An institution which was at the beginning of no use or force cannot acquire force from after matter. Dig. 50, 17, 210.

Quæ ab initio non valent, ex post facto convalescere non possunt. Things invalid from the beginning cannot be made valid by subsequent act. Tray. Lat. Max. 482.

Quæ accessionum locum obtinent, extinguuntur cum principales res peremptæ fuerint. Things which hold the place of accessories are extinguished when the principal things are destroyed. 2 Poth. Obl. 202; Broom, Max. 496.

Quæ ad unum finem loquuta sunt, non debent ad alium detorqueri. 4 Coke, 14. Those words which are spoken to one end ought not to be perverted to another.

Quæ cohærent personæ a persona separari nequeunt. Things which cohere to, or are closely connected with, the person, cannot be separated from the person. Jenk. Cent. p. 28, case 53.

Quæ communi lege derogant stricte interpretantur. [Statutes] which derogate from the common law are strictly interpreted. Jenk. Cent. p. 221, case 72.

Quæ contra rationem juris introducta sunt, non debent trahi in consequentiam. 12 Coke, 75. Things introduced contrary to the reason of law ought not to be drawn into a precedent.

Quæ dubitationis causa tollendæ inseruntur communem legem non lædunt. Co. Litt. 205. Things which are inserted for the purpose of removing doubt hurt not the common law.

Quæ dubitationis tollendæ causa contractibus inseruntur, jus commune non lædunt. Particular clauses inserted in agreements to avoid doubts and ambiguity do not prejudice the general law. Dig. 50, 17, 81.

QUÆ EST EADEM. Lat. Which is the same. Words used for alleging that the trespass or other fact mentioned in the plea is the same as that laid in the declaration, where, from the circumstances, there is an apparent difference between the two. 1 Chit. Pl. *582.

Quæ in curia regis acta sunt rite agi præsumuntur. 3 Bulst. 43. Things done in the king's court are presumed to be rightly done.

Quæ in partes dividi nequeunt solida a singulis præstantur. 6 Coke, 1. Services which are incapable of division are to be performed in whole by each individual.

Quæ in testamento ita sunt scripta ut intelligi non possint, perinde sunt ac si scripta non essent. Things which are so written in a will that they cannot be understood, are the same as if they had not been written at all. Dig. 50, 17, 73, 3.

Quæ incontinenti fiunt inesse videntur. Things which are done incontinently [or simultaneously with an act] are supposed to be inherent [in it; to be a constituent part of it.] Co. Litt. 236*b*.

Quæ inter alios acta sunt nemini nocere debent, sed prodesse possunt. 6 Coke, 1. Transactions between strangers ought to hurt no man, but may benefit.

Quæ legi communi derogant non sunt trahenda in exemplum. Things derogatory to the common law are not to be drawn into precedent. Branch. Princ.

Quæ legi communi derogant stricte interpretantur. Jenk. Cent. 29. Those things which are derogatory to the common law are to be strictly interpreted.

Quæ mala sunt inchoata in principio vix bono peraguntur exitu. 4 Coke, 2. Things bad in principle at the commencement seldom achieve a good end.

QUÆ NIHIL FRUSTRA. Lat. Which [does or requires] nothing in vain. Which requires nothing to be done, that is, to no purpose. 2 Kent, Comm. 53.

Quæ non fieri debent, facta valent. Things which ought not to be done are held valid when they have been done. Tray. Lat. Max. 484.

Quæ non valeant singula, juncta juvant. Things which do not avail when separate, when joined avail. 3 Bulst. 132; Broom, Max. 588.

QUÆ PLURA. Lat. In old English practice. A writ which lay where an inquisition had been made by an escheator in any county of such lands or tenements as any man died seised of, and all that was in his possession was imagined not to be found by the office; the writ commanding the escheator to inquire *what more* (*quæ plura*) lands and tenements the party held on the day when he died, etc. Fitzh. Nat. Brev. 255*a*; Cowell.

Quæ præter consuetudinem et morem majorum fiunt neque placent neque recta videntur. Things which are done contrary to the custom of our ancestors neither please nor appear right. 4 Coke, 78.

Quæ propter necessitatem recepta sunt, non debent in argumentum trahi. Things which are admitted on the ground of necessity ought not to be drawn into question. Dig. 50, 17, 162.

Quæ rerum natura prohibentur nulla lege confirmata sunt. Things which are forbidden by the nature of things are [can be] confirmed by no law. Branch, Princ. Positive laws are framed after the laws of nature and reason. Finch, Law, 74.

Quæ singula non prosunt, juncta juvant. Things which taken singly are of no avail afford help when taken together. Tray. Lat. Max. 486.

Quæ sunt minoris culpæ sunt majoris infamiæ. [Offenses] which are of a lower grade of guilt are of a higher degree of infamy. Co. Litt. 6b.

Quæcunque intra rationem legis inveniuntur intra legem ipsam esse judicantur. Things which are found within the reason of a law are supposed to be within the law itself. 2 Inst. 689.

Quælibet concessio domini regis capi debet stricte contra dominum regem, quando potest intelligi duabus viis. 3 Leon. 243. Every grant of our lord the king ought to be taken strictly against our lord the king, when it can be understood in two ways.

Quælibet concessio fortissime contra donatorem interpretanda est. Every grant is to be interpreted most strongly against the grantor. Co. Litt. 183a.

Quælibet jurisdictio cancellos suos habet. Jenk. Cent. 137. Every jurisdiction has its own bounds.

Quælibet pardonatio debet capi secundum intentionem regis, et non ad deceptionem regis. 3 Bulst. 14. Every pardon ought to be taken according to the intention of the king, and not to the deception of the king.

Quælibet pœna corporalis, quamvis minima, major est qualibet pœna pecuniaria. 3 Inst. 220. Every corporal punishment, although the very least, is greater than any pecuniary punishment.

Quæras de dubiis legem bene discere si vis. Inquire into doubtful points if you wish to understand the law well. Litt. § 443.

QUÆRE. A query; question; doubt. This word, occurring in the syllabus of a reported case or elsewhere, shows that a question is propounded as to what follows, or that the particular rule, decision, or statement is considered as open to question.

Quære de dubiis, quia per rationes pervenitur ad legitimam rationem. Inquire into doubtful points, because by reasoning we arrive at legal reason. Litt. § 377.

QUÆRENS. A plaintiff; the plaintiff.

QUÆRENS NIHIL CAPIAT PER BILLAM. The plaintiff shall take nothing by his bill. A form of judgment for the defendant. Latch, 133.

QUÆRENS NON INVENIT PLEGIUM. L. Lat. The plaintiff did not find a pledge. A return formerly made by a sheriff to a writ requiring him to take security of the plaintiff to prosecute his claim. Cowell.

Quærere dat sapere quæ sunt legitima vere. Litt. § 443. To inquire into them, is the way to know what things are truly lawful.

QUÆSTA. An indulgence or remission of penance, sold by the pope.

QUÆSTIO. In Roman law. Anciently a species of commission granted by the *comitia* to one or more persons for the purpose of inquiring into some crime or public offense and reporting thereon. In later times, the *quæstio* came to exercise plenary criminal jurisdiction, even to pronouncing sentence, and then was appointed periodically, and eventually became a *permanent* commission or regular criminal tribunal, and was then called "*quæstio perpetua.*" See Maine, Anc. Law, 369–372.

In medieval law. The question; the torture; inquiry or inquisition by inflicting the torture.

QUÆSTIONARII. Those who carried *quæsta* about from door to door.

QUÆSTIONES PERPETUÆ, in Roman law, were commissions (or courts) of inquisition into crimes alleged to have been committed. They were called "*perpetuæ,*" to distinguish them from *occasional* inquisitions, and because they were permanent courts for the trial of offenders. Brown.

QUÆSTOR. Lat. A Roman magistrate, whose office it was to collect the public revenue. Varro de L. L. iv. 14.

QUÆSTOR SACRI PALATII. Lat. Quæstor of the sacred palace. An officer of the imperial court at Constantinople, with powers and duties resembling those of a chancellor. Calvin.

QUÆSTUS. That estate which a man has by acquisition or purchase, in contradistinction to "*hæreditas,*" which is what he has by descent. Glan. 1, 7, c. 1.

QUAKER. This, in England, is the statutory, as well as the popular, name of a member of a religious society, by themselves denominated "Friends."

QUALE JUS. Lat. In old English law. A judicial writ, which lay where a man of religion had judgment to recover land before execution was made of the judgment. It went forth to the escheator between judgment and execution, to inquire what *right* the religious person had to recover, or whether the judgment were obtained by the collusion of the parties, to the intent that the lord might not be defrauded. Reg. Jud. 8.

QUALIFICATION. The possession by an individual of the qualities, properties, or circumstances, natural or adventitious, which are inherently or legally necessary to render him eligible to fill an office or to perform a public duty or function. Thus, the ownership of a freehold estate may be made the qualification of a voter; so the possession of a certain amount of stock in a corporation may be the qualification necessary to enable one to serve on its board of directors.

Qualification for office is "endowment, or accomplishment that fits for an office; having the legal requisites, endowed with qualities suitable for the purpose." 64 Mo. 89.

Also a modification or limitation of terms or language; usually intended by way of restriction of expressions which, by reason of their generality, would carry a larger meaning than was designed.

QUALIFIED. Adapted; fitted; entitled; as an elector to vote. Applied to one who has taken the steps to prepare himself for an appointment or office, as by taking oath, giving bond, etc. Pub. St. Mass. p. 1294.

Also limited; restricted; confined; modified; imperfect, or temporary.

The term is also applied in England to a person who is enabled to hold two benefices at once.

QUALIFIED ELECTOR means a person who is legally qualified to vote, while a "legal voter" means a qualified elector who does in fact vote. 28 Wis. 358.

QUALIFIED FEE. In English law. A fee having a qualification subjoined thereto, and which must be determined whenever the qualification annexed to it is at an end; otherwise termed a "base fee." 2 Bl. Comm. 109; 1 Steph. Comm. 225. An interest which may continue forever, but is liable to be determined, without the aid of a conveyance, by some act or event, circumscribing its continuance or extent. 4 Kent, Comm. 9.

QUALIFIED INDORSEMENT. A transfer of a bill of exchange or promissory note to an indorsee, without any liability to the indorser. The words usually employed for this purpose are "*sans recours,*" without recourse. 1 Bouv. Inst. no. 1138.

QUALIFIED OATH. A circumstantial oath.

QUALIFIED PROPERTY. A temporary or special interest in a thing, liable to be totally divested on the happening of some particular event. 2 Kent, Comm. 347.

Such property as is not in its nature permanent, but may sometimes subsist, and at other times not subsist; *e. g.*, the property which a man may have in wild animals which he has caught and holds, and which is only coterminous with his possession, or the limited and special property of a bailee or pledgee. 2 Bl. Comm. 391-396.

QUALIFIED VOTER. A person qualified to vote generally. 9 Colo. 629, 21 Pac. Rep. 473. A person qualified and actually voting. 111 U. S. 565, 4 Sup. Ct. Rep. 539.

QUALIFY. To make one's self fit or prepared to exercise a right, office, or franchise. To take the steps necessary to prepare one's self for an office or appointment, as by taking oath, giving bond, etc. Pub. St. Mass. p. 1294.

Also to limit; to modify; to restrict. Thus, it is said that one section of a statute qualifies another.

Qualitas quæ inesse debet, facile præsumitur. A quality which ought to form a part is easily presumed.

QUALITY. In respect to persons, this term denotes comparative rank; state or condition in relation to others; social or civil position or class. In pleading, it means an attribute or characteristic by which one thing is distinguished from another.

QUALITY OF ESTATE. The period when, and the manner in which, the right of enjoying an estate is exercised. It is of two kinds: (1) The period when the right of enjoying an estate is conferred upon the owner, whether at present or in future; and (2) the manner in which the owner's right of enjoyment of his estate is to be exercised, whether solely, jointly, in common, or in coparcenary. Wharton.

Quam longum debet esse rationabile tempus non definitur in lege, sed pendet ex discretione justiciariorum. Co. Litt. 56. How long *reasonable time* ought to be, is not defined by law, but depends upon the discretion of the judges.

Quam rationabilis debet esse finis, non definitur, sed omnibus circumstantiis inspectis pendet ex justiciariorum discretione. What a reasonable fine ought to be is not defined, but is left to the discretion of the judges, all the circumstances being considered. 11 Coke, 44.

QUAMDIU. Lat. As long as; so long as. A word of limitation in old conveyances. Co. Litt. 235*a*.

QUAMDIU SE BENE GESSERIT. As long as he shall behave himself well; during good behavior; a clause frequent in letters patent or grants of certain offices, to secure them so long as the persons to whom they are granted shall not be guilty of abusing them, the opposite clause being "*durante bene placito*," (during the pleasure of the grantor.)

Quamvis aliquid per se non sit malum, tamen, si sit mali exempli, non est faciendum. Although a thing may not be bad in itself, yet, if it is of bad example, it is not to be done. 2 Inst. 564.

Quamvis lex generaliter loquitur, restringenda tamen est, ut, cessante ratione, ipsa cessat. Although a law speaks generally, yet it is to be restrained, so that when its reason ceases, it should cease also. 4 Inst. 330.

Quando abest provisio partis, adest provisio legis. When the provision of the party is wanting, the provision of the law is at hand. 6 Vin. Abr. 49; 13 C. B. 960.

QUANDO ACCIDERINT. Lat. When they shall come in. The name of a judgment sometimes given against an executor, especially on a plea of *plene administravit*, which empowers the plaintiff to have the benefit of assets which may at any time thereafter come to the hands of the executor.

Quando aliquid mandatur, mandatur et omne per quod pervenitur ad illud. 5 Coke, 116. When anything is commanded, everything by which it can be accomplished is also commanded.

Quando aliquid prohibetur ex directo, prohibetur et per obliquum. Co. Litt. 223. When anything is prohibited directly, it is prohibited also indirectly.

Quando aliquid prohibetur, prohibetur et omne per quod devenitur ad illud. When anything is prohibited, everything by which it is reached is prohibited also. 2 Inst. 48. That which cannot be done directly shall not be done indirectly. Broom, Max. 489.

Quando aliquis aliquid concedit, concedere videtur et id sine quo res uti non potest. When a person grants anything, he is supposed to grant that also without which the thing cannot be used. 3 Kent, Comm. 421. When the use of a thing is granted, everything is granted by which the grantee may have and enjoy such use. Id.

Quando charta continet generalem clausulam, posteaque descendit ad verba specialia quæ clausulæ generali sunt consentanea, interpretanda est charta secundum verba specialia. When a deed contains a general clause, and afterwards descends to special words which are agreeable to the general clause, the deed is to be interpreted according to the special words. 8 Coke, 154*b*.

Quando de una et eadem re duo onerabiles existunt, unus, pro insufficientia alterius, de integro onerabitur. When there are two persons liable for one and the same thing, one of them, in case of default of the other, shall be charged with the whole. 2 Inst. 277.

Quando dispositio referri potest ad duas res ita quod secundum relationem unam vitietur et secundum alteram utilis sit, tum facienda est relatio ad illam ut valeat dispositio. 6 Coke, 76. When a disposition may refer to two things, so that by the former it would be vitiated, and by the latter it would be preserved, then the relation is to be made to the latter, so that the disposition may be valid.

Quando diversi desiderantur actus ad aliquem statum perficiendum, plus respicit lex actum originalem. When different acts are required to the formation of any estate, the law chiefly regards the original act. 10 Coke, 49*a*. When to the perfection of an estate or interest divers acts or things are requisite, the law has more regard to the original act, for that is the fundamental part on which all the others are founded. Id.

Quando jus domini regis et subditi concurrunt, jus regis præferri debet. 9 Coke, 129. When the right of king and of subject concur, the king's right should be preferred.

Quando lex aliquid alicui concedit, concedere videtur et id sine quo res ipsæ esse non potest. 5 Coke, 47. When the law gives a man anything, it gives him that also without which the thing itself cannot exist.

Quando lex aliquid alicui concedit, omnia incidentia tacite conceduntur. 2 Inst. 326. When the law gives anything to any one, all incidents are tacitly given.

Quando lex est specialis, ratio autem generalis, generaliter lex est intelligenda. When a law is special, but its reason [or object] general, the law is to be understood generally. 2 Inst. 83.

Quando licet id quod majus, videtur et licere id quod minus. Shep. Touch. 429. When the greater is allowed, the less is to be understood as allowed also.

Quando mulier nobilis nupserit ignobili, desinit esse nobilis nisi nobilitas nativa fuerit. 4 Coke, 118. When a noble woman marries a man not noble, she ceases to be noble, unless her nobility was born with her.

Quando plus fit quam fieri debet, videtur etiam illud fieri quod faciendum est. When more is done than ought to be done, that at least shall be considered as performed which should have been performed, [as, if a man, having a power to make a lease for ten years, make one for twenty years, it shall be void only for the surplus.] Broom, Max. 177; 5 Coke, 115; 8 Coke, 85*a*.

Quando quod ago non valet ut ago, valeat quantum valere potest. When that which I do does not have effect as I do it, let it have as much effect as it can. 16 Johns. 172, 178; 3 Barb. Ch. 242, 261.

Quando res non valet ut ago, valeat quantum valere potest. When a thing is of no effect as I do it, it shall have effect as far as [or in whatever way] it can. Cowp. 600.

Quando verba et mens congruunt, non est interpretationi locus. When the words and the mind agree, there is no place for interpretation.

Quando verba statuti sunt specialia, ratio autem generalis, generaliter statutum est intelligendum. When the words of a statute are special, but the reason or object of it general, the statute is to be construed generally. 10 Coke, 101*b*.

QUANTI MINORIS. The name of an action in the civil law, (and in Louisiana,) brought by the purchaser of an article, for a reduction of the agreed price on account of defects in the thing which diminish its value.

QUANTUM DAMNIFICATUS? How much damnified? The name of an issue directed by a court of equity to be tried in a court of law, to ascertain the amount of compensation to be allowed for damage.

QUANTUM MERUIT. As much as he deserved. In pleading. The common count in an action of *assumpsit* for work and labor, founded on an implied *assumpsit* or promise on the part of the defendant to pay the plaintiff *as much as he* reasonably *deserved* to have for his labor. 3 Bl. Comm. 161; 1 Tidd, Pr. 2.

Quantum tenens domino ex homagio, tantum dominus tenenti ex dominio debet præter solam reverentiam; mutua debet esse dominii et homagii fidelitatis connexio. Co. Litt. 64. As much as the tenant by his homage owes to his lord, so much is the lord, by his lordship, indebted to the tenant, except reverence alone; the tie of dominion and of homage ought to be mutual.

QUANTUM VALEBANT. As much as they were worth. In pleading. The common count in an action of *assumpsit* for goods sold and delivered, founded on an implied *assumpsit* or promise, on the part of the defendant, to pay the plaintiff *as much as* the goods *were* reasonably *worth*. 3 Bl. Comm. 161; 1 Tidd, Pr. 2.

QUARANTINE. A period of time (theoretically forty days) during which a vessel, coming from a place where a contagious or infectious disease is prevalent, is detained by authority in the harbor of her port of destination, or at a station near it, without being permitted to land or to discharge her crew or passengers. Quarantine is said to have been first established at Venice in 1484. Baker, Quar. 3.

In real property. The space of forty days during which a widow has a right to remain in her late husband's principal mansion immediately after his death. The right of the widow is also called her "quarantine."

QUARE. Lat. Wherefore; for what reason; on what account. Used in the Latin form of several common-law writs.

QUARE CLAUSUM FREGIT. Lat. Wherefore he broke the close. That species of the action of trespass which has for its object the recovery of damages for an unlawful entry upon another's land is termed "trespass *quare clausum fregit;*" "breaking a close" being the technical expression for an unlawful entry upon land. The language of the declaration in this form of action is "that the defendant, with force and arms, broke and entered the close" of the plaintiff. The phrase is often abbreviated to "*qu. cl. fr.*" Brown.

QUARE EJECIT INFRA TERMINUM. Wherefore he ejected within the term. In old practice. A writ which lay for a lessee where he was ejected before the expiration of his term, in cases where the wrong-doer or ejector was not himself in possession of the lands, but his feoffee or another claiming under him. 3 Bl. Comm. 199, 206; Reg. Orig.. 227; Fitzh. Nat. Brev. 197 S.

QUARE IMPEDIT. Wherefore he hinders. In English practice. A writ or action which lies for the patron of an advowson, where he has been disturbed in his right of patronage; so called from the emphatic words of the old form, by which the disturber was summoned to answer *why he hinders* the plaintiff. 3 Bl. Comm. 246, 248.

QUARE INCUMBRAVIT. In English law. A writ which lay against a bishop who, within six months after the vacation of a benefice, conferred it on his clerk, while two others were contending at law for the right of presentation, calling upon him to show cause why he had incumbered the church. Reg. Orig. 32. Abolished by 3 & 4 Wm. IV. c. 27.

QUARE INTRUSIT. A writ that formerly lay where the lord proffered a suitable marriage to his ward, who rejected it, and entered into the land, and married another, the value of his marriage not being satisfied to the lord. Abolished by 12 Car. II. c. 24.

QUARE NON ADMISIT. In English law. A writ to recover damages against a bishop who does not admit a plaintiff's clerk. It is, however, rarely or never necessary; for it is said that a bishop, refusing to execute the writ *ad admittendum clericum,* or making an insufficient return to it, may be fined. Wats. Cler. Law, 302.

QUARE NON PERMITTIT. An ancient writ, which lay for one who had a right to present to a church for a turn against the proprietary. Fleta, l. 5, c. 6.

QUARE OBSTRUXIT. Wherefore he obstructed. In old English practice. A writ which lay for one who, having a liberty to pass through his neighbor's ground, could not enjoy his right because the owner had so obstructed it. Cowell.

QUARENTENA TERRÆ. A furlong. Co. Litt. 5*b*.

QUARREL. This word is said to extend not only to real and personal actions, but also to the causes of actions and suits; so that by the release of all "quarrels," not only actions pending, but also causes of action and suit, are released; and "quarrels," "controversies," and "debates" are in law considered as having the same meaning. Co. Litt. 8, 153; Termes de la Ley.

QUARRY. In mining law. An open excavation where the works are visible at the surface; a place or pit where stone, slate, marble, etc., is dug out or separated from a mass of rock. Bainb. Mines, 2.

QUART. A liquid measure, containing one-fourth part of a gallon.

QUARTER. The fourth part of a thing, especially of a year. Also a length of four inches.

QUARTER-DAY. The four days in the year upon which, by law or custom, moneys payable in quarter-yearly installments are collectible, are called "quarter-days."

QUARTER-DOLLAR. A siver coin of the United States, of the value of twenty-five cents.

QUARTER-EAGLE. A gold coin of the United States, of the value of two and a half dollars.

QUARTER OF A YEAR. Ninety-one days. Co. Litt. 135*b*.

QUARTER-SALES. In New York law. A species of fine on alienation, being one-fourth of the purchase money of an estate, which is stipulated to be paid back on alienation by the grantee. The expressions "tenth-sales," etc., are also used, with similar meanings. 7 Cow. 285.

QUARTER SEAL. In Scotch law. A seal kept by the director of the chancery; in shape and impression the fourth part of the great seal, and called in statutes the "testimonial" of the great seal. Bell.

QUARTER SESSIONS. In English law. A criminal court held before two or more justices of the peace, (one of whom must be of the quorum,) in every county, once in every quarter of a year. 4 Bl. Comm. 271; 4 Steph. Comm. 335.

In American law. Courts established in some of the states, to be holden four times in the year, invested with criminal jurisdiction, usually of offenses less than felony, and sometimes with the charge of certain administrative matters, such as the care of public roads and bridges.

QUARTERING. In English criminal law. The dividing a criminal's body into quarters, after execution. A part of the punishment of high treason. 4 Bl. Comm. 93.

QUARTERING SOLDIERS. The act of a government in billeting or assigning soldiers to private houses, without the consent of the owners of such houses, and requiring such owners to supply them with board or lodging or both.

QUARTERIZATION. Quartering of criminals.

QUARTERLY COURTS. A system of courts in Kentucky possessing a limited original jurisdiction in civil cases and appellate jurisdiction from justices of the peace.

QUARTO DIE POST. Lat. On the fourth day after. Appearance day, in the former English practice, the defendant being allowed four days, inclusive, from the return of the writ, to make his appearance.

QUASH. To overthrow; to abate; to annul; to make void. Spelman; 3 Bl. Comm. 303.

QUASI. Lat. As if; as it were; analogous to. This term is used in legal phraseology to indicate that one subject resembles another, with which it is compared, in certain characteristics, but that there are also intrinsic differences between them.

It is exclusively a term of classification. Prefixed to a term of Roman law, it implies that the conception to which it serves as an index is connected with the conception with which the comparison is instituted by a strong superficial analogy or resemblance. It negatives the notion of identity, but points out that the conceptions are sufficiently similar for one to be classed as the sequel to the other. Maine, Anc. Law, 332. Civilians use the expressions "*quasi contractus*," "*quasi delictum*," "*quasi possessio*," "*quasi traditio*," etc.

QUASI AFFINITY. In the civil law. The affinity which exists between two persons, one of whom has been betrothed to a kinsman of the other, but who have never been married.

QUASI CONTRACT. In the civil law. A contractual relation arising out of transactions between the parties which give them mutual rights and obligations, but do not involve a specific and express convention or agreement between them; a species of implied contract.

Quasi contracts are the lawful and purely voluntary acts of a man, from which there results any obligation whatever to a third person, and sometimes a reciprocal obligation between the parties. Civil Code La. art. 2293.

Persons who have not contracted with each other are often regarded by the Roman law, under a certain state of facts, as if they had actually concluded a convention between themselves. The legal relation which then takes place between these persons, which has always a similarity to a contract obligation, is therefore termed "*obligatio quasi ex contractu.*" Such a relation arises from the conducting of affairs without authority, (*negotiorum gestio,*) from the payment of what was not due, (*solutio indebiti,*) from tutorship and curatorship, and from taking possession of an inheritance. Mackeld. Rom. Law, § 491.

QUASI CORPORATIONS. Organizations resembling corporations; municipal societies or similar bodies which, though not true corporations in all respects, are yet recognized, by statutes or immemorial usage, as persons or aggregate corporations, with precise duties which may be enforced, and privileges which may be maintained, by suits at law. They may be considered *quasi* corporations, with limited powers, co-extensive with the duties imposed upon them by statute or usage, but restrained from a general use of the authority which belongs to those metaphysical persons by the common law. 13 Mass. 199.

QUASI CRIMES. This term embraces all offenses not crimes or misdemeanors, but that are in the nature of crimes,—a class of offenses against the public which have not been declared crimes, but wrongs against the general or local public which it is proper should be repressed or punished by forfeitures and penalties. This would embrace all *qui tam* actions and forfeitures imposed for the neglect or violation of a public duty. A *quasi* crime would not embrace an indictable offense, whatever might be its grade, but simply forfeitures for a wrong done to the public, whether voluntary or involuntary, where a penalty is given, whether recoverable by criminal or civil process. 68 Ill. 375.

QUASI DELICT. In the civil law. An act whereby a person, without malice, but by fault, negligence, or imprudence not legally excusable, causes injury to another.

They were four in number, viz.: (1) *Qui judex litem suam fecit*, being the offense of partiality or excess in the *judex*, (juryman;) *e. g.*, in assessing the damages at a figure in excess of the extreme limit permitted by the formula. (2) *Dejectum effusumve aliquid*, being the tort committed by one's servant in emptying or throwing something out of an attic or upper story upon a person passing beneath. (3) *Damnum infectum*, being the offense of hanging dangerous articles over the heads of persons passing along the king's highway. (4) Torts committed by one's agents (*e. g.*, stable-boys, shop-managers, etc.) in the course of their employment. Brown.

QUASI DEPOSIT. In the law of bailment. A kind of implied or involuntary deposit, which takes place where a party comes lawfully to the possession of another person's property, by finding it. Story, Bailm. § 85.

QUASI DERELICT. In admiralty law. When a vessel, without being abandoned, is no longer under the control or direction of those on board, (as where part of the crew are dead, and the remainder are physically and mentally incapable of providing for their own safety,) she is said to be *quasi derelict*. 1 Newb. Adm. 449.

QUASI EASEMENT. An "easement," in the proper sense of the word, can only exist in respect of two adjoining pieces of land occupied by different persons, and can only impose a negative duty on the owner of the servient tenement. Hence an obligation on the owner of land to repair the fence between his and his neighbor's land is not a true easement, but is sometimes called a "*quasi* easement." Gale, Easem. 516; Sweet.

QUASI ENTAIL. An estate *pur autre vie* may be granted. not only to a man and his heirs, but to a man and the heirs of his body, which is termed a "*quasi* entail;" the interest so granted not being properly an estate-tail, (for the statute *De Donis* applies only where the subject of the entail is an estate of inheritance,) but yet so far in the nature of an estate-tail that it will go to the heir of the body as special occupant during the life of the *cestui que vie*, in the same manner as an estate of inheritance would descend, if limited to the grantee and the heirs of his body. Wharton.

QUASI FEE. An estate gained by wrong; for wrong is unlimited and uncontained within rules. Wharton.

QUASI OFFENSE. One which is imputed to the person who is responsible for its injurious consequences, not because he himself committed it, but because the perpetrator of it is presumed to have acted under his commands.

QUASI PARTNERS. Partners of lands, goods, or chattels who are not actual partners are sometimes so called. Poth. de Société, App. no. 184.

QUASI PERSONALTY. Things which are movable in point of law, though fixed to things real, either actually, as emblements, (*fructus industriales*,) fixtures, etc.; or fictitiously, as chattels-real, leases for years, etc.

QUASI POSSESSION is to a right what possession is to a thing; it is the exercise or enjoyment of the right, not necessarily the continuous exercise, but such an exercise as shows an intention to exercise it at any time when desired. Sweet.

QUASI POSTHUMOUS CHILD. In the civil law. One who, born during the life of his grandfather or other male ascendant, was not his heir at the time he made his testament, but who by the death of his father became his heir in his life-time. Inst. 2, 13, 2; Dig. 28, 3, 13.

QUASI PURCHASE. In the civil law. A purchase of property not founded on the actual agreement of the parties, but on conduct of the owner which is inconsistent with any other hypothesis than that he intended a sale.

QUASI REALTY. Things which are fixed in contemplation of law to realty, but movable in themselves, as heir-looms, (or limbs of the inheritance,) title-deeds, court rolls, etc. Wharton.

QUASI TENANT AT SUFFERANCE. An under-tenant, who is in possession at the determination of an original lease, and is permitted by the reversioner to hold over.

QUASI TORT, though not a recognized term of English law, may be conveniently used in those cases where a man who has not committed a tort is liable as if he had. Thus, a master is liable for wrongful acts done by his servant in the course of his employment. Broom, Com. Law, 690; Underh. Torts, 29.

QUASI TRADITIO. In the civil law. A supposed or implied delivery of property from one to another. Thus, if the purchaser of an article was already in possession of it before the sale, his continuing in possession is considered as equivalent to a fresh delivery of it, delivery being one of the necessary elements of a sale; in other words, a *quasi traditio* is predicated.

QUASI TRUSTEE. A person who reaps a benefit from a breach of trust, and so becomes answerable as a trustee. Lewin, Trusts, (4th Ed.) 592, 638.

QUASI USUFRUCT. In the civil law. Originally the usufruct gave no right to the substance of the thing, and consequently none to its consumption; hence only an inconsumable thing could be the object of it, whether movable or immovable. But in later times the right of usufruct was, by analogy, extended to consumable things, and therewith arose the distinction between true and *quasi* usufructs. See Mackeld. Rom. Law, § 307.

QUATER COUSIN. A cousin in the fourth degree. "The very name of '*cater*' or (as it is more properly wrote) '*quater*' cousins is grown into a proverb, to express, by way of irony, the last and most trivial degree of intimacy and regard." Bl. Law Tracts, 6.

QUATUOR PEDIBUS CURRIT. Lat. It runs upon four feet; it runs upon all fours. See ALL-FOURS.

QUATUORVIRI. In Roman law. Magistrates who had the care and inspection of roads. Dig. 1, 2, 3, 30.

QUAY. A wharf for the loading or unloading of goods carried in ships. This word is sometimes spelled "key."

The popular and commercial signification of the word "quay" involves the notion of a space of ground appropriated to the public use; such use as the convenience of commerce requires. 10 Pet. 662, 715.

QUE EST LE MESME. L. Fr. Which is the same. A term used in actions of trespass, etc. See QUÆ EST EADEM.

QUE ESTATE. L. Fr. Whose estate. A term used in pleading, particularly in claiming prescription, by which it is alleged that the plaintiff and those former owners *whose estate* he has have immemorially exercised the right claimed. This was called "prescribing in a *que* estate."

QUEAN. A worthless woman; a strumpet. Obsolete.

QUEEN. A woman who possesses the sovereignty and royal power in a country under a monarchical form of government. The wife of a king.

QUEEN ANNE'S BOUNTY. A fund created by a charter of Queen Anne, (confirmed by St. 2 Ann. c. 11,) for the augmentation of poor livings, consisting of all the revenue of first fruits and tenths, which was vested in trustees forever. 1 Bl. Comm. 286.

QUEEN CONSORT. In English law. The wife of a reigning king. 1 Bl. Comm. 218.

QUEEN DOWAGER. In English law. The widow of a king. 1 Bl. Comm. 223.

QUEEN-GOLD. A royal revenue belonging to every queen consort during her marriage with the king, and due from every person who has made a voluntary fine or offer to the king of ten marks or upwards, in consideration of any grant or privilege conferred by the crown. It is now quite obsolete. 1 Bl. Comm. 220-222.

QUEEN REGNANT. In English law. A queen who holds the crown in her own right; as the first Queen Mary, Queen Elizabeth, Queen Anne, and the present Queen Victoria. 1 Bl. Comm. 218; 2 Steph. Comm. 465.

QUEEN'S ADVOCATE. An English advocate who holds, in the courts in which the rules of the canon and civil law prevail, a similar position to that which the attorney general holds in the ordinary courts, *i. e.*, he acts as counsel for the crown in ecclesiastical, admiralty, and probate cases, and ad vises the crown on questions of international law. In order of precedence it seems that he ranks after the attorney general. 3 Steph. Comm. 275*n.*

QUEEN'S BENCH. The English court of king's bench is so called during the reign of a queen. 3 Steph. Comm. 403. See KING'S BENCH.

QUEEN'S CORONER AND ATTORNEY. An officer of the court of queen's bench, usually called "the master of the crown office," whose duty it is to file informations at the suit of a private subject by direction of the court. 4 Bl. Comm. 308, 309; 4 Steph. Comm. 374, 378.

QUEEN'S (or KING'S) COUNSEL. In English law. Barristers called within the bar, and selected to be the queen's (or king's) counsel, learned in the law; answering in some measure, to the advocates of the revenue, (*advocati fisci,*) among the Romans. They cannot be employed in any cause against the crown, without special license. 3 Bl. Comm. 27; 3 Steph. Comm. 386.

QUEEN'S EVIDENCE. When several persons are charged with a crime, and one of them gives evidence against his accomplices, on the promise of being granted a pardon, he is said to be admitted queen's or (in America) state's evidence. 4 Steph. Comm. 395; Sweet.

QUEEN'S PRISON. A jail which used to be appropriated to the debtors and criminals confined under process or by authority of the superior courts at Westminster, the high court of admiralty, and also to persons imprisoned under the bankrupt law.

QUEEN'S PROCTOR. A proctor or solicitor representing the crown in the former practice of the courts of probate and divorce. In petitions for dissolution of marriage, or for declarations of nullity of marriage, the queen's proctor may, under the direction of the attorney general, and by leave of the court, intervene in the suit for the purpose of proving collusion between the parties. Mozley & Whitley.

QUEEN'S REMEMBRANCER. An officer of the central office of the English supreme court. Formerly he was an officer of the exchequer, and had important duties to perform in protecting the rights of the crown; *e. g.*, by instituting proceedings for the recovery of land by writs of intrusion, (*q. v.*,) and for the recovery of legacy and succession duties; but of late years administrative changes have lessened the duties of the office. Sweet.

QUEM REDITUM REDDIT. An old writ which lay where a rent-charge or other rent which was not rent service was granted by fine holding of the grantor. If the tenant would not attorn, then the grantee might have had this writ. Old Nat. Brev. 126.

Quemadmodum ad quæstionem facti non respondent judices, ita ad quæstionem juris non respondent juratores. In the same manner that judges do not answer to questions of fact, so jurors do not answer to questions of law. Co. Litt. 295.

QUERELA. An action preferred in any court of justice. The plaintiff was called "*querens,*" or complainant, and his brief, complaint, or declaration was called "*querela.*" Jacob.

QUERELA CORAM REGE A CONCILIO DISCUTIENDA ET TERMINANDA. A writ by which one is called to justify a complaint of a trespass made to the king himself, before the king and his council. Reg. Orig. 124.

QUERELA INOFFICIOSI TESTAMENTI. In the civil law. A species of action allowed to a child who had been unjustly disinherited, to set aside the will, founded on the presumption of law, in such cases, that the parent was not in his right mind. Calvin.; 2 Kent, Comm. 327; Bell.

QUERENS. A plaintiff; complainant; inquirer.

QUESTA. In old records. A quest; an inquest, inquisition, or inquiry, upon the oaths of an impaneled jury. Cowell.

QUESTION. A method of criminal examination heretofore in use in some of the countries of continental Europe, consisting of the application of torture to the supposed criminal, by means of the rack or other engines, in order to extort from him, as the condition of his release from the torture, a confession of his own guilt or the names of his accomplices.

In evidence. An interrogation put to a witness, for the purpose of having him declare the truth of certain facts as far as he knows them. As to *leading* questions, see that title.

In practice. A point on which the parties are not agreed, and which is submitted to the decision of a judge and jury.

QUESTMAN, or QUESTMONGER. In old English law. A starter of lawsuits, or prosecutions; also a person chosen to inquire into abuses, especially such as relate to weights and measures; also a church-warden.

QUESTORES PARRICIDII. In Roman law. Certain officers, two in number, who were deputed by the *comitia*, as a kind of commission, to search out and try all cases of parricide and murder. They were probably appointed annually. Maine, Anc. Law, 370.

QUESTUS EST NOBIS. A writ of nuisance, which, by 15 Edw. I., lay against him to whom a house or other thing that caused a nuisance descended or was alienated; whereas, before that statute the action lay only against him who first levied or caused the nuisance to the damage of his neighbor. Cowell.

Qui abjurat regnum amittit regnum, sed non regem; patriam, sed non patrem patriæ. 7 Coke, 9. He who abjures the realm leaves the realm, but not the king; the country, but not the father of the country.

Qui accusat integræ famæ sit, et non criminosus. Let him who accuses be of clear fame, and not criminal. 3 Inst. 26.

Qui acquirit sibi acquirit hæredibus. He who acquires for himself acquires for his heirs. Tray. Lat. Max. 496.

Qui adimit medium dirimit finem. He who takes away the mean destroys the end. Co. Litt. 161*a*. He that deprives a man of the mean by which he ought to come to a thing deprives him of the thing itself. Id.; Litt. § 237.

Qui aliquid statuerit, parte inaudita altera, æquum licet dixerit, haud æquum fecerit. He who determines any matter without hearing both sides, though he may have decided right, has not done justice. 6 Coke, 52*a*; 4 Bl. Comm. 283.

Qui alterius jure utitur, eodem jure uti debet. He who uses the right of another ought to use the same right. Poth. Traité De Change, pt. 1, c. 4, § 114; Broom, Max. 473.

Qui approbat non reprobat. He who approbates does not reprobate, [*i. e.*, he cannot both accept and reject the same thing.]

Qui bene distinguit bene docet. 2 Inst. 470. He who distinguishes well teaches well.

Qui bene interrogat bene docet. He who questions well teaches well. 3 Bulst. 227. Information or express averment may be effectually conveyed in the way of interrogation. Id.

Qui cadit a syllaba cadit a tota causa. He who fails in a syllable fails in his whole cause. Bract. fol. 211.

Qui concedit aliquid, concedere videtur et id sine quo concessio est irrita, sine quo res ipsa esse non potuit. 11 Coke, 52. He who concedes anything is considered as conceding that without which his concession would be void, without which the thing itself could not exist.

Qui concedit aliquid concedit omne id sine quo concessio est irrita. He who grants anything grants everything without which the grant is fruitless. Jenk. Cent. p. 32, case 63.

Qui confirmat nihil dat. He who confirms does not give. 2 Bouv. Inst. no. 2069.

Qui contemnit præceptum contemnit præcipientem. He who contemns [contemptuously treats] a command contemns the party who gives it. 12 Coke, 97.

Qui cum alio contrahit, vel est, vel esse debet non ignarus conditionis ejus. He who contracts with another either is or ought to be not ignorant of his condition. Dig. 50, 17, 19; Story, Confl. Laws, § 76.

Qui dat finem, dat media ad finem necessaria. He who gives an end gives the means to that end. 3 Mass. 129.

Qui destruit medium destruit finem. He who destroys the mean destroys the end. 10 Coke, 51*b*; Co. Litt. 161*a*; Shep. Touch. 342.

Qui doit inheriter al pere doit inheriter al fitz. He who would have been heir to the father shall be heir to the son. 2 Bl. Comm. 223; Broom, Max. 517.

Qui evertit causam, evertit causatum futurum. He who overthrows the cause overthrows its future effects. 10 Coke, 51.

Qui ex damnato coitu nascuntur inter liberos non computentur. Those who are born of an unlawful intercourse are not reckoned among the children. Co. Litt. 8*a;* Broom, Max. 519.

Qui facit per alium facit per se. He who acts through another acts himself, [*i. e.*, the acts of an agent are the acts of the principal.] Broom, Max. 818, et seq.; 1 Bl. Comm. 429; Story, Ag. § 440.

Qui habet jurisdictionem absolvendi, habet jurisdictionem ligandi. He who has jurisdiction to loosen, has jurisdiction to bind. 12 Coke, 60. Applied to writs of prohibition and consultation, as resting on a similar foundation. Id.

Qui hæret in litera hæret in cortice. He who considers merely the letter of an instrument goes but skin deep into its meaning. Co Litt. 289; Broom, Max. 685.

Qui ignorat quantum solvere debeat, non potest improbus videre. He who does not know what he ought to pay, does not want probity in not paying. Dig. 50, 17, 99.

Qui in jus dominiumve alterius succedit jure ejus uti debet. He who succeeds to the right or property of another ought to use his right, [*i. e.*, holds it subject to the same rights and liabilities as attached to it in the hands of the assignor.] Dig. 50, 17, 177; Broom, Max. 473, 478.

Qui in utero est pro jam nato habetur, quoties de ejus commodo quæritur. He who is in the womb is held as already born, whenever a question arises for his benefit.

Qui jure suo utitur, nemini facit injuriam. He who uses his legal rights harms no one. 8 Gray, 424. See Broom, Max. 379.

Qui jussu judicis aliquod fecerit non videtur dolo malo fecisse, quia parere necesse est. Where a person does an act by command of one exercising judicial authority, the law will not suppose that he acted from any wrongful or improper motive, because it was his bounden duty to obey. 10 Coke, 76; Broom, Max. 93.

Qui male agit odit lucem. He who acts badly hates the light. 7 Coke, 66.

Qui mandat ipse fecissi videtur. He who commands [a thing to be done] is held to have done it himself. Story, Bailm. § 147.

Qui melius probat melius habet. He who proves most recovers most. 9 Vin. Abr. 235.

Qui molitur insidias in patriam id facit quod insanus nauta perforans navem in qua vehitur. He who betrays his country is like the insane sailor who bores a hole in the ship which carries him. 3 Inst. 36.

Qui non cadunt in constantem virum vani timores sunt æstimandi. 7 Coke, 27. Those fears are to be esteemed vain which do not affect a firm man.

Qui non habet, ille non dat. He who has not, gives not. He who has nothing to give, gives nothing. A person cannot convey a right that is not in him. If a man grant that which is not his, the grant is void. Shep. Touch. 243; Watk. Conv. 191.

Qui non habet in ære, luat in corpore, ne quis peccetur impune. He who cannot pay with his purse must suffer in his person, lest he who offends should go unpunished. 2 Inst. 173; 4 Bl. Comm. 20.

Qui non habet potestatem alienandi habet necessitatem retinendi. Hob. 336. He who has not the power of alienating is obliged to retain.

Qui non improbat, approbat. 3 Inst. 27. He who does not blame, approves.

Qui non libere veritatem pronunciat proditor est veritatis. He who does not freely speak the truth is a betrayer of the truth.

Qui non negat fatetur. He who does not deny, admits. A well-known rule of pleading. Tray. Lat. Max. 503.

Qui non obstat quod obstare potest, facere videtur. He who does not prevent [a thing] which he can prevent, is considered to do [as doing] it. 2 Inst. 146.

Qui non prohibet id quod prohibere potest assentire videtur. 2 Inst. 308. He who does not forbid what he is able to prevent, is considered to assent.

Qui non propulsat injuriam quando potest, infert. Jenk. Cent. 271. He who does not repel an injury when he can, induces it.

Qui obstruit aditum, destruit commodum. He who obstructs a way, passage, or entrance destroys a benefit or convenience. Co. Litt. 161*a*. He who prevents another from entering upon land destroys the benefit which he has from it. Id.

Qui omne dicit nihil excludit. 4 Inst. 81. He who says all excludes nothing.

Qui parcit nocentibus innocentes punit. Jenk. Cent. 133. He who spares the guilty punishes the innocent.

Qui peccat ebrius luat sobrius. He who sins when drunk shall be punished when sober. Cary, 133; Broom, Max. 17.

Qui per alium facit per seipsum facere videtur. He who does a thing by an agent is considered as doing it himself. Co. Litt. 258; Broom, Max. 817.

Qui per fraudem agit frustra agit. 2 Rolle, 17. What a man does fraudulently he does in vain.

Qui potest et debet vetare, jubet. He who can and ought to forbid a thing [if he do not forbid it] directs it. 2 Kent, Comm. 483, note.

Qui primum peccat ille facit rixam. Godb. He who sins first makes the strife.

Qui prior est tempore potior est jure. He who is before in time is the better in right. Priority in time gives preference in law. Co. Litt. 14*a*; 4 Coke, 90*a*. A maxim of very extensive application, both at law and in equity. Broom, Max. 353–362; 1 Story, Eq. Jur. § 64*d*; Story, Bailm. § 312.

Qui pro me aliquid facit mihi fecisse videtur. 2 Inst. 501. He who does anything for me appears to do it to me.

Qui providet sibi providet hæredibus. He who provides for himself provides for his heirs.

Qui rationem in omnibus quærunt rationem subvertunt. They who seek a reason for everything subvert reason. 2 Coke, 75; Broom, Max. 157.

Qui sciens solvit indebitum donandi consilio id videtur fecisse. One who knowingly pays what is not due is supposed to have done it with the intention of making a gift. 17 Mass. 388.

Qui semel actionem renunciaverit amplius repetere non potest. He who has once relinquished his action cannot bring it again. 8 Coke, 59*a*. A rule descriptive of the effect of a *retraxit* and *nolle prosequi*.

Qui semel est malus, semper præsumitur esse malus in eodem genere. He who is once criminal is presumed to be always criminal in the same kind or way. Cro. Car. 317; Best, Ev. 345.

Qui sentit commodum sentire debet et onus. He who receives the advantage ought also to suffer the burden. 1 Coke, 99; Broom, Max. 706-713.

Qui sentit onus sentire debet et commodum. 1 Coke, 99*a*. He who bears the burden of a thing ought also to experience the advantage arising from it.

Qui tacet, consentire videtur. He who is silent is supposed to consent. The silence of a party implies his consent. Jenk. Cent. p. 32, case 64; Broom, Max. 138, 787.

Qui tacet consentire videtur, ubi tractatur de ejus commodo. 9 Mod. 38. He who is silent is considered as assenting, when his interest is at stake.

Qui tacet non utique fatetur, sed tamen verum est eum non negare. He who is silent does not indeed confess, but yet it is true that he does not deny. Dig. 50, 17, 142.

QUI TAM. Lat. "Who as well ———." An action brought by an informer, under a statute which establishes a penalty for the commission or omission of a certain act, and provides that the same shall be recoverable in a civil action, part of the penalty to go to any person who will bring such action and the remainder to the state or some other institution, is called a "*qui tam* action;" because the plaintiff states that he sues *as well* for the state as for himself.

Qui tardius solvit, minus solvit. He who pays more tardily [than he ought] pays less [than he ought.] Jenk. Cent. 58.

Qui timent, cavent vitant. They who fear, take care and avoid. Branch, Princ.

Qui totum dicit nihil excipit. He who says all excepts nothing.

Qui vult decipi, decipiatur. Let him who wishes to be deceived, be deceived. Broom, Max. 782, note; 1 De Gex, M. & G. 687, 710; Shep. Touch. 56.

QUIA. Lat. Because; whereas; inasmuch as.

QUIA DATUM EST NOBIS INTELLIGI. Because it is given to us to understand. Formal words in old writs.

QUIA EMPTORES. "Because the purchasers." The title of the statute of Westm. 3, (18 Edw. I. c. 1.) This statute took from the tenants of common lords the feudal liberty they claimed of disposing of part of their lands to hold of themselves, and, instead of it, gave them a general liberty to sell all or any part, to hold of the next superior lord, which they could not have done before without consent. The effect of this statute was twofold: (1) To facilitate the alienation of fee-simple estates; and (2) to put an end to the creation of any new manors, *i. e.*, tenancies in fee-simple of a subject. Brown.

QUIA ERRONICE EMANAVIT. Because it issued erroneously, or through mistake. A term in old English practice. Yel. 83.

QUIA TIMET. Lat. Because he fears or apprehends. In equity practice. The technical name of a bill filed by a party who seeks the aid of a court of equity, *because he fears* some future probable injury to his rights or interests. 2 Story, Eq. Jur. § 826.

QUIBBLE. A cavilling or verbal objection. A slight difficulty raised without necessity or propriety.

QUICK. Living; alive. "*Quick* chattels must be put in pound-overt that the owner may give them sustenance; dead need not." Finch, Law, b. 2, c. 6.

QUICK WITH CHILD. See QUICKENING.

QUICKENING. In medical jurisprudence. The first motion of the *fœtus* in the womb felt by the mother, occurring usually about the middle of the term of pregnancy.

Quicquid acquiritur servo acquiritur domino. Whatever is acquired by the servant is acquired for the master. Pull. Accts. 38, note. Whatever rights are acquired by an agent are acquired for his principal. Story, Ag. § 403.

Quicquid demonstratæ rei additur satis demonstratæ frustra est. Whatever is added to demonstrate anything already sufficiently demonstrated is surplusage. Dig. 33, 4, 1, 8; Broom, Max. 630.

Quicquid est contra normam recti est injuria. 3 Bulst. 313. Whatever is against the rule of right is a wrong.

Quicquid in excessu actum est, lege prohibetur. 2 Inst. 107. Whatever is done in excess is prohibited by law.

Quicquid judicis auctoritati subjicitur novitati non subjicitur. Whatever is subject to the authority of a judge is not subject to innovation. 4 Inst. 66.

Quicquid plantatur solo, solo cedit. Whatever is affixed to the soil belongs to the soil. Broom, Max. 401-431.

Quicquid solvitur, solvitur secundum modum solventis; quicquid recipitur, recipitur secundum modum recipientis. Whatever money is paid, is paid according to the direction of the payer; whatever money is received, is received according to that of the recipient. 2 Vern. 606; Broom, Max. 810.

Quicunque habet jurisdictionem ordinariam est illius loci ordinarius. Co. Litt. 344. Whoever has an ordinary jurisdiction is ordinary of that place.

Quicunque jussu judicis aliquid fecerit non videtur dolo malo fecisse, quia parere necesse est. 10 Coke, 71. Whoever does anything by the command of a judge is not reckoned to have done it with an evil intent, because it is necessary to obey.

QUID JURIS CLAMAT. In old English practice. A writ which lay for the grantee of a reversion or remainder, where the particular tenant would not attorn, for the purpose of compelling him. Termes de la Ley; Cowell.

QUID PRO QUO. What for what; something for something. Used in law for the giving one valuable thing for another. It is nothing more than the mutual consideration which passes between the parties to a contract, and which renders it valid and binding. Cowell.

Quid sit jus, et in quo consistit injuria, legis est definire. What constitutes right, and what injury, it is the business of the law to declare. Co. Litt. 158*b*.

QUIDAM. Lat. Somebody. This term is used in the French law to designate a person whose name is not known.

Quidquid enim sive dolo et culpa venditoris accidit in eo venditor securus est. For concerning anything which occurs without deceit and wrong on the part of the vendor, the vendor is secure. 4 Pick. 198.

QUIET ENJOYMENT. A covenant, usually inserted in leases and conveyances on the part of the grantor, promising that the tenant or grantee shall enjoy the possession of the premises in peace and without disturbance, is called a covenant "for quiet enjoyment."

Quieta non movere. Not to unsettle things which are established. 28 Barb. 9, 22.

QUIETARE. To quit, acquit, discharge, or save harmless. A formal word in old deeds of donation and other conveyances. Cowell.

QUIETE CLAMANTIA. In old English law. Quitclaim. Bract. fol. 33*b*.

QUIETE CLAMARE. To quitclaim or renounce all pretensions of right and title. Bract. fols. 1, 5.

QUIETUS. In old English law. Quit; acquitted; discharged. A word used by the clerk of the pipe, and auditors in the exchequer, in their acquittances or discharges given to accountants; usually concluding with an *abinde recessit quietus*, (hath gone quit thereof,) which was called a "*quietus est*." Cowell.

In modern law, the word denotes an acquittance or discharge; as of an executor or administrator, (4 Mass. 133; 3 Fla. 233,) or of a judge or attorney general, (3 Mod. 99.)

QUIETUS REDDITUS. In old English law. Quitrent. Spelman. See QUITRENT.

Quilibet potest renunciare juri pro se introducto. Every one may renounce or relinquish a right introduced for his own benefit. 2 Inst. 183; Wing. Max. p. 483, max. 123; 4 Bl. Comm. 317.

QUILLE. In French marine law. Keel; the keel of a vessel. Ord. Mar. liv. 3, tit. 6, art. 8.

QUINQUE PORTUS. In old English law. The Cinque Ports. Spelman.

QUINQUEPARTITE. Consisting of five parts; divided into five parts.

QUINSTEME, or QUINZIME. Fifteenths; also the fifteenth day after a festival. 13 Edw. 1. See Cowell.

QUINTAL, or KINTAL. A weight of one hundred pounds. Cowell.

QUINTO EXACTUS. In old practice. Called or exacted the fifth time. A return made by the sheriff, after a defendant had been proclaimed, required, or exacted in five county courts successively, and failed to appear, upon which he was outlawed by the coroners of the county. 3 Bl. Comm. 283.

QUIRE OF DOVER. In English law. A record in the exchequer, showing the tenures for guarding and repairing Dover Castle, and determining the services of the Cinque Ports. 3 How. State Tr. 868.

QUIRITARIAN OWNERSHIP. In Roman law. Ownership held by a title recognized by the municipal law, in an object also recognized by that law, and in the strict character of a Roman citizen. "Roman law originally only recognized one kind of dominion, called, emphatically, 'quiritary dominion.' Gradually, however, certain real rights arose which, though they failed to satisfy all the elements of the definition of quiritary dominion, were practically its equivalent, and received from the courts a similar protection. These real rights might fall short of quiritary dominion in three respects: (1) Either in respect of the persons in whom they resided; (2) or of the subjects to which they related; or (3) of the title by which they were acquired." In the latter case, the ownership was called "bonitarian," *i. e.*, "the property of a Roman citizen, in a subject capable of quiritary property, acquired by a title not known to the civil law, but introduced by the prætor and protected by his *imperium* or supreme executive power;" *e. g.*, where *res mancipi* had been transferred by mere tradition. Poste's Gaius' Inst. 186.

Quisquis erit qui vult juris-consultus haberi continuet studium, velit a quocunque doceri. Jenk. Cent. Whoever wishes to be a juris-consult, let him continually study, and desire to be taught by every one.

Quisquis præsumitur bonus; et semper in dubiis pro reo respondendum. Every one is presumed good; and in doubtful cases the resolution should be ever for the accused.

QUIT. Clear; discharged; free; also spoken of persons absolved or acquitted of a charge.

QUITCLAIM, *v*. In conveyancing. To release or relinquish a claim; to execute a deed of quitclaim. See QUITCLAIM, *n*.

QUITCLAIM, *n*. A release or acquittance given to one man by another, in respect of any action that he has or might have against him. Also acquitting or giving up one's claim or title. Termes de la Ley; Cowell.

QUITCLAIM DEED. A deed of conveyance operating by way of release; that is, intended to pass any title, interest, or claim which the grantor may have in the premises, but not professing that such title is valid, nor containing any warranty or covenants for title. See 3 Me. 445.

QUITRENT. Certain established rents of the freeholders and ancient copyholders of manors are denominated "quitrents," because thereby the tenant goes quit and free of all other services. 3 Cruise, Dig. 314.

QUITTANCE. An abbreviation of "acquittance;" a release, (*q. v.*)

QUO ANIMO. Lat. With what intention or motive. Used sometimes as a substantive, in lieu of the single word "*animus*," design or motive. "The *quo animo* is the real subject of inquiry." 1 Kent, Comm. 77.

QUO JURE. In old English practice. A writ which lay for one that had land in which another claimed common, to compel the latter to show *by what title* he claimed it. Cowell; Fitzh. Nat. Brev. 128, F.

Quo ligatur, eo dissolvitur. 2 Rolle, 21. By the same mode by which a thing is bound, by that is it released.

QUO MINUS. A writ upon which all proceedings in the court of exchequer were formerly grounded. In it the plaintiff suggests that he is the king's debtor, and that the defendant has done him the injury or damage complained of, *quo minus sufficiens existit*, by which *he is less able* to pay the king's debt. This was originally requisite in order to give jurisdiction to the court of exchequer; but now this suggestion is a mere form. 3 Bl. Comm. 46.

Also, a writ which lay for him who had a grant of house-bote and hay-bote in another's woods, against the grantor making such waste as that the grantee could not enjoy his grant. Old Nat. Brev. 148.

Quo modo quid constituitur eodem modo dissolvitur. Jenk. Cent. 74. In the same manner by which anything is constituted by that it is dissolved.

QUO WARRANTO. In old English practice. A writ, in the nature of a writ of right for the king, against him who claimed or usurped any office, franchise, or liberty, to inquire *by what authority* he supported his claim, in order to determine the right. It lay also in case of non-user, or long neglect of a franchise, or misuser or abuse of it; being a writ commanding the defendant to show *by what warrant* he exercises such a franchise, having never had any grant of it, or having forfeited it by neglect or abuse. 3 Bl. Comm. 262.

In England, and quite generally throughout the United States, this writ has given place to an "information in the nature of a *quo warranto*," which, though in form a criminal proceeding, is in effect a civil remedy similar to the old writ, and is the method now usually employed for trying the title to a corporate or other franchise, or to a public or corporate office.

QUOAD HOC. Lat. As to this; with respect to this; so far as this in particular is concerned.

A prohibition *quoad hoc* is a prohibition as to certain things among others. Thus, where a party was complained against in the ecclesiastical court for matters cognizable in the temporal courts, a prohibition *quoad* these matters issued, *i. e.*, *as to such matters* the party was prohibited from prosecuting his suit in the ecclesiastical court. Brown.

QUOAD SACRA. As to sacred things; for religious purposes.

Quocumque modo velit; quocumque modo possit. In any way he wishes; in any way he can. 14 Johns. 484, 492.

Quod a quoque pœnæ nomine exactum est id eidem restituere nemo cogitur. That which has been exacted as a penalty no one is obliged to restore. Dig. 50, 17, 46.

Quod ab initio non valet in tractu temporis non convalescet. That which is bad in its commencement improves not by lapse of time. 4 Coke, 2; Broom, Max. 178.

Quod ad jus naturale attinet omnes homines æquales sunt. All men are equal as far as the natural law is concerned. Dig. 50, 17, 32.

Quod ædificatur in area legata cedit legato. Whatever is built on ground given by will goes to the legatee. Broom, Max. 424.

Quod alias bonum et justum est, si per vim vel fraudem petatur, malum et injustum efficitur. 3 Coke, 78. What otherwise is good and just, if it be sought by force and fraud, becomes bad and unjust.

Quod alias non fuit licitum, necessitas licitum facit. What otherwise was not lawful, necessity makes lawful. Fleta, lib. 5, c. 23, § 14.

Quod approbo non reprobo. What I approve I do not reject. I cannot approve and reject at the same time. I cannot take the benefit of an instrument, and at the same time repudiate it. Broom, Max. 712.

Quod attinet ad jus civile, servi pro nullis habentur, non tamen et jure naturali, quia, quod ad jus naturale attinet, omnes homines æquali sunt. So far as the civil law is concerned, slaves are not reckoned as persons, but not so by natural law, for, so far as regards natural law, all men are equal. Dig. 50, 17, 32.

QUOD BILLA CASSETUR. That the bill be quashed. The common-law form of a judgment sustaining a plea in abatement, where the proceeding is by bill, *i. e.*, by a *capias* instead of by original writ.

QUOD CLERICI BENEFICIATI DE CANCELLARIA. A writ to exempt a clerk of the chancery from the contribution towards the proctors of the clergy in parliament, etc. Reg. Orig. 261.

QUOD CLERICI NON ELIGANTUR IN OFFICIO BALLIVI, etc. A writ which lay for a clerk, who, by reason of some land he had, was made, or was about to be made, bailiff, beadle, reeve, or some such officer, to obtain exemption from serving the office. Reg. Orig. 187.

QUOD COMPUTET. That he account. Judgment *quod computet* is a preliminary or interlocutory judgment given in the action of account-render (also in the case of creditors' bills against an executor or administrator,) directing that accounts be taken before a master or auditor.

Quod constat clare non debet verificari. What is clearly apparent need not be proved. 10 Mod. 150.

Quod constat curiæ opere testium non indiget. That which appears to the court needs not the aid of witnesses. 2 Inst. 662.

Quod contra legem fit pro infecto habetur. That which is done against law is regarded as not done at all. 4 Coke, 31*a*.

Quod contra rationem juris receptum est, non est producendum ad consequentias. That which has been received against the reason of the law is not to be drawn into a precedent. Dig. 1, 3, 14.

QUOD CUM. In pleading. For that whereas. A form of introducing matter of inducement in certain actions, as *assumpsit* and case.

Quod datum est ecclesiæ, datum est Deo. 2 Inst. 2. What is given to the church is given to God.

Quod demonstrandi causa additur rei satis demonstratæ, frustra fit. 10 Coke, 113. What is added to a thing sufficiently palpable, for the purpose of demonstration, is vain.

Quod dubitas, ne feceris. What you doubt of, do not do. In a case of moment, especially in cases of life, it is safest to hold that in practice which hath least doubt and danger. 1 Hale, P. C. 300.

QUOD EI DEFORCEAT. In English law. The name of a writ given by St. Westm. 2, 13 Edw. I. c. 4, to the owners of a particular estate, as for life, in dower, by the curtesy, or in fee-tail, who were barred of the right of possession by a recovery had against them through their default or non-appearance in a possessory action, by which the right was restored to him who had been thus unwarily deforced by his own default. 3 Bl. Comm. 193.

Quod est ex necessitate nunquam introducitur, nisi quando necessarium. 2 Rolle, 502. That which is of necessity is never introduced, unless when necessary.

Quod est inconveniens aut contra rationem non permissum est in lege. Co. Litt. 178*a*. That which is inconvenient or against reason is not permissible in law.

Quod est necessarium est licitum. What is necessary is lawful. Jenk. Cent. p. 76, case 45.

Quod factum est, cum in obscuro sit, ex affectione cujusque capit interpretationem. When there is doubt about an act, it receives interpretation from the (known) feelings of the actor. Dig. 50, 17, 68, 1.

Quod fieri debet facile præsumitur. Halk. 153. That which ought to be done is easily presumed.

Quod fieri non debet, factum valet. That which ought not to be done, when done, is valid. Broom, Max. 182.

QUOD FUIT CONCESSUM. Which was granted. A phrase in the reports, signifying that an argument or point made was conceded or acquiesced in by the court.

Quod in jure scripto "jus" appellatur, id in lege Angliæ "rectum" esse dicitur. What in the civil law is called "*jus,*" in the law of England is said to be "*rectum,*" (right.) Co. Litt. 260; Fleta, l. 6, c. 1, § 1.

Quod in minori valet valebit in majori; et quod in majori non valet nec valebit in minori. Co. Litt. 260*a*. That which is valid in the less shall be valid in the greater; and that which is not valid in the greater shall neither be valid in the less.

Quod in uno similium valet valebit in altero. That which is effectual in one of two like things shall be effectual in the other. Co. Litt. 191*a*.

Quod inconsulto fecimus, consultius revocemus. Jenk. Cent. 116. What we have done without due consideration, upon better consideration we may revoke.

Quod initio vitiosum est non potest tractu temporis convalescere. That which is void from the beginning cannot become valid by lapse of time. Dig. 50, 17, 29.

Quod ipsis qui contraxerunt obstat, et successoribus eorum obstabit. That which bars those who have made a contract will bar their successors also. Dig. 50, 17, 143.

QUOD JUSSU. Lat. In the civil law. The name of an action given to one who had contracted with a son or slave, *by order* of the father or master, to compel such father or master to stand to the agreement. Hallifax, Civil Law, b. 3, c. 2, no. 3; Inst. 4, 7, 1.

Quod jussu alterius solvitur pro eo est quasi ipsi solutum esset. That which is paid by the order of another is the same as though it were paid to himself. Dig. 50, 17, 180.

Quod meum est sine facto meo vel defectu meo amitti vel in alium transferri non potest. That which is mine cannot be lost or transferred to another without my alienation or forfeiture. Broom, Max. 465.

Quod meum est sine me auferri non potest. That which is mine cannot be taken away without me, [without my assent.] Jenk. Cent. p. 251, case 41.

Quod minus est in obligationem videtur deductum. That which is the less is held to be imported into the contract; (*e. g.*, A. offers to hire B.'s house at six hundred dollars, at the same time B. offers to let it for five hundred dollars; the contract is for five hundred dollars.) 1 Story, Cont. 481.

Quod naturalis ratio inter omnes homines constituit, vocatur jus gentium. That which natural reason has established among all men is called the "law of nations." 1 Bl. Comm. 43; Dig. 1, 1, 9; Inst. 1, 2, 1.

Quod necessarie intelligitur non deest. 1 Bulst. 71. That which is necessarily understood is not wanting.

Quod necessitas cogit, defendit. Hale, P. C. 54. That which necessity compels, it justifies.

Quod non apparet non est; et non apparet judicialiter ante judicium. 2 Inst. 479. That which appears not is not; and nothing appears judicially before judgment.

Quod non capit Christus, capit fiscus. What Christ [the church] does not take the treasury takes. Goods of a *felo de se* go to the king. A maxim in old English law. Yearb. P. 19 Hen. VI. 1.

QUOD NON FUIT NEGATUM. Which was not denied. A phrase found in the old reports, signifying that an argument or proposition was not denied or controverted by the court. Latch, 213.

Quod non habet principium non habet finem. Wing. Max. 79; Co. Litt. 345*a*. That which has not beginning has not end.

Quod non legitur, non creditur. What is not read is not believed. 4 Coke, 304.

Quod non valet in principali, in accessorio seu consequenti non valebit; et quod non valet in magis propinquo non valebit in magis remoto. 8 Coke, 78. That which is not good against the principal will not be good as to accessories or consequences; and that which is not of force in regard to things near it will not be of force in regard to things remote from it.

QUOD NOTA. Which note; which mark. A reporter's note in the old books, directing attention to a point or rule. Dyer, 23.

Quod nullius esse potest id ut alicujus fieret nulla obligatio valet efficere. No agreement can avail to make that the property of any one which cannot be acquired as property. Dig. 50, 17, 182.

Quod nullius est, est domini regis. That which is the property of nobody belongs to our lord the king. Fleta, lib. 1, c. 3; Broom, Max. 354.

Quod nullius est, id ratione naturali occupanti conceditur. That which is the property of no one is, by natural reason, given to the [first] occupant. Dig. 41, 1, 3; Inst. 2, 1, 12. Adopted in the common law. 2 Bl. Comm. 258.

Quod nullum est, nullum producit effectum. That which is null produces no effect. Tray. Leg. Max. 519.

Quod omnes tangit ab omnibus debet supportari. That which touches or concerns all ought to be supported by all. 3 How. State Tr. 878, 1087.

QUOD PARTES REPLACITENT. That the parties do replead. The form of the judgment on award of a repleader. 2 Salk. 579.

QUOD PARTITIO FIAT. That partition be made. The name of the judgment in a suit for partition, directing that a partition be effected.

Quod pendet non est pro eo quasi sit. What is in suspense is considered as not existing during such suspense. Dig. 50, 17, 169, 1.

Quod per me non possum, nec per alium. What I cannot do by myself, I cannot by another. 4 Coke, 24*b*; 11 Coke, 87*a*.

Quod per recordum probatum, non debet esse negatum. What is proved by record ought not to be denied.

QUOD PERMITTAT. That he permit. In old English law. A writ which lay for the heir of him that was disseised of his common of pasture, against the heir of the disseisor. Cowell.

QUOD PERMITTAT PROSTERNERE. That he permit to abate. In old practice. A writ, in the nature of a writ of right, which lay to abate a nuisance. 3 Bl. Comm. 221.

QUOD PERSONA NEC PREBENDARII, etc. A writ which lay for spiritual persons, distrained in their spiritual possessions, for payment of a fifteenth with the rest of the parish. Fitzh. Nat. Brev. 175. Obsolete.

Quod populus postremum jussit, id jus ratum esto. What the people have last enacted, let that be the established law. A law of the Twelve Tables, the principle of which is still recognized. 1 Bl. Comm. 89.

Quod primum est intentione ultimum est in operatione. That which is first in intention is last in operation. Bac. Max.

Quod principi placuit legis habet vigorem. That which has pleased the prince has the force of law. The emperor's pleasure has the force of law. Dig. 1, 4, 1; Inst. 1, 2, 6. A celebrated maxim of imperial law.

Quod prius est verius est; et quod prius est tempore potius est jure. Co. Litt. 347. What is first is true; and what is first in time is better in law.

Quod pro minore licitum est et pro majore licitum est. 8 Coke, 43. That which is lawful as to the minor is lawful as to the major.

QUOD PROSTRAVIT. That he do abate. The name of a judgment upon an indictment for a nuisance, that the defendant abate such nuisance.

Quod pure debetur præsenti die debetur. That which is due unconditionally is due now. Tray. Leg. Max. 519.

Quod quis ex culpa sua damnum sentit non intelligitur damnum sentire. The damage which one experiences from his own fault is not considered as his damage. Dig. 50, 17, 203.

Quod quis sciens indebitum debit hac mente, ut postea repeteret, repetere non potest. That which one has given, knowing it not to be due, with the intention of redemanding it, he cannot recover back. Dig. 12, 6, 50.

Quod quisquis norit in hoc se exerceat. Let every one employ himself in what he knows. 11 Coke, 10.

QUOD RECUPERET. That he recover. The ordinary form of judgments for the plaintiff in actions at law. 1 Archb. Pr. K. B. 225; 1 Burrill, Pr. 246.

Quod remedio destituitur ipsa re valet si culpa absit. That which is without remedy avails of itself, if there be no fault in the party seeking to enforce it. Broom, Max. 212.

Quod semel aut bis existit prætereunt legislatores. Legislators pass over what happens [only] once or twice. Dig. 1, 3, 6; Broom, Max. 46.

Quod semel meum est amplius meum esse non potest. Co. Litt. 49*b*. What is once mine cannot be more fully mine.

Quod semel placuit in electione, amplius displicere non potest. Co. Litt. 146. What a party has once determined, in a case where he has an election, cannot afterwards be disavowed.

QUOD SI CONTINGAT. That if it happen. Words by which a condition might formerly be created in a deed. Litt. § 330.

Quod sub certa forma concessum vel reservatum est non trahitur ad valorem vel compensationem. That which is granted or reserved under a certain form is not [permitted to be] drawn into valuation or compensation. Bac. Max. 26, reg. 4. That which is granted or reserved in a certain specified form must be taken as it is granted, and will not be permitted to be made the subject of any adjustment or compensation on the part of the grantee. 2 Hill, 423.

Quod subintelligitur non deest. What is understood is not wanting. 2 Ld. Raym. 832.

Quod tacite intelligitur deesse non videtur. What is tacitly understood is not considered to be wanting. 4 Coke, 22*a*.

Quod vanum et inutile est, lex non requirit. Co. Litt. 319. The law requires not what is vain and useless.

QUOD VIDE. Which see. A direction to the reader to look to another part of the book, or to another book, there named, for further information.

Quod voluit non dixit. What he intended he did not say, or express. An answer sometimes made in overruling an argument that the law-maker or testator *meant* so and so. 1 Kent, Comm. 468, note; 1 Johns. Ch. 235.

Quodcunque aliquis ob tutelam corporis sui fecerit, jure id fecisse videtur. 2 Inst. 590. Whatever any one does in defense of his person, that he is considered to have done legally.

Quodque dissolvitur eodem modo quo ligatur. 2 Rolle, 39. In the same manner that a thing is bound, in the same manner it is unbound.

QUONIAM ATTACHIAMENTA. (Since the attachments.) One of the oldest books in the Scotch law. So called from the two first words of the volume. Jacob; Whishaw.

QUORUM. When a committee, board of directors, meeting of shareholders, legislative or other body of persons cannot act unless a certain number at least of them are present, that number is called a "quorum." Sweet.

Quorum prætextu nec auget nec minuit sententiam, sed tantum confirmat præmissa. Plowd. 52. "*Quorum prætextu*" neither increases nor diminishes a sentence, but only confirms that which went before.

QUOT. In old Scotch law. A twentieth part of the movable estate of a person dying, which was due to the bishop of the diocese within which the person resided. Bell.

QUOTA. A proportional part or share; the proportional part of a demand or liability, falling upon each of those who are collectively responsible for the whole.

QUOTATION. 1. The production to a court or judge of the exact language of a statute, precedent, or other authority, in support of an argument or proposition advanced.

2. The transcription of part of a literary composition into another book or writing.

3. A statement of the market price of one or more commodities; or the price specified to a correspondent.

Quoties dubia interpretatio libertatis est, secundum libertatem respondendum erit. Whenever the interpretation of liberty is doubtful, the answer should be on the side of liberty. Dig. 50, 17, 20.

Quoties idem sermo duas sententias exprimit, ea potissimum excipiatur, quæ rei gerendæ aptior est. Whenever the same language expresses two meanings, that should be adopted which is the better fitted for carrying out the subject-matter. Dig. 50, 17, 67.

Quoties in stipulationibus ambigua oratio est, commodissimum est id accipi quo res de qua agitur in tuto sit. Whenever the language of stipulations is ambiguous, it is most fitting that that [sense] should be taken by which the subject-matter may be protected. Dig. 45, 1, 80.

Quoties in verbis nulla est ambiguitas, ibi nulla expositio contra verba fienda est. Co. Litt. 147. When in the words there is no ambiguity, then no exposition contrary to the words is to be made.

QUOTUPLEX. Of how many kinds; how many fold. A term of frequent occurrence in Sheppard's Touchstone.

QUOUSQUE. Lat. How long; how far; until. In old conveyances it is used as a word of limitation. 10 Coke, 41.

QUOVIS MODO. Lat. In whatever manner.

Quum de lucro duorum quæratur, melior est causa possidentis. When the question is as to the gain of two persons, the title of the party in possession is the better one. Dig. 50, 17, 126, 2.

Quum in testamento ambigue aut etiam perperam scriptum est, benigne interpretari et secundum id quod credible et cogitatum, credendum est. When in a will an ambiguous or even an erroneous expression occurs, it should be construed liberally and in accordance with what is thought the probable meaning of the testator. Dig. 34, 5, 24; Broom, Max. 437.

Quum principalis causa non consistit ne ea quidem quæ sequuntur locum habent. When the principal does not hold, the incidents thereof ought not to obtain. Broom, Max. 496.

Quum quod ago non valet ut ago, valeat quantum valere potest. 1 Vent. 216. When what I do is of no force as to the purpose for which I do it, let it be of force to as great a degree as it can.

R.

R. In the signatures of royal persons, "R." is an abbreviation for "*rex*" (king) or "*regina*" (queen.)

R. G. An abbreviation for *Regula Generalis*, a general rule or order of court; or for the plural of the same.

R. L. This abbreviation may stand either for "Revised Laws" or "Roman law."

R. S. An abbreviation for "Revised Statutes."

RACE. A tribe, people, or nation, belonging or supposed to belong to the same stock or lineage. "*Race*, color, or previous condition of servitude." Const. U. S., Am. XV.

RACE-WAY. An artificial canal dug in the earth; a channel cut in the ground. 26 Minn. 17, 1 N. W. Rep. 48. The channel for the current that drives a water-wheel. Webster.

RACHAT. In French law. The right of repurchase which, in English and American law, the vendor may reserve to himself. It is also called "*réméré*." Brown.

RACHATER. L. Fr. To redeem; to repurchase, (or buy back.) Kelham.

RACHETUM. In Scotch law. Ransom; corresponding to Saxon "*weregild*," a pecuniary composition for an offense. Skene; Jacob.

RACHIMBURGII. In the legal polity of the Salians and Ripuarians and other Germanic peoples, this name was given to the judges or assessors who sat with the count in his *mallum*, (court,) and were generally associated with him in other matters. Spelman.

RACK. An engine of torture anciently used in the inquisitorial method of examining persons charged with crime, the office of which was to break the limbs or dislocate the joints.

RACK-RENT. A rent of the full value of the tenement, or near it. 2 Bl. Comm. 43.

RACK-VINTAGE. Wines drawn from the lees. Cowell.

RADICALS. A political party. The term arose in England, in 1818, when the popular leaders, Hunt, Cartwright, and others, sought to obtain a radical reform in the representative system of parliament. Bolingbroke (Disc. Parties, Let. 18) employs the term in its present accepted sense: "Such a remedy might have wrought a *radical* cure of the evil that threatens our constitution," etc. Wharton.

RADOUB. In French law. A term including the repairs made to a ship, and a fresh supply of furniture and victuals, munitions, and other provisions required for the voyage. 3 Pard. Droit Commer. § 602.

RAFFLE. A kind of lottery in which several persons pay, in shares, the value of something put up as a stake, and then determine by chance (as by casting dice) which one of them shall become the sole possessor of it. Webster.

A raffle may be described as a species of "adventure or hazard," but is held not to be a lottery. 2 Mill, Const. 130.

RAGEMAN. A statute, so called, of justices assigned by Edward I. and his council, to go a circuit through all England, and to hear and determine all complaints of injuries done within five years next before Michaelmas, in the fourth year of his reign. Spelman.

Also a rule, form, regimen, or precedent.

RAGMAN'S ROLL, or RAGIMUND'S ROLL. A roll, called from one Ragimund, or Ragimont, a legate in Scotland, who, summoning all the beneficed clergymen in that kingdom, caused them on oath to give in the true value of their benefices, according to which they were afterwards taxed by the court of Rome. Wharton.

RAILROAD. A road or way on which iron or steel rails are laid for wheels to run on, for the conveyance of heavy loads in cars or carriages propelled by steam or other motive power.

Whether or not this term includes roads operated by horse-power, electricity, cable-lines, etc., will generally depend upon the context of the statute in which it is found. The decisions on this point are at variance.

RAILWAY COMMISSIONERS. A body of three commissioners appointed under the English regulation of railways act, 1873, principally to enforce the provisions of the railway and canal traffic act, 1854, by compelling railway and canal companies to give reasonable facilities for traffic, to abstain from giving unreasonable preference to any company or person, and to forward through traffic at through rates. They also have the supervision of working agreements between companies. Sweet.

RAISE. To create. A use may be raised; *i. e.*, a use may be created. Also to infer; to create or bring to light by construction or interpretation.

RAISE A PRESUMPTION. To give occasion or ground for a presumption; to be of such a character, or to be attended with such circumstances, as to justify an inference or presumption of law. Thus, a person's silence, in some instances, will "raise a presumption" of his consent to what is done.

RAISE AN ISSUE. To bring pleadings to an issue; to have the effect of producing an issue between the parties pleading in an action.

RAISE REVENUE. To levy a tax, as a means of collecting revenue; to bring together, collect, or levy revenue. The phrase does not imply an increase of revenue. 58 Ala. 557.

RAISING A PROMISE. By this phrase is meant the act of the law in extracting from the facts and circumstances of a particular transaction a promise which was implicit therein, and postulating it as a ground of legal liability.

RAISING A USE. Creating, establishing, or calling into existence a use. Thus, if a man conveyed land to another in fee, without any consideration, equity would presume that he meant it to be to the use of himself, and would therefore raise an implied use for his benefit. Brown.

RAISING AN ACTION, in Scotland, is the institution of an action or suit.

RAISING MONEY. To raise money is to realize money by subscription, loan, or otherwise.

RAISING PORTIONS. When a landed estate is settled on an eldest son, it is generally burdened with the payment of specific sums of money in favor of his brothers and sisters. A direction to this effect is called a direction for "raising portions for younger children;" and, for this purpose, it is usual to demise or lease the estate to trustees for a term of years, upon trust to raise the required portions by a sale or mortgage of the same. Mozley & Whitley.

RAN. Sax. In Saxon and old English law. Open theft, or robbery.

RANGE. In the government survey of the United States, this term is used to denote one of the divisions of a state, and designates a row or tier of townships as they appear on the map.

RANGER. In forest law. A sworn officer of the forest, whose office chiefly consists in three points: To walk daily through his charge to see, hear, and inquire as well of trespasses as trespassers in his bailiwick; to drive the beasts of the forest, both of venery and chace, out of the deafforested into the forested lands; and to present all trespassers of the forest at the next courts holden for the forest. Cowell.

RANK, *n.* The order or place in which certain officers are placed in the army and navy, in relation to others.

RANK, *adj.* In English law. Excessive; too large in amount; as a *rank modus.* 2 Bl. Comm. 30.

RANK MODUS. One that is too large. Rankness is a mere rule of evidence, drawn from the improbability of the fact, rather than a rule of law. 2 Steph. Comm. 729.

RANKING OF CREDITORS is the Scotch term for the arrangement of the property of a debtor according to the claims of the creditors, in consequence of the nature of their respective securities. Bell. The corresponding process in England is the marshalling of securities in a suit or action for redemption or foreclosure. Paterson.

RANSOM. In international law. The redemption of captured property from the hands of an enemy, particularly of property captured at sea. 1 Kent, Comm. 104.

A sum paid or agreed to be paid for the redemption of captured property. 1 Kent, Comm. 105.

A "ransom," strictly speaking, is not a recapture of the captured property. It is rather a purchase of the right of the captors at the time, be it what it may; or, more properly, it is a relinquishment of all the interest and benefit which the captors might acquire or consummate in the property, by a regular adjudication of a prize tribunal, whether it be an interest *in rem*, a lien, or a mere title to expenses. In this respect, there seems to be no difference between the case of a ransom of an enemy or a neutral. 2 Gall. 325.

In old English law. A sum of money paid for the pardoning of some great offense. The distinction between ransom and amerciament is said to be that ransom was the redemption of a corporal punishment, while amerciament was a fine or penalty directly imposed, and not in lieu of another punishment. Cowell; 4 Bl. Comm. 380.

Ransom was also a sum of money paid for the redemption of a person from captivity or imprisonment. Thus one of the feudal "aids" was to ransom the lord's person if taken prisoner. 2 Bl. Comm. 63.

RANSOM BILL. A contract by which a captured vessel, in consideration of her release and of safe-conduct for a stipulated course and time, agrees to pay a certain sum as ransom.

RAPE. In criminal law. The unlawful carnal knowledge of a woman by a man forcibly and against her will. Code Ga. § 4349.

In English law. An intermediate division between a shire and a hundred; or a division of a county, containing several hundreds. 1 Bl. Comm. 116; Cowell. Apparently peculiar to the county of Sussex.

RAPE OF THE FOREST. In old English law. Trespass committed in a forest by violence. Cowell.

RAPE-REEVE. In English law. The chief officer of a rape, (*q. v.*) 1 Bl. Comm. 116.

RAPINE. In criminal law. Plunder; pillage; robbery. In the civil law, *rapina* is defined as the forcible and violent taking of another man's movable property with the criminal intent to appropriate it to the robber's own use. A prætorian action lay for this offense, in which quadruple damages were recoverable. Gaius, lib. 3, § 209; Inst. 4, 2; Mackeld. Rom. Law, § 481; Heinecc. Elem. § 1071.

RAPPORT À SUCCESSION. In French law and in Louisiana. A proceeding similar to hotchpot; the restoration to the succession of such property as the heir may have received by way of advancement from the decedent, in order that an even division may be made among all the co-heirs. Civil Code La. art. 1305.

RAPTOR. In old English law. A ravisher. Fleta, lib. 2, c. 52, § 12.

RAPTU HÆREDIS. In old English law. A writ for taking away an heir holding in socage, of which there were two sorts: One when the heir was married; the other when he was not. Reg. Orig. 163.

RAPUIT. Lat. In old English law. Ravished. A technical word in old indictments. 2 East, 30.

RASURE. The act of scraping, scratching, or shaving the surface of a written instrument, for the purpose of removing certain letters or words from it. It is to be distinguished from "obliteration," as the latter word properly denotes the crossing out of a word or letter by drawing a line through it with ink. But the two expressions are often used interchangeably. See 18 Johns. 499.

RASUS. In old English law. A rase; a measure of onions, containing twenty flones, and each flonis twenty-five heads. Fleta, lib. 2, c. 12, § 12.

RATABLE ESTATE. Within the meaning of a tax law, this term means "taxable estate;" the real and personal property which the legislature designates as "taxable." 55 Vt. 546.

RATAM REM HABERE. Lat. In the civil law. To hold a thing ratified; to ratify or confirm it. Dig. 46, 8, 12, 1.

RATE. Proportional or relative value, measure, or degree; the proportion or standard by which quantity or value is adjusted. Thus, the *rate* of interest is the proportion or ratio between the principal and interest. So the buildings in a town are *rated* for insurance purposes; *i. e.*, classified and individually estimated with reference to their insurable qualities. In this sense also we speak of articles as being in "first-rate" or "second-rate" condition.

Absolute measure, value, or degree. Thus, we speak of the *rate* at which public lands are sold, of the *rates* of fare upon railroads, etc.

The term is also used as the synonym of "tax;" that is, a sum assessed by governmental authority upon persons or property, by proportional valuation, for public purposes. It is chiefly employed in this sense in England, but is there usually confined to taxes of a local nature, or those raised by the parish; such as the poor-rate, borough-rate, etc.

It sometimes occurs in a connection which gives it a meaning synonymous with "assessment;" that is, the apportionment of a tax among the whole number of persons who are responsible for it, by estimating the value of the taxable property of each, and making a proportional distribution of the whole amount. Thus we speak of "rating" persons and property.

RATE OF EXCHANGE. In commercial law. The actual price at which a bill, drawn in one country upon another country, can be bought or obtained in the former country at any given time. Story, Bills, § 31.

RATE-TITHE. In English law. When any sheep, or other cattle, are kept in a parish for less time than a year, the owner must pay tithe for them *pro rata*, according to the custom of the place. Fitzh. Nat. Brev. 51.

RATIFICATION. The confirmation of a previous act done either by the party himself or by another; confirmation of a voidable act. See Story, Ag. §§ 250, 251; 2 Kent, Comm. 237.

This is where a person adopts a contract or other transaction which is not binding on him, because it was entered into by an unauthorized agent or the like. Leake, Cont. 268.

RATIFICATION OF TREATIES. See TREATY.

RATIHABITIO. Lat. Confirmation, agreement, consent, approbation of a contract.

Ratihabitio mandato æquiparatur. Ratification is equivalent to express command. Dig. 46, 3, 12, 4; Broom, Max. 867.

RATIO. Rate; proportion; degree. Reason, or understanding. Also a cause, or giving judgment therein.

RATIO DECIDENDI. The ground of decision. The point in a case which determines the judgment.

Ratio est formalis causa consuetudinis. Reason is the formal cause of custom.

Ratio est legis anima; mutata legis ratione mutatur et lex. 7 Coke, 7. Reason is the soul of law; the reason of law being changed, the law is also changed.

Ratio est radius divini luminis. Co. Litt. 232. Reason is a ray of the divine light.

Ratio et auctoritas, duo clarissima mundi lumina. 4 Inst. 320. Reason and authority, the two brightest lights of the world.

RATIO LEGIS. The reason or occasion of a law; the occasion of making a law. Bl. Law Tracts, 3.

Ratio legis est anima legis. Jenk. Cent. 45. The reason of law is the soul of law.

Ratio potest allegari deficiente lege; sed ratio vera et legalis, et non apparens. Co. Litt. 191. Reason may be alleged when law is defective; but it must be true and legal reason, and not merely apparent.

RATIONABILE ESTOVERIUM. A Latin phrase equivalent to "alimony."

RATIONABILI PARTE BONORUM. A writ that lay for the wife against the executors of her husband, to have the third part of his goods after his just debts and funeral expenses had been paid. Fitzh. Nat. Brev. 122.

RATIONALIBUS DIVISIS. An abolished writ which lay where two lords, in divers towns, had seigniories adjoining, for him who found his waste by little and little to have been encroached upon, against the other, who had encroached, thereby to rectify their bounds. Cowell.

RATIONE IMPOTENTIÆ. Lat. On account of inability. A ground of qualified property in some animals *feræ naturæ;* as in the young ones, while they are unable to fly or run. 2 Bl. Comm. 3 4.

RATIONE MATERIÆ. Lat. By reason of the matter involved; in consequence of, or from the nature of, the subject-matter.

RATIONE PERSONÆ. Lat. By reason of the person concerned; from the character of the person.

RATIONE PRIVILEGII. Lat. This term describes a species of property in wild animals, which consists in the right which, by a peculiar franchise anciently granted by the English crown, by virtue of its prerogative, one man may have of killing and taking such animals on the land of another. 106 E. C. L. 870.

RATIONE SOLI. Lat. On account of the soil; with reference to the soil. Said to be the ground of ownership in bees. 2 Bl. Comm. 393.

RATIONE TENURÆ. L. Lat. By reason of tenure; as a consequence of tenure. 3 Bl. Comm. 230.

RATIONES. In old law. The pleadings in a suit. *Rationes exercere*, or *ad rationes stare*, to plead.

RATTENING is where the members of a trade union cause the tools, clothes, or other property of a workman to be taken away or hidden, in order to compel him to join the union or cease working. It is an offense punishable by fine or imprisonment. 38 & 39 Vict. c. 86, § 7. Sweet.

RAVISHED. In criminal practice. A material word in indictments for rape. Whart. Crim. Law, § 401.

RAVISHMENT. In criminal law. An unlawful taking of a woman, or of an heir in ward. Rape.

RAVISHMENT DE GARD. L. Fr. An abolished writ which lay for a guardian by knight's service or in socage, against a person who took from him the body of his ward. Fitzh. Nat. Brev. 140; 12 Car. II. c. 3.

RAVISHMENT OF WARD. In English law. The marriage of an infant ward without the consent of the guardian.

RAZE. To erase. 3 How. State Tr. 156.

RAZON. In Spanish law. Cause, (*causa*.) Las Partidas, pt. 4, tit. 4, l. 2.

RE. Lat. In the matter of; in the case of. A term of frequent use in designating judicial proceedings, in which there is only one party. Thus, "*Re* Vivian" signifies "In the matter of Vivian," or in "Vivian's Case."

RE. FA. LO. The abbreviation of "*recordari facias loquelam*," (*q. v.*)

Re, verbis, scripto, consensu, traditione, junctura vestes sumere pacta solent. Compacts usually take their clothing from the thing itself, from words, from writing, from consent, from delivery. Plowd. 161.

READERS. In the middle temple, those persons were so called who were appointed to deliver lectures or "readings" at certain periods during term. The clerks in holy orders who read prayers and assist in the performance of divine service in the chapels of the several inns of court are also so termed. Brown.

READING-IN. In English ecclesiastical law. The title of a person admitted to a rectory or other benefice will be divested unless within two months after actual possession he publicly read in the church of the benefice, upon some Lord's day, and at the appointed times, the morning and evening service, according to the book of common prayer; and afterwards, publicly before the congregation, declare his assent to such book; and also publicly read the thirty-nine articles in the same church, in the time of common prayer, with declaration of his assent thereto; and moreover, within three months after his admission, read upon some Lord's day in the same church, in the presence of the congregation, in the time of divine service, a declaration by him subscribed before the ordinary, of conformity to the Liturgy, together with the certificate of the ordinary of its having been so subscribed. 2 Steph. Comm. (7th Ed.) 687; Wharton.

REAFFORESTED. Where a deafforested forest is again made a forest. 20 Car. II. c. 3.

REAL. In common law. Relating to *land*, as distinguished from personal property. This term is applied to lands, tenements, and hereditaments.

In the civil law. Relating to a *thing*, (whether movable or immovable,) as distinguished from a person.

REAL ACTION. At the common law. One brought for the specific recovery of lands, tenements, or hereditaments. Steph. Pl. 3.

Among the civilians, real actions, otherwise called "vindications," were those in which a man demanded something that was his own. They were founded on dominion, or *jus in re*.

The real actions of the Roman law were not, like the real actions of the common law, confined to real estate, but they included personal, as well as real, property. Wharton.

REAL ASSETS. Lands or real estate in the hands of an heir, chargeable with the payment of the debts of the ancestor. 2 Bl. Comm. 244, 302.

REAL BURDEN. In Scotch law. Where a right to lands is expressly granted under the burden of a specific sum, which is declared a burden on the lands themselves, or where the right is declared null if the sum be not paid, and where the amount of the sum, and the name of the creditor in it, can be discovered from the records, the burden is said to be real. Bell.

REAL CHATTELS. Such as concern, or savor of, the realty, such as leasehold estates; interests issuing out of, or annexed to, real estate; such chattel interests as devolve after the manner of realty. 2 Bl. Comm. 386. See CHATTELS.

REAL CHYMIN. L. Fr. In old English law. The royal way; the king's highway, (*regia via.*)

REAL COMPOSITION. An agreement made, in England, between the owner of land and the incumbent of a parish, with the consent of the ordinary and the patron of the living, that the land shall for the future be discharged from payment of tithes, by reason of some land or other real recompense given in lieu and satisfaction thereof. But since the statute 13 Eliz. c. 10, no real composition can be made for any longer term than three lives or twenty-one years, and such compositions are now rarely heard of. 2 Bl. Comm. 28.

REAL CONTRACT. In the civil law. A contract in which the obligation arose from the thing (*ex re*) itself, which was the subject of it. Inst. 3, 14, 2; Id. 3, 15. Real contracts were those in which, besides the consent of the parties, the delivery of some *thing* was required to perfect the obligation. Hallifax, Civil Law, b. 2, c. 15, no. 1.

In common law. A contract respecting real property; as a lease of land for years. 3 Coke, 22*a*.

REAL COVENANT A covenant whereby a man binds himself to pass a real thing, as lands or tenements; as a covenant to levy a fine, etc. Shep. Touch. 161.

A covenant, the obligation of which is so connected with the realty that he who has the latter is either entitled to the benefit of or liable to perform the other. 2 Bl. Comm. 304, (Coleridge's note.)

A covenant by which the covenantor binds his heirs. 2 Bl. Comm. 304.

REAL ESTATE. Landed property, including all estates and interests in lands which are held for life or for some greater estate, and whether such lands be of freehold or copyhold tenure. Wharton.

REAL-ESTATE AGENT. Any person whose business it is to sell, or offer for sale, real estate for others, or to rent houses, stores, or other buildings, or real estate, or to collect rent for others. Act July 13, 1866, 49; 14 St. at Large, 118.

REAL-ESTATE BROKER. One who engages in the purchase and sale of real estate as a business and occupation, and so holds himself out to the public in that character and capacity. 26 Pa. St. 138.

REAL EVIDENCE. All evidence of which any object belonging to the class of *things* is the source, *persons* also included, in respect of such properties as belong to them in common with things. Best, Ev. 26.

REAL INJURY. In the civil law. An injury arising from an unlawful *act*, as distinguished from a verbal injury, which was done by *words*. Hallifax, Civil Law, b. 2, c. 15, nn. 3, 4.

REAL ISSUE. An issue formed in a regular manner in a regular suit for the purpose of determining an actual controversy; as distinguished from a *feigned* issue, (*q. v.*)

REAL LAW. At common law. The body of laws relating to real property. This use of the term is popular rather than technical.

In the civil law. A law which relates to specific property, whether movable or immovable.

Laws purely real directly and indirectly regulate property, and the rights of property, without intermeddling with or changing the state of the person. Wharton.

REAL PARTY. In statutes requiring suits to be brought in the name of the "real party in interest," this term means the person who is actually and substantially interested in the subject-matter, as distinguished from one who has only a nominal, formal, or technical interest in it or connection with it.

REAL PRIVILEGE. In English law. A privilege granted to, or concerning, a particular place or locality.

REAL PROPERTY. A general term for lands, tenements, and hereditaments; property which, on the death of the owner intestate, passes to his heir. Real property is either corporeal or incorporeal. See Code N. Y. § 462.

REAL REPRESENTATIVE. He who represents or stands in the place of another, with respect to his real property, is so termed, in contradistinction to him who stands in the place of another, with regard to his personal property, and who is termed the "personal representative." Thus the heir is the real representative of his deceased ancestor. Brown.

REAL RIGHT. In Scotch law. That which entitles him who is vested with it to possess the subject as his own, and, if in the possession of another, to demand from him its actual possession. *Real* rights affect the subject itself; *personal* are founded in obligation. Erskine, Inst. 3, 1, 2.

REAL SECURITY. The security of mortgages or other liens or incumbrances upon land. See 2 Atk. 806.

REAL SERVITUDE. In the civil law. A right which one estate or piece of land (*prædium*) owes to another estate. See PRÆDIAL SERVITUDE.

REAL STATUTES. In the civil law. Statutes which have principally for their object, property, and which do not speak of persons, except in relation to property. Story, Confl. Laws, § 13.

REAL THINGS, (or THINGS REAL.) In common law. Such things as are permanent, fixed, and immovable, which cannot be carried out of their place; as lands and tenements. 2 Bl. Comm. 15. Things substantial and immovable, and the rights and profits annexed to or issuing out of them. 1 Steph. Comm. 156.

REAL WARRANDICE. In Scotch law. An infeoffment of one tenement given in security of another.

REAL WRONG. In old English law. An injury to the freehold.

REALITY. In foreign law. That quality of laws which concerns property or things, (*quæ ad rem spectant.*) Story, Confl. Laws, § 16.

REALIZE. To convert any kind of property into money; but especially to receive the returns from an investment.

REALM. A kingdom; a country. 1 Taunt. 270; 4 Camp. 289.

REALTY. A brief term for real property; also for anything which partakes of the nature of real property.

REAPPRAISER. A person who, in certain cases, is appointed to make a revaluation or second appraisement of imported goods at the custom-house.

REASON. A faculty of the mind by which it distinguishes truth from falsehood, good from evil, and which enables the possessor to deduce inferences from facts or from propositions. Webster.

REASONABLE. Agreeable to reason; just; proper. Ordinary or usual.

REASONABLE ACT. Such as may fairly, justly, and reasonably be required of a party.

REASONABLE AID. A duty claimed by the lord of the fee of his tenants, holding by knight service, to marry his daughter, etc. Cowell.

REASONABLE AND PROBABLE CAUSE. Such grounds as justify any one in suspecting another of a crime, and giving him in custody thereon. It is a defense to an action for false imprisonment.

REASONABLE CARE. Such a degree of care, precaution, or diligence as may fairly and properly be expected or required, having regard to the nature of the action, or of the subject-matter, and the circumstances surrounding the transaction.

"Reasonable care and skill" is a relative phrase, and, in its application as a rule or measure of duty, will vary in its requirements, according to the circumstances under which the care and skill are to be exerted. 4 Allen, 268.

REASONABLE DILIGENCE. A fair, proper, and due degree of care and activity, measured with reference to the particular circumstances; such diligence, care, or attention as might be expected from a man of ordinary prudence and activity.

REASONABLE DOUBT. This is a term often used, probably pretty well understood, but not easily defined. It does not mean a mere possible doubt, because everything relating to human affairs, and depending on moral evidence, is open to some possible or imaginary doubt. It is that state of the case which, after the entire comparison and consideration of all the evidence, leaves the minds of jurors in that condition that they cannot say they feel an abiding conviction to a moral certainty of the truth of the charge. 26 N. J. Law, 601, 615.

A reasonable doubt is deemed to exist, within the rule that the jury should not convict unless satisfied beyond a reasonable doubt, when the evidence is not sufficient to satisfy the judgment of the truth of a proposition with such certainty that a prudent man would feel safe in acting upon it in his own important affairs. 23 Ind. 170.

REASONABLE NOTICE. Such notice or information of a fact as may fairly and properly be expected or required in the particular circumstances.

REASONABLE PART. In old English law. That share of a man's goods which the law gave to his wife and children after his decease. 2 Bl. Comm. 492.

REASONABLE SKILL. Such skill as is ordinarily possessed and exercised by persons of common capacity, engaged in the same business or employment. 6 Metc. (Mass.) 26.

REASONABLE TIME. Such length of time as may fairly, properly, and reasonably be allowed or required, having regard to the nature of the act or duty, or of the subject-matter, and to the attending circumstances. It is a maxim of English law that "how long a 'reasonable time' ought to be is not defined in law, but is left to the discretion of the judges." Co. Litt. 50.

REASSURANCE. This is where an insurer procures the whole or a part of the sum which he has insured (*i. e.*, contracted to pay in case of loss, death, etc.) to be insured again to him by another person. Sweet.

REATTACHMENT. A second attachment of him who was formerly attached, and dismissed the court without day, by the not coming of the justices, or some such casualty. Reg. Orig. 35.

REBATE. Discount; reducing the interest of money in consideration of prompt payment.

REBEL. The name of rebels is given to all subjects who unjustly take up arms against the ruler of the society, [or the lawful and constitutional government,] whether their view be to deprive him of the supreme authority or to resist his lawful commands in some particular instance, and to impose conditions on him. Vatt. Law Nat. bk. 3, § 288.

REBELLION. Deliberate, organized resistance, by force and arms, to the laws or operations of the government, committed by a subject.

In old English law, the term "rebellion" was also applied to contempt of a court manifested by disobedience to its process, particularly of the court of chancery. If a defendant refused to appear, after attachment and proclamation, a "commission of rebellion" issued against him. 3 Bl. Comm. 444.

REBELLION, COMMISSION OF. In equity practice. A process of contempt issued on the non-appearance of a defendant.

REBELLIOUS ASSEMBLY. In English law. A gathering of twelve persons or more, intending, going about, or practicing unlawfully and of their own authority to change any laws of the realm; or to destroy the inclosure of any park or ground inclosed, banks of fish-ponds, pools, conduits, etc., to the intent the same shall remain void; or that they shall have way in any of the said grounds; or to destroy the deer in any park, fish in ponds, coneys in any warren, dove-houses, etc.; or to burn sacks of corn; or to abate rents or prices of victuals, etc. See Cowell.

REBOUTER. To repel or bar. The action of the heir by the warranty of his ancestor is called "to rebut or repel." 2 Co. Litt. 247.

REBUS SIC STANTIBUS. Lat. At this point of affairs; in these circumstances.

REBUT. In pleading and evidence. To rebut is to defeat or take away the effect of something. Thus, when a plaintiff in an action produces evidence which raises a presumption of the defendant's liability, and the defendant adduces evidence which shows that the presumption is ill-founded, he is said to "rebut it." Sweet.

In the old law of real property, to rebut was to repel or bar a claim. Thus, when a person was sued for land which had been warranted to him by the plaintiff or his ancestor, and he pleaded the warranty as a defense to the action, this was called a "rebutter." Co. Litt. 365*a;* Termes de la Ley.

REBUT AN EQUITY. To defeat an apparent equitable right or claim, by the introduction of evidence showing that, in the particular circumstances, there is no ground for such equity to attach, or that it is overridden by a superior or countervailing equity. See 2 Whart. Ev. § 973.

REBUTTABLE PRESUMPTION. In the law of evidence. A presumption which may be rebutted by evidence. Otherwise called a "disputable" presumption. A species of legal presumption which holds good until disproved. Best, Pres. § 25; 1 Greenl. Ev. § 33.

REBUTTAL. The introduction of rebutting evidence; the stage of a trial at which such evidence may be introduced; also the rebutting evidence itself.

REBUTTER. In pleading. A defendant's answer of fact to a plaintiff's surrejoinder; the third pleading in the series on the part of the defendant. Steph. Pl. 59; 3 Bl. Comm. 310.

REBUTTING EVIDENCE. Evidence offered on the part of the plaintiff (or prosecution) for the purpose of contradicting or counteracting the evidence adduced by the defendant.

That which is given by one party in a cause, to explain, repel, counteract, or disprove evidence produced by the other party. Wharton.

RECALL. In international law. To summon a diplomatic minister back to his home court, at the same time depriving him of his office and functions.

RECALL A JUDGMENT. To revoke, cancel, vacate, or reverse a judgment, for matters of fact; when it is annulled by reason of errors of law, it is said to be "reversed."

RECAPTION. A retaking, or taking back. A species of remedy by the mere act of the party injured, (otherwise termed "reprisal,") which happens when any one has deprived another of his property in goods or chattels personal, or wrongfully detains one's wife, child, or servant. In this case, the owner of the goods, and the husband, parent, or master may lawfully claim and retake them, wherever he happens to find them, so it be not in a riotous manner, or attended with a breach of the peace. 3 Inst. 134; 3 Bl. Comm. 4; 3 Steph. Comm. 358.

It also signifies the taking a second distress of one formerly distrained during the plea grounded on the former distress.

Also a writ to recover damages for him whose goods, being distrained for rent in service, etc., are distrained again for the same cause, pending the plea in the county court, or before the justice. Fitzh. Nat. Brev. 71.

RECAPTURE. The taking from an enemy, by a friendly force, a vessel previously taken for prize by such enemy.

Receditur a placitis juris, potius quam injuriæ et delicta maneant impunita. Positive rules of law [as distinguished from maxims or conclusions of reason] will be receded from, [given up or dispensed with,] rather than that crimes and wrongs should remain unpunished. Bac. Max. 55, reg. 12.

RECEIPT. A receipt is the written acknowledgment of the receipt of money, or a thing of value, without containing any affirmative obligation upon either party to it; a mere admission of a fact, in writing. 53 Ind. 574.

A receipt may be defined to be such a written acknowledgment by one person of his having received money from another as will be *prima facie* evidence of that fact in a court of law. 10 Ohio, 75.

Also the act or transaction of accepting or taking anything delivered.

In old practice. Admission of a party to defend a suit, as of a wife on default of the husband in certain cases. Litt. § 668; Co. Litt. 352*b*.

RECEIPTOR. A name given in some of the states to a person who receives from the sheriff goods which the latter has seized under process of garnishment, on giving to the sheriff a bond conditioned to have the property forthcoming when demanded or when execution issues. Story, Bailm. § 124.

RECEIVER. A receiver is an indifferent person between the parties appointed by the court to collect and receive the rents, issues, and profits of land, or the produce of personal estate, or other things which it does not seem reasonable to the court that either party should do; or where a party is incompetent to do so, as in the case of an infant. The remedy or the appointment of a receiver is one of the very oldest in the court of chancery, and is founded on the inadequacy of the remedy to be obtained in the court of ordinary jurisdiction. Bisp. Eq. § 576.

One who receives money to the use of another to render an account. Story, Eq. Jur. § 446.

In criminal law. One who receives stolen goods from thieves, and conceals them. Cowell. This was always the prevalent sense of the word in the common as well as the civil law.

RECEIVER GENERAL OF THE DUCHY OF LANCASTER. An officer of the duchy court, who collects all the revenues, fines, forfeitures, and assessments within the duchy.

RECEIVER GENERAL OF THE PUBLIC REVENUE. In English law. An officer appointed in every county to receive the taxes granted by parliament, and remit the money to the treasury.

RECEIVER OF FINES. An English officer who receives the money from persons who compound with the crown on original writs sued out of chancery. Wharton.

RECEIVERS AND TRIERS OF PETITIONS. The mode of receiving and trying petitions to parliament was formerly judicial rather than legislative, and the triers were committees of prelates, peers, and judges, and, latterly, of the members generally. Brown.

RECEIVER'S CERTIFICATE. A non-negotiable evidence of debt, or debenture, issued by authority of a court of chancery, as a first lien upon the property of a debtor corporation in the hands of a receiver. Beach, Rec. § 379.

RECEIVERS OF WRECK. Persons appointed by the English board of trade. The duties of a receiver of wreck are to take steps for the preservation of any vessel stranded or in distress within his district; to receive and take possession of all articles washed on shore from the vessel; to use force for the suppression of plunder and disorder; to institute an examination on oath with respect to the vessel; and, if necessary, to sell the vessel, cargo, or wreck. Sweet.

RECEIVING STOLEN GOODS. The short name usually given to the offense of receiving any property with the knowledge that it has been feloniously or unlawfully stolen, taken, extorted, obtained, embezzled, or disposed of. Sweet.

RECENS INSECUTIO. In old English law. Fresh suit; fresh pursuit. Pursuit of a thief immediately after the discovery of the robbery. 1 Bl. Comm. 297.

RÉCÉPISSÉ DE COTISATION. In French law. A receipt setting forth the extent of the interest subscribed by a member of a mutual insurance company. Arg. Fr. Merc. Law, 571.

RECEPTUS. In the civil law. The name sometimes given to an arbitrator, because he had been received or chosen to settle the differences between the parties. Dig. 4, 8; Cod. 2, 56.

RECESSION. The act of ceding back; the restoration of the title and dominion of a territory, by the government which now holds it, to the government from which it was obtained by cession or otherwise. 2 White, Recop. 516.

RECESSUS MARIS. In old English law. A going back; reliction or retreat of the sea.

RECHT. Ger. Right; justice; equity; the whole body of law; unwritten law; law; also a right.

There is much ambiguity in the use of this term, an ambiguity which it shares with the French "*droit*," the Italian "*diritto*," and the English "right." On the one hand, the term "*recht*" answers to the Roman "*jus*," and thus indicates law in the abstract, considered as the foundation of all rights, or the complex of underlying moral principles which impart the character of justice to all positive law, or give it an ethical content. Taken in this abstract sense, the term may be an adjective, in which case it is equivalent to the English "just," or a noun, in which case it may be paraphrased by the expressions "justice," "morality," or "equity." On the other hand, it serves to point out *a* right; that is, a power, privilege, faculty, or demand, inherent in one person, and incident upon another. In the latter signification "*recht*" (or "*droit*," or "*diritto*," or "right") is the correlative of "duty" or "obligation." In the former sense, it may be considered as opposed to wrong, injustice, or the absence of law. The word "*recht*" has the further ambiguity that it is used in contradistinction to "*gesetz*," as "*jus*" is opposed to "*lex*," or the unwritten law to enacted law. See DROIT; JUS; RIGHT.

RECIDIVE. In French law. The state of an individual who commits a crime or misdemeanor, after having once been condemned for a crime or misdemeanor; a relapse. Dalloz.

RECIPROCAL CONTRACT. A contract, the parties to which enter into mutual engagements. A mutual or bilateral contract.

RECIPROCITY. Mutuality. The term is used in international law to denote the relation existing between two states when each of them gives the subjects of the other certain privileges, on condition that its own subjects shall enjoy similar privileges at the hands of the latter state. Sweet.

RECITAL. The formal statement or setting forth of some matter of fact, in any deed or writing, in order to explain the reasons upon which the transaction is founded. The recitals are situated in the premises of a deed, that is, in that part of a deed between the date and the *habendum*, and they usually commence with the formal word "whereas." Brown.

The formal preliminary statement in a deed or other instrument, of such deeds, agreements, or matters of fact as are necessary to explain the reasons upon which the transaction is founded. 2 Bl. Comm. 298.

In pleading. The statement of matter as introductory to some positive allegation, beginning in declarations with the words, "For that *whereas*." Steph. Pl. 388, 389.

RECITE. To state in a written instrument facts connected with its inception, or reasons for its being made.

RECKLESSNESS. Rashness; heedlessness; wanton conduct. The state of mind accompanying an act, which either pays no regard to its probably or possibly injurious consequences, or which, though foreseeing such consequences, persists in spite of such knowledge.

RECLAIM. To claim or demand back; to ask for the return or restoration of a thing; to insist upon one's right to recover that which was one's own, but was parted with conditionally or mistakenly; as, to *reclaim* goods which were obtained from one under false pretenses.

In feudal law, it was used of the action of a lord pursuing, prosecuting, and recalling his vassal, who had gone to live in another place, without his permission.

In international law, it denotes the demanding of a thing or person to be delivered up or surrendered to the government or state to which either properly belongs, when, by an irregular means, it has come into the possession of another. Wharton.

In the law of property. Spoken of animals, to reduce from a wild to a tame or domestic state; to tame them. In an analogous sense, to reclaim land is to reduce marshy or swamp land to a state fit for cultivation and habitation.

In Scotch law. To appeal. The reclaiming days in Scotland are the days allowed to a party dissatisfied with the judgment of the lord ordinary to appeal therefrom to the inner house; and the petition of appeal is called the reclaiming "bill," "note," or "petition." Mozley & Whitley; Bell.

RECLAIMED ANIMALS. Those that are made tame by art, industry, or education, whereby a qualified property may be acquired in them.

RECLAIMING BILL. In Scotch law. A petition of appeal or review of a judgment of the lord ordinary or other inferior court. Bell.

RECOGNITION. Ratification; confirmation; an acknowledgment that something done by another person in one's name had one's authority.

An inquiry conducted by a chosen body of men, not sitting as part of the court, into the facts in dispute in a case at law; these "recognitors" preceded the jurymen of modern times, and reported their recognition or verdict to the court. Stim. Law Gloss.

RECOGNITIONE ADNULLANDA PER VIM ET DURITIEM FACTA. A writ to the justices of the common bench for sending a record touching a recognizance, which the recognizor suggests was acknowledged by force and duress; that if it so appear the recognizance may be annulled. Reg. Orig. 183.

RECOGNITORS. In English law. The name by which the jurors impaneled on an assize are known. See RECOGNITION.

The word is sometimes met in modern books, as meaning the person who enters into a recognizance, being thus another form of recognizor.

RECOGNIZANCE. An obligation of record, entered into before some court of record, or magistrate duly authorized, with condition to do some particular act; as to appear at the assizes, or criminal court, to keep the peace, to pay a debt, or the like. It resembles a bond, but differs from it in being an acknowledgment of a former debt upon record. 2 Bl. Comm. 341.

In criminal law, a person who has been found guilty of an offense may, in certain cases, be required to enter into a recognizance by which he binds himself to keep the peace for a certain period. Sweet.

In the practice of several of the states, a recognizance is a species of bail-bond or security, given by the prisoner either on being bound over for trial or on his taking an appeal.

RECOGNIZE. To try; to examine in order to determine the truth of a matter. Also to enter into a recognizance.

RECOGNIZEE. He to whom one is bound in a recognizance.

RECOGNIZOR. He who enters into a recognizance.

RECOLEMENT. In French law. This is the process by which a witness, who has given his deposition, reads the same over and scrutinizes it, with a view to affirming his satisfaction with it as it stands, or to making such changes in it as his better recollection may suggest to him as necessary to the truth. This is necessary to the validity of the deposition. See Poth. Proc. Crim. § 4, art. 4.

RECOMMENDATION. In feudal law. A method of converting allodial land into feudal property. The owner of the allod surrendered it to the king or a lord, doing homage, and received it back as a benefice or feud, to hold to himself and such of his heirs as he had previously nominated to the superior.

The act of one person in giving to another a favorable account of the character, responsibility, or skill of a third.

RECOMMENDATORY. Precatory, advisory, or directory. Recommendatory words in a will are such as do not express the testator's command in a peremptory form, but advise, counsel, or suggest that a certain course be pursued or disposition made.

RECOMPENSATION. In Scotland, where a party sues for a debt, and the defendant pleads compensation, *i. e.*, set-off, the plaintiff may allege a compensation on his part; and this is called a "recompensation." Bell.

RECOMPENSE. A reward for services; remuneration for goods or other property.

RECOMPENSE OR RECOVERY IN VALUE. That part of the judgment in a "common recovery" by which the tenant is declared entitled to recover lands of equal value with those which were warranted to him and lost by the default of the vouchee. See 2 Bl. Comm. 358-359.

RECONCILIATION. The renewal of amicable relations between two persons who had been at enmity or variance; usually implying forgiveness of injuries on one or both sides. It is sometimes used in the law of divorce as a term synonymous or analogous to "condonation."

RECONDUCTION. In the civil law. A renewing of a former lease; relocation. Dig. 19, 2, 13, 11; Code Nap. arts. 1737-1740.

RECONSTRUCTION. The name commonly given to the process of reorganizing, by acts of congress and executive action, the governments of the states which had passed ordinances of secession, and of re-establishing their constitutional relations to the national government, restoring their representation in congress, and effecting the necessary changes in their internal government, after the close of the civil war.

RECONTINUANCE seems to be used to signify that a person has recovered an incorporeal hereditament of which he had been wrongfully deprived. Thus, "A. is disseised of a mannor, whereunto an advowson is appendant, an estranger [*i. e.*, neither A. nor the disseisor] usurpes to the advowson; if the disseisee [A.] enter into the mannor, the advowson is recontinued again, which was severed by the usurpation. * * * And so note a diversitie between a recontinuance and a remitter; for a remitter cannot be properly, unlesse there be two titles; but a recontinuance may be where there is but one." Co. Litt. 363*b*; Sweet.

RECONVENIRE. Lat. In the canon and civil law. To make a cross-demand upon the actor, or plaintiff. 4 Reeve, Eng. Law, 14, and note, (*r*.)

RECONVENTION. In the civil law. An action by a defendant against a plaintiff in a former action; a cross-bill or litigation.

The term is used in practice in the states of Louisiana and Texas, derived from the *reconventio* of the civil law. Reconvention is not identical with set-off, but more extensive. See 6 Tex. 414; 5 Tex. 501, 504.

RECONVERSION. That imaginary process by which a prior constructive conversion is annulled, and the converted property restored in contemplation of law to its original state.

RECONVEYANCE takes place where a mortgage debt is paid off, and the mortgaged property is conveyed again to the mortgagor or his representatives free from the mortgage debt. Sweet.

RECOPILACION DE INDIAS. A collection of Spanish colonial law, promulgated A. D. 1680. See Schm. Civil Law, Introd. 94.

RECORD, *v.* To register or enroll; to write out on parchment or paper, or in a book, for the purpose of preservation and perpetual memorial; to transcribe a document, or enter the history of an act or series of acts, in an official volume, for the purpose of giving notice of the same, of furnishing authentic evidence, and for preservation.

RECORD, *n.* A written account of some act, transaction, or instrument, drawn up, under authority of law, by a proper officer, and designed to remain as a memorial or permanent evidence of the matters to which it relates.

There are three kinds of records, viz.: (1) *judicial*, as an attainder; (2) *ministerial*, on oath, being an office or inquisition found; (3) by way of *conveyance*, as a deed enrolled. Wharton.

In practice. A written memorial of all the acts and proceedings in an action or suit, in a court of record. The record is the official and authentic history of the cause, consisting in entries of each successive step in the proceedings, chronicling the various acts of the parties and of the court, couched in the formal language established by usage, terminating with the judgment rendered in the cause, and intended to remain as a perpetual and unimpeachable memorial of the proceedings and judgment.

At common law, "record" signifies a *roll of parchment* upon which the proceedings and transactions of a court are entered or drawn up by its officers, and which is then deposited in its treasury *in perpetuam rei memoriam*. 3 Steph. Comm. 583; 3 Bl. Comm. 24. A court of record is that where the acts and judicial proceedings are enrolled in parchment for a perpetual memorial and testimony, which rolls are called the "records of the court," and are of such high and supereminent authority that their truth is not to be called in question. 34 Cal. 422.

In the practice of appellate tribunals, the word "record" is generally understood to mean the history of the proceedings on the trial of the action below, (with the pleadings, offers, objections to evidence, rulings of the court, exceptions, charge, etc.,) in so far as the same appears in the record furnished to the appellate court in the paper-books or other transcripts. Hence, derivatively, it means the aggregate of the various judicial steps taken on the trial below, in so far as they were taken, presented, or allowed in the formal and proper manner necessary to put them upon the record of the court. This is the meaning in such phrases as "no error in the record," "contents of the record," "outside the record," etc.

RECORD AND WRIT CLERK. Four officers of the court of chancery were designated by this title, whose duty it was to file bills brought to them for that purpose. Business was distributed among them according to the initial letter of the surname of the first plaintiff in a suit. Hunt, Eq.

These officers are now transferred to the high court of justice under the judicature acts.

RECORD COMMISSION. The name of a board of commissioners appointed for the purpose of searching out, classifying, indexing, or publishing the public records of a state or county.

RECORD, CONVEYANCES BY. Extraordinary assurances; as private acts of parliament, and royal grants.

RECORD, COURTS OF. Those whose judicial acts and proceedings are enrolled in parchment, for a perpetual memorial and testimony, which rolls are called the "records of the court," and are of such high and supereminent authority that their truth is not to be called in question. Every court of record has authority to fine and imprison for contempt of its authority. 3 Broom & H. Comm. 21, 30.

RECORD, DEBTS OF. Those which appear to be due by the evidence of a court of record; such as a judgment, recognizance, etc.

RECORD OF NISI PRIUS. In English law. An official copy or transcript of the proceedings in an action, entered on parchment and "sealed and passed," as it is termed, at the proper office; it serves as a warrant to the judge to try the cause, and is the only document at which he can judicially look for information as to the nature of the proceedings and the issues joined. Brown.

RECORD, TRIAL BY. A species of trial adopted for determining the existence or non-existence of a record. When a record is asserted by one party to exist, and the opposite party denies its existence under the form of a traverse that there is no such record remaining in court as alleged, and issue is joined thereon, this is called an "issue of *nul tiel record*," and in such case the court awards a trial by inspection and examination of the record. Upon this the party affirming its existence is bound to produce it in court on a day given for the purpose, and, if he fails to do so, judgment is given for his adversary. Co. Litt. 117*b*, 260*a*; 3 Bl. Comm. 331.

Recorda sunt vestigia vetustatis et veritatis. Records are vestiges of antiquity and truth. 2 Rolle, 296.

RECORDARE. In American practice. A writ to bring up judgments of justices of the peace. 3 Jones, (N. C.) 491.

RECORDARI FACIAS LOQUELAM. In English practice. A writ by which a suit or plaint in replevin may be removed from a county court to one of the courts of Westminster Hall. 3 Bl. Comm. 149; 3 Steph. Pl. 522, 666. So termed from the emphatic words of the old writ, by which the sheriff was commanded to *cause the plaint to be recorded*, and to have the record before the superior court. Reg. Orig. 5*b*.

RECORDATUR. In old English practice. An entry made upon a record, in order to prevent any alteration of it. 1 Ld. Raym. 211.

An order or allowance that the verdict returned on the *nisi prius* roll be recorded.

RECORDER, *v*. L. Fr. In Norman law To recite or testify on recollection what had previously passed in court. This was the duty of the judges and other principal persons who presided at the *placitum;* thence called "*recordeurs*." Steph. Pl., Append. note 11.

RECORDER, *n*. In old English law. A barrister or other person learned in the law, whom the mayor or other magistrate of any city or town corporate, having jurisdiction or a court of record within their precincts, associated to him for his better direction in matters of justice and proceedings according to law. Cowell.

The name "recorder" is also given to a magistrate, in the judicial systems of some of the states, who has a criminal jurisdiction analogous to that of a police judge or other committing magistrate, and usually a limited civil jurisdiction, and sometimes authority conferred by statute in special classes of proceedings.

Also an officer appointed to make record or enrolment of deeds and other legal instruments authorized by law to be recorded.

RECORDER OF LONDON. One of the justices of oyer and terminer, and a justice of the peace of the *quorum* for putting the laws in execution for the preservation of the peace and government of the city. Being the mouth of the city, he delivers the sentences and judgments of the court therein, and also certifies and records the city customs, etc. He is chosen by the lord mayor and aldermen, and attends the business of the city when summoned by the lord mayor, etc. Wharton.

RECORDING ACTS. Statutes enacted in the several states relative to the official recording of deeds, mortgages, bills of sale, chattel mortgages, etc., and the effect of such records as notice to creditors, purchasers, incumbrancers, and others interested.

RECOUP, or RECOUPE. To deduct, defalk, discount, set off, or keep back; to withhold part of a demand.

RECOUPMENT. In practice. Defalcation or discount from a demand. A keeping back something which is due, because there is an equitable reason to withhold it. Tomlins.

Recoupment is a right of the defendant to have a deduction from the amount of the plaintiff's damages, for the reason that the plaintiff has not complied with the cross-obligations or independent covenants arising under the same contract. Code Ga. 1882, § 2909.

It is keeping back something which is due because there is an equitable reason to withhold it; and is now uniformly applied where a man brings an action for breach of a contract between him and the defendant; and where the latter can show that some stipulation in the same contract was made by the plaintiff, which he has violated, the defendant may, if he choose, instead of suing in his turn, *recoupe* his damages arising from the breach committed by the plaintiff, whether they be liquidated or not. 22 Wend. 155. See 3 Ohio St. 341; 12 Ark. 702; 28 Vt. 415.

In speaking of matters to be shown in defense, the term "recoupment" is often used as synonymous with "reduction." The term is of French origin, and signifies cutting again, or cutting back, and, as a defense, means the cutting back on the plaintiff's claim by the defendant. Like reduction, it is of necessity limited to the amount of the plaintiff's claim. It is properly applicable to a case where the same contract imposes mutual duties and obligations on the two parties, and one seeks a remedy for the breach of duty by the second, and the second meets the demand by a claim for the breach of duty by the first. 46 Vt. 207.

"Recoupment" differs from "set-off" in this respect: that any claim or demand the defendant may have against the plaintiff may be used as a set-off, while it is not a subject for recoupment unless it grows out of the very same transaction which furnishes the plaintiff's cause of action. The term is, as appears above, synonymous with "*reduction;*" but the latter is not a technical term of the law; the word "defalcation," in one of its meanings, expresses the same idea, and is used interchangeably with recoupment. Recoupment, as a remedy, corresponds to the *reconvention* of the civil law.

RECOURSE. The phrase "without recourse" is used in the form of making a qualified or restrictive indorsement of a bill or note. By these words the indorser signifies that, while he transfers his property in the instrument, he does not assume the responsibility of an indorser.

RECOUSSE. Fr. In French law. Recapture. Emerig. Traité des Assur. c. 12, § 23.

RECOVEREE. In old conveyancing. The party who suffered a common recovery.

RECOVERER. The demandant in a common recovery, after judgment has been given in his favor.

RECOVERY. In its most extensive sense, a recovery is the restoration or vindication of a right existing in a person, by the formal judgment or decree of a competent court, at his instance and suit, or the obtaining, by such judgment, of some right or property which has been taken or withheld from him. This is also called a "true" recovery, to distinguish it from a "feigned" or "common" recovery. See COMMON RECOVERY.

RECREANT. Coward or craven. The word pronounced by a combatant in the trial by battel, when he acknowledged himself beaten. 3 Bl. Comm. 340.

RECRIMINATION. A charge made by an accused person against the accuser; in particular a counter-charge of adultery or cruelty made by one charged with the same offense in a suit for divorce, against the person who has charged him or her. Wharton.

Recrimination is a showing by the defendant of any cause of divorce against the plaintiff, in bar of the plaintiff's cause of divorce. Civil Code Cal. § 122.

RECRUIT. A newly-enlisted soldier.

RECTA PRISA REGIS. In old English law. The king's right to prisage, or taking of one butt or pipe of wine before and another behind the mast, as a custom for every ship laden with wines. Cowell.

RECTIFICATION. **Rectification of instrument.** In English law. To rectify is to correct or define something which is erroneous or doubtful. Thus, where the parties to an agreement have determined to embody its terms in the appropriate and conclusive form, but the instrument meant to effect this purpose (*e. g.*, a conveyance, settlement, etc.) is, by mutual mistake, so framed as not to express the real intention of the parties, an action may be brought in the chancery division of the high court to have it rectified. Sweet.

Rectification of boundaries. An action to rectify or ascertain the boundaries of two adjoining pieces of land may be brought in the chancery division of the high court. Id.

Rectification of register. The rectification of a register is the process by which a person whose name is wrongly entered on (or omitted from) a register may compel the keeper of the register to remove (or enter) his name. Id.

RECTIFIER. As used in the United States internal revenue laws, this term is not confined to a person who runs spirits through charcoal, but is applied to any one who rectifies or purifies spirits in any manner whatever, or who makes a mixture of spirits with anything else, and sells it under any name. 3 Ben. 73.

RECTITUDO. Right or justice; legal dues; tribute or payment. Cowell.

RECTO, BREVE DE. A writ of right, which was of so high a nature that as other writs in real actions were only to recover the possession of the land, etc., in question, this aimed to recover the seisin and the property, and thereby both the rights of possession and property were tried together. Cowell.

RECTO DE ADVOCATIONE ECCLESIÆ. A writ which lay at common law, where a man had right of advowson of a church, and, the parson dying, a stranger had presented. Fitzh. Nat. Brev. 30.

RECTO DE CUSTODIA TERRÆ ET HÆREDIS. A writ of right of ward of the land and heir. Abolished.

RECTO DE DOTE. A writ of right of dower, which lay for a widow who had received part of her dower, and demanded the residue, against the heir of the husband or his guardian. Abolished. See 23 & 24 Vict. c. 126, § 26.

RECTO DE DOTE UNDE NIHIL HABET. A writ of right of dower whereof the widow had nothing, which lay where her deceased husband, having divers lands or tenements, had assured no dower to his wife, and she thereby was driven to sue for her thirds against the heir or his guardian. Abolished.

RECTO DE RATIONABILI PARTE. A writ of right, of the reasonable part, which lay between privies in blood; as brothers in gavelkind, sisters, and other coparceners, for land in fee-simple. Fitzh. Nat. Brev. 9.

RECTO QUANDO (or QUIA) DOMINUS REMISIT CURIAM. A writ of right, when or because the lord had remitted his court, which lay where lands or tenements in the seigniory of any lord were in demand by a writ of right. Fitzh. Nat. Brev. 16.

RECTO SUR DISCLAIMER. An abolished writ on disclaimer.

RECTOR. In English law. He that has full possession of a parochial church. A rector (or parson) has, for the most part, the whole right to all the ecclesiastical dues in his parish; while a *vicar* has an appropriator over him, entitled to the best part of the profits, to whom the vicar is, in effect, perpetual curate, with a standing salary. 1 Bl. Comm. 384, 388.

RECTOR PROVINCIÆ. Lat. In Roman law. The governor of a province. Cod. 1, 40.

RECTOR SINECURE. A rector of a parish who has not the cure of souls. 2 Steph. Comm. 683.

RECTORIAL TITHES. Great or predial tithes.

RECTORY. An entire parish church, with all its rights, glebes, tithes, and other profits whatsoever; otherwise commonly called a "benefice."

A rector's manse, or parsonage house. Spelman.

RECTUM. Lat. Right; also a trial or accusation. Bract.; Cowell.

RECTUM ESSE. To be right in court.

RECTUM ROGARE. To ask for right; to petition the judge to do right.

RECTUM, STARE AD. To stand trial or abide by the sentence of the court.

RECTUS IN CURIA. Right in court. The condition of one who stands at the bar, against whom no one objects any offense. When a person outlawed has reversed his outlawry, so that he can have the benefit of the law, he is said to be "*rectus in curia.*" Jacob.

RECUPERATIO. Lat. In old English law. Recovery; restitution by the sentence of a judge of a thing that has been wrongfully taken or detained. Co. Litt. 154*a*.

Recuperatio, i. e., ad rem, per injuriam extortam sive detentam, per sententiam judicis restitutio. Co. Litt. 154*a*. Recovery, *i. e.*, restitution by sentence of a judge of a thing wrongfully extorted or detained.

Recuperatio est alicujus rei in causam, alterius adductæ per judicem acquisitio. Co. Litt. 154*a*. Recovery is the acquisition by sentence of a judge of anything brought into the cause of another.

RECUPERATORES. In Roman law. A species of judges first appointed to decide controversies between Roman citizens and strangers concerning rights requiring speedy remedy, but whose jurisdiction was gradually extended to questions which might be brought before ordinary judges. Mackeld. Rom. Law, § 204.

Recurrendum est ad extraordinarium quando non valet ordinarium. We must have recourse to what is extraordinary, when what is ordinary fails.

RECUSANTS. In English law. Persons who willfully absent themselves from their parish church, and on whom penalties were imposed by various statutes passed during the reigns of Elizabeth and James I. Wharton.

Those persons who separate from the church established by law. Termes de la Ley. The term was practically restricted to Roman Catholics.

RECUSATIO TESTIS. Lat. In the civil law. Rejection of a witness, on the ground of incompetency. Best, Ev. Introd. 60, § 60.

RECUSATION. In the civil law. A species of exception or plea to the jurisdiction, to the effect that the particular judge is disqualified from hearing the cause by reason of interest or prejudice. Poth. Proc. Civile, pt. 1, c. 2, § 5.

The challenge of jurors. Code Prac. La. arts. 499, 500. An act, of what nature soever it may be, by which a strange heir, by deeds or words, declares he will not be heir. Dig. 29, 2, 95.

RED, RAED, or REDE. Sax. Advice; counsel.

RED BOOK OF THE EXCHEQUER. An ancient record, wherein are registered the holders of lands *per baroniam* in the time of Henry II., the number of hides of land in certain counties before the Conquest, and the ceremonies on the coronation of Eleanor, wife of Henry III. Jacob; Cowell.

RED-HANDED. With the marks of crime fresh on him.

RED TAPE. In a derivative sense, order carried to fastidious excess; system run out into trivial extremes. 55 Ga. 434.

REDDENDO SINGULA SINGULIS. By referring each to each; referring each phrase or expression to its appropriate object. A rule of construction.

REDDENDUM. In conveyancing. Rendering; yielding. The technical name of that clause in a conveyance by which the grantor creates or reserves some new thing to himself, out of what he had before granted; as "*rendering* therefor yearly the sum of ten shillings, or a pepper-corn," etc. That clause in a lease in which a rent is reserved to the lessor, and which commences with the word "*yielding.*" 2 Bl. Comm. 299.

REDDENS CAUSAM SCIENTIÆ. Giving the reason of his knowledge.

In Scotch practice. A formal phrase used in depositions, preceding the statement of the reason of the witness' knowledge. 2 How. State Tr. 715.

Reddere, nil aliud est quam acceptum restituere; seu, reddere est quasi retro dare, et redditur dicitur a redeundo, quia retro it. Co. Litt. 142. To render is nothing more than to restore that which has been received; or, to render is as it were to give back, and it is called "rendering" from "returning," because it goes back again.

REDDIDIT SE. He has rendered himself.

In old English practice. A term applied to a principal who had rendered himself in discharge of his bail. Holthouse.

REDDITARIUS. In old records. A renter; a tenant. Cowell.

REDDITARIUM. In old records. A rental, or rent-roll. Cowell.

REDDITION. A surrendering or restoring; also a judicial acknowledgment that the thing in demand belongs to the demandant, and not to the person surrendering. Cowell.

REDEEM. To buy back. To liberate an estate or article from mortgage or pledge by paying the debt for which it stood as security. To repurchase in a literal sense; as, to redeem one's land from a tax-sale.

REDEEMABLE. 1. Subject to an obligation of redemption; embodying, or conditioned upon, a promise or obligation of redemption; convertible into coin; as, a "redeemable currency."

2. Subject to redemption; admitting of redemption or repurchase; given or held under conditions admitting of reacquisition by purchase; as, a "redeemable pledge."

REDEEMABLE RIGHTS. Rights which return to the conveyor or disposer of land, etc., upon payment of the sum for which such rights are granted. Jacob.

REDELIVERY. A yielding and delivering back of a thing.

REDEMISE. A regranting of land demised or leased.

REDEMPTION. A repurchase; a buying back. The act of a vendor of property in buying it back again from the purchaser at the same or an enhanced price.

The right of redemption is an agreement or paction, by which the vendor reserves to himself the power of taking back the thing sold by returning the price paid for it. Civil Code La. art. 2567.

The process of annulling and revoking a conditional sale of property, by performance of the conditions on which it was stipulated to be revocable.

The process of cancelling and annulling a defeasible title to land, such as is created by a mortgage or a tax-sale, by paying the debt or fulfilling the other conditions.

The liberation of a chattel from pledge or pawn, by paying the debt for which it stood as security.

Repurchase of notes, bills, or other evidences of debt, (particularly bank-notes and paper-money,) by paying their value in coin to their holders.

REDEMPTION, EQUITY OF. See EQUITY OF REDEMPTION.

REDEMPTION OF LAND-TAX. In English law. The payment by the landowner of such a lump sum as shall exempt his land from the land-tax. Mozley & Whitley.

REDEMPTIONES. In old English law. Heavy fines. Distinguished from *misericordia,* (which see.)

REDEUNDO. Lat. Returning; in returning; while returning. 2 Strange, 985.

REDEVANCE. In old French and Canadian law. Dues payable by a tenant to his lord, not necessarily in money.

REDHIBERE. Lat. In the civil law. To have again; to have back; to cause a seller to have again what he had before.

REDHIBITION. In the civil law. The avoidance of a sale on account of some vice or defect in the thing sold, which renders it either absolutely useless or its use so inconvenient and imperfect that it must be supposed that the buyer would not have purchased it had he known of the vice. Civil Code La. art. 2520.

REDHIBITORY ACTION. In the civil law. An action for redhibition. An action to avoid a sale on account of some vice or defect in the thing sold, which renders its use impossible, or so inconvenient and imperfect that it must be supposed the buyer would not have purchased it had he known of the vice. Civil Code La. art. 2520.

REDHIBITORY DEFECT (or VICE.) In the civil law. A defect in an article sold, for which the seller may be compelled to take it back; a defect against which the seller is bound to warrant. Poth. Cont. Sale, no. 203.

REDISSEISIN. In old English law. A second disseisin of a person of the same tenements, and by the same disseisor, by whom he was before disseised. 3 Bl. Comm. 188.

REDITUS ALBI. White rent; blanche farm; rent payable in silver or other money.

REDITUS ASSISUS. A set or standing rent.

REDITUS CAPITALES. Chief rent paid by freeholders to go quit of all other services.

REDITUS NIGRI. Black rent; black mail; rent payable in provisions, corn, labor, etc.; as distinguished from "money rent," called "*reditus albi.*"

REDITUS QUIETI. Quitrents, (*q. v.*)

REDITUS SICCUS. Rent seck, (*q. v.*)

REDMANS. Men who, by the tenure or custom of their lands, were to ride with or for the lord of the manor, about his business. Domesday.

REDOBATORES. In old English law. Those that buy stolen cloth and turn it into some other color or fashion that it may not be recognized. Redubbers.

REDRAFT. In commercial law. A draft or bill drawn in the place where the original bill was made payable and where it went to protest, on the place where such original bill was drawn, or, when there is no regular commercial intercourse rendering that practicable, then in the next best or most direct practicable course. 1 Bell, Comm. 406.

REDRESS. The receiving satisfaction for an injury sustained.

REDUBBERS. In criminal law. Those who bought stolen cloth and dyed it of another color to prevent its being identified were anciently so called. Cowell; 3 Inst. 134.

REDUCE. In Scotch law. To rescind or annul.

REDUCTIO AD ABSURDUM. In logic. The method of disproving an argument by showing that it leads to an absurd consequence.

REDUCTION. In Scotch law. An action brought for the purpose of rescinding, annulling, or cancelling some bond, contract, or other instrument in writing. 1 Forb. Inst. pt. 4, pp. 158, 159.

In French law. Abatement. When a parent gives away, whether by gift *inter vivos* or by legacy, more than his *portion disponible,* (*q. v.,*) the donee or legatee is required to submit to have his gift reduced to the legal proportion.

REDUCTION EX CAPITE LECTI. By the law of Scotland the heir in heritage was entitled to reduce all voluntary deeds granted to his prejudice by his predecessor within sixty days preceding the predecessor's death; provided the maker of the deed, at its date, was laboring under the disease of which he died, and did not subsequently go to kirk or market unsupported. Bell.

REDUCTION IMPROBATION. In Scotch law. One form of the action of reduction in which falsehood and forgery are alleged against the deed or document sought to be set aside.

REDUCTION INTO POSSESSION. The act of exercising the right conferred by a chose in action, so as to convert it into a chose in possession; thus, a debt is reduced into possession by payment. Sweet.

REDUNDANCY. This is the fault of introducing superfluous matter into a legal instrument; particularly the insertion in a pleading of matters foreign, extraneous, and irrelevant to that which it is intended to answer.

RE-ENTRY. The entering again into or resuming possession of premises. Thus in leases there is a proviso for re-entry of the lessor on the tenant's failure to pay the rent or perform the covenants contained in the lease, and by virtue of such proviso the lessor may take the premises into his own hands again if the rent be not paid or covenants performed; and this resumption of possession is termed "re-entry." 2 Cruise, Dig. 8; Cowell.

RE-EXAMINATION. An examination of a witness after a cross-examination, upon matters arising out of such cross-examination.

RE-EXCHANGE. The damages or expenses caused by the dishonor and protest of a bill of exchange in a foreign country, where it was payable, and by its return to the place where it was drawn or indorsed, and its being there taken up.

RE-EXTENT. In English practice. A second extent made upon lands or tenements, upon complaint made that the former extent was partially performed. Cowell.

REEVE. In old English law. A ministerial officer of justice. His duties seem to have combined many of those now confided to the sheriff or constable and to the justice of the peace. He was also called, in Saxon, "*gerefa.*"

REFALO. A word composed of the three initial syllables "*re.*" "*fa.*" "*lo.*," for "*recordari facias loquelam,*" (*q. v.*) 2 Sell. Pr. 160.

REFARE. To bereave, take away, rob. Cowell.

REFECTION. In the civil law. Reparation; re-establishment of a building. Dig. 19, 1, 6, 1.

REFER. 1. When a case or action involves matters of account or other intricate details which require minute examination, and for that reason are not fit to be brought before a jury, it is usual to *refer* the whole case, or some part of it, to the decision of an auditor or referee, and the case is then said to be referred.

Taking this word in its strict, technical use, it relates to a mode of determining questions which is distinguished from "arbitration," in that the latter word imports submission of a controversy without any lawsuit having been brought, while "reference" imports a lawsuit pending, and an issue framed or question raised which (and not the controversy itself) is sent out. Thus, arbitration is resorted to instead of any judicial proceeding; while reference is one mode of decision employed in the course of a judicial proceeding. And "reference" is distinguished from "hearing or trial," in that these are the ordinary modes of deciding issues and questions in and by the courts, with aid of juries when proper; while reference is an employment of non-judicial persons—individuals not integral parts of the court—for the decision of particular matters inconvenient to be heard in actual court. Abbott.

2. To point, allude, direct, or make reference to. This is the use of the word in conveyancing and in literature, where a word or sign introduced for the purpose of directing the reader's attention to another place in the deed, book, document, etc., is said to "refer" him to such other connection.

REFEREE. In practice. A person to whom a cause pending in a court is referred by the court, to take testimony, hear the parties, and report thereon to the court. See REFER.

REFERENCE. In contracts. An agreement to submit to arbitration; the act of parties in submitting their controversy to chosen referees or arbitrators.

In practice. The act of sending a cause pending in court to a referee for his examination and decision. See REFER.

In commercial law. The act of sending or directing one person to another, for information or advice as to the character, solvency, standing, etc., of a third person, who desires to open business relations with the first, or to obtain credit with him.

REFERENCE IN CASE OF NEED. When a person draws or indorses a bill of exchange, he sometimes adds the name of a person to whom it may be presented "in case of need;" *i. e.*, in case it is dishonored by the original drawee or acceptor. Byles, Bills, 261.

REFERENCE TO RECORD. Under the English practice, when an action is commenced, an entry of it is made in the cause-book according to the year, the initial letter of the surname of the first plaintiff, and the place of the action, in numerical order among those commenced in the same year, *e. g.*, "1876, A. 26;" and all subsequent documents in the action (such as pleadings and affidavits) bear this mark, which is called the "reference to the record." Sweet.

REFERENDARIUS. An officer by whom the order of causes was laid before the Roman emperor, the desires of petitioners made known, and answers returned to them. Vicat, Voc. Jur.; Calvin.

REFERENDARY. In Saxon law. A master of requests; an officer to whom petitions to the king were referred. Spelman.

REFERENDO SINGULA SINGULIS. Lat. Referring individual or separate words to separate subjects; making a distributive reference of words in an instrument; a rule of construction.

REFERENDUM. In international law. A communication sent by a diplomatic representative to his home government, in regard to matters presented to him which he is unable or unwilling to decide without further instructions.

In the modern constitutional law of Switzerland, the *referendum* is a method of submitting an important legislative measure to a direct vote of the whole people. See PLEBISCITE.

REFORM. To correct, rectify, amend, remodel. Instruments *inter partes* may be *reformed*, when defective, by a court of equity. By this is meant that the court, after ascertaining the real and original intention of the parties to a deed or other instrument, (which intention they failed to sufficiently express, through some error, mistake of fact, or inadvertence,) will decree that the instrument be held and construed as if it fully and technically expressed that intention.

It is to be observed that "reform" is seldom, if ever, used of the correction of defective pleadings, judgments, decrees or other judicial proceedings; "amend" being the proper term for that use. Again, "amend" seems to connote the idea of improving that which may have been well enough before, while "reform" might be considered as properly applicable only to something which before was quite worthless.

REFORM ACTS. A name bestowed on the statutes 2 Wm. IV. c. 45, and 30 & 31 Vict. c. 102, passed to amend the representation of the people in England and Wales; which introduced extended amendments into the system of electing members of the house of commons.

REFORMATION. See REFORM.

REFORMATORY. This term is of too wide and uncertain signification to support a bequest for the building of a "boys' reformatory." It includes all places and institutions in which efforts are made either to cultivate the intellect, instruct the conscience, or improve the conduct; places in which persons voluntarily assemble, receive instruction, and submit to discipline, or are detained therein for either of these purposes by force. 49 Conn. 35.

REFORMATORY SCHOOLS. In English law. Schools to which convicted juvenile offenders (under sixteen) may be sent by order of the court before which they are tried, if the offense be punishable with penal servitude or imprisonment, and the sentence be to imprisonment for ten days or more. Wharton.

REFRESHER. In English law. A further or additional fee to counsel in a long case, which may be, but is not necessarily, allowed on taxation.

REFRESHING THE MEMORY. The act of a witness who consults his documents, memoranda, or books, to bring more distinctly to his recollection the details of past events or transactions, concerning which he is testifying.

REFUND. To repay or restore; to return money had by one party of another.

REFUNDING BOND. A bond given to an executor by a legatee, upon receiving payment of the legacy, conditioned to *refund* the same, or so much of it as may be necessary, if the assets prove deficient.

REFUNDS. In the laws of the United States, this term is used to denote sums of money received by the government or its officers which, for any cause, are to be refunded or restored to the parties paying them; such as excessive duties or taxes, duties paid on goods destroyed by accident, duties received on goods which are re-exported, etc.

REFUSAL. The act of one who has, by law, a right and power of having or doing something of advantage, and declines it.

REFUTANTIA. In old records. An acquittance or acknowledgment of renouncing all future claim. Cowell.

REG. GEN. An abbreviation of "*Regula Generalis*," a general rule, (of court.)

REG. JUD. An abbreviation of "*Registrum Judiciale*," the register of judicial writs.

REG. LIB. An abbreviation of "*Registrarii Liber*," the register's book in chancery, containing all decrees.

REG. ORIG. An abbreviation of "*Registrum Originale*," the register of original writs.

REG. PL. An abbreviation of "*Regula Placitandi*," rule of pleading.

REGAL FISH. Whales and sturgeons.

REGALE. In old French law. A payment made to the *seigneur* of a fief, on the election of every bishop or other ecclesiastical feudatory, corresponding with the relief paid by a lay feudatory. Steph. Lect. 235.

REGALE EPISCOPORUM. The temporal rights and privileges of a bishop. Cowell.

REGALIA seems to be an abbreviation of "*jura regalia*," royal rights, or those rights which a king has by virtue of his prerogative. Hence owners of counties palatine were formerly said to have "*jura regalia*" in their counties as fully as the king in his palace. 1 Bl. Comm. 117.

Some writers divide the royal prerogative into *majora* and *minora regalia*, the former including the regal dignity and power, the latter the revenue or fiscal prerogatives of the crown. 1 Bl. Comm. 117.

REGALIA FACERE. To do homage or fealty to the sovereign by a bishop when he is invested with the regalia.

REGALITY. A territorial jurisdiction in Scotland conferred by the crown. The lands were said to be given *in liberam regalitatem*, and the persons receiving the right were termed "lords of regality." Bell.

REGARD. In old English law. Inspection; supervision. Also a reward, fee, or perquisite.

REGARD, COURT OF. In forest law. A tribunal held every third year, for the lawing or expeditation of dogs, to prevent them from chasing deer. Cowell.

REGARD OF THE FOREST. In old English law. The oversight or inspection of it, or the office and province of the regarder, who is to go through the whole forest, and every bailiwick in it, before the holding of the sessions of the forest, or justice-seat, to see and inquire after trespassers, and for the survey of dogs. Manwood.

REGARDANT. A term which was applied, in feudal law, to a villein annexed to a manor, and having charge to do all base services within the same, and to see the same freed from all things that might annoy his lord. Such a villein *regardant* was thus opposed to a villein *en gros*, who was transferable by deed from one owner to another. Cowell; 2 Bl.Comm. 93.

REGARDER OF A FOREST. An ancient officer of the forest, whose duty it was to take a view of the forest hunts, and to inquire concerning trespasses, offenses, etc. Manwood.

REGE INCONSULTO. Lat. In English law. A writ issued from the sovereign to the judges, not to proceed in a cause which may prejudice the crown, until advised. Jenk. Cent. 97.

REGENCY. Rule; government; kingship. The man or body of men intrusted with the vicarious government of a kingdom during the minority, absence, insanity, or other disability of the king.

REGENT. A governor or ruler. One who vicariously administers the government of a kingdom, in the name of the king, during the latter's minority or other disability.

A master, governor, director, or superintendent of a public institution, particularly a college or university.

Regia dignitas est indivisibilis, et quælibet alia derivativa dignitas est similiter indivisibilis. 4 Inst. 243. The kingly power is indivisible, and every other derivative power is similarly indivisible.

REGIA VIA. In old English law. The royal way; the king's highway. Co. Litt. 56*a*.

REGIAM MAJESTATEM. A collection of the ancient laws of Scotland. It is said to have been compiled by order of David I., king of Scotland, who reigned from A. D. 1124 to 1153. Hale, Com. Law, 271.

REGICIDE. The murder of a sovereign; also the person who commits such murder.

REGIDOR. In Spanish law. One of a body, never exceeding twelve, who formed a part of the *ayuntamiento*. The office of regidor was held for life; that is to say, during the pleasure of the supreme authority. In most places the office was purchased; in some cities, however, they were elected by persons of the district, called "*capitulares.*" 12 Pet. 442, note.

RÉGIME. In French law. A system of rules or regulations.

RÉGIME DOTAL. In French law. The *dot*, being the property which the wife brings to the husband as her contribution to the support of the burdens of the marriage, and which may either extend as well to future as to present property, or be expressly confined to the present property of the wife, is subject to certain regulations which are summarized in the phrase "*régime dotal.*" The husband has the entire administration during the marriage; but, as a rule, where the *dot* consists of immovables, neither the husband nor the wife, nor both of them together, can either sell or mortgage it. The *dot* is returnable upon the dissolution of the marriage, whether by death or otherwise. Brown.

RÉGIME EN COMMUNAUTÉ. In French law. The community of interests between husband and wife which arises upon their marriage. It is either (1) legal or (2) conventional, the former existing in the absence of any "agreement" properly so called, and arising from a mere declaration of community; the latter arising from an "agreement," properly so called. Brown.

REGIMIENTO. In Spanish law. The body of regidores, who never exceeded twelve, forming a part of the municipal council, or *ayuntamiento,* in every capital of a jurisdiction. 12 Pet. 442, note.

REGINA. The queen.

REGIO ASSENSU. A writ whereby the sovereign gives his assent to the election of a bishop. Reg. Orig. 294.

REGISTER. An officer authorized by law to keep a record called a "register" or "registry;" as the register for the probate of wills.

A book containing a record of facts as they occur, kept by public authority; a register of births, marriages, and burials.

REGISTER OF PATENTS. A book of patents, directed by St. 15 & 16 Vict. c. 83, § 34, passed in 1852, to be kept at the specification office, for public use. 2 Steph. Comm. 29, note *t.*

REGISTER OF SHIPS. A register kept by the collectors of customs, in which the names, ownership, and other facts relative to merchant vessels are required by law to be entered. This register is evidence of the nationality and privileges of an American ship. The certificate of such registration, given by the collector to the owner or master of the ship, is also called the "ship's register." Rapalje & Lawrence.

REGISTER OF WRITS. A book preserved in the English court of chancery, in which were entered the various forms of original and judicial writs.

REGISTERED VOTERS. In Virginia, this term refers to the persons whose names are placed upon the registration books provided by law as the sole record or memorial of the duly qualified voters of the state. 76 Va. 719.

REGISTER'S COURT. In American law. A court in the state of Pennsylvania which has jurisdiction in matters of probate.

REGISTRANT. One who registers; particularly, one who registers anything (*e. g.*, a trade-mark) for the purpose of securing a right or privilege granted by law on condition of such registration.

REGISTRAR. An officer who has the custody or keeping of a registry or register. This word is used in England; "register" is more common in America.

REGISTRAR GENERAL. In English law. An officer appointed by the crown under the great seal, to whom, subject to such regulations as shall be made by a principal secretary of state, the general superintendence of the whole system of registration of births, deaths, and marriages is intrusted. 3 Steph. Comm. 234.

REGISTRARIUS. In old English law. A notary; a registrar or register.

REGISTRATION. Recording; inserting in an official register.

REGISTRUM BREVIUM. The register of writs, (*q. v.*)

REGISTRY. A register, or book authorized or recognized by law, kept for the recording or registration of facts or documents.

In commercial law. The registration of a vessel at the custom-house, for the purpose of entitling her to the full privileges of a British or American built vessel. 3 Kent, Comm. 139; Abb. Shipp. 58-96.

REGISTRY OF DEEDS. The system or organized mode of keeping a public record of deeds, mortgages, and other instruments affecting title to real property.

REGIUS PROFESSOR. A royal professor or reader of lectures founded in the universities by the king. Henry VIII. founded in each of the universities five professorships, viz., of divinity, Greek, Hebrew, law, and physic. Cowell.

REGLAMENTO. In Spanish colonial law. A written instruction given by a competent authority, without the observance of any peculiar form. Schm. Civil Law, Introd. 93, note.

REGNAL YEARS. Statutes of the British parliament are usually cited by the name and year of the sovereign in whose reign they were enacted, and the successive years of the reign of any king or queen are denominated the "regnal years." For convenience in determining the date of statutes so cited, a "Table of British Regnal Years" is prefixed to this volume.

REGNANT. One having authority as a king; one in the exercise of royal authority.

REGNI POPULI. A name given to the people of Surrey and Sussex, and on the seacoasts of Hampshire. Blount.

REGNUM ECCLESIASTICUM. The ecclesiastical kingdom. 2 Hale, P. C. 324.

Regnum non est divisibile. Co. Litt. 165. The kingdom is not divisible.

REGRANT. In the English law of real property, when, after a person has made a grant, the property granted comes back to him, (*e. g.*, by escheat or forfeiture,) and he grants it again, he is said to regrant it. The phrase is chiefly used in the law of copyholds.

REGRATING. In old English law. The offense of buying or getting into one's hands at a fair or market any provisions, corn, or other dead victual, with the intention of selling the same again in the same fair or market, or in some other within four miles thereof, at a higher price. The offender was termed a "regrator." 3 Inst. 195.

REGRESS is used principally in the phrase "free entry, egress, and regress" but it is also used to signify the re-entry of a person who has been disseised of land. Co. Litt. 318*b*.

REGULA. Lat. In practice. A rule. *Regula generalis*, a general rule; a standing rule or order of a court. Frequently abbreviated, "*Reg. Gen.*"

REGULA CATONIANA. Lat. In Roman law. The rule of Cato. A rule respecting the validity of dispositions by will. See Dig. 34, 7.

Regula est, juris quidem ignorantiam cuique nocere, facti vero ignorantiam non nocere. Cod. 1, 18, 10. It is a rule, that every one is prejudiced by his ignorance of law, but not by his ignorance of fact.

REGULÆ GENERALES. General rules, which the courts promulgate from time to time for the regulation of their practice.

REGULAR. According to rule; as distinguished from that which violates the rule or follows no rule.

According to rule; as opposed to that which constitutes an exception to the rule, or is not within the rule.

REGULAR CLERGY. In old English law. Monks who lived *secundum regulas* (according to the *rules*) of their respective houses or societies were so denominated, in contradistinction to the parochial clergy, who performed their ministry in the world, *in seculo*, and who from thence were called "secular" clergy. 1 Chit. Bl. 387, note.

REGULAR DEPOSIT. A strict or special deposit; a deposit which must be returned *in specie; i. e.*, the thing deposited must be returned.

REGULAR ELECTION. A general, usual, or stated election. When applied to elections, the terms "regular" and "general" are used interchangeably and synonymously. The word "regular" is used in reference to a general election occurring throughout the state. 45 Mo. 47.

REGULAR NAVIGATION. In this phrase, the word "regular" may be used in contradistinction to "occasional," rather than to "unlawful," and refer to vessels that, alone or with others, constitute lines, and not merely to such as are regular in the sense of being properly documented under the laws of the country to which they belong. 16 Op. Attys. Gen. 276.

REGULAR PROCESS. Such as is issued according to rule and the prescribed practice, or which emanates, lawfully and in a proper case, from a court or magistrate possessing jurisdiction.

REGULAR SESSION. An ordinary, general, or stated session, (as of a legislative body,) as distinguished from a special or extra session.

Regulariter non valet pactum de re mea non alienanda. Co. Litt. 223. It is a rule that a compact not to alienate my property is not binding.

REGULARS. Those who profess and follow a certain rule of life, (*regula*,) belong to a religious order, and observe the three approved vows of poverty, chastity, and obedience. Wharton.

REGULATE. The power to regulate commerce, vested in congress, is the power to prescribe the rules by which it shall be governed, that is, the conditions upon which it shall be conducted, to determine when it shall be free, and when subject to duties or other exactions. The power also embraces within its control all the instrumentalities by which that commerce may be carried on, and the means by which it may be aided and encouraged. 114 U. S. 203, 5 Sup. Ct. Rep. 826.

REGULATION. The act of regulating; a rule or order prescribed for management or government; a regulating principle; a precept. Webster.

REGULUS. Lat. In Saxon law. A title sometimes given to the earl or *comes*, in old charters. Spelman.

REHABERE FACIAS SEISINAM. When a sheriff in the "*habere facias seisinam*" had delivered seisin of more than he ought, this judicial writ lay to make him restore seisin of the excess. Reg. Jud. 13, 51, 54.

REHABILITATE. In Scotch and French criminal law. To reinstate a criminal in his personal rights which he has lost by a judicial sentence. Brande.

REHABILITATION. In French and Scotch criminal law. The reinstatement of a criminal in his personal rights which he has lost by a judicial sentence. Brande.

In old English law. A papal bull or brief for re-enabling a spiritual person to exercise his function, who was formerly disabled; or a *restoring* to a former *ability*. Cowell.

REHEARING. In equity practice. A second hearing of a cause, for which a party who is dissatisfied with the decree entered on the former hearing may apply by petition. 3 Bl. Comm. 453.

REI INTERVENTUS. Lat. Things intervening; that is, things done by one of the parties to a contract, in the faith of its validity, and with the assent of the other party, and which have so affected his situation that the other will not be allowed to repudiate his obligation, although originally it was imperfect, and he might have renounced it. 1 Bell, Comm. 328, 329.

Rei turpis nullum mandatum est. The mandate of an immoral thing is void. Dig. 17, 1, 6, 3. A contract of mandate requiring an illegal or immoral act to be done has no legal obligation. Story, Bailm. § 158.

REIF. A robbery. Cowell.

REIMBURSE. The primary meaning of this word is "to pay back." 83 Pa. St. 264. It means to make return or restoration of an equivalent for something paid, expended, or lost; to indemnify, or make whole.

REINSTATE. To place again in a former state, condition, or office; to restore to a state or position from which the object or person had been removed. See 15 Ct. Cl. 22.

REINSURANCE. A contract of reinsurance is one by which an insurer procures a third person to insure him against loss or liability by reason of such original insurance. Civil Code Cal. § 2646.

Reipublicæ interest voluntates defunctorum effectum sortiri. It concerns the state that the wills of the dead should have their effect.

REISSUABLE NOTES. Bank-notes which, after having been once paid, may again be put into circulation.

REJOIN. In pleading. To answer a plaintiff's replication in an action at law, by some matter of fact.

REJOINDER. In common-law pleading. The second pleading on the part of the defendant, being his answer of matter of fact to the plaintiff's replication.

REJOINING GRATIS. Rejoining voluntarily, or without being required to do so by a rule to rejoin. When a defendant was under terms to rejoin *gratis*, he had to deliver a rejoinder, without putting the plaintiff to the necessity and expense of obtaining a rule to rejoin. 10 Mees. & W. 12; Lush, Pr. 396; Brown.

Relatio est fictio juris et intenta ad unum. Relation is a fiction of law, and intended for one thing. 3 Coke, 28.

Relatio semper fiat ut valeat dispositio. Reference should always be had in such a manner that a disposition in a will may avail. 6 Coke, 76.

RELATION. 1. A relative or kinsman; a person connected by consanguinity or affinity.

2. The connection of two persons, or their situation with respect to each other, who are associated, whether by the law, by their own agreement, or by kinship, in some social *status* or union for the purposes of domestic life; as the relation of guardian and ward, husband and wife, master and servant, parent and child; so in the phrase "domestic relations."

3. In the law of contracts, when an act is done at one time, and it operates upon the thing as if done at another time, it is said to do so by relation; as, if a man deliver a deed as an escrow, to be delivered, by the party holding it, to the grantor, on the performance of some act, the delivery to the latter will have relation back to the first delivery. Termes de la Ley.

4. A recital, account, narrative of facts; information given. Thus, suits by *quo warranto* are entitled "on the relation of" a private person, who is called the "relator." But in this connection the word seems also to involve the idea of the suggestion, instigation, or instance of the relator.

5. In the civil law, the term "relation" was used to designate the report of the facts and law in a pending case, made by the judges to the emperor, for the purpose of obtaining his opinion on the questions of law involved, in the form of an imperial rescript. This proceeding might be resorted to in cases where no law seemed applicable, or where there were great difficulties in its interpretation, until it was abolished by Justinian. Nov. 125.

Relation never defeats collateral acts. 18 Vin. Abr. 292.

Relation shall never make good a void grant or devise of the party. 18 Vin. Abr. 292.

RELATIONS. A term which, in its widest sense, includes all the kindred of the person spoken of. 2 Jarm. Wills, 661.

RELATIVE. A kinsman; a person connected with another by blood or affinity.

A person or thing having relation or connection with some other person or thing; as, relative rights, relative powers, *infra.*

RELATIVE FACT. In the law of evidence. A fact having relation to another fact; a minor fact; a circumstance.

RELATIVE POWERS. Those which relate to land; so called to distinguish them from those which are collateral to it.

RELATIVE RIGHTS. Those rights of persons which are incident to them as members of society, and standing in various relations to each other. 1 Bl. Comm. 123. Those rights of persons in private life which arise from the civil and domestic relations. 2 Kent, Comm. 1.

Relative words refer to the next antecedent, unless the sense be thereby impaired. Noy, Max. 4; Wing. Max. 19; Broom, Max. 606; Jenk. Cent. 180.

Relativorum, cognito uno, cognoscitur et alterum. Cro. Jac. 539. Of relatives, one being known, the other is also known.

RELATOR. The person upon whose complaint, or at whose instance, an information or writ of *quo warranto* is filed, and who is *quasi* the plaintiff in the proceeding.

RELATRIX. In practice. A female relator or petitioner.

RELAXARE. In old conveyancing. To release. *Relaxavi, relaxasse,* have released. Litt. § 445.

RELAXATIO. In old conveyancing. A release; an instrument by which a person relinquishes to another his right in anything.

RELAXATION. In old Scotch practice. Letters passing the signet by which a debtor was relaxed [released] from the horn; that is, from personal diligence. Bell.

RELEASE. 1. Liberation, discharge, or setting free from restraint or confinement. Thus, a man unlawfully imprisoned may obtain his *release* on *habeas corpus.*

2. The relinquishment, concession, or giving up of a right, claim, or privilege, by the person in whom it exists or to whom it accrues, to the person against whom it might have been demanded or enforced.

3. The abandonment to (or by) a person called as a witness in a suit of his interest in the subject-matter of the controversy, in order to qualify him to testify, under the common-law rule.

4. A receipt or certificate given by a ward to the guardian, on the final settlement of the latter's accounts, or by any other beneficiary on the termination of the trust administration, relinquishing all and any further rights, claims, or demands, growing out of the trust or incident to it.

5. In admiralty actions, when a ship, cargo, or other property has been arrested, the owner may obtain its release by giving bail, or pay-

ing the value of the property into court. Upon this being done he obtains a release, which is a kind of writ under the seal of the court, addressed to the marshal, commanding him to release the property. Sweet.

6. **In estates.** The conveyance of a man's interest or right which he hath unto a thing to another that hath the possession thereof or some estate therein. Shep. Touch. 320. The relinquishment of some right or benefit to a person who has already some interest in the tenement, and such interest as qualifies him for receiving or availing himself of the right or benefit so relinquished. Burt. Real Prop. 12.

A conveyance of an ulterior interest in lands or tenements to a particular tenant, or of an undivided share to a co-tenant, (the releasee being in either case in privity of estate with the releasor,) or of the right, to a person wrongfully in possession. 1 Steph. Comm. 479.

RELEASE BY WAY OF ENLARGING AN ESTATE. A conveyance of the ulterior interest in lands to the particular tenant; as, if there be tenant for life or years, remainder to another in fee, and he in remainder releases all his right to the particular tenant and his heirs, this gives him the estate in fee. 1 Steph. Comm. 480; 2 Bl. Comm. 324.

RELEASE BY WAY OF ENTRY AND FEOFFMENT. As if there be two joint disseisors, and the disseisee releases to one of them, he shall be sole seised, and shall keep out his former companion; which is the same in effect as if the disseisee had entered and thereby put an end to the disseisin, and afterwards had enfeoffed one of the disseisors in fee. 2 Bl. Comm. 325.

RELEASE BY WAY OF EXTINGUISHMENT. As if my tenant for life makes a lease to A. for life, remainder to B. and his heirs, and I release to A., this extinguishes my right to the reversion, and shall inure to the advantage of B.'s remainder, as well as of A.'s particular estate. 2 Bl. Comm. 325.

RELEASE BY WAY OF PASSING A RIGHT. As if a man be disseised and releaseth to his disseisor all his right, hereby the disseisor acquires a new right, which changes the quality of his estate, and renders that lawful which before was tortious or wrongful. 2 Bl. Comm. 325.

RELEASE BY WAY OF PASSING AN ESTATE. As, where one of two coparceners releases all her right to the other, this passes the fee-simple of the whole. 2 Bl. Comm. 324, 325.

RELEASE TO USES. The conveyance by a deed of release to one party to the use of another is so termed. Thus, when a conveyance of lands was effected, by those instruments of assurance termed a lease and release, from A. to B. and his heirs, to the use of C. and his heirs, in such case C. at once took the whole fee-simple in such lands; B., by the operation of the statute of uses, being made a mere conduit-pipe for conveying the estate to C. Brown.

RELEASEE. The person to whom a release is made.

RELEASER, or RELEASOR. The maker of a release.

RELEGATIO. Lat. A kind of banishment known to the civil law, which differed from "*deportatio*" in leaving to the person his rights of citizenship.

RELEGATION. In old English law. Banishment for a time only. Co. Litt. 133.

RELEVANCY. As a quality of evidence, "relevancy" means applicability to the issue joined. Relevancy is that which conduces to the proof of a pertinent hypothesis; a pertinent hypothesis being one which, if sustained, would logically influence the issue. Whart. Ev. § 20.

In Scotch law, the relevancy is the justice or sufficiency in law of the allegations of a party. A plea to the relevancy is therefore analogous to the demurrer of the English courts.

RELEVANT. Applying to the matter in question; affording something to the purpose.

RELICT. This term is applied to the survivor of a pair of married people, whether the survivor is the husband or the wife; it means the relict of the united pair, (or of the marriage union,) not the relict of the deceased individual. 42 Ohio St. 101.

RELICTA VERIFICATIONE. Where a judgment was confessed by *cognovit actionem* after plea pleaded, and the plea was withdrawn, it was called a "confession" or "*cognovit actionem relicta verificatione.*" Wharton.

RELICTION. An increase of the land by the sudden withdrawal or retrocession of the sea or a river.

RELIEF. 1. In feudal law. A sum payable by the new tenant, the duty being incident to every feudal tenure, by way of fine or composition with the lord for taking up the estate which was lapsed or fallen in by the death of the last tenant. At one time the amount was arbitrary, but afterwards the relief of a knight's fee became fixed at one hundred shillings. 2 Bl. Comm. 65.

2. "Relief" also means deliverance from oppression, wrong, or injustice. In this sense it is used as a general designation of the assistance, redress, or benefit which a complainant seeks at the hands of a court, particularly in equity. It may be thus used of such remedies as specific performance, or the reformation or rescission of a contract; but it does not seem appropriate to the awarding of money damages.

3. The assistance or support, pecuniary or otherwise, granted to indigent persons by the proper administrators of the poor-laws, is also called "relief."

RELIEVE. In feudal law, relieve is to depend; thus, the seigniory of a tenant *in capite* relieves of the crown, meaning that the tenant holds of the crown. The term is not common in English writers. Sweet.

RELIGION, OFFENSES AGAINST. In English law. They are thus enumerated by Blackstone: (1) Apostasy; (2) heresy; (3) reviling the ordinances of the church; (4) blasphemy; (5) profane swearing; (6) conjuration or witchcraft; (7) religious imposture; (8) simony; (9) profanation of the Lord's day; (10) drunkenness; (11) lewdness. 4 Bl. Comm. 43.

RELIGIOUS. When religious books or reading are spoken of, those which tend to promote the religion taught by the Christian dispensation must be considered as referred to, unless the meaning is so limited by associated words or circumstances as to show that the speaker or writer had reference to some other mode of worship. 72 Me. 500.

RELIGIOUS HOUSES. Places set apart for pious uses; such as monasteries, churches, hospitals, and all other places where charity was extended to the relief of the poor and orphans, or for the use or exercise of religion.

RELIGIOUS IMPOSTORS. In English law. Those who falsely pretend an extraordinary commission from heaven, or terrify and abuse the people with false denunciations of judgment; punishable with fine, imprisonment, and infamous corporal punishment. 4 Broom & H. Comm. 71.

RELIGIOUS MEN. Such as entered into some monastery or convent. In old English deeds, the vendee was often restrained from aliening to "Jews or religious men" lest the lands should fall into mortmain. Religious men were civilly dead. Blount.

RELIGIOUS SOCIETY. A body of persons associated together for the purpose of maintaining religious worship. A church and society are often united in maintaining worship, and in such cases the society commonly owns the property, and makes the pecuniary contract with the minister. But, in many instances, societies exist without a church, and churches without a society. 16 Gray, 330; 9 Cush. 188.

RELIGIOUS USE. See CHARITABLE USES.

RELINQUISHMENT. In practice. A forsaking, abandoning, renouncing, or giving over a right.

RELIQUA. The remainder or debt which a person finds himself debtor in upon the balancing or liquidation of an account. Hence *reliquary*, the debtor of a *reliqua;* as also a person who only pays piece-meal. Enc. Lond.

RELIQUES. Remains; such as the bones, etc., of saints, preserved with great veneration as sacred memorials. They have been forbidden to be used or brought into England. St. 3 Jac. I. c. 26.

RELOCATIO. In the civil law. A renewal of a lease on its determination. It may be either express or tacit; the latter is when the tenant holds over with the knowledge and without objection of the landlord. Mackeld. Rom. Law, § 412.

RELOCATION. In Scotch law. A reletting or renewal of a lease; a *tacit relocation* is permitting a tenant to hold over without any new agreement.

REMAINDER. The remnant of an estate in land, depending upon a particular prior estate created at the same time and by the same instrument, and limited to arise immediately on the determination of that estate, and not in abridgment of it. 4 Kent, Comm. 197.

An estate limited to take effect and be enjoyed after another estate is determined. As, if a man seised in fee-simple grants lands to A. for twenty years, and, after the determination of the said term, then to B. and his heirs forever, here A. is tenant for years, *remainder* to B. in fee. 2 Bl. Comm. 164.

An estate in remainder is one limited to be enjoyed after another estate is determined, or at a time specified in the future. An estate in reversion is the residue of an estate, usually the fee left in the grantor and his heirs after the determination of a particular estate which he has granted out of it. The rights of the reversioner are the same as those of a vested remainder-man in fee. Code Ga. 1882, § 2263.

Remainders are either *vested* or *contingent*. A vested remainder is one limited to a certain person at a certain time, or upon the happening of a necessary event. A contingent remainder is one limited to an uncertain person, or upon an event which may or may not happen. Code Ga. 1882, § 2265.

A "vested" remainder, whereby a present interest passes to the party, though to be enjoyed in future, is where the estate is invariably fixed, to remain to a determinate person, after the particular estate is spent. A "contingent" remainder, whereby no present interest passes, is where the estate in remainder is limited to take effect, either to a dubious and uncertain person or upon a dubious and uncertain event; so that the particular estate may chance to be determined, and the remainder never take effect. 2 Bl. Comm. 168, 169.

Cross-remainders. Cross-remainders arise when land is given in undivided shares to two persons, A. and B., for particular estates, in such a manner that, upon the determination of the particular estates in A.'s share, the whole of the land goes to B., and *vice versa*, the remainder-man or reversioner not being let in till the determination of all the particular estates in both shares. Sweet.

Remainder to a person not of a capacity to take at the time of appointing it, is void. Plowd. 27.

REMAINDER-MAN. One who is entitled to the remainder of the estate after a particular estate carved out of it has expired.

REMAND. To remand a prisoner, after a preliminary or partial hearing before a court or magistrate, is to send him back to custody, to be kept until the hearing is resumed or the trial comes on.

REMANDING A CAUSE. Remitting or sending it back to the court from which it was removed, appealed, or transferred into another court, in order that some further action may be taken upon it in the original form.

REMANENT PRO DEFECTU EMPTORUM. In practice. The return made by the sheriff to a writ of execution when he has not been able to sell the property seized, that the same *remains unsold for want of buyers*.

REMANENTIA. In old English law. A remainder. Spelman. A perpetuity, or perpetual estate. Glan. lib. 7, c. 1.

REMANET. A remnant; that which remains. Thus the causes of which the trial is deferred from one term to another, or from one sitting to another, are termed "*remanets.*" 1 Archb. Pr. 375.

REMEDIAL. 1. Affording a remedy; giving the means of obtaining redress.

2. Of the nature of a remedy; intended to remedy wrongs or abuses, abate faults, or supply defects.

3. Pertaining to or affecting the remedy, as distinguished from that which affects or modifies the right.

REMEDIAL STATUTE. A statute providing a remedy for an injury, as distinguished from a penal statute. A statute giving a party a mode of remedy for a wrong, where he had none, or a different one, before. 1 Chit. Bl. 86, 87, notes.

Remedial statutes are those which are made to supply such defects, and abridge such superfluities, in the common law, as arise either from the general imperfection of all human laws, from change of time and circumstances, from the mistakes and unadvised determinations of unlearned (or even learned) judges, or from any other cause whatsoever. 1 Bl. Comm. 86.

Remedies for rights are ever favorably extended. 18 Vin. Abr. 521.

REMEDY. Remedy is the means by which the violation of a right is prevented, redressed, or compensated. Remedies are of four kinds: (1) By act of the party injured, the principal of which are defense, recaption, distress, entry, abatement, and seizure; (2) by operation of law, as in the case of retainer and remitter; (3) by agreement between the parties, *e. g.*, by accord and satisfaction and arbitration; and (4) by judicial remedy, *e. g.*, action or suit. Sweet.

Also a certain allowance to the master of the mint, for deviation from the standard weight and fineness of coins. Enc. Lond.

REMEDY OVER. A person who is primarily liable or responsible, but who, in turn, can demand indemnification from another, who is responsible to him, is said to have a "remedy over." For example, a city, being compelled to pay for injuries caused by a defect in the highway, has a "remedy over" against the person whose act or negligence caused the defect, and such person is said to be "liable over" to the city. 2 Black, Judgm. § 575.

REMEMBRANCER. The remembrancer of the city of London is parliamentary solicitor to the corporation, and is bound to attend all courts of aldermen and common council when required. Pull. Laws & Cust. Lond. 122.

REMEMBRANCERS. In English law. Officers of the exchequer, whose duty it is to put in remembrance the lord treasurer and the justices of that court of such things as are to be called and dealt in for the benefit of the crown. Jacob.

RÉMÉRÉ. In French law. Redemption; right of redemption. A sale *à réméré* is a species of conditional sale with right of repurchase. An agreement by which the vendor reserves to himself the right to take back the thing sold on restoring the price paid, with costs and interest. Duverger.

REMISE. To remit or give up. A formal word in deeds of release and quitclaim. Litt. § 445; Co. Litt. 264*b*.

REMISE DE LA DETTE. In French law. The release of a debt.

REMISSION. In the civil law. A release of a debt. It is *conventional*, when it is expressly granted to the debtor by a creditor having a capacity to alienate; or *tacit*, when the creditor voluntarily surrenders to his debtor the original title, under private signature constituting the obligation. Civil Code La. art. 2195.

"Remission" also means forgiveness or condonation of an offense or injury.

At common law. The act by which a forfeiture or penalty is forgiven. 10 Wheat. 246.

Remissius imperanti melius paretur. 3 Inst. 233. A man commanding not too strictly is better obeyed.

REMISSNESS. This term imports the doing of the act in question in a tardy, negligent, or careless manner; but it does not apply to the entire omission or forbearance of the act. 6 Abb. Pr. (N. S.) 423.

REMIT. To send or transmit; as to *remit* money.

To give up; to annul; to relinquish; as to *remit* a fine.

REMITMENT. The act of sending back to custody; an annulment. Wharton.

REMITTANCE. Money sent by one person to another, either in specie, bill of exchange, check, or otherwise.

REMITTEE. A person to whom a remittance is made. Story, Bailm. § 75.

REMITTER. The relation back of a later defective title to an earlier valid title. *Remitter* is where he who has the true property or *jus proprietatis* in lands, but is out of possession thereof, and has no right to enter without recovering possession in an action, has afterwards the freehold cast upon him by some subsequent and of course defective title. In this case he is *remitted*, or sent back by operation of law, to his ancient and more certain title. The right of entry which he has gained by a bad title shall be *ipso facto* annexed to his own inherent good one; and his defeasible estate shall be utterly defeated and annulled by the instantaneous act of law, without his participation or consent. 3 Bl. Comm. 19.

REMITTIT DAMNA. Lat. An entry on the record, by which the plaintiff declares that he remits a part of the damages which have been awarded him.

REMITTITUR DAMNA. Lat. In practice. An entry made on record, in cases where a jury has given greater damages than a plaintiff has declared for, remitting the excess. 2 Tidd, Pr. 896.

REMITTITUR OF RECORD. The returning or sending back by a court of appeal of the record and proceedings in a cause, after its decision thereon, to the court whence the appeal came, in order that the cause may be tried anew, (where it is so ordered,) or that judgment may be entered in accordance with the decision on appeal, or execution be issued, or any other necessary action be taken in the court below.

REMITTOR. A person who makes a remittance to another.

REMONSTRANCE. Expostulation; showing of reasons against something proposed; a representation made to a court or legislative body wherein certain persons unite in urging that a contemplated measure be not adopted or passed.

REMOTE. Damage is said to be too remote to be actionable when it is not the legal and natural consequence of the act complained of.

REMOTENESS. Want of close connection between a wrong and the injury, as cause and effect, whereby the party injured cannot claim compensation from the wrongdoer. Wharton.

REMOTENESS OF EVIDENCE. When the fact or facts proposed to be established as a foundation from which indirect evidence may be drawn, by way of inference, have not a visible, plain, or necessary connection with the proposition eventually to be proved, such evidence is rejected for "remoteness." See 2 Whart. Ev. § 1226, note.

Remoto impedimento, emergit actio. The impediment being removed, the action rises. When a bar to an action is removed, the action rises up into its original efficacy. Shep. Touch. 150; Wing. 20.

REMOVAL FROM OFFICE. The act of a person or body, having lawful authority thereto, in depriving one of an office to which he was appointed or elected.

REMOVAL OF CAUSES. The transfer of a cause from one court to another; commonly used of the transfer of the jurisdiction and cognizance of an action commenced but not finally determined, with all further proceedings therein, from one trial court to another trial court. More particularly, the transfer of a cause, before trial or final hearing thereof, from a state court to the United States circuit court, under the acts of congress in that behalf.

REMOVAL OF PAUPER. The actual transfer of a pauper, by order of a court having jurisdiction, from a poor district in which he has no settlement, but upon which he has become a charge, to the district of his domicile or settlement.

REMOVAL, ORDER OF. 1. An order of court directing the removal of a pauper from the poor district upon which he has illegally become a charge to the district in which he has his settlement.

2. An order made by the court *a quo*, directing the transfer of a cause therein depending, with all future proceedings in such cause, to another court.

REMOVER. In practice. A transfer of a suit or cause out of one court into another, which is effected by writ of error, *certiorari*, and the like. 11 Coke, 41.

REMUNERATION. Reward; recompense; salary. Dig. 17, 1, 7.

The word "remuneration" means a *quid pro quo*. If a man gives his services, whatever consideration he gets for giving his services seems to me a remuneration for them. Consequently, I think, if a person was in the receipt of a payment, or in the receipt of a percentage, or any kind of payment which would not be an actual money payment, the amount he would receive annually in respect of this would be "remuneration." 1 Q. B. Div. 663, 664.

RENANT, or RENIANT. In old English law. Denying. 32 Hen. VIII. c. 2.

RENCOUNTER. A sudden meeting; as opposed to a duel, which is deliberate.

RENDER, *v.* In practice. To give up; to yield; to return; to surrender. Also to pay or perform; used of rents, services, and the like.

RENDER, *n.* In feudal law, "render" was used in connection with rents and heriots. Goods subject to rent or heriot-service were said to lie in *render*, when the lord might not only seize the identical goods, but might also distrain for them. Cowell.

RENDEZVOUS. Fr. A place appointed for meeting. Especially used of places appointed for the assembling of troops, the coming together of the ships of a fleet, or the meeting of vessels and their convoy.

RENEGADE. One who has changed his profession of faith or opinion; one who has deserted his church or party.

RENEWAL. The act of renewing or reviving. The substitution of a new grant, engagement, or right, in place of one which has expired, of the same character and on the same terms and conditions as before; as, the renewal of a note, a lease, a patent.

RENOUNCE. To reject; cast off; repudiate; disclaim; forsake; abandon; divest one's self of a right, power, or privilege. Usually it implies an affirmative act of disclaimer or disavowal.

RENOUNCING PROBATE. In English practice. Refusing to take upon one's self the office of executor or executrix. Refusing to take out probate under a will wherein one has been appointed executor or executrix. Holthouse.

RENOVARE. Lat. In old English law. To renew. *Annuatim renovare*, to renew annually. A phrase applied to profits which are taken and the product renewed again. Amb. 131.

RENT. At common law. A certain profit issuing yearly out of lands and tenements corporeal; a species of incorporeal hereditament. 2 Bl. Comm. 41. A compensation or return yielded periodically, to a certain amount, out of the profits of some corporeal hereditaments, by the tenant thereof. 2 Steph. Comm. 23. A certain yearly profit in money, provisions, chattels, or labor, issuing out of lands and tenements, in retribution for the use. 3 Kent, Comm. 460.

The compensation, either in money, provisions, chattels, or labor, received by the owner of the soil from the occupant thereof. Jack. & G. Landl. & Ten. § 38.

A fee-farm rent is one issuing out of an estate in fee, of at least one-fourth of the value of the lands, at the time of its reservation.

See, also, GROUND-RENT; RACK-RENT.

In Louisiana. The contract of *rent of lands* is a contract by which one of the parties conveys and cedes to the other a tract of land, or any other immovable property, and stipulates that the latter shall hold it as owner, but reserving to the former an annual rent of a certain sum of money, or of a certain quantity of fruits, which the other party binds himself to pay him. It is of the essence of this conveyance that it be made in perpetuity. If it be made for a limited time, it is a lease. Civil Code La. arts. 2779, 2780.

RENT-CHARGE. This arises where the owner of the rent has no future interest or reversion in the land. It is usually created by deed or will, and is accompanied with powers of distress and entry.

Rent must be reserved to him from whom the state of the land moveth. Co. Litt. 143.

RENT-ROLL. A list of rents payable to a particular person or public body.

RENT SECK. Barren rent; a rent reserved by deed, but without any clause of distress. 2 Bl. Comm. 42; 3 Kent, Comm. 461.

RENT-SERVICE. This consisted of fealty, together with a certain rent, and was the only kind of rent originally known to the common law. It was so called because it was given as a compensation for the services to which the land was originally liable. Brown.

RENTAGE. Rent.

RENTAL. (Said to be corrupted from "rent-roll.") In English law. A roll on which the rents of a manor are registered or set down, and by which the lord's bailiff collects the same. It contains the lands and tenements let to each tenant, the names of the tenants, and other particulars. Cunningham; Holthouse.

RENTAL BOLLS. In Scotch law. When the tithes (tiends) have been liquidated and settled for so many bolls of corn yearly. Bell.

RENTAL-RIGHTS. In English law. A species of lease usually granted at a low rent and for life. Tenants under such leases were called "rentalers" or "kindly tenants."

RENTE. In French law. *Rente* is the annual return which represents the revenue of a capital or of an immovable alienated. The constitution of *rente* is a contract by which one of the parties lends to the other a capital which he agrees not to recall, in consideration of the borrower's paying an annual interest. It is this interest which is called "*rente.*" Duverger. The word is therefore nearly synonymous with the English "annuity."

"*Rentes,*" is the term applied to the French government funds, and "*rentier*" to a fundholder or other person having an income from personal property. Wharton.

RENTE FONCIÈRE. In French law. A rent which issues out of land, and it is of its essence that it be perpetual, for, if it be made but for a limited time, it is a lease. It may, however, be extinguished. Civil Code La. art. 2780.

RENTE VIAGÈRE. In French law. That species of *rente*, the duration of which depends upon the contingency of the death of one or more persons indicated in the contract. The uncertainty of the time at which such death may happen causes the *rente viagère* to be included in the number of aleatory contracts. Duverger. It is an annuity for life. Civil Code La. art. 2764.

RENTS, ISSUES, AND PROFITS more commonly signify in the books a chattel real interest in land; a kind of estate growing out of the land, for life or years, producing an annual or other rent. 26 Vt. 746.

RENTS OF ASSIZE. The certain and determined rents of the freeholders and ancient copyholders of manors are called "rents of assize," apparently because they were assized or made certain, and so distinguished from a *redditus mobilis*, which was a variable or fluctuating rent. 3 Cruise, Dig. 314; Brown.

RENTS RESOLUTE. Rents anciently payable to the crown from the lands of abbeys and religious houses; and after their dissolution, notwithstanding that the lands were demised to others, yet the rents were still reserved and made payable again to the crown. Cowell.

RENUNCIATION. The act of giving up a right. See RENOUNCE.

REO ABSENTE. Lat. The defendant being absent; in the absence of the defendant.

REPAIRS. Restoration to soundness; supply of loss; reparation; work done to an estate to keep it in good order.

"Repair" means to restore to its former condition; not to change either the form or material of a building. 63 Pa. St. 162.

REPARATION. The redress of an injury; amends for a wrong inflicted.

REPARATIONE FACIENDA. For making repairs. The name of an old writ which lay in various cases; as if, for instance, there were three tenants in common of a mill or house which had fallen into decay, and one of the three was willing to repair it, and the other two not; in such case the party who was willing to repair might have this writ against the others. Cowell; Fitzh. Nat. Brev. 127.

REPATRIATION takes place when a person who has been expatriated regains his nationality.

REPEAL. The abrogation or annulling of a previously existing law by the enactment of a subsequent statute which declares that the former law shall be revoked and abrogated, (which is called "express" repeal,) or which contains provisions so contrary to or irreconcilable with those of the earlier law that only one of the two statutes can stand in force, (called "implied" repeal.)

Repellitur a sacramento infamis. An infamous person is repelled or prevented from taking an oath. Co. Litt. 158; Bract. fol. 185.

Repellitur exceptione cedendarum actionum. He is defeated by the plea that the actions have been assigned. 1 Johns. Ch. 409, 414.

REPERTORY. In French law. The inventory or minutes which notaries make of all contracts which take place before them. Merl. Repert.

REPETITION. In the civil law. A demand or action for the restoration of money paid under mistake, or goods delivered by mistake or on an unperformed condition. Dig. 12, 6. See SOLUTIO INDEBITI.

In Scotch law. The act of reading over a witness' deposition, in order that he may adhere to it or correct it at his choice. The same as *recolement* (*q. v.*) in the French law. 2 Benth. Jud. Ev. 239.

REPETITUM NAMIUM. A repeated, second, or reciprocal distress; withernam. 3 Bl. Comm. 148.

REPETUNDÆ, or PECUNIÆ REPETUNDÆ. In Roman law. The terms used to designate such sums of money as the *socii* of the Roman state, or individuals, claimed to recover from *magistratus, judices*, or *publici curatores*, which they had improperly taken or received in the *provinciæ*, or in the *urbs Roma*, either in the discharge of their *jurisdictio*, or in their capacity of *judices*, or in respect of any other public function. Sometimes the word "*repetundæ*" was used to express the illegal act for which compensation was sought. Wharton.

REPETUNDARUM CRIMEN. In Roman law. The crime of bribery or extortion in a magistrate, or person in any public office. Calvin.

REPLEAD. To plead anew; to file new pleadings.

REPLEADER. When, after issue has been joined in an action, and a verdict given thereon, the pleading is found (on examination) to have miscarried and failed to effect its proper object, viz., of raising an apt and material question between the parties, the court will, on motion of the unsuccessful party, award a *repleader*; that is, will order the parties to plead *de novo* for the purpose of obtaining a better issue. Brown.

Judgment of repleader differs from a judgment *non obstante veredicto*, in this: that it is allowed by the court to do justice between the parties where the defect is in the form or manner of stating the right, and the issue joined is on an immaterial point, so that it cannot tell for whom to give judgment; while judgment *non obstante* is given only where it is clearly apparent to the court that the party who has succeeded has, upon his own showing, no merits, and cannot have by any manner of statement. 1 Chit. Pl. 687, 688.

REPLEGIARE. To replevy; to redeem a thing detained or taken by another by putting in legal sureties.

REPLEGIARE DE AVERIIS. In old English practice. Replevin of cattle. A writ brought by one whose cattle were distrained, or put in the pound, upon any cause by another, upon surety given to the sheriff to prosecute or answer the action in law. Cowell.

REPLEGIARI FACIAS. You cause to be replevied. In old English law. The original writ in the action of replevin; superseded by the statute of Marlbridge, c. 21. 3 Bl. Comm. 146.

REPLETION. In canon law. Where the revenue of a benefice is sufficient to fill or occupy the whole right or title of the graduate who holds it. Wharton.

REPLEVIABLE, or REPLEVISABLE. Property is said to be repleviable or replevisable when proceedings in replevin may be resorted to for the purpose of trying the right to such property.

REPLEVIN. A personal action *ex delicto* brought to recover possession of goods unlawfully taken, (generally, but not only, applicable to the taking of goods distrained for rent,) the validity of which taking it is the mode of contesting, if the party from whom the goods were taken wishes to have them back *in specie*, whereas, if he prefer to have damages instead, the validity may be contested by action of trespass or unlawful distress. The word means a redelivery to the owner of the pledge or thing taken in distress. Wharton.

REPLEVISH. In old English law. To let one to mainprise upon surety. Cowell.

REPLEVISOR. The plaintiff in an action of replevin.

REPLEVY. This word, as used in reference to the action of replevin, signifies to redeliver goods which have been distrained, to the original possessor of them, on his pledging or giving security to prosecute an action against the distrainor for the purpose of trying the legality of the distress. It has also been used to signify the bailing or liberating a man from prison on his finding bail to answer for his forthcoming at a future time. Brown.

REPLIANT, or REPLICANT. A litigant who replies or files or delivers a replication.

REPLICARE. Lat. In the civil law and old English pleading. To reply; to answer a defendant's plea.

REPLICATIO. Lat. In the civil law and old English pleading. The plaintiff's answer to the defendant's exception or plea; corresponding with and giving name to the *replication* in modern pleading. Inst. 4, 14, pr.

REPLICATION. In pleading. A reply made by the plaintiff in an action to the defendant's plea, or in a suit in chancery to the defendant's answer.

REPLY. In its general sense, a reply is what the plaintiff, petitioner, or other person who has instituted a proceeding says in answer to the defendant's case. Sweet.

On trial or argument. When a case is tried or argued in court, the speech or argument of the plaintiff in answer to that of the defendant is called his "reply."

Under the practice of the chancery and common-law courts, to reply is to file or deliver a replication, (*q. v.*)

Under codes of reformed procedure, "reply" is very generally the name of the pleading which corresponds to "replication" in common-law or equity practice.

REPONE. In Scotch practice. To replace; to restore to a former state or right. 2 Alis. Crim. Pr. 351.

REPORT. An official or formal statement of facts or proceedings.

In practice. The formal statement in writing made to a court by a master in chancery, a clerk, or referee, as the result of his inquiries into some matter referred to him by the court.

The name is also applied (usually in the plural) to the published volumes, appearing periodically, containing accounts of the various cases argued and determined in the courts, with the decisions thereon.

Lord Coke defines "report" to be "a public relation, or a bringing again to memory cases judicially argued, debated, resolved, or adjudged in any of the king's courts of justice, together with such causes and reasons as were delivered by the judges of the same." Co. Litt. 293.

REPORT OF COMMITTEE. The report of a legislative committee is that communication which the chairman of the committee makes to the house at the close of the investigation upon which it has been engaged. Brown.

REPORT OFFICE. A department of the English court of chancery. The suitors' account there is discontinued by the 15 & 16 Vict. c. 87, § 36.

REPORTER. A person who reports the decisions upon questions of law in the cases adjudged in the several courts of law and equity. Wharton.

REPORTS, THE. The name given, *par excellence*, to Lord Coke's Reports, from 14 Eliz. to 13 Jac. I., which are cited as "Rep." or "Coke." They are divided into thirteen parts, and the modern editions are in six volumes, including the index.

REPOSITION OF THE FOREST. In old English law. An act whereby certain forest grounds, being made *purlieu* upon view, were by a second view laid to the forest again, put back into the forest. Manwood; Cowell.

REPOSITORIUM. A storehouse or place wherein things are kept; a warehouse. Cro. Car. 555.

REPRESENT. To exhibit; to expose before the eyes. To represent a thing is to produce it publicly. Dig. 10, 4, 2, 3.

To represent a person is to stand in his place; to supply his place; to act as his substitute.

REPRESENTATION. In contracts. A statement made by one of two contracting parties to the other, before or at the time of making the contract, in regard to some fact, circumstance, or state of facts pertinent to the contract, which is influential in bringing about the agreement.

In insurance. A collateral statement, either by writing not inserted in the policy or by parol, of such facts or circumstances, relative to the proposed adventure, as are necessary to be communicated to the underwriters, to enable them to form a just estimate of the risks. 1 Marsh. Ins. 450.

The allegation of any facts, by the applicant to the insurer, or *vice versa*, preliminary to making the contract, and directly bearing upon it, having a plain and evident tendency to induce the making of the policy. The statements may or may not be in writing, and may be either express or by obvious implication. 11 Cush. 324; 12 Md. 348.

In relation to the contract of insurance, there is an important distinction between a representation and a warranty. The former, which precedes the contract of insurance, and is no part of it, need be only materially true; the latter is a part of the contract, and must be exactly and literally fulfilled, or else the contract is broken and inoperative. 21 Conn. 19.

In the law of distribution and descent. The principle upon which the issue of a deceased person take or inherit the share of an estate which their immediate ancestor would have taken or inherited, if living; the taking or inheriting *per stirpes*. 2 Bl. Comm. 217, 517.

In Scotch law. The name of a plea or statement presented to a lord ordinary of the court of session, when his judgment is brought under review.

REPRESENTATION OF PERSONS. A fiction of the law, the effect of which is to put the representative in the place, degree, or right of the person represented. Civil Code La. art. 894.

REPRESENTATIVE. Representation is the act of one person representing or standing in the place of another; and he who so represents or stands in the place of another is termed his "representative." Thus, an heir is the representative of the ancestor, and an executor is the representative of the testator, the heir standing in the place of his deceased ancestor with respect to his realty, the executor standing in the place of his deceased testator with respect to his personalty; and hence the heir is frequently denominated the "real" representative, and the executor the "personal" representative. Brown; 39 Barb. 516; 2 Steph. Comm. 243.

In constitutional law, representatives are those persons chosen by the people to represent their several interests in a legislative body.

REPRESENTATIVE ACTION OR SUIT. A representative action or suit is one brought by a member of a class of persons on behalf of himself and the other members of the class. In the proceedings before judgment the plaintiff is, as a rule, *dominus litis*, (*q. v.*,) and may discontinue or compromise the action as he pleases. Sweet.

REPRESENTATIVE DEMOCRACY. A form of government where the powers of the sovereignty are delegated to a body of men, elected from time to time, who exercise them for the benefit of the whole nation. 1 Bouv. Inst. no. 31.

REPRESENTATIVE PEERS. Those who, at the commencement of every new parliament, are elected to represent Scotland and Ireland in the British house of lords; sixteen for the former and twenty-eight for the latter country. Brown.

REPRIEVE. In criminal law. The withdrawing of a sentence of death for an interval of time, whereby the execution is suspended. 4 Bl. Comm. 394.

REPRIMAND. A public and formal censure or severe reproof, administered to a person in fault by his superior officer or by a body to which he belongs. Thus, a member of a legislative body may be reprimanded by the presiding officer, in pursuance of a vote of censure, for improper conduct in the house. So a military officer, in some cases, is punished by a reprimand administered by his commanding officer, or by the secretary of war.

REPRISALS. The forcibly taking a thing by one nation which belonged to another, in return or satisfaction for an injury committed by the latter on the former. Vattel, b. 2, c. 18, s. 342.

REPRISES. In English law. Deductions and duties which are yearly paid out of a manor and lands, as rent-charge, rent seck, pensions, corrodies, annuities, etc., so that, when the clear yearly value of a manor is spoken of, it is said to be so much per annum *ultra reprisas*,—besides all *reprises*. Cowell.

Reprobata pecunia liberat solventem. Money refused [the refusal of money tendered] releases him who pays, [or tenders it.] 9 Coke, 79*a*.

REPROBATION. In ecclesiastical law. The interposition of objections or exceptions; as, to the competency of witnesses, to the due execution of instruments offered in evidence, and the like.

REPROBATOR, ACTION OF. In Scotch law. An action or proceeding intended to convict a witness of perjury, to which the witness must be made a party. Bell.

REP-SILVER. In old records. Money paid by servile tenants for exemption from the customary duty of *reaping* for the lord. Cowell.

REPUBLIC. A commonwealth; a state in which the exercise of the sovereign power is lodged in representatives elected by the people. Webster.

In a wider sense, the state, the common weal, the whole organized political community, without reference to the form of government.

REPUBLICAN GOVERNMENT. A government in the republican form; a government of the people; a government by representatives chosen by the people. Cooley, Const. Law, 194.

REPUBLICATION. The re-execution or re-establishment by a testator of a will which he had once revoked.

A second publication of a will, either expressly or by construction.

REPUDIATE. To put away, reject, disclaim, or renounce a right, duty, obligation, or privilege.

REPUDIATION. Rejection; disclaimer; renunciation; the rejection or refusal of an offered or available right or privilege, or of a duty or relation.

The refusal on the part of a state or government to pay its debts, or its declaration that its obligations, previously contracted, are no longer regarded by it as of binding force.

In the civil law. The casting off or putting away of a woman betrothed; also, but less usually, of a wife; divorcement.

In ecclesiastical law. The refusal to accept a benefice which has been conferred upon the party repudiating.

REPUDIUM. Lat. In Roman law. A breaking off of the contract of espousals, or of a marriage intended to be solemnized. Sometimes translated "divorce;" but this was not the proper sense. Dig. 50, 16, 191.

REPUGNANCY. An inconsistency, opposition, or contrariety between two or more clauses of the same deed or contract, or between two or more material allegations of the same pleading.

REPUGNANT. That which is contrary to what is stated before, or insensible. A repugnant condition is void.

Reputatio est vulgaris opinio ubi non est veritas. Et vulgaris opinio est duplex, scil.: Opinio vulgaris orta inter graves et discretos homines, et quæ vultum veritatis habet; et opinio tantum orta inter leves et vulgares homines, absque specie veritatis. Reputation is common opinion where there is not truth. And common opinion is of two kinds, to-wit: Common reputation arising among grave and sensible men, and which has the appearance of truth; and mere opinion arising among foolish and ignorant men, without any appearance of truth. 4 Coke, 107.

REPUTATION. A person's credit, honor, character, good name. Injuries to one's reputation, which is a personal right, are defamatory and malicious words, libels, and malicious indictments or prosecutions.

Reputation of a person is the estimate in which he is held by the public in the place where he is known. 1 Denio, 347.

In the law of evidence, matters of public and general interest, such as the boundaries of counties or towns, rights of common, claims of highway, etc., are allowed to be proved by general reputation; *e. g.*, by the declaration of deceased persons made *ante litem motam*, by old documents, etc., notwithstanding the general rule against secondary evidence. Best, Ev. 632.

REPUTED. Accepted by general, vulgar, or public opinion. Thus, land may be reputed part of a manor, though not really so, and a certain district may be reputed a parish or a manor, or be a parish or a manor in reputation, although it is in reality no parish or manor at all. Brown.

REPUTED MANOR. Whenever the demesne lands and the services become absolutely separated, the manor ceases to be a manor in reality, although it may (and usually does) continue to be a manor in reputation, and is then called a "reputed manor," and it is also sometimes called a "seigniory in gross." Brown.

REPUTED OWNER. He who has the general credit or reputation of being the owner or proprietor of goods is said to be the reputed owner. This phrase is chiefly used in English bankruptcy practice, where the bankrupt is styled the "reputed owner" of goods lawfully in his possession, though the real owner may be another person.

The word "reputed" has a much weaker sense than its derivation would appear to warrant; importing merely a supposition or opinion derived or made up from outward appearances, and often unsupported by fact. The term "reputed owner" is frequently employed in this sense. 2 Steph. Comm. 206.

REQUEST. An asking or petition; the expression of a desire to some person for something to be granted or done; particularly for the payment of a debt or performance of a contract.

The two words, "request" and "require," as used in notices to creditors to present claims against an estate, are of the same origin, and virtually synonymous. 8 Hun, 300.

In pleading. The statement in the plaintiff's declaration that the particular payment or performance, the failure of which constitutes the cause of action, was duly requested or demanded of the defendant.

REQUEST, LETTERS OF. In English law. Many suits are brought before the Dean of the Arches as original judge, the cognizance of which properly belongs to inferior jurisdictions within the province, but in respect of which the inferior judge has waived his jurisdiction under a certain form of proceeding known in the canon law by the denomination of "letters of request." 3 Steph. Comm. 306.

REQUEST NOTE. In English law. A note requesting permission to remove dutiable goods from one place to another without paying the excise.

REQUESTS, COURTS OF. See COURTS OF REQUESTS.

REQUISITION. A demand in writing, or formal request or requirement.

In international law. The formal demand by one government upon another, or by the governor of one of the United States upon the governor of a sister state, of the surrender of a fugitive criminal.

In Scotch law. A demand made by a creditor that a debt be paid or an obligation fulfilled. Bell.

REQUISITIONS ON TITLE, in English conveyancing, are written inquiries made by the solicitor of an intending purchaser of land, or of any estate or interest therein, and addressed to the vendor's solicitor, in respect of some apparent insufficiency in the abstract of title. Mozley & Whitley.

REREFIEFS. In Scotch law. Inferior fiefs; portions of a fief or feud granted out to inferior tenants. 2 Bl. Comm. 57.

Rerum ordo confunditur si unicuique jurisdictio non servetur. 4 Inst. Proœm. The order of things is confounded if every one preserve not his jurisdiction.

Rerum progressus ostendunt multa, quæ in initio præcaveri seu prævideri non possunt. 6 Coke, 40. The progress of events shows many things which, at the beginning, could not be guarded against or foreseen.

Rerum suarum quilibet est moderator et arbiter. Every one is the regulator and disposer of his own property. Co. Litt. 223*a*.

RES. Lat. In the civil law. A thing; an object. As a term of the law, this word has a very wide and extensive signification, including not only things which are objects of property, but also such as are not capable of individual ownership. See Inst. 2, 1, pr. And in old English law it is said to have a general import, comprehending both corporeal and incorporeal things of whatever kind, nature, or species. 3 Inst. 182. See Bract. fol. 7*b*.

By "*res*," according to the modern civilians, is meant everything that may form an *object* of rights, in opposition to "*persona*," which is regarded as a *subject* of rights. "*Res*," therefore, in its general meaning, comprises *actions* of all kinds; while in its restricted sense it comprehends every object of right, except actions. Mackeld. Rom. Law, § 146. This has reference to the fundamental division of the Institutes, that all law relates either to *persons*, to *things*, or to *actions*. Inst. 1, 2, 12.

In modern usage, the term is particularly applied to an object, subject-matter, or *status*, considered as the defendant in an action, or as the object against which, directly, proceedings are taken. Thus, in a prize case, the captured vessel is "the *res*." And proceedings of this character are said to be *in rem*. (See IN PERSONAM; IN REM.) "*Res*" may also denote the action or proceeding, as when a cause, which is not between adversary parties, is entitled "*In re* ———."

Res accendent lumina rebus. One thing throws light upon others. 4 Johns. Ch. 149.

RES ACCESSORIA. In the civil law. An accessory thing; that which belongs to a principal thing, or is in connection with it.

Res accessoria sequitur rem principalem. Broom, Max. 491. The accessory follows the principal.

RES ADJUDICATA. See RES JUDICATA.

RES CADUCA. In the civil law. A fallen or escheated thing; an escheat. Hallifax, Civil Law, b. 2, c. 9, no. 60.

RES COMMUNES. In the civil law. Things common to all; that is, those things which are used and enjoyed by every one, even in single parts, but can never be exclusively acquired as a whole, *e. g.*, light and air. Inst. 2, 1, 1; Mackeld. Rom. Law, § 169.

RES CONTROVERSA. In the civil law. A matter controverted; a matter in controversy; a point in question; a question for determination. Calvin.

RES CORONÆ. In old English law. Things of the crown; such as ancient manors, homages of the king, liberties, etc. Fleta, lib. 3, c. 6, § 3.

RES CORPORALES. In the civil law. Corporeal things; things which can be touched, or are perceptible to the senses. Dig. 1, 8, 1, 1; Inst. 2, 2; Bract. fols. 7*b*, 10*b*, 13*b*.

Res denominatur a principali parte. 9 Coke, 47. The thing is named from its principal part.

Res est misera ubi jus est vagum et incertum. 2 Salk. 512. It is a wretched state of things when law is vague and mutable.

RES FUNGIBILES. In the civil law. Fungible things, (*q. v.*)

RES FURTIVÆ. In Scotch law. Goods which have been stolen. Bell.

Res generalem habet significationem quia tam corporea quam incorporea, cujuscunque sunt generis, naturæ, sive speciei, comprehendit. 3 Inst. 182. The word "thing" has a general signification, because it comprehends corporeal and incorporeal objects, of whatever nature, sort, or species.

RES GESTÆ. Things done; transactions; essential circumstances surrounding the subject. The circumstances, facts, and declarations which grow out of the main fact, are contemporaneous with it, and serve to illustrate its character. 46 Conn. 464.

RES IMMOBILES. In the civil law. Immovable things; including land and that which is connected therewith, either by nature or art, such as trees and buildings. Mackeld. Rom. Law, § 160.

RES INCORPORALES. In the civil law. Incorporeal things; things which cannot be touched; such as those things which consist in right. Inst. 2, 2; Bract. fols. 7*b*, 10*b*. Such things as the mind alone can perceive.

RES INTEGRA. A whole thing; a new or unopened thing. The term is applied to those points of law which have not been decided, which are untouched by *dictum* or decision. 3 Mer. 269.

RES INTER ALIOS ACTA. A thing done between others, or between third parties or strangers.

Res inter alios acta alteri nocere non debet. Things done between strangers ought not to injure those who are not parties to them. Co. Litt. 132; Broom, Max. 954, 967.

Res inter alios judicatæ nullum aliis præjudicium faciunt. Matters adjudged in a cause do not prejudice those who were not parties to it. Dig. 44, 2, 1.

RES IPSA LOQUITUR. The thing speaks for itself. A phrase used in actions for injury by negligence where no proof of negligence is required beyond the accident itself, which is such as necessarily to involve negligence; *e. g.*, a collision between two trains upon a railway. Wharton.

RES JUDICATA. A matter adjudged; a thing judicially acted upon or decided; a thing or matter settled by judgment. A phrase of the civil law, constantly quoted in the books. 2 Kent, Comm. 120.

Res judicata facit ex albo nigrum; ex nigro, album; ex curvo, rectum; ex recto, curvum. A thing adjudged makes white, black; black, white; the crooked, straight; the straight, crooked. 1 Bouv. Inst. no. 840.

Res judicata pro veritate accipitur. A matter adjudged is taken for truth. Dig. 50, 17, 207. A matter decided or passed upon by a court of competent jurisdiction is received as evidence of truth. 2 Kent, Comm. 120.

RES MANCIPI. In Roman law. Certain classes of things which could not be aliened or transferred except by means of a certain formal ceremony of conveyance called "*mancipatio*," (*q. v.*) These included land, houses, slaves, horses, and cattle. All other things were called "*res nec mancipi.*" The distinction was abolished by Justinian.

RES MOBILES. In the civil law. Movable things; things which may be transported from one place to another, without injury to their substance and form. Things corresponding with the chattels personal of the common law. 2 Kent, Comm. 347.

RES NOVA. A new matter; a new case; a question not before decided.

RES NULLIUS. The property of nobody. A thing which has no owner, either because a former owner has finally abandoned it, or because it has never been appropriated by any person, or because (in the Roman law) it is not susceptible of private ownership.

Res per pecuniam æstimatur, et non pecunia per rem. 9 Coke, 76. The value of a thing is estimated according to its worth in money, but the value of money is not estimated by reference to a thing.

RES PERIIT DOMINO. A phrase used to express that, when a thing is lost or destroyed, it is lost to the person who was the owner of it at the time. Broom, Max. 238.

RES PRIVATÆ. In the civil law. Things the property of one or more individuals. Mackeld. Rom. Law, § 157.

Res propria est quæ communis non est. A thing is private which is not common. 8 Paige, 261, 270.

RES PUBLICÆ. Things belonging to the public; public property; such as the sea, navigable rivers, highways, etc.

Res quæ intra præsidia perductæ nondum sunt, quanquam ab hostibus occupatæ, ideo postliminii non egent, quia dominum nondum maturunt ex gentium jure. Things which have not yet been introduced within the enemy's lines, although held by the enemy, do not need the fiction of postliminy on this account, because their ownership by the law of nations has not yet changed. Gro. de Jure B. l. 3, c. 9, § 16; Id. l. 3, c. 6, § 3.

RES QUOTIDIANÆ. Every-day matters; familiar points or questions.

RES RELIGIOSÆ. Things pertaining to religion. In Roman law, especially, burial-places, which were regarded as sacred, and could not be the subjects of commerce.

Res sacra non recipit æstimationem. A sacred thing does not admit of valuation. Dig. 1, 8, 9, 5.

RES SACRÆ. In the civil law. Sacred things. Things consecrated by the pontiffs to the service of God; such as sacred edifices, and gifts or offerings. Inst. 2, 1, 8. Chalices, crosses, censers. Bract. fol. 8.

RES SANCTÆ. In the civil law. Holy things; such as the walls and gates of a city. Inst. 2, 1, 10. Walls were said to be holy, because any offense against them was punished capitally. Bract. fol. 8.

Res sua nemini servit. 4 Macq. H. L. Cas. 151. No one can have a servitude over his own property.

Res transit cum suo onere. The thing passes with its burden. Where a thing has been incumbered by mortgage, the incumbrance follows it wherever it goes. Bract. fols. 47*b*, 48.

RES UNIVERSITATIS. In the civil law. Things belonging to a community, (as, to a municipality,) the use and enjoyment of which, according to their proper purpose, is free to every member of the community, but which cannot be appropriated to the exclusive use of any individual; such as the public buildings, streets, etc. Inst. 2, 1, 6; Mackeld. Rom. Law, § 170.

RES, VARIETIES OF. These have been variously divided and classified in law, *e. g.*, in the following ways: (1) Corporeal and incorporeal things; (2) movables and immovables; (3) *res mancipi* and *res nec mancipi;* (4) things real and things personal; (5) things in possession and choses (*i. e.*, things) in action; (6) fungible things and things not fungible, (*fungibiles vel non fungibiles;*) and (7) *res singulæ* (*i. e.*, individual objects) and *universitates rerum*, (*i. e.*, aggregates of things.) Also persons are for some purposes and in certain respects regarded as things. Brown.

RESALE is where a person who has sold goods or other property to a purchaser sells them again to some one else. Sometimes a vendor reserves the right of reselling if the purchaser commits default in payment of the purchase money, and in some cases (*e. g.*, on a sale of perishable articles) the vendor may do so without having reserved the right. Sweet.

RESCEIT. In old English practice. An admission or receiving a third person to plead his right in a cause formerly commenced between two others; as, in an action by tenant for life or years, he in the reversion might come in and pray to be received to defend the land, and to plead with the demandant. Cowell.

RESCEIT OF HOMAGE. The lord's receiving homage of his tenant at his admission to the land. Kitch. 148.

RESCIND. To abrogate, annul, avoid, or cancel a contract; particularly, nullifying a contract by the act of a party.

RESCISSIO. Lat. In the civil law. An annulling; avoiding, or making void; abrogation; rescission. Cod. 4, 44.

RESCISSION. Rescission, or the act of rescinding, is where a contract is canceled, annulled, or abrogated by the parties, or one of them.

In Spanish law, nullity is divided into absolute and relative. The former is that which arises from a law, whether civil or criminal, the principal motive for which is the public interest; and the latter is that which affects only certain individuals. "Nullity" is not to be confounded with "rescission." Nullity takes place when the act is affected by a radical vice, which prevents it from producing any effect; as where an act is in contravention of the laws or of good morals, or where it has been executed by a person who cannot be supposed to have any will, as a child under the age of seven years, or a madman, (*un nino o demente.*) Rescission is where an act, valid in appearance, nevertheless conceals a defect, which may make it null, if demanded by any of the parties; as, for example, mistake, force, fraud, deceit, want of sufficient age, etc. Nullity relates generally to public order, and cannot therefore be made good either by ratification or prescription; so that the tribunals ought, for this reason alone, to decide that the null act can have no effect, without stopping to inquire whether the parties to it have or have not received any injury. Rescission, on the contrary, may be made good by ratification or by the silence of the parties; and neither of the parties can demand it, unless he can prove that he has received some prejudice or sustained some damage by the act. 1 Cal. 281, citing Escriche.

RESCISSORY ACTION. In Scotch law. One to rescind or annul a deed or contract.

RESCOUS. Rescue. The taking back by force goods which had been taken under a distress, or the violently taking away a man who is under arrest, and setting him at liberty, or otherwise procuring his escape, are both so denominated. This was also the name of a writ which lay in cases of rescue. Co. Litt. 160; 3 Bl. Comm. 146; Fitzh. Nat. Brev. 100; 6 Mees. & W. 564.

RESCRIPT. In canon law. A term including any form of apostolical letter emanating from the pope. The answer of the pope in writing. Dict. Droit Can.

In the civil law. A species of imperial constitutions, being the answers of the prince in individual cases, chiefly given in response to inquiries by parties in relation to litigated suits, or to inquiries by the judges, and which became rules for future litigated or doubtful legal questions. Mackeld. Rom. Law, § 46.

At common law. A counterpart, duplicate, or copy.

In American law. A written order from the court to the clerk, giving directions concerning the further disposition of a case. Pub. St. Mass. p. 1295.

The written statement by an appellate court of its decision in a case, with the reasons therefor, sent down to the trial court.

RESCRIPTION. In French law. A rescription is a letter by which one requests some one to pay a certain sum of money, or to account for him to a third person for it. Poth. Cont. de Change, no. 225.

RESCRIPTUM. In the civil law. A species of imperial constitution, in the form of an answer to some application or petition; a rescript. Calvin.

RESCUE. The act of forcibly and intentionally delivering a person from lawful arrest or imprisonment, and setting him at liberty. 4 Bl. Comm. 131; Code Ga. § 4478.

The unlawfully or forcibly taking back goods which have been taken under a distress for rent, damage feasant, etc.

In admiralty and maritime law. The deliverance of property taken as prize, out of the hands of the captors, either when the captured party retake it by their own efforts, or when, pending the pursuit or struggle, the party about to be overpowered receive reinforcements, and so escape capture.

RESCUSSOR. In old English law. A rescuer; one who commits a rescous. Cro. Jac. 419; Cowell.

RESCYT. L. Fr. Resceit; receipt; the receiving or harboring a felon, after the commission of a crime. Britt. c. 23.

RESEALING WRIT. In English law. The second sealing of a writ by a master so as to continue it, or to cure it of an irregularity.

RESERVANDO. Reserving. In old conveyancing. An apt word of reserving a rent. Co. Litt. 47*a*.

Reservatio non debet esse de proficuis ipsis, quia ea conceduntur, sed de reditu novo extra proficua. A reservation ought not to be of the profits themselves, because they are granted, but from the new rent, apart from the profits. Co. Litt. 142.

RESERVATION. A clause in a deed or other instrument of conveyance by which the grantor creates, and reserves to himself, some right, interest, or profit in the estate granted, which had no previous existence as such, but is first called into being by the instrument reserving it; such as rent, or an easement.

A reservation is something taken from the whole thing covered by the general terms making the grant, and cuts down and lessens the grant from what it would be except for the reservation. 44 Vt. 416.

A "reservation" should be carefully distinguished from an "exception," the difference between the two being this: By an exception, the grantor withdraws from the effect of the grant some part of the thing itself which is *in esse*, and included under the terms of the grant, as one acre from a certain field, a shop or mill standing within the limits of the granted premises, and the like; whereas, a reservation, though made to the grantor, lessor, or the one creating the estate, is something arising out of the thing granted not then *in esse*, or some new thing created or reserved, issuing or coming out of the thing granted, and not a part of the thing itself, nor of anything issuing out of another thing. 3 Washb. Real Prop. 645.

In public land laws of the United States, a reservation is a tract of land, more or less considerable in extent, which is by public authority withdrawn from sale or settlement, and appropriated to specific public uses; such as parks, military posts, Indian lands, etc.

In practice, the reservation of a point of law is the act of the trial court in setting it aside for future consideration, allowing the trial to proceed meanwhile as if the question had been settled one way, but subject to alteration of the judgment in case the court *in banc* should decide it differently.

RESET. The receiving or harboring an outlawed person. Cowell.

RESET OF THEFT. In Scotch law. The receiving and keeping stolen goods, knowing them to be stolen, with a design of feloniously retaining them from the real owner. Alis. Crim. Law, 328.

RESETTER. In Scotch law. A receiver of stolen goods, knowing them to have been stolen.

RESIANCE. Residence, abode, or continuance.

RESIANT. In old English law. Continually dwelling or abiding in a place; resident; a resident. Kitchin, 33; Cowell.

RESIANT ROLLS. Those containing the resiants in a tithing, etc., which are to be called over by the steward on holding courts leet.

RESIDENCE. Living or dwelling in a certain place permanently or for a considerable length of time. The place where a man makes his home, or where he dwells permanently or for an extended period of time.

The difference between a residence and a domicile may not be capable of easy definition; but every one can see at least this distinction: A person domiciled in one state may, for temporary reasons, such as health, reside for one or more years in some other place deemed more favorable. He does not, by so doing, forfeit his domicile in the first state, or, in any proper sense, become a non-resident of it, unless some intention, manifested by some act, of abandoning his residence in the first state is shown. 1 Mo. App. 404.

"Residence" means a fixed and permanent abode or dwelling-place for the time being, as contradistinguished from a mere temporary locality of existence. So does "inhabitancy;" and the two are distinguishable in this respect from "domicile." 8 Wend. 134.

As they are used in the New York Code of Procedure, the terms "residence" and "resident" mean legal residence; and legal residence is the place of a man's fixed habitation, where his political rights are to be exercised, and where he is liable to taxation. 16 How. Pr. 77.

RESIDENT. One who has his residence in a place.

"Resident" and "inhabitant" are distinguishable in meaning. The word "inhabitant" implies a more fixed and permanent abode than does "resident;" and a resident may not be entitled to all the privileges or subject to all the duties of an inhabitant. 19 Wend. 11.

Also a tenant, who was obliged to reside on his lord's land, and not to depart from the same; called, also, "*homme levant et couchant,*" and in Normandy, "*resseant du fief.*"

RESIDENT FREEHOLDER. In the Wisconsin highway laws, a person who resides in the town in question, and owns a freehold interest in lands situate therein. 29 Wis. 419.

RESIDENT MINISTER. In international law. A public minister who resides at a foreign court. Resident ministers are ranked in the third class of public ministers. Wheat. Int. Law, 264, 267.

RESIDUAL. Relating to the residue; relating to the part remaining.

RESIDUARY. Pertaining to the residue; constituting the residue; giving or bequeathing the residue; receiving or entitled to the residue.

RESIDUARY ACCOUNT. In English practice. The account which every executor and administrator, after paying the debts and particular legacies of the deceased, and before paying over the residuum, must pass before the board of inland revenue. Mozley & Whitley.

RESIDUARY CLAUSE. The clause in a will by which that part of the property is disposed of which remains after satisfying previous bequests and devises.

RESIDUARY DEVISEE. The person named in a will, who is to take all the real property remaining over and above the other devises.

RESIDUARY ESTATE. The remaining part of a testator's estate and effects, after payment of debts and legacies; or that portion of his estate which has not been particularly devised or bequeathed.

RESIDUARY LEGATEE. The person to whom a testator bequeaths the residue of his personal estate, after the payment of such other legacies as are specifically mentioned in the will. Toller, 269.

RESIDUE. The surplus of a testator's estate remaining after all the debts and particular legacies have been discharged. 2 Bl. Comm. 514.

The "residue" of a testator's estate and effects means what is left after all liabilities are discharged, and all the purposes of the testator, specifically expressed in his will, are carried into effect. 3 Jones, Eq. 302.

RESIDUUM. That which remains after any process of separation or deduction; a residue or balance. That which remains of a decedent's estate, after debts have been paid and legacies deducted.

Resignatio est juris proprii spontanea refutatio. Resignation is a spontaneous relinquishment of one's own right. Godb. 284.

RESIGNATION. The act by which an officer renounces the further exercise of his office and returns the same into the hands of those from whom he received it.

In ecclesiastical law. Resignation is where a parson, vicar, or other beneficed clergyman voluntarily gives up and surrenders his charge and preferment to those from whom he received the same. It is usually done by an instrument attested by a notary. Phillim. Ecc. Law, 517.

In Scotch law. The return of a fee into the hands of the superior. Bell.

RESIGNATION BOND. A bond or other engagement in writing taken by a patron from the clergyman presented by him to a living, to resign the benefice at a future period. This is allowable in certain cases under St. 9 Geo. IV. c. 94, passed in 1828. 2 Steph. Comm. 721.

RESIGNEE. One in favor of whom a resignation is made. 1 Bell, Comm. 125*n*.

RESILIRE. Lat. In old English law. To draw back from a contract before it is made binding. Bract. fol. 38.

RESIST. To oppose. This word properly describes an opposition by direct action and *quasi* forcible means. 37 Wis. 196.

RESISTANCE. The act of resisting opposition; the employment of forcible means to prevent the execution of an endeavor in which force is employed.

RESOLUCION. In Spanish colonial law. An opinion formed by some superior authority on matters referred to its decision, and forwarded to inferior authorities for their instruction and government. Schm. Civil Law, 93, note 1.

RESOLUTION. The determination or decision, in regard to its opinion or intention, of a deliberative or legislative body, public assembly, town council, board of directors or the like. Also a motion or formal proposition offered for adoption by such a body.

In legislative practice. The term is usually employed to denote the adoption of a motion, the subject-matter of which would not properly constitute a statute; such as a mere expression of opinion; an alteration of the rules; a vote of thanks or of censure, etc.

In practice. The judgment of a court. 5 Mod. 438; 10 Mod. 209.

In the civil law. The cancellation or annulling, by the act of parties or judgment of a court, of an existing contract which was valid and binding, in consequence of some cause or matter arising after the making of the agreement, and not in consequence of any inherent vice or defect, which, invalidating the contract from the beginning, would be ground for rescission. 7 Toullier, no. 551.

RESOLUTIVE. In Scotch conveyancing. Having the quality or effect of resolving or extinguishing a right. Bell.

Resoluto jure concedentis resolvitur jus concessum. The right of the grantor being extinguished, the right granted is extinguished. Mackeld. Rom. Law, 179; Broom, Max. 467.

RESOLUTORY CONDITION. A resolutory or dissolving condition is that which, when accomplished, operates the revocation of the obligation, placing matters in the same state as though the obligation had not existed. It does not suspend the execution of the obligation. It only obliges the creditor to restore what he has received in case the event provided for in the condition takes place. Civil Code La. art. 2045.

RESORT, *v.* To go back. "It resorted to the line of the mother." Hale, Com. Law, c. 11.

RESORT, *n.* A court whose decision is final and without appeal is, in reference to the particular case, said to be a "court of last resort."

RESOURCES. Money or any property that can be converted into supplies; means of raising money or supplies; capabilities of raising wealth or to supply necessary wants; available means or capability of any kind. 3 Mont. 386; Webster.

RESPECTU COMPUTI VICECOMITIS HABENDO. A writ for respiting a sheriff's account addressed to the treasurer and barons of the exchequer. Reg. Orig. 139.

RESPECTUS. In old English and Scotch law. Respite; delay; continuance of time; postponement.

Respiciendum est judicanti ne quid aut durius aut remissius constituatur quam causa deposcit; nec enim aut severitatis aut clementiæ gloria affectanda est. The judge must see that no order be made or judgment given or sentence passed either more harshly or more mildly than the case requires; he must not seek renown, either as a severe or as a tender-hearted judge.

RESPITE. The temporary suspension of the execution of a sentence; a reprieve; a delay, forbearance, or continuation of time. 62 Pa. St. 55; 4 Bl. Comm. 394.

Continuance. In English practice, a jury is said, on the record, to be "respited" till the next term. 3 Bl. Comm. 354.

In the civil law. A *respite* is an act by which a debtor, who is unable to satisfy his debts at the moment, transacts (compromises) with his creditors, and obtains from them time or delay for the payment of the sums which he owes to them. The respite is either voluntary or forced. It is *voluntary* when all the creditors consent to the proposal, which the debtor makes, to pay in a limited time the whole or a part of the debt. It is *forced* when a part of the creditors refuse to accept the debtor's proposal, and when the latter is obliged to compel them by judicial authority to consent to what the others have determined, in the cases directed by law. Civil Code La. arts. 3084, 3085.

RESPITE OF APPEAL. Adjourning an appeal to some future time. Brown.

RESPITE OF HOMAGE. To dispense with the performance of homage by tenants who held their lands in consideration of performing homage to their lords. Cowell.

RESPOND. 1. To make or file an answer to a bill, libel, or appeal, in the character of a respondent, (*q. v.*)

2. To be liable or answerable; to make satisfaction or amends; as, to "respond in damages."

RESPONDE BOOK. In Scotch practice. A book kept by the directors of chancery, in which are entered all non-entry and relief duties payable by heirs who take precepts from chancery. Bell.

RESPONDEAT OUSTER. Upon an issue in law arising upon a dilatory plea, the form of judgment for the plaintiff is that the defendant answer over, which is thence called a judgment of "*respondeat ouster.*" This not being a final judgment, the pleading is resumed, and the action proceeds. Steph. Pl. 115; 3 Bl. Comm. 303.

Respondeat raptor, qui ignorare non potuit quod pupillum alienum abduxit. Hob. 99. Let the ravisher answer, for he cannot be ignorant that he has taken away another's ward.

Respondeat superior. Let the master answer. This maxim means that a master is liable in certain cases for the wrongful acts of his servant, and a principal for those of his agent. Broom, Max. 843.

RESPONDENT. The party who makes an answer to a bill or other proceeding in chancery.

The party who appeals against the judgment of an inferior court is termed the "appellant;" and he who contends against the appeal, the "respondent." The word also denotes the person upon whom an ordinary petition in the court of chancery (or a libel in admiralty) is served, and who is, as it were, a defendant thereto. The terms "respondent" and "co-respondent" are used in like manner in proceedings in the divorce court. Brown.

In the civil law. One who answers or is security for another; a fidejussor. Dig. 2, 8, 6.

RESPONDENTIA. The hypothecation of the cargo or goods on board a ship as security for the repayment of a loan, the term "bottomry" being confined to hypothecations of the ship herself; but now the term "respondentia" is seldom used, and the expression "bottomry" is generally employed, whether the vessel or her cargo or both be the security. Maude & P. Shipp. 433; Smith, Merc. Law, 416.

Respondentia is a contract by which a cargo, or some part thereof, is hypothecated as security for a loan, the repayment of which is dependent on maritime risks. Civil Code Cal. § 3036; Civil Code Dak. § 1796.

The word "respondentia" properly applies to the loan of money upon merchandise laden on board a ship, the repayment whereof is made to depend upon the safe arrival of the merchandise at the destined port. Newb. Adm. 514, 516.

Respondera son soveraigne. His superior or master shall answer. Articuli sup. Chart. c. 18.

RESPONDERE NON DEBET. Lat. In pleading. The prayer of a plea where the defendant insists that he ought not to answer, as when he claims a privilege; for example, as being a member of congress or a foreign ambassador. 1 Chit. Pl. *433.

RESPONSA PRUDENTUM. Answers of jurists; responses given upon cases or questions of law referred to them, by certain learned Roman jurists, who, though not magistrates, were authorized to render such opinions. These *responsa* constituted one of the most important sources of the earlier Roman law, and were of great value in developing its scientific accuracy. They held much the same place of authority as our modern precedents and reports.

RESPONSALIS. In old English law. One who appeared for another.

In ecclesiastical law. A proctor.

RESPONSALIS AD LUCRANDUM VEL PETENDUM. He who appears and answers for another in court at a day assigned; a proctor, attorney, or deputy. 1 Reeve, Eng. Law, 169.

RESPONSIBILITY. The obligation to answer for an act done, and to repair any injury it may have caused.

RESPONSIBLE. To say that a person is "responsible" means that he is able to pay a sum for which he is or may become liable, or to discharge an obligation which he may be under. 26 N. H. 527.

RESPONSIBLE GOVERNMENT. This term generally designates that species of governmental system in which the responsibility for public measures or acts of state rests upon the ministry or executive council, who are under an obligation to resign when disapprobation of their course is expressed by a vote of want of confidence, in the legislative assembly, or by the defeat of an important measure advocated by them.

Responsio unius non omnino audiatur. The answer of one witness shall not be heard at all. A maxim of the Roman law of evidence. 1 Greenl. Ev. § 260.

RESPONSIVE. Answering; constituting or comprising a complete answer. A "responsive allegation" is one which directly answers the allegation it is intended to meet.

RESSEISER. The taking of lands into the hands of the crown, where a general livery or *ouster le main* was formerly misused.

REST. In the trial of an action, a party is said to "rest," or "rest his case," when he intimates that he has produced all the evidence he intends to offer at that stage, and submits the case, either finally, or subject to his right to afterwards offer rebutting evidence.

RESTAMPING WRIT. Passing it a second time through the proper office, whereupon it receives a new stamp. 1 Chit. Arch. Pr. 212.

RESTAUR, or RESTOR. The remedy or recourse which assurers have against each other, according to the date of their assurances, or against the master, if the loss arise through his default, as through ill loading, want of caulking, or want of having the vessel tight; also the remedy or recourse a person has against his guarantor or other person who is to indemnify him from any damage sustained. Enc. Lond.

RESTAURANT. This term, as currently understood, means only, or chiefly, an eating-house; but it has no such fixed and definite legal meaning as necessarily to exclude its being an "inn" in the legal sense. 10 Fed. Rep. 4.

RESTITUTIO IN INTEGRUM. Lat. In the civil law. Restoration or restitution to the previous condition. This was effected by the prætor on equitable grounds, at the prayer of an injured party, by rescinding or annulling a contract or transaction valid by the strict law, or annulling a change in the legal condition produced by an omission, and restoring the parties to their previous situation or legal relations. Dig. 4, 1; Mackeld. Rom. Law, § 220.

The restoration of a cause to its first state, on petition of the party who was cast, in order to have a second hearing. Hallifax, Civil Law, b. 3, c. 9, no. 49.

RESTITUTION. In maritime law. When a portion of a ship's cargo is lost by jettison, and the remainder saved, and the articles so lost are replaced by a general contribution among the owners of the cargo, this is called "restitution."

In practice. The return of something to the owner of it or to the person entitled to it.

If, after money has been levied under a writ of execution, the judgment be reversed by writ of error, or set aside, the party against whom the execution was sued out shall have *restitution*. 2 Tidd, Pr. 1033; 1 Burrill, Pr. 292. So, on conviction of a felon, immediate *restitution* of such of the goods stolen as are brought into court will be ordered to be made to the several prosecutors. 4 Steph. Comm. 434.

In equity. Restitution is the restoration of both parties to their original condition, (when practicable,) upon the rescission of a contract for fraud or similar cause.

RESTITUTION OF CONJUGAL RIGHTS. In English ecclesiastical law. A species of matrimonial cause or suit which is brought whenever either a husband or wife is guilty of the injury of subtraction, or lives separate from the other without any sufficient reason; in which case the ecclesiastical jurisdiction will compel them to come together again, if either party be weak enough to desire it, contrary to the inclination of the other. 3 Bl. Comm. 94.

RESTITUTION OF MINORS. In Scotch law. A minor on attaining majority may obtain relief against a deed previously executed by him, which may be held void or voidable according to circumstances. This is called "restitution of minors." Bell.

RESTITUTION, WRIT OF. In practice. A writ which lies, after the reversal of a judgment, to restore a party to all that he has lost by occasion of the judgment. 2 Tidd, Pr. 1186.

RESTITUTIONE EXTRACTI AB ECCLESIA. A writ to restore a man to the church, which he had recovered for his sanctuary, being suspected of felony. Reg. Orig. 69.

RESTITUTIONE TEMPORALIUM. A writ addressed to the sheriff, to restore the temporalities of a bishopric to the bishop elected and confirmed. Fitzh. Nat. Brev. 169.

RESTRAIN. To limit, confine, abridge, narrow down, or restrict.

To prohibit from action; to put compulsion upon; to restrict; to hold or press back. To enjoin, (in equity.)

RESTRAINING ORDER. An order in the nature of an injunction. The term is applied in England to an order restraining the Bank of England, or some public company, from allowing any dealing with some stock or shares specified in the order. It is granted on motion or petition. Hunt, Eq. p. 216.

RESTRAINING POWERS. Restrictions or limitations imposed upon the exercise of a power by the donor thereof.

RESTRAINING STATUTE. A statute which restrains the common law, where it is too lax and luxuriant. 1 Bl. Comm. 87. Statutes restraining the powers of corporations in regard to leases have been so called in England. 2 Bl. Comm. 319, 320.

RESTRAINT. Confinement, abridgment, or limitation. Prohibition of action; holding or pressing back from action. Hindrance, confinement, or restriction of liberty.

"What, then, according to a common understanding, is the meaning of the term 'restraint?' Does it imply that the limitation, restriction, or confinement must be imposed by those who are in possession of the person or thing which is limited, restricted, or confined, or is the term satisfied by a restriction created by the application of external force? If, for example, a town be besieged, and the inhabitants confined within its walls by the besieging army, if, in attempting to come out, they are forced back, would it be inaccurate to say that they are restrained within those limits? The court believes that it would not; and, if it would not, then with equal propriety may it be said, when a port is blockaded, that the vessels within are confined, or restrained from coming out. The blockading force is not in possession of the vessels inclosed in the harbor, but it acts upon and restrains them. It is a *vis major*, applied directly and effectually to them, which prevents them from coming out of port. This appears to the court to be, in correct language, 'a restraint,' by the power imposing the blockade; and when a vessel, attempting to come out, is boarded and turned back, this restraining force is practically applied to such vessel." 3 Wheat. 189.

The terms "restraint" and "detention of princes," as used in policies of marine insurance, have the same meaning,—that of the effect of superior force, operating directly on the vessel. So long as a ship is under restraint, so long she is detained; and, whenever she is detained, she is under restraint. 6 Mass. 102.

RESTRAINT OF MARRIAGE. A contract, covenant, bond, or devise is "in restraint of marriage" when its conditions unreasonably hamper or restrict the party's freedom to marry, or his choice, or unduly postpone the time of his marriage.

RESTRAINT OF TRADE. A contract is void, as being "in restraint of trade," when by it a person binds himself to abstain everywhere from the exercise of a particular lawful trade, business, or avocation.

RESTRAINT ON ALIENATION is where property is given to a married woman to her separate use, without power of alienation.

RESTRICTION. In the case of land registered under the English land transfer act, 1875, a restriction is an entry on the register made on the application of the registered proprietor of the land, the effect of which is to prevent the transfer of the land or the creation of any charge upon it, unless notice of the application for a transfer or charge is sent by post to a certain address, or unless the consent of a certain person or persons to the transfer or charge is obtained, or unless some other thing is done. Sweet.

RESTRICTIVE INDORSEMENT. An indorsement may be so worded as to restrict the further negotiability of the instrument, and it is then called a "restrictive indorsement." Thus, "Pay the contents to J. S. only," or "to J. S. for my use," are restrictive indorsements, and put an end to the negotiability of the paper. 1 Daniel, Neg. Inst. § 698.

RESTS. Periodical balancings of an account, (particularly in mortgage and trust accounts,) made for the purpose of converting interest into principal, and charging the party liable thereon with compound interest. Mozley & Whitley.

RESULT. In law, a thing is said to result when, after having been ineffectually or only partially disposed of, it comes back to its former owner or his representatives. Sweet.

RESULTING TRUST. One that arises by implication of law, or by the operation and construction of equity, and which is established as consonant to the presumed intention of the parties as gathered from the nature of the transaction.

RESULTING USE. A use raised by equity for the benefit of a feoffor who has made a voluntary conveyance to uses without any declaration of the use. 2 Washb. Real Prop. 100.

A resulting use arises where the legal seisin is transferred, and no use is expressly declared, nor any consideration nor evidence of intent to direct the use. The use then remains in the original grantor, for it cannot be supposed that the estate was intended to be given away, and the statute immediately transfers the legal estate to such resulting use. Wharton.

RESUMMONS. In practice. A second summons. The calling a person a second time to answer an action, where the first summons is defeated upon any occasion; as the death of a party, or the like. Cowell.

RESUMPTION. In old English law. The taking again into the king's hands such lands or tenements as before, upon false suggestion, or other error, he had delivered to the heir, or granted by letters patent to any man. Cowell.

RESURRENDER. Where copyhold land has been mortgaged by surrender, and the mortgagee has been admitted, then, on the mortgage debt being paid off, the mortgagor is entitled to have the land reconveyed to him, by the mortgagee surrendering it to the lord to his use. This is called a "resurrender." 2 Dav. Conv. 1332*n*.

RETAIL. To sell by small parcels, and not in the gross. To sell in small quantities. 7 Metc. (Mass.) 308; 5 Mart. (N. S.) 297.

RETAILER OF MERCHANDISE. A merchant who buys articles in gross or merchandise in large quantities, and sells the same by single articles or in small quantities.

RETAIN. In practice. To engage the services of an attorney or counsellor to manage a cause. See RETAINER, 2.

RETAINER. 1. The right of retainer is the right which the executor or administrator of a deceased person has to retain out of the assets sufficient to pay any debt due to him from the deceased in priority to the other creditors whose debts are of equal degree. 3 Steph. Comm. 263.

2. In English practice, a "retainer," as applied to counsel, is commonly used to signify a notice given to a counsel by an attorney on behalf of the plaintiff or defendant in an action, in order to secure his services as advocate when the cause comes on for trial. Holthouse.

3. A servant, not menial or familiar,—that is, not continually dwelling in the house of his master, but only wearing his livery, and attending sometimes upon special occasions, —is, in old English usage, called a "retainer." Cowell.

RETAINING A CAUSE. In English practice. The act of one of the divisions of the high court of justice in retaining jurisdiction of a cause wrongly brought in that division instead of another. Under the judicature acts of 1873 and 1875, this may be done, in some cases, in the discretion of the court or a judge.

RETAINING FEE. A fee given to counsel on engaging his services for the trial of the cause.

RETAKING. The taking one's goods, from another, who without right has taken possession thereof.

RETALIATION. The *lex talionis*, (*q. v.*)

RETALLIA. In old English law. Retail; the cutting up again, or division of a commodity into smaller parts.

RETENEMENTUM. In old English law. Restraint; detainment; withholding.

RETENTION. In Scotch law. A species of lien; the right to retain possession of a chattel until the lienor is satisfied of his claim upon the article itself or its owner.

RETINENTIA. A retinue, or persons retained by a prince or nobleman. Cowell.

RETIRE. As applied to bills of exchange, this word is ambiguous. It is commonly used of an indorser who takes up a bill by handing the amount to a transferee, after which the indorser holds the instrument with all his remedies intact. But it is sometimes used of an acceptor, by whom, when a bill is taken up or retired at maturity, it is in effect paid, and all the remedies on it extinguished. Byles, Bills, 215.

RETONSOR. L. Lat. In old English law. A clipper of money. Fleta, lib. 1, c. 20, § 122.

RETORNA BREVIUM. The return of writs. The indorsement by a sheriff or other officer of his doings upon a writ.

RETORNO HABENDO. A writ that lies for the distrainor of goods (when, on replevin brought, he has proved his distress to be a lawful one) against him who was so distrained, to have them returned to him according to law, together with damages and costs. Brown.

RETORSION. In international law. A species of retaliation, which takes place where a government, whose citizens are subjected to severe and stringent regulation or harsh treatment by a foreign government, employs measures of equal severity and harshness upon the subjects of the latter government found within its dominions. See Vattel, lib. 2, c. 18, § 341.

RETOUR. In Scotch law. To return a writ to the office in chancery from which it issued.

RETOUR OF SERVICE. In Scotch law. A certified copy of a verdict establishing the legal character of a party as heir to a decedent.

RETOUR SANS FRAIS. In French law. A formula put upon a bill of exchange to signify that the drawer waives protest, and will not be responsible for costs arising thereon. Arg. Fr. Merc. Law, 573.

RETOUR SANS PROTÊT. Fr. Return without protest. A request or direction by a drawer of a bill of exchange that, should the bill be dishonored by the drawee, it may be returned without protest.

RETRACT. To take back. To retract an offer is to withdraw it before acceptance, which the offerer may always do.

RETRACTATION, in probate practice, is a withdrawal of a renunciation, (*q. v.*)

RETRACTO O TANTEO. In Spanish law. The right of revoking a contract of sale; the right of redemption of a thing sold. White, New Recop. b. 2, tit. 13, c. 2, § 4.

RETRACTUS AQUÆ. The ebb or return of a tide. Cowell.

RETRACTUS FEUDALIS. In old Scotch law. The power which a superior possessed of paying off a debt due to an adjudging creditor, and taking a conveyance to the adjudication. Bell.

RETRAIT. Fr. In old French and Canadian law. The taking back of a fief by the seignior, in case of alienation by the vassal. A right of pre-emption by the seignior, in case of sale of the land by the grantee.

RETRAXIT. Lat. In practice. An open and voluntary renunciation by a plaintiff of his suit in court, made when the trial is called on, by which he forever loses his action, or is barred from commencing another action for the same cause. 3 Bl. Comm. 296; 2 Archb. Pr. K. B. 250.

A *retraxit* is the open, public, and voluntary renunciation by the plaintiff, in open court, of his suit or cause of action, and if this is done by the plaintiff, and a judgment entered thereon by the defendant, the plaintiff's right of action is forever gone. Code Ga. 1882, § 3445.

"RETREAT TO THE WALL." In the law relating to homicide in self-defense, this phrase means that the party must avail himself of any apparent and reasonable avenues of escape by which his danger might be averted, and the necessity of slaying his assailant avoided. 57 Cal. 120.

RETRIBUTION. This word is sometimes used in law, though not commonly in modern times, as the equivalent of "recompense," or a payment or compensation for services, property, use of an estate, or other value received.

RETRO. Lat. Back; backward; behind. *Retrofeodum*, a rerefief, or *arriere* fief. Spelman.

RETROACTIVE has the same meaning as "retrospective," (*q. v.*)

RETROCESSION. In the civil law. When the assignee of heritable rights conveys his rights back to the cedent, it is called a "retrocession." Ersk. Inst. 3, 5, 1.

RETROSPECTIVE. Looking back; contemplating what is past.

RETROSPECTIVE LAW. A law which looks backward or contemplates the past; one which is made to affect acts or facts transpiring, or rights accruing, before it came into force. Every statute which takes away or impairs vested rights acquired under existing laws, or creates a new obligation, imposes a new duty, or attaches a new disability in respect to transactions or considerations already past, must be deemed *retrospective*. 2 Gall. 139. See Ex post Facto.

RETTE. L. Fr. An accusation or charge. St. Westm. 1, c. 2.

RETURN. The act of a sheriff, constable, or other ministerial officer, in delivering back to the court a writ, notice, or other paper, which he was required to serve or execute, with a brief account of his doings under the mandate, the time and mode of service or execution, or his failure to accomplish it, as the case may be. Also the indorsement made by the officer upon the writ or other paper, stating what he has done under it, the time and mode of service, etc.

The report made by the court, body of magistrates, returning board, or other authority charged with the official counting of the votes cast at an election.

In English practice, the election of a member of parliament is called his "return."

RETURN-BOOK. The book containing the list of members returned to the house of commons. May, Parl. Pr.

RETURN-DAY. The day named in a writ or process, upon which the officer is required to return it.

RETURN IRREPLEVISABLE. A writ allowed by the statute of Westm. 2, c. 2, to a defendant who had had judgment upon verdict or demurrer in an action of replevin, or after the plaintiff had, on a writ of second deliverance, become a second time nonsuit in such action. By this writ the goods were returned to the defendant, and the plaintiff was restrained from suing out a fresh replevin. Previously to this statute, an unsuccessful plaintiff might bring actions of replevin *in infinitum*, in reference to the same matter. 3 Bl. Comm. 150.

RETURN OF PREMIUM. The repayment of the whole or a ratable part of the premium paid for a policy of insurance, upon the cancellation of the contract before the time fixed for its expiration.

RETURN OF WRITS. In practice. A short account, in writing, made by the sheriff, or other ministerial officer, of the manner in which he has executed a writ. Steph. Pl. 24.

RETURNABLE. In practice. To be returned; requiring a return. When a writ is said to be "returnable" on a certain day, it is meant that on that day the officer must return it.

RETURNING BOARD. This is the official title in some of the states of the board of canvassers of elections.

RETURNING FROM TRANSPORTATION. Coming back to England before the term of punishment is determined.

RETURNING OFFICER. The official who conducts a parliamentary election in England. The sheriff in counties, and the mayor in boroughs. Wharton.

RETURNUM AVERIORUM. A judicial writ, similar to the *retorno habendo*. Cowell.

RETURNUM IRREPLEGIABILE. A judicial writ addressed to the sheriff for the final restitution or return of cattle to the owner when unjustly taken or distrained, and so found by verdict. It is granted after a nonsuit in a second deliverance. Reg. Jud. 27.

REUS. Lat. In the civil and canon law. The defendant in an action or suit.

A person judicially accused of a crime; a person criminally proceeded against. Hallifax, Civil Law, b. 3, c. 13, no. 7.

A party to a suit, whether plaintiff or defendant; a litigant. This was the ancient sense of the word. Calvin.

A party to a contract. *Reus stipulandi*, a party stipulating; the party who asked the question in the form prescribed for stipulations. *Reus promittendi*, a party promising; the party who answered the question.

Reus excipiendo fit actor. The defendant, by excepting or pleading, becomes a plaintiff; that is, where, instead of simply denying the plaintiff's action, he sets up some new matter in defense, he is bound to establish it by proof, just as a plaintiff is bound to prove his cause of action. Bounier, Tr. des Preuves, §§ 152, 320; Best, Ev. p. 294, § 252.

Reus læsæ majestatis punitur ut pereat unus ne pereant omnes. A traitor is punished that one may die lest all perish. 4 Coke, 124.

REUS PROMITTENDI. See Reus Stipulandi.

REUS STIPULANDI. In the civil law. The party to a stipulation is so called if he is the creditor or obligee, and the debtor or obligor to such a stipulation is called the "*reus promittendi.*" Where there are several creditors or several debtors jointly entitled to or jointly liable under a stipulation, they were respectively called "*correi;*" *i. e.*, joint *rei*. Brown.

REVE. In old English law. The bailiff of a franchise or manor; an officer in parishes within forests, who marks the commonable cattle. Cowell.

REVE MOTE. In Saxon law. The court of the *reve, reeve*, or *shire reeve*. 1 Reeve, Eng. Law, 6.

REVEL. A criminal complaint charged that the defendant did "revel, quarrel, commit mischief, and otherwise behave in a disorderly manner." *Held*, that the word "revel" has a definite meaning; *i. e.*, "to behave in a noisy, boisterous manner, like a bacchanal." 12 R. I. 309.

REVELAND. The land which in Domesday is said to have been "thane-land," and afterwards converted into "reveland." It seems to have been land which, having reverted to the king after the death of the thane, who had it for life, was not granted out to any by the king, but rested in charge upon the account of the reve or bailiff of the manor. Spel. Feuds, c. 24.

REVELS. Sports of dancing, masking, etc., formerly used in princes' courts, the inns of court, and noblemen's houses, commonly performed by night. There was an officer to order and supervise them, who was entitled the "master of the revels." Cowell.

REVENDICATION. In the civil law. The right of a vendor to reclaim goods sold out of the possession of the purchaser, where the price was not paid. Story, Confl. Laws, § 401.

REVENUE. As applied to the income of a government, this is a broad and general term, including all public moneys which the state collects and receives, from whatever source and in whatever manner. 22 Kan. 712.

It also designates the income of an individual or private corporation.

REVENUE LAW. Any law which provides for the assessment and collection of a tax to defray the expenses of the government is a revenue law. Such legislation is commonly referred to under the general term "revenue measures," and those measures include all the laws by which the government provides means for meeting its expenditures. 1 Woolw. 178.

REVENUE SIDE OF THE EXCHEQUER. That jurisdiction of the court of exchequer, or of the exchequer division of the high court of justice, by which it ascertains and enforces the proprietary rights of the crown against the subjects of the realm. The practice in revenue cases is not affected by the orders and rules under the judicature act of 1875. Mozley & Whitley.

REVERSAL. The annulling or making void a judgment on account of some error or irregularity. Usually spoken of the action of an appellate court.

In international law. A declaration by which a sovereign promises that he will observe a certain order or certain conditions, which have been once established, notwithstanding any changes that may happen to cause a deviation therefrom. Bouvier.

REVERSE, REVERSED. A term frequently used in the judgments of an appellate court, in disposing of the case before it. It then means "to set aside; to annul; to vacate." 7 Kan. 254.

REVERSER. In Scotch law. The proprietor of an estate who grants a wadset (or mortgage) of his lands, and who has a right, on repayment of the money advanced to him, to be replaced in his right. Bell.

REVERSIO. L. Lat. In old English law. The returning of land to the donor. Fleta, lib. 3, cc. 10, 12.

Reversio terræ est tanquam terra revertens in possessione donatori, sive hæredibus suis post donum finitum. Co. Litt. 142. A reversion of land is, as it were, the return of the land to the possession of the donor or his heirs after the termination of the estate granted.

REVERSION. **In real property law.** A reversion is the residue of an estate left by operation of law in the grantor or his heirs, or in the heirs of a testator, commencing in possession on the determination of a particular estate granted or devised. How. St. Mich. 1882, § 5528; Civil Code Cal. § 768; 2 Bl. Comm. 175.

When a person has an interest in lands, and grants a portion of that interest, or, in other terms, a less estate than he has in himself, the possession of those lands shall, on the determination of the granted interest or estate, return or revert to the grantor. This interest is what is called the "grantor's reversion," or, more properly, his "right of reverter," which, however, is deemed an actual estate in the land. Watk. Conv. 16.

Where an estate is derived, by grant or otherwise, out of a larger one, leaving in the original owner an ulterior estate immediately expectant on that which is so derived, the ulterior interest is called the "reversion." 1 Steph. Comm. 290.

A *reversion* is the residue of an estate left in the grantor, to commence in possession after the determination of some particular estate; while a *remainder* is an estate limited to take effect and be enjoyed after another estate is determined. 26 N. J. Law, 525.

In personalty. "Reversion" is also used to denote a reversionary interest; *e. g.*, an interest in personal property subject to the life interest of some other person.

In Scotch law. A reversion is a right of redeeming landed property which has been either mortgaged or adjudicated to secure the payment of a debt. In the former case, the reversion is called "conventional;" in the latter case, it is called "legal;" and the period of seven years allowed for redemption is called the "legal." Bell; Paterson.

REVERSIONARY. That which is to be enjoyed in reversion.

REVERSIONARY INTEREST. The interest which a person has in the reversion of lands or other property. A right to the future enjoyment of property, at present in the possession or occupation of another. Holthouse.

REVERSIONARY LEASE. One to take effect *in futuro*. A second lease, to commence after the expiration of a former lease. Wharton.

REVERSIONER. A person who is entitled to an estate in reversion. By an extension of its meaning, one who is entitled to any future estate or any property in expectancy.

REVERT. To revert is to return. Thus, when the owner of an estate in land has granted a smaller estate to another person, on the determination of the latter estate, the land is said to "revert" to the grantor. Sweet.

REVERTER. Reversion. A possibility of reverter is that species of reversionary interest which exists when the grant is so limited that it may possibly terminate. 1 Washb. Real Prop. 63. See FORMEDON IN THE REVERTER.

REVEST. To vest again. A seisin is said to *revest*, where it is acquired a second time by the party out of whom it has been divested. 1 Rop. Husb. & Wife, 353.

It is opposed to "divest." The words "revest" and "divest" are also applicable to the mere right or title, as opposed to the possession. Brown.

REVESTIRE. In old European law. To return or resign an investiture, seisin, or possession that has been received; to reinvest; to re-enfeoff. Spelman.

REVIEW. A reconsideration; second view or examination; revision; consideration for purposes of correction. Used especially of the examination of a cause by an appellate court, and of a second investigation of a proposed public road by a jury of viewers.

REVIEW, BILL OF. In equity practice. A bill, in the nature of a writ of error, filed to procure an examination and alteration or reversal of a decree made upon a former bill, which decree has been signed and enrolled. Story, Eq. Pl. § 403.

REVIEW, COMMISSION OF. In English ecclesiastical law. A commission formerly sometimes granted, in extraordinary cases, to revise the sentence of the court of delegates, when it was apprehended they had been led into a material error. 3 Bl. Comm. 67.

REVIEW, COURT OF. In England. A court established by 1 & 2 Wm. IV. c. 56, for the adjudicating upon such matters in bankruptcy as before were within the jurisdiction of the lord chancellor. It was abolished in 1847.

REVIEWING TAXATION. The retaxing or re-examining an attorney's bill of costs by the master. The courts sometimes order the masters to review their taxation, when, on being applied to for that purpose, it appears that items have been allowed or disallowed on some erroneous principle, or under some mistaken impression. 1 Archb. Pr. K. B. 55.

REVILING CHURCH ORDINANCES. An offense against religion punishable in England by fine and imprisonment. 4 Steph. Comm. 208.

REVIVAL. The process of renewing the operative force of a judgment which has remained dormant or unexecuted for so long a time that execution cannot be issued upon it without new process to reanimate it.

The act of renewing the legal force of a contract or obligation, which had ceased to be sufficient foundation for an action, on account of the running of the statute of limitations, by giving a new promise or acknowledgment of it.

REVISE. To review, re-examine for correction; to go over a thing for the purpose of amending, correcting, rearranging, or otherwise improving it; as, to revise statutes, or a judgment.

REVISED STATUTES. A body of statutes which have been revised, collected, arranged in order, and re-enacted as a whole. This is the legal title of the collections of compiled laws of several of the states, and also of the United States. Such a volume is usually cited as "Rev. Stat.," "Rev. St.," or "R. S."

REVISING ASSESSORS. In English law. Two officers elected by the burgesses of non-parliamentary municipal boroughs for the purpose of assisting the mayor in revising the parish burgess lists. Wharton.

REVISING BARRISTERS. In English law. Barristers appointed to revise the list of voters for county and borough members of parliament, and who hold courts for that purpose throughout the county. St. 6 Vict. c. 18.

REVISING BARRISTERS' COURTS. In English law. Courts held in the autumn throughout the country, to revise the list of voters for county and borough members of parliament.

REVIVE. To renew, revivify; to make one's self liable for a debt barred by the statute of limitations by acknowledging it; or for a matrimonial offense, once condoned, by committing another.

REVIVOR, BILL OF. In equity practice. A bill filed for the purpose of reviving or calling into operation the proceedings in a suit when, from some circumstance, (as the death of the plaintiff,) the suit had abated.

REVIVOR, WRIT OF. In English practice. Where it became necessary to revive a judgment, by lapse of time, or change by death, etc., of the parties entitled or liable to execution, the party alleging himself to be entitled to execution might sue out a writ of revivor in the form given in the act, or apply to the court for leave to enter a suggestion upon the roll that it appeared that he was entitled to have and issue execution of the judgment, such leave to be granted by the court or a judge upon a rule to show cause, or a summons, to be served according to the then present practice. C. L. P. Act, 1852, § 129.

REVOCABLE. Susceptible of being revoked.

REVOCATION. The recall of some power, authority, or thing granted, or a destroying or making void of some deed that had existence until the act of revocation made it void. It may be either *general*, of all acts and things done before; or *special*, to revoke a particular thing. 5 Coke, 90.

Revocation by act of the party is an intentional or voluntary revocation. The principal instances occur in the case of authorities and powers of attorney and wills.

A revocation in law, or constructive revocation, is produced by a rule of law, irrespectively of the intention of the parties. Thus, a power of attorney is in general revoked by the death of the principal. Sweet.

REVOCATION OF PROBATE is where probate of a will, having been granted, is afterwards recalled by the court of probate, on proof of a subsequent will, or other sufficient cause.

REVOCATIONE PARLIAMENTI. An ancient writ for recalling a parliament. 4 Inst. 44.

REVOCATUR. Lat. It is recalled. This is the term, in English practice, appropriate to signify that a judgment is annulled or set aside for error in fact; if for error in law, it is then said to be *reversed*.

REVOKE. To call back; to recall; to annul an act by calling or taking it back.

REVOLT. The endeavor of the crew of a vessel, or any one or more of them, to overthrow the legitimate authority of her commander, with intent to remove him from his command, or against his will to take possession of the vessel by assuming the government and navigation of her, or by transferring their obedience from the lawful commander to some other person. 11 Wheat. 417.

REWARD. A recompense or premium offered by government or an individual in return for special or extraordinary services to be performed, or for special attainments or achievements, or for some act resulting to the benefit of the public; as, a reward for useful inventions, for the discovery and apprehension of criminals, for the restoration of lost property.

REWME. In old records. Realm, or kingdom.

REX. Lat. The king. The king regarded as the party prosecuting in a criminal action; as in the form of entitling such actions, "Rex v. Doe."

Rex debet esse sub lege quia lex facit regem. The king ought to be under the law, because the law makes the king. 1 Bl. Comm. 239.

Rex est legalis et politicus. Lane, 27. The king is both a legal and political person.

Rex est lex vivens. Jenk. Cent. 17. The king is the living law.

Rex est major singulis, minor universis. Bract. l. 1, c. 8. The king is greater than any single person, less than all.

Rex hoc solum non potest facere quod non potest injuste agere. 11 Coke, 72. The king can do everything but an injustice.

Rex non debit esse sub homine, sed sub Deo et sub lege, quia lex facit regem. Bract. fol. 5. The king ought to be under no man, but under God and the law, because the law makes a king. Broom, Max. 47.

Rex non potest peccare. The king cannot do wrong; the king can do no wrong. 2 Rolle, 304. An ancient and fundamental principle of the English constitution. Jenk. Cent. p. 9, case 16; 1 Bl. Comm. 246.

Rex nunquam moritur. The king never dies. Broom, Max. 50; Branch, Max. (5th Ed.) 197; 1 Bl. Comm. 249.

RHANDIR. A part in the division of Wales before the Conquest; every township comprehended four gavels, and every gavel had four rhandirs, and four houses or tenements constituted every rhandir. Tayl. Hist. Gav. 69.

RHODIAN LAWS. This, the earliest code or collection of maritime laws, was formulated by the people of the island of Rhodes, who, by their commercial prosperity and the superiority of their navies, had acquired the sovereignty of the seas. Its date is very uncertain, but is supposed (by Kent and others) to be about 900 B. C. Nothing of it is now extant except the article on jettison, which has been preserved in the Roman collections. (Dig. 14, 2, "*Lex Rhodia de Jactu.*") Another code, under the same name, was published in more modern times, but is generally considered, by the best authorities, to be spurious. See Schomberg, Mar. Laws Rhodes, 37, 38; 3 Kent, Comm. 3, 4; Azuni, Mar. Law, 265–296.

RIAL. A piece of gold coin current for 10s., in the reign of Henry VI., at which time there were half-rials and quarter-rials or rial-farthings. In the beginning of Queen Elizabeth's reign, golden rials were coined at 15s. a piece; and in the time of James I. there were rose-rials of gold at 30s. and spur-rials at 15s. Lown. Essay Coins, 38.

RIBAUD. A rogue; vagrant; whoremonger; a person given to all manner of wickedness. Cowell.

RIBBONMEN. Associations or secret societies formed in Ireland, having for their object the dispossession of landlords by murder and fire-raising. Wharton.

RICHARD ROE, otherwise TROUBLESOME. The casual ejector and fictitious defendant in ejectment, whose services are no longer invoked.

RICOHOME. Span. In Spanish law. A nobleman; a count or baron. 1 White, Recop. 36.

RIDER. A rider, or rider-roll, signifies a schedule or small piece of parchment annexed to some part of a roll or record. It is frequently familiarly used for any kind of a schedule or writing annexed to a document which cannot well be incorporated in the body of such document. Thus, in passing bills through a legislature, when a new clause is added after the bill has passed through committee, such new clause is termed a "rider." Brown.

RIDER-ROLL. In old English practice. A schedule or small piece of parchment added to some part of a roll or record. Cowell; Blount. A supplementary roll. 2 Tidd, Pr. 730.

RIDGLING. A half-castrated horse. 4 Tex. App. 221.

RIDING ARMED. In English law. The offense of riding or going armed with dangerous or unusual weapons is a misdemeanor tending to disturb the public peace by terrifying the good people of the land. 4 Steph. Comm. 357.

RIDING CLERK. In English law. One of the six clerks in chancery who, in his turn for one year, kept the controlment books of all grants that passed the great seal. The six clerks were superseded by the clerks of records and writs.

RIDINGS, (corrupted from *trithings.*) The names of the parts or divisions of Yorkshire, which, of course, are three only, viz., East Riding, North Riding, and West Riding.

RIEN. Nothing. It appears in a few law French phrases.

RIEN CULP. L. Fr. In old pleading. Not guilty.

RIEN DIT. L. Fr. In old pleading. Says nothing, (*nil dicit.*)

RIEN LUY DOIT. L. Fr. In old pleading. Owes him nothing. The plea of *nil debet.*

RIENS EN ARRERE. L. Fr. Nothing in arrear. A plea in an action of debt for arrearages of account. Cowell.

RIENS LOUR DEUST. L. Fr. Not their debt. The old form of the plea of *nil debet.* 2 Reeve, Eng. Law, 332.

RIENS PASSA PER LE FAIT. L. Fr. Nothing passed by the deed. A plea by which a party might avoid the operation of a deed, which had been enrolled or acknowledged in court; the plea of *non est factum* not being allowed in such case.

RIENS PER DISCENT. L. Fr. Nothing by descent. The plea of an heir, where he is sued for his ancestor's debt, and has no land from him by descent, or assets in his hands. Cro. Car. 151; 1 Tidd, Pr. 645; 2 Tidd, Pr. 937.

RIER COUNTY. In old English law. After-county; *i. e.,* after the end of the county court. A time and place appointed by the sheriff for the receipt of the king's money after the end of his county, or county court. Cowell.

RIFLETUM. A coppice or thicket. Cowell.

RIGA. In old European law. A species of service and tribute rendered to their lords by agricultural tenants. Supposed by Spelman to be derived from the name of a certain portion of land, called, in England, a "rig" or "ridge," an elevated piece of ground, formed out of several furrows. Burrill.

RIGGING THE MARKET. A term of the stock-exchange, denoting the practice of inflating the price of given stocks, or enhancing their quoted value, by a system of pretended purchases, designed to give the air of an unusual demand for such stocks. See L. R. 13 Eq. 447.

RIGHT. As a *noun,* and taken in an *abstract* sense, the term means justice, ethical correctness, or consonance with the rules of law or the principles of morals. In this signification it answers to one meaning of the Latin "*jus,*" and serves to indicate law in the abstract, considered as the foundation of all rights, or the complex of underlying moral principles which impart the character of justice to all positive law, or give it an ethical content.

As a *noun,* and taken in a *concrete* sense, a right signifies a power, privilege, faculty, or demand, inherent in one person and incident upon another. "Rights" are defined generally as "powers of free action." And the primal rights pertaining to men are undoubtedly enjoyed by human beings purely as such, being grounded in personality, and existing antecedently to their recognition by positive law. But leaving the abstract moral sphere, and giving to the term a juristic content, a "right" is well defined as "a capacity residing in one man of controlling, with the assent and assistance of the state, the actions of others." Holl. Jur. 69.

The noun substantive "a right" signifies that which jurists denominate a "faculty;" that which resides in a determinate person, by virtue of a given law, and which avails against a person (or answers to a duty lying on a person) other than the person in whom it resides. And the noun substantive "rights" is the plural of the noun substantive "a right." But the expression "right," when it is used as an adjective, is equivalent to the adjective "just," as the adverb "rightly" is equivalent to the adverb "justly." And, when used as the abstract name corresponding to the adjective "right," the noun substantive "right" is synonymous with the noun substantive "justice." Aust. Jur. § 264, note.

In a narrower signification, the word denotes an interest or title in an object of property; a just and legal claim to hold, use, or enjoy it, or to convey or donate it, as he may please. See Co. Litt. 345*a*.

The term "right," in civil society, is defined to mean that which a man is entitled to have, or to do, or to receive from others within the limits prescribed by law. 6 Neb. 40.

That which one person ought to have or receive from another, it being withheld from him, or not in his possession. In this sense, "right" has the force of "claim," and is properly expressed by the Latin "*jus.*" Lord Coke considers this to be the proper signification of the word, especially in writs and pleadings, where an *estate is turned to a right;* as by discontinuance, disseisin, etc. Co. Litt. 345*a*.

Classification. Rights may be described as *perfect* or *imperfect*, according as their action or scope is clear, settled, and determinate, or is vague and unfixed.

Rights are either *in personam* or *in rem*. A right *in personam* is one which imposes an obligation on a definite person. A right *in rem* is one which imposes an obligation on persons generally; *i. e.*, either on all the world or on all the world except certain determinate persons. Thus, if I am entitled to exclude all persons from a given piece of land, I have a right *in rem* in respect of that land; and, if there are one or more persons, A., B., and C., whom I am not entitled to exclude from it, my right is still a right *in rem*. Sweet.

Rights may also be described as either *primary* or *secondary*. *Primary* rights are those which can be created without reference to rights already existing. *Secondary* rights can only arise for the purpose of protecting or enforcing primary rights. They are either preventive (protective) or remedial (reparative.) Sweet.

Preventive or *protective secondary* rights exist in order to prevent the infringement or loss of primary rights. They are judicial when they require the assistance of a court of law for their enforcement, and extrajudicial when they are capable of being exercised by the party himself. *Remedial* or *reparative secondary* rights are also either judicial or extrajudicial. They may further be divided into (1) rights of restitution or restoration, which entitle the person injured to be replaced in his original position; (2) rights of enforcement, which entitle the person injured to the performance of an act by the person bound; and (3) rights of satisfaction or compensation. Id.

With respect to the ownership of external objects of property, rights may be classed as *absolute* and *qualified*. An absolute right gives to the person in whom it inheres the uncontrolled dominion over the object at all times and for all purposes. A qualified right gives the possessor a right to the object for certain purposes or under certain circumstances only. Such is the right of a bailee to recover the article bailed when it has been unlawfully taken from him by a stranger.

Rights are also either *legal* or *equitable*. The former is the case where the person seeking to enforce the right for his own benefit has the legal title and a remedy at law. The latter are such as are enforceable only in equity; as, at the suit of *cestui que trust*.

There is also a classification of rights, with respect to the constitution of civil society. Thus, according to Blackstone, "the rights of persons, considered in their natural capacities, are of two sorts,—*absolute* and *relative;* absolute, which are such as appertain and belong to particular men, merely as individuals or single persons; relative, which are incident to them as members of society, and standing in various relations to each other." 1 Bl. Comm. 123.

Rights are also classed as *natural*, *civil*, and *political*.

We mean by *natural* rights those which, by fair deduction from the present physical, moral, social, and religious characteristics of man, he must be invested with, and which he ought to have realized for him in a jural society, in order to fulfill the ends to which his nature calls him. Wools. Pol. Science, I. 26.

Political rights consist in the power to participate, directly or indirectly, in the establishment or administration of government.

Civil rights are such as belong to every citizen of the state or country, or, in a wider sense, to all its inhabitants, and are not connected with the organization or administration of government. These rights are such as belong to the juristic personality of the individual, or pertain to him as a member of the community. They include the right of freedom, of property, of marriage, of protection by the laws, etc.

As an *adjective*, the term "right" means just, morally correct, consonant with ethical principles or rules of positive law. It is the opposite of wrong, unjust, illegal.

"Right" is used in law, as well as in ethics, as opposed to "wrong." Thus, a person may acquire a title by wrong.

In old English law. The term denoted an accusation or charge of crime. Fitzh. Nat. Brev. 66 F.

See, also, DROIT; JUS; RECHT.

RIGHT CLOSE, WRIT OF. An abolished writ which lay for tenants in ancient demesne, and others of a similar nature, to try the right of their lands and tenements in the court of the lord exclusively. 1 Steph. Comm. 224.

RIGHT IN ACTION. This is a phrase frequently used in place of *chose in action*, and having an identical meaning.

RIGHT IN COURT. See RECTUS IN CURIA.

RIGHT OF ACTION. The right to bring suit; a legal right to maintain an action, growing out of a given transaction or state of facts and based thereon.

By the old writers "right of action" is commonly used to denote that a person has lost a right of entry, and has nothing but a right of action left. Co. Litt. 363*b*.

RIGHT OF DISCUSSION. In Scotch law. The right which the cautioner (surety) has to insist that the creditor shall do his best to compel the performance of the contract by the principal debtor, before he shall be called upon. 1 Bell, Comm. 347.

RIGHT OF DIVISION. In Scotch law. The right which each of several cautioners (sureties) has to refuse to answer for more than his own share of the debt. To entitle the cautioner to this right the other cautioners must be solvent, and there must be no words in the bond to exclude it. 1 Bell, Comm. 347.

RIGHT OF ENTRY. A right of entry is the right of taking or resuming possession of land by entering on it in a peaceable manner.

RIGHT OF HABITATION. In Louisiana. The right to occupy another man's house as a dwelling, without paying rent or other compensation. Civil Code La. art. 623.

RIGHT OF POSSESSION. The right to possession which may reside in one man, while another has the actual possession, being the right to enter and turn out such actual occupant; *e. g.*, the right of a disseisee. An apparent right of possession is one which may be defeated by a better; an actual right of possession, one which will stand the test against all opponents. 2 Bl. Comm. 196.

RIGHT OF PROPERTY. The mere right of property in land; the abstract right which remains to the owner after he has lost the right of possession, and to recover which the writ of right was given. United with possession, and the right of possession, this right constitutes a complete title to lands, tenements, and hereditaments. 2 Bl. Comm. 197.

RIGHT OF RELIEF. In Scotch law. The right of a cautioner (surety) to demand reimbursement from the principal debtor when he has been compelled to pay the debt. 1 Bell, Comm. 347.

RIGHT OF REPRESENTATION AND PERFORMANCE. By the acts 3 & 4 Wm. IV. c. 15, and 5 & 6 Vict. c. 45, the author of a play, opera, or musical composition, or his assignee, has the sole right of representing or causing it to be represented in public at any place in the British dominions during the same period as the copyright in the work exists. The right is distinct from the copyright, and requires to be separately registered. Sweet.

RIGHT OF SEARCH. In international law. The right of one vessel, on the high seas, to stop a vessel of another nationality and examine her papers and (in some cases) her cargo. Thus, in time of war, a vessel of either belligerent has the right to search a neutral ship, encountered at sea, to ascertain whether the latter is carrying contraband goods.

RIGHT OF WAY. The right of passage or of way is a servitude imposed by law or by convention, and by virtue of which one has a right to pass on foot, or horseback, or in a vehicle, to drive beasts of burden or carts, through the estate of another. When this servitude results from the law, the exercise of it is confined to the wants of the person who has it. When it is the result of a contract, its extent and the mode of using it is regulated by the contract. Civil Code La. art. 722.

"Right of way," in its strict meaning, is the right of passage over another man's ground; and in its legal and generally accepted meaning, in reference to a *railway*, it is a mere easement in the lands of others, obtained by lawful condemnation to public use or by purchase. It would be using the term in an unusual sense, by applying it to an absolute purchase of the fee-simple of lands to be used for a railway or any other kind of a way. 50 Wis. 76, 5 N. W. Rep. 482.

RIGHT PATENT. An obsolete writ, which was brought for lands and tenements, and not for an advowson, or common, and lay only for an estate in fee-simple, and not for him who had a lesser estate; as tenant in tail, tenant in frank marriage, or tenant for life. Fitzh. Nat. Brev. 1.

RIGHT TO BEGIN. On the hearing or trial of a cause, or the argument of a demurrer, petition, etc., the right to begin is the right of first addressing the court or jury.

The right to begin is frequently of importance, as the counsel who begins has also the right of replying or having the last word after the counsel on the opposite side has addressed the court or jury. Sweet.

RIGHT TO REDEEM. The term "right of redemption," or "right to redeem," is familiarly used to describe the estate of the debtor when under mortgage, to be sold at auction, in contradistinction to an absolute estate, to be set off by appraisement. It would be more consonant to the legal character of this interest to call it the "debtor's estate subject to mortgage." 3 Metc. (Mass.) 86.

RIGHT, WRIT OF. A procedure for the recovery of real property after not more than sixty years' adverse possession; the highest writ in the law, sometimes called, to distinguish it from others of the droitural class, the "writ of right proper." Abolished by 3 & 4 Wm. IV. c. 27. 3 Steph. Comm. 392.

RIGHTS OF PERSONS. Rights which concern and are annexed to the *persons* of men. 1 Bl. Comm. 122.

RIGHTS OF THINGS. Such as a man may acquire over external objects, or things unconnected with his person. 1 Bl. Comm. 122.

RIGHTS, PETITION OF. See PETITION OF RIGHTS.

RIGOR JURIS. Lat. Strictness of law. Latch, 150. Distinguished from *gratia curiæ*, favor of the court.

RING. A clique; an exclusive combination of persons for illegitimate or selfish purposes; as to control elections or political affairs, distribute offices, obtain contracts, control the market or the stock-exchange, etc.

RING-DROPPING. A trick variously practised. 'One mode is as follows, the circumstances being taken from 2 East, P. C. 678: The prisoner, with accomplices, being with their victim, pretend to find a ring wrapped in paper, appearing to be a jeweler's receipt for a "rich, brilliant diamond ring." They offer to leave the ring with the victim if he will deposit some money and his watch as a security. He lays down his watch and money, is beckoned out of the room by one of the confederates, while the others take away his watch, etc. This is a larceny.

RINGING THE CHANGE. In criminal law. A trick practised by a criminal, by which, on receiving a good piece of money in payment of an article, he pretends it is not good, and, changing it, returns to the buyer a spurious coin. See 2 Leach, 786; Bouvier.

RINGING UP. A custom among commission merchants and brokers (not unlike the clearing-house system) by which they exchange contracts for sale against contracts for purchase, or reciprocally cancel such contracts, adjust differences of price between themselves, and surrender margins. See 11 Biss. 60; 31 Fed. Rep. 12.

RINGS, GIVING. In English practice. A custom observed by serjeants at law, on being called to that degree or order. The rings are given to the judges, and bear certain mottoes, selected by the serjeant about to take the degree. Brown.

RIOT. In criminal law. A tumultuous disturbance of the peace by three persons or more, assembling together of their own authority, with an intent mutually to assist each other against any who shall oppose them, in the execution of some enterprise of a private nature, and afterwards actually executing the same in a violent and turbulent manner, to the terror of the people, whether the act intended were of itself lawful or unlawful. Hawk. P. C. c. 65, § 1; 2 McCord, 117; 1 Hill, (S. C.) 361.

When three or more persons together, and in a violent or tumultuous manner, assemble together to do an unlawful act, or together do a lawful act in an unlawful, violent, or tumultuous manner, to the disturbance of others, they are guilty of a riot. Rev. Code Iowa, 1880, § 4067.

Any use of force or violence, disturbing the public peace, or any threat to use such force or violence, if accompanied by immediate power of execution, by two or more persons acting together, and without authority of law, is a riot. Pen. Code Cal. § 404.

RIOT ACT. A celebrated English statute, which provides that, if any twelve persons or more are unlawfully assembled and disturbing the peace, any sheriff, under-sheriff, justice of the peace, or mayor may, by proclamation, command them to disperse, (which is familiarly called "reading the riot act,") and that if they refuse to obey, and remain together for the space of one hour after such proclamation, they are all guilty of felony. The act is 1 Geo. I. St. 2, c. 5.

RIOTOSE. L. Lat. Riotously. A formal and essential word in old indictments for riots. 2 Strange, 834.

RIOTOUS ASSEMBLY. In English criminal law. The unlawful assembling of twelve persons or more, to the disturbance of the peace, and not dispersing upon proclamation. 4 Bl. Comm. 142; 4 Steph. Comm. 273.

RIOTOUSLY. A technical word, properly used in indictments for riot. It of itself implies force and violence. 2 Chit. Crim. Law, 489.

RIPA. Lat. The banks of a river, or the place beyond which the waters do not in their natural course overflow.

RIPARIA. A medieval Latin word, which Lord Coke takes to mean water running between two banks; in other places it is rendered "bank."

RIPARIAN. Belonging or relating to the bank of a river; of or on the bank.

RIPARIAN NATIONS. In international law. Those who possess opposite banks or different parts of banks of one and the same river.

RIPARIAN OWNER. A riparian proprietor; one who owns land on the bank of a river.

RIPARIAN PROPRIETOR. An owner of land, bounded generally upon a stream of water, and as such having a qualified property in the soil to the thread of the stream with the privileges annexed thereto by law. 22 Pick. 355.

RIPARIAN RIGHTS. The rights of the owners of lands on the banks of watercourses, relating to the water, its use, ownership of soil under the stream, accretions, etc.

Riparum usus publicus est jure gentium, sicut ipsius fluminis. The use of river-banks is by the law of nations public, like that of the stream itself. Dig. 1, 8, 5, pr.; Fleta, l. 3, c. 1, § 5.

RIPTOWELL, or REAPTOWEL. A gratuity or reward given to tenants after they had reaped their lord's corn, or done other customary duties. Cowell.

RIPUARIAN LAW. An ancient code of laws by which the Ripuarii, a tribe of Franks who occupied the country upon the Rhine, the Meuse, and the Scheldt, were governed. They were first reduced to writing by Theodoric, king of Austrasia, and completed by Dagobert. Spelman.

RIPUARIAN PROPRIETORS. Owners of lands bounded by a river or watercourse.

RISCUS. L. Lat. In the civil law. A chest for the keeping of clothing. Calvin.

RISK. In insurance law; the danger or hazard of a loss of the property insured; the casualty contemplated in a contract of insurance; the degree of hazard; and, colloquially, the specific house, factory, ship, etc., covered by the policy.

RISKS OF NAVIGATION. It is held that this term is not the equivalent of "perils of navigation," but is of more comprehensive import than the latter. 48 N. Y. 419.

RISTOURNE. Fr. In insurance law; the dissolution of a policy or contract of insurance for any cause. Emerig. Traité des Assur. c. 16.

RITE. Lat. Duly and formally; legally; properly; technically.

RIVAGE. In French law. The shore, as of the sea.

In English law. A toll anciently paid to the crown for the passage of boats or vessels on certain rivers. Cowell.

RIVEARE. To have the liberty of a river for fishing and fowling. Cowell.

RIVER. A natural stream of water, of greater volume than a creek or rivulet, flowing in a more or less permanent bed or channel, between defined banks or walls, with a current which may either be continuous in one direction or affected by the ebb and flow of the tide.

Rivers are public or private; and of public rivers some are navigable and others not. The common-law distinction is that navigable rivers are those only wherein the tide ebbs and flows. But, in familiar usage, any river is navigable which affords passage to ships and vessels, irrespective of its being affected by the tide.

RIXA. Lat. In the civil law. A quarrel; a strife of words. Calvin.

RIXATRIX. In old English law. A scold; a scolding or quarrelsome woman. 4 Bl. Comm. 168.

ROAD. A way or passage; a line of travel or communication extending from one town or place to another.

"Road" and "way" are not synonymous terms. "Road" is used to designate the land over which a way, public or private, is established. 3 Nev. 361.

Roads are of two kinds,—*public* and *private*. Public roads are those which are made use of as highways, which are generally furnished and kept up by the owners of the estates adjacent to them. Private roads are those which are only open for the benefit of certain individuals, to go from and to their homes, for the service of their lands, and for the use of some estates exclusively. Civil Code La. art. 704.

In maritime law. An open passage of the sea that receives its denomination commonly from some part adjacent, which, though it lie out at sea, yet, in respect of the situation of the land adjacent, and the depth and wideness of the place, is a safe place for the common riding or anchoring of ships; as Dover road, Kirkley road, etc. Hale de Jure Mar. pt. 2, c. 2.

ROADSTED. In maritime law. A known general station for ships, notoriously used as such, and distinguished by the name; and not any spot where an anchor will find bottom and fix itself. 1 C. Rob. Adm. 232.

ROBBATOR. In old English law. A robber. *Robbatores et burglatores*, robbers and burglars. Bract. fol. 115*b*.

ROBBER. One who commits a robbery.

ROBBERY. Robbery is the felonious taking of personal property in the possession of another, from his person or immediate presence, and against his will, accomplished by means of force or fear. Pen. Code Cal. § 211; 1 Hawk. P. C. 25; 4 Bl. Comm. 243; 3 Wash. C. C. 209; 15 Ind. 288; 16 Miss. 401.

Robbery is the wrongful, fraudulent, and violent taking of money, goods, or chattels, from the person of another by force or intimidation, without the consent of the owner. Code Ga. 1882, § 4389.

Robbery is where a person, either with violence or with threats of injury, and putting the person robbed in fear, takes and carries away a thing which is on the body, or in the immediate presence of the person from whom it is taken, under such circumstances that, in the absence of violence or threats, the act committed would be a theft. Steph. Crim. Dig. 208; 2 Russ. Crimes, 78.

ROBE. Fr. A word anciently used by sailors for the cargo of a ship. The Italian "*roba*" had the same meaning.

ROBERDSMEN. In old English law. Persons who, in the reign of Richard I., committed great outrages on the borders of England and Scotland. Said to have been the followers of Robert Hood, or Robin Hood. 4 Bl. Comm. 246.

ROD. A lineal measure of sixteen feet and a half, otherwise called a "perch."

ROD KNIGHTS. In feudal law. Certain servitors who held their land by serving their lords on horseback. Cowell.

ROGARE. Lat. In Roman law. To ask or solicit. *Rogare legem*, to ask for the adoption of a law, *i. e.*, to propose it for enactment, to bring in a bill. In a derivative sense, to vote for a law so proposed; to adopt or enact it.

ROGATIO. Lat. In Roman law. An asking for a law; a proposal of a law for adoption or passage. Derivatively, a law passed by such a form.

ROGATIO TESTIUM, in making a nuncupative will, is where the testator formally calls upon the persons present to bear witness that he has declared his will. Williams, Ex'rs, 116; Browne, Prob. Pr. 59.

ROGATION WEEK. The second week before Whitsunday, thus called from three fasts observed therein, the Monday, Tuesday, and Wednesday, called "Rogation days," because of the extraordinary prayers then made for the fruits of the earth, or as a preparation for the devotion of Holy Thursday. Wharton.

Rogationes, quæstiones, et positiones debent esse simplices. Hob. 143. Demands, questions, and claims ought to be simple.

ROGATOR. Lat. In Roman law. The proposer of a law or rogation.

ROGATORY LETTERS. A commission from one judge to another requesting him to examine a witness.

ROGO. Lat. In Roman law. I ask; I request. A precatory expression often used in wills. Dig. 30, 108, 13, 14.

ROGUE. In English criminal law. An idle and disorderly person; a trickster; a wandering beggar; a vagrant or vagabond. 4 Bl. Comm. 169.

ROLE D'ÉQUIPAGE. In French mercantile law. The list of a ship's crew; a muster roll.

ROLL. A schedule of parchment which may be turned up with the hand in the form of a pipe or tube. Jacob.

A schedule or sheet of parchment on which legal proceedings are entered. Thus, in English practice, the roll of parchment on which the issue is entered is termed the "issue roll." So the rolls of a manor, wherein the names, rents, and services of the tenants are copied and enrolled, are termed the "court rolls." There are also various other rolls; as those which contain the records of the court of chancery, those which contain the registers of the proceedings of old parliaments, called "rolls of parliament," etc. Brown.

In English practice, there were formerly a great variety of these rolls, appropriated to the different proceedings; such as the *warrant of attorney* roll, the *process* roll, the *recognizance* roll, the *imparlance* roll, the *plea* roll, the *issue* roll, the *judgment* roll, the *scire facias* roll, and the roll of proceedings on writs of *error*. 2 Tidd, Pr. 729, 730.

In modern practice, the term is sometimes used to denote a record of the proceedings of a court or public office. Thus, the "judgment roll" is the file of records comprising the pleadings in a case, and all the other proceedings up to the judgment, arranged in order. In this sense the use of the word has survived its appropriateness; for such records are no longer prepared in the form of a roll.

ROLLING STOCK. The portable or movable apparatus and machinery of a railroad, particularly such as moves on the road, viz., engines, cars, tenders, coaches, and trucks.

ROLLING STOCK PROTECTION ACT. The act of 35 & 36 Vict. c. 50, passed to protect the rolling stock of railways from distress or sale in certain cases.

ROLLS, MASTER OF THE. See MASTER OF THE ROLLS.

ROLLS OF PARLIAMENT. The manuscript registers of the proceedings of old parliaments; in these rolls are likewise a great many decisions of difficult points of law, which were frequently, in former times, referred to the determination of this supreme court by the judges of both benches, etc.

ROLLS OF THE EXCHEQUER. There are several in this court relating to the revenue of the country.

ROLLS OF THE TEMPLE. In English law. In each of the two Temples is a roll called the "calves-head roll," wherein every bencher, barrister, and student is taxed yearly; also meals to the cook and other officers of the houses, in consideration of a dinner of calves-head, provided in Easter term. Orig. Jur. 199.

ROLLS OFFICE OF THE CHANCERY. In English law. An office in Chancery Lane, London, which contains rolls and records of the high court of chancery, the master whereof is the second person in the chancery, etc. The rolls court was there held, the master of the rolls sitting as judge; and that judge still sits there as a judge of the chancery division of the high court of justice. Wharton.

ROMA PEDITÆ. Pilgrims that traveled to Rome on foot.

ROMAN CATHOLIC CHARITIES ACT. The statute 23 & 24 Vict. c. 134, providing a method for enjoying estates given upon trust for Roman Catholics, but invalidated by reason of certain of the trusts being superstitious or otherwise illegal. 3 Steph. Comm. 76.

ROMAN LAW. This term, in a general sense, comprehends all the laws which prevailed among the Romans, without regard to the time of their origin, including the collections of Justinian.

In a more restricted sense, the Germans understand by this term merely the law of Justinian, as adopted by them. Mackeld. Rom. Law, § 18.

In England and America, it appears to be customary to use the phrase, indifferently with "the civil law," to designate the whole system of Roman jurisprudence, including the *Corpus Juris Civilis;* or, if any distinction is drawn, the expression "civil law" denotes the system of jurisprudence obtaining in those countries of continental Europe which have derived their juridical notions and principles from the Justinian collection, while "Roman law" is reserved as the proper appellation of the body of law developed under the government of Rome from the earliest times to the fall of the empire.

ROME-SCOT, or ROME-PENNY. Peter-pence, (*q. v.*) Cowell.

ROMNEY MARSH. A tract of land in the county of Kent, England, containing twenty-four thousand acres, governed by certain ancient and equitable laws of sewers, composed by Henry de Bathe, a venerable judge in the reign of king Henry III.; from which laws all commissioners of sewers in England may receive light and direction. 3 Bl. Comm. 73, note *t;* 4 Inst. 276.

ROOD OF LAND. The fourth part of an acre in square measure, or one thousand two hundred and ten square yards.

ROOT. The under-ground portion of a tree or plant, which serves to support and nourish it.

ROOT OF DESCENT. The same as "stock of descent."

ROOT OF TITLE. The document with which an abstract of title properly commences is called the "root" of the title. Sweet.

ROS. A kind of rushes, which some tenants were obliged by their tenure to furnish their lords withal. Cowell.

ROSLAND. Heathy ground, or ground full of ling; also watery and moorish land. 1 Inst. 5.

ROSTER. A list of persons who are to perform certain legal duties when called upon in their turn. In military affairs it is a table or plan by which the duty of officers is regulated.

ROTA. L. Lat. Succession; rotation. "*Rota* of presentations;" "*rota* of the terms." 2 W. Bl. 772, 773.

The name of two ancient courts, one held at Rome and the other at Genoa.

ROTA. Span. In Spanish law. Obliterated. White, New Recop. b. 3, tit. 7, c. 5, § 2.

ROTHER-BEASTS. A term which includes oxen, cows, steers, heifers, and such like horned animals. Cowell.

ROTTEN BOROUGHS. Small boroughs in England, which prior to the reform act, 1832, returned one or more members to parliament.

ROTTEN CLAUSE. A clause sometimes inserted in policies of marine insurance, to the effect that "if, on a regular survey, the ship shall be declared unseaworthy by reason of being *rotten* or unsound," the insurers shall be discharged. 1 Phil. Ins. § 849.

ROTULUS WINTONIÆ. The roll of Winton. An exact survey of all England, made by Alfred, not unlike that of Domesday; and it was so called because it was kept at Winchester, among other records of the kingdom; but this roll time has destroyed. Ingulph. Hist. 516.

ROTURE. Fr. In old French and Canadian law. A free tenure without the privilege of nobility; the tenure of a free commoner.

ROTURIER. Fr. In old French and Canadian law. A free tenant of land on services exigible either in money or in kind. Steph. Lect. 229. A free commoner; one who held of a superior, but could have no inferior below him.

ROUND-ROBIN. A circle divided from the center, like Arthur's round table, whence its supposed origin. In each compartment is a signature, so that the entire circle, when filled, exhibits a list, without priority being given to any name. A common form of round-robin is simply to write the names in a circular form. Wharton.

ROUP. In Scotch law. A sale by auction. Bell.

ROUT. A rout is an unlawful assembly which has made a motion towards the execution of the common purpose of the persons assembled. It is, therefore, between an unlawful assembly and a riot. Steph. Crim. Dig. 41.

Whenever two or more persons, assembled and acting together, make any attempt or advance toward the commission of an act which would be a riot if actually committed, such assembly is a rout. Pen. Code Cal. § 406.

ROUTE. Fr. In French insurance law. The way that is taken to make the voyage insured. The direction of the voyage assured.

ROUTOUSLY. In pleading. A technical word in indictments, generally coupled with the word "riotously." 2 Chit. Crim. Law, 488.

ROY. L. Fr. The king.

Roy est l'original de touts franchises. Keilw. 138. The king is the origin of all franchises.

Roy n'est lie per ascun statute si il ne soit expressment nosme. The king is not bound by any statute, unless expressly named. Jenk. Cent. 307; Broom, Max. 72.

Roy poet dispenser ove malum prohibitum, mais non malum per se. Jenk. Cent. 307. The king can grant a dispensation for a *malum prohibitum*, but not for a *malum per se*.

ROYAL ASSENT. The royal assent is the last form through which a bill goes previously to becoming an act of parliament. It is, in the words of Lord Hale, "the complement and perfection of a law." The royal assent is given either by the queen in person or by royal commission by the queen herself, signed with her own hand. It is rarely given in person, except when at the end of the session the queen attends to prorogue parliament, if she should do so. Brown.

ROYAL BURGHS. Boroughs incorporated in Scotland by royal charter. Bell.

ROYAL COURTS OF JUSTICE. Under the statute 42 & 43 Vict. c. 78, § 28, this is the name given to the buildings, together with all additions thereto, erected under the courts of justice building act, 1865, (28 & 29 Vict. c. 48,) and courts of justice concentration (site) act, 1865, (28 & 29 Vict. c. 49.) Brown.

ROYAL FISH. Whale and sturgeon: so called in English law, as belonging to the king by prerogative, when thrown ashore, or caught near the coast. A branch of the king's ordinary revenue. 1 Bl. Comm. 290; 2 Steph. Comm. 554.

ROYAL GRANTS. Conveyances of record, in England. They are of two kinds: (1) Letters patent; and (2) letters close, or writs close. 1 Steph. Comm. 615-618.

ROYAL HONORS. In the language of diplomacy, this term designates the privilege enjoyed by every empire or kingdom in Europe, by the pope, the grand duchies of Germany, and the Germanic and Swiss confederations, to precedence over all others who do not enjoy the same rank, with the exclusive right of sending to other states public ministers of the first rank, as ambassadors, together with other distinctive titles and ceremonies. Wheat. Int. Law, pt. 2, c. 3, § 2.

ROYAL MINES. Mines of silver and gold belonged to the king of England, as part of his prerogative of coinage, to furnish him with material. 1 Bl. Comm. 294.

ROYALTIES. Regalities; royal property.

ROYALTY. A payment reserved by the grantor of a patent, lease of a mine, or similar right, and payable proportionately to the use made of the right by the grantee.

Royalty also sometimes means a payment which is made to an author or composer by an assignee or licensee in respect of each copy of his work which is sold, or to an inventor in respect of each article sold under the patent. Sweet.

RUBRIC. Directions printed in books of law and in prayer-books, so termed because they were originally distinguished by red ink.

RUBRIC OF A STATUTE. Its title, which was anciently printed in red letters. It serves to show the object of the legislature, and thence affords the means of interpreting the body of the act; hence the phrase, of an argument, "*a rubro ad nigrum.*" Wharton.

RUDENESS. Roughness; incivility; violence. Touching another with rudeness may constitute a battery.

RUINA. Lat. In the civil law. Ruin; the falling of a house. Dig. 47, 9.

RULE, *v.* This verb has two significations: (1) to command or require by a rule of court; as, to rule the sheriff to return the writ, to rule the defendant to plead. (2) To settle or decide a point of law arising upon a trial at *nisi prius;* and, when it is said of a judge presiding at such a trial that he "ruled" so and so, it is meant that he laid down, settled, or decided such and such to be the law.

RULE, *n.* 1. An established standard, guide, or regulation; a principle or regulation set up by authority, prescribing or directing action or forbearance; as, the rules of a legislative body, of a company, court, public office, of the law, of ethics.

2. A regulation made by a court of justice or public office with reference to the conduct of business therein.

3. An order made by a court, at the instance of one of the parties to a suit, commanding a ministerial officer, or the opposite party, to do some act, or to show cause why some act should not be done. It is usually upon some interlocutory matter, and has not the force or solemnity of a decree or judgment.

4. "Rule" sometimes means a rule of law. Thus, we speak of the rule against perpetuities; the rule in Shelley's Case, etc.

RULE ABSOLUTE. One which commands the subject-matter of the rule to be forthwith enforced. It is usual, when the party has failed to show sufficient cause against a rule *nisi*, to "make the rule absolute," *i. e.*, imperative and final.

RULE-DAY. In practice. The day on which a rule is returnable, or on which the act or duty enjoined by a rule is to be performed.

RULE IN SHELLEY'S CASE. A celebrated rule in English law, propounded in Lord Coke's reports in the following form: That whenever a man, by any gift or conveyance, takes an estate of freehold, and in the same gift or conveyance an estate is limited, either mediately or immediately, to his heirs in fee or in tail, the word "heirs" is a word of *limitation* and not of *purchase*. In other words, it is to be understood as expressing the quantity of estate which the party is to take, and not as conferring any distinct estate on the persons who may become his representatives. 1 Coke, 104*a*; 1 Steph. Comm. 308.

RULE NISI. A rule which will become imperative and final *unless* cause be shown against it. This rule commands the party to show cause why he should not be compelled to do the act required, or why the object of the rule should not be enforced.

RULE OF 1756. A rule of international law, first practically established in 1756, by which neutrals, in time of war, are prohibited from carrying on with a belligerent power a trade which is not open to them in time of peace. 1 Kent, Comm. 82.

RULE OF COURSE. There are some rules which the courts authorize their officers to grant as a matter of course, without formal application being made to a judge in open court, and these are technically termed, in English practice, "side-bar rules," because formerly they were moved for by the the attorneys at the side bar in court. They are now generally termed "rules of course." Brown.

RULE OF LAW. A legal principle, of general application, sanctioned by the recognition of authorities, and usually expressed in the form of a maxim or logical proposition. Called a "rule," because in doubtful or unforeseen cases it is a guide or norm for their decision. Toullier, tit. prel. no. 17.

RULE OF PROPERTY. A settled rule or principle, resting usually on precedents or a course of decisions, regulating the ownership or devolution of property.

RULE OF THE ROAD. The popular English name for the regulations governing the navigation of vessels in public waters, with a view to preventing collisions. Sweet.

RULE TO PLEAD. A rule of court, taken by a plaintiff as of course, requiring the defendant to plead within a given time, on pain of having judgment taken against him by default.

RULE TO SHOW CAUSE. A rule commanding the party to appear and show cause why he should not be compelled to do the act required, or why the object of the rule should not be enforced; a rule *nisi*, (*q. v.*)

RULES. In American practice. This term is sometimes used, by metonymy, to denote a time or season in the judicial year when motions may be made and rules taken; as special terms or argument-days, or even the vacations, as distinguished from the regular terms of the courts for the trial of causes; and, by a further extension of its meaning, it may denote proceedings in an action taken out of court. Thus, "an irregularity committed *at rules* may be corrected at the next term of the court." 12 Grat. 312.

RULES OF A PRISON. Certain limits without the walls, within which all prisoners in custody in civil actions were allowed to live, upon giving sufficient security to the marshal not to escape.

RULES OF COURT. The rules for regulating the practice of the different courts, which the judges are empowered to frame and put in force as occasion may require, are termed "rules of court." Brown.

RULES OF PRACTICE. Certain orders made by the courts for the purpose of regulating the practice in actions and other proceedings before them.

RULES OF THE KING'S BENCH PRISON. In English practice. Certain limits beyond the walls of the prison, within which all prisoners in custody in civil actions were allowed to live, upon giving security by bond, with two sufficient sureties, to the marshal, not to escape, and paying him a certain percentage on the amount of the debts for which they were detained. Holthouse.

RUMOR. Flying or popular report; a current story passing from one person to another without any known authority for the truth of it. Webster. It is not generally admissible in evidence.

RUN, *v.* To have currency or legal validity in a prescribed territory; as, the writ *runs* throughout the county.

To have applicability or legal effect during a prescribed period of time; as, the statute of limitations has *run* against the claim.

To follow or accompany; to be attached to another thing in pursuing a prescribed course or direction; as, the covenant *runs* with the land.

RUN, *n.* In American law. A water-course of small size. 2 Bibb, 354.

RUNCARIA. In old records. Land full of brambles and briars. 1 Inst. 5*a*.

RUNCINUS. In old English law. A load-horse; a sumpter-horse or cart-horse.

RUNDLET, or RUNLET. A measure of wine, oil, etc., containing eighteen gallons and a half. Cowell.

RUNNING ACCOUNT. An open unsettled account, as distinguished from a stated and liquidated account. "Running accounts mean mutual accounts and reciprocal demands between the parties, which accounts and demands remain open and unsettled." 1 Ind. 335.

RUNNING AT LARGE. This term is applied to wandering or straying animals.

RUNNING DAYS. Days counted in their regular succession on the calendar, including Sundays and holidays.

RUNNING OF THE STATUTE OF LIMITATIONS. A metaphorical expression, by which is meant that the time mentioned in the statute of limitations is considered as passing. 1 Bouv. Inst. no. 861.

RUNNING POLICY. A running policy is one which contemplates successive insurances, and which provides that the object of the policy may be from time to time defined, especially as to the subjects of insurance, by additional statements or indorsements. Civil Code Cal. § 2597.

RUNNING WITH THE LAND. A covenant is said to run with the land when either the liability to perform it or the right to take advantage of it passes to the assignee of that land. Brown.

RUNNING WITH THE REVERSION. A covenant is said to "run with the reversion" when either the liability to perform it or the right to take advantage of it passes to the assignee of that reversion. Brown.

RUNRIG LANDS. Lands in Scotland where the ridges of a field belong alternatively to different proprietors. Anciently this kind of possession was advantageous in giving a united interest to tenants to resist inroads. By the act of 1695, c. 23, a division of these lands was authorized, with the exception of lands belonging to corporations. Wharton.

RUPEE. A silver coin of India, rated at 2s. for the current, and 2s. 3d. for the Bombay, rupee.

RUPTUM. Lat. In the civil law. Broken. A term applied to a will. Inst. 2, 17, 3.

RURAL DEANERY. The circuit of an archdeacon's and rural dean's jurisdictions. Every rural deanery is divided into parishes. See 1 Steph. Comm. 117.

RURAL DEANS. In English ecclesiastical law. Very ancient officers of the church, almost grown out of use, until about the middle of the present century, about which time they were generally revived, whose deaneries are as an ecclesiastical division of the diocese or archdeaconry. They are deputies of the bishop, planted all round his diocese, to inspect the conduct of the parochial clergy, to inquire into and report dilapidations, and to examine candidates for confirmation, armed in minuter matters with an inferior degree of judicial and coercive authority. Wharton.

RURAL SERVITUDE. In the civil law. A servitude annexed to a rural estate, (*prædium rusticum.*)

RUSE DE GUERRE. Fr. A trick in war; a stratagem.

RUSTICI. Lat. In feudal law. Natives of a conquered country.

In old English law. Inferior country tenants, churls, or chorls, who held cottages and lands by the services of plowing, and other labors of agriculture, for the lord. Cowell.

RUSTICUM JUDICIUM. In maritime law. A rough or rude judgment or decision. A judgment in admiralty dividing the damages caused by a collision between the two ships. 3 Kent, Comm. 231; Story, Bailm. § 608*a*.

RUTA. In the civil law. Things extracted from land; as sand, chalk, coal, and such other matters.

RUTA ET CÆSA. In the civil law. Things dug, (as sand and lime,) and things cut, (as wood, coal, etc.) Dig. 19, 1, 17, 6. Words used in conveyancing.

RYOT. In India. A peasant, subject, or tenant of house or land. Wharton.

RYOT-TENURE. A system of land-tenure, where the government takes the place of land-owners and collects the rent by means of tax gatherers. The farming is done by poor peasants, (ryots,) who find the capital, so far as there is any, and also do the work. The system exists in Turkey, Egypt, Persia, and other Eastern countries, and in a modified form in British India. After slavery, it is accounted the worst of all systems, because the government can fix the rent at what it pleases, and it is difficult to distinguish between rent and taxes.

S.

S. As an abbreviation, this letter stands for "section," "statute," and various other words of which it is the initial.

S. B. An abbreviation for "senate bill."

S. C. An abbreviation for "same case." Inserted between two citations, it indicates that the same case is reported in both places. It is also an abbreviation for "supreme court," and for "select cases;" also for "South Carolina."

S. D. An abbreviation for "southern district."

S. F. S. An abbreviation in the civil law for "*sine fraude sua,*" (without fraud on his part.) Calvin.

S. L. An abbreviation for "session [or statute] laws."

S. P. An abbreviation of "*sine prole,*" without issue. Also an abbreviation of "same principle," or "same point," indicating, when inserted between two citations, that the second involves the same doctrine as the first.

S. V. An abbreviation for "*sub voce,*" under the word; used in references to dictionaries, and other works arranged alphabetically.

SABBATH. One of the names of the first day of the week; more properly called "Sunday," (*q. v.*)

SABBATH-BREAKING. The offense of violating the laws prescribed for the observance of Sunday.

SABBATUM. The Sabbath; also peace. Domesday.

SABBULONARIUM. A gravel pit, or liberty to dig gravel and sand; money paid for the same. Cowell.

SABINIANS. A school or sect of Roman jurists, under the early empire, founded by Ateius Capito, who was succeeded by M. Sabinus, from whom the name.

SABLE. The heraldic term for black. It is called "Saturn," by those who blazon by planets, and "diamond," by those who use the names of jewels. Engravers commonly represent it by numerous perpendicular and horizontal lines, crossing each other. Wharton.

SABURRA. L. Lat. In old maritime law. Ballast.

SAC. In old English law. A liberty of holding pleas; the jurisdiction of a manor court; the privilege claimed by a lord of trying actions of trespass between his tenants, in his manor court, and imposing fines and amerciaments in the same.

SACABURTH, SACABERE, SAKABERE. In old English law. He that is robbed, or by theft deprived of his money or goods, and puts in surety to prosecute the felon with fresh suit. Bract. fol. 154*b*.

SACCABOR. In old English law. The person from whom a thing had been stolen, and by whom the thief was freshly pursued. Bract. fol. 154*b*. See SACABURTH.

SACCULARII. In Roman law. Cutpurses. 4 Steph. Comm. 125.

SACCUS. L. Lat. In old English law. A sack. A quantity of wool weighing thirty or twenty-eight stone. Fleta, l. 2, c. 79, § 10.

SACCUS CUM BROCHIA. In old English law. A service or tenure of finding a sack and a broach (pitcher) to the sovereign for the use of the army. Bract. l. 2, c. 16.

SACQUIER. In maritime law. The name of an ancient officer, whose business was to load and unload vessels laden with salt, corn, or fish, to prevent the ship's crew defrauding the merchant by false tale, or cheating him of his merchandise otherwise. Laws Oleron, art. 11; 1 Pet. Adm. Append. 25.

SACRA. Lat. In Roman law. The right to participate in the sacred rites of the city. Butl. Hor. Jur. 27.

SACRAMENTALES. In feudal law. Compurgators; persons who came to purge a defendant by their oath that they believed him innocent.

SACRAMENTI ACTIO. In the older practice of the Roman law, this was one of the forms of *legis actio*, consisting in the deposit of a stake or juridical wager. See SACRAMENTUM.

SACRAMENTUM. Lat. **In Roman law.** An oath, as being a very sacred thing; more particularly, the oath taken by soldiers to be true to their general and their country. Ainsw. Lex.

In one of the formal methods of beginning an action at law (*legis actiones*) known to the early Roman jurisprudence, the *sacramentum* was a sum of money deposited in court by each of the litigating parties, as a kind of wager or forfeit, to abide the result of the suit. The successful party received back his stake; the losing party forfeited his, and it was paid into the public treasury, to be expended for sacred objects, (*in sacris rebus,*) whence the name. See Mackeld. Rom. Law, § 203.

In common law. An oath. Cowell.

SACRAMENTUM DECISIONIS. The voluntary or decisive oath of the civil law, where one of the parties to a suit, not being able to prove his case, offers to refer the decision of the cause to the oath of his adversary, who is bound to accept or make the same offer on his part, or the whole is considerd as confessed by him. 3 Bl. Comm. 342.

SACRAMENTUM FIDELITATIS. In old English law. The oath of fealty. Reg. Orig. 303.

Sacramentum habet in se tres comites,—veritatem, justitiam, et judicium; veritas habenda est in jurato; justitia et justicium in judice. An oath has in it three component parts,—truth, justice, and judgment; truth in the party swearing; justice and judgment in the judge administering the oath. 3 Inst. 160.

Sacramentum si fatuum fuerit, licet falsum, tamen non committit perjurium. 2 Inst. 167. A foolish oath, though false, makes not perjury.

SACRILEGE. In English criminal law. Larceny from a church. 4 Steph. Comm. 164. The crime of breaking a church or chapel, and stealing therein. 1 Russ. Crimes, 843.

In old English law. The desecration of anything considered holy; the alienation to lay-men or to profane or common purposes of what was given to religious persons and to pious uses. Cowell.

SACRILEGIUM. In the civil law. The stealing of sacred things, or things dedicated to sacred uses; the taking of things out of a holy place. Calvin.

SACRILEGUS. In the civil and common law. A sacrilegious person; one guilty of sacrilege.

Sacrilegus omnium prædonum cupiditatem et scelera superat. 4 Coke, 106. A sacrilegious person transcends the cupidity and wickedness of all other robbers.

SACRISTAN. A sexton, anciently called "*sagerson,*" or "*sagiston;*" the keeper of things belonging to divine worship.

SADBERGE. A denomination of part of the county palatine of Durham. Wharton.

SÆMEND. In old English law. An umpire, or arbitrator.

Sæpe constitutum est, res inter alios judicatas aliis non præjudicare. It has often been settled that matters adjudged between others ought not to prejudice those who were not parties. Dig. 42, 1, 63.

Sæpe viatorem nova, non vetus, orbita fallit. 4 Inst. 34. A new road, not an old one, often deceives the traveler.

Sæpenumero ubi proprietas verborum attenditur, sensus veritatis amittitur. Oftentimes where the propriety of words is attended to, the true sense is lost. Branch, Princ.; 7 Coke, 27.

SÆVITIA. Lat. In the law of divorce. Cruelty; anything which tends to bodily harm, and in that manner renders cohabitation unsafe. 1 Hagg. Const. 458.

SAFE-CONDUCT. A guaranty or security granted by the king under the great seal to a stranger, for his safe coming into and passing out of the kingdom. Cowell.

One of the papers usually carried by vessels in time of war, and necessary to the safety of neutral merchantmen. It is in the nature of a license to the vessel to proceed on a designated voyage, and commonly contains the name of the master, the name, description, and nationality of the ship, the voyage intended, and other matters.

SAFE-PLEDGE. A surety given that a man shall appear upon a certain day. Bract. l. 4, c. 1.

SAFEGUARD. In old English law. A special privilege or license, in the form of a writ, under the great seal, granted to strangers seeking their right by course of law within the king's dominions, and apprehending violence or injury to their persons or property from others. Reg. Orig. 26.

SAGAMAN. A tale-teller; a secret accuser.

SAGES DE LA LEY. L. Fr. Sages of the law; persons learned in the law. A term applied to the chancellor and justices of the king's bench.

SAGIBARO. In old European law. A judge or justice; literally, a man of causes, or having charge or supervision of causes. One who administered justice and decided causes in the *mallum*, or public assembly. Spelman.

SAID. Before mentioned. This word is constantly used in contracts, pleadings, and other legal papers, with the same force as "aforesaid."

SAIGA. In old European law. A German coin of the value of a penny, or of three pence.

SAIL. In insurance law. To put to sea; to begin a voyage. The least locomotion, with readiness of equipment and clearance, satisfies a warranty to *sail*. 3 Barn. & Adol. 514.

SAILING. When a vessel quits her oorings, in complete readiness for sea, and is the actual and real intention of the master to proceed on the voyage, and she is afterwards stopped by head winds and comes to anchor, still intending to proceed as soon as wind and weather will permit, this is a sailing on the voyage within the terms of a policy of insurance. 20 Pick. 278.

SAILING INSTRUCTIONS. Written or printed directions, delivered by the commanding officer of a convoy to the several masters of the ships under his care, by which they are enabled to understand and answer his signals, to know the place of rendezvous appointed for the fleet in case of dispersion by storm, by an enemy, or otherwise. Without sailing instructions no vessel can have the protection and benefit of convoy. Marsh. Ins. 368.

SAILORS. Seamen; mariners.

SAINT MARTIN LE GRAND, COURT OF. An ancient court in London, of local importance, formerly held in the church from which it took its name.

SAINT SIMONISM. An elaborate form of non-communistic socialism. It is a scheme which does not contemplate an equal, but an unequal, division of the produce. It does not propose that all should be occupied alike, but differently, according to their vocation or capacity; the function of each being assigned, like grades in a regiment, by the choice of the directing authority, and the remuneration being by salary, proportioned to the importance, in the eyes of that authority, of the function itself, and the merits of the person who fulfills it. 1 Mill, Pol. Econ. 258.

SAIO. In Gothic law. The ministerial officer of a court or magistrate, who brought parties into court and executed the orders of his superior. Spelman.

SAISIE-ARRÊT. In French law. An attachment of property in the possession of a third person.

SAISIE-EXÉCUTION. In French law. A writ resembling that of *fieri facias;* defined as that species of execution by which a creditor places under the hand of justice (custody of the law) his debtor's movable property liable to seizure, in order to have it sold, so that he may obtain payment of his debt out of the proceeds. Dalloz, Dict.

SAISIE-FORAINE. In French law. A species of foreign attachment; that which a creditor, by the permission of the president of a tribunal of first instance or a *juge de paix*, may exercise, without preliminary process, upon the effects, found within the commune where he lives, belonging to his foreign debtor. Dalloz, Dict.

SAISIE-GAGERIE. In French law. A conservatory act of execution, by which the owner or principal lessor of a house or farm causes the furniture of the house or farm leased, and on which he has a lien, to be seized; similar to the *distress* of the common law. Dalloz, Dict.

SAISIE-IMMOBILIÈRE. In French law. The proceeding by which a creditor places under the hand of justice (custody of the law) the immovable property of his debtor, in order that the same may be sold, and that he may obtain payment of his debt out of the proceeds. Dalloz, Dict.

SAKE. In old English law. A lord's right of amercing his tenants in his court. Keilw. 145.

Acquittance of suit at county courts and hundred courts. Fleta, l. 1, c. 47, § 7.

SALADINE TENTH. A tax imposed in England and France, in 1188, by Pope Innocent III., to raise a fund for the crusade undertaken by Richard I. of England and

Philip Augustus of France, against Saladin, sultan of Egypt, then going to besiege Jerusalem. By this tax every person who did not enter himself a crusader was obliged to pay a tenth of his yearly revenue and of the value of all his movables, except his wearing apparel, books, and arms. The Carthusians, Bernardines, and some other religious persons were exempt. Gibbon remarks that when the necessity for this tax no longer existed, the church still clung to it as too lucrative to be abandoned, and thus arose the tithing of ecclesiastical benefices for the pope or other sovereigns. Enc. Lond.

SALARIUM. Lat. In the civil law. An allowance of provisions. A stipend, wages, or compensation for service. An annual allowance or compensation. Calvin.

SALARY. A recompense or consideration made to a person for his pains and industry in another person's business; also wages, stipend, or annual allowance. Cowell.

An annual compensation for services rendered; a fixed sum to be paid by the year for services.

"Salary" signifies the periodical compensation to men in official and some other situations. The word is derived from "*salarium*," which is from the word "*sal*," salt, that being an article in which the Roman soldiers were paid. 10 Ind. 88.

SALE. A contract between two parties, called, respectively, the "seller" (or vendor) and the "buyer," (or purchaser,) by which the former, in consideration of the payment or promise of payment of a certain price in money, transfers to the latter the title and the possession of an object of property. See Pard. Droit Commer. § 6; 2 Kent, Comm. 363; Poth. Cont. Sale, § 1.

Sale is a contract by which, for a pecuniary consideration called a "price," one transfers to another an interest in property. Civil Code Cal. § 1721.

The contract of sale is an agreement by which one gives a thing for a price in current money, and the other gives the price in order to have the thing itself. Three circumstances concur to the perfection of the contract, to-wit, the thing sold, the price, and the consent. Civil Code La. art. 2439.

A transmutation of property from one man to another in consideration of some price or recompense in value. 2 Bl. Comm. 446.

"Sale" is a word of precise legal import, both at law and in equity. It means, at all times, a contract between parties to give and to pass rights of property for money, which the buyer pays or promises to pay to the seller for the thing bought and sold. 8 How. 495, 544; (Or.) 26 Pac. Rep. 565.

Synonyms. The contract of "sale" is distinguished from "barter" (which applies only to goods) and "exchange," (which is used of both land and goods,) in that both the latter terms denote a commutation of property for property; *i. e.*, the price or consideration is always paid in money if the transaction is a sale, but, if it is a barter or exchange, it is paid in specific property susceptible of valuation. "Sale" differs from "gift" in that the latter transaction involves no return or recompense for the thing transferred. But an onerous gift sometimes approaches the nature of a sale, at least where the charge it imposes is a payment of money. "Sale" is also to be discriminated from "bailment;" and the difference is to be found in the fact that the contract of bailment always contemplates the return to the bailor of the specific article delivered, either in its original form or in a modified or altered form, or the return of an article which, though not identical, is of the same class, and is equivalent. But sale never involves the return of the article itself, but only a consideration in money. This contract differs also from "accord and satisfaction;" because in the latter the object of transferring the property is to compromise and settle a claim, while the object of a sale is the price given.

SALE AND RETURN. This is a species of contract by which the seller (usually a manufacturer or wholesaler) delivers a quantity of goods to the buyer, on the understanding that, if the latter should desire to retain or use or resell any portion of such goods; he will consider such part as having been sold to him, and will pay their price, and the balance he will return to the seller, or hold them, as bailee, subject to his order.

SALE IN GROSS. The term "sale in gross," when applied to the thing sold, means a sale by the tract, without regard to quantity, and is in that sense a contract of hazard. 77 Va. 616.

SALE-NOTE. A memorandum of the subject and terms of a sale, given by a broker or factor to the seller, who bailed him the goods for that purpose, and to the buyer, who dealt with him. Also called "bought and sold notes."

SALE ON CREDIT. A sale of property accompanied by delivery of possession, but where payment of the price is deferred to a future day.

SALE ON APPROVAL. A species of conditional sale, which is to become absolute only in case the buyer, on trial, approves or is satisfied with the article sold. The approval, however, need not be express; it may be inferred from his keeping the goods beyond a reasonable time. Benj. Sales, § 911.

SALE WITH ALL FAULTS. On what is called a "sale with all faults," unless the seller fraudulently and inconsistently represents the article sold to be faultless, or contrives to conceal any fault from the purchaser, the latter must take the article for better or worse. 3 Camp. 154; Brown.

SALET. In old English law. A headpiece; a steel cap or morion. Cowell.

SALFORD HUNDRED COURT OF RECORD. An inferior and local court of record having jurisdiction in personal actions where the debt or damage sought to be recovered does not exceed £50, if the cause of action arise within the hundred of Salford. St. 31 & 32 Vict. c. 130; 2 Exch. Div. 346.

SALIC LAW. A body of law framed by the Salian Franks, after their settlement in Gaul under their king Pharamond, about the beginning of the fifth century. It is the most ancient of the barbarian codes, and is considered one of the most important compilations of law in use among the feudal nations of Europe. See LEX SALICA.

In French jurisprudence. The name is frequently applied to that fundamental law of France which excluded females from succession to the crown. Supposed to have been derived from the sixty-second title of the Salic Law, "De Alode." Brande.

SALOON does not necessarily import a place to sell liquors. It may mean a place for the sale of general refreshments. 26 Mich. 325.

"Saloon" has not acquired the legal signification of a house kept for retailing intoxicating liquor. It may mean a room for the reception of company, for exhibition of works of art, etc. 36 Tex. 364.

SALOON-KEEPER. This expression has a definite meaning, namely, a retailer of cigars, liquors, etc. 105 Mass. 40.

SALT DUTY IN LONDON. A custom in the city of London called "granage," formerly payable to the lord mayor, etc., for salt brought to the port of London, being the twentieth part. Wharton.

SALT SILVER. One penny paid at the feast day of St. Martin, by the tenants of some manors, as a commutation for the service of carrying their lord's salt from market to his larder. Paroch. Antiq. 496.

SALUS. Lat. Health; prosperity; safety.

Salus populi suprema lex. The welfare of the people is the supreme law. Bac. Max. reg. 12; Broom, Max. 1–10; Montesq. Esprit des Lois, lib. 26, c. 23; 13 Coke, 139.

Salus reipublicæ suprema lex. The welfare of the state is the supreme law. 4 Cush. 71; 1 Gray, 386; Broom, Max. 366.

Salus ubi multi consiliarii. 4 Inst. 1. Where there are many counselors, there is safety.

SALUTE. A gold coin stamped by Henry V. in France, after his conquests there, whereon the arms of England and France were stamped quarterly. Cowell.

SALVA GARDIA. L. Lat. Safeguard. Reg. Orig. 26.

SALVAGE. In maritime law. A compensation allowed to persons by whose assistance a ship or its cargo has been saved, in whole or in part, from impending danger, or recovered from actual loss, in cases of shipwreck, derelict, or recapture. 3 Kent, Comm. 245.

In the older books of the law, (and sometimes in modern writings,) the term is also used to denote the goods or property saved.

EQUITABLE SALVAGE. By analogy, the term "salvage" is sometimes also used in cases which have nothing to do with maritime perils, but in which property has been preserved from loss by the last of several advances by different persons. In such a case, the person making the last advance is frequently entitled to priority over the others, on the ground that, without his advance, the property would have been lost altogether. This right, which is sometimes called that of "equitable salvage," and is in the nature of a lien, is chiefly of importance with reference to payments made to prevent leases or policies of insurance from being forfeited, or to prevent mines and similar undertakings from being stopped or injured. See 1 Fish. Mortg. 149; 3 Ch. Div. 411; L. R. 14 Eq. 4; 7 Ch. Div. 825.

SALVAGE CHARGES. This term includes all the expenses and costs incurred in the work of saving and preserving the property which was in danger. The salvage charges ultimately fall upon the insurers.

SALVAGE LOSS. In the language of marine underwriters, this term means the difference between the amount of salvage, after deducting the charges, and the original value of the property insured.

SALVAGE SERVICE. In maritime law. Any service rendered in saving property on the sea, or wrecked on the coast of the sea. 1 Sum. 210.

SALVIAN INTERDICT. See INTERDICTUM SALVIANUM.

SALVO. Lat. Saving; excepting; without prejudice to. *Salvo me et hæredibus meis*, except me and my heirs. *Salvo jure cujuslibet*, without prejudice to the rights of any one.

SALVOR. A person who, without any particular relation to a ship in distress, proffers useful service, and gives it as a volunteer adventurer, without any pre-existing covenant that connected him with the duty of employing himself for the preservation of that ship. 10 Pet. 122.

SALVUS PLEGIUS. L. Lat. A safe pledge; called, also, "*certus plegius*," a sure pledge. Bract. fol. 160*b*.

SAME. The word "same" does not always mean "identical," not different or other. It frequently means of the kind or species, not the specific thing. 40 Iowa, 487, 493.

SAMPLE. A specimen; a small quantity of any commodity, presented for inspection or examination as evidence of the quality of the whole; as a sample of cloth or of wheat.

SAMPLE, SALE BY. A sale at which only a sample of the goods sold is exhibited to the buyer.

SANÆ MENTIS. Lat. In old English law. Of sound mind. Fleta, lib. 3, c. 7, § 1.

SANCTIO. Lat. In the civil law. That part of a law by which a penalty was ordained against those who should violate it. Inst. 2, 1, 10.

SANCTION. In the original sense of the word, a "sanction" is a penalty or punishment provided as a means of enforcing obedience to a law. In jurisprudence, a law is said to have a sanction when there is a state which will intervene if it is disobeyed or disregarded. Therefore international law has no legal sanction. Sweet.

In a more general sense, a "sanction" has been defined as a conditional evil annexed to a law to produce obedience to that law; and, in a still wider sense, a "sanction" means simply an authorization of anything. Occasionally, "sanction" is used (*e. g.*, in Roman law) to denote a statute, the part (penal clause) being used to denote the whole. Brown.

The vindicatory part of a law, or that part which ordains or denounces a penalty for its violation. 1 Bl. Comm. 56.

SANCTUARY. In old English law. A consecrated place which had certain privileges annexed to it, and to which offenders were accustomed to resort for refuge, because they could not be arrested there, nor the laws be executed.

SAND-GAVEL. In old English law. A payment due to the lord of the manor of Rodley, in the county of Gloucester, for liberty granted to the tenants to dig sand for their common use. Cowell.

SANE. Of natural and normal mental condition; healthy in mind.

SANE MEMORY. Sound mind, memory, and understanding. This is one of the essential elements in the capacity of contracting; and the absence of it in lunatics and idiots, and its immaturity in infants, is the cause of their respective incapacities or partial incapacities to bind themselves. The like circumstance is their ground of exemption in cases of crime. Brown.

SANG, or SANC. In old French. Blood.

SANGUINE, or MURREY. An heraldic term for "blood-color," called, in the arms of princes, "dragon's tail," and, in those of lords, "sardonyx." It is a tincture of very infrequent occurrence, and not recognized by some writers. In engraving, it is denoted by numerous lines in saltire. Wharton.

SANGUINEM EMERE. Lat. In feudal law. A redemption by villeins, of their blood or tenure, in order to become freemen.

Sanguinis conjunctio benevolentia devincit homines et caritate. A tie of blood overcomes men through benevolence and family affection. 5 Johns. Ch. 1, 13.

SANGUIS. Lat. In the civil and old English law. Blood; consanguinity.

The right or power which the chief lord of the fee had to judge and determine cases where blood was shed. Mon. Ang. t. i. 1021.

SANIS. A kind of punishment among the Greeks; inflicted by binding the malefactor fast to a piece of wood. Enc. Lond.

SANITARY AUTHORITIES. In English law. Bodies having jurisdiction over their respective districts in regard to sewerage, drainage, scavenging, the supply of water, the prevention of nuisances and offensive trades, etc., all of which come under the head of "sanitary matters" in the special sense of the word. Sanitary authorities also have jurisdiction in matters coming under the head of "local government." Sweet.

SANITY. Sound understanding; the reverse of insanity, (*q. v.*)

SANS CEO QUE. L. Fr. Without this. See ABSQUE HOC.

SANS FRAIS. Fr. Without expense. See RETOUR SANS PROTÊT.

SANS IMPEACHMENT DE WAST. L. Fr. Without impeachment of waste. Litt. § 152. See ABSQUE IMPETITIONE VASTI.

SANS JOUR. Fr. Without day; *sine die.*

SANS NOMBRE. Fr. A term used in relation to the right of putting animals on a common. The term "common *sans nombre*" does not mean that the beasts are to be innumerable, but only indefinite; not certain. Willes, 227.

SANS RECOURS. Fr. Without recourse. See INDORSEMENT.

Sapiens incipit a fine, et quod primum est in intentione, ultimum est in executione. A wise man begins with the last, and what is first in intention is last in execution. 10 Coke, 25.

Sapiens omnia agit cum consilio. A wise man does everything advisedly. 4 Inst. 4.

Sapientia legis nummario pretio non est æstimanda. The wisdom of the law cannot be valued by money. Jenk. Cent. 168.

Sapientis judicis est cogitare tantum sibi esse permissum, quantum commissum et creditum. It is the part of a wise judge to think that a thing is permitted to him, only so far as it is committed and intrusted to him. 4 Inst. 163. That is, he should keep his jurisdiction within the limits of his commission.

SARCULATURA. L. Lat. In old records. Weeding corn. A tenant's service of weeding for the lord. Cowell.

SART. In old English law. A piece of woodland, turned into arable. Cowell.

SARUM. In old records. The city of Salisbury in England. Spelman.

SASINE. In Scotch law. The symbolical delivery of land, answering to the livery of seisin of the old English law. 4 Kent, Comm. 459.

SASSE. In old English law. A kind of wear with flood-gates, most commonly in cut rivers, for the shutting up and letting out of the water, as occasion required, for the more ready passing of boats and barges to and fro; a lock; a turnpike; a sluice. Cowell.

SASSONS. The corruption of Saxons. A name of contempt formerly given to the English, while they affected to be called "Angles;" they are still so called by the Welsh.

SATISDARE. Lat. In the civil law. To guaranty the obligation of a principal.

SATISDATIO. Lat. In the civil law. Security given by a party to an action, as by a defendant, to pay what might be adjudged against him. Inst. 4, 11; 3 Bl. Comm. 291.

SATISFACTION. The act of satisfying a party by paying what is due to him, (as on a mortgage, lien, or contract,) or what is awarded to him, by the judgment of a court or otherwise. Thus, a judgment is satisfied by the payment of the amount due to the party who has recovered such judgment, or by his levying the amount.

In practice. An entry made on the record, by which a party in whose favor a judgment was rendered declares that he has been satisfied and paid.

In equity. The doctrine of satisfaction in equity is somewhat analogous to performance in equity, but differs from it in this respect: that satisfaction is always something given either in whole or in part as a substitute or equivalent for something else, and not (as in performance) something that may be construed as the identical thing covenanted to be done. Brown.

SATISFACTION PIECE. In practice. A memorandum in writing, entitled in a cause, stating that satisfaction is acknowledged between the parties, plaintiff and defendant. Upon this being duly acknowledged and filed in the office where the record of the judgment is, the judgment becomes satisfied, and the defendant discharged from it. 1 Archb. Pr. 722.

Satisfaction should be made to that fund which has sustained the loss. 4 Bouv. Inst. no. 3731.

SATISFACTORY EVIDENCE. That which is sufficient to induce a belief that the thing is true; in other words, it is credible evidence. 3 Bouv. Inst. no. 3049.

SATISFIED TERM. A term of years in land is thus called when the purpose for which it was created has been satisfied or executed before the expiration of the set period.

SATISFIED TERMS ACT. The statute 8 & 9 Vict. c. 112, passed to abolish satisfied outstanding terms of years in land. By this act, terms which shall henceforth become attendant upon the inheritance, either by express *declaration* or construction of law, are to cease and determine. This, in effect, abolishes outstanding terms. 1 Steph. Comm. 380–382; Williams, Real Prop. pt. 4, c. 1.

SATISFY, in technical use, generally means to comply actually and fully with a demand; to extinguish, by payment or performance.

Satius est petere fontes quam sectari rivulos. Lofft, 606. It is better to seek the source than to follow the streamlets.

SATURDAY'S STOP. In old English law. A space of time from even-song on Saturday till sun-rising on Monday, in which it was not lawful to take salmon in Scotland and the northern parts of England. Cowell.

SAUNKEFIN. L. Fr. End of blood; failure of the direct line in successions. Spelman; Cowell.

SAUVAGINE. L. Fr. Wild animals.

SAUVEMENT. L. Fr. Safely. *Sauvement gardes,* safely kept. Britt. c. 87.

SAVE. To except, reserve, or exempt; as where a statute "saves" vested rights. To toll, or suspend the running or operation of; as to "save" the statute of limitations.

SAVER DEFAULT. L. Fr. In old English practice. To excuse a default. Termes de la Ley.

SAVING THE STATUTE OF LIMITATIONS. A creditor is said to "save the statute of limitations" when he saves or preserves his debt from being barred by the operation of the statute. Thus, in the case of a simple contract debt, if a creditor commence an action for its recovery within six years from the time when the cause of action accrued, he will be in time to save the statute. Brown.

SAVINGS BANK. An institution in the nature of a bank, formed or established for the purpose of receiving deposits of money, for the benefit of the persons depositing, to accumulate the produce of so much thereof as shall not be required by the depositors, their executors or administrators, at compound interest, and to return the whole or any part of such deposit, and the produce thereof, to the depositors, their executors or administrators, deducting out of such produce so much as shall be required for the necessary expenses attending the management of such institution, but deriving no benefit whatever from any such deposit or the produce thereof. Grant, Banks, 546.

SAVOUR. To partake the nature of; to bear affinity to.

SAVOY. One of the old privileged places, or sanctuaries. 4 Steph. Comm. 227*n*.

SAXON LAGE. The laws of the West Saxons. Cowell.

SAY ABOUT. This phrase, like "more or less," is frequently introduced into conveyances or contracts of sale, to indicate that the quantity of the subject-matter is uncertain, and is only estimated, and to guard the vendor against the implication of having warranted the quantity.

SAYER. In Hindu law. Variable imposts distinct from land, rents, or revenues; consisting of customs, tolls, licenses, duties on goods; also taxes on houses, shops, bazaars, etc. Wharton.

SC. An abbreviation for "*scilicet,*" that is to say.

SCABINI. In old European law. The judges or assessors of the judges in the court held by the count. Assistants or associates of the count; officers under the count. The permanent selected judges of the Franks. Judges among the Germans, Franks, and Lombards, who were held in peculiar esteem. Spelman.

SCACCARIUM. A chequered cloth resembling a chess-board which covered the table in the exchequer, and on which, when certain of the king's accounts were made up, the sums were marked and scored with counters. Hence the court of exchequer, or *curia scaccarii,* derived its name. 3 Bl. Comm. 44.

SCALAM. At the scale; the old way of paying money into the exchequer. Cowell.

SCALE. In early American law. To adjust, graduate, or value according to a scale. 2 Wash. (Va.) 5, 6.

SCAMNUM CADUCUM. In old records, the cucking-stool, (*q. v.*) Cowell.

SCANDAL. Defamatory reports or rumors; aspersion or slanderous talk, uttered recklessly or maliciously.

In pleading. "Scandal consists in the allegation of anything which is unbecoming the dignity of the court to hear, or is contrary to good manners, or which charges some person with a crime not necessary to be shown in the cause; to which may be added that any unnecessary allegation, bearing cruelly upon the moral character of an individual, is also scandalous." Daniell, Ch. Pr. 290.

SCANDALOUS MATTER. In equity pleading. See SCANDAL.

SCANDALUM MAGNATUM. In English law. Scandal or slander of great men or nobles. Words spoken in derogation of a peer, a judge, or other great officer of the realm, for which an action lies, though it is now rarely resorted to. 3 Bl. Comm. 123; 3 Steph. Comm. 473.

SCAPELLARE. In old European law. to chop; to chip or haggle. Spelman.

SCAPHA. Lat. In Roman law. A boat; a lighter. A ship's boat.

SCAVAGE, SCHEVAGE, SCHEWAGE, or SHEWAGE. A kind of toll or custom, exacted by mayors, sheriffs, etc., of merchant strangers, for wares showed or offered for sale within their liberties. Prohibited by 19 Hen. VII. c. 7. Cowell.

SCAVAIDUS. The officer who collected the scavage money. Cowell.

SCEATTA. A Saxon coin of less denomination than a shilling. Spelman.

SCEPPA SALIS. An ancient measure of salt, the quantity of which is now not known. Wharton.

SCHAR-PENNY, SCHARN-PENNY, or SCHORN-PENNY. A small duty or compensation. Cowell.

SCHEDULE. A sheet of paper or parchment annexed to a statute, deed, answer in equity, deposition, or other instrument, exhibiting in detail the matters mentioned or referred to in the principal document.

A list or inventory; the paper containing an inventory.

In practice. When an indictment is returned from an inferior court in obedience to a writ of *certiorari*, the statement of the previous proceedings sent with it is termed the "schedule." 1 Saund. 309*a*, n. 2.

In constitutional law. A schedule is a statement annexed to a constitution newly adopted by a state, in which are described at length the particulars in which it differs from the former constitution, or which contains provisions for the adjustment of matters affected by the change from the old to the new constitution.

SCHEME. In English law, a scheme is a document containing provisions for regulating the management or distribution of property, or for making an arrangement between persons having conflicting rights. Thus, in the practice of the chancery division, where the execution of a charitable trust in the manner directed by the founder is difficult or impracticable, or requires supervision, a scheme for the management of the charity will be settled by the court. Tud. Char. Trusts, 257; Hunt, Eq. 248; Daniell, Ch. Pr. 1765.

SCHETES. Usury. Cowell.

SCHIREMAN. In Saxon law. An officer having the civil government of a *shire*, or county; an earl. 1 Bl. Comm. 398.

SCHIRRENS-GELD. In Saxon law. A tax paid to sheriffs for keeping the shire or county court. Cowell.

SCHISM-BILL. In English law. The name of an act passed in the reign of Queen Anne, which restrained Protestant dissenters from educating their own children, and forbade all tutors and schoolmasters to be present at any conventicle or dissenting place of worship. The queen died on the day when this act was to have taken effect, (August 1, 1714,) and it was repealed in the fifth year of Geo. I. Wharton.

SCHOOL. An institution of learning of a lower grade, below a college or a university. A place of primary instruction. The term generally refers to the common or public schools, maintained at the expense of the public.

SCHOOL BOARD. A board of municipal officers charged with the administration of the affairs of the public schools. They are commonly organized under the general laws of the state, and fall within the class of *quasi* corporations, sometimes coterminous with a county or borough, but not necessarily so. The members of the school board are sometimes termed "school directors," or the official style may be "the board of school directors." The circuit of their territorial jurisdiction is called a "school-district," and each school-district is usually a separate taxing district for school purposes.

SCHOOL DIRECTORS. See SCHOOL BOARD.

SCHOOL-DISTRICT. See SCHOOL BOARD.

SCHOOL-MASTER. One employed in teaching a school.

SCHOUT. In Dutch law. An officer of a court whose functions somewhat resemble those of a sheriff.

SCI. FA. An abbreviation for "*scire facias*, (*q. v.*)

SCIENDUM. In English law. The name given to a clause inserted in the record by which it is made "known that the justice here in court, in this same term, delivered a writ thereupon to the deputy-sheriff of the county aforesaid, to be executed in due form of law." Lee. Dict. "Record."

SCIENDUM EST. Lat. It is to be known; be it remarked. In the books of the civil law, this phrase is often found at the beginning of a chapter or paragraph, by way of introduction to some explanation, or directing attention to some particular rule.

SCIENTER. Lat. Knowingly. The term is used in pleading to signify an allegation (or that part of the declaration or indictment which contains it) setting out the defendant's previous knowledge of the cause which led to the injury complained of, or rather his previous knowledge of a state of facts which it was his duty to guard against, and his omission to do which has led to the injury complained of. The insertion of such an allegation is called "laying the action (or indictment) with a *scienter*." And the term is frequently used to signify the defendant's guilty knowledge.

Scienti et volenti non fit injuria. Bract. fol. 20. An injury is not done to one who knows and wills it.

Scientia sciolorum est mixta ignorantia. 8 Coke, 159. The knowledge of smatterers is diluted ignorance.

Scientia utrimque par pares contrahentes facit. Equal knowledge on both sides makes contracting parties equal. 3 Burrows, 1905. An insured need not mention what the underwriter knows, or what he ought to know. Broom, Max. 772.

SCILICET. Lat. To-wit; that is to say. A word used in pleadings and other instruments, as introductory to a more particular statement of matters previously mentioned in general terms. Hob. 171, 172.

SCINTILLA. Lat. A spark; a remaining particle; the least particle.

SCINTILLA JURIS. In real property law. A spark of right or interest. By this figurative expression was denoted the small particle of interest which, by a fiction of law, was supposed to remain in a feoffee to uses, sufficient to support contingent uses afterwards coming into existence, and thereby enable the statute of uses (27 Hen. VIII. c. 10) to execute them. See 2 Washb. Real Prop. 125; 4 Kent, Comm. 238.

SCINTILLA OF EVIDENCE. The doctrine that where there is *any* evidence, however slight, *tending* to support a material issue, the case must go to the jury, since they are the exclusive judges of the weight of the evidence. 43 Ga. 323; 106 Mass. 271; 40 Mo. 151.

Scire debes cum quo contrahis. You ought to know with whom you deal. 11 Mees. & W. 405, 632; 13 Mees. & W. 171.

Scire et scire debere æquiparantur in jure. To know a thing, and to be bound to know it, are regarded in law as equivalent. Tray. Leg. Max. 551.

SCIRE FACIAS. Lat. In practice. A judicial writ, founded upon some record, and requiring the person against whom it is brought to show cause why the party bringing it should not have advantage of such record, or (in the case of a *scire facias* to repeal letters patent) why the record should not be annulled and vacated. 2 Archb. Pr. K. B. 86; Pub. St. Mass. p. 1295.

The most common application of this writ is as a process to revive a judgment, after the lapse of a certain time, or on a change of parties, or otherwise to have execution of the judgment, in which cases it is merely a continuation of the original action. It is used more rarely as a mode of proceeding against special bail on their recognizance, and as a means of repealing letters patent, in which cases it is an original proceeding. 2 Archb. Pr. K. B. 86.

SCIRE FACIAS AD AUDIENDUM ERRORES. The name of a writ which is sued out after the plaintiff in error has assigned his errors. Fitzh. Nat. Brev. 20.

SCIRE FACIAS AD DISPROBANDUM DEBITUM. The name of a writ in use in Pennsylvania, which lies by a defendant in foreign attachment against the plaintiff, in order to enable him, within a year and a day next ensuing the time of payment to the plaintiff in the attachment, to disprove or avoid the debt recovered against him. Bouvier.

SCIRE FACIAS AD REHABENDAM TERRAM. A *scire facias ad rehabendam terram* lies to enable a judgment debtor to recover back his lands taken under an *elegit* when the judgment creditor has satisfied or been paid the amount of his judgment. Chit. 692; Fost. on Sci. Fa. 58.

SCIRE FACIAS FOR THE CROWN. In English law. The summary proceeding by extent is only resorted to when a crown debtor is insolvent, or there is good ground for supposing that the debt may be lost by delay. In ordinary cases where a debt or duty appears by record to be owing to the crown, the process for the crown is a writ of *sci. fa. quare executionem non;* but should the defendant become insolvent pending this writ, the crown may abandon the proceeding and resort to an extent. Wharton.

SCIRE FACIAS QUARE RESTITUTIONEM NON. This writ lies where execution on a judgment has been levied, but the money has not been paid over to the plaintiff, and the judgment is afterwards reversed in error or on appeal; in such a case a *scire facias* is necessary before a writ of restitution can issue. Chit. 582; Fost. on Sci. Fa. 64.

SCIRE FACIAS SUR MORTGAGE. A writ of *scire facias* issued upon the default of a mortgagor to make payments or observe conditions, requiring him to show cause why the mortgage should not be foreclosed, and the mortgaged property taken and sold in execution.

SCIRE FACIAS SUR MUNICIPAL CLAIM. A writ of *scire facias*, authorized to be issued, in Pennsylvania, as a means of enforcing payment of a municipal claim (*q. v.*) out of the real estate upon which such claim is a lien.

SCIRE FECI. Lat. In practice. The name given to the sheriff's return to a writ of *scire facias* that he has caused notice to be given to the party or parties against whom the writ was issued. 2 Archb. Pr. K. B. 98, 99.

SCIRE FIERI INQUIRY. In English law. The name of a writ formerly used to recover the amount of a judgment from an executor.

Scire leges non hoc est verba earum tenere, sed vim ac potestatem. To know the laws is not to observe their mere words, but their force and power; [that is, the essential meaning in which their efficacy resides.] Dig. 1, 3, 17; 1 Kent, Comm. 462.

Scire proprie est rem ratione et per causam cognoscere. To know properly is to know a thing in its reason, and by its cause. We are truly said to know anything, where we know the true cause thereof. Co. Litt. 183*b*.

SCIREWYTE. In old English law. A tax or prestation paid to the sheriff for holding the assizes or county courts. Cowell.

SCISSIO. Lat. In old English law. A cutting. *Scissio auricularum*, cropping of the ears. An old punishment. Fleta, lib. 1, c. 38, § 10.

SCITE, or SITE. The sitting or standing on any place; the seat or situation of a capital messuage, or the ground whereon it stands. Jacob.

SCOLD. A troublesome and angry woman, who, by brawling and wrangling among her neighbors, breaks the public peace, increases discord, and becomes a public nuisance to the neighborhood. 4 Steph. Comm. 276.

SCOT. In old English law. A tax, or tribute; one's *share* of a contribution.

SCOT AND LOT. In English law. The name of a customary contribution, laid upon all the subjects according to their ability. Brown.

SCOT AND LOT VOTERS. In English law. Voters in certain boroughs entitled to the franchise in virtue of their paying this contribution. 2 Steph. Comm. 360.

SCOTAL. In old English law. An extortionate practice by officers of the forest who kept ale-houses, and compelled the people to drink at their houses for fear of their displeasure. Prohibited by the charter of the forest, c. 7. Wharton.

SCOTCH MARRIAGES. See GRETNA GREEN.

SCOTCH PEERS. Peers of the kingdom of Scotland; of these sixteen are elected to parliament by the rest and represent the whole body. They are elected for one parliament only.

SCOTS. In English law. Assessments by commissioners of sewers.

SCOTTARE. To pay scot, tax, or customary dues. Cowell.

SCOUNDREL. An opprobious epithet, implying rascality, villainy, or a want of honor or integrity. In slander, this word is not actionable *per se.* 2 Bouv. Inst. 2250.

SCRAMBLING POSSESSION. By this term is meant a struggle for possession on the land itself, not such a contest as is waged in the courts. 54 Cal. 176.

SCRAWL. A word used in some of the United States for scrowl or scroll. "The word 'seal,' written in a *scrawl* attached to the name of an obligor, makes the instrument a specialty." 2 Fla. 418.

SCRIBA. A scribe; a secretary. *Scriba regis*, a king's secretary; a chancellor. Spelman.

Scribere est agere. To write is to act. Treasonable words set down in writing amount to overt acts of treason. 2 Rolle, 89; 4 Bl. Comm. 80; Broom, Max. 312, 967.

SCRIP. Certificates of ownership, either absolute or conditional, of shares in a public company, corporate profits, etc. Pub. St. Mass. 1882, p. 1295.

A scrip certificate (or shortly "scrip") is an acknowledgment by the projectors of a company or the issuers of a loan that the person named therein (or more commonly the holder for the time being of the certificate) is entitled to a certain specified number of shares, debentures, bonds, etc. It is usually given in exchange for the letter of allotment, and in its turn is given up for the shares, debentures, or bonds which it represents. Lindl. Partn. 127; Sweet.

SCRIPT. Where instruments are executed in part and counterpart, the original or principal is so called.

In English probate practice. A will, codicil, draft of will or codicil, or written instructions for the same. If the will is destroyed, a copy or any paper embodying its contents becomes a script, even though not made under the direction of the testator. Browne, Prob. Pr. 280.

Scriptæ obligationes scriptis tolluntur, et nudi consensus obligatio contrario consensu dissolvitur. Written obligations are superseded by writings, and an obligation of naked assent is dissolved by assent to the contrary.

SCRIPTORIUM. In old records. A place in monasteries, where writing was done. Spelman.

SCRIPTUM. A writing; something written. Fleta, l. 2, c. 60, § 25.

SCRIPTUM INDENTATUM. A writing indented; an indenture or deed.

SCRIPTUM OBLIGATORIUM. A writing obligatory. The technical name of a bond in old pleadings. Any writing under seal.

SCRIVENER. A writer; scribe; conveyancer. One whose occupation is to draw contracts, write deeds and mortgages, and prepare other species of written instruments.

Also an agent to whom property is intrusted by others for the purpose of lending it out at an interest payable to his principal, and for a commission or bonus for himself, whereby he gains his livelihood. These are called "money scriveners." In order to make a man a money scrivener he must carry on the business of being intrusted with other people's money to lay out for them as occasion offers. 3 Camp. 534; 9 Dow, 882; Brown.

SCROLL. A mark intended to supply the place of a seal, made with a pen or other instrument of writing.

A paper or parchment containing some writing, and rolled up so as to conceal it.

SCROOP'S INN. An obsolete law society, also called "Serjeants' Place," opposite to St. Andrew's Church, Holborn, London.

SCRUET-ROLL. In old practice. A species of roll or record, on which the bail on *habeas corpus* was entered.

SCRUTATOR. Lat. In old English law. A searcher or bailiff of a river; a water-bailiff, whose business was to look to the king's rights, as his wrecks, his flotsam, jetsam, water-strays, royal fishes. Hale, de Jure Mar. pars 1, c. 5.

SCUSSUS. In old European law. Shaken or beaten out; threshed, as grain. Spelman.

SCUTAGE. In feudal law. A tax or contribution raised by those that held lands by knight's service, towards furnishing the king's army, at the rate of one, two, or three marks for every knight's fee.

A pecuniary composition or commutation made by a tenant by knight-service in lieu of actual service. 2 Bl. Comm. 74.

A pecuniary aid or tribute originally reserved by particular lords, instead or in lieu of personal service, varying in amount according to the expenditure which the lord had to incur in his personal attendance upon the king in his wars. Wright, Ten. 121–134.

SCUTAGIO HABENDO. A writ that anciently lay against tenants by knight's service to serve in the wars, or send sufficient persons, or pay a certain sum. Fitzh. Nat. Brev. 83.

SCUTE. A French coin of gold, coined A. D. 1427, of the value of 3s. 4d.

SCUTELLA. A scuttle; anything of a flat or broad shape like a shield. Cowell.

SCUTELLA ELEEMOSYNARIA. An alms-basket.

SCUTIFER. In old records. Esquire; the same as "armiger." Spelman.

SCUTUM ARMORUM. A shield or coat of arms. Cowell.

SCYRA. In old English law. Shire; county; the inhabitants of a county.

SCYREGEMOTE. In Saxon law. The meeting or court of the shire. This was the most important court in the Saxon polity, having jurisdiction of both ecclesiastical and secular causes. Its meetings were held twice in the year. Its Latin name was "*curia comitatis.*"

SE DEFENDENDO. Lat. In defending himself; in self-defense. Homicide committed *se defendendo* is excusable.

SEA. The ocean; the great mass of water which surrounds the land.

SEA-BATTERIES. Assaults by masters in the merchant service upon seamen at sea.

SEA-BED. All that portion of land under the sea that lies beyond the sea-shore.

SEA-BRIEF. See SEA-LETTER.

SEA-GREENS. In the Scotch law. Grounds overflowed by the sea in spring tides. Bell.

SEA-LAWS. Laws relating to the sea, as the laws of Oleron, etc.

SEA-LETTER. A species of manifest, containing a description of the ship's cargo, with the port from which it comes and the port of destination. This is one of the documents necessary to be carried by all neutral vessels, in the merchant service, in time of war, as an evidence of their nationality. 4 Kent, Comm. 157.

SEA-REEVE. An officer in maritime towns and places who took care of the maritime rights of the lord of the manor, and watched the shore, and collected wrecks for the lord. Tomlins.

SEA ROVERS. Pirates and robbers at sea.

SEA-SHORE. The margin of the sea in its usual and ordinary state. When the tide is out, low-water mark is the margin of the sea; and, when the sea is full, the margin is high-water mark. The sea-shore is therefore all the ground between the ordinary high-water mark and low-water mark. It cannot be considered as including any ground always covered by the sea, for then it would have no definite limit on the sea-board. Neither can it include any part of the upland, for the same reason. 6 Mass. 439; 15 Me. 237.

That space of land over which the waters of the sea are spread in the highest water during the winter season. Civil Code La. art. 442.

SEAL. An impression upon wax, wafer, or some other tenacious substance capable of being impressed. 5 Johns. 239; 4 Kent, Comm. 452.

A seal is a particular sign, made to attest, in the most formal manner, the execution of an instrument. Code Civil Proc. Cal. § 1930.

Merlin defines a seal to be a plate of metal with a flat surface, on which is engraved the arms of a prince or nation, or private individual, or other device, with which an impression may be made on wax or other substance on paper or parchment, in order to authenticate them. The impression thus made is also called a "seal." Répert. *mot* "*Sceau.*"

SEAL DAYS. In English practice. Motion days in the court of chancery, so called because every motion had to be stamped with the seal, which did not lie in court in the ordinary sittings out of term. Wharton.

SEAL OFFICE. In English practice. An office for the sealing of judicial writs.

SEAL-PAPER. In English law. A document issued by the lord chancellor, previously to the commencement of the sittings, detailing the business to be done for each day in his court, and in the courts of the lords justices and vice-chancellors. The master of the rolls in like manner issued a seal-paper in respect of the business to be heard before him. Smith, Ch. Pr. 9.

"SEALED AND DELIVERED." These words, followed by the signatures of the witnesses, constitute the usual formula for the attestation of conveyances.

SEALED INSTRUMENT. An instrument of writing to which the party to be bound has affixed, not only his name, but also his seal, or (in those jurisdictions where it is allowed) a scroll, (*q. v.*)

SEALING. By seals, in matters of succession, is understood the placing, by the proper officer, of seals on the effects of a succession for the purpose of preserving them, and for the interest of third persons. The seals are affixed by order of the judge having jurisdiction. Civil Code La. art. 1075.

SEALING A VERDICT. When the jury have agreed upon a verdict, if the court is not in session at the time, they are permitted (usually) to put their written finding in a sealed envelope, and then separate. This verdict they return when the court again convenes. The verdict thus returned has the same effect, and must be treated in the same manner, as if returned in open court before any separation of the jury had taken place. The process is called "sealing a verdict." 8 Ohio, 408.

SEALING UP. Where a party to an action has been ordered to produce a document part of which is either irrelevant to the matters in question or is privileged from production, he may, by leave of the court, seal up that part, if he makes an affidavit stating that it is irrelevant or privileged. Daniell, Ch. Pr. 1681. The sealing up is generally done by fastening pieces of paper over the part with gum or wafers. Sweet.

SEALS. In Louisiana. Seals are placed upon the effects of a deceased person, in certain cases, by a public officer, as a method of taking official custody of the succession. See SEALING.

SEAMEN. Sailors; mariners; persons whose business is navigating ships. Commonly exclusive of the officers of a ship.

SEANCE. In French law. A session; as of some public body.

SEARCH. In international law. The right of search is the right on the part of ships of war to visit and search merchant vessels during war, in order to ascertain whether the ship or cargo is liable to seizure. Resistance to visitation and search by a neutral vessel makes the vessel and cargo liable to confiscation. Numerous treaties regulate the manner in which the right of search must be exercised. Man. Int. Law. 433; Sweet.

In criminal law. An examination of a man's house or other buildings or premises, or of his person, with a view to the discovery of contraband or illicit or stolen property, or some evidence of guilt to be used in the prosecution of a criminal action for some crime or offense with which he is charged.

In practice. An examination of the official books and dockets, made in the process of investigating a title to land, for the purpose of discovering if there are any mortgages, judgments, tax-liens, or other incumbrances upon it.

SEARCH-WARRANT. A search-warrant is an order in writing, issued by a justice or other magistrate, in the name of the state, directed to a sheriff, constable, or other officer, commanding him to search a specified house, shop, or other premises, for personal property alleged to have been stolen, or for unlawful goods, and to bring the same, when found, before the magistrate, and usually also the body of the person occupying the premises, to be dealt with according to law. Pen. Code Cal. § 1523; Code Ala. 1886, § 4727; Rev. Code Iowa, 1880, § 4629.

SEARCHER. In English law. An officer of the customs, whose duty it is to examine and search all ships outward bound, to ascertain whether they have any prohibited or uncustomed goods on board. Wharton; Jacob.

SEATED LAND. Land that is occupied, cultivated, improved, reclaimed, farmed, or used as a place of residence. Residence without cultivation, or cultivation without residence, or both together, impart to land the character of being seated. The term is used, as opposed to "unseated land," in Pennsylvania tax laws. See 6 Watts, 269.

SEAWAN. The name used by the Algonquin Indians for the shell beads (or wampum) which passed among the Indians as money. Webster.

SEAWORTHINESS. In marine insurance. A warranty of seaworthiness means that the vessel is competent to resist the ordinary attacks of wind and weather, and is competently equipped and manned for the voyage, with a sufficient crew, and with sufficient means to sustain them, and with a captain of general good character and nautical skill. 3 Kent, Comm. 287.

A warranty of seaworthiness extends not only to the condition of the structure of the ship itself, but requires that it be properly laden, and provided with a competent master, a sufficient number of competent officers and seamen, and the requisite appurtenances and equipments, such as ballast, cables and anchors, cordage and sails, food, water, fuel, and lights, and other necessary or proper stores and implements for the voyage. Civil Code Cal. § 2684.

The term "seaworthy" is somewhat equivocal. In its more literal sense, it signifies capable of navigating the sea; but, more exactly, it implies a condition to be and remain in safety, in the condition she is in, whether at sea, in port, or on a railway, stripped and under repairs. If, when the policy attaches, she is in a suitable place, and capable, when repaired and equipped, of navigating the sea, she is seaworthy. But where a vessel is warranted seaworthy for a specified voyage, the place and usual length being given, something more is implied than mere physical strength and capacity; she must be suitably officered and manned, supplied with provisions and water, and furnished with charts and instruments, and, especially in time of war, with documents necessary to her security against hostile capture. 12 Cush. 517, 521.

The term "seaworthy," as used in the law and practice of insurance, does not mean, as the term would seem to imply, capable of going to sea or of being navigated on the sea; it imports something very different, and much more, viz., that she is sound, staunch, and strong, in all respects, and equipped, furnished, and provided with officers and men, provisions and documents, for a certain service. In a policy for a definite voyage, the term "seaworthy" means "sufficient for such a vessel and voyage." 12 Cush. 517, 536.

SEAWORTHY. This adjective, applied to a vessel, signifies that she is properly constructed, prepared, manned, equipped, and provided, for the voyage intended. See SEAWORTHINESS.

SEBASTOMANIA. In medical jurisprudence. Religious insanity; demonomania.

SECK. A want of remedy by distress. Litt. § 218. See RENT. Want of present fruit or profit, as in the case of the reversion without rent or other service, except fealty. Co. Litt. 151*b*, n. 5.

SECOND COUSINS. Persons who are related to each other by descending from the same great-grandfather or great-grandmother. L. R. 19 Ch. Div. 204.

SECOND DELIVERANCE. In practice. A writ allowed a plaintiff in replevin, where the defendant has obtained judgment for return of the goods, by default or nonsuit, in order to have the same distress again delivered to him, on giving the same security as before. 3 Bl. Comm. 150; 3 Steph. Comm. 668.

SECOND DISTRESS. A supplementary distress for rent in arrear, allowed by law in some cases, where the goods seized under the first distress are not of sufficient value to satisfy the claim.

SECOND-HAND EVIDENCE. Evidence which has passed through one or more media before reaching the witness; *hearsay* evidence.

SECOND SURCHARGE. In English law. The surcharge of a common a second time, by the same defendant against whom the common was before admeasured, and for which the *writ of second surcharge* was given by the statute of Westminster, 2. 3 Bl. Comm. 239.

SECONDARY. In English practice. An officer of the courts of king's bench and common pleas; so called because he was *second* or next to the chief officer. In the king's bench he was called "Master of the King's Bench Office," and was a deputy of the prothonotary or chief clerk. 1 Archb. Pr. K. B. 11, 12. By St. 7 Wm. IV. and 1 Vict. c. 30, the office of secondary was abolished.

An officer who is next to the chief officer. Also an officer of the corporation of London, before whom inquiries to assess damages are held, as before sheriffs in counties. Wharton.

SECONDARY CONVEYANCES. The name given to that class of conveyances which presuppose some other conveyance precedent, and only serve to enlarge, confirm, alter, restrain, restore, or transfer the interest granted by such original conveyance. 2 Bl. Comm. 324. Otherwise termed "derivative conveyances," (*q. v.*)

SECONDARY EVIDENCE. That species of evidence which becomes admissible, as being the next best, when the primary or best evidence of the fact in question is lost or inaccessible; as when a witness details orally the contents of an instrument which is lost or destroyed.

SECONDARY USE. A use limited to take effect in derogation of a preceding estate, otherwise called a "shifting use," as a conveyance to the use of A. and his heirs, with a proviso that, when B. returns from India, then to the use of C. and his heirs. 1 Steph. Comm. 546.

SECONDS. In criminal law. Those persons who assist, direct, and support others engaged in fighting a duel.

SECRET COMMITTEE. A secret committee of the house of commons is a committee specially appointed to investigate a certain matter, and to which secrecy being deemed necessary in furtherance of its objects, its proceedings are conducted with closed doors, to the exclusion of all persons not members of the committee. All other committees are open to members of the house, although they may not be serving upon them. Brown.

SECRET EQUITY. An equitable claim or right, the knowledge of which has been confined to the parties for and against whom it exists, or which has been concealed from one or several persons interested in the subject-matter.

SECRET LIEN. A lien reserved by the vendor of chattels, who has delivered them to the vendee, to secure the payment of the price, which is concealed from all third persons.

SECRET PARTNERSHIP. One where the existence of certain persons as partners is not avowed to the public by any of the partners. 49 N. H. 225.

SECRET TRUSTS. Where a testator gives property to a person, on a verbal promise by the legatee or devisee that he will hold it in trust for another person, this is called a "secret trust." Sweet.

SECRETARY. The secretary of a corporation or association is an officer charged with the direction and management of that part of the business of the company which is concerned with keeping the records, the official correspondence, with giving and receiving notices, countersigning documents, etc.

The name "secretary" is also given to several of the heads of executive departments in the government of the United States; as the "Secretary of War," "Secretary of the Interior," etc. It is also the style of some of the members of the English cabinet; as the "Secretary of State for Foreign Affairs." There are also secretaries of embassies and legations.

SECRETARY OF DECREES AND INJUNCTIONS. An officer of the English court of chancery. The office was abolished by St. 15 & 16 Vict. c. 87, § 23.

SECRETARY OF EMBASSY. A diplomatic officer appointed as secretary or assistant to an ambassador or minister plenipotentiary.

SECRETARY OF LEGATION. An officer employed to attend a foreign mission and to perform certain duties as clerk.

SECRETARY OF STATE. In American law. This is the title of the chief of the executive bureau of the United States called the "Department of State." He is a member of the cabinet, and is charged with the general administration of the international and diplomatic affairs of the government. In many of the state governments there is an executive officer bearing the same title and exercising important functions.

In English law. The secretaries of state are cabinet ministers attending the sovereign for the receipt and dispatch of letters, grants, petitions, and many of the most important affairs of the kingdom, both foreign and domestic. There are five principal secretaries, —one for the home department, another for foreign affairs, a third for the colonies, a fourth for war, and a fifth for India. Wharton.

SECRETE. To conceal or hide away. Particularly, to put property out of the reach of creditors, either by corporally hiding it, or putting the title in another's name, or otherwise hindering creditors from levying on it or attaching it.

SECT. "A religious sect is a body or number of persons united in tenets, but constituting a distinct organization or party, by holding sentiments or doctrines different from those of other sects or people." 16 Nev. 385.

SECTA. In old English law. Suit; attendance at court; the plaintiff's suit or following, *i. e.*, the witnesses whom he was required, in the ancient practice, to bring with him and produce in court, for the purpose of confirming his claim, before the defendant was put to the necessity of answering the declaration. See 3 Bl. Comm. 295, 344; Bract. fol. 214*a*. A survival from this proceeding is seen in the formula still used at the end of declarations, "and therefore he brings his suit," (*et inde producit sectam.*)

This word, in its secondary meaning, signifies suit in the courts; lawsuit.

SECTA AD CURIAM. A writ that lay against him who refused to perform his suit either to the county court or the court-baron. Cowell.

SECTA AD FURNUM. In old English law. Suit due to a man's public oven or bake-house. 3 Bl. Comm. 235.

SECTA AD JUSTICIAM FACIENDAM. In old English law. A service which a man is bound to perform by his fee.

SECTA AD MOLENDINUM. A writ which lay for the owner of a mill against the inhabitants of a place where such mill is situated, for not doing suit to the plaintiff's mill; that is, for not having their corn ground at it. Brown.

SECTA AD TORRALE. In old English law. Suit due to a man's kiln or malt-house. 3 Bl. Comm. 235.

SECTA CURIÆ. In old English law. Suit of court; attendance at court. The service, incumbent upon feudal tenants, of attending the lord at his court, both to form a jury when required, and also to answer for their own actions when complained of.

Secta est pugna civilis; sicut actores armantur actionibus, et, quasi, gladiis accinguntur, ita rei muniuntur exceptionibus, et defenduntur, quasi, clypeis. Hob. 20. A suit is a civil warfare; for as the plaintiffs are armed with actions, and, as it were, girded with swords, so the defendants are fortified with pleas, and are defended, as it were, by shields.

SECTA FACIENDA PER ILLAM QUÆ HABET ENICIAM PARTEM. A writ to compel the heir, who has the elder's part of the co-heirs, to perform suit and services for all the coparceners. Reg. Orig. 177.

Secta quæ scripto nititur a scripto variari non debet. Jenk. Cent. 65. A suit which is based upon a writing ought not to vary from the writing.

SECTA REGALIS. A suit so called by which all persons were bound twice in the year to attend in the sheriff's tourn, in order that they might be informed of things relating to the public peace. It was so called because the sheriff's tourn was the king's leet, and it was held in order that the people might be bound by oath to bear true allegiance to the king. Cowell.

SECTA UNICA TANTUM FACIENDA PRO PLURIBUS HÆREDITATIBUS. A writ for an heir who was distrained by the lord to do more suits than one, that he should be allowed to do one suit only in respect of the land of divers heirs descended to him. Cowell.

SECTATORES. Suitors of court who, among the Saxons, gave their judgment or verdict in civil suits upon the matter of fact and law. 1 Reeve, Eng. Law, 22.

SECTION. In text-books, codes, statutes, and other juridical writings, the smallest distinct and numbered subdivisions are commonly called "sections," sometimes "articles," and occasionally "paragraphs."

SECTION OF LAND. In American land law. A division or parcel of land, on the government survey, comprising one square mile or 640 acres. Each "township" (six miles square) is divided by straight lines into thirty-six sections, and these are again divided into half-sections and quarter-sections.

The general and proper acceptation of the terms "section," "half," and "quarter section," as well as their construction by the general land department, denotes the land in the sectional and subdivisional lines, and not the exact quantity which a perfect admeasurement of an unobstructed surface would declare. 21 Ark. 327.

SECTIS NON FACIENDIS. A writ which lay for a dowress, or one in wardship, to be free from suit of court. Cowell.

SECTORES. Lat. In Roman law. Purchasers at auction, or public sales.

SECULAR. Not spiritual; not ecclesiastical; relating to affairs of the present world.

SECULAR CLERGY. Parochial clergy who performed their ministry *in seculo*, and were contradistinguished from the regular clergy. Steph. Comm. 681, note.

SECUNDUM. Lat. In the civil and common law. According to. *Secundum bonos mores*, according to good usages; according to established custom; regularly; orderly. Calvin.

SECUNDUM ÆQUUM ET BONUM. According to what is just and right.

SECUNDUM ALLEGATA ET PROBATA. According to what is alleged and proved; according to the allegations and proofs. 15 East, 81; 1 Sum. 375.

SECUNDUM ARTEM. According to the art, trade, business, or science.

SECUNDUM CONSUETUDINEM MANERII. According to the custom of the manor.

SECUNDUM FORMAM CHARTÆ. According to the form of the charter, (deed.)

SECUNDUM FORMAM DONI. According to the form of the gift or grant. See FORMEDON.

SECUNDUM FORMAM STATUTI. According to the form of the statute.

SECUNDUM LEGEM COMMUNEM. According to the common law.

Secundum naturam est commoda cujusque rei eum sequi, quem sequuntur incommoda. It is according to nature that the advantages of anything should attach to him to whom the disadvantages attach. Dig. 50, 17, 10.

SECUNDUM NORMAM LEGIS. According to the rule of law; by the intendment and rule of law.

SECUNDUM REGULAM. According to the rule; by rule.

SECUNDUM SUBJECTAM MATERIAM. According to the subject-matter. 1 Bl. Comm. 229. All agreements must be construed *secundum subjectam materiam* if the matter will bear it. 2 Mod. 80, arg.

SECURE. To give security; to assure of payment, performance, or indemnity; to guaranty or make certain the payment of a debt or discharge of an obligation. One "secures" his creditor by giving him a lien, mortgage, pledge, or other security, to be used in case the debtor fails to make payment.

SECURED CREDITOR. A creditor who holds some special pecuniary assurance of payment of his debt, such as a mortgage or lien.

SECURITAS. In old English law. Security; surety.

In the civil law. An acquittance or release. Spelman; Calvin.

SECURITATEM INVENIENDI. An ancient writ, lying for the sovereign, against any of his subjects, to stay them from going out of the kingdom to foreign parts; the ground whereof is that every man is bound to serve and defend the commonwealth as the crown shall think fit. Fitzh. Nat. Brev. 115.

SECURITATIS PACIS. In old English law. Security of the peace. A writ that lay for one who was threatened with death or bodily harm by another, against him who so threatened. Reg. Orig. 88.

SECURITY. Protection; assurance; indemnification. The term is usually applied to an obligation, pledge, mortgage, deposit, lien, etc., given by a debtor in order to make sure the payment or performance of his debt, by furnishing the creditor with a resource to be used in case of failure in the principal obligation. The name is also sometimes given to one who becomes surety or guarantor for another.

SECURITY FOR COSTS. In practice. A security which a defendant in an action may require of a plaintiff who does not reside within the jurisdiction of the court, for the payment of such costs as may be awarded to the defendant. 1 Tidd, Pr. 534.

SECURITY FOR GOOD BEHAVIOR. A bond or recognizance which the magistrate exacts from a defendant brought before him on a charge of disorderly conduct or threatening violence, conditioned upon his being of good behavior, or keeping the peace, for a prescribed period, towards all people in general and the complainant in particular.

Securius expediuntur negotia commissa pluribus, et plus vident oculi quam oculus. 4 Coke, 46*a*. Matters intrusted to several are more securely dispatched, and eyes see more than eye, [*i. e.*, "two heads are better than one."]

SECUS. Lat. Otherwise; to the contrary. This word is used in the books to indicate the converse of a foregoing proposition, or the rule applicable to a different state of facts, or an exception to a rule before stated.

SED NON ALLOCATUR. Lat. But it is not allowed. A phrase used in the old reports, to signify that the court disagreed with the arguments of counsel.

SED PER CURIAM. Lat. But by the court ———. This phrase is used in the reports to introduce a statement made by the court, on the argument, at variance with the propositions advanced by counsel, or the opinion of the whole court, where that is different from the opinion of a single judge immediately before quoted.

SED QUÆRE. Lat. But inquire; examine this further. A remark indicating, briefly, that the particular statement or rule laid down is doubted or challenged in respect to its correctness.

SED VIDE. Lat. But see. This remark, followed by a citation, directs the reader's attention to an authority or a statement which conflicts with or contradicts the statement or principle laid down.

SEDATO ANIMO. Lat. With settled purpose. 5 Mod. 291.

SEDE PLENA. The see being filled. A phrase used when a bishop's see is not vacant.

SEDENTE CURIA. The court sitting; during the sitting of the court.

SEDERUNT, ACTS OF. In Scotch law. Certain ancient ordinances of the court of session, conferring upon the courts power to establish general rules of practice. Bell.

SEDES. Lat. A see; the dignity of a bishop. 3 Steph. Comm. 65.

SEDGE FLAT, like "sea-shore," imports a tract of land below high-water mark. 34 Conn. 421.

SEDITION. An insurrectionary movement tending towards treason, but wanting an overt act; attempts made by meetings or speeches, or by publications, to disturb the tranquillity of the state.

The distinction between "sedition" and "treason" consists in this: that though the ultimate object of sedition is a violation of the public peace, or at least such a course of measures as evidently engenders it, yet it does not aim at direct and open violence against the laws or the subversion of the constitution. Alis. Crim. Law, 580.

In Scotch law. The raising commotions or disturbances in the state. It is a revolt against legitimate authority. Ersk. Inst. 4, 4, 14.

In English law. Sedition is the offense of publishing, verbally or otherwise, any words or document with the intention of exciting disaffection, hatred, or contempt against the sovereign, or the government and constitution of the kingdom, or either house of parliament, or the administration of justice, or of exciting her majesty's subjects to attempt, otherwise than by lawful means, the alteration of any matter in church or state, or of exciting feelings of ill will and hostility between different classes of her majesty's subjects. Sweet.

SEDUCE. To entice a woman to the commission of fornication or adultery, by persuasion, solicitation, promises, bribes, or otherwise; to corrupt; to debauch.

The word "seduce," when used with reference to the conduct of a man towards a woman, has a precise and determinate signification, and "*ex vi termini*" implies the commission of fornication. An information for the crime of seduction need not charge the offense in any other words. 27 Conn. 319.

SEDUCING TO LEAVE SERVICE. An injury for which a master may have an action on the case.

SEDUCTION. The act of a man in enticing a woman to commit unlawful sexual intercourse with him, by means of persuasion, solicitation, promises, bribes, or other means without the employment of force.

In order to constitute seduction, the defendant must use insinuating arts to overcome the opposition of the seduced, and must by his wiles and persuasions, without force, debauch her. This is the ordinary meaning and acceptation of the word "seduce." 6 Rob. (N. Y.) 150.

SEE. The circuit of a bishop's jurisdiction; or his office or dignity, as being bishop of a given diocese.

SEIGNIOR, in its general signification, means "lord," but in law it is particularly applied to the lord of a fee or of a manor; and the fee, dominions, or manor of a seignior is thence termed a "seigniory," *i. e.*, a lordship. He who is a lord, but of no manor, and therefore unable to keep a court, is termed a "seignior in gross." Kitch. 206; Cowell.

SEIGNIOR IN GROSS. A lord without a manor, simply enjoying superiority and services. Cowell.

SEIGNIORAGE. A royalty or prerogative of the sovereign, whereby an allowance of gold and silver, brought in the mass to be exchanged for coin, is claimed. Cowell. Mintage; the charge for coining bullion into money at the mint.

SEIGNIORESS. A female superior.

SEIGNIORY. In English law. A lordship; a manor. The rights of a lord, as such, in lands.

SEISED IN DEMESNE AS OF FEE. This is the strict technical expression used to describe the ownership in "an estate in fee-simple in possession in a corporeal hereditament." The word "seised" is used to express the "seisin" or owner's possession of a freehold property; the phrase "in demesne," or "in his demesne," (*in dominico suo*) signifies that he is seised as owner of the land itself, and not merely of the seigniory or services; and the concluding words, "as of fee," import that he is seised of an estate of inheritance in fee-simple. Where the subject is incorporeal, or the estate expectant on a precedent freehold, the words "in his demesne" are omitted. (Co. Litt. 17*a;* Fleta, l. 5, c. 5, § 18; Bract. l. 4, tr. 5, c. 2, § 2.) Brown.

SEISI. In old English law. Seised; possessed.

SEISIN. The completion of the feudal investiture, by which the tenant was admitted into the feud, and performed the rights of homage and fealty. Stearns, Real Act. 2.

Possession with an intent on the part of him who holds it to claim a freehold interest. 8 N. H. 58; 1 Washb. Real Prop. 35.

Upon the introduction of the feudal law into England, the word "seisin" was applied only to the possession of an estate of freehold, in contradistinction to that precarious kind of possession by which tenants in villeinage held their lands, which was considered to be the possession of those in whom the freehold continued. The word still retains its original signification, being applied exclusively to the possession of land of a freehold tenure, it being inaccurate to use the word as expressive of the possession of leaseholds or terms of years, or even of copyholds. Brown.

Under our law, the word "seisin" has no accurately defined technical meaning. At common law, it imported a feudal investiture of title by actual possession. With us it has the force of possession under some legal title or right to hold. This possession, so far as possession alone is involved, may be shown by parol; but, if it is intended to show possession under a legal title, then the title must be shown by proper conveyance for that purpose. 49 Ala. 603.

Every person in whom a seisin is required by any of the provisions of this chapter shall be deemed to have been seised, if he may have had any right, title, or interest in the inheritance. Code N. C. 1883, § 1281, rule 12.

Seisin in fact is possession with intent on the part of him who holds it to claim a freehold interest. *Seisin in law* is a right of immediate possession according to the nature of the estate. 1 Washb. Real Prop. 33, 34.

Seisin is of two kinds: Seisin in law arises when the grantor of real estate gives the right of present possession to the grantee; seisin in deed is the actual possession of freehold estate. 2 MacArthur, 60.

Quasi seisin. *Quasi* seisin is the possession which a copyholder has of the land to which he has been admitted. The freehold in copyhold lands being in the lord, the copyholder cannot have seisin of them in the proper sense of the word, but he has a customary or *quasi* seisin, analogous to that of a freeholder. Williams, Seis. 126; Sweet.

Equitable seisin. Equitable seisin is analogous to legal seisin; *i. e.*, it is seisin of an equitable estate in land. Thus, a mortgagor is said to have equitable seisin of the land by receipt of the rents. Sweet.

SEISIN, LIVERY OF. Delivery of possession; called, by the feudists, "investiture."

SEISIN OX. In Scotch law. A perquisite formerly due to the sheriff when he gave possession to an heir holding crown lands. It was long since converted into a payment in money, proportioned to the value of the estate. Bell.

SEISINA. L. Lat. Seisin.

Seisina facit stipitem. Seisin makes the stock. 2 Bl. Comm. 209; Broom, Max. 525, 528.

SEISINA HABENDA. A writ for delivery of seisin to the lord, of lands and tenements, after the sovereign, in right of his prerogative, had had the year, day, and waste on a felony committed, etc. Reg Orig. 165.

SEIZIN. See SEISIN.

SEIZING OF HERIOTS. Taking the best beast, etc., where an heriot is due, on the death of the tenant. 2 Bl. Comm. 422.

SEIZURE. In practice. The act performed by an officer of the law, under the authority and exigence of a writ, in taking into the custody of the law the property, real or personal, of a person against whom the judgment of a competent court has passed, condemning him to pay a certain sum of money, in order that such property may be sold, by authority and due course of law, to satisfy the judgment. Or the act of taking possession of goods in consequence of a violation of public law.

Seizure, even though hostile, is not necessarily capture, though such is its usual and probable result. The ultimate act or adjudication of the state, by which the seizure has been made, assigns the proper and conclusive quality and denomination to the original proceeding. A condemnation asserts a capture *ab initio;* an award of restitution pronounces upon the act as having been not a valid act of capture, but an act of temporary seizure only. 3 Mass. 443.

In the law of copyholds. Seizure is where the lord of copyhold lands takes possession of them in default of a tenant. It is either seizure *quousque* or absolute seizure.

SELDA. A shop, shed, or stall in a market; a wood of sallows or willows; also a saw-pit. Co. Litt. 4.

SELECT COUNCIL. The name given, in some states, to the upper house or branch of the council of a city.

SELECTI JUDICES. In Roman law. Judges who were selected very much like our juries. They were returned by the prætor, drawn by lot, subject to be challenged, and sworn. 3 Bl. Comm. 366.

SELECTMEN. The name of certain municipal officers, in the New England states, elected by the towns to transact their general public business, and possessing certain executive powers.

SELF-DEFENSE. In criminal law. The protection of one's person or property against some injury attempted by another. The right of such protection. An excuse for the use of force in resisting an attack on the person, and especially for killing an assailant. See Whart. Crim. Law, §§ 1019-1026.

SELF-MURDER, or SELF-SLAUGHTER. See FELO DE SE; SUICIDE.

SELF-REGARDING EVIDENCE. Evidence which either serves or disserves the party is so called. This species of evidence is either self-serving (which is not in general receivable) or self-disserving, which is invariably receivable, as being an admission against the party offering it, and that either in court or out of court. Brown.

SELION OF LAND. In old English law. A ridge of ground rising between two furrows, containing no certain quantity, but sometimes more and sometimes less. Termes de la Ley.

SELL. To dispose of by sale, (*q. v.*)

SELLER. One who sells anything; the party who transfers property in the contract of sale. The correlative is "buyer," or "purchaser." Though these terms are not inapplicable to the persons concerned in a transfer of real estate, it is more customary to use "vendor" and "vendee" in that case.

SEMAYNE'S CASE. This case decided, in 2 Jac. I., that "every man's house [meaning his dwelling-house only] is his castle," and that the defendant may not break open outer doors in general, but only inner doors, but that (after request made) he may break open even outer doors to find goods of another wrongfully in the house. Brown.

SEMBLE. L. Fr. It seems; it would appear. This expression is often used in the reports to preface a statement by the court upon a point of law which is not directly decided, when such statement is intended as an intimation of what the decision would be if the point were necessary to be passed upon. It is also used to introduce a suggestion by the reporter, or his understanding of the point decided when it is not free from obscurity.

Semel civis semper civis. Once a citizen always a citizen. Tray. Lat. Max. 555.

Semel malus semper præsumitur esse malus in eodem genere. Whoever is once bad is presumed to be so always in the same kind of affairs. Cro. Car. 317.

SEMESTRIA. In the civil law. The collected decisions of the emperors in their councils.

SEMI-MATRIMONIUM. Lat. In Roman law. Half-marriage. Concubinage was so called. Tayl. Civil Law, 273.

SEMI-PLENA PROBATIO. Lat. In the civil law. Half-full proof; half-proof. 3 Bl. Comm. 370. See HALF-PROOF.

SEMINARIUM. Lat. In the civil law. A nursery of trees. Dig. 7, 1, 9, 6.

SEMINARY. A place of education. Any school, academy, college, or university in which young persons are instructed in the several branches of learning which may qualify them for their future employments. Webster.

The word is said to have acquired no fixed and definite legal meaning. 12 N. Y. 229.

SEMINAUFRAGIUM. In maritime law. Half-shipwreck, as where goods are cast overboard in a storm; also where a ship has been so much damaged that her repair costs more than her worth. Wharton.

SEMITA. In old English law. A path. Fleta, l. 2, c. 52, § 20.

SEMPER. Lat. Always. A word which introduces several Latin maxims, of which some are also used without this prefix.

Semper in dubiis benigniora præferenda sunt. In doubtful cases, the more favorable constructions are always to be preferred. Dig. 50, 17, 56.

Semper in dubiis id agendum est, ut quam tutissimo loco res sit bona fide contracta, nisi quum aperte contra leges scriptum est. In doubtful cases, such a course should always be taken that a thing contracted *bona fide* should be in the safest condition, unless when it has been openly made against law. Dig. 34, 5, 21.

Semper in obscuris, quod minimum est sequimur. In obscure constructions we always apply that which is the least obscure. Dig. 50, 17, 9; Broom, Max. 687*n*.

Semper in stipulationibus, et in ceteris contractibus, id sequimur quod actum est. In stipulations and in other contracts we follow that which was done, [we are governed by the actual state of the facts.] Dig. 50, 17, 34.

Semper ita fiat relatio ut valeat dispositio. Reference [of a disposition in a will] should always be so made that the disposition may have effect. 6 Coke, 76*b*.

Semper necessitas probandi incumbit ei qui agit. The claimant is always bound to prove, [the burden of proof lies on the actor.]

SEMPER PARATUS. The name of a plea by which the defendant alleges that he has always been ready to perform what is demanded of him. 3 Bl. Comm. 303.

Semper præsumitur pro legitimatione puerorum. The presumption always is in favor of the legitimacy of children. 5 Coke, 98*b*; Co. Litt. 126*a*.

Semper præsumitur pro matrimonio. The presumption is always in favor of the validity of a marriage.

Semper præsumitur pro negante. The presumption is always in favor of the one who denies. See 10 Clark & F. 534; 3 El. & Bl. 723.

Semper præsumitur pro sententia. The presumption always is in favor of a sentence. 3 Bulst. 42; Branch, Princ.

Semper qui non prohibet pro se intervenire, mandare creditur. He who does not prohibit the intervention of another in his behalf is supposed to authorize it. 2 Kent, Comm. 616; Dig. 14, 6, 16; Id. 46, 3, 12, 4.

Semper sexus masculinus etiam femininum sexum continet. The masculine sex always includes the feminine. Dig. 32, 62.

Semper specialia generalibus insunt. Specials are always included in generals. Dig. 50, 17, 147.

SEN. This is said to be an ancient word, which signified "justice." Co. Litt. 61*a*.

SENAGE. Money paid for synodals.

SENATE. In American law. The name of the upper chamber, or less numerous branch, of the congress of the United States. Also the style of a similar body in the legislatures of several of the states.

In Roman law. The great administrative council of the Roman commonwealth.

SENATOR. In Roman law. A member of the *senatus*.

In old English law. A member of the royal council; a king's councillor.

In American law. One who is a member of a senate, either of the United States or of a state.

Senatores sunt partes corporis regis. Senators are part of the body of the king. Staundef. 72, E.; 4 Inst. 53, in marg.

SENATORS OF THE COLLEGE OF JUSTICE. The judges of the court of session in Scotland are called "Senators of the College of Justice."

SENATUS. Lat. In Roman law. The senate; the great national council of the Roman people.

The place where the senate met. Calvin.

SENATUS CONSULTUM. In Roman law. A decision or decree of the Roman senate, having the force of law, made without the concurrence of the people. These enactments began to take the place of laws enacted by popular vote, when the commons had grown so great in number that they could no longer be assembled for legislative purposes.

Mackeld. Rom. Law, § 33; Hunter, Rom. Law, xlvii; Inst. 1, 2, 5.

SENATUS CONSULTUM MARCIANUM. In Roman law. A decree of the senate, in relation to the celebration of the Bacchanalian mysteries, enacted in the consulate of Q. Marcius and S. Postumus.

SENATUS CONSULTUM ORFICIANUM. In Roman law. An enactment of the senate (Orficius being one of the consuls and Marcus Antoninus emperor) for admitting both sons and daughters to the succession of a mother dying intestate. Inst. 3, 4, pr.

SENATUS CONSULTUM PEGASIANUM. In the civil law. The Pegasian decree of the senate. A decree enacted in the consulship of Pegasus and Pusio, in the reign of Vespasian, by which an heir, who was requested to restore an inheritance, was allowed to retain one-fourth of it for himself. Inst. 2, 23, 5.

SENATUS CONSULTUM TREBELLIANUM. Lat. In Roman law. A decree of the senate (named from Trebellius, in whose consulate it was enacted) by which it was provided that, if an inheritance was restored under a trust, all actions which, by the civil law, might be brought by or against the heir should be given to and against him to whom the inheritance was restored. Inst. 2, 23, 4; Dig. 36, 1.

SENATUS CONSULTUM ULTIMÆ NECESSITATIS. A decree of the senate of the last necessity. The name given to the decree which usually preceded the nomination of a dictator. 1 Bl. Comm. 136.

SENATUS CONSULTUM VELLEIANUM. In the civil law. The Velleian decree of the senate. A decree enacted in the consulship of Velleius, by which married women were prohibited from making contracts. Story, Confl. Laws, § 425.

SENATUS DECRETA. In the civil law. Decisions of the senate. Private acts concerning particular persons merely.

SENDA. In Spanish law. A path; the right of a path. The right of foot or horse path. White, New Recop. b. 2, tit. 6, § 1.

SENESCALLUS. In old English law. A seneschal; a steward; the steward of a manor. Fleta, l. 2, c. 72.

SENESCHAL. In old European law. A title of office and dignity, derived from the middle ages, answering to that of steward or high steward in England. Seneschals were originally the lieutenants of the dukes and other great feudatories of the kingdom, and sometimes had the dispensing of justice and high military commands.

SENESCHALLO ET MARESHALLO QUOD NON TENEAT PLACITA DE LIBERO TENEMENTO. A writ addressed to the steward and marshal of England, inhibiting them to take cognizance of an action in their court that concerns freehold. Reg. Orig. 185. Abolished.

SENEUCIA. In old records. Widowhood. Cowell.

SENILE DEMENTIA. That peculiar decay of the mental faculties which occurs in extreme old age, and in many cases much earlier, whereby the person is reduced to second childhood, and becomes sometimes wholly incompetent to enter into any binding contract, or even to execute a will. It is the recurrence of second childhood by mere decay. 1 Redf. Wills, 63.

SENILITY. Incapacity to contract arising from the impairment of the intellectual faculties by old age.

SENIOR. Lord; a lord. Also the elder. An addition to the name of the elder of two persons having the same name.

SENIOR COUNSEL. Of two or more counsel retained on the same side of a cause, he is the "senior" who is the elder, or more important in rank or estimation, or who is charged with the more difficult or important parts of the management of the case.

SENIOR JUDGE. Of several judges composing a court, the "senior" judge is the one who holds the oldest commission, or who has served the longest time under his present commission.

SENIORES. In old English law. Seniors; ancients; elders. A term applied to the great men of the realm. Spelman.

SENORIO. In Spanish law. Dominion or property.

SENSU HONESTO. In an honest sense. To interpret words *sensu honesto* is to take them so as not to impute impropriety to the persons concerned.

Sensus verborum est anima legis. 5 Coke, 2. The meaning of the words is the spirit of the law.

Sensus verborum est duplex,—mitis et asper; et verba semper accipienda sunt in mitiori sensu. 4 Coke, 13. The meaning of words is two-fold,—mild and harsh; and words are always to be received in their milder sense.

Sensus verborum ex causa dicendi accipiendus est; et sermones semper accipiendi sunt secundum subjectam materiam. The sense of words is to be taken from the occasion of speaking them; and discourses are always to be interpreted according to the subject-matter. 4 Coke, 13*b*. See 2 Kent, Comm. 555.

SENTENCE. The judgment formally pronounced by the court or judge upon the defendant after his conviction in a criminal prosecution, awarding the punishment to be inflicted. The word is properly confined to this meaning. In *civil* cases, the terms "judgment," "decision," "award," "finding," etc., are used.

Ecclesiastical. In ecclesiastical procedure, "sentence" is analogous to "judgment" (*q. v.*) in an ordinary action. A definite sentence is one which puts an end to the suit, and regards the principal matter in question. An interlocutory sentence determines only some incidental matter in the proceedings. Phillim. Ecc. Law, 1260.

SENTENCE OF DEATH RECORDED. In English practice. The recording of a sentence of death, not actually pronounced, on the understanding that it will not be executed. Such a record has the same effect as if the judgment had been pronounced and the offender reprieved by the court. Mozley & Whitley. The practice is now disused.

SENTENTIA. Lat. In the civil law. (1) Sense; import; as distinguished from mere words. (2) The deliberate expression of one's will or intention. (3) The sentence of a judge or court.

Sententia a non judice lata nemini debet nocere. A sentence pronounced by one who is not a judge should not harm any one. Fleta, l. 6, c. 6, § 7.

Sententia contra matrimonium nunquam transit in rem judicatam. 7 Coke, 43. A sentence against marriage never becomes a matter finally adjudged, *i. e., res judicata*.

Sententia facit jus, et legis interpretatio legis vim obtinet. Ellesm. Post. N. 55. Judgment creates right, and the interpretation of the law has the force of law.

Sententia facit jus, et res judicata pro veritate accipitur. Ellesm. Post. N. 55. Judgment creates right, and what is adjudicated is taken for truth.

Sententia interlocutoria revocari potest, definitiva non potest. Bac. Max. 20. An interlocutory judgment may be recalled, but not a final.

Sententia non fertur de rebus non liquidis. Sentence is not given upon matters that are not clear. Jenk. Cent. p. 7, case 9.

SEPARALITER. Separately. Used in indictments to indicate that two or more defendants were charged separately, and not jointly, with the commission of the offense in question.

SEPARATE ACKNOWLEDGMENT. An acknowledgment of a deed or other instrument, made by a married woman, on her examination by the officer separate and apart from her husband.

SEPARATE ACTION. As opposed to a *joint* action, this term signifies an action brought for himself alone by each of several complainants who are all concerned in the same transaction, but cannot legally join in the suit.

SEPARATE COVENANT. A several covenant; one which binds the several covenantors each for himself, but not jointly.

SEPARATE DEMISE IN EJECTMENT. A demise in a declaration in ejectment used to be termed a "separate demise" when made by the lessor separately or individually, as distinguished from a demise made jointly by two or more persons, which was termed a "joint demise." No such demise, either separate or joint, is now necessary in this action. Brown.

SEPARATE ESTATE. The individual property of one of two persons who stand in a social or business relation, as distinguished from that which they own jointly or are jointly interested in.

Thus, "separate estate," within the meaning of the bankrupt law, is that in which each partner is separately interested at the time of the bankruptcy. The term can only be applied to such property as belonged to one or more of the partners, to the exclusion of the rest. 11 N. B. R. 221.

The separate estate of a married woman is that which belongs to her, and over which her husband has no right in equity. It may consist of lands or chattels. 4 Barb. 407.

SEPARATE EXAMINATION. The interrogation of a married woman, who appears before an officer for the purpose of acknowledging a deed or other instrument, conducted by such officer in private or out of the hearing of her husband, in order to ascertain if she acts of her own will and without compulsion or constraint of the husband.

Also the examination of a witness in private or apart from, and out of the hearing of, the other witnesses in the same cause.

SEPARATE MAINTENANCE. An allowance made to a woman by her husband on their agreement to live separately. This must not be confused with "alimony," which is judicially awarded upon granting a divorce.

SEPARATE TRIAL. The separate and individual trial of each of several persons jointly accused of a crime.

SEPARATIM. In old conveyancing. Severally. A word which made a several covenant. 5 Coke, 23*a*.

SEPARATION. A cessation of cohabitation of husband and wife by mutual agreement.

SEPARATION A MENSA ET THORO. A partial dissolution of the marriage relation.

SEPARATION OF PATRIMONY. In Louisiana probate law. The creditors of the succession may demand, in every case and against every creditor of the heir, a separation of the property of the succession from that of the heir. This is what is called the "separation of patrimony." The object of a separation of patrimony is to prevent property out of which a particular class of creditors have a right to be paid from being confounded with other property, and by that means made liable to the debts of another class of creditors. Civil Code La. art. 1444.

SEPARATION ORDER. In England, where a husband is convicted of an aggravated assault upon his wife, the court or magistrate may order that the wife shall be no longer bound to cohabit with him. Such an order has the same effect as a judicial decree of separation on the ground of cruelty. It may also provide for the payment of a weekly sum by the husband to the wife and for the custody of the children. Sweet.

SEPARATISTS. Seceders from the Church of England. They, like Quakers, solemnly affirm, instead of taking the usual oath, before they give evidence.

SEPES. Lat. In old English law. A hedge or inclosure. The inclosure of a trench or canal. Dig. 43, 21, 4.

SEPTENNIAL ACT. In English law. The statute 1 Geo. I. St. 2, c. 38. The act by which a parliament has continuance for seven years, and no longer, unless sooner dissolved; as it always has, in fact, been since the passing of the act. Wharton.

SEPTUAGESIMA. The third Sunday before *Quadragesima* Sunday in Lent, being about the seventieth day before Easter.

SEPTUM. Lat. In Roman law. An inclosure; an inclosed place where the people voted; otherwise called "*ovile.*"

In old English law. An inclosure or close. Cowell.

SEPTUNX. In Roman law. A division of the *as*, containing seven *unciæ*, or duodecimal parts; the proportion of seven-twelfths. Tayl. Civil Law, 492.

SEPULCHRE. A grave or tomb. The place of interment of a dead human body. The violation of sepulchres is a misdemeanor at common law.

SEPULTURA. An offering to the priest for the burial of a dead body.

Sequamur vestigia patrum nostrorum. Jenk. Cent. Let us follow the footsteps of our fathers.

SEQUATUR SUB SUO PERICULO. In old English practice. A writ which issued where a sheriff had returned *nihil*, upon a *summoneas ad warrantizandum*, and after an *alias* and *pluries* had been issued. So called because the tenant lost his lands without any recovery in value, unless upon that writ he brought the vouchee into court. Rosc. Real Act. 268; Cowell.

SEQUELA. L. Lat. In old English law. Suit; process or prosecution. *Sequela causæ*, the process of a cause. Cowell.

SEQUELA CURIÆ. Suit of court. Cowell.

SEQUELA VILLANORUM. The family retinue and appurtenances to the goods and chattels of villeins, which were at the absolute disposal of the lord. Par. Antiq. 216.

SEQUELS. Small allowances of meal, or manufactured victual, made to the servants at a mill where corn was ground, by tenure, in Scotland. Wharton.

SEQUESTER, *v.* **In the civil law.** To renounce or disclaim, etc. As when a widow came into court and disclaimed having anything to do with her deceased husband's estate, she was said to sequester. The word more commonly signifies the act of taking in execution under a writ of sequestration. Brown.

To deposit a thing which is the subject of a controversy in the hands of a third person, to hold for the contending parties.

To take a thing which is the subject of a controversy out of the possession of the contending parties, and deposit it in the hands of a third person. Calvin.

In equity practice. To take possession of the property of a defendant, and hold it in the custody of the court, until he purges himself of a contempt.

In English ecclesiastical practice. To gather and take care of the fruits and profits of a vacant benefice, for the benefit of the next incumbent.

In international law. To confiscate; to appropriate private property to public use; to seize the property of the private citizens of a hostile power, as when a belligerent nation sequesters debts due from its own subjects to the enemy. See 1 Kent, Comm. 62.

SEQUESTER, *n.* Lat. In the civil law. A person with whom two or more contending parties deposited the subject-matter of the controversy.

SEQUESTRARI FACIAS. In English ecclesiastical practice. A process in the nature of a *levari facias*, commanding the bishop to enter into the rectory and parish church, and to take and sequester the same, and hold them until, of the rents, tithes, and profits thereof, and of the other ecclesiastical goods of a defendant, he have levied the plaintiff's debt. 3 Bl. Comm. 418; 2 Archb. Pr. 1284.

SEQUESTRATIO. In the civil law. The separating or setting aside of a thing in controversy, from the possession of both parties that contend for it. It is two-fold,—*voluntary*, done by consent of all parties; and *necessary*, when a judge orders it. Brown.

SEQUESTRATION. In equity practice. A writ authorizing the taking into the custody of the law of the real and personal estate (or rents, issues, and profits) of a defendant who is in contempt, and holding the same until he shall comply. It is sometimes directed to the sheriff, but more commonly to four commissioners nominated by the complainant. 3 Bl. Comm. 444.

In Louisiana. A mandate of the court, ordering the sheriff, in certain cases, to take in his possession, and to keep, a thing of which another person has the possession, until after the decision of a suit, in order that it be delivered to him who shall be adjudged entitled to have the property or possession of that thing. This is what is properly called a "judicial sequestration." Code. Prac. La. art. 269.

In contracts. A species of deposit which two or more persons, engaged in litigation about anything, make of the thing in contest with an indifferent person who binds himself to restore it, when the issue is decided, to the party to whom it is adjudged to belong. Civil Code La. art. 2973.

In English ecclesiastical law. The act of the ordinary in disposing of the goods and chattels of one deceased, whose estate no one will meddle with. Cowell. Or, in other words, the taking possession of the property of a deceased person, where there is no one to claim it.

Also, where a benefice becomes vacant, a sequestration is usually granted by the bishop to the church-wardens, who manage all the profits and expenses of the benefice, plow and sow the glebe, receive tithes, and provide for the necessary cure of souls. Sweet.

In international law. The seizure of the property of an individual, and the appropriation of it to the use of the government.

Mayor's court. In the mayor's court of London, "a sequestration is an attachment of the property of a person in a warehouse or other place belonging to and abandoned by him. It has the same object as the ordinary attachment, viz., to compel the appearance of the defendant to an action," and, in default, to satisfy the plaintiff's debt by appraisement and execution. Id.

SEQUESTRATOR. One to whom a sequestration is made. One appointed or chosen to perform a sequestration, or execute a writ of sequestration.

SEQUESTRO HABENDO. In English ecclesiastical law. A judicial writ for the discharging a sequestration of the profits of a church benefice, granted by the bishop at the sovereign's command, thereby to compel the parson to appear at the suit of another. Upon his appearance, the parson may have this writ for the release of the sequestration. Reg. Jud. 36.

Sequi debet potentia justitiam non præcedere. 2 Inst. 454. Power should follow justice, not precede it.

SERF. In the feudal polity, the serfs were a class of persons whose social condition was servile, and who were bound to labor and onerous duties at the will of their lords. They differed from slaves only in that they were bound to their native soil, instead of being the absolute property of a master.

SERGEANT. In military law. A non-commissioned officer, of whom there are several in each company of infantry, troop of cavalry, etc. The term is also used in the organization of a municipal police force.

SERGEANT AT ARMS. See SERJEANT AT ARMS.

SERGEANT AT LAW. See SERJEANT AT LAW.

SERIATIM. Lat. Severally; separately; individually; one by one.

SERIOUS. Important; weighty; momentous, and not trifling; as in the phrases "serious bodily harm," "serious personal injury," etc. 74 Ill. 231; 13 Wall. 230.

SERJEANT AT ARMS. An executive officer appointed by, and attending on, a legislative body, whose principal duties are to execute its warrants, preserve order, and arrest offenders.

SERJEANT AT LAW. A barrister of the common-law courts of high standing, and of much the same rank as a doctor of law is in the ecclesiastical courts. These serjeants seem to have derived their title from the old knights templar, (among whom there existed a peculiar class under the denomination of "*frères sergens,*" or "*fratres servientes,*") and to have continued as a separate fraternity from a very early period in the history of the legal profession. The barristers who first assumed the old monastic title were those who practiced in the court of common pleas, and until a very recent period (the 25th of April, 1834, 9 & 10 Vict. c. 54) the serjeants at law always had the exclusive privilege of practice in that court. Every judge of a common-law court, previous to his elevation to the bench, used to be created a serjeant at law; but since the judicature act this is no longer necessary. Brown.

SERJEANT OF THE MACE. In English law. An officer who attends the lord mayor of London, and the chief magistrates of other corporate towns. Holthouse.

Serjeantia idem est quod servitium. Co. Litt. 105. Serjeanty is the same as service.

SERJEANTS' INN. The inn to which the serjeants at law belonged, near Chancery lane; formerly called "Faryndon Inn."

SERJEANTY. A species of tenure by knight service, which was due to the king only, and was distinguished into grand and petit serjeanty. The tenant holding by grand serjeanty was bound, instead of attending the king generally in his wars, to do some honorary service to the king in person, as to carry his banner or sword, or to be his butler, champion, or other officer at his coronation. Petit serjeanty differed from grand serjeanty, in that the service rendered to the king was not of a personal nature, but consisted in rendering him annually some small implement of war, as a bow, sword, arrow, lance, or the like. Cowell; Brown.

SERMENT. In old English law. Oath; an oath.

Sermo index animi. 5 Coke, 118. Speech is an index of the mind.

Sermo relatus ad personam intelligi debet de conditione personæ. Language which is referred to a person ought to be understood of the condition of the person. 4 Coke, 16.

Sermones semper accipiendi sunt secundum subjectam materiam, et conditionem personarum. 4 Coke, 14. Language is always to be understood according to its subject-matter, and the condition of the persons.

SERRATED. Notched on the edge; cut in notches like the teeth of a saw. This was anciently the method of trimming the top or edge of a deed of indenture. See INDENT, v.

SERVAGE, in feudal law, was where a tenant, besides payment of a certain rent, found one or more workmen for his lord's service. Tomlins.

Servanda est consuetudo loci ubi causa agitur. The custom of the place where the action is brought is to be observed. 3 Johns. Ch. 190, 219.

SERVANT. A servant is one who is employed to render personal services to his employer, otherwise than in the pursuit of an independent calling, and who in such service remains entirely under the control and direction of the latter, who is called his master. Civil Code Cal. § 2009.

Servants or domestics are those who receive wages, and stay in the house of the person paying and employing them for his services or that of his family; such are valets, footmen, cooks, butlers, and others who reside in the house. Civil Code La. art. 3205.

Free servants are in general all free persons who let, hire, or engage their services to another in the state, to be employed therein at any work, commerce, or occupation whatever for the benefit of him who has contracted with them, for a certain price or retribution, or upon certain conditions. Civil Code La. art. 163.

Servants are of two kinds,—menial servants, being persons retained by others to live within the walls of the house, and to perform the work and business of the household; and persons employed by men of trades and professions under them, to assist them in their particular callings. Mozley & Whitley.

SERVE. In Scotch practice. To render a verdict or decision in favor of a person claiming to be an heir; to declare the fact of his heirship judicially. A jury are said to *serve* a claimant *heir*, when they find him to be heir, upon the evidence submitted to them. Bell.

As to serving papers, etc., see SERVICE OF PROCESS.

SERVI. Lat. **In old European law.** Slaves; persons over whom their masters had absolute dominion.

In old English law. Bondmen; servile tenants. Cowell.

SERVI REDEMPTIONE. Criminal slaves in the time of Henry I. 1 Kemble, Sax. 197, (1849.)

SERVICE. **In contracts.** The being employed to serve another; duty or labor to be rendered by one person to another.

The term is used also for employment in one of the offices, departments, or agencies of the government; as in the phrases "civil service," "public service," etc.

In feudal law. Service was the consideration which the feudal tenants were bound to render to the lord in recompense for the lands they held of him. The services, in respect of their quality, were either free or base services, and, in respect of their quantity and the time of exacting them, were either certain or uncertain. 2 Bl. Comm. 60.

SERVICE BY PUBLICATION. In practice. Service of a summons or other process upon an absent or non-resident defendant, by publishing the same as an advertisement in a designated newspaper, with such other efforts to give him actual notice as the particular statute may prescribe.

SERVICE OF AN HEIR. An old form of Scotch law, fixing the right and character of an heir to the estate of his ancestor. Bell.

SERVICE OF PROCESS. The service of writs, summonses, rules, etc., signifies the delivering to or leaving them with the party to whom or with whom they ought to be delivered or left; and, when they are so delivered, they are then said to have been served. Usually a copy only is served and the original is shown. Brown.

SERVICE, SECULAR. Worldly service, as contrasted with spiritual or ecclesiastical. Cowell.

SERVICES FONCIERS. These are, in French law, the easements of English law. Brown.

SERVIDUMBRE. In Spanish Law. A servitude. The right and use which one man has in the buildings and estates of another, to use them for the benefit of his own. Las Partidas, 3, 31, 1.

SERVIENS AD CLAVAM. Serjeant at mace. 2 Mod. 58.

SERVIENS AD LEGEM. In old English practice. Serjeant at law.

SERVIENS DOMINI REGIS. In old English law. King's serjeant; a public officer, who acted sometimes as the sheriff's deputy, and had also judicial powers. Bract. fols. 145*b*, 150*b*, 330, 358.

SERVIENT. Serving; subject to a service or servitude. A *servient* estate is one which is burdened with a servitude.

SERVIENT TENEMENT. An estate in respect of which a service is owing, as the *dominant tenement* is that to which the service is due.

Servile est expilationis crimen; sola innocentia libera. 2 Inst. 573. The crime of theft is slavish; innocence alone is free.

Servitia personalia sequuntur personam. 2 Inst. 374. Personal services follow the person.

SERVITIIS ACQUIETANDIS. A judicial writ for a man distrained for services to one, when he owes and performs them to another, for the acquittal of such services. Reg. Jud. 27.

SERVITIUM. In feudal and old English law. The duty of obedience and performance which a tenant was bound to render to his lord, by reason of his fee. Spelman.

SERVITIUM FEODALE ET PRÆDIALE. A personal service, but due only by reason of lands which were held in fee. Bract. l. 2, c. 16.

SERVITIUM FORINSECUM. Forinsic, foreign, or extra service; a kind of service that was due to the king, over and above (*foris*) the service due to the lord.

Servitium, in lege Angliæ, regulariter accipitur pro servitio quod per tenentes dominis suis debetur ratione feodi sui. Co. Litt. 65. Service, by the law of England, means the service which is due from the tenants to the lords, by reason of their fee.

SERVITIUM INTRINSECUM. Intrinsic or ordinary service; the ordinary service due the chief lord, from tenants within the fee. Bract. fols. 36, 36*b*.

SERVITIUM LIBERUM. A service to be done by feudatory tenants, who were called "*liberi homines*," and distinguished from vassals, as was their service, for they were not bound to any of the base services of plowing the lord's land, etc., but were to find a man and horse, or go with the lord into the army, or to attend the court, etc. Cowell.

SERVITIUM MILITARE. Knight-service; military service. 2 Bl. Comm. 62.

SERVITIUM REGALE. Royal service, or the rights and preogatives of manors which belong to the king as lord of the same, and which were generally reckoned to be six, viz.: Power of judicature, in matters of property; power of life and death, in felonies and murder; a right to waifs and strays; assessments; minting of money; and assise of bread, beer, weights, and measures. Cowell.

SERVITIUM SCUTI. Service of the shield; that is, knight-service.

SERVITIUM SOKÆ. Service of the plow; that is, socage.

SERVITOR. A serving-man; particularly applied to students at Oxford, upon the foundation, who are similar to sizars at Cambridge. Wharton.

SERVITORS OF BILLS. In old English practice. Servants or messengers of the marshal of the king's bench, sent out with bills or writs to summon persons to that court. Now more commonly called "tipstaves." Cowell.

SERVITUDE. 1. The condition of being bound to service; the state of a person who is subjected, voluntarily or otherwise, to another person as his servant.

2. A charge upon one estate for the benefit of another. A species of incorporeal right derived from the civil law, resembling and answering to the *easement* of the common law. 3 Kent, Comm. 434.

The term "servitude," in its original and popular sense, signifies the duty of service, or rather the condition of one who is liable to the performance of services. The word, however, in its legal sense, is applied figuratively to things. When the freedom of ownership in land is fettered or restricted, by reason of some person, other than the owner thereof, having some right therein, the land is said to "serve" such person. The restricted condition of the ownership or the right which forms the subject-matter of the restriction is termed a "servitude," and the land so burdened with another's right is termed a "servient tenement," while the land belonging to the person enjoying the right is called the "dominant tenement." The word "servitude" may be said to have both a positive and a negative signification; in the former sense denoting the restrictive right belonging to the entitled party; in the latter, the restrictive duty entailed upon the proprietor or possessor of the servient land. Brown.

All servitudes which affect lands may be divided into two kinds,—*personal* and *real*. Personal servitudes are those attached to the person for whose benefit they are established, and terminate with his life. This kind of servitude is of three sorts,—usufruct, use, and habitation. Real servitudes, which are also called "predial" or "landed" servitudes, are those which the owner of an estate enjoys on a neighboring estate for the benefit of his own estate. They are called "predial" or "landed" servitudes because, being established for the benefit of an estate, they are rather due to the estate than to the owner personally. Civil Code La. art. 646.

Real servitudes are divided, in the civil law, into *rural* and *urban* servitudes. Rural servitudes are such as are established for the benefit of a landed estate; such, for example, as a right of way over the servient tenement, or of access to a spring, a coal-mine, a sand-pit, or a wood that is upon it. Urban servitudes are such as are established for the benefit of one building over another. (But the buildings need not be in the city, as the name would apparently imply.) They are such as the right of support, or of view, or of drip or sewer, or the like. See Mackeld. Rom. Law, § 316, et seq.

SERVITUS. Lat. In the civil law. Slavery; bondage; the state of service. Defined as "an institution of the conventional law of nations, by which one person is subjected to the dominion of another, contrary to natural right." Inst. 1, 3, 2.

Also a service or servitude; an easement.

SERVITUS ACTUS. The servitude or right of walking, riding, or driving over another's ground. Inst. 2, 3, pr. A species of right of way.

SERVITUS ALTIUS NON TOLLENDI. The servitude of not building higher. A right attached to a house, by which its proprietor can prevent his neighbor from building his own house higher. Inst. 2, 3, 4.

SERVITUS AQUÆ DUCENDÆ. The servitude of leading water; the right of leading water to one's own premises through another's land. Inst. 2, 3, pr.

SERVITUS AQUÆ EDUCENDÆ. The servitude of leading off water; the right of leading off the water from one's own onto another's ground. Dig. 8, 3, 29.

SERVITUS AQUÆ HAURIENDÆ. The servitude or right of draining water from another's spring or well. Inst. 2, 3, 2.

SERVITUS CLOACÆ MITTENDÆ. The servitude or right of having a sewer through the house or ground of one's neighbor. Dig. 8, 1, 7.

Servitus est constitutio jure gentium qua quis domino alieno contra naturam subjicitur. Slavery is an institution by the law of nations, by which a man is subjected to the dominion of another, contrary to nature. Inst. 1, 3, 2; Co. Litt. 116.

SERVITUS FUMI IMMITTENDI. The servitude or right of leading off smoke or vapor through the chimney or over the ground of one's neighbor. Dig. 8, 5, 8, 5-7.

SERVITUS ITINERIS. The servitude or privilege of walking, riding, and being carried over another's ground. Inst. 2, 3, pr. A species of right of way.

SERVITUS LUMINUM. The servitude of lights; the right of making or having windows or other openings in a wall belonging to another, or in a common wall, in order to obtain light for one's building. Dig. 8, 2, 4.

SERVITUS NE LUMINIBUS OFFICIATUR. A servitude not to hinder lights: the right of having one's lights or windows unobstructed or darkened by a neighbor's building, etc. Inst. 2, 3, 4.

SERVITUS NE PROSPECTUS OFFENDATUR. A servitude not to obstruct one's prospect, *i. e.*, not to intercept the view from one's house. Dig. 8, 2, 15.

SERVITUS ONERIS FERENDI. The servitude of bearing weight; the right to let one's building rest upon the building, wall, or pillars of one's neighbor. Mackeld. Rom. Law, § 317.

SERVITUS PASCENDI. The servitude of pasturing; the right of pasturing one's cattle on another's ground; otherwise called "*jus pascendi.*" Inst. 2, 3, 2.

SERVITUS PECORIS AD AQUAM ADPULSAM. A right of driving one's cattle on a neighbor's land to water.

SERVITUS PRÆDII RUSTICI. The servitude of a rural or country estate; a rural servitude. Inst. 2, 3, pr., and 3.

SERVITUS PRÆDII URBANI. The servitude of an urban or city estate; an urban servitude. Inst. 2, 3, 1.

SERVITUS PRÆDIORUM. A prædial servitude; a service, burden, or charge upon one estate for the benefit of another. Inst. 2, 3, 3.

SERVITUS PROJICIENDI. The servitude of projecting; the right of building a projection from one's house in the open space belonging to one's neighbor. Dig. 8, 2, 2.

SERVITUS PROSPECTUS. A right of prospect. This may be either to give one a free prospect over his neighbor's land or to prevent a neighbor from having a prospect over one's own land. Dig. 8, 2, 15; Domat. 1, 1, 6.

SERVITUS STILLICIDII. The right of drip; the right of having the water drip from the eaves of one's house upon the house or ground of one's neighbor. Inst. 2, 3, 1, 4; Dig. 8, 2, 2.

SERVITUS TIGNI IMMITTENDI. The servitude of letting in a beam; the right of inserting beams in a neighbor's wall. Inst. 2, 3, 1, 4; Dig. 8, 2, 2.

SERVITUS VIÆ. The servitude or right of way; the right of walking, riding, and driving over another's land. Inst. 2, 3, pr.

SERVUS. Lat. In the civil and old English law. A slave; a bondman. Inst. 1, 3, pr.; Bract. fol. 4*b*.

SESS. In English law. A tax, rate, or assessment.

SESSIO. Lat. In old English law. A sitting; a session. *Sessio parliamenti*, the sitting of parliament. Cowell.

SESSION. The sitting of a court, legislature, council, commission, etc., for the transaction of its proper business. Hence, the period of time, within any one day, during which such body is assembled in form, and engaged in the transaction of business, or, in a more extended sense, the whole space of time from its first assembling to its prorogation or adjournment *sine die*.

SESSION, COURT OF. The supreme civil court of Scotland, instituted A. D. 1532, consisting of thirteen (formerly fifteen) judges, viz., the lord president, the lord justice clerk, and eleven ordinary lords.

SESSION, GREAT, OF WALES. A court which was abolished by St. 1 Wm. IV. c. 70. The proceedings now issue out of the courts at Westminster, and two of the judges of the superior courts hold the circuits in Wales and Cheshire, as in other English counties. Wharton.

SESSION LAWS. The name commonly given to the body of laws enacted by a state legislature at one of its annual or biennial sessions. So called to distinguish them from the "compiled laws" or "revised statutes" of the state.

SESSION OF THE PEACE, in English law, is a sitting of justices of the peace for the exercise of their powers. There are four kinds,—petty, special, quarter, and general sessions.

SESSIONAL ORDERS. Certain resolutions which are agreed to by both houses at the commencement of every session of the English parliament, and have relation to the business and convenience thereof; but they are not intended to continue in force beyond the session in which they are adopted. They are principally of use as directing the order of business. Brown.

SESSIONS. A sitting of justices in court upon their commission, or by virtue of their appointment, and most commonly for the trial of criminal cases. The title of several courts in England and the United States, chiefly those of criminal jurisdiction. Burrill.

SET. This word appears to be nearly synonymous with "lease." A lease of mines is frequently termed a "mining set." Brown.

SET ASIDE. To set aside a judgment, decree, award, or any proceedings is to cancel, annul, or revoke them at the instance of a party unjustly or irregularly affected by them.

SET DOWN. To set down a cause for trial or hearing at a given term is to enter its title in the calendar, list, or docket of causes which are to be brought on at that term.

SET OF EXCHANGE. In mercantile law. Foreign bills are usually drawn in duplicate or triplicate, the several parts being called respectively "first of exchange," "second of exchange," etc., and these parts together constitute a "set of exchange." Any one of them being paid, the others become void.

SET-OFF. A counter-claim or cross-demand; a claim or demand which the defendant in an action sets off against the claim of the plaintiff, as being his due, whereby he may extinguish the plaintiff's demand, either in whole or in part, according to the amount of the set-off.

Set-off is a defense which goes not to the justice of the plaintiff's demand, but sets up a demand against the plaintiff to counterbalance his in whole or in part. Code Ga. 1882, § 2899.

For the distinction between set-off and recoupment, see RECOUPMENT.

"Set-off" differs from a "lien," inasmuch as the former belongs exclusively to the remedy, and is merely a right to insist, if the party think proper to do so, when sued by his creditor on a counter-demand, which can only be enforced through the medium of judicial proceedings; while the latter is, in effect, a substitute for a suit. 2 Op. Attys. Gen. 677.

SET OUT. In pleading. To recite or narrate facts or circumstances; to allege or aver; to describe or to incorporate; as, to set out a deed or contract.

SET UP. To bring forward or allege, as something relied upon or deemed sufficient; to propose or interpose, by way of defense, explanation, or justification; as, to set up the statute of limitations, *i. e.*, offer and rely upon it as a defense to a claim.

SETTER. In Scotch law. The granter of a tack or lease. 1 Forb. Inst. pt. 2, p. 153.

SETTLE. To adjust, ascertain, or liquidate; to pay. Parties are said to *settle* an account when they go over its items and ascertain and agree upon the balance due from one to the other. And, when the party indebted pays such balance, he is also said to settle it. 9 Wis. 38.

To settle property is to limit it, or the income of it, to several persons in succession, so that the person for the time being in the possession or enjoyment of it has no power to deprive the others of their right of future enjoyment. Sweet.

To settle a document is to make it right in form and in substance. Documents of difficulty or complexity, such as mining leases, settlements by will or deed, partnership agreements, etc., are generally settled by counsel. Id.

The term "settle" is also applied to paupers.

SETTLE UP. A term, colloquial rather than legal, which is applied to the final collection, adjustment, and distribution of the estate of a decedent, a bankrupt, or an insolvent corporation. It includes the processes of collecting the property, paying debts and charges, and turning over the balance to those entitled to receive it.

SETTLEMENT. In conveyancing. A disposition of property by deed, usually through the medium of a trustee, by which its enjoyment is limited to several persons in succession, as a wife, children, or other relatives.

In contracts. Adjustment or liquidation of mutual accounts; the act by which parties who have been dealing together arrange their accounts and strike a balance. Also full and final payment or discharge of an account.

The term also signifies a right acquired by a person, by continued residence for a given length of time in a town or district, to claim aid or relief under the poor-laws in case of his becoming a pauper.

SETTLEMENT, ACT OF. The statute 12 & 13 Wm. III. c. 2, by which the crown of England was limited to the house of Hanover, and some new provisions were added at the same time for the better securing the religion, laws, and liberties.

SETTLEMENT, DEED OF. A deed made for the purpose of settling property, *i. e.*, arranging the mode and extent of the enjoyment thereof. The party who settles property is called the "settlor;" and usually his wife and children or his creditors or his near relations are the beneficiaries taking interests under the settlement. Brown.

SETTLEMENT, EQUITY OF. The equitable right of a wife, when her husband sues in equity for the reduction of her equitable estate to his own possession, to have the whole or a portion of such estate settled upon herself and her children. Also a similar right now recognized by the equity courts as directly to be asserted against the husband. Also called the "wife's equity."

SETTLER. A person who, for the purpose of acquiring a pre-emption right, has gone upon the land in question, and is actually resident there. See 27 Minn. 222, 6 N. W. Rep. 615.

SETTLING A BILL OF EXCEPTIONS. When the bill of exceptions prepared for an appeal is not accepted as correct by the respondent, it is *settled* (*i. e.*, adjusted and finally made conformable to the truth) by being taken before the judge who presided at the trial, and by him put into a form agreeing with his minutes and his recollection.

SETTLING DAY. The day on which transactions for the "account" are made up on the English stock-exchange. In consols they are monthly; in other investments, twice in the month.

SETTLING INTERROGATORIES. The determination by the court of objections to interrogatories and cross-interrogatories prepared to be used in taking a deposition.

SETTLING ISSUES. In English practice. Arranging or determining the form of the issues in a cause. "Where, in any action, it appears to the judge that the statement of claim or defense or reply does not sufficiently disclose the issues of fact between the parties, he may direct the parties to prepare issues; and such issues shall, if the parties differ, be *settled* by the judge." Judicature Act 1875, schedule, art. 19.

SEVER. To separate. When two joint defendants separate in the action, each pleading separately his own plea and relying upon a separate defense, they are said to *sever*.

SEVERABLE. Admitting of severance or separation, capable of being divided; capable of being severed from other things to which it was joined, and yet maintaining a complete and independent existence.

SEVERAL. Separate; individual; independent. In this sense the word is distinguished from "joint." Also exclusive; individual; appropriated. In this sense it is opposed to "common."

SEVERAL ACTIONS. Where a separate and distinct action is brought against each of two or more persons who are all liable to the plaintiff in respect to the same subject-matter, the actions are said to be "several." If all the persons are joined as defendants in one and the same action, it is called a "joint" action.

SEVERAL COUNTS. Where a plaintiff has several distinct causes of action, he is allowed to pursue them cumulatively in the same action, subject to certain rules which the law prescribes. Wharton.

SEVERAL COVENANT. A covenant by two or more, separately; a covenant made so as to bind the parties to it severally, or individually.

SEVERAL DEMISES. In English practice. In the action of ejectment, it was formerly customary, in case there were any doubt as to the legal estate being in the plaintiff, to insert in the declaration several demises from as many different persons; but this was rendered unnecessary by the provisions of the common-law procedure acts.

SEVERAL FISHERY. A fishery of which the owner is also the owner of the soil, or derives his right from the owner of the soil. 2 Bl. Comm. 39, 40; 1 Steph. Comm. 671, note.

SEVERAL INHERITANCE. An inheritance conveyed so as to descend to two persons severally, by moieties, etc.

SEVERAL ISSUES. This occurs where there is more than one issue involved in a case. 3 Steph. Comm. 560.

SEVERAL TAIL. An entail severally to two; as if land is given to two men and their wives, and to the heirs of their bodies begotten; here the donees have a joint estate for their two lives, and yet they have a several inheritance, because the issue of the one shall have his moiety, and the issue of the other the other moiety. Cowell.

SEVERAL TENANCY. A tenancy which is separate, and not held jointly with another person.

SEVERALTY. A state of separation. An estate in *severalty* is one that is held by a person in his own right only, without any other person being joined or connected with him, in point of interest, during his estate therein. 2 Bl. Comm. 179.

The term "severalty" is especially applied, in England, to the case of adjoining meadows undivided from each other, but belonging, either permanently or in what are called "shifting severalties," to separate owners, and held in severalty until the crops have been carried, when the whole is thrown open as pasture for the cattle of all the owners, and in some cases for the cattle of other persons as well; each owner is called a "severalty owner," and his rights of pasture are called "severalty rights," as opposed to the rights of persons not owners. Cooke, Incl. Acts, 47, 163*n*.

SEVERANCE. In pleading. Separation; division. The separation by defendants in their pleas; the adoption, by several defendants, of separate pleas, instead of joining in the same plea. Steph. Pl. 257.

In estates. The destruction of any one of the unities of a joint tenancy. It is so called because the estate is no longer a joint tenancy, but is severed.

The word "severance" is also used to signify the cutting of the crops, such as corn, grass, etc., or the separating of anything from the realty. Brown.

SEWARD, or SEAWARD. One who guards the sea-coast; *custos maris*.

SEWER. A fresh-water trench or little river, encompassed with banks on both sides, to drain off surplus water into the sea. Cowell. Properly, a trench artificially made for the purpose of carrying water into the sea, (or a river or pond.) Crabb, Real Prop. § 113.

In its modern and more usual sense, a "sewer" means an under-ground or covered channel used for the drainage of two or more separate buildings, as opposed to a "drain," which is a channel used for carrying off the drainage of one building or set of buildings in one curtilage. Sweet.

SEWERS, COMMISSIONERS OF. In English law. The court of commissioners of sewers is a temporary tribunal erected by virtue of a commission under the great seal. Its jurisdiction is to overlook the repairs of sea-banks and sea-walls, and the cleansing of public rivers, streams, ditches, and other conduits whereby any waters are carried off, and is confined to such county or particular district as the commission expressly names. Brown.

SEX. The distinction between male and female; or the property or character by which an animal is male or female. Webster.

SEXAGESIMA SUNDAY. The second Sunday before Lent, being about the sixtieth day before Easter.

SEXHINDENI. In Saxon law. The middle thanes, valued at 600s.

SEXTANS. Lat. In Roman law. A subdivision of the *as*, containing two *unciæ;* the proportion of two-twelfths, or one-sixth. 2 Bl. Comm. 462, note.

SEXTARY. In old records. An ancient measure of liquids, and of dry commodities; a quarter or seam. Spelman.

SEXTERY LANDS. Lands given to a church or religious house for maintenance of a sexton or sacristan. Cowell.

SEXTUS DECRETALIUM. Lat. The sixth (book) of the decretals; the sext, or sixth decretal. So called because appended, in the body of the canon law, to the five books of the decretals of Gregory IX.; it consists of a collection of supplementary decretals, and was published A. D. 1298. Butl. Hor. Jur. 172; 1 Bl. Comm. 82.

SHACK. In English law. The straying and escaping of cattle out of the lands of their owners into other uninclosed land; an intercommoning of cattle. 2 H. Bl. 416.

It sometimes happens that a number of adjacent fields, though held in severalty, *i. e.*, by separate owners, and cultivated separately, are, after the crop on each parcel has been carried in, thrown open as pasture to the cattle of all the owners. "Arable lands cultivated on this plan are called 'shack fields,' and the right of each owner of a part to feed cattle over the whole during the autumn and winter is known in law as 'common of shack,' a right which is distinct in its nature from common because of vicinage, though sometimes said to be nearly identical with it." Elton, Commons, 30; Sweet.

SHACK, COMMON OF. The right of persons occupying lands lying together in the same common field, to turn out their cattle after harvest to feed promiscuously in such field.

SHALL. As against the government, the word "shall," when used in statutes, is to be construed as "may," unless a contrary intention is manifest. 95 U. S. 170.

SHAM PLEA. A false plea; a plea of false or fictitious matter, subtly drawn so as to entrap an opponent, or create delay. 3 Chit. Pr. 729, 730.

A vexatious or false defense, resorted to under the old system of pleading for purposes of delay and annoyance. Steph. Pl. 383.

Mr. Chitty defines sham pleas to be pleas so palpably and manifestly untrue that the court will assume them to be so; pleas manifestly absurd. When answers or defenses admit of lawyer-like argument, such as courts should listen to, they are not "sham," in the sense of the statute. When it needs argument to prove that an answer or demurrer is frivolous, it is not frivolous, and should not be stricken off. To warrant this summary mode of disposing of a defense, the mere reading of the pleadings should be sufficient to disclose, without deliberation and without a doubt, that the defense is sham or irrelevant. 40 Wis. 559.

SHARE. A portion of anything. When a whole is divided into shares, they are not necessarily equal.

In the law of corporations and joint-stock companies, a share is a definite portion of the capital of a company.

SHARE AND SHARE ALIKE. In equal shares or proportions.

SHARE-CERTIFICATE. A share-certificate is an instrument under the seal of the company, certifying that the person therein named is entitled to a certain number of shares; it is *prima facie* evidence of his title thereto. Lindl. Partn. 150, 1187.

SHARE-WARRANT. A share-warrant to bearer is a warrant or certificate under the seal of the company, stating that the bearer of the warrant is entitled to a certain number or amount of fully paid up shares or stock. Coupons for payment of dividends may be annexed to it. Delivery of the share-warrant operates as a transfer of the shares or stock. Sweet.

SHAREHOLDER. In the strict sense of the term, a "shareholder" is a person who has agreed to become a member of a corporation or company, and with respect to whom all the required formalities have been gone through; *e. g.*, signing of deed of settlement, registration, or the like. A shareholder by estoppel is a person who has acted and been treated as a shareholder, and consequently has the same liabilities as if he were an ordinary shareholder. Lindl. Partn. 130.

SHARP. A "sharp" clause in a mortgage or other security (or the whole instrument described as "sharp") is one which empowers the creditor to take prompt and summary action upon default in payment or breach of other conditions.

SHARPING CORN. A customary gift of corn, which, at every Christmas, the farmers in some parts of England give to their smith for sharpening their plow-irons, harrow-tines, etc. Blount.

SHASTER. In Hindu law. The instrument of government or instruction; any book of instructions, particularly containing Divine ordinances. Wharton.

SHAVE. While "shave" is sometimes used to denote the act of obtaining the property of another by oppression and extortion, it may be used in an innocent sense to denote the buying of existing notes and other securities for money, at a discount. Hence to charge a man with using money for shaving is not libelous *per se*. 2 Denio, 300.

SHAW. In old English law. A wood. Co. Litt. 4*b*.

SHAWATORES. Soldiers. Cowell.

SHEADING. A riding, tithing, or division in the Isle of Man, where the whole island is divided into six sheadings, in each of which there is a coroner or chief constable appointed by a delivery of a rod at the Tinewald court or annual convention. King, Isle of Man, 7.

SHEEP. A wether more than a year old. 4 Car. & P. 216.

SHEEP-HEAVES. Small plots of pasture, in England, often in the middle of the waste of a manor, of which the soil may or may not be in the lord, but the pasture is private property, and leased or sold as such. They principally occur in the northern counties, (Cooke, Incl. Acts 44,) and seem to be corporeal hereditaments, (Elton, Commons, 35,) although they are sometimes classed with rights of common, but erroneously, the right being an exclusive right of pasture. Sweet.

SHEEP-SILVER. A service turned into money, which was paid in respect that anciently the tenants used to wash the lord's sheep. Wharton.

SHEEP-SKIN. A deed; so called from the parchment it was written on.

SHEEP-WALK. A right of sheep-walk is the same thing as a fold-course, (*q. v.*) Elton, Commons, 44.

SHELLEY'S CASE, RULE IN. "When the ancestor, by any gift or conveyance, taketh an estate of freehold, and in the same gift or conveyance an estate is limited, either mediately or immediately, to his heirs in fee or in tail, the 'heirs' are words of limitation of the estate, and not words of purchase." 1 Coke, 104.

Intimately connected with the quantity of estate which a tenant may hold in realty is the antique feudal doctrine generally known as the "Rule in Shelley's Case," which is reported by Lord Coke in 1 Coke, 93*b*, (23 Eliz. in C. B.) This rule was not first laid down or established in that case, but was then simply admitted in argument as a well-founded and settled rule of law, and has always since been quoted as the "Rule in Shelley's Case." Wharton.

SHEPWAY, COURT OF. A court held before the lord warden of the Cinque Ports. A writ of error lay from the mayor and jurats of each port to the lord warden in this court, and thence to the queen's bench. The civil jurisdiction of the Cinque Ports is abolished by 18 & 19 Vict. c. 48.

SHEREFFE. The body of the lordship of Cærdiff in South Wales, excluding the members of it. Powel, Hist. Wales, 123.

SHERIFF. In American law. The chief executive and administrative officer of a county, being chosen by popular election. His principal duties are in aid of the criminal courts and civil courts of record; such as serving process, summoning juries, executing judgments, holding judicial sales, and the like. He is also the chief conservator of the peace within his territorial jurisdiction.

In English law. The sheriff is the principal officer in every county, and has the transacting of the public business of the county. He is an officer of great antiquity, and was also called the "shire-reeve," "reeve," or "bailiff." He is called in Latin "*vice-comes*," as being the deputy of the earl or *comes*, to whom anciently the custody of the shire was committed. The duties of the sheriff principally consist in executing writs, precepts, warrants from justices of the peace for the apprehension of offenders, etc. Brown.

In Scotch law. The office of sheriff differs somewhat from the same office under the English law, being, from ancient times, an office of important judicial power, as well as ministerial. The sheriff exercises a jurisdiction of considerable extent, both of civil and criminal character, which is, in a proper sense, judicial, in addition to powers resembling those of an English sheriff. Tomlins; Bell.

SHERIFF CLERK. The clerk of the sheriff's court in Scotland.

SHERIFF DEPUTE. In Scotch law. The principal sheriff of a county, who is also a judge.

SHERIFF-GELD. A rent formerly paid by a sheriff, and it is prayed that the sheriff in his account may be discharged thereof. Rot. Parl. 50 Edw. III.

SHERIFF-TOOTH. In English law. A tenure by the service of providing entertainment for the sheriff at his county-courts; a common tax, formerly levied for the sheriff's diet. Wharton.

SHERIFF'S COURT. The court held before the sheriff's deputy, that is, the under-sheriff, and wherein actions are brought for recovery of debts under £20. Writs of inquiry are also brought here to be executed. The sheriff's court for the county of Middlesex is that wherein damages are assessed in proper cases after trial at Westminster. Brown.

SHERIFF'S COURT IN LONDON. See CITY OF LONDON COURT.

SHERIFF'S JURY. In practice. A jury composed of no determinate number, but which may be more or less than twelve, summoned by the sheriff for the purposes of an inquisition or inquest of office. 3 Bl. Comm. 258.

SHERIFF'S OFFICERS. Bailiffs, who are either bailiffs of hundreds or bound-bailiffs.

SHERIFF'S SALE. A sale of property, conducted by a sheriff, or sheriff's deputy, in virtue of his authority as an officer holding process.

SHERIFF'S TOURN. A court of record in England, held twice every year, within a month after Easter and Michaelmas, before the sheriff, in different parts of the county. It is, indeed, only the *turn* or rotation of the sheriff to keep a court-leet in each respective hundred. It is the great court-leet of the county, as the county court is the court-baron; for out of this, for the ease of the sheriff, was taken the court-leet or view of frank-pledge. 4 Bl. Comm. 273.

SHERIFFALTY. The time of a man's being sheriff. Cowell. The term of a sheriff's office.

SHERIFFWICK. The jurisdiction of a sheriff. Called, in modern law, "bailiwick." The office of a sheriff.

SHERRERIE. A word used by the authorities of the Roman Church, to specify contemptuously the technical parts of the law, as administered by non-clerical lawyers. Wharton.

SHEWER. In the practice of the English high court, when a view by a jury is ordered, persons are named by the court to show the property to be viewed, and are hence called "shewers." There is usually a shewer on behalf of each party. Archb. Pr. 339, et seq.

SHEWING. In English law. To be quit of attachment in a court, in plaints shewed and not avowed. Obsolete.

SHIFTING CLAUSE. A shifting clause in a settlement is a clause by which some other mode of devolution is substituted for that primarily prescribed. Examples of shifting clauses are: The ordinary name and arms clause, and the clause of less frequent occurrence by which a settled estate is destined as the foundation of a second family, in the event of the elder branch becoming otherwise enriched. These shifting clauses take effect under the statute of uses. Sweet.

SHIFTING USE. A use which is so limited that it will be made to shift or transfer itself, from one beneficiary to another, upon the occurrence of a certain event after its creation. For example, an estate is limited to the use of A. and his heirs, provided that, upon the return of B. from Rome, it shall be to the use of C. and his heirs; this is a shifting use, which transfers itself to C.

when the event happens. 1 Steph. Comm. 503; 2 Bl. Comm. 335.

These shifting uses are common in all settlements; and, in marriage settlements, the first use is always to the owner in fee till the marriage, and then to other uses. The fee remains with the owner until the marriage, and then it *shifts* as uses arise. 4 Kent, Comm. 297.

SHILLING. In English law. The name of an English coin, of the value of one-twentieth part of a pound. This denomination of money was also used in America, in colonial times, but was not everywhere of uniform value.

SHIN-PLASTER. Formerly, a jocose term for a bank-note greatly depreciated in value; also for paper money of a denomination less than a dollar. Webster. See 2 Ind. 483.

SHIP, *v.* In maritime law. To put on board a ship; to send by ship.

To engage to serve on board a vessel as a seaman.

SHIP, *n.* A vessel of any kind employed in navigation. In a more restricted and more technical sense, a three-masted vessel navigated with sails.

The term "ship" or "shipping," when used in this Code, includes steam-boats, sailing vessels, canal-boats, barges, and every structure adapted to be navigated from place to place for the transportation of merchandise or persons. Civil Code Cal. § 960.

Nautical men apply the term "ship" to distinguish a vessel having three masts, each consisting of a lower mast, a topmast, and a top-gallant mast, with their appropriate rigging. In familiar language, it is usually employed to distinguish any large vessel, however rigged. It is also frequently used as a general designation for all vessels navigated with sails; and this is the sense in which it is employed in law. Tomlins.

SHIP-BREAKING. In Scotch law. The offense of breaking into a ship. Arkley, 461.

SHIP-BROKER. An agent for the transaction of business between ship-owners and charterers or those who ship cargoes.

SHIP-CHANDLERY. This is a term of extensive import, and includes everything necessary to furnish and equip a vessel, so as to render her seaworthy for the intended voyage. Not only stores, stoves, hardware, and crockery have been held to be within the term, but muskets and other arms also, the voyage being round Cape Horn to California, in the course of which voyage arms are sometimes carried for safety. 1 Wall. Jr. 368.

SHIP-DAMAGE. In the charter-parties with the English East India Company, these words occur. Their meaning is, damage from negligence, insufficiency, or bad stowage in the ship. Abb. Shipp. 204.

SHIP-MASTER. The captain or master of a merchant ship, appointed and put in command by the owner, and having general control of the vessel and cargo, with power to bind the owner by his lawful acts and engagements in the management of the ship.

SHIP-MONEY. In English law. An imposition formerly levied on port-towns and other places for fitting out ships; revived by Charles I., and abolished in the same reign. 17 Car. I. c. 14.

SHIP'S BILL. The copy of the bill of lading retained by the master is called the "ship's bill." It is not authoritative as to the terms of the contract of affreightment; the bill delivered to the shipper must control, if the two do not agree. 14 Wall. 98.

SHIP'S HUSBAND. In maritime law. A person appointed by the several part-owners of a ship, and usually one of their number, to manage the concerns of the ship for the common benefit. Generally understood to be the general agent of the owners in regard to all the affairs of the ship in the home port. Story, Ag. § 35; 3 Kent, Comm. 151.

SHIP'S PAPERS. The papers which must be carried by a vessel on a voyage, in order to furnish evidence of her national character, the nature and destination of the cargo, and of compliance with the navigation laws.

The ship's papers are of two sorts: Those required by the law of a particular country; such as the certificate of registry, license, charter-party, bills of lading and of health, required by the law of England to be on board all British ships. Those required by the law of nations to be on board neutral ships, to vindicate their title to that character; these are the passport, sea-brief, or sea-letter, proofs of property, the muster-roll or *rôle d'equipage*, the charter-party, the bills of lading and invoices, the log-book or ship's journal, and the bill of health. 1 Marsh. Ins. c. 9, § 6.

SHIPPED. This term, in common maritime and commercial usage, means "placed on board of a vessel for the purchaser or consignee, to be transported at his risk." 10 Gray, 262.

SHIPPER. 1. The owner of goods who intrusts them on board a vessel for delivery abroad, by charter-party or otherwise.

2. Also, a Dutch word, signifying the master of a ship. It is mentioned in some of the statutes; is now generally called "skipper." Tomlins.

SHIPPING. Ships in general; ships or vessels of any kind intended for navigation. Relating to ships; as, shipping interest, shipping affairs, shipping business, shipping concerns. Putting on board a ship or vessel, or receiving on board a ship or vessel. Webster; Worcester.

The "law of shipping" is a comprehensive term for all that part of the maritime law which relates to ships and the persons employed in or about them. It embraces such subjects as the building and equipment of vessels, their registration and nationality, their ownership and inspection, their employment, (including charter-parties, freight, demurrage, towage, and salvage,) and their sale, transfer, and mortgage; also, the employment, rights, powers, and duties of masters and mariners; and the law relating to ship-brokers, ship-agents, pilots, etc.

SHIPPING ARTICLES. A written agreement between the master of a vessel and the mariners, specifying the voyage or term for which the latter are shipped, and the rate of wages.

SHIPPING COMMISSIONER. An officer of the United States, appointed by the several circuit courts, within their respective jurisdictions, for each port of entry (the same being also a port of ocean navigation) which, in the judgment of such court, may require the same; his duties being to supervise the engagement and discharge of seamen; to see that men engaged as seamen report on board at the proper time; to facilitate the apprenticing of persons to the marine service; and other similar duties, such as may be required by law. Rev. St. U. S. §§ 4501-4508.

SHIPWRECK. The demolition or shattering of a vessel, caused by her driving ashore or on rocks and shoals in the mid-seas, or by the violence of winds and waves in tempests. 2 Arn. Ins. p. 734.

SHIRE. In English law. A county. So called because every county or shire is divided and parted by certain metes and bounds from another. Co. Litt. 50*a*.

SHIRE-CLERK. He that keeps the county court.

SHIRE-MAN, or SCYRE-MAN. Before the Conquest, the judge of the county, by whom trials for land, etc., were determined. Tomlins; Mozley & Whitley.

SHIRE-MOTE. The assize of the shire, or the assembly of the people, was so called by the Saxons. It was nearly, if not exactly, the same as the *scyregemote*, and in most respects corresponded with what were afterwards called the "county courts." Brown.

SHIRE-REEVE. In Saxon law. The reeve or bailiff of the shire. The *viscount* of the Anglo-Normans, and the *sheriff* of later times. Co. Litt. 168*a*.

SHOOFAA. In Mohammedan law. Preemption, or a power of possessing property which has been sold, by paying a sum equal to that paid by the purchaser. Wharton.

SHOP. A building in which goods and merchandise are sold at retail.

Strictly, a shop is a place where goods are sold by retail, and a store a place where goods are deposited; but, in this country, shops for the sale of goods are frequently called "stores." 15 Gray, 197.

SHOP-BOOKS. Books of original entry kept by tradesmen, shop-keepers, mechanics, and the like, in which are entered their accounts and charges for goods sold, work done, etc.

SHOPA. In old records, a shop. Cowell.

SHORE. Land on the margin of the sea, or a lake or river.

In common parlance, the word "shore" is understood to mean the line that separates the tide-water from the land about it, wherever that line may be, and in whatever stage of the tide. The word "shore," in its legal and technical sense, indicates the lands adjacent to navigable waters, where the tide flows and reflows, which at high tides are submerged, and at low tides are bare. 23 N. J. Law, 624, 683.

Sea-shore is that space of land over which the waters of the sea spread in the highest water, during the winter season. Civil Code La. art. 451.

When the sea-shore is referred to as a boundary, the meaning must be understood to be the margin of the sea in its usual and ordinary state; the ground between the ordinary high-water mark and low-water mark is the shore. Hence a deed of land bounded at or by the "shore" will convey the flats as appurtenant. 6 Mass. 435.

SHORT CAUSE. A cause which is not likely to occupy a great portion of the time of the court, and which may be entered on the list of "short causes," upon the application of one of the parties, and will then be heard more speedily than it would be in its regular order. This practice obtains in the English chancery and in some of the American states.

SHORT ENTRY. A custom of bankers of entering on the customer's pass-book the amount of notes deposited for collection, in such a manner that the amount is not carried to the latter's general balance until the notes are paid. See ENTERING SHORT.

SHORT LEASE. A term applied colloquially, but without much precision, to a lease for a short term, (as a month or a year,) as distinguished from one running for a long period.

SHORT NOTICE. In practice. Notice of less than the ordinary time; generally of half that time. 2 Tidd, Pr. 757.

SHORT SUMMONS. A process, authorized in some of the states, to be issued against an absconding, fraudulent, or non-resident debtor, which is returnable within a less number of days than an ordinary writ of summons.

SHORTFORD. An old custom of the city of Exeter. A mode of foreclosing the right of a tenant by the chief lord of the fee, in cases of non-payment of rent. Cowell.

SHOW. Although the words "show" and "indicate" are sometimes interchangeable in popular use, they are not always so. To "show" is to make apparent or clear by evidence; to prove; while an "indication" may be merely a symptom; that which points to or gives direction to the mind. 104 Pa. St. 133.

SHOW CAUSE. To show cause against a rule *nisi*, an order, decree, execution, etc., is to appear as directed, and present to the court such reasons and considerations as one has to offer why it should not be confirmed, take effect, be executed, or as the case may be.

SHRIEVALTY. The office of sheriff; the period of that office.

SHYSTER. A "pettifogging shyster" is an unscrupulous practitioner who disgraces his profession by doing mean work, and resorts to sharp practice to do it. 40 Mich. 251. See, also, 34 Minn. 342, 25 N. W. Rep. 710.

Si a jure discedas, vagus eris, et erunt omnia omnibus incerta. If you depart from the law, you will go astray, and all things will be uncertain to everybody. Co. Litt. 227*b*.

SI ACTIO. Lat. The conclusion of a plea to an action when the defendant demands judgment, if the plaintiff ought to have his action, etc. Obsolete.

Si alicujus rei societas sit et finis negotio impositus est, finitur societas. If there is a partnership in any matter, and the business is ended, the partnership ceases. 16 Johns. 438, 489.

Si aliquid ex solemnibus deficiat, cum æquitas poscit, subveniendum est. If any one of certain required forms be wanting, where equity requires, it will be aided. 1 Kent, Comm. 157. The want of some of a neutral vessel's papers is strong presumptive evidence against the ship's neutrality, yet the want of any one of them is not absolutely conclusive. Id.

SI ALIQUID SAPIT. If he knows anything; if he is not altogether devoid of reason.

Si assuetis mederi possis, nova non sunt tentanda. If you can be relieved by accustomed remedies, new ones should not be tried. 10 Coke, 142*b*. If an old wall can be repaired, a new one should not be made. Id.

SI CONSTET DE PERSONA. If it be certain who is the person meant.

SI CONTINGAT. If it happen. Words of condition in old conveyances. 10 Coke, 42*a*.

SI FECERIT TE SECURUM. If [he] make you secure. In practice. The initial and emphatic words of that description of original writ which directs the sheriff to cause the defendant to appear in court, without any option given him, provided the plaintiff gives the sheriff security effectually to prosecute his claim. 3 Bl. Comm. 274.

Si ingratum dixeris, omnia dixeris. If you affirm that one is ungrateful, in that you include every charge. A Roman maxim. Tray. Lat. Max.

SI ITA EST. If it be so. Emphatic words in the old writ of *mandamus* to a judge, commanding him, if the fact alleged be truly stated, (*si ita est,*) to affix his seal to a bill of exceptions. 5 Pet. 192.

Si meliores sunt quos ducit amor, plures sunt quos corrigit timor. If those are better who are led by love, those are the greater number who are corrected by fear. Co. Litt. 392.

Si non appareat quid actum est, erit consequens ut id sequamur quod in regione in qua actum est frequentatur. If it does not appear what was agreed upon, the consequence will be that we must follow that which is the usage of the place where the agreement was made. Dig. 50, 17, 34.

SI NON OMNES. In English practice. A writ of association of justices whereby, if all in commission cannot meet at the day assigned, it is allowed that two or more may proceed with the business. Cowell; Fitzh. Nat. Brev. 111 C.

Si nulla sit conjectura quæ ducat alio, verba intelligenda sunt ex proprietate, non grammatica sed populari ex usu. If there be no inference which leads to a different result, words are to be understood according to their proper meaning, not in a grammatical, but in a popular and ordinary, sense. 2 Kent, Comm. 555.

SI PARET. If it appears. In Roman law. Words used in the formula by which the prætor appointed a judge, and instructed him how to decide the cause.

Si plures sint fidejussores, quotquot erunt numero, singuli in solidum tenentur. If there are more sureties than one, how many soever they shall be, they shall each be held for the whole. Inst. 3, 20, 4.

SI PRIUS. In old practice. If before. Formal words in the old writs for summoning juries. Fleta, l. 2, c. 65, § 12.

Si quid universitati debetur singulis non debetur, nec quod debet universitas singuli debent. If anything be owing to an entire body, it is not owing to the individual members; nor do the individuals owe that which is owing by the entire body. Dig. 3, 4, 7, 1.

Si quidem in nomine, cognomine, prænomine legatarii testator erraverit, cum de persona constat, nihilominus valet legatum. Although a testator may have mistaken the *nomen, cognomen*, or *prænomen* of a legatee, yet, if it be certain who is the person meant, the legacy is valid. Inst. 2, 20, 29; Broom, Max. 645.

SI QUIS. In the civil law. If any one. Formal words in the prætorian edicts. The word "*quis*," though masculine in form, was held to include women. Dig. 50, 16, 1.

Si quis custos fraudem pupillo fecerit, a tutela removendus est. Jenk. Cent. 39. If a guardian do fraud to his ward, he shall be removed from his guardianship.

Si quis prægnantem uxorem reliquit, non videtur sine liberis decessisse. If a man leave his wife pregnant, he shall not be considered to have died without children. A rule of the civil law.

Si quis unum percusserit, cum alium percutere vellet, in felonia tenetur. 3 Inst. 51. If a man kill one, meaning to kill another, he is held guilty of felony.

SI RECOGNOSCAT. If he acknowledge. In old practice. A writ which lay for a creditor against his debtor for money numbered (*pecunia numerata*) or counted; that is, a specific sum of money, which the debtor had acknowledged in the county court, to owe him, as received *in pecuniis numeratis*. Cowell.

Si suggestio non sit vera, literæ patentes vacuæ sunt. 10 Coke, 113. If the suggestion be not true, the letters patent are void.

SIB. Sax. A relative or kinsman. Used in the Scotch tongue, but not now in English.

SIC. Lat. Thus; so; in such manner.

Sic enim debere quem meliorem agrum suum facere ne vicini deteriorem faciat. Every one ought so to improve his land as not to injure his neighbor's. 3 Kent, Comm. 441. A rule of the Roman law.

Sic interpretandum est ut verba accipiantur cum effectu. 3 Inst. 80. [A statute] is to be so interpreted that the words may be taken with effect.

SIC SUBSCRIBITUR. In Scotch practice. So it is subscribed. Formal words at the end of depositions, immediately preceding the signature. 1 How. State Tr. 1379.

Sic utere tuo ut alienum non lædas. Use your own property in such a manner as not to injure that of another. 9 Coke, 59; 1 Bl. Comm. 306; Broom, Max. 365.

SICH. A little current of water, which is dry in summer; a water furrow or gutter. Cowell.

SICIUS. A sort of money current among the ancient English, of the value of 2d.

SICKNESS. Disease; malady; any morbid condition of the body (including insanity) which, for the time being, hinders or prevents the organs from normally discharging their several functions. L. R. 8 Q. B. 295.

SICUT ALIAS. As at another time, or heretofore. This was a second writ sent out when the first was not executed. Cowell.

SICUT ME DEUS ADJUVET. Lat. So help me God. Fleta, l. 1, c. 18, § 4.

Sicut natura nil facit per saltum, ita nec lex. Co. Litt. 238. In the same way as nature does nothing by a bound, so neither does the law.

SIDE. The same court is sometimes said to have different *sides;* that is, different provinces or fields of jurisdiction. Thus, an admiralty court may have an "instance side," distinct from its powers as a prize court; the "crown side," (criminal jurisdiction) is to be distinguished from the "plea side," (civil jurisdiction;) the same court may have an "equity side" and a "law side."

SIDE-BAR RULES. In English practice. There are some rules which the courts authorize their officers to grant as a matter of course without formal application being made to them in open court, and these are technically termed "side-bar rules," because formerly they were moved for by the attorneys at the side bar in court; such, for instance, was the rule to plead, which was an order or command of the court requiring a defendant to plead within a specified number of days. Such also were the rules to reply, to rejoin, and many others, the granting of which depended upon settled rules of practice rather than upon the discretion of the courts, all of which are rendered unnecessary by recent statutory changes. Brown, voc. "Rule."

SIDE REPORTS. A term sometimes applied to unofficial volumes or series of reports, as contrasted with those prepared by the official reporter of the court, or to collections of cases omitted from the official reports.

SIDESMEN. In ecclesiastical law. These were originally persons whom, in the ancient episcopal synods, the bishops were wont to summon out of each parish to give information of the disorders of the clergy and people, and to report heretics. In process of time they became standing officers, under the title of "synodsmen," "sidesmen," "or "quest-men." The whole of their duties seems now to have devolved by custom upon the church-wardens of a parish. 1 Burn, Ecc. Law, 399.

SIDEWALK. A walk for foot passengers at the side of a street or road. See 11 Kan. 391; 69 N. Y. 250.

SIEN. An obsolete form of the word "scion," meaning offspring or descendant. Co. Litt. 123*a*.

SIERVO. Span. In Spanish law. A slave. Las Partidas, pt. 4, tit. 21, l. 1.

SIETE PARTIDAS. Span. Seven parts. See LAS PARTIDAS.

SIGHT. When a bill of exchange is expressed to be payable "at sight," it means on presentment to the drawee.

SIGIL. Seal; signature.

SIGILLUM. Lat. In old English law. A seal.

Sigillum est cera impressa, quia cera sine impressione non est sigillum. A seal is a piece of wax impressed, because wax without an impression is not a seal. 3 Inst. 169.

SIGLA. Lat. In Roman law. Marks or signs of abbreviation used in writing. Cod. 1, 17, 11, 13.

SIGN. To affix one's name to a writing or instrument, for the purpose of authenticating it, or to give it effect as one's act.

To "sign" is merely to write one's name on paper, or declare assent or attestation by some sign or mark, and does not, like "subscribe," require that one should write at the bottom of the instrument signed. 6 N. Y. 9, 13; 4 Edw. 102.

SIGN-MANUAL. In English law. The signature or subscription of the king is termed his "sign-manual." There is this difference between what the sovereign does under the sign manual and what he or she does under the great seal, viz., that the former is done as a personal act of the sovereign; the latter as an act of state. Brown.

SIGNATORIUS ANNULUS. Lat. In the civil law. A signet-ring; a seal-ring. Dig. 50, 16, 74.

SIGNATURE. In ecclesiastical law. The name of a sort of rescript, without seal, containing the supplication, the signature of the pope or his delegate, and the grant of a pardon.

In contracts. The act of writing one's name upon a deed, note, contract, or other instrument, either to identify or authenticate it, or to give it validity as one's own act. The name so written is also called a "signature."

SIGNET. A seal commonly used for the sign manual of the sovereign. Wharton. The signet is also used for the purpose of civil justice in Scotland. Bell.

SIGNIFICATION. In French law. The notice given of a decree, sentence, or other judicial act.

SIGNIFICAVIT. In ecclesiastical law. When this word is used alone, it means the bishop's certificate to the court of chancery in order to obtain the writ of excommunication; but, where the words "*writ of significavit*" are used, the meaning is the same as "*writ de excommunicato capiendo.*" Shelf. Mar. & Div. 502. Obsolete.

SIGNING JUDGMENT. In English practice. The signature or allowance of the proper officer of a court, obtained by the party entitled to judgment in an action, expressing generally that judgment is given in his favor, and which stands in the place of its actual delivery by the judges themselves. Steph. Pl. 110, 111.

In American practice. Signing judgment means a signing of the judgment record itself, which is done by the proper officer, on the margin of the record, opposite the entry of the judgment. 1 Burrill, Pr. 268.

SIGNUM. Lat. **In the Roman and civil law.** A sign; a mark; a seal. The seal of an instrument. Calvin.

A species of proof. By "*signa*" were meant those species of *indicia* which come more immediately under the cognizance of the senses; such as stains of blood on the person of the accused. Best, Pres. 13, note *f*.

In Saxon law. The sign of a cross prefixed as a sign of assent and approbation to a charter or deed.

SILENCE. The state of a person who does not speak, or of one who refrains from speaking. In the law of estoppel, "silence" implies knowledge and an opportunity to act upon it. 99 U. S. 581.

Silent leges inter arma. The power of law is suspended during war. Bacon.

SILENTIARIUS. In English law. One of the privy council; also an usher, who sees good rule and silence kept in court. Wharton.

SILK GOWN. Used especially of the gowns worn by queen's counsel; hence, "to take silk" means to attain the rank of queen's counsel. Mozley & Whitley.

SILVA. Lat. In the civil law. Wood; a wood.

SILVA CÆDUA. In the civil law. That kind of wood which was kept for the purpose of being cut.

In English law. Under wood; coppice wood. 2 Inst. 642; Cowell. All small wood and under timber, and likewise timber when cut down, under twenty years' growth; titheable wood. 3 Salk. 347.

SIMILAR. This word is often used to denote a partial resemblance only; but it is also often used to denote sameness in all essential particulars. Thus, a statutory provision in relation to "previous conviction of a *similar* offense" may mean conviction of an offense identical in kind. 127 Mass. 454.

SIMILITER. Lat. In pleading. Likewise; the like. The name of the short formula used either at the end of pleadings or by itself, expressive of the acceptance of an issue of fact tendered by the opposite party; otherwise termed a "joinder in issue." Steph. Pl. 57, 237.

Similitudo legalis est casuum diversorum inter se collatorum similis ratio; quod in uno similium valet, valebit in altero. Dissimilium, dissimilis est ratio. Legal similarity is a similar reason which governs various cases when compared with each other; for what avails in one similar case will avail in the other. Of things dissimilar, the reason is dissimilar. Co. Litt. 191.

Simonia est voluntas sive desiderium emendi vel vendendi spiritualia vel spiritualibus adhærentia. Contractus ex turpi causa et contra bonos mores. Hob. 167. Simony is the will or desire of buying or selling spiritualities, or things pertaining thereto. It is a contract founded on a bad cause, and against morality.

SIMONY. In English ecclesiastical law. The corrupt presentation of any one to an ecclesiastical benefice for money, gift, or reward. 2 Bl. Comm. 278. An unlawful contract for presenting a clergyman to a bene-

fice. The buying or selling of ecclesiastical preferments or of things pertaining to the ecclesiastical order. Hob. 167.

SIMPLA. Lat. In the civil law. The single value of a thing. Dig. 21, 2, 37, 2.

SIMPLE. Pure; unmixed; not compounded; not aggravated; not evidenced by sealed writing or record.

SIMPLE AVERAGE. Particular average, (*q. v.*)

SIMPLE BATTERY. In criminal law and torts. A beating of a person, not accompanied by circumstances of aggravation, or not resulting in grievous bodily injury.

SIMPLE CONTRACT. A contract that is not a specialty. A contract, the evidence of which is merely oral or in writing, not under seal nor of record. 1 Chit. Cont. 1.

SIMPLE CONTRACT DEBT. One where the contract upon which the obligation arises is neither ascertained by matter of record nor yet by deed or special instrument, but by mere oral evidence the most simple of any, or by notes unsealed, which are capable of a more easy proof, and therefore only better than a verbal promise. 2 Bl. Comm. 466.

SIMPLE DEPOSIT. A deposit made, according to the civil law, by one or more persons having a common interest.

SIMPLE INTEREST. Interest computed merely upon the principal sum due, and not compounded.

SIMPLE LARCENY. Larceny which is not complicated or aggravated with acts of violence. Larceny from the person, or with force and violence, is called "compound" larceny.

SIMPLE OBLIGATION. In the civil law. An obligation which does not depend for its execution upon any event provided for by the parties, or which is not agreed to become void on the happening of any such event. Civil Code La. art. 2015.

SIMPLE TRUST. A simple trust corresponds with the ancient use, and is where property is simply vested in one person for the use of another, and the nature of the trust, not being qualified by the settler, is left to the construction of law. It differs from a *special trust*. 2 Bouv. Inst. no. 1896.

SIMPLE WARRANDICE. In Scotch law. An obligation to warrant or secure from all subsequent or future deeds of the grantor. A simple warranty against the grantor's own acts. Whishaw.

SIMPLEX. Lat. Simple; single; pure; unqualified.

SIMPLEX BENEFICIUM. In ecclesiastical law. A minor dignity in a cathedral or collegiate church, or any other ecclesiastical benefice, as distinguished from a cure of souls. It may therefore be held with any parochial cure, without coming under the prohibitions against pluralities. Wharton.

Simplex commendatio non obligat. Mere recommendation [of an article] does not bind, [the vendor of it.] Dig. 4, 3, 37; 2 Kent, Comm. 485; Broom, Max. 781.

SIMPLEX DICTUM. In old English practice. Simple averment; mere assertion without proof.

Simplex et pura donatio dici poterit, ubi nulla est adjecta conditio nec modus. A gift is said to be pure and simple when no condition or qualification is annexed. Bract. 1.

SIMPLEX JUSTITIARIUS. In old records. Simple justice. A name sometimes given to a puisne justice. Cowell.

SIMPLEX LOQUELA. In old English practice. Simple speech; the mere declaration or *plaint* of a plaintiff.

SIMPLEX OBLIGATIO. A single obligation; a bond without a condition. 2 Bl. Comm. 340.

SIMPLEX PEREGRINATIO. In old English law. Simple pilgrimage. Fleta, l. 4, c. 2, § 2.

Simplicitas est legibus amica; et nimia subtilitas in jure reprobatur. 4 Coke, 8. Simplicity is favorable to the laws; and too much subtlety in law is to be reprobated.

SIMPLICITER. Lat. Simply; without ceremony; in a summary manner.

Directly; immediately; as distinguished from inferentially or indirectly.

By itself; by its own force; *per se*.

SIMUL CUM. Lat. Together with. In actions of tort and in prosecutions, where several persons united in committing the act complained of, some of whom are known and others not, it is usual to allege in the declaration or indictment that the persons therein named did the injury in question, "together with (*simul cum*) other persons unknown."

SIMUL ET SEMEL. Lat. Together and at one time.

SIMULATE. To feign, pretend, or counterfeit. To engage, usually with the co-operation or connivance of another person, in an act or series of acts, which are apparently transacted in good faith, and intended to be followed by their ordinary legal consequences, but which in reality conceal a fraudulent purpose of the party to gain thereby some advantage to which he is not entitled, or to injure, delay, or defraud others.

SIMULATED FACT. In the law of evidence. A fabricated fact; an appearance given to things by human device, with a view to deceive and mislead. Burrill, Circ. Ev. 131.

SIMULATED JUDGMENT. One which is apparently rendered in good faith, upon an actual debt, and intended to be collected by the usual process of law, but which in reality is entered by the fraudulent contrivance of the parties, for the purpose of giving to one of them an advantage to which he is not entitled, or of defrauding or delaying third persons.

SIMULATED SALE. One which has all the appearance of an actual sale in good faith, intended to transfer the ownership of property for a consideration, but which in reality covers a collusive design of the parties to put the property beyond the reach of creditors, or proceeds from some other fraudulent purpose.

SIMULATIO LATENS. Lat. A species of feigned disease, in which disease is actually present, but where the symptoms are falsely aggravated, and greater sickness is pretended than really exists. Beck, Med. Jur. 3.

SIMULATION. In the civil law. Misrepresentation or concealment of the truth; as where parties pretend to perform a transaction different from that in which they really are engaged. Mackeld. Rom. Law, § 181.

In French law. Collusion; a fraudulent arrangement between two or more persons to give a false or deceptive appearance to a transaction in which they engage.

SINDERESIS. "A natural power of the soul, set in the highest part thereof, moving and stirring it to good, and abhorring evil. And therefore *sinderesis* never sinneth nor erreth. And this *sinderesis* our Lord put in man, to the intent that the order of things should be observed. And therefore *sinderesis* is called by some men the 'law of reason,' for it ministereth the principles of the law of reason, the which be in every man by nature, in that he is a reasonable creature." Doct. & Stud. 39.

SINE ANIMO REVERTENDI. Without the intention of returning. 1 Kent, Comm. 78.

SINE ASSENSU CAPITULI. Without the consent of the chapter. In old English practice. A writ which lay where a dean, bishop, prebendary, abbot, prior, or master of a hospital aliened the lands holden in the right of his house, abbey, or priory, without the consent of the chapter; in which case his successor might have this writ. Fitzh. Nat. Brev. 194, I; Cowell.

SINE CONSIDERATIONE CURIÆ. Without the judgment of the court. Fleta, lib. 2, c. 47, § 13.

SINE DECRETO. Without authority of a judge. 2 Kames, Eq. 115.

SINE DIE. Without day; without assigning a day for a further meeting or hearing. Hence, a final adjournment; final dismissal of a cause. *Quod eat sine die*, that he go without day; the old form of a judgment for the defendant, *i. e.*, a judgment discharging the defendant from any further appearance in court.

SINE HOC QUOD. L. Lat. Without this, that. A technical phrase in old pleading, of the same import with the phrase "*absque hoc quod.*"

SINE NUMERO. Without stint or limit. A term applied to common. Fleta, lib. 4, c. 19, § 8.

Sine possessione usucapio procedere non potest. There can be no prescription without possession.

SINE PROLE. Without issue. Used in genealogical tables, and often abbreviated into "*s. p.*"

SINE QUA NON. Without which not. That without which the thing cannot be. An indispensable requisite or condition.

SINECURE. In ecclesiastical law. When a rector of a parish neither resides nor performs duty at his benefice, but has a vicar under him endowed and charged with the cure thereof, this is termed a "sinecure." Brown.

An ecclesiastical benefice without cure of souls.

In popular usage, the term denotes an office which yields a revenue to the incumbent, but makes little or no demand upon his time or attention.

SINGLE ADULTERY. In some jurisdictions, a distinction is made between "double" and "single" adultery, the former being committed where both the parties are married to other persons, the latter where only one is so married.

SINGLE BILL. One without any condition, and which does not depend upon any future event to give it validity.

SINGLE BOND. A deed whereby the obligor obliges himself, his heirs, executors, and administrators, to pay a certain sum of money to the obligee at a day named, without terms of defeasance.

SINGLE COMBAT, TRIAL BY. See BATTLE.

SINGLE DEMISE. A declaration in ejectment might contain either one demise or several. When it contained only one, it was called a "declaration with a single demise."

SINGLE ENTRY. In book-keeping. An entry made to charge or to credit an individual or thing, as distinguished from double entry, which is an entry of both the debit and credit accounts of a transaction.

SINGLE ESCHEAT. When all a person's movables fall to the crown, as a casualty, because of his being declared rebel. Wharton.

SINGLE ORIGINAL. An original instrument which is executed singly, and not in duplicate.

SINGULAR. Each; as in the expression "all and singular." Also, individual.

SINGULAR SUCCESSOR. A term borrowed from the civil law, denoting a person who succeeds to the rights of a former owner in a single article of property, (as by purchase,) as distinguished from a *universal* successor, who succeeds to all the rights and powers of a former owner, as in the case of a bankrupt or intestate estate.

SINGULAR TITLE. The title by which a party acquires property as a singular successor.

SINKING FUND. The aggregate of sums of money (as those arising from particular taxes or sources of revenue) set apart and invested, usually at fixed intervals, for the extinguishment of the debt of a government or corporation, by the accumulation of interest.

SIPESSOCUA. In old English law. A franchise, liberty, or hundred.

SIST, *v.* In Scotch practice. To stay proceedings. Bell.

SIST, *n.* In Scotch practice. A stay or suspension of proceedings; an order for a stay of proceedings. Bell.

SISTER. A woman who has the same father and mother with another, or has one of them only. The word is the correlative of "brother."

SIT. To hold a session, as of a court, grand jury, legislative body, etc. To be formally organized and proceeding with the transaction of business.

SITHCUNDMAM. The high constable of a hundred.

SITTINGS. In practice. The holding of a court, with full form, and before all the judges; as a *sitting in banc.* 3 Steph. Comm. 423.

The holding of a court of *nisi prius* by one or more of the judges of a superior court, instead of the ordinary *nisi prius* judge. 3 Steph. Comm. 422.

SITTINGS AFTER TERM. Sittings *in banc* after term were held by authority of the St. 1 & 2 Vict. c. 32. The courts were at liberty to transact business at their sittings as in term-time, but the custom was to dispose only of cases standing for argument or judgment. Wharton.

SITTINGS IN BANK or BANC. The sessions of a court, with the full bench present, for the purpose of determining matters of law argued before them.

SITTINGS IN CAMERA. See CHAMBERS.

SITUS. Lat. Site; position; location; the place where a thing is, considered, for example, with reference to jurisdiction over it.

Sive tota res evincatur, sive pars, habet regressum emptor in venditorem. The purchaser who has been evicted in whole or in part has an action against the vendor. Dig. 21, 2, 1; Broom, Max. 768.

SIX ACTS, THE. The acts passed in 1819, for the pacification of England, are so called. They, in effect, prohibited the training of persons to arms; authorized general searches and seizure of arms; prohibited meetings of more than fifty persons for the discussion of public grievances; repressed with heavy penalties and confiscations seditious and blasphemous libels; and checked pamphleteering by extending the newspaper stamp duty to political pamphlets. Brown.

SIX ARTICLES, LAWS OF. A celebrated act entitled "An act for abolishing diversity of opinion," (31 Hen. VIII. c. 14,) enforcing conformity to six of the strongest points in the Roman Catholic religion, under the severest penalties; repealed by St. 1 Eliz. c. 1. 4 Reeve, Eng. Law, 378.

SIX CLERKS. In English practice. Officers of the court of chancery, who received and filed all bills, answers, replications, and other papers, signed office copies of pleadings, examined and signed dockets of decrees, etc., and had the care of all records in their office. Holthouse; 3 Bl. Comm. 443. They were abolished by St. 5 Vict. c. 5.

SIX-DAY LICENSE. In English law. A liquor license, containing a condition that the premises in respect of which the license is granted shall be closed during the whole of Sunday, granted under section 49 of the licensing act, 1872, (35 & 36 Vict. c. 94.)

SIXHINDI. Servants of the same nature as rod knights, (*q. v.*) Anc. Inst. Eng.

SKELETON BILL. One drawn, indorsed, or accepted in blank.

SKILLED WITNESSES. Witnesses who are allowed to give evidence on matters of opinion and abstract fact.

SLADE. In old records. A long, flat, and narrow piece or strip of ground. Paroch. Antiq. 465.

SLAINS. See LETTERS OF SLAINS.

SLANDER. In torts. Oral defamation; the speaking of false and malicious words concerning another, whereby injury results to his reputation.

SLANDER OF TITLE. This is a statement of something tending to cut down the extent of title to some estate vested in the plaintiff. Such statement, in order to be actionable, must be false and malicious; *i. e.*, both untrue and done on purpose to injure the plaintiff. Damage must also have resulted from the statement. Brown.

SLANDERER. One who maliciously and without reason imputes a crime or fault to another of which he is innocent. See SLANDER.

SLAVE. A person who is wholly subject to the will of another; one who has no freedom of action, but whose person and services are wholly under the control of another. Webster.

One who is under the power of a master, and who belongs to him; so that the master may sell and dispose of his person, of his industry, and of his labor, without his being able to do anything, have anything, or acquire anything, but what must belong to his master. Civil Code La. art. 35.

SLAVE-TRADE. The traffic in slaves, or the buying and selling of slaves for profit.

SLAVERY. The condition of a slave; that civil relation in which one man has absolute power over the life, fortune, and liberty of another.

SLAY. This word, in an indictment, adds nothing to the force and effect of the word "kill," when used with reference to the taking of human life. It is particularly applicable to the taking of human life in battle; and, when it is not used in this sense, it is synonymous with "kill." 32 La. Ann. 351.

SLEDGE. A hurdle to draw traitors to execution. 1 Hale, P. C. 82.

SLEEPING PARTNER. A dormant partner; one whose name does not appear in the firm, and who takes no active part in the business, but who has an interest in the concern, and shares the profits, and thereby becomes a partner, either absolutely, or as respects third persons.

SLEEPING RENT. In English law. An expression frequently used in coal-mine leases and agreements for the same. It signifies a fixed or dead, *i. e.*, certain, rent, as distinguished from a rent or royalty varying with the amount of coals gotten, and is payable although the mine should not be worked at all, but should be sleeping or dead, whence the name. Brown.

SLIGHT CARE. See CARE; DILIGENCE; NEGLIGENCE.

SLIGHT NEGLIGENCE. Slight negligence is not slight want of ordinary care contributing to the injury, which would defeat an action for negligence. Slight negligence is defined to be only an absence of that degree of care and vigilance which persons of extraordinary prudence and foresight are accustomed to use. 43 Wis. 512. See CARE; DILIGENCE; NEGLIGENCE.

SLIP. 1. In negotiations for a policy of insurance, in England, the agreement is in practice concluded between the parties by a memorandum called the "slip," containing the terms of the proposed insurance, and initialed by the underwriters. Sweet.

2. Also that part of a police court which is divided off from the other parts of the court, for the prisoner to stand in. It is frequently called the "dock." Brown.

SLIPPA. A stirrup. There is a tenure of land in Cambridgeshire by holding the sovereign's stirrup. Wharton.

SLOUGH. An arm of a river, flowing between islands and the main-land, and separating the islands from one another. Sloughs have not the breadth of the main river, nor does the main body of water of the stream flow through them. 55 Iowa, 565, 8 N. W. Rep. 443.

SLOUGH SILVER. A rent paid to the castle of Wigmore, in lieu of certain days' work in harvest, heretofore reserved to the lord from his tenants. Cowell.

SLUICEWAY. An artificial channel into which water is let by a sluice. Specifically, a trench constructed over the bed of a stream, so that logs or lumber can be floated down to a convenient place of delivery. Webster. See 29 Minn. 416, 13 N. W. Rep. 192.

SMAKA. In old records. A small, light vessel; a smack. Cowell.

SMALL DEBTS COURTS. The several county courts established by St. 9 & 10 Vict. c. 95, for the purpose of bringing justice home to every man's door.

SMALL TITHES. All personal and mixed tithes, and also hops, flax, saffrons, potatoes, and sometimes, by custom, wood. Otherwise called "privy tithes." 2 Steph. Comm. 726.

SMART-MONEY. Vindictive or exemplary damages.

SMOKE-FARTHINGS. In old English law. An annual rent paid to cathedral churches; another name for the pentecostals or customary oblations offered by the dispersed inhabitants within a diocese, when they made their processions to the mother cathedral church. Cowell.

SMOKE-SILVER. In English law. A sum paid to the ministers of divers parishes as a modus in lieu of tithe-wood. Blount.

SMUGGLE. The act, with intent to defraud, of bringing into the United States, or, with like intent, attempting to bring into the United States, dutiable articles, without passing the same, or the package containing the same, through the custom-house, or submitting them to the officers of the revenue for examination. 18 U. S. St. at Large, 186.

"The word is a technical word, having a known and accepted meaning. It implies something illegal, and is inconsistent with an innocent intent. The idea conveyed by it is that of a secret introduction of goods, with intent to avoid payment of duties." 13 Blatchf. 184.

SMUGGLING. The offense of importing prohibited articles, or of defrauding the revenue by the introduction of articles into consumption, without paying the duties chargeable upon them. It may be committed indifferently either upon the excise or customs revenue. Wharton.

SNOTTERING SILVER. A small duty which was paid by servile tenants in Wylegh to the abbot of Colchester. Cowell.

SO. This term is sometimes the equivalent of "hence," or "therefore," and it is thus understood whenever what follows is an illustration of, or conclusion from, what has gone before. 33 Ind. 431.

SO HELP YOU GOD. The formula at the end of a common oath.

SOBRE. Span. Above; over; upon. 15 Tex. 586, 592.

SOBRE-JUEZES. In Spanish law. Superior judges. Las Partidas, pt. 3, tit. 4, l. 1.

SOBRINI and SOBRINÆ. Lat. In the civil law. The children of cousins german in general.

SOC, SOK, or SOKA. In Saxon law. Jurisdiction; a power or privilege to administer justice and execute the laws; also a shire, circuit, or territory. Cowell.

SOCA. A seigniory or lordship, enfranchised by the king, with liberty of holding a court of his *socmen* or *socagers; i. e.*, his tenants.

SOCAGE. Socage tenure, in England, is the holding of certain lands in consideration of certain inferior services of husbandry to be performed by the tenant to the lord of the fee. "Socage," in its most general and extensive signification, seems to denote a tenure by any certain and determinate service. And in this sense it is by the ancient writers constantly put in opposition to tenure by chivalry or knight-service, where the render was precarious and uncertain. Socage is of two sorts,—free socage, where the services are not only certain, but honorable; and villein socage, where the services, though certain, are of baser nature. Such as hold by the former tenure are also called in Glanvil and other authors by the name of "*liberi sokemanni*," or tenants in fee socage. By the statute 12 Car. 2, c. 24, all the tenures by knight-service were, with one or two immaterial exceptions, converted into free and common socage. See Cowell; Bract. l. 2, c. 35; 2 Bl. Comm. 79; Fleta, lib. 3, c. 14, § 9; Litt. § 117; Glan. l. 3, c. 7.

SOCAGER. A tenant by socage.

Socagium idem est quod servitum socæ; et soca, idem est quod caruca. Co. Litt. 86. Socage is the same as service of the soc; and soc is the same thing as a plow.

SOCER. In the civil law. A wife's father; a father-in-law. Calvin.

SOCIALISM. A scheme of government aiming at absolute equality in the distribution of the physical means of life and enjoyment. It is on the continent employed in a larger sense; not necessarily implying communism, or the entire abolition of private property, but applied to any system which requires that the land and the instruments of production should be the property, not of individuals, but of communities or associations or of the government. 1 Mill, Pol. Econ. 248.

SOCIEDAD. In Spanish law. Partnership. Schm. Civil Law, 153, 154.

SOCIEDAD ANONIMA. In Spanish and Mexican law. A business corporation. "By the corporate name, the shareholders' names are unknown to the world; and, so far as their connection with the corporation is concerned, their own names may be said to be anonymous, that is, nameless. Hence the derivation of the term 'anonymous' as applied to a body of persons associated together in the form of a company to transact any given business under a company name which does not disclose any of their own." Hall, Mex. Law, § 749.

SOCIETAS. Lat. In the civil law. Partnership; a partnership; the contract of partnership. Inst. 3, 26. A contract by which the goods or labor of two or more are united in a common stock, for the sake of sharing in the gain. Hallifax, Civil Law, b. 2, c. 18, no. 12.

SOCIETAS LEONINA. In Roman law. That kind of society or partnership by which the entire profits belong to some of the partners, in exclusion of the rest. So called in allusion to the fable of the lion, who, having entered into partnership with other animals for the purpose of hunting, appropriated all the prey to himself. It was void. Wharton.

SOCIETAS NAVALIS. A naval partnership; an association of vessels; a number of ships pursuing their voyage in company, for purposes of mutual protection.

SOCIÉTÉ. Fr. In French law. Partnership. See COMMENDAM.

SOCIÉTÉ ANONYME. In French law. An association where the liability of all the partners is limited. It had in England until lately no other name than that of "chartered company," meaning thereby a joint-stock company whose shareholders, by a charter from the crown, or a special enactment of the legislature, stood exempted from any liability for the debts of the concern, beyond the amount of their subscriptions. 2 Mill, Pol. Econ. 485.

SOCIÉTÉ EN COMMANDITE. In Louisiana. A partnership formed by a contract by which one person or partnership agrees to furnish another person or partnership a certain amount, either in property or money, to be employed by the person or partnership to whom it is furnished, in his or their own name or firm, on condition of receiving a share in the profits, in the proportion determined by the contract, and of being liable to losses and expenses to the amount furnished and no more. Civil Code La. art. 2810.

SOCIETY. An association or company of persons (generally not incorporated) united together for any mutual or common purpose. In a wider sense, the community or public; the people in general.

Socii mei socius meus socius non est. The partner of my partner is not my partner. Dig. 50, 17, 47, 1.

SOCIUS. In the civil law. A partner.

SOCMAN. A socager.

SOCMANRY. Free tenure by socage.

SOCNA. A privilege, liberty, or franchise. Cowell.

SOCOME. A custom of grinding corn at the lord's mill. Cowell. Bond-socome is where the tenants are bound to it. Blount.

SODOMITE. One who has been guilty of sodomy.

SODOMY. The crime against nature; carnal copulation, against the order of nature, by man with man, or in the same unnatural manner with woman, or with a beast. Code Ga. § 4352.

SOIL. The surface, or surface-covering of the land, not including minerals beneath it or grass or plants growing upon it. But in a wider (and more usual) sense, the term is equivalent to "land," and includes all that is below, upon, or above the surface.

SOIT BAILE AUX COMMONS. L. Fr. Let it be delivered to the commons. The form of indorsement on a bill when sent to the house of commons. Dyer, 93*a*.

SOIT BAILE AUX SEIGNEURS. L. Fr. Let it be delivered to the lords. The form of indorsement on a bill in parliament when sent to the house of lords. Hob. 111*a*.

SOIT DROIT FAIT AL PARTIE. L. Fr. In English law. Let right be done to the party. A phrase written on a petition of right, and subscribed by the king.

SOIT FAIT COMME IL EST DESIRE. L. Fr. Let it be as it is desired. The royal assent to private acts of parliament.

SOJOURNING. This term means something more than "traveling," and applies to a temporary, as contradistinguished from a permanent, residence. 1 Wheat. 5.

SOKE-REEVE. The lord's rent gatherer in the soca. Cowell.

SOKEMANRIES. Lands and tenements which were not held by knight-service, nor by grand serjeanty, nor by petit, but by simple services; being, as it were, lands enfranchised by the king or his predecessors from their ancient demesne. Their tenants were *sokemans*. Wharton.

SOKEMANS. In English law. Those who held their lands in socage. 2 Bl. Comm. 100.

Sola ac per se senectus donationem testamentum aut transactionem non vitiat. Old age does not alone and of itself vitiate a will or gift. 5 Johns. Ch. 148, 158.

SOLAR. In Spanish law. Land; the demesne, with a house, situate in a strong or fortified place. White, New Recop. b. 1, tit. 5, c. 3, § 2.

SOLAR DAY. That period of time which begins at sunrise and ends at sunset. Co. Litt. 135*a*.

SOLAR MONTH. A calendar month, (*q. v.*)

SOLARIUM. Lat. In the civil law. A rent paid for the ground, where a person built on the public land. A ground rent. Spelman; Calvin.

SOLATIUM. Compensation. Damages allowed for injury to the feelings.

SOLD NOTE. A note given by a broker, who has effected a sale of merchandise, to the buyer, stating the fact of sale, quantity, price, etc. Story, Ag. § 28.

SOLDIER. A military man; a private in the army.

SOLE. Single; individual; separate; the opposite of joint; as a *sole tenant*.

Comprising only one person; the opposite of aggregate; as a *sole corporation*.

Unmarried; as a *feme sole*.

SOLE CORPORATION. A corporation comprising one person and his successors, who are incorporated by law, in order to give them some legal capacities and advantages, particularly that of perpetuity, which in their natural persons they could not have had; as the sovereign, bishop, parson, etc. 1 Steph. Comm. 358; 3 Steph. Comm. 4.

SOLE TENANT. He that holds lands by his own right only, without any other person being joined with him. Cowell.

SOLEMN. Formal; in regular form; with all the forms of a proceeding.

SOLEMN FORM. There are two kinds of probate, namely, probate in common form, and probate in solemn form. Probate in common form is granted in the registry, without any formal procedure in court, upon an *ex parte* application made by the executor. Probate in solemn form is in the nature of a final decree pronounced in open court, all parties interested having been duly cited. The difference between the effect of probate in common form and probate in solemn form is that probate in common form is revocable, whereas probate in solemn form is irrevocable, as against all persons who have been cited to see the proceedings, or who can be proved to have been privy to those proceedings, except in the case where a will of subsequent date is discovered, in which case probate of an earlier will, though granted in solemn form, would be revoked. Coote, Prob. Pr. (5th Ed.) 237–239; Mozley & Whitley.

SOLEMN WAR. A war made in form by public declaration; a war solemnly declared by one state against another.

SOLEMNES LEGUM FORMULÆ. In the civil law. Solemn forms of laws; forms of forensic proceedings and of transacting legal acts. One of the sources of the unwritten law of Rome. Butl. Hor. Jur. 47.

SOLEMNITAS ATTACHIAMENTORUM. In old English practice. Solemnity or formality of attachments. The issuing of attachments in a certain formal and regular order. Bract. fols. 439, 440; 1 Reeve, Eng. Law, 480.

Solemnitates juris sunt observandæ. The solemnities of law are to be observed. Jenk. Cent. 13.

SOLEMNITY. A rite or ceremony; the formality established by law to render a contract, agreement, or other act valid.

SOLEMNIZE. To solemnize, spoken of a marriage, means no more than to enter into a marriage contract, with due publication, before third persons, for the purpose of giving it notoriety and certainty; which may be before any persons, relatives, friends, or strangers, competent to testify to the facts. 11 N. J. Law, 12, 19.

SOLICITATION. Asking; enticing; urgent request. Thus "solicitation of chastity" is the asking or urging a woman to surrender her chastity. The word is also used in such phrases as "solicitation to larceny," to bribery, etc.

SOLICITOR. In English law. A legal practitioner in the court of chancery. The words "solicitor" and "attorney" are commonly used indiscriminately, although they are not precisely the same, an attorney being a practitioner in the courts of common law, a solicitor a practitioner in the courts of equity. Most attorneys take out a certificate to practice in the courts of chancery, and therefore become solicitors also, and, on the other hand, most, if not all, solicitors take out a certificate to practice in the courts of common law, and therefore become attorneys also. Brown.

SOLICITOR GENERAL. In English law. One of the principal law officers of the crown, associated in his duties with the attorney general, holding office by patent during the pleasure of the sovereign, and having a right of preaudience in the courts. 3 Bl. Comm. 27.

SOLICITOR OF THE SUPREME COURT. The solicitors before the supreme courts, in Scotland, are a body of solicitors entitled to practice in the court of session, etc. Their charter of incorporation bears date August 10, 1797.

SOLICITOR OF THE TREASURY. An officer of the United States attached to the department of justice, having general charge of the law business appertaining to the treasury.

SOLICITOR TO THE SUITORS' FUND. An officer of the English court of chancery, who is appointed in certain cases guardian *ad litem*.

SOLIDUM. Lat. In the civil law. A whole; an entire or undivided thing.

SOLIDUS LEGALIS. A coin equal to 13s. 4d. of the present standard. 4 Steph. Comm. 119*n*.

SOLINUM. In old English law. Two plow-lands, and somewhat less than a half. Co. Litt. 5*a*.

Solo cedit quod solo inædificatur. That which is built upon the soil belongs to the soil. The proprietor of the soil becomes also proprietor of the building erected upon it. Mackeld. Rom. Law, § 275.

Solo cedit quod solo implantatur. That which is planted in the soil belongs to the soil. The proprietor of the soil becomes also the proprietor of the seed, the plant, and the tree, as soon as these have taken root. Mackeld. Rom. Law, § 275.

SOLUM PROVINCIALE. In Roman law. The *solum italicum* (an extension of the old *Ager Romanus*) admitted full ownership, and of the application to it of *usucapio;* whereas the *solum provinciale* (an extension of the old *Ager Publicus*) admitted of a possessory title only, and of *longi temporis possessio* only. Justinian abolished all distinctions between the two, sinking the *italicum* to the level of the *provinciale.* Brown.

Solum rex hoc non facere potest, quod non potest injuste agere. 11 Coke, 72. This alone the king cannot do, he cannot act unjustly.

Solus Deus facit hæredem, non homo. Co. Litt. 5. God alone makes the heir, not man.

SOLUTIO. Lat. In civil law. Payment, satisfaction, or release; any species of discharge of an obligation accepted as satisfactory by the creditor. The term refers not so much to the counting out of money as to the substance of the obligation. Dig. 46, 3, 54; Id. 50, 16, 176.

SOLUTIO INDEBITI. Lat. In the civil law. Payment of what was not due. From the payment of what was not due arises an obligation *quasi ex contractu.* When one has erroneously given or performed something to or for another, for which he was in no wise bound, he may redemand it, as if he had only lent it. The term "*solutio indebiti*" is here used in a very wide sense, and includes also the case where one performed labor for another, or assumed to pay a debt for which he was not bound, or relinquished a right or released a debt, under the impression that he was legally bound to do so. Mackeld. Rom. Law, § 500.

Solutio pretii emptionis loco habetur. The payment of the price [of a thing] is held to be in place of a purchase, [operates as a purchase.] Jenk. Cent. p. 56, case 2; 2 Kent, Comm. 387.

SOLUTIONE FEODI MILITIS PARLIAMENTI, or FEODI BURGENSIS PARLIAMENTI. Old writs whereby knights of the shire and burgesses might have recovered their wages or allowance if it had been refused. 35 Hen. VIII. c. 11.

SOLUTUS. In the civil law. Loosed; freed from confinement; set at liberty. Dig. 50, 16, 48.

In Scotch practice. Purged. A term used in old depositions.

SOLVABILITÉ. Fr. In French law. Ability to pay; solvency. Emerig. Traité des Assur. c. 8, § 15.

SOLVENCY. Ability to pay; present ability to pay; ability to pay one's debts out of one's own present means.

SOLVENDO. Lat. Paying. An apt word of reserving a rent in old conveyances. Co. Litt. 47*a*.

SOLVENDO ESSE. To be in a state of solvency; *i. e.*, able to pay.

Solvendo esse nemo intelligitur nisi qui solidum potest solvere. No one is considered to be solvent unless he can pay all that he owes. Dig. 50, 16, 114.

SOLVENT. A solvent person is one who is able to pay all his just debts in full out of his own present means. See Dig. 50, 16, 114.

SOLVERE. Lat. To pay; to comply with one's engagement; to do what one has undertaken to do; to release one's self from obligation, as by payment of a debt. Calvin.

SOLVERE PŒNAS. Lat. To pay the penalty.

SOLVIT. Lat. He paid; paid. 10 East, 206.

SOLVIT AD DIEM. He paid at the day. The technical name of the plea, in an action of debt on bond, that the defendant paid the money *on the day* mentioned in the condition. 1 Archb. N. P. 220, 221.

SOLVIT ANTE DIEM. A plea that the money was paid before the day appointed.

SOLVIT POST DIEM. He paid after the day. The plea in an action of debt on bond that the defendant paid the money *after the day* named for the payment, and before the commencement of the suit. 1 Archb. N. P. 222.

Solvitur adhuc societas etiam morte socii. A partnership is moreover dissolved by the death of a partner. Inst. 3, 26, 5; Dig. 17, 2.

Solvitur eo ligamine quo ligatur. In the same manner that a thing is bound it is unloosed. 4 Johns. Ch. 582.

SOMERSETT'S CASE. A celebrated decision of the English king's bench, in 1771, that slavery no longer existed in England in any form, and could not for the future exist on English soil, and that any person brought into England as a slave could not be thence removed except by the legal means applicable in the case of any free-born person.

SOMMATION. In French law. A demand served by a *huissier*, by which one party calls upon another to do or not to do a certain thing. This document has for its object to establish that upon a certain date the demand was made. Arg. Fr. Merc. Law, 574.

SOMNAMBULISM. Sleep-walking. Whether this condition is anything more than a co-operation of the voluntary muscles with the thoughts which occupy the mind during sleep is not settled by physiologists. Wharton.

SON. An immediate male descendant; the correlative of "father." Technically a word of purchase, unless explained.

SON. Fr. His. Her. See Civil Code La. art. 3522.

SON ASSAULT DEMESNE. L. Fr. His own assault. A plea which occurs in the actions of trespass and trespass on the case, by which the defendant alleges that it was the plaintiff's own original assault that occasioned the trespass for which he has brought the action, and that what the defendant did was merely in his own defense. Steph. Pl. 186.

SON-IN-LAW. The husband of one's daughter.

SONTAGE. A tax of forty shillings anciently laid upon every knight's fee. Cowell.

SONTICUS. Lat. In the civil law. Hurtful; injurious; hindering; excusing or justifying delay. *Morbus sonticus* is any illness of so serious a nature as to prevent a defendant from appearing in court and to give him a valid excuse. Calvin.

SOON. If there is no time specified for the performance of an act, or if it is specified that it is to be performed *soon*, the law implies that it is to be performed within a reasonable time. 14 Kan. 232.

SOREHON, or SORN. An arbitrary exaction, formerly existing in Scotland and Ireland. Whenever a chieftain had a mind to revel, he came down among the tenants with his followers, by way of contempt called "*Gilliwitfitts*," and lived on free quarters. Wharton; Bell.

SORNER. In Scotch law. A person who takes meat and drink from others by force or menaces, without paying for it. Bell.

SOROR. Lat. In the civil law. Sister; a sister. Inst. 3, 6, 1.

SORORICIDE. The killing or murder of a sister; one who murders his sister. This is not a technical term of the law.

SORS. Lat. In the civil law. Lot; chance; fortune; hazard; a lot, made of wood, gold, or other material. Money borrowed, or put out at interest. A principal sum or fund, such as the capital of a partnership. Ainsworth; Calvin.

In old English law. A principal lent on interest, as distinguished from the interest itself.

A thing recovered in action, as distinguished from the costs of the action.

SORTITIO. Lat. In the civil law. A drawing of lots. *Sortitio judicum* was the process of selecting a number of judges, for a criminal trial, by drawing lots.

SOUGH. In English law. A drain or water-course. The channels or water-courses used for draining mines are so termed; and those mines which are near to any given sough, and lie within the same level, and are benefited by it, are technically said to lie within the title of that sough. 5 Mees. & W. 228; Brown.

SOUL SCOT. A mortuary, or customary gift due ministers, in many parishes of England, on the death of parishioners. It was originally voluntary and intended as amends for ecclesiastical dues neglected to be paid in the life-time. 2 Bl. Comm. 425.

SOUND, *v.* To have reference or relation to; to aim at. An action is technically said to *sound in damages* where it is brought not for the specific recovery of a thing, but for damages only. Steph. Pl. 105.

SOUND, *adj.* Whole; in good condition; marketable. So used in warranties of chattels.

SOUND AND DISPOSING MIND AND MEMORY. This phrase is often used in the law of wills, to signify testamentary capacity.

SOUND MIND. This term denotes the normal condition of the human mind,—that state in which its faculties of perception and judgment are ordinarily well developed, and not impaired by mania, insanity, or dementia.

SOUNDING IN DAMAGES. When an action is brought, not for the recovery of lands, goods, or sums of money, (as is the case in real or mixed actions or the personal action of debt or detinue,) but for damages only, as in covenant, trespass, etc., the action is said to be "sounding in damages." Steph. Pl. 116.

SOUNDNESS. General health; freedom from any permanent disease. 1 Car. & M. 291.

SOURCES OF THE LAW. The origins from which particular positive laws derive their authority and coercive force. Such are constitutions, treaties, statutes, usages, and customs.

In another sense, the authoritative or reliable works, records, documents, edicts, etc., to which we are to look for an understanding of what constitutes the law. Such, for example, with reference to the Roman law, are the compilations of Justinian and the treatise of Gaius; and such, with reference to the common law, are especially the ancient reports and the works of such writers as Bracton, Littleton, Coke, "Fleta," and others.

SOUS SEING PRIVE. In French law. Under private signature; under the private signature of the parties. A contract or instrument thus signed is distinguished from an "authentic act," which is formally concluded before a notary or judge. Civil Code La. art. 2240.

SOUTH. L. Fr. Under. Bendloe, 33.

SOUTH SEA FUND. The produce of the taxes appropriated to pay the interest of such part of the English national debt as was advanced by the South Sea Company and its annuitants. The holders of South Sea annuities have been paid off, or have received other stock in lieu thereof. 2 Steph. Comm. 578.

SOVEREIGN. A chief ruler with supreme power; a king or other ruler with limited power.

In English law. A gold coin of Great Britain, of the value of a pound sterling.

SOVEREIGN POWER, or SOVEREIGNTY. That power in a state to which none other is superior or equal.

SOVEREIGN STATES. States whose subjects or citizens are in the habit of obedience to them, and which are not themselves subject to any other (or paramount) state in any respect. The state is said to be semi-sovereign only, and not sovereign, when in any respect or respects it is liable to be controlled (like certain of the states in India) by a paramount government, (*e. g.*, by the British empire.) Brown.

"In the intercourse of nations, certain states have a position of entire independence of others, and can perform all those acts which it is possible for any state to perform in this particular sphere. These same states have also entire power of self-government; that is, of independence upon all other states as far as their own territory and citizens not living abroad are concerned. No foreign power or law can have control except by convention. This power of independent action in external and internal relations constitutes complete sovereignty." Wools. Pol. Science, i. 204.

SOVEREIGNTY. The possession of sovereign power; supreme political authority; paramount control of the constitution and frame of government and its administration; the self-sufficient source of political power, from which all specific political powers are derived; the international independence of a state, combined with the right and power of regulating its internal affairs without foreign dictation; also a political society, or state, which is sovereign and independent.

"The freedom of the nation has its correlate in the sovereignty of the nation. Political sovereignty is the assertion of the self-determinate will of the organic people, and in this there is the manifestation of its freedom. It is in and through the determination of its sovereignty that the order of the nation is constituted and maintained." Mulford, Nation, p. 129.

"If a determinate human superior, not in a habit of obedience to a like superior, receive habitual obedience from the bulk of a given society, that determinate superior is sovereign in that society, and the society (including the superior) is a society political and independent." Aust. Jur.

SOVERTIE. In old Scotch law. Surety. Skene.

SOWLEGROVE. February; so called in South Wales. Cowell.

SOWMING AND ROWMING. In Scotch law. Terms used to express the form by which the number of cattle brought upon a common by those having a servitude of pasturage may be justly proportioned to the rights of the different persons possessed of the servitude. Bell.

SOWNE. In old English law. To be leviable. An old exchequer term applied to sheriff's returns. 4 Inst. 107; Cowell; Spelman.

SPADARIUS. A sword-bearer. Blount.

SPADONES. In the civil law. Impotent persons. Those who, on account of their temperament or some accident they have suffered, are unable to procreate. Inst. 1, 11, 9; Dig. 1, 7, 2, 1.

SPARSIM. Lat. Here and there; scattered; at intervals. For instance, trespass to realty by cutting timber *sparsim* (here and there) through a tract.

SPATÆ PLACITUM. A court for the speedy execution of justice upon military delinquents. Cowell.

SPEAK. In practice. To argue. "The case was ordered to be *spoke to* again." 10 Mod. 107. See IMPARLANCE; SPEAKING WITH PROSECUTOR.

SPEAKER. This is the official designation of the president or chairman of certain legislative bodies, particularly of the house of representatives in the congress of the United States, of one or both branches of several of the state legislatures, and of the two houses of the British parliament.

The term "speaker," as used in reference to either of the houses of parliament, signifies the functionary acting as chairman. In the commons his duties are to put questions, to preserve order, and to see that the privileges of the house are not infringed; and, in the event of the numbers being even on a division, he has the privilege of giving the casting vote. The speaker of the lords is the lord chancellor or the lord keeper of the great seal of England, or, if he be absent, the lords may choose their own speaker. The duties of the speaker of the lords are principally confined to putting questions, and the lord chancellor has no more to do with preserving order than any other peer. Brown.

SPEAKING DEMURRER. In pleading. One which alleges new matter in addition to that contained in the bill as a cause for demurrer. 4 Brown, Ch. 254; 2 Ves. Jr. 83.

SPEAKING WITH PROSECUTOR. A method of compounding an offense, allowed in the English practice, where the court permits a defendant convicted of a misdemeanor to speak with the prosecutor before judgment is pronounced; if the prosecutor declares himself satisfied, the court may inflict a trivial punishment. 4 Steph. Comm. 261.

SPECIAL. Relating to or designating a species, kind, or sort; designed for a particular purpose; confined to a particular purpose, object, person, or class. The opposite of "general."

SPECIAL ACCEPTANCE. The qualified acceptance of a bill of exchange, as where it is accepted as payable at a particular place "and not elsewhere."

SPECIAL ACT. A private statute; an act which operates only upon particular persons or private concerns. 1 Bl. Comm. 86; 103 U. S. 454.

SPECIAL ADMINISTRATION. Authority to administer upon some few particular effects of a decedent, as opposed to authority to administer his whole estate.

SPECIAL AGENT. One authorized to transact only a particular business for his principal, as distinguished from a general agent.

SPECIAL ALLOCATUR. The special allowance of a writ (particularly a writ of error) which is required in some particular cases.

SPECIAL ALLOWANCES. In English practice. In taxing the costs of an action as between party and party, the taxing officer is, in certain cases, empowered to make special allowances; *i. e.*, to allow the party costs which the ordinary scale does not warrant. Sweet.

SPECIAL APPEARANCE. In practice. One which is made for some specific purpose only, and does not extend to all the purposes of the suit.

SPECIAL ASSUMPSIT. An action of *assumpsit* is so called where the declaration sets out the precise language or effect of a special contract, which forms the ground of action; as distinguished from a *general assumpsit*, in which the technical claim is for a debt alleged to grow out of the contract, not the agreement itself.

SPECIAL BAIL. In practice. Bail to the action, given by a defendant as a security to abide the event of it.

Also a person who enters into a recognizance to answer for the appearance of another.

SPECIAL BAILIFF. A deputy-sheriff, appointed at the request of a party to a suit, for the special purpose of serving or executing some writ or process in such suit.

SPECIAL BASTARD. One born of parents before marriage, the parents afterwards intermarrying. By the civil and Scotch law he would be then legitimated.

SPECIAL CALENDAR, DOCKET, OR PAPER. A calendar or list of causes, containing those set down specially for hearing, trial, or argument.

SPECIAL CASE. In English practice. When a trial at *nisi prius* appears to the judge to turn on a point of law, the jury may find a general verdict, subject to the opinion of the court above, upon what is termed a "special case" to be made; that is, upon a written statement of all the facts of the case drawn up for the opinion of the court *in banc*, by the counsel and attorneys on either side, under correction of the judge at *nisi prius*. The party for whom the general verdict is so given is in such case not entitled to judgment till the court *in banc* has decided on the special case; and, according to the result of that decision, the verdict is ultimately entered either for him or his adversary. Brown.

SPECIAL CHARGE. In practice A charge or instruction given by the court to the jury, upon some particular point or question involved in the case, and usually in response to counsel's request for such instruction.

SPECIAL CLAIM. In English law. A claim not enumerated in the orders of 22d April, 1850, which required the leave of the court of chancery to file it. Such claims are abolished.

SPECIAL COMMISSION. In English law. An extraordinary commission of oyer and terminer and gaol delivery, issued by the crown to the judges when it is necessary that offenses should be immediately tried and punished. Wharton.

SPECIAL CONSTABLE. One who has been appointed and sworn in as a constable only for some special occasion; as, to assist in quelling an apprehended or existing riot.

SPECIAL CONTRACT. A contract under seal; a specialty; as distinguished from one merely oral or in writing not sealed. But in common usage this term is often used to denote an express or explicit contract, one which clearly defines and settles the reciprocal rights and obligations of the parties, as distinguished from one which must be made out, and its terms ascertained, by the inference of the law from the nature and circumstances of the transaction.

SPECIAL COUNT. As opposed to the common counts, in pleading, a special count is a statement of the actual facts of the particular case.

SPECIAL COVENANT. In real property law, covenants are divided into *general* and *special;* the former relating to land generally, and placing the covenantee in the position of a specialty creditor only; the latter relating to particular lands, and giving the covenantee a lien thereon. Brown.

SPECIAL CUSTOM. A particular or local custom; one which, in respect to the sphere of its observance, does not extend throughout the entire state or country, but is confined to some particular district or locality. 1 Bl. Comm. 67; 23 Me. 95.

SPECIAL DAMAGE. The damages which a plaintiff seeks to recover are either general or special. General damages are such as the law implies or presumes to have resulted from the wrong complained of. Special damages are such as really and in fact resulted, but are not implied by law, and are either superadded to general damages arising from an act injurious in itself or are such as arise from an act indifferent and not actionable in itself, but injurious only in its consequences. Brown.

Special damage, as contradistinguished from general damage, is that which is the natural, but not the necessary, consequence of the act complained of. 6 Wall. 578.

SPECIAL DEMURRER. One which excepts to the sufficiency of the pleadings on the opposite side, and shows specifically the nature of the objection, and the particular ground of the exception. 3 Bouv. Inst. no. 3022.

SPECIAL DEPOSIT. A deposit in which the identical thing deposited is to be returned to the depositor. Distinguished from an irregular deposit.

SPECIAL DEPUTY. One constituted or appointed, not to perform the general duties of the officer whose deputy he is, but for the specific purpose of doing some one or more acts in the place and stead of such officer.

SPECIAL ELECTION. An election for a particular emergency; out of the regular course; as one held to fill a vacancy arising by death of the incumbent of the office.

SPECIAL ERRORS. Special pleas in error are such as, instead of joining in error, allege some extraneous matter as a ground of defeating the writ of error, *e. g.*, a release of errors, expiration of the time within which error might be brought, or the like. To these, the plaintiff in error may either reply or demur.

SPECIAL EXAMINER. In English law. Some person, not one of the examiners of the court of chancery, appointed to take evidence in a particular suit. This may be done when the state of business in the examiner's office is such that it is impossible to obtain an appointment at a conveniently early day, or when the witnesses may be unable to come to London. Hunt. Eq. pt. I. c. 5, § 2.

SPECIAL EXECUTOR. One whose power and office are limited, either in respect to the time or place of their exercise, or restricted to a particular portion of the decedent's estate.

SPECIAL FINDING. A specific expression of their conviction, made by a jury in relation to some matter of fact constituting a part of the general issue or question submitted to them.

SPECIAL GUARANTY. A guaranty which is available only to the particular person to whom it is offered or addressed; as distinguished from a *general* guaranty, which will operate in favor of any person who may accept it.

SPECIAL GUARDIAN. One who has special or limited powers and duties with respect to his ward; as, a guardian who has the custody of the estate but not of the person, or *vice versa*, or a guardian *ad litem*.

SPECIAL IMPARLANCE. In pleading. An imparlance which contains the clause, "saving to himself all advantages and exceptions, as well to the writ as to the declaration aforesaid." 2 Chit. Pl. 407.

SPECIAL INDORSEMENT. An indorsement *in full*, which specifically names the indorsee.

SPECIAL INDORSEMENT OF WRIT. In English practice. The writ of summons in an action may, under Order iii. 6, be indorsed with the particulars of the amount sought to be recovered in the action, after giving credit for any payment or set-off; and this special indorsement (as it is called) of the writ is applicable in all actions where the plaintiff seeks merely to recover a debt or liquidated demand in money payable by the defendant, with or without interest, arising upon a contract, express or implied, as, for instance, on a bill of exchange, promissory note, check, or other simple contract debt, or on a bond or contract under seal for payment of a liquidated amount of money, or on a statute where the sum sought to be recovered is a fixed sum of money or in the nature of a debt, or on a guaranty, whether under seal or not. Brown.

SPECIAL INJUNCTION. An injunction obtained only on motion and petition, usually with notice to the other party.

An injunction by which parties are restrained from committing waste, damage, or injury to property. 4 Steph. Comm. 12, note *z*.

SPECIAL ISSUE. In pleading. An issue produced upon a special plea. So called as being usually more specific and particular than the general issues. Steph. Pl. 162.

SPECIAL JURISDICTION. A court authorized to take cognizance of only some few kinds of causes or proceedings expressly designated by statute is called a "court of special jurisdiction."

SPECIAL JURY. In practice. A jury ordered by the court, on the motion of either party, in cases of unusual importance or intricacy. Called, from the manner in which it is constituted, a "struck jury." 3 Bl. Comm. 357.

A jury composed of persons above the rank of ordinary freeholders; usually summoned to try questions of greater importance than those usually submitted to common juries. Brown.

SPECIAL LAW. A special law is such as, at common law, the courts would not notice, unless it were pleaded and proved like any other fact. 24 Ind. 34.

A law, framed in general terms, restricted to no locality, and operating equally upon all of a group of objects, which, having regard to the purposes of the legislation, are distinguished by characteristics sufficiently marked and important to make them a class by themselves, is not a special or local law, but a general law. 40 N. J. Law, 123.

SPECIAL LEGACY. A "specific legacy" (*q. v.*) is sometimes so called.

SPECIAL LICENSE. In English law. One granted by the archbishop of Canterbury to authorize a marriage at any time or place whatever. 2 Steph. Comm. 247, 255.

SPECIAL LIEN. Another term for a *particular* lien.

SPECIAL LIMITATION. A qualification serving to mark out the bounds of an estate, so as to determine it *ipso facto* in a given event, without action, entry, or claim, before it would, or might, otherwise expire by force of, or according to, the general limitation. 59 Pa. St. 340.

SPECIAL MALICE. In criminal law. Particular or personal malice; that is, hatred, ill-will, or a vindictive disposition against a particular individual.

SPECIAL MATTER. Under a plea of the general issue, the defendant is allowed to give special matter in evidence, usually after notice to the plaintiff of the nature of such matter, thus sparing him the necessity of pleading it specially. 3 Bl. Comm. 306.

SPECIAL MEETING. In the law of corporations. A meeting called for special purposes; one limited to particular business; a meeting for those purposes of which the parties have had special notice. 1 Exch. 505; 11 Vt. 391.

SPECIAL MOTION. A motion addressed to the discretion of the court, and which must be heard and determined; as distinguished from one which may be granted of course.

SPECIAL NON EST FACTUM. A form of the plea of *non est factum*, in debt on a specialty, by which the defendant alleges that, although he executed the deed, yet it is in law "not his deed," because of certain special circumstances which he proceeds to set out; as, where he delivered the deed as an escrow, and it was turned over to the plaintiff prematurely or without performance of the condition.

SPECIAL OCCUPANT. A person having a special right to enter upon and occupy lands granted *pur auter vie*, on the death of the tenant, and during the life of *cestui que vie*. Where the grant is to a man *and his heirs* during the life of *cestui que vie*, the *heir* succeeds as special occupant, having a special exclusive right by the terms of the original grant. 2 Bl. Comm. 259; 1 Steph. Comm. 416.

SPECIAL OWNER. One who has a special interest in an article of property, amounting to a qualified ownership of it, such, for example, as a bailee's lien; as distinguished from the *general* owner, who has the primary or residuary title to the same thing.

SPECIAL PAPER. A list kept in the English courts of common law, and now in the queen's bench, common pleas, and exchequer divisions of the high court, in which list demurrers, special cases, etc., to be argued are set down. It is distinguished from the new trial paper, peremptory paper, crown paper, revenue paper, etc., according to the practice of the particular division. Wharton.

SPECIAL PARTNER. A member of a limited partnership, who furnishes certain funds to the common stock, and whose liability extends no further than the fund furnished. A partner whose responsibility is restricted to the amount of his investment. 3 Kent, Comm. 34.

SPECIAL PARTNERSHIP. At common law. One formed for the prosecution of a special branch of business, as distinguished from the general business of the parties, or for one particular venture or subject.

Under statutes. A limited partnership, (*q. v.*)

SPECIAL PLEA. A special kind of plea in bar, distinguished by this name from the general issue, and consisting usually of some new affirmative matter, though it may also be in the form of a traverse or denial. See Steph. Pl. 52, 162.

SPECIAL PLEA IN BAR. One which advances new matter. It differs from the general, in this: that the latter denies some material allegation, but never advances new matter. Gould, Pl. c. 2, § 38.

SPECIAL PLEADER. In English practice. A person whose professional occupation is to give verbal or written opinions upon statements made verbally or in writing, and to draw pleadings, civil or criminal, and such practical proceedings as may be out of the usual course. 2 Chit. Pr. 42.

SPECIAL PLEADING. When the allegations (or "pleadings," as they are called) of the contending parties in an action are not of the general or ordinary form, but are of a more complex or special character, they are denominated "special pleadings;" and, when a defendant pleads a plea of this description, (*i. e.*, a special plea,) he is said to plead specially, in opposition to pleading the general issue. These terms have given rise to the popular denomination of that science which, though properly called "pleading," is generally known by the name of "special pleading." Brown.

The allegation of special or new matter in opposition or explanation of the last previous averments on the other side, as distinguished from a direct denial of matter previously alleged by the opposite party. Gould, Pl. c. 1, § 18.

In popular language, the adroit and plausible advocacy of a client's case in court. Stimson, Law Gloss.

SPECIAL PRIVILEGE. In constitutional law. A right, power, franchise, immunity, or privilege granted to, or vested in, a person or class of persons, to the exclusion of others, and in derogation of common right. See 1 Dak. 118; 1 Utah, 108.

SPECIAL PROCEEDING. This phrase has been used in the New York and other codes of procedure as a generic term for all civil remedies which are not ordinary actions. Code Proc. N. Y. § 3.

SPECIAL PROPERTY. Property of a qualified, temporary, or limited nature; as distinguished from absolute, general, or unconditional property. Such is the property of a bailee in the article bailed, of a sheriff in goods temporarily in his hands under a levy, of the finder of lost goods while looking for the owner, of a person in wild animals which he has caught.

SPECIAL REQUEST. A request actually made, at a particular time and place. This term is used in contradistinction to a general request, which need not state the time when nor place where made. 3 Bouv Inst. no. 2843.

SPECIAL RESTRAINT OF TRADE. One which forbids the person to employ his talents, capital, or industry in a designated trade or business, either for a limited time or within a prescribed area or district.

SPECIAL RETAINER. An engagement or retainer of an attorney or solicitor for a special and designated purpose; as, to prepare and try a particular case.

SPECIAL RULE. Rules granted without any motion in court, or when the motion is only assumed to have been made, and is not actually made, are called "common" rules; while the rules granted upon motion actually made to the court in term, or upon a judge's order in vacation, are termed "special" rules. Brown.

The term may also be understood as opposed to "general" rule; in which case it means a particular direction, in a matter of practice, made for the purposes of a particular case.

SPECIAL SERVICE. In Scotch law. That form of service by which the heir is served to the ancestor who was feudally vested in the lands. Bell.

SPECIAL SESSIONS. In English law. A meeting of two or more justices of the peace held for a special purpose, (such as the licensing of alehouses,) either as required by statute or when specially convoked, which can only be convened after notice to all the other magistrates of the division, to give them an opportunity of attending. Stone, J. Pr. 52, 55.

SPECIAL STATUTE. One which operates only upon particular persons and private concerns. 1 Bl. Comm. 86. Distinguished from a general or public statute. See SPECIAL ACT.

SPECIAL TAIL. Where an estate tail is limited to the children of two given parents, as to A. and the heirs of his body by B., his wife. 1 Steph. Comm. 244.

SPECIAL TERM. In New York practice, that branch of the court which is held by a single judge for hearing and deciding in the first instance motions and causes of equitable nature is called the "special term," as opposed to the "general term," held by three judges (usually) to hear appeals. Abbott.

SPECIAL TERMS. Peculiar or unusual conditions imposed on a party before granting some application to the favor of the court.

SPECIAL TRAVERSE. In pleading. A peculiar form of traverse or denial, the design of which, as distinguished from a *common* traverse, is to explain or qualify the denial, instead of putting it in the direct and absolute form. It consists of an affirmative and a negative part, the first setting forth the new affirmative matter tending to explain or qualify the denial, and technically called the "inducement," and the latter constituting the direct denial itself, and technically called the "*absque hoc.*" Steph. Pl. 169-180.

SPECIAL TRUST. Where the machinery of a trust is introduced for the execution of some purpose particularly pointed out, and the trustee is not a mere passive depositary of the estate, but is called upon to exert himself actively in the execution of the settlor's intention; as, where a conveyance is to trustees upon trust to sell for payment of debts.

Special trusts have been divided into (1) ministerial (or instrumental) and (2) discretionary. The former, such as demand no further exercise of reason or understanding than every intelligent agent must necessarily employ; the latter, such as cannot be duly administered without the application of a certain degree of prudence and judgment. 2 Bouv. Inst. no. 1896.

SPECIAL VERDICT. In practice. A special finding of the facts of a case by a jury, leaving to the court the application of the law to the facts thus found. 1 Archb. Pr. K. B. 213; 3 Bl. Comm. 377.

SPECIAL WARRANTY. A clause of warranty inserted in a deed of lands, by which the grantor covenants, for himself and his heirs, to "warrant and forever defend" the title to the same, to the grantee and his heirs, etc., against all persons claiming "by, through, or under" the grantor or his heirs. If the warranty is against the claims of all persons whatsoever, it is called a "general" warranty, (*q. v.*)

Specialia generalibus derogant. Special words derogate from general words. A special provision as to a particular subject-matter is to be preferred to general language, which might have governed in the absence of such special provision. L. R. 1 C. P. 546.

SPECIALTY. A writing sealed and delivered, containing some agreement. A writing sealed and delivered, which is given as a security for the payment of a debt, in which such debt is particularly specified. Bac. Abr. "Obligation," A.

A specialty is a contract under seal, and is considered by law as entered into with more solemnity, and, consequently, of higher dignity than ordinary simple contracts. Code Ga. 1882, § 2717.

SPECIALTY DEBT. A debt due or acknowledged to be due by deed or instrument under seal. 2 Bl. Comm. 465.

SPECIE. 1. Coin of the precious metals, of a certain weight and fineness, and bearing the stamp of the government, denoting its value as currency. 5 Hill, 523, 536.

2. When spoken of a contract, the expression "performance *in specie*" means strictly, or according to the exact terms. As applied to things, it signifies individuality or identity. Thus, on a bequest of a specific picture, the legatee would be said to be entitled to the delivery of the picture *in specie; i. e.*, of the very thing. Whether a thing is due *in genere* or *in specie* depends, in each case, on the will of the transacting parties. Brown.

SPECIES. Lat. In the civil law. Form; figure; fashion or shape. A form or shape given to materials.

A particular thing; as distinguished from "*genus.*"

SPECIES FACTI. Lat. In Scotch law. The particular criminal act charged against a person.

SPECIFIC. Having a certain form or designation; observing a certain form; particular; precise.

SPECIFIC DEVISES are devises of lands particularly specified in the terms of the devise, as opposed to general and residuary devises of land, in which the local or other particular descriptions are not expressed. For example, "I devise my Hendon Hall estate" is a specific devise; but "I devise all my lands," or, "all other my lands," is a *general* devise or a *residuary* devise. But all devises are (in effect) specific, even residuary devises being so. L. R. 3 Ch. 420; Id. 136.

SPECIFIC LEGACY. A legacy or gift by will of a particular specified thing, as of a horse, a piece of furniture, a term of years, and the like.

In a strict sense, a legacy of a particular chattel, which is specified and distinguished from all other chattels of the testator of the same kind; as of a horse of a certain color.

A legacy of a quantity of chattels described collectively; as a gift of all the testator's pictures. Ward, Leg. 16–18.

A legacy is general, where its amount or value is a charge upon the general assets in the hands of the executors, and where, if these are sufficient to meet all the provisions in the will, it must be satisfied; it is specific, when it is limited to a particular thing, subject, or chose in action, so identified as to render the bequest inapplicable to any other; as the bequest of a horse, a picture, or jewel, or a debt due from a person named, and, in special cases, even of a sum of money. 3 Duer, 477, 543.

SPECIFIC PERFORMANCE. Performance of a contract in the specific form in which it was made, or according to the precise terms agreed upon. This is frequently compelled by a bill in equity filed for the purpose. 2 Story, Eq. Pl. § 712, et seq.

The doctrine of specific performance is that, where damages would be an inadequate compensation for the breach of an agreement, the contractor will be compelled to perform specifically what he has agreed to do. Sweet.

SPECIFICATIO. Lat. In the civil law. Literally, a making of form; a giving of form to materials. That mode of acquiring property through which a person, by transforming a thing belonging to another, especially by working up his materials into a new species, becomes proprietor of the same. Mackeld. Rom. Law, § 271.

SPECIFICATION. As used in the law relating to patents and in building contracts, the term denotes a particular or detailed statement of the various elements involved.

In military law. The clear and particular description of the charges preferred against a person accused of a military offense. Tytler, Mil. Law, 109.

SPECIMEN. A sample; a part of something intended to exhibit the kind and quality of the whole.

SPECULATION. In commerce. The act or practice of buying lands, goods, etc., in expectation of a rise of price and of selling them at an advance, as distinguished from a regular trade, in which the profit expected is the difference between the retail and wholesale prices, or the difference of price in the place where the goods are purchased, and the place where they are to be carried for market. Webster.

SPECULATIVE DAMAGES. Prospective or anticipated damages from the same acts or facts constituting the present cause of action, but which depend upon future developments which are contingent, conjectural, or improbable.

SPECULUM. Lat. Mirror or looking-glass. The title of several of the most ancient law-books or compilations. One of the ancient Icelandic books is styled "*Speculum Regale.*"

SPEEDY EXECUTION. An execution which, by the direction of the judge at *nisi prius*, issues forthwith, or on some early day fixed upon by the judge for that purpose after the trial of the action. Brown.

SPEEDY TRIAL. In criminal law. As secured by constitutional guaranties, a speedy trial means a trial conducted according to fixed rules, regulations, and proceedings of law, free from vexatious, capricious, and oppressive delays manufactured by the ministers of justice. 8 Eng. (Ark.) 720; 10 Miss. 497; 3 Mont. 512.

SPELLING. The formation of words by letters; orthography. Incorrect spelling does not vitiate a written instrument if the intention clearly appears.

SPENDTHRIFT. A person who by excessive drinking, gaming, idleness, or debauchery of any kind shall so spend, waste, or lessen his estate as to expose himself or his family to want or suffering, or expose the town to charge or expense for the support of himself or family. Rev. St. Vt. c. 65, § 9; 57 N. H. 54.

The word "spendthrift," in all the provisions relating to guardians and wards, contained in this or any other statute, is intended to include every person who is liable to be put under guardianship, on account of excessive drinking, gaming, idleness, or debauchery. How. St. Mich. 1882, § 6340.

SPERATE. That of which there is hope. Thus a debt which one may hope to recover may be called "sperate," in opposition to "desperate." See 1 Chit. Pr. 520.

SPES ACCRESCENDI. Lat. Hope of surviving. 3 Atk. 762; 2 Kent, Comm. 424.

Spes est vigilantis somnium. Hope is the dream of the vigilant. 4 Inst. 203.

Spes impunitatis continuum affectum tribuit delinquendi. The hope of impunity holds out a continual temptation to crime. 3 Inst. 236.

SPES RECUPERANDI. Lat. The hope of recovery or recapture; the chance of retaking property captured at sea, which prevents the captors from acquiring complete ownership of the property until they have definitely precluded it by effectual measures. 1 Kent, Comm. 101.

SPIGURNEL. The sealer of the royal writs.

SPINSTER. The addition given, in legal proceedings, and in conveyancing, to a woman who never has been married.

SPIRITUAL CORPORATIONS. Corporations, the members of which are entirely spiritual persons, and incorporated as such, for the furtherance of religion and perpetuating the rights of the church.

SPIRITUAL COURTS. In English law. The ecclesiastical courts, or courts Christian. See 3 Bl. Comm. 61.

SPIRITUAL LORDS. The archbishops and bishops of the house of lords. 2 Steph. Comm. 328.

SPIRITUALITIES OF A BISHOP. Those profits which a bishop receives in his ecclesiastical character, as the dues arising from his ordaining and instituting priests, and such like, in contradistinction to those profits which he acquires in his temporal capacity as a baron and lord of parliament, and which are termed his "temporalities," consisting of certain lands, revenues, and lay fees, etc. Cowell.

SPIRITUALITY OF BENEFICES. In ecclesiastical law. The tithes of land, etc. Wharton.

SPIRITUOUS LIQUORS. These are inflammable liquids produced by distillation, and forming an article of commerce. 1 Exch. 281.

The phrase "spirituous liquor," in a penal statute, cannot be extended beyond its exact literal sense. Spirit is the name of an inflammable liquor produced by distillation. Wine is the fermented juice of the grape, or a preparation of other vegetables by fermentation; hence the term does not include wine. 5 Blackf. 118.

SPITAL, or SPITTLE. A charitable foundation; a hospital for diseased people. Cowell.

SPLITTING A CAUSE OF ACTION. Dividing a single cause of action, claim, or demand into two or more parts, and bringing suit for one of such parts only, intending to reserve the rest for a separate action. The plaintiff who does this is bound by his first judgment, and can recover no more. 2 Black, Judgm. § 734.

SPOLIATION. In English ecclesiastical law. An injury done by one clerk or incumbent to another, in taking the fruits of his benefice without any right to them, but under a pretended title. 3 Bl. Comm. 90, 91.

The name of a suit sued out in the spiritual court to recover for the fruits of the church or for the church itself. Fitzh. Nat. Brev. 85.

In torts. Destruction of a thing by the act of a stranger; as the erasure or alteration of a writing by the act of a stranger is called "spoliation." This has not the effect to destroy its character or legal effect. 1 Greenl. Ev. § 566.

SPOLIATOR. It is a maxim of law, bearing chiefly on evidence, but also upon the value generally of the thing destroyed, that everything most to his disadvantage is to be presumed against the destroyer, (*spoliator,*) *contra spoliatorem omnia præsumuntur.* 1 Smith, Lead. Cas. 315.

Spoliatus debet ante omnia restitui. A party despoiled [forcibly deprived of possession] ought first of all to be restored. 2 Inst. 714; 4 Reeve, Eng. Law, 18.

SPOLIUM. In the civil and common law. A thing violently or unlawfully taken from another.

SPONDEO. Lat. In the civil law. I undertake; I engage. Inst. 3, 16, 1.

SPONDES? SPONDEO. Lat. Do you undertake? I do undertake. The most common form of verbal stipulation in the Roman law. Inst. 3, 16, 1.

Spondet peritiam artis. He promises the skill of his art; he engages to do the work in a skillful or workmanlike manner. 2 Kent, Comm. 588. Applied to the engagements of workmen for hire. Story, Bailm. § 428.

SPONSALIA, STIPULATIO SPONSALITIA. Lat. In the civil law. Espousal; betrothal; a reciprocal promise of future marriage.

SPONSIO. Lat. In the civil law. An engagement or undertaking; particularly such as was made in the form of an answer to a formal interrogatory by the other party. Calvin.

An engagement to pay a certain sum of money to the successful party in a cause. Calvin.

SPONSIO JUDICIALIS. Lat. In Roman law. A judicial wager corresponding in some respects to the "feigned issue" of modern practice.

SPONSIO LUDICRA. Lat. In Scotch law. A trifling or ludicrous engagement, such as a court will not sustain an action for. 1 Kames, Eq. Introd. 34.

In the civil law. An informal undertaking, or one made without the usual formula of interrogation. Calvin.

SPONSIONS. In international law. Agreements or engagements made by certain public officers (as generals or admirals in time of war) in behalf of their governments, either without authority or in excess of the authority under which they purport to be made, and which therefore require an express or tacit ratification.

SPONSOR. A surety; one who makes a promise or gives security for another, particularly a godfather in baptism.

In the civil law. One who intervenes for another voluntarily and without being requested.

SPONTE OBLATA. A free gift or present to the crown.

Sponte virum mulier fugiens et adultera facta, dote sua careat, nisi sponsi sponte retracta. Co. Litt. 32*b*. Let a woman leaving her husband of her own accord, and committing adultery, lose her dower, unless taken back by her husband of his own accord.

SPORTULA. Lat. In Roman law. A largess, dole, or present; a pecuniary donation; an official perquisite; something over and above the ordinary fee allowed by law. Inst. 4, 6, 24.

SPOUSALS. In old English law. Mutual promises to marry.

SPOUSE-BREACH. In old English law. Adultery. Cowell.

SPRING. A fountain of water; an issue of water from the earth, or the basin of water at the place of its issue. Webster. A natural chasm in which water has collected, and from which it either is lost by percolation or rises in a defined channel. 41 Law T. (N. S.) 457.

SPRING-BRANCH. In American land law. A branch of a stream, flowing from a spring. 12 Grat. 196.

SPRINGING USE. A use limited to arise on a future event where no preceding use is limited, and which does not take effect in derogation of any other interest than that which results to the grantor, or remains in him in the mean time. 2 Washb. Real Prop. 281.

SPUILZIE. In Scotch law. The taking away or meddling with movables in another's possession, without the consent of the owner or authority of law. Bell.

SPURIOUS. Not proceeding from the true source; not genuine; counterfeited. "A *spurious* bank-bill may be a legitimate impression from the genuine plate, but it must have the signatures of persons not the officers of the bank whence it purports to have issued, or else the names of fictitious persons. A spurious bill, also, may be an illegitimate impression from a genuine plate, or an impression from a counterfeit plate, but it must have such signatures or names as we have just indicated. A bill, therefore, may be both counterfeit and forged, or both counterfeit and spurious, but it cannot be both forged and spurious." 1 Ohio St. 187.

SPURIUS. Lat. In the civil law. A bastard; the offspring of promiscuous cohabitation.

SPY. A person sent into an enemy's camp to inspect their works, ascertain their strength and their intentions, watch their movements, and secretly communicate inteligence to the proper officer. By the laws of war among all civilized nations, a spy is punished with death. Webster. See Vattel, 3, 179.

SQUATTER. In American law. One who settles on another's land, particularly on public lands, without a title.

SQUIRE. A contraction of "esquire."

SS. An abbreviation used in that part of a record, pleading, or affidavit, called the "statement of the venue." Commonly translated or read, "to-wit," and supposed to be a contraction of "*scilicet*."

STAB. A wound inflicted by a thrust with a pointed weapon.

STABILIA. A writ called by that name, founded on a custom in Normandy, that where a man in power claimed lands in the possession of an inferior, he petitioned the prince that it might be put into his hands till the right was decided, whereupon he had this writ. Wharton.

Stabit præsumptio donec probetur in contrarium. A presumption will stand good till the contrary is proved. Hob. 297; Broom, Max. 949.

STABLE-STAND. In forest law. One of the four evidences or presumptions whereby a man was convicted of an intent to steal the king's deer in the forest. This was when a man was found at his *standing* in the forest with a cross-bow or long-bow bent, ready to shoot at any deer, or else standing close by a tree with grey-hounds in a leash, ready to slip. Cowell; Manwood.

STABULARIUS. Lat. In the civil law. A stable-keeper. Dig. 4, 9, 4, 1.

STACHIA. In old records. A dam or head made to stop a water-course. Cowell.

STAFF-HERDING. The following of cattle within a forest.

STAGE-RIGHT is a word which it has been attempted to introduce as a substitute for "the right of representation and performance," but it can hardly be said to be an accepted term of English or American law. Sweet.

STAGIARIUS. A resident. Cowell.

STAGNUM. In old English law. A pool, or pond. Co. Litt. 5*a*.

STAKE. A deposit made to answer an event, as on a wager.

STAKEHOLDER primarily means a person with whom money is deposited pending the decision of a bet or wager, (*q. v.*,) but it is more often used to mean a person who holds money or property which is claimed by rival claimants, but in which he himself claims no interest. Sweet.

STALE. In Saxon law. Larceny. Wharton.

STALE DEMAND. A demand or claim which has not been pressed or asserted for a long time, so long, in fact, that a court of equity will refuse to enforce it.

STALLAGE. The liberty or right of pitching or erecting stalls in fairs or markets, or the money paid for the same. 1 Steph. Comm. 664.

STALLARIUS. In Saxon law. The *præfectus stabuli*, now master of the horse. Sometimes one who has a stall in a fair or market.

STAMP. An impression made by public authority, in pursuance of law, upon paper or parchment, upon which certain legal proceedings, conveyances, or contracts are required to be written, and for which a tax or duty is exacted.

A small label or strip of paper, bearing a particular device, printed and sold by the government, and required to be attached to mail-matter, and to some other articles subject to duty or excise.

STAMP ACTS. In English law. Acts regulating the stamps upon deeds, contracts, agreements, papers in law proceedings, bills and notes, letters, receipts, and other papers.

STAMP DUTIES. In English law. Duties imposed upon and raised from stamps upon parchment and paper, and forming a branch of the perpetual revenue of the kingdom. 1 Bl. Comm. 323.

STANCE. In Scotch law. A resting place; a field or place adjoining a drove-road, for resting and refreshing sheep and cattle on their journey. 7 Bell, App. Cas. 53, 57, 58.

STAND. To abide; to submit to; as "to *stand* a trial."

To remain as a thing is; to remain in force. Pleadings demurred to and held good are allowed to *stand*.

To appear in court.

STANDARD. An ensign or flag used in war.

STANDARD OF WEIGHT, or MEASURE. A weight or measure fixed and prescribed by law, to which all other weights and measures are required to correspond.

STANDING ASIDE JURORS. A practice by which, on the drawing of a jury for a criminal trial, the prosecuting officer puts aside a juror, provisionally, until the panel is exhausted, without disclosing his reasons, instead of being required to challenge him and show cause. The statute 33 Edw. I. deprived the crown of the power to challenge jurors without showing cause, and the practice of standing aside jurors was adopted, in England, as a method of evading its provisions.

STANDING BY is used in law as implying knowledge, under such circumstances as rendered it the duty of the possessor to communicate it; and it is such knowledge, and not the mere fact of "standing by," that lays the foundation of responsibility. 8 Blackf. 45.

The phrase does not import an actual presence, "but implies knowledge under such circumstances as to render it the duty of the possessor to communicate it." 6 Ind. 289.

STANDING MUTE. A prisoner, arraigned for treason or felony, was said to "stand mute," when he refused to plead, or answered foreign to the purpose, or, after a plea of not guilty, would not put himself upon the country.

STANDING ORDERS are rules and forms regulating the procedure of the two houses of parliament, each having its own. They are of equal force in every parliament, except so far as they are altered or suspended from time to time. Cox, Inst. 136; May, Parl. Pr. 185.

STANDING SEISED TO USES. A covenant to stand seised to uses is one by which the owner of an estate covenants to hold the same to the use of another person, usually a relative, and usually in consideration of blood or marriage. It is a species of conveyance depending for its effect on the statute of uses.

STANNARIES. A district which includes all parts of Devon and Cornwall where some tin work is situate and in actual operation. The tin miners of the stannaries have certain peculiar customs and privileges.

STANNARY COURTS. Courts in Devonshire and Cornwall for the administration of justice among the miners and tinners. These courts were held before the lord warden and his deputies by virtue of a privilege granted to the workers of the tin-mines there, to sue and be sued in their own courts only, in order that they might not be drawn away from their business by having to attend lawsuits in distant courts. Brown.

STAPLE. **In English law.** A mart or market. A place where the buying and selling of wool, lead, leather, and other articles were put under certain terms. 2 Reeve, Eng. Law, 393.

In international law. The right of staple, as exercised by a people upon foreign merchants, is defined to be that they may not allow them to set their merchandises and wares to sale but in a certain place. This practice is not in use in the United States. 1 Chit. Com. Law, 103.

STAPLE INN. An inn of chancery. See INNS OF CHANCERY.

STAR-CHAMBER was a court which originally had jurisdiction in cases where the ordinary course of justice was so much obstructed by one party, through writs, combination of maintenance, or overawing influence that no inferior court would find its process obeyed. The court consisted of the privy council, the common-law judges, and (it seems) all peers of parliament. In the reign of Henry VIII. and his successors, the jurisdiction of the court was illegally extended to such a degree (especially in punishing disobedience to the king's arbitrary proclamations) that it became odious to the nation, and was abolished. 4 Steph. Comm. 310; Sweet.

STARE DECISIS. Lat. To stand by decided cases; to uphold precedents; to maintain former adjudications. 1 Kent, Comm. 477.

STARE IN JUDICIO. Lat. To appear before a tribunal, either as plaintiff or defendant.

STARR, or STARRA. The old term for contract or obligation among the Jews, being a corruption from the Hebrew word "*shetar*," a covenant. By an ordinance of Richard I., no starr was allowed to be valid, unless deposited in one of certain repositories established by law, the most considerable of which was in the king's exchequer at Westminster; and Blackstone conjectures that the room in which these chests were kept was thence called the "starr-chamber." 4 Bl. Comm. 266, 267, note *a*.

Stat pro ratione voluntas. The will stands in place of a reason. 1 Barb. 408, 411; 16 Barb. 514, 525.

Stat pro ratione voluntas populi. The will of the people stands in place of a reason. 25 Barb. 276, 344.

STATE, *v.* To express the particulars of a thing in writing or in words; to set down or set forth in detail.

To set down in gross; to mention in general terms, or by way of reference; to refer. 6 Hill, 300.

STATE, *n.* A body politic, or society of men, united together for the purpose of promoting their mutual safety and advantage, by the joint efforts of their combined strength. Cooley, Const. Lim. 1.

One of the component commonwealths or states of the United States of America.

The people of a state, in their collective capacity, considered as the party wronged by a criminal deed; the public; as in the title of a cause, "The State *vs.* A. B."

The section of territory occupied by one of the United States.

STATE OF FACTS. Formerly, when a master in chancery was directed by the court of chancery to make an inquiry or investigation into any matter arising out of a suit, and which could not conveniently be brought before the court itself, each party in the suit carried in before the master a statement showing how the party bringing it in represented the matter in question to be; and this statement was technically termed a "state of facts," and formed the ground upon which the evidence was received, the evidence being, in fact, brought by one party or the other, to prove his own or disprove his opponent's state of facts. And so now, a state of facts means the statement made by any one of his version of the facts. Brown.

STATE OF FACTS AND PROPOSAL. In English lunacy practice, when a person has been found a lunatic, the next step is to submit to the master a scheme called a "state of facts and proposal," showing what is the position in life, property, and income of the lunatic, who are his next of kin and heir at law, who are proposed as his committees, and what annual sum is proposed to be allowed for his maintenance, etc. From the state of facts and the evidence adduced in support of it, the master frames his report. Elmer, Lun. 22; Pope, Lun. 79; Sweet.

STATE OF THE CASE. A narrative of the facts upon which the plaintiff relies, substituted for a more formal declaration, in suits in the inferior courts. The phrase is used in New Jersey.

STATE TRIAL. A trial for a political offense.

STATE TRIALS. A work in thirty-three volumes octavo, containing all English trials for offenses against the state and others partaking in some degree of that character, from the ninth year of Hen. II. to the first of Geo. IV.

STATED. Settled; closed. An account *stated* means an account settled, and at an end. Pull. Acc'ts, 33. "In order to constitute an account *stated*, there must be a statement of some certain amount of money being due, which must be made either to the party himself or to some agent of his." 5 Mees. & W. 667.

STATED TERM. A regular or ordinary term or session of a court for the dispatch of its general business, held at the time fixed by law or rule; as distinguished from a *special* term, held out of the due order or for the transaction of particular business.

STATEMENT. In a general sense, an allegation; a declaration of matters of fact. The term has come to be used of a variety of formal narratives of facts, required by law in various jurisdictions as the foundation of judicial or official proceedings.

STATEMENT OF AFFAIRS. In English bankruptcy practice, a bankrupt or debtor who has presented a petition for liquidation or composition must produce at the first meeting of creditors a statement of his affairs, giving a list of his creditors, secured and unsecured, with the value of the securities, a list of bills discounted, and a statement of his property. Sweet.

STATEMENT OF CLAIM. A written or printed statement by the plaintiff in an action in the English high court, showing the facts on which he relies to support his claim against the defendant, and the relief which he claims. It is delivered to the defendant or his solicitor. The delivery of the statement of claim is usually the next step after appearance, and is the commencement of the pleadings. Sweet.

STATEMENT OF DEFENSE. In the practice of the English high court, where the defendant in an action does not demur to the whole of the plaintiff's claim, he delivers a pleading called a "statement of defense." The statement of defense deals with the allegations contained in the statement of claim, (or the indorsement on the writ, if there is no statement of claim,) admitting or denying them, and, if necessary, stating fresh facts in explanation or avoidance of those alleged by the plaintiff. Sweet.

STATEMENT OF PARTICULARS. In English practice, when the plaintiff claims a debt or liquidated demand, but has not indorsed the writ specially, (*i. e.*, indorsed on it the particulars of his claim under Order iii. r. 6,) and the defendant fails to appear, the plaintiff may file a statement of the particulars of his claim, and after eight days enter judgment for the amount, as if the writ had been specially indorsed. Court Rules, xiii. 5; Sweet.

STATESMAN. A freeholder and farmer in Cumberland. Wharton.

STATIM. Lat. Forthwith; immediately. In old English law, this term meant either "at once," or "within a legal time," *i. e.*, such time as permitted the legal and regular performance of the act in question.

STATING AN ACCOUNT. Exhibiting, or listing in their order, the items which make up an account.

STATING PART OF A BILL. That part of a bill in chancery in which the plaintiff states the facts of his case; it is distinguished from the *charging* part of the bill and from the *prayer*.

STATION. In the civil law. A place where ships may ride in safety. Dig. 50, 16, 59.

STATIONERS' HALL. In English law. The hall of the stationers' company, at which every person claiming copyright in a book must register his title, in order to be able to bring actions against persons infringing it. 2 Steph. Comm. 37-39.

STATIONERY OFFICE. In English law. A government office established as a department of the treasury, for the purpose of supplying government offices with stationery and books, and of printing and publishing government papers.

STATIST. A statesman; a politician; one skilled in government.

STATISTICS. That part of political science which is concerned in collecting and arranging facts illustrative of the condition and resources of a state. The subject is sometimes divided into (1) historical statistics, or facts which illustrate the former condition of a state; (2) statistics of population; (3) of revenue; (4) of trade, commerce, and navigation; (5) of the moral, social, and physical condition of the people. Wharton.

STATU LIBER. Lat. In Roman law. One who is made free by will under a condition; one who has his liberty fixed and appointed at a certain time or on a certain condition. Dig. 40, 7.

STATU LIBERI. Lat. In Louisiana. Slaves for a time, who had acquired the right of being free at a time to come, or on a condition which was not fulfilled, or in a certain event which had not happened, but who in the mean time remained in a state of slavery. Civil Code La. (Ed. 1838,) art. 37.

STATUS. The *status* of a person is his legal position or condition. Thus, when we say that the *status* of a woman after a decree *nisi* for the dissolution of her marriage with her husband has been made, but before it has been made absolute, is that of a married woman, we mean that she has the same legal rights, liabilities, and disabilities as an ordinary married woman. The term is chiefly applied to persons under disability, or persons who have some peculiar condition which prevents the general law from applying to them in the same way as it does to ordinary persons. Sweet.

There are certain rights and duties, with certain capacities and incapacities to take rights and incur duties, by which persons, as subjects of law, are variously determined to certain classes. The rights, duties, capacities, or incapacities which determine a given person to any of these classes, constitute a condition or *status* with which the person is invested. Aust. Jur. § 973.

STATUS DE MANERIO. The assembly of the tenants in the court of the lord of a manor, in order to do their customary suit.

STATUS OF IRREMOVABILITY. In English law. The right acquired by a pauper, after one year's residence in any parish, not to be removed therefrom.

STATUS QUO. Lat. The existing state of things at any given date. *Status quo ante bellum*, the state of things before the war.

Statuta pro publico commodo late interpretantur. Jenk. Cent. 21. Statutes made for the public good ought to be liberally construed.

Statuta suo cluduntur territorio, nec ultra territorium disponunt. Statutes are confined to their own territory, and have no extraterritorial effect. 4 Allen, 324.

STATUTABLE, or STATUTORY, is that which is introduced or governed by statute law, as opposed to the common law or equity. Thus, a court is said to have statutory jurisdiction when jurisdiction is given to it in certain matters by act of the legislature.

STATUTE, *v.* In old Scotch law. To ordain, establish, or decree.

STATUTE, *n.* An act of the legislature; a particular law enacted and established by the will of the legislative department of government, expressed with the requisite formalities.

Statutes are public and private. A private statute is one which concerns only certain designated individuals, and affects only their private rights. All other statutes are public. Code Civil Proc. Cal. § 1898.

In foreign and civil law. Any particular municipal law or usage, though resting for its authority on judicial decisions, or the practice of nations. 2 Kent, Comm. 456. The whole municipal law of a particular state, from whatever source arising. Story, Confl. Laws, § 12.

"Statute" also sometimes means a kind of bond or obligation of record, being an abbreviation for "statute merchant" or "statute staple," (*q. v.*)

For different kinds of statutes, see AFFIRMATIVE STATUTE; DECLARATORY STATUTE; ENABLING STATUTE; NEGATIVE STAT-

UTE; PENAL STATUTE; PRIVATE STATUTE; PUBLIC STATUTE; REMEDIAL STATUTE.

STATUTE FAIR. In English law. A fair at which laborers of both sexes stood and offered themselves for hire; sometimes called also "Mop."

STATUTE-MERCHANT. In English law. A security for a debt acknowledged to be due, entered into before the chief magistrate of some trading town, pursuant to the statute 13 Edw. I. *De Mercatoribus*, by which not only the body of the debtor might be imprisoned, and his goods seized in satisfaction of the debt, but also his lands might be delivered to the creditor till out of the rents and profits of them the debt be satisfied. 2 Bl. Comm. 160. Now fallen into disuse. 1 Steph. Comm. 287.

STATUTE OF ACCUMULATIONS. In English law. The statute 39 & 40 Geo. III. c. 98, forbidding the accumulation, beyond a certain period, of property settled by deed or will.

STATUTE OF ALLEGIANCE DE FACTO. An act of 11 Hen. VII. c. 1, requiring subjects to give their allegiance to the actual king for the time being, and protecting them in so doing.

STATUTE OF DISTRIBUTIONS. A law prescribing the manner of the distribution of the estate of an intestate among his heirs or relatives. Such statutes exist in all the states.

STATUTE OF ELIZABETH. In English law. The statute 13 Eliz. c. 5, against conveyances made in fraud of creditors.

STATUTE OF FRAUDS. See FRAUDS, STATUTE OF.

STATUTE OF GLOUCESTER. In English law. The statute 6 Edw. I. c. 1, A. D. 1278. It takes its name from the place of its enactment, and was the first statute giving costs in actions. 3 Bl. Comm. 399.

STATUTE OF LIMITATIONS. A statute prescribing limitations to the right of action on certain described causes of action; that is, declaring that no suit shall be maintained on such causes of action unless brought within a specified period after the right accrued.

STATUTE OF USES. See USE.

STATUTE OF WILLS. In English law. The statute 32 Hen. VIII. c. 1, which enacted that all persons being seised in fee-simple (except *femes covert*, infants, idiots, and persons of non-sane memory) might, by will and testament in writing, devise to any other person, except to bodies corporate, two-thirds of their lands, tenements, and hereditaments, held in chivalry, and the whole of those held in socage. 2 Bl. Comm. 375.

STATUTE ROLL. A roll upon which an English statute, after receiving the royal assent, was formerly entered.

STATUTE-STAPLE. In English law. A security for a debt acknowleged to be due, so called from its being entered into before the mayor of the *staple*, that is to say, the grand mart for the principal commodities or manufactures of the kingdom, formerly held by act of parliament in certain trading towns. In other respects it resembled the *statute-merchant*, (*q. v.*,) but like that has now fallen into disuse. 2 Bl. Comm. 160; 1 Steph. Comm. 287.

STATUTES AT LARGE. Statutes printed in full and in the order of their enactment, in a collected form, as distinguished from any digest, revision, abridgment, or compilation of them. Thus the volumes of "United States Statutes at Large," contain all the acts of congress in their order.

The name is also given to an authentic collection of the various statutes which have been passed by the British parliament from very early times to the present day.

Statutes in derogation of common law must be strictly construed. 1 Grant, Cas. 57; Cooley, Const. Lim. 75, note.

STATUTI. Lat. In Roman law. Licensed or registered advocates; members of the college of advocates. The number of these was limited, and they enjoyed special privileges from the time of Constantine to that of Justinian.

STATUTORY EXPOSITION. When the language of a statute is ambiguous, and any subsequent enactment involves a particular interpretation of the former act, it is said to contain a *statutory* exposition of the former act. Wharton.

STATUTORY OBLIGATION. An obligation—whether to pay money, perform certain acts, or discharge certain duties—which is created by or arises out of a statute, as distinguished from one founded upon acts between parties or jural relationships.

STATUTORY RELEASE. A conveyance which superseded the old compound assurance by lease and release. It was created by St. 4 & 5 Vict. c. 21, which abolished the lease for a year.

STATUTUM. Lat. In the civil law. Established; determined. A term applied to judicial action. Dig. 50, 16, 46, pr.

In old English law. A statute; an act of parliament.

Statutum affirmativum non derogat communi legi. Jenk Cent. 24. An affirmative statute does not derogate from the common law.

STATUTUM DE MERCATORIBUS. The statute of Acton Burnell, (*q. v.*)

Statutum ex gratia regis dicitur, quando rex dignatur cedere de jure suo regio, pro commodo et quiete populi sui. 2 Inst. 378. A statute is said to be by the grace of the king, when the king deigns to yield some portion of his royal rights for the good and quiet of his people.

Statutum generaliter est intelligendum quando verba statuti sunt specialia, ratio autem generalis. When the words of a statute are special, but the reason of it general, the statute is to be understood generally. 10 Coke, 101.

STATUTUM HIBERNIÆ DE COHÆREDIBUS. The statute 14 Hen. III. The third public act in the statute-book. It has been pronounced not to be a statute. In the form of it, it appears to be an instruction given by the king to his justices in Ireland, directing them how to proceed in a certain point where they entertained a doubt. It seems the justices itinerant in that country had a doubt, when land descended to sisters, whether the younger sisters ought to hold of the eldest, and do homage to her for their several portions, or of the chief lord, and do homage to him; and certain knights had been sent over to know what the practice was in England in such a case. 1 Reeve, Eng. Law, 259.

STATUTUM SESSIONUM. In old English law. The statute session; a meeting in every hundred of constables and householders, by custom, for the ordering of servants, and debating of differences between masters and servants, rating of wages, etc. 5 Eliz. c. 4.

Statutum speciale statuto speciali non derogat. Jenk. Cent. 199. One special statute does not take from another special statute.

STATUTUM WALLIÆ. The statute of Wales. The title of a statute passed in the twelfth year of Edw. I., being a sort of constitution for the principality of Wales, which was thereby, in a great measure, put on the footing of England with respect to its laws and the administration of justice. 2 Reeve, Eng. Law. 93, 94.

STAURUM. In old records. A store, or stock of cattle. A term of common occurrence in the accounts of monastic establishments. Spelman; Cowell.

STAY. In practice. A stopping; the act of arresting a judicial proceeding, by the order of a court.

STAY LAWS. Acts of the legislature prescribing a stay of execution in certain cases, or a stay of foreclosure of mortgages, or closing the courts for a limited period, or providing that suits shall not be instituted until a certain time after the cause of action arose, or otherwise suspending legal remedies; designed for the relief of debtors, in times of general distress or financial trouble.

STAY OF EXECUTION. The stopping or arresting of execution on a judgment, that is, of the judgment-creditor's right to issue execution, for a limited period. This is given by statute in many jurisdictions, as a privilege to the debtor, usually on his furnishing bail for the debt, costs, and interest. Or it may take place by agreement of the parties.

STAY OF PROCEEDINGS. The temporary suspension of the regular order of proceedings in a cause, by direction or order of the court, usually to await the action of one of the parties in regard to some omitted step or some act which the court has required him to perform as incidental to the suit; as where a non-resident plaintiff has been ruled to give security for costs.

STEAL. This term is commonly used in indictments for larceny, ("take, *steal*, and carry away,") and denotes the commission of theft. But, in popular usage, "stealing" seems to be a wider term than "larceny," inasmuch as it may include the unlawful appropriation of things which are not technically the subject of larceny, *e. g.*, immovables.

STEALING CHILDREN. See KIDNAPPING.

STEALTH. Theft is so called by some ancient writers. "Stealth is the wrongful taking of goods without pretense of title." Finch, Law, b. 3, c. 17.

STEELBOW GOODS. In Scotch law. Corns, cattle, straw, and implements of husbandry delivered by a landlord to his tenant, by which the tenant is enabled to stock and labor the farm; in consideration of which be becomes bound to return articles equal in quantity and quality, at the expiry of the lease. Bell.

STELLIONATAIRE. In French law. A party who fraudulently mortgages property to which he has no title.

STELLIONATE. In Scotch law. The crime of aliening the same subject to different persons. 2 Kames, Eq. 40.

STELLIONATUS. Lat. In the civil law. A general name for any kind of fraud not falling under any specific class. But the term is chiefly applied to fraud practiced in the sale or pledging of property; as, selling the same property to two different persons, selling another's property as one's own, placing a second mortgage on property without disclosing the existence of the first, etc.

STENOGRAPHER. One who is skilled in the art of short-hand writing; one whose business is to write in short-hand.

STEP-DAUGHTER. The daughter of one's wife by a former husband, or of one's husband by a former wife.

STEP-FATHER. The man who marries a widow, she having a child by her former marriage, is step-father to such child.

STEP-MOTHER. The woman who marries a widower, he having a child by his former wife, becomes step-mother to such child.

STEP-SON. The son of one's wife by a former husband, or of one's husband by a former wife.

STERBRECHE, or STREBRICH. The breaking, obstructing, or straitening of a way. Termes de la Ley.

STÈRE. A French measure of solidity, used in measuring wood. It is a cubic meter.

STERILITY. Barrenness; incapacity to produce a child.

STERLING. In English law. Current or standard coin, especially silver coin; a standard of coinage.

STET BILLA. If the plaintiff in a plaint in the mayor's court of London has attached property belonging to the defendant and obtained execution against the garnishee, the defendant, if he wishes to contest the plaintiff's claim, and obtain restoration of his property, must issue a *scire facias ad disprobandum debitum;* if the only question to be tried is the plaintiff's debt, the plaintiff in appearing to the *scire facias* prays *stet billa* "that his bill original," *i. e.*, his original plaint, "may stand, and that the defendant may plead thereto." The action then proceeds in the usual way as if the proceedings in attachment (which are founded on a fictitious default of the defendant in appearing to the plaint) had not taken place. Brand, F. Attachm. 115; Sweet.

STET PROCESSUS. *Stet processus* is an entry on the roll in the nature of a judgment of a direction that all further proceedings shall be stayed, (*i. e.*, that the process may stand,) and it is one of the ways by which a suit may be terminated by an act of the party, as distinguished from a termination of it by judgment, which is the act of the court. It was used by the plaintiff when he wished to suspend the action without suffering a nonsuit. Brown.

STEVEDORE. A person employed in loading and unloading vessels.

STEWARD. This word signifies a man appointed in the place or stead of another, and generally denotes a principal officer within his jurisdiction. Brown.

STEWARD OF A MANOR. An important officer who has the general management of all forensic matters connected with the manor of which he is steward. He stands in much the same relation to the lord of the manor as an under-sheriff does to the sheriff. Cowell.

STEWARD OF ALL ENGLAND. In old English law. An officer who was invested with various powers; among others, to preside on the trial of peers.

STEWARD OF SCOTLAND. An officer of the highest dignity and trust. He administered the crown revenues, superintended the affairs of the household, and possessed the privilege of holding the first place in the army, next to the king, in the day of battle. From this office the royal house of Stuart took its name. But the office was sunk on their advancement to the throne, and has never since been revived. Bell.

STEWARD OF THE HOUSEHOLD. See MARSHALSEA.

STEWARTRY, in Scotch law, is said to be equivalent to the English "county." See Brown.

STEWS. Certain brothels anciently permitted in England, suppressed by Henry VIII. Also, breeding places for tame pheasants.

STICK. In the old books. To stop; to hesitate; to accede with reluctance. "The court *stuck* a little at this exception." 2 Show. 491.

STICKLER. (1) An inferior officer who cuts wood within the royal parks of Clarendon. Cowell. (2) An arbitrator. (3) An obstinate contender about anything.

STIFLING A PROSECUTION. Agreeing, in consideration of receiving a pecuniary or other advantage, to abstain from prosecuting a person for an offense not giving rise to a civil remedy; *e. g.*, perjury. Sweet.

STILLICIDIUM. Lat. In the civil law. The drip of water from the eaves of a house. The servitude *stillicidii* consists in the right to have the water drip from one's eaves upon the house or ground of another. The term "*flumen*" designated the rain-water collected from the roof, and carried off by the gutters, and there is a similar easement of having it discharged upon the adjoining estate. Mackeld. Rom. Law, § 317, par. 4.

STINT. In English law. Limit; a limited number. Used as descriptive of a species of common. See COMMON SANS NOMBRE.

STIPEND. A salary; settled pay.

In English and Scotch law. A provision made for the support of the clergy.

STIPENDIARY ESTATES. Estates granted in return for services, generally of a military kind. 1 Steph. Comm. 174.

STIPENDIARY MAGISTRATES. In English law. Paid magistrates; appointed in London and some other cities and boroughs, and having in general the powers and jurisdiction of justices of the peace.

STIPENDIUM. Lat. In the civil law. The pay of a soldier; wages; stipend. Calvin.

STIPES. Lat. In old English law. Stock; a stock; a source of descent or title. *Communis stipes*, the common stock. Fleta, lib. 6, c. 2.

STIPITAL. Relating to *stirpes*, roots, or stocks. "Stipital distribution" of property is distribution *per stirpes;* that is, by right of representation.

STIPULATED DAMAGE. Liquidated damage, (*q. v.*)

STIPULATIO. Lat. In the Roman law, *stipulatio* was the verbal contract, (*verbis obligatio*,) and was the most solemn and formal of all the contracts in that system of jurisprudence. It was entered into by question and corresponding answer thereto, by the parties, both being present at the same time, and usually by such words as "*spondes? spondeo*," "*promittis? promitto*," and the like. Brown.

STIPULATIO AQUILIANA. Lat. In Roman law. A particular application of the *stipulatio*, which was used to collect together into one verbal contract all the liabilities of every kind and quality of the debtor, with a view to their being released or discharged by an *acceptilatio*, that mode of discharge being applicable only to the verbal contract. Brown.

STIPULATION. A material article in an agreement.

In practice. An engagement or undertaking in writing, to do a certain act; as to try a cause at a certain time. 1 Burrill, Pr. 389.

The name "stipulation" is familiarly given to any agreement made by the attorneys engaged on opposite sides of a cause, (especially if in writing,) regulating any matter incidental to the proceedings or trial, which falls within their jurisdiction. Such, for instance, are agreements to extend the time for pleading, to take depositions, to waive objections, to admit certain facts, to continue the cause.

In admiralty practice. A recognizance of certain persons (called in the old law "*fide jussors*") in the nature of bail for the appearance of a defendant. 3 Bl. Comm. 108.

STIPULATOR. In the civil law. The party who asked the question in the contract of stipulation; the other party, or he who answered, being called the "promissor." But, in a more general sense, the term was applied to both the parties. Calvin.

STIRPS. Lat. A root or stock of descent or title. Taking property by right of representation is called "succession *per stirpes*," in opposition to taking in one's own right, or as a principal, which is termed "taking *per capita.*"

STOCK. **In mercantile law.** The goods and wares of a merchant or tradesman, kept for sale and traffic.

In a larger sense. The capital of a merchant or other person, including his merchandise, money, and credits, or, in other words, the entire property employed in business. 2 Wis. 42, 56, 57.

In corporation law. A right to partake, according to the amount of the party's subscription, of the surplus profits obtained from the use and disposal of the capital stock of the company. Ang. & A. Corp. § 557.

The capital stock of a corporation is that money or property which is put into a fund by those who by subscription therefor become members of the corporate body. 75 N. Y. 216.

When the word "stock," as used in reference to a corporation, means anything else than the capital of the company, it cannot refer to anything else than the interests of the shareholders or individuals. Such interests are called "stock;" and the sum total of them is appropriately enough called the "stock" of a corporation. 23 N. Y. 192, 220.

The funded indebtedness of a state or government, also, is often represented by stocks, shares of which are held by its creditors at interest.

In the law of descent. The term is used, metaphorically, to denote the original progenitor of a family, or the ancestor from whom the persons in question are all descended; such descendants being called "branches."

STOCK ASSOCIATION. A joint-stock company, (*q. v.*)

STOCK-BROKER. One who buys and sells stock as the agent of others.

STOCK-EXCHANGE. A voluntary association of persons (not usually a corporation) who, for convenience in the transaction of business with each other, have associated themselves to provide a common place for the transaction of their business; an association of stock-brokers. Dos Passos, Stock-Brok. 14.

The building or room used by an association of stock-brokers for meeting for the transaction of their common business.

STOCK-JOBBER. A dealer in stock; one who buys and sells stock on his own account on speculation.

STOCK-NOTE. The term "stock-note" has no technical meaning, and may as well apply to a note given on the sale of stock which the bank had purchased or taken in the payment of doubtful debts as to a note given on account of an original subscription to stock. 12 Ill. 402.

STOCKHOLDER. A person who owns shares of stock in a corporation or joint-stock company.

The owners of shares in a corporation which has a capital stock are called "stockholders." If a corporation has no capital stock, the corporators and their successors are called "members." Civil Code Dak. § 392.

STOCKS. A machine consisting of two pieces of timber, arranged to be fastened together, and holding fast the legs of a person placed in it. This was an ancient method of punishment.

STOP ORDER. The name of an order grantable in English chancery practice, to prevent drawing out a fund in court to the prejudice of an assignee or lienholder.

STOPPAGE. In the civil law. Compensation or set-off.

STOPPAGE IN TRANSITU. The act by which the unpaid vendor of goods stops their progress and resumes possession of them, while they are in course of transit from him to the purchaser, and not yet actually delivered to the latter.

The right of stoppage *in transitu* is that which the vendor has, when he sells goods on credit to another, of resuming the possession of the goods while they are in the possession of a carrier or middle-man, in the transit to the consignee or vendee, and before they arrive into his actual possession, or the destination he has appointed for them on his becoming bankrupt and insolvent. 2 Kent. Comm. 702.

Stoppage *in transitu* is the right which arises to an unpaid vendor to resume the possession, with which he has parted, of goods sold upon credit, before they come into the possession of a buyer who has become insolvent, bankrupt, or pecuniarily embarrassed. 57 N. H. 454.

STORE. Storing is the keeping merchandise for safe custody, to be delivered in the same condition as when received, where the safe-keeping is the principal object of deposit, and not the consumption or sale. 3 N. Y. 122; 16 Barb. 119.

STORES. The supplies of different articles provided for the subsistence and accommodation of a ship's crew and passengers.

STOUTHRIEFF. In Scotch law. Formerly this word included every species of theft accompanied with violence to the person, but of late years it has become the *vox signata* for forcible and masterful depredation within or near the dwelling-house; while robbery has been more particularly applied to violent depredation on the highway, or accompanied by house-breaking. Alis. Prin. Scotch Law, 227.

STOWAGE. In maritime law. The storing, packing, or arranging of the cargo in a ship, in such a manner as to protect the goods from friction, bruising, or damage from leakage.

Money paid for a room where goods are laid; housage. Wharton.

STOWE. In old English law. A valley. Co. Litt. 4*b*.

STRADDLE. In stock-brokers' parlance the term means the double privilege of a "put" and a "call," and secures to the holder the right to demand of the seller at a certain price within a certain time a certain number of shares of specified stock, or to require him to take, at the same price within the same time, the same shares of stock. 83 N. Y. 95.

STRAMINEUS HOMO. A man of straw, one of no substance, put forward as bail or surety.

STRAND. A shore or bank of the sea or a river. Cowell.

STRANDING. In maritime law. The drifting, driving, or running aground of a ship on a shore or strand. *Accidental* stranding takes place where the ship is driven on shore by the winds and waves. *Voluntary* stranding takes place where the ship is run on shore either to preserve her from a worse fate or for some fraudulent purpose. Marsh. Ins. bk. 1, c. 12, § 1.

STRANGER IN BLOOD. Any person not within the consideration of natural love and affection arising from relationship.

STRANGERS. By this term is intended third persons generally. Thus the persons bound by a fine are parties, privies, and strangers; the parties are either the cognizors or cognizees; the privies are such as are in any way related to those who levy the fine, and claim under them by any right of blood, or other right of representation; the strangers are all other persons in the world, except only the parties and privies. In its general legal signification the term is opposed to the word "privy." Those who are in no way parties to a covenant, nor bound by it, are also said to be strangers to the covenant. Brown.

STRATAGEM. A deception either by words or actions, in times of war, in order to obtain an advantage over an enemy.

STRATOCRACY. A military government; government by military chiefs of an army.

STRATOR. In old English law. A surveyor of the highways.

STRAW BAIL. Nominal or worthless bail. Irresponsible persons, or men of no property, who make a practice of going bail for any one who will pay them a fee therefor.

STRAY. See ESTRAY.

STREAM. A current of water; a body of flowing water. The word, in its ordinary sense, includes rivers. But Callis defines a stream "a current of waters running over the level at random, and not kept in with banks or walls." Call. Sew. [83,] 133.

STREAMING FOR TIN. The process of working tin in Cornwall and Devon. The right to stream must not be exercised so as to interfere with the rights of other private individuals; *e. g.*, either by withdrawing or by polluting or choking up the water-courses or waters of others; and the statutes 23 Hen. VIII. c. 8, and 27 Hen. VIII. c. 23, impose a penalty of £20 for the offense. Brown.

STREET. A public thoroughfare or highway in a city or village. It differs from a country highway.

STREIGHTEN. In the old books. To narrow or restrict. "The *habendum* should not *streighten* the devise." 1 Leon. 58.

STREPITUS. In old records. Estrepement or strip; a species of waste or destruction of property. Spelman.

STREPITUS JUDICIALIS. Turbulent conduct in a court of justice. Jacob.

STRICT CONSTRUCTION. Construction of a statute or other instrument according to its letter, which recognizes nothing that is not expressed, takes the language used in its exact and technical meaning, and admits no equitable considerations or implications.

STRICT SETTLEMENT. This phrase was formerly used to denote a settlement whereby land was limited to a parent for life, and after his death to his first and other sons or children in tail, with trustees interposed to preserve contingent remainders. 1 Steph. Comm. 332, 333.

STRICTI JURIS. Lat. Of strict right or law; according to strict law. "A license is a thing *stricti juris;* a privilege which a man does not possess by his own right, but it is conceded to him as an indulgence, and therefore it is to be strictly observed." 2 Rob. Adm. 117.

STRICTISSIMI JURIS. Lat. Of the strictest right or law. "Licenses being matter of special indulgence, the application of them was formerly *strictissimi juris.*" 1 Edw. Adm. 328.

STRICTO JURE. Lat. In strict law. 1 Kent, Comm. 65.

STRICTUM JUS. Lat. Strict right or law; the rigor of the law as distinguished from equity.

STRIKE. The act of a body of workmen employed by the same master, in stopping work all together at a prearranged time, and refusing to continue until higher wages, or shorter time, or some other concession is granted to them by the employer.

STRIKE OFF. In common parlance, and in the language of the auction-room, property is understood to be "struck off" or "knocked down," when the auctioneer, by the fall of his hammer, or by any other audible or visible announcement, signifies to the bidder that he is entitled to the property on paying the amount of his bid, according to the terms of the sale. 7 Hill, 439.

In practice. A court is said to "strike off" a case when it directs the removal of the case from the record or docket, as being one over which it has no jurisdiction and no power to hear and determine it.

STRIKING A DOCKET. In English practice. The first step in the proceedings in bankruptcy, which consists in making affidavit of the debt, and giving a bond to follow up the proceedings with effect. 2 Steph. Comm. 199. When the affidavit and bond are delivered at the bankrupt office, an entry is made in what is called the "docket-book," upon which the petitioning creditor is said to have *struck a docket.* Eden, Bankr. 51, 52.

STRIKING A JURY. The selecting or nominating a jury of twelve men out of the whole number returned as jurors on the panel. It is especially used of the selection of a *special* jury, where a panel of forty-eight is prepared by the proper officer, and the parties, in turn, strike off a certain number of names, until the list is reduced to twelve. A jury thus chosen is called a "struck jury."

STRIKING OFF THE ROLL. The disbarring of an attorney or solicitor.

STRIP. The act of spoiling or unlawfully taking away anything from the land, by the tenant for life or years, or by one holding an estate in the land less than the entire fee. Pub. St. Mass. 1882, p. 1295.

STRONG HAND. The words "with strong hand" imply a degree of criminal force, whereas the words *vi et armis* ("with force and arms") are mere formal words in the action of trespass, and the plaintiff is not bound to prove any force. The statutes relating to forcible entries use the words "with a strong hand" as describing that degree of force which makes an entry or detainer of lands criminal. Brown.

STRUCK. In pleading. A word essential in an indictment for murder, when the death arises from any wounding, beating, or bruising. 1 Bulst. 184; 5 Coke, 122; 3 Mod. 202.

STRUCK JURY. In practice. A special jury. So called because constituted by *striking out* a certain number of names from a prepared list. See STRIKING A JURY.

STRUMPET. A whore, harlot, or courtesan. This word was anciently used for an addition. It occurs as an addition to the name of a woman in a return made by a jury in the sixth year of Henry V. Wharton.

STUFF GOWN. The professional robe worn by barristers of the outer bar; viz., those who have not been admitted to the rank of queen's counsel. Brown.

STULTIFY. To make one out mentally incapacitated for the performance of an act.

STULTILOQUIUM. In old English law. Vicious pleading, for which a fine was imposed by King John, supposed to be the origin of the fines for *beau-pleader.* Crabb, Eng. Law, 135.

STUMPAGE. The sum agreed to be paid to an owner of land for trees standing (or lying) upon his land, the purchaser being permitted to enter upon the land and to cut down and remove the trees; in other words, it is the price paid for a license to cut. 67 Me. 478.

STUPRUM. Lat. In the civil law. Unlawful intercourse with a woman. Distinguished from adultery as being committed with a virgin or widow. Dig. 48, 5, 6.

STURGEON. A royal fish which, when either thrown ashore or caught near the coast, is the property of the sovereign. 2 Steph. Comm. 19*n*, 540.

STYLE. As a verb, to call, name, or entitle one; as a noun, the title or appellation of a person.

SUA SPONTE. Lat. Of his or its own will or motion; voluntarily; without prompting or suggestion.

SUABLE. That which may be sued.

SUAPTE NATURA. Lat. In its own nature. *Suapte natura sterilis*, barren in its own nature and quality; intrinsically barren. 5 Maule & S. 170.

SUB. Lat. Under; upon.

SUB-BALLIVUS. In old English law. An under-bailiff; a sheriff's deputy. Fleta, lib. 2, c. 68, § 2.

SUB-BOIS. Coppice-wood. 2 Inst. 642.

SUB COLORE JURIS. Lat. Under color of right; under a show or appearance of right or rightful power.

SUB CONDITIONE. Upon condition. The proper words to express a condition in a conveyance, and to create an estate upon condition.

SUB DISJUNCTIONE. In the alternative. Fleta, lib. 2, c. 60, § 21.

SUB JUDICE. Under or before a judge or court; under judicial consideration; undetermined. 12 East, 409.

SUB MODO. Under a qualification; subject to a restriction or condition.

SUB NOMINE. Under the name; in the name of; under the title of.

SUB PEDE SIGILLI. Under the foot of the seal; under seal. 1 Strange, 521.

SUB POTESTATE. Under, or subject to, the power of another; used of a wife, child, slave, or other person not *sui juris*.

SUB SALVO ET SECURO CONDUCTU. Under safe and secure conduct. 1 Strange, 430. Words in the old writ of *habeas corpus*.

SUB SILENTIO. Under silence; without any notice being taken. Passing a thing *sub silentio* may be evidence of consent.

SUB SPE RECONCILIATIONIS. Under the hope of reconcilement. 2 Kent, Comm. 127.

SUB SUO PERICULO. At his own risk. Fleta, lib. 2, c. 5, § 5.

SUBAGENT. An under-agent; a substituted agent; an agent appointed by one who is himself an agent. 2 Kent, Comm. 633.

SUBALTERN. An inferior or subordinate officer. An officer who exercises his authority under the superintendence and control of a superior.

SUBCONTRACT. A contract subordinate to another contract, made or intended to be made between the contracting parties, on one part, or some of them, and a stranger. 1 H. Bl. 37, 45.

Where a person has contracted for the performance of certain work, (*e. g.*, to build a house,) and he in turn engages a third party to perform the whole or a part of that which is included in the original contract, (*e. g.*, to do the carpenter work,) his agreement with such third person is called a "subcontract," and such person is called a "subcontractor."

SUBDITUS. Lat. In old English law. A vassal; a dependent; any one under the power of another. Spelman.

SUBDIVIDE. To divide a part into smaller parts; to separate into smaller divisions. As, where an estate is to be taken by some of the heirs *per stirpes*, it is divided and subdivided according to the number of takers in the nearest degree and those in the more remote degree respectively.

SUBDUCT. In English probate practice, to subduct a *caveat* is to withdraw it.

SUBHASTARE. Lat. In the civil law. To sell at public auction, which was done *sub hasta*, under a spear; to put or sell under the spear. Calvin.

SUBHASTATIO. Lat. In the civil law. A sale by public auction, which was done *under a spear*, fixed up at the place of sale as a public sign of it. Calvin.

SUBINFEUDATION. The system which the feudal tenants introduced of granting smaller estates out of those which they held of their lord, to be held of themselves as inferior lords. As this system was proceeding downward *ad infinitum*, and depriving the lords of their feudal profits, it was entirely suppressed by the statute *Quia Emptores*, 18 Edw. I. c. 1., and instead of it alienation in the modern sense was introduced, so that thenceforth the alienee held of the same chief lord and by the same services that his alienor before him held. Brown.

SUBJECT. **In logic.** That concerning which the affirmation in a proposition is made; the first word in a proposition.

An individual matter considered as the object of legislation. The constitutions of several of the states require that every act of the legislature shall relate to but one *subject*, which shall be expressed in the title of the statute.

In constitutional law. One that owes allegiance to a sovereign and is governed by his laws. The natives of Great Britain are *subjects* of the British government. Men in free governments are subjects as well as *citizens;* as citizens they enjoy rights and franchises; as subjects they are bound to obey the laws. Webster. The term is little used, in this sense, in countries enjoying a republican form of government.

In Scotch law. The thing which is the object of an agreement.

SUBJECTION. The obligation of one or more persons to act at the discretion or according to the judgment and will of others.

SUBJECT-MATTER. The thing in controversy, or the matter spoken or written about.

Sublata causa tollitur effectus. Co. Litt. 303. The cause being removed the effect ceases.

Sublata veneratione magistratuum, respublica ruit. When respect for magistrates is taken away, the commonwealth falls. Jenk. Cent. p. 43, case 81.

Sublato fundamento cadit opus. Jenk. Cent. 106. The foundation being removed, the superstructure falls.

Sublato principali, tollitur adjunctum. When the principal is taken away, the incident is taken also. Co. Litt. 389*a*.

SUBLEASE. A lease by a tenant to another person of a part of the premises held by him; an under-lease.

SUBMISSION. A yielding to authority. A citizen is bound to submit to the laws; a child to his parents.

In practice. A *submission* is a covenant by which persons who have a lawsuit or difference with one another name arbitrators to decide the matter, and bind themselves reciprocally to perform what shall be arbitrated. Civil Code La. art. 3099.

In maritime law. Submission on the part of the vanquished, and complete possession on the part of the victor, transfer property as between belligerents. 1 Gall. 532.

SUBMISSION BOND. The bond by which the parties agree to submit their matters to arbitration, and by which they bind themselves to abide by the award of the arbitrator, is commonly called a "submission bond." Brown.

SUBMIT. To propound; as an advocate *submits* a proposition for the approval of the court.

Applied to a controversy, it means to place it before a tribunal for determination.

SUBMORTGAGE. When a person who holds a mortgage as security for a loan which he has made, procures a loan to himself from a third person, and pledges his mortgage as security, he effects what is called a "submortgage."

SUBNERVARE. To ham-string by cutting the sinews of the legs and thighs.

It was an old custom *meretrices et impudicas mulieres subnervare*. Wharton.

SUBNOTATIONS. In the civil law. The answers of the prince to questions which had been put to him respecting some obscure or doubtful point of law.

SUBORN. In criminal law. To procure another to commit perjury. Steph. Crim. Law, 74.

SUBORNATION OF PERJURY. In criminal law. The offense of procuring another to take such a false oath as would constitute perjury in the principal.

SUBORNER. One who suborns or procures another to commit any crime, particularly to commit perjury.

SUBPŒNA. The process by which the attendance of a witness is required is called a "subpœna." It is a writ or order directed to a person, and requiring his attendance at a particular time and place to testify as a witness. It may also require him to bring with him any books, documents, or other things under his control which he is bound by law to produce in evidence. Code Civil Proc. Cal. § 1985.

In chancery practice. A mandatory writ or process directed to and requiring one or more persons to appear at a time to come and answer the matters charged against him or them.

SUBPŒNA AD TESTIFICANDUM. Subpœna to testify. The common subpœna requiring the attendance of a witness on a trial, inquisition, or examination. 3 Bl. Comm. 369.

SUBPŒNA DUCES TECUM. A subpœna used, not only for the purpose of compelling witnesses to attend in court, but also requiring them to *bring with them* books or documents which may be in their possession, and which may tend to elucidate the subject-matter of the trial. Brown; 3 Bl. Comm. 382.

SUBREPTIO. Lat. In the civil law. Obtaining gifts of escheat, etc., from the king by concealing the truth. Bell; Calvin.

SUBREPTION. In French law. The fraud committed to obtain a pardon, title, or grant, by alleging facts contrary to truth.

SUBROGATION. The substitution of one thing for another, or of one person into the place of another with respect to rights, claims, or securities.

Subrogation denotes the putting a third person who has paid a debt in the place of the creditor to whom he has paid it, so as that he may exercise against the debtor all the rights which the creditor, if unpaid, might have done. It is of two kinds,—either conventional or legal; the former being where the subrogation is express, by the acts of the creditor and the third person; the latter being (as in the case of sureties) where the subrogation is implied by the law. Brown.

The equity by which a person who is secondarily liable for a debt, and has paid it, is put in the place of the creditor, so as to entitle him to make use of all the securities and remedies possessed by the creditor, in order to enforce the right of exoneration as against the principal debtor, or of contribution against others who are liable in the same rank as himself. Bisp. Eq. § 335.

SUBROGEE. A person who is subrogated; one who succeeds to the rights of another by subrogation.

SUBSCRIBE. In the law of contracts. To write under; to write the name under; to write the name at the bottom or end of a writing. 45 Ind. 213; 26 Wend. 341.

SUBSCRIBER. One who writes his name under a written instrument; one who affixes his signature to any document, whether for the purpose of authenticating or attesting it, of adopting its terms as his own expressions, or of binding himself by an engagement which it contains.

SUBSCRIBING WITNESS. He who witnesses or attests the signature of a party to an instrument, and in testimony thereof subscribes his own name to the document.

A subscribing witness is one who sees a writing executed, or hears it acknowledged, and at the request of the party thereupon signs his name as a witness. Code Civil Proc. Cal. § 1935.

SUBSCRIPTIO. Lat. In the civil law. A writing under, or under-writing; a writing of the name under or at the bottom of an instrument by way of attestation or ratification; subscription.

That kind of imperial constitution which was granted in answer to the prayer of a petitioner who was present. Calvin.

SUBSCRIPTION. The act of writing one's name under a written instrument; the affixing one's signature to any document, whether for the purpose of authenticating or attesting it, of adopting its terms as one's own expressions, or of binding one's self by an engagement which it contains.

Subscription is the act of the hand, while attestation is the act of the senses. To subscribe a paper published as a will is only to write on the same paper the name of the witness; to attest a will is to know that it was published as such, and to certify the facts required to constitute an actual and legal publication. 42 Wis. 66, 76.

A written contract by which one engages to contribute a sum of money for a designated purpose, either gratuitously, as in the case of subscribing to a charity, or in consideration of an equivalent to be rendered, as a subscription to a periodical, a forthcoming book, a series of entertainments, or the like.

SUBSCRIPTION LIST. A list of subscribers to some agreement with each other or a third person.

SUBSELLIA. Lat. In Roman law. Lower seats or benches, occupied by the *judices* and by inferior magistrates when they sat in judgment, as distinguished from the *tribunal* of the prætor. Calvin.

Subsequens matrimonium tollit peccatum præcedens. A subsequent marriage [of the parties] removes a previous fault, *i. e.*, previous illicit intercourse, and legitimates the offspring. A rule of Roman law.

SUBSEQUENT CONDITION. See CONDITION SUBSEQUENT.

SUBSIDY. In English law. An aid, tax, or tribute granted by parliament to the king for the urgent occasions of the kingdom, to be levied on every subject of ability, according to the value of his lands or goods. Jacob.

In American law. A grant of money made by government in aid of the promoters of any enterprise, work, or improvement in which the government desires to participate, or which is considered a proper subject for state aid, because likely to be of benefit to the public.

In international law. The assistance given in money by one nation to another to enable it the better to carry on a war, when such nation does not join directly in the war. Vattel, bk. 3, § 82.

SUBSTANCE. Essence; the material or essential part of a thing, as distinguished from "form."

SUBSTANTIAL DAMAGES. A sum, assessed by way of damages, which is worth having; opposed to nominal damages, which are assessed to satisfy a bare legal right. Wharton.

SUBSTANTIVE LAW. That part of the law which the courts are established to administer, as opposed to the rules according to which the substantive law itself is administered. That part of the law which creates, defines, and regulates rights, as opposed to *adjective* or remedial law, which prescribes the method of enforcing rights or obtaining redress for their invasion.

SUBSTITUTE. One appointed in the place or stead of another, to transact business for him; a proxy.

A person hired by one who has been drafted into the military service of the country, to go to the front and serve in the army in his stead.

SUBSTITUTED EXECUTOR. One appointed to act in the place of another executor upon the happening of a certain event; *e. g.*, if the latter should refuse the office.

SUBSTITUTED SERVICE. In English practice. Service of process made under authorization of the court upon some other person, when the person who should be served cannot be found or cannot be reached.

In American law. Service of process upon a defendant in any manner, authorized by statute, other than personal service within the jurisdiction; as by publication, by mailing a copy to his last known address, or by personal service in another state.

SUBSTITUTES. In Scotch law. The person first called or nominated in a tailzie (entailment of an estate upon a number of heirs in succession) is called the "institute" or "heir-institute;" the rest are called "substitutes."

SUBSTITUTIO HÆREDIS. Lat. In Roman law, it was competent for a testator after instituting a *hæres* (called the "*hæres institutus*") to substitute another (called the "*hæres substitutus*") in his place in a certain event. If the event upon which the substitution was to take effect was the refusal of the instituted heir to accept the inheritance at all, then the substitution was called "*vulgaris*," (or common;) but if the event was the death of the infant (*pupillus*) after acceptance, and before attaining his majority, (of fourteen years if a male, and of twelve years if a female,) then the substitution was called "*pupillaris*," (or for minors.) Brown.

SUBSTITUTION. In the civil law. The putting one person in place of another; particularly, the act of a testator in naming a second devisee or legatee who is to take the bequest either on failure of the original devisee or legatee or after him.

In Scotch law. The enumeration or designation of the heirs in a settlement of property. Substitutes in an entail are those heirs who are appointed in succession on failure of others.

SUBSTITUTIONAL, SUBSTITUTIONARY. Where a will contains a gift of property to a class of persons, with a clause providing that on the death of a member of the class before the period of distribution his share is to go to his issue, (if any,) so as to substitute them for him, the gift to the issue is said to be substitutional or substitutionary. A bequest to such of the children of A. as shall be living at the testator's death, with a direction that the issue of such as shall have died shall take the shares which their parents would have taken, if living at the testator's death, is an example. Sweet.

SUBSTRACTION. In French law. The fraudulent appropriation of any property, but particularly of the goods of a decedent's estate.

SUBTENANT. An under-tenant.

SUBTRACTION. The offense of withholding or withdrawing from another man what by law he is entitled to. There are various descriptions of this offense, of which the principal are as follows: (1) Subtraction of suit and services, which is a species of injury affecting a man's real property, and consists of a withdrawal of (or a neglect to perform or pay) the fealty, suit of court, rent, or services reserved by the lessor of the land. (2) Subtraction of tithes is the withholding from the parson or vicar the tithes to which he is entitled, and this is cognizable in the ecclesiastical courts. (3) Subtraction of conjugal rights is the withdrawing or withholding by a husband or wife of those rights and privileges which the law allows to either party. (4) Subtraction of legacies is the withholding or detaining of legacies by an executor. (5) Subtraction of church rates, in English law, consists in the refusal to pay the amount of rate at which any individual parishioner has been assessed for the necessary repairs of the parish church. Brown.

SUBTRACTION OF CONJUGAL RIGHTS. The act of a husband or wife living separately from the other without a lawful cause. 3 Bl. Comm. 94.

SUBURBANI. Lat. In old English law. Husbandmen.

SUBVASSORES. In old Scotch law. Base holders; inferior holders; they who held their lands of knights. Skene.

SUCCESSIO. Lat. In the civil law. A coming in place of another, on his decease; a coming into the estate which a deceased person had at the time of his death. This was either by virtue of an express appointment of the deceased person by his *will*, (*ex testamento*,) or by the general appointment of law in case of *intestacy*, (*ab intestato*.) Inst. 2, 9, 7; Heinecc. Elem. lib. 2, tit. 10.

SUCCESSION. In the civil law and in Louisiana. 1. The *fact* of the transmission of the rights, estate, obligations, and charges of a deceased person to his heir or heirs.

2. The *right* by which the heir can take possession of the decedent's estate. The right of the heir to step into the place of the deceased, with respect to the possession, control, enjoyment, administration, and settlement of all the latter's property, rights, obligations, charges, etc.

3. The *estate* of a deceased person, comprising all kinds of property owned or claimed by him, as well as his debts and obligations, and considered as a legal entity (according to the notion of the Roman law) for certain purposes, such as collecting assets and paying debts.

Succession is the transmission of the rights and obligations of the deceased to the heirs.

Succession signifies also the estates, rights, and charges which a person leaves after his death, whether the property exceeds the charges or the charges exceed the property, or whether he has only left charges without any property.

The succession not only includes the rights and obligations of the deceased as they exist at the time of his death, but all that has accrued thereto since the opening of the succession, as also the new charges to which it becomes subject.

Finally, succession signifies also that right by which the heir can take possession of the estate of the deceased, such as it may be. Civil Code La. arts. 871-874.

Succession is the coming in of another to take the property of one who dies without disposing of it by will. Civil Code Cal. § 1383; Civil Code Dak. § 776.

Testamentary succession is that which results from the institution of heir, contained in a testament executed in the form prescribed by law. *Legal* succession is that which the law has established in favor of the nearest relation of the deceased. *Irregular* succession is that which is established by law in favor of certain persons, or of the state, in default of heirs either legal or instituted by testament. Civil Code La. arts. 876-878.

In common law. The right by which one set of men may, by succeeding another set, acquire a property in all the goods, movables, and other chattels of a corporation. 2 Bl. Comm. 430. The power of perpetual *succession* is one of the peculiar properties of a corporation. 2 Kent, Comm. 267.

SUCCESSION DUTY. In English law. This is a duty, (varying from one to ten per cent.,) payable under the statute 16 & 17 Vict. c. 51, in respect chiefly of real estate and leaseholds, but generally in respect of all property (not already chargeable with legacy duty) devolving upon any one in consequence of any death. Brown.

SUCCESSION TAX. A tax imposed upon the succession to, or devolution of, real property by devise, deed, or intestate succession. See 4 Cliff. 103; 76 Va. 929.

SUCCESSOR. One who succeeds to the rights or the place of another; particularly, the person or persons who constitute a corporation after the death or removal of those who preceded them as corporators.

One who has been appointed or elected to hold an office after the term of the present incumbent.

Succurritur minori; facilis est lapsus juventutis. A minor is [to be] aided; a mistake of youth is easy, [youth is liable to err.] Jenk. Cent. p. 47, case 89.

SUCKEN, SUCHEN. In Scotch law. The whole lands astricted to a mill; that is, the lands of which the tenants are obliged to send their grain to that mill. Bell.

SUDDER. In Hindu law. The best; the fore-court of a house; the chief seat of government, contradistinguished from "*mofussil*," or interior of the country; the presidency. Wharton.

SUE. To prosecute by law; to commence legal proceedings against a party. It is applied almost exclusively to the institution and prosecution of a civil action.

SUE OUT. To obtain by application; to petition for and take out. Properly the term is applied only to the obtaining and issuing of such process as is only accorded upon an application first made; but conventionally it is also used of the taking out of process which issues of course. The term is occasionally used of instruments other than writs. Thus, we speak of "suing out" a pardon.

SUERTE. In Spanish law. A small lot of ground. 5 Tex. 83.

SUFFER. To suffer an act to be done, by a person who can prevent it, is to permit or consent to it; to approve of it, and not to hinder it. It implies a willingness of the mind. 19 Conn. 505; 17 Blatchf. 330.

SUFFERANCE. Toleration; negative permission by not forbidding; passive consent; license implied from the omission or neglect to enforce an adverse right.

SUFFERANCE, TENANCY AT. This is the least and lowest estate which can subsist in realty. It is in strictness not an estate, but a mere possession only. It arises when a person, after his right to the occupation, under a lawful title, is at an end, continues (having no title at all) in possession of the land, without the agreement or disagreement of the person in whom the right of possession resides. 2 Bl. Comm. 150.

SUFFERANCE WHARVES. In English law. These are wharves in which goods may be landed before any duty is paid. They are appointed for the purpose by the commissioners of the customs. 2 Steph. Comm. 500, note.

SUFFERENTIA PACIS. A grant or sufferance of peace or truce.

SUFFERING A RECOVERY. A recovery was effected by the party wishing to convey the land *suffering* a fictitious action to be brought against him by the party to whom the land was to be conveyed, (the demandant,) and allowing the demandant to recover a judgment against him for the land in question. The vendor, or conveying party, in thus assisting or permitting the demandant so to recover a judgment against him, was thence technically said to "suffer a recovery." Brown.

SUFFRAGAN. Bishops who in former times were appointed to supply the place of others during their absence on embassies or other business were so termed. They were consecrated as other bishops were, and were anciently called "*chorepiscopi*," or "bishops of the county," in contradistinction to the regular bishops of the city or see. The practice of creating *suffragan* bishops, after having long been discontinued, was recently revived; and such bishops are now permanently "assistant" to the bishops. Brown.

A suffragan is a titular bishop ordained to aid and assist the bishop of the diocese in his spiritual function; or one who supplieth the place instead of the bishop, by whose suffrage ecclesiastical causes or matters committed to him are to be adjudged, acted on, or determined. Some writers call these suffragans by the name of "subsidiary bishops." Tomlins.

SUFFRAGE. A vote; the act of voting; the right or privilege of casting a vote at public elections. The last is the meaning of the term in such phrases as "the extension of the suffrage," "universal suffrage," etc.

SUFFRAGIUM. Lat. In Roman law. A vote; the right of voting in the assemblies of the people.

Aid or influence used or promised to obtain some honor or office; the purchase of office. Cod. 4, 3.

SUGGESTIO FALSI. Lat. Suggestion or representation of that which is false; false representation. To recite in a deed that a will was duly executed, when it was not, is *suggestio falsi;* and to conceal from the heir that the will was not duly executed is *suppressio veri.* 1 P. Wms. 240.

SUGGESTION. In practice. A statement, formally entered on the record, of some fact or circumstance which will materially affect the further proceedings in the cause, or which is necessary to be brought to the knowledge of the court in order to its right disposition of the action, but which, for some reason, cannot be pleaded. Thus, if one of the parties dies after issue and before trial, his death may be *suggested* on the record.

SUGGESTIVE INTERROGATION. A phrase which has been used by some writers to signify the same thing as "leading question." 2 Benth. Jud. Ev. b. 3, c. 3. It is used in the French law.

SUI GENERIS. Lat. Of its own kind or class; *i. e.*, the *only one* of its own kind; peculiar.

SUI HÆREDES. Lat. In the civil law. One's own heirs; proper heirs. Inst. 2, 19, 2.

SUI JURIS. Lat. Of his own right; possessing full social and civil rights; not under any legal disability, or the power of another, or guardianship.

Having capacity to manage one's own affairs; not under legal disability to act for one's self. Story, Ag. § 2.

SUICIDE. Suicide is the willful and voluntary act of a person who understands the physical nature of the act, and intends by it to accomplish the result of self-destruction. 10 Amer. Law Reg. (N. S.) 101.

Suicide is the deliberate termination of one's existence, while in the possession and enjoyment of his mental faculties. Self-killing by an insane person is not suicide. 4 Hill, 73; 8 N. Y. 299.

SUING AND LABORING CLAUSE is a clause in an English policy of marine insurance, generally in the following form: "In case of any loss or misfortune, it shall be lawful for the assured, their factors, servants and assigns, to sue, labor, and travel for, in, and about the defense, safeguard, and recovery of the" property insured, "without prejudice to this insurance; to the charges whereof we, the assurers, will contribute." The object of the clause is to encourage the assured to exert themselves in preserving the property from loss. Sweet.

SUIT. In old English law. The witnesses or followers of the plaintiff. 3 Bl. Comm. 295. See SECTA.

Old books mention the word in many connections which are now disused,—at least, in the United States. Thus, "suit" was used of following any one, or in the sense of pursuit; as in the phrase "making fresh suit." It was also used of a petition to the king or lord. "Suit of court" was the attendance which a tenant owed at the court of his lord. "Suit covenant" and "suit custom" seem to have signified a right to one's attendance, or one's obligation to attend, at the lord's court, founded upon a known covenant, or an immemorial usage or practice of ancestors. "Suit regal" was attendance at the sheriff's tourn or leet, (his court.) "Suit of the king's peace" was pursuing an offender, — one charged with breach of the peace. Abbott.

In modern law. "Suit" is a generic term, of comprehensive signification, and applies to any proceeding in a court of justice in which the plaintiff pursues, in such court, the remedy which the law affords him for the redress of an injury or the recovery of a right. 10 Ill. App. 333; 2 Pet. 449; Co. Litt. 291*a*.

It is, however, seldom applied to a criminal prosecution. And it is sometimes restricted to the designation of a proceeding in equity, to distinguish such proceeding from an action at law.

SUIT OF COURT. This phrase denoted the duty of attending the lord's court, and, in common with fealty, was one of the incidents of a feudal holding. Brown.

SUIT OF THE KING'S PEACE. The pursuing a man for breach of the king's peace by treasons, insurrections, or trespasses. Cowell.

SUIT SILVER. A small sum of money paid in lieu of attendance at the court-baron. Cowell.

SUITAS. Lat. In the civil law. The condition or quality of a *suus hæres*, or proper heir. Hallifax, Civil Law, b. 2, c. 9, no. 11; Calvin.

SUITE. Those persons who by his authority *follow* or attend an ambassador or other public minister.

SUITOR. A party to a suit or action in court. In its ancient sense, "suitor" meant one who was bound to attend the county court; also one who formed part of the *secta*.

SUITORS' DEPOSIT ACCOUNT. Formerly suitors in the English court of chancery derived no income from their cash paid into court, unless it was invested at their request and risk. Now, however, it is provided by the court of chancery (funds) act, 1872, that all money paid into court, and not required by the suitor to be invested, shall be placed on deposit and shall bear interest at two per cent. per annum for the benefit of the suitor entitled to it. Sweet.

SUITORS' FEE FUND. A fund in the English court of chancery into which the fees of suitors in that court were paid, and out of which the salaries of various officers of the court were defrayed. Wharton.

SUITORS' FUND IN CHANCERY. In England. A fund consisting of moneys which, having been paid into the court of chancery, are placed out for the benefit and better security of the suitors, including interest from the same. By St. 32 & 33 Vict. c. 91, § 4, the principal of this fund, amounting to over £3,000,000, was transferred to the commissioners for the reduction of the national debt. Mozley & Whitley.

SULCUS. A small brook or stream of water. Cowell.

SULLERY. A plow-land. 1 Inst. 5.

SUM. In English law. A summary or abstract; a compendium; a collection. Several of the old law treatises are called "sums." Lord Hale applies the term to summaries of statute law. Burrill.

SUMAGE. Toll for carriage on horseback. Cowell.

Summa caritas est facere justitiam singulis, et omni tempore quando necesse fuerit. The greatest charity is to do justice to every one, and at any time whenever it may be necessary. 11 Coke, 70.

Summa est lex quæ pro religione facit. That is the highest law which favors religion. 10 Mod. 117, 119; Broom, Max. 19.

Summa ratio est quæ pro religione facit. That consideration is strongest which determines in favor of religion. Co. Litt. 341*a;* Broom, Max. 19.

SUMMARY, *n.* An abridgment; brief; compendium; also a short application to a court or judge, without the formality of a full proceeding. Wharton.

SUMMARY, *adj.* Immediate; peremptory; off-hand; without a jury; provisional; statutory.

SUMMARY ACTIONS. In Scotch law. Those which are brought into court not by summons, but by petition, corresponding to summary proceedings in English courts. Bell; Brown.

SUMMARY CONVICTION. The conviction of a person, (usually for a minor misdemeanor,) as the result of his trial before a magistrate or court, without the intervention of a jury, which is authorized by statute in England and in many of the states.

In these proceedings there is no intervention of a jury, but the party accused is acquitted or condemned by the suffrage of such person only as the statute has appointed to be his judge. A conviction reached on such a magistrate's trial is called a "summary conviction." Brown.

SUMMARY JURISDICTION. The jurisdiction of a court to give a judgment or make an order itself forthwith; *e. g.*, to commit to prison for contempt; to punish malpractice in a solicitor; or, in the case of justices of the peace, a jurisdiction to convict an offender themselves instead of committing him for trial by a jury. Wharton.

SUMMARY PROCEDURE ON BILLS OF EXCHANGE. This phrase refers to the statute 18 & 19 Vict. c. 67, passed in 1855, for the purpose of facilitating the remedies on bills and notes by the prevention of frivolous or fictitious defenses. By this statute, a defendant in an action on a bill or note, brought within six months after it has become payable, is prohibited from defending the action without the leave of the court or a judge. See 2 Steph. Comm. 118, note; Lush, Pr. 1027.

SUMMARY PROCEEDING. Any proceeding by which a controversy is settled, case disposed of, or trial conducted, in a prompt and simple manner, without the aid of a jury, without presentment or indictment, or in other respects out of the regular course of the common law.

In procedure, proceedings are said to be summary when they are short and simple in comparison with regular proceedings; *i. e.*, in comparison with the proceedings which alone whould have been applicable, either in the same or analogous cases, if summary proceedings had not been available. Sweet.

SUMMER-HUS SILVER. A payment to the lords of the wood on the Wealds of Kent, who used to visit those places in summer, when their under-tenants were bound to prepare little summer-houses for their reception, or else pay a composition in money. Cowell.

SUMMING UP, on the trial of an action by a jury, is a recapitulation of the evidence adduced, in order to draw the attention of the jury to the salient points. The counsel for each party has the right of summing up his evidence, if he has adduced any, and the judge finally sums up the whole in his charge to the jury. Smith, Act. 157.

SUMMON. In practice. To serve a summons; to cite a defendant to appear in court to answer a suit which has been begun against him; to notify the defendant that an action has been instituted against him, and that he is required to answer to it at a time and place named.

SUMMONEAS. L. Lat. In old practice. A writ of summons; a writ by which a party was summoned to appear in court.

SUMMONERS. Petty officers, who cite and warn persons to appear in any court. Fleta, lib. 9.

SUMMONITIO. L. Lat. In old English practice. A summoning or summons; a writ by which a party was summoned to appear in court, of which there were various kinds. Spelman.

Summonitiones aut citationes nullæ liceant fieri intra palatium regis. 3 Inst. 141. Let no summonses or citations be served within the king's palace.

SUMMONITORES SCACCARII. Officers who assisted in collecting the revenues by citing the defaulters therein into the court of exchequer.

SUMMONS. In practice. A writ, directed to the sheriff or other proper officer, requiring him to notify the person named that an action has been commenced against him in the court whence the writ issues, and that he is required to appear, on a day named, and answer the complaint in such action.

Civil actions in the courts of record of this state shall be commenced by the service of a summons. Code N. Y. § 127.

In Scotch law. A writ passing under the royal signet, signed by a writer to the signet, and containing the grounds and conclusions of the action, with the warrant for citing the defender. This writ corresponds to the writ of summons in English procedure. Bell; Paters. Comp.

SUMMONS AND ORDER. In English practice. In this phrase the summons is the application to a common-law judge at chambers in reference to a pending action, and upon it the judge or master makes the order. Mozley & Whitley.

SUMMONS AND SEVERANCE. The proper name of what is distinguished in the books by the name of "summons and severance" is "severance;" for the summons is only a process which must, in certain cases, issue before judgment of severance can be given; while severance is a judgment by which, where two or more are joined in an action, one or more of these is enabled to proceed in such action without the other or others. Jacob.

SUMMUM JUS. Lat. Strict right; extreme right. The extremity or rigor of the law.

Summum jus, summa injuria; summa lex, summa crux. Extreme law (rigor of law) is the greatest injury; strict law is great punishment. Hob. 125. That is, insistence upon the full measure of a man's strict legal rights may work the greatest injury to others, unless equity can aid.

SUMNER, or SOMPNOUR. One who cites or summons. Cowell.

SUMPTUARY LAWS. Laws made for the purpose of restraining luxury or extravagance, particularly against inordinate expenditures in the matter of apparel, food, furniture, etc.

SUNDAY. The first day of the week is designated by this name; also as the "Lord's Day," and as the "Sabbath."

SUO NOMINE. Lat. In his own name.

SUO PERICULO. Lat. At his own peril or risk.

SUPELLEX. Lat. In Roman law. Household furniture. Dig. 33, 10.

SUPER. Lat. Upon; above; over.

SUPER ALTUM MARE. L. Lat. On the high sea. Hob. 212; 2 Ld. Raym. 1453.

Super fidem chartarum, mortuis testibus, erit ad patriam de necessitate recurrendum. Co. Litt. 6. The truth of charters is necessarily to be referred to a jury, when the witnesses are dead.

SUPER-JURARE. Over-swearing. A term anciently used when a criminal endeavored to excuse himself by his own oath or the oath of one or two witnesses, and the crime objected against him was so plain and notorious that he was convicted on the oaths of many more witnesses. Wharton.

SUPER PRÆROGATIVA REGIS. A writ which formerly lay against the king's tenant's widow for marrying without the royal license. Fitzh. Nat. Brev. 174.

SUPER STATUTO. A writ, upon the statute 1 Edw. III, c. 12, that lay against the king's tenant holding in chief, who aliened the king's land without his license.

SUPER STATUTO DE ARTICULIS CLERI. A writ which lay against a sheriff or other officer who distrained in the king's highway, or on lands anciently belonging to the church.

SUPER STATUTO FACTO POUR SENESCHAL ET MARSHAL DE ROY, etc. A writ which lay against a steward or marshal for holding plea in his court, or for trespass or contracts not made or arising within the king's household. Wharton.

SUPER STATUTO VERSUS SERVANTES ET LABORATORES. A writ which lay against him who kept any servants who had left the service of another contrary to law.

SUPER VISUM CORPORIS. Lat. Upon view of the body. When an inquest is held over a body found dead, it must be *super visum corporis.*

SUPERARE RATIONES. In old Scotch law. To have a balance of account due to one; to have one's expenses exceed the receipts.

SUPERCARGO. An agent of the owner of goods shipped as cargo on a vessel, who has charge of the cargo on board, sells the same to the best advantage in the foreign market, buys a cargo to be brought back on the return voyage of the ship, and comes home with it.

SUPERFICIARIUS. Lat. In the civil law. He who has built upon the soil of another, which he has hired for a number of years or forever, yielding a yearly rent. Dig. 43, 18, 1. In other words, a tenant on ground-rent.

SUPERFICIES. Lat. In the civil law. The alienation by the owner of the surface of the soil of all rights necessary for building on the surface, a yearly rent being generally reserved; also a building or erection. Sandars' Just. Inst. (5th Ed.) 133.

Superflua non nocent. Superfluities do not prejudice. Jenk. Cent. 184. Surplusage does not vitiate.

SUPERFLUOUS LANDS, in English law, are lands acquired by a railway company under its statutory powers, and not required for the purposes of its undertaking. The company is bound within a certain time to sell such lands, and, if it does not, they vest in and become the property of the owners of the adjoining lands. Sweet.

SUPERFŒTATION. In medical jurisprudence. The formation of a *fœtus* as the result of an impregnation occurring after another impregnation, but before the birth of the offspring produced by it. Webster.

SUPERINDUCTIO. Lat. In the civil law. A species of obliteration. Dig. 28, 4, 1, 1.

SUPERINSTITUTION. The institution of one in an office to which another has been previously instituted; as where A. is admitted and instituted to a benefice upon one title, and B. is admitted and instituted on the title or presentment of another. 2 Cro. Eliz. 463.

A church being full by institution, if a second institution is granted to the same church this is a superinstitution. Wharton.

SUPERINTENDENT REGISTRAR. In English law. An officer who superintends the registers of births, deaths, and marriages. There is one in every poor-law union in England and Wales.

SUPERIOR. Higher; more elevated in rank or office. Possessing larger power. Entitled to command, influence, or control over another.

In estates, some are superior to others. An estate entitled to a servitude or easement over another estate is called the "superior" or "dominant," and the other, the "inferior" or "servient," estate. 1 Bouv. Inst. no. 1612.

In the feudal law, until the statute *quia emptores* precluded subinfeudations, (*q. v.*,) the tenant who granted part of his estate to be held of and from himself as lord was called a "superior."

SUPERIOR AND VASSAL. In Scotch law. A feudal relation corresponding with the English "lord and tenant." Bell.

SUPERIOR COURTS. In English law. The courts of the highest and most extensive jurisdiction, viz., the court of chancery and the three courts of common law, *i. e.*, the queen's bench, the common pleas, and the exchequer, which sit at Westminster, were commonly thus denominated. But these courts are now united in the supreme court of judicature.

In American law. Courts of general or extensive jurisdiction, as distinguished from the inferior courts. As the *official style* of a tribunal, the term "superior court" bears a different meaning in different states. In some it is a court of intermediate jurisdiction between the trial courts and the chief appellate court; elsewhere it is the designation of the ordinary *nisi prius* courts; in Delaware it is the court of last resort.

SUPERIORITY. In Scotch law. The *dominium directum* of lands, without the profit. 1 Forb. Inst. pt. 2, p. 97.

SUPERNUMERARII. Lat. In Roman law. Advocates who were not registered or enrolled and did not belong to the college of advocates. They were not attached to any local jurisdiction. See STATUTI.

SUPERONERATIO. Surcharging a common; *i. e.*, putting in beasts of a number or kind other than the right of common allows.

SUPERONERATIONE PASTURÆ. A judicial writ that lay against him who was impleaded in the county court for the surcharge of a common with his cattle, in a case where he was formerly impleaded for it in the same court, and the cause was removed into one of the superior courts.

SUPERPLUSAGIUM. In old English law. Overplus; surplus; residue or balance. Bract. fol. 301; Spelman.

SUPERSEDE. To annul; to stay; to suspend. Thus, it is said that the proceedings of outlawry may be superseded by the entry of appearance before the return of the exigent, or that the court would supersede a fiat in bankruptcy, if found to have been improperly issued. Brown.

SUPERSEDEAS. Lat. In practice. A writ ordering the suspension or superseding of another writ previously issued. It directs the officer to whom it is issued to refrain from executing or acting under another writ which is in his hands or may come to him.

By a conventional extension of the term it has come to be used as a designation of the *effect* of any proceeding or act in a cause which, of its own force, causes a suspension or stay of proceedings. Thus, when we say that a writ of error is a *supersedeas*, we merely mean that it has the same effect, of suspending proceedings in the court below, which would have been produced by a writ of *supersedeas*.

SUPERSTITIOUS USE. In English law. When lands, tenements, rents, goods, or chattels are given, secured, or appointed for and towards the maintenance of a priest or chaplain to say mass, for the maintenance of a priest or other man to pray for the soul of any dead man in such a church or elsewhere, to have and maintain perpetual obits, lamps, torches, etc., to be used at certain times to help to save the souls of men out of purgatory,—in such cases the king, by force of several statutes, is authorized to direct and appoint all such uses to such purposes as are truly charitable. Bac. Abr. "Charitable Uses."

SUPERVISOR. A surveyor or overseer; a highway officer. Also, in some states, the chief officer of a town; one of a board of county officers.

SUPERVISORS OF ELECTION. Persons appointed and commissioned by the judge of the circuit court of the United States in cities or towns of over 20,000 inhabitants upon the written application of two citizens, or in any county or parish of any congressional district upon that of ten citizens, to attend at all times and places fixed for the registration of voters for representatives and delegates in congress, and supervise the registry and mark the list of voters is such manner as will in their judgment detect and expose the improper removal or addition of any name. Rev. St. U. S. § 2011, et seq.

SUPPLEMENT, LETTERS OF. In Scotch practice. A process by which a party not residing within the jurisdiction of an inferior court may be cited to appear before it. Bell.

SUPPLEMENTAL. Something added to supply defects in the thing to which it is added, or in aid of which it is made.

SUPPLEMENTAL AFFIDAVIT. An affidavit made in addition to a previous one, in order to supply some deficiency in it.

SUPPLEMENTAL ANSWER. One which was filed in chancery for the purpose of correcting, adding to, and explaining an answer already filed. Smith, Ch. Pr. 334.

SUPPLEMENTAL BILL. In equity pleading. A bill filed in addition to an original bill, in order to supply some defect in its original frame or structure. It is the appropriate remedy where the matter sought to be supplied cannot be introduced by amendment. Story, Eq. Pl. §§ 332–338.

SUPPLEMENTAL BILL, BILL IN THE NATURE OF A. See BILL IN THE NATURE, etc.

SUPPLEMENTAL CLAIM. A further claim which was filed when further relief was sought after the bringing of a claim. Smith, Ch. Pr. 655.

SUPPLEMENTAL COMPLAINT. Under the codes of practice obtaining in some of the states, this name is given to a complaint filed in an action, for the purpose of supplying some defect or omission in the original complaint, or of adding something to it which could not properly be introduced by amendment.

SUPPLETORY OATH. In the modern practice of the civil law, they do not allow a less number than two witnesses to be "*plena probatio*," (full proof,) calling the testimony of one "*semi-plena probatio*" only, (half-proof,) on which no sentence can be founded. In order to supply the other half of proof, they admit the party himself (plaintiff or defendant) to be examined in his own behalf, and the oath administered to him for that purpose is called the "suppletory oath," because it supplies the necessary *quantum* of proof on which to found the sentence. 3 Bl. Comm. 370.

This term, although without application in American law, in its original sense, is sometimes used as a designation of a party's oath required to be taken in authentication or support of some piece of documentary evidence which he offers; *e. g.*, his books of account.

SUPPLIANT. The actor in, or party preferring, a petition of right.

SUPPLICATIO. Lat. In the civil law. A petition for pardon of a first offense; also a petition for reversal of judgment; also equivalent to "*duplicatio*," which corresponds to the common law rejoinder. Calvin.

SUPPLICAVIT. In English law. The name of a writ issuing out of the king's bench or chancery for taking sureties of the peace. It is commonly directed to the justices of the peace, when they are averse to acting in the affair in their judicial capacity. 4 Bl. Comm. 253.

SUPPLICIUM. Lat. In the civil law. Punishment; corporal punishment for crime. Death was called "*ultimum supplicium*," the last or extreme penalty.

SUPPLIES. In English law. The "supplies" in parliamentary proceedings signify the sums of money which are annually voted by the house of commons for the maintenance of the crown and the various public services. Jacob; Brown.

SUPPLY, COMMISSIONERS OF. Persons appointed to levy the land-tax in Scotland, and to cause a valuation roll to be annually made up, and to perform other duties in their respective counties. Bell.

SUPPLY, COMMITTEE OF. In English law. All bills which relate to the public income or expenditure must originate with the house of commons, and all bills authorizing expenditure of the public money are based upon resolutions moved in a committee of supply, which is always a committee of the whole house. Wharton.

SUPPORT, *v.* To support a rule or order is to argue in answer to the arguments of the party who has shown cause against a rule or order *nisi*.

SUPPORT, *n.* The right of support is an easement consisting in the privilege of resting the joists or beams of one's house upon, or inserting their ends into, the wall of an adjoining house belonging to another owner. It may arise either from contract or prescription. 3 Kent, Comm. 436.

Support also signifies the right to have one's ground supported so that it will not cave in, when an adjoining owner makes an excavation.

SUPPRESSIO VERI. Lat. Suppression or concealment of the truth. "It is a rule of equity, as well as of law, that a *suppressio veri* is equivalent to a *suggestio falsi;* and where either the suppression of the truth or the suggestion of what is false can be proved, in a fact material to the contract, the party injured may have relief against the contract." 18 Johns. 405.

Suppressio veri, expressio falsi. Suppression of the truth is [equivalent to] the expression of what is false. 11 Wend. 374, 417.

Suppressio veri, suggestio falsi. Suppression of the truth is [equivalent to] the suggestion of what is false. 23 Barb. 521, 525.

SUPRA. Lat. Above; upon. This word occurring by itself in a book refers the reader to a previous part of the book, like "*ante;*" it is also the initial word of several Latin phrases.

SUPRA PROTEST. In mercantile law. A term applied to an acceptance of a bill by a third person, after protest for non-acceptance by the drawee. 3 Kent, Comm. 87.

SUPRA-RIPARIAN. Upper riparian; higher up the stream. This term is applied to the estate, rights, or duties of a riparian proprietor whose lana is situated at a point nearer the source of the stream than the estate with which it is compared.

Suprema potestas seipsam dissolvere potest. Supreme power can dissolve itself. Bac. Max.

SUPREMACY. The state of being supreme, or in the highest station of power; paramount authority; sovereignty; sovereign power.

SUPREMACY, ACT OF. The English statute 1 Eliz. c. 1, whereby the supremacy and autonomy of the crown in spiritual or ecclesiastical matters was declared and established.

SUPREMACY, OATH OF. An oath to uphold the supreme power of the kingdom of England in the person of the reigning sovereign.

SUPREME COURT. A court of high powers and extensive jurisdiction, existing in most of the states. In some it is the official style of the chief appellate court or court of last resort. In others (as New Jersey and New York) the supreme court is a court of general original jurisdiction, possessing also (in New York) some appellate jurisdiction, but not the court of last resort.

SUPREME COURT OF ERRORS. In American law. An appellate tribunal, and the court of last resort, in the state of Connecticut.

SUPREME COURT OF JUDICATURE. The court formed by the English judicature act, 1873, (as modified by the judicature act, 1875, the appellate jurisdiction act, 1876, and the judicature acts of 1877, 1879, and 1881,) in substitution for the various superior courts of law, equity, admiralty, probate, and divorce, existing when the act was passed, including the court of appeal in chancery and bankruptcy, and the exchequer chamber. It consists of two permanent divisions, viz., a court of original jurisdiction, called the "high court of justice," and a court of appellate jurisdiction, called the "court of appeal." Its title of "supreme" is now a misnomer, as the superior appellate jurisdiction of the house of lords and privy council, which was originally intended to be transferred to it, has been allowed to remain. Sweet.

SUPREME COURT OF THE UNITED STATES. The court of last resort in the federal judicial system. It is vested by the constitution with original jurisdiction in all cases affecting ambassadors, public ministers, and consuls, and those in which a state is a party, and appellate jurisdiction over all other cases within the judicial power of the United States, both as to law and fact, with such exceptions and under such regulations as congress may make. Its appellate powers extend to the subordinate federal courts, and also (in certain cases) to the supreme courts of the several states. The court is composed of a chief justice and eight associate justices.

SUPREME JUDICIAL COURT. In American law. An appellate tribunal, and the court of last resort, in the states of Maine, Massachusetts, and New Hampshire.

SUPREME POWER. The highest authority in a state, all other powers in it being inferior thereto.

SUPREMUS. Lat. Last; the last.

Supremus est quem nemo sequitur. He is last whom no one follows. Dig. 50, 16, 92.

SUR. Fr. On; upon; over. In the titles of real actions "*sur*" was used to point out what the writ was founded upon. Thus, a real action brought by the owner of a reversion or seigniory, in certain cases where his tenant repudiated his tenure, was called "a writ of right *sur disclaimer*." So, a writ of entry *sur disseisin* was a real action to recover the possession of land from a disseisor. Sweet.

SUR CUI ANTE DIVORTIUM. See CUI ANTE DIVORTIUM.

SUR CUI IN VITA. A writ that lay for the heir of a woman whose husband had aliened her land in fee, and she had omitted to bring the writ of *cui in vita* for the recovery thereof; in which case her heir might have this writ against the tenant after her decease. Cowell. See CUI IN VITA.

SUR DISCLAIMER. A writ in the nature of a writ of right brought by the lord against a tenant who had disclaimed his tenure, to recover the land.

SURCHARGE, *v.* To put more cattle upon a common than the herbage will sustain or than the party has a right to do. 3 Bl. Comm. 237.

In equity practice. To show that a particular item, in favor of the party surcharging, ought to have been included, but was not, in an account which is alleged to be settled or complete.

SURCHARGE, *n.* An overcharge; an exaction, impost, or incumbrance beyond what is just and right, or beyond one's authority or power. "Surcharge" may mean a second or further mortgage. Wharton.

SURCHARGE AND FALSIFY. This phrase, as used in the courts of chancery, denotes the liberty which these courts will occasionally grant to a plaintiff, who disputes an account which the defendant alleges to be settled, to scrutinize particular items therein without opening the entire account. The showing an item for which credit ought to have been given, but was not, is to surcharge the account; the proving an item to have been inserted wrongly is to falsify the account. Brown.

SURDUS. Lat. In the civil law. Deaf; a deaf person. Inst. 2, 12, 3. *Surdus et mutus*, a deaf and dumb person.

SURENCHÈRE. In French law. A party desirous of repurchasing property at auction before the court, can, by offering one-tenth or one-sixth, according to the case, in addition to the price realized at the sale, oblige the property to be put up once more at auction. This bid upon a bid is called a "*surenchère.*" Arg. Fr. Merc. Law, 575.

SURETY. A surety is one who at the request of another, and for the purpose of securing to him a benefit, becomes responsible for the performance by the latter of some act in favor of a third person, or hypothecates property as security therefor. Civil Code Cal. § 2831; Civil Code Dak. § 1673.

A surety is defined as a person who, being liable to pay a debt or perform an obligation, is entitled, if it is enforced against him, to be indemnified by some other person who ought himself to have made payment or performed before the surety was compelled to do so. 35 Mich. 42.

SURETY COMPANY. A company, usually incorporated, whose business is to assume the responsibility of a surety on the bonds of officers, trustees, executors, guardians, etc., in consideration of a fee proportioned to the amount of the security required.

SURETY OF THE PEACE. Surety of the peace is a species of preventive justice, and consists in obliging those persons whom there is a probable ground to suspect of future misbehavior, to stipulate with, and to give full assurance to, the public that such offense as is apprehended shall not take place, by finding pledges or securities for keeping the peace, or for their good behavior. Brown.

SURETYSHIP. The contract of suretyship is that whereby one obligates himself to pay the debt of another in consideration of credit or indulgence, or other benefit given to his principal, the principal remaining bound therefor. It differs from a *guaranty* is this: that the consideration of the latter is a benefit flowing to the guarantor. Code Ga. 1882, § 2148.

Suretyship is an accessory promise by which a person binds himself for another already bound, and agrees with the creditor to satisfy the obligation, if the debtor does not. Civil Code La. art. 3035.

A contract of suretyship is a contract whereby one person engages to be answerable for the debt, default, or miscarriage of another. Pitm. Princ. & Sur. 1, 2.

For the distinctions between "suretyship" and "guaranty," see GUARANTY, *n.*

SURGEON. One whose profession or occupation is to cure diseases or injuries of the body by manual operation; one whose occupation is to cure local injuries or disorders, whether by manual operation, or by medication and constitutional treatment. Webster.

SURMISE. Formerly where a defendant pleaded a local custom, for instance, a custom of the city of London, it was necessary for him to "surmise," that is, to suggest that such custom should be certified to the court by the mouth of the recorder, and without such a surmise the issue was to be tried by the country as other issues of fact are. 1 Burrows, 251; Vin. Abr. 246.

A surmise is something offered to a court to move it to grant a prohibition, *audita querela*, or other writ grantable thereon. Jacob.

In ecclesiastical practice, an allegation in a libel is called a "surmise." A collateral surmise is a surmise of some fact not appearing in the libel. Phillim. Ecc. Law, 1445.

SURNAME. The family name; the name over and above the Christian name. The part of a name which is not given in baptism; the last name; the name common to all members of a family.

SURPLICE FEES. In English ecclesiastical law. Fees payable on ministerial offices of the church; such as baptisms, funerals, marriages, etc.

SURPLUS. That which remains of a fund appropriated for a particular purpose; the remainder of a thing; the overplus; the residue.

SURPLUSAGE. In pleading. Allegations of matter wholly foreign and impertinent to the cause. All matter beyond the circumstances necessary to constitute the action.

SURPLUSAGE OF ACCOUNTS. A greater disbursement than the charge of the accountant amounts unto. In another sense, "surplusage" is the remainder or overplus of money left. Jacob.

Surplusagium non nocet. Surplusage does no harm. 3 Bouv. Inst. no. 2949; Broom, Max. 627.

SURPRISE. In equity practice. The act by which a party who is entering into a contract is taken unawares, by which sudden confusion or perplexity is created, which renders it proper that a court of equity should relieve the party so surprised. 2 Brown, Ch. 150.

Anything which happens without the agency or fault of the party affected by it, tending to disturb and confuse the judgment, or to mislead him, and of which the opposite party takes an undue advantage, is in equity a surprise, and one species of fraud for which relief is granted. Code Ga. 1882, § 3180.

The situation in which a party is placed, without any default of his own, which will be injurious to his interests. 8 Mart. (N. S.) 407.

There does not seem anything technical or peculiar in the word "surprise," as used in courts of equity. Where a court of equity relieves on the ground of surprise, it does so upon the ground that the party has been taken unawares, and that he has acted without due deliberation, and under confused and sudden impressions. 1 Story, Eq. Jur. § 120, note.

In law. The general rule is that when a party or his counsel is "taken by surprise," in a material point or circumstance which could not have been anticipated, and when want of skill, care, or attention cannot be justly imputed, and injustice has been done, a new trial should be granted. Hill. New Trials, 521.

SURREBUTTER. In pleading. The plaintiff's answer of fact to the defendant's rebutter. Steph. Pl. 59.

SURREJOINDER. In pleading. The plaintiff's answer of fact to the defendant's rejoinder. Steph. Pl. 59.

SURRENDER. A yielding up of an estate for life or years to him who has an immediate estate in reversion or remainder, by which the lesser estate is merged in the greater by mutual agreement. Co. Litt. 337*b*.

An assurance restoring or yielding up an estate, the operative verbs being "surrender and yield up." The term is usually applied to the giving up of a lease before the expiration of it. Wharton.

The giving up by bail of their principal into custody, in their own discharge. 1 Burrill, Pr. 394.

Of charter. A corporation created by charter may give up or "surrender" its charter to the people, unless the charter was granted under a statute, imposing indefeasible duties on the bodies to which it applies. Grant, Corp. 45.

SURRENDER BY BAIL. The act, by bail or sureties in a recognizance, of giving up their principal again into custody.

SURRENDER BY OPERATION OF LAW. This phrase is properly applied to cases where the tenant for life or years has been a party to some act the validity of which he is by law afterwards estopped from disputing, and which would not be valid if his particular estate continued to exist.

SURRENDER OF COPYHOLD. The mode of conveying or transferring copyhold property from one person to another is by means of a surrender, which consists in the yielding up of the estate by the tenant into the hands of the lord for such purposes as are expressed in the surrender. The process in most manors is for the tenant to come to the steward, either in court or out of court, or else to two customary tenants of the same manor, provided there be a custom to warrant it, and there, by delivering up a rod, a glove, or other symbol, as the custom directs, to resign into the hands of the lord, by the hands and acceptance of his steward, or of the said two tenants, all his interest and title to the estate, in trust, to be again granted out by the lord to such persons and for such uses as are named in the surrender, and as the custom of the manor will warrant. Brown.

SURRENDER OF CRIMINALS. The act by which the public authorities deliver a person accused of a crime, and who is found in their jurisdiction, to the authorities within whose jurisdiction it is alleged the crime has been committed.

SURRENDER OF A PREFERENCE. In bankruptcy practice. The surrender to the assignee in bankruptcy, by a preferred creditor, of anything he may have received under his preference and any advantage it gives him, which he must do before he can share in the dividend. 1 Dill. 544.

SURRENDER TO USES OF WILL. Formerly a copyhold interest would not pass by will unless it had been surrendered to the use of the will. By St. 55 Geo. III. c. 192, this is no longer necessary. 1 Steph. Comm. 639; Mozley & Whitley.

SURRENDEREE. The person to whom a surrender is made.

SURRENDEROR. One who makes a surrender. One who yields up a copyhold estate for the purpose of conveying it.

SURREPTITIOUS. Stealthily or fraudulently done, taken away, or introduced.

SURROGATE. In English law. One that is substituted or appointed in the room of another, as by a bishop, chancellor, judge, etc.; especially an officer appointed to dispense licenses to marry without banns. 2 Steph. Comm. 247.

In American law. The name given in some of the states to the judge or judicial officer who has the administration of probate matters, guardianships, etc.

SURROGATE'S COURT. In the United States. A state tribunal, with similar jurisdiction to the *court of ordinary, court of probate*, etc., relating to matters of probate, etc. 2 Kent, Comm. 409, note *b*.

SURSISE. L. Fr. In old English law. Neglect; omission; default; cessation.

SURSUM REDDERE. In old conveyancing. To render up; to surrender.

SURSUMREDDITIO. A surrender.

SURVEY. The process by which a parcel of land is measured and its contents ascertained; also a statement of the result of such survey, with the courses and distances and the quantity of the land.

In insurance law, the term "the survey" has acquired a general meaning, inclusive of what is commonly called the "application," which contains the questions propounded on behalf of the company, and the answers of the assured. 25 Wis. 291.

SURVEY OF A VESSEL. A public document, looked to both by underwriters and owners, as affording the means of ascertaining, at the time and place, the state and condition of the ship and other property at hazard. 3 Sum. 43.

SURVEYOR. One who makes surveys of land; one who has the overseeing or care of another person's land or works.

SURVEYOR OF HIGHWAYS. In English law. A person elected by the inhabitants of a parish, in vestry assembled, to survey the highways therein. He must possess certain qualifications in point of property; and, when elected, he is compellable, unless he can show some grounds of exemption, to take upon himself the office. Mozley & Whitley.

SURVEYOR OF THE PORT. A revenue officer of the United States appointed for each of the principal ports of entry, whose duties chiefly concern the importations at his station and the determination of their amount and valuation. Rev. St. U. S. § 2627.

SURVIVOR. One who survives another; one who outlives another; one of two or more persons who lives after the death of the other or others.

SURVIVORSHIP. The living of one of two or more persons after the death of the other or others.

Survivorship is where a person becomes entitled to property by reason of his having survived another person who had an interest in it. The most familiar example is in the case of joint tenants, the rule being that on the death of one of two joint tenants the whole property passes to the survivor. Sweet.

SUS. PER COLL. An abbreviation of "*suspendatur per collum*," let him be hanged by the neck. Words formerly used in England in signing judgment against a prisoner who was to be executed; being written by the judge in the margin of the sheriff's calendar or list, opposite the prisoner's name. 4 Bl. Comm. 403.

SUSPEND. To forbid an attorney or solicitor or ecclesiastical person from practicing for an interval of time.

SUSPENDER. In Scotch law. He in whose favor a suspension is made.

SUSPENSE. When a rent, profit *à prendre*, and the like, are, in consequence of the unity of possession of the rent, etc., of the land out of which they issue, not *in esse* for a time, they are said to be in suspense, *tunc dormiunt;* but they may be revived or awakened. Co. Litt. 313*a*.

SUSPENSION. A temporary stop of a right, of a law, and the like. Thus, we speak of a *suspension* of the writ of *habeas corpus*, of a statute, of the power of alienating an estate, of a person in office, etc.

Suspension of a right in an estate is a temporary or partial withholding of it from use or exercise. It differs from extinguishment, because a suspended right is susceptible of being revived, which is not the case where the right was extinguished.

In ecclesiastical law. An ecclesiastical censure, by which a spiritual person is either interdicted the exercise of his ecclesiastical function or hindered from receiving the profits of his benefice. It may be partial or total, for a limited time, or forever, when it is called "deprivation" or "amotion." Ayl. Par. 501.

In Scotch law. A stay of execution until after a further consideration of the cause. Ersk. Inst. 4, 3, 5.

SUSPENSION OF ARMS. An agreement between belligerents, made for a short time or for a particular place, to cease hostilities.

SUSPENSION, PLEAS IN, were those which showed some matter of temporary incapacity to proceed with the action or suit. Steph. Pl. 45.

SUSPENSIVE CONDITION. The obligation contracted on a suspensive condition is that which depends, either on a future and uncertain event, or on an event which has actually taken place, without its being yet known to the parties. In the former case, the obligation cannot be executed till after the event; in the latter, the obligation has its effect from the day on which it was contracted, but it cannot be enforced until the event be known. Civil Code La. art. 2043.

SUSPICION. The act of suspecting, or the state of being suspected; imagination, generally of something ill; distrust; mistrust; doubt. 66 Ga. 348.

SUTHDURE. The south door of a church, where canonical purgation was performed, and plaints, etc., were heard and determined. Wharton.

SUTLER. A person who, as a business, follows an army and sells provisions and liquor to the troops.

SUUM CUIQUE TRIBUERE. Lat. To render to every one his own. One of the three fundamental maxims of the law laid down by Justinian.

SUUS HÆRES. Lat. In the civil law. Those descendants who were under the power of the deceased at the time of his death, and who are most nearly related to him. Calvin.

SUUS JUDEX. Lat. In old English law. A proper judge; a judge having cognizance of a cause. Literally, one's own judge. Bract. fol. 401.

SUZEREIGN. L. Fr. In French and feudal law. The immediate vassal of the king; a crown vassal.

SWAIN; SWAINMOTE. See SWEIN; SWEINMOTE.

SWARF-MONEY. Warth-money, or guard-money paid in lieu of the service of castle-ward. Cowell.

SWEAR. 1. To put on oath; to administer an oath to a person.

2. To take an oath; to become bound by an oath duly administered.

3. To use profane language. Swearing, in this sense, is made a punishable offense in many jurisdictions.

SWEARING THE PEACE. Showing to a magistrate that one has just cause to be afraid of another in consequence of his menaces, in order to have him bound over to keep the peace.

SWEEPING. Comprehensive; including in its scope many persons or objects; as a sweeping objection.

SWEIN. In old English law. A freeman or freeholder within the forest.

SWEINMOTE. In forest law. A court holden before the verderors, as judges, by the steward of the sweinmote, thrice in every year, the *sweins* or freeholders within the forest composing the jury. Its principal jurisdiction was—*First*, to inquire into the oppressions and grievances committed by the officers of the forest; and, *secondly*, to receive and try presentments certified from the court of attachments in offenses against vert and venison. 3 Bl. Comm. 72.

SWELL. To enlarge or increase. In an action of tort, circumstances of aggravation may "swell" the damages.

SWIFT WITNESS. A term colloquially applied to a witness who is unduly zealous or partial for the side which calls him, and who betrays his bias by his extreme readiness to answer questions or volunteer information.

SWINDLING. Cheating and defrauding grossly with deliberate artifice. 2 Port. (Ala.) 157.

By the statute, "swindling" is defined to be the acquisition of personal or movable property, money, or instrument of writing conveying or securing a valuable right, by means of some false or deceitful pretense or device, or fraudulent representation, with intent to appropriate the same to the use of the party so acquiring, or of destroying or impairing the rights of the party justly entitled to the same. (Pen. Code, art. 790.) 10 Tex. App. 285.

SWOLING OF LAND. So much land as one's plow can till in a year; a hide of land. Cowell.

SWORN BROTHERS. In old English law. Persons who, by mutual oaths, covenant to share in each other's fortunes.

SWORN CLERKS IN CHANCERY. Certain officers in the English court of chancery, whose duties were to keep the records, make copies of pleadings, etc. Their offices were abolished by St. 5 & 6 Vict. c. 103.

SYB AND SOM. A Saxon form of greeting, meaning peace and safety.

SYLLABUS. A head-note; a note prefixed to the report of an adjudged case, containing an epitome or brief statement of the rulings of the court upon the point or points decided in the case.

SYLLOGISM. In logic. The full logical form of a single argument. It consists of three propositions, (two premises and the conclusion,) and these contain three terms, of which the two occurring in the conclusion are brought together in the premises by being referred to a common class.

SYLVA CÆDUA. Lat. In ecclesiastical law. Wood of any kind which was kept on purpose to be cut, and which, being cut, grew again from the stump or root. Lynd. Prov. 190; 4 Reeve, Eng. Law, 90.

SYMBOLÆOGRAPHY. The art or cunning rightly to form and make written instruments. It is either judicial or extrajudicial; the latter being wholly occupied with such instruments as concern matters not yet judicially in controversy, such as instruments of agreements or contracts, and testaments or last wills. Wharton.

SYMBOLIC DELIVERY. The constructive delivery of the subject-matter of a sale, where it is cumbersome or inaccessible, by the actual delivery of some article which is conventionally accepted as the symbol or representative of it, or which renders access to it possible, or which is evidence of the purchaser's title to it.

SYMBOLUM ANIMÆ. A mortuary, or soul-scot.

SYMOND'S INN. Formerly an inn of chancery.

SYNALLAGMATIC CONTRACT. In the civil law. A bilateral or reciprocal contract, in which the parties expressly enter into mutual engagements, each binding himself to the other. Poth. Obl. no. 9.

SYNCOPARE. To cut short, or pronounce things so as not to be understood. Cowell.

SYNDIC. In the civil law. An advocate or patron; a burgess or recorder; an agent or attorney who acts for a corporation or university; an actor or procurator; an assignee. Wharton.

In French law. The person who is commissioned by the courts to administer a bankruptcy. He fulfills the same functions as the trustee in English law, or assignee in America. The term is also applied to the person appointed to manage the affairs of a corporation. See 9 Pet. 182.

SYNDICATE. A university committee. A combination of persons or firms united for the purpose of enterprises too large for individuals to undertake; or a group of financiers who buy up the shares of a company in order to sell them at a profit by creating a scarcity. Mozley & Whitley.

SYNDICOS. One chosen by a college, municipality, etc., to defend its cause. Calvin.

SYNGRAPH. The name given by the canonists to deeds of which both parts were written on the same piece of parchment, with some word or letters of the alphabet written between them, through which the parchment was cut in such a manner as to leave half the word on one part and half on the other. It thus corresponded to the chirograph or indenture of the common law. 2 Bl. Comm. 295, 296.

A deed or other written instrument under the hand and seal of all the parties.

SYNOD. A meeting or assembly of ecclesiastical persons concerning religion; being the same thing, in Greek, as convocation in Latin. There are four kinds: (1) A general or universal synod or council, where bishops of all nations meet; (2) a national synod of the clergy of one nation only; (3) a provincial synod, where ecclesiastical persons of a province only assemble, being now what is called the "convocation;" (4) a diocesan synod, of those of one diocese.

A synod in Scotland is composed of three or more presbyteries. Wharton.

SYNODAL. A tribute or payment in money paid to the bishop or archdeacon by the inferior clergy, at the Easter visitation.

SYNODALES TESTES. Synods-men (corrupted into sidesmen) were the urban and rural deans, now the church-wardens.

T.

T. As an abbreviation, this letter usually stands for either "Territory," "Trinity," "term," "*tempore*," (in the time of,) or "title."

Every person who was convicted of felony, short of murder, and admitted to the benefit of clergy, was at one time marked with this letter upon the brawn of the thumb. The practice is abolished. 7 & 8 Geo. IV. c. 27.

By a law of the Province of Pennsylvania, A. D. 1698, it was provided that a convicted thief should wear a badge in the form of the letter "T.," upon his left sleeve, which badge should be at least four inches long and of a color different from that of his outer garment. Linn, Laws Prov. Pa. 275.

T. R. E. An abbreviation of "*Tempore Regis Edwardi*," (in the time of King Edward,) of common occurrence in Domesday, when the valuation of manors, as it was in the time of Edward the Confessor, is recounted. Cowell.

TABARD. A short gown; a herald's coat; a surcoat.

TABARDER. One who wears a tabard or short gown; the name is still used as the title of certain bachelors of arts on the old foundation of Queen's College, Oxford. Enc. Lond.

TABELLA. Lat. In Roman law. A tablet. Used in voting, and in giving the verdict of juries; and, when written upon, commonly translated "ballot." The laws which introduced and regulated the mode of voting by ballot were called "*leges tabellariæ*." Calvin.; 1 Kent, Comm. 232, note.

TABELLIO. In Roman law. An officer corresponding in some respects to a notary. His business was to draw legal instruments, (contracts, wills, etc.,) and witness their execution. Calvin.

TABERNACULUM. In old records. A public inn, or house of entertainment. Cowell.

TABERNARIUS. Lat. In the civil law. A shop-keeper. Dig. 14, 3, 5, 7.

In old English law. A taverner or tavern-keeper. Fleta, lib. 2, c. 12, § 17.

TABLE. A synopsis or condensed statement, bringing together numerous items or details so as to be comprehended in a single view; as genealogical tables, exhibiting the names and relationships of all the persons composing a family; life and annuity tables, used by actuaries; interest tables, etc.

TABLE DE MARBRE. Fr. In old French law. Table of Marble; a principal seat of the admiralty, so called. These Tables de Marbre are frequently mentioned in the Ordonnance of the Marine. Burrill.

TABLE OF CASES. An alphabetical list of the adjudged cases cited, referred to, or digested in a legal text-book, volume of reports, or digest, with references to the sections, pages, or paragraphs where they are respectively cited, etc., which is commonly either prefixed or appended to the volume.

TABLE RENTS. In English law. Payments which used to be made to bishops, etc., reserved and appropriated to their table or house-keeping. Wharton.

TABLEAU OF DISTRIBUTION. In Louisiana. A list of creditors of an insolvent estate, stating what each is entitled to. 4 Mart. (N. S.) 535.

TABULA. Lat. In the civil law. A table or tablet; a thin sheet of wood, which, when covered with wax, was used for writing.

TABULA IN NAUFRAGIO. Lat. A plank in a shipwreck. This phrase is used metaphorically to designate the power subsisting in a third mortgagee, who took without notice of the second mortgage, to acquire the first incumbrance, attach it to his own, and thus squeeze out and get satisfaction, before the second is admitted to the fund. 1 Story, Eq. Jur. § 414; 2 Ves. Ch. 573.

TABULÆ. Lat. In Roman law. Tables. Writings of any kind used as evidences of a transaction. Brissonius.

TABULÆ NUPTIALES. In the civil law. A written record of a marriage; or the agreement as to the *dos*.

TABULARIUS. Lat. A notary, or tabellio. Calvin.

TAC, TAK. In old records. A kind of customary payment by a tenant. Cowell.

TAC FREE. In old records. Free from the common duty or imposition of *tac*. Cowell.

TACIT. Silent; not expressed; implied or inferred; manifested by the refraining from contradiction or objection; inferred from the situation and circumstances, in the absence of express matter. Thus, *tacit* consent is consent inferred from the fact that the party kept silence when he had an opportunity to forbid or refuse.

TACIT LAW. A law which derives its authority from the common consent of the people without any legislative enactment. 1 Bouv. Inst. no. 120.

TACIT MORTGAGE. In the law of Louisiana. The law alone in certain cases gives to the creditor a mortgage on the property of his debtor, without it being requisite that the parties should stipulate it. This is called "legal mortgage." It is called also "tacit mortgage," because it is established by the law without the aid of any agreement. Civil Code La. art. 3311.

TACIT RELOCATION. In Scotch law. The tacit or implied renewal of a lease, inferred when the landlord, instead of warning a tenant to remove at the stipulated expiration of the lease, has allowed him to continue without making a new agreement. Bell, "Relocation."

TACIT TACK. In Scotch law. An implied tack or lease; inferred from a tacksman's possessing peaceably after his tack is expired. 1 Forb. Inst. pt. 2, p. 153.

Tacita quædam habentur pro expressis. 8 Coke, 40. Things unexpressed are sometimes considered as expressed.

TACITE. Lat. Silently; impliedly; tacitly.

TACITURNITY. In Scotch law, this signifies laches in not prosecuting a legal claim, or in acquiescing in an adverse one. Mozley & Whitley.

TACK, *v*. To annex some junior lien to a first lien, thereby acquiring priority over an intermediate one.

TACK, *n*. In Scotch law. A term corresponding to the English "lease," and denoting the same species of contract.

TACK DUTY. Rent reserved upon a lease.

TACKING. The uniting securities given at different times, so as to prevent any intermediate purchaser from claiming a title to redeem or otherwise discharge one lien, which is prior, without redeeming or discharging the other liens also, which are subsequent to his own title. 1 Story, Eq. Jur. § 412.

The term is particularly applied to the action of a third mortgagee who, by buying the first lien and uniting it to his own, gets priority over the second mortgagee.

TACKSMAN. In Scotch law. A tenant or lessee; one to whom a *tack* is granted. 1 Forb. Inst. pt. 2, p. 153.

TACTIS SACROSANCTIS. In old English law. Touching the holy evangelists. Fleta, lib. 3, c. 16, § 21. "A bishop may swear *visis evangeliis*, [looking at the Gospels,] and not *tactis*, and it is good enough." Freem. 133.

TACTO PER SE SANCTO EVANGELIO. Having personally touched the holy Gospel. Cro. Eliz. 105. The description of a corporal oath.

TAIL. Limited; abridged; reduced; curtailed, as a fee or estate in fee, to a certain order of succession, or to certain heirs.

TAIL AFTER POSSIBILITY OF ISSUE EXTINCT. A species of estate tail which arises where one is tenant in special tail, and a person from whose body the issue was to spring dies without issue, or, having left issue, that issue becomes extinct. In either of these cases the surviving tenant in special tail becomes "tenant in tail after possibility of issue extinct." 2 Bl. Comm. 124.

TAIL, ESTATE IN. An estate of inheritance, which, instead of descending to heirs generally, goes to the heirs of the donee's body, which means his lawful issue, his children, and through them to his grandchildren in a direct line, so long as his posterity endures in a regular order and course of descent, and upon the death of the first owner without issue, the estate determines. 1 Washb. Real Prop. *72.

An estate tail is a freehold of inheritance, limited to a person and the heirs of his body, general or special, male or female, and is the creature of the statute *de Donis*. The estate, provided the entail be not barred, reverts to the donor or reversioner, if the donee die without leaving descendants answering to the condition annexed to the estate upon its creation, unless there be a limitation over to a third person on default of such descendants, when it vests in such third person or remainder-man. Wharton.

TAIL FEMALE. When lands are given to a person and the *female* heirs of his or her body, this is called an "estate tail female," and the male heirs are not capable of inheriting it.

TAIL GENERAL. An estate in tail granted to one "and the heirs of his body begotten," which is called "tail general" because, how often soever such donee in tail be married, his issue in general by all and every such marriage is, in successive order, capable of inheriting the estate tail *per formam doni.* 2 Bl. Comm. 113.

This is where an estate is limited to a man and the heirs of his body, without any restriction at all; or, according to some authorities, with no other restriction than that in relation to sex. Thus, tail male general is the same thing as tail male; the word "general," in such case, implying that there is no other restriction upon the descent of the estate than that it must go in the male line. So an estate in tail female general is an estate in tail female. The word "general," in the phrase, expresses a purely negative idea, and may denote the absence of any restriction, or the absence of some given restriction which is tacitly understood. Mozley & Whitley.

TAIL MALE. When lands are given to a person and the *male* heirs of his or her body, this is called an "estate tail male," and the female heirs are not capable of inheriting it.

TAIL SPECIAL. An estate in tail where the succession is restricted to certain heirs of the donee's body, and does not go to all of them in general; *e. g.*, where lands and tenements are given to a man and "the heirs of his body on Mary, his now wife, to be begotten;" here no issue can inherit but such special issue as is engendered between them two, not such as the husband may have by another wife, and therefore it is called "special tail." 2 Bl. Comm. 113.

It is defined by Cowell as the limitation of lands and tenements to a man and his wife and the heirs of their two bodies. But the phrase need not be thus restricted. Tail special, in its largest sense, is where the gift is restrained to certain heirs of the donor's body, and does not go to all of them in general. Mozley & Whitley.

TAILAGE. A piece cut out of the whole; a share of one's substance paid by way of tribute; a toll or tax. Cowell.

TAILLE. Fr. In old French law. A tax or assessment levied by the king, or by any great lord, upon his subjects, usually taking the form of an imposition upon the owners of real estate. Brande.

In old English law. The fee which is opposed to fee-simple, because it is so minced or pared that it is not in the owner's free power to dispose of it, but it is, by the first giver, cut or divided from all other, and tied to the issue of the donee,—in short, an estate-tail. Wharton.

TAILZIE. In Scotch law. An entail. A tailzied fee is that which the owner, by exercising his inherent right of disposing of his property, settles upon others than those to whom it would have descended by law. 1 Forb. Inst. pt. 2, p. 101.

TAINT. A conviction of felony, or the person so convicted. Cowell.

TAKE. 1. To lay hold of; to gain or receive into possession; to seize; to deprive one of the possession of; to assume ownership. Thus, it is a constitutional provision that a man's property shall not be *taken* for public uses without just compensation. 9 Ind. 433.

2. To obtain or assume possession of a chattel unlawfully, and without the owner's consent; to appropriate things to one's own use with felonious intent. Thus, an actual *taking* is essential to constitute larceny. 4 Bl. Comm. 430.

3. To seize or apprehend a person; to arrest the body of a person by virtue of lawful process. Thus, a *capias* commands the officer to *take* the body of the defendant.

4. To acquire the title to an estate; to receive an estate in lands from another person by virtue of some species of title. Thus, one is said to "*take* by purchase," "*take* by descent," "*take* a life-interest under the devise," etc.

5. To receive the verdict of a jury; to superintend the delivery of a verdict; to hold a court. The commission of assize in England empowers the judges to *take the assizes;* that is, according to its ancient meaning, to take the verdict of a peculiar species of jury called an "assize;" but, in its present meaning, "to hold the assizes." 3 Bl. Comm. 59, 185.

TAKE UP. A party to a negotiable instrument, particularly an indorser or acceptor, is said to "take up" the paper, or to "retire" it, when he pays its amount, or substitutes other security for it, and receives it again into his own hands.

TAKER. One who takes or acquires; particularly, one who takes an estate by devise. When an estate is granted subject to a remainder or executory devise, the devisee of the immediate interest is called the "first taker."

TAKING. In criminal law and torts. The act of laying hold upon an article, with or without removing the same.

TALE. In old pleading. The plaintiff's count, declaration, or narrative of his case. 3 Bl. Comm. 293.

The count or counting of money. Said to be derived from the same root as "tally." Cowell. Whence also the modern word "teller."

TALES. Lat. Such; such men. When, by means of challenges or any other cause, a sufficient number of unexceptionable jurors does not appear at the trial, either party may pray a "tales," as it is termed; that is, a supply of *such* men as are summoned on the first panel in order to make up the deficiency. Brown.

TALES DE CIRCUMSTANTIBUS. So many of the by-standers. The emphatic words of the old writ awarded to the sheriff to make up a deficiency of jurors out of the persons present in court. 3 Bl. Comm. 365.

TALESMAN. A person summoned to act as a juror from among the by-standers in the court.

TALIO. Lat. In the civil law. Like for like; punishment in the same kind; the punishment of an injury by an act of the same kind, as an eye for an eye, a limb for a limb, etc. Calvin.

Talis interpretatio semper fienda est, ut evitetur absurdum et inconveniens, et ne judicium sit illusorium. 1 Coke, 52. Interpretation is always to be made in such a manner that what is absurd and inconvenient may be avoided, and the judgment be not illusory.

Talis non est eadem; nam nullum simile est idem. 4 Coke, 18. What is like is not the same; for nothing similar is the same.

Talis res, vel tale rectum, quæ vel quod non est in homine adtunc superstite sed tantummodo est et consistit in consideratione et intelligentia legis, et quod alii dixerunt talem rem vel tale rectum fore in nubibus. Such a thing or such a right as is not vested in a person then living, but merely exists in the consideration and contemplation of law [is said to be in abeyance,] and others have said that such a thing or such a right is in the clouds. Co. Litt. 342.

TALITER PROCESSUM EST. Upon pleading the judgment of an inferior court, the proceedings preliminary to such judgment, and on which the same was founded, must, to some extent, appear in the pleading, but the rule is that they may be alleged with a general allegation that "such proceedings were had," instead of a detailed account of the proceedings themselves, and this general allegation is called the "*taliter processum est.*" A like concise mode of stating former proceedings in a suit is adopted at the present day in chancery proceedings upon petitions and in actions in the nature of bills of revivor and supplement. Brown.

TALLAGE. A word used metaphorically for a share of a man's substance paid by way of tribute, toll, or tax, being derived from the French "*tailler*," which signifies to cut a piece out of the whole. Cowell.

TALLAGERS. Tax or toll gatherers; mentioned by Chaucer.

TALLAGIUM. A term including all taxes. 2 Inst. 532.

TALLAGIUM FACERE. To give up accounts in the exchequer, where the method of accounting was by tallies.

TALLATIO. A keeping account by tallies. Cowell.

TALLEY, or TALLY. A stick cut into two parts, on each whereof is marked, with notches or otherwise, what is due between debtor and creditor. It was the ancient mode of keeping accounts. One part was held by the creditor, and the other by the debtor. The use of tallies in the exchequer was abolished by St. 23 Geo. III. c. 82, and the old tallies were ordered to be destroyed by St. 4 & 5 Wm. IV. c. 15. Wharton.

TALLIA. L. Lat. A tax or tribute; tallage; a share taken or *cut out* of any one's income or means. Spelman.

TALLY TRADE. A system of dealing by which dealers furnish certain articles on credit, upon an agreement for the payment of the stipulated price by certain weekly or monthly installments. McCul. Dict.

TALTARUM'S CASE. A case reported in Yearb. 12 Edw. IV. 19-21, which is regarded as having established the foundation of common recoveries.

TAM QUAM. A phrase used as the name of a writ of error from inferior courts, when the error is supposed to be as well in giving the judgment as in awarding execution upon it. (*Tam in redditione judicii, quam in adjudicatione executionis.*)

A *venire tam quam* was one by which a jury was summoned, *as well* to try an issue *as* to inquire of the damages on a default. 2 Tidd, Pr. 722, 895.

TAME. Domesticated; accustomed to man; reclaimed from a natural state of wildness. In the Latin phrase, tame animals are described as *domitæ naturæ.*

TAMEN. Lat. Notwithstanding; nevertheless; yet.

TANGIBLE PROPERTY. Property which may be touched; such as is perceptible to the senses; corporeal property, whether real or personal. The phrase is used in opposition to such species of prope ty as patents, franchises, copyrights, rents, ways, and incorporeal property generally.

TANISTRY. In old Irish law. A species of tenure, founded on ancient usage, which allotted the inheritance of lands, castles, etc., to the "oldest and worthiest man of the deceased's name and blood." It was abolished in the reign of James I. Jacob; Wharton.

TANNERIA. In old English law. Tannery; the trade or business of a tanner. Fleta, lib. 2, c. 52, § 35.

TANTEO. Span. In Spanish law. Preemption. White, New Recop. b. 2, tit. 2, c. 3.

TANTO, RIGHT OF. In Mexican law. The right enjoyed by an usufructuary of property, of buying the property at the same price at which the owner offers it to any other person, or is willing to take from another. Civil Code Mex. art. 992.

Tantum bona valent, quantum vendi possunt. Shep. Touch. 142. Goods are worth so much as they can be sold for.

TARDE VENIT. Lat. In practice. The name of a return made by the sheriff to a writ, when it came into his hands too late to be executed before the return-day.

TARE. A deficiency in the weight or quantity of merchandise by reason of the weight of the box, cask, bag, or other receptacle which contains it and is weighed with it. Also an allowance or abatement of a certain weight or quantity which the seller makes to the buyer, on account of the weight of such box, cask, etc. See TRET.

TARIFF. A cartel of commerce, a book of rates, a table or catalogue, drawn usually in alphabetical order, containing the names of several kinds of merchandise, with the duties or customs to be paid for the same, as settled by authority, or agreed on between the several princes and states that hold commerce together. Enc. Lond.

The list or schedule of articles on which a duty is imposed upon their importation into the United States, with the rates at which they are severally taxed. Also the custom or duty payable on such articles. And, derivatively, the system or principle of imposing duties on the importation of foreign merchandise.

TASSUM. In old English law. A heap; a hay-mow, or hay-stack. *Fœnum in tassis*, hay in stacks. Reg. Orig. 96.

TATH. In the counties of Norfolk and Suffolk, the lords of manors anciently claimed the privilege of having their tenants' flocks or sheep brought at night upon their own demesne lands, there to be folded for the improvement of the ground, which liberty was called by the name of the "tath." Spelman.

TAURI LIBERI LIBERTAS. A common bull; because he was free to all the tenants within such a manor, liberty, etc.

TAUTOLOGY. Describing the same thing twice in one sentence in equivalent terms; a fault in rhetoric. It differs from repetition or iteration, which is repeating the same sentence in the same or equivalent terms; the latter is *sometimes* either excusable or necessary in an argument or address: the former (tautology) never. Wharton.

TAVERN. A place of entertainment; a house kept up for the accommodation of strangers. Originally, a house for the retailing of liquors to be drunk on the spot. Webster.

The word "tavern," in a charter provision authorizing municipal authorities to "license and regulate taverns," includes hotels. "Tavern," "hotel," and "public house" are, in this country, used synonymously; and while they entertain the traveling public, and keep guests, and receive compensation therefor, they do not lose their character, though they may not have the privilege of selling liquors. 46 Mo. 593.

TAVERN-KEEPER. One who keeps a tavern. One who keeps an inn; an innkeeper.

TAVERNER. In old English law. A seller of wine; one who kept a house or shop for the sale of wine.

TAX, *v*. To impose a tax; to enact or declare that a pecuniary contribution shall be made by the persons liable, for the support of government. Spoken of an individual, to be taxed is to be included in an assessment made for purposes of taxation.

In practice. To assess or determine; to liquidate, adjust, or settle. Spoken particularly of *taxing costs*, (*q. v.*)

TAX, *n*. Taxes are a ratable portion of the produce of the property and labor of the individual citizens, taken by the nation, in the exercise of its sovereign rights, for the support of government, for the administration of the laws, and as the means for continuing in operation the various legitimate functions of the state. Black, Tax Titles, § 2.

Taxes are the enforced proportional contribution of persons and property, levied by the authority of the state for the support of the government, and for all public needs; portions of the property of the citizen, demanded and received by the government, to be disposed of to enable it to discharge its functions. 58 Me. 590.

In a general sense, a tax is any contribution imposed by government upon individuals, for the use and service of the state, whether under the name of toll, tribute, tallage, gabel, impost, duty, custom, excise, subsidy, aid, supply, or other name. Story, Const. § 950.

By the concurrent opinion of lawyers, judges, lexicographers, and political economists, as well as by the general and popular understanding, taxes are burdens or charges imposed by the legislature upon persons or property to raise money for public purposes, or to accomplish some governmental end. 27 Iowa, 28.

A tax is a pecuniary burden, imposed for the support of government. 17 Wall. 322.

Taxes are classified as *direct*, which includes those which are assessed upon the property, person, business, income, etc., of those who pay them; and *indirect*, or those which are levied on commodities before they reach the consumer, and are paid by those upon whom they ultimately fall, not as taxes, but as part of the market price of the commodity. Cooley, Tax'n, 6.

Synonyms. In a broad sense, *taxes* undoubtedly include *assessments*, and the right to impose assessments has its foundation in the taxing power of the government; and yet, in practice and as generally understood, there is a broad distinction between the two terms. "Taxes," as the term is generally used, are public burdens imposed generally upon the inhabitants of the whole state, or upon some civil division thereof, for governmental purposes, without reference to peculiar benefits to particular individuals or property. "Assessments" have reference to impositions for improvements which are specially beneficial to particular individuals or property, and which are imposed in proportion to the particular benefits supposed to be conferred. They are justified only because the improvements confer special benefits, and are just only when they are divided in proportion to such benefits. 84 N. Y. 112.

A charge imposed by law upon the assessed value of all property, real and personal, in a district, is a tax, and not an assessment, although the purpose be to make a local improvement on a road. 46 Cal. 553.

Taxes differ from *subsidies*, in being certain and orderly, and from forced contributions, etc., in that they are levied by authority of law, and by some rule of proportion which is intended to insure uniformity of contribution, and a just apportionment of the burdens of government. Cooley, Tax'n, 2.

The words "tax" and "excise," although often used as synonymous, are to be considered as having entirely distinct and separate significations. The former is a charge apportioned either among the whole people of the state, or those residing within certain districts, municipalities, or sections. It is required to be imposed, as we shall more fully explain hereafter, so that, if levied for the public charges of government, it shall be shared according to the estate, real and personal, which each person may possess; or, if raised to defray the cost of some local improvement of a public nature, it shall be borne by those who will receive some special and peculiar benefit or advantage which an expenditure of money for a public object may cause to those on whom the tax is assessed. An excise, on the other hand, is of a different character. It is based on no rule of apportionment or equality whatever. It is a fixed, absolute, and direct charge laid on merchandise, products, or commodities, without any regard to the amount of property belonging to those on whom it may fall, or to any supposed relation between money expended for a public object and a special benefit occasioned to those by whom the charge is to be paid. 11 Allen, 274.

TAX-DEED. The conveyance given upon a sale of lands made for non-payment of taxes; the deed whereby the officer of the law undertakes to convey the title of the proprietor to the purchaser at the tax-sale.

TAX-LEVY. The total sum to be raised by a tax. Also the bill, enactment, or measure of legislation by which an annual or general tax is imposed.

TAX-LIEN. A statutory lien, existing in favor of the state or municipality, upon the lands of a person charged with taxes, binding the same either for the taxes assessed upon the specific tract of land or (in some jurisdictions) for all the taxes due from the individual, and which may be foreclosed for non-payment, by judgment of a court or sale of the land.

TAX-PAYER. A person chargeable with a tax; one from whom government demands a pecuniary contribution towards its support.

TAX-PAYERS' LISTS. Written exhibits required to be made out by the taxpayers resident in a district, enumerating all the property owned by them and subject to taxation, to be handed to the assessors, at a specified date or at regular periods, as a basis for assessment and valuation.

TAX PURCHASER. A person who buys land at a tax-sale; the person to whom land, at a tax-sale thereof, is struck down.

TAX-SALE. A sale of land for unpaid taxes; a sale of property, by authority of law, for the collection of a tax assessed upon it, or upon its owner, which remains unpaid.

TAX-TITLE. The title by which one holds land which he purchased at a tax-sale. That species of title which is inaugurated by a successful bid for land at a collector's sale of the same for non-payment of taxes, completed by the failure of those entitled to redeem within the specified time, and evidenced by the deed executed to the tax purchaser, or his assignee, by the proper officer.

TAXA. L. Lat. A tax. Spelman.

In old records. An allotted piece of work; a task.

TAXABLE. Subject to taxation; liable to be assessed, along with others, for a share in a tax. Persons subject to taxation are sometimes called "taxables;" so property which may be assessed for taxation is said to be taxable.

Applied to costs in an action, the word means proper to be taxed or charged up; legally chargeable or assessable.

TAXARE. Lat. To rate or value. Calvin.

To tax; to lay a tax or tribute. Spelman.

In old English practice. To assess; to rate or estimate; to moderate or regulate an assessment or rate.

TAXATI. In old European law. Soldiers of a garrison or fleet, assigned to a certain station. Spelman.

TAXATIO. Lat. In Roman law. Taxation or assessment of damages; the assessment, by the judge, of the amount of damages to be awarded to a plaintiff, and particularly in the way of reducing the amount claimed or sworn to by the latter.

TAXATIO ECCLESIASTICA. The valuation of ecclesiastical benefices made through every diocese in England, on occasion of Pope Innocent IV. granting to King Henry III. the tenth of all spirituals for three years. This taxation was first made by Walter, bishop of Norwich, delegated by the pope to this office in 38 Hen. III., and hence called "*Taxatio Norwicencis.*" It is also called "Pope Innocent's Valor." Wharton.

TAXATIO EXPENSARUM. In old English practice. Taxation of costs.

TAXATIO NORWICENSIS. A valuation of ecclesiastical benefices made through every diocese in England, by Walter, bishop of Norwich, delegated by the pope to this office in 38 Hen. III. Cowell.

TAXATION. The imposition of a tax; the act or process of imposing and levying a pecuniary charge or enforced contribution, ratable, or proportioned to value or some other standard, upon persons or property, by or on behalf of a government or one of its divisions or agencies, for the purpose of providing revenue for the maintenance and expenses of government.

The term "taxation," both in common parlance and in the laws of the several states, has been ordinarily used, not to express the idea of the sovereign power which is exercised, but the exercise of that power for a particular purpose, viz., to raise a revenue for the general and ordinary expenses of the government, whether it be the state, county, town, or city government. But there is another class of expenses, also of a public nature, necessary to be provided for, peculiar to the local government of counties, cities, towns, and even smaller subdivisions, such as opening, grading, improving in various ways, and repairing, highways and streets, and constructing sewers in cities, and canals and ditches for the purpose of drainage in the country. They are generally of peculiar local benefit. These burdens have always, in every state, from its first settlement, been charged upon the localities benefited, and have been apportioned upon various principles; but, whatever principle of apportionment has been adopted, they have been known, both in the legislation and ordinary speech of the country, by the name of "assessments." Assessments have also, very generally, if not always, been apportioned upon principles different from those adopted in "taxation," in the ordinary sense of that term; and any one can see, upon a moment's reflection, that the apportionment, to bear equally, and do substantial justice to all parties, must be made upon a different principle from that adopted in "taxation," so called. 28 Cal. 356.

The differences between taxation and taking property in right of eminent domain are that taxation exacts money or services from individuals, as and for their respective shares of contribution to any public burden; while private property taken for public use, by right of eminent domain, is taken, not as the owner's share of contribution to a public burden, but as so much beyond his share, and for which compensation must be made. Moreover, taxation operates upon a community, or upon a class of persons in a community, and by some rule of apportionment; while eminent domain operates upon an individual, and without reference to the amount or value exacted from any other individual, or class of individuals. 4 N. Y. 419.

TAXATION OF COSTS. In practice. The process of ascertaining and charging up the amount of costs in an action to which a party is legally entitled, or which are legally chargeable. And, in English practice, the process of examining the items in an attorney's bill of costs and making the proper deductions, if any.

TAXERS. Two officers yearly chosen in Cambridge, England, to see the true gauge of all the weights and measures.

TAXING DISTRICT. The district throughout which a particular tax or assessment is ratably apportioned and levied upon the inhabitants; it may comprise the whole state, one county, a city, a ward, or part of a street.

TAXING MASTERS. Officers of the English supreme court, who examine and allow or disallow items in bills of costs.

TAXING OFFICER. Each house of parliament has a taxing officer, whose duty it is to tax the costs incurred by the promoters or opponents of private bills. May, Parl. Pr. 843.

TAXING POWER. The power of any government to levy taxes.

TAXT-WARD. An annual payment made to a superior in Scotland, instead of the duties due to him under the tenure of ward-holding. Abolished. Wharton.

TEAM, or THEAME. In old English law. A royalty or privilege granted, by royal charter, to a lord of a manor, for the having, restraining, and judging of bondmen and villeins, with their children, goods, and chattels, etc. Glan. lib. 5, c. 2.

TEAM. Within the meaning of an exemption law, a "team" consists of either one or two horses, with their harness and the vehicle to which they are customarily attached for use. 32 Barb. 291; 31 N. Y. 655.

TEAM WORK. Within the meaning of an exemption law, this term means work done by a team as a substantial part of a man's business; as in farming, staging, express carrying, drawing of freight, peddling, or the transportation of material used or dealt in as a business. 49 Vt. 375.

TEAMSTER. One who drives horses in a wagon for the purpose of carrying goods for hire. He is liable as a common carrier. Story, Bailm. § 496.

TECHNICAL. Belonging or peculiar to an art or profession. Technical terms are frequently called in the books "words of art."

TECHNICAL MORTGAGE. A true and formal mortgage, as distinguished from other instruments which, in some respects, have the character of equitable mortgages. 50 Md. 514.

TEDDING. Spreading. Tedding grass is spreading it out after it is cut in the swath. 10 East, 5.

TEDING-PENNY. In old English law. A small tax or allowance to the sheriff from each tithing of his county towards the charge of keeping courts, etc. Cowell.

TEEP. In Hindu law. A note of hand; a promissory note given by a native banker or money-lender to *zemindars* and others, to enable them to furnish government with security for the payment of their rents. Wharton.

TEGULA. In the civil law. A tile. Dig. 19, 1, 18.

TEIND COURT. In Scotch law. A court which has jurisdiction of matters relating to *teinds*, or tithes.

TEIND MASTERS. Those entitled to tithes.

TEINDS. In Scotch law. A term corresponding to tithes (*q. v.*) in English ecclesiastical law.

TEINLAND. Sax. In old English law. Land of a thane or Saxon noble; land granted by the crown to a thane or lord. Cowell; 1 Reeve, Eng. Law, 5.

TELEGRAM. A telegraphic dispatch; a message sent by telegraph.

TELEGRAPH. In the English telegraph act of 1863, the word is defined as "a wire or wires used for the purpose of telegraphic communication, with any casing, coating, tube, or pipe inclosing the same, and any apparatus connected therewith for the purpose of telegraphic communication." St. 26 & 27 Vict. c. 112, § 3.

TELEGRAPHIÆ. Written evidence of things past. Blount.

TELEPHONE. In a general sense, the name "telephone" applies to any instrument or apparatus which transmits sound beyond the limits of ordinary audibility. But, since the recent discoveries in telephony, the name is technically and primarily restricted to an instrument or device which transmits sound by means of electricity and wires similar to telegraphic wires. In a secondary sense, however, being the sense in which it is most commonly understood, the word "telephone" constitutes a generic term, having reference generally to the art of telephony as an institution, but more particularly to the apparatus, as an entirety, ordinarily used in the transmission, as well as in the reception, of telephonic messages. 105 Ind. 261, 5 N. E. Rep. 178.

TELLER. One who numbers or counts. An officer of a bank who receives or pays out money. Also one appointed to count the votes cast in a deliberative or legislative assembly or other meeting. The name was also given to certain officers formerly attached to the English exchequer.

The teller is a considerable officer in the exchequer, of which officers there are four, whose office is to receive all money due to the king, and to give the clerk of the pells a bill to charge him therewith. They also pay to all persons any money payable by the king, and make weekly and yearly books of their receipts and payments, which they deliver to the lord treasurer. Cowell; Jacob.

TELLERS IN PARLIAMENT. In the language of parliament, the "tellers" are the members of the house selected to count the members when a division takes place. In the house of lords a division is effected by the "non-contents" remaining within the bar, and the "contents" going below it, a teller being appointed for each party. In the commons the "ayes" go into the lobby at one end of the house, and the "noes" into the lobby at the other end, the house itself being perfectly empty, and two tellers being appointed for each party. May, Parl. Pr.; Brown.

TELLIGRAPHUM. An Anglo-Saxon charter of land. 1 Reeve, Eng. Law, c. 1, p. 10.

TELLWORC. That labor which a tenant was bound to do for his lord for a certain number of days.

TEMENTALE, or TENEMENTALE. A tax of two shillings upon every plow-land; a decennary.

TEMERE. Lat. In the civil law. Rashly; inconsiderately. A plaintiff was said *temere litigare* who demanded a thing out of malice, or sued without just cause, and who could show no ground or cause of action. Brissonius.

TEMPEST. A violent or furious storm; a current of wind rushing with extreme violence, and usually accompanied with rain or snow. See 29 U. C. C. P. 84.

TEMPLARS. A religious order of knighthood, instituted about the year 1119, and so called because the members dwelt in a part of the temple of Jerusalem, and not far from the sepulcer of our Lord. They entertained Christian strangers and pilgrims charitably, and their profession was at first to defend travelers from highwaymen and robbers. The order was suppressed A. D. 1307, and their substance given partly to the knights of St. John of Jerusalem, and partly to other religious orders. Brown.

TEMPLE. Two English inns of court, thus called because anciently the dwelling place of the Knights Templar. On the suppression of the order, they were purchased by some professors of the common law, and converted into *hospitia* or inns of court. They are called the "Inner" and "Middle Temple," in relation to Essex House, which was also a part of the house of the Templars, and called the "Outer Temple," because situated without Temple Bar. Enc. Lond.

TEMPORAL LORDS. The peers of England; the bishops are not in strictness held to be peers, but merely lords of parliament. 2 Steph. Comm. 330, 345.

TEMPORALIS. Lat. In the civil law. Temporary; limited to a certain time.

TEMPORALIS ACTIO. Lat. An action which could only be brought within a certain period.

TEMPORALIS EXCEPTIO. Lat. A temporary exception which barred an action for a time only.

TEMPORALITIES. In English law. The lay fees of bishops, with which their churches are endowed or permitted to be endowed by the liberality of the sovereign, and in virtue of which they become barons and lords of parliament. Spelman.

TEMPORALITY. The laity; secular people.

TEMPORARY. That which is to last for a limited time only, as distinguished from that which is perpetual, or indefinite, in its duration.

TEMPORE. Lat. In the time of. Thus, the volume called "Cases *tempore* Holt" is a collection of cases adjudged in the king's bench during the time of Lord Holt. Wall. Rep. 398.

TEMPORIS EXCEPTIO. Lat. In the civil law. A plea of time; a plea of lapse of time, in bar of an action. Corresponding to the plea of prescription, or the statute of limitations, in our law. See Mackeld. Rom. Law, § 213.

TEMPUS. Lat. In the civil and old English law. Time in general. A time limited; a season; *e. g., tempus pessonis*, mast time in the forest.

TEMPUS CONTINUUM. Lat. In the civil law. A continuous or absolute period of time. A term which begins to run from a certain event, even though he for whom it runs has no knowledge of the event, and in which, when it has once begun to run, all the days are reckoned as they follow one another in the calendar. Dig. 3, 2, 8; Mackeld. Rom. Law, § 195.

Tempus enim modus tollendi obligationes et actiones, quia tempus currit contra desides et sui juris contemptores. For time is a means of destroying obligations and actions, because time runs against the slothful and contemners of their own rights. Fleta, l. 4, c. 5, § 12.

TEMPUS SEMESTRE. Lat. In old English law. The period of six months or half a year, consisting of one hundred and eighty-two days. Cro. Jac. 166.

TEMPUS UTILE. Lat. In the civil law. A profitable or advantageous period of time. A term which begins to run from a certain event, only when he for whom it runs has obtained a knowledge of the event, and in which, when it has once begun to run, those days are not reckoned on which one has no *experiundi potestas; i. e.*, on which one cannot prosecute his rights before a court. Dig. 3, 6, 6; Mackeld. Rom. Law, § 195.

TENANCY is the relation of a tenant to the land which he holds. Hence it signifies (1) the estate of a tenant, as in the expressions "joint tenancy," "tenancy in common;" (2) the term or interest of a tenant for years or at will, as when we say that a lessee must remove his fixtures during his tenancy. Sweet.

TENANCY, JOINT. See JOINT TENANCY.

TENANT. In the broadest sense, one who holds or possesses lands or tenements by any kind of right or title, whether in fee, for life, for years, at will, or otherwise. Cowell.

In a more restricted sense, one who holds lands of another; one who has the temporary use and occupation of real property owned by another person, (called the "landlord,") the duration and terms of his tenancy being usually fixed by an instrument called a "lease."

The word "tenant" conveys a much more comprehensive idea in the language of the law than it does in its popular sense. In popular language it is used more particularly as opposed to the word "landlord," and always seems to imply that the land or property is not the tenant's own, but belongs to some other person, of whom he immediately holds it. But, in the language of the law, every possessor of landed property is called a "tenant" with reference to such property, and this, whether such landed property is absolutely his own, or whether he merely holds it under a lease for a certain number of years. Brown.

In feudal law. One who holds of another (called "lord" or "superior") by some service; as fealty or rent.

One who has actual possession of lands claimed in suit by another; the defendant in a real action. The correlative of "demandant." 3 Bl. Comm. 180.

Strictly speaking, a "tenant" is a person who holds land; but the term is also applied by analogy to personalty. Thus we speak of a person being tenant for life, or tenant in common, of stock. Sweet.

TENANT A VOLUNTE. L. Fr. A tenant at will.

TENANT AT SUFFERANCE. One that comes into the possession of land by lawful title, but holds over by wrong, after the determination of his interest. 4 Kent, Comm. 116; 2 Bl. Comm. 150.

TENANT AT WILL "is where lands or tenements are let by one man to another, to have and to hold to him at the will of the lessor, by force of which lease the lessee is in possession. In this case the lessee is called 'tenant at will,' because he hath no certain nor sure estate, for the lessor may put him out at what time it pleaseth him." Litt. § 68; Sweet.

TENANT BY COPY OF COURT ROLL (shortly, "tenant by copy") is the old-fashioned name for a copyholder. Litt. § 73.

TENANT BY THE CURTESY. One who, on the death of his wife seised of an estate of inheritance, after having by her issue born alive and capable of inheriting her estate, holds the lands and tenements for the term of his life. Co. Litt. 30*a*; 2 Bl. Comm. 126.

TENANT BY THE MANNER. One who has a less estate than a fee in land which remains in the reversioner. He is so called because in avowries and other pleadings it is specially shown in what manner he is tenant of the land, in contradistinction to the *veray tenant*, who is called simply "tenant." Ham. N. P. 393.

TENANT FOR LIFE. One who holds lands or tenements for the term of his own life, or for that of any other person, (in which case he is called "*pur auter vie*,") or for more lives than one. 2 Bl. Comm. 120.

TENANT FOR YEARS. One who has the temporary use and possession of lands or tenements not his own, by virtue of a lease or demise granted to him by the owner, for a determinate period of time, as for a year or a fixed number of years. 2 Bl. Comm. 140.

TENANT FROM YEAR TO YEAR. One who holds lands or tenements under the demise of another, where no certain term has been mentioned, but an annual rent has been reserved. See 1 Steph. Comm. 271; 4 Kent, Comm. 111, 114.

One who holds over, by consent given either expressly or constructively, after the determination of a lease for years. 4 Kent, Comm. 112.

TENANT IN CAPITE. In feudal and old English law. Tenant in chief; one who held immediately under the king, in right of his crown and dignity. 2 Bl. Comm. 60.

TENANT IN COMMON. Tenants in common are generally defined to be such as hold the same land together by several and distinct titles, but by unity of possession, because none knows his own severalty, and therefore they all occupy promiscuously. 2 Bl. Comm. 191.

A tenancy in common is where two or more hold the same land, with interests accruing under different titles, or accruing under the same title, but at different periods, or conferred by words of limitation importing that the grantees are to take in distinct shares. 1 Steph. Comm. 323.

TENANT IN DOWER. This is where the husband of a woman is seised of an estate of inheritance and dies; in this case the wife shall have the third part of all the lands and tenements whereof he was seised at any time during the coverture, to hold to herself for life, as her dower. Co. Litt. 30; 2 Bl. Comm. 129.

TENANT IN FEE-SIMPLE, (or **TENANT IN FEE.**) He who has lands, tenements, or hereditaments, to hold to him and his heirs forever, generally, absolutely, and simply; without mentioning *what* heirs, but referring that to his own pleasure, or to the disposition of the law. 2 Bl. Comm. 104; Litt. § 1.

TENANT IN SEVERALTY is he who holds lands and tenements in his own right only, without any other person being joined or connected with him in point of interest during his estate therein. 2 Bl. Comm. 179.

TENANT IN TAIL. One who holds an estate in fee-tail, that is, an estate which, by the instrument creating it, is limited to some particular heirs, exclusive of others; as to the heirs of *his body* or to the heirs, *male* or *female*, of his body.

TENANT IN TAIL AFTER POSSIBILITY OF ISSUE EXTINCT. See TAIL AFTER POSSIBILITY, etc.

TENANT IN TAIL EX PROVISIONE VIRI. Where an owner of lands, upon or previously to marrying a wife, settled lands upon himself and his wife, and the heirs of their two bodies begotten, and then died, the wife, as survivor, became tenant in tail of the husband's lands, in consequence of the husband's provision, (*ex provisione viri.*) Originally, she could bar the estate-tail like any other tenant in tail; but the husband's intention having been merely to provide for her during her widowhood, and not to enable her to bar his children of their inheritance, she was very early restrained from so doing, by the statute 32 Hen. VII. c. 36. Brown.

TENANT OF THE DEMESNE. One who is tenant of a mesne lord; as, where A. is tenant of B., and C. of A., B. is the lord, A. the mesne lord, and C. tenant of the demesne. Ham. N. P. 392, 393.

TENANT PARAVAILE. The under-tenant of land; that is, the tenant of a tenant; one who held of a mesne lord.

TENANT-RIGHT. 1. A kind of customary estate in the north of England, falling under the general class of copyhold, but distinguished from copyhold by many of its incidents.

2. The so-called tenant-right of renewal is the expectation of a lessee that his lease will be renewed, in cases where it is an established practice to renew leases from time to time, as in the case of leases from the crown, from ecclesiastical corporations, or other collegiate bodies. Strictly speaking, there can be no right of renewal against the lessor without an express compact by him to that effect, though the existence of the custom often influences the price in sales.

3. The Ulster tenant-right may be described as a right on the tenant's part to sell his holding to the highest bidder, subject to the existing or a reasonable increase of rent from time to time, as circumstances may require, with a reasonable veto reserved to the landlord in respect of the incoming tenant's character and solvency. Mozley & Whitley.

TENANT TO THE PRÆCIPE. Before the English fines and recoveries act, if land was conveyed to a person for life with remainder to another in tail, the tenant in tail in remainder was unable to bar the entail without the concurrence of the tenant for life, because a common recovery could only be suffered by the person seised of the land. In such a case, if the tenant for life wished to concur in barring the entail, he usually conveyed his life-estate to some other person, in order that the *præcipe* in the recovery might be issued against the latter, who was therefore called the "tenant to the *præcipe.*" Williams, Seis. 169; Sweet.

TENANT'S FIXTURES. This phrase signifies things which are fixed to the freehold of the demised premises, but which the tenant may detach and take away, provided he does so in season. 4 Gray, 256, 270.

TENANTABLE REPAIR. Such a repair as will render a house fit for present habitation.

TENANTS BY THE VERGE "are in the same nature as tenants by copy of court roll, [*i. e.*, copyholders.] But the reason why they be called 'tenants by the verge' is for that, when they will surrender their tenements into the hands of their lord to the use of another, they shall have a little rod (by the custome) in their hand, the which they shall deliver to the steward or to the bailife, * * * and the steward or bailife, according to the custome, shall deliver to him that taketh the land the same rod, or another rod, in the name of seisin; and for this cause they are called 'tenants by the verge,' but they have no other evidence [title-deed] but by copy of court roll." Litt. § 78; Co. Litt. 61*a*.

TENCON. L. Fr. A dispute; a quarrel. Kelham.

TEND. In old English law. To tender or offer. Cowell.

TENDER. An offer of money; the act by which one produces and offers to a person holding a claim or demand against him the amount of money which he considers and admits to be due, in satisfaction of such claim or demand, without any stipulation or condition.

Tender, in pleading, is a plea by defendant that he has been always ready to pay the debt demanded, and before the commencement of the action tendered it to the plaintiff, and now brings it into court ready to be paid to him, etc. Brown.

Legal tender. Money is said to be legal tender when a creditor cannot refuse to accept it in payment of a debt.

TENDER OF AMENDS. An offer by a person who has been guilty of any wrong or breach of contract to pay a sum of money by way of amends. If a defendant in an action make tender of amends, and the plaintiff decline to accept it, the defendant may pay the money into court, and plead the payment into court as a satisfaction of the plaintiff's claim. Mozley & Whitley.

TENDER OF ISSUE. A form of words in a pleading, by which a party offers to refer the question raised upon it to the appropriate mode of decision. The common tender of an issue of fact by a defendant is expressed by the words, "and of this he puts himself upon the country." Steph. Pl. 54, 230.

TENEMENT. This term, in its vulgar acceptation, is only applied to houses and other buildings, but in its original, proper, and legal sense it signifies everything that may be *holden*, provided it be of a permanent nature, whether it be of a substantial and sensible, or of an unsubstantial, ideal, kind. Thus, *liberum tenementum*, frank tenement, or freehold, is applicable not only to lands and other solid objects, but also to offices, rents, commons, advowsons, franchises, peerages, etc. 2 Bl. Comm. 16.

"Tenement" is a word of greater extent than "land," including not only land, but rents, commons, and several other rights and interests issuing out of or concerning land. 1 Steph. Comm. 158, 159.

Its original meaning, according to some, was "house" or "homestead." Jacob. In modern use it also signifies rooms let in houses. Webster.

TENEMENTAL LAND. Land distributed by a lord among his tenants, as opposed to the demesnes which were occupied by himself and his servants. 2 Bl. Comm. 90.

TENEMENTIS LEGATIS. An ancient writ, lying to the city of London, or any other corporation, (where the old custom was that men might devise by will lands and tenements, as well as goods and chattels,) for the hearing and determining any controversy touching the same. Reg. Orig. 244.

TENENDAS. In Scotch law. The name of a clause in charters of heritable rights, which derives its name from its first words, "*tenendas prædictas terras;*" it points out the superior of whom the lands are to be holden, and expresses the particular tenure. Ersk. Inst. 2, 3, 24.

TENENDUM. Lat. To hold; to be holden. The name of that formal part of a deed which is characterized by the words "to hold." It was formerly used to express the tenure by which the estate granted was to be held; but, since all freehold tenures have been converted into socage, the *tenendum* is of no further use, and is therefore joined in the *habendum*, — "to have and to hold." 2 Bl. Comm. 298; 4 Cruise, Dig. 26.

TENENS. A tenant; the defendant in a real action.

TENENTIBUS IN ASSISÂ NON ONERANDIS. A writ that formerly lay for him to whom a disseisor had alienated the land whereof he disseised another, that he should not be molested in assize for damages, if the disseisor had wherewith to satisfy them. Reg. Orig. 214.

TENERE. Lat. In the civil law. To hold; to hold fast; to have in possession; to retain.

In relation to the doctrine of possession, this term expresses merely the fact of manual detention, or the corporal possession of any object, without involving the question of title; while *habere* (and especially *possidere*) denotes the maintenance of possession by a lawful claim; *i. e.*, *civil* possession, as distinguished from mere *natural* possession.

TENERI. The Latin name for that clause in a bond in which the obligor expresses that he is "held and firmly bound" to the obligee, his heirs, etc.

TENET; TENUIT. Lat. He holds; he held. In the Latin forms of the writ of waste against a tenant, these words introduced the allegation of tenure. If the tenancy still existed, and recovery of the land was sought, the former word was used, (and the writ was said to be "in the *tenet.*") If the tenancy had already determined, the latter term was used, (the writ being described as "in the *tenuit*,") and then damages only were sought.

TENHEDED, or TIENHEOFED. In old English law. A dean. Cowell.

TENMENTALE. The number of ten men, which number, in the time of the Saxons, was called a "decennary;" and ten decennaries made what was called a "hundred." Also a duty or tribute paid to the crown, consisting of two shillings for each plowland. Enc. Lond.

TENNE. A term of heraldry, meaning orange color. In engravings it should be represented by lines in bend sinister crossed by others bar-ways. Heralds who blazon by the names of the heavenly bodies, call it "dragon's head," and those who employ jewels, "jacinth." It is one of the colors called "stainand." Wharton.

TENOR. A term used in pleading to denote that an exact copy is set out. 1 Chit. Crim. Law, 235.

By the tenor of a deed, or other instrument in writing, is signified the matter contained therein, according to the true intent and meaning thereof. Cowell.

"Tenor," in pleading a written instrument, imports that the very words are set out. "Purport" does not import this, but is equivalent only to "substance." 5 Blackf. 458; 1 Cush. 46; 5 Wend. 271.

The action of proving the tenor, in Scotland, is an action for proving the contents and purport of a deed which has been lost. Bell.

In chancery pleading. A certified copy of records of other courts removed into chancery by *certiorari*. Gres. Eq. Ev. 309.

Tenor est qui legem dat feudo. It is the tenor [of the feudal grant] which regulates its effect and extent. Craigius, Jus Feud. (3d Ed.) 66; Broom, Max. 459.

TENORE INDICTAMENTI MITTENDO. A writ whereby the record of an indictment, and the process thereupon, was called out of another court into the queen's bench. Reg. Orig. 69.

TENORE PRÆSENTIUM. By the tenor of these presents, *i. e.*, the matter contained therein, or rather the intent and meaning thereof. Cowell.

TENSERIÆ. A sort of ancient tax or military contribution. Wharton.

TENTATES PANIS. The essay or assay of bread. Blount.

TENTERDEN'S ACT. In English law. The statute 9 Geo. IV. c. 14, taking its name from Lord Tenterden, who procured its enactment, which is a species of extension of the statute of frauds, and requires the reduction of contracts to writing.

TENTHS. In English law. A temporary aid issuing out of personal property, and granted to the king by parliament; formerly the real tenth part of all the movables belonging to the subject. 1 Bl. Comm. 308

In English ecclesiastical law. The tenth part of the annual profit of every living in the kingdom, formerly paid to the pope, but by statute 26 Hen. VIII. c. 3, transferred to the crown, and afterwards made a part of the fund called "Queen Anne's Bounty." 1 Bl. Comm. 284-286.

TENUIT. A term used in stating the tenure in an action for waste done after the termination of the tenancy. See TENET.

TENURA. In old English law. Tenure.

Tenura est pactio contra communem feudi naturam ac rationem, in contractu interposita. Wright, Ten. 21. Tenure is a compact contrary to the common nature and reason of the fee, put into a contract.

TENURE. The mode or system of holding lands or tenements in subordination to some superior, which, in the feudal ages, was the leading characteristic of real property.

Tenure is the direct result of feudalism, which separated the *dominium directum*, (the dominion of the soil,) which is placed mediately or immediately in the crown, from the *dominium utile*, (the possessory title,) the right to the use and profits in the soil, designated by the term "seisin," which is the highest interest a subject can acquire. Wharton.

Wharton gives the following list of tenures which were ultimately developed:

LAY TENURES.

I. Frank tenement, or freehold. (1) The military tenures (abolished, except grand serjeanty, and reduced to free socage tenures) were: Knight service proper, or tenure in chivalry; grand serjeanty; cornage. (2) Free socage, or plow-service; either petit sorjeanty, tenure in burgage, or gavelkind.

II. Villeinage. (1) Pure villeinage, (whence copyholds at the lord's [nominal] will, which is regulated according to custom.) (2) Privileged villeinage, sometimes called "villein socage," (whence tenure in ancient demesne, which is an exalted species of copyhold, held according to custom, and not according to the lord's will,) and is of three kinds: Tenure in ancient demesne; privileged copyholds, customary freeholds, or free copyholds; copyholds of base tenure.

SPIRITUAL TENURES.

I. Frankalmoigne, or free alms.
II. Tenure by divine service.

Tenure, in its general sense, is a mode of holding or occupying. Thus, we speak of the tenure of an office, meaning the manner in which it is held, especially with regard to time, (tenure for life, tenure during good behavior,) and of tenure of land in the sense of occupation or tenancy, especially with reference to cultivation and questions of political economy; *e. g.*, tenure by peasant proprietors, cottiers, etc. Sweet.

TENURE BY DIVINE SERVICE is where an ecclesiastical corporation, sole or aggregate, holds land by a certain divine service; as, to say prayers on a certain day in every year, "or to distribute in almes to an hundred poore men an hundred pence at such a day." Litt. § 137.

TENURE OF OFFICE. See TENURE.

TERCE. In Scotch law. Dower; a widow's right of dower, or a right to a life-estate in a third part of the lands of which her husband died seised.

TERCER. In Scotch law. A widow that possesses the third part of her husband's land, as her legal jointure. 1 Kames, Eq. pref.

TERM. A word or phrase; an expression; particularly one which possesses a fixed and known meaning in some science, art, or profession.

In the civil law. A space of time granted to a debtor for discharging his obligation. Poth. Obl. pt. 2, c. 3, art. 3, § 1. Civil Code La. art. 2048.

In estates. "Term" signifies the bounds, limitation, or extent of time for which an estate is granted; as when a man holds an estate for any limited or specific number of years, which is called his "term," and he himself is called, with reference to the term he so holds, the "termor," or "tenant of the term."

Of court. The word "term," when used with reference to a court, signifies the space of time during which the court holds a session. A *session* signifies the time during the term when the court sits for the transaction of business, and the session commences when the court convenes for the term, and continues until final adjournment, either before or at the expiration of the term. The *term* of the court is the time prescribed by law during which it may be in *session*. The *session* of the court is the time of its actual sitting. 19 Tex. App. 433.

TERM ATTENDANT ON THE INHERITANCE. See ATTENDANT TERMS.

TERM FEE. In English practice. A certain sum which a solicitor is entitled to charge to his client, and the client to recover, if successful, from the unsuccessful party; payable for every term in which any proceedings subsequent to the summons shall take place. Wharton.

TERM FOR DELIBERATING. By "term for deliberating" is understood the time given to the beneficiary heir, to examine if it be for his interest to accept or reject the succession which has fallen to him. Civil Code La. art. 1033.

TERM FOR YEARS. An *estate for years* and the *time* during which such estate is to be held are each called a "term;" hence the term may expire before the time, as by a surrender. Co. Litt. 45.

TERM IN GROSS. A term of years is said to be either in gross (outstanding) or attendant upon the inheritance. It is outstanding, or in gross, when it is unattached or disconnected from the estate or inheritance, as where it is in the hands of some third party having no interest in the inheritance; it is attendant, when vested in some trustee in trust for the owner of the inheritance. Brown.

TERM OF LEASE. The word "term," when used in connection with a lease, means the period which is granted for the lessee to occupy the premises, and does not include the time between the making of the lease and the tenant's entry. 5 N. Y. 463.

TERM PROBATORY. The period of time allowed to the promoter of an ecclesiastical suit to produce his witnesses, and prove the facts on which he rests his case. Coote, Ecc. Pr. 240, 241.

TERM TO CONCLUDE. In English ecclesiastical practice. An appointment by the judge of a time at which both parties are understood to renounce all further exhibits and allegations.

TERM TO PROPOUND ALL THINGS. In English ecclesiastical practice. An appointment by the judge of a time at which both parties are to exhibit all the acts and instruments which make for their respective causes.

TERMES DE LA LEY. Terms of the law. The name of a lexicon of the law French words and other technicalities of legal language in old times.

TERMINABLE PROPERTY. This name is sometimes given to property of such a nature that its duration is not perpetual or indefinite, but is limited or liable to terminate upon the happening of an event or the expiration of a fixed term; *e. g.*, a leasehold, a life-annuity, etc.

TERMINATING BUILDING SOCIETIES. Societies, in England, where the members commence their monthly contributions on a particular day, and continue to pay them until the realization of shares to a given amount for each member, by the advance of the capital of the society to such members as required it, and the payment of interest as well as principal by them, so as to insure such realization within a given period of years. They have been almost superseded by permanent building societies. Wharton.

TERMINER. L. Fr. To determine. See OYER AND TERMINER.

TERMINI. Lat. Ends; bounds; limiting or terminating points.

TERMINO. In Spanish law. A common; common land. Common because of vicinage. White, New Recop. b. 2, tit. 1, c. 6, § 1, note.

TERMINUM. A day given to a defendant. Spelman.

TERMINUM QUI PRETERIIT, WRIT OF ENTRY AD. A writ which lay for the reversioner, when the possession was withheld by the lessee, or a stranger, after the determination of a lease for years. Brown.

TERMINUS. Boundary; a limit, either of space or time.

The phrases "*terminus a quo*" and "*terminus ad quem*" are used, respectively, to designate the starting point and terminating point of a private way. In the case of a street, road, or railway, either end may be, and commonly is, referred to as the "terminus."

Terminus annorum certus debet esse et determinatus. Co. Litt. 45. A term of years ought to be certain and determinate.

Terminus et feodum non possunt constare simul in una eademque persona. Plowd. 29. A term and the fee cannot both be in one and the same person at the same time.

TERMINUS HOMINIS. In English ecclesiastical practice. A time for the determination of appeals, shorter than the *terminus juris*, appointed by the judge. Hallifax, Civil Law, b. 3, c. 11, no. 36.

TERMINUS JURIS. In English ecclesiastical practice. The time of one or two years, allowed by law for the determination of appeals. Hallifax, Civil Law, b. 3, c. 11, no. 38.

TERMOR. He that holds lands or tenements for a term of years or life. But we generally confine the application of the word to a person entitled for a term of years. Mozley & Whitley.

TERMS. In the law of contracts. Conditions; propositions stated or promises made which, when assented to or accepted by another, settle the contract and bind the parties. Webster.

TERMS, TO BE UNDER. A party is said to be *under terms* when an indulgence is granted to him by the court in its discretion, on certain conditions. Thus, when an injunction is granted *ex parte*, the party obtaining it is put *under terms* to abide by such order as to damages as the court may make at the hearing. Mozley & Whitley.

TERRA. Lat. Earth; soil; arable land. Kennett, Gloss.

TERRA AFFIRMATA. Land let to farm.

TERRA BOSCALIS. Woody land.

TERRA CULTA. Cultivated land.

TERRA DEBILIS. Weak or barren land.

TERRA DOMINICA, or INDOMINICATA. The demesne land of a manor. Cowell.

TERRA EXCULTABILIS. Land which may be plowed. Mon. Ang. i. 426.

TERRA EXTENDENDA. A writ addressed to an escheator, etc., that he inquire and find out the true yearly value of any land, etc., by the oath of twelve men, and to certify the extent into the chancery. Reg. Writs, 293.

TERRA FRUSCA, or FRISCA. Fresh land, not lately plowed. Cowell.

TERRA HYDATA. Land subject to the payment of hydage. Selden.

TERRA LUCRABILIS. Land gained from the sea or inclosed out of a waste. Cowell.

Terra manens vacua occupanti conceditur. 1 Sid. 347. Land lying unoccupied is given to the first occupant.

TERRA NORMANORUM. Land held by a Norman. Paroch. Antiq. 197.

TERRA NOVA. Land newly converted from wood ground or arable. Cowell.

TERRA PUTURA. Land in forests, held by the tenure of furnishing food to the keepers therein. 4 Inst. 307.

TERRA SABULOSA. Gravelly or sandy ground.

TERRA SALICA. In Salic law. The land of the house; the land within that inclosure which belonged to a German house. No portion of the inheritance of Salic land passes to a woman, but this the male sex acquires; that is, the sons succeed in that inheritance. Lex Salic. tit. 62, § 6.

TERRA TESTAMENTALIS. Gavelkind land, being disposable by will. Spelman.

TERRA VESTITA. Land sown with corn. Cowell.

TERRA WAINABILIS. Tillable land. Cowell.

TERRA WARRENATA. Land that has the liberty of free-warren.

TERRÆ DOMINICALES REGIS. The demesne lands of the crown.

TERRAGE. In old English law. A kind of tax or charge on land; a boon or duty of plowing, reaping, etc. Cowell.

TERRAGES. An exemption from all uncertain services. Cowell.

TERRARIUS. In old English law. A landholder.

TERRE-TENANT. He who is literally in the occupation or possession of the land, as distinguished from the owner out of possession. But, in a more technical sense, the person who is seised of the land, though not in actual occupancy of it. 4 Watts & S. 256; 1 Eden, 177.

TERRIER. In English law. A land-roll or survey of lands, containing the quantity of acres, tenants' names, and such like; and in the exchequer there is a terrier of all the glebe lands in England, made about 1338. In general, an ecclesiastical terrier contains a detail of the temporal possessions of the church in every parish. Cowell; Tomlins; Mozley & Whitley.

TERRIS BONIS ET CATALLIS REHABENDIS POST PURGATIONEM. A writ for a clerk to recover his lands, goods, and chattels, formerly seized, after he had cleared himself of the felony of which he was accused, and delivered to his ordinary to be purged. Reg. Orig.

TERRIS ET CATALLIS TENTIS ULTRA DEBITUM LEVATUM. A judicial writ for the restoring of lands or goods to a debtor who is distrained above the amount of the debt. Reg. Jud.

TERRIS LIBERANDIS. A writ that lay for a man convicted by attaint, to bring the record and process before the king, and take a fine for his imprisonment, and then to deliver to him his lands and tenements again, and release him of the strip and waste. Reg. Orig. 232. Also it was a writ for the delivery of lands to the heir, after homage and relief performed, or upon security taken that he should perform them. Id. 293.

TERRITORIAL, TERRITORIALITY. These terms are used to signify connection with, or limitation with reference to, a particular country or territory. Thus, "territorial law" is the correct expression for the law of a particular country or state, although "municipal law" is more common. "Territorial waters" are that part of the sea adjacent to the coast of a given country which is by international law deemed to be within the sovereignty of that country, so that its courts have jurisdiction over offenses committed on those waters, even by a person on board a foreign ship. Sweet.

TERRITORIAL COURTS. The courts established in the territories of the United States.

TERRITORY. A part of a country separated from the rest, and subject to a particular jurisdiction.

In American law. A portion of the United States, not within the limits of any state, which has not yet been admitted as a state of the Union, but is organized, with a separate legislature, and with executive and judicial officers appointed by the president.

TERRITORY OF A JUDGE. The territorial jurisdiction of a judge; the bounds, or district, within which he may lawfully exercise his judicial authority.

TERROR. Alarm; fright; dread; the state of mind induced by the apprehension of hurt from some hostile or threatening event or manifestation; fear caused by the appearance of danger. In an indictment for riot, it must be charged that the acts done were "to the *terror* of the people."

TERTIA DENUNCIATIO. Lat. In old English law. Third publication or proclamation of intended marriage.

TERTIUS INTERVENIENS. Lat. In the civil law. A third person intervening; a third person who comes in between the parties to a suit; one who interpleads. Gilbert's Forum Rom. 47.

TEST. To bring one to a trial and examination, or to ascertain the truth or the quality or fitness of a thing.

Something by which to ascertain the truth respecting another thing.

TEST ACT. The statute 25 Car. II. c. 2, which directed all civil and military officers to take the oaths of allegiance and supremacy, and make the declaration against transubstantiation, within six months after their admission, and also within the same time receive the sacrament according to the usage of the Church of England, under penalty of £500 and disability to hold the office. 4 Bl. Comm. 58, 59. This was abolished by St. 9 Geo. IV. c. 17, so far as concerns receiving the sacrament, and a new form of declaration was substituted.

TEST ACTION. An action selected out of a considerable number of suits, concurrently depending in the same court, brought by several plaintiffs against the same defendant, or by one plaintiff against different defendants, all similar in their circumstances, and embracing the same questions, and to be supported by the same evidence, the selected action to go first to trial, (under an order of court equivalent to consolidation,) and its decision to serve as a *test* of the right of recovery in the others, all parties agreeing to be bound by the result of the test action.

TEST OATH. An oath required to be taken as a criterion of the fitness of the person to fill a public or political office; but particularly an oath of fidelity and allegiance (past or present) to the established government.

TESTA DE NEVIL. An ancient and authentic record in two volumes, in the custody of the queen's remembrancer in the exchequer, said to be compiled by John de Nevil, a justice itinerant, in the eighteenth and twenty-fourth years of Henry III. Cowell. These volumes were printed in 1807, under the authority of the commissioners of the public records, and contain an account of fees held either immediately of the king or of others who held of the king *in capite;* fees holden in frankalmoigne; serjeanties holden of the king; widows and heiresses of tenants *in capite*, whose marriages were in the gift of the king; churches in the gift of the king; escheats, and sums paid for scutages and aids, especially within the county of Hereford. Cowell; Wharton.

TESTABLE. A person is said to be testable when he has capacity to make a will; a man of twenty-one years of age and of sane mind is testable.

TESTACY. The state or condition of leaving a will at one's death. Opposed to "intestacy."

TESTAMENT. A disposition of personal property to take place after the owner's decease, according to his desire and direction.

A testament is the act of last will, clothed with certain solemnities, by which the testator disposes of his property, either universally, or by universal title, or by particular title. Civil Code La. art. 1571.

Strictly speaking, the term denotes only a will of personal property; a will of land not being called a "testament." The word "testament" is now seldom used, except in the heading of a formal will, which usually begins: "This is the last will and testament of me, A. B.," etc. Sweet.

Testament is the true declaration of a man's last will as to that which he would have to be done after his death. It is compounded, according to Justinian, from *testatio mentis;* but the better opinion is that it is a simple word formed from the Latin *testor*, and not a compound word. Mozley & Whitley.

Testamenta cum duo inter se pugnantia reperiuntur, ultimum ratum est; sic est, cum duo inter se pugnantia reperiuntur in eodem testamento. Co. Litt. 112. When two conflicting wills are found, the last prevails; so it is when two conflicting clauses occur in the same will.

Testamenta latissimam interpretationem habere debent. Jenk. Cent. 81. Wills ought to have the broadest interpretation.

TESTAMENTARY. Pertaining to a will or testament; as *testamentary* causes. Derived from, founded on, or appointed by a testament or will; as a *testamentary* guardian, letters *testamentary*, etc.

A paper, instrument, document, gift, appointment, etc., is said to be "testamentary" when it is written or made so as not to take effect until after the death of the person making it, and to be revocable and retain the property under his control during his life, although he may have believed that it would operate as an instrument of a different character. Sweet.

TESTAMENTARY CAPACITY. That measure of mental ability which is recognized in law as sufficient for the making a will.

TESTAMENTARY CAUSES. In English law. Causes or matters relating to the probate of wills, the granting of administrations, and the suing for legacies, of which the ecclesiastical courts have jurisdiction. 3 Bl. Comm. 95, 98.

Testamentary causes are causes relating to the validity and execution of wills. The phrase is generally confined to those causes which were formerly matters of ecclesiastical jurisdiction, and are now dealt with by the court of probate. Mozley & Whitley.

TESTAMENTARY GUARDIAN. A guardian appointed by the last will of a father for the person and real and personal estate of his child until the latter arrives of full age. 1 Bl. Comm. 462; 2 Kent, Comm. 224.

TESTAMENTARY PAPER. An instrument in the nature of a will; an unprobated will; a paper writing which is of the character of a will, though not formally such, and which, if allowed as a testament, will have the effect of a will upon the devolution and distribution of property.

TESTAMENTI FACTIO. Lat. In the civil law. The ceremony of making a testament, either as testator, heir, or witness.

TESTAMENTUM. Lat. In the civil law. A testament; a will, or last will.

In old English law. A testament or will; a disposition of property made in contemplation of death. Bract. fol. 60.

A general name for any instrument of conveyance, including deeds and charters, and so called either because it furnished written *testimony* of the conveyance, or because it was authenticated by witnesses, (*testes.*) Spelman.

Testamentum est voluntatis nostræ justa sententia, de eo quod quis post mortem suam fieri velit. A testament is the just expression of our will concerning that which any one wishes done after his death, [or, as Blackstone translates, "the legal declaration of a man's intentions which he wills to be performed after his death."] Dig. 28, 1, 1; 2 Bl. Comm. 499.

Testamentum, i. e., testatio mentis, facta nullo præsente metu periculi, sed cogitatione mortalitatis. Co. Litt. 322. A testament, *i. e.*, the witnessing of one's intention, made under no present fear of danger, but in expectancy of death.

TESTAMENTUM INOFFICIOSUM. Lat. In the civil law. An inofficious testament, (*q. v.*)

Testamentum omne morte consummatur. Every will is perfected by death. A will speaks from the time of death only. Co. Litt. 232.

TESTARI. Lat. In the civil law. To testify; to attest; to declare, publish, or make known a thing before witnesses. To make a will. Calvin.

TESTATE. One who has made a will; one who dies leaving a will.

TESTATION. Witness; evidence.

TESTATOR. One who makes or has made a testament or will; one who dies leaving a will. This term is borrowed from the civil law. Inst. 2, 14, 5, 6.

Testatoris ultima voluntas est perimplenda secundum veram intentionem suam. Co. Litt. 322. The last will of a testator is to be thoroughly fulfilled according to his real intention.

TESTATRIX. A woman who makes a will; a woman who dies leaving a will; a female testator.

TESTATUM. **In practice.** When a writ of execution has been directed to the sheriff of a county, and he returns that the defendant is not found in his bailiwick, or that he has no goods there, as the case may be, then a second writ, reciting this former writ and the sheriff's answer to the same, may be directed to the sheriff of some other county wherein the defendant is supposed to be, or to have goods, commanding him to execute the writ as it may require; and this second writ is called a "*testatum*" writ, from the words with which it concludes, viz.: "Whereupon, on behalf of the said plaintiff, *it is testified* in our said court that the said defendant is [or has goods, etc.] within your bailiwick."

In conveyancing. That part of a deed which commences with the words, "This indenture witnesseth."

TESTATUM WRIT. In practice. A writ containing a *testatum* clause; such as a *testatum capias*, a *testatum fi. fa.*, and a *testatum ca. sa.* See TESTATUM.

TESTATUS. Lat. In the civil law. Testate; one who has made a will. Dig. 50, 17, 7.

TESTE MEIPSO. Lat. In old English law and practice. A solemn formula of attestation by the sovereign, used at the conclusion of charters, and other public instruments, and also of original writs out of chancery. Spelman.

TESTE OF A WRIT. In practice. The concluding clause, commencing with the word "Witness," etc. A writ which bears the teste is sometimes said to be *tested*.

"Teste" is a word commonly used in the last part of every writ, wherein the date is contained, beginning with the words, "*Teste meipso,*" meaning the sovereign, if the writ be an original writ, or be issued in the name of the sovereign; but, if the writ be a judicial writ, then the word "Teste" is followed by the name of the chief judge of the court in which the action is brought, or, in case of a vacancy of such office, in the name of the senior puisne judge. Mozley & Whitley.

TESTED. To be tested is to bear the teste, (*q. v.*)

TESTES. Lat. Witnesses.

Testes ponderantur, non numerantur. Witnesses are weighed, not numbered. That is, in case of a conflict of evidence, the truth is to be sought by weighing the credibility of the respective witnesses, not by the mere numerical preponderance on one side or the other.

Testes qui postulat debet dare eis sumptus competentes. Whosoever demands witnesses must find them in competent provision.

TESTES, TRIAL PER. A trial had before a judge without the intervention of a jury, in which the judge is left to form in his own breast his sentence upon the credit of the witnesses examined; but this mode of trial, although it was common in the civil law, was seldom resorted to in the practice of the common law, but it is now becoming common when each party waives his right to a trial by jury. Brown.

Testibus deponentibus in pari numero, dignioribus est credendum. Where the witnesses who testify are in equal number, [on both sides,] the more worthy are to be believed. 4 Inst. 279.

TESTIFY. To bear witness; to give evidence as a witness; to make a solemn declaration, under oath or affirmation, in a judicial inquiry, for the purpose of establishing or proving some fact.

Testimonia ponderanda sunt, non numeranda. Evidence is to be weighed, not enumerated.

TESTIMONIAL. Besides its ordinary meaning of a written recommendation to character, "testimonial" has a special meaning, under St. 39 Eliz. c. 17, § 3, passed in 1597, under which it signified a certificate under the hand of a justice of the peace, testifying the place and time when and where a soldier or mariner landed, and the place of his dwelling or birth, unto which he was to pass, and a convenient time limited for his passage. Every idle and wandering soldier or mariner not having such a testimonial, or willfully exceeding for above fourteen days the time limited thereby, or forging or counterfeiting such testimonial, was to suffer death as a felon, without benefit of clergy. This act was repealed, in 1812, by St. 52 Geo. III. c. 31. Mozley & Whitley.

TESTIMONIAL PROOF. In the civil law. Proof by the evidence of witnesses, *i. e.*, parol evidence, as distinguished from proof by written instruments, which is called "literal" proof.

TESTIMONIES. In Spanish law. An attested copy of an instrument by a notary.

TESTIMONIUM CLAUSE. In conveyancing. That clause of a deed or instrument with which it concludes: "In witness whereof, the parties to these presents have hereunto set their hands and seals."

TESTIMONY. Evidence of a witness; evidence given by a witness, under oath or affirmation; as distinguished from evidence derived from writings, and other sources.

Testimony is not synonymous with *evidence*. It is but a species, a class, or kind of evidence. Testimony is the evidence given by witnesses. Evidence is whatever may be given to the jury as tending to prove a case. It includes the testimony of witnesses, documents, admissions of parties, etc. 13 Ind. 389. See EVIDENCE.

TESTIS. Lat. A witness; one who gives evidence in court, or who witnesses a document.

Testis de visu præponderat aliis. 4 Inst. 279. An eye-witness is preferred to others.

Testis lupanaris sufficit ad factum in lupanari. Moore, 817. A lewd person is a sufficient witness to an act committed in a brothel.

Testis nemo in sua causa esse potest. No one can be a witness in his own cause.

Testis oculatus unus plus valet quam auriti decem. 4 Inst. 279. One eye-witness is worth more than ten ear-witnesses.

TESTMOIGNE. An old law French term, denoting evidence or testimony.

Testmoignes ne poent testifier le negative, mes l'affirmative. Witnesses cannot testify to a negative; they must testify to an affirmative. 4 Inst. 279.

TEST-PAPER. In practice. A paper or instrument shown to a jury as evidence. A term used in the Pennsylvania courts. 7 Pa. St. 428.

TEXT-BOOK. A legal treatise which lays down principles or collects decisions on any branch of the law.

TEXTUS ROFFENSIS. In old English law. The Rochester text. An ancient manuscript containing many of the Saxon laws, and the rights, customs, tenures, etc., of the church of Rochester, drawn up by Ernulph, bishop of that see from A. D. 1114 to 1124. Cowell.

THANAGE OF THE KING. A certain part of the king's land or property, of which the ruler or governor was called "thane." Cowell.

THANE. An Anglo-Saxon nobleman; an old title of honor, perhaps equivalent to "baron." There were two orders of thanes, —the king's thanes and the ordinary thanes. Soon after the Conquest this name was disused. Cowell.

THANELANDS. Such lands as were granted by charter of the Saxon kings to their thanes with all immunities, except from the *trinoda necessitas*. Cowell.

THANESHIP. The office and dignity of a thane; the seigniory of a thane.

That which I may defeat by my entry I make good by my confirmation. Co. Litt. 300.

THAVIES INN. An inn of chancery. See INNS OF CHANCERY.

THE. An article which particularizes the subject spoken of. "Grammatical niceties should not be resorted to without necessity; but it would be extending liberality to an unwarrantable length to confound the articles 'a' and 'the.' The most unlettered persons understand that 'a' is indefinite, but 'the' refers to a certain object." Per Tilghman, C. J., 2 Bin. 516.

The fund which has received the benefit should make the satisfaction. 4 Bouv. Inst. no. 3730.

THEATER. Any edifice used for the purpose of dramatic or operatic or other representations, plays, or performances, for admission to which entrance-money is received, not including halls rented or used occasionally for concerts or theatrical representations. Act Cong. July 13, 1866, § 9, (14 St. at Large, 126.)

THEFT. An unlawful felonious taking away of another man's movable and personal goods against the will of the owner. Jacob.

Theft is the fraudulent taking of corporeal personal property belonging to another, from his possession, or from the possession of some person holding the same for him, without his consent, with intent to deprive the owner of the value of the same, and to appropriate it to the use or benefit of the person taking. 1 Tex. App. 65.

In Scotch law. The secret and felonious abstraction of the property of another for sake of lucre, without his consent. Alis. Crim. Law, 250.

THEFT-BOTE. The offense committed by a party who, having been robbed and knowing the felon, takes back his goods again, or receives other amends, upon an agreement not to prosecute.

Theft-bote est emenda furti capta, sine consideratione curiæ domini regis. 3 Inst. 134. Theft-bote is the paying money to have goods stolen returned, without having any respect for the court of the king.

THELONIO IRRATIONABILI HABENDO. A writ that formerly lay for him that had any part of the king's demesne in fee-farm, to recover reasonable toll of the king's tenants there, if his demesne had been accustomed to be tolled. Reg. Orig. 87.

THELONIUM. An abolished writ for citizens or burgesses to assert their right to exemption from toll. Fitzh. Nat. Brev. 226.

THELONMANNUS. The toll-man or officer who receives toll. Cowell.

THELUSSON ACT. The statute 39 & 40 Geo. III. c. 98, which restricted accumulations to a term of twenty-one years from the testator's death. It was passed in consequence of litigation over the will of one Thelusson.

THEME. In Saxon law. The power of having jurisdiction over naifs or villeins, with their suits or offspring, lands, goods, and chattels. Co. Litt. 116*a*.

THEMMAGIUM. A duty or acknowledgment paid by inferior tenants in respect of theme or team. Cowell.

THEN. This word, as an adverb, means "at that time," referring to a time specified, either past or future. It has no power in itself to fix a time. It simply refers to a time already fixed. 16 S. C. 329. It may also denote a contingency, and be equivalent to "in that event." 20 N. J. Law, 505.

THENCE. In surveying, and in descriptions of land by courses and distances, this word, preceding each course given, imports that the following course is continuous with the one before it. 141 Mass. 66, 6 N. E. Rep. 702.

THEOCRACY. Government of a state by the immediate direction of God, (or by the assumed direction of a supposititious divinity,) or the state thus governed.

THEODEN. In Saxon law. A husbandman or inferior tenant; an under-thane. Cowell.

THEODOSIAN CODE. See CODEX THEODOSIANUS.

THEOF. In Saxon law. Offenders who joined in a body of seven to commit depredations. Wharton.

THEOWES, THEOWMEN, or THEWS. In feudal law. Slaves, captives, or bondmen. Spel. Feuds, c. 5.

THEREUPON. At once; without interruption; without delay or lapse of time. 133 Mass. 205.

THESAURER. Treasurer. 3 State Tr. 691.

THESAURUS, THESAURIUM. The treasury; a treasure.

THESAURUS ABSCONDITUS. In old English law. Treasure hidden or buried. Spelman.

Thesaurus competit domino regi, et non domino liberatis, nisi sit per verba specialia. Fitz. Coron. 281. A treasure belongs to the king, and not to the lord of a liberty, unless it be through special words.

THESAURUS INVENTUS. In old English law. Treasure found; treasure-trove. Bract. fols. 119*b*, 122.

Thesaurus inventus est vetus dispositio pecuniæ, etc., cujus non extat modo memoria, adeo ut jam dominum non habeat. 3 Inst. 132. Treasure-trove is an ancient hiding of money, etc., of which no recollection exists, so that it now has no owner.

Thesaurus non competit regi, nisi quando nemo scit qui abscondit thesaurum. 3 Inst. 132. Treasure does not belong to the king, unless no one knows who hid it.

Thesaurus regis est vinculum pacis et bellorum nervus. Godb. 293. The king's treasure is the bond of peace and the sinews of war.

THESMOTHETE. A law-maker; a lawgiver.

THETHINGA. A tithing.

THIA. Lat. In the civil and old European law. An aunt.

THIEF. One who has been guilty of larceny or theft. The term covers both compound and simple larceny. 1 Hill, 25.

THINGS. The most general denomination of the subjects of property, as contradistinguished from *persons*. 2 Bl. Comm. 16.

The word "estate" in general is applicable to anything of which riches or fortune may consist. The word is likewise relative to the word "things," which is the second object of jurisprudence, the rules of which are applicable to persons, things, and actions. Civil Code La. art. 448.

Such permanent objects, not being persons, as are sensible, or perceptible through the senses. Aust. Jur. § 452.

A "thing" is the object of a right; *i. e.*, whatever is treated by the law as the object over which one person exercises a right, and with reference to which another person lies under a duty. Holl. Jur. 83.

Things are the subjects of dominion or property, as distinguished from *persons*. They are distributed into three kinds: (1) Things real or immovable, comprehending lands, tenements, and hereditaments; (2) things personal or movable, comprehending goods and chattels; and (3) things mixed, partaking of the characteristics of the two former, as a title-deed, a term for years. The civil law divided things into corporeal (*tangi possunt*) and incorporeal (*tangi non possunt.*) Wharton.

Things accessory are of the nature of the principal. Finch, Law, b. 1, c. 3, n. 25.

Things are construed according to that which was the cause thereof. Finch, Law, b. 1, c. 3, n. 4.

Things are dissolved as they be contracted. Finch, Law, b. 1, c. 3, n. 7.

Things grounded upon an ill and void beginning cannot have a good perfection. Finch, Law, b. 1, c. 3, n. 8.

THINGS IN ACTION. A thing in action is a right to recover money or other personal property by a judicial proceeding. Civil Code Cal. § 953. See CHOSE IN ACTION.

Things in action, entry, or re-entry cannot be granted over. 19 N. Y. 100, 103.

Things incident cannot be severed. Finch, Law, b. 3, c. 1, n. 12.

Things incident pass by the grant of the principal. 25 Barb. 284, 310.

Things incident shall pass by the grant of the principal, but not the principal by the grant of the incident. Co. Litt. 152*a*, 151*b*; Broom, Max. 433.

THINGS PERSONAL. Goods, money, and all other movables, which may attend the owner's person wherever he thinks proper to go. 2 Bl. Comm. 16. Things personal consist of goods, money, and all other movables, and of such rights and profits as relate to movables. 1 Steph. Comm. 156.

THINGS REAL. Such things as are permanent, fixed, and immovable, which cannot be carried out of their place; as lands and tenements. 2 Bl. Comm. 16. This definition has been objected to as not embracing incorporeal rights. Mr. Stephen defines *things real* to "consist of things substantial and immovable, and of the rights and profits annexed to or issuing out of these." 1 Steph. Comm. 156. *Things real* are otherwise described to consist of lands, tenements, and hereditaments.

THINGUS. In Saxon law. A thane or nobleman; knight or freeman. Cowell.

THINK. In a special finding by a jury, this word is equivalent to "believe," and expresses the conclusion of the jury with sufficient positiveness. 59 Iowa, 414, 13 N. W. Rep. 424.

THIRD-NIGHT-AWN-HINDE. By the laws of St. Edward the Confessor, if any man lay a third night in an inn, he was called a "third-night-awn-hinde," and his host was answerable for him if he committed any offense. The first night, forman-night, or uncuth, (unknown,) he was reckoned a stranger; the second night, twa-night, a guest; and the third night, an awn-hinde, a domestic. Bract. l. 3.

THIRD PARTIES. A term used to include all persons who are not parties to the contract, agreement, or instrument of writing by which their interest in the thing conveyed is sought to be affected. 1 Mart. (N. S.) 384.

THIRD PENNY. A portion (one-third) of the amount of all fines and other profits of the county court, which was reserved for the earl, in the early days when the jurisdiction of those courts was extensive, the remainder going to the king.

THIRDBOROUGH, or THIRDBOROW. An under-constable. Cowell.

THIRDINGS. The third part of the corn growing on the land, due to the lord for a heriot on the death of his tenant, within the manor of Turfat, in Hereford. Blount.

THIRDS. The designation, in colloquial language, of that portion of a decedent's personal estate (one-third) which goes to the widow where there is also a child or children.

THIRLAGE. In Scotch law. A servitude by which lands are astricted or "thirled" to a particular mill, to which the possessors must carry the grain of the growth of the astricted lands to be ground, for the payment of such duties as are either expressed or implied in the constitution of the right. Ersk. Inst. 2, 9, 18.

THIRTY-NINE ARTICLES. See ARTICLES OF RELIGION.

THIS. When "this" and "that" refer to different things before expressed, "this" refers to the thing last mentioned, and "that" to the thing first mentioned. 66 Pa. St. 251.

THIS DAY SIX MONTHS. Fixing "this day six months," or "three months," for the next stage of a bill, is one of the modes in which the house of lords and the house of commons reject bills of which they disapprove. A bill rejected in this manner cannot be reintroduced in the same session. Wharton.

THISTLE-TAKE. It was a custom within the manor of Halton, in Chester, that if, in driving beasts over a common, the driver permitted them to graze or take but a thistle, he should pay a halfpenny a-piece to the lord of the fee. And at Fiskerton, in Nottinghamshire, by ancient custom, if a native or a cottager killed a swine above a year old, he paid to the lord a penny, which purchase of leave to kill a hog was also called "thistle-take." Cowell.

THOROUGHFARE. The term means, according to its derivation, a street or passage *through* which one can *fare*, (travel;) that is, a street or highway affording an unobstructed exit at each end into another street or public passage. If the passage is closed at one end, admitting no exit there, it is called a "*cul de sac.*"

THRAVE. In old English law. A measure of corn or grain, consisting of twenty-four sheaves or four shocks, six sheaves to every shock. Cowell.

THREAD. A middle line; a line running through the middle of a stream or road. See FILUM; FILUM AQUÆ; FILUM VIÆ.

THREAT. In criminal law. A menace; a declaration of one's purpose or intention to work injury to the person, property, or rights of another.

A threat has been defined to be any menace of such a nature and extent as to unsettle the mind of the person on whom it operates, and to take away from his acts that free, voluntary action which alone constitutes consent. Abbott.

THREATENING LETTERS. Sending threatening letters is the name of the offense of sending letters containing threats of the kinds recognized by the statute as criminal.

THREE-DOLLAR PIECE. A gold coin of the United States, of the value of three dollars; authorized by the seventh section of the act of Feb. 21, 1853.

THRENGES. Vassals, but not of the lowest degree; those who held lands of the chief lord.

THRITHING. In Saxon and old English law. The third part of a county; a division of a county consisting of three or more hundreds. Cowell. Corrupted to the modern "riding," which is still used in Yorkshire. 1 Bl. Comm. 116.

THROAT. In medical jurisprudence. The front or anterior part of the neck. Where one was indicted for murder by "cutting the throat" of the deceased, it was held that the word "throat" was not to be confined to that part of the neck which is scientifically so called, but must be taken in its common acceptation. 6 Car. & P. 401.

THROUGH. This word is sometimes equivalent to "over;" as in a statute in reference to laying out a road "through" certain grounds. 119 Ill. 147, 7 N. E. Rep. 627.

THROW OUT. To ignore, (a bill of indictment.)

THRUSTING. Within the meaning of a criminal statute, "thrusting" is not necessarily an attack with a pointed weapon; it means pushing or driving with force, whether the point of the weapon be sharp or not. 33 La. Ann. 1224.

THRYMSA. A Saxon coin worth fourpence. Du Fresne.

THUDE-WEALD. A woodward, or person that looks after a wood.

THURINGIAN CODE. One of the "barbarian codes," as they are termed; supposed by Montesquieu to have been given by Theodoric, king of Austrasia, to the Thuringians, who were his subjects. Esprit des Lois, lib. 28, c. 1.

THWERTNICK. In old English law. The custom of giving entertainments to a sheriff, etc., for three nights.

TICK. A colloquial expression for credit or trust; credit given for goods purchased.

TICKET. In contracts. A slip of paper containing a certificate that the person to whom it is issued, or the holder, is entitled to some right or privilege therein mentioned or described; such, for example, are railroad tickets, theater tickets, pawn tickets, lottery tickets, etc.

In election law. A ticket is a paper upon which is written or printed the names of the persons for whom the elector intends to vote, with a designation of the office to which each person so named is intended by him to be chosen. Pol. Code Cal. § 1185.

TICKET OF LEAVE. In English law. A license or permit given to a convict, as a reward for good conduct, particularly in the penal settlements, which allows him to go at large, and labor for himself, before the expiration of his sentence, subject to certain specific conditions, and revocable upon subsequent misconduct.

TICKET-OF-LEAVE MAN. A convict who has obtained a ticket of leave.

TIDAL. In order that a river may be "tidal" at a given spot, it may not be necessary that the water should be salt, but the spot must be one where the tide, in the ordinary and regular course of things, flows and reflows. 8 Q. B. Div. 630.

TIDE. The ebb and flow of the sea.

TIDE-WATER. Water which falls and rises with the ebb and flow of the tide. The term is not usually applied to the open sea, but to coves, bays, rivers, etc.

TIDESMEN, in English law, are certain officers of the custom-house, appointed to watch or attend upon ships till the customs are paid; and they are so called because they go aboard the ships at their arrival in the mouth of the Thames, and come up with the tide. Jacob.

TIE, *v.* To bind. "The parson is not *tied* to find the parish clerk." 1 Leon. 94.

TIE, *n.* When, at an election, neither candidate receives a májority of the votes cast, but each has the same number, there is said to be a "tie." So when the number of votes cast in favor of any measure, in a legislative or deliberative body, is equal to the number cast against it.

TIEL. L. Fr. Such. *Nul tiel record,* no such record.

TIEMPO INHABIL. Span. A time of inability; a time when the person is not able to pay his debts, (when, for instance, he may not alienate property to the prejudice of his creditors.) The term is used in Louisiana. 3 Mart. (N. S.) 270; 4 Mart. (N. S.) 292.

TIERCE. L. Fr. Third. *Tierce mein,* third hand. Britt. c. 120.

TIERCE. A liquid measure, containing the third part of a pipe, or forty-two gallons.

TIGH. In old records. A close or inclosure; a croft. Cowell.

TIGHT. As colloquially applied to a note, bond, mortgage, lease, etc., this term signifies that the clauses providing the creditor's remedy in case of default (as, by foreclosure, execution, distress, etc.) are summary and stringent.

TIGNI IMMITTENDI. Lat. In the civil law. The name of a servitude which is the right of inserting a beam or timber from the wall of one house into that of a neighboring house, in order that it may rest on the latter, and that the wall of the latter may bear this weight. Wharton. See Dig. 8, 2, 36.

TIGNUM. A civil-law term for building material; timber.

TIHLER. In old Saxon law. An accusation.

TILLAGE. A place tilled or cultivated; land under cultivation, as opposed to lands lying fallow or in pasture.

TIMBER. Wood felled for building or other such like use. In a legal sense it generally means (in England) oak, ash, and elm, but in some parts of England, and generally in America, it is used in a wider sense, which is recognized by the law.

The term "timber," as used in commerce, refers generally only to large sticks of wood, squared or capable of being squared for building houses or vessels; and certain trees only having been formerly used for such purposes, namely, the oak, the ash, and the elm, they alone were recognized as timber trees. But the numerous uses to which wood has come to be applied, and the general employment of all kinds of trees for some valuable purpose, has wrought a change in the general acceptation of terms in connection therewith, and we find that Webster defines "timber" to be "that sort of wood which is proper for buildings or for tools, utensils, furniture, carriages, fences, ships, and the like." This would include all sorts of wood from which any useful articles may be made, or which may be used to advantage in any class of manufacture or construction. 14 Fed. Rep. 824.

TIMBER-TREES. Oak, ash, elm, in all places, and, by local custom, such other trees as are used in building. 2 Bl. Comm. 281. See TIMBER.

TIMBERLODE. A service by which tenants were bound to carry timber felled from the woods to the lord's house. Cowell.

TIME. The measure of duration.

The word is expressive both of a precise *point* or *terminus* and of an *interval* between two points.

In pleading. A point in or space of duration at or during which some fact is alleged to have been committed.

TIME-BARGAIN. In the language of the stock exchange, a time-bargain is an agreement to buy or sell stock at a future time, or within a fixed time, at a certain price. It is in reality nothing more than a bargain to pay differences.

TIME IMMEMORIAL. Time whereof the memory of a man is not to the contrary.

TIME OF MEMORY. In English law. Time commencing from the beginning of the reign of Richard I. 2 Bl. Comm. 31.

Lord Coke defines *time of memory* to be "when no man alive hath had any proof to the contrary, nor hath any conusance to the contrary." Co. Litt. 86*a*, 86*b*.

TIME OUT OF MEMORY. Time beyond memory; time out of mind; time to which memory does not extend.

TIME-POLICY. A policy of marine insurance in which the risk is limited, not to a given voyage, but to a certain fixed term or period of time.

TIME, REASONABLE. "Reasonable time" has never been held to be any determined number of days or years as applied to every case, like the statute of limitations, but must be decided in each case upon all the elements of it which affect that question. 91 U. S. 591.

TIME THE ESSENCE OF THE CONTRACT. A case in which "time is of the essence of the contract" is one where the parties evidently contemplated a punctual performance, at the precise time named, as vital to the agreement, and one of its essential elements. Time is *not* of the essence of the contract in any case where a moderate delay in performance would not be regarded as an absolute violation of the contract.

TIMOCRACY. An aristocracy of property; government by men of property who are possessed of a certain income.

Timores vani sunt æstimandi qui non cadunt in constantem virum. 7 Coke, 17. Fears which do not assail a resolute man are to be accounted vain.

TINBOUNDING is a custom regulating the manner in which tin is obtained from waste-land, or land which has formerly been waste-land, within certain districts in Cornwall and Devon. The custom is described in the leading case on the subject as follows: "Any person may enter on the waste-land of another, and may mark out by four corner boundaries a certain area. A written description of the plot of land so marked out with metes and bounds, and the name of the person, is recorded in the local stannaries court, and is proclaimed on three successive court-days. If no objection is sustained by any other person, the court awards a writ to the bailiff to deliver possession of the said 'bounds of tin-work' to the 'bounder,' who thereupon has the exclusive right to search for, dig, and take for his own use all tin and tin-ore within the inclosed limits, paying as a royalty to the owner of the waste a certain proportion of the produce under the name of 'toll-tin.'" 10 Q. B. 26, cited in Elton Commons, 113. The right of tinbounding is not a right of common, but is an interest in land, and, in Devonshire, a corporeal hereditament. In Cornwall tin bounds are personal estate. Sweet.

TINEL. L. Fr. A place where justice was administered. Kelham.

TINEMAN. Sax. In old forest law. A petty officer of the forest who had the care of vert and venison by night, and performed other servile duties.

TINET. In old records. Brush-wood and thorns for fencing and hedging. Cowell; Blount.

TINEWALD. The ancient parliament or annual convention in the Isle of Man, held upon Midsummer-day, at St. John's chapel. Cowell.

TINKERMEN. Fishermen who destroyed the young fry on the river Thames by nets and unlawful engines. Cowell.

TINNELLUS. In old Scotch law. The sea-mark; high-water mark. Tide-mouth. Skene.

TINPENNY. A tribute paid for the liberty of digging in tin-mines. Cowell.

TINSEL OF THE FEU. In Scotch law. The loss of the feu, from allowing two years of feu duty to run into the third unpaid. Bell.

TIPPLING HOUSE. A place where intoxicating drinks are sold in drams or small quantities to be drunk on the premises, and where men resort for drinking purposes. See 47 Ill. 370.

TIPSTAFF. In English law. An officer appointed by the marshal of the king's bench to attend upon the judges with a kind of rod or staff tipped with silver, who take into their custody all prisoners, either committed or turned over by the judges at their chambers, etc. Jacob.

In American law. An officer appointed by the court, whose duty is to wait upon the court when it is in session, preserve order, serve process, guard juries, etc.

TITHE RENT-CHARGE. A rent-charge established in lieu of tithes, under the tithes commutation act, 1836, (St. 6 & 7 Wm. IV. c. 71.) As between landlord and tenant, the tenant paying the tithe rent-charge is entitled, in the absence of express agreement, to deduct it from his rent, under section 70 of the above act. And a tithe rent-charge unpaid is recoverable by distress as rent in arrear. Mozley & Whitley.

TITHE-FREE. Exempted from the payment of tithes.

TITHER. One who gathers tithes.

TITHES. In English law. The *tenth* part of the increase, yearly arising and renewing from the profits of lands, the stock upon lands, and the personal industry of the inhabitants. 2 Bl. Comm. 24. A species of incorporeal hereditament, being an ecclesiastical inheritance collateral to the estate of the land, and due only to an ecclesiastical person by ecclesiastical law. 1 Crabb, Real Prop. § 133.

Prædial tithes are such as arise immediately from the ground; as grain of all sorts, hay, wood, fruits, and herbs. *Mixed tithes* are such as do not arise immediately from the ground, but from things nourished by the ground; as calves, lambs, chickens, colts, milk, cheese, and eggs. *Personal tithes* are such as arise by the industry of man, being the tenth part of the clear gain, after charges deducted. 1 Crabb, Real Prop. § 133.

TITHING. One of the civil divisions of England, being a portion of that greater division called a "hundred." It was so called because ten freeholders with their families composed one. It is said that they were all knit together in one society, and bound to the king for the peaceable behavior of each other. In each of these societies there was one chief or principal person, who, from his office, was called "teothing-man," now "tithing-man." Brown.

TITHING-MAN. In Saxon law. This was the name of the head or chief of a decennary. In modern English law, he is the same as an under-constable or peace-officer.

In modern law. A constable. "After the introduction of justices of the peace, the offices of constable and *tithing-man* became so similar that we now regard them as precisely the same." Willc. Const. Introd.

In New England. A parish officer annually elected to preserve good order in the church during divine service, and to make complaint of any disorderly conduct. Webster.

TITHING-PENNY. In Saxon and old English law. Money paid to the sheriff by the several tithings of his county. Cowell.

TITIUS. In Roman law. A proper name, frequently used in designating an indefinite or fictitious person, or a person referred to by way of illustration. "Titius" and "Seius," in this use, correspond to "John Doe" and "Richard Roe," or to "A. B" and "C. D."

TITLE. The radical meaning of this word appears to be that of a mark, style, or designation; a distinctive appellation; the name by which anything is known. Thus, in the law of persons, a title is an appellation of dignity or distinction, a name denoting the social rank of the person bearing it; as "duke" or "count." So, in legislation, the title of a statute is the heading or preliminary part, furnishing the name by which the act is individually known. It is usually prefixed to the statute in the form of a brief summary of its contents; as "An act for the prevention of gaming." Again, the title of a patent is the short description of the invention, which is copied in the letters patent from the inventor's petition; *e. g.*, "a new and improved method of drying and preparing malt." Johns. Pat. Man. 90.

In the law of trade-marks, a title may become a subject of property; as one who has adopted a particular title for a newspaper, or other business enterprise, may, by long and prior user, or by compliance with statutory provisions as to registration and notice, acquire a right to be protected in the exclusive use of it. Abbott.

The title of a book, or any literary composition, is its name; that is, the heading or caption prefixed to it, and disclosing the distinctive appellation by which it is to be known. This usually comprises a brief description of its subject-matter and the name of its author.

"Title" is also used as the name of one of the subdivisions employed in many literary works, standing intermediate between the divisions denoted by the term "books" or "parts," and those designated as "chapters" and "sections."

In real property law. Title is the means whereby the owner of lands has the just possession of his property. Co. Litt. 345; 2 Bl. Comm. 195.

Title is the means whereby a person's right to property is established. Code Ga. 1882, § 2348.

Title may be defined generally to be the evidence of right which a person has to the possession of property. The word "title" certainly does not merely signify the right which a person has to the possession of property; because there are many instances in which a person may have the right to the possession of property, and at the same time have no title to the same. In its ordinary legal acceptation, however, it generally seems to imply a right of possession also. It therefore appears, on the whole, to signify the outward evidence of the right, rather than the mere right itself. Thus, when it is said that the "most imperfect degree of title consists in the mere naked possession or actual occupation of an estate," it means that the mere circumstance of occupying the estate is the weakest species of evidence of the occupier's right to such possession. The word is defined by Sir Edward Coke thus: *Titulus est justa causa possidendi id quod nostrum est,* (1 Inst. 34;) that is to say, the ground, whether purchase, gift, or other such ground of acquiring; "*titulus*" being distinguished in this respect from "*modus acquirendi,*" which is the *traditio, i. e.,* delivery or conveyance of the thing. Brown.

Title is when a man hath lawful cause of entry into lands whereof another is seised; and it signifies also the means whereby a man comes to lands or tenements, as by feoffment, last will and testament, etc. The word "title" includes a right, but is the more general word. Every right is a title, though every title is not a right for which an action lies. Jacob.

A *title* is a lawful cause or ground of possessing that which is ours. An *interest,* though primarily it includes the terms "estate," "right," and "title," has latterly come often to mean less, and to be the same as "concern," "share," and the like. 73 N. Y. 456.

The investigation of titles is one of the principal branches of conveyancing, and in that practice the word "title" has acquired the sense of "history," rather than of "right." Thus, we speak of an abstract of title, and of investigating a title, and describe a document as forming part of the title to property. Sweet.

In pleading. The right of action which the plaintiff has. The declaration must show the plaintiff's title, and, if such title be not shown in that instrument, the defect cannot be cured by any of the future pleadings. Bac. Abr. "Pleas," etc., B 1.

In procedure, every action, petition, or other proceeding has a title, which consists of the name of the court in which it is pending, the names of the parties, etc. Administration actions are further distinguished by the name of the deceased person whose estate is being administered. Every pleading, summons, affidavit, etc., commences with the title. In many cases it is sufficient to give what is called the "short title" of an action, namely, the court, the reference to the record, and the surnames of the first plaintiff and the first defendant. Sweet.

TITLE, COVENANTS FOR. Covenants usually inserted in a conveyance of land, on the part of the grantor, and binding him for the completeness, security, and continuance of the title transferred to the grantee. They comprise "covenants for seisin, for right to convey, against incumbrances, for quiet enjoyment, sometimes for further assurance, and almost always of warranty." Rawle, Cov. § 21.

TITLE-DEEDS. Deeds which constitute or are the evidence of title to lands.

TITLE OF A CAUSE. The distinctive appellation by which any cause in court, or other juridical proceeding, is known and discriminated from others.

TITLE OF AN ACT. The heading, or introductory clause, of a statute, wherein is briefly recited its purpose or nature, or the subject to which it relates.

TITLE OF CLERGYMEN, (to orders.) Some certain place where they may exercise their functions; also an assurance of being preferred to some ecclesiastical benefice. 2 Steph. Comm. 661.

TITLE OF DECLARATION. That preliminary clause of a declaration which states the name of the court and the term to which the process is returnable.

TITLE OF ENTRY. The right to enter upon lands. Cowell.

TITLE TO ORDERS. In English ecclesiastical law, a title to orders is a certificate of preferment or provision required by the thirty-third canon, in order that a person may be admitted into holy orders, unless he be a fellow or chaplain in Oxford or Cambridge, or master of arts of five years' standing in either of the universities, and living there at his sole charges; or unless the bishop himself intends shortly to admit him to some benefice or curacy. 2 Steph. Comm. 661.

TITULADA. In Spanish law. Title. White, New Recop. b. 1, tit. 5, c. 3, § 2.

TITULARS OF ERECTION. Persons who in Scotland, after the Reformation, obtained grants from the crown of the monasteries and priories then erected into temporal lordships. Thus the titles formerly held by the religious houses, as well as the property of the lands, were conferred on these grantees, who were also called "lords of erection" and "titulars of the teinds." Bell.

TITULUS. Lat. **In the civil law.** Title; the source or ground of possession; the means whereby possession of a thing is acquired, whether such possession be lawful or not.

In old ecclesiastical law. A temple or church; the material edifice. So called because the priest in charge of it derived therefrom his name and *title*. Spelman.

Titulus est justa causa possidendi id quod nostrum est; dicitur a tuendo. 8 Coke, 153. A title is the just right of possessing that which is our own; it is so called from "*tuendo*," defending.

TO. This is a word of exclusion, when used in describing premises; it excludes the terminus mentioned. 69 Me. 514.

TO HAVE AND TO HOLD. The words in a conveyance which show the estate intended to be conveyed. Thus, in a conveyance of land in fee-simple, the grant is to "A. and his heirs, to have and to hold the said [land] unto and to the use of the said A., his heirs and assigns forever." Williams, Real Prop. 198.

Strictly speaking, however, the words "to have" denote the estate to be taken, while the words "to hold" signify that it is to be held of some superior lord, *i. e.*, by way of tenure, (*q. v.*) The former clause is called the "*habendum;*" the latter, the "*tenendum.*" Co. Litt. 6*a*.

TOALIA. A towel. There is a tenure of lands by the service of waiting with a towel at the king's coronation. Cowell.

TOBACCONIST. Any person, firm, or corporation whose business it is to manufacture cigars, snuff, or tobacco in any form. Act of congress of July 13, 1866, § 9; 14 St. at Large, 120.

TOFT. A place or piece of ground on which a house formerly stood, which has been destroyed by accident or decay. 2 Broom & H. Comm. 17.

TOFTMAN. In old English law. The owner of a toft. Cowell; Spelman.

TOGATI. Lat. In Roman law. Advocates; so called under the empire because they were required, when appearing in court to plead a cause, to wear the *toga*, which had then ceased to be the customary dress in Rome. Vicat.

TOKEN. A sign or mark; a material evidence of the existence of a fact. Thus, cheating by "false tokens" implies the use of fabricated or deceitfully contrived material objects to assist the person's own fraud and falsehood in accomplishing the cheat.

TOKEN-MONEY. A conventional medium of exchange consisting of pieces of metal, fashioned in the shape and size of coins, and circulating among private persons, by consent, at a certain value. No longer permitted or recognized as money. 2 Chit. Com. Law, 182.

TOLERATION. The allowance of religious opinions and modes of worship in a state which are contrary to, or different from, those of the established church or belief. Webster.

TOLERATION ACT. The statute 1 W. & M. St. 1, c. 18, for exempting Protestant dissenters from the penalties of certain laws is so called. Brown.

TOLL, *v.* To bar, defeat, or take away; thus, to toll the entry means to deny or take away the right of entry.

TOLL, *n.* **In English law.** Toll means an excise of goods; a seizure of some part for permission of the rest. It has two significations: A liberty to buy and sell within the precincts of the manor, which seems to import as much as a fair or market; a tribute or custom paid for passage. Wharton.

A Saxon word, signifying, properly, a payment in towns, markets, and fairs for goods and cattle bought and sold. It is a reasonable sum of money due to the owner of the fair or market, upon sale of things tollable within the same. The word is used for a liberty as well to take as to be free from toll. Jacob.

In modern English law. A reasonable sum due to the lord of a fair or market for things sold there which are tollable. 1 Crabb, Real Prop. p. 350, § 683.

In contracts. A sum of money for the use of something, generally applied to the consideration which is paid for the use of a road, bridge, or the like, of a public nature.

TOLL AND TEAM. Sax. Words constantly associated with Saxon and old English grants of liberties to the lords of manors. Bract. fols. 56, 104*b*, 124*b*, 154*b*. They appear to have imported the privileges of having a market, and jurisdiction of villeins. See TEAM.

TOLL-GATHERER. The officer who takes or collects toll.

TOLL-THOROUGH. In English law. A toll for passing through a highway, or over a ferry or bridge. Cowell. A toll paid to a town for such a number of beasts, or for every beast that goes through the town, or over a bridge or ferry belonging to it. Com. Dig. "Toll," C. A toll claimed by an individual where he is bound to repair some particular highway. 3 Steph. Comm. 257.

TOLL-TRAVERSE. In English law. A toll for passing over a private man's ground. Cowell. A toll for passing over the private soil of another, or for driving beasts across his ground. Cro. Eliz. 710.

TOLL-TURN. In English law. A toll on beasts returning from a market. 1 Crabb, Real Prop. p. 101, § 102. A toll paid at the return of beasts from fair or market, though they were not sold. Cowell.

TOLLAGE. Payment of toll; money charged or paid as toll; the liberty or franchise of charging toll.

TOLLBOOTH. A prison; a customhouse; an exchange; also the place where goods are weighed. Wharton.

TOLLDISH. A vessel by which the toll of corn for grinding is measured.

Tolle voluntatem et erit omnis actus indifferens. Take away the will, and every action will be indifferent. Bract. fol. 2.

TOLLER. One who collects tribute or taxes.

TOLLERE. Lat. In the civil law. To lift up or raise; to elevate; to build up.

TOLLS. In a general sense, tolls signify any manner of customs, subsidy, prestation, imposition, or sum of money demanded for exporting or importing of any wares or merchandise to be taken of the buyer. 2 Inst. 58.

TOLLSESTER. An old excise; a duty paid by tenants of some manors to the lord for liberty to brew and sell ale. Cowell.

TOLSEY. The same as "tollbooth." Also a place where merchants meet; a local tribunal for small civil causes held at the Guildhall, Bristol.

TOLT. A writ whereby a cause depending in a court baron was taken and removed into a county court. Old Nat. Brev. 4.

TOLTA. Wrong; rapine; extortion. Cowell.

TON. A measure of weight; differently fixed, by different statutes, at two thousand pounds avoirdupois, (1 Rev. St. N. Y. 609, § 35,) or at twenty hundred-weights, each hundred-weight being one hundred and twelve pounds avoirdupois, (Rev. St. U. S. § 2951.)

TONNAGE. The capacity of a vessel for carrying freight or other loads, calculated in tons. But the way of estimating the tonnage varies in different countries. In England, tonnage denotes the actual weight in tons which the vessel can safely carry; in America, her carrying capacity estimated from the cubic dimensions of the hold. See 40 N. Y. 259.

The "tonnage" of a vessel is her capacity to carry cargo, and a charter of "the whole tonnage" of a ship transfers to the charterer only the space necessary for that purpose. 103 Mass. 405.

The tonnage of a vessel is her internal cubical capacity, in tons. 94 U. S. 238.

TONNAGE DUTY. In English law. A duty imposed by parliament upon merchandise exported and imported, according to a certain rate upon every ton. Brown.

In American law. A tax laid upon vessels according to their tonnage or cubical capacity.

A tonnage duty is a duty imposed on vessels in proportion to their capacity. The vital principle of a tonnage duty is that it is imposed, whatever the subject, solely according to the rule of weight, either as to the capacity to carry or the actual weight of the thing itself. 94 U. S. 238.

The term "tonnage duty," as used in the constitutional prohibition upon state laws imposing tonnage duties, describes a duty proportioned to the tonnage of the vessel; a certain rate on each ton. But it is not to be taken in this restricted sense in the constitutional provision. The general prohibition upon the states against levying duties on imports or exports would have been ineffectual if it had not been extended to duties on the ships which serve as the vehicles of conveyance. The prohibition extends to any duty on the ship, whether a fixed sum upon its whole tonnage or a sum to be ascertained by comparing the amount of tonnage with the rate of duty. 6 Wall. 31.

A tonnage tax is defined to be a duty levied on a vessel according to the tonnage or capacity. It is a tax upon the boat as an instrument of navigation, and not a tax upon the property of a citizen of the state. 6 Biss. 505.

TONNAGE-RENT. When the rent reserved by a mining lease or the like consists of a royalty on every ton of minerals gotten in the mine, it is often called a "tonnage-rent." There is generally a dead rent in addition. Sweet.

TONNAGIUM. In old English law. A custom or impost upon wines and other merchandise exported or imported, according to a certain rate per ton. Spelman; Cowell.

TONNETIGHT. In old English law. The quantity of a ton or tun, in a ship's freight or bulk, for which tonnage or tunnage was paid to the king. Cowell.

TONODERACH. In old Scotch law. A thief-taker.

TONSURA. Lat. In old English law. A shaving, or polling; the having the crown of the head shaven; tonsure. One of the peculiar badges of a clerk or clergyman.

TONSURE. In old English law. A being shaven; the having the head shaven; a shaven head. 4 Bl. Comm. 367.

TONTINE. In French law. A species of association or partnership formed among persons who are in receipt of perpetual or life annuities, with the agreement that the shares or annuities of those who die shall accrue to the survivors. This plan is said to be thus named from Tonti, an Italian, who invented it in the seventeenth century. The principle is used in some forms of life insurance. Merl. Repert.

TOOK AND CARRIED AWAY. In criminal pleading. Technical words necessary in an indictment for simple larceny.

TOOL. The usual meaning of the word "tool" is "an instrument of manual operation;" that is, an instrument to be used and managed by the hand instead of being moved and controlled by machinery. 124 Mass. 420.

TOP ANNUAL. In Scotch law. An annual rent out of a house built in a burgh. Whishaw. A duty which, from the act 1551, c. 10, appears to have been due from certain lands in Edinburgh, the nature of which is not now known. Bell.

TORT. Wrong; injury; the opposite of right. So called, according to Lord Coke, because it is *wrested*, or crooked, being contrary to that which is right and straight. Co. Litt. 158*b*.

In modern practice, *tort* is constantly used as an English word to denote a wrong or wrongful act, for which an action will lie, as distinguished from a *contract*. 3 Bl. Comm. 117.

A tort is a legal wrong committed upon the person or property independent of contract. It may be either (1) a direct invasion of some legal right of the individual; (2) the infraction of some public duty by which special damage accrues to the individual; (3) the violation of some private obligation by which like damage accrues to the individual. In the former case, no special damage is necessary to entitle the party to recover. In the two latter cases, such damage is necessary. Code Ga. 1882, § 2951.

TORT-FEASOR. A wrong-doer; one who commits or is guilty of a tort.

TORTIOUS. Wrongful; of the nature of a tort. Formerly certain modes of conveyance (*e. g.*, feoffments, fines, etc.) had the effect of passing not merely the estate of the person making the conveyance, but the whole fee-simple, to the injury of the person really entitled to the fee; and they were hence called "tortious conveyances." Litt. § 611; Co. Litt. 271*b*, n. 1; 330*b*, n. 1. But this operation has been taken away. Sweet.

Tortura legum pessima. The torture or wresting of laws is the worst [kind of torture.] 4 Bacon's Works, 434.

TORTURE. In old criminal law. The question; the infliction of violent bodily pain upon a person, by means of the rack, wheel, or other engine, under judicial sanction and superintendence, in connection with the interrogation or examination of the person, as a means of extorting a confession of guilt, or of compelling him to disclose his accomplices.

TORY. Originally a nickname for the wild Irish in Ulster. Afterwards given to, and adopted by, one of the two great parliamentary parties which have alternately governed Great Britain since the Revolution in 1688. Wharton.

The name was also given, in America, during the struggle of the colonies for independence, to the party of those residents who favored the side of the king and opposed the war.

TOT. In old English practice. A word written by the foreign opposer or other officer opposite to a debt due the king, to denote that it was a *good* debt; which was hence said to be *totted*.

TOTA CURIA. L. Lat. In the old reports. The whole court.

TOTAL LOSS. In marine insurance, a total loss is the entire destruction or loss, to the insured, of the subject-matter of the policy, by the risks insured against. An *actual* total loss is the absolute destruction or perishing of the subject, so that nothing remains of it. A *constructive* total loss occurs where the damage to the property is such that, although it may still subsist *in specie*, or there may be salvage from it or claims or equities growing out of the circumstances of its loss, the assured has the right, either by express stipulation or implication of law, to abandon and surrender to the underwriters the surviving portion of the property, or his rights and claims in regard to it, and thereupon recover the same amount of insurance as under an actual total loss.

In fire insurance, a total loss is the complete destruction of the insured property by fire, so that nothing of value remains from it; as distinguished from a *partial* loss, where the property is damaged, but not entirely destroyed.

Total loss, in marine insurance, signifies the total destruction of the thing insured, or such damage to the thing insured as renders it, though it may specifically remain, of little or no value to the owner. 1 Mass. 264.

An *actual* total loss is where the vessel ceases to exist *in specie*, and becomes a "mere congeries of planks," incapable of being repaired; or where, by the peril insured against, it is placed beyond the control of the insured and beyond his power of recovery. A *constructive* loss is where the vessel remains *in specie*, and is susceptible of repairs or recovery, but at an expense, according to the rule of the English common law, exceeding its value when restored. 25 Ohio St. 64.

The words "total loss," in their literal sense, mean complete physical annihilation and destruction of the thing, but, in a sense adopted in insurance, they signify a loss which is total to the owner; as where the goods are seized and taken away, or have been rendered worthless for the uses or purposes for which they are designed. 3 Rob. Adm. 528.

TOTIDEM VERBIS. In so many words.

TOTIES QUOTIES. As often as occasion shall arise.

TOTIS VIRIBUS. With all one's might or power; with all his might; very strenuously.

TOTTED. A good debt to the crown, *i. e.*, a debt paid to the sheriff, to be by him paid over to the king. Cowell; Mozley & Whitley.

Totum præfertur unicuique parti. 3 Coke, 41. The whole is preferable to any single part.

TOUCH. In insurance law. To stop at a port. If there be liberty granted by the policy to *touch*, or to *touch and stay*, at an intermediate port on the passage, the better opinion now is that the insured may *trade* there, when consistent with the object and the furtherance of the adventure, by breaking bulk, or by discharging and taking in cargo, provided it produces no unnecessary delay, nor enhances nor varies the risk. 3 Kent, Comm. 314.

TOUCHING A DEAD BODY. It was an ancient superstition that the body of a murdered man would bleed freshly when touched by his murderer. Hence, in old criminal law, this was resorted to as a means of ascertaining the guilt or innocence of a person suspected of the murder.

TOUJOURS ET UNCORE PRIST. L. Fr. Always and still ready. This is the name of a plea of tender.

TOUR D'ECHELLE. In French law. An easement consisting of the right to rest ladders upon the adjoining estate, when necessary in order to repair a party-wall or buildings supported by it.

Also the vacant space surrounding a building left unoccupied in order to facilitate its reparation when necessary. Merl. Repert.

TOURN. In old English law. A court of record, having criminal jurisdiction, in each county, held before the sheriff, twice a year, in one place after another, following a certain circuit or rotation.

TOUT. Fr. All; whole; entirely. *Tout temps prist*, always ready.

Tout ce que la loi ne defend pas est permis. Everything is permitted which is not forbidden by law.

TOUT TEMPS PRIST. L. Fr. Always ready. The emphatic words of the old plea of tender; the defendant alleging that he has always been ready, and still is ready, to discharge the debt. 3 Bl. Comm. 303; 2 Salk. 622.

TOUT UN SOUND. L. Fr. All one sound; sounding the same; *idem sonans*.

Toute exception non surveillée tend à prendre la place du principe. Every exception not watched tends to assume the place of the principle.

TOWAGE. The act or service of towing ships and vessels, usually by means of a small steamer called a "tug." That which is given for towing ships in rivers.

Towage is the drawing a ship or barge along the water by another ship or boat, fastened to her, or by men or horses, etc., on land. It is also money which is given by bargemen to the owner of ground next a river, where they tow a barge or other vessel. Jacob.

TOWAGE SERVICE. In admiralty law. A service rendered to a vessel, by towing, for the mere purpose of expediting her voyage, without reference to any circumstances of danger. It is confined to vessels that have received no injury or damage. 1 W. Rob. 177; 9 Fed. Rep. 53.

TO-WIT. That is to say; namely; *scilicet; videlicet*.

TOWN. In English law. Originally, a vill or tithing; but now a generic term, which comprehends under it the several species of cities, boroughs, and common towns. 1 Bl. Comm. 114.

In American law. A civil and political division of a state, varying in extent and importance, but usually one of the divisions of a county. In the New England states, the town is the political unit, and is a municipal corporation. In some other states, where the county is the unit, the town is merely one of its subdivisions, but possesses some powers of local self-government. In still other states, such subdivisions of a county are called "townships," and "town" is the name of a village, borough, or smaller city.

A village and a town are not identical. A village is ordinarily less than a town, and more occupied by agriculturists; yet the two cannot be definitely distinguished by the size of the place or employment of the inhabitants. 46 Iowa, 256.

TOWN CAUSE. In English practice. A cause tried at the sittings for London and Middlesex. 3 Steph. Comm. 517.

TOWN-CLERK. In those states where the *town* is the unit for local self-government, the town-clerk is a principal officer who keeps the records, issues calls for town-meetings, and performs generally the duties of a secretary to the political organization.

TOWN COLLECTOR. One of the officers of a town charged with collecting the taxes assessed for town purposes.

TOWN COMMISSIONER. In some of the states where the town is the political unit, the town commissioners constitute a board of administrative officers, charged with the general management of the town's business.

TOWN-CRIER. An officer in a town whose business it is to make proclamations.

TOWN-HALL. The building maintained by a town for town-meetings and the offices of the municipal authorities.

TOWN-MEETING. Under the municipal organization of the New England states, the town-meeting is a legal assembly of the qualified voters of a town, held at stated intervals or on call, for the purpose of electing town officers, and of discussing and deciding on questions relating to the public business, property, and expenses of the town.

TOWN ORDER or WARRANT. An official direction in writing by the auditing officers of a town, directing the treasurer to pay a sum of money.

TOWN POUND. A place of confinement maintained by a town for estrays.

TOWN PURPOSE. When it is said that taxation by a town, or the expenditure of the town's money, must be for town purposes, it is meant that the purposes must be public with respect to the town; *i. e.*, concern the welfare and advantage of the town as a whole.

TOWN-REEVE. The reeve or chief officer of a town.

TOWN TAX. Such tax as a town may levy for its peculiar expenses; as distinguished from a county or state tax.

TOWN TREASURER. The treasurer of a town which is an organized municipal corporation.

TOWNSHIP. 1. In surveys of the public land of the United States, a "township" is a division of territory six miles square, containing thirty-six sections.

2. In some of the states, this is the name given to the civil and political subdivisions of a county. See TOWN.

TOWNSHIP TRUSTEE. One of a board of officers to whom, in some states, affairs of a township are intrusted.

TOXICAL. Poisonous; containing poison.

TOXICOLOGY. The science of poisons.

TRABES. Lat. In the civil law. A beam or rafter of a house. Calvin.

In old English law. A measure of grain, containing twenty-four sheaves; a thrave. Spelman.

TRACEA. In old English law. The track or trace of a felon, by which he was pursued with the hue and cry; a foot-step, hoof-print, or wheel-track. Bract. fols. 116, 121*b*.

TRACT. A lot, piece, or parcel of land, of greater or less size, the term not importing, in itself, any precise dimension. See 28 N. J. Law, 45.

Tractent fabrilia fabri. Let smiths perform the work of smiths. 3 Co. Epist.

TRADAS IN BALLIUM. You deliver to bail. In old English practice. The name of a writ which might be issued in behalf of a party who, upon the writ *de odio et atia*, had been found to have been maliciously accused of a crime, commanding the sheriff that, if the prisoner found twelve good and lawful men of the county who would be mainpernors for him, he should *deliver* him *in bail* to those twelve, until the next assize. Bract. fol. 123; 1 Reeve, Eng. Law, 252.

TRADE. The act or business of exchanging commodities by barter; or the business of buying and selling for money; traffic; barter. Webster.

The business which a person has learned and which he carries on for procuring subsistence, or for profit; occupation, particularly mechanical employment; distinguished from the liberal arts and learned professions, and from agriculture. Id.

Traffic; commerce; exchange of goods for other goods, or for money. All wholesale trade, all buying in order to sell again by wholesale, may be reduced to three sorts: The home trade, the foreign trade of consumption, and the carrying trade. 2 Smith, Wealth Nat. b. 2, c. 5.

TRADE DOLLAR. A silver coin of the United States, of the weight of four hundred and twenty grains, troy. Rev. St. § 3513.

TRADE-MARK. A distinctive mark, motto, device, or emblem, which a manufacturer stamps, prints, or otherwise affixes to the goods he produces, so that they may be identified in the market, and their origin be vouched for.

TRADE-MARKS REGISTRATION ACT, 1875. This is the statute 38 & 39 Vict. c. 91, amended by the acts of 1876 and 1877. It provides for the establishment of a register of trade-marks under the superintendence of the commissioners of patents, and for the registration of trade-marks as belonging to particular classes of goods, and for their assignment in connection with the goodwill of the business in which they are used. Sweet.

TRADE-NAME. A trade-name is a name which by user and reputation has acquired the property of indicating that a certain trade or occupation is carried on by a particular person. The name may be that of a person, place, or thing, or it may be what is called a "fancy name," (*i. e.*, a name having no sense as applied to the particular trade,) or word invented for the occasion, and having no sense at all. Seb. Trade-Marks, 37. Sweet.

TRADE UNION. A combination or association of men employed in the same trade, (usually a manual or mechanical trade,) united for the purpose of regulating the customs and standards of their trade, fixing prices or hours of labor, influencing the relations of employer and employed, enlarging or maintaining their rights and privileges, and other similar objects.

TRADE-UNION ACT. The statute 34 & 35 Vict. c. 31, passed in 1871, for the purpose of giving legal recognition to trade unions, is known as the "trade-union act," or "trade-union funds protection act." It provides that the members of a trade union shall not be prosecuted for conspiracy merely by reason that the rules of such union are in restraint of trade; and that the agreements of trade unions shall not on that account be void or voidable. Provisions are also made with reference to the registration and registered offices of trade unions, and other purposes connected therewith. Mozley & Whitley.

TRADE USAGE. The usage or customs commonly observed by persons conversant in, or connected with, a particular trade.

TRADER. A person engaged in trade; one whose business is to buy and sell merchandise, or any class of goods, deriving a profit from his dealings. 2 Kent, Comm. 389; 80 N. C. 481.

TRADESMAN. In England, a shop-keeper; a small shop-keeper.

In the United States, a mechanic or artificer of any kind, whose livelihood depends upon the labor of his hands. 4 Pa. St. 472.

"Primarily the words 'trader' and 'tradesman' mean one who trades, and they have been treated by the courts in many instances as synonymous. But, in their general application and usage, I think they describe different vocations. By 'tradesman' is usually meant a shop-keeper. Such is the definition given the word in Burrill's Law Dictionary. It is used in this sense by Adam Smith. He says, (Wealth of Nations:) 'A tradesman in London is obliged to hire a whole house in that part of the town where his customers live. His shop is on the ground floor,' etc. Dr. Johnson gives it the same meaning, and quotes Prior and Goldsmith as authorities." 7 Biss. 155.

TRADICION. Span. In Spanish law. Delivery. White, New Recop. b. 2, tit. 2, c. 9.

TRADITIO. Lat. In the civil law. Delivery; transfer of possession; a derivative mode of acquiring, by which the owner of a corporeal thing, having the right and the will of aliening it, transfers it for a lawful consideration to the receiver. Heinecc. Elem. lib. 2, tit. 1, § 380.

TRADITIO BREVI MANU. In the civil law. A species of constructive or implied delivery. When he who already holds possession of a thing in another's name agrees with that other that thenceforth he shall possess it in his own name, in this case a delivery and redelivery are not necessary. And this species of delivery is termed "*traditio brevi manu.*" Mackeld. Rom. Law, § 284.

TRADITIO CLAVIUM. In the civil law. Delivery of keys; a symbolical kind of delivery, by which the ownership of merchandise in a warehouse might be transferred to a buyer. Inst. 2, 1, 44.

TRADITIO LONGA MANU. In the civil law. A species of delivery which takes place where the transferor places the article in the hands of the transferee, or, on his order, delivers it at his house. Mackeld. Rom. Law, § 284.

Traditio loqui facit chartam. Delivery makes a deed speak. 5 Coke, 1*a*. Delivery gives effect to the words of a deed. Id.

Traditio nihil amplius transferre debet vel potest, ad eum qui accipit, quam est apud eum qui tradit. Delivery ought to, and can, transfer nothing more to him who receives than is with him who delivers. Dig. 41, 1, 20, pr.

TRADITIO REI. Delivery of the thing. See 5 Maule & S. 82.

TRADITION. Delivery. A close translation or formation from the Latin "*traditio.*" 2 Bl. Comm. 307.

The tradition or delivery is the transferring of the thing sold into the power and possession of the buyer. Civil Code La. art. 2477.

TRADITOR. In old English law, A traitor; one guilty of high treason. Fleta, lib. 1, c. 21, § 8.

TRADITUR IN BALLIUM. In old practice. Is delivered to bail. Emphatic words of the old Latin bail-piece. 1 Salk. 105.

TRAFFIC. Commerce; trade; dealings in merchandise, bills, money, and the like.

TRAHENS. Lat. In French law. The drawer of a bill. Story, Bills, § 12, note.

TRAIL - BASTON. Justices of trailbaston were justices appointed by King Edward I., during his absence in the Scotch and French wars, about the year 1305. They were so styled, says Hollingshed, for trailing or drawing the staff of justice. Their office was to make inquisition, throughout the kingdom, of all officers and others, touching extortion, bribery, and such like grievances, of intruders into other men's lands, barrators, robbers, breakers of the peace, and divers other offenders. Cowell; Tomlins.

TRAINBANDS. The militia; the part of a community trained to martial exercises.

TRAISTIS. In old Scotch law. A roll containing the particular dittay taken up upon malefactors, which, with the *porteous*, is delivered by the justice clerk to the coroner, to the effect that the persons whose names are contained in the porteous may be attached, conform to the dittay contained in the traistis. So called, because committed to the *traist*, [trust,] faith, and credit of the clerks and coroner. Skene; Burrill.

TRAITOR. One who, being trusted, betrays; one guilty of treason.

TRAITOROUSLY. In criminal pleading. An essential word in indictments for treason. The offense must be laid to have been committed *traitorously*. Whart. Crim. Law, 100.

TRAJECTITIUS. Lat. In the civil law. Sent across the sea.

TRAM-WAYS. Rails for conveyance of traffic along a road not owned, as a railway is, by those who lay down the rails and convey the traffic. Wharton.

TRAMP. A strolling beggar; a vagrant or vagabond.

TRANSACT. In Scotch law. To compound. Amb. 185.

TRANSACTIO. Lat. In the civil law. The settlement of a suit or matter in controversy, by the litigating parties, between themselves, without referring it to arbitration. Hallifax, Civil Law, b. 3, c. 8, no. 14. An agreement by which a suit, either pending or about to be commenced, was forborne or discontinued on certain terms. Calvin.

TRANSACTION. In the civil law. A transaction or compromise is an agreement between two or more persons, who, for preventing or putting an end to a lawsuit, adjust their differences by mutual consent, in the manner which they agree on, and which every one of them prefers to the hope of gaining, balanced by the danger of losing. This contract must be reduced into writing. Civil Code La. art. 3071.

In common law. Whatever may be done by one person which affects another's rights, and out of which a cause of action may arise. 18 Kan. 406.

"Transaction" is a broader term than "contract." A contract is a transaction, but a transaction is not necessarily a contract. 70 Cal. 113, 11 Pac. Rep. 599.

TRANSCRIPT. An official copy of certain proceedings in a court. Thus, any person interested in a judgment or other record of a court can obtain a transcript of it.

TRANSCRIPTIO PEDIS FINIS LEVATI MITTENDO IN CANCELLARIUM. A writ which certified the foot of a fine levied before justices in eyre, etc., into the chancery. Reg. Orig. 669.

TRANSCRIPTIO RECOGNITIONIS FACTÆ CORAM JUSTICIARIIS ITINERANTIBUS, Etc. An old writ to certify a cognizance taken by justices in eyre, Reg. Orig. 152.

TRANSFER, *v.* To carry or pass over; to pass a thing over to another; to convey.

TRANSFER, *n.* The passing of a thing or of property from one person to another; alienation; conveyance. 2 Bl. Comm. 294.

Transfer is an act of the parties, or of the law, by which the title to property is conveyed from one living person to another. Civil Code Cal. § 1039.

In procedure, "transfer" is applied to an action or other proceeding, when it is taken from the jurisdiction of one court or judge, and placed under that of another.

TRANSFER OF A CAUSE. The removal of a cause from the jurisdiction of one court or judge to another by lawful authority.

TRANSFERABLE. A term used in a *quasi* legal sense, to indicate that the character of assignability or negotiability attaches to the particular instrument, or that it may pass from hand to hand, carrying all rights of the original holder. The words "not transferable" are sometimes printed upon a ticket, receipt, or bill of lading, to show that the same will not be good in the hands of any person other than the one to whom first issued.

TRANSFEREE. He to whom a transfer is made.

TRANSFERENCE. In Scotch law. The proceeding to be taken upon the death of one of the parties to a pending suit, whereby the action is transferred or continued, in its then condition, from the decedent to his representatives. Transference is either *active* or *passive;* the former, when it is the pursuer (plaintiff) who dies; the latter, upon the death of the defender. Ersk. Inst, 4, 1, 60.

The transferring of a legacy from the person to whom it was originally given to another; this is a species of ademption, but the latter is the more general term, and includes cases not covered by the former.

TRANSFERROR. One who makes a transfer.

Transferuntur dominia sine titulo et traditione, per usucaptionem, scil, per longam continuam et pacificam possessionem. Co. Litt. 113. Rights of dominion are transferred without title or delivery, by usucaption, to-wit, long and quiet possession.

TRANSFRETATIO. Lat. In old English law. A crossing of the strait, [of Dover;] a passing or sailing over from England to France. The royal passages or voyages to Gascony, Brittany, and other parts of France were so called, and time was sometimes computed from them.

TRANSGRESSIO. In old English law. A violation of law. Also trespass; the action of trespass.

Transgressio est cum modus non servatur nec mensura, debit enim quilibet in suo facto modum habere et mensuram. Co. Litt. 37. Transgression is when neither mode nor measure is preserved, for every one in his act ought to have a mode and measure.

TRANSGRESSIONE. In old English law. A writ or action of trespass.

Transgressione multiplicata, crescat pœnæ inflictio. When transgression is multiplied, let the infliction of punishment be increased. 2 Inst. 479.

TRANSHIPMENT. In maritime law. The act of taking the cargo out of one ship and loading it in another.

TRANSIENT. In poor-laws. A "transient person" is not exactly a person on a journey from one known place to another, but rather a wanderer ever on the tramp. 6 Vt. 203; 51 Vt. 423.

In Spanish law. A "transient foreigner" is one who visits the country, without the intention of remaining. 10 Tex. 170.

TRANSIRE, *v.* Lat. To go, or pass over; to pass from one thing, person, or place to another.

TRANSIRE, *n.* In English law. A warrant or permit for the custom-house to let goods pass.

Transit in rem judicatam. It passes into a matter adjudged; it becomes converted into a *res judicata* or judgment. A contract upon which a judgment is obtained is said to pass *in rem judicatam.* 2 Sumn. 436; 3 East, 251; 18 Johns. 480.

Transit terra cum onere. Land passes subject to any burden affecting it. Co. Litt. 231*a;* Broom, Max. 495, 706.

TRANSITIVE COVENANT. One which binds not only the covenantor, but also passes over, with obligatory force, to his representatives.

TRANSITORY. Passing from place to place; that may pass or be changed from one place to another; not confined to one place; the opposite of "local."

TRANSITORY ACTION. Actions are said to be either local or transitory. An action is "local," when the principal facts on which it is founded pertain to a particular place. An action is termed "transitory," when the principal fact on which it is founded is of a transitory kind, and might be supposed to have happened anywhere; and therefore all actions founded on debts, contracts, and such like matters relating to the person or personal property, come under this latter denomination. Steph. Pl. 316, 317.

TRANSITUS. Lat. Passage from one place to another; transit. *In transitu,* on the passage, transit, or way. 2 Kent, Comm. 543.

TRANSLADO. Span. A transcript.

TRANSLATION. The reproduction in one language of a book, document, or speech delivered in another language.

The transfer of property; but in this sense it is seldom used. 2 Bl. Comm. 294.

In ecclesiastical law. As applied to a bishop, the term denotes his removal from one diocese to another.

TRANSLATITIUM EDICTUM. In Roman law. The prætor, on his accession to office, did not usually publish an entirely new edict, but retained the whole or a part of that promulgated by his predecessor, as being of an approved or permanently useful character. The portion thus repeated or handed down from year to year was called the "*edictum translatitium.*" See Mackeld. Rom. Law, § 36.

TRANSLATIVE FACT. A fact by means of which a right is transferred or passes from one person to another; one, that is, which fulfills the double function of terminating the right of one person to an object, and of originating the right of another to it.

TRANSMISSION. In the civil law. The right which heirs or legatees may have of passing to their successors the inheritance or legacy to which they were entitled, if they happen to die without having exercised their rights. Domat, liv. 3, t. 1, s. 10; 4 Toullier, no. 186; Dig. 50, 17, 54; Code, 6, 51.

TRANSPORT. In old New York law. A conveyance of land.

TRANSPORTATION. The removal of goods or persons from one place to another, by a carrier.

In criminal law. A species of punishment consisting in removing the criminal from his own country to another, (usually a penal colony,) there to remain in exile for a prescribed period.

TRANSUMPTS. In Scotch law, an action of transumpt is an action competent to any one having a partial interest in a writing, or immediate use for it, to support his title or defenses in other actions. It is directed against the custodier of the writing, calling upon him to exhibit it, in order that a transumpt, *i. e.*, a copy, may be judicially made and delivered to the pursuer. Bell.

TRASLADO. In Spanish law. A copy. a sight. White, New Recop. b. 3, tit. 7, c. 3.

A copy of a document taken by the notary from the original, or a subsequent copy taken from the protocol, and not a copy taken directly from the matrix or protocol. (Tex.) 16 S. W. Rep. 54.

TRASSANS. Drawing; one who draws. The drawer of a bill of exchange.

TRASSATUS. One who is drawn, or drawn upon. The drawee of a bill of exchange. Heinecc. de Camb. c. 6, §§ 5, 6.

TRAVAIL. The act of child-bearing. A woman is said to be in her travail from the time the pains of child-bearing commence until her delivery. 5 Pick. 63.

TRAVEL. To go from one place to another at a distance; to journey; spoken of voluntary change of place.

TRAVELER. The term is used in a broad sense to designate those who patronize inns. Traveler is one who travels in any way. Distance is not material. A townsman or neighbor may be a traveler, and therefore a guest at an inn, as well as he who comes from a distance or from a foreign country. 35 Conn. 185.

TRAVERSE. In the language of pleading, a traverse signifies a denial. Thus, where a defendant denies any material allegation of fact in the plaintiff's declaration, he is said to traverse it, and the plea itself is thence frequently termed a "traverse." Brown.

A *common* traverse is a simple and direct denial of the material allegations of the opposite pleading, concluding to the country, and without inducement or *absque hoc*. Gould, Pl. 7, 11.

A *general* traverse is one preceded by a general inducement, and denying all that is last before alleged on the opposite side, in general terms, instead of pursuing the words of the allegation which it denies. Id. 7, 5.

A *special* traverse is one which commences with the words "*absque hoc*," and pursues the material portion of the words of the allegation which it denies. Id. 7, 6.

A traverse upon a traverse is one growing out of the same point or subject-matter as is embraced in a preceding traverse on the other side. Id. 7, 42*n*.

In criminal practice. To put off or delay the trial of an indictment till a succeeding term. More properly, to deny or take issue upon an indictment. 4 Bl. Comm. 351.

TRAVERSE JURY. A petit jury; a trial jury; a jury impaneled to try an action or prosecution, as distinguished from a grand jury.

TRAVERSE OF INDICTMENT or PRESENTMENT. The taking issue upon and contradicting or denying some chief point of it. Jacob.

TRAVERSE OF OFFICE. The proving that an inquisition made of lands or goods by the escheator is defective and untruly made. Tomlins.

It is the challenging, by a subject, of an inquest of office, as being defective and untruly made. Mozley & Whitley.

TRAVERSER. In pleading. One who traverses or denies. A prisoner or party indicted; so called from his traversing the indictment.

TRAVERSING NOTE. This is a pleading in chancery, and consists of a denial put in by the plaintiff on behalf of the defendant, generally denying all the statements in the plaintiff's bill. The effect of it is to put the plaintiff upon proof of the whole contents of his bill, and is only resorted to for the purpose of saving time, and in a case where the plaintiff can safely dispense with an answer. A copy of the note must be served on the defendant. Brown.

TREACHER, TRECHETOUR, or TREACHOUR. A traitor.

TREAD-MILL, or TREAD-WHEEL, is an instrument of prison discipline, being a wheel or cylinder with an horizontal axis, having steps attached to it, up which the prisoners walk, and thus put the axis in motion. The men hold on by a fixed rail, and, as their weight presses down the step upon which they tread, they ascend the next step, and thus drive the wheel. Enc. Brit.

TREASON. The offense of attempting to overthrow the government of the state to which the offender owes allegiance; or of betraying the state into the hands of a foreign power. Webster.

In England, treason is an offense particularly directed against the person of the sovereign, and consists (1) in compassing or imagining the death of the king or queen, or their eldest son and heir; (2) in violating the king's companion, or the king's eldest daughter unmarried, or the wife of the king's eldest son and heir; (3) in levying war against the king in his realm; (4) in adhering to the king's enemies in his realm, giving to them aid and comfort in the realm or elsewhere; and (5) slaying the chancellor, treasurer, or the king's justices of the one bench or the other, justices in eyre, or justices of assize, and all other justices assigned to hear and determine, being in their places doing their offices. 4 Steph. Comm. 185–193; 4 Bl. Comm. 76–84.

"Treason against the United States shall consist only in levying war against them, or in adhering to their enemies, giving them aid and comfort." U. S. Const. art. 3, § 3, cl. 1.

TREASON-FELONY, under the English statute 11 & 12 Vict. c. 12, passed in 1848, is the offense of compassing, devising, etc., to depose her majesty from the crown; or to levy war in order to intimidate either house of parliament, etc., or to stir up foreigners by any printing or writing to invade the kingdom. This offense is punishable with penal servitude for life, or for any term not less than five years, etc., under statutes 11 & 12 Vict. c. 12, § 3; 20 & 21 Vict. c. 3, § 2; 27 & 28 Vict. c. 47, § 2. By the statute first above mentioned, the government is enabled to treat as felony many offenses which must formerly have been treated as high treason. Mozley & Whitley.

TREASONABLE. Having the nature or guilt of treason.

TREASURE. A treasure is a thing hidden or buried in the earth, on which no one can prove his property, and which is discovered by chance. Civil Code La. art. 3423, par. 2. See TREASURE-TROVE.

TREASURE-TROVE. Literally, treasure found. Money or coin, gold, silver, plate or bullion *found* hidden in the earth or other private place, the owner thereof being unknown. 1 Bl. Comm. 295. Called in Latin "*thesaurus inventus;*" and in Saxon "*fynderinga.*"

TREASURER. An officer of a public or private corporation, company, or government, charged with the receipt, custody, and disbursement of its moneys or funds.

TREASURER, LORD HIGH. Formerly the chief treasurer of England, who had charge of the moneys in the exchequer, the chançellor of the exchequer being under him. He appointed all revenue officers and escheators, and leased crown lands. The office is obsolete, and his duties are now performed by the lords commissioners of the treasury. Stim. Gloss.

TREASURER OF A COUNTY. See COUNTY TREASURER.

TREASURER'S REMEMBRANCER. In English law. He whose charge was to put the lord treasurer and the rest of the judges of the exchequer in remembrance of such things as were called on and dealt in for the sovereign's behoof. There is still one in Scotland. Wharton.

TREASURY. A place or building in which stores of wealth are reposited; particularly, a place where the public revenues are deposited and kept, and where money is disbursed to defray the expenses of government. Webster.

That department of government which is charged with the receipt, custody, and disbursement (pursuant to appropriations) of the public revenues or funds.

TREASURY BENCH. In the English house of commons, the first row of seats on the right hand of the speaker is so called, because occupied by the first lord of the treasury or principal minister of the crown. Brown.

TREASURY CHEST FUND. A fund, in England, originating in the unusual balances of certain grants of public money, and which is used for banking and loan purposes by the commissioners of the treasury. Its amount was limited by St. 24 & 25 Vict. c. 127, and has been further reduced to one million pounds, the residue being transferred to the consolidated fund, by St. 36 & 37 Vict. c. 56. Wharton.

TREATY. In international law. An agreement between two or more independent states. Brande. An agreement, league, or contract between two or more nations or sovereigns, formally signed by commissioners properly authorized, and solemnly ratified by the several sovereigns or the supreme power of each state. Webster.

In private law, "treaty" signifies the discussion of terms which immediately precedes the conclusion of a contract or other transaction. A warranty on the sale of goods, to be valid, must be made during the "treaty" preceding the sale. Chit. Cont. 419; Sweet.

TREATY OF PEACE. A treaty of peace is an agreement or contract made by belligerent powers, in which they agree to lay down their arms, and by which they stipulate the conditions of peace and regulate the manner in which it is to be restored and supported. Vattel, b. 4, c. 2, § 9.

TREBELLANIC PORTION. "In consequence of this article, the trebellanic portion of the civil law—that is to say, the portion of the property of the testator which the instituted heir had a right to detain when he was charged with a *fidei commissa* or fiduciary bequest—is no longer a part of our law." Civil Code La. art. 1520, par. 3.

TREBLE COSTS. In practice. A rate of costs given in certain actions, consisting, according to its technical import, of the common costs, half of these, and half of the latter. 2 Tidd, Pr. 988. The word "treble," in this application, is not understood in its literal sense of thrice the amount of single costs, but signifies merely the addition together of the three sums fixed as above. Id. Treble costs have been abolished in England, by St. 5 & 6 Vict. c. 97.

In American law. In Pennsylvania the rule is different. When an act of assembly gives treble costs, the party is allowed three times the usual costs, with the exception that the fees of the officers are not to be trebled when they are not regularly or usually payable by the defendant. 2 Rawle, 201.

TREBLE DAMAGES. In practice. Damages given by statute in certain cases, consisting of the single damages found by the jury, actually tripled in amount. The usual practice has been for the jury to find the single amount of the damages, and for the court, on motion, to order that amount to be trebled. 2 Tidd, Pr. 893, 894.

TREBUCKET. A tumbrel, castigatory, or cucking-stool.

TREET. In old English law. Fine wheat.

TREMAGIUM, TREMESIUM. The season or time of sowing summer corn, being about March, the third month, to which the word may allude. Cowell.

Tres faciunt collegium. Three make a corporation; three members are requisite to constitute a corporation. Dig. 50, 16, 8; 1 Bl. Comm. 469.

TRESAEL. L. Fr. A great-great-grandfather. Britt. c. 119. Otherwise written "*tresaiel*," and "*tresayle*." 3 Bl. Comm. 186; Litt. § 20.

TRESAYLE. An abolished writ sued on ouster by abatement, on the death of the grandfather's grandfather.

TRESPASS. Any misfeasance or act of one man whereby another is injuriously treated or damnified. 3 Bl. Comm. 208.

An injury or misfeasance to the person, property, or rights of another person, done with force and violence, either actual or implied in law.

In the strictest sense, an entry on another's ground, without a lawful authority, and doing some damage, however inconsiderable, to his real property. 3 Bl. Comm. 209.

Trespass, in its most comprehensive sense, signifies any transgression or offense against the law of nature, of society, or of the country in which we live; and this, whether it relates to a man's person or to his property. In its more limited and ordinary sense, it signifies an injury committed with violence, and this violence may be either actual or implied; and the law will imply violence though none is actually used, when the injury is of a direct and immediate kind, and committed on the person or tangible and corporeal property of the plaintiff. Of actual violence, an assault and battery is an instance; of implied, a peaceable but wrongful entry upon a person's land. Brown.

A *continuing* trespass is one which is permanent in its nature; as, where a person builds on his own land so that part of the building overhangs his neighbor's land.

In practice. A form of action, at the common law, which lies for redress in the shape of money damages for any unlawful injury done to the plaintiff, in respect either to his person, property, or rights, by the immediate force and violence of the defendant.

TRESPASS DE BONIS ASPORTATIS. (Trespass for goods carried away.) In practice. The technical name of that species of action of trespass for injuries to personal property which lies where the injury consists in *carrying away* the goods or property. See 3 Bl. Comm. 150, 151.

TRESPASS FOR MESNE PROFITS. A form of action supplemental to an action of ejectment, brought against the tenant in possession to recover the profits which he has wrongfully received during the time of his occupation. 3 Bl. Comm. 205.

TRESPASS ON THE CASE. The form of action, at common law, adapted to the recovery of damages for some injury resulting to a party from the wrongful act of another, unaccompanied by direct or immediate force, or which is the indirect or secondary consequence of such act. Commonly called, by abbreviation, "Case."

TRESPASS QUARE CLAUSUM FREGIT. "Trespass wherefore he broke the close." The common-law action for damages for an unlawful entry or trespass upon the plaintiff's land. In the Latin form of the writ, the defendant was called upon to show why he broke the plaintiff's close; *i. e.*, the real or imaginary structure inclosing the land, whence the name. It is commonly abbreviated to "*trespass qu. cl. fr.*"

TRESPASS TO TRY TITLE. The name of the action used in several of the states for the recovery of the possession of real property, with damages for any trespass committed upon the same by the defendant.

TRESPASS VI ET ARMIS. Trespass with force and arms. The common-law action for damages for any injury committed by the defendant with direct and immediate force or violence against the plaintiff or his property.

TRESPASSER. One who has committed trespass; one who unlawfully enters or intrudes upon another's land, or unlawfully and forcibly takes another's personal property.

TRESPASSER AB INITIO. Trespasser from the beginning. A term applied to a tort-feasor whose acts relate back so as to make a previous act, at the time innocent, unlawful; as, if he enter peaceably, and subsequently commit a breach of the peace, his entry is considered a trespass. Stim. Gloss.

TRESTORNARE. In old English law. To turn aside; to divert a stream from its course. Bract. fols. 115, 234*b*. To turn or alter the course of a road. Cowell.

TRESVIRI. Lat. In Roman law. Officers who had the charge of prisons, and the execution of condemned criminals. Calvin.

TRET. An allowance made for the water or dust that may be mixed with any commodity. It differs from *tare*, (*q. v.*)

TRETHINGA. In old English law. A trithing; the court of a trithing.

TREYT. Withdrawn, as a juror. Written also *treat*. Cowell.

TRIA CAPITA, in Roman law, were *civitas, libertas,* and *familia; i. e.,* citizenship, freedom, and family rights.

TRIAL. The examination before a competent tribunal, according to the law of the land, of the facts or law put in issue in a cause, for the purpose of determining such issue. 32 Cal. 267; 4 Mason, 232; 39 Ind. 1.

A trial is the judicial examination of the issues between the parties, whether they be issues of law or of fact. Code N. Y. § 252; Code N. C. § 397.

The examination of a cause, civil or criminal, before a judge who has jurisdiction over it, according to the laws of the land. 1 Inst. 124.

TRIAL AT BAR. A species of trial now seldom resorted to, excepting in cases where the matter in dispute is one of great importance and difficulty. It is a trial which takes place before all the judges at the bar of the court in which the action is brought. Brown. See 2 Tidd, Pr. 747; Steph. Pl. 84.

TRIAL AT NISI PRIUS. In practice. The ordinary kind of trial which takes place at the sittings, assizes, or circuit, before a single judge. 2 Tidd, Pr. 751, 819.

TRIAL BY CERTIFICATE. A form of trial allowed in cases where the evidence of the person certifying was the only proper criterion of the point in dispute. Under such circumstances, the issue might be determined by the certificate alone, because, if sent to a jury, it would be conclusive upon them, and therefore their intervention was unnecessary. Tomlins.

TRIAL BY GRAND ASSIZE is a peculiar mode of trial allowed in writs of right. See ASSIZE; GRAND ASSIZE.

TRIAL BY INSPECTION OR EXAMINATION is a form of trial in which the judges of the court, upon the testimony of their own senses, decide the point in dispute.

TRIAL BY JURY. A trial in which the issues of fact are to be determined by the verdict of a jury of twelve men, duly selected, impaneled, and sworn.

The terms "jury" and "trial by jury" are, and for ages have been, well known in the language of the law. They were used at the adoption of the constitution, and always, it is believed, before that time, and almost always since, in a single sense. A jury for the trial of a cause was a body of twelve men, described as upright, well-qualified, and lawful men, disinterested and impartial, not of kin nor personal dependents of either of the parties, having their homes within the jurisdictional limits of the court, drawn and selected by officers free from all bias in favor of or against either party, duly impaneled under the direction of a competent court, sworn to render a true verdict according to the law and the evidence given them, who, after hearing the parties and their evidence, and receiving the instructions of the court relative to the law involved in the trial, and deliberating, when necessary, apart from all extraneous influences, must return their unanimous verdict upon the issue submitted to them. All the books of the law describe a trial jury substantially as we have stated it; and a "trial by jury" is a trial by such a body so constituted and conducted. 11 Nev. 60.

TRIAL BY PROVISO. A proceeding allowed where the plaintiff in an action desists from prosecuting his suit, and does not bring it to trial in convenient time. The defendant, in such case, may take out the *venire facias* to the sheriff, containing these words, "*proviso quod,*" etc., *i. e.,* provided that. If plaintiff take out any writ to that purpose, the sheriff shall summon but one jury on them both. This is called "going to trial by proviso." Jacob, tit. "Proviso."

TRIAL BY THE RECORD. A form of trial resorted to where issue is taken upon a plea of *nul tiel record*, in which case the party asserting the existence of a record as pleaded is bound to produce it in court on a day assigned. If the record is forthcoming, the issue is tried by inspection and examination of it. If the record is not produced, judgment is given for his adversary. 3 Bl. Comm. 330.

TRIAL BY WAGER OF BATTEL. This was a species of trial introduced into England, among other Norman customs, by William the Conqueror, in which the person accused fought with his accuser, under the apprehension that Heaven would give the victory to him who was in the right. 3 Bl. Comm. 337–341.

TRIAL BY WAGER OF LAW. In old English law. A method of trial, where the defendant, coming into court, made oath that he did not owe the claim demanded of him, and eleven of his neighbors, as compurgators, swore that they believed him to speak the truth. 3 Bl. Comm. 343. See WAGER OF LAW.

TRIAL BY WITNESSES. The name "trial *per testes*" has been used for a trial without the intervention of a jury, is the only method of trial known to the civil law, and is adopted by depositions in chancery. The judge is thus left to form, in his own breast, his sentence upon the credit of the witnesses examined. But it is very rarely used at common law. Tomlins.

TRIAL LIST. A list of cases marked down for trial for any one term.

TRIAL WITH ASSESSORS. Admiralty actions involving nautical questions, *e. g.*, actions of collision, are generally tried in England before a judge, with Trinity Masters sitting as assessors. Rosc. Adm. 179.

Triatio ibi semper debet fieri, ubi juratores meliorem possunt habere notitiam. Trial ought always to be had where the jurors can have the best information. 7 Coke, 1.

TRIBUERE. Lat. In the civil law. To give; to distribute.

TRIBUNAL. The seat of a judge; the place where he administers justice; a judicial court; the bench of judges.

In Roman law. An elevated seat occupied by the prætor, when he judged, or heard causes in form. Originally a kind of stage made of wood in the form of a square, and movable, but afterwards built of stone in the form of a semi-circle. Adams, Rom. Ant. 132, 133.

TRIBUNAUX DE COMMERCE. In French law. Certain courts composed of a president, judges, and substitutes, which take cognizance of all cases between merchants, and of disagreements among partners. Appeals lie from them to the courts of justice. Brown.

TRIBUTE. A contribution which is raised by a prince or sovereign from his subjects to sustain the expenses of the state.

A sum of money paid by an inferior sovereign or state to a superior potentate, to secure the friendship or protection of the latter. Brande.

TRICESIMA. An ancient custom in a borough in the county of Hereford, so called, because thirty burgesses paid 1d. rent for their houses to the bishop, who was lord of the manor. Wharton.

TRIDING-MOTE. The court held for a triding or trithing. Cowell.

TRIDUUM. In old English law. The space of three days. Fleta, lib. 1, c. 31, § 7.

TRIENNIAL ACT. An act limiting the duration of every parliament to three years, unless sooner dissolved. It was passed by the long parliament in 1640, and afterwards repealed, and the term was fixed at seven years by the septennial act, (St. 1 Geo. I. St. 2, c. 38.)

TRIENS. Lat. **In Roman law.** A subdivision of the *as*, containing four *unciæ;* the proportion of four-twelfths or one-third. 2 Bl. Comm. 462, note *m*. A copper coin of the value of one-third of the *as*. Brande.

In feudal law. Dower or third. 2 Bl. Comm. 129.

TRIGAMUS. In old English law. One who has been thrice married; one who, at different times and successively, has had three wives; a trigamist. 3 Inst. 88.

TRIGILD. In Saxon law. A triple gild, geld, or payment; three times the value of a thing, paid as a composition or satisfaction. Spelman.

TRINEPOS. Lat. In the civil law. A great-grandson's or great-granddaughter's great-grandson. A male descendant in the sixth degree. Inst. 3, 6, 4.

TRINEPTIS. Lat. In the civil law. A great-grandson's or great-granddaughter's great-granddaughter. A female descendant in the sixth degree. Inst. 3, 6, 4.

TRINITY HOUSE. In English law. A society at Deptford Strond, incorporated by Hen. VIII. in 1515, for the promotion of commerce and navigation by licensing and regulating pilots, and ordering and erecting beacons, light-houses, buoys, etc. Wharton.

TRINITY MASTERS are elder brethren of the Trinity House. If a question arising in an admiralty action depends upon technical skill and experience in navigation, the judge or court is usually assisted at the hearing by two Trinity Masters, who sit as assessors, and advise the court on questions of a nautical character. Williams & B. Adm. Jur. 271; Sweet.

TRINITY SITTINGS. Sittings of the English court of appeal and of the high court of justice in London and Middlesex, commencing on the Tuesday after Whitsun week, and terminating on the 8th of August.

TRINITY TERM. One of the four terms of the English courts of common law, beginning on the 22d day of May, and ending on the 12th of June. 3 Steph. Comm. 562.

TRINIUMGELDUM. In old European law. An extraordinary kind of composition for an offense, consisting of *three times nine*, or twenty-seven times the single geld or payment. Spelman.

TRINODA NECESSITAS. In Saxon law. A threefold necessity or burden. A term used to denote the three things from contributing to the performance of which no lands were exempted, viz., *pontis reparatio*, (the repair of bridges,) *arcis constructio*, (the building of castles,) *et expeditio contra hostem*, (military service against an enemy.) 1 Bl. Comm. 263, 357.

TRIORS. In practice. Persons who are appointed to try challenges to jurors, *i. e.*, to hear and determine whether a juror challenged for favor is or is not qualified to serve.

The lords chosen to try a peer, when indicted for felony, in the court of the lord high steward, are also called "triors." Mozley & Whitley.

TRIPARTITE. In conveyancing. Of three parts; a term applied to an indenture to which there are three several parties, (of the first, second, and third parts,) and which is executed in triplicate.

TRIPLICACION. L. Fr. In old pleading. A rejoinder in pleading; the defendant's answer to the plaintiff's replication. Britt. c. 77.

TRIPLICATIO. In the civil law. The reply of the plaintiff to the rejoinder of the defendant. It corresponds to the surrejoinder of common law. Inst. 4, 14; Bract. l. 5, t. 5, c. 1.

TRIPLUM. Lat. In the civil law. The triple value of a thing. *Actio in triplum*, an action for the triple value. Inst. 4, 6, 21, 24.

TRIPLY. In Scotch practice. A pleading corresponding with the Latin "*triplicatio*," from which the term also was taken. 3 How. State Tr. 478, 637, 638.

TRISTRIS. In old forest law. A freedom from the duty of attending the lord of a forest when engaged in the chase. Spelman.

TRITAVIA. Lat. In the civil law. A great-grandmother's great-grandmother; the female ascendant in the sixth degree.

TRITAVUS. Lat. In the civil law. A great-grandfather's great-grandfather; the male ascendant in the sixth degree.

TRITHING. In Saxon law. One of the territorial divisions of England, being the *third* part of a county, and comprising three or more hundreds. Within the trithing there was a court held (called "trithing-mote") which resembled the court-leet, but was inferior to the county court.

TRITHING-MOTE. The court held for a trithing or riding.

TRITHING-REEVE. The officer who superintended a trithing or riding.

TRIUMVIR. In old English law. A trithing man or constable of three hundred Cowell.

TRIUMVIRI CAPITALES. In Roman law. Officers who had charge of the prison, through whose intervention punishments were inflicted. They had eight lictors to execute their orders. Vicat, Voc. Jur.

TRIVERBIAL DAYS. In the civil law. Juridical days; days allowed to the prætor for deciding causes; days on which the prætor might speak the *three* characteristic *words* of his office, viz., *do, dico, addico*. Calvin.

Otherwise called "*dies fasti.*" 3 Bl. Comm. 424, and note *u*.

TRIVIAL. Trifling; inconsiderable; of small worth or importance. In equity, a demurrer will lie to a bill on the ground of the *triviality* of the matter in dispute, as being below the dignity of the court. 4 Bouv. Inst. no. 4237.

TRONAGE. In English law. A customary duty or toll for weighing wool; so called because it was weighed by a common *trona*, or beam. Fleta, lib. 2, c. 12.

TRONATOR. A weigher of wool. Cowell.

TROPHY MONEY. Money formerly collected and raised in London, and the several counties of England, towards providing harness and maintenance for the militia, etc.

TROVER. In common-law practice, the action of trover (or trover and conversion) is a species of action on the case, and originally lay for the recovery of damages against a person who had *found* another's goods and wrongfully converted them to his own use. Subsequently the allegation of the loss of the goods by the plaintiff and the finding of them by the defendant was merely fictitious, and the action became the remedy for any wrongful interference with or detention of the goods of another. 3 Steph. Comm. 425. Sweet.

TROY WEIGHT. A weight of twelve ounces to the pound, having its name from Troyes, a city in Aube, France.

TRUCE. In international law. A suspension or temporary cessation of hostilities by agreement between belligerent powers; an armistice. Wheat. Int. Law, 442.

TRUCE OF GOD. In medieval law. A truce or suspension of arms promulgated by the church, putting a stop to private hostilities at certain periods or during certain sacred seasons.

TRUCK ACT. In English law. This name is given to the statute 1 & 2 Wm. IV. c. 37, passed to abolish what is commonly called the "truck system," under which employers were in the practice of paying the wages of their work people in goods, or of requiring them to purchase goods at certain shops. This led to laborers being compelled to take goods of inferior quality at a high price. The act applies to all artificers, workmen, and laborers, except those engaged in certain trades, especially iron and metal works, quarries, cloth, silk, and glass manufactories. It does not apply to domestic or agricultural servants. Sweet.

TRUE. Conformable to fact; correct; exact; actual; genuine; honest.

"In one sense, that only is *true* which is conformable to the actual state of things. In that sense, a statement is untrue which does not express things exactly as they are. But in another and broader sense, the word 'true' is often used as a synonym of 'honest,' 'sincere,' 'not fraudulent.'" 111 U. S. 345, 4 Sup. Ct. Rep. 466.

TRUE BILL. In criminal practice. The indorsement made by a grand jury upon a bill of indictment, when they find it sustained by the evidence laid before them, and are satisfied of the truth of the accusation. 4 Bl. Comm. 306.

TRUE, PUBLIC, AND NOTORIOUS. These three qualities used to be formally predicated in the libel in the ecclesiastical courts, of the charges which it contained, at the end of each article severally. Wharton.

TRUST. An equitable or beneficial right or title to land or other property, held for the beneficiary by another person, in whom resides the legal title or ownership, recognized and enforced by chancery courts.

An obligation upon a person, arising out of a confidence reposed in him, to apply property faithfully, and according to such confidence. Willis, Trustees, c. 1, p. 2.

"A trust, in the general and enlarged sense, is a right on the part of the *cestui que trust* to receive the profits, and to dispose of the lands in equity." 4 Kent, Comm. 304.

Classification. Trusts are either *express* or *implied;* the former being trusts which are created in so many fit and appropriate terms; the latter being trusts founded on the presumable, though unexpressed, intention of the party who creates them.

Express trusts are those created and manifested by agreement of the parties. Implied trusts are such as are inferred by law from the nature of the transaction, or the conduct of the parties. Code Ga. 1882, § 2309.

Trusts are also either *executed* or *executory*. An executed trust is one which the person creating it has fully and finally declared, whence also it is called a "complete" trust; while an executory trust is one which the person creating it has not fully or finally declared, but has given merely an outline of it by way of direction to the conveyancer, whence also it is called sometimes an "incomplete" and sometimes a "directory" trust. Brown.

Trusts are again classified as *special* (or

active) and *simple*, (or passive, or dry.) The special trust is where the machinery of a trustee is introduced for the execution of some purpose particularly pointed out, and the trustee is not, as before, a mere passive depositary of the estate, but is called upon to exert himself actively in the execution of the settlor's intention; as where a conveyance is to trustees upon trust to sell for payment of debts. Lewin, Trusts, 18. A simple trust is one which requires the performance of no duty by the trustee to carry out the trust, but by force of which the mere legal title rests in the trustee.

Trusts are also either *voluntary* or *involuntary*. A voluntary trust is an obligation arising out of a personal confidence reposed in, and voluntarily accepted by, one for the benefit of another. An involuntary trust is one which is created by operation of law. Civil Code Cal. §§ 2216, 2217.

According to another use of the term, "voluntary trusts" are such as are made in favor of a volunteer; that is, a person who gives nothing in exchange for the trust, but receives it as a pure gift. And in this use the term is distinguished from "trusts for value," the latter being such as are in favor of purchasers, mortgagees, etc.

Constructive trusts are such as are founded neither on an expressed nor on any presumable intention of the party, but which are raised by construction of equity without any regard to intention, and simply for the purpose of satisfying the demands of justice and good conscience. Brown.

Public trusts. "By 'public' must be understood such as are constituted for the benefit either of the public at large or of some considerable portion of it answering a particular description. To this class belong all trusts for *charitable* purposes, and indeed 'public trusts' and 'charitable trusts' may be considered in general as synonymous expressions." Lewin, Trusts, 20.

Private trusts. "In private trusts the beneficial interest is vested absolutely in one or more individuals, who are, or within a certain time may be, definitely ascertained, and to whom, therefore, collectively, unless under some legal disability, it is, or within the allowed limit will be, competent to control, modify, or determine the trust." Lewin, Trusts, 20.

For a discussion of the differences between "trust" and "use," see 50 N. H. 491.

In mercantile law. An organization of persons or corporations, formed mainly for the purpose of regulating the supply and price of commodities, etc.

TRUST-DEED. 1. A species of mortgage given to a trustee for the purpose of securing a numerous class of creditors, as the bondholders of a railroad corporation, with power to foreclose and sell on failure of the payment of their bonds, notes, or other claims.

2. In some of the states, and in the District of Columbia, a trust-deed is a security resembling a mortgage, being a conveyance of lands to trustees to secure the payment of a debt, with a power of sale upon default, and upon a trust to apply the net proceeds to paying the debt and to turn over the surplus to the grantor.

TRUSTEE. The person appointed, or required by law, to execute a trust; one in whom an estate, interest, or power is vested, under an express or implied agreement to administer or exercise it for the benefit or to the use of another.

"Trustee" is also used in a wide and perhaps inaccurate sense, to denote that a person has the duty of carrying out a transaction, in which he and another person are interested, in such manner as will be most for the benefit of the latter, and not in such a way that he himself might be tempted, for the sake of his personal advantage, to neglect the interests of the other. In this sense, directors of companies are said to be "trustees for the shareholders." Sweet.

TRUSTEE ACTS. The statutes 13 & 14 Vict. c. 60, passed in 1850, and 15 & 16 Vict. c. 55, passed in 1852, enabling the court of chancery, without bill filed, to appoint new trustees in lieu of any who, on account of death, lunacy, absence, or otherwise, are unable or unwilling to act as such; and also to make vesting orders by which legal estates and rights may be transferred from the old trustee or trustees to the new trustee or trustees so appointed. Mozley & Whitley.

TRUSTEE EX MALEFICIO. A person who, being guilty of wrongful or fraudulent conduct, is held by equity to the duty and liability of a trustee, in relation to the subject-matter, to prevent him from profiting by his own wrong.

TRUSTEE IN BANKRUPTCY. A trustee in bankruptcy is a person in whom the property of a bankrupt is vested in trust for the creditors.

TRUSTEE PROCESS. The name given, in the New England states, to the process of garnishment or foreign attachment.

TRUSTEE RELIEF ACTS. The statute 10 & 11 Vict. c. 96, passed in 1847, and statute 12 & 13 Vict. c. 74, passed in 1849, by which a trustee is enabled to pay money into court, in cases where a difficulty arises respecting the title to the trust fund. Mozley & Whitley.

TRUSTER. In Scotch law. The maker or creator of a trust.

TRUSTIS. In old European law. Trust; faith; confidence; fidelity.

TRUSTOR. A word occasionally, though rarely, used as a designation of the creator, donor, or founder of a trust.

TRY. To examine judicially; to examine and investigate a controversy, by the legal method called "trial," for the purpose of determining the issues it involves.

TUAS RES TIBI HABETO. Lat. Have or take your things to yourself. The form of words by which, according to the old Roman law, a man divorced his wife. Calvin.

TUB. In mercantile law. A measure containing sixty pounds of tea, and from fifty-six to eighty-six pounds of camphor. Jacob.

TUB-MAN. In English law. A barrister who has a preaudience in the exchequer, and also one who has a particular place in court, is so called. Brown.

TUCHAS. In Spanish law. Objections or exceptions to witnesses. White, New Recop. b. 3, tit. 7, c. 10.

TUERTO. In Spanish law. Tort. Las Partidas, pt. 7, tit. 6, l. 5.

TUG. A steam vessel built for towing; synonymous with "tow-boat."

TULLIANUM. Lat. In Roman law. That part of a prison which was under ground. Supposed to be so called from Servius Tullius, who built that part of the first prison in Rome. Adams, Rom. Ant. 290.

TUMBREL. A castigatory, trebucket, or ducking-stool, anciently used as a punishment for common scolds.

TUMULTUOUS PETITIONING. Under St. 13 Car. II. St. 1, c. 5, this was a misdemeanor, and consisted in more than twenty persons signing any petition to the crown or either house of parliament for the alteration of matters established by law in church or state, unless the contents thereof had been approved by three justices, or the majority of the grand jury at assizes or quarter sessions. No petition could be delivered by more than ten persons. 4 Bl. Comm. 147; Mozley & Whitley.

TUN. A measure of wine or oil, containing four hogsheads.

TUNGREVE. A town-reeve or bailiff. Cowell.

TURBA. Lat. In the civil law. A multitude; a crowd or mob; a tumultuous assembly of persons. Said to consist of ten or fifteen, at the least. Calvin.

TURBARY. Turbary, or common of turbary, is the right or liberty of digging turf upon another man's ground. Brown.

TURN, or TOURN. The great court-leet of the county, as the old county court was the court-baron. Of this the sheriff is judge, and the court is incident to his office: wherefore it is called the "sheriff's tourn;" and it had its name originally from the sheriff making a turn of circuit about his shire, and holding this court in each respective hundred. Wharton.

TURNED TO A RIGHT. This phrase means that a person whose estate is divested by usurpation cannot expel the possessor by mere entry, but must have recourse to an action, either possessory or droitural. Mozley & Whitley.

TURNKEY. A person, under the superintendence of a jailer, who has the charge of the keys of the prison, for the purpose of opening and fastening the doors.

TURNPIKE. A gate set across a road, to stop travelers and carriages until toll is paid for the privilege of passage thereon.

TURNPIKE ROADS. These are roads on which parties have by law a right to erect gates and bars, for the purpose of taking toll, and of refusing the permission to pass along them to all persons who refuse to pay. 6 Mees. & W. 428.

A turnpike road is a public highway, established by public authority for public use, and is to be regarded as a public easement, and not as private property. The only difference between this and a common highway is that, instead of being made at the public expense in the first instance, it is authorized and laid out by public authority, and made at the expense of individuals in the first instance; and the cost of construction and maintenance is reimbursed by a toll, levied by public authority for the purpose. 16 Pick. 175.

TURPIS. Lat. In the civil law. Base; mean; vile; disgraceful; infamous; unlawful. Applied both to things and persons. Calvin.

TURPIS CAUSA. Lat. A base cause; a vile or immoral consideration; a consideration which, on account of its immorality, is not allowed by law to be sufficient either to support a contract or found an action; *e. g.*, future illicit intercourse.

TURPIS CONTRACTUS. Lat. An immoral or iniquitous contract.

Turpis est pars quæ non convenit cum suo toto. The part which does not agree with its whole is of mean account, [entitled to small or no consideration.] Plowd. 101; Shep. Touch. 87.

TURPITUDE. Everything done contrary to justice, honesty, modesty, or good morals is said to be done with turpitude.

TURPITUDO. Lat. Baseness; infamy; immorality; turpitude.

Tuta est custodia quæ sibimet creditur. Hob. 340. That guardianship is secure which is intrusted to itself alone.

TUTELA. Lat. In the civil law. Tutelage; that species of guardianship which continued to the age of puberty; the guardian being called "*tutor*," and the ward, "*pupillus*." 1 Dom. Civil Law, b. 2, tit. 1, p. 260.

TUTELA LEGITIMA. Lat. In the civil law. Legal tutelage; tutelage created by act of law, as where none had been created by testament. Inst. 1, 15, pr.

TUTELA TESTAMENTARIA. Lat. In the civil law. Testamentary tutelage or guardianship; that kind of tutelage which was created by will. Calvin.

TUTELÆ ACTIO. Lat. In the civil law. An action of tutelage; an action which lay for a ward or pupil, on the termination of tutelage, against the *tutor* or guardian, to compel an account. Calvin.

TUTELAGE. Guardianship; state of being under a guardian.

TUTELAM REDDERE. Lat. In the civil law. To render an account of tutelage. Calvin. *Tutelam reposcere*, to demand an account of tutelage.

TUTEUR. In French law. A kind of guardian.

TUTUER OFFICIEUX. In French law, a person over fifty years of age may be appointed a tutor of this sort to a child over fifteen years of age, with the consent of the parents of such child, or, in their default, the *conseil de famille*. The duties which such a tutor becomes subject to are analogous to those in English law of a person who puts himself *in loco parentis* to any one. Brown.

TUTEUR SUBROGÉ. In French law. The title of a second guardian appointed for an infant under guardianship. His functions are exercised in case the interests of the infant and his principal guardian conflict. Code Nap. 420; Brown.

Tutius erratur ex parte mitiore. 3 Inst. 220. It is safer to err on the gentler side.

Tutius semper est errare acquietando, quam in puniendo, ex parte misericordiæ quam ex parte justitiæ. It is always safer to err in acquitting than punishing, on the side of mercy than on the side of justice. Branch, Princ.; 2 Hale, P. C. 290; Broom, Max. 326; 9 Metc. (Mass.) 116.

TUTOR. In the civil law. This term corresponds nearly to "guardian," (*i. e.*, a person appointed to have the care of the person of a minor and the administration of his estate,) except that the guardian of a minor who has passed a certain age is called "curator," and has powers and duties differing somewhat from those of a tutor.

By the laws of Louisiana, minors under the age of fourteen years, if males, and under the age of twelve years, if females, are, both as to their persons and their estates, placed under the authority of a tutor. Above that age, and until their majority or emancipation, they are placed under the authority of a curator. Civil Code La. 1838, art. 263.

TUTOR ALIENUS. In English law. The name given to a stranger who enters upon the lands of an infant within the age of fourteen, and takes the profits. Co. Litt. 89*b*, 90*a*.

TUTOR PROPRIUS. The name given to one who is rightly a guardian in socage, in contradistinction to a *tutor alienus*.

TUTORSHIP. The office and power of a tutor.

TUTORSHIP BY NATURE. After the dissolution of marriage by the death of either husband or wife, the tutorship of minor children belongs of right to the surviving mother or father. This is what is called "tutorship by nature." Civil Code La. art. 250.

TUTORSHIP BY WILL. The right of appointing a tutor, whether a relation or a stranger, belongs exclusively to the father or mother dying last. This is called "tutorship by will," because generally it is given by testament; but it may likewise be given by any declaration by the surviving father or mother, executed before a notary and two witnesses. Civil Code La. art. 257.

TUTRIX. A female tutor.

TWA NIGHT GEST. In Saxon law. A guest on the second night. By the laws of Edward the Confessor it was provided that a man who lodged at an inn, or at the house of another, should be considered, on the first night of his being there, a stranger, (*uncuth;*) on the second night, a guest; on the third night, a member of the family. This had reference to the responsibility of the host or entertainer for offenses committed by the guest.

TWELFHINDI. The highest rank of men in the Saxon government, who were valued at 1200s. If any injury were done to such persons, satisfaction was to be made according to their worth. Cowell.

TWELVE TABLES. The earliest statute or code of Roman law, framed by a commission of ten men, B. C. 450, upon the return of a commission of three who had been sent abroad to study foreign laws and institutions. The Twelve Tables consisted partly of laws transcribed from the institutions of other nations, partly of such as were altered and accommodated to the manners of the Romans, partly of new provisions, and mainly, perhaps, of laws and usages under their ancient kings. They formed the source and foundation for the whole later development of Roman jurisprudence. They exist now only in fragmentary form. See 1 Kent, Comm. 520.

TWELVE-DAY WRIT. A writ issued under the St. 18 & 19 Vict. c. 67, for summary procedure on bills of exchange and promissory notes, abolished by rule of court in 1880. Wharton.

TWELVE - MONTH, in the singular number, includes all the year; but *twelve months* are to be computed according to twenty-eight days for every month. 6 Coke, 62.

TWICE IN JEOPARDY. See JEOPARDY; ONCE IN JEOPARDY.

TWYHINDI. The lower order of Saxons, valued at 200s. in the scale of pecuniary mulcts inflicted for crimes. Cowell.

TYBURN TICKET. A certificate which was given to the prosecutor of a felon to conviction.

TYHTLAN. In Saxon law. An accusation, impeachment, or charge of any offense.

TYLWITH. Brit. A tribe or family branching or issuing out of another. Cowell.

TYRANNY. Arbitrary or despotic government; the severe and autocratic exercise of sovereign power, either vested constitutionally in one ruler, or usurped by him by breaking down the division and distribution of governmental powers.

TYRANT. A despot; a sovereign or ruler, legitimate or otherwise, who uses his power unjustly and arbitrarily, to the oppression of his subjects.

TYRRA, or TOIRA. A mount or hill. Cowell.

TYTHE. Tithe, or tenth part.

TYTHING. A company of ten; a district; a tenth part. See TITHING.

TZAR, TZARINA. The emperor and empress of Russia. See CZAR.

U.

U. B. An abbreviation for "Upper Bench."

U. C. An abbreviation for "Upper Canada," used in citing the reports.

U. R. Initials of "*uti rogas*," be it as you desire, a ballot thus inscribed, by which the Romans voted in favor of a bill or candidate. Tayl. Civil Law, 191.

U. S. An abbreviation for "United States."

UBERRIMA FIDES. Lat. The most abundant good faith; absolute and perfect candor or openness and honesty; the absence of any concealment or deception, however slight.

Ubi aliquid conceditur, conceditur et id sine quo res ipsa esse non potest. When anything is granted, that also is granted without which the thing granted cannot exist. Broom, Max. 483; 13 Mees. & W. 706.

Ubi aliquid impeditur propter unum, eo remoto, tollitur impedimentum. Where anything is impeded by one single cause, if that be removed, the impediment is removed. Branch, Princ., citing 5 Coke, 77*a*.

Ubi cessat remedium ordinarium, ibi decurritur ad extraordinarium. Where the ordinary remedy fails, recourse must be had to an extraordinary one. 4 Coke, 92*b*.

Ubi culpa est, ibi pœna subesse debet. Where the crime is committed, there ought the punishment to be undergone. Jenk. Cent. 325.

Ubi damna dantur, victus victori in expensis condemnari debet. Where damages are given, the vanquished party ought to be condemned in costs to the victor. 2 Inst. 289.

Ubi eadem ratio, ibi eadem lex; et de similibus idem est judicium. 7 Coke, 18. Where the same reason exists, there the same law prevails; and, of things similar, the judgment is similar.

Ubi et dantis et accipientis turpitudo versatur, non posse repeti dicimus; quotiens autem accipientis turpitudo versatur, repeti posse. Where there is turpitude on the part of both giver and receiver, we say it cannot be recovered back; but as often as the turpitude is on the side of the receiver [alone] it can be recovered back. 17 Mass. 562.

Ubi factum nullum, ibi fortia nulla. Where there is no principal fact, there can be no accessory. 4 Coke, 426.

Ubi jus, ibi remedium. Where there is a right, there is a remedy. Broom, Max. 191, 204; 1 Term R. 512; Co. Litt. 197*b*.

Ubi jus incertum, ibi jus nullum. Where the law is uncertain, there is no law.

Ubi lex aliquem cogit ostendere causam, necesse est quod causa sit justa et legitima. Where the law compels a man to show cause, it is necessary that the cause be just and lawful. 2 Inst. 289.

Ubi lex est specialis, et ratio ejus generalis, generaliter accipienda est. 2 Inst. 43. Where the law is special, and the reason of it general, it ought to be taken as being general.

Ubi lex non distinguit, nec nos distinguere debemus. Where the law does not distinguish, neither ought we to distinguish. 7 Coke, 5*b*.

Ubi major pars est, ibi totum. Where the greater part is, there the whole is. That is, majorities govern. Moore, 578.

Ubi non adest norma legis, omnia quasi pro suspectis habenda sunt. When the law fails to serve as a rule, almost everything ought to be suspected. Bac. Aphorisms, 25.

Ubi non est annua renovatio, ibi decimæ non debent solvi. Where there is no annual renovation, there tithes ought not to be paid.

Ubi non est condendi auctoritas, ibi non est parendi necessitas. Dav. Ir. K. B. 69. Where there is no authority for establishing a rule, there is no necessity of obeying it.

Ubi non est directa lex, standum est arbitrio judicis, vel procedendum ad similia. Ellesm. Post. N. 41. Where there is no direct law, the opinion of the judge is to be taken, or references to be made to similar cases.

Ubi non est lex, ibi non est transgressio, quoad mundum. Where there is no law, there is no transgression, so far as relates to the world. 4 Coke, 16*b*.

Ubi non est manifesta injustitia, judices habentur pro bonis viris, et judicatum pro veritate. Where there is no manifest injustice, the judges are to be regarded as honest men, and their judgment as truth. 1 Johns. Cas. 341, 345.

Ubi non est principalis, non potest esse accessorius. 4 Coke, 43. Where there is no principal, there cannot be an accessory.

Ubi nulla est conjectura quæ ducat alio, verba intelligenda sunt ex proprietate, non grammatica, sed populari ex usu. Where there is nothing to call for a different construction, [the] words [of an instrument] are to be understood, not according to their strict grammatical meaning, but according to their popular and ordinary sense. Grot. de Jure B. lib. 2, c. 16.

Ubi nullum matrimonium, ibi nulla dos. Where there is no marriage, there is no dower. Bract. fol. 92; 2 Bl. Comm. 130.

Ubi periculum, ibi et lucrum collocatur. He at whose risk a thing is, should receive the profits arising from it.

Ubi pugnantia inter se in testamento juberentur, neutrum ratum est. Where repugnant or inconsistent directions are contained in a will, neither is valid. Dig. 50, 17, 188, pr.

Ubi quid generaliter conceditur inest hæc exceptio, si non aliquid sit contra jus fasque. 10 Coke, 78. Where a thing is conceded generally this exception is implied: that there shall be nothing contrary to law and right.

Ubi quis delinquit, ibi punietur. Where a man offends, there he shall be punished. 6 Coke, 47*b*. In cases of felony, the trial shall be always by the common law in the same place where the offense was, and shall not be supposed in any other place. Id.

UBI RE VERA. Where in reality; when in truth or in point of fact. Cro. Eliz. 645; Cro. Jac. 4.

Ubi verba conjuncta non sunt sufficit alterutrum esse factum. Dig. 50, 17, 110, 3. Where words are not conjoined, it is enough if one or other be complied with.

UBIQUITY. Omnipresence; presence in several places, or in all places, at one time. A fiction of English law is the "legal ubiquity" of the sovereign, by which he is constructively present in all the courts. 1 Bl. Comm. 270.

UDAL. A term mentioned by Blackstone as used in Finland to denote that kind of right in real property which is called, in English law, "allodial." 2 Bl. Comm. 45, note *f*.

UKAAS, UKASE. The name of a law or ordinance made by the czar of Russia.

ULLAGE. In commercial law. The amount wanting when a cask, on being gauged, is found not to be completely full.

ULNA FERREA. In old English law. The iron ell; the standard ell of iron, kept in the exchequer for the rule of measure.

ULNAGE. Alnage, (which see.)

ULTIMA RATIO. Lat. The last argument; the last resort; the means last to be resorted to.

Ultima voluntas testatoris est perimplenda secundum veram intentionem suam. Co. Litt. 322. The last will of a testator is to be fulfilled according to his true intention.

ULTIMATE FACTS. In pleading and practice. Facts in issue; opposed to probative or evidential facts, the latter being such as serve to establish or disprove the issues. 2 Utah, 379.

ULTIMATUM. Lat. The last. The final and ultimate proposition made in negotiating a treaty, or a contract, or the like.

ULTIMUM SUPPLICIUM. Lat. The extreme punishment; the extremity of punishment; the punishment of death. 4 Bl. Comm. 17.

Ultimum supplicium esse mortem solam interpretamur. The extremest punishment we consider to be death alone. Dig. 48, 19, 21.

ULTIMUS HÆRES. Lat. The last or remote heir; the lord. So called in contradistinction to the *hæres proximus* and the *hæres remotior*. Dalr. Feud. Prop. 110.

ULTRA. Lat. Beyond; outside of; in excess of.

Damages *ultra*, damages beyond a sum paid into court.

ULTRA MARE. Beyond sea. One of the old essoins or excuses for not appearing in court at the return of process. Bract. fol. 338.

Ultra posse non potest esse, et vice versa. What is beyond possibility cannot exist, and the reverse, [what cannot exist is not possible.] Wing. Max. 100.

ULTRA REPRISES. After deduction of drawbacks; in excess of deductions or expenses.

ULTRA VIRES. A term used to express the action of a corporation which is beyond the powers conferred upon it by its charter, or the statutes under which it was instituted. 13 Amer. Law Rev. 632.

"*Ultra vires*" is also sometimes applied to an act which, though within the powers of a corporation, is not binding on it because the consent or agreement of the corporation has not been given in the manner required by its constitution. Thus, where a company delegates certain powers to its directors, all acts done by the directors beyond the scope of those powers are *ultra vires*, and not binding on the company, unless it subsequently ratifies them. Sweet.

ULTRONEOUS WITNESS. In Scotch law. A volunteer witness; one who appears to give evidence without being called upon. 2 Alis. Crim. Pr. 393.

UMPIRAGE. The decision of an umpire. The word "umpirage," in reference to an umpire, is the same as the word "award," in reference to arbitrators; but "award" is commonly applied to the decision of the umpire also.

UMPIRE. When matters in dispute are submitted to two or more arbitrators, and they do not agree in their decision, it is usual for another person to be called in as "umpire," to whose sole judgment it is then referred. Brown.

Un ne doit prise advantage de son tort demesne. 2 And. 38, 40. One ought not to take advantage of his own wrong.

Una persona vix potest supplere vices duarum. 7 Coke, 118. One person can scarcely supply the places of two. See 9 H. L. Cas. 274.

UNA VOCE. Lat. With one voice; unanimously; without dissent.

UNALIENABLE. Incapable of being aliened, that is, sold and transferred.

UNANIMITY. Agreement of all the persons concerned, in holding one and the same opinion or determination of any matter or question; as the concurrence of a jury in deciding upon their verdict.

UNASCERTAINED DUTIES. Payment in gross, on an estimate as to amount, and where the merchant, on a final liquidation, will be entitled by law to allowances or deductions which do not depend on the rate of duty charged, but on the ascertainment of the quantity of the article subject to duty. 5 Blatchf. 274.

UNAVOIDABLE ACCIDENT. Not necessarily an accident which it was physically impossible, in the nature of things, for the person to have prevented, but one not occasioned in any degree, either remotely or directly, by the want of such care or skill as the law holds every man bound to exercise. 8 Wend. 473.

UNCEASESATH. In Saxon law. An oath by relations not to avenge a relation's death. Blount.

UNCERTAINTY. Such vagueness, obscurity, or confusion in any written instrument, *e. g.*, a will, as to render it unintelligible to those who are called upon to execute or interpret it, so that no definite meaning can be extracted from it.

UNCIA. Lat. In Roman law. An ounce; the twelfth of the Roman "*as*," or pound. The twelfth part of anything; the proportion of one-twelfth. 2 Bl. Comm. 462, note *m*.

UNCIA AGRI, UNCIA TERRÆ. These phrases often occur in the charters of the British kings, and signify some measure or quantity of land. It is said to have been the quantity of twelve *modii*; each *modius* being possibly one hundred feet square. Jacob.

UNCIARIUS HÆRES. Lat. In Roman law. An heir to one-twelfth of an estate or inheritance. Calvin.

UNCLE. The brother of one's father or mother.

UNCONSCIONABLE BARGAIN. A contract which no man in his senses, not under delusion, would make, on the one hand, and which no fair and honest man would accept, on the other. 4 Bouv. Inst. no. 3848.

UNCONSTITUTIONAL. That which is contrary to the constitution. The opposite of "constitutional."

UNCORE PRIST. L. Fr. Still ready. A species of plea or replication by which the party alleges that he is still ready to pay or perform all that is justly demanded of him. In conjunction with the phrase "*tout temps prist,*" it signifies that he has always been and still is ready.

UNCUTH. In Saxon law. Unknown; a stranger. A person entertained in the house of another was, on the first night of his entertainment, so called. Bract. fol. 124*b*.

UNDE NIHIL HABET. Lat. In old English law. The name of the writ of dower, which lay for a widow, where *no dower* at all had been assigned her within the time limited by law. 3 Bl. Comm. 183.

UNDEFENDED. A term sometimes applied to one who is obliged to make his own defense when on trial, or in a civil cause. A cause is said to be undefended when the defendant makes default, in not putting in an appearance to the plaintiff's action; in not putting in his statement of defense; or in not appearing at the trial either personally or by counsel, after having received due notice. Mozley & Whitley.

UNDER AND SUBJECT. Words frequently used in conveyances of land which is subject to a mortgage, to show that the grantee takes subject to such mortgage. 27 Amer. Law Reg. (N. S.) 337.

UNDER-CHAMBERLAINS OF THE EXCHEQUER. Two officers who cleaved the tallies written by the clerk of the tallies, and read the same, that the clerk of the pell and comptrollers thereof might see their entries were true. They also made searches for records in the treasury, and had the custody of Domesday Book. Cowell. The office is now abolished.

UNDER-LEASE. In conveyancing. A lease granted by one who is himself a lessee for years, for any fewer or less number of years than he himself holds. If a deed passes *all* the estate or time of the termor, it is an *assignment;* but, if it be for a *less* portion of time than the whole term, it is an *under-lease,* and leaves a reversion in the termor. 4 Kent, Comm. 96.

UNDER-SHERIFF. An officer who acts directly under the sheriff, and performs all the duties of the sheriff's office, a few only excepted where the personal presence of the high-sheriff is necessary. The sheriff is civilly responsible for the acts or omissions of his under-sheriff. Mozley & Whitley.

A distinction is made between this officer and a *deputy,* the latter being appointed for a special occasion or purpose, while the former discharges, in general, all the duties required by the sheriff's office.

UNDER-TENANT. A tenant under one who is himself a tenant; one who holds by under-lease.

UNDER-TUTOR. In Louisiana. In every tutorship there shall be an under-tutor, whom it shall be the duty of the judge to appoint at the time letters of tutorship are certified for the tutor. It is the duty of the under-tutor to act for the minor whenever the interest of the minor is in opposition to the interest of the tutor. Civil Code La. 1838, arts. 300, 301.

UNDER-TREASURER OF ENGLAND. He who transacted the business of the lord high treasurer.

UNDERLIE THE LAW. In Scotch criminal procedure, an accused person, in appearing to take his trial, is said "to compear and underlie the law." Mozley & Whitley.

UNDERSTANDING. In the law of contracts. This is a loose and ambiguous term, unless it be accompanied by some expression to show that it constituted a meeting of the minds of parties upon something respecting which they intended to be bound. 25 Conn. 529. But it may denote an informal agreement, or a concurrence as to its terms. See 47 Wis. 507.

UNDERSTOOD. The phrase "it is understood," when employed as a word of contract in a written agreement, has the same force as the words "it is agreed." 14 Gray, 165.

UNDERTAKING. A promise, engagement, or stipulation. Each of the promises made by the parties to a contract, considered independently and not as mutual, may, in this sense, be denominated an "undertaking."

"Undertaking" is frequently used in the special sense of a promise given in the course of legal proceedings by a party or his counsel, generally as a condition to obtaining some concession from the court or the opposite party. Sweet.

UNDERTOOK. Agreed; assumed. This is the technical word to be used in alleging the promise which forms the basis of an action of *assumpsit.*

UNDERWRITER. The person who insures another in a fire or life policy; the insurer.

A person who joins with others in entering into a marine policy of insurance as insurer.

UNDIVIDED. An undivided right or title, or a title to an undivided portion of an estate, is that owned by one of two or more tenants in common or joint tenants before partition.

UNDRES. Minors or persons under age not capable of bearing arms. Fleta, l. 1, c. 9; Cowell.

UNDUE INFLUENCE. Undue influence consists (1) in the use, by one in whom a confidence is reposed by another, or who holds a real or apparent authority over him, of such confidence or authority, for the purpose of obtaining an unfair advantage over him; (2) in taking an unfair advantage of another's weakness of mind; or (3) in taking a grossly oppressive and unfair advantage of another's necessities or distress. Civil Code Dak. § 886.

Undue influence at elections is where any one interferes with the free exercise of a voter's franchise, by violence, intimidation, or otherwise. It is a misdemeanor. 1 Russ. Crimes, 321; Steph. Crim. Dig. 79.

UNGELD. In Saxon law. An outlaw; a person whose murder required no composition to be made, or *weregeld* to be paid, by his slayer.

UNICA TAXATIO. The obsolete language of a special award of *venire*, where, of several defendants, one pleads, and one lets judgment go by default, whereby the jury, who are to try and assess damages on the issue, are also to assess damages against the defendant suffering judgment by default. Wharton.

UNIFORM. A statute is general and uniform in its operation when it operates equally upon all persons who are brought within the relations and circumstances provided for. 20 Iowa, 338.

UNIFORMITY. In taxation. Uniformity in taxation implies equality in the burden of taxation, which cannot exist without uniformity in the mode of assessment, as well as in the rate of taxation. Further, the uniformity must be co-extensive with the territory to which it applies. And it must be extended to all property subject to taxation, so that all property may be taxed alike and equally. 3 Ohio St. 15.

UNIFORMITY, ACT OF, which regulates the terms of membership in the Church of England and the colleges of Oxford and Cambridge, (St. 13 & 14 Car. II. c. 4.) See St. 9 & 10 Vict. c. 59. The act of uniformity has been amended by the St. 35 & 36 Vict. c. 35, which *inter alia* provides a shortened form of morning and evening prayer. Wharton.

UNIFORMITY OF PROCESS ACT. The English statute of 2 Wm. IV. c. 39, establishing a uniform process for the commencement of actions in all the courts of law at Westminster. 3 Steph. Comm. 566.

UNIGENITURE. The state of being the only begotten.

UNILATERAL. One-sided.

UNILATERAL CONTRACT. In the civil law. When the party to whom an engagement is made makes no express agreement on his part, the contract is called "unilateral," even in cases where the law attaches certain obligations to his acceptance. Civil Code La. art. 1765.

UNINTELLIGIBLE. That which cannot be understood.

UNIO. Lat. In canon law. A consolidation of two churches into one. Cowell.

UNIO PROLIUM. Lat. Uniting of offspring. A method of adoption, chiefly used in Germany, by which step-children (on either or both sides of the house) are made equal, in respect to the right of succession, with the children who spring from the marriage of the two contracting parties. See Heinecc. Elem. § 188.

UNION. In English poor-law. A union consists of two or more parishes which have been consolidated for the better administration of the poor-law therein.

In ecclesiastical law. A union consists of two or more benefices which have been united into one benefice. Sweet.

In public law. A popular term in America for the United States; also, in Great Britain, for the consolidated governments of England and Scotland, or for the political tie beween Great Britain and Ireland.

In Scotch law. A "clause of union" is a clause in a feoffment by which two estates, separated or not adjacent, are united as one, for the purpose of making a single seisin suffice for both.

UNION-JACK. The national flag of Great Britain and Ireland, which combines the banner of St. Patrick with the crosses of St. George and St Andrew. The word "jack" is most probably derived from the surcoat, charged with a red cross, anciently used by the English soldiery. This appears to have been called a "*jacque*," whence the word "jacket," anciently written "*jacquit*." Some, however, without a shadow of evidence, derive the word from "*Jacques*," the first alteration having been made in the reign of King James I. Wharton.

UNION OF CHURCHES. A combining and consolidating of two churches into one. Also it is when one church is made subject to another, and one man is rector of both; and where a conventual church is made a cathedral. Tomlins.

UNITAS PERSONARUM. Lat. The unity of persons, as that between husband and wife, or ancestor and heir.

UNITED STATES BONDS. Obligations for payment of money which have been at various times issued by the government of the United States.

UNITED STATES COMMISSIONERS. Each circuit court of the United States may appoint, in different parts of the district for which it is held, as many discreet persons as it may deem necessary, who shall be called "commissioners of the circuit court," and shall exercise the powers which are or may be conferred upon them. Rev. St. U. S. § 627.

UNITED STATES NOTES. Promissory notes, resembling bank-notes, issued by the government of the United States.

UNITY. In the law of estates. The peculiar characteristic of an estate held by several in joint tenancy, and which is fourfold, viz., unity of interest, unity of title, unity of time, and unity of possession. In other words, joint tenants have one and the same interest, accruing by one and the same conveyance, commencing at one and the same time, and held by one and the same undivided possession. 2 Bl. Comm. 180.

UNITY OF INTEREST. This term is applied to joint tenants, to signify that no one of them can have a greater interest in the property than each of the others, while, in the case of tenants in common, one of them may have a larger share than any of the others. Williams, Real Prop. 134, 139.

UNITY OF POSSESSION. Joint possession of two rights by several titles. As if I take a lease of land from a person at a certain rent, and afterwards I buy the fee-simple of such land, by this I acquire unity of possession, by which the lease is extinguished. Cowell; Brown.

It is also one of the essential properties of a joint estate, each of the tenants having the entire possession as well of every parcel as of the whole. 2 Bl. Comm. 182.

UNITY OF SEISIN is where a person seised of land which is subject to an easement, *profit à prender*, or similar right, also becomes seised of the land to which the easement or other right is annexed. Sweet.

UNITY OF TIME. One of the essential properties of a joint estate; the estates of the tenants being vested at one and the same period. 2 Bl. Comm. 181.

UNITY OF TITLE is applied to joint tenants, to signify that they hold their property by one and the same title, while tenants in common may take property by several titles. Williams, Real Prop. 134.

Unius omnino testis responsio non audiatur. The answer of one witness shall not be heard at all; the testimony of a single witness shall not be admitted under any circumstances. A maxim of the civil and canon law. Cod. 4, 20, 9; 3 Bl. Comm. 370; Best, Ev. p. 426, § 390, and note.

Uniuscujusque contractus initium spectandum est, et causa. The commencement and cause of every contract are to be regarded. Dig. 17, 1, 8; Story, Bailm. § 56.

UNIVERSAL AGENT. One who is appointed to do all the acts which the principal can personally do, and which he may lawfully delegate the power to another to do. Story, Ag. 18.

UNIVERSAL LEGACY. In the civil law. A testamentary disposition by which the testator gives to one or several persons the whole of the property which he leaves at his decease. Civil Code La. art. 1606.

UNIVERSAL PARTNERSHIP. One in which the partners jointly agree to contribute to the common fund of the partnership the whole of their property, of whatever character, and future, as well as present. Poth. Société, 29.

UNIVERSAL REPRESENTATION. In Scotch law. A term applied to the representation by an heir of his ancestor. Bell.

Universalia sunt notiora singularibus. 2 Rolle, 294. Things universal are better known than things particular.

UNIVERSITAS. Lat. In the civil law. A corporation aggregate. Dig. 3, 4, 7. Literally, a whole formed out of many individuals. 1 Bl. Comm. 469.

UNIVERSITAS FACTI. Lat. In the civil law. A plurality of corporeal things of the same kind, which are regarded as a whole; *e. g.*, a herd of cattle, a stock of goods. Mackeld. Rom. Law, § 162.

UNIVERSITAS JURIS. Lat. In the civil law. A quantity of things of all sorts, corporeal as well as incorporeal, which, taken together, are regarded as a whole; *e. g.*, an inheritance, an estate. Mackeld. Rom. Law, § 162.

UNIVERSITAS RERUM. Lat. In the civil law. Literally, a whole of things. Several single things, which, though not mechanically connected with one another, are, when taken together, regarded as a whole in any legal respect. Mackeld. Rom. Law, § 162.

UNIVERSITY. An institution of higher learning, consisting of an assemblage of colleges united under one corporate organization and government, affording instruction in the arts and sciences and the learned professions, and conferring degrees.

UNIVERSITY COURT. See CHANCELLOR'S COURTS IN THE TWO UNIVERSITIES.

UNIVERSUS. Lat. The whole; all together. Calvin.

UNJUST. Contrary to right and justice, or to the enjoyment of his rights by another, or to the standards of conduct furnished by the laws.

UNKOUTH. Unknown. The law French form of the Saxon "uncouth." Britt. c. 12.

UNLAGE. Sax. An unjust law.

UNLARICH. In old Scotch law. That which is done without law or against law. Spelman.

UNLAW. In Scotch law. A witness was formerly inadmissible who was not worth the king's *unlaw; i. e.*, the sum of £10 Scots, then the common fine for absence from court and for small delinquencies. Bell.

UNLAWFUL. That which is contrary to law.

"Unlawful" and "illegal" are frequently used as synonymous terms, but, in the proper sense of the word, "unlawful," as applied to promises, agreements, considerations, and the like, denotes that they are ineffectual in law because they involve acts which, although not illegal, *i. e.*, positively forbidden, are disapproved of by the law, and are therefore not recognized as the ground of legal rights, either because they are immoral or because they are against public policy. It is on this ground that contracts in restraint of marriage or of trade are generally void. Sweet.

UNLAWFUL ASSEMBLY. At common law. The meeting together of three or more persons, to the disturbance of the public peace, and with the intention of co-operating in the forcible and violent execution of some unlawful private enterprise. If they take steps towards the performance of their purpose, it becomes a *rout;* and, if they put their design into actual execution, it is a *riot.* 4 Bl. Comm. 146.

Any meeting of great numbers of people, with such circumstances of terror as cannot but endanger the public peace, and raise fears and jealousies among the subjects of the realm. 4 Steph. Comm. 254.

UNLAWFULLY. The term is commonly used in indictments for statutory crimes, to show that the act constituting the offense was in violation of a positive law, especially where the statute itself uses the same phrase.

UNLIQUIDATED. Not ascertained in amount; not determined; remaining unassessed or unsettled; as unliquidated damages.

UNNATURAL OFFENSE. The infamous crime against nature; *i. e.*, sodomy or buggery.

Uno absurdo dato, infinita sequuntur. 1 Coke, 102. One absurdity being allowed, an infinity follows.

UNO ACTU. Lat. In a single act; by one and the same act.

UNO FLATU. Lat. In one breath. 3 Man. & G. 45. *Uno flatu, et uno intuitu,* at one breath, and in one view. 3 Story, 504.

UNQUES. L. Fr. Ever; always. *Ne unques*, never.

UNQUES PRIST. L. Fr. Always ready. Cowell. Another form of *tout temps prist.*

UNSEATED LAND. A phrase used in the Pennsylvania tax laws to describe land which, though owned by a private person, has not been reclaimed, cultivated, improved, occupied, or made a place of residence. See SEATED LAND.

UNSEAWORTHY. See SEAWORTHY.

UNSOLEMN WAR. War denounced without a declaration; war made not upon general but special declaration; imperfect war. 1 Hill, 409.

UNSOUND MIND. A person of unsound mind is an adult who from infirmity of mind is incapable of managing himself or his affairs. The term, therefore, includes insane persons, idiots, and imbeciles. Sweet.

UNTHRIFT. A prodigal; a spendthrift. 1 Bl. Comm. 306.

UNTIL. This term generally excludes the day to which it relates; but it will be construed otherwise, if required by the evident intention of the parties. 120 Mass. 95.

Unumquodque dissolvitur eodem ligamine quo ligatur. Every obligation is dissolved by the same solemnity with which it is created. Broom, Max. 884.

Unumquodque eodem modo quo colligatum est, dissolvitur,—quo constituitur, destruitur. Everything is dissolved by the same means by which it is put together,—destroyed by the same means by which it is established. 2 Rolle, 39; Broom, Max. 891.

Unumquodque est id quod est principalius in ipso. Hob. 123. That which is the principal part of a thing is the thing itself.

Unumquodque principiorum est sibimetipsi fides; et perspicua vera non sunt probanda. Every general principle [or maxim of law] is its own pledge or warrant; and things that are clearly true are not to be proved. Branch; Co. Litt. 11.

UNUS NULLUS RULE, THE. The rule of evidence which obtains in the civil law, that the testimony of *one* witness is equivalent to the testimony of *none*. Wharton.

UNWHOLESOME FOOD. Food not fit to be eaten; food which if eaten would be injurious.

UNWRITTEN LAW. See LEX NON SCRIPTA.

UPLIFTED HAND. The hand raised towards the heavens, in one of the forms of taking an oath, instead of being laid upon the Gospels.

UPPER BENCH. The court of king's bench, in England, was so called during the interval between 1649 and 1660, the period of the commonwealth, Rolle being then chief justice. See 3 Bl. Comm. 202.

UPSET PRICE. In sales by auctions, an amount for which property to be sold is put up, so that the first bidder at that price is declared the buyer. Wharton.

UPSUN. In Scotch law. Between the hours of sunrise and sunset. Poinding must be executed with *upsun.* 1 Forb. Inst. pt. 3, p. 32.

URBAN SERVITUDE. City servitudes, or servitudes of houses, are called "urban." They are the easements appertaining to the building and construction of houses; as, for instance, the right to light and air, or the right to build a house so as to throw the rain-water on a neighbor's house. Mozley & Whitley.

URBS. Lat. In Roman law. A city, or a walled town. Sometimes it is put for *civitas*, and denotes the inhabitants, or both the city and its inhabitants; *i. e.*, the municipality or commonwealth. By way of special pre-eminence, *urbs* meant the city of Rome. Ainsworth.

URE. L. Fr. Effect; practice. *Mis en ure*, put in practice; carried into effect. Kelham.

USAGE. Usage is a reasonable and lawful public custom concerning transactions of the same nature as those which are to be effected thereby, existing at the place where the obligation is to be performed, and either known to the parties, or so well established, general, and uniform that they must be presumed to have acted with reference thereto. Civil Code Dak. § 2119.

This word, as used in English law, differs from "custom" and "prescription," in that no man may claim a rent common or other inheritance by usage, though he may by prescription. Moreover, a usage is local in all cases, and must be proved; whereas, a custom is frequently general, and as such is noticed without proof. "Usage," in French law, is the "*usus*" of Roman law, and corresponds very nearly to the tenancy at will or on sufferance of English law. Brown.

"Usage," in its most extensive meaning, includes both custom and prescription; but, in its narrower signification, the term refers to a general habit, mode, or course of procedure. A usage differs from a custom, in that it does not require that the usage should be immemorial to establish it; but the usage must be known, certain, uniform, reasonable, and not contrary to law. 3 Brewst. 452.

"Usage" is also called a "custom," though the latter word has also another signification; it is a long and uniform practice, applied to habits, modes, and courses of dealing. It relates to modes of action, and does not comprehend the mere adoption of certain peculiar doctrines or rules of law. 7 Allen, 29.

USAGE OF TRADE. A course of dealing; a mode of conducting transactions of a particular kind, proved by witnesses testifying of its existence and uniformity from their knowledge obtained by observation of what is practiced by themselves and others in the trade to which it relates. 115 Mass. 535.

USANCE. In mercantile law. The common period fixed by the usage or custom or habit of dealing between the country where a bill is drawn, and that where it is payable, for the payment of bills of exchange. It means, in some countries, a month, in others two or more months, and in others half a month. Story, Bills, §§ 50, 144, 332.

USE. A confidence reposed in another, who was made tenant of the land, or terretenant, that he would dispose of the land according to the intention of the *cestui que use*, or him to whose use it was granted, and suffer him to take the profits. 2 Bl. Comm. 328.

A right in one person, called the "*cestui que use*," to take the profits of land of which another has the legal title and possession, together with the duty of defending the same, and of making estates thereof according to the direction of the *cestui que use*. Bouvier.

Use is the right given to any one to make a gratuitous use of a thing belonging to another, or to exact such a portion of the fruit it produces as is necessary for his personal wants and those of his family. Civil Code La. art. 626.

Uses and *trusts* are not so much different things as different aspects of the same subject. A use regards principally the beneficial interest; a trust regards principally the nominal ownership. The usage of the two terms is, however, widely different. The word "use" is employed to denote either an estate vested since the statute of uses, and by force of that statute, or to denote such an estate created before that statute as, had it been created since, would have become a legal estate by force of the statute. The word "trust" is employed since that statute to denote the relation between the party invested with the legal estate (whether by force of that statute or independently of it) and the party beneficially entitled, who has hitherto been said to have the equitable estate. Mozley & Whitley.

In conveyancing "use" literally means "benefit;" thus, in an an ordinary assignment of chattels, the assignor transfers the property to the assignee for his "absolute use and benefit." In the expressions "separate use," "superstitious use," and "charitable use," "use" has the same meaning. Sweet.

In the civil law. A right of receiving so much of the natural profits of a thing as is necessary to daily sustenance. It differs from "usufruct," which is a right not only to use, but to enjoy. 1 Browne, Civil & Adm. Law, 184.

As to the various kinds of uses, see CHARITABLE USE; CONSTRUCTIVE USE; CONTINGENT USE; RESULTING USE; SHIFTING USE; SPRINGING USE; SUPERSTITIOUS USE.

USE AND OCCUPATION. This is the name of an action, being a variety of *assumpsit*, to be maintained by a landlord against one who has had the occupation and enjoyment of an estate, under a contract to pay therefor, express or implied, but not under such a lease as would support an action specifically for rent.

USEE. A person for whose use a suit is brought; otherwise termed the "use-plaintiff."

USEFUL. By "useful," in the patent law, is meant not an invention in all cases superior to the modes now in use for the same purposes, but "useful," in contradistinction to frivolous and mischievous, invention. 1 Mass. 182, 186.

By "useful" is meant such an invention as may be applied to some beneficial use in society, in contradistinction to an invention which is injurious to the morals, the health, or the good order of society. 1 Mass. 302.

USER. The actual exercise or enjoyment of any right or property. It is particularly used of franchises.

USER DE ACTION. L. Fr. In old practice. The pursuing or bringing an action. Cowell.

USHER. This word is said to be derived from "*huissier*," and is the name of a subordinate officer in some English courts of law. Archb. Pr. 25.

USHER OF THE BLACK ROD. The gentleman usher of the black rod is an officer of the house of lords appointed by letters patent from the crown. His duties are, by himself or deputy, to desire the attendance of the commons in the house of peers when the royal assent is given to bills, either by the queen in person or by commission, to execute orders for the commitment of persons guilty of breach of privilege, and also to assist in the introduction of peers when they take the oaths and their seats. Brown.

USO. In Spanish law. Usage; that which arises from certain things which men say and do and practice uninterruptedly for a great length of time, without any hindrance whatever. Las Partidas, pt. 1, tit. 2, l. 1.

USQUE. Lat. Up to; until. This is a word of exclusion, and a release of all demands *usque ad* a certain day does not cover a bond made on that day. 2 Mod. 280.

USQUE AD FILUM AQUÆ, OR VIÆ. Up to the middle of the stream or road.

USUAL COVENANTS. An agreement on the part of a seller of real property to give the usual covenants binds him to insert in the grant covenants of "seisin," "quiet enjoyment," "further assurance," "general warranty," and "against incumbrances." Civil Code Cal. § 1733.

The result of the authorities appears to be that in a case where the agreement is silent as to the particular covenants to be inserted in the lease, and provides merely for the lease containing "usual covenants," or, which is the same thing, in an open agreement without any reference to the covenants, and there are no special circumstances justifying the introduction of other covenants, the following are the only ones which either party can insist upon, namely: Covenants by the lessee (1) to pay rent; (2) to pay taxes, except such as are expressly payable by the landlord; (3) to keep and deliver up the premises in repair; and (4) to allow the lessor to enter and view the state of repair; and the usual qualified covenant by the lessor for quiet enjoyment by the lessee. 7 Ch. Div. 561.

USUAL TERMS. A phrase in the common-law practice, which meant pleading issuably, rejoining *gratis*, and taking short notice of trial. When a defendant obtained further time to plead, these were the terms usually imposed. Wharton.

USUARIUS. Lat. In the civil law. One who had the mere use of a thing belonging to another for the purpose of supplying his daily wants; a usuary. Dig. 7, 8, 10, pr.; Calvin.

USUCAPIO, or USUCAPTIO. A term of Roman law used to denote a mode of acquisition of property. It corresponds very nearly to the term "prescription." But the prescription of Roman law differed from that of the English law, in this: that no *mala fide* possessor (*i. e.*, person in possession knowingly of the property of another) could, by however long a period, acquire title by possession merely. The two essential requisites to *usucapio* were *justa causa* (*i. e.*, title) and *bona fides*, (*i. e.*, ignorance.). The term "*usucapio*" is sometimes, but erroneously, written "*usucaptio*." Brown.

Usucapio constituta est ut aliquis litium finis esset. Prescription was instituted that there might be some end to litigation. Dig. 41, 10, 5; Broom, Max. 894, note.

USUFRUCT. In the civil law. The right of enjoying a thing, the property of which is vested in another, and to draw from the same all the profit, utility, and advantage which it may produce, provided it be without altering the substance of the thing. Civil Code La. art. 533.

USUFRUCTUARY. In the civil law. One who has the usufruct or right of enjoying anything in which he has no property. 18 Tex. 628.

USUFRUIT. In French law. The same as the *usufruct* of the English and Roman law.

USURA. Lat. In the civil law. Money given for the use of money; interest. Commonly used in the plural, "*usuræ*." Dig. 22, 1.

Usura est commodum certum quod propter usum rei mutuatæ recipitur. Sed secundario spirare de aliqua retributione, ad voluntatem ejus qui mutuatus est, hoc non est vitiosum. Usury is a certain benefit which is received for the use of a thing lent. But to have an understanding, [literally, to breathe or whisper,] in an incidental way, about some compensation to be made at the pleasure of the borrower, is not lawful. Branch, Princ.; 5 Coke, 70*b*; Glan. lib. 7, c. 16.

USURA MANIFESTA. Manifest or open usury; as distinguished from *usura velata*, veiled or concealed usury, which consists in giving a bond for the loan, in the amount of which is included the stipulated interest.

USURA MARITIMA. Interest taken on bottomry or respondentia bonds, which is proportioned to the risk, and is not affected by the usury laws.

USURARIUS. In old English law. A usurer. Fleta, lib. 2, c. 52, § 14.

USURIOUS. Pertaining to usury; partaking of the nature of usury; involving usury; tainted with usury; as, a usurious contract.

USURPATIO. Lat. In the civil law. The interruption of a usucaption, by some act on the part of the real owner. Calvin.

USURPATION. Torts. The unlawful assumption of the use of property which belongs to another; an interruption or the disturbing a man in his right and possession. Tomlins.

In public law. The unlawful seizure or assumption of sovereign power; the assumption of government or supreme power by force or illegally, in derogation of the constitution and of the rights of the lawful ruler.

USURPATION OF ADVOWSON. An injury which consists in the absolute ouster or dispossession of the patron from the advowson or right of presentation, and which happens when a stranger who has no right presents a clerk, and the latter is thereupon admitted and instituted. Brown.

USURPATION OF FRANCHISE or OFFICE. The unjustly intruding upon or exercising any office, franchise, or liberty belonging to another.

USURPED POWER. In insurance. An invasion from abroad, or an internal rebellion, where armies are drawn up against each other, when the laws are silent, and when the firing of towns becomes unavoidable. These words cannot mean the power of a common mob. 2 Marsh. Ins. 791.

USURPER. One who assumes the right of government by force, contrary to and in violation of the constitution of the country.

USURY. In old English law. Interest of money; increase for the loan of money; a reward for the *use* of money. 2 Bl. Comm. 454.

In modern law. Unlawful interest; a premium or compensation paid or stipulated to be paid for the use of money borrowed or returned, beyond the rate of interest established by law. Webster.

An unlawful contract upon the loan of money, to receive the same again with exorbitant increase. 4 Bl. Comm. 156.

Usury is the reserving and taking, or contracting to reserve and take, either directly or by indirection, a greater sum for the use of money than the lawful interest. Code Ga. 1882, § 2051. See 11 Bush, 180; 11 Conn. 487.

USUS. Lat. In Roman law. A precarious enjoyment of land, corresponding with the right of *habitatio* of houses, and being closely analogous to the tenancy at sufferance or at will of English law. The *usuarius* (*i. e.*, tenant by *usus*) could only hold on so long as the owner found him convenient, and had to go so soon as ever he was in the owner's way, (*molestus*.) The *usuarius* could not have a friend to share the produce. It was scarcely permitted to him (Justinian says) to have even his wife with him on the land; and he could not let or sell, the right being strictly personal to himself. Brown.

USUS BELLICI. Lat. In international law. Warlike uses or objects. It is the *usus bellici* which determine an article to be contraband. 1 Kent, Comm. 141.

Usus est dominium fiduciarium. Bac. St. Uses. Use is a fiduciary dominion.

Usus et status sive possessio potius differunt secundum rationem fori, quam secundum rationem rei. Bac. St. Uses. Use and estate, or possession, differ more in the rule of the court than in the rule of the matter.

USUS FRUCTUS. Lat. In Roman law. Usufruct; usufructuary right or possession. The temporary right of using a thing, without having the ultimate property, or full dominion, of the substance. 2 Bl. Comm. 327.

UT CURRERE SOLEBAT. Lat. As it was wont to run; applied to a water-course.

UT DE FEODO. L. Lat. As of fee.

UT HOSPITES. Lat. As guests. 1 Salk. 25, pl. 10.

Ut pœna ad paucos, metus ad omnes perveniat. That the punishment may reach a few, but the fear of it affect all. A maxim in criminal law, expressive of one of the principal objects of human punishment. 4 Inst. 6; 4 Bl. Comm. 11.

Ut res magis valeat quam pereat. That the thing may rather have effect than be destroyed. 11 Allen, 445; 100 Mass. 113; 108 Mass. 373.

Ut summæ potestatis regis est posse quantum velit, sic magnitudinis est velle quantum possit. 3 Inst. 236. As the highest power of a king is to be able to do all he wishes, so the highest greatness of him is to wish all he is able to do.

UTAS. In old English practice. Octave; the octave; the eighth day following any term or feast. Cowell.

UTERINE. Born of the same mother. A uterine brother or sister is one born of the same mother, but by a different father.

UTERO-GESTATION. Pregnancy.

UTERQUE. Lat. Both; each. "The justices, being in doubt as to the meaning of this word in an indictment, demanded the opinions of grammarians, who delivered their opinions that this word doth aptly signify *one of them.*" 1 Leon. 241.

UTFANGTHEF. In Saxon and old English law. The privilege of a lord of a manor to judge and punish a thief dwelling out of his liberty, and committing theft without the same, if he were caught within the lord's jurisdiction. Cowell.

UTI. Lat. In the civil law. To use. Strictly, to use for necessary purposes; as distinguished from "*frui,*" to enjoy. Heinecc. Elem. lib. 2, tit. 4, § 415.

UTI FRUI. Lat. In the civil law. To have the full use and enjoyment of a thing, without damage to its substance. Calvin.

UTI POSSIDETIS. Lat. In the civil law. A species of interdict for the purpose of retaining possession of a thing, granted to one who, at the time of contesting suit, was in possession of an immovable thing, in order that he might be declared the legal possessor. Hallifax, Civil Law, b. 3, c. 6, no. 8.

In international law. A phrase used to signify that the parties to a treaty are to retain possession of what they have acquired by force during the war. Wheat. Int. Law, 627.

UTI ROGAS. Lat. In Roman law. The form of words by which a vote in favor of a proposed law was orally expressed. *Uti rogas, volo vel jubeo,* as you ask, I will or order; I vote as you propose; I am for the law. The letters "U. R." on a ballot expressed the same sentiment. Adams, Rom. Ant. 98, 100.

Utile per inutile non vitiatur. The useful is not vitiated by the useless. Surplusage does not spoil the remaining part if that is good in itself. Dyer, 392; Broom, Max. 627.

UTILIDAD. Span. In Spanish law. The profit of a thing. White, New Recop. b. 2, tit. 2, c. 1.

UTILIS. Lat. In the civil law. Useful; beneficial; equitable; available. *Actio utilis,* an equitable action. Calvin. *Dies utilis,* an available day.

UTLAGATUS. In old English law. An outlawed person; an outlaw.

Utlagatus est quasi extra legem positus. Caput gerit lupinum. 7 Coke, 14. An outlaw is, as it were, put out of the protection of the law He bears the head of a wolf.

Utlagatus pro contumacia et fuga, non propter hoc convictus est de facto principali. Fleta. One who is outlawed for contumacy and flight is not on that account convicted of the principal fact.

UTLAGE. L. Fr. An outlaw. Britt. c. 12.

UTLESSE. An escape of a felon out of prison.

UTRUBI. In the civil law. The name of a species of interdict for retaining a thing, granted for the purpose of protecting the possession of a movable thing, as the *uti possidetis* was granted for an immovable. Inst. 4, 15, 4; Mackeld. Rom. Law, § 260.

In Scotch law. An interdict as to movables, by which the colorable possession of a *bona fide* holder is continued until the final settlement of a contested right; corresponding to *uti possidetis* as to heritable property. Bell.

UTRUMQUE NOSTRUM. Both of us. Words used formerly in bonds.

UTTER. To put or send into circulation; to publish or put forth. To utter and publish an instrument is to declare or assert, directly or indirectly, by words or actions, that it is good; uttering it is a declaration that it is good, with an intention or offer to pass it. Whart. Crim. Law, § 703.

To utter, as used in a statute against forgery and counterfeiting, means to offer, whether accepted or not, a forged instrument, with the representation, by words or actions, that the same is genuine. 48 Mo. 520.

UTTER BAR. In English law. The bar at which those barristers, usually junior men, practice who have not yet been raised to the dignity of queen's counsel. These junior barristers are said to plead without the bar; while those of the higher rank are admitted to seats within the bar, and address the court or a jury from a place reserved for them, and divided off by a bar. Brown.

UTTER BARRISTER. In English law. Those barristers who plead without the bar, and are distinguished from benchers, or those who have been readers, and who are allowed to plead within the bar, as the king's counsel are. Cowell.

UXOR. Lat. In the civil law. A wife; a woman lawfully married.

Uxor et filius sunt nomina naturæ. Wife and son are names of nature. 4 Bac. Works, 350.

Uxor non est sui juris, sed sub potestate viri. A wife is not her own mistress, but is under the power of her husband. 3 Inst. 108.

Uxor sequitur domicilium viri. A wife follows the domicile of her husband. Tray. Lat. Max. 606.

UXORICIDE. The killing of a wife by her husband; one who murders his wife. Not a technical term of the law.

V.

V. As an abbreviation, this letter may stand for "Victoria," "volume," or "verb;" also "*vide*" (see) and "*voce*" (word.)

It is also a common abbreviation of "*versus,*" in the titles of causes, and reported cases.

V. C. An abbreviation for "vice-chancellor."

V. C. C. An abbreviation for "vice-chancellor's court."

V. E. An abbreviation for "*venditioni exponas,*" (*q. v.*)

V. G. An abbreviation for "*verbi gratia,*" for the sake of example.

VACANCY. A place which is empty. The term is principally applied to an interruption in the incumbency of an office.

The term "vacancy" applies not only to an interregnum in an existing office, but it aptly and fitly describes the condition of an office when it is first created, and has been filled by no incumbent. 89 Pa. St. 426.

VACANT POSSESSION. An estate which has been abandoned, vacated, or forsaken by the tenant.

VACANT SUCCESSION. A succession is called "vacant" when no one claims it, or when all the heirs are unknown, or when all the known heirs to it have renounced it. Civil Code La. art. 1095.

VACANTIA BONA. Lat. In the civil law. Goods without an owner, or in which no one claims a property; escheated goods. Inst. 2, 6, 4; 1 Bl. Comm. 298.

VACATE. To annul; to cancel or rescind; to render an act void; as, to vacate an entry of record, or a judgment.

VACATIO. Lat. In the civil law. Exemption; immunity; privilege; dispensation; exemption from the burden of office. Calvin.

VACATION. That period of time between the end of one term of court and the beginning of another.

Vacation also signifies, in ecclesiastical law, that a church or benefice is vacant; *e. g.*, on the death or resignation of the incumbent, until his successor is appointed. 2 Inst. 359; Phillim. Ecc. Law, 495.

VACATUR. In practice. A rule or order by which a proceeding is vacated; a vacating.

VACATURA. An avoidance of an ecclesiastical benefice. Cowell.

VACCARIA. In old English law. A dairy-house. Co. Litt. 5*b*.

VACCINATION. Inoculation with the cow-pox. The English statute 30 & 31 Vict. c. 84, § 16, requires the vaccination of every child born in England, within three months of its birth.

VACUA POSSESSIO. The vacant possession, *i. e.*, free and unburdened possession, which (*e. g.*) a vendor had and has to give to a purchaser of lands.

VACUUS. Lat. In the civil law. Empty; void; vacant; unoccupied. Calvin.

VADES. Lat. In the civil law. Pledges; sureties; bail; security for the appearance of a defendant or accused person in court. Calvin.

VADIARE DUELLUM. L. Lat. In old English law. To wage or gage the *duellum;* to wage battel; to give pledges mutually for engaging in the trial by combat.

VADIMONIUM. Lat. In Roman law. Bail or security; the giving of bail for appearance in court; a recognizance. Calvin.

VADIUM. Lat. A pledge; security by pledge of property.

VADIUM MORTUUM. A mortgage or *dead pledge;* a security given by the borrower of a sum of money, by which he grants to the lender an estate in fee, on condition that, if the money be not repaid at the time appointed, the estate so put in pledge shall continue to the lender as dead or gone from the mortgagor. 2 Bl. Comm. 157.

VADIUM PONERE. To take bail for the appearance of a person in a court of justice. Tomlins.

VADIUM VIVUM. A species of security by which the borrower of a sum of money made over his estate to the lender until he had received that sum out of the issues and profits of the land. It was so called because neither the money nor the lands were lost, and were not left in dead pledge, but this was a *living* pledge, for the profits of the land were constantly paying off the debt. Litt. § 206; 1 Pow. Mortg. 3; Termes de la Ley.

VADLET. In old English law. The king's eldest son; hence the valet or knave follows the king and queen in a pack of cards. Bar. Obs. St. 344.

VADUM. In old records, a ford, or wading place. Cowell.

VAGABOND. One that wanders about, and has no certain dwelling; an idle fellow. Jacob.

Vagabonds are described in old English statutes as "such as wake on the night and sleep on the day, and haunt customable taverns and ale-houses and routs about; and no man wot from whence they came, nor whither they go." 4 Bl. Comm. 169.

Vagabundum nuncupamus eum qui nullibi domicilium contraxit habitationis. We call him a "vagabond" who has acquired nowhere a domicile of residence. Phillim. Dom. 23, note.

VAGRANT. A wandering, idle person; a strolling or sturdy beggar. A general term, including, in English law, the several classes of idle and disorderly persons, rogues, and vagabonds, and incorrigible rogues. 4 Steph. Comm. 308, 309.

VAGRANT ACT. In English law. The statute 5 Geo. IV. c. 83, which is an act for the punishment of idle and disorderly persons. 2 Chit. St. 145.

VALE. In Spanish law. A promissory note. White, New Recop. b. 3, tit. 7, c. 5, § 3.

Valeat quantum valere potest. It shall have effect as far as it can have effect. Cowp. 600; 4 Kent, Comm. 493; Shep. Touch. 87.

VALEC, VALECT, or VADELET. In old English law. A young gentleman; also a servitor or gentleman of the chamber. Cowell.

VALENTIA. The value or price of anything.

VALESHERIA. In old English law. The proving by the kindred of the slain, one on the father's side, and another on that of the mother, that a man was a Welshman. Wharton.

VALET, was anciently a name denoting young gentlemen of rank and family, but afterwards applied to those of lower degree, and is now used for a menial servant, more particularly occupied about the person of his employer. Cab. Lawy. 800.

VALID. Of binding force. A deed, will, or other instrument, which has received all the formalities required by law, is said to be valid.

VALIDITY. This term is used to signify legal sufficiency, in contradistinction to mere regularity. "An official sale, an order, judgment, or decree may be regular,—the whole practice in reference to its entry may be correct,—but still invalid, for reasons going behind the regularity of its forms." 1 Flip. 487.

VALOR BENEFICIORUM. L. Lat. The value of every ecclesiastical benefice and preferment, according to which the first fruits and tenths are collected and paid. It is commonly called the "king's books," by which the clergy are at present rated. 2 Steph. Comm. 533; Wharton.

VALOR MARITAGII. Lat. Value of the marriage. In feudal law, the guardian in chivalry had the right of tendering to his infant ward a suitable match, without "disparagement," (inequality,) which, if the infants refused, they forfeited the value of the marriage (*valor maritagii*) to their guardian; that is, so much as a jury would assess, or any one would *bona fide* give, to the guardian for such an alliance. 2 Bl. Comm. 70; Litt. § 110.

A writ which lay against the ward, on coming of full age, for that he was not married, by his guardian, for the *value of the marriage*, and this though no convenient marriage had been offered. Termes de la Ley.

VALUABLE CONSIDERATION. The distinction between a *good* and a *valuable* consideration is that the former consists of blood, or of natural love and affection; as when a man grants an estate to a near relation from motives of generosity, prudence, and natural duty; and the latter consists of such a consideration as money, marriage which is to follow, or the like, which the law esteems an equivalent given for the grant. 2 Bl. Comm. 297.

A valuable consideration is a thing of value parted with, or a new obligation assumed, at the time of obtaining a thing, which is a substantial compensation for that which is obtained thereby. It is also called simply "value." Civil Code Dak. § 2121.

VALUATION. The act of ascertaining the worth of a thing. The estimated worth of a thing.

VALUATION LIST. In English law. A list of all the ratable hereditaments in a parish, showing the names of the occupier, the owner, the property, the extent of the property, the gross estimated rental, and the ratable value; prepared by the overseers of each parish in a union under section 14 of the union assessment committee act, 1862, (St. 25 & 26 Vict. c. 103,) for the purposes of the poor rate. Wharton.

VALUE. The utility of an object in satisfying, directly or indirectly, the needs or desires of human beings, called by economists "value in use;" or its worth consisting in the power of purchasing other objects, called "value in exchange." Also the estimated or appraised worth of any object of property, calculated in money.

The term is also often used as an abbreviation for "valuable consideration," especially in the phrases "purchaser for value," "holder for value," etc.

VALUE RECEIVED. A phrase usually employed in a bill of exchange or promissory note, to denote that a consideration has been given for it.

VALUED POLICY. A policy is called "valued," when the parties, having agreed upon the value of the interest insured, in order to save the necessity of further proof have inserted the valuation in the policy, in the nature of liquidated damages. 1 Duer, Ins. 97.

VALUER. A person whose business is to appraise or set a value upon property.

VALVASORS, or VIDAMES. An obsolete title of dignity next to a peer. 2 Inst. 667; 2 Steph. Comm. 612.

Vana est illa potentia quæ nunquam venit in actum. That power is vain [idle or useless] which never comes into action, [which is never exercised.] 2 Coke, 51.

Vani timores sunt æstimandi, qui non cadunt in constantem virum. Those are to be regarded as idle fears which do not affect a steady [firm or resolute] man. 7 Coke, 27.

Vani timoris justa excusatio non est. A frivolous fear is not a legal excuse. Dig. 50, 17, 184; 2 Inst. 483.

VANTARIUS. L. Lat. In old records. A fore-footman. Spelman; Cowell.

VARDA. In old Scotch law. Ward; custody; guardianship. Answering to "*warda*," in old English law. Spelman.

VARENNA. In old Scotch law. A warren. Answering to "*warenna*," in old English law. Spelman.

VARIANCE. In pleading and practice. A discrepancy or disagreement between two instruments or two steps in the same cause, which ought by law to be entirely consonant. Thus, if the evidence adduced by the plaintiff does not agree with the allegations of his declaration, it is a variance; and so if the statement of the cause of action in the declaration does not coincide with that given in the writ.

VARRANTIZATIO. In old Scotch law. Warranty.

VAS. Lat. In the civil law. A pledge; a surety; bail or surety in a criminal proceeding or civil action. Calvin.

VASSAL. In feudal law. A feudal tenant or grantee; a feudatory; the holder of a fief on a feudal tenure, and by the obligation of performing feudal services. The correlative term was "lord."

VASSALAGE. The state or condition of a vassal.

VASSELERIA. The tenure or holding of a vassal. Cowell.

VASTUM. L. Lat. A waste or common lying open to the cattle of all tenants who have a right of commoning. Cowell.

VASTUM FORESTÆ VEL BOSCI. In old records. Waste of a forest or wood. That part of a forest or wood wherein the trees and underwood were so destroyed that it lay in a manner waste and barren. Paroch. Antiq. 351, 497; Cowell.

VAUDERIE. In old European law. Sorcery; witchcraft; the profession of the Vaudois.

VAVASORY. The lands that a vavasour held. Cowell.

VAVASOUR. One who was in dignity next to a baron. Britt. 109; Bract. lib. 1, c. 8. One who held of a baron. Enc. Brit.

VEAL-MONEY. The tenants of the manor of Bradford, in the county of Wilts, paid a yearly rent by this name to their lord, in lieu of veal paid formerly in kind. Wharton.

VECORIN. In old Lombardic law. The offense of stopping one on the way; forestalling. Spelman.

VECTIGAL JUDICIARIUM. Lat. Fines paid to the crown to defray the expenses of maintaining courts of justice. 3 Salk. 33.

Vectigal, origine ipsa, jus Cæsarum et regum patrimoniale est. Dav. 12. Tribute, in its origin, is the patrimonial right of emperors and kings.

VECTIGALIA. In Roman law. Customs-duties; taxes paid upon the importation or exportation of certain kinds of merchandise. Cod. 4, 61.

VECTURA. In maritime law. Freight.

VEHICLE. The word "vehicle" includes every description of carriage or other artificial contrivance used, or capable of being used, as a means of transportation on land. Rev. St. U. S. § 4.

VEHMGERICHT. See FEHMGERICHT.

VEIES. L. Fr. Distresses forbidden to be replevied; the refusing to let the owner have his cattle which were distrained. Kelham.

VEJOURS. Viewers; persons sent by the court to take a view of any place in question, for the better decision of the right. It signifies, also, such as are sent to view those that *essoin* themselves *de malo lecti*, (*i. e.*, excuse themselves on ground of illness) whether they be in truth so sick as that they cannot appear, or whether they do counterfeit. Cowell.

VELABRUM. In old English law. A toll-booth. Cro. Jac. 122.

VELITIS JUBEATIS QUIRITES? Lat. Is it your will and pleasure, Romans? The form of proposing a law to the Roman people. Tayl. Civil Law, 155.

Velle non creditur qui obsequitur imperio patris vel domini. He is not presumed to consent who obeys the orders of his father or his master. Dig. 50, 17, 4.

VELTRARIA. The office of dog-leader, or courser. Cowell.

VELTRARIUS. One who leads greyhounds. Blount.

VENAL. Something that is bought; capable of being bought; offered for sale; mercenary. Used in an evil sense, such purchase or sale being regarded as corrupt and illegal.

VENARIA. Beasts caught in the woods by hunting.

VENATIO. Hunting. Cowell.

VEND. To sell; to transfer the ownership of an article to another for a price in money. The term is not commonly applied to the sale of real estate, although its derivatives "vendor" and "vendee" are.

VENDEE. A purchaser or buyer; one to whom anything is sold. Generally used of the transferee of real property, one who acquires chattels by sale being called a "buyer."

Vendens eandem rem duobus falsarius est. He is fraudulent who sells the same thing twice. Jenk. Cent. 107.

VENDIBLE. Fit or suitable to be sold; capable of transfer by sale; merchantable.

VENDITÆ. In old European law. A tax upon things sold in markets and public fairs. Spelman.

VENDITIO. Lat. In the civil law. In a strict sense, sale; the act of selling; the contract of sale, otherwise called "*emptio venditio.*" Inst. 3, 24. Calvin.

In a large sense. Any mode or species of alienation; any contract by which the property or ownership of a thing may be transferred. Id.

VENDITION. Sale; the act of selling.

VENDITIONI EXPONAS. Lat. You expose to sale. This is the name of a writ of execution, requiring a sale to be made, directed to a sheriff when he has levied upon goods under a *fieri facias*, but returned that they remained unsold for want of buyers; and in some jurisdictions it is issued to cause a sale to be made of lands, seized under a former writ, after they have been condemned or passed upon by an inquisition. Frequently abbreviated to "*vend. ex.*"

VENDITOR. Lat. A seller; a vendor. Inst. 3, 24; Bract. fol. 41.

VENDITOR REGIS. In old English law. The king's seller or salesman; the person who exposed to sale those goods and chattels which were seized or distrained to answer any debt due to the king. Cowell.

VENDITRIX. Lat. A female vendor. Cod. 4, 51, 3.

VENDOR. The person who transfers property by sale, particularly real estate, "seller" being more commonly used for one who sells personalty.

He is the vendor who negotiates the sale, and becomes the recipient of the consideration, though the title comes to the vendee from another source, and not from the vendor. 53 Miss. 685.

VENDOR AND PURCHASER ACT. The act of 37 & 38 Vict. c. 78, which substitutes forty for sixty years as the root of title, and amends in other ways the law of vendor and purchaser. Mozley & Whitley.

VENDOR'S LIEN. A lien for purchase money remaining unpaid, allowed in equity to the vendor of land, when the statement of receipt of the price in the deed is not in accordance with the fact.

Also, a lien existing in the unpaid vendor of chattels, the same remaining in his hands, to the extent of the purchase price, where the sale was for cash, or on a term of credit which has expired, or on an agreement by which the seller is to retain possession. 1 Pars. Cont. 563; 93 U. S. 631.

VENDUE. A sale; generally a sale at public auction; and more particularly a sale so made under authority of law, as by a constable, sheriff, tax collector, administrator, etc.

VENDUE MASTER. An auctioneer.

VENIA. A kneeling or low prostration on the ground by penitents; pardon.

VENIA ÆTATIS. A privilege granted by a prince or sovereign, in virtue of which a person is entitled to act, *sui juris*, as if he were of full age. Story, Confl. Laws, § 74.

Veniæ facilitas incentivum est delinquendi. 3 Inst. 236. Facility of pardon is an incentive to crime.

VENIRE. Lat. To come; to appear in court. This word is sometimes used as the name of the writ for summoning a jury, more commonly called a "*venire facias.*"

VENIRE FACIAS. Lat. In practice. A judicial writ, directed to the sheriff of the county in which a cause is to be tried, commanding him that he *cause to come* before the court, on a certain day therein mentioned, twelve good and lawful men of the body of his county, qualified according to law, by whom the truth of the matter may be the better known, and who are in no wise of kin either to the plaintiff or to the defendant, to make a jury of the country between the parties in the action, because as well the plaintiff as the defendant, between whom the matter in variance is, have put themselves upon that jury, and that he return the names of the jurors, etc. 2 Tidd, Pr. 777, 778; 3 Bl. Comm. 352.

VENIRE FACIAS AD RESPONDENDUM. A writ to summon a person, against whom an indictment for a misdemeanor has been found, to appear and be arraigned for the offense. A justice's warrant is now more commonly used. Archb. Crim. Pl. 81; Sweet.

VENIRE FACIAS DE NOVO. A fresh or new *venire*, which the court grants when there has been some impropriety or irregularity in returning the jury, or where the verdict is so imperfect or ambiguous that no judgment can be given upon it, or where a judgment is reversed on error, and a new trial awarded.

VENIRE FACIAS JURATORES was a judicial writ directed to the sheriff, when issue was joined in an action, commanding him to cause to come to Westminster, on such a day, twelve free and lawful men of his county by whom the truth of the matter at issue might be better known. This writ was abolished by section 104 of the common-law procedure act, 1852, and by section 105 a precept issued by the judges of assize is substituted in its place. The process so substituted is sometimes loosely spoken of as a "*venire.*" Brown.

VENIRE FACIAS TOT MATRONAS. A writ to summon a jury of matrons to execute the writ *de ventre inspiciendo*.

VENIREMAN. A member of a panel of jurors; a juror summoned by a writ of *venire facias*.

VENIT ET DEFENDIT. In old pleading. Comes and defends. The proper words of appearance and defense in an action. 1 Ld. Raym. 117.

VENIT ET DICIT. In old pleading. Comes and says. 2 Salk. 544.

VENTE. In French law. Sale; contract of sale.

VENTE À RÉMÉRÉ. In French law. A conditional sale, in which the seller reserves the right to redeem or repurchase at the same price.

VENTER, VENTRE. The belly or womb. The term is used in law as designating the maternal parentage of children. Thus, where in ordinary phraseology we should say that A. was B.'s child by his first wife, he would be described in law as "by the first *venter.*" Brown.

VENTRE INSPICIENDO. In old English law. A writ that lay for an heir presumptive, to cause an examination to be made of the widow in order to determine whether she were pregnant or not, in cases where she was suspected of a design to bring forward a supposititious heir. 1 Bl. Comm. 456.

VENUE. In pleading and practice. A neighborhood; the neighborhood, place, or county in which an injury is declared to have been done, or fact declared to have happened. 3 Bl. Comm. 294.

Venue also denotes the county in which an action or prosecution is brought for trial, and which is to furnish the panel of jurors. To "change the venue" is to transfer the cause for trial to another county or district.

In the common-law practice, the venue is that part of the declaration in an action which designates the county in which the action is to be tried. Sweet.

VERAY. L. Fr. True. An old form of *vrai*. Thus, *veray*, or true, *tenant*, is one who holds in fee-simple; *veray tenant by the manner*, is the same as tenant by the manner, (*q. v.*,) with this difference only: that the fee-simple, instead of remaining in the lord, is given by him or by the law to another. Ham. N. P. 393, 394.

Verba accipienda sunt cum effectu, ut sortiantur effectum. Words are to be received with effect, so that they may produce effect. Bac. Max.

Verba accipienda sunt secundum subjectam materiam. 6 Coke, 62. Words are to be understood with reference to the subject-matter.

Verba æquivoca, ac in dubio sensu posita, intelliguntur digniori et potentiori sensu. Equivocal words, and such as are put in a doubtful sense, are [to be] understood in the more worthy and effectual sense. 6 Coke, 20*a*.

Verba aliquid operari debent; debent intelligi ut aliquid operentur. 8 Coke, 94. Words ought to have some operation; they ought to be interpreted in such a way as to have some operation.

Verba artis ex arte. Terms of art should be explained from the art. 2 Kent, Comm. 556, note.

VERBA CANCELLARIÆ. Words of the chancery. The technical style of writs framed in the office of chancery. Fleta, lib. 4, c. 10, § 3.

Verba chartarum fortius accipiuntur contra proferentem. The words of charters are to be received more strongly against the grantor. Co. Litt. 36; Broom, Max. 594.

Verba cum effectu accipienda sunt. Bac. Max. 3. Words ought to be used so as to give them their effect.

Verba currentis monetæ, tempus solutionis designant. Dav. 20. The words "current money" designate current at the time of payment.

Verba debent intelligi cum effectu, ut res magis valeat quam pereat. Words ought to be understood with effect, that a thing may rather be preserved than destroyed. 2 Smith, Lead. Cas. 530.

Verba debent intelligi ut aliquid operentur. Words ought to be understood so as to have some operation. 8 Coke, 94*a*.

Verba dicta de persona intelligi debent de conditione personæ. Words spoken of a person are to be understood of the condition of the person. 2 Rolle, 72.

Verba fortius accipiuntur contra proferentem. Words are to be taken most strongly against him who uses them. Bac. Max. 11, reg. 3.

Verba generalia generaliter sunt intelligenda. 3 Inst. 76. General words are to be generally understood.

Verba generalia restringuntur ad habilitatem rei vel aptitudinem personæ. General words must be narrowed either to the nature of the subject-matter or to the aptitude of the person. Broom, Max. 646.

Verba illata (relata) inesse videntur. Words referred to are to be considered as if incorporated. Broom, Max. 674, 677; 11 Mees. & W. 183.

Verba in differenti materia per prius, non per posterius, intelligenda sunt. Words on a different subject are to be understood by what precedes, not by what comes after. A maxim of the civil law. Calvin.

Verba intelligenda sunt in casu possibili. Words are to be understood in [of] a possible case. A maxim of the civil law. Calvin.

Verba intentioni, non e contra, debent inservire. 8 Coke, 94. Words ought to be made subservient to the intent, not the intent to the words.

Verba ita sunt intelligenda, ut res magis valeat quam pereat. The words [of an instrument] are to be so understood, that the subject-matter may rather be of force than perish, [rather be preserved than destroyed; or, in other words, that the instrument may have effect, if possible.] Bac. Max. 17, in reg. 3; Plowd. 156; 2 Bl. Comm. 380; 2 Kent, Comm. 555.

Verba mere æquivoca, si per communem usum loquendi in intellectu certo sumuntur, talis intellectus præferendus est. [In the case of] words merely equivocal, if they are taken by the common usage of speech in a certain sense, such sense is to be preferred. A maxim of the civil law. Calvin.

Verba nihil operari melius est quam absurde. It is better that words should have no operation at all than [that they should operate] absurdly. A maxim of the civil law. Calvin.

Verba non tam intuenda, quam causa et natura rei, ut mens contrahentium ex eis potius quam ex verbis appareat. The words [of a contract] are not so much to be looked at as the cause and nature of the thing, [which is the subject of it,] in order that the intention of the contracting parties may appear rather from them than from the words. Calvin.

Verba offendi possunt, imo ab eis recedere licet, ut verba ad sanum intellectum reducantur. Words may be opposed, [taken in a contrary sense,] nay, we may disregard them altogether, in order that the [general] words [of an instrument] may be restored to a sound meaning. A maxim of the civilians. Calvin.

Verba ordinationis quando verificari possunt in sua vera significatione, trahi ad extraneum intellectum non debent. When the words of an ordinance can be carried into effect in their own true meaning, they ought not to be drawn to a foreign intendment. A maxim of the civilians. Calvin.

Verba posteriora propter certitudinem addita, ad priora quæ certitudine indigent, sunt referenda. Subsequent words, added for the purpose of certainty, are to be referred to the preceding words which require the certainty. Wing. Max. 167, max. 53; Broom, Max. 586.

VERBA PRECARIA. Lat. In the civil law. Precatory words; words of trust, or used to create a trust.

Verba pro re et subjecta materia accipi debent. Words ought to be understood in favor of the thing and subject-matter. A maxim of the civilians. Calvin.

Verba quæ aliquid operari possunt non debent esse superflua. Words which can have any kind of operation ought not to be [considered] superfluous. Calvin.

Verba, quantumvis generalia, ad aptitudinem restringantur, etiamsi nullam aliam paterentur restrictionem. Words, howsoever general, are restrained to fitness, (*i. e.*, to harmonize with the subject-matter,) though they would bear no other restriction. Spiegelius.

Verba relata hoc maxime operantur per referentiam, ut in eis inesse videntur. Related words [words connected with others by reference] have this particular operation by the reference, that they are considered as being inserted in those [clauses which refer to them.] Co. Litt. 9*b*, 359*a*. Words to which reference is made in an instrument have the same effect and operation as if they were inserted in the clauses referring to them. Broom, Max. 673.

Verba secundum materiam subjectam intelligi nemo est qui nesciat. There is no one who does not know that words are to be understood according to their subject-matter. Calvin.

Verba semper accipienda sunt in mitiori sensu. Words are always to be taken in the milder sense. 4 Coke, 13*a*.

Verba strictæ significationis ad latam extendi possunt, si subsit ratio. Words of a strict or narrow signification may be extended to a broad meaning, if there be ground in reason for it. A maxim of the civilians. Calvin.

Verba sunt indices animi. Words are the indices or indicators of the mind or thought. Latch, 106.

VERBAL. Parol; by word of mouth; as, verbal agreement; verbal evidence.

VERBAL NOTE. A memorandum or note, in diplomacy, not signed, sent when an affair has continued a long time without any reply, in order to avoid the appearance of an urgency which perhaps is not required; and, on the other hand, to guard against the supposition that it is forgotten, or that there is an intention of not prosecuting it any further. Wharton.

VERBAL PROCESS. In Louisiana. *Procès verbal*, (*q. v.*)

Verbis standum ubi nulla ambiguitas. One must abide by the words where there is no ambiguity. Tray. Lat. Max. 612.

Verbum imperfecti temporis rem adhuc imperfectam significat. The imperfect tense of the verb indicates an incomplete matter. 6 Wend. 103, 120.

VERDEROR. An officer of the king's forest, who is sworn to maintain and keep the assizes of the forest, and to view, receive, and enroll the attachments and presentments of all manner of trespasses of vert and venison in the forest. Manw. c. 6, § 5.

VERDICT. In practice. The formal and unanimous decision or finding of a jury, impaneled and sworn for the trial of a cause, upon the matters or questions duly submitted to them upon the trial.

A verdict is the honest accord of twelve intelligent minds upon the issue submitted to them. 26 Ind. 366.

The word "verdict" has a well-defined signification in law. It means the decision of a jury, and it never means the decision of a court or a referee or a commissioner. In common language, the word "verdict" is sometimes used in a more extended sense, but in law it is always used to mean the decision of a jury; and we must suppose that the legislature intended to use the word as it is used in law. 25 Kan. 656.

The verdict of a jury is either *general* or *special*. A general verdict is that by which they pronounce generally upon all or any of the issues, either in favor of the plaintiff or defendant; a special verdict is that by which the jury finds the facts only, leaving the judgment to the court. The special verdict must present the conclusions of fact as established by the evidence, and not the evidence to prove them; and those conclusions of fact must be so presented as that nothing shall remain to the court but to draw from them conclusions of law. Code Civil Proc. Cal. § 624; Gen. St. Minn. 1878, c. 66, § 235.

A general verdict is that by which the jury pronounce generally upon all or any of the issues, either in favor of the plaintiff or defendant. A special verdict is that by which the jury find the facts only, leaving the judgment to the court. Code N. Y. § 260. See 28 Conn. 144; 8 Ga. 208; 1 Litt. 376; Co. Litt. 228; 4 Bl. Comm. 461.

A verdict is also either *public* or *privy*. A public verdict is one delivered in open court. It is called a "privy verdict" when the judge has left or adjourned the court, and the jury, being agreed, in order to be delivered from their confinement obtain leave to give their verdict privily to the judge out of court, which privy verdict, however, is of no force unless afterwards affirmed by a public verdict given openly in court. Boote, Suit Law, 273.

A *partial* verdict, in criminal practice, is where the jury convict the prisoner on part of the indictment, and acquit him as to the residue. Archb. Crim. Pl. 170.

VERDICT SUBJECT TO OPINION OF COURT. A verdict returned by the jury, the entry of judgment upon which is subject to the determination of points of law reserved by the court upon the trial.

VEREBOT. Sax. In old records. A packet-boat or transport vessel. Cowell.

VEREDICTUM. L. Lat. In old English law. A verdict; a declaration of the truth of a matter in issue, submitted to a jury for trial.

Veredictum, quasi dictum veritatis; ut judicium quasi juris dictum. Co. Litt. 226. The verdict is, as it were, the *dictum* of truth; as the judgment is the *dictum* of law.

VERGE, or VIRGE. The compass of the queen's court, which bounds the jurisdiction of the lord steward of the household; it seems to have been twelve miles about. Britt. 68. A quantity of land from fifteen to thirty acres. 28 Edw. I. Also a stick, or rod, whereby one is admitted tenant to a copyhold estate. Old Nat. Brev. 17.

VERGELT. In Saxon law. A mulct or fine for a crime. See WEREGILD.

VERGENS AD INOPIAM. L. Lat. In Scotch law. Verging towards poverty; in declining circumstances. 2 Kames, Eq. 8.

VERGERS. In English law. Officers who carry white wands before the justices of either bench. Cowell. Mentioned in Fleta, as officers of the king's court, who oppressed the people by demanding exorbitant fees. Fleta, lib. 2, c. 38.

VERIFICATION. In pleading. A certain formula with which all pleadings containing new affirmative matter must conclude, being in itself an averment that the party pleading is ready to establish the truth of what he has set forth.

In practice. The examination of a writing for the purpose of ascertaining its truth; or a certificate or affidavit that it is true.

"Verification" is not identical with "authentication." A notary may verify a mortgagee's written statement of the actual amount of his claim, but need not authenticate the act by his seal. 19 Ohio St. 291.

VERIFY. To confirm or substantiate by oath; to show to be true. Particularly used of making formal oath to accounts, petitions, pleadings, and other papers.

The word "verify" sometimes means to confirm and substantiate by oath, and sometimes by argument. When used in legal proceedings it is generally employed in the former sense. 3 How. Pr. 284.

Veritas, a quocunque dicitur, a Deo est. 4 Inst. 153. Truth, by whomsoever pronounced, is from God.

Veritas demonstrationis tollit errorem nominis. The truth of the description removes an error in the name. 1 Ld. Raym. 303.

Veritas habenda est in juratore; justitia et judicium in judice. Truth is the desideratum in a juror; justice and judgment in a judge. Bract. fol. 185*b*.

Veritas nihil veretur nisi abscondi. Truth fears nothing but to be hid. 9 Coke, 20*b*.

Veritas nimium altercando amittitur. Truth is lost by excessive altercation. Hob. 344.

Veritas, quæ minime defensatur opprimitur; et qui non improbat, approbat. 3 Inst. 27. Truth which is not sufficiently defended is overpowered; and he who does not disapprove, approves.

Veritatem qui non libere pronunciat proditor est veritatis. 4 Inst. Epil. He who does not freely speak the truth is a betrayer of truth.

VERITY. Truth; truthfulness; conformity to fact. The records of a court "import uncontrollable verity." 1 Black, Judgm. § 276.

VERNA. In the civil law. A slave born in his master's house.

VERSARI. Lat. In the civil law. To be employed; to be conversant. *Versari male in tutela*, to misconduct one's self in a guardianship. Calvin.

VERSUS. Lat. Against. In the title of a cause, the name of the plaintiff is put first, followed by the word "*versus*," then the defendant's name. Thus, "Fletcher *versus* Peck," or "Fletcher *against* Peck." The word is commonly abbreviated "*vs.*" or "*v.*"

VERT. Everything bearing green leaves in a forest.

Also that power which a man has, by royal grant, to cut green wood in a forest.

Also, in heraldry, green color, called "venus" in the arms of princes, and "emerald" in those of peers, and expressed in engravings by lines in bend. Wharton.

VERUS. Lat. True; truthful; genuine; actual; real; just.

VERY LORD AND VERY TENANT. They that are immediate lord and tenant one to another. Cowell.

VESSEL. A ship, brig, sloop, or other craft used in navigation. The word is more comprehensive than "ship."

The word "vessel" includes every description of water-craft or other artificial contrivances used, or capable of being used, as a means of transportation on water. Rev. St. U. S. § 3.

"Vessel," in the provision of the code of Louisiana that commercial partners are those who are engaged in "carrying personal property for hire in ships or other vessels," means any structure which is made to float upon the water, for purposes of commerce or war, whether impelled by wind, steam, or oars. 27 La. Ann. 607.

VEST. To accrue to; to be fixed: to take effect; to give a fixed and indefeasible right. An estate is vested in possession when there exists a right of present enjoyment; and an estate is vested in interest when there is a present fixed right of future enjoyment. Fearne, Rem. 2.

To clothe with possession; to deliver full possession of land or of an estate; to give seisin; to enfeoff. Spelman.

VESTA. The crop on the ground. Cowell.

VESTED ESTATE or INTEREST. Any estate, property, or interest is called "vested," whether in possession or not, which is not subject to any condition precedent and unperformed. The interest may be either a present and immediate interest, or it may be a future but uncontingent, and therefore transmissible, interest. Brown.

VESTED IN INTEREST. A legal term applied to a present fixed right of future enjoyment; as reversions, vested remainders, such executory devises, future uses, conditional limitations, and other future interests as are not referred to, or made to depend on, a period or event that is uncertain. Wharton.

VESTED IN POSSESSION. A legal term applied to a right of present enjoyment actually existing.

VESTED INTEREST. A future interest is vested when there is a person in being who would have a right, defeasible or indefeasible, to the immediate possession of the property, upon the ceasing of the intermediate or precedent interest. Civil Code Cal. § 694.

VESTED LEGACY. A legacy is said to be vested when the words of the testator making the bequest convey a transmissible interest, whether present or future, to the legatee in the legacy. Thus a legacy to one to be paid when he attains the age of twenty-one years is a vested legacy, because it is given unconditionally and absolutely, and therefore vests an immediate interest in the legatee, of which the enjoyment only is deferred or postponed. Brown.

VESTED REMAINDER. An estate by which a present interest passes to the party, though to be enjoyed *in futuro*, and by which the estate is invariably fixed to remain to a determinate person after the particular estate has been spent. 2 Bl. Comm. 168.

VESTED RIGHTS. In constitutional law. Rights which have so completely and definitively accrued to or settled in a person that they are not subject to be defeated or canceled by the act of any other private person, and which it is right and equitable that the government should recognize and protect, as being lawful in themselves, and settled according to the then current rules of law, and of which the individual could not be deprived arbitrarily without injustice, or of which he could not justly be deprived otherwise than by the established methods of procedure and for the public welfare.

VESTIGIUM. Lat. In the law of evidence, a vestige, mark, or sign; a trace, track, or impression left by a physical object. Fleta, l. 1, c. 25, § 6.

VESTING ORDER. In English law. An order which may be granted by the chancery division of the high court of justice, (and formerly by chancery,) passing the legal estate in lieu of a conveyance. Commissioners also, under modern statutes, have similar powers. St. 15 & 16 Vict. c. 55; Wharton.

VESTRY. The place in a church where the priest's vestures are deposited. Also an assembly of the minister, church-wardens, and parishioners, usually held in the vestry of the church, or in a building called a "vestry-hall," to act upon business of the church. Mozley & Whitley.

VESTRY CESS. A rate levied in Ireland for parochial purposes, abolished by St. 27 Vict. c. 17.

VESTRY-CLERK. An officer appointed to attend vestries, and take an account of their proceedings, etc.

VESTRY-MEN. A select number of parishioners elected in large and populous parishes to take care of the concerns of the parish; so called because they used ordinarily to meet in the vestry of the church. Cowell.

VESTURA. A crop of grass or corn. Also a garment; metaphorically applied to a possession or seisin.

VESTURA TERRÆ. In old English law. The vesture of the land; that is, the corn, grass, underwood, sweepage, and the like. Co. Litt. 4*b*.

VESTURE. In old English law. Profit of land. "How much the *vesture* of an acre is worth." Cowell.

VESTURE OF LAND. A phrase including all things, trees excepted, which grow upon the surface of the land, and clothe it externally. Ham. N. P. 151.

VETERA STATUTA. Lat. Ancient statutes. The English statutes from *Magna Charta* to the end of the reign of Edward II. are so called; those from the beginning of the reign of Edward III. being contradistinguished by the appellation of "*Nova Statuta.*" 2 Reeve, Eng. Law, 85.

VETITUM NAMIUM. Where the bailiff of a lord distrains beasts or goods of another, and the lord forbids the bailiff to deliver them when the sheriff comes to make replevin, the owner of the cattle may demand satisfaction in *placitum de vetito namio.* 2 Inst. 140; 2 Bl. Comm. 148.

VETO. Lat. I forbid. The veto-power is a power vested in the executive officer of some governments to declare his refusal to assent to any bill or measure which has been passed by the legislature. It is either absolute or qualified, according as the effect of its exercise is either to destroy the bill finally, or to prevent its becoming law unless again passed by a stated proportion of votes or with other formalities. Or the veto may be merely suspensive.

VETUS JUS. Lat. The old law. A term used in the civil law, sometimes to designate the law of the Twelve Tables, and sometimes merely a law which was in force previous to the passage of a subsequent law. Calvin.

VEX. To harass, disquiet, annoy; as by repeated litigation upon the same facts.

VEXARI. Lat. To be harassed, vexed, or annoyed; to be prosecuted; as in the maxim, *Nemo debet bis vexari pro una et eadem causa,* no one should be twice prosecuted for one and the same cause.

VEXATA QUÆSTIO. Lat. A vexed question; a question often agitated or discussed, but not determined or settled; a question or point which has been differently determined, and so left doubtful. 7 Coke, 45*b;* 3 Burrows, 1547.

VEXATION. The injury or damage which is suffered in consequence of the tricks of another.

VEXATIOUS. A proceeding is said to be vexatious when the party bringing it is not acting *bona fide,* and merely wishes to annoy or embarrass his opponent, or when it is not calculated to lead to any practical result. Such a proceeding is often described as "frivolous and vexatious," and the court may stay it on that ground. Sweet.

VEXED QUESTION. A question or point of law often discussed or agitated, but not determined or settled.

VI AUT CLAM. Lat. In the civil law. By force or covertly. Dig. 43, 24.

VI BONORUM RAPTORUM. Lat. In the civil law. Of goods taken away by force. The name of an action given by the prætor as a remedy for the violent taking of another's property. Inst. 4, 2; Dig. 47, 8.

VI ET ARMIS. Lat. With force and arms. See TRESPASS.

VIA. Lat. **In the civil law.** Way; a road; a right of way. The right of walking, riding, and driving over another's land. Inst. 2, 3, pr. A species of rural servitude, which included *iter* (a footpath) and *actus,* (a driftway.)

In old English law. A way; a public road; a foot, horse, and cart way. Co. Litt. 56*a*.

Via antiqua via est tuta. The old way is the safe way. 1 Johns. Ch. 527, 530.

VIA PUBLICA. Lat. In the civil law. A public way or road, the land itself belonging to the public. Dig. 43, 8, 2, 21.

VIA REGIA. Lat. In English law. The king's highway for all men. Co. Litt. 56*a*. The highway or common road, called "the king's" highway, because authorized by him and under his protection. Cowell.

Via trita est tutissima. The trodden path is the safest. 10 Coke, 142; Broom, Max. 134.

VIABILITY. Capability of living. A term used to denote the power a new-born child possesses of continuing its independent existence.

VIABLE. Capable of life. This term is applied to a newly-born infant, and especially to one prematurely born, which is not only born alive, but in such a state of organic development as to make possible the continuance of its life.

VIÆ SERVITUS. Lat. A right of way over another's land.

VIAGÈRE RENTE. In French law. A rent-charge or annuity payable for the life of the annuitant.

VIANDER. In old English law. A returning officer. 7 Mod. 13.

VIATOR. Lat. In Roman law. A summoner or apparitor; an officer who attended on the tribunes and ædiles.

VICAR. One who performs the functions of another; a substitute. Also the incumbent of an appropriated or impropriated ecclesiastical benefice, as distinguished from the incumbent of a non-appropriated benefice, who is called a "rector." Wharton.

VICAR GENERAL. An ecclesiastical officer who assists the archbishop in the discharge of his office.

VICARAGE. In English ecclesiastical law. The living or benefice of a vicar, as a parsonage is of a parson. 1 Bl. Comm. 387, 388.

VICARIAL TITHES. Petty or small tithes payable to the vicar. 2 Steph. Comm. 681.

VICARIO, etc. An ancient writ for a spiritual person imprisoned, upon forfeiture of a recognizance, etc. Reg. Orig. 147.

Vicarius non habet vicarium. A deputy has not [cannot have] a deputy. A delegated power cannot be again delegated. Broom, Max. 839.

VICE. A fault, defect, or imperfection. In the civil law, redhibitory vices are such faults or imperfections in the subject-matter of a sale as will give the purchaser the right to return the article and demand back the price.

VICE. Lat. In the place or stead. *Vice mea,* in my place.

VICE-ADMIRAL. An officer in the (English) navy next in rank after the admiral.

VICE-ADMIRALTY COURTS. In English law. Courts established in the queen's possessions beyond the seas, with jurisdiction over maritime causes, including those relating to prize. 3 Steph. Comm. 435; 3 Bl. Comm. 69.

VICE-CHAMBERLAIN. A great officer under the lord chamberlain, who, in the absence of the lord chamberlain, has the control and command of the officers appertaining to that part of the royal household which is called the "chamber." Cowell.

VICE-CHANCELLOR. In English law. A judge of the court of chancery, acting as assistant to the lord chancellor, and holding a separate court, from whose judgment an appeal lay to the chancellor. 3 Steph. Comm. 418.

VICE-CHANCELLOR OF THE UNIVERSITIES. See CHANCELLOR OF THE UNIVERSITIES.

VICE-COMES. A title formerly bestowed on the sheriff of a county, when he was regarded as the deputy of the count or earl.

Vice-comes dicitur quod vicem comitis suppleat. Co. Litt. 168. "*Vice-comes*" [sheriff] is so called because he supplies the place of the "*comes,*" [earl.]

VICE-COMES NON MISIT BREVE. The sheriff hath not sent the writ. The form of continuance on the record after issue and before trial. 7 Mod. 349; 11 Mod. 231.

VICE-COMITISSA. In old English law. A viscountess. Spelman.

VICE-CONSTABLE OF ENGLAND. An ancient officer in the time of Edward IV.

VICE-CONSUL. In international law. A commercial agent who acts in the place or stead of a consul, or has charge of a portion of his territory.

In old English law. The deputy or substitute of an earl, (*comes,*) who was anciently called "consul;" answering to the more modern "*vice-comes.*" Burrill.

VICE-DOMINUS. A sheriff.

VICE-DOMINUS EPISCOPI. The vicar general or commissary of a bishop. Blount.

VICE-GERENT. A deputy or lieutenant.

VICE-JUDEX. In old Lombardic law. A deputy judge.

VICE-MARSHAL. An officer who was appointed to assist the earl marshal.

VICE-PRESIDENT OF THE UNITED STATES. The title of the second officer, in point of rank, in the executive branch of the government of the United States.

VICE VERSA. Lat. Conversely; in inverted order; in reverse manner.

VICEROY. A person clothed with authority to act in place of the king; hence, the usual title of the governor of a dependency.

VICINAGE. Neighborhood; near dwelling; vicinity. 2 Bl. Comm. 33; Cowell.

VICINETUM. The neighborhood; vicinage; the venue. Co. Litt. 158*b*.

Vicini viciniora præsumuntur scire. 4 Inst. 173. Persons living in the neighborhood are presumed to know the neighborhood.

VICIOUS INTROMISSION. In Scotch law. A meddling with the movables of a deceased, without confirmation or probate of his will or other title. Wharton.

VICIS ET VENELLIS MUNDANDIS. An ancient writ against the mayor or bailiff of a town, etc., for the clean keeping of their streets and lanes. Reg. Orig. 267.

VICOUNTIEL, or VICONTIEL. Anything that belongs to the sheriffs, as *vicontiel writs; i. e.*, such as are triable in the sheriff's court. As to vicontiel rents, see St. 3 & 4 Wm. IV. c. 99, §§ 12, 13, which places them under the management of the commissioners of the woods and forests. Cowell.

VICOUNTIEL JURISDICTION. That jurisdiction which belongs to the officers of a county; as sheriffs, coroners, etc.

VICTUALLER. In English law. A person authorized by law to keep a house of entertainment for the public; a publican. 9 Adol. & E. 423.

VICTUS. Lat. In the civil law. Sustenance; support; the means of living.

VIDAME. In French feudal law. Originally, an officer who represented the bishop, as the viscount did the count. In process of time, these dignitaries erected their offices into fiefs, and became feudal nobles, such as the *vidame* of Chartres, Rheims, etc., continuing to take their titles from the seat of the bishop whom they represented, although the lands held by virtue of their fiefs might be situated elsewhere. Brande; Burrill.

VIDE. Lat. A word of reference. *Vide ante*, or *vide supra*, refers to a previous passage, *vide post*, or *vide infra*, to a subsequent passage, in a book.

Videbis ea sæpe committi quæ sæpe vindicantur. 3 Inst. Epil. You will see these things frequently committed which are frequently punished.

VIDELICET. Lat. The words "to-wit," or "that is to say," so frequently used in pleading, are technically called the "*videlicet*" or "*scilicet;*" and when any fact alleged in pleading is preceded by, or accompanied with, these words, such fact is, in the language of the law, said to be "laid under a *videlicet.*" The use of the *videlicet* is to point out, particularize, or render more specific that which has been previously stated in general language only; also to explain that which is doubtful or obscure. Brown.

Videtur qui surdus et mutus ne poet faire alienation. It seems that a deaf and dumb man cannot alienate. 4 Johns. Ch. 444; Brooke, Abr. "Eschete," pl. 4.

VIDIMUS. An *inspeximus*, (*q. v.*) Barring, Ob. St. 5.

VIDUA REGIS. In old English law. A king's widow. The widow of a tenant *in capite*. So called, because she was not allowed to marry a second time without the king's permission; obtaining her dower also from the assignment of the king, and having the king for her patron and defender. Spelman.

VIDUITATIS PROFESSIO. The making a solemn profession to live a sole and chaste woman.

VIDUITY. Widowhood.

VIE. Fr. Life; occurring in the phrases *cestui que vie, pur autre vie*, etc.

VIEW. The right of prospect; the outlook or prospect from the windows of one's house. A species of urban servitude which prohibits the obstruction of such prospect. 3 Kent. Comm. 448.

We understand by *view* every opening which may more or less facilitate the means of looking out of a building. *Lights* are those openings which are made rather for the admission of light than to look out of. Civil Code La. art. 715.

Also an inspection of property in controversy, or of a place where a crime has been committed, by the jury previously to the trial.

VIEW AND DELIVERY. When a right of common is exercisable not over the whole waste, but only in convenient places indicated from time to time by the lord of the manor or his bailiff, it is said to be exercisable after "view and delivery." Elton, Commons, 233.

VIEW, DEMAND OF. In real actions, the defendant was entitled to demand a *view*, that is, a sight of the thing, in order to ascertain its identity and other circumstances. As, if a real action were brought against a tenant, and such tenant did not exactly know what land it was that the demandant asked, then he might pray the view, which was that he might see the land which the demandant claimed. Brown.

VIEW OF AN INQUEST. A view or inspection taken by a jury, summoned upon an inquisition or inquest, of the place or property to which the inquisition or inquiry refers. Brown.

VIEW OF FRANKPLEDGE. In English law. An examination to see if every freeman above twelve years of age within the district had taken the oath of allegiance, and found nine freemen pledges for his peaceable demeanor. 1 Reeve, Eng. Law, 7.

VIEWERS. Persons who are appointed by a court to make an investigation of certain matters, or to examine a particular locality, (as, the proposed site of a new road,) and to report to the court the result of their inspection, with their opinion on the same.

In old practice. Persons appointed under writs of view to testify the view. Rosc. Real Act. 253.

VIF-GAGE. In old English law. A *vivum vadium* or living pledge, as distinguished from a *mortgage* or dead pledge. Properly, an estate given as security for a debt, the debt to be satisfied out of the rents, issues, and profits.

VIGIL. The eve or next day before any solemn feast.

VIGILANCE. Watchfulness; precaution; a proper degree of activity and promptness in pursuing one's rights or guarding them from infraction, or in making or discovering opportunities for the enforcement of one's lawful claims and demands. It is the opposite of *laches.*

Vigilantibus et non dormientibus jura subveniunt. The laws aid those who are vigilant, not those who sleep upon their rights. 2 Inst. 690; 7 Allen, 493; Broom, Max. 892.

VIGOR. Lat. Strength; virtue; force; efficiency. *Proprio vigore,* by its own force.

VIIS ET MODIS. Lat. In the ecclesiastical courts, service of a decree or citation *viis et modis, i. e.,* by all "ways and means" likely to affect the party with knowledge of its contents, is equivalent to substituted service in the temporal courts, and is opposed to personal service. Phillim. Ecc. Law, 1258, 1283.

VILL. In old English law, this word was used to signify the parts into which a hundred or wapentake was divided. It also signifies a town or city.

Villa est ex pluribus mansionibus vicinata, et collata ex pluribus vicinis, et sub appellatione villarum continentur burgi et civitates. Co. Litt. 115. Vill is a neighborhood of many mansions, a collection of many neighbors, and under the term of "vills" boroughs and cities are contained.

VILLA REGIA. Lat. In Saxon law. A royal residence. Spelman.

VILLAGE. Any small assemblage of houses for dwellings or business, or both, in the country, whether they are situated upon regularly laid out streets and alleys or not, constitutes a village. 27 Ill. 48.

VILLAIN. An opprobrious epithet, implying great moral delinquency, and equivalent to knave, rascal, or scoundrel. The word is libelous. 1 Bos. & P. 331.

VILLANIS REGIS SUBTRACTIS REDUCENDIS. A writ that lay for the bringing back of the king's bondmen, that had been carried away by others out of his manors whereto they belonged. Reg. Orig. 87.

VILLANUM SERVITIUM. In old English law. Villein service. Fleta, lib. 3, c. 13, § 1.

VILLEIN. A person attached to a manor, who was substantially in the condition of a slave, who performed the base and servile work upon the manor for the lord, and was, in most respects, a subject of property and belonging to him. 1 Washb. Real Prop. 26.

VILLEIN IN GROSS. In old English law. A villein who was annexed to the person of the lord, and transferable by deed from one owner to another. 2 Bl. Comm. 93.

VILLEIN REGARDANT. A villein annexed to the manor of land; a serf.

VILLEIN SERVICES. In old English law. Base services, such as villeins performed. 2 Bl. Comm. 93. They were not, however, exclusively confined to villeins, since they might be performed by freemen, without impairing their free condition. Bract. fol. 24*b*.

VILLEIN SOCAGE. In feudal and old English law. A species of tenure in which the services to be rendered were certain and determinate, but were of a base or servile nature; *i. e.,* not suitable to a man of free and honorable rank. This was also called "privileged villeinage," to distinguish it from "pure villeinage," in which the services were not certain, but the tenant was obliged to do whatever he was commanded. 2 Bl. Comm. 61.

VILLENAGE. A servile kind of tenure belonging to lands or tenements, whereby the tenant was bound to do all such services as the lord commanded, or were fit for a villein to do. Cowell. See VILLEIN.

VILLENOUS JUDGMENT. A judgment which deprived one of his *libera lex,* whereby he was discredited and disabled as a juror or witness; forfeited his goods and chattels and lands for life; wasted the lands, razed the houses, rooted up the trees, and committed his body to prison. It has become obsolete. 4 Bl. Comm. 136; 4 Steph. Comm. 230; 4 Broom & H. Comm. 153. Wharton.

Vim vi repellere licet, modo fiat moderamine inculpatæ tutelæ, non ad sumendam vindictam, sed ad propulsandam injuriam. It is lawful to repel force by force, provided it be done with the moderation of blameless defense, not for the purpose of taking revenge, but to ward off injury. Co. Litt. 162*a*.

VINAGIUM. A payment of a certain quantity of wine instead of rent for a vineyard. 2 Mon. Ang. p. 980.

VINCULACION. In Spanish law. An entail. Schm. Civil Law, 308.

VINCULO. In Spanish law. The bond, chain, or tie of marriage. White, New Recop. b. 1, tit. 6, c. 1, § 2.

VINCULO MATRIMONII. See A VINCULO MATRIMONII; DIVORCE.

VINCULUM JURIS. Lat. In the Roman law, an obligation is defined as a *vinculum juris, i. e.*, "a bond of law," whereby one party becomes or is bound to another to do something according to law.

VINDEX. Lat. In the civil law. A defender.

VINDICARE. Lat. In the civil law. To claim, or challenge; to demand one's own; to assert a right in or to a thing; to assert or claim a property in a thing; to claim a thing as one's own. Calvin.

VINDICATIO. Lat. In the civil law. The claiming a thing as one's own; the asserting of a right or title in or to a thing.

VINDICATORY PARTS OF LAWS. The sanction of the laws, whereby it is signified what evil or penalty shall be incurred by such as commit any public wrongs, and transgress or neglect their duty. 1 Steph. Comm. 37.

VINDICTA. In Roman law. A rod or wand; and, from the use of that instrument in their course, various legal acts came to be distinguished by the term; *e. g.*, one of the three ancient modes of manumission was by the *vindicta;* also the rod or wand intervened in the progress of the old action of *vindicatio*, whence the name of that action. Brown.

VINDICTIVE DAMAGES. Exemplary or punitive damages; damages given on the principle of punishing the defendant, over and above compensating the plaintiff.

VIOL. Fr. In French law. Rape. Barring, Ob. St. 139.

VIOLATION. Injury; infringement; breach of right, duty, or law. Ravishment; seduction. The statute 25 Edw. III. St. 5, c. 2, enacts that any person who shall *violate* the king's companion shall be guilty of high treason.

VIOLATION OF SAFE CONDUCTS. An offense against the laws of nations. 4 Steph. Comm. 217.

VIOLENCE. The term "violence" is synonymous with "physical force," and the two are used interchangeably, in relation to assaults, by elementary writers on criminal law. 31 Conn. 212.

VIOLENT DEATH. Death caused by violent external means, as distinguished from natural death, caused by disease or the wasting of the vital forces.

VIOLENT PRESUMPTION. In the law of evidence. Proof of a fact by the proof of circumstances which necessarily attend it. 3 Bl. Comm. 371. Violent presumption is many times equal to full proof. Id.

VIOLENT PROFITS. Mesne profits in Scotland. "They are so called because due on the tenant's forcible or unwarrantable detaining the possession after he ought to have removed." Ersk. Inst. 2, 6, 54; Bell.

Violenta præsumptio aliquando est plena probatio. Co. Litt. 6*b*. Violent presumption is sometimes full proof.

VIOLENTLY. By the use of force; forcibly; with violence. The term is used in indictments for certain offenses.

Viperina est expositio quæ corrodit viscera textus. 11 Coke, 34. It is a poisonous exposition which destroys the vitals of the text.

Vir et uxor censentur in lege una persona. Jenk. Cent. 27. Husband and wife are considered one person in law.

Vir et uxor sunt quasi unica persona, quia caro et sanguis unus; res licet sit propria uxoris, vir tamen ejus custos, cum sit caput mulieris. Co. Litt. 112.

Man and wife are, as it were, one person, because only one flesh and blood; although the property may be the wife's, the husband is keeper of it, since he is the head of the wife.

Vir militans Deo non implicetur secularibus negotiis. Co. Litt. 70. A man fighting for God must not be involved in secular business.

VIRES. Lat. (The plural of "*vis.*") Powers; forces; capabilities; natural powers; powers granted or limited. See ULTRA VIRES.

Vires acquirit eundo. It gains strength by continuance. 1 Johns. Ch. 231, 237.

VIRGA. In old English law. A rod or staff; a rod or ensign of office. Cowell.

VIRGA TERRÆ, (or VIRGATA TERRÆ.) In old English law. A yard-land; a measure of land of variable quantity, containing in some places twenty, in others twenty-four, in others thirty, and in others forty, acres. Cowell; Co. Litt. 5*a*.

VIRGATA REGIA. In old English law. The verge; the bounds of the king's household, within which the court of the steward had jurisdiction. Crabb, Eng. Law, 185.

VIRGATE. A yard-land.

VIRGE, TENANT BY. A species of copyholder, who holds by the virge or rod.

VIRGO INTACTA. A pure virgin.

VIRIDARIO ELIGENDO. A writ for choice of a verderer in the forest. Reg. Orig. 177.

VIRILIA. The privy members of a man, to cut off which was felony by the common law, though the party consented to it. Bract. l. 3, 144; Cowell.

VIRTUE. The phrase "by virtue" differs in meaning from "under color." For instance, the proper fees are received *by virtue* of the office; extortion is *under color* of the office. Any rightful act in office is by virtue of the office. A wrongful act in office may be under color of the office. Phil. Law, 380.

VIRTUTE CUJUS. Lat. By virtue whereof. This was the clause in a pleading justifying an entry upon land, by which the party alleged that it was in virtue of an order from one entitled that he entered. Wharton.

VIRTUTE OFFICII. Lat. By virtue of his office. By the authority vested in him as the incumbent of the particular office.

VIS. Lat. Any kind of force, violence, or disturbance relating to a man's person or his property.

VIS ABLATIVA. In the civil law. Ablative force; force which is exerted in taking away a thing from another. Calvin.

VIS ARMATA. In the civil and old English law. Armed force; force exerted by means of arms or weapons.

VIS CLANDESTINA. In old English law. Clandestine force; such as is used by night. Bract. fol. 162.

VIS COMPULSIVA. In the civil and old English law. Compulsive force; that which is exerted to compel another to do an act against his will; force exerted by menaces or terror.

VIS DIVINA. In the civil law. Divine or superhuman force; the act of God.

VIS ET METUS. In Scotch law. Force and fear. Bell.

VIS EXPULSIVA. In old English law. Expulsive force; force used to expel another, or put him out of his possession. Bracton contrasts it with "*vis simplex,*" and divides it into expulsive force with arms, and expulsive force without arms. Bract. fol. 162.

VIS EXTURBATIVA. In the civil law. Exturbative force; force used to thrust out another. Force used between two contending claimants of possession, the one endeavoring to thrust out the other. Calvin.

VIS FLUMINIS. In the civil law. The force of a river; the force exerted by a stream or current; water-power.

VIS IMPRESSA. The original act of force out of which an injury arises, as distinguished from "*vis proxima,*" the proximate force, or immediate cause of the injury. 2 Greenl. Ev. § 224.

VIS INERMIS. In old English law. Unarmed force; the opposite of "*vis armata.*" Bract. fol. 162.

VIS INJURIOSA. In old English law. Wrongful force; otherwise called "*illicita,*" (unlawful.) Bract. fol. 162.

VIS INQUIETATIVA. In the civil law. Disquieting force. Calvin. Bracton defines it to be where one does not permit another to use his possession quietly and in peace. Bract. fol. 162.

VIS LAICA. In old English law. Lay force; an armed force used to hold possession of a church. Reg. Orig. 59, 60.

Vis legibus est inimica. 3 Inst. 176. Violence is inimical to the laws.

VIS LICITA. In old English law. Lawful force. Bract. fol. 162.

VIS MAJOR. A greater or superior force; an irresistible force. This term is much used in the law of bailments to denote the interposition of violence or coercion proceeding from human agency, (wherein it differs from the "act of God,") but of such a character and strength as to be beyond the powers of resistance or control of those against whom it is directed; for example, the attack of the public enemy or a band of pirates.

In the civil law, this term is sometimes used as synonymous with "*vis divina,*" or the act of God. Calvin.

VIS PERTUBATIVA. In old English law. Force used between parties contending for a possession.

VIS PROXIMA. Immediate force. See VIS IMPRESSA.

VIS SIMPLEX. In old English law. Simple or mere force. Distinguished by Bracton from "*vis armata,*" and also from "*vis expulsiva.*" Bract. fol. 162.

VISA. An official indorsement upon a document, passport, commercial book, etc., to certify that it has been examined and found correct or in due form.

VISCOUNT. A degree of English nobility, next below that of earl.

An old title of the sheriff.

VISÉ. An indorsement made on a passport by the proper authorities, denoting that it has been examined, and that the person who bears it is permitted to proceed on his journey. Webster.

VISIT. In international law. The right of visit or visitation is the right of a cruiser or war-ship to stop a vessel sailing under another flag on the high seas, and send an officer to such vessel to ascertain whether her nationality is what it purports to be. It is exercisable only when suspicious circumstances attend the vessel to be visited; as when she is suspected of a piratical character.

VISITATION. Inspection; superintendence; direction; regulation. A power given by law to the founders of all eleemosynary corporations. 2 Kent, Comm. 300-303; 1 Bl. Comm. 480, 481. In England, the visitation of ecclesiastical corporations belongs to the ordinary. Id.

VISITATION BOOKS. In English law. Books compiled by the heralds, when progresses were solemnly and regularly made into every part of the kingdom, to inquire into the state of families, and to register such marriages and descents as were verified to them upon oath; they were allowed to be good evidence of pedigree. 3 Bl. Comm. 105; 3 Steph. Comm. 724.

VISITOR. An inspector of the government of corporations, or bodies politic. 1 Bl. Comm. 482.

Visitor is an inspector of the government of a corporation, etc. The ordinary is visitor of spiritual corporations. But corporations instituted for private charity, if they are lay, are visitable by the founder, or whom he shall appoint; and from the sentence of such visitor there lies no appeal. By implication of law, the founder and his heirs are visitors of lay foundations, if no particular person is appointed by him to see that the charity is not perverted. Jacob.

The term "visitor" is also applied to an official appointed to see and report upon persons found lunatics by inquisition, and to a person appointed by a school board to visit houses and see that parents are complying with the provisions in reference to the education of their children. Mozley & Whitley.

VISITOR OF MANNERS. The regarder's office in the forest. Manw. i. 195.

VISNE. L. Fr. The neighborhood; vicinage; venue.

VISUS. Lat. In old English practice. View; inspection, either of a place or person.

VITIATE. To impair; to make void or voidable; to cause to fail of force or effect; to destroy or annul, either entirely or in part, the legal efficacy and binding force of an act or instrument; as when it is said that fraud *vitiates* a contract.

VITILITIGATE. To litigate cavilously.

VITIOUS INTROMISSION. In Scotch law. An unwarrantable intermeddling with the movable estate of a person deceased, without the order of law. Ersk. Prin. b. 3, tit. 9, § 25. The irregular intermeddling with the effects of a deceased person, which subjects the party to the whole debts of the deceased. 2 Kames, Eq. 327.

VITIUM CLERICI. In old English law. The mistake of a clerk; a clerical error.

Vitium clerici nocere non debet. Jenk. Cent. 23. A clerical error ought not to hurt.

Vitium est quod fugi debet, nisi, rationem non invenias, mox legem sine ratione esse clames. Ellesm. Post. N. 86. It is a fault which ought to be avoided, that if you cannot discover the reason you should presently exclaim that the law is without reason.

VITIUM SCRIPTORIS. In old English law. The fault or mistake of a writer or copyist; a clerical error. Gilb. Forum Rom. 185.

VITRICUS. Lat. In the civil law. A step-father; a mother's second husband. Calvin.

VIVA AQUA. Lat. In the civil law. Living water; running water; that which issues from a spring or fountain. Calvin.

VIVA PECUNIA. Lat. Cattle, which obtained this name from being received during the Saxon period as money upon most occasions, at certain regulated prices. Cowell.

VIVA VOCE. Lat. With the living voice; by word of mouth. As applied to the examination of witnesses, this phrase is equivalent to "orally." It is used in contradistinction to evidence on affidavits or depositions. As descriptive of a species of voting, it signifies voting by speech or outcry, as distinguished from voting by a written or printed ballot.

VIVARIUM. Lat. In the civil law. An inclosed place, where live wild animals are kept. Calvin.; Spelman.

VIVARY. In English law. A place for keeping wild animals alive, including fishes; a fish pond, park, or warren.

VIVUM VADIUM. See VADIUM VIVUM.

Vix ulla lex fieri potest quæ omnibus commoda sit, sed si majori parti prospiciat, utilis est. Scarcely any law can be made which is adapted to all, but, if it provide for the greater part, it is useful. Plowd. 369.

VIZ. A contraction for *videlicet*, to-wit, namely, that is to say.

VOCABULA ARTIS. Lat. Words of art; technical terms.

Vocabula artium explicanda sunt secundum definitiones prudentum. Terms of arts are to be explained according to the definitions of the learned or skilled [in such arts.] Bl. Law Tracts, 6.

VOCARE AD CURIAM. In feudal law. To summon to court. Feud. Lib. 2, tit. 22.

VOCATIO IN JUS. Lat. A summoning to court. In the earlier practice of the Roman law, (under the *legis actiones*,) the creditor orally called upon his debtor to go with him before the prætor for the purpose of determining their controversy, saying, "*In jus eamus; in jus te voco.*" This was called "*vocatio in jus.*"

VOCIFERATIO. Lat. In old English law. Outcry; hue and cry. Cowell.

VOCO. Lat. In the civil and old English law. I call; I summon; I vouch. *In jus voco te*, I summon you to court; I summon you before the prætor. The formula by which a Roman action was anciently commenced. Adams, Rom. Ant. 242.

VOID. Null; ineffectual; nugatory; having no legal force or binding effect; unable, in law, to support the purpose for which it was intended.

"Void" does not always imply entire nullity; but it is, in a legal sense, subject to large qualifications in view of all the circumstances calling for its application, and the rights and interests to be affected in a given case. 50 N. H. 538, 552.

"Void," as used in statutes and by the courts, does not usually mean that the act or proceeding is an absolute nullity. 50 Mo. 284.

There is this difference between the two words "void" and "voidable:" *void* means that an instrument or transaction is so nugatory and ineffectual that nothing can cure it; *voidable*, when an imperfection or defect can be cured by the act or confirmation of him who could take advantage of it. Thus, while acceptance of rent will make good a voidable lease, it will not affirm a void lease. Wharton.

The true distinction between void and voidable acts, orders, and judgments is that the former can always be assailed in any proceeding, and the latter only in a direct proceeding. 42 Ala. 462.

The term "void," as applicable to conveyances or other agreements, has not at all times been used with technical precision, nor restricted to its peculiar and limited sense, as contradistinguished from "voidable;" it being frequently introduced, even by legal writers and jurists, when the purpose is nothing further than to indicate that a contract was invalid, and not binding in law. But the distinction between the terms "void" and "voidable," in their application to contracts, is often one of great practical importance; and, whenever entire technical accuracy is required, the term "void" can only be properly applied to those contracts that are of no effect whatsoever, such as are a mere nullity, and incapable of confirmation or ratification. 6 Metc. (Mass.) 415.

Void in part, void in toto. 15 N. Y. 9, 96.

Void things are as no things. 9 Cow. 778, 784.

VOIDABLE. That may be avoided, or declared void; not absolutely void, or void in itself. Most of the acts of infants are *voidable* only, and not absolutely void. 2 Kent, Comm. 234. See VOID.

VOIDANCE. The act of emptying; ejection from a benefice.

VOIR DIRE. L. Fr. To speak the truth. This phrase denotes the preliminary examination which the court may make of one presented as a witness, where his competency, interest, etc., is objected to.

VOITURE. Fr. Carriage; transportation by carriage.

VOLENS. Lat. Willing. He is said to be willing who either expressly consents or tacitly makes no opposition. Calvin.

Volenti non fit injuria. He who consents cannot receive an injury. Broom, Max. 268, 269, 271, 395; Shelf. Mar. & Div. 449; Wing. Max. 482; 4 Term R. 657.

Voluit, sed non dixit. He willed, but he did not say. He may have intended so, but he did not say so. A maxim frequently used in the construction of wills, in answer to arguments based upon the supposed intention of a testator. 2 Pow. Dev. 625; 4 Kent, Comm. 538.

VOLUMEN. Lat. In the civil law. A volume; so called from its form, being *rolled* up.

VOLUMUS. Lat. We will; it is our will. The first word of a clause in the royal writs of protection and letters patent. Cowell.

VOLUNTARIUS DÆMON. A voluntary madman. A term applied by Lord Coke to a drunkard, who has voluntarily contracted madness by intoxication. Co. Litt. 247; 4 Bl. Comm. 25.

VOLUNTARY. Free; without compulsion or solicitation.

Without consideration; without valuable consideration; gratuitous.

VOLUNTARY ANSWER, in the practice of the court of chancery, was an answer put in by a defendant, when the plaintiff had filed no interrogatories which required to be answered. Hunt, Eq.

VOLUNTARY ASSIGNMENT. An assignment for the benefit of his creditors made by a debtor voluntarily; as distinguished from a compulsory assignment which takes place by operation of law in proceedings in bankruptcy or insolvency.

Presumably it means an assignment of a debtor's property in trust to pay his debts generally, in distinction from a transfer of property to a particular creditor in payment of his demand, or to a conveyance by way of collateral security or mortgage. 10 Paige, Ch. 445.

VOLUNTARY CONFESSION. A confession of guilt made spontaneously by an accused person, and not induced by either promises or threats.

VOLUNTARY CONVEYANCE. A conveyance without valuable consideration; such as a deed or settlement in favor of a wife or children.

VOLUNTARY COURTESY. A voluntary act of kindness; an act of kindness performed by one man towards another, of the free will and inclination of the doer, without any previous request or promise of reward made by him who is the object of the courtesy; from which the law will not imply a promise of remuneration. Holthouse.

VOLUNTARY DEPOSIT. In the civil law of bailment. A deposit arising from the mere consent and agreement of parties, as distinguished from a necessary deposit, which was made upon some sudden emergency, or from some pressing necessity. Dig. 16, 3, 2; Story, Bailm. § 44.

VOLUNTARY ESCAPE. In practice. An escape of a person from custody by the express consent of his keeper. 3 Bl. Comm. 415. An escape in consequence of the sheriff, or his officer, permitting a party to go at large. 1 Archb. Pr. K. B. 85.

VOLUNTARY IGNORANCE. This exists where a party might, by taking reasonable pains, have acquired the necessary knowledge, but has neglected to do so.

VOLUNTARY JURISDICTION. In English law. A jurisdiction exercised by certain ecclesiastical courts, in matters where there is no opposition. 3 Bl. Comm. 66. The opposite of *contentious* jurisdiction, (*q. v.*)

In Scotch law. One exercised in matters admitting of no opposition or question, and therefore cognizable by any judge, and in any place, and on any lawful day. Bell.

VOLUNTARY MANSLAUGHTER. In criminal law. Manslaughter committed voluntarily upon a sudden heat of the passions; as if, upon a sudden quarrel, two persons fight, and one of them kills the other. 4 Bl. Comm. 190, 191.

VOLUNTARY NONSUIT. In practice. The abandonment of his cause by a plaintiff, and an agreement that a judgment for costs be entered against him. 3 Bouv. Inst. no. 3306.

VOLUNTARY OATH. Such as a person may take in extrajudicial matters, and not regularly in a court of justice, or before an officer invested with authority to administer the same. Brown.

VOLUNTARY PAYMENT. A payment made by a debtor of his own will and choice, as distinguished from one exacted from him by process of execution or other compulsion.

VOLUNTARY REDEMPTION, in Scotch law, is when a mortgagee receives the sum due into his own hands, and discharges the mortgage, without any consignation. Bell.

VOLUNTARY SALE. One made freely, without constraint, by the owner of the thing sold. 1 Bouv. Inst. no. 974.

VOLUNTARY SETTLEMENT. A settlement of property upon a wife or other beneficiary, made gratuitously or without valuable consideration.

VOLUNTARY TRUST. See TRUST.

VOLUNTARY WASTE. Active or positive waste; waste done or committed, in contradistinction to that which results from mere negligence, which is called "permissive" waste. 2 Bouv. Inst. no. 2394.

Voluntas donatoris in charta doni sui manifeste expressa observetur. Co. Litt. 21. The will of the donor manifestly expressed in his deed of gift is to be observed.

Voluntas est justa sententia de eo quod quis post mortem suam fieri velit. A will is an exact opinion or determination concerning that which each one wishes to be done after his death.

Voluntas et propositum distinguunt maleficia. The will and the proposed end distinguish crimes. Bract. fols. 2*b*, 136*b*.

Voluntas facit quod in testamento scriptum valeat. Dig. 30, 1, 12, 3. It is intention which gives effect to the wording of a will.

Voluntas in delictis, non exitus spectatur. 2 Inst. 57. In crimes, the will, and not the consequence, is looked to.

Voluntas reputatur pro facto. The intention is to be taken for the deed. 3 Inst. 69; Broom, Max. 311.

Voluntas testatoris est ambulatoria usque ad extremum vitæ exitum. 4 Coke, 61. The will of a testator is ambulatory until the latest moment of life.

Voluntas testatoris habet interpretationem latam et benignam. Jenk. Cent. 260. The intention of a testator has a broad and benignant interpretation.

Voluntas ultima testatoris est perimplenda secundum veram intentionem suam. Co. Litt. 322. The last will of the testator is to be fulfilled according to his true intention.

VOLUNTEER. In conveyancing, one who holds a title under a voluntary conveyance, *i. e.*, one made without consideration, good or valuable, to support it.

A person who gives his services without any express or implied promise of remuneration in return is called a "volunteer," and is entitled to no remuneration for his services, nor to any compensation for injuries sustained by him in performing what he has undertaken. Sweet.

In military law, the term designates one who freely and voluntarily offers himself for service in the army or navy; as distinguished from one who is compelled to serve by draft or conscription, and also from one entered by enlistment in the standing army.

VOTE. Suffrage; the expression of his will, preference, or choice, formally manifested by a member of a legislative or deliberative body, or of a constituency or a body of qualified electors, in regard to the decision to be made by the body as a whole upon any proposed measure or proceeding, or the selection of an officer or representative. And the aggregate of the expressions of will or choice, thus manifested by individuals, is called the "vote of the body."

VOTER. One who has the right of giving his voice or suffrage.

VOTES AND PROCEEDINGS. In the houses of parliament the clerks at the tables make brief entries of all that is actually done; and these minutes, which are printed from day to day for the use of members, are called the "votes and proceedings of parliament." From these votes and proceedings the journals of the house are subsequently prepared, by making the entries at greater length. Brown.

VOTUM. Lat. A vow or promise. *Dies votorum*, the wedding day. Fleta l. 1, c. 4.

VOUCH. To call upon; to call in to warranty; to call upon the grantor or warrantor to defend the title to an estate.

To vouch is to call upon, rely on, or quote as an authority. Thus, in the old writers, to vouch a case or report is to quote it as an authority. Co. Litt. 70*a*.

VOUCHEE. In common recoveries, the person who is called to warrant or defend the title is called the "vouchee." 2 Bouv. Inst. no. 2093.

VOUCHER. A receipt, acquittance, or release, which may serve as evidence of payment or discharge of a debt, or to certify the correctness of accounts. An account-book containing the acquittances or receipts showing the accountant's discharge of his obligations. 1 Metc. (Mass.) 218.

The term "voucher," when used in connection with the disbursements of moneys, implies some written or printed instrument in the nature of a receipt, note, account, bill of particulars, or something of that character which shows on what account or by what authority a particular payment has been made, and which may be kept or filed away by the party receiving it, for his own convenience or protection, or that of the public. 107 Ill. 504.

In old conveyancing. The person on whom the tenant calls to defend the title to the land, because he warranted the title to him at the time of the original purchase.

VOUCHER TO WARRANTY. The calling one who has warranted lands, by the party warranted, to come and defend the suit for him. Co. Litt. 101*b*.

Vox emissa volat; litera scripta manet. The spoken word flies; the written letter remains. Broom, Max. 666.

VOX SIGNATA. In Scotch practice. An emphatic or essential word. 2 Alis. Crim. Pr. 280.

VOYAGE. In maritime law. The passing of a vessel by sea from one place, port, or country to another. The term is held to include the enterprise entered upon, and not merely the route. 113 Mass. 326.

VOYAGE INSURED. In insurance law. A transit at sea from the *terminus a quo* to the *terminus ad quem*, in a prescribed course of navigation, which is never set out in any policy, but virtually forms parts of all policies, and is as binding on the parties thereto as though it were minutely detailed. 1 Arn. Ins. 333.

VRAIC. Seaweed. It is used in great quantities by the inhabitants of Jersey and Guernsey for manure, and also for fuel by the poorer classes.

VS. An abbreviation for *versus*, (against,) constantly used in legal proceedings, and especially in entitling cases.

Vulgaris opinio est duplex, viz., orta inter graves et discretos, quæ multum veritatis habet, et opinio orta inter leves et vulgares homines absque specie veritatis. 4 Coke, 107. Common opinion is of two kinds, viz., that which arises among grave and discreet men, which has much truth in it, and that which arises among light and common men, without any appearance of truth.

VULGARIS PURGATIO. In old English law. Common purgation; a name given to the trial by *ordeal*, to distinguish it from the canonical purgation, which was by the oath of the party. 4 Bl. Comm. 342.

VULGO CONCEPTI. Lat. In the civil law. Spurious children; bastards.

VULGO QUÆSITI. Lat. In the civil law. Spurious children; literally, gotten from the people; the offspring of promiscuous cohabitation, who are considered as having no father. Inst. 3, 4, 3; Id. 3, 5, 4.

W.

W. As an abbreviation, this letter frequently stands for "William," (king of England,) "Westminster," "west," or "western."

W. D. An abbreviation for "Western District."

WACREOUR. L. Fr. A vagabond, or vagrant. Britt. c. 29.

WADSET. In Scotch law. The old term for a mortgage. A right by which lands or other heritable subjects are impignorated by the proprietor to his creditor in security of his debt. Wadsets are usually drawn in the form of mutual contracts, in which one party sells the land, and the other grants the right of reversion. Ersk. Inst. 2, 8, 3.

WADSETTER. In Scotch law. A creditor to whom a wadset is made, corresponding to a mortgagee.

WAFTORS. Conductors of vessels at sea. Cowell.

WAGA. In old English law. A weigh; a measure of cheese, salt, wool, etc., containing two hundred and fifty-six pounds avoirdupois. Cowell; Spelman.

WAGE. In old English practice. To give security for the performance of a thing. Cowell.

WAGER. A wager is a contract by which two or more parties agree that a certain sum of money or other thing shall be paid or delivered to one of them on the happening of an uncertain event. 75 Ill. 554; 44 How. Pr. 207; 18 Ind. 18.

WAGER OF BATTEL. The trial by wager of battel was a species of trial introduced into England, among other Norman customs, by William the Conqueror, in which the person accused fought with his accuser, under the apprehension that Heaven would give the victory to him who was in the right. 3 Bl. Comm. 337. It was abolished by St. 59 Geo. III. c. 46.

WAGER OF LAW. In old practice. The giving of *gage* or sureties by a defendant in an action of debt that at a certain day assigned he would *make his law;* that is, would take an oath in open court that he did not owe the debt, and at the same time bring with him eleven neighbors, (called "compurgators,") who should avow upon their oaths that they believed in their consciences that he said the truth. Glanv. lib. 1, c. 9, 12; Bract. fol. 156*b;* Britt. c. 27; 2 Bl. Comm. 343; Cro. Eliz. 818.

WAGER POLICY. In the law of insurance. An insurance upon a subject-matter in which the party assured has no real, valuable, or insurable interest.

A mere wager policy is that in which the party assured has no interest in the thing assured, and could sustain no possible loss by the event insured against, if he had not made such wager. 2 Mass. 1.

WAGERING CONTRACT. One in which the parties stipulate that they shall gain or lose, upon the happening of an uncertain event, in which they have no interest except that arising from the possibility of such gain or loss. 89 Pa. St. 89.

WAGES. The compensation agreed upon by a master to be paid to a servant, or any other person hired to do work or business for him.

In maritime law. The compensation allowed to seamen for their services on board a vessel during a voyage.

In political economy. The reward paid, whether in money or goods, to human exertion, considered as a factor in the production of wealth, for its co-operation in the process.

"Three factors contribute to the production of commodities,—nature, labor, and capital. Each must have a share of the product as its reward, and this share, if it is just, must be proportionate to the several contributions. The share of the natural agents is rent; the share of labor, *wages;* the share of capital, interest. The clerk receives a salary; the lawyer and doctor, fees; the manufacturer, profits. Salary, fees, and profits are so many forms of wages for services rendered." De Laveleye, Pol. Econ.

WAGONAGE. Money paid for carriage in a wagon.

WAGON. A common vehicle for the transportation of goods, wares, and merchandise of all descriptions. The term does not include a hackney-coach. 5 Cal. 418.

WAIF. Waifs are goods found, but claimed by nobody; that of which every one waives the claim. Also, goods stolen and waived, or thrown away by the thief in his flight, for fear of being apprehended. Wharton.

Waifs are to be distinguished from *bona fugitiva*, which are the goods of the felon himself, which he abandons in his flight from justice. Brown.

WAIN-BOTE. Timber for wagons or carts.

WAINABLE. In old records. That may be plowed or manured; tillable. Cowell; Blount.

WAINAGE. In old English law. The team and instruments of husbandry belonging to a countryman, and especially to a villein who was required to perform agricultural services.

WAINAGIUM. What is necessary to the farmer for the cultivation of his land. Barring. Ob. St. 12.

WAITING CLERKS. Officers whose duty it formerly was to wait in attendance upon the court of chancery. The office was abolished in 1842 by St. 5 & 6 Vict. c. 103. Mozley & Whitley.

WAIVE, *v.* To abandon or throw away; as when a thief, in his flight, throws aside the stolen goods, in order to facilitate his escape, he is technically said to *waive* them.

In modern law, to renounce, repudiate, or surrender a claim, a privilege, a right, or the opportunity to take advantage of some defect, irregularity, or wrong.

A person is said to waive a benefit when he renounces or disclaims it, and he is said to waive a tort or injury when he abandons the remedy which the law gives him for it. Sweet.

WAIVE, *n.* A woman outlawed. The term is, as it were, the feminine of "outlaw," the latter being always applied to a man; "waive," to a woman. Cowell.

WAIVER. The renunciation, repudiation, abandonment, or surrender of some claim, right, privilege, or of the opportunity to take advantage of some defect, irregularity, or wrong.

The passing by of an occasion to enforce a legal right, whereby the right to enforce the same is lost; a common instance of this is where a landlord waives a forfeiture of a lease by receiving rent, or distraining for rent, which has accrued due after the breach of covenant causing the forfeiture became known to him. Wharton.

This word is commonly used to denote the declining to take advantage of an irregularity in legal proceedings, or of a forfeiture incurred through breach of covenants in a lease. A gift of goods may be *waived* by a disagreement to accept; so a plaintiff may commonly sue in contract *waiving* the tort. Brown.

WAIVER OF TORT. The election, by an injured party, for purposes of redress, to treat the facts as establishing an implied contract, which he may enforce, instead of an injury by fraud or wrong, for the committing of which he may demand damages, compensatory or exemplary. 1 Hun, 630.

WAKEMAN. The chief magistrate of Ripon, in Yorkshire.

WAKENING. In Scotch law. The revival of an action. A process by which an action that has lain over and not been insisted in for a year and a day, and thus technically said to have "fallen asleep," is wakened, or put in motion again. 1 Forb. Inst. pt. 4, p. 170; Ersk. Prin. 4, 1, 33.

WALAPAUZ. In old Lombardic law. The disguising the head or face, with the intent of committing a theft.

WALENSIS. In old English law. A Welshman.

WALESCHERY. The being a Welshman. Spelman.

WALISCUS. In Saxon law. A servant, or any ministerial officer. Cowell.

WALKERS. Foresters who have the care of a certain space of ground assigned to them. Cowell.

WALL. An erection of stone, brick, or other material, raised to some height, and intended for purposes of security or inclosure. In law, this term occurs in such compounds as "ancient wall," "party-wall," "division-wall," etc.

WALLIA. In old English law. A wall; a sea-wall; a mound, bank, or wall erected in marshy districts as a protection against the sea. Spelman.

WAMPUM. Beads made of shells, used as money by the North American Indians, and which continued current in New York as late as 1693.

WAND OF PEACE. In Scotch law. A wand or staff carried by the messenger of a court, and which, when deforced, (that is, hindered from executing process,) he breaks, as a symbol of the deforcement, and protest for remedy of law. 2 Forb. Inst. 207.

WANLASS. An ancient customary tenure of lands; *i. e.*, to drive deer to a stand that the lord may have a shot. Blount, Ten. 140.

WANTAGE. In marine insurance. Ullage; deficiency in the contents of a cask or vessel caused by leaking. 107 Mass. 140.

WANTON. Regardless of another's rights.

WANTONNESS. Reckless sport; willfully unrestrained action, running immoderately into excess. 75 Pa. St. 330.

A licentious act by one man towards the person of another, without regard to his rights; as, for example, if a man should attempt to pull off another's hat against his will, in order to expose him to ridicule, the offense would be an assault, and if he touched him it would amount to a *battery*. Bouvier.

WAPENTAKE. In English law. A local division of the country; the name is in use north of the Trent to denote a hundred. The derivation of the name is said to be from "weapon" and "take," and indicates that the division was originally of a military character. Cowell; Brown.

Also a hundred court.

WAR. A state of forcible contention; an armed contest between nations; a state of hostility between two or more nations or states. Gro. de Jur. B. lib. 1, c. 1.

Every connection by force between two nations, in external matters, under the authority of their respective governments, is a public war. If war is declared in form, it is called "solemn," and is of the perfect kind; because the whole nation is at war with another whole nation. When the hostilities are limited as respects places, persons, and things, the war is properly termed "imperfect war." 4 Dall. 37, 40.

A *civil* war is one which takes place between a state, as such, and a party, class, or section of its own citizens. It is public on the part of the established government, and private on the part of the people resisting its authority, but both the parties are entitled to all the rights of war as against each other, and even as respects neutral nations. Dana's Wheat. Int. Law, § 296.

WAR, ARTICLES OF. See ARTICLES OF WAR.

WAR-OFFICE. In England. A department of state from which the sovereign issues orders to his forces. Wharton.

WARD. 1. Guarding; care; charge; as, the ward of a castle; so in the phrase "watch and ward."

2. A division in the city of London committed to the special ward (guardianship) of an alderman.

3. A territorial division is adopted in most American cities, by which the municipality is separated into a number of precincts or districts called "wards" for purposes of police, sanitary regulations, prevention of fires, elections, etc.

4. A corridor, room, or other division of a prison, hospital, or asylum.

5. An infant placed by authority of law under the care of a guardian.

The person over whom or over whose property a guardian is appointed is called his "ward." Civil Code Cal. § 237.

WARD-CORN. In old English law. The duty of keeping watch and *ward*, with a *horn* to blow upon any occasion of surprise. 1 Mon. Ang. 976.

WARD-FEGH. Sax. In old records. Ward-fee; the value of a ward, or the money paid to the lord for his redemption from wardship. Blount.

WARD-HOLDING. In old Scotch law. Tenure by military service; the proper feudal tenure of Scotland. Abolished by St. 20 Geo. II. c. 50. Ersk. Prin. 2, 4, 1.

WARD IN CHANCERY. An infant who is under the superintendence of the chancellor.

WARD-MOTE. In English law. A court kept in every ward in London, commonly called the "ward-mote court," or "inquest." Cowell.

WARD-PENNY. In old English law. Money paid to the sheriff or castellains, for the duty of watching and warding a castle. Spelman.

WARD-STAFF. In old records. A constable's or watchman's staff. Cowell.

WARD-WIT. In old English law. Immunity or exemption from the duty or service of ward, or from contributing to such service. Spelman. Exemption from amercement for not finding a man to do ward. Fleta, lib. 1, c. 47, § 16.

WARDA. L. Lat. In old English law. Ward; guàrd; protection; keeping; custody. Spelman.

A ward; an infant under wardship. Id.

In old Scotch law. An award; the judgment of a court.

WARDAGE. Money paid and contributed to watch and ward. Domesday.

WARDEN. A guardian; a keeper. This is the name given to various officers.

WARDEN OF THE CINQUE PORTS. In English law. The title of the governor or presiding officer of the Cinque Ports, (*q. v.*)

WARDS AND LIVERIES. In English law. The title of a court of record, established in the reign of Henry VIII. See COURT OF WARDS AND LIVERIES.

WARDS OF ADMIRALTY. Seamen are sometimes thus designated, because, in view of their general improvidence and rashness, the admiralty courts are accustomed to scrutinize with great care their bargains and engagements, when brought before them, with a view to protecting them against imposition and overreaching.

WARDSHIP. In military tenures, the right of the lord to have custody, as guardian, of the body and lands of the infant heir, without any account of profits, until he was twenty-one, or she sixteen. In socage the guardian was accountable for profits; and he was not the lord, but the nearest relative to whom the inheritance could not descend, and the wardship ceased at fourteen. In copyholds, the lord was the guardian, but was perhaps accountable for profits. Stim. Gloss. See 2 Bl. Comm. 67.

WARDSHIP IN CHIVALRY. An incident to the tenure of knight-service.

WARDSHIP IN COPYHOLDS. The lord is guardian of his infant tenant by special custom.

WARECTARE. L. Lat. In old English law. To fallow ground; or plow up land (designed for wheat) in the spring, in order to let it lie fallow for the better improvement. Fleta, lib. 2, c. 33; Cowell.

WAREHOUSE. A place adapted to the reception and storage of goods and merchandise. 23 Me. 47.

WAREHOUSE BOOK. A book used by merchants to contain an account of the quantities of goods received, shipped, and remaining in stock.

WAREHOUSE RECEIPT. A receipt given by a warehouseman for goods received by him on storage in his warehouse.

WAREHOUSE SYSTEM. A system of public stores or warehouses, established or authorized by law, in which an importer may deposit goods imported, in the custody of the revenue officers, paying storage, but not being required to pay the customs duties until the goods are finally removed for consumption in the home market, and with the privilege of withdrawing the goods from store for the purpose of re-exportation without paying any duties.

WAREHOUSEMAN. The owner of a warehouse; one who, as a business, and for hire, keeps and stores the goods of others.

WARNING, under the old practice of the English court of probate, was a notice given by a registrar of the principal registry to a person who had entered a *caveat*, warning him, within six days after service, to enter an appearance to the *caveat* in the principal registry, and to set forth his interest, concluding with a notice that in default of his doing so the court would proceed to do all such acts, matters, and things as should be necessary. By the rules under the judicature acts, a writ of summons has been substituted for a warning. Sweet.

WARNISTURA. In old records. Garniture; furniture; provision. Cowell.

WARNOTH. In old English law. An ancient custom, whereby, if any tenant holding of the Castle of Dover failed in paying his rent at the day, he should forfeit double, and, for the second failure, treble, etc. Cowell.

WARP. A rope attached to some fixed point, used for moving a ship. Pub. St. Mass. 1882, p. 1297.

WARRANDICE. In Scotch law. Warranty; a clause in a charter or deed by which the grantor obliges himself that the right conveyed shall be effectual to the receiver. Ersk. Prin. 2, 3, 11. A clause whereby the granter of a charter obliges himself to warrant or make good the thing granted to the receiver. 1 Forb. Inst. pt. 2, p. 113.

WARRANT, *v.* In conveyancing. To assure the title to property sold, by an express covenant to that effect in the deed of conveyance. To stipulate by an express covenant that the title of a grantee shall be good, and his possession undisturbed.

In contracts. To engage or promise that a certain fact or state of facts, in relation to the subject-matter, is, or shall be, as it is represented to be.

WARRANT, *n.* 1. A writ or precept from a competent authority in pursuance of law, directing the doing of an act, and addressed to an officer or person competent to do the act, and affording him protection from damage, if he does it. 71 N. Y. 376.

2. Particularly, a writ or precept issued by a magistrate, justice, or other competent authority, addressed to a sheriff, constable, or other officer, requiring him to arrest the body of a person therein named, and bring him before the magistrate or court, to answer, or to be examined, touching some offense which he is charged with having committed. See, also, BENCH-WARRANT; SEARCH-WARRANT.

3. A warrant is an order by which the drawer authorizes one person to pay a particular sum of money. 2 Kan. 130.

4. An authority issued to a collector of taxes, empowering him to collect the taxes extended on the assessment roll, and to make distress and sale of goods or land in default of payment.

5. An order issued by the proper authorities of a municipal corporation, authorizing the payee or holder to receive a certain sum out of the municipal treasury.

6. A *land-warrant* is a warrant issued at the local land-offices of the United States to purchasers of public lands, on the surrender of which, at the general land-office at Washington, they receive a conveyance from the general government.

WARRANT IN BANKRUPTCY. A warrant issued, upon an adjudication in bankruptcy, directing the marshal to take possession of the bankrupt's property, notify creditors, etc.

WARRANT OF ATTORNEY. In practice. A written authority, directed to any attorney or attorneys of any court of record, to appear for the party executing it, and receive a declaration for him in an action at the suit of a person named, and thereupon to confess the same, or to suffer judgment to pass by default; and it also usually contains a release of errors. 2 Burrill, Pr. 239.

WARRANT OF COMMITMENT. A warrant of commitment is a written authority committing a person to custody.

WARRANT OFFICERS. In the United States navy, these are a class of inferior officers who hold their rank by virtue of a written warrant instead of a commission, including boatswains, gunners, carpenters, etc.

WARRANT TO SUE AND DEFEND. In old practice. A special warrant from the crown, authorizing a party to appoint an attorney to sue or defend for him. 3 Bl. Comm. 25.

A special authority given by a party to his attorney, to commence a suit, or to appear and defend a suit, in his behalf. These warrants are now disused, though formal entries of them upon the record were long retained in practice. 1 Burrill, Pr. 39.

WARRANTEE. A person to whom a warranty is made.

WARRANTIA CHARTÆ. In old practice. Warranty of charter. A writ which lay for one who, being enfeoffed of lands or tenements, with a clause of warranty, was afterwards impleaded in an assize or other action in which he could not vouch to warranty. In such case, it might be brought against the warrantor, to compel him to assist the tenant with a good plea or defense, or else to render damages and the value of the land, if recovered against the tenant. Cowell; 3 Bl. Comm. 300.

WARRANTIA CUSTODIÆ. An old English writ, which lay for him who was challenged to be a ward to another, in respect to land said to be holden by knight-service; which land, when it was bought by the ancestors of the ward, was warranted free from such thraldom. The writ lay against the warrantor and his heirs. Cowell.

WARRANTIA DIEI. A writ which lay for a man who, having had a day assigned him personally to appear in court in any action in which he was sued, was in the mean time, by commandment, employed in the king's service, so that he could not come at the day assigned. It was directed to the justices that they might not record him in default for that day. Cowell.

WARRANTIZARE. In old conveyancing. To warrant; to bind one's self, by covenant in a deed of conveyance, to defend the grantee in his title and possession.

Warrantizare est defendere et acquietare tenentem, qui warrantum vocavit, in seisina sua; et tenens de re warranti

excambium habebit ad valentiam. Co. Litt. 365. To warrant is to defend and insure in peace the tenant, who calls for warranty, in his seisin; and the tenant in warranty will have an exchange in proportion to its value.

WARRANTOR. One who makes a warranty. Shep. Touch. 181.

Warrantor potest excipere quod querens non tenet terram de qua petit warrantiam, et quod donum fuit insufficiens. Hob. 21. A warrantor may object that the complainant does not hold the land of which he seeks the warranty, and that the gift was insufficient.

WARRANTY. In real property law. A real covenant by the grantor of lands, for himself and his heirs, to warrant and defend the title and possession of the estate granted, to the grantee and his heirs, whereby, either upon voucher, or judgment in the writ of *warrantia chartæ*, and the eviction of the grantee by paramount title, the grantor was bound to recompense him with other lands of equal value. Co. Litt. 365*a*.

Lineal warranty existed when the heir derived title to the land warranted either from or through the ancestor who made the warranty.

Collateral warranty existed when the heir's title was not derived from the warranting ancestor, and yet it barred the heir from claiming the land by any collateral title, upon the presumption that he might thereafter have assets by descent from or through the ancestor; and it imposed upon him the obligation of giving the warrantee other lands in case of eviction, provided he had assets. 2 Bl. Comm. 301, 302.

In sales of personal property. A warranty is a statement or representation made by the seller of goods, contemporaneously with and as a part of the contract of sale, though collateral to the express object of it, having reference to the character, quality, or title of the goods, and by which he promises or undertakes to insure that certain facts are or shall be as he then represents them. The warranty may be either *express* or *implied*. It is the former when created by the apt and explicit statements of the seller; the latter, when the law derives it by implication or inference from the nature of the transaction, or the relative situation or circumstances of the parties.

A warranty is an engagement by which a seller assures to a buyer the existence of some fact affecting the transaction, whether past, present, or future. Civil Code Cal. § 1763.

In contracts. An undertaking or stipulation, in writing, or verbally, that a certain fact in relation to the subject of a contract is or shall be as it is stated or promised to be.

A warranty differs from a representation in that a warranty must always be given contemporaneously with, and as part of, the contract; whereas a representation precedes and induces to the contract. And, while that is their difference in nature, their difference in consequence or effect is this: that, upon breach of warranty, (or false warranty,) the contract remains binding, and damages only are recoverable for the breach; whereas, upon a false representation, the defrauded party may elect to avoid the contract, and recover the entire price paid. Brown.

The same transaction cannot be characterized as a warranty and a fraud at the same time. A warranty rests upon contract, while fraud or fraudulent representations have no element of contract in them, but are essentially a tort. When judges or law-writers speak of a fraudulent warranty, the language is neither accurate nor perspicuous. If there is a breach of warranty, it cannot be said that the warranty was fraudulent, with any more propriety than any other contract can be said to have been fraudulent, because there has been a breach of it. On the other hand, to speak of a false representation as a contract or warranty, or as tending to prove a contract or warranty, is a perversion of language and of correct ideas. 39 Ind. 81.

A *continuing* warranty is one which applies to the whole period during which the contract is in force. Thus, an undertaking in a charter-party that a vessel shall continue to be of the same class that she was at the time the charter-party was made is a continuing warranty. Sweet.

In insurance. In the law of insurance, "warranty" means any assertion or undertaking on the part of the assured, whether expressed in the contract or capable of being annexed to it, on the strict and literal truth or performance of which the liability of the underwriter is made to depend. Maude & P. Shipp. 377; Sweet.

WARRANTY DEED. One which contains a covenant of warranty.

WARRANTY, VOUCHER TO. In old practice. The calling a warrantor into court by the party warranted, (when tenant in a real action brought for recovery of such lands,) to defend the suit for him. Co. Litt. 101*b*.

WARREN. A term in English law for a place in which birds, fishes, or wild beasts are kept.

A franchise or privilege, either by prescription or grant from the king, to keep beasts and fowls of warren, which are hares, coneys, partridges, pheasants, etc.

Also any place to which such privilege extends. Mozley & Whitley.

WARSCOT. In Saxon law. A customary or usual tribute or contribution towards armor, or the arming of the forces.

WARTH. In old English law. A customary payment, supposed to be the same with *ward-penny*. Spelman; Blount.

WASH. A shallow part of a river or arm of the sea.

WASHING-HORN. The sounding of a horn for washing before dinner. The custom was formerly observed in the Temple.

WASHINGTON, TREATY OF. A treaty signed on May 8, 1871, between Great Britain and the United States of America, with reference to certain differences arising out of the war between the northern and southern states of the Union, the Canadian fisheries, and other matters. Wharton.

WASTE. Spoil or destruction, done or permitted, to lands, houses, gardens, trees, or other corporeal hereditaments, by the tenant thereof, to the prejudice of the heir, or of him in reversion or remainder. 2 Bl. Comm. 281.

Waste is a spoil and destruction of an estate, either in houses, woods, or lands, by demolishing, not the temporary profits only, but the very substance of the thing, thereby rendering it wild and desolate, which the common law expresses very significantly by the word "*vastum.*" 3 Bl. Comm. 223.

Waste is a lasting damage to the reversion caused by the destruction, by the tenant for life or years, of such things on the land as are not included in its temporary profits. 29 Mo. 325.

Voluntary waste is active or positive waste, waste done or committed, consisting in some act of destruction or devastation.

Permissive waste is such as is merely suffered or permitted by the tenant, and consists in the neglect or omission to do what will prevent injury; as, to suffer a house to go to decay for the want of repair.

Equitable waste (which is voluntary only) is an unconscientious abuse of the privilege of non-impeachability for waste at common law, whereby a tenant for life, without impeachment of waste, will be restrained from committing willful, destructive, malicious, or extravagent waste, such as pulling down houses, cutting timber of too young a growth, or trees planted for ornament, or for shelter of premises. Wharton.

In old English criminal law. A prerogative or liberty, on the part of the crown, of committing *waste* on the lands of felons, by pulling down their houses, extirpating their gardens, plowing their meadows, and cutting down their woods. 4 Bl. Comm. 385.

WASTE-BOOK. A book used by merchants, to receive rough entries or memoranda of all transactions in the order of their occurrence, previous to their being posted in the journal. Otherwise called a "blotter."

WASTE, WRIT OF. See WRIT OF WASTE.

WASTORS. In old statutes. A kind of thieves.

WATCH, *v.* To keep guard; to stand as sentinel; to be on guard at night, for the preservation of the peace and good order.

WATCH, *n.* A body of constables on duty on any particular night.

WATCH AND WARD. "Watch" denotes keeping guard during the night; "ward," by day.

WATCHMAN. An officer in many cities and towns, whose duty it is to watch during the night and take care of the property of the inhabitants.

WATER-BAILIFF. The title of an officer, in port towns in England, appointed for the searching of ships. Also of an officer belonging to the city of London, who had the supervising and search of the fish brought thither. Cowell.

WATER-BAYLEY. In American law. An officer mentioned in the colony laws of New Plymouth, (A. D. 1671,) whose duty was to collect dues to the colony for fish taken in their waters. Probably another form of *water-bailiff*. Burrill.

WATER-COURSE. A running stream of water; a body of running water; a natural stream, including rivers, creeks, runs, and rivulets.

There must be a stream usually flowing in a particular direction, though it need not flow continually. It may sometimes be dry. It must flow in a definite channel, having a bed, sides, or banks, and usually discharge itself into some other stream or body of water. It must be something more than a mere surface drainage over the entire face of a tract of land, occasioned by unusual freshets or other extraordinary causes. It does not include the water flowing in the hollows or ravines in land, which is the mere surface-water from rain or melting snow, and is discharged through them from a higher to a lower level, but which at other times are destitute of water. Such hollows or ravines are not, in legal contemplation, water-courses. 27 Wis. 661.

WATER-GAGE. A sea-wall or bank to restrain the current and overflowing of the water; also an instrument to measure water. Cowell.

WATER-GAVEL. In old records. A gavel or rent paid for fishing in or other benefit received from some river or water. Cowell; Blount.

WATER-MARK. A mark indicating the highest point to which water rises, or the lowest point to which it sinks.

WATER-MEASURE. In old statutes. A measure greater than Winchester measure by about three gallons in the bushel. Cowell.

WATER-ORDEAL. In Saxon and old English law. The ordeal or trial by water. The *hot-water* ordeal was performed by plunging the bare arm up to the elbow in boiling water, and escaping unhurt thereby. 4 Bl. Comm. 343. The *cold-water* ordeal was performed by casting the person suspected into a river or pond of cold water, when, if he floated therein, without any action of swimming, it was deemed an evidence of his guilt; but, if he sunk, he was acquitted. Id.

WATER-POWER. The water-power to which a riparian owner is entitled consists of the fall in the stream, when in its natural state, as it passes through his land, or along the boundary of it; or, in other words, it consists of the difference of level between the surface where the stream first touches his land, and the surface where it leaves it. 3 Rawle, 90.

WATERGANG. A Saxon word for a trench or course to carry a stream of water, such as are commonly made to drain water out of marshes. Cowell.

WATERSCAPE. An aqueduct or passage for water.

WATERING STOCK. In the language of brokers, adding to the capital stock of a corporation by the issue of new stock, without increasing the real value represented by the capital.

WAVESON. In old records. Such goods as, after a wreck, swim or float on the waves. Jacob.

WAX SCOT. A duty anciently paid twice a year towards the charge of wax candles in churches. Spelman.

WAY. A passage, path, road, or street. In a technical sense, a *right* of passage over land.

A right of way is the privilege which an individual, or a particular description of persons, as the inhabitants of a village, or the owners or occupiers of certain farms, have of going over another's ground. It is an incorporeal hereditament of a real nature, entirely different from a public highway. Cruise, Dig. tit. 24, § 1.

The term "way" is derived from the Saxon, and means a right of use for passengers. It may be private or public. By the term "right of way" is generally meant a private way, which is an incorporeal hereditament of that class of easements in which a particular person, or particular description of persons, have an interest and a right, though another person is the owner of the fee of the land in which it is claimed. 43 Ind. 455.

WAY-BILL. A writing in which is set down the names of passengers who are carried in a public conveyance, or the description of goods sent with a common carrier by land. Wharton.

WAY-GOING CROP. A crop of grain sown by a tenant for a term certain, during his tenancy, but which will not ripen until after the expiration of his lease; to this, by custom in some places, the tenant is entitled.

WAYLEAVE is a right of way over or through land for the carriage of minerals from a mine or quarry. It is an easement, being a species of the class called "rights of way," and is generally created by express grant or reservation. Sweet.

WAYNAGIUM. Implements of husbandry. 1 Reeve, Eng. Law, c. 5, p. 268.

WAYS AND MEANS. In a legislative body, the "committee on ways and means" is a committee appointed to inquire into and consider the methods and sources for raising revenue, and to propose means for providing the funds needed by the government.

WAYWARDENS. The English highway acts provide that in every parish forming part of a highway district there shall annually be elected one or more waywardens. The waywardens so elected, and the justices for the county residing within the district, form the highway board for the district. Each waywarden also represents his parish in regard to the levying of the highway rates, and in questions arising concerning the liability of his parish to repairs, etc. Sweet.

WEALD. Sax. A wood; the woody part of a country.

WEALREAF. In old English law. The robbing of a dead man in his grave.

WEALTH. All material objects, capable of satisfying human wants, desires, or tastes, having a value in exchange, and upon which human labor has been expended; *i. e.*, which have, by such labor, been either reclaimed from nature, extracted or gathered from the earth or sea, manufactured from raw materials, improved, adapted, or cultivated.

"The aggregate of all the things, whether material or immaterial, which contribute to comfort and enjoyment, which cannot be obtained without more or less labor, and which are objects of frequent barter and sale, is what we usually call 'wealth.'" Bowen, Pol. Econ.

WEAPON. An instrument used in fighting; an instrument of offensive or defensive combat. The term is chiefly used, in law, in the statutes prohibiting the carrying of "concealed" or "deadly" weapons.

WEAR, or WEIR. A great dam or fence made across a river, or against water, formed of stakes interlaced by twigs of osier, and accommodated for the taking of fish, or to convey a stream to a mill. Cowell; Jacob.

WEAR AND TEAR. "Natural wear and tear" means deterioration or depreciation in value by ordinary and reasonable use of the subject-matter. 20 N. J. Law, 548.

WED. Sax. A covenant or agreement. Cowell.

WEDBEDRIP. Sax. In old English law. A customary service which tenants paid to their lords, in cutting down their corn, or doing other harvest duties; as if a *covenant* to *reap* for the lord at the time of his *bidding* or commanding. Cowell.

WEEK. Seven days of time.

WEHADINC. In old European law. The judicial combat, or duel; the trial by battel.

WEIGHAGE. In English law. A duty or toll paid for weighing merchandise. It is called "*tronage*" for weighing wool at the king's beam, or "*pesage*" for weighing other avoirdupois goods. 2 Chit. Com. Law, 16.

WEIGHT OF EVIDENCE. The balance or preponderance of evidence; the inclination of the greater amount of credible evidence, offered in a trial, to support one side of the issue rather than the other.

The "weight" or "preponderance of proof" is a phrase constantly used, the meaning of which is well understood and easily defined. It indicates clearly to the jury that the party having the burden of proof will be entitled to their verdict, if, on weighing the evidence in their minds, they shall find the greater amount of credible evidence sustains the issue which is to be established before them. 9 Gray, 393.

WEIGHTS OF AUNCEL. See AUNCEL WEIGHT.

WEIR. A fence or an inclosure of twigs, set in a stream to catch fish. Pub. St. Mass. p. 1297.

WELL, *adj.* **In marine insurance.** A term used as descriptive of the safety and soundness of a vessel, in a warranty of her condition at a particular time and place; as, "warranted *well* at ——— on ———."

In the old reports. Good, sufficient, unobjectionable in law; the opposite of "ill."

WELL, *n.* A well, as the term is used in a conveyance, is an artificial excavation and erection in and upon land, which necessarily, from its nature and the mode of its use, includes and comprehends the substantial occupation and beneficial enjoyment of the whole premises on which it is situated. 6 Gray, 107, 110.

WELL KNOWING. A phrase used in pleading as the technical expression in laying a *scienter*, (*q. v.*)

WELSH MORTGAGE. In English law. A species of security which partakes of the nature of a mortgage, as there is a debt due, and an estate is given as security for the repayment, but differs from it in the circumstances that the rents and profits are to be received without account till the principal money is paid off, and there is no remedy to enforce payment, while the mortgagor has a perpetual power of redemption. It is now rarely used. 1 Pow. Mortg. 373*a*.

WEND. In old records. A large extent of ground, comprising several *juga;* a perambulation; a circuit. Spelman; Cowell.

WERA, or WERE. The estimation or price of a man, especially of one slain. In the criminal law of the Anglo-Saxons, every man's life had its value, called a "were," or "*capitis æstimatio.*"

WEREGELT THEF. Sax. In old English law. A robber who might be ransomed. Fleta, lib. 1, c. 47, § 13.

WEREGILD, or WERGILD. This was the price of homicide, or other atrocious personal offense, paid partly to the king for the loss of a subject, partly to the lord for the loss of a vassal, and partly to the next of kin of the injured person. In the Anglo-Saxon laws, the amount of compensation varied with the degree or rank of the party slain. Brown.

WERELADA. A purging from a crime by the oaths of several persons, according to the degree and quality of the accused. Cowell.

WERGELT. In old Scotch law. A sum paid by an offender as a compensation or satisfaction for the offense; a weregild, or wergild.

WERP-GELD. Belg. In European law. Contribution for jettison; average.

WESTMINSTER. A city immediately adjoining London, and forming a part of the metropolis; formerly the seat of the superior courts of the kingdom.

WESTMINSTER CONFESSION. A document containing a statement of religious doctrine, concocted at a conference of British and continental Protestant divines at Westminster, in the year 1643, which subsequently became the basis of the Scotch Presbyterian Church. Wharton.

WESTMINSTER THE FIRST. The statute 3 Edw. I., A. D. 1275. This statute, which deserves the name of a code rather than an act, is divided into fifty-one chapters. Without extending the exemption of churchmen from civil jurisdiction, it protects the property of the church from the violence and spoliation of the king and the nobles, provides for freedom of popular elections, because sheriffs, coroners, and conservators of the peace were still chosen by the freeholders in the county court, and attempts had been made to influence the election of knights of the shire, from the time when they were instituted. It contains a declaration to enforce the enactment of *Magna Charta* against excessive fines, which might operate as perpetual imprisonment; enumerates and corrects the abuses of tenures, particularly as to marriage of wards; regulates the levying of tolls, which were imposed arbitrarily by the barons and by cities and boroughs; corrects and restrains the powers of the king's escheator and other officers; amends the criminal law, putting the crime of rape on the footing to which it has been lately restored, as a most grievous, but not capital, offense; and embraces the subject of procedure in civil and criminal matters, introducing many regulations to render it cheap, simple, and expeditious. 1 Camp. Lives Ld. Ch. p. 167; 2 Reeve, Eng. Law, c. 9, p. 107. Certain parts of this act are repealed by St. 26 & 27 Vict. c. 125. Wharton.

WESTMINSTER THE SECOND. The statute 13 Edw. I. St. 1, A. D. 1285, otherwise called the "Statute *de Donis Conditionalibus.*" See 2 Reeve, Eng. Law, c. 10, p. 163. Certain parts of this act are repealed by St. 19 & 20 Vict. c. 64, and St. 26 & 27 Vict. c. 125. Wharton.

WESTMINSTER THE THIRD, STATUTE OF. A statute passed in the eighteenth year of Edward I. More commonly known as the "Statute of *Quia Emptores*, (*q. v.*) See Barring. Ob. St. 167-169.

WEST SAXON LAGE. The laws of the West Saxons, which obtained in the counties to the south and west of England, from Kent to Devonshire. Blackstone supposes these to have been much the same with the laws of Alfred, being the municipal law of the far most considerable part of his dominions, and particularly including Berkshire, the seat of his peculiar residence. 1 Bl. Comm. 65.

WETHER. A castrated ram, at least one year old. In an indictment it may be called a "sheep." 4 Car. & P. 216.

WHALE. A royal fish, the head being the king's property, and the tail the queen's. 2 Steph. Comm. 19, 448, 540.

WHALER. A vessel employed in the whale fishery.

WHARF. A perpendicular bank or mound of timber, or stone and earth, raised on the shore of a harbor, river, canal, etc., or extending some distance into the water, for the convenience of lading and unlading ships and other vessels. Webster.

A broad, plain place near a river, canal, or other water, to lay wares on that are brought to or from the water. Cowell.

A wharf is a structure erected on a shore below high-water mark, and sometimes extending into the channel, for the laying vessels along-side to load or unload, and on which stores are often erected for the reception of cargoes. 6 Mass. 332.

WHARFAGE. Money paid for landing wares at a wharf, or for shipping or taking goods into a boat or barge from thence. Cowell.

Strictly speaking, "wharfage" is money due, or money actually paid, for the privilege of landing goods upon, or loading a vessel while moored from, a wharf. 1 Brown, Adm. 37.

WHARFINGER. One who owns or keeps a wharf for the purpose of receiving and shipping merchandise to or from it for hire.

WHEEL. An engine of torture used in medieval Europe, on which a criminal was bound while his limbs were broken one by one till he died.

WHEELAGE. Duty or toll paid for carts, etc., passing over certain ground. Cowell.

WHEN AND WHERE. Technical words in pleading, formerly necessary in making *full defense* to certain actions.

WHENEVER. This word, though often used as equivalent to "as soon as," is also often used where the time intended by it is, and will be until its arrival, or for some uncertain period, at least, indeterminate. 14 R. I. 188.

WHEREAS. A word which implies a recital of a past fact. The word "whereas," when it renders the deed senseless or repugnant, may be struck out as impertinent, and shall not vitiate a deed in other respects sensible.

WHIG. This name was applied in Scotland, A. D. 1648, to those violent Covenanters who opposed the Duke of Hamilton's invasion of England in order to restore Charles I. The appellation of "Whig" and "Tory" to political factions was first heard of in A. D. 1679, and, though as senseless as any cant terms that could be devised, they became instantly as familiar in use as they have since continued. 2 Hall. Const. Hist. c. 12; Wharton.

WHIPPING. A mode of punishment, by the infliction of stripes, occasionally used in England and in a few of the American states.

WHIPPING-POST. A post or stake to which a criminal is tied to undergo the punishment of whipping. This penalty is now abolished, except in a few states.

WHITE. A Mongolian is not a "white person," within the meaning of the term as used in the naturalization laws of the United States; the term applies only to persons of the Caucasian race. 5 Sawy. 155.

WHITE ACRE. A fictitious name given to a piece of land, in the English books, for purposes of illustration.

WHITE BONNET. In Scotch law. A fictitious offerer or bidder at a roup or auction sale. Bell.

WHITE MEATS. In old English law. Milk, butter, cheese, eggs, and any composition of them. Cowell.

WHITE RENTS. In English law. Rents paid in silver, and called "white rents," or "*redditus albi*," to distinguish them from rents payable in corn, labor, provisions, etc., called "black-rent" or "black-mail."

WHITE SPURS. A kind of esquires. Cowell.

WHITEFRIARS. A place in London between the Temple and Blackfriars, which was formerly a sanctuary, and therefore privileged from arrest. Wharton.

WHITEHART SILVER. A mulct on certain lands in or near to the forest of Whitehart, paid into the exchequer, imposed by Henry III. upon Thomas de la Linda, for killing a beautiful white hart which that king before had spared in hunting. Camd. Brit. 150.

WHITSUN FARTHINGS. Pentecostals, (*q. v.*)

WHITSUNTIDE. The feast of Pentecost, being the fiftieth day after Easter, and the first of the four cross-quarter days of the year. Wharton.

WHITTANWARII. In old English law. A class of offenders who whitened stolen ox-hides and horse-hides so that they could not be known and identified.

WHOLE BLOOD. Kinship by descent from the same father and mother; as distinguished from *half* blood, which is the relationship of those who have one parent in common, but not both.

WHOLESALE. To sell by wholesale is to sell by large parcels, generally in original packages, and not by retail.

WHORE. A whore is a woman who practices unlawful commerce with men, particularly one who does so for hire; a harlot; a concubine; a prostitute. 43 Iowa, 183.

WIC. A place on the sea-shore or the bank of a river.

WICA. A country house or farm. Cowell.

WICK. Sax. A village, town, or district. Hence, in composition, the territory over which a given jurisdiction extends. Thus, "bailiwick" is the territorial jurisdiction of a bailiff or sheriff or constable. "Sheriffwick" was also used in the old books.

WIDOW. A woman whose husband is dead, and who has not married again. The "king's widow" was one whose deceased husband had been the king's tenant *in capite;* she could not marry again without the royal permission.

WIDOW-BENCH. The share of her husband's estate which a widow is allowed besides her jointure.

WIDOW'S CHAMBER. In London, the apparel of a widow and the furniture of her chamber, left by her deceased husband, is so called, and the widow is entitled to it. 2 Bl. Comm. 518.

WIDOW'S QUARANTINE. In old English law. The space of forty days after the death of a man who died seised of lands, during which his widow might remain in her husband's capital mansion-house, without rent, and during which time her dower should be assigned. 2 Bl. Comm. 135.

WIDOW'S TERCE. In Scotch law. The right which a wife has after her husband's death to a third of the rents of lands in which her husband died infeft; dower. Bell.

WIDOWER. A man whose wife is dead, and who has not remarried.

WIDOWHOOD. The state or condition of being a widow. An estate is sometimes settled upon a woman "during widowhood," which is expressed in Latin, "*durante viduitate.*"

WIFA. L. Lat. In old European law. A mark or sign; a mark set up on land, to denote an exclusive occupation, or to prohibit entry. Spelman.

WIFE. A woman who has a husband living and undivorced. The correlative term is "husband."

WIFE'S EQUITY. When a husband is compelled to seek the aid of a court of equity for the purpose of obtaining the possession or control of his wife's estate, that court will recognize the right of the wife to have a suitable and reasonable provision made, by settlement or otherwise, for herself and her children, out of the property thus brought within its jurisdiction. This right is called the "wife's equity," or "equity to a settlement." See 2 Kent, Comm. 139.

WIGREVE. In old English law. The overseer of a wood. Cowell.

WILD ANIMALS, (or animals *feræ naturæ.*) Animals of an untamable disposition.

WILD LAND. Land in a state of nature, as distinguished from improved or cultivated land. 4 Cow. 203.

WILD'S CASE, RULE IN. A devise to B. and his children or issue, B. having no issue at the time of the devise, gives him an estate tail; but, if he have issue at the time, B. and his children take joint estates for life. 6 Coke, 16*b;* Tudor, Lead. Cas. Real Prop. 542, 581.

WILL. A will is the legal expression of a man's wishes as to the disposition of his property after his death. Code Ga. 1882, § 2394; Swinb. Wills, § 2.

An instrument in writing, executed in form of law, by which a person makes a disposition of his property, to take effect after his death.

Except where it would be inconsistent with the manifest intent of the legislature, the word "will" shall extend to a testament, and to a codicil, and to an appointment by will, or by writing in the nature of a will, in exercise of a power; and also to any other testamentary disposition. Code Va. 1887, § 2511.

A will is an instrument by which a person makes a disposition of his property, to take effect after his decease, and which is, in its own nature, ambulatory and revocable during his life. It is this ambulatory quality which forms the characteristic of wills; for though a disposition by deed may postpone the possession or enjoyment, or even the vesting, until the death of the disposing party, yet the postponement is in such case produced by the express terms, and does not result from the nature of the instrument. 45 Miss. 641.

A will, when it operates upon personal property, is sometimes called a "testament," and when upon real estate, a "devise;" but the more general and the more popular denomination of the instrument embracing equally real and personal estate is that of "last will and testament." 4 Kent, Comm. 501.

In criminal law. The power of the mind which directs the action of a man.

In Scotch practice. That part or clause of a process which contains the mandate or command to the officer. Bell.

WILL, ESTATE AT. This estate entitles the grantee or lessee to the possession of land during the pleasure of both the grantor and himself, yet it creates no sure or durable right, and is bounded by no definite limits as to duration. It must be at the reciprocal will of both parties, (for, if it be at the will of the lessor only, it is a lease for life,) and the dissent of either determines it. Wharton.

WILLA. In Hindu law. The relation between a master or patron and his freedman, and the relation between two persons who had made a reciprocal testamentary contract. Wharton.

WILLFUL. Proceeding from a conscious motion of the will; intending the result which actually comes to pass; designed; intentional; malicious.

A willful differs essentially from a negligent act. The one is positive and the other negative. Intention is always separated from negligence by a precise line of demarkation. 38 N. Y. Super. Ct. 317.

In common parlance, "willful" is used in the sense of "intentional," as distinguished from "accidental" or "involuntary." But language of a statute affixing a punishment to acts done willfully may be restricted to such acts done with an unlawful intent. 29 N. J. Law, 96.

WILLFUL NEGLECT. Willful neglect is the neglect of the husband to provide for his wife the common necessaries of life, he having the ability to do so; or it is the failure to do so by reason of idleness, profligacy, or dissipation. Civil Code Cal. § 105.

WILLFULLY. Intentionally. In charging certain offenses, it is required that they should be stated to be *willfully* done. Archb. Crim. Pl. 51, 58; Leach, 556.

WILLS ACT. In England. 1. The statute 32 Hen. VIII. c. 1, passed in 1540, by which persons seised in fee-simple of lands holden in socage tenure were enabled to devise the same at their will and pleasure, except to bodies corporate; and those who held estates by the tenure of chivalry were enabled to devise two-third parts thereof.

2. The statute 7 Wm. IV. & 1 Vict. c. 26, passed in 1837, and also called "Lord Langdale's Act." This act permits of the disposition by will of every kind of interest in real and personal estate, and provides that all wills, whether of real or of personal estate, shall be attested by two witnesses, and that such attestation shall be sufficient. Other important alterations are effected by this statute in the law of wills. Mozley & Whitley.

WINCHESTER MEASURE. The standard measure of England, originally kept at Winchester. 1 Bl. Comm. 274.

WINCHESTER, STATUTE OF. A statute passed in the thirteenth year of the reign of Edward I., by which the old Saxon law of police was enforced, with many additional provisions. 2 Reeve, Eng. Law, 163; Crabb, Hist. Eng. Law, 189.

WINDING UP. The name applied in England to the process of settling the accounts and liquidating the assets of a partnership or company, for the purpose of making distribution and dissolving the concern.

WINDING-UP ACTS. In English law. General acts of parliament, regulating settlement of corporate affairs on dissolution.

WINDOW. An opening made in the wall of a house to admit light and air, and to furnish a view or prospect. The use of this word in law is chiefly in connection with the doctrine of ancient lights and other rights of adjacent owners.

WINDOW TAX. A tax on windows, levied on houses which contained more than six windows, and were worth more than £5 per annum; established by St. 7 Wm. III. c. 18. The St. 14 & 15 Vict. c. 36, substituted for this tax a tax on inhabited houses. Wharton.

WINDSOR FOREST. A royal forest founded by Henry VIII.

WINTER CIRCUIT. An occasional circuit appointed for the trial of prisoners, in England, and in some cases of civil causes, between Michaelmas and Hilary terms.

WINTER HEYNING. The season between 11th November and 23d April, which is excepted from the liberty of commoning in certain forests. St. 23 Car. II. c. 3.

WISBY, LAWS OF. The name given to a code of maritime laws promulgated at Wisby, then the capital of Gothland, in Sweden, in the latter part of the thirteenth century. This compilation resembled the laws of Oleron in many respects, and was early adopted, as a system of sea laws, by the commercial nations of Northern Europe. It formed the foundation for the subsequent code of the Hanseatic League. A translation of the Laws of Wisby may be seen in the appendix to 1 Pet. Adm. And see 3 Kent, Comm. 13.

WISTA. In Saxon law. Half a hide of land, or sixty acres.

WIT. To know; to learn; to be informed. Used only in the infinitive, *to-wit*, which term is equivalent to "that is to say," "namely," or "*videlicet*."

WITAM. The purgation from an offense by the oath of the requisite number of witnesses.

WITAN. In Saxon law. Wise men; persons of information, especially in the laws; the king's advisers; members of the king's council; the optimates, or principal men of the kingdom. 1 Spence, Eq. Jur. 11, note.

WITCHCRAFT. Under Sts. 33 Hen. VIII. c. 8, and 1 Jac. I. c. 12, the offense of witchcraft, or supposed intercourse with evil spirits, was punishable with death. These acts were not repealed till 1736. 4 Bl. Comm. 60, 61.

WITE. Sax. A punishment, pain, penalty, mulct, or criminal fine. Cowell.

WITEKDEN. A taxation of the West Saxons, imposed by the public council of the kingdom.

WITENA DOM. In Saxon law. The judgment of the county court, or other court of competent jurisdiction, on the title to property, real or personal. 1 Spence, Eq. Jur. 22.

WITENAGEMOTE. "The assembly of wise men." This was the great national council or parliament of the Saxons in England, comprising the noblemen, high ecclesiastics, and other great thanes of the kingdom, advising and aiding the king in the general administration of government.

WITENS. The chiefs of the Saxon lords or thanes, their nobles, and wise men.

WITH ALL FAULTS. This phrase, used in a contract of sale, implies that the purchaser assumes the risk of all defects and imperfections, provided they do not destroy the identity of the thing sold.

WITH STRONG HAND. In pleading. A technical phrase indispensable in describing a forcible entry in an indictment. No other word or circumlocution will answer the same purpose 8 Term. R 357.

WITHDRAWING A JUROR. In practice. The withdrawing of one of the twelve jurors from the box, with the result that, the jury being now found to be incomplete, no further proceedings can be had in the cause. The withdrawing of a juror is always by the agreement of the parties, and is frequently done at the recommendation of the judge, where it is doubtful whether the action will lie; and in such case the consequence is that each party pays his own costs. It is, however, no bar to a future action for the same cause. 2 Tidd, Pr. 861, 862; 1 Archb. Pr. K. B. 196.

WITHDRAWING RECORD. In practice. The withdrawing by a plaintiff of the *nisi prius* or trial record filed in a cause, just before the trial is entered upon, for the purpose of preventing the cause from being tried. This may be done before the jury are sworn, and afterwards, by consent of the defendant's counsel. 2 Tidd, Pr. 851; 1 Archb. Pr. K. B. 189; 3 Chit. Pr. 870.

WITHERNAM. In practice. A taking by way of reprisal; a taking or a reprisal of other goods, in lieu of those that were formerly taken and eloigned or withholden. 2 Inst. 141. A reciprocal distress, in lieu of a previous one which has been eloigned. 3 Bl. Comm. 148.

WITHERSAKE. An apostate, or perfidious renegade. Cowell.

WITHOUT DAY. A term used to signify that an adjournment or continuance is indefinite or final, or that no subsequent time is fixed for another meeting, or for further proceedings. See SINE DIE.

WITHOUT IMPEACHMENT OF WASTE. The effect of the insertion of this clause in a lease for life is to give the tenant the right to cut timber on the estate, without making himself thereby liable to an action for waste.

WITHOUT PREJUDICE. Where an offer or admission is made "without prejudice," or a motion is denied "without prejudice," it is meant as a declaration that no rights or privileges of the party concerned are to be considered as thereby waived or lost except in so far as may be expressly conceded or decided.

WITHOUT RECOURSE. This phrase, used in making a qualified indorsement of a negotiable instrument, signifies that the indorser means to save himself from liability to subsequent holders, and is a notification that, if payment is refused by the parties primarily liable, recourse cannot be had to him.

WITHOUT RESERVE. A term applied to a sale by auction, indicating that no price is reserved.

WITHOUT STINT. Without limit; without any specified number.

WITHOUT THIS, THAT. In pleading. Formal words used in pleadings by way of *traverse,* particularly by way of *special* traverse, (*q. v.*,) importing an express denial of some matter of fact alleged in a previous pleading. Steph. Pl. 168, 169, 179, 180.

WITNESS, *v.* To subscribe one's name to a deed, will, or other document, for the purpose of attesting its authenticity, and proving its execution, if required, by bearing witness thereto.

WITNESS, *n.* In the primary sense of the word, a witness is a person who has knowledge of an event. As the most direct mode of acquiring knowledge of an event is by seeing it, "witness" has acquired the sense of a person who is present at and observes a transaction. Sweet.

A witness is a person whose declaration under oath (or affirmation) is received as evidence for any purpose, whether such declaration be made on oral examination or by deposition or affidavit. Code Civil Proc. Cal. § 1878; Gen. St. Minn. 1878, c. 73, § 6.

One who is called upon to be present at a transaction, as a wedding, or the making of a will, that he may thereafter, if necessary, testify to the transaction.

In conveyancing. One who sees the execution of an instrument, and subscribes it, for the purpose of confirming its authenticity by his testimony.

WITNESSING PART, in a deed or other formal instrument, is that part which comes after the recitals, or, where there are no recitals, after the parties. It usually commences with a reference to the agreement or intention to be effectuated, then states or refers to the consideration, and concludes with the operative words and parcels, if any. Where a deed effectuates two distinct objects, there are two witnessing parts. 1 Dav. Prec. Conv. 63, et seq.; Sweet.

WITTINGLY means with knowledge and by design, excluding only cases which are the result of accident or forgetfulness, and including cases where one does an unlawful act through an erroneous belief of his right. 44 Conn. 357.

WOLD. Sax. In England. A down or champaign ground, hilly and void of wood. Cowell; Blount.

WOLF'S HEAD. In old English law. This term was used as descriptive of the condition of an outlaw. Such persons were said to carry a wolf's head, (*caput lupinum;*) for if caught alive they were to be brought to the king, and if they defended themselves they might be slain and their heads carried to the king, for they were no more to be accounted of than wolves. Termes de la Ley, "Woolferthfod."

WOMEN. All the females of the human species. All such females who have arrived at the age of puberty. Dig. 50, 16, 13.

WONG. Sax. In old records. A field. Spelman; Cowell.

WOOD-CORN. In old records. A certain quantity of oats or other grain, paid by customary tenants to the lord, for liberty to pick up dead or broken wood. Cowell.

WOOD-GELD. In old English law. Money paid for the liberty of taking wood in a forest. Cowell.

Immunity from such payment. Spelman.

WOOD-MOTE. In forest law. The old name of the court of attachments; otherwise called the "Forty-Days Court." Cowell; 3 Bl. Comm. 71.

WOOD PLEA COURT. A court held twice in the year in the forest of Clun, in Shropshire, for determining all matters of wood and agistments. Cowell.

WOOD-STREET COMPTER. The name of an old prison in London.

WOODS. A forest; land covered with a large and thick collection of natural forest trees. The old books say that a grant of "all his woods" (*omnes boscos suos*) will pass the land, as well as the trees growing upon it. Co. Litt. 4*b*.

WOODWARDS. Officers of the forest, whose duty consists in looking after the wood and vert and venison, and preventing offenses relating to the same. Manw. 189.

WOOL-SACK. The seat of the lord chancellor of England in the house of lords, being a large square bag of wool, without back or arms, covered with red cloth. Webster; Brande.

WORDS OF LIMITATION. In a conveyance or will, words which have the effect of marking the duration of an estate are termed "words of limitation." Thus, in a grant to A. and his heirs, the words "and his heirs" are words of limitation, because they show that A. is to take an estate in fee-simple, and do not give his heirs anything. Fearne, Rem. 78.

WORDS OF PROCREATION. To create an estate tail by deed, it is necessary that words of procreation should be used in order to confine the estate to the descendants of the first grantee, as in the usual form of limitation,—"to A. and the heirs of his body." Sweet.

WORDS OF PURCHASE. Words of purchase are words which denote the person who is to take the estate. Thus, if I grant land to A. for twenty-one years, and after the determination of that term to A.'s heirs, the word "heirs" does not denote the duration of A.'s estate, but the person who is to take the remainder on the expiration of the term, and is therefore called a "word of purchase." Williams, Real Prop.; Fearne, Rem. 76, et seq.

WORK AND LABOR. The name of one of the common counts in actions of *assumpsit*, being for work and labor done and materials furnished by the plaintiff for the defendant.

WORK-BEAST, or WORK-HORSE. These terms mean an animal of the horse kind, which can be rendered fit for service, as well as one of maturer age and in actual use. 8 Bush, 587.

WORK-HOUSE. A place where convicts (or paupers) are confined and kept at labor.

WORKING DAYS. In settling lay-days, or days of demurrage, sometimes the contract specifies "working days;" in the computation, Sundays and custom-house holidays are excluded. 1 Bell, Comm. 577.

WORKMAN. One who labors; one who is employed to do business for another.

WORLD. This term sometimes denotes all persons whatsoever who may have, claim, or acquire an interest in the subject-matter; as in saying that a judgment *in rem* binds "all the world."

WORSHIP. The act of offering honor and adoration to the Divine Being. Religious exercises participated in by a number of persons assembled for that purpose, the disturbance of which is a statutory offense in many states.

In English law. A title of honor or dignity used in addresses to certain magistrates and other persons of rank or office.

WORT, or WORTH. A curtilage or country farm.

WORTHIEST OF BLOOD. In the English law of descent. A term applied to males, expressive of the preference given to them over females. See 2 Bl. Comm. 234-240.

WORTHING OF LAND. A certain quantity of land so called in the manor of Kingsland, in Hereford. The tenants are called "worthies." Wharton.

WOUND. In criminal cases, the definition of a "wound" is an injury to the person by which the skin is broken. 22 Mo. 451; 6 Car. & P. 684.

"In legal medicine, the term 'wound' is used in a much more comprehensive sense than in surgery. In the latter, it means strictly a solution of continuity; in the former, injuries of every description that affect either the hard or the soft parts; and accordingly under it are comprehended bruises, contusions, fractures, luxations," etc. 2 Beck, Med. Jur. 106.

WOUNDING. An aggravated species of assault and battery, consisting in one person giving another some dangerous hurt. 3 Bl. Comm. 121.

Wreccum maris significat illa bona quæ naufragio ad terram pelluntur. A wreck of the sea signifies those goods which are driven to shore from a shipwreck.

WRECK. At common law. Such goods as after a shipwreck are cast upon the land by the sea, and, as lying within the territory of some county, do not belong to the jurisdiction of the admiralty, but to the common law. 2 Inst. 167; 1 Bl. Comm. 290.

Goods cast ashore from a wrecked vessel, where no living creature has escaped from the wreck alive; and which are forfeited to the crown, or to persons having the franchise of wreck. Cowell.

In American law. Goods cast ashore by the sea, and not claimed by the owner within a year, or other specified period; and which, in such case, become the property of the state. 2 Kent, Comm. 322.

In maritime law. A ship becomes a wreck when, in consequence of injuries received, she is rendered absolutely unnavigable, or unable to pursue her voyage, without repairs exceeding the half of her value. 6 Mass. 479.

WRECK COMMISSIONERS are persons appointed by the English lord chancellor under the merchant shipping act, 1876, (section 29,) to hold investigations at the request of the board of trade into losses, abandonments, damages, and casualties of or to ships on or near the coast of the United Kingdom, whereby loss of life is caused. Sweet.

WRECKFREE. Exempt from the forfeiture of shipwrecked goods and vessels to the king. Cowell.

WRIT. A precept in writing, couched in the form of a letter, running in the name of the king, president, or state, issuing from a court of justice, and sealed with its seal, addressed to a sheriff or other officer of the law, or directly to the person whose action the court desires to command, either as the commencement of a suit or other proceeding or as incidental to its progress, and requiring the performance of a specified act, or giving authority and commission to have it done.

In regard to the division and classification of writs, see CLOSE WRITS; JUDICIAL WRITS; ORIGINAL WRITS; PATENT WRITS; PREROGATIVE WRITS.

In old English law. An instrument in the form of a letter; a letter or letters of attorney. This is a very ancient sense of the word.

In the old books, "writ" is used as equivalent to "action;" hence writs are sometimes divided into real, personal, and mixed.

In Scotch law. A writing; an instrument in writing, as a deed, bond, contract, etc. 2 Forb. Inst. pt. 2, pp. 175-179.

WRIT DE BONO ET MALO. See DE BONO ET MALO; ASSIZE.

WRIT DE HÆRETICO COMBURENDO. In English law. The name of a writ formerly issued by the secular courts, for the execution, by burning, of a man who had been convicted in the ecclesiastical courts of heresy.

WRIT DE RATIONABILI PARTE BONORUM. A writ which lay for a widow, against the executor of her deceased husband, to compel the executor to set off to her a third part of the decedent's personalty, after payment of his debts. Fitzh. Nat. Brev. 122, L.

WRIT OF ASSISTANCE. A writ issuing out of chancery in pursuance of an order, commanding the sheriff to eject the defendant from certain lands and to put the plaintiff in possession; also an ancient writ issuing out of the exchequer. Mozley & Whitley.

WRIT OF ASSOCIATION. In English practice. A writ whereby certain persons (usually the clerk of assize and his subordinate officers) are directed to associate themselves with the justices and serjeants; and they are required to admit the said persons into their society in order to take the assizes. 3 Bl. Comm. 59.

WRIT OF ATTACHMENT. A writ employed to enforce obedience to an order or judgment of the court. It commands the sheriff to attach the disobedient party and to have him before the court to answer his contempt. Smith, Act. 176.

WRIT OF CONSPIRACY. A writ which anciently lay against persons who had conspired to injure the plaintiff, under the same circumstances which would now give him an action on the case.

WRIT OF COVENANT. A writ which lies where a party claims damages for breach of covenant; *i. e.*, of a promise under seal.

WRIT OF DEBT. A writ which lies where the party claims the recovery of a debt; *i. e.*, a liquidated or certain sum of money alleged to be due to him.

WRIT OF DECEIT. The name of a writ which lies where one man has done anything in the name of another, by which the latter is damnified and deceived. Fitzh. Nat. Brev. 95, E.

WRIT OF DELIVERY. A writ of execution employed to enforce a judgment for the delivery of chattels. It commands the sheriff to cause the chattels mentioned in the writ to be returned to the person who has obtained the judgment; and, if the chattels cannot be found, to distrain the person against whom the judgment was given until he returns them. Smith, Act. 175; Sweet.

WRIT OF DETINUE. A writ which lies where a party claims the specific recovery of goods and chattels, or deeds and writings, detained from him. This is seldom used; trover is the more frequent remedy, in cases where it may be brought. Bouvier.

WRIT OF DOWER. This is either a writ of dower *unde nihil habet*, which lies for a widow, commanding the tenant to assign her dower, no part of which has yet been set off to her; or a writ of *right of dower*, whereby she seeks to recover the remainder of the dower to which she is entitled, part having been already received from the tenant.

WRIT OF EJECTMENT. The writ in an action of ejectment, for the recovery of lands. See EJECTMENT.

WRIT OF ENTRY. A real action to recover the possession of land where the tenant (or owner) has been disseised or otherwise wrongfully dispossessed. If the disseisor has aliened the land, or if it has descended to his heir, the writ of entry is said to be in the *per*, because it alleges that the defendant (the alienee or heir) obtained possession *through* the original disseisor. If two alienations (or descents) have taken place, the writ is in the *per* and *cui*, because it alleges that the defendant (the second alienee) obtained possession *through* the first alienee, *to whom* the original disseisor had aliened it. If more than two alienations (or descents) have taken place, the writ is in the *post*, because it simply alleges that the defendant acquired possession *after* the original disseisin. Co. Litt. 238*b;* 3 Bl. Comm. 180. The writ of entry was abolished, with other real actions, in England, by St. 3 & 4 Wm. IV. c. 27, § 36, but is still in use in a few of the states of the Union. Sweet.

WRIT OF ERROR. A writ issued from a court of appellate jurisdiction, directed to the judge or judges of a court of record, requiring them to remit to the appellate court the record of an action before them, in which a final judgment has been entered, in order that examination may be made of certain errors alleged to have been committed, and that the judgment may be reversed, corrected, or affirmed, as the case may require.

A writ of error is defined to be a commission by which the judges of one court are authorized to examine a record upon which a judgment was given in another court, and, on such examination, to affirm or reverse the same, according to law. 6 Wheat. 409.

WRIT OF EXECUTION. A writ to put in force the judgment or decree of a court.

WRIT OF FALSE JUDGMENT. A writ which appears to be still in use to bring appeals to the English high court from inferior courts not of record proceeding according to the course of the common law. Archb. Pr. 1427.

WRIT OF FORMEDON. A writ which lies for the recovery of an estate by a person claiming as issue in tail, or by the remainder-man or reversioner after the termination of the entail. See FORMEDON.

WRIT OF INQUIRY. In common-law practice. A writ which issues after the plaintiff in an action has obtained a judgment by default, on an unliquidated claim, directing the sheriff, with the aid of a jury, to inquire into the amount of the plaintiff's demand and assess his damages.

WRIT OF MAINPRIZE. In English law. A writ directed to the sheriff, (either generally, when any man is imprisoned for a bailable offense and bail has been refused, or specially, when the offense or cause of commitment is not properly bailable below,) commanding him to take sureties for the prisoner's appearance, commonly called "mainpernors," and to set him at large. 3 Bl. Comm. 128.

WRIT OF MESNE. In old English law. A writ which was so called by reason of the words used in the writ, namely, "*Unde idem A. qui medius est inter C. et præfatum B.;*" that is, A., who is mesne between C., the lord paramount, and B., the tenant paravail. Co. Litt. 100*a*.

WRIT OF POSSESSION. This is the writ of execution employed to enforce a judgment to recover the possession of land. It commands the sheriff to enter the land and give possession of it to the person entitled under the judgment. Smith, Act. 175.

WRIT OF PRÆCIPE. This writ is also called a "writ of covenant," and is sued out by the party to whom lands are to be conveyed by fine, the foundation of which is a supposed agreement or covenant that the one shall convey the land to the other. 2 Bl. Comm. 349.

WRIT OF PREVENTION. This name is given to certain writs which may be issued in anticipation of suits which may arise. Co. Litt. 100.

WRIT OF PROCLAMATION. In English law. By the statute 31 Eliz. c. 3, when an *exigent* is sued out, a writ of proclamation shall issue at the same time, commanding the sheriff of the county where the defendant dwells to make three proclamations thereof, in places the most notorious, and most likely to come to his knowledge, a month before the outlawry shall take place. 3 Bl. Comm. 284.

WRIT OF PROTECTION. In England, the queen may, by her writ of protection, privilege any person in her service from arrest in civil proceedings during a year and a day; but this prerogative is seldom, if ever, exercised. Archb. Pr. 687. See Co. Litt. 130*a*.

WRIT OF QUARE IMPEDIT. See QUARE IMPEDIT.

WRIT OF RECAPTION. If, pending an action of replevin for a distress, the defendant distrains again for the same rent or service, the owner of the goods is not driven to another action of replevin, but is allowed a writ of recaption, by which he recovers the goods and damages for the defendant's contempt of the process of the law in making a second distress while the matter is *sub judice.* Woodf. Landl. & Ten. 484.

WRIT OF RESTITUTION. A writ which is issued on the reversal of a judgment commanding the sheriff to restore to the defendant below the thing levied upon, if it has not been sold, and, if it has been sold, the proceeds. Bac. Abr. "Execution," Q.

WRIT OF RIGHT. This was a writ which lay for one who had the right of property, against another who had the right of possession and the actual occupation. The writ properly lay only to recover corporeal hereditaments for an estate in fee-simple; but there were other writs, said to be "in the nature of a writ of right," available for the recovery of incorporeal hereditaments or of lands for a less estate than a fee-simple. Brown.

In another sense of the term, a "writ of right" is one which is grantable as a matter of right, as opposed to a "prerogative writ," which is issued only as a matter of grace or discretion.

WRIT OF SUMMONS. The writ by which, under the English judicature acts, all actions are commenced.

WRIT OF TOLT. In English law. The name of a writ to remove proceedings on a writ of right patent from the court-baron into the county court.

WRIT OF TRIAL. In English law. A writ directing an action brought in a superior court to be tried in an inferior court or before the under-sheriff, under St. 3 & 4 Wm. IV. c. 42. It is now superseded by the county courts act of 1867, c. 142, § 6, by which a defendant, in certain cases, is enabled to obtain an order that the action be tried in a county court. 3 Steph. Comm. 515, n.; Mozley & Whitley.

WRIT OF WASTE. The name of a writ to be issued against a tenant who has committed waste of the premises. There are several forms of this writ. Fitzh. Nat. Brev. 125.

WRIT PRO RETORNO HABENDO. A writ commanding the return of the goods to the defendant, upon a judgment in his favor in replevin, upon the plaintiff's default.

WRITER OF THE TALLIES. In England. An officer of the exchequer whose duty it was to write upon the tallies the letters of tellers' bills.

WRITER TO THE SIGNET. In Scotch law. An officer nearly corresponding to an attorney at law, in English and American practice. "Writers to the signet," called also "clerks to the signet," derive their name from the circumstance that they were anciently clerks in the office of the secretary of state, by whom writs were prepared and issued under the royal *signet* or seal; and, when the signet became employed in judicial proceedings, they obtained a monopoly of the privileges of acting as agents or attorneys before the court of session. Brande, voc. "Signet."

WRITING. The expression of ideas by letters visible to the eye. 14 Johns. 491. The giving an outward and objective form to a contract, will, etc., by means of letters or marks placed upon paper, parchment, or other material substance.

In the most general sense of the word, "writing" denotes a document, whether manuscript or printed, as opposed to mere spoken words. Writing is essential to the validity of certain contracts and other transactions. Sweet.

WRITING OBLIGATORY. The technical name by which a *bond* is described in pleading.

WRITTEN LAW. One of the two leading divisions of the Roman law, comprising the *leges, plebiscita, senatus-consulta, principum placita, magistratuum edicta,* and *responsa prudentum.* Inst. 1, 2, 3.

Statute law; law deriving its force from express legislative enactment. 1 Bl. Comm. 62, 85.

WRONG. An injury; a tort; a violation of right or of law.

The idea of *rights* naturally suggests the correlative one of *wrongs;* for every right is capable of being violated. A right to receive payment for goods sold (for example) implies a wrong on the part of him who owes, but withholds the price; a right to live in personal security, a wrong on the part of him who commits personal violence. And therefore, while, in a general point of view, the law is intended for the establishment and maintenance of *rights*, we find it, on closer examination, to be dealing both with rights and wrongs. It first fixes the character and definition of rights, and then, with a view to their effectual security, proceeds to define wrongs, and to devise the means by which the latter shall be prevented or redressed. 1 Steph. Comm. 126.

WRONG-DOER. One who commits an injury; a *tort-feasor.*

WRONGFULLY INTENDING. In the language of pleading, this phrase is appropriate to be used in alleging the malicious motive of the defendant in committing the injury which forms the cause of action.

WRONGOUS. In Scotch law. Wrongful; unlawful; as *wrongous* imprisonment. Ersk. Prin. 4, 4, 25.

WURTH. In Saxon law. Worthy; competent; capable. *Atheswurthe,* worthy of oath; admissible or competent to be sworn. Spelman.

WYTE. In old English law. Acquittance or immunity from amercement.

X.

XENODOCHIUM. In the civil and old English law. An inn allowed by public license, for the entertainment of strangers, and other guests. Calvin.; Cowell.

A hospital; a place where sick and infirm persons are taken care of. Cowell.

XENODOCHY. Reception of strangers; hospitality. Enc. Lond.

XYLON. A punishment among the Greeks answering to our stocks. Wharton.

Y.

YA ET NAY. In old records. Mere assertion and denial, without oath.

YACHT. A light sea-going vessel, used only for pleasure-trips, racing, etc. Webster. See 22 St. at Large, 566; Rev. St. U. S. §§ 4215–4218.

YARD. A measure of length, containing three feet, or thirty-six inches.

A piece of land inclosed for the use and accommodation of the inhabitants of a house.

YARDLAND, or *virgata terræ*, is a quantity of land, said by some to be twenty acres, but by Coke to be of uncertain extent.

YEA AND NAY. Yes and no. According to a charter of Athelstan, the people of Ripon were to be believed in all actions or suits upon their yea and nay, without the necessity of taking any oath. Brown.

YEAR. The period in which the revolution of the earth round the sun, and the accompanying changes in the order of nature, are completed. Generally, when a statute speaks of a year, twelve calendar, and not lunar, months are intended. Cro. Jac. 166. The year is either astronomical, ecclesiastical, or regnal, beginning on the 1st of January, or 25th of March, or the day of the sovereign's accession. Wharton.

YEAR AND DAY. This period was fixed for many purposes in law. Thus, in the case of an estray, if the owner did not claim it within that time, it became the property of the lord. So the owners of wreck must claim it within a year and a day. Death must follow upon wounding within a year and a day if the wounding is to be indicted as murder. Also, a year and a day were given for prosecuting or avoiding certain legal acts; *e. g.*, for bringing actions after entry, for making claim for avoiding a fine, etc. Brown.

YEAR BOOKS. Books of reports of cases in a regular series from the reign of the English King Edward I., inclusive, to the time of Henry VIII., which were taken by the prothonotaries or chief scribes of the courts, at the expense of the crown, and published annually; whence their name, "Year Books." Brown.

YEAR, DAY, AND WASTE. In English law. An ancient prerogative of the king, whereby he was entitled to the profits, for a year and a day, of the lands of persons attainted of petty treason or felony, together with the right of wasting the tenements, afterwards restoring the property to the lord of the fee. Abrogated by St. 54 Geo. III. c. 145. Wharton.

YEAR TO YEAR, TENANCY FROM. This estate arises either expressly, as when land is let from year to year; or by a general parol demise, without any determinate interest, but reserving the payment of an annual rent; or impliedly, as when property is occupied generally under a rent payable yearly, half-yearly, or quarterly; or when a tenant holds over, after the expiration of his term, without having entered into any new contract, and pays rent, (before which he is tenant on sufferance.) Wharton.

YEARS, ESTATE FOR. See ESTATE FOR YEARS.

YEAS AND NAYS. The affirmative and negative votes on a bill or measure before a legislative assembly. "Calling the yeas and nays" is calling for the individual and oral vote of each member, usually upon a call of the roll.

YEME. In old records. Winter; a corruption of the Latin "*hieme.*"

YEOMAN. In English law. A commoner; a freeholder under the rank of gentleman. Cowell. A man who has free land of forty shillings by the year; who was anciently thereby qualified to serve on juries, vote for knights of the shire, and do any other act, where the law requires one that is *probus et legalis homo.* 1 Bl. Comm. 406, 407.

This term is occasionally used in American law, but without any definite meaning.

YEOMANRY. The collected body of yeomen.

YEOMEN OF THE GUARD. Properly called "yeomen of the guard of the royal household;" a body of men of the best rank under the gentry, and of a larger stature than ordinary, every one being required to be six feet high. Enc. Lond.

YEVEN, or YEOVEN. Given; dated. Cowell.

YIELD, in the law of real property, is to perform a service due by a tenant to his lord. Hence the usual form of reservation of a rent in a lease begins with the words "yielding and paying." Sweet.

YIELDING AND PAYING. In conveyancing. The initial words of that clause in leases in which the rent to be paid by the lessee is mentioned and reserved.

YOKELET. A little farm, requiring but a yoke of oxen to till it.

YORK, CUSTOM OF. A custom of the province of York in England, by which the effects of an intestate, after payment of his debts, are in general divided according to the ancient universal doctrine of the *pars rationabilis;* that is, one-third each to the widow, children, and administrator. 2 Bl. Comm. 518.

YORK, STATUTE OF. An important English statute passed at the city of York, in the twelfth year of Edward II., containing provisions on the subject of attorneys, witnesses, the taking of inquests by *nisi prius*; etc. 2 Reeve, Eng. Law, 299-302.

YORKSHIRE REGISTRIES. The registries of titles to land provided by acts of parliament for the ridings of the county of York in England. These resemble the offices for the registration or recording of deeds commonly established in the several counties of the states.

YOUNGER CHILDREN. This phrase, when used in English conveyancing with reference to settlements of land, signifies all such children as are not entitled to the rights of an eldest son. It therefore includes daughters, even those who are older than the eldest son. Mozley & Whitley.

YOUTH. This word may include children and youth of both sexes. 2 Cush. 519, 528.

YULE. The times of Christmas and Lammas.

YVERNAIL BLE. L. Fr. Winter grain. Kelham.

Z.

ZEALOT. This word is commonly taken in a bad sense, as denoting a separatist from the Church of England, or a fanatic. Brown.

ZEALOUS WITNESS. An untechnical term denoting a witness, on the trial of a cause, who manifests a partiality for the side calling him, and an eager readiness to tell anything which he thinks may be of advantage to that side.

ZEIR. O. Sc. Year. "*Zeir* and day" Bell.

ZEMINDAR. In Hindu law. Landkeeper. An officer who under the Mohammedan government was charged with the financial superintendence of the lands of a district, the protection of the cultivators, and the realization of the government's share of its produce, either in money or kind. Wharton.

ZETETICK. Proceeding by inquiry. Enc. Lond.

ZIGARI, or ZINGARI. Rogues and vagabonds in the middle ages; from Zigi, now Circassia.

ZOLL-VEREIN. A union of German states for uniformity of customs, established in 1819. It continued until the unification of the German empire, including Prussia, Saxony, Bavaria, Wurtemberg, Baden, Hesse-Cassel, Brunswick, and Mecklenburg-Strelitz, and all intermediate principalities. It has now been superseded by the German empire; and the federal council of the empire has taken the place of that of the Zoll-Verein. Wharton.

ZYGOCEPHALUM. In the civil law. A measure or quantity of land. Nov. 17, c. 8. As much land as a yoke of oxen could plow in a day. Calvin.

ZYGOSTATES. In the civil law. A weigher; an officer who held or looked to the balance in weighing money between buyer and seller; an officer appointed to determine controversies about the weight of money. Spelman.

ZYTHUM. Lat. A liquor or beverage made of wheat or barley. Dig. 33, 6, 9, pr.

WEST PUBLISHING CO., PRINTERS AND STEREOTYPERS, ST. PAUL, MINN.